The New York Times 2004 ALMANAC

Edited by John W. Wright
WITH EDITORS AND REPORTERS OF
The Times

PENGUIN REFERENCE

PENGUIN REFERENCE BOOKS
Published by the Penguin Group
Penguin Putnam Inc., 375 Hudson Street, New York, New York 10014, U.S.A.
Penguin Books Ltd, 80 Strand, London WC2R 0RL, England
Penguin Books Australia Ltd, 250 Camberwell Road, Camberwell, Victoria 3124, Australia
Penguin Books Canada Ltd, 10 Alcorn Avenue, Toronto, Ontario, Canada M4V 3B2
Penguin Books India (P) Ltd, 11 Community Centre, Panchsheel Park, New Delhi – 110 017, India
Penguin Books (N.Z.) Ltd, Cnr Rosedale and Airborne Roads, Albany, Auckland, New Zealand
Penguin Books (South Africa) (Pty) Ltd, 24 Sturdee Avenue, Rosebank, Johannesburg 2196, South Africa

Penguin Books Ltd, Registered Offices: Harmondsworth, Middlesex, England

Published in 2003 by Penguin Reference Books, a member of Penguin Putnam Inc.

10 9 8 7 6 5 4 3 2 1

ISBN 0 14 20.0367 0
ISSN 1523-7079

Printed in the United States of America
Set in Utopia and Optima

Designed by Virginia Norey

Please direct all comments to:

The New York Times Almanac
122 East 42nd Street
New York, New York 10168

CONTRIBUTORS AND STAFF

General Editor
John W. Wright

Executive Editor
John Rosenthal

Senior Editors and Writers
Bryan Bunch, John Connelly, Jeffrey Hacker, Alan Joyce, John Major, Allison Paxton Paine, Lincoln Paine, Patricia Szczerba, Jenny Tesar

Contributing Editors
Abigail Elbow, Alice Finer, Glen Gendzel, Deborah Kaple, Jerold Kappes, Michael Kaufman, Thomas LaRosa, Steven Lichtman, David Major, Lisa Renaud

Researchers and Fact Checkers
James Garver, William T. LeGro, Susan McMichaels, Robert L. Spring, Laura Stickney, Victoria Vine

Data Entry
Arlene Jacks, Dorothy Green

The New York Times
Thomas K. Carley, President, News Services; Nancy Lee, Vice President, Business Development; Susan Chira, Editorial Director, Book Development; Mitchel Levitas, Book Development

Editors
Laura Chang, Renee Murawski, David Rampe, David Stout

Correspondents
Daniel Altman, Lawrence K. Altman, M.D., Ed Andrews, Elizabeth Becker, James Bennet, Keith Bradsher, John M. Broder, Chris Buckley, Laurie Goodstein, Michael Gordon, Denise Grady, Linda Greenhouse, David Halbfinger, Carl Hulse, Stephen Labaton, Marc Lacey, Warren E. Leary, Neil A. Lewis, Eric Lipton, Gretchen Morgenson, Timothy L. O'Brien, Dennis Overbye, Robert Pear, Lydia Polgreen, Andrew C. Revkin, Larry Rohter, David E. Sanger, Somini Sengupta, Thom Shanker, Philip Shenon, Richard W. Stevenson, John Noble Wilford, Edward Wyatt, Kate Zernike

Maps
Steve Hadermeyer, John Papasian

CONTENTS

PART I: ALMANAC OF THE YEAR
Late Breaking News & 2003 Nobel Prizes iv-vi
Chronology of the Year's Events 1-10
Obituaries 2002-03 11-16
Major News Stories of 2001-02 17-36
Calendar of the Year 37-49
Understanding Calendars 37-41
Holidays and Holy Days 42-47
Astronomical Events, 2002 47-49

PART II: THE UNITED STATES
U.S. Geography 50-57
U.S. History 58-123
Documents of U.S. History 58-67
Chronology of U.S. History 68-85
Biographies of U.S. Presidents 86-100
Presidential Elections, 1796-2000 101-12
Political Office Holders 112-19
The U.S. Supreme Court 120-23
The Federal Government 124-68
The Judicial Branch 124-25
The Legislative Branch 125-31
The Executive Branch 131-39
Federal Employees and Budget 139-46
National Defense 146-55
Social Insurance Programs 155-63
Internal Revenue Service 163-66
U.S. Postal Service 167-68
States, Territories, and Possessions 169-210
The Fifty States 169-203
State Government Finances 204-6
U.S. Territories and Possessions 207-10
Cities and Counties in the U.S. 211-59
The 50 Largest Cities, 2000 212-30
Cities in America 231-41
City Finances 242-43
Metropolitan Statistical Areas (MSAs) 244-57
Counties in America 258-59
The American People Today 260-301
The Census 260-67
U.S. Population by Race & Hispanic Origin 267-75
U.S. Population by Age and Sex 276-78
Vital Statistics 278-83
Households and Families 284-86
Housing 287-92
Immigration 293-300
Sex in America 300-301
Agriculture 302-04
Crime and Punishment 305-15
Economy and Business 316-53
The U.S. Economy 316-38
U.S. Business 339-50
Advertising 351-53
Education 354-60
Energy 361-64
Health and Medicine 365-85
The Media 386-400
The Print Media 386-92
The Electronic Media 393-400
Religion in America 401-406
Transportation 407-15

PART III: THE WORLD
World History 416-39
Rulers of the World 440-46
World Geography 447-64
Climate and Weather 465-71
World Population 472-78
World Health 478-86
World Religions 486-92
Major Languages of the World 493
World Energy 494-97
The Global Military Situation 498-501
The Global Economy 502-16
Nations of the World 517-697
Territories of the World 698-707
The United Nations 708-714
International Organizations 715

PART IV: SCIENCE AND TECHNOLOGY
Science 716-71
Astronomy 716-38
Earth Sciences 738-46
Chemistry 746-52
Physics 752-58
Life Sciences 758-63
Mathematics 763-67
Standard Weights and Measures 767-71
The Environment 772-86
Endangered Species 782-86
Technology 787-812
Computers 795-99
Telecommunications 800-05
The Internet 806-12

PART V: AWARDS AND PRIZES
Awards in the Arts and Entertainment 813-38
Pulitzer Prizes 839-54
The Nobel Prizes 854-68

PART VI: SPORTS
College Sports 869-78
International Sports 879-86
The Olympic Sports 887-905
Professional Sports 906-72
Football 923-34
Basketball 934-41
Ice Hockey 942-47
Baseball 947-72

INDEX 973-1002

MAPS
Immediately follow page 618
Africa • Asia and the Pacific • Australia
Canada • Europe • Mexico, Central America & the Caribbean • Middle East
Nations of the former Soviet Union
South America • United States physical
United States political • World

Late Breaking News

Bolivian President Resigns After Month of Turmoil

After nearly a month of increasingly violent clashes between Indian demonstrators and army troops that left more than 80 people dead, Bolivia's Gonzalo Sánchez de Lozada resigned on October 17, 2003 as president of South America's poorest country. Mr. Sánchez de Lozada became the fourth South American president forced from office by popular unrest since 2000, joining Jamil Mahuad of Ecuador, Alberto Fujimori of Peru, and Fernando de la Rua of Argentina. Unpopular economic policies caused the downfall in each case except Mr. Fujimori's.

Mr. Sánchez de Lozada was an advocate of free-market policies, and had come under increasing criticism for a proposal to export natural gas to the U.S. through a port in Chile, Bolivia's traditional enemy. A week before his resignation, he ordered troops to quell the uprisings. The resulting violence and deaths eviscerated Mr. Sánchez de Lozada's political support; his popularity plunged to single digits.

In his resignation letter, he blamed his downfall on a "seditious" movement that sought to overturn the mandate voters had given him in an election just 15 months earlier. He also warned that the crisis was not over. "The dangers that hang over our fatherland continue intact."

Political leaders in Bolivia expressed relief at the resignation, gratified that both a coup and a constitutional crisis had been averted. Senate President Hormando Vaca Díaz, who presided over the joint session of Congress that voted to accept the president's resignation, described it as "a solution that is not ideal, but which preserves the constitutional order, which had been at risk."

Mr. Sánchez de Lozada fled to the United States after his resignation.

As dictated by the Bolivian constitution, Mr. Sánchez de Lozada was replaced by his vie president, Carlos Mesa. Mr. Sánchez de Lozada chose Mr. Mesa specifically because he belonged to no political party and had never held public office. During his time as vice president, he clashed frequently with entrenched political leaders, including the president.

Mr. Mesa's chances to restore order to the chaotic nation seemed tenuous. "Few times has the nation confronted a moment like this," said the 50-year-old former historian and television journalist after his swearing-in. "Give us some space, some time to work." Evo Morales, leader of the Movement Toward Socialism and the runner-up in the 2002 election, appeared ready to do exactly that. "I think it is important to give him a grace period," Mr. Morales said.

But Bolivia's other powerful indigenous leader, Felipe Quispe, whose organization began the nationwide strike that led to Mr. Sánchez de Lozada's ouster, was less sanguine about the new president. He refused to pledge his support to Mr. Mesa, and continued to demand that the new government meet all 72 of his demands. He also insisted that Mr. Mesa schedule new elections as soon as possible rather than serving out the remainder of his five-year term, a demand that Mr. Mesa agreed to in his inaugural speech.

Security Council Approves Iraq Plan

The United Nations Security Council unanimously approved an American and British resolution authorizing a U.S..-led multinational force in Iraq on October 16, 2003. The measure set a December 15 deadline for the Iraqi Governing Council to put forth a timetable for creating a constitution and democratic government.

The vote was something of a triumph for the Bush administration, which had been isolated by the U.N. after ignoring the Security Council's desire not to invade Iraq. The Security Council's approval gives the U.S. and Britain authority to carry out their vision of Iraq's political future while creating a U.N.-authorized multinational force under U.S. command.

Despite agreeing to the resolution, France, Germany, and Pakistan, among others, indicated that the plan was still too flawed to compel any contributions of troops or money beyond current levels. Russia, France, and Germany, the three leading opponents of the war, issued a joint statement saying "We believe that the resolution should have gone further on two major issues: First the role of the United Nations, in particular in the political process, and second, the pace of the transfer of responsibilities to the Iraqi people."

In a blow to Pres. Bush's plans, the U.S. Senate insisted that Iraq repay up to $10 billion of the president's proposed $87 billion in reconstruction aid. A bipartisan coalition of moderate senators (51-47) said they did not think American taxpayers should bear the entire brunt of rebuilding Iraq.

A week later, at an international conference in Madrid, however, the White House succeeded in winning $13 billion in commitments for reconstruction of water, power, health care, and other Iraqi systems. Most of the aid will come not as grants from individual countries, but in the form of loans from the International Monetary Fund and the World Bank. The emphasis on loans, rather than grants, is expected to encourage Congress to strengthen its insistence that at least some U.S. aid to Iraq be repaid, rather than granted.

Contributions from Arab nations were lower than expected, primarily because of antipathy toward the U.S. over the war on Iraq and the collapse of the Middle East peace negotiations. The United Arab Emirates offered $200 million to $250 million, Kuwait pledged $500 million, and Saudi Arabia offered $1 billion in low-cost loans and an additional $500 million to finance Saudi export credits.

Senate Approves Late-Term Abortion Ban; Florida Governor Inserts Feeding Tube

The Senate on October 21, 2003, approved legislation that makes it a crime to perform a specific type of late-term abortion. Seventeen Democrats joined with 47 Republicans to ensure passage of the bill. Pres. Bush promised to sign it when he returned from his trip to Asia.

Both sides of the abortion debate said the vote was a historic turning point in the controversy that has lingered ever since the Supreme Court established a constitutional right to abortion in the 1973 case *Roe v. Wade*.

Abortion rights advocates promised to challenge the new law. In 2000, the Supreme Court rejected a similar law in Nebraska, saying it was overly broad. The high Court said the Nebraska law was unconstitutional because it did not make exceptions for the health of the woman, a provision that is also lacking from the new federal legislation.

On the same day the U.S. Senate passed the abortion legislation, Florida Gov. Jeb Bush inserted himself into a controversy involving a woman in a persistent vegetative state whose husband had asked to remove a feeding tube that was keeping her alive. After the Florida state legislature hastily passed a rule that allowed him to do so, Gov. Bush, the president's brother, ordered the feeding tube re-inserted, overruling both her husband's wishes and several years of court rulings.

Iran Agrees to Inspections Of Nuclear Sites by U.N.

After months of resistance, Iran finally agreed on Oct. 21, 2003, to stricter international inspections of its nuclear sites, and to suspend production of enriched uranium, which can be used to develop nuclear weapons. It did not agree, however, to suspend its uranium enriching processes, or to surprise inspections of its nuclear installations, as mandated by the Nuclear Nonproliferation Treaty of 1986.

The agreement resulted from an unusual visit by the foreign ministers of three European countries: France, Germany, and Britain. The U.S. State Department, meanwhile, remained skeptical whether Iran would actually follow through on its pledge, and discounted the diplomacy of the three European nations.

Wildfires Force Thousands of Californians To Flee Their Homes

Wildfires roared across Southern California in the last week of October, 2003, forcing tens of thousands of people to flee residential areas less than 50 miles outside of Los Angeles and San Diego. By Sunday, October 26, the fires had burned more than 275,000 acres, and caused 13 deaths. At least 850 homes had been confirmed destroyed, but because there were so many areas that firefighters couldn't even reach, the total was expected to be much higher.

The fires were fueled by warm Santa Ana winds gusting up to 60 miles per hour, exacerbated by extremely low humidity. The most destructive fire, in the San Bernardino National Forest north and east of Los Angeles, was worsened by more than a million mature pine trees killed over the previous year by drought and a bark beetle infestation. The U.S. Forest Service estimated the fire front at close to 40 miles.

Ash and soot descended like snow in suburbs north and east of Los Angeles and San Diego. In areas close to the fire, the ground was covered by more than a half-inch of ash.

Outgoing Gov. Gray Davis declared states of emergency in San Bernardino, Ventura, Los Angeles, and San Diego Counties, and asked Pres. Bush for federal assistance. Davis described the fires as the worst in California in a decade..

Russia Arrests Oil Tycoon

Government security agents in Moscow on October 25 arrested Russia's richest man, oil baron Mikhail B. Khodorkovsky, and jailed him on charges of fraud and tax evasion. The arrest of the 40-year-old Mr. Khodorkovsky, heightens longstanding tensions between the government of Russian President Vladimir V. Putin and Russia's oligarchy, which grabbed cheap assets in rigged auctions after the collapse of the Soviet Union in 1991.

Many of the oligarchs fled Russia soon afterward, but Mr. Khodorkovsky remained. He has openly financed opposition parties for parliamentary elections scheduled for November, and for presidential elections expected in March.

Mr. Putin's heavy-handed move could spell disaster for foreign investment in Russia. Some analysts were predicting that the Russian stock market could drop 10 percent as a result, and that oil stocks would remain under pressure for months. The United States ambassador to Russia, Alexander Vershbow, said on Sunday that Mr. Khodorkovsky's areest "could negatively affect Russia's investment climate" and "raise new doubts among both foreign companies and potential investors."

Ironically, the Khodorkovsky arrest follows a year-long campaign by the Russian government to woo foreign investors into Russia's oil sector. For more than a year, the Russians have tried to portray themselves as a more stable supplier of oil than the Middle East, and the government and private companies both have shown a greater willingness to cooperate with foreigners.

China Sends a Man Into Space

China joined the U.S. and Russia as the only nations with space programs on October 15, 2003, when the spacecraft Shenzhou 5 took off from the Gobi Desert and landed in Mongolia 21 hours later after orbiting the earth 14 times. Astronaut Yang Liwei became a national hero overnight, and Chinese government officials trumpeted the accomplishment as an indication of China's technological savvy. In an attempt to instill good will and inspire nationalism in a citizenry that has come to regard the Communist Party as increasingly irrelevant, the government started talking about establishing a small space laboratory in future years, followed by missions to the Moon and to Mars.

"The successful launching of the Shenzhou 5 manned spacecraft is a glory for our great motherland," President Hu Jintao said in comments issued by the New China News Agency, "and it signifies that our country has scored an initial victory in this first effort at manned space flight. It also signifies the Chinese people have made another historically significant step forward in their progress toward conquering the summit of world science and technology."

Strife in Zimbabwe Takes Toll on Its Wildlife, Too

The economic decline of Zimbabwe, once one of Africa's most prosperous states, became so acute in October, 2003 that thousands of hungry families turned to the country's safari animals as a source of food. Conservationists estimate that as many as two-thirds of the animals on Zimbabwean game farms and wildlife conservancies have been wiped out. Hunting and tourism, which once brought in millions of foreign capital into Zimbabwe, slowed to a trickle.

The bleak outlook for Zimbabwe comes as a result of a five-year-old program to seize land from white owners and redistribute it. But the best farmland was given to cabinet ministers and other political supporters of Pres. Robert Mugabe, while the land given to thousands of peasants was too poor to support crops, forcing them to resort to poaching. In the last year, foreign investment disappeared. Just 1 in 10 workers now holds a steady job. In a nation that exported beef and wheat in 2000, four million people — one-third of the population —now subsist on foreign food donations. According to the U.N., 40 percent of Zimbabwe's children suffer from malnutrition.

"Zimbabwe was probably the best hunting land in Africa," said a former conservancy operator, who refused to be identified. "I suppose it's improved in some respects," he added, "Because there's nothing left to kill."

Pujols, Rodriguez Win Hank Aaron Awards
Major League Baseball named St. Louis's Albert Pujols (NL) and Texas's Alex Rodríguez (AL) as the winners of the 2003 Hank Aaron Awards, given annually to the best overall hitter in each league.

LATE-BREAKING OBITUARIES

Madame Chiang Kai-shek, 105, Chinese politician; one of the pivotal figures in the struggle between the Nationalists and the Communists during post-imperial China. She wielded immense influence in Nationalist China before she and her husband were forced by the Communist victory into exile in Taiwan, where she presided as the grande dame of Nationalist politics for years. Of old age, New York City, Oct. 23, 2003.

Hicks, Louise Day, 87, Boston public school official and City Council member prominent for her vocal opposition to the court-ordered busing that polarized the city in the 1960's. Of undisclosed causes, South Boston, Oct. 22, 2003.

The Nobel Prizes, 2003

CHEMISTRY

Peter Agre, 54, (U.S.), Johns Hopkins University, "for the discovery of water channels in cell membranes." **Roderick MacKinnon,** 47 (U.S.), Howard Hughes Medical Institute, Rockefeller University, New York, "for structural and mechanistic studies of ion channels." Their discoveries clarified how salts (ions) and water are transported out of and into the cells of the body, which consists of about 70% salt water. Their scholarship is of great importance to understanding of diseases of the kidneys, heart, muscles, and nervous system. This year's prize illustrates how contemporary biochemistry reaches down to the atomic level in its quest to understand the fundamental processes of life.

ECONOMIC SCIENCES

Robert F. Engle, 60, (U.S.) New York University, "for methods of analyzing economic time series with time-varying volatility (ARCH)" and **Clive W. J. Granger,** 69, U.K., University of California-San Diego, "for methods of analyzing economic time series with common trends (cointegration)." Engle's concept of autoregressive conditional heteroskedasticity (ARCH) allows researchers to compare data across different periods even if periodic fluctuations over time are not consistent. Granger's scholarship has become invaluable in analyzing systems where variations in the short run are influenced by large random disturbances or where long-run dynamics are restricted by economic equilibrium relationships. Examples include the relations between wealth and consumption, exchange rates and price levels, and short and long-term interest rates.

LITERATURE

J. M. Coetzee, 63, South Africa, "who in innumerable guises portrays the surprising involvement of the outsider." A fundamental theme of John Maxwell Coetzee's writing is the distinction between right and wrong, which while crystal clear, can be seen to serve no end. His novels have often focused on his South Africa's apartheid system, which in his view, could occur anywhere. In 1999, Coetzee became the first author to win the Booker Award twice; he won in 1983 for *The Life and Times of Michael K.* and in 1999 for *Disgrace.*

PEACE

Shirin Ebadi, 56, (Iran) "for her efforts for democracy and human rights," especially on the struggle for the rights of women and children. Ebadi, a Muslim woman, has worked to unify the notions of Islam and fundamental human rights. As a lawyer, judge, writer, and activist, she has spoken out strongly in Iran and far beyond its borders, without concern for threats to her personal safety. One of her strongest beliefs is that no society shall be labeled civilized unless it respects the basic rights of women and children.

PHYSICS

Alexei A. Abrikosov, 75, (U.S. and Russia) Argonne National Laboratory, Argonne, Illinois; **Vitaly L. Ginzburg,** 87, (Russia) former Head of the Theory Group at the P.N. Lebedev Physical Institute, Moscow; and **Anthony J. Leggett,** 65, (U.S. and U.K.), MacArthur Professor at the University of Illinois at Urbana-Champaign, "for pioneering contributions to the theory of superconductors and superfluids." Superconducting material is used in magnetic resonance imaging for medical examinations and particle accelerators. Knowledge about superfluid liquids can give us deeper insight into the ways in which matter behaves in its lowest and most ordered state.

PHYSIOLOGY OR MEDICINE

Paul C. Lauterbur, 74, (U.S.) University of Illinois-Urbana, and **Peter Mansfield,** 70, (U.K.) University of Nottingham, School of Physics and Astronomy, "for their discoveries concerning magnetic resonance imaging." MRI is now a routine method of medical diagnostics—more than 60 million MRIs are performed each year, replacing several much more invasive modes of examination. Lauterbur discovered the possibility of creating two-dimensional pictures by introducing gradients into the magnetic field. Mansfield showed how signals could be analysed mathematically, and how extremely fast imaging could be achieved.

Part I

THE ALMANAC OF THE YEAR

Chronology of the Year Nov. 1, 2002–Oct. 2003

NOVEMBER 2002

1 In a victory for Microsoft, a federal judge approves the company's antitrust settlement with the Justice Dept. and rejects nearly all of the tougher sanctions sought by a coalition of state attorneys general.

2 A new government in the Indian-governed portion of Kashmir is sworn in. The government is a coalition whose two largest parties are the Indian National Congress and the People's Democratic Party.

3 Using a missile fired by an unmanned Predator aircraft, the C.I.A. kills a senior leader of Al Qaeda and five low-level associates in Yemen.

By a sound margin, Turkish voters elect a new party led by a former Islamist who quickly emphasizes his support for a modern, secular Turkey committed to joining Europe and continuing strong relations with the U.S.

4 On the eve of Election Day, Pres. Bush campaigns in four battleground states for the House and Senate, imploring voters to send him "some allies" and vote Republican.

5 In mid-term elections, Republicans retain control of the House and recapture the Senate, with victories in North Carolina, South Carolina, New Hampshire and Tennessee.

Israeli Prime Minister Ariel Sharon calls for new elections eight months early after failing to form a new coalition government.

6 The U.S. presents the U.N. Security Council with its final proposal for a resolution on Iraq that gives the country a last chance to disarm through rigorous weapons inspections or face an American-led war.

7 Attorney General John Ashcroft approves Virginia as the site for the first trials of sniper suspects John Muhammad and John Malvo.

8 The U.N. Security Council unanimously adopts a resolution on Iraq that Pres. Bush calls a "final test" of Saddam Hussein's willingness to disarm.

9 Pres. Bush approves a final war plan for Iraq that would begin with an air campaign and follow with swift ground actions and strikes.

Dozens of tornadoes slice their way from Louisiana to Pennsylvania, carving up farmland and forests and nearly erasing whole communities in Alabama, Tennessee and Ohio, killing 36.

10 Arab governments voice collective support for new weapons inspections inside Iraq, but call for Arab experts to be included in the inspections.

11 Iraq is reported to have ordered large quantities of atropine, a drug that can be used to counter the effects of nerve gas, mainly from suppliers in Turkey.

12 Al Jazeera, the Arab satellite television network, broadcasts an audiotape it claims was recorded by Osama bin Laden in which he praises recent terrorist attacks in Moscow and Bali, and threatens further bloodshed over Iraq.

13 In a letter to the U.N., Iraqi officials reluctantly agree to weapons inspections and say that they will "deal with" the Security Council resolution obligating the country to disarm, yet express hostility towards the U.S. and repeatedly deny that Iraq possesses weapons of mass destruction.

14 Nancy Pelosi (D-Calif.) wins election as House Minority leader, becoming the first woman to head a party in Congress.

15 Hu Jintao is named chief of the Chinese Communist Party.

16 Senior government officials announce that the Bush administration has begun to monitor Iraqis in the U.S. in an effort to identify domestic terrorist threats posed by Hussein sympathizers.

17 Western and Indonesian officials reveal that the al Qaeda network is planning to strike at Western students at international schools in Jakarta.

18 A special federal appeals court rules that the Justice Dept. has broad new powers under the anti-terrorism bill enacted last year to use wiretaps obtained for intelligence operations to prosecute terrorists.

19 After months of debate, the Senate votes 90-9 to create the Department of Homeland Security, expected to employ 170,000.

A tanker carrying 20 million gallons of oil splits in two and sinks off the coast of Galicia in Northern Spain, threatening hundreds of miles of Spanish coastline.

20 At a NATO summit meeting in Prague, Bush vows that Saddam Hussein will face "the severest of consequences" if he does not fully disclose Iraq's inventory of weapons by Dec. 8, the deadline set by the U.N.

Scientists announce that they have created a vaccine that appears to prevent cervical cancer.

21 American officials report that a suspected senior leader of Al Qaeda described as chief of operations in the Persian Gulf has been captured.

22 A draft report by the joint Congressional committee on the Sept. 11 attacks concludes that the F.B.I. and C.I.A. did not aggressively pursue leads that might have linked the terrorists to Saudi Arabia.

The Bush administration announces that the E.P.A. will loosen its industrial air pollution rules.

23 The Justice Dept. plans to assign federal lawyers in counterintelligence to terrorism task forces in New York and Washington to help secure secret warrants against suspects.

24 Islamic militants attack a Hindu temple complex in Kashmir, killing at least 10 people and wounding more than 40.

25 Pres. Bush creates the Dept. of Homeland Security and names as its secretary Tom Ridge, the former Pennsylvania governor who has been the White House's domestic security coordinator.

26 Pres. Bush signs legislation requiring that the federal government pick up most of the insurance losses in the case of a catastrophic terrorist attack.

27 After a nearly four-year hiatus, U.N. arms inspectors begin a search for banned weapons programs in Iraq, checking three sites with no reported Iraqi resistance.

28 In coordinated assaults in the Kenyan city of Mombasa, terrorists fire shoulder-launched missiles at an Israeli passenger jet and three suicide bombers detonate explosives at the doors of an Israeli-owned hotel, killing 13.

30 The U.S. is installing a new command center at a heavily guarded base in Qatar that would serve as the main headquarters in the case of a war with Iraq.

DECEMBER

1 Arab leaders from countries neighboring Iraq indicate willingness to support an American military effort to remove Saddam Hussein from power. But to prevent public anger, they caution that any such campaign should be a part of a U.N. demand for disarmament, not a unilateral action.
2 U.S. intelligence officials say they have evidence linking al Qaeda to the terrorist attacks in Mombasa, Kenya, the week before.
3 Turkey says it won't allow the U.S. to station troops there in the event of an attack on Iraq.
4 A federal panel rejects United Airlines's plea for $1.8 billion in loan guarantees that would have helped the airline avoid filing for bankruptcy.
6 In a sign of impatience with the struggling economy, Pres. Bush dismisses two of his top economic advisors: Treasury Secretary Paul H. O'Neill, and National Economic Council Director Lawrence B. Lindsey.
8 Pres. Bush says he will choose John W. Snow, the chairman of the CSX Railroad Corp., to replace Paul H. O'Neill as Treasury Secretary.
9 United Airlines, the nation's second-largest carrier, becomes the biggest airline ever to seek bankruptcy protection from its creditors.
10 Pres. Bush chooses William H. Donaldson, the former chairman of the New York Stock Exchange, to head the S.E.C.
11 Pres. Bush announces plans to vaccinate more than a million military, health care, and emergency personnel against smallpox. The decision reflects the administration's belief that the dangers of a biological terrorist attack outweigh the risks of side effects presented by inoculation.
12 North Korea says it will reactivate a nuclear reactor it had shut down under a 1994 agreement.
13 Boston's Cardinal Bernard F. Law becomes the highest-ranking American prelate to lose his job because of a scandal. Over his 18 year-tenure, Law repeatedly allowed priests accused of sexual abuse to remain in the ministry. (see "Major News Stories of the Year.")
14 Pres. Bush unveils a list of terrorist leaders that he has authorized the C.I.A. to kill if capturing them proves impractical and civilian casualties can be minimized. The list includes Osama bin Laden and other Al Qaeda leaders.
16 Pres. Bush names former N.J. Gov. Thomas H. Kean to head the commission investigating the Sept. 11 attacks, after Henry Kissinger withdrew.
17 Pres. Bush orders the Pentagon to deliver an antimissile system within two years. A week earlier, the Pentagon's latest $100 million prototype missed its intended target by hundreds of miles.
19 The country's biggest brokerage firms agree to pay nearly $1 billion in fines, ending inquiries into whether they misled investors and gave favored clients special access to initial public offerings.
Roh Moo Hyun, who promised increased engagement with North Korea and greater autonomy from the U.S., is elected president of South Korea.
20 Trent Lott (R-Miss.) gives up his position as Senate Majority Leader, clearing the way for Bill Frist (R-Tenn.), the White House's choice. Lott failed to outrun a controversy he ignited two weeks earlier by praising Strom Thurmond's 1948 segregationist presidential candidacy.
23 North Korea reopens a plutonium reprocessing plant that had been sealed in 1994 by international weapons inspectors.
24 In an effort to improve relations with the U.S., China releases its most prominent political prisoner. Xu Wenli had spent 16 of the past 21 years in prison for his advocacy of civil liberties.
27 Suicide bombers kill at least 46 people at the headquarters of Chechnya's pro-Russian government in Grozny. It is the worst bombing in Chechnya in more than three years.
28 Leaders of the pilots' and flight attendants' unions agree to short-term wage cuts that will allow United Airlines to avoid bankruptcy.
Saudi Arabia says it will allow the U.S. to use its airspace and bases in the event of a U.S. attack on Iraq.
29 Kenyans overwhelmingly elect opposition leader Mwai Kibaki as their next president, repudiating 24 years of rule by Daniel arap Moi and the 39-year reign of Moi's KANU party, which had ruled Kenya since independence in 1963.
30 Tyco International admits that it used accounting tricks to inflate its earnings by nearly $400 million, and acknowledges that financial abuse at the company was not limited to its former chief executive Dennis L. Kozlowski.
31 The U.S. Army deploys more than 15,000 soldiers to Kuwait in the largest military buildup since the Persian Gulf War.
Nine northeastern states file a lawsuit against the government's new air pollution rules, claiming that they will roll back the Clean Air Act.

JANUARY 2003

1 Luis Inacio da Silva, leader of the left-wing Workers Party, takes office as Brazil's president, promising a crusade against hunger, corruption, and injustice. (see "Major News Stories of the Year.")
2 Pres. Bush announces his plan for sweeping, long-term changes to Medicare, including a prescription drug benefit for the elderly.
J.P. Morgan announces it will receive $580 million from insurers in a settlement of a dispute involving Morgan's handling of loans to Enron.
3 Pres. Bush proposes a $600 million tax cut over the next 10 years in an effort to stimulate the sagging economy.
5 Pres. Bush announces a plan to eliminate taxes on stock dividends altogether, costing the government more than $300 billion over 10 years.
6 The Republican Party chooses New York City as the site for its 2004 national convention for the first time ever.
9 North Korea says it is withdrawing from the Nuclear Nonproliferation Treaty, claiming self-defense because it is "most seriously threatened" by the U.S.
10 The Labor Department reports that the country lost more than 100,000 jobs in December, 2002, indicating a jobless recovery.
11 Illinois Gov. George Ryan commutes all 167 death sentences in the state to life in prison, citing fundamental questions of fairness in the Illinois capital punishment system.
The Pentagon deploys more than 60,000 troops to the Persian Gulf, bringing the total there to nearly 150,000, or enough to attack Iraq.
12 Stephen M. Case quits as chairman of AOL Time Warner. Case, who engineered AOL's takeover of the media giant, had been blamed for the company's sagging fortunes since then.
14 Seven former employees of the Datek online trading company agree to pay $70 million in fines for illegal trading and fraudulent bookkeeping during the stock market boom of the 1990s.
15 The White House estimates a budget deficit of $200 billion this fiscal year and $300 billion the next year. These figures do not include the cost of an attack on Iraq, estimated at $50 billion or more.

16 U.N. weapons inspectors find empty chemical warheads in southern Iraq.
18 Tens of thousands of demonstrators fill the mall in Washington, D.C., protesting the Bush administration's threats to attack Iraq.
19 U.S. officials reveal that Russian spies secretly placed nuclear detection devices inside North Korea during the 1990s to help the C.I.A. track North Korea's weapons program.
20 France warns the U.S., in unusually blunt terms, that an attack on Iraq is not justified, and that it will not support any U.N. resolution authorizing military action there.

In a reversal, Turkey says it will permit American troops to use Turkish bases for an attack on Iraq.
21 Pres. Bush says Iraq is not complying with demands that it disarm, and expresses frustration with France and other nations calling for more time and diplomacy, rather than a rush to war.
22 The White House says it will allow religious groups to use federal funds to construct buildings where religious services are held, if some part of the building is used for social programs.
24 The Pension Guaranty Benefit Corporation, the agency that insures the pensions of more than 40 million Americans, admits that it has squandered its entire $8 billion surplus in one year.
25 Ivory Coast President Laurent Gbagbo agrees to a peace plan ending the country's four-month-long civil war, and appoints a new prime minister to lead a reconciliation government. (see "Major News Stories of the Year.")
26 Sec. of State Colin Powell says the U.S. will go to war alone in Iraq, even as weapons inspectors claim they need more time before making an evaluation of Iraq's chemical and nuclear arsenals.
27 Hans Blix, one of the chief U.N. weapons inspectors, sharply criticizes Iraq's failure to cooperate with inspections
28 In his State of the Union address, Pres. Bush pledges to disarm Iraq and also rebuild the U.S. economy. He contends that U.S. intelligence shows Iraq aiding and protecting terrorists.

Israel's Prime Minister Ariel Sharon and his conservative Likud Party overwhelmingly defeat the Labor party in parliamentary elections, indicating voters' preference for a hawkish response to renewed conflict with Palestinians.
29 Ted Turner steps down as vice chairman of AOL Time Warner in the wake of an announcement that the company was writing down its value by $45 billion.
30 Pres. Bush says Iraq has "weeks, not months" to disarm or face an invasion.

American spy satellites over North Korea produce photos apparently showing trucks moving 8,000 nuclear fuel rods out of storage and into position to create a half dozen nuclear weapons.
31 The Bush administration proposes fundamental changes to Medicaid that would give the states greater control over how to administer benefits to millions of recipients.

FEBRUARY

1 The space shuttle Columbia breaks up over Texas upon re-entry , killing all seven aboard. (see "Major News Stories of the Year.")

Opposition leaders in Venezuela agree to scale back the 62-day-long general strike that was intended to force the resignation of Pres. Hugo Chavez, but has instead crippled businesses.
2 German voters show their dissatisfaction with Chancellor Gerhard Schröder by giving the main opposition parties big gains in state elections.
3 Pres. Bush submits to Congress a $2.23 trillion budget that includes tax cuts for the wealthy, increases in spending on defense and NASA, and more than $300 billion in deficits over each of the next two years. It does not, however, include the cost of war with Iraq.
4 Pres. Bush says the U.S. will continue to support manned exploration of space, the space shuttle Columbia disaster notwithstanding.
5 The U.S. economy falls into its worst hiring slump in nearly 20 years; business leaders see no end to the decline in employment.
6 NASA agrees to transfer authority for the investigation of the Columbia disaster to an independent review board. The space agency now says it had not ruled out a broken off piece of foam as a culprit in the explosion.
7 The leaders of France and China refuse to support Pres. Bush's call for a U.N. resolution of war against Iraq, saying they want weapons inspections to continue.

Pres. Bush places the nation on "high" terror alert, claiming that Al Qaeda is planning attacks on U.S. targets. Homeland Security Secretary Tom Ridge causes panic by advising Americans to buy duct tape to seal up their houses.

Hamas leader Sheik Ahmed Yassin urges Muslims worldwide to retaliate against "Western interests" if the U.S. attacks Iraq.
8 Defense Sec. Donald Rumsfeld goes to Munich to challenge the U.N. and NATO to join the U.S. in its plans to disarm Iraq through military action; thousands protest his appearance.

Saudi Arabian leaders announce a long-range plan to introduce democratic reforms, limit the clergy's power, and disengage militarily from the U.S.
10 France, Germany, and Belgium join forces with Russia to oppose a NATO effort to begin military planning for a strike against Iraq and the defense of Turkey. Turkey takes the unusual step of invoking a clause of the NATO treaty that requires the entire organization to consult when any member feels its security threatened.
11 Federal Reserve Chairman Alan Greenspan criticizes Pres. Bush's budget, saying the economy does not need tax cuts, and that the deficits could multiply rapidly.
12 State and local governments say they are still unprepared to deal with a terrorist attack because Washington has not distributed more than $3.5 billion in federal anti-terrorism aid promised shortly after the Sept. 11 attacks.
13 Despite the Bush administration's vigorous campaign for attacking Iraq, 59 percent of Americans believe the president should give U.N. weapons inspectors more time.
14 At the U.N., French Foreign Minister Dominique de Villepin tells U.S. Sec. of State Colin Powell that weapons inspections had not failed, and there was no cause for war yet.
15 Millions of demonstrators in dozens of cities around the world take to the streets to protest the Bush administration's plans to invade Iraq.
16 NATO agrees to bolster Turkey in the event of an American war on Iraq, ending a dispute that had pitted the U.S. against France and Germany.
17 London begins imposing $8 fees for driving cars into the city in an effort to fight gridlock.
18 Pres. Bush likens anti-war protests by millions around the world to a focus group. He says the rallies will not dissuade him from attacking Iraq.
20 A fire rips through a crowded Rhode Island nightclub, killing 100 people, after the band performing set off fireworks on the stage.

22 International weapons inspectors report that Iran has built facilities for enriching uranium, a major step toward developing nuclear weapons.
24 Flaunting its lack of concern about international opinion, North Korea test fires a missile for the first time in three years.
25 A panel of 17 experts convened by the National Academy of Sciences strongly faults Pres. Bush's proposal for studying the risks of global warming, saying it "lacks most of the elements of a strategic plan," especially funding.
27 Daniel Libeskind's design for reconstructing the World Trade Center is chosen from the competition's seven finalists. (See "Major News Stories of the Year.")
28 A Federal Appeals Court in California affirms a decision banning the forced recitation of the Pledge of Allegiance because of its inclusion of the words "under God."

MARCH

1 Authorities in Pakistan capture Khalid Shaikh Mohammed, the Al Qaeda terrorist suspected of masterminding the Sept. 11, 2001 attacks.

Turkey's Parliament votes to refuse to allow U.S. troops to use the country as a base for the U.S.'s planned attack on Iraq. U.S. officials pressure the defense minister to lobby his parliament for a second vote.
2 Tens of thousands of Pakistanis protest the impending war with Iraq, and urge their president not to accede to the U.S.
3 North Korean fighter jets intercept an American spy plane over the East Sea. Though no shots are fired, the incident raises fears of an escalation of tensions between the two nations.
4 The House Budget Committee revises its estimates of the cost of Pres. Bush's tax-cutting proposals, saying they will cause the deficit to grow by an additional 15 percent, or $30 billion, pushing the total shortfall to nearly $400 billion.
5 Russia and France make clear that they will use their veto power to prevent a U.N. Security Council resolution authorizing an attack on Iraq.
6 Air Force Sec. James Roche says the Air Force has investigated 54 reports of sexual assault or rape over the past 10 years.

Pres. Bush holds a rare prime-time news conference to insist that Saddam Hussein poses a security risk to America. He says "we really don't need anybody's permission to defend the U.S."
7 The Labor Department reports that 308,000 jobs were lost in February, the worst decline in employment since Sept. 11.
8 The C.I.A. warns that terrorists in Iraq are planning attacks against U.S. and allied forces within the country after the likely U.S. invasion.

P.L.O. leader Yasir Arafat nominates his deputy Mahmoud Abbas, a critic of the Palestinian uprising, to the new post of Palestinian prime minister.
10 The Bush administration announces changes that will give the Occupational Health and Safety Administration authority to punish companies that consistently violate workplace safety rules.
11 Bob Ney (R-Ohio) orders House of Representatives dining rooms to change the name of French fries to "freedom fries" to express his displeasure with France's refusal to support U.S. plans to invade Iraq.
12 Elizabeth Smart, a 15-year-old girl kidnapped from her Utah bedroom nine months earlier, is found alive and returned to her family.

Serbian prime minister Zoran Djindjic is assassinated by a sniper believed to be a member of an organized crime syndicate whose leader Mr. Djindjic was planning to arrest for war crimes.
13 China reveals plans to send its first astronauts into space on its Shenzhou spacecraft.
14 NASA announces that space shuttle flights will resume as early as fall 2003.
15 The World Health Organization takes the unusual step of warning of a "worldwide health threat" against SARS. (See "Major News Stories of the Year.")
16 China appoints Wen Jiabao prime minister, succeeding Zhu Rongji, and completing a transition of power that began in the fall of 2002.
17 Pres. Bush issues an ultimatum to Saddam Hussein, giving the Iraqi leader 48 hours to go into exile or face an invasion by U.S.-led forces. U.S. stocks rally more than three percent on the news.
18 Saddam Hussein rejects Pres. Bush's ultimatum. Thousands flee Baghdad for the relative safety of Kurdish-controlled areas in the north.
19 Pres. Bush orders the invasion of Iraq. Missiles begin raining on Baghdad, but apparently fail to kill Saddam Hussein, who makes a televised address hours later, urging Iraqis to "draw your swords" against invaders. (see "Major News Stories of the Year.")

The Senate defeats the Bush administration's plan to drill for oil in Alaska's Arctic National Wildlife Refuge.
20 U.S. air strikes continue to pound Baghdad, bringing the first casualties of the war. U.S.-led forces encounter little resistance.
21 U.S. forces devastate parts of Baghdad as thousands of troops sweep into South Iraq.

An Illinois judge orders Philip Morris to pay $10.1 billion in damages for defrauding consumers into believing that its "light" cigarettes were less dangerous than full-tar cigarettes.
22 U.S. and British ground troops reach the outskirts of Basra, the largest city in southern Iraq. Millions of protesters rally in the streets of New York and other cities to protest the U.S. invasion.
23 U.S. forces in Iraq suffer their heaviest casualties yet, as two dozen soldiers are missing or killed by Iraqi ambushes.
24 Pres. Bush asks Congress for $75 billion to pay for the war in Iraq. The sum will cover expenses only through the end of fiscal year (Sept. 30) and does not include any money for reconstruction.
25 The Senate narrowly votes to cut Pres. Bush's tax plan in half, from $726 billion to $350 billion.

The Air Force Academy replaces its top four officers in the wake of a rape and sexual abuse scandal there.
26 One thousand American paratroopers land in Kurdish-held Northern Iraq, opening a second front in the U.S.-led invasion of Iraq.
27 Richard N. Perle resigns as chairman of a Pentagon advisory board amid conflict of interest charges stemming from his relationship with a private defense contractor. He does not, however, resign from the board itself.
28 Serbian police say they have found the body of former Pres. Ivan Stambolic; they say he had been executed by the special police just before the ouster of his former ally Slobodan Milosevic.
29 The director of the Centers for Disease Control warns of the potential for SARS, to infect "large numbers of people." (See "Major News Stories of the Year.")
30 Defense Sec. Donald Rumsfeld defends the progress of the invasion of Iraq. He insists that he and his commanders had not underestimated the number of ground troops needed.

31 Army field commanders question the management of Defense Sec. Donald Rumsfeld. "He wanted to fight this war on the cheap," says one.

APRIL

1 U.S. forces advance on the "red zone" around Baghdad defended by Iraq's Republican Guard.

Prosecutors in Tulia, Texas admit that they had made a disastrous mistake in convicting 38 people, most of them black, on the basis of uncorroborated testimony of one undercover officer.

2 U.S. Army and Marine forces close to within 20 miles of Baghdad after destroying two divisions of the Iraqi Republican Guard.

3 Millions of Spaniards take to the streets to condemn Prime Minister Jose Maria Aznar for his support of George W. Bush.

4 U.S. troops encircle Baghdad, isolating the capital in preparation of taking control of the city.

5 U.S. tanks roll into Baghdad, taking its defenders by surprise.

6 Additional U.S. divisions enter Baghdad and begin a push into Basra.

SARS becomes an international epidemic, with 2,416 cases worldwide, causing 89 deaths, according to the World Health Organization.

7 U.S. Air Force bombers drop four 2,000-pound bombs on a Baghdad neighborhood in an attempt to kill Saddam Hussein and his sons.

The U.S. Supreme Court says states may ban cross-burning if prosecutors can prove that it is meant to intimidate.

8 U.S. forces tighten the noose around Baghdad, taking parts of the city in street-to-street fighting.

9 Hoping to remind people of the toppling of Lenin's statue in Russia, American marines pull down a statue of Saddam Hussein in Baghdad.

10 Kurdish fighters take control of Kirkuk, Northern Iraq's oil capital, alarming Turkish officials, who oppose the idea of a separate Kurdish state.

11 Mayhem replaces warfare in Baghdad. Looting, angry mobs, and assassinations grip the city.

12 Congress approves $79 billion to pay for the war in Iraq.

13 Canadian scientists say they have broken the genetic code of the SARS virus.

14 The Pentagon says major combat operations are ended in Iraq after U.S. forces take control of Tikrit, the last remaining Iraqi stronghold.

15 Jay Garner, a retired general, is chosen to oversee the U.S.-led reconstruction of Iraq.

16 Pres. Bush calls on the U.N. to lift 12 years of economic sanctions against Iraq now that the regime of Saddam Hussein is ended.

17 The Bush administration awards the first major Iraq reconstruction contract to the Bechtel Group in a deal worth $680 million.

Ontario takes the extraordinary step of asking anyone who has even one symptom of SARS to stay home for a few days in hopes of preventing an outbreak over the Easter holiday weekend.

18 Shiite and Sunni Muslims join together to protest both the United States and Saddam Hussein. Ahmad Chalabi, an Iraqi exile backed by the Pentagon, emerges from well-guarded seclusion to stake his claim on the country's future.

India's Prime Minister Atal Bihari Vajpayee reaches out to Pakistan, addressing a public rally in Kashmir, a territory claimed by both countries.

20 The U.S. lowers its profile in Iraq, pulling out Marines and replacing them with Army forces.

China admits that the number of SARS cases is much higher than previously reported. Beijing says 339 cases are confirmed and another 402 are suspected.

21 Hundreds of thousands of Shiite pilgrims travel to the holy city of Karbala to partake in rituals that had been banned under Saddam Hussein.

22 Pres. Bush gives Federal Reserve Chairman Alan Greenspan a vote of confidence, effectively giving Greenspan the decision about whether to accept a fifth term as head of the central bank.

Nigerian Pres. Olusegun Obasanjo wins re-election in a vote that international observers call corrupt and opposition parties call "frivolous."

The record industry files copyright infringement lawsuits against four college students who operated Web sites that enable file-sharing.

23 The W.H.O. adds Toronto to its list of places that travelers should avoid because of SARS.

The U.S. warns Iran not to interfere with its efforts to build an "Islamic democracy" in Iraq.

24 North Korea announces that it has nuclear weapons and has begun making weapons-grade plutonium. (See "Major News Stories of the Year.")

Iraq's Deputy Prime Minister Tariq Aziz surrenders to American forces in Baghdad.

25 Beijing issues a quarantine for more than 4,000 residents in fear of SARS.

26 Pres. Bush triples the size of the team searching for Iraq's elusive weapons of mass destruction.

27 Sinn Fein president Gerry Adams says the Irish Republican Army will fully disarm as long as the other parties to the Northern Ireland peace accord fulfill their obligations.

28 The nation's 10 largest investment banks sign a $1.4 billion agreement with the S.E.C. intended to end conflicts of interest between their banking and analysis divisions. (See "Major News Stories of the Year.")

29 The U.S. announces it will withdraw all combat forces from Saudi Arabia by midsummer, ending a decade of military operations there.

MAY

1 George W. Bush flies onto the deck of the U.S.S. *Abraham Lincoln* to declare the end to major combat operations in Iraq.

2 The Labor Dept. reports that the unemployment rate rose from 5.8 to 6 percent in March, equaling an eight-year high.

William J. Bennett, a moral crusader, reveals that he has lost more than $8 million gambling.

Indian Prime Minister Atal Bihari Vajpayee restores diplomatic and air links with Pakistan.

4 Pres. Bush attempts to round up international support for preventing North Korea from exporting nuclear material.

5 An official at Iraq's central bank says Saddam Hussein's son Qusay walked off with nearly $1 billion in cash in the hours before American bombs started falling on Baghdad.

6 Pres. Bush appoints retired diplomat L. Paul Bremer to succeed Lt. Gen Jay Garner as the official in charge of rebuilding Iraq. The move indicates a shift of emphasis toward civilian rule.

7 The Bush administration asks the International Atomic Energy Agency to declare that Iran has violated the Nuclear Nonproliferation Treaty, which could lead to U.N. economic sanctions.

8 The U.S., Britain, and Spain ask the U.N. to endorse American and British control of Iraq's political and economic development for at a year.

10 *The New York Times* reveals that Jayson Blair, a writer who recently resigned, had committed frequent acts of plagiarism and fabrication while covering news events.

12 Seven Americans and 14 others are killed in four separate truck bombings in Saudi Arabia.
13 France says it will respond to a U.N. call for troops to end the fighting in Congo.
14 Federal officials begin a criminal investigation of McWane Inc. Since 1995, the company has suffered more than 4,600 worker injuries and has been cited for more than 800 safety and environmental violations.
15 The Senate passes a $350 billion tax cut plan that would reduce and ultimately eliminate taxes on stock dividends before restoring them in 2007.
16 A federally financed study of 76,000 students nationwide shows that drug testing in schools does not deter drug use among teenagers.
17 The Moroccan government says that five suicide bombings in Casablanca the night before are the work of an organization with ties to Al Qaeda.
18 Palestinian suicide attacks kill nine bystanders in Jerusalem, causing Prime Minister Ariel Sharon to repudiate the mideast road map.
19 MCI, formerly Worldcom, agrees to pay a $500 million fine to settle S.E.C. fraud accusations. The money will ultimately be given to investors.

White House spoeksman Ari Fleischer announces his resignation.
20 A case of mad cow disease in Canada prompts the U.S. to ban imports of Canadian beef.
21 Christie Todd Whitman, who was constantly at odds with the Bush administration, resigns as administrator of the E.P.A.

A devastating earthquake rumbles through Algeria, causing more than 2,000 deaths and injuring over 8,000 people.
22 Archaeologists say looters in Iraq are walking off with countless urns, statues, vases, and other artifacts dating as far back as 3,000 years, to the ancient civilizations of Babylon and Sumer.
23 Scientists in Hong Kong identify SARS in three animal species, causing speculation that the disease may have come from a non-human species, and making it more difficult to contain.
24 Nestor Kirchner takes office as Argentina's sixth president in the last 18 months.
26 The U.N. pleads for troops and financial aid to restore some semblance of order in Congo, where a four-year war has killed more than three million.
27 The Supreme Court rules (6-3) that workers can sue states for violating their federally guaranteed right to take time off for family emergencies.
28 A last-minute revision in the Pres. Bush's tax cut prevents millions of minimum-wage families from receiving a promised $400 child credit. Pres. Bush signs the bill into law anyway.
29 Microsoft agrees to pay AOL Time Warner $750 million to end a long-running Internet browser war. The deal will make it easier for AOL users to work with Microsoft's Explorer browser.
30 U.S. and Philippine officials say Mindanao has become a major training center for Al Qaeda affiliates in southeast Asia.
31 Robert Eric Rudolph, suspected of the 1996 bombing at the Atlanta Olympic Games as well as attacks on three abortion clinics, is captured in Murphy, N.C. (see "Major News Stories of the Year.")

Burmese opposition leader Daw Aung San Suu Kyi and 19 members of her party are taken into custody after a clash between pro-democracy and the military government's forces left four people dead and 50 injured.

JUNE

1 The National Drought Mitigation Center reports that 11 Western states are experiencing extreme or exceptional drought conditions. The governors of Arizona and Utah declare emergency drought areas in order to seek federal aid.
2 An internal Justice Dept. report criticizes the F.B.I.'s roundup of illegal immigrants after the Sept. 11 attacks. Many people with no connection to terrorism were left to languish in jail for months in unduly harsh conditions.
3 In the government's first major terrorism trial since Sept. 11, two Arab immigrants are convicted and two are cleared of federal charges that they conspired to attack American airports, military installations, and targets like Disneyland.
4 Style maven Martha Stewart is indicted on charges of conspiracy, obstruction of justice, and securities fraud in connection with insider trading of ImClone Systems stock in 2001.
5 Howell Raines and Gerald Boyd, two top editors of *The New York Times*, resign after five weeks of turmoil at the newspaper, sparked by the Jayson Blair plagiarism scandal.

Attorney General John Ashcroft urges Congress to grant law enforcement officials even greater powers to pursue terrorism suspects.
6 The U.S. unemployment rate rises to 6.1 percent, its highest level in nine years.
7 Idaho Senator Larry Craig blocks the promotions of 850 Air Force officers, including pilots who fought in Iraq, in order to obtain four cargo planes for the Idaho Air National Guard.

Polish voters overwhelmingly approve entry into the European Union.
8 In an attempt to derail the peace process, Palestinian gunmen from Hamas, Islamic Jihad and the Al Aksa Martyrs Brigade attack an Israeli army outpost, killing four soldiers.
9 Mortgage giant Freddie Mac fires its president, David Glenn, charging that he failed to cooperate with an internal investigation into its accounting practices.
10 An Israeli attack in Gaza, designed to kill a Hamas leader, draws an unusually stern rebuke from the Bush administration, which fears the cycle of violence will undermine the peace process.
11 A Palestinian suicide bomber blows up a bus in Jerusalem, killing 16. Hamas claims responsibility.
12 The Guidant Corp. pleads guilty to 10 felony counts, admitting that it lied to the government and hid thousands of serious health problems, including 12 deaths, caused by one of its devices.
13 Huge antigovernment riots continue for a fourth day in Iran, with protesters calling for more social, economic and political freedom.
14 Thousands of U.S. troops carry out extensive raids across Iraq, arresting dozens of Baath Party members loyal to Saddam Hussein.
16 Twelve Texas inmates are released on bond after an investigation of a fraudulent drug sweep in 1999 that led to the conviction of 38 people, most of them black. The convictions rested on the testimony of one racist undercover agent.
17 A federal appeals court rules that the Justice Dept. was within its rights to withhold the names of more than 700 people arrested on immigration violations in connection with the Sept. 11 attacks.
18 A former agency official releases edited drafts of an E.P.A. report that shows the White House removed data on global warming.

Thomas O'Brien, Bishop of the Phoenix Diocese, resigns in the wake of a sexual abuse scandal and his own arrest in a fatal hit-and-run accident.

U.S. forces in Iraq capture Abd Hamid Mahmoud al-Tikrit, one of Saddam Hussein's closest aides, who was fourth on their most-wanted list.

19 Federal law enforcement officials announce that they have uncovered a plot by al Qaeda to destroy the Brooklyn Bridge.
20 Defense Dept. officials report that a captured aide to Saddam Hussein has told interrogators that the Iraqi dictator fled to Syria.
21 In Congo, the commander of a French-led emergency force gives tribal fighters besieging the town of Bunia 72 hours to withdraw or disarm.
23 The Supreme Court (5-4) backs affirmative action in a case involving admissions at the University of Michigan. In a separate decision, the court upholds a federal law requiring public libraries to install Internet pornography filters on their computers (see "Major News Stories of the Year.")
24 The World Health Organization announces that China has effectively controlled SARS. (See "Major News Stories of the Year.")
26 The Supreme Court votes 6-3 to overrule a Texas sodomy law, legalizing gay sexual conduct.

The National Governors Association reports that 46 states remain locked in budget disputes despite record tax increases and service cuts.
28 In the disputed territory of Kashmir, two suspected terrorists kill 12 Indian soldiers and wound seven during a visit to the region by Indian President A.P.J. Abdul Kalam.
29 Israeli troops withdraw from portions of the Gaza Strip, returning the areas to Palestinian control after the three leading Palestinian militant factions declare a suspension of violence.

JULY

1 Half a million demonstrators in Hong Kong demand the protection of civil liberties, protesting government plans to impose stringent internal-security laws demanded by China.
2 The European Parliament approves legislation to require strict labels for food and feed made with genetically modified ingredients.
3 The U.S. unemployment rate rises to 6.4 percent, the highest level in nine years, as the economy shed 30,000 jobs in June.
4 Suspected Islamic militants attack a mosque in Quetta, Pakistan, killing 47 Shiite Muslims and wounding 65 others.
5 A bomb explodes at a graduation ceremony for the first American-trained class of Iraqi police officers, killing seven police recruits.
7 The White House acknowledges for the first time that Pres. Bush relied on less-than-accurate intelligence when he declared that Saddam Hussein tried to purchase uranium from Africa.
8 The federal commission investigating the Sept. 11 attacks says that its work is hampered by intransigence by executive branch agencies, notably the Pentagon and the Justice Dept.

Pres. Bush begins a tour of Africa with a pledge to work closely with African nations to help them build a peaceful and prosperous future. But he will not commit to sending U.S. peacekeeping troops to Liberia.
9 In Senate hearings, Gen. Tommy Franks says that it is unlikely that U.S. troop levels in Iraq will be reduced "for the foreseeable future."
10 Indonesian police arrest nine suspected Jemaah Islaniyah militants linked to the 2002 bombing of a Bali nightclub that killed more than 200 people.
12 A group of Iraqi political parties and former exiles reach agreement on a list of 25 Iraqis to comprise a new governing council.
13 Iraq's new governing council convenes. In its first act, the Council abolishes six national holidays that had been celebrated under Saddam Hussein, and declares a new national day.
14 North Korea tells the Bush administration it has finished making enough plutonium to build six nuclear bombs.
15 The White House projects a $455 billion budget deficit for 2003, the largest in U.S. history.
16 The commander of Allied forces in Iraq, Gen. John Abizaid, cautions that U.S. troops may need to spend yearlong tours there, double the normal duration of Army forces on peacekeeping duty.
17 Congo's main rebel leaders are sworn in as vice presidents in a power-sharing government intended to end the nation's five-year civil war.
18 L.A. Lakers star Kobe Bryant is charged with sexually assaulting a 19-year-old woman at a resort in Colorado. Bryant admits to having sex with the woman but insists that it was consensual.

David Kelly, a British arms expert at the center of a dispute over whether the British government hyped intelligence reports on Iraq's weapons programs, is found dead in an apparent suicide.
19 U.S. and Asian intelligence officials reveal evidence that North Korea has built a second, secret plant for producing weapons-grade plutonium.
20 A report by internal investigators at the Justice Dept. cites dozens of cases in which department employees have been accused of civil rights violations involving enforcement of the Patriot Act.
21 As U.S. Marines arrive in Monrovia to protect the U.S. embassy and evacuate foreigners from the besieged capital, enraged Liberians lay the mutilated bodies of loved ones by the embassy gate and plead for U.S. assistance.
22 U.S. troops find and kill Saddam Hussein's two eldest sons in a fierce firefight. Uday and Qusay Hussein were notorious for torture.
23 In a stunning rebuke to the F.C.C., the House votes 400-21 to block a new rule that would allow the nation's largest television networks to own more local stations.
24 A joint Congressional report castigates the F.B.I. and C.I.A. for failing to heed and share warnings before the Sept. 11 attacks. The Bush administration deletes as classified information 28 pages about the role of Saudi Arabia, which, according to those who have seen it, details millions of dollars that the Saudis funneled to organizations that may have financed the terrorist attacks.
26 Federal prosecutors open an investigation into charges that MCI, the nation's second-largest long-distance carrier, defrauded other telephone companies of hundreds of millions of dollars over nearly a decade by disguising long-distance calls as local calls to avoid paying special access tariffs to local carriers across the country.
27 At least 40 retired Argentine military officials accused of human rights violations during the 1976-1983 dictatorship are in custody in Argentina to face trial in Europe after Argentina's new government moves to strip them of their immunity from extradition.
28 J.P. Morgan Chase and Citigroup, the two largest banks in the nation, agree to pay $300 million in fines to settle accusations that they aided Enron in misrepresenting its true financial condition for years before the company collapsed.
29 Pres. Bush refuses to declassify the 28-page section of a Congressional report on the Sept. 11 attacks that centers on accusations about Saudi Arabia's role in financing the hijackings.
30 In his first full news conference in five months, Pres. Bush rejects criticism that he exaggerated the urgency of going to war with Iraq.

The A.C.L.U. and six Muslim groups file the first constitutional challenge to the USA Patriot Act, arguing that the law gives federal agents virtually unchecked authority to spy on Americans.
31 John Poindexter resigns from the Defense Dept. after an outcry over his plan for a terrorism futures-trading market, which would have rewarded investors who forecast terrorist attacks, assassinations and coups.

AUGUST

1 The Labor Dept. announces that the U.S. economy shed 44,000 jobs in July.
4 West African peacekeeping troops arrive in Liberia, seeking to quell months of heavy fighting in the country's bloody civil war.
5 Episcopal leaders approve the election of the denomination's first openly gay bishop.
6 Arnold Schwarzenegger shakes up the California recall election by announcing he will run for governor.
7 A car bomb explodes outside the Jordanian embassy in Baghdad, killing 11 people.

Lt. Gov. Cruz Bustamante enters the California recall election, presenting himself as a Democratic back-up choice should the recall succeed.
8 Pentagon officials refuse U.N. pleas to expand the number of U.S. peacekeeping troops in Liberia.
9 Ending years of legal challenges from environmental groups, the U.S. Army begins incinerating the first of millions of pounds of U.S. stores of chemical weapons in Alabama.
10 Iraqis riot for the second consecutive day in Basra over fuel shortages.
11 Charles Taylor resigns as president of Liberia and enters exile in Nigeria, raising hopes for peace after 14 years of civil war. (See "Major News Stories of the Year.")
13 The Bush administration rejects the idea of giving the U.N. an expanded role in the occupation of Iraq.

California officials certify the final ballot for the gubernatorial recall election, listing 135 candidates. The list includes actors, comedians, activists, and a porn star.
14 The largest power blackout in American history hits eight Northeastern states and parts of Canada as a surge of electricity takes out the region's aging power grid. The blackout strands thousands of travelers, halts commerce, and causes major disruptions. (See "Major News Stories of the Year.")
15 Power is gradually restored to New York and other major Northeastern cities.
16 Electricity returns to Detroit, the last major metropolitan area to recover from the blackout.
17 In one turbulent day in Iraq, guerillas blow up a major pipeline supplying water to Baghdad, set fires along an oil pipeline, and launch a mortar attack on a prison that leaves six Iraqis dead and 59 wounded.
18 Republican lawmakers and the White House dismiss calls for a separate bill to upgrade the nation's electrical grid, preferring to combine the measure with a broader and more controversial energy bill.

France's director general for health resigns after the country's death toll from a major heat wave reaches over 5,000. French prime minister Jean-Pierre Raffarin blames the crisis on the failure of French families to care for their elderly relatives.
19 In the deadliest attack on a U.N. installation in the organization's history, a massive truck bomb demolishes U.N. headquarters in Baghdad, killing 17 people (including Sergio de Mello, the secretary general's special representative in Iraq) and wounding at least 100, most of them aid workers.
21 Israeli forces kill a top Hamas leader in Gaza. In response, Hamas and Islamic Jihad formally abandon their cease-fire with Israel.
22 Experts race to stop the SoBig computer virus, which wreaks havoc on PCs and corporate computer systems. The cyber attack follows the spread of the Blaster worm, which infected computer systems worldwide.

Federal mortgage giant Freddie Mac agrees to remove its C.E.O. as regulators probe his involvement in a major accounting scandal.
23 John Geoghan, the former Catholic priest who was convicted in 1998 of sexual abuse, is murdered by a fellow inmate in a Massachusetts prison.
24 An Israeli air strike in Gaza City kills four members of the Palestinian group Hamas.
25 Twin car-bomb blasts in Bombay kill 52 people and wound at least 135.
26 Contradicting optimistic projections by the White House, the Congressional Budget Office warns that the annual deficit will likely hit $480 billion in 2004, and could push the overall national debt to $5.8 trillion by 2013.

An International Atomic Energy Association report states that inspectors have found traces of enriched uranium at a facility in Iran, raising the possibility that Tehran has already produced weapons-grade nuclear materials.

The death toll of 139 American troops in Iraq since Pres. Bush declared victory on May 1 surpasses the G.I. death toll incurred during the war.
27 Over the protests of environmental groups, the Bush administration relaxes clear-air rules, allowing older industrial plants to make upgrades without installing pollution controls.
28 Gen. John Abizaid, the top American commander in Iraq, insists that no more U.S. troops are needed, while urging Muslim countries like Pakistan and Turkey to send peacekeeping forces.

A government-appointed truth commission issues a report stating that more than 69,000 people were killed in Peru during two decades of civil unrest between 1980 and 2000—more than twice previous estimates.

North Korea warns that it may soon test an atomic bomb to prove that it has become a nuclear power.
29 A powerful car bomb explodes outside the holiest Shiite shrine in Iraq, killing 95 people.

The French Ministry of Health announces that the country's death toll from an August heat wave has topped 11,000.
30 North Korea announces that it sees no purpose in continuing nuclear talks and has no choice but to strengthen its nuclear deterrent.
31 U.S. officials acknowledge that the Taliban is regrouping and attacking in their former stronghold of southern and eastern Afghanistan.

SEPTEMBER

1 Pres. Bush defends his tax cuts and asserts that they have prevented the economic downturn from becoming worse.

The Iraqi Governing Council appoints a 25-member cabinet to begin taking over day-to-day control of the government.
2 The Bush administration relaxes rules requiring hospitals to treat patients in need of emergency care, regardless of their ability to pay.

3 A federal appeals court blocks the F.C.C. from enacting widely opposed rules that would make it easier for the nation's largest media conglomerates to add new markets and new businesses.

State Senator John Whitmire returns to Texas, ending a month-long stalemate caused when Democrats fled to New Mexico to deny Republicans a quorum to vote on redistricting Texas's U.S. Congressional districts, which had already been redrawn just two years earlier.

4 Miguel Estrada, nominated by Pres. Bush to a federal appeals court post, withdraws his name after his appointment was blocked by a Democratic filibuster in the Senate.

5 The Labor Dept. announces that the U.S. economy lost 93,000 jobs in August.

6 Palestinian Prime Minister Mahmoud Abbas resigns, dealing a major blow to the prospects for peace in the Mideast.

7 Pres. Bush addresses the nation, requesting $87 billion in emergency spending for the reconstruction of Iraq and Afghanistan. The figure comes on top of $79 billion already spent, taking Congress by surprise.

8 The recording industry files 261 lawsuits against people it accused of sharing copyrighted music over the Internet. Industry officials had delayed such action for fear of alienating consumers, but felt they had to take action to stem the widespread practice of file-swapping, which has significantly cut into music sales.

A funeral is held in Brooklyn for the last New York firefighter killed at the World Trade Center.

9 The Archdiocese of Boston agrees to pay $85 million to settle some 550 lawsuits by victims who were sexually abused by priests.

Senior Pentagon officials testify at Congressional hearings, stating that U.S. forces are straining to meet their missions in Iraq. The Army announces that their tours of duty for 20,000 Army Reserve and National Guard troops will be extended to as long as a year.

A new study indicates that U.S. employees are paying 48 percent more in out-of-pocket expenses for health insurance than they did three years ago.

10 Pres. Bush uses the eve of the Sept. 11 anniversary to call for a significant expansion of law enforcement powers under the USA Patriot Act.

A new videotape of Osama bin Laden is aired on Al Jazeera.

11 Swedish Foreign Minister Anna Lindh, who opposed Sweden's proposed adoption of the euro, dies of wounds she received when an unidentified man stabbed her in a store.

The Israeli government decides in principle to "remove" Yasir Arafat, threatening the Palestinian leader with exile, arrest, or death. The Bush administration and other governments condemn the move as harmful to the peace process.

12 A firefight in the Iraqi city of Falluja escalates into chaos, as U.S. troops kill eight Iraqi policemen and a Jordanian security guard.

13 Talks at the U.N. fail to produce a consensus on a U.S.-backed proposal designed to enlist more international support of its occupation of Iraq. France continues to insist that Iraq's transition to self-rule should be overseen by the U.N.

14 Delegates from developing nations walk out of World Trade Organization talks in Mexico, accusing wealthy nations of failure to compromise on issues like farm subsidies. The collapse of negotiations means that the group will fail to reach a new agreement dismantling global trade barriers.

Sec. of State Colin Powell cautions against rushing Iraq to self-rule too quickly, a move that he fears would not be seen as legitimate.

Swedes vote overwhelmingly to reject adopting the euro.

15 A three-judge panel of the Ninth Circuit Court of Appeals orders that the recall election of California Gov. Gray Davis be delayed, ruling that the Oct. 7 date does not give several counties with large minority populations enough time to replace aging punch-card voting machines.

16 The Senate votes 55-40 to overturn all of the new F.C.C. regulations that would make it easier for the nation's largest media conglomerates to grow even bigger.

17 New York Stock Exchange chairman Richard Grasso resigns in the wake of furor over his $139.5 million compensation package. Critics questioned the propriety of such lavish pay being set by directors representing some of the companies Grasso was responsible for regulating.

Wesley Clark, a four-star general and the former Supreme Allied Commander for NATO, shakes up the race for the Democratic presidential nomination by declaring his candidacy.

The Bill & Melinda Gates Foundation donates $51 million to create 67 small, theme-based public high schools in New York City with no more than 500 students each.

18 Hurricane Isabel slams into North Carolina's Outer Banks and roars north into Virginia, knocking out power to more than two million people, and shutting down the federal government.

19 Hurricane Isabel peters out over Canada, after causing two dozen deaths and major flooding in Virginia and Maryland.

JetBlue Airways admits that it violated its own privacy policies by providing a Pentagon contractor with information on more than a million passengers as part of a program to track terrorists and other "high-risk" passengers. The contractor used the information to identify passengers' Social Security numbers and financial histories.

20 An Islamic U.S. Army chaplain who ministered to detainees at Guantánamo Bay, Cuba, is arrested on suspicion that he was sympathetic to the Islamic militants held there, most of whom were captured in the days after Sept. 11.

Prime Minister Junichuro Koizumi is reelected as leader of Japan's governing Liberal Democratic Party in a decisive victory.

21 John Reed, former chief executive of Citigroup, is named interim chairman of the New York Stock Exchange. He pledges to reform the Exchange's practices.

22 Attorney General John Ashcroft issues a policy directive that makes it more difficult for federal prosecutors to seek plea bargains.

Officials report that soaring health costs and a growing fiscal crisis have forced most states to reduce Medicaid by scaling back eligibility, cutting benefits, increasing co-payments, and freezing or reducing payments to care providers.

23 The full U.S. Court of Appeals for the Ninth Circuit puts the California governor's recall election back on its original schedule.

In an address to the U.N. General Assembly, Pres. Bush defends the war in Iraq, saying he had acted to protect "the credibility of the United Nations." In a separate speech, U.N. Secretary General Kofi Annan warns that nations that "reserve the right to act unilaterally" present "a fundamental challenge to the principles on which . . . world peace and stability have rested for 58 years."

An Air Force translator serving at the U.S. prison camp for captured militants and suspected terrorists at Guantánamo Bay, Cuba, is arrested and charged with espionage and passing military secrets to Syria.

24 A draft of a report by David Kay, the American leading the hunt for weapons of mass destruction in Iraq, indicates that no illicit weapons have been found after a four-month search.

OPEC announces a cut in oil production commencing Nov. 1, sending oil prices up sharply.

25 Secretary of State Colin Powell says the U.S. will set a deadline of six months for Iraqi leaders to draft a new constitution, and the U.S. will not transfer sovereignty to Iraqi authorities until then.

A Nigerian woman whose case had caused an international outcry after she was sentenced to death by stoning for adultery is acquitted by the highest Islamic court in her state.

26 The Census Bureau reports that the number of Americans living in poverty increased by 1.7 million in 2002, and the median household income declined by 1.1 percent.

A U.S. Court of Appeals says World Trade Center leaseholder Larry Silverstein is entitled to $3.5 billion in insurance payouts, not the $7 billion he had sought by claiming that the Sept. 11 attacks were two separate terrorist incidents. The ruling raises additional questions about how much money will be available for rebuilding.

27 Justice Dept. officials acknowledge that the government has begun using the Patriot Act, which grants law enforcement expanded powers for fighting terrorism, in a wide range of criminal investigations that are unrelated to terrorism.

Russian Pres. Vladimir Putin, meeting with Pres. Bush, says Russia will encourage Iran to comply with weapons inspections but will proceed with plans to help Iran build a nuclear reactor.

28 Leaders of the House Intelligence Committee criticize the Bush administration's use of intelligence about the existence of weapons of mass destruction to justify the war in Iraq.

29 The Census Bureau reports a sharp increase in the number of Americans without health insurance, with the total now at 43.6 million, or 15.2 percent of the population.

The White House denies that Karl Rove, senior advisor to Pres. Bush, illegally revealed the name of an undercover C.I.A. operative to retaliate against her husband, who criticized the case for going to war against Iraq.

30 A civilian Arabic-language translator who had helped to interview suspected Al Qaeda and Taliban militants becomes the third person arrested in connection with possible espionage at the military prison at Guantánamo Bay, Cuba.

OCTOBER

1 Democrats in Congress say John Ashcroft's deep political ties to the Bush administration (political advisor Karl Rove was a paid consultant to three political campaigns in Missouri) present a clear conflict of interest for the Attorney General in investigating who might have leaked the identity of an undercover C.I.A. officer.

2 A federal judge in Virginia rules out the death penalty in the trial of Zacarias Moussaoui, the so-called 20th hijacker. The judge also bars prosecutors from linking Moussaoui to the Sept. 11 attacks because they refused to let him interview captured terrorists who might aid in his defense.

A *New York Times*/CBS News poll shows a drop in Americans' confidence in Pres. Bush. For the first time, more people disapprove than approve of his foreign policy, while his disapproval ratings on the economy jump to 56 percent.

3 The day after the government's chief weapons inspector in Iraq says there is no evidence of weapons of mass destruction anywhere in the country, Pres. Bush says the inspector's report justifies the decision to invade Iraq.

4 A Pentagon task force contradicts assertions by the Bush administration that Iraq's oil, and not American taxpayers, would cover the cost of rebuilding the country. The report says Iraq's production capacity had decreased by more than 25 percent because of a decade of trade embargos.

Police in New York tranquilize a 400-pound Bengal tiger and remove it from a public housing apartment in Manhattan.

5 A day after suicide bomber kills at least 19 Jews and Arabs at a restaurant in Haifa, Israel attacks what it calls a terrorist training camp deep inside Syria.

Roy Horn, of the Las Vegas entertainment duo Siegfried and Roy, is in critical condition after being attacked by one of the tigers in the act.

6 Akhmad Kadyrov, the candidate favored by the Kremlin, wins election as president of Chechnya, in a vote that independent experts say was most likely rigged.

7 Californians vote to recall Gov. Gray Davis from office and to replace him with former bodybuilder-turned-actor Arnold Schwarzenegger (See "Major News Stories of the Year.").

8 Philadelphia and federal officials uncover a listening device that had been planted by F.B.I. agents in the office of Mayor John F. Street, a Democrat in a bitter race for re-election.

9 A new drug regimen is found to greatly reduce the risk of recurrence of breast cancer in postmenopausal women.

10 Conservative radio commentator Rush Limbaugh, who has regularly told his listeners that drug users should be jailed, admits that he is addicted to painkillers and will check into a rehab clinic.

11 Republicans in the Texas state senate, at the urging of U.S. House Majority Leader Tom DeLay, force through a measure to redraw the state's congressional districts in a way that they believe will produce more Republicans in the U.S. Congress.

13 Bolivian President Gonzalo Sánchez de Lozada remains defiant, even as protesters calling for his resignation clash with government troops in La Paz, resulting in 14 deaths. The president's popularity is at eight percent. (See "Major News Stories of the Year."

14 China sends a man into orbit, joining the U.S. and Russia as the only countries to do so. The spacecraft *Shenzhou 5* will orbit the earth 14 times.

Charles Gyude Bryant, a businessman, takes office in Liberia, replacing an interim government that was appointed when warlord-turned-president Charles G. Taylor finally went into exile (See "Major News Stories of the Year").

15 New York City's Staten Island Ferry crashes into a pier, killing 10 people.

An advisory panel to the Food and Drug Administration recommends lifting the 11-year-old ban on silicone breast implants, contingent on several conditions. The panel's recommendation is usually tantamount to approval by the F.D.A.

Obituaries November 1, 2002–October 31, 2003

Abplanalp, Robert, 81, Bronx-born inventor who made millions with an improved aerosol valve, enabling him to befriend and bankroll Pres. Nixon before and after White House years. Of cancer, Bronxville, N.Y., Aug. 30, 2003.
Adams, Lucian, 80, Medal of Honor hero in WWII for killing nine German machine-gunners, opening supply lines for isolated G.I. unit. Cause undisclosed, San Antonio, Tex., March 31, 2003.
Agnelli, Giovanni, 81, Italian business magnate, head of Fiat (Fabbrica Italiana Automobili Torino, 1899); transformed private family auto company into worldwide firm encompassing banking, media, armaments and many other fields; international society figure and political power in Italy. Of prostate cancer,Turin, Italy, Jan. 24, 2003.
Amin, Idi, ca. 78, African despot whose military career started with British colonial forces and ended with brutal rule of Uganda 1971-79, marked by economic devastation and killing of as many as 300,000 people; judged both mad and cunning. Of multiple organ failure, in exile, Jidda, Saudi Arabia, Aug, 16, 2003.
Aptheker, Herbert, 87, Brooklyn-born historian whose books, defined by Marxist views, include three-volume history of the Negro people and edition of W.E.B. Du Bois's letters. Cause undisclosed, Mountain View, Calif., March 17, 2003.
Arledge, Roone, 71, U.S. TV executive who transformed sports and news coverage at ABC through the 1960's and 70's, bringing *Monday Night Football* and the Olympics into prime-time popularity, and creating magazine news shows such as *20/20* and *Nightline*. Of cancer, New York, Dec. 5, 2002.
Atkins, Dr. Robert C., 72, U.S. diet guru to millions, whose best-selling books favor consuming protein over carbohydrates, from *Diet Revolution* (1972) to *Atkins for Life* (2003). Of head injuries after a fall, New York, April 17, 2003.
Axelrod, George, 81, U.S. playwright and screenwriter whose whimsical outlook lit up Broadway in 1952 with *The Seven Year Itch*; films include *Breakfast at Tiffany's* and *The Manchurian Candidate*. At home, Los Angeles, June 21, 2003.
Beach, Edward L., 84, Navy captain who led 1960 voyage of nuclear submarine *Triton*, history's first undersea circumnavigation, following Magellan's 16th-century path; accomplished author, best known for *Run Silent, Run Deep*. Of cancer, at home, Washington, D.C., Dec. 1, 2002.
Berrigan, Philip, 79, U.S. pacifist and ex-priest; led opposition to the Vietnam War by raiding draft boards and destroying records, notably in Catonsville, Md. (the "Catonsville Nine"), along with his brother Rev. Daniel Berrigan, S.J. Of cancer, Baltimore, Md., Dec. 6, 2002.
Bettger, Lyle, 88, U.S. actor whose icy smooth villains were familiar faces in western and noir films of 50's and 60's; later played good guys on TV. Of natural causes, Atascadero, Calif., Sept. 24, 2003.
Biller, Moe, 87, New York-born president of American Postal Workers Union 1980-2001; known for tough bargaining tactics and 1970 illegal strike that led to post office reorganization as public corporation. Of heart disease, New York, Sept. 5, 2003.
Bonds, Bobby, 57, 1970's baseball star, mostly as Giants outfielder, who hit over 30 home runs and stole over 30 bases five times; father of Barry Bonds. Of cancer, San Francisco, Aug. 23, 2003.
Bracken, Eddie, 87, New York-born actor from childhood, best remembered as the hapless hero of two 1940's comedies by Preston Sturges, *The Miracle of Morgan's Creek* and *Hail the Conquering Hero*; also successful in TV and theater touring companies. Of natural causes, Montclair, N.J. Nov. 14, 2002.
Brakhage, Stan, 70, U.S. filmmaker whose extensive work has been described more as poetry and abstract painting than narrative, with such subjects as *Mothlight* and *The Text of Light*; influential teacher and author. Of cancer, Victoria, British Columbia, March 9, 2003.
Brian, Mary, 96, Texas-born star of silent films (*Peter Pan*) who moved gracefully into talkies and on to postwar *Dragnet*; best remembered for early talkie *The Virginian*, opposite Gary Cooper. Of natural causes, Del Mar, Calif., Dec. 30, 2002.
Brinkley, David, 82, U.S. newsman whose collaboration with Chet Huntley set a lasting pattern for TV journalism, going back to popular coverage of the 1956 political conventions; his dry delivery and wry wit endured on *David Brinkley's Journal* and *This Week*. Houston, June 11, 2003.
Brockhouse, Bertram, 85, Canadian scientist, co-winner of 1994 Nobel Prize in Physics for experiments using neutron beams bouncing off atomic nuclei to measure underlying structure of matter. Cause undisclosed, Hamilton, Ontario, Oct.13, 2003.
Bronson, Charles, 81, U.S. actor who was a success in Europe before achieving American stardom for his brawny roles in the five violent *Death Wish* movies, as well as *The Great Escape* and *The Dirty Dozen*. Of pneumonia, Los Angeles, Aug. 30, 2003.
Brooks, Herb, 66, U.S. hockey coach who led U.S. "miracle" team to gold medal victory over Soviet team in 1980 Olympic Games; coach of championship University of Minnesota teams. Of auto accident injuries, Minneapolis-St. Paul, Aug. 11, 2003.
Brown, Dee, 94, U.S. writer of numerous works, many about the American West, most notably *Bury My Heart at Wounded Knee*, 1970 best seller that transformed understanding of treatment of native Americans in last half of 19th century. At home, Little Rock, Ark., Dec. 12, 2002.
Brumel, Valery, 60, Russian Olympic high jump champion, silver medal Rome 1960, gold medal Tokyo 1964; career ended in1965 motorcycle accident. Cause undisclosed, Moscow, Jan. 26, 2003.
Buchholz, Horst, 69, German actor known for early 60's American films *The Magnificent Seven* and *One, Two, Three*; played teenage rebels in German films. After surgery, Berlin, March 3, 2003.
Carter, Benny, 95, jazz master, virtuoso of alto sax and other instruments, leader of big bands 1920's to 40's, influential music arranger for radio, TV and movies; numerous awards include 1996 Kennedy Center Honors and 2000 National Medal of Arts. Of natural causes, Los Angeles, July 12, 2003.
Carter, Nell, 54, U.S. singer who won a 1978 Tony Award for her snappy renditions of Fats Waller songs in *Ain't Misbehavin'*, leading to TV sitcom success with *Gimme a Break*. Of a probable brain aneurysm, Beverly Hills, Calif., Jan. 23, 2003.
Cash, Johnny, 71, U.S. country music star whose legendary recordings tell stories of hardscrabble lives—railroad and farm workers, convicts, cow-

boys—"I Walk the Line" and "Folsom Prison Blues" among 1,500 others. Of diabetes, Nashville, Tenn., Sept. 13, 2003.

Cash, June Carter, 73, country music star with her mother and sisters, then with husband, Johnny Cash, and his touring show, often featuring her songs, such as "Ring of Fire;" acting credits include TV's *Little House on the Prairie* and the movie *The Apostle*. After heart surgery, Nashville, May 15, 2003.

Coburn, James, 74, U.S. actor whose sly delivery made him a popular action hero or villain in numerous films, including *The Magnificent Seven, Major Dundee, Our Man Flint* and *Charade*; Oscar for supporting role in *Affliction* (1999). Of cardiac arrest, Los Angeles, Nov. 18, 2002.

Coors, Joseph Sr., 85, scion of beer-making family who popularized brand nationwide and bankrolled such conservative causes as the Heritage Foundation and Ronald Reagan's presidential run. Of lymphatic cancer, Rancho Mirage, Calif., March 15, 2003.

Crenna, Richard, 76, U.S. actor who started as a child on radio with *Burns and Allen* and *Our Miss Brooks* and moved on to TV and movies in wide-ranging roles, including the *Rambo* series and most recently *Judging Amy*. Of pancreatic cancer, Los Angeles, Jan. 17, 2003.

Cronyn, Hume, 91, Canadian-born U.S. actor whose character-driven roles energized stage and screen for more than 60 years; Tony Award winner for Polonius to Richard Burton's Hamlet; best known onstage for acting with wife, Jessica Tandy, in *The Fourposter, A Delicate Balance* and *The Gin Game*, both receiving first Tony for lifetime achievement. At home, Fairfield, Conn., June 15, 2003.

Cruz, Celia, 77, Cuban singer whose extravagant dresses and wigs matched the powerful rasp of her voice as she belted out salsa, mambo and cha-cha, along with her signature shout, "Azucar" ("Sugar"); 2000 Grammy winner; awarded 1994 National Medal of Arts. After brain tumor surgery, at home, Fort Lee, N.J. July 16, 2003.

Davis, Raymond, 88, Marine general awarded Medal of Honor in Korean War, among other decorations, for rescue mission under fire; Marine assistant commandant 1971. At home, Conyers, Ga., Sept. 3, 2003.

DeBusschere, Dave, 62, Detroit-born Hall of Fame basketball star hailed for defensive skills and leadership that led Knicks to only N.B.A. championships, 1970, 1973. Of a heart attack, New York, May 14, 2003.

Dillon, C. Douglas, 93, Wall Street banker who served as Pres. Eisenhower's ambassador to France and Pres. Kennedy's secretary of the treasury. Of old age, New York, Jan 10, 2003.

Djindjic, Zoran, 50, Serbian prime minister, part of democratically elected government opposed by nationalist forces. Assassinated, Belgrade, Serbia, March 15, 2003.

Doby, Larry, 79, Hall of Fame and seven-time All-Star baseball player, first black in American League, signing with Cleveland Indians in 1947; second black manager, Chicago White Sox 1978. Of cancer, at home, Montclair, N.J., June 18, 2003.

Doerr, Harriet, 92, U.S. writer at age 73 won American Book Award for first fiction with *Stones for Ibarra*; several sharply observed novels and short stories followed. At home, Pasadena, Calif., Nov. 24, 2002.

Douglass, Charles, 93, TV technician who invented a Laff Box in early 1950's; now a computerized laugh track that "enhances" many a sitcom. Of natural causes, Templeton, Calif., April 8, 2003.

Dugan, Alan, 80, Brooklyn-born poet whose verse plumbs the depths of everyday living in coarse, vivid, yet eloquent language; Pulitzer Prize and National Book Award winner. Of pneumonia, Truro, Mass., Sept. 3, 2003.

Eban, Abba, 87, Israeli diplomat whose gracefully forceful rhetoric helped cement the fledgling nation's establishment and right to exist from 1948 on; born in S. Africa and raised in England, he served in several ministerial posts, most notably as Israel's voice at the U.N. after the 1967 war. Of natural causes, Tel Aviv, Nov. 17, 2002.

Ebsen, Buddy, 95, U.S. character actor best known as TV's Jed Clampett in *The Beverly Hillbillies* and private eye *Barnaby Jones*. Of natural causes, Torrance, Calif., July 6, 2003.

Falkenburg, Jinx, 84, U.S. cover girl and radio/TV personality; first "Miss Rheingold," 1941 beer promotion that led to small movie roles; best known for pioneer talk show broadcasts with husband, Tex McCrary. Of natural causes, Manhasset, N.Y., Aug. 27, 2003.

Fast, Howard, 88, U.S. writer of more than 80 books, many best-selling novels, such as *Freedom Road* and *Spartacus*; blacklisted in 1950's due to Communist Party membership, which he later recanted. Of natural causes, Old Greenwich, Conn., March 12, 2003.

Fiedler, Leslie, 85, idiosyncratic U.S. literary critic and teacher who enjoyed stirring up academic controversy by delving into psychological and sexual areas others ignored; most notable work, *Love and Death in the American Novel* (1960). Of natural causes, Buffalo, N.Y., Jan. 29, 2003.

Foss, Joe, 87, World War II flying ace awarded Medal of Honor; South Dakota Republican governor 1954-58; American Football League commissioner 1959-66; National Rifle Association president 1988-90. Cause undisclosed, Scottsdale Ariz., Jan. 1, 2003.

Freeman, Orville, 84, Minnesota governor 1956-60; secretary of agriculture under Pres. Kennedy and Johnson, promoted food stamps and food safety. Of Alzheimer's disease, Minneapolis, Feb. 20, 2003.

Galtieri, Leopoldo, 76, Argentine military dictator for eight months in 1982 when he seized Falkland Islands but bowed to British supremacy within weeks; later served five years in prison. Cause and place undisclosed, Jan. 12, 2003.

Gardner, Herb, 68, Brooklyn-born playwright whose Broadway hits featured crotchety oddballs you could love, notably in *A Thousand Clowns* (1962) and Tony winner *I'm Not Rappaport* (1985). Of lung disease, at home, New York, Sept. 24, 2003.

Gavilan, Kid (Gerardo Gonzalez), 77, Cuban Hall of Fame boxer who won the welterweight championship in 1951; his colorful bolo punch energized fans in 1943-58 career of 107 wins. Of a heart attack, Miami, Feb. 13, 2003.

Getty, J. Paul Jr., 70, U.S.-born oil heir who became a philanthropic British citizen after youthful years of partying and drug abuse; his many charities were rewarded with an honorary knighthood in 1986. Of infection, London, April 17, 2003.

Gibb, Maurice, 53, English-born singer/composer with brothers Robin and Barry as the Bee Gees; many hit records in 70's disco era, most memorably for *Saturday Night Fever* soundtrack. Of cardiac arrest, Miami, Jan.12, 2003.

Gibson, Althea, 76, U.S. tennis star, raised in Harlem, the first black to win Wimbledon and the U.S. title at Forest Hills; five Grand Slam titles in 1950's. Of respiratory illness, East Orange, N.J., Sept. 28, 2003.

Gillman, Sid, 91, U.S. football coach, member of college and pro Halls of Fame; celebrated as the "father of modern-day passing," most notably with the San Diego Chargers, 1960-71. Of a probable aneurysm, Los Angeles, Jan. 3, 2003.

Gionfriddo, Al, 81, Brooklyn Dodger outfielder remembered for catching Joe DiMaggio's 415-foot drive in Game 6 of the 1947 World Series. Of a heart attack, Solvang, Calif., March 14, 2003.

Good, Robert A., 81, U.S. physician and scientist who identified the thymus gland as source of immunology defenses; led team that performed first bone marrow transplant, 1968. Of cancer, at home, St. Petersburg, Fla., June 13, 2003.

Griffiths, Martha, 91, Democratic representative from Michigan 1955-74; a sharp-tongued legislator, she was responsible for adding the word "sex" to "race, religion or national origin"in the 1964 Civil Rights Act. Of natural causes, Armada, Mich., April 22, 2003.

Hackett, Buddy, 78, Brooklyn-born comedian whose squashed-up face was familiar to TV and nightclub audiences in1950's and 60's; on Broadway in *Lunatics and Lovers* and *I Had a Ball*; movies include *The Music Man*. Cause undisclosed, Malibu, Calif., June 30, 2003.

Hall, Conrad, 76, Tahiti-born U.S. cinematographer; best known for Oscar-winning *Butch Cassidy and the Sundance Kid* (1969), *American Beauty* (1999) and posthumously for *Road to Perdition* (2003). Of bladder cancer, Santa Monica, Calif., Jan. 4, 2003.

Hargrove, Marion, 83, whose breezy account of barracks life, *See Here, Private Hargrove*, became 1940's best seller; later wrote TV and movie scripts. Of pneumonia, Long Beach, Calif., Aug. 23, 2003.

Harrison, Lou, 85, U.S. composer who championed union of music of Asia and the West as well as causes for peace and gay brotherhood; works range from opera and concertos to ballet scores and music for special instruments such as the gamelan. Of a heart attack, Layfayette, Ind., Feb. 2, 2003.

Hartke, Vance, 84, Indiana Democratic senator 1958-77; liberal supporter of social programs, he broke with Pres. Johnson and opposed involvement in Vietnam. Of a heart attack, Fairfax, Va., July 27, 2003.

Heilbrun, Carolyn, 77, U.S. writer known to academics for scholarly works on feminist topics and to a wider public for murder mysteries written by "Amanda Cross." A suicide, at home, New York, Oct. 9, 2003.

Hepburn, Katharine, 96, arguably the last Hollywood Golden Age star; she turned "box-office poison" into a six-decade career on stage and screen, always playing a vivacious yet vulnerable woman, most memorably in nine films with Spencer Tracy, her real-life love; winner of a record four Oscars, for *Morning Glory* (1933), *Guess Who's Coming to Dinner* (1967), *The Lion in Winter* (1968) and *On Golden Pond* (1981); stage credits include *The Philadelphia Story*. At home, Old Saybrook, Conn., June 29, 2003.

Hill, George Roy, 81, U.S. stage and film director who went from TV to Hollywood to direct a wide variety of films, notably *Butch Cassidy and the Sundance Kid* and *The Sting*, both Oscar winners for best direction and best picture. Of Parkinson's disease, New York, Dec. 27, 2002.

Hiller, Wendy, 90, vivacious British stage and film actress who created distinctive Shavian heroines onscreen, Eliza Doolittle and Major Barbara; Oscar winner for *Separate Tables* (1958). At home, Beaconsfield, England, May 14, 2003.

Hines, Gregory, 57, New York-born tap-dancer whose adroit elegance led to success as an actor on stage and screen; 1992 Tony winner playing Jelly Roll Morton in *Jelly's Last Jam*; films include *The Cotton Club* and *White Nights*. Of cancer, Los Angeles, Aug. 9, 2003.

Hines, Jerome, 81, longtime Metropolitan Opera bass 1946-87, 868 performances in 45 roles, notably Mussorgsky's Boris Gudonov and Wagner's Wotan; treasured for a resonant voice that searched deeply into characterization. Cause undisclosed, New York, Feb. 4, 2003.

Hirschfeld, Al, 99, U.S. artist whose singular style of line-drawn caricatures chronicled Broadway for most of 20th century; captured personalities in a few deft strokes, hiding daughter's name, Nina, in each drawing. Of natural causes, New York, Jan. 22, 2003.

Hope, Bob, 100, British-born U.S. comedian whose breezy style with wisecracks brought universal stardom in a long career that spanned vaudeville, Broadway, radio, movies and television, with many tours abroad entertaining G.I.'s; movies include seven "Road" films with Bing Crosby and Dorothy Lamour; many awards include medals from Presidents Eisenhower, Kennedy and Clinton, as well as five special Oscars. At home, Toluca Lake, Calif., July 27, 2003.

Hoyte, Desmond, 73, president of Guyana 1984-92; London-trained lawyer who opened nation to electoral democracy and Western economic aid. Of heart failure, Georgetown, Dec. 22, 2002.

Hunter, Kim, 79, U. S. actress, the original Stella in *A Streetcar Named Desire* on stage and screen, to Marlon Brando's loutish Stanley Kowalski; also remembered as the ape who played up to Charlton Heston in *Planet of the Apes*. Of a heart attack, New York, Sept. 11, 2002.

Illich, Ivan, 76, Vienna-born ex-priest and writer, he ministered to Hispanic parishioners in New York and Puerto Rico in the 1950's and 60's, then turned against Vatican bureaucracy and elitism and wrote numerous works that preached a philosophy that ran against the grain, notably *DeSchooling Society* (1971). Cause undisclosed, Bremen, Germany, Dec. 2, 2002.

Izetbegovic, Alija, 78, Muslim leader, Bosnia president when 1992 independence plunged unstable state into chaos of Balkan rivalries and war; signed 1995 Dayton accords; resigned 2000. Of heart disease, Sarajevo, Oct. 19, 2003.

Jackson, Maynard H. Jr., 65, Atlanta's first black mayor, won first of three terms in 1973; advocating affirmative action programs, he presided over construction of Atlanta's international airport; helped promote Atlanta as host of '96 Olympics. Of a heart attack, Washington, D.C., June, 23, 2003.

Jenkins, Roy, 82, Welsh-born Labor politician whose long-held moderate views were finally realized in the Blair New Labor Party; 1981 founder of the Social Democratic Party, and author of 1997 biography of Churchill. Of natural causes, Oxfordshire, England, Jan. 5, 2003.

Katz, Sir Bernard, 92, German-born scientist, 1970 Nobel Prize co-winner for work describing the flow of electrical charges between nerves and muscles, experiments that led to better understanding of drug addiction and mental illness. Of natural causes, London, April 20, 2003.

Kazan, Elia, 94, Greek-born, New York-educated director whose masterly control of actors shone in such hits as *A Streetcar Named Desire* and *Death of a Salesman* onstage and *Gentleman's Agreement* and *On the Waterfront* on screen; three-time Tony winner, his many films won 20 Oscars; 1999 Oscar for lifetime achievement, denounced by some since Kazan had named friends as Communists to Congress in 1950's. At home, New York, Sept. 28, 2003.

Kerr, Jean, 80, U.S. writer who found droll humor in the glamour of theater and the routine of suburbia; her best-selling *Please Don't Eat the Daisies* (1957) went to the movies and TV; *Mary, Mary* ran for 1,500 Broadway performances;often collaborated with husband, drama critic Water Kerr. Of pneumonia, White Plains, N.Y., Jan. 5, 2003.

King, Earl, 69, New Orleans-born blues singer and composer of numerous hits recorded by Jimi Hendrix, Fats Domino and others, many popular at Mardi Gras. Of diabetes complications, New Orleans, April 17, 2003.

Knott, Frederick, 86, British playwright who scored on Broadway with two long-running hits, *Dial M for Murder* and *Wait Until Dark*, both later made into successful movies. Of natural causes, New York, Dec. 17, 2002.

Koppett, Leonard, 79, Moscow-born New York sportswriter for the *Times, Herald Tribune* and *Post* whose many articles and books on baseball and basketball not only reported events but also interpreted them. Of a heart attack, San Francisco, June 22, 2003.

Lagardère, Jean-Luc, 75, French industrialist and engineer whose executive reach encompassed Airbus, Hachette publishing and telecommunications. Of neurological disease, Paris, March 14, 2003.

Lansdale, John Jr., 91, Army lieutenant colonel who led search for German atomic bomb material and scientists in April 1945 to head off its capture by Soviets. At home, Annapolis, Md., Aug. 22, 2003.

Larrabee, Mike, 69, track champion who won two gold medals in 1964 Tokyo Olympics—400 meters and 1,600 meter relay—near age 31. Of cancer, Santa Maria, Calif., April 22. 2003.

LeFrak, Samuel J., 85, New York real estate mogul who built thousands of middle-class apartments, most notably Lefrak City in Queens and Gateway Plaza in lower Manhattan; an avid art collector and major philanthropist. Of natural causes, New York, April 16, 2003.

Littlewood, Joan, 87, British director and producer who revolutionized English theater in the 1950's and 60's with such spirited productions as *Oh What a Lovely War*, which presented World War I in lively vaudeville style. Of natural causes, London, Sept. 20, 2002.

Long, Russell B., 84, Louisiana Democratic senator 1948-86, son of Huey Long; wily debater who mastered Senate rules and the tax code, often to the benefit of business and industry; assistant majority leader 1965-69. Cause undisclosed, Washington D.C., May 9, 2003.

Longden, Johnny, 96, British-born jockey who won Triple Crown riding Count Fleet in 1943, highlight of a career that ran from 1927 to 1966, with 6,032 winners. After a stroke, Banning, Calif., Feb. 14, 2003.

MacGregor, Clark, 80, Republican Minnesota congressman 1962-70 who went on to manage Pres. Nixon's 1972 re-election campaign but remained untouched by Watergate scandal. Cause undisclosed, Pompano Beach, Fla., Feb. 10, 2003.

MacKenzie, Gisele, 76, Canadian-born singer whose warm voice and personality brought U.S. radio and TV stardom on *Your Hit Parade* and her own shows; often played violin and traded jokes with Jack Benny. Of colon cancer, Burbank, Calif., Sept. 6, 2003.

Maddox, Lester, 87, Georgia governor 1966-70, he parlayed refusal to serve blacks at his Atlanta restaurant into a determined stand against desegregation and civil rights that won him the governorship; later attempts to gain office failed. Cause undisclosed, Atlanta, June 25, 2003.

Marshall, Burke, 80, assistant attorney general for civil rights in Kennedy and Johnson administrations; his understated approach led to advances in national crises such as desegregation of University of Mississippi and 1964 Civil Rights Act. Of a bone marrow disorder, at home, Newton, Conn., June 2, 2003.

Matta (Roberto Echaurren), 91, Chilean-born Surrealist artist who lived mostly in France; paintings delve into the unconscious world of dreams and influenced many other artists, even some Abstract Expressionists. At home, Tarquinia, Italy, Nov. 23, 2002.

Mauldin, Bill, 81, Pulitzer Prize-winning creator of Willie and Joe, the cartoon G.I.s who stood for all the men who slogged on to victory over Axis forces and their own smug officers in World War II; syndicated cartoons skewered public pomposity for 50 years. Of pneumonia and Alzheimer's disease,Newport Beach, Calif., Jan. 22, 2003.

McClendon, Sarah, 92, Texas-born news gadfly who covered the White House in a loud voice that vexed presidents from Franklin Roosevelt to George W. Bush. Of natural causes, Washington, D.C., Jan. 8, 2003.

McCrary, Tex (John Reagan), 92, Texas-born journalist, one of the first talk-show hosts on radio and TV; scored political coup by encouraging Dwight Eisenhower to enter 1952 presidential race. At home, New York, July 29, 2003.

McNally, Dave, 60, All-Star and World Series pitcher for Baltimore Orioles; made baseball history in 1975 by refusing to re-sign, leading to free agency. Of lung cancer, Billings, Mont., Dec. 1, 2003.

Merton, Robert K., 92, U.S. sociologist of wide-ranging interests who gave the world "role models" and "focus groups" in a series of studies, the best known being *On the Shoulders of Giants*. Of cancer, at home, New York, Feb. 23, 2003.

Metcalfe, Ben, 83, Canadian journalist who turned to environmental issues and became one of the founders of Greenpeace in 1970. Of a heart attack, Vancouver Island, British Columbia, Oct. 14, 2003.

Meyer, Helen Honig, 95, Brooklyn-born publishing executive at Dell who led company's growth from pulps and comics to literary paperbacks and hardcovers; one of the first women at the top in publishing. Of natutral causes, Livingston, N.J., April 21, 2003.

Mink, Patsy, 74, Hawaii Democratic congresswoman 1965-77 and since 1990; liberal supporter of women's causes, notably Title IX, and labor and civil rights; early opponent of Vietnam War. Of viral pneumonia, Honolulu, Sept. 28, 2002.

Modigliani, Franco, 85, Rome-born lawyer turned economist, M.I.T. professor, awarded 1985 Nobel Prize for new insights into peoples' savings and corporate debt; outspoken against anti-Semitism and fascism. At home, Cambridge, Mass., Sept. 25, 2003.

Moore, Rev. Paul Jr., 83, 13th Episcopal bishop of New York 1972-89, strong advocate of liberal agenda in support of the poor and against greed and racism; one of the first to ordain women. Of brain and lung cancer, New York, May 1, 2003.

Mosley, Lady Diana, 93, British socialite, one of the famously witty and stylish Mitford sisters; left husband for British fascist Oswald Mosley, befriending and supporting Hitler. At home, Paris, Aug. 11, 2003.

Moynihan, Daniel Patrick, 76, Democratic New York senator, 1977-2001, Harvard professor, ambassador to India and the U.N.; a novel thinker about race, poverty and international intelligence, he also gave practical solutions to problems of urban decay and preservation; remembered for wit and political savvy. Of ruptured appendix complications, Washington, D.C., March 26, 2003.

Ne Win, 81, Burmese general whose authoritarian government held power 1962-88, a time of failure of once-prosperous economy; rule ended with demonstrations that led to present repressive regime. At home, Yangon, Dec. 5, 2002.

O'Connor, Donald, 78, Chicago-born song and dance man from age three in vaudeville, to movies, stage and TV; films include dancing with partner Peggy Ryan and chatting with Francis the talking mule, but best known as Gene Kelly's agile sidekick who could "Make 'Em Laugh" in *Singin' in the Rain*. Cause undisclosed, Woodland Hills, Calif., Sept. 27, 2003.

Olatunji, Babatunde, 76, Nigerian drummer whose 1959 album *Drums of Passion* introduced U.S. audiences and many musicians to the percussive power of African music; played at Radio City Music Hall and 1964 World's Fair. Of diabetes, Salinas, Calif., April 6, 2003.

Omarr, Sydney, 76, Philadelphia-born syndicated astrologer whose advice in 200 newspapers and yearly books (50 million copies sold) was devoured by anxious readers. Of a heart attack, Santa Monica, Calif., Jan. 2, 2003.

Palmer, Robert, 54, British singer of many styles including rock, blues and reggae; best known for 1985 album *Riptide*, featuring hit song "Addicted to Love." Of a heart attack, Paris, Sept. 26, 2003.

Parker, Suzy, 69, U.S. fashion model whose lithe figure and striking cheekbones graced magazine covers in the 1950's; one of the first supermodels, posing in a bikini and earning $100 an hour. The inspiration for Audrey Hepburn's character in *Funny Face*, she made a few films, including *The Best of Everything* in 1959. Cause undisclosed, Montecito, Calif., May 3, 2003.

Paycheck, Johnny (Donald Eugene Lytle), 64, U.S. country singer whose ups and downs with the law and alcohol made for a checkered career through 60's, 70's and 80's; remembered for hit record "Take This Job and Shove It." Of respiratory failure, Nashville, Tenn., Feb. 19, 2003.

Peck, Gregory, 87, U.S. movie giant whose gentlemanly grace illuminated a wide variety of roles—mad Captain Ahab in *Moby Dick*, an earnest journalist battling anti-Semitism in *Gentleman's Agreement*, and most notably, lawyer Atticus Finch battling racism in *To Kill a Mockingbird*, his Oscar winner; liberal activist; awarded Presidential Medal of Freedom and American Film Institute Life Achievement honors. At home, Los Angeles, June 12, 2003.

Peugeot, Pierre, 70, French industrialist whose astute leadership turned the family name automaker into a leading European giant, second after Volkswagen. Cause undisclosed, Paris, Dec. 1, 2002.

Phillips, Sam, 80, U.S. music producer whose Sun Records helped popularize rock 'n' roll and make stars of Elvis Presley, Roy Orbison and many others. Of respiratory illness, Memphis, July 30, 2003.

Phillips, William, 94, New York-born publisher who founded and led *Partisan Review*, an intellectual journal which featured such writers as Lionel Trilling, Bernard Malamud and Susan Sontag, and explored the political and ideological battles of the 1940's, 50's and 60's. Of natural causes, New York, Sept. 13, 2002.

Plimpton, George, 76, New York editor and writer whose *Paris Review* has featured new fiction and must-read interviews for 50 years; also known for his literary salons and many amateur stabs at sports, from football to boxing. At home, of a heart attack, New York, Sept. 26, 2003.

Postman, Neil, 72, New York writer and teacher whose many books attack television and promote educational reform, e.g. *The Disappearance of Childhood* (1962) and *Teaching As a Subversive Activity* (1969). Of lung cancer, Flushing, Queens, New York, Oct. 5, 2003.

Prigogine, Ilya, 86, Russian-born Belgian scientist awarded 1977 Nobel Prize in Chemistry for work describing complexity in physical systems. Cause undisclosed, Brussels, May 29, 2003.

Rawls, John, 81, influential Harvard philosopher who called for a return to the social contract of Hobbes and Locke, whereby justice is realized by the least advantaged; though belittled by conservatives, his 1971 *A Theory of Justice* sold 200,000 copies. Of heart failure after earlier stroke, Lexington, Mass., Nov. 24, 2002.

Regan, Donald, 84, U.S. banker who headed Merrill Lynch; influential supply-side Treasury secretary under Pres. Reagan and later controversial chief of staff, resigning after discord with Nancy Reagan and as Congress investigated Iran-Contra. Of cancer, Williamsburg, Va., June 10, 2003.

Reisz, Karel, 76, Czech-born film and stage director whose films *Saturday Night and Sunday Morning* and *Morgan!* established the British New Wave; later films include *The French Lieutenant's Woman* and *Sweet Dreams*. Of a blood disorder, London, Nov. 27, 2002.

Riefenstahl, Leni, 101, German filmmaker and photographer best known for the creativity and propaganda found in *Triumph of the Will* and *Olympia*, her documentaries of Hitler's Nuremburg 1934 rally and the 1936 Olympics. At home, south of Munich, Sept. 8, 2003.

Ritter, John, 54, Emmy-winning actor, son of singing cowboy Tex Ritter, who excelled at playing the daffy friend or dad on sitcoms, most notably in *Three's Company* (1978-84) and most recently in *8 Simple Rules for Dating My Teenage Daughter*. On the set of that show, of sudden aortic failure, Burbank, Calif., Sept. 11, 2003.

Robbins, Frederick C., 86, U.S. medical scientist and educator, 1954 Nobel Prize winner for research describing test-tube growth of polio virus, leading to development of effective vaccines; similar work led to recent identification of SARS virus. Of natural causes, Cleveland, Aug. 4, 2003.

Rogers, Fred, 74, TV's "Mister Rogers," whose "Neighborhood" was a place where millions of children enjoyed songs and stories and learned how to get along in a world that isn't always agreeable; Protestant minister turned TV icon since 1954. Of stomach cancer, Pittsburgh, Feb. 27, 2003.

Rostow, Walt, 86, U.S. professor and author of more than 30 books on history and economics, best remembered as adviser to Presidents Kennedy and Johnson and avid proponent of Vietnam War. Cause undisclosed, Feb. 13, 2003.

Said, Edward, 67, Jerusalem-born Columbia University professor, author of literary and political works that spell out his view of East/West power struggle, notably *Orientalism* (1978); strong voice for Palestinian independence. Of leukemia, New York, Sept. 24, 2003.

Schlesinger, John, 77, British director of stark, character-driven films of London life such as *Darling* and *Sunday, Bloody Sunday*; best known for first American film, 1969 Oscar-winning *Midnight Cowboy*. After earlier stroke, Palm Springs, Calif., July 25, 2003.

Schonberg, Harold C., 87, influential New York music critic for the *Times* 1960-80, whose direct and self-assured style won a 1971 Pulitzer Prize; noted for favoring emotional Romantic music over more rational serialism. Of natural causes, New York, July 26, 2003.

Schramm, Tex, 83, U.S. pro football executive, led Dallas Cowboys from 1960 start through rise to fame as "America's Team" until 1989; advocate of AFL–NFL merger and such innovations as instant replay. At home, Dallas, July 15, 2003.

Scribner, Belding H., 82, U.S. physician who invented the U-shaped shunt that allowed long-term survival on kidney dialysis. Of accidental drowning, Portage Bay, Wash., June 19, 2003.

Shields, Carol, 68, U.S.-born Canadian writer of novels and short stories that sketch drama of ordinary life, e.g. the Pulitzer Prize-winning *Stone Diaries*. Of breast cancer, Victoria, B.C., July 16, 2003.

Shoemaker, Bill, 72, Texas-born jockey ("The Shoe") who won 11 Triple Crown races and 8,833 winners overall in 1949-90 career; successfully trained horses after 1991 auto accident left him paralyzed. At home, San Marino, Calif., Oct. 12, 2003.

Simmons, Richard W., 89, U.S. actor who played Sergeant Preston of the Yukon in the 1950's TV series, as well as many movie roles for 40 years. At home, Oceanside, Calif., Jan. 11, 2003.

Simone, Nina, 70, U.S. singer of a wide range of styles, jazz, blues, art songs and Gershwin, whose "I Loves You, Porgy" was her first and only Top 20 hit; also known for her outspoken views on civil rights and racism. Cause undisclosed, near Marseille, France, April 21, 2003.

Sisulu, Walter, 90, South African leader who was both mentor and partner to Nelson Mandela in the long struggle to overcome apartheid; a political prisoner for 26 years, he helped lead the African National Congress to the establishment of a democratic government in 1994. Of natural causes, Johannesburg, May 5, 2003.

Stack, Robert, 84, U.S. actor who won an Emmy playing Eliot Ness on *The Untouchables*, 1959-63; later narrated *Unsolved Mysteries*; films include *The High and the Mighty* and *Written on the Wind*. Of heart failure, at home, Los Angeles, May 15, 2003.

Steig, William, 95, Brooklyn-born cartoonist and writer whose wise guy kids and spurned lovers have amused *New Yorker* readers since 1930. Many children's books include *Shrek!*, made into 2001 Oscar winner. Of natural causes, Boston, Oct. 3, 2003.

Stone, Peter, 73, U.S. writer for stage and screen who won an Oscar for *Father Goose*, and three Tonys, for *Woman of the Year*, *Titanic*, and most notably for *1776*, the clever musical about the signing of the Declaration of Independence. Of pulmonary fibrosis, New York, April 26, 2003.

Strummer, Joe (John Graham Mellor), 50, British singer/composer who led The Clash, a popular 70's and 80's punk-rock group that featured songs of rebellion and political angst; later had movie roles and a radio show. Of a heart attack, Somerset, England, Dec. 22, 2002.

Teller, Edward, 95, Hungarian-born physicist who led development of hydrogen bomb in 1952; outspoken foe of Soviet threat, he testified against atomic bomb developer Robert Oppenheimer on security grounds. At home, Palo Alto, Calif., Sept. 9, 2003.

Thatcher, Sir Denis, 88, British oil executive, was best known as the assiduous, sometimes testy husband of Prime Minister Margaret Thatcher. After bypass surgery, London, June 26, 2003.

Thurmond, Strom, 100, South Carolina senator 1954–2002, the record for Senate service; originally a Democrat who ran against Pres. Truman as a "Dixiecrat" in 1948, he switched parties in 1964, paving the way for G.O.P. success in the once-solid South; best known for opposition to integration and civil rights laws, though he disclaimed racism. At home, Edgefield, S.C., June 26, 2003.

Trevor-Roper, Hugh, 89, British historian whose *Last Days of Hitler* was a 1947 best seller, but Oxford repute declined in 1983 when he verified phony Hitler diaries. Of natural causes, Oxford, England, Jan. 26, 2003.

Tureck, Rosalyn, 88, Chicago-born Bach specialist on piano and harpsichord whose performances, recordings and teaching sparked revival of interest in the composer of "The Well-Tempered Klavier" and "Goldberg Variations." At home, Bronx, N.Y., July 17, 2003.

Uris, Leon, 78, U.S. writer of such best-selling novels as *Battle Cry*, *Exodus* and *Trinity*; his success stemmed from rigorous research and gripping narrative style. Of kidney failure, at home, Shelter Island, N.Y., June 21, 2003.

Varnedoe, Kirk, 57, U.S. art critic and historian whose writing and lectures on modernism advanced him to chief curator of the Museum of Modern Art, transforming its collection. Of colon cancer, New York, Aug. 14, 2003.

White, Barry, 58, Texas-born singer whose resonant bass pulsed through popular bedroom ballads of the disco 70's, such as "Can't Get Enough of Your Love, Babe." Of kidney failure, Los Angeles, July 4, 2003.

Williams, Sir Bernard, 73, British philosopher, viewed morality as intertwined with history and culture, notably in 1985 study, *Ethics and the Limits of Philosophy*; left England, disaffected by Thatcher government in 1980's to teach at Berkeley. Of cancer, Oxford, June 10, 2003.

Wilson, Kemmons, 90, U.S. builder and founder of the Holiday Inn chain in 1951, growing into thousands of motels worldwide. At home, Memphis, Tenn., Feb. 12, 2003.

Wilson, Sloan, 83, U.S. novelist best known for *Man in the Gray Flannel Suit* (1955), which evokes postwar corporate culture and social climbing; popular 1956 movie. Of Alzheimer's disease, Colonial Beach, Va., May 25, 2003.

Winsor, Kathleen, 83, U.S. writer who practically invented the bodice-ripper best seller with *Forever Amber* in 1944, a rigorously researched tale of Amber's many loves in the racy Restoration. At home, New York, May 26, 2003.

Ziegler, Ron, 63, U.S. public relations and advertising figure who served as press secretary during Nixon presidency; remembered for tenacious defense of president as Watergate scandal unfolded. Of a heart attack, Coronado, Calif., Feb. 10, 2003.

Zindel, Paul, 66, Staten Island-born science teacher turned playwright who won 1971 Pulitzer Prize for *The Effect of Gamma Rays on Man-in-the-Moon Marigolds*, about growing up scientifically gifted in a dysfunctional family. Of cancer, New York, March 27, 2003.

Major News Stories of 2002-2003

By Correspondents of The New York Times

INTERNATIONAL NEWS

THE WAR IN IRAQ

After the terrorist attacks of Sept. 11, 2001, and the war in Afghanistan, President George W. Bush declared a doctrine justifying pre-emptive strikes against any nation thought to be threatening the United States with unconventional arms, and Iraq quickly came into sight.

The administration's determination to invade Iraq led to a diplomatic crisis with the United Nations in 2003, a six-week war and a lingering and bloody aftermath, which continues. Also, lasting questions remained about the principal premise of the war, that Saddam Hussein possessed weapons of mass destruction.

U.S. Forces Defeat Saddam, Then Face Guerrilla Attacks

The military campaign to topple Saddam Hussein's regime was very different from Desert Storm, the 1991 American-level military operation to evict Iraqi forces from Kuwait. Instead of assembling a massive ground force, as happened in 1991, this American-led invasion force consisted primarily of two Army divisions, with a Marine Expeditionary Force and a British Armored Division.

And instead of conducting a lengthy air campaign before the ground attack, this time the allied land assault and air attacks were nearly simultaneous.

The new approach reflected Defense Secretary Donald Rumsfeld's emphasis on transforming the military, a push to get the armed forces to take full advantage of their superior technology, precision air power and reconnaissance. According to Mr. Rumsfeld, the United States could defeat its foes with smaller and more deployable ground forces.

But critics, such as retired general Barry R. McCaffrey, who led the 24th Mechanized Division in the 1991 war, complained that the invasion force this time was too small for the task at hand, which included protecting long supply lines, seizing an enemy capital and stabilizing a nation the size of California. The debate over the force used in the war continued well after the main fighting was over.

The war began on March 19, 2003, when President Bush ordered a surprise air strike to try to kill Mr. Hussein and his top aides. The decapitation strike was carried out in the Dora Farms area of Baghdad where Mr. Hussein was believed to be holding a meeting in a bunker. The attack failed and it was later determined that there was no bunker there.

The Iraqis responded by firing surface-to-surface missiles at American forces in Kuwait. A small number of oil wells in the Rumaillah oil field were set on fire. That was worrisome to American commanders, since the Bush administration was determined to safeguard Iraq's oil wealth on the assumption (which later turned out to be doubtful) that it would be used to pay for the nation's reconstruction. To prevent any further destruction of the oil fields, the ground attack was moved forward a day, to March 20. The main air assault began a day later.

The plan was to conduct the ground attack on two main axes. In keeping with the allied strategy, the main ground attack was led by the U.S. Army's V Corps, using the 3rd Infantry Division, the 101st Airborne Division and the 11th Attack Helicopter Regiment.

The V Corps initially meant to seize the bridge that crossed the Euphrates River near Nasiriyah. After that, the V Corps planned to conduct a feint east of the Euphrates to persuade the Iraqis that the Army planned a direct attack on Baghdad, by moving up Highways 1 and 8 to the capital. The main V Corps invasion route was to the west of the Euphrates, then moving through the Karbala gap, in southern Iraq.

While the V Corps attacked, the 1st Marine Expeditionary Force was to mount a supporting attack to the east. Its force included the 1st Marine Division, a large Marine Air Wing, as well as the British ground forces. Its initial objective was to secure the Rumaillah oil field and the port of Umm Qasr. The Marines would then advance past Nasiriyah and head toward Al Kut before moving onto Baghdad.

The allies also hoped to mount an important attack from Turkey. But the Turkish parliament refused to approve the deployment of American troops, despite promises of billions of dollars in American aid. So the plan for opening a northern front was scaled back.

The Army's 4th Infantry Division was redirected to Kuwait, where it belatedly joined in the main attack from the south. Special operations forces, the Army's 173 Brigade and Marines from the 26th Marine Expeditionary Unit were deployed in the north, where they were to stabilize the region and discourage ethnic violence.

When the war began, allied commanders thought that the main resistance would come from the Republican Guard divisions that defended the approaches to Baghdad. The Medina Republican Guard was a particular worry. What allied commanders did not foresee was that Saddam Hussein's regime would try to block the advance by ordering paramilitary style attacks using fighters based in Nasariyah, Najaf and other southern towns.

These paramilitary forces included fighters from the Saddam Fedayeen, as well as foreign fighters recruited from Syria and other Arab countries. Mr. Hussein's apparent aim was to draw the allies into urban warfare in the south. His hope was that this would bog down the allied attack and produce enough allied casualties to turn the American public against the war. The presence of the paramilitary forces also was intended to deter the Shiite population from rebelling as they had after the 1991 war.

The Iraqi strategy caused the American and British forces to change their tactics. Instead of bypassing Iraq's southern cities on the way to Baghdad, American commanders decided that they needed to fight in the south to clean out the paramilitary forces.

Soldiers from the Army's Airborne Division, which had been held in reserve, were assigned to the V Corps to help out. Meanwhile, the British forces were assigned the mission of taking Basra, Iraq's second-largest city.

The allied forces withstood the urban warfare. After a delay of several days to consolidate logistics and deal with the paramilitary forces in the south, the Americans continued their advance toward Baghdad.

Still, the war had its costs. In one notorious episode, an American transportation company stumbled into an enemy-controlled area of Nasiriya on March 23. Jessica Lynch, a private and five fellow soldiers were captured and 11 soldiers were killed. On April 3, Army forces seized Saddam International Airport, which was renamed Baghdad International Airport. On April 5, a battalion from the 2nd Brigade of the 3rd Infantry Division drove through Baghdad in a show of force. More than 1,000 Iraqis were reported killed during the raid.

On April 7, the Second Brigade raced into central Baghdad and stayed. The same day, a B-1 bomber dropped four 2,000-pound bombs in a house in the Mansour district of Baghdad where Saddam was believed to be hiding. But neither he nor his sons proved to be there. U.S. Marines arrived in Baghdad two days later. Tikrit, Saddam's hometown, was later taken by the Marines without much of a fight.

As the conventional forces advanced, special operations forces fought in western Iraq. One of their missions was to prevent the possible launch of Scud missiles against Israel. No Scud missiles were found. Nor were allied fighters attacked with chemical or biological arms despite intelligence reports that they had been deployed and likely to be used in combat. The extensive precautions taken by allied forces — vaccinations and protective bulky chemical suits — turned out not to be necessary.

After the regime collapsed, Baghdad became the scene of widespread looting, which the overstretched invading forces failed to foresee or prevent. The United States had limited its air strikes as a way to avoid extensive damage to Iraq's electrical system and other key elements of its infrastructure. But the looting — which targeted banks, offices, shops and even the main archeological musem — produced the sort of physical and psychological damage that Washington war planners had hoped to avoid.

After the war, a document from the Iraqi Intelligence Service was discovered that called for a campaign of economic sabotage in the event the regime was overthrown.

President Bush declared an end to combat operations in a May 1 address on the deck of the Abraham Lincoln aircraft carrier. But guerrilla attacks continued, as did the coalition casualties.

Mr. Hussein's sons, Qusay and Uday — Qusay was second on the list of the most wanted in the American formulation (a deck of illustrated playing cards), as the Ace of Clubs, and Uday was third as the Ace of Hearts — were discovered in Mosul and killed by troops from the 101st Airborne in a ferocious battle on July 22. American officials hoped that their deaths would demoralize the guerrilla fighters and decrease the attacks against allied troops. But the attacks continued unabated.

The ongoing turmoil was hazardous to groups the United States was counting on for support. On Aug. 29, for example, in Najaf, in the south, a car bomb exploded outside the holiest Shiite shrine, killing upwards of a hundred people, including the most prominent Shiite cleric cooperating with United States forces in Iraq. He was Ayatollah Muhammad Bakr al-Hakim, a longtime leader of the opposition to Saddam Hussein. The United Nations compound also was bombed on Aug. 19, leaving more than 20 people dead, including a prominent U.N. diplomat.

While the Americans tried to subdue guerrilla attacks, the Iraqis took the first tentative steps toward self-government. Iraq's American-appointed Governing Council delegated a committee to figure out how to write a constitution, a task the Americans wanted to see completed in just six months. But the attempt simply to figure out procedures exposed the deep divisions between the majority Shiites, the Sunnis — who were themselves bitterly divided — and Kurds.

In all, 138 American service personnel died from the beginning of the invasion until President Bush's announcement that the major combat phase was over. Of these, 115 were directly due to combat. The total doubled by early October, to 332, though fewer died as a direct result of combat. Among British military personnel, 51 soldiers were killed during the war and in the first four months of post-war operations.

— Michael Gordon

At the U.N., Bitterness Persists After the War

When the Security Council took up the matter of Saddam Hussein's Iraq back in January, the stage was set for a diplomatic clash of major proportions. And that is exactly what happened.

The French, Russians, and Chinese opposed an American-led military strike to oust Mr. Hussein and bring an end to a despotic regime that sat atop a gusher of oil. The Germans also wanted to give peace a chance, but unlike the others, Germany does not have a membership and veto power on the Security Council, and unlike France and Russia, did not have significant oil concessions in Iraq.

The United States — impatient, oil-savvy, and in preemptive mode — was buttressed by its Security Council colleague, Britain, and by a consortium of lesser entities, including Belgium, Poland and Spain. As diplomats debated the finer points of international affairs, and the role of the U.N., the organization itself was oddly on the sidelines. The Secretary General, Kofi Annan, did not play a forceful role in that debate and whatever leverage he might have wielded did not make itself felt.

By the time the United States decided to invade Iraq in March, with or without U.N. approval, the world body appeared crippled. It had failed as an institution to rise to the Iraqi occasion and its future role as a broker of international differences seemed clouded, at best. Then the war began, without quite coming to an end.

The United States launched an impressive blitz and toppled Mr. Hussein in short order. But the occupation of Iraq proved to be a much more costly affair than the White House's master planners had anticipated. At first, in the heady days of late April and May, when Saddam statues were toppling across Iraq, the United States appeared poised to make changes in the Middle Eastern status quo.

In that context, the United Nations seemed left out. Then as the summer wore on, Iraq's electricity and water failed, and the American body bags piled up. With the new landscape, the U.N. took tentative steps back into Iraq, setting up shop there under the guidance of one its top trouble-shooters, Sergio

Vieira de Mello. The United Nations' mission wasn't entirely clear, but the Americans weren't dismissing the institution anymore.

Then the United Nations itself became a target. On Aug. 19, a suicide bomber demolished the United Nations compound in Baghdad, killing Mr. de Mello, among others.The attack shattered the U.N. and its self-image as an unpolitical agent of fairness and development. Some United Nations staffers began leaving Iraq, an exodus that swelled after subsequent attacks on its Baghdad headquarters.

In September, Pres. Bush returned to New York, hat in hand. He wanted a United Nations resolution to encourage its members to contribute money and troops to the Iraqi reconstruction effort — a sharp reversal from the we-can-go-it-alone attitude the White House had brandished months earlier.

Mr. Annan argued that pre-emptive military strikes against any country ran counter to hard-won lessons about the balance of power and peace on the world. Mr. Bush left New York empty-handed, after conducting fence-mending meetings with the French and Germans.

But they and Russia insisted that the United States act much faster to turn over power to the Iraqis. The French president, Jacques Chirac, called first for a symbolic transfer of sovereignty to the existing 25-member Iraqi Governing Council, followed by the gradual ceding of real power over the next six to nine months. Meanwhile, the Iraqi Governing Council lobbied for a greater role in running the nation.

U.S. Sec. of State Colin L. Powell said that while "We are anxious to remove the burden from ourselves," the Bush administration argued that prudence required a slower, step-by-step turnover of governing responsibility to Iraqis. Finally, in early October, Mr. Annan voiced his reluctance to play a supporting role in Washington's blueprint for a longer political transition. The administration was dismayed as the secretary-general's position emboldened critics of the American approach, jeopardizing a new resolution.

Meanwhile, the cost to the U.S. was growing, both in lives and money. Pres. Bush asked Congress to approve $87 billion to cover military costs in Iraq and Afghanistan, of which some $20.3 billion was for rebuilding Iraq's civic institutions such as police training, a new army, prisons and a justice system, and the oil fields. Democrats and even Republicans complained about the $20.3 billion proposal, and began whittling it back.

The administration's admitted failure in early October to find weapons of mass destruction — the major justification for the war — along with the request for the $87 billion took a serious toll in public support for the president's policies. A *New York Times*/CBS News Poll found that just 45 percent of Americans had confidence in Mr. Bush's ability to deal wisely with an international crisis, down from 66 percent in April.

With matters so unsettled, and with an eye on national elections a year away, the White House ordered a major reorganization of efforts to stop the violence in Iraq and Afghanistan and to speed the reconstruction of both countries. From now on, responsibility for ending attacks on U.S. soldiers and rebuilding both nations would rest squarely with Condoleezza Rice, the national security adviser. "This puts accountability right into the White House," a senior administration official said.

—*Timothy L. O'Brien*

After Months of Looking, No Evidence of Mass Weapons

In making the case for invading Iraq, Bush administration officials (like their British allies) insisted that they had compelling evidence that Saddam Hussein possessed weapons of mass destruction, the programs to develop them further and the immediate means to use them.

On Oct. 10 and 11, 2002, Mr.Bush won authorization for the war by big margins in the House and Senate, with overwhelming Republican approval and substantial Democratic support. The House voted 296 to 133 to give the President a broad mandate to topple Saddam Hussein; the Senate vote was 77 to 23.

But after the war, following an intensive but futile nationwide search for Iraqi weapons of mass destruction, critics in both parties began to question the premise for military action. Democrats and several Republicans asked whether intelligence had been colored in order to sway public opinion and make the case for attack more convincing. Responding to the charge, Pres. Bush, Vice Pres. Cheney and Defense Sec. Donald H. Rumsfeld expressed unwavering confidence that, given sufficient time and stability, Iraqis would come forward to provide conclusive evidence of the feared weapons programs, especially if they felt confident that the Hussein regime was gone forever.

But by late September, an interim report by David Kay, the former United Nations weapon inspector selected by the administration to lead a new search for illicit arms, declared that his teams had found none of the unconventional weapons cited as a principal reason for invasion. However, the teams said, there were signs of substances and equipment with civilian uses but which also may play a role in chemical or biological arms.

Perhaps the most scrutinized statement by the administration on the Iraqi threat came from Pres. Bush himself, delivering his State of the Union message on Jan. 28. "The British government has learned that Saddam Hussein recently sought significant quantities of uranium from Africa," Mr. Bush said, making the case that Iraq posed an imminent threat worthy of taking the nation to war.

The African country in question was Niger, and Central Intelligence Agency officials had concluded that the report was dubious. In fact, a similar reference had been removed from a previous presidential speech. Eight days after the State of the Union speech, Sec. of State Colin L. Powell presented the United Nations with detailed assessments culled from American intelligence to show that Iraq had preserved and hidden the capability to produce terror weapons, but he omitted the uranium allegation.

The controversy over quoting the British intelligence dossier badly tarnished the president's wartime ally, Prime Minister Tony Blair. Britain began a formal inquiry after the death of David Kelly, a British weapons expert whose body was discovered on July 18 in the woods, his wrist slashed in an apparent suicide. Dr. Kelly was identified as a source for a BBC report suggesting that the Blair government had exaggerated Baghdad's nuclear threat.

The White House itself came under suspicion when the Justice Department began an investigation into whether administration officials had leaked the identity of an undercover C.I.A. agent whose husband, Joseph C. Wilson IV, a former ambassador, had investigated the Niger claim for the C.I.A. in 2002 and said publicly that it was unfounded. By late summer, intelligence officials acknowledged that little new evidence had flowed to American agencies in the five years since United Nations inspectors left Iraq, creating an intelligence vacuum.

Mr. Rumsfeld went to Capitol Hill and offered a new analysis of the pre-war intelligence estimates. "The coalition did not act in Iraq because we had discovered dramatic new evidence of Iraq's pursuit of weapons of mass murder," he said. "We acted because we saw the existing evidence in a new light, through the prism of our experience on Sept. 11." The chance that Mr. Hussein might make common cause with terrorists who showed no compunction about attacking civilians in the United States accelerated the need for action, Mr. Rumsfeld argued.

"Intelligence doesn't necessarily mean something is true," Gen. Richard B. Myers, chairman of the Joint Chiefs of Staff, said at a Pentagon briefing after major combat had ended in Iraq. "You know, it's your best estimate of the situation. It doesn't mean it's a fact. I mean, that's not what intelligence is."

And even with inspectors failing to find any actual weapons in Iraq, Pres. Bush declared on Oct. 3 that preliminary findings of active research projects and efforts to obtain missiles justified the war, and showed that "Saddam Hussein was a danger to the world." Hence, the war was justified, he argued.

— *Thom Shanker*

Bush Plunges Into Mideast, But the Violence Goes On

Having set out as president to avoid any such entanglement, George W. Bush plunged into the thicket of Middle East diplomacy, seeking to capitalize on the war in Iraq and to stabilize the region.

But despite what seemed like momentum toward ending the three-year conflict in Israel, Gaza and the West Bank, and even toward achieving peace and Palestinian statehood, Israeli and Palestinian leaders made only grudging concessions under an international plan that came to be called the road map. By autumn 2003, the violence had resumed, the new Palestinian government had collapsed and Israel, with its military options seemingly depleted, threatened to "remove" Mr. Arafat by exile, prison or death.

The first government to change in the region was the Israeli one led by Prime Minister Ariel Sharon. His "unity" coalition fell apart in autumn 2002 after the left-of-center Labor Party bolted. In elections on Jan. 28, Mr. Sharon led his rightist Likud party to a crushing victory. Labor refused to join a new coalition, and Mr. Sharon turned to hard-right parties supportive of settlements in the West Bank and Gaza and opposed to Palestinian statehood.

Mr. Sharon did not substantially change his policies toward the Palestinians. Israel remained in military control of the West Bank. In 2002, after a series of Palestinian attacks, Israel had taken back areas it had previously ceded to Palestinian control under the Oslo accords.

The Bush administration was showing increasing interest in proceeding with the road map, which was drafted in December 2002 by a diplomatic "Quartet" — the United States, the United Nations, the European Union and Russia. The three-phase plan called for reciprocal, simultaneous concessions that would not only end the conflict but also resolve disputes that had divided the two sides for generations. It envisioned a comprehensive Arab-Israeli peace and a Palestinian state alongside Israel in 2005.

Mr. Sharon worked for numerous changes, arguing that the plan endangered Israeli security. For its part, Palestinian leaders set about forming a new government, Mr. Bush's condition for introducing the plan. Under intense international pressure, as well as domestic pressure for civic reform, Mr. Arafat agreed on March 18 to legislation that would give substantial authority to a prime minister, at least on paper. He appointed Mahmoud Abbas as prime minister, a longtime ally and P.L.O. official backed by the Bush administration and Israel as a critic of the armed Palestinian uprising.

After haggling with Mr. Arafat over a cabinet — a fight that set a pattern — Mr. Abbas was confirmed by the Palestinian parliament on April 29. He denounced terrorism "by any party and in all its shapes" and appealed for a "lasting peace" with Israel.

Mr. Abbas said that Hamas and other violent organizations should compete as political parties for Palestinian leadership, not maintain unilateral policies toward Israel. "On this land and for this people, there is only one authority, one law and one democratic and national decision that applies to us all," he said, staking out a position very different than Mr. Arafat's.

Shortly after Mr. Abbas addressed Palestinians and diplomats in Ramallah, a suicide bomber exploded in a Tel Aviv bar, killing three people.

Mr. Sharon was also coming under pressure from Washington and from Israel's economic stagnation. On May 25, his government gave qualified backing to the road map. It was the first time an Israeli government officially endorsed the idea of eventual Palestinian statehood.

The next day, Mr. Sharon, an architect of the settlement movement, shocked Israelis by referring to Israel's presence in the West Bank and Gaza, which it captured in the Six-Day War of 1967, as "occupation." Many Jews regard that land as their Biblical birthright. He used the word occupation four times that day, but after a storm of criticism, he resisted using it again.

Mr. Bush formally presented the road map on June 4, and on June 29, Hamas, Islamic Jihad and Fatah, the mainstream faction of Mr. Arafat and Mr. Abbas, declared a unilateral suspension of attacks on Israelis. Mr. Abbas, who had almost no popular support, hoped this cease-fire would buy him time to negotiate gains from Israel and consolidate his government without immediately confronting violent groups.

That same night, April 29, Israel withdrew its forces and checkpoints from parts of Gaza, permitting Palestinians to travel more freely there than they had in more than two years. A few days later, Israel also returned policing responsibility for Bethlehem, in the West Bank, to the governing Palestinian Authority.

But, arguing that Hamas was using the declared ceasefire to re-arm, Israel resisted further withdrawals before the Palestinian Authority began dismantling militant groups and collecting their weapons. Israel also continued its raids into Palestinian areas in search of accused suspects.

In the peace plan's first phase, the Palestinian Authority was supposed to begin taking such steps against militants. But Mr. Abbas argued that he lacked the support to do so, particularly while Israel was resisting its own concessions. Israel was supposed to dismantle the dozens of settlement "outposts" built under Mr. Sharon, the clusters of trailers on West Bank hilltops set up by settlers to tighten their grip on the land. It dismantled only a small number. It also did not take the mandated step of freezing the growth of settlements. Israel did release some Palestinian prisoners, but Palestinian leaders dismissed that step.

Israel also continued building its barrier of concrete, fencing, ditches and barbed wire against West Bank Palestinians, in some areas seizing large swaths of West Bank land to do so.

Mr. Abbas's position became increasingly precarious. Mr. Arafat refused to hand over control of all the security forces. The cease-fire also began to unravel. Hamas and Islamic Jihad said they would make exceptions and retaliate for any lethal Israeli raids.

Then, on Aug. 19, a Hamas suicide bomber blew himself apart on a Jerusalem bus, killing 23 people, including several children. Israel froze all contacts with the Palestinian Authority and embarked on what it called "all-out" war on Hamas. On Aug. 21, Israel killed a top Hamas political leader, Ismail Abu Shanab, with an air strike in Gaza City. Israeli forces moved back into Gaza.

By early September, Mr. Abbas had had enough. On Sept. 6, he resigned, blaming primarily Israel but also Mr. Arafat as undermining him, and blaming the Bush administration for not pressing Israel. Mr. Arafat quickly appointed the speaker of the Palestinian parliament, Ahmed Qurei, as the new prime minister.

As Mr. Qurei struggled to form a new government, Israel focused blame for the disintegration on Mr. Arafat. On Sept. 11, it declared him "an absolute obstacle" and said it would "act to remove" him.

But if that decision was intended to sideline Mr. Arafat, it backfired, bringing waves of criticism from around the world and demonstrations of support for Mr. Arafat from his own people. The domestic demands for Palestinian reform that helped bring Mr. Abbas into office had also been stifled. Mr. Arafat, at 74, once again presented himself as a besieged leader defying Israel on his people's behalf.

—James Bennet

North Korean Nuclear Threat Makes America Pay Attention

Even as Washington invaded Iraq and then struggled to manage the occupation, the Bush Administration faced a huge challenge on the other side of the world: stopping North Korea from producing nuclear weapons. Such a development would change the balance of power — and of terror — in Asia.

The crisis began in October 2002, when Washington presented evidence to the North Koreans that they had secretly begun a program to enrich uranium in violation of a nuclear "freeze" agreement they signed with the Clinton administration in 1994. North Korean officials angrily conceded that the program had begun, and said they were within their rights to develop a "self-defensive weapon."

Mr. Bush responded by cutting off oil shipments to North Korea, which had been America's part of the 1994 bargain. On New Year's Eve, North Korea kicked out of the country the small number of international nuclear inspectors who had lived at the country's Yongbyon nuclear plant.

Through the winter and spring, the North restarted its nuclear reactor at Yongbyon, and at the reprocessing plant that can turn spent nuclear fuel into weapons-grade plutonium. But while American satellites could detect activity at the reprocessing facility, they could not tell how much plutonium it was producing. When American negotiators met the North Koreans in late spring in Beijing, in a meeting arranged by China, North Korea said its manufacturing of nuclear weapons material was almost finished, a statement the C.I.A. deemed to be a bluff.

But in private, American officials feared that sooner or later North Korea would complete the job. Richard Armitage, the deputy secretary of state, warned Congress that his big fear was that North Korea might not bother to produce a weapon, but would simply sell its plutonium to the highest bidder.

All this seemed far more urgent than the situation in Iraq, but the Administration avoided using the word "crisis," for fear that North Korea's strategy was to create a situation that forced the United States into concessions.

"Why tell the other guy he's gotten your attention so much?" Mr. Armitage asked in congressional testimony. But clearly, the other guy had, and the administration was deeply divided. People inside the Pentagon urged no negotiations, hoping to force North Korea's collapse. The State Department urged one-on-one talks, as the North Koreans demanded, saying that they might be willing to trade away their nuclear capability and noting that military options to take out that capability were impractical, because the United States did not know where all of North Korea's nuclear infrastructure was located.

Mr. Bush chose another path. He said the United States would talk to North Korea only if there were others in the room, specifically Japan, South Korea, China and Russia. The idea was to isolate North Korea, and make it plain that no country in the region would prop up the regime if it continues to issue threats. The first round of these multi-player talks did take place, in Beijing, over three days that ended Aug. 29.

By autumn, the administration was claiming a victory of sorts, saying the world had made it clear that a nuclear capability would not be tolerated. American negotiators even described to the North Koreans a vague vision of what good things could come their way, in the form of relaxed sanctions and eventually a peace treaty ending the Korean war (none was signed in 1953).

But there was little evidence that Kim Jong Il, the country's reclusive leader, was about to allow in inspectors, disclose all its nuclear infrastructure or give up his trump card — the nuclear weapons that make the world pay attention.

—David E. Sanger

Warlord President Exits, Leaving Liberia Shattered

Liberia was founded by Americans in the anxious pre-Emancipation days of the 19th century, becoming black Africa's first independent republic in 1847. But it has been marked by intermittent civil war since 1989. The chief protagonist was the American-educated warlord-turned-president, Charles G. Taylor.

Ending a bloody chapter in the country's history, on Aug. 11 Mr. Taylor stepped down from the presidency and accepted asylum in Nigeria. He had been squeezed out by an arms embargo, a fierce rebel uprising and a war crimes indictment in connection with his alleged role in fomenting war in neighboring Sierra Leone.

Mr. Taylor, who attended college in the Boston area, broke out of an American prison in 1985 while awaiting extradition to Liberia on embezzlement charges. In 1989, he set off a guerrilla uprising against President Samuel K. Doe, a former army sergeant who came to power in a military coup and who became one of Washington's staunchest allies in the late cold war years.

After fueling a seven-year civil war, Mr. Taylor assumed the presidency in 1997. One of his campaign slogans was: "He killed my ma. He killed my pa. I'll vote for him." Mr. Taylor's troubles began anew in 1999 when a new rebel movement, largely a regrouping of his past enemies, sprung up with the blessings of neighboring Guinea.

The rebel group, calling itself Liberians United for Reconciliation and Democracy, took over a vast swath of the country's northeast and, starting in June 2003, made several bloody bids for the capital, Monrovia.

By July the city was divided in half. Disease and hunger was rampant. Mortar shells and stray bullets killed and maimed an untold number of civilians. The war displaced more than half of the country's three million citizens. All the while, a second rebel group, the Movement for Democracy in Liberia, emerged from the southeast, taking over huge stretches of timber regions.

With no ideological motivations to speak of, the warring factions fought for control of a trove of natural resources, chief among them timber, gold and diamonds. Liberia is also the site of the world's largest rubber plantation, owned by Firestone.

The Liberian war spread guns and young disaffected gunmen across the region, fueling conflicts in Sierra Leone, Guinea and Ivory Coast. The International Crisis Group, a research and advocacy organization, has singled out Liberia as the "eye of the regional storm."

Mr. Taylor's long-time ally and vice president, Moses Blah, took over the presidency on Aug. 11, the day Mr. Taylor left the country. A power-sharing deal provided for a transitional government to take over in mid-October, until elections can be scheduled.

Pres. George W. Bush had been under competing pressure for and against intervention to restore security to Liberia. He said American involvement would be limited to helping West African peacekeepers, who began arriving in early August. Some 200 American marines did enter the country later that month but most stayed only briefly, disappointing many Liberians.

— Somini Sengupta

Ivory Coast, an Oasis of Calm, Disintegrates Into Civil War

Ivory Coast, once an island of prosperity and peace in troubled West Africa, was partitioned by a grizzly civil war that began with a failed coup on Sept. 19, 2002.

At the heart of the dispute in the former French colony is the notion of "Ivoirite," literally, Ivoirianness. Its proponents view it as a term of national pride; critics say it feeds xenophobia.

The world's largest cocoa exporter, Ivory Coast was once a haven for African migrant workers entering from neighboring Burkina Faso, Mali and Liberia. But constitutional revisions in July 2000 imposed new restrictions on immigrants and their children, tightening the rules on who could vote, own property and run for national election. Of particular concern was a provision that required both parents of a presidential candidate to have been born in the Ivory Coast.

That provision excluded a popular Northerner named Allasane Ouattara in the last presidential elections, in 2000. At the time, a Southerner named Laurent Gbagbo was elected to the presidency. Critics say the polls were rigged.

What began as an uprising by disaffected soldiers in September 2002 quickly grew into a full-scale civil war that tore the country in half, with rebel factions controlling the north and President Gbagbo's loyalists controlling the south, including the port city and commercial capital, Abidjan. As in the rest of West Africa, the war in Ivory Coast became marked by ragged bands of Kalashnikov-toting child soldiers, civilian massacres and mass graves.

A French-brokered peace accord was signed on Jan. 25, 2003, providing for a power-sharing deal between the warring factions. But Mr. Gbagbo's supporters opposed the accord. Riots broke out in Abidjan, and fighting continued in the interior over the next several months. A transitional government, with representatives from rebel and government factions, was established in May. But disputes continued over key cabinet posts and tensions continued to run high about the resumption of war.

France, the former colonial power here, deployed a 4,000-strong force to police the truce. Elections are scheduled for 2005.

— Somini Sengupta

Bush Visits Nigeria, An Unsettled Giant

Nigeria, which has been ruled by military dictators for so much of its history, held a presidential election in April 2003 that gave Olusegun Obasanjo, himself a former military ruler but now a civilian, another four years in office.

The polling was marred by charges of rigging and intimidation, but the fact that an election happened at all was noteworthy. Coups have long been the way that leaders have been replaced in Africa's most populous country. Since the country began its experiment with civilian government in 1999, Nigeria has barely held together.

The country has been torn by religious and ethnic violence. But its oil wealth and regional clout make it one of America's most important allies in sub-Saharan Africa. President Bush, on a five-nation tour of Africa in July, included a stop in Abuja, Nigeria's shiny capital. After visiting Senegal, South Africa, Botswana and Uganda, Mr. Bush said in Nigeria that America would not allow terrorists to establish a foothold in Africa.

"Several African governments face particular dangers from terrorists, and the United States is working closely with those nations to fight terror," Mr. Bush said. "And we will do more. We will not allow terrorists to threaten the African peoples or to use Africa as a base to threaten the world."

— Marc Lacey

South America Takes A Turn to the Left

South America took a turn to the left in 2003, as mounting discontent after more than a decade of economic stagnation resulted in the elections of presidents critical of free-market capitalism in Argentina, Brazil, Ecuador and Paraguay. But the head of state who began that trend in 1999, Hugo Chavez of Venezuela, found himself increasingly under siege when he failed to deliver prosperity.

With the Bush administration increasingly focused on its war on terrorism, complaints of neglect by Washington and investors, as well as overt anti-American sentiment, grew throughout the region, even in Chile, which signed a free-trade agreement with the United States in 2003.

A new generation of leaders seized on that dissatisfaction, each in a somewhat different way and with strikingly diverse results during their first year in power.

After winning more than 52 million votes late in 2002 and becoming Brazil's first working-class president, Luiz Inacio Lula da Silva emerged as the new beacon for the Latin American left and a source of alarm on the right. A labor leader born into rural poverty, Mr. da Silva promised a new era of social justice and equality and placed former guerrillas in positions of prominence in his cabinet.

After taking power on Jan. 1, 2003, though, Mr. da Silva proved to be more bark than bite. He formed a coalition in Congress with centrist parties and pursued market-friendly economic policies that were almost identical to those of his predecessor, slashing pension benefits and outlays on social programs to increase the government's budget surplus and thus avoid problems with the International Monetary Fund. [See separate story below.]

Ecuador's new president also surprised skeptics by pursuing a conservative strategy, at least at first. Col. Lucio Gutierrez, an admirer of Hugo Chavez, had led an unsuccessful coup attempt in 2000 and was jailed, but defeated a billionaire banana grower after two rounds of voting late in 2002. Upon taking office early in 2003, he immediately made friendly overtures to the United States and Wall Street.

In contrast, Argentina's new president, a Peronist from Patagonia named Nestor Kirchner, took a more confrontational course. Elected with just 22 percent of the vote after a former president, Carlos Menem, withdrew from a runoff, he vowed at his inauguration in late May to shake things up and restore national morale, and soon did just that.

Mr. Kirchner's initial focus was the painful legacy of human rights abuses left by the military dictatorship, which killed as many as 30,000 people before it was forced from power 20 years ago, a subject that had been swept under the rug in recent years. He purged the military high command, pressured Congress into rescinding a pair of amnesty laws, and backed the imprisonment and trial of those responsible for broad rights abuses.

His popularity soared even further after he refused to accept the terms proposed by the I.M.F. for a long-term agreement and briefly defaulted on a $2.9 billion loan repayment in September 2003. That forced Argentina's international creditors to back down from demands for heightened fiscal austerity and compensation to banks and utilities for losses they suffered in the collapse of the economy in December 2001.

But in Venezuela, Mr. Chavez's hold on power faced growing challenges, first in the form of a general strike, led by business and labor groups that accused him of trying to install a pro-Cuban dictatorship. Then, after that effort failed early in 2003, a petition campaign for a recall election obtained 3.2 million signatures. In September, though, the document was ruled invalid, auguring even greater political divisions and social tensions ahead.

Neighboring Colombia also continued in crisis, with no signs of an end to the guerrilla conflict that has plagued the country since the 1960's and killed more than 40,000 people. The Bush administration's support for the conservative president, Alvaro Uribe, held steady, with Washington valuing him as one of its few Latin American allies in the war on terrorism. But neither Mr. Uribe or leftist insurgent groups appeared ready to return to the negotiating table.

—Larry Rohter

Up From Poverty, Brazil's Leader Maneuvers a Moderate Course

Latin America has never known a political leader quite like Luiz Inacio Lula da Silva, who was sworn in as president of Brazil, the region's largest nation, on Jan. 1, 2003. Numerous other political figures have claimed to speak in the name of the poor and disenfranchised, but Mr. da Silva is the first head of state in modern times to have emerged from the most downtrodden segment of the masses, who make up the majority of the continent's population.

Mr. da Silva came to attention a quarter of a century ago as a labor leader in the industrial suburbs around São Paulo, South America's largest city. He came from peasant stock. He was born in 1945 in the interior of Pernambuco, an arid agricultural state, and as a child worked as a farmhand before moving south, like millions of other poor Brazilians seeking work, with his mother and six siblings, settling in São Paulo.

There he sold candy and fruit and shined shoes before dropping out of school at 12 to work in a metalworking factory, where he was trained to be a lathe operator and lost a finger in an accident. He later joined the labor movement and was arrested as a subversive by the military dictatorship then in power. After his release in 1980, he helped found the leftist Workers Party, which chose him as its presidential candidate in three unsuccessful campaigns before he scored a landslide victory in October 2002.

The experience of having shared poverty and deprivation has helped Mr. da Silva create a deep bond with the electorate, a connection that has been strengthened by his plain-spoken style of expression and a willingness to show emotion in public.

Over the years, Mr. da Silva professes to have moved toward the political center, to the point that he now claims never to have been a leftist at all. Whatever the political shift, his enduring and wide-ranging appeal stems from the personally empathy he evokes in his countrymen.

—Larry Rohter

Hong Kong Backs Down On Tough Security Law

A huge crowd marched in Hong Kong on July 1, 2003, the sixth anniversary of the territory's handover by Britain to Chinese rule, to protest the local government's plans for new security legislation. The police estimated that the crowd peaked at 350,000 three hours into the seven-hour march, while organizers put the total at 500,000 during the entire gathering. Either way, it was the biggest demonstration anywhere in the People's Republic of China since the Tiananmen Square protests in 1989.

The government of Chief Executive Tung Chee-hwa tried to push the security bill through the Legislative Council to comply with its interpretation of Article 23 of the Basic Law, the legal framework for Hong Kong negotiated between Britain and China before the handover. The Basic Law requires Hong Kong to enact legislation against treason, secession, sedition, subversion and the theft of state secrets.

But democracy activists contended that the government's bill, drafted the previous autumn and winter, was unnecessary, given British laws still on the books, and went too far. The most controversial provision would have allowed the government to ban groups in Hong Kong with links to organizations banned in mainland China for reasons of national security.

Mr. Tung stripped the banning provision from the bill on July 5. He also deleted a provision allowing the police to conduct searches and make seizures without a warrant during urgent national security investigations. He added a clause regarding the theft of state secrets to allow journalists and others to argue in court that they were acting in the public interest by publicizing government information.

James Tien, the chairman of one of the two pro-government political parties, the Liberal Party, quit Mr. Tung's cabinet on the evening of July 6, saying his party could not support the bill in the legislature. Lacking the votes for passage, Mr. Tung announced early the following morning that he would postpone the bill but set no timetable.

The other pro-government party, the Democratic Alliance for the Betterment of Hong Kong, urged Mr. Tung on Aug. 21 to postpone the bill until after the next Legislative Council elections in the summer of 2004, fearing losses then if the issue remained in the news. Mr. Tung ended up withdrawing the bill on Sept. 5, and declined to say whether he would introduce it again before his term expires in 2007.

At smaller rallies on July 9 and July 13, tens of thousands called for more democracy. The public had chosen only 24 of the 60 Legislative Council members; industries and professions chose another 30, while an 800-member Election Committee, which also selects the chief executive, chose six. In the elections in 2004, the general public will choose 30 members and the Election Committee will no longer choose any.

Mr. Tung said that in 2004 or 2005 he would study proposals for the public to vote in 2007 on his successor as chief executive, and to elect all members of the legislature starting in 2008.

— Keith Bradsher

China's Orderly Transition Elevates New Leaders

In late 2002 and early 2003, China's ruling Communist Party underwent the most extensive peaceful handover of power in its history. At the Party's 16th Congress in November 2002, all but one of the seven members of the Party's top leading group, the Standing Committee, retired from their positions on the committee. The exception was Hu Jintao who, as long expected, was installed as the new general secretary, replacing Jiang Zemin.

But Mr. Jiang retained his post as chairman of the Central Military Commission, leaving him leader of China's military and in a powerful position to shape policies and personnel decisions.

Mr. Hu, an engineer by training, had been groomed for succession from 1992, when he was appointed to the central leadership after serving as the top provincial official in Gansu and then Tibet. He earned a reputation as a cautious, deferential politician, but since becoming general secretary he has sought to put his personal stamp on power with a series of speeches casting himself as a practical, caring leader. On March 15, 2003, Parliament elected a new state president, prime minister and cabinet, thus completing the handover of power to a new generation. Mr. Jiang retired as president, handing the largely ceremonial position over to Mr. Hu. Zhu Rongji retired as prime minister and was replaced by Wen Jiabao, who had served as a deputy prime minister since 1998.

Mr. Wen was trained as a geologist and earned a reputation as a disciplined, unruffled administrator. He and Mr. Hu have largely held to the same policies as the previous leaders, focusing on economic development. But the two men have also sought to assuage popular discontent with the party by adopting a more populist, compassionate tone and promising to devote more money to welfare and jobs growth.

— Chris Buckley

Major Failure Ends World Trade Talks

The failure of the World Trade Organization to agree on a draft program to reform agriculture and other issues at Cancun, Mexico was a major setback for the world trading system and fed a growing sense of protectionism.

It was seen as a defeat for developing nations who had joined together as a bloc to push for agricultural reform and for the world's wealthier nations who were hoping that new openings in trade would give a boost to their sputtering economies by expanding the global marketplace.

The trade ministers gathered in September 2003 to approve a mid-term program for completing this round of trade talks that began in Doha, Qatar in November 2001 and was dedicated to helping developing nations. The breaking point came when Europe upset some of the developing world by asking the trade organization to expand its rules to cover four new areas.

But the heart of the talks was an attempt to convince the world's richest nations, especially the United States and those in the European Union, to cut back the more than $300 billion they give their farmers in annual subsidies. They were also aimed at eliminating Europe's export subsidies on agricultural products and to reduce their tariffs that block food imports from developing nations.

Together, these policies make agriculture the most protected sector in rich nations and create the most unjust trade barriers for poor and developing countries whose best chance of trading their way out of poverty is through their agricultural sector.

But the United States wanted some of the wealthier nations like Brazil, China and India to agree to further open up their markets to agricultural goods and rejected a proposal to compensate four poor African nations for the harm caused by cotton subsidies given to some of America's richest farmers.

Experts at the World Bank and the Organization for Economic Cooperation and Development also tried to convince Europe and the United States to reduce their farm subsidies. But with the 2004 elections looming in the United States, Pres. Bush was reluctant to alienate agribusinesses that benefit from the taxpayer subsidies.

— Elizabeth Becker

NATIONAL NEWS

Californians Recall Governor, Elect Arnold Schwarzenegger

A storm of public anxiety and anger drove California Governor Gray Davis into early retirement as voters used the state's recall provision to remove him from office only 11 months after he was elected to a second term. They chose as his replacement Republican Arnold Schwarzenegger, the Austrian-born bodybuilder and action movie actor making his first run for public office.

The recall election, on Oct. 7, culminated a madcap 11-week campaign featuring a deeply unpopular Democratic governor fighting for his political life, 135 self-nominated candidates to replace him, numerous court challenges, $40 million worth of television advertising and almost daily surprises. Because of the novelty of the recall contest and Mr. Schwarzenegger's global celebrity, the race attracted worldwide attention and was covered with the intensity of the final weeks of a presidential campaign.

It was the first time a California governor had been recalled, despite 31 previous attempts, none of which qualified for the ballot. Mr. Davis became only the second governor in American history to be removed from office by voters, joining in ignominy Lynn J. Frazier of North Dakota, who was recalled in 1921.

The recall ballot posed two questions: Should Governor Davis be recalled? Who should replace him? Voters rejected Mr. Davis by 55.4 percent to 44.6 percent, with support for the recall cutting across party, gender, ethnic and geographic lines. A quarter of those identifying themselves as Democrats voted to recall Mr. Davis, who had won statewide office five times over the previous 28 years.

Mr. Schwarzenegger's victory was as sweeping as Mr. Davis's defeat. Running as a moderate Republican, Mr. Schwarzenegger beat his closest challenger, the Democratic lieutenant governor, Cruz M. Bustamante, by 48 percent to 31 percent. His margin of victory exceeded expectations and came despite accusations of sexual harassment and groping leveled against him by 15 women in the last days of the campaign.

Shortly after Mr. Davis was elected to a second four-year term in November 2002, winning a surprisingly narrow victory over a political novice, Bill Simon Jr., Republican political consultants and an anti-tax crusader named Ted Costa began exploring the possibility of recalling the governor. Their main complaint was that Mr. Davis had underestimated the size of the state's budget deficit during the fall campaign. By winter, it was clear that the state faced a $38 billion gap between expected revenues and planned spending, the largest state budget deficit in the nation's history.

The recall effort was disorganized and underfunded until Darrell Issa, a conservative Republican member of Congress from San Diego County, put up nearly $2 million of his personal fortune to hire professional signature-gatherers. Within weeks, recall proponents had far more than the 900,000 signatures they needed to put the recall question to voters.

The threshold for qualifying for the replacement ballot was low — 65 signatures and a $3,500 filing fee. Potential candidates poured into county elections offices: strippers, washed-up actors, single-issue fanatics and a middle-aged sumo wrestler. Mr. Davis and his advisers tried to keep credible Democrats off the ballot, and they were successful, with the exception of Mr. Bustamante, who saw the compressed election as his best shot at capturing the top office.

The Republican ballot was crowded with well-known candidates, including Mr. Simon, Mr. Issa, State Senator Tom McClintock and Peter Ueberroth, the former commissioner of major league baseball. But Mr. Schwarzenegger transformed the race with his surprise announcement of his candidacy on the "Tonight Show" three days before the filing deadline. Mr. Issa immediately dropped out. Mr. Simon and Mr. Ueberroth followed several weeks later. Mr. McClintock stayed in to the end, despite the pleas of his fellow Republicans to clear the field for the movie superstar. Mr. McClintock ultimately came in third, with 13 percent of the vote.

— *John M. Broder*

Huge Blackout Spreads From Midwest to East Coast

North America in August 2003 suffered the worst blackout in its history, after a cascading series of power line and electricity plant failures that started in the Midwest somehow then managed, within a few minutes, to wipe out power for tens of millions of people in the northeast. Power went out in areas from Toronto to New Jersey

Thousands were trapped, at least temporarily, in stalled subways cars and elevators; Amtrak trains north of Philadelphia stopped running, airports were hobbled, traffic lights went dark; cell phone systems were overloaded. As the sun went down and power remained out, millions spent a mid-August night in stifling-hot homes and apartments without lights, air conditioning or fans. Candles, flashlights and battery-powered radios suddenly became the most important household amenities.

The impact was the greatest in cities like New York, Detroit, Toronto, Ottawa and Cleveland, as urbanites learned just how fundamental electricity is in their lives. In New York, thousands of commuters, stranded in Manhattan without subways or commuter rail, were forced to sleep in building lobbies, station waiting areas, or flat on their backs on sidewalks. Others walked for miles on foot to reach home. Water supplies in Detroit and Cleveland, meanwhile, were threatened because of failed pumping stations.

At least four deaths, two in New York City and two in Canada, were attributed to the power failure, which started at 4:10 p.m. on Aug. 14, a Thursday. Other deaths were blamed on carbon monoxide poisonings tied to use of poorly ventilated generators. But the proper use of generators saved countless other lives, as hospitals throughout the region generally reported having a sufficient backup power supply to keep vital pumps and other equipment running. Many office buildings and hotels — better prepared after the 2001 terrorist attacks — also had generators available to keep basic building systems functioning.

Power would be restored for most of the region by Friday night, as the 290 electricity generation units that had been shut down were brought back on line, one at a time, and power was again sent across the 34,000 miles worth of transmission lines that had been knocked out of service. Even before all the lights were back on the finger pointing started. By Saturday, the sequence of events that led to the massive blackout started to become clear.

A series of power line failures early in the afternoon in northern Ohio, as well as the unexpected shutdown of several power generation units in the area, created an unstable condition that utility plant operators and regulators failed to detect quickly enough to isolate and counteract. FirstEnergy Corp, an Akron-based company that had recently suffered a string of embarrassing slips, including the shutdown of one of its Ohio nuclear power plants after a football-sized, acid-burned cavity was found in the reactor lid, took most of the heat over the blackout. Computer problems at its control center meant its crews were largely unaware of the impending catastrophe. Staff at the regional organization charged with ensuring the reliable delivery of power — Midwest Independent Transmission System Operator — also failed to detect warning signs.

Ultimately, once enough lines in northern Ohio had failed, the spread of the blackout took only a few minutes. By 4:09 p.m., with northern Ohio now cut off from power plants in southern Ohio, a surge in demand for replacement power hit Michigan, and then reached into Canada and around into New York. Power plants throughout the region, detecting this surge and other abnormalities, shut down automatically to prevent equipment damage. Between 4:11 and 4:15, large swaths of Michigan, Ohio, New York, New Jersey, Pennsylvania and Ontario and Quebec, as well as pieces of Connecticut, Massachusetts and Vermont went black.

A flurry of investigations ensued. And in Washington, debate intensified over legislative proposals to change the way the electricity industry is regulated or to increase the available supply of power. By the fall, though, the progress was slowed by partisan disputes over how best to deliver on what so far has been elusive goal in the United States: permanently preventing another major regional blackout.

There was at least one redeeming aspect of the whole affair: There was no repeat of the widespread looting and arson that marred the last major New York City blackout, in July 1977. The city's calm response this time — one of the most characteristic scenes during this blackout was the crowds gathered outside of candle-lit Manhattan bars, or residential neighborhoods, chatting, laughing and looking up at the star-filled sky — demonstrated that somehow New York City in the three decades since the last blackout had become a decidedly more civil place.

— Eric Lipton

Homeland Security Gets Shaky Start

The government's newest Cabinet agency, the Department of Homeland Security, opened for business on Jan. 24, drawing together more than 170,000 employees from 22 existing federal agencies into a new super-department given respnsibility, above all else, for protecting American soil from terrorist attack. In terms of the number of government workers affected, it was the largest reorganization of the government since the creation of the Defense Department in 1947.

Agencies as diverse the Customs Service, the Secret Service, the Coast Guard and most of what had been the Immigration and Naturalization Service suddenly had a new home. Two days earlier, on Jan. 22, Tom Ridge, the former Republican governor of Pennsylvania, was unanimously confirmed by the Senate as the nation's first Secretary of Homeland Security. Mr. Ridge's swearing-in and the department's birth ended one set of debates — between politicians and policymakers who felt that the government needed a special domestic security agency, and opponents who felt the new department would create confusion and that its huge size would make it unmanageable.

But the department's creation set off a new set of policy battles, many focused on whether the new department and Mr. Ridge had the money and other resources to do the job of preventing new terrorist attacks. The Bush administration set the department's first annual budget at about $37 billion, 7 percent more than was spent on the agency's programs when they were housed in different agencies the year before.

The White House said the money was more than adequate, since there had already been a big boost in domestic security spending by the federal government in the panicky months after the Sept. 11, 2001, terror attacks. Many members of Congress, Democrats and Republicans alike, disagreed, vowing to push more money into the department during the appropriations season in the fall. On April 12, Congress approved an additional $1.5 billion in domestic counterterrorism spending. City and state governments continued to complain throughout the year, however, that they were seeing little of the federal money they were promised to protect their communities from terrorist attack.

The department got off to an inauspicious start when, on Feb. 10, department officials released a detailed set of instructions to the public on how they should prepare for the possibility of a terrorist attack, urging families to prepare a "disaster supply kit" that included duct tape and plastic sheeting for use in sealing windows and doors against chemical or biological weapons.

The warning created a near-panic in some communities, with people rushing to supermarkets and hardware stores to stock up on duct tape, sheeting and other supplies. The episode also prompted a round of jokes at the department's expenses from late-night television comedians who were already making fun of the department's color-coded terrorism alert system.

The department got an early test of its capabilities in the weeks before the American invasion of Iraq, when Mr. Ridge and others warned that terrorists might try to strike against Americans in the opening days of the war, claiming they were acting to avenge Iraq. On March 17, two days ahead of the invasion, the department raised the color-coded alert level to orange, or "high risk" from yellow, or "elevated risk," and called on the nation's governors to deploy National Guard troops and state police to protect government buildings and other sites that might be obvious terrorist targets. The war and the weeks following the collapse of the Saddam Hussein government passed without any sort of domestic terrorist incident.

— Philip Shenon

Campaign Finance Reform Faces New Obstacles

The Watergate scandal, with its episodes of easy cash disbursements to dirty tricksters from unaccounted funds, spurred passage of laws, notably the Federal Election and Campaign Act, designed to reform the system. But the desire of large donors to give to politicians and the desire of politicians to receive was not so easily deterred. In 1979, regulators allowed an exemption to the strict limits on donations was forged that allowed the nation's wealthiest individuals, labor unions and corporations to continue to shower the political system with millions of dollars.

The limits on contributions to individuals were sidestepped by donating to national or local party organizations which were then supposed to use these funds to build the party or get out the vote. But these unlimited "soft money" donations proved to be just a backdoor way of helping candidates.

Soft-money accounts grew by huge amounts in recent presidential elections: the total raised by both parties went from $86 million in 1992 to $495 million in 2000.

But in March 2002, a law designed to eliminate soft money donations was passed as momentum from corporate scandals lifted the measure over the objections of many Republicans, and some Democrats, who for years had beaten back the legislation.

The law, known as McCain-Feingold after its sponsors, was quickly challenged in court, with opponents arguing that it abridged the free speech rights of donors, while supporters said that it fostered "meaningful representation," the ability of those who do not make large contributions to have their voices heard.

The Supreme Court held an extraordinary session on Sept. 8, 2003, weeks before its traditional opening on the first Monday of October, to hear arguments over a challenge to the law in order to have a ruling in place as soon as possible for the coming campaigns. Given the complexity of the McCain-Feingold law and the arguments, no one dared predict when or how the Court might rule.

—Neil A. Lewis

New Tax Cuts Amidst Record High Deficit

With the economy still struggling to recover from the recession of 2001, the federal government cut taxes in 2003 for the third time in three years, and the federal budget deficit rose to an all-time high.

The tax cut was a big political victory for Pres. Bush and his fellow Republicans on Capitol Hill, and was cast by them as an effort to help bring down the stubbornly high unemployment rate. But the economy continued to shed jobs through most of the year, and the expansion of the budget deficit—in part because of the tax cut—gave Democrats an opportunity to accuse the administration of fiscal mismanagement. Keenly aware that his prospects for re-election could hinge in large part on the economy, Mr. Bush wasted no time in proposing what he has always sold as the best economic cure-all, a big tax cut. On Jan. 7, in a speech in Chicago, Mr. Bush called for a package of tax reductions for individuals and small businesses that the White House initially valued at $670 billion over 10 years; the pricetag was later found by Congress's Joint Committee on Taxation to be $726 billion. His plan would have reduced personal income tax rates, provided an additional $400-per-child rebate to many families, eliminated the taxation of stock dividends and created incentives for small businesses to buy equipment.

Mr. Bush's proposal ran into trouble in the Senate, where a small group of moderate Republicans said the tax cut was too big given the deterioration of the government's fiscal health. Lacking the votes to get anything bigger through Congress, Republican leaders scaled Mr. Bush's plan back to $350 billion over 10 years, in part by agreeing to reduce rather than eliminate taxes on dividends but also by making some of the other tax cuts temporary. The House passed the final version at that level in the early morning hours of May 23 on a vote of 231-200. The Senate followed suit later that day by a 51-50 margin, with Vice President Dick Cheney casting the tie-breaking vote. Mr. Bush signed it into law on May 28.

Democrats immediately made an issue of the legislation's failure to provide the $400 per child credit to low income working families who do not pay federal income taxes, a controversy that dragged into the fall. But the bigger question was whether the tax cut would live up to the administration's promise that it would create jobs.

The unemployment rate, which stood at 4.1 percent when Mr. Bush took office, rose from 5.7 percent in January 2003 to 6.4 percent in June. By October it had declined slightly to 6.1 percent, but the economy had also lost 2.8 million non-farm jobs during Mr. Bush's presidency, a record that Democrats said was grounds for voting him out of office.

By late summer there were signs that the economy was reviving. But economists said increased economic growth would probably bring the unemployment rate down only slowly — a prediction of considerable concern to Mr. Bush as he developed a re-election campaign strategy for 2004.

The combination of the economic slowdown, the tax cuts and the growth of government spending on the military and homeland security led the budget deficit to rise to a projected $401 billion in the fiscal year ended Sept. 30 from $158 billion a year earlier, according to the Congressional Budget Office in a report issued Aug. 26. At $401 billion, the deficit would exceed the previous record of $290 billion in 1992. But measured another way — as a percentage of total economic output — the deficit for the year ended Sept. 30, at 3.7 percent, remained well below the record of 6 percent, set in 1983.

Still, Democrats said Mr. Bush had squandered the nation's fiscal health for decades to come, and in the process had created a spending squeeze on education, health care and other programs. Some of the Democratic presidential candidates advocated rolling back all of the tax cuts enacted under Mr. Bush; others called for a partial repeal.

— Richard W. Stevenson

Democrats Change Lineup Along With Some Issues

Faced with a popular war-time president and Republican majorities in the House and Senate, Democrats struggled to define their differences with President Bush while not appearing weak on national security issues.

As the start of armed conflict with Iraq approached, leading Democrats continued to urge restraint and called for President Bush to work through the United Nations, saying he had not justified a pre-emptive strike. "Obviously, the case has not been made," Representative Nancy Pelosi of California, the House Democratic leader, said on March 6.

Senate Democratic Leader Tom Daschle of South Dakota came under heavy Republican criticism after a speech before a labor audience on March 17 when he said the president had failed miserably at trying to achieve a diplomatic solution in Iraq, the same day the president issued a final ultimatum to Saddam Hussein. Mr. Daschle did not retract his comments, but the backlash muffled him and other Democrats as the war proceeded, and they left much of the criticism of the war effort to others for months.

Democrats tried to challenge Republicans on domestic issues, but complaints about the economy and the rising federal deficit were slow to pierce the focus on the conflict overseas. On the rare occasions when House Democrats appeared to muster the votes to defeat Republicans on social or spending issues, the Republican leadership pulled the matter from the floor.

In the Senate, Democrats had slightly more muscle under the rules and were able to thwart Republicans on some key initiatives like new limits on medical malpractice suits. They also held together to block a handful of conservative judicial nominations from getting confirmation votes on the Senate floor, a stalemate that led Miguel Estrada, a federal appeals court nominee, to ask on Sept. 3 that his name be withdrawn.

After unsuccessfully fighting Mr. Bush's tax cuts approved in late May, Democrats suddenly found themselves with a potent issue as the result of a last-minute change in the tax package. As they worked out the final details, Republican authors eliminated a special tax credit of up to $400 per child for thousands of low-income families. Democrats seized on the omission as evidence of what they had been saying all along: that the administration's tax package was weighted to benefit the more affluent.

Republicans disputed that assertion, saying many of the families that would not get the credit paid no income tax to begin with. But, sensing the political ramifications, the White House urged Congress to restore the credit. House Republicans, however, wanted it put back only as a larger package and negotiations over extending the credit bogged down.

Bolstered by their party's presidential contenders, Congressional Democrats also sought to highlight the loss of American jobs, particularly in the manufacturing sector, under President Bush. After polls showed public resistance to Mr. Bush's request for $87 billion for military operations and reconstruction in Iraq and Afghanistan, Democrats stepped up their complaints about Iraq policy and compared the overseas spending with unmet domestic needs.

The Democratic presidential primary was roiled on Sept. 17 when Wesley K. Clark, the former Army general and NATO commander, entered the race and immediately moved into the top tier of candidates. Other Democrats questioned his party credentials given his past backing for Republican candidates and sought to exploit his inexperience on domestic issues.Former Vermont Governor Howard Dean, who successfully mined the Internet for contributions to his presidential campaign, came under frequent fire from competitors Representative Richard A. Gephardt of Missouri and Senator John Kerry of Massachusetts, who felt threatened by Mr. Dean in the early Iowa and New Hampshire primaries respectively.

In Congress, party strategists acknowledged Democrats faced a difficult task adding to their numbers in the House and Senate in the 2004 elections let alone recapturing the majority in either the Senate or House.

— Carl Hulse

Presidential Politics: The Rove Factor at Midterm

For Pres. Bush and his chief political adviser, Karl Rove, 2003 was in many ways about setting the table for 2004, and the president's re-election campaign. As the end of the year approached, they had achieved mixed success on this score.

Mr. Bush began the year with much of the country unified behind him in support of the war in Iraq – and many of his prospective Democratic challengers befuddled as they as they struggled to figure out how to challenge this policy. By the time Mr. Bush went on national television on Sept. 7 to request $87 billion for military and reconstruction efforts in Iraq and Afghanistan, the Democratic presidential candidates were unified in assailing Mr. Bush's post-war effort, and polls were suggesting that the war might not prove to be the political benefit that he had hoped.

Indeed, the event that had once seemed sure to find its way into one of Mr. Bush's reelection commercials – his orchestrated landing on the carrier Abraham Lincoln on May 1, where he proclaimed the fall of Baghdad – became by the year's end a symbol of the war's persistence

On the domestic front, Mr. Bush used the year to bolster his standing with his conservative base, rallying behind positions that he presumably would prefer not to emphasize in the midst of an election when he is appealing to centrist voters.

On Jan. 16, the Bush Administration filed a friend of the court brief with the Supreme Court, contending that the admission programs at the University of Michigan's undergraduate and law schools were quota systems and should be overturned. (The court ultimately rejected the argument). Mr. Bush won approval of $350 billion in tax cuts in May; it was about half of the $726 billion he had sought, but it won him applause from conservative groups that had been concerned about what they saw as creeping spending by the Bush White House.

In July, Mr. Bush said he supported some sort of legislation that would bar marriages by homosexuals. And he repeatedly reiterated his opposition to abortion rights, pressing Congress to approve a ban on late-term abortions. (The fact that the Supreme Court adjourned without any announced resignations — apparently sparing Mr. Bush from the battle over abortion that seems almost certain to overshadow whomever Mr. Bush nominates for the seat — saved him some trouble.)

Yet Mr. Bush occasionally strayed beyond tending the base. He pushed for the inclusion of prescription drug benefits in Medicare legislation, setting off a long battle in Congress. A victory there would strip from Democrats one of the most potent issues they had used against Republicans. And when the Supreme Court ruled in favor of the University of Michigan admission programs, Mr. Bush issued a statement praising the ruling, notwithstanding the brief his White House had filed.

— Daniel Altman

Team Effort Underway Rebuilding Ground Zero

In the second year after the terrorist attack on the World Trade Center, a competition was begun to design a memorial to the victims of the Sept. 11 attacks, and Daniel Libeskind, a Polish-born immigrant to the Bronx, was chosen as the architect of the master plan for the rebuilding of the trade center.

Months after the public resoundingly rejected six initial plans to rebuild the trade center, seven teams of renowned architects unveiled new visions for site on Dec. 18. The results were as astounding as the previous designs were dull, from Sir Norman Foster's "kissing towers," evocative of both the twin towers and a double helix, to the matrix design of Richard Meier and Peter Eisenman, which some observers compared to a giant tic-tac-toe.

The designs of two teams stood above the rest, however, to emerge as finalists. One was the World Cultural Center, twin, circular towers with arts buildings nestled high in their scaffolding, designed by Think, a team that included the architects Rafael Viñoly and Frederic Schwartz.

Though the Think design was preferred by some rebuilding officials, on Feb. 26, Gov. George E. Pataki and Mayor Michael R. Bloomberg chose the other finalist, Studio Daniel Libeskind, as the winner.

Mr. Libeskind's design, which he calls Memory Foundations, leaves open a 5-acre pit at the heart of the trade center site, encompassing the footprints of the twin towers and exposing the vast foundation walls of the former complex. Those walls, designed to hold back the underground waters of the Hudson River, held fast through the destruction and collapse of the towers. To Mr. Libeskind, they represented the foundations of democracy, which also were shaken but held fast that fateful day.

Even before the selection of the winning design, construction was underway within the World Trade Center site, as the Port Authority of New York & New Jersey raced to restore service on the PATH commuter line, which crosses beneath the Hudson River to New Jersey. A temporary station was scheduled to open in November 2003.

On April 23, Mr. Pataki outlined an accelerated schedule to get the rebuilding underway, calling for the laying in August 2004 of the cornerstone of the first commercial building to be constructed on the site, the iconic 1,776-foot tower. The entire complex of office buildings, cultural buildings and a transportation hub is expected to cost more than $10 billion.

And although Mr. Libeskind won the competition to design the site, plenty of other hands will be involved in the rebuilding. On July 16, Larry A. Silverstein, the developer who leased the commercial rights to the trade center, won an agreement to have his chosen architect, David M. Childs, serve as the lead designer of the 1,776-foot tower. Mr. Libeskind will serve as a consultant and set the guidelines for the building's floor sizes and general outline.

On July 31, Santiago Calatrava, a renowned Spanish architect known for his train stations and bridges around the world, was chosen by the Port Authority to design the new transportation terminal at the site.

While the influence of other architects will be felt within the framework of Mr. Libeskind's design, Mr. Pataki and other rebuilding officials said they were dedicated to preserving the Libeskind vision. As part of that effort, they also announced in July that they would try to buy the site of the heavily damaged Deutsche Bank building, located across the street from the trade center.

That building would be torn down and replaced with new office space that is part of Mr. Libeskind's design, thus relieving the crowding of the commercial buildings that will encircle the memorial area.

By the deadline of June 30, 5,200 entries had been submitted in the competition to design the memorial for ground zero. A 13-member jury began painstakingly reviewing each entry in August, planning to name a group of finalists in the fall and a winning design sometime after that.

—Edward Wyatt

No Compromise Yet In Prescription Drug Debate

Congress spent most of the year wrangling over prescription drugs, trying to figure out how to help older Americans cope with the rising cost of their medicines.

President Bush set the tone in his State of the Union address, saying, "All seniors should have the choice of a health care plan that provides prescription drugs." He fleshed out his ideas five weeks later in "a framework to modernize and improve Medicare."

The administration proposal offered Medicare coverage of prescription drugs to people who join private insurance plans. The president also offered more modest assistance — a drug discount card and protection against high out-of-pocket drug costs — to people who remain in the traditional Medicare program.

About 88 percent of the 40 million Medicare beneficiaries are in the traditional fee-for-service program, which generally does not pay for outpatient prescription drugs.

At least 25 percent of the elderly have no drug coverage from any source. Even those who buy private insurance to supplement Medicare and those who receive coverage from former employers may be required to pay a substantial share of their drug costs.

Congress quickly rejected the idea of any disparity in drug coverage for Medicare beneficiaries in the traditional program and those in private health plans. Democrats accused the administration of trying to privatize Medicare and coerce the elderly into managed care.

Republicans from rural states said they doubted that private plans would serve their constituents. "We need a universal drug benefit so seniors who want to stay in traditional Medicare get a prescription drug plan that's just as good" as that available in private plans, said Senator Charles E. Grassley, Republican of Iowa, the chairman of the Finance Committee. With that issue settled, Congress still had to work out many details, including the structure of the drug benefit. President Bush and Congress agreed to spend $400 billion over 10 years. To stay within that limit, lawmakers decided to provide coverage for initial drug expenses and catastrophic costs, but left beneficiaries to pay all drug bills in the middle. The Senate and the House passed separate drug bills on June 27. The Senate vote, 76 to 21, was overwhelmingly bipartisan. The House bill passed by a single vote, 216 to 215, with only nine Democrats voting for it.

To get the bill through the House, Republican leaders persuaded a Republican, Representative Jo Ann Emerson of Missouri, to switch her vote. But she extracted a promise: the House would hold a separate vote on a bill allowing Americans — consumers, pharmacists and wholesalers — to import less expensive prescription drugs from Canada and Europe.

That bill was adamantly opposed by the Bush administration and the pharmaceutical industry. Both argued that the bill would allow the sale of unsafe, adulterated and counterfeit drugs, including products made elsewhere and shipped through Canada.

But the House approved that bill by a vote of 243 to 186 on July 25. "We did this against an army of 600-plus lobbyists and millions of dollars of misinformation," Mrs. Emerson said.

Yet the differences between the Senate and House bills were so significant, and the issues so complicated, that as summer turned to fall there was still no final legislation for Pres. Bush to sign.

—Robert Pear

A Year of Pain and Healing For Roman Catholic Church

Leaders of the Roman Catholic Church in the United States worked to repair the damage to their church after a year of scandal over revelations that bishops had covered up the sexual abuse of minors by priests. Catholic dioceses set up review boards to hear accusations, and to implement abuse awareness and prevention programs. New bishops replaced two brought down by scandal. And many bishops moved to settle lawsuits with accusers. But it was still a traumatic year for the church as more accusations became public, more priests were removed from ministry or put on trial, and grand juries and prosecutors issued reports accusing bishops of failure to prevent the abuse.

A Long Island, N.Y., grand jury issued a report in February accusing the Diocese of Rockville Centre, the nation's sixth largest, of protecting sexually abusive priests for decades and tricking victims into silence. But, as in many states, the grand jury said that no indictments were possible because of the statute of limitations. In Los Angeles, a bishop and three former vicars testified before a grand jury about possible abuse by 17 other priests. And in Boston, where the scandal erupted in 2002, Cardinal Bernard Law testified before a criminal grand jury, even though he had already resigned as archbishop in December 2002 in the furor over clergy abuse.

In an unprecedented arrangement, the bishop of Phoenix, Thomas J. O'Brien, avoided criminal charges by striking a plea bargain in June, admitting he had reassigned abusive priests to parishes, and agreeing to submit some administrative functions of the diocese to external supervision. Two weeks later, Bishop O'Brien was accused of hitting and killing a pedestrian, then driving away from the scene. He was charged with leaving the scene of an accident, and resigned on June 18.

Leadership of the Phoenix Diocese was assumed temporarily by Archbishop Michael Sheehan, who years before had taken over the New Mexico Diocese after its bishop was caught in a sexual abuse scandal. In the Boston Archdiocese, one of the most prominent positions in the American church, the Vatican gave the top post to Bishop Sean Patrick O'Malley, a Franciscan priest who had formerly shepherded two other dioceses shaken by clergy sex abuse. Within days of his installation on July 30, Bishop O'Malley moved to settle sexual abuse lawsuits with hundreds of plaintiffs.

The bishops suffered harsh criticism from a high-profile layman whom they had entrusted to help restore their credibility. Former Oklahoma Governor Frank Keating, whom the bishops had appointed in 2002 to lead a board of prominent lay Catholics to monitor the church's recovery, likened the bishops to the Mafia in their inclination for secrecy. But most of the other board members thought his remarks extreme and unhelpful, and Mr. Keating resigned on June 16. The board members continued their work, which included several major studies on the causes and extent of the crisis. They contracted with researchers at the John Jay College of Criminal Justice in New York City to find out the extent of abuse by priests going back 50 years. The researchers asked dioceses to complete detailed surveys, and some bishops balked. The board also hired investigators, many of them former F.B.I. officials, to find out whether each diocese had instituted the reforms that the bishops had promised.

On Aug. 23, the former Boston priest John J. Geoghan, who was convicted of molesting a boy and was accused of molesting nearly 150 others, was slain in a Massachusetts prison. Mr. Geoghan had been in protective custody, but prison authorities say he was strangled in his cell by another inmate, Joseph L. Druce, who was serving a life sentence for strangling a truck driver he believed to be gay.

—***Laurie Goodstein***

States Face Budget Shortfalls

Governors, state budget officials and lawmakers faced the most challenging time in years in 2003 in trying to manage state spending. Reflecting a sour national economy, plunging state tax revenues and rising social service costs, state budgets declined in absolute terms during the 2002-03 fiscal year for the first time since the recession of the early 1980's.

Thirty-seven states were forced to trim budgets enacted in 2002, reducing spending by a total of $14.5 billion, the largest mid-year spending cuts in at least 27 years, according to the National Association of State Budget Officers. Governors and legislators adopted a variety of tactics to address the problem, including spending cuts, tax and fee increases and drawing down emergency or "rainy day" funds. In 2000, following the late-1990's boom in technology and other sectors, states had nearly $50 billion in reserves. By mid-2003, all but $6 billion of that had been spent.

For the 2003-04 fiscal year, a large number of states resorted to increases in taxes and fees to try to bring their budgets into balance. Connecticut enacted a one-time increase in the state's inheritance tax, New Jersey raised taxes on casino profits, and Michigan and Kansas accelerated property tax collections to give state treasurers an increase in cash flow. Fees rose on studded tires in Alaska, mobile-home inspections in Florida, traffic fines in Iowa and birth certificates in New York.

California faced by far the worst fiscal crisis of all the states. California entered the current fiscal year facing a $38.2 billion budget shortfall, larger than the deficits of all the other states combined. The state particularly suffered from the collapse of the dot-com bubble, which slashed state revenue from income and capital gains taxes by more than $15 billion from the 1999-2000 peak. Bond rating agencies downgraded the state's credit to the lowest in the nation, just two notches above junk-bond status.

After a bitter debate and threatened shutdown of many government services, Gov. Gray Davis and the Democrat-dominated state Legislature agreed in late July to a 2003-04 budget that contains no new taxes. The compromise budget relied on deep cuts in education and health care and more than $11 billion in new borrowing. The plan left the state with an $8 billion deficit that will have to be addressed next year.

—***John M. Broder***

Suspect in Olympics Bombing Is Captured in North Carolina

One of the most exhaustive manhunts in American history came to an end just before sunrise on May 31 when a rookie patrolman in Murphy, N.C., spotted a man lurking near a Dumpster behind a discount store. The man turned out to be Eric R. Rudolph, 36, the fugitive charged in the bombing at the 1996 Olympics and a string of other blasts.

The authorities say Mr. Rudolph was the man who planted the knapsack that exploded in Centennial Olympic Park in Atlanta on July 27, 1996, drilling nails and shrapnel into a crowd, killing a woman and injuring more than 100 other people.

Six months later, on Jan. 16, 1997, two bombs ripped through a crowd outside an Atlanta medical clinic where doctors perform abortions, injuring seven people. On Feb. 21, 1997, a bomb at a gay nightclub in Atlanta injured five, and a second bomb, intended for rescue workers, exploded while being handled by a police robot.

On Jan. 29, 1998, a bomb blew up outside an abortion clinic in Birmingham, Ala. An off-duty police officer, Robert D. Sanderson, was killed and a nurse, Emily Lyons, was maimed. Only then was Mr. Rudolph identified: he was seen walking away from the blast, investigators said, and someone noted his North Carolina license plate.

Despite a massive search, which was revived in July 1998 — when he emerged bedraggled from the woods and made contact with the owner of a health-food store 20 miles from Murphy — Mr. Rudolph managed to elude hundreds of officers equipped with high-tech sensors and detection gadgetry. When finally captured, Mr. Rudolph told the authorities he had been living all along in a mountaintop clearing near Andrews, N.C., but investigators suspected he had been helped by sympathetic local residents.

— David Halbfinger

Nightclub Fire Kills 100

It began like any rock and roll show, with flashing lights, thumping drums and grinding guitar. But moments after the headline act, Great White, took the stage on Feb. 20, the Station nightclub, a small roadhouse in the working class town of West Warwick, R.I., was engulfed in flames ignited by a pyrotechnic display. By the end of the night, it was clear that a tragedy of unimaginable proportions had unfolded. Eventually, 100 people died of injuries sustained that night, the worst nightclub fire in at least 25 years.

At least 350 people were packed into the club when Great White took the stage just after 11 p.m., with lead singer Jack Russell singing the opening lines of the song "Desert Moon." Pyrotechnic devices set up on the stage sent a shower of sparks to the ceiling, setting alight the black soundproofing foam that covered the walls. The polyurethane foam quickly sending a wave of flame across the ceiling and walls of the club.

The fire moved so quickly that many people, caught in a mad rush of bodies struggling to escape, died jammed in the main doorway. Within minutes the entire wood frame structure had burned to its cinder block foundation. A grandfather clause in the state fire code allowed the Station's owners, brothers Michael and Jeff Derderian, to operate the club without sprinklers.

The investigation immediately centered on whether the band had secured permission to set off fireworks in the small club and whether the Derderian brothers were criminally responsible for the deaths. Town officials said they have no record of the club seeking a permit. Rhode Island's attorney general convened a grand jury and the state fined the owners more than $1 million for fire code violations and for failing to carry worker's compensation insurance. No criminal charges had been filed as of October 2003, but state officials said the investigation was continuing.

—Lydia Polgreen

Battle Over Gay Marriage

Churches, courts and politicians debated whether gays should be allowed to marry as a growing number of states and cities extended legal benefits to same-sex couples.

On March 4, the Supreme Judicial Court in Massachusetts, the state's highest, heard arguments in *Goodridge v. Department of Public Health*, a case brought on behalf of seven gay and lesbian couples who had been denied marriage licenses. A ruling in favor of the couples would make the state the only one to recognize gay marriage.

The debate peaked in June with two court decisions, including one in neighboring Canada, where on June 10, the highest court in Ontario ruled that a federal ban on same-sex marriage was unconstitutional. Prime Minister Jean Chretien said his government would not appeal the decision and introduced legislation to allow same-sex marriage across Canada. On June 26, the United States Supreme Court, in a 6-to-3 decision, overturned a Texas law that criminalized sodomy. Justice Antonin Scalia, in a dissent, warned that gay marriage would be the logical next step, and gay rights advocates and conservative groups alike vowed to use the decision, *Lawrence v. Texas*, to wage a state-by-state battle over allowing gays to marry.

Senate Majority Leader Bill Frist, a Tennessee Republican, responded by advocating a constitutional amendment defining marriage as between a man and a woman. Gay rights groups pressed Democratic presidential candidates to support gay marriage — which most refused to do. On July 30, President Bush said government lawyers were looking into ways to ensure that the word "marriage" would apply legally only to heterosexual unions. The following day, the Vatican issued a strongly worded document exhorting Roman Catholic lawmakers and others to fight legislation allowing gay marriage. The document was issued under the explicit direction of Pope John Paul II, and in the United States, archbishops in several dioceses instructed priests to preach from their pulpits against gay marriage.

On Aug. 6, the bishops of the Episcopal Church rejected a proposal to draft an official liturgy for gay marriages, but the next day, approved a resolution saying that local dioceses could allow clergy to bless same-sex unions.

By late summer, about 100 couples from the United States had crossed into Canada to be married. But lawyers warned that those marriages would not be recognized in the United States. And while gay rights advocates were predicting that a decision in their favor in the Massachusetts case could set a precedent for gay marriage in other states, 37 states and the federal government have so-called Defense of Marriage Acts, which recognize only marriages between a man and a woman.

— Kate Zernike

Supreme Court Decisions 2002-03

It was a Supreme Court term to remember, rich in drama and impact, both symbolic and real. During the term that began Oct. 7, 2002 and ended June 26, 2003, the justices chose sides on two divisive social issues: the use of race in university admissions and the right of gay men and lesbians to sexual intimacy in their own homes without the prospect of criminal prosecution.

The decisions were notable not only for their outcomes but for the sweeping language employed to justify those results. In *Grutter v. Bollinger*, decided on June 23 by a vote of 5 to 4, the court reaffirmed the constitutionality of affirmative action for the purpose of achieving and maintaining racial diversity on campus. In *Lawrence v. Texas*, decided June 26, the court invalidated a Texas criminal sodomy law and declared that gays "are entitled to respect for their private lives," in the words of Justice Anthony M. Kennedy's majority opinion. The 6-to-3 decision entailed a stunning repudiation of a 1986 ruling, *Bowers v. Hardwick*, in which the court had dismissed as "facetious" the claim to a right of sexual privacy asserted by a gay man in Georgia.

The 2002-2003 term was notable in other respects. It brought an unexpected pause in the Rehnquist Court's federalism revolution. In *Nevada Department of Human Resources v. Hibbs*, decided on May 27, a 6-to-3 majority opinion written by Chief Justice William H. Rehnquist himself rejected the claim that states are immune from suit by their employees under the Family and Medical Leave Act of 1993. This statute requires employers, including state agencies, to give their employees up to 12 weeks of unpaid leave to handle family emergencies. Nevada argued that Congress lacked authority to breach the states' constitutional immunity from suit, an immunity the Supreme Court itself had significantly enhanced in recent decisions shielding states from employees' lawsuits complaining of disability and age discrimination.

But this case was different, Chief Justice Rehnquist said, because the law's goal was to combat discrimination against women in the workplace by acknowledging that men as well as women had responsibilities at home that might require time off from their jobs. Because the 14th Amendment gives Congress special authority to address sex discrimination, Congress could appropriately open the states to suit, the court concluded.

In the area of criminal law, the court rejected two challenges to California' "three strikes and you're out" law for repeat offenders, the harshest such law in the country, under which a third offense, even a nonviolent property crime, can result in a prison sentence of 25 yeas to life. In *Ewing v. California*, the law was challenged by a man who received 25 years without parole for stealing two golf clubs. *In Lockyer v. Andrade*, a shoplifter who stole videos worth $150 received 50 years without parole. A pair of 5-to-4 decisions issued on March 5 rejected the argument that these sentences were so disproportionate as to violate the Eighth Amendment's prohibition against cruel and unusual punishment.

In a free speech case, the court voted 6 to 3 to uphold the Children's Internet Protection Act, a new law requiring public libraries, as a condition of receiving the federal grants on which many depend, to install antipornography filers on all computers providing Internet access. Librarians themselves were in the forefront of the challenge to this law, arguing in a suit filed before it took effect that it would turn them into unwilling censors. The decision in *United States v. American Library Association*, issued June 23, left open the prospect that if the statute proved unduly burdensome once it took effect, the court might be open to hearing a new challenge.

The term was an important one for the business community. The court placed new limits on punitive damages in a decision issued April 7, overturning a $145-million punitive award against the State Farm insurance company by a Utah jury that had assessed compensatory damages of only $1 million. The Supreme Court's 6-to-3 decision in *State Farm v. Campbell* declared the 145:1 ratio to be "irrational and arbitrary." While not setting a ceiling on punitive damages, the 6-to-3 majority opinion said the ratio should be small, perhaps no greater than 1:1.

The court handed a big victory to Hollywood studios and other corporate copyright holders by uphold a disputed 20-year extension of existing copyrights. The court's 7-to-2 decision in *Eldred v. Ashcroft* was issued Jan. 15.

No matter what else the court accomplished, there was little doubt that the term would be known for the two late-June decisions on affirmative action and gay rights. The affirmative action case challenged the admissions policy at the University of Michigan Law School, a competitive institution that gives special consideration to members of "under-representative minority groups:" blacks, Hispanics, and American Indians. A disappointed white applicant, Barbara Grutter, brought a lawsuit claiming the policy violated her right to equal protection. Rejecting this argument, Justice Sandra Day O'Connor's majority opinion was a forceful endorsement of the role of racial diversity on campus in opening doors and achieving a more equal society. At the same time, the court made clear that race cannot be used in a "mechanical" way. In a companion case, *Gratz v. Bollinger*, the court voted 6 to 3 to reject Michigan's undergraduate admissions policy, which awarded minority applicants an automatic 20 points on a 150-point scale.

The majority opinion in the gay rights case was notable for its embrace of an expansive view of the meaning of the Constitution's due process guarantee, as well as for its approving reference to a decision in support of gay rights by the European Court of Human Rights. Texas was one of 13 states to make sodomy among consenting adults a crime, and one of only four to apply such a law exclusively to same-sex partners. The law was challenged by two men, John G. Lawrence and Tyron Garner, who were arrested in Mr. Lawrence's Houston apartment after the police entered on a false tip about the presence of a gun.

The court's summer recess was unusually short: instead of waiting until the traditional first Monday in October, the justices met in special session on Sept. 8 to hear arguments on the constitutionality of the new federal campaign finance law, with a decision anticipated by early 2004.

—Linda Greenhouse

BUSINESS AND ECONOMY

Asians Prop Up Strong Dollar, Badly Hurting U.S. Exports

Something strange happened this year to the foreign-exchange rate of the dollar: American leaders began to wish it would go down. From the steel towns of Pennsylvania to furniture makers in North Carolina, manufacturers and politicians across the country angrily complained that American business was being crippled by the high value of the dollar and the artificially low value of Asian currencies — especially that of the Chinese yuan.

In a major departure from policies of the past decade, the Bush Administration put public pressure on China and Japan to let their currencies rise in value against the dollar. Officially, Administration officials insisted they merely wanted Asian central banks to intervene less in currency markets and adopt more "flexible" exchange rates. But the real complaint was that Asian central banks were intervening in the markets to keep their own currencies weak. A weak currency makes a country's exports cheap in other markets, and critics of China have charged that its currency is undervalued by as much as 40 percent against the dollar.

This was one issue on which European leaders were entirely on the same side as the Americans.

The dollar had already fallen sharply against the euro, which had made European exports to the United States more expensive. With Asian currencies still weak, European leaders complained that their products were being squeezed on all fronts at once. The reasons for American fixation on China were not hard to identify. As almost anybody who shops at Wal-Mart or Kmart has discovered, Chinese products are flooding into the United States at levels that seemed inconceivable just a few years ago. The United States' trade deficit with China exceeded $100 billion last year — bigger than the U.S. trade deficit with Japan or the entire European Union. American manufacturers, meanwhile, have shed more than two million jobs in the past three years. Many of those jobs went directly to China, as American manufacturers either moved their own operations or bought more of their components from Chinese suppliers.

In pressuring Asian countries to let their currencies rise against the dollar, the Bush Administration tacitly broke with the "strong dollar" policies championed throughout the Clinton administration. The Bush Administration has shown no inclination to push the dollar down by intervening in the markets itself. But a passive acceptance of the dollar's weakness is at least as significant. Most economists have been convinced for years that the dollar was ready for a fall, because the United States has a huge trade deficit and a growing fiscal deficit that can only be financed by borrowing money from abroad. Indeed, the United States is now the world's biggest net borrower by a wide margin.

But in a globalized world, there is no such thing as a perfect exchange rate. American consumers have been huge beneficiaries of low-cost imports. And even though American manufacturers have lost ground to imports, a big share of those imports are coming from their own subsidiaries in places like China.

— Ed Andrews

Corporate Scandals Grow and Grow

If United States investors expected corporate scandals to abate in 2003, they were sorely — and quickly — disappointed. Not only were further shenanigans at Enron, Worldcom and the nation's top brokerage firms disclosed in disturbing detail throughout the year, unsavory practices came to light at industries and institutions that had previously been considered exemplary.

The mutual fund industry, for example, came under intense scrutiny in an investigation by Eliot Spitzer, the New York Attorney General. The investigation, made public in early September, found that several funds had given preferential treatment to large investors in exchange for gaining access to these investors' money. One fund allowed an investor to trade fund shares after the market closed, which is illegal, enabling the investor to profit on news disclosed after trading hours.

The New York Stock Exchange and its chairman, Richard A. Grasso, also came under attack when the board disclosed that it had approved a contract for Mr. Grasso that paid him $140 million in compensation and retirement benefits. The firestorm over the payment, which was decided by the compensation committee of the exchange's board, a group dominated by the very brokerage firms and financial institutions policed by the exchange's regulatory unit, forced Mr. Grasso to resign in mid-September.

As the year began, many investors hoped that a 2002 law known as Sarbanes-Oxley, designed to make corporate executives more accountable to their shareholders, would improve financial disclosure at companies and encourage their managers to behave more ethically. A new cop on the Wall Street beat arrived in February when William H. Donaldson, a former brokerage firm executive, became the chairman of the Securities and Exchange Commission. Congress voted to give the commission a big increase in funding and Mr. Donaldson quickly increased his staff of lawyers and accountants watching over corporate America.

But in April, 10 of the nation's largest brokerage firms agreed to pay $1.4 billion to settle a series of cases brought by regulators who contended that the firms published overly optimistic research reports recommending stocks to their customers to curry favor with the corporations issuing the shares. Earning future investment banking fees was the idea behind the research reports that always urged investors to buy and never advised the sale of a stock. Prosecutors produced hundreds of emails showing analysts privately deriding companies whose shares they public recommended.

As a result of the settlement, Henry Blodget, the former internet analyst at Merrill Lynch, and Jack B. Grubman, a former telecommunications analyst at Salomon Smith Barney, paid a total of $19 million in fines and were barred from the securities industry.

As the year progressed, prosecutors continued to build their case against the management of Enron, the rogue energy trading company that had failed in the fall of 2001. In September 2003, Ben F. Glisan Jr., a former treasurer at the company, pleaded guilty to conspiring to commit fraud and began serving a five-year jail sentence. He was the first Enron executive to go to prison.

But prosecutors amassing evidence in the Enron investigation also expanded their reach to include the big banks and brokerage firms that helped the company hide the truth about its precarious financial condition. Previously, such institutions had been shielded from prosecution in fraud cases, but in July, Robert M. Morgenthau, the New York district attorney, reached a settlement with Citigroup and J.P. Morgan Chase in which the banks paid fines and penalties of $300 million without admitting or denying that they had helped Enron mislead investors.

Other executives donned pinstripes last year. In May, Samuel Waksal, the former chief executive of Imclone, a biotechnology company, pleaded guilty to securities fraud and perjury related to sales of ImClone stock he made for himself and family members at the end of 2001. He was sentenced to seven years in prison.

And Martha Stewart, a friend of Mr. Waksal, was indicted in June for securities fraud and obstruction of justice related to her own sales of ImClone stock. She pleaded not guilty; her trial is to begin in January 2004.

—Gretchen Morgenson

Furor Mounts Over New Media Ownership Rules

After more than a year of study, the Federal Communications Commission relaxed many of the media ownership rules that had limited the nation's largest media conglomerates from growing larger and entering new fields. The decision, one of the most significant deregulatory steps undertaken during the Bush administration, was adopted by a bitterly divided commission on June

2. It followed heavy lobbying by broadcasters, television networks and newspaper publishers that had long chafed under restrictions.

But the rules provoked an outpouring of criticism from an ideologically diverse array of organizations, from the National Rifle Association and the United States Conference of Catholic Bishops to the National Organization for Women and the Leadership Conference on Civil Rights. The broadcasting industry was deeply divided as well. The networks favored the rules that enabled them to buy more stations, while the smaller affiliate broadcast stations lobbied heavily to try to prevent the networks from expanding. The architect of the new rules, F.C.C. chairman Michael K. Powell, had maintained that the new rules were necessary to preserve free over-the-air television and as a response to a series of court decisions that had questioned the constitutionality of some of the old rules.

But the critics maintained that the new rules would lead to a wave of media consolidation that would reduce the number of diverse voices on the airwaves, limit competition in the industry, and discourage coverage of local news events as conglomerates bought small town stations and newspapers. No sooner had the rules been adopted than critics began working Congress and the courts to try to get some or all of them repealed. On Sept. 3, a federal appeals court in Philadelphia blocked the rules from being imposed to consider a challenge to them by a group of small radio stations. On Sept. 16, the Senate voted, 55 to 40, to approve a resolution of disapproval that, if it became law, would effectively reverse the commission. Republican leaders in the House of Representatives vowed to keep the measure from reaching the floor, and the White House threatened to veto it. Still, the lawmakers opposed to the new rules vowed to continue to take steps to block the commission.

—Stephen Labaton

SCIENCE AND MEDICINE

Another Space Shuttle Is Lost, And NASA's "Culture" Is Blamed

Bright clumps of smoldering debris streaked across the clear, cool Western sky the morning of Feb. 1. At the end of a successful 16-day research mission, the space shuttle Columbia had disintegrated on re-entering the atmosphere, just 16 minutes before it was to land at the Kennedy Space Center in Florida, leaving a swath of wreckage across east Texas and Louisiana.

Lost aboard Columbia was its crew of seven, a multicultural group of astronauts: Rick D. Husband, the mission commander; William C. McCool, the shuttle pilot; and the mission specialists, David M. Brown, Michael P. Anderson, Laurel B. Clark, Kalpana Chawla and Ilan Ramon, the first astronaut from Israel.

The Columbia Accident Investigation Board, an independent panel appointed by the National Aeronautics and Space Administration (NASA), concluded after a seven-month investigation that the shuttle was mortally wounded shortly after liftoff in an incident few took seriously at the time. A large piece of insulating foam that had dislodged from its main fuel tank struck the leading edge of the left wing 81 seconds into the flight, punching a hole in the craft's thermal protection system. This breach allowed the superhot gases of re-entry to destroy the wing from the inside.

But the board said in a scathing 248-page report, released on Aug. 26, that blunders and organizational problems within NASA were equally at fault. The report said the space agency had a "broken safety culture" that delayed addressing "routine problems that were not defined as a threat to mission safety," like foam-shedding, if they threatened the launching schedule.

The factors that led to the loss of Columbia echoed those that underlay the explosion of the shuttle Challenger on Jan. 16, 1986, the board said. By the time of Columbia's last launching, the bad habits "that were in effect at the time of the Challenger accident — like inadequate concern over deviations from expected performance, a silent safety program and schedule pressure — had returned to NASA," and "history became cause."

Sean O'Keefe, the NASA administrator, replied, "We get it," and promised to follow the board's 29 recommendations, 15 of which had to be carried out before the next shuttle flight. NASA replaced most of the management of the shuttle program, established a new safety and engineering center to actively pursue safety issues throughout the agency and appointed a panel of outside experts to monitor its compliance with return-to-flight recommendations, including developing ways to assess and repair a shuttle's heat protection system during flights.

The space agency said it hoped to resume shuttle flights sometime during 2004, primarily to continue building and supplying the International Space Station. While the investigation board said shuttles could be operated safely for a few more years with sufficient diligence, it urged NASA to retire them as soon as possible in favor of newer, safer spacecraft.

—Warren E. Leary

A Mystery Virus Kills Hundreds, But Doctors Identify and Contain It

On March 12, the World Health Organization (W.H.O.) issued a rare global health alert, saying an illness that started with nonspecific flulike symptoms and often led to severe pneumonia had been reported from Vietnam and Hong Kong. There, it was striking a relatively large number of doctors and nurses. The death rate was high.

In another warning three days later, on March 15, the United Nations agency in Geneva declared the respiratory illness "a worldwide health threat." W.H.O. named the mysterious illness SARS, for severe acute respiratory syndrome, and urged all countries to help in controlling it.

Symptoms included high fever, headache, muscle aches, sore throat and dry cough. Severely ill patients were short of breath. The illness did not respond to anti-viral and antibiotic drugs. W.H.O. recommended that doctors isolate infected patients and that health workers take extraordinary precautions in caring for them by wearing masks, gowns and gloves. Epidemiologists traced individuals who had contact with a case and ordered them to stay at home in quarantine.

Acting with uncharacteristic speed and suspecting that a virus caused the illness, W.H.O. organized a collaborative network of scientists to identify the virus and seek its source in nature. In a month, the network of scientists identified a previously unknown member of the coronavirus family as the cause of SARS.

As travelers from infected areas carried the SARS virus to more countries, including Canada, W.H.O.

issued travel advisories for first time in its 55-year history. The warnings set off international alarms and created economic and political havoc in many countries, emptying hotels, canceling flights for lack of passengers, and discouraging travel.

Medical detectives traced the origins of the epidemic to Guangdong province in southern China, where it apparently began in the fall of 2002. The illness broke out of China when a doctor who had cared for a SARS patient in Guangdong fell ill while staying at the Metropole Hotel in nearby Hong Kong. There the doctor inadvertently spread the virus to other guests and visitors, who, in turn, passed it on to other people.

The Chinese government reluctantly admitted in March that the illness had affected 305 people, a third of them doctors and nurses, in Guangdong. But as Chinese doctors described many more cases in Beijing that the government had not reported to W.H.O., the world learned that the Chinese government had lied and withheld crucial information about SARS from the agency. In April, Chinese officials reversed themselves and agreed to cooperate with the W.H.O.

On July 5, W.H.O. declared that the human-to-human chain of infection had been broken, ending the epidemic — for the moment, at least. SARS had killed 774 people out of 8,099 reported cases, a death rate of 9.6 percent. China and Hong Kong reported the most, 5,327 and 1,755 respectively. Canada reported 151 cases, including 43 deaths — an unusually high death rate. But the United States escaped with 29 cases without a fatality, and health officials offer no better explanation than luck.

In continuing research, scientists have been seeking the source of the SARS virus in nature. In preliminary reports, Chinese scientists said they found a SARS virus that is nearly identical to the human one among palm civet cats and other exotic animals sold for food in markets in Guangdong. Scientists are maintaining a vigil for the possible return of SARS. As of September, only one new SARS case had been identified, in a worker who contracted it while working in a laboratory in Singapore.

— Lawrence K. Altman, M.D.

U.N. Says War on AIDS Is Lagging, And Declares a Global Emergency

On Sept. 22, in the first report card on its two-year-old commitment to defeat AIDS, the United Nations gave the world's countries generally low marks in their efforts to overcome ignorance about the disease and provide access to prevention and treatment measures. The report card arose from a General Assembly special session on AIDS in June 2001 — the first ever held on a health issue — in which member nations agreed that defeating AIDS would take commitment, resources and action.

The U.N. estimates that 42 million people are infected with H.I.V., half of them women, and that the vast majority live in sub-Saharan Africa. Without an expanded response, the United Nations estimates that an additional 45 million people will become infected with H.I.V. by 2010.

At the same follow-up session on Sept. 22, the World Health Organization declared that the failure to deliver AIDS drugs to impoverished people is so grave that it has become a global health emergency. The agency, a Geneva-based unit of the United Nations, announced plans to provide AIDS drugs to three million people, mostly in sub-Saharan Africa, by the end of 2005. The number of people in these countries who would receive drugs under the W.H.O. plan would be nearly four times the total to be covered by 2005 under all existing programs, including President Bush's $15 billion initiative to treat two million people in 14 countries by 2008. The W.H.O. plans to adapt many of the rapid response skills it learned in controlling the SARS epidemic and in responding to health emergencies in Afghanistan, Iraq and Liberia, said Dr. Jong Wook Lee, its new director general.

W.H.O. said that at least three million people need to receive such therapy by 2005 to avert an enormous catastrophe. If the 34 countries with the highest H.I.V. rates each get 50 percent of those who require treatment into treatment by the end of 2005, W.H.O. said it believes that it can reach 92 percent of its goal.

— Lawrence K. Altman, M.D.

Global Warnings on Global Warming; In the U.S., Calls for More Research

On Jan. 2, researchers published a paper in the journal *Nature* that was the most comprehensive report yet showing that many species worldwide were being affected by of warming temperatures and that the warming was at least partly caused by humans. The report documented dozens of instances in which global warming was altering ecosystems.

The Bush administration continued to express skepticism that rising temperatures had been caused by heat-trapping smokestack and tailpipe emissions and to insist on the need for additional research. In June, the White House cut a section on global warming from an otherwise comprehensive report by the Environmental Protection Agency on environmental trends. In July, it unveiled a plan for four years of research on climate change, although it committed no new money to the effort.

At the same time, other industrialized countries began moving to adhere to the Kyoto Protocol, the 1997 treaty to curb emissions of heat-trapping gases. The treaty has been rejected by President Bush. In July, the European Union created the first international trading system for credits earned by countries that make deep cuts in their emissions. July saw at least one sign that international efforts could help curb a global environmental problem, when scientists reported the first evidence that a ban on ozone-destroying chemicals was measurably slowing the deterioration of the protective ozone shield high in the atmosphere.

— Andrew C. Revkin

Ancient Skulls From Ethiopia Show a Familiar Face: Ours

In the 160,000-year-old fossilized skulls of two adults and a child found in Ethiopia, scientists think they see for the first time the faces of the immediate ancestors of modern humans.

Except for a few archaic characteristics, the skulls are readily recognizable. They are longer than their Neanderthal contemporaries from Eurasia or earlier ancestors. Their midfaces are broad, but the nasal bones are tall and narrow. The brow ridges are less prominent than those displayed in skulls from earlier branches of the family tree. And the cranial vaults are higher and within modern dimensions.

An international team led by Dr. Tim D. White, University of California, announced the discovery on June 11. They said it was a major step in establishing the time for the emergence of anatomically modern *Homo sapiens*. Attempts to determine when that fateful transition occurred had been frustrated by a complete gap in fossil evidence between 100,000 and 300,000 years ago.

The latest find dates almost precisely from the time when genetic researchers determined that an African "Eve" gave rise to all modern humans. It also appeared to confirm the theory that *Homo sapiens* with almost entirely human characteristics had already evolved in Africa before Neanderthals evolved into their classic form, meaning that Neanderthals could not have been direct forebears of today's humans.

A leading paleoanthropologist, Dr. Chris Stringer of the Natural History Museum in London, hailed the findings as "some of the most significant discoveries in early *Homo sapiens* so far."

Noting a few variations from the modern human skull, the discoverers decided to designate the specimens a subspecies. They are *Homo sapiens idaltu,* not quite fully modern humans, *Homo sapiens sapiens. Idaltu* means elder in the local Ethiopian language.

—John Noble Wilford

Call it Methuselah: Astronomers Find a 12-Billion-Year-Old Planet

Astronomers reported on July 10, 2003 that they had found the oldest known planet, a huge gaseous object almost three times as old as Earth and nearly as old as the universe itself. The discovery of what is being called the Methuselah planet has challenged scientists to rethink theories of how, when and where planets form.

Detected by NASA's Hubble Space Telescope, the planet orbits two burned-out stars in a region of primitive stars 7,200 light-years away. The planet, 2.5 times as massive as Jupiter, appears to have formed 12.7 billion years ago, within a billion years of the origin of the universe in the theorized Big Bang. The Sun and its planets are 4.6 billion years old.

The planet exists in an unlikely place. Such early stars were presumably formed before subsequent generations of stars had produced the abundance of heavy elements needed to make planets. These metallic elements, including iron, silicon and carbon, are cooked in stellar nuclear furnaces and accumulate from the ashes of dying stars, which are recycled in new stars and their families of planets. Recently detected planets beyond the solar system are all orbiting younger, relatively metal-rich stars.

If planets were proliferating billions of years earlier than previously thought, scientists said, they may be more abundant than anyone imagined.

—John Noble Wilford

A Baby Picture of the Universe In the Afterglow of the Big Bang

The strangeness of the universe clicked into sharp focus on February 11, 2003, when astronomers showed off their best picture ever of the infant cosmos. Recorded by a satellite known as the Wilkinson Microwave Anisotropy Probe, it shows the pattern of heat and density in the afterglow of the Big Bang, when the universe was only 380,000 years old, with 40 times the resolution of a previous all-sky map produced by NASA's COBE satellite.

Reading between the splotches and ripples, the international team led by Dr. Charles L. Bennett of the Goddard Space Fight Center, which built and operated the satellite, were able to compute the parameters that describe the universe with a precision of a few percent.

Those numbers gave credence to an increasingly strange view that has emerged of the cosmos in recent years, one in which most matter is invisible and of unknown composition and in which an even more mysterious "dark energy" is accelerating the expansion of the universe, pushing us faster and faster into a dark frozen future.

The universe is 13.7 billion years old, plus or minus 1 percent. Atoms make up only 4 percent of its weight, the dark matter 23 percent and the dark energy — an unknown repulsion apparently residing in empty space — a whopping 73 percent. The first stars ignited when the universe was only 200 million years old, suggesting that dark matter is something that clumps quickly and densely. And the universe will expand forever.

Scientists said the new picture would be the foundation of cosmology for the rest of the decade. Dr. John Bahcall of the Institute for Advanced Study in Princeton said, "We live in an implausible crazy universe, but one whose defining characteristics we now know."

—Dennis Overbye

Treatment to Prevent Premature Births; Warnings on Blood Pressure, Hormones

Doctors conducting a nationwide study announced on Feb. 6, 2003 that they had devised the first treatment ever to succeed in preventing premature births. In pregnant women who had already had one premature baby and therefore were at high risk of having another, weekly shots of a form of the hormone progesterone lowered the rate of premature births by more than a third. Nearly half a million babies are born too early in the United States every year. Prematurity is a leading cause of newborn death, cerebral palsy, mental retardation, hearing loss and blindness.

Millions of people who in the past would have been told that their blood pressure was normal or "high normal" should now be told that they actually have "prehypertension," which threatens their health, according to guidelines issued on May 14 by government health experts. The new category includes 45 million Americans whose blood pressure is 120 to 139 millimeters of mercury systolic (top number) or 80 to 90 diastolic (bottom number). People with readings in this range do not have high blood pressure yet and do not need medication. But they are likely to develop high blood pressure, and should try to lower their pressure by losing excess weight, exercising more, quitting smoking, cutting back on salt, having no more than one or two alcoholic drinks a day and eating more fruits, vegetables and low-fat dairy foods.

Several studies added to the bad news that has been piling up about hormone therapy for postmenopausal women. All the studies used Prempro, the most widely prescribed hormone combination, which contains estrogen and progestin, a form of progesterone. On March 17, a large federal study reported that contrary to widely held beliefs, hormone therapy did not make women feel more energetic or less depressed, or help them enjoy sex more or sleep better. Another large study, reported May 28, found that the treatment doubled the risk of Alzheimer's disease and other types of dementia in women who began taking it at age 65 or older. On June 25, doctors reported that hormone therapy not only stimulates the growth of breast cancer, but also makes tumors harder to detect on mammograms, leading to dangerous delays in diagnosis.

—Denise Grady

Calendar of the Year

UNDERSTANDING CALENDARS

The day Earth turns at a fairly steady pace about the imaginary line that defines the North and South Poles. This line through the poles is called Earth's *axis*. Each turn about the axis, called a *rotation*, takes slightly less than 24 hours. Since Earth is also traveling around the Sun, however, the time from noon to noon is longer than the time it takes for one rotation—about 3 minutes and 56 seconds longer, or almost exactly 24 hours. The time from noon to noon changes slightly during the year, depending on where Earth is in its path. If you average all the days in a year, the mean time from noon to noon is exactly 24 hours.

The year All the nine planets of the solar system travel in nearly circular paths, called *orbits*, around the Sun. Each trip around the Sun is called a *revolution*. The planets all revolve in the same direction, which can be observed from Earth by noting the position the Sun has among the background stars, which are traditionally grouped into constellations. (Since you can't see the Sun and stars at the same time, you can observe where the Sun rises or sets each day and then note the stars that appear in the same region.) Over the course of a year, the Sun appears to pass through the 12 constellations that make up the zodiac.

Earth's trip around the Sun, reflected in the Sun's trip through the zodiac, takes about 365.25 days. This varies slightly from time to time, so astronomers add or delete a second in some years to keep their records in tune with Earth's motion. (see also "Precession of the equinoxes" below).

Seasons The seasons mark the change in the pattern of daylight over the course of the year. Because the Earth is tilted with respect to its path around the Sun, different parts receive different amounts of sunlight during Earth's annual orbit, the time we know as a year. Between late September (around the 21st) and late March, Earth's Northern Hemisphere is tilted away from the Sun. This period constitutes the fall and winter seasons for the Northern Hemisphere, during which there are fewer than 12 hours of daylight each day. For the rest of the year, spring and summer, the Northern Hemisphere is tilted toward the Sun, and daylight hours constitute more than half of each day. In the Southern Hemisphere, this situation is reversed: spring and summer last from late September to late March, while fall and winter make up the other half of the year.

At the points of transition from long days and short nights to short days and long nights and vice versa, the *equinoxes* occur—the two days of the year when periods of daylight and darkness are equal. The *vernal equinox*, marking the first day of spring, takes place on or around March 21 in the Northern Hemisphere, while the *autumnal equinox*, marking the beginning of fall, is on or around September 21. Officially, summer begins on the day of the longest daytime during the year, about June 21 in the Northern Hemisphere, called the *summer solstice*. The *winter solstice*, about December 21 in the Northern Hemisphere, has the shortest amount of daylight and the longest night of the year. The word *solstice* means "standing still Sun." These two days are so called because the apparent movement of where the Sun rises or sets reaches its extreme positions on the solstices and then reverses direction.

Precession of the equinoxes Ancient Greek astronomers determined that the direction of Earth's axis is constantly, but very slowly, changing in a regular pattern. The kind of change is similar to the way a spinning top slowly leans one way then another as its axis changes direction. This movement of the Earth is caused by several factors, the most dominant being one called *precession*. The precession of the Earth results from its not being a perfect sphere. Earth's diameter is about 27 miles greater from one side of the equator to the other than it is from one pole to the other. (Earth is oblate, or fat around the middle, as a result of its rotation.)

Picture Earth without considering its revolution. Keep Earth's center in the same place mentally, and think about how the axis changes position during precession. Any point on Earth's axis (except the center of the planet) moves in a slow circle as a result of precession. This movement is so slow that it takes 26,000 years for a point to return to its original spot. In the meantime, the axis gradually changes its position in relation to the stars. While what we call the North Star (officially known as Polaris) is currently positioned above the North Pole about one degree off center, over time the axis will shift, so that about A.D. 15,000 the star Vega will be above the North Pole within about four degrees of that axis. By about A.D. 28,000, Polaris will have returned to its present position.

As the precession continues, one of its effects is to change the times of the year that seasons occur. Our calendar is corrected for this; if it were not, the vernal equinox would, over 13,000 years, shift from around March 21 to about September 21, the date at which the autumnal equinox is now. For this reason, the precession of the Earth is generally known as the precession of the equinoxes.

Although the precession of the equinoxes is slow, it can be easily observed. The year of about 365.25 days is the time it takes from one vernal equinox to the next. Because of the precession of the equinoxes, however, the time it takes the Sun to appear in the same position with respect to the

Solar Phenomena: The Seasons, 2004

Solar phenomenon	Month	Day	Hour	Min
Perigee[1]	Jan.	4	18	—
Vernal equinox	Mar.	20	06	49
Summer solstice	June	21	00	57
Apogee[2]	July	5	11	—
Autumnal equinox	Sept.	22	16	30
Winter solstice	Dec.	21	12	42

Note: Shown in Universal time (UT). To convert to local time, see "Timing Planetary Phenomena." 1. Sun closest to the Earth (91.4 million miles). 2. Sun farthest from the Earth (94.5 million miles).
Source: U.S. Naval Observatory, *Astronomical Phenomena for the Year 2004* (2001)

stars is 20 minutes, 24 seconds longer than the period from one equinox to the next. For this reason, accurate star maps have to specify both the date and the year for which they are intended.

Lunar Calendar

There is some evidence that very early humans (c. 25,000 B.C.) used marks on bone to indicate the passage of time, which they may have measured by the Moon's phases. A calendar for the year can be based upon the Moon's phases, which gives a year of 12 periods from new moon to new moon (hence the word *month*) lasting about 354 days. This is about 11 days shorter than the time it takes Earth to revolve around the Sun. The Chinese, who still use a version of this calendar, resolve the discrepancy by inserting extra months at fixed intervals to bring the lunar and solar years into alignment. The Chinese year is divided into months that are either 29 or 30 days long, since the time from new moon to new moon is approximately 29.5 days. The New Year begins at the first new moon over China between Jan. 21 and Feb. 19, and is celebrated for a four-day period. Each year has both a number and a name. The year 2004, or 4641 in the Chinese era, is the Year of the Monkey.

Solar Calendar

The ancient Egyptians were the first people known to have instituted a solar calendar. In actuality, their calendar might be called a stellar calendar, since the year began with the rising of Sirius (the brightest star in the sky) at the same place the Sun rises, which generally happened at the same time the Nile flooded. The Egyptians determined that a year was 365 days, about one-quarter of a day short of the true solar year, so gradually the Egyptian calendar no longer coincided with the seasons. Historical records reveal when the Egyptian calendar and the rising of Sirius coincided, from which astronomers inferred that the Egyptian calendar must have been instituted in either 4241 B.C. or 2773 B.C. The Egyptian calendar had 12 months of 30 days and five days of festival, a system adopted by various early cultures, although some continued to use lunar calendars.

Julian Calendar

In 46 B.C., Julius Caesar realized that various parts of the land controlled by Rome used different calendars, so he asked the astronomer Sosigenes to develop a uniform calendar. Sosigenes proposed that since the year was 365.25 days long (though not exactly), a 365-day calendar be kept with one day added (a leap day) every fourth year. When Caesar introduced the new system, he also added days to the year 46 B.C. to bring the seasons in line with the calendar. With a total of 445 days, 46 B.C. is the longest calendar year on record. A year at that time began in what we call March, and the months were numbered. *September, October, November,* and *December* derive from this system and mean "seventh," "eighth," "ninth," and "tenth" months respectively.

There was a little further adjustment of the calendar, however, by Augustus Caesar, the first Roman emperor. The name of the fifth month was changed from Quintilis to July to honor Julius Caesar, and Augustus named the sixth month August after himself. So that August would not be shorter than 31-day July, Augustus borrowed a day from February.

Because of the Roman Empire's great sphere of influence, the Julian calendar became the ordinary calendar of Western nations.

Julian Day Count

A year after the Gregorian calendar was first instituted, Joseph Justus Scaliger developed a system of counting days instead of years, which is still used by astronomers. Called the Julian Day Count (after his father Julius Caesar Scaliger), it begins with 1 on Jan. 1, 4713 B.C. On this date, the Julian calendar, the lunar calendar and the Roman tax system (which had its own calendar) all coincided—something that won't happen again until A.D. 3267. Each day within such a 7,980-year period is numbered.

Gregorian Calendar

From at least A.D. 730, it was known that the solar year—measured from vernal equinox to vernal equinox—was somewhat short of 365.25 days. Each century the solar year gets about half a second shorter. In 1990 the solar year was calculated at 365 days, 5 hours, 48 minutes, and 45.5 seconds long, not 365¼ days, which is what the Julian calendar assumes. Because the date of Easter was slipping, Pope Gregory XIII instituted calendar reform in 1582. He proclaimed that the day following Oct. 4 would be Oct. 15, which dropped 10 days from the year. Furthermore, on the advice of astronomer Christoph Clavius, the new calendar would be kept in line by omitting the leap year in century years unless they were divisible by 400. Thus 1900 was not a leap year in the Gregorian calendar, but 2000 was.

Most Roman Catholic countries and some other Western countries adopted the new system, but England did not. Finally, in 1752, England and its colonies adopted the Gregorian calendar, but they had to drop 11 days to fit common Western practice. It was at this time that New Year's Day in England was moved from Mar. 25 to Jan. 1, changing the number of the year for the almost three months affected. Thus George Washington was born according to the Julian calendar on Feb. 11, 1731, but he came to celebrate his birthday on Feb. 22, 1732 according to the Gregorian calendar.

Because the solar year is shortening, astronomers today keep the Gregorian calendar in line by making a one-second adjustment, as needed, usually on Dec. 31 at midnight, whenever the error's accumulation nears one second.

When Did the Third Millennium Begin?

Did the third millennium begin on January 1, 2000, January 1, 2001, or an entirely different day? The answer depends on how you count your years. If you believe that our calendar began in the year 1, rather than the year 0, then a thousand years did not pass until the end of the year 1000, and the third millennium didn't start until 2001.

But by that logic, the 1990s wouldn't have begun until 1991, and would have included the year 2000. Yet we routinely consider years ending in 0 to be the first year of a decade rather than the last, so why should it be any different for millennia? Also, calendars are an inexact science and plenty of shifting of days, months, and years, have been perpetrated over the years by kings, emperors and popes. The Jewish calendar counted more than 3,700 years before Western calendars counted their first, while the Chinese celebrated the third millennium more than 1,600 years ago.

Perpetual Calendar, 1775–2050

A perpetual calendar lets you find the day of the week for any date in any year. Since January 1 may fall on any of the seven days of the week, and may be a leap or non-leap year, 14 different calendars are possible. The number next to each year corresponds to one of the 14 calendars. For example, in 1776, calendar 9 (a leap year in which Jan. 1 fell on a Monday) was used; July 4 of that year was a Thursday. Calendar 3 was used in 2002; Calendar 4 will be used in 2003.

Year	No.	Year	No.	Year	No.	Year	No.	Year	No.	Year	No.	Year	No.
1775	1	1815	1	1855	2	1895	3	1935	3	1975	4	2015	5
1776	9	1816	9	1856	10	1896	11	1936	11	1976	12	2016	13
1777	4	1817	4	1857	5	1897	6	1937	6	1977	7	2017	1
1778	5	1818	5	1858	6	1898	7	1938	7	1978	1	2018	2
1779	6	1819	6	1859	7	1899	1	1939	1	1979	2	2019	3
1780	14	1820	14	1860	8	1900	2	1940	9	1980	10	2020	11
1781	2	1821	2	1861	3	1901	3	1941	4	1981	5	2021	6
1782	3	1822	3	1862	4	1902	4	1942	5	1982	6	2022	7
1783	4	1823	4	1863	5	1903	5	1943	6	1983	7	2023	1
1784	12	1824	12	1864	13	1904	13	1944	14	1984	8	2024	9
1785	7	1825	7	1865	1	1905	1	1945	2	1985	3	2025	4
1786	1	1826	1	1866	2	1906	2	1946	3	1986	4	2026	5
1787	2	1827	2	1867	3	1907	3	1947	4	1987	5	2027	6
1788	10	1828	10	1868	11	1908	11	1948	12	1988	13	2028	14
1789	5	1829	5	1869	6	1909	6	1949	7	1989	1	2029	2
1790	6	1830	6	1870	7	1910	7	1950	1	1990	2	2030	3
1791	7	1831	7	1871	1	1911	1	1951	2	1991	3	2031	4
1792	8	1832	8	1872	9	1912	9	1952	10	1992	11	2032	12
1793	3	1833	3	1873	4	1913	4	1953	5	1993	6	2033	7
1794	4	1834	4	1874	5	1914	5	1954	6	1994	7	2034	1
1795	5	1835	5	1875	6	1915	6	1955	7	1995	1	2035	2
1796	13	1836	13	1876	14	1916	14	1956	8	1996	9	2036	10
1797	1	1837	1	1877	2	1917	2	1957	3	1997	4	2037	5
1798	2	1838	2	1878	3	1918	3	1958	4	1998	5	2038	6
1799	3	1839	3	1879	4	1919	4	1959	5	1999	6	2039	7
1800	4	1840	11	1880	12	1920	12	1960	13	2000	14	2040	8
1801	5	1841	6	1881	7	1921	7	1961	1	2001	2	2041	3
1802	6	1842	7	1882	1	1922	1	1962	2	2002	3	2042	4
1803	7	1843	1	1883	2	1923	2	1963	3	2003	4	2043	5
1804	8	1844	9	1884	10	1924	10	1964	11	2004	12	2044	13
1805	3	1845	4	1885	5	1925	5	1965	6	2005	7	2045	1
1806	4	1846	5	1886	6	1926	6	1966	7	2006	1	2046	2
1807	5	1847	6	1887	7	1927	7	1967	1	2007	2	2047	3
1808	13	1848	14	1888	8	1928	8	1968	9	2008	10	2048	11
1809	1	1849	2	1889	3	1929	3	1969	4	2009	5	2049	6
1810	2	1850	3	1890	4	1930	4	1970	5	2010	6	2050	7
1811	3	1851	4	1891	5	1931	5	1971	6	2011	7		
1812	11	1852	12	1892	13	1932	13	1972	14	2012	8		
1813	6	1853	7	1893	1	1933	1	1973	2	2013	3		
1814	7	1854	1	1894	2	1934	2	1974	3	2014	4		

1

JANUARY

S	M	T	W	T	F	S
1	2	3	4	5	6	7
8	9	10	11	12	13	14
15	16	17	18	19	20	21
22	23	24	25	26	27	28
29	30	31				

FEBRUARY

S	M	T	W	T	F	S
			1	2	3	4
5	6	7	8	9	10	11
12	13	14	15	16	17	18
19	20	21	22	23	24	25
26	27	28				

MARCH

S	M	T	W	T	F	S
			1	2	3	4
5	6	7	8	9	10	11
12	13	14	15	16	17	18
19	20	21	22	23	24	25
26	27	28	29	30	31	

APRIL

S	M	T	W	T	F	S
						1
2	3	4	5	6	7	8
9	10	11	12	13	14	15
16	17	18	19	20	21	22
23	24	25	26	27	28	29
30						

MAY

S	M	T	W	T	F	S
	1	2	3	4	5	6
7	8	9	10	11	12	13
14	15	16	17	18	19	20
21	22	23	24	25	26	27
28	29	30	31			

JUNE

S	M	T	W	T	F	S
				1	2	3
4	5	6	7	8	9	10
11	12	13	14	15	16	17
18	19	20	21	22	23	24
25	26	27	28	29	30	

JULY

S	M	T	W	T	F	S
						1
2	3	4	5	6	7	8
9	10	11	12	13	14	15
16	17	18	19	20	21	22
23	24	25	26	27	28	29
30	31					

AUGUST

S	M	T	W	T	F	S
		1	2	3	4	5
6	7	8	9	10	11	12
13	14	15	16	17	18	19
20	21	22	23	24	25	26
27	28	29	30	31		

SEPTEMBER

S	M	T	W	T	F	S
					1	2
3	4	5	6	7	8	9
10	11	12	13	14	15	16
17	18	19	20	21	22	23
24	25	26	27	28	29	30

OCTOBER

S	M	T	W	T	F	S
1	2	3	4	5	6	7
8	9	10	11	12	13	14
15	16	17	18	19	20	21
22	23	24	25	26	27	28
29	30	31				

NOVEMBER

S	M	T	W	T	F	S
			1	2	3	4
5	6	7	8	9	10	11
12	13	14	15	16	17	18
19	20	21	22	23	24	25
26	27	28	29	30		

DECEMBER

S	M	T	W	T	F	S
					1	2
3	4	5	6	7	8	9
10	11	12	13	14	15	16
17	18	19	20	21	22	23
24	25	26	27	28	29	30
31						

2

JANUARY

S	M	T	W	T	F	S
	1	2	3	4	5	6
7	8	9	10	11	12	13
14	15	16	17	18	19	20
21	22	23	24	25	26	27
28	29	30	31			

FEBRUARY

S	M	T	W	T	F	S
				1	2	3
4	5	6	7	8	9	10
11	12	13	14	15	16	17
18	19	20	21	22	23	24
25	26	27	28			

MARCH

S	M	T	W	T	F	S
				1	2	3
4	5	6	7	8	9	10
11	12	13	14	15	16	17
18	19	20	21	22	23	24
25	26	27	28	29	30	31

APRIL

S	M	T	W	T	F	S
1	2	3	4	5	6	7
8	9	10	11	12	13	14
15	16	17	18	19	20	21
22	23	24	25	26	27	28
29	30					

MAY

S	M	T	W	T	F	S
		1	2	3	4	5
6	7	8	9	10	11	12
13	14	15	16	17	18	19
20	21	22	23	24	25	26
27	28	29	30	31		

JUNE

S	M	T	W	T	F	S
					1	2
3	4	5	6	7	8	9
10	11	12	13	14	15	16
17	18	19	20	21	22	23
24	25	26	27	28	29	30

JULY

S	M	T	W	T	F	S
1	2	3	4	5	6	7
8	9	10	11	12	13	14
15	16	17	18	19	20	21
22	23	24	25	26	27	28
29	30	31				

AUGUST

S	M	T	W	T	F	S
			1	2	3	4
5	6	7	8	9	10	11
12	13	14	15	16	17	18
19	20	21	22	23	24	25
26	27	28	29	30	31	

SEPTEMBER

S	M	T	W	T	F	S
						1
2	3	4	5	6	7	8
9	10	11	12	13	14	15
16	17	18	19	20	21	22
23	24	25	26	27	28	29
30						

OCTOBER

S	M	T	W	T	F	S
	1	2	3	4	5	6
7	8	9	10	11	12	13
14	15	16	17	18	19	20
21	22	23	24	25	26	27
28	29	30	31			

NOVEMBER

S	M	T	W	T	F	S
				1	2	3
4	5	6	7	8	9	10
11	12	13	14	15	16	17
18	19	20	21	22	23	24
25	26	27	28	29	30	

DECEMBER

S	M	T	W	T	F	S
						1
2	3	4	5	6	7	8
9	10	11	12	13	14	15
16	17	18	19	20	21	22
23	24	25	26	27	28	29
30	31					

3

JANUARY

S	M	T	W	T	F	S
		1	2	3	4	5
6	7	8	9	10	11	12
13	14	15	16	17	18	19
20	21	22	23	24	25	26
27	28	29	30	31		

FEBRUARY

S	M	T	W	T	F	S
					1	2
3	4	5	6	7	8	9
10	11	12	13	14	15	16
17	18	19	20	21	22	23
24	25	26	27	28		

MARCH

S	M	T	W	T	F	S
					1	2
3	4	5	6	7	8	9
10	11	12	13	14	15	16
17	18	19	20	21	22	23
24	25	26	27	28	29	30
31						

APRIL

S	M	T	W	T	F	S
	1	2	3	4	5	6
7	8	9	10	11	12	13
14	15	16	17	18	19	20
21	22	23	24	25	26	27
28	29	30				

MAY

S	M	T	W	T	F	S
			1	2	3	4
5	6	7	8	9	10	11
12	13	14	15	16	17	18
19	20	21	22	23	24	25
26	27	28	29	30	31	

JUNE

S	M	T	W	T	F	S
						1
2	3	4	5	6	7	8
9	10	11	12	13	14	15
16	17	18	19	20	21	22
23	24	25	26	27	28	29
30						

JULY

S	M	T	W	T	F	S
	1	2	3	4	5	6
7	8	9	10	11	12	13
14	15	16	17	18	19	20
21	22	23	24	25	26	27
28	29	30	31			

AUGUST

S	M	T	W	T	F	S
				1	2	3
4	5	6	7	8	9	10
11	12	13	14	15	16	17
18	19	20	21	22	23	24
25	26	27	28	29	30	31

SEPTEMBER

S	M	T	W	T	F	S
1	2	3	4	5	6	7
8	9	10	11	12	13	14
15	16	17	18	19	20	21
22	23	24	25	26	27	28
29	30					

OCTOBER

S	M	T	W	T	F	S
		1	2	3	4	5
6	7	8	9	10	11	12
13	14	15	16	17	18	19
20	21	22	23	24	25	26
27	28	29	30	31		

NOVEMBER

S	M	T	W	T	F	S
					1	2
3	4	5	6	7	8	9
10	11	12	13	14	15	16
17	18	19	20	21	22	23
24	25	26	27	28	29	30

DECEMBER

S	M	T	W	T	F	S
1	2	3	4	5	6	7
8	9	10	11	12	13	14
15	16	17	18	19	20	21
22	23	24	25	26	27	28
29	30	31				

4

JANUARY

S	M	T	W	T	F	S
			1	2	3	4
5	6	7	8	9	10	11
12	13	14	15	16	17	18
19	20	21	22	23	24	25
26	27	28	29	30	31	

FEBRUARY

S	M	T	W	T	F	S
						1
2	3	4	5	6	7	8
9	10	11	12	13	14	15
16	17	18	19	20	21	22
23	24	25	26	27	28	

MARCH

S	M	T	W	T	F	S
						1
2	3	4	5	6	7	8
9	10	11	12	13	14	15
16	17	18	19	20	21	22
23	24	25	26	27	28	29
30	31					

APRIL

S	M	T	W	T	F	S
		1	2	3	4	5
6	7	8	9	10	11	12
13	14	15	16	17	18	19
20	21	22	23	24	25	26
27	28	29	30			

MAY

S	M	T	W	T	F	S
				1	2	3
4	5	6	7	8	9	10
11	12	13	14	15	16	17
18	19	20	21	22	23	24
25	26	27	28	29	30	31

JUNE

S	M	T	W	T	F	S
1	2	3	4	5	6	7
8	9	10	11	12	13	14
15	16	17	18	19	20	21
22	23	24	25	26	27	28
29	30					

JULY

S	M	T	W	T	F	S
		1	2	3	4	5
6	7	8	9	10	11	12
13	14	15	16	17	18	19
20	21	22	23	24	25	26
27	28	29	30	31		

AUGUST

S	M	T	W	T	F	S
					1	2
3	4	5	6	7	8	9
10	11	12	13	14	15	16
17	18	19	20	21	22	23
24	25	26	27	28	29	30
31						

SEPTEMBER

S	M	T	W	T	F	S
	1	2	3	4	5	6
7	8	9	10	11	12	13
14	15	16	17	18	19	20
21	22	23	24	25	26	27
28	29	30				

OCTOBER

S	M	T	W	T	F	S
			1	2	3	4
5	6	7	8	9	10	11
12	13	14	15	16	17	18
19	20	21	22	23	24	25
26	27	28	29	30	31	

NOVEMBER

S	M	T	W	T	F	S
						1
2	3	4	5	6	7	8
9	10	11	12	13	14	15
16	17	18	19	20	21	22
23	24	25	26	27	28	29
30						

DECEMBER

S	M	T	W	T	F	S
	1	2	3	4	5	6
7	8	9	10	11	12	13
14	15	16	17	18	19	20
21	22	23	24	25	26	27
28	29	30	31			

5

JANUARY

S	M	T	W	T	F	S
				1	2	3
4	5	6	7	8	9	10
11	12	13	14	15	16	17
18	19	20	21	22	23	24
25	26	27	28	29	30	31

FEBRUARY

S	M	T	W	T	F	S
1	2	3	4	5	6	7
8	9	10	11	12	13	14
15	16	17	18	19	20	21
22	23	24	25	26	27	28

MARCH

S	M	T	W	T	F	S
1	2	3	4	5	6	7
8	9	10	11	12	13	14
15	16	17	18	19	20	21
22	23	24	25	26	27	28
29	30	31				

APRIL

S	M	T	W	T	F	S
			1	2	3	4
5	6	7	8	9	10	11
12	13	14	15	16	17	18
19	20	21	22	23	24	25
26	27	28	29	30		

MAY

S	M	T	W	T	F	S
					1	2
3	4	5	6	7	8	9
10	11	12	13	14	15	16
17	18	19	20	21	22	23
24	25	26	27	28	29	30
31						

JUNE

S	M	T	W	T	F	S
	1	2	3	4	5	6
7	8	9	10	11	12	13
14	15	16	17	18	19	20
21	22	23	24	25	26	27
28	29	30				

JULY

S	M	T	W	T	F	S
			1	2	3	4
5	6	7	8	9	10	11
12	13	14	15	16	17	18
19	20	21	22	23	24	25
26	27	28	29	30	31	

AUGUST

S	M	T	W	T	F	S
						1
2	3	4	5	6	7	8
9	10	11	12	13	14	15
16	17	18	19	20	21	22
23	24	25	26	27	28	29
30	31					

SEPTEMBER

S	M	T	W	T	F	S
		1	2	3	4	5
6	7	8	9	10	11	12
13	14	15	16	17	18	19
20	21	22	23	24	25	26
27	28	29	30			

OCTOBER

S	M	T	W	T	F	S
				1	2	3
4	5	6	7	8	9	10
11	12	13	14	15	16	17
18	19	20	21	22	23	24
25	26	27	28	29	30	31

NOVEMBER

S	M	T	W	T	F	S
1	2	3	4	5	6	7
8	9	10	11	12	13	14
15	16	17	18	19	20	21
22	23	24	25	26	27	28
29	30					

DECEMBER

S	M	T	W	T	F	S
		1	2	3	4	5
6	7	8	9	10	11	12
13	14	15	16	17	18	19
20	21	22	23	24	25	26
27	28	29	30	31		

6

JANUARY

S	M	T	W	T	F	S
					1	2
3	4	5	6	7	8	9
10	11	12	13	14	15	16
17	18	19	20	21	22	23
24	25	26	27	28	29	30
31						

FEBRUARY

S	M	T	W	T	F	S
	1	2	3	4	5	6
7	8	9	10	11	12	13
14	15	16	17	18	19	20
21	22	23	24	25	26	27
28						

MARCH

S	M	T	W	T	F	S
	1	2	3	4	5	6
7	8	9	10	11	12	13
14	15	16	17	18	19	20
21	22	23	24	25	26	27
28	29	30	31			

APRIL

S	M	T	W	T	F	S
				1	2	3
4	5	6	7	8	9	10
11	12	13	14	15	16	17
18	19	20	21	22	23	24
25	26	27	28	29	30	

MAY

S	M	T	W	T	F	S
						1
2	3	4	5	6	7	8
9	10	11	12	13	14	15
16	17	18	19	20	21	22
23	24	25	26	27	28	29
30	31					

JUNE

S	M	T	W	T	F	S
		1	2	3	4	5
6	7	8	9	10	11	12
13	14	15	16	17	18	19
20	21	22	23	24	25	26
27	28	29	30			

JULY

S	M	T	W	T	F	S
				1	2	3
4	5	6	7	8	9	10
11	12	13	14	15	16	17
18	19	20	21	22	23	24
25	26	27	28	29	30	31

AUGUST

S	M	T	W	T	F	S
1	2	3	4	5	6	7
8	9	10	11	12	13	14
15	16	17	18	19	20	21
22	23	24	25	26	27	28
29	30	31				

SEPTEMBER

S	M	T	W	T	F	S
			1	2	3	4
5	6	7	8	9	10	11
12	13	14	15	16	17	18
19	20	21	22	23	24	25
26	27	28	29	30		

OCTOBER

S	M	T	W	T	F	S
					1	2
3	4	5	6	7	8	9
10	11	12	13	14	15	16
17	18	19	20	21	22	23
24	25	26	27	28	29	30
31						

NOVEMBER

S	M	T	W	T	F	S
	1	2	3	4	5	6
7	8	9	10	11	12	13
14	15	16	17	18	19	20
21	22	23	24	25	26	27
28	29	30				

DECEMBER

S	M	T	W	T	F	S
			1	2	3	4
5	6	7	8	9	10	11
12	13	14	15	16	17	18
19	20	21	22	23	24	25
26	27	28	29	30	31	

7

JANUARY

S	M	T	W	T	F	S
						1
2	3	4	5	6	7	8
9	10	11	12	13	14	15
16	17	18	19	20	21	22
23	24	25	26	27	28	29
30	31					

FEBRUARY

S	M	T	W	T	F	S
		1	2	3	4	5
6	7	8	9	10	11	12
13	14	15	16	17	18	19
20	21	22	23	24	25	26
27	28					

MARCH

S	M	T	W	T	F	S
		1	2	3	4	5
6	7	8	9	10	11	12
13	14	15	16	17	18	19
20	21	22	23	24	25	26
27	28	29	30	31		

APRIL

S	M	T	W	T	F	S
					1	2
3	4	5	6	7	8	9
10	11	12	13	14	15	16
17	18	19	20	21	22	23
24	25	26	27	28	29	30

MAY

S	M	T	W	T	F	S
1	2	3	4	5	6	7
8	9	10	11	12	13	14
15	16	17	18	19	20	21
22	23	24	25	26	27	28
29	30	31				

JUNE

S	M	T	W	T	F	S
			1	2	3	4
5	6	7	8	9	10	11
12	13	14	15	16	17	18
19	20	21	22	23	24	25
26	27	28	29	30		

JULY

S	M	T	W	T	F	S
					1	2
3	4	5	6	7	8	9
10	11	12	13	14	15	16
17	18	19	20	21	22	23
24	25	26	27	28	29	30
31						

AUGUST

S	M	T	W	T	F	S
	1	2	3	4	5	6
7	8	9	10	11	12	13
14	15	16	17	18	19	20
21	22	23	24	25	26	27
28	29	30	31			

SEPTEMBER

S	M	T	W	T	F	S
				1	2	3
4	5	6	7	8	9	10
11	12	13	14	15	16	17
18	19	20	21	22	23	24
25	26	27	28	29	30	

OCTOBER

S	M	T	W	T	F	S
						1
2	3	4	5	6	7	8
9	10	11	12	13	14	15
16	17	18	19	20	21	22
23	24	25	26	27	28	29
30	31					

NOVEMBER

S	M	T	W	T	F	S
		1	2	3	4	5
6	7	8	9	10	11	12
13	14	15	16	17	18	19
20	21	22	23	24	25	26
27	28	29	30			

DECEMBER

S	M	T	W	T	F	S
				1	2	3
4	5	6	7	8	9	10
11	12	13	14	15	16	17
18	19	20	21	22	23	24
25	26	27	28	29	30	31

8

JANUARY

S	M	T	W	T	F	S
1	2	3	4	5	6	7
8	9	10	11	12	13	14
15	16	17	18	19	20	21
22	23	24	25	26	27	28
29	30	31				

FEBRUARY

S	M	T	W	T	F	S
			1	2	3	4
5	6	7	8	9	10	11
12	13	14	15	16	17	18
19	20	21	22	23	24	25
26	27	28	29			

MARCH

S	M	T	W	T	F	S
					1	2
3	4	5	6	7	8	9
10	11	12	13	14	15	16
17	18	19	20	21	22	23
24	25	26	27	28	29	30
31						

APRIL

S	M	T	W	T	F	S
	1	2	3	4	5	6
7	8	9	10	11	12	13
14	15	16	17	18	19	20
21	22	23	24	25	26	27
28	29	30				

MAY

S	M	T	W	T	F	S
			1	2	3	4
5	6	7	8	9	10	11
12	13	14	15	16	17	18
19	20	21	22	23	24	25
26	27	28	29	30	31	

JUNE

S	M	T	W	T	F	S
						1
2	3	4	5	6	7	8
9	10	11	12	13	14	15
16	17	18	19	20	21	22
23	24	25	26	27	28	29
30						

JULY

S	M	T	W	T	F	S
	1	2	3	4	5	6
7	8	9	10	11	12	13
14	15	16	17	18	19	20
21	22	23	24	25	26	27
28	29	30	31			

AUGUST

S	M	T	W	T	F	S
				1	2	3
4	5	6	7	8	9	10
11	12	13	14	15	16	17
18	19	20	21	22	23	24
25	26	27	28	29	30	31

SEPTEMBER

S	M	T	W	T	F	S
1	2	3	4	5	6	7
8	9	10	11	12	13	14
15	16	17	18	19	20	21
22	23	24	25	26	27	28
29	30					

OCTOBER

S	M	T	W	T	F	S
		1	2	3	4	5
6	7	8	9	10	11	12
13	14	15	16	17	18	19
20	21	22	23	24	25	26
27	28	29	30	31		

NOVEMBER

S	M	T	W	T	F	S
					1	2
3	4	5	6	7	8	9
10	11	12	13	14	15	16
17	18	19	20	21	22	23
24	25	26	27	28	29	30

DECEMBER

S	M	T	W	T	F	S
1	2	3	4	5	6	7
8	9	10	11	12	13	14
15	16	17	18	19	20	21
22	23	24	25	26	27	28
29	30	31				

9

JANUARY
S	M	T	W	T	F	S
	1	2	3	4	5	6
7	8	9	10	11	12	13
14	15	16	17	18	19	20
21	22	23	24	25	26	27
28	29	30	31			

FEBRUARY
S	M	T	W	T	F	S
				1	2	3
4	5	6	7	8	9	10
11	12	13	14	15	16	17
18	19	20	21	22	23	24
25	26	27	28	29		

MARCH
S	M	T	W	T	F	S
					1	2
3	4	5	6	7	8	9
10	11	12	13	14	15	16
17	18	19	20	21	22	23
24	25	26	27	28	29	30
31						

APRIL
S	M	T	W	T	F	S
	1	2	3	4	5	6
7	8	9	10	11	12	13
14	15	16	17	18	19	20
21	22	23	24	25	26	27
28	29	30				

MAY
S	M	T	W	T	F	S
			1	2	3	4
5	6	7	8	9	10	11
12	13	14	15	16	17	18
19	20	21	22	23	24	25
26	27	28	29	30	31	

JUNE
S	M	T	W	T	F	S
						1
2	3	4	5	6	7	8
9	10	11	12	13	14	15
16	17	18	19	20	21	22
23	24	25	26	27	28	29
30						

JULY
S	M	T	W	T	F	S
	1	2	3	4	5	6
7	8	9	10	11	12	13
14	15	16	17	18	19	20
21	22	23	24	25	26	27
28	29	30	31			

AUGUST
S	M	T	W	T	F	S
				1	2	3
4	5	6	7	8	9	10
11	12	13	14	15	16	17
18	19	20	21	22	23	24
25	26	27	28	29	30	31

SEPTEMBER
S	M	T	W	T	F	S
1	2	3	4	5	6	7
8	9	10	11	12	13	14
15	16	17	18	19	20	21
22	23	24	25	26	27	28
29	30					

OCTOBER
S	M	T	W	T	F	S
		1	2	3	4	5
6	7	8	9	10	11	12
13	14	15	16	17	18	19
20	21	22	23	24	25	26
27	28	29	30	31		

NOVEMBER
S	M	T	W	T	F	S
					1	2
3	4	5	6	7	8	9
10	11	12	13	14	15	16
17	18	19	20	21	22	23
24	25	26	27	28	29	30

DECEMBER
S	M	T	W	T	F	S
1	2	3	4	5	6	7
8	9	10	11	12	13	14
15	16	17	18	19	20	21
22	23	24	25	26	27	28
29	30	31				

10

JANUARY
S	M	T	W	T	F	S
		1	2	3	4	5
6	7	8	9	10	11	12
13	14	15	16	17	18	19
20	21	22	23	24	25	26
27	28	29	30	31		

FEBRUARY
S	M	T	W	T	F	S
					1	2
3	4	5	6	7	8	9
10	11	12	13	14	15	16
17	18	19	20	21	22	23
24	25	26	27	28	29	

MARCH
S	M	T	W	T	F	S
						1
2	3	4	5	6	7	8
9	10	11	12	13	14	15
16	17	18	19	20	21	22
23	24	25	26	27	28	29
30	31					

APRIL
S	M	T	W	T	F	S
		1	2	3	4	5
6	7	8	9	10	11	12
13	14	15	16	17	18	19
20	21	22	23	24	25	26
27	28	29	30			

MAY
S	M	T	W	T	F	S
				1	2	3
4	5	6	7	8	9	10
11	12	13	14	15	16	17
18	19	20	21	22	23	24
25	26	27	28	29	30	31

JUNE
S	M	T	W	T	F	S
1	2	3	4	5	6	7
8	9	10	11	12	13	14
15	16	17	18	19	20	21
22	23	24	25	26	27	28
29	30					

JULY
S	M	T	W	T	F	S
		1	2	3	4	5
6	7	8	9	10	11	12
13	14	15	16	17	18	19
20	21	22	23	24	25	26
27	28	29	30	31		

AUGUST
S	M	T	W	T	F	S
					1	2
3	4	5	6	7	8	9
10	11	12	13	14	15	16
17	18	19	20	21	22	23
24	25	26	27	28	29	30
31						

SEPTEMBER
S	M	T	W	T	F	S
	1	2	3	4	5	6
7	8	9	10	11	12	13
14	15	16	17	18	19	20
21	22	23	24	25	26	27
28	29	30				

OCTOBER
S	M	T	W	T	F	S
			1	2	3	4
5	6	7	8	9	10	11
12	13	14	15	16	17	18
19	20	21	22	23	24	25
26	27	28	29	30	31	

NOVEMBER
S	M	T	W	T	F	S
						1
2	3	4	5	6	7	8
9	10	11	12	13	14	15
16	17	18	19	20	21	22
23	24	25	26	27	28	29
30						

DECEMBER
S	M	T	W	T	F	S
	1	2	3	4	5	6
7	8	9	10	11	12	13
14	15	16	17	18	19	20
21	22	23	24	25	26	27
28	29	30	31			

11

JANUARY
S	M	T	W	T	F	S
			1	2	3	4
5	6	7	8	9	10	11
12	13	14	15	16	17	18
19	20	21	22	23	24	25
26	27	28	29	30	31	

FEBRUARY
S	M	T	W	T	F	S
						1
2	3	4	5	6	7	8
9	10	11	12	13	14	15
16	17	18	19	20	21	22
23	24	25	26	27	28	29

MARCH
S	M	T	W	T	F	S
1	2	3	4	5	6	7
8	9	10	11	12	13	14
15	16	17	18	19	20	21
22	23	24	25	26	27	28
29	30	31				

APRIL
S	M	T	W	T	F	S
			1	2	3	4
5	6	7	8	9	10	11
12	13	14	15	16	17	18
19	20	21	22	23	24	25
26	27	28	29	30		

MAY
S	M	T	W	T	F	S
					1	2
3	4	5	6	7	8	9
10	11	12	13	14	15	16
17	18	19	20	21	22	23
24	25	26	27	28	29	30
31						

JUNE
S	M	T	W	T	F	S
	1	2	3	4	5	6
7	8	9	10	11	12	13
14	15	16	17	18	19	20
21	22	23	24	25	26	27
28	29	30				

JULY
S	M	T	W	T	F	S
			1	2	3	4
5	6	7	8	9	10	11
12	13	14	15	16	17	18
19	20	21	22	23	24	25
26	27	28	29	30	31	

AUGUST
S	M	T	W	T	F	S
						1
2	3	4	5	6	7	8
9	10	11	12	13	14	15
16	17	18	19	20	21	22
23	24	25	26	27	28	29
30	31					

SEPTEMBER
S	M	T	W	T	F	S
		1	2	3	4	5
6	7	8	9	10	11	12
13	14	15	16	17	18	19
20	21	22	23	24	25	26
27	28	29	30			

OCTOBER
S	M	T	W	T	F	S
				1	2	3
4	5	6	7	8	9	10
11	12	13	14	15	16	17
18	19	20	21	22	23	24
25	26	27	28	29	30	31

NOVEMBER
S	M	T	W	T	F	S
1	2	3	4	5	6	7
8	9	10	11	12	13	14
15	16	17	18	19	20	21
22	23	24	25	26	27	28
29	30					

DECEMBER
S	M	T	W	T	F	S
		1	2	3	4	5
6	7	8	9	10	11	12
13	14	15	16	17	18	19
20	21	22	23	24	25	26
27	28	29	30	31		

12

JANUARY
S	M	T	W	T	F	S
				1	2	3
4	5	6	7	8	9	10
11	12	13	14	15	16	17
18	19	20	21	22	23	24
25	26	27	28	29	30	31

FEBRUARY
S	M	T	W	T	F	S
1	2	3	4	5	6	7
8	9	10	11	12	13	14
15	16	17	18	19	20	21
22	23	24	25	26	27	28
29						

MARCH
S	M	T	W	T	F	S
	1	2	3	4	5	6
7	8	9	10	11	12	13
14	15	16	17	18	19	20
21	22	23	24	25	26	27
28	29	30	31			

APRIL
S	M	T	W	T	F	S
				1	2	3
4	5	6	7	8	9	10
11	12	13	14	15	16	17
18	19	20	21	22	23	24
25	26	27	28	29	30	

MAY
S	M	T	W	T	F	S
						1
2	3	4	5	6	7	8
9	10	11	12	13	14	15
16	17	18	19	20	21	22
23	24	25	26	27	28	29
30	31					

JUNE
S	M	T	W	T	F	S
		1	2	3	4	5
6	7	8	9	10	11	12
13	14	15	16	17	18	19
20	21	22	23	24	25	26
27	28	29	30			

JULY
S	M	T	W	T	F	S
				1	2	3
4	5	6	7	8	9	10
11	12	13	14	15	16	17
18	19	20	21	22	23	24
25	26	27	28	29	30	31

AUGUST
S	M	T	W	T	F	S
1	2	3	4	5	6	7
8	9	10	11	12	13	14
15	16	17	18	19	20	21
22	23	24	25	26	27	28
29	30	31				

SEPTEMBER
S	M	T	W	T	F	S
			1	2	3	4
5	6	7	8	9	10	11
12	13	14	15	16	17	18
19	20	21	22	23	24	25
26	27	28	29	30		

OCTOBER
S	M	T	W	T	F	S
					1	2
3	4	5	6	7	8	9
10	11	12	13	14	15	16
17	18	19	20	21	22	23
24	25	26	27	28	29	30
31						

NOVEMBER
S	M	T	W	T	F	S
	1	2	3	4	5	6
7	8	9	10	11	12	13
14	15	16	17	18	19	20
21	22	23	24	25	26	27
28	29	30				

DECEMBER
S	M	T	W	T	F	S
			1	2	3	4
5	6	7	8	9	10	11
12	13	14	15	16	17	18
19	20	21	22	23	24	25
26	27	28	29	30	31	

13

JANUARY
S	M	T	W	T	F	S
					1	2
3	4	5	6	7	8	9
10	11	12	13	14	15	16
17	18	19	20	21	22	23
24	25	26	27	28	29	30
31						

FEBRUARY
S	M	T	W	T	F	S
	1	2	3	4	5	6
7	8	9	10	11	12	13
14	15	16	17	18	19	20
21	22	23	24	25	26	27
28	29					

MARCH
S	M	T	W	T	F	S
		1	2	3	4	5
6	7	8	9	10	11	12
13	14	15	16	17	18	19
20	21	22	23	24	25	26
27	28	29	30	31		

APRIL
S	M	T	W	T	F	S
					1	2
3	4	5	6	7	8	9
10	11	12	13	14	15	16
17	18	19	20	21	22	23
24	25	26	27	28	29	30

MAY
S	M	T	W	T	F	S
1	2	3	4	5	6	7
8	9	10	11	12	13	14
15	16	17	18	19	20	21
22	23	24	25	26	27	28
29	30	31				

JUNE
S	M	T	W	T	F	S
			1	2	3	4
5	6	7	8	9	10	11
12	13	14	15	16	17	18
19	20	21	22	23	24	25
26	27	28	29	30		

JULY
S	M	T	W	T	F	S
					1	2
3	4	5	6	7	8	9
10	11	12	13	14	15	16
17	18	19	20	21	22	23
24	25	26	27	28	29	30
31						

AUGUST
S	M	T	W	T	F	S
	1	2	3	4	5	6
7	8	9	10	11	12	13
14	15	16	17	18	19	20
21	22	23	24	25	26	27
28	29	30	31			

SEPTEMBER
S	M	T	W	T	F	S
				1	2	3
4	5	6	7	8	9	10
11	12	13	14	15	16	17
18	19	20	21	22	23	24
25	26	27	28	29	30	

OCTOBER
S	M	T	W	T	F	S
						1
2	3	4	5	6	7	8
9	10	11	12	13	14	15
16	17	18	19	20	21	22
23	24	25	26	27	28	29
30	31					

NOVEMBER
S	M	T	W	T	F	S
		1	2	3	4	5
6	7	8	9	10	11	12
13	14	15	16	17	18	19
20	21	22	23	24	25	26
27	28	29	30			

DECEMBER
S	M	T	W	T	F	S
				1	2	3
4	5	6	7	8	9	10
11	12	13	14	15	16	17
18	19	20	21	22	23	24
25	26	27	28	29	30	31

14

JANUARY
S	M	T	W	T	F	S
						1
2	3	4	5	6	7	8
9	10	11	12	13	14	15
16	17	18	19	20	21	22
23	24	25	26	27	28	29
30	31					

FEBRUARY
S	M	T	W	T	F	S
		1	2	3	4	5
6	7	8	9	10	11	12
13	14	15	16	17	18	19
20	21	22	23	24	25	26
27	28	29				

MARCH
S	M	T	W	T	F	S
			1	2	3	4
5	6	7	8	9	10	11
12	13	14	15	16	17	18
19	20	21	22	23	24	25
26	27	28	29	30	31	

APRIL
S	M	T	W	T	F	S
						1
2	3	4	5	6	7	8
9	10	11	12	13	14	15
16	17	18	19	20	21	22
23	24	25	26	27	28	29
30						

MAY
S	M	T	W	T	F	S
	1	2	3	4	5	6
7	8	9	10	11	12	13
14	15	16	17	18	19	20
21	22	23	24	25	26	27
28	29	30	31			

JUNE
S	M	T	W	T	F	S
				1	2	3
4	5	6	7	8	9	10
11	12	13	14	15	16	17
18	19	20	21	22	23	24
25	26	27	28	29	30	

JULY
S	M	T	W	T	F	S
						1
2	3	4	5	6	7	8
9	10	11	12	13	14	15
16	17	18	19	20	21	22
23	24	25	26	27	28	29
30	31					

AUGUST
S	M	T	W	T	F	S
		1	2	3	4	5
6	7	8	9	10	11	12
13	14	15	16	17	18	19
20	21	22	23	24	25	26
27	28	29	30	31		

SEPTEMBER
S	M	T	W	T	F	S
					1	2
3	4	5	6	7	8	9
10	11	12	13	14	15	16
17	18	19	20	21	22	23
24	25	26	27	28	29	30

OCTOBER
S	M	T	W	T	F	S
1	2	3	4	5	6	7
8	9	10	11	12	13	14
15	16	17	18	19	20	21
22	23	24	25	26	27	28
29	30	31				

NOVEMBER
S	M	T	W	T	F	S
			1	2	3	4
5	6	7	8	9	10	11
12	13	14	15	16	17	18
19	20	21	22	23	24	25
26	27	28	29	30		

DECEMBER
S	M	T	W	T	F	S
					1	2
3	4	5	6	7	8	9
10	11	12	13	14	15	16
17	18	19	20	21	22	23
24	25	26	27	28	29	30
31						

HOLIDAYS AND HOLY DAYS

▶FEDERAL HOLIDAYS IN THE U.S.

Congress and the president have designated 10 days as federal holidays. Although these are so widely observed as to be considered "national" holidays, they technically apply only to federal employees and the District of Columbia. It is up to the individual states to designate their own holidays. When a federal holiday falls on a Saturday or a Sunday, it is observed on the preceding Friday or the following Monday.

New Year's Day (January 1) The observance of the New Year dates back to pre-Christian times when rites were performed to ensure the return of spring.

Martin Luther King, Jr., Day (Third Monday in January) Before his assassination in 1968, Martin Luther King, Jr., was the foremost civil rights leader of the 1950s and 1960s, and in 1964 he won the Nobel Peace Prize. In 1983, Congress set aside this day to celebrate his life and accomplishments.

Washington's Birthday (Third Monday in February) Originally celebrated on the actual birthday of America's first president (February 22), this holiday was officially moved in 1971 to the third Monday in February to create a three-day weekend. It is sometimes known as Presidents' Day, because the birthday of Abraham Lincoln (Feb. 12) is so close.

Memorial Day (Last Monday in May) Memorial Day (also known as Decoration Day) honors soldiers fallen in battle. Dating from the Civil War, it is traditionally marked with parades and memorial services.

Independence Day (Fourth of July) The most important U.S. holiday, Independence Day commemorates the signing of the Declaration of Independence on July 4, 1776, an event that marked America's birth as a free nation. The holiday was first observed in 1777 and is celebrated with fireworks, parades, and oratory.

Labor Day (First Monday in September) The idea of Peter J. McGuire, president of the United Brotherhood of Carpenters and Joiners of America, the official observance of a day celebrating the American worker was signed into law on June 28, 1894.

Columbus Day (Second Monday in October) On Oct. 12, 1492, Christopher Columbus and his crew landed in the Bahama Islands after sailing across the Atlantic. First celebrated in 1792, Columbus Day was not officially recognized until 1909. Its observance is of special national pride to Italian-Americans who claim the Genoese Columbus for their own.

Veterans' Day (Nov. 11) Armistice Day, which marked the end of World War I on Nov. 11, 1918, was made a legal holiday in 1938. The name was changed to Veterans' Day in 1954 to honor all of America's veterans.

Thanksgiving (Fourth Thursday in November) Thanksgiving Day was first observed in Plymouth Colony (Massachusetts) in 1621, the year in which the Pilgrims landed in the New World and gave thanks for their first harvest and for the new land they had colonized. President Lincoln proclaimed Thanksgiving a national holiday in 1863.

Christmas is celebrated December 25. (See also "Christian Holy Days.")

▶U.S. MINOR HOLIDAYS AND OCCASIONS

April Fool's Day (April 1) A day for practical jokes, the origins of April Fool's Day are obscure, but it bears some resemblance to an ancient Roman festival honoring the goddess of nature.

Arbor Day (Last Friday in April) Dedicated to trees and their preservation. Its observance is meant to encourage preservation of the environment. Internationally it is observed on December 22.

Armed Forces Day (Third Saturday in May) A day to honor of the members of the United States Armed Forces.

Citizenship Day (September 17) First observed by presidential proclamation in 1952, Citizenship Day falls on the same day as the old Constitution Day, which it replaces, but the name of which is still in use.

Daylight Saving Time The idea of moving clocks ahead one hour to capture more daylight on summer evenings dates back to colonial times—Benjamin Franklin first suggested it in a 1784 essay—but it did not become a nationwide practice until the Uniform Time Act of 1966 (effective April of 1967). During World War I, World War II, and the energy crisis of 1973–74, the U.S. adopted daylight saving time all year round to save money on fuel. Daylight saving time is not observed in Hawaii, the Eastern time zone portion of Indiana, most of Arizona (except on the Navajo Indian Reservation) or in the territories of American Samoa, Guam, Puerto Rico and the Virgin Islands. By law, daylight saving time begins at 2 A.M. on the first Sunday in April and ends at 2 A.M. on the last Sunday in October, when clocks are turned back one hour. Remember to "Spring ahead, Fall back."

Election Day (Tuesday after first Monday in November) In years evenly divisible by four, presidential elections are held; in years evenly divisible by two, elections for all members of the House of Representatives and for one-third of the members of the Senate are held.

Father's Day (Third Sunday in June) Father's Day was first observed in West Virginia in 1908, but it was not until 1972 that the president signed a Congressional resolution designating its official observance. Father's Day is a uniquely American institution.

Flag Day (June 14) The first observance of Flag Day was in 1877, the centenary of the adoption of the Flag Resolution, which adopted the design of the American flag flown today. President Truman signed the Flag Day Bill in 1949.

Important Dates in the U.S. and Canada, 2003-08

Event	2003	2004[1]	2005	2006	2007	2008[1]
New Year's Day[2]	Jan. 1	Jan. 1	Jan. 1	Jan. 1	Jan. 1	Jan.1
Martin Luther King Day[2]	Jan. 20	Jan. 19	Jan. 17	Jan. 16	Jan. 15	Jan. 21
Groundhog Day	Feb. 2	Feb. 2	Feb. 2	Feb. 2	Feb. 2	Feb. 2
St. Valentine's Day	Feb. 14	Feb. 14	Feb. 14	Feb. 14	Feb. 14	Feb. 14
Susan B. Anthony Day	Feb. 15	Feb. 15	Feb. 15	Feb. 15	Feb. 15	Feb. 15
Washington's Birthday[2]	Feb. 17	Feb. 16	Feb. 21	Feb. 20	Feb. 19	Feb. 18
Mardi Gras	Mar. 4	Feb. 24	Feb. 8	Feb. 28	Feb. 20	Feb. 5
St. Patrick's Day	Mar. 17	Mar. 17	Mar. 17	Mar. 17	Mar. 17	Mar. 17
April Fool's Day	Apr. 1	Apr. 1	Apr. 1	Apr. 1	Apr. 1	Apr. 1
Daylight Saving begins	Apr. 6	Apr. 4	Apr. 3	Apr. 2	Apr. 1	Apr. 6
Arbor Day	Apr. 25	Apr. 30	Apr. 29	Apr. 28	Apr. 27	Apr. 26
National Teacher Day	May 6	May 4	May 3	May 2	May 8	May 6
Mother's Day[2]	May 11	May 9	May 8	May 14	May 13	May 11
Armed Forces Day	May 17	May 15	May 21	May 20	May 19	May 17
Victoria Day3	May 19	May 24	May 23	May 22	May 21	May 19
National Maritime Day	May 22	May 22	May 22	May 22	May 22	May 22
Memorial Day[2]	May 26	May 31	May 30	May 29	May 28	May 26
Flag Day	June 14	June 14	June 14	June 14	June 14	June 14
Father's Day	June 15	June 20	June 19	June 18	June 17	June 15
Canada Day[3]	July 1	July 1	July 1	July 1	July 1	July 1
Independence Day[2]	July 4	July 4	July 4	July 4	July 4	July 4
Labor Day[2, 3]	Sept. 1	Sept. 6	Sept. 5	Sept. 4	Sept. 3	Sept. 1
Citizenship Day	Sept. 17	Sept. 17	Sept. 17	Sept. 17	Sept. 17	Sept. 17
Columbus Day[2]	Oct. 13	Oct. 11	Oct. 10	Oct. 9	Oct. 8	Oct. 13
Thanksgiving Day[3] (Can.)	Oct. 13	Oct. 11	Oct. 10	Oct. 9	Oct. 8	Oct. 13
United Nations Day	Oct. 24	Oct. 24	Oct. 24	Oct. 24	Oct. 24	Oct. 24
Daylight Saving ends	Oct. 26	Oct. 31	Oct. 30	Oct. 29	Oct. 28	Oct. 26
Halloween	Oct. 31	Oct. 31	Oct. 31	Oct. 31	Oct. 31	Oct. 31
Election Day (U.S.)	Nov. 4	Nov. 2	Nov. 8	Nov. 7	Nov. 6	Nov. 4
Veterans'(Armistice) Day[2]	Nov. 11	Nov. 11	Nov. 11	Nov. 11	Nov. 11	Nov. 11
Remembrance Day[3]	Nov. 11	Nov. 11	Nov. 11	Nov. 11	Nov. 11	Nov. 11
Thanksgiving Day[2] (U.S.)	Nov. 27	Nov. 25	Nov. 24	Nov. 23	Nov. 22	Nov. 27
Christmas Day[2, 3]	Dec. 25	Dec. 25	Dec. 25	Dec. 25	Dec. 25	Dec. 25
Boxing Day[3]	Dec. 26	Dec. 26	Dec. 26	Dec. 26	Dec. 26	Dec. 26
Kwanzaa[4]	Dec. 26	Dec. 26	Dec. 26	Dec. 26	Dec. 26	Dec. 26
New Year's Eve	Dec. 31	Dec. 31	Dec. 31	Dec. 31	Dec. 31	Dec. 31

1. Leap year; February has 29 days. 2. Federal holiday in U.S. 3. Federal holiday in Canada. 4. First day of seven-day holiday.

Groundhog Day (February 2) On this day the groundhog peeks out of his burrow to look for his shadow. If he sees his shadow, six weeks of winter will follow; if he doesn't, spring is just around the corner.

Halloween (October 31) All Hallow's Eve (the day before the feast of All Saints in the Christian calendar) began as a pagan custom honoring the dead and a celebration of autumn. The wearing of costumes can be traced back to medieval religious practice in which parishioners dressed as saints and angels and paraded through the churchyard. The modern practice of "trick or treat" is of American origin with no apparent historical basis.

Kwanzaa (or Kwanza) This secular celebration by African-Americans commemorates their African heritage and emphasizes the role of family and community. It begins on Dec. 26 and lasts for seven days; on each day one candle of a candelabrum is lighted. Kwanzaa was developed by Maulana Karenga and was first observed in 1966.

Mother's Day (Second Sunday in May) Conceived by Anne M. Jarvis of Philadelphia, where it was first observed, as a day for children to pay tribute to their mothers, this was declared a national holiday by presidential proclamation in 1914.

National Maritime Day (May 22) Designated by presidential proclamation in 1935, this commemorates the anniversary of the departure of the SS *Savannah* on the first successful transoceanic voyage of a steam-powered vessel, in 1819. It is also a day of remembrance of merchant mariners who died in defense of their country.

National Teacher Day (Tuesday of first full week in May) This is a day when students and communities around the country honor their teachers and the teaching profession.

St. Patrick's Day (March 17) A day in honor of Ireland's patron saint, St. Patrick's Day is a religious, political and social event rolled into one. In Ireland, St. Patrick is honored by church ceremonies and a three-day period of devotion. In the United States, March 17 is celebrated with parades and the "wearing of the green."

St. Valentine's Day (February 14) Originally an occasion to honor two Christian saints martyred by the Roman Emperor Claudius (214–270), since the Middle Ages St. Valentine's Day has been dedicated to lovers, probably because it is believed to be the day that birds choose their mates.

Susan B. Anthony Day (February 15) Anthony (1820–1906) was one of the first women's rights advocates, working especially for equal suffrage—that is, the right to vote. She was a cofounder and later president of the National Woman Suffrage Association.

United Nations Day (October 24) This commemorates the ratification of the United Nations Charter on this date in 1945 by the five permanent members of the Security Council and a majority of the other Charter signatories.

▶CHRISTIAN HOLY DAYS

Christmas is the celebration of Christ's birth. The exact date of his birth is unknown, but the date of December 25 was probably chosen because it coincided with the ancient mid-winter celebrations honoring pagan deities. The 12 days of Christmas fall between Christmas and Epiphany (January 6), the day the Wise Men visited the Christ child.

Advent, a religious season that begins on the Sunday nearest Nov. 30 and lasts until Christmas, both celebrates the birth of Jesus and anticipates His second coming. At one time Advent was a solemn season observed by fasting, but this is no longer the case.

Easter is the most important holy day in the Christian religion. It is the celebration of Christ's Resurrection from the dead, which gave Christians the hope of salvation and eternal life. Although Easter is only one day, the full observance of the holy day spans from Septuagesima Sunday (70 days before Easter Sunday), which may fall as early as January, to Pentecost, which can occur as late as June.

Easter always falls on the first Sunday after the first full moon after the vernal equinox on March 21. Thus, Easter can fall no earlier than March 23 (if the first full moon is a Saturday March 22) and no later than April 24 (if the first full moon is a Sunday, April 17).

Mardi Gras (Shrove Tuesday; Fat Tuesday) Originally a day of penance, the last day before the beginning of Lent is now celebrated with feasting and merrymaking.

Ash Wednesday derives its name from the rite of burning the palms carried on the Palm Sunday of the year before and using the ashes to mark worshippers' foreheads with a cross.

Lent, a 40-day period of fasting and penitence beginning on Ash Wednesday and ending on Easter Sunday, Lent is traditionally observed by fasting, performing acts of charity, and by giving up certain pleasures and amusements.

Palm Sunday, the Sunday before Easter, celebrates Jesus' triumphant entry into Jerusalem where palm branches were spread before Him to honor His path.

Holy (Maundy) Thursday, is the anniversary of the Last Supper. The traditional services mark three events that occurred during the week before Jesus was crucified: He washed the feet of His 12 disciples; He instituted the Eucharist (the sacrament of Holy Communion); and He was arrested and imprisoned.

Good Friday marks the day of Christ's Crucifixion. The holy day is observed with fasting, mourning, and penitence.

Holy Saturday is the day that anticipates the Resurrection. In the Catholic church, special vigils are held on Holy Saturday evening.

Easter Sunday marks the day of Christ's Resurrection. Many worshippers celebrate the holy day with sunrise services, a custom believed to be inspired by the example of Mary Magdalene, who went to Christ's tomb "early, while it was yet dark."

Pentecost (literally, "fiftieth day") is the end of the full ecclesiastical observance of Easter. It takes place on the seventh Sunday after Easter Sunday and commemorates the descent of the Holy Spirit upon the Apostles.

The Annunciation This holy day marks the archangel Gabriel's announcement to Mary that she would conceive and give birth to Jesus. It is celebrated by Roman Catholics on March 25; it is not observed by Protestant denominations.

Trinity Sunday The Sunday after Pentecost, this occasion honors the Father, Son and Holy Spirit. It was declared a part of the church calendar in 1334 by Pope John XXII and is observed by Roman Catholics and by some Protestant denominations.

Corpus Christi This feast celebrates the presence of the body (*corpus*) of Christ in the Eucharist. At one time this was the principal feast of the church year, but today it is observed only by Catholic churches. Corpus Christi is celebrated on the Thursday following Trinity Sunday.

All Saints' Day, celebrated on November 1, honors all of the Christian saints. In America, many churches mark the Sunday nearest November 1 as a day to pay tribute to those who have died during the year. All Saints' Day is observed primarily by Roman Catholics.

Holy Days of Obligation are feast days in the Catholic calendar observed by attendance at Mass and rest from unnecessary work. Six holy days of obligation are observed in the United States:

1. Solemnity of Mary, Jan. 1 (formerly, Christ's circumcision, the first shedding of his blood, was commemorated on this day).
2. Ascension (of Jesus to Heaven), 40 days after Easter
3. Assumption of the Blessed Virgin into Heaven, Aug. 15
4. All Saints' Day, Nov. 1
5. Mary's Immaculate Conception (honoring the Mother of God as the only person conceived without original sin), Dec. 8
6. Christmas, Dec. 25

Calendar of Christian Holy Days

Year A.D.	Ash Wednesday	Good Friday	Easter Sunday	Pentecost	Trinity Sunday	Advent
2003	March 5	April 18	April 20	June 8	June 15	Nov. 30
2004	Feb. 25	April 9	April 11	May 30	June 6	Nov. 28
2005	Feb. 9	March 25	March 27	May 15	May 22	Nov. 27
2006	March 1	April 14	April 16	June 4	June 11	Dec. 3
2007	Feb. 21	April 6	April 8	May 27	June 3	Dec. 2
2008	Feb. 6	Mar. 21	Mar. 23	May 11	May 18	Nov. 30

▶THE JEWISH CALENDAR

The months of the Jewish year are Tishri, Heshvan, Kislev, Tebet, Shebat, Adar, Nisan, Iyar, Sivan, Tammuz, Ab and Elul. The Jewish era dates from the year of the creation (*anno mundii* or A.M.), which is equal to 3761 B.C.), thus 5764 began in 2003 and ends in 2004 of the Gregorian calendar. (Tishri, the first month of the Jewish year, falls in either September or October of the Gregorian calendar.)

Because the Jewish calendar is a blend of solar and lunar calendars, there are intercalated months to keep the lunar and solar years in alignment. (Intercalation is the insertion of an extra day, month, or other unit—February 29 in a leap year, for example—into a calendar). The intercalated month is called Adar Sheni or Veadar—Second Adar.

▶JEWISH HOLY DAYS

Sabbath is the first and most important Jewish holy day, occurring each week from sundown Friday to sundown Saturday. It is a day of rest and spiritual growth, given to men and women so they will remember the sweetness of freedom and keep it. Sabbath takes precedence over all other observances.

Rosh Hashanah (New Year) held to be the birthday of the world, is also called the Day of Judgment and Remembrance, and the day of the shofar—a ram's horn—which is blown to remind Jews of Abraham's willingness to sacrifice his son Isaac. The holiday takes place on the first and second days of Tishri (in September or October).

Yom Kippur (Day of Atonement) concludes the 10 days of repentance that Rosh Hashanah begins and takes place from sundown on the ninth day of Tishri until sundown on the 10th. The observance begins with the recitation of the most famous passage in the Jewish liturgy—*Kol Nidre*—which nullifies unfulfilled vows made in the past year. The entire day is spent praying and fasting.

Sukkoth (Tabernacles) is a harvest festival celebrated from the 15th through the 22nd of Tishri. Sukkoth also commemorates the journey of the Jewish people through the wilderness to the land of Israel. Jewish families take their meals this week in a roughly constructed *sukkah* (booth)—a reminder of an agricultural society, of the Exodus, and of how precarious and fragile life can be. On the Simchath Torah, the 23rd of Tishri, a congregation finishes reading the last book of the Torah and immediately starts again with the first.

Hanukkah (Chanukah, Feast of Dedication; Festival of Lights) The importance of the eight-day feast, which begins on the 25th day of Kislev, is its commemoration of the first war in human history fought in the cause of religious freedom. The Maccabees vanquished not just the military threat to Judaism, but the internal forces for assimilation into the Hellenistic culture of Israel's rulers. Jews light candles for eight nights to mark a miracle: a day's supply of oil, found in the recaptured Temple, which according to religious myth, burned for eight days.

Purim (Feast of Lots) set on the 14th day of Adar, is another celebration of survival, noting the events described in the Book of Esther. At Purim, Jews rejoice at Queen Esther's and her cousin Mordecai's defeat of Haman, the Persian King Ahaseurus's advisor who plotted to slaughter all the Persian Jews around 400 B.C.

Calendar of Jewish Holy Days, 5762–69

Year AM	Rosh Hashanah[1]	Yom Kippur	Sukkoth[1]	Hanukkah[1]	Purim	Pesach[1]	Shabuoth[1]
5764	Sept. 27, 2003	Oct. 6, 2003	Oct. 11, 2003	Dec. 20, 2003	Mar. 7, 2004	Apr. 6, 2004	May 26, 2004
5765	Sept. 16, 2004	Sept. 25, 2004	Sept. 30, 2004	Dec. 8, 2004	Mar. 25, 2005	Apr. 24, 2005	June 13, 2005
5766	Oct. 4, 2005	Oct. 13, 2005	Oct. 18, 2005	Dec. 26, 2005	Mar. 14, 2006	Apr. 13, 2006	June 2, 2006
5767	Sept. 23, 2006	Oct. 2, 2006	Oct. 7, 2006	Dec. 15, 2996	Mar. 4, 2007	Apr. 3, 2007	May 23, 2007
5768	Sept. 13, 2007	Sept. 22, 2007	Sept. 27, 2007	Dec. 4, 2007	Mar. 21, 2008	Apr. 20, 2008	June 9, 2008
5769	Sept. 30, 2008	Oct. 9, 2008	Oct. 14, 2008	Dec. 21, 2008	Mar. 10, 2009	April 9, 2009	May 29, 2009

Note: The Jewish day begins and ends at sundown. Thus, all holidays begin at sundown of the day preceding the date shown.
1. Multi-day holiday; first day of holiday shown. **Source:** B'nai B'rith.

Chinese Years, 1900–2019

The Chinese New Year is the second New Moon after the winter solstice. The Chinese Year 4699 began on February 12, 2002; Chinese Year 4700 begins on February 1, 2003 and ends January 21, 2004.

Year of the Rat	1900	1912	1924	1936	1948	1960	1972	1984	1996	2008
. . . Ox	1901	1913	1925	1937	1949	1961	1973	1985	1997	2009
. . . Tiger	1902	1914	1926	1938	1950	1962	1974	1986	1998	2010
. . . Hare (Rabbit)	1903	1915	1927	1939	1951	1963	1975	1987	1999	2011
. . . Dragon	1904	1916	1928	1940	1952	1964	1976	1988	2000	2012
. . . Snake	1905	1917	1929	1941	1953	1965	1977	1989	2001	2013
. . . Horse	1906	1918	1930	1942	1954	1966	1978	1990	2002	2014
. . . Sheep(Goat)	1907	1919	1931	1943	1955	1967	1979	1991	2003	2015
. . . Monkey	1908	1920	1932	1944	1956	1968	1980	1992	2004	2016
. . . Rooster	1909	1921	1933	1945	1957	1969	1981	1993	2005	2017
. . . Dog	1910	1922	1934	1946	1958	1970	1982	1994	2006	2018
. . . Pig	1911	1923	1935	1947	1959	1971	1983	1995	2007	2019

Pesach (Passover) beginning on the 15th day of Nisan and lasting seven days, commemorates the exodus of the Hebrews from Egypt in about 1300 B.C. The name, Passover, also recalls God's sparing (passing over) the Jewish first-born during the plagues upon the land brought by God through Moses. The holiday is marked by eating only unleavened foods, participating in a *seder*, or special meal, and reading the *Haggadah*, the story of the Hebrews' deliverance from Egypt.

Shabuoth (Feast of Weeks) is observed on the sixth or seventh day of Sivan. Originally an agricultural festival, Shabuoth is a celebration of the revelation of the Torah at Mt. Sinai, by which God established his covenant with the Jewish people.

▶THE ISLAMIC CALENDAR

The 12 months of the Islamic year are: Muharram, Safar, Rab'i I, Rab'i II, Jomada I, Jomada II, Rajab, Sha'ban, Ramadan, Shawwal, Dhu al-Qa'dah, Dhu al-Hijja. The Islamic calendar is based on a lunar year of 12 months of 30 and 29 days (alternating every month) and the year is equal to 354 days. It runs in cycles of 30 years, of which the 2nd, 5th, 7th, 10th, 13th, 16th, 18th, 21st, 24th, 26th, and 29th are leap years. Leap years have 355 days, the extra day being added to the last month, Dhu al-Hijja. There are no intercalated months or leap years, so the Islamic year does not keep a constant relationship to the solar year—which dictates the seasons—and months occur about 10 or 11 days earlier than in the year before.

The caliph Abu Bakr adopted A.D. 622, the year of the *hejira* (Mohammed's migration from Mecca to Medina), as the first year of Islam. However, dating of the Muslim era varies throughout the Islamic world. In some countries, the year of the Muslim era is obtained by subtracting 622 from the Gregorian year; 2004 A.D. equals 1382 A.H. (anno hegirae, in the year of the hejira).

Other countries (Saudi Arabia, Yemen, and the principalities of the Persian Gulf) continue to use a purely lunar year. To approximate the Muslim era equivalent of the Gregorian year, subtract 622 (the year of hejira in the Gregorian calendar) from the current year, and multiply the result by 1.031 (days in the year of the Gregorian calendar divided by days in the lunar year): 2004 A.D. = (2004-622) x 1.031 = 1425 A.H. The accompanying calendar uses this method of calculation.

▶MUSLIM HOLY DAYS

Ramadan the ninth month of the Islamic calendar, is the Islamic faith's holiest period. To honor the month in which the Koran was revealed, all adult Muslims of sound body and mind fast, eschewing food, water, or even a kiss between the hours of sunrise and sunset. Exempted from the fast are women in menstruation or childbirth bleeding, the chronically ill, or people on a journey, all of whom must make up the fast days at a later date.

Id al-Fitr This day of feasting is celebrated at the end of Ramadan. To mark the fast's break, worshippers also attend an early morning service, Salat-ul-'Id, at which they give alms in staple foodstuffs or their monetary value.

Id al-Adha The Feast of Sacrifice takes place on the 10th day of Dhu al-Hijja, the last month of the year and the season of the haj, or pilgrimage. The day begins with a service in the mosques or other places of gathering, and for those who are not pilgrims, continues with the ritual slaughter of a sheep in commemoration of God's ransom of Abraham's son from sacrifice. At least a third of the meat of the animal is to be given in charity.

Fridays At noontime, Muslims attend mosque or comparable gathering places to say the congregational Friday prayer that ends the week. While Friday is the holy day of the weekly Muslim calendar, it is not a Sabbath comparable to Christian Sundays or Jewish Saturdays, and there are no restrictions on work or other worldly enterprises.

▶THE HINDU YEAR

The Hindu year consists of 12 months: Caitra, Vaisakha, Jyaistha, Asadha, Sravana, Bhadrapada, Asvina, Karttika, Margasivsa, Pansa, Magha and Phalguna. Calendrically, holidays are of two types, lunar and solar. Solar holidays in the Hindu calendar include:

Mesasamkranti The beginning of the new astrological year, when the Sun enters the constellation Aries.

Makaraj-Samkranti The winter solstice, when the sun enters the constellation Capricorn.

Mahavisuva Day is New Year's Eve.

Principal holidays determined by the lunar year are:

Ramanavami (Caitra 9), celebrates the birth of Rama, in Hindu folklore, the epitome of chivalry, courage and obedience to sacred law. Considered an incarnation of Vishnu, his name is synonymous with God.

Rathayatra (Asadha 2), the pilgrimage of the chariot festival of Orissa.

Janmastami (Sravana 8), The birthday of Krishna, an incarnation of the supreme deity,

Calendar of Muslim Holy Days

Year A.H. (A.D.)	New Year's Day 1 Muharram	1 Ramadan	Id al-Fitr, 1 Shawwal	Id al-Adha, 10 Dhu al-Hijja
1424 (2003-04)	March 4, 2003	Oct. 27, 2003	Nov. 25, 2003	Feb. 1, 2004
1425 (2004-05)	Feb. 22, 2004	Oct. 16, 2004	Nov. 14, 2004	Jan. 21, 2005
1426 (2005-06)	Feb. 10, 2005	Oct. 5, 2005	Nov. 4, 2005	Jan. 11, 2006
1427 (2006-07)	Jan. 31, 2006	Sept. 24, 2006	Oct. 24, 2006	Dec. 2, 2006
1428 (2007-08)	Jan. 20, 2007	Sept. 13, 2007	Oct. 13, 2007	Dec. 20, 2007

Note: The Islamic calendar is based on calculation and depends on actual sighting of the moon. Therefore the dates above are estimates. For exact dates, contact your local masjid, organization, or scholar. **Source:** Islamic Shura Council of North America. www.moonsighting.com.

Vishnu, celebrated as a philosopher-king and hero.

Dasahra (Asvina 7-10), commemorates Rama's victory over the demon Ravana.

Laksmipuja (Asvina 15), honors Laksmi, goddess of good fortune.

Dipavali (Karttika 15), festival of lights and exchanging of presents.

Mahasivaratri (Magha 13), which honors the god Shiva, one of the three supreme Hindu gods. Shiva, whose name means "Auspicious One," is a god of both reproduction and destruction.

Months of the Year

Gregorian	Hebrew	Hindu	Muslim
January	Shebat	Magha	*Muharram*
February	Adar	Phalguna	Safar
March	Nisan	*Caitra*	Rab'i I
April	Iyar	Vaisakha	Rab'i II
May	Sivan	Jyaistha	Jomada I
June	Tammuz	Asadha	Jomada II
July	Ab	Sravana	Rajab
August	Elul	Bhadrapada	Sha'ban
September	*Tishri*	Asvina	Ramadan
October	Heshvan	Karttika	Shawwal
November	Kislev	Margasivsa	Dhu al-Qa'dah
December	Tebet	Pansa	Dhu al-Hijja

Note: The months of the traditional (lunar) Muslim calendar occur at different times every year. Months in italics indicate the first month of the year in the respective calendars.

Birthstones

Month	Stone
January	Garnet
February	Amethyst
March	Aquamarine, Bloodstone
April	Diamond
May	Emerald
June	Alexandrite, Moonstone, Pearl
July	Ruby
August	Peridot, Sardonyx
September	Sapphire
October	Opal, Tourmaline
November	Topaz
December	Turquoise, Lapis Lazuli

Astrological Calendar

Dates	Sign
January 20 - February 18	Aquarius, the water bearer
February 19-March 20	Pisces, the fishes
March 21-April 19	Aries, the ram
April 20-May 20	Taurus, the bull
May 21-June 20	Gemini, the twins
June 21-July 22	Cancer, the crab
July 23-August 22	Leo, the lion
August 23-September 22	Virgo, the virgin
September 23-October 22	Libra, the scales
October 23-November 21	Scorpio, the scorpion
November 22-December 21	Sagittarius, the archer
December 22-January 19	Capricorn, the goat

Wedding Anniversaries

Anniversary	Type of gift	Anniversary	Type of gift
1st	Paper	**14th**	Ivory
2nd	Cotton	**15th**	Crystal
3rd	Leather	**20th**	China
4th	Fruit, flowers	**25th**	Silver
5th	Wood	**30th**	Pearl
6th	Sugar	**35th**	Coral
7th	Copper, wool	**40th**	Ruby
8th	Bronze, pottery	**45th**	Sapphire
9th	Pottery, willow	**50th**	Gold
10th	Tin	**55th**	Emerald
11th	Steel	**60th**	Diamond
12th	Silk, linen	**70th**	Platinum
13th	Lace		

ASTRONOMICAL EVENTS, 2004

The main astronomical events included in this section are the phases of the Moon, the Moon's perigee (when it is closest to the Earth) and apogee (when it is farthest away), lunar and solar eclipses, and the visibility of the planets.

▶PHASES OF THE MOON

The relative position of the Earth, Moon and Sun affect what, if any, part of the Moon we can see illuminated by the Sun during our night. A *new moon* occurs when the Moon is precisely aligned between the Earth and the Sun, making the Moon invisible from the Earth. When the Moon is at *first quarter* (90° from the Sun relative to the Earth), its sunlit part appears in the shape of a D (in the Southern Hemisphere, a backward D). A *full moon*, when the Moon shows an almost fully illuminated face, occurs when the Moon is 180° around the sky from the Sun. The *last quarter* (or third quarter) occurs when the Moon is again moving toward a position between the Earth and the Sun, and it appears as a backward D (a normal D in the Southern Hemisphere). Intermediate phases are the *crescent moon*—between the new Moon and first quarter, and between the last quarter and new Moon; and the *gibbous moon*, occurring between the half and the full Moon. The full cycle from one phase through all the other phases takes about 29.53 days and is called a *lunation*.

▶VISIBILITY OF THE PLANETS, 2004

Mercury can only be seen low in the east before sunrise, or low in the west after sunset (about the time of the beginning or end of twilight). It is visible in the mornings between the following approximate dates: Jan. 2-Feb. 21, April 26-June 11, Sept. 1-Sept. 25, and Dec. 16-Dec. 31. The planet is brighter at the end of each period (the best con-

Phases of the Moon, 2004

New moon				First quarter				Full moon				Last quarter			
Month	d	h	m	Month	d	h	m	Month	d	h	m	Month	d	h	m
Jan.	21	21	05	**Jan.**	29	06	03	**Jan.**	7	15	40	**Jan.**	15	04	46
Feb.	20	09	18	**Feb.**	28	03	24	**Feb.**	6	08	47	**Feb.**	13	13	40
Mar.	20	22	41	**Mar.**	28	23	48	**Mar.**	6	23	14	**Mar.**	13	21	01
Apr.	19	13	21	**Apr.**	27	17	32	**Apr.**	5	11	03	**Apr.**	12	03	46
May	19	04	52	**May**	27	07	57	**May**	4	20	33	**May**	11	11	04
June	17	20	27	**June**	25	19	08	**June**	3	04	20	**June**	9	20	02
July	17	11	24	**July**	25	03	37	**July**	2	11	09	**July**	9	07	34
								July	31	18	05				
Aug.	16	01	24	**Aug.**	23	10	12	**Aug.**	30	02	22	**Aug.**	7	22	01
Sept.	14	14	29	**Sept.**	21	15	54	**Sept.**	28	13	09	**Sept.**	6	15	11
Oct.	14	02	48	**Oct.**	20	21	59	**Oct.**	28	03	07	**Oct.**	6	10	12
Nov.	12	14	27	**Nov.**	19	05	50	**Nov.**	26	20	07	**Nov.**	5	05	53
Dec.	12	01	29	**Dec.**	18	16	40	**Dec.**	26	15	06	**Dec.**	5	00	53

Note: Shown in Universal Time (UT). To convert to local time, see "Timing Planetary Phenomena."
Source: U.S. Naval Observatory, *Astronomical Phenomena for the Year 2004* (2001).

ditions in northern latitudes occur in mid-September and late December, and in southern latitudes in mid-May). It is visible in the evenings between the following approximate dates: March 14-April 9, June 26-Aug. 17, Oct. 20-Dec. 4. The planet is brighter at the beginning of each period (the best conditions in northern latitudes occur from late March to early April, and in southern latitudes from mid-July to early August.)

Venus is a brilliant object in the evening sky from the beginning of the year until early June, when it becomes too close to the Sun for observation. In mid-June, it reappears in the morning sky, where it stays until the end of the year. Venus is in conjunction with Saturn on Sept. 1, Jupiter on Nov. 14, Mars on Dec. 5, and Mercury on Dec. 29. Venus transits the Sun's disk on June 8 from 05:14 to 11:26; the event is visible from Alaska, Australasia except New Zealand, Asia, Indian Ocean, Africa, Europe, Greenland, South America except the southern part, and North America except the western part.

Mars can only be seen in the evening sky for the first seven months of the year, as it moves through Pisces, Aries, Taurus, (passing 7° N of Aldebaran on Apr. 7), Gemini (passing 6° S of Pollux on June 14), Cancer and into Leo in late July. It soon becomes too close to the Sun for observation until late Oct. when it reappears in the morning sky in Virgo. It passes 3° N of Spica on Oct. 31, moves into Libra in late Nov. and into Scorpius at the end of Dec. Mars is in conjunction with Saturn on May 24, with Mercury on July 10 and Aug. 17 and with Venus on Dec. 5.

Jupiter can be seen in January and February for more than half the night in Leo. Its westward elongation gradually increases until it is at opposition on March 4, when it can be seen throughout the night. Its eastward elongation then gradually decreases until by early June it can be seen only in the evening sky. In early September it becomes too close to the Sun for observation until early October when it reappears in the morning sky in Virgo, where it remains for the rest of the year. Jupiter is in conjunction with Venus on Nov. 4.

Visibility of the Planets, 2004

Planet	Morning Twilight	Evening Twilight
Venus	June 15-Dec. 31	Jan. 1-June 2
Mars	Oct. 30-Dec. 31	Jan. 1-July 31
Jupiter	Jan. 1-March 4 Oct. 5-Dec. 31	March 4-Sept. 8
Saturn	July 27-Dec. 31	Jan. 1-June 20

Source: U.S. Naval Observatory, *Astronomical Phenomena for the Year 2004* (2001).

Saturn is in Gemini throughout the year. It can be seen for more than half the night until early April, after which it can be seen only in the evening sky. In the second half of June it becomes too close to the Sun for observation. It reappears in the morning sky in late July. It passes 7° S of Pollux on Sept. 12 and from late Oct. can be seen for more than half the night. Saturn is in conjunction with Mars on May 24 and with Venus on Sept. 1.

Uranus is visible for the first month of the year in the evening sky in Aquarius and remains in this constellation throughout the year. From the beginning of February it becomes too close to the Sun for observation until it reappears in the morning sky in mid-March. It is at opposition on August 27, and in December it can be seen only in the evening sky.

Neptune is visible for the first half of January in the evening sky in Capricornus, where it remains throughout the year. It then becomes too close to the Sun for observation until late February, when it reappears in the morning sky. It is at opposition on Aug. 6, and from early November can be seen only in the evening sky.

Do not confuse

(1) Mars with Saturn from mid-May to early June when Saturn is the brighter object, and with Mercury during the second week of July when Mercury is the brighter object.

(2) Venus with Saturn from late August to early September, with Jupiter in early November, with

Mars in late November to mid-December and with Mercury in late December; on all occasions Venus is the brighter object.

▶TIMING PLANETARY PHENOMENA

The times for astronomical data shown here are expressed in Universal Time (UT) which is the standard time of the Greenwich meridian (0° of longitude) also known as Greenwich mean time (GMT). To convert to local time, determine your longitude and subtract 1 hour for every 15° of longitude west of 0°; or add 1 hour for every 15° of longitude east of 0°.

The first new moon of 2004 occurs Jan. 21 at 2105 hours in UT. The equivalent time in New York (74°W) is 5 hours earlier, or Jan. 20 at 1605 hours (4:05 P.M.); in Chicago (87°W), 6 hours earlier, or Jan. 20 at 3:05 P.M.; in Denver (105°W), 7 hours earlier, or Jan. 20 at 2:05 P.M.; and in San Francisco (122°W), 8 hours earlier, or Jan. 20 at 1:05 P.M. (To obtain the P.M. equivalent of UT times later than 1200, subtract 12.) Note that local clock times may differ from these standard times, especially in summer when clocks are often advanced by 1 hour.

▶ECLIPSES

Eclipses of the Moon

A lunar eclipse occurs when the Sun, Earth and Moon are in a straight line and the shadow of the Earth falls on the Moon. There are three kinds of lunar eclipse. A *total eclipse* occurs when the Moon passes completely into the Earth's total umbra, or shadow, so the Sun cannot be seen from the Moon. A *partial eclipse* occurs when only part of the Earth's umbra falls across the Moon and the Sun is partially visible from some places on the Moon. A *penumbral eclipse* occurs when only the Earth's penumbra (partial shadow) shades the Moon; and from the Moon one's view of the Sun would be only partially blocked by the Earth. It is usually difficult to detect a penumbral eclipse from the Earth.

During 2004, there will be two total eclipses of the Moon. (All times shown in universal time (UT). To convert to local time, see *Timing Planetary Phenomena.*)

May 4, 2004–Total eclipse of the Moon

Moon enters penumbra 17:50.8; Moon enters totality 19:52.0; middle of eclipse 20:30.1; Moon leaves totality 21:08.3; Moon leaves penumbra 23:09.5; magnitude of the eclipse: 1.309.

The beginning of the umbral phase will be visible in most of Asia, Europe, Africa and Antarctica; Indonesia, Australia and New Zealand; and the eastern South Atlantic Ocean, the Indian Ocean and the western Pacific Ocean. The end will be visible in Africa, Europe, western Asia, western Australia, Antarctica, most of South America, the eastern North Atlantic Ocean, the South Atlantic Ocean, the Indian Ocean and part of the South Pacific ocean.

October 28, 2004–Total Eclipse of the Moon

Moon enters penumbra 0:05.5; Moon enters totality 2:23.4; middle of eclipse 3:04.0; Moon leaves totality 3:44.6; Moon leaves penumbra 6:02.7; magnitude of the eclipse: 1.313.

The beginning of the umbral phase will be visible in Africa, Europe, Greenland, the Arctic region, North America except the extreme northwest, Central America, South America, extreme western Asia, part of Queen Maud Land and the peninsula of Antarctica, the Atlantic Ocean, the eastern South Pacific Ocean, and the western Indian Ocean. The end will be visible in North America, the Arctic region, Greenland, Central America, South America, Europe, western Africa, Antarctic peninsula, the eastern Pacific Ocean, and the Atlantic Ocean.

Eclipses of the Sun

A solar eclipse occurs when the Moon passes between the Earth and the Sun; there are three types. A total eclipse occurs when the Moon's shadow completely covers the Sun and the sky turns dark. Total eclipses occur along a narrow path (typically 100-200 miles wide) called the track of totality and last only a few minutes at any point on the track. A partial eclipse occurs when the Moon covers only a portion of the Sun. A total eclipse may be only partial in less than optimum viewing locations. An annular (ring-shaped) eclipse occurs when the Moon is too far from the Earth to completely cover the Sun, so that at the height of the eclipse, a ring of light surrounds the Moon.

In 2004, there will be two partial eclipses of the Sun; only the second eclipse will be visible from the U.S., and only in parts of Alaska.

April 19, 2004–Partial Eclipse of the Sun.

Eclipse begins 11:29.9; greatest eclipse 13:33.9; eclipse ends 15:38.5.

This eclipse will be a southern hemisphere event, visible from southern Africa (including Angola, Madagascar, Mozambique, South Africa, Zambia and Zimbabwe) and parts of Antarctica.

October 14, 2004–Partial Eclipse of the Sun

Eclipse begins 22:19; greatest eclipse 22:49:17; eclipse ends 23:19.

This eclipse will be visible from the northern hemisphere. Northeastern Asia (including Japan, North and South Korea, and parts of China) and the Pacific Ocean will fall within the Moon's penumbral shadow, as will Hawaii and parts of Alaska.

Part II

THE UNITED STATES

U.S. Geography

The United States of America shares the North American continent with Canada, Mexico and the Central American nations. The 48 conterminous states lie in a broad land mass from approximately 24°N to 49°N from south to north, and 67°W to 124°W from east to west. It is bordered on the north by Canada, on the south by Mexico and the Gulf of Mexico, on the east by the Atlantic Ocean, and on the west by the Pacific Ocean. The two nonconterminous states of Alaska and Hawaii are located to the northwest on the North American continent, and in the Pacific Ocean Basin approximately 2,400 miles southwest of the state of California, respectively.

▶POLITICAL-GEOGRAPHIC DIVISIONS

The Bureau of the Census groups the states in a number of divisions and sub-divisions.

Northeast

New England Maine, New Hampshire, Vermont, Massachusetts, Rhode Island, Connecticut.
Middle Atlantic New York, New Jersey, Pennsylvania.

Midwest

East North Central Ohio, Indiana, Illinois, Michigan, Wisconsin.
West North Central Minnesota, Iowa, Missouri, North Dakota, South Dakota, Nebraska, Kansas.

South

South Atlantic Delaware, Maryland, District of Columbia, Virginia, West Virginia, North Carolina, South Carolina, Georgia, Florida.
East South Central Kentucky, Tennessee, Alabama, Mississippi.
West South Central Arkansas, Louisiana, Oklahoma, Texas.

Pacific

Mountain Montana, Idaho, Wyoming, Colorado, New Mexico, Arizona, Utah, Nevada.
Pacific Washington, Oregon, California, Alaska, Hawaii.

▶PHYSIOGRAPHIC REGIONS

The physiographic regions, or the primary geological features and landforms, of the United States are:

Atlantic and Gulf Coast Plains

These run from the islands of southern New England, Cape Cod, and Long Island, through New Jersey, Delaware, Maryland, Virginia, North Carolina, South Carolina, Georgia, Florida, Alabama, Mississippi, Louisiana, Texas; includes lower Mississippi Valley in Arkansas, Missouri, Tennessee.

Appalachian System

The Appalachian System is divided into five parts:
New England White Mountains (New Hampshire), Green Mountains (Vermont), Champlain Lowland and Hudson Valley (Vermont, New York), Catskill Mountains (New York).
The Piedmont Pennsylvania, Virginia, North Carolina, South Carolina, Georgia, Alabama.
Great Smoky and Blue Ridge Mountains Pennsylvania (Poconos), [discontinuous], Virginia, North Carolina, Georgia.
Ridge and Valley Pennsylvania, West Virginia, Virginia, Kentucky, Tennessee, Alabama.
Appalachian Plateau Pennsylvania, Ohio, West Virginia, Kentucky, Tennessee, Alabama.

Canadian (or Laurentian) Shield

This region covers much of eastern Canada and extends into the U.S. in two places:
Adirondack Mountains New York.
Superior Upland Upper Michigan, Wisconsin, Minnesota.

Central Lowland

The Central Lowland includes most of the U.S. interior, and is divided into four parts:
Interior Lowlands Ohio, Kentucky, Tennessee.
Mississippi Great Lakes Basin Ohio, Indiana, Illinois, Michigan, Wisconsin, Iowa, North Dakota, South Dakota.
Interior Highlands Ozark Mountains: Missouri, Arkansas, Oklahoma; Ouachita Mountains: Arkansas, Oklahoma.
Great Plains North Dakota, South Dakota, Nebraska, Kansas, Oklahoma, Texas, Montana, Wyoming, Colorado, New Mexico.

Cordilleran Province

Rocky Mountains New Mexico, Colorado, Wyoming, Montana.

Intermontane Range

This range is divided into four sections:
Colorado Plateau Colorado, Utah, New Mexico, Arizona (including Grand Canyon).
Basin and Range Plateau Nevada, Utah (including Wasatch Range).
Desert Basin and Range California (including Death Valley), Arizona.
Snake and Columbia River Basins Idaho, Washington, Oregon.

U.S. Geographic Extremes

Because the Aleutian Islands wrap around the Greenwich Meridian, Alaska technically contains both the easternmost and westernmost points in the United States.

Extreme	Contiguous 48 states (Long. or Lat.)	U.S. (Long. or Lat.)[1]
North	Northwest Angle Inlet, Minn. 49° 23' N	Point Barrow, Alaska, 71° 23' N
South	Key West, Fla. 24° 33' N	Ka Lae, Hawaii 18° 55' N
East	West Quoddy Head, Maine, 66° 57' W	Pochnoi Point, Alaska, 179° 52' E
West	Capa Alava, Wash. 124° 44' W	Amatignak Island, Alaska 179° 09' W

1. U.S. states only; does not include U.S. territories and possessions. **Source:** U.S. Geological Survey, *Elevations and Distances in the United States,* online edition. http://mapping.usgs.gov/mac/isb/pubs/booklets/elvadist/elvadist.html.

Pacific Coastlands
This region is divided into four sections, three oriented north-south, the other east-west.
Cascade Mountains and Sierra Nevada Washington, Oregon, California, Nevada.
Puget Sound, Willamette Valley, and Central Valley Washington, Oregon, California.
Coast Ranges Washington, Oregon, California.
Los Angeles Extension Tehachapi Mountains (east-west), San Gabriel Mountains and San Bernardino Mountains.

▶NATIONAL PARK SYSTEM

The National Park System of the U.S. began in March 1872 with the establishment of the Yellowstone National Park in the Territories of Montana and Wyoming, "as a public park or pleasuring ground for the benefit and enjoyment of the people" and was placed "under exclusive control of the Secretary of the Interior." The founding of Yellowstone began a worldwide national park movement and today more than 100 countries contain some 1,200 national parks or equivalent preserves.

President Woodrow Wilson created the National Park Service as a bureau within the Department of the Interior in 1916, and charged it with protecting the 35 national parks and monuments then in existence. Today, the U.S. National Park System comprises 385 areas covering more than 79 million acres (3 percent of total U.S. area) in 49 states (there are no areas in Delaware), the District of Columbia, Guam, Puerto Rico, Saipan and the Virgin Islands. Additions to the National Park System are generally made through acts of Congress, and national parks can be created only through such acts. But under the Antiquities Act of 1906, the president has authority to proclaim national monuments on lands already under Federal jurisdiction.

The diversity of the parks managed by the National Park Service (NPS) is reflected in the variety of titles given to them. Although the system is best known for its scenic National Parks, more than half the areas of the National Park System preserve places, and commemorate persons, events, and activities important in the nation's history. Brief definitions of each type of park follow, together with the number of areas and total federal acreage. An additional 11 areas such as the White House, the National Mall, etc., totaling nearly 40,000 acres of federal land were without designation.

National battlefields/battlefield parks/battlefield site/military parks cover a variety of areas associated with U.S. military history (Antietam National Battlefield, Maryland). (1 battlefield site, 1 acre; 9 military parks, 36,338 acres; 11 battlefields, 12,289 acres; 3 battlefield parks, 8,713 acres)

National Capital Parks include more than 346 sites (The Ellipse; Lafayette Park) throughout the Washington, D.C., area. (6,482 acres)

National historical parks are areas of greater physical extent and complexity than historic sites (Nez Perce, Idaho). (41; 119,049 acres)

National historic sites include areas of prehistoric and modern historical interest (Tuskegee Institute, Mississippi), archaeological sites, historic structures and the like. Because it is of importance to both the U.S. and Canada, St. Croix Island (28 acres) is designated an International Historic Site. (77; 21,677 acres)

National lakeshores/seashores (Cape Cod NS, Massachusetts; Pictured Rocks NL, Michigan) preserve shoreline areas and offshore islands while providing water-oriented recreation. (4 lakeshores, 145,641 acres; 10 seashores, 479,054 acres)

National memorial designates an area or structure that is commemorative in nature (Mt. Rushmore, South Dakota). (29; 8,081 acres)

National monuments are intended to preserve at least one nationally significant resource (Rainbow Bridge, Utah). They are usually smaller than national parks and lack the diversity of attractions. (75; 2,157,574 acres)

National parks contain a variety of resources and encompass large land and water areas (Grand Canyon, Arizona) to help provide adequate protection of resources. (56; 49,638,564 acres)

National parkways are ribbons of land flanking roadways (Natchez Trace, Mississippi, Alabama and Tennessee) that offer an opportunity for leisurely driving through areas of scenic interest. (4; 163,940 acres)

National preserves serve primarily to protect certain resources (Big Thicket, Texas). Activities like hunting and fishing or mineral extraction may be permitted. (18; 22,027,743 acres)

National recreation areas were originally areas surrounding reservoirs (Lake Mead, Nevada and Arizona), but now include other lands and waters set aside for recreational use. . (18; 3,389,572 acres)

National reserves are similar to the preserves, but are administered by state or local authorities (City of Rocks, Idaho). (2; 11,440 acres)

National rivers/wild and scenic riverways preserve ribbons of land bordering free-flowing streams that have not been dammed, channelized, or otherwise altered (Delaware River, Pennsylvania and New Jersey). Activities such as hiking, boating and hunting may be permitted. (5 National Rivers; 312,161 acres; 10 National Wild & Scenic Riverways; 73,892 acres)

National scenic trails are usually long-distance footpaths winding through areas of natural beauty (Appalachian Trail, Maine to Georgia). (3; 166,922 acres)

National wilderness areas are designated under the Wilderness Act of 1964, which provides that "there shall be no commercial enterprise and no permanent road within any wilderness area . . . and (except for emergency uses) no temporary road, no use of motor vehicles, motorized equipment or motorboats, no landing of aircraft, no other form of mechanical transport, and no structure or installation." Wilderness areas are usually part of other larger entities.

In addition to the National Park System, there are three groups of areas that are closely linked in importance and purpose to NPS-managed areas.

Affiliated areas (designated by Act of Congress, 1970) are areas in the U.S. and Canada that preserve significant areas outside the National Park System but that rely on NPS assistance.

U.S. National Parks: Acreage, Visits, and Overnight Stays, 1990–2002

National Park, State	Acres under Federal protection, 2002	Visits ('000s) 1990	Visits ('000s) 2000	Visits ('000s) 2002	Overnight stays ('000s) 1990	Overnight stays ('000s) 2000	Overnight stays ('000s) 2002
Acadia, Maine	46,051	2,413	2,469	2,559	223	146	156
Arches, Utah	76,353	621	786	770	58	46	47
Badlands, South Dakota	232,822	1,326	1,106	909	35	54	41
Big Bend, Texas	775,279	257	262	328	215	186	205
Biscayne, Florida	170,956	573	393	513	29	N.A.	N.A.
Black Canyon of the Gunnison, Colo.	30,045	(1)	192	174	(1)	14	12
Bryce Canyon, Utah	35,833	863	1,099	886	144	145	132
Canyonlands, Utah	337,570	277	402	367	78	108	92
Capitol Reef, Utah	241,234	562	613	526	48	42	43
Carlsbad Caverns, New Mexico	46,427	747	469	476	(x)	(x)	(x)
Channel Islands, California	79,019	144	483	614	32	101	143
Crater Lake, Oregon	183,224	385	427	457	45	73	78
Cuyahoga Valley, Ohio	19,408	(1)	3,325	3,218	(1)	6	8
Death Valley, California-Nevada	3,291,779	(1)	1,179	898	(1)	225	189
Denali, Alaska	4,724,788	547	364	311	118	121	52
Dry Tortugas, Florida	61,481	19	84	80	25	41	27
Everglades, Florida	1,398,617	958	995	969	128	106	111
Gates of the Arctic, Alaska	7,266,102	1	12	7	5	1	3
Glacier Bay, Alaska	3,222,858	204	385	408	36	44	17
Glacier, Montana	1,013,154	1,987	1,729	1,906	330	309	322
Grand Canyon, Arizona	1,180,863	3,777	4,460	4,002	908	1085	1,143
Grand Teton, Wyoming	307,654	1,588	2,590	2,613	597	532	545
Great Basin, Nevada	77,180	65	81	86	44	32	37
Great Smoky Mountain, Tennessee-North Carolina	521,225	8,152	10,176	9,316	463	421	393
Guadalupe Mountains, Texas	86,190	193	199	203	18	20	20
Haleakala, Hawaii	28,969	1,261	1,620	1,521	19	24	22
Hawaii Volcanoes, Hawaii	207,643	1,097	1,515	1,111	112	110	117
Hot Springs, Arkansas	4,898	1,123	1,338	1,440	8	4	6
Isle Royale, Michigan	539,282	23	21	19	56	61	58
Joshua Tree, California	733,496	(1)	1,234	1,178	(1)	245	278
Katmai, Alaska	3,611,609	41	72	59	12	29	28
Kenai Fjords, Alaska	601,839	66	255	252	1	4	4
Kings Canyon, California	461,845	1,063	529	545	302	217	199
Kobuk Valley, Alaska	1,669,933	3	3	4	(x)	(x)	(x)
Lake Clark, Alaska	2,226,807	10	6	4	1	2	2
Lassen Volcanic, California	106,368	461	375	388	113	79	87
Mammoth Cave, Kentucky	52,003	1,925	1,749	1,891	98	89	88
Mesa Verde, Colorado	51,891	611	452	406	159	82	73
Mount Rainier, Washington	235,625	1,327	1,345	1,310	184	196	190
North Cascades, Washington	504,634	456	26	21	97	19	18
Olympic, Washington	913,520	2,795	3,328	3,691	404	506	418
Petrified Forest, Arizona	93,533	845	605	572	1	2	2
Redwood, California	77,729	348	383	405	16	59	38
Rocky Mountain, Colorado	265,397	2,647	3,185	2,988	209	232	206
Saguaro, Arizona	87,526	(1)	765	615	(1)	2	1
Sequoia, California	403,876	1,064	839	920	345	252	246
Shenandoah, Virginia	198,202	1,772	1,420	1,389	323	284	286
Theodore Roosevelt, North Dakota	69,702	461	432	472	26	28	26
Virgin Island, U.S. Virgin Islands	12,913	665	704	693	173	215	267
Voyageurs, Minnesota	133,075	224	227	238	47	18	19
Wind Cave, South Dakota	28,295	586	669	810	11	10	9
Wrangell-St. Elias, Alaska	7,662,670	36	28	40	3	2	N.A.
Yellowstone, Montana-Wyoming	2,219,789	2,824	2,838	2,974	1,345	1,191	1,285
Yosemite, California	759,530	3,125	3,401	3,362	2,220	1,633	1,701
Zion, Utah	143,060	2,102	2,432	2,593	292	243	246
Total National Parks	**49,533,773**	**54,619**	**66,076**	**66,509**	**10,156**	**9,696**	**3,232**
Total National Parks System[2]	**78,810,679**	**255,655**	**285,891**	**277,300**	**17,625**	**15,726**	**15,062**

Note: (x) = less than 1,000. Visit and overnight stay data often varies from year to year because of special events such as anniversaries and natural disasters. 1. Area was not a National Park in year shown. 2. Includes National Historic Sites, National Memorials, National Seashores, National Parkways, and other areas under the jurisdiction of the National Park Service. **Source:** *U.S. National Park Service Statistical Abstract 2002* (2003).

Wild and Scenic Rivers System (designated by Act of Congress, 1968) preserves undeveloped rivers as free-flowing streams accessible for public use. Wild rivers are free of dams and generally accessible only by trails; scenic rivers have relatively primitive shorelines and are largely undeveloped but may be accessible by road.

State Parks and Recreation Areas by State, 2003

State	Areas	Total Acreage	Visitors ('000s) Day	Overnight	Total[1]	Revenues ('000s)	Revenues as percent of operating expenses
U.S. Total	**5,655**	**13,162,230**	**689,998**	**67,657**	**757,655**	**$715,110**	**35.4%**
Alabama	24	49,710	4,002	1,115	5,117	24,095	78.5
Alaska	140	3,325,939	3,580	702	4,282	2,341	34.7
Arizona	31	58,512	1,743	667	2,410	7,055	17.7
Arkansas	50	51,239	7,627	590	8,217	13,739	42.2
California	273	1,456,732	78,332	6,917	85,249	39,080	21.4
Colorado	113	365,142	10,299	799	11,098	15,165	64.6
Connecticut	132	200,458	8,539	461	9,000	3,741	38.5
Delaware	29	22,039	3,049	157	3,206	8,323	46.2
Florida	151	591,525	16,072	1,662	17,734	31,925	45.4
Georgia	70	81,218	13,417	1,205	14,622	26,037	46.4
Hawaii	67	28,002	6,296	44	6,340	1,795	23.5
Idaho	32	44,643	2,146	350	2,496	3,427	16.7
Illinois	307	306,066	42,428	906	43,334	6,020	12.6
Indiana	33	178,937	14,635	2,384	17,019	33,514	78.7
Iowa	174	63,200	14,776	662	15,438	3,386	33.4
Kansas	24	32,300	4,148	3,841	7,989	4,891	69.3
Kentucky	49	44,209	6,694	1,178	7,872	52,185	66.6
Louisiana	56	38,267	1,153	854	2,007	4,183	1.4
Maine	127	96,686	2,266	287	2,553	2,214	30.6
Maryland	51	266,136	9,545	793	10,338	15,065	31.4
Massachusetts	238	293,821	11,048	835	11,883	8,211	9.1
Michigan	102	284,977	20,234	5,062	25,296	32,848	51.4
Minnesota	133	267,209	7,179	895	8,074	12,118	24.9
Mississippi	28	24,287	3,318	906	4,224	6,645	43.5
Missouri	83	138,522	16,592	1,167	17,759	7,527	15.1
Montana	374	65,839	1,023	175	1,198	1,464	20.8
Nebraska	85	134,200	8,219	1,582	9,801	14,626	59.1
Nevada	24	132,524	3,116	169	3,285	2,019	25.5
New Hampshire	89	84,547	6,533	246	6,779	7,979	100.0
New Jersey	116	376,532	14,594	444	15,038	8,163	8.5
New Mexico	31	90,693	1,569	2,353	3,922	4,317	25.6
New York	830	1,158,960	52,823	4,040	56,863	65,994	29.2
North Carolina	59	168,241	12,261	497	12,758	3,712	11.8
North Dakota	30	17,276	943	153	1,096	1,170	41.7
Ohio	74	204,557	53,756	3,489	57,245	26,974	44.4
Oklahoma	50	71,667	12,774	1,283	14,057	24,008	53.4
Oregon	231	95,463	37,133	2,305	39,438	15,425	42.2
Pennsylvania	119	289,362	34,760	1,866	36,626	15,362	21.2
Rhode Island	74	8,748	6,913	356	7,269	3,839	67.1
South Carolina	55	80,459	6,862	1,288	8,150	16,537	69.0
South Dakota	129	105,386	8,091	730	8,821	8,473	63.6
Tennessee	53	144,013	25,215	1,059	26,274	32,403	49.6
Texas	124	668,269	13,806	3,283	17,089	25,428	25.6
Utah	46	114,532	4,752	1,188	5,940	8,212	36.5
Vermont	98	68,859	491	502	993	6,191	93.1
Virginia	37	62,236	6,135	721	6,856	8,584	28.8
Washington	259	262,134	46,724	2,140	48,864	13,818	23.6
West Virginia	47	195,831	6,640	676	7,316	19,214	63.3
Wisconsin	68	132,725	13,893	1,635	15,528	14,395	43.3
Wyoming	36	119,266	1,788	995	2,783	1,268	23.1

1. Includes overnight visitors. **Source:** National Association of State Park Directors (Tucson, Ariz.), *2003 Annual Information Exchange.*

National Trails System (designated by National Trails System Act of 1968) includes trails in both urban and rural settings for persons of all ages, interests, skills, and physical abilities. The Appalachian Trail and the Pacific Crest were the first two trails designated under the National Trails System. Today, there are more than 800 trails, in every state, Puerto Rico and the District of Columbia, totaling more than 9,000 miles in length.

Source: National Park Service, *The National Parks: Index*

▶RIVERS AND LAKES

Major Navigable Waterways of the United States The U.S inland and intracoastal waterway system handles over 500 million tons of traffic each year, carried by a fleet of more than 5,000 towboats and 31,000 barges on over 11,000 miles of primary channels. Ninety percent of these channels have depths of between 9 and 14 feet. Maintenance and improvement of the waterways—including channel dredging, bridge and levee maintenance, and the construction of canals and locks—are in large measure the responsibility of the U.S. Army Corps of Engineers. The 522-mile New York State Barge Canal System is the only major nonFederal waterway in the country.

Mississippi River System The major inland river transportation network is the Mississippi River and its tributaries. This north-south-oriented system includes the Mississippi River, the Ohio River System, the Illinois Waterway, and the Arkansas and Missouri rivers, among others. In this system there are about 7,000 miles of heavily used, improved navigable channels, 85 percent of which have at least nine-foot navigable channel depths.

Intracoastal Waterways At its mouth, the Mississippi River is intersected by the Gulf Intracoastal Waterway (GIWW), which parallels the Gulf Coast for 1,180 miles from St. Marks River, Florida, to Brownsville, Texas, at the Mexican border. The GIWW is intersected by a number of river systems in addition to the Mississippi, including the Mobile River, the Apalachicola and the Houston Ship Channel.

This network of major inland and coastal waterways connects some of the largest Gulf Coast ports—New Orleans, La.; Houston, Beaumont and Corpus Christi, Tex.; and Mobile, Ala.—with some of the largest inland ports—St. Louis, Mo.; Pittsburgh, Pa.; Huntington, W. Va.; Cincinnati, Ohio; Memphis, Tenn; and Chicago, Ill. The 40-foot controlling depth of the Mississippi River between the Gulf of Mexico and Baton Rouge allows ocean shipping to join the barge traffic, making this segment especially vital to both the domestic and foreign commerce of the United States.

The Atlantic Intracoastal Waterway provides 1,329 miles of protected channels for commercial and recreational navigation along the Atlantic Coast from Key West, Fla., to Norfolk, Va. Partially protected segments of the waterway continue north from Norfolk along the Delmarva Peninsula, the New Jersey coast and Long Island. Among the major Atlantic Coast ports located along this waterway are Miami, Savannah, Baltimore, Philadelphia and New York/New Jersey.

Pacific Coast In comparison with the Mississippi River system and the intracoastal waterways of the Atlantic and Gulf coasts, the inland and coastal waterways of the Pacific are few. Shallow draft waterways include the Columbia-Snake Waterway and the Willamette River above Portland, Oreg.; the Sacramento River above Sacramento, Calif.; the San Joaquin River above Stockton, Calif.; and a few short navigable rivers stretching along the Washington and Oregon coasts.

The accompanying table shows the major navigable rivers in the United States, their total length, the distance commercially navigable, the body of water they flow into, and the head of navigation—the upriver point beyond which commercial ships cannot pass—and the states through or by which the rivers pass, from source to mouth.

Great Lakes and St. Lawrence Seaway The Great Lakes have been crucial to the development of the United States. They were the highways along which people and finished goods moved west, and along which raw materials such as lumber, minerals, and grains were transported to eastern markets. Later, the cities of the Great Lakes, such as Chicago, Duluth, Detroit and Buffalo, became important centers of finance, industry, and trade in their own right. So important was the maritime trade of the Lakes that in the 1890s, Chicago was the fourth-largest port in the world, despite being closed by ice for as many as five months a year.

An early obstacle to Great Lakes navigation was the fact that the lakes are not all at the same elevation: there is a difference of 354 feet between the level of the westernmost Lake Superior and easternmost Lake Ontario, and there is another 246 feet descent from Lake Ontario down the St. Lawrence River where it empties into the Atlantic Ocean. (It is 2,342 miles from Duluth, Minnesota, at the western end of Lake Superior, to the mouth of the St. Lawrence.)

The first canal (1799) was built on the St. Mary's River between Lake Superior and Lake Huron. (Today, there are two Sault Sainte Marie [or Soo] Canals—along the 70-mile river.) In 1825, the United States opened the way between the upper Lakes (all but Lake Ontario) and the Atlantic via the 175-mile Erie Canal between Buffalo, on Lake Erie, and Albany, on the Hudson River north of New York City. Canada followed with the 27-mile Welland Canal (1833) connecting Welland on Lake Erie and St. Catharine's on Lake Ontario.

The most ambitious undertaking was the construction of the St. Lawrence Seaway, a joint Canadian-American effort to open the entire length of the St. Lawrence and the Great Lakes to oceangoing navigation. Started in 1955 and opened to navigation in 1959, the seaway's system of canals and locks allows ships of up to 730 feet in length and 27 feet draft to sail the entire 2,342 miles from the mouth of the St. Lawrence to Duluth, Minn., at the western end of Lake Superior. The seaway also provides hydroelectric power for Canada and the United States.

The Panama Canal One of the great engineering feats of the world, the 44-mile Panama Canal bisects the continents of North and South America, making it possible for ships to sail between the Atlantic and Pacific oceans without rounding

The Great Lakes

Lake	Area (sq. mi)	Area (sq. km)	Depth (feet)	Depth (meters)	Height above sea level (feet)	Height above sea level (meters)
Erie	9,940	25,745	210	64	571	174
Huron	23,010	59,596	750	229	577	176
Michigan	22,400	58,016	923	281	577	176
Ontario	7,540	19,529	802	244	246	75
Superior	31,820	82,414	1,333	406	600	183

Source: U.S. Environmental Protection Agency and Environment Canada, *The Great Lakes: An Environmental Atlas and Resource Book* (1987).

the treacherous Cape Horn at the tip of South America. The U.S. government began construction of the canal in 1904, and it was opened to commercial navigation Aug. 15, 1914. For inter-ocean shippers, the savings in distance and time afforded by the canal are enormous. A ship sailing from New York to San Francisco via the Panama Canal travels a distance of 5,264 miles, a savings of more than 7,800 miles—or about 20 days— over the 13,100-mile route around Cape Horn. The minimum depth of the canal is 41 feet, the minimum width 300 feet, and the highest elevation above sea level 85 feet.

The Canal Zone, a 10-mile-wide strip of land around the canal in the Republic of Panama was acquired in 1903 by the United States, who governed it until 1979. The Panama Canal Treaty of 1977 abolished the Canal Zone as an independent political entity, but the canal's maintenance and operation remained the responsibility of the U.S. Panama Canal Commission until 1999, when the Republic of Panama assumed full responsibility.

Land Cover and Use, by State, 1997 (thousands of acres)

			Non-Federal land areas				
State	Total surface area[1]	Federal land area	Developed[2]	Rural cropland	Rural pastureland	Rural rangeland	Rural forestland
United States	**1,941,827**	**452,913**	**104,812**	**374,690**	**119,144**	**402,976**	**398,409**
Alabama	33,424	2,240	2,410	2,919	3,527	68	21,073
Arizona	72,964	30,634	1,675	1,204	67	32,114	4,262
Arkansas	34,037	3,997	1,501	7,582	5,453	73	14,765
California	101,510	48,584	5,687	9,561	1,065	17,457	14,295
Colorado	66,625	24,145	1,706	8,860	1,269	23,855	3,729
Connecticut	3,195	143	897	199	107	—	1,729
Delaware	1,534	321	238	472	23	—	347
Florida	37,534	6,938	5,449	2,719	4,177	3,193	12,255
Georgia	37,741	3,177	4,238	4,661	2,853	—	21,216
Hawaii	4,163	446	186	244	89	946	1,514
Idaho	53,488	34,120	811	5,500	1,253	6,478	3,942
Illinois	36,059	1,252	3,262	23,954	2,525	—	3,631
Indiana	23,158	858	2,356	13,358	1,818	—	3,638
Iowa	36,017	663	1,803	25,262	3,554	—	2,084
Kansas	52,661	1,064	2,882	26,460	2,213	15,179	1,290
Kentucky	25,863	1,815	1,955	5,151	5,613	—	10,440
Louisiana	31,377	5,063	1,693	5,568	2,376	280	13,114
Maine	20,966	1,457	747	419	82	—	17,633
Maryland	7,870	1,832	1,291	1,598	454	—	2,331
Massachusetts	5,339	477	1,549	271	114	—	2,657
Michigan	37,349	4,385	3,764	8,439	2,004	—	16,238
Minnesota	54,010	6,484	2,361	21,328	3,423	—	14,830
Mississippi	30,527	2,632	1,656	5,296	3,699	—	16,019
Missouri	44,614	2,766	2,653	13,710	10,947	98	12,118
Montana	94,110	28,150	881	15,086	3,495	37,016	5,279
Nebraska	49,510	1,139	1,268	19,421	1,976	22,864	799
Nevada	70,763	60,315	416	711	271	8,300	297
New Hampshire	5,941	1,000	642	132	92	—	3,875
New Jersey	5,216	679	1,849	574	109	—	1,625
New Mexico	77,823	26,603	1,325	1,842	207	40,276	4,915
New York	31,361	1,495	3,373	5,375	2,627	—	17,533
North Carolina	33,709	5,284	4,181	5,539	1,980	—	15,678
North Dakota	45,251	2,834	1,152	24,991	1,105	10,551	443
Ohio	26,445	781	3,797	11,504	1,980	—	6,984
Oklahoma	44,738	2,230	1,997	9,709	7,933	13,974	7,254
Oregon	62,161	32,088	1,296	3,800	1,905	9,556	12,295
Pennsylvania	28,995	1,204	4,336	5,245	1,812	—	15,306
Rhode Island	813	154	205	20	24	—	381
South Carolina	19,939	1,857	2,325	2,542	1,182	—	10,958
South Dakota	49,358	3,991	1,035	16,738	2,078	21,764	532
Tennessee	26,974	2,020	2,618	4,566	4,985	—	11,736
Texas	171,052	7,062	8,984	26,762	15,807	95,323	10,627
Utah	54,339	36,079	760	1,676	695	10,720	1,830
Vermont	6,154	659	346	601	342	—	4,118
Virginia	27,087	4,604	2,805	2,879	3,071	—	13,030
Washington	44,035	13,478	2,214	6,689	1,200	5,744	12,666
West Virginia	15,508	1,385	986	848	1,503	—	10,472
Wisconsin	35,920	3,142	2,543	10,537	2,882	—	13,634
Wyoming	62,603	29,184	716	2,171	1,181	27,150	995

Note: U.S. Totals exclude Alaska and the District of Columbia. 1. Includes water area and minor land cover and uses not shown separately. 2. Includes urban and built-up areas in units of 10 acres or greater, and rural tranpsortation areas.
Source: U.S. Department of Agriculture, National Resource and Conservation Service and Iowa State University, *Statistical Laboratory, Summary Report,* 1997 National Resources Inventory, December, 1999.

Major Navigable Rivers in the U.S.

Ultimate outflow/river	Length (miles)	Navigable length (miles)	Mouth to head of navigation	States/provinces (from source to mouth)
ATLANTIC OCEAN				
St. Lawrence	760	760	Gulf of St. Lawrence to Lake Ontario	N.Y.; Ontario, Quebec (Canada)
Cape Cod Canal	17	17	Sandwich to Buzzards Bay, Mass.	Mass.
Connecticut	407	52	Long Island Sound to Hartford, Conn.	N.H., Vt., Mass., Conn.
Hudson	306	134	New York Bay to Troy Lock, N.Y. New York State Barge Canal links to Lake Erie (353 mi. Troy to Buffalo), and to Lakes Champlain, Ontario, Cayuga, Seneca.	N.Y.
Delaware	367	77	Delaware Bay to Trenton, N.J.	N.Y., Pa., N.J., Del.
Chesapeake and Delaware Canal	14	14	Delaware Bay to Chesapeake Bay	Del., Md.
Potomac	287	101	Chesapeake Bay to Washington, D.C.	Va., Md., D.C.
James	340	87	Chesapeake Bay to Richmond, Va.	Va.
Roanoke	410	112	Atlantic Ocean to Altavista, N.C.	Va., N.C.
Cape Fear	202	111	Atlantic Ocean to Fayetteville, N.C.	N.C.
Savannah	314	181	Atlantic Ocean to Augusta, Ga.	S.C., Ga.
Saint Johns	285	160	Atlantic Ocean to Lake Harney	Fla.
GULF OF MEXICO				
Chattahoochee	436	194	Apalachicola River to Columbus, Ga.	Ga., Ala.
Apalachicola	90	90	Gulf of Mexico to Chattahoochee, Fla.	Fla.
Mobile	45	45	Mobile Bay to confluence of Alabama and Tombigbee rivers	Ala.
Alabama	318	305	Mobile River to Montgomery, Ala.	Ala.
Tombigbee	362	362	Mobile River to Amory, Miss. Linked to Tennessee River by Tennessee-Tombigbee Waterway (253 mi.)	Miss., Ala.
Black Warrior	217	217	Tombigbee River to Birmingham, Ala.	Ala.
Houston Ship Channel	57	57	Galveston Bay to Houston, Tex.	Tex.
Rio Grande[1]	1,885	13	Gulf of Mexico to Brownsville, Tex.	Colo., N.Mex., Tex., Mexico
MISSISSIPPI RIVER SYSTEM				
Mississippi	2,348	1,807	Gulf of Mexico to Minneapolis, Minn.,	Minn., Wis., Iowa, Ill., Mo., Ky., Tenn., Ark., Miss., La
EASTERN TRIBUTARIES OF THE MISSISSIPPI				
Illinois	273	273	Mississippi River to Joliet. Also linked to Mississippi by Illinois and Mississippi Canal (La Salle to Rockport); and to Lake Michigan (at Chicago, Calumet, East Chicago Gary) by Illinois Waterway	Ill.
Ohio	981	981	Mississippi River to Pittsburgh, Pa.	Pa., Ohio, W.Va., Ind., Ky., Ill.
Monongahela	129	129	Ohio River to Fairmont, W.Va.	W.Va., Pa.
Allegheny	325	72	Ohio River to East Brady, Pa.	N.Y., Pa.
Kanawha	97	91	Ohio River to Charleston, W.Va.	W.Va.
Kentucky	259	82	Ohio River to Beattyville, Ky.	Ky.
Green	360	103	Ohio River to Bowling Green, Ky.	Ky.
Cumberland	694	387	Ohio River to Burnside, Ky.	Ky., Tenn.
Tennessee	652	648	Ohio River to Knoxville, Tenn.	Tenn., Ala., Miss., Ky.
Yazoo	169	165	Mississippi River to Greenwood, Miss.	Miss.
WESTERN TRIBUTARIES OF THE MISSISSIPPI				
Missouri	2,315	735	Mississippi River to Ponca, Nebr.	Mont., N.Dak., S.Dak., Nebr., Iowa, Kans., Mo.
Arkansas	1,396	448	McClellan-Kerr Arkansas River System from Mississippi River to Catoosa, Okla., incorporates sections of White, Arkansas, Verdigris rivers.	Colo., Kans., Okla., Ark.,
Ouachita[2]	605	351	Mississippi River to Camden, Ark.	Ark., La.
Red	1,018	236	Mississippi River to Shreveport, La.	N.Mex., Tex., Okla., Ark., La.
Atchafalaya[3]	220	220	Atchafalaya Bay to Mississippi River	La.
PACIFIC OCEAN				
San Joaquin	340	103	Sacramento River to Hills Ferry, Calif.	Calif.
Sacramento	374	163	San Francisco Bay to Chico Landing, Calif.	Calif.
Columbia	1,210	285	Pacific Ocean to Pasco, Wash.	British Col. (Can.), Wash., Oreg.
Snake	1,083	192	Columbia River to Johnson Bar Landing,	Wyo., Idaho, Oreg., Wash.
Willamette	294	133	Columbia River to Harrisburg, Oreg.	Oreg.

Note: All distances given in nautical miles except for the Mississippi River and its tributaries: 1 nautical mile = 1.151 statute miles. 1. In Mexico known as the Río Bravo or Río Bravo del Norte. 2. Lower 57 miles known as the Black River. 3. Flows from the Mississippi River to the Gulf of Mexico.
Source: National Oceanic and Atmospheric Administration, *Distances Between United States Ports, 1987* (1987).

Extreme Elevations of States and Outlying Areas

State	Highest Point: Name	Elevation: Feet	Elevation: Meters	Lowest Point: Name	Elevation: Feet	Elevation: Meters
United States	**Mount McKinley, Alaska**	**20,320**	**6,198**	**Death Valley, Calif.**	**-282**	**-86**
Alabama	Cheaha Mountain	2,405	733	Gulf of Mexico	Sea level	
Alaska	Mount McKinley	20,320	6,198	Pacific Ocean	Sea level	
Arizona	Humphreys Peak	12,633	3,853	Colorado River	70	21
Arkansas	Magazine Mountain	2,753	840	Ouachita River	55	17
California	Mount Whitney	14,494	4,419	Death Valley	-282	-86
Colorado	Mount Elbert	14,433	4,402	Arkansas River	3,315	1,011
Connecticut	Mount Frissell, South slope	2,380	726	Long Island Sound	Sea level	
Delaware	Ebright Rd., New Castle Co.	448	137	Atlantic Ocean	Sea level	
Dist. of Columbia	Tenleytown	410	125	Potomac River	1	0.3
Florida	Sec.30,T6N,R20W, Walton Co.	345	105	Atlantic Ocean	Sea level	
Georgia	Brasstown Bald	4,784	1,459	Atlantic Ocean	Sea level	
Hawaii	Mauna Kea	13,806	4,211	Pacific Ocean	Sea level	
Idaho	Borah Peak	12,662	3,862	Snake River	710	217
Illinois	Charles Mound	1,235	377	Mississippi River	279	85
Indiana	Franklin Township, Wayne Co.	1,257	383	Ohio River	320	98
Iowa	Sec. 29, T100N, R41W Osceola Co.	1,670	509	Mississippi River	480	146
Kansas	Mount Sunflower	4,039	1,232	Verdigris River	679	207
Kentucky	Black Mountain	4,139	1,262	Mississippi River	257	78
Louisiana	Driskill Mountain	535	163	New Orleans	-8	-2
Maine	Mount Katahdin	5,267	1,606	Atlantic Ocean	Sea level	
Maryland	Backbone Mountain	3,360	1,025	Atlantic Ocean	Sea level	
Massachusetts	Mount Greylock	3,487	1,064	Atlantic Ocean	Sea level	
Michigan	Mount Arvon	1,979	604	Lake Erie	571	174
Minnesota	Eagle Mountain, Cook Co.	2,301	702	Lake Superior	600	183
Mississippi	Woodall Mountain	806	246	Gulf of Mexico	Sea level	
Missouri	Taum Sauk Mountain	1,772	540	St. Francis River	230	70
Montana	Granite Peak	12,799	3,904	Kootenai River	1,800	549
Nebraska	Johnson Township, Kimball Co.	5,424	1,653	Missouri River	840	256
Nevada	Boundary Peak	13,140	4,007	Colorado River	479	146
New Hampshire	Mount Washington	6,288	1,918	Atlantic Ocean	Sea level	
New Jersey	High Point	1,803	550	Atlantic Ocean	Sea level	
New Mexico	Wheeler Peak	13,161	4,014	Red Bluff Reservoir	2,842	867
New York	Mount Marcy	5,344	1,630	Atlantic Ocean	Sea level	
North Carolina	Mount Mitchell	6,684	2,039	Atlantic Ocean	Sea level	
North Dakota	White Butte, Slope Co.	3,506	1,069	Red River	750	229
Ohio	Campbell Hilll	1,549	472	Ohio River	455	139
Oklahoma	Black Mesa	4,973	1,517	Little River	289	88
Oregon	Mount Hood	11,239	3,428	Pacific Ocean	Sea level	
Pennsylvania	Mount Davis	3,213	980	Delaware River	Sea level	
Rhode Island	Jerimoth Hill	812	248	Atlantic Ocean	Sea level	
South Carolina	Sassafras Mountain	3,560	1,086	Atlantic Ocean	Sea level	
South Dakota	Harney Peak	7,242	2,209	Big Stone Lake	966	295
Tennessee	Clingmans Dome	6,643	2,026	Mississippi River	178	54
Texas	Guadalupe Peak	8,749	2,668	Gulf of Mexico	Sea level	
Utah	Kings Peak	13,528	4,126	Beaverdam Creek	2,000	610
Vermont	Mount Mansfield	4,393	1,340	Lake Champlain	95	29
Virginia	Mount Rogers	5,729	1,747	Atlantic Ocean	Sea level	
Washington	Mount Rainier	14,410	4,395	Pacific Ocean	Sea level	
West Virginia	Spruce Knob	4,861	1,483	Potomac River	240	73
Wisconsin	Timms Hill	1,951	595	Lake Michigan	579	177
Wyoming	Gannett Peak	13,804	4,210	Belle Fourche River	3,099	945
Puerto Rico	Cerro de Punta	4,390	1,339	Atlantic Ocean	Sea level	
Amer. Samoa	Lata Mountain	3,160	964	Pacific Ocean	Sea level	
Guam	Mount Lamlam	1,332	405	Pacific Ocean	Sea level	
Virgin Islands	Crown Mountain	1,556	475	Atlantic Ocean	Sea level	

Note: Sec. denotes section; T, township; R, range; N, north; W, west.
Source: U.S. Geological Survey, *Elevations and Distances in the United States* (2000).

U.S. History

DOCUMENTS OF U.S. HISTORY

▶THE DECLARATION OF INDEPENDENCE

After a year of war with Britain, American patriots were driven to make the final break in 1776. On June 7, before the Continental Congress in Philadelphia, Richard Henry Lee of Virginia proposed a declaration that the colonies "are, and of right ought to be, free and independent States." A committee of five, headed by Thomas Jefferson, was appointed to draw up the formal Declaration of Independence on June 10. The committee brought its version, mainly the work of Jefferson, back to Congress on June 28. Congress voted unanimously to declare independence on July 2, and after making several changes in the Jefferson committee's draft, they unanimously adopted the Declaration of Independence on July 4. Copies of the Declaration were dispatched to the states for approval. Charles Carroll of Maryland was the last surviving signer of the Declaration when he died on November 14, 1832. The original document is on display today at the National Archives in Washington, D.C.

In Congress, July 4, 1776,
THE UNANIMOUS DECLARATION
OF THE
THIRTEEN UNITED STATES
OF AMERICA,

When in the Course of human events, it becomes necessary for one people to dissolve the political bands which have connected them with another, and to assume among the Powers of the earth, the separate and equal station to which the Laws of Nature and of Nature's God entitle them, a decent respect to the opinions of mankind requires that they should declare the causes which impel them to the separation.

We hold these truths to be self-evident, that all men are created equal, that they are endowed by their Creator with certain unalienable Rights, that among these are Life, Liberty and the pursuit of Happiness. That to secure these rights, Governments are instituted among Men, deriving their just powers from the consent of the governed. That whenever any Form of Government becomes destructive of these ends, it is the Right of the People to alter or to abolish it, and to institute new Government, laying its foundation on such principles and organizing its powers in such form, as to them shall seem most likely to effect their Safety and Happiness. Prudence, indeed, will dictate that governments long established should not be changed for light and transient causes; and accordingly all experience hath shown, that mankind are more disposed to suffer, while evils are sufferable, than to right themselves by abolishing the forms to which they are accustomed. But when a long train of abuses and usurpations, pursuing invariably the same Object evinces a design to reduce them under absolute Despotism, it is their right, it is their duty, to throw off such Government, and to provide new Guards for their future security. Such has been the patient sufferance of these Colonies; and such is now the necessity which constrains them to alter their former Systems of Government. The history of the present King of Great Britain is a history of repeated injuries and usurpations, all having in direct object the establishment of an absolute Tyranny over these States. To prove this, let Facts be submitted to a candid world.

He has refused his Assent to Laws, the most wholesome and necessary for the public good.

He has forbidden his Governors to pass Laws of immediate and pressing importance, unless suspended in their operation till his Assent should be obtained; and when so suspended, he has utterly neglected to attend to them.

He has refused to pass other Laws for the accommodation of large districts of people, unless those people would relinquish the right of Representation in the Legislature, a right inestimable to them and formidable to tyrants only.

He has called together legislative bodies at places unusual, uncomfortable, and distant from the depository of their Public Records, for the sole purpose of fatiguing them into compliance with his measures.

He has dissolved Representative Houses repeatedly, for opposing with manly firmness his invasions on the rights of the people.

He has refused for a long time, after such dissolutions, to cause others to be elected; whereby the Legislative Powers, incapable of Annihilation, have returned to the People at large for their exercise; the State remaining in the mean time exposed to all the dangers of invasion from without, and convulsions within.

He has endeavoured to prevent the population of these States; for that purpose obstructing the Laws of Naturalization of Foreigners; refusing to pass others to encourage their migration hither, and raising the conditions of new Appropriations of Lands.

He has obstructed the Administration of Justice, by refusing his Assent to Laws for establishing Judiciary Powers.

He has made Judges dependent on his Will alone, for the tenure of their offices, and the amount and payment of their salaries.

He has erected a multitude of New Offices, and sent hither swarms of Officers to harass our People, and eat out their substance.

He has kept among us, in times of peace, Standing Armies without the Consent of our legislature.

He has affected to render the Military independent of and superior to the Civil Power.

He has combined with others to subject us to a jurisdiction foreign to our constitution, and unacknowledged by our laws; giving his Assent to their acts of pretended legislation:

For quartering large bodies of armed troops among us:

For protecting them, by a mock Trial, from Punishment for any Murders which they should commit on the Inhabitants of these States:

For cutting off our Trade with all parts of the world:

For imposing taxes on us without our consent:

For depriving us in many cases, of the benefits of Trial by Jury:

For transporting us beyond Seas to be tried for pretended offences:

For abolishing the free System of English Laws in a neighbouring Province, establishing therein an Arbitrary government, and enlarging its Boundaries so as to render it at once an example and fit instrument for introducing the same absolute rule into these Colonies:

For taking away our Charters, abolishing our most valuable Laws, and altering fundamentally the forms of our Government:

For suspending our own legislature, and declaring themselves invested with Power to legislate for us in all cases whatsoever.

He has abdicated Government here, by declaring us out of his Protection and waging War against us.

He has plundered our seas, ravaged our Coasts, burnt our towns, and destroyed the lives of our people.

He is at this time transporting large armies of foreign mercenaries to compleat the works of death, desolation and tyranny, already begun with circumstances of Cruelty & perfidy scarcely paralleled in the most barbarous ages, and totally unworthy of the Head of a civilized nation.

He has constrained our fellow Citizens taken Captive on the high Seas to bear Arms against their Country, to become the executioners of their friends and Brethren, or to fall themselves by their Hands.

He has excited domestic insurrections amongst us, and has endeavoured to bring on the inhabitants of our frontiers, the merciless Indian Savages, whose known rule of warfare, is an undistinguished destruction of all ages, sexes and conditions.

In every stage of these Oppressions We have Petitioned for Redress in the most humble terms: Our repeated Petitions have been answered only by repeated injury. A prince, whose character is thus marked by every act which may define a Tyrant, is unfit to be the ruler of a free People.

Nor have We been wanting in attention to our British brethren. We have warned them from time to time of attempts by their legislature to extend an unwarrantable jurisdiction over us. We have reminded them of the circumstances of our emigration and settlement here. We have appealed to their native justice and magnanimity, and we have conjured them by the ties of our common kindred to disavow these usurpations, which would inevitably interrupt our connections and correspondence. They too have been deaf to the voice of justice and of consanguinity. We must, therefore, acquiesce in the necessity, which denounces our Separation and hold them, as we hold the rest of mankind, Enemies in War, in Peace Friends.

We, therefore, the Representatives of the United States of America, in General Congress, Assembled, appealing to the Supreme Judge of the world for the rectitude of our intentions, do, in the Name, and by Authority of the good People of these Colonies, solemnly publish and declare, That these United Colonies are, and of Right ought to be Free and Independent States; that they are Absolved from all Allegiance to the British Crown, and that all political connection between them and the State of Great Britain, is and ought to be totally dissolved; and that as Free and Independent States, they have full Power to levy War, conclude Peace, contract Alliances, establish Commerce, and to do all other Acts and Things which Independent States may of right do. And for the support of this Declaration, with a firm reliance on the Protection of Divine Providence, we mutually pledge to each other our Lives, our Fortunes and our sacred Honor.

▶THE U.S. CONSTITUTION

During and after the Revolution, the United States was governed by the Continental Congress under the Articles of Confederation, which delegated very limited powers to the national government and reserved the rest to the states. Economic chaos, political confusion, and widespread dissatisfaction with the lack of central authority peaked after Shays's Rebellion in 1786. George Washington lent his prestige to the call for a convention to consider a new form of government. Congress endorsed the plan on February 21, 1787, "for the sole and express purpose of revising the Articles of Confederation." All states but Rhode Island sent delegates to the convention, which opened in Philadelphia on May 14. The delegates moved at once to discard the Articles, draw up a new Constitution, and conduct their meetings in secrecy, while Washington presided and James Madison took notes. A long summer of debate and compromise finally produced the document that most of the delegates signed on September 17. Congress ordered the Constitution sent to the states for ratification on September 28, requiring approval by at least nine of them to validate the new charter. Whether the Constitution would be adopted was in doubt until June 21, 1788, when New Hampshire became the ninth state to ratify it. The Constitution went into effect on March 4, 1789. All of the original 13 states eventually ratified the Constitution, ending with Rhode Island on May 29, 1790. The U.S. Constitution remains the world's oldest written constitution.

Preamble

We, the People of the United States, in Order to form a more perfect Union, establish Justice, insure domestic Tranquillity, provide for the common defence, promote the general Welfare, and secure the Blessings of Liberty to ourselves and our Posterity, do ordain and establish this Constitution for the United States of America.

Article I

Section 1 All legislative powers herein granted shall be vested in a Congress of the United States, which shall consist of a Senate and House of Representatives.

Section 2 [1] The House of Representatives shall be composed of members chosen every second year by the people of the several States, and the electors in each State shall have the qualifications requisite for electors of the most numerous branch of the State legislature.

[2] No person shall be a Representative who shall not have attained to the age of twenty-five years, and been seven years a citizen of the United States, and who shall not, when elected, be an inhabitant of that State in which he shall be chosen.

[3] Representatives and direct taxes shall be apportioned among the several States which may be included within this Union, according to their respective numbers, which shall be determined by adding to the whole number of free persons, including those bound to service for a term of years, and excluding Indians not taxed, three-fifths of all other persons. The actual enumeration shall be made within three years after the first meeting of the Congress of the United States, and within every subsequent term of ten years, in such manner as they shall by law direct. The number of Representatives shall not exceed one for every thirty thousand, but each State shall have at least one Representative; and until such enumeration shall be made, the State of New Hampshire shall

Signers of the Declaration of Independence

Delegate	State	Born/Died	Delegate	State	Born/Died
Adams, John	Massachusetts	1735–1826	**Lynch, Thomas, Jr.**	South Carolina	1749–1779
Adams, Samuel	Massachusetts	1722–1803	**McKean, Thomas**	Delaware	1734–1817
Bartlett, Josiah	New Hampshire	1729–1795	**Middleton, Arthur**	South Carolina	1742–1787
Braxton, Carter	Virginia	1736–1797	**Morris, Lewis**	New York	1726–1798
Carroll, Charles	Maryland	1737–1832	**Morris, Robert**	Pennsylvania	1734–1806
Chase, Samuel	Maryland	1741–1811	**Morton, John**	Pennsylvania	1724–1777
Clark, Abraham	New Jersey	1726–1794	**Nelson, Thomas Jr.**	Virginia	1738–1789
Clymer, George	Pennsylvania	1739–1813	**Paca, William**	Maryland	1740–1799
Ellery, William	Rhode Island	1727–1820	**Paine, Robert Treat**	Massachusetts	1731–1814
Floyd, William	New York	1734–1821	**Penn, John**	North Carolina	1741–1788
Franklin, Benjamin	Pennsylvania	1706–1790	**Read, George**	Delaware	1733–1798
Gerry, Elbridge	Massachusetts	1744–1814	**Rodney, Caesar**	Delaware	1728–1784
Gwinnett, Button	Georgia	1732–1777	**Ross, George**	Pennsylvania	1730–1779
Hall, Lyman	Georgia	1724–1790	**Rush, Benjamin**	Pennsylvania	1745–1813
Hancock, John	Massachusetts	1737–1793	**Rutledge, Edward**	South Carolina	1749–1800
Harrison, Benjamin	Virginia	1726–1791	**Sherman, Roger**	Connecticut	1721–1793
Hart, John	New Jersey	? –1779	**Smith, James**	Pennsylvania	1713–1806
Hewes, Joseph	North Carolina	1730–1779	**Stockton, Richard**	New Jersey	1730–1781
Heyward, Thomas, Jr.	South Carolina	1746–1809	**Stone, Thomas**	Maryland	1743–1787
Hooper, William	North Carolina	1742–1790	**Taylor, George**	Pennsylvania	1716–1781
Hopkins, Stephen	Rhode Island	1707–1785	**Thornton, Matthew**	New Hampshire	1714–1803
Hopkinson, Francis	New Jersey	1737–1791	**Walton, George**	Georgia	1741–1804
Huntington, Samuel	Connecticut	1731–1796	**Whipple, William**	New Hampshire	1730–1785
Jefferson, Thomas	Virginia	1743–1826	**Williams, William**	Connecticut	1731–1811
Lee, Richard Henry	Virginia	1732–1794	**Wilson, James**	Pennsylvania	1742–1798
Lee, Francis Lightfoot	Virginia	1734–1797	**Witherspoon, John**	New Jersey	1723–1794
Lewis, Francis	New York	1713–1803	**Wolcott, Oliver**	Connecticut	1726–1797
Livingston, Philip	New York	1716–1778	**Wythe, George**	Virginia	1726–1806

be entitled to choose three; Massachusetts, eight; Rhode Island and Providence Plantations, one; Connecticut, five; New York, six; New Jersey, four; Pennsylvania, eight; Delaware, one; Maryland, six; Virginia, ten; North Carolina, five; South Carolina, five; and Georgia, three.

[4] When vacancies happen in the representation from any State, the executive authority thereof shall issue writs of election to fill such vacancies.

[5] The House of Representatives shall choose their Speaker and other officers, and shall have the sole power of impeachment.

Section 3 [1] The Senate of the United States shall be composed of two Senators from each State, chosen by the legislature thereof for six years; and each Senator shall have one vote.

[2] Immediately after they shall be assembled in consequence of the first election, they shall be divided as equally as may be into three classes. The seats of the Senators of the first class shall be vacated at the expiration of the second year, of the second class at the expiration of the fourth year, and of the third class at the expiration of the sixth year, so that one-third may be chosen every second year; and if vacancies happen by resignation or otherwise during the recess of the legislature of any State, the executive thereof may make temporary appointments until the next meeting of the legislature, which shall then fill such vacancies.

[3] No person shall be a Senator who shall not have attained to the age of thirty years, and been nine years a citizen of the United States, and who shall not, when elected, be an inhabitant of that State for which he shall be chosen.

[4] The Vice-President of the United States shall be President of the Senate, but shall have no vote, unless they be equally divided.

[5] The Senate shall choose their other officers and also a President pro tempore in the absence of the Vice-President, or when he shall exercise the office of President of the United States.

[6] The Senate shall have the sole power to try all impeachments. When sitting for that purpose, they shall be on oath or affirmation. When the President of the United States is tried, the Chief Justice shall preside; and no person shall be convicted without the concurrence of two-thirds of the members present.

[7] Judgment in cases of impeachment shall not extend further than to removal from office, and disqualification to hold and enjoy any office of honor, trust, or profit under the United States; but the party convicted shall, nevertheless, be liable and subject to indictment, trial, judgment, and punishment, according to law.

Section 4 [1] The times, places, and manner of holding elections for Senators and Representatives shall be prescribed in each State by the legislature thereof; but the Congress may at any time by law make or alter such regulations, except as to the places of choosing Senators.

[2] The Congress shall assemble at least once in every year, and such meeting shall be on the first Monday in December, unless they shall by law appoint a different day.

Section 5 [1] Each House shall be the judge of the elections, returns, and qualification of its own members, and a majority of each shall constitute a quorum to do business; but a smaller number may adjourn from day to day, and may be authorized to compel the attendance of absent members, in such manner, and under such penalties, as each House may provide.

[2] Each House may determine the rules of its proceedings, punish its members for disorderly behavior, and with the concurrence of two-thirds, expel a member.

[3] Each House shall keep a journal of its proceedings, and from time to time publish the

same, excepting such parts as may in their judgment require secrecy, and the yeas and nays of the members of either House on any question shall, at the desire of one-fifth of those present, be entered on the journal.

[4] Neither House, during the session of Congress, shall, without the consent of the other, adjourn for more than three days, nor to any other place than that in which the two Houses shall be sitting.

Section 6 [1] The Senators and Representatives shall receive a compensation for their services, to be ascertained by law and paid out of the Treasury of the United States. They shall, in all cases except treason, felony, and breach of the peace, be privileged from arrest during their attendance at the session of their respective Houses, and in going to and returning from the same; and for any speech or debate in either House they shall not be questioned in any other place.

[2] No Senator or Representative shall, during the time for which he was elected, be appointed to any civil office under the authority of the United States, which shall have been created, or the emoluments whereof shall have been increased during such time; and no person holding any office under the United States shall be a member of either House during his continuance in office.

Section 7 [1] All bills for raising revenue shall originate in the House of Representatives; but the Senate may propose or concur with amendments as on other bills.

[2] Every bill which shall have passed the House of Representatives and the Senate shall, before it becomes a law, be presented to the President of the United States; if he approves he shall sign it, but if not he shall return it, with his objections, to that House in which it shall have originated, who shall enter the objections at large on their journal and proceed to reconsider it. If after such reconsideration two-thirds of that House shall agree to pass the bill, it shall be sent, together with the objections, to the other House, by which it shall likewise be reconsidered, and if approved by two-thirds of that House it shall become a law. But in all such cases the vote of both Houses shall be determined by yeas and nays, and the names of the persons voting for and against the bill shall be entered on the journal of each House respectively. If any bill shall not be returned by the President within ten days (Sundays excepted) after it shall have been presented to him, the same shall be a law, in like manner as if he had signed it, unless the Congress by their adjournment prevent its return, in which case it shall not be a law.

[3] Every order, resolution or vote to which the concurrence of the Senate and House of Representatives may be necessary (except on a question of adjournment) shall be presented to the President of the United States; and before the same shall take effect shall be approved by him, or being disapproved by him, shall be repassed by two-thirds of the Senate and House of Representatives, according to the rules and limitations prescribed in the case of a bill.

Section 8 [1] The Congress shall have power to lay and collect taxes, duties, imposts and excises, to pay the debts and provide for the common defense and general welfare of the United States; but all duties, imposts and excises shall be uniform throughout the United States;

[2] To borrow money on the credit of the United States;

[3] To regulate commerce with foreign nations, and among the several States, and with the Indian tribes;

[4] To establish an uniform rule of naturalization, and uniform laws on the subject of bankruptcies throughout the United States;

[5] To coin money, regulate the value thereof, and of foreign coin, and fix the standard of weights and measures;

[6] To provide for the punishment of counterfeiting the securities and current coin of the United States;

[7] To establish post offices and post roads;

[8] To promote the progress of science and useful arts by securing for limited times to authors and inventors the exclusive right to their respective writings and discoveries;

[9] To constitute tribunals inferior to the Supreme Court;

[10] To define and punish piracies and felonies committed on the high seas and offenses against the law of nations.

[11] To declare war, grant letters of marque and reprisal, and make rules concerning captures on land and water;

[12] To raise and support armies, but no appropriation of money to that use shall be for a longer term than two years;

[13] To provide and maintain a navy;

[14] To make rules for the government and regulation of the land and naval forces;

[15] To provide for calling forth the militia to execute the laws of the Union, suppress insurrections, and repel invasions;

[16] To provide for organizing, arming and disciplining the militia, and for governing such part of them as may be employed in the service of the United States, reserving to the States respectively the appointment of the officers, and the authority of training the militia according to the discipline prescribed by Congress;

[17] To exercise exclusive legislation in all cases whatsoever over such district (not exceeding ten miles square) as may, by cession of particular States and the acceptance of Congress, become the seat of the Government of the United States, and to exercise like authority over all places purchased by the consent of the legislature of the State in which the same shall be, for the erection of forts, magazines, arsenals, dockyards, and other needful buildings;

[18] To make all laws which shall be necessary and proper for carrying into execution the foregoing powers, and all other powers vested by this Constitution in the Government of the United States, or in any department or officer thereof.

Section 9 [1] The migration or importation of such persons as any of the States now existing shall think proper to admit shall not be prohibited by the Congress prior to the year one thousand eight hundred and eight, but a tax or duty may be imposed on such importation, not exceeding ten dollars for each person.

[2] The privilege of the writ of habeas corpus shall not be suspended, unless when in cases of rebellion or invasion the public safety may require it.

[3] No bill of attainder or ex post facto law shall be passed.

[4] No capitation or other direct tax shall be laid, unless in proportion to the census or enumeration hereinbefore directed to be taken.

[5] No tax or duty shall be laid on articles exported from any State.

[6] No preference shall be given by any regulation of commerce or revenue to the ports of one State

over those of another; nor shall vessels bound to or from one State be obliged to enter, clear or pay duties in another.

[7] No money shall be drawn from the Treasury but in consequence of appropriations made by law; and a regular statement and account of the receipts and expenditures of all public money shall be published from time to time.

[8] No title of nobility shall be granted by the United States; and no person holding any office of profit or trust under them shall, without the consent of the Congress, accept of any present, emolument, office, or title of any kind whatever from any king, prince, or foreign state.

Section 10 [1] No State shall enter into any treaty, alliance, or confederation; grant letters of marque and reprisal; coin money, emit bills of credit, make anything but gold and silver coin a tender in payment of debts; pass any bill of attainder, ex post facto law or law impairing the obligation of contracts, or grant any title of nobility.

[2] No State shall, without the consent of the Congress, lay any imposts or duties on imports or exports, except what may be absolutely necessary for executing its inspection laws; and the net produce of all duties and imposts, laid by any State on imports or exports, shall be for the use of the Treasury of the United States; and all such laws shall be subject to the revision and control of the Congress.

[3] No State shall, without the consent of Congress, lay any duty of tonnage, keep troops and ships of war in time of peace, enter into any agreement or compact with another State or with a foreign power, or engage in war, unless actually invaded or in such imminent danger as will not admit of delay.

Article II

Section 1 [1] The executive power shall be vested in a President of the United States of America. He shall hold his office during the term of four years, and together with the Vice-President, chosen for the same term, be elected as follows:

[2] Each State shall appoint, in such manner as the legislature thereof may direct, a number of Electors, equal to the whole number of Senators and Representatives to which the State may be entitled in the Congress; but no Senator or Representative, or person holding an office of trust or profit under the United States shall be appointed an Elector.

[3] The Electors shall meet in their respective States and vote by ballot for two persons, of whom one at least shall not be an inhabitant of the same State with themselves. And they shall make a list of all the persons voted for, and of the number of votes for each; which list they shall sign and certify, and transmit sealed to the seat of government of the United States, directed to the President of the Senate. The President of the Senate shall, in the presence of the Senate and House of Representatives, open all the certificates, and the votes shall then be counted. The person having the greatest number of votes shall be the President, if such number be a majority of the whole number of Electors appointed; and if there be more than one who have such majority, and have an equal number of votes, then the House of Representatives shall immediately choose by ballot one of them for President; and if no person have a majority, then from the five highest on the list the said House shall in like manner choose the President. But in choosing the President the votes shall be taken by States, the representation from each State having one vote; a quorum for this purpose shall consist of a member or members from two-thirds of the States, and a majority of all the States shall be necessary to a choice. In every case, after the choice of the President, the person having the greatest number of votes of the Electors shall be the Vice-President. But if there should remain two or more who have equal votes, the Senate shall choose from them by ballot the Vice-President.

[4] The Congress may determine the time of choosing the Electors and the day on which they shall give their votes, which day shall be the same throughout the United States.

[5] No person except a natural-born citizen, or citizen of the United States at the time of the adoption of this Constitution, shall be eligible to the office of President; neither shall any person be eligible to that office who shall not have attained to the age of thirty-five years, and been fourteen years a resident within the United States.

[6] In case of the removal of the President from office, or of his death, resignation, or inability to discharge the powers and duties of the said office, the same shall devolve on the Vice-President, and the Congress may by law provide for the case of removal, death, resignation, or inability, both of the President and Vice-President, declaring what officer shall then act as President, and such officer shall act accordingly until the disability be removed or a President shall be elected.

[7] The President shall, at stated times, receive for his services a compensation, which shall neither be increased nor diminished during the period for which he shall have been elected, and he shall not receive within that period any other emolument from the United States or any of them.

[8] Before he enter on the execution of his office he shall take the following oath or affirmation: "I do solemnly swear (or affirm) that I will faithfully execute the office of President of the United States, and will to the best of my ability preserve, protect, and defend the Constitution of the United States."

Section 2 [1] The President shall be Commander-in-Chief of the Army and Navy of the United States, and of the militia of the several States when called into the actual service of the United States; he may require the opinion, in writing, of the principal officer in each of the executive departments, upon any subject relating to the duties of their respective offices, and he shall have power to grant reprieves and pardons for offenses against the United States, except in cases of impeachment.

[2] He shall have power, by and with the advice and consent of the Senate, to make treaties, provided two-thirds of the Senators present concur; and he shall nominate, and, by and with the advice and consent of the Senate, shall appoint ambassadors, other public ministers and consuls, judges of the Supreme Court, and all other officers of the United States whose appointments are not herein otherwise provided for, and which shall be established by law; but the Congress may by law vest the appointment of such inferior officers, as they think proper, in the President alone, in the courts of law, or in the heads of departments.

[3] The President shall have power to fill up all vacancies that may happen during the recess of the Senate, by granting commissions which shall expire at the end of their next session.

Section 3 He shall from time to time give to the Congress information of the state of the Union, and recommend to their consideration such measures as he shall judge necessary and expedient; he may, on extraordinary occasions, convene both Houses, or either of them, and in case of disagreement between them with respect to the time of adjournment, he may adjourn them to such time as he shall think proper; he shall receive ambassadors and other public ministers; he shall take care that the laws be faithfully executed, and shall commission all the officers of the United States.

Section 4 The President, Vice-President and all civil officers of the United States shall be removed from office on impeachment for and conviction of treason, bribery, or other high crimes and misdemeanors.

Article III

Section 1 The judicial power of the United States shall be vested in one Supreme Court, and in such inferior courts as the Congress may from time to time ordain and establish. The judges, both of the Supreme and inferior courts, shall hold their offices during good behavior, and shall, at stated times, receive for their services a compensation which shall not be diminished during their continuance in office.

Section 2 [1] The judicial power shall extend to all cases, in law and equity, arising under this Constitution, the laws of the United States, and treaties made, or which shall be made, under their authority; to all cases affecting ambassadors, other public ministers, and consuls; to all cases of admiralty and maritime jurisdiction; to controversies to which the United States shall be a party; to controversies between two or more States; between a State and citizens of another State; between citizens of different States; between citizens of the same State claiming lands under grants of different States, and between a State, or the citizens thereof, and foreign states, citizens, or subjects.

[2] In all cases affecting ambassadors, other public ministers and consuls, and those in which a State shall be party, the Supreme Court shall have original jurisdiction. In all the other cases before mentioned the Supreme Court shall have appellate jurisdiction, both as to law and fact, with such exceptions and under such regulations as the Congress shall make.

[3] The trial of all crimes, except in cases of impeachment, shall be by jury; and such trial shall be held in the State where the said crimes shall have been committed; but when not committed within any State, the trial shall be at such place or places as the Congress may by law have directed.

Section 3 [1] Treason against the United States shall consist only in levying war against them, or in adhering to their enemies, giving them aid and comfort. No person shall be convicted of treason unless on the testimony of two witnesses to the same overt act, or on confession in open court.

[2] The Congress shall have power to declare the punishment of treason, but no attainder of treason shall work corruption of blood or forfeiture except during the life of the person attained.

Article IV

Section 1 Full faith and credit shall be given in each State to the public acts, records, and judicial proceedings of every other State. And the Congress may by general laws prescribe the manner in which such acts, records, and proceedings shall be proved, and the effect thereof.

Section 2 [1] The citizens of each State shall be entitled to all privileges and immunities of citizens in the several States.

[2] A person charged in any State with treason, felony, or other crime, who shall flee from justice, and be found in another State, shall, on demand of the executive authority of the State from which he fled, be delivered up, to be removed to the State having jurisdiction of the crime.

[3] No person held to service or labor in one State, under the laws thereof, escaping into another, shall, in consequence of any law or regulation therein, be discharged from such service or labor, but shall be delivered up on claim to the party to whom such service or labor may be due.

Section 3 [1] New States may be admitted by the Congress into this Union; but no new State shall be formed or erected within the jurisdiction of any other State; nor any State be formed by the junction of two or more States or parts of States, without the consent of the legislatures of the States concerned as well as of the Congress.

[2] The Congress shall have power to dispose of and make all needful rules and regulations respecting the territory or other property belonging to the United States; and nothing in this Constitution shall be so construed as to prejudice any claims of the United States or of any particular State.

Section 4 The United States shall guarantee to every State in this Union a republican form of government, and shall protect each of them against invasion, and on application of the legislature, or of the executive (when the legislature cannot be convened), against domestic violence.

Article V

The Congress, whenever two-thirds of both Houses shall deem it necessary, shall propose amendments to this Constitution, or, on the application of the legislatures of two-thirds of the several States, shall call a convention for proposing amendments, which in either case shall be valid to all intents and purposes as part of this Constitution, when ratified by the legislatures of three-fourths of the several States, or by conventions in three-fourths thereof, as the one or the other mode of ratification may be proposed by the Congress; provided that no amendment which may be made prior to the year one thousand eight hundred and eight shall in any manner affect the first and fourth clauses in the Ninth Section of the First Article; and that no State, without its consent shall be deprived of its equal suffrage in the Senate.

Article VI

[1] All debts contracted and engagements entered into, before the adoption of this Constitution, shall be as valid against the United States under this Constitution as under the Confederation.

[2] This Constitution, and the laws of the United States which shall be made in pursuance thereof, and all treaties made, or which shall be made, under the authority of the United States, shall be the supreme law of the land; and the judges in every State shall be bound thereby, anything in the Constitution or laws of any State to the contrary notwithstanding.

[3] The Senators and Representatives before mentioned and the members of the several State legislatures, and all executive and judicial officers both of the United States and of the several States, shall be bound by oath or affirmation to support

this Constitution; but no religious test shall ever be required as a qualification to any office or public trust under the United States.

Article VII

The ratification of the conventions of nine States shall be sufficient for the establishment of this Constitution between the States so ratifying the same.

Amendments to the Constitution

[The first 10 amendments, known collectively as The Bill of Rights, were adopted in 1791.]

Amendment I

Congress shall make no law respecting an establishment of religion, or prohibiting the free exercise thereof; or abridging the freedom of speech or of the press; or the right of the people peaceably to assemble, and to petition the government for a redress of grievances.

Amendment II

A well-regulated militia being necessary to the security of a free State, the right of the people to keep and bear arms shall not be infringed.

Amendment III

No soldier shall, in time of peace, be quartered in any house without the consent of the owner, nor in time of war, but in a manner to be prescribed by law.

Amendment IV

The right of the people to be secure in their persons, houses, papers, and effects, against unreasonable searches and seizures, shall not be violated, and no warrants shall issue but upon probable cause, supported by oath or affirmation, and particularly describing the place to be searched, and the persons or things to be seized.

Amendment V

No person shall be held to answer for a capital, or otherwise infamous crime, unless on a presentment or indictment of a grand jury, except in cases arising in the land or naval forces, or in the militia, when in actual service in time of war or public danger; nor shall any person be subject for the same offense to be twice put in jeopardy of life or limb; nor shall be compelled in any criminal case to be a witness against himself, nor be deprived of life, liberty or property, without due process of law; nor shall private property be taken for public use without just compensation.

Amendment VI

In all criminal prosecutions, the accused shall enjoy the right to a speedy and public trial, by an impartial jury of the State and district wherein the crime shall have been committed, which district shall have been previously ascertained by law, and to be informed of the nature and cause of the accusation; to be confronted with the witnesses against him; to have compulsory process for obtaining witnesses in his favor, and to have the assistance of counsel for his defense.

Amendment VII

In suits at common law, where the value in controversy shall exceed twenty dollars, the right of trial by jury shall be preserved, and no fact tried by a jury shall be otherwise re-examined in any court of the United States, than according to the rules of the common law.

Amendment VIII

Excessive bail shall not be required, nor excessive fines imposed, nor cruel and unusual punishments inflicted.

Amendment IX

The enumeration in the Constitution of certain rights shall not be construed to deny or disparage others retained by the people.

Amendment X

The powers not delegated to the United States by the Constitution, nor prohibited by it to the States, are reserved to the States respectively, or to the people.

Amendment XI [Adopted Jan. 8, 1798]

The judicial power of the United States shall not be construed to extend to any suit in law or equity, commenced or prosecuted against one of the United States by citizens of another State, or by citizens or subjects of any foreign state.

Amendment XII [Adopted Sept. 25, 1804]

[1] The Electors shall meet in their respective States and vote by ballot for President and Vice-President, one of whom, at least, shall not be an inhabitant of the same State with themselves; they shall name in their ballots the person voted for as President, and in distinct ballots the person voted for as Vice-President, and they shall make distinct lists of all persons voted for as President and of all persons voted for as Vice-President, and of the number of votes for each; which lists they shall sign and certify, and transmit sealed to the seat of the government of the United States, directed to the President of the Senate. The President of the Senate shall, in the presence of the Senate and House of Representatives, open all the certificates and the votes shall then be counted. The person having the greatest number of votes for President shall be the President, if such number be a majority of the whole number of Electors appointed; and if no person have such majority, then from the persons having the highest numbers not exceeding three on the list of those voted for as President, the House of Representatives shall choose immediately, by ballot, the President. But in choosing the President the votes shall be taken by States, the representation from each State having one vote; a quorum for this purpose shall consist of a member or members from two-thirds of the States, and a majority of all the States shall be necessary to a choice. And if the House of Representatives shall not choose a President whenever the right of choice shall devolve upon them, before the fourth day of March next following, then the Vice-President shall act as President, as in the case of the death or other constitutional disability of the President.

[2] The person having the greatest number of votes as Vice-President shall be the Vice-President, if such number be a majority of the whole number of Electors appointed; and if no person have a majority, then from the two highest numbers on the list the Senate shall choose the Vice-President; a quorum for the purpose shall consist of two-thirds of the whole number of Senators, and a majority of the whole number shall be necessary to a choice. But no person constitutionally ineligible to the office of President shall be eligible to that of Vice-President of the United States.

Amendment XIII [Adopted Dec. 18, 1865]

Section 1 Neither slavery nor involuntary servitude, except as a punishment for crime whereof the party shall have been duly convicted, shall exist within the United States, or any place subject to their jurisdiction.

Section 2 Congress shall have power to enforce this article by appropriate legislation.

Amendment XIV [Adopted July 28, 1868]

Section 1 All persons born or naturalized in the United States, and subject to the jurisdiction thereof, are citizens of the United States and of the State wherein they reside. No State shall make or enforce any law which shall abridge the privileges or immunities of citizens of the United States; nor shall any State deprive any person of life, liberty or property, without due process of law; nor deny to any person within its jurisdiction the equal protection of the laws.

Section 2 Representatives shall be apportioned among the several States according to their respective numbers, counting the whole number of persons in each State, excluding Indians not taxed. But when the right to vote at any election for the choice of Electors for President and Vice-President of the United States, Representatives in Congress, the executive and judicial officers of a State, or the members of the legislature thereof, is denied to any of the male inhabitants of such State, being twenty-one years of age, and citizens of the United States, or in any way abridged except for participation in rebellion or other crime, the basis of representation therein shall be reduced in the proportion which the number of such male citizens shall bear to the whole number of male citizens twenty-one years of age in such State.

Section 3 No person shall be a Senator or Representative in Congress, or elector of President and Vice-President, or hold any office, civil or military, under the United States or under any State, who, having previously taken an oath as a member of Congress, or as an officer of the United States, or as a member of any State legislature, or as an executive or judicial officer of any State, to support the Constitution of the United States, shall have engaged in insurrection or rebellion against the same, or given aid or comfort to the enemies thereof. But Congress may, by a vote of two-thirds of each House, remove such disability.

Section 4 The validity of the public debt of the United States, authorized by law, including debts incurred for payment of pensions and bounties for services in suppressing insurrection or rebellion, shall not be questioned. But neither the United States nor any State shall assume or pay any debt or obligation incurred in aid of insurrection or rebellion against the United States, or any claim for the loss or emancipation of any slave; but all such debts, obligations, and claims shall be held illegal and void.

Section 5 The Congress shall have power to enforce, by appropriate legislation, the provisions of this article.

Amendment XV [Adopted Mar. 30, 1870]

Section 1 The right of citizens of the United States to vote shall not be denied or abridged by the United States or by any State on account of race, color, or previous condition of servitude.

Section 2 The Congress shall have power to enforce this article by appropriate legislation.

Amendment XVI [Adopted Feb. 25, 1913]

The Congress shall have power to lay and collect taxes on incomes, from whatever source derived, without apportionment among the several States, and without regard to any census or enumeration.

Amendment XVII [Adopted May 31, 1913]

Section 1 The Senate of the United States shall be composed of two Senators from each State, elected by the people thereof, for six years; and each Senator shall have one vote. The electors in each State shall have the qualifications requisite for electors of the most numerous branch of the State legislatures.

Section 2 When vacancies happen in the representation of any State in the Senate, the executive authority of such State shall issue writs of election to fill such vacancies: Provided, that the legislature of any State may empower the executive thereof to make temporary appointments until the people fill the vacancies by election as the legislature may direct.

Section 3 This amendment shall not be so construed as to affect the election or term of any Senator chosen before it becomes valid as part of the Constitution.

Amendment XVIII [Adopted Jan. 29, 1919]

Section 1 After one year from the ratification of this article the manufacture, sale or transportation of intoxicating liquors within, the importation thereof into, or the exportation thereof from the United States and all territory subject to the jurisdiction thereof, for beverage purposes, is hereby prohibited.

Section 2 The Congress and the several States shall have concurrent power to enforce this article by appropriate legislation.

Section 3 This article shall be inoperative unless it shall have been ratified as an amendment to the Constitution by the legislatures of the several States, as provided in the Constitution, within seven years from the date of the submission hereof to the States by the Congress.

Amendment XIX [Adopted Aug. 26, 1920]

Section 1 The right of citizens of the United States to vote shall not be denied or abridged by the United States or by any State on account of sex.

Section 2 Congress shall have power to enforce this article by appropriate legislation.

Amendment XX [Adopted Feb. 6, 1933]

Section 1 The terms of the President and Vice-President shall end at noon on the 20th day of January, and the terms of Senators and Representatives at noon on the 3d day of January, of the years in which such terms would have ended if this article had not been ratified; and the terms of their successors shall then begin.

Section 2 The Congress shall assemble at least once in every year, and such meeting shall begin at noon on the 3d day of January, unless they shall by law appoint a different day.

Section 3 If, at the time fixed for the beginning of the term of the President, the President-elect shall have died, the Vice-President-elect shall become President. If a President shall not have been chosen before the time fixed for the beginning of his term or if the President-elect shall have failed to qualify, then the Vice-President-elect shall act as President until a President shall have qualified; and the Congress may by law provide for the case wherein neither a President-elect nor a Vice-President-elect shall have qualified, declaring who shall then act as President, or the manner in which one who is to act shall be selected, and such person shall act accordingly until a President or Vice-President shall have qualified.

Section 4 The Congress may by law provide for the case of the death of any of the persons from whom the House of Representatives may choose a President whenever the right of choice shall have devolved upon them, and for the case of death of any of the persons from whom the Senate may choose a Vice-President whenever the right of choice shall have devolved upon them.

Section 5 Sections 1 and 2 shall take effect on the 15th day of October following the ratification of this article.

Section 6 This article shall be inoperative unless it shall have been ratified as an amendment to the Constitution by the legislatures of three-fourths of the several States within seven years from the date of its submission.

Amendment XXI [Adopted Dec. 5, 1933]

Section 1 The eighteenth article of amendment to the Constitution of the United States is hereby repealed.

Section 2 The transportation or importation into any State, territory, or possession of the United States for delivery or use therein of intoxicating liquors, in violation of the laws thereof, is hereby prohibited.

Section 3 This article shall be inoperative unless it shall have been ratified as an amendment to the Constitution by conventions in the several States, as provided in the Constitution, within seven years from the date of the submission hereof to the States by the Congress.

Amendment XXII [Adopted Feb. 26, 1951]

Section 1 No person shall be elected to the office of President more than twice, and no person who has held the office of President, or acted as President, for more than two years of a term to which some other person was elected President shall be elected to the office of President more than once. But this Article shall not apply to any person holding the office of President when this Article was proposed by the Congress, and shall not prevent any person who may be holding the office of President, or acting as President, during the term within which this Article becomes operative from holding the office of President or acting as President during the remainder of such term.

Section 2 This article shall be inoperative unless it shall have been ratified as an amendment to the Constitution by the legislatures of three-fourths of the several States within seven years from the date of its submission to the States by the Congress.

Amendment XXIII [Adopted Apr. 3, 1961]

Section 1 The District constituting the seat of Government of the United States shall appoint in such manner as the Congress may direct:

A number of electors of President and Vice President equal to the whole number of Senators and Representatives in Congress to which the District would be entitled if it were a State, but in no event more than the least populous State; they shall be in addition to those appointed by the States, but they shall be considered, for the purposes of the election of President and Vice-President, to be electors appointed by a State; and they shall meet in the District and perform such duties as provided by the twelfth article of amendment.

Section 2 The Congress shall have power to enforce this article by appropriate legislation.

Amendment XXIV [Adopted Jan. 23, 1964]

Section 1 The right of citizens of the United States to vote in any primary or other election for President or Vice-President, for electors for President or Vice-President, or for Senator or Representative in Congress, shall not be denied or abridged by the United States or any State by reason of failure to pay any poll tax or other tax.

Section 2 The Congress shall have power to enforce this article by appropriate legislation.

Amendment XXV [Adopted Feb. 10, 1967]

Section 1 In case of the removal of the President from office or of his death or resignation, the Vice-President shall become President.

Section 2 Whenever there is a vacancy in the office of the Vice-President, the President shall nominate a Vice-President who shall take office upon confirmation by a majority vote of both Houses of Congress.

Section 3 Whenever the President transmits to the President pro tempore of the Senate and the Speaker of the House of Representatives his written declaration that he is unable to discharge the powers and duties of his office, and until he transmits to them a written declaration to the contrary, such powers and duties shall be discharged by the Vice-President as Acting President.

Section 4 Whenever the Vice-President and a majority of either the principal officers of the executive departments or of such other body as Congress may by law provide, transmit to the President pro tempore of the Senate and the Speaker of the House of Representatives their written declaration that the President is unable to discharge the powers and duties of his office, the Vice-President shall immediately assume the powers and duties of the office as Acting President.

Thereafter, when the President transmits to the President pro tempore of the Senate and the Speaker of the House of Representatives his written declaration that no inability exists, he shall resume the powers and duties of his office unless the Vice-President and a majority of either the principal officers of the executive department or of such other body as Congress may by law provide, transmit within four days to the President pro tempore of the Senate and the Speaker of the House of Representatives their written declaration that the President is unable to discharge the powers and duties of his office. Thereupon Congress shall decide the issue, assembling within forty-eight hours for that purpose if not in session. If the Congress, within twenty-one days after receipt of the latter written declaration, or, if Congress is not in session, within twenty-one days after Congress is required to assemble, determines by two-thirds vote of both Houses that the President is unable to discharge the powers and duties of his office, the Vice-President shall continue to discharge the same as Acting President; otherwise the President shall resume the powers and duties of his office.

Amendment XXVI [Adopted June 30, 1971]

Section 1 The right of citizens of the United States, who are eighteen years of age or older, to vote shall not be denied or abridged by the United States or by any State on account of age.

Section 2 The Congress shall have power to enforce this article by appropriate legislation.

Amendment XXVII [Adopted May 18, 1992]

No law, varying the compensation for the services of the Senators and Representatives, shall take effect until an election of Representatives shall have intervened.

▶THE EMANCIPATION PROCLAMATION

On July 22, 1862, Abraham Lincoln read to his cabinet a preliminary draft of an emancipation proclamation. Secretary of State William Seward suggested that the proclamation not be issued until a military victory had been won. The battle of Antietam gave Lincoln his desired opportunity, and on Sept. 22, he read to his cabinet a second draft of the proclamation. After some changes this was issued as a preliminary proclamation; the formal and definite proclamation came Jan. 1, 1863.

A Proclamation.

Whereas on the 22nd day of September, A.D. 1862, a proclamation was issued by the President of the United States, containing among other things, the following, to wit:

"That on the 1st day of January, A.D. 1863, all persons held as slaves within any State or designated part of a State the people whereof shall then be in rebellion against the United States shall be then, thenceforward, and forever free; and the executive government of the United States, including the military and naval authority thereof, will recognize and maintain the freedom of such persons and will do no act or acts to repress such persons, or any of them, in any efforts they may make for their actual freedom.

"That the executive will on the 1st day of January aforesaid, by proclamation, designate the States and parts of States, if any, in which the people thereof, respectively, shall then be in rebellion against the United States; and the fact that any State or the people thereof shall on that day be in good faith represented in the Congress of the United States by members chosen thereto at elections wherein a majority of the qualified voters of such States shall have participated shall, in the absence of strong countervailing testimony, be deemed conclusive evidence that such State and the people thereof are not then in rebellion against the United States."

Now, therefore, I, Abraham Lincoln, President of the United States, by virtue of the power in me vested as Commander-in-Chief of the Army and Navy of the United States in time of actual armed rebellion against the authority and government of the United States, and as a fit and necessary war measure for suppressing said rebellion, do, on this 1st day of January, A.D. 1863, and in accordance with my purpose so to do, publicly proclaimed for the full period of one hundred days from the first day above mentioned, order and designate as the States and parts of States wherein the people thereof, respectively, are this day in rebellion against the United States the following, to wit:

Arkansas, Texas, Louisiana (except the parishes of St. Bernard, Plaquemines, Jefferson, St. John, St. Charles, St. James, Ascension, Assumption, Terrebonne, Lafourche, St. Mary, St. Martin, and Orleans, including the city of New Orleans), Mississippi, Alabama, Florida, Georgia, South Carolina, North Carolina, and Virginia (except the forty-eight counties designated as West Virginia, and also the counties of Berkeley, Accomac, Northhampton, Elizabeth City, York, Princess Anne, and Norfolk, including the cities of Norfolk and Portsmouth), and which excepted parts are for the present left precisely as if this proclamation were not issued.

And by virtue of the power and for the purpose aforesaid, I do order and declare that all persons held as slaves within said designated States and parts of States are, and henceforward shall be, free; and that the Executive Government of the United States, including the military and naval authorities thereof, will recognize and maintain the freedom of said persons.

And I hereby enjoin upon the people so declared to be free to abstain from all violence, unless in necessary self-defense; and I recommend to them that, in all cases when allowed, they labor faithfully for reasonable wages.

And I further declare and make known that such persons of suitable condition will be received into the armed service of the United States to garrison forts, positions, stations, and other places, and to man vessels of all sorts in said service.

And upon this act, sincerely believed to be an act of justice, warranted by the Constitution upon military necessity, I invoke the considerate judgment of mankind and the gracious favor of Almighty God.

▶THE GETTYSBURG ADDRESS

Abraham Lincoln's most famous and most eloquent words were delivered on Nov. 19, 1863, at the dedication of the cemetery that held the remains of the 45,000 soldiers who fell at the Battle of Gettysburg, a significant Union victory.

"Fourscore and seven years ago our fathers brought forth on this continent, a new nation, conceived in Liberty, and dedicated to the proposition that all men are created equal.

"Now we are engaged in a great civil war, testing whether that nation or any nation so conceived and so dedicated, can long endure. We are met on a great battle-field of that war. We have come to dedicate a portion of that field, as a final resting place for those who here gave their lives that that nation might live. It is altogether fitting and proper that we should do this.

"But, in a larger sense, we can not dedicate—we can not consecrate—we can not hallow—this ground. The brave men, living and dead, who struggled here, have consecrated it, far above our poor power to add or detract. The world will little note, nor long remember what we say here, but it can never forget what they did here. It is for us the living, rather, to be dedicated here to the unfinished work which they who fought here have thus far so nobly advanced. It is rather for us to be here dedicated to the great task remaining before us—that from these honored dead we take increased devotion to that cause for which they gave the last full measure of devotion—that we here highly resolve that these dead shall not have died in vain—that this nation, under God, shall have a new birth of freedom—and that government of the people, by the people, for the people, shall not perish from the earth."

▶PLEDGE OF ALLEGIANCE

The original version of the Pledge of Allegiance appeared in the September 8, 1892, issue of *Youth's Companion* magazine. Authorship was in dispute between magazine staffers Francis Bellamy and James B. Upham until 1939, when the United States Flag Association declared Bellamy the author, and the Library of Congress concurred in 1957. Congress mandated two wording changes in the original version by substituting "the flag of the United States of America" for "my flag" in 1923, and adding "under God" in 1954. Public schools throughout the United States made the daily Pledge of Allegiance obligatory, and students who refused were expelled until the Supreme Court ruled in *West Virginia Board of Education v. Barnette* (1943) that the First Amendment protected the "right of silence" as well as freedom of speech.

"I pledge allegiance to the flag of the United States of America, and to the Republic, for which it stands, one nation, under God, indivisible, with liberty and justice for all."

CHRONOLOGY OF U.S. HISTORY

c. 1000 Viking explorer Leif Ericson explores North American coast and founds temporary colony called Vinland.
1492 On first voyage to America, Christopher Columbus lands at San Salvador island in Bahamas.
1493 Pope Alexander VI divides New World between Spain and Portugal.
1497 John Cabot claims Newfoundland for King Henry VII of England.
1499 Florentine merchant Amerigo Vespucci visits New World and begins writing popular accounts of his voyages.
1506 Columbus dies poor and embittered, convinced he found a new route to Asia and refusing to believe he discovered new continent.
1507 German mapmaker Martin Waldseemüller, after reading Vespucci's descriptions of the New World, names it "America" after him.
1513 Juan Ponce de León discovers Florida. Vasco Nuñez de Balboa crosses Panama and sights Pacific Ocean.
1519 Hernán Cortés lands in Mexico.
1520 Ferdinand Magellan, leader of the first expedition to circumnavigate the globe, discovers the South American straits that bear his name. In 1521, he is killed in the Philippines by natives.
1522 Cortés captures Mexico City and conquers Aztec empire.
1524 Giovanni de Verrazano, commissioned by King Francis I of France, discovers New York harbor and Hudson River.
1534 Jacques Cartier of France explores coast of Newfoundland and Gulf of St. Lawrence.
1536 Traveling overland from Gulf of Mexico, Alvar Núñez Cabeza de Vaca reaches Gulf of California.
1539 Fernando de Soto conquers Florida and begins three-year trek across Southeast.
1540 Francisco Vásquez de Coronado explores Southwest, discovering Grand Canyon and introducing horses to North America.
1541 Coronado discovers Mississippi River.
1542 João Rodrígues Cabrilho explores coast of California, missing San Francisco Bay.
1565 Don Pedro Menéndez de Aviles founds first permanent European settlement in North America at St. Augustine, Florida.
1572 Sir Francis Drake of England makes first voyage to America, landing in Panama.
1576 English explorer Martin Frobisher searches for Northwest Passage.
1577 Drake begins voyage of plunder around the world.
1579 Drake lands north of San Francisco Bay and claims region for Queen Elizabeth I.
1584 Sir Walter Raleigh discovers Roanoke Island. He names land Virginia, after Queen Elizabeth.
1585 Raleigh establishes England's first American colony at Roanoke.
1586 Drake evacuates surviving Roanoke settlers.
1587 Raleigh resettles Roanoke with 150 new colonists. Virginia Dare first child of English parents born in America.
1591 Relief expedition returns to the Roanoke colony; all settlers disappeared without trace.
1602 Captain Bartholomew Gosnold, first Englishman to set foot in New England, explores Cape Cod and Martha's Vineyard.
1603 Samuel de Champlain of France explores St. Lawrence Seaway, later founds Quebec.
1607 First permanent English settlement in America established at Jamestown, Virginia. Only 32 of original 105 colonists survive first winter.
1608 Captain John Smith imprisoned by Indians and saved by Pocahontas, daughter of Chief Powhatan.
1609 Henry Hudson sets out in search of Northwest Passage. Champlain sails into Great Lakes.
1611 Hudson cast adrift by mutinous crewmen to die in bay named after him.
1612 First Dutch trading post appears on Manhattan Island.
1616 Smallpox epidemic decimates Indian tribes from Maine to Rhode Island.
1619 Dutch traders bring first African slaves to Virginia for sale. Americans hold first election when Virginia planters vote for House of Burgesses.
1620 Pilgrims and others arrive in Plymouth, Massachusetts, aboard *Mayflower.* They draw up the Mayflower Compact.
1622 Most of Virginia colony wiped out in an Indian attack.
1624 King James I revokes Virginia's charter and makes it royal colony.
1626 The Dutch colony of New Amsterdam founded on Manhattan Island, bought from Indians for about $24.
1630 John Winthrop sets sail for Massachusetts with 900 Puritans and others, beginning Great Migration to New England.
1632 King Charles I of England grants Lord Baltimore charter to establish colony in Maryland.
1634 Massachusetts adopts representative government. Jean Nicolet of France begins trading with Indians in Wisconsin.
1635 Roger Williams, banished from Massachusetts, founds dissident colony of Rhode Island.
1636 New Englanders massacre hundreds of Indians in Pequot War. Harvard College established.
1638 First Swedish colony founded in Delaware.
1639 "Oath of a Free Man" the first English document printed in America. First public school appears in Dorchester, first post office in Boston, and Connecticut writes first colonial constitution.
1644 Indians make last unsuccessful attempt to expel English settlers from Virginia. First American ship built in Boston.
1647 Margaret Brent of Maryland first American woman to demand right to vote. Massachusetts passes first compulsory education law. First witchcraft execution occurs in Hartford, Conn.
1648 Boston shoemakers and coopers establish first American labor unions.
1651 Parliament passes first Navigation Act regulating colonial trade.
1652 Rhode Island first colony to outlaw slavery. First American coins minted in Boston.
1654 Jacob Barsimon, first American Jew, arrives in New Amsterdam, followed by 23 more Jews from Brazil.
1655 Dutch colonists capture Swedish colony in Delaware. Lady Deborah Moody of Long Island first American woman to vote.
1656 First Quakers arrive in America; imprisoned in Boston, beaten, and deported.
1659 Massachusetts hangs two Quakers on Boston Common.

1660 Parliament forbids Americans to export goods to countries other than England. Massachusetts outlaws celebration of Christmas.
1661 Virginia becomes the first colony to recognize slavery as legal.
1662 Connecticut granted royal charter. Massachusetts appoints official press censors and institutes half-way covenant.
1663 Parliament requires colonial imports from Europe to pass first through England. King Charles II grants charters to Carolina and Rhode Is-
land
1664 New Amsterdam captured by Richard Nicolls, who renames it New York. New Jersey established.
1670 Charles Town, later called Charleston, first permanent settlement in Carolina.
1672 Parliament tightens trade restrictions on colonies and appoints American customs collectors.
1673 French explorers Jacques Marquette and Louis Joliet paddle down Mississippi River to Arkansas. Regular mail service begins between Boston and New York. Dutch forces recapture New York.
1674 Treaty of Westminster restores New York to England. King Louis XIV of France sends Sieur de La Salle to explore Mississippi River.
1675 Thousands die in King Philip's War between New Englanders and five Indian tribes.
1676 Bacon's Rebellion overthrows government of Virginia and burns down Jamestown.
1680 New Hampshire separated from Massachusetts and made royal colony.
1681 King Charles II names William Penn proprietor of Pennsylvania.
1682 Penn founds Philadelphia. Sieur de La Salle claims North American interior for France, naming it Louisiana.
1683 First German-Americans, group of Mennonites, arrive in Philadelphia.
1684 King Charles II revokes Massachusetts charter.
1686 King James II appoints Sir Edmund Andros governor-general of Dominion of New England, dissolving colonial governments.
1688 Quakers publish first anti-slavery tracts in Pennsylvania.
1689 Andros surrenders to Boston mobs and colonial self-government is reestablished. Jacob Leisler seizes power in New York uprising. King William's War begins in America.
1690 Massachusetts issues first colonial paper money. American campaigns against French Canada fail. French and Indians burn Schenectady, N.Y.
1691 Jacob Leisler surrenders and is hanged. Massachusetts rechartered with religious freedom.
1692 Witchcraft hysteria breaks out in Salem, Mass., leading to 20 executions.
1693 College of William and Mary chartered, the second college in America.
1695 New York City organizes public relief for poor and homeless.
1696 Parliament places more commercial restrictions on colonies. American merchants join slave trade.
1697 Treaty of Ryswick ends King William's War.
1701 Antoine de la Mothe Cadillac establishes French outpost at Detroit, Michigan. Yale College founded. Delaware separated from Pennsylvania.
1702 Queen Anne's War breaks out.
1704 *Boston News-Letter* first regularly published newspaper in America.
1710 German Migration to America begins. British and American forces capture Port Royal, Nova Scotia.
1711 Anglo-American attack on Quebec fails. Tuscarora Indian War breaks out in North Carolina.
1712 Militia quell slave rebellion in New York City. Pennsylvania prohibits importing slaves.
1713 Treaty of Utrecht ends Queen Anne's War.
1716 First American theater built in Williamsburg, Va. Slavery introduced to French Louisiana.
1718 Jean Baptiste le Moyne founds French city of New Orleans.
1721 Sir Robert Walpole loosens colonial trade restrictions with policy of "salutary neglect."
1722 France declares New Orleans capital of Louisiana.
1723 America's first business corporation chartered in Connecticut.
1724 France expels all Jews from Louisiana.
1728 First American synagogue built in New York City.
1729 North and South Carolina receive royal charters.
1731 Benjamin Franklin founds first American library in Philadelphia.
1732 King George II grants charter to Georgia. Only Catholic church in colonial America opens in Philadelphia. Benjamin Franklin begins publishing *Poor Richard's Almanac.* George Washington born in Virginia.
1733 Parliament passes the Molasses Act, taxing imports from non-British sugar islands.
1734 Beginning of Great Awakening, widespread religious revival.
1735 French begin settling in Illinois.
1737 Boston holds its first public celebration of St. Patrick's Day.
1739 War of Jenkin's Ear begins. South Carolina slaves mount Stono Rebellion. French explorers Pierre and Paul Mallet discover Rocky Mountains.
1741 Danish navigator Vitus Bering, hired by Peter the Great of Russia, explores coast of Alaska. *American Magazine,* first in colonies, begins publishing in Philadelphia. Slave insurrection panic sweeps New York City.
1742 First sugar cane planted in Louisiana.
1744 King George's War breaks out.
1745 British and Americans capture Fort Louisbourg on Cape Breton Island. French and Indians raid Maine.
1748 Treaty of Aix-la-Chapelle ends King George's War and returns Fort Louisbourg to France.
1751 Parliament forbids New England colonies to issue paper money.
1752 Benjamin Franklin conducts famous kite experiment. Liberty bell is cracked in Philadelphia.
1753 Governor Dinwiddie of Virginia sends George Washington into Ohio country to demand withdrawal of French. First steam engine arrives in America.
1754 Washington skirmishes with French patrol, touching off French and Indian War. Franklin presents Albany Plan of Union for colonies.
1755 Quakers withdraw from Pennsylvania assembly rather than vote for military spending. Washington leads retreat from Battle of the Wilderness.
1758 British and American forces lose Battle of Ticonderoga, but capture Louisbourg and Fort

Duquesne. New Jersey sets aside first Indian reservation for Onami tribe.
1759 General Wolfe defeats General Montcalm as British capture Quebec. Both generals fall in battle.
1760 After fall of Montreal, all of New France surrenders to Britain. King George III crowned in England.
1762 King Louis XV of France secretly cedes Louisiana to Spain.
1763 Treaty of Paris ends French and Indian War. France cedes Canada to Britain. King George III prohibits Americans to settle in West. Conspiracy of Pontiac threatens frontier.
1764 Parliament passes Sugar Act and forbids all colonies to issue paper money. French settlers found St. Louis. "Paxton Boys" march on Philadelphia. In Boston, James Otis protests, "no taxation without representation."
1765 Parliament passes Stamp Act (tax on newspapers, legal documents, etc.) and Quartering Act (requiring housing of British soldiers in homes). Sons of Liberty organize resistance and non-importation throughout colonies. Stamp Act Congress meets in New York.
1766 Parliament repeals the Stamp Act, but passes Declaratory Act affirming its right to pass laws binding on colonies. Chief Pontiac makes peace.
1767 Parliament enacts Townshend Duties and suspends New York assembly for resisting Quartering Act.
1768 "Regulators" rebel in North Carolina. Boston riots against Townshend Duties.
1769 Daniel Boone explores Kentucky. Father Junipero Serra founds San Diego, first Spanish mission in California. Gaspar de Portola sails into San Francisco Bay.
1770 Five Americans perish in Boston Massacre (Mar. 5). Parliament repeals Townshend Duties, except tax on tea.
1772 Rhode Island mob burns British revenue ship *Gaspee*. Boston appoints first Committee of Correspondence.
1773 Parliament passes Tea Act, leading to Boston Tea Party (Dec. 16).
1774 Parliament passes "Intolerable Acts" punishing colonists for Tea Party. Boston is occupied by British forces. First Continental Congress meets in Philadelphia.
1775 American Revolution begins with Battle of Lexington and Concord (Apr. 19). Second Continental Congress appoints George Washington as commander of Continental Army. British win Battle of Bunker Hill. First abolition society organized in Pennsylvania.
1776 Tom Paine's *Common Sense* published. Declaration of Independence signed. Congress adopts name, "United States of America." British occupy New York City. Washington crosses Delaware to win Battle of Trenton, N.J.
1777 Americans win battles at Princeton and Saratoga. British occupy Philadelphia. Congress adopts Stars and Stripes flag and endorses Articles of Confederation. Washington's army spends winter at Valley Forge, Pa.
1778 France makes alliance with U.S. and declares war on Britain. When French fleet arrives, British evacuate Philadelphia.
1779 Congress offers to make peace in exchange for independence. British withdraw from New York City.
1780 Pennsylvania first state to abolish slavery. British occupy Charleston, S.C. Washington quells Continental Army mutiny. Benedict Arnold defects to British.
1781 French and American victory at Battle of Yorktown ends the American Revolution. Articles of Confederation take effect. Los Angeles founded by Spanish missionaries.
1782 Parliament votes for peace with U.S. Negotiations in Paris lead to provisional Anglo-American peace treaty. Virginia permits owners to free their slaves. First English Bible printed in America.
1783 Massachusetts, Connecticut, and Rhode Island abolish slavery. Treaty of Paris signed (Sept. 3), officially ending American Revolution . Washington retires to Mount Vernon, Va.
1784 Congress ratifies Treaty of Paris. Spain closes Mississippi River to American trade. First bale of American cotton shipped to Britain.
1785 First state university chartered in Georgia.
1786 Virginia proclaims religious freedom. Shays's Rebellion put down in Massachusetts. Annapolis Convention calls for revising Articles of Confederation. New Jersey abolishes slavery.
1787 Convention in Philadelphia writes Constitution. Congress passes Northwest Ordinance and submits Constitution for state approval.
1788 Constitution ratified by New Hampshire (June 21), the ninth state to do so thereby marking its final approval.
1789 Constitution takes effect (March 4). George Washington wins first presidential election unopposed. Federal government begins meeting in New York City. Congress enacts first Federal tariff.
1790 First antislavery petitions are submitted to Congress. Temporary capital moved to Philadelphia. Pope Pius VI appoints John Carroll first Catholic bishop in U.S. First U.S. census lists population at 3,929,625.
1791 Congress sets up First Bank of the United States and first internal revenue law, a tax on whiskey. Vermont enters union as 14th state. Bill of Rights takes effect. Pres. Washington selects site of new U.S. capital on the Potomac River.
1792 New York stock traders begin meeting under a tree on Wall Street. Pres. Washington is unanimously reelected. Construction begins on White House.
1793 Eli Whitney invents cotton gin. Congress passes first Fugitive Slave Act. Pres. Washington holds first official cabinet meeting and lays cornerstone for Capitol. Britain begins confiscating American ships trading with France.
1794 Pres. Washington defeats Whiskey Rebellion in Pennsylvania. U.S. and Britain sign Jay's Treaty. Ohio Indians defeated at Battle of Fallen Timbers.
1795 Georgia stung by scandal of Yazoo land frauds. Senate ratifies Jay's Treaty with Britain.
1796 Pres. Washington delivers "Farewell Address." France begins to confiscate ships trading with Britain.
1797 France insults American diplomats in XYZ Affair. Spanish begin building Mission San Juan Capistrano in California.
1798 Georgia last state to abolish slave trade. Congress passes Alien and Sedition Acts. U.S. renounces alliance with France as unofficial naval war breaks out.
1799 Russian-American trading company set up in Alaska. New York abolishes slavery.
1800 Library of Congress founded. Convention of 1800 signed, ending quasi-war between U.S. and France. Spain secretly cedes Louisiana to France. Congress begins meeting in Washington.

1801 Election of Thomas Jefferson results in first transfer of executive power between rival parties. Congress takes jurisdiction over District of Columbia. Tripoli pirates declare war on U.S.
1802 U.S. Military Academy established at West Point, N.Y.
1803 Louisiana Purchase from France doubles size of the U.S. Federal outpost founded at Fort Dearborn, Illinois, future site of Chicago.
1804 Lewis and Clark expedition sets out from St. Louis. Alexander Hamilton killed in duel with Aaron Burr.
1805 Barbary War with Tripoli ends.
1806 Congress authorizes construction of Cumberland Road. Noah Webster's first dictionary published.
1807 Britain and France enact blockades in Europe, confiscating American trading ships. British attack USS *Chesapeake*. Embargo Act forbids all American exports.
1808 Congress declares end to African slave trade.
1809 Embargo Act replaced with Non-Intercourse Act, outlawing exports to Britain and France. First steamboat sea voyage made from New York City to Philadelphia.
1810 Pres. Madison annexes West Florida.
1811 Worst earthquake in U.S. history rocks Ohio-Mississippi valleys. Russians settle at Ft. Ross, California. First Bank of the United States fails to obtain recharter. Gen. William Henry Harrison defeats Indians at Battle of Tippecanoe.
1812 War of 1812 begins by close vote in Congress. New England resists war. British clamp blockade on U.S. ports, capture Detroit, and repel American attack on Canada at Queenstown.
1813 Americans regain Detroit, attack Toronto and Ft. George in Canada, but surrender to British at Beaver Dams, Ontario. Captain Oliver H. Perry wins control of the Great Lakes. British and Indians burn Buffalo, N.Y.
1814 British destroy Fort Oswego, N.Y., and set fire to Washington, D.C. Francis Scott Key writes "The Star Spangled Banner." New Englanders opposed to war meet secretly at Hartford Convention. First textile mill established at Waltham, Mass. Treaty of Ghent ends War of 1812.
1815 General Andrew Jackson routs British at Battle of New Orleans, before news arrives that War of 1812 is over.
1816 Congress charters Second Bank of the U.S.
1817 Rush-Bagot Treaty between Britain and U.S. demilitarizes Great Lakes. New York Stock and Exchange Board organized. Work begins on Erie Canal. Indian attack starts Seminole War in Florida.
1818 Cumberland Road opens. Congress adopts present format for American flag. Canadian boundary dispute with Britain settled.
1819 Panic of 1819 plunges South and West into depression. U.S. obtains Florida from Spain in Adams-Onís Treaty, settling border of Louisiana. *Savannah* makes first successful trans-Atlantic crossing under steam power.
1820 Missouri Compromise solves crisis over admission of Missouri as slave state. Abolitionists begin colonizing freed slaves to Africa.
1821 First Catholic cathedral in U.S. built in Baltimore.
1822 Denmark Vesey and 36 others executed for organizing rebel slave conspiracy in Charleston, S.C.
1823 Monroe Doctrine, masterminded by Secy. of State John Quincy Adams, announced by Pres. Monroe.
1824 Russia and U.S. settle territorial disputes in Pacific Northwest. First presidential nominating convention held in Utica, N.Y.
1825 John Quincy Adams chosen president in infamous "Corrupt Bargain" with Henry Clay, who becomes Secy. of State. Erie Canal opened. Mexico invites Americans to settle in Texas.
1826 Anti-Mason party organized. John Adams and Thomas Jefferson die on 50th anniversary of Declaration of Independence. Jedediah Smith leads first overland expedition to California.
1827 U.S. and Britain agree to joint occupation of Pacific Northwest.
1828 Congress passes protectionist "Tariff of Abominations" over Southern protests.
1829 Mexico refuses Pres. Jackson's offer to buy Texas.
1830 Webster-Hayne Debate in U.S. Senate reveals sectional tension. Church of Latter-Day Saints (the Mormons) founded by Joseph Smith in Fayette, N.Y. Mexico forbids further American immigration to Texas.
1831 Nat Turner leads bloodiest of all slave rebellions, killing 57 whites in Virginia.
1832 Black Hawk War fought in Illinois and Wisconsin. First nationwide Democratic Party convention held in Baltimore. Pres. Jackson vetoes bill to recharter national bank. South Carolina nullifies "Tariff of Abominations."
1833 Massachusetts last state to end tax support for churches. Congress lowers tariff and passes "Force Bill" to pressure South Carolina, which rescinds nullification. American Anti-Slavery Society organized.
1834 Whig party organized by Senators Henry Clay and Daniel Webster in opposition to Pres. Jackson. Anti-abolitionist riots break out in New York and Philadelphia.
1835 Samuel Morse invents telegraph. National debt completely paid off. Pres. Jackson survives first attempt to assassinate a president. Second Seminole War begins in Florida.
1836 Samuel Colt invents revolver. Texas declares independence from Mexico and requests U.S. annexation. Mexican army captures Alamo, but Texans are victorious at San Jacinto.
1837 Panic of 1837 begins lengthy depression.
1838 Joshua Giddings of Ohio is first abolitionist elected to Congress. Trans-Atlantic steamship service established. Congress blocks abolitionist petitions with "Gag Rule."
1839 Abner Doubleday of Cooperstown, N.Y., codifies rules of baseball. Congress outlaws dueling in Washington, D.C.
1840 "Log Cabin Campaign" between William Henry Harrison and Martin Van Buren begins era of mass political participation. Liberty Party founded by abolitionists in Albany, N.Y.
1841 First emigrant train of 48 covered wagons arrives in California. Pres. Harrison dies after month in office. First Japanese immigrant arrives in New Bedford, Mass.
1842 Webster-Ashburton Treaty settles Canada boundary disputes between U.S. and Britain. U.S. accidentally seizes California, then returns it with apology to Mexico.
1843 End of Second Seminole War. B'Nai B'rith founded in New York. Mormons begin practicing polygamy.
1844 Baptists first church to split North and South over slavery. Samuel Morse sends first tele-

graph message. James K. Polk, first "Dark horse" candidate, elected President.

1845 "Potato Famine" begins massive Irish immigration. U.S. annexes Texas, over Mexican protests. U.S. Naval Academy opens at Annapolis, Md.

1846 Mexican War begins when U.S. troops are attacked in disputed Texas territory. American settlers in California stage Bear Flag Revolt. Oregon Treaty gives U.S. sole possession of Pacific Northwest up to 49th parallel. First recorded baseball game played in Hoboken, N.J.

1847 Wilmot Proviso, forbidding slavery expansion, passes House and sets off wave of panic in South. General Winfield Scott conquers Mexico City. Brigham Young leads Mormons to Utah. Abraham Lincoln of Illinois arrives in Congress.

1848 Treaty of Guadalupe-Hidalgo ends Mexican War, ceding Southwest to U.S. Revolution of 1848 begins wave of German immigration. New York-Chicago telegraph line completed. Chicago Board of Trade established. Free Soil party organized. Gold discovered in California. First Chinese immigrants arrive in San Francisco. Lucretia Mott and Elizabeth Cady Stanton hold first Women's Rights Convention in Seneca Falls, N.Y.

1849 Gold Rush brings hundreds of thousands to California. Elizabeth Blackwell first American woman to receive medical degree.

1850 Sen. Henry Clay's Compromise of 1850 solves crisis over slavery expansion. Clayton-Bulwer Treaty pledges Anglo-American cooperation in building any Central American canal.

1851 Y.M.C.A. established. Northern mobs resist Fugitive Slave Act. Maine is first state to pass prohibition laws. *New York Times* founded. Herman Melville's *Moby Dick* published.

1852 Harriet Beecher Stowe's *Uncle Tom's Cabin* published.

1853 U.S. buys Gila River valley from Mexico in Gadsden Purchase. Native American, or "Know-Nothing," party founded. Commodore Matthew C. Perry opens trade with Japan.

1854 Congress passes Kansas-Nebraska Act, setting off mass protests across North. Republican Party founded. U.S. threatens to seize Cuba from Spain in Ostend Manifesto.

1855 "Bleeding Kansas" fighting begins as pro-slavery and anti-slavery settlers hold rival state conventions. First railroad train crosses Mississippi River at Rock Island, Ill., into Davenport, Iowa.

1856 Cong. Preston Brooks of South Carolina beats Sen. Charles Sumner of Massachusetts unconscious on Senate floor. John Brown leads Pottawatomie massacre in Kansas. First Republican national convention in Pittsburgh, Pa., in February.

1857 New York-St. Louis railroad completed. Supreme Court hands down controversial *Dred Scott* decision protecting slavery. Panic of 1857 sends North into depression.

1858 Lincoln-Douglas Debates dramatize issue of slavery expansion in Illinois race for Senate. First trans-Atlantic telegraph cable laid.

1859 John Brown's raid on Harper's Ferry arsenal to launch abolitionist war against slavery ends in his capture and execution. Slave insurrection panic sweeps South. Comstock Silver Lode discovered in Nevada. First producing oil well in U.S. flows in Titusville, Pa.

1860 Democratic Party splits into Northern and Southern wings. South Carolina is first state to secede from Union after victory of Abraham Lincoln. Crittenden Compromise fails to preserve Union. Pony Express begins mail delivery between California and Missouri.

1861 Civil War begins with attack on Ft. Sumter, South Carolina (Apr. 12). Pres. Lincoln calls for 75,000 volunteers to suppress rebellion. Jefferson Davis of Mississippi elected President of Confederate States of America. New York-San Francisco telegraph link completed. Yale awards first American Ph.D. Congress enacts first federal income tax.

1862 Congress issues "greenbacks," subsidizes transcontinental railroad, abolishes slavery in District of Columbia, and passes Homestead Act. Pres. Lincoln issues Emancipation Proclamation after Battle of Antietam, bloodiest of Civil War.

1863 Emancipation Proclamation takes effect (Jan. 1). Union victories at Vicksburg, Miss., and Gettysburg, Pa., signal turning point of Civil War. West Virginia secedes from Virginia and rejoins Union. Hundreds killed in New York City draft riot. Pres. Lincoln proclaims Thanksgiving national holiday.

1864 Pres. Lincoln names General Ulysses S. Grant as commander of Union armies. General William T. Sherman destroys Atlanta and conducts "March to the Sea." Confederate army of General Robert E. Lee crippled in Wilderness Campaign. Cheyenne and Arapaho Indians slaughtered in Sand Creek Massacre in Colorado.

1865 General Lee surrenders to General Grant at Appomattox Court House, Virginia (Apr. 9). Pres. Lincoln assassinated by John Wilkes Booth in Washington, D.C. (Apr. 14). Confederacy dissolved, ending Civil War. Pres. Johnson proclaims amnesty for most rebels. Slavery outlawed by adoption of Thirteenth Amendment. Ku Klux Klan founded in Pulaski, Tenn.

1866 In the struggle over Reconstruction policy, Congress overrides Pres. Johnson's vetoes of Civil Rights Act and New Freedmen's Bureau Bill. Whites riot in New Orleans to protest black suffrage. Grand Army of the Republic organized by Union veterans.

1867 Congress takes control of Reconstruction in the South by passing First Reconstruction Act over Pres. Johnson's veto and Tenure of Office Act. U.S. purchases Alaska from Russia for $7.2 million (2¢ an acre). Farmers organize Patrons of Husbandry, beginning Granger movement.

1868 Pres. Johnson is impeached in the House (Feb. 24), but acquitted in the Senate by a single vote (May 16). U.S. and China sign Burlingame Treaty to allow immigration. Fourteenth Amendment grants equal citizenship and protection to freedmen (July 28). Half a million black votes help elect Gen. Ulysses S. Grant to the presidency. The typewriter invented.

1869 "Hard Money" prevails when Congress passes Public Credit Act, promising repayment of government debts in gold. Transcontinental railroad completed with golden spike between Union Pacific and Central Pacific lines at Promontory Point, Utah (May 10). Jay Gould and James Fisk cause financial panic by trying to corner gold market on "Black Friday" (Sept. 24). Knights of Labor union organized. National Women's Suffrage Association formed in New York. Wyoming Territory grants first U.S. women's suffrage.

1870 Fifteenth Amendment guarantees right to vote for all U.S. citizens, though only Wyoming and Utah territories allow women's suffrage (Mar. 30). Congress passes first Ku Klux Act to enforce Fifteenth Amendment. First black senator and black congressman are elected.

1871 Congress passes second Ku Klux Klan Act to enforce Fourteenth Amendment in the South. *New York Times* begins exposé of Boss William Marcy Tweed, leading to overthrow of Tammany Hall ring. Most of Chicago destroyed in the Great Fire (Oct. 8-11). Anti-Chinese race riots in Los Angeles.

1872 Crédit Mobilier scandal implicates Vice President Schuyler Colfax and embarrasses Grant administration. Yellowstone National Park created. Susan B. Anthony arrested for leading suffragists to the polls. Montgomery Ward opens for business in Chicago.

1873 Silver withdrawn from money supply in the "Crime of '73." Congressmen raise their own salaries 50 percent, and double president's pay in "Salary Grab" Act. Panic of 1873, triggered by failure of Jay Cooke's banking house, begins depression of 1870s. New York Stock Exchange forced to close for 10 days. Great Bonanza silver lode discovered in Nevada. San Francisco installs first cable cars.

1874 Granger movement begins passing railroad regulations in Midwestern states. Women's Christian Temperance Union founded in Cleveland, Ohio. Greenback Party formed in Indianapolis. Black rioters attack courthouse in Vicksburg, Miss. Chautauqua movement begins bringing educational speakers to rural communities across the country.

1875 Congress passes Specie Resumption Act to reduce money supply by redeeming greenbacks for gold, and Civil Rights Act to guarantee equal rights for freedmen. Whiskey Ring scandal casts further pall on Grant administration. Archbishop John McCloskey of New York first American bishop. *Aristides* wins first Kentucky Derby at Churchill Downs, Ky.

1876 U.S. awards patent to Alexander Graham Bell for the telephone. Gen. George A. Custer and 265 men are massacred by Sioux at Little Big Horn, S. Dak. (June 25). Democrat Samuel Tilden outpolls Republican Rutherford B. Hayes as presidential election is thrown into the House (Nov. 7). Baseball's National League established. Kappa Alpha opens first fraternity house at Williams College. Central Park in New York completed.

1877 Congress appoints Electoral Commission to solve impasse over disputed 1876 election. House votes 185 to 184 to declare Rutherford Hayes president, three days before his inauguration (Mar. 2). Reconstruction officially ends with withdrawal of federal troops from the South (Apr. 24). Pres. Hayes sends in troops as Great Railroad Strike paralyzes much of the country. Anti-Chinese riots break out in San Francisco.

1878 Sen. A. A. Sargent introduces Women's Suffrage Amendment in Congress (Jan. 10). Greenback-Labor Party formed in Toledo, Ohio. Limited coinage of silver resumes with Bland-Allison Act. American Bar Association organized in Saratoga, N.Y. Edison Electric begins operating in New York City. New Haven, Conn. sets up first commercial telephone network.

1879 U.S. resumes specie payments for greenbacks. F.W. Woolworth opens his first store in Utica, N.Y. First Church of Christ, Scientist, founded in Boston. Thomas Edison invents light bulb. California adopts state constitution forbidding employment of Chinese labor.

1880 Pres. Hayes declares U.S. must control any Isthmian canal. U.S. and China agree to Chinese Exclusion Treaty. National Farmers' Alliance organized in Chicago. American branch of Salvation Army founded in Philadelphia, Pa. Census lists U.S. population over 50 million for first time (50,155,783).

1881 Pres. Garfield assassinated by Charles Guiteau in Washington, D.C. (July 2—dies Sept. 19). Clara Barton creates American Red Cross. Booker T. Washington founds Tuskegee Institute for black education in Alabama. Russian Jews begin immigrating to U.S. to escape pogroms.

1882 John D. Rockefeller organizes Standard Oil trust, first such combination. Congress passes first Chinese Exclusion Act (May 10), and legislates first immigration restrictions: no paupers, convicts, or mental defectives. Knights of Columbus founded with permission from Roman Catholic Church.

1883 Congress passes Pendleton Act, requiring civil service competition for Federal jobs. Brooklyn Bridge opened in New York. Supreme Court strikes down Civil Rights Act of 1875. New York-Chicago telephone service begins. Ohio River floods devastate Cincinnati. U.S. Navy builds its first steel ships. Railroads agree on Standard Time zones for North America.

1884 "Mugwumps" bolt Republican Party. Statue of Liberty cornerstone laid (Aug. 5). Belva A. Lockwood of Equal Rights Party first woman candidate for president. Grover Cleveland of New York first Democrat elected president since Civil War. Home Insurance Building of Chicago first skyscraper in the world. Moses Fleetwood Walker first black professional baseball player.

1885 Washington Monument completed after 36 years of construction. U.S. Marines land in Panama (Apr. 24). Senate refuses to ratify treaty for building a canal across Nicaragua. Congress outlaws building fences on public lands in the West. Josiah Strong's best-seller *Our Country* argues for American imperialism.

1886 Knights of Labor rail strike sets off national wave of strikes for eight-hour day. Haymarket Riot in Chicago leads to execution of seven anarchists. Statue of Liberty dedicated (Oct. 28). American Federation of Labor founded in Columbus, Ohio. Indian wars end with capture of Geronimo.

1887 Congress creates Interstate Commerce Commission, first federal regulatory agency, but with weak enforcement powers. Congress distributes reservation land to Indians, also bans opium imports. First electric trolley line built in Richmond, Va. U.S. Navy leases base at Pearl Harbor, Hawaii.

1888 Snow falls for 36 hours in New York, killing 400 people in "Great Blizzard of '88" (Mar. 12). First secret ballot election held in Louisville, Ky. George Eastman markets first Kodak camera. National Geographic Society founded in Washington, D.C. Edward Bellamy's utopian novel, Looking Backward, a sensational best-seller.

1889 Four new states—N.Dak., S.Dak., Mont., Wash.—all admitted in one day (Feb. 22). Oklahoma Land Rush results as former Indian territory is opened for settlement (Apr. 22). Johnstown Flood claims thousands of lives in Pennsylvania (May 31). Kansas passes first antitrust law. Jane Addams founds Hull House in Chicago.

1890 Congress passes Sherman Antitrust Act (July 2) and Sherman Silver Purchase Act. Wyoming admitted as first state with women's suffrage (July 10). Sioux uprising ends at Battle of Wounded Knee (Dec. 29). Yosemite National Park created. Mississippi leads South in disfranchising black voters. Jacob Riis's *How the Other*

Half Lives awakens Americans to urban poverty. Navy wins 24-0 in first Army-Navy football game.
1891 New Orleans mob lynches 11 Italian immigrants. People's, or Populist, Party organized in Cincinnati. U.S. and Chile nearly go to war over death of two American sailors in Valparaiso (Oct. 16). Dr. James A. Naismith invents basketball in Springfield, Mass. Thomas Edison patents first American-made motion picture camera.
1892 Populist candidate James B. Weaver of Iowa receives over a million votes for president. Violent strikes break out among steel workers in Homestead, Pa., and silver miners in Coeur d'Alene, Idaho. Chinese immigrants forced to register with Federal government. First gasoline-powered American automobile built in Chicopee, Mass. Boll weevil first appears in Texas.
1893 U.S. gold reserve falls below $100 million (Apr. 21). Panic of 1893, touched off by New York stock market crash (June 27), begins second-worst depression in U.S. history. Congress repeals Sherman Silver Purchase Act (Oct. 30). Mormon Temple dedicated in Salt Lake City, Utah.
1894 Coxey's Army of unemployed march on Washington, D.C. (Apr. 30). U.S. Treasury issues two $50 million bond offerings to shore up dwindling gold reserves. Congress enacts first peacetime Federal income tax, denounced as "socialism, communism, devilism" (Aug. 27). Pullman strike paralyzes railroads across the country.
1895 J.P. Morgan bails out U.S. Treasury, faced with a gold drain. "Silver Democrats" appeal for unlimited silver coinage as way out of depression. Supreme Court rules income tax unconstitutional (May 20). First professional football game played in Latrobe, Pa.
1896 Supreme Court approves segregation (*Plessy vs. Ferguson*). William Jennings Bryan, "Silver Democrat" of Nebraska, wins nomination with "Cross of Gold" speech. Gold discovered in Klondike, Alaska, defusing the money question (Aug. 16). American athletes win nine of 12 events at first Olympics. Henry Ford builds his first automobile. First American motion pictures appear in theaters. "The Yellow Kid," first comic strip, begins running in *New York World*.
1897 U.S. offers to mediate Cuban rebellion, lodges official complaint against Spanish brutality. "Yellow press" newspapers keep up assault on Spain. First American subway completed in Boston.
1898 After mysterious explosion of battleship *Maine* in Havana (Feb. 15), Spanish-American War breaks out (Apr. 21). Commodore George Dewey destroys Spanish fleet at Manila Bay (May 1); U.S. takes Manila (Aug. 13). After Battle of San Juan Hill (July 1), Spanish garrison at Santiago, Cuba, surrenders (July 17). U.S. takes Cuba, Puerto Rico, Guam, Wake Island, and Philippines from Spain in Treaty of Paris (Dec. 10). Senate agrees to annex Hawaii.
1899 Philippine Revolt against U.S. rule erupts. Sec. of State John Hay issues Open Door notes to European powers and Japan, requesting no spheres of influence in China (Sept. 6). U.S. and Germany agree to partition Samoan Islands. Congress investigates incompetence in War Department, revealed during Spanish-American War.
1900 "Hard Money" triumphs as U.S. returns to single gold standard (Mar. 14). Puerto Rico and Hawaii become U.S. territories (Apr. 12 & Apr. 30). U.S. troops relieve foreign legations under siege in Peking, China, during Boxer Rebellion. Olds Company opens first Detroit auto factory. Carrie Nation leads hatchet-wielding women into Kansas saloons to smash liquor barrels.
1901 J.P. Morgan creates U.S. Steel, first billion-dollar corporation. U.S. retains control over Cuba with Platt Amendment. Pres. McKinley shot by anarchist Leon Czolgosz in Buffalo, N.Y. (Sept. 6—dies Sept. 14). Hay-Paunceforte Treaty secures British approval for a U.S.-built canal in Panama (Nov. 18). First great Texas oil strike made near Beaumont, Tex. Pres. Roosevelt promises to "speak softly and carry a big stick."
1902 End of Philippine Insurrection. Reclamation Act initiates Federal policy of conservation of natural resources (June 17). Congress declares Philippines an unorganized territory whose inhabitants are not U.S. citizens (July 1). First Rose Bowl game played. Pres. Roosevelt helps mediate Pennsylvania coal strike.
1903 Pres. Roosevelt helps Panama gain independence from Colombia, then negotiates treaty to build Panama Canal. Orville and Wilbur Wright conduct first powered flight near Kitty Hawk, N.C. (Dec. 17). *The Great Train Robbery,* first feature-length motion picture, released. Wisconsin holds first primary elections. Ford Motor Company formed. Boston defeats Pittsburgh in first baseball World Series.
1904 Supreme Court upholds antitrust dissolution of Northern Securities company (Mar. 14). "Roosevelt Corollary" to Monroe Doctrine justifies U.S. intervention to keep other powers out of Western hemisphere. New York state enacts first speed limit: 20 mph Deaf, dumb, and blind, Helen Keller graduates from Radcliffe College.
1905 Supreme Court disallows limits on length of working day. Industrial Workers of the World, a radical labor union, formed in Chicago. Pres. Roosevelt mediates Treaty of Portsmouth, ending Russo-Japanese War. Black leaders hold Niagara Falls Conference, calling for equal rights.
1906 San Francisco destroyed by earthquake and fire (Apr. 18-19). Congress passes Pure Food and Drug Act and Meat Inspection Act. Race riot breaks out in Atlanta (Sept. 22). Japan protests segregation of Asian students in California schools (Oct. 25). Pres. Roosevelt first American to win the Nobel Peace Prize, and first sitting president to leave U.S. on visit to Panama.
1907 Panic of 1907 triggers crash on Wall Street (Mar. 13) and run on banks across the country. Pres. Roosevelt orders exclusion of Japanese laborers (Mar. 14). Congress outlaws corporate contributions to political campaigns. Hundreds killed in coal mine explosions in Monongah, W. Va., and Jacobs Creek, Pa. All-time record 1,285,349 immigrants arrive in one year.
1908 U.S. and Japan conclude "Gentleman's Agreement" limiting immigration. Ford Model T appears on the market (Oct. 1). Root-Takahira Agreement promises U.S. and Japan will respect each other's interests in Pacific. Pres. Roosevelt appoints National Conservation Commission. Federal Bureau of Investigation established. New York City outlaws women smoking in public.
1909 Robert E. Peary plants American flag at North Pole (Apr. 6). Pres. Taft opens 700,000 acres for settlement in the West. W.E.B. DuBois founds National Association for the Advancement of Colored People (NAACP), advocating racial equality.
1910 Theodore Roosevelt calls for "New Nationalism" in a speech at Ossawatomie, Kans. *Los Angeles Times* building destroyed by terrorist bomb (Oct. 1). Glacier National Park created.

Mann Act cracks down on "white slave" trade. Boy Scouts of America chartered.

1911 Pres. Taft orders U.S. troops to border during Mexican Revolution. Supreme Court upholds antitrust breakups of Standard Oil and American Tobacco. Calbraith P. Rodgers makes first transcontinental airplane flight. U.S. bankers take control of Nicaragua's finances. Steel magnate Andrew Carnegie donates $125 million for philanthropic purposes.

1912 *Titanic* sinks on maiden voyage from England (Apr. 15). Progressive, or "Bull Moose," Party founded by Theodore Roosevelt, who survives an assassination attempt by John Schrank in Milwaukee (Oct. 14). Massachusetts adopts first minimum wage law. U.S. Marines land in Honduras, Cuba, Nicaragua, and Santo Domingo. Textile strike in Lawrence, Mass.

1913 Sixteenth Amendment empowers Federal government to collect income taxes (Feb. 25). Seventeenth Amendment allows for popular election of U.S. senators (May 31). Congress creates Federal Reserve system. Ford Motor Company introduces assembly line. John D. Rockefeller donates $100 million to philanthropic Rockefeller Foundation. Grand Central Station opens in New York City.

1914 Pres. Wilson nearly goes to war with Mexico over arrests of American sailors in Tampico. U.S. Navy shells Vera Cruz and lands Marines in retaliation (Apr. 21). U.S. declares neutrality in World War I (Aug. 4). Congress passes Clayton Act, toughening antitrust standards. Congress proclaims Mother's Day.

1915 *The Birth of a Nation,* first movie blockbuster. Pres. Wilson strongly protests German sinking of *Lusitania* with 128 Americans aboard (May 7). U.S. Marines land in Haiti (July 28). Ku Klux Klan revived in Atlanta, Ga. Coast-to-coast long distance telephone service begins.

1916 House-Grey Memorandum warns Germany that refusal to negotiate may bring U.S. into World War I. Gen. John Pershing chases Pancho Villa into Mexico after border raid on Columbus, N.Mex. (Mar. 15). U.S. acquires Virgin Islands from Denmark for $25 million. Jeanette Rankin of Montana first woman elected to Congress. Louis D. Brandeis first Jewish member of Supreme Court. Margaret Sanger opens first birth control clinic in Brooklyn, N.Y. National Park Service created.

1917 Germany resumes unrestricted submarine warfare, leading U.S. to sever diplomatic relations (Feb. 3). Gen. John Pershing withdraws from Mexico. Zimmerman Telegram reveals German overtures to Mexico in case of war (Feb. 24). U.S. merchant ships armed for self-defense against German submarines (Mar. 13). After Pres. Wilson proclaims "the world must be made safe for democracy," Congress declares war on Germany (Apr. 6) and Austria-Hungary (Dec. 7). Prohibition begins as wartime conservation measure.

1918 Pres. Wilson announces U.S. war aims in "Fourteen Points" speech (Jan. 8). U.S. troops join Allied intervention in Russian Revolution (Aug. 2). Congress passes Sedition Act. Over a million U.S. troops participate in month-long Meuse-Argonne campaign (Sept. 26-Nov. 11). Republicans win control of Congress, a rebuke to Pres. Wilson . Armistice Day ends World War I (Nov. 11) as mass celebrations break out across the country. Pres. Wilson goes to Europe for peace conference. Supreme Court approves draft laws and strikes down child labor laws. Influenza epidemic takes hundreds of thousands American lives.

1919 Eighteenth Amendment establishes Prohibition (Jan. 29). Strike wave sweeps country, triggering "Red Scare." American Communist Party organized in Chicago. Race riots in Washington, D.C., and Chicago. Pres. Wilson suffers incapacitating stroke (Sept. 26). Volstead Act implements national Prohibition enforcement. Senate rejects Versailles Treaty and League of Nations (Nov. 19). Grand Canyon National Park created. New York-Chicago daily airmail service begins.

1920 Attorney General A. Mitchell Palmer stages "Palmer Raids," arresting and deporting thousands of radicals and immigrants. Sacco and Vanzetti are arrested for murder in Braintree, Mass. Supreme Court upholds Prohibition. Nineteenth Amendment establishes women's suffrage (Aug. 26). National League of Women Voters organized. First regular radio broadcasts begin in East Pittsburgh, Pa. Pres. Wilson receives Nobel Peace Prize. U.S. population, more urban than rural for first time, tops 100 million (105,710,620).

1921 Pres. Harding, promising a "return to normalcy," takes office. U.S. negotiates separate peace with Germany, Austria, and Hungary. Ku Klux Klan spreads terror in the South. Jack Dempsey defeats Georges Carpentier in first million-dollar prize fight.

1922 Washington Conference concludes with nine international treaties to limit naval arms race, relax tensions in the Pacific, and protect China. Supreme Court upholds women's suffrage. Lincoln Memorial dedicated in Washington, D.C. (May 30). Pres. Harding vetoes "Bonus Bill" for World War I veterans. Congress passes joint resolution in favor of Jewish homeland in Palestine (Sept. 21). First commercial radio show broadcast in New York.

1923 Last U.S. occupation troops leave Germany (Jan. 10). Senate begins investigating corruption in Veterans Bureau and Teapot Dome oil leases (Oct. 25). Pres. Harding dies mysteriously of "apoplexy" in San Francisco (Aug. 2). Pres. Coolidge's address to Congress, calling for economy in government, first radio broadcast of a presidential speech (Dec. 6). Oklahoma declares martial law to crack down on Ku Klux Klan. Yankee Stadium opens.

1924 Congress provides bonuses for World War I veterans over Pres. Coolidge's veto. Congress passes Immigration Act, imposing strict national quota system. European powers accept Dawes Plan for repayment of war debts and reparations. U.S. Marines withdraw from Santo Domingo. Coast-to-coast air mail service begins.

1925 Tennessee outlaws teaching evolution in school, leading to the Scopes Trial in Dayton, Tenn. (July 10-21). Ku Klux Klan marches on Washington, D.C. (Aug. 8) Nellie Tayloe Ross of Wyoming first woman governor. Florida land boom draws hordes of speculators. Chicago gang wars break out as Al Capone consolidates bootlegging operations.

1926 Treasury Sec. Andrew Mellon's drastic tax cuts approved. Admiral Richard E. Byrd and Floyd Bennett first to fly over North Pole (May 9). Henry Ford institutes 8-hour day and 5-day work week at Ford Motor Company factories. Hurricane sweeps Florida, killing 372 people. Book of the Month Club founded. U.S. Marines return to Nicaragua.

1927 Charles Lindbergh completes non-stop solo flight from New York to Paris (May 20-21), returns home to huge welcoming crowds. Sacco and Vanzetti executed in Massachusetts, despite international protests. *The Jazz Singer* with Al Jolson becomes first "talkie" motion picture (Oct. 6). Mississippi River floods causes $300 million damage. Ford Model A unveiled. Mechanical cotton picker invented. New York-London commercial telephone service begins.

1928 U.S. joins fourteen countries in signing Kellogg-Briand Pact for the "outlawry of war" (Aug. 27). Clark Memorandum disavows future U.S. interventions in Latin America. Pres. Coolidge refuses to aid American farmers mired in agricultural depression. Walt Disney creates "Steamboat Willie," first Mickey Mouse cartoon. George Eastman demonstrates color motion picture technology. Republicans promise "a chicken in every pot, a car in every garage."

1929 St. Valentine's Day Massacre claims six lives in Chicago gang wars. Young Plan replaces Dawes Plan for payment of war debts and reparations. Albert B. Fall, former secretary of the Interior, found guilty in Teapot Dome scandal. Stock market crash on "Black Tuesday" (Oct. 29) ushers in Great Depression.

1930 Wave of bank failures sweeps U.S., wiping out millions of savings accounts and leading to private hoarding of gold. U.S., Britain, and Japan sign London Naval Treaty limiting naval arms race (Apr. 22). Hawley-Smoot Tariff raises barriers to world trade, worsening Depression. Congress creates Veteran's Administration (July 3).

1931 World War I veterans are offered "Bonus Loans" to combat Depression. "Star Spangled Banner" becomes national anthem. "Scottsboro Boys" arrested for rape in Alabama. Empire State Building, tallest building in the world, opens in New York City. Pres. Hoover declares moratorium on international debt and reparations payments.

1932 Stimson Doctrine condemns Japanese invasion of China. Congress approves Reconstruction Finance Corporation to help recovery. Norris-LaGuardia act restricts use of injunctions against labor strikes. Franklin D. Roosevelt wins presidential election in a landslide, promising a "New Deal." Stock market drops to 10% of its 1929 value. "Bonus Army" of poor veterans marches on Washington, D.C. Amelia Earhart first woman to fly solo across the Atlantic.

1933 Giuseppe Zangara kills Chicago Mayor Anton J. Cermak in a Miami, Fla., motorcade, narrowly missing president-elect Franklin D. Roosevelt (Feb. 15). Banks are closed for four days by presidential order (Mar. 5). During "Hundred Days" (Mar. 9-June 16), Pres. Roosevelt pushes New Deal through Congress, conducts first "Fireside Chat" on radio, and takes U.S. off gold standard. Prohibition repealed (Mar. 22). U.S. recognizes Soviet Union (Nov. 16). U.S. Marines withdraw from Nicaragua. Frances Perkins, Sec. of Labor, becomes first woman cabinet member.

1934 Dust storms inundate Southwest, driving "Okies" and "Arkies" to California. General strike paralyzes San Francisco (July 16). John Dillinger, public enemy number one, killed by FBI agents (July 22). Sen. Gerald P. Nye of North Dakota begins investigating role of U.S. munitions manufacturers in World War I. U.S. releases Cuba from Platt Amendment. U.S. troops withdraw from Haiti.

1935 Supreme Court invalidates National Industrial Recovery Act. Pres. Roosevelt pushes more "Second New Deal" legislation through Congress, notably the Wagner Act protecting unions, Social Security Act, and "Soak the Rich" Wealth Tax Act. Sen. Huey P. Long of Louisana assassinated (Sept. 8). Congress of Industrial Organization (CIO) formed (Nov. 9). Congress passes first Neutrality Act. Alcoholics Anonymous founded.

1936 Congress passes second Neutrality Act. France, Britain, and U.S. sign New London Naval Treaty (Mar. 25). U.S. declares neutrality in Spanish Civil War (Aug. 7). CIO auto workers begin sit-down strikes in Flint, Mich. *Life* magazine begins publishing. Jesse Owens wins four gold medals at "Nazi Olympics" in Berlin.

1937 Congress passes third Neutrality Act. Pres. Roosevelt proposes controversial "court-packing" plan. German dirigible *Hindenburg* explodes and burns in Lakehurst, N.J. (May 6). Pres. Roosevelt angers isolationists with "Quarantine Speech" (Oct. 5). Japanese planes sink U.S. Navy gunboat *Panay* in China (Dec. 12). Slow recovery ends abruptly as Depression worsens.

1938 Pres. Roosevelt calls for military buildup. Mexico seizes U.S.-owned oil wells. Rep. Martin Dies of Texas begins House Un-American Activities Committee (HUAC) investigations of Communists and Fascists. Howard Hughes sets record for around-the-world flight in less than four days (July 14). "Invasion from Mars" radio broadcast by Orson Welles causes widespread panic (Oct. 30). Hurricane devastates Atlantic coast, killing 700.

1939 Supreme Court upholds Tennessee Valley Authority. Pan Am begins first regular trans-Atlantic passenger service. U.S. declares neutrality in World War II (Sept. 5). Congress passes fourth Neutrality Act, approving Pres. Roosevelt's request for "cash-and-carry" arms sales to belligerents. First nylon stockings appear on the market.

1940 As World War II engulfs Europe, Pres. Roosevelt announces U.S. move from "neutrality" to "non-belligerency" (June 10). U.S. and Britain conclude Destroyers-for-Bases deal. Congress enacts peacetime draft (Sept. 16) and massive increases in military spending. Over 16 million men register for draft as embargo on strategic exports takes effect. Roosevelt, reelected to an unprecedented third term, calls for U.S. to become "the arsenal of democracy" (Dec. 20).

1941 Congress appropriates $7 billion in Lend-Lease aid to Britain. German submarine sinks merchant ship Robin Moor, first U.S. casualty of war (May 21). Pres. Roosevelt responds by declaring "unlimited national emergency" (May 27), freezing German and Italian assets in U.S. (June 14), and promising aid to Soviet Union (June 24). Pres. Roosevelt freezes Japanese assets in retaliation for invasion of Indochina. U.S. Navy is ordered to "shoot on sight" at German warships. Japanese planes attack Pearl Harbor, Hawaii, killing 2,400 U.S. servicemen and civilians (Dec. 7). U.S. declares war on Japan (Dec. 10) and on Germany and Italy (Dec. 11).

1942 Roosevelt creates War Production Board, calls for mass mobilization, and puts New Deal on hold. U.S. troops land in North Ireland, first to arrive in Europe (Jan. 26). Pres. Roosevelt approves internment of Japanese-Americans for duration of war (Feb. 20). Japanese submarine shells an oil refinery in Santa Barbara, Calif. (Feb. 23). Maj. James H. Doolittle stages carrier-launched bombing raid on Tokyo (Apr. 18). U.S. armed forces surrender in Philippines (May 6), but win major naval victories over Japan in Coral Sea (May 4-8) and at Midway (June 3-6). U.S. offensive begins in Pacific with invasion of Guadalcanal Island (Aug. 7). First all-U.S. bombing attack launched against German forces at Rouen, France (Aug. 17). Congress approves "Victory Tax" on wartime incomes. Allies land 400,000 men in North Africa (Nov. 7-8). Eight German saboteurs apprehended in New York; six executed. Cocoanut Grove nightclub fire in Boston kills 492.

1943 Congress appropriates $100 billion for war effort. Roosevelt and Churchill demand "unconditional surrender" at Casablanca conference in Morocco. U.S. Marines drive last Japanese from Guadalcanal (Feb. 9). U.S. troops defeated in first battle with Germans at Kasserine Pass, Tunisia (Feb. 20). Pres. Roosevelt declares wage-and-price freeze to stem inflation. U.S. and Britain invade Sicily (July 10) and Italy proper (Sept. 3). Roosevelt and Churchill meet with Chiang Kai-Shek of China in Cairo, Egypt (Nov. 22), and with Josef Stalin of Soviet Union in Teheran, Iran (Dec. 4-6). Gen. Dwight D. Eisenhower named Supreme Commander of Allied forces in Europe.

1944 U.S. and British planes begin around-the-clock bombing of Berlin. Allied forces land at Anzio, Italy (Jan. 22). Congress approves $1.35 billion for United Nations Relief and Reconstruction Agency, first U.S. foreign aid (Mar. 29). Allied forces enter Rome (June 5) as reconquest of Europe begins with D-Day invasion of Normandy (June 6). Allied breakout from Normandy sends German forces reeling across France (July 25). Postwar financial arrangements made at an international conference in Bretton Woods, N.H. (July 1-22). Plans for United Nations made at Dumbarton Oaks conference (Aug. 21-Oct. 7). Gen. Douglas MacArthur begins reconquest of Philippines with landings at Leyte Gulf (Oct. 20). Congress passes Servicemen's Readjustment Act, known as "GI Bill of Rights." Roosevelt wins fourth term.

1945 Roosevelt, Churchill and Stalin meet for last time at Yalta in Soviet Crimea to begin postwar planning (Feb. 4–11). Allied forces cross Rhine River and drive into heart of Germany (Mar. 7). U.S. air raids destroy Tokyo (Mar. 10–11). Pres. Roosevelt dies suddenly of cerebral hemorrhage in Warm Springs, Ga. (Apr. 12). Germany surrenders, ending war in Europe (May 7). Fifty nations sign United Nations Charter (June 26). First atomic explosion occurs in test at Alamagordo, N. Mex. (July 16). Pres. Truman meets with Churchill and Stalin at Potsdam, Germany (July 17–Aug. 2). Atomic bombs dropped on Hiroshima (Aug. 6) and Nagasaki (Aug. 9); Japan surrenders (Aug. 14), ending World War II. Council of Allied Foreign Ministers meets in London, unable to agree on peace treaty (Dec. 16–27). Empire State Building hit by B-25 bomber in heavy fog.

1946 Strike wave sweeps U.S., idling 4.6 million U.S. workers. Congress passes Employment Act, committing Federal government to postwar economic management. Churchill warns Americans about Communist expansion with "Iron Curtain" speech in Fulton, Mo. (Mar. 5). Pres. Truman seizes control of railroads and coal mines during strikes. U.S. presents Baruch Plan for international control of atomic energy, grants independence to Philippines (July 4), and agrees to loan Britain $3.5 billion for postwar reconstruction. Paris Peace Conference ends in failure (July 29–Oct. 15). Congress creates Atomic Energy Commission. U.N. General Assembly begins meeting in New York.

1947 Council of Foreign Ministers meets in Moscow, again unable to agree on peace treaty (Mar. 10–Apr. 24). Pres. Truman announces Truman Doctrine, promising aid to countries threatened by subversion (May 12). Sec. of State George C. Marshall announces Marshall Plan for reconstruction of Europe (June 5). Republican-dominated Congress restricts union organizing with Taft-Hartley Act. House Un-American Activities Committee (HUAC) begins investigating Communism in Hollywood (Oct. 20). Texas City, Tex., wiped out when a ship explodes, killing over 500 people. Jackie Robinson of Brooklyn Dodgers breaks color line in baseball.

1948 Postwar inflation keeps prices rising fast. Congress approves $5.3 billion for Marshall Plan aid to Europe with Foreign Assistance Act. U.S. recognizes new state of Israel (May 14) and admits 205,000 war refugees from Europe. Britain and U.S. begin airlifting supplies into West Berlin after Soviets cut off all traffic into city (June 26). Pres. Truman orders peacetime draft and desegregation of U.S. armed forces. HUAC charges Alger Hiss with spying for Soviet Union. Pres. Truman wins upset reelection victory over New York Gov. Thomas E. Dewey. Idlewild International Airport, world's largest, opens in New York.

1949 Pres. Truman calls for "Fair Deal" domestic programs and "Point Four" foreign aid programs. U.S., Canada, and 10 Western European nations sign treaty that will lead to North Atlantic Treaty Organization (NATO). Berlin Airlift ends when Soviets finally lift blockade (May 12). Pres. Truman announces Soviet atomic bomb test (Sept. 23). Eleven U.S. Communist leaders convicted of conspiring to overthrow government. Steel strike idles half a million workers nationwide (Oct. 1-Nov. 11). *Lucky Lady II* of U.S. Air Force completes first nonstop around-the-world flight.

1950 Sen. Joseph R. McCarthy of Wisconsin issues his first accusations of Communists in government at a speech in Wheeling, W. Va. North Korea invades South Korea, beginning Korean War (June 25). Pres. Truman orders U.S. intervention (June 27), obtains U.N. support (July 7), asks Congress for a $10 billion rearmament program (July 20), and calls up reserves (Aug. 4). Inchon landing begins rout of North Korean invaders (Sept. 15). U.N. troops recapture Seoul (Sept. 26) and invade North Korea (Oct. 7). Congress passes Internal Security Act, requiring registration of Communist organizations, over Pres. Truman's veto (Sept. 23). Puerto Rican nationalists nearly assassinate Pres. Truman in Washington (Nov. 11). After China intervenes in the Korean War, Pres. Truman proclaims a national emergency (Dec. 16).

1951 Gen. Dwight D. Eisenhower comes out of retirement to accept command of Allied forces in Europe (Apr. 4). Julius and Ethel Rosenberg sentenced to death for spying (Apr. 5). Pres. Truman removes Gen. Douglas MacArthur from command in Korea for insubordination (Apr. 11). MacArthur returns to the U.S., greeted by exultant crowds, to deliver address to Congress. Missouri River floods devastate Kansas City, causing over $1 billion in damages (July 11–25). U.S. concludes a mutual defense pact with Australia and New Zealand, and signs a peace treaty with Japan (Sept. 8). Congress passes the Mutual Security Act, providing $7 billion for foreign aid and military cooperation with pro-U.S. nations. CBS transmits first color television broadcast from New York.

1952 Pres. Truman seizes steel mills paralyzed by strikes (Apr. 8). U.S., Britain and France sign a peace treaty with West Germany (May 26). Construction begins on USS *Nautilus,* first atomic submarine. Supreme Court upholds barring subversives from teaching in schools. Sen. Richard M. Nixon of California, Republican candidate for Vice President, delivers "Checkers Speech" on national television to explain his "secret slush fund." Republicans win control of White House and both houses of Congress for first time since 1928. U.S. announces first successful hydrogen bomb test at Eniwetok Atoll in Marshall Islands (Nov. 16).

1953 Thirteen more Communist leaders are convicted of conspiring to overthrow the government. Julius and Ethel Rosenberg are executed in Ossining, N.Y. (June 19). Pres. Eisenhower lifts wage and price controls, increases U.S. support for French war effort in Indochina, negotiates armistice ending Korean War (June 27). Congress creates Department of Health, Education, and Welfare (Apr. 1). U.S. pledges aid to Spain in exchange for military bases (Sept. 26). Major Chuck Yeager of the U.S. Air Force sets new air speed record in rocket-powered X-1 jet plane.

1954 Sec. of State John Foster Dulles vows "massive retaliation" against Soviet aggression (Jan. 12). Puerto Rican nationalists shoot five Congressmen on the floor of the House of Representatives (Mar. 1). U.S. negotiates the Southeast Asia Treaty Organization (SEATO) security pact (Sept. 8). Supreme Court orders school desegregation in *Brown v. Board of Education* (May 17). CIA helps overthrow the Arbenz government in Guatemala (June 29). gress passes Communist Control Act. Senate censures Sen. Joseph McCarthy.

1955 Pres. Eisenhower promises to use atomic weapons in case of war and conducts first televised press conference. U.S., Soviet Union, and Allies agree on Austrian peace treaty to end occupation. Supreme Court orders school desegregation to proceed "with all deliberate speed." Interstate Commerce Commission orders desegregation on interstate trains and buses. AFL and CIO labor federations merge to form the AFL-CIO, with 15 million members. Dr. Jonas Salk perfects polio vaccine. Dr. Martin Luther King, Jr., leads bus boycott in Montgomery, Ala.

1956 Pres. Eisenhower refuses to intervene against Soviet invasion of Hungary and exerts pressure on Allies to withdraw from Suez. Congressmen signing Southern Manifesto promise "massive resistance" to school desegregation. Atomic Energy Commission approves commercial nuclear power plants. Congress passes Highway Act, appropriating $32 billion for construction of a vast nationwide road system. TWA and United airliners collide in midair and crash into Grand Canyon, killing 128 people (June 30). First trans-Atlantic telephone cable begins operating.

1957 Pres. Eisenhower announces Eisenhower Doctrine, promising aid to any Middle Eastern country threatened by Communism. McClellan Committee begins investigating corruption and racketeering in International Brotherhood of Teamsters union. Sen. J. Strom Thurmond of South Carolina sets all-time filibuster record (24 hours, 27 minutes) with speech against civil rights (Aug. 30). Congress nevertheless approves the first Civil Rights Act since Reconstruction (Sept. 9). Pres. Eisenhower sends troops to Little Rock, Ark., to enforce Federal desegregation order (Sept. 24). First underground atomic test conducted in Nevada (Sept. 19).

1958 In response to Soviet launch of *Sputnik*, U.S. launches *Explorer I*, first American satellite; Congress creates National Aeronautics and Space Administration (NASA). Vice President Richard M. Nixon nearly killed by angry mob in Caracas, Venezuela. At request of weak government in Beirut, Pres. Eisenhower orders U.S. Marines to land in Lebanon (July 15). Nuclear submarine *Nautilus* performs first undersea crossing of North Pole (Aug. 5). Presidential assistant Sherman Adams forced to resign in scandal over accepting favors (Sept. 22).

1959 Fidel Castro's takeover of Cuba begins rapid deterioration of U.S.-Cuba relations (Jan. 1). Alaska becomes 49th state (Jan. 3), and Hawaii becomes 50th state (Aug. 21). Joint U.S.-Canada St. Lawrence Seaway project completed. Congress passes the Landrum-Griffin Act to suppress racketeering in labor unions. Vice Pres. Richard M. Nixon holds impromptu "kitchen debate" in Moscow with Soviet Premier Nikita Khrushchev. Charles Van Doren testifies that his victory on the "$64,000 Question" TV game show was fixed.

1960 U.S. and Japan conclude new security treaty (Jan. 19). Black students stage first sit-in at a Woolworth's lunch counter in Greensboro, N.C. (Feb. 1). U-2 spy plane, with American pilot Francis Gary Powers, is shot down over the Soviet Union (May 1). Congress passes second Civil Rights Act since Reconstruction. Congress investigates "payola" in the radio industry, leading to the arrest of Alan Freed, "father of rock 'n' roll." After Cuba rejects American protests over confiscated property, Pres. Eisenhower imposes trade embargo. John F. Kennedy and Richard M. Nixon hold first televised presidential campaign debates. Kennedy wins election by 0.3 percent of popular vote, closest presidential election since 1884 (Nov. 8).

1961 Pres. Eisenhower breaks diplomatic relations with Cuba, warns Americans to beware of "military-industrial complex." CIA-backed Bay of Pigs invasion fails to overthrow Castro regime in Cuba (Apr. 17). Commander Alan B. Shephard, Jr., U.S. Navy, first American in space on *Mercury* rocket (May 5). Soviet construction of Berlin Wall creates temporary crisis (Aug. 13). Pres. Kennedy creates Peace Corps and Alliance for Progress. American families advised to build nuclear fallout shelters. "Freedom Rides" civil rights protests broken up by riots in Anniston and Birmingham, Ala. American Medical Association reports link between smoking and heart disease. National Council of Churches endorses birth control for families.

1962 Lt. Col. John H. Glenn, Jr., first American to orbit Earth. Pres. Kennedy convinces steel companies to rescind price increases. U.S. conducts first successful test of sea-launched long-range ballistic missile with nuclear warhead. Pres. Kennedy sends U.S. marshals to protect James H. Meredith, a black student at University of Mississippi. U.S. extends a $100 million emergency loan to the United Nations. Threat of nuclear war during Cuban Missile Crisis averted when Soviet Union agrees to withdraw missiles from Cuba (Oct. 22-28). Rachel Carson's *Silent Spring* draws attention to environmental crisis.

1963 Pres. Kennedy proposes the Medicare program. U.S., Great Britain, and the Soviet Union conclude the Nuclear Test-Ban Treaty outlawing atmospheric testing (July 25). "Hot line" between Washington and Moscow put in place. Civil rights movement reaches a climax with mass demonstrations in Birmingham, Ala., and epic March on Washington, where Martin Luther King delivers his "I Have a Dream" speech (Aug. 28). Pres. Kennedy is assassinated in Dallas, Tex., by Lee Harvey Oswald (Nov. 22), who is murdered by Jack Ruby (Nov. 24).

1964 Pres. Johnson, taking up Pres. Kennedy's cause, calls for a "War on Poverty." Supreme Court orders states to redraw Congressional boundaries to ensure fair representation. Alaska declared disaster area after major earthquake rocks Anchorage (Mar. 28). Mississippi "Freedom Summer" begins with murder of three civil rights workers (June 22). Pres. Johnson pushes landmark Civil Rights and Economic Opportunity acts through Congress. After alleged North Vietnamese attack on U.S. Navy destroyers, Congress passes Tonkin Gulf Resolution giving Pres. Johnson free hand in Vietnam (Aug. 7). Warren Commission reports there was no conspiracy to assassinate Pres. Kennedy (Sept. 27). The Rev. Martin Luther King Jr. wins Nobel Peace Prize.

1965 Pres. Johnson calls for the "Great Society." Black nationalist Malcolm X is assassinated in New York City (Feb. 21). Pres. Johnson orders U.S. Marines into South Vietnam (Mar. 8) and into Santo Domingo (Apr. 38). U.S. troops authorized to undertake offensive operations in South Vietnam (June 8). Martin Luther King leads civil rights marches from Selma to Montgomery, Ala., and in white neighborhoods of Chicago. Congress approves Medicare (July 30) and Voting Rights Act (Aug. 6). The Watts Riot in Los Angeles leaves 34 dead and over $200 million in damage (Aug. 11-16), accelerating wave of ghetto riots. Tornadoes sweep Midwest, killing 271 and injuring 5,000.

1966 Pres. Johnson orders first B-52 strategic bombing raids on North Vietnam (Apr. 12). Supreme Court rules police must advise suspects of their rights. Cesar Chavez leads United Farm Workers strike and boycott against California grape growers. Stokeley Carmichael of Student Non-Violent Coordinating Committee demands "Black Power." Congress enacts safety standards for automobiles. Edward W. Brooke of Massachusetts is first black senator since Reconstruction. U.S. troops in Vietnam increase from 215,000 to over 400,000.

1967 Green Bay defeats Kansas City in first ever Super Bowl. Hundreds of thousands of anti-war protesters march on Washington (Apr. 15 & Oct. 21–22). Pres. Johnson announces U.S. troop level will reach 525,000 by end of 1968. Worst race riot in U.S. history erupts in Detroit (July 23), leaving 43 dead, while riot in Newark, N.J., (July 12) kills another 26. Sen. Eugene McCarthy (D-Minn.) announces antiwar candidacy for president (Nov. 30). U.S. agrees to refrain from placing nuclear weapons in space and joins General Agreement on Tariffs and Trade (GATT). Albert DeSalvo, the "Boston Strangler," sentenced to life in prison. Thurgood Marshall becomes first black justice on Supreme Court.

1968 North Korea seizes USS *Pueblo,* holding 82 crewmen hostage (Jan. 23). North Vietnam and Viet Cong launch massive Tet Offensive (Jan. 30). Pres. Johnson makes surprise announcement that he will not seek re-election (Mar. 31). Martin Luther King assassinated by James Earl Ray in Memphis, Tenn. (Apr. 4). Washington-Hanoi peace talks begin in Paris (May 10). After winning California primary, Sen. Robert F. Kennedy of New York murdered by Sirhan Sirhan in Los Angeles (June 5). U.S. signs Nuclear Non-Proliferation Treaty. Democratic Convention in Chicago marred by riots and police violence against antiwar demonstrators. Shirley Chisholm of New York is the first black woman elected to Congress. *Apollo VIII* completes first moon orbit.

1969 Oil spill off Santa Barbara, Calif., draws attention to need for environmental protection (Feb. 5). Pres. Nixon asks Congress to fund Anti-Ballistic Missile program as "safeguard" for strategic defense. U.S. losses in Vietnam exceed losses in Korean War. Sen. Edward M. Kennedy (D-Mass.) drives off a bridge at Chappaquiddick, Mass., killing Mary Jo Kopechne (July 18). Neil Armstrong and Buzz Aldrin of Apollo XI are first men to walk on the moon (July 20). Hurricane Camille claims over 300 victims in the South. Trial of Chicago Seven begins. Woodstock music festival near Bethel, N.Y., draws 400,000 young fans (Aug. 15–18). Vietnam Moratorium and "March Against Death" antiwar demonstrations draw hundreds of thousands to Washington. U.S. and the Soviet Union begin Strategic Arms Limitation Talks (SALT) in Helsinki, Finland.

1970 Pres. Nixon calls for "Vietnamization" to decrease U.S. involvement in war. U.S. bombing of North Vietnam escalates dramatically; nationwide protests break out when U.S. invades Cambodia (Apr. 29). Four students are killed and nine wounded by National Guard units at Kent State University in Ohio (May 4). SALT negotiations reopen in Vienna, Austria. Lt. William L. Calley court-martialed for massacre of 102 civilians in My Lai South Vietnam (Nov. 12). Supreme Court upholds new 18-year-old voting age (Dec. 21). Congress creates Environmental Protection Agency, passes Water Quality Improvement Act, Air Quality Control Act, and Occupational Safety and Health Act.

1971 Pres. Nixon proposes federal revenue sharing with states. Charles Manson and three women followers convicted for Tate-LaBianca murders in Los Angeles (Jan. 25). Major earthquake rocks Southern California, killing 64 and injuring over 1,000 (Feb. 9). Supreme Court approves busing to achieve school integration. Indian occupation of Alcatraz Island in San Francisco Bay comes to an end. Prison riot in Attica, N.Y., kills 43 inmates and guards. *New York Times* begins publishing "Pentagon Papers," top-secret history of Vietnam War (June 13). U.S. devalues dollar (Dec. 18). U.S. troops in Vietnam reach 139,000; U.S. air attacks are heaviest since 1968.

1972 Nixon first president to visit China (Feb. 21–28) and the Soviet Union (May 22–30). Airlines begin screening passengers to prevent hijackings. Congress passes Equal Rights Amendment and submits it to states for ratification. Gov. George Wallace of Alabama shot and seriously wounded by Arthur Bremer while campaigning for president in Laurel, Md. (May 15). Five men arrested for breaking into Democratic National Committee headquarters at the Watergate complex in Washington (June 17). Federal grand jury indicts five burglars and two former White House aides in Watergate trial (Sept. 15). Pres. Nixon angers farmers with the "Great Grain Robbery," a secret deal to sell wheat at discount to Soviet Union. National Security Advisor Henry Kissinger announces "peace is at hand" in Vietnam in time for Pres. Nixon to carry 49 states in election. U.S. troops in Vietnam fall to 69,000 as Nixon orders resumption of heavy bombing of North Vietnam (Dec. 18).

1973 Supreme Court overturns state restrictions on abortions (Roe vs. Wade). U.S. signs Paris peace accords ending Vietnam War (Jan. 27). Trial of Watergate burglars reveals conspiracy to conceal White House involvement. Top presidential aides H.R. Haldeman, John Ehrlichman, John Dean, and Attorney General Richard Kleindienst resign amid charges of White House cover-up (Apr. 30). Sen. Sam Ervin of North Carolina chairs Senate investigation of Watergate scandal (May

17–Nov. 15). Pres. Nixon fires Watergate Special Prosecutor Archibald Cox and others in "Saturday Night Massacre" (Oct. 20). Vice President Spiro Agnew resigns after threat of prosecution for tax evasion (Oct. 10). Gasoline prices skyrocket after Arab nations embargo oil exports to U.S. in retaliation for U.S. aid to Israel in Yom Kippur War (Oct. 17). Pres. Nixon turns over first White House tapes, which include mysterious 18 1/2 minute gap (Nov. 26). Gerald R. Ford of Michigan sworn in as first vice president chosen under 25th Amendment (Dec. 6). Indians defy Federal authority in Wounded Knee, S.D.

1974 Arab oil embargo of U.S. lifted (Mar. 18). Supreme Court rules that Pres. Nixon must submit all White House tapes to Special Prosecutor Leon Jaworski (July 24). House Judiciary Committee votes three articles of impeachment (July 24–30). Pres. Nixon releases transcripts of tapes that show he ordered cover-up (Aug. 5). Citing "political" difficulties, Pres. Nixon resigns (Aug. 8), elevating Vice Pres. Ford to presidency (Aug. 9). Pres. Ford shocks nation by pardoning Nixon for all crimes (Sept. 8). Pres. Ford meets with Soviet Premier Leonid Brezhnev in Vladivostock to approve SALT treaty (Nov. 23–24). Newspaper heiress Patty Hearst kidnapped in Berkeley, Calif., by radical Symbionese Liberation Army.

1975 Nixon aides convicted of obstructing justice in Watergate investigation (Jan. 1). Last Americans evacuate Saigon as South Vietnam falls to North Vietnamese invasion (Apr. 30). Cambodia seizes USS *Mayaguez* (May 12), and Pres. Ford orders rescue operation (May 14). Apollo-Soyuz, joint Soviet-American space mission, achieves link-up in space (July 17). Lynette "Squeaky" Fromme and Sarah Jane Moore attempt to assassinate Pres. Ford in separate California incidents (Sept. 5 & Sept. 22). Congress votes to admit women to Army, Navy, and Air Force academies. House Democrats dismantle seniority system. Church Committee discovers CIA helped overthrow Salvador Allende of Chile and plotted to assassinate Fidel Castro of Cuba.

1976 Congress repeatedly overrides Pres. Ford's vetoes of bills providing for jobs, health, education, and welfare programs. Supreme Court upholds death penalty (July 3). Bicentennial of U.S. celebrated coast to coast. Jimmy Carter defeats Pres. Ford as voters hold Ford responsible for pardoning Richard Nixon. Justice Department begins probing South Korean bribery of Congressmen and other officials. *Viking I* and *Viking II* space probes land on Mars, transmit scientific data and color photographs back to Earth. "Legionnaire's Disease" breaks out at Philadelphia American Legion convention, killing 29. Hundreds of West Point cadets found to have cheated on exams.

1977 Pres. Carter pardons Vietnam War draft evaders, threatens to reduce foreign aid for countries violating human rights, calls for "moral equivalent of war" in energy conservation, and signs Panama Canal treaty (Sept. 7). U.S. declares 200-mile sovereignty zone in Atlantic and Pacific oceans to exclude foreign fishing vessels. Power blackout sets off arson and looting spree in New York City (July 13–14). Oil begins flowing through the Alaska pipeline. Pres. Carter accuses oil industry of "the biggest rip-off in history" (Oct. 13). ABC mini-series *Roots*, draws 130 million viewers.

1978 Pres. Carter postpones production of neutron bomb. California voters approve Proposition 13, reducing property taxes and setting off a nationwide "taxpayers' revolt." Supreme Court gives limited approval to affirmative action programs, but disallows quotas for college admissions (June 28). In private talks with Anwar Sadat and Menachem Begin, Pres. Carter mediates peace between Egypt and Israel with landmark Camp David Accords (Sept. 17). Nearly one thousand American followers of the Rev. Jim Jones commit mass suicide in Jonestown, Guiana, after cult members murder Rep. Leo Ryan of California and others (Nov. 18). House investigations of John F. Kennedy and Martin Luther King assassinations conclude that conspiracies were probable in both cases (Dec. 30). Federal loan guarantees rescue New York City from financial crisis.

1979 U.S. resumes diplomatic relations with China (Jan 1). Worst nuclear accident in U.S. history takes place at Three Mile Island power plant near Harrisburg, Pa. Pres. Carter and Soviet Premier Leonid Brezhnev sign SALT II treaty in Vienna (June 18). The Shah of Iran and Anastasio Somoza of Nicaragua, both U.S.-supported dictators, flee revolutions in their countries. Iranian militants seize U.S. Embassy in Teheran, taking 66 American hostages and demanding return of the Shah from U.S. (Nov. 4). They release 13 hostages, all blacks or women. Pres. Carter deports illegal Iranian students, freezes Iranian assets, and bars oil imports from Iran. Inflation reaches highest level in 33 years as Organization of Petroleum Exporting Countries doubles price of oil.

1980 Canadian embassy officials help six Americans escape from Iran (Jan. 29). In response to Soviet invasion of Afghanistan, Pres. Carter embargoes grain and high technology exports to Soviet Union, approves arms sales to China, and secures U.S. boycott of Olympics in Moscow. Congress grants Pres. Carter's request for Crude Oil Windfall Profits Tax and for resumption of Selective Service draft registration. Pres. Carter's secret rescue mission for American hostages in Iran fails when a U.S. Navy helicopter crashes in desert, killing eight servicemen (Apr. 24). Mt. St. Helens erupts in Washington state, killing 26 people and causing $2.7 billion in damage (May 18). Banking and trucking industries deregulated. FBI's "Abscam" operation implicates over 30 public officials, including a senator and seven congressmen, for accepting bribes.

1981 Minutes after Pres. Reagan is sworn in, Iran releases 52 American hostages after 444 days in captivity. Pres. Reagan shot by John Hinckley in Washington (Mar. 30), but makes full recovery. *Columbia* completes first successful space shuttle mission (Apr. 12–14). Federal air traffic controllers go on strike and lose jobs when Pres. Reagan fires all 13,000 of them. Sandra Day O'Connor unanimously confirmed as first woman justice of Supreme Court. Pres. Reagan lifts grain embargo against Soviet Union, but imposes new sanctions after Poland declares martial law. Congress accepts Pres. Reagan's plans for tax cuts, lower domestic spending, and major defense buildup. U.S. sends military advisors and aid to El Salvador.

1982 Ending 13-year antitrust suit, AT&T agrees to surrender control of local Bell System phone companies in return for expansion into new businesses (Jan. 8). Pres. Reagan calls for "New Federalism," transferring programs to state and local control. Unemployment exceeds 10% for first time since Great Depression, and Federal budget deficit exceeds $100 billion a year for first time ever. After a decade, Equal Rights Amendment fails, falling three states short of ratification.

1983 Inflation slows as oil prices decline sharply. Congress agrees to bail out the Social Security system, and admits internment of Japanese-Americans during World War II was unjust. National Commission on Excellence in Education reports U.S. is a "nation at risk" because of inferior elementary and secondary schools. Sally Ride is first American woman astronaut, aboard space shuttle *Challenger*. Pres. Reagan strongly condemns Soviet Union for shooting down Korean airliner with 269 people aboard (Sept. 1). U.S. Marines join multinational peacekeeping force in Beirut, Lebanon, where Muslim terrorists kill 240 of them in suicide bombing (Oct. 23). U.S. invades Grenada to overthrow Cuban-backed regime (Oct. 25). Pres. Reagan calls for large-scale funding of Strategic Defense Initiative, or "Star Wars."
1984 Economic recovery begins as unemployment falls, inflation rate declines, economic growth accelerates, and U.S. dollar soars on international markets. Pres. Reagan orders U.S. Marines out of Lebanon (Feb. 7). The Rev. Jesse Jackson mounts first major challenge by black candidate for major party nomination. Rep. Geraldine Ferraro, (D-N.Y.) becomes first woman to receive major party nomination for vice president. Soviet bloc countries boycott Los Angeles Olympics. Pres. Reagan wins landslide re-election over Democratic challenger Walter Mondale.
1985 Pres. Reagan calls for more tax and budget cuts to sustain economic growth (Feb. 4–6). Despite worldwide protests, Pres. Reagan delivers address at Bitburg cemetery in West Germany, where Nazi SS troops are buried (May 5). Muslim terrorists hijack TWA airliner (June 14), kill one American hostage, then release rest in Beirut (June 30). Palestinian terrorists kill an American hostage aboard hijacked Italian cruise ship *Achille Lauro* (Oct. 9). Pres. Reagan and Soviet Premier Mikhail Gorbachev hold their first summit meeting in Geneva (Nov. 19–21). Pres. Reagan signs Gramm-Rudman Act, requiring automatic spending cuts if Congress cannot reduce burgeoning Federal deficit.
1986 Space shuttle *Challenger* explodes in midair over Florida, killing six astronauts and a civilian passenger (Jan. 28). Investigations reveal NASA relaxed safety regulations to speed up launch date. U.S. Navy repels attack by Libyan forces during maneuvers in Gulf of Sidra (Mar. 24). Pres. Reagan blames Libya for death of two Americans in terrorist bombing of West Berlin disco, then orders retaliatory air raids on Tripoli and Benghazi (Apr. 14). Second Reagan-Gorbachev summit in Reykjavik, Iceland, reaches impasse over arms control and "Star Wars" (Oct. 12). Congress approves sweeping revision of U.S. tax structure. Democrats regain control of Senate. Pres. Reagan denies trading arms for hostages as Iran-Contra scandal breaks (Nov. 19). Wall Street financier Ivan Boesky fined $100 million for illegal insider trading on stock market.
1987 Pres. Reagan submits first trillion-dollar U.S. budget to Congress as national debt mounts steadily. Stock market closes above 2000 for first time in U.S. history. Tower Commission inquiry into Iran-Contra affair criticizes White House staff and Pres. Reagan's "management style." U.S.-Japan trade war erupts. After Pres. Reagan orders U.S. Navy into Persian Gulf to escort Kuwaiti oil tankers, an Iraqi warplane accidentally attacks USS *Stark*, killing 37 sailors (May 27). Bernhard Goetz acquitted of major charges in New York City "Subway Vigilante" shootings. Stock market crashes 508 points in one day, an all-time record, jolting markets around the world (Oct. 16). Third Reagan-Gorbachev summit in Washington produces agreement to dismantle medium-range missiles in Europe (Dec. 8).
1988 U.S. pressure on ruler Manuel Noriega to step down plunges Panama into economic turmoil. After Iran lays mines in Persian Gulf, U.S. Navy warships and planes destroy two Iranian oil platforms and repel Iranian counterattacks (Apr. 18–19). USS *Vincennes* accidentally shoots down Iranian passenger plane, killing 290 people (July 3). George Bush becomes first sitting vice president elected president since 1836. Terrorist bomb aboard Pan Am Flight 103 kills all 259 aboard, mostly Americans, and 11 on the ground in Lockerbie, Scotland (Dec. 21). Drexel Burnham Lambert agrees to pay all-time record $650 million penalty for securities fraud (Dec. 21).
1989 Exxon *Valdez* supertanker spills over 11 million gallons of oil off Alaska coast (Mar. 24). HUD scandal reveals fraud, mismanagement, and influence-peddling. House speaker Jim Wright and Democartic majority whip Tony Coelho resign over ethics violations. Supreme Court upholds the right to burn U.S. flag. Pres. Bush signs $300 billion savings-and-loan bailout (Aug. 9). Severe earthquake, second worst in U.S. history, inflicts $6 billion damage and leaves 62 dead in San Francisco Bay area (Oct. 17). L. Douglas Wilder of Virginia is the first black elected governor (Nov. 7). After Panama declares a "state of war" with the U.S., Pres. Bush sends 24,000 U.S. troops to overthrow the Noriega regime and install a popularly elected government (Dec. 20).
1990 After Iraq invades Kuwait (Aug. 2), U.S. launches Operation Desert Shield: more than 200,000 U.S. troops move into Saudi Arabia. The Navy blockades all oil exports from Iraq and all imports except food. Pres. Bush refuses any compromise with Iraq's dictator, Saddam Hussein, and works with U.N. Security Council to condemn invasion and impose stringent economic sanctions. Bush and Gorbachev meet twice: U.S. agrees to some economic aid, grants USSR most favored nation trade status. Pres. Bush breaks campaign pledge of "no new taxes." A major flaw in the $1.5 bil. Hubble Space Telescope is discovered shortly after its deployment. Drexel Burnham Lambert defaults on $100 mil. in loans; Michael Milken, head of junk bond department, is fined $600 mil. and sentenced to jail.
1991 U.S. Operation Desert Storm quickly and decisively drives Iraq's armed forces out of Kuwait. The ground war lasts only 100 hours. Bush and Gorbachev sign first nuclear arms reduction treaty (July 31) as U.S.S.R. continues to crumble. U.S. establishes diplomatic relations with former Soviet republics, Estonia, Latvia, and Lithuania. Unemployment rate rises to highest level in a decade. Interest rates are cut to lowest levels in 20 years. Senate's confirmation of Clarence Thomas's nomination to the Supreme Court is delayed by Anita Hill's luridly detailed charges (Oct. 6) of sexual harassment 10 years earlier. Oliver North and John Poindexter are exonerated in connection with the Iran-contra scandal. Four white Los Angeles policemen indicted for videotaped beating of black motorist Rodney King.
1992 The Americans with Disabilities Act, the most sweeping anti-discrimination legislation since the Civil Rights Act of 1964 guarantees equal access for the disabled (Jan. 26). Pres. Bush and

Russian Pres. Boris Yeltsin issue joint statement officially ending the cold war (Feb.1). Riots erupt in Los Angeles after an all-white jury acquits four L.A. police officers of beating Rodney King (April 29-May 4); more than 50 people are killed, 2,000 injured, and over 7,000 arrested. Federal Reserve cuts discount rate to 3 percent, its lowest rate since 1963, after unemployment skyrockets to 7.8 percent, its highest level since 1983. Bill Clinton defeats Pres. George Bush and billionaire-populist third-party candidate Ross Perot to become the 42nd President. Pres. Bush commits at least 28,000 U.S. troops to protect the delivery of relief supplies to Somalia (Dec. 3). IBM announces it will cut 25,000 more jobs in 1993 in the wake of $6 billion losses, the biggest loss ever for an American corporation. Pres. Bush pardons six Reagan Administration officials for their involvement in the Iran-Contra scandal.

1993 More than 120 nations, including the U.S. and Russia, agree to ban production, stockpiling, and use of all chemical weapons and to destroy them all within 10 years. Hillary Rodham Clinton becomes the first First Lady to have an office in the White House. She chairs a committee to overhaul the nation's health care system. Sears Roebuck and Co. ceases publication of the Sears Catalog after 97 years. Family Leave Act guarantees workers up to 12 weeks of unpaid leave for medical emergencies. A car bomb rips through the garage at New York's World Trade Center, killing 7, and injuring 1,000 (Feb. 26). Four federal agents are killed in a gunfight with cult leader David Koresh. After a 51-day standoff, Koresh sets the buildings on fire, killing himself and 86 followers (April 19). "The worst storm of the century" according to the National Weather Service pelts the mid-Atlantic and Northeast with as much as 40 inches of snow, killing at least 104 people. The Supreme Court rules (9-0) that public school systems must permit religious groups to use their buildings after hours if they allow community groups to do so. Law enforcement officials root out a Muslim extremist group plotting to bomb the UN, federal office buildings, and the Lincoln and Holland tunnels, and to assassinate prominent politicians (June 24). The Supreme Court rules (5-4) that legislative districts drawn to increase black representation can violate the constitutional rights of white voters. Pres. Clinton signs the Brady Bill, requiring background checks before gun purchases. The U.S. and Europe sign the General Agreement of Tariffs and Trade (GATT), substantially reducing tariffs on trade. The Pentagon rules that gays and lesbians may serve in the military, but may not proclaim their sexual orientation. Astronauts restore full vision to the Hubble Space Telescope.

1994 Federated Department Stores acquires R.H. Macy & Company, creating the largest department store chain in America. Iran-contra prosecutor Lawrence E. Walsh finds no evidence that Pres. Reagan or Vice Pres. Bush broke the law. All four men on trial for the World Trade Center bombing are found guilty and sentenced to 240 years in prison. Rodney King wins $3.8 mil. in damages for his 1991 beating by the L.A. police. L.A. police charge former football star O.J. Simpson with murdering his ex-wife Nicole Brown and Ron Goldman. Simpson leads police on a bizarre 60-mile low-speed car chase (televised live on all major networks) before surrendering (June 17). The dollar dips below 100 Japanese yen, a post-World War II low (June 21). Major league baseball players' strike results in the cancellation of the World Series for the first time ever (Aug. 11). The number of inmates in U.S. prisons tops one million, giving the U.S. the highest incarceration rate in the world. Republicans take control of both Houses of Congress for the first time in 40 years (Nov. 8).

1995 The Congressional Accountability Act ends Congress's exemption from laws against workplace harassment and discrimination. A federal judge issues an injunction against major league baseball owners for unfair labor practices, ending the longest players' strike in sports history. A massive car bomb blows up a Federal building in Oklahoma City, killing 169 people (April 19). The Supreme Court (5-4) overturns term limits on Congressional offices in 23 states, and rules (5-4) that affirmative action programs can only survive constitutional scrutiny if they are "narrowly tailored" to accomplish a "compelling governmental interest." The Walt Disney Company acquires Capital Cities/ABC. A federal grand jury indicts Timothy J. McVeigh and Terry L. Nichols on charges of blowing up the Oklahoma City Federal Building. The Chase Manhattan Corporation merges with the Chemical Banking Corporation, creating the largest bank in the nation. Sheik Omar Abdel Rahman and nine militant Muslim followers are convicted of conspiring to blowup the United Nations and assassinate political leaders. A mostly black Los Angeles jury finds O.J. Simpson not guilty of murdering his ex-wife Nicole Brown Simpson and Ron Goldman. (Oct. 3). Pres. Clinton dispatches 20,000 U.S. troops to Bosnia as part of an international deployment to end the four-year civil war in the Balkans.

1996 Congress votes to return hundreds of thousands of workers to their jobs and to reopen nonessential government offices that had closed for three weeks in the budget impasse. Pres. Clinton offers a plan to balance the budget within seven years, but promising smaller tax cuts (Jan. 5-6). The Hubble Space Telescope returns the first-ever images of Pluto, and pictures showing the existence of more than 50 billion galaxies, or five times the number previously thought to exist. According to the new information, the Sun is one of 100 billion stars in the Milky Way. Congress approves a vast bill rewriting laws governing the telecommunications industries, deregulating cable television, and increasing competition among local phone companies. The Liggett Group becomes the first U.S. cigarette manufacturer to agree to a settlement in a giant class action suit against the tobacco industry. Pres. Clinton signs the line-item veto, which allows the president to invalidate certain bills without negating entire packages of legislation. Pres. Clinton signs legislation allowing workers to take their health insurance with them when they change or leave jobs and to restrict insurers' ability to deny policies to workers with preexisting medical conditions. The worst drought since the Dust Bowl era of the 1930s plagues the southwest, bankrupting more than 10,000 farmers. The gap between the richest 20 percent of Americans and everybody else has reaches a postwar high (June 18). TWA Flight 800 explodes in midair, killing all 230 aboard (July 17). A pipe bomb blows up in Atlanta's Olympic Park during the Olympics, killing one woman and injuring more than 100. Pres. Clinton signs welfare reform legislation, ending more than 60 years of federal cash assistance (July 31). Pres. Clinton signs the Defense of Marriage Act, denying Federal recognition to same-sex marriages, (Sept. 21).

1997 The Dow Jones Industrial Average breaks 7,000 in Feb., and 8,000 in July. Mergers and acquisitions by major corporations reach record levels: notably Dean Witter and Morgan Stanley, Lockheed Martin and Northrup Grumman, World Com and MCI. Madeleine Albright becomes the first woman Sec. of State. A civil jury finds O.J. Simpson liable in the killings of his ex-wife and her friend and orders Simpson to pay $33.5 million in damages to their families. The Senate unanimously approves a very broad investigation into White House and Congressional campaign fund-raising (March 11). Comet Hale-Bopp, with its brilliant 31-million-mile tail, makes continuous appearances from March to May. The Senate approves (74-26) the Chemical Weapons Convention prohibiting the production and storage of poison gas. The Supreme Court rules unanimously that a sitting president can be sued for actions outside the scope of his official duties thereby allowing the Paula Jones sexual harassment suit to proceed. After a five-week trial, Timothy J. McVeigh is found guilty in the 1995 bombing of the Federal building in Oklahoma City that killed 168 (June 2); he is sentenced to death. A separate jury convicts Terry L. Nichols of conspiracy and manslaughter, but not murder; he is sentenced to life in prison. The tobacco industry agrees to pay $368.5 bil. over 25 years to compensate states for the cost of smoking-related illnesses. Mars Pathfinder, a robotic spacecraft, arrives on Mars (July 4), and sends back panoramic pictures of the landscape. IBM Computer, Deep Blue, defeats world chess champion Garry Kasparov. Atty. Gen. Janet Reno absolves Pres. Clinton of criminal wrongdoing because the Justice Department found no credible evidence he broke any campaign finance laws. The Hubble Space Telescope returns pictures of a star as bright as 10 million suns. Thirty Wall Street brokerages agree to pay $900 million to end a civil suit contending they conspired for years to fix prices on the Nasdaq stock market.

1998 Bill Clinton becomes the first sitting president to submit as a defendant in civil court when he denies charges that he sexually harassed Paula Jones when he was governor of Arkansas (Jan. 17) Under oath, and later in a national television address (Jan. 26), Clinton also denies having sexual relations with White House intern Monica Lewinsky. In exchange for immunity, Lewinsky later testifies that she had an affair with the president. Texas executes a woman, convicted murderer Karla Faye Tucker, for the first time since the Civil War. SBC Communications acquires Ameritech Corp. for $62 bil., creating the nation's largest local phone company. Astronomers detect a titanic explosion in the outer reaches of the cosmos rivaled only by the Big Bang. Pres. Clinton signs legislation to make the I.R.S. more friendly to citizens. The federal government and 20 states file antitrust lawsuits against Microsoft, accusing it of attempting to control access to the Internet. Pictures from the Hubble Space Telescope show the first image of a planet outside our solar system (May 28). Scientists break the code of the tuberculosis bacterium, a germ that kills more people in the world than any other infectious agent. The Supreme Court (6-3) overturns the Line Item Veto. Two powerful bombs explode outside the U.S. Embassies in Kenya and Tanzania, killing at least 190 people and wounding nearly 5,000 (Aug. 7). Pres. Clinton testifies that he had an "inappropriate" relationship with Monica Lewinsky. Later he goes on national TV to confess he had lied in January (Aug. 17). The Republican-controlled House Judiciary Committee votes along party lines to begin an impeachment investigation. Pres. Clinton announces a record budget surplus of about $70 bil., the first since 1969. The nation's four largest cigarette makers agree to pay $206 billion to resolve all remaining state claims over smoking-related health costs; the settlement does not shield them from punitive damages or class action suits. The House of Representatives, strictly along party lines, approves two articles of impeachment against Pres. Clinton: perjury and obstruction of justice (Dec. 19).

1999 The top two organizers of the 2002 Winter Olympics resign after investigators discover they bribed International Olympic Committee members in Salt Lake City's bid for the games. In the first presidential impeachment trial in 131 years, the Senate acquits Pres. Clinton on both articles of impeachment, falling short of even a majority vote on either charge (Feb. 12). NATO forces begin dropping bombs on Serbian forces occupying Kosovo (Mar. 24). Astronomers announce the detection of three large planets around a solar-type star, providing the first solid evidence that our solar system is no singular phenomenon (April 15). In the deadliest school massacre in U.S. history, two teenagers in Littleton, Colo. kill 12 students and one teacher (April 20). Texas Gov. George W. Bush declares he will not accept Federal matching funds, opting to use his $37 mil. campaign war chest instead. The FCC relaxes rules that had prevented a single company from owning multiple radio stations in the same city or from controlling too much of the cable industry; the decision allows AT&T to own more than a third of the nation's TV, phone, and high-speed Internet service franchises. Viacom Inc. acquires CBS Corp. for $37.3 billion. A Federal judge rules that integration of the Charlotte-Mecklenburg School District is no longer necessary, ending court-ordered busing approved by the Supreme Court in 1971 (Sept. 10). Senate Republicans again kill legislation to reform the nation's campaign finance system (Oct. 19). Congress repeals the 1933 Glass-Steagall Act, which had prevented the securities, banking, and insurance industries from expanding into one another's businesses. Thousands of demonstrators wreak havoc on a Seattle meeting of the World Trade Organization, protest the WTO's policies on the environment and international labor. A federal grand jury in New Mexico indicts Wen Ho Lee, a nuclear weapons engineer, on 59 counts of illegally removing highly classified material from the Los Alamos weapons laboratory. Jimmy Carter officially hands over control of the Panama Canal to Panama (Dec. 14).

2000 America Online buys Time Warner for $165 bil. in the biggest merger in history (Jan 10). The U.S. government concedes that workers making nuclear weapons have been exposed to dangerous radiation and chemicals (Jan 28). Illinois Gov. George Ryan halts all executions in his state citing a "shameful record of convicting innocent people and putting them on death row." (Jan 31). Four white New York City police officers are acquitted of all charges in the shooting of African immigrant Amadou Diallo (Feb 25). Two New York City police officers are convicted of covering up a brutal assault on Abner Louima (Mar 6). Two of the nation's largest and oldest newspaper companies, the Tribune Co. and the Times Mirror Co. merge. Armed U.S. immigration agents storm a

Miami house and remove six-year-old Cuban refugee Elián González so he can be returned to his father in Cuba (Apr 22). A Federal judge orders the breakup of Microsoft, saying the severe remedy was necessary because the software giant "has proved untrustworthy." Two rival groups of scientists announce that they have deciphered the human genome (June 26). The Supreme Court rules that the government cannot prohibit doctors from performing the so-called "partial-birth abortion," and that the Boy Scouts of America have a constitutional right to exclude gay members. Demand for electricity soars in California and the state nearly runs out of power. Vice Pres. Al Gore picks Connecticut Sen. Joseph Lieberman to be his running mate, the first time a Jew will be on the ticket of a major party. The Firestone tire company admits that millions of tires seemed prone to flinging off their treads and announces it will replace the 6.5 million tires still on the road (Aug. 9). The U.S. government agrees to drop virtually its entire case against Wen-Ho Lee, the Chinese-American scientist the F.B.I. had accused of stealing nuclear weapons secrets. The independent prosecutor in the Whitewater investigation concludes that there is insufficient evidence to show that Bill or Hillary Clinton committed any crimes (Sept. 20). The F.D.A. approves the marketing of the abortion-inducing pill RU486 (Sept. 28). The U.S. Navy destroyer *Cole*, refueling in Yemen, is rocked by a terrorist bomb, killing 17 sailors (Oct. 12). Hillary Rodham Clinton wins the New York Senate race, becoming the only First Lady ever to hold public office. Vice Pres. Al Gore holds a slim lead in the national popular vote for president, but the Electoral College remains undecided because Florida's outcome is too close to call. After a machine recount, Florida officials declare Bush to be the winner of the state's electoral votes but Democrats head to state court to contest the certification (Nov. 26). The Florida Supreme Court orders the immediate recount of disputed ballots across the state (Dec. 8). In its first-ever decision relating to a presidential election, a bitterly divided U.S. Supreme Court (5-4) ends the Florida recounts, handing the state, and thus the election, to Bush. (Dec. 1-12). Gore concedes the following day. The Supreme Court reaffirms the Fourth Amendment prohibition against unlawful searches and seizures in a ruling that bars police drug roadblocks. Pres. Clinton issues an executive order creating the largest U.S. nature preserve, encompassing 84 million acres around the northwestern Hawaiian Islands (Dec. 4). The Census Bureau announces that the U.S. population is 281,421,906 people, or more than 6 million above recent predictions.

2001 California begins rolling blackouts, affecting hundreds of thousands of people. Two teams of U.S. scientists report that they have slowed light to a stop and released it again (Jan. 17). In his final hours in office, Pres. Clinton issues pardons to more than 100 people. F.B.I. agent Robert Hanssen is arrested on charges of spying for Russia (Feb. 20). The U.S. bans imports of European animal products due to fears of foot-and-mouth disease (Mar. 13). A Chinese fighter jet collides with a U.S. Navy spy plane near the Chinese coast; after an emergency landing on Hainan island the U.S. crew is taken into Chinese custody (Apr. 1) and later released. California's largest utility files for bankruptcy (Apr. 6). The mayor of Cincinnati declares a state of emergency after violence spreads after the shooting of a black teenager by police (Apr. 12). The U.S. is voted off the U.N. Human Rights Commission (May 3). The F.B.I. says thousands of pages of materials about the Oklahoma City bombing were never given to Timothy J. McVeigh's defense lawyers (May 10). McVeigh is nevertheless executed (June 11). Congress passes a $1.35 trillion tax cut (May 26). A federal jury in New York convicts four men of conspiring with Osama bin Laden in the 1988 bombing of U.S. embassies in Kenya and Tanzania (May 29). The Bush administration says it will halt aerial bombing runs on the Puerto Rican island of Vieques by May 2003 (June 13). Arthur Andersen settles a civil fraud suit brought by the S.E.C. and has agreed to pay a $7 mil. penalty (June 20). The Federal Reserve cuts its benchmark interest rate for the sixth time this year (June 27). Surgeons in Louisville, Ky. announce that they have placed the fully implantable artificial heart in a human being (July 3). Pres. Bush allows tax dollars to be used for research into stem cells for human embryos, but limits usage to cells already extracted (Aug. 9). In the worst terrorist attack in U.S. history, hijackers crash two U.S. airliners into the World Trade Center, destroying both buildings and killing nearly 3,000 people. A third hijacked plane crashes into the Pentagon, and a fourth crashes in western Pennsylvania (Sept. 11). Pres. Bush blames Osama bin Laden, says he wants the Al Qaeda leader captured "dead or alive," and calls up 35,000 military reservists. The Taliban refuses to turn bin Laden over to U.S. authorities (Sept. 17). Pres. Bush pledges an attack on Afghanistan unless it surrenders bin Laden, and warns of a long campaign against terrorism (Sept. 20). Congress overwhelmingly passes a $15 billion package to bail out the ailing airlines industry. They also agree to set up an open-ended federal fund to compensate victims of the 9/11 attacks. Pres. Bush orders a freeze on all assets in the U.S. of suspected terrorist groups and individuals (Sept. 24). An employee of a South Florida tabloid publisher dies of inhalation anthrax (Oct. 5). The U.S. and Great Britain launch a series of air attacks against Afghanistan (Oct. 7). A letter filled with anthrax-laden powder contaminates a Senate office building and leads to 31 anthrax exposures (Oct. 15). The unemployment rate jumps to 5.4 percent in October, its highest level since 1996. The Justice Dept. and Microsoft settle their antitrust lawsuit. (Nov. 2). An American Airlines jet crashes in New York, killing all 260 people on board (Nov. 12). The U.S. and Russia pledge significant cuts in their nuclear arsenals over the next decade. Pres. Bush signs an executive order allowing foreigners accused of terrorism to be tried in special military tribunals. The Justice Department asks law enforcement offices to pick up and question 5,000 men, mostly from the Middle East, who entered the country legally in the last two years (Nov. 13). The Enron Corporation files the largest corporate bankruptcy in U.S. history (Dec. 2). The U.S. government files its first criminal charges related to the Sept. 11 attacks, against a French-Moroccan man believed to be the 20th hijacker (Dec. 11). Pres. Bush announces that America has formally withdrawn from the 1972 Antiballistic Missile treaty. (Dec. 13). American officials claim they have destroyed the Al Qaeda network in Afghanistan (Dec. 16). A man on an American Airlines flight is subdued by passengers after he tries to ignite explosives concealed in his shoes (Dec. 22).

2002 The U.S. begins transporting Taliban and Al Qaeda prisoners from Afghanistan to a detention center in Guantanamo Bay, Cuba. Pres. Bush says the Geneva Convention will apply to Taliban captives, but not to Al Qaeda detainees. A Massachusetts man is convicted of manslaughter in the beating death of another father in an argument over their sons' hockey practice. Pres. Bush faints and bruises his face after choking on a pretzel. Defrocked priest John Geoghan, accused of molesting 130 children over three decades, is sentenced to 10 years in prison for fondling a 10-year-old boy; the Boston Archidocese agrees to pay $10 million to the victims. Kmart files for bankruptcy protection in the largest ever filing by a retailer. Ken Lay resigns as Enron's chairman; he asserts his Fifth Amendment rights before the Senate Commerce Committee against charges that Enron executives intentionally inflated profits to enrich themselves at the expense of stockholders. In his first State of the Union address, Pres. Bush calls Iran, Iraq and North Korea the "axis of evil" (Jan. 23). Pres. Bush visits New York and restates his pledge to provide at least $20 billion in aid to help rebuild the city from the Sept. 11 attacks. The General Accounting Office sues Vice Pres. Dick Cheney for access to records from his energy policy meetings in 2001 (Feb. 22). U.S. officials say new evidence suggests that Osama bin Laden is still alive, but American intelligence doesn't know where he is. In hopes of propping up the ailing U.S. steel industry, Pres. Bush imposes tariffs of up to 30 percent on many types of imported steel. The *Journal of Genetic Counseling* reports that children of first cousins bear relatively little increased risk of birth defects. The Senate votes to prevent oil and gas drilling in the Arctic National Wildlife Refuge (Apr. 18). Congress passes a $100 million farm bill to raise subsidies to the largest grain and cotton farmers. After victims of sexual abuse by clergymen say the church is to blame, the U.S. Conference of Catholic Bishops decide to bar any priest who has ever abused a minor from ministerial duties. A federal jury in Houston convicts Arthur Andersen of obstruction of justice for shredding documents and impeding the Enron investigation (Jun. 15). The Supreme Court declares that the Constitution bars the execution of mentally retarded offenders, and that juries, rather than judges, must decide if a convicted murderer should get the death penalty. Acknowledging that they overstated cash flow by $7.1 billion, WorldCom submits the largest bankruptcy filing in U.S. history (Jul. 21). Pres. Bush vows "to hold people accountable." In two 5-4 decisions, the Supreme Court upholds a voucher plan to use public money for religious school tuition, and to permit random drug testing in public schools. (Jun. 27). The White House says the deficit will reach $165 billion in 2002, ending four years of budget surpluses (Jul. 12). Pfizer acquires Pharmacia for $60 billion, making it the world's largest drug company. American citizen John Walker Lindh pleads guilty to two felony counts and will serve 20 years in prison for conspiring with Afghanistan's Taliban to kill Americans (Jul. 15). Reviews of 11 locations in Afghanistan reveal that the U.S. air strikes there resulted in as many as 400 civilian deaths. The House of Representatives expels James A. Traficant (D-Ohio), who was convicted in April for bribery, racketeering and corruption. Rescue workers in Pennsylvania succeed in bringing nine trapped miners above ground to safety (Jul. 28). Surgeons at Mattel Children's Hospital at UCLA successfully separate twins joined at the head (Aug. 6) US Airways, the nation's sixth-largest airline, files for bankruptcy (Aug. 10). A federal appeals court in Cincinnati unanimously declares that the Bush administration illegally held hundreds of deportation hearings in secret (Aug. 26). The Senate votes (87-6) to allow airline pilots to carry guns in the cockpits (Sept. 5). Investigators reveal that Tyco agreed to pay chief financial officer Mark Swartz $44.8 million in severance, even after Swartz was indicted for defrauding investors of $600 million. Federal authorities arrest five Arab men outside Buffalo, N.Y., alleging that they were part of a terrorist cell operating in the U.S. (Sept. 13). The Census Bureau reports that the number of people living in poverty in the U.S. increased in 2001 for the first time in eight years (Sept. 24). The Senate votes (77-23) to authorize Pres. Bush to use military force against Iraq (Oct. 10). Former president Jimmy Carter receives the Nobel Peace Prize. The Bush administration says it will scrap the 1994 arms control accord with North Korea (Oct. 19). After a month-long manhunt, Maryland police arrest two men in connection with 10 sniper shootings around the Washington, D.C. area. A federal judge approves Microsoft's antitrust settlement with the Justice Dept., rejecting tougher sanctions sought by a coalition of state attorneys general. Republicans regain a majority control in the Senate, giving the G.O.P. control of all three branches of government. The U.S. gives the U.N. a final chance to disarm Iraq through weapons inspections or else face an American-led war invasion (Nov. 6). Nancy Pelosi (D-Calif.) becomes House Democratic leader; she is the first woman to head a party in Congress (Nov. 14). Congress approves creation of the Department of Homeland Security, expected to employ 170,000; Pres. Bush names former Pennsylvania governor Tom Ridge the first secretary. A joint Congressional committee on the Sept. 11 attacks reports that the F.B.I. and C.I.A. did not aggressively pursue leads that might have linked the terrorists to Saudi Arabia (Nov. 22). U.S. intelligence officials say they have evidence linking al Qaeda to the terrorist attacks in Mombasa, Kenya (Dec. 2). An international group of scientists reveal that the mouse genome and human genome are remarkably similar, a discovery that is expected to speed efforts to understand the human genome and the genetic roots of disease. Thirteen years after convicting five Harlem teens for the brutal rape of a Central Park jogger, prosecutors in New York reveal DNA evidence linking the attack to a serial rapist who had confessed to the crime in January, 2002 (Dec. 5). United Airlines, the nation's second-largest carrier, becomes the biggest airline ever to seek bankruptcy protection (Dec. 9). Boston's Cardinal Bernard F. Law becomes the highest-ranking American Catholic to lose his job because of a scandal. Over his 18-year tenure, Law repeatedly allowed sexually abusive priests to remain in the ministry, simply moving them from parish to parish without telling parishioners or law enforcement officials. Robert L. Johnson, the founder of Black Entertainment Television, becomes the first African-American to own a major sports franchise, After praising Strom Thurmond's 1948 segregationist presidential candidacy, Trent Lott (R-Miss.) loses his position as Senate majority leader to White house favorite Bill Frist (R-Tenn.). Nearly two dozen U.S. cities pass resolutions to prevent the federal government from violating civil liberties in its war against terrorism.

BIOGRAPHIES OF U.S. PRESIDENTS

1. George Washington (1789–97)

Born in Westmoreland County, Virginia, on Feb. 22, 1732, the first president, with a love for the land, trained as a surveyor in his teens. At age 16 he went to live with his brother Lawrence, who built Mount Vernon. Lawrence died only four years later, leaving his property to George, who went on to become one of Virginia's foremost landowners, ultimately acquiring more than 100,000 acres in Virginia and what is now West Virginia. In 1753 Washington joined the French and Indian War as an officer in the Virginia militia and fought bravely if poorly. The war provided Washington with the beginnings of his anti-British sentiments, exposing him to the arrogance of his British commanders. Upon returning to plantation life, and marrying Martha Custis, in 1759, Washington's resentment of the British was further fueled by their commercial restrictions. With the passage of the Stamp Act of 1765, Washington joined opposition to imperial rule in the Virginia House of Burgesses, becoming ever more active in resisting the British. He went as a delegate to the Continental Congress, which chose him to command the Continental Army when war with Britain broke out in 1775. Washington proved an uncommonly resourceful general, keeping his ragtag army together through years of defeat, retreat, and hard winters to outlast the British and finally prevail at Yorktown in 1781. Here, as in all his life, Washington earned respect for his judgment, dignity, and bearing. Retiring to Mount Vernon after the war, the general quashed suggestions that he assume military dictatorship of the fledgling republic, not wanting to subvert the very principles for which the Americans had fought. But because of his belief in a strong central government, Washington felt compelled to return to public life to salvage his country from the chaotic Articles of Confederation. In 1787 he presided over the Constitutional Convention in Philadelphia, which framed the presidency with him in mind, the only president ever elected unanimously in the electoral college (twice).

Washington's renowned judgment equaled the task of setting presidential precedent, for, as he wrote, "It is devoutly wished on my part, that these precedents may be fixed on true principles." His first act as president was to urge adoption of the Bill of Rights. Other notable achievements included national unity, quelling the Whiskey Rebellion, bolstering the treasury with a national bank, settling Jay's Treaty of commerce with Britain, and maintaining neutrality in the French Revolution. Washington successfully implemented executive power and quieted fears and suspicions of executive tyranny. But he regretted the rivalry between Thomas Jefferson and Alexander Hamilton, which led to the birth of political parties in his own cabinet; Washington feared that allegiance to "factions" would someday eclipse the guiding light of patriotism. After refusing a third term in 1796, Washington in his Farewell Address warned against party spirit, sectionalism, and "entangling alliances" with other nations. He died on Dec. 14, 1799, "first in war, first in peace, and first in the hearts of his countrymen," as his friend Henry Lee eulogized him.

2. John Adams (1797–1801)

A fifth-generation American directly descended from a Mayflower passenger, John Adams was born on Oct. 30, 1735, in Braintree, Massachusetts. At Harvard Adams considered the ministry but turned to law. He joined his cousin Sam Adams as an early opponent of the Stamp Act of 1765, organizing the Sons of Liberty and defending Americans accused of smuggling. Yet he also defended the British soldiers brought to trial for the Boston Massacre in 1770. In the Revolution, Adams persuaded the Continental Congress to commission George Washington as commander in chief, declare independence, and put stars and stripes on the flag. He wrote the Massachusetts state constitution in 1779 and negotiated peace with Britain in 1782. The first vice president, Adams called that position the "most insignificant office that ever the invention of man contrived or his imagination conceived."

Elected president as a Federalist in 1796, Adams retained Washington's cabinet, but Alexander Hamilton turned the party against him for refusing to make war on France. Adams built up the navy and kept the peace, but disaffecting the Federalists and signing the Alien and Sedition Acts (1798) politically weakened "His Rotundity." Adams lost the 1800 election to the increasingly popular Thomas Jefferson. The first president to reside in the White House, Adams lived to be 90, able to see his son John Quincy Adams elected the sixth president in 1824. John Adams died on the same day that Thomas Jefferson did: July 4, 1826, the 50th anniversary of the Declaration of Independence they both signed.

3. Thomas Jefferson (1801–09)

Thomas Jefferson was born on Apr. 13, 1743, in Albemarle County, Virginia, son of a self-made Virginian who died when Jefferson was 14. Jefferson graduated from William and Mary in 1762, began practicing law in 1767, and joined the Virginia House of Burgesses in 1769. With his pen Jefferson sharply criticized British rule, winning a place on Virginia's Committee of Correspondence to keep in touch with patriots in other colonies. His writings amassed great respect, earning him the right, as a delegate to the Continental Congress in 1776, to draft the Declaration of Independence. He then returned to Virginia as wartime governor, narrowly escaping capture when British troops destroyed his home. Congress sent Jefferson to Europe in 1784; he was minister to France during the Constitutional Convention and the early French Revolution, an event that affected him profoundly. As secretary of state under Washington, Jefferson's faith in democracy and states' rights clashed repeatedly with Alexander Hamilton's pursuit of central executive power. Jefferson resigned in 1793 and led opposition to the Federalists, whom Jefferson called "monarchists in principle." As vice president after 1796, Jefferson speeded the Federalists' downfall by secretly authoring the Kentucky Resolutions, critical of the Alien and Sedition Acts.

The House of Representatives chose Jefferson (ironically, with Hamilton's support) over Aaron Burr, whose electoral votes for president equaled his in 1800. "We are all Republicans—we are all Federalists," appealed Jefferson in his inaugural address, easing the transfer of power. In his first term, Jefferson slashed the budget, lowered taxes, reduced the national debt, and sent marines to fight Barbary pirates. Despite some concern over his constitutional authority to make the acquisition, Jefferson's greatest feat was the Louisiana Purchase from France in 1803, which doubled the size of the United States. "The less said about the constitutional difficulties, the better," wrote Jefferson, sending Lewis and Clark to explore the new lands. In his second term, Jefferson's unpopular Embargo Act (1807) was an attempt to avoid war with Britain or France, but it ruined American merchants. Retiring to Monticello in 1809, Jefferson busied himself with inventions and designing the University of Virginia. He died on the 50th anniversary of the Declaration of Independence, July 4, 1826. His broad interests spanned music, science, architecture, agronomy, and the classics, as well as politics and government.

4. James Madison (1809–17)

James Madison was born to a wealthy family on Mar. 16, 1751, in Port Conway, Virginia. A Princeton graduate, Madison attended the first Virginia state convention in 1776, drafting a bill that guaranteed religious liberty. As the youngest member of the Continental Congress in 1780, he led the movement to revise the Articles of Confederation. At the Constitutional Convention in Philadelphia in 1787, Madison's Virginia Plan became the pivot of discussion. Madison, dubbed the Father of the Constitution, tirelessly directed debate and applied his political wisdom. His voluminous notes provide the best record of the convention. Madison helped ratify the Constitution by coauthoring *The Federalist* (1787–88) with John Jay and Alexander Hamilton. A four-term congressman, Madison drafted the Bill of Rights and cofounded the Democratic-Republican party. In 1794 he married a young and ebullient widow, Dolley Payne Todd, an especially popular first lady. Madison led the opposition to the Federalists' Alien and Sedition Acts with the Virginia Resolutions, arguing the acts were unconstitutional attacks on liberty. Jefferson chose Madison as his secretary of state and later as his successor. Madison easily won the election of 1808. Britain and France preyed on American shipping throughout Madison's first term. Pushed by war hawks in Congress, Madison asked for a declaration of war to defend American rights against British outrages. Reelected despite numerous American defeats in the War of 1812, Madison barely escaped Washington as the British burned the White House. Yet he persisted in "Mr. Madison's War" until the Peace of Ghent (1814) and belated victory at New Orleans (1815) vindicated him. War expenses forced Madison to recharter the national bank and raise the tariff, contrary to his Jeffersonian principles. But by 1817 Madison could retire confident of secure independence, surging nationalism, and the total collapse of his Federalist opponents who had opposed the war. He died on June 28, 1836, having outlived all the Founding Fathers. Madison's presidency pales beside his greatest contributions—the Constitution and the Bill of Rights.

5. James Monroe (1817–25)

The last Revolutionary hero and member of the "Virginia Dynasty" to become president, James Monroe was born on Apr. 28, 1758, in Westmoreland County, Virginia. He left the College of William and Mary to answer the call to arms in 1775. Wounded at Trenton, Monroe fought courageously and rose to lieutenant colonel under Gen. Washington. He learned law as an aide to Thomas Jefferson, who helped Monroe into Congress and the Senate. Much diplomatic experience followed Monroe's appointment as minister to France in 1794. Governor of Virginia from 1799 to 1802, Monroe returned to Europe to negotiate the Louisiana Purchase and later served in Britain and Spain. James Madison appointed him secretary of state in 1811 and secretary of war in 1814. Chosen to succeed Madison, Monroe won the 1816 election and presided over the Era of Good Feeling, a period marked by minimal sectional or partisan discord. Monroe bought Florida from Spain in 1819, and his popularity survived the Panic of 1819 as well as rancorous debates over the admission of Missouri as a slave state. Monroe toured the nation to jubilant crowds, winning reelection with all but one electoral vote in 1820. John Quincy Adams, his secretary of state, suggested Monroe proclaim American opposition to European encroachment in the Western Hemisphere, which he did in 1823; decades later this became known as the Monroe Doctrine. After retiring, Monroe became a regent of the University of Virginia (1826) and a member of the Virginia constitutional convention of 1829. Because of lack of attention over the years, his private affairs had suffered greatly, and Monroe discovered he was lapsing into bankruptcy. He sold his plantation and died all but penniless on Independence Day, July 4, 1831.

6. John Quincy Adams (1825–29)

The first president's son to become president, John Quincy Adams was born on July 11, 1767, in Braintree, Massachusetts. A true child of the Revolution, Adams watched the Battle of Bunker Hill while holding his mother's hand, and he spent his teens in Europe with his father, John Adams, on diplomatic missions for the new nation. He entered Harvard in 1785, already an experienced diplomat fluent in seven languages. After a brief career as a Boston lawyer, Adams was minister to Holland in 1794 and to Prussia in 1797. As a Federalist, Adams was elected to the Senate in 1803, but after supporting Thomas Jefferson, he had to resign. James Madison made Adams minister to Russia in 1809, in time to witness Napoleon's invasion. Then Adams helped negotiate the Peace of Ghent (1814) before serving as ambassador to England, the second of three Adams generations to hold that post. James Monroe recalled Adams from Europe—where he had spent most of his life—to appoint him secretary of state in 1817, and in that post, Adams purchased Florida from Spain, patched relations with Britain, and conceived the Monroe Doctrine.

Running for president in 1824, Adams was beaten by Andrew Jackson in both popular and electoral votes; but with Henry Clay's support, the House of Representatives chose Adams for president. No one ever became president with less than Adams's 31 percent of the vote, yet he refused to conciliate his foes or even act like a politician. Adams posed above politics and made no effort to deal with Congress or use patronage. Consequently, elaborate plans for internal improvements and national academies came to naught. Adams, like his father, failed to win a second term, as Jackson gained revenge at the polls in 1828. Massachusetts rescued Adams from despair by sending him to Congress in 1830, and "Old Man Eloquent" remained a powerful antislavery leader until he collapsed on the floor of the House at age 80; he died in the Speaker's Room on Feb. 23, 1848. John Quincy Adams, who considered himself a failure as president, worked for the first 11 presidents and numbers among the most important architects of early American foreign policy.

7. Andrew Jackson (1829–37)

Born to Scotch-Irish immigrants in Waxhaw, South Carolina, on Mar. 15, 1767, Andrew Jackson was the first first-generation American to become president, as well as the first president from the western frontier and the first of seven to be born in a log cabin. Orphaned at 15, he was by then already a Revolutionary veteran, a former prisoner of war, and scarred by the saber of a British officer whose boots he refused to clean. Jackson read law and made his way to the Tennessee frontier, marrying Rachel Donelson Robards in 1791. She neglected to divorce her first husband, but Jackson challenged to a duel anyone who questioned his marriage, once even killing a man on the field of honor. Jackson's frontier law practice prospered, and Tennessee elected him its first congressman in 1796. He served only briefly in the Senate; Washington so disgusted the rough-hewn Jackson that he resigned. Back in Tennessee, Jackson became a respected judge and honorary major general of the militia. In the War of 1812, Jackson led troops to victory at the Battle of New Orleans (1815), his men routing British invaders twice their number.

"Old Hickory" was now a national icon, reentering the Senate in 1823 and running for president as a hero above party. Jackson won more popular and electoral votes than anyone in 1824 but lost when the election was thrown into the House and Henry Clay supported John Quincy Adams. Vowing revenge against the politicians, Jackson swept to victory in 1828 as the "people's choice" reform candidate. Jackson's wife died on the eve of his inauguration. As president, Jackson aggrandized the power of his office on behalf of the common man by expanding suffrage, rotating officeholders (the "spoils system"), and economizing in government. Under Jackson the Federal government completely paid off the national debt. Jackson vetoed Federal road-building and banking—yet he asserted Federal authority by ordering troops to South Carolina in the Nullification Crisis of 1832–33. The Whig party arose in opposition to "King Andrew I," especially to his high-handed veto of the national bank, but voters endorsed Jackson's war on privilege by reelecting him in 1832. In his second term, Jackson seized land from the Native Americans, ignoring the Supreme Court, and he recognized Texas in hopes of taking more land from Mexico. He became the first president to ride a train (1833) and to survive an assassination attempt (1835). After placing his friend Martin Van Buren in the White House, Jackson retired to the Hermitage, his plantation in Tennessee. He remained quite influential behind the scenes, persuading the Democrats to discard Van Buren and nominate James K. Polk in 1844. Jackson finally succumbed to dropsy and old wounds on June 8, 1845.

8. Martin Van Buren (1837–41)

The first president to have played no part in the Revolution, Martin Van Buren was born to a Dutch family in Kinderhook, New York, on Dec. 5, 1782. Apprenticed to a lawyer at 14, Van Buren took to law and politics—so well, in fact, that he came to be called the Little Magician. By 1821 staunch party loyalty elevated him to the Senate, where Van Buren led northern supporters of Andrew Jackson and guided his victory in 1828. Brief service as New York governor ended when Jackson appointed him secretary of state in 1829. Van Buren helped build the Democratic party, and Jackson made him vice president in 1832. As Jackson's heir apparent, Van Buren won the 1836 election, but two months after he took office, the Panic of 1837 launched a severe depression that spoiled his presidency. "Martin Van Ruin" responded by creating the independent treasury system, but his lack of popularity was beyond repair. He made enemies in the North by protecting slavery and in the South by refusing to annex Texas. Though the self-made son of an innkeeper, Van Buren was cast by his opponents as an aristocrat. In 1844 Van Buren lost the Democratic nomination when Jackson abandoned him over the Texas issue. Then, in 1848 Van Buren guaranteed a Democratic defeat by founding the Free Soil party and running for president, which split the decisive New York vote. Van Buren died a Unionist on July 24, 1862, the only president whose life touched both the Revolution and the Civil War.

9. William Henry Harrison (1841)

Son of a signatory of the Declaration of Independence and grandfather of a president, William Henry Harrison was born in Charles City County, Virginia, on Feb. 9, 1773. Campaign legend held that his birthplace was a log cabin, but in fact it was a plantation mansion. Harrison left medical school to join the army and fight Native Americans in the Northwest in 1791. After an illustrious military career, he served in Congress (1816–19), the U.S. Senate (1825–28), and as ambassador to Colombia (1828–29) before falling victim to Andrew Jackson's spoils system. Harrison fit Whig designs of defeating Jacksonians with a war hero of their own and received the Whig nomination to face Martin Van Buren in 1840. Harrison's campaign sidestepped issues to cast him as a plain frontiersman who guzzled hard cider while Van Buren sipped champagne. In the first modern election full of hoopla and hype, "Tippecanoe and Tyler Too"—the Whig slogan—linked Harrison's most famous victory with his obscure running mate. A huge turnout gave Harrison the victory at age 67, the oldest president until Ronald Reagan. Harrison delivered a record 8,500-word inaugural address hatless and coatless on a drizzly winter day. He caught a cold from which he never recovered and succumbed to pneumonia on Apr, 4, 1841. He was the first president to die in the White House—where he lived for only 31 days. His grandson, Benjamin Harrison, was the 23rd president.

10. John Tyler (1841–45)

The first vice president to become president by succession, the first president to see impeachment proposed against him, and the only president to change parties in office, John Tyler was born on Mar. 29, 1790, in Charles City County, Virginia. He was a Virginia legislator, congressman, senator, and governor before the Whigs chose him as William Henry Harrison's running mate in 1840. Though a strict constructionist and states' rights advocate, Tyler earned the Whigs' favor by opposing Andrew Jackson. But as president after Harrison's death, "His Accidency" earned their ire by vetoing, in mid-1842, two tariff bills vital to the Whig party. Eventually, his cabinet resigned and his party expelled him. Outraged members of Congress called for his impeachment. On July 10, 1842, John Minor Botts, a Whig representative from Richmond, Va., proposed the appointment of a special committee to investigate Tyler's conduct in office with an eye toward impeachment. The proposal was defeated on Jan. 10, 1843, by a vote of 127 to 83. This was the first time presidential impeachment proceedings were introduced in Congress. Tyler concluded the Webster-Ashburton Treaty (1842), which adjusted the northeastern boundary of the United States, and the Texas annexation (1845), but without popular or partisan support, he was powerless and decided against running for reelection. A veto on his last day in office became the first ever to be overridden. Tyler died on Jan. 18, 1862, awaiting his seat in the Confederate Congress.

11. James Knox Polk (1845–49)

The first dark-horse president, James Knox Polk was born in Mecklenburg County, North Carolina, on Nov. 2, 1795. A star orator in Tennessee politics, Polk idolized Andrew Jackson. "Young Hickory" took Jackson's old seat in Congress in 1825 and was reelected seven times. Polk was Speaker of the House from 1835 to 1839 and governor of Tennessee until 1841. He lost two bids for reelection, and his political career seemed over when the Democrats nominated him for president in 1844. Polk's name had not even appeared on the first seven ballots, but the deadlocked convention latched onto Polk as a pro-expansion dark horse. In the election he defeated Henry Clay by 1.5 percent of the vote on a platform that ignored slavery. From his inaugural address onward, Polk pursued expansion in the West. In 1846, he bluffed the British into believing the United States would go to war over Oregon, extracting a treaty for it. When Mexico attacked U.S. troops in disputed Texas territory, Polk called it an invasion and got a declaration of war. The ensuing Mexican War (1846–48) won California and the Southwest for the United States in the Treaty of Guadalupe-Hidalgo. Polk declined a second term, having fulfilled the nation's "Manifest Destiny" to span the continent. The last strong president before Abraham Lincoln, Polk added a million square miles to the United States. But the issue of slavery in the new territories split the Democrats and soon the whole country. "The presidency is not a bed of roses," complained Polk, who left the White House totally exhausted and died three months later, on June 15, 1849.

12. Zachary Taylor (1849–50)

Zachary Taylor, the first president to have no previous political experience, was born on Nov. 24, 1784, in Montebello, Virginia. His father was a colonel in the Revolutionary War, and Taylor—along with four brothers—served as a professional soldier for nearly 40 years. After distinguished service against the British and Native Americans, Gen. Taylor's finest hour came during the Mexican War, when he captured Monterrey and smashed Gen. Santa Ana's much larger army at the Battle of Buena Vista (1847). Though Taylor had never held office or even voted, the Whigs eagerly nominated "Old Rough and Ready" for president in 1848; Taylor, like William Henry Harrison, was an apolitical war hero above the slavery controversy. He won the election when the new Free Soil party siphoned off Democratic votes, but Taylor took office with Congress in chaos over the admission of California as a free state. Taylor opposed the Compromise of 1850 and probably would have vetoed it, but he died suddenly of acute indigestion on July 9, 1850. (A long, hot Fourth of July at Washington Monument ceremonies had no doubt contributed to his weakened state.) Backers of the compromise rejoiced that Taylor's death saved the Union. Taylor was both the last of eight slave owners and the last Whig to be elected president.

13. Millard Fillmore (1850–53)

Born in a log cabin on Jan. 7, 1800, Millard Fillmore was the son of a poor farmer in Locke Township, New York. Apprenticed to a cloth maker in his youth, Fillmore struggled for an education and got a job teaching even though he never attended college. Clerking for a judge taught Fillmore enough law to join the bar at age 23, and he became a prosperous New York attorney. Fillmore entered politics as an Anti-Mason and was a four-term congressman when the Whigs made him Zachary Taylor's vice president in 1848. Dignified good looks were Fillmore's main political asset; he was quite unprepared for the presidency when Taylor died suddenly in 1850. Fillmore delayed civil war another decade by signing the Compromise of 1850, but he lost the nomination in 1852 when the Whigs turned to Gen. Winfield Scott, yet another genial war hero and their last candidate. In 1856 Fillmore ran again for president as candidate of the American, or "Know Nothing," party. Fillmore hoped to unite the country behind anti-Catholicism and nativism, submerging the slavery issue, but he carried only Maryland. Though a Unionist in the Civil War, Fillmore denounced Abraham Lincoln and remained sharply critical of Republicans until his death on Mar. 8, 1874.

14. Franklin Pierce (1853–57)

Son of a Revolutionary War hero, Franklin Pierce was born in Hillsboro, New Hampshire, on Nov. 23, 1804—the first president born in the 19th century. A leader of Jacksonian Democrats in Congress in the 1830s, Pierce had been absent from national politics for a decade when the deadlocked Democratic convention nominated him for president on the 49th ballot in 1852. A dark horse candidate, Pierce won enough southern votes to defeat Gen. Winfield Scott, his Mexican War commander, becoming the youngest president as of that date. Pierce greatly hastened the coming of the Civil War by signing the Kansas-Nebraska Act (1854), which repealed the Missouri Compromise and reopened the dangerous issue of slavery expansion. He continually appeased the South by backing proslavery ruffians in "Bleeding Kansas," encouraging slavery expansionists who coveted Cuba, and buying the land known as the Gadsen Purchase from Mexico for a southern railroad. As a result Pierce's party lost elections to Republicans who charged that "slave power" controlled the White House. In 1856 Pierce became the only elected president to be denied his own party's renomination. During the Civil War, Pierce criticized the Emancipation Proclamation and was nearly lynched by angry New Englanders. He died a forgotten, depressed alcoholic, in Concord, New Hampshire, on Oct. 8, 1869, the only president from New Hampshire.

15. James Buchanan (1857–61)

Considered one of the worst presidents because of his lack of good judgment and moral courage, and also the only bachelor president, James Buchanan was born in Mercersburg, Pennsylvania, on Apr. 23, 1791. A lawyer and veteran of the War of 1812, Buchanan compiled more than 40 years of public service as legislator and diplomat.

The Democrats nominated Buchanan in 1856 largely because he was in England during the Kansas-Nebraska debate and thus remained untainted by either side of the issue. Millard Fillmore's "Know-Nothing" candidacy helped Buchanan defeat John C. Frémont, the first Republican candidate for president. Buchanan favored "popular sovereignty" over slavery in the territories and was the last of the Doughfaces, or northern politicians submissive to the South. Few Americans shared Buchanan's faith that the Supreme Court's Dred Scott decision (1857) would end conflict over slavery expansion "speedily and finally." When it did not, Buchanan tried to close the issue himself by urging that Kansas be admitted as a slave state—an even worse miscalculation. Democrats deserted him, and Republicans won the House in 1858, but Buchanan's vetoes and southern votes in the Senate stalemated the government. He inadvertently helped Abraham Lincoln win in 1860 by refusing to conciliate his own party. The secession crisis paralyzed Buchanan, who denied both the southern right to secede and the Federal government's right to do anything about it; he was relieved to hand Lincoln the reins. Buchanan died on June 1, 1868. On the day before, he predicted that "history will vindicate my memory," but historians continue mainly to denigrate him.

16. Abraham Lincoln (1861–65)

A largely unpopular president until he was assassinated (the first assassinated president), Abraham Lincoln was born in a log cabin in Hodgenville, Kentucky, on Feb. 12, 1809. He accumulated barely a year's total education while growing up, though he did learn to write and developed a fondness for reading. Family moves took him to Indiana and then to Illinois by the time he was 21. At age 19 Lincoln had worked his way down the Mississippi and came away appalled at slavery. He served in the Black Hawk War (1832) before losing an election for the state legislature. A failed storekeeper, Lincoln worked odd jobs while he taught himself law, sometimes walking 20 miles to borrow books. He finally made the state legislature in 1834 as a Whig, and in 1842 married Mary Todd, having canceled their engagement once before.

Elected to Congress in 1846, Lincoln denounced James K. Polk for precipitating the Mexican War. He returned to his Springfield, Ill., law practice after only one term. But the repeal of the Missouri Compromise shocked Lincoln back into politics, and he helped organize the Illinois Republicans. An unsuccessful candidate for the Senate in 1858, Lincoln drew national attention in debates with Stephen A. Douglas, the nation's leading Democrat. Lincoln was rewarded with his party's nomination for president in 1860, the least objectionable candidate among several more prominent Republicans. He defeated three opponents in the election, though his name did not even appear on the ballot in the South. As Southern states left the Union, Lincoln preached conciliation and promised no harm to slavery—but he vowed to crush secession and forced the issue at Ft. Sumter. After early reverses in the Civil War, Lincoln decided slavery had to be abolished altogether to restore the Union, and he issued the Emancipation Proclamation (1862). Lincoln's management of the war was thwarted by incompetent generals, feuding politicians, and his own inexperience, which matched that of his troops. Yet, like them, Lincoln learned on the job, settling on Ulysses S. Grant as his top general by 1864. The powers of the presidency expanded dramatically under Lincoln, who stretched the Constitution on behalf of the war effort. Lincoln defeated Gen. George McClellan for reelection in 1864, vowing to "bind up the nation's wounds." Before he had the chance, Lincoln was shot on Good Friday, five days after the war's end, by John Wilkes Booth, an arch-Confederate. Lincoln died the next morning, on Apr. 15, 1865. His martyrdom spurred the vengefulness of Reconstruction, ironically against Lincoln's own wishes. Millions of Americans lined the 1,700-mile route of Lincoln's funeral train, their mournful cries resounding all the way back to Illinois. Lincoln's prestige has grown with time, until many have come to regard him as the greatest president.

17. Andrew Johnson (1865–69)

The first president to be impeached, Andrew Johnson was born in Raleigh, North Carolina, on Dec. 29, 1808, the son of a poor laborer. No president could claim humbler origins: Johnson's father died when he was three, his mother worked as a washerwoman, and he never attended a day of school in his life. As a teenager he ran away to Tennessee, opened a successful tailor's shop, and got elected mayor of Greeneville by age 21. A fiery Democratic stump speaker, Johnson's attacks on Whigs and rich planters won him a seat in the state legislature in 1835 and in Congress in 1843, made him governor in 1853, and took him to the Senate in 1857. Alone among 22 southern senators, Johnson stayed loyal to the Union in 1861, though a mob of Virginians nearly lynched him for it. Lincoln appointed Johnson military governor of Tennessee, and he was nominated for vice president on the "National Union" ticket in 1864. Suddenly made president by Lincoln's assassination, Johnson vowed to carry on Lincoln's policy of leniency toward the South, but radical Republican opposition and his own coarse ineptitude led to serious clashes with Congress. Johnson vetoed 29 bills and was overridden 15 times, more than any other president to that time. A former slave owner, Johnson resisted Republican efforts to aid the freedmen. His only victory was the unpopular purchase of Alaska in 1867. Congress systematically stripped him of power until Johnson fought back by removing his disloyal secretary of war, Edwin M. Stanton. Impeached in the House for defying the Tenure of Office Act, Johnson was tried in the Senate and acquitted by a single vote on May 26, 1868. Few presidents were so stymied in office. Tennessee helped vindicate Johnson by making him the only former president elected to the Senate, he died a few months later, on July 31, 1875.

18. Ulysses S. Grant (1869–77)

A better general than president, Ulysses Simpson Grant was born in Point Pleasant, Ohio, on Apr. 27, 1822. Having barely passed West Point's height requirement for entrance, Grant attended the academy and graduated in the middle of his class in 1843. Fifty of Grant's classmates fought with or against him as Civil War generals. He served under Gen. Zachary Taylor in the Mexican War before marrying his sweetheart, Julia Dent, in 1848. Assigned to isolated posts after 1852, Grant grew bored away from his family and reportedly turned to heavy drinking. Finally resigning from the army in 1854, he went to Missouri, only to fail in farming and real estate. When the Civil War began, Grant was working in his younger brother's leather shop in Galena, Ill. He received a commission and rose rapidly to brigadier general. U.S. Grant acquired the nickname Unconditional Surrender for his string of western victories, notably at Vicksburg and Chattanooga in 1863. Once Abraham Lincoln made him supreme commander in 1864, Grant opened a relentless offensive that quickly ended the war. He personally accepted Gen. Robert E. Lee's surrender at Appomattox in 1865. After feuding with Andrew Johnson, Grant joined the Republicans and was elected president in 1868. Grant pressed radical Reconstruction in the South with mixed results. Corruption—notably the Jay Gould (1869), Crèdit Mobilier (1872), and Whiskey Ring (1875) scandals—marred Grant's presidency; nevertheless, he easily won reelection in 1872. The Panic of 1873 triggered a deep economic depression that dissuaded Grant from a third term in 1876. Reconsidering in 1880, he sought the Republican nomination again and nearly succeeded. Afterward Grant retired and went bankrupt. To provide for his family, he began writing his memoirs. Developing cancer, Grant valiantly hung on to finish the project, which would earn him some literary fame and his family half a million dollars. He died on July 23, 1885, just four days after completing his autobiography.

19. Rutherford B. Hayes (1877–81)

Rutherford Birchard Hayes was born a frail child on Oct. 4, 1822, in Delaware, Ohio, where he was raised by his mother. After attending Harvard Law School, he set up a successful Cincinnati law practice in 1849. Hayes defended fugitive slaves and helped found the Ohio Republicans. In 1852 he married Lucy Ware Webb, the first college graduate first lady. A decorated Civil War veteran, Hayes was wounded five times and promoted to general. From 1868 to 1876 he served as governor of Ohio. Republicans turned to Hayes as a scandal-free hero in 1876 and nominated him for president. He lost the election to Samuel Tilden of the Democrats, but Republicans in Congress disputed enough state vote totals to connive "Rutherfraud" into office with the support of southern Democrats. Hayes's first acts were to appoint an ex-Confederate to his cabinet and to withdraw Federal troops from the South. He never overcame the resulting stigma of political bargain, and facing a Democratic Congress, Hayes seemed destined for a weak presidency. Yet he put the nation back on the gold standard, put down railroad strikes, reformed the civil service, and banished liquor from the White House before keeping his promise to serve only one term. Hayes viewed the return of prosperity and Republican majorities in Congress as personal triumphs. He worked quietly for charitable causes until his death on Jan. 17, 1893.

20. James A. Garfield (1881)

The last log cabin president, James Abram Garfield was born near Orange, Ohio, on Nov. 19, 1831, and like Rutherford B. Hayes, Garfield was raised by his mother. Garfield graduated from Williams College in 1856, became a classics professor, president of Hiram College, a lawyer, and at age 30 the youngest Union general in the Civil War. Garfield left the battlefield in 1864 to enter Congress, where he remained until the Republicans nominated him for president in 1880, a dark-horse compromise between Grant and James G. Blaine. Garfield defeated Gen. Winfield Scott Hancock of the Democrats by 0.1 percent of the vote in a campaign stressing tariffs. Republicans immediately swarmed to Garfield, demanding patronage for their rival "Stalwart" and "Half-Breed" factions. After only four months in office, Garfield was shot in a train station by Charles J. Guiteau, a disappointed Stalwart office-seeker. Garfield died 80 days later, on Sept. 19, 1881, the second presidential assassination ending the second-shortest presidency. When hordes of Republican hopefuls had besieged the White House begging for jobs, Garfield had exclaimed: "My God! What is there in this place that a man should ever want to get in it?"

21. Chester A. Arthur (1881–85)

Chester Alan Arthur was born a preacher's son on Oct. 5, 1829, in Fairfield, Vermont. He grew up in Vermont and in New York to become an ardent abolitionist like his father. A true machine politician, Arthur worked for Republican candidates in New York and enjoyed several patronage jobs during the Civil War. Ulysses S. Grant appointed him collector of the port of New York in 1871, and Arthur prospered there until 1879, when Rutherford B. Hayes removed him in the name of reform. In 1880 "Half-Breed" Republicans nominated Arthur for vice president in a conciliatory gesture to his "Stalwart" faction. "The office of Vice President is a greater honor than I ever dreamed of attaining," he said. But Arthur acceded to the presidency on Sept. 19, 1881, when another Stalwart assassinated James A. Garfield. Perhaps shamed into supporting civil service reform, Arthur signed the Pendleton Act (1883) and rooted out post office graft. Democrats in Congress thwarted the rest of Arthur's initiatives; Republicans, whose calls for spoils Arthur ignored, denied him renomination in 1884. He lost a Senate race in New York and died two years later, on Nov. 18, 1886. Arthur was the last of three presidents in the single year 1881.

22, 24. Grover Cleveland (1885–89; 1893–97)

The only president to serve two nonconsecutive terms, Stephen Grover Cleveland was a minister's son, born in Caldwell, New Jersey, on Mar. 18, 1837. The family moved to New York, where Cleveland's uncle made him a lawyer. He showed scant interest in politics until Buffalo elected him mayor in 1881, and the next year Cleveland became governor. His war on corrupt Tammany Hall made Cleveland the perfect Democratic reform candidate for president in 1884. During the election campaign, backers of James G. Blaine, the Republican candidate, accused Cleveland of fathering an illegitimate child. He admitted it and won anyway—by 0.3 percent of the vote—but not before the Republicans came up with the immortal campaign chant "Ma! Ma! Where's my Pa?/Gone to the White House,/Ha! Ha! Ha!" The first Democratic president after the Civil War, Cleveland pushed for civil service reform and lower tariffs. In the first White House wedding, Cleveland married Frances Folsom in 1886. Cleveland cast over 300 vetoes—more than twice the combined total of all previous presidents. He cut Civil War pensions, seized 81 million acres of unused land from railroads, and signed the Interstate Commerce Act (1887). Defeated in the 1888 election, Cleveland claimed there was "no happier man in the United States"; yet four years later he won a rematch with Benjamin Harrison. Back in the White House, Cleveland underwent a secret operation to remove his cancerous upper jaw. His tight-money policies did nothing to help the depression after the Panic of 1893. Cleveland sent Federal troops to break up the Pullman strike (1894) and supported William McKinley, a Republican, for president in 1896. "I have tried so hard to do right," Cleveland said on his deathbed on June 24, 1908.

23. Benjamin Harrison (1889–93)

Benjamin Harrison was born on Aug. 20, 1833, at the North Bend, Ohio, farm of his grandfather William Henry Harrison, the ninth president. He took up the law in Indiana before joining the Union Army in 1862. Harrison finished the Civil War a brigadier general and returned to Indiana, where he was a prominent Republican, defeated for governor in 1876 but elected senator in 1881. A colorless compromise candidate for president, Harrison won the 1888 election despite receiving fewer popular votes than Grover Cleveland. Harrison bowed to the "Billion Dollar Congress" of free-spending Republicans who escalated Civil War pensions, transportation subsidies, naval construction, and spoils patronage. The McKinley Tariff, the Sherman Anti-Trust Act, the Sherman Silver Purchase Act (all 1890), and Secretary of State James G. Blaine's vigorous foreign policy were hallmarks of Harrison's administration, which oversaw the admission of six new states. Democrats won back Congress in 1890 and the White House in 1892, when Harrison lost to Cleveland in their rematch. A legal expert, Harrison taught at Stanford University and defended Venezuela in a boundary dispute with Britain before his death, on Mar. 13, 1901. Harrison referred to the White House as "my jail."

25. William McKinley (1897–1901)

The last Civil War veteran to become president, William McKinley was born in Niles, Ohio, on Jan. 29, 1843, son of an iron founder. A college dropout, McKinley was a post office clerk when the Civil War began. He volunteered as a private and mustered out as a 22-year-old major. McKinley studied law and was elected to Congress in 1876. A longtime Republican floor leader, he authored the record-high McKinley Tariff of 1890, before losing his seat that same year. Ohio millionaire Marcus Hanna, McKinley's political manager, engineered two governor's terms for him and funded McKinley's run for the presidency in 1896. William Jennings Bryan opposed him on a free-silver platform, but McKinley's dignified front porch campaign stressed sound money, tariffs, and the "full dinner pail." He won the election with the first popular majority since Grant's reelection. Strongly probusiness, McKinley raised the tariff still higher and reluctantly led the country into the Spanish-American War (1898). By acquiring the Philippines and other islands, the country became a world power under McKinley, who went on to proclaim the open-door policy in China. McKinley defeated Bryan by an even larger margin in 1900 and was enjoying great popularity when anarchist Leon Czolgosz shot him in Buffalo, N.Y. McKinley died two weeks later, on Sept. 14, 1901.

26. Theodore Roosevelt (1901–09)

Theodore Roosevelt was born in New York City on Oct. 27, 1858, the only president born there. A small, sickly child plagued by asthma, Roosevelt overcame a pampered youth to live the "strenuous life:" he boxed, hiked, hunted, rode horses, and climbed the Matterhorn. After graduating Phi Beta Kappa from Harvard in 1880, he attended Columbia Law School and became the youngest member of New York's legislature. Rich men of his day did not consider politics a suitable avocation, but Roosevelt desperately wanted "to be of the governing class." His first wife, Alice Hathaway Lee, died on the same day his mother died in 1884. Roosevelt wrote books and ran a cattle ranch in North Dakota until he married Edith Kermit Carow in 1886 and they moved to Oyster Bay, N.Y. During the Spanish-American War, Roosevelt left a job at the Navy Department in 1898 to lead the Rough Riders volunteer regiment in Cuba, achieving glory in the Battle of San Juan Hill. Elected governor of New York immediately upon returning home, Roosevelt was named William McKinley's running mate, in 1900. Roosevelt learned of McKinley's death while on a mountain-climbing expedition.

The youngest president at 42, "T.R." promised a Square Deal to close the gap between capital and labor. He mounted well-publicized campaigns against big business and successfully arbitrated major strikes. "Teddy's" popularity soared when he humbled billionaire J.P. Morgan in the Northern Securities case, and a record plurality reelected him in 1904. Roosevelt signed progressive laws to regulate railroads, inspect food and drugs, and create more than 150 million acres of national parks and forests. No less vigorous in foreign policy, Roosevelt's corollary to the Monroe Doctrine asserted the country would intervene to prevent European involvement in Latin America. For helping to end the RussoJapanese War, Roosevelt became the first American to win the Nobel Prize, but he considered the Panama Canal his greatest achievement. Roosevelt kept his pledge not to seek a third term in 1908—but in 1912 he ran against his chosen successor, William Howard Taft. Denied his party's nomination, Roosevelt survived an assassination attempt and won more than four million votes as the Progressive, or Bull Moose, candidate. During World War I, Roosevelt bitterly denounced the neutrality policy of Woodrow Wilson, who then denied Roosevelt's request to lead troops in France. While laying plans for another run at the White House, Roosevelt died suddenly of a cardiac embolism on Jan. 6, 1919. "No president has ever enjoyed himself as much as I have," he once said.

27. William Howard Taft (1909–13)

By far the largest president at over 330 pounds, William Howard Taft was born in Cincinnati, Ohio, on Sept. 15, 1857. He graduated from Yale in 1878, then followed his father into law and Republican politics: "I always had my plate right side up when offices were falling," Taft wrote. William McKinley sent him to govern the Philippines in 1900, and Theodore Roosevelt appointed him secretary of war in 1904. Taft traveled around the world as Roosevelt's personal emissary, becoming T.R.'s chosen successor in 1908. As president, Taft tried to carry on Roosevelt's policies, but he wrecked the Republican party by alienating progressives from conservative "Stand-Patters" over tariff and conservation issues. Taft initiated the income tax and pursued antitrust suits against big business—but generally he sided with wealthy interests. An infuriated Roosevelt challenged Taft unsuccessfully for the Republican nomination in 1912, then outpolled him in the election, giving Woodrow Wilson the victory. With eight electoral votes, Taft suffered the worst-ever defeat for an incumbent president. But the better part of his career lay ahead: Taft, always more comfortable as a jurist, taught law at Yale until he was appointed chief justice of the United States in

1921. He served with distinction, alternating a liberal nationalism in economic affairs with political and social conservatism. Taft died on Mar. 8, 1930. Never nostalgic for the White House, Taft once said, "I don't remember that I ever was president."

28. Woodrow Wilson (1913–21)

Born on Dec. 28, 1856, in Staunton, Virginia, the son of a Presbyterian minister, Thomas Woodrow Wilson grew up in Virginia, Georgia, South Carolina, and North Carolina—the first southern president since Andrew Jackson. Probably dyslexic, Wilson was slow to read; yet he became the most highly educated president. Graduated from Princeton in 1879, Wilson studied law before taking a Ph.D. in political science at Johns Hopkins in 1886. He taught at Bryn Mawr and Wesleyan University before Princeton appointed him professor in 1890. Wilson attracted the attention of Democratic bosses after he was elected Princeton's president in 1902, and they persuaded him to run for New Jersey governor in 1910. A strong progressive, Wilson won easily—and then turned on party bosses by sponsoring anti-machine reforms. In 1912 the Democrats nominated Wilson for president on the 46th ballot, and he won, with Theodore Roosevelt and William Howard Taft splitting the Republican vote.

Wilson's expert knowledge of government and strong party leadership pushed the Underwood Tariff, the Federal Reserve Act, the Federal Trade Commission, and the Clayton Antitrust Act through Congress by 1914. Restoring competition to the monopoly-plagued economy was the goal of Wilson's "New Freedom," until war in Europe made neutrality his top priority. German attacks on Allied ships carrying Americans strained Wilson's commitment, but he was narrowly reelected in 1916 on the slogan "He Kept Us Out of the War." After Germany spurned Wilson's mediation and resumed attacks on Allied shipping, Congress declared war at Wilson's behest in April 1917. World War I would "make the world safe for democracy," Wilson vowed, and he issued "Fourteen Points" for a just peace. After the armistice in November 1918, Wilson became the first president to visit Europe, when he attended the Paris peace conference that produced the Versailles Treaty. Wilson's dream of "peace without vengeance" was frustrated at Versailles, where he compromised away his Fourteen Points to obtain the League of Nations for collective security. In July 1919, Wilson returned home to face hostile Republicans in the Senate, where his treaty languished. On a nationwide speaking tour, Wilson collapsed from exhaustion in Colorado and suffered a paralytic stroke in October 1919. Wilson, all but incapacitated, refused to compromise as the Senate rejected the Versailles Treaty. Wilson's second wife, Edith Bolling Galt, whom he married in 1915, shielded the disabled president from the press and politicians until the end of his term in 1921. Woodrow Wilson died in his sleep on Feb. 3, 1924, frustrated by his own country's refusal to join the League of Nations.

29. Warren G. Harding (1921–23)

The first president born after the Civil War, Warren Gamaliel Harding was born in Blooming Grove, Ohio, which earlier had been named Corsica, on Nov. 2, 1865. He taught, studied law, and sold insurance before following his father into the newspaper business. Marriage to Florence DeWolfe, a wealthy widow, in 1891 helped finance Harding's paper, the Marion Star. A staunch Republican, Harding's probusiness editorials got him elected state senator and lieutenant governor. Although defeated for governor in 1910, Harding was elected senator four years later. Republicans turned to him in 1920 as a compromise candidate for president, the "best of the second-raters"; his good looks were expected to win over women first-time voters. Elected by an unprecedented 61 percent majority, Harding promised a return to "normalcy" for Americans tired of war and Woodrow Wilson. Harding's administration featured higher tariffs, lower taxes, and immigration restriction—but perhaps most notably, pervasive corruption and incompetence by Harding's crooked appointees. Harding was disturbed by the dishonesty of "my God-damn friends," two of whom committed suicide to avoid prosecution. While visiting San Francisco, Harding died suddenly of an embolism on Aug. 2, 1923. Scandals involving secret love affairs, official graft, and the vast Teapot Dome swindle erupted soon thereafter. Mrs. Harding zealously tracked down Harding's letters and destroyed them, leaving him the most enigmatic president, and certainly one of the worst.

30. Calvin Coolidge (1923–29)

The only president to share the nation's birthday, John Calvin Coolidge was born in Plymouth, Vermont, on July 4, 1872. Descended from a long line of New Englanders, he graduated from Amherst in 1895, practiced law in Massachusetts, and entered Republican politics in 1899. Coolidge rose slowly through a succession of state offices until he was elected governor of Massachusetts in 1918. Acclaimed for crushing the Boston police strike in 1919, Coolidge became the unexpected Republican vice-presidential nominee in 1920. After Warren G. Harding's death while still in office, Coolidge's own father swore him in as the new president. "Silent Cal" was the butt of jokes for his laconic utterances, but his minimalist approach to government fit the public mood, and he restored respectability to the White House, tainted by Harding's corrupt appointees and all-night poker parties. Instead of the whiskey that once flowed freely there, ice water in paper cups was served to visitors. Coolidge, untouched by leftover scandals, won the election in his own right in 1924. Pronouncing that the "business of America is business," he ushered in the heady years of Coolidge Prosperity, as the stock market soared higher and higher. Coolidge ignored foreign affairs and made frugality his trademark, slashing the budget at the expense of farmers and veterans, even driving out a White House cook who could not abide Coolidge's cost cutting. "It's a pretty good idea to get out when they still want you," Coolidge said, surprising the nation at the peak of his success by declining to run again in 1928. A popular president, Coolidge was safely out of politics when the Great Depression arrived. He died on Jan. 5, 1933, on the eve of the New Deal.

31. Herbert Hoover (1929–33)

Born in West Branch, Iowa, on Aug. 10, 1874, Herbert Clark Hoover was the first president from west of the Mississippi. Orphaned at eight and raised by Quaker relatives in Iowa and Oregon, Hoover joined the first graduating class of Stanford University in 1895. He became a world-famous mining engineer and a multimillionaire by age 40. In World War I, Hoover helped rescue

Americans stranded in Europe, distributed food supplies to occupied Belgium, and convinced the nation to save food ("Hooverize") for the war effort. Hoover was Woodrow Wilson's economic adviser at Versailles, and he organized relief for famine-struck Russia during the revolution. Joining the Republicans in 1919, Hoover earned prominence as the secretary of commerce in the 1920s and was elected president in 1928—the only electoral victory of his life. He promised a "chicken in every pot," but a few months later, the Wall Street crash brought on the Great Depression. Paralyzed by his conservative instincts, Hoover could not halt the spread of bank failures, bankruptcy, unemployment, and despair. Government should not get involved, he believed, and public relief would ruin American morals—so Hoover called for a balanced budget while promising the return of prosperity. He sent tanks to disperse veterans begging for pensions, and shantytowns across the country were dubbed Hoovervilles. Massively defeated by Franklin D. Roosevelt in 1932, Hoover called the New Deal "socialistic, collectivistic, fascistic and communistic." For decades Americans blamed Hoover for the depression and criticized his hard-hearted refusal to help the needy. Hoover lived another 31 years, the longest postpresidential lifespan, and he salvaged his reputation with more relief work after World War II. In retirement Hoover chaired two bipartisan commissions on government reorganization, issuing many important recommendations for Federal reform. Boulder Dam on the Colorado River was renamed to honor Hoover before he died, at age 90, on Oct. 20, 1964.

32. Franklin D. Roosevelt (1933–45)

The only president elected more than twice, Franklin Delano Roosevelt was born to a wealthy Hyde Park, New York, family on Jan. 30, 1882. He followed his cousin, Theodore Roosevelt, into Harvard and Columbia Law School—but not into the Republican party. F.D.R. was a Democratic state senator, assistant secretary of the navy, and nominee for vice president in 1920. Paralyzed by polio in 1921, Roosevelt learned to walk with braces and canes. As governor of New York after 1928, he pioneered unemployment relief in the Great Depression, earning him the Democratic nomination for president in 1932. Herbert Hoover, brooding and baffled by the depression, posed little challenge to the beaming, magnetic Roosevelt, who won the election by 23 million to 16 million votes. F.D.R. promised vague but bold experimentation ("above all, try something"), and as he took office in the worst inaugural crisis since Abraham Lincoln's, he assured Americans they had "nothing to fear but fear itself." F.D.R.'s first 100 days set a breakneck pace as compliant congressmen approved his New Deal for relief and recovery. Major landmarks were the National Industrial Recovery Act, the Agricultural Adjustment Act, the Tennessee Valley Authority, the Works Progress Administration, the National Labor Relations Act (Wagner Act), and the Social Security Act (1933–35). Though often contradictory and ineffective, the New Deal established the Federal government's responsibility for protecting farmers, workers, and the unemployed while actively regulating the economy to prevent another crash. F.D.R.'s high-profile "fireside chats," public works projects, and Social Security programs overcame despair and restored public confidence in the economy and government.

Reelected by a huge margin in 1936, Roosevelt proved incapable of ending the depression, as he ran afoul of the "nine old men" on the Supreme Court. Almost as many Americans called Roosevelt a Communist as praised him for rescuing the common man. Despite alienating many voters with his court-packing plan and "soak the rich" taxes, F.D.R. won an unprecedented third term in 1940. As war loomed in Europe, F.D.R. used his mastery of public opinion to lead Americans away from isolation, helping Britain with the destroyers-for-bases deal (1940) and Lend-Lease Act (1941) even before Pearl Harbor. World War II then occupied F.D.R.'s full attention as he shelved the New Deal and orchestrated the mammoth war effort. Roosevelt crisscrossed the globe to meet with Allied leaders and kept close personal control of diplomacy and grand strategy. He rallied a powerful sense of national purpose in the war, winning his fourth election in 1944. Together with Winston Churchill and Josef Stalin, F.D.R. planned a postwar peace of UN cooperation. Just after the Yalta Conference, Roosevelt died suddenly of a cerebral hemorrhage on Apr. 12, 1945, days before the war's end. His wife of 40 years, Eleanor Roosevelt, easily the most influential first lady, led her husband's campaign on behalf of disadvantaged Americans and continued it long after his death.

33. Harry S Truman (1945–53)

A plain midwestern farmer and World War I artilleryman, Harry S Truman (the S does not stand for a middle name) was born on May 8, 1884, in Lamar, Missouri. After his Kansas City haberdashery failed, Truman entered politics as a Democrat in the 1920s, and the local Pendergast machine arranged his election to the Senate as a New Dealer in 1934. National attention came to Truman when he headed a congressional committee investigating government waste during World War II. When Franklin D. Roosevelt needed a new vice president in 1944, he chose Truman. After only a few weeks in office, Truman had the presidency thrust upon him by Roosevelt's sudden death in April 1945. "Pray for me, boys," he told his first press conference. Utterly unprepared, Truman did not even know about the atomic bomb project, but he vowed to carry on Roosevelt's policies. Truman proved a remarkably capable chief executive. In his first four months, Truman approved the United Nations, accepted the German surrender, met with Allied leaders at Potsdam, and ordered atomic bombs dropped on Japan. As the Cold War commenced, Truman talked tough with the Soviets, accusing them of breaking agreements and intimidating helpless neighbors. In 1947 he proclaimed the Truman Doctrine, promising U.S. aid to threatened countries, and the Marshall Plan to aid European recovery and contain communism. The next year Truman ordered the Berlin airlift when the Soviets cut off West Berlin, and he promised to help Third World countries with the Point Four program. No less assertive at home, Truman made progress on civil rights, subdued restive unions, and prevented the Republican-controlled Congress from dismantling the New Deal—a specter that he effectively raised to win surprise reelection in 1948. Truman committed the country to the NATO alliance in 1949 and sent troops to South Korea when Communist armies invaded in 1950. But as Congress rejected Truman's ambitious Fair Deal domestic program and the Korean War bogged down, Truman's last years were barren. He had more vetoes overridden than all presidents but Andrew Johnson, and his poll ratings were lower than all but

Jimmy Carter's. Truman, who initially raised fears of subversion with his loyalty program, could not quell the Red Scare that swept his party from power in 1952, as Republicans hammered away on the theme that Democrats were "soft on communism." Truman was convinced that he saved the world from communism, prevented World War III, and could have won another term if he chose to run in 1952. "He did his damndest" was the only eulogy Harry Truman desired on his death, on Dec. 26, 1972. Out of favor when he left office, Truman gained rising respect after his death.

34. Dwight D. Eisenhower (1953–61)

The last war hero president, Dwight David Eisenhower was born in Denison, Texas, on Oct. 14, 1890, and grew up poor in Kansas. A military history buff, Eisenhower graduated with the 1915 class of West Point that produced 59 generals. He married Mamie Doud, his wife of 52 years, and spent World War I as a tank-training instructor. Eisenhower, only a major at age 40, rose rapidly during World War II, promoted past 350 senior officers to become commander of U.S. forces in Europe in 1942. By the end of 1944, he was the first U.S. five-star general and Supreme Allied Commander, taking the German surrender in May 1945. By that point a global celebrity, Eisenhower was army chief of staff until 1948, when he resigned to become president of Columbia University. Pres. Truman named him to command NATO forces in 1950, but two years later, Eisenhower retired again to take the Republican nomination and run for president against Adlai E. Stevenson.

"Ike" became perhaps the most popular president in U.S. history, though many questioned his lax work habits, detached management style, and baffling speeches. Prominent millionaires in Eisenhower's cabinet and archconservatives such as Sec. of State John Foster Dulles seemed to have free rein, and Eisenhower acquiesced in Sen. Joe McCarthy's wild charges of subversion. His administration stockpiled atomic weapons and promised "massive retaliation" against Soviet aggression—yet did nothing when the Red Army rolled into Hungary in 1956. Eisenhower did end the Korean War, concluded several alliance agreements, and cut the defense budget. The "Eisenhower Doctrine" promised U.S. aid to Middle Eastern countries fighting communism. When Britain, France, and Israel invaded the Suez Canal in 1956, Eisenhower led UN condemnation and forced them to withdraw, though he sent U.S. Marines into Lebanon two years later. He began heavy U.S. involvement in Vietnam by backing the French and then the puppet Diem regime. At home Eisenhower promised to scale back the government—yet he expanded Social Security; created the Department of Health, Education, and Welfare; and spent billions on public housing and freeways. He pointedly stressed religious devotion. The Supreme Court's *Brown* decision, which Eisenhower deeply regretted, inaugurated the civil rights movement. Eisenhower defeated Stevenson again in 1956, but Soviet domination of space, revolution in Cuba, embarrassment over the Soviets' shooting down of a U.S. spy plane, and his own ill health marred his second term. Eisenhower reluctantly sent paratroopers to enforce desegregation in Little Rock, Ark., in 1957. Democrats controlled Congress for all but two years of Eisenhower's presidency. In retirement Eisenhower approved of U.S. intervention in Vietnam and counseled presidents until his death on Mar. 28, 1969.

35. John F. Kennedy (1961–63)

The youngest man elected president, the only Roman Catholic, and the first born in the 20th century, John Fitzgerald Kennedy was born in Brookline, Massachusetts, on May 29, 1917, to a family of Irish politicos. His father, Joseph P. Kennedy, was ambassador to England and one of the richest men in America. Kennedy attended Dexter and Choate Academies, the London School of Economics, and Princeton before graduating from Harvard in 1940. A patrol boat commander in World War II, Kennedy was decorated for bravery in saving the lives of wounded crew members. Kennedy's father arranged his election to Congress, where he served three undistinguished terms before entering the Senate in 1952. In 1953, he married wealthy socialite Jacqueline Bouvier, and in 1957, he won the Pulitzer Prize for *Profiles in Courage*, a study of principled politicians. In 1960, running on a platform that lambasted Republicans for insufficient anticommunism and "vigor," Kennedy became the first candidate to utilize the presidential primary system to defeat three prominent opponents for the Democratic nomination. In the general election, Kennedy edged sitting vice president Richard M. Nixon by the narrowest of margins: 118,000 votes out of 69 million cast. The campaign was the first to feature televised presidential debates, in which Kennedy's poise, polish, and charisma were an invaluable asset.

During the campaign, Kennedy had pledged a New Frontier, but his social programs languished in Congress. Undaunted, he plunged into foreign affairs, his primary interest. Just after taking office, he approved the disastrous Bay of Pigs invasion, and a year later, he terrified the world by confronting the Soviets over the presence of their missiles in Cuba. He visited the Berlin Wall and expressed solidarity with Germans under the Russian gun. But he also set up the Washington-Moscow hotline, and signed the Nuclear Test Ban Treaty (1963).

Thousands of U.S. troops went to Vietnam as Kennedy escalated the commitment to containing communism. Kennedy vastly increased spending for defense and space programs, vowing to put a man on the Moon. He also engineered a $10 billion tax cut that eventually brought prosperity and increased revenues. As racial unrest spread, Kennedy cautiously supported the civil rights movement, introducing sweeping legislation that would not pass in his lifetime—nor would his plans for aid to education and medical care for the elderly reach fruition before his death. In a Dallas, Tex., motorcade on Nov. 22, 1963, he was fatally shot. Kennedy's alleged assassin, Lee Harvey Oswald, a left-wing ex-marine, was in turn murdered by Jack Ruby two days later. While doubts persisted that Oswald acted alone, Kennedy's martyrdom helped realize his legislative legacy, and subsequent revelation of his many peccadilloes have not tarnished the "Kennedy myth."

36. Lyndon B. Johnson (1963–69)

The eighth vice president to succeed by death of a president, Lyndon Baines Johnson was born on his father's Texas ranch near Stonewall on Aug. 27, 1908. He worked his way through Southwest Texas State Teachers College, taught briefly, then took a job in Washington—where he would live for all but two years until he left the White House. Government fascinated Johnson, and he reveled in making connections, marrying heiress Claudia Alta "Lady Bird" Taylor after a two-month courtship in 1934. An ardent New Dealer, Johnson won election to Congress as a Democrat in 1937. Reelected three times without opposition, Johnson became the first congressman to volunteer for combat in World War II, winning a Silver Star before returning to Washington. In 1948, on his second try, "Landslide Lyndon" was elected to the Senate by just 87 votes. Hard work and Texas oil money made Johnson the youngest Senate majority leader by 1955. A huge man, Johnson's powers of persuasion were legendary, but he failed in his bid for the Democratic nomination for president in 1960. Johnson accepted John F. Kennedy's offer of the vice presidency and campaigned hard in the South to aid their narrow victory. Made president a thousand days later by the tragedy in Dallas, Johnson vowed to continue Kennedy's programs, pushing them through Congress with surprising ease. Notable were the Civil Rights Act outlawing segregation and the Equal Opportunity Act, which declared "war on poverty." After less than a year in office, Johnson defeated Barry Goldwater by the biggest plurality in history.

Now president in his own right, Johnson unveiled plans for a Great Society free from poverty and discrimination and passed the Education Act, Medical Care Act, and the Voting Rights Act in 1965. But Johnson came to grief in Vietnam, where he broke his 1964 campaign promise not to send "American boys to fight Asian wars." Earlier administrations committed the U.S. to defending South Vietnam, but Johnson intervened massively to prove American credibility to allies and enemies alike. Following the Tonkin Gulf incident (1964), Johnson steadily expended American power and lives in Vietnam, but victory, or a means to achieve it, never came within reach—despite the presence of over half a million U.S. troops by 1968. Johnson's presidency unraveled as American losses mounted, antiwar protests grew strident, race riots exploded in inner cities across the nation, and the government developed a credibility gap. Virtually a prisoner of the White House, Johnson faced a war he could neither win nor leave behind and a nation more deeply divided than at any time since the Civil War. In March 1968 Johnson effectively resigned by announcing he would not seek another term. He retired to his sprawling Texas ranch and stayed out of politics until his death, on Jan. 22, 1973.

37. Richard M. Nixon (1969–74)

The only president to resign from office, Richard Milhous Nixon was born in Yorba Linda, California, to a poor Quaker family on Jan. 9, 1913. A graduate of Whittier College and Duke University Law School, Nixon married Thelma "Pat" Ryan in 1940, saw noncombat service in World War II, and rode into Congress on the Republican wave of 1946. He gained fame in the anti-Communist trial of Alger Hiss before entering the Senate in 1950. Dwight D. Eisenhower made Nixon his running mate in 1952, but Nixon was nearly forced to resign for accepting questionable contributions. He appealed for national exoneration in the televised "Checkers" speech. A well-traveled vice president, Nixon almost lost his life to hostile Latin American mobs in 1958, and he waged an impromptu debate in Moscow with Soviet premier Nikita Khrushchev in 1959. Eisenhower's obvious successor in 1960, Nixon narrowly lost the election to John F. Kennedy, and when he lost a California gubernatorial race in 1962, his career seemed over. Yet he practiced law in New York until the Republicans nominated him again in 1968. To a nation riven by the Vietnam War, Nixon promised "law and order," appealing to calm and unity against a background of riots, assassinations, and protest. Nixon defeated Hubert H. Humphrey with the smallest victor's share of the vote since 1912.

Vowing to "bring us together," Nixon tried to thwart the bureaucracy and Democrats in Congress by centralizing executive power. To control inflation, he ordered wage-price controls and devalued the dollar for the first time since the depression. Seeking "peace with honor" in Vietnam, Nixon built up the South Vietnamese army and withdrew U.S. troops—while massively escalating bombing of North Vietnam. Antiwar protests reached fever pitch when the United States invaded Cambodia in 1970. Nixon responded with appeals to the "silent majority," attacks on press freedom, and clandestine harassment of administration critics. High points of his first administration were the Apollo moon landing in 1969, Nixon's pathbreaking visit to China in 1972, and the first Strategic Arms Limitation Treaty with the Soviet Union. Twelve days after announcing "peace is at hand" in Vietnam, Nixon was reelected by a landslide, carrying an unprecedented 49 states. During the campaign five burglars were arrested in the Democratic party headquarters, and by early 1973, they were linked to the White House. The ensuing "Watergate" scandal exposed the Nixon administration's rampant corruption, illegality, and deceit. Nixon himself downplayed the scandal as mere politics, but when his aides resigned in disgrace, Nixon's role in ordering an illegal cover-up came to light in the press, courts, and congressional investigations. Nixon evaded taxes, accepted illicit campaign contributions, ordered secret bombings, and harassed opponents with executive agencies, wiretaps, and break-ins. Vice Pres. Spiro T. Agnew resigned in October 1973 for accepting bribes, but Nixon hung on to power, claiming, "I am not a crook," as the House began impeachment proceedings. Subpoenas and Supreme Court orders forced Nixon to release tapes of his White House conversations authorizing the Watergate cover-up. Ultimately, he resigned to avoid impeachment for obstruction of justice, abuse of power, and contempt of Congress. Claiming to have lost his "political base," Nixon announced his resignation on national television on Aug. 9, 1974. He never admitted wrongdoing, though he later conceded errors of judgment. Saved by a blanket pardon from Gerald R. Ford, his second vice president, Nixon retired to California, later moving to New Jersey. He dedicated the remainder of his life to unsullying his name, while becoming a foreign policy adviser to presidents until his death at the age of 81 in 1994.

38. Gerald R. Ford (1974–77)

The only vice president and president never elected to either office, Gerald Rudolph Ford was born in Omaha, Nebraska, on July 14, 1913. An Eagle Scout, he grew up in Michigan and attended the University of Michigan on a football scholarship, playing on the national championship teams of 1932 and 1933. After graduating in 1935, Ford coached football and boxing at Yale while attending law school. In the navy he earned 10 battle stars in the Pacific during World War II. Ford was elected to Congress in 1948 as a Republican. He would be reelected 12 times, never by less than 60 percent. His solid conservative record elevated him to House Republican minority leader by 1965. For supporting Richard M. Nixon, Ford was rewarded with the vice presidency in December

1973, replacing Spiro T. Agnew under the 25th Amendment. "I do not think the public would stand for it," Ford said at his confirmation hearings, when asked if he would ever pardon Nixon. For eight months Ford stayed loyal to Nixon, until his resignation made Ford the new president on Aug. 9, 1974. Ford announced "our long national nightmare is over," but a month later he shocked the nation by giving Nixon a blanket pardon. Ford denied any deal had been made, but his public standing never recovered. He struggled with huge Democratic majorities in Congress to stem soaring inflation and unemployment, casting 66 vetoes in all. In the Mayaguez incident, Ford sent the marines to rescue 39 Americans captured by Cambodia.

Breaking a 1973 pledge, Ford decided to seek reelection, and while campaigning, he survived two assassination attempts by California women. Ford was far behind Jimmy Carter in the polls, but he carried four more states than Carter in the election—which Ford lost by 57 electoral votes. It was the first defeat of an incumbent president since Herbert Hoover's.

39. Jimmy Carter (1977–81)

James Earl Carter, the first deep-southerner elected president in 128 years, was born in Plains, Georgia, on Oct. 1, 1924. He grew up on a farm with no plumbing or electricity but realized his dream of attending the U.S. Naval Academy. Carter graduated in 1946 and married Rosalynn Smith. He joined the submarine fleet and studied nuclear physics, leaving the Navy in 1953 to run the family peanut business. He was elected to the Georgia state senate in 1962. Defeated for governor in 1966, Carter campaigned constantly for the next four years, winning on his second try in 1970. Carter reorganized the government and hired more blacks, declaring that the "time for racial discrimination is over." A month before leaving office in 1974, Carter was the first Democrat to announce his candidacy for president in 1976, again campaigning constantly. "Jimmy Who?" burst into headlines by winning narrow pluralities over nine rivals in early primaries. Carter's grinning, homespun style and earnest vows of honesty ("I will never lie to you") struck a chord with voters after Watergate. Carter won the nomination and defeated incumbent Gerald R. Ford by 2 percent of the vote. Lack of Washington connections helped his candidacy but not his presidency, for Carter never shook his image as the provincial amateur. Democratic majorities in Congress ignored Carter's pleas for tax reform and a long-range energy policy. Transportation deregulation, environmental protection, and new departments of energy and education were Carter's main domestic achievements.

But as federal spending mounted and oil prices doubled, most Americans blamed Carter for runaway inflation. His 20 percent approval rating in August 1979 was the lowest ever recorded. In foreign affairs Carter obtained a Panama Canal treaty, normalized relations with China, and mediated the Camp David peace accords between Israel and Egypt. He moved toward closer relations with the Soviet Union, signing the SALT II treaty in 1979, but the Soviet invasion of Afghanistan led Carter to embargo grain sales to the USSR and to order a boycott of the 1980 Moscow Olympics. The Carter Doctrine announced the United States would defend the Persian Gulf, where ironically, Carter soon met his downfall in the Iran hostage crisis. Early public support for Carter's restraint gradually withered under the glare of relentless media coverage. Carter himself became a hostage of Iran, trapped in the White House as Edward Kennedy nearly deprived him of the Democratic nomination. In April 1980, Carter approved a military rescue mission whose tragic failure reinforced his image of incompetence and weakness, which Republican candidate Ronald Reagan exploited, winning the election in a landslide. Carter left the White House discredited, his informal style ridiculed as inappropriate. In later years he won recognition as a trustworthy international negotiator.

40. Ronald Reagan (1981–89)

Ronald Wilson Reagan was born in Tampico, Illinois, on Feb. 6, 1911. Reagan was a radio sports announcer when he made his first movie in 1937. Over 50 more films would follow in Reagan's prolific Hollywood career. In 1940 he married actress Jane Wyman, who divorced him in 1948. During World War II, Reagan made propaganda films for the U.S. Army, and after the war he became president of the Screen Actors Guild. Then a Democrat, Reagan assailed Communists in Hollywood. He married Nancy Davis, another actress, in 1952. As his movie career waned, Reagan espoused conservative causes, switching to the Republican party in 1960. Reagan made a dramatic speech at the end of the 1964 campaign, and despite his total lack of experience he was elected governor of California in 1966 by a million votes. As governor, Reagan broke all promises by raising taxes, increasing spending, and expanding the state government—yet he easily won reelection in 1970. He made unsuccessful runs for the Republican presidential nomination in 1968 and 1976 before winning it in 1980. He swept past Jimmy Carter in the crushing "Reagan Revolution" of 1980, carrying 44 states and making huge Republican gains in Congress.

"Reaganomics" promised to cut taxes and social spending while vastly increasing the defense budget and somehow balancing the budget. Congress was unmoved until Mar. 20, 1981, when a crazed youth named John Hinckley shot Reagan twice in the chest. Reagan's good humor and rapid recovery charmed Americans—especially the press, which had questioned his age and health. Reagan then prevailed over Congress to pass mammoth tax cuts. The national debt began its meteoric rise under Reagan as defense spending outweighed cuts in social programs. By 1986 the U.S. had become a net borrower for the first time since World War I, but falling oil prices slowed inflation and rekindled economic growth, for which Reagan took credit. Calling the Soviet Union an "evil empire," Reagan built up the armed forces, deployed U.S. nuclear missiles in Europe, and began the Strategic Defense Initiative. He sent U.S. Marines to Lebanon, where 240 of them died in a terrorist attack. To halt the spread of communism, Reagan ordered the invasion of Grenada and isolated the Sandinista government of Nicaragua. Reelected by another landslide in 1984, with the economy booming and his public esteem high, Reagan seemed headed for an even more successful second term. He ordered bombing raids on Libya and met with Soviet leader Mikhail Gorbachev, eventually producing historic arms control agreements. But in 1987 Reagan's invincible popularity finally succumbed to the Iran-Contra scandal: White House staff had secretly sold arms to Iran in hopes of freeing American hostages held in Lebanon, using the profits illegally to fund Contra fighters in Nicaragua. Many top Reagan aides had to resign, but more damaging was the president's apparent loss of control over his own administration.

Reagan left office with the highest approval rating of any departing president since FDR. As the Iran-Contra trials continued in 1990, Reagan was ordered to testify under oath about his role in the scandal; he responded 130 times with "I don't recall" or "I don't remember." In 1995, he revealed he was suffering from Alzheimer's disease.

41. George H. Bush (1989–93)

The first sitting vice president elected president in over 150 years, George Herbert Walker Bush was born in Milton, Massachusetts, on June 12, 1924. His father was former U.S. Senator Prescott Sheldon Bush (R-Conn., 1952-63) As a Navy pilot during World War II, Bush was shot down over the Pacific and rescued at sea. He married Barbara Pierce, a Smith College student, on Jan. 6, 1945, and graduated Phi Beta Kappa in economics from Yale in 1948. Bush spurned an offer from his millionaire father's Wall Street firm to pursue a career in the Texas oil fields that eventually made him a millionaire in his own right.

Running on a conservative anti-Communist and anti-civil rights platform, Bush won the Republican nomination for Senate in 1964 and again in 1970, but lost the general election both times. In between, he was elected to Congress from a wealthy suburban Houston district. Presidents Richard Nixon and Gerald Ford rewarded the Republican party loyalist with appointed offices, including U.S. ambassador to the United Nations (1971), chairman of the Republican National Committee (1973), and director of the C.I.A. (1976). After losing the Republican presidential nomination to Ronald Reagan in 1980, Bush accepted Reagan's offer to join him on the winning ticket.

One of the few members of Reagan's staff to emerge unscathed by the Iran-Contra affair, Bush bested Bob Dole for the Republican nomination in 1988. With Reagan's endorsement, Bush defeated Massachusetts governor Michael S. Dukakis, renewing the Reagan pledge of "no new taxes" and vowing to uphold the Reagan legacy of less government, strong defense, and family values. He declared war on "this scourge" of drugs by creating an office of National Drug Control Policy within the White House. Bush's first official act was to proclaim January 20 as the "National Day of Prayer."

Bush suffered early criticism for lack of leadership. For months, many key administration posts went unfilled, and the Senate rejected John Tower as Bush's nominee for defense secretary. But Bush struck back with major initiatives, including major arms control proposals and two summit meetings with Soviet premier Mikhail Gorbachev. In December 1989, Bush ordered the invasion of Panama, he said, to protect U.S. citizens and overthrow the regime of Gen. Manuel Noriega.

As one eastern bloc country after another opted for democracy in 1989 and 1990, Bush enjoyed the highest public approval rating of any postwar president. This popularity gave him the political leverage to renege on his campaign pledge of "no new taxes." His popularity rose to record levels when he ordered Operation Desert Storm to liberate Kuwait from Iraqi occupation. But it later became apparent that Bush had ordered a cease-fire much too early, allowing Saddam Hussein to retain power in Iraq.

Throughout 1991, as the Soviet Union was crumbling, Bush acted quickly and decisively to support those republics seeking independence, and to provide food and medical supplies where needed. He and Gorbachev declared an end to the arms race by signing the first nuclear arms reduction pact in July.

Bush had less success on the domestic front. In spring of 1992, his approval rating dipped below 40 percent, reflecting the deepening economic recession that drove unemployment levels to their highest level in a decade. Bush was challenged first in the primaries and then in the general election by opponents who made the economy the central issue of their campaigns. Bush survived a vicious attack from the right wing of his party to win the Republican nomination. But unable to get the economy on course, Bush lost to Bill Clinton in a three-way race that saw independent candidate Ross Perot capture nearly 20 percent of the vote. It marked only the 10th time that an incumbent president had been unseated.

42. Bill Clinton (1993–2001)

William Jefferson Clinton was born in tiny Hope, Arkansas, on Aug. 19, 1946. His father, William Jefferson Blythe 3d, was killed before his son was born, leaving his wife, Virginia, to raise their son alone. Four years later, she married Roger Clinton; Bill assumed his stepfather's surname. After graduating from Georgetown University, Bill Clinton went to Oxford University on a Rhodes scholarship and then to Yale Law School, where he met Hillary Rodham, whom he married in 1973.

Clinton was elected Arkansas attorney general in 1976, and two years later became the nation's youngest governor in 40 years. In 1980 he lost, a victim of the Reagan Republican landslide. But in 1982, Clinton won his old job back, and over the next decade helped Arkansas to transform its economy. He became a leading figure among the so-called New Democrats, who called for welfare reform, smaller government, and other Reagan-like ideas.

In 1992, Clinton emerged as a shaky frontrunner among six Democratic hopefuls for the presidential nomination. Allegations that he had extramarital affairs, dodged the draft during the Vietnam War, and smoked marijuana threatened to derail his campaign. But as the candidate with the most money and the best-articulated campaign strategy—creating more jobs—Clinton was able to stay in the race the longest, fending off all rivals long before the Democratic convention. In a three-way race against the incumbent George Bush and the billionaire populist Ross Perot, who ran as an independent, Clinton garnered 366 of the 538 electoral votes, despite winning only 43 percent of the popular vote.

Clinton entered office hoping that a Democratic president and a Democratic Congress could untangle the gridlock that had paralyzed Washington for 12 years. But his first act as president, a pledge to end the ban on lesbians and gay men in the armed forces, met with heavy resistance from top military leaders. And his economic stimulus package fell to defeat in the face of a remarkable Republican filibuster in the Senate.

During his second 100 days, he signed the family leave bill, lifted restrictions on abortion counseling at federally funded clinics, and laid the groundwork for the North American Free Trade Agreement. The passage of his first budget—with Vice Pres. Al Gore casting the deciding vote in the Senate—started the nation on the road to recovery from the burden of the enormous deficits created by the Reagan and Bush administrations. In the ensuing economic prosperity, the 5 to 8 percent increase on the tax rates of the wealthiest Americans as well as a surge in capital gains taxes from the booming stock markets generated so much income for the Treasury that deficits turned to surpluses by 1998.

Clinton had several early successes on the foreign policy front, assuring the stability of Russia's government, and negotiating a peace treaty between Israel and the P.L.O. that recognized Palestinian self-rule in Gaza and part of the West Bank. Clinton's handling of the escalating conflict in Bosnia (placing the issue in the hands of the U.N.) allowed him to avoid engagement while placing the responsibility for inaction squarely on the European nations.

On the domestic front, however, Clinton found little support for his programs. A complex plan (devised by a committee headed by First Lady Hillary Rodham Clinton) called for guaranteed health coverage to all Americans. But it also promised a huge government bureaucracy that opponents claimed would be less efficient than the post office. Politicians of all stripes responded with half a dozen rival plans, with the end result that no reform took place.

In the 1994 midterm elections, the G.O.P. captured both Houses of Congress for the first time in more than 40 years. New House Speaker Newt Gingrich proclaimed a Republican revolution, and Clinton barely raised a contrary voice. In 1995 Republicans in Congress also opened hearings on the Clintons' controversial investment in a land deal known as Whitewater.

As he prepared for a second term, Clinton's approval ratings rebounded. He took centrist positions on issues like abortion and affirmative action, and signed the Republican welfare bill that ended 60-year-old guarantees for poor people. With the stock market soaring, unemployment falling, and inflation firmly in check, Clinton won re-election almost effortlessly against Senator Bob Dole.

During Clinton's second term, the Whitewater scandal came back to haunt him in an unexpected way. Failing to uncover anything directly implicating the President or Mrs. Clinton in connection with the land deal, independent counsel Kenneth Starr expanded his inquiry far beyond its original scope and unearthed evidence of an affair between Clinton and a young White House intern, Monica Lewinsky. Clinton emphatically denied the allegation, and then, as the first sitting president ever subpoenaed to testify before a federal grand jury, he lied under oath about the affair. Clinton later admitted that he had had an "inappropriate" relationship with Monica Lewinsky.

Clinton's admission did little to hurt his approval ratings, which remained high, because of the strong economy. In the 1998 elections, Democrats gained five seats in the House. Despite polls indicating that an overwhelming majority of Americans wanted Congress to drop the Lewinsky matter, the Republican-controlled House approved two articles of impeachment articles—perjury and obstruction of justice—against Clinton, making him the first president impeached since Andrew Johnson in 1868. The month-long Senate trial was filled with legal wrangling on all sides, but in the end, not even a simple majority could be mustered for either impeachment article, far short of the two-thirds needed for conviction.

The day after his acquittal, Clinton sent 4,000 troops to Kosovo as part of a NATO peacekeeping force. Congress approved more than $12 billion to fund the action, and after 72 days of air strikes, Serbian Pres. Slobodan Milosevic agreed to withdraw all military forces from Kosovo. On the domestic front, Clinton and the Republican Congress battled over how to spend the first budget surplus since 1969, resulting in a stalemate whose effect was that the money went to paying off the most important component of the national debt: the $3.6 trillion in Treasury bonds.

Clinton spent much of his final year on a global "farewell tour" trying to shore up his legacy. He successfully shepherded a bill through Congress granting China permanent trade status, but was unable to broker a lasting peace in the Middle East, despite a major summit at Camp David with Palestinian leader Yasir Araft and Israeli Prime Minister Ehud Barak.

Clinton stayed in the spotlight even after he left office. Hillary's brother Hugh Rodham was found to have accepted $400,000 in return for lobbying for presidential pardons for two felons. More troubling, however, was Clinton's last-minute pardon of fugitive businessman Marc Rich, wanted for years on charges of tax evasion and illegal business deals with Iran.

43. George W. Bush (2001-)

The election of George Walker Bush in 2000 was unusual in several ways. Like John Quincy Adams, the only other son of a president to win the White House, Bush lost the popular vote (by some 500,000 votes to Vice Pres. Al Gore). And he didn't capture a majority in the Electoral College until five weeks after the election, when the U.S. Supreme Court, in an unprecedented ruling on a state election process, voted 5-4 to suspend recounts in Florida, which Bush appeared to win by less than 1,000 votes.

Bush was born on July 6, 1946 in New Haven, Connecticut. His family moved to Texas when he was nearly 2, but in the family tradition, he went back east for prep school (at Phillips Andover), and then to Yale University, where he had an undistinguished academic career.

In 1968, at the height of the Vietnam War, Bush entered the Texas National Guard and spent two years learning to fly. His sudden departure from that unit has never been fully explained. In 1973 he attended Harvard Business School, received an M.B.A. in 1975 and returned to Texas to enter the oil business.

After marrying Laura Welch in 1977, he made his first bid for public office, a 1978 campaign for a Congressional seat, which ended in defeat. After the campaign, Bush returned to his oil business, amassing a great personal fortune even though his business steadily lost money until it was bought out in 1986. Meanwhile Bush's parents set up a 1985 meeting with evangelist Billy Graham, which ultimately led the younger Bush to give up alcohol and devote himself to a more serious practice of Christianity. In 1989, he joined a family friend in purchasing the Texas Rangers baseball team, paying his share with funds borrowed against stock in his former oil company.

In 1994, Bush surprisingly challenged Ann Richards, the popular incumbent governor of Texas. Despite his lack of political experience,

Bush's down-home style won him the office. Four years later, he became the first Texas governor elected to a second consecutive four-year term. That same year, he and his partners sold the Rangers, with the governor realizing a profit of more than $14 million.

Advisers convinced him that 2000 was the right time to run for president. He had more than enough money, and the Republican party lacked any single strong candidate. Before he had even committed to the race, he was the clear favorite in the polls and huge sums of money flowed into his campaign treasury from corporations and wealthy Republicans. Bush lost the New Hampshire primary in a bruising, bitter fight with Senator John McCain of Arizona, but he rebounded to capture 9 of 13 Super Tuesday states, effectively clinching the nomination. In the general election, Bush's campaign promised to restore dignity to the White House and pledged a huge tax cut intended to give a large part of the projected budget surplus back to the taxpayers.

In the general election Bush and Vice Pres. Al Gore both tried to appeal to moderate voters, Bush calling himself a "compassionate conservative," Gore pledging to preserve Social Security. Although Gore unquestionably won the national popular vote, Florida (with its 25 votes in the Electoral College) held the key to the election. After two recounts and the counting of absentee ballots, Bush led in Florida by fewer than 1,000 votes out of six million cast, but allegations of confusing ballots, defective voting machines, faulty absentee ballots from the military, and illegal barring of many voters threw the process into chaos. Bush remained calm, almost aloof during this time as his supporters continued to assert that he had won the election. The race finally ended on December 12, when the U.S. Supreme Court ordered an end to the recounts, delivering Florida and the White House to Bush. Gore conceded the next day.

Bush's first 100 days in office were less bipartisan than he pledged during the campaign. His cabinet appointees were largely Republicans from his father's staff, but his appointment of fundamentalist Christian John Ashcroft as attorney general proved very controversial. Democrats vigorously opposed Ashcroft for his strong right-wing positions on issues like abortion and the death penalty, but they eventually confirmed him. On his first day in office, Bush moved to block federal aid to foreign groups that offered counseling or any other assistance to women in obtaining abortions. Days later, he announced his commitment to channeling more federal aid to faith-based service organizations, raising fears that the traditional separation of church and state would disappear.

He angered environmentalists, first reneging on a campaign pledge to regulate carbon dixoide emissions by U.S. power plants, then refusing to join the Kyoto accord to prevent global warming, and finally pursuing an energy policy short on conservation and long on drilling for oil and gas in Alaska.

The Republicans lost control of the Senate in June, 2001, when Vermont's James Jeffords quit the Republican party to become an Independent, but not before five Senate Democrats crossed party lines to approve Bush's $1.35 billion tax cut. Less than three months later, however, the administration released budget projections that showed the budget surplus dwindling rapidly.

Within days the terrorist attacks of September 11th transformed the Bush presidency. Bush accused Osama bin Laden of masterminding the hijackings (urging his capture, "dead or alive"), and persuaded Congress (with only one dissenting vote) to give him "all necessary and appropriate force" to respond to the terrorist attacks. Bush vowed a U.S. military response that will demolish terrorist networks worldwide, and promised to "end" nations that harbored terrorists.

Since Afghanistan was known to be bin Laden's chief sponsor, in late October of 2001 the U.S. mounted an invasion, and with the help of troops from Afghanistan's rebel Northern Alliance, the attack routed the Taliban in less than three months. Bush's popularity ratings rose above 80 percent.

In his January 2002 State of the Union address, Bush shocked the international community by identifying Iran, Iraq and North Korea as "an axis of evil" that threatened the world although he offered no evidence that they were involved in the Sept. 11th attacks. Over the next year the administration redefined two centuries of U.S. policy by declaring it had the right to preemptively attack any nation that posed a threat to its security. Iraq became the first target of that doctrine and by the summer of 2002 Bush was urging the U.N. Security Council to approve military action to remove Saddam Hussein from power because he was building weapons of mass destruction. Over the next six months U.N. weapons inspectors sought out these weapons but found none and the U.N. proposed a continuation of inspections. Bush refused and on March 20 he ordered the world's most powerful military machine to launch a devastating attack (then called "shock and awe") on what proved to be a weak and disorganized Iraqi military. After only three weeks the U.S., with some help from Great Britain, toppled the regime but was now left alone to rebuild a devastated country. Within a few months Bush's approval ratings began to plummet in part because no weapons of mass destruction were found and credible evidence showed that the intelligence data had been grossly exaggerated.

Domestically Bush continued to press for deep tax cuts at the highest income levels and a way to stimulate a sluggish economy so deficits continued to soar. Although he first opposed a separate Dept. of Homeland Security as proposed by the Democrats Bush eventually agreed to approve it creating an enormous new government agency (more than 170,000 employees). Bush also approved the Patriot Act which despite overwhelming congressional approval brought strong criticism from civil libertarians for giving the Justice Dept. unprecedented powers in conducting investigations and interrogations of suspected terrorists.

For additional information about the Bush presidency, see Part I: "The Almanac of the Year."

Presidential Elections, 1796–2000

George Washington of Virginia ran unopposed for president in 1789 and 1792. He received 69 and 132 electoral votes in those years, respectively. John Adams of Massachusetts was elected vice president in both years, receiving 34 and 77 electoral votes.

1796

Party	Candidate	Popular vote	Percent	Electoral vote
Federalist	John Adams (Mass.)	N.A.	N.A.	71
	and Thomas Pinckney (S.C.)	N.A.	N.A.	59
Democratic-Republican	Thomas Jefferson (Va.)	N.A.	N.A.	68
	and Aaron Burr (N.Y.)	N.A.	N.A.	30

Key Issues Washington set a precedent by refusing to run for a third term. Though the Founders hoped to avoid parties, factions developed around Hamilton and Jefferson during Washington's first term. Hamilton's Federalists supported a strong central government that would play a major role in the national economy and represent the commercial interests of the north. Jefferson's Republicans advocated states' rights and the agrarian interests of the south. **Regional Influences** Though led by Hamilton, the Federalists nominated the more moderate Adams. Jefferson's strength in the south was balanced by Adams's power in the north. Eleven Federalist electors in New Hampshire failed to vote for Pinckney, their party's vice-presidential nominee, giving the position to Jefferson.

1800

Party	Candidate	Popular vote	Percent	Electoral vote
Democratic-Republican	Thomas Jefferson (Va.)	N.A.	N.A.	73
	and Aaron Burr (N.Y.)	N.A.	N.A.	73
Federalist	John Adams (Mass.)	N.A.	N.A.	65
	and Charles C. Pinckney (S.C.)	N.A.	N.A.	64
Federalist	John Jay (N.Y.)	N.A.	N.A.	1

Key Issues Adams divided the Federalists by keeping the U.S. out of war with France over seizures of American ships by the French. In the meantime the Republicans under Jefferson organized nationally. They accused the Federalists of aristocratic and monarchical leanings, citing large taxes levied to maintain a standing army and navy, the Alien and Sedition Acts seeking to silence the administration's critics, and suppression of the Whiskey Rebellion. **Regional Influences** The Republicans again carried the South, but also won New York through the efforts of vice-presidential nominee Burr. The election was thrown into the House when Jefferson and Burr received an equal number of electoral votes. With Hamilton's support, Jefferson won the election in the Federalist-dominated House.

1804

Party	Candidate	Popular vote	Percent	Electoral vote
Democratic-Republican	Thomas Jefferson (Va.)	N.A.	N.A.	162
	and George Clinton (N.Y.)	N.A.	N.A.	162
Federalist	Charles C. Pinckney (S.C.)	N.A.	N.A.	14
	and Rufus King (N.Y.)	N.A.	N.A.	14

Key Issues In 1804 Vice President Burr, a northern Republican, joined with a group of northeastern Federalists in a plot to unite New York and New England in a separate nation. The plot was exposed, discrediting the Federalists. Jefferson, already popular for his personal qualities as well as the Louisiana Purchase, swept to an easy victory. **Regional Influences** Jefferson lost only three states, and even swept all of New England with the exception of Connecticut.

1808

Party	Candidate	Popular vote	Percent	Electoral vote[1]
Democratic-Republican	James Madison (Va.)	N.A.	N.A.	122
	and George Clinton (N.Y.)	N.A.	N.A.	113
Federalist	Charles C. Pinckney (S.C.)	N.A.	N.A.	47
	and Rufus King (N.Y.)	N.A.	N.A.	47

Key Issues Jefferson reinforced the two-term precedent by refusing to run for a third term. Madison, his chosen successor, easily won the Republican nomination and the presidency. **Regional Influences** Pinckney and the Federalists regained most of the New England votes lost four years earlier and increased their strength in Congress due to commercial opposition to the embargo imposed by Jefferson on the export of American goods to warring European nations.

[1]Clinton received six electoral votes for president. Madison and James Monroe of Virginia both received three electoral votes for vice-president.

1812

Party	Candidate	Popular vote	Percent	Electoral vote
Democratic-Republican	James Madison (Va.)	N.A.	N.A.	128
	and Elbridge Gerry (Mass.)	N.A.	N.A.	131
Federalist	DeWitt Clinton (N.Y.)	N.A.	N.A.	89
	and Jared Ingersoll (Pa.)	N.A.	N.A.	86

Key Issues The election was a referendum on Madison's bid for a declaration of war against Great Britain in response to Britain's attempts to block the sale of southern raw materials in European markets. A vote for Madison was a vote for war, a vote for Clinton a vote for peace. **Regional Influences** Commercial interests in the northeast opposed war with Great Britain. The original 13 states were evenly split in the election, favoring Madison 90-89. New England, except Vermont, voted for Clinton, as did a majority of the Middle Atlantic states. The South voted unanimously for Madison. But all of the western states voted for Madison and thus for war.

1816

Party	Candidate	Popular vote	Percent	Electoral vote
Democratic-Republican	James Monroe (Va.)	N.A.	N.A.	183
	and D. D. Tompkins (N.Y.)	N.A.	N.A.	183
Federalist	Rufus King (N.Y.)	N.A.	N.A.	34
	and John E. Howard (Md.)	N.A.	N.A.	22

Key Issues Nationalism triumphed after the war with Britain, a time of national and economic growth that saw establishment of an expanded standing army, central bank, Federal tariff and large internal improvements despite opposition from northeastern Federalists. **Regional Influences** Monroe, Madison's chosen successor, won a landslide victory that seemed to validate Madison's nationalistic program, which called for a stronger standing army, a protective tariff, uniform currency and a nationwide system of roads and canals, including the Cumberland Road. The Federalists won only three states, all in New England.

1820

Party	Candidate	Popular vote	Percent	Electoral vote
Democratic-Republican	James Monroe (Va.)	N.A.	N.A.	231
	and D.D. Tompkins (N.Y.)	N.A.	N.A.	218
Democratic-Republican	John Q. Adams (Mass.)	N.A.	N.A.	1

Key Issues The election was held at the height of the "Era of Good Feelings," though sectional differences over slavery earlier in the year led to the Missouri Compromise, which in its final version resulted in the admittance of Missouri as a slave state with the provision that it allow free Negroes of other states to retain their freedom while in Missouri. The Federalists ceased to exist as a functioning party by the time of the election and failed to run a candidate against Monroe. **Regional Influences** Monroe ran unopposed for reelection. One elector from New Hampshire voted for Adams so that only Washington would hold the honor of being elected to the presidency by a unanimous vote.

1824

Party	Candidate	Popular vote	Per-cent	Elec-toral vote
Democratic-Republican	John Q. Adams (Mass.)	113,122	30.92	84
Democratic-Republican	Andrew Jackson (Tenn.)	151,271	41.34	99
Democratic-Republican	William H. Crawford (Ga.)	40,876	11.17	41
Democratic-Republican	Henry Clay (Ky.)	47,531	12.99	37
Other		13,053	3.57	—
	Total Vote	365,833		
	Jackson Plurality	38,149		

Key Issues Personalities dominated an election in which all four candidates ran as Democratic-Republicans. Crawford, Monroe's treasury secretary, won the nomination of the party's congressional caucus. But few attended the caucus and most electors were chosen by state legislatures. Crawford later suffered a stroke and was not a serious candidate. John C. Calhoun of South Carolina ran unopposed for vice president. **Regional Influences** Each candidate represented his region Adams the commercial northeast, Crawford the cotton south, Clay and Jackson the agrarian west. Jackson, a hero of the War of 1812 and battles against Indians, won a clear plurality of the popular vote and was the only candidate with support outside his home region. But no candidate won a majority of the electoral vote and the election was decided in the House, where Speaker Clay's support gave the victory to Adams.

1828

Party	Candidate	Popular vote	Per-cent	Elec-toral vote
Democratic-	Andrew Jackson (Tenn.)	642,553	55.97	178
Republican	and John C. Calhoun (S.C.)			171
National-	John Q. Adams (Mass.)	500,987	43.63	83
Republican	and Richard Rush (Pa.)			83
Other		4,568	0.40	—
	Total Vote	1,148,018		
	Jackson Plurality	141,656		

Key Issues Personalities again overshadowed issues. The Jackson campaign catered to popular prejudices, portraying the contest as one between democracy and aristocracy. The Jackson coalition was a forerunner of the modern Democratic Party and reestablished two-party politics in the U.S. **Regional Influences** Jackson won the south and west easily, and appealed to discontented laborers in the north. Adams carried only New England, New Jersey, Maryland and Delaware.

1832

Party	Candidate	Popular vote	Per-cent	Elec-toral vote
Democrat	Andrew Jackson (Tenn.)	701,780	54.23	219
	and Martin Van Buren (N.Y.)			189
National-	Henry Clay (Ky.)	484,205	37.42	49
Republican	and John Sergeant (Pa.)			49
Anti-	William Wirt (Md.)	100,715	7.78	7
Masonic	and Amos Ellmaker (Pa.)			7
Independent	John Floyd (Va.)	—	—	11
	and Henry Lee (Mass.)			11
Other		7,273	0.56	—
	Total Vote	1,293,973		
	Jackson Plurality	217,575		

Key Issues The Anti-Masons, the first third-party in American politics, began in opposition to secret societies in particular and privileged groups in general, but were at heart an anti-Jackson party. The two established parties followed the Anti-Masons lead by holding national nominating conventions to select a presidential nominee. While Jackson's opposition to the Bank of the United States was made an issue by the two major parties, the election was more a referendum on Jackson himself. **Regional Influences** Anti-Masonic strength was concentrated in rural sections of New England and the Middle Atlantic states. In those states National-Republicans and Anti-Masons supported the same ticket. With the forces against him divided, Jackson won easily. Clay won only half of the New England states, Wirt won only Vermont. Jackson captured Maine and New Hampshire. In South Carolina, where electors still were chosen by the legislature, nullificationists cast their ballots for Floyd.

1836

Party	Candidate	Popular vote	Per-cent	Elec-toral vote
Democrat	Martin Van Buren (N.Y.)	764,716	50.83	170
	and Richard M. Johnson (Ky.)	147		
Whig	William Henry Harrison (Ohio)	550,816	36.63	73
Whig	Hugh L. White (Tenn.)	146,107	9.72	26
Whig	Daniel Webster (Mass.)	41,201	2.74	14
	Willie P. Mangum (N.C.)	—	—	11
Other		1,234	0.08	—
	Total Vote	1,503,534		
	Van Buren Plurality	213, 360		

Key Issues Jackson's heavy-handed tactics, especially in his successful battle against the national bank, led the National-Republicans to rename themselves Whigs, after the 18th-century British party that tried to lessen the power of the crown. But lacking effective national leadership and divided along sectional lines, the anti-Jackson forces could not agree on a single candidate or platform and instead ran three regional candidates. **Regional Influences** Whig strategy was to throw the election into the House, where they could unite around a single candidate. Webster was to win New England, Harrison the west and Lawson the south. Van Buren, forced on the Democrats by Jackson, foiled the plan by picking up enough states throughout the nation to win by a slim majority. Johnson fell one electoral vote short of a majority for vice president and was selected by the Senate. The South Carolina legislature cast its votes for Mangum.

1840

Party	Candidate	Popular vote	Per-cent	Elec-toral vote
Whig	William Henry Harrison (Ohio) and John Tyler (Va.)	1,275,390	52.88	234
Democrat	Martin Van Buren (N.Y.)	1,128,854	46.81	60
Liberty	James G. Birney (N.Y.)	6,797	0.28	—
Other		767	0.03	—
	Total Vote	2,411,808		
	Harrison Plurality	146,536		

Key Issues With the country still reeling from the Panic of 1837, the Democrats were on the defensive. Though differences prevented them from writing a platform, the Whigs rallied around Harrison. In a campaign notable for its absence of issues, the Whigs turned the tables on Jackson's party. Harrison, despite his wealthy origins, was portrayed as the "log-cabin, hard-cider candidate" opposing the allegedly aristocratic Van Buren. The Democrats left the selection of a vice-presidential candidate to each state. **Regional Influences** Van Buren won only seven states, just one outside of the south or west. Harrison was long associated with the west and Tyler was a conservative Southerner and friend of Henry Clay. For the first time, active two-party politics was established across the nation. The 68-year-old Harrison caught a severe cold after delivering a lengthy Inaugural Address in the rain and died one month into his term.

1844

Party	Candidate	Popular vote	Per-cent	Elec-toral vote
Democrat	James K. Polk (Tenn.) and George M. Dallas (Pa.)	1,339,494	49.54	170
Whig	Henry Clay (Ky.) and Theodore Frelinghuysen (N.J.)	1,300,004	48.08	
Abolitionist	James G. Birney (N.Y.)	62,103	2.30	—
Other		2,058	0.08	—
	Total Vote	2,703,659		
	Polk Plurality	39,490		

Key Issues Manifest Destiny, the goal of a U.S. stretching from the Atlantic to the Pacific, was the central issue because of the question of the annexation of Texas. With the election approaching, opponents of slavery lead the Senate to reject a treaty between Texas and the Tyler Administration that would have preserved Texan slavery and made it a U.S. territory. The two leading presidential candidates, Clay and Van Buren, sought to smother the Texas issue by ignoring it. But Polk snatched the Democratic nomination with his clear and vocal advocacy of annexation of Texas and general territorial expansion. **Regional Influences** Expansionism was immensely popular, especially in the south and west, where memories of the depression following 1837 added to the attraction of new, vast, and open public lands. Support for manifest destiny more than made up for anti-slavery sentiment elsewhere and Polk won a narrow plurality but a clear victory.

1848

Party	Candidate	Popular vote	Per-cent	Elec-toral vote
Whig	Zachary Taylor (La.) and Millard Fillmore (N.Y.)	1,361,393	47.28	163
Democrat	Lewis Cass (Mich.) and William O. Butler (Ky.)	1,223,460	42.49	127
Free Soil	Martin Van Buren (N.Y.) and Charles Francis Adams (Mass.)	291,501	10.12	—
Other		2,830	0.10	—
	Total Vote	2,879,184		
	Taylor Plurality	137,933		

Key Issues The Wilmot Proviso, calling for a ban on extension of slavery into territories acquired in the Mexican War, dominated the election. But both major parties evaded the issue. Slavery foes banded together to form the Free Soil Party, which won no electoral votes but drew enough popular support away from the Democrats to throw the election to "Old Rough and Ready," Zachary Taylor, a slave-holder. Taylor died in July 1850. **Regional Influences** Both major parties balanced their tickets with a Northerner and Southerner. Free Soilers were mostly Northern Democrats, anti-slavery Whigs and abolitionists. There was no distinct pattern in the Electoral College following a lackluster campaign. Free Soil strength in New York gave the state and the election to the Whigs.

1852

Party	Candidate	Popular vote	Per-cent	Elec-toral vote
Democrat	Franklin Pierce (N.H.) and William R. D. King (Ala.)	1,607,510	50.84	254
Whig	Winfield Scott (Va.) and William A. Graham (N.C.)	1,386,942	43.87	42
Free Soil	John P. Hale (N.H.) and George Washington Julian (Ind.)	155,210	4.91	—
Other		12,168	0.38	—
	Total Vote	3,161,830		
	Pierce Plurality	220,568		

Key Issues The election was a referendum on the Compromise of 1850, in which Congress voted to admit California as a free state, create the territories of New Mexico and Utah with no restriction on slavery, abolish the slave trade in the District of Columbia, purchase disputed land from Texas on behalf of New Mexico, and toughen the Fugitive Slave Act. The Democrats strongly endorsed the Compromise, but the bitterly divided Whigs only vaguely accepted it. **Regional Influences** The Democrats won a resounding electoral victory, capturing 27 states to the four taken by the Whigs Massachusetts, Vermont, Kentucky and Tennessee. Free Soilers returned to the Democrats and the Whigs never again were a political force in a nation which believed the slave question was behind it.

1856

Party	Candidate	Popular vote	Per-cent	Elec-toral vote
Democrat	James Buchanan (Pa.) and John C. Breckinridge (Ky.)	1,836,072	45.28	174
Republican	John C. Fremont (Calif.) and William L. Dayton (N.J.)	1,342,345	33.11	114
Whig	Millard Fillmore (N.Y.) and Andrew J. Donelson (Tenn.)	873,053	21.53	8
Other		3,177	0.08	—
	Total Vote	4,054,647		
	Buchanan Plurality	493,727		

Key Issues The Democrats firmly endorsed "popular sovereignty" even though it led to great turmoil in the territory of Kansas. But they chose as their nominee Buchanan, largely because he had been out of the country and was untainted by "Bleeding Kansas" battle, which pitted supporters and foes of slavery trying to organize the territory into a slave or free state. The Republicans, a new party of northern Whigs and Democrats committed to the containment of slavery ran Fremont, a popular general and explorer. **Regional Influences** Fremont carried all but five of the free states. But Buchanan won all of the south in addition to the five northern states and was elected. Fillmore, supported by the Know-Nothings and Whig remnants, only won Maryland but strongly challenged the Democrats in the south.

1860

Party	Candidate	Popular vote	Per-cent	Elec-toral vote
Republican	Abraham Lincoln (Ill.) and Hannibal Hamlin (Maine)	1,865,908	39.82	180
Democrat	Stephen A. Douglas (Ill.) and Herschel V. Johnson (Ga.)	1,380,202	29.46	12
Democrat	John C. Breckinridge (Ky.) and Joseph Lane (Oreg.)	848,019	18.09	72
Constitutional Union and	John Bell (Tenn.) Edward Everett (Mass.)	590,901	12.61	39
Other		531	0.01	—
	Total Vote	4,685,561		
	Lincoln Plurality	485,706		

Key Issues Sectional differences over slavery came to a head in 1860. The Democrats could not agree on a candidate and split into northern and southern factions. The Northerners backed Douglas and popular sovereignty, the Southerners Breckinridge and Federal protection of slavery in the territories. The Republicans, virtually all Northerners, were a pro-tariff, nationalistic party that opposed the extension of slavery but did not seek to overturn it where it already existed. Bell, the candidate of Whigs and Know-Nothings who backed Fillmore in 1856, were a compromise party expressing support for preservation of the Union. **Regional Influences** In effect there were two separate contests in 1860 Lincoln versus Douglas in the north, Breckinridge versus Bell in the south. Free states outnumbered slave states and cast half again as many electoral votes. Lincoln won every northern state except New Jersey and, though not even on the ballot in 10 southern states, was elected president. Breckinridge captured 11 of the 15 southern states. The four southern states won by Douglas and Bell were in the upper south.

1864

Party	Candidate	Popular vote	Per-cent	Elec-toral vote
Republican	Abraham Lincoln (Ill.) and Andrew Johnson (Tenn.)	2,218,388	55.02	212
Democrat	George B. McClellan (N.Y.) and George H. Pendleton (Ohio)	1,812,807	44.96	21
	Total Vote	4,031,887		
	Lincoln Plurality	405,581		

Key Issues Lincoln's renomination was not assured. Radical Republicans thought he was not aggressive enough in his conduct of the war or plans for the eventual peace, but moderation ultimately prevailed. The Republicans ran as the Union Party and nominated Johnson, a pro-Union Democrat, for vice president. The Democrats ran a peace campaign, calling the war a failure. But McClellan, a popular general, broke with his party's platform and denied the war was a failure, denouncing members of his party who seemed to advocate peace at any price. He opposed emancipation as a goal of the war. **Regional Influences** Military victories around election time helped the embattled incumbent. Lincoln won a convincing popular and electoral victory with the support of middle-class professionals, farmers, laborers and the strongly pro-Union voters who voted for Bell four years earlier. McClellan was strongest in areas carried by Breckinridge four years before. Eleven Confederate states did not participate in the election.

1868

Party	Candidate	Popular vote	Per-cent	Electoral vote
Republican	Ulysses S. Grant (Ohio) and Schuyler Colfax (Ind.)	3,013,650	52.66	214
Democrat	Horatio S. Seymour (N.Y.) and Francis P. Blair (Mo.)	2,708,744	47.34	80
Other		46	—	—
	Total Vote	5,722,440		
	Grant Plurality	304,906		

Key Issues The Republicans waved the "bloody shirt" of the war and ran on their program of Radical Reconstruction. While calling for Negro suffrage in the south, the Republicans asserted it was a matter for individual northern states to decide for themselves. Democrats ran against Reconstruction, declaring that the question of Negro suffrage should be decided by individual southern states as well. **Regional Influences** Despite Grant's popularity, the Republicans were just able to win the election. Seymour carried only eight states, though he did well in the states won by Grant. Without black votes in the South, Grant would not have received a majority of the popular vote. The votes of the "unreconstructed" states of Mississippi, Texas and Virginia were not counted.

1872

Party	Candidate	Popular vote	Per-cent	Electoral vote
Republican	Ulysses S. Grant (Ohio) and Henry Wilson (Mass.)	3,598,235	55.63	286
Liberal Republican/ Democrat	Horace Greeley (N.Y.) and Benjamin Gratz Brown (Mo.)	2,834,761	43.83	—
Straight Democrat	Charles O'Conor (N.Y.)	18,602	—	
	Other	16,081	0.25	—
	Total Vote	6,467,679		
	Grant Plurality	763,474		

Key Issues Liberal Republicans broke with Grant over corruption in his administration, high tariffs and continued Radical Reconstruction. They nominated Greeley, editor of the *New York Tribune*. The Democrats endorsed Greeley and the Liberal platform. But the great scandals of the Grant administration were not yet revealed and the Republicans again waved the bloody shirt to victory. **Regional Influences** Greeley carried only two states in the lower South and four border states. He died shortly after the election (Nov. 29, 1872) and his electoral votes went to other candidates: Thomas Hendricks, Indiana, 42; Benjamin Gratz Brown, Missouri, 18; Charles J. Jenkins, Georgia, 2; and David Davis, Illinois, 1.

> ***"Great men are not chosen president, firstly because great men are rare in politics; secondly, because the method of choice does not bring them to the top; thirdly, because they are not, in quiet times, absolutely necessary."***
>
> **–English jurist, historian, and diplomat James Bryce, *The American Commonwealth* (1888)**

1876

Party	Candidate	Popular vote	Per-cent	Electoral vote
Republican	Rutherford B. Hayes (Ohio) and William A. Wheeler (N.Y.)	4,034,311	47.95	185
Democrat	Samuel J. Tilden (N.Y.) and Thomas A. Hendricks (Ind.)	4,288,546	50.97	184
Greenback	Peter Cooper (N.Y.)	75,973	0.90	—
Other		14,271	0.17	
	Total Vote	8,413,101		
	Tilden Plurality	254,235		

Key Issues The Republicans were in trouble as 1876 approached due to rampant corruption in the Grant administration and the economic depression that followed the Panic of 1873. Hayes, a three-term Ohio governor known for his unassailable integrity, was nominated to run against the favored Democrat, Tilden, a New York reform governor whose reputation was made in opposition to the Tweed political machine. Both men espoused conservative economics. Cooper and the Greenbacks advocated currency expansion. **Regional Influences** As Election Day approached, Tilden could count on winning all of the south except for the three states still controlled by Republican carpetbaggers: South Carolina, Louisiana, and Florida. He seemed assured of victory when those states appeared to vote for him along with several northern states, including New York and New Jersey. But Republicans claimed South Carolina, Louisiana and Florida for Hayes, arguing that thousands of blacks who would have voted for Hayes were barred from voting there. Election boards in those Republican-controlled states gave Hayes the needed majority, and thus the election. In the uproar that followed Congress set up an Election Commission to validate the returns. The commission voted strictly along party lines, eight to seven, to give the election to Hayes. Despite charges that Republicans stole the election, Hayes later was inaugurated peaceably after he let it be known that as president he would end military reconstruction by withdrawing Federal troops from the south and that he would restore "efficient local government" to the south.

1880

Party	Candidate	Popular vote	Per-cent	Electoral vote
Republican	James A. Garfield (Ohio) and Chester A. Arthur (N.Y.)	4,461,158	48.27	214
Democrat	Winfield S. Hancock (Pa.) and William H. English (Ind.)	4,444,260	48.25	155
Greenback	James B. Weaver (Iowa) and Benjamin J. Chambers (Tex.)	305,997	3.32	—
Other		14,005	0.15	—
	Total Vote	9,210,420		
	Garfield Plurality	1,898		

Key Issues With the war and Reconstruction behind, no major issues arose over which the major parties disagreed. The Democrats, the party of secession 20 year earlier, nominated General Hancock to help combat the stigma of treason. Garfield made a protectionist tariff central to his campaign. **Regional Influences** The balance between Republican strength in the Midwest and west and Democratic strength in the south resulted in a plurality of less than 2,000 for Garfield out of more than 9 million votes cast. Four months into his term Garfield was shot by a disappointed office-seeker.

1884

Party	Candidate	Popular vote	Per-cent	Electoral vote
Democrat	Grover Cleveland (N.Y.) and Thomas A. Hendricks (Ind.)	4,874,621	48.50	219
Republican	James G. Blaine (Maine) and John A. Logan (Ill.)	4,848,936	48.25	182
Greenback	Benjamin F. Butler (Mass.)	175,096	1.74	—
Prohibition	John P. St. John (Kans.)	147,482	1.47	—
Other		3,619	0.04	—
	Total Votes	10,049,754		
	Cleveland Plurality	25,685		

Key Issues The private lives and morals of the candidates were the focus of a campaign notable for mudslinging. Blaine was accused of accepting bribes from a railroad company for whom he obtained a federal grant and Republicans taunted Cleveland for fathering a son out of wedlock. Still, Cleveland, known for his independence and integrity in public life, attracted the votes of many liberal Republicans and reformers unable to stomach Blaine, a Radical Republican leader. **Regional Influences** Cleveland carried all of the southern states as well as the key swing states of Indiana, New Jersey, Connecticut and New York, becoming the first Democrat elected president since the Civil War. Cleveland carried his home state of New York and its 36 electoral votes by less than 1,200 votes.

1888

Party	Candidate	Popular vote	Per-cent	Electoral vote
Republican	Benjamin Harrison (Ind.) and Levi P. Morton (N.Y.)	5,443,892	47.82	233
Democrat	Grover Cleveland (N.Y.) and Allen G. Thurman (Ohio)	5,534,488	48.62	168
Prohibition	Clinton B. Fisk (N.J.)	249,813	2.19	—
Union Labor	Alson J. Streeter (Ill.)	146,602	1.29	—
Other		8,519	0.07	—
	Total Votes	11,383,320		
	Cleveland Plurality	90,596		

Key Issues Cleveland made tariff reform central to his administration, seeking to lower existing high tariffs. The Republicans campaigned on the need to maintain high wages by keeping a high tariff on imported goods. **Regional Influences** Despite the emphasis on the tariff, Cleveland still carried such manufacturing states as New Jersey and Connecticut as well as most of the south. But though Cleveland won 90,000 more popular votes than Harrison, the Republican carried the pro-tariff swing states of Indiana and New York by slight margins to win the election in the electoral college in one of the most corrupt campaigns in history.

1892

Party	Candidate	Popular vote	Per-cent	Electoral vote
Democrat	Grover Cleveland (N.Y.) and Adlai E. Stevenson (Ill.)	5,551,883	46.05	277
Republican	Benjamin Harrison (Indiana) and Whitelaw Reid (N.Y.)	5,179,244	42.96	145
Populist	James B. Weaver (Iowa) and James G. Field (Virginia)	1,024,280	8.50	22
Prohibition	John Bidwell (California)	270,770	2.25	—
Other		29,920	0.25	
	Total Votes	12,056,097		
	Cleveland Plurality	372,639		

Key Issues Cleveland and Harrison again fought a battle over the tariff, which the Republicans drastically raised in 1890. Both men were out of touch with the growing agrarian and populist discontent. Weaver, campaigning for free silver, became the first third-party candidate to gain electoral votes since the war. **Regional Influences** Cleveland improved upon his 1884 and 1888 showings to win the most decisive presidential victory in 20 years. This time he carried the swing states of New York, New Jersey, Connecticut and Indiana as well as the traditionally Republican states of Illinois, California and Wisconsin.

1896

Party	Candidate	Popular vote	Per-cent	Electoral vote
Republican	William McKinley (Ohio) and Garret A. Hobart (N.J.)	7,108,480	51.01	271
Democrat/ Populist	William J. Bryan (Nebr.) and Democrat Arthur Sewall (Me.) and Populist Thomas E. Watson (Ga.)	6,511,495	46.73	176 149
National Democrat	John M. Palmer (Ill.)	133,435	0.96	—
Prohibition	Joshua Levering (Md.)	125,072	0.90	—
Other		57,256	0.41	—
	Total Votes	13,935,738		
	McKinley Plurality	596,985		

Key Issues The Democrats absorbed Populist energies and abandoned the conservatism of Cleveland by nominating Bryan and adopting key elements of the Populist program, especially the call for free silver. The pro-tariff and pro-gold Republicans led by McKinley and Mark Hanna outspent the Democrats by almost 12 to 1. In losing, Bryan amassed more votes than any victorious candidate before him. **Regional Influences** Bryan did not carry a single state north of Virginia or east of Missouri. His hold on the agricultural south and west was broken by Republican victories in Maryland, Delaware, West Virginia, Kentucky, California and Oregon. Bryan, failing to appeal to labor, carried no industrial or urban states.

1900

Party	Candidate	Popular vote	Per-cent	Electoral vote
Republican	William McKinley (Ohio) and Theodore Roosevelt (N.Y.)	7,218,039	51.67	292
Democrat	William J. Bryan (Nebr.) and Adlai E. Stevenson (Ill.)	6,358,345	45.51	155
Prohibition	John C. Woolley (Ill.)	209,004	1.50	—
Social Democrat	Eugene V. Debs (Ind.)	86,935	0.62	—
Other		98,147	0.70	—
	Total Vote	13,970,470		
	McKinley Plurality	859,694		

Key Issues Imperialism in the Philippines joined free silver and the tariff as the key issues in a replay of the 1896 election. Bryan tried to unite the silver interests in the west and south with supporters of the gold standard in a coalition against imperialism, which the Democratic platform called the "paramount issue" of the campaign. But voters did not desert McKinley in a time of prosperity. **Regional Influences** Bryan carried only the Solid South and four silver states in the west, and was defeated in the silver states of Kansas, South Dakota, Utah and Wyoming as well as his home state of Nebraska. Both houses of Congress were led by significant Republican majorities.

1904

Party	Candidate	Popular vote	Per-cent	Electoral vote
Republican	Theodore Roosevelt (N.Y.) and Charles W. Fairbanks (Ind.)	7,626,593	56.41	336
Democrat	Alton B. Parker (N.Y.) and Henry G. Davis (W. Va.)	5,082,898	37.60	140
Socialist	Eugene V. Debs (Ind.)	402,489	2.98	—
Prohibition	Silas C. Swallow (Pa.)	258,596	1.91	—
Other		148,388	1.10	—
	Total Votes	13,518,964		
	Roosevelt Plurality	2,543,695		

Key Issues Roosevelt stole the mantle of reform from the Democrats with his campaigns against the "malefactors of great wealth." The Democrats turned to the right by nominating the lackluster Parker, a judge with close ties to Wall Street. Parker turned his back on Bryan Democrats by renouncing free silver. **Regional Influences** Roosevelt won a landslide victory based largely on his own personality and popularity. The Democrats won only 13 states, none outside the south.

1908

Party	Candidate	Popular vote	Per-cent	Electoral vote
Republican	William H. Taft (Ohio) and James S. Sherman (N.Y.)	7,662,258	51.58	321
Democrat	William J. Bryan (Nebr.) and John W. Kern (Ind.)	6,406,801	43.05	162
Socialist	Eugene V. Debs (Ind.)	420,380	2.82	—
Prohibition	Eugene W. Chafin (Ill.)	252,821	1.70	—
Other		126,474	0.85	—
	Total Vote	14,882,734		
	Taft Plurality	1,269,457		

Key Issues The immensely popular Roosevelt declined to run. Taft, his secretary of war and handpicked successor, debated Bryan over who was better qualified to complete TR's progressive program. Bryan abandoned silver and courted labor but ran a lackluster losing campaign. **Regional Influences** Bryan again carried the South. But the appeal of Roosevelt's reform programs helped the Republicans to do well in the west and Taft's background as a Yale graduate and Federal jurist enabled him to carry the east as well.

1912

Party	Candidate	Popular vote	Per-cent	Elec-toral vote
Democrat	Woodrow Wilson (N.J.) and Thomas Marshall (Ind.)	6,293,152	41.84	435
Progressive	Theodore Roosevelt (N.Y.) and Hiram Johnson (Calif.)	4,119,207	27.39	88
Republican	William H. Taft (Ohio) and James S. Sherman (N.Y.)	3,486,333	23.18	8
Socialist	Eugene V. Debs (Ind.)	900,369	5.99	—
Other		241,902	1.61	—
	Total Vote	15,040,963		
	Wilson Plurality	2,173,945		

Key Issues Taft's conservatism and political ineptitude led Roosevelt to challenge him within the party from the left. Unable to wrest the nomination from Taft, Roosevelt ran a third-party campaign. The election boiled down to a contest between Roosevelt and Wilson and their respective conceptions of progressivism. Roosevelt's "New Nationalism" called for strong Federal regulations to control the trusts and big businesses. Wilson's "New Freedom" sought instead to revive competition through vigorous application of anti-trust laws. The Progressives advocated a broad array of social reforms to be implemented by the Federal government while the Democrats emphasized the primacy of the states in such matters. **Regional Influences** Though he amassed fewer votes than did Bryan in 1908, Wilson took advantage of the split in the Republican ranks to win a decisive plurality of the vote. He did best in traditional Democratic states, but was able to win most traditionally Republican states as well. Roosevelt won only 6 states, including California, which he carried by fewer than 200 votes. Taft carried Utah and Vermont. The Democrats also won control of both houses of Congress, their best overall performance since the Civil War.

1916

Party	Candidate	Popular vote	Per-cent	Elec-toral vote
Democrat	Woodrow Wilson (N.J.) and Thomas Marshall (Ind.)	9,126,300	49.24	277
Republican	Charles Evans Hughes (N.Y.) and Charles W. Fairbanks (Ind.)	8,546,789	46.11	254
Socialist	Allen L. Benson (N.Y.)	589,924	3.18	—
Prohibition	James F. Hanly (Ind.)	221,030	1.19	—
Other		50,979	0.28	—
	Total Vote	18,535,022		
	Wilson Plurality	579,511		

Key Issues The campaign was a referendum on Wilson's first term, his program of domestic reform, and his policy toward the war in Europe. He ran a peace campaign with the slogan "He kept us out of war" and attracted the votes of many Bull Moosers. Voters who felt Wilson was either too harsh or too lenient toward Germany tended to vote Republican. Irish-American and German-American extremists, virulently opposed to aiding Great Britain, embarrassed Hughes with their vocal support. A coalition of labor, farmers, reformers, and intellectuals won the election for Wilson. **Regional Influences** Hughes, a former reform governor of New York who left the Supreme Court to challenge Wilson, carried all of the east except New Hampshire and all of the Old Northwest except Ohio. But the South was again solid for the Democrats and so was every state west of the Mississippi except Minnesota, Iowa, South Dakota and Oregon, which Wilson lost by close margins. The electoral vote was the closest since 1876.

1920

Party	Candidate	Popular vote	Per-cent	Elec-toral vote
Republican	Warren G. Harding (Ohio) and Calvin Coolidge (Mass.)	16,133,314	60.30	404
Democrat	James M. Cox (Ohio) and Franklin D. Roosevelt (N.Y.)	9,140,884	34.17	127
Socialist	Eugene V. Debs (Ind.)	913,664	3.42	—
Farmer-Labor	Parley P. Christensen (Utah)	264,540	0.99	—
Other		301,384	1.13	—
	Total Vote	26,753,786		
	Harding Plurality	6,992,430		

Key Issues The voters turned against Wilsonian progressivism and internationalism by electing Harding, a vacuous party hack who promised a "return to normalcy" after the turbulent years of domestic reform and world war. The undistinguished Cox ran in support of the League of Nations and little else. **Regional Influences** Harding carried every state outside of the south, except Tennessee. The Republicans added to their majorities in both houses of Congress, regained in 1918.

1924

Party	Candidate	Popular vote	Per-cent	Elec-toral vote
Republican	Calvin Coolidge (Mass.) and Charles G. Dawes (Ohio)	15,717,553	54.00	382
Democrat	John W. Davis (N.Y.) and Charles W. Bryan (Nebr.)	8,386,169	28.84	136
Progressive Socialist	Robert M. LaFollette (Wis.) and Burton K. Wheeler (Mont.)	4,814,050	16.56	13
Other		158,187	0.55	—
	Total Vote	29,075,959		
	Coolidge Plurality	7,331,384		

Key Issues The country "kept cool with Coolidge" as the Democrats could not overcome prosperity or themselves. Davis, a conservative Wall Street lawyer, was a compromise nominee selected by a bitterly divided party after 103 ballots. Reformers, labor and farmers flocked to the LaFollette candidacy. **Regional Influences** All 12 of the Democratic states were from the south. LaFollette's 13 electoral votes came from his home of Wisconsin.

1928

Party	Candidate	Popular vote	Per-cent	Elec-toral vote
Republican	Herbert C. Hoover (Calif.) and Charles E. Curtis (Kans.)	21,411,911	58.20	444
Democrat	Alfred E. Smith (N.Y.) and Joseph T. Robinson (Ark.)	15,000,185	40.77	87
Socialist	Norman Thomas (N.Y.)	266,453	0.72	—
Worker's	William Z. Foster (Ill.)	48,170	0.13	—
Other		63,565	0.17	—
	Total Vote	36,790,364		
	Hoover Plurality	6,411,806		

Key Issues Booze, bigotry, Tammany and prosperity did in the Democrats. Rural America would not vote for an anti-Prohibition, big-city, Catholic machine politician, despite Smith's success as governor of New York, especially while the Republicans could convincingly cite the success of their economic leadership. **Regional Influences** The solid south was shattered as Hoover Democrats gave Republicans the states of Virginia, North Carolina, Tennessee, Florida and Texas for the first time since Reconstruction. Smith lost his own state and every western and border state. But Smith set the stage for the New Deal coalition with the votes of urban ethnics, he carried the nation's 12 largest cities, all of which had been won by the Republicans four years earlier. The Democrats also won votes in the traditionally Republican west among farmers unsure about prosperity.

1932

Party	Candidate	Popular vote	Per-cent	Elec-toral vote
Democrat	Franklin D. Roosevelt (N.Y.) and John Nance Garner (Tex.)	22,825,016	57.42	472
Republican	Herbert C. Hoover (Calif.) and Charles E. Curtis (Kans.)	15,758,397	39.64	59
Socialist	Norman Thomas (N.Y.)	883,990	2.22	—
Communist	William Z. Foster (Ill.)	102,221	0.26	—
Other		179,758	0.45	—
	Total Vote	39,749,382		
	Roosevelt Plurality	7,066,619		

Key Issues The Democrats won by blaming the Republicans for the Great Depression. Roosevelt was the first presidential nominee of a major party to address his nominating convention, pledging to help "the forgotten man at the bottom of the economic pyramid." In a vague and contradictory platform, the Democrats promised to balance the Federal budget by drastically reducing expenses and vowed to spend Federal dollars to attack the nation's economic woes. **Regional Influences** Roosevelt lost only six states, Maine, New Hampshire, Vermont, Connecticut, Delaware and Pennsylvania, carrying all of the agricultural West and South. He put the finishing touches on the New Deal coalition by also improving upon Smith's margins of victory in the nation's big cities.

1936

Party	Candidate	Popular vote	Per-cent	Elec-toral vote
Democrat	Franklin D. Roosevelt (N.Y.) and John Nance Garner (Tex.)	27,747,636	60.79	523
Republican	Alfred M. Landon (Kans.) and Frank Knox (Ill.)	16,679,543	36.54	8
Union	William Lemke (N.Dak.)	892,492	1.96	—
Socialist	Norman Thomas (N.Y.)	187,785	0.41	—
Other		134,847	0.30	—
	Total Vote	45,642,303		
	Roosevelt Plurality	11,068,093		

Key Issues Despite intense opposition to the New Deal, its great public appeal was confirmed in the most one-sided election since 1820 and sweeping victories for the Democrats in Congress. The populist forces of the late Huey Long coalesced around Lemke but failed to gather widespread support. **Regional Influences** Roosevelt carried every state except Maine and Vermont. The New Deal coalition was at its height as every large city voted overwhelmingly for FDR. The middle-class, farmers in the west and south, big-city ethnics, labor and reform intellectuals flocked to the Democrats. Northern Blacks also began to vote heavily Democratic for the first time.

1940

Party	Candidate	Popular vote	Per-cent	Elec-toral vote
Democrat	Franklin D. Roosevelt (N.Y.) and Henry A. Wallace (Iowa)	27,263,448	54.70	449
Republican	Wendell L. Willkie (Ind.) and Charles L. McNary (Oreg.)	22,336,260	44.82	82
Socialist	Norman Thomas (N.Y.)	116,827	0.23	—
Prohibition	Roger W. Babson (Mass.)	58,685	0.12	—
Other		65,223	0.13	—
	Total Vote	49,840,443		
	Roosevelt Plurality	4,927,188		

Key Issues With war raging in Europe the electorate turned its attention from domestic to foreign affairs. The international scene led the Democrats to break with tradition and renominate FDR for a third term. The Republicans turned to businessman and political neophyte Willkie, a charismatic former Democrat. Willkie's internationalism and the pledge of both candidates to keep the U.S. out of the war minimized the role of foreign policy in the campaign. **Regional Influences** Willkie carried only 10 states, mostly in the Midwest. But Roosevelt's percentage of the popular vote was markedly down from 1936.

1944

Party	Candidate	Popular vote	Per-cent	Elec-toral vote
Democrat	Franklin D. Roosevelt (N.Y.) and Harry S Truman (Mo.)	25,611,936	53.39	432
Republican	Thomas E. Dewey (N.Y.) and John W. Bricker (Ohio)	22,013,372	45.89	99
Socialist	Norman Thomas (N.Y.)	79,100	0.16	—
Prohibition	Claude A. Watson (Calif.)	74,733	0.16	—
Other		195,778	0.41	—
	Total Vote	47,974,819		
	Roosevelt Plurality	3,598,564		

Key Issues With both candidates supporting New Deal social legislation and an international organization to maintain the peace after the war, the nation chose to let FDR lead America into the post-war era. Big-city bosses and southern conservatives, with FDR's private support, ousted Wallace from the ticket in favor of Truman. **Regional Influences** Roosevelt won 36 states and the Democrats improved their control over Congress and the nation's statehouses. The Republicans only won a handful of western and New England states.

1948

Party	Candidate	Popular vote	Per-cent	Elec-toral vote
Democrat	Harry S Truman (Mo.) and Alben W. Barkley (Ky.)	24,105,587	49.51	303
Republican	Thomas E. Dewey (N.Y.) and Earl Warren (Calif.)	21,970,017	45.12	189
States' Rights	Strom Thurmond (S.C.) and Fielding L. Wright (Miss.)	1,169,134	2.40	39
Progressive	Henry A. Wallace (Iowa) and Glen H. Taylor (Idaho)	1,157,057	2.38	—
Other		290,647	0.60	—
	Total Vote	48,692,442		
	Truman Plurality	2,135,570		

Key Issues The Republicans were sure of victory after 16 years of Democratic rule and the desertion of the Democrats by conservative Southern Dixiecrats and the ultra-liberal Wallace faction. But Dewey's dour personality and Truman's intense whistle-stop campaign against the "do-nothing, good-for-nothing" Republican 80th Congress resulted in one of the biggest upsets in presidential history. **Regional Influences** Dewey captured all of the Middle Atlantic and New England states, except Massachusetts and Connecticut, along with the Dakotas, Nebraska and Kansas in the Midwest and Oregon in the northwest. Thurmond won South Carolina, Mississippi, Alabama and Louisiana in the Deep South.

1952

Party	Candidate	Popular vote	Per-cent	Elec-toral vote
Republican	Dwight D. Eisenhower (Kans.) and Richard M. Nixon (Calif.)	33,936,137	55.13	442
Democrat	Adlai E. Stevenson (Ill.) and John J. Sparkman (Ala.)	27,314,649	44.38	89
Progressive	Vincent W. Hallinan (Calif.)	140,416	0.23	—
Prohibition	Stuart Hamblen (Calif.)	73,413	0.12	—
Other		86,503	0.14	—
	Total Vote	61,551,118		
	Eisenhower Plurality	6,621,485		

Key Issues Popular war hero Eisenhower swept to victory after uniting the internationalist and isolationist factions of the Republican party. He routed the Democrats by promising to kick out alleged crooks and communists in Washington, wage a more aggressive fight against communists worldwide and "go to Korea," implying that he had a plan to end the war there. **Regional Influences** Stevenson, who appealed to northern liberals as well as southern states' rights Democrats, carried only nine states in the south. The Republicans also won slight majorities in both houses of Congress and were in control of the national government for the first time in 20 years.

1956

Party	Candidate	Popular vote	Percent	Electoral vote
Republican	Dwight D. Eisenhower (Kans.) and Richard M. Nixon (Calif.)	35,585,247	57.37	457
Democrat	Adlai E. Stevenson (Ill.) and Estes Kefauver (Tenn.)	26,030,172	41.97	73
Constitution/ States' Rights	T. Coleman Andrews (Va.)	108,055	0.17	—
Socialist-Labor	Eric Hass (New York)	44,300	0.07	—
Other		257,600	0.42	—
	Total Vote	62,025,372		
	Eisenhower Plurality	9,555,073		

Key Issues Eisenhower won an easy victory in a rematch of the 1952 election. His popularity did not translate into victories for his party elsewhere, as Democrats increased their control of Congress, regained in 1954, and their hold on the nation's governorships. **Regional Influences** Winning even more handsomely than he did in 1952, Eisenhower lost only seven southern states.

1960

Party	Candidate	Popular vote	Percent	Electoral vote
Democrat	John F. Kennedy (Mass.) and Lyndon B. Johnson (Tex.)	34,221,344	49.72	303
Republican	Richard M. Nixon (Calif.) and Henry Cabot Lodge (Mass.)	34,106,671	49.55	219
Socialist-Labor	Eric Hass (N.Y.)	47,522	0.07	—
Other		337,175	0.48	15
Unpledged		116,248	0.17	—
	Total Vote	68,828,960		
	Kennedy Plurality	114,673		

Key Issues Kennedy called for the government to play a larger role in stimulating the national economy in order to fund domestic social programs as well as to sustain a defense build-up and keep ahead militarily of the Soviet Union. The election was the first in which there were nationally televised debates between the two candidates. Kennedy's slick television performance played a role in his narrow triumph. **Regional Influences** The Democrats won a thin victory by narrowly defeating the Republicans in the Middle Atlantic states, the Deep South, Illinois and Texas. Nixon carried most of the Midwest, border and western states. Conservative Democratic Senator Harry F. Byrd of Virginia received 15 electoral votes: all eight of Mississippi's, six of Alabama's 11, and one of Oklahoma's eight.

1964

Party	Candidate	Popular vote	Percent	Electoral vote
Democrat	Lyndon B. Johnson (Tex.) and Hubert H. Humphrey (Minn.)	43,126,584	61.05	486
Republican	Barry M. Goldwater (Ariz.) and William E. Miller (N.Y.)	27,177,838	38.47	52
Socialist-Labor	Eric Hass (N.Y.)	45,187	0.06	—
Socialist Workers	Clifton DeBerry (N.Y.)	32,701	0.05	—
Other		258,794	0.37	—
	Total Vote	70,641,104		
	Johnson Plurality	15,948,746		

Key Issues Johnson ran for election in his own right on the basis of his Great Society domestic programs. The reactionary Goldwater campaigned against the New Deal and for the bombing of North Vietnam. **Regional Influences** Johnson won all but six states—Goldwater's home state of Arizona and five states in the Deep South—in the biggest popular and electoral landslide since 1936. Forty new Northern Democrats were elected to the House on LBJ's coattails.

1968

Party	Candidate	Popular vote	Percent	Electoral vote
Republican	Richard M. Nixon (Calif.) and Spiro T. Agnew (Md.)	31,785,148	43.42	301
Democrat	Hubert H. Humphrey (Minn.) and Edmund S. Muskie (Maine)	31,274,503	42.72	191
American Independent	George C. Wallace (Ala.) and Curtis LeMay (Ohio)	901,151	13.53	46
Socialist-Labor	Henning A. Blomen (Mass.)	52,591	0.07	—
Other		189,977	0.20	—
	Total Vote	73,203,370		
	Nixon Plurality	510,645		

Key Issues With the country divided over Vietnam, Humphrey failed to emerge from the shadow of the unpopular Johnson, while the previously hawkish Nixon pledged to end the war and hinted that he had a secret plan to do so. Wallace attacked Federal encroachment on states' rights, desegregation, "pointy-headed" intellectuals and the administration's timidity in Vietnam, in an effort to capture blue-collar votes. **Regional Influences** Barely more than 500,000 votes separated Nixon and Humphrey, but the Republican edge in the Electoral College was comfortable and the combined anti-Democratic vote amounted to a repudiation of the Johnson-Humphrey Administration. Humphrey's strength was in the eastern seaboard states. Wallace won five states in the Deep South.

1972

Party	Candidate	Popular vote	Percent	Electoral vote
Republican	Richard M. Nixon (Calif.) and Spiro T. Agnew (Md.)	47,170,179	60.69	520
Democrat	George S. McGovern (S.Dak.) and R. Sargent Shriver (Md.)	29,171,791	37.53	17
American Independent	John G. Schmitz (Calif.)	1,090,673	1.40	—
People's	Benjamin Spock	78,751	0.10	—
Other		216,196	0.28	(1)
	Total Vote	77,727,590		
	Nixon Plurality	17,998,388		

Key Issues Seeking to create a Republican majority by converting Wallace Democrats, Nixon pursued a "Southern strategy" of denouncing busing, the welfare state, the media and intellectuals. McGovern was unable to overcome an image of radicalism furthered by Republican charges that he was the candidate of "acid, abortion, and amnesty." **Regional Influences** The GOP's Southern strategy was aided by an assassination attempt on Wallace that knocked him out of the race. Nixon lost only Massachusetts and the District of Columbia, but Democrats added to their majority in the Senate and maintained control of the House.

[1]The Libertarian slate of John Hospers and Theodora Nathan received 1 electoral vote from a Republican elector in Virginia.

1976

Party	Candidate	Popular vote	Percent	Electoral vote
Democrat	Jimmy Carter (Ga.) and Walter F. Mondale (Minn.)	40,830,763	50.06	297
Republican	Gerald R. Ford (Mich.) and Robert Dole (Kans.)	39,147,793	48.00	240[1]
Independent	Eugene J. McCarthy (Minn.)	756,691	0.93	—
Libertarian	Roger MacBride (Va.)	173,011	0.21	—
Other		647,631	0.79	—
	Total Vote	81,555,889		
	Carter Plurality	1,682,970		

Key Issues In the wake of Watergate, Carter ran a moralistic campaign as a political outsider. Vague on issues, he railed against the Washington bureaucracy and vowed to lead "a government that is as good and honest and decent . . . as filled with love as are the American people." He also promised Americans that he would never lie to them. **Regional Influences** Ford nearly overcame a huge early deficit in the polls. But Carter's background as a southern moderate enabled him to eke out a victory through wins in northern, southern and border states.

[1]Ronald Reagan received one electoral vote from an elector in Washington.

1980

Party	Candidate	Popular vote	Per-cent	Elec-toral vote
Republican	Ronald Reagan (Calif.) and George Bush (Tex.)	43,901,812	50.75	489
Democrat	Jimmy Carter (Ga.) and Walter F. Mondale (Minn.)	35,483,820	41.02	49
Indepen-dent	John B. Anderson (Ill.) and Patrick J. Lucey (Wis.)	5,719,722	6.61	—
Libertarian	Edward E. Clark (Calif.)	921,188	1.06	—
Other		486,754	0.56	—
	Total Vote	86,513,296		
	Reagan Plurality	8,417,992		

Key Issues Inflation, an energy shortage, the taking of American hostages by Iran and a strong primary challenge from Edward Kennedy of Massachusetts weakened Carter. Reagan, promising to get government "off the backs fo the American people," pledged to cut taxes, increase defense spending, and balance the federal budget. Anderson, a Republican, ran as an independent to the left of both Carter and Reagan. **Regional Influences** Reagan swept to a landslide win in the Electoral College as Carter carried only six states and Washington, D.C.

1984

Party	Candidate	Popular vote	Per-cent	Elec-toral vote
Republican	Ronald Reagan (Calif.) and George Bush (Tex.)	54,450,603	58.78	525
Democrat	Walter F. Mondale (Minn.) and Geraldine Ferraro (N.Y.)	37,573,671	40.56	13
Libertarian	David Bergland (Calif.)	227,949	0.25	—
Other		570,343	0.61	
	Total Vote	92,628,458		
	Reagan Plurality	16,876,932		

Key Issues The economy was flying after emerging in late 1983 from the worst economic downturn since the Great Depression. Reagan, whose commercials proclaimed it was "morning in America," ridiculed Mondale as an old-fashioned "tax-and-spend, gloom-and-doom" Democrat. Controversy over her husband's finances blunted Ferraro's appeal as the first woman on a major party ticket. **Regional Influences** Mondale carried only his home state of Minnesota and the District of Columbia as Reagan won the greatest electoral victory in American history and the fifth highest share of the popular vote.

1988

Party	Candidate	Popular vote	Per-cent	Elec-toral vote
Republican	George Bush (Tex.) and J. Danforth Quayle (Ind.)	48,881,011	53.37	426
Democrat	Michael S. Dukakis (Mass.) and Lloyd Bentsen (Tex.)	41,828,350	45.67	111[1]
Libertarian	Ron Paul (Texas)	431,499	0.47	—
New Alliance	Lenora Fulani (New York)	218,159	0.24	—
Other		226,852	0.25	—
	Total Vote	91,585,871		
	Bush Plurality	7,052,661		

Key Issues Trailing Dukakis by 17 points in early summer, Bush made an issue of his opponent's "liberalism," depicting the Massachusetts governor as soft on crime. Bush made a household name out of Willie Horton, a black Massachusetts prison inmate who raped a woman while on a prison furlough. Bush also called Dukakis a card-carrying member of the American Civil Liberties Union and said that he didn't share the same values as the American people. Dukakis' failure to respond to those charges and to shed the "liberal" label until late in the campaign ultimately doomed his candidacy, despite Bush's links to the Iran-Contra scandal and to Panama's drug-running leader, Gen. Mañuel Noriega. **Regional Influences** Dukakis won the District of Columbia and only 10 states: Washington, Oregon, Hawaii, New York, Minnesota, Wisconsin, Iowa, New York, West Virginia, Rhode Island and his home state of Massachusettts. Bush easily captured the formerly Democratic "solid South."

[1]Bentsen received one electoral vote for President.

1992

Party	Candidate	Popular vote	Per-cent	Elec-toral vote
Democrat	Bill Clinton (Ark.) and Al Gore (Tenn.)	44,908,233	42.95	370
Republican	George Bush (Tex.) and J. Danforth Quayle (Ind.)	39,102,282	37.40	168
Indepen-dent	Ross H. Perot (Tex.) and James H. Stockdale (Calif.)	19,721,433	18.86	—
Other		820,788	0.79	
	Total Vote	104,552,736		
	Clinton Plurality	5,805,951		

Key Issues Bush's approval ratings were sky high as little as 13 months before the election, but a flagging economy and a national debt that wouldn't go away spelled his downfall in a three-way race that saw billionaire Ross Perot capture more votes than any third-party candidate since Theodore Roosevelt in 1912. Excitement for Perot, who entered the race in March, quit in July, and re-entered the campaign in October, brought a record 102 million people to the polls. Clinton ran especially strong among women, who supported his stances in favor of abortion rights and a strong defense of the environment. **Regional Influences** Perot's presence prevented either major party candidate from capturing an outright majority in every state except New York, Maryland, Arkansas (all of which went for Clinton) and Mississippi (which supported Bush). But Clinton won pluralities in California, Georgia, Illinois, Massachusetts, Michigan, Minnesota, Missouri, New Jersey, Ohio, Pennsylvania, Tennessee, Washington and Wisconsin. The only states with double-digit electoral votes in Bush's column were Florida, Indiana, North Carolina, Texas and Virginia.

1996

Party	Candidate	Popular vote	Per-cent	Elec-toral vote
Democrat	Bill Clinton (Ark.) and Al Gore (Tenn.)	47,402,357	49.24	379
Republican	Bob Dole (Kans.) and Jack Kemp (N.Y.)	39,198,755	40.71	159
Reform	Ross H. Perot and Patrick Choate	8,085,402	8.40	--
Green	Ralph Nader	684,902	0.71	--
Libertarian	Harry Browne	485,798	0.50	--
Other		420,009	0.44	--
	Total Vote	96,277,223		
	Clinton Plurality	8,203,602		

[1]Other includes write-ins and "none of the above."

Key Issues Clinton easily won re-election, campaigning on the strong economy and declining crime rates. Less than half of the voting age population went to the polls, the lowest number since 1924. Among those who did vote, Clinton ran strong with women, Asian-Americans, and Hispanics, and captured about half of the voters who described themselves as Independents. Dole's refusal to contravene his own party's strict stand against abortion hurt him dearly among women, who overwhelmingly chose Clinton. Perot's presence in the race prevented Clinton from winning an outright majority, but was not nearly as influential as it had been four years earlier. **Regional Influences** The president carried 31 states, including New York, California, Florida, Illinois and Pennsylvania. Dole won 19 states, including Texas, Virginia, North Carolina, Georgia, and Indiana, as well as his home state of Kansas.

2000

Party	Candidate	Popular vote	Percent	Electoral vote
Republican	George W. Bush (Tex.) and Dick Cheney (Wyo.)	50,455,156	47.87	271
Democrat	Al Gore (Tenn.) and Joe Lieberman (Conn.)	50,992,335	48.38	266[1]
Green	Ralph Nader and Winona LaDuke	2,882,897	2.74	--
Reform	Pat Buchanan and Ezola Foster	448,892	0.42	--
Libertarian	Harry Browne	384,429	0.36	--
Other		232,932	0.23	--
	Total Vote	105,396,641		
	Gore Plurality	537,179		

1. One elector from the District of Columbia abstained.

▶THE ELECTORAL COLLEGE

The Electoral College is the body of electors chosen by all of the states that ultimately is responsible for selecting the president of the United States. The Framers did not want the nation's Chief Executive chosen by either the national legislature or the people directly. Instead they set up the Electoral College, under Article II, sections 2 and 3 of the Constitution to provide for indirect election of the president: "Each State shall appoint, in such manner as the legislature thereof may direct, a number of Electors, equal to the whole number of Senators and Representatives to which the State may be entitled in the Congress; but no Senator or Representative, or person holding an office of trust or profit under the United States, shall be appointed an Elector."

Electors were supposed to be distinguished, enlightened citizens who would cast a disinterested vote for president. From the start, however, electors have been instruments of partisan passions. At first, most state legislatures were responsible for choosing electors. By 1828, however, all states except South Carolina allowed electors to be chosen by direct popular election. (In South Carolina, the legislature continued to select electors until the Civil War.) When electors began to be selected by popular vote, parties presented slates of candidates for presidential electors who were tacitly pledged to support the party's nominees for president and vice president. This is how the practice began of states voting as a unit. Subsequently, many states passed laws requiring their electors to vote as a bloc. Where it is not required by law, it is customary for all of a state's electors to vote for the candidate receiving a plurality of the popular vote in that state. The names of the candidates for electors may or may not appear on the ballot alongside the names of the candidates to whom they are pledged. Voters really vote for presidential electors, though, even when they seem to be casting a ballot for a presidential candidate.

The presidential electors chosen by the voters in November meet in their state capitals on the first Monday after the second Wednesday in December to cast their vote for president and vice president. The results of this balloting are sent to the president of the U.S. Senate, the directors of the U.S. General Services Administration, the state's secretary of state, and to the judge of the Federal District Court of the district in which the electors gathered. Sealed state ballots are opened and counted at a joint session of Congress on January 6 following the election year.

Originally electors voted for two individuals for president on a single ballot. The winner of a majority of the vote was elected president, the runner-up vice president. The Framers fully expected there to be many elections in which no candidate would gain a majority of the vote and the president would have to be selected by the House of Representatives, where each state delegation would cast a single vote. But in 1789 and 1792 every elector voted for George Washington. In both years John Adams was the runner-up and, thus, vice president.

Problems inherent in this system became apparent once Washington was no longer a candidate. In 1796, Adams and Thomas Jefferson finished first and second in the balloting and were elected

Voter Turnout in Presidential Elections, 1928–2000

Year	Total Vote	Voting Age Population		Registered Voters	
		Number	Percent Voting	Number[1]	Percent Voting
1928	36,879,414	71,185,000	51.8%	N/A	N/A
1932	39,816,522	75,768,000	52.6	N/A	N/A
1936	45,646,817	80,354,000	56.8	N/A	N/A
1940	49,815,312	84,728,000	58.8	N/A	N/A
1944	48,025,684	95,573,000	56.1	N/A	N/A
1948	48,833,680	95,573,000	51.1	N/A	N/A
1952	61,551,919	99,929,000	61.6	N/A	N/A
1956	62,033,908	104,515,000	59.4	N/A	N/A
1960	68,838,204	109,159,000	63.06	N/A	N/A
1964	70,644,592	114,090,000	61.92	73,715,818	95.83%
1968	73,211,875	120,328,186	60.84	81,658,180	89.65
1972	77,718,554	140,776,000	55.21	97,328,541	79.85
1976	81,555,789	152,309,190	53.55	105,037,986	77.64
1980	86,515,221	164,597,000	52.56	113,043,734	76.53
1984	92,652,680	174,466,000	53.11	124,150,614	74.63
1988	91,594,693	182,778,000	50.11	126,379,628	72.48
1992	104,405,155	189,529,000	55.09	133,821,178	78.01
1996	96,456,345	196,511,000	49.08	146,211,960	65.97
2000	105,586,274	205,815,000	51.30	156,421,311	67.50

Source: Federal Election Commission. www.fec.gov

president and vice president, respectively, despite being fierce foes. By 1800, two formal parties had evolved which nominated a single candidate for both president and vice president. A Federalist elector purposely failed to vote for the party's vice presidential nominee, Thomas Pinckney, in order to assure a potential majority for Adams. But overzealous Republican electors all voted for both Jefferson and the party's vice presidential nominee, Aaron Burr. Both men received the same majority of the electoral vote and the election had to be decided by the House, where Jefferson won. This led to adoption of the Twelfth Amendment to the Constitution, implemented in 1804, which requires electors to cast separate ballots for president and vice president. If no candidate achieves a majority of the electoral vote for vice president, the position is filled by the Senate with each senator casting a single ballot. This has happened only once, when the Senate selected Richard M. Johnson after he fell one electoral vote short of a majority for vice president in 1836.

The 2000 Presidential Election

	REPUBLICAN George W. Bush/ Dick Cheney			DEMOCRAT Al Gore/ Joseph Lieberman			GREEN Ralph Nader/ Winona LaDuke	
State	Popular Vote	Percent	Electoral Vote	Popular Vote	Percent	Electoral Vote	Popular Vote	Percent
Alabama	941,173	56.48%	9	692,611	41.57%	—	18,323	1.10%
Alaska	167,398	58.62	3	79,004	27.67	—	28,747	10.07
Arizona	781,652	51.02	8	685,341	44.73	—	45,645	2.98
Arkansas	472,940	51.31	6	422,768	45.86	—	13,421	1.46
California	4,567,429	41.65	—	5,861,203	53.45	54	418,707	3.82
Colorado	883,748	50.75	8	738,227	42.39	—	91,434	5.25
Connecticut	561,094	38.44	—	816,015	55.91	8	64,452	4.42
Delaware	137,288	41.90	—	180,068	54.96	3	8,307	2.54
Dist. of Columbia	18,073	8.95	—	171,923	85.16	2[1]	10,576	5.24
Florida	2,912,790	48.85	25	2,912,253	48.84	—	97,488	1.63
Georgia	1,419,720	54.67	13	1,116,230	42.98	—	13,432	0.52
Hawaii	137,845	37.46	—	205,286	55.79	4	21,623	5.88
Idaho	336,937	67.17	4	138,637	27.64	—	12,292	2.45
Illinois	2,019,421	42.58	—	2,589,026	54.60	22	103,759	2.19
Indiana	1,245,836	56.65	12	901,980	41.01	—	18,531	0.84
Iowa	634,373	48.22	—	638,517	48.54	7	29,374	2.23
Kansas	622,332	58.04	6	399,276	37.24	—	36,086	3.37
Kentucky	872,492	56.50	8	638,898	41.37	—	23,192	1.50
Louisiana	927,871	52.55	9	792,344	44.88	—	20,473	1.16
Maine	286,616	43.97	—	319,951	49.09	4	37,127	5.70
Maryland	813,797	40.28	—	1,140,782	56.46	10	53,768	2.66
Massachusetts	878,502	32.50	—	1,616,487	59.8	12	173,564	6.42
Michigan	1,953,139	46.15	—	2,170,418	51.28	18	84,165	1.99
Minnesota	1,109,659	45.50	—	1,168,266	47.91	10	126,696	5.20
Mississippi	572,844	57.62	7	404,614	40.70	—	8,122	0.82
Missouri	1,189,924	50.42	11	1,111,138	47.08	—	38,515	1.63
Montana	240,178	58.44	3	137,126	33.36	—	24,437	5.95
Nebraska	433,862	62.25	5	231,780	33.25	—	24,540	3.52
Nevada	301,575	49.52	4	279,978	45.98	—	15,008	2.46
New Hampshire	273,559	48.07	4	266,348	46.80	—	22,198	3.90
New Jersey	1,284,173	40.29	—	1,788,850	56.13	15	94,554	2.97
New Mexico	286,417	47.85	—	286,783	47.91	5	21,251	3.55
New York	2,403,374	35.23	—	4,107,697	60.21	33	244,030	3.58
North Carolina	1,631,163	56.03	14	1,257,692	43.20	—	0	0.00
North Dakota	174,852	60.66	3	95,284	33.06	—	9,486	3.29
Ohio	2,350,363	49.99	21	2,183,628	46.44	—	117,799	2.51
Oklahoma	744,337	60.31	8	474,276	38.43	—	0	0.00
Oregon	713,577	46.52	—	720,342	46.96	7	77,357	5.04
Pennsylvania	2,281,127	46.43	—	2,485,967	50.60	23	103,392	2.10
Rhode Island	130,555	31.91	—	249,508	60.99	4	25,052	6.12
South Carolina	785,937	56.84	8	565,561	40.90	—	20,200	1.46
South Dakota	190,700	60.30	3	118,804	37.56	—	0	0.00
Tennessee	1,061,949	51.15	11	981,720	47.28	—	19,781	0.95
Texas	3,799,639	59.30	32	2,433,746	37.98	—	137,994	2.15
Utah	515,096	66.83	5	203,053	26.34	—	35,850	4.65
Vermont	119,775	40.70	—	149,022	50.63	3	20,374	6.92
Virginia	1,437,490	52.47	13	1,217,290	44.44	—	59,398	2.17
Washington	1,108,864	44.58	—	1,247,652	50.16	11	103,002	4.14
West Virginia	336,475	51.92	5	295,497	45.59	—	10,680	1.65
Wisconsin	1,237,279	47.61	—	1,242,987	47.83	11	94,070	3.62
Wyoming	147,947	67.76	3	60,481	27.70	—	4,625	2.12
Total	**50,455,156**	**47.87%**	**271**	**50,992,335**	**48.38%**	**266**	**2,882,897**	**2.74%**

1. One elector from the District of Columbia abstained. **Source:** Federal Election Commission. www.fec.gov

Today, 270 votes are required to reach a majority in the Electoral College. There have been two elections in which no candidate received a majority of the electoral vote. In 1824, no candidate achieved a majority of the vote, and in 1876, disputed results in several states prevented either Rutherford B. Hayes or Samuel J. Tilden from achieving a majority. John Quincy Adams and Hayes won those contests, respectively. A candidate also can be elected president despite losing the popular vote. This occurred, again in 1824 and 1876, when the House selected Adams and Hayes, though they lost the popular vote to Andrew Jackson and Tilden, respectively; in 1888, when Benjamin Harrison was elected over Grover Cleveland despite receiving a minority of the popular vote; and in 2000, when George W. Bush lost the popular vote by more than 400,000 votes to Al Gore, but won enough states for an Electoral College victory.

▶THE FEDERAL ELECTION CAMPAIGN ACT

In 1971 Congress passed the Federal Election Campaign Act to deal with various aspects of campaign financing. The law was amended and strengthened in 1974 and 1976, and the Federal Election Commission (FEC) was established to administer the law, which affects candidates for the U.S. House of Representatives, the U.S. Senate, and the presidency. The act requires disclosure of sources and uses of funds for federal elections, provides public financing for presidential elections, and sets limits on campaign contributions. The specific requirements of each of these three parts of the act are detailed below.

Public disclosure Candidates for federal office and the political committees that support them must register and file periodic disclosures of their campaign finance activities with the clerk of the House, the secretary of the Senate, or the FEC. These reports are available to the public within 48 hours of their disclosure. A candidate is defined as one who has raised or spent more than $5,000 in any given year in campaigning for federal office. A political committee, also known as a Political Action Committee (PAC) is defined as a club, committee, association, or organization that receives contributions or makes expenditures of more than $1,000 to a federal candidate in any calendar year. PACs are subject to different contirbution limits than are individuals.

Public financing Public financing is provided for eligible presidential candidates in primary and general elections, and for national party committees for the nominating conventions. Financing is given in the form of matching payments to primary candidates, public grants to nominees in the general election, and public grants to the national party committees for the conventions. The money for public financing is raised by the Presidential Election Campaign Fund, which collects three dollars from the tax payment of every taxpayer who checks off this box on his or her federal income tax return.

Contribution limits and prohibitions The Federal Election Campaign Act capped contributions to individual candidates at $1,000 per two-year election cycle, and donations to national political party committees to $20,000 per year. But a 1978 FEC ruling opened a loophole that allowed national political parties to accept unlimited "soft money" contributions from corporations, unions, and individuals, which did not count against the $20,000 limit. In theory, soft money contributions were supposedly limited to general party-building activities, but in practice, these monies were almost always spent in support of specific candidates for office.

After years of failed attempts, Congress in 2002 finally passed a campaign finance reform bill that closed the soft money loophole. The legislation, which took effect after the 2002 elections (subject to review by the Supreme Court) doubled the contribution limit to $2,000 per candidate per election cycle, raised the cap on hard money contributions to national political parties to $25,000 per year, and increased the limit on contributions to state and local political parties (for get-out-the-vote and voter registration efforts) from $5,000 to $10,000 per year. In addition, the law prohibits unions, corporations, and nonprofit groups from paying for so-called "issue ads" advocating the election or defeat of specific candidates within 60 days of a general election and 30 days of a primary. These ads must now be paid for only with regulated hard money.

POLITICAL OFFICE HOLDERS

▶THE VICE PRESIDENCY

Unlike the office of the president, that of the vice president has sometimes been left vacant after the death of the vice president, or his assumption

Campaign Contribution Limits

Type of Contribution	Individuals Old	Individuals New	PACs Old	PACs New
Contributions directly to political candidates	$1,000 per election cycle	$2,000 per election cycle	$5,000 per election cycle	$5,000 per election cycle
Hard money contributions to national party committees	$20,000 per year	$25,000 per year	$15,000 per year	$15,000 per year
Soft money contributions to national party committees	*UNLIMITED*	*BANNED*	*UNLIMITED*	*BANNED*
Contributions to state and local party committees	$5,000 per year	$10,000 per year	$5,000 per year	$5,000 per year
Total contributions	**$25,000 per year**	**$95,000 per cycle**	*UNLIMITED*	*UNLIMITED*

Note: The new limits took effect November 6, 2002, pending review by the U.S. Supreme Court, and will be indexed for inflation. An election cycle is two years. **Source:** Federal Elecion Commission.

of higher office on the death of the president. Until adoption of the 25th Amendment to the Constitution in 1967, there was no provision to fill a vacancy in the vice presidency. Under the amendment, the president must name a vice president when the office is vacant, and the nominee must pass a majority vote of approval in both houses of Congress. Gerald Ford, Richard Nixon's choice to replace Spiro Agnew after the latter's resignation in 1973, was the first vice president to gain the office under the amendment. The second was Nelson Rockefeller, whom Ford nominated to the position after he became president upon Nixon's resignation the following year. While the 25th Amendment does not supersede the presidential order of succession, it decreases the likelihood of the office's ever falling to the speaker of the House or a sitting cabinet member.

Vice Presidents of the United States

Name	Party	Tenure	State, birth-death
1. John Adams	Fed.	1789–97	Mass., 1735–1826
2. Thomas Jefferson	D-R	1797–1801	Va., 1743–1826
3. Aaron Burr	D-R	1801–05	N.Y., 1756–1836
4. George Clinton	D-R	1805–13†	N.Y., 1739–1812
5. Elbridge Gerry	D-R	1813–17†	Mass., 1744–1814
6. Daniel D. Tompkins	D-R	1817–25	N.Y., 1774–1825
7. John C. Calhoun	D-R	1825–33[1]	S.C., 1782–1850
8. Martin Van Buren	D	1833–37	N.Y., 1782–1862
9. Richard M. Johnson	D	1837–41[2]	Ky., 1780–1850
10. John Tyler	Whig	1841[3]	Va., 1790–1862
11. George M. Dallas	D	1845–49	Pa., 1792–1864
12. Millard Fillmore	Whig	1849–50[4]	N.Y., 1800–74
13. William R. King	D	1853–57†	Ala., 1786–1853
14. John C. Breckenridge	D	1857–61	Ky., 1821–75
15. Hannibal Hamlin	R	1861–65	Maine, 1809–91
16. Andrew Johnson	D	1865[5]	Tenn., 1808–75
17. Schuyler Colfax	R	1869–73	Ind., 1823–85
18. Henry Wilson	R	1873–77†	Mass., 1812–75
19. William A. Wheeler	R	1877–81	N.Y., 1819–87
20. Chester A. Arthur	R	1881[6]	N.Y., 1829–86
21. Thomas A. Hendricks	D	1885†	Ind., 1819–85
22. Levi P. Morton	R	1889–93	N.Y., 1824–1920
23. Adlai E. Stevenson	D	1893–97	Ill., 1835–1914
24. Garret A. Hobart	R	1897–1901†	N.J., 1844–99
25. Theodore Roosevelt	R	1901[7]	N.Y., 1858–1919
26. Charles W. Fairbanks	R	1905–09	Ind., 1852–1918
27. James S. Sherman	R	1909–13†	N.Y., 1855–1912
28. Thomas R. Marshall	D	1913–21	Ind., 1854–1925
29. Calvin Coolidge	R	1921–23[8]	Mass., 1872–1933
30. Charles G. Dawes	R	1925–29	Ill., 1865–1951
31. Charles Curtis	R	1929–33	Kans., 1860–1936
32. John Nance Garner	D	1933–41	Tex., 1868–1967
33. Henry A. Wallace	D	1941–45	Iowa, 1888–1965
34. Harry S Truman	D	1945[9]	Mo., 1884–1972
35. Alben W. Barkley	D	1949–53	Ky., 1877–1956
36. Richard M. Nixon	R	1953–61	Calif., 1913–95
37. Lyndon B. Johnson	D	1961–63[10]	Tex., 1908–73
38. Hubert H. Humphrey	D	1965–69	Minn., 1911–78
39. Spiro T. Agnew	R	1969–73[11]	Md., 1918–96
40. Gerald R. Ford	R	1973–74[12]	Mich., 1913–
41. Nelson A. Rockefeller	R	1974–77[13]	N.Y., 1908–79
42. Walter F. Mondale	D	1977–81	Minn., 1928–
43. George Bush	R	1981–89	Tex., 1924–
44. J. Danforth Quayle	R	1989–93	Ind., 1947–
45. Albert Gore	D	1993–2001	Tenn., 1948–
46. Richard Cheney	R	2001–	Wyo., 1941–

Notes: Fed. = Federalist. D = Democrat. D-R = Democratic-Republican. R = Republican. † = Died in office. 1. Resigned to become senator from South Carolina (1832-43). 2. Voted in by senate after no candidate for vice president gained a majority in the electoral college. 3. Became president after Benjamin Harrison's death. 4. Became president after Zachary Taylor's death. 5. Nominated by Republicans to run with Abraham Lincoln on the Union ticket; became president after Lincoln's assassination. 6. Became president after James Garfield's assassination. 7. Became president after William McKinley's assassination. 8. Became president after Warren Harding's death. 9. Became president after Franklin D. Roosevelt's death. 10. Became president after John F. Kennedy's assassination. 11. Resigned while under investigation for receiving kickbacks as governor of Maryland. 12. First vice president named under terms of the 25th amendment; assumed presidency after Richard Nixon resigned. 13. Named vice president by Ford.

Speakers of the U.S. House of Representatives

Name	Party	State	Dates in Office
1. Frederick A.C. Muhlenberg	D-R	Pa.	1789–91
2. Jonathan Trumbull	Fed.	Conn.	1791–93
3. Frederick A. C. Muhlenberg	D-R	Pa.	1793–95
4. Jonathan Dayton	Fed.	N.J.	1795–97
5. George Dent	Fed.	Md.	1797–99
6. Theodore Sedgwick	Fed.	Mass.	1799–1801
7. Nathaniel Macon	D-R	N.C.	1801–07
8. Joseph B. Varnum	D-R	Mass.	1807–11
9. Henry Clay	D-R	Ky.	1811–14
10. Langdon Cheves	D-R	S.C.	1814–15
11. Henry Clay	D-R	Ky.	1815–20
12. John W. Taylor	D-R	N.Y.	1820–21
13. Philip Barbour	D-R	Va.	1821–23
14. Henry Clay	D-R	Ky.	1823-25
15. John W. Taylor	D-R	N.Y.	1825–27
16. Andrew Stevenson	D	Va.	1827–34
17. John Bell	D	Tenn.	1834–35
18. James K. Polk	D	Tenn.	1835–39
19. Robert M.T. Hunter	NP	Va.	1839–41
20. John White	Whig	Ky.	1841–43
21. John W. Jones	D	Va.	1843–45
22. John W. Davis	D	Ind.	1845–47
23. Robert C. Winthrop	Whig	Mass.	1847–49
24. Howell Cobb	D	Ga.	1849–51
25. Linn Boyd	D	Ky.	1851–55
26. Nathaniel Banks	R	Mass.	1855–57
27. James L. Orr	D	S.C.	1857–59
28. William Pennington	Whig	N.J.	1859–61
29. Galusha A. Grow	R	Pa.	1861–63
30. Schuyler Colfax	R	Ind.	1863–69
31. James G. Blaine	R	Maine	1869–75
32. Michael C. Kerr	D	Ind.	1875–76
33. Samuel J. Randall	D	Pa.	1876–81
34. J. Warren Keifer	R	Ohio	1881–83
35. John G. Carlisle	D	Ky.	1883–89
36. Thomas B. Reed	R	Maine	1889–91
37. Charles F. Crisp	D	Ga.	1891–95
38. Thomas B. Reed	R	Maine	1895–99
39. David B. Henderson	R	Iowa	1899–1903
40. Joseph G. Cannon	R	Ill.	1903–11
41. Champ Clark	D	Mo.	1911–19
42. Frederick H. Gillett	R	Mass.	1919–25
43. Nicholas Longworth	R	Ohio	1925–31
44. John Nance Garner	D	Tex.	1931–33
45. Henry T. Rainey	D	Ill.	1933–34
46. Joseph W. Byrns	D	Tenn.	1935–36
47. William B. Bankhead	D	Ala.	1936–39
48. Sam Rayburn	D	Tex.	1940–46
49. Joseph W. Martin Jr.	R	Mass.	1947–49
50. Sam Rayburn	D	Tex.	1949–52
51. Joseph W. Martin Jr.	R	Mass.	1953–54
52. Sam Rayburn	D	Tex.	1955–61
53. John W. McCormack	D	Mass.	1962–71
54. Carl B. Albert	D	Okla.	1971–76
55. Thomas P. O'Neill Jr.	D	Mass.	1977–87
56. James C. Wright Jr.	D	Tex.	1987–89
57. Thomas S. Foley	D	Wash.	1989–95
58. Newt Gingrich	R	Ga.	1995–99
59. J. Dennis Hastert	R	Ill.	1999–

Notes: D = Democrat. Fed. = Federalist. R = Republican.

▶ PRESIDENTIAL ORDER OF SUCCESSION

Article II of the Constitution gives to Congress the power to determine the presidential order of succession should both the president and vice president die, become incapacitated or be disqualified from office. The present law, passed in 1947, puts the Speaker of the House first in line to the presidency, followed by the president pro tempore of the Senate. The order of succession then goes through the members of the Cabinet, in the order in which the executive departments were established:

(1) Secretary of State, (2) Secretary of the Treasury, (3) Secretary of Defense, (4) Attorney General, (5) Secretary of the Interior, (6) Secretary of Agriculture, (7) Secretary of Commerce, (8) Secretary of Labor, (9) Secretary of Health and Human Services, (10) Secretary of Housing and Urban Development, (11) Secretary of Transportation, (12) Secretary of Energy, (13) Secretary of Education, (14) Secretary of Veterans' Affairs (15) Secretary of Homeland Security. The following sentence, composed of words using the first letter (or letters) of each cabinet department, is often used as a mnemonic device to remember the order: See The Dog Jump In A Circle; Leave HEr HOuse To ENtertain EDucated Veterans' HOmes. (State, Treasury, Justice, Interior, Agriculture, Commerce, Labor, HEalth and Human Services, HOusing and Urban Development, Transportation, ENergy, EDucation, Veterans Affairs, Homeland Security.

Until the 1970 legislation removing the Postmaster General from the Cabinet and establishing an independent Postal Service, the Postmaster General was fifth in line to the presidency. The heads of new departments are automatically added to the line of succession as the new departments are created.

A Cabinet member must be a natural-born U.S. citizen and at least 35 years old in order to become acting president. If a Cabinet member next-in-line to fill a presidential vacancy were not yet 35, the presidency would pass to the next Cabinet member in the order of succession who had attained that age.

Cabinet Members

Washington Administration (1789-97)

Secretary of State	Thomas Jefferson	1789–93
	Edmund Randolph	1794–95
	Timothy Pickering	1795–97
Secretary of Treasury	Alexander Hamilton	1789–95
	Oliver Wolcott	1795–97
Secretary of War	Henry Knox	1789–94
	Timothy Pickering	1795
	James McHenry	1796–97
Attorney General	Edmund Randolph	1789–93
	William Bradford	1794–95
	Charles Lee	1795–97
Postmaster General	Samuel Osgood	1789–91
	Timothy Pickering	1791–94
	Joseph Habersham	1795–97

John Adams Administration (1797–1801)

Secretary of State	Timothy Pickering	1797–1800
	John Marshall	1800–1801
Secretary of Treasury	Oliver Wolcott	1797–1800
	Samuel Dexter	1800–1801
Secretary of War	James McHenry	1797–1800
	Samuel Dexter	1800–1801
Attorney General	Charles Lee	1797–1801
Postmaster General	Joseph Habersham	1797–1801
Secretary of Navy	Benjamin Stoddert	1798–1801

Jefferson Administration (1801–09)

Secretary of State	James Madison	1801–09
Secretary of Treasury	Samuel Dexter	1801
	Albert Gallatin	1801–09
Secretary of War	Henry Dearborn	1801–09
Attorney General	Levi Lincoln	1801–05
	Robert Smith	1805
	John Breckinridge	1805–06
	Caesar Rodney	1807–09
Postmaster General	Joseph Habersham	1801
	Gideon Granger	1801–09
Secretary of Navy	Robert Smith	1801–09

Madison Administration (1809–17)

Secretary of State	Robert Smith	1809–11
	James Monroe	1811–17
Secretary of Treasury	Albert Gallatin	1809–13
	George Campbell	1814
	Alexander Dallas	1814–16
	William Crawford	1816–17
Secretary of War	William Eustis	1809–13
	John Armstrong	1813–14
	James Monroe	1814–15
	William Crawford	1815–17
Attorney General	Caesar Rodney	1809–11
	William Pinkney	1811–14
	Richard Rush	1814–17
Postmaster General	Gideon Granger	1809–14
	Return Meigs	1814–17
Secretary of Navy	Paul Hamilton	1809–13
	William Jones	1813–14
	Benjamin Crowninshield	1814–17

Monroe Administration (1817–25)

Secretary of State	John Quincy Adams	1817–25
Secretary of Treasury	William Crawford	1817–25
Secretary of War	George Graham	1817
	John C. Calhoun	1817–25
Attorney General	Richard Rush	1817
	William Wirt	1817–25
Postmaster General	Return Meigs	1817–23
	John McLean	1823–25
Secretary of Navy	Benjamin Crowninshield	1817–18
	Smith Thompson	1818–23
	Samuel Southard	1823–25

John Quincy Adams Administration (1825–29)

Secretary of State	Henry Clay	1825–25
Secretary of Treasury	Richard Rush	1825–25
Secretary of War	James Barbour	1825–29
	Peter Porter	1828–29
Attorney General	William Wirt	1825–29
Postmaster General	John McLean	1825–29
Secretary of Navy	Samuel Southard	1825–29

Jackson Administration (1829–37)

Secretary of State	Martin Van Buren	1829–33
	Edward Livingston	1831–33
	Louis McLane	1833–34
	John Forsyth	1834–37
Secretary of Treasury	Samuel Ingham	1829–31
	Louis McLane	1831–33
	William Duane	1833
	Roger B. Taney	1833–34
	Levi Woodbury	1834–37
Secretary of War	John H. Eaton	1829–31

	Lewis Cass	1831–37
	Benjamin Butler	1837
Attorney General	John M. Berrien	1829–31
	Roger B. Taney	1831–33
	Benjamin Butler	1833–37
Postmaster General	William Barry	1829–35
	Amos Kendall	1835–37
Secretary of Navy	John Branch	1829–31
	Levi Woodbury	1831–34
	Mahlon Dickerson	1834–37

Van Buren Administration (1837–41)

Secretary of State	John Forsyth	1837–41
Secretary of Treasury	Levi Woodbury	1837–41
Secretary of War	Joel Poinsett	1837–41
Attorney General	Benjamin Butler	1837–38
	Felix Grundy	1838–40
	Henry D. Gilpin	1840–41
Postmaster General	Amos Kendall	1837–40
	John M. Niles	1840–41
Secretary of Navy	Mahlon Dickerson	1837–38
	James Paulding	1838–41

William Harrison Administration (1841)

Secretary of State	Daniel Webster	1841
Secretary of Treasury	Thomas Ewing	1841
Secretary of War	John Bell	1841
Attorney General	John J. Crittenden	1841
Postmaster General	Francis Granger	1841
Secretary of Navy	George Badger	1841

Tyler Administration (1841–45)

Secretary of State	Daniel Webster	1841–43
	Hugh S. Legaré	1843
	Abel P. Upshur	1843–44
	John C. Calhoun	1844–45
Secretary of Treasury	Thomas Ewing	1841
	Walter Forward	1841–43
	John C. Spencer	1843–44
	George Bibb	1844–45
Secretary of War	John Bell	1841
	John C. Spencer	1841–43
	James M. Porter	1843–44
	William Wilkins	1844–45
Attorney General	John J. Crittenden	1841
	Hugh S. Legaré	1841–43
	John Nelson	1843–45
Postmaster General	Francis Granger	1841
	Charles Wickliffe	1841
Secretary of Navy	George Badger	1841
	Abel P. Upshur	1841
	David Henshaw	1843–44
	Thomas Gilmer	1844
	John Y. Mason	1844–45

Polk Administration (1845–49)

Secretary of State	James Buchanan	1845–49
Secretary of Treasury	Robert J. Walker	1845–49
Secretary of War	William L. Marcy	1845–49
Attorney General	John Y. Mason	1845–46
	Nathan Clifford	1846–48
	Isaac Toucey	1848–49
Postmaster General	Cave Johnson	1845–49
Secretary of Navy	George Bancroft	1845–46
	John Y. Mason	1846–49

Taylor Administration (1849–50)

Secretary of State	John M. Clayton	1849–50
Secretary of Treasury	William Meredith	1849–50
Secretary of War	George Crawford	1849–50
Attorney General	Reverdy Johnson	1849–50
Postmaster General	Jacob Collamer	1849–50
Secretary of Navy	William Preston	1849–50
Secretary of Interior	Thomas Ewing	1849–50

Fillmore Administration (1850–53)

Secretary of State	Daniel Webster	1850–52
	Edward Everett	1852–53
Secretary of Treasury	Thomas Corwin	1850–53
Secretary of War	Charles Conrad	1850–53
Attorney General	John J. Crittenden	1850–53
Postmaster General	Nathan Hall	1850–52
	Sam D. Hubbard	1852–53
Secretary of Navy	William A. Graham	1852–53
	John P. Kennedy	1852–53
Secretary of Interior	Thomas McKennan	1850
	Alexander Stuart	1850–53

Pierce Administration (1853–57)

Secretary of State	William L. Marcy	1853–57
Secretary of Treasury	James Guthrie	1853–57
Secretary of War	Jefferson Davis	1853–57
Attorney General	Caleb Cushing	1853–57
Postmaster General	James Campbell	1853–57
Secretary of Navy	James C. Dobbin	1853–57
Secretary of Interior	Robert McClelland	1853–57

Buchanan Administration (1857–61)

Secretary of State	Lewis Cass	1857–60
	Jeremiah S. Black	1860–61
Secretary of Treasury	Howell Cobb	1857–60
	Philip Thomas	1860–61
	John A. Dix	1861
Secretary of War	John B. Floyd	1857–61
	Joseph Holt	1861
Attorney General	Jeremiah S. Black	1857–60
	Edwin M. Stanton	1860–61
Postmaster General	Aaron W. Brown	1857–59
	Joseph Holt	1859–61
	Horatio King	1861
Secretary of Navy	Isaac Toucey	1857–61
Secretary of Interior	Jacob Thompson	1857–61

Lincoln Administration (1861–65)

Secretary of State	William H. Seward	1861–65
Secretary of Treasury	Salmon P. Chase	1861–65
	William P. Fessenden	1864–65
	Hugh McCulloch	1865
Secretary of War	Simon Cameron	1861–62
	Edwin M. Stanton	1862–65
Attorney General	Edward Bates	1861–64
	James Speed	1864–65
Postmaster General	Horatio King	1861
	Montgomery Blair	1861–64
	William Dennison	1864–65
Secretary of Navy	Gideon Welles	1861–65
Secretary of Interior	Caleb B. Smith	1861–63
	John P. Usher	1863–65

Andrew Johnson Administration (1865–69)

Secretary of State	William H. Seward	1865–69
Secretary of Treasury	Hugh McCulloch	1865–69
Secretary of War	Edwin M. Stanton	1865–67
	Ulysses S. Grant	1867–68
	Lorenzo Thomas	1868
	John M. Schofield	1868–69
Attorney General	James Speed	1865–66
	Henry Stanbery	1866–68
	William M. Evarts	1868–69

Postmaster General	William Dennison	1865–66
	Alexander Randall	1866–69
Secretary of Navy	Gideon Welles	1865–69
Secretary of Interior	John P. Usher	1865
	James Harlan	1865–66
	Orville H. Browning	1866–69

Grant Administration (1869–77)

Secretary of State	Elihu B. Washburne	1869
	Hamilton Fish	1869–77
Secretary of Treasury	George S. Boutwell	1869–73
	William Richardson	1873–74
	Benjamin Bristow	1874–76
	Lot M. Morrill	1876–77
Secretary of War	John A. Rawlins	1869
	William T. Sherman	1869
	William W. Belknap	1869–76
	Alphonso Taft	1876
	James D. Cameron	1876–77
Attorney General	Ebenezer Hoar	1869–70
	Amos T. Ackerman	1870–71
	G. H. Williams	1871–75
	Edwards Pierrepont	1875–76
	Alphonso Taft	1876–77
Postmaster General	John A. J. Creswell	1869–74
	James W. Marshall	1874
	Marshall Jewell	1874–76
	James N. Tyner	1876–77
Secretary of Navy	Adolph E. Borie	1869
	George M. Robeson	1869–77
Secretary of Interior	Jacob D. Cox	1869–70
	Columbus Delano	1870–75
	Zachariah Chandler	1875–77

Hayes Administration (1877–81)

Secretary of State	William M. Evarts	1877–81
Secretary of Treasury	John Sherman	1877–81
Secretary of War	George W. McCrary	1877–79
	Alex Ramsey	1879–81
Attorney General	Charles Devens	1877–81
Postmaster General	David M. Key	1877–80
	Horace Maynard	1880–81
Secretary of Navy	Richard W. Thompson	1877–80
	Nathan Goff, Jr.	1881
Secretary of Interior	Carl Schurz	1877–81

Garfield Administration (1881)

Secretary of State	James G. Blaine	1881
Secretary of Treasury	William Windom	1881
Secretary of War	Robert T. Lincoln	1881
Attorney General	Wayne MacVeagh	1881
Postmaster General	Thomas L. James	1881
Secretary of Navy	William H. Hunt	1881
Secretary of Interior	Samuel J. Kirkwood	1881

Arthur Administration (1881–85)

Secretary of State	F. T. Frelinghuysen	1881–85
Secretary of Treasury	Charles J. Folger	1881–84
	Walter Q. Gresham	1884
	Hugh McCulloch	1884–85
Secretary of War	Robert T. Lincoln	1881–85
Attorney General	Benjamin H. Brewster	1881–85
Postmaster General	Timothy O. Howe	1881–83
	Walter Q. Gresham	1883–84
	Frank Hatton	1884–85
Secretary of Navy	William H. Hunt	1881–82
	William E. Chandler	1882–85
Secretary of Interior	Samuel J. Kirkwood	1881–82
	Henry M. Teller	1882–85

Cleveland Administration (1885–89)

Secretary of State	Thomas F. Bayard	1885–89
Secretary of Treasury	Daniel Manning	1885–87
	Charles S. Fairchild	1887–89
Secretary of War	William C. Endicott	1885–89
Attorney General	Augustus H. Garland	1885–89
Postmaster General	William F. Vilas	1885–88
	Don M. Dickinson	1888–89
Secretary of Navy	William C. Whitney	1885–89
Secretary of Interior	Lucius Q. C. Lamar	1885–88
	William F. Vilas	1888–89
Secretary of Agriculture	Norman J. Colman	1889

Benjamin Harrison Administration (1889–93)

Secretary of State	James G. Blaine	1889–92
	John W. Foster	1892–93
Secretary of Treasury	William Windom	1889–91
	Charles Foster	1891–93
Secretary of War	Redfield Proctor	1889–91
	Stephen B. Elkins	1891–93
Attorney General	William H. H. Miller	1889–91
Postmaster General	John Wanamaker	1889–93
Secretary of Navy	Benjamin F. Tracy	1889–93
Secretary of Interior	John W. Noble	1889–93
Secretary of Agriculture	Jeremiah M. Rusk	1889–93

Cleveland Administration (1893–97)

Secretary of State	Walter Q. Gresham	1893–95
	Richard Olney	1895–97
Secretary of Treasury	John G. Carlisle	1893–97
Secretary of War	Daniel S. Lamont	1893–97
Attorney General	Richard Olney	1893–95
	James Harmon	1895–97
Postmaster General	Wilson S. Bissell	1893–95
	William L. Wilson	1895–95
Secretary of Navy	Hilary A. Herbert	1893–97
Secretary of Interior	Hoke Smith	1893–96
	David R. Francis	1896–97
Secretary of Agriculture	Julius S. Morton	1893–97

McKinley Administration (1897–1901)

Secretary of State	John Sherman	1897–98
	William R. Day	1898
	John Hay	1898–1901
Secretary of Treasury	Lyman J. Gage	1897–1901
Secretary of War	Russell A. Alger	1897–99
	Elihu Root	1899–1901
Attorney General	Joseph McKenna	1897–98
	John W. Griggs	1898–1901
	Philander C. Knox	1901
Postmaster General	James A. Gary	1897–98
	Charles E. Smith	1898–1901
Secretary of Navy	John D. Long	1897–1901
Secretary of Interior	Cornelius N. Bliss	1897–99
	Ethan A. Hitchcock	1899–1901
Secretary of Agriculture	James Wilson	1897–1901

Theodore Roosevelt Administration (1901–09)

Secretary of State	John Hay	1901–05
	Elihu Root	1905–09
	Robert Bacon	1909
Secretary of Treasury	Lyman J. Gage	1901–02
	Leslie M. Shaw	1902–07
	George B. Cortelyou	1907–09
Secretary of War	Elihu Root	1901–04
	William H. Taft	1904–08
	Luke E. Wright	1908–09
Attorney General	Philander C. Knox	1901–04
	William H. Moody	1904–06
	Charles J. Bonaparte	1906–09

Postmaster General	Charles E. Smith	1901–02
	Henry C. Payne	1902–04
	Robert J. Wynne	1904–05
	George B. Cortelyou	1905–07
	George von L. Meyer	1907–09
Secretary of Navy	John D. Long	1901–02
	William H. Moody	1902–04
	Paul Morton	1904–05
	Charles J. Bonaparte	1905–06
	Victor H. Metcalf	1906–08
	Truman H. Newberry	1908–09
Secretary of Interior	Ethan A. Hitchcock	1901–07
	James R. Garfield	1907–09
Secretary of Agriculture	James Wilson	1901–09
Secretary of Labor and Commerce	George B. Cortelyou	1903–04
	Victor H. Metcalf	1904–06
	Oscar S. Straus	1906–09
	Charles Nagel	1909

Taft Administration (1909–13)

Secretary of State	Philander C. Knox	1909–13
Secretary of Treasury	Franklin MacVeagh	1909–13
Secretary of War	Jacob M. Dickinson	1909–11
	Henry L. Stimson	1911–13
Attorney General	George W. Wickersham	1909–13
Postmaster General	Frank H. Hitchcock	1909–13
Secretary of Navy	George von L. Meyer	1909–13
Secretary of Interior	Richard A. Ballinger	1909–11
	Walter Fisher	1911–13
Secretary of Agriculture	James Wilson	1909–13
Secretary of Labor and Commerce	Charles Nagel	1909–13

Wilson Administration (1913–21)

Secretary of State	William J. Bryan	1913–15
	Robert Lansing	1915–20
	Bainbridge Colby	1920–21
Secretary of Treasury	William G. McAdoo	1913–18
	Carter Glass	1918–20
	David F. Houston	1920–21
Secretary of War	Lindley M. Garrison	1913–16
	Newton D. Baker	1916–21
Attorney General	James C. McReynolds	1913–14
	Thomas W. Gregory	1914–19
	A. Mitchell Palmer	1919–21
Postmaster General	Albert S. Burleson	1913–21
Secretary of Navy	Josephus Daniels	1913–21
Secretary of Interior	Franklin K. Lane	1913–20
	John B. Payne	1920–21
Secretary of Agriculture	David F. Houston	1913–20
	Edwin T. Meredith	1920–21
Secretary of Commerce	William C. Redfield	1913–19
Secretary of Labor	William B. Wilson	1913–21

Harding Administration (1921–23)

Secretary of State	Charles E. Hughes	1921–23
Secretary of Treasury	Andrew Mellon	1921–23
Secretary of War	John W. Weeks	1921–23
Attorney General	Harry M. Daugherty	1921–23
Postmaster General	Will H. Hays	1921–22
	Hubert Work	1922–23
	Harry S. New	1923
Secretary of Navy	Edwin Denby	1921–23
Secretary of Interior	Albert B. Fall	1921–23
	Hubert Work	1923
Secretary of Agriculture	Henry C. Wallace	1921–23
Secretary of Commerce	Herbert C. Hoover	1921–23
Secretary of Labor	James J. Davis	1921–23

Coolidge Administration (1923–29)

Secretary of State	Charles E. Hughes	1923–25
	Frank B. Kellogg	1925–29
Secretary of Treasury	John W. Weeks	1923–25
	Dwight F. Davis	1925–29
Attorney General	Henry M. Daugherty	1923–24
	Harlan F. Stone	1923–25
	John G. Sargent	1925–29
Postmaster General	Harry S. New	1923–29
Secretary of Navy	Edwin Denby	1923–24
	Curtis D. Wilbur	1924–29
Secretary of Interior	Hubert Work	1923–28
	Roy O. West	1928–29
Secretary of Agriculture	Henry C. Wallace	1923–24
	Howard M. Gore	1924–25
	William M. Jardine	1925–29
Secretary of Commerce	Herbert C. Hoover	1923–28
	William F. Whiting	1928–29
Secretary of Labor	James J. Davis	1923–29

Hoover Administration (1929–33)

Secretary of State	Henry L. Stimson	1929–33
Secretary of Treasury	Andrew Mellon	1929–32
	Ogden L. Mills	1932–33
Secretary of War	James W. Good	1929
	Patrick J. Hurley	1929–33
Attorney General	William D. Mitchell	1929–33
Postmaster General	Walter F. Brown	1929–33
Secretary of Navy	Charles F. Adams	1929–33
Secretary of Interior	Ray L. Wilbur	1929–33
Secretary of Agriculture	Arthur M. Hyde	1929–33
Secretary of Commerce	Robert P. Lamont	1929–32
	Roy D. Chapin	1932–33
Secretary of Labor	James J. Davis	1929–30
	William N. Doak	1930–33

Franklin D. Roosevelt Administration (1933–45)

Secretary of State	Cordell Hull	1933–44
	Edward R. Stettinius, Jr.	1944–45
Secretary of Treasury	William H. Woodin	1933–34
	Henry Morgenthau, Jr.	1934–45
Secretary of War	George H. Dern	1933–36
	Henry A. Woodring	1936–40
	Henry L. Stimson	1940–45
Attorney General	Homer S. Cummings	1933–39
	Frank Murphy	1939–40
	Robert H. Jackson	1940–41
	Francis Biddle	1941–45
Postmaster General	James A. Farley	1933–40
	Frank C. Walker	1940–45
Secretary of Navy	Claude A. Swanson	1933–40
	Charles Edison	1940
	Frank Knox	1940–44
	James V. Forrestal	1944–45
Secretary of Interior	Harold L. Ickes	1933–45
Secretary of Agriculture	Henry A. Wallace	1933–40
	Claude R. Wickard	1940–45
Secretary of Commerce	Daniel C. Roper	1933–39
	Harry L. Hopkins	1939–40
	Jesse Jones	1940–45
	Henry A. Wallace	1945
Secretary of Labor	Frances Perkins	1933–45

Truman Administration (1945–53)

Secretary of State	Edward R. Stettinius, Jr.	1945
	James F. Byrnes	1945–47
	George C. Marshall	1947–49
	Dean G. Acheson	1949–53
Secretary of Treasury	Fred M. Vinson	1945–46
	John W. Snyder	1946–53
Secretary of War	Robert P. Patterson	1945–47
	Kenneth C. Royall	1947

Attorney General	Tom C. Clark	1945–49
	J. Howard McGrath	1949–52
	James P. McGranery	1952–53
Postmaster General	Frank C. Walker	1945
	Robert E. Hannegan	1945–47
	Jesse M. Donaldson	1947–53
Secretary of Navy	James V. Forrestal	1945–47
Secretary of Interior	Harold L. Ickes	1945–46
	Julius A. Krug	1946–49
	Oscar L. Chapman	1949–53
Secretary of Agriculture	Clinton P. Anderson	1945–48
	Charles F. Brannan	1948–53
Secretary of Commerce	Henry A. Wallace	1945–46
	W. Averell Harriman	1946–48
	Charles W. Sawyer	1948–53
Secretary of Labor	Lewis B. Schwellenbach	1945–48
	Maurice J. Tobin	1948–53
Secretary of Defense	James V. Forrestal	1947–49
	Louis A. Johnson	1949–50
	George C. Marshall	1950–51
	Robert A. Lovett	1951–53

Eisenhower Administration (1953–61)

Secretary of State	John Foster Dulles	1953–59
	Christian A. Herter	1959–61
Secretary of Treasury	George M. Humphrey	1953–57
	Robert B. Anderson	1957–61
Attorney General	Herbert Brownell, Jr.	1953–58
	William P. Rogers	1958–61
Postmaster General	Arthur E. Summerfield	1953–61
Secretary of Interior	Douglas McKay	1953–56
	Fred A. Seaton	1956–61
Secretary of Agriculture	Ezra T. Benson	1953–61
Secretary of Commerce	Sinclair Weeks	1953–58
	Lewis L. Strauss	1958–59
	Frederick H. Mueller	1959–61
Secretary of Labor	Martin P. Durkin	1953
	James P. Mitchell	1953–61
Secretary of Defense	Charles E. Wilson	1953–57
	Neil H. McElroy	1957–59
	Thomas S. Gates, Jr.	1959–61
Secretary of Health, Education, and Welfare	Oveta Culp Hobby	1953–55
	Marion B. Folsom	1955–58
	Arthur S. Flemming	1958–61

Kennedy Administration (1961–63)

Secretary of State	Dean Rusk	1961–63
Secretary of Treasury	C. Douglas Dillon	1961–63
Attorney General	Robert F. Kennedy	1961–63
Postmaster General	J. Edward Day	1961–63
	John A. Gronouski	1963
Secretary of Interior	Stewart L. Udall	1961–63
Secretary of Agriculture	Orville L. Freeman	1961–63
Secretary of Commerce	Luther H. Hodges	1961–63
Secretary of Labor	Arthur J. Goldberg	1961–62
	W. Willard Wirtz	1962–63
Secretary of Defense	Robert S. McNamara	1961–63
Secretary of Health, Education, and Welfare	Abraham A. Ribicoff	1961–62
	Anthony J. Celebrezze	1962–63

Lyndon Johnson Administration (1963–69)

Secretary of State	Dean Rusk	1963–69
Secretary of Treasury	C. Douglas Dillon	1963–65
	Henry H. Fowler	1965–69
Attorney General	Robert F. Kennedy	1963–64
	Nicholas Katzenbach	1965–66
	Ramsey Clark	1967–69
Postmaster General	John A. Gronouski	1963–65
	Lawrence F. O'Brien	1965–68
	Marvin Watson	1968–69
Secretary of Interior	Stewart L. Udall	1963–69
Secretary of Agriculture	Orville L. Freeman	1963–69
Secretary of Commerce	Luther H. Hodges	1963–64
	John T. Connor	1964–67
	Alexander B. Trowbridge	1967–68
	Cyrus R. Smith	1968–69
Secretary of Labor	W. Willard Wirtz	1963–69
Secretary of Defense	Robert F. McNamara	1963–68
	Clark Clifford	1968–69
Secretary of Health, Education, and Welfare	Anthony J. Celebrezze	1963–65
	John W. Gardner	1965–68
	Wilbur J. Cohen	1968–69
Secretary of Housing & Urban Development	Robert C. Weaver	1966–69
	Robert C. Wood	1969
Secretary of Transportation	Alan S. Boyd	1967–69

Nixon Administration (1969–74)

Secretary of State	William P. Rogers	1969–73
	Henry A. Kissinger	1973–74
Secretary of Treasury	David M. Kennedy	1969–70
	John B. Connally	1971–72
	George P. Shultz	1972–74
	William E. Simon	1974
Attorney General	John N. Mitchell	1969–72
	Richard G. Kleindienst	1973–73
	Elliot L. Richardson	1973
	William B. Saxbe	1973–74
Postmaster General	Winton M. Blount	1969–71
Secretary of Interior	Walter J. Hickel	1969–70
	Rogers Morton	1971–74
Secretary of Agriculture	Clifford M. Hardin	1969–71
	Earl L. Butz	1971–74
Secretary of Commerce	Maurice H. Stans	1969–72
	Peter G. Peterson	1972–73
	Frederick B. Dent	1973–74
Secretary of Labor	George P. Shultz	1969–70
	James D. Hodgson	1970–73
	Peter J. Brennan	1973–74
Secretary of Defense	Melvin R. Laird	1969–73
	Elliot L. Richardson	1973
	James R. Schlesinger	1973–74
Secretary of Health, Education, and Welfare	Robert H. Finch	1969–70
	Elliot L. Richardson	1970–73
	Caspar W. Weinberger	1973–74
Secretary of Housing & Urban Development	George Romney	1969–73
	James T. Lyon	1973–74
Secretary of Transportation	John A. Volpe	1969–73
	Claude S. Brinegar	1973–74

Ford Administration (1974–77)

Secretary of State	Henry A. Kissinger	1974–77
Secretary of Treasury	William E. Simon	1974–77
Attorney General	William Saxbe	1974–75
	Edward Levi	1975–77
Secretary of Interior	Rogers Morton	1974–75
	Stanley K. Hathaway	1975
	Thomas Kleppe	1975–77
Secretary of Agriculture	Earl L. Butz	1974–76
	John A. Knebel	1976–77
Secretary of Commerce	Frederick B. Dent	1974–75
	Rogers Morton	1975–76
	Elliot L. Richardson	1976–77
Secretary of Labor	Peter J. Brennan	1974–75
	John T. Dunlop	1975–76
	W. J. Usery	1976–77
Secretary of Defense	James R. Schlesinger	1974–75
	Donald Rumsfeld	1975–77
Secretary of Health, Education, and Welfare	Caspar Weinberger	1974–75
	Forrest D. Mathews	1975–77
Secretary of Housing & Urban Development	James T. Lynn	1974–75
	Carla A. Hills	1975–77
Secretary of Transportation	William T. Coleman	1975–77

Carter Administration (1977-81)

Secretary of State	Cyrus R. Vance	1977–80
	Edmund Muskie	1980–81
Secretary of Treasury	W. Michael Blumenthal	1977–79
	G. William Miller	1979–81
Attorney General	Griffin Bell	1977–79
	Benjamin R. Civiletti	1979–81
Secretary of Interior	Cecil D. Andrus	1977–81
Secretary of Agriculture	Robert Bergland	1977–81
Secretary of Commerce	Juanita M. Kreps	1977–79
	Philip M. Klutznick	1979–81
Secretary of Labor	F. Ray Marshall	1977–81
Secretary of Defense	Harold Brown	1977–81
Secretary of Health, Education, and Welfare	Joseph A. Califano	1977–79
	Patricia R. Harris	1979–80
Secretary of Health & Human Services[1]	Patricia R. Harris	1980–81
Secretary of Housing & Urban Development	Patricia R. Harris	1977–79
	Moon Landrieu	1979–81
Secretary of Transportation	Brock Adams	1977–79
	Neil E. Goldschmidt	1979–81
Secretary of Energy	James R. Schlesinger	1977–79
	Charles W. Duncan	1979–81
Secretary of Education[1]	Shirley M. Hufstedler	1980–81

1. The Dept. of Health, Education, and Welfare was split into the Dept. of Education and the Dept. of Health and Human Services on May 4, 1980.

Reagan Administration (1981–89)

Secretary of State	Alexander M. Haig	1981–82
	George P. Shultz	1982–89
Secretary of Treasury	Donald Regan	1981–85
	James A. Baker, III	1985–89
Secretary of Defense	Caspar Weinberger	1981–87
	Frank Carlucci	1987–89
Attorney General	William F. Smith	1981–85
	Edwin A. Meese, III	1985–88
	Richard L. Thornburgh	1988–89
Secretary of Interior	James Watt	1981–83
	William P. Clark, Jr.	1983–85
	Donald P. Hodel	1985–89
Secretary of Agriculture	John Block	1981–86
	Richard E. Lyng	1986–89
Secretary of Commerce	Malcolm Baldrige	1981–87
	C. William Verity Jr	1987-89
Secretary of Labor	Raymond Donovan	1981–85
	William E. Brock	1985–89
Secretary of Health & Human Services	Richard Schweiker	1981–83
	Margaret Heckler	1983–85
	Otis R. Bowen	1985–89
Secretary of Housing & Urban Development	Samuel Pierce	1981–89
Secretary of Transportation	Drew Lewis	1981–83
	Elizabeth Dole	1983–89
Secretary of Energy	James Edwards	1981–82
	Donald P. Hodel	1982–85
	John S. Herrington	1985–89
Secretary of Education	Terrel H. Bell	1981–85
	William J. Bennett	1985–89

George Bush Administration (1989–93)

Secretary of State	James A. Baker III	1989–92
	Lawrence Eagleburger	1992–93
Secretary of Treasury	Nicholas F. Brady	1989–93
Secretary of Defense	Dick Cheney	1989–93
Attorney General	Richard L. Thornburgh	1989–91
	William P. Barr	1991–93
Secretary of Interior	Manuel Lujan	1989–93
Secretary of Agriculture	Clayton K. Yeutter	1989–91
	Edward Madigan	1991–93
Secretary of Commerce	Robert A. Mosbacher	1989–91
	Barbara Franklin	1991–93
Secretary of Labor	Elizabeth Hanford Dole	1989–90
	Lynn Martin	1990–93
Secretary of Health & Human Services	Louis Sullivan	1989–93
Secretary of Housing & Urban Development	Jack F. Kemp	1989–93
Secretary of Transportation	Samuel K. Skinner	1989–91
	Andrew Card	1991–93
Secretary of Energy	James D. Watkins	1989–93
Secretary of Education	Lauro D. Cavazos	1989–90
	Lamar Alexander	1990–93
Secretary of Veterans' Affairs	Edward J. Derwinski	1989–92
	Anthony J. Principi	1992–93

Clinton Administration (1993–2001)

Secretary of State	Warren M. Christopher	1993–97
	Madeleine K. Albright	1997–2001
Secretary of Treasury	Lloyd Bentsen	1993–94
	Robert E. Rubin	1994–99
	Lawrence H. Summers	1999–2001
Secretary of Defense	Les Aspin	1993–94
	William Perry	1994–97
	William S. Cohen	1997–2001
Attorney General	Janet Reno	1993–2001
Secretary of Interior	Bruce Babbitt	1993–2001
Secretary of Agriculture	Mike Espy	1993–94
	Dan Glickman	1995–2001
Secretary of Commerce	Ronald H. Brown	1993–96
	Mickey Kantor	1996–97
	William M. Daley	1997–2000
	Norman Y. Mineta	2000–2001
Secretary of Labor	Robert B. Reich	1993–97
	Alexis M. Herman	1997–2001
Secretary of Health & Human Services	Donna E. Shalala	1993–2001
Secretary of Housing & Urban Development	Henry G. Cisneros	1993–97
	Andrew M. Cuomo	1997–2001
Secretary of Transportation	Federico F. Peña	1993–97
	Rodney E. Slater	1997–2001
Secretary of Energy	Hazel O'Leary	1993–97
	Federico F. Peña	1997–98
	Bill Richardson	1998–2001
Secretary of Education	Richard W. Riley	1993–2001
Secretary of Veterans' Affairs	Jesse Brown	1993–97
	Hershel Gober, acting	1997–98
	Togo D. West Jr.	1998–99
	Hershel Gober, acting	1999–2001

George W. Bush Administration (2001–)

Secretary of State	Colin Powell	2001–
Secretary of Treasury	Paul O'Neill	2001–02
	John Snow	2003-
Secretary of Defense	Donald Rumsfeld	2001–
Attorney General	John Ashcroft	2001–
Secretary of Interior	Gale Norton	2001–
Secretary of Agriculture	Ann Veneman	2001–
Secretary of Commerce	Donald Evans	2001–
Secretary of Labor	Elaine Chao	2001–
Secretary of Health & Human Services	Tommy Thompson	2001–
Secretary of Housing & Urban Development	Mel Martinez	2001–
Secretary of Transportation	Norman Mineta	2001–
Secretary of Energy	Spencer Abraham	2001–
Secretary of Education	Rod Paige	2001–
Secretary of Veterans' Affairs	Anthony Principi	2001–
Secretary of Homeland Security	Tom Ridge	2002-

THE U.S. SUPREME COURT

▶IMPORTANT SUPREME COURT DECISIONS

Marbury v. Madison (1803) The Court struck down a law "repugnant to the constitution" for the first time and set the precedent for judicial review of acts of Congress. In a politically ingenious ruling on the Judiciary Act of 1789, Chief Justice John Marshall asserted the Supreme Court's power "to say what the law is," while avoiding a confrontation with President Thomas Jefferson. Not until the *Dred Scott* case of 1857 would another Federal law be ruled unconstitutional.

Fletcher v. Peck (1810) The Court ruled that Georgia could not deprive land speculators of their title, even though the previous owners had obtained the land from the state through fraud and bribery. Arising from the infamous Yazoo land frauds of 1795, this decision followed the Constitution's obligation of contracts clause and was the first time the Court invalidated a state law.

Dartmouth College v. Woodward (1819) The Court encouraged business investment with this decision by treating corporate charters as fully protected contracts. Not even the state legislatures that originally granted them could tamper with charters to private corporations, unless they retained the power to do so. Dartmouth College remained a private institution despite New Hampshire's attempt to take it over. This decision, which opened the way for abuse of corporate privileges, would later be modified in the *Charles River Bridge* (1837) and *Munn v. Illinois* (1877) cases.

McCulloch v. Maryland (1819) "Broad," as opposed to "strict," construction of the Constitution received high court approval in Chief Justice John Marshall's opinion upholding the constitutionality of the national bank against a Maryland challenge. This ruling enhanced Federal governmental authority by liberally interpreting the power of Congress to make laws "necessary and proper" for its specified powers. At a time when states were trying to tax the Bank of the United States out of existence, this decision also forbade such state interference with the Federal government. "The power to tax," Marshall wrote, "involves the power to destroy."

Cohens v. Virginia (1821) With this ruling, the Court reiterated its power to hear appeals from state courts, and affirmed the national supremacy of Federal judicial power. Virginia's conviction of the Cohens for selling lottery tickets in violation of state law was upheld, but so too was the Cohens' right to appeal to the Court, which Virginia had challenged. Critics of judicial "consolidationalism" were reminded of the Court's comprehensive powers as the ultimate appellate court for all Americans.

Gibbons v. Ogden (1824) In a dispute arising from a New York ferry monopoly, the Court ruled that states could not restrain interstate commerce in any way, and that congressional power to regulate interstate commerce "does not stop at the jurisdictional lines of the several states." The decision helped prevent interstate trade wars, quite common under the Articles of Confederation, from breaking out under the Constitution. Chief Justice Marshall's opinion also confirmed the broad potential power of the Constitution's commerce clause.

Charles River Bridge v. Warren Bridge (1837) A key decision for economic development, this case arose when state-chartered proprietors of a Boston toll bridge objected that a new state-chartered bridge across the Charles River would put them out of business. Chief Justice Roger B. Taney, in his first constitutional ruling, held that state charters implied no vested rights and that ambiguities must be construed in favor of the public, which would benefit from the new toll-free bridge. This decision balanced private property rights against the public welfare.

Dred Scott v. Sanford (1857) Dred Scott, a Missouri slave, sued for his liberty after his owner took him into free territory. The Court ruled that Congress could not bar slavery in the territories. Scott remained a slave because the Missouri Compromise of 1820, prohibiting slavery from part of the Louisiana Purchase, violated the Fifth Amendment by depriving slave owners of their right to enjoy property without due process of law. Scott himself could not even sue, for he was held to be property, not a citizen. This decision sharpened sectional conflict by sweeping away legal barriers to the expansion of slavery.

Ex Parte Milligan (1866) President Abraham Lincoln's suspension of some civil liberties during the Civil War was attacked in this decision, which upheld the right of *habeas corpus*. The Court ruled that the president could not hold military tribunals in areas remote from battle and where civil courts were open and functioning. Milligan's conviction by such a Civil War tribunal in Indianapolis, was overturned. The Constitution, admonished the Court, applies "at all times, and under all circumstances."

Slaughter-House Cases (1873) In its first ruling on the Fourteenth Amendment, the Court held that Louisiana's grant of a butcher monopoly did not violate the privileges and immunities of competitors, nor deny them equal protection of the laws, nor deprive them of property without due process. Only a few rights deriving from "Federal citizenship" were subject to Federal protection, while states still protected most civil and property rights. Federal protection of civil rights, even for former slaves, was very narrowly interpreted in this ruling. But this decision broadly upheld business regulation by states until *Santa Clara Co. v. Southern Pacific Railroad Co.* (1886) applied the Fourteenth Amendment to defense of corporate property rights.

Chief Justices of the United States

Chief Justice	Tenure[1]	Appointed by
John Jay	1789–1795	George Washington
John Rutledge[3]	1795	George Washington
Oliver Ellsworth	1796–1800	George Washington
John Marshall[4]	1801–35	John Adams
Roger B. Taney	1836–64	Andrew Jackson
Salmon P. Chase	1864–73	Abraham Lincoln
Morrison R. Waite	1874–88	Ulysses S. Grant
Melville W. Fuller	1888–1910	Grover Cleveland
Edward D. White	1910–21	William Howard Taft
William Howard Taft[5]	1921–30	Warren G. Harding
Charles Evans Hughes[2]	1930–41	Herbert Hoover
Harlan F. Stone[2]	1941–46	Franklin D. Roosevelt
Fred M. Vinson	1946–53	Harry S Truman
Earl Warren	1953–69	Dwight D. Eisenhower
Warren E. Burger	1969–87	Richard M. Nixon
William H. Rehnquist[2]	1987–	Ronald Reagan

1. Dates are for tenure as Chief Justice. For complete tenure on Supreme Court, see "Supreme Court Justices." 2. Served as Associate Justice prior to appointment as Chief Justice. 3. Served one term, but appointment not confirmed by Senate. 4. Longest tenure as Chief Justice. 5. Formerly served as 27th president of the United States.

***Munn v. Illinois* (1877)** This decision, in one of the "Granger Cases," enabled states to regulate private property in the public interest when the public had an interest in that property. The Court held that Illinois laws setting maximum rates for grain storage did not violate the Fourteenth Amendment's ban on deprivation of property without due process of law, and did not restrain interstate commerce. But for the next half century, the Court imposed the burden of proof on the states for their regulatory laws.

***Civil Rights Cases* (1883)** Racial equality was postponed 80 years by this decision, which struck down the Civil Rights Act of 1875 and allowed for private segregation. The Fourteenth Amendment's guarantee of equal protection, the Court ruled, applied against state action—but not against private individuals, whose discrimination unaided by the states was beyond Federal control. Segregation of public facilities was approved soon afterward in *Plessy v. Ferguson* (1896).

Justices of the Supreme Court of the United States, 1789–2003

Name	Tenure	Appointed by
Baldwin, Henry	1830–44	Andrew Jackson
Barbour, Philip P.	1836–41	Andrew Jackson
Black, Hugo L.	1937–71	Franklin D. Roosevelt
Blackmun, Harry A.	1970–94	Richard M. Nixon
Blair, John	1789–96	George Washington
Blatchford, Samuel	1882–93	Chester A. Arthur
Bradley, Joseph P.	1870–92	Ulysses S. Grant
Brandeis, Louis D.	1916–39	Woodrow Wilson
Brennan, William J., Jr.	1956–90	Dwight D. Eisenhower
Brewer, David J.	1889–1910	Benjamin Harrison
Breyer, Stephen G.	1994–	Bill Clinton
Brown, Henry B.	1890–1906	Benjamin Harrison
Burger, Warren E.[1]	1969–87	Richard M. Nixon
Burton, Harold H.	1945–58	Harry S Truman
Butler, Pierce	1922–39	Warren G. Harding
Byrnes, James F.	1941–42	Franklin D. Roosevelt
Campbell, John A.	1853–61	Franklin Pierce
Cardozo, Benjamin N.	1932–38	Herbert Hoover
Catron, John	1837–65	Martin Van Buren
Chase, Salmon P.[1]	1864–73	Abraham Lincoln
Chase, Samuel	1796–1811	George Washington
Clark, Tom C.	1949–67	Harry S Truman
Clarke, John H.	1916–22	Woodrow Wilson
Clifford, Nathan	1858–81	James J. Buchanan
Curtis, Benjamin R.	1851–57	Millard Fillmore
Cushing, William	1789–1810	George Washington
Daniel, Peter V.	1841–60	Martin Van Buren
Davis, David	1862–77	Abraham Lincoln
Day, William R.	1903–22	Theodore Roosevelt
Douglas, William O.[2]	1939–75	Franklin D. Roosevelt
Duval, Gabriel	1811–36	James Madison
Ellsworth, Oliver[1]	1796–1800	George Washington
Field, Stephen J.	1863–97	Abraham Lincoln
Fortas, Abe	1965–69	Lyndon B. Johnson
Frankfurter, Felix	1939–62	Franklin D. Roosevelt
Fuller, Melville W.[1]	1888–1910	Grover Cleveland
Ginsburg, Ruth Bader	1993–	Bill Clinton
Goldberg, Arthur J.	1962–65	John F. Kennedy
Gray, Horace	1881–1902	Chester A. Arthur
Grier, Robert C.	1846–70	James K. Polk
Harlan, John Marshall	1877–1911	Rutherford B. Hayes
Harlan, John Marshall[3]	1955–71	Dwight D. Eisenhower
Harrison, Robert H.	1789–90	George Washington
Holmes, Oliver Wendell	1902–32	Theodore Roosevelt
Hughes, Charles Evans[1,4]	1910–16	William Howard Taft
	1930–41	Herbert Hoover
Hunt, Ward	1872–82	Ulysses S. Grant
Iredell, James	1790–99	George Washington
Jackson, Howell E.	1893–95	Benjamin Harrison
Jackson, Robert H.	1941–54	Franklin D. Roosevelt
Jay, John[1]	1789–95	George Washington
Johnson, Thomas	1791–93	George Washington
Johnson, William	1804–34	Thomas Jefferson
Kennedy, Anthony M.	1987–	Ronald Reagan
Lamar, Joseph R.	1911–16	William Howard Taft
Lamar, Lucius Q. C.	1888–93	Grover Cleveland
Livingston, H. Brockholst	1806–23	Thomas Jefferson
Lurton, Horace H.	1910–14	William Howard Taft
Marshall, John[1]	1801–35	John Adams
Marshall, Thurgood	1967–92	Lyndon B. Johnson
Matthews, Stanley	1881–89	James A. Garfield
McKenna, Joseph	1898–1925	William McKinley
McKinley, John	1837–52	Martin Van Buren
McLean, John	1829–61	Andrew Jackson
McReynolds, James C.	1914–41	Woodrow Wilson
Miller, Samuel F.	1862–90	Abraham Lincoln
Minton, Sherman	1949–56	Harry S Truman
Moody, William H.	1906–10	Theodore Roosevelt
Moore, Alfred	1799–1804	John Adams
Murphy, Frank	1940–49	Franklin D. Roosevelt
Nelson, Samuel	1845–72	John Tyler
O'Connor, Sandra Day	1981–	Ronald Reagan
Paterson, William	1793–1806	George Washington
Peckham, Rufus W.	1895–1910	Grover Cleveland
Pitney, Mahlon	1912–22	William Howard Taft
Powell, Lewis F., Jr.	1972–87	Richard M. Nixon
Reed, Stanley F.	1938–57	Franklin D. Roosevelt
Rehnquist, William H.[1]	1972–	Richard M. Nixon
Roberts, Owen J.	1930–45	Herbert Hoover
Rutledge, John[1]	1789–91	George Washington
	1795	George Washington
Rutledge, Wiley B.	1943–49	Franklin D. Roosevelt
Sanford, Edward T.	1923–30	Warren G. Harding
Scalia, Antonin	1986–	Ronald Reagan
Shiras, George	1892–1903	Benjamin Harrison
Souter, David H.	1990–	George Bush
Stevens, John Paul	1975–	Gerald R. Ford
Stewart, Potter	1959–81	Dwight D. Eisenhower
Stone, Harlan F.[1]	1925–46	Calvin Coolidge
Story, Joseph	1811–45	James Madison
Strong, William	1870–80	Ulysses S. Grant
Sutherland, George	1922–38	Warren G. Harding
Swayne, Noah H.	1862–81	Abraham Lincoln
Taft, William Howard[1,5]	1921–30	Warren G. Harding
Taney, Roger B.[1]	1836–64	Andrew Jackson
Thomas, Clarence	1991–	George Bush
Thompson, Smith	1823–43	James Monroe
Todd, Thomas	1807–26	Thomas Jefferson
Trimble, Robert	1826–28	John Quincy Adams
Van Devanter, Willis	1910–37	William Howard Taft
Vinson, Fred M.[1]	1946–53	Harry S Truman
Waite, Morrison R.[1]	1874–88	Ulysses S. Grant
Warren, Earl[1]	1953–69	Dwight D. Eisenhower
Washington, Bushrod	1798–1829	John Adams
Wayne, James M.	1835–67	Andrew Jackson
White, Byron R.	1962–93	John F. Kennedy
White, Edward D.[1]	1894–1921	Grover Cleveland
Whittaker, Charles E.	1957–62	Dwight D. Eisenhower
Wilson, James	1789–98	George Washington
Woodbury, Levi	1845–51	James K. Polk
Woods, William B.	1880–87	Rutherford B. Hayes

Note: Dates reflect complete tenure on the Supreme Court, including tenure as Chief Justice. 1. See "Chief Justices of the United States" for dates of tenure and appointment as Chief Justice. 2. Longest-serving justice. 3. The two Harlans were grandfather and grandson. 4. Stepped down as Associate Justice to run for president in 1916; later appointed Chief Justice. 5. Formerly served as 27th U.S. president

United States v. E.C. Knight Co. (1895) The first ruling on the Sherman Antitrust Act of 1890, this decision curtailed Federal regulation of monopolies by placing national manufacturers beyond the reach of the Constitution's commerce clause. Only the actual interstate commerce of monopolies, not their production activities, was subject to Federal control. The Court's distinction between production and commerce impeded Federal regulation of manufacturing until *National Labor Relations Board v. Jones & Laughlin Steel Corp.* (1937).

Plessy v. Ferguson (1896) The "separate but equal" doctrine supporting public segregation by law received the Court's approval in this ruling, which originated with segregated railroad cars in Louisiana. The Court held that as long as equal accommodations were provided, segregation was not discrimination and did not deprive blacks of equal protection of the laws under the Fourteenth Amendment. This decision was overturned in *Brown v. Board of Education* (1954).

Lochner v. New York (1905) This decision struck down a New York law placing limits on maximum working hours for bakers. The law violated the Fourteenth Amendment by restricting individual "freedom of contract" to buy and sell labor, and was an excessive use of state police power, the Court held. The ruling was soon modified in *Muller v. Oregon* (1908), which approved state-regulated limits on women's labor after the Court used sociological and economic data to consider the health and morals of women workers.

Standard Oil Co. of New Jersey v. United States (1911) Federal efforts to break up monopolies under the Sherman Antitrust Act had to follow the "rule of reason," according to this ruling. Only those combinations in restraint of trade which were contrary to the public interest, and therefore unreasonable, were illegal. Although the Taft administration's prosecution of Standard Oil was upheld, breaking up one of the nation's leading monopolies, further antitrust suits were impaired by this decision, which facilitated the 1920s merger movement.

Schenk v. United States (1919) The Court unanimously held that World War I limits on freedom of speech did not violate the First Amendment—if the speech in question represented a "clear and present danger." That famous doctrine of Justice Oliver Wendell Holmes, which approved the arrest of a draft resister for handing out pamphlets to soldiers in wartime, became an important standard for interpreting the First Amendment. But in subsequent cases of this period, the Court added that the mere "bad tendency" of speech to cause danger could be grounds for censorship.

Schechter Poultry Corp. v. United States (1935) At the height of its assault on the New Deal, the Court struck down the National Industrial Recovery Act in the famous "Sick Chicken Case." The NIRA was found to delegate excessive legislative regulatory powers to the executive without constitutional authority, and to regulate commerce within states in violation of the commerce clause. Schechter's kosher chicken supply house in New York did not have to abide by the NIRA's rigid industry codes, the Court ruled.

National Labor Relations Board v. Jones & Laughlin Steel Corp. (1937) Under pressure from the public and President Franklin D. Roosevelt, the Court abruptly reversed itself and began approving New Deal legislation. In this case, laws protecting unions and barring "unfair labor practices" were upheld by the "stream of commerce" doctrine that employers who sold their goods and obtained their raw materials through interstate commerce were subject to Federal regulation. This ruling overturned *U.S. v. E.C. Knight Co.* (1895) and became the basis for the expansive understanding of the commerce power.

West Virginia Board of Education v. Barnette (1943) The Court reversed its earlier ruling in *Minersville School District v. Gobitis* (1940), which had required Jehovah's Witnesses to salute the flag in school. In this case, also brought against a Jehovah's Witness, the Court recognized that refusing to salute the flag did not violate anyone's rights, and that the First Amendment protected the "right of silence" as well as freedom of speech.

Korematsu v. United States (1944) President Franklin D. Roosevelt's Executive Order No. 9066, which approved the West Coast evacuation and internment of 120,000 Japanese-Americans during World War II, was upheld on the grounds of "military necessity" in this ruling. The Court was reluctant to interfere with executive authority in time of national emergency. But in *Ex parte Endo* (1944), the Court held that persons of proven loyalty should not be interned. In August 1988, Congress made a formal apology to former internees and appropriated $1.25 billion in compensation for the 60,000 survivors.

Dennis v. United States (1951) At the height of the postwar "Red Scare," the Court upheld the conviction of 11 American Communist leaders under the Smith Act of 1940, which made it a crime to belong to organizations teaching or advocating the violent overthrow of the government. The "clear and present danger" doctrine could be disregarded, the Court held, if "the gravity of the 'evil,' discounted by its improbability, justifies such invasion of free speech as is necessary to avoid the evil." Over 100 Communists were indicted as a result, effectively destroying the Communist Party as a political force.

Youngstown Sheet and Tube Co. v. Sawyer (1952) During the Korean War, when President Harry S Truman seized steel plants to keep them operating despite a strike, the Court held that his action was an unconstitutional usurpation of legislative authority. Only an act of Congress, not the president's inherent executive powers or military powers as commander-in-chief, could justify such a sizeable confiscation of property, despite the wartime emergency.

Brown v. Board of Education of Topeka (1954) Chief Justice Earl Warren led the Court unanimously to decide that segregated schools violated the equal protection clause of the Fourteenth Amendment. The "separate but equal" doctrine of *Plessy v. Ferguson* (1896) was overruled after a series of cases dating back to *Missouri ex. rel. Gaines v. Canada* (1938) had already limited it. "Separate educational facilities are inherently unequal," held the Court. Efforts to desegregate southern schools after the *Brown* decision met with massive resistance for many years.

Baker v. Carr (1962) Overrepresentation of rural districts in state legislatures, which effectively disfranchised millions of voters, led the Court to abandon its traditional non-interference in drawing legislative boundaries. Tennessee citizens deprived of full representation by "arbitrary and capricious" malapportionment were denied equal protection under the Fourteenth Amendment, ruled the Court. All states eventually reapportioned their legislatures in conformance with the "one man, one vote" doctrine of *Reynolds v. Sims* (1964).

Gideon v. Wainwright (1963) Reversing an earlier ruling in *Betts v. Brady* (1942), the Court held that the Sixth Amendment guaranteed access to qualified counsel, which was "fundamental to a fair trial." Gideon was entitled to a retrial because Florida failed to provide him with an attorney. After this decision, states were required to furnish public defenders for indigent defendants in felony cases. In *Argersinger v. Hamlin* (1972), the ruling was extended to all cases that might result in imprisonment.

Heart of Atlanta Motel, Inc. v. United States (1964) The Court upheld Title II of the Civil Rights Act of 1964, outlawing private discrimination in public accommodations, as a legitimate exertion of Federal power over interstate commerce. Congress had "ample power" to forbid racial discrimination in facilities that affected commerce by serving interstate travelers. The Heart of Atlanta Motel was located on two interstate highways, so the Court could sidestep the *Civil Rights Cases* (1883) protection of private discrimination to overrule it.

Griswold v. Connecticut (1965) In striking down an 1879 Connecticut law against the use of contraceptives, the Court established a "right to privacy" that was implied by, though not specifically enumerated in the First, Third, Fourth, Fifth, Ninth, and Fourteenth Amendments. The case is most notable for laying the groundwork for other legal challenges invoking this newfound right to privacy. Foremost among them is the 1973 *Roe v. Wade* decision allowing women to choose abortion.

South Carolina v. Katzenbach (1966) Federal intervention on behalf of voting rights was upheld in this decision. South Carolina sued the Attorney General, contending that the 1965 Voting Rights Act encroached on the reserved powers of the states, treated the states unequally, and violated separation of powers. Chief Justice Warren ruled that the Fifteenth Amendment gave Congress broad powers to "use any rational means to effectuate the constitutional prohibition of racial discrimination in voting." After this decision, blacks registered and voted in massive numbers in the South.

Miranda v. Arizona (1966) Expanding upon *Gideon v. Wainwright* (1963) and *Escobedo v. Illinois* (1964), the Court set forth stringent interrogation procedures for criminal suspects to protect their Fifth Amendment freedom from self-incrimination. Miranda's confession to kidnapping and rape was obtained without counsel and without his having been advised of his right to silence, so it was ruled inadmissable as evidence. This decision obliged police to advise suspects of their rights upon taking them into custody.

New York Times Co. v. United States (1971) When the *New York Times* and the *Washington Post* published the top-secret "Pentagon Papers" in 1971, revealing government duplicity in the Vietnam War, the Nixon administration obtained an injunction against the *Times* on grounds of national security. But in a brief *per curiam* opinion, the Court observed that in this case, the government had not met the "heavy burden of showing justification" for "prior restraint" on freedom of the press.

Roe v. Wade (1973) In a controversial ruling, the Court held that state laws restricting abortion were an unconstitutional invasion of a woman's right to privacy. Only in the last trimester of pregnancy, when the fetus achieved viability outside the womb, might states regulate abortion—except when the life or health of the mother was at stake. In *Planned Parenthood of Central Missouri v. Danforth* (1976), the Court added that wives did not need their husbands' consent to obtain abortions.

United States v. Nixon (1974) In a unanimous ruling, the Court held that the secret White House recordings of President Richard M. Nixon's conversations with aides were subject to subpoena in the Watergate coverup trial. Nixon's claim to "executive privilege" was rejected as invalid because military and national security issues were not at stake, and Chief Justice Warren Burger cited *Marbury v. Madison* (1803) to assert the Court's primacy in constitutional issues. Once the tapes were released, documenting Nixon's obstruction of justice, the president resigned to avoid impeachment.

University of California Regents v. Bakke (1978) Twice refused admission to medical school, Bakke sued the University of California for giving "affirmative action" preference to less-qualified black applicants. In an ambiguous 5-4 ruling, the Court agreed that Bakke's right to equal protection had been denied, that he should be admitted, and that affirmative action quotas should be discarded. But at the same time, the Court recognized race as "a factor" in admissions and hiring decisions. Affirmative action could continue as long as rigid quotas did not constitute, in effect, "reverse discrimination."

Immigration and Naturalization Service v. Chadha (1983) The legislative veto, contained in hundreds of Federal statutes since 1932, was disallowed in this decision. Congress exceeded its constitutional powers when it blocked the Attorney General's suspension of a deportation order for Jagdish Rai Chadha, a Kenyan student who overstayed his visa. The Court held that the Immigration and Nationality Act's legislative veto provision violated the constitutional separation of powers. Chief Justice Burger recognized that Congress would prefer to delegate authority to the executive branch and reserve the right to veto administrative regulations, but "we have not found a better way to preserve freedom" than the separation of powers.

Bowers v. Hardwick (1986) In a controversial 5-4 decision applauded by fundamentalists but protested by gay activists, the Court ruled that the constitutional right to privacy does not protect homosexual relations, even between consenting adults in their own homes. Georgia's law against oral and anal sex, passed in 1816, could be applied to homosexuals (the Court declined to rule on whether heterosexuals might also be prosecuted). The decision raised fears of bedroom patrols and sexual surveillance, despite a right to privacy in intimate personal matters established in cases dating back to the 1920s. Justice Byron White ruled that "none of the rights announced in those cases bears any resemblance to the claimed constitutional right of homosexuals to engage in acts of sodomy."

Bush v. Gore (2000) For the first time in the nation's history, the Court found itself in the position of deciding a presidential election. With Florida's decisive 25 electoral votes hanging in the balance, Vice Pres. Al Gore filed suit in state court to begin a recount of ballots in several counties where machines were unable to determine the voter's selection. Texas Gov. George W. Bush appealed the decision to the Supreme Court, which ruled that because there were no uniform standards for how to conduct a recountt, doing so would violate the Fourteenth Amendment's guarantee of equal protection. The highly controversial 5-4 decision ended the recount 36 days after Election Day, and with it, Gore's chance of winning the presidency.

The Federal Government

In their desire to create a government based on an elaborate system of "checks and balances," the Founding Fathers divided the sources of power into three separate and distinct branches of government—the legislative, the judicial, and the executive. The fundamental purpose, organization, and workings of these three branches are set down in the first three articles of the Constitution. Despite the passing of more than two centuries, the creation of dozens of departments, agencies, and commissions, the ongoing employment of almost 2.5 million civilian workers, and the presence of a standing peacetime military force of some 1.5 million, this structure remains essentially unchanged.

Below is a list of every major body within the Federal Government. Wherever possible, a Web home page is included. Every entry mentions the date each entity was founded and summarizes its official function. (The primary source of this information is the National Archives and Records Administration, Office of the Federal Register, *U.S. Government Manual*.)

THE JUDICIAL BRANCH

▶SUPREME COURT OF THE UNITED STATES

United States Supreme Court Building, 1 First St. NE, Washington, DC 20543. (202) 479-3000. www.supremecourtus.gov. Created by Judiciary Act of September 24, 1789 in accordance with Article III, section 1 of the Constitution. Composed of the chief justice and a number of associate justices to be fixed by Congress. Justices (including the chief justice) are chosen by the president with the advice and consent of the Senate and have lifetime tenure. Court terms begin the first Monday of October and usually last until the end of June. In recent years, the Court has seen the size of its docket nearly double (from 4,212 cases in 1970 to more than 9,000 in 2002), but it has heard fewer and fewer of these cases (see the accompanying table).

▶LOWER COURTS

U.S. Courts of Appeals

These intermediate appellate courts were created by act of March 3, 1891, to relieve the Supreme Court of having to reconsider all trials originally decided by federal courts. Decisions of these courts are final except when law provides for direct review by the Supreme Court. Each of the 50 states is assigned to one of the following judicial circuits that compose the Court of Appeals system.

District of Columbia Circuit: Washington, D.C.
First Circuit: Maine, Massachusetts, New Hampshire, Rhode Island, Puerto Rico.

The Supreme Court, 2003-04

Name	Appointed by	Born	Law school
William H. Rehnquist (chief justice)	Nixon, 1972; Reagan, 1986	1924	Stanford
John Paul Stevens	Ford, 1975	1920	Northwestern
Sandra Day O'Connor	Reagan, 1981	1930	Stanford
Antonin Scalia	Reagan, 1986	1936	Harvard
Anthony M. Kennedy	Reagan, 1987	1936	Harvard
David H. Souter	Bush, 1990	1939	Harvard
Clarence Thomas	Bush, 1991	1948	Yale
Ruth Bader Ginsburg	Clinton, 1993	1933	Columbia
Stephen G. Breyer	Clinton, 1994	1938	Harvard

Cases Before U.S. Supreme Court, U.S. Courts of Appeals, and U.S. District Courts, 1970–2002

Status	1970	1980	1990	1995	2000	2001	2002
U.S. Supreme Court[1]							
Total cases on docket	4,212	5,144	6,316	7,565	8,445	8,965	9,176
Cases argued	151	154	125	90	83	86	88
Number of signed opinions	109	123	112	75	79	83	85
U.S. Courts of Appeals							
Cases commenced	11,662	23,200	40,898	49,671	54,967	57,464	57,555
Cases terminated	10,699	20,887	38,520	50,085	56,512	57,422	56,583
Cases disposed of[1]	6,139	10,607	21,006	28,187	27,516	28,840	22,502
Median months to final disposition[2]	8.2	8.9	10.1	10.5	11.6	10.9	10.7
U.S. District Courts							
Civil cases commenced[3]	87,300	168,800	217,900	239,013	259,517	250,907	274,841
Trials[3, 4]	8,000	10,100	9,200	7,700	5,780	6,513	6,015
Percent reaching trial	10.0%	6.5%	4.3%	3.4%	2.2%	2.6%	2.4%
Criminal cases commenced[3, 5]	38,100	28,000	46,500	44,200	62,745	62,708	67,000
Defendants disposed of	36,400	36,600	56,500	55,300	75,071	74,650	78,835
Not convicted	8,200	8,000	9,800	9,000	8,035	7,919	7,953
Convicted	28,200	28,600	46,700	46,300	67,036	67,731	70,882

Note: Data are for the 12 months ending on September 30 of year shown. 1. Terminated on the merits after hearing or submission. Beginning 1980, data not comparable with earlier years due to changes in criteria. 2. Prior to 1985, the figure is from filing of complete record to final disposition; beginning 1985, figure is from filing notice of appeal to final disposition. 3. Figures rounded in source. 4. A trial is defined as a contested proceeding (other than a hearing on a motion) before either court or jury in which evidence is introduced and final judgment sought. 5. Excludes transfers. **Source:** Administrative Office of the U.S. Courts, *Annual Report of the Director.*

Second Circuit: Connecticut, New York, Vermont
Third Circuit: Delaware, New Jersey, Pennsylvania, Virgin Islands
Fourth Circuit: Maryland, North Carolina, South Carolina, Virginia, West Virginia
Fifth Circuit: Louisiana, Mississippi, Texas
Sixth Circuit: Kentucky, Michigan, Ohio, Tennessee
Seventh Circuit: Illinois, Indiana, Wisconsin
Eighth Circuit: Arkansas, Iowa, Minnesota, Missouri, Nebraska, North Dakota, South Dakota
Ninth Circuit: Alaska, Arizona, California, Guam, Hawaii, Idaho, Montana, Nevada, Northern Mariana Islands, Oregon, Washington
Tenth Circuit: Colorado, Kansas, New Mexico, Oklahoma, Utah, Wyoming
Eleventh Circuit: Alabama, Florida, Georgia
Federal Circuit

U.S. District Courts These are trial courts of general Federal jurisdiction. There are 89 courts in the 50 states, including at least one in each state and the District of Columbia. Each court has from 2 to 28 federal district judgeships, depending on the amount of work within the territory. Overall, there are 610 permanent district judges in the 50 states, 15 in the District of Columbia and seven in Puerto Rico. Usually one judge is required to decide a case, but in some limited cases it is required that three judges be called together to comprise the court.

Administrative Office of the U.S. Courts One Columbus Circle NE, Washington, DC 20544. (202)-502-2600. www.uscourts.gov. Created by act of Aug. 7, 1939. Its areas of primary concern are administering courts, supervising probation office, and overseeing administration of bankruptcy courts, magistrate offices, and public defender's offices.

Federal Judicial Center Thurgood Marshall Federal Judiciary Building, One Columbus Circle NE, Washington, DC 20002-8003. (202)-502-4000. www.fjc.gov. Created by act of Dec. 20, 1967. Its mission is to further the development and adoption of improved judicial administration in U.S. courts. The Chief Justice of the Supreme Court is the permanent chairman of the center's Board of Directors.

United States Sentencing Commission. Suite 2-500, South Lobby, One Columbus Circle NE, Washington, DC 20002-8002. (202)-502-4500. wwww.ussc.gov. Created by the Sentencing Reform Act of 1984. Establishes sentencing guidelines (including forms and severity of punishment) for federal offenses.

THE LEGISLATIVE BRANCH

Architect of the Capitol U.S. Capitol Building, Washington, DC 20515. (202) 228-1793. www.aoc.gov. First Architect appointed in 1793 by President. Permanent authority for care of Capitol established by Act of August 15, 1876. Responsible for care and maintenance of Capitol building and grounds, Library of Congress buildings, and U.S. Supreme Court building. Operates Senate and House restaurants. Maintains, operates, and cares for House and Senate office buildings. Plans future construction, renovation, reconstruction, and alterations to existing buildings.

U.S. Botanic Garden Director's Office: 245 First Street SW, Washington, DC 20024. (202) 226-8333. www.aoc.gov. Conservatory: Maryland Avenue-First to Second Streets SW; Washington, D.C. 20024. (202) 225-6646. Created in 1820. Collects, cultivates, and grows vegetable and plant matter of this and other countries for exhibition and display. Provides study materials on vegetable and plant matter for students, botanists, horticulturists, floriculturists, and garden clubs.

General Accounting Office (GAO) 441 G Street NW Washington, DC 20548. (202) 512-3000. www.gao.gov. Created in 1921 by Budget and Accounting Act. Provides legal, accounting, auditing, and claims settlement services for Congress. Facilitates more efficient government operations.

Government Printing Office (GPO) 732 North Capitol Street NW, Washington, DC 20401. (202) 512-0000. www.gpo.gov. Created June 23, 1860 by Congressional Joint Resolution 25. Provides printing and binding services for Congress and the departments and establishments of the Federal Government. Furnishes blank paper, ink, and supplies to all agencies. Prepares and distributes catalogs and Government publications.

Library of Congress 101 Independence Ave. SE Washington, DC 20540. (202) 707-5000. www.loc.gov. Created by law of April 24, 1800. Librarian appointed by the President. Buys books necessary for use by Congress and/or other governmental agencies. National library of the United States. Develops and maintains national book classification systems such as the Library of Congress and Dewey Decimal systems. Maintains and publishes The National Union Catalogs.

Congressional Budget Office (CBO) Second and D Streets SW Washington, DC 20515. (202) 226-2600. www.cbo.gov. Created by Congressional Budget Act of 1974. Provides Congress with basic budget data. Analyzes and evaluates alternative fiscal and budgetary policy options and programs and makes recommendations to Congress. Publishes annual report on the budget.

How A Bill Becomes Law

Usually bills are raised in any of the various committees of the Senate or House of Representatives. If the bill is supported by a majority of the committee, it is brought to the floor of the house in which it originated, and voted upon. If it gains majority support in the full Senate or House, the other house of Congress votes on it. If the bill is passed in both the Senate and House, it is sent to the President, who may either sign it, veto it, or not act on it.

If the president signs it or refuses to act within 10 days and the Congress is still in session, the bill becomes law. If the president vetoes it, it is returned to the Senate and the House for another vote; a two-thirds majority in each house is then required to overturn the presidential veto. However, if the president refuses to act on a bill and Congress adjourns before the end of the 10-day period, the legislation is dead. This is known as a pocket veto.

Occasionally, bills are raised on the floor of the Senate or the House, in which case the first step of committee voting is avoided and the legislation process begins with the full Senate or House Vote. All other processes remain the same.

How to Contact Your Senator or Representative

To contact any senator, call (202)-224-3121. More information about the Senate is available on the Internet at **www.senate.gov.** To reach a Representative, call (202)-225-3121. More information about the House is available on the Internet at **www.house.gov**

The 108th Congress of the United States

The upper house of the U.S. Congress, the Senate, is composed of 100 members: two from each state. Members are elected to six-year terms. One-third of the Senate faces re-election every two years. Senators must have been U.S. citizens for at least nine years and must be at least 30 years old. In the table below, the senior senator is listed first.

The lower house of government is known as the House of Representatives, and is composed of 435 members. The number of representatives from each state is determined by population every 10 years; every state is entitled to at least one representative. The entire House faces re-election every two years. Representatives must have been U.S. citizens for at least seven years and must be at least 25 years old.

In addition to state representatives, there are delegates from the District of Columbia, American Samoa, Guam, and the Virgin Islands, and a resident commissioner from Puerto Rico. They may take part in floor debates, but they may not vote.

Senate Offices

President	Dick Cheney (R-Wyoming)
Majority Leader	Bill Frist (R-Tennessee)
Majority Whip	Mitch McConnell (R-Kentucky)
Majority Leader	Tom DeLay (R-Texas)
Minority Whip	Harry Reid (D-Nevada)

House Offices

Speaker	J. Dennis Hastert (R-Illinois)
Majority Whip	Roy Blunt (R-Missouri)
Minority Leader	Tom Daschle (D-South Dakota)
Minority Leader	Nancy Pelosi (D-California)
Minority Whip	Steny Hoyer (D-Maryland)

Alabama
Richard C. Shelby (R)
Jeff Sessions (R)

Alaska
Ted Stevens (R)
Lisa Murkowski (R)

Arizona
John McCain (R)
Jon Kyl (R)

Arkansas
Blanche Lincoln (D)
Mark Pryor (D)

California
Dianne Feinstein (D)
Barbara Boxer (D)

Colorado
Ben Nighthorse Campbell (R)
Wayne A. Allard (R)

Connecticut
Christopher J. Dodd (D)
Joseph I. Lieberman (D)

Delaware
Joseph R. Biden Jr. (D)
Thomas R. Carper (D)

Florida
Bob Graham (D)
Bill Nelson (D)

Georgia
Zell Miller (D)
Saxby Chambliss (R)

Hawaii
Daniel K. Inouye (D)
Daniel K. Akaka (D)

Idaho
Larry E. Craig (R)
Mike Crapo (R)

Illinois
Peter Fitzgerald (R)
Richard J. Durbin (D)

Indiana
Richard G. Lugar (R)
Evan Bayh (D)

Iowa
Chuck Grassley (R)
Tom Harkin (D)

Kansas
Pat Roberts (R)
Sam Brownback (R)

Kentucky
Mitch McConnell (R)
Jim Bunning (R)

Louisiana
John B. Breaux (D)
Mary Landrieu (D)

Maine
Olympia J. Snowe (R)
Susan Collins (R)

Maryland
Paul S. Sarbanes (D)
Barbara A. Mikulski (D)

Massachusetts
Edward M. Kennedy (D)
John F. Kerry (D)

Michigan
Carl Levin (D)
Debbie Stabenow (D)

Minnesota
Mark Dayton (D)
Norm Coleman (R)

Mississippi
Thad Cochran (R)
Trent Lott (R)

Missouri
Christopher S. Bond (R)
James Talent (R)

Montana
Max Baucus (D)
Conrad R. Burns (R)

Nebraska
Charles Hagel (R)
Ben Nelson (D)

Nevada
Harry Reid (D)
John Ensign (R)

New Hampshire
Judd Gregg (R)
John Sununu (R)

New Jersey
Jon Corzine (D)
Frank Lautenberg (D)

New Mexico
Pete V. Domenici (R)
Jeff Bingaman (D)

New York
Charles Schumer (D)
Hillary Rodham Clinton (D)

North Carolina
John Edwards (D)
Elizabeth Dole (R)

North Dakota
Kent Conrad (D)
Byron L. Dorgan (D)

Ohio
Mike DeWine (R)
George Voinovich (R)

Oklahoma
Don Nickles (R)
James Inhofe (R)

Oregon
Ron Wyden (D)
Gordon Smith (R)

Pennsylvania
Arlen Specter (R)
Rick Santorum (R)

Rhode Island
Jack Reed (D)
Lincoln Chafee (R)

South Carolina
Ernest F. Hollings (D)
Lindsey Graham (R)

South Dakota
Thomas A. Daschle (D)
Tim Johnson (D)

Tennessee
William H. Frist (R)
Lamar Alexander (R)

Texas
Kay Bailey Hutchison (R)
John Cornyn (R)

Utah
Orrin G. Hatch (R)
Robert F. Bennett (R)

Vermont
Patrick J. Leahy (D)
James M. Jeffords (I)

Virginia
John W. Warner (R)
George Allen (R)

Washington
Patty Murray (D)
Maria Cantwell (D)

West Virginia
Robert C. Byrd (D)
John D. Rockefeller IV (D)

Wisconsin
Herb Kohl (D)
Russell D. Feingold (D)

Wyoming
Craig Thomas (R)
Mike Enzi (R)

Note: The senior senator is listed first.

THE HOUSE OF REPRESENTATIVES

District	City	Representative
Alabama		
1st	Mobile	Jo Bonner (R)
2nd	Montgomery	Terry Everett (R)
3rd	Auburn	Mike Rogers (R)
4th	Gadsden	Robert B. Aderholt (R)
5th	Huntsville	Robert E. (Bud) Cramer Jr. (D)
6th	Hoover	Spencer Bachus (R)
7th	Birmingham	Artur Davis (D)
Alaska		
1st	At-Large	Don Young (R)
Arizona		
1st	Flagstaff	Rick Renzi (R)
2nd	Peoria	Trent Franks (R)
3rd	Paradise Valley	John B. Shadegg (R)
4th	Phoenix	Ed Pastor (D)
5th	Scottsdale	J. D. Hayworth (R)
6th	Mesa	Jeff Flake (R)
7th	Tucson	Raúl M. Grijalva (D)
8th	Sierra Vista	Jim Kolbe (R)
Arkansas		
1st	Jonesboro	Marion Berry (D)
2nd	Little Rock	Vic Snyder (D)
3rd	Fort Smith	John Boozman (R)
4th	Pine Bluff	Mike Ross (D)
California		
1st	Napa	Mike Thompson (D)
2nd	Redding	Wally Herger (R)
3rd	Citrus Heights	Doug Ose (R)
4th	Roseville	John T. Doolittle (R)
5th	Sacramento	Robert T. Matsui (D)
6th	Santa Rosa	Lynn C. Woolsey (D)
7th	Concord	George Miller (D)
8th	San Francisco	Nancy Pelosi (D)
9th	Oakland	Barbara Lee (D)
10th	Fairfield	Ellen O. Tauscher (D)
11th	Tracy	Richard W. Pombo (R)
12th	Daly City	Tom Lantos (D)
13th	Fremont	Fortney Pete Stark (D)
14th	Redwood City	Anna G. Eshoo (D)
15th	Santa Clara	Michael M. Honda (D)
16th	San Jose	Zoe Lofgren (D)
17th	Salinas	Sam Farr (D)
18th	Stockton	Dennis A. Cardoza (D)
19th	Turlock	George Radanovich (R)
20th	Fresno	Calvin M. Dooley (D)
21st	Visalia	Devin Nunes (R)
22nd	Bakersfield	William M. Thomas (R)
23rd	Oxnard	Lois Capps (D)
24th	Thousand Oaks	Elton Gallegly (R)
25th	Santa Clarita	Howard "Buck" McKeon (R)
26th	Rancho Cucamonga	David Dreier (R)
27th	Reseda	Brad Sherman (D)
28th	San Fernando	Howard L. Berman (D)
29th	Glendale	Adam B. Schiff (D)
30th	Santa Monica	Henry A. Waxman (D)
31st	Hollywood	Xavier Becerra (D)
32nd	El Monte	Hilda L. Solis (D)
33rd	Culver City	Diane E. Watson (D)
34th	Los Angeles	Lucille Roybal-Allard (D)
35th	Inglewood	Maxine Waters (D)
36th	Torrance	Jane Harman (D)
37th	Compton	Juanita Millender-McDonald(D)
38th	Pomona	Grace F. Napolitano (D)
39th	South Gate	Linda T. Sánchez (D)
40th	Fullerton	Edward R. Royce (R)
41st	Hesperia	Jerry Lewis (R)
42nd	Chino	Gary G. Miller (R)
43rd	San Bernardino	Joe Baca (D)
44th	Riverside	Ken Calvert (R)
45th	Moreno Valley	Mary Bono (R)
46th	Long Beach	Dana Rohrabacher (R)
47th	Santa Ana	Loretta Sanchez (D)
48th	Irvine	Christopher Cox (R)
49th	Oceanside	Darrell E. Issa (R)
50th	Escondido	Randy "Duke" Cunningham (R)
51st	Chula Vista	Bob Filner (D)
52nd	El Cajon	Duncan Hunter (R)
53rd	San Diego	Susan A. Davis (D)
Colorado		
1st	Denver	Diana DeGette (D)
2nd	Westminster	Mark Udall (D)
3rd	Pueblo	Scott McInnis (R)
4th	Fort Collins	Marilyn N. Musgrave (R)
5th	Colorado Springs	Joel Hefley (R)
6th	Littleton	Thomas G. Tancredo (R)
7th	Aurora	Bob Beauprez (R)
Connecticut		
1st	Hartford	John B. Larson (D)
2nd	Norwich	Rob Simmons (R)
3rd	New Haven	Rosa L. DeLauro (D)
4th	Bridgeport	Christopher Shays (R)
5th	Waterbury	Nancy L. Johnson (R)
Delaware		
1st	At-Large	Michael N.Castle (R)
Florida		
1st	Pensacola	Jeff Miller (R)
2nd	Tallahassee	Allen Boyd (D)
3rd	Jacksonville	Corrine Brown (D)
4th	Jacksonville Beach	Ander Crenshaw (R)
5th	Zephyrhills	Ginny Brown-Waite (R)
6th	Ocala	Cliff Stearns (R)
7th	Deltona	John L.Mica (R)
8th	Orlando	Ric Keller (R)
9th	Clearwater	Michael Bilirakis (R)
10th	Largo	C.W. Bill Young (R)
11th	Tampa	Jim Davis (D)
12th	Lakeland	Adam H. Putnam (R)
13th	Sarasota	Katherine Harris (R)
14th	Cape Coral	Porter J. Goss (R)
15th	Palm Bay	Dave Weldon (R)
16th	Port St. Lucie	Mark Foley (R)
17th	Pembroke Pines	Kendrik B. Meek (D)
18th	Miami Beach	Ileana Ros-Lehtinen (R)
19th	Coral Springs	Robert Wexler (D)
20th	Fort Lauderdale	Peter Deutsch (D)
21st	Hialeah	Lincoln Diaz-Balart (R)
22nd	West Palm Beach	E. Clay Shaw Jr. (R)
23rd	Sunrise	Alcee L.Hastings (D)
24th	Port Orange	Tom Feeney (R)
25th	Homestead	Mario Diaz-Balart (R)
Georgia		
1st	Hinesville	Jack Kingston (R)
2nd	Columbus	Sanford D. Bishop Jr. (D)
3rd	Macon	Jim Marshall (D)
4th	North Atlanta	Denise L. Majette (D)
5th	Atlanta	John Lewis (D)
6th	Roswell	Johnny Isakson (R)

District City		Representative
7th	Lawrenceville	John Linder (R)
8th	Griffiin	Mac Collins (R)
9th	Monroe	Charlie Norwood (R)
10th	Dalton	Nathan Deal (R)
11th	Marietta	Phil Gingrey (R)
12th	Augusta	Max Burns (R)
13th	Forest Park	David Scott (D)
Hawaii		
1st	Honolulu	Neil Abercrombie (D)
2nd	Outer Islands	Ed Case (D)
Idaho		
1st	Boise	C. L. "Butch" Otter (R)
2nd	Pocatello	Michael K. Simpson (R)
Illinois		
1st	Tinley Park	Bobby L. Rush (D)
2nd	Calumet City	Jesse L. Jackson Jr. (D)
3rd	Oak Lawn	William O. Lipinski (D)
4th	Chicago	Luis V. Gutierrez (D)
5th	Elmwood Park	Rahm Emanuel (D)
6th	Mount Prospect	Henry J. Hyde (R)
7th	Oak Park	Danny K. Davis (D)
8th	Schaumburg	Philip M. Crane (R)
9th	Evanston	Janice D. Schakowsky (D)
10th	Waukegan	Mark Steven Kirk (R)
11th	Joliet	Jerry Weller (R)
12th	Belleville	Jerry F. Costello (D)
13th	Naperville	Judy Biggert (R)
14th	Aurora	J. Dennis Hastert (R)
15th	Springfield	Timothy V. Johnson (R)
16th	Rockford	Donald A. Manzullo (R)
17th	Decatur	Lane Evans (D)
18th	Peoria	Ray LaHood (R)
19th	Collinsville	John Shimkus (R)
Indiana		
1st	Gary	Peter J. Visclosky (D)
2nd	South Bend	Chris Chocola (R)
3rd	Fort Wayne	Mark E. Souder (R)
4th	Lafayette	Steve Buyer (R)
5th	Carmel	Dan Burton (R)
6th	Muncie	Mike Pence (R)
7th	Indianapolis	Julia Carson (D)
8th	Evansville	John N. Hostettler (R)
9th	Bloomington	Baron P. Hill (D)
Iowa		
1st	Davenport	Jim Nussle (R)
2nd	Cedar Rapids	James A. Leach (R)
3rd	Des Moines	Leonard L. Boswell (D)
4th	Ames	Tom Latham (R)
5th	Sioux City	Steve King (R)
Kansas		
1st	Salina	Jerry Moran (R)
2nd	Topeka	Jim Ryun (R)
3rd	Overland Park	Dennis Moore (D)
4th	Wichita	Todd Tiahrt (R)
Kentucky		
1st	Hopkinsville	Ed Whitfield (R)
2nd	Owensboro	Ron Lewis (R)
3rd	Louisville	Anne M. Northrup (R)
4th	Covington	Ken Lucas (D)
5th	Somerset	Harold Rogers (R)
6th	Lexington	Ernie Fletcher (R)

District City		Representative
Louisiana		
1st	Slidell	David Vitter (R)
2nd	New Orleans	William J. Jefferson (D)
3rd	New Iberia	W.J. (Billy) Tauzin (R)
4th	Shreveport	Jim McCrery (R)
5th	Monroe	Rodney Alexander (D)
6th	Baton Rouge	Richard H. Baker (R)
7th	Lafayette	Christopher John (D)
Maine		
1st	Portland	Thomas H. Allen (D)
2nd	Bangor	Michael H. Michaud (D)
Maryland		
1st	Salisbury	Wayne T. Gilchrest (R)
2nd	Towson	C. A. Dutch Ruppersberger (D)
3rd	Annapolis	Benjamin L. Cardin (D)
4th	Germantown	Albert Russell Wynn (D)
5th	Bowie	Steny H. Hoyer (D)
6th	Frederick	Roscoe G. Bartlett (R)
7th	Baltimore	Elijah E. Cummings (D)
8th	Rockville	Chris Van Hollen (D)
Massachusetts		
1st	Leominster	John W. Olver (D)
2nd	Springfield	Richard E. Neal (D)
3rd	Worcester	James P. McGovern (D)
4th	New Bedford	Barney Frank (D)
5th	Lowell	Martin T.Meehan (D)
6th	Lynn	John F. Tierney (D)
7th	Waltham	Edward J. Markey (D)
8th	Cambridge	Michael E. Capuano (D)
9th	Boston	Stephen F. Lynch (D)
10th	Quincy	William D. Delahunt (D)
Michigan		
1st	Upper Peninsula	Bart Stupak (D)
2nd	Muskegon	Peter Hoekstra (R)
3rd	Grand Rapids	Vernon J. Ehlers (R)
4th	Midland	Dave Camp (R)
5th	Flint	Dale E. Kildee (D)
6th	Kalamazoo	Fred Upton (R)
7th	Battle Creek	Nick Smith (R)
8th	Lansing	Mike Rogers (R)
9th	Farmington Hills	Joe Knollenberg (R)
10th	Sterling Heights	Candice S. Miller (R)
11th	Livonia	Thaddeus G. McCotter (R)
12th	Warren	Sander M. Levin (D)
13th	Detroit	Carolyn C. Kilpatrick (D)
14th	Dearborn	John Conyers Jr. (D)
15th	Ann Arbor	John D. Dingell (D)
Minnesota		
1st	Rochester	Gil Gutknecht (R)
2nd	Eagan	John Kliine (R)
3rd	Bloomington	Jim Ramstad (R)
4th	St. Paul	Betty McCollum (D)
5th	Minneapolis	Martin Olav Sabo (D)
6th	St. Cloud	Mark R. Kennedy (R)
7th	Moorhead	Colin C. Peterson (D)
8th	Duluth	James L. Oberstar (D)
Mississippi		
1st	Tupelo	Roger F. Wicker (R)
2nd	Jackson	Bennie G. Thompson (D)
3rd	Meridian	Charles "Chip" Pickering (R)
4th	Gulfport	Gene Taylor (D)

District	City	Representative
Missouri		
1st	St. Louis	Wm. Lacy Clay (D)
2nd	St. Charles	W. Todd Akin (R)
3rd	Webster Groves	Richard A. Gephardt (D)
4th	Jefferson City	Ike Skelton (D)
5th	Kansas City	Karen McCarthy (D)
6th	St. Joseph	Sam Graves (R)
7th	Springfield	Roy Blunt (R)
8th	Cape Girardeau	Jo Ann Emerson (R)
9th	Columbia	Kenny C. Hulshof (R)
Montana		
1st	At-Large	Dennis R. Rehberg (R)
Nebraska		
1st	Lincoln	Doug Bereuter (R)
2nd	Omaha	Lee Terry (R)
3rd	Grand Island	Tom Osbourne (R)
Nevada		
1st	Las Vegas	Shelley Berkley (D)
2nd	Reno	Jim Gibbons (R)
3rd	Henderson	Jon C. Porter (R)
New Hampshire		
1st	Manchester	Jeb Bradley (R)
2nd	Nashua	Charles F. Bass (R)
New Jersey		
1st	Camden	Robert E. Andrews (D)
2nd	Vineland	Frank A. LoBiondo (R)
3rd	Cherry Hill	Jim Saxton (R)
4th	Trenton	Christopher H. Smith (R)
5th	Paramus	Scott Garrett (R)
6th	New Brunswick	Frank Pallone Jr. (D)
7th	Westfield	Mike Ferguson (R)
8th	Paterson	Bill Pascrell Jr. (D)
9th	Hackensack	Steven R. Rothman (D)
10th	Newark	Donald M. Payne (D)
11th	Morristown	Rodney P. Frelinghuysen (R)
12th	Princeton	Rush D. Holt (D)
13th	Jersey City	Robert Menendez (D)
New Mexico		
1st	Albuquerque	Heather Wilson (R)
2nd	Las Cruces	Joseph R. Skeen (R)
3rd	Santa Fe	Tom Udall (D)
New York		
1st	Coram	Timothy H. Bishop (D)
2nd	Brentwood	Steve Israel (D)
3rd	Long Beach	Peter T. King (R)
4th	Hempstead	Carolyn McCarthy (D)
5th	Great Neck	Gary L. Ackerman (D)
6th	Queens	Gregory W. Meeks (D)
7th	Flushing	Joseph Crowley (D)
8th	Manhattan, West	Jerrold Nadler (D)
9th	Brooklyn	Anthony D. Weiner (D)
10th	Brooklyn Heights	Edolphus Towns (D)
11th	Flatbush	Major R. Owens (D)
12th	Brooklyn	Nydia M. Velázquez (D)
13th	Staten Island	Vito Fossella (R)
14th	Manhattan, East	Carolyn B. Maloney (D)
15th	Harlem	Charles B. Rangel (D)
16th	Bronx	José E. Serrano (D)
17th	Mount Vernon	Eliot L. Engel (D)
18th	New Rochelle	Nita M. Lowey (D)
19th	Peekskill	Sue W. Kelly (R)
20th	Saratoga Springs	Johnn E. Sweeney (R)
21st	Albany	Michael R. McNulty (D)
22nd	Binghamton	Maurice D. Hinchey (D)
23rd	Watertown	John M. McHugh (R)
24th	Utica	Sherwood L. Boehlert (R)
25th	Syracuse	James T. Walsh (R)
26th	North Tonawanda	Thomas M. Reynolds (R)
27th	Buffalo	Jack Quinn (R)
28th	Rochester	Louise McIntosh Slaughter (D)
29th	Elmira	Amo Houghton (R)
North Carolina		
1st	Rocky Mount	Frank W. Ballance Jr. (D)
2nd	Raleigh	Bob Etheridge (D)
3rd	Jacksonville	Walter B. Jones (R)
4th	Durham	David E. Price (D)
5th	Statesville	Richard Burr (R)
6th	Burlington	Howard Coble (R)
7th	Fayetteville	Mike McIntyre (D)
8th	Concord	Robin Hayes (R)
9th	Gastonia	Sue Wilkins Myrick (R)
10th	Hickory	Cass Ballenger (R)
11th	Asheville	Charles H. Taylor (R)
12th	Charlotte	Melvin L. Watt (D)
13th	Greensboro	Brad Miller (D)
North Dakota		
1st	At-Large	Earl Pomeroy (D)
Ohio		
1st	Cincinnati	Steve Chabot (R)
2nd	Portsmouth	Rob Portman (R)
3rd	Dayton	Michael R. Turner (R)
4th	Mansfield	Michael G. Oxley (R)
5th	Bowling Green	Paul E. Gillmor (R)
6th	Athens	Ted Strickland (D)
7th	Springfield	David L. Hobson (R)
8th	Hamilton	John A. Boehner (R)
9th	Toledo	Marcy Kaptur (D)
10th	Parma	Dennis J. Kucinich (D)
11th	Cleveland	Stephanie Tubbs Jones (D)
12th	Westerville	Patrick J. Tiberi (R)
13th	Akron	Sherrod Brown (D)
14th	Mentor	Steven C. LaTourette (R)
15th	Columbus	Debra Pryce (R)
16th	Canton	Ralph Regula (R)
17th	Youngstown	Tim Ryan (D)
18th	Newark	Robert W. Ney (R)
Oklahoma		
1st	Tulsa	John Sullivan (R)
2nd	Muskogee	Brad Carson (D)
3rd	Stillwater	Frank D. Lucas (R)
4th	Norman	Tom Cole (R)
5th	Oklahoma City	Ernest J. Istook (R)
Oregon		
1st	Portland	David Wu (D)
2nd	Medford	Greg Walden (R)
3rd	Gresham	Earl Blumenauer (D)
4th	Eugene	Peter A. DeFazio (D)
5th	Salem	Darlene Hooley (D)
Pennsylvania		
1st	Philadelphia	Robert A. Brady (D)
2nd	W. Philadelphia	Chaka Fattah (D)
3rd	Erie	Phil Enlish (R)
4th	Plum	Melissa A. Hart (R)
5th	State College	John Peterson (R)
6th	Norristown	Jim Gerlack (R)

District	City	Representative
7th	Radnor	Curt Weldon (R)
8th	Bristol	James C. Greenwood (R)
9th	Altoona	Bill Shuster (R)
10th	Williamsport	Don Sherwood (R)
11th	Scranton	Paul E. Kanjorski (D)
12th	Johnstown	John P. Murtha (D)
13th	Lansdale	Joseph M. Hoeffel (D)
14th	Pittsburgh	Michael F. Doyle (D)
15th	Allentown	Patrick J. Toomey (R)
16th	Reading	Joseph R. Pitts (R)
17th	Harrisburg	Tim Holden (D)
18th	Bethel Park	Tim Murphy (R)
19th	York	Todd Russell Platts (R)
Rhode Island		
1st	Providence	Patrick J. Kennedy (D)
2nd	Warwick	James R. Langevin (D)
South Carolina		
1st	Charleston	Henry E. Brown Jr. (R)
2nd	Columbia	Joe Wilson (R)
3rd	Aiken	J. Gresham Barrett (R)
4th	Greenville	Jim DeMint (R)
5th	Rock Hill	John M. Spratt Jr. (D)
6th	Sumter	James E. Clyburn (D)
South Dakota		
1st	At-Large	William J. Janklow (R)
Tennessee		
1st	Johnson	William L. Jenkins (R)
2nd	Knoxville	John J. Duncan Jr. (R)
3rd	Chattanooga	Zach Wamp (R)
4th	Franklin	Lincoln Davis (D)
5th	Nasvhille	Jim Cooper (D)
6th	Murfreesboro	Bart Gordon (D)
7th	Germantown	Marsha Blackburn (R)
8th	Clarksville	John S. Tanner (D)
9th	Memphis	Harold E. Ford Jr. (D)
Texas		
1st	Texarkana	Max Sandlin (D)
2nd	Huntsville	Jim Turner (D)
3rd	Plano	Sam Johnson (R)
4th	Tyler	Ralph M. Hall (D)
5th	Mesquite	Jeb Hensarling (R)
6th	Mansfield	Joe Barton (R)
7th	Hunters Creek	John Abney Culberson (R)
8th	Conroe	Kevin Brady (R)
9th	Beaumont	Nick Lampson (D)
10th	Austin	Lloyd Doggett (D)
11th	Waco	Chet Edwards (D)
12th	N. Richland Hills	Kay Granger (R)
13th	Amarillo	Mac Thornberry (R)
14th	Victoria	Ron Paul (R)
15th	McAllen	Rubén Hinojosa (D)
16th	El Paso	Silvestre Reyes (D)
17th	Abilene	Charles W. Stenholm (D)
18th	Houston	Sheila Jackson-Lee (D)
19th	Lubbock	Randy Neugebauer (R)
20th	San Antonio	Charles A. Gonzalez (D)
21st	New Braunfels	Lamar S. Smith (R)
22nd	Sugar Land	Tom DeLay (R)
23rd	Laredo	Henry Bonilla (R)
24th	Fort Worth	Martin Frost (D)

District	City	Representative
25th	Baytown	Chris Bell (D)
26th	Denton	Michael C. Burgess (R)
27th	Corpus Christi	Solomon P. Ortiz (D)
28th	Schertz	Ciro D. Rodriguez (D)
29th	Pasadena	Gene Green (D)
30th	Dallas	Eddie Bernice Johnson (D)
31st	Round Rock	John R. Carter (R)
32nd	Carrollton	Pete Sessions (R)
Utah		
1st	Ogden	Rob Bishop (R)
2nd	Salt Lake City	Jim Matheson (D)
3rd	West Valley City	Chris Cannon (R)
Vermont		
1st	At-Large	Bernard Sanders (I)
Virginia		
1st	Fredericksburg	Jo Ann Davis (R)
2nd	Virginia Beach	Edward L. Schrock (R)
3rd	Norfolk	Robert C. Scott (D)
4th	Chesapeake	J. Randy Forbes (R)
5th	Danville	Virgil H. Goode Jr. (R)
6th	Roanoke	Bob Goodlatte (R)
7th	Richmond	Eric Cantor (R)
8th	Arlington	James P. Moran (D)
9th	Blacksburg	Rick Boucher (D)
10th	Manassas	Frank R. Wolf (R)
11th	Fairfax	Tom Davis (R)
Washington		
1st	Shoreline	Jay Inslee (D)
2nd	Everett	Rick Larsen (D)
3rd	Vancouver	Brian Baird (D)
4th	Yakima	Doc Hastings (R)
5th	Spokane	George R. Nethercutt Jr. (R)
6th	Tacoma	Norman D. Dicks (D)
7th	Seattle	Jim McDermott (D)
8th	Bellevue	Jennifer Dunn (R)
9th	Federal Way	Adam Smith (D)
West Virginia		
1st	Wheeling	Alan B. Mollohan (D)
2nd	Charleston	Shelley Moore Capito (R)
3rd	Huntington	Nick J. Rahall, II (D)
Wisconsin		
1st	Kenosha	Paul Ryan (R)
2nd	Madison	Tammy Baldwin (D)
3rd	Eau Claire	Ron Kind (D)
4th	Milwaukee	Gerald D. Kleczka (D)
5th	Waukesha	F. James Sensenbrenner (R)
6th	Oshkosh	Thomas Petri (R)
7th	Wausau	David R. Obey (D)
8th	Green Bay	Mark Green (R)
Wyoming		
1st	At Large	Barbara Cubin (R)
NON-VOTING REPRESENTATIVES		
American Samoa		Eni F. H. Faleomavaega (D)
Dist. of Columbia		Eleanor Holmes Norton (D)
Guam		Madeleine Z. Bordallo (D)
Puerto Rico		Aníbal Acevedo-Vilá (D)
Virgin Islands		Donna M. Christian-Green (D)

Note: D = Democrat; I= Independent; R = Republican. **Source:** Clerk of the U.S. House of Representatives.

Congressional Reapportionment, 2000-02

As a result of population shifts reported in the 2000 Census, a total of eight states gained representatives (four of them gained two), while 10 states lost representatives (two states lost two each). States cannot have fewer than one representative, so even though North Dakota experienced a much lower growth rate than New York, it could not lose its sole member of Congress, whereas New York lost two representatives. The table below shows states gaining and losing representation. States were reapportioned prior to the November, 2002 elections, and took effect in January, 2003.

States Gaining Representatives

Arizona	+2	California	+1
Florida	+2	Colorado	+1
Georgia	+2	Nevada	+1
Texas	+2	North Carolina	+1

States Losing Representatives

New York	-2	Michigan	-1
Pennsylvania	-2	Mississippi	-1
Connecticut	-1	Ohio	-1
Illinois	-1	Oklahoma	-1
Indiana	-1	Wisconsin	-1

Source: U.S. Census Bureau.

THE EXECUTIVE BRANCH

▶EXECUTIVE OFFICE OF THE PRESIDENT

White House Office 1600 Pennsylvania Ave. NW, Washington, DC 20500 (202) 456-1414. www.whitehouse.gov. Serves president in performance of duties incident to his office. Maintains communication with Congress, individual members of Congress, heads of executive agencies, media, and public.

Office of the Vice President of the United States Eisenhower Executive Office Building, Washington, DC 20501. (202) 456-7549. www.whitehouse.gov/vicepresident. Vice president participates in cabinet meetings and is, by statute, a member of National Security Council and board of regents of the Smithsonian Institution; serves as president of Senate; empowered to succeed to presidency pursuant to Article II and the 20th and 25th amendments to the Constitution.

Council of Economic Advisers 1800 G St. NW; Washington, DC 20502. (202) 395-5084. www.whitehouse.gov/cea. Created by Employment Act of 1946. Council's three members—appointed by president—analyze the various segments of the economy, appraise and assess existing economic programs, recommend new economic programs, and assist in preparation President's economic reports to Congress.

Council on Environmental Quality 722 Jackson Place NW, Washington DC 20503. (202) 395-5750. www.whitehouse.gov/ceq. Eisenhower Executive Office Building, Room 360, Washington DC 20501. (202) 456-6224. Created by National Environmental Policy Act of 1969. Recommends national policies to improve quality of environment. Analyzes environmental changes and trends. Assesses and evaluates existing environmental programs. Assists president in compiling annual environmental quality report to Congress.

National Security Council (NSC) Eisenhower Executive Office Building, Washington DC 20504. (202) 456-9301. www.whitehouse.gov/nsc. Created by National Security Act of 1947. Chaired by president. Members include vice president and secretaries of state and defense. Chairman of Joint Chiefs of Staff is statutory military adviser; CIA director is intelligence adviser. Advises president on integration of domestic, foreign, and military policies relating to national security.

Office of Administration Eisenhower Executive Office Building, 725 17th St. NW, Washington, DC 20503. (202) 456-2861. www.whitehouse.gov/oa. Created December 12, 1977 by Reorganization Plan No. 1. Provides administrative services to all units within executive office except those in direct support of president.

Office of Management and Budget (OMB) 725 17th St. NW, Washington, DC 20503. (202)-395-3080. www.whitehouse.gov/omb. Created July 1, 1970. Assists president in reviewing and assessing efficiency of structure and management of executive branch. Expands interagency cooperation. Assists president in preparing Government's budget and fiscal program. Supervises, controls, and administers the budget. Coordinates departmental advice and makes recommendations to president based on this advice. Plans, conducts, and promotes evaluation efforts to help president assess program objectives, performance, and efficiency. Keeps president informed of work planned and performed by the various Government agencies.

Office of National Drug Control Policy 750 17th St. NW, Washington, DC, 20503. (202) 395-6700. www.whitehousedrugpolicy.gov. Created by National Narcotics Leadership Act of 1988. Coordinates Federal, state and local efforts to control illegal drug abuse and devises national strategies to ensure that national anti-drug activities are carried out effectively.

Office of Policy Development Eisenhower Executive Office Building, Washington, DC 20502. Composed of the *Domestic Policy Council* (202-456-5594) www.whitehouse.gov/dpc, *National Economic Council* (202-456-2800), and *Office of National AIDS Policy* (202-456-7320) which are responsible for advising and assisting the president in the formulation, coordination, and implementation of domestic and economic policy.

Office of Science and Technology Policy Eisenhower Executive Office Building, Washington, DC 20502. (202) 395-7347. www.ostp.gov. Created May 11, 1976. Serves as source of scientific, engineering, and technological analysis and expertise for president with respect to public policy in areas of economy, national security, health, foreign relations, and environment. Appraises sale, quality and effectiveness of U.S. efforts in science and technology.

Office of the U.S. Trade Representative 600 17th St. NW, Washington, DC 20508. (202) 395-3230. www.ustr.gov. Created as Office of the Special Representative for Trade Negotiations, Jan. 15, 1963. Congress made it agency of executive office under Trade Act of 1974. Sets and administers overall trade policy. Representative is chief U.S. representative for all activities of the General Agreement on Tariffs and Trade (GATT) and at discussions, meetings, and negotiations in most conferences in which trade and commodity are issues.

▶DEPARTMENT OF AGRICULTURE (USDA)

14th St. and Independence Ave. SW, Washington, DC 20250. (202) 720-2791. www.usda.gov. Created May 15, 1862; incorporated into cabinet, Feb. 8, 1889. Improves and maintains farm income, develops agricultural markets abroad, curbs poverty, hunger, and malnutrition. Through inspection and grading services, safeguard standards of quality in the nation's food supply. The dept. was reorganized in 1994 into eight program or mission areas: *Rural Development, Alternative Agricultural Research & Commercialization Center, Marketing & Regulatory Programs, Food Safety, Food Nutrition & Consumer Services, Farm & Foreign Agriculture Services, Research Education & Economics,* and *Natural Resources & Environment.* Each program area may be further divided into more specific agencies, such as the Rural Housing Service or the Food Safety and Inspection Service.

The Cabinet

The president is the administrative head of the executive branch of the Federal Government. A creation of custom and tradition dating back to George Washington's administration, the cabinet functions at the pleasure of the president. Its purpose is to advise the president on any subject on which he requests information. The cabinet is composed of the heads of the 15 executive departments and certain other executive officials to whom the president accords cabinet rank. In the Bush Administration, cabinet-level rank has been accorded to the officials listed below (as of September 29, 2003)

President George W. Bush
Vice President Dick Cheney

Office	Officer
Secretary of State	Colin Powell
Secretary of the Treasury	John Snow
Secretary of Defense	Donald Rumsfeld
Attorney General (Dept. of Justice)	John Ashcroft
Secretary of the Interior	Gale Norton
Secretary of Agriculture	Ann Veneman
Secretary of Commerce	Donald Evans
Secretary of Labor	Elaine Chao
Secretary of Health and Human Services	Tommy Thompson
Secretary of Housing and Urban Development	Melquiades Martinez
Secretary of Transportation	Norman Mineta
Secretary of Energy	Spencer Abraham
Secretary of Education	Roderick Paige
Secretary of Veterans Affairs	Anthony Principi
Secretary of Homeland Security	Tom Ridge
White House Chief of Staff	Andrew H. Card
Administrator, Environmental Protection Agency	Marianne Lamont Horinko, Acting
Director, Office of Management and Budget	Joshua B. Bolten
U.S. Trade Representative	Robert B. Zoellick
Director, Office of National Drug Control Policy	John Walters

Source: White House Press Office.

▶DEPARTMENT OF COMMERCE

14th St. between Constitution and Pennsylvania Avenues NW, Washington, DC 20230. (202) 482-2000. www.doc.gov. Created Feb. 14, 1903 as part of Dept. of Commerce and Labor. Redesignated Dept. of Commerce Mar. 4, 1913. Promotes international trade, economic growth, and technological advancement through encouragement of competitive free-enterprise system, prevention of unfair trade, granting of patents, promotion of tourism and assistance in the growth of minority businesses. The department is divided into 12 operating units; only the major agencies are described in detail below.

Bureau of the Census www.census.gov. Created Mar. 6, 1902 by act of Congress. Collects, tabulates, and publishes census statistics about America, its people, and its economy. Statistics are used by Congress, president, and public to aid development and evaluation of public policy. Population and housing censuses are performed every 10 years. Censuses of agriculture, state and local governments, manufacturers, mineral industries, distributive trades, and construction and transportation industries are performed every five years. Special censuses are performed on demand from state and local governments.

Economic Development Administration (EDA) www.doc.gov/eda. Created by Public Works and Economic Development Act of 1965. Promotes new jobs, protects existing jobs, and stimulates job growth in areas where unemployment is high or incomes are low.

International Trade Administration (ITA) www.ita.gov. Created Jan. 2, 1980. Promotes world trade and strengthens U.S. position in relation to world trade and investment.

Minority Business Development Agency (MBDA) www.mbda.gov. Created Nov. 1, 1979. Promotes minority business. Ensures effective, equitable, and competitive participation by minority business in free enterprise system.

National Oceanic and Atmospheric Administration (NOAA) www.noaa.gov. Created Oct. 3, 1970. Investigates and maps oceans of world. Discovers, utilizes, and conserves living resources of oceans. Monitors and predicts conditions of atmosphere, sun, and oceans; warns against deterioration of these conditions arising from natural and manmade events and circumstances. Provides weather reports and forecasts. Forecasts floods, hurricanes and other weather-related natural disasters.

Technology Administration www.technology.gov. Created by Congress in 1988 and includes the Office of Technology, National Technical Information Service, and the National Institute of Standards and Technology. Works with U.S. industries to promote competitiveness and to maximize the impact of technology on economic growth.

▶DEPARTMENT OF DEFENSE (DOD)

The Pentagon, Washington, DC 20301-1155. (703) 545-6700. www.defenselink.mil. Created by National Security Act Amendments of 1949. Provides necessary military forces to deter war and protect security of the country. The three armed forces departments and the Organization of the Joint Chiefs of Staff make up the military side of the Defense Dept. (Additional information can be found later in "National Defense.")

Organization of the Joint Chiefs of Staff Consists of Chairman of Joint Chiefs of Staff, the chiefs of staff of the three armed forces departments, and the Commandant of the Marine Corps. Advises and assists president and secretary of defense on most military issues. Assists president and secretary of defense in planning, direction, and allocation of strategic resources. Compares strengths and capabilities of American forces with those of potential adversaries.

Department of the Air Force www.af.mil. Created Sept. 18, 1947 by National Security Act of 1947. Works in conjunction with other armed forces to protect peace and security of the U.S. Focuses on air missions and protecting American interests from invasion by air.

Department of the Army www.army.mil. U.S. Army created June 14, 1775 by Continental Congress. Dept. of the Army created 1947 by National Security Act of 1947. Organizes, trains, and equips active and reserve forces to protect peace, security, welfare, and defense of the U.S. Its mission focuses on land operations and maneuvers.

Department of the Navy www.navy. mil. U.S. Navy created Oct. 13, 1775, by Continental Congress. Dept. of the Navy created Apr. 30, 1798. Protects U.S. from attack by sea. Encompasses Marine Corps. Maintains freedom of the seas.

▶DEPARTMENT OF EDUCATION

400 Maryland Ave. SW, Washington, DC 20202. (800) USA-LEARN. www. ed.gov. Created Oct. 17, 1979, by Dept. of Education Organization Act. Establishes policy for, administers, and coordinates almost all federal assistance to education.

▶DEPARTMENT OF ENERGY (DOE)

1000 Independence Ave. SW, Washington, DC 20585. (202) 586-5000. www.doe.gov. Created Oct. 1, 1977, by Dept. of Energy Organization Act. Coordinates and administrates energy functions of Federal Government, including research and development of energy technology, marketing federal power, energy conservation, nuclear weapons and energy regulation.

▶DEPARTMENT OF HEALTH AND HUMAN SERVICES (HHS)

200 Independence Ave. SW, Washington, DC 20201. (202) 619-0257. www.dhhs.gov. Created Apr. 11, 1953, as Dept. of Health, Education, and Welfare. Re-designated Dept. of Health and Human Services Oct. 17, 1979, by Dept. of Education Organization Act. Advises president in formulation of public policy regarding health, welfare, and income and security programs. The department is divided into 12 major administrations and agencies; only the major agencies are described in detail below

Administration for Children and Families (ACF) www.acf.dhhs.gov. Created April 15, 1991. Administers child welfare services, foster care and child care programs, the Head Start Program, and other family preservation and support services.

Centers for Disease Control and Prevention (CDC) www.cdc.gov. Reorganized, Nov. 9, 1995. Responsible for protecting the public health by preventing and controlling diseases.

Centers for Medicare and Medicaid Services (CMS) www.cms.hhs.gov. (Formerly Health Care Financing Administration; Reorganized June 14, 2001. Oversees Medicare and Medicaid Health Insurance and grant programs. (See the section on "Social Insurance Programs" for additional information about these programs).

Food and Drug Administration (FDA) www.fda.gov. Created by Agriculture Appropriation Act of 1931; reorganized into HHS Dept. Nov. 9, 1995. It protects the health of the nation against impure and unsafe foods, drugs, cosmetics and other hazards.

Health Care Financing Administration (HCFA) www.hcfa.gov. Created Mar. 8, 1977. Oversees Medicare and Medicaid Health Insurance and grant programs. (See the section on "Social Insurance Programs" for additional information about these programs).

National Institutes of Health (NIH) www.nih.gov. Reorganized, Nov. 1995. The principal biomedical research agency of the Federal Government, its mission is to employ science in the pursuit of knowledge to improve human health conditions.

Substance Abuse and Mental Health Services Administration www.samhsa.gov. Disseminates accurate and up-to-date information on and provides leadership in the prevention and treatment of addictive and mental disorders.

▶DEPARTMENT OF HOUSING AND URBAN DEVELOPMENT (HUD)

451 Seventh St. SW, Washington, DC 20410. (202) 708-1422. www.hud.gov. Created Nov. 9, 1965, by Dept. of Housing and Urban Development Act. Administers mortgage programs to help families become homeowners. Fosters construction of new housing and renovation of existing rental housing. Provides aid for low-income families who cannot afford their rent. Enacts programs to prevent housing discrimination. Encourages strong private sector housing industry.

▶DEPARTMENT OF THE INTERIOR

1849 C St. NW, Washington, DC 20240. (202) 208-3171. www.doi.gov. Created Mar. 3, 1849. Principal U.S. conservation agency. Directs use and conservation of public lands and natural resources; administers over 500 million acres of Federal land and has trust responsibilities for approximately 50 million acres, mostly Indian reservations. Prescribes use of land and water resources, fish and wildlife, national parks and historic places, and mineral resources; aids in preservation of American Indian reservation communities.

United States Fish and Wildlife Service www.fws.gov. Conserves and protects fish and wildlife and their habitats. Assesses environmental impact of pesticides, thermal pollution, hydroelectric dams and nuclear power sites.

National Park Service www.nps.gov. Created Aug. 25, 1916. Administers, protects, and maintains diverse system of national parks, monuments, historic areas and recreation areas; encourages understanding of the historic value of these sites through lectures, tours and exhibits.

U.S. Geological Survey www.usgs.gov. Created Mar. 3, 1879. Identifies and classifies land, water, energy, and mineral resources. Investigates potential hazards such as earthquakes and volcanoes. Conducts topographic mapping.

Bureau of Indian Affairs *(The BIA website as well as the BIA mail servers have been made temporarily unavailable due to the Cobell Litigation, a suit brought against the DOI in 1996 and ongoing today. 202-208-3710 is the public affairs number for the BIA.)* Created 1824 as part of Dept. of War. Transferred to Dept. of Interior in 1849. Trains American Indian and Alaska native peoples to manage their own affairs under trust relationship to Federal Government. Facilitates public and private aid to advancement of these peoples.

Bureau of Land Management (BLM) www.blm.gov. Created July 16, 1946, by consolidation of the General Land Office and the Grazing Service. Manages 270 million acres of public lands primarily in Far West and in Alaska. Resources in these lands include timber, oil, gas, hard minerals and wildlife habitats.

▶DEPARTMENT OF JUSTICE

950 Pennsylvania Ave. NW, Washington, DC 20530. (202) 514-2000. www.usdoj.gov. Created June 22, 1870. Enforces the law in the public interest. Ensures fair competition in free enterprise system; enforces drug, immigration, and naturalization laws; conducts all Supreme Court suits in which U.S. is party or is concerned. Advises president on legal matters.

Federal Bureau of Investigation (FBI) www.fbi.gov. Created 1908. Principal investigative bureau of Justice Dept. Investigates violations of Federal law. Areas of primary concern are organized crime (including drug trafficking), terrorism, white-collar crime, and foreign counterintelligence.

Bureau of Prisons www.bop.gov. Imprisons and rehabilitates criminals convicted of Federal crimes and sentenced to serve time in federal prison.

United States Marshals Service www.usdoj.gov/marshals. Provides security and support to federal court system. Apprehends federal fugitives. Ensures safety of federal witnesses. Executes court orders and arrest warrants. Maintains custody, manages, and sells property seized from criminals.

Immigration and Naturalization Service (INS) *(On March 1, 2003, the Immigration and Naturalization Service became part of the U.S. Department of Homeland Security and its functions were divided into various bureaus of that department. Its new Web address is: www.bcis.gov.)* Created Mar. 3, 1891. Controls immigration into U.S. by facilitating entry to qualified persons and denying admission to unqualified aliens. Deports illegal aliens already in U.S. Encourages and facilitates naturalization and citizenship.

Drug Enforcement Administration (DEA) www.dea.gov. Created July 1973. Investigates interstate drug-trafficking. Enforces Government regulations regarding manufacture, distribution, sale and dispensing of controlled substances.

▶DEPARTMENT OF LABOR

200 Constitution Ave NW, Washington, DC 20210. (202) 693-5000. www.dol.gov. Created Mar. 4, 1913. Improves welfare and working conditions of wage earners. Guarantees minimum wages and overtime pay as well as unemployment insurance and workers' compensation. Prevents employment discrimination. Protects pension rights. Provides for job training programs. Pays special attention to labor-related needs of minority workers, old and young, women and disabled people.

Employee Benefits Security Administration (EBSA) www.dol.gov/ebsa. (Formerly Pension and Welfare Benefits Administration. Created Sept. 2, 1974, by Employment Retirement Income Security Act of 1974 (ERISA). Requires private pension and welfare plan administrators to give participants summaries of pension and welfare plans. Keeps summaries on file. Regulates financial operations of pension and welfare plans.

Employment and Training Administration (ETA) www.doleta.gov. Provides employment security through unemployment insurance, worker dislocation programs and federal-state employment service system. Trains or retrains and finds employment for disadvantaged workers through Job Training Partnership Act (JTPA).

Occupational Safety and Health Administration (OSHA) www.osha.gov. Created 1970 by Occupational Safety and Health Act. Promotes safety and health standards in workplace. Issues regulations, conducts investigations, issues citations, and proposes penalties for violations of health standards and regulations.

Bureau of Labor Statistics (BLS) www.bls.gov. Data-gathering agency. Collects, processes, interprets, and distributes data involving employment, unemployment, wages, family income and expenditures, worker's compensation, industrial relations, productivity and technological change.

Veteran's Employment and Training Service (VETS) www.dol.gov/vets. Maximizes training and employment opportunities for veterans and disabled. Ensures that legislation involving veterans is carried out by local public employment services and by private enterprise.

▶DEPARTMENT OF STATE

2201 C Street NW; Washington, DC 20520. (202) 647-4000. www.state.gov. Created July 27, 1789, as Dept. of Foreign Affairs. Renamed Dept. of State Sept. 15, 1789. Advises president on foreign policy. Formulates and executes policy to protect and defend American interests overseas. Negotiates treaties and agreements with foreign countries. Oversees and administers overseas information and cultural programs, including Voice of America and Fulbright scholarship program.

United States Mission to the United Nations Represents U.S. at U.N.. Carries out U.S. foreign policy as it relates to U.N.

Foreign Service Maintains relations with more than 140 nations around world. Reports to State Dept. on developments relating to safety and welfare of U.S., its citizens, and their interests. Ambassadors to each country are personal representatives of the president and have full responsibility for carrying out U.S. foreign policy within the country. Ambassadors negotiate agreements between host country and U.S., explain and administer U.S. foreign policy, and maintain relations with government and public of host country.

▶DEPARTMENT OF TRANSPORTATION

400 Seventh St. SW, Washington, DC 20590. (202) 366-4000. www.dot.gov. Created Oct. 15, 1966. Establishes nation's comprehensive transportation policy. Several umbrella administrations are responsible for highway planning, development, and construction; urban mass transit; railroads; aviation; and the safety of waterways, ports, highways, and oil and gas pipelines.

United States Coast Guard www.uscg.mil. Created Jan. 28, 1915. Included in Dept. of Transportation Apr. 1, 1967. Coast Guard is at all times a branch of armed forces and a service with Dept. of Transportation except when operating as part of Navy during war. Primary maritime law enforcement agency for U.S. Suppresses drug smuggling and trafficking. Licenses marine vessels. Administers and inspects violations of safety standards for design, construction, equipment and maintenance of commercial marine vessels and offshore structures in U.S. waters. Provides search and rescue functions for saving lives and property in U.S. waters. Operates ice-breaking vessels to facilitate marine transportation.

Federal Aviation Administration (FAA) www.faa.gov. Created 1958 by Federal Aviation Act. Included in Dept. of Transportation in 1967. Regulates air commerce in effort to promote safety and secure national defense interests. Directs use of navigable U.S. airspace. Develops and operates system of air traffic control for both civil and military aircraft. Regulates aircraft noise.

Federal Highway Administration (FHWA) www.fhwa.dot.gov. Included in Dept. of Transportation in 1967 by Dept. of Transportation Act. Promotes highway safety. Provides aid for construction and maintenance of state and Federal highway systems.

Federal Railroad Administration (FRA) www.fra.dot.gov. Created by Dept. of Transportation Act of 1966. Administers and enforces railroad safety regulations such as track maintenance, inspection and equipment standards, and operating practices.

National Highway Traffic Safety Administration www.nhtsa.dot.gov. Created by Highway Safety Act of 1970. Research and development programs are aimed at reducing number of highway collisions, reducing severity of injuries and economic loss involved in highway accidents, and reducing fatalities resulting from highway crashes.

Federal Transit Administration www.fta.dot.gov. Created July 1, 1968. Improves equipment and methods used in urban mass transit. Encourages planning of cost-effective mass transit systems. Provides economic and technical assistance for mass transit programs.

Maritime Administration (MARAD) www.marad.dot.gov. Created May 24, 1950. Included in Dept. of Transportation Aug. 6, 1981, by Maritime Act of 1981. Constructs or supervises construction of U.S. flag merchant ships for federal government. Generates business for U.S. ships. Develops ports and facilities for maritime transport.

Saint Lawrence Seaway Development Corporation www.seaway.dot.gov. Created May 13, 1954. Owns, develops, maintains, and operates St. Lawrence Seaway between Montreal and Lake Erie within territorial limits of U.S. Provides safe and efficient waterway for maritime commerce.

Bureau of Transportation Statistics www.bts.gov. Created by Transportation Efficiency Act of 1991. Compiles, analyzes and disseminates statistics and other information on the nation's transportation systems.

▶DEPARTMENT OF THE TREASURY

1500 Pennsylvania Ave. NW, Washington, DC 20220. (202) 622-2000. www.treas.gov. Created Sept. 2, 1789. Formulates and recommends economic, financial, tax, and fiscal policies. Acts as financial agent for U.S. Government. Manufactures coins and currency.

Bureau of Alcohol, Tobacco and Firearms www.atf.treas.gov/. Created July 1, 1972. Enforces and administers laws regulating production, use, distribution, and sale of alcohol and tobacco products, firearms, and explosives. Bureau's objectives are to eliminate illegal trafficking, possession and use of firearms and explosives, to suppress illegal alcohol and tobacco trafficking, and to ensure safety of storage facilities for explosives.

United States Customs Service www.customs.treas.gov/. Created Mar. 3, 1927 as Bureau of Customs. Re-designated Customs Service Apr. 4, 1973. Collects revenue from imports. Enforces customs treaties. Assesses and collects customs duties, excise taxes, fees, and penalties on imported merchandise. Seizes contraband including narcotics and illegal drugs. Processes people, mail, carriers, and cargo in and out of U.S. Apprehends violators of U.S. customs regulations and

Money Men

The first U.S. paper money was printed in 1862. Until then, state banks printed their own notes, but there were no federal bills. The Secretary of the Treasury selects the designs shown on United States currency and coinage. In 1862, Treasury Secretary Salmon Chase put his face on the first U.S. notes in an attempt to further his political ambitions. To this day, he remains on the front of the $10,000 bill, though it is no longer in circulation.

Federal law prohibits portraits of living persons from appearing on Government Securities. Therefore, the portraits on our currency notes and coins are of deceased persons whose places in history the American people know well. The basic designs of all denominations of U.S. paper currency in circulation today were selected in 1928.

Note	Portrait, Importance
$ 1	George Washington, 1st President
$ 2	Thomas Jefferson, 3rd President.
$ 5	Abraham Lincoln, 16th President
$ 10	Alexander Hamilton, 1st Sec. of Treasury
$ 20	Andrew Jackson, 7th President
$ 50	Ulysses Grant, 18th President
$100	Ben Franklin, Statesman
$500[1]	William McKinley, 25th President
$1000[1]	Grover Cleveland, 22nd/24th President
$5000[1]	James Madison, 4th President
$10,000[1]	Salmon Chase, Sec. of Treasury in 1862
$100,000[2]	Woodrow Wilson, 28th President

1. No longer in circulation. 2. This note never appeared in general circulation, and was only used in transactions between Federal Reserve Banks. **Source:** U.S. Bureau of Engraving and Printing. www.moneyfactory.com

related laws including copyright, patent and trademark, and import quotas. Suppresses traffic of illegal narcotics, pornography, counterfeit monetary instruments; quarantines animals, plants, and foods.

Bureau of Engraving and Printing www.bep.treas.gov/. Created July 11, 1862. Designs, prints, and finishes Federal Reserve notes, U.S. postage stamps, identification cards, and Treasury securities. Inhibits counterfeiting of these documents.

Internal Revenue Service (IRS) www.irs. gov. Created July 1, 1862. Administers and enforces internal revenue laws except those relating to alcohol, tobacco, firearms and explosives. Determines, assesses, and collects federal tax revenues from public. Encourages, assesses, and enforces compliance with tax laws.

United States Mint www.usmint.gov/. Mint of the United States created Apr. 2, 1792. Bureau of the Mint created Feb. 12, 1873. Renamed United States Mint Jan. 9, 1984. Manufactures and distributes coins for circulation through Federal Reserve Banks. Mints foreign coins. Processes gold and silver bullion. Manufactures national medals, proof coin sets, and commemorative coins for sale to public.

Bureau of the Public Debt www.publicdebt. treas.gov/. Created June 30, 1940. Manages public debt. Offers public debt securities. Audits retired securities and interest coupons. Maintains accounting control over public debt receipts and expenditures, securities, and interest costs. Adjudicates claims of lost, stolen or destroyed securities.

United States Secret Service www.treas. gov.usss/. Protects president and vice president (and president-elect and vice president-elect) of U.S. and their families. Protects former presidents and their wives until their death. Protects distinguished foreign visitors and U.S. officials abroad at direction of president. Detects and apprehends counterfeiters. Suppresses forgery of government securities and documents.

Office of Thrift Supervision (OTS) 1700 G St., NW, Washington, DC 20552. (202) 906-6000. www.ots.treas.gov. Created by the Financial Institutions Reform, Recovery and Enforcement Act, Aug. 9, 1989. Established by Congress as part of a reorganization of the thrift regulatory structure, the OTS has authority to charter federal thrift institutions, and to serve as the primary regulator of federal- and state-chartered thrifts belonging to the Savings Association Insurance Fund (SAIF).

▶DEPARTMENT OF VETERANS AFFAIRS

810 Vermont Ave. NW, Washington, DC 20420. (202) 273-4800. www.va.gov. Created by Dept. of Veterans Affairs Act of 1988; predecessor Veterans Administration created 1930. Administers benefit programs for veterans and their families, including military-related death or disability compensation, pensions, education and rehabilitation, home loan guaranty, medical care programs, and the National Cemetery System.

Veterans Health Administration Provides hospital, nursing home and outpatient care to eligible veterans. Operates over 100 medical centers, nearly 400 outpatient clinics, over 100 nursing home care units and many Vietnam Veteran Outreach Centers.

Veterans Benefit Administration Has responsibility for claims for disability compensation and pension, specially adapted housing and automobiles, special clothing allowances, and emergency officers' retirement pay, survivors' claims for death compensation, dependency and indemnity compensation, burial and plot allowance claims, and reimbursement for headstones.

▶INDEPENDENT ESTABLISHMENTS & GOVERNMENT CORPORATIONS

African Development Foundation 1400 Eye St. NW, Washington, DC 20005. (202) 673-3916. www.adf.gov. Created in 1984 by African Development Foundation Act. Nonprofit Government corporation. Through grants, loans, and loan guarantees, aids self-help efforts by poor people in African countries.

AMTRAK (National Railroad Passenger Corporation) 60 Massachusetts Ave. NE, Washington, DC 20002. (202) 906-3000. www. amtrak.com. Created by Rail Passenger Service Act of 1970. Develops, operates, and improves inter-city rail passenger service to create national rail transportation system.

Central Intelligence Agency (CIA) Washington, DC 20505. (703) 482-1100. www.cia.gov. Created by National Security Act of 1947. Under direction of president and National Security Council. Advises NSC on intelligence matters of national security. Collects, evaluates, and disseminates intelligence information relating to national security and to drug production and trafficking. Collects, produces and disseminates counterintelligence and foreign intelligence here (in conjunction with FBI) and abroad. Conducts special activities as directed by president. Protects security of its activities, information, and personnel by necessary and appropriate means.

Commodity Futures Trading Commission (CFTC) 1155 21st St. NW, Washington, DC 20581. (202) 418-5000. www.cftc.gov/. Created May 14, 1973 by Commodity Futures Act of 1973. Regulates trading on the 11 U.S. futures exchanges. Regulates activities of commodity exchange members, public brokerage houses, commodity trading advisers and other related employees.

Consumer Product Safety Commission (CPSC) East-West Towers, 4330 East-West Highway, Bethesda, Md. 20814. www.cpsc.gov. (301) 504-7908. Created May 14, 1973 by Consumer Product Safety Act. Protects public from unreasonable risk of injury from consumer products. Develops, enforces, and evaluates safety standards for consumer products.

Corporation for National Community Service 1201 New York Ave. NW, Washington, DC 20525. (202) 606-5000. www.nationalservice. org. Created by National and Community Service Act of 1993. Incorporates programs previously administered by ACTION. Administers agencies such as AmeriCorps and AmeriCorps VISTA, which encourage and provide national and community service by volunteers, schools, and retired and senior volunteers.

Defense Nuclear Facilities Safety Board 625 Indiana Ave. NW, Suite 700, Washington, D.C. 20004. (202) 694-7000. www.dnfsb.gov. Created by Atomic Energy Act of 1954; established as independent agency Sept. 29, 1988. Reviews and evaluates standards for defense nuclear facilities of the Department of Energy. Investigates practices that may imperil public health and safety.

Environmental Protection Agency (EPA) 41200 Pennsylvania Avenue NW., Washington, DC 20460-0001. (202) 272-0167 www.epa.gov. Created Dec. 2, 1970. Protects and enhances environment. Controls and reduces pollution of air and water. Regulates solid-waste disposal and use of pesticides, radiation and toxic substances.

Equal Employment Opportunity Commission (EEOC) 1801 L St. NW, Washington, DC 20507. (202) 663-4900. www.eeoc.gov. Created July 2, 1965, by Title VII of Civil Rights Act of 1964. Protects against discrimination based on race, color, handicap, religion, sex, age and national origin in hiring, promoting, firing, wages, testing, training, apprenticeship and all other terms and conditions of employment.

Export-Import Bank of the United States 811 Vermont Ave. NW, Washington, DC 20571. (800) 565-EXIM. www.exim.gov. Created Feb. 2, 1934. Facilitates and aids exports of U.S. goods and services through loans, loan guarantees and insurance to exporters and private banks.

Farm Credit Administration 1501 Farm Credit Drive, McLean, VA 22102-5090. (877) 322-6253. www.fca.gov. Created by Farm Credit Act of 1971. Regulates and examines programs, banks, associations, and organizations of the Farm Credit System, which provides credit to farmers, ranchers, producers of farm products, rural home owners, and associations and organizations of farmers, ranchers, and farm-equipment producers.

Federal Communications Commission (FCC) 445 12th St. SW, Washington, DC 20554. (888) 225-5322. www.fcc.gov. Created by Communications Act of 1934. Regulates interstate and foreign communications by radio, television, wire and cable. Oversees development of broadcast services and the rapid and efficient provision of telephone and telegraph services nationwide.

Federal Deposit Insurance Corporation (FDIC) 550 17th St. NW, Washington, DC 20429. (877)-275-3342. www.fdic.gov. Created June 16, 1933, by Federal Reserve Act. Protects money supply by insuring deposits in and reviewing operations of state-chartered banks that are not members of the Federal Reserve System. Assumed responsibility for insuring savings and loan institutions formerly insured by defunct Federal Savings and Loan Insurance Corp. (FSLIC) in 1989.

Federal Election Commission (FEC) 999 E St. NW, Washington, DC 20463. (800) 424-9530. www.fec.gov. Created by Federal Election Campaign Act of 1971. Provides public funding for presidential elections. Ensures public disclosure of campaign finance activities. Administers and enforces contribution and spending limits for Federal elections. (See also "U.S. Presidential Elections.")

Federal Emergency Management Agency (FEMA) 500 C St. SW, Washington, DC 20472. (202) 646-4600. www.fema.gov Created Mar. 31, 1979. Provides single point of accountability for all federal emergency preparedness, mitigation, and response activities. Facilitates most efficient use of resources in cases of natural or man-made emergencies.

Federal Housing Finance Board 1777 F St. NW, Washington, DC 20006. (202) 408-2500. www.fhfb.gov. Created August 9, 1989. Responsible for the administration and enforcement of the Federal Home Loan Bank Act, ensuring that banks carry out their housing finance and community investment mission

Federal Labor Relations Authority (FLRA) 607 14th St. NW, Washington, DC 20424. (202) 482-6560. www.flra.gov. Created Jan. 1, 1979. Protects rights of federal employees to organize, bargain collectively, and participate in labor organizations. Oversees rights and obligations of federal employees and the labor organizations that represent them.

Federal Maritime Commission 800 North Capitol St. NW, Washington, D.C. 20573-0001. (202) 523-5707. www.fmc.gov. Created August 12, 1961. Regulates waterborne foreign commerce, insures that U.S. international trade is open to all nations on fair and equitable terms, and protects against unauthorized, concerted activity in U.S. waterborne commerce.

Federal Mediation and Conciliation Service 2100 K. St. NW, Washington, D.C. 20427. (202) 606-8100. www.fmcs.gov. Created in 1947 by Labor Management Relations Act. Promotes development of stable labor management relations. Prevents or minimizes work stoppages by helping to settle disputes and by advocating collective bargaining, mediation, and arbitration.

Federal Reserve System Board of Governors of Federal Reserve System. 20th St. and Constitution Ave. NW, Washington, DC 20551. (202) 452-3000. www.federalreserve.gov. Created Dec. 23, 1913, by Federal Reserve Act. Central Bank of U.S. Administers and creates national credit and monetary policy. Regulates money supply. Maintains soundness of banking industry. (See also the section on "The U.S. Economy").

Federal Trade Commission (FTC) 600 Pennsylvania Ave. NW, Washington, DC 20580. (202) 326-2222. www.ftc.gov. Created in 1914 by Federal Trade Commission Act and Clayton Act. Maintains free and fair competition in free enterprise system. Breaks up monopolies. Seeks to prevent corruption, restraints on trade, and unfair trade practices.

General Services Administration (GSA) 1800 F St. NW, Washington, DC 20405. (202) 708-5082. www.gsa. gov. Created July 1, 1949, by Federal Property and Administrative Services Act of 1949. Establishes policy for and manages Government property and records, construction of buildings, distribution of supplies, and other Government services. Its services are divided among four service agencies: the *Information Resources Management Services*, the *Federal Supply Service*, the *Public Buildings Service (PBS)*, and the *Federal Property Resources Service (FPRS)*.

Inter-American Foundation 901 North Stuart St., Arlington, VA 22203. (703) 306-4301. www.iaf.gov. Created by Congress in 1969. Supports social and economic development in Latin America and Caribbean. Makes grants to self-help organizations for the poor.

National Aeronautics and Space Administration (NASA) 300 E. Street SW, Washington, DC 20546. (202) 358-0000. www.nasa. gov. Created by National Aeronautics and Space Act of 1958. Develops, constructs, tests, and operates vehicles for in-flight research within and outside Earth's atmosphere. Disseminates information about space exploration and agency's activities.

National Archives and Records Administration (NARA) 8601 Adelphi Rd., College Park, Md. 20740-6001. (866)-272-6272. www.nara. gov. Created Oct. 19, 1984. Establishes policy for managing records of U.S. government and making them available to public. Maintains 11 regional archives and 14 federal records centers, as well as 11 presidential libraries or collections.

National Capital Planning Commission Suite 500, 401 Ninth St. NW, Washington, DC 20576. (202) 482-7200. www.ncpc.gov. Created as a park planning agency by act of June 6, 1924. Serves as the central planning agency for development activities for federal lands in the National Capital region in and around Washington.

National Credit Union Administration (NCUA) 1775 Duke St., Alexandria, VA 22314-3428. (703) 518-6300. www.ncua.gov. Created Mar. 10, 1970. Charters, insures, supervises and examines federal credit unions. Administers National Credit Union Share Insurance Fund. Supplies emergency loans to credit unions through Central Liquidity Facility.

National Foundation on the Arts and the Humanities 1100 Pennsylvania Ave. NW, Washington, DC 20506. Created in 1965. Its three divisions encourage and support national progress in humanities and arts. The *National Endowment for the Arts (NEA)* (202-682-5400; ww.arts.gov) fosters professional excellence in arts. The *National Endowment for the Humanities (NEH)* (202-606-8400; www.neh.gov) is an independent grant-making agency that supports research, education, and public programs in humanities. The *Institute of Museum and Library Services (IMS)* (202-606-8536; www.imls.gov) assists museums in maintaining, increasing, and improving services to public.

National Labor Relations Board (NLRB) 1099 14th Street NW, Washington, DC 20570. (202) 273-1000. www.nlrb.gov. Created by National Labor Relations Act of 1935 (also known as Wagner Act). Administers Federal labor law. Safeguards employees' rights to organize, conducts elections to determine whether workers want unions as their bargaining representative, and prevents or remedies unfair labor practices.

National Mediation Board 1301 K Street NW, Suite 250 East, Washington, DC 20572. (202) 692-5000. www.nmb.gov. Created June 21, 1934, by amendment to Railway Labor Act. Resolves and investigates representation disputes in railroad and airline industries that could interrupt flow of commerce and endanger national economy.

National Science Foundation (NSF) 4201 Wilson Blvd., Arlington, VA 22230. (703) 292-5111; www.nsf.gov. Created by National Science Foundation Act of 1950. Promotes progress of science and engineering through support of research and education programs.

National Transportation Safety Board (NTSB) 490 L'Enfant Plaza SW, Washington, DC 20594. (202) 314-6000. www.ntsb.gov. Created Apr. 1, 1975, by Independent Safety Board Act of 1974. Ensures safe operation of all types of transportation in U.S. Investigates accidents, conducts studies, and makes policy recommendations to government agencies, transportation industry and others.

Nuclear Regulatory Commission (NRC) Washington, DC 20555. (301) 415-7000. www.nrc.gov. Created by Energy Reorganization Act of 1974. Licenses and regulates uses of civilian nuclear energy to protect public health and environment. Sets licensing regulations, issues licenses for, and inspects construction, ownership, and operation of nuclear reactors and other nuclear materials.

Office of Personnel Management (OPM) 1900 E St. NW, Washington, DC 20415. (202) 606-1800. www.opm.gov. Created Jan. 1, 1979. Recruits, examines, trains, and promotes people for Government jobs, regardless of race, religion, sex, political influence and other nonmerit factors. Provides direct benefits, including health and life insurance, to employees and to retired employees and their survivors.

Overseas Private Investment Corporation (OPIC) 1100 New York Ave. NW, Washington, DC 20527. (202) 336-8400. www.opic.gov. Established as an independent agency in 1998. Promotes economic growth in developing countries by encouraging U.S. private investment in those nations.

Office of Special Counsel Suite 300, 1730 M Street NW., Washington, DC 20036-4505. (800) 872-9855. www.osc.gov. Created Jan. 1, 1979. Investigates allegations of certain activities prohibited by civil service laws, rules, or regulations before the Merit Sysems Protection Board. Protects whistleblowers from reprisals by their employers or former employers.

Peace Corps 1111 20th St. NW, Washington, DC 20526. (202) 692-2000. www.peacecorps.gov. Created by Peace Corps Act of 1961. Promotes world peace and friendship. Helps people of other countries develop manpower by bringing U.S. volunteers abroad to participate in public works programs. Emphasis placed on helping the poorest areas of countries served by the Peace Corps.

Pension Benefit Guaranty Corporation (PBGC) 1200 K St. NW, Washington, DC 20005. (202) 326-4000. www.pbgc.gov. Created Sept. 2, 1974, by Title IV of Employee Retirement Income Security Act of 1974. Guarantees payment of nonforfeitable pension benefits in covered private sector defined benefit pension plans.

Postal Rate Commission 1333 H St. NW, Washington, DC 20268-0001. (202) 789-6800. www.prc.gov. Created Aug. 12, 1970, by Postal Reorganization Act. Recommends changes in postal rates, fees, services, programs, studies and mail classification schedules. Hears complaints about postal rates, services, and fees.

Securities and Exchange Commission (SEC) 450 Fifth St. NW, Washington, DC 20549. (202) 942-4150. www.sec.gov. Created July 2, 1934 by Securities Exchange Act of 1934. Provides fullest possible disclosure to the public of securities sales, operations, and registrations. Protects public against malpractice in securities and financial markets.

Selective Service System National Headquarters, Arlington, VA 22209-2425. (703) 605-4000. www.sss.gov. Created June 24, 1948, by Military Selective Service Act. Requires registration, and maintains list of males age 18-26 eligible to serve in armed forces in case of national security emergency.

Small Business Administration (SBA) 409 Third St. SW, Washington, DC 20416. (202) 205-6600. www.sba.gov. Created by Small Business Act of 1953. Aids, counsels, makes loans to and protects interests of small businesses; ensures that they receive a fair amount of government purchases and contracts.

Social Security Administration 6401 Security Blvd., Baltimore, MD 21235. (410) 965-1234. www.ssa.gov. Created July 16, 1946; made independent agency by Social Security Independence Act of 1994. Manages the nation's social insurance program, consisting of retirement, survivors, and disability insurance programs, commonly known as Social Security. Also administers the Supplemental Security Income program for the aged, blind, and disabled. Studies poverty and recommends solutions. Assigns Social Security numbers to all U.S. workers.

Tennessee Valley Authority (TVA) 400 West Summit Hill Dr., Knoxville, TN 37902. (865) 632-2101. 1 Massachusetts Ave. NW, Washington, DC 20444-0001. (202)-898-2999. www.tva.gov. Created May 18, 1933. Government-owned corporation. Conducts resource development programs for advancement of growth in Tennessee Valley region. Controls floods, develops navigation, produces electric power, develops fertilizer, improves recreation, and develops forestry and wildlife.

United States Agency for International Development (AID) 1300 Pennsylvania Ave. NW, Washington, DC 20523-0001. (202) 712-0000. www.usaid.gov. Established as independent agency in 1998. Administers foreign economic and humanitarian assistance programs in the developing world, Central and Eastern Europe, and the countries of the former Soviet Union.

United States Commission on Civil Rights 624 Ninth St. NW, Washington, DC 20425. (202) 376-8177. www.usccr.gov. Created by Civil Rights Act of 1957. Collects and studies information on discrimination based on race, color, religion, age, sex, handicap or national origin. Assures equal protection in voting rights and enforcement of civil rights laws. Promotes equal opportunity in education, employment, and housing.

United States International Trade Commission 500 E St. SW, Washington, DC 20436. (202) 205-2000. www.usitc.gov. Created Sept. 8, 1916. Furnishes studies, reports, and recommendations regarding international trade and tariffs to president, Congress, and other government agencies.

United States Postal Service 475 L'Enfant Plaza SW, Washington, DC 20260-0010. (202) 268-2000. www.usps.gov. Created Aug. 12, 1970, by Postal Reorganization Act. Provides mail processing and delivery service to individuals and businesses in U.S. Protects mail from loss or theft and apprehends violators of postal laws.

FEDERAL EMPLOYEES AND BUDGET

▶FEDERAL JOBS AND SALARIES

As of March 31, 2002 (the latest year available), there were 1,681,537 full-time non-postal federal civilian employees. Nearly 97 percent of the federal civilian workforce was employed in the United States; 12,049 (0.7 percent) worked in U.S. territories, and 40,742 (2.4 percent) worked in foreign countries. The majority of government employees worked in metropolitan statistical areas, led by the Washington, D.C., MSA, with 272,941, or 16.2 percent of the total.

Four executive departments accounted for nearly 70 percent of the federal civilian workforce. The Department of Defense employed 635,774 civilians (37.8 percent of the total), Veterans Affairs employed 199,191 (11.8 percent), the Treasury 156,848 (9.3 percent), and Justice 125,127 or 7.4 percent).

Federal government civilian employees are paid according to a number of different systems: the General Schedule (GS), Federal Wage Systems, and other acts and administratively determined systems. Overall, the average salary for full-time civilian government employees was $55,715. Employees under the General Schedule on average earned more than those on Federal Wage Systems ($54,329 to $39,892), but not as much as employees covered by other acts and administrative determinations, who averaged $74,771. Average salaries by major geographic areas were: United States, $55,932; Washington, D.C. area, $71,139; foreign countries, $50,870; and U.S. territories, $42,852.

White-Collar Employees

General Schedule After declining for four straight years, the number of white-collar employees increased for the second straight year, from 1,219,441 in 2001 to 1,238,182 in 2002. There are 15 grades broadly defined in terms of responsibility, difficulty, and qualifications; within each grade there are 10 steps. Within-grade advancement occurs on a fixed schedule, though employees demonstrating "high-quality performance"

The Federal Government: Employees and Budget, 1901–2003

		Budget (millions)		
Year	Number of employees[1]	Receipts	Outlays	Surplus or deficit (-)
1901	239,476	$588	$525	$63
1910	388,708	676	694	-18
1920	655,265	6,649	6,358	291
1930	601,319	4,058	3,320	738
1940	1,042,420	6,548	9,468	-2,920
1945	3,816,310	45,159	92,712	-47,553
1950	1,960,708	39,443	42,562	-3,119
1960	2,398,704	92,492	92,191	301
1970	2,984,574	192,807	195,649	-2,842
1980	2,875,866	517,112	590,941	-73,830
1990	3,128,267	1,031,969	1,253,165	-221,195
1995	2,920,277	1,351,830	1,515,802	-163,972
1998	2,789,532	1,721,798	1,652,585	69,213
1999	2,749,239	1,827,454	1,701,891	125,563
2000	2,702,258	2,025,218	1,788,826	236,392
2001	2,693,929	1,991,194	1,863,895	127,299
2002	2,695,536	1,853,173	2,010,975	-157,802
2003[2]	N.A.	1,836,218	2,140,377	-304,159

1. Paid civilians only. 2. Projected. **Source:** Office of Management and Budget, *Budget of the United States Government, FY 2004*.

can receive "quality step increases." In all, General Schedule employees make up more than three-quarters of all civilians employed by the government.

Foreign Service Personnel and Veterans Affairs There were 3,834 Foreign Service Officers in 2002, with an average salary of $87,972. Non-officers in the foreign service numbered 7,845 and averaged $58,133 in salary. The pay system of the Department of Veterans Affairs covered 7,505 physicians and dentists with an average salary of $106,676; 304 podiatrists and optometrists ($95,629); 31,560 nurses ($60,683); and 1,267 physicians' assistants ($71,352).

Executive Schedule (EX) and Senior Executive Service (ES) The very top executives in the executive branch are paid under a system known as the Executive Schedule (EX). Broadly speaking, the five Executive Schedule levels include the following job titles: level I, cabinet members; level II, deputy secretaries of major departments; level III, presidential advisors, chief administrators of major independent agencies, and under secretaries; level IV, assistant secretaries, deputy under secretaries, and general counsels in executive departments; and level V, deputy assistant secretaries, administrators, commissioners,

Salaries of Federal Officials, 2002-03

To prevent themselves from having to vote publicly on raising their own pay, Congress in 1999 passed a law that gives legislators an automatic annual cost of living increase unless they actively vote against such a raise. Salaries in the judicial branch are pegged to those in Congress, so whenever legislators get a raise, so does the judiciary.

Branch/Official	2002 Salary	2003 Salary
Executive branch		
President	$400,000	$400,000
Vice President	192,600	198,600
Legislative branch		
Senate		
President pro tempore	$166,700	$171,900
Majority and minority leaders	166,700	171,900
Senators	150,000	154,700
House of Representatives		
Speaker of the House	$192,600	$198,600
Minority and majority leaders	166,700	171,900
Representatives	150,000	154,700
Judicial branch		
Chief Justice	$192,600	$198,600
Associate justices	184,400	190,100
Circuit judges	159,100	164,000
District judges	150,000	150,700

Source: Office of Personnel Management, Compensation Administration.

Federal Government Pay Systems, 2002

Grade	Employees	Mean Salary
General Schedule		
GS-1	397	$16,636
GS-2	1,657	19,229
GS-3	11,666	21,850
GS-4	51,485	25,158
GS-5	109,238	29,038
GS-6	83,511	32,964
GS-7	127,818	36,463
GS-8	48,958	41,235
GS-9	127,840	44,022
GS-10	15,221	49,863
GS-11	169,945	53,485
GS-12	205,120	64,299
GS-13	168,881	77,004
GS-14	76,866	91,724
GS-15	39,579	110,065
Total	**1,238,182**	**$54,329**
Senior Level (SL)	500	$99,096-130,000[1]
Executive Schedule (EX)		
Level I	17	166,700
Level II	36	150,000
Level III	99	138,200
Level IV	275	130,000
Level V	19	121,600
Total	**446**	**$134,978**
Senior Executive Service (ES)		
ES-1	814	113,000
ES-2	925	118,300
ES-3	1,051	123,700
ES-4	2,589	129,800
ES-5	1,108	130,000
ES-6	509	130,000
Total	**6,996**	**$135,717**

Note: As of March 31. 1. Mean salary not available. Salary range shown. **Source:** U.S. Office of Personnel Management, *Pay Structure of the Federal Civil Service 2002,* (2003).

U.S. Federal Employment, 1992–2002

Description	1992	2000	2001	2002
Executive branch civilian employment[1]	**2,226,778**	**1,778,138**	**1,791,810**	**1,818,260**
U.S. Postal Service[2]	792,049	860,777	847,870	811,691
Military personnel on active duty[3]	1,847,600	1,426,338	1,427,723	1,456,093
Department of Defense	1,808,131	1,384,338	1,385,116	1,411,634
Department of Transportation (Coast Guard)	39,469	36,157	36,580	38,238
Total executive branch employment	4,866,427	4,065,253	4,067,403	4,086,044
Legislative branch	38,509	31,157	30,439	30,886
Judicial branch	27,987	32,186	33,810	34,699
Total federal employment	**4,932,923**	**4,128,596**	**4,131,652**	**4,151,629**

Note: 1.Excludes Postal Service employees. 2. Includes Postal Rate Commission. 3. Excludes reserve components.
Source: Office of Management and Budget, *Budget of the United States Government, FY 2004.*

and directors. Executive Schedule employment in 2002 was 446, more than double what it was the year before, with an average salary of $134,978. The Senior Executive Service (ES) covers most managerial and policy positions in the executive branch that do not require Senate confirmation. In 2002, there were 6,966 employees covered by ES (up from 6,719 in 2001); salaries averaged $135,717.

Government Employment and Population, 1962–2002

Fiscal year	Government employment: Federal executive branch[1] ('000s)	Total Federal personnel ('000s)	State and local governments ('000s)	All governmental units ('000s)	Executive branch employment as a percent of all governmental units[1]	Executive branch employment per 1,000 population[1]
1962	2,485	5,354	6,549	11,903	20.9%	13.3%
1965	2,496	5,215	7,696	12,911	19.3	12.8
1970[2]	2,944	6,085	9,822	15,907	18.5	14.4
1975	2,848	5,061	11,937	16,998	16.8	13.2
1980[2]	2,821	4,965	13,375	18,340	15.4	12.4
1985	3,008	5,256	13,519	18,775	16.0	12.6
1990[2]	3,067	5,234	15,219	20,453	15.0	12.3
1995	2,858	4,475	16,484	20,959	13.6	10.7
2000[2]	2,639	4,129	17,925	22,054	12.0	9.4
2001[2]	2,640	4,132	18,317	22,449	11.8	9.3
2002	2,630	4,152	18,642	22,794	11.5	9.1

1. Civilian employment only, including full-time permanent, temporary, part-time, and intermittent employees in the executive branch, including the Postal Service, and beginning in 1970, includes various disadvantaged worker-trainee programs. 2. Includes temporary employees in the decennial census. **Source:** Office of Management and Budget, *Budget of the United States Government, FY 2004.*

Federal Government Employment and Outlays, by Branch and Agency, 1990–2003

Agency	Employment 2001[1]	Outlays (millions of dollars) 1990	2000	2002	2003[2]
Legislative branch	30,886	$2,241	$2,911	$3,218	$3,961
Judicial branch	34,699	1,646	4,086	4,823	5,419
Executive branch[3]	1,749,900	—	—	—	—
Executive Office of the President	N.A.	158	283	451	334
Department of Agriculture	97,000	46,012	75,663	68,731	72,773
Department of Commerce	34,900	3,734	7,807	5,314	5,790
Department of Defense[4] (military functions)	649,900	289,755	281,223	331,951	358,155
Department of Defense (civil functions)	N.A.	21,692	32,864	35,157	40,148
Department of Education	4,500	22,972	33,900	46,282	59,481
Department of Energy	15,800	12,084	15,010	17,681	19,796
Department of Health and Human Services	59,000	175,531	382,626	465,812	502,013
Department of Homeland Security	81,300	N.A.	N.A.	17,476	28,155
Dept. of Housing and Urban Development	10,000	20,167	30,828	31,885	37,987
Department of the Interior	70,300	5,825	8,029	9,739	10,357
Department of Justice	97,300	6,507	20,064	21,112	22,156
Department of Labor	17,000	25,215	31,876	64,704	70,746
Department of State	28,600	4,802	6,850	9,453	10,977
Department of Transportation	61,200	28,650	45,965	56,104	52,280
Department of the Treasury	115,900	255,172	390,677	370,558	368,803
Department of Veterans Affairs	208,900	28,998	47,087	50,884	56,946
Environmental Protection Agency	17,500	5,108	7,238	7,450	7,958
General Services Administration	12,400	–93	28	–677	424
National Aeronautics & Space Administration (NASA)	18,700	12,429	13,442	14,430	14,599
Office of Personnel Management	2,800	31,949	48,660	52,512	55,793
Small Business Administration	4,000	692	–421	493	1,553
Social Security Administration (off-budget)	63,100	244,998	396,169	442,425	465,404
Totals[5, 6]	**1,815,465**	**$1,253,198**	**$1,788,773**	**$2,010,975**	**$2,140,377**

Note: Outlays are the measure of Government spending--payments to liquidate obligations (other than the repayment of debt), net of cash, and offsetting collections. Outlays are generally recorded on a cash basis, but also include many cash-equivalent transactions and interest accrued on public issues of the public debt. 1. Employment figures exclude developmental positions under the Worker-Trainee Opportunity Program; participants in the Cooperative Education Program; disadvantaged summer and part-time workers under such Office of Personnel Management programs as Summer Aides, stay-in-school, and junior fellowship; and certain statutory exemptions. Figures for executive branch rounded at source. 2. Estimate. 3. Civilian employment. 4. By law (10 U.S.C. Chapter 4, section 140b) the Department of Defense is exempt from full-time equivalent employment controls. Data shown are estimated. 5. Employment totals do not include FDIC or U.S. Postal Service. 6. Outlay totals do not account for undistributed offsetting receipts.
Source: Office of Management and Budget, *Budget of the United States Government, FY 2004*

Special rates The government has difficulty recruiting and retaining qualified personnel in certain occupations and for certain locations with higher competitive salaries. To alleviate this problem, the Office of Personnel Management has the authority to establish special rates for certain white-collar positions. The number of white-collar employees receiving special-rate salaries varies from year to year; in 2002, it was 191,171, up from 184,867 in 2001.

Blue-Collar Employees

As of March 31, 2002, the federal government employed 193,021 workers (11.5 percent of the civilian government workforce) in blue-collar (trades and labor) occupations. The vast majority of these employees worked in the United States, mostly for the Defense Department (73.4 percent). The Department of Veterans Affairs employed 24,982 blue-collar workers (12.9 percent of the total).

The Congressional Budget Process

On or before	Action to be completed
First Monday in February	President submits his budget. Congressional committees have six weeks to submit views and estimates to Budget Committees.
February 15	Congressional Budget Office submits report to budget committees.
April 1	Senate budget committee reports concurrent resolution on the budget.
April 15	Congress completes action on concurrent resolution on the budget.
May 15	Annual appropriation bills may be considered in the House.
June 10	House Appropriations Committee reports last annual appropriations bill.
June 15	Congress completes action on reconciliation legislation.
June 30	House completes action on annual appropriation bills.
October 1	Fiscal year begins.

1. A concurrent resolution sets levels for new budget authority and outlays, direct loan obligations, primary loan guarantee commitments, the amount by which Federal revenues should be increased or decreased, the budget surplus or deficit, the public debt, and so on. **Source**: Committee on Ways and Means, U.S. House of Representatives, *Overview of Entitlement Programs,* (annual).

Blue-collar pay rates are governed by federal Wage Systems and determined on a prevailing rate basis by pay locality. The worldwide average salary for the blue-collar workforce in 2001 was $39,892. Salaries were highest in the United States (where they averaged $40,040) and lowest in foreign countries, (where they averaged just $32,713). Blue-collar salaries averaged $41,195 in the Washington D.C. metropolitan area, but only $29,444 in U.S. territories and possessions.

▶SURPLUS, WHAT SURPLUS?

After 30 years of annual budget deficits, the federal government recorded a budget surplus in 1998, and posted a record $236.4 billion surplus in 2000. But even four consecutive years of annual surpluses (a feat not seen since before the Depression) did little to dent the immense federal debt run up during the Reagan Administration. In 2002, the gross federal debt was more than $6 trillion, or more than six times what it was in 1980, and the surpluses didn't even equal the net interest payments on this huge debt. (see the U.S. Economy for an explanation of the difference between deficits and the debt). In 2003, the government is expected to run a record budget deficit of more than $300 billion.

▶GLOSSARY OF FEDERAL BUDGET TERMS

Budget authority The term budget authority means the authority provided by law to incur financial obligations that result in immediate or future outlays involving government funds or to collect offsetting receipts.

Budget deficit/surplus A budget deficit occurs when government outlays exceed government receipts; a surplus occurs when receipts exceed outlays. The record budget surplus was $236.4 billion (in 2000); the record deficit is the $300.4 billion scheduled for Fiscal 2003.

Fiscal year The federal government's fiscal year begins Oct. 1 and ends Sept. 30 of the next calendar year; so, FY 2003 began Oct. 1, 2003, and ends Sept. 30, 2004.

Intergovernmental expenditure/revenue Amounts paid to or received from other governments either in the form of shared revenues and grants-in-aid, as reimbursements for performance of general government activities or for specific services such as care of prisoners for the paying government, or in lieu of taxes.

Federal Government Receipts by Source, 1934-2003 (billions of dollars)

Year	Individual income taxes	Corporation income taxes[1]	Social insurance & retirement receipts	Excise taxes	Other[2]	Total
1934	$0.4	$0.3	(3)	$1.4	$0.8	**$3.0**
1940	0.9	1.2	$1.8	2.0	0.7	**6.5**
1950	15.8	10.4	4.3	7.6	1.4	**39.4**
1960	40.7	21.5	14.7	11.7	3.9	**92.5**
1970	90.4	32.8	44.3	15.7	9.5	**192.8**
1980	244.1	64.6	157.8	24.3	26.3	**517.1**
1990	466.9	93.5	380.0	35.3	56.2	**1,032.0**
2000	1,004.5	207.3	652.9	68.9	91.8	**2,025.2**
2001	994.4	151.1	694.0	66.1	85.6	**1,991.0**
2002	858.3	148.0	700.8	67.0	79.1	**1,853.2**
2003[4]	849.1	143.2	726.6	68.4	48.9	**1,836.2**

1. Beginning in 1990 includes trust fund receipts for the hazardous substance Superfund. 2. Includes estate and gift taxes, customs duties and fees, federal reserve deposits, and other. 3. Less than $100 million. 4. Estimate.
Source: Office of Management and Budget, *Budget of the United States Government, FY 2004.*

Off-budget/on-budget Some presentations in the federal budget distinguish on-budget totals from off-budget totals. On-budget totals reflect the transactions of all federal government entities except those excluded from the budget totals by law, the two Social Security trust funds (old-age and survivors insurance and the federal disability insurance trust funds), and the Postal Service fund. Off-budget totals reflect the transactions of government entities excluded from the on-budget totals by law.

Offsetting collections Offsetting collections are collections from the public that result from business-type or market-oriented activities and collections; examples include proceeds from the sale of electric power by the Tennessee Valley Authority, voluntary medical insurance premiums paid to the supplementary medical insurance trust fund, and the sale of postage stamps.

Outlays Budget outlays are expenditures and net lending of funds under budget authority during the fiscal year. They constitute the spending side

Outlays by Budget Enforcement Act Category, 1970-2003 (billions)

Category	1970	1980	1990	2000	2001	2002	2003[1]
Total Outlays	**$195.6**	**$590.9**	**$1,253.2**	**$1,788.8**	**$1,863.9**	**$2,011.0**	**$2,140.4**
Discretionary outlays	120.3	276.3	500.6	614.8	649.3	734.4	791.4
National defense	81.9	134.6	300.1	295.0	306.1	348.9	375.7
Non-defense, international	4.0	12.8	19.1	21.3	22.5	26.2	27.6
Non-defense, domestic	34.4	128.9	181.4	298.6	320.8	359.2	388.1
Mandatory outlays	61.0	262.1	568.2	951.0	1,008.4	1,105.7	1,187.5
Social Security	29.6	117.1	246.5	406.0	429.4	452.5	474.5
Deposit Insurance	-0.5	-0.4	57.9	-3.1	–1.4	–1.0	0.1
Means-tested entitlements[2]	10.1	45.0	94.1	226.3	241.5	269.9	293.4
Other	30.4	120.4	206.4	364.2	386.0	432.1	469.8
Undistributed offsetting receipts[3]	-8.6	-19.9	-36.7	-42.6	–47.0	–47.8	–50.3
Net interest	14.4	52.5	184.4	223.0	206.2	171.0	161.4

1. Estimate. 2. Includes Medicaid, food stamps, family support assistance (AFDC), supplemental security income (SSI), child nutrition programs, earned income tax credits, and veterans' pensions. 3. Includes asset sales.
Source: Office of Management and Budget, *Budget of the United States Government, FY 2004.*

Budget Outlays and Percent Distribution, by Function, 1970–2002

Function	1970	1980	1990	1995	2000	2002
		Millions of dollars				
National defense	**$81,692**	**$133,995**	**$299,331**	**$272,066**	**$294,495**	**348,555**
Human resources	**75,349**	**313,374**	**619,329**	**923,765**	**1,115,481**	**1,317,852**
Education, training, employment and social services	8,634	31,843	38,755	54,263	53,754	70,544
Health	5,907	23,169	57,716	115,418	154,533	196,545
Medicare	6,213	32,090	98,102	159,855	197,113	230,855
Income Security	15,655	86,540	147,076	220,493	253,575	312,511
Social Security	30,270	118,547	248,623	335,846	409,423	456,413
Veterans benefits & services	8,669	21,185	29,058	37,890	47,083	50,984
Physical resources	**15,574**	**65,985**	**126,039**	**59,142**	**84,665**	**104,405**
Energy	997	10,156	3,341	4,936	–1,060	483
Natural resources and environment	3,065	13,858	17,080	21,915	25,031	29,454
Commerce and housing credit	2,112	9,390	67,600	-17,808	3,211	–385
Transportation	7,008	21,329	29,485	39,350	46,854	61,862
Community and regional development	2,392	11,252	8,498	10,641	10,629	12,991
Net interest	**14,380**	**52,538**	**184,380**	**232,169**	**222,951**	**170,951**
Other functions	**17,286**	**44,996**	**60,734**	**73,150**	**113,762**	**117,018**
International affairs	4,330	12,714	13,764	16,434	17,216	22,357
General science, space, & technology	4,511	5,832	14,444	16,724	18,637	20,772
Agriculture	5,166	8,839	11,958	9,778	36,641	22,188
Administration of justice	959	4,584	9,993	16,216	27,995	34,316
General government	2,320	13,028	10,575	13,998	13,273	17,385
Total[1]	**$195,649**	**$590,947**	**$1,253,198**	**$1,515,837**	**$1,788,773**	**2,010,975**
		As percentage of total				
National defense	41.8%	22.7%	23.9%	17.9%	16.5%	17.3%
Human resources	38.5	53.0	49.4	60.9	62.4	65.5
Physical resources	8.0	11.2	10.1	3.9	4.7	5.2
Net interest	7.4	8.9	14.7	15.3	12.5	8.5
Other functions	8.8	7.6	4.8	4.8	6.4	5.8

1. Includes undistributed offsetting receipts not shown separately.
Source: Office of Management and Budget, *Budget of the United States Government, FY 2004.*

of the budget and are compared to receipts in calculating the budget surplus or deficit.

Receipts Budget receipts constitute the income side of the budget and are composed almost entirely of taxes or other compulsory payments to the government. They are compared to outlays in calculating the budget surplus or deficit.

Trust fund In the federal budget, a trust fund means only that the law requires that funds must be accounted for separately and used only for specified purposes. The largest trust funds are those for civil service and military retirement, Social Security, Medicare and unemployment insurance. These are financed largely by Social Security taxes and contributions and payments from the general fund. There are also major trust funds for transportation and bank deposit insurance which are financed by user charges.

User charges These are charges for services rendered, collected in the form of taxes, such as highway excise taxes to fund the highway trust fund.

Federal Government Finances, 2000-03 (in millions of dollars)

Category	2000	2001	2002	2003[1]
RECEIPTS, TOTAL	**$2,025,218**	**$1,991,194**	**$1,853,173**	**$1,836,218**
Individual income taxes, total	**1,004,462**	**994,339**	**858,345**	**849,053**
Corporation income taxes, total	**207,289**	**151,075**	**148,044**	**143,186**
Social insurance and retirement receipts, total	**652,852**	**693,967**	**700,760**	**726,593**
Employment and general retirement:	620,451	661,442	668,547	687,832
Old-age and survivors insurance (Off-budget)	411,677	434,057	440,541	454,405
Disability insurance (Off-budget)	68,907	73,462	74,780	77,160
Hospital insurance	135,529	149,651	149,049	152,275
Railroad retirement:	4,338	4,272	4,177	3,992
Unemployment insurance:	27,640	27,812	27,619	34,230
Other retirement:	4,761	4,713	4,594	4,531
Federal employees' retirement—employee share	4,691	4,647	4,533	4,479
Non-Federal employees retirement[2]	70	66	61	52
Excise taxes, total	**68,865**	**66,232**	**66,989**	**68,416**
Federal funds, total	22,692	24,286	24,017	24,871
Alcohol taxes	8,140	7,624	7,764	7,840
Tobacco taxes	7,221	7,396	8,274	8,158
Transportation fuels tax	819	1,150	814	869
Telephone and teletype services	5,670	5,769	5,829	6,205
Ozone depleting chemicals and products	125	32	N.A.	N.A.
Other Federal fund excise taxes	717	2,315	1,336	1,799
Trust funds, total	46,173	41,946	42,972	43,545
Highway	34,972	31,469	32,603	32,815
Airport and airway	9,739	9,191	9,031	9,381
Aquatic resources	342	358	386	393
Black lung disability insurance	518	522	567	561
Inland waterway	101	113	95	88
Hazardous substance superfund	2	2	N.A.	N.A.
Vaccine injury compensation	133	112	109	124
Leaking underground storage tank	184	179	181	183
Estate and gift taxes, total	**29,010**	**28,400**	**26,507**	**20,209**
Customs duties, total	**19,914**	**19,369**	**18,602**	**19,052**
Miscellaneous receipts, total	**42,826**	**37,812**	**33,926**	**34,709**
OUTLAYS, TOTAL	**$1,788,826**	**$1,863,895**	**$2,010,975**	**$2,140,377**
National defense, total	**294,495**	**305,500**	**348,555**	**376,286**
Department of Defense—Military, total	281,223	291,015	331,951	358,155
Military Personnel	75,950	73,977	86,799	92,687
Operation and Maintenance	105,870	112,015	130,005	136,284
Procurement	51,696	54,986	62,515	63,220
Research, Development, Test, and Evaluation	37,606	40,459	44,389	52,838
Military Construction	5,109	4,977	5,052	6,001
Family Housing	3,413	3,516	3,736	4,151
Other	1,579	1,085	–545	2,974
Atomic energy defense activities	12,161	13,005	14,877	16,348
Defense-related activities	1,111	1,480	1,727	1,783
International affairs, total	**17,216**	**16,493**	**22,357**	**20,735**
International development and humanitarian assistance	6,518	7,191	7,821	8,662
International security assistance	6,387	6,560	7,907	6,765
Conduct of foreign affairs	4,709	5,050	7,068	8,138
Foreign information and exchange activities	817	804	906	876
International financial programs	-1,215	–3,112	–1,345	–3,706
General science, space and technology, total	**18,637**	**19,789**	**20,772**	**21,699**
General science and basic research	6,210	6,553	7,299	8,087
Space flight, research, and supporting activities	12,427	13,236	13,473	13,612
Energy, total	**-1,060**	**39**	**483**	**708**
Energy supply	-2,118	–1,116	–796	–648

Category	2000	2001	2002	2003[1]
Energy conservation	666	760	878	847
Emergency energy preparedness	162	159	169	177
Energy information, policy, and regulation	230	236	232	332
Natural resources and environment, total	**25,031**	**25,623**	**29,454**	**30,578**
Water resources	5,081	5,240	5,570	5,296
Conservation and land management	6,770	7,109	9,797	9,889
Recreational resources	2,550	2,339	2,750	3,067
Pollution control and abatement	7,402	7,562	7,615	8,121
Other natural resources	3,228	3,373	3,722	4,205
Agriculture, total	**36,641**	**26,397**	**22,188**	**20,847**
Farm income stabilization	33,452	22,698	18,364	16,305
Agricultural research and services	3,189	3,699	3,824	4,542
Commerce and housing credit, total	**3,211**	**5,883**	**–385**	**1,262**
Mortgage credit	-3,335	–1,164	–7,006	–4,328
Postal Service	2,129	2,395	207	–4,161
Deposit insurance	-3,051	–1,443	–1,021	141
Other advancement of commerce	7,468	6,095	7,435	9,610
Transportation, total	**46,854**	**54,449**	**61,862**	**64,228**
Ground transportation	31,697	35,804	40,158	37,813
Air transportation	10,571	13,975	16,538	20,281
Water transportation	4,394	4,401	5,059	5,749
Other transportation	192	269	107	385
Community and regional development, total	**10,629**	**11,907**	**12,991**	**18,459**
Community development	5,480	5,313	5,998	7,621
Area and regional development	2,538	2,759	2,633	2,841
Disaster relief and insurance	2,611	3,835	4,360	7,997
Education, training, employment, and social services, total	**53,754**	**57,143**	**70,544**	**86,252**
Elementary, secondary, and vocational education	20,578	22,858	25,879	32,798
Higher education	10,116	9,568	17,049	22,918
Research and general education aids	2,532	2,777	2,928	3,065
Training and employment	6,772	7,186	8,348	9,916
Other labor services	1,199	1,274	1,439	1,599
Social services	12,557	13,480	14,901	15,956
Health, total	**154,533**	**172,270**	**196,545**	**223,068**
Health care services	136,230	151,911	172,598	196,054
Health research and training	15,979	17,926	21,356	24,122
Consumer and occupational health and safety	2,324	2,433	2,591	2,892
Medicare, total	**197,113**	**217,384**	**230,855**	**244,667**
Income security, total	**253,525**	**269,615**	**312,511**	**330,120**
General retirement and disability insurance (excluding social security)	5,152	5,761	5,741	6,589
Federal employee retirement and disability	77,152	80,972	83,361	86,342
Unemployment compensation	23,012	30,242	53,267	56,313
Housing assistance	28,800	30,091	33,061	34,199
Food and nutrition assistance	32,483	34,053	38,150	42,982
Other income security	86,926	88,496	98,931	103,695
Social security, total	**409,436**	**432,958**	**456,413**	**478,471**
Veterans benefits and services, total	**47,083**	**45,039**	**50,984**	**57,070**
Income security for veterans	24,872	23,202	27,433	30,272
Veterans education, training and rehabilitation	1,342	1,371	1,884	2,477
Hospital and medical care for veterans	19,516	20,907	22,217	23,372
Veterans housing	342	–904	–959	277
Other veterans benefits and services	1,011	463	409	672
Administration of justice, total	**27,995**	**29,660**	**34,316**	**36,142**
Federal law enforcement activities	11,617	12,000	14,663	15,269
Federal litigative and judicial activities	7,762	8,299	9,137	9,497
Federal correctional activities	3,707	4,206	4,748	5,444
Criminal justice assistance	4,909	5,155	5,768	5,932
General government, total	**13,273**	**14,589**	**17,385**	**18,998**
Legislative functions	2,222	2,311	2,637	3,242
Executive direction and management	456	457	639	579
Central fiscal operations	8,345	9,206	10,269	10,418
General property and records management	225	196	–10	1,195
Central personnel management	184	184	47	212
General purpose fiscal assistance	2,084	2,308	2,404	2,462
Other general government	2,241	1,809	2,291	2,084
Deductions for offsetting receipts	-2,484	–1,882	–892	–1,194
Net interest, total	**223,041**	**206,168**	**170,951**	**161,441**

1. Estimate. 2 Represents employer and employee contributions to the civil service retirement and disability fund for covered employees of Government-sponsored, privately owned enterprises and the District of Columbia municipal government.
Source: Office of Management and Budget, *Budget of the United States Government, FY 2004*

Federal Government Dollar, Fiscal Year 2003

Revenues: $1,922 billion | **Outlays $2,229 billion**

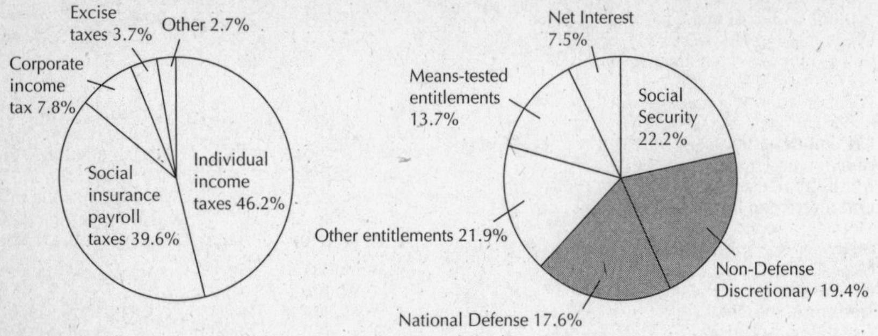

Note: Gray-shaded areas are discretionary outlays. All other outlays are mandatory.
Source: Office of Management and Budget, *Budget of the United States Government, FY 2004.*

Federal Budget Outlays for National Defense Functions, 1962–2002 (billions of dollars)

Function	1962	1970	1980	1990	2000	2002	2003[1]
Military personnel	$16,331	$29,032	$40,897	$75,622	$75,950	$86,799	$92,687
Percent of defense budget	31.2%	35.4%	30.5%	25.2%	25.8%	24.9%	24.6%
Operations & maintenance	$11,594	$21,609	$44,788	$88,340	$105,870	130,005	136,284
Procurement	14,532	21,584	29,021	80,972	51,696	62,515	63,220
Research, development, test and evaluation	6,319	7,166	13,127	37,458	37,606	44,389	52,838
Military construction	1,347	1,168	2,450	5,080	5,109	5,052	6,001
Family housing	259	614	1,680	3,501	3,413	3,736	4,151
Other	–271	–1,050	–1,050	–1,218	1,579	–545	2,974
Total outlays[2]	**$52,345**	**$81,692**	**$133,995**	**$299,331**	**$294,495**	**$348,555**	**$376,286**

1. Estimate. 2. Includes atomic energy defense activities and other defense-related activities not shown separately.
Source: Office of Management and Budget, *Budget of the United States Government, FY 2004.*

NATIONAL DEFENSE

In 2003, the United States spent $376 billion to keep 1.4 million people in active military service and to build and maintain the greatest arsenal of weapons ever known.

Since the end of World War II, a large percentage of people and material have been committed to regions around the world that the government has determined are vital to U.S. interests. Between 1961 and 1980, the defense budget averaged around $200 billion annually (in 1982 constant dollars)—even during the Vietnam War. In 1981, however, the Reagan administration began a massive defense buildup that swelled successive defense budgets to unprecedented peacetime levels and in the process helped to quadruple the annual federal deficit in less than five years.

When the cold war ended, the defense budget started to recede from its previous high of $303 billion in 1989. But since 1998, the amount spent on the military has been increasing again; by 2002, the defense budget was expected to set a new record of nearly $350 billion. The U.S. remains committed to maintaining active duty and reserve forces sufficient for quick and effective response to crises around the world, but after the terror attacks in 2001, military leaders of the only remaining superpower urged a major expansion and thorough reorganization of all branches of the military to better confront the threat of terrorism and the proliferation of weapons of mass destruction.

The defense establishment The earliest precursor to the Department of Defense was the War Department, established by Congress in 1789; a separate Navy Department was created in 1798. These were merged under the National Security Act of 1947 and subsequent amendments. By 1949 the secretary of defense was established as the principal assistant to the president on defense matters in charge of the Defense Department.

The Department of Defense (DoD) is a cabinet-level organization responsible for providing the military forces needed to deter war and protect the security of the United States. The major elements of these forces are the Army, Navy, Air Force, and Marine Corps. Under the president, who is also the commander-in-chief, the secretary of defense exercises direction, authority and control over the Department of Defense, which includes the three military departments, the Joint Chiefs of Staff and Joint Staff, nine unified commands, 15 defense agencies, and seven DoD field activities.

The four armed services are subordinate to the military departments, which are responsible for recruiting, training and equipping their forces. The Marine Corps is the second armed service in the Department of the Navy. (A fifth armed service, the U.S. Coast Guard, joined the Department of Homeland Security in 2003.)

Chain of command Operational command of U.S. combat forces is assigned to the nation's unified and specified commands. The chain of command runs from the president to the secretary of defense, through the Joint Chiefs of Staff to the commanders-in-chief of the unified and specified commands. (The four service secretaries are not part of this chain of command.) A *unified command* is composed of forces from two or more services, has a broad and continuing mission and is normally organized on a geographical basis.

▶U.S. ARMY

In peacetime, the primary mission of the continental U.S. armies is to train reserves and national guard, plan for mobilization, and coordinate domestic emergency relief efforts. The largest unit is a numbered *army,* such as the Fifth Army. (In time of war, two or three armies may be brought under a single command in an *army*

Chairmen of the Joint Chiefs of Staff, 1949–2003

General of the Army Omar N. Bradley, USA	1949–53
Adm. Arthur W. Radford, USN	1953–57
Gen. Nathan F. Twining, USAF	1957–60
Gen. Lyman L. Lemnitzer, USA	1960–62
Gen. Maxwell D. Taylor, USA	1962–64
Gen. Earle G. Wheeler, USA	1964–70
Adm. Thomas H. Moorer, USN	1970–74
Gen. George S. Brown, USAF	1974–78
Gen. David C. Jones, USAF	1978–82
Gen. John W. Vessey Jr., USA	1982–85
Adm. William J. Crowe, USN	1985–89
Gen. Colin L. Powell, USA	1989–93
Gen. John Shalikashvili, USA	1993–97
Gen. H. Hugh Shelton, USA	1997–2001
Gen. Richard B. Myers, USAF	2001-present

Defense Establishment Employees, 2002

Branch	Active Duty[1] Officers	Enlisted	Total	Civilian employees
Army	78,158	404,304	486,542	223,450
Navy[2]	54,780	325,996	385,051	195,851
Marine Corps	18,288	155,445	173,733	N.A.
Air Force	72,032	292,061	368,251	159,781
Total DoD	223,258	1,177,806	1,413,577	683,347[3]

Note: As of September 30, 2002. 1. Includes Academy Cadets and Midshipmen, not shown separately. 2. Includes Marine Corps civilian personnel. 3. Includes other Defense Dept. organizations. **Source:** U.S. Dept. of Defense, *Selected Manpower Statistics, Fiscal Year 2002* (2003). www.defenselink.mil.

Military Personnel on Active Duty, 1789–2002

Year/War	Total
1789	718
1795	5,296
1801	7,108
1810	11,554
War of 1812 (1812-15)	
1812	12,631
1813	25,152
1814	46,858
1815	40,885
1820	15,113
1830	11,942
1840	21,616
Mexican War (1846-48)	
1846	39,165
1847	57,761
1848	60,308
1850	20,824
1860	27,958
Civil War (1861-65)	
1861	217,112
1862	673,124
1863	960,061
1864	1,031,724
1865	1,062,848
1870	50,348
1880	37,894
1890	38,666
Spanish-American War (1898)	
1898	235,785
1900	139,344
1915	174,112
World War I (1917-18)	
1917	643,833
1918	2,897,167
1919	1,172,602
1920	343,302
1930	255,648
1940	458,365
World War II (1941-46)	
1941	1,801,101
1942	3,858,791
1943	9,044,745
1944	11,451,719
1945	12,123,455
1946	3,030,088
Korean Conflict (1950-53)	
1950	1,460,261
1951	3,249,455
1952	3,635,912
1953	3,555,067
1960	2,476,435
Vietnam Conflict (1964-73)	
1964	2,687,409
1965	2,655,389
1966	3,094,058
1967	3,376,880
1968	3,547,902
1969	3,460,162
1970	3,066,294
1975	2,128,120
1980	2,050,627
1985	2,151,032
Operation Desert Storm (1990-91)	
1990	2,043,705
1991	1,985,555
1995	1,518,224
2000	1,384,338
2001	1,385,116
2002	1,411,200

Note: Figures in italics are wartime years. Totals exclude Coast Guard.
Source: Bureau of the Census, *Statistical History of the U.S.* (1976) and U.S. Dept. of Defense, unpublished statistics.

group.) An *army* is made up of two or more corps plus a headquarters (HQ) unit; a *corps* is made up of two to five divisions and an HQ.

There are 10 active and 8 reserve divisions in the U.S. Army combat forces. The *division* is a self-sufficient force, typically consisting of three *brigades* (each comprising three to five battalions) and various combat support elements. A *brigade* is made up of two or more regiments or battalions; a *regiment*, of subordinate units such as battalions, companies or squadrons; a *battalion*, of four or more companies; a *company* of several

U.S. Unified Command Structure

Unified Command and Area of Responsibility	Headquarters
U.S. Northern Command (USNORTHCOM)	**Peterson Air Force Base, Colo.**
Coordinating homeland defense forces in North America, parts of the Caribbean and contiguous Atlantic and Pacific waters	
U.S. Joint Forces Command (USJFCOM)	**Norfolk, Va.**
Updating and transforming the military	
U.S. European Command (USEUCOM)	**Stuttgart-Vaihingen, Germant**
Atlantic from the East Coast to the shores of Europe; primary responsibility for Russia	
U.S. Pacific Command (USPACOM)	**Honolulu, Hawaii**
Pacific Ocean, Australia, Antarctica and Asia	
U.S. Central Command (USCENTCOM)	**MacDill Air Force Base, Fla.**
Middle East and Eastern Europe	
U.S. Southern Command (USSOUTHCOM)	**Miami, Fla.**
South America, parts of Central America and the Carribean	
U.S. Special Operations Command	**MacDill Air Force Base, Fla.**
U.S. Transportation Command	**Scott Air Force Base, Ill.**
U.S. Strategic Command	**Offutt Air Force Base, Neb.**

Major U.S. Army Forces

Unit	Headquarters
Forces Command	**Ft. McPherson, Ga.**
Central Command/Third U.S. Army	Ft. McPherson, Ga.
First U.S. Army	Ft. Gillem, Ga.
Fifth U.S. Army	Ft. Sam Houston, Tex.
I Corps	Ft. Lewis, Wash.
III Corps, "Phantom Corps"	Ft. Hood, Tex.
XVIII Airborne Corps	Ft. Bragg, N.C.
U.S. Army Network Enterprise Technology	Command/9th Army Signal Command
32nd Army Air and Missile Defense Command	Ft. Bliss, Texas
7th Transportation Group	Ft. Eustis, Va.
Army Special Operations Command (USASOC)	**Ft. Bragg, N.C.**
Training and Doctrine Command	**Ft. Monroe, Va.**
U.S. Army Space and Missile Defense Command (USASMDC)	**Arlington, Va.**
Army Intelligence and Security Command (INSCOM)	**Ft. Belvoir, Va.**
Criminal Investigation Command (CID)	**Ft. Belvoir, Va.**
Military Traffic Management Command (MTMC)	**Alexandria, Va.**
Military District of Washington (MDW)	**Washington, D.C.**
U.S. Army Europe (USAREUR) & 7th Army	**Heidelberg, Germany**
V Corps	Heidelberg, Germany
U.S. Army Pacific (USARPAC)	**Ft. Shafter, Hawaii**
U.S. Army, Japan/ 9th Theater Army Area	Command Camp Zama, Japan
U.S. Army, Alaska	Ft. Wainwright, Alaska
25th Infantry Division (light)/U.S. Army Hawaii	Schofield Barracks, Hawaii
8th Army (EUSA)	**Seoul, South Korea**
U.S. Army South	**Ft. Buchanon, Puerto Rico**
National Guard divisions:	
28th Infantry Division, "Keystone"	Harrisburg, Pa.
29th Infantry Division (light), "Blue and Grey"	Ft. Belvoir, Va.
34th Infantry Division	St. Paul, Minn.
35th Infantry Division (mech.), "Santa Fe"	Ft. Leavenworth, Kans.
38th Infantry Division, "Cyclone"	Indianapolis, Ind.
40th Infantry Division (mech.), "Sunshine"	Los Alamitos, Calif.
42nd Infantry Division, "Rainbow"	Troy, N.Y.
49th Armored Division, "Lone Star"	Austin, Tex.

Source: U.S. Army Force Command.

platoons; and a *platoon* of four squads. A *squad* consists of about 10 soldiers.

▶U.S. MARINE CORPS

Marine Corps organization emphasizes the close integration of air-ground operations for service with the U.S. fleet and for the conduct of land operations essential to the prosecution of a naval campaign. All Marines serve "at the pleasure of the president," and the Corps's mission includes "performing such other duties as the President may direct."

The smallest tactical unit of Marine Corps infantry is the *fire team*, which consists of 4 Marines. A *squad* is made up of three fire teams, and there are three squads to a *platoon*, three platoons to a *company*, three companies to a *battalion*, three battalions to a *regiment*, three regiments to a *brigade*, and three brigades to a *division*.

These components are organized into three basic organizational structures called *Marine air-ground task forces*, or MAGTFs. The largest—about 47,500 personnel—is the *Marine Expeditionary Force* (MEF), which consists of a Marine air wing (330 planes), a Marine division, and a force service support group. The *Marine Expeditionary Brigade* (MEB) consists of a Marine

Major Naval Operating Forces

Name	Headquarters
Pacific Fleet	Pearl Harbor, Hawaii
Third Fleet	San Diego, Calif.
Seventh Fleet	Yokosuka, Japan
Atlantic Fleet	Norfolk, Va.
Second Fleet	Norfolk, Va.
U.S. Naval Forces Europe	London, England
Sixth Fleet	Gaeta, Italy
Military Sealift Command	Washington, D.C.
Naval Reserve Force	New Orleans, La.
Mine Warfare Command	Ingleside, Texas
Operational and Test Evaluation Force	Norfolk, Va.
Naval Forces Central Command	Manama, Bahrain
Fifth Fleet	Manama, Bahrain
Naval Special Warfare Command	Coronado, Calif.

Source: U.S. Dept. of Defense, *Defense Almanac*. www.defenselink.mil.

U.S. Service Academies

U.S. Military Academy, West Point, NY 10996; (Founded, 1802).

U.S. Naval Academy, Annapolis, MD 21402; (1845).

U.S. Air Force Academy, Colorado Springs, CO 80840; (1954).

U.S. Coast Guard Academy, New London, CT 06320; (1876).

U.S. Merchant Marine Academy, Kings Point, NY 11024; (1943).

Major Coast Guard Commands

Name	Headquarters
Coast Guard Headquarters	Washington, D.C.
Atlantic Area	Portsmouth, Va.
1st District	Boston, Mass.
5th District	Portsmouth, Va.
7th District	Miami, Fla.
8th District	New Orleans, La.
9th District	Cleveland, Ohio
Pacific Area	Alameda, Calif.
11th District	Alameda, Calif.
13th District	Seattle, Wash.
14th District	Honolulu, Hawaii
17th District	Juneau, Alaska

Source: U.S. Coast Guard.

Major Marine Corps Commands

Name	Headquarters
Fleet Marine Force, Atlantic	Camp Lejeune, N.C.
Fleet Marine Force, Pacific	Camp H.M. Smith, Hawaii
Marine Corps Combat Development Command	Quantico, Va.
Marine Corps Systems Command	Quantico, Va.
I Marine Expeditionary Force	Camp Pendleton,Calif.
II Marine Expeditionary Force	Camp Lejeune, N.C.
III Marine Expeditionary Force	Camp Butler, Okinawa, Japan
Marine Corps Air Ground Combat Center	Twentynine Palms, Calif.
Marine Reserve Forces	New Orleans, La.

Source: U.S. Dept. of Defense, *Defense Almanac*. www.defenselink.mil.

Major Air Force Units

Name	Headquarters/Location
Air Combat Command	Langley AFB, Hampton, Va.
Air Force Materiel Command	Wright-Patterson AFB, Dayton, Ohio
Air Force Space Command	Peterson AFB, Colorado Spring, Colo.
Air Force Special Operations Command	Hurlburt Field, Fort Walton Beach, Fla.
Air Mobility Command	Scott AFB, Belleville, Ill.
Air Education and Training Command	Randolph AFB, San Antonio, Texas
Pacific Air Forces	Hickam AFB, Honolulu, Hawaii
U.S. Air Forces, Europe	Ramstein AB, Ramstein, Germany

Note: AB = air base; AFB = air force base; RAF = Royal Air Force (UK). **Source:** U.S. Dept. of Defense, *Defense Almanac*, www.defenselink.mil

air group (150 planes), a regimental landing group and a brigade service support group—about 15,000 personnel. The smallest and most responsive Marine force, the *Marine Expeditionary Unit* (MEU), consists of about 2,500 personnel and is made up of a helicopter squadron, a battalion landing team, and a unit service support group. MEUs are sea-based, can be airlifted and they are equipped and trained to be self-sustaining in the field for up to 15 days.

▶U.S. NAVY

The ships of the U.S. Navy are organized into the Pacific Fleet, the Atlantic Fleet, and U.S. Naval Forces Europe. These are composed of numbered fleets which consist of *carrier battle groups, battleship surface action groups* and one or more *underway replenishment groups.* Smaller subdivisions of naval forces are the *flotilla* consisting of two or more squadrons; a *squadron,* of two or more divisions; and a *division,* normally made up of four ships.

A naval *task force* designates a collection of ships under a single command designed to accomplish a particular tactical or strategic purpose. An *amphibious squadron* consists of amphibious assault ships, amphibious transport docks, dock landing ships and tank landing ships, and transports troops and equipment necessary for an assault landing from the sea.

▶U.S. COAST GUARD

A successor to the Revenue Marine established in 1790, the primary function of the Coast Guard is to enforce federal maritime law. For most of its history, the Coast Guard served as part of the Department of Transportation during peacetime and as part of the Navy during wartime. On January 24, 2003, the Coast Guard became part of the newly created Department of Homeland Security, though it may still operate as an element of the Defense Department in the event of war or at the President's direction.

▶U.S. AIR FORCE

The Air Force is organized into a number of commands. Within commands concerned with the strategic or tactical operation of aircraft, the primary subdivisions are indicated by the term air force prefaced by a number, as the Eighth Air Force. Such an *air force* is comprised of wings; a *wing* consists of two or more groups or squadrons; a *group* consists of two or more squadrons; and a *squadron* is made up of two or more flights. A *flight* is the basic tactical unit and consists of four or more planes.

▶SPECIAL OPERATIONS FORCES (SOF)

A unified command whose elements are drawn from the four major services, the special operations

U.S. Service and Casualties in Major Wars and Conflicts

War or conflict	Number serving	Battle deaths	Other deaths	Wounds not mortal
Revolutionary War (1775–83)				
Army	N.A.	4,044	N.A.	6,004
Navy	N.A.	342	N.A.	114
Marines	N.A.	49	N.A.	70
Total	N.A.	4,435	N.A.	6,188
War of 1812 (1812–15)				
Army	N.A.	1,950	N.A.	4,000
Navy	N.A.	265	N.A.	439
Marines	N.A.	45	N.A.	66
Total	286,730	2,260	N.A.	4,505
Mexican War (1846–48)				
Army	N.A.	1,721	11,550	4,102
Navy	N.A.	1	N.A.	3
Marines	N.A.	11	N.A.	47
Total	78,718	1,733	11,550	4,152
Civil War (1861–65)[1]				
Army	2,128,948	138,154	221,374	280,040
Navy	84,415[2]	2,112	2,411	1,710
Marines	—	148	312	131
Total	2,213,363	140,414	224,097	281,881
Spanish-American War (1898)				
Army	280,564	369	2,061	1,594
Navy	22,875	10	0	47
Marines	3,321	6	0	21
Total	306,760	385	2,061	1,662
World War I (1917–1918)				
Army	4,057,101	50,510	55,868	193,663
Navy	599,051	431	6,856	819
Marines	78,839	2,461	390	9,520
Total	4,734,991	53,402	63,114	204,002
World War II (1941–46)				
Army	11,260,000	234,874	83,400	565,861
Navy	4,183,466	36,950	25,664	37,778
Marines	669,100	19,733	4,778	67,207
Total	16,112,566	291,557	113,842	670,846
Korean Conflict (1950–53)				
Army	2,834,000	27,709	806	77,596
Navy	1,177,000	468	939	1,576
Marines	424,000	4,267	1,261	23,744
Air Force	1,285,000	1,302	243	368
Total	5,720,000	33,746	3,249	103,284
Vietnam Conflict (1964–73)				
Army	4,368,000	30,905	7,275	96,802
Navy	1,842,000	1,631	925	4,178
Marines	794,000	13,081	1,754	51,392
Air Force	1,740,000	1,738	842	931
Total	8,744,000	47,355	10,796	153,303
Operation Desert Storm (1990–91)[3]				
Army	782,000	98	126	354
Navy	669,000	5	50	12
Marines	213,000	24	44	92
Air Force	561,000	20	15	9
Total	2,225,000	147	235	467

Note: N.A. = not available. Prior to World War I, dates are approximate. Actual period covered for World War I: Apr. 6, 1917-Nov. 11, 1918; World War II: Dec. 7, 1941-Dec. 31, 1946; Korea: June 25, 1950-July 27, 1953; Vietnam: Aug. 4, 1964-Jan. 27, 1973. 1. Union Forces only; authoritative statistics for Confederate forces not available. Estimates of the number who served range from 600,000 to 1.5 million. *The Final Report of the Provost Marshal General, 1863-1866* indicated 133,821 Confederate deaths (74,524 battle and 59,297 other) based upon incomplete returns. In addition, an estimated 26,000-31,000 Confederate prisoners died in prisons. 2. Includes Navy and Marines. 3. DMDC, Sept. 9, 1991. Deployment figures changed continuously throughout the operation and have since, and have depended on, among other things, the timely reporting and posting of data.
Source: U.S. Dept. of Defense, *Defense Almanac.* www.defenselink.mil.

forces are designated to achieve military objectives of a limited and specific nature. Among the various elements of the SOF are: *Army* special forces; Rangers; psychological operations, civil affairs, and special operations aviation units; *Navy* SEAL and SEAL delivery vehicle teams; and *Air Force* Twenty-third Air Force special operations force.

▶RESERVE FORCES

The United States has always relied on reserve forces that can be called to active duty or mobilized to deal with emergencies beyond the capacities of active forces. The reserve forces constitute the initial and primary augmentation of active forces in any emergency requiring rapid expansion of those forces.

U.S. Armed Forces Worldwide, 2002

Region/Area	Army	Navy	Marine Corps	Air Force	Total
United States and Territories[1]	**386,335**	**344,694**	**141,677**	**301,021**	**1,173,727**
Continental United States	350,134	195,148	133,605	278,425	957,312
Alaska	6,817	98	26	9,574	16,515
Hawaii	16,157	8,511	5,554	4,619	34,841
Guam	31	1,576	6	1,687	3,300
Johnston Atoll	1	0	0	18	19
Puerto Rico	797	1,627	23	68	2,515
Transients	12,375	12,025	2,463	6,628	33,491
Afloat	0	125,706	0	0	125,706
Europe[1]	**65,569**	**12,707**	**4,458**	**34,667**	**117,401**
Belgium[2]	867	103	28	518	1,516
Bosnia and Herzegovina	3,024	0	29	47	3,100
France[2]	17	12	24	54	107
Germany[2]	55,816	300	242	15,647	72,005
Greece[2]	80	424	21	73	598
Hungary[2]	5	0	7	6	18
Iceland[2]	3	1,047	59	650	1,759
Italy[2]	3,040	5,423	65	4,599	13,127
Portugal[2]	17	54	6	964	1,041
Serbia (includes Kosovo)	1,612	1	5	3	1,621
Spain[2]	46	1,381	630	271	2,328
Turkey[2]	119	23	25	1,706	1,873
United Kingdom[2]	462	1,195	92	9,595	11,344
Afloat	0	2,681	3,035	0	5,716
Former Soviet Union[1]	**31**	**5**	**76**	**16**	**128**
East Asia and Pacific[1]	**30,810**	**19,936**	**21,826**	**23,717**	**96,289**
Australia	16	71	20	70	177
Japan	1,884	6,492	19,124	14,126	41,626
Korea, Republic of	28,810	353	142	9,420	38,725
Philippines	10	6	101	9	126
Singapore	6	91	26	42	165
Thailand	40	10	28	27	105
Afloat	0	12,887	2,320	0	15,207
North Africa, Near East, South Asia[1]	**1,519**	**2,381**	**1,953**	**7,844**	**13,697**
Algeria	1	0	6	1	8
Bahrain	19	1,199	556	24	1,798
Diego Garcia	3	528	0	27	558
Egypt	339	8	38	55	440
India	5	1	11	4	21
Israel	6	3	18	13	40
Kuwait	757	7	1,185	1,147	3,096
Oman	3	1	9	208	221
Pakistan	4	2	20	6	32
Saudi Arabia	297	29	35	5,753	6,114
United Arab Emirates	3	7	8	573	591
Afloat	0	586	0	0	586
Sub-Saharan Africa[1]	**53**	**7**	**200**	**21**	**281**
Western Hemisphere[1]	**332**	**610**	**380**	**362**	**1,684**
Canada	14	47	10	80	151
Colombia	14	3	16	7	40
Cuba(Guantanamo)	7	478	164	1	650
Honduras	195	2	9	204	410
Peru	7	12	17	5	41
Afloat	0	17	0	0	17
Total, Foreign Countries	**98,909**	**39,596**	**32,341**	**66,627**	**237,473**
Total, Worldwide	**485,244**	**384,290**	**174,018**	**367,648**	**1,411,200**
Ashore	**485,244**	**241,590**	**168,663**	**367,648**	**1,263,145**
Afloat	**0**	**142,700**	**5,355**	**0**	**148,055**

Note: Note: As of Dec. 31, 2002. 1. Includes other countries not shown separately. 2. Member of NATO Europe.
Source: U.S. Dept. of Defense. *Defense Almanac.* www.defenselink.mil.

There are seven reserve components: Army National Guard, Army Reserve, Naval Reserve, Marine Corps Reserve, Air National Guard, Air Force Reserve, and Coast Guard Reserve. All National Guard and Reserve personnel are assigned to one of three categories: the Ready Reserve, the Standby Reserve, or the Retired Reserve. All National Guard members are in the Ready Reserve. The Ready Reserve consists of the Selected Reserve, the Individual Ready Reserve, and the Inactive National Guard. Some reservists are organized in units, others train as individuals. All are subject to orders for active duty in time of war or national emergency.

In addition, members of the Selected Reserve may be ordered to active duty under implementation of the presidential call-up authority, under which the president can activate up to 200,000 members of the Selected Reserve involuntarily, for operational missions, for not more than 90 days, without declaring a national emergency.

Top 10 Defense Contractors, 2001-02

2002 Rank, Company (2001 rank)	Awards (billions) 2001	2002
1. Lockheed Martin Corp. (1)	$14.7	$17.0
2. Boeing Company (2)	13.3	16.6
3. Northrop Grumman Corp. (5)	5.2	8.7
4. Raytheon Company (4)	5.6	7.0
5. General Dynamics Corp. (6)	4.9	7.0
6. United Technologies Corp. (7)	3.8	3.6
7. Science Applications Int'l. Corp. (9)	1.7	2.1
8. TRW Incorporated (8)	1.9	2.0
9. Health Net, Inc.(12)	0.9	1.7
10. L-3 Communications Holdings, Inc (26)	0.5	1.7

Source: Source: U.S. Dept. of Defense, Directorate for Information Operations and Reports. www.dior.whs.mil/peidhome/procstat/p01/fy2002/top100.htm

Major Weapon Systems and Combat Forces, 1980–2001

Weapon or force	1980	1990	1999	2000	2001
STRATEGIC (NUCLEAR) FORCES					
Land-based ICBMs					
Minuteman	1,000	950	500	500	500
Peacekeeper	0	50	50	50	50
Heavy bombers[1]					
B-52	241	154	56	56	56
B-1	0	90	74	80	82
B-2 (stealth bomber)	0	0	13	16	16
Submarine-Launched Ballistic Missiles[2]					
Poseidon (C-3 and C-4)[3]	336	368	0	0	0
Trident (C-4 and D-5)	0	216	432	432	432
GENERAL PURPOSE FORCES					
Active land forces					
Army divisions	16	18	10	10	10
Marine Corps divisions	3	3	3	3	3
Army Separate brigades[4]	8	8	3	3	3
Army Special Forces groups	2	5	7	7	7
Army Ranger regiment	0	1	1	1	1
Active tactical air forces (PAA/squadrons)					
Air Force attack and fighter aircraft	1,608/74	1,722/76	936/49	936/47	906/45
Navy attack and fighter aircraft	696/60	622/57	432/36	432/36	432/36
Marine Corps attack and fighter aircraft	329/25	334/24	308/21	308/21	308/21
Naval forces					
Strategic forces ships	48	39	18	18	18
Battle forces ships	384	412	256	259	259
Support forces ships	41	65	25	25	25
Reserve forces ships	6	31	18	16	15
Total battle forces deployable	479	547	317	318	317
Coastal defense, mine warfare, and other	52	19	22	22	22
AIRLIFT AND SEALIFT FORCES					
Intertheater airlift (PMAI)[5]					
C-5	70	109	104	104	104
C-141	234	234	136	104	88
KC-10	0	57	54	54	54
C-17	0	0	37	46	58
Intratheater airlift (PMAI)[5]					
C-130[6]	482	460	425	425	418
Sealift ships[7]					
Tankers, active	21	28	10	10	10
Cargo, active	23	40	49	52	57
Ready Reserve Force (RRF)	24	96	87	87	87

Note: PMAI = primary mission aircraft inventory. 1. Excludes backup and attrition reserve aircraft. 2. Number operational. 3. C-3 missiles were removed from Poseidon submarines in September of 1992. 4. Includes the Eskimo scout group and the armored cavalry regiments. 5. Excludes development/test and training aircraft. 6. Excludes Dept. of Navy aircraft. 7. Includes fast sealift ships, afloat prepositioned force ships, and common user (charter) ships. **Source:** U.S. Dept. of Defense, *Defense Almanac.* www.defenselink.mil.

Minorities in Uniform, 2000

Service	Black Americans		Hispanic Americans		Other[1]		Total	
	Number	Percent	Number	Percent	Number	Percent	Number	Percent
Officers, Total	**18,309**	**8.5%**	**8,269**	**3.8%**	**11,150**	**5.2%**	**37,728**	**17.5%**
Army	9,162	12.0	3,105	4.1	4,075	5.3	16,342	21.4
Navy	3,524	6.7	2,732	5.2	2,653	5.0	8,909	16.9
Marines	1,341	7.5	914	5.1	599	3.3	2,854	15.9
Air Force	4,282	6.3	1,518	2.2	3,823	5.6	9,623	14.1
Enlisted, Total	**254,509**	**22.3%**	**99,297**	**8.7%**	**73,888**	**6.5%**	**427,694**	**37.5%**
Army	115,240	29.2	34,232	8.7	26,388	6.7	175,860	44.6
Navy	62,974	20.3	29,630	9.5	27,568	8.9	120,172	38.7
Marines	25,023	16.4	20,174	13.2	7,185	4.7	52,382	34.4
Air Force	51,272	18.2	15,261	5.4	12,747	4.5	79,280	28.1
DoD Total	**272,818**	**20.1%**	**107,566**	**7.9%**	**85,038**	**6.3%**	**465,422**	**34.4%**

Note: As of September 5, 2000. 1. Includes Native Americans, Alaskan Natives, and Pacific Islanders.
Source: U.S. Dept. of Defense, *Defense 2000*. www.defenselink.mil.

Guard and Reserve Forces, 2002

Status	Army National Guard	Army Reserve	Naval Reserve	Marine Corps Reserve	Air National Guard	Air Force Reserve	Total DoD	Coast Guard Reserve
Selected Reserve								
Officers	29,023	37,710	18,060	3,370	13,928	17,295	119,386	1,035
Warrant Officers	7,426	2,714	206	391	—	—	10,737	167
Enlisted	314,627	166,258	69,692	36,144	98,127	59,315	744,163	6,614
Total	351,076	206,682	87,958	39,905	112,055	76,610	874,286	7,816
Individual Ready Reserve/Inactive National Guard								
Officers	333	25,295	14,695	3,257	—	10,275	53,855	159
Warrant Officers	70	2,160	10	71	—	—	2,311	38
Enlisted	2,739	111,191	56,435	54,711	—	30,809	255,885	4,920
Total	3,142	138,646	71,140	58,039	—	41,084	312,051	5,117
Total Ready Reserve								
Officers	29,356	63,005	32,755	6,627	13,928	27,570	173,241	1,194
Warrant Officers	7,496	4,874	216	462	—	—	13,048	205
Enlisted	317,366	277,449	126,127	90,855	98,127	90,124	1,000,048	11,534
Total	**354,218**	**345,328**	**159,098**	**97,944**	**112,055**	**117,694**	**1,186,337**	**12,9331**

Note: As of September 30, 2002. **Source:** U.S. Dept. of Defense, *Selected Manpower Statistics, Fiscal Year 2002* (2003). www.defenselink.mil.

Women in Uniform: Female Active Duty Military Personnel 1945–2002

Year	Total DoD	Army		Navy		Marine Corps.		Air Force	
		Officers	Enlisted	Officers	Enlisted	Officers	Enlisted	Officers	Enlisted
1945	266,256	62,775	93,095	19,188	72,833	809	17,556	N.A.	N.A.
1950	22,069	4,431	6,551	2,447	2,746	45	535	1,532	3,782
1960	31,550	4,263	8,279	2,711	5,360	123	1,488	3,675	5,651
1970	41,479	5,248	11,476	2,888	5,795	299	2,119	4,667	8,987
1975	96,868	4,594	37,701	3,676	17,498	345	2,841	4,981	25,232
1980	171,418	7,609	61,729	4,877	30,103	487	6,219	8,493	51,901
1985	211,606	10,828	68,419	6,913	45,690	654	9,041	11,927	58,134
1990	227,018	12,404	71,217	7,808	52,099	677	8,679	13,331	60,803
1995	196,116	10,786	57,260	7,899	47,931	690	7,403	12,068	52,079
2000	202,601	10,814	62,889	7,846	43,760	932	9,530	11,819	55,011
2002	212,266	11,543	63,222	8,189	47,330	998	9,475	12,912	58,597

Source: U.S. Dept. of Defense, *Selected Manpower Statistics,* Fiscal Year 2002 (2003). www.defenselink.mil.

▶NUCLEAR FORCES

Nuclear forces are classified as either strategic or nonstrategic. The strategic triad—a cornerstone of post–World War II U.S. defense—is composed of land-based missile forces, including intercontinental ballistic missiles (ICBMs); submarine-launched ballistic missiles (SLBMs); and manned aircraft of the strategic bomber force. Nonstrategic nuclear weapons are shorter-range weapons that can be deployed on the battlefield and include sea-launched cruise missiles, artillery-fired atomic projectiles, and dual-capable (conventional and nuclear) aircraft.

Department of Defense Contract Awards, Payroll, and Civilian and Military Personnel by State, 2002

State	Payroll[1] ('000s)	Contract awards[2] ('000s)	Personnel[3]	
			Military	Civilian
Alabama	$2,714,4789	$4,671,560	11,354	20,474
Alaska	1,044,376	911,379	15,906	4,204
Arizona	2,187,684	6,685,404	22,448	8,290
Arkansas	848,525	833,141	4,855	3,686
California	12,389,975	23,816,177	123,948	58,076
Colorado	2,686,331	2,623,565	29,733	10,183
Connecticut	581,052	5,638,585	4,239	2,497
Delaware	370,597	135,060	3,899	1,429
District of Columbia	1,676,392	2,420,198	12,767	15,640
Florida	7,545,843	7,072,528	55,815	27,144
Georgia	5,494,660	5,814,189	64,392	31,167
Hawaii	2,842,371	1,433,119	34,608	16,508
Idaho	424,501	160,697	4,251	1,472
Illinois	2,437,665	2,005,762	25,036	12,780
Indiana	1,052,263	1,860,428	1,041	8,719
Iowa	331,487	552,234	447	1,546
Kansas	1,243,767	1,222,935	15,819	5,603
Kentucky	2,034,428	2,268,260	34,081	8,348
Louisiana	1,530,774	1,682,812	16,541	7,440
Maine	658,632	1,107,663	2,689	5,791
Maryland	4,219,937	6,505,462	30,928	32,090
Massachusetts	942,402	4,928,676	2,427	6,829
Michigan	1,011,905	2,179,870	1,173	8,038
Minnesota	526,232	1,528,525	702	2,576
Mississippi	1,518,240	2,271,530	14,005	9,289
Missouri	1,749,732	5,755,990	16,119	9,330
Montana	322,022	128,624	3,512	1,187
Nebraska	729,654	306,122	7,793	3,365
Nevada	904,882	359,262	8,461	2,072
New Hampshire	291,671	605,698	326	1,051
New Jersey	1,579,586	3,452,131	6,306	13,943
New Mexico	1,161,017	823,396	11,254	6,704
New York	2,075,117	4,434,731	20,882	11,220
North Carolina	5,163,465	1,520,130	94,296	16,444
North Dakota	389,682	206,758	7,465	1,621
Ohio	2,469,274	3,444,496	6,899	22,080
Oklahoma	2,553,211	1,572,682	23,664	21,972
Oregon	642,383	404,145	705	3,121
Pennsylvania	2,488,636	4,570,861	3,098	24,920
Rhode Island	573,191	364,616	2,974	4,346
South Carolina	2,634,884	1,138,083	37,943	9,370
South Dakota	276,280	190,931	3,350	1,219
Tennessee	1,281,800	1,304,693	2,554	5,496
Texas	9,414,371	13,699,670	115,100	37,238
Utah	1,262,729	1,509,359	5,447	14,725
Vermont	128,436	383,948	61	567
Virginia	13,038,690	18,128,348	90,851	77,119
Washington	4,381,655	2,789,477	38,521	23,259
West Virginia	335,143	169,542	558	1,783
Wisconsin	532,458	1,064,759	532	3,074
Wyoming	255,570	79,204	3,292	1,004
Total U.S.	**$114,950,056**	**$158,737,415**	**1,045,067**	**628,049**

1. Payroll estimates cover active duty military and direct hire civilian personnel, including Army Corps of Engineers. 2. Military awards for supplies, services and construction; expenditures relating to awards may extend over several years. Net value of contracts of over $25,000 for work in each state; the state in which the prime contractor is located is not necessarily the state in which the subcontracted work is done.

Source: U.S. Dept. of Defense, *Selected Manpower Statistics, Fiscal Year 2002 (2003)*. www.defenselink.mil.

Active Duty, Monthly Basic Pay Table

Pay Grade	Army Rank	Years of Service: 2	10	20	26
	Commissioned Officers				
0-10	General, Admiral	—	—	$11,875	$11,875
0-9	Lieut. General, Vice-Admiral	—	—	10,564	11,320
0-8	Maj. General, Rear Admiral	$7,719	$8,547	10,004	10,256
0-7	Brig. General, Commodore	6,499	7,340	9,051	9,097
0-6	Colonel, Captain	5,057	5,672	7,233	7,990
0-5	Lt. Colonel, Commander	4,323	5,223	6,329	6,520
0-4	Major, Lt. Commander	3,833	4,954	5,528	5,528
0-3	Captain, Lieutenant	3,300	4,406	4,736	4,736
0-2	1st Lieutenant, Lieut. (J.G.)	2,865	3,481	3,481	3,481
0-1	2nd Lieutenant, Ensign	2,272	2,747	2,747	2,747
	Warrant Officers				
W-5	Chief Warrant Officer	—	—	$5,169	$5,703
W-4	Chief Warrant Officer	$3,236	$3,891	4,664	5,138
W-3	Chief Warrant Officer	2,862	3,467	4,202	4,548
W-2	Chief Warrant Officer	2,554	3,148	3,706	3,957
W-1	Warrant Officer	2,308	2,888	3,410	3,410
	Enlisted Personnel				
E-9	Sgt. Major, Master C.P.O.	—	$3,564	$4,181	$4,757
E-8	Master Sgt., Senior C.P.O.	—	3,061	3,626	4,099
E-7	Sgt.1st Class, Chief Petty Officer	$2,258	2,753	3,183	3,671
E-6	Staff Sgt., Petty Officer 1st Class	1,948	2,477	2,710	2,710
E-5	Sergeant, Petty Officer 2d Class	1,734	2,237	2,283	2,283
E-4	Corporal, Petty Officer 3d Class	1,580	1,824	1,824	1,824
E-3	Pvt. 1st Class, Seaman	1,442	1,529	1,529	1,529
E-2	Private, Seaman	1,290	1,290	1,290	1,290
E-1	Recruit, Seaman Recruit	1,151	1,151	1,151	1,151

Note: Effective Jan. 1, 2003. Numbers rounded to nearest dollar. N.A.: Not Applicable
Source: U.S. Department of Defense.

SOCIAL INSURANCE PROGRAMS

In order to provide a "safety net" for the disadvantaged, the elderly, and the disabled, the federal government administers a range of social insurance and social assistance programs. Many of these programs are administered by the Social Security Administration, which became an independent government agency in 1995. But many cabinet-level departments, other independent government agencies, and state government human services agencies also run programs such as food stamps (Dept. of Agriculture), public housing (Dept. of Housing and Urban Development), and programs for veterans (Dept. of Veterans Affairs).

Social Insurance Programs: Beneficiaries and Payments, 2001

Program	Beneficiaries ('000s)	Benefits (billions)
OASDI	**45,878**	**$ 425.8**
Medicare	**40,000**	**N.A.**
Medicaid	**34,300**	**N.A.**
Food Stamps	**17,313**	**15,547.0**
Welfare	**5,363**	**10,124.0**
Supplemental Security Insurance	**6,800**	**33,060.0**

Note: OASDI = Old Age, Survivors, and Disability Insurance.
Sources: Social Security Administration; Administration on Children and Families; Health Care Financing Administration.

Social insurance programs were not developed all at once to fulfill a specific agenda of national need. Rather they are a hodgepodge of legislation passed (and often altered) over the years to meet the needs of particular groups of citizens at particular times. In what the government calls "social insurance programs," certain risks—injury, disability, unemployment, old age, and death—are lumped together. "Premiums," usually in the form of a payroll tax, are paid by employees and/or their employers. The benefit is paid, regardless of other financial resources (other than earnings), when one of those "risks" occurs.

▶SOCIAL SECURITY

The Depression proved that the traditional support systems—the family, private charities, and local government—failed in nationwide economic hard times. Many old people had exhausted their savings and were destitute; in fact, during the Depression less than 10 percent of the aged left estates large enough to be probated. This led to the enactment of one of the most comprehensive pieces of legislation ever passed by Congress, the Social Security Act.

Signed into law by Franklin Roosevelt on August 14, 1935, the Social Security Act established two social insurance programs: a federal system of old-age benefits for retired workers in commerce and industry and a federal-state system of unemployment insurance. The law also provided for federal matching grants-in-aid to states to help them assist the needy aged, the blind, and children. Today, in the words of former Social Security Commissioner Dorcas R. Hardy, it is "the most complex Government program that God and Congress ever created."

SOCIAL SERVICE PROGRAMS INFORMATION

Information about social service programs can be obtained from the following government agencies:

Aid to Families with Dependent Children (AFDC) This program was abolished under the Welfare Reform Act of 1996. It was replaced with the Temporary Assistance to Needy Families (TANF) program. Information is available from the Administration for Children and Families, U.S. Dept. of Health and Human Services. (202)-401-9200. **www.acf.dhhs.gov**
Black lung program Office of Workers Compensation Programs, U.S. Dept. of Labor. (202)-693-0046. **www.dol.gov/dol/esa/public/owcp-org.htm**
Food Stamps Food and Consumer Service, U.S. Dept. of Agriculture. (703) 305-2276. **www.usda.gov/fcs/fcs.htm**
Head Start Administration for Children and Families, U.S. Dept. of Health and Human Services. (202)-401-9200. **www.acf.dhhs.gov**
Medicaid Health Care Financing Administration, U.S. Dept. of Health and Human Services. (410) 786-3151. **www.ssa.gov/hcfa/hcfahp2.html**
Medicare (HI) Health Care Financing Administration, U.S. Dept. of Health and Human Services. (410) 786-3151. **www.ssa.gov/hcfa/hcfahp2.html**
Social Security (OASDI) Social Security Administration. (410) 965-7700. **www.ssa.gov/**
Special nutrition programs Food and Consumer Service, U.S. Dept. of Agriculture. (703) 305-2276. **www.usda.gov/fcs/fcs.htm**
Supplemental Security Income (SSI) Social Security Administration. (410) 965-7700. **www.ssa.gov**
Temporary disability insurance Office of Workers Compensation Programs, U.S. Dept. of Labor. (202)-219-7503. **www.dol.gov/dol/esa/public/owcp-org.htm**
Unemployment insurance Office of Workers Compensation Programs, U.S. Dept. of Labor. (202)-219-7503. **www.dol.gov/dol/esa/public/owcp-org.htm**
Veterans' benefits U.S. Dept. of Veterans Affairs. (202) 273-5700. **www.va.gov**

The first payments of monthly benefits were made in 1940. Major changes in the scope of Social Security were made in 1956, when the program was broadened through the addition of disability insurance; in 1965, through the addition of Medicare and Medicaid; in 1970, when the black lung program was developed to provide benefits to coal miners (and their survivors) who suffer from pneumoconiosis (black lung disease); in 1974, when Social Security insurance was taken over by the Social Security Administration; and in 1972 Congress authorized provisions for cost-of-living increases. In 1983, amendments provided for the taxing of up to one-half of benefits for certain upper-income beneficiaries.

Workers and their employers each contribute an equal amount to the Social Security program to pay for retirement, disability, and Medicare benefits. The amount deducted from paychecks increased steadily from 1983 before levelling off in 1990 at 7.65 percent. Employers must contribute the same amount. Self-employed workers, who are both employee and employer, pay both shares, or a total of 15.3 percent. Contributions are limited to the first $76,200 of earnings although Medicare taxes continue at a rate of 1.45 percent each for employer and employee (twice that amount for the self-employed) for all earnings above that amount.

Old Age, Survivors and Disability Insurance (OASDI)

This program's basic principles are that benefits are related to earnings in covered work, benefits are paid regardless of income from savings, pensions, etc. and universal compulsory coverage is to assure a base of economic security. Monthly benefits are payable at age 65 to workers who are eligible, and lump sum payments are made to the estates of workers who die before reaching 65. The addition of disability insurance in 1956 and hospital insurance in 1965 broadened the program's scope, and in 1972 Congress authorized provisions for cost-of-living increases. The 1983 amendments improved the program's financial footing with tax rate increases in self-employment tax rates, and taxing up to one-half of benefits for certain upper-income beneficiaries.

To receive Social Security benefits, you must have worked for 10 years in a job in which you contributed to the fund. Your social Security benefit is not directly dependent on the number of years you worked. Rather it is based on your average earnings over your working liftetime. The average recipient receives benefits equivalent to 42 percent of an average working year's earnings. Because Social Security is designed to benefit low-income workers, people in upper-income brackets generally receive a lower percentage of their working year's earnings when they collect their benefits. However, you can still earn money while collecting Social Security. In 2003, recipients under age 65 may earn up to $11,280 ($940/month) before their benefits are reduced; after that amount, $1 is withheld for every $2 earned. In the year they turn 65, recipients may earn up to $30,000; after that, benefits are reduced $1 for every $3 earned. Beginning in the month they turn 65, recipients may earn any amount of money while collecting Social Security benefits.

You may start collecting Social Security as early as age 62, but you will receive only 80 percent of the amount you would have received if you retired at age 65. The normal retirement age will be increased

OASDI Beneficiaries and Benefit Payments, 2003

Type of Beneficiaries	Number ('000s)	Monthly rate (millions)	Average monthly benefit
Retired workers	29,353	$26,380	$899
Dependents of retired workers[1]	3,127	1,404	442
Disabled workers	5,730	4,805	839
Dependents of disabled workers[1]	1,708	416	230
Survivors of deceased workers[1]	6,835	5,277	—
Total monthly beneficiaries	**46,753**	**38,282**	—

Note: OASDI = old-age, survivors and disability insurance. 1. Benefits vary depending on relationship to beneficiary. Range of benefits shown. **Source**: Social Security Administration, *Fact Sheet on OASDI*

Approximate Monthly Retirement, Disability, and Survivor Benefits

Worker's age, 2003	Worker's family	Insured worker's earnings, 2003: $20,000	$40,000	$60,000	$84,900 or more
Retirement Benefits[1]					
45	Retired worker only	$876	$1,409	$1,699	$1,977
	Worker and spouse[2]	1,314	2,113	2,548	2,965
55	Retired worker only	876	1,409	1,697	1,925
	Worker and spouse[2]	1,314	2,113	2,545	2,887
65	Retired worker only	820	1,323	1,536	1,660
	Worker and spouse[2]	1,230	1,984	2,304	2,490
Disability Benefits[3]					
25	Disabled worker only	$876	$1,409	$1,699	$1,921
	Disabled, with dependents[4]	1,314	2,114	2,549	2,882
35	Disabled worker only	876	1,409	1,699	1,932
	Disabled, with dependents[4]	1,314	2,114	2,549	2,899
45	Disabled worker only	876	1,409	1,699	1,918
	Disabled, with dependents[4]	1,314	2,114	2,549	2,878
55	Disabled worker only	876	1,409	1,684	1,847
	Disabled, with dependents[4]	1,314	2,114	2,527	2,771
64	Disabled worker only	839	1,351	1,572	1,689
	Disabled, with dependents[4]	1,259	2,027	2,359	2,547
Survivor benefits[5]					
35	Spouse and 1 child[6]	$1,314	$2,114	$2,549	$2,912
	Spouse and 2 children[7]	1,461	2,473	2,975	3,398
	1 child only	657	1,057	1,274	1,456
	Spouse at age 60[8]	626	1,008	1,215	1,388
45	Spouse and 1 child[6]	1,314	2,114	2,549	2,880
	Spouse and 2 children[7]	1,461	2,473	2,975	3,361
	1 child only	657	1,057	1,274	1,440
	Spouse at age 60[8]	626	1,008	1,215	1,373
55	Spouse and 1 child[6]	1,314	2,114	2,527	2,771
	Spouse and 2 children[7]	1,461	2,473	2,949	3,234
	1 child only	657	1,057	1,263	1,385
	Spouse at age 60[8]	626	1,008	1,204	1,321

Note: Assumes steady earnings; actual benefits depend on the pattern of past and future earnings. 1. If worker retires at normal retirement age with steady lifetime earnings. 2. Spouse is assumed to be the same age as the worker. Spouse may qualify for a higher retirement benefit based on his or her own work record. 3. For workers with steady earnings and disabled in 2003. 4. Includes spouse and child, the maximum family benefit. 5. For workers with steady earnings who died in 2003; benefits are based on 2002 earnings. 6. Benefits are the same for two children if no parent survives or if the surviving parent has substantial earnings. 7. Equals maximum family benefit. 8. Spouse is assumed to be age 60 in year of worker's death. **Source**: Social Security Administration, *Social Security: Understanding the Benefits* (2003).

Medicare: Recipients and Benefits, 1975–2001

Category	1975	1980	1985	1990	1995	2000	2001
Hospital Insurance (HI)							
Total enrolled ('000s)	23,842	28,067	30,627	33,719	37,108	39,200	39,567
Aged	21,795	25,104	27,683	30,464	32,742	33,833	34,028
Disabled	2,047	2,963	2,944	3,255	4,366	5,367	5,539
Total Beneficiaries ('000s)	5,419	6,745	6,840	7,042	8,000	N.A.	N.A.
Aged	4,963	6,024	6,168	6,367	7,080	N.A.	N.A.
Disabled	456	721	672	675	920	820[2]	N.A.
Average annual benefit	$434	$863	$1,587	$1,970	$3,063	$3,282	$3,417
Aged	432	853	1,563	1,947	3,078	3,324	3,469
Disabled	460	948	1,808	2,176	2,955	3,021	3,102
Supplementary Medical Insurance (SMI)							
Total enrolled	23,339	27,399	29,983	32,629	35,616	37,360	37,668
Aged	21,504	24,680	27,311	29,686	31,742	32,590	32,741
Disabled	1,835	2,719	2,672	2,943	3,874	4,770	4,927
Total Beneficiaries	12,559	17,768	22,132	26,871	29,774	N.A.	N.A.
Aged	11,762	16,099	20,199	24,687	26,681	N.A.	N.A.
Disabled	797	1,669	1,933	2,184	3,093	3,615[2]	N.A.
Average annual benefit	$161	$374	$734	$1,282	$1,788	$2,451	$2,733
Aged	153	348	705	1,250	1,728	2,656	2,700
Disabled	259	610	1,022	1,603	2,282	2,422	2,954

1. Estimate. 2. Beneficiary numbers for 1999 and 2000 include only those receiving care under Fee For Service programs. A small number of beneficiaries who received benefits under managed care programs are not included in this figure.
Source: Health Care Financing Administration, Division of Budget, 2002.

gradually from 65 to 67, beginning in the year 2003. See the accompanying table for approximate monthly retired, disabled and survivor benefits.

If you become disabled—defined as having a physical or mental impairment that permanently prevents you from doing any substantial work (i.e. worth more than $780 a month, or $1,300 for the blind)—you are eligible for additional benefits after six months. See the accompanying table for examples of disability benefits.

Additional benefits are also paid to the survivors of workers eligible for Social Security. Widows and widowers over the age of 60, children under the age of 18, and certain other survivors each generally receive amounts equivalent to 75 percent to 100 percent of the worker's Social Security benefit. There is, however, a per-family benefit limit, usually equal to 150-180 percent of the worker's benefit rate.

The OASDI programs are financed from taxes collected on earnings in covered jobs from employees and employers, which are deposited in two separate trust funds. The money received by the trust funds can be used only to pay OASDI benefits and operating expenses.

Medicare

The Social Security Amendments of 1965 established two contributory health insurance programs designed to provide assistance for medical expenses for the aged and disabled. The first is a compulsory program of hospital insurance (HI) which provides basic protection against the costs of inpatient hospital services and related post-hospital care, including home health services, part-time nursing care, and physical therapy. This is commonly referred to as Part A. Persons reaching age 65 without qualifying for HI may voluntarily enroll by paying a monthly premium ($316 per month, or $175 per month for individuals with 39 to 40 quarters of Medicare-covered employment). In 2002, HI paid all hospital bills for the first 60 days after the patient paid a deductible of $840. For days 61–90, the patient was responsible for a co-payment of $210 per day; beyond 90 days (for up to 60 additional days), the patient paid $420 per day. For nursing homes, the first 20 days have no deductible, but $105 a day thereafter, up to 100 days.

The second health program, called Part B, is supplementary medical insurance (SMI) coverage, a voluntary program in which enrolled individuals pay a monthly premium. The program's coverage includes physician's and surgeon's services, outpatient services, laboratory tests, ambulance services, surgical dressings, home health services, and comprehensive outpatient services. The premium in 2003 was $58.70 per month after the patient has paid the deductible ($100); Part B pays for 80 percent of covered services.

As with OASDI, hospital insurance is financed by a tax on earnings: of the 7.65 percent tax on earnings (FICA) deducted from employee paychecks, 1.45 percent is for hospital insurance and 6.2 percent is for OASDI.

Some private companies also contract with Medicare to offer Medicare+Choice ("Medicare plus Choice") health plans, which take two different forms: managed care plans, and private fee-for-service plans. These plans generally offer extra benefits (prescription drugs, eye exams, extra hospital days) in addition to basic Medicare benefits and may reduce out-of-pocket costs, but doctor choice is usually limited in comparison to Medicare. Private insurance companies also sell ten standardized Medigap policies (called "A"

Supplemental Security Insurance Beneficiaries and Benefits, 1975–2001

	Beneficiaries				Benefits (millions)			
			State Supplement				State Supplement	
Year	Total[1]	Federal SSI	Federally administered	State administered	Total	Federal SSI	Federally administered	State administered
Total								
1975	4,359,625	3,893,419	1,684,018	303,391	$5,878.2	$4,313.5	$1,402.5	$162.2
1980	4,194,100	3,682,411	1,684,765	249,474	7,941.7	5,866.4	1,848.3	226.1
1990	4,888,180	4,412,131	2,058,273	285,530	16,598.7	12,893.8	3,239.2	465.7
2000	6,685,169	6,319,907	2,480,637	682,867	31,564.4	27,290.2	3,381.5	892.7
2001	6,775,548	6,410,138	2,520,005	689,163	33,060.8	28,705.5	3,460.4	895.0
Aged								
1975	2,333,685	2,024,765	843,917	184,679	$2,604.8	$1,843.0	$ 673.5	$ 88.3
1980	1,838,381	1,533,366	702,763	134,555	2,734.3	1,860.2	756.8	117.2
1990	1,484,160	1,256,623	649,530	115,890	3,736.1	2,521.4	1,038.0	176.7
2000	1,327,567	1,186,309	622,668	144,644	4,811.0	3,595.4	942.5	283.1
2001	1,304,273	1,164,825	620,952	143,654	4,958.6	3,708.5	955.5	294.6
Blind								
1975	75,315	68,375	31,376	4,933	$130.9	$ 92.4	$34.8	$3.7
1980	79,139	68,945	36,214	3,649	190.1	131.5	54.3	4.2
1990	84,109	74,781	40,334	3,042	334.1	238.4	90.5	5.2
2000	79,295	72,931	35,940	4,645	394.5	312.1	73.7	8.6
2001	79,058	72,811	35,708	4,564	407.4	323.9	74.7	8.7
Disabled								
1975	11,950,625	1,800,279	808,725	113,504	$3,142.5	$2,378.1	$ 694.2	$ 70.2
1980	2,276,130	2,080,100	945,788	104,367	5,013.9	3,874.7	1,037.1	102.2
1990	3,319,911	3,080,727	1,368,409	166,598	12,520.6	10,134.0	2,110.6	275.9
2000	5,270,126	5,060,667	1,822,029	325,916	26,198.4	23,399.4	2,365.2	479.6
2001	5,384,121	5,172,502	1,863,345	333,294	27,611.3	24,695.6	2,430.1	485.6

1. Total beneficiaries includes some people who receive both Federal SSI and a state supplement.
Source: Social Security Administration, *Social Security Bulletin, Annual Statistical Supplement.*

through "J") which offer more health insurance coverage than the basic Medicare program. In general, you must have Medicare Parts A and B in order to buy a Medigap policy; it is illegal for an insurance company to sell Medigap coverage to a person who already participates in Medicare+Choice.

(Medicaid, a separate program that helps the financially needy of all ages pay for health care, is not a part of Social Security. It is discussed in "Other Income Support Programs," below).

Supplemental Security Income (SSI)

In 1974, Congress replaced the federal-state programs for needy aged (over 65 years old), blind, and disabled people with a single Federal Supplementary Security Income program. SSI eligibility depends on whether you work and in what state you live. In addition, SSI recipients may have no more than $2,000 in assets ($3,000 for married couples), though houses and cars are not usually counted as assets in this equation. The qualifying standards for disability benefits are the same as those used for the Social Security disability insurance program. Nearly 6.8 million people received SSI benefits in 2001; the basic monthly federal benefit as of January 1, 2003 was the same in all states: $552 for one person and $829 for a couple. States have the option of supplementing Federal SSI under their own programs administered. More than 2.5 million persons received state supplements in 2001; the average payment was about $113.

Black Lung Program

Established by the Federal Coal Mine Health and Safety Act of 1969, this provides monthly cash benefits to coal miners who are totally disabled because of "black lung" disease (pneumoconiosis) and to survivors of miners who die from this disease. Benefits are paid mostly out of a trust fund financed by an excise tax on coal. The monthly benefit in 2003 ranged from $534 for a single recipient to $1,069 for a recipient with three or more dependents. The number of beneficiaries continues to decline as older beneficiaries are dying in greater numbers than new claimants are entering the program. A total of 89,355 miners, widows, and their dependents received a total of $460 million in 2003, down from $1.0 billion in 1985, when 294,846 people were receiving benefits.

Social Security and You

While Social Security benefits are automatic for all people who hold a Social Security card and who are eligible for programs, the Social Security Administration (SSA) recommends that workers check the agency's records of their earnings every three to five years. If their records are not accurate—the SSA says that 1 percent of eligible wages are not credited to workers' records—your benefits could be lower than you deserve.

To find out what your earnings are, pick up a Personal Earnings and Benefit Estimate Statement (PEBES). This, as well as free booklets detailing eligibility requirements and benefit payments, is available at any of the more than 1,300 local SSA offices nationwide. They are also available by calling 1-800-234-5SSA, 1-800-772-1212, or on the Internet at www.ssa.gov.

▶OTHER INCOME SUPPORT PROGRAMS

Welfare

The Social Security Act of 1935 included a provision authorizing Aid to Families with Dependent Children (AFDC), commonly known as "welfare." Benefits were limited to families with children under 18. But in the much-ballyhooed 1996 welfare reform effort, the federal government ended more than 60 years of guaranteed assistance to the needy, and replaced it with a system of block grants to the states, who could use the money to enact their own welfare programs. The Temporary Assistance to Needy Families (TANF) Block Grant replaced AFDC on July 1, 1997. TANF gives states broad discretion to determine eligibility and benefit levels. However, families may not receive benefits for longer than 60 months, unwed teenage parents must stay in school and live at home, and people convicted of drug-related felonies are banned from receiving TANF or Food Stamp benefits. In addition, non-working adults must participate in community service within two months of receiving benefits, and must find work within two years. Parents with children under age 1 are exempt from the work requirements (under age 6 if child care is not available).

Welfare reform has succeeded in reducing the number of people receiving government assistance. In 2001, the total number of people receiving welfare benefits had dropped to 5.4 million, its lowest level in over 30 years. That's a 60 percent drop from the all-time high of 14.4 million reached in March, 1994. Reform has most benefited white families. They made up 38 percent of all welfare families in 1990, but only 30 percent in 2001. Over the same period, the percentage of welfare families that were black declined only from 40 percent to 39 percent, while the percentage of Hispanic families increased dramatically, from 16.6 percent to 26 percent. Among welfare recipients, the employment rate has also increased dramatically, from 11 percent in 1996 to 27 percent in 2001.

Medicaid

Enacted jointly with Medicare in 1965, Medicaid provides federal matching funds to states to help pay the cost of medical care and services for low-income persons. Payments are made to suppliers of the care and service. To be eligible for matching funds, a state Medicaid program must cover all persons who receive assistance under TANF. (Most SSI recipients are also covered.) In 1998, 40.6 million aged, blind, disabled or poor persons with families received Medicaid benefits at a total

Welfare Beneficiaries and Benefits, 1970–2001

Year	Average monthly beneficiaries ('000s)			Benefits	
	Recipients	Families	Children	Total (millions)	Average monthly benefit
1970	7,429	1,909	5,494	$ 4,082	$178
1975	11,067	3,269	7,821	8,153	208
1980	10,597	3,574	7,220	11,540	269
1985	10,813	3,692	7,165	14,580	329
1990	11,460	3,974	7,755	18,539	389
1995	13,652	4,876	9,274	22,032	377
1997	10,381	3,734	N.A.	N.A.	359
1998	8,347	3,050	6,034	12,926	353
1999	6,822	2,553	5,120	10,929	357
2000	5,778	2,216	4,268	10,490	395
2001	5,363	2,104	3,987	10,124	401

Note: "Welfare" refers to the Aid to Families with Dependent Children (AFDC) program through 1996; in 1997, AFDC was renamed Temporary Assistance to Needy Families (TANF), and many more restrictions were added. **Source:** Administration for Children and Families, unpublished data.

cost to state and federal governments of $142 billion. Medicaid may also pay the premiums for supplementary medical insurance and the deductible and co-insurance cost of hospital insurance. Medicaid also covers some medical services that Medicare does not.

Food Stamps

By providing eligible applicants with coupons to buy food, this program enables families in need to purchase a nutritionally adequate diet. In general, a household is considered eligible if it has less than $2,000 in liquid assets, or if 30 percent of its countable cash income is insufficient to purchase an adequate low-cost diet as defined by the U.S. Department of Agriculture (USDA) "Thrifty Food Plan." The Food Stamp Act of 1964 set eligibility requirements for food stamp program participants and provides coupons through state and local agencies that are used to buy food in approved retail stores. States delegate varying degrees of authority to counties and cities, but the federal government finances 100 percent of the state-issued food benefits and part of the state's administrative costs. The Omnibus Budget Reconciliation Act of 1982 tightened eligibility and authorized pilot projects in which recipients lose their stamps if they don't work at least 20 hours a week.

Special nutrition programs

The USDA administers a number of programs designed to help safeguard the health and well-being of the nation's children by assisting the states in providing adequate meals to all children at a

Federal Food Assistance Programs, 1970–2001

Program	1970	1980	1990	1995	2000	2001
Participants (millions)						
Food stamps	4.3	21.1	20.1	26.6	17.1	17.3
National school lunch program1	22.4	26.6	24.1	25.7	27.2	28.0
School breakfast1	0.5	3.6	4.1	6.3	7.6	8.1
Women-infants-children2	—	1.9	4.5	6.9	7.2	7.5
Child and adult care3	0.1	0.7	1.5	2.4	2.7	2.9
Federal cost (millions)						
Food stamps	$4,624	$8,721	$14,187	$22,765	$14,985	$15,547
National school lunch program1	300	2,279	3,214	4,466	6,149	6,856
School breakfast2	11	288	596	1,048	1,393	1,567
Women-infants-children	—	584	1,637	2,516	3,981	4,342
Child and adult care3	6	236	720	1,296	1,684	1,854

1. Average monthly participation during school year. Covers public and private elementary and secondary schools and residential child care institutions. Costs do not include the value of USDA donated commodities. 2. WIC serves pregnant and postpartum women, infants, and children up to age five. 3. Provides year-round subsidies to feed preschool children in child care centers and family day care programs. Certain care centers serving disabled or elderly adults also receive meal subsidies.
Source: U.S. Dept. of Agriculture, Annual Historical Review of Food and Nutrition Service Programs, annual, and unpublished data.

Medicaid Enrollment, Beneficiaries and Payments, 1975–2003

Year	Aged	Blind/Disabled	Dependent children under 21	Adults in families with dependent children	Other/ Unknown	Total
Enrollment (millions)						
1975	N.A.	N.A.	N.A.	N.A.	N.A.	N.A.
1980	N.A.	N.A.	N.A.	N.A.	N.A.	N.A.
1985	N.A.	N.A.	N.A.	N.A.	N.A.	N.A.
1990	3.1	3.8	10.7	4.9	0.5	22.9
1995	3.7	5.8	16.5	6.7	0.6	33.4
2000	3.9	6.8	16.7	6.7	N.A.	34.0
2003	4.3	7.7	19.6	8.8	N.A.	40.4
Beneficiaries (millions)						
1975	3.7	2.4	9.8	4.7	1.9	22.4
1980	3.4	2.8	9.3	4.8	1.5	21.6
1985	3.1	3.0	9.8	5.5	1.2	21.8
1990	3.2	3.7	11.2	6.0	1.1	25.3
1995	4.2	6.0	17.6	7.8	0.6	36.3
2000	4.5	7.5	21.5	9.0	N.A.	42.5
2003	5.0	8.5	25.2	12.0	N.A.	50.7
Payments (millions)						
1975	$4,358	$3,145	$2,186	$2,062	$492	$12,242
1980	9,926	9,455	3,508	3,763	552	27,204
1985	14,096	13,452	4,414	4,746	798	37,508
1990	21,508	24,403	9,100	8,590	1,051	64,859
1995	36,527	49,418	17,976	13,511	1,499	120,141
2000	N.A.	N.A.	N.A.	N.A.	N.A.	N.A.
2003	N.A.	N.A.	N.A.	N.A.	N.A.	N.A.

Note: Figures are in current dollars. A small number of recipients are in more than one category. 1. Figures for blind were combined with those for the disabled in 1997. **Source:** Health Care Financing Administration.

moderate cost. The programs include the National School Lunch Program, the School Breakfast Program, the Summer Food Service Program, the Child Care Food Program, the Special Milk Program, and the Special Supplemental Food Program for Women, Infants, and Children (WIC) Program. The nutrition program for the elderly requires no income test, but preference is given to those with the greatest need.

Housing subsidies

The federal government has traditionally provided housing aid directly to lower-income households in the form of rental and mortgage-interest subsidies. The primary purposes are to improve housing quality and to reduce housing costs for lower-income households. Other goals include promoting residential construction, expanding housing opportunities for disadvantaged groups and groups with special housing needs, promoting neighborhood preservation and revitalization, increasing homeownership, and empowering the poor to become homeowners.

Most housing aid is targeted to very-low-income renters through two basic types of rental assistance programs. Project-based aid is typically tied to projects specifically produced for lower-income households through new construction or substantial renovation. Almost all project-based aid is provided through production-oriented programs, including the public-housing program, the section 8 new construction and substantial rehabilitation program, and the section 236 mortgage-interest-subsidy program (administered by the Department of Housing and Urban Development), and the section 515 mortgage-interest-subsidy program administered by the Farmers Home Administration.

Household-based subsidies permit renters to choose from standard housing units in the existing private housing stock. Rental assistance programs generally reduce tenants' rent payments to 30 percent of their income, with the Government paying the balance of the contract rents.

The federal government also assists some lower- and moderate-income households in becoming homeowners by making long-term commitments to reduce their mortgage interest. These generally reduce mortgage payments, property taxes and insurance costs to a fixed percentage of income, ranging from 20 percent to 28 percent.

The total number of households receiving assistance has increased substantially, from 3.2 million in 1977 to 5.7 million in 1995. Total outlays for housing aid rose from $2.9 billion in 1977 to an estimated 26.0 billion in 1996; outlays per unit rose from $1,160 to $5,480 over the same period.

Housing for the homeless

HUD funding for homeless programs is made available to state and local governments, Indian tribes, and nonprofit organizations. The specific programs are the Emergency Shelter Grants (ESG) Program, the Supportive Housing Demonstration Program, the Shelter-Plus-Care Homeless Rental Housing Assistance, and the HUD-Owned Single Property Disposition Program.

Head Start

Head Start provides a wide range of services to children of low-income families (and their families) up to the age of five. Its goals are to improve the social competence, learning skills, and health and nutrition status of low-income children so that they can begin school on an equal footing with their more advantaged peers. The services include cognitive and language development, medical, dental, and mental health services (including screening and immunizations), and nutritional and social services. Parental involvement is extensive, through both volunteer participation and employment of parents as Head Start staff.

At least 90 percent of Head Start children come from families with incomes at or below the poverty line, and at least 10 percent of enrollment slots in each state must be available to disabled children. In 2002, more than 910,000 children were served in Head Start programs, at a total federal cost of $6.5 billion, or an average cost of $7,166 per child. The program has served a total of 21.2 million children since it began in 1965. Since 1980, the children served by Head Start have

Head Start Participation and Funding, 1966–2002

Year	Enrollment	Appropriations
1966	733,000	$198,900,000
1970	477,400	325,700,000
1980	376,300	735,000,000
1990	540,930	1,552,000,000
1995	750,696	3,534,128,000
1998	822,316	4,347,433,000
1999	826,016	4,658,151,448
2000	857,664	5,267,000,000
2001	905,235	6,200,000,000
2002	912,345	6,538,000,000

1. Estimate. **Source:** U.S. Dept of Health and Human Services, Administration for Children and Families. www.acf.hhs.gov.

U.S. Weighted Average Poverty Thresholds by Family Size, 1960–2002

Year	Maximum yearly family income						
	1 person	2 people	3 people	4 people	5 people	6 people	7 people
1960	$1,490	$1,924	$2,359	$3,022	$3,560	$4,002	$4,921[1]
1970	1,954	2,525	3,099	3,968	4,680	5,260	6,468[1]
1980	4,190	5,363	6,565	8,414	9,966	11,269	12,761
1990	6,652	8,509	10,419	13,359	15,792	17,839	20,241
1995	7,763	9,933	12,158	15,569	18,408	20,804	23,552
1998	8,316	10,634	13,003	16,660	19,680	22,228	25,257
1999	8,501	10,869	13,290	17,029	20,127	22,727	25,912
2000	8,794	11,239	13,738	17,603	21,819	23,528	26,754
2001	**9,039**	**11,569**	**14,128**	**18,104**	**21,405**	**24,195**	**27,517**
2002	**9,182**	**11,752**	**14,351**	**18,390**	**21,743**	**24,578**	**27,952**

1. Seven or more people. **Source:** U.S. Bureau of the Census, 2003.

grown younger, less black, and more Hispanic. Five-year-olds made up 21 percent of the Head Start population in 1980; in 2002 they constituted only 5 percent. Meanwhile, three-year-olds increased from 24 to 36 percent over the same period. In 1980, 19 percent of Head Start children were Hispanic; in 2001, 30 percent were Hispanic, while black Head Start children declined from 42 to 33 percent over the same period.

Poverty income guidelines

The poverty income guidelines are used to determine whether a person or family is eligible for assistance under a particular federal program. The poverty threshold is established each year by increasing the previous year's threshold by the change in the Consumer Price Index. The original poverty threshold was devised in 1960 and was equal to three times the amount of money to buy the cheapest "nutritionally adequate" diet as dictated by the Department of Agriculture.

Unemployment Compensation

The Social Security Act provided an inducement to states to enact unemployment insurance laws, and by 1937 all 48 states, the territories of Alaska and Hawaii, and the District of Columbia had passed such laws. All contributions collected under state laws are deposited in the unemployment trust fund of the U.S. Treasury, but each state maintains a separate account. A state may withdraw money from its account only to pay benefits. Each state has major responsibility for the content and development of its unemployment insurance law. Nationwide, Unemployment covers about 125 million workers.

Workers must be ready, able and willing to work and must be registered for work at a state public employment office. A worker's benefit is based on his or her employment in covered work over a prior performance period. No state can deny benefit to a claimant if he or she refuses to accept a new job under substandard labor conditions or where he or she would be required to join a company union.

For the 12-month period ending July 31, 2003, 10.2 million people made initial unemployment claims and nearly 4.4 million exhausted their compensation. The average weekly benefit was $260 and the average duration of benefit was 16.1 weeks, making the average total benefit $4,186. The weekly benefit varies from state to state, but the general formula is designed to compensate for between 50 percent and 70 percent of average weekly pretax wage, up to a state-determined minimum.

Workers' compensation

Social insurance began in the United States with worker's compensation. A law covering federal civilian employees was passed in 1908; the first state compensation law to be held constitutional was enacted in 1911. These laws made industry responsible for the compensation of workers (or their survivors) injured or killed while on the job. A worker incurring an occupational injury is compensated regardless of fault or blame in the accident. A separate federal program enacted in 1969 protects coal miners (see "Black lung program" below).

Workers' compensation is almost exclusively financed by employers on the principle that the cost of work-related accidents is part of the expense of production. Every state except Texas mandates coverage under workers' compensation for private employees. Certain categories of workers, usually domestic, agricultural, and casual laborers, are often exempted from this requirement. Employers can use private insurance companies or can qualify as self-insurers. Workers' compensation covered nearly 127 million workers in 2001, or about 97 percent of the civilian labor force. The cash benefit for temporary total disability, permanent, total or partial disability, or death of a breadwinner is usually about two-thirds of weekly earnings at the time of the accident. Most state laws pay temporary disability benefits for as long as the disability lasts and the condition has not been stabilized to the point where no further improvement can result from medical treatment. Total benefit payments under workers' compensation programs in 2001 were $49.4 billion, up from $47.7 billion in 2000.

Permanent partial disability compensation for specific, or "schedule" injuries (for clearly measurable matters) is generally subject to different (usually lower) dollar maximums and is determined without regard to loss of earning power. Compensation for "nonschedule" injuries (injuries to head, back, nervous system) is the difference between wages before and after impairment. Death benefits are related to earnings and graduated by the number of dependents. Medical benefits are furnished without limit as to time or amount for accidental injuries. Temporary Disability Insurance provides coverage against the risk of lost wages due to short-term nonoccupational disability. The Federal Unemployment Tax Act permits states where employees make contributions under the unemployment insurance program to use some or all of those contributions for disability benefits. It is estimated that about two-thirds of the nation's wage and salary earners in private employment have some protection through various voluntary and governmental group arrangements. In general the benefit amount for a week is intended to replace at least half the weekly wage loss for a maximum of 26 to 39 weeks per year.

▶VETERANS' BENEFITS

The tradition of veterans' benefits dates to the 18th century, when the Continental Congress provided disability pensions for veterans of the Revolutionary War. Today, the Department of Veterans Affairs (DVA) offers a wide range of services and benefits to eligible veterans, their dependents, and their survivors.

After years of decreasing in numbers (from about 29.5 million in 1975 to 25.5 million in 2000), the veteran population marked a small uptick in 2001 to 26.1 million. Nearly 75 percent of them served during a war or official period of conflict. The number of veterans age 65 or older is increasing very rapidly, and the use and cost of medical care are expected to grow more rapidly in the near future than those of other veterans' benefits and services. Compensation and pension caseloads are decreasing steadily due to beneficiary deaths, terminations for excess incomes, and age limitation for dependents. The number of trainees under the Montgomery GI bill will increase as more veterans become eligible.

Veterans who have incurred injuries or illness while in service are entitled to service-connected compensation. The amounts are determined by disability ratings. Death compensation or dependency and indemnity compensation is paid to survivors of veterans who died as a result of service-connected causes.

War veterans who have become permanently and totally disabled from non-service-connected causes, and to survivors of war veterans may receive means-tested veterans' pensions. Benefits are based on family size, and the pensions provide a floor of income.

Medical programs The VA operates 163 hospital centers, 137 nursing homes, 43 domiciliaries, and more than 850 community-based ambulatory care and outpatient clinics. In 2002, the VA treated about 564,700 patients in VA hospitals, 50,267 in nursing homes, and 22,541 in domiciliaries. The VA extends free priority care to service-connected disabled veterans, to veterans in special categories, and to needy non-service-connected veterans. As facilities and other resources permit, the VA provides care to non-service-connected veterans with incomes that exceed the mandatory care income limits.

Housing and loan programs Since 1944, when the Montgomery GI bill began helping veterans buy homes, the VA has guaranteed more than 16.9 million loans totaling over $748 billion; in fiscal 2002, the VA guaranteed 320,000 loans totaling $40.5 billion. The maximum guaranty is as follows: 50 percent of the loan amount for loans of $45,000 or less; for loans between $45,001 and $144,000, a minimum of $22,500 and a maximum of 40 percent of the loan up to $36,000; and a maximum guaranty of 25 percent of loans over $144,000, up to $60,000.

Other veterans' programs The GI Bill has also provided education and training programs to more than 21 million veterans since 1944, at a total cost of more than $75 billion. Contributions are required, and veterans can receive a basic educational benefit of up to $400 per month for 36 months while in an educational program.

The Veterans Job Training Act program provides payments to defray training costs of employers who hire certain veterans of the Korean conflict or Vietnam era who have been unemployed for long periods of time.

Veterans Benefits and Services: Outlays and Recipients, 1975–2002

Fiscal year	Compensation and pensions	Readjustment, education, job training	Medical programs	Housing loans
Outlays (millions)				
1975	$ 7,860	$4,593	$3,665	N.A.
1980	11,688	2,342	6,515	N.A.
1985	14,714	1,059	9,547	N.A.
1990	15,241	278	12,134	N.A.
1995	18,966	1,124	15,981	N.A.
1997	19,389	1,167	17,149	27,042
1998	19,700	1,429	17,441	37,906
1999	21,800	N.A.	18,300	54,000
2000	21,500	N.A.	19,400	23,300
2002	25,000	N.A.	N.A.	40,500
Recipients ('000s)				
1975	4,855	2,804	1,985	290
1980	4,646	1,232	2,671	297
1985	4,005	491	2,963	179
1990	3,614	329	3,018	196
1995	3,332	476	2,859	263
1997	2,200	297	3,142	261
1998	2,700	297	3,431	344
1999	2,700	288	3,600	486
2000	2,700	279	3,800	200
2002	3,300	325	4,500	320

Source: *Facts About the Depratment of Veterans Affairs* (1975-2002).

THE INTERNAL REVENUE SERVICE

Founded in 1862, the Internal Revenue Service (I.R.S.) is the office of the Department of the Treasury charged with collecting federal taxes. The Constitution empowers Congress to levy excise taxes and—in emergencies—to raise direct taxes. Congress's right to levy taxes on the income of individuals and corporations was contested throughout the 19th century, but that authority was written into the Constitution with the passage of the 16th Amendment in 1913. Today, the source of most of the federal government's revenues are the individual income tax, corporate income tax, excise taxes, estate taxes, and gift taxes. The I.R.S. is responsible for these taxes as well as for collecting employee and employer payments for social insurance and retirement insurance (see "Social Insurance Programs").

In 1998, Congress enacted a major overhaul of the I.R.S. in hopes of transforming the agency from a menacing symbol of Government authority into a resource for taxpayers trying to cope with the increasingly bewildering tax code. The legislation established an outside board with broad authority to supervise the I.R.S.'s operations, and perhaps more important, shifted the burden of proof in tax dispute cases to the I.R.S. (previously, taxpayers had to prove their innocence). Initial reaction to the legislation was overwhelmingly favorable. But tax experts correctly predicted the law would give scofflaws greater incentive to cheat on their taxes. Property seizures dropped by 98 percent between 1997 and 1999, garnishments of bank accounts and paychecks were a quarter of their level two years earlier, and tax liens, which insure that back taxes are paid when properties are sold, were down by 67 percent.

But the most damaging change was the anti-harassment section of the legislation, which tax collectors say has thwarted them from collecting taxes from delinquent filers. Several I.R.S. agents said they no longer pursued outstanding tax bills vigorously because they feared losing their jobs under the anti-harassment policy. In 1998, the I.R.S. gave up on collecting back taxes from just 98 taxpayers; in 2000, the agency wrote off $2.5 billion in back taxes owed by more than 650,000 delinquent taxpayers.

The decline in aggressive pursuit of tax cheats actually began even before the new law went into effect. In 1996, the I.R.S. audited 2.13 million of the 155 million tax returns filed, a rate of 1.38 percent. Two years later, the agency examined only half as many returns (1.36 million, out of a total of

161 million filed, or 0.8 percent). Almost all of the decrease in audits came in individual returns. The I.R.S. audited just under 2 million individual returns in 1996; that number dropped to 1.2 million in 1998 and plunged again to only 815,057 in 2000. The agency also eased up on corporate tax filings. In 1996, it audited 69,650 corporate returns (2.67 percent); corporate audits fell to 54,051 returns (2.1 percent) in 1998 and 23,268 returns (0.95 percent) in 2000.

The shift can also be seen in the number and distribution of I.R.S. employees. Between 1995 and 2002 the number of tax returns increased by 13 percent, but the I.R.S.'s auditing staff shrunk by 29 percent. However, in 2002 the agency announced a renewed focus on audits: it planned to retrain several hundred agents as fraud specialists, reintroduce random audits (last conducted in 1998), and devote more attention to wealthy taxpayers suspected of hiding income. In 2001 it examined 34 percent of the 10,908 returns filed by corporations with total revenues of $250 million or more, resulting in $13.6 billion in additional taxes and penalties, or more than $700,000 per audit. The other closely monitored group of tax returns is from estates valued at $5 million or

Tax Returns Processed, 1990–2002

Type of return	Number of returns ('000s)				
	1990	1995	2000	2001	2002
Individual income tax (Form 1040 series)	112,492	116,298	127,590	129,783	130,905
Individual estimated tax (Form 1040ES)	38,188	35,475	39,230	37,470	33,817
Fiduciary (Form 1041 series)	2,702	3,187	3,530	3,868	3,684
Fiduciary estimated tax (Form 1041ES)	651	583	892	885	670
Partnership (Form 1065)	1,741	1,572	2,048	2,134	2,236
Corporation (Forms 1120 series, 1066)	4,311	4,781	5,458	5,491	5,711
Estate tax (Forms 706, 706NA)	59	83	121	122	121
Gift tax (Form 709)	146	215	305	304	279
Employment taxes (Forms 94X series, CT-1, 1042)	28,914	29,006	28,911	28,899	29,141
Exempt organizations (Forms 990 series, 4720, 5227)	484	560	707	715	748
Employee plans (Form 5500 series)	1,016	1,262	1,164	883	–
Excise taxes (Forms 720, 730, 2290, 11C)	840	787	916	765	885
Supplemental documents (1040X, 2688, 4868, 7004, 1041A)	10,170	11,937	15,260	16,609	18,413
Total tax returns	**201,715**	**205,747**	**226,130**	**227,929**	**226,609**

Source: Internal Revenue Service, *2002 Data Book* (2003).

Tax Rate Schedules, 2003

Taxable income	What you pay
Single Individual	
$0-$7,000	10% of sum over $0
$7,000–$28,400	$700.00 + 15% of sum over $7,000
$28,400- $68,800	$3,910 + 25% of sum over $28,400
$68,800-$143,500	$14,010 + 28% of sum over $68,800
$143,500- $311,950	$34,926 + 33% of sum over $143,500
over $311,950	$90,514.50 + 35% of sum over $311,950
Heads of Households	
$0- $10,000	10% of sum over $0
$10,000–$38,050	$1,000 + 15% of sum over $10,000
$38,050- $98,250	$5,207.50 + 25% of sum over $38,050
$98,250- $159,100	$20,257.50 + 28% of sum over $98,250
$159,100- $311,950	$37,295.50 + 33% of sum over $159,100
over $311,950	$87,736 + 35% of sum over $311,950
Married individuals filing jointly, or qualifying widow(er)	
$0- $14,000	10% of sum over $0
$14,000–$56,800	$1,400 + 15% of sum over $14,000
$56,800- $114,650	$7,820 + 25% of sum over $56,800
$114,650- $174,700	$22,282.50 + 28% of sum over $114,650
$174,700- $311,950	$39,096.50 + 33% of sum over $174,700
over $311,950	$84,389 + 35% of sum over $311,950
Married, Filing Separate Return	
$0- $7,000	10% of sum over $0
$7,000–$28,400	$700 + 15% of sum over $7,000
$28,400- $57,325	$3,910 + 25% of sum over $28,400
$57,325- $87,350	$11,141.25 + 28% of sum over $57,325
$87,350- $155,975	$19,548.25 + 33% of sum over $87,350
over $155,975	$42,194.50 + 35% of sum over $155,975

Note: Preliminary figures, subject to review by the Office of Management & Budget. **Source:** Internal Revenue Service.

more. There were 5,738 such returns filed in 2001; the I.R.S. examined 26.9 percent of them, resulting in $976.1 million in additional taxes and penalties ($631,917 per examination).

This shift in emphasis may not have hurt the Federal coffers, but the Bush administration's emphasis on tax cuts almost certainly has. Total I.R.S. tax collections (as well as tax per capita) reached all-time highs in 2000 and 2001 (See the accompanying table), but then dropped to pre-2000 levels in 2002.

▶TAX CHANGES IN 2003

In 2003, President Bush signed the Jobs and Growth Tax Relief Reconciliation Act, lowering three of the top four income tax rates (35 percent, 30 percent, and 27 percent) by two full percentage points, and the highest rate (38.6 percent) by 3.6 percentage points. The Act also expanded the 15 percent rate bracket for married taxpayers to twice that of single filers; increased the maximum taxable income subject to the lowest (10 percent) tax rate; and increased the maximum child tax credit from $600 to $1,000. In the summer of 2003, a new round of child tax credit checks was sent out as an advance against 2003 tax payments.

▶PRINCIPAL DEDUCTIONS

Taxes: Taxpayers who pay a state and/or local tax may deduct this amount from their federal tax payment. In addition, in Alabama, Iowa, Louisiana, Missouri, Oklahoma, Oregon and Utah, taxpayers may deduct their federal income tax before calculating their state tax payments.

Personal exemptions: Taxpayers are allowed to claim personal exemptions for the taxpayer and each dependent claimed in filing income tax. Congress determines the amount (since 1990, pegged to the inflation rate) allowable for deductions on personal and other exemptions. Because the personal exemption is the same for a single person as for a married couple, the tax schedule effectively dissuades people from getting married. For several years, politicians have discussed eliminating the so-called marriage tax penalty, but to date have not remedied this situation.

Interest expenses: The most common interest deduction is on home mortgages, thus making the cost of owning a home more affordable to most Americans. Although politically very popular, the mortgage deduction is what experts call an "upside-down" subsidy because the more a taxpayer earns, the greater the tax cut yielded. In re-

Returns Filed and Examined, and Additional Taxes and Penalties, 2001

Type of return	Total returns filed, 2001[1]	Total returns examined, 2001	Percent examined	Additional taxes and penalties (thousands)[2]	Average tax and penalty per return[3]
All returns, total	**171,140,558**	**826,979**	**.48**	**20,998,475**	**—**
Individual, total	**141,389,658**	**800,753**	**.57**	**20,310,343**	**39,924**
1040A, income under $25,000	40,560,604	289,136	.71	819,403	7,504
Non 1040A, income under $25,000	14,106,067	90,781	.64	323,167	10,822
income $25,000-$50,000	30,720,483	71,966	.23	174,515	5,369
income $50,000-$100,000	24,702,589	69,620	.28	220,642	8,031
income $100,000 and over	10,692,928	80,483	.75	1,070,820	30,628
Schedule C—receipts under $25,000	2,541,662	67,876	2.67	167,426	10,874
Schedule C—receipts $25,000-$100,000	3,425,939	40,530	1.18	193,398	11,507
Schedule C—receipts $100,000 and over	2,059,115	29,848	1.45	637,952	26,722
Schedule F—receipts under $100,000	367,420	1,709	.47	4,279	9,224
Schedule F—receipts $100,000 and over	268,140	1,932	.72	24,884	21,255
Corporation, total	**2,411,981**	**23,410**	**.97**	**14,738,381**	**105,130**
No balance sheet	293,983	2,729	.93	67,881	47,863
Under $250,000	1,395,497	3,343	.24	40,147	12,391
$250,000-$1 mil.	417,973	3,177	.76	57,175	18,222
$1 mil-$ 5 mil.	191,456	3,990	2.08	96,725	24,499
$5 mil-$10 mil.	30,570	1,416	4.63	53,897	38,719
$10 mil-$50 mil.	32,570	2,540	7.80	256,958	99,168
$50 mil-$100 mil.	8,057	865	10.74	106,093	123,257
$100 mil-$250 mil.	8,067	1,289	15.98	295,793	214,945
$250 mil. and over	10,908	3,749	34.37	13,668,201	709,580
Form 1120F	22,900	312	1.36	95,511	114,119
Fiduciary	**3,918,918**	**7,206**	**.18**	**98,339**	**17,888**
Estate, total	**122,412**	**7,151**	**5.84**	**1,432,090**	**200,229**
Gross estate under $1 mil.	56,704	1,241	2.19	33,863	27,287
Gross estate $1 mil.-$5 mil.	59,970	4,365	7.28	422,097	96,700
Gross estate $5 mil. and over	5,738	1,545	26.93	976,130	631,917
Gift	**303,800**	**1,899**	**.63**	**405,047**	**213,309**
Employment	**28,935,800**	**17,252**	**.06**	**357,892**	**11,546**
Excise	**815,100**	**8,426**	**1.03**	**130,550**	**12,775**
Miscellaneous taxable[4]	**—**	**548**	**—**	**199,691**	**32,081**
Partnerships	**2,165,011**	**5,543**	**.26**	**—**	**—**
S-Corporations	**3,022,589**	**11,646**	**.39**	**—**	**—**

Note: Totals may not add due to rounding. 1. Calendar year. 2. Recommended. 3. Includes only returns reviewed by revenue agents. Additional taxes and penalties were recovered through reviews of individual returns by tax auditors and service centers. 4. Includes taxable small business corporations (1120S). **Source:** Internal Revenue Service, *2002 Data Book* (2003).

cent years, 20 percent of the tax savings from home mortgage interest has gone to taxpayers earning more than $200,000.

Medical expenses: Although almost all medical expenses are deductible, it is difficult to take a deduction because your combined expenses for the year must total 7.5 percent of your adjusted gross income. So, for someone with an adjusted gross income of $25,000, medical expenses would have to exceed $1,875 not covered by any medical insurance.

▶ ELECTRONIC FILING

The number of people filing their tax returns electronically has jumped dramatically in the 1990s. Just over 4 million individuals filed electronically in 1990; by 1993, that number had tripled to 12.3 million; and by 2002 it nearly quadrupled again, reaching 46.8 million.

▶ CHECK BOXES

In 2002, 11 million people checked the little box authorizing the I.R.S. to send a portion of their tax to the Presidential Election Campaign Fund. That meant $67.0 million went to that fund. Since 1972, more than $1.2 billion has gone to public financing of presidential elections.

Internal Revenue Collections, Costs, and Tax Per Capita, 1960–2002

Fiscal year	Collections ('000s)	Cost of collecting $100	Tax per capita
1960	$91,774,803	$ 0.40	$ 507.97
1965	114,434,634	0.52	588.95
1970	195,722,096	0.45	955.31
1975	293,822,726	0.54	1,375.84
1980	519,375,273	0.44	2,275.66
1985	742,871,541	0.48	3,098.99
1990	1,056,365,652	0.52	4,222.00
1995	1,375,731,835	0.54	5,216.70
1999	1,904,151,888	0.43	6,957.79
2000	2,096,916,925	0.39	7,595.24
2001	2,128,831,182	0.41	7,448.90
2002	2,016,627,269	0.45	6,967.40

Note: In current dollars.
Source: Internal Revenue Service, *2002 Data Book* (2003).

Internal Revenue Collections, 2002

Type of return	Gross collections	Refunds[1]	Net collections	
			Amount	Percent of total
Corporation income taxes	$211,437,773,000	$66,757,609,000	$144,679,991,000	8.3
Individual income taxes2	1,037,733,908,000	210,159,025,000	827,574,883,000	47.8
Employment taxes, total	688,077,238,000	3,943,671,000	684,133,567,000	39.5
Estate and gift taxes	27,241,515,000	803,406,000	26,438,109,000	1.5
Excise taxes	52,136,835,000	2,248,229,000	49,888,606,000	2.9
Grand total	**$2,016,627,269,000**	**$283,911,940,000**	**$1,732,715,156,000**	**100.0**

Note: 1. Excludes excise taxes paid to the Customs Service and Bureau of Alcohol, Tobacco and Firearms. Does not include interest paid on refunds. 2. Includes Presidential Election Campaign Fund contributions of $61.0 million. **Source:** Internal Revenue Service, *2002 Data Book* (2003).

I.R.S. Collections by Principal Sources, 1961–2002 (thousands of dollars)

Year	Total Internal Revenue collections	Corporate income & profits tax	Individual income tax	Employment taxes	Estate and gift taxes	Excise taxes
1961	**$94,401,086**	$21,764,940	$46,153,001	$12,502,451	$ 1,916,392	$12,064,302
1970	**195,722,096**	35,036,983	103,651,585	37,449,188	3,680,076	15,904,264
1980	**519,375,273**	72,379,610	287,547,782	128,330,480	6,498,381	24,619,021
1990	**1,056,365,652**	110,016,539	540,228,408	367,219,321	11,761,939	27,139,445
1995	**1,375,731,835**	174,422,173	675,779,337	465,405,305	15,144,394	44,980,627
1998	**1,769,408,739**	213,270,011	928,065,856	557,799,193	24,630,962	45,642,716
1999	**1,904,151,888**	216,324,889	1,002,185,765	598,669,865	28,385,607	58,585,763
2000	**2,096,916,925**	235,654,894	1,137,077,702	639,651,814	29,721,620	54,810,895
2001	**2,128,831,182**	186,731,643	1,178,209,880	682,222,895	29,247,916	52,418,848
2002	**2,016,627,269**	211,437,773	1,037,733,908	688,077,238	25,532,186	52,136,835

Note: In current dollars. **Source:** Internal Revenue Service, *2002 Data Book* (2003).

Average Itemized Deductions By Income Level, 2000

Adjusted gross income ranges	Percent itemizing deductions	Average deduction for:				
		Medical	Taxes	Gifts	Interest	Total
0- $15,000	3.56%	$7,500	$1,963	$1,350	$5,958	$11,522
$15,000- $30,000	14.64	5,137	2,200	1,619	5,866	10,627
$30,000- $50,000	36.66	4,992	2,991	1,774	6,247	11,770
$50,000-$100,000	69.58	5,950	4,918	2,282	7,544	15,228
$100,000-$200,000	90.49	10,494	9,262	3,727	10,806	23,500
$200,000 or more	92.46	32,259	36,592	19,454	21,735	64,996

Note: 2000 data based on tax returns for the 1999 tax year. **Source:** Research Institute of America, *Federal Taxes Weekly Alert*, July, 2001.

THE U.S. POSTAL SERVICE

With more than 750,000 employees moving more than 200 billion pieces of mail annually, the U.S. Postal Service provides one of the most vital government services. What most people don't realize is that it's done at a cost to the consumer significantly less than in any other industrial nation, and that for first-class mail, the on-time delivery rate is still over 95 percent for local mail and 90 percent for cross-country.

First established by the Continental Congress in 1775, the Postal Service was made part of the federal system in the Constitution and the office of postmaster general established in George Washington's very first cabinet. In 1969, however, in response to vociferous complaints of mismanagement, waste, unreliable service and staggering financial losses, the Nixon administration reorganized the service as an independent establishment within the executive branch. The Postal Service Act of 1969 removed the postmaster general from the cabinet and created a self-supporting postal corporation owned by the federal government and vested power in an 11-member Board of Governors, nine of whom are appointed by the president with the consent of the Senate; these in turn appoint the postmaster general who serves as the CEO of the postal service; the 11th member of the board is chosen by the other 10 and serves as deputy postmaster general.

Finally, the 1969 law established an independent Postal Rate Commission of five members, appointed by the president, to recommend postal rates and classifications for adoption by the Board of Governors. Under this agreement, the Postal Service turned a profit five times in the early 1980s. But between 1989 and 1994, the Postal Service lost money every year. A 1995 hike in the price of stamps helped create record-level profits in 1995, 1996, and 1997, more than wiping out the $2.6 billion lost between 1993 and 1994. But this didn't stop the Board of Governors from approving a one-cent hike in the price of stamps in 1999 and another one-cent hike two years later. Measured in constant dollars, the real cost of a stamp in 2001 was 7 cents, a penny less than in 1971.

Postage rates If you know the weight of a package, you can determine the amount of postage you will need before going to the post office. Point your browser to http://postcalc.usps.gov.

In 2002, the Postal Service delivered nearly 203 billion pieces of mail, down from a record 208 billion pieces in 2000; it delivers more mail each day than Federal Express delivers all year. If the Postal Service were privately held, its $66.5 billion in 2002 revenues would have ranked it among the top 12 *Fortune* 500 companies in the U.S. and among the top 40 companies in the world.

However, by the end of 2002, the Postal Service's full-time labor force had fallen to a seven-year low, a number of "behind-the-scenes" postal facilities had been closed, and the agency posted a

Domestic Postage Rates

Weight up to	Rate	Weight up to	Rate	Weight up to	Rate
1 oz.	$0.37	**6 oz.**	$1.52	**11 oz.**	2.67
2 oz.	0.60	**7 oz.**	1.75	**12 oz.**	2.90
3 oz.	0.83	**8 oz.**	1.98	**13 oz.**	3.13
4 oz.	1.06	**9 oz.**	2.21	**over 13 oz.:**	
5 oz.	1.29	**10 oz.**	2.44	UsePriority Mail	

Post cards 23 cents. Post cards cannot exceed 4.25" x 6", nor be smaller than 3.5" x 5".

Priority mail Priority mail is a zone-based domestic service providing two-day delivery to all major parts of the U.S. For local delivery and in Zones 1–3, rates for packages are as follows:

Weight up to	Rate	Weight up to	Rate
1 lb.	$3.85	**4 lbs.**	$5.30
2 lbs.	3.95	**5 lbs.**	5.85
3 lbs.	4.75	**5-70 lbs.**	6.30-38.45

For packages weighing more than one pound, rates depend on the zone. The maximum weight is 70 pounds.

Express mail is an overnight and second-day delivery service available every day of the year for items up to 70 lbs. in weight and 108 in. in combined length and girth. The post office will pick up packages to be sent by express mail a $10.25 fee (per pickup, not per package). Call 1-800-222-1811.

Weight up to	Rate	Weight up to	Rate
8 oz.	$13.65	**3 lbs.**	$21.05
2 lbs.	17.85	**4-70 lbs.**	24.20-133.20

Parcel Post This is a zone-based class of mail for sending books, circulars, catalogs, other printed matter, and merchandise-weighing not more than 70 pounds. Parcel Post must measure 130 inches or less in combined length and girth. A regular package up to a pound is $3.69 or $3.75; the maximum rate is $43.68 for a 70-pound package sent to zone 8. Oversized parcels are charged approximately three times the maximum rates.

Source: U.S. Postal Service. www.usps.gov

International Postage Rates

Type/ Weight up to	Canada	Mexico	Europe	Australia, Japan & New Zealand	All other countries
Airmail letters					
1.0 oz	$0.60	$0.60	$0.80	$0.80	$0.80
2.0 oz	0.85	0.85	1.60	1.70	1.55
3.0 oz	1.10	1.25	2.40	2.60	2.30
4.0 oz	1.35	1.65	3.20	3.50	3.05
8.0 oz	2.35	3.25	6.40	7.10	6.05
Postcards	0.50	0.50	0.70	0.70	0.70

Source: U.S. Postal Service. www.usps.gov

Volume and Revenue of Mail by Type, 1990–2002

Type of Service	Millions of pieces 1990	1996	2000	2002	Revenues (millions) 2000	2002
First-class	89,269	98,216	103,526	102,379	$35,516	$36,483
Priority mail	518	937	1,222	998	4,837	4,723
Express mail	59	58	71	61	996	911
Mailgrams	14	4	4	3	1	1
Periodicals	10,682	10,126	10,365	9,690	2,171	2,165
Standard Mail	63,725	71,686	90,057	87,231	15,193	15,819
Parcel Post	663	949	1,128	1,075	1,912	2,080
International surface	166	104	79	39	180	150
International air	632	949	1,021	865	1,477	1,429
U.S. Postal Service	538	360	363	425	N.A.	N.A.
Free for the blind	35	50	47	57	N.A.	N.A.
Total mail	166,301	183,439	207,882	202,822	$62,284	$63,761

Source: U.S. Postal Service, *2002 Annual Report.*

Postal Abbreviations for States and Territories

State	Abb.	State	Abb.
Alabama	AL	**Nevada**	NV
Alaska	AK	**New Hampshire**	NH
Arizona	AZ	**New Jersey**	NJ
Arkansas	AR	**New Mexico**	NM
California	CA	**New York**	NY
Colorado	CO	**North Carolina**	NC
Connecticut	CT	**North Dakota**	ND
Delaware	DE	**Ohio**	OH
District of Columbia	DC	**Oklahoma**	OK
		Oregon	OR
Florida	FL	**Pennsylvania**	PA
Georgia	GA	**Rhode Island**	RI
Hawaii	HI	**South Carolina**	SC
Idaho	ID	**South Dakota**	SD
Illinois	IL	**Tennessee**	TN
Indiana	IN	**Texas**	TX
Iowa	IA	**Utah**	UT
Kansas	KS	**Vermont**	VT
Kentucky	KY	**Virginia**	VA
Louisiana	LA	**Washington**	WA
Maine	ME	**West Virginia**	WV
Maryland	MD	**Wisconsin**	WI
Massachusetts	MA	**Wyoming**	WY
Michigan	MI	**American Samoa**	AS
Minnesota	MN	**Guam**	GU
Mississippi	MS	**Northern Mariana Islands**	CM
Missouri	MO		
Montana	MT	**Puerto Rico**	PR
Nebraska	NE	**Virgin Islands**	VI

Postal Service Employees and Offices, 1990–2002

Category	1990	2002
Employees		
Headquarters (Washington, D.C.)	2,291	1,712
Field support units	5,691	3,848
Inspection services (field)	4,259	3,875
Area offices	N.A.	2,107
Postmasters	26,995	25,771
Supervisors, managers	43,458	37,829
Professional, administrative, and technical personnel	9,793	9,661
Clerks	290,380	256,656
Nurses	286	173
Mail Handlers	51,123	59,259
City delivery carriers	236,081	233,639
Motor vehicle operators	7,308	9,092
Rural delivery carriers (full-time)	42,252	60,817
Special delivery messengers	2,012	—
Building and equipment maintenance personnel	33,323	42,275
Vehicle maintenance personnel	4,874	5,513
Total career employees	**760,668**	**752,949**
Non-career employees (casuals)	26,829	19,065
Offices, stations and branches	**40,067**	**37,683**
Post offices	28,959	27,791
Stations and branches	11,108	9,892
Classified stations and branches	5,008	5,900
Contract stations and branches	4,397	2,500
Community post offices	1,703	1,492

Source: U.S. Postal Service, *2002 Annual Report.*

deficit of $1 billion for the fiscal year ending September 30. In mid-2003, the President's Commission on the United States Postal Service issued a report addressing these issues and recommending strategies for the Postal Service's future, including an overhaul of the nation's sprawling network of post offices and new responses to the "electronic diversion of mail" (e-mail, electronic bill payment, and the like). The commission cited the Internet as a primary cause of the decline in first-class mail, which traditionally accounts for more than half of Postal Service revenues.

ZIP Codes There are about 42,000 separate ZIP codes in the U.S.; the number is constantly changing. A national ZIP code directory is available in every post office. Directory assistance telephone operators can also provide ZIP code information. You can also find ZIP codes for almost any address at **www.cedar.buffalo.edu/adserv.html,** a site run by the State University of New York at Buffalo. The site also shows maps of the surrounding area.

The price of a first-class letter is 19 cents in Mexico, 24 cents in Australia, 36 cents in Italy, 40 cents in France and Great Britain, 50 cents in Germany, 52 cents in Switzerland, 74 cents in Japan, and 37 cents in the U.S.

States, Territories, and Possessions

This section, a compilation of history and statistics about the 50 United States, the District of Columbia, and U.S. territories and possessions, includes a brief history of each state and territory; its official motto and other emblems; a summary of geographic, demographic and economic facts; and a list of prominent natives, places, and dates.

Statistical sources include the U.S. Census Bureau's 2000 decennial census and *The Statistical Abstract* (annual); the Council of State Government's *Book of the States* and *State Elective Officials and the Legislatures*; and the Bureau of Economic Analysis's *Survey of Current Business.*

The headings for demographic statistics in the paragraphs on People and Language conform to U.S. Census Bureau usage, except "Black" is used as short for Black or African American, "Indian" is used for American Indian and Alaska Native, and "Pacific Islander" is used for Native Hawaiian and other Pacific Islander. Note that Hispanics may be of any race.

Estimates of the Resident Population by State, 1990-2000

State	Population ('000s) 2000 Census	1990 Census	Change 1990 to 2000 Number	Percent
United States	**281,422**	**248,710**	**32,712**	**13.2%**
Alabama	4,447	4,041	407	10.1
Alaska	627	550	77	14.0
Arizona	5,131	3,665	1,465	40.0
Arkansas	2,673	2,351	323	13.7
California	33,872	29,760	4,112	13.8
Colorado	4,301	3,294	1,007	30.6
Connecticut	3,406	3,287	118	3.6
Delaware	784	666	117	17.6
District of Columbia	572	607	-35	-5.7
Florida	15,982	12,938	3,044	23.5
Georgia	8,186	6,478	1,708	26.4
Hawaii	1,212	1,108	103	9.3
Idaho	1,294	1,007	287	28.5
Illinois	12,419	11,431	989	8.6
Indiana	6,080	5,544	536	9.7
Iowa	2,926	2,777	150	5.4
Kansas	2,688	2,478	211	8.5
Kentucky	4,042	3,685	356	9.7
Louisiana	4,469	4,220	249	5.9
Maine	1,275	1,228	47	3.8
Maryland	5,296	4,781	515	10.8
Massachusetts	6,349	6,016	333	5.5
Michigan	9,938	9,295	643	6.9
Minnesota	4,919	4,375	544	12.4
Mississippi	2,845	2,573	271	10.5
Missouri	5,595	5,117	478	9.3
Montana	902	799	103	12.9
Nebraska	1,711	1,578	133	8.4
Nevada	1,998	1,202	796	66.3
New Hampshire	1,236	1,109	127	11.4
New Jersey	8,414	7,730	684	8.9
New Mexico	1,819	1,515	304	20.1
New York	18,976	17,990	986	5.5
North Carolina	8,049	6,629	1,421	21.4
North Dakota	642	639	3	0.5
Ohio	11,353	10,847	506	4.7
Oklahoma	3,451	3,146	305	9.7
Oregon	3,421	2,842	579	20.4
Pennsylvania	12,281	11,882	399	3.4
Rhode Island	1,048	1,003	45	4.5
South Carolina	4,012	3,487	525	15.1
South Dakota	755	696	59	8.5
Tennessee	5,689	4,877	812	16.7
Texas	20,852	16,987	3,865	22.8
Utah	2,233	1,723	510	29.6
Vermont	609	563	46	8.2
Virginia	7,079	6,187	891	14.4
Washington	5,894	4,867	1,027	21.1
West Virginia	1,808	1,793	15	0.8
Wisconsin	5,364	4,892	472	9.6
Wyoming	494	454	40	8.9

Note: Includes armed forces residing in each state.
Source: U.S. Bureau of the Census, 2001. www.census.gov

▶ALABAMA

The memory of the Native American presence is particularly strong in Alabama. Trade with the Northeast via the Ohio River valley began during the Burial Mound Period (1000 B.C.–A.D. 700) and continued until European contact. Meso-American influence is evident in the agrarian Mississippian culture that followed. Pressured by white settlers in the early 19th century, the Creeks warred against the U.S. government until defeated by General Andrew Jackson.

The cradle of the Confederacy during the Civil War, Alabama was at stage center in the civil rights movement of the 1950's and 1960's. Although cotton is still a major crop, the northern part of the state around Birmingham is a major industrial area with abundant coal, iron ore, limestone, and electricity from the TVA. Increasingly urban—70 percent of the population lived in rural areas 50 years ago, compared with less than 40 percent today—Alabama's economy is progressing slowly, although it still ranks near last in taxes and in money spent on education.

Name Probably after Alabama tribe. **Nickname** Yellowhammer State, Heart of Dixie. **Capital** Montgomery. **Entered union** Dec. 14, 1819 (22nd). **Motto** "We dare defend our rights."

Emblems **Bird** Yellowhammer. **Dance** Square dance. **Game bird** Wild turkey. **Fish** Tarpon. **Fossil** *Basilosaurus oetoides.* **Mineral** Hematite. **Nut** Pecan. **Song** "Alabama." **Stone** Marble. **Tree** Southern (longleaf) pine.

Land **Total area** 52,419 sq. mi (30th), incl. 1,675 sq. mi. inland water. **Borders** Tenn., Ga., Fla., Gulf of Mexico, Miss. **Rivers** Alabama, Chattahoochee, Mobile, Tennessee, Tennessee-Tombigbee Waterway, Tensaw, Tombigbee. **Lakes** Guntersville, Pickwick, Wheeler, Wilson (all formed by Tennessee Valley Authority [TVA]); Dannelly Res., Martin, Lewis Smith, Weiss. **Mountains** Cumberland, Lookout, Raccoon, Sand.

Elected officials Gov. Bob Riley (R, term exp. 2006) Lt. Gov. Lucy Baxley (D). Sec. State Nancy Worley (D). Atty. Gen. William Pryor (R).

People (July, 2002 est.) 4,486,508 (23rd). Race/Hispanic Origin (2000 Census): White 71.1%. Black 26.0%. Indian 0.5%. Asian 0.7%. Other 0.7%. Two or more races 1.0%. Hispanic 1.7%.

Cities (2002) Birmingham 239,416. Montgomery 201,425. Mobile 194,862. Huntsville 162,536. Tuscaloosa 79,149. Hoover 64,265. Dothan 58,998. Decatur 53,941. Auburn 45,389. Gadsden 37,966.

Business **Gross State Product, 2001:** $121.49 bil. (25th). **Leading Sectors of GSP (2001):** Services 18.10%; Manufacturing 17.80%; Government 15.88%. ***Fortune* 500 Companies (2003):** 6: Saks, Caremark Rx, Healthsouth, Regions Financial, Southtrust Corp., Amsouth Bancorp.

Famous natives Hank Aaron, baseball player. Tallulah Bankhead, actress. William B. Bankhead, politician. Hugo L. Black, jurist. Wernher von Braun (b. Germany), rocket scientist. Nat "King" Cole, singer. Red Eagle (William Weatherfield), Creek leader. W.C. Handy, musician. Frank M. Johnson, Jr., jurist. Helen Keller, author. Coretta Scott (Mrs. Martin Luther) King, reformer. Harper Lee, author. Joe Louis, boxer. Jesse Owens, runner. Leroy Robert "Satchell" Paige, baseball player. Walker Percy, author. George Wallace, politician. Hank Williams, singer.

Noteworthy places Alabama Deep Sea Fishing Rodeo, Dauphin Island. Alabama Space and Rocket Center, U.S. Space Camp, Huntsville. Battleship USS *Alabama*, Mobile. Birmingham Museum of Art. First White House of the Confederacy, Montgomery. Horseshoe Bend Natl. Military Park. Mound State Monument Archaeological Museum, Moundville. Museum of Natural History, Univ. Alabama, Tuscaloosa. Point Clear (resort). Russell Cave Natl. Monument. Tuskegee Institute.

Memorable events Humans first inhabit Russell Cave c. 6000 B.C. Temple Mound culture flourishes around Moundville, A.D. 1200–1500. First Europeans in Mobile Bay 1519. Hernando de Soto's battle with Tuscaloosa possibly bloodiest encounter ever between Europeans and Native Americans in U.S. 1540. Spanish at Mobile Bay 1599. Pierre Le Moyne, sieur d'Iberville, establishes first permanent colony at Mobile 1711. Treaty of Paris gives Mobile to Britain 1763. U.S. control recognized 1783. Chickasaws, Choctaws, and Cherokees cede lands to U.S. 1805. First Baptist Church established 1808. Gen. Andrew Jackson defeats Creek Indian Confederacy at Horseshoe Bend 1814. Cotton principal cash crop 1820's. Beginning of coal and iron mining and steel manufacturing 1850's. Alabama secedes from Union; first capital of Confederate States of America at Montgomery 1861. Battle of Mobile Bay 1864. Readmitted to Union 1868. Booker T. Washington founds Tuskegee Institute 1881. Destruction of cotton crops by boll weevils leads to diversification of rural economy 1915. Tennessee Valley Authority enacted by Congress 1933. Montgomery bus boycott 1955. Freedom march from Selma to Montgomery 1965.

Tourist information (800) ALABAMA. **www.alabama.gov.**

▶ALASKA

One-fifth the size of the entire lower 48 states, Alaska is a vast, geographically varied wilderness. The coast from the Bering Sea to the Arctic was originally inhabited by Eskimos and Aleuts, while inland and to the south were Athapascans and people of the Northwest Indian culture. Russian fur traders in the 1740's were the first Europeans to recognize the region's commercial potential, and the Russian Orthodox faith is still found in the old territorial capital of Sitka (New Archangel).

Russia sold Alaska to the United States in 1867 for $7.2 million—2 cents an acre—and Alaska experienced successive booms in furs, fishing and whaling, and gold. Discovery of oil on the North Slope near Prudhoe Bay in 1968 and completion of an 800-mile trans-Alaska pipeline a decade later made oil production the centerpiece of the state's economy in the 1980's. Although the population has grown by more than 10 percent during the 1990's, the number of people per square mile remains below 1.5. In recent years, tourism based on the state's extraordinary beauty, has grown substantially and now many Alaskans oppose proposed oil exploration at the Arctic National

Population Density of U.S. States, 1980–2000

State	Population per square mile 1980	1990	2000
U.S. Total	64.1	70.4	79.6
Alabama	76.7	79.6	87.6
Alaska	0.7	1.0	1.1
Arizona	23.9	32.3	45.2
Arkansas	43.9	45.1	51.3
California	151.7	191.0	217.2
Colorado	27.9	31.8	41.5
Connecticut	641.4	678.5	702.9
Delaware	304.0	340.8	401.1
District of Columbia	10,397.9	9,884.4	9,316.4
Florida	180.7	239.9	296.4
Georgia	94.3	111.8	141.4
Hawaii	150.2	172.5	188.6
Idaho	11.4	12.2	15.6
Illinois	205.6	205.6	223.4
Indiana	153.1	154.6	169.5
Iowa	52.1	49.7	52.4
Kansas	28.9	30.3	32.9
Kentucky	92.1	92.8	101.7
Louisiana	96.5	96.9	102.6
Maine	36.5	39.8	41.3
Maryland	431.4	489.1	541.9
Massachusetts	732.0	767.6	809.8
Michigan	163.0	163.6	175.0
Minnesota	51.2	55.0	61.8
Mississippi	53.7	54.9	60.6
Missouri	71.4	74.3	81.2
Montana	5.4	5.5	6.2
Nebraska	20.4	20.5	22.3
Nevada	7.3	10.9	18.2
New Hampshire	102.6	123.7	137.8
New Jersey	992.7	1,044.3	1,134.4
New Mexico	10.7	12.5	15.0
New York	371.8	381.0	401.9
North Carolina	120.7	136.1	165.2
North Dakota	9.5	9.3	9.3
Ohio	263.7	264.9	277.3
Oklahoma	44.1	45.8	50.3
Oregon	27.4	29.6	35.6
Pennsylvania	264.7	265.1	274.0
Rhode Island	906.4	960.3	1,003.2
South Carolina	103.6	115.8	133.2
South Dakota	9.1	9.2	9.9
Tennessee	111.4	118.3	138.0
Texas	54.3	64.9	79.6
Utah	17.8	21.0	27.2
Vermont	55.3	60.8	65.8
Virginia	135.0	156.3	178.8
Washington	62.1	73.1	88.6
West Virginia	81.0	74.5	75.1
Wisconsin	86.6	90.1	98.8
Wyoming	4.8	4.7	5.1

Note: Persons per square mile for all years calculated on the basis of land area data from the 1990 census.
Source: U.S. Bureau of the Census, 2002. www.census.gov

Wildlife Refuge. The memory of the *Exxon Valdez* oil spill into Prince William Sound in 1989 has had a powerful effect.

Name From Aleut *alaska* and Eskimo *alakshak*, both meaning "mainland." **Nickname** "The Last Frontier." **Capital** Juneau. **Entered union** Jan. 3, 1959 (49th). **Motto** "North to the future."

Emblems **Bird** Willow ptarmigan. **Fish** King salmon. **Flower** Forget-me-not. **Gem** Jade. **Marine mammal** Bowhead whale. **Mineral** Gold. **Song** "Alaska's Flag." **Sport** Mushing (dog-team racing). **Tree** Sitka spruce.

Land **Total area** 663,267 sq. mi (1st), incl. 91,316 sq. mi. inland water. **Borders** Arctic Ocean (Chukchi Sea, Beaufort Sea), Yukon, British Columbia, Pacific Ocean, Bering Strait. **Rivers** Colville, Porcupine, Noatak, Yukon, Susitna, Copper, Kobuk, Koyukuk, Kuskokwim, Tanana. **Mountains** Alaska Range (Mt. McKinley 20,320 ft., highest in North America), Aleutian Range, Brooks Range, Kuskokwim, St. Elias. **Other notable features** Aleutian Islands, Alexander Archipelago, Kodiak Island, Nunivak Island, Point Barrow (71°23'N), Pribilof Islands, Seward Peninsula, St. Lawrence Island.

Elected officials Gov. Frank Murkowski (R, term exp. 2006). Lt. Gov. Loren Leman (R). Atty. Gen. Gregg D. Renkes (R)

People (July, 2002 est.) 643,786 (47th). Race/Hispanic Origin (2000 Census): White 69.3%. Black 3.5%. Indian 15.6%. Asian 4.0%. Pacific Islander 0.5%. Other 1.6%. Two or more races 5.4%. Hispanic 4.1%.

Cities (2002) Anchorage 268,983. Fairbanks 30,780. Juneau 30,751. Sitka 8,835. Ketchikan 7,922. Kenai 6,942. Kodiak 6,334. Bethel 5,471. Wasilla 5,469. Barrow 4,581.

Business **Gross State Product, 2001:** $28.58 bil. (45th). **Leading Sectors of GSP (2001):** Mining 19.56%; Government 19.50%; Oil and gas extraction 17.12%. ***Fortune* 500 Companies (2003):** 0.

Famous natives Aleksandr Baranov (b. Russia), first governor of Russian America. Vitus Bering (b. Denmark), explorer. Ernest Gruening (b. N.Y.), governor. Carl Ben Eielson, bush pilot. Walter Hickel (b. Kans.), governor.

Noteworthy places Aniakchak Natl. Monument. Bering Land Bridge Natl. Preserve. Cape Krusenstern Natl. Monument. Denali Natl. Park (formerly Mt. McKinley Natl. Park). Gates of the Arctic Natl. Park. Glacier Bay Natl. Park. Katmai Natl. Park (Valley of Ten Thousand Smokes). Kenai Fjords Natl. Park. Klondike Gold Rush Natl. Hist. Park. Kobuk Valley Natl. Park. Lake Clark Natl. Park. Little Diomede Island—2.5 mi. from Big Diomede Island (Russia). Sitka Natl. Hist. Park. St. Michael's Cathedral, Sitka. Wrangell–St. Elias Natl. Park.

Memorable events Earliest migration from Asia to Americas across Bering Sea land bridge, c. 15,000 years ago. Alaska inhabited by Tlingits, Tinnehs, Aleuts, and Eskimos. Peter the Great sponsors expedition to find land opposite Siberia 1728. Bering expedition lands near Mt. Elias; begins Pacific Northwest fur trade with Europe and Asia 1741. Russians establish first European settlement at Three Saints Bay 1784. Russian-American Company chartered 1799. Baranov's massacre of Tlingits at Sitka 1802. Gold discovered at Stikine Creek (1861), Juneau (1880), Fortymile Creek (1886), Nome (1898), Fairbanks (1903). Russians sell Alaska to U.S. for $7.2 million 1867. First salmon cannery established 1878. Japanese occupy Agattu, Attu, and Kiska islands 1942–43. Alaskans vote for statehood 1946. Statehood 1959. Earthquake destroys Anchorage, Northwest Panhandle, and Cook Inlet; tsunami wipes out Valdez; coast sinks 32 ft. at Kodiak and Seward and rises 16 ft. at Cordova 1964. Oil discovered on North Slope 1968. Alaska Native Claims Settlement Act gives Alaska's Native Americans 44 million acres for native landholdings 1971. Completion of 789-mi. pipeline to Valdez 1977. Population growth of 32.8% highest in U.S. 1980–86. *Exxon Valdez* spills 10 million gallons of oil into Prince William Sound off Valdez — worst oil spill in U.S. history 1989.

Tourist information (907) 929-2200. **www.state.ak.us.**

▶ARIZONA

The Hopi village of Oraibi is the oldest continuously inhabited town in the United States, and today vast tracts of Arizona are reserved for Apaches, Hopis, Navajos, Papagos and other Native Americans. Last of the 48 conterminous states admitted to the union, Arizona was sparsely settled until the advent of air conditioning in the postwar years made it habitable and a popular destination for retirees. More recently, there has been a boom in manufacturing and light industry, and in the last decade, population growth has been among the highest in the nation. Mexican-Americans are an important political force.

As in most southwestern states, water scarcity is a major problem. Arizona draws 2.8 million acre-feet of water from the Colorado River, whose water it shares with 5 other states and Mexico.

Name Probably from the Pima or Papago for "place of small springs." **Nickname** Grand Canyon State. **Capital** Phoenix. **Entered union** Feb. 14, 1912 (48th). **Motto** *Ditat deus* (God enriches).

Emblems **Bird** Cactus wren. **Flower** Blossom of the saguaro cactus. **Gemstone** Turquoise. **Official neck wear** Bolo tie. **Songs** "Arizona March Song," "Arizona." **Tree** Palo verde.

Land **Total area** 113,998 sq. mi (6th), incl. 364 sq. mi. inland water. **Borders** Utah, Colo., N.Mex., Sonora, Baja California Norte, Calif., Nev. **Rivers** Colorado, Gila, Little Colorado, Salt, Zuni. **Lakes** Havasu, Mead, Mohave, Powell, Roosevelt, San Carlos. **Mountains** Black, Gila, Hualpai, Mohawk, San Francisco Peaks (Humphreys Peak 12,633 ft.). **Other notable features** Grand Canyon, Kaibab Plateau, Painted and Sonoran Deserts, Petrified Forest.

Elected officials Gov. Janet Napolitano (D, term exp. 2006). Atty. Gen. Terry Goddard (D). Sec. State Janice Brewer (R).

People (July, 2002 est.) 5,456,453 (19th). Race/Hispanic Origin (2000 Census): White 75.5%. Black 3.1%. Indian 5.0%. Asian 1.8%. Pacific Islander 0.1%. Other 11.6%. Two or more races 2.9%. Hispanic 25.3%.

Cities (2002) Phoenix 1,371,960. Tucson 503,151. Mesa 426,841. Glendale 230,564. Scottsdale 215,779. Chandler 202,016. Tempe 159,508. Gilbert 135,005. Peoria 123,239. Yuma 80,358.

Business **Gross State Product, 2001:** $160.69 bil. (23rd). **Leading Sectors of GSP (2001):** Services 21.46%; Finance, insurance, and real estate 19.53%; Manufacturing 13.51%. ***Fortune* 500 Companies (2003):** 3: Avnet, Allied Waste Industries, Phelps Dodge.

Famous natives Bruce Babbitt, politician. Cesar Chavez, labor leader. Cochise, Apache chief. Andrew Ellicott Douglass (b. Vt.), dendrochronologist. Wyatt Earp (b. Ill.), lawman. Barry Goldwater, politician. Goyathlay (Geronimo), Apache chieftain. Carl T. Hayden, congressman. Eusebio Kino (b. Italy), missionary. Sandra Day O'Connor, ju-

rist. William H. Rehnquist, jurist. Linda Ronstadt, singer. Morris Udall, politician.
Noteworthy Places Canyon de Chelly Natl. Monument. Casa Grande Ruins Natl. Monument. Chiricahua Natl. Monument. Ft. Bowie. Grand Canyon Natl. Park. Heard Museum, Phoenix. London Bridge, Lake Havasu City. Montezuma Castle Natl. Monument. Navajo Natl. Monument. Organ Pipe Cactus Natl. Monument. Painted Desert. Petrified Forest Natl. Park. Pipe Spring Natl. Monument. Saguaro Natl. Monument. Slot canyons, Upper and Lower Antelope Canyons, near Page. Sunset Crater Natl. Monument. Taliesin West, near Scottsdale. Tonto Natl. Monument. Tumacacori Natl. Monument. Tuzigoot Natl. Monument. Walnut Canyon Natl. Monument. Wupatki Natl. Monument.
Memorable events Apaches and Navajos absorb Pueblos c. A.D. 1000. Alvar Núñez Cabeza de Vaca, first Spanish explorer 1536. Marcos de Niza 1539. Ruled as part of New Spain 1598–1821. First missionaries among Hopis 1638. Tubac first European settlement 1752. Tucson founded 1776. Apaches wipe out settlements under Mexican control, except Tucson 1821. Northern part ceded to U.S. following Mexican War 1848. Area south of Gila River to U.S. after Gadsden Purchase 1853. Territory 1863. Southern Pacific Railroad reaches Tucson 1880. Apaches subjugated 1886. Congress refuses to grant statehood 1906. Roosevelt Dam and Reservoir built on Salt River 1911. Native Americans given right to vote 1948. Glen Canyon Dam built on Colorado River 1964. Population growth of 24.3 percent is second highest in U.S., 1990–97.
Tourist information (888) 520-3434. **www.az.gov.**

▶ARKANSAS

First inhabited by bluff dwellers 10,000 years ago, the Boston and Ouachita mountains of western Arkansas are the only mountains between the Appalachians and the Rockies. By the time of the Hernando De Soto expedition of 1541, Arkansas was inhabited by a variety of peoples: the agrarian Quapaws to the south, the Caddo to the west and south, the Osage to the north, and the Chickasaw and Choctaw in the northeast. The Arkansas Post, the first permanent settlement in the Mississippi Valley, became the pillar of the French claim to the region that became the Louisiana Purchase.

Not fully part of the deep south, and cut off geographically from the Midwest, Arkansas has developed slowly. Although cotton was a mainstay of the economy and Arkansas joined the Confederacy during the Civil War, it was the first southern state to have integrated public colleges after World War II, a fact overshadowed by Gov. Orville Faubus's resistance to the integration of the Little Rock public schools. In recent years, Arkansas has attracted manufacturing and industry, but has one of the highest rural populations and ranks low in services, income, and education attainment.

Name From term for Quapaw tribe given by other Indians. **Nickname** Land of Opportunity. **Capital** Little Rock. **Entered union** June 15, 1836 (25th). **Motto** *Regnat populus* (Let the people rule).
Emblems **Bird** Mockingbird. **Flower** Apple blossom. **Gem** Diamond. **Song** "Arkansas." **Tree** Pine.
Land **Total area** 53,179 sq. mi (29th), incl. 1,110 sq. mi. inland water. **Borders** Mo., Tenn, Miss., La., Tex., Okla. **Rivers** Arkansas, Mississippi, Ouachita, Red, St. Francis, White. **Lakes** Beaver, Bull Shoals, Chicot, Dardanelle, Greers Ferry, Greeson, Norfolk, Ouachita. **Other notable features** Ozark Mts.
Elected officials Gov. Mike Huckabee (R, term exp. 2006). Lt. Gov. Winthrop P. Rockefeller (R). Sec. State Charlie Daniels (D). Atty. Gen. Mike Beebe (D).
People (July, 2002 est.) 2,710,079 (33rd). Race/Hispanic Origin (2000 Census): White 80.0%. Black 15.7%. Indian 0.7%. Asian 0.8%. Pacific Islander 0.1%. Other 1.3%. Two or more races 1.3%. Hispanic 3.2%.
Cities (2002) Little Rock 184,055. Fort Smith 81,519. Fayetteville 60,732. North Little Rock 60,007. Jonesboro 56,888. Pine Bluff 54,169. Springdale 50,941. Conway 45,915. Rogers 41,545. Hot Springs 36,356.
Business **Gross State Product, 2001:** $67.91 bil. (34th). **Leading Sectors of GSP (2001):** Manufacturing 19.34%; Services 16.95%; Government 13.07%. ***Fortune* 500 Companies (2003):** 5: Wal-Mart Stores, Tyson Foods, Dillard's, Alltel, Murphy Oil.
Famous natives Maya Angelou, author. Linda Bloodworth-Thomason, television producer/director. Glen Campbell, singer. Hattie W. Caraway, first woman senator. Johnny Cash, singer. Eldridge Cleaver, author. Bill Clinton, U.S. president. William Fulbright (b. Mo.), politician. Alan Ladd, actor. Douglas MacArthur, general. Dick Powell, actor. Brooks Robinson, baseball player. Winthrop Rockefeller (b. N.Y.), politician/philanthropist. Edward Durrell Stone, architect. C. Vann Woodward, historian.
Noteworthy places Arkansas Post Natl. Monument (first permanent French settlement in lower Mississippi Valley). Buffalo Natl. River. Crater of Diamonds State Park, Murfreesboro. Eureka Springs. Ft. Smith Natl. Hist. Site. Hot Springs Natl. Park. Pea Ridge Natl. Military Park.
Memorable Events Bluff-dwellers present c. A.D. 500, followed by mound-building cultures. Hernando de Soto explores for Spain 1541. Jacques Marquette and Louis Jolliet explore for France 1673. René-Robert de La Salle meets Quapaws 1682. Henri de Tonti founds Arkansas Post on Arkansas River 1686. Ceded from France to Spain 1782; to France 1800; to U.S. 1803. Territory 1819. Admitted to Union as slave state, under terms of 1820 Missouri Compromise, 1836. Secedes from Union 1861. Fall of Little Rock to Union army 1863. Readmitted to Union 1868. Bauxite discovered 1887. Oil production begins 1920's. Federal troops called to Little Rock to ensure high school desegregation 1957. Winthrop Rockefeller (b. N.Y.) first Republican governor since Reconstruction 1966. McClellan-Kerr Arkansas River Navigation System links Arkansas and Oklahoma to Mississippi River system 1971. Governor Bill Clinton Elected U.S. President 1992.
Tourist information (800) NATURAL. **www.arkansas.com.**

▶CALIFORNIA

Before the arrival of Europeans, no area of comparable size in North America was home to a greater variety of languages and cultures than what is now California, and today the state's population is more diverse than that of any other. In 2001, non-Hispanic whites became a minority of California's population; by 2040, demographers project that the majority of Californians will be Hispanic.

The largest state by population since the 1960's, California gained seven Congressional representatives in the 1990 Census redistricting, and one more in 2000. By some estimates, California is the sixth largest economic power in the world.

Despite these attractions, and the state's rugged terrain and dramatic vistas, California has problems. The state's position as a leader in agriculture masks an alarming lack of water. It already draws off 4.4 million acre-feet annually from the Colorado River, mostly for irrigating the Imperial Valley—a desert when settlers crossed it 150 years ago. Almost the entire flow of the San Joaquin River is similarly diverted for the Central Valley. This inefficient use of water leaves less and less for consumption by people, whose numbers have leaped from 15 million in 1960 to over 32 million today.

Of more immediate concern is the threat of earthquakes. California has already suffered eight major earthquakes in this century. The 1906 quake destroyed San Francisco, and the Loma Prieta earthquake on October 17, 1989—one of the most powerful quakes in U.S. history—killed 67 people, left 48,000 people homeless and resulted in $10 billion of property damage. Like surfers waiting for the perfect wave, scientists are still bracing for "the big one."

Name Probably from mythical island in García Ordoñez de Montalvo's 16th-century romance, *The Deeds of Esplandián*. **Nickname** Golden State. **Capital** Sacramento. **Entered union** Sept. 9, 1850 (31st). **Motto** "Eureka" (I have found it).

Emblems **Animal** California grizzly bear (extinct). **Bird** California valley quail. **Fish** California golden trout. **Flower** Golden poppy. **Fossil** California saber-toothed cat. **Gemstone** Benitoite. **Insect** California dog-face butterfly. **Marine mammal** California gray whale. **Mineral** Gold. **Reptile** California desert tortoise. **Rock** Serpentine. **Song** "I Love You, California." **Tree** California redwood.

Land **Total area** 163,696 sq. mi (3rd), incl. 7,736 sq. mi. inland water. **Borders** Oreg., Nev., Ariz., Baja California Norte, Pacific Ocean. **Rivers** American, Colorado, Colorado River Aqueduct, Eel, Friant-Kern Canal, Klamath, Russian, Sacramento, Salinas, San Joaquin. **Lakes** Clear, Goose, Honey, Mono, Owens, Salton Sea, Shasta, Tahoe. **Mountains** Coast Ranges, Klamath, Lassen Peak, Sierra Nevada (Mt. Whitney 14,494 ft.). **Other notable features** Catalina Islands, Death Valley (282 ft. below sea level), San Francisco Bay, San Joaquin Valley.

Elected officials Gov. Arnold Schwarzenegger (R term exp. 2006). Lt. Gov. Cruz Bustamante (D) Sec. State Kevin Shelley (D). Atty. Gen. Bill Lockyer (D).

People (July, 2002 est.) 35,116,033 (1st). Race/Hispanic Origin (2000 Census): White 59.5%. Black 6.7%. Indian 1.0%. Asian 10.9%. Pacific Islander 0.3%. Other 16.8%. Hispanic 32.4%.

Cities (2002) Los Angeles 3,798,981. San Diego 1,259,532. San Jose 900,443. San Francisco 764,049. Long Beach 472,412. Fresno 445,227. Sacramento 435,245. Oakland 402,777. Santa Ana 343,413. Anaheim 332,642.

Business Gross State Product, 2001: $1,359.27 bil. (1st). **Leading Sectors of GSP (2001):** Services 23.99%; Finance, insurance, and real estate 23.36%; Real estate 16.21%. ***Fortune* 500 Companies (2003):** 56: including ChevronTexaco, Hewlett-Packard, McKesson, Safeway, Wells Fargo, Intel, Walt Disney, Ingram Micro, PG&E Corp., Cisco Systems, Solectron, Sun Microsystems, Occidental Petroleum, Gap, Northrop Grumman, Wellpoint Health Networks, Edison International, Tenet Healthcare, Pacificare Health Systems, Oracle, Applied Materials, Gateway, Unocal, Apple Computer, Charles Schwab, Dole Food, Levi Strauss.

Famous natives Ansel Adams, photographer. Dave Brubeck, musician. Luther Burbank (b. Mass.), horticulturist. John Cage, composer. Joe DiMaggio, baseball player. Robert Frost, poet. Ernest and Julio Gallo (b. Italy), vintners. Pancho Gonzales, tennis player. Samuel Ichiye Hayakawa, politician/educator. William Randolph Hearst, publisher. Steve Jobs, computer scientist. Billie Jean King, tennis player. Allen Lockheed, aviator. Jack London, author. Paul Masson (b. France), vintner. Marilyn Monroe, actress. John Muir (b. Scotland), naturalist. Richard M. Nixon, U.S. president. John Northrop, aviator. Adlai Stevenson, politician. John Steinbeck, author. Levi Strauss (b. Germany), clothier. Edward Teller (b. Hungary), nuclear physicist. Shirley Temple, actress. Earl Warren, politician/jurist.

Noteworthy places Big Sur, Monterey. Cabrillo Natl. Monument. California Academy of Sciences, San Francisco. California Palace of the Legion of Honor, San Francisco. Channel Islands Natl. Park. Devils Postpile Natl. Monument. Death Valley Natl. Monument. Disneyland. Fine Arts Museum of San Francisco. Fishermen's Wharf, San Francisco. Hollywood. Huntington Library and Botanical Gardens, San Marino. J. Paul Getty Museum, Malibu. Joshua Tree Natl. Monument. Kings Canyon Natl. Park. Lassen Volcanic Natl. Park. Lava Beds Natl. Monument. Los Angeles Co. Museum of Art. Muir Woods Natl. Monument. Mt. Palomar Observatory. Natl. Maritime Museum, San Francisco. Natural History Museum, Los Angeles. Natural History Museum of San Diego. Norton Simon Museum of Art at Pasadena. Pinnacles Natl. Monument. Redwood Natl. Park. Rosicrucian Egyptian Museum, San José. San Diego Museum of Art. San Diego Museum of Man. San Diego Zoo. San Francisco Museum of Modern Art. Sequoia Natl. Park. Southwest Museum (Casa de Adobe), Los Angeles. Yosemite Natl. Park.

Memorable events João Rodrigues Cabrilho lands at San Diego Bay 1542. Francis Drake lands north of San Francisco Bay 1579. Junípero Serra founds missions at San Diego (1769), Monterey (1770), San Luis Obispo (1772), and San Juan Capistrano (1776). California declares allegiance to independent Mexico 1821. First wagon train from Missouri 1841. Gold discovered north of Los Angeles 1842. California declares itself independent republic 1846. Gold found at John Sutter's mill; nine days later, by Treaty of Guadalupe Hidalgo, Mexico cedes California to U.S. 1848. Announcement of gold discovery brings 80,000 'Forty-niners. Gold rush peaks 1852. Transcontinental telegraph completed 1861. Transcontinental railway completed 1869. U.S. Congress enacts Chinese Exclusion Act, prohibiting immigration of Chinese laborers 1882, 1892, and 1902; Act repealed 1943. San Francisco earthquake kills 452, destroys 28,000 buildings 1906. Webb Alien Land Law prohibits Japanese from holding land 1913. Los Angeles has one car for every three people, twice national average, 1925. Dust Bowl immigrants 1930. Hollywood produces bulk of movies for U.S. theaters, which number more than banks 1940. Most populous state 1963. Proposition 13 limits property tax, 1978. Loma Prieta earthquake registers 7.1 on Richter scale — second most powerful in U.S. history; 67 dead, 48,000 homeless, and $10 billion in property damage, 1989. Riots in Los Angeles kill 60 and cause $1 billion in damage, 1992.

Tourist information (800) TO-CALIF. **www.state.ca.us.**

▶COLORADO

The native peoples of Colorado were the Plains Indians (Arapahoe and Cheyenne) to the east and Great Basin Indians (Utes) to the west. This pre-Columbian division of the land is reflected today in Colorado's economy, which is a mix of agriculture and technology in the east and mining and ski tourism in the mountains. During the oil price shocks of the 1970's, shale-oil production on the Western Slope created a boom comparable to Colorado's silver and lead boom in the late 19th century. During the 1990's, strong job growth has attracted many young people: the population has increased by more than 18 percent, while the percentage of people over 65 has fallen to 10 percent, one of the lowest in the nation. While a state of great natural beauty, it must cope with a high altitude that almost doubles the effect of auto emissions. Economic development means in large part resource extraction and requires more and more water, whose limited supply poses a great question for the future.

Name For Spanish for the color red. **Nickname** Centennial State. **Capital** Denver. **Entered union** Aug. 1, 1876 (38th). **Motto** *Nil sine numine* (Nothing without providence).

Emblems **Animal** Rocky Mountain bighorn sheep. **Bird** Lark bunting. **Flower** Rocky Mountain Columbine. **Gem** Aquamarine. **Song** "Where the Columbines Grow." **Tree** Colorado blue spruce.

Land **Total area** 104,094 sq. mi (8th), incl. 376 sq. mi. inland water. **Borders** Wyo., Nebr., Kans., N.Mex., Ariz., Utah. **Rivers** Arkansas, Colorado, Green, Platte, Rio Grande. **Lakes** Blue Mesa, Dillon, Granby. **Mountains** Front Range, Laramie, Sangre de Cristo, San Juan, Sawatch Range (Mt. Elbert 14,443 ft.).

Elected officials Gov. Bill Owens (R, term exp. 2006). Lt. Gov. Jane Norton (R). Sec. State Donetta Davidson (R). Atty. Gen. Ken Salazar (D).

People (July, 2002 est.) 4,506,542 (22nd). Race/Hispanic Origin (2000 Census): White 82.8%. Black 3.8%. Indian 1.0%. Asian 2.2%. Pacific Islander 0.1%. Other 7.2%. Two or more races 2.8%. Hispanic 17.1%.

Cities (2002) Denver 560,415. Colorado Springs 371,182. Aurora 286,028. Lakewood 143,754. Fort Collins 124,665. Westminster 103,599. Pueblo 103,411. Arvada 102,190. Centennial 99,447. Boulder 94,167.

Business **Gross State Product, 2001:** $173.77 bil. (21st). **Leading Sectors of GSP (2001):** Services 24.09%; Finance, insurance, and real estate 18.31%; Government 11.82%. ***Fortune* 500 Companies (2003):** 6: Qwest Communications, First Data, Echostar Communications, Ball, Adolph Coors, Level 3 Communications

Famous natives Charlie Bent (b. Va.), trapper. "Unsinkable" Molly Brown, *Titanic* survivor. Scott Carpenter, astronaut. Lon Chaney, actor. Jack Dempsey, boxer. Mamie Eisenhower, first lady. Douglas Fairbanks, actor. Scott Hamilton, ice skater. Anne Parrish, novelist. Lowell Thomas, journalist. Byron R. White, jurist.

Noteworthy Places Black Canyon of the Gunnison National Park. Buffalo Bill grave site, Evergreen. Central City Opera House. Colorado Springs Fine Arts Center. Denver Art Museum. Denver Mint. Denver Museum of Natural History. Dinosaur Natl. Monument. Florissant Fossil Beds Natl. Monument. Garden of the Gods, Colorado Springs. Great Sand Dunes Natl. Monument. Hovenweep Natl. Monument. Mesa Verde Natl. Park. Molly Brown House, Denver. Pikes Peak. Red Rocks Amphitheater. Rocky Mountain Natl. Park, Aspen. Rocky Mountain Natl. Park. U.S. Air Force Academy, Colorado Springs. U.S. Olympic Headquarters, Colorado Springs. Yucca House Natl. Monument.

Memorable events Pueblos build cliff dwellings near Mesa Verde through 1200's. Arapahos and Cheyennes settle area after 13th century. France abandons claims 1763. Juan de Uribarri explores area 1786. Spain restores area to France 1801. To United States as part of Louisiana Purchase 1803. Zebulon Pike explores for United States 1806. Kit Carson and other scouts explore and trade with Native Americans 1810's–20's. Native Americans form alliance at Brent's Fork 1840. John Frémont's explorations 1842–53. Present territorial limits after Mexican War 1848. First permanent settlement at San Luis 1851. Gold found west of Denver—"Pikes Peak or Bust"—1858. Mineral springs bring first tourists 1861. Homestead Act encourages farming 1862. U.S. Army kills 400 Cheyenne at Sand Creek Massacre 1864. Utes and Cheyennes fight white settlement through 1870's. John Wesley Powell and nine others navigate Colorado River from the Green River branch in Wyoming to the end of Grand Canyon in Arizona 1869. Railroad link to Denver 1870. Silver and lead discoveries 1875. Uranium discovered near Grand Junction 1946. U.S. Air Force Academy founded Denver 1954; to Colorado Springs 1958. Shale oil boom on Western Slope 1974 and 1979. Accumulation of nuclear waste threatens suspension of operations at Rocky Flats 1988.

Tourist information (800) COLORADO. **www.colorado.com.**

▶CONNECTICUT

Called the "arsenal of the nation" during the Revolution, Connecticut remained in modern times the leader among the 50 states in defense-contract dollars per capita. In recent years, this has caused a serious dislocation in the economy as the nation downsizes its military capabilities. Still, as home to over a dozen *Fortune* 500 companies(including several major insurance companies), and with easy access to New York City, Connecticut remains the state with the highest per capita income in the country.

Severe budget deficits in 1991 forced passage of a state income tax and helped to reveal the disparities in wealth between the very rich suburbs and the decaying industrial cities such as Bridgeport. As the economy is being retooled, population has actually declined slightly.

Name From Mahican word meaning "beside the long tidal river." **Nicknames** Constitution State, Nutmeg State. **Capital** Hartford. **Entered union** Jan. 9, 1788 (5th). **Motto** *Qui transtulit sustinet* (He who transplanted still sustains).

Emblems **Animal** Sperm whale. **Bird** American robin. **Flower** Mountain laurel. **Hero** Nathan Hale. **Insect** European praying mantis. **Mineral** Garnet. **Ship** USS *Nautilus*. **Song** "Yankee Doodle." **Tree** White oak.

Land **Total area** 5,543 sq. mi (48th), incl. 699 sq. mi. inland water **Borders** Mass., R.I., Long Island Sound, N.Y. **Rivers** Connecticut, Housatonic, Mianus, Naugatuck, Thames. **Lakes** Bantam, Barkhamstead, Candlewood, Waramaug. **Other notable features** Berkshire Hills, Long Island Sound.

Elected officials Gov. John G. Rowland (R, term exp. 2003). Lt. Gov. M. Jodi Rell (R). Sec. State Susan Bysiewicz (D). Atty. Gen. Richard Blumenthal (D).

People (July, 2002 est.) 3,460,503 (29th). Race/Hispanic Origin (2000 Census): White 81.6%. Black 9.1%. Indian 0.3%. Asian 2.4%. Other 4.3%. Two or more races 2.2%. Hispanic 9.4%.
Cities (2002) Bridgeport 140,104. Hartford 124,558. New Haven 124,176. Stamford 119,850. Waterbury 107,883. Norwalk 84,127. Danbury 76,917. New Britain 71,589. Bristol 60,541. Meriden 58,675.
Business **Gross State Product, 2001:** $166.17 bil. (22nd). **Leading Sectors of GSP (2001):** Finance, insurance, and real estate 30.97%; Services 21.46%; Real estate 15.82%. ***Fortune* 500 Companies (2003):** 13: General Electric, United Technologies, International Paper, Aetna, Xerox, Hartford Financial Services, Northeast Utilities, Praxair, Pitney Bowes, Oxford Health Plans, Meadwestvaco, Emcor Group, Asbury Automotive Group.
Famous natives Benedict Arnold, traitor. P.T. Barnum, showman. Lyman Beecher, theologian. John Brown, abolitionist. Samuel Colt, inventor. Jonathan Edwards, theologian. Charles Goodyear, inventor. Nathan Hale, patriot. Katharine Hepburn, actress. Charles Ives, composer. J.P. Morgan, financier. Ralph Nader, consumer advocate. Frederick Law Olmsted, landscape architect. Harriet Beecher Stowe, author. John Trumbell, artist. Noah Webster, lexicographer. Eli Whitney, inventor.
Noteworthy places Charles Ives Center, Danbury. Eugene O'Neill Memorial Theater Center, Waterford. Gilette Castle. Housatonic State Park. Mark Twain House, Hartford. Mystic Marinelife Aquarium. Mystic Seaport. Norwalk Maritime Center. U.S. Coast Guard Academy. USS *Nautilus*, New London. Wadsworth Atheneum, Hartford. Whitney Museum of Modern Art, Stamford. Yale Center for British Art, New Haven. Yale University, New Haven.
Memorable events Adriaen Block claims for Dutch 1614. First English settlement in Windsor 1633. Royal charter of 1662 hidden in Charter Oak 1687. *Hartford Courant*, oldest continuously published newspaper in U.S., first published 1764. Samuel Colt develops six-shooter 1835. Horace Wells uses first anesthesia 1844. Elias Howe invents sewing machine 1845. U.S. Coast Guard Academy founded New London 1876. First woman governor elected in her own right, Ella T. Grasso, 1974.
Tourist information (800) CT-BOUND. **www.state.ct.us.**

▶DELAWARE

The du Pont family has enjoyed a political and economic prominence in Delaware unmatched in the history of the other 49 states. Seven generations ago E.I. du Pont de Nemours and Co. was founded as a gunpowder mill, then grew into a monopoly, and in the wake of World War I, diversified into today's giant, with interests in banking, media, and real estate. Only half the size of Los Angeles County, Delaware was called the corporate state by Ralph Nader's "raiders" in 1973. Its liberal incorporation laws have led more than half the Fortune 500 companies to incorporate there. (A total of more than 170,000 corporations are incorporated in Delaware). It was one of the few states to prosper even during the recessions of the early 1980's and early 1990's.

Name For Thomas West, Lord De La Warre, colonial governor of Virginia. **Nicknames** First State, Diamond State. **Capital** Dover. **Entered union** Dec. 7, 1787 (1st). **Motto** "Liberty and Independence."
Emblems **Bird** Blue hen chicken. **Fish** Weakfish. **Flower** Peach blossom. **Insect** Ladybug. **Rock** Sillimanite. **Song** "Our Delaware." **Tree** American holly.
Land **Total area** 2,489 sq. mi (49th), incl. 536 sq. mi. inland water. **Borders** Pa., N.J., Atlantic Ocean, Md. **Rivers** Chesapeake & Delaware Canal, Delaware, Nanticoke.
Elected officials Gov. Ruth Ann Minner (D, term exp. 2005). Lt. Gov. John Carney (D). Sec. State Harriet Smith Windsor (D). Atty. Gen. M. Jane Brady (R).
People (July, 2002 est.) 807,385 (45th). Race/Hispanic Origin (2000 Census): White 74.6%. Black 19.2%. Indian 0.3%. Asian 2.1%. Other 2.0%. Two or more races 1.7%. Hispanic 4.8%.
Cities (2002) Wilmington 72,503. Dover 32,581. Newark 29,798.
Business **Gross State Product, 2001:** $40.51 bil. (43rd). **Leading Sectors of GSP (2001):** Finance, insurance, and real estate 43.14%; Depository and nondepository i...?? 30.64%; Depository institutions 30.12%. ***Fortune* 500 Companies (2003):** 3: DuPont Nemours, MBNA, Hercules
Famous natives Valerie Bertinelli, actress. John Dickinson (b. Md.), Penman of the Revolution. Eleuthère I. du Pont, manufacturer. Pierre S. ("Pete") du Pont, politician. Morgan Edwards, founder of Brown University (R.I.). Thomas Macdonough, navy officer. Howard Pyle, illustrator. Edward R. Squibb, physician/manufacturer. Christopher Ward, historian.
Noteworthy places Brandywine Zoo, Wilmington. Delaware Art Museum, Wilmington. Delaware State Museum, Dover. Dover Downs International Speedway. Grand Opera House, Wilmington. Hagley Museum, Wilmington. Rehoboth Beach.
Memorable events Dutch arrive 1631. Swedes establish first permanent settlement at Wilmington 1638. Captured by Dutch 1655. To England 1664. Part of territory granted to William Penn 1682. Breaks off from Pennsylvania; first to ratify Constitution 1787. E.I. du Pont de Nemours Co. founded 1802. Railroad connects Wilmington to Philadelphia and Baltimore 1838. Though slave state, sides with Union during Civil War 1861–65. Delaware last state to abolish whipping post (last used 1952) 1972.
Tourist information (800) 441-8846. **www.visitdelaware.com.**

▶DISTRICT OF COLUMBIA

Chosen as the site for the nation's capital by George Washington, Washington, D.C., was carved out of land ceded by Maryland and Virginia. Although under Federal jurisdiction, the District has petitioned for statehood as New Columbia. In 1961 Congress enacted the 23rd Amendment granting citizens of D.C. the right to vote in Presidential elections for the first time, and 10 years later gave the District a nonvoting delegate to the House of Representatives. The District's largest employer is the federal government, and printing is the largest industry. Pres. John F. Kennedy called it a city of "Southern efficiency and Northern charm," but since his time, the city has become a leading patron of the arts. The problems of any large city are made worse by the city's largely transient population of government workers. The city, as the seat of the U.S. Government is a mecca for tourists from around the world, and more than 17 million people visit it each year.

Name After Christopher Columbus; Columbia was commonly used for the United States before 1800. **Nickname** None. **Capital** Washington. **Became capital** Dec. 1, 1800. **Motto** *Justitia omnibus* (Justice for all).
Emblems **Bird** Wood thrush. **Flower** American beauty rose. **Tree** Scarlet oak.
Land **Total area** 68 sq. mi., incl. 7 sq. mi. inland water. **Borders** Md., Va. **Rivers** Anacostia, Potomac.
Elected officials Mayor Anthony A. Williams (D, term exp. 2006).
People (July, 2002 est.) 570,898 (N.A.) Race/Hispanic Origin (2000 Census): White 30.8%. Black 60.0%. Indian 0.3%. Asian 2.7%. Pacific Islander 0.1%. Other 3.8%. Two or more races 2.4%. Hispanic 7.9%.
Business **Gross State Product, 2001:** $64.46 bil. (N.A.). **Leading Sectors of GSP (2001):** Services 37.65%; Government 35.18%; Federal, civilian(?) 30.07%. ***Fortune* 500 Companies (2003):** 3: Fannie Mae, Danaher, Pepco Holdings.
Famous natives Edward Albee, playwright. Carl Bernstein, journalist. John Foster Dulles, politician. Duke Ellington, composer. J. Edgar Hoover, FBI director. Marjorie Kinnan Rawlings, novelist. John Philip Sousa, composer.
Noteworthy places The Capitol. Chesapeake & Ohio Canal Natl. Hist. Park. Corcoran Gallery of Art. Dumbarton Oaks. FDR Memorial. Folger Shakespeare Library. Freer Gallery of Art. Hirshhorn Museum. Jefferson Memorial. Kennedy Center. Korean War Veterans Memorial. Library of Congress. Lincoln Memorial. Natl. Air and Space Museum. Natl. Gallery of Art. Natl. Museum of African Art. Natl. Museum of American Art. Natl. Museum of American History. Natl. Museum of Natural History. Natl. Portrait Gallery. Naval Observatory. Navy Memorial Museum. Renwick Gallery. Smithsonian Institution. Vietnam Veterans Memorial. Washington Monument. Washington Zoo. White House. Woodrow Wilson House.
Memorable events Originally part of Maryland. Congress approves plan to secure land for seat of Federal Government, no more than 10 miles square, on land in Virginia and Maryland 1787. George Washington commissions Pierre Charles l'Enfant to lay out city 1791. Government moves 1800. British sail up the Potomac and burn capital 1814. Virginia reclaims its half of District 1846. President Abraham Lincoln assassinated 1865. Coxey's Army marches on Washington 1894. The Bonus Army—17,000 veterans—marches on Washington 1932. Led by Martin Luther King, Jr., 200,000 march for Civil Rights 1963. One hundred thousand protest Vietnam War 1971. Democratic party headquarters at Watergate burglarized by men linked to President Richard M. Nixon's reelection effort 1972. Congress grants limited self-rule; mayor and city council elected 1975.
Tourist information (202) 789-7000. **www.washington.org.**

▶FLORIDA

A vast network of swamps, rivers, and lakes, much of Florida is barely above sea level. Florida is home to Disney World, Cypress Gardens, the wealth-laden resort of Palm Beach, the *National Enquirer*, and the Okefenokee Swamp. The pleasant climate and proximity to the Caribbean and Latin America have attracted tourists, large populations of the elderly (almost 19 percent of the population is over 65) and immigrants. Over the last two decades, it has been one of the fastest-growing states. The growth has brought with it, however, attendant increases in drug trafficking, racial disturbances, and environmental damage to such wildlife as the crocodile, alligator, and the Florida panther.

Name By Juan Ponce de León for Pascua Florida (Easter festival of the flowers). **Nickname** Sunshine State. **Capital** Tallahassee. **Entered union** Mar. 3, 1845 (27th). **Motto** "In God We Trust." **Poet laureate** Dr. Edmund Skellings.
Emblems **Animal** Florida panther. **Beverage** Orange juice. **Bird** Mockingbird. **Flower** Orange blossom. **Freshwater fish** Florida largemouth bass. **Gem** Moonstone. **Marine mammals** Dolphin, manatee. **Saltwater fish** Atlantic sailfish. **Shell** Horse conch. **Song** "Old Folks at Home" ("Swanee River"). **Stone** Agatized coral. **Tree** Sabal palmetto palm.
Land **Total area** 65,755 sq. mi (22nd), incl. 11,828 sq. mi. inland water. **Borders** Ga., Atlantic Ocean, Gulf of Mexico, Ala. **Rivers** Apalachicola, Caloosahatchee, Indian, Kissimmee, Perdido, St. Johns, St. Mary's, Suwanee, Withlacoochee. **Lakes** Apopka, George, Okeechobee, Seminole. **Other notable features** Everglades, Florida Keys, Okefenokee Swamp.
Elected officials Gov. John Ellis "Jeb" Bush (R, term exp. 2006). Lt. Gov. Toni Jennings (R). Sec. State Glenda Hood (R). Atty. Gen. Charlie Crist (R).
People (July, 2002 est.) 16,713,149 (4th). Race/Hispanic Origin (2000 Census): White 78.0%. Black 14.6%. Indian 14.6%. Asian 0.3%. Pacific Islander 0.1%. Other 3.0%. Two or more races 2.4%. Hispanic 16.8%.
Cities (2000) Jacksonville 735,617. Miami 362,470. Tampa 303,447. St. Petersburg 248,232. Hialeah 226,419. Orlando 185,951. Fort Lauderdale 152,397. Tallahassee 150,624. Hollywood 139,357. Pembroke Pines 137,427.
Business **Gross State Product, 2001:** $491.49 bil. (4th). **Leading Sectors of GSP (2001):** Services 25.62%; Finance, insurance, and real estate 22.08%; Real estate 14.52%. ***Fortune* 500 Companies (2003):** 11: AutoNation, Tech Data, Publix Super Markets, Winn-Dixie Stores, Office Depot, FPL Group, Lennar, Ryder System, Jabil Circuit, Darden Restaurants, Hughes Supply
Famous natives Mary Bethune, educator/reformer. Faye Dunaway, actress. Chris Evert, tennis player. Zora Neale Hurston, writer. James Weldon Johnson, lawyer/novelist. Osceola, Seminole chief. Sidney Poitier, actor. A. Philip Randolph, labor leader. Edmund Kirby Smith, Confederate general. Joseph Warren "Vinegar Joe" Stillwell, army officer. Ben Vereen, actor/singer.
Noteworthy places Biscayne Natl. Park. Castillo de San Marcos, St. Augustine. Everglades Natl. Park. Florida State Museum, Gainesville. Ft. Jefferson Natl. Monument. Ft. Matanzas Natl. Monument. Kennedy Space Center, Cape Canaveral. Ringling Museum, Sarasota. St. Augustine. Walt Disney World/EPCOT Center, Orlando.
Memorable events Juan Ponce de León claims Florida for Spain 1513. French stake claim for Florida 1562; build Ft. Caroline 1564. Pedro Menéndez de Avilés founds St. Augustine, first permanent European settlement in U.S. 1565. Spain cedes Florida to United States 1819. Seminole War 1835–42. State secedes from Union 1861. Readmitted 1868. Carl Fisher begins to develop Miami Beach as resort 1912. Florida's first paper mill opens expanding forest industry 1931. More than 100,000 Cuban refugees enter United States, most through Florida, during Mariel boat lift 1980. Army Corps of Engineers announce plans to let Kissimmee River, canalized in 1971, return to natural course to Lake Okeechobee; the largest back-to-nature project ever undertaken in U.S. -

1990. Hurricane Andrew causes $10 billion in damage to South Florida 1992.
Tourist information (888) 735-2872. **www.myflorida.com or www.flausa.com.**

▶GEORGIA

The largest state east of the Mississippi River, Georgia is diverse in its terrain, embracing the woods of the Blue Ridge Mountains to the north and the alligators of the Okefenokee Swamp in the south. Though two-thirds of the population are urban dwellers, Georgia's farms rank at or near the top in poultry production and are leading producers of pecans, cattle, hogs, and peanuts. Atlanta, the largest city in the South, elected Andrew Young the first black member of the U.S. Congress and Maynard Jackson the first black mayor from the South since Reconstruction. Today divisions linger in Georgia, the cities favoring a progressive stance and the rural areas clinging to some of the ways of the Old South. Some of those divisions came to a peaceful resolution in early 2001, when the state redesigned its flag to reduce the size and prominence of the Confederate cross.

Name For King George II of England 1732. **Nicknames** Empire State of the South, Peach State. **Capital** Atlanta. **Entered union** Jan. 2, 1788 (4th). **Motto** "Wisdom, justice, moderation."
Emblems **Bird** Brown thrasher. **Fish** Largemouth bass. **Flower** Cherokee rose. **Fossil** Shark tooth. **Gem** Quartz. **Insect** Honeybee. **Songs** "Georgia," "Georgia on My Mind." **Tree** Live oak. **Wildflower** Azalea.
Land **Total area** 59,425 sq. mi (24th), incl. 1,519 sq. mi. inland water. **Borders** Tenn., N.C., S.C., Atlantic Ocean, Fla., Ala. **Rivers** Altamaha, Apalachicola, Chattahoochee, Flint, Ocmulgee, Oconee, Savannah, Suwanee. **Lakes** Clark Hill, Harding, Hartwell, Seminole, Sidney Lanier, Sinclair, Walter F. George, West Point Lake. **Other notable features** Blue Ridge Mountains (Mount Enotah 4,784 ft.), Okefenokee Swamp.
Elected officials Gov. Sonny Perdue (R, term exp. 2007). Lt. Gov. Mark Taylor (D). Sec. State Cathy Cox (D). Atty. Gen. Thurbert E. Baker (D).
People (July, 2002 est.) 8,560,310 (10th). Race/Hispanic Origin (2000 Census): White 65.1%. Black 28.7%. Indian 0.3%. Asian 2.1%. Pacific Islander 0.1%. Two or more races 1.4%. Hispanic 5.3%.
Cities (2002) Atlanta 424,868. Augusta 193,101. Columbus 185,948. Savannah 127,691. Athens 102,663. Macon 95,862. Roswell 79,031. Albany 76,325. Marietta 62,020. Warner Robins 52,565.
Business **Gross State Product, 2001:** $299.87 bil. (10th). **Leading Sectors of GSP (2001):** Services 20.38%; Finance, insurance, and real estate 16.33%; Manufacturing 14.50%. ***Fortune* 500 Companies (2003):** 14: Home Depot, Mirant, United Parcel Service, Georgia-Pacific, Bellsouth, Coca-Cola, Coca-Cola Enterprises, Delta Airlines, Southern, AFLAC, Suntrust Banks, Genuine Parts, Cox Communications, Mohawk Industries.
Famous natives James Brown, singer. Erskine Caldwell, author. James Earl ("Jimmy") Carter, U.S. president. Ray Charles, musician. Ty Cobb, baseball player. James Dickey, poet. Martin Luther King, Jr., minister/reformer. Sidney Lanier, author. Little Richard, musician. Carson McCullers, author. Alexander McGillivray, Creek chief. Margaret Mitchell, author. Elijah Muhammad, religious leader. Flannery O'Connor, author. Burt Reynolds, actor. Jackie Robinson, baseball player. Tomochichi, Yamacraw chief. Ted Turner (b. Ohio), businessman. Joanne Woodward, actress.
Noteworthy places Chickamauga and Chattanooga Natl. Military Park. Confederate Memorial, Stone Mountain. Ft. Frederica Natl. Monument. Ft. Pulaski Natl. Monument. High Museum of Art, Atlanta. Martin Luther King Natl. Hist. Site., Atlanta. Ocmulgee Natl. Monument. Okefenokee Swamp. Savannah Historic District.
Memorable events Hernando de Soto explores region 1540. Cotton gin invented 1793. Georgia expels Cherokee Indian tribes on Trail of Tears 1832–38. Secedes from Union 1860. Gen. William T. Sherman's 60,000 troops cut 60-mi. swathe in their "march to the sea" 1864. Formula for Coca-Cola developed by chemist in search of cure for hangover 1886. Cyclone kills 1,000 in Charleston, S.C., and Savannah 1893. Franklin D. Roosevelt dies at the Little White House, Warm Springs 1945. First state to give vote to 18-year-olds 1948. Emory University designated to receive $100-million philanthropic gift from Robert W. Woodruff 1979. Dept. of Justice rules that state's process for electing superior court judges violates 1965 Voting Rights Act 1990. Summer Olympics held in Atlanta 1996.
Tourist information (800) VISIT-GA. **www.georgiaonmymind.org.**

▶HAWAII

What the air conditioner did for the Sunbelt, the jetliner has done for Hawaii, the last state to enter the Union. Because of the jet, Hawaii is a possible vacation spot for millions and welcomes 20 times the air travelers of 25 years ago. Tourism is Hawaii's key industry, attracting more than 6.5 million visitors to the state each year. Recent economic problems in Japan have had a negative effect on Hawaii's tourism numbers, and the state economy has suffered greatly as a result. Thousands of miles from both California and mainland Asia, Hawaii was originally peopled by Polynesian seafarers around A.D. 500 and has the richest ethnic mix of any state, with the lowest percentage of whites and highest percentages of Asians. It was partly fear of this diversity that stalled its statehood. A link between the United States and Asia, Hawaii is the center of U.S. defense in the Pacific and is home to 100,000 veterans, three-quarters of them veterans of Vietnam. Hawaii produces large quantities of pineapples and sugar cane, and efforts are under way to harness thermal electric power from Mauna Loa volcano.

Name Of unknown origin, perhaps from Hawaii Loa, traditional discoverer of islands, or from Hawaiki, the traditional Polynesian homeland. **Nicknames** Aloha State, Paradise of the Pacific. **Capital** Honolulu. **Entered union** Aug. 21, 1959 (50th). **Motto** *Ua mau ke ea o ka aina i ke pono* (The life of the land is perpetuated in righteousness).
Emblems **Bird** Nene (Hawaiian goose). **Fish** Humuhumunukunukuapuaa (reef triggerifish). **Flower** Pua aloalo (hibiscus). **Song** "Hawaii Ponoi." **Tree** Kukui (candlenut).
Land **Total area** 10,931 sq. mi (43rd), incl. 4,508 sq. mi. inland water. Surrounded by Pacific Ocean. **Rivers** Kaukonahua Stream, Wailuku Stream. **Lakes** Halulu, Kolekole, Salt Lake, Waiia Res. **Other notable features** Pearl Harbor. Hualalai, Kilauea, Mauna Kea (13,796 ft.), and Mauna Loa volcanoes. **Main islands** Hawaii, Kauai, Lanai, Maui, Molokai, Oahu.
Elected officials Gov. Linda Lingle (R, term exp. 2006). Lt. Gov/Sec. State, James Aiona, Jr. (R). Atty. Gen. Mark Bennett (R).
People (July, 2002 est.) 1,244,898 (42nd). Race/Hispanic Origin (2000 Census): White 24.3%.

Black 1.8%. Indian 0.3%. Asian 41.6%. Pacific Islander 9.4%. Other 1.3%. Two or more races 21.4%. Hispanic 7.2%.
Cities (2002) Honolulu 378,155. Hilo 40,759. Kailua 36,513. Kaneohe 34,970. Waipahu 33,108. Pearl City 30,976. Waimalu 29,371. Mililani Town 28,608. Kahului 20,146. Kihei 16,749. (Note: The Census Bureau does not keep statistics on cities other than Honolulu between decennial censuses because most Hawaiian cities are not incorporated).
Business **Gross State Product, 2001:** $43.71 bil. (39th). **Leading Sectors of GSP (2001):** Finance, insurance, and real estate 23.01%; Services 22.92%; Government 21.51%. ***Fortune* 500 Companies (2003):** 0.
Famous natives Bernice P. Bishop, philanthropist. Sanford B. Dole, statehood advocate. Charlotte (b. Ohio) and Luther Halsey Gulick, Camp Fire Girls founders. Don Ho, singer. Daniel J. Inouye, politician. Duke Kahanamoku, swimmer. Victoria Kaiulani, last heiress presumptive to Hawaiian throne. Kamehameha I, king. Kamehameha III, king. Liliuokalani, queen. Bette Midler, singer.
Noteworthy places Bernice P. Bishop Museum, Honolulu. Diamond Head. Haleakala Natl. Park, Maui. Hawaii Volcanoes Natl. Park (Kilauea and Mauna Loa), Hawaii. Iolani Palace, Honolulu. Kaloko-Honokohau Natl. Hist. Park, Molokai. Natl. Cemetery of the Pacific and USS *Arizona* Memorial. Polynesian Cultural Center, Laiea. Pu'uhonua o Honaunau Natl. Hist. Park, Hawaii.
Memorable events Polynesians first arrive 6th century. Second wave of Polynesians arrive 10th century. Captain James Cook first European to visit islands 1778; killed on Hawaii 1779. Sugar production begins 1835. Land reform ends feudal system 1848. Monarchy rule ends in revolution 1893. Becomes U.S. Territory 1900. Japanese attack Pearl Harbor 1941. Statehood 1959.
Tourist information (800) GOHAWAII. **www.gohawaii.com.**

▶IDAHO

Home to some of the most isolated and rugged country in the United States, Idaho's diversified economy has traditionally been based on lumber and potatoes (more than 13 billion pounds in 1993). In the 1980's these were augmented by a number of small high-tech industries fleeing the high cost of business in California. During the 1990's the population has grown rapidly (20 percent by 1997).

Name Means "gem of the mountains." **Nickname** Gem State. **Capital** Boise. **Entered union** July 3, 1890 (43rd). **Motto** *Esto perpetua* (May it last forever).
Emblems **Bird** Mountain bluebird. **Flower** Syringa. **Gem** Star garnet. **Horse** Appaloosa. **Song** "Here We Have Idaho." **Tree** Western white pine.
Land **Total area** 83,570 sq. mi (14th), incl. 823 sq. mi. inland water. **Borders** British Columbia, Mont., Wyo., Utah, Nev., Oreg., Wash. **Rivers** Bear, Clearwater, Payette, Salmon, Snake. **Lakes** American Falls Res., Coeur d'Alene, Pend Oreille. **Mountains** Bitterroot Range, Centennial, Clearwater, Salmon River, Sawtooth Range (Castle Peak 11,820 ft.), Wasatch Range. **Other notable features** Grand Canyon of the Snake River.
Elected officials Gov. Dirk Kempthorne (R, term exp. 2006). Lt. Gov. Jim Risch (R). Sec. State Ben Ysursa (R). Atty. Gen. Lawrence Wasden (R).
People (July, 2002 est.) 1,341,131 (39th). Race/Hispanic Origin (2000 Census): White 91.0%. Black 0.4%. Indian 1.4%. Asian 0.9%. Pacific Islander 0.1%. Other 4.2%. Two or more races 2.0%. Hispanic 7.9%.
Cities (2002) Boise City 189,847. Nampa 60,259. Pocatello 51,242. Idaho Falls 51,096. Meridian 39,067. Coeur d'Alene 36,259. Twin Falls 35,633. Lewiston 30,487. Caldwell 29,466. Moscow 21,674.
Business **Gross State Product, 2001:** $36.91 bil. (41st). **Leading Sectors of GSP (2001):** Services 17.98%; Manufacturing 17.80%; Government 14.08%. ***Fortune* 500 Companies (2003):** 4: 3: Albertson's, Boise Cascade, Washington Group Intl.
Famous natives Joseph, Nez Percé chief. Ezra Taft Benson, politician. Gutzon Borglum, sculptor. Frank Church, politician. Ezra Pound, poet. Harmon Killebrew, baseball player. Jerry Kramer, football player. Sacagawea (Bird Woman), Shoshone interpreter. Lana Turner, actress.
Noteworthy places Craters of the Moons Natl. Monument. Hell's Canyon Natl. Recreation Area. Nez Percé Natl. Hist. Park. Sawtooth Natl. Recreation Area. Sun Valley ski resort. Yellowstone Natl. Park.
Memorable events Lewis and Clark expedition 1805. Becomes part of U.S. when Idaho Treaty concluded with Britain 1846. Gold Rush 1860. Nez Percé War 1877. Statehood 1890. World's first breeder reactor built at Idaho Falls, 1951. Snake River opened to navigation, linking Lewiston to Pacific Ocean at Astoria, Oregon, 1975. New Teton River Dam collapses as it is being filled for first time; 10 dead, $400 million in damage 1976.
Tourist information (800) 635-7820. **www.visitid.org.**

▶ILLINOIS

The Illinois economy is enormously productive and diverse. While Chicago is a leader in world finance and trade, the southern part of the state has rich farmlands (the state is second to Iowa in corn and soybean exports) and mineral deposits (both coal and gas — there are especially rich coal deposits in the southeast region around Cairo, known as Little Egypt). Manufacturing centers on Chicago, Rockford—the state's second-largest city—and Springfield, the capital. Chicago is also a major transportation hub with extensive rail networks, an international port serving ships from both the Atlantic and Gulf of Mexico, and the largest airport in the country.

Name Corruption of *iliniwek* ("tribe of the superior men"), natives of region at time of earliest French explorations. **Nickname** Prairie State. **Capital** Springfield. **Entered union** Dec. 3, 1818 (21st). **Motto** "State sovereignty—national unity." **Slogan** "Land of Lincoln."
Emblems **Animal** White-tailed deer. **Bird** Cardinal. **Flower** Violet. **Insect** Monarch butterfly. **Mineral** Fluorite. **Song** "Illinois." **Tree** White oak.
Land **Total area** 57,914 sq. mi (25th), incl. 2,331 sq. mi. inland water. **Borders** Wis., Lake Michigan, Ind., Ky., Mo., Iowa. **Rivers** Fox, Illinois, Illinois Waterway, Kankakee, Kaskaskia, Mississippi, Ohio, Rock, Vermillion, Wabash. **Lakes** Carlyle, Crab Orchard. **Other notable features** Charles Mound (1,235 ft.), Little Egypt.
Elected officials Gov. Rod Blagojevich (D, term exp. 2006). Lt. Gov. Pat Quinn (D). Sec. State Jesse White (D). Atty. Gen. Lisa Madigan (D).
People (July, 2002 est.) 12,600,620 (5th). Race/Hispanic Origin (2000 Census): White 73.5%. Black 15.1%. Indian 0.2%. Asian 3.4%. Other 5.8%. Two or more races 1.9%. Hispanic 12.3%.
Cities (2002) Chicago 2,886,251. Aurora 156,974. Rockford 151,068. Naperville 135,389.

Joliet 118,423. Peoria 112,670. Springfield 111,834. Elgin 96,539. Waukegan 91,323. Cicero 84,254.
Business **Gross State Product, 2001:** $475.54 bil. (5th). **Leading Sectors of GSP (2001):** Services 22.73%; Finance, insurance, and real estate 22.10%; Manufacturing 14.37%. ***Fortune* 500 Companies (2003):** 36 including Boeing, State Farm Insurance, Sears Roebuck, Motorola, Allstate, Walgreen, Bank One Corp., Caterpillar, Archer Daniels Midland, Sara Lee, Abbott Laboratories, UAL, Exelon, McDonald's, Household International, Deere, Illinois Tool Works, Smurfit-Stone Container, Aon, Baxter International.
Famous natives Jane Addams, reformer (Nobel Peace Prize, 1930). Ernie Banks, baseball player. Saul Bellow, author (Nobel Prize, 1976). Harry A. Blackmun, jurist. Ray Bradbury, author. Gwendolyn Brooks, poet. William Jennings Bryan, politician. Edgar Rice Burroughs, novelist. St. Frances Xavier Cabrini (b. Italy). Clarence Darrow, lawyer. Miles Davis, musician. John Dos Passos, novelist. Enrico Fermi (b. Italy), nuclear physicist (Nobel Prize, 1938). Robert Louis ("Bob") Fosse, choreographer. Milton Friedman, economist (Nobel Prize, 1976). Benny Goodman, musician. Ernest Hemingway, novelist. Charlton Heston, actor. William Holden, actor. Abraham Lincoln, U.S. President (b. Kentucky). Vachel Lindsay, poet. Archibald MacLeish, poet. Ludwig Mies van der Rohe (b. Germany), architect. Charles W. Post, cereal manufacturer. Ronald Reagan, U.S. president. Carl Sandburg, poet. Albert G. Spalding, merchant. John Paul Stevens, jurist. Gloria Swanson, actress.
Noteworthy places Art Institute of Chicago. Crab Orchard Wildlife Refuge. Dickson Mounds Museum, Lewistown. Field Museum of Natural History, Chicago. Ft. Chartres. Ft. Kaskaskia. Ft. Massac. Frank Lloyd Wright Historic District, Oak Park. Illinois State Museum, Springfield. Lincoln Home Natl. Hist. Park, Springfield. Mormon Settlement, Nauvoo. Morton Arboretum, Lisle. Museum of Science and Industry, Chicago. Shawnee Natl. Forest. Starved Rock State Park.
Memorable events French missionary explorers Jacques Marquette and Louis Jolliet in Illinois 1673. Cahokia first European settlement 1699. Territory to England after French and Indian War 1763. Chicago founded by Jean-Baptiste Point du Sable 1779. Illinois and Michigan Canal links Lake Michigan and Mississippi River 1848. Lincoln-Douglas Debates at Springfield 1860. Half of Chicago destroyed by great fire 1871. Terrorist bombing leaves nine dead and 130 wounded in Haymarket affair, Chicago 1886. Columbia Exposition, Chicago 1893. First successful nuclear chain reaction created at University of Chicago 1942. Riots at Democratic National Convention in Chicago 1968. Sears Tower, world's tallest building (1,454 ft.), completed in Chicago 1973. Mississippi and Illinois rivers flood and cause $1.5 billion in damage 1993.
Tourist information (800) 2-CONNECT. **www.enjoyillinois.com.**

▶INDIANA

Indiana is strong in both farms and manufacturing. Its southern half has large coal deposits and produces most of the limestone quarried in the United States. To the north the fertile land helps make Indiana one of the primary farm-belt states. Indiana is also very much a part of the industrial Midwest, where unemployment is always a threat, especially in the heavily industrial areas of Gary and Indianapolis (the latter of which has developed into a center for high-tech industries through the 1980's and 1990's). These geographic divisions have parallels in the political history of the state, which during the Civil War was Union in the north and Confederate in the south.

Name For the land of Indians by early settlers, who found many distinct tribes living in region. **Nickname** Hoosier State. **Capital** Indianapolis. **Entered union** Dec. 11, 1816 (19th). **Motto** "The Crossroads of America."
Emblems **Bird** Cardinal. **Flower** Peony. **Poem** "Indiana." **Song** "On the Banks of the Wabash, Far Away." **Stone** Indiana limestone. **Tree** Tulip tree.
Land **Total area** 36,418 sq. mi (38th), incl. 551 sq. mi. inland water. **Borders** Lake Michigan, Mich., Ohio, Ky., Ill. **Rivers** Kankakee, Ohio, Tippecanoe, Wabash, White, Whitewater. **Lakes** Freeman, Shafer.
Elected officials Gov. Frank O'Bannon (D, term exp. 2005). Lt. Gov. Joseph Kernan (D). Sec. State Todd Rokita (R). Atty. Gen. Steve Carter (R).
People (July, 2002 est.) 6,159,068 (14th). Race/Hispanic Origin (2000 Census): White 87.5%. Black 8.4%. Indian 0.3%. Asian 1.0%. Other 1.6%. Two or more races 1.2%. Hispanic 3.5%.
Cities (2002) Indianapolis 783,612. Fort Wayne 210,070. Evansville 119,081. South Bend 106,558. Gary 100,945. Hammond 81,413. Bloomington 69,987. Muncie 67,195. Lafayette 60,594. Anderson 58,853.
Business **Gross State Product, 2001:** $189.92 bil. (15th). **Leading Sectors of GSP (2001):** Manufacturing 27.19%; Durable Goods 18.94%; Services 18.06%. ***Fortune* 500 Companies (2003):** 5: 6: Eli Lilly, Anthem, Nisource, Conseco, Cummins, Guidant.
Famous natives Larry Bird, basketball player. Hoagy Carmichael, composer. Eugene V. Debs, politician/organizer. Theodore Dreiser, author. Benjamin Harrison, U.S. president. Jimmy Hoffa, union leader. Michael Jackson, singer. David Letterman, comedian. Carole Lombard, actress. Cole Porter, composer. Ernie Pyle, journalist. Knute Rockne (b. Norway), football coach. Paul Samuelson, economist (Nobel Prize, 1960). Booth Tarkington, author. Kurt Vonnegut, author. Wendell L. Willkie, politician. Wilbur Wright, aviatior.
Noteworthy places Ernie Pyle birthplace, Dana. George Rogers Clark Natl. Hist. Park, Vincennes. Benjamin Harrison home, Indianapolis. Hoosier Natl. Forest. Indiana Dunes Natl. Lakeshore. Indianapolis Motor Speedway and Museum. Indianapolis Museum of Art. New Harmony village. Notre Dame Univ., South Bend. Old state capital, Corydon. Wilbur Wright State Memorial, Millville. Wyandotte Cave. Tippecanoe sites.
Memorable events Mound Builders present c. A.D. 1000. René-Robert Cavelier de La Salle explores for French 1679–87. French near Vincennes from c. 1700. French cede territory to British 1763. Gen. Ambrose Clark captures Ft. Vincennes 1779. Territory ceded to U.S. 1783; included in Northwest Territory 1787. Miamis defeat U.S. twice in 1790. Gen. Anthony Wayne defeats Miamis at Battle of Fallen Timbers 1794. Territory included in Indiana Territory 1800. Gen. William Henry Harrison defeats Tecumseh's Indian Confederation at Tippecanoe 1811. Statehood 1816. Studebaker wagon company founded in South Bend 1852. U.S. Steel establishes mill at company-built town of Gary 1906. First Indianapolis 500 run 1911. Only a dozen companies producing cars, down from a pre-World War I peak of 375, 1920. Studebaker, last Indiana-based car maker, closes 1963.
Tourist information (888) ENJOYIN. **www.enjoyin.com.**

▶IOWA

Iowa lies between the two great rivers of the central United States, the Mississippi and the Missouri, with a quarter of the nation's richest and deepest topsoil. Iowa's farmers lead the country in the production of corn, and Iowa is also a big producer of hogs, cattle, and other livestock. With about 75 percent of Iowans employed in agriculture-related industries and 90 percent of the land farmed, Iowa can be deeply affected by natural disasters such as droughts and floods. Yet more than 100 *Fortune* 500 Companies have production facilities in this farm state. Industrial production has risen since World War II. Iowans send abroad a quarter of the food they produce. As a result, this traditionally Republican state is better attuned to world developments than one might suspect.

Name For Iowa tribe. **Nickname** Hawkeye State. **Capital** Des Moines. **Entered union** Dec. 28, 1846 (29th). **Motto** "Our liberties we prize and our rights we will maintain."

Emblems **Bird** Eastern goldfinch. **Flower** Wild rose. **Song** "The Song of Iowa." **Stone** Geode. **Tree** Oak.

Land **Total area** 56,272 sq. mi (26th), incl. 402 sq. mi. inland water. **Borders** Minn., Wis., Ill., Mo., Nebr., S.Dak. **Rivers** Big Sioux, Des Moines, Mississippi, Missouri. **Lakes** Okoboji, Rathburn Res., Red Rock, Saylorville Res., Spirit, Storm. **Other notable features** Ocheyedan Mound (1,675 ft.).

Elected officials Gov. Tom Vilsack (D, term exp. 2006). Lt. Gov. Sally Pederson (D). Sec. State Patty Judge (D). Atty. Gen. Thomas J. Miller (D).

People (July, 2002 est.) 2,936,760 (30th). Race/Hispanic Origin (2000 Census): White 93.9%. Black 2.1%. Indian 0.3%. Asian 1.3%. Other 1.3%. Two or more races 1.1%. Hispanic 2.8%.

Cities (2002) Des Moines 198,076. Cedar Rapids 122,514. Davenport 97,777. Sioux City 84,131. Waterloo 67,742. Iowa City 63,816. Council Bluffs 58,640. Dubuque 57,031. Ames 50,913. West Des Moines 49,961.

Business **Gross State Product, 2001:** $90.94 bil. (30th). **Leading Sectors of GSP (2001):** Manufacturing 21.02%; Services 17.82%; Finance, insurance, and real estate 16.05%. ***Fortune* 500 Companies (2003):** 2: Principal Financial, Maytag.

Famous natives Norman E. Borlaug, agronomist (Nobel Peace Prize, 1970). William F. ("Buffalo Bill") Cody, scout/showman. George Gallup, pollster. Josiah B. Grinnell (b. Vt.), abolitionist. Herbert Hoover, U.S. president. Harry L. Hopkins, politician. John L. Lewis, labor leader. John R. Mott, religious leader. Billy Sunday, baseball player/evangelist. John Wayne, actor. Meredith Wilson, composer. Grant Wood, painter.

Noteworthy places Amana Colonies. Davenport Art Gallery. Des Moines Art Center. Effigy Mounds Natl. Monument, Marquette. Ft. Dodge Hist. Museum. Herbert Hoover birthplace and library, West Branch. Natl. Rivers Hall of Fame, Dubuque. Putnam Museum, Davenport.

Memorable events Mound Builders present c. A.D. 1000. Jacques Marquette and Louis Jolliet claim land for France 1673. Part of Louisiana Purchase 1803. Part of Missouri Territory 1812–21. Black Hawk Wars 1832, 1834–37. First permanent settlement at Dubuque 1833. Organized as Iowa Territory (incl. parts of Minnesota, North Dakota, and South Dakota) 1838. Statehood 1846. Capital moved from Iowa City to Des Moines 1857. Fifty percent of Iowa's farms foreclosed during depression 1929–35. Iowa's urban population exceeds rural for first time 1960. Population loss of 7.9 percent in the 1980's. Floods cause $2.2 billion in damage 1993.

Tourist information (800) 345-IOWA. **www.traveliowa.com.**

▶KANSAS

Kansas burst on the American scene as the territory called Bleeding Kansas, seething with conflict over the spread of slavery. Victorious New England abolitionists imprinted the state with the Puritan ethic. They were early supporters of prohibition, partly to discourage foreign newcomers. Kansas suffered enormously during the Great Depression and "Dust Bowl" days of the 1930's but rebounded strongly during the war. Wichita's aircraft industries, vital to the war effort, helped the Kansas economy to remain strong in the postwar years as family farming declined dramatically. Today Kansas remains a primary producer of wheat, cattle, and other agricultural products. Its manufacturing base still includes extensive aircraft industries, and it leads the states in the production of helium. The geographic center of the continental U.S. is near Lebanon.

Name For Kansa or Kaw, "people of the south wind." **Nickname** Sunflower State. **Capital** Topeka. **Entered union** Jan. 29, 1861 (34th). **Motto** *Ad astra per aspera* (To the stars through adversity).

Emblems **Animal** American buffalo. **Bird** Western meadowlark. **Flower** Wild native sunflower. **March** "The Kansas March." **Song** "Home on the Range." **Tree** Cottonwood.

Land **Total area** 82,277 sq. mi (15th), incl. 462 sq. mi. inland water. **Borders** Nebr., Mo., Okla., Colo. **Rivers** Arkansas, Kansas, Missouri, Republican, Saline, Smoky Hill, Solomon. **Lakes** Kanapolis, Malvern, Perry, Pomona, Tuttle Creek, Waconda. **Other notable features** Flint Hills.

Elected officials Gov. Kathleen Sebelius (D, term exp. 2006). Lt. Gov. John Moore (D). Sec. State Ron Thornburgh (R). Atty. Gen. Phil Kline (R).

People (July, 2002 est.) 2,715,884 (32nd). Race/Hispanic Origin (2000 Census): White 86.1%. Black 5.7%. Indian 0.9%. Asian 1.7%. Other 3.4%. Two or more races 2.1%. Hispanic 7.0%.

Cities (2002) Wichita 355,126. Overland Park 158,430. Kansas City 146,978. Topeka 122,103. Olathe 101,413. Lawrence 81,604. Shawnee 52,715. Salina 45,969. Manhattan 43,794. Lenexa 41,249.

Business **Gross State Product, 2001:** $87.20 bil. (31st). **Leading Sectors of GSP (2001):** Services 17.81%; Manufacturing 16.12%; Government 13.77%. ***Fortune* 500 Companies (2003):** 2: Sprint, Yellow.

Famous natives "Buffalo Bill" Cody. Walter Chrysler, carmaker. Robert Dole, politician. Amelia Earhart, aviator. Dwight David Eisenhower (b. Tex.), general/U.S. president. Dennis Hopper, actor. William Inge, playwright. Nancy Landon Kassebaum, politician. Alf Landon, politician. Edgar Lee Masters, poet. James Naismith, inventor of basketball. Carry Nation (b. Ky.), prohibitionist. Charlie ("Bird") Parker, musician. Damon Runyon, writer. Gale Sayers, football player. William Allen White, the Sage of Emporia, editor.

Noteworthy places Agricultural Hall of Fame, Kansas City. Dodge City. Eisenhower Center, Abilene. Ft. Larned. Ft. Leavenworth. Ft. Riley. Ft. Scott. John Brown's Cabin, Osawatomie. Kansas Cosmosphere and Space Discovery Center, Hutchinson. Kansas State Historical Society Museum, Topeka. Wichita Art Museum.

Memorable events First major expedition to region under Francisco Vásquez de Coronado 1540–41. La Salle claims territory including

Kansas for France 1682. Part of Louisiana Purchase 1803. Area visited by Meriwether Lewis and George Rogers Clark (1803), Zebulon Pike (1806), and Stephen H. Long (1819). Santa Fe Trail crosses Kansas 1821. Fts. Leavenworth (1827), Scott (1842), and Riley (1853) established to protect pioneers on Santa Fe and Oregon trails. Organized as Territory by Kansas-Nebraska Act 1854, which repealed Missouri Compromise of 1820. "Bleeding Kansas" scene of free vs. slave rivalry 1854–56. Statehood 1861. Introduction of winter wheat makes Kansas leading U.S. wheat producer 1870. Airplane manufacturing starts in Wichita 1919. World-famous Menninger Foundation for mental health founded 1919. "Dust Bowl" drought drives thousands of farmers off the land, especially in western Kansas, 1934–35. Murder of Clutter family by Richard E. Hickock and Perry E. Smith at Holcomb (later the subject of Truman Capote's *In Cold Blood*,) 1959.

Tourist information (800) 252-6727. **www.travelks.com.**

▶KENTUCKY, COMMONWEALTH OF

First pioneered by English immigrants in the mid-17th century, Kentucky's golden age as a choice frontier destination in the early 1800's was brought to an end by the Civil War. During the Civil War, the Bluegrass gentry supported the Confederacy, while the Appalachian backwoods men enlisted in the Union Army. Many took advantage of their uniforms to settle old accounts, and the social order was often threatened before the turn of the century. Though the state is known today for its bourbon and horse breeding, many Kentuckians make their living from the land as tobacco farmers or coal miners. The Appalachian part of the state in the east delivers about 20 percent of the nation's coal, but its economic problems remain acute, despite vast expenditures during the "war on poverty."

Name Corruption of the Iroquois *kenta-ke* (meadow land) or Wyandot *kah-ten-tah-teh* (land of tomorrow). **Nickname** Bluegrass State. **Capital** Frankfort. **Entered union** June 1, 1792 (15th). **Motto** "United we stand, divided we fall."

Emblems **Bird** Cardinal. **Colors** Blue and gold. **Fish** Bass. **Flower** Goldenrod. **Song** "My Old Kentucky Home." **Tree** Tulip poplar. **Wild animal** Gray squirrel.

Land **Total area** 40,409 sq. mi (37th), incl. 681 sq. mi. inland water. **Borders** Ind., Ohio, W.Va., Va., Tenn., Mo., Ill. **Rivers** Cumberland, Kentucky, Licking, Ohio, Tennessee. **Lakes** Barkley, Barren River Res., Dewey, Grayson Res., Laurel Res., Nolin Res., Rough Res. **Mountains** Appalachian (Black Mt. 4,145 ft.), Cumberland. **Other notable features** Tennessee Valley.

Elected officials Gov. Paul E. Patton (D, term exp. 2003). Lt. Gov. Stephen L. Henry, M.D. (D). Sec. State John Y. Brown III (D). Atty. Gen. A.B. Chandler (D).

People (July, 2002 est.) 4,092,891 (26th). Race/Hispanic Origin (2000 Census): White 90.1%. Black 7.3%. Indian 0.2%. Asian 0.7%. Other 0.6%. Two or more races 1.1%. Hispanic 1.5%.

Cities (2002) Lexington-Fayette 260,512. Louisville 251,399. Owensboro 54,176. Bowling Green 50,226. Covington 42,983. Hopkinsville 29,279. Richmond 28,093. Frankfort 27,660. Henderson 27,426. Jeffersontown 26,156.

Business **Gross State Product, 2001:** $120.27 bil. (27th). **Leading Sectors of GSP (2001):** Manufacturing 25.19%; Services 16.70%; Durable Goods 15.79%. ***Fortune* 500 Companies (2003):** 5: Humana, Ashland, Lexmark International, Kindred Healthcare, Yum! Brands.

Famous natives Muhammad Ali, boxer. Alben W. Barkley, politician. Daniel Boone (b. Pa.), frontiersman. Louis D. Brandeis, jurist. Kit Carson, frontiersman. Henry Clay, politician. Jefferson Davis, president of Confederate States of America. D.W. Griffith, director. John Marshall Harlan, jurist. Abraham Lincoln, U.S. president. Col. Harland Sanders, entrepreneur. Frederick M. Vinson, jurist. Robert Penn Warren, author.

Noteworthy places Abraham Lincoln birthplace, Hodgenville. Churchill Downs, Louisville. George S. Patton, Jr. Military Museum, Fort Knox. J.B. Speed Art Museum, Louisville. Land Between the Lakes Natl. Rec. Area. Mammoth Cave Natl. Park. My Old Kentucky Home, Bardstown. Old Ft. Harrod State Park.

Memorable events English enter territory through Cumberland Gap 1750. Territory included in area ceded by French 1763. Daniel Boone leads expeditions into region 1769. First settlement Harrodsburg 1774. Daniel Boone blazes Wilderness Trail through Cumberland Gap, establishes Ft. Boonesborough 1775. Organized as a county of Virginia 1776. British support Indian resistance ("Dark and Bloody Wars") until George Rogers Clark captures British forts in Indiana and Illinois 1778. Included as part of United States after Revolution 1783. Virginia approves separate statehood, achieved 1792. First steamboat reaches Louisville from New Orleans 1815. Invaded by Confederate armies 1862. Kentucky Derby first run at Louisville 1875. State has highest per capita income of southern states 1900; ranks last among all 48 states in per capita income 1940. Farm population decreases by 76%, and total number of farms by 53%, 1945–80.

Tourist information (800) 225-TRIP or (800) 255-PARK. **www.kytourism.com.**

▶LOUISIANA

European influences and ethnic diversity distinguish Louisiana from the rest of the nation. When Louisiana entered the Union in 1812, it brought with it a French legal system and a bilingualism that still survive. African-Americans, Cajuns and Creoles have contributed to its distinctive music and cuisine. The state has rich farmland, more oil and gas reserves than any other state but Texas, and in New Orleans an international port that serves the most extensive river system in North America.

The "devil's bargain" with the petrochemical industry struck by charismatic populist governor Huey Long (assassinated in 1935) brought needed jobs to the state. But the environmental impact of 100 loosely regulated petrochemical plants on the Mississippi River between New Orleans and Baton Rouge is being assessed only now. The state's reliance on the petroleum industry was felt when a downturn in oil prices in the 1980's led to massive unemployment. Economic diversification is under way, especially in field of tourism.

Name For King Louis XIV. **Nickname** Pelican State. **Capital** Baton Rouge. **Entered union** Apr. 30, 1812 (18th). **Motto** "Union, justice, confidence."

Emblems **Bird** Eastern brown pelican. **Colors** Gold, white, and blue. **Crustacean** Crawfish. **Dog** Catahoula leopard. **Flower** Magnolia. **Fossil** Petrified palmwood. **Gem** Agate. **Insect** Honeybee. **Songs** "Give Me Louisiana," "You Are My Sunshine." **Tree** Bald cypress.

Land **Total area** 51,840 sq. mi (31st), incl. 8,278 sq. mi. inland water. **Borders** Ark., Miss., Gulf of

Mexico, Tex. **Rivers** Atchafalaya, Mississippi, Ouachita, Pearl, Red, Sabine. **Lakes** Bistineau, Borgne, Caddo, Catahoula, Grand, Maurepas, Pontchartrain, Salvador, White. **Other notable features** Bayou Barataria, Bayou Bodcau, Bayou D'Arbonne, Driskill Mt. (535 ft.).

Elected officials Gov. Mike Foster Jr. (D, term exp. 2004). Lt. Gov. Kathleen B. Blanco (D). Sec. State W. Fox McKeithen (R). Atty. Gen. Richard Ieuyob (D).

People (July, 2002 est.) 4,482,646 (24th). Race/Hispanic Origin (2000 Census): White 63.9%. Black 32.5%. Indian 0.6%. Asian 1.2%. Other 0.7%. Two or more races 1.1%. Hispanic 2.4%.

Cities (2002) New Orleans 484,674. Baton Rouge 225,702. Shreveport 199,033. Lafayette 111,272. Lake Charles 70,726. Kenner 70,502. Bossier City 57,156. Monroe 52,360. Alexandria 45,856. New Iberia 35,506.

Business **Gross State Product, 2001:** $148.70 bil. (24th). **Leading Sectors of GSP (2001):** Mining 28.11%; Oil and gas extraction 18.77%; Services 16.82%. ***Fortune* 500 Companies (2003):** 2: Entergy, Shaw Group.

Famous natives Louis "Satchmo" Armstrong, jazz musician. Pierre Beauregard, Confederate general. Terry Bradshaw, football player. Braxton Bragg, Confederate general. Truman Capote, author. Clyde Cessna, aviator. Michael DeBakey, surgeon. Fats Domino, singer. Lillian Hellman, author. Mahalia Jackson, singer. Jean Baptiste Le Moyne, sieur de Bienville (b. Canada), founded New Orleans. Jerry Lee Lewis, singer. Huey P. Long, senator. Ferdinand Joseph La Menthe "Jelly Roll" Morton, musician. Leonidas K. Polk, clergyman/Confederate general. Henry Miller Shreve (b. NJ), riverboat captain. Edward D. White, Jr., jurist.

Noteworthy places Avery Island. Cabildo, New Orleans. French Quarter, New Orleans. Garden District, New Orleans. Hodges Gardens, Natchitoches. Jean Lafitte Natl. Hist. Park, Chalmette. Kent House Museum, Alexandria. Longfellow-Evangeline State Commemorative Area, St. Martinsville. Louisiana Maritime Museum, Baton Rouge. New Orleans Museum of Art.

Memorable events Area first visited by Alonso Alvarez de Piñeda 1519. Claimed by René-Robert Cavelier de La Salle for France 1682. New Orleans founded 1718. French crown colony 1731. Four thousand Acadians (Cajuns) from Nova Scotia forcibly transported by British to Louisiana and settled in Bayou Teche 1755. Lands west of Mississippi given to Spain for help in French and Indian War 1763. Lands east of Mississippi ceded to Britain 1763. Same lands retroceded to France 1800. Jefferson negotiates Louisiana Purchase; U.S. acquires 885,000 sq. mi. for $15 million 1803. Statehood 1812. Andrew Jackson beats British at Battle of New Orleans 1815. State secedes 1861. Surrenders to Union forces 1862. Readmitted to Union 1868. Petroleum discovered 1901. Huey "The Kingfish" Long elected to Senate 1928; assassinated 1935. Racial designation law of 1970 repealed 1983.

Tourist information (800) 33-GUMBO. **www.louisianatravel.com.**

▶MAINE

Down-Easters—the original Puritans as well as the later French Canadians—are distinct from the New Englanders of Maine's economically more vital sister states. Their land, especially the coast, is rugged, and the living everywhere is hard. Maine touches only one other state, and it has an end-of-the-line feel to it. Lumbering, fishing, and potato farming were the traditional industries. More than half of the state is still unorganized territory largely owned by paper companies. In the 18th century, canneries, textiles, and shoe factories developed. Recently Maine's economy has combined light industry and tourism that is moving it into the mainstream. The modern Maine entrepreneur, often an out-of-stater, seeks an economy based on small industries and more in keeping with Maine's independent spirit.

Name Either for Maine in France or to distinguish mainland from islands in the Gulf of Maine. **Nickname** Pine Tree State. **Capital** Augusta. **Entered union** Mar. 15, 1820 (23rd). **Motto** *Dirigo* (I direct).

Emblems **Animal** Moose. **Bird** Chickadee. **Fish** Landlocked salmon. **Flower** White pinecone and tassel. **Insect** Honeybee. **Mineral** Tourmaline. **Song** "State of Maine Song." **Tree** Eastern white pine.

Land **Total area** 35,385 sq. mi (39th), incl. 4,523 sq. mi. inland water. **Borders** Quebec, New Brunswick, Atlantic Ocean, N.H. **Rivers** Alagash, Androscoggin, Aroostock, Kennebec, Machias, Penobscot, Piscataqua, Salmon Falls, St. John. **Lakes** Chamberlain, Chesuncook, Grand, Moosehead, Rangeley, Sebago. **Other notable features** Longfellow Mts. (Mt. Katahadin 5,268 ft.), Mt. Desert Island, Penobscot Bay.

Elected officials Gov. John Baldacci (D, term exp. 2006). Sec. State Dan A. Gwadowsky (D). Atty. Gen. G. Steven Rowe (D).

People (July, 2002 est.) 1,294,464 (40th). Race/Hispanic Origin (2000 Census): White 96.9%. Black 0.5%. Indian 0.6%. Asian 0.7%. Other 0.2%. Two or more races 1.0%. Hispanic 0.7%.

Cities (2002) Portland 64,249. Lewiston 34,690. Bangor 31,473. South Portland 23,324. Auburn 23,203. Biddeford 20,942. Augusta 18,560. Saco 17,634. Westbrook 16,103. Waterville 15,629.

Business **Gross State Product, 2001:** $37.45 bil. (44th). **Leading Sectors of GSP (2001):** Services 21.28%; Finance, insurance, and real estate 19.21%; Government 14.41%. ***Fortune* 500 Companies (2003):** 0.

Famous natives Cyrus H.K. Curtis, publisher. Hannibal Hamlin, politician. Sarah Orne Jewett, novelist. Henry Wadsworth Longfellow, poet. Sir Hiram and Hudson Maxim, inventors. Edna St. Vincent Millay, poet. Edmund S. Muskie, politician. John Knowles Paine, composer. Kenneth Roberts, novelist. Edward Arlington Robinson, poet. Nelson Rockefeller, politician. Marguerite Yourcenar (b. France), author.

Noteworthy places Acadia National Park, Mt. Desert Island. Allagash National Wilderness Waterway. Boothbay Railway Museum Campobello-Longfellow House, Portland. Maine Maritime Museum, Bath. Portland Art Museum Roosevelt-Campobello Intl. Park, Campobello Island. St. Croix Island Natl. Monument.

Memorable events Vikings explore coast c. A.D.1000. Bartholomew Gosnold sails along coast 1602. French settlers at St. Croix River 1604. Included in grant to Plymouth Company 1606. Monhegan Island and Saco settled 1622. Annexed to Massachusetts Colony 1652. French attack northern territory intermittently through 1713. Statehood 1820. Border with Canada settled 1842. First state prohibition law enacted 1851. Penobscot and Passamaquoddy tribes file claim against state for $300 million compensation for land seized in violation of 1790 Indian Non-Intercourse Act, 1972; settled for $81.5 million 1980.

Tourist information (800) 533-9595. **www.visitmaine.com.**

▶MARYLAND

Maryland wraps like a fishhook from the Atlantic Ocean around the fish-rich Chesapeake Bay and into the Cumberland Mountains in the northwest. Baltimore—full of urban problems but newly redeveloped with urban homesteading and shopsteading—holds the center. The suburbs of Baltimore and Washington seem far removed from the Delmarva (**del**aware, **mar**yland, **v**irgini**a**) peninsula with its watermen hanging on to an older way of life. Terrain, cultures, and history are a border state's mix of North and South. Founded as a haven for Catholics, Maryland's population is still 20 percent Catholic.

Name For Henrietta Maria, queen consort of Charles I. **Nicknames** Old Line State, Free State. **Capital** Annapolis. **Entered union** Apr. 28, 1788 (7th). **Motto** *Fatti maschii, parole femine* (Manly deeds, womanly words).

Emblems **Bird** Baltimore oriole. **Dog** Chesapeake Bay retriever. **Fish** Rockfish. **Flower** Black-eyed Susan. **Fossil** *Ecphora quadricostata* (extinct snail). **Insect** Baltimore checkerspot butterfly. **Song** "Maryland, My Maryland." **Sport** Jousting. **Tree** White oak.

Land **Total area** 12,407 sq. mi (42nd), incl. 2,633 sq. mi. inland water. **Borders** Pa., Del., Atlantic Ocean, Va., D.C., W.Va. **Rivers** Chester, Choptank, Nanticoke, Patapsco, Patuxent, Pocomoke, Potomac, Susquehanna. **Other notable features** Allegheny Mts., Blue Ridge Mts., Chesapeake Bay.

Elected officials Gov. Robert Ehrlich (R, term exp. 2006). Lt. Gov. Michael Steele (R). Sec. State R. Karl Aumann (R). Atty. Gen. J. Joseph Curran, Jr. (D).

People (July, 2002 est.) 5,458,137 (18th). Race/Hispanic Origin (2000 Census): White 64.0%. Black 27.9%. Indian 0.3%. Asian 4.0%. Other 1.8%. Two or more races 2.0%. Hispanic 4.3%.

Cities (2002). Baltimore 651,154. Gaithersburg 56,300. Frederick 56,063. Rockville 52,573. Bowie 52,123. Hagerstown 36,659. Annapolis 36,196. College Park 25,320. Salisbury 24,645. Greenbelt 22,006.

Business **Gross State Product, 2001:** $195.01 bil. (16th). **Leading Sectors of GSP (2001):** Services 24.89%; Finance, insurance, and real estate 21.55%; Government 17.58%. ***Fortune* 500 Companies (2003):** 7: Lockheed Martin, Allegheny Energy, Marriott International, Black & Decker, Constellation Energy, Host Marriott, Coventry Healthcare.

Famous natives Russell Baker, journalist. Benjamin Banneker, surveyor. Eubie Blake, pianist. Rachel Carson, biologist/author. Stephen Decatur, navy officer. Frederick Douglass, abolitionist. Billie Holiday, singer. Johns Hopkins, financier/philanthropist. Francis Scott Key, lawyer/poet. Thurgood Marshall, jurist. H.L. Mencken, writer. Charles Willson Peale, artist. William Pinckney, statesman. James Rouse, urban planner. Babe Ruth, baseball player. Upton Sinclair, author. Roger B. Taney, jurist. Harriet Tubman, abolitionist. John Waters, filmmaker.

Noteworthy places Aberdeen Proving Ground. Antietam Natl. Battlefield, Sharpsburg. Assateague Island Natl. Seashore. Natl. Aquarium in Baltimore. Baltimore Museum of Art. Baltimore Museum of Industry. Calvert Marine Museum, Solomons. Chesapeake & Ohio Canal Natl. Hist. Park. Chesapeake Bay Maritime Museum, St. Michaels. Ft. McHenry Natl. Monument, Baltimore. Harpers Ferry Natl. Hist. Park. Liberty ship *John W. Brown*, Baltimore. St. Marys City. State House, Annapolis. U.S. Naval Academy, Annapolis. USS *Constellation*, Baltimore. Walters Art Gallery, Baltimore.

Memorable events John Smith explores area 1608. William Claiborne sets up trading post on Kent Island 1631. Land granted to Cecilius Calvert, Lord Baltimore, 1632. Leonard Calvert and 200 Roman Catholic settlers land on Blakistone Island 1634. Mason Dixon Line establishes northern boundary of state 1763–67; later identified as boundary between slave and nonslave states. Francis Scott Key composes "The Star Spangled Banner" after British fail to take Ft. McHenry 1814. U.S. Naval Academy founded Annapolis 1845. State under federal military control during Civil War 1861–65. First state to adopt income tax 1938. Alabama Gov. George C. Wallace shot while campaigning in Democratic presidential primary 1972.

Tourist Information (800) MD-IS-FUN. **www.mdisfun.org.**

▶MASSACHUSETTS, COMMONWEALTH OF

Massachusetts is rich in the history of the early American republic. The Boston Tea Party, the "shot heard round the world" from Lexington and Concord, and the Battle of Bunker Hill are American folklore. So is the feast of Thanksgiving, first celebrated by the Puritans at Plymouth. Fishing, trade, textiles and leather industries were the backbone of Massachusetts's 19th-century economy. In the 1980's, Boston's Route 128 became the East Coast counterpart to California's Silicon Valley, with some of the nation's most advanced computer and electronic research and manufacturing. The state's "economic miracle" of the 1980's ended abruptly, and Massachusetts endured a severe downturn during the recession of the early 1990's. It recently rebounded, along with most of the nation.

A staple of the Massachusetts scene is education, in which the state is a national leader. Boston alone boasts such institutions as Harvard University (founded 1636), M.I.T., Northeastern, Brandeis, Boston University, Boston College, Wellesley and Tufts. To the west are the University of Massachusetts, Amherst, Williams, Smith and Mt. Holyoke.

Name For Massachuset tribe, whose name means "at or about the great hill." **Nickname** Bay State. **Capital** Boston. **Entered union** Feb. 6, 1788 (6th). **Motto** *Ense petit placidam sub libertate quietem* (By the sword we seek peace, but peace only under liberty).

Emblems **Beverage** Cranberry juice. **Bird** Chickadee. **Building & monument stone** Granite. **Dog** Boston terrier. **Explorer rock** Dighton Rock. **Fish** Cod. **Flower** Mayflower. **Folk song** "Massachusetts." **Gem** Rhodonite. **Heroine** Deborah Samson. **Historical rock** Plymouth Rock. **Horse** Morgan. **Insect** Ladybug. **Marine mammal** Right whale. **Mineral** Babingtonite. **Poem** "Blue Hills of Massachusetts." **Rock** Roxbury pudding stone. **Song** "All Hail to Massachusetts." **Stone** Granite. **Tree** American elm.

Land **Total area** 10,555 sq. mi (44th), incl. 2,715 sq. mi. inland water. **Borders** Vt., N.H., Atlantic Ocean, R.I., Conn., N.Y. **Rivers** Cape Cod Canal, Connecticut, Merrimack, Taunton. **Other notable features** Buzzard's Bay, Cape Ann, Cape Cod, Cape Cod Bay, Connecticut Valley, Elizabeth Islands, Martha's Vineyard, Monomoy Island, Nantucket Island.

Elected officials Gov. Mitt Romney (R, term exp. 2006). Lt. Gov. Kerry Healey (R). Sec. of Commonwealth William Francis Galvin (D). Atty. Gen. Thomas Reilly (D).

People (July, 2002 est.) 6,427,801 (13th). Race/Hispanic Origin (2000 Census): White 84.5%. Black 5.4%. Indian 0.2%. Asian 3.8%. Other 3.7%. Two or more races 2.3%. Hispanic 2.3%.

Cities (2002) Boston 589,281. Worcester 174,962. Springfield 151,915. Lowell 104,901. Cambridge 101,807. Brockton 95,437. New Bedford 94,088. Fall River 92,660. Lynn 89,590. Quincy 89,187.

Business **Gross State Product, 2001:** $287.80 bil. (11th). **Leading Sectors of GSP (2001):** Services 27.76%; Finance, insurance, and real estate 25.67%; Real estate 14.48%. ***Fortune* 500 Companies (2003):** 13: Mass. Mutual Life Insurance, FleetBoston Financial, Raytheon, Liberty Mutual Insurance Group, Staples, TJX, John Hancock Financial Services, Gillette, EMC, State Street Corp., BJ's Wholesale Club, Allmerica Financial, Reebok International

Famous natives John Adams, U.S. president. John Quincy Adams, U.S. president. Samuel Adams, patriot. Horatio Alger, clergyman/author. Susan B. Anthony, suffragette. Clara Barton, nurse. Leonard Bernstein, composer. George Herbert Walker Bush, U.S. president. John ("Johnny Appleseed") Chapman, pioneer. Richard Cardinal Cushing, prelate. Bette Davis, actress. Emily Dickinson, poet. Ralph Waldo Emerson, author. Marshall Field, merchant. R. Buckminster Fuller, inventor/engineer. John Hancock, patriot. Oliver Wendell Holmes, jurist. Winslow Homer, painter. John F. Kennedy, U.S. president. Jack Kerouac, author. Cotton Mather, theologian. Samuel Eliot Morison, historian. Samuel Morse, inventor. Thomas P. "Tip" O'Neill, congressman. Edgar Allan Poe, poet/author. Paul Revere patriot/silversmith. Louis Sullivan, architect. Henry David Thoreau, author.

Noteworthy places Addison Gallery of American Art, Andover. Arnold Arboretum, Boston. Arthur M. Sackler Museum, Cambridge. Berkshires Museum, Pittsfield. Boston Museum of Fine Arts. Boston Natl. Hist. Park (incl. Bunker Hill, Charlestown Navy Yard, Old North Church). Busch-Reisinger Museum, Cambridge. Cape Cod Natl. Seashore. Clark Art Institute, Williamsburg. Fogg Art Museum, Boston. Gardner Art Museum, Boston. Hancock Shaker Village. Lowell Natl. Hist. Park. Minute Man Natl. Hist. Park, Lexington and Concord. Nantucket Hist. Society. Old Sturbridge Village. Peabody Museum, Salem. Plimoth Plantation, Plymouth. Tanglewood Music Festival, Lenox. *U.S.S. Constitution* ("Old Ironsides"), Charlestown. Walden Pond. Woods Hole Oceanographic Institute. Worcester Art Museum.

Memorable events Pilgrims land at Plymouth 1620. First Thanksgiving celebrated 1621. Harvard College founded 1636. Region acquires province of Maine 1652. Colonists battle Wampanoags in King Philip's War 1655–56. Boston Massacre 1770. Boston Tea Party protests taxation 1773. Battles at Lexington, Concord, and Bunker Hill 1775. Shays's Rebellion 1785–86. Maine becomes a separate state 1820. Massachusetts receives influx of Irish immigrants fleeing famine 1845. Textile workers' strike at Lawrence brings International Workers of the World (IWW) to prominence in East 1912. Cape Cod Canal completed 1914. International protest follows trial and execution of anarchists Nicola Sacco and Bartolomeo Vanzetti for robbery and murder 1920; names cleared by governor's proclamation 1970. Eleven robbers steal $2.7 million from Brink's North Terminal Garage 1950. Martha's Vineyard and Nantucket symbolically vote to secede from state 1973.

Tourist information (800) 227-MASS. **www.massvacation.com.**

▶MICHIGAN

The automobile is the single commodity with which Michigan is most identified, and it is the home of General Motors and Ford, the nation's two largest automakers. More than 50 percent of Michiganders live in the southeastern corner of the state, where the car industry flourishes. In the Upper Peninsula, across the Straits of Mackinac, lumber and copper have been the principal commodities from the 19th century, and the northern part of the Lower Peninsula boasts rich farmland. Michigan's boundaries include parts of four of the five Great Lakes, and it has more coastline than any state except Alaska. Michigan has had an outstanding reputation in higher education, and the University of Michigan at Ann Arbor and Michigan State are helping to foster the state's high-tech industries. But the state's heavy reliance on auto manufacturing makes the state vulnerable to economic downturns, as well as the general contraction of the American industry.

Name From the Fox *mesikami*, "large lake." **Nicknames** Wolverine State, Lake State. **Capital** Lansing. **Entered union** Jan. 26, 1837 (26th). **Motto** *Si quaeris peninsulam amoenam circumspice* (If you are looking for a beautiful peninsula, look around you).

Emblems **Bird** Robin. **Fish** Trout. **Flower** Apple blossom. **Gem** Chlorastrolite. **Insect** Dragonfly. **Song** "Michigan, My Michigan." **Stone** Petoskey stone. **Tree** White pine.

Land **Total area** 96,716 sq. mi (11th), incl. 39,912 sq. mi. inland water. **Borders** Lake Superior, Ontario, Lake Huron, Lake Erie, Ohio, Ind., Lake Michigan, Wisc. **Rivers** Brule, Detroit, Kalamazoo, Menominee, Montreal, Muskegon, St. Joseph, St. Mary's. **Lakes** Burt, Higgins, Houghton, Huron, Manistique, Michigan, Mullett, St. Clair, Superior. **Other notable features** Isle Royale, Mt. Curwood (1,980 ft.), Saginaw Bay, Traverse Bay, Whitefish Bay.

Elected officials Gov. Jennifer Granholm (D, term exp. 2006). Lt. Gov. John Cherry (D). Sec. State Terri Land (R). Atty. Gen. Mike Cox (R).

People (July, 2002 est.) 10,050,446 (8th). Race/Hispanic Origin (2000 Census): White 80.2%. Black 14.2%. Indian 0.6%. Asian 1.8%. Other 1.3%. Two or more races 1.9%. Hispanic 3.3%.

Cities (2002) Detroit 925,051. Grand Rapids 196,595. Warren 137,672. Sterling Heights 126,146. Flint 121,763. Lansing 118,588. Ann Arbor 115,213. Livonia 100,341. Dearborn 97,833. Westland 86,282.

Business **Gross State Product, 2001:** $320.47 bil. (9th). **Leading Sectors of GSP (2001):** Manufacturing 23.07%; Services 20.72%; Durable goods 17.40%. ***Fortune* 500 Companies (2003):** 25: General Motors, Ford Motor, Kmart, Dow Chemical, Delphi, Visteon, Lear, CMS Energy, Whirlpool, Kellogg, Masco, DTE Energy, Arvinmeritor, United Auto Group, Federal-Mogul, Pulte Homes, Kelly Services, Comerica, Steelcase, Spartan Stores, Borders Group, American Axle & Manufacturing, Collins & Aikman, Auto-Owners Insurance, Stryker

Famous natives Ralph J. Bunche, statesman (Nobel Peace Prize, 1950). Paul de Kruif, bacteriologist. Thomas Dewey, politician. Herbert H. Dow

(b. Canada), chemical manufacturer. Edna Ferber, author. Gerald Ford (b. Neb.) U.S. president. Henry Ford, industrialist. Edgar Guest, journalist/poet. Robert Ingersoll, industrialist. Will Kellogg, businessman/philanthopist. Charles A. Lindbergh, aviator. Madonna, singer. Antoine de La Mothe, sieur de Cadillac (b. France), founded Detroit. Pontiac, Ottawa chief. William Upjohn, drug manufacturer. **Noteworthy places** Detroit Historical Society. Detroit Institute of Arts. Dossin Great Lakes Museum, Detroit. Great Lakes Indian Interpretive Museum, Detroit. Greenfield Village, Dearborn. Historic Ft. Wayne, Detroit. Isle Royale Natl. Park. Mackinac Island. Pictured Rocks Natl. Lakeshore, Lake Superior. Sleeping Bear Dunes Natl. Lakeshore, Lake Superior.
Memorable events French explorers in region 1634. Jacques Marquette settles Sault Ste. Marie 1668. Detroit founded as French military post 1701. Region ceded to England 1763; to United States 1783. Included in Northwest Territory but British maintain control until 1796. Michigan Territory 1805. First steamboat on Great Lakes reaches Detroit 1818. Statehood 1837. First state to outlaw capital punishment 1846. Republican party organized at Jackson 1854. Canals at Sault Ste. Marie link Lakes Superior and Huron 1855. Ransom E. Olds and Henry Ford, working independently, develop gasoline-powered car 1896. United Auto Workers first to use sit-down strike successfully in contract negotiations 1935. Race riot, one of the worst in U.S. history, leaves 43 dead and $200 million in damages in Detroit 1967. Congress authorizes $1.5 billion in federal loan guarantees to bail out Chrysler Corporation 1979.
Tourist information (888) 784-7328. **www.michigan.org.**

▶MINNESOTA

A land of at least 10,000 lakes, Minnesota is a magnet for those who love the outdoors. It is also home to the largest Scandinavian populations in the United States. Originally exploited for its wealth of lumber and iron—the Mesabi Range still produces much of the nation's iron ore—Minnesota also has highly developed agribusinesses (especially dairy products), manufacturing and transportation industries. Minneapolis and St. Paul are at the north end of the Mississippi River system, and Duluth at the westernmost point of Lake Superior is the largest U.S. inland port. Minnesota has one of the best state school systems.

Name From the Sioux *minisota*, "sky-tinted waters." **Nicknames** North Star State, Gopher State, Land of 10,000 Lakes. **Capital** St. Paul. **Entered union** May 11, 1858 (32rd). **Motto** *L'étoile du nord* (Star of the north).
Emblems **Bird** Common loon. **Beverage** Milk. **Fish** Walleye. **Flower** Pink and white lady's slipper. **Gem** Lake Superior agate. **Grain** Wild rice. **Mushroom** Morel, or sponge mushroom. **Song** "Hail, Minnesota!." **Tree** Red pine.
Land **Total area** 86,939 sq. mi (12th), incl. 7,329 sq. mi. inland water. **Borders** Manitoba, Ontario, Lake Superior, Wisc., Iowa, S.Dak., N.Dak. **Rivers** Minnesota, Mississippi, Red River of the North, St. Croix. **Lakes** Itasca, Lake of the Woods, Leech, Mille Lacs, Red, Winnibigoshish. **Other notable features** Mesabi Range.
Elected officials Gov. Tim Pawlenty (R, term exp. 2006). Lt. Gov. Carol Molnau (R) Sec. State Mary Kiffmeyer (R). Atty. Gen. Mike Hatch (D).
People (July, 2001 est.) 4,972,294 (21st). Race/Hispanic Origin (2000 Census): White 89.4%. Black 3.5%. Indian 1.1%. Asian 2.9%. Other 1.3%. Two or more races 1.7%. Hispanic 2.9%.
Cities (2002) Minneapolis 375,635. St. Paul 284,037. Rochester 90,515. Duluth 86,419. Bloomington 84,092. Brooklyn Park 68,128. Plymouth 67,304. Eagan 64,407. Coon Rapids 62,239. Burnsville 60,033.
Business **Gross State Product, 2001:** $188.05 bil. (17th). **Leading Sectors of GSP (2001):** Services 21.58%; Finance, insurance, and real estate 19.33%; Manufacturing 15.85%. ***Fortune* 500 Companies (2003):** 18: Target, UnitedHealth Group, Supervalu, U.S. Bancorp, Best Buy, Xcel Energy, Northwest Airlines, St. Paul Cos., Cenex Harvest States, General Mills, Medtronic, Hormel Foods, Nash Finch, Pepsiamericas, C.H. Robinson Worldwide, 3M, Land O'Lakes, Ecolab.
Famous natives Warren Burger, jurist. Bob Dylan, musician. F. Scott Fitzgerald, novelist. Judy Garland, actress. J. Paul Getty, businessman. Garrison Keillor, humorist. Sinclair Lewis, author (Nobel Prize, 1930). Paul Manship, sculptor. William and Charles Mayo, surgeons. Eugene McCarthy, politician. Walter F. Mondale, politician. Charles Schulz, cartoonist. Richard W. Sears, merchant.
Noteworthy places Boundary Waters Canoe Area. Grand Portage Natl. Monument. International Falls. Lake Itasca State Park (headwaters of Mississippi). Mall of America. Mayo Clinic, Rochester. Minneapolis Institute of Arts. Minnehaha Falls, Minneapolis. Minnesota Zoo, Apple Valley. Pipestone Natl. Monument. Tyrone Guthrie Theater, Minneapolis. Voyageurs Natl. Park. Walker Art Center, Minneapolis.
Memorable events Pierre Esprit Radisson and Médard Chouart des Groselliers visit area 1654–60. René-Robert de La Salle and Louis Hennepin explore upper Mississippi 1680. Daniel Greysolon, sieur de Duluth, claims region for France 1679. Area east of Mississippi to Britain 1763; to United States 1783. Western region of state as part of Louisiana Purchase 1803. Britain cedes northern strip to United States 1818. Ft. Snelling built 1820. Northern border settled by Ashburton Treaty 1842. Minnesota Territory created 1849. Statehood 1858. Sioux driven from state after uprising led by Chief Little Crow 1862. Iron ore deposits discovered in Mesabi Range 1890. Democratic party merges with Farmer-Labor party 1944.
Tourist information (800) 657-3700. **www.exploreminnesota.com.**

▶MISSISSIPPI

Mississippi's rank as the poorest state in the nation can be traced to the Civil War. Before the Civil War, Mississippi was the fifth-wealthiest state in the nation. The war cost the state 30,000 men. Plantation owners who survived the war were virtually bankrupted by the emancipation of the slaves, and Union troops under Sherman and others left widespread destruction in their wake. The increasingly harsh race-laws passed around 1900 also cost the state in the emigration of almost half a million (75 percent blacks, 25 percent whites) in the 1940's. Compounding all this was the fact that until World War II, Mississippi had virtually no urban center such as Jackson to attract or sustain major industry. In race relations particularly, Mississippi has made vast improvements, and there have been substantial gains in education and the attraction of out-of-state companies, especially light industry.

Name From the Ojibwa *misi sipi*, "great river." **Nickname** Magnolia State. **Capital** Jackson. **En-**

tered union Dec. 10, 1817 (20th). **Motto** *Virtute et armis* (By virtue and arms).
Emblems **Beverage** Milk. **Bird** Mockingbird. **Fish** Largemouth or black bass. **Flower** Magnolia. **Fossil** Prehistoric whale. **Insect** Honeybee. **Mammal** White-tailed deer. **Song** "Go, Mississippi." **Stone** Petrified wood. **Tree** Magnolia. **Waterfowl** Wood duck. **Water mammal** Porpoise.
Land **Total area** 48,430 sq. mi (32nd), incl. 1,523 sq. mi. inland water. **Borders** Tenn., Ala., Gulf of Mexico, La., Ark. **Rivers** Big Black, Mississippi, Pearl, Tennessee, Yazoo. **Lakes** Arkabutla, Grenada, Ross Barnett Res., Sardis. **Other notable features** Pontotoc Ridge.
Elected officials Gov. Ronnie Musgrove (D, term exp. 2004). Lt. Gov. Amy Tuck (D). Sec. State Eric Clark (D). Atty. Gen. Mike Moore (D).
People (July, 2002 est.) 2,871,782 (31st). Race/Hispanic Origin (2000 Census): White 61.4%. Black 36.3%. Indian 0.4%. Asian 0.7%. Other 0.5%. Two or more races 0.7%. Hispanic 1.4%.
Cities (2002) Jackson 180,881. Gulfport 72,511. Biloxi 49,809. Hattiesburg 45,773. Greenville 40,286. Meridian 39,518. Tupelo 34,975. Southaven 33,161. Vicksburg 26,226. Pascagoula 25,990.
Business **Gross State Product, 2001:** $67.13 bil. (35th). **Leading Sectors of GSP (2001):** Services 17.95%; Manufacturing 17.94%; Government 17.15%. ***Fortune* 500 Companies (2003):** 0.
Famous natives Medgar Evers, civil rights leader. William Faulkner, novelist. Shelby Foote, historian. Jim Henson, puppeteer. B.B. King, musician. Elvis Presley, singer. Leontyne Price, opera singer. Jerry Rice, football player. John C. Stennis, politician. Conway Twitty, singer. Muddy Waters, musician. Eudora Welty, novelist. Ben Ames Williams, novelist. Tennessee Williams, playwright. Richard Wright, author.
Noteworthy places Delta Blues Museum, Clarksdale. Natchez Trace Natl. Parkway. Seafood Industry Museum, Biloxi. Tupelo Natl. Battlefield. Vicksburg Natl. Military Park.
Memorable events Hernando de Soto's expedition travels through Mississippi 1540–41. René-Robert Cavelier de La Salle claims Mississippi valley for France 1682. Pierre Le Moyne, sieur d'Iberville builds Ft. Maurepas on Biloxi Bay 1699. Natchez (Ft. Rosalie) established 1716. France cedes territory to Britain 1763. Mississippi Territory (including presentday Alabama) created 1798. Statehood (Natchez first capital) 1817. Secedes from Union; Jefferson Davis becomes president of Confederacy 1861. Siege of Vicksburg 1863. Petroleum discovered 1939. Gov. Ross R. Barnett found guilty of contempt in preventing desegregation of University of Mississippi; James H. Meredith first black enrolled at University of Mississippi 1962. Civil rights leader Medgar Evers assassinated in Jackson and buried in Arlington National Cemetery 1963. White civil rights workers James Cheney, Andrew Goodman, and Michael Schwener killed 1964.
Tourist information (800) WARMEST. **www.visitmississippi.org.**

▶MISSOURI

Missouri is remarkable for the number and variety of its neighbors—southern states (Arkansas, Kentucky, and Tennessee), midwestern states (Illinois and Iowa), and Plains states (Oklahoma, Nebraska, and Kansas). For Missouri, geography was destiny. Still one of the country's most important inland ports, St. Louis was founded at the confluence of the Missouri and Mississippi rivers and became the gateway to the West; and Independence (now part of metropolitan Kansas City) got its start provisioning wagons for the Oregon and Santa Fe trails. The Pony Express from St. Joseph to Sacramento began in 1860, and the first attempt at airmail service was tried in St. Louis in 1911. While farming and livestock are still important to the state's economy, manufacturing and services are now the biggest sectors.

Name From the Iliniwek *missouri*, "owner of big canoes." **Nickname** Show Me State. **Capital** Jefferson City. **Entered union** Aug. 10, 1821 (24th). **Motto** *Salus populi suprema lex esto* (The welfare of the people shall be the supreme law).
Emblems **Bird** Bluebird. **Flower** Hawthorne. **Insect** Honeybee. **Mineral** Galena. **Rock** Mozarkite. **Song** "Missouri Waltz." **Tree** Dogwood.
Land **Total area** 69,704 sq. mi (21st), incl. 818 sq. mi. inland water. **Borders** Iowa, Ill., Ky., Tenn., Ark., Okla., Kans., Nebr. **Rivers** Des Moines, Mississippi, Missouri, Osage, St. Francis. **Lakes** Bull Shoals, Clearwater, Lake of the Ozarks, Lake of the Woods, Table, Wappapella. **Other notable features** Ozark Mts. (Taum Sauk Mt. 1,772 ft.).
Elected officials Gov. Bob Holden (D, term exp. 2005). Lt. Gov. Joe Maxwell (D). Sec. State Matt Blunt (R). Atty. Gen. Jeremiah W. Nixon (D).
People (July, 2002 est.) 5,672,579 (17th). Race/Hispanic Origin (2000 Census): White 84.9%. Black 11.2%. Indian 0.4%. Asian 1.1%. Pacific Islander 0.1%. Other 0.8%. Two or more races 1.5%. Hispanic 2.1%.
Cities (2002) Kansas City 443,471. St. Louis 338,353. Springfield 151,010. Independence 113,027. Columbia 86,981. Lee's Summit 74,948. St. Joseph 73,148. St. Charles 60,755. O'Fallon 59,678. St. Peters 53,596.
Business **Gross State Product, 2001:** $181.49 bil. (18th). **Leading Sectors of GSP (2001):** Services 21.29%; Manufacturing 16.77%; Finance, insurance, and real estate 16.34%. ***Fortune* 500 Companies (2003):** 12: Aquila, Emerson Electric, May Department Stores, Anheuser-Busch, Farmland Industries, Express Scripts, Graybar Electric, Ameren, Leggett & Platt, Charter Communications, Interstate Bakeries, H&R Block.
Famous natives Thomas Hart Benton, painter. Yogi Berra, baseball player. George Caleb Bingham (b. Va.), painter. Omar Bradley, general. Adophus Busch (b. Germany), brewer. George Washington Carver, botanist. Walter Cronkite, journalist. Walt Disney, film producer. T.S. Eliot, poet. Walker Evans, photographer. Langston Hughes, poet. Jesse James, outlaw. Marianne Moore, poet. Reinhold Niebuhr, theologian. J.C. Penny, businessman. John J. "Black Jack" Pershing, soldier. Joseph Pulitzer (b. Hungary), publisher. Ginger Rogers, dancer. Casey Stengel, baseball player. Virgil Thompson, composer. Harry S Truman, U.S. president. Mark Twain, writer. Tom Watson, golfer. Shelley Winters, actress.
Noteworthy places Churchill Memorial, Gateway Arch, St. Louis. George Washington Carver Natl. Monument, Diamond. Harry S Truman Library, Independence. Mark Twain Area, Hannibal. Nelson-Atkins Museum of Art, Kansas City. Pony Express Museum, St. Joseph. St. Louis Art Museum. Wilson's Creek Natl. Battlefield. Cahokia Mounds State Historic Site, near St. Louis.
Memorable events French miners and hunters settle at Ste. Genevieve 1735. Pierre Laclade settles St. Louis 1765. New Madrid earthquakes (8.6 on Richter scale) rock buildings as far away as Baltimore 1811-12. Statehood 1821. Mis-

souri legislature split over secesssion: minority party adopts secession ordinance; Missouri admitted to Confederacy; majority party remains loyal to Union 1861. Jesse James killed by fellow gang member at St. Joseph 1882. Lake of the Ozarks formed after completion of Bagnell Dam on Missouri River 1931. Winston Churchill delivers "iron curtain" speech at Fulton 1952. Gateway Arch, 630 ft. high, opens at St. Louis 1964. St. Louis population declines 53 percent 1950–90. Floods cause $3 billion in damage 1993.
Tourist information (800) 877-1234. **www.visitmo.com.**

▶MONTANA

Mountains account for only the western two-fifths of "Big Sky Country," where copper mining, lumber and tourism are the chief industries. The eastern portion of the state is part of the Great Plains, devoted to agriculture and ranching. For many years Montana was in the grip of the Anaconda Copper Mining Company, which virtually owned the state government and took most of its profits out of the state. After Anaconda's demise in the 1970's, Montana developed some of the most stringent environmental laws in the West. In recent years, many famous Hollywood stars, as well as media mogul Ted Turner, have bought large tracts of land in western Montana.

Name From Spanish *montaña*, "mountainous." **Nicknames** Treasure State, Big Sky Country. **Capital** Helena. **Entered union** Nov. 8, 1889 (41st). **Motto** *Oro y plata* (Gold and silver).
Emblems Bird Western meadowlark. **Fish** Blackspotted cutthroat trout. **Flower** Bitterroot. **Gems** Yogo sapphire, Montana agate. **Grass** Bluebunch wheatgrass. **Song** "Montana." **State ballad** "Montana Melody." **Tree** Ponderosa pine.
Land Total area 147,042 sq. mi (4th), incl. 1,490 sq. mi. inland water. **Borders** British Columbia, Alberta, Saskatchewan, N.Dak., S.Dak., Wyo., Idaho. **Rivers** Kootenai, Milk, Missouri, Musselshell, Powder, Yellowstone. **Lakes** Bighorn, Canyon Ferry, Elwell, Flathead, Ft. Peck. **Mountains** Absaroka Range, Beartooth Range (Granite Peak 12,799 ft.), Big Belt, Bitterroot Range, Centennial, Crazy, Lewis Range, Little Belt. **Other notable features** Continental Divide, Missoula Valley.
Elected officials Gov. Judy Martz (R, term exp. 2005). Lt. Gov. Karl Ohs (R). Sec. State Bob Brown (R). Atty. Gen. Mike McGrath (D).
People (July, 2002 est.) 909,453 (44th). Race/Hispanic Origin (2000 Census): White 90.6%. Black 0.3%. Indian 6.2%. Asian 0.5%. Pacific Islander 0.1%. Other 0.6%. Two or more races 1.7%. Hispanic 2.0%.
Cities (2002) Billings 92,008. Missoula 59,518. Great Falls 56,046. Butte-Silver Bow 32,716. Bozeman 29,459. Helena 26,353. Kalispell 15,463. Havre 9,621. Anaconda-Deer Lodge County 9,417. Miles City 8,487.
Business Gross State Product, 2001: $22.64 bil. (47th). **Leading Sectors of GSP (2001):** Services 21.22%; Government 17.12%; Finance, insurance, and real estate 14.14%. ***Fortune* 500 Companies (2003): 0.**
Famous natives Gary Cooper, actor. Marcus Daly (b. Ireland), mine owner. Chet Huntley, journalist. Myrna Loy, actress. Mike Mansfield (b. N.Y.), politician/diplomat. Jeanette Rankin, politician/reformer. Charles M. Russell, artist.
Noteworthy places Big Hole Natl. Battlefield. Bob Marshall Wilderness. Charles M. Russell Museum, Great Falls. Custer Battlefield Natl. Monument. Ft. Union Trading Post Natl. Hist. Site. Lewis and Clark Caverns State Park. Museum of the Plains Indian, Browning. Natl. Bison Range. Waterton-Glacier International Peace Park. World Museum of Mining, Butte. Yellowstone Natl. Park.
Memorable events French explorers and trappers visit region 1740's. Large part of state in Louisiana Purchase 1803. Lewis and Clark expedition 1805–6. Ft. Benton first permanent settlement 1846. Western part of state included in Washington Territory 1853 and 1859; eastern part in Nebraska (1854) and Dakota (1861) territories. Gold discovered at Bannack (1862) and Alder Gulch (1863). Organized as Montana Territory 1864. Dakota and Cheyenne defeat U.S. troops under Gen. William Armstrong Custer at Battle of Little Bighorn 1876. Under Chief Joseph, Nez Percé beat U.S. Army at Big Hole Basin 1877. Marcus Daly discovers copper near Butte 1880's. Statehood 1889. Homesteaders enter state 1909. Ft. Peck Dam completed 1940. Anaconda Copper Mining, dominant in Montana industry and politics since 1915, closes mining operations at Butte 1983. Elizabeth Prophet (Guru Ma) convinces 3,000 disciples of the Church Universal and Triumphant to await nuclear cataclysm in underground shelters in Paradise Valley while state bureaucrats worried over sewage facilities 1990.
Tourist information (800) VISIT-MT, (800) 548-3390. **www.state.mt.us.**

▶NEBRASKA

Although set aside as Indian territory in 1834 and made off-limits to white settlement, thousands of whites crossed the region along the Independence, Mormon and Oregon trails. Eventually Congress opened the land to settlement, which accelerated after the Homestead Act of 1862 and the coming of the railroads. The newcomers took up ranching and farming under hard conditions. The winter of 1886–87 killed thousands of cattle and drove many large-scale ranchers into bankruptcy, while the dust bowl of the 1930's spurred a mass exodus. Significant industry did not develop until World War II, when many war-related industries and army airfields moved to the center of the country. Nebraska is among the leading agricultural states, especially in the production of corn for grain and livestock. A state constitutional amendment passed in 1982 prevents the sale of farmlands and ranch lands from being sold to anyone other than a Nebraska family farm corporation.

Name From the Oto *nebrathka*, "flat water." **Nickname** Cornhusker State. **Capital** Lincoln. **Entered union** Mar. 1, 1867 (37th). **Motto** "Equality before the law."
Emblems Bird Western meadowlark. **Flower** Goldenrod. **Fossil** Mammoth. **Gem** Blue agate. **Grass** Little blue stem. **Insect** Honeybee. **Mammal** White-tailed deer. **Rock** Prairie agate. **Soil** Soils of the Holdrege series. **Song** "Beautiful Nebraska." **Tree** Western cottonwood.
Land Total area 77,354 sq. mi (16th), incl. 481 sq. mi. inland water. **Borders** S.Dak., Iowa, Mo., Kans., Colo., Wyo. **Rivers** Missouri, North Platte, Republican, South Platte. **Lakes** Harlan Co. Res., Lewis and Clark Lake. **Other notable features** Pine Ridge, Sand Hills.
Elected officials Gov. Mike Johanns (R, term exp. 2006). Lt. Gov. David Heineman (R). Sec. State John A. Gale (R). Atty. Gen. Jon Bruning (R).
People (July, 2002 est.) 1,729,180 (38th). Race/Hispanic Origin (2000 Census): White 89.6%. Black 4.0%. Indian 0.9%. Asian 1.3%. Other 2.8%. Two or more races 1.4%. Hispanic 5.5%.

Cities (2002) Omaha 399,357. Lincoln 232,362. Bellevue 46,217. Grand Island 43,010. Kearney 27,910. Fremont 25,188. Norfolk 24,183. Hastings 23,908. North Platte 23,674. Columbus 20,877.
Business **Gross State Product, 2001:** $56.97 bil. (36th). **Leading Sectors of GSP (2001):** Services 20.25%; Finance, insurance, and real estate 15.77%; Government 14.40%. ***Fortune* 500 Companies (2003):** 5: Berkshire Hathaway, Conagra, Union Pacific, Mutual of Omaha Insurance, Peter Kiewitt Sons'.
Famous natives Fred Astaire, dancer. Marlon Brando, actor. William Jennings Bryan, politician. Johnny Carson (b. Iowa), comedian. Willa Cather (b. Va.), author. Loren Eiseley, anthropologist. The Rev. Edward J. Flanagan (b. Ireland), reformer. Henry Fonda, actor. Rollin Kirby, cartoonist. Melvin Laird, politician. Harold Lloyd, actor. Mahpiua Luta (Red Cloud), Oglala Sioux chief. Malcolm X, religious leader. Roscoe Pound, educator.
Noteworthy places Agate Fossil Beds Natl. Monument. Arbor Lodge State Park, Nebraska City. Boys Town, Omaha. Buffalo Bill Ranch State Hist. Park. Chimney Rock Hist. Site. Homestead Natl. Monument, Beatrice. Oregon Trail. Pioneer Village, Minden. Scotts Bluff Natl. Monument. Stuhr Museum of the Prairie Pioneer, Grand Island.
Memorable events Acquired as part of Louisiana Purchase 1803. Separate territory created by Kansas-Nebraska Act 1854. Size reduced after creation of Colorado and Dakota territories 1861. Statehood 1867. To encourage tree planting, becomes first state to observe Arbor Day 1872. Adopts unicameral legislature 1937. Oil discovered 1939. Population peaks at 1,605,000 1984–85.
Tourist information (877) NEBRASKA. **www.visitnebraska.org.**

▶NEVADA

Set in the Great Basin desert, Nevada is one of the most barren places in North America, and the state receives less rainfall than any other. First explored by Europeans in 1776, it was 75 years before anyone thought of establishing a town in the area, and it did not last a decade. Miners came to Nevada early, but the discovery of the Comstock Lode in 1859 brought thousands. To add free-state Congressional votes, Nevada was hustled into the Union in 1864, three years before its boundaries were settled. That boom was over by the 1870's, and it took more gold and silver strikes in the early 1900's, as well as the discovery of copper, to get the economy rolling again. The mainstay of the economy since World War II has been the gambling industry, which generates virtually half of all tax revenues. During the 1990's, Nevada has been the fastest growing state in the union, with skyrocketing tourism fueling much of the growth.

Name From Spanish, meaning "snow-covered sierra." **Nicknames** Sagebrush State, Silver State. **Capital** Carson City. **Entered union** Oct. 31, 1864 (36th). **Motto** "All for our country."
Emblems **Animal** Desert bighorn sheep. **Bird** Mountain bluebird. **Flower** Sagebrush. **Fossil** Icthyosaur. **Grass** Indian ricegrass. **Metal** Silver. **Song** "Home Means Nevada." **Tree** Single-leaf piñon.
Land **Total area** 110,561 sq. mi (7th), incl. 735 sq. mi. inland water. **Borders** Oreg., Idaho, Utah, Ariz., Calif. **Rivers** Colorado, Humboldt. **Lakes** Pyramid, Walker, Winnemucca. **Other notable features** Black Rock Desert, Carson Sink, Humboldt Salt Marsh, Mojave Desert.
Elected officials Gov. Kenny Guinn (R, term exp. 2006). Lt. Gov. Lorraine Hunt (R). Sec. State Dean Heller (R). Atty. Gen. Brian Sandoval (R).
People (July, 2002 est.) 2,173,491 (35th). Race/Hispanic Origin (2000 Census): White 75.2%. Black 6.8%. Indian 1.3%. Asian 4.5%. Pacific Islander 0.4%. Other 8.0%. Two or more races 3.8%. Hispanic 19.7%.
Cities (2002) Las Vegas 508,604. Henderson 206,153. Reno 190,248. North Las Vegas 135,902. Sparks 73,730. Carson City 54,311. Elko 16,278. Boulder City 15,364. Mesquite 11,264.
Business **Gross State Product, 2001:** $79.22 bil. (32nd). **Leading Sectors of GSP (2001):** Services 31.82%; Finance, insurance, and real estate 18.76%; Hotels and other lodging places 14.31%. ***Fortune* 500 Companies (2003):** 4: Park Place Entertainment, Sierra Pacific Resources, MGM Mirage, Harrah's Entertainment.
Famous natives Andre Agassi, tennis player. Walter Van Tilburg Clark (b. Me.), author. Sarah Winnemucca Hopkins, interpeter/teacher. John William MacKay, miner. William Morris Stewart (b. N.Y.), lawyer/senator.
Noteworthy places Death Valley Natl. Monument. Las Vegas. Lehman Caves Natl. Monument. Valley of the Fire State Park, Overton.
Memorable events Francisco Tomás Garcés explores area 1775–76. Jedediah Smith, trader, crosses region 1826–27. Old Spanish Trail (1830) and California Trail (1833) cross region. John Frémont explores area 1843–45. To United States after Mexican War 1846. Genoa, first settlement in Nevada, founded as Mormon Station 1849. Gold of Comstock Lode discovered 1859. Organized as separate territory 1861. Statehood 1864. Nevada legalizes gambling 1931. Hoover Dam built on Colorado River 1935. Nuclear tests begun at Yucca Flats 1951. Population grows more than 550 percent 1950–88, and 25 percent in 1990's.
Tourist information (800) NEVADA8. **www.state.nv.us.**

▶NEW HAMPSHIRE

New Hampshire has a disproportionate influence on presidential elections because by state law its primary must fall at least one week before any other state's (though Iowa's caucuses can come earlier). Through independence the mainstays of the economy were fishing, trade and farming. Boston proved more suitable for trade, and New Hampshire's stubborn land was outproduced by the more fertile valleys to the south and west. The state's economy receded until the beginning of the Industrial Revolution, when there was tremendous growth in textile-producing mill towns in the Merrimack River Valley. The mills began to close after World War I, and the economy faltered again. Improvement came as high-tech firms from Boston sought refuge in New Hampshire's favorable tax climate. The state's economy was pummeled by the severe New England recession in the early 1990's, but has rebounded since.

Name For English county of Hampshire. **Nickname** Granite State. **Capital** Concord. **Entered union** June 21, 1788 (9th). **Motto** "Live free or die."
Emblems **Amphibian** Spotted newt. **Bird** Purple finch. **Flower** Purple lilac. **Gem** Smoke quartz. **Insect** Ladybug. **Mineral** Beryl. **Song** "Old New Hampshire." **Tree** White birch.
Land **Total area** 9,350 sq. mi (46th), incl. 382 sq. mi. inland water. **Borders** Quebec, Maine, Atlantic Ocean, Mass., Vt. **Rivers** Connecticut, Mer-

rimack, Piscataqua, Saco, Salmon Falls. **Lakes** First Connecticut, Francis, Newfound, Ossipee, Sunapee, Winnipesaukee. **Other notable features** Isles of Shoals, White Mts. (Mt. Washington 6,288 ft., highest peak in Northeast).

Elected officials Gov. Craig Benson (R, two-year term exp. 2004). Sec. State William Gardner (D). Atty. Gen. Peter Heed (R).

People (July, 2002 est.) 1,275,056 (41st). Race/Hispanic Origin (2000 Census): White 96.0%. Black 0.7%. Indian 0.2%. Asian 1.3%. Other 0.6%. Two or more races 1.1%. Hispanic 1.7%.

Cities (2002) Manchester 108,398. Nashua 87,705. Concord 41,404. Rochester 29,350. Dover 27,784. Keene 22,714. Portsmouth 21,408. Laconia 16,949. Claremont 13,195. Lebanon 12,788.

Business **Gross State Product, 2001:** $47.18 bil. (38th). **Leading Sectors of GSP (2001):** Finance, insurance, and real estate 24.99%; Services 21.57%; Manufacturing 16.13%. ***Fortune* 500 Companies (2003):** 1: Fisher Scientific Intl.

Famous natives Salmon P. Chase, jurist. Ralph Adams Cram, architect. Mary Baker Eddy, founder, Church of Christ, Scientist. Daniel Chester French, sculptor. Horace Greeley, journalist. Sarah Buell Hale, author. Franklin Pierce, U.S. president. Augustus Saint-Gaudens (b. Ireland), sculptor. Alan Shepard, astronaut. Daniel Webster, politician. Eleazar Wheelock (b. Conn.), Dartmouth founder.

Noteworthy places Currier Gallery of Art, Manchester. The Flume (gorge). Franconia Notch. Isles of Shoals. Lake Winnipesaukee. Mt. Washington. Shaker Village, Canterbury. St. Gaudens Natl. Hist. Site. Strawberry Bank. White Mountains Natl. Forest.

Memorable events Martin Pring sails along coast 1603. Champlain explores area 1604. John Smith visits Isles of Shoals 1614. Included in king's grant to John Mason and Sir Ferdinando Gorges 1622. First settlers at Little Harbor, near Portsmouth 1623. Made separate royal province 1679, though under Massachusetts governor 1699–1741. Rogers's Rangers halt Indian raids 1759. New Hampshire patriots seize British fort at Portsmouth and drive out Royal governor 1775. Province relinquishes claims to New Connecticut (Vermont) 1782. First textile mill built 1803. Treaty of Portsmouth ends Russo-Japanese War 1905. Bretton Woods conference leads to establishment of International Monetary Fund 1944. First state to adopt lottery to support public education 1963.

Tourist information (800) FUN-IN-NH. **www.visitnh.gov.**

▶NEW JERSEY

With the entire state population classified as living in metro areas, New Jersey is the most densely populated state, 15 times the national average. The image survives of New Jersey as a chemical-industrial wasteland south of New York Harbor. Pharmaceuticals and chemicals are in fact New Jersey's leading products, but the next most important industry is tourism, because of the money tourists spend at the gaming tables of Atlantic City. What earns New Jersey its nickname, the Garden State, is its extensive small-scale agriculture, which produces tomatoes, dairy products, asparagus, blueberries, corn and poultry.

New Jersey lies on a plain between Philadelphia and New York City, two larger neighbors that have overshadowed New Jersey on the national scene since colonial days. Yet during the Revolution, more than 100 battles were fought on New Jersey soil, and today the overwhelming majority of containerized shipping in the Port of New York and New Jersey is shipped from New Jersey terminals. Per capita income is always among the top five in the nation.

Name After English Channel Island of Jersey. **Nickname** Garden State. **Capital** Trenton. **Entered union** Dec. 18, 1787 (3rd). **Motto** "Liberty and prosperity."

Emblems **Animal** Horse. **Bird** Eastern goldfinch. **Flower** Violet. **Insect** Honeybee. **Memorial tree** Dogwood. **Tree** Red oak.

Land **Total area** 8,721 sq. mi (47th), incl. 1,304 sq. mi. inland water. **Borders** N.Y., Atlantic Ocean, Del., Pa. **Rivers** Delaware, Hackensack, Hudson, Passaic. **Lakes** Greenwood, Hopatcong, Round Valley Res., Spruce Run. **Other notable features** Delaware Water Gap, Kittatinny Mts., Palisades, Pine Barrens, Ramapo Mts.

Elected officials Gov. James E. McGreevey (D, term exp. 2006). Sec. Regena L. Thomas (D). Atty. Gen. Peter Harvey (D)

People (July, 2002 est.) 8,590,300 (9th). Race/Hispanic Origin (2000 Census): White 72.6%. Black 13.6%. Indian 0.2%. Asian 5.7%. Other 5.4%. Two or more races 2.5%. Hispanic 13.3%.

Cities (2002) Newark 277,000. Jersey City 240,100. Paterson 150,750. Elizabeth 123,279. Trenton 85,650. Camden 79,685. Clifton 79,626. East Orange 69,750. Passaic 68,445. Union City 66,902.

Business **Gross State Product, 2001:** $365.39 bil. (8th). **Leading Sectors of GSP (2001):** Finance, insurance, and real estate 24.66%; Services 22.85%; Real estate 15.71%. ***Fortune* 500 Companies (2003):** 21: Merck, Johnson & Johnson, Prudential Financial, Lucent Technologies, Honeywell International, Pharmacia, Wyeth, Toys "R" Us, Public Service Enterprise Group, Schering-Plough, Chubb, American Standard, Automatic Data Processing, Avaya, Campbell Soup, Engelhard, Pathmark Stores, Becton Dickinson, Quest Diagnostics, Sealed Air, AT&T, CIT Group.

Famous natives Count Basie, jazz musician. William J. Brennan, jurist. Aaron Burr, politician. Grover Cleveland, U.S. president. James Fenimore Cooper, novelist/historian. Stephen Crane, author. Thomas Edison, inventor. Albert Einstein (b. Germany), nuclear physicist. Waldo Frank, author. Joyce Kilmer, poet. Jerry Lewis, actor. Jack Nicholson, actor. Zebulon Pike, explorer. Molly Pitcher, Revolutionary War heroine. Paul Robeson, actor/singer. Walter Schirra, astronaut. Frank Sinatra, singer. Alfred Stieglitz, photographer. Meryl Streep, actress. Aaron Montgomery Ward, merchant. William Carlos Williams, poet.

Noteworthy places Atlantic City. Cape May Historic District. Edison Natl. Hist. Site, West Orange. Lakehurst Naval Air Station. Liberty State Park, Jersey City. Morristown Natl. Hist. Park. Newark Museum. Palisades Interstate Park. Pine Barrens wilderness area. Princeton University. Walt Whitman House, Camden.

Memorable events Giovanni de Verrazano explores 1524. Hudson explores up Hudson River 1609. Dutch settlers establish Ft. Nassau 1623. New Jersey taken over by British and organized as colony under Sir George Carteret 1665. Major battles of Revolution at Trenton (1776), Princeton (1777), and Monmouth (1778). Women given vote at Elizabethtown 1800. Voting rights restricted to men 1807. Adopts state constitution 1844. Passenger ship *Morro Castle* burns off Asbury Park; 134

die 1934. Dirigible *Hindenburg* explodes while mooring at Lakehurst; 36 die 1937. New Jersey Turnpike linking New York City and Philadelphia opens 1952. Five days of race riots in Newark leave 26 dead 1967. Gambling legalized in Atlantic City 1978. State enacts strictest gun legislation in United States 1990.
Tourist information (800) VISITNJ. **www.visitnj.org.**

▶NEW MEXICO

The development problem of the western states is shared by New Mexico, which of all states has the smallest percentage of its area covered by water. Rich in other resources, it is the uranium capital of the world. The state mineral tax brings in a large percentage of state revenues, some of which goes into permanent endowments. Distribution of wealth in New Mexico remains uneven, but Hispanics, who tend to register as Democrats, vote in roughly the same ways as Anglos. A higher percentage of Native Americans live in New Mexico than in any other state.

Today, mining's influence on the state economy has waned in favor of service industry jobs. Despite the enormous governmental investment in research at Los Alamos, where the atom bomb was born, the highly classified nature of this work limits the development of related industry.

Name By Spanish explorers after Mexico. **Nickname** Land of Enchantment. **Capital** Santa Fe. **Entered union** Jan. 6, 1912 (47th). **Motto** *Crescit eundo* (It grows as it goes).
Emblems **Animal** Black bear. **Bird** Roadrunner (chaparral bird). **Fish** Cutthroat trout. **Flower** Yucca. **Fossil** *Coelphysis* dinosaur. **Gem** Turquoise. **Songs** "O, Fair New Mexico," "Así es Nuevo Mejico." **Tree** Piñon. **Vegetables** Frijole, chili.
Land **Total area** 121,589 sq. mi (5th), incl. 234 sq. mi. inland water. **Borders** Colo., Okla., Tex., Chihuahua, Ariz. **Rivers** Gila, Pecos, Rio Grande, Zuni. **Lakes** Conchas Res., Eagle Nest, Elephant Butte Res., Navajo Res., Ute Res. **Mountains** Chuska, Guadalupe, Sacramento, San Andres, Sangre de Cristo. **Other notable features** Carlsbad Caverns, Continental Divide, Staked Plain.
Elected officials Gov. Bill Richardson (D, term exp. 2006). Lt. Gov. Diane Denish (D). Sec. State Rebecca Vigil-Giron (D). Atty. Gen. Patricia Madrid (D).
People (July, 2002 est.) 1,855,059 (36th). Race/Hispanic Origin (2000 Census): White 66.8%. Black 1.9%. Indian 9.5%. Asian 1.1%. Pacific Islander 0.1%. Other 17.0%. Two or more races 3.6%. Hispanic 42.1%.
Cities (2002) Albuquerque 463,874. Las Cruces 475,015. Santa Fe 65,127. Rio Rancho 56,614. Roswell 44,058. Farmington 40,563. Alamogordo 35,107. Clovis 32,511. Hobbs 28,479. Carlsbad 25,196.
Business **Gross State Product, 2001:** $55.43 bil. (37th). **Leading Sectors of GSP (2001):** Services 18.30%; Government 18.05%; Manufacturing 13.61%. ***Fortune* 500 Companies (2003):** 0.
Famous natives William "Billy the Kid" Bonney (b. N.Y.), outlaw. Peter Hurd, artist. Archbishop Jean Baptiste Lamy (b. France), missionary. Georgia O'Keeffe (b. Wis.), artist. Popé, Tewa Pueblo chief. Harrison Schmitt, astronaut.
Noteworthy places Aztec Ruins Natl. Monument. Bandelier Natl. Monument. Capulin Mt. Natl. Monument. Carlsbad Caverns Natl. Park. Chaco Culture Natl. Hist. Park. El Morro Natl. Monument. Ft. Union Natl. Monument. Gila Cliff Dwellings Natl. Monument. Museum of New Mexico, Santa Fe. Pecos Mission. Salinas Mission. Santa Fe Opera. Wheelwright Museum of the American Indian, Santa Fe. White Sands Natl. Monument.
Memorable events Marcos de Niza enters Zuni country 1539. Juan de Oñate establishes first Spanish settlement on Rio Grande near Espanola 1598. Santa Fe founded; becomes capital of New Mexico 1710. Santa Fe Trail from Independence, Missouri, completed; Mexico secedes from Spain 1821. Manuel Armijo suppresses revolt against Mexican rule (1837); defeats invasion from Republic of Texas (1841). Land annexed by United States after Mexican-American War 1848. Organized as territory with Arizona and part of Colorado 1850. Lincoln County War pits cattlemen against merchants 1878–81. Statehood; 17 killed in raid by Pancho Villa 1912. Los Alamos selected as first research and development facility for nuclear weapons 1942. First atom bomb exploded at Alamagordo Air Base 1945.
Tourist information (800) 545-2040. **www.newmexico.org.**

▶NEW YORK

New York's greatest and most inviting asset has always been its strategic location and long arteries into the hinterland. New York Bay is one of the great natural harbors of the world, and the broad Hudson River is one of the most fortunately placed. After the opening of the Erie Canal between the Hudson and Lake Erie in 1825, New York City became the trading center for the Midwest as well as the Hudson Valley and the Atlantic Coast. Buffalo also experienced a boom, becoming a major Great Lakes industrial port. New York is still the first state in number of manufacturing establishments and employees. Wall Street alone employs half a million people.

Although New York's population grew by nearly half a million people between 1980 and 1990, its relatively slow rate of growth resulted in a loss of three Congressional seats—an indication of the change in the state's political clout. As its place among the 50 states has fallen by some measures, New York City's worldwide importance in business, culture and communications has risen.

Name For Duke of York, later James II, of England. **Nickname** Empire State. **Capital** Albany. **Entered union** July 26, 1788 (11th). **Motto** *Excelsior* (Higher).
Emblems **Animal** Beaver. **Beverage** Milk. **Bird** Bluebird. **Fish** Brook or speckled trout. **Flower** Rose. **Fossil** Prehistoric crab (*Eurypterus remipes*). **Fruit** Apple. **Gem** Garnet. **Song** "I Love New York." **Tree** Sugar maple.
Land **Total area** 54,556 sq. mi (27th), incl. 7,342 sq. mi. inland water. **Borders** Lake Ontario, Ontario, Quebec, Vt., Mass., Conn., Atlantic Ocean, N.J., Pa., Lake Erie. **Rivers** Allegheny, Delaware, Genesee, Hudson, Mohawk, New York State Barge Canal, Niagara, St. Lawrence, Susquehanna. **Lakes** Cayuga, Champlain, Chautauqua, Erie, George, Oneida, Ontario, Seneca. **Mountains** Adirondack (Mt. Marcy 5,344 ft.), Allegheny, Berkshire Hills, Catskill, Kittatinny, Ramapo. **Other notable features** Hudson Valley, Mohawk Valley, Niagara Falls, Palisades, Thousand Islands.
Elected officials Gov. George E. Pataki (R, term exp. 2006). Lt. Gov. Mary Donohue (R). Sec. State Randy A. Daniels (D). Atty. Gen. Eliot Spitzer (D).
People (July, 2002 est.) 19,157,532 (3rd). Race/Hispanic Origin (2000 Census): White 67.9%. Blac, 15.9%. Indian 0.4%. Asian 5.5%.

Other 7.1%. Two or more races 3.1%. Hispanic 15.1%.

Cities (2002) New York 8,084,316. Buffalo 287,698. Rochester 217,158. Yonkers 197,234. Syracuse 145,164. Albany 93,779. New Rochelle 72,472. Mount Vernon 68,615. Schenectady 61,420. Utica 59,947.

Business **Gross State Product, 2001:** $826.49 bil. (2nd). **Leading Sectors of GSP (2001):** Finance, insurance, and real estate 34.23%; Services 23.01%; Real Estate 14.10%. ***Fortune* 500 Companies (2003):** 52: including Citigroup, International Business Machines, Verizon Communications, American International Group, J.P. Morgan Chase, Morgan Stanley Dean Witter, Merrill Lynch, AOL Time Warner, Pfizer, MetLife, Goldman Sachs Group, Pepsico, New York Life Insurance, TIAA-CREF, Viacom, American Express, Lehman Brothers Holdings, Bristol-Myers Squibb, Eastman Kodak, Marsh & McLennan, Colgate-Palmolive, Corning, Avon Products, Foot Locker, Liz Claiborne, New York Times, Altria Group, Loews.

Famous natives Woody Allen, director. John Jacob Astor (b. Germany), merchant. Humphrey Bogart, actor. George Burns, actor. Aaron Copland, composer. Agnes de Mille, choreographer. George Eastman, camera inventor. Millard Fillmore, U.S. president. Lou Gehrig, baseball player. George Gershwin, composer. Julia Ward Howe, reformer. Washington Irving, author. Henry James, author. Vince Lombardi, football coach. Groucho Marx, comedian. Herman Melville, author. Ogden Nash, poet/humorist. Eugene O'Neill, playwright. Otetiani "Red Jacket", Seneca chief. Channing E. Phillips, minister/reformer. John D. Rockefeller, industrialist. Norman Rockwell, illustrator. Richard Rodgers, composer. Franklin Delano Roosevelt, U.S. president. Theodore Roosevelt, U.S. president. Jonas Salk, physician. Elizabeth Ann Seton, first American saint. Elizabeth Cady Stanton, suffragette. James Johnson Sweeney, art critic. Martin Van Buren, U.S. president. Mae West, actress. E.B. White, author. Walt Whitman, poet.

Noteworthy places Albright-Knox Gallery of American Art, Buffalo. American Merchant Marine Museum, Kings Point. Baseball Hall of Fame, Cooperstown. Bear Mt. State Park. Buffalo Museum of Science. Corning Glass Center, Corning. Erie Canal Museum, Syracuse. Farmers' Museum, Cooperstown. Fenimore House, Cooperstown. Franklin D. Roosevelt Natl. Hist. Site, Hyde Park. Ft. Stanwix Natl. Monument, Rome. Ft. Ticonderoga. Hudson Valley. Mohawk Valley. Niagara Falls. Palisades Interstate Park. Saratoga Natl. Hist. Park. Vanderbilt Museum, Hyde Park. U.S. Military Academy, West Point. Women's Rights Natl. Hist. Park, Seneca Falls. **New York City** American Academy of Arts & Sciences. American Museum of Natural History. Bronx Zoo. Brooklyn Botanical Garden. Brooklyn Museum. Cathedral of St. John the Divine. Cooper-Hewitt Museum. Federal Hall. Fraunces Tavern. Frick Collection. Guggenheim Museum. Hispanic Society of America. Jewish Museum. Lincoln Center for the Performing Arts. Metropolitan Museum of Art. Museum of Modern Art. Museum of the American Indian. N.Y. Public Library. N.Y. Stock Exchange. Rockefeller Center. South Street Seaport Museum. Statue of Liberty. United Nations.

Memorable events Giovanni de Verrazano sails into New York Bay 1524. Samuel de Champlain sails down the St. Lawrence River 1603. Henry Hudson sails up Hudson River 1609. Dutch establish Ft. Orange (Albany) 1614. Peter Minuit buys Manhattan Island and founds colony of New Amsterdam 1625. British take New Amsterdam and name it New York 1664. Ethan Allen takes Ft. Ticonderoga 1775. George Washington inaugurated president New York City 1789. U.S. Military Academy founded West Point 1802. Erie Canal opened 1825. Statue of Liberty dedicated 1886. New York City includes Manhattan, Bronx, Queens, Brooklyn, and Staten Island 1898. President William McKinley assassinated in Buffalo 1901. UN headquarters established at New York City 1945. St. Lawrence Seaway opened 1959. One-fourth of New York City below poverty level 1984.

Tourist information (800) CALL-NYS. **www.iloveny.com.**

▶NORTH CAROLINA

At the time of the Revolution, tobacco and rice plantations dominated the economy of the eastern part of the state, which in turn dominated the legislature. Next to last to ratify the Constitution, North Carolina was the last Southern state to secede from the Union. The Civil War cost North Carolina dearly; reconstruction was short-lived, and blacks were effectively disenfranchised again by the turn of the century. Since World War II, the state has grown increasingly prosperous, especially in the "academic triangle" that encloses the University of North Carolina at Chapel Hill, Duke, and North Carolina State. The traditional industries of textiles, furniture, and tobacco still lead, partly because of diversification within them. North Carolina benefits from the general Sunbelt boom and from an influx of foreign capital; it maintains a healthy manufacturing sector, and has enjoyed steady economic growth in the 1990's.

Name For King Charles I (Carolus is Latin for Charles). **Nicknames** Tarheel State, Old North State. **Capital** Raleigh. **Entered union** Nov. 21, 1789 (12th). **Motto** *Esse quam videri* (To be rather than to seem).

Emblems **Bird** Cardinal. **Fish** Channel bass. **Flower** Dogwood. **Insect** Honeybee. **Precious stone** Emerald. **Reptile** Eastern box turtle. **Rock** Granite. **Shell** Scotch bonnet. **Song** "The Old North State." **Tree** Pine.

Land **Total area** 53,819 sq. mi (28th), incl. 5,108 sq. mi. inland water. **Borders** Va., Atlantic Ocean, S.C., Tenn., Georgia. **Rivers** Pee Dee, Roanoke, Yadkin. **Lakes** Buggs Island, High Rock, Mattamuskeet, Norman, Waccamaw. **Mountains** Black, Blue Ridge, Great Smoky, Unaka. **Other notable features** Great Dismal Swamp, Mount Mitchell, Outer Banks, Pamlico Sound.

Elected officials Gov. Michael F. Easley (D, term exp. 2005). Lt. Gov. Beverly Purdue (D). Sec. State Elaine Marshall (D). Atty. Gen. Roy Cooper (D).

People (July, 2002 est.) 8,320,146 (11th). Race/Hispanic Origin (2000 Census): White 72.1%. Black 21.6%. Indian 1.2%. Asian 1.4%. Other 2.3%. Two or more races 1.3%. Hispanic 4.7%.

Cities (2002) Charlotte 580,597. Raleigh 306,944. Greensboro 228,217. Durham 195,914. Winston-Salem 188,934. Fayetteville 124,286. Cary 98,041. Wilmington 90,644. High Point 90,639. Asheville 69,193.

Business **Gross State Product, 2001:** $275.62 bil. (12th). **Leading Sectors of GSP (2001):** Manufacturing 21.38%; Finance, insurance, and real estate 18.98%; Services 17.41%. ***Fortune* 500 Companies (2003):** 14: Duke Energy, Bank of America Corp., Wachovia Corp., Lowe's, R.J.

Reynolds Tobacco, Progress Energy, Sonic Automotive, BB&T Corp., VF, Nucor, Goodrich, SPX, Family Dollar Stores, Jefferson-Pilot.

Famous natives Benjamin Newton Duke and James Buchanan Duke, industrialists/philanthropists. Richard J. Gatling, inventor. Billy Graham, minister. Andy Griffith, actor. O. Henry, writer. Andrew Johnson, U.S. president. William Rufus King, politician. Charles Kuralt, journalist. Meadowlark Lemon, athlete. Dolley Madison, First Lady. Thelonius Monk, musician. Edward R. Murrow, journalist. James Knox Polk, U.S. president. Moses Waddell, Confederate general. Thomas Wolfe, author.

Noteworthy places Bennett Place. Blue Ridge Natl. Parkway. Cape Hatteras and Cape Lookout Natl. Seashore. Carl Sandburg home, Hendersonville. Ft. Raleigh. Great Smoky Mountains Natl. Park. Great Smoky Mountains Natl. Hist. Park. Guilford Courthouse Natl. Military Park. Mint Museum, Charlotte. Moores Creek Natl. Battlefield. North Carolina Maritime Museum, Beaufort. North Carolina Museum of Art, Raleigh. Roanoke Island. Wright Brothers Natl. Memorial, Kitty Hawk.

Memorable events Part of Carolina grant given to eight noblemen by Charles II 1663. Culpepper's Rebellion in reaction to unfair tax collection policies 1677. Tuscarora lose war against European immigrants 1713. Proprietors sell rights to Crown; becomes royal province 1729. Mecklenburg Declaration (1775), forerunner of Declaration of Independence. Becomes first colony to sanction explicitly declaration of independence from Britain in Apr. 1776. Gen. Charles Cornwallis wins Battle of Guilford Courthouse, but British lose control of colony 1781. Ratifies Constitution 1789. Gives up claims to western territories, now part of Tennessee 1790. Establishes first state university system in United States 1829. Cherokees driven out of North Carolina to Oklahoma 1838. Secedes 1861. Readmitted to Union 1868. American Tobacco Company founded 1890. Wright brothers launch first successful airplane at Kitty Hawk 1903. Confrontation between Ku Klux Klan and anti-Klan demonstrators leaves five dead; 12 Klansmen charged with first-degree murder 1979.

Tourist information (800) VISIT-NC. **www.visitnc.com.**

▶NORTH DAKOTA

The first permanent settlers in North Dakota were Scots-Canadians who settled at Pembina on the Red River near the Canadian border, and who traded primarily with Winnipeg and St. Paul. The arrival of the Northern Pacific Railway in 1872 created a surge of huge farms, many of which were wiped out by drought and harsh winters in the 1880's. There followed a huge influx of Norwegians and Germans whose influence is still very apparent today. North Dakota's economy is heavily agricultural and leads the nation in production of wheat. Farming is centered in the fertile Red River of the North Valley, with livestock throughout the rest of the state.

Name For northern section of Dakota territory; *dakota* is Sioux word for "allies." **Nicknames** Sioux State, Peace Garden State, Flickertail State. **Capital** Bismarck. **Entered union** Nov. 2, 1889 (39th). **Motto** "Liberty and union, now and forever, one and inseparable."

Emblems **Beverage** Milk. **Bird** Western meadowlark. **Fish** Northern pike. **Flower** Wild prairie rose. **Fossil** Teredo petrified wood. **Grass** Western wheatgrass. **March** "Spirit of North Dakota." **Song** "North Dakota Hymn." **Tree** American elm.

Land **Total area** 70,700'sq. mi (19th), incl. 1,724 sq. mi. inland water. **Borders** Saskatchewan, Manitoba, Minn., S.Dak., Mont. **Rivers** Missouri, Red River of the North. **Lakes** Ashtabula, Devils, Oahe, Sakakawea. **Other notable features** Geographical center of North America, Missouri Plateau, Red River Valley, Rolling Drift Prairie.

Elected officials Gov. John Hoeven (R, term exp. 2004). Lt. Gov. Jack Dalrymple (R). Sec. State Alvin A. Jaegar (R). Atty. Gen. Wayne Stenehjem (R).

People (July, 2002 est.) 634,110 (48th). Race/Hispanic Origin (2000 Census): White 92.4%. Black 0.6%. Indian 4.9%. Asian 0.6%. Other 0.4%. Two or more races 1.2%. Hispanic 1.2%.

Cities (2002) Fargo 91,240. Bismarck 56,234. Grand Forks 48,546. Minot 35,617. Mandan 16,769. West Fargo 15,801. Dickinson 15,679. Jamestown 15,115. Williston 12,376. Wahpeton 8,586.

Business **Gross State Product, 2001:** $19.01 bil. (50th). **Leading Sectors of GSP (2001):** Services 19.27%; Government 15.60%; Finance, insurance, and real estate 14.58%. ***Fortune* 500 Companies (2003):** 0.

Famous natives Angie Dickinson, actress. John Bernard Flannagan, sculptor. Louis L'Amour, novelist. Peggy Lee, singer. Roger Maris, baseball player. Eric Sevareid, broadcaster. Vihjalmur Stefansson (b. Canada), ethnologist. Lawrence Welk, entertainer.

Noteworthy places Ft. Abraham Lincoln State Park. Ft. Union Trading Post Natl. Hist. Site. International Peace Garden. Knife River Indian Villages Natl. Hist. Site. Theodore Roosevelt Natl. Park, the Badlands.

Memorable events Pierre Gaultier de Varennes, sieur de Vérendrye first European to visit area 1738. United States acquires half of territory in Louisiana Purchase 1803. Meriwether Lewis and William Clark expedition builds Ft. Mandan 1804–5. First permanent settlement at Pembina 1812. Britain cedes western half of state to United States 1818. Missouri River steamboats reach territory 1838. First railroad arrives 1873. Statehood 1889. First state to hold presidential primary 1912. Garrison Dam completed forming Lake Sakakawea; gambling (blackjack) legalized 1981. Red River floods, devastating agriculture, 1997.

Tourist information (800) HELLO-ND. **www.ndtourism.com.**

▶OHIO

The first settlements in Ohio were Marietta, in 1788, and Cincinnati in 1789, on the Ohio River, but significant migration into the state didn't occur until after the War of 1812. Shipping flourished in the 1820's and 1830's thanks to a network of canals connecting the Ohio and Lake Erie. Since 1959 the St. Lawrence Seaway has helped keep Ohio among the top five exporting states. Heavy industry also flourished in the northern cities that had access to coal and iron ore from the Lake Superior region. The 1870's saw the development of a manufacturing base that later became an integral part of the automotive industry. Although Ohio's economy has traditionally been well balanced between agriculture, industry, mining, and trade, the recession of the early 1980's weakened manufacturing, triggered flight from the industrial cities, and saw a dramatic shift to a service economy and to high-tech industry.

Name From the Iroquois *oheo,* "beautiful." **Nickname** Buckeye State. **Capital** Columbus. **Entered union** Mar. 1, 1803 (17th). **Motto** "With God, all things are possible."

Emblems **Beverage** Tomato juice. **Bird** Cardinal. **Flower** Scarlet carnation. **Gem** Ohio flint. **Insect** Ladybug. **Song** "Beautiful Ohio." **Tree** Buckeye.

Land **Total area** 44,825 sq. mi (34th), incl. 3,877 sq. mi. inland water. **Borders** Mich., Lake Erie, Pa., W.Va., Ky., Ind. **Rivers** Cuyahoga, Maumee, Miami, Muskingum, Ohio, Sandusky, Scioto. **Lakes** Berlin Res., Dillon Res., Erie, Mosquito Res., St. Mary's.

Elected officials Gov. Bob Taft (R, term exp. 2006). Lt. Gov. Jennette Bradley (R). Sec. State. J. Kenneth Blackwell (R). Atty. Gen. Jim Petro (R).

People (July, 2002 est.) 11,421,267 (7th). Race/Hispanic Origin (2000 Census): White 85.0%. Black 11.5%. Indian 0.2%. Asian 1.2%. Other 0.8%. Two or more races 1.4%. Hispanic 1.9%.

Cities (2002) Columbus 725,228. Cleveland 467,851. Cincinnati 323,885. Toledo 309,106. Akron 214,349. Dayton 162,669. Parma 84,534. Youngstown 80,026. Canton 79,772. Lorain 67,704.

Business **Gross State Product, 2001:** $373.71 bil. (7th). **Leading Sectors of GSP (2001):** Manufacturing 21.30%; Services 19.61%; Finance, insurance, and real estate 17.78%. ***Fortune* 500 Companies (2003):** 28, including American Electric Power, Kroger, Cardinal Health, Procter & Gamble, Federated Department Stores, Nationwide, Goodyear Tire & Rubber, Cinergy, Dana, Limited, National City Corp., FirstEnergy, Progressive, Keycorp, Eaton, Fifth Third Bancorp, Owens-Illinois, Parker Hannifin, NCR, Sherwin-Williams.

Famous natives Sherwood Anderson, writer. Neil Armstrong, astronaut. George Bellows, artist. Ambrose Bierce, author. George Armstrong Custer, army officer. Paul Laurence Dunbar, poet. Thomas A. Edison, inventor. James A. Garfield, U.S. president. John Glenn, astronaut/politician. Ulysses S. Grant, U.S. president/general. Zane Grey, author. Warren G. Harding, U.S. president. Benjamin Harrison, U.S. president. Rutherford B. Hayes, U.S. president. Bob Hope, entertainer. William McKinley, U.S. president. Annie Oakley, markswoman. Ransom Eli Olds, carmaker. Eddie Rickenbacker, pilot. William Sherman, army officer. William Howard Taft, U.S. president/chief justice. Art Tatum, pianist. Tecumseh, Shawnee chief. James Thurber, humorist. Orville Wright, airplane inventor.

Noteworthy places Air Force Museum, Dayton. Cleveland Museum of Art. Cleveland Museum of Natural History. Columbus Museum of Art. Great Lakes Historical Society Museum, Vermilion. Mound City Group Natl. Monument, Chillicothe. Neil Armstrong Air and Space Museum, Wapakoneta. Ohio River Museum, Marietta. Pro Football Hall of Fame, Canton. Toledo Museum of Art.

Memorable events Hopewell Mound-Builders present throughout state prior to arrival of Miamis, Shawnees, Wyandots, and Delawares. Conflicting claims by France, Virginia, Connecticut, and New York 1609–1786. René-Roger Cavelier de La Salle visits region 1669–70. To Britain 1763. To United States after 1783. Becomes part of Northwest Territory 1787. First settlement at Marietta 1788. Gen. "Mad" Anthony Wayne beats Tecumseh at Battle of Fallen Timbers 1794. Enters Union 1803. Harrison beats Tecumseh at Battle of Tippecanoe 1811. Oliver Hazard Perry beats British fleet at Battle of Put-in-Bay 1813. Ohio and Erie Canal completed 1832. Dayton flood kills 400 in Miami River Valley; damage put at $100 million 1913. Carl B. Stokes elected mayor of Cleveland, first black mayor of major U.S. city 1967. Four students protesting Vietnam War killed by National Guard at Kent State University 1970.

Tourist information (800) BUCKEYE. **www.state.oh.us.**

▶OKLAHOMA

French trappers entered the region of Oklahoma in the 1700's. In 1830 the land was designated the Indian Country, set aside for members of the Cherokees, Chickasaw, Choctaw, Creek, and Seminole deported from the southeast by the Indian Removal Act of 1830. These "Five Civilized Tribes," among others, fared well until the Civil War. They supported the Confederacy (some were actually slave-holders), and in 1868 Col. George Armstrong Custer led a massacre of Cheyenne at the Battle of the Washita. Twenty years later the government abrogated its treaty commitments and opened the territory to settlement. Today the state has a distinctly southern character. The region bordering the Red River is known as "Little Dixie," and as many as two-thirds of all Oklahomans consider themselves born-again Christians.

Oklahoma has a diversified economy. The state led the country in oil and gas production through the 1920's. Agriculture was hit heavily by the dust bowl of the 1930's, and thousands of "Okies" fled west. While agriculture and petroleum are still vital to the economy, manufacturing is increasingly important. The state is crossed by two of the country's longest rivers. The Arkansas links Catoosa (near Tulsa) to the Gulf of Mexico and the Mississippi River system; but the Red River is not navigable in Oklahoma, and dissolved salts make it useless for agriculture, industry or residential purposes.

Name From the Choctaw *okla humma,* "land of the red people." **Nickname** Sooner State. **Capital** Oklahoma City. **Entered union** Nov. 16, 1907 (46th). **Motto** *Labor omnia vincit* (Work overcomes all obstacles).

Emblems **Animal** American buffalo. **Bird** Scissor-tailed flycatcher. **Colors** Green and white. **Fish** White bass. **Floral emblem** Mistletoe. **Grass** Indian grass. **Poem** "Howdy Folks." **Reptile** Collared lizard (mountain boomer). **Song** "Oklahoma!" **Stone** Barite rose (rose rock). **Tree** Redbud. **Waltz** "Oklahoma Wind."

Land Total area 69,898 sq. mi (20th), incl. 1,231 sq. mi. inland water. **Borders** Kans., Mo., Ark., Tex., N.Mex., Colo. **Rivers** Arkansas, Canadian, Cimarron, Red. **Lakes** Canton, Lake o' the Cherokees, Oologah, Texoma. **Other notable features** Ouachita Mts., Ozark Plateau, Staked Plain, Wichita Mts.

Elected officials Gov. Brad Henry (D, term exp. 2006). Lt. Gov. Mary Fallin (R). Sec. State M. Susan Savage (D). Atty. Gen. Drew Edmondson (D).

People (July, 2002 est.) 3,493,714 (28th). Race/Hispanic Origin (2000 Census): White 76.2%. Black 7.6%. Indian 7.9%. Asian 1.4%. Pacific Islander 0.1%. Other 2.4%. Two or more races 4.5%. Hispanic 5.2%.

Cities (2002) Oklahoma City 519,034. Tulsa 391,098. Norman 97,831. Lawton 91,333. Broken Arrow 80,088. Edmond 70,540. Midwest City 54,503. Enid 46,531. Moore 43,739. Stillwater 40,586.

Business **Gross State Product, 2001:** $93.86 bil. (29th). **Leading Sectors of GSP (2001):** Services 18.73%; Government 16.81%; Manufacturing 13.89%. ***Fortune* 500 Companies (2003):** 4:

Phillips Petroleum, Williams, Oneok, Kerr-McGee, OGE Energy, Devon Energy.

Famous natives Ralph Ellison, author. Woody Guthrie, reformer/musician. Patrick J. Hurley, diplomat. Karl Jansky, electrical engineer. Mickey Mantle, baseball player. Wiley Post, aviator. Tony Randall, actor. Oral Roberts, evangelist. Will Rogers, humorist. Maria Tallchief, ballerina. Jim Thorpe, athlete.

Noteworthy places American Indian Hall of Fame, Anadarko. Chisholm Trail Museum, Kingfisher. Ft. Gibson Stockade, Muskogee. Natl. Cowboy Hall of Fame, Oklahoma City. Ouachita Natl. Forest. Pioneer Woman Museum, Ponca City. Will Rogers Memorial, Claremore.

Memorable events Francisco Vásquez de Coronado expedition in territory 1541. Except for panhandle, becomes part of Louisiana purchase 1803. Region made Indian Territory (not organized) in 1830 and becomes home of "Five Civilized Tribes"—Cherokee, Choctaw, Chickasaw, Creek, and Seminole—after they left the southeast on Trail of Tears 1828–46. United States acquires panhandle with annexation of Texas 1845. Territory opened to homesteaders 1889. Commercial oil well at Bartlesville 1897. Indian Territory and Oklahoma Territory merged and granted statehood 1907. Gov. John C. Walton impeached after declaring martial law to quell violence 1923. McClellan-Kerr Arkansas River Navigation system links Oklahoma to Mississippi, making Catoosa (Tulsa) major inland port 1971. Timothy McVeigh blows up Federal Building in Oklahoma City, killing 168 people 1995.

Tourist information (800) 652-6552. **www.state.ok.us.**

▶OREGON

Although the Lewis and Clark expedition reached the mouth of the Columbia River in 1805, interest in the area was kindled by the Hudson's Bay Company and later by Jason Lee, a Methodist minister who settled near Salem in 1834. After the decline of the fur trade, lumbering became the most important industry in Oregon. Though lumbering and related industries are still leading employers—the state is the leading grower of Christmas trees—Oregon has benefited from the arrival of smaller computer and electronics firms leaving California in search of a more favorable business climate. Traditionally progressive, it is one of most active states in the environmental protection movement. Only one-third of the population is affiliated with an organized religion.

Name Unknown origin, first applied to Columbia River. **Nickname** Beaver State. **Capital** Salem. **Entered union** Feb. 14, 1859 (33rd). **Motto** "She flies with her own wings." **Poet laureate** William E. Stafford.

Emblems **Animal** Beaver. **Bird** Western meadowlark. **Dance** Square dance. **Fish** Chinook salmon. **Flower** Oregon grape. **Insect** Swallowtail butterfly. **Song** "Oregon, My Oregon." **Stone** Thunderegg. **Tree** Douglas fir.

Land **Total area** 98,381 sq. mi (9th), incl. 2,384 sq. mi. inland water. **Borders** Wash., Idaho, Nev., Calif., Pacific Ocean. **Rivers** Columbia, Snake, Willamette. **Mountains** Cascade Range, Coast Range, Klamath. **Other notable features** Willamette Valley.

Elected officials Gov. Ted Kulongoski (D, term exp. 2006). Sec. State Bill Bradbury (D). Atty. Gen. Hardy Myers (D).

People (July, 2002 est.) 3,521,515 (27th). Race/Hispanic Origin (2000 Census): White 86.6%. Black 1.6%. Indian 1.3%. Asian 3.0%. Pacific Islander 0.2%. Other 4.2%. Two or more races 3.1%. Hispanic 8.0%.

Cities (2002) Portland 539,438. Salem 140,977. Eugene 140,395. Gresham 94,706. Beaverton 79,768. Hillsboro 75,945. Medford 64,653. Bend 57,010. Springfield 54,035. Corvallis 49,781.

Business **Gross State Product, 2001:** $120.06 bil. (26th). **Leading Sectors of GSP (2001):** Manufacturing 25.50%; Durable Goods 22.00%; Services 18.20%. ***Fortune* 500 Companies (2003):** 2: Nike, Willamette Industries.

Famous natives In-mut-too-yah-lat-lat (Joseph), Nez Percé chief. Ursula LeGuin (b. Calif.), author. Edwin Markham, poet. Dr. John McLoughlin, fur trader, "Father of Oregon". Linus Pauling, chemist. John Reed, author. William Simon U'Ren (b. Wis.), lawyer/reformer.

Noteworthy places Bonneville Dam, Columbia River. Columbia River Gorge. Columbia River Museum, Astoria. Crater Lakes Natl. Park. Ft. Clatsop Natl. Monument. Hells Canyon. High Desert Museum, Bend. John Day Fossil Beds Natl. Monument. Mt. Hood. Oregon Caves Natl. Monument. Oregon Dunes Natl. Recreation Area. Point Perpetua. Timberline Lodge.

Memorable events Sir Francis Drake turns away from fogbound coast of Pacific Northwest 1578. Capt. James Cook visits 1778. Mouth of Columbia River explored by Capt. Robert Gray, who claims region for U.S. 1792. Meriwether Lewis and George Rogers Clark expedition arrives at mouth of Columbia 1805. Claims to Oregon Territory, from California border to Alaska and east to Montana and Wyoming, relinquished by Spain (1819), Russia (1825), and Britain (1846). First settlers arrive Willamette Valley 1843. Organized as territory 1848. Statehood 1859. Railroad arrives 1883. Bonneville Dam completed 1937. Following severe rain and snow that claim 40 lives, Oregon declared disaster area 1964. First state to enact "bottle law" 1972. Snake River opened to navigation, linking Astoria to Lewiston, Idaho, 1975.

Tourist information (800) 547-7842. **www.traveloregon.com.**

▶PENNSYLVANIA, COMMONWEALTH OF

William Penn and his Quakers encouraged settlement and religious tolerance, and Pennsylvania was the first state to abolish slavery. In the late colonial period, Philadelphia was the cultural capital of the colonies. The first Continental Congress convened there in 1774, and it was for a decade the U.S. capital. With access to both the Great Lakes and to the Atlantic, Pennsylvanians took a lead in opening up the Midwest. Its resources include large coal deposits—which contribute to its iron-making capabilities—lumber, textiles, and leather. Leadership in these sectors lasted well into the 20th century, when Pennsylvania lost ground to Sunbelt states. As in many states, there has been growth in tourist and service industries, though machinery production and trade continue to expand significantly.

Name For Adm. William Penn, father of William Penn, founder of commonwealth. **Nickname** Keystone State. **Capital** Harrisburg. **Entered union** Dec. 12, 1787 (2nd). **Motto** "Virtue, liberty and independence."

Emblems **Animal** White-tailed deer. **Beautification and conservation plant** Penngift crown vetch. **Beverage** Milk. **Bird** Ruffed grouse. **Dog** Great Dane. **Fish** Brook trout. **Flower** Mountain laurel. **Insect** Firefly. **Tree** Hemlock.

Land **Total area** 46,055 sq. mi (33rd), incl. 1,239 sq. mi. inland water. **Borders** N.Y., N.J., Del., Md., W.Va., Ohio, Lake Erie. **Rivers** Allegheny, Delaware, Juniata, Monongahela, Ohio, Schuylkill, Susquehanna. **Lakes** Allegheny Res., Erie, Pymatuning Res., Shenango Res. **Mountains** Allegheny, Kittatinny, Laurel Hills, Pocono.

Elected officials Gov. Edward Rendell (D, term exp. 2006). Lt. Gov. Catherine Knoll (D). Sec. Commonwealth Pedro Cortes (D). Atty. Gen. D. Michael Fisher (R).

People (July, 2002 est.) 12,335,091 (6th). Race/Hispanic Origin (2000 Census): White 85.4%. Black 10.0%. Indian 0.1%. Asian 1.8%. Other 1.5%. Two or more races 1.2%. Hispanic 3.2%.

Cities (2002) Philadelphia 1,492,231. Pittsburgh 327,898. Allentown 106,105. Erie 102,122. Reading 80,494. Scranton 74,712. Bethlehem 71,749. Lancaster 55,628. Harrisburg 78,540. Altoona 48,490.

Business **Gross State Product, 2001:** $408.38 bil. (6th). **Leading Sectors of GSP (2001):** Services 23.65%; Finance, insurance, and real estate 19.42%; Manufacturing 16.72%. ***Fortune* 500 Companies (2003):** 27, including ALCOA, Cigna, AmerisourceBergen, Rite Aid, Sunoco, Comcast, H.J. Heinz, PPG Industries, Aramark, Crown Cork & Seal, PNC Financial Services Group, Unisys, Rohm & Haas, PPL, Air Products & Chemicals, IKON Office Solutions, Hershey Foods, Jones Apparel Group, Mellon Financial Corp.

Famous natives Louisa May Alcott, author. Maxwell Anderson, playwright. James Buchanan, U.S. president. Alexander Calder, sculptor. Andrew Carnegie (b. Scotland), industrialist/philanthropist. Mary Cassatt, painter. Wilt Chamberlain, basketball player. Bill Cosby, comedian/philanthropist. Stephen Foster, songwriter. Benjamin Franklin (b. Mass.), inventor/statesman. Robert Fulton, inventor. Milton S. Hershey, chocolatier. George C. Marshall, statesman. Andrew W. Mellon, financier/philanthropist. Robert E. Peary, explorer. Betsy Ross, patriot. Andy Warhol, artist. Johnny Weismuller, swimmer/actor. Benjamin West, painter.

Noteworthy places Academy of Natural Sciences, Philadelphia. Carnegie Institute, Pittsburgh. Delaware Water Gap Natl. Recreation Area. Ft. Necessity Natl. Battlefield. Franklin Institute, Philadelphia. Gettysburg Battlefield. Hugh Moore Hist. Park and Museums, Easton. Independence Natl. Hist. Park, Philadelphia. Liberty Bell, Carpenters Hall, Philadelphia. Pennsylvania Academy of Fine Arts, Philadelphia. Pennsylvania Dutch Country. Philadelphia Museum of Art. Pine Creek Gorge. Rodin Museum, Philadelphia. Valley Forge Natl. Hist. Park.

Memorable events Cornelis Jacobssen sails into Delaware Bay 1614. Swedes settle at Tinicum Island 1643. Charles II grants proprietary charter to William Penn 1681. First U.S. hospital established, in Philadelphia, 1751. Mason-Dixon Line establishes southern boundary of state 1763–67—later boundary between slave and nonslave states. Declaration of Independence (1776) and Constitution (1787) signed in Philadelphia. Becomes first state to abolish slavery 1780. Bank of North America becomes first bank chartered in United States 1781. Philadelphia capital of United States 1790–1800. First iron furnace in U.S. 1792. First oil well in the world driven near Titusville 1859. Battle of Gettysburg turning point in Civil War; Lincoln's Gettysburg Address 1863. Centennial Exhibition at Philadelphia 1876. Johnstown flood—worst in U.S. history—kills 2,200 people 1889. Pinkerton detectives kill 12 strikers at Homestead steel works near Pittsburgh 1892. Twenty coal miners killed during strike for eight-hour day and other concessions 1897. More than 500 injured during three-day race riot in Philadelphia 1964. Partial meltdown at Three Mile Island forces closure of nuclear reactor 1979. Storage tank spills 713,000 gallons diesel fuel into Monongahela River, disrupting water supplies in Pennsylvania, West Virginia, and Ohio 1988.

Tourist information (800) VISIT-PA. **www.experiencepa.com.**

▶RHODE ISLAND AND PROVIDENCE PLANTATIONS

Giovanni de Verrazano was the first European to record visiting the area of Narragansett Bay, the prominent inlet that almost splits the eastern third of the state from the rest. The first settlers were followers of Roger Williams, who left the restrictive religious atmosphere of the Puritan Massachusetts Bay Colony to found Providence in 1636. Rhode Island is the site of the first U.S. Baptist church, at Providence, and at Newport the first Quaker meetinghouse and the first synagogue. It was the last of the 13 original colonies to ratify the Constitution, the centralized federalism of which many Rhode Islanders objected to. The development of 19th-century Rhode Island was influenced by immigration and the Industrial Revolution; the state's leading manufacturers are still silver, jewelry and textiles. Although it ranks 43rd in population, Rhode Island is second in population density (behind New Jersey) at 947.6 people per square mile.

Name For Rhode Island in Narragansett Bay, named in turn for Mediterranean island of Rhodes. **Nicknames** Ocean State, Little Rhody. **Capital** Providence. **Entered union** May 29, 1790 (13th). **Motto** "Hope."

Emblems **Bird** Rhode Island red. **Flower** Violet. **Mineral** Bowenite. **Rock** Cumberlandite. **Song** "Rhode Island." **Tree** Red maple.

Land **Total area** 1,545 sq. mi (50th), incl. 500 sq. mi. inland water. **Borders** Mass., Atlantic Ocean, Conn. **Rivers** Blackstone, Pawcatuck, Providence, Sakonnet. **Other notable features** Block Island, Narragansett Bay, Aquidneck Island.

Elected officials Gov. Donald Carcieri (R, term exp. 2006). Lt. Gov. Charles Fogarty (D). Sec. State Matthew Brown (D). Atty. Gen. Patrick Lynch (D).

People (July, 2002 est.) 1,069,725 (43rd). Race/Hispanic Origin (2000 Census): White 85.0%. Black 4.5%. Indian 0.5%. Asian 2.3%. Pacific Islander 0.1%. Other 5.0%. Two or more races 2.7%. Hispanic 8.7%.

Cities (2002) Providence 175,901. Warwick 87,039. Cranston 81,113. Pawtucket 74,033. East Providence 49,658. Woonsocket 43,879. Newport 26,312. Central Falls 19,168.

Business **Gross State Product, 2001:** $36.94 bil. (42nd). **Leading Sectors of GSP (2001):** Finance, insurance, and real estate 29.60%; Services 21.52%; Real estate 14.35%. ***Fortune* 500 Companies (2003):** 2: CVS, Textron.

Famous natives George M. Cohan, actor/producer. Nathanael Greene, army officer. Galway Kinell, poet. Metacomet (King Philip), Wam-

panoag chief. Oliver H. Perry and Matthew C. Perry, naval officers. Gilbert Stuart, portraitist.
Noteworthy places Brown University, Providence. First Baptist Church in North America (1638), Providence. Hoffenreffer Museum of Anthropology, Bristol. John Carter Brown Library, Providence. Rhode Island School of Design, Providence. Nathanael Greene homestead, Coventry. Museum of Yachting, Newport. Newport mansions. Tennis Hall of Fame, Newport. Touro Synagogue (oldest extant in North America), Newport.
Memorable events Roger Williams, expelled from Massachusetts Bay Colony, settles in Providence 1636. Other religious exiles settle in Portsmouth (1638), Newport (1639), and Warwick (1642). King Philip's War 1675–76. First Quaker meetinghouse in North America founded 1699. First colony to renounce allegiance to Britain 1776. Last colony to ratify Constitution 1790. Dorr's Rebellion achieves liberalization of state constitution, which had remained unchanged since 1663, 1842. America's Cup Race held in Newport for first time 1930. Newport Bridge across Narragansett Bay completed 1969. *Australia II* first non-U.S. boat to win America's Cup in 132 years 1983.
Tourist information (800) 556-2484. **www.visitrhodeisland.com.**

▶SOUTH CAROLINA

South Carolina's early economy was based on rice—its plantations worked by slaves—though tobacco later played a major role. As was true in North Carolina, many settlers made their way into the back country where they eked out a living as tenant farmers. During the Revolution, Ft. Charlotte was the first British installation to fall to Colonial troops, and at the outbreak of the Civil War, Ft. Sumter was the first Union installation to fall to Confederate forces. While agriculture remained a staple of the state's economy through the close of the 19th century, textile manufacture took over in the early 20th century. The postwar era has seen the rapid expansion of the chemical and paper industries, as well as large-scale development of the Atlantic Coast ports of Charleston, Georgetown, and Port Royal.

Name For King Charles II (Carolus is Latin for Charles). **Nickname** Palmetto State. **Capital** Columbia. **Entered union** May 23, 1788 (8th). **Motto** *Animis opibusque parati* (Prepared in mind and deed); *Dum spiro spero* (While I breathe I hope). **Poet laureate** Helen von Kolnitz Hyer.
Emblems **Animal** White-tailed deer. **Beverage** Milk. **Bird** Carolina wren. **Dance** Shag. **Dog** Boykin spaniel. **Fish** Striped bass. **Flower** Yellow jessamine. **Fruit** Peach. **Shell** Lettered olive. **Song** "Carolina." **Stone** Blue granite. **Tree** Palmetto. **Wild game Bird** Wild turkey.
Land **Total area** 32,020 sq. mi (40th), incl. 1,911 sq. mi. inland water. **Borders** N.C., Atlantic Ocean, Ga. **Rivers** Catawba, Congaree, Edisto, Pee Dee, Savannah, Tugalos, Wateree. **Lakes** Greenwood, Hartwell, Keowee, Marion, Murray, Santee Res., Wylie. **Other notable features** Blue Ridge Mts., Congaree Swamp, Sea Islands.
Elected officials Gov. Mark Sanford (R, term exp. 2006). Lt. Gov. Andre Bauer (R). Sec. State J. Mark Hammond (R). Atty. Gen. Henry McMaster (R).
People (July, 2002 est.) 4,107,183 (25th). Race/Hispanic Origin (2000 Census): White 67.2%. Black 29.5%. Indian 0.3%. Asian 0.9%. Other 1.0%. Two or more races 1.0%. Hispanic 2.4%.
Cities (2002) Columbia 117,394. Charleston 98,795. North Charleston 80,691. Greenville 56,181. Rock Hill 54,606. Mount Pleasant 53,096. Sumter 39,382. Spartanburg 39,068. Hilton Head Island 34,601. Goose Creek 30,179.
Business **Gross State Product, 2001:** $115.20 bil. (28th). **Leading Sectors of GSP (2001):** Manufacturing 20.07%; Services 17.00%; Government 15.54%. ***Fortune* 500 Companies (2003):** 1: Scana.
Famous natives James F. Byrnes, politician/jurist. John C. Calhoun, politician. Dizzy Gillespie, musician. Althea Gibson, athlete. DuBose Heyward, author. Andrew Jackson, U.S. president. Eartha Kitt, singer. James Longstreet, army officer. Francis Marion, army officer/politician. Charles C. Pinckney and Thomas Pinckney, diplomats. Edward Rutledge and John Rutledge, politicians. Strom Thurmond, politician.
Noteworthy places Charleston Museum (1773, oldest in United States). Congaree Swamp Natl. Monument. Cowpens Natl. Battlefield. Ft. Moultrie, Ft. Johnson, and Ft. Sumter Natl. Monument, Charleston. Hilton Head Island. Kings Mountain Natl. Military Park. Ninety-Six Natl. Hist. Site, Greenwood. Patriots Point Maritime Museum, Charleston. Sea Islands. Spoleto Music Festival, Charleston.
Memorable events Spanish visit 1521. French Huguenots at Port Royal 1562. Included in Carolina grant by Charles II 1663. Charleston founded 1680. Becomes royal province 1729. Ratifies Constitution 1787. *Best Friend of Charleston,* first American steam locomotive built for passenger use 1833. First state to secede from Union Dec. 20, 1860. Confederate forces attack Ft. Sumter Apr. 12, 1861. Secession repealed 1865. Readmitted to Union 1868. Cyclone kills 1,000 in Savannah, Georgia, and Charleston 1893. Savannah River nuclear plant begins production near Aiken 1951; closed for safety reasons 1988. Hurricane Hugo kills 24 and causes $700 million in property damage 1989. BMW opens plant in Spartanburg 1994.
Tourist information (800) SC-SMILE. **www.discoversouthcarolina.com.**

▶SOUTH DAKOTA

The United States did not organize the Dakota Territory until 1861, and even then interest in the region was scant until gold was discovered in 1874. The majority of those who remained after the gold rush turned to cattle ranching, which was a mainstay of the economy through the first half of the 20th century. The manufacturing base was developed after four major dams were built on the Missouri River in the 1930's. They provided hydroelectric power and increased irrigation along the Missouri, which cuts the state in half. Concerned especially over the abrogation of 19th-century treaties, the American Indian Movement (AIM) took over the courthouse at Wounded Knee for 10 weeks in 1973. While U.S. courts have found in favor of the Sioux in several cases concerning the earlier treaties, many maintain that the settlements were insufficient.

Name For southern section of Dakota territory; *dakota* is Sioux word for "allies." **Nicknames** Coyote State, Sunshine State. **Capital** Pierre. **Entered union** Nov. 2, 1889 (40th). **Motto** "Under God the people rule."
Emblems **Animal** Coyote. **Bird** Chinese ring-necked pheasant. **Fish** Walleye. **Flower** Pasque .
Land **Total area** 77,116 sq. mi (17th), incl. 1,232 sq. mi. inland water. **Borders** N.Dak., Minn., Iowa, Nebr., Wyo., Mont. **Rivers** Cheyenne, James, Missouri, Moreau, White. **Lakes** Belle Fourche Res., Big Stone, Traverse. **Other notable features** Badlands, Black Hills (Harney Peak 7,242 ft.).

Elected officials Gov. M. Michael Rounds (R, term exp. 2006). Lt. Gov. Dennis Daugaard (R). Sec. State Chris Nelson (R). Atty. Gen. Larry Long (R).
People (July, 2002 est.) 761,063 (46th). Race/Hispanic Origin (2000 Census): White 88.7%. Black 0.6%. Indian 8.3%. Asian 0.6%. Other 0.5%. Two or more races 1.3%. Hispanic 1.4%.
Cities (2002) Sioux Falls 130,491. Rapid City 60,262. Aberdeen 24,312. Watertown 20,191. Brookings 18,703. Mitchell 14,626. Pierre 14,012. Yankton 13,440. Huron 11,569.Vermillion 10,065.
Business **Gross State Product, 2001:** $24.25 bil. (46th). **Leading Sectors of GSP (2001):** Finance, insurance, and real estate 22.07%; Services 17.32%; Depository and nondepository 13.94%. ***Fortune* 500 Companies (2003):** 0.
Famous natives Tom Brokaw, journalist. Martha "Calamity" Jane Burk (b. Mo.), frontierswoman. Alvin Hansen, economist. Hubert H. Humphrey, politician. Ernest O. Lawrence, physicist (Nobel Prize, 1939). George McGovern, politician. Ta-sunko-witko (Crazy Horse), Oglala Sioux chief. Tatanka Iyotake (Sitting Bull), Sioux chief.
Noteworthy places Badlands Natl. Park. Crazy Horse State Memorial, Custer. Custer State Park. Ft. Sisseton. Geographical center of the United States. Jewel Cave Natl. Monument. Mount Rushmore. Natl. Memorial. Wind Cave Natl. Park.
Memorable events French visit region 1742–43. To United States in Louisiana Purchase 1803. Ft. Pierre first permanent settlement 1817. Part of Dakota Territory 1861. Gold discovered in Black Hills 1874. Divided from North Dakota; statehood 1889. U.S. troops massacre Sioux at Battle of Wounded Knee 1890.
Tourist information (800) SDAKOTA. **www.travelsd.com.**

▶TENNESSEE

At first claimed by Virginia and later by North Carolina, Tennessee had its first great pioneer in Daniel Boone, who traversed the region in the 1760's. Political attitudes in the 18th century were shaped by the land, with the cotton and tobacco growers in the fertile western part of the state favoring slavery and the backwoods people of the eastern hills opposed to it. The Cherokees were removed to Oklahoma by the federal government in the 1830's. The state was captured by Union troops in 1862 and put under the governorship of Andrew Johnson, later a U.S. president.

Its economy was radically altered in the 1930's and 1940's by the creation of the Tennessee Valley Authority, which provided abundant energy for industry, and to a lesser extent by the location of the government's first uranium enrichment facility at Oak Ridge during World War II. The state's leading industries are textiles, food processing, and chemicals, and there is considerable lead and coal mining in the east.

Name For Tenase, principal village of Cherokees. **Nickname** Volunteer State. **Capital** Nashville. **Entered union** June 1, 1796 (16th). **Motto** "Agriculture and commerce." **Slogan** "Tennessee—America at its best." **Poet laureate** Richard M. ("Pek") Gunn.
Emblems **Animal** Raccoon. **Bird** Mockingbird. **Folk dance** Square dance. **Cultivated flower** Iris. **Gem** Tennessee pearl. **Insects** Ladybug, firefly. **Poem** "Oh Tennessee, My Tennessee." **Public school song** "My Tennessee." **Rock** Limestone agate. **Songs** "When It's Iris Time in Tennessee," "The Tennessee Waltz," My Homeland, Tennessee," "Rocky Top." **Tree** Tulip poplar. **Wildflower** Passion flower.
Land **Total area** 42,143 sq. mi (36th), incl. 926 sq. mi. inland water. **Borders** Ky., Va., N.C., Ga., Ala., Miss., Ark., Mo. **Rivers** Clinch, Cumberland, Mississippi, Tennessee. **Lakes** Boone, Center Hill, Cherokee, Dale Hollow, Douglass, J. Percy Priest, Watauga. **Other notable features** Cumberland Mts., Great Smoky Mts., Tennessee Valley, Unaka Mts.
Elected officials Gov. Phil Bredesen (D, term exp. 2006). Lt. Gov. John S. Wilder (D). Sec. State Riley C. Darnell (D). Atty. Gen. Paul Summers (D).
People People (July, 2002 est.) 5,797,289 (16th). Race/Hispanic Origin (2000 Census): White 80.2%. Black 16.4%. Indian 0.3%. Asian 1.0%. Other 1.0%. two or more races 1.1%. Hispanic 2.2%.
Cities (2002) Memphis 648,882. Nashville-Davidson 545,915. Knoxville 173,661. Chattanooga 155,404. Clarksville 105,898. Murfreesboro 74,894. Jackson 60,635. Johnson City 56,767. Franklin 45,175. Kingsport 44,362.
Business Gross State Product, 2001: $182.52 bil. (19th). **Leading Sectors of GSP (2001):** Services 21.73%; Manufacturing 18.72%; Finance, insurance, and real estate 15.09%. ***Fortune* 500 Companies (2003):** 6: FedEx, HCA, UnumProvident, Eastman Chemical, Dollar General, AutoZone.
Famous natives James Agee, author. Davy Crockett, frontiersman. David Farragut, naval officer. Aretha Franklin, singer. Morgan Freeman, actor. Al Gore, (b. Washington, D.C.), politician. Cordell Hull, statesman (Nobel Peace Prize, 1945). Dolly Parton, singer. Sikawyi (Sequoya), Cherokee scholar. Alvin York, soldier.
Noteworthy places American Museum of Science and Energy, Oak Ridge. Andrew Johnson Natl. Hist. Site, Greenville. Chickamauga and Chattanooga Natl. Military Park. Cumberland Natl. Hist. Park. Ft. Donelson Natl. Military Park. Grand Old Opry, Nashville. Great Smoky Mountains Natl. Park. The Hermitage (Andrew Jackson home), Nashville. Lookout Mountain, Chattanooga. The Parthenon, Nashville. Shiloh Natl. Military Park, Pittsburgh Landing. Stones River Natl. Battlefield, Murfreesboro.
Memorable events De Soto expedition passes through region 1540. French claim territory as part of Louisiana; English claim territory as part of Carolina grant 1663. French claim given up after French and Indian War 1763. State of Franklin established in what is now eastern Tennessee 1784–87. Organized as Territory South of the Ohio 1790. Statehood 1796. Secedes from Union 1861. Battles of Shiloh (1862), Chattanooga (1863), Stones River (1863), and Nashville (1864). Readmitted to Union 1866. Clarence Darrow defends John T. Scopes for violating ban on teaching evolution in public schools; loses case 1925. Congress creates Tennessee Valley Authority 1933. First operational nuclear reactor at Oak Ridge 1943. Martin Luther King assassinated at Memphis 1968. World's Fair held in Knoxville 1982.
Tourist information (800) 836-6200. **www.state.tn.us.**

▶TEXAS

The land that is Texas today was originally part of Spain's holdings in Mexico. After Mexico won independence, the new government invited U.S. citizens to settle there. After many clashes between the Mexican and Anglo cultures, Texas broke away and for 10 years was an independent country before becoming a state in 1845. Modern Texas was made by oil, discovered at Spindletop in 1901, and the state's economy has been tied to the oil market ever since. After World War II, the Texas economy soared, bringing both prosperity and an unprecedented population boom. With the oil glut of the early 1980's, growth came to a halt, causing a drastic realignment of economic priorities. Unemployment jumped more than 20 percent during the 1980's, and remained higher than the national average in 1990, a year that saw many bank failures. The economy has been forced to diversify; currently the petroleum industry accounts for only 7 percent of state revenues, down from 25 percent a decade before. Texas has enormous resources ranging from cotton, cattle and timber to aerospace, computers and electronics. The largest of the 48 conterminous states, Texas's image as a state of wide-open spaces is understandable, but fully 80 percent of its people live in metropolitan areas, and Dallas, Houston and San Antonio are among the nation's 10 largest cities. Twenty-five percent of the population is Hispanic; the majority of those are Mexican-American.

Name From the Caddo *tavshas*, "friends." **Nickname** Lone Star State. **Capital** Austin. **Entered union** Dec. 29, 1845 (28th). **Motto** "Friendship."

Emblems Bird Mockingbird. **Dish** Chili. **Flower** Bluebonnet. **Gem** Topaz. **Grass** Sideoats grama. **Songs** "Texas, Our Texas," "The Eyes of Texas." **Stone** Palmwood. **Tree** Pecan.

Land Total area 268,581 sq. mi (2nd), incl. 6,784 sq. mi. inland water. **Borders** Okla., Ark., La., Gulf of Mexico, Tamaulipas, Coahuila, Chihuahua, N.Mex. **Rivers** Brazos, Colorado, Natchez, Red, Rio Grande, Sabine, Trinity. **Lakes** Sam Rayburn Res., Texoma, Toledo Bend Res. **Other notable features** Balcones Escarpment, Diablo Sierra, Edwards Plateau, Guadalupe Mts., Staked Plain, Stockton Plateau.

Elected officials Gov. Rick Perry (R, term exp. 2006). Lt. Gov. David Dewhurst (R). Sec. State Gwyn Shea (R). Atty. Gen. Greg Abbott (R).

People (July, 2002 est.) 21,779,893 (2nd). Race/Hispanic Origin (2000 Census): White 71.0%. Black 11.5%. Indian 0.6%. Asian 2.7%. Pacific Islander 0.1%. Other 11.7%. Two or more races 2.5%. Hispanic 32.0%.

Cities (2002) Houston 2,009,834. Dallas 1,211,467. San Antonio 1,194,222. Austin 671,873. El Paso 577,415. Fort Worth 567,516. Arlington 349,944. Corpus Christi 278,520. Plano 238,091. Garland 219,646.

Business Gross State Product, 2001: $763.87 bil. (3rd). **Leading Sectors of GSP (2001):** Services 20.48%; Finance, insurance, and real estate 15.48%; Manufacturing 12.27%. ***Fortune* 500 Companies (2003):** 45, including Exxon Mobil, El Paso, Reliant Energy, SBC Communications, Dynegy, Marathon Oil, ConocoPhillips, J.C. Penney, Dell Computer, TXU, Sysco, Electronic Data Systems, AMR, Fleming, Valero Energy, Kimberly-Clark, Halliburton, Waste Management, Texas Instruments, Southwest Airlines, RadioShack, AdvancePCS, USAA.

Famous natives Stephen Austin (b. Va.), pioneer. James "Jim" Bowie (b. Ky.), army officer. Carol Burnett, comedian. J. Frank Dobie, folklorist. Dwight D. Eisenhower, U.S. president/general. Samuel Houston (b. Va.), president Republic of Texas/governor State of Texas. Howard Hughes, industrialist/aviator. Lyndon Baines Johnson, U.S. president. Janis Joplin, singer. Barbara Jordan, politician. Audie Murphy, soldier/actor. Chester Nimitz, navy officer. Katherine Anne Porter, author. Samuel T. Rayburn, politician. Mildred "Babe" Didrikson Zaharias, athlete.

Noteworthy places The Alamo, San Antonio. Alibates Flint Quarries Natl. Monument. Big Bend Natl. Park. Ft. Davis. Galveston Historical Foundation. Guadalupe Mountains Natl. Park. Houston Museum of Fine Arts. Lyndon B. Johnson Natl. Hist. Park, Johnson City. Lyndon B. Johnson Space Center, Houston. Old Stone Ft., Nacogdoches. Padre Island Natl. Seashore. San Antonio Missions Natl. Hist. Park. Texas Ranger Museum, Waco.

Memorable events Alonzo Alvarez de Piñeda sails along coast 1519. Estevanico blazes trail through West Texas 1539. Spanish establish settlement at Ysleta near El Paso 1682. René-Robert Cavalier de La Salle attempts to found colony on Matagorda Bay, establishing claim to region for France 1685. Effective Spanish occupation 1715. United States acquires French claim to region with Louisiana Purchase 1803. United States relinquishes claim to Spain 1819. Americans move into region in early 19th century. Mexico, of which Texas is a province, wins independence from Spain 1821. Declaration of Independence from Mexico; Santa Anna victor at Battle of the Alamo; Sam Houston victor at Battle of San Jacinto; founding of Republic of Texas 1836. Texas granted statehood by United States 1845. Secedes from Union 1861; readmitted 1870. Hurricane kills 6,000 at Galveston 1900. NASA Space Center opens at Houston 1962. Pres. Kennedy assassinated at Dallas 1963. Price of oil plunges during 1980's, crippling state economy.

Tourist information (800) 888-8TEX, ext. 728. **www.traveltex.com.**

▶UTAH

In the middle of the Great Basin between the Rocky Mountains and the Sierra Nevada, Utah was an arid and uninviting region. After Joseph Smith, the founder of the Church of Jesus Christ of Latter-day Saints (Mormons), was shot in Illinois, Brigham Young led his people west, ultimately to the Salt Lake Valley in 1847. The chief obstacle to statehood was polygamy, which the church eventually renounced. There was an influx of non-Mormons after the discovery of silver in 1863, but Mormons still comprise two-thirds of the state's population, and the state remains conservative in outlook. Although the federal government is a major employer, government policy has lately been challenged by increased concern over the issues of chemical weapons testing, the MX missile, and disposal of nuclear waste from the Rocky Mountain Arsenal in neighboring Colorado.

Name For Ute Indians. **Nicknames** Beehive State, Mormon State. **Capital** Salt Lake City. **Entered Union** Jan. 4, 1896 (45th). **Motto:** "Industry."

Emblems Animal Elk. **Bird** California Gull. **Emblem** Beehive **Fish** Rainbow Trout **Flower** Sego lily. **Gem** Topaz. **Song** "Utah, We Love Thee." **Tree** Blue spruce.

Land Total area 84,899 sq. mi (13th), incl. 2,755 sq. mi. inland water. **Borders** Idaho, Wyo., Colo., Ariz., Nev. **Rivers** Bear, Colorado, Green, Sevier. **Lakes** Bear, Great Salt, Utah. **Mountains** La Sal, Uinta (Kings Peak 13,528 ft.) Wasatch Range. **Other notable features** Great Salt Lake Desert (Bonneville Salt Flats) Kaibab Plateau.

Elected officials Gov. Michael O. Leavitt (R, term exp. 2005). Lt. Gov./Sec. State Olene Walker (R). Atty. Gen. Mark Shurtleff (R).

People (July, 2002 est.) 2,316,256 (34th). Race/Hispanic Origin (2000 Census): White 89.2%. Black 0.8%. Indian 1.3%. Asian 1.7%. Pacific Islander 0.7%. Other 4.2%. Two or more races 2.1%. Hispanic 9.0%.

Cities (2002) Salt Lake City 181,266. West Valley City 111,254. Provo 105,170. Sandy 89,244. Orem 83,662. Ogden 78,641. West Jordan 73,355. Layton 60,064. Taylorsville 59,115. St. George 54,049.
Business **Gross State Product, 2001:** $70.41 bil. (33rd). **Leading Sectors of GSP (2001):** Services 20.59%; Finance, insurance, and real estate 20.08%; Government 14.65%. ***Fortune* 500 Companies (2003):** 1: Autoliv.
Famous natives Maud Adams, actress. John Moses Browning, inventor. Philo Farnsworth, engineer. Merlin Olsen, football player/actor. Ivy Baker Priest, U.S. treasurer. Brigham Young (b. Vt.), religious leader. Loretta Young, actress.
Noteworthy places Arches Natl. Park. Bryce Canyon Natl. Park. Canyonlands Natl. park. Capitol Reef Natl. Park. Cedar Breaks Natl. Monument. Dinosaur Natl. Monument. Flaming Gorge Dam Natl. Monument. Great Salt Lake. Lake Powell Natl. Monument. Monument Valley. Mormon Tabernacle, Salt Lake City. Natural Bridges Natl. Monument. Promontory Point. Rainbow Bridge Natl. Monument. Temple Square, Salt Lke City. Timpanogas Cave Natl. Monument. Zion Natl. Park.
Memorable events First visted probably by explorers from Coronado expedition 1540. Silvestre Vélez de Escalante and Francisco Atanasio Dominguez explore for Spain 1776. James Bridger discovers Great Salt Lake 1824. Led by Brigham Young, Mormons reach Great Salt Lake 1847. United States acquires Utah region from Mexico 1848. Mormons organize state of Deseret 1849; Congress refuses to recognize and instead organizes Territory of Utah 1850. Silver discovered at Little Cottonwood Canyon 1868. First transcontinental railroad completed with driving of golden spike at Promontory Point 1869. Mormon church renounces polygamy 1890, paving way to statehood 1896. Uranium discovered near Moab 1952. Winter Olympics held in Salt Lake City 2002.
Tourist Information (800) 200-1160. **www.utah.gov.**

▶VERMONT

Originally claimed by both New Hampshire and New York, Vermont's independence was asserted by Ethan Allen. His Green Mountain Boys rid the state of New Yorkers in 1770, fought well against the British in the Revolution, and declared the independent republic of New Connecticut in 1777. Allen was eventually overthrown, and Vermont joined the Union in 1791.

Vermont traditionally has strong ties to Canada, and there was an influx of French-Canadians as Vermont began to develop its manufacturing base in the mid-19th century. Vermont's politics have always been characterized by tolerance and progressivism. As New Connecticut, it abolished slavery and allowed universal male suffrage. Vermont's environmental concerns focus on acid rain and the degree to which development (especially by the tourist industry) should infringe on the state's remaining unspoiled land.

Name From French *vert mont*, "green mountain." **Nickname** Green Mountain State. **Capital** Montpelier. **Entered Union** Mar. 4, 1791 (14th). **Motto** "Freedom and unity."
Emblems **Animal** Morgan horse. **Beverage** Milk. **Bird** Hermit thrush. **Cold-Water Fish** Brook trout. **Flower** Red Clover. **Insect** Honeybee. Song "Hail, Vermont!" **Tree** Sugar Maple. **Warm-Water Fish** Walleye pike.
Land **Total Area** 9,614 sq. mi (45th), incl. 365 sq. mi. inland water. **Borders** Quebec, N.H., Mass., N.Y. **Rivers** Connecticut, Lamoille, Otter Creek, Poultney, White, Winooski. **Lakes** Bomoseen, Champlain, Memphremagog, Willoughby. **Other Notable Features** Grand Isle, Green Mts. (Mt. Mansfield 4,393 ft.), Taconic Mts.
Elected officials Gov. James Douglas (R, two-year term exp. 2004). Lt. Gov. Brian Dubie (R). Sec. State Deborah Markowitz (D). Atty. Gen. William H. Sorrell (D).
People (July, 2002 est.) 616,592 (49th). Race/Hispanic Origin (2000 Census): White 96.8%. Black 0.5%. Indian 0.4%. Asian 0.9%. Other 0.2%. Two or more races 1.2%. Hispanic 0.9%.
Cities (2002) Burlington 39,466. Rutland 17,098. South Burlington 15,870.
Business **Gross State Product, 2001:** $19.15 bil. (49th). **Leading Sectors of GSP (2001):** Services 22.88%; Finance, insurance, and real estate 18.41%; Manufacturing 15.66%. ***Fortune* 500 Companies (2003):** 0.
Famous natives Ethan Allen (b. Conn.), army officer. Chester A. Arthur, U.S. President. Calvin Coolidge, U.S. president. John Deere, industrialist. George Dewey, naval officer. John Dewey, philosopher. Stephen Douglas, politician. James Fisk, financier. Robert Frost (b. Calif.), poet. Rudy Vallee, singer.
Noteworthy places Bennington Battleground/Monument. Calvin Coolidge Homestead, Plymouth. Maple Grove Maple Museum, Rock of Ages Tourist Center, Graniteville. Shelburne Museum. St. Johnsbury. Vermont Marble Exhibit, Proctor.
Memorable events Samuel de Champlain explores for France 1609. First French settlement at Ste. Anne 1666. First English settlers build Ft. Drummer near Brattleboro 1724. Bennington settled 1761. Ethan Allen organizes Green Mountain Boys 1764. Green Mountain Boys capture Ft. Ticonderoga and Ft. Crown Point 1775. Gen. John Stark defeats British general John Burgoyne near Bennington; constitution abolishes slavery and grants universal male suffrage 1777. Claims to area relinquished by Massachusetts (1781), New Hampshire (1782), and New York (1790). First state admitted after original 13 1791. MacDonough defeats British Lake Champlain fleet 1814. Canal between Hudson River and Lake Champlain gives Vermont direct access to port of New York 1823. Confederate soldiers steal $400,000 from St. Albans bank 1864. State recognizes "civil unions" giving gay and lesbian couples virtually all the benefits of marriage 2000.
Tourist Information (800) VERMONT. **www.vermontvacation.com.**

▶VIRGINIA, COMMONWEALTH OF

The first successful English settlement in America was at Jamestown in 1607. The differences between the Virginia colonists and those of Massachusetts were pronounced, and the commercial southern planter class shared little of their New England counterparts' religious zeal. Virginia bred its own strain of independence, and it was the fiery Patrick Henry who heralded the American Revolution with the cry "Give me liberty or give me death." Seven of the first 12 presidents were from Virginia. With an economy very dependent on labor-intensive tobacco in the mid-19th century, Virginia seceded from the Union over the slavery issue, despite the misgivings of many, including Robert E. Lee. After the war Virginia developed an increasingly diversified industrial and manufacturing base that survives today, with food products, tobacco, and chemicals leading the way. Despite the dramatic decline of the American merchant marine, Virginia's shipbuilding industry in Newport News flourished in the 1980's, thanks to the Pentagon's commitment to a 600-ship navy. Norfolk is also one of the country's leading commercial ports.

Name For Elizabeth I, called Virgin Queen. **Nicknames** Old Dominion, Mother of Presidents, Mother of States. **Capital** Richmond. **Entered union** June 25, 1788 (10th). **Motto** *Sic semper tyrannis* (Thus always to tyrants).

Emblems **Beverage** Milk. **Bird** Cardinal. **Dog** Foxhound. **Flower** Dogwood. **Shell** Oyster. **Song** "Carry Me Back to Old Virginia." **Tree** Dogwood.

Land **Total area** 42,774 sq. mi (35th), incl. 3,180 sq. mi. inland water. **Borders** Md., D.C., Atlantic Ocean, N.C., Tenn., Ky., W.Va. **Rivers** James, Potomac, Rappahannock, Roanoke, Shenandoah, York. **Lakes** Buggs Island, Claytor, Gaston, Leesville. **Mountains** Allegheny, Blue Ridge, Cumberland, Unaka. **Other notable features** Great Dismal Swamp, Shenandoah Valley.

Elected officials Gov. Mark Warner (D, term exp. 2006). Lt. Gov. Tim Kaine (D). Sec. Commonwealth Anita A. Rimler (D). Atty. Gen. Jerry W. Kilgore (R).

People (July, 2002 est.) 7,293,542 (12th). Race/Hispanic Origin (2000 Census): White 72.3%. Black 19.6%. Indian 0.3%. Asian 3.7%. Pacific Islander 0.1%. Other 2.0%. Two or more races 2.0%. Hispanic 4.7%.

Cities (2002) Virginia Beach 433,934. Norfolk 239,036. Chesapeake 206,665. Richmond 197,456. Newport News 180,272. Hampton 145,921. Alexandria 130,084. Portsmouth 99,790. Roanoke 93,873. Suffolk 69,966.

Business **Gross State Product, 2001:** $273.07 bil. (13th). **Leading Sectors of GSP (2001):** Services 23.63%; Finance, insurance, and real estate 18.97%; Government 17.67%. ***Fortune* 500 Companies (2003):** 18: Freddie Mac, Circuit City Stores, General Dynamics, Dominion Resources, AES, US Airways Group, CSX, Nextel Communications, Capital One Financial, Gannett, Norfolk Southern, Smithfield Foods, Pittston, Owens & Minor, Performance Food Group, Advance Auto Parts, SLM, NVR.

Famous natives Richard E. Byrd, explorer/aviator. William Clark, explorer. Jerry Falwell, evangelist. William Henry Harrison, U.S. president. Patrick Henry, Revolutionary patriot. Thomas Jefferson, U.S. president. Joseph E. Johnston, Confederate general. John Paul Jones (b. Scotland), navy officer. Robert E. Lee, Confederate general. Meriwether Lewis, explorer. James Madison, U.S. president. John Marshall, jurist. Cyrus Hall McCormick, inventor. James Monroe, U.S. president. Walter Reed, doctor. Pat Robertson, evangelist/politician. Bill "Bojangles" Robinson, dancer. George C. Scott, actor. Thomas Sumter, army officer. Zachary Taylor, U.S. president. John Tyler, U.S. president. Booker T. Washington, educator. George Washington, U.S. president. Woodrow Wilson, U.S. president.

Noteworthy places Appomattox Courthouse Natl. Hist Park. Arlington Natl. Cemetery. Booker T. Washington Natl. Monument, Roanoke. Colonial Natl. Hist. Park (incl. Jamestown, Yorktown & Williamsburg). Fredericksburg and Spotsylvania Natl. Military Park. George Washington birthplace, Frederick Co. Harpers Ferry Natl. Hist. Site. The Mariners' Museum, Newport News. Monticello, Charlottesville. Mount Vernon. Petersburg Natl. Battlefield. Robert E. Lee Memorial, Lexington. Shenandoah Natl. Park. Virginia Beach. Virginia Museum of Fine Arts. Wolf Trap Farm for the Performing Arts, Reston.

Memorable events John Smith founds Jamestown, first permanent settlement in North America, 1607. John Rolfe marries Pocahontas, daughter of Powhatan, leader of so-called Powhatan Confederacy 1614. First English women arrive at Jamestown; House of Burgesses established 1619. Northampton Declaration first resistance to taxation without representation 1653. College of William and Mary founded 1693. First state to establish Committee of Correspondence 1773. American Revolution ends with Charles Cornwallis's surrender to George Washington at Yorktown 1781. Nat Turner's slave revolt 1831. State secedes from Union 1861. Civil War ends with Robert E. Lee's surrender to Ulysses S. Grant at Appomattox Courthouse 1865. Readmitted to Union 1870. Norfolk Naval Base founded 1917. John D. Rockefeller, Jr. restores Colonial Williamsburg 1926. E. Claiborne Robins donates $50 million to University of Richmond 1969. Douglas Wilder becomes nation's first black governor 1989.

Tourist information (800) VISIT-VA. **www.virginia.org.**

▶WASHINGTON

The northwest corner of the continental U.S. was originally the locus of a rich Native American culture noted today primarily for its ornately carved canoes and totem poles. In 1792, Boston merchant Capt. Robert Gray began a trade in sea otter pelts; but the first permanent settlers in the region did not establish themselves for almost 50 years. Agriculture and lumbering were, and remain, mainstays of the state's economy—the farming regions in the east, rich in dairy products, fruit and wheat, and the lumber industry in the western part of the state rely heavily on exports to the Far East. This geographic split reflects the weather patterns: eastern Washington rarely gets more than 10 inches of rain in a year, while on the Pacific coast almost 40 inches is the average.

Since World War I, Puget Sound has been a center of heavy industry and shipbuilding, and 60 percent of the population is concentrated in the region. Boeing maintains one of the country's largest airplane-manufacturing plants in the Seattle-Tacoma area, and Microsoft, the world's leading software company, is located in Redmond. The industrial work force was open to progressive and sometimes radical unionism, and the International Workers of the World (Wobblies) had their national headquarters at Seattle. Before statehood the territorial government pioneered women's suffrage, but Congress declared the women's right to vote unconstitutional.

Name For George Washington. **Nickname** Evergreen State. **Capital** Olympia. **Entered union** Nov. 11, 1889 (42nd). **Motto** *Alki* (By and by).

Emblems **Bird** Willow goldfinch. **Fish** Steelhead trout. **Flower** Western rhododendron. **Gem** Petrified wood. **Song** "Washington, My Home." **Tree** Western hemlock.

Land **Total area** 71,300 sq. mi (18th), incl. 4,756 sq. mi. inland water. **Borders** British Columbia, Idaho, Oreg., Pacific Ocean. **Rivers** Chehalis, Columbia, Pend Oreille, Snake, Yakima. **Lakes** Baker, Bank, Chelan, Franklin D. Roosevelt, Ross, Rufus Woods. **Mountains** Cascade Range, Coast Range, Kettle River Range, Olympic. **Other notable features** Puget Sound, San Juan Islands, Strait of Juan de Fuca.

Elected officials Gov. Gary Locke (D, term exp. 2005). Lt. Gov. Brad Owen (D). Sec. State Sam Reed (D). Atty. Gen. Christine Gregoire (D).
People (July, 2002 est.) 6,068,996 (15th). Race/Hispanic Origin (2000 Census): White 81.8%. Black 3.2%. Indian 1.6%. Asian 5.5%. Pacific Islander 0.4%. Other 3.9%. Two or more races 3.6%. Hispanic 7.5%.
Cities (2002) Seattle 570,426. Tacoma 197,553. Spokane 196,305. Vancouver 149,811. Bellevue 112,894. Everett 97,088. Federal Way 82,174. Kent 81,724. Yakima 73,298. Bellingham 70,480.
Business **Gross State Product, 2001:** $222.95 bil. (14th). **Leading Sectors of GSP (2001):** Services 23.38%; Finance, insurance, and real estate 18.41%; Government 13.82%. ***Fortune* 500 Companies (2003):** 11: Costco Wholesale, Microsoft, Washington Mutual, Weyerhauser, Safeco, Paccar, Nordstrom, Airborne, Amazon.com, AT&T Wireless Services, Starbucks.
Famous natives Harry L. "Bing" Crosby, singer. Merce Cunningham, choreographer. Bill Gates, businessman. Jimi Hendrix, guitarist. Henry M. "Scoop" Jackson, politician. Robert Joffrey, choreographer. Gary Larson, cartoonist. Edward R. Murrow, reporter (b. North Carolina). Theodore Roethke (b. Mich.), poet. Marcus Whitman (b. N.Y.), missionary/pioneer.
Noteworthy places Grand Coulee Dam. Klondike Gold Rush Natl. Hist. Park, Seattle. Mount Rainier Natl. Park. Mount Saint Helens Natl. Monument. North Cascades Natl. Park. Olympic Natl. Park. San Juan Islands Natl. Hist. Park. Seattle Art Museum.
Memorable events Sir Francis Drake skirts coast of Pacific Northwest 1579. Juan de Fuca sails into straits now bearing his name. Bruno de Heceta lands at Hoh River 1775. Capt. James Cook arrives 1778. Capt. Robert Gray discovers mouth of Columbia River, which he names for his ship; George Vancouver explores Puget Sound 1792. Lewis and Clark expedition winters at Columbia River 1805. Marcus Whitman, Protestant Mission Board, settles near Walla Walla 1836. Territorial status 1853. Northern Pacific railroad reaches Puget Sound 1883. Alaska-Yukon-Pacific Exposition at Seattle 1909. Grand Coulee Dam, largest concrete hydroelectric dam in United States, completed 1941. Hanford works atomic energy plant opens 1943. Upholding treaty provisions from Washinton's days as a territory, a decision awards Native Americans half the catch of Northwest salmon and steelhead 1974. Mt. Saint Helens erupts, killing 61, 1980. Washington Public Power Supply System (known as "whoops") defaults on $8.25 billion bond issue 1983. Reports linking growth-enhancing chemical Alar to cancer generate $140 million loss for Washington's apple growers 1988.
Tourist information (800) 544-1800. **access.tourism.wa.gov.**

▶WEST VIRGINIA

When Virginia seceded in 1861, its western counties reorganized and in 1863 were admitted to the Union as a separate state. Despite the rugged terrain, through which transportation has always been difficult, farming remained the backbone of the economy until the close of the 19th century, when coal mining and other extractive industries developed. After World War II, the manufacturing base developed to include steel and chemical manufacturing. Even with vast natural resources, West Virginia has long been one of the poorest states in the union. Population losses since the 1950's have been pronounced, and the 8 percent loss between 1980 and 1990 was the highest in the country. There is low participation in the workforce by women and educational achievement is well below the national average.

Name for western part of Virginia. **Nickname** Mountain State. **Capital** Charleston. **Entered union** June 20, 1863 (35th). **Motto** *Montani semper liberi* (Mountaineers are always free).
Emblems **Animal** Black bear. **Bird** Cardinal. **Colors** Old gold and blue. **Fish** Brook trout. **Flower** *Rhododendron maximum* (big laurel). **Fruit** Apple. **Songs** "The West Virginia Hills," "West Virginia, My Home Sweet Home," "This Is My West Virginia." **Tree** Sugar maple.
Land **Total area** 24,230 sq. mi (41st), incl. 152 sq. mi. inland water. **Borders** Ohio, Pa., Md., Va., Ky. **Rivers** Big Sandy, Guayandotte, Kanawha, Little Kanawha, Monongahela, Ohio, Potomac. **Lakes** Summersville Dam. **Mountains** Allegheny, Blue Ridge, Cumberland.
Elected officials Gov. Bob Wise, Jr. (D, term exp. 2005). Lt. Gov. Earl Ray Tomblin (D). Sec. State Joe Manchin III (D). Atty. Gen. Darrell V. McGraw (D).
People (July, 2002 est.) 1,801,873 (37th). Race/Hispanic Origin (2000 Census): White 95.0%. Black 3.2%. Indian 0.2%. Asian 0.5%. Other 0.2%. Two or more races 0.9%. Hispanic 0.7%.
Cities (2002) Charleston 51,702. Huntington 49,910. Parkersburg 32,299. Wheeling 30,367. Morgantown 27,342. Weirton 20,027. Fairmont 19,026. Beckley 17,006. Clarksburg 16,498. Martinsburg 15,119.
Business **Gross State Product, 2000:** $42.27 bil. (40th). **Leading Sectors of GSP (2000):** Services 18.26%; Government 16.07%; Manufacturing 15.99%. ***Fortune* 500 Companies (2003):** 0.
Famous natives Newton D. Baker, politician. Pearl Buck, novelist (Nobel Prize, 1938). John W. Davis, politician. Dwight Whitney Morrow, lawyer/diplomat. Michael Owens, manufacturer. Walter Reuther, labor leader. Cyrus Vance, statesman. Jerry West, basketball player. Charles "Chuck" Yeager, pilot.
Noteworthy places Cass Scenic Railroad. Harpers Ferry Natl. Hist. Park. Monongahela Natl. Forest. New River Gorge Bridge. Science and Cultural Center, Charleston.
Memorable events First permanent settlement by Morgan Morgan at Mill Creek 1731. Coal discovered on Coal River 1742. Wheeling Convention repudiates act of secession; forms new state of Kanahwa 1861. Enters Union as West Virginia 1863. Population peaks at 2.5 million 1950. Unemployment jumps 8.6% to 18.0%, highest in nation, 1980–83.
Tourist information (800) CALL-WVA. **www.callwva.com.**

▶WISCONSIN

The indigenous people of the region had a largely agricultural economy, but the fur trade drew Europeans into the region. Native resistance to white settlement was strong and not overcome until the Black Hawk Wars of 1832. In the early 19th century, German, Scandinavian, and Dutch farmers migrated to the region in large numbers. Many social welfare policies now common to the nation as a whole—including aid to dependent children, workmen's compensation, and old-age assistance—were pioneered in Wisconsin. Although manufacturing accounts for the lion's share of Wisconsin's profits, agriculture is extremely important, and the state is the nation's leading producer of dairy products. There are major shipping facilities at Superior, Green Bay, and Milwaukee.

Name From the Ojibwa *wishkonsing*, "place of the bearer." **Nickname** Badger State. **Capital** Madison. **Entered union** May 29, 1848 (30th). **Motto** "Forward."

Emblems **Animal** Badger. **Bird** Robin. **Domestic animal** Dairy cow. **Fish** Muskellunge. **Flower** Wood violet. **Insect** Honeybee. **Mineral** Galena. **Rock** Red granite. **Soil** Antigo silt loam. **Song** "On, Wisconsin!" **Symbol of peace** Mourning dove. **Tree** Sugar maple. **Wildlife animal** White-tailed deer.

Land **Total area** 65,498 sq. mi (23rd), incl. 11,188 sq. mi. inland water. **Borders** Minn., Lake Superior, Mich., Lake Michigan, Ill., Iowa. **Rivers** Black, Chippewa, Menominee, Mississippi, St. Croix, Wisconsin. **Lakes** Chippewa, Du Bay, Mendota, Michigan, Superior, Winnebago. **Other notable features** Apostle Islands, Door Peninsula, Green Bay.

Elected officials Gov. Jim Doyle (D, term exp. 2006). Lt. Gov. Barbara Lawton (D). Sec. State Douglas La Follette (D). Atty. Gen. Peg Lautenschlager (D).

People (July, 2002 est.) 5,441,196 (20th). Race/Hispanic Origin (2000 Census): White 88.9%. Black 5.7%. Indian 0.9%. Asian 1.7%. Other 1.6%. Two or more races 1.2%. Hispanic 3.6%.

Cities (2002) Milwaukee 590,895. Madison 215,211. Green Bay 101,515. Kenosha 92,513. Racine 80,712. Appleton 70,633. Waukesha 66,186. Oshkosh 63,464. Eau Claire 62,361. Janesville 60,921.

Business **Gross State Product, 2001:** $173.48 bil. (20th). **Leading Sectors of GSP (2001):** Manufacturing 25.38%; Services 18.21%; Finance, insurance, and real estate 15.81%. ***Fortune* 500 Companies (2003):** 11: Johnson Controls, Northwestern Mutual, Manpower, Kohl's, American Family Insurance Group, Rockwell Automation, Wisconsin Energy, Roundy's, Shopko Stores, Harley-Davidson, Thrivent Financial for Lutherans.

Famous natives King Camp Gillette, inventor/businessman. Eric Heiden, speed skater. Harry Houdini (b. Hungary), magician. Robert La Follette, politician. Liberace (Wladziu Valentino), pianist. Alfred Lunt, actor. Joseph R. McCarthy, politician. Spencer Tracy, actor. Thorstein Veblen, economist. Orson Welles, director. Laura Ingalls Wilder, novelist. Thornton Wilder, author. Frank Lloyd Wright, architect.

Noteworthy places Apostle Island Natl. Lakeshore. Chequamegon Natl. Forest. Circus World Museum, Baraboo. Door County Peninsula. Ice Age Natl. Scientific Reserve. Manitowoc Maritime Museum. Milwaukee Art Museum. Milwaukee Public Museum. Nicolet Natl. Forest. Old Wade House and Carriage Museum, Greenbush. Old World Wisconsin, Eagle. Villa Louis, Prairie du Chien. Wisconsin Dells.

Memorable events Jean Nicolet lands at Green Bay 1634. French establish mission and trading post near Ashland 1634. British take control of region 1763. Land ceded to United States 1787, but U.S. control not established until after War of 1812. Becomes independent Territory 1836. Statehood 1848. More than 800 die in forest fire near Peshtigo 1871. First hydroelectric plant completed at Appleton 1882. Ringling Brothers circus formed at Baraboo 1884. First state to enact income tax 1911. Milwaukee transfers more than 11,000 students between city and surburban schools 1986.

Tourist information (800) 432-TRIP or (800) 372-2737. **www.travelwisconsin.com.**

▶WYOMING

Tens of thousands of migrants traveled through the region along the Oregon Trail, but few settled the land until Ft. Laramie was built in 1834. Territorial status came in 1869. Wyoming was the first state to give the vote to women, and in 1925 Nellie Tayloe Ross became the first woman governor following the death of her husband. Cattle ranching is the traditional mainstay of the economy. The state ranks second in uranium output, petroleum and coal production have become increasingly important. Wyoming is best known for its natural wonders. Yellowstone National Park—the site of Old Faithful—is the oldest and largest national park in the country. Following a decade-long mining boom in the 1970's and 1980's, Wyoming's population declined, and it has fallen behind even Alaska in total population. Although the population has increased in the 1990's, there are still no more than five people per square mile.

Name From the Delaware *maugh-wau-wa-ma*, "large plains" or "mountains and valleys alternating." **Nickname** Equality State. **Capital** Cheyenne. **Entered union** July 10, 1890 (44th). **Motto** "Equal rights."

Emblems **Bird** Meadowlark. **Flower** Indian paintbrush. **Gem** Jade. **Song** "Wyoming." **Tree** Cottonwood.

Land Total area 97,814 sq. mi (10th), incl. 713 sq. mi. inland water. **Borders** Mont., S.Dak., Nebr., Colo., Utah, Idaho. **Rivers** Bighorn, Green, North Platte, Powder, Snake, Yellowstone. **Lakes** Bighorn, Yellowstone. **Mountains** Absaroka, Bighorn, Black Hills, Laramie, Owl Creek, Teton Range, Wind River Range, Wyoming Range.

Elected officials Gov. Dave Freudenthal (D, term exp. 2006). Sec. State Joseph B. Meyer (R). Atty. Gen. Pat Crank (D).

People (July, 2002 est.) 498,703 (50th). Race/Hispanic Origin (2000 Census): White 92.1%. Black 0.8%. Indian 2.3%. Asian 0.6%. Pacific Islander 0.1%. Other 2.5%. Two or more races 1.8%. Hispanic 6.4%.

Cities (2002) Cheyenne 53,658. Casper 50,024. Laramie 26,885. Gillette 21,130. Rock Springs 18,464. Sheridan 15,946. Green River 11,628. Evanston 11,448.

Business **Gross State Product, 2001:** $19.29 bil. (48th). **Leading Sectors of GSP (2001):** Mining 24.35%; Transportation & utilities 13.61%; Government 13.42%. ***Fortune* 500 Companies (2003):** 0.

Famous natives James Bridger (b. Va.), pioneer. J.C. Penney, businessman. Jackson Pollock, painter. Nellie Tayloe Ross (b. Mo.), politician.

Noteworthy places Bighorn Canyon Natl. Rec. Area. Buffalo Bill Museum, Cody. Devil's Tower Natl. Monument. Ft. Bridger State Park. Ft. Laramie Natl. Hist. Site. Fossil Butte Natl. Monument. Grand Teton Natl. Park. Medicine Wheel Natl. Hist. Landmark, near Lovell. Natl. Elk Refuge. Yellowstone Natl. Park (Old Faithful).

Memorable events Part of Louisiana Territory claimed for France 1682. Pierre Gaultier de Varennes, sieur de Vérendrye explores region for France 1743. Region to United States with Louisiana Purchase 1803. John Colter crosses area of Yellowstone 1807–08. Indian Wars follow massacre of army detachments 1854 and 1866.

Wyoming Territory organized 1868. Women's suffrage adopted permanently (first instance in United States); Union Pacific railroad crosses state 1869. Yellowstone, world's first national park, opens 1872. White mob kills 28 Chinese miners and burns Chinatown in Rock Springs 1885. Statehood 1890. Nellie Tayloe Ross first woman governor 1925. First Intercontinental Ballistic Missile (ICBM) base opens near Cheyenne 1951. Fires consume 1.6 million acres of land in and around Yellowstone Park 1988.

Tourist information (800) CALL-WYO. **www.wyomingtourism.org.**

Revenues and Expenditures of State Governments, 2001

State	Revenues		Expenditures	
	Total ('000s)	Per capita (rank)	Total ('000s)	Per capita (rank)
Alabama	$17,859,889	$3,996.40 (28)	$16,718,151	$3,740.92 (34)
Alaska	6,185,917	9,756.97 (1)	9,047,480	14,270.47 (1)
Arizona	15,488,897	2,918.58 (49)	17,143,148	3,230.29 (46)
Arkansas	10,330,394	3,833.17 (33)	10,597,097	3,932.13 (30)
California	176,080,892	5,089.04 (12)	170,470,259	4,926.89 (12)
Colorado	19,774,425	4,462.75 (20)	15,685,926	3,540.04 (40)
Connecticut	17,750,445	5,167.52 (10)	18,189,210	5,295.26 (7)
Delaware	5,114,008	6,416.57 (2)	4,311,551	5,409.73 (5)
Florida	46,370,565	2,832.14 (50)	50,264,767	3,069.98 (49)
Georgia	25,250,019	3,003.81 (48)	27,860,155	3,314.32 (44)
Hawaii	6,591,146	5,371.76 (5)	6,792,058	5,535.50 (3)
Idaho	5,286,097	4,001.59 (27)	4,951,659	3,748.42 (33)
Illinois	47,348,197	3,781.80 (34)	45,170,257	3,607.85 (37)
Indiana	20,766,968	3,389.42 (42)	21,583,665	3,522.71 (41)
Iowa	10,255,453	3,497.77 (39)	12,271,461	4,185.36 (24)
Kansas	8,713,237	3,224.74 (43)	10,196,910	3,773.84 (32)
Kentucky	18,550,297	4,558.93 (19)	17,330,724	4,259.21 (22)
Louisiana	17,811,457	3,984.67 (29)	16,410,263	3,671.20 (36)
Maine	5,207,414	4,055.62 (25)	5,737,911	4,468.78 (19)
Maryland	20,938,683	3,887.61 (32)	21,484,098	3,988.88 (29)
Massachusetts	29,303,913	4,578.02 (18)	32,435,081	5,067.19 (8)
Michigan	43,346,782	4,332.08 (21)	46,657,684	4,662.97 (14)
Minnesota	26,135,477	5,242.82 (8)	24,612,196	4,937.25 (11)
Mississippi	11,692,949	4,088.44 (24)	11,727,422	4,100.50 (26)
Missouri	20,133,937	3,571.75 (38)	18,888,113	3,350.74 (43)
Montana	4,224,359	4,667.80 (15)	4,048,049	4,472.98 (18)
Nebraska	5,943,922	3,455.77 (41)	6,111,217	3,553.03 (38)
Nevada	6,643,897	3,166.78 (44)	6,747,035	3,215.94 (47)
New Hampshire	4,574,828	3,633.70 (37)	4,411,243	3,503.77 (42)
New Jersey	42,788,178	5,027.40 (13)	37,659,554	4,424.81 (21)
New Mexico	9,099,224	4,969.54 (14)	9,173,756	5,010.24 (10)
New York	112,438,570	5,891.77 (3)	106,598,603	5,585.76 (2)
North Carolina	32,202,748	3,924.29 (31)	31,626,851	3,854.11 (31)
North Dakota	3,373,244	5,295.52 (6)	2,897,950	4,549.37 (17)
Ohio	52,802,649	4,635.88 (16)	47,880,092	4,203.70 (23)
Oklahoma	12,745,926	3,673.18 (36)	11,416,492	3,290.06 (45)
Oregon	18,218,617	5,245.79 (7)	16,321,295	4,699.48 (13)
Pennsylvania	45,887,490	3,729.78 (35)	51,488,402	4,185.03 (25)
Rhode Island	5,483,128	5,172.76 (9)	5,350,551	5,047.69 (9)
South Carolina	16,865,229	4,151.95 (23)	18,078,717	4,450.69 (20)
South Dakota	3,170,959	4,183.32 (22)	2,690,165	3,549.03 (39)
Tennessee	17,344,232	3,016.91 (47)	18,385,079	3,197.96 (48)
Texas	65,525,245	3,066.08 (46)	64,685,858	3,026.81 (50)
Utah	9,131,656	4,006.87 (26)	9,253,469	4,060.32 (27)
Vermont	3,143,100	5,127.41 (11)	3,370,929	5,499.07 (4)
Virginia	22,760,130	3,162.45 (45)	26,786,593	3,721.91 (35)
Washington	23,646,114	3,945.62 (30)	27,824,006	4,642.75 (15)
West Virginia	8,296,556	4,606.64 (17)	7,300,483	4,053.57 (28)
Wisconsin	18,826,011	3,482.43 (40)	24,857,238	4,598.08 (16)
Wyoming	2,880,176	5,830.32 (4)	2,645,226	5,354.71 (6)
United States	**$1,180,303,656**	**$4,145.14 (N.A.)**	**$1,184,146,099**	**$4,158.63 (N.A.)**

Source: U.S. Bureau of the Census, Governments Division, *State Government Finances*.

STATE GOVERNMENT FINANCES

▶REVENUES AND EXPENDITURES

Revenues Revenue of state governments from all sources in 2001 was $1.18 trillion, a 6 percent drop from the previous year. Taxes accounted for 47 percent, or $560 billion of the total state general revenue. Another 26 percent of state revenues came from the federal government. Individual income taxes made up 18 percent of general revenue, while sales taxes and gross receipts accounted for about 15 percent, while. Charges were responsible for 8 percent of state revenues.

Expenditures State government expenditures in 2001 totaled $1.18 trillion, an increase of 9.3 percent from the amount spent in 2000. State general expenditures amounted to $1.04 billion, 8 percent more than the previous year. The leading expenditure categories, by function, were education services (32 percent), public welfare programs (22 percent), highways (7 percent) and health and hospitals (7 percent).

State Tax Collections Per Capita, By Type, 2002

State	Total taxes[1]	Property taxes	Sales taxes	Licenses	Income taxes: Individual	Income taxes: Corporate
United States	**$1,853.50**	**$32.89**	**$906.74**	**$122.06**	**$642.93**	**$89.95**
Alabama	1,533.25	43.49	754.05	88.04	534.90	71.91
Alaska	1,692.34	77.13	220.65	115.13	N.A.	418.26
Arizona	1,553.57	60.34	982.01	49.60	383.15	63.46
Arkansas	1,857.55	179.66	955.42	86.69	549.15	59.42
California	2,214.24	55.57	874.30	162.12	941.07	151.87
Colorado	1,536.25	N.A.	628.99	61.69	771.27	45.54
Connecticut	2,610.25	N.A.	1,305.05	116.90	1,064.94	43.19
Delaware	2,692.15	N.A.	399.85	966.54	887.61	311.68
Florida	1,484.82	25.59	1,132.05	93.15	N.A.	72.93
Georgia	1,608.84	6.32	702.96	57.73	757.87	66.36
Hawaii	2,747.75	N.A.	1,701.30	89.81	892.92	42.28
Idaho	1,693.40	N.A.	832.41	165.73	628.11	57.24
Illinois	1,782.47	4.51	879.60	151.92	551.66	163.61
Indiana	1,622.74	0.67	866.93	48.66	574.90	108.32
Iowa	1,704.69	N.A.	864.38	176.99	602.48	30.07
Kansas	1,770.46	20.10	895.53	84.68	682.96	44.90
Kentucky	1,948.42	106.97	914.04	131.74	654.39	73.82
Louisiana	1,638.76	7.38	935.07	114.83	396.98	58.99
Maine	2,029.28	37.19	955.81	114.90	828.77	59.77
Maryland	1,982.60	49.98	860.93	79.87	861.90	65.85
Massachusetts	2,305.58	0.01	810.67	77.89	1,231.05	126.37
Michigan	2,175.43	188.13	1,001.87	129.08	609.45	205.49
Minnesota	2,577.11	1.62	1,148.81	172.11	1,084.67	108.13
Mississippi	1,646.68	0.43	1,108.48	104.94	343.03	68.19
Missouri	1,529.92	3.61	729.86	82.06	637.35	53.29
Montana	1,586.37	199.57	407.72	219.34	569.10	74.96
Nebraska	1,730.60	3.69	870.51	113.21	667.05	62.24
Nevada	1,815.20	51.81	1,535.78	201.87	N.A.	N.A.
New Hampshire	1,477.52	393.48	474.79	134.50	56.02	295.92
New Jersey	2,133.66	0.38	1,021.79	111.43	795.90	128.20
New Mexico	1,955.76	28.45	982.65	92.39	529.84	67.02
New York	2,258.23	N.A.	684.89	54.29	1,334.91	117.86
North Carolina	1,867.19	N.A.	788.75	106.26	873.21	80.30
North Dakota	1,762.00	2.17	977.71	162.10	314.76	78.83
Ohio	1,717.55	1.62	771.73	136.80	729.83	66.63
Oklahoma	1,732.45	N.A.	650.52	235.68	654.35	49.72
Oregon	1,459.41	N.A.	184.66	140.96	1,043.57	55.73
Pennsylvania	1,794.52	4.13	887.56	168.48	545.98	97.16
Rhode Island	1,988.93	1.06	1,084.98	86.44	769.84	26.43
South Carolina	1,399.64	3.10	768.85	75.66	475.39	52.91
South Dakota	1,283.20	N.A.	1,021.17	174.83	N.A.	53.28
Tennessee	1,345.06	N.A.	1,042.88	144.21	25.23	86.76
Texas	1,316.00	N.A.	1,082.52	173.46	N.A.	N.A.
Utah	1,694.71	N.A.	873.41	63.74	693.06	47.92
Vermont	2,487.84	785.46	858.98	112.39	607.28	60.50
Virginia	1,752.39	2.82	655.69	74.41	920.10	42.31
Washington	2,080.83	240.14	1,639.46	103.94	N.A.	N.A.
West Virginia	1,971.15	2.12	1,065.96	96.93	574.22	122.18
Wisconsin	2,171.18	16.85	997.51	119.64	914.07	95.86
Wyoming	2,194.50	288.70	1,090.52	190.67	N.A.	N.A.

1. Includes other taxes not shown separately. **Source:** U.S. Bureau of the Census, *State Government Tax Collections, 2002.*

Summary of State Government Finances, 1995–2001

Item	Amount (millions) 1995	2001
TOTAL REVENUES	**$903,756**	**$1,180,304**
General Revenue	739,016	1,049,296
Intergovernmental revenue	215,558	305,619
Taxes	399,148	559,679
Sales and gross receipts	222,934	179,319
Individual income	125,610	208,079
Corporation net income	29,075	31,687
Other Taxes	21,528	29,028
Current charges	64,774	93,050
Miscellaneous general revenue	59,536	90,948
Utility revenue	3,845	6,930
Liquor stores revenue	3,073	4,092
Insurance trust revenue	157,821	119,985
TOTAL EXPENDITURES	**$836,894**	**$1,184,146**
Intergovernmental expenditure	240,978	350,323
Direct expenditure	595,916	833,823
Current operation	396,035	578,320
Capital outlay	57,829	81,976
Insurance benefits and repayments	93,282	118,833
Assistance and subsidies	23,511	23,496
Interest on debt	25,259	31,198
Exhibit: Salaries and wages	125,432	165,751

Item	Amount (millions) 1995	2001
General expenditure	$733,503	$1,043,334
Intergovernmental expenditure	240,978	350,323
Direct expenditure	492,525	693,011
General expenditure, by function:		
Education	249,670	374,539
Public Welfare	194,854	260,310
Hospitals	29,139	34,538
Health	30,865	43,716
Highways	57,374	78,786
Police protection	6,451	10,145
Correction	26,069	38,165
Natural resources	12,534	17,309
Parks and recreation	3,403	5,441
Governmental administration	26,078	38,052
Interest on general debt	24,485	30,452
Other and unallocable	72,648	111,880
Utility expenditure	7,586	18,632
Liquor stores expenditure	2,522	3,347
Insurance trust expenditure	93,282	118,833
Debt at end of fiscal year	**$427,239**	**$576,599**
Cash and Security holdings	**$1,388,527**	**$2,537,489**

Source: U.S. Bureau of the Census, Governments Division, *State Government Finances.*

State Government Individual Income Taxes, 2002

State	Taxable income rate range	Taxable income brackets: Lowest: amount under	Highest: amount over
Alabama[1,2]	2.0-5.0%	$ 500	$ 3,000
Arizona	2.87-5.04	10,000	150,000
Arkansas	1.0-7.0	3,299	27,500
California	1.0-9.3	5,748	37,725
Colorado	4.63% on modified federal tax liability		
Connecticut	3.0-4.5	10,000	10,000
Delaware	2.2-5.95	5,000	60,000
District of Columbia	5.0-9.3	10,000	30,000
Georgia	1.0-6.0	750	7,000
Hawaii	1.4-8.25	2,000	40,000
Idaho[2]	1.6-7.8	1,056	21,129
Illinois	3.0% of taxable net income		
Indiana	23.4% of federal adjusted gross income		
Iowa[1]	0.36-8.98	1,148	51,660
Kansas	3.5-6.45	15,000	30,000
Kentucky	2.0-6.0	3,000	8,000
Louisiana[1]	2.0-6.0	10,000	51,000
Maine	2.0-8.5	4,200	16,700
Maryland[2]	2.0-4.75	1,000	3,000
Massachusetts	5.3% of taxable income		
Michigan	24.2% of federal adjusted gross income		
Minnesota	5.35-7.85	18,710	61,460
Mississippi	3.0-5.0	10,000	10,000
Missouri[1,2]	1.5-6.0	1,000	9,000
Montana[1]	2.0-11.0	2,200	76,200
Nebraska	2.56-6.84	2,400	26,500
New Hampshire	5.0% on dividend and interest income over $2,400		
New Jersey	1.4-6.37	20,000	75,001
New Mexico	1.7-8.2	5,500	65,000
New York[2]	4.0-6.85	8,000	20,000
North Carolina	6.0-7.75	12,750	120,000
North Dakota	2.1-5.54	27,050	297,350
Ohio[2]	0.74-7.5	5,000	200,000
Oklahoma[1]	0.5-7.0	1,000	10,000
Oregon[1,2]	5.0-9.0	2,500	6,250
Pennsylvania[2]	2.8% on taxable income		
Rhode Island	3.8-10.098	1,035	297,350
South Carolina	2.5-7.0	2,340	11,700
Tennessee	6.0% on interest and dividend income		
Utah[1]	2.3-7.0	863	4,313
Vermont	24% of federal income tax liability		
Virginia	2.0-5.75	3,000	17,000
West Virginia	3.0-6.5	10,000	60,000
Wisconsin	4.6-6.75	8,430	126,420

Note: Rates and brackets shown are for single taxpayers. Brackets for married taxpayers filing jointly are usually double those shown. Alaska, Florida, Nevada, South Dakota, Texas, Washington, and Wyoming have no state income tax. 1. State with a provision that allows the taxpayer to deduct fully the federal income tax payment. 2. States in which one or more local governments levy a local income tax.
Source: Government of the District of Columbia, Dept. of Finance and Revenue, *Tax Rates and Tax Burdens in the District of Columbia: A Nationwide Comparison* (January, 2003)

Composition of State Legislatures, 2003-04

State or other jurisdiction	Senate			House		
	Demo-crats	Repub-licans	Total	Demo-crats	Repub-licans	Total
Alabama	**25**	10	35	**64**	41	105
Alaska	8	**12**	20	13	**27**	40
Arizona	13	**17**	30	24	**36**	60
Arkansas	**27**	8	35	**70**	30	100
California	**25**	15	40	**50**	30	80
Colorado	17	**18**	35	28	**37**	65
Connecticut	**21**	15	36	**100**	51	151
Delaware	**13**	8	21	15	**26**	41
Florida	14	**25**	40[1]	43	**77**	120
Georgia	**32**	24	56	**105**	74	180[1]
Hawaii	**22**	3	25	**32**	19	51
Idaho	3	**31**	35[2]	9	**61**	70
Illinois	27	**32**	59	**62**	56	118
Indiana	18	**32**	50	**52**	46	100[2]
Iowa	20	**30**	50	44	**56**	100
Kansas	10	**30**	40	46	**79**	125
Kentucky	18	**20**	38	**66**	34	100
Louisiana	**25**	14	39	**71**	34	105
Maine	**17**	16	35[1,2]	**81**	69	151[1]
Maryland	**33**	14	47	**106**	35	141
Massachusetts	**32**	6	402	**136**	22	160[2]
Michigan	16	**22**	38	52	**57**	110[2]
Minnesota	**37**	27	67[1,2]	64	**70**	134
Mississippi	**34**	18	52	**86**	33	122[1]
Missouri	14	**18**	34[2]	**87**	76	163
Montana	19	**31**	50	42	**58**	100
Nebraska	Nonpartisan		49	Unicameral		
Nevada	9	**12**	21	**27**	15	42
New Hampshire	11	**13**	24	142	**255**	400[1,2]
New Jersey	20	20	40	**44**	36	80
New Mexico	**24**	18	42	**42**	28	70
New York	25	**37**	62	**99**	51	150
North Carolina	**35**	15	50	**62**	58	120
North Dakota	17	**32**	47	29	**69**	94
Ohio	11	**21**	33[2]	39	**59**	99[2]
Oklahoma	**30**	18	48	**52**	48	101[2]
Oregon	14	**16**	30	28	**32**	60
Pennsylvania	21	**29**	50	98	**104**	203[2]
Rhode Island	**32**	6	38	**87**	13	75
South Carolina	21	**25**	46	53	**71**	124
South Dakota	11	**24**	35	20	**50**	70
Tennessee	**18**	15	33	**57**	41	99[2]
Texas	15	15	2	**78**	71	150[2]
Utah	9	**20**	29	24	**51**	75
Vermont	**16**	13	30[2]	62	**82**	150[1,2]
Virginia	18	**22**	40	34	**64**	100[1]
Washington	**25**	24	49	**50**	48	98
West Virginia	**28**	6	34	**75**	25	100
Wisconsin	**18**	15	33	43	**56**	99
Wyoming	10	**20**	30	14	**46**	60
Dist./Columbia[3]	**11**	2	13	Unicameral		
Amer. Samoa	Nonpartisan		18	Nonpartisan		21
Guam	7	**8**	15	Unicameral		
No. Mariana Isl.	2	**5**	91	1	**16**	18[1]
Puerto Rico	**19**	8	28[1]	**30**	20	51[1]
U.S. Virgin Isl.	**7**	0	15[1]	Unicameral		

Note: As of February, 2003. Numbers in bold indicates the party in the majority. 1. Includes one or more Independent or other third-party legislator . 2. Includes one or more vacancy. 3. Council of the District of Columbia. **Source:** Council of State Governments, *The Book of the States*, 2003.

Salaries of Major State Administrative Officials, 2003-04

State	Governor	Lieutenant governor	Secretary of state	Attorney general
Alabama	$101,432	$48,620	$66,722	$124,951
Alaska	83280	77,712	(1)	88,548
Arizona	95,000	(2)	70,000	90,000
Arkansas	71,738	34,673	43,000	59,781
California	175,000	131,250	123,750	148,750
Colorado	90,000	68,500	68,500	80,000
Connecticut	150,000	77,756	50,000	81,562
Delaware	114,000	60,000	103,900	114,400
Florida	120,171	115,112	116,056	118,957
Georgia	127,303	83,148	112,776	125,871
Hawaii	94,780	90,041	(1)	85,302
Idaho	98,500	26,000	80,000	88,500
Illinois	150,691	115,235	123,700	132,963
Indiana	95,000	76,000	66,000	79,400
Iowa	107,482	76,698	82,940	105,430
Kansas	95,446	26,967	74,148	85,267
Kentucky	103,018	87,580	82,521	87,580
Louisiana	95,000	85,008	85,000	85,000
Maine	70,000	(4)	N.A.	78,062
Maryland	120,000	100,000	70,000	100,000
Massachusetts	135,000	120,000	120,000	122,500
Michigan	177,000	123,000	124,900	124,900
Minnesota	120,303	62,980	66,169	93,000
Mississippi	101,800	60,000	75,000	90,800
Missouri	120,087	77,184	90,471	104,332
Montana	88,190	62,471	67,512	75,550
Nebraska	65,000	47,000	52,000	64,500
Nevada	117,000	50,000	80,000	110,000
New Hampshire	100,690	(4)	65,540	85,753
New Jersey[3]	157,000	(4)	137,165	137,165
New Mexico	90,000	65,000	65,000	72,500
New York	179,000	151,500	120,800	151,500
North Carolina	118,430	104,523	94,552	104,523
North Dakota	83,013	64,452	68,000	71,076
Ohio	126,485	73,715	90,725	93,434
Oklahoma	101,140	75,530	90,000	94,349
Oregon	93,600	(4)	72,000	77,200
Pennsylvania	144,416	119,300	102,343	118,262
Rhode Island	95,000	80,000	80,000	85,000
South Carolina	106,078	44,737	92,007	92,007
South Dakota	95,389	12,6355	64,812	80,995
Tennessee	85,000	49,500	127,308	118,416
Texas	115,345	99,122	117,546	92,217
Utah	93,600	78,200	(1)	84,600
Vermont	88,026	50,253	75,317	90,272
Virginia[3]	124,885	36,321	12,479	110,667
Washington	139,087	72,705	89,004	126,443
West Virginia	90,000	(4)	65,000	75,000
Wisconsin	122,406	69,379	62,549	127,868
Wyoming	130,000	(4)	110,000	89,067

1. Lieutenant governor also serves as secretary of state. 2. Secretary of state also serves as lieutenant governor. 3. Data for officials other than governor is for 2000-01. 4. No lieutenant governor. Speaker or President of the Senate next in line of succession to the governorship. 5. Annual salary for duties as presiding officer of the Senate.
Source: Council of State Governments, *The Book of the States*, 2003.

U.S. TERRITORIES AND POSSESSIONS

The United States administers a number of overseas territories and commonwealth states under a variety of circumstances. The provisions of the Northwest Ordinance of 1787 established the system under which territories of the United States can achieve statehood. In order to elect a territorial legislature and send a nonvoting delegate to Congress, a territory must contain 5,000 inhabitants of voting age; it is eligible for statehood when the population numbers 60,000.

▶AMERICAN SAMOA

Territory of American Samoa

Geography **Location:** seven islands (Tutuila, Ta'u, Olosega, Ofu, Aunun, Rose, Swain's) in southern central Pacific Ocean. **Boundaries:** Hawaii about 2,300 mi. (3,700 km) to NNE, Cook Islands to E, Tonga to SW, Western Samoa to W. **Total area:** 76.1 sq. mi. (199 sq km). **Coastline:** 72 mi. (116 km). **Comparative area:** slightly larger than Washington, DC. **Land use:** 5% arable land; 10% permanent crops; 0% meadows and pastures; 70% forest and woodland; 15% other. **Major cities:** (1980 census) Pago Pago (capital) 3,075.

People **Population:** 67,084 (July 2001 est.) **Nationality:** noun—American Samoan(s); adjective—American Samoan. **Ethnic groups:** 89% Samoan (Polynesian), 2% Caucasian, 4% Tongan, 5% other. **Languages:** Samoan (closely related to Hawaiian and other Polynesian languages) and English; most people are bilingual. **Religions:** 50% Christian Congregationalist, 20% Roman Catholic, 30% mostly Protestant denominations and other.

Government **Type:** unincorporated and unorganized territory of U.S. **Constitution:** ratified 1966, in effect 1967. **National holiday:** Flag Day, Apr. 17 (1900). **Heads of Government:** Tauese P. Sunia, Governor (since Jan. 1997). **Structure:** executive—governor is popularly elected to four-year term and exercises authority under direction of U.S. Secretary of Interior; legislative—bicameral legislature (Fono) with 18 member Senate chosen by county councils to serve four-year terms and House of Representatives with 20 members popularly elected to serve two-year terms, plus a nonvoting delegate from Swain's Island; judicial—High Court with chief justice and associate justices appointed by U.S. Secretary of Interior.

Economy **Monetary unit:** U.S. dollar. **Budget:** (1996-97 est.) income: $121 mil.; expend.: 127 mil. **GDP:** $500 mil.; $8,000 per capita (2000 est.). **Chief crops:** bananas, coconuts, vegetables, taro, breadfruit, yams, copra, pineapples, papayas. **Natural resources:** pumice and pumicite. **Major industries:** tuna canneries, handicrafts. **Labor force:** 14,400 (1996) 33% government, 34% tuna canneries, 33% other. **Exports:** $500 mil. (1998); 93% canned tuna. **Imports:** $471 mil. (1996); 56% material for canneries, 8% food, 7% petroleum products, 6% machinery and parts. **Major trading partners:** (1992) *exports:* 99.6% U.S.; *imports*: 62% U.S., 9% Japan, 11% Australia, 7% New Zealand, 4% Fiji, 7% other.

American Samoa consists of seven islands between 14° and 15°S, and 168° and 171°W. It was first peopled by Polynesians in the first millennium B.C. The first European to visit the islands was Louis Antoine de Bougainville, who came in 1768 and called them "The Islands of the Navigators," in recognition of the islanders' seamanship. American whalers and missionaries began visiting the islands in the 1830's, and the United States secured trading privileges by treaty in 1878. In 1889, the United States, Britain, and Germany established tripartite control of the islands. The High Chiefs of Tutuila ceded the islands of Tutuila and Aunun to the United States in 1900, and the High Chiefs of the Manu'a islands ceded those of Tau, Ofu, Olosega, and Rose in 1904. Swain's Island became part of American Samoa in 1925.

The islands have been administered by Department of Interior since 1904. American Samoa is an unincorporated and unorganized territory of the United States,with its own government but under the plenary authority of the Department of the Interior.

▶BAKER AND HOWLAND ISLANDS

About 1,600 mi. (2,575 km) southwest of Hawaii and 1,000 miles west of Jarvis Island are Baker Island (0°14'N, 176°28'W) and Howland Island (0°48'N, 176°38'W, 40 miles north of Baker). Discovered in 1842, the two coral atolls were worked for guano until about 1890. Great Britain claimed them in 1889, but the U.S. made them territories in 1935 and sent colonists to them. With an area about of about 1 sq. mi. each, neither is inhabited today. Both are unincorporated territories administered by the U.S. Fish and Wildlife Service as part of the National Wildlife Refuge.

▶GUAM

Territory of Guam

Geography **Location:** southernmost and largest of Mariana Islands in western North Pacific Ocean; Agaña 13°28'N, 144°45'E. **Boundaries:** Tokyo, Japan about 1,350 mi. (2,170 km) to N, Honolulu, Hawaii 3,300 mi. (5,955 km) to ENE; Federated States of Micronesia to S, Philippines to W across Philippine Sea. **Total area:** 209 sq. mi. (541 sq km). **Coastline:** 78 mi. (125.5 km). **Comparative area:** Three times size of Washington, D.C. **Land use:** 18% forest and woodland; 15% meadows and pastures; 11% arable land; 11% permanent crops; 45% other. **Major cities:** Agaña (capital).

People **Population:** 157,557 (July 2001 est.) **Nationality:** noun—Guamanian(s); adjective—Guamanian. **Ethnic groups:** 47% Chamorro, 25% Filipino, 10% Caucasian, 18% Chinese, Japanese, Korean, other. **Languages:** English, Chamorro, and Japanese. **Religions:** 85% Roman Catholic, 15% other.

Government **Type:** organized, unincorporated territory of U.S. **Constitution:** Organic Act of Aug. 1, 1950. **National holiday:** Guam Discovery Day, first Monday in Mar. **Heads of Government:** Carl Gutierrez, governor (since Nov. 8, 1994). **Structure:** executive—governor elected to 4-year term; legislative—unicameral; Senate has 15 members elected for 2-year terms; judicial—U.S. District Court, Guam Superior Court.

Economy **Monetary unit:** U.S. dollar. **Budget:** (2000) ***revenuse:*** $605.3 mil.; ***expend.:*** $654.2 mil. **GDP:** $3.2 bil., $21,000 per capita (2000 est.). **Chief crops:** fruits, copra, vegetables, eggs; relatively undeveloped with most food imported.

Livestock: poultry, pigs, cows. **Natural resources:** fishing (largely undeveloped), tourism (especially from Japan). **Major industries:** U.S. military, tourism, construction, transshipment services, concrete products, printing and publishing, food processing, textiles. **Labor force:** 60,000 (2000 est.) ; 40% private services, 26% government, 24% trade, 10% industry. **Exports:** $75.7 mil. (f.o.b., 1999) mostly transshipments of refined petroleum products, construction materials, fish, food and beverage products. **Imports:** $203 mil. (f.o.b. 1999); petroleum and petroleum products; food, manufactured goods. **Major trading partners:** *exports*: 25% U.S., 63% Trust Territory of the Pacific Islands, 12% other; *imports*: 23% U.S., 19% Japan, 58% other.

Guam was inhabited by Chamorros from the Malay Peninsula as early as 1500 B.C. The first European to stop at Guam was Ferdinand Magellan in 1521. Spanish colonization began with the arrival of Jesuit missionaries in 1668. By 1700 pestilence and insurrection had reduced the Chamorro population from 50,000 to about 2,000. Guam was ceded to the United States in 1899. In 1941 it was occupied by Japan—the only inhabited territory of the U.S. to be seized by enemy forces during World War II. It was retaken by the Americans in 1944. Though unincorporated, the Congressionally approved Guam Organic Act provides for a republican form of government with executive, legislative, and judicial branches.

More than one million tourists visit Guam annually, but the impact of military downsizing will nevertheless cause new economic problems.

▶JARVIS ISLAND, KINGMAN REEF, AND PALMYRA ATOLL

Jarvis Island (0°23'S, 160°02'W, about 1,510 mi. S of Hawaii), Kingman Reef (6°24'N, 162°22'W, about 1,070 mi. SSW of Hawaii), and Palmyra Atoll (5°52'N, 162°05'W, about 1,100 mi. SSW of Hawaii) in the Line Island group.

Discovered in 1798, Kingman Reef (0.4 sq. mi.; 1 sq km) was annexed by the U.S. in 1922, and used as an aviation station during the 1930's. Discovered in 1802, Palmyra Atoll consists of about 50 islets with a combined area of four square miles. It was annexed by the Kingdom of Hawaii in 1862, by Great Britain in 1889, and claimed by the U.S. in 1912. Privately owned, it is administered by the Department of the Navy, as is Kingman Reef. Jarvis Island was claimed by the U.S. in 1857, annexed by Great Britain in 1889, and reclaimed by the U.S. in 1935. Its rich guano deposits were worked by U.S. and British companies in the late 19th century.

▶JOHNSTON ATOLL

Geography **Location:** Johnston Island and Sand Island (uninhabited) in central Pacific Ocean. **Boundaries:** Honolulu, Hawaii about 825 mi. (1,330 km) to ENE, Marshall Islands to SW. **Total area:** 1.1 sq. mi. (2.8 sq km). **Coastline:** 6.21 mi. (10 km). **Comparative area:** about 4.7 times size of The Mall in Washington, DC. **Land use:** 0% arable land; 0% permanent crops; 0% meadows and pastures; 0% forest and woodland; 100% other. **Major cities:** none.

People **Population:** 970 (Jan. 2001), all U.S. government personnel and contractors.

Government **Type:** unincorporated territory of U.S.

Johnston Atoll (16°45N, 169°32'W) , 820 miles SW of Hawaii) includes Johnston, Hikina, and Akan Islands, with a total area of 1.1 square miles. Claimed by the U.S. in 1858, Johnston Atoll is manned and administered by the U.S. Defense Special Weapons Agency and managed jointly as a National Wildlife Refuge by the DSWA and the Fish and Wildlife Service.

▶MIDWAY ISLANDS

Geography **Location:** Sand Island and Eastern Island in northern Pacific Ocean; 28°15'N, 177°25'W. **Boundaries:** Honolulu, Hawaii about 1,460 mi. (2,350 km) to SE, Marshall Islands to SW. **Total area:** 2.0 sq. mi. (5.2 sq km). **Coastline:** 9.3 mi. (15.0 km). **Comparative area:** about nine times size of The Mall in Washington, DC. **Land use:** 0% arable land; 0% permanent crops; 0% meadows and pastures; 0% forest and woodland; 100% other. **Major cities:** none.

People **Population:** 150 U.S. Fish and Wildlife Service personnel (July, 2001 est.). No indigenous population. **Nationality:** noun—Midway Islander(s); adjective—Midway Island. **Languages:** English. **Religions:** Christianity.

Government **Type:** unincorporated territory of U.S.

Economy **Monetary unit:** U.S. dollar. **Major industries:** support of National Wildlife Refuge activities.

Midway Atoll consists of Eastern Island and Sand Island. Although they are part of the Leeward Islands—the westernmost islands of the Hawaiian chain—they are not part of the state of Hawaii. They were the site of the Battle of Midway, June 1942, a turning point in the Pacific theater of World War II. The islands continued to serve as a naval station until 1993; since 1996, it has been managed by the U.S. Fish and Wildlife Service as a National Wlidlife Refuge open to the public for snorkeling, scuba diving, and sportfishing.

▶NAVASSA

Located in the Caribbean between the islands of Jamaica and Haiti and 100 mi (160km) south of the U.S. Naval Base at Guantánamo, Cuba, Navassa was claimed by the U.S. in 1856. It is uninhabited except for a lighthouse under U.S. Coast Guard administration. The island is about 2 sq. mi. (5.2 sq km).

▶NORTHERN MARIANA ISLANDS

Commonwealth of the Northern Mariana Islands (CNMI)

Geography **Location:** Fourteen major islands (including Saipan, Rota, and Tinian) in western central Pacific Ocean. Saipan 15°13'N, 145°44'E. **Boundaries:** Japan to N; Honolulu, Hawaii about 3,500 mi. (5,635 km) to E; Guam to SW; Philippines to W across Philippine Sea. **Total area:** 293 sq. mi. (759 sq km). **Coastline:** undetermined. **Comparative area:** slightly more than 2.5 times size of Washington, D.C. **Land use:** 19% meadows and pastures, 21% arable land, 60% other. **Major cities:** (1990 census) Saipan (capital) 38,896.

People **Population:** 74,612 (July 2001 est.) **Nationality:** undetermined. **Ethnic groups:** Chamorro majority; Carolinians, other Micronesians; Caucasian, Japanese, Chinese, Korean. **Languages:** English, Chamorro, Carolinian; 86 percent speak a language other than English at home. **Religions:** Christian (Roman Catholic majority); some traditional beliefs.

Government **Type:** commonwealth associated with U.S. **Constitution:** Covenant Agreement effective Nov. 3, 1986. **National holiday:** Commonwealth Day, Jan. 8. **Heads of Government:** Pedro P. Tenorio, governor (since January, 1998). **Structure:** executive—governor elected by popular vote; legislative—bicameral legislature (nine-member Senate elected for four-year term, 15-member House of Representatives elected for two-year term; judiciary—U.S. District Court, Commonwealth Trial Court, Commonwealth Appeals Court.

Economy **Monetary unit:** U.S. dollar. **Budget:** (1996) ***revenues:*** $221 mil. ***expend:*** 213 mil. **GDP:** $900 mil., $12,500 per capita (2000). **Chief crops:** coconuts, fruits, vegetables. **Livestock:** cattle. **Natural resources:** arable land, fish. **Major industries:** tourism, construction, light industry, handicrafts. **Labor force:** 7,476 total indigenous labor force, 2,699 unemployed, 22,560 foreign workers (1995). **Exports:** $N.A. garments. **Imports:** $N.A. food, construction equipment and materials, petroleum products. **Major trading partners:** U.S., Japan.

Running north from the island of Guam across a 600-mile-long archipelago in the Pacific Island group known as Micronesia, the islands of the Northern Marianas (CNMI) were originally settled by Pacific argonauts as early as 1500 B.C. Ferdinand Magellan landed at Saipan in 1521, introducing Western culture to the region. The Spanish took control of the archipelago in 1565 and ruled until 1898, when Germany took over the islands. After World War I, the League of Nations mandated the Marianas to Japan, who developed extensive sugar processing works on Saipan. Allied forces took the Marianas in 1944.

In 1947, the islands were included in the United Nations Trust Territory of the Pacific and placed under U.S. administration. In 1976, the CNMI adopted its own constitution. A mutually approved Covenant to Establish a Commonwealth was implemented by the Marianas and the United States in 1986. The Northern Marianas are subject to provisions of U.S. law, except regarding customs, minimum wages, immigration, and taxation. The people are, as a rule, U.S. citizens. The CNMI benefits from substantially from United States assistance.

▶PUERTO RICO

Commonwealth of Puerto Rico

Geography **Location:** large island of Puerto Rico, together with Vieques, Culebra, and many smaller islands, in northeastern Caribbean Sea. San Juan 18° 29'N, 66° 08'W **Boundaries:** Atlantic Ocean to N, Virgin Islands to E, Caribbean Sea to S, Dominican Republic 50 mi. (80 km) to W. **Total land area:** 3,459 sq. mi. (8,959 sq km). **Coastline:** 311 mi. (501 km). **Comparative area:** slightly less than three times size of Rhode Island. **Land use:** 26% pastures; 16% forest and woodland; 5% permanent crops; 4% arable land; 49% other; **Major cities:** (2000 Census) San Juan (capital) 421,958, Bayamón 203,499, Carolina 168,164, Ponce 155,038, Caguas 88,680

People **Population:** 3,808,610 (2000 Census). **Nationality:** noun—Puerto Rican(s); adjective—Puerto Rican. **Ethnic groups:** almost entirely Hispanic. **Languages:** Spanish (official), English. **Religions:** mostly Christian, 85% Roman Catholic, 15% Protestant denominations and other.

Government **Type:** commonwealth associated with U.S. **Constitution:** effective July 25, 1952. **National holiday:** U.S. Independence Day, July 4. **Heads of Government:** Sila Calderon, governor, since Jan. 2001. **Structure:** executive—governor elected by direct vote to four-year term; legislative—bicameral legislature (Senate with 28 members, House of Representatives with 54 members, all elected by popular vote to four-year terms); judiciary—Supreme Court appointed by governor.

Economy **Monetary unit:** U.S. dollar. **Budget:** (FY99/00) ***income:*** $6.7 bil.; ***expend.:*** $9.6 bil. **GDP:** $38.1 bil., $9,800 per capita (1999 est.). **Chief crops:** sugarcane, coffee, pineapples, plantains, bananas (imports a large share of food needs). **Livestock:** cattle, chickens. **Natural resources:** copper, nickel; potential for crude oil. **Major industries:** manufacturing of pharmaceuticals, electronics, apparel, food products, instruments, tourism. **Labor force:** (2000); industry 20%, services 77%, 9.5% unemployed. **Exports:** $38.5 bil. (f.o.b. 2000); pharmaceuticals, electronics, apparel, canned tuna, rum, beverage concentrates, medical equipment, tourism. **Imports:** $27 bil. (c.i.f. 2000); chemicals, machinery and equipment, clothing, food, fish, petroleum products. **Major trading partners:** (1999 est.) *exports:* 88% U.S; *imports:* 60% U.S.

Puerto Rico was initially peopled by the Igneri and Taíno tribes. The island's first European visitor was Christopher Columbus, who landed on the island in 1493. In 1508, Juan Ponce de Léon led the first settlers to San Juan, and by 1514 the Taíno population had dropped from an estimated 30,000 to 4,000. In the 17th and 18th centuries, Puerto Rico was invaded by both English and Danish forces, and though San Juan was captured or burned several times, the Spanish maintained control.

The Spanish constitution granted Puerto Ricans citizenship in 1812, but a revolution was put down in 1868. Spain granted Puerto Rico self-government in 1897 but this was repealed when sovereignty was transferred to the U.S. after the Spanish-American War. Despite early attempts to Americanize Puerto Rico, including an effort to make English the official language and granting citizenship in 1917, the Popular Democratic Party, founded in 1938, brought about a change in political status from that of a U.S. colony to an autonomous commonwealth in 1952.

Governed under the Puerto Rican Federal Relations Act and a constitution modeled on that of the U.S., Puerto Rico is nonetheless an autonomous political entity in voluntary association with the U.S. Despite dramatic increases in industrial development since the 1950's, Puerto Rico suffered from net outward migration until 1988.

Puerto Ricans remain almost equally divided between those who favor statehood and those who favor maintaining commonwealth status, with those seeking independence constituting a vocal but small minority. The statehood-minded argue that limited citizenship is disadvantageous since it allows them to be drafted into the U.S. military but they cannot vote in national elections. The other side fears the burden of full U.S. taxes. In the most recent balloting on the issue, held December 13, 1998, 50.2 percent of Puerto Ricans voted for "none of the above," an option that maintained Puerto Rico's commonwealth status; 46.5 percent voted for statehood, while 2.5 percent preferred independence.

▶VIRGIN ISLANDS

Virgin Islands of the United States

Geography **Location:** three main inhabited islands (St. Croix, St. Thomas and St. John) and about 50 smaller islands, mostly uninhabited, in northeastern Caribbean Sea. Charlotte Amalie 18°22'N, 64°56'W. **Boundaries:** British Virgin Islands to N, Netherlands Antilles to E, Caribbean Sea to S, Puerto Rico about 40 mi. (64 km) to W. **Total area:** 136 sq. mi. (352 sq km). **Coastline:** 117 mi. (188 km). **Comparative area:** twice the size of Washington, DC. **Land use:** 26% meadows and pastures; 15% arable land; 6% permanent crops; 6% forest and woodland; 47% other. **Major cities:** (1990 census) Charlotte Amalie (capital) 12,331; Christiansted 2,555; Frederiksted 1,064.

People **Population:** 122,211 (July 2001). **Nationality:** noun—Virgin Islander(s); adjective—Virgin Islander. **Ethnic groups:** 74% West Indian (45% born in Virgin Islands, 29% born elsewhere in West Indies), 13% U.S. mainland, 5% Puerto Rican, 8% other; 80% black, 15% white, 5% other; 14% of Hispanic origin. **Languages:** English (official), Spanish, Creole. **Religions:** 42% Baptist, 34% Roman Catholic, 17% Episcopalian, 7% other.

Government **Type:** organized, unincorporated territory of U.S. **Constitution:** Revised Organic Act of July 22, 1954 serves as constitution. **National holiday:** Transfer Day (from Denmark to U.S.), Mar. 31. **Heads of Government:** Dr. Charles Wesley Turnbull, governor (since Jan. 1999). **Structure:** executive—governor elected to four-year term; unicameral legislature—senate with 15 members elected to two-year terms; judiciary—two U.S. district courts.

Economy **Monetary unit:** U.S. dollar. **Budget:** (1992) ***income:*** $364.4 mil.; ***expend.:*** $364.4 mil. **GDP:** $1.8 bil., $15,000 per capita (2000). **Chief crops:** fruit, vegetables, sorghum. **Livestock:** Senepol cattle. **Natural resources:** sun, sand, sea, surf. **Major industries:** tourism, petroleum refining, watch assembly, rum distilling, construction, pharmaceuticals, textiles, electronics. **Labor force:** 47,443 (1990); 79% services, 20% industry, 1.2% agriculture; 4.9% unemployment. **Exports:** $N.A.; refined petroleum products to U.S. **Imports:** $N.A.; 82% crude petroleum for refining. **Major trading partners:** ***exports:*** U.S., Puerto Rico; imports: U.S., Puerto Rico.

The Virgin Islands of the United States (USVI) consists of more than 50 islands located about 40 miles east of Puerto Rico, and about 1,730 east-southeast of Miami. Excavations have revealed evidence of human habitation in the Virgin Islands from as early as A.D. 100. By 1493, when Christopher Columbus landed in the islands—which he named for the virgin martyr St. Ursula—they were inhabited by Carib Indians who were driven out by the Spanish in 1555.

In 1672, St. Thomas was settled by the Danish West India Company. The Danes laid claim to St. John in 1683 and purchased St. Croix from the French in 1773. The United States purchased the Virgin Islands from Denmark for $25 million in 1917, and they were made a territory under the jurisdiction of the Navy. U.S. citizenship was granted in 1927, and the Department of the Interior assumed administration of the islands in 1931. The first governor elected by popular vote was installed in 1970, and an independent constitution was voted down by the electorate 1979.

The primary industry is tourism, which accounts for 70 percent of GDP and employs 70 percent of the work force. Inernational business and financial services are increasingly important.

▶WAKE ISLANDS

Geography **Location:** three islands (Wake, Wilkes, and Peale) in North Pacific Ocean; Wake 19°18'N, 166°36'E. **Boundaries:** Honolulu, Hawaii 2,3000 mi. (3,700 km) to E, Marshall Islands to S, Guam about 1,280 mi. (2,060 km) to W. **Total area:** 2.5 sq. mi. (6.5 sq km). **Coastline:** 12 mi. (19.3 km) **Comparative area:** about 11 times size of the Mall in Washington, D.C. **Land use:** 0% arable land; 0% permanent crops; 0% meadows and pastures; 0% forest and woodland; 100% other. **Major cities:** none.

People **Population:** no indigenous inhabitants; temporary population of 123 civilian contractors and one U.S. Army civilian. (Jan. 2001).

Government **Type:** unincorporated territory of U.S., administered by U.S. Air Force.

The Wake Island group was first discovered by British captain William Wake in 1796. It was chartered by Capt. Charles Wilkes's surveying expedition, which was accompanied by a naturalist named Peale. Annexed by the United States in 1898, Wake became a civil aviation station in the 1930's, and was captured by the Japanese shortly after Pearl Harbor. It was retaken in 1944. Formerly an important commercial aviation base, it is now used only by some commercial cargo planes and for emergency landings.

Resident Population of U.S. Territories, 1960–2020 (in thousands)

Territory	1960	1970	1980	1990	2000	2010[1]	2020[1]
Puerto Rico	2,358	2,7122	3,210	3,537	3,916	4,088	4,196
Guam	67	86	107	134	155	184	211
Virgin Islands	33	63	100	104	121	133	144
American Samoa	20	27	32	47	65	81	95
Northern Mariana Islands	9	12	17	44	72	99	123

1. Projected. **Source:** U.S. Census Bureau, International Data Base.

Cities and Counties in the U.S.

Included here is basic information about population change, cost of living, and government finances in major U.S. cities, metropolitan statistical areas and counties. In addition, there are brief descriptions of the 50 largest cities—from Albuquerque to Wichita. Statistical sources include the U.S. Census Bureau's decennial census, *City Government Finances, County Government Finances,* and the *Statistical Abstract of the United States* (all annual publications).

▶FORMS OF LOCAL GOVERNMENT

In addition to the one federal and 50 state governments, the Bureau of the Census recognizes five basic types of organized local government. In addition to these, which are authorized in state constitutions and statutes, some local governments operate under a "home-rule charter" the form and organization of which are specified by locally approved charters rather than by general or special state law. The number of local governments and officials continues to skyrocket even as the size of the federal bureaucracy shrinks. In 1997, there were a total of 87,453 state and local governments compared with 85,006 five years earlier.

Counties

County governments are established to provide general government; and include those governments designated as boroughs in Alaska, parishes in Louisiana, and counties in the other states. In 1997, there were 3,043 county governments; the most common forms are:

Council-commission A county government without a chief executive but with an elected governing body that shares administrative responsibility with officials elected or appointed to specific positions.

Council-administrator A county government with an elected governing body responsible for overall policy, and an appointed administrator (sometimes called a county manager, county commissioner, or county judge) responsible for administration. The powers of the administrator under this form of government may vary widely.

Council-elected executive A county government with an elected governing body and an elected chief executive—sometimes called a president or a chairperson of the board. The powers of the executive under this form of government may vary widely.

Municipalities

Municipal governments are established to provide general government for a specific concentration of population in a defined area and include those governments designated as cities, villages, boroughs (except in Alaska), and towns (except in the six New England states, Minnesota, New York and Wisconsin). In 1997, there were 19,372 municipal governments; the most common forms are:

Mayor-council A municipal government with an elected mayor and an elected council or other governing body. In some mayor-council municipalities, the mayor is the chief executive, with broad powers. In some other mayor-council cities, the mayor has limited powers.

Council-manager A municipal government with an elected council or other governing body responsible for overall policy, and an appointed manager responsible for administration. The council may select a chairperson from among their own number who may be designated as the mayor.

Commission A municipal government with an elected board of commissioners responsible for overall policy. Each commissioner is responsible for administration of one or more departments of the municipal government. The board may select a chairperson from among their own number who may be designated as the mayor.

Towns

Township governments are established to provide general government for areas defined without regard to population concentration and include those governments designated as towns in Connecticut, Maine (including organized plantations), Massachusetts, Minnesota, New Hampshire (including organized locations), New York, Rhode Island, Vermont, and Wisconsin, and townships in other states. In 1997, there were 16,629 township governments; the most common forms are:

Town meeting A township government in which an annual town meeting of resident voters makes basic policy. An elected board (often called "a board of selectmen" or "township supervisors") is responsible for day-to-day administration of the township.

Representative town meeting A township government in which a town meeting composed of elected representatives of the resident voters makes basic policy. This form of government is usually found in more populous towns or townships. An elected board (often called "a board of selectmen" or "township supervisors") is responsible for day-to-day administration of the township.

School districts

School district governments are organized local entities providing public elementary, secondary and/or higher education which, under state law, have sufficient administrative and fiscal autonomy to qualify as separate governments. Excludes "dependent public school systems" of county, township or state governments. In 1997, there were 13,726 school district governments.

Special district governments

All organized local entities other than the four categories listed above, authorized by state law to provide only one or a limited number of designated functions, and with sufficient administrative and fiscal autonomy to qualify as separate governments; known by a variety of titles, including districts, authorities, boards, commissions, etc., as specified in the state legislation. In 1997, there were 34,683 special district governments.

Source: U.S. Bureau of the Census.

THE 50 LARGEST CITIES, 2000

Between 1990 and 2000, the westward movement of the U.S. population again revealed its strength as three cities in the so-called Rust Belt (Buffalo, Cincinnati, Pittsburgh and Toledo) fell from the list of the 50 largest cities in the U.S. They were replaced by Colorado Springs, Las Vegas, Mesa, Ariz. and Wichita, Kansas.

Among the largest cities in the U.S., however, no city came close to Las Vegas in terms of population growth. Between 1990 and 2000, its population increased from 258,295 to 478,434, leapfrogging more than 30 cities in going from the 63rd largest city to the 32nd.

Following are brief descriptions of the 50 largest cities in the U.S. according to numbers from the 2000 Census. They are set forth in alphabetical order. Several tables showing the growth of major cities in America follow this section. See also the section on Metropolitan Statistical Areas (MSAs) later in this chapter.

▶ALBUQUERQUE, NEW MEXICO

Seventy million years ago, earthquakes and volcanoes pushed the land that is now Albuquerque above the sea, forming the Rio Grande Valley and a ring of mountain ranges. Even today, the 10,000-foot-high Sandia Mountains are rising slowly and the Rio Grande Valley continues gradually to deepen. During the Ice Age, Sandia Man roamed the area hunting mastodon and buffalo, and some 3,000 years ago, the Anasazi built stone and adobe cities which still stand. The 1530's marked the arrival of Spanish conquistadors and missionaries.

Founded as a Spanish Villa in 1706, when 35 families moved to the land along the Rio Grande, Albuquerque was named by Don Francisco Cuervo y Valdez in honor of the Duke of Albuquerque, King Phillip's Viceroy of New Spain. Indian raids arrested the villa's expansion, and 100 years after its founding, its population numbered a mere 2,200. Benefitting from their proximity to the Santa Fe Trail, the people farmed, raised cattle, marketed wool and adobe for building, and ran trading posts, military supply depots, saloons, hotels, and mercantile businesses. The introduction of the railroad in 1880 spurred Albuquerque's growth, and the 1940 population of 35,000 has since grown more than tenfold.

Today, Albuquerque occupies a central position along the Rio Grande Research Corridor, which stretches from Los Alamos to Las Cruces, and is home to the University of New Mexico and such major high-tech installments as GTE Communications, UNISYS, GE, and Sandia National Laboratories. Albuquerque's cultural and historical attractions include the Albuquerque Museum, the Indian Pueblo Culture Center, the Maxwell Museum of Anthropology, the National Atomic Museum, and Petroglyph National Monument.

Population 448,607 (2000). Rank: 35th. Race/Hispanic Origin (2000): White 71.6%. Black 3.1%. Indian 3.9%. Asian 2.2%. Pacific Islander 0.1%. Other 14.8%. Two or more races 4.3%. Hispanic 39.9%.

Location: 35°05'N, 106°47'W. County: Bernalillo.

Terrain and climate Elev.: 5,300 ft. Area: 127.2 sq. mi. (329.4 sq km). Avg. daily min. temp.: Jan.: 22.3°F/-5.3°C; avg. daily max. July: 92.8°F/33.7°C. Avg. annual: rainfall, 8.12"; snowfall, 11"; clear days, 71; precipitation days, 135.

Government Form: mayor and council. Mayor Martin Chavez. (505) 768-3000. **www.cabq.gov**

Visitor info: (505) 842-9918 or (800) 284-2282. **www.cabq.gov**

▶ATLANTA, GEORGIA

Atlanta, the capital and largest city of Georgia, lies at the base of the Blue Ridge Mountains, near the Chattahoochee River. First settled in 1836, the area became the terminus for the Georgia Railroad in 1845 and took the name Atlanta. The population grew to 15,000 by 1861, and during the Civil War, Atlanta became a strategic Confederate depot and collection point for recruits, establishing it as one of the most important cities of the Confederacy and making it a vital objective during Gen. William Tecumseh Sherman's infamous "March to the Sea" in 1864. After two months of bitter battle, Sherman took the city on Sept. 1 and burned most of it to the ground. After the war, the ravaged city was rebuilt; it became the state capital in 1868.

The leading city of the "New South," Atlanta is a the chief commercial hub of the southeastern United States. Atlanta is nicknamed the "City Without Limits" because there are no major rivers, mountains, or coastlines to retard its burgeoning growth into the ever-expanding suburbs. Several *Fortune* 500 Companies have their headquarters in Atlanta (including Coca-Cola and United Parcel Service) as do CNN and the U.S. Centers for Disease Control. Hartsfield Atlanta International (the major hub for Delta Airlines) is the world's busiest airport, giving rise to the saying, "whether you're going to heaven or hell, you still have to change planes in Atlanta."

The city is also an important educational and cultural center, home to more than 30 institutions of higher learning, including Georgia Tech, Emory University, and Morehouse and Spelman Colleges. The Jimmy Carter Presidential Library is here, as is the grave of the Rev. Martin Luther King Jr.

The 1996 Summer Olympics thrust Atlanta into the international spotlight, and helped fuel the city's economic future. The Olympiad added hundreds of thousands of jobs (most of them permanent) and an estimated $500 million in construction to Atlanta's economy. It also brought Centennial Olympic Park and Turner Field to the downtown landscape.

Population 416,474 (2000). Rank: 39th. Race/Hispanic Origin (2000): White 33.2%. Black 61.4%. Indian 0.2%. Asian 1.9%. Other 2.0%. Two or more races 1.2%. Hispanic 4.5%.

Location: 33°50'N, 84°24'W. County: Fulton.

Terrain and climate Elev.: 1,034 ft. Area: 131.2 sq. mi. (339.80 sq km). Avg. daily min. temp.: Jan.: 32.6°F/0.3°C; avg. daily max. July: 87.9°F/31°C. Avg. annual: rainfall, 48.61"; snowfall, 2"; clear days, 108; precipitation days, 116.

Government Form: mayor and council. Mayor Shirley Franklin. (404) 330-6100. **www.atlantaga.gov**

Visitor info: (800) ATLANTA. **www.atlanta.net**

▶AUSTIN, TEXAS

Austin, the capital of Texas, lies about 80 miles northeast of San Antonio on the banks of the Colorado River. First inhabited by nomadic Indian tribes, the area had as its first permanent European settler Jacob Harrell, in 1835, who established the town of Waterloo. In 1839, it was chosen as the site of the Texas Republic's capital and was renamed after Stephen F. Austin, who brought the first Anglo settlers to Texas in the 1820s. After 1845, when Texas gained admission into the Union, Austin began to flourish, and by 1930 it had grown into a major regional center with a population of 75,000.

Originally a business and distribution center serving the farmers of the Blackland Prairies to the east, Austin's farmers produce cotton, maize, corn, livestock, and poultry. Traditional industries such as meat packing, canning, and furniture manufacturing have been outstripped by the high-tech companies that have helped to nearly double the population since 1970. The city's economic landscape has for decades been defined by the state government (responsible for 131,000 jobs, or one-fourth of Austin's workforce). The University of Texas, founded in 1881 in Austin, boasts the highest endowment of any U.S. university—a legacy of the Texas oil fields. As the University developed into a first-class institution (with 50,000 students) feeding the city's cultural and economic life, and with the influx of electronics and computer companies, Austin has prospered into a metropolis of national, even worldwide, scope.

In recent years, the university's academic excellence and Austin's reputation for liberalism and progressivism (coffeehouses are more common here than cowboy hats) have attracted both the arts and high-tech companies such as Dell Computer, Motorola, 3M, IBM, and Texas Instruments.

Population 656,562 (2000). Rank: 16th. Race/Hispanic Origin (2000): White 65.4%. Black 10.0%. Indian 0.6%. Asian 4.7%. Pacific Islander 0.1%. Other 16.2%. Two or more races 3.0%. Hispanic 30.5%.

Location: 30°20'N, 97°45W. Counties: Travis, Williamson

Terrain and climate Elev.: 570 ft. Area: 232 sq. mi. (600.9 sq km). Avg. daily min. temp.: Jan.: 38.8°F/3.8°C; avg. daily max. July: 95.4°F/35.2°C. Avg. annual: rainfall, 31.50"; snowfall, 1"; clear days, 115; precipitation days, 82.

Government Form: council and manager. Mayor Will Wynn. (512) 974-2250. www.ci.austin.tx.us

Visitor info: (866) GO-AUSTIN or (512)583-7234. **www.austintexas.org.**

▶BALTIMORE, MARYLAND

One of America's most active seaports since Colonial days and chartered in 1729 as a major conduit of tobacco exportation, Baltimore was named after the founder of the colony of Maryland, George Calvert, Lord Baltimore. By the time of the Revolutionary War, it earned fame as an important commercial and maritime center, and ships sailing from Baltimore plied their trade with northern Europe, the Mediterranean and the Caribbean. Chartered as a city in 1797, Baltimore's commercial activity began to surge, spurred by its burgeoning iron and copper industries, its proximity to the nation's capital, and the arrival of the Baltimore and Ohio Railroad, which developed links to the Midwest. However, the deep, divisive passions of the Civil War stunted growth and it would take years before the city recovered.

A fire in 1904 destroyed almost every building in the downtown area, providing impetus for needed revitalization. The two world wars renewed demands for Baltimore's port facilities and fostered development of a solid heavy industrial base. After World War II, however, the city's infrastructure aged and decayed. Today, Baltimore remains a large port and industrial city with one of the largest steel plants in the world (Bethlehem Steel's Sparrow Point works). Much of the city has been rebuilt through urban renewal efforts, including the nationally acclaimed Inner Harbor Project, and Oriole Park at Camden Yards. The population seems to have stabilized after a loss of almost 20 percent in 1960.

Among the city's historic sites is Fort McHenry, where Francis Scott Key wrote "The Star-Spangled Banner." Baltimore is home to St. Mary's Seminary and University (1791), Johns Hopkins University (1876), and the University of Baltimore (1925), among other noted institutions of higher learning.

Population 651,154 (2000). Rank: 17th. Race/Hispanic Origin (2000): White 31.6%. Black 64.3%. Indian 0.3%. Asian 1.5%. Other 0.7%. Two or more races 1.5%. Hispanic 1.7%.

Location: 39°18'N, 76°37'W. County: independent city within Baltimore County.

Terrain and climate Elev.: 155 ft. Area: 80.3 sq. mi. (208 sq km). Avg. daily min. temp.: Jan.: 24.3°F/-4.2°C; avg. daily max. July: 87.1°F/30.6°C. Avg. annual: rainfall, 43.39"; snowfall, 22"; clear days, 106; precipitation days, 112.

Government Form: mayor and council. Mayor Martin O'Malley. (410) 396-3835. **www.baltimorecity.gov**

Visitor info: (877) BALTIMORE. **www.baltimore.org.**

▶BOSTON, MASSACHUSETTS

Named for the English port from which many Puritan immigrants to America came, Boston was first settled in 1630 under the leadership of John Winthrop. As the capital of the Massachusetts Bay Colony, it quickly became the cultural and mercantile capital of the New England colonies. Bostonians never wholly embraced British authority, and they provided the earliest challenges to British rule in their reaction to the Stamp Act (1765) and the Boston Tea Party (1773). The colonists killed in the Boston Massacre (1770) were the first to fall in the years immediately preceding the American Revolution.

With the end of the Revolution, Boston merchants found themselves shut out of English ports by prohibitive tariffs, and in their quest for new markets for American goods opened American trade to the Orient and India. In the 19th century, Boston benefitted early from the industrial revolution, and from several waves of immigration, particularly blacks from the southern states, and Irish and Italians from Europe.

Although Boston's preeminence in trade and industry did not survive the 19th century, it continues to be a major center for banking and financial services. Since World War II its suburbs have flourished as a center of research and development and of the computer industry—Route 128 was the East Coast's answer to California's Silicon Valley during the 1980's—spurring investment in downtown Boston. As the gateway to New England and the birthplace of the Revolution, Boston is also a center for tourism.

Perhaps most important to its identity is Boston's wealth of educational, cultural, and religious tolerance. Harvard University (across the Charles River in Cambridge, 1636) is the country's oldest, and Roxbury Latin (1645) the country's oldest privately endowed secondary school. Today Boston is home to more than 30 colleges and universities, as well as to some of the finest cultural institutions in the country, including the American Academy of Arts and Sciences (1780), the Massachusetts Historical Society (1791), the Boston Athenaeum (1807), the Boston Public Library (the nation's first, 1854), the Boston Museum of Fine Arts (1870), and the Boston Symphony (1881). Boston is also home to three major medical schools and 27 hospitals including the world famous Massachusetts General and Brigham and Women's.

Population 589,141 (2000). Rank: 20th. Race/Hispanic Origin (2000): White 54.5%. Black 25.3%. Indian 0.4%. Asian 7.5%. Pacific Islander 0.1%. Other 7.8%. Two or more races 4.4%. Hispanic 14.4%.

Location: 42°20'N, 71°05'W. County: Suffolk.

Terrain and climate Elev.: 10 ft. Area: 47.2 sq. mi. (122.2 sq km). Avg. daily min. temp.: Jan.: 22.8°F/-5.1°C; avg. daily max. July: 81.8°F/27.6°C. Avg. annual: rainfall, 43.81"; snowfall, 42"; clear days, 99; precipitation days, 128.

Government Form: mayor and council. Mayor Thomas M. Menino. (617) 635-4500. **www.cityofboston.gov**

Visitor info: (888) 733-2678 or (617) 536-4100. **www.bostonusa.com**

▶CHARLOTTE, NORTH CAROLINA

An area of lush green foothills lying at the southernmost tip of the Carolina Piedmont, Charlotte has long been a crossroads city and an important distribution point for the surrounding farmlands. About 250 years ago, Scotch-Irish settlers retracing old Catawba Indian trading routes established a settlement where the paths crossed, and in 1762 it was named Charlotte, after the new bride of King George III. Remembering Gen. Cornwallis's reference to Charlotte as a "hornet's nest" while his army briefly occupied it during the American Revolution, the city adopted the symbol as its emblem.

The discovery of a 17-pound gold nugget in 1799 triggered a gold rush, and although the mines dotting the landscape boosted business, the California gold rush in the mid-1800's lured away prospectors, putting Charlotte on its future course as a top cotton producer. A leading city of the Confederacy in the Civil War, Charlotte hosted the last full meeting of the Confederate cabinet in 1865. The Queen City's second population surge has occurred over the past 20 years. Charlotte is now the country's second-largest banking center, with two of the country's top 10 banks (Bank of America and Wachovia) making their headquarters there. Charlotte is also the home of Duke Energy, one of the largest electric utilities in the United States, and the teachers' pension fund TIAA-CREF.

Recently, the city's economic base has diversified beyond the production of chemicals, foodstuffs, machinery, metals, and textiles, and matured into a major center of world trade and technology, with more than 160 multinational companies engaging in such businesses as microelectronics, insurance, machining and biomedical supplies. North Carolina's status as a right-to-work state has given Charlotte the country's second-lowest unionization rate (less than 4 percent). Located at the intersection of Interstates I-77 and I-85, Charlotte is a key distribution hub, equidistant from the northwestern, midwestern, and southern Florida markets. The Carolina Panthers and the Charlotte Motor Speedway, are all sources of the city's legendary civic pride and boosterism.

Population 540,828 (2000). Rank: 26th. Race/Hispanic Origin (2000): White 58.3%. Black 32.7%. Indian 0.3%. Asian 3.4%. Pacific Islander 0.1%. Other 3.6%. Two or more races 1.7%. Hispanic 7.4%.

Location: 35°16'N, 80°46'W. County: Mecklenburg.

Terrain and climate Elev.: 665 ft. Area: 152.1 sq. mi. (393.9 sq km). Avg. daily min. temp.: Jan.: 30.7°F/-0.7°C; avg. daily max. July: 88.3°F/31.2°C. Avg. annual: rainfall, 43.16"; snowfall, 6"; clear days, 111; precipitation days, 111.

Government Form: council and manager. Mayor Patrick McCrory. (704) 336-2241. **www.charmeck.org**

Visitor Info: (800) 231-4636 or (704) 331-2700. **www.visitcharlotte.org.**

▶CHICAGO, ILLINOIS

Chicago extends roughly 26 miles along the southwestern shoreline of Lake Michigan. The city has historically been a major transportation hub and gateway to the Great Plains, and continues to be one today with major air, rail, and highway hubs. Nineteen trunk-line railroad routes converge at Chicago, linking it with every major U.S. and Canadian city. The city has three major airports, including O'Hare, the second-busiest in the nation. It is also the terminus for major interstate highways running east-west and north-south.

Historically, Chicago's rise parallels the growth of the American republic to the west. Chicago was first settled in 1779, when Jean Baptiste Point de Sable built a house on the site. In 1803, federal troops built a stockade named Fort Dearborn, but by 1830 only 12 families had settled in the area. In the 1830's, however, the population grew rapidly as Americans spread westward, and the city of Chicago was incorporated in 1837 with a population of 4,170. Chicago then began to grow into a bustling Great Lakes port, connected to the Mississippi via a system of rivers and canals.

Chicago has maintained its strategic importance despite changes in transportation technology and remains today a prosperous city. Over the years, Chicago has been noted as a hotbed of labor reform, the center of violent organized crime gang wars during the prohibition era, and a prime example of the good and the bad of American city machine politics. But despite its checkered past, it has grown into the wealthiest and most vibrant city in the Midwest with hardly a sign of the rust belt malaise plaguing many of its sister cities. Chicago has grown into a financial center with three of the nation's four largest futures exchanges and the world's largest listed stock options exchange.

Chicago also far outstrips other midwestern cities in cultural, entertainment, recreational and commercial facilities. Major attractions include the Museum of Science and Industry, the Field Museum of Natural History, the Chicago Historical Society, the Lincoln Park Zoo, the Chicago Lyric Opera Company, the Chicago Symphony Orchestra and the Chicago Art Institute. Downtown Chicago currently has three of the tallest manmade structures in the world—the Sears Tower (1,454 ft. high), the John Hancock Building (1,127 ft.) and the Amoco Building (1,136 ft.). It is also home to the world's tallest apartment complex, the 70-story Lake Point Tower and the world's largest commercial building, the Merchandise Mart.

Population 2,896,016 (2000). Rank: 3rd. Race/Hispanic Origin (2000): White 42.0%. Black 36.8%. Indian 0.4%. Asian 4.3%. Pacific Islander 0.1%. Other 13.6%. Two or more races 2.9%. Hispanic 26.0%.

Location: 41°53'N, 87°40'W. County: Cook.

Terrain and climate Elev.: 623 ft. Area: 228.1 sq. mi. (590.8 sq km). Avg. daily min. temp.: Jan.: 13.6°F/-10.2°C; avg. daily max. July: 83.3°F/28.5°C. Avg. annual: rainfall, 33.34"; snowfall, 40"; clear days, 94; precipitation days, 123.

Government Form: mayor and council. Mayor Richard M. Daley. (312) 744-4000. **www.cityofchicago.org**
Visitor info: (877) CHICAGO. or (312) 744-2400. **www.877chicago.com.**

▶CLEVELAND, OHIO

The heart of the largest metropolitan area in Ohio, Cleveland was founded in 1796 and named after Moses Cleaveland, a surveyor with the Connecticut Land Company, which administered the state of Connecticut's lingering claim on 3.5 million acres of what is now Ohio (the Western Reserve). A frontier village at the mouth of the Cuyahoga River on Lake Erie, Cleveland was transformed into the business and manufacturing center of northern Ohio by the opening of the Erie Canal in 1825, and the Ohio and Erie Canal, which linked Cleveland with Portsmouth on the Ohio River. When the Soo Locks opened Lake Superior to trade with the Lower Lakes in 1855, Cleveland became a major shipping center for ore, lumber, copper, coal and farm produce.

During the Civil War, the city's iron ore and coal deposits were mined for steel production and commercial activity increased to meet the Union's increased demands for heavy machinery, railroad equipment and ships. In the postwar years, Cleveland's mills and factories expanded even further to satisfy the increased needs of the new cities and farms springing up in the wake of westward migration.

Although heavy manufacturing still employs about 20 percent of the city's workforce, the national trend toward a service economy had a severe impact on the local economy, and the population of the Cleveland metropolitan area declined from a high of 2.8 million in 1970 to only 1.8 million today. Nonetheless, Cleveland is still home to many large industrial companies. There are also many medical and industrial research firms, most notably the world-famous Cleveland Clinic and NASA's Lewis Research Center.

Cleveland's industrial strength manifests itself in its flourishing cultural institutions, including the Cleveland Play House, the oldest repertory house in the nation, the world-famous Cleveland Orchestra, the Cleveland Institute of Art, the Cleveland Museum of Natural History, Western Reserve Historical Society, the Cleveland Health Museum, the Allen Memorial Medical Library and the Cleveland Zoo.

Population 478,403 (2000). Rank: 33rd. Race/Hispanic Origin (2000): White 41.5%. Black 51.0%. Indian 0.3%. Asian 1.3%. Other 3.6%. Two or more races 2.2%. Hispanic 7.3%.
Location: 41°28'N, 81°43'W. County: Cuyahoga.
Terrain and climate Elev.: 805 ft. Area: 79 sq. mi. (204.6 sq km). Avg. daily min. temp.: Jan.: 18.5°F/-7.5°C; avg. daily max. July: 81.7°F/27.6°C. Avg. annual: rainfall, 35.40"; snowfall, 52"; clear days, 70; precipitation days, 156.
Government Form: mayor and council. Mayor Jane L. Campbell. (216) 664-2000. **www.city.cleveland.oh.us**
Visitor Info: (800) 321-1001 or (216) 621-4110. **www.travelcleveland.com**

▶COLORADO SPRINGS, COLORADO

Colorado's second-largest city lies on the eastern edge of the Rocky Mountains, some 60 miles south of Denver. Most of the city is nestled among rolling hills with views of the 14,110–foot Pikes Peak to the west. General William Jackson Palmer was the first to recognize the area's natural beauty when he founded the city in 1871. In its early years, it was popular with Europeans, especially Britons, and the city acquired the nickname Little London.

The city's first big boom came during the 1890's, when gold was discovered in nearby Cripple Creek in 1891. The gold rush ended in 1917, when the U.S. began coining money with silver. Since the beginning of World War II, the military has been a major presence in Colorado Springs, beginning with the establishment of Fort Carson in 1942 and continuing with the location of the Air Force Academy, several Air Force bases and the North American Aerospace Defense Command (NORAD) over the years since then.

The city's manufacturing base experienced record growth during the 1960's and 70's due to Colorado Springs' low cost of living and sunny weather patterns (the city has hundreds of clear days and receives less snow than Denver or Minneapolis). Semiconductors, electronic equipment, computers and plastics are among the major manufacturing industries.

Leading an expansion of the service industry in the Pikes Peak region, the United States Olympic Committee has its headquarters in Colorado Springs, as well as its Olympic Training Center, the world's premier multi-sport training facility.

Colorado Springs also prides itself on its extremely clean air. According to local officials, the city's pollen counts are among the lowest in the country, providing relief to people suffering from asthma, nasal allergies, and other respiratory ailments.

Population 360,890 (2000). Rank: 48th. Race/Hispanic Origin (2000): White 80.7%. Black 6.6%. Indian 0.9%. Asian 2.8%. Pacific Islander 0.2%. Other 5.0%. Two or more races 3.9%. Hispanic 12.0%.
Location: 38°48'N, 104°42'W. County: El Paso.
Terrain and climate Elev. 6,145 ft. Area 183.2 sq. mi. (474.5 sq km). Avg. daily min. temp.: Jan.: 16.1°F/–8.8°C; avg. daily max. July: 86.5°F/30.3°C. Avg. annual: rainfall, 16.24"; snowfall, 51"; clear days, 129; precipitation days, 98.
Government Form: council and manager. Mayor Lionel Rivera.. (719) 385-CITY. **www.springsgov.com**
Visitor info: (800) 888-4748. **www.coloradosprings-travel.com.**

▶COLUMBUS, OHIO

The Ohio legislature designated a site along the banks of the Scioto River in the center of the state as the capital in 1812, and named it Columbus in honor of the famous explorer of the New World. From the first, the city exploited its status as the seat of government and its prime location in the middle of the nation's growing network of roads, canals and highways. Incorporated in 1834, Columbus became a thriving hub of agricultural trade.

Between 1850 and 1900, its population grew from 17,800 to over 100,000. Because of the many carriage factories, in the 19th century Columbus was known as the "Buggy Capital of the World." Five railroads passed through the city, so banks soon began to spring up, making Columbus a financial center for the surrounding farm counties.

As in the 19th century, Columbus's modern economy is built on government, agriculture, local finance, and education. In 1950, to counter the trend of suburbanization, the city developed a policy of annexation of surrounding communities. Because it is less reliant on heavy industry than other midwestern cities, it has weathered the decline of the rust belt better than most and it remains a bustling metropolis. In the 1980's, the city realized the creation of more than $780 million in new development and about 100,000 new jobs.

Ohio State University, one of the nation's largest universities, opened as the Ohio Agricultural and Mechanical College in 1870, and the city today has a rich academic community that includes the Ohio Dominican College (whose origins date to 1868), the Columbus College of Art and Design and the Ohio Institute of Technology. Business leaders and politicians have joined in an effort to make the city a center for the arts, refurbishing three theaters and building a complex of three more.

Population 711,470 (2000). Rank: 15th. Race/Hispanic Origin (2000): White 67.9%. Black 24.5%. Indian 0.3%. Asian 3.4%. Pacific Islander 0.1%. Other 1.2%. Two or more races 2.6%. Hispanic 2.5%.

Location: 39°57'N, 83°01'W. Counties: Fairfield, Franklin.

Terrain and climate Elev.: 833 ft. Area: 186.8 sq. mi. (483.8 sq km). Avg. daily min. temp.: Jan.: 19.4°F/-7°C; avg. daily max. July: 84.4°F/29.1°C. Avg. annual: rainfall, 36.97"; snowfall, 28"; clear days, 75; precipitation days, 136.

Government Form: mayor and council. Mayor Michael B. Coleman. (614) 645-7671. **www.cityofcolumbus.org**

Visitor info: (800) 345-4FUN. **www.experiencecolumbus.com.**

▶DALLAS, TEXAS

First settled in 1841 by John Neely Bryan, a Tennessee trader and lawyer, Dallas stretches about 30 miles east of Forth Worth on the Trinity River. Named in 1846 after James K. Polk's vice president, George Mifflin Dallas, it was chartered as a city in 1871. Though it grew substantially with the arrival of railroads in 1872, the population numbered a mere 92,000 in 1910.

Located in the heart of the northern Texas oil belt, Dallas today thrives on a diverse economic base, which, in addition to oil and natural gas, includes production of brick clay and the raw materials for Portland cement, and cotton, grains, fruits, beef, dairy cattle, hogs, sheep and poultry from the farms that surround the city. One of the largest inland cotton markets, and a leading distributor of farm goods and machinery, Dallas also serves as the southwest's banking center with major banks, insurance companies, and the Federal Reserve Bank for the Eleventh District. Key manufacturing industries include aerospace, electronics, transportation equipment, machinery, food and related products, and apparel. Among its leading high-tech employers are Texas Instruments and Electronic Data Systems.

Some of Dallas's distinguished universities are Southern Methodist, Southwestern Medical School of the University of Texas, the Dallas Theological Seminary and Graduate School of Theology, and the Baylor University Schools of Dentistry and Nursing. The Dallas Symphony Orchestra, the Dallas Theater Center, the Dallas Civic Opera, the Dallas Historical Society Museum in the Texas Hall of State, and the Dallas Garden Center, contribute to the city's rich cultural life. Fair Park, the site of the annual State Fair of Texas, remains the most widely attended state fair in the country.

Population 1,188,580 (2000). Rank: 8th. Race/Hispanic Origin (2000): White 50.8%. Black 25.9%. Indian 0.5%. Asian 2.7%. Other 17.2%. Two or more races 2.7%. Hispanic 35.6%.

Location: 32°50'N, 96°50'W. Counties: Collin, Dallas, Denton, Kaufman, Rockwall.

Terrain and climate Elev.: 596 ft. Area: 331.4 sq. mi. (858.3 sq km). Avg. daily min. temp.: Jan.: 33.9°F/1°C; avg. daily max. July: 97.8°F/36.5°C. Avg. annual: rainfall, 34.16"; snowfall, 3"; clear days, 138; precipitation days, 79.

Government Form: council and manager. Mayor Laura Miller. (214) 670-5111. **www.dallascityhall.com.**

Visitor info: (800) CDALLAS or (214) 571-1000 **www.visitdallas.com**

▶DENVER, COLORADO

Denver was born during the great "Pikes Peak or Bust" gold rush of 1859 when small flakes of placer gold were found where the South Platte River meets Cherry Creek. In its first few years, the city survived a flood, several major fires, Indian attacks, and an invasion by Confederate soldiers during the Civil War. With the discovery of more gold in the Rocky Mountains, Denver became a boom town. Saloons, gambling halls, and wagon trains lined the mud-filled streets and just about every outlaw, desperado, and lawman in the West made at least one visit to the city. The turn of the century brought respectability and the wealth of the mountains was poured into parks, fountains, tree-lined streets, and elaborate mansions.

During the oil crisis of the late 1970's and early 80's, Denver experienced a second boom when it became a corporate center for oil-from-shale companies working the Western Slope of the Rockies. Then one of the fastest-growing cities in the United States, in 1983, it doubled its office space as part of a five-year building campaign that added 16 skyscrapers, a $76 million pedestrian mall, and an $80 million performing arts center. Expansion was slowed by the energy glut of the mid-1980's, but it has rebounded dramatically in the 1990's and the population grew by close to 10,000 per year in the first few years of the 1990's.

In 1993, the Colorado Rockies baseball team drew more than four million fans to a converted football stadium. And in 1995, after countless setbacks stemming from problems with its automated baggage system, the much-heralded Denver International Airport finally opened its doors, thus completing the final chapter of a vastly overbudget boondoggle.

Denver's population is among the youngest in the nation, and the youthful flavor of the city is very evident. Denver leads the nation in movie attendance and has more sporting goods stores per resident than any city in the world. The city's 205 parks are so active that a speed limit was recently instituted—for bicycles.

Population 554,636 (2000). Rank: 25th. Race/Hispanic Origin (2000): White 65.3%. Black 11.1%. Indian 1.3%. Asian 2.8%. Pacific Islander 0.1%. Other 15.6%. Two or more races 3.7%. Hispanic 31.7%.

Location: 39°45'N, 105°00'W. County: Denver.

Terrain and climate Elev.: 5,280 ft. Area: 106.8 sq. mi. (276.6 sq km). Avg. daily min. temp.: Jan.: 15.9°F/-8.9°C; avg. daily max. July: 88°F/31°C. Avg. annual: rainfall, 15.31"; snowfall, 60"; clear days, 115; precipitation days, 88.

Government Form: mayor and council. Mayor John Hickenlooper. (720) 865-9000. **www.denvergov.org.**

Visitor info: (800) 233-6837 or (303)-892-1505. **www.denver.org**

▶DETROIT, MICHIGAN

Founded in 1701 by Antoine de La Mothe, sieur de Cadillac, Detroit lies on the Detroit River between

Lake Erie and Lake Huron. Named Fort Pontchartrain-du-Détroit (of the strait), the oldest permanent settlement on the Great Lakes flourished as a trading post for trappers, under French control (to 1760), then British (to 1796) and then American.

The first steamboat reached Detroit from Buffalo in 1818, but it was the easy access to eastern markets via the Erie Canal in 1825 that allowed Detroit to exploit the abundant natural resources in the Michigan peninsula and fostered its emergence as a modern industrial giant in the post-Civil War years. Tenth among cities in the value of its manufactures by 1899, Detroit's main exports included iron ore, copper, lead, salt, and fish. The development of the automotive industry, which eventually became centered in Detroit, propelled Detroit to number three by the 1920's. While Detroit is the home of General Motors, Chrysler, and Ford, recently the automotive industry has been as much a curse as a blessing, for every setback to any of the "Big Three" is felt throughout the Motor City.

Despite the fact that it still ranks high in industrial manufacturing, Detroit has been plagued by urban decline. The relatively low standard of living among the predominantly black inhabitants ignited riots in the 1940's and 1960's, and the city's crime rate is today among the highest in the nation. However, it was Detroit blacks who gave rise to one of the most sensational expressions of popular culture in the 1960's. Founded in 1960, the Tamla Motown label propelled the Jackson 5, the Supremes, and Stevie Wonder—among others—to world renown, and in the process created one of the largest black-owned businesses in the country.

The city's rich and diverse cultural institutions include the Detroit Institute of Arts (which contains one of the largest collections of American art in the world in addition to extensive European holdings), the Detroit Symphony, the Cranbrook Academy of Art, and the 1,000-acre Belle Isle Park, situated on an island in the Detroit River and featuring beaches, a yacht basin, a zoo, an aquarium, and a botanical gardens. In 2000, Detroit became the first U.S. city to see its population drop below one million.

Population 951,270 (2000). Rank: 10th. Race/Hispanic Origin (2000): White 12.3%. Black 81.6%. Indian 0.3%. Asian 1.0%. Other 2.5%. Two or more races 2.3%. Hispanic 5.0%.
Location: 42°23'N, 83°05'W. County: Wayne.
Terrain and climate Elev.: 581 ft. Area: 135.6 sq. mi. (351.2 sq km). Avg. daily min. temp.: Jan.: 16.1°F/-8.8°C; avg. daily max. July: 83.1°F/28.3°C. Avg. annual: rainfall, 30.97"; snowfall, 39"; clear days, 75; precipitation days, 133.
Government Form: mayor and council. Mayor Kwame Kilpatrick (313) 224-3270. **www.ci.detroit.mi.us**
Visitor info: (800) DETROIT or (313) 202-1800. **www.visitdetroit.com**

▶EL PASO, TEXAS

The largest Texas city bordering Mexico, El Paso sits in the western part of the state on the northern bank of the Rio Grande across from Juarez. A major port of entry, with the biggest commercial and manufacturing base in the area, the city encompasses a region of mines, oil fields, livestock ranches, and farms (principal crops: pecans, fruit, cotton, alfalfa, onions, lettuce, chiles). Important industries include metals smelting and refining, oil and gas refining, textiles, meat packing, and food processing. The city is also home to the University of Texas, at El Paso.

In 1536, Alvar Núñez Cabeza de Vaca crossed the Rio Grande, becoming the first European to set foot in the area, but settlement did not follow until 1659, with the establishment of both El Paso del Norte on the southern bank of the Rio Grande, and the Mission of Guadalupe. In 1682, settlers from New Mexico founded Ysleta, an area within the current city limits of El Paso, but permanent settlement did not begin until the arrival of Juan Maria Ponce de Leon in 1827. Incorporated as a city in 1873, El Paso grew into a major industrial center with the introduction of the railroads in 1881.

El Paso's access to sources of cheap labor complemented its mining, refining, and agricultural activities and helped build the city's manufacturing base. In recent years, however, the movement of manufacturing back to Mexico, where labor costs are far less, has created some concern for that portion of the economy. El Paso's proximity to Juarez, Mexico, makes it a vibrant tourist haven, and its pleasant climate, combined with its position on the immigration route from Latin America, have made El Paso one of the fastest-growing cities in the U.S. El Paso also has the highest percentage of citizens with Hispanic ancestry of any American city with over half a million people.

Population 563,662 (2000). Rank: 23rd. Race/Hispanic Origin (2000): White 73.3%. Black 3.1%. Indian 0.8%. Asian 1.1%. Pacific Islander 0.1%. Other 18.2%. Two or more races 3.4%. Hispanic 76.6%.
Location: 31°50'N, 106°30'W. County: El Paso.
Terrain and climate Elev.: 3,700 ft. Area: 239.7 sq. mi. (620.8 sq km). Avg. daily min. temp.: Jan.: 30.4°F/-0.8°C; avg. daily max. July: 95.3°F/35.1°C. Avg. annual: rainfall, 7.82"; snowfall, 5"; clear days, 194; precipitation days, 45.
Government Form: mayor and council. Mayor: Joe Wardy. (915) 541-4000. **www.ci.elpaso.tx.us**
Visitor info: (800) 351-6024 or (915) 534-0600. **www.visitelpaso.com/**

▶FORT WORTH, TEXAS

Named in 1849 after Gen. William J. Worth, commander of the U.S. Army in Texas, Forth Worth originally served to protect settlers from Indian attacks. It grew slowly mainly as a stopover on the cattle drives along the Chisholm Trail until the Texas and Pacific Railroad reached the city in 1871. Stockyards sprang up, making Fort Worth a conduit of cattle shipping, and with the building of a grain elevator, it developed into a milling center as well. By the turn of the century, it had also emerged as a flourishing meat packing market. Oil was discovered in 1917, bringing prosperity and transforming the city into a major refining center with a dozen operating facilities. The two world wars introduced military installations (particularly airfields) to the area. Fort Worth is the sixth largest city in Texas, boasting the state's three finest art museums and a network of parks with total acreage second only to Chicago's.

Population 534,694 (2000). Rank: 27th. Race/Hispanic Origin (2000): White 59.7%. Black 20.3%. Indian 0.6%. Asian 2.6%. Pacific Islander 0.1%. Other 14.0%. Two or more races 2.7%. Hispanic 29.8%.
Location 32°45'N, 97°25'W. County: Tarrant.
Terrain and climate Elev.: 670 ft. Area: 258.5 sq. mi. (670.3 sq km). Avg. daily min. temp.: Jan.: 33.9°F/1°C; avg. daily max. July: 97.8°F/36.5°C. Avg. annual: rainfall, 29.45"; snowfall, 1.4"; clear days, 137; precipitation days, 78.
Government Form: council and manager. Mayor Michael J. Moncrief. (817) 871-8888. **www.fortworth.org.**
Visitor info: (800) 433-5747 or (817) 336-8791.

www.fortworth.com.

▶FRESNO, CALIFORNIA

Fresno grew up around a train station established in 1872 for what became the Southern Pacific Railway. The city was incorporated in 1874. With the introduction of irrigation to the fertile San Joaquin Valley in the 1880's, the small city thrived at the center of a healthy agricultural economy. Today Fresno County is the number one producer of agricultural products in the nation—and the world—and averages more than $2 billion a year in the production and processing of 200 commercial crops, including grapes (for wine and raisins), melon, cotton, alfalfa, barley, grains, cattle, sheep, and poultry.

Fresno's population grew 63 percent between 1980 and 1990, and in the 1980's it was the ninth fastest growing city in the United States and by far the fastest growing of the nation's 50 largest cities.

Located in central California, Fresno—the name is Spanish for ash tree—is a gateway to the Sierra Nevadas, and it is less than 90 minutes from three national parks—Kings Canyon (55 miles), Sequoia (85 miles) and Yosemite (92 miles). Among the attractions to be found within the city limits are the Fresno Art Museum, the Fresno Zoo, the Kearney Mansion Museum (restored home of Theo Kearney, "Raisin King of California"), the Fresno Metropolitan Museum, and the Discovery Center. There are also 10 colleges and universities including a campus of California State University and Fresno City College.

Population 427,652 (2000). Rank: 37th. Race/Hispanic Origin (2000): White 50.2%. Black 8.4%. Indian 1.6%. Asian 11.2%. Pacific Islander 0.1%. Other 23.4%. Two or more races 5.2%. Hispanic 39.9%.

Location 36°47'N, 119°50'W. County: Fresno.

Terrain and climate Elev. 328 ft.; Area: 99.4 sq. mi. (257 sq. km). Avg. daily min. temp. Jan.: 37.4°/3°C; avg. daily max. July: 98°.7F/37°C. Avg. annual rainfall: 10"; snowfall 0"; clear days: 200; precipitation days: 44.

Government Form: council and manager. Mayor: Alan Autrey. (559) 498-1560. **www.ci.fresno.ca.us.**

Visitor info: (800) 788-0836 or (559) 233-0836. **www.fresnocvb.org.**

▶HONOLULU, HAWAII

First visited by Europeans in 1794, Honolulu, meaning "sheltered harbor," has attracted droves of visitors ever since. Situated on Oahu Island, it benefits from a large bay fully protected by coral reefs and its large port facilities. Because of its hospitable climate, the beaches of Waikiki, its majestic mountains, and exotic locale, tourism is Honolulu's major industry; several million visitors come annually, mainly from the U.S. mainland and the Far East, particularly from Japan.

The defense industry is the second mainstay of Honolulu's economy, as the U.S. has long maintained major installations around the island, including the naval base at Pearl Harbor, Hickam Air Force Base, and the U.S. Army's Schofield Barracks and Fort Shafter. Honolulu also serves as the center for Hawaii's export crops—sugar, pineapple, and molasses—and is the principal port for the import of much of the island state's necessities.

Population 371,657 (2000). Rank: 46th. Race/Hispanic Origin (2000): White 19.7%. Black 1.6%. Indian 0.2%. Asian 55.9%. Pacific Islander 6.8%. Other 0.9%. Two or more races 14.9%. Hispanic 4.4%.

Location: 21°19'N, 157°52'W. County: Honolulu.

Terrain and climate Elev.: 15 ft. Area: 25.3 sq. mi. (65.52 sq km). Avg. daily min. temp.: Jan.: 65.3°F/18.5°C; avg. daily max. July: 87.1°F/30.6°C. Avg. annual rainfall: 23.47"; snowfall: 0"; clear days: 90; precipitation days: 102.

Government Form: mayor and council. Mayor Jeremy Harris. (808) 523-4141. **www.co.honolulu.hi.us**

Visitor info: (877) 525-OAHU. **www.gohawaii.com**

▶HOUSTON, TEXAS

On August 30, 1836, brothers August C. and John K. Allen founded this city and named it after Sam Houston, the first president of the Republic of Texas. The Allens paid just over $1.40 per share for 6,642 acres of land near the headwaters of Buffalo Bayou about 50 miles inland from the Gulf of Mexico. Houston's proximity to Stephen Austin's central Texas colonies gave it great potential as a marketing and distribution site. Incorporated in 1837, the city served as capital of the Republic of Texas until 1840. When the first railroad in Texas began operating out of Houston in 1853, the city developed into a major agricultural center while the discovery of oil in southeast Texas at Spindletop in 1901, and the opening of the man-made Houston Ship Channel in 1914, stimulated petroleum refining and metal fabricating. During World War II, petrochemical production began on a large scale, and with the building of NASA's $761 million complex in the early 1960's (now known as the Johnson Space Center), Houston took center stage as the main player in manned spacecraft.

A major corporate and international business center—more than a dozen *Fortune* 500 companies are based here—present-day Houston has successfully limited its dependence on the energy economy. The Port of Houston is the eighth largest in the world in terms of tonnage handled; the city is also home to four of the nation's 10 major liquid gas pipelines. The presence of the Texas Medical Center also makes Houston a vital U.S. center for the practice and progress of modern high-tech medicine. The Center's 39 institutions occupy in excess of 550 acres and employ more than 50,000 workers. Houston's total health employment exceeds 100,000.

Population 1,953,631 (2000). Rank: 4th. Race/Hispanic Origin (2000): White 49.3%. Black 25.3%. Indian 0.4%. Asian 5.3%. Pacific Islander 0.1%. Other 16.5%. Two or more races 3.1%. Hispanic 37.4%.

Location: 29°50'N, 95°20'W. Counties: Fort Bend, Harris, Montgomery.

Terrain and climate Elev.: 49 ft. Area: 572.7 sq. mi. (1,483.3 sq km). Avg. daily min. temp.: Jan.: 40.8°F/4.8°C; avg. daily max. July: 93.6°F/34.2°C. Avg. annual rainfall: 44.77"; snowfall: 0"; clear days: 94; precipitation days: 107.

Government Form: mayor and council. Mayor Lee P. Brown. (713) 247-1000. **www.cityofhouston.gov.**

Visitor info: (800) 4HOUSTON. **www.houston-spacecityusa.com**

▶INDIANAPOLIS, INDIANA

Indianapolis, the capital of Indiana and a major commercial center in the country's heartland, is intersected by more highways than any other in the nation, earning it the name, the "Crossroads of America." Fifty percent of America's population is within a day's drive of the city, a geographic asset that makes it a focal point of transportation and manufacturing.

The first European-American settlement, established in 1820 where Fall Creek meets the White River, was chosen as the location of Indiana's capital in 1825. The state government created jobs triggering an expanding population that further swelled with the routing of the National Road (U.S. 40) in 1830. Development mushroomed in 1839 with the building of the Central Canal on the White River, providing a vital transportation link and the necessary water power to run factories, sawmills, and paper mills. Maintenance of the canal, however, proved impossible, and the town declined until the introduction of the railroad. By 1853, railroad lines fed into Indianapolis from every corner of the nation and at one point, nearly 200 trains passed through daily. At the turn of the century, Indianapolis had emerged as a sophisticated city with sidewalks and streetcars. The city's economy prospered during the early stages of the automotive industry, producing more than 50 types of car—including the Duesenberg, the Marmon, and the Stutz—before Detroit gained ascendancy.

Having survived the decline in heavy industry and the flight of the affluent to the suburbs, Indianapolis remains a hub of manufacturing and transportation, with a bustling wheat, soybean, and livestock market. Key industries include electronics, metal fabrication, pharmaceuticals, and transportation equipment. Downtown Indianapolis has enjoyed a renaissance with the construction of a convention center, the Hoosier Dome, Market Square Arena, and the refurbishment of Union Station. But the city's premier attraction remains the Indianapolis 500, the annual Memorial Day weekend auto race, first held in 1911.

Population 791,926 (2000). Rank: 12th. Race/Hispanic Origin (2000): White 69.3%. Black 25.3%. Indian 0.3%. Asian 1.4%. Pacific Islander 0.0%. Other 2.0%. Two or more races 1.6%. Hispanic 3.9%.
Location 39°42'N, 86°10'W. County: Marion.
Terrain and climate Elev.: 808 ft. Area: 352 sq. mi. (911.7 sq km). Avg. daily min. temp.: Jan.: 17.8°F/-7.8°C; avg. daily max. July: 85.2°F/29.5°C. Avg. annual rainfall: 39.12"; snowfall: 21"; clear days: 90; precipitation days: 122.
Government Form: mayor and council. Mayor: Bart Peterson. (317) 327-4MAC. **www.indygov.org**
Visitor info: 1-800-323-4639 or (317) 639-4282. **www.visitindy.info.**

▶JACKSONVILLE, FLORIDA

The first Europeans to visit the area were French Huguenots who in 1564 established a colony at Fort Caroline on the Saint Johns River in northeast Florida. The Spanish destroyed the fort in the following year. Permanent settlement began in 1816, and in 1822 Jacksonville was laid out and named for then Maj. Gen. Andrew Jackson, who had led the U.S. campaign to take Florida from the Spanish. Growth was slow until after the Civil War. After World War II, several large naval bases were located here and by 1960 the population was over 200,000. In 1968, the population jumped to more than 500,000 when it was consolidated with Duval County, and Jacksonville became one of the largest cities by area in the U.S.

Florida's largest city, Jacksonville is a major regional center for commerce, industry, finance, and medicine. After years of improvements on its harbor, 25 miles west from the mouth of the Saint Johns, it has grown into a major port of entry and it is the primary distribution center for the region. Jacksonville has also emerged as a leading resort with extensive recreational and convention facilities. Among its amenities are the Haydon Burns Library, the Cummer Gallery of Art, the Jacksonville Art Museum, the Jacksonville Zoological Park, the Saint Johns River Park, and Fort Caroline National Memorial, site of the first European colony in Florida. Among its leading educational institutions are Jacksonville University and the University of Northern Florida.

Population 735,617 (2000). Rank: 14th. Race/Hispanic Origin (2000): White 64.5%. Black 29.0%. Indian 0.3%. Asian 2.8%. Pacific Islander 0.1%. Other 1.3%. Two or more races 2.0%. Hispanic 4.2%.
Location: 30°15'N, 81°38'W. County: Duval.
Terrain and climate Elev.: 31 ft. Area: 840 sq. mi. (1,967.6 sq km). Avg. daily min. temp.: Jan.: 41.7°F/ °C; avg. daily max. July: 90.7°F/29.5°C. Avg. annual rainfall: 52.77"; snowfall: 0"; clear days: 98; precipitation days: 116.
Government Form: mayor and council. Mayor John A. Delaney. (904) 630-2489 www.coj.net
Visitor info: 1-800-733-2668 or (904) 353-9736. www.visitjacksonville.com

▶KANSAS CITY, MISSOURI

Kansas City was begun as a trading outpost by the French fur trader François Chouteau in 1821. In 1833, the town of Westport was founded nearby, and in 1850 the City of Kansas received its first charter. (Its name was changed to Kansas City in 1889.)

Situated at the confluence of the Kansas and Missouri rivers, Kansas City prospered early on as a river port and as the terminus of the Santa Fe and Oregon trails. With the arrival of the railroad in 1866, Kansas City's status as a major commercial hub was assured. Thanks to its central location and the development of excellent and diversified transportation and storage facilities, Kansas City is one of the nation's key markets for agricultural and livestock products, as well as for the distribution of heavy agricultural machinery. The Kansas City Board of Trade is one of the largest grain and commodities trading markets in the world. Other major industries are greeting card publishing, telecommunications, and high-tech manufacturing, especially instrument landing systems for airplanes. Kansas City is also home to the 10th Federal Reserve Bank.

An early oasis of culture in the midst of an unsettled, untamed prairie (the city once boasted two opera houses), Kansas City remains a mecca of the arts, with cultural offerings like the Kansas City Art Institute, the Nelson Atkins Museum of Art, the Kansas City Symphony, the Lyric Opera, and the Missouri Repertory Theatre. The city's beginnings are preserved in the Lone Jack Civil War Museum and Missouri Town 1855, and it is the site of the annual American Royal Livestock, Horse Show, and Rodeo, held as part of the annual convention of the Future Farmers of America. Among its institutes of higher learning are Rockhurst College (1916), the University of Missouri-Kansas City, and the DeVry Institute of Technology.

Population 441,545 (2000). Rank: 36th. Race/Hispanic Origin (2000): White 60.7%. Black 31.2%. Indian 0.5%. Asian 1.9%. Pacific Islander 0.1%. Other 3.2%. Two or more races 2.4%. Hispanic 6.9%.
Location: 39°07'N, 94°38'W. Counties: Cass, Clay, Jackson, and Platte.
Terrain and climate Elev.: 744 ft. Area: 316.4 sq. mi. (819.5 sq km). Avg. daily min. temp.: Jan.: 17.2°F/-8.2°C; avg. daily max. July: 88.5°F/31.3°C. Avg. annual rainfall: 29.27"; snowfall: 5.9"; clear days: 132; precipitation days: 97.

Government Form: council and manager. Mayor Kay Barnes. (816) 513-3500. www.kcmo.org.
Visitor info: (800) 767-7700. www.visitkc.com

▶LAS VEGAS, NEVADA

Las Vegas was originally settled by Mormons in 1855, but its modern history began in 1931, when Nevada legalized gambling and liberalized marriage and divorce laws. From then until 1978 (when Atlantic City re-opened its casinos), Las Vegas prospered while it enjoyed a monopoly on casino gambling in the U.S. Since 1980, it has been one of America's fastest-growing cities, more than doubling in size between 1980 and 1996. There were 164,674 people living in Las Vegas in 1980; by 1996 the city's population had climbed to 376,906. The 2000 Census has the city's population nearing the 500,000 mark. Las Vegas is growing so fast, it prints phone books twice a year.

To be sure, gambling has fueled this growth—gaming revenues topped $6 billion in 1997—but the city's expansion has come even as dozens of other cities across the country have legalized casino gambling on riverboats, at Native American reservations, or even in the French Quarter of New Orleans. Las Vegas has thrived because of a mix of gambling, nightlife, shopping, and an unequivocal commitment to excess. Since 1993, five major resorts have been torn down, only to make way for newer, bigger properties. The nation's 10 biggest hotels (including the 5,000-room MGM Grand) are all here. Over the past decade, the city has built hotels replicating New York City, Paris, Venice (complete with canals through the desert landscape), and the pyramids of Egypt.

More than 30 million visitors (including 3 million conventioneers) travel to Las Vegas each year. With all this tourism have come tens of thousands of new jobs and new housing (an average of 578 new homes per month). Because the city is laid out in a desert, there are few geographical barriers to limit urban expansion, except the availability of drinking water. The city is beginning to confront problems of urban sprawl such as traffic, air pollution, and distribution of resources such as schools and water.

Population 478,434 (2000). Rank: 32nd. Race/Hispanic Origin (2000): White 69.9%. Black 10.4%. Indian 0.7%. Asian 4.8%. Pacific Islander 0.4%. Other 9.7%. Two or more races 4.1%. Hispanic 23.6%.
Location: 36° 05'N, 115°10'W. County: Clark.
Terrain and climate Elev.: 2,162 ft. Area: 83.3 sq. mi. (215.7 sq km). Avg. daily min. temp.: Jan.: 33.6°F/0.9°C; avg. daily max. July: 105.9°F/41.1°C. Avg. annual rainfall: 4"; snowfall: 1"; clear days: 211; precipitation days: 26.
Government Form: Council and manager. Mayor Oscar B. Goodman. (702) 229–6241. www.ci.las-vegas.nv.us.
Visitor info: (877) VISIT-LV or (702) 892–7575. www.vegasfreedom.com.

▶LONG BEACH, CALIFORNIA

Originally the site of an Indian trading camp, by the end of the 18th century the area of what is now Long Beach was part of the Spanish Ranchos Los Alamitos and Cerritos. In 1881, William E. Willmore began development of the land as a resort (which he named for himself). When first incorporated in 1888, the town was named Long Beach after its 8.5 miles of Pacific beachfront. Content to remain a resort community, Long Beach saw its fortunes rewritten in 1921 when extensive petroleum deposits were discovered at Signal Hill. Today, industry is a major presence in Long Beach—especially ship repair, transportation, oil refining, and marine research; in addition, the Navy maintains a large base and dry dock.

Among the cultural and recreational attractions Long Beach boasts are its own Museum of Art, the Terrace Theater, home of the Long Beach Symphony Orchestra, and the Long Beach Community Playhouse. Popular tourist attractions include Los Cerritos (a Spanish adobe house which dates to 1844), the Aquarium of the Pacific, and the magnificent ocean liner *Queen Mary* which today serves as a floating maritime museum, convention center, and hotel. Long Beach is also the site of a Formula 1 Grand Prix every spring. Disneyland is in nearby Anaheim.

Population: 461,522 (2000). Rank: 34th. Race/Hispanic Origin (2000): White 45.2%. Black 14.9%. Indian 0.8%. Asian 12.0%. Pacific Islander 1.2%. Other 20.6%. Two or more races 5.3%. Hispanic 35.8%.
Location: 33°46'N, 118°10'W. County: Los Angeles.
Terrain and climate Elev.: 35 ft. Area: 49.8 sq. mi. (129 sq km). Avg. daily min. temp.: Jan.: 44.3°F/6.8°C; avg. daily max. July: 83°F/28.3°C. Avg. annual rainfall: 12"; snowfall: 0"; clear days: 143; precipitation days: 35.
Government Form: council and manager. Mayor Beverly O'Neill. (562) 570-6801. www.ci.long-beach.ca.us.
Visitor info: (800) 4LB-STAY or (562) 436-3645. www.visitlongbeach.com

▶LOS ANGELES, CALIFORNIA

In pre-Spanish days, the area of Los Angeles was inhabited by approximately 4,000 Indians representing some 30 tribes. The village of Yang-na, with a population of 300, was located in what is now downtown Los Angeles, in the vicinity of Alameda and Commercial Streets. In October of 1542, João Rodrigues Cabrilho, a Portuguese explorer in the employ of Spain, became the first European to set foot on Los Angeles soil, but 200 years passed before a land expedition under the command of Gaspar de Portola crossed the territory on the way from Monterey to San Diego, in 1769.

The establishment of the Mission of San Gabriel (destined to become the largest of the Franciscan Missions) followed and in 1781, the Spanish Governor Felipe Neve founded the city of El Pueblo de Nuestra Señora de los Angeles de Porciuncula ("The Village of Our Lady of the Angels") as part of a plan to colonize California. Spanish rule continued until 1822 when Spain relinquished her holdings in western America, prompting California to pledge her allegiance to the Mexican empire. With the Treaty of Guadalupe Hidalgo (1848) the U.S. acquired all of California from Mexico and in 1850 Los Angeles was incorporated as a city. Introduction of the Southern Pacific Railroad in 1876 sparked a 12-year land boom, promoting the city's growth. By 1892, Los Angeles thrived as a center of oil production and in 1899 work began on the largest man-made deep-water facility in the world. Emerging as the motion picture capital of the world by 1910, industry accelerated in the 1920's and today L.A. ranks as one of the three great industrial cities in the country.

A thriving metropolis, Los Angeles boasts one of the finest highway systems in the world, handling about 6 million cars registered in its five-county area—a car for every two people, the highest ratio in the world. Three transcontinental railway systems terminate in L.A., about 40 certified air carriers fly to all parts of the world, its harbors have 46 miles of waterfront, and the city has the largest trucking center in the west. L.A. remains the world's movie mecca, teeming with studios, stars, and the starstruck.

Los Angelenos live with daily problems of smog, traffic jams, spectacular traffic accidents, and the ever-present threats of mud slides, fires, floods, high winds, and earthquakes. But the year-round sunshine, and the number of beaches and mountain areas, all within an easy drive, tend to ameliorate one's anxiety.

Population 3,694,820 (2000). Rank: 2nd. Race/Hispanic Origin (2000): White 46.9%. Black 11.2%. Indian 0.8%. Asian 10.0%. Pacific Islander 0.2%. Other 25.7%. Two or more races 5.2%. Hispanic 46.5%.

Location: 34°00'N, 118°10'W. County: Los Angeles.

Terrain and climate Elev.: 104 ft. Area: 465.9 sq. mi. (1206.7 sq km). Avg. daily min. temp.: Jan.: 47.3°F/8.5°C; avg. daily max. July: 75.3°F/24°C. Avg. annual rainfall: 14.85"; snowfall: 0"; clear days: 143; precipitation days: 35.

Government Form: mayor and council. Mayor James K. Hahn. (213) 978-0600. **www.lacity.org**

Visitor info: (800) 228-2450. **www.visitlanow.com**

▶MEMPHIS, TENNESSEE

The first settlers in the area of Memphis arrived on the bluffs overlooking the Mississippi River more than 1,000 years ago. The Chickasaw forcibly displaced these people and then lived there for eight centuries until 1838, when the U.S. government scattered the entire tribe to Oklahoma and parts further west so its citizens could develop the land. The Spanish explorer Hernando de Soto first set eyes on the bluffs in 1541. Other explorers passed through over the next century and in 1739 the French built Fort Assumption. The French, Spanish, and the Chickasaw fought over the land for the balance of the 18th century until it became a part of the U.S. in 1797. The area's original American owners, Gen. James Winchester, Judge John Overton, and Gen. Andrew Jackson (who later sold his share and went on to become President), established the town in 1819, and named it Memphis, after the ancient Egyptian city on the Nile.

Riverboatmen gave young Memphis a reputation for brawls and bawdiness, while mosquitoes gave it a history of yellow fever epidemics, which in the 1880's claimed more than half the city's population and jeopardized its charter. A sewage system, the first of its kind, helped finally conquer the epidemic. Between the river traffic and cotton crops, the city prospered, attracting Irish and German immigrants, and by the 20th century was on its way to becoming the unofficial capital of the mid-south. Elvis Presley, who expanded the city's rhythm and blues tradition to become the world's first rock-and-roll idol, remains the city's most enduring contribution to popular culture. In 1991, the Lorraine Motel, where civil rights leader Dr. Martin Luther King Jr. was assassinated in 1968, was opened as the National Civil Rights Museum. In recent years the city's central location has helped it to attract major corporations, most notably FedEx and Northwest Airlines.

Population 650,100 (2000). Rank: 18th. Race/Hispanic Origin (2000): White 34.4%. Black 61.4%. Indian 0.2%. Asian 1.5%. Pacific Islander 0.0%. Other 1.5%. Two or more races 1.0%. Hispanic 3.0%.

Location: 35'07'N, 90°00'W. County: Shelby.

Terrain and climate Elev.: 307 ft. Area: 264.1 sq. mi. (684 sq km). Avg. daily min. temp.: Jan.: 30.9°F/-0.6°C; avg. daily max. July: 91.5°F/33°C. Avg. annual rainfall: 51.57"; snowfall: 6"; clear days: 118; precipitation days: 106.

Government Form: mayor and council. Mayor: Willie W. Herenton. (901) 576-6000. **www.cityofmemphis.org.**

Visitor info: (800) 873-6282 or (901) 543-5300. **www.memphistravel.com.**

▶MESA, ARIZONA

Just 15 miles east of Phoenix is Mesa, a one-time suburb that has quickly climbed onto the list of the nation's largest cities. Arizona's third largest city grew by 24.5 percent between 1990 and 1998. There are solid reasons for Mesa's growth: low costs of doing business; a reasonable tax structure; a skilled and well-educated workforce; low crime rate; superior schools; affordable housing; and an abundant water supply. Founded in 1878 and incorporated in 1883, Mesa is the Spanish word for "table top," describing a flat-topped, raised area. The first settlers built homes and farms on a mesa above the surrounding area.

Population 396,375 (2000). Rank: 42nd. Race/Hispanic Origin (2000): White 81.7%. Black 2.5%. Indian 1.7%. Asian 1.5%. Pacific Islander 0.2%. Other 9.7%. Two or more races 2.8%. Hispanic 19.7%.

Location: 33°N, 112°W. County: Maricopa.

Terrain and climate Elev.: 1,241 ft. Area: 124.62 sq. mi. Avg. daily min temp.: Jan.: 35.6°F/2°C; avg. daily max. July: 104.3°F/40.16°C. Avg. annual: rainfall, 7.52"; snowfall, 0"; clear days, 320; precipitation days, 45.

Government Form: mayor and city council. Mayor Keno Hawker. (480) 644-2388. **www.cityofmesa.org**

Visitor info: (480) 827-4700 or (800) 283-6372. www.visitmesa.com

▶MIAMI, FLORIDA

Miami, the most southerly major city in the continental U.S., sits about two degrees north of the Tropic of Cancer, a location that has made it a long-standing resort haven. Miami in the 1980's also thrived as a major hub of commerce and as a population center for Latin American immigrants, particularly those arriving from Cuba, whose ambition and business acumen contributed to the city's prosperity. While tourists still generate over 60 percent of the area's economic activity, many other areas of enterprise, such as construction, light industry, and agriculture (limes, tomatoes, avocados, mangoes and beans) have flourished.

Miami (whose name is thought to derive from the Indian mayami, meaning "big water"), dates back to the 16th century when Native Americans occupied the southern part of Florida. Fort Dallas, built near the mouth of the Miami River in 1836 as a base of war against the Seminoles, became the first permanent European-American settlement. The building of the Florida East Coast Railroad, coinciding with Miami's incorporation as a city in 1896 (population 343), offered ready access to the area. Resort hotels quickly cropped up and Miami, along with the rest of Florida, enjoyed great success. In 1926, a severe hurricane submerged much of its land under water, abruptly ending Miami's prosperity, but the city managed to steadily grow by draining and developing swampland. After World War II, new resorts rose up, and Miami thrived both as a haven for older retirees and a refuge for a substantial number of Cubans fleeing Castro's repressive regime. In 2000, the city attracted national media attention during the Elian Gonzalez controversy. Gonzalez, a five-year-old Cuban refugee, became the center of a custody battle between Cuba and the U.S. when he survived a raft crossing from Cuba to Florida, but his mother did not.

Today Miami bills itself as the "Gateway of the Americas," where the value of exports and imports has increased by over 20 percent a year for the last decade and foreign banking has expanded rapidly.

Population 362,470 (2000). Rank: 47th. Race/Hispanic Origin (2000): White 66.6%. Black 22.3%. Indian 0.2%. Asian 0.7%. Other 5.4%. Two or more races 4.7%. Hispanic 65.8%.

Location: 25°45'N, 80°15'W. County: Dade.

Terrain and climate Elev.: 12 ft. Area: 34.3 sq. mi. (88.8 sq km). Avg. daily min. temp.: Jan.: 59.2°F/15.1°C; avg. daily max. July: 88.7°F/31.5°C. Avg. annual rainfall: 57.55"; snowfall: 0"; clear days: 76; precipitation days: 129.

Government Form: council and manager. Mayor: Manuel A. Diaz. (305) 250-5300. **www.ci.miami.fl.us.**

Visitor info: (800) 933-8448 or (305) 539-3000. **www.miamiandbeaches.com.**

▶MILWAUKEE, WISCONSIN

During the 1670's the French explorers Jacques Marquette and Louis Joliet were the first Europeans to visit the site of present-day Milwaukee, an area on the western shore of Lake Michigan at the confluence of the Menomonee and Kinnickinnic Rivers. In 1795, Jacques Vicau of the North West Company established a trading post and in 1818, Solomon Laurent Juneau, the first permanent settler, founded Milwaukee (from the Indian term millioke, meaning "beautiful land"). From the 1840's on, large numbers of German immigrants came to the city, making up over 60 percent of the 1850 population; today, an estimated one-third of the city's residents are of German descent.

A flourishing agricultural center, Milwaukee had by the Civil War become the largest wheat market in the world. Its industrial base expanded after the war and by 1940 the city ranked fourth in manufacturing among U.S. cities. Still one of the most vigorous producers of durable goods, especially automotive parts, construction and road building equipment, diesel and gasoline engines, tractors, and outboard motors, Milwaukee also emerged as a major meat-packing center. Reflecting its German heritage, the city developed a thriving brewing industry with several of the largest beer-producing companies in the U.S. (though almost all have since disappeared). A major Great Lakes and international port, Milwaukee handles several international steamship lines.

Population 596,974 (2000). Rank: 19th. Race/Hispanic Origin (2000): White 50.0%. Black 37.3%. Indian 0.9%. Asian 2.9%. Pacific Islander 0.1%. Other 6.1%. Two or more races 2.7%. Hispanic 12.0%.

Location: 43°09'N, 87°58'W. County: Milwaukee.

Terrain and climate Elev.: 581 ft. Area: 95.8 sq. mi. (248.1 sq km). Avg. daily min. temp.: Jan.: 11.3°F/-11.5°C; avg. daily max. July: 79.8°F/26.5°C. Avg. annual rainfall: 30.94"; snowfall: 45"; clear days: 96; precipitation days: 122.

Government Form: mayor and council. Mayor: John O. Norquist. (414) 286-2200. **www.milwaukee.gov**

Visitor info: (800) 554-1448 or (414) 273-7222. **www.milwaukee.org**

▶MINNEAPOLIS, MINNESOTA

With an average annual temperature of 45° F, Minneapolis is the second coldest city in the U.S. But despite its arctic winters, it is one of the most desirable cities in the U.S. It sits astride the Mississippi River, near the headwaters of the Minnesota River, about 350 miles northwest of Chicago. While it is the largest commercial metropolis in the north between Milwaukee and Seattle, no single industry dominates, although many large computer and electronics companies make Minneapolis their home. A regional banking center and the site of the Federal Reserve Bank for the Ninth District, Minneapolis has the world's largest cash grain exchange, the world's four largest wheat-flour-milling companies, and provides the upper Midwest with truck, barge, and air transport.

In 1682 Father Louis Hennepin, the French priest who explored the Mississippi, was the first European to set eyes on the Falls of St. Anthony, the future site of Minneapolis. Unsettled until Fort Snelling was built in 1819 to protect the fur traders from the Sioux and Chippewa, the town of St. Anthony began growing up on one side of the Mississippi and a second settlement sprang up on the other. The two were consolidated in 1872; the new name was a hybrid of the Indian word minne, meaning "water," and the Greek word for "city," polis. Minneapolis blossomed on the basis of its flour and lumber milling. By century's end, the forests to the north had been depleted, but flour milling continues as a thriving industry to this day.

Long considered a center of progressive political and social thinking, it is a mecca of education and culture. Minneapolis contains the main campus of the University of Minnesota, and boasts the Minnesota Orchestra and the Minneapolis Institute of the Arts. A haven for outdoor enthusiasts, the park system numbers 153 parks encompassing 6,000 acres, and with 12 lakes within its city limits, Minneapolis has 10 percent of its surface covered by water. Despite all this, the city has been steadily losing population (160,000 since 1950) to suburban areas.

Population 382,618 (2000). Rank: 45th. Race/Hispanic Origin (2000): White 65.1%. Black 18.0%. Indian 2.2%. Asian 6.1%. Pacific Islander 0.1%. Other 4.1%. Two or more races 4.4%. Hispanic 7.6%.

Location: 44°58'N, 93°20'W. County: Hennepin.

Terrain and climate Elev.: 828 ft. Area: 55.1 sq. mi. (142.7 sq km). Avg. daily min. temp.: Jan.: 2.4°F/-16.4°C; avg. daily max. July: 83.4°F/28.5°C. Avg. annual rainfall: 26.36"; snowfall: 46"; clear days: 100; precipitation days: 113.

Government Form: mayor and council. Mayor: R.T. Rybak. (612) 673-2100. **www.ci.minneapolis.mn.us**

Visitor info: (888) 676-6757 **www.minneapolis.org.**

▶NASHVILLE, TENNESSEE

In the winter of 1779–80, settlers from North Carolina, led by James Robertson, arrived at a place on the Cumberland River called Big Salt Lick, and built forts on both sides of the river, one of which they named Nashborough, after Gen. Francis Nash of the Revolutionary Army. Adopting the name Nashville in 1784, the settlement was chartered as a city in 1806, became state capital in 1843, and prospered until the Civil War as the northern terminus of the Natchez Trace, a 500-mile road to Natchez, Mississippi. The site of one of the war's last major battles in December 1864, the city underwent a long period of rebuilding and by the end of the century, the population reached 81,000. The city continued to grow, doubling in population by World War II, and has experienced even greater expansion since that time.

While best known as a major center of both the recording and music-publishing industries, Nashville enjoys a widely diversified economic foundation and serves as a distribution and marketing point for the upper southern region of the U.S. Several religious organizations and their publishing operations are headquartered here, and the city is home to more than a dozen institutions of higher learning, including Vanderbilt University, Fisk University, and Tennessee State University. With a growing base of manufacturing, especially in the automotive sector, and with the insurance and banking industries firmly entrenched, Nashville leaders project a prosperous future. As home of the Grand Ole Opry, Nashville has also developed into a regional tourist and convention attraction. A full-scale replica of the Greek temple the Parthenon is a noted site.

Population 569,891 (2000). Rank: 22nd. Race/Hispanic Origin (2000): White 67.0%. Black 25.9%. Indian 0.3%. Asian 2.3%. Pacific Islander 0.1%. Other 2.4%. Two or more races 2.0%. Hispanic 4.6%.

Location: 36°12'N, 86°46'W. County: Davidson.

Terrain and climate Elev.: 605 ft. Area: 479.5 sq. mi. (1241.9 sq km). Avg. daily min. temp.: Jan.: 27.8°F/-2.3°C; avg. daily max. July: 89.8°F/32.1°C. Avg. annual rainfall: 48.49"; snowfall: 10.7"; clear days: 103; precipitation days: 119.

Government Form: mayor and council. Mayor: Bill Purcell. (615) 862-6000. **www.nashville.org.**

Visitor info: (800) 657-6910 or (615) 743-3000. **www.nashvillecvb.com.**

▶NEW ORLEANS, LOUISIANA

Founded in 1718 by Jean Baptiste le Moyne and named Ville d'Orléans after the regent of France, the city of New Orleans is one of the nation's most distinctive cities. Situated only 110 miles from the mouth of the Mississippi River, it has long been a major international port (it ranks second in the nation today), and thanks to overlapping waves of French, Spanish, African-American, and Anglo-American immigrants, it has one of the most richly textured cultures of any city in North America. It is geographically distinct, too, in that much of it is below sea level; the almost constant threat of flooding is mitigated by an intricate network of canals and levees.

After half a century under French rule, New Orleans became the capital of Spanish Louisiana in 1763. It was briefly under French rule again (1800–1803) before being acquired by the United States as part of the Louisiana Purchase. Although Louisiana was admitted as a state in 1815, New Orleans continues to reflect its Spanish and French heritage in its architecture, cuisine, and its flamboyant Mardi Gras celebration in the days leading up to the beginning of Lent. African-American traditions are strong here, too, and Dixieland jazz—long heralded as a uniquely American music—is a fusion of African and European styles.

In addition to being a major port for the export of cotton, rice, petroleum products, iron, steel, and corn, and the import of sugar, bananas, coffee, bauxite, and molasses, New Orleans is a major center for offshore drilling in the Gulf of Mexico. In recent years its industrial sector, with an emphasis on aerospace research and technology, petroleum refinement, and shipbuilding, has been strong.

A major tourist attraction in its own right, the city includes among its special points of interest St. Louis Cathedral, the French Market, Preservation Hall and Dixieland Hall, and the Presbytère—all in the French Quarter—as well as the celebrated residential architecture of the Garden District, the New Orleans Museum of Art, the Confederate Museum, and Audubon Park Zoo. Among its educational institutions are Tulane University, Sophie Newcomb College, and Dillard University.

Population 484,674 (2000). Rank: 31st. Race/Hispanic Origin (2000): White 28.1%. Black 67.3%. Indian 0.2%. Asian 2.3%. Pacific Islander 0.0%. Other 0.9%. Two or more races 1.3%. Hispanic 3.1%.

Location: 30°00'W., 90°05'W. Parish: Orleans.

Terrain and climate Elev.: 30 ft. Area: 199.4 sq. mi. (516.4 sq km). Avg. daily min. temp.: Jan.: 43°F/6.1°C; avg. daily max.: July: 90.7°F/32.6°C. Avg. annual rainfall: 59.74"; snowfall: 0.2"; clear days: 109; precipitation days: 113.

Government Form: mayor and council. Mayor: C. Ray Nagin. (504) 565-6400. **www.new-orleans.la.us.**

Visitor info: (800) 672-6124. **www.www.visitneworleans.info.**

▶NEW YORK CITY, NEW YORK

Even before the arrival of Europeans in North America, the waters that today make New York one of the world's foremost ports—and the foremost city in the United States—were the scene of lively trade between the predominant Algonquian tribes in the region. The city's modern history dates to 1524 when the Florentine explorer, Giovanni de Verrazano, sailed into New York Bay. In 1609, Henry Hudson, an English navigator sailing for the Dutch East India Company, explored the river that bears his name today. In 1625, the Dutch West India Company purchased Manhattan and established Nieuw Amsterdam, which quickly became a profitable trading post. Dutch settlers soon expanded beyond the original colony settling Breukelen, Nieuw Harlem, Bronck, and Staaten Eylandt. Taken by the British in 1664 (the Dutch briefly regained control in 1673-74), and renamed for the Duke of York, the town continued to prosper.

As resentment of British authority grew, New York became a seat of colonial discontent, participating in actions against the Stamp Act (1763) and tea tax (1773). But after the Battle of Long Island and Washington's retreat in August 1776, the British held New York through the end of the war. Yet Washington was inaugurated president at Federal Hall (today the site of the second Federal Reserve Bank) on Wall Street, and from 1789-90 New York was the nation's capital.

Industry and trade expanded dramatically after the opening of the Erie Canal from Troy (150 miles up the Hudson River) and Buffalo (350 miles west of Troy) gave New York direct access to the raw materials and the markets of the Great Lakes states. In the mid-19th century, New York became the primary port of immigration to the U.S. and many of the millions of immigrants who came to America carved out distinctly ethnic neighborhoods throughout the city in a patchwork that survives to the present.

In 1898, an act of the state legislature created "Greater New York," and today New York's population is greater than that of Los Angeles and Chicago (the second and third largest cities in the country) combined. Even if they were separate cities, four of New York boroughs would rank in the top 10—Brooklyn fourth (2.3 million), Queens fifth (1.9 million), Manhattan eighth (1.5 million), and the Bronx ninth (1.2 million).

New York's attractions are seemingly innumerable—enough to draw over 17 million visitors annually—but they include 150 museums, 400 art galleries, dozens of Broadway theaters, and scores of concert halls, clubs, and dance halls. In addition, there are close to 1,000 landmark buildings, more than 50 landmark interiors, and more than 50 historic districts. (A list of attractions can be found under "New York State.") The city leads the nation in the arts, fashion, advertising, banking and financial services, publishing, broadcasting, and certain service industries; it is also the home of the General Assembly of the United Nations. There are 87 colleges and universities here, including Columbia University, New York University, Long Island University, Brooklyn College, Fordham University, the Pratt Institute of Technology, the Juilliard School, and the School of Visual Arts. Manufactured goods include apparel, chemicals, metal products, and printing.

New York City was the site of the worst terrorist attack in U.S. history on Sept. 11, 2001, when two hijacked commercial jets crashed into the twin towers of the World Trade Center, causing the complete collapse of both buildings and killing more than 2,800 people.

Population 8,008,278 (2000). Rank: 1st. Race/Hispanic Origin (2000): White 44.7%. Black 26.6%. Indian 0.5%. Asian 9.8%. Pacific Islander 0.1%. Other 13.4%. Two or more races 4.9%. Hispanic 27.0%.

Location: 40°45'N, 74°00'W. Counties: Bronx, Kings, New York, Queens, and Richmond.

Terrain and climate Elev.: 87 ft. Area: 301.5 sq. mi. (780.9 sq km). Avg. daily min. temp.: Jan.: 25.6°F/-3.5°C; avg. daily max. July: 85.3°F/29.6°C. Avg. annual rainfall: 44.12"; snowfall: 29"; clear days: 107; precipitation days: 121.

Government Form: mayor and council. Mayor: Michael R. Bloomberg. (212) 788-9600. **http://home.nyc.gov.**

Visitor info: (212) 484-1200. **www.nycvisit.com.**

▶OAKLAND, CALIFORNIA

The first European-American to settle present-day Oakland was Dom Luis Maria Peralta, who established the 44,000-acre settlement called Rancho San Antonio in 1820. Its first real growth began with the establishment of ferry service to San Francisco in 1852, though the ferry's importance was overshadowed by Oakland's selection as the western terminus of the first transcontinental railroad in 1869. The city remained in the economic shadow of its more sophisticated neighbor across the Bay until the San Francisco earthquake of 1906 drove 100,000–150,000 people to Oakland for shelter. An estimated 65,000 of these are thought to have settled there permanently, providing an impetus for a long period of growth as an international port and industrial center.

A major commercial and cultural center with a container port ranked 10th in the world, Oakland is also the major northern hub of the California freeway system, which is integrated into the Bay Area Rapid Transit (BART) system. It has also become the premier biotechnology center in the region, and it is home to regional and international headquarters for firms in finance, medicine, telecommunications, international trade, and heavy industry.

Long a primarily industrial urban center, Oakland has pumped hundreds of millions of dollars into development of its downtown area and the Jack London waterfront—named for the author who spent his youth on the Oakland docks. Oakland embraces a racially and culturally diverse populace. Oakland sustained heavy damage in the 1989 Loma Prieta earthquake. Two years later, almost to the day, the worst fire in California history leveled more than 1,000 buildings in the Oakland Hills neighborhood, killing 14 people and inflicting more than $1.5 billion in damage.

Population 399,484 (2000). Rank: 41st. Race/Hispanic Origin (2000): White 31.3%. Black 35.7%. Indian 0.7%. Asian 15.2%. Pacific Islander 0.5%. Other 11.7%. Two or more races 5.0%. Hispanic 21.9%.

Location: 37°50'N, 122°18'W. County: Alameda.

Terrain and climate Elev.: 42 ft. Area: 53.9 sq. mi. (139.6 sq km). Avg. daily min. temp.: Jan.: 43.4°F/6.3°C; avg. daily max. July: 70.6°F/29.6°C. Avg. annual rainfall: 18.03"; snowfall: N.A.; clear days: N.A; precipitation days: N.A.

Government Form: council and manager. Mayor: Jerry Brown. (510) 238-3141. **www.oaklandnet.com.**

Visitor info: (800) 262-5526 or (510) 839-9000. **www.oaklandcvb.com.**

▶OKLAHOMA CITY, OKLAHOMA

Oklahoma City quite literally sprang up during the Great Land Rush of 1889 and, by presidential proclamation, opened for European-American settlement officially on April 22 of that year. At day's end, approximately 10,000 settlers had moved in—the greatest one-day non-annexation population increase in the history of cities. Oklahoma became a state in 1907 and Oklahoma City its capital in 1910, by which time the population had swelled to about 64,000. Since then, it has become Oklahoma's largest city, its leading commercial center, and home to the National Cowboy Hall of Fame.

Oklahoma City's economy, based on oil and livestock, thrives on petroleum production, meat processing, and the breeding of stocker and feeder cattle. The city hosts a flourishing printing and publishing industry and manufactures a diversity of products including automobiles, electronic equipment, computers, communications switches, and oil well supplies. As a vital banking center serving the central and western regions of the state, Oklahoma City boasts a Federal Reserve branch bank. On a somewhat less positive note, Oklahoma City reportedly sparked the "go-go" banking syndrome that characterized the 1970's oil boom, when Penn Square Bank's ill-advised oil patch loans nearly devastated the U.S. banking system.

Oklahoma City was the site of one of the deadliest terrorist bombings in U.S. history on April 19, 1995, when a 5,000-pound car bomb ripped a huge hole in the Alfred Murrah Federal Building, killing 169 people, including 15 children in a day care center within the building.

Population 506,132 (2000). Rank: 29th. Race/Hispanic Origin (2000): White 68.4%. Black 15.4%. Indian 3.5%. Asian 3.5%. Pacific Islander 0.1%. Other 5.3%. Two or more races 3.9%. Hispanic 10.1%.

Location: 35°25'N, 97°30'W. Counties: Canadian, Cleveland, McClain, Oklahoma.

Terrain and climate Elev.: 1,304 ft. Area: 604 sq. mi. (1,564.4 sq km). Avg. daily min. temp.: Jan.: 25.2°F/-3.7°C; avg. daily max. July: 93.5°F/34.1°C. Avg. annual: rainfall, 30.89"; snowfall, 9"; clear days, 141; precipitation days, 81.

Government Form: council and manager. Mayor: Kirk Humphries. (405) 297-3884 or (405) 297-2535. **www.okc.gov**

Visitor info: (800) 225-5652 or (405) 297-8912. **www.okccvb.org.**

▶OMAHA, NEBRASKA

Permanent settlement in what is now Omaha began with a fur-trading post established shortly after the Lewis and Clark expedition passed through the area in 1804. In 1820, the government built Ft. Atkinson, and the surrounding community became a major stop on both the Mormon and the Lewis and Clark trails, and was incorporated as a city in 1854. After strong lobbying by citizens of Council Bluffs, Iowa, just across the Missouri River to the east, Omaha (the name means "above all others on the stream") became the eastern terminus of the Union-Pacific transcontinental railroad, the country's first, in 1869. Within six years, the population grew to 39,000 and by the turn of the century, it had passed the 100,000 mark.

As a major transportation hub of the Midwest—Omaha today boasts seven major railroads and the recently expanded Port of Omaha services a dozen barge lines—the city became a major distribution center for meat and grain, living up to its motto "We feed the world" (ConAgra is based here). Its major food products include pasta, potato chips, coffee, pancake mixes, frozen dinners, and Omaha steaks. With dozens of *Fortune* 500 manufacturing operations, and a healthy publishing industry (roughly one out of every four manufacturers is either a publisher or printer), Omaha's diversified economy also has strong roots in insurance (Mutual of Omaha), communications, direct mail/telemarketing, and sophisticated medical facilities are centered at the medical schools of Creighton University and the University of Nebraska. Since 1989 employment in the metro area has grown by 15 percent, while the unemployment rate, one of the lowest in the nation, has been less than 3 percent for several years.

Among its performing arts institutions are the Omaha Symphony, Opera/Omaha, the Omaha Ballet, the Orpheum Theater, and the Omaha Community Playhouse. Museums and historic sites include the Boys Town Hall of Fame, the Henry Doorly Zoo and Aquarium, the Great Plains Black Museum, the historic ships *U.S.S. Hazard* and *U.S.S. Marlin*, and the Old Market, a mixed-use National Historic District on the Missouri River.

Population 390,007 (2000). Rank: 44th. Race/Hispanic Origin (2000): White 78.4%. Black 13.3%. Indian 0.7%. Asian 1.7%. Pacific Islander 0.1%. Other 3.9%. Two or more races 1.9%. Hispanic 7.5%.

Location: 41°15'N, 95°55'W. County: Douglas.

Terrain and climate Elev.: 982 ft. Area: 99.3 sq. mi. (257.2 sq km). Avg. daily min. temp.: Jan.: 10.2°F/-12.1°C; avg. daily max. July: 88.5°F/31.3°C. Avg. annual rainfall: 30.34"; snowfall: 32"; clear days: 113; precipitation days: 99.

Government Form: mayor and council. Mayor: Mike Fahey. (402) 444-5000. **www.ci.omaha.ne.us**

Visitor info: (866) YES-OMAHA. **www.visit omaha.com.**

▶PHILADELPHIA, PENNSYLVANIA

In 1632, a small contingent of Swedes and Finns came to the land where the Schuylkill River meets the Delaware and founded New Sweden. In 1655, Peter Stuyvesant seized New Sweden for the Dutch, inciting conflict with the British until the Dutch relinquished their rights to the territory in 1673. Nine years later, William Penn established a town between the Schuylkill and the Delaware Rivers, named it Philadelphia, "the city of brotherly love," and in two years it evolved into an active settlement of about 2,500 people, most of them Quakers.

In the mid-1700's, Benjamin Franklin began shaping the destiny of Philadelphia by presiding over the founding of the University of Pennsylvania, the Pennsylvania Hospital, and a fire insurance company (the last two were firsts for the young nation). Under his guidance, Philadelphia became the premier colonial city for the arts and the home of many famous educators, scientists, mathematicians, authors, and painters. In addition, a total of 17 libraries were founded at this time. The meeting place of the Continental Congress and the site of the signing of the Declaration of Independence, Philadelphia was the nation's capital from 1790 to 1800, when the federal government moved permanently to Washington, D.C.

Throughout the 19th century, the influx first of Irish and German, then Jewish, Italian, Polish, and Slavic immigrants from Europe, and blacks from the South, helped build the city's industrial base. Today, Philadelphia ranks high among U.S. cities in oil refining; other principal industries are electrical machinery, automobile and truck bodies, petrochemicals, metalworking, and scientific instruments. But many other businesses have left the city and unemployment and poverty have taken a heavy toll in recent years. Since 1990, the city has lost almost 7 percent of its population.

Population 1,517,550 (2000). Rank: 5th. Race/Hispanic Origin (2000): White 45.0%. Black 43.2%. Indian 0.3%. Asian 4.5%. Other 4.8%. Two or more races 2.2%. Hispanic 8.5%.

Location: 40°00'N, 75°10'W. County: Philadelphia.

Terrain and climate Elev.: 28 ft. Area: 136 sq. mi. (352.2 sq km). Avg. daily min. temp.: Jan.: 23.8°F/-4.5°C; avg. daily max. July: 86.1°F/30°C. Avg. annual rainfall: 41.42"; snowfall: 20"; clear days: 92; precipitation days: 116.

Government Form: mayor and council. Mayor: John F. Street. (215) 686-1776. **www.phila.gov.**

Visitor info: (800) CALL-PHL or (215) 636-3300. **www.gophila.com.**

▶PHOENIX, ARIZONA

Arizona's capital and its largest city sits in the Salt River Valley in a former desert that has become a prosperous agricultural area because of a network of irrigated dams located northeast of the city. Long a resort area owing to its mild climate, Phoenix has recently emerged as a lively commercial and agricultural center as well. A flourishing high-tech haven attracting businesses engaged in electronics, communications, and research and development, the city also has a strong manufacturing base that includes airplane parts, electronic equipment, agricultural chemicals, radios, air conditioners, and leather goods. Among its agricultural products are lettuce, melons, vegetables, grapefruit, oranges, lemons, and olives.

While Phoenix benefits from modern irrigation efforts, the Hohokam Indian people dug the area's first irrigation ditches in the 3rd century, B.C. and developed an extensive network of canals that lasted until their culture's decline in A.D. 1400. The area was not resettled until 1864, when a hay camp was established to supply Camp McDowell 30 miles away. Jack Weilling and "Lord Darrell" Dupa rebuilt the old Indian irrigation ditches in 1867, and named the site Phoenix, after the mythical bird that rose from its own ashes. The settlement grew as a trading post, was incorporated as a city in 1881, became capital of the territory in 1889 and the state capital when Arizona was admitted to the Union in 1912.

With the westward exodus from the snowbelt states, and the perfecting of air conditioning to make the summer heat bearable, the small 1950's resort city of 106,818 people has since swelled almost tenfold. In the 1980's, Phoenix's population grew 24.5 percent from 789,704 to just under a

million. Growth between 1990 and 2000 was even faster (34 percent).
Population 1,321,045 (2000). Rank: 6th. Race/Hispanic Origin (2000): White 71.1%. Black 5.1%. Indian 2.0%. Asian 2.0%. Pacific Islander 0.1%. Other 16.4%. Two or more races 3.3%. Hispanic 34.1%.
Location: 33°30'N, 112°04'W. County: Maricopa.
Terrain and climate Elev.: 1,117 ft. Area: 375 sq. mi. (971.3 sq km). Avg. daily min. temp.: Jan.: 44.4°F/6.8°C; avg. daily max. July: 107.5°F/41°C. Avg. annual rainfall: 7.11"; snowfall: 0"; clear days: 214; precipitation days: 34.
Government Form: Mayor and council. Mayor: Skip Rimsza. (602) 262-7111. **www.phoenix.gov.**
Visitor info: (877) CALL-PHX or (602) 254-6500. **www.visitphoenix.com.**

▶PORTLAND, OREGON

Portland's renowned beauty is a result of its unique natural setting, which offers a view of the Cascade Mountains and Mt. Hood to the east, Mt. Adams to the northeast, and Mt. St. Helens and Mt. Rainier to the north. Eleven bridges span the Willamette River, which divides the city into east and west sections.

Indian traders traveling between Oregon City and Vancouver carved out an acre of land by the Willamette River 12 miles north of Oregon City, which became known as The Clearing. In 1884 William Overton claimed the 640 acres surrounding the area, which he then sold to Asa Lovejoy and Francis W. Pettygrove, who set out to build a city. Winning a coin toss, Pettygrove named the city-to-be after his hometown in Maine.

As a vital port of entry (the coast's only freshwater port) with a large inland harbor, Portland is a leader in the shipping of lumber, flour, and grain, and has blossomed into Oregon's largest city. Main industries also include paper and pulp, mining, high-technology equipment, and aerospace. Portland enjoys a flourishing arts community and its residents partake of the beaches and ski slopes within easy driving distance.
Population 529,121 (2000). Rank: 28th. Race/Hispanic Origin (2000): White 77.9%. Black 6.6%. Indian 1.1%. Asian 6.3%. Pacific Islander 0.4%. Other 3.5%. Two or more races 4.1%. Hispanic 6.8%.
Location: 45°35'N, 122°40'W. Counties: Clackamas, Multnomah, Washington.
Terrain and climate Elev.: 39 ft. Area: 113.9 sq. mi. (295 sq km). Avg. daily min. temp.: Jan.: 33.5°F/0.8°C; avg. daily max. July: 79.5°F/26.3°C. Avg. annual rainfall: 37.39"; snowfall: 7"; clear days: 69; precipitation days: 152.
Government Form: commission. Mayor: Vera Katz. (503) 823-4000. **www.portlandonline.com.**
Visitor info: (877) PORTLAND. **www.travelportland.com.**

▶SACRAMENTO, CALIFORNIA

The capital of California and its seventh largest city, Sacramento sits 75 miles northeast of San Francisco at the confluence of the American and Sacramento rivers. A wholesale and retail center for the surrounding rich farmland, the city includes among its main commercial enterprises food processing and canning, and one of the world's largest almond-shelling plants.

Receiving a land grant from the Mexican government in 1839, Swiss-American John Augustus Sutter founded a colony called New Helvetia, and when Fort Sutter was constructed in 1844, it became one of California's chief trading posts. Established soon after the discovery of gold in 1848, Sacramento grew to 7,000 residents by 1850, became state capital in 1854, and in 1863 was incorporated as a city.

The "Gateway to the Goldfields," "Old Sacramento" became a pivotal point of commerce in the 1860's, connected to the mining towns by the American River, and transporting produce from the farms and orchards lining the banks of the Sacramento River. Sailors stopping in San Francisco visited Sacramento to replenish their stocks of fresh produce and to entertain themselves in the saloons and gambling halls. The wealthy lived in great mansions by the river and the cobblestone streets, gaslights, and wood sidewalks imbued the town with a touch of civility. Today's Sacramento, appreciated for its subtle, quiet charms, boasts 120 parks, hiking and biking trails along the American River Parkway, a large collection of art galleries, two symphony orchestras, ballet, theater and opera companies, and a number of jazz clubs and coffee houses.
Population 407,018 (2000). Rank: 40th. Race/Hispanic Origin (2000): White 48.3%. Black 15.5%. Indian 1.3%. Asian 16.6%. Pacific Islander 0.9%. Other 11.0%. Two or more races 6.4%. Hispanic 21.6%.
Location: 38°33'N, 121°30'W. County: Sacramento.
Terrain and climate Elev.: 25 ft. Area: 97.3 sq. mi. (252 sq km). Avg. daily min. temp.: Jan.: 37.9°F/3.2°C; avg. daily max. July: 93.3°F/34°C. Avg. annual rainfall: 17.87"; snowfall: 0.1"; clear days: 193; precipitation days: 57.
Government Form: council and manager. Mayor: Heather Fargo. (916) 808-5704. **www.cityofsacramento.org.**
Visitor info: (800) 292-2334 or (916) 264-7777. **www.sacramentocvb.org.**

▶SAN ANTONIO, TEXAS

San Antonio, the third-largest city in Texas, lies in the state's south-central region at the edge of the Gulf Coastal Plain 140 miles from the Gulf of Mexico. Its economy thrives on agriculture, livestock, and the activity of the wholesale traders who dominate the commerce of southwestern Texas and northern Mexico. It is also a regional leader in biotechnology. Adding further stimulus to the economy are five major military installations—Fort Sam Houston, Randolph Air Force Base, Kelly Air Force Base, Lackland Air Force Base, and Brooks Air Force Base. The military contributes approximately $3 billion annually to the area economy.

The founding of the mission of San Antonio de Valero (later known as the Alamo) and the Presidio of San Antonio in 1718 represented the area's first permanent settlement. When 56 settlers from the Canary Islands joined the original coterie of ranchmen, missionaries, and soldiers, they formed the first municipal organization in Texas, called the villa of San Fernando de Bexar, which became a city in 1809, and suffered under Mexican rule until the battle of San Jacinto in 1836. With the influx of American pioneers and German immigrants (following Texas's statehood in 1845), the population grew to over 96,000 by 1910, and has since increased nearly tenfold. By 1998 it had reached 1.1 million, up 22 percent since 1990.

Today San Antonio is a popular haven for vacationers, with over 10 million visitors per year. San Antonio's attractions include the Alamo and its four sister missions, the Riverwalk along the San Antonio River, Breckenridge Park (home of one of America's largest zoos), Sea World of Texas; La Villita, the Tower of the Americas, and the Spanish Governor's Palace.

Population 1,144,646 (2000). Rank: 9th. Race/Hispanic Origin (2000): White 67.7%. Black 6.8%. Indian 0.8%. Asian 1.6%. Pacific Islander 0.1%. Other 19.3%. Two or more races 3.7%. Hispanic 58.7%.
Location: 29°30'N, 98°30'W. County: Bexar.
Terrain and climate Elev.: 701 ft. Area: 304.5 sq. mi. (788.7 sq km). Avg. daily min. temp.: Jan.: 39°F/3.8°C; avg. daily max. July: 96.3°F/35.7°C. Avg. annual rainfall: 29.13"; snowfall: 0.5"; clear days: 110; precipitation days: 81.
Government Form: council and manager. Mayor: Ed Garza. (210) 207-7060. **www.sanantonio.gov.**
Visitor info: (800) 447-3372 or (210) 270-8700. **www.sanantoniovisit.com.**

▶SAN DIEGO, CALIFORNIA

Sixty years after João Rodrigues Cabrilho first sailed into San Diego Bay, Sebastian Vizcaino embarked from Spain with three ships to explore the coast of California, and in November 1602 anchored on the lee of what is now known as Point Loma. When he finished charting the bay two days later, he changed its original name, San Miguel, to San Diego, in honor of the saint San Diego de Alcalal de Henares, In 1769, Father Junipero Serra established California's first mission, the Mission San Diego de Alcala.

Compared to its sister cities to the north—Los Angeles and San Francisco—San Diego developed slowly, despite its large and hospitable harbor. In 1887, the city became the southern terminus for the Santa Fe Railroad, but floods soon washed out the tracks and trackbeds, and the railroad was rebuilt to terminate in L.A. which had a new man-made harbor. This put San Diego at an almost insurmountable disadvantage. With its industrial development stunted, San Diego welcomed the establishment of a U.S. Navy base during World War I; since then, about a quarter of the Navy's seagoing vessels and roughly 20 percent of the Marine Corps' forces have been located there. Jonas Salk's work on polio and the emergence of the University of California at San Diego have earned the city the reputation as a premier biomedical research center, luring billions of dollars in development and research grants.

San Diego, a picturesque city with many tourist attractions, enjoys an average of 350 days of sunshine, enticing both residents and visitors to its 70 beaches and the parks, resorts, and health spas lining its great bay. Coronado Island is a popular attraction. Balboa Park, host to international expositions in 1915 and 1935, contains the San Diego Zoo, one of the finest in the nation. The pleasure boats berthed at the city's numerous yacht clubs offer a curious contrast to the naval warships moored nearby. San Diego was the site of the 1992 America's Cup yacht races.

Population 1,223,400 (2000). Rank: 7th. Race/Hispanic Origin (2000): White 60.2%. Black 7.9%. Indian 0.6%. Asian 13.6%. Pacific Islander 0.5%. Other 12.4%. Two or more races 4.8%. Hispanic 25.4%.
Location: 32°43'N, 117°10'W. County: San Diego.
Terrain and climate Elev.: 13 ft. Area: 329 sq. mi. (852.1 sq km). Avg. daily min. temp.: Jan.: 48.4°F/9.1°C; avg. daily max. July: 75.6°F/24.2°C. Avg. annual rainfall: 9.32"; snowfall: 0"; clear days: 150; precipitation days: 41.
Government Form: council and manager. Mayor: Dick Murphy. (619) 236-5555. **www.sandiego.gov**
Visitor info: (619) 236-1212. **www.sandiego.org.**

▶SAN FRANCISCO, CALIFORNIA

Located near the Golden Gate, the strait between San Francisco Bay and the Pacific Ocean, fog-bound San Francisco hid from some of the greatest European navigators to explore the West Coast. João Rodrigues Cabrilho discovered the Farrallon Islands just off the coast in 1542 and Sir Francis Drake landed a few miles north of the Golden Gate in 1579. Yet it was another 200 years before Don Gasper de Portola sailed into the Bay, followed six years later by Don Juan Manuel Ayala who established a town and mission.

Neither the Spanish nor (after 1821) the Mexican governments were very keen on capitalizing on San Francisco's temperate and strategic location, and when Captain John Montgomery raised the American flag there on July 9, 1846, the community consisted of only 840 people. The discovery of gold at Sutter's mill in 1848, and the gold rush of 1849—which brought 40,000 of the hopeful to California, most by ship—catapulted San Francisco onto the world map, and the following year it was incorporated as a city.

San Francisco continued to prosper as a major transportation and industrial center, but in 1906 an earthquake registering 8.6 on the Richter scale claimed 452 lives, 28,000 buildings, and losses totalling approximately $350 million. San Francisco rose from the ashes to become a thriving, multifaceted, cosmopolitan city and one of the country's leaders in world trade. Another major earthquake, measuring 7.1 on the Richter scale, struck on Oct. 17, 1989, causing extensive damage and 67 deaths in the region, but did not devastate the city as thoroughly as the 1906 tremor.

San Francisco today is a port of call for more than 40 steamship lines which import approximately $25 billion worth of goods from more than 300 ports around the world. A major international financial center, it is the headquarters of three of the nation's largest banks, the 12th Federal Reserve District, and the Pacific Stock Exchange. There are also more than 650 insurance companies, and the city is a haven for venture capitalists and entrepreneurs: more than 90 percent of its businesses have fewer than 25 employees. There are also several U.S. military installations in the area.

Well known for its spirit of individualism, San Francisco was a haven for the beat movement of the 1950's, and the capital of the hippie movement of the 1960's was the Haight-Ashbury district. Its more traditional arts institutions include the San Francisco Ballet, the San Francisco Opera, the San Francisco Symphony, and the American Conservatory Theater. Among its leading educational institutions are the University of San Francisco, the Heald Institute of Technology, the University of California, the San Francisco Art Institute, the San Francisco Conservatory of Music, and the San Francisco College of Mortuary Science. Among its many museums are the National Maritime Historic Park, the Fine Arts Museum, and the California Palace of the Legion of Honor. Other attractions include its historic cable cars (first used in 1873), Chinatown, and Fisherman's Wharf.

Population 776,733 (2000). Rank: 13th. Race/Hispanic Origin (2000): White 49.7%. Black 7.8%. Indian 0.4%. Asian 30.8%. Pacific Islander 0.5%. Other 6.5%. Two or more races 4.3%. Hispanic 14.1%.
Location: 37°47'N, 122°30'W. County: San Francisco.
Terrain and climate Elev.: 155 ft. Area: 46.4 sq. mi. (120.2 sq km). Avg. daily min. temp.: Jan.: 41.5°F/5.2°C; avg. daily max. July: 71°F/21°C. Avg. annual rainfall: 19.71"; snowfall: 0"; clear days:

162; precipitation days: 67.
Government Form: mayor and council. Mayor: Willie L. Brown Jr. (415) 554-6141. **www.ci.sf.ca.us**
Visitor info: (415) 391-2000. **www.sfvisitor.org.**

▶SAN JOSE, CALIFORNIA

Located at the southern end of San Francisco Bay, about 45 miles south of San Francisco, San Jose was the first non-religious European community founded in California. Pueblo de San Jose de Guadalupe was settled in 1777 by enterprising farmers who sought to make themselves and the region independent of Mexico and the Spanish mission network for their supplies. Fruit and olive trees, hides, tallow, livestock, grain, and lively retail activity all contributed to San Jose's early prosperity, and it was the first state capital (1849–52).

San Jose remained an agricultural center until World War II, when industry and technology began to expand. The rapid growth of innovative industry over the last 20 years, taking its lead from research and development begun at nearby Stanford University in the 1930's, changed the area dramatically. With the revolution in high technology, Santa Clara County became known as Silicon Valley, excelling in the production of information systems, personal computers, peripherals, and fostering a burgeoning semi-conductor industry. At the same time, financial services, real estate, construction, and retail industries all flourished.

More than 2,600 high-tech companies employing 250,000 people are located in San Jose, and one-third of the labor force works in manufacturing, a very high proportion in post-industrial America. Santa Clara County has the highest median family income in California, and median housing prices in San Jose are perennially among the highest in the nation.

Population 894,943 (2000). Rank: 11th. Race/Hispanic Origin (2000): White 47.5%. Black 3.5%. Indian 0.8%. Asian 26.9%. Pacific Islander 0.4%. Other 15.9%. Two or more races 5.0%. Hispanic 30.2%.
Location: 37°20'N, 121°53'W. County: Santa Clara.
Terrain and climate Elev.: 65 ft. Area: 169.2 sq. mi. (438.2 sq km). Avg. daily min. temp.: Jan.: 41.1°F/5°C; avg. daily max.: July: 81.5°F/27.5°C. Avg. annual rainfall: 13.86"; snowfall: 0"; clear days: N.A.; precipitation days: N.A.
Government Form: council and manager. Mayor: Ron Gonzales. (408) 277-4237. **www.ci.san-jose.ca.us.**
Visitor info: (888) SAN JOSE. **www.sanjose.org.**

▶SEATTLE, WASHINGTON

Located on the protected waters of Puget Sound, Seattle was the first European-American settlement established in the Pacific Northwest north of the Columbia River. Starting out at Alki Point in 1851, the settlers moved to what is now known as Pioneer Square. Befriended by the Suquamish Chief Sealth (Seattle is a loose approximation of his name), the people turned to lumber harvesting and log milling, which formed the backbone of the city's economy.

With the completion of the Great Northern Railway in 1893 and the Alaska gold rush of 1897, when Seattle became "the Gateway to the Klondike," the city was transformed into a metropolis of merchants and entrepreneurs. Even as gold fever abated, and despite a devastating fire in 1899, the city prospered as a major port to the Orient and as an industrial center. In 1909 Seattle was the site of the Alaska-Yukon-Pacific Exposition. The completion of the Panama Canal in 1914 brought even more business to the already bustling port. Two years later, a small company began building two-seater biplanes; in time the little company became Boeing, the world's largest producer of commercial planes, and the largest employer (more than 80,000 people) in the Seattle area. In 2001, the company stunned the Emerald City by announcing that it was moving its corporate headquarters (and 500 jobs) to Chicago.

Endowed with spectacular natural beauty, with the broad expanse of Puget Sound before it, and the snow-capped peaks of the Cascade Mountains and Mt. Rainier visible to the south and east, the Seattle area offers a wide variety of outdoor activities, from skiing and hiking to fishing and boating. A second international exposition, the Seattle World's Fair in 1962, helped establish the city's reputation as a center of technology, trade, industry, and tourism. In 1974 Bill Gates and Paul Allen founded Microsoft and Seattle has since been seen as the hub of the computer world. The leading cultural programs are put on by the Seattle Symphony Orchestra, the Seattle Opera Association, and the Seattle Repertory Theater. Other attractions include the Seattle Art Museum, Pioneer Square, Pike Place Market, the historic ships on Lake Union, and Woodland Park and Zoo, as well as the many events at the 74-acre Seattle Convention Center, whose buildings (including the famed Space Needle), and park-like grounds and fountains are legacies of the World's Fair. Among the 20 universities and colleges in the area are the University of Washington and Seattle Pacific University.

Population 563,374 (2000). Rank: 24th. Race/Hispanic Origin (2000): White 70.1%. Black 8.4%. Indian 1.0%. Asian 13.1%. Pacific Islander 0.5%. Other 2.4%. Two or more races 4.5%. Hispanic 5.3%.
Location: 47°41'N, 122°15'W. County: King.
Terrain and climate Elev.: 450 ft. Area: 83.6 sq. mi. (216.5 sq km). Avg. daily min. temp.: Jan.: 34.3°F/1.2°C; avg. daily max.: July: 75.2°F/24°C. Avg. annual rainfall: 38.85"; snowfall: 15"; clear days: 57; precipitation days: 160.
Government Form: mayor and council. Mayor: Greg Nickels. (206) 684-4000. **www.cityofseattle.net.**
Visitor info: (206) 461-5840. **www.seeseattle.org.**

▶ST. LOUIS, MISSOURI

St. Louis is one of the nation's major centers of transportation, manufacturing, commerce, and education. With abundant water and electric power, a workforce of over a million people in the metropolitan area, and a location in an area rich in mineral resources, St. Louis ranks as one of the top 10 industrial areas in the country. It is also one of the nation's busiest river ports, the third-largest rail center, the eighth-largest trucking center, and has the sixth-busiest airport. Aircraft, automobiles, printing, beer, and chemicals are among the principal products. The metropolitan area boasts five universities, 23 colleges, and seven junior colleges. St. Louis University, oldest west of the Mississippi, founded in 1818, and Washington University are world famous for their medical schools and research programs and their Nobel Prize winners.

For the 40 years after its founding in 1764 by Pierre Laclade, St. Louis was a French settlement and trading post, outfitting fur trading expeditions up the Missouri River. With the Louisiana Purchase in 1803, St. Louis came under American control. The city was incorporated in 1823 with a population of almost 5,000. The first steamboat docked at St. Louis in 1817 and steamboats then became a vital part of the city's growth. Fueled by settlers from the East and by waves of Irish and German immigrants attracted by the prosperity of the river trade, the city's population grew rapidly. In 1870, St. Louis had 311,000 people, and it was the country's third largest city after New York and Philadelphia. The population continued to grow to a peak of 856,800 in 1950, but the post-World War II flight to the suburbs hit St. Louis hard, reducing its population by almost half.

The downtown St. Louis area has many landmarks and historic buildings. The Old Cathedral, completed in 1834, and the Old Courthouse, where the Dred Scott case was first tried, have been preserved as part of the Jefferson National Expansion Memorial. Atop the famous Gateway Arch, the observation room provides a panoramic view of the city. Kiel Auditorium contains a 3,500-seat opera house and a 10,000-seat convention hall. Forest Park, site of the 1904 Louisiana Purchase Exposition (also known as the St. Louis World's Fair), contains the St. Louis Zoo, McDonnell Planetarium, and the Jewel Box, an all-glass floral display house. St. Louis is also the home of the Missouri Botanical Gardens, which features the Climatron—a geodesic dome with rare orchids and other tropical plants—and the largest Japanese garden in the United States. The St. Louis Symphony (founded in 1880) is the country's second oldest and is housed in the Powell Symphony Hall.

Population 348,189 (2000). Rank: 49th. Race/Hispanic Origin (2000): White 43.8%. Black 51.2%. Indian 0.3%. Asian 2.0%. Other 0.8%. Two or more races 1.9%. Hispanic 2.0%.

Location: 38°40'N, 90°12'W. County: independent city.

Terrain and climate Elev.: 564 ft. Area: 61.4 sq. mi. (159 sq km). Avg. daily min. temp.: Jan.: 19.9°F/-6.7°C; avg. daily max. July: 89°F/31°C. Avg. annual rainfall: 33.91"; snowfall: 18"; clear days: 105; precipitation days: 108.

Government Form: mayor and council. Mayor: Francis Slay. (314) 622-4000. **http://stlouis.missouri.org.**

Visitor info: (800) 325-7692 or (314) 421-1023. **www.explorestlouis.com.**

▶TUCSON, ARIZONA

The first European to travel through the area that is now Tucson was the Jesuit missionary Eusebio Kino, in 1692. In 1700 the mission of San Xavier del Bac was established among the Papago Indians nearby. It was not until 1776, however, that the Spanish established a permanent settlement, taking its name from the Papago *Stjukshon* (or *Chuk Shon*), meaning "village of the dark spring at the foot of the mountain." Tucson remained under Spanish and Mexican control until acquired by the U.S. government as part of the Gadsden Purchase in 1853. During the Civil War it was under Confederate control, but from 1867 to 1877 it was the territorial capital.

Despite the arrival of the Southern Pacific railroad in 1880 and the discovery of extensive copper deposits in southern Arizona, neither the city's location nor its natural resources much stimulated its economy. It was best known as a winter and health resort, and as a commercial hub for the surrounding agricultural and mining industries. In 1950, the population was only 45,500.

The last half-century has seen a dramatic change. One of the many beneficiaries of the exodus from the industrial states to the Sunbelt, Tucson's population has grown almost tenfold in that period, and in the last decade Tucson added 20,000 manufacturing jobs. Surrounded by a wealth of natural beauty, the city is still appealing to retirees and tourists, as is reflected in the many golf courses, ranches, and resorts in and around Tucson. It is ringed by four mountain ranges: the Rincon, Santa Catalina, Tucson, and Santa Rita. Other natural wonders include Sabino Canyon (which has the only year-round stream in the region), the Saguaro National Monument (a preserve for Saguaro cacti), and Tucson Mountain Park, home of the Arizona-Sonora Desert Museum. The University of Arizona is located in Tucson, and the Davis-Mothan Air Force Base and Kitts Peak Observatory are nearby.

Population 486,699 (2000). Rank: 30th. Race/Hispanic Origin (2000): White 70.2%. Black 4.3%. Indian 2.3%. Asian 2.5%. Pacific Islander 0.2%. Other 16.8%. Two or more races 3.8%. Hispanic 35.7%.

Location: 32°14'N, 110°59'W. County: Pima.

Terrain and climate Elev.: 2,584 ft. Area: 125 sq. mi. (324.8 sq km). Avg. daily min. temp.: Jan.: 38.1°F/3.3°C; avg. daily max. July: 98.5°F/3.3°C. Avg. annual rainfall: 11.14"; snowfall: 2"; clear days: 198; precipitation days: 50.

Government Form: council and manager. Mayor: Bob Walkup. (520) 791-4201. **www.ci.tucson.az.us.**

Visitor info: (800) 638-8350 or (520) 624-1817. **www.visittucson.org.**

▶TULSA, OKLAHOMA

Tulsa was first settled by Indian nations forced out of the South Atlantic States by the Indian Removal Act of 1830. The name they chose for their new home was Tulsey Town, a corruption of *Tullahassee,* meaning "old town." The name Tulsa was made official with the establishment of a post office in 1879. In 1900, Tulsa's population numbered less than 2,000, but the discovery of extensive oil fields at the turn of the century, beginning with the Glenn Pool and Red Fork strikes, started Tulsa on the way from a small Indian settlement to a sizable metropolis. By 1907, its population had increased to 7,298, and by 1920 it was 10 times that. Soon Tulsa was "the Oil Capital of the World."

While still heavily involved in the oil and gas industry—it remains the home of about 500 oil-related companies—modern Tulsa is a far more diverse city than its oil patch origins. Among Tulsa's top employers are regional, national and international firms involved in aviation and aerospace, energy, computer technology, insurance, telecommunications, health care, and electronic equipment. The Port of Catoosa, which opened in 1972 after the completion of the 445-mile Arkansas-Mississippi Waterway, is a major inland port which provides Tulsa with a direct link to the Mississippi River system and the Gulf of Mexico.

While growing in business, Tulsa has preserved the cultural heritage of its early oil barons and workers as well as that of its original Indian settlers. Thomas Gilcrease, a Creek Indian, became a millionaire with the Glenn Pool oil strike, and founded the Thomas Gilcrease Institute of American History and Art, devoted to the American Indian. The Tulsa Opera Company was founded in the early 1900's, and along with the city's philharmonic, ballet, and theaters, it gives Tulsa just cause to lay claim to being the cultural capital of Oklahoma. Tulsans also honor their roots through rodeos and regional music festivals. In addition, representatives of the state's 65 Indian tribes gather in Tulsa each summer for their annual powwow. Among Tulsa's colleges and universities are the University of Tulsa and Oral Roberts University.

Population 393,049 (2000). Rank: 43rd. Race/Hispanic Origin (2000): White 70.1%. Black 15.5%. Indian 4.7%. Asian 1.8%. Pacific Islander 0.1%. Other 3.5%. Two or more races 4.4%. Hispanic 7.2%.
Location: 36°10'N, 96°00'W. Counties: Osage, Tulsa.
Terrain and climate Elev.: 676 ft. Area: 186.1 sq. mi. (482 sq km). Avg. daily min. temp.: Jan.: 24.8°F/-4°C; avg. daily max. July: 93.9°F/34.3°C. Avg. annual rainfall: 38.77"; snowfall: 9"; clear days: 127; precipitation days: 90.
Government Form: commission. Mayor: Bill La Fortune. (918) 596-2100. **www.cityoftulsa.org**
Visitor info: (800) 558-3311 or (918) 585-1201. **www.visittulsa.com.**

▶VIRGINIA BEACH, VIRGINIA

Throughout much of its history—which dates to the the landing of the Jamestown colonists at Point Henry in 1607—Virginia Beach was overshadowed by its northern neighbor, Norfolk, which with its magnificent harbor was long the home of many shipping and naval enterprises at the mouth of Chesapeake Bay. But Virginia Beach has seen remarkable change in the last two decades.

In 1970, Virginia Beach's population was 172,000, only slightly more than half that of Norfolk. By 1990, it had grown 128 percent, to 393,000, and surpassing Norfolk as the state's largest city, a distinction it still holds today, though growth cooled to a 8.2 percent between 1990 and 2000. Local initiative accounts for most of this growth: in the same period Norfolk's population fell 10 percent. A dominant presence is the U.S. Navy, which has three bases—Oceana Naval Air Station, Little Creek Naval Amphibious Base, and the Dam Neck Fleet Training Center—and which together with the U.S. Army's Fort Story employs 36,000 military and civilian personnel.

With 38 miles of Atlantic shoreline, 28 miles of public beaches, and the Seashore State Park—2,700 acres of shady upland woods, cypress swamps, and Spanish moss—the city continues to depend on tourism as a major factor in its economy, attracting 2.5 million visitors a year. The city's main industries, which include marine and engineering services, construction, communications, and electronics, occupy 10 industrial/business parks, including four built by the Virginia Beach Development Authority.

Among Virginia Beach's outstanding historic and recreational attractions are the Virginia Marine Science Museum, the Adam Thoroughgood House (c. 1680, one of the oldest brick houses in North America), the Old Cape Henry Lighthouse, authorized by the first Congress in 1790, and the statue of Admiral Compte de Grasse whose defeat of the British at the Battle of the Virginia Capes brought about the defeat of Gen. Cornwallis at Yorktown and the end of the American Revolution in 1781.

Population 425,257 (2000). Rank: 38th. Race/Hispanic Origin (2000): White 71.4%. Black 19.0%. Indian 0.4%. Asian 4.9%. Pacific Islander 0.1%. Other 1.5%. Two or more races 2.7%. Hispanic 4.2%.
Location: 36°54'N, 75°58'W. County: independent city.
Terrain and climate Elev.: 12 ft. Area: 225.9 sq. mi. (585.1 sq km). Avg. daily min. temp.: Jan.: 31.7°F/-0.1°C; avg. daily max. July: 86.9°F/30.5°C. Avg. annual rainfall: 45.22"; snowfall: 7"; clear days: 110; precipitation days: 115.
Government Form: council and manager. Mayor: Meyera E. Oberndorf. (757) 427-4581. **www.vbgov.com.**
Visitor info: (800) VA-BEACH. **www.vbfun.com.**

▶WASHINGTON, D.C.

[*For description, see District of Columbia entry in "States, Territories, and Possessions."*]

Population 572,059 (2000). Rank: 21st. Race/Hispanic Origin (2000): White 30.8%. Black 60.0%. Indian 0.3%. Asian 2.7%. Pacific Islander 0.1%. Other 3.8%. Two or more races 2.4%. Hispanic 7.9%.
Location: 38°52'N, 77°00'W. County: independent city.
Terrain and climate Elev.: 30 ft. Area: 62.7 sq. mi. (162.4 sq km). Avg. daily min. temp.: Jan.: 27.5°F/-2.5°C; avg. daily max. July: 87.9°F/31°C. Avg. annual rainfall: 39"; snowfall: 16"; clear days: 101; precipitation days: 111.
Government Form: mayor and council. Mayor: Anthony A. Williams. (202) 727-1000. **www.dc.gov.**
Visitor info: (202) 789-7000. **www.washington.org.**

▶WICHITA, KANSAS

Initially settled by Indians during the Civil War who had migrated from Oklahoma, Wichita, which takes its name from the Indian tribe, was officially founded in 1864 as a trading post along the Chisholm Trail, an important cattle route, and was incorporated in 1871. In 1872 the Santa Fe Rail Line reached the city, further cementing its role as a major cattle shipping center, although by 1875 cattle movement was obstructed by farmers' fences, and flour milling and retail trade began to flourished. The discovery of oil nearby in 1915 and the pioneering of aircraft manufacture in the 1920's quickly brought industrial growth to the city, and Wichita is now dominated by aircraft and aerospace equipment manufacture (including Beech Aircraft Corp., Cessna Aircraft Co., Gates Learjet Corp., and the Boeing Military Airplane company), along with oil refining, grain processing and storage, and livestock marketing.

Wichita is home to Friends University (1898), Kansas Newman College (formerly Sacred Heart College, 1933), and Wichita State University (1895). McDonnell Air Force Base is located nearby. Culturally, the city features the Wichita Art Museum (housing one of the country's largest American art collections), the Kansas Coliseum, and the Wichita Symphony Orchestra.

Population 344,284 (2000). Rank: 50th. Race/Hispanic Origin (2000): White 75.2%. Black 11.4%. Indian 1.2%. Asian 4.0%. Pacific Islander 0.1%. Other 5.1%. Two or more races 3.1%. Hispanic 9.6%.
Location: 37°42'N, 97°20'W. County: Sedgwick.
Terrain and climate Elev.: 387.1 ft. Area: 140.2 sq. mi. (363.1sq km). Avg. daily min. temp.: Jan.: 19.2°F/-7.1°C; avg. daily max. July: 92.8°F/33.8°C. Avg. annual rainfall: 29"; snowfall: 16"; clear days: 279; precipitation days: 86.
Government Form: council and manager. Mayor: Bob Knight. 316-268-4331. **www.wichita.gov**
Visitor info: (800) 288-9424 or (316) 265-2800. **www.visitwichita.com.**

CITIES IN AMERICA

The number of large U.S. cities continues to grow. The 2000 Census recorded 243 cities with populations over 100,000, up from 199 such places in 1990.

The number of very large cities also continues to grow. In 1990, the only cities with more than a million residents were New York, Los Angeles, Chicago, Houston, Philadelphia, Detroit, Dallas and San Diego. In the 2000 Census, Detroit's population dropped below a million (mostly from flight to the suburbs), but Phoenix, and San Antonio topped a million.

New York, the nation's largest city, grew by 685,000 people between censuses, with most of that growth coming in the latter half of the decade. Meanwhile, Los Angeles, which declined in population early in the decade, grew by an overall 479,000 people.

Major U.S. Cities: Population, Population Change, Population Density, and Land Area, 1970–2000

City (Rank, 2000)	Population ('000s) 1970	1980	1990	2000	Percent change 1990-2000	Population per sq. mi. 1990	Land area (sq.mi.) 1990
Abilene, Texas (197)	90	98	107	116	8.7%	1,035	103.1
Akron, Ohio (82)	275	237	223	217	-2.7	3,586	62.2
Albuquerque, N.Mex. (35)	245	332	385	449	16.6	2,909	132.2
Alexandria, Va. (170)	111	103	111	128	15.4	7,267	15.3
Allentown, Pa. (219)	110	104	105	107	1.5	5,949	17.7
Amarillo, Texas (120)	127	149	158	174	10.2	1,793	87.9
Anaheim, Calif. (56)	166	219	266	328	23.1	6,014	44.3
Anchorage , Alaska[1] (66)	48	174	226	260	15.0	133	1,697.7
Ann Arbor, Mich. (199)	100	108	110	114	4.0	4,231	25.9
Arlington, Texas (54)	90	160	262	333	27.2	2,814	93.0
Arvada, Colo. (235)	N.A.	N.A.	89	102	14.5	N.A.	N.A.
Athens-Clarke County, Ga.[1] (237)	N.A.	N.A.	46	101	121.9	N.A.	N.A.
Atlanta, Ga. (40)	495	425	394	416	5.7	2,990	131.8
Augusta-Richmond County, Ga.[1] (91)	N.A.	N.A.	45	200	347.5	N.A.	N.A.
Aurora, Colo. (62)	75	159	222	276	24.4	1,676	132.5
Aurora, Ill. (151)	N.A.	N.A.	100	143	43.6	N.A.	N.A.
Austin, Texas (16)	254	346	466	657	41.0	2,138	217.8
Bakersfield, Calif. (70)	70	106	175	247	41.3	1,904	91.8
Baltimore, Md. (17)	905	787	736	651	-11.5	9,108	80.8
Baton Rouge, La. (75)	166	220	220	228	3.8	2,969	74.0
Bayamon, Puerto Rico (86)	N.A.	N.A.	202	203	0.7	N.A.	N.A.
Beaumont, Texas (200)	118	118	114	114	-0.4	1,427	80.1
Bellevue, Wash. (210)			87	110	26.1		
Berkeley, Calif. (231)	114	103	103	103	0.0	9,783	10.5
Birmingham, Ala. (72)	301	284	266	243	-8.7	1,791	148.5
Boise City, Idaho (108)	75	102	126	186	47.8	2,726	46.1
Boston, Mass. (20)	641	563	574	589	2.6	11,860	48.4
Bridgeport, Conn. (156)	157	143	142	140	-1.5	8,855	16.0
Brownsville, Texas (155)	N.A.	N.A.	99	140	41.2	N.A.	N.A.
Buffalo, N.Y. (59)	463	358	328	293	-10.8	8,083	40.6
Burbank, Calif. (243)	N.A.	N.A.	94	100	7.1	N.A.	N.A.
Cambridge, Mass. (238)	N.A.	N.A.	96	101	5.8	N.A.	N.A.
Cape Coral, Fla. (234)	N.A.	N.A.	75	102	36.4	N.A.	N.A.
Carolina , Puerto Rico (125)	N.A.	N.A.	162	168	3.5	N.A.	N.A.
Carrollton, Texas (209)	N.A.	N.A.	82	110	33.4	N.A.	N.A.
Cedar Rapids, Iowa (185)	111	110	109	121	11.0	2,033	53.5
Chandler, Ariz. (116)	N.A.	N.A.	91	177	95.0	N.A.	N.A.
Charlotte, N.C. (26)	241	315	396	541	36.6	2,272	174.3
Chattanooga, Tenn. (132)	120	170	152	156	2.0	1,288	118.4
Chesapeake, Va. (93)	90	114	152	199	31.1	446	340.7
Chicago, Ill. (3)	3,369	3,005	2,784	2,896	4.0	12,251	227.2
Chula Vista, Calif. (122)	68	84	135	174	28.4	4,661	29.0
Cincinnati, Ohio (55)	454	385	364	331	-9.0	4,717	77.2
Clarksville, Tenn. (228)	N.A.	N.A.	75	103	37.0	N.A.	N.A.
Clearwater, Fla. (212)	N.A.	N.A.	99	109	10.1	N.A.	N.A.
Cleveland, Ohio (33)	751	574	506	478	-5.4	6,565	77.0
Colorado Springs, Colo. (49)	136	215	281	361	28.4	1,535	183.2
Columbia, S.C. (195)	114	101	98	116	18.6	884	117.1
Columbus, Ga. [1] (106)	155	169	179	186	3.9	827	216.1
Columbus, Ohio (15)	540	565	633	711	12.4	3,315	190.9
Concord, Calif. (181)	85	104	111	122	9.4	3,773	29.5
Coral Springs, Fla. (190)	N.A.	N.A.	79	118	48.0	N.A.	N.A.
Corona, Calif. (174)	N.A.	N.A.	76	125	64.2	N.A.	N.A.
Corpus Christi, Texas (61)	205	232	257	277	7.8	1,907	135.0

City (Rank, 2000)	Population ('000s) 1970	1980	1990	2000	Percent change 1990-2000	Population per sq. mi. 1990	Land area (sq.mi.) 1990
Costa Mesa, Calif. (213)	N.A.	N.A.	96	109	12.8%	N.A.	N.A.
Dallas, Texas (8)	844	905	1,007	1,189	18.0	2,943	342.4
Daly City, Calif. (227)	N.A.	N.A.	92	104	12.3	N.A.	N.A.
Dayton, Ohio (126)	243	194	182	166	-8.7	3,310	55.0
Denver, Colo.[1] (25)	515	493	468	555	18.6	3,051	153.3
Des Moines, Iowa (95)	201	191	193	199	2.8	2,567	75.3
Detroit, Mich. (10)	1,514	1,203	1,028	951	-7.5	7,410	138.7
Downey, Calif. (216)	N.A.	N.A.	91	107	17.4	N.A.	N.A.
Durham, N.C. (105)	95	101	137	187	36.9	1,972	69.3
El Monte, Calif. (196)	70	79	106	116	9.2	11,175	9.5
El Paso, Texas (23)	322	425	515	564	9.4	2,100	245.4
Elizabeth, N.J. (186)	113	106	110	121	9.6	8,929	12.3
Erie, Pa. (226)	129	119	109	104	-4.6	4,944	22.0
Escondido, Calif. (164)	37	64	109	134	22.9	3,048	35.6
Eugene, Oreg. (160)	79	106	113	138	22.4	2,962	38.0
Evansville, Ind. (182)	139	130	126	122	-3.7	3,102	40.7
Fayetteville, N.C. (184)	N.A.	N.A.	76	121	59.9	N.A.	N.A.
Flint, Mich. (175)	193	160	141	125	-11.2	4,161	33.8
Fontana, Calif. (167)	N.A.	N.A.	88	129	47.3	N.A.	N.A.
Fort Collins, Colo. (189)	N.A.	N.A.	88	119	35.2	N.A.	N.A.
Fort Lauderdale, Fla. (134)	140	153	149	152	2.0	4,753	31.4
Fort Wayne, Ind. (85)	178	172	173	206	18.9	2,762	62.7
Fort Worth, Texas (27)	393	385	448	535	19.5	1,592	281.1
Fremont, Calif. (87)	101	132	173	203	17.3	2,250	77.0
Fresno, Calif. (37)	166	217	354	428	20.7	3,573	99.1
Fullerton, Calif. (173)	86	102	114	126	10.4	5,160	22.1
Garden Grove, Calif. (127)	121	123	143	165	15.5	7,974	17.9
Garland, Texas (83)	81	139	181	216	19.4	3,150	57.4
Gary, Ind. (230)	175	152	117	103	-11.9	2,322	50.2
Gilbert town, Ariz. (208)	N.A.	N.A.	29	110	275.8	N.A.	N.A.
Glendale, Ariz. (81)	36	97	148	219	47.7	2,837	52.2
Glendale, Calif. (100)	133	139	180	195	8.3	5,882	30.6
Grand Prairie, Texas (172)	N.A.	N.A.	100	127	27.9	N.A.	N.A.
Grand Rapids, Mich. (96)	198	182	189	198	4.6	4,273	44.3
Green Bay, Wisc. (233)	N.A.	N.A.	96	102	6.1	N.A.	N.A.
Greensboro, N.C. (78)	144	156	184	224	22.0	2,304	79.8
Hampton, Va. (147)	121	123	134	146	9.5	2,583	51.8
Hartford, Conn. (183)	158	136	140	122	-13.0	8,077	17.3
Hayward, Calif. (154)	93	94	111	140	25.6	2,560	43.5
Henderson, Nevada (118)	N.A.	N.A.	65	175	170.1	N.A.	N.A.
Hialeah, Fla. (76)	102	145	188	226	20.4	9,772	19.2
Hollywood, Fla. (157)	107	121	122	139	14.5	4,464	27.3
Honolulu, Hawaii[2] (47)	325	365	365	372	1.7	4,400	85.7
Houston, Texas (4)	1,234	1,595	1,631	1,954	19.8	3,021	539.9
Huntington Beach, Calif. (103)	116	171	182	190	4.4	6,871	26.4
Huntsville, Ala. (130)	139	143	160	158	-1.0	973	164.4
Independence, Mo. (202)	112	112	112	113	0.9	1,436	78.2
Indianapolis , Ind. (12)	737	701	742	792	6.7	2,022	361.7
Inglewood, Calif. (204)	90	94	110	113	2.7	11,952	9.2
Irvine, Calif. (150)	(3)	62	110	143	29.7	2,607	42.3
Irving, Texas (102)	97	110	155	192	23.6	2,293	67.6
Jackson, Miss. (111)	154	203	197	184	-6.3	1,804	109.0
Jacksonville, Fla. (14)	504	541	635	736	15.8	837	758.7
Jersey City, N.J. (73)	260	224	229	240	5.0	15,337	14.9
Joliet, Ill. (221)	N.A.	N.A.	77	106	38.2	N.A.	N.A.
Kansas City, Kans. (146)	168	161	150	147	-1.9	1,390	107.8
Kansas City, Mo. (36)	507	448	435	442	1.5	1,397	311.5
Knoxville, Tenn. (119)	175	175	165	174	5.3	2,135	77.2
Lafayette, La. (207)	N.A.	N.A.	94	110	16.7	N.A.	N.A.
Lakewood, Colo. (148)	93	114	126	144	14.0	3,100	40.8
Lancaster, Calif. (188)	N.A.	N.A.	97	119	22.0	N.A.	N.A.
Lansing, Mich. (187)	131	130	127	119	-6.4	3,755	33.9
Laredo, Texas (117)	69	91	123	177	43.7	3,739	32.9
Las Vegas, Nevada (32)	126	165	258	478	85.2	3,100	83.3
Lexington-Fayette, Ky. (65)	108	204	225	261	15.6	792	284.5
Lincoln, Neb. (77)	150	172	192	226	17.5	3,033	63.3
Little Rock, Ark. (112)	132	159	176	183	4.2	1,709	102.9
Livonia, Mich. (242)	110	105	101	101	-0.3	2,823	35.7
Long Beach, Calif. (34)	359	361	429	462	7.5	8,586	50.0
Los Angeles, Calif. (2)	2,812	2,969	3,485	3,695	6.0	7,426	469.3
Louisville, Ky. (67)	362	299	269	256	-4.8	4,341	62.1
Lowell, Mass. (222)	94	92	103	105	1.7	7,506	13.8

City (Rank, 2000)	Population ('000s) 1970	1980	1990	2000	Percent change 1990-2000	Population per sq. mi. 1990	Land area (sq.mi.) 1990
Lubbock, Texas (92)	149	174	186	200	7.2%	1,789	104.1
Madison, Wisc. (84)	172	171	191	208	8.8	3,300	57.8
Manchester, N.H. (218)	N.A.	N.A.	100	107	7.5	N.A.	N.A.
McAllen, Texas (220)	N.A.	N.A.	84	106	26.7	N.A.	N.A.
Memphis, Tenn. (18)	624	646	610	650	6.5	2,384	256.0
Mesa, Ariz. (43)	63	152	288	396	37.6	2,653	108.6
Mesquite, Texas (176)	55	67	101	125	22.7	2,369	42.8
Miami, Fla. (48)	335	347	359	362	1.1	10,074	35.6
Milwaukee, Wisc. (19)	717	636	628	597	-5.0	6,537	96.1
Minneapolis, Minn. (46)	434	371	368	383	3.9	6,706	54.9
Mobile, Ala. (94)	190	200	196	199	1.3	1,663	118.0
Modesto, Calif. (104)	62	107	165	189	14.6	5,458	30.2
Montgomery, Ala. (89)	133	178	187	202	7.7	1,389	135.0
Moreno Valley, Calif. (152)	(3)	(3)	119	142	19.9	2,418	49.1
Naperville, Ill. (169)	N.A.	N.A.	85	128	50.4	N.A.	N.A.
Nashville-Davidson, Tenn.[1] (22)	426	456	511	570	11.6	1,032	473.3
New Haven, Conn. (179)	138	126	130	124	-5.2	6,922	18.9
New Orleans, La. (31)	593	558	497	485	-2.5	2,751	180.7
New York, N.Y. (1)	7,896	7,072	7,323	8,008	9.4	23,701	309.0
Newark, N.J. (64)	382	329	275	274	-0.6	11,554	23.8
Newport News, Va. (115)	138	145	170	180	5.9	2,510	68.3
Norfolk, Va. (74)	308	267	261	234	-10.3	4,856	53.8
North Las Vegas, Nevada (198)	N.A.	N.A.	48	115	142.1	N.A.	N.A.
Norwalk, Calif. (229)	N.A.	N.A.	94	103	9.6	N.A.	N.A.
Oakland, Calif. (42)	362	339	372	399	7.3	6,640	56.1
Oceanside, Calif. (128)	40	77	128	161	25.4	3,164	40.5
Oklahoma City, Okla. (29)	368	404	445	506	13.8	731	608.2
Omaha, Neb. (45)	347	314	336	390	16.1	3,336	100.7
Ontario, Calif. (131)	64	89	133	158	18.6	3,624	36.8
Orange, Calif. (168)	77	91	111	129	16.4	4,741	23.3
Orlando, Fla. (107)	99	128	165	186	12.9	2,448	67.3
Overland Park, Kans. (143)	78	82	112	149	33.4	2,007	55.7
Oxnard, Calif. (124)	71	108	142	170	19.8	5,843	24.4
Palmdale, Calif. (194)	N.A.	N.A.	69	117	69.5	N.A.	N.A.
Pasadena, Calif. (163)	113	118	132	134	1.8	5,724	23.0
Pasadena, Texas (153)	90	113	119	142	18.7	2,726	43.8
Paterson, N.J. (142)	145	138	141	149	5.9	16,693	8.4
Pembroke Pines, Fla. (161)	N.A.	N.A.	65	137	110.0	N.A.	N.A.
Peoria, Ariz. (214)	N.A.	N.A.	51	108	114.1	N.A.	N.A.
Peoria, Ill. (203)	127	124	114	113	-0.5	2,776	40.9
Philadelphia, Pa. [1] (5)	1,949	1,688	1,586	1,518	-4.3	11,734	135.1
Phoenix, Ariz. (6)	584	790	983	1,321	34.3	2,342	419.9
Pittsburgh, Pa. (53)	520	424	370	335	-9.5	6,649	55.6
Plano, Texas (79)	18	72	129	222	72.5	1,929	66.3
Pomona, Calif. (141)	87	93	132	149	13.5	5,770	22.8
Ponce, Puerto Rico (133)	N.A.	N.A.	159	155	-2.6	N.A.	N.A.
Portland, Oreg. (28)	380	368	437	529	21.0	3,508	124.7
Portsmouth, Va. (241)	111	105	104	101	-3.2	3,139	33.1
Providence, R.I. (121)	179	157	161	174	8.0	8,707	18.5
Provo, Utah (223)	N.A.	N.A.	87	105	21.1	N.A.	N.A.
Pueblo, Colo. (236)	N.A.	N.A.	99	102	3.5	N.A.	N.A.
Raleigh, N.C. (63)	123	150	208	276	32.8	2,395	88.1
Rancho Cucamonga,Calif. (171)	(3)	55	101	128	26.0	2,682	37.8
Reno, Nevada (114)	73	101	134	180	34.8	2,328	57.5
Richmond, Va. (97)	249	219	203	198	-2.6	3,374	60.1
Riverside, Calif. (68)	140	171	227	255	12.7	2,916	77.7
Rochester, N.Y. (80)	295	242	232	220	-5.1	6,435	35.8
Rockford, Ill. (140)	147	140	139	150	7.7	3,110	45.0
Sacramento, Calif. (41)	257	276	369	407	10.2	3,836	96.3
Salem, Oreg. (162)	69	89	108	137	27.0	2,595	41.5
Salinas, Calif. (138)	59	80	109	151	38.9	5,839	18.6
Salt Lake City, Utah (113)	176	163	160	182	13.6	1,467	109.0
San Antonio, Texas (9)	654	786	936	1,145	22.3	2,810	333.0
San Bernardino, Calif. (110)	107	119	164	185	12.9	2,980	55.1
San Diego, Calif. (7)	697	876	1,111	1,223	10.2	3,428	324.0
San Francisco, Calif. [1] (13)	716	679	724	777	7.3	15,502	46.7
San Jose, Calif. (11)	460	629	782	895	14.4	4,568	171.3
San Juan , Puerto Rico (39)	N.A.	N.A.	427	422	-1.1	N.A.	N.A.
Santa Ana, Calif. (52)	156	204	294	338	15.1	10,842	27.1
Santa Clara, Calif. (232)	N.A.	N.A.	94	102	9.3	N.A.	N.A.
Santa Clarita, Calif. (137)	(3)	(3)	111	151	36.6	2,733	40.5
Santa Rosa, Calif. (144)	50	83	113	148	30.3	3,362	33.7

City (Rank, 2000)	Population ('000s) 1970	1980	1990	2000	Percent change 1990-2000	Population per sq. mi. 1990	Land area (sq.mi.) 1990
Savannah, Ga. (166)	118	142	138	132	-4.4%	2,204	62.6
Scottsdale, Ariz. (88)	68	89	130	203	55.8	706	184.4
Seattle, Wash. (24)	531	494	516	563	9.1	6,154	83.9
Shreveport, La. (90)	182	206	199	200	0.8	2,013	98.6
Simi Valley, Calif. (206)	60	78	100	111	11.1	3,034	33.0
Sioux Falls, SD (178)	72	81	101	124	23.0	2,236	45.1
South Bend, Ind. (215)	126	110	106	108	2.2	2,897	36.4
Spokane, Wash. (99)	171	171	177	196	10.4	3,169	55.9
Springfield, Ill. (205)	92	100	105	111	5.9	2,474	42.5
Springfield, Mass. (135)	164	152	157	152	-3.1	4,890	32.1
Springfield, Mo. (136)	120	133	140	152	7.9	2,068	68.0
St. Louis, Mo. (50)	622	453	397	348	-12.2	6,405	61.9
St. Paul, Minn. (60)	310	270	272	287	5.5	5,157	52.8
St. Petersburg, Fla. (69)	216	239	239	248	4.0	4,059	59.2
Stamford, Conn. (191)	109	102	108	117	8.4	2,865	37.7
Sterling Heights, Mich. (177)	61	109	118	124	5.7	3,215	36.6
Stockton, Calif. (71)	110	150	211	244	15.6	4,013	52.6
Sunnyvale, Calif. (165)	96	107	117	132	12.4	5,353	21.9
Syracuse, N.Y. (145)	197	170	164	147	-10.1	6,528	25.1
Tacoma, Wash. (101)	154	159	177	194	9.6	3,677	48.1
Tallahassee, Fla. (139)	73	82	125	151	20.7	1,972	63.3
Tampa, Fla. (58)	278	272	280	303	8.4	2,577	108.7
Tempe, Ariz. (129)	64	107	142	159	11.8	3,590	39.5
Thousand Oaks, Calif. (192)	36	77	104	117	12.1	2,104	49.6
Toledo, Ohio (57)	383	355	333	314	-5.8	4,132	80.6
Topeka, Kans. (180)	125	119	120	122	2.1	2,173	55.2
Torrance, Calif. (159)	135	130	133	138	3.6	6,487	20.5
Tucson, Ariz. (30)	263	331	405	487	20.1	2,594	156.3
Tulsa, Okla. (44)	330	361	367	393	7.0	2,001	183.5
Vallejo, Calif. (193)	72	80	109	117	6.9	3,613	30.2
Vancouver, Wash. (149)	N.A.	N.A.	46	144	209.5	N.A.	N.A.
Ventura, Calif. (240)	N.A.	N.A.	93	101	9.0	N.A.	N.A.
Virginia Beach, Va. (38)	172	262	393	425	8.2	1,583	248.3
Waco, Texas (201)	95	101	104	114	9.8	1,367	75.8
Warren, Mich. (158)	179	161	145	138	-4.6	4,226	34.3
Washington, D.C. (21)	757	638	607	572	-5.7	9,883	61.4
Waterbury, Conn. (217)	108	103	109	107	-1.6	3,815	28.6
West Covina, Calif. (224)	N.A.	N.A.	96	105	9.4	N.A.	N.A.
West Valley City, Utah (211)	N.A.	N.A.	87	109	25.2	N.A.	N.A.
Westminster, Colo. (239)	N.A.	N.A.	75	101	35.3	N.A.	N.A.
Wichita Falls, Texas (225)	N.A.	N.A.	96	104	8.2	N.A.	N.A.
Wichita, Kans. (51)	277	280	304	344	13.2	2,640	115.1
Winston-Salem, N.C. (109)	134	132	143	186	29.5	2,018	71.1
Worcester, Mass. (123)	177	162	170	173	1.7	4,520	37.6
Yonkers, N.Y. (98)	204	195	188	196	4.3	10,403	18.1

Note: Cities over 100,000 population. 1. Represents the portion of a consolidated city not within one or more separately incorporated areas. 2. Data represent the census designated place of Honolulu, as delineated by the State of Hawaii. 3. Not incorporated
Source: U.S. Bureau of the Census, Statistical Abstract of the United States 1990 (1990), and Release (2001).

Cities, by Population Size, 1960–90

Population size	Number of Cities 1960	1970	1980	1990	Population (mil.) 1960	1970	1980	1990	Percent of Total 1960	1970	1980	1990
Total	**18,088**	**18,666**	**19,097**	**19,262**	**115.9**	**131.9**	**140.3**	**152.9**	**100%**	**100%**	**100%**	**100%**
1 million +	5	6	6	8	17.5	18.8	17.5	20.0	15.1	14.2	12.5	13.0
500,000-1 million	16	20	16	15	11.1	13.0	10.9	10.1	9.6	9.8	7.8	6.6
250,000-500,000	30	30	33	41	10.8	10.5	11.8	14.2	9.3	7.9	8.4	9.3
100,000-250,000	79	97	114	131	11.4	13.9	16.6	19.1	9.8	10.5	11.8	12.5
50,000-100,000	180	232	250	309	12.5	16.2	17.6	21.2	10.8	12.2	12.3	13.9
25,000-50,000	366	455	526	567	12.7	15.7	18.4	20.0	11.0	11.9	13.1	13.0
10,000-25,000	978	1,127	1,260	1,290	15.1	17.6	19.8	20.3	13.1	13.3	14.1	13.3
<10,000	16,434	16,699	16,892	16,901	24.9	26.4	28.0	28.2	21.5	20.0	20.0	18.4

Source: U.S. Bureau of the Census, *Statistical Abstract of the United States* (annual).

Resident Population of Major U.S Cities by Race and Hispanic Origin, 2000

Geographic area	Total population	Black	American Indian	Asian	Native Hawaiian	Some other race	Two or more races	Hispanic or Latino (any race)
Abilene, Texas	115,930	8.8%	0.6%	1.3%	0.1%	8.7%	2.4%	19.4%
Akron, Ohio	217,074	28.5	0.3	1.5	-	0.4	2.1	1.2
Albuquerque, N.Mex.	448,607	3.1	3.9	2.2	0.1	14.8	4.3	39.9
Alexandria, Va.	128,283	22.5	0.3	5.7	0.1	7.4	4.3	14.7
Allentown, Pa.	106,632	7.8	0.3	2.3	0.1	13.4	3.6	24.4
Amarillo, Texas	173,627	6.0	0.8	2.1	-	11.3	2.3	21.9
Anaheim, Calif.	328,014	2.7	0.9	12.0	0.4	24.2	5.0	46.8
Anchorage, Alaska	260,283	5.8	7.3	5.5	0.9	2.2	6.0	5.7
Ann Arbor, Mich.	114,024	8.8	0.3	11.9	-	1.2	3.1	3.3
Arlington, Texas	332,969	13.7	0.5	6.0	0.1	8.9	2.9	18.3
Arlington, Va.	189,453	9.3	0.3	8.6	0.1	8.3	4.3	18.6
Arvada, Colo.	102,153	0.7	0.7	2.2	0.1	3.1	2.3	9.8
Athens, Ga.	101,489	27.3	0.2	3.1	-	3.1	1.4	6.3
Atlanta, Ga.	416,474	61.4	0.2	1.9	-	2.0	1.2	4.5
Augusta, Ga.	199,775	49.8	0.3	1.5	0.1	1.0	1.8	2.8
Aurora, Colo.	276,393	13.4	0.8	4.4	0.2	8.1	4.2	19.8
Aurora, Ill.	142,990	11.1	0.4	3.1	-	14.5	2.9	32.6
Austin, Texas	656,562	10.0	0.6	4.7	0.1	16.2	3.0	30.5
Bakersfield, Calif.	247,057	9.2	1.4	4.3	0.1	18.7	4.4	32.5
Baltimore, Md.	651,154	64.3	0.3	1.5	-	0.7	1.5	1.7
Baton Rouge, La.	227,818	50.0	0.2	2.6	-	0.5	1.0	1.7
Beaumont, Texas	113,866	45.8	0.2	2.5	-	3.5	1.5	7.9
Bellevue, Wash.	109,569	2.0	0.3	17.4	0.2	2.5	3.2	5.3
Berkeley, Calif.	102,743	13.6	0.5	16.4	0.1	4.6	5.6	9.7
Birmingham, Ala.	242,820	73.5	0.2	0.8	-	0.6	0.8	1.6
Boise City, Idaho	185,787	0.8	0.7	2.1	0.2	1.7	2.4	4.5
Boston, Mass.	589,141	25.3	0.4	7.5	0.1	7.8	4.4	14.4
Bridgeport, Conn.	139,529	30.8	0.5	3.3	0.1	14.8	5.6	31.9
Brownsville, Texas	139,722	0.4	0.4	0.5	-	14.7	2.3	91.3
Buffalo, N.Y.	292,648	37.2	0.8	1.4	-	3.7	2.5	7.5
Burbank, Calif.	100,316	2.1	0.5	9.2	0.1	9.9	6.0	24.9
Cambridge, Mass.	101,355	11.9	0.3	11.9	0.1	3.2	4.6	7.4
Cape Coral, Fla.	102,286	2.0	0.3	0.9	0.1	2.2	1.6	8.3
Carrollton, Texas	109,576	6.3	0.5	10.9	0.1	7.7	2.7	19.5
Cedar Rapids, Iowa	120,758	3.7	0.3	1.8	0.1	0.6	1.8	1.7
Chandler, Ariz.	176,581	3.5	1.2	4.2	0.1	10.8	3.0	21.0
Charlotte, N.C.	540,828	32.7	0.3	3.4	0.1	3.6	1.7	7.4
Chattanooga, Tenn.	155,554	36.1	0.3	1.5	0.1	1.0	1.3	2.1
Chesapeake, Va.	199,184	28.5	0.4	1.8	0.1	0.7	1.6	2.0
Chicago, Ill.	2,896,016	36.8	0.4	4.3	0.1	13.6	2.9	26.0
Chula Vista, Calif.	173,556	4.6	0.8	11.0	0.6	22.1	5.8	49.6
Cincinnati, Ohio	331,285	42.9	0.2	1.5	-	0.6	1.7	1.3
Clarksville, Tenn.	103,455	23.2	0.5	2.2	0.3	2.6	3.3	6.0
Clearwater, Fla.	108,787	9.8	0.3	1.6	0.1	2.5	1.8	9.0
Cleveland, Ohio	478,403	51.0	0.3	1.3	-	3.6	2.2	7.3
Colorado Springs, Colo.	360,890	6.6	0.9	2.8	0.2	5.0	3.9	12.0
Columbia, S.C.	116,278	46.0	0.3	1.7	0.1	1.4	1.4	3.0
Columbus, Ga.	186,291	43.7	0.4	1.5	0.1	1.9	1.9	4.5
Columbus, Ohio	711,470	24.5	0.3	3.4	0.1	1.2	2.6	2.5
Concord, Calif.	121,780	3.0	0.8	9.4	0.5	9.7	5.9	21.8
Coral Springs, Fla.	117,549	9.2	0.2	3.5	0.1	3.0	2.5	15.5
Corona, Calif.	124,966	6.4	0.9	7.5	0.3	17.5	5.3	35.7
Corpus Christi, Texas	277,454	4.7	0.6	1.3	0.1	18.6	3.1	54.3
Costa Mesa, Calif.	108,724	1.4	0.8	6.9	0.6	16.6	4.3	31.8
Dallas, Texas	1,188,580	25.9	0.5	2.7	-	17.2	2.7	35.6
Daly City, Calif.	103,621	4.6	0.4	50.7	0.9	11.3	6.2	22.3
Dayton, Ohio	166,179	43.1	0.3	0.6	-	0.7	1.8	1.6
Denver, Colo.	554,636	11.1	1.3	2.8	0.1	15.6	3.7	31.7
Des Moines, Iowa	198,682	8.1	0.4	3.5	-	3.5	2.2	6.6
Detroit, Mich.	951,270	81.6	0.3	1.0	-	2.5	2.3	5.0
Downey, Calif.	107,323	3.8	0.9	7.7	0.2	29.1	4.9	57.9
Durham, N.C.	187,035	43.8	0.3	3.6	-	4.7	1.9	8.6
East Los Angeles, Calif.	124,283	0.4	1.3	0.8	0.1	54.0	4.2	96.8
El Monte, Calif.	115,965	0.8	1.4	18.5	0.1	39.3	4.3	72.4
El Paso, Texas	563,662	3.1	0.8	1.1	0.1	18.2	3.4	76.6
Elizabeth, N.J.	120,568	20.0	0.5	2.3	-	15.5	5.9	49.5
Erie, Pa.	103,717	14.2	0.2	0.7	-	1.9	2.3	4.4
Escondido, Calif.	133,559	2.3	1.2	4.5	0.2	19.2	4.8	38.7
Eugene, Oreg.	137,893	1.3	0.9	3.6	0.2	2.2	3.7	5.0

Geographic area	Total population	Black	American Indian	Asian	Native Hawaiian	Some other race	Two or more races	Hispanic or Latino (any race)
Evansville, Ind.	121,582	10.9%	0.2%	0.7%	-	0.5%	1.4%	1.1%
Fayetteville, N.C.	121,015	42.4	1.1	2.2	0.2%	2.5	2.8	5.7
Flint, Mich.	124,943	53.3	0.6	0.4	-	1.1	3.1	3.0
Fontana, Calif.	128,929	11.8	1.1	4.4	0.3	31.9	5.4	57.7
Fort Collins, Colo.	118,652	1.0	0.6	2.5	0.1	3.6	2.5	8.8
Fort Lauderdale, Fla.	152,397	28.9	0.2	1.0	-	1.8	3.8	9.5
Fort Wayne, Ind.	205,727	17.4	0.4	1.6	-	2.9	2.3	5.8
Fort Worth, Texas	534,694	20.3	0.6	2.6	0.1	14.0	2.7	29.8
Fremont, Calif.	203,413	3.1	0.5	37.0	0.4	5.5	5.8	13.5
Fresno, Calif.	427,652	8.4	1.6	11.2	0.1	23.4	5.2	39.9
Fullerton, Calif.	126,003	2.3	0.7	16.1	0.2	14.8	4.0	30.2
Garden Grove, Calif.	165,196	1.3	0.8	30.9	0.7	15.4	4.1	32.5
Garland, Texas	215,768	11.9	0.6	7.3	0.1	12.0	2.9	25.6
Gary, Ind.	102,746	84.0	0.2	0.1	-	2.0	1.7	4.9
Gilbert, Ariz.	109,697	2.4	0.6	3.6	0.1	4.8	2.8	11.9
Glendale, Ariz.	218,812	4.7	1.5	2.7	0.1	12.0	3.5	24.8
Glendale, Calif.	194,973	1.3	0.3	16.1	0.1	8.6	10.1	19.7
Grand Prairie, Texas	127,427	13.5	0.8	4.4	0.1	15.9	3.3	33.0
Grand Rapids, Mich.	197,800	20.4	0.7	1.6	0.1	6.6	3.2	13.1
Green Bay, Wisc.	102,313	1.4	3.3	3.8	-	3.7	2.0	7.1
Greensboro, N.C.	223,891	37.4	0.4	2.8	-	2.1	1.7	4.4
Hampton, Va.	146,437	44.7	0.4	1.8	0.1	1.0	2.4	2.8
Hartford, Conn.	121,578	38.1	0.5	1.6	0.1	26.5	5.4	40.5
Hayward, Calif.	140,030	11.0	0.8	19.0	1.9	16.8	7.5	34.2
Henderson, Nevada	175,381	3.8	0.7	4.0	0.4	3.2	3.5	10.7
Hialeah, Fla.	226,419	2.4	0.1	0.4	-	5.5	3.6	90.3
Hollywood, Fla.	139,357	12.1	0.3	2.0	0.1	4.0	3.3	22.5
Honolulu, Hawaii	371,657	1.6	0.2	55.9	6.8	0.9	14.9	4.4
Houston, Texas	1,953,631	25.3	0.4	5.3	0.1	16.5	3.1	37.4
Huntington Beach, Calif.	189,594	0.8	0.6	9.3	0.2	5.8	3.9	14.7
Huntsville, Ala.	158,216	30.2	0.5	2.2	0.1	0.7	1.8	2.0
Independence, Mo.	113,288	2.6	0.6	0.7	0.5	1.4	2.3	3.7
Indianapolis, Ind.	791,926	25.3	0.3	1.4	-	2.0	1.6	3.9
Inglewood, Calif.	112,580	47.1	0.7	1.1	0.4	27.4	4.2	46.0
Irvine, Calif.	143,072	1.4	0.2	29.8	0.1	2.5	4.8	7.4
Irving, Texas	191,615	10.2	0.6	8.2	0.1	13.4	3.2	31.2
Jackson, Miss.	184,256	70.6	0.1	0.6	-	0.2	0.7	0.8
Jacksonville, Fla.	735,617	29.0	0.3	2.8	0.1	1.3	2.0	4.2
Jersey City, N.J.	240,055	28.3	0.4	16.2	0.1	15.1	5.8	28.3
Joliet, Ill.	106,221	18.2	0.3	1.1	-	9.0	2.1	18.4
Kansas City, Kans.	146,866	30.1	0.8	1.7	-	8.6	3.0	16.8
Kansas City, Mo.	441,545	31.2	0.5	1.9	0.1	3.2	2.4	6.9
Knoxville, Tenn.	173,890	16.2	0.3	1.5	-	0.7	1.6	1.6
Lafayette, La.	110,257	28.5	0.2	1.4	-	0.6	1.0	1.9
Lakewood, Colo.	144,126	1.5	1.1	2.7	0.1	4.9	2.6	14.5
Lancaster, Calif.	118,718	16.0	1.0	3.8	0.2	11.1	5.0	24.1
Lansing, Mich.	119,128	21.9	0.8	2.8	0.1	4.5	4.6	10.0
Laredo, Texas	176,576	0.4	0.4	0.5	-	13.9	2.5	94.1
Las Vegas, Nevada	478,434	10.4	0.7	4.8	0.4	9.7	4.1	23.6
Lexington-Fayette, Ky.	260,512	13.5	0.2	2.5	-	1.2	1.6	3.3
Lincoln, Neb.	225,581	3.1	0.7	3.1	0.1	1.8	2.0	3.6
Little Rock, Ark.	183,133	40.4	0.3	1.7	-	1.3	1.3	2.7
Livonia, Mich.	100,545	0.9	0.2	1.9	-	0.3	1.1	1.7
Long Beach, Calif.	461,522	14.9	0.8	12.0	1.2	20.6	5.3	35.8
Los Angeles, Calif.	3,694,820	11.2	0.8	10.0	0.2	25.7	5.2	46.5
Louisville, Ky.	256,231	33.0	0.2	1.4	-	0.7	1.7	1.9
Lowell, Mass.	105,167	4.2	0.2	16.5	-	6.5	3.9	14.0
Lubbock, Texas	199,564	8.7	0.6	1.5	-	14.3	2.0	27.5
Madison, Wisc.	208,054	5.8	0.4	5.8	-	1.7	2.3	4.1
Manchester, N.H.	107,006	2.1	0.3	2.3	-	1.8	1.7	4.6
McAllen, Texas	106,414	0.6	0.4	1.9	-	15.8	2.7	80.3
Memphis, Tenn.	650,100	61.4	0.2	1.5	-	1.5	1.0	3.0
Mesa, Ariz.	396,375	2.5	1.7	1.5	0.2	9.7	2.8	19.7
Mesquite, Texas	124,523	13.3	0.6	3.7	0.1	6.4	2.3	15.7
Metairie, La.	146,136	6.8	0.3	2.8	-	1.9	1.7	7.3
Miami, Fla.	362,470	22.3	0.2	0.7	-	5.4	4.7	65.8
Milwaukee, Wisc.	596,974	37.3	0.9	2.9	0.1	6.1	2.7	12.0
Minneapolis, Minn.	382,618	18.0	2.2	6.1	0.1	4.1	4.4	7.6
Mobile, Ala.	198,915	46.3	0.2	1.5	-	0.5	1.0	1.4
Modesto, Calif.	188,856	4.0	1.2	6.0	0.5	12.7	5.9	25.6
Montgomery, Ala.	201,568	49.6	0.2	1.1	-	0.4	1.0	1.2

Geographic area	Total population	Black	American Indian	Asian	Native Hawaiian	Some other race	Two or more races	Hispanic or Latino (any race)
Moreno Valley, Calif.	142,381	19.9%	0.9%	5.9%	0.5%	20.1%	5.8%	38.4%
Naperville, Ill.	128,358	3.0	0.1	9.6	-	0.8	1.2	3.2
Nashville-Davidson, Tenn..	569,891	25.9	0.3	2.3	0.1	2.4	2.0	4.6
New Haven, Conn.	123,626	37.4	0.4	3.9	0.1	10.9	3.9	21.4
New Orleans, La.	484,674	67.3	0.2	2.3	-	0.9	1.3	3.1
New York, N.Y.	8,008,278	26.6	0.5	9.8	0.1	13.4	4.9	27.0
Bronx borough	1,332,650	35.6	0.9	3.0	0.1	24.7	5.8	48.4
Brooklyn borough	2,465,326	36.4	0.4	7.5	0.1	10.1	4.3	19.8
Manhattan borough	1,537,195	17.4	0.5	9.4	0.1	14.1	4.1	27.2
Queens borough	2,229,379	20.0	0.5	17.6	0.1	11.7	6.1	25.0
Staten Island borough	443,728	9.7	0.2	5.7	-	4.1	2.7	12.1
Newark, N.J.	273,546	53.5	0.4	1.2	-	14.0	4.4	29.5
Newport News, Va.	180,150	39.1	0.4	2.3	0.1	1.8	2.8	4.2
Norfolk, Va.	234,403	44.1	0.5	2.8	0.1	1.7	2.5	3.8
North Las Vegas, Nevada	115,488	19.0	0.8	3.2	0.5	15.8	4.7	37.6
Norwalk, Calif.	103,298	4.6	1.2	11.5	0.4	32.7	4.7	62.9
Oakland, Calif.	399,484	35.7	0.7	15.2	0.5	11.7	5.0	21.9
Oceanside, Calif.	161,029	6.3	0.9	5.5	1.3	14.5	5.2	30.2
Oklahoma City, Okla.	506,132	15.4	3.5	3.5	0.1	5.3	3.9	10.1
Omaha, Neb.	390,007	13.3	0.7	1.7	0.1	3.9	1.9	7.5
Ontario, Calif.	158,007	7.5	1.1	3.9	0.4	34.1	5.3	59.9
Orange, Calif.	128,821	1.6	0.8	9.3	0.2	13.8	3.8	32.2
Orlando, Fla.	185,951	26.9	0.3	2.7	0.1	5.4	3.5	17.5
Overland Park, Kans.	149,080	2.5	0.3	3.8	-	1.2	1.4	3.8
Oxnard, Calif.	170,358	3.8	1.3	7.4	0.4	40.4	4.7	66.2
Palmdale, Calif.	116,670	14.5	1.0	3.8	0.2	20.4	5.2	37.7
Paradise, Nevada	186,070	6.6	0.8	6.5	0.6	8.4	4.7	23.5
Pasadena, Calif.	133,936	14.4	0.7	10.0	0.1	16.0	5.4	33.4
Pasadena, Texas	141,674	1.6	0.7	1.8	-	21.3	3.1	48.2
Paterson, N.J.	149,222	32.9	0.6	1.9	0.1	27.6	6.2	50.1
Pembroke Pines, Fla.	137,427	13.3	0.2	3.8	-	3.7	3.5	28.2
Peoria, Ariz.	108,364	2.8	0.7	1.9	0.1	7.1	2.5	15.4
Peoria, Ill.	112,936	24.8	0.2	2.3	-	1.2	2.2	2.5
Philadelphia, Pa.	1,517,550	43.2	0.3	4.5	-	4.8	2.2	8.5
Phoenix, Ariz.	1,321,045	5.1	2.0	2.0	0.1	16.4	3.3	34.1
Pittsburgh, Pa.	334,563	27.1	0.2	2.7	-	0.7	1.6	1.3
Plano, Texas	222,030	5.0	0.4	10.2	-	3.9	2.3	10.1
Pomona, Calif.	149,473	9.6	1.3	7.2	0.2	34.9	5.0	64.5
Portland, Oreg.	529,121	6.6	1.1	6.3	0.4	3.5	4.1	6.8
Portsmouth, Va.	100,565	50.6	0.5	0.8	0.1	0.6	1.6	1.7
Providence, R.I.	173,618	14.5	1.1	6.0	0.2	17.6	6.1	30.0
Provo, Utah	105,166	0.5	0.8	1.8	0.8	5.1	2.4	10.5
Pueblo, Colo.	102,121	2.4	1.7	0.7	0.1	15.2	3.7	44.1
Raleigh, N.C.	276,093	27.8	0.4	3.4	-	3.2	1.9	7.0
Rancho Cucamonga, Calif.	127,743	7.9	0.7	6.0	0.3	13.3	5.4	27.8
Reno, Nevada	180,480	2.6	1.3	5.3	0.6	9.3	3.6	19.2
Richmond, Va.	197,790	57.2	0.2	1.2	0.1	1.5	1.5	2.6
Riverside, Calif.	255,166	7.4	1.1	5.7	0.4	21.0	5.1	38.1
Rochester, N.Y.	219,773	38.5	0.5	2.2	-	6.6	3.8	12.8
Rockford, Ill.	150,115	17.4	0.3	2.2	-	4.8	2.5	10.2
Sacramento, Calif.	407,018	15.5	1.3	16.6	0.9	11.0	6.4	21.6
Salem, Oreg.	136,924	1.3	1.5	2.4	0.5	7.9	3.4	14.6
Salinas, Calif.	151,060	3.3	1.3	6.2	0.3	38.7	5.1	64.1
Salt Lake City, Utah	181,743	1.9	1.3	3.6	1.9	8.5	3.5	18.8
San Antonio, Texas	1,144,646	6.8	0.8	1.6	0.1	19.3	3.7	58.7
San Bernardino, Calif.	185,401	16.4	1.4	4.2	0.4	27.1	5.3	47.5
San Diego, Calif.	1,223,400	7.9	0.6	13.6	0.5	12.4	4.8	25.4
San Francisco, Calif.	776,733	7.8	0.4	30.8	0.5	6.5	4.3	14.1
San Jose, Calif.	894,943	3.5	0.8	26.9	0.4	15.9	5.0	30.2
Santa Ana, Calif.	337,977	1.7	1.2	8.8	0.3	40.6	4.6	76.1
Santa Clara, Calif.	102,361	2.3	0.5	29.3	0.4	6.9	5.0	16.0
Santa Clarita, Calif.	151,088	2.1	0.6	5.2	0.1	8.5	3.9	20.5
Santa Rosa, Calif.	147,595	2.2	1.4	3.8	0.3	10.3	4.4	19.2
Savannah, Ga.	131,510	57.1	0.2	1.5	0.1	0.9	1.3	2.2
Scottsdale, Ariz.	202,705	1.2	0.6	2.0	0.1	2.3	1.7	7.0
Seattle, Wash.	563,374	8.4	1.0	13.1	0.5	2.4	4.5	5.3
Shreveport, La.	200,145	50.8	0.3	0.8	-	0.4	1.0	1.6
Simi Valley, Calif.	111,351	1.3	0.7	6.3	0.1	6.5	3.7	16.8
Sioux Falls S. Dak.	123,975	1.8	2.1	1.2	0.1	1.2	1.7	2.5
South Bend, Ind.	107,789	24.6	0.4	1.2	0.1	4.9	2.8	8.5
Spokane, Wash.	195,629	2.1	1.8	2.2	0.2	0.9	3.4	3.0

Geographic area	Total population	Black	American Indian	Asian	Native Hawaiian	Some other race	Two or more races	Hispanic or Latino (any race)
Spring Valley, Nevada	117,390	5.3%	0.6%	11.2%	0.5%	5.1%	4.7%	13.8%
Springfield, Ill.	111,454	15.3	0.2	1.5	-	0.5	1.5	1.2
Springfield, Mass.	152,082	21.0	0.4	1.9	0.1	16.4	4.0	27.2
Springfield, Mo.	151,580	3.3	0.8	1.4	0.1	0.9	2.0	2.3
St. Louis, Mo.	348,189	51.2	0.3	2.0	-	0.8	1.9	2.0
St. Paul, Minn.	287,151	11.7	1.1	12.4	0.1	3.8	3.9	7.9
St. Petersburg, Fla.	248,232	22.4	0.3	2.7	0.1	1.1	2.2	4.2
Stamford, Conn.	117,083	15.4	0.2	5.0	-	6.5	3.1	16.8
Sterling Heights, Mich.	124,471	1.3	0.2	4.9	-	0.3	2.5	1.3
Stockton, Calif.	243,771	11.2	1.1	19.9	0.4	17.3	6.8	32.5
Sunnyvale, Calif.	131,760	2.2	0.5	32.3	0.3	7.2	4.3	15.5
Sunrise Manor, Nevada	156,120	12.9	1.0	5.4	0.5	10.1	4.7	26.0
Syracuse, N.Y.	147,306	25.3	1.1	3.4	-	2.2	3.6	5.3
Tacoma, Wash.	193,556	11.2	2.0	7.6	0.9	2.9	6.3	6.9
Tallahassee, Fla.	150,624	34.2	0.2	2.4	0.1	1.0	1.7	4.2
Tampa, Fla.	303,447	26.1	0.4	2.2	0.1	4.2	2.9	19.3
Tempe, Ariz.	158,625	3.7	2.0	4.7	0.3	8.5	3.3	17.9
Thousand Oaks, Calif.	117,005	1.1	0.5	5.9	0.1	4.5	2.8	13.1
Toledo, Ohio	313,619	23.5	0.3	1.0	-	2.3	2.6	5.5
Topeka, Kans.	122,377	11.7	1.3	1.1	-	4.1	3.3	8.9
Torrance, Calif.	137,946	2.2	0.4	28.6	0.3	4.6	4.7	12.8
Tucson, Ariz.	486,699	4.3	2.3	2.5	0.2	16.8	3.8	35.7
Tulsa, Okla.	393,049	15.5	4.7	1.8	0.1	3.5	4.4	7.2
Vallejo, Calif.	116,760	23.7	0.7	24.2	1.1	7.9	6.6	15.9
Vancouver, Wash.	143,560	2.5	1.0	4.5	0.5	2.9	3.8	6.3
Ventura, Calif.	100,916	1.4	1.2	3.0	0.2	11.1	4.3	24.3
Virginia Beach, Va.	425,257	19.0	0.4	4.9	0.1	1.5	2.7	4.2
Waco, Texas	113,726	22.6	0.5	1.4	0.1	12.4	2.3	23.6
Warren, Mich.	138,247	2.7	0.4	3.1	-	0.3	2.2	1.4
Washington, D.C.	572,059	60.0	0.3	2.7	0.1	3.8	2.4	7.9
Waterbury, Conn.	107,271	16.3	0.4	1.5	0.1	10.9	3.7	21.8
West Covina, Calif.	105,080	6.4	0.8	22.7	0.2	21.2	4.9	45.7
West Valley City, Utah	108,896	1.1	1.2	4.3	2.9	8.7	3.5	18.5
Westminster, Colo.	100,940	1.2	0.7	5.5	0.1	5.5	2.8	15.2
Wichita Falls, Texas	104,197	12.4	0.9	2.2	0.1	6.4	3.0	14.0
Wichita, Kans.	344,284	11.4	1.2	4.0	0.1	5.1	3.1	9.6
Winston-Salem, N.C.	185,776	37.1	0.3	1.1	-	4.3	1.6	8.6
Worcester, Mass.	172,648	6.9	0.4	4.9	0.1	7.2	3.4	15.1
Yonkers, N.Y	196,086	16.6	0.4	4.9	-	13.4	4.4	25.9

Note: Black includes African-American. Native American includes Alaska Native. Native Hawaiian Includes other Pacific Islander. Cities with populations over 100,000 as of April 1, 2000. **Source:** U.S. Bureau of the Census, Press Release, 2001.

Population Change in the 75 Largest U.S. Cities, 1980–2000

City (2000 Rank)	Population			Percent change,	Change, 1990–2000	
	1980	1990	2000	1980–2000	Number	Percent
Albuquerque, N.Mex (35)	332,920	384,736	448,607	15.6%	63,871	16.6%
Anaheim, Calif. (56)	219,494	266,406	328,014	21.4	61,608	23.1
Anchorage, Alaska (66)	174,731	226,338	260,283	29.5	33,945	15.0
Arlington, Texas (54)	160,113	261,721	332,969	63.5	71,248	27.2
Atlanta, Ga. (40)	425,022	394,017	416,474	-7.3	22,457	5.7
Aurora, Colo. (62)	158,588	222,103	276,393	40.1	54,290	24.4
Austin, Texas (16)	345,890	465,622	656,562	34.6	190,940	41.0
Bakersfield, Calif. (70)	N.A.	174,820	247,057	N.A.	72,237	41.3
Baltimore, Md. (17)	786,741	736,014	651,154	-6.4	-84,860	-11.5
Baton Rouge, La. (75)	220,394	219,531	227,818	-0.4	8,287	3.8
Birmingham, Ala. (72)	284,413	265,968	242,820	-6.5	-23,148	-8.7
Boston, Mass. (20)	562,994	574,283	589,141	2.0	14,858	2.6
Buffalo, N.Y (59)	357,870	328,123	292,648	-8.3	-35,475	-10.8
Charlotte, N.C (26)	315,474	395,934	540,828	25.5	144,894	36.6
Chicago, Ill. (3)	3,005,072	2,783,726	2,896,016	-7.4	112,290	4.0
Cincinnati, Ohio (55)	385,409	364,040	331,285	-5.5	-32,755	-9.0
Cleveland, Ohio (33)	573,822	505,616	478,403	-11.9	-27,213	-5.4
Colorado Springs, Colo. (49)	215,105	281,140	360,890	30.7	79,750	28.4
Columbus, Ohio (15)	565,021	632,910	711,470	12.0	78,560	12.4

City (2000 Rank)	Population 1980	Population 1990	Population 2000	Percent change, 1980–2000	Change, 1990–2000 Number	Change, 1990–2000 Percent
Corpus Christi, Texas (61)	232,134	257,453	277,454	10.9%	20,001	7.8%
Dallas, Texas (8)	904,599	1,006,877	1,188,580	11.3	181,703	18.0
Denver, Colo. (25)	492,686	467,610	554,636	-5.1	87,026	18.6
Detroit, Mich. (10)	1,203,368	1,027,974	951,270	-14.6	-76,704	-7.5
El Paso, Texas (23)	425,259	515,342	563,662	21.2	48,320	9.4
Fort Worth, Texas (27)	385,164	447,619	534,694	16.2	87,075	19.5
Fresno, Calif. (37)	217,491	354,202	427,652	62.9	73,450	20.7
Honolulu, Hawaii. (47)	365,048	365,272	371,657	0.1	6,385	1.7
Houston, Texas (4)	1,595,138	1,630,553	1,953,631	2.2	323,078	19.8
Indianapolis, Ind. (12)	711,539	741,952	791,926	4.3	49,974	6.7
Jacksonville, Fla. (14)	571,003	635,230	735,617	17.9	100,387	15.8
Jersey City, N.J. (73)	223,532	228,537	240,055	2.2	11,518	5.0
Kansas City, Mo. (36)	448,028	435,146	441,545	-2.9	6,399	1.5
Las Vegas, Nev. (32)	164,674	258,295	478,434	56.9	220,139	85.2
Lexington-Fayette, Ky. (65)	204,165	225,366	260,512	10.4	35,146	15.6
Long Beach, Calif. (34)	361,498	429,433	461,522	18.8	32,089	7.5
Los Angeles, Calif. (2)	2,968,528	3,485,557	3,694,820	17.4	209,422	6.0
Louisville, Ky. (67)	298,694	269,063	256,231	-9.9	-12,832	-4.8
Memphis, Tenn. (18)	646,174	610,337	650,100	-5.5	39,763	6.5
Mesa, Ariz. (43)	152,404	288,091	396,375	89.0	108,284	37.6
Miami, Fla. (48)	346,681	358,548	362,470	3.4	3,922	1.1
Milwaukee, Wis. (19)	636,297	628,088	596,974	-1.3	-31,114	-5.0
Minneapolis, Minn. (46)	370,951	368,383	382,618	-0.7	14,235	3.9
Nashville, Tenn. (22)	477,811	510,784	569,891	6.9	59,107	11.6
New Orleans, La. (31)	557,927	496,938	484,674	-10.9	-12,264	-2.5
New York, N.Y. (1)	7,071,639	7,322,564	8,008,278	3.5	685,714	9.4
Newark, N.J. (64)	329,248	275,221	273,546	-16.4	-1,675	-0.6
Norfolk, Va. (74)	266,979	261,229	234,403	-2.2	-26,826	-10.3
Oakland, Calif. (42)	339,337	372,242	399,484	9.7	27,242	7.3
Oklahoma City, Okla. (29)	404,014	444,719	506,132	10.1	61,413	13.8
Omaha, Nebr. (45)	313,939	335,795	390,007	7.0	54,212	16.1
Philadelphia, Pa. (5)	1,688,210	1,585,577	1,517,550	-6.1	-68,027	-4.3
Phoenix, Ariz. (6)	789,704	983,403	1,321,045	24.5	337,642	34.3
Pittsburgh, Pa. (53)	423,959	369,879	334,563	-12.8	-35,316	-9.5
Portland, Oreg. (28)	368,148	437,319	529,121	18.8	91,802	21.0
Raleigh, N.C. (63)	150,255	207,951	276,093	38.4	68,142	32.8
Riverside, Calif. (68)	170,591	226,505	255,166	32.8	28,661	12.7
Sacramento, Calif. (41)	275,741	369,365	407,018	34.0	37,653	10.2
San Antonio, Texas (9)	785,940	935,933	1,144,646	19.1	208,713	22.3
San Diego, Calif. (7)	875,538	1,110,549	1,223,400	26.8	112,851	10.2
San Francisco, Calif. (13)	678,974	723,959	776,733	6.6	52,774	7.3
San Jose, Calif. (11)	629,400	782,248	894,943	24.3	112,695	14.4
San Juan, Puerto Rico (39)	N.A.	426,832	421,958	N.A.	-4,874	-1.1
Santa Ana, Calif. (52)	204,023	293,742	337,977	44.0	44,235	15.1
Seattle, Wash. (24)	493,846	516,259	563,374	4.5	47,115	9.1
St. Louis, Mo. (50)	452,801	396,685	348,189	-12.4	-48,496	-12.2
St. Paul, Minn. (60)	270,320	272,235	287,151	0.7	14,916	5.5
St. Petersburg, Fla. (69)	238,647	238,629	248,232	-0.0	9,603	4.0
Stockton, Calif. (71)	148,283	210,943	243,771	42.3	32,828	15.6
Tampa, Fla. (58)	271,577	280,015	303,447	3.1	23,432	8.4
Toledo, Ohio (57)	354,635	332,943	313,619	-6.1	-19,324	-5.8
Tucson, Ariz. (30)	330,537	405,390	486,699	22.6	81,309	20.1
Tulsa, Okla. (44)	360,919	367,302	393,049	1.8	25,747	7.0
Virginia Beach, Va. (38)	262,199	393,069	425,257	49.9	32,188	8.2
Washington, D.C (21)	638,432	606,900	572,059	-4.9	-34,841	-5.7
Wichita, Kans. (51)	279,838	304,011	344,284	8.6	40,273	13.2

Source: U.S. Bureau of the Census, 2000.

Population of the 50 Largest Cities, 1950–2000

2000 Rank, City	1950	1960	1970[1]	1980[1]	1990	2000	Population change, 1990–2000
1. New York, N.Y.	7,891,957	7,781,984	7,896,000	7,072,000	7,322,564	8,008,278	685,714
2. Los Angeles, Calif.	1,970,358	2,479,015	2,812,000	2,969,000	3,485,557	3,694,820	209,422
3. Chicago, Ill.	3,620,962	3,550,404	3,369,000	3,005,000	2,783,726	2,896,016	112,290
4. Houston, Texas	596,163	938,219	1,234,000	1,595,000	1,630,864	1,953,631	323,078
5. Philadelphia, Pa.	2,071,605	2,002,512	1,949,000	1,688,000	1,585,577	1,517,550	-68,027
6. Phoenix, Ariz.	(2)	439,170	584,000	790,000	984,309	1,321,045	337,642
7. San Diego, Calif.	334,387	573,224	697,000	876,000	1,110,623	1,223,400	112,851
8. Dallas, Texas	434,462	679,684	844,000	905,000	1,007,618	1,188,580	181,703
9. San Antonio, Texas	408,442	587,718	654,000	786,000	935,393	1,144,646	208,713
10. Detroit, Mich.	1,849,568	1,670,144	1,514,000	1,203,000	1,027,974	951,270	-76,704
11. San Jose, Calif.	(2)	(2)	460,000	629,000	782,224	894,943	112,695
12. Indianapolis, Ind.[3]	427,173	476,258	737,000	701,000	731,278	791,926	49,974
13. San Francisco, Calif.	775,357	742,855	716,000	679,000	723,959	776,733	52,774
14. Jacksonville, Fla.[3]	204,517	(2)	504,000	541,000	635,230	735,617	100,387
15. Columbus, Ohio	375,901	471,316	540,000	565,000	632,945	711,470	78,560
16. Austin, Texas	(2)	(2)	254,000	346,000	472,020	656,562	190,940
17. Baltimore, Md.	949,708	939,024	905,000	787,000	736,014	651,154	-84,860
18. Memphis, Tenn.	396,000	497,524	624,000	646,000	618,652	650,100	39,763
19. Milwaukee, Wisc.	637,392	741,324	717,000	636,000	628,088	596,974	-31,114
20. Boston, Mass.	801,444	697,197	641,000	563,000	574,283	589,141	14,858
21. Washington, D.C.	802,178	763,956	757,000	638,000	606,900	572,059	-34,841
22. Nashville, Tenn.[3]	(2)	(2)	426,000	456,000	488,366	569,891	59,107
23. El Paso, Texas	(2)	276,687	322,000	425,000	515,342	563,662	48,320
24. Seattle, Wash.	467,591	557,087	531,000	494,000	516,259	563,374	47,115
25. Denver, Colo.	415,786	493,887	515,000	493,000	467,610	554,636	87,026
26. Charlotte, N.C.	(2)	(2)	241,000	315,000	419,558	540,828	144,894
27. Fort Worth, Texas	278,778	356,268	393,000	385,000	447,619	534,694	87,075
28. Portland, Oreg.	373,628	372,676	380,000	368,000	485,975	529,121	91,802
29. Oklahoma City, Okla.	243,504	324,253	368,000	404,000	444,724	506,132	61,413
30. Tucson, Ariz.	(2)	(2)	263,000	331,000	415,444	486,699	81,309
31. New Orleans, La.	570,445	627,525	593,000	558,000	496,938	484,674	-12,264
32. Las Vegas, Nev.	(2)	(2)	(2)	(2)	258,295	478,434	220,139
33. Cleveland, Ohio	914,808	876,050	751,000	574,000	505,616	478,403	-27,213
34. Long Beach, Calif.	250,767	344,168	359,000	361,000	429,321	461,522	32,089
35. Albuquerque, N.Mex.	(2)	(2)	245,000	332,000	384,619	448,607	63,871
36. Kansas City, Mo.	456,622	475,539	507,000	448,000	434,829	441,545	6,399
37. Fresno, Calif.	(2)	(2)	166,000	217,000	354,091	427,652	73,450
38. Virginia Beach, Va.	(2)	(2)	172,000	262,000	393,089	425,257	32,188
39. Atlanta, Ga.	332,314	487,455	495,000	425,000	394,017	416,474	22,457
40. Sacramento, Calif.	(2)	(2)	257,000	276,000	369,365	407,018	37,653
41. Oakland, Calif.	384,575	367,548	362,000	339,000	372,242	399,484	27,472
42. Mesa, Ariz.	(2)	(2)	(2)	(2)	288,091	396,375	108,284
43. Tulsa, Okla.	(2)	261,685	330,000	361,000	367,302	393,049	25,747
44. Omaha, Neb.	251,117	301,598	347,000	314,000	335,795	390,007	54,212
45. Minneapolis, Minn.	521,718	482,872	434,000	371,000	368,383	382,618	14,235
46. Honolulu, Hawaii[4]	248,034	294,194	325,000	365,000	365,272	371,657	6,385
47. Miami, Fla.	249,276	291,688	335,000	347,000	358,548	362,470	3,922
48. Colorado Springs, Colo.	(2)	(2)	(2)	(2)	281,140	360,890	79,750
49. St. Louis, Mo.	856,796	750,026	622,000	453,000	396,685	348,189	-48,496
50. Wichita, Kans.	(2)	(2)	(2)	279,838	304,011	344,284	40,273

Note: 1. Figure rounded in source. 2. City was not one of the 50 largest that year. 3. City is part of a consolidated city-county government; populations of the other incorporated places in the county have been excluded from the population totals shown here. 4. Not incorporated as a city, but recognized for census purposes as large urban places. Honolulu CDP is coextensive with Honolulu Judicial District within the City and County of Honolulu. **Source:** U.S. Bureau of the Census, 2001

25 Fastest-Growing Major Cities in the U.S., 1990–2000

City	Population 1990	Population 2000	Change, 1990–2000 Number	Change, 1990–2000 Percent	Overall rank, 2000
1. Augusta, Ga.	44,639	199,775	155,136	347.5%	91
2. Gilbert, Ariz.	29,188	109,697	80,509	275.8	208
3. Vancouver, Wash.	46,380	143,560	97,180	209.5	149
4. Henderson, Nev.	64,942	175,381	110,439	170.1	118
5. North Las Vegas, Nev.	47,707	115,488	67,781	142.1	198
6. Athens, Ga.	45,734	101,489	55,755	121.9	237
7. Peoria, Ariz.	50,618	108,364	57,746	114.1	214
8. Pembroke Pines, Fla.	65,452	137,427	71,975	110.0	161
9. Chandler, Ariz.	90,533	176,581	86,048	95.0	116
10. Las Vegas, Nevada	258,295	478,434	220,139	85.2	32
11. Plano, Texas	128,713	222,030	93,317	72.5	79
12. Palmdale, Calif.	68,842	116,670	47,828	69.5	194
13. Corona, Calif.	76,095	124,966	48,871	64.2	174
14. Fayetteville, N.C.	75,695	121,015	45,320	59.9	184
15. Scottsdale, Ariz.	130,069	202,705	72,636	55.8	88
16. Naperville, Ill.	85,351	128,358	43,007	50.4	169
17. Coral Springs, Fla.	79,443	117,549	38,106	48.0	190
18. Boise City, Idaho	125,738	185,787	60,049	47.8	108
19. Glendale, Ariz.	148,134	218,812	70,678	47.7	81
20. Fontana, Calif.	87,535	128,929	41,394	47.3	167
21. Laredo, Texas	122,899	176,576	53,677	43.7	117
22. Aurora, Ill.	99,581	142,990	43,409	43.6	151
23. Bakersfield, Calif.	174,820	247,057	72,237	41.3	70
24. Brownsville, Texas	98,962	139,722	40,760	41.2	155
25. Austin, Texas	465,622	656,562	190,940	41.0	16

Note: Cities over 100,000 population. **Source:** U.S. Bureau of the Census.

25 Fastest-Declining Major U.S. Cities, 1990–2000

City	Population 1990	Population 2000	Change, 1990–2000 Number	Change, 1990–2000 Percent	Overall rank, 2000
1. Hartford, Conn.	139,739	121,578	-18,161	-13.0%	183
2. St. Louis, Miss.	396,685	348,189	-48,496	-12.2	50
3. Gary, Ind.	116,646	102,746	-13,900	-11.9	230
4. Baltimore, Md.	736,014	651,154	-84,860	-11.5	17
5. Flint, Mich.	140,761	124,943	-15,818	-11.2	175
6. Buffalo, N.Y.	328,123	292,648	-35,475	-10.8	59
7. Norfolk, Va.	261,229	234,403	-26,826	-10.3	74
8. Syracuse, N.Y.	163,860	147,306	-16,554	-10.1	145
9. Pittsburgh, Penn.	369,879	334,563	-35,316	-9.5	53
10. Cincinnati, Ohio	364,040	331,285	-32,755	-9.0	55
11. Dayton, Ohio	182,044	166,179	-15,865	-8.7	126
12. Birmingham, Ala.	265,968	242,820	-23,148	-8.7	72
13. Detroit, Mich.	1,027,974	951,270	-76,704	-7.5	10
14. Lansing, Mich.	127,321	119,128	-8,193	-6.4	187
15. Jackson, Miss.	196,637	184,256	-12,381	-6.3	111
16. Toledo, Ohio	332,943	313,619	-19,324	-5.8	57
17. Washington, D.C.	606,900	572,059	-34,841	-5.7	21
18. Cleveland, Ohio	505,616	478,403	-27,213	-5.4	33
19. New Haven, Conn.	130,474	123,626	-6,848	-5.2	179
20. Rochester, N.Y.	231,636	219,773	-11,863	-5.1	80
21. Milwaukee, Wis.	628,088	596,974	-31,114	-5.0	19
22. Louisville, Ky.	269,063	256,231	-12,832	-4.8	67
23. Erie, Penn.	108,718	103,717	-5,001	-4.6	226
24. Warren, Mich.	144,864	138,247	-6,617	-4.6	158
25. Savannah, Ga.	137,560	131,510	-6,050	-4.4	166

Note: Cities over 100,000 population. **Source:** U.S. Bureau of the Census.

CITY FINANCES

▶TAX BURDENS AND PROGRESSIVITY IN MAJOR U.S. CITIES

Tax rates differ widely not only from state to state and city to city, but also from one income level to another. Any tax system in which the percentage of taxes paid rises with the income level is said to be *progressive*. A system where the percentage tax burden is the same at all income levels is said to be *proportional*. And a system in which the percentage of taxes paid decreases as income rises is said to be *regressive*. Because progressivity is measured as the ratio of one tax rate to another, progressivity does not necessarily reflect the actual tax burden.

State and Local Taxes for Families by Income Level in Selected Cities, 2002

City	$25,000		$50,000		$75,000		$100,000	
	Percent[1]	Amount	Percent[1]	Amount	Percent[1]	Amount	Percent[1]	Amount
Albuquerque, N.Mex.	5.9%	$1,482	7.4%	$3,721	8.5%	$6,389	8.9%	$8,934
Anchorage, Alaska	4.7	1,164	4.3	2,144	4.3	3,243	4.1	4,073
Atlanta, Ga.	8.1	2,035	10.3	5,137	11.4	8,514	11.5	11,550
Baltimore, Md.	7.1	1,776	11.2	5,615	11.9	8,962	11.9	11,904
Billings, Mont.	5.2	1,303	6.1	3,025	7.5	5,648	8.1	8,114
Birmingham, Ala.	8.9	2,228	8.5	4,274	8.6	6,452	8.4	8,427
Boise City, Idaho	4.4	1,101	7.2	3,576	9.2	6,881	9.6	9,621
Boston, Mass.	7.1	1,763	9.0	4,496	9.6	7,189	9.5	9,520
Bridgeport, Conn.	15.3	3,814	14.8	7,389	17.2	12,919	17.3	17,297
Burlington, Vt.	7.7	1,919	9.1	4,539	9.5	7,088	9.9	9,877
Charleston, W.Va.	6.5	1,625	7.1	3,538	8.0	6,031	8.4	8,435
Charlotte, N.C.	7.3	1,836	8.9	4,457	9.9	7,413	10.3	10,279
Cheyenne, Wyo.	3.7	927	3.4	1,685	3.5	2,644	3.4	3,393
Chicago, Ill.	9.3	2,320	9.5	4,734	10.0	7,489	9.7	9,655
Columbia, S.C.	5.6	1,398	8.2	4,116	9.5	7,088	9.9	9,882
Columbus, Ohio	8.3	2,064	9.1	4,544	9.9	7,391	10.2	10,185
Denver, Colo.	5.2	1,309	6.7	3,347	7.5	5,656	7.5	7,534
Des Moines, Iowa	7.5	1,871	9.1	4,525	10.1	7,558	10.4	10,409
Detroit, Mich.	8.5	2,114	9.3	4,656	9.8	7,362	11.0	11,036
Fargo, N. Dak.	6.8	1,693	6.9	3,468	7.2	5,403	7.3	7,314
Honolulu, Hawaii	7.1	1,763	8.0	3,999	8.9	6,668	9.0	9,037
Houston, Tex.	6.2	1,562	6.0	3,020	6.3	4,698	5.9	5,937
Indianapolis, Ind.	7.2	1,798	7.6	3,786	7.9	5,896	7.8	7,753
Jackson, Miss.	6.1	1,537	7.7	3,834	8.6	6,472	9.1	9,050
Jacksonville, Fla.	4.3	1,070	4.6	2,309	5.0	3,758	4.8	4,817
Kansas City, Mo.	7.2	1,791	8.6	4,275	9.1	6,808	9.1	9,125
Las Vegas, Nev.	5.9	1,487	5.2	2,595	5.2	3,928	4.9	4,911
Little Rock, Ark.	7.6	1,905	8.4	4,200	9.2	6,885	9.4	9,419
Los Angeles, Calif.	8.6	2,154	8.7	4,354	10.3	7,705	11.2	11,246
Louisville, Ky.	8.8	2,207	10.1	5,066	10.6	7,984	10.8	10,751
Manchester, N.H.	7.0	1,748	6.4	3,224	6.5	4,893	6.2	6,192
Memphis, Tenn.	6.8	1,699	6.1	3,063	6.2	4,656	5.8	5,847
Milwaukee, Wis.	7.7	1,935	10.4	5,189	11.4	8,562	11.5	11,466
Minneapolis, Minn.	5.6	1,412	8.5	4,249	9.0	6,767	9.8	9,756
New Orleans, La.	4.6	1,138	7.2	3,578	8.2	6,148	8.2	8,205
New York, N.Y.	5.6	1,408	10.8	5,400	12.7	9,546	13.4	13,398
Newark, N.J.	14.7	3,682	14.1	7,069	14.4	10,808	14.1	14,125
Oklahoma City, Okla.	7.3	1,825	8.3	4,129	9.1	6,858	8.9	8,891
Omaha, Nebr.	7.2	1,788	8.3	4,152	9.5	7,110	9.8	9,790
Philadelphia, Pa.	11.0	2,760	13.2	6,581	13.0	9,763	12.6	12,629
Phoenix, Ariz.	6.7	1,676	7.6	3,820	7.6	5,733	8.5	8,506
Portland, Maine	7.0	1,758	9.3	4,674	10.9	8,163	11.3	11,295
Portland, Oreg.	9.0	2,241	10.2	5,095	11.0	8,220	11.1	11,112
Providence, R.I.	8.6	2,152	10.4	5,221	10.6	7,917	11.5	11,511
Salt Lake City, Utah	6.9	1,733	9.1	4,544	9.7	7,304	9.6	9,637
Seattle, Wash.	7.4	1,841	6.7	3,355	6.8	5,077	6.4	6,366
Sioux Falls, S.Dak.	5.8	1,462	5.3	2,640	5.3	4,002	5.0	5,006
Virginia Beach, Va.	7.2	1,795	7.9	3,958	8.4	6,336	8.5	8,490
Washington, D.C.	6.5	1,632	9.3	4,631	10.4	7,797	10.7	10,702
Wichita, Kans.	4.2	1,041	6.5	3,275	7.7	5,802	8.2	8,187
Wilmington, Del.	5.7	1,414	7.1	3,547	7.8	5,876	8.0	8,007
51 city average[2]	**7.1%**	**$1,787**	**8.3%**	**$4,153**	**9.0%**	**$6,774**	**9.2%**	**$9,188**

Note: Tax burdens computed for a family of four. The four major taxes compared are the individual income tax, real property taxes on residential property, general sales and use taxes, and various automobile taxes, including the gasoline tax, registration fees, excise taxes, and personal property taxes. 1. Percentage of income. 2. Average of the largest city in each state plus the District of Columbia.
Source: Government of the District of Columbia, Dept. of Finance and Revenue, *Tax Rates and Tax Burdens in the District of Columbia: A Nationwide Comparison* (2003).

Several factors contribute to the progressivity of a tax system. A graduated individual income tax rate combined with exemptions and credits to lessen the regressiveness of the property tax will increase the progressivity of a tax system. Progressivity can be lessened by a lack of an individual income tax as well as by reliance on regressive taxes such as the sales tax and certain automobile taxes. The upper and lower income levels chosen for comparison also affect progressiveness.

Tax Progressivity of U.S. Cities, 2002

Most progressive	Index	Least progressive	Index
New York City, N.Y.	0.399	Las Vegas, Nev.	1.309
Boise City, Idaho	0.440	Sioux Falls, S.Dak.	1.259
Wichita, Kans.	0.488	Seattle, Wash.	1.241
New Orleans, La.	0.537	Memphis, Tenn.	1.236
Columbia, S.C.	0.548	Anchorage, Alaska	1.222
Average progressivity[1]			**0.809**

Note: An index coefficient of less than 1.000 indicates a progressive tax system; an index coefficient of greater than one indicates a regressive tax system. A proportional system is indicated by a coefficient of 1.000. 1. The average of the largest city in each state plus the District of Columbia. **Source:** Government of the District of Columbia, *Tax Rates and Tax Burdens in the District of Columbia:* (2003).

20 Best-Paid U.S. Mayors, 2002

Rank, Mayor	City	Salary
1. Richard M. Daley	Chicago	$170,000
2. Michael R. Bloomberg	New York	165,000
3. Lee P. Brown	Houston	160,500
4. Kwame Kilpatrick	Detroit	157,300
5. James K.Hahn	Los Angeles	147,390
6. Sharpe James	Newark, N.J.	147,000
7. Willie L. Brown Jr.	San Francisco	146,891
8. John F. Street	Philadelphia	135,000
9. John A. Delaney	Jacksonville	127,230
10. Greg Nickels	Seattle	126,616
11. Martin O'Malley	Baltimore	125,000
11. Thomas M. Menino	Boston	125,000
13. John O. Norquist	Milwaukee	115,851
14. John Spencer	Yonkers, N.Y.	115,000
15. Willie W. Herenton	Memphis	110,000
15. Dick A. Greco	Tampa, Fla.	110,000
15. Victor H. Ashe	Knoxville, Tenn.	110,000
18. Michael B. Coleman	Columbus, Ohio	107,087
19. Wellington E. Webb	Denver	103,056
20. William A. Johnson Jr.	Rochester, N.Y	102,678

Note: This table is based on information submitted by the cities and therefore is unable to rank mayor's salaries for cities that did not voluntarily provide it. **Source:** U.S. Conference of Mayors.

The Cost of Living Index in Selected U.S. Cities, 2002

Urban area	Composite index (100%)	Grocery items (16%)	Housing (28%)	Utilities (8%)	Trans-portation (10%)	Health care (5%)	Misc. goods & services (33%)
Atlanta, Ga.	**100.1**	102.4	103.1	88.9	103.3	102.3	98.0
Baltimore, Md.	**94.2**	91.5	89.1	105.7	98.4	92.7	96.0
Boston, Mass.	**146.2**	111.6	210.7	164.7	120.7	133.7	113.5
Charlotte, N.C.	**96.0**	100.8	90.7	88.6	101.2	94.2	98.7
Chicago, Ill.	**147.2**	118.5	233.1	108.8	120.3	132.0	107.8
Cincinnati, Ohio	**96.8**	97.7	90.6	114.8	92.5	90.2	99.7
Cleveland, Ohio	**106.2**	108.1	102.4	134.1	107.9	111.1	100.4
Dallas, Texas	**98.6**	98.9	93.3	99.2	102.5	99.4	101.6
Denver, Colo.	**107.4**	109.9	117.7	86.5	109.4	123.2	99.7
Detroit, Mich.	**106.8**	107.4	123.2	93.2	100.7	114.1	96.6
Fort Worth, Texas	**95.2**	93.9	92.5	95.6	103.5	91.1	96.2
Houston, Texas	**94.2**	91.1	81.9	108.6	105.4	105.9	97.4
Indianapolis, Ind.	**95.7**	94.7	93.2	108.2	94.8	95.7	95.5
Kansas, City, Mo.	**98.5**	98.6	94.2	94.5	101.3	102.1	101.8
Los Angeles-Long, Beach, Calif.	**138.0**	111.8	210.3	101.9	108.8	114.3	110.4
Memphis, Tenn.	**88.4**	91.4	81.8	78.3	97.3	87.6	92.4
Miami/Dade County, Fla.	**104.0**	102.7	95.3	112.0	112.8	122.2	104.5
Milwaukee, Wisc.	**101.7**	97.0	110.9	99.5	102.2	95.6	97.6
Minneapolis, Minn.	**109.4**	99.3	115.9	100.7	112.2	120.4	108.5
New Orleans, La.	**99.0**	100.9	92.6	112.8	105.0	101.7	98.1
New York (Manhattan), N.Y.	**228.2**	143.2	449.8	154.5	120.5	176.9	139.5
Orlando, Fla.	**98.3**	101.9	87.3	105.5	94.8	102.6	104.4
Philadelphia, Pa.	**119.5**	108.6	134.0	126.0	119.2	97.5	114.3
Phoenix, Ariz.	**99.2**	101.6	93.8	93.8	107.1	113.0	99.5
Pittsburgh, Pa.	**99.8**	102.8	89.2	132.2	104.7	89.0	99.7
Portland, Oreg.	**103.2**	107.9	92.1	93.7	114.8	116.1	107.0
Sacramento, Calif.	**118.6**	122.2	124.7	122.9	117.2	146.6	106.8
San Antonio, Texas	**89.7**	88.3	85.9	78.6	77.3	98.3	98.6
San Diego, Calif.	**128.0**	122.5	162.2	108.9	121.8	128.3	108.0
San Francisco, Calif.	**182.5**	121.9	343.8	103.9	136.1	154.9	112.4
Seattle, Wash.	**115.4**	114.1	138.9	82.3	114.3	126.3	102.7
St. Louis, Mo.	**98.8**	92.8	94.4	100.0	105.6	103.0	102.4
Tampa, Fla.	**97.5**	100.0	95.1	88.9	103.2	101.2	98.2
Washington, DC	**125.7**	116.4	153.5	104.7	120.5	121.1	114.1

Note: : Metropolitan areas with more than 1.5 million population. Percentage figures in parentheses show relative weight of component indexes used in calculating composite cost of living index. Figures are averages for second quarter 2001 through first quarter 2002. **Source:** *ACCRA Cost of Living Index* (2002).

METROPOLITAN STATISTICAL AREAS (MSAs)

Because population patterns don't conform strictly to city boundaries, statisticians have devised a way of measuring city populations to include people who live around an urban area but whose address is outside the city limits. Known as Metropolitan Statistical Areas (or MSAs), these measures give a much more accurate reflection of how many people actually live in the area than do city population figures. For example, the city of Boston is relatively small: just 589,000 people lived in Boston proper, according to the 2000 Census, making it the 20th-largest city in America. But the Boston metropolitan area, which includes suburbs ranging from Rhode Island to New Hampshire, is the seventh-largest in the country, with a total population of 5.5 million within an hour's commute of the Hub. On the other hand, the population of San Diego proper was more than 1.2 million in 2000, making it the seventh-largest city in the U.S., but the entire San Diego metro area was only 2.8 million, or 17th-largest in the country.

The United States Office of Management and Budget (OMB) first defined metropolitan areas in 1949, subsequently changed the designation to "standard metropolitan area," "standard metropolitan statistical area," and finally "metropolitan statistical area" in 1983.

Defining MSAS, CMSAs, and PMSAs

Currently, the OMB distinguishes between MSAs, consolidated metropolitan statistical areas (CMSAs), and primary metropolitan statistical areas (PMSAs).

Metropolitan Statistical Areas (MSAs) are defined as an area that includes at least one city with 50,000 or more inhabitants, or a Census Bureau-defined urbanized area (of at least 50,000 inhabitants) and a total metropolitan population of at least 100,000. An MSA includes the county in which the central city is located plus any adjacent counties in which at least 50 percent of the population lives in the urbanized area. Additional "outlying counties" are included in the MSA if they meet specified requirements of commuting to the central counties and other selected requirements of metropolitan character (such as population density and percent urban). In New England, MSAs are defined in terms of cities and towns rather than counties.

Consolidated Metropolitan Statistical Areas (PMSAs) are defined as MSAs with populations of one million or more that also contain separate component areas that can each be identified as smaller urban areas, or *Primary Metropolitan Statistical Areas (PMSAs)*. For example, the New York CMSA includes the Primary MSAs of Nassau and Suffolk Counties on Long Island, Bergen and Passaic Counties in Northern New Jersey, and Bridgeport and Milford Counties in Connecticut. PMSAs, like the CMSAs that contain them, are composed of entire counties, except in New England where they are composed of cities and towns.

The 2000 Census counted 280 MSAs in the U.S (down from 284 in 1990), including 20 CMSAs. Although MSAs take up only about 16 percent of the country's land area, they are home to more than 75 percent of all Americans.

According to the 2000 Census, the U.S. population living in all metropolitan areas totaled 229,192,836, an increase of more than 36 million people (19.3 percent) since 1990. That's a significant increase over the previous decade, when MSAs grew by only 11.6 percent. The 1950 Census indicated that there were 14 metropolitan areas of at least one million population; these areas had a combined population of about 45 million people, or less than 30 percent of the national total. By the 1990 Census, the number of MSAs with a million people had grown to 39, with a combined population of 124.8 million people, or 50.2 percent of the U.S. total. By 2000, there were an even 50 MSAs with more than a million people, with a total population of 164.0 million people, or 58.2 percent of the national total.

Population of Metropolitan Statistical Areas, 1990–2000

Metropolitan Statistical Area	1990	2000	Change 1990–2000 Number	Change 1990–2000 Percent	CMSA/MSA rank 1990	CMSA/MSA rank 2000
Abilene, Tex. MSA	119,655	126,555	6,900	5.8%	235	230
Aguadilla, P.R. MSA	128,172	146,424	18,252	14.2	N.A.	210
Albany, Ga. MSA	112,561	120,822	8,261	7.3	248	238
Albany-Schenectady-Troy, N.Y. MSA	861,424	875,583	14,159	1.6	48	57
Albuquerque, N.Mex. MSA	589,131	712,738	123,607	21.0	77	62
Alexandria, La. MSA	131,556	126,337	-5,219	-4.0	210	231
Allentown-Bethlehem-Easton, Pa. MSA	595,081	637,958	42,877	7.2	58	66
Altoona, Pa. MSA	130,542	129,144	-1,398	-1.1	219	226
Amarillo, Tex. MSA	187,547	217,858	30,311	16.2	164	160
Anchorage, Alaska MSA	226,338	260,283	33,945	15.0	143	140
Anniston, Ala. MSA	116,034	112,249	-3,785	-3.3	241	249
Appleton-Oshkosh-Neenah, Wis. MSA	315,121	358,365	43,244	13.7	114	117
Asheville, N.C. MSA	191,774	225,965	34,191	17.8	171	157
Athens, Ga. MSA	126,262	153,444	27,182	21.5	182	198
Atlanta, Ga. MSA	2,959,950	4,112,198	1,152,248	38.9	12	11
Auburn-Opelika, Ala. MSA	87,146	115,092	27,946	32.1	N.A.	244
Augusta-Aiken, Ga.-S.C. MSA	395,065	477,441	62,257	15.0	91	87
Austin-San Marcos, Tex. MSA	846,227	1,249,763	403,536	47.7	52	38
Bakersfield, Calif. MSA	543,477	661,645	118,168	21.7	68	65

Metropolitan Statistical Area	1990	2000	Change 1990–2000 Number	Change 1990–2000 Percent	CMSA/MSA rank 1990	CMSA/MSA rank 2000
Baton Rouge, La. MSA	528,264	602,894	74,630	14.1%	71	70
Bangor, Maine MSA	91,629	90,864	-765	-0.8	268	267
Beaumont-Port Arthur, Tex. MSA	361,226	385,090	23,864	6.6	102	107
Bellingham, Wash. MSA	127,780	166,814	39,034	30.5	221	188
Benton Harbor, Mich. MSA	161,378	162,453	1,075	0.7	177	192
Billings, Mont. MSA	113,419	129,352	15,933	14.0	246	225
Biloxi-Gulfport-Pascagoula, Miss. MSA	312,368	363,988	51,620	16.5	156	114
Binghamton, N.Y. MSA	264,497	252,320	-12,177	-4.6	127	143
Birmingham, Ala. MSA	840,140	921,106	80,966	9.6	46	55
Bismarck, N.Dak. MSA	83,831	94,719	10,888	13.0	273	264
Bloomington, Ind. MSA	108,978	120,563	11,585	10.6	251	239
Bloomington-Normal, Ill. MSA	129,180	150,433	21,253	16.5	220	203
Boise City, Idaho MSA	295,851	432,345	136,494	46.1	154	97
Boston-Worcester-Lawrence, Mass.-N.H.-Maine-Conn. CMSA	5,455,403	5,819,100	363,697	6.7	7	7
Boston, Mass.-N.H. PMSA	3,227,707	3,406,829	179,122	5.5	N.A.	N.A.
Brockton, Mass. PMSA	236,409	255,459	19,050	8.1	N.A.	N.A.
Fitchburg-Leominster, Mass. PMSA	138,165	142,284	4,119	3.0	N.A.	N.A.
Lawrence, Mass.-N.H. PMSA	353,232	396,230	42,998	12.2	N.A.	N.A.
Lowell, Mass.-N.H. PMSA	280,578	301,686	21,108	7.5	N.A.	N.A.
Manchester, N.H. PMSA	173,783	198,378	24,595	14.2	N.A.	N.A.
Nashua, N.H. PMSA	168,233	190,949	22,716	13.5	N.A.	N.A.
New Bedford, Mass. PMSA	175,641	175,198	-443	-0.3	N.A.	N.A.
Portsmouth-Rochester, N.H.-Maine PMSA	223,271	240,698	17,427	7.8	N.A.	N.A.
Worcester, Mass.-Conn. PMSA	478,384	511,389	33,005	6.9	N.A.	N.A.
Brownsville-Harlingen-San Benito, Tex. MSA	260,120	335,227	75,107	28.9	129	122
Bryan-College Station, Tex. MSA	121,862	152,415	30,553	25.1	229	200
Buffalo-Niagara Falls, N.Y. CMSA	1,189,288	1,170,111	-19,177	-1.6	33	43
Burlington, Vt. MSA	151,506	169,391	17,885	11.8	212	186
Canton-Massillon, Ohio MSA	394,106	406,934	12,828	3.3	93	101
Casper, Wyo. MSA	61,226	66,533	5,307	8.7	283	279
Cedar Rapids, Iowa MSA	168,767	191,701	22,934	13.6	174	173
Champaign-Urbana, Ill. MSA	173,025	179,669	6,644	3.8	172	178
Charleston-N. Charleston, S.C. MSA	506,875	549,033	42,158	8.3	73	77
Charleston, W.Va. MSA	250,454	251,662	1,208	0.5	134	144
Charlotte-Gastonia-Rock Hill, N.C.-S.C. MSA	1,162,093	1,499,293	337,200	29.0	34	34
Charlottesville, Va. MSA	131,107	159,576	28,469	21.7	214	194
Chattanooga, Tenn.-Ga. MSA	424,347	465,161	40,814	9.6	82	90
Cheyenne, Wyo. MSA	73,142	81,607	8,465	11.6	281	275
Chicago-Gary-Kenosha, Ill.-Ind.-Wis. CMSA	8,239,820	9,157,540	917,720	11.1	3	3
Chicago, Ill. PMSA	7,410,858	8,272,768	861,910	11.6	N.A.	N.A.
Gary, Ind. PMSA	604,526	631,362	26,836	4.4	N.A.	N.A.
Kankakee, Ill. PMSA	96,255	103,833	7,578	7.9	N.A.	N.A.
Kenosha, Wis. PMSA	128,181	149,577	21,396	16.7	N.A.	N.A.
Chico-Paradise, Calif. MSA	182,120	203,171	21,051	11.6	167	167
Cincinnati-Hamilton, Ohio-Ky.-Ind. CMSA	1,817,571	1,979,202	161,631	8.9	23	24
Cincinnati, Ohio-Ky.-Ind. PMSA	1,526,092	1,646,395	120,303	7.9	N.A.	N.A.
Hamilton-Middletown, Ohio PMSA	291,479	332,807	41,328	14.2	N.A.	N.A.
Clarksville-Hopkinsville, Tenn.-Ky. MSA	169,439	207,033	37,594	22.2	173	166
Cleveland-Akron, Ohio CMSA	2,859,644	2,945,831	86,187	3.0	13	16
Akron, Ohio PMSA	657,575	694,960	37,385	5.7	N.A.	N.A.
Cleveland-Lorain-Elyria, Ohio PMSA	2,202,069	2,250,871	48,802	2.2	N.A.	N.A.
Colorado Springs, Colo. MSA	397,014	516,929	119,915	30.2	90	81
Columbia, Mo. MSA	112,379	135,454	23,075	20.5	249	221
Columbia, S.C. MSA	453,331	536,691	83,360	18.4	79	80
Columbus, Ga.-Ala. MSA	260,860	274,624	13,764	5.3	136	138
Columbus, Ohio MSA	1,345,450	1,540,157	194,707	14.5	29	33
Corpus Christi, Tex.	349,894	380,783	30,889	8.8	105	109
Corvallis, Oreg. MSA	70,811	78,153	7,342	10.4	N.A.	277
Cumberland, Md.-W.Va. MSA	101,643	102,008	365	0.4	259	259
Dallas-Fort Worth, Tex. CMSA	4,037,282	5,221,801	1,184,519	29.3	9	9
Dallas, Tex. PMSA	2,676,248	3,519,176	842,928	31.5	N.A.	N.A.
Fort Worth-Arlington, Tex. PMSA	1,361,034	1,702,625	341,591	25.1	N.A.	N.A.
Danville, Va. MSA	108,711	110,156	1,445	1.3	252	253
Davenport-Rock Island-Moline, Iowa-Ill. MSA	350,861	359,062	8,201	2.3	104	116
Dayton-Springfield, Ohio MSA	951,270	950,558	-712	-0.1	44	53
Daytona Beach, Fla. MSA	399,413	493,175	93,762	23.5	96	83
Decatur, Ala. MSA	131,556	145,867	14,311	10.9	211	211
Decatur, Ill. MSA	117,206	114,706	-2,500	-2.1	239	246

Metropolitan Statistical Area	1990	2000	Change 1990–2000 Number	Change 1990–2000 Percent	CMSA/MSA rank 1990	CMSA/MSA rank 2000
Denver-Boulder-Greeley, Colo. CMSA	1,980,140	2,581,506	601,366	30.4%	22	19
Boulder-Longmont, Colo. PMSA	225,339	291,288	65,949	29.3	N.A.	N.A.
Denver, Colo. PMSA	1,622,980	2,109,282	486,302	30.0	N.A.	N.A.
Greeley, Colo. PMSA	131,821	180,936	49,115	37.3	N.A.	N.A.
Des Moines, Iowa MSA	392,928	456,022	63,094	16.1	94	91
Detroit-Ann Arbor-Flint, Mich. CMSA	5,187,171	5,456,428	269,257	5.2	6	8
Ann Arbor, Mich. PMSA	490,058	578,736	88,678	18.1	N.A.	N.A.
Detroit, Mich. PMSA	4,266,654	4,441,551	174,897	4.1	N.A.	N.A.
Flint, Mich. PMSA	430,459	436,141	5,682	1.3	N.A.	N.A.
Dothan, Ala. MSA	130,964	137,916	6,952	5.3	215	219
Dover, Del. MSA	110,993	126,697	15,704	14.1	N.A.	229
Dubuque, Iowa MSA	86,403	89,143	2,740	3.2	271	269
Duluth-Superior, Minn.-Wis. MSA	239,971	243,815	3,844	1.6	140	149
Eau Claire, Wis. MSA	137,543	148,337	10,794	7.8	204	206
El Paso, Tex. MSA	591,610	679,622	88,012	14.9	66	64
Elkhart-Goshen, Ind. MSA	156,198	182,791	26,593	17.0	183	176
Elmira, N.Y. MSA	95,195	91,070	-4,125	-4.3	266	266
Enid, Okla. MSA	56,735	57,813	1,078	1.9	284	280
Erie, Pa. MSA	275,572	280,843	5,271	1.9	124	137
Eugene-Springfield, Oreg. MSA	282,912	322,959	40,047	14.2	119	125
Evansville-Henderson, Ind.-Ky. MSA	278,990	296,195	17,205	6.2	121	133
Fargo-Moorhead, N.Dak.-Minn. MSA	153,296	174,367	21,071	13.7	185	182
Fayetteville, N.C. MSA	274,566	302,963	28,397	10.3	125	131
Fayetteville-Springdale-Rogers, Ark. MSA	210,908	311,121	100,213	47.5	247	130
Flagstaff, Ariz.-Utah MSA	101,760	122,366	20,606	20.2	N.A.	237
Florence, Ala. MSA	131,327	142,950	11,623	8.9	213	213
Florence, S.C. MSA	114,344	125,761	11,417	10.0	245	233
Fort Collins-Loveland, Colo. MSA	186,136	251,494	65,358	35.1	165	145
Fort Myers-Cape Coral, Fla. MSA	335,113	440,888	105,775	31.6	110	95
Fort Pierce-Port St. Lucie, Fla. MSA	251,071	319,426	68,355	27.2	133	127
Fort Smith, Ark.-Okla. MSA	175,911	207,290	31,379	17.8	169	165
Fort Walton Beach, Fla. MSA	143,776	170,498	26,722	18.6	198	184
Fort Wayne, Ind. MSA	456,281	502,141	45,860	10.1	100	82
Fresno, Calif. MSA	755,580	922,516	166,936	22.1	59	54
Gadsden, Ala. MSA	99,840	103,459	3,619	3.6	260	257
Gainesville, Fla. MSA	181,596	217,955	36,359	20.0	155	159
Glens Falls, N.Y. MSA	118,539	124,345	5,806	4.9	238	234
Goldsboro, N.C. MSA	104,666	113,329	8,663	8.3	N.A.	247
Grand Forks, N.Dak.-Minn. MSA	103,181	97,478	-5,703	-5.5	282	262
Grand Junction, Colo. MSA	93,145	116,255	23,110	24.8	N.A.	243
Grand Rapids-Muskegon-Holland, Mich. MSA	937,891	1,088,514	150,623	16.1	57	48
Great Falls, Mont. MSA	77,691	80,357	2,666	3.4	279	276
Green Bay, Wis. MSA	194,594	226,778	32,184	16.5	158	156
Greensboro—Winston-Salem—High Point, N.C. MSA	1,050,304	1,251,509	201,205	19.2	45	37
Greenville, N.C. MSA	107,924	133,798	25,874	24.0	N.A.	222
Greenville-Spartanburg-Anderson, S.C. MSA	830,563	962,441	131,878	15.9	62	52
Harrisburg-Lebanon-Carlisle, Pa. MSA	587,986	629,401	41,415	7.0	67	67
Hartford, Conn. MSA	1,157,585	1,183,110	25,525	2.2	36	42
Hattiesburg, Miss. MSA	98,738	111,674	12,936	13.1	N.A.	250
Hickory-Morganton-Lenoir, N.C. MSA	292,409	341,851	49,442	16.9	148	120
Honolulu, Hawaii MSA	836,231	876,156	39,925	4.8	51	56
Houma, La. MSA	182,842	194,477	11,635	6.4	166	170
Houston-Galveston-Brazoria, Tex. CMSA	3,731,131	4,669,571	938,440	25.2	10	10
Brazoria, Tex. PMSA	191,707	241,767	50,060	26.1	N.A.	N.A.
Galveston-Texas City, Tex. PMSA	217,399	250,158	32,759	15.1	N.A.	N.A.
Houston, Tex. PMSA	3,322,025	4,177,646	855,621	25.8	N.A.	N.A.
Huntington-Ashland, W.Va.-Ky.-Ohio MSA	312,529	315,538	3,009	1.0	115	128
Huntsville, Ala. MSA	293,047	342,376	49,329	16.8	141	119
Indianapolis, Ind. MSA	1,380,491	1,607,486	226,995	16.4	31	29
Iowa City, Iowa MSA	96,119	111,006	14,887	15.5	265	251
Jackson, Mich. MSA	149,756	158,422	8,666	5.8	191	195
Jackson, Miss. MSA	395,396	440,801	45,405	11.5	92	96
Jackson, Tenn. MSA	90,801	107,377	16,576	18.3	278	254
Jacksonville, Fla. MSA	906,727	1,100,491	193,764	21.4	47	46
Jacksonville, N.C. MSA	149,838	150,355	517	0.3	190	204
Jamestown, N.Y. MSA	141,895	139,750	-2,145	-1.5	202	217
Janesville-Beloit, Wis. MSA	139,510	152,307	12,797	9.2	203	201
Johnson City-Kingsport-Bristol, Tenn.-Va. MSA	436,047	480,091	44,044	10.1	81	85

Metropolitan Statistical Area	1990	2000	Change 1990–2000 Number	Change 1990–2000 Percent	CMSA/MSA rank 1990	CMSA/MSA rank 2000
Johnstown, Pa. MSA	241,247	232,621	-8,626	-3.6%	138	155
Jonesboro, Ark. MSA	68,956	82,148	13,192	19.1	N.A.	274
Joplin, Mo. MSA	134,910	157,322	22,412	16.6	207	196
Kalamazoo-Battle Creek, Mich. MSA	429,453	452,851	23,398	5.4	146	92
Kansas City, Mo.-Kans. MSA	1,582,875	1,776,062	193,187	12.2	25	26
Killeen-Temple, Tex. MSA	255,301	312,952	57,651	22.6	131	129
Knoxville, Tenn. MSA	585,960	687,249	101,289	17.3	65	63
Kokomo, Ind. MSA	96,946	101,541	4,595	4.7	263	260
La Crosse, Wis.-Minn. MSA	116,401	126,838	10,437	9.0	262	228
Lafayette, La. MSA	344,953	385,647	40,694	11.8	153	106
Lafayette, Ind. MSA	161,572	182,821	21,249	13.2	218	175
Lake Charles, La. MSA	168,134	183,577	15,443	9.2	175	174
Lakeland-Winter Haven, Fla. MSA	405,382	483,924	78,542	19.4	87	84
Lancaster, Pa. MSA	422,822	470,658	47,836	11.3	85	89
Lansing-East Lansing, Mich. MSA	432,674	447,728	15,054	3.5	83	93
Laredo, Tex. MSA	133,239	193,117	59,878	44.9	208	171
Las Cruces, N.Mex. MSA	135,510	174,682	39,172	28.9	206	181
Las Vegas, Nev.-Ariz. MSA	852,737	1,563,282	710,545	83.3	53	32
Lawrence, Kans. MSA	81,798	99,962	18,164	22.2	275	261
Lawton, Okla. MSA	111,486	114,996	3,510	3.1	250	245
Lewiston-Auburn, Maine MSA	93,679	90,830	-2,849	-3.0	269	268
Lexington, Ky. MSA	405,936	479,198	73,262	18.0	106	86
Lima, Ohio MSA	154,340	155,084	744	0.5	184	197
Lincoln, Nebr. MSA	213,641	250,291	36,650	17.2	151	147
Little Rock-North Little Rock, Ark. MSA	513,117	583,845	70,728	13.8	72	74
Longview-Marshall, Tex. MSA	193,801	208,780	14,979	7.7	176	164
Los Angeles-Riverside-Orange County, Calif. CMSA	14,531,529	16,373,645	1,842,116	12.7	2	2
Los Angeles-Long Beach, Calif. PMSA	8,863,164	9,519,338	656,174	7.4	N.A.	N.A.
Orange County, Calif. PMSA	2,410,556	2,846,289	435,733	18.1	N.A.	N.A.
Riverside-San Bernardino, Calif. PMSA	2,588,793	3,254,821	666,028	25.7	N.A.	N.A.
Ventura, Calif. PMSA	669,016	753,197	84,181	12.6	N.A.	N.A.
Louisville, Ky.-Ind. MSA	948,829	1,025,598	76,769	8.1	43	50
Lubbock, Tex. MSA	222,636	242,628	19,992	9.0	147	151
Lynchburg, Va. MSA	193,928	214,911	20,983	10.8	200	161
Macon, Ga. MSA	290,909	322,549	31,640	10.9	120	126
Madison, Wis. MSA	367,085	426,526	59,441	16.2	99	98
Mansfield, Ohio MSA	174,007	175,818	1,811	1.0	223	179
Mayaguez, P.R. MSA	237,143	253,347	16,204	6.8	N.A.	142
McAllen-Edinburg-Mission, Tex. MSA	383,545	569,463	185,918	48.5	95	75
Medford-Ashland, Oreg. MSA	146,389	181,269	34,880	23.8	196	177
Melbourne-Titusville-Palm Bay, Fla. MSA	398,978	476,230	77,252	19.4	89	88
Memphis, Tenn.-Ark.-Miss. MSA	1,007,306	1,135,614	128,308	12.7	41	44
Merced, Calif. MSA	178,403	210,554	32,151	18.0	168	163
Miami-Fort Lauderdale, Fla. CMSA	3,192,582	3,876,380	683,798	21.4	11	12
Fort Lauderdale, Fla. PMSA	1,255,488	1,623,018	367,530	29.3	N.A.	N.A.
Miami, Fla. PMSA	1,937,094	2,253,362	316,268	16.3	N.A.	N.A.
Milwaukee-Racine, Wis. CMSA	1,607,183	1,689,572	82,389	5.1	24	27
Milwaukee-Waukesha, Wis. PMSA	1,432,149	1,500,741	68,592	4.8	N.A.	N.A.
Racine, Wis. PMSA	175,034	188,831	13,797	7.9	N.A.	N.A.
Minneapolis-St. Paul, Minn.-Wis. MSA	2,538,834	2,968,806	429,972	16.9	16	15
Missoula, Mont. MSA	78,687	95,802	17,115	21.8	N.A.	263
Mobile, Ala. MSA	476,923	540,258	63,335	13.3	78	79
Modesto, Calif. MSA	370,522	446,997	76,475	20.6	97	94
Monroe, La. MSA	142,191	147,250	5,059	3.6	201	209
Montgomery, Ala. MSA	292,517	333,055	40,538	13.9	117	123
Muncie, Ind. MSA	119,659	118,769	-890	-0.7	234	242
Myrtle Beach, S.C. MSA	144,053	196,629	52,576	36.5	N.A.	169
Naples, Fla. MSA	152,099	251,377	99,278	65.3	186	146
Nashville, Tenn. MSA	985,026	1,231,311	246,285	25.0	40	39
New London-Norwich, Conn.-R.I. MSA	290,734	293,566	2,832	1.0	126	134
New Orleans, La. MSA	1,285,270	1,337,726	52,456	4.1	32	35
New York-Northern New Jersey-Long Island, N.Y.-N.J.-Conn.-Pa. PMSA	19,549,649	21,199,865	1,650,216	8.4	1	1
Bergen-Passaic, N.J. PMSA	1,278,440	1,373,167	94,727	7.4	N.A.	N.A.
Bridgeport, Conn. PMSA	443,722	459,479	15,757	3.6	N.A.	N.A.
Danbury, Conn. PMSA	193,597	217,980	24,383	12.6	N.A.	N.A.
Dutchess County, N.Y. PMSA	259,462	280,150	20,688	8.0	N.A.	N.A.
Jersey City, N.J. PMSA	553,099	608,975	55,876	10.1	N.A.	N.A.
Middlesex-Somerset-Hunterdon, N.J. PMSA	1,019,835	1,169,641	149,806	14.7	N.A.	N.A.

Metropolitan Statistical Area	1990	2000	Change 1990–2000 Number	Change 1990–2000 Percent	CMSA/MSA rank 1990	CMSA/MSA rank 2000
Monmouth-Ocean, N.J. PMSA	986,327	1,126,217	139,890	14.2%	N.A.	N.A.
Nassau-Suffolk, N.Y. PMSA	2,609,212	2,753,913	144,701	5.5	N.A.	N.A.
New Haven-Meriden, Conn PMSA	530,180	542,149	11,969	2.3	N.A.	N.A.
New York, N.Y. PMSA	8,546,846	9,314,235	767,389	9.0	N.A.	N.A.
Newark, N.J. PMSA	1,915,928	2,032,989	117,061	6.1	N.A.	N.A.
Newburgh, N.Y.-Pa. PMSA	335,613	387,669	52,056	15.5	N.A.	N.A.
Stamford-Norwalk, Conn. PMSA	329,935	353,556	23,621	7.2	N.A.	N.A.
Trenton, N.J. PMSA	325,824	350,761	24,937	7.7	N.A.	N.A.
Waterbury, Conn.	221,629	228,984	7,355	3.3	N.A.	N.A.
Norfolk-Virginia Beach-Newport News, Va.-N.C. MSA	1,443,244	1,569,541	126,297	8.8	28	31
Ocala, Fla. MSA	194,833	258,916	64,083	32.9	157	141
Odessa-Midland, Tex. MSA	225,545	237,132	11,587	5.1	236	152
Oklahoma City, Okla. MSA	958,839	1,083,346	124,507	13.0	42	49
Omaha, Nebr.-Iowa MSA	639,580	716,998	77,418	12.1	63	61
Orlando, Fla. MSA	1,224,852	1,644,561	419,709	34.3	37	28
Owensboro, Ky. MSA	87,189	91,545	4,356	5.0	270	265
Panama City, Fla. MSA	126,994	148,217	21,223	16.7	222	207
Parkersburg-Marietta, W.Va.-Ohio MSA	149,169	151,237	2,068	1.4	192	202
Pensacola, Fla. MSA	344,406	412,153	67,747	19.7	107	100
Peoria-Pekin, Ill. MSA	339,172	347,787	8,215	2.4	108	118
Philadelphia-Wilmington-Atlantic City, Pa.-N.J.-Del.-Md. CMSA	5,892,937	6,188,463	295,526	5.0	5	6
Atlantic-Cape May, N.J. PMSA	319,416	354,878	35,462	11.1	N.A.	N.A.
Philadelphia, Pa.-N.J. PMSA	4,922,175	5,100,931	178,756	3.6	N.A.	N.A.
Vineland-Millville-Bridgeton, N.J. PMSA	138,053	146,438	8,385	6.1	N.A.	N.A.
Wilmington-Newark, Del.-Md. PMSA	513,293	586,216	72,923	14.2	N.A.	N.A.
Phoenix-Mesa, Ariz. MSA	2,238,480	3,251,876	1,013,396	45.3	20	14
Pine Bluff, Ark. MSA	85,487	84,278	-1,209	-1.4	272	272
Pittsburgh, Pa. MSA	2,394,811	2,358,695	-36,116	-1.5	19	22
Pittsfield, Mass. MSA	88,695	84,699	-3,996	-4.5	277	271
Pocatello, Idaho MSA	66,026	75,565	9,539	14.4	N.A.	278
Ponce, P.R. MSA	342,660	361,094	18,434	5.4	N.A.	115
Portland, Maine MSA	221,095	243,537	22,442	10.2	150	150
Portland-Salem, Oreg.-Wash. CMSA	1,793,476	2,265,223	471,747	26.3	27	23
Portland-Vancouver, Oreg.-Wash. PMSA	1,515,452	1,918,009	402,557	26.6	N.A.	N.A.
Salem, Oreg. PMSA	278,024	347,214	69,190	24.9	N.A.	N.A.
Providence-Fall River-Warwick, R.I.-Mass. MSA	1,134,350	1,188,613	54,263	4.8	35	40
Provo-Orem, Utah MSA	263,590	368,536	104,946	39.8	128	112
Pueblo, Colo. MSA	123,051	141,472	18,421	15.0	226	215
Punta Gorda, Fla. MSA	110,975	141,627	30,652	27.6	N.A.	214
Raleigh-Durham-Chapel Hill, N.C. MSA	855,545	1,187,941	332,396	38.9	54	41
Rapid City, S.Dak. MSA	81,343	88,565	7,222	8.9	276	270
Reading, Pa. MSA	336,523	373,638	37,115	11.0	109	110
Redding, Calif. MSA	147,036	163,256	16,220	11.0	194	190
Reno, Nev. MSA	254,667	339,486	84,819	33.3	132	121
Richland-Kennewick-Pasco, Wash. MSA	150,033	191,822	41,789	27.9	189	172
Richmond-Petersburg, Va. MSA	865,640	996,512	130,872	15.1	49	51
Roanoke, Va. MSA	224,477	235,932	11,455	5.1	144	153
Rochester, Minn. MSA	106,470	124,277	17,807	16.7	256	235
Rochester, N.Y. MSA	1,062,470	1,098,201	35,731	3.4	39	47
Rockford, Ill. MSA	329,676	371,236	41,560	12.6	118	111
Rocky Mount, N.C. MSA	133,235	143,026	9,791	7.3	N.A.	212
Sacramento-Yolo, Calif. CMSA	1,481,102	1,796,857	315,755	21.3	26	25
Sacramento, Calif. PMSA	1,340,010	1,628,197	288,187	21.5	N.A.	N.A.
Yolo, Calif. PMSA	141,092	168,660	27,568	19.5	N.A.	N.A.
Saginaw-Bay City-Midland, Mich. MSA	399,320	403,070	3,750	0.9	88	102
Salinas, Calif. MSA	355,660	401,762	46,102	13.0	103	103
Salt Lake City-Ogden, Utah MSA	1,072,227	1,333,914	261,687	24.4	38	36
San Angelo, Tex. MSA	98,458	104,010	5,552	5.6	261	256
San Antonio, Tex. MSA	1,324,749	1,592,383	267,634	20.2	30	30
San Diego, Calif. MSA	2,498,016	2,813,833	315,817	12.6	15	17
San Francisco-Oakland-San Jose, Calif. CMSA	6,253,311	7,039,362	786,051	12.6	4	5
Oakland, Calif. PMSA	2,082,914	2,392,557	309,643	14.9	N.A.	N.A.
San Francisco, Calif. PMSA	1,603,678	1,731,183	127,505	8.0	N.A.	N.A.
San Jose, Calif. PMSA	1,497,577	1,682,585	185,008	12.4	N.A.	N.A.
Santa Cruz-Watsonville, Calif. PMSA	229,734	255,602	25,868	11.3	N.A.	N.A.
Santa Rosa, Calif. PMSA	388,222	458,614	70,392	18.1	N.A.	N.A.
Vallejo-Fairfield-Napa, Calif. PMSA	451,186	518,821	67,635	15.0	N.A.	N.A.

Metropolitan Statistical Area	1990	2000	Change 1990–2000 Number	Change 1990–2000 Percent	CMSA/MSA rank 1990	CMSA/MSA rank 2000
San Juan-Caguas-Arecibo, P.R. CMSA	2,270,808	2,450,292	179,484	7.9%	N.A.	20
Arecibo, P.R. PMSA	155,005	174,300	19,295	12.4	N.A.	N.A.
Caguas, P.R. PMSA	279,501	308,365	28,864	10.3	N.A.	N.A.
San Juan-Bayamon, P.R. PMSA	1,836,302	1,967,627	131,325	7.2	N.A.	N.A.
San Luis Obispo-Atascadero-Pasa Robles, Calif. MSA	217,162	246,681	29,519	13.6	N.A.	148
Santa Barbara-Santa Maria-Lompoc, Calif. PMSA	369,608	399,347	29,739	8.0	98	104
Santa Fe, N.Mex. MSA	117,043	147,635	30,592	26.1	240	208
Sarasota-Bradenton, Fla. MSA	489,483	589,959	100,476	20.5	123	73
Savannah, Ga. MSA	258,060	293,000	34,090	13.5	137	135
Scranton-Wilkes-Barre-Hazleton, Pa. MSA	638,466	624,776	-13,690	-2.1	55	68
Seattle-Tacoma-Bremerton, Wash. CMSA	2,970,328	3,554,760	584,432	19.7	14	13
Bremerton, Wash. PMSA	189,731	231,969	42,238	22.3	N.A.	N.A.
Olympia, Wash. PMSA	161,238	207,355	46,117	28.6	N.A.	N.A.
Seattle-Bellevue-Everett, Wash. PMSA	2,033,156	2,414,616	381,460	18.8	N.A.	N.A.
Tacoma, Wash. PMSA	586,203	700,820	114,617	19.6	N.A.	N.A.
Sharon, Pa. MSA	121,003	120,293	-710	-0.6	231	240
Sheboygan, Wis. MSA	103,877	112,646	8,769	8.4	257	248
Sherman-Denison, Tex. MSA	95,021	110,595	15,574	16.4	267	252
Shreveport-Bossier City, La. MSA	376,330	392,302	15,972	4.2	111	105
Sioux City, Iowa-Nebr. MSA	115,018	124,130	9,112	7.9	244	236
Sioux Falls, S.Dak. MSA	139,236	172,412	33,176	23.8	224	183
South Bend, Ind. MSA	247,052	265,559	18,507	7.5	135	139
Spokane, Wash. MSA	361,364	417,939	56,575	15.7	101	99
Springfield, Ill. MSA	189,550	201,437	11,887	6.3	161	168
Springfield, Mass. MSA	587,884	591,932	4,048	0.7	70	72
Springfield, Mo. MSA	264,346	325,721	61,375	23.2	139	124
St. Cloud, Minn. MSA	148,976	167,392	18,416	12.4	159	187
St. Joseph, Mo. MSA	97,715	102,490	4,775	4.9	274	258
St. Louis, Mo.-Ill. MSA	2,492,525	2,603,607	111,082	4.5	17	18
State College, Pa. MSA	123,786	135,758	11,972	9.7	225	220
Steubenville-Weirton, Ohio-W.Va. MSA	142,523	132,008	-10,515	-7.4	199	223
Stockton-Lodi, Calif. MSA	480,628	563,598	82,970	17.3	76	76
Sumter, S.C. MSA	102,637	104,646	2,009	2.0	N.A.	255
Syracuse, N.Y. MSA	742,177	732,117	-10,060	-1.4	61	60
Tallahassee, Fla. MSA	233,598	284,539	50,941	21.8	142	136
Tampa-St. Petersburg-Clearwater, Fla. MSA	2,067,959	2,395,997	328,038	15.9	21	21
Terre Haute, Ind. MSA	147,585	149,192	1,607	1.1	216	205
Texarkana, Tex.-Texarkana, Ark. MSA	120,132	129,749	9,617	8.0	233	224
Toledo, Ohio MSA	614,128	618,203	4,075	0.7	64	69
Topeka, Kans. MSA	160,976	169,871	8,895	5.5	179	185
Tucson, Ariz. MSA	666,880	843,746	176,866	26.5	60	58
Tulsa, Okla. MSA	708,954	803,235	94,281	13.3	56	59
Tuscaloosa, Ala. MSA	150,522	164,875	14,353	9.5	188	189
Tyler, Tex. MSA	151,309	174,706	23,397	15.5	187	180
Utica-Rome, N.Y. MSA	316,633	299,896	-16,737	-5.3	113	132
Victoria, Tex. MSA	74,361	84,088	9,727	13.1	280	273
Visalia-Tulare-Porterville, Calif. MSA	311,921	368,021	56,100	18.0	116	113
Waco, Tex. MSA	189,123	213,517	24,394	12.9	162	162
Washington-Baltimore, D.C.-Md.-Va.-W.Va. CMSA	4,223,485	4,923,153	699,668	16.6	8	4
Baltimore, Md. PMSA	2,382,172	2,552,994	170,822	7.2	N.A.	N.A.
Hagerstown, Md. PMSA	121,393	131,923	10,530	8.7	N.A.	N.A.
Washington, D.C.-Md.-Va.-W.Va. PMSA	4,223,485	4,923,153	699,668	16.6	N.A.	N.A.
Waterloo-Cedar Falls, Iowa MSA	123,798	128,012	4,214	3.4	195	227
Wausau, Wis. MSA	115,400	125,834	10,434	9.0	242	232
West Palm Beach-Boca Raton, Fla. MSA	863,518	1,131,184	267,666	31.0	50	45
Wheeling, W.Va.-Ohio MSA	159,301	153,172	-6,129	-3.8	180	199
Wichita Falls, Tex. MSA	130,351	140,518	10,167	7.8	228	216
Wichita, Kans. MSA	485,270	545,220	59,950	12.4	75	78
Williamsport, Pa. MSA	118,710	120,044	1,334	1.1	237	241
Wilmington, N.C. MSA	171,269	233,450	62,181	36.3	232	154
Yakima, Wash. MSA	188,823	222,581	33,758	17.9	163	158
York, Pa. MSA	339,574	381,751	42,177	12.4	86	108
Youngstown-Warren, Ohio MSA	600,895	594,746	-6,149	-1.0	74	71
Yuba City, Calif. MSA	122,643	139,149	16,506	13.5	227	218
Yuma, Ariz. MSA	106,895	160,026	53,131	49.7	254	193

Note: CMSA = consolidated metropolitan statistical area; MSA = metropolitan statistical area; PMSA = primary metropolitan statistical area; N.A. = not applicable. **Source**: U.S. Bureau of the Census release, 2001.

Population of U.S. Metropolitan Areas by Race and Hispanic Origin, 2000

Metropolitan area	Total	White	Black	Indian/ Alaska Native	Asian	Pacific Islander	Other	Two or more races	Hispanic
Abilene, Texas MSA	126,555	80.6%	6.7%	0.6%	1.2%	0.1%	8.3%	2.4%	17.6%
Albany, Ga. MSA	120,822	46.9	51.0	0.2	0.6	0.0	0.5	0.7	1.3
Albany–Schenectady–Troy, N.Y. MSA	875,583	89.4	6.1	0.2	1.8	0.0	0.9	1.5	2.7
Albuquerque, N.Mex. MSA	712,738	69.6	2.5	5.6	1.7	0.1	16.3	4.2	41.6
Alexandria, La. MSA	126,337	66.5	30.4	0.7	0.9	0.0	0.4	1.0	1.4
Allentown–Bethlehem–Easton, Pa. MSA	637,958	89.8	3.0	0.2	1.6	0.0	3.9	1.5	7.9
Altoona, Pa. MSA	129,144	97.6	1.2	0.1	0.4	0.0	0.1	0.6	0.5
Amarillo, Texas MSA	217,858	79.1	5.9	0.8	1.8	0.0	10.3	2.1	19.6
Anchorage, Alaska MSA	260,283	72.2	5.8	7.3	5.5	0.9	2.2	6.0	5.7
Anniston, Ala. MSA	112,249	78.9	18.5	0.4	0.6	0.1	0.6	1.0	1.6
Appleton–Oshkosh–Neenah, Wis. MSA	358,365	94.6	0.8	0.9	2.0	0.0	0.7	0.9	1.9
Asheville, N.C. MSA	225,965	89.8	6.9	0.4	0.6	0.0	1.1	1.2	2.7
Athens, Ga. MSA	153,444	73.2	20.5	0.2	2.4	0.0	2.5	1.2	5.1
Atlanta, Ga. MSA	4,112,198	63.0	28.9	0.3	3.3	0.0	2.8	1.7	6.5
Auburn–Opelika, Ala. MSA	115,092	74.1	22.7	0.2	1.6	0.0	0.5	0.9	1.4
Augusta–Aiken, Ga.–S.C. MSA	477,441	61.5	34.4	0.3	1.5	0.1	0.9	1.5	2.4
Austin–San Marcos, Texas MSA	1,249,763	72.5	8.0	0.6	3.5	0.1	12.8	2.6	26.2
Bakersfield, Calif. MSA	661,645	61.6	6.0	1.5	3.4	0.1	23.2	4.1	38.4
Bangor, Maine MSA	90,864	95.6	0.7	1.3	1.0	0.0	0.3	1.1	0.7
Barnstable–Yarmouth, Mass. MSA	162,582	94.4	1.7	0.6	0.6	0.0	1.1	1.6	1.3
Baton Rouge, La. MSA	602,894	64.9	31.9	0.2	1.5	0.0	0.5	0.9	1.8
Beaumont–Port Arthur, Texas MSA	385,090	68.2	24.8	0.4	2.1	0.0	3.1	1.4	8.0
Bellingham, Wash. MSA	166,814	88.4	0.7	2.8	2.8	0.1	2.5	2.7	5.2
Benton Harbor, Mich. MSA	162,453	79.7	15.9	0.4	1.1	0.0	1.1	1.6	3.0
Billings, Mont. MSA	129,352	92.8	0.4	3.1	0.5	0.0	1.3	1.9	3.7
Biloxi–Gulfport–Pascagoula, Miss.MSA	363,988	76.0	19.3	0.4	2.0	0.1	0.8	1.4	2.3
Binghamton, N.Y. MSA	252,320	92.6	2.7	0.2	2.3	0.0	0.7	1.5	1.8
Birmingham, Ala. MSA	921,106	67.3	30.1	0.3	0.8	0.0	0.7	0.8	1.8
Bismarck, N.Dak. MSA	94,719	95.2	0.2	3.0	0.4	0.0	0.2	0.9	0.7
Bloomington, Ind. MSA	120,563	90.8	3.0	0.3	3.4	0.0	0.9	1.6	1.9
Bloomington–Normal, Ill. MSA	150,433	89.2	6.2	0.2	2.1	0.0	1.0	1.4	2.5
Boise City, Idaho MSA	432,345	89.9	0.5	0.7	1.5	0.1	4.9	2.4	8.8
Boston–Worcester–Lawrence, Mass.–N.H.–Maine–Conn. CMSA	5,819,100	85.1	5.1	0.2	4.0	0.0	3.3	2.2	6.2
Boston, MA–NH PMSA	3,406,829	82.5	7.0	0.2	4.9	0.0	3.0	2.4	5.9
Brockton, MA PMSA	255,459	82.4	7.6	0.2	1.3	0.0	5.0	3.5	3.7
Fitchburg–Leominster, MA PMSA	142,284	89.5	2.6	0.2	2.3	0.0	3.4	2.0	8.3
Lawrence, MA–NH PMSA	396,230	85.6	1.7	0.3	2.1	0.0	8.1	2.1	14.0
Lowell, MA–NH PMSA	301,686	85.9	1.9	0.2	7.6	0.0	2.5	2.0	5.7
Manchester, NH PMSA	198,378	94.4	1.3	0.3	1.7	0.0	1.1	1.3	3.0
Nashua, NH PMSA	190,949	93.4	1.3	0.2	2.4	0.0	1.5	1.1	3.4
New Bedford, MA PMSA	175,198	85.9	2.7	0.4	0.7	0.0	6.4	3.8	5.9
Portsmouth–Rochester, NH–ME PMSA	240,698	96.5	0.7	0.2	1.3	0.0	0.3	1.0	1.0
Worcester, MA–CT PMSA	511,389	88.7	3.0	0.3	3.0	0.0	3.2	1.9	7.1
Brownsville–Harlingen–San Benito, Texas MSA	335,227	80.3	0.5	0.4	0.5	0.0	16.0	2.3	84.3
Bryan–College Station, Texas MSA	152,415	74.5	10.7	0.4	4.0	0.1	8.4	2.0	17.9
Buffalo–Niagara Falls, N.Y. MSA	1,170,111	83.8	11.7	0.7	1.3	0.0	1.2	1.3	2.9
Burlington, Vt. MSA	169,391	95.2	0.8	0.5	1.8	0.0	0.3	1.4	1.0
Canton–Massillon, Ohio MSA	406,934	90.8	6.7	0.2	0.5	0.0	0.3	1.4	0.9
Casper, Wyo. MSA	66,533	94.2	0.8	1.0	0.4	0.0	1.9	1.7	4.9
Cedar Rapids, Iowa MSA	191,701	93.9	2.6	0.2	1.4	0.0	0.5	1.4	1.4
Champaign–Urbana, Ill. MSA	179,669	78.8	11.2	0.2	6.5	0.0	1.3	2.0	2.9
Charleston–North Charleston, S.C. MSA	549,033	65.1	30.8	0.4	1.3	0.1	1.0	1.3	2.4
Charleston, W.Va. MSA	251,662	92.0	5.7	0.2	0.8	0.0	0.2	1.1	0.6
Charlotte–Gastonia–Rock Hill, N.C.–S.C. MSA	1,499,293	73.6	20.5	0.4	1.9	0.0	2.3	1.2	5.1
Charlottesville, Va. MSA	159,576	80.6	14.0	0.2	2.9	0.0	0.8	1.5	2.2
Chattanooga, Tenn.–Ga. MSA	465,161	82.8	14.2	0.3	1.0	0.0	0.6	1.0	1.5
Cheyenne, Wyo. MSA	81,607	88.9	2.6	0.8	1.0	0.1	4.0	2.6	10.9
Chicago–Gary–Kenosha, Ill.–Ind.–Wis. CMSA	9,157,540	66.8	18.6	0.3	4.2	0.0	7.7	2.2	16.4
Chicago, IL PMSA	8,272,768	65.8	18.9	0.3	4.6	0.0	8.2	2.3	17.1
Gary, IN PMSA	631,362	73.4	19.7	0.3	0.8	0.0	4.1	1.7	10.5

Metropolitan area	Total	White	Black	Indian/ Alaska Native	Asian	Pacific Islander	Other	Two or more races	Hispanic
Kankakee, IL PMSA	103,833	79.9%	15.5%	0.2%	0.7%	0.0%	2.4%	1.4%	4.8%
Kenosha, WI PMSA	149,577	88.4	5.1	0.4	0.9	0.0	3.3	1.9	7.2
Chico–Paradise, Calif. MSA	203,171	84.5	1.4	1.9	3.3	0.1	4.8	3.9	10.5
Cincinnati–Hamilton, Ohio–Ky.–Ind. CMSA	1,979,202	85.3	11.7	0.2	1.2	0.0	0.5	1.1	1.1
Cincinnati, OH–KY–IN PMSA	1,646,395	84.1	13.0	0.2	1.2	0.0	0.4	1.1	1.1
Hamilton–Middletown, OH PMSA	332,807	91.2	5.3	0.2	1.5	0.0	0.6	1.1	1.4
Clarksville–Hopkinsville, Tenn.–Ky. MSA	207,033	72.0	20.8	0.5	1.5	0.2	2.2	2.7	5.0
Cleveland–Akron, Ohio CMSA	2,945,831	79.0	16.8	0.2	1.3	0.0	1.2	1.5	2.7
Akron, OH PMSA	694,960	85.9	11.0	0.2	1.3	0.0	0.3	1.3	0.8
Cleveland–Lorain–Elyria, OH PMSA	2,250,871	76.9	18.5	0.2	1.4	0.0	1.4	1.6	3.3
Colorado Springs, Colo. MSA	516,929	81.2	6.5	0.9	2.5	0.2	4.7	3.9	11.3
Columbia, Mo. MSA	135,454	85.4	8.5	0.4	3.0	0.0	0.7	1.9	1.8
Columbia, S.C. MSA	536,691	63.9	32.1	0.3	1.4	0.1	1.0	1.2	2.4
Columbus, Ga.–Ala. MSA	274,624	54.4	40.4	0.4	1.3	0.1	1.7	1.7	4.0
Columbus, Ohio MSA	1,540,157	81.3	13.4	0.3	2.4	0.0	0.8	1.9	1.8
Corpus Christi, Texas MSA	380,783	72.9	4.0	0.6	1.1	0.1	18.2	3.1	54.7
Corvallis, Oreg. MSA	78,153	89.2	0.8	0.8	4.5	0.2	1.9	2.6	4.7
Cumberland, Md.–W.Va. MSA	102,008	93.9	4.6	0.1	0.4	0.0	0.2	0.8	0.7
Dallas–Fort Worth, Texas CMSA	5,221,801	69.5	13.8	0.6	3.7	0.1	9.9	2.4	21.5
Dallas, TX PMSA	3,519,176	67.2	15.1	0.6	4.0	0.1	10.7	2.4	23.0
Fort Worth–Arlington, TX PMSA	1,702,625	74.3	11.2	0.6	3.2	0.1	8.3	2.4	18.2
Danville, Va. MSA	110,156	65.7	32.6	0.2	0.4	0.0	0.4	0.7	1.2
Davenport–Moline–Rock Island, Iowa–Ill. MSA	359,062	88.4	6.0	0.3	1.2	0.0	2.5	1.7	5.8
Dayton–Springfield, Ohio MSA	950,558	82.3	14.2	0.2	1.2	0.0	0.5	1.5	1.2
Daytona Beach, Fla. MSA	493,175	86.2	9.2	0.3	1.0	0.0	1.7	1.4	6.4
Decatur, Ala. MSA	145,867	83.3	11.7	1.8	0.4	0.1	1.0	1.7	2.8
Decatur, Ill. MSA	114,706	83.5	14.1	0.2	0.6	0.0	0.3	1.4	1.0
Denver–Boulder–Greeley, Colo. CMSA	2,581,506	80.6	4.6	0.9	2.8	0.1	8.1	2.9	18.5
Boulder–Longmont, CO PMSA	291,288	88.5	0.9	0.6	3.1	0.1	4.7	2.2	10.5
Denver, CO PMSA	2,109,282	79.4	5.5	0.9	3.0	0.1	8.1	3.0	18.8
Greeley, CO PMSA	180,936	81.7	0.6	0.9	0.8	0.1	13.3	2.7	27.0
Des Moines, Iowa MSA	456,022	89.8	4.1	0.2	2.3	0.1	2.1	1.5	4.2
Detroit–Ann Arbor–Flint, Mich. CMSA	5,456,428	73.1	21.1	0.4	2.4	0.0	1.1	2.1	2.9
Ann Arbor, MI PMSA	578,736	85.3	7.3	0.4	3.7	0.0	1.2	2.0	3.1
Detroit, MI PMSA	4,441,551	71.2	22.9	0.3	2.3	0.0	1.1	2.1	2.9
Flint, MI PMSA	436,141	75.3	20.4	0.6	0.8	0.0	0.8	2.2	2.3
Dothan, Ala. MSA	137,916	73.5	23.1	0.5	0.8	0.1	0.7	1.4	2.0
Dover, Del. MSA	126,697	73.5	20.7	0.6	1.7	0.0	1.3	2.2	3.2
Dubuque, Iowa MSA	89,143	97.1	0.9	0.1	0.6	0.1	0.5	0.8	1.2
Duluth–Superior, Minn.–Wis. MSA	243,815	94.9	0.8	2.0	0.7	0.0	0.2	1.4	0.8
Eau Claire, Wis. MSA	148,337	96.0	0.4	0.5	1.9	0.0	0.3	0.9	0.8
El Paso, Texas MSA	679,622	73.9	3.1	0.8	1.0	0.1	17.9	3.2	78.2
Elkhart–Goshen, Ind. MSA	182,791	86.4	5.2	0.3	0.9	0.0	5.4	1.8	8.9
Elmira, N.Y. MSA	91,070	91.0	5.8	0.2	0.8	0.0	0.7	1.4	1.8
Enid, Okla. MSA	57,813	88.7	3.3	2.1	0.8	0.5	2.0	2.6	4.1
Erie, Pa. MSA	280,843	90.9	6.1	0.2	0.7	0.0	0.9	1.2	2.2
Eugene–Springfield, Oreg. MSA	322,959	90.6	0.8	1.1	2.0	0.2	1.9	3.3	4.6
Evansville–Henderson, Ind.–Ky. MSA	296,195	91.8	6.1	0.2	0.6	0.0	0.3	0.9	0.9
Fargo–Moorhead, N.Dak.–Minn. MSA	174,367	94.8	0.7	1.2	1.1	0.0	0.8	1.3	1.9
Fayetteville, N.C. MSA	302,963	55.2	34.9	1.5	1.9	0.3	3.1	3.1	6.9
Fayetteville–Springdale–Rogers, Ark. MSA	311,121	89.4	1.3	1.4	1.3	0.3	4.2	2.0	8.5
Flagstaff, Ariz.–Utah MSA	122,366	64.7	1.0	27.2	0.8	0.1	4.0	2.3	10.5
Florence, Ala. MSA	142,950	85.7	12.5	0.3	0.3	0.0	0.4	0.8	1.1
Florence, S.C. MSA	125,761	58.7	39.3	0.2	0.7	0.0	0.4	0.7	1.1
Fort Collins–Loveland, Colo. MSA	251,494	91.4	0.7	0.7	1.6	0.1	3.4	2.2	8.3
Fort Myers–Cape Coral, Fla. MSA	440,888	87.7	6.6	0.3	0.8	0.0	3.1	1.6	9.5
Fort Pierce–Port St. Lucie, Fla. MSA	319,426	83.4	11.4	0.3	0.8	0.1	2.5	1.5	7.9
Fort Smith, Ark.–Okla. MSA	207,290	82.2	4.0	5.1	2.3	0.0	2.6	3.8	4.9
Fort Walton Beach, Fla. MSA	170,498	83.4	9.1	0.6	2.5	0.1	1.3	3.0	4.3
Fort Wayne, Ind. MSA	502,141	88.1	7.5	0.3	1.0	0.0	1.6	1.4	3.3
Fresno, Calif. MSA	922,516	55.4	5.1	1.7	7.1	0.1	25.7	4.8	44.0
Gadsden, Ala. MSA	103,459	82.9	14.7	0.3	0.4	0.0	0.7	0.9	1.7
Gainesville, Fla. MSA	217,955	73.5	19.3	0.2	3.5	0.0	1.4	2.0	5.7

Metropolitan area	Total	White	Black	Indian/ Alaska Native	Asian	Pacific Islander	Other	Two or more races	Hispanic
Glens Falls, N.Y. MSA	124,345	96.2%	1.8%	0.2%	0.4%	0.0%	0.5%	0.8%	1.5%
Goldsboro, N.C. MSA	113,329	61.3	33.0	0.4	1.0	0.0	3.1	1.3	4.9
Grand Forks, N.Dak.–Minn. MSA	97,478	93.4	1.0	2.0	0.8	0.1	1.3	1.5	2.9
Grand Junction, Colo. MSA	116,255	92.3	0.5	0.9	0.5	0.1	3.7	2.0	10.0
Grand Rapids–Muskegon–Holland, Mich. MSA	1,088,514	85.7	7.3	0.5	1.6	0.0	3.0	1.9	6.3
Great Falls, Mont. MSA	80,357	90.7	1.1	4.2	0.8	0.1	0.7	2.4	2.4
Green Bay, Wis. MSA	226,778	91.1	1.2	2.3	2.2	0.0	1.9	1.3	3.8
Greensboro–Winston-Salem–High Point, N.C. MSA	1,251,509	74.4	20.2	0.4	1.4	0.0	2.4	1.2	5.0
Greenville, N.C. MSA	133,798	62.1	33.6	0.3	1.1	0.0	1.8	1.1	3.2
Greenville–Spartanburg–Anderson, S.C. MSA	962,441	79.0	17.5	0.2	1.2	0.0	1.1	1.0	2.7
Harrisburg–Lebanon–Carlisle, Pa. MSA	629,401	87.8	7.8	0.1	1.5	0.0	1.4	1.3	3.1
Hartford, Conn. MSA	1,183,110	80.7	9.5	0.2	2.2	0.0	5.2	2.1	9.6
Hattiesburg, Miss.MSA	111,674	71.7	26.3	0.2	0.7	0.0	0.4	0.7	1.2
Hickory–Morganton–Lenoir, N.C. MSA	341,851	87.5	6.9	0.2	2.3	0.1	2.0	1.0	4.0
Honolulu, Hawaii MSA	876,156	21.3	2.4	0.2	46.0	8.9	1.3	19.9	6.7
Houma, La. MSA	194,477	78.1	15.4	3.9	0.7	0.0	0.6	1.2	1.5
Houston–Galveston–Brazoria, Texas CMSA	4,669,571	62.6	16.9	0.4	4.9	0.1	12.4	2.7	28.9
Brazoria, TX PMSA	241,767	77.1	8.5	0.5	2.0	0.0	9.6	2.2	22.8
Galveston–Texas City, TX PMSA	250,158	72.7	15.4	0.5	2.1	0.0	7.2	2.1	18.0
Houston, TX PMSA	4,177,646	61.1	17.5	0.4	5.2	0.1	12.9	2.8	29.9
Huntington–Ashland, W.Va.–Ky.–Ohio MSA	315,538	96.2	2.2	0.2	0.4	0.0	0.1	0.8	0.7
Huntsville, Ala. MSA	342,376	74.3	21.0	0.7	1.6	0.1	0.7	1.7	2.0
Indianapolis, Ind. MSA	1,607,486	82.1	13.9	0.2	1.2	0.0	1.3	1.3	2.7
Iowa City, Iowa MSA	111,006	90.1	2.9	0.3	4.1	0.0	1.0	1.5	2.5
Jackson, Mich. MSA	158,422	88.5	7.9	0.4	0.5	0.0	0.8	1.7	2.2
Jackson, Miss.MSA	440,801	52.6	45.6	0.1	0.7	0.0	0.3	0.6	1.0
Jackson, Tenn. MSA	107,377	68.5	29.2	0.2	0.6	0.0	0.6	0.9	1.6
Jacksonville, Fla. MSA	1,100,491	72.6	21.7	0.3	2.3	0.1	1.2	1.8	3.8
Jacksonville, N.C. MSA	150,355	72.1	18.5	0.7	1.7	0.2	3.6	3.2	7.2
Jamestown, N.Y. MSA	139,750	94.0	2.2	0.4	0.4	0.0	1.7	1.2	4.2
Janesville–Beloit, Wis. MSA	152,307	91.0	4.6	0.3	0.8	0.0	1.8	1.5	3.9
Johnson City–Kingsport–Bristol, Tenn.–Va. MSA	480,091	96.2	2.1	0.2	0.4	0.0	0.3	0.7	0.9
Johnstown, Pa. MSA	232,621	96.3	2.4	0.1	0.3	0.0	0.3	0.6	0.8
Jonesboro, Ark. MSA	82,148	89.3	7.8	0.3	0.6	0.0	0.9	1.1	2.1
Joplin, Mo. MSA	157,322	92.8	1.2	1.6	0.6	0.1	1.4	2.2	3.0
Kalamazoo–Battle Creek, Mich. MSA	452,851	84.9	9.3	0.6	1.4	0.0	1.6	2.1	3.6
Kansas City, Mo.–Kans. MSA	1,776,062	80.8	12.8	0.5	1.6	0.1	2.3	2.0	5.2
Killeen–Temple, Texas MSA	312,952	63.9	20.8	0.8	2.4	0.5	8.0	3.8	15.7
Knoxville, Tenn. MSA	687,249	91.3	5.8	0.3	1.0	0.0	0.5	1.1	1.3
Kokomo, Ind. MSA	101,541	91.1	5.5	0.3	0.9	0.0	0.8	1.4	1.9
La Crosse, Wis.–Minn. MSA	126,838	94.8	0.8	0.4	2.7	0.0	0.2	0.9	0.9
Lafayette, La. MSA	385,647	69.7	28.2	0.2	0.7	0.0	0.4	0.8	1.3
Lafayette, Ind. MSA	182,821	89.9	2.1	0.3	3.7	0.0	2.8	1.3	5.6
Lake Charles, La. MSA	183,577	73.6	24.0	0.3	0.6	0.0	0.4	1.0	1.3
Lakeland–Winter Haven, Fla. MSA	483,924	79.6	13.5	0.4	0.9	0.0	3.8	1.7	9.5
Lancaster, Pa. MSA	470,658	91.5	2.8	0.1	1.4	0.0	2.9	1.3	5.7
Lansing–East Lansing, Mich. MSA	447,728	84.4	8.1	0.5	2.6	0.0	1.9	2.4	4.7
Laredo, Texas MSA	193,117	82.2	0.4	0.5	0.4	0.0	14.0	2.5	94.3
Las Cruces, N.Mex. MSA	174,682	67.8	1.6	1.5	0.8	0.1	24.7	3.6	63.4
Las Vegas, Nev.–Ariz. MSA	1,563,282	73.8	8.1	1.0	4.7	0.4	8.0	4.0	20.6
Lawrence, Kans. MSA	99,962	86.1	4.2	2.6	3.1	0.1	1.2	2.7	3.3
Lawton, Okla. MSA	114,996	65.2	19.0	5.1	2.1	0.4	3.5	4.7	8.4
Lewiston–Auburn, Maine MSA	90,830	96.8	0.7	0.3	0.6	0.0	0.3	1.3	1.0
Lexington, Ky. MSA	479,198	86.4	9.5	0.2	1.6	0.0	1.0	1.3	2.5
Lima, Ohio MSA	155,084	88.9	8.6	0.2	0.5	0.0	0.5	1.3	1.2
Lincoln, Nebr. MSA	250,291	90.1	2.8	0.6	2.9	0.1	1.7	1.9	3.4
Little Rock–North Little Rock, Ark. MSA	583,845	74.5	21.9	0.4	1.0	0.0	0.9	1.3	2.1
Longview–Marshall, Texas MSA	208,780	74.6	19.5	0.5	0.5	0.0	3.6	1.3	7.1
Los Angeles–Riverside–Orange County, Calif. CMSA	16,373,645	55.1	7.6	0.9	10.4	0.3	21.0	4.7	40.3
Los Angeles–Long Beach, Calif. PMSA	9,519,338	48.7	9.8	0.8	11.9	0.3	23.5	4.9	44.6

Metropolitan area	Total	White	Black	Indian/ Alaska Native	Asian	Pacific Islander	Other	Two or more races	Hispanic
Orange County, Calif. PMSA	2,846,289	64.8%	1.7%	0.7%	13.6%	0.3%	14.8%	4.1%	30.8%
Riverside–San Bernardino, Calif. PMSA	3,254,821	62.1	7.7	1.2	4.2	0.3	19.8	4.7	37.8
Ventura, CA PMSA	753,197	69.9	1.9	0.9	5.3	0.2	17.7	3.9	33.4
Louisville, Ky.–Ind. MSA	1,025,598	82.8	13.9	0.2	1.1	0.0	0.6	1.3	1.6
Lubbock, Texas MSA	242,628	74.3	7.7	0.6	1.3	0.0	14.1	2.0	27.5
Lynchburg, Va. MSA	214,911	79.6	17.9	0.3	0.7	0.0	0.4	1.0	1.0
Macon, Ga. MSA	322,549	59.2	37.5	0.2	1.1	0.0	0.7	1.1	2.1
Madison, Wis. MSA	426,526	89.0	4.0	0.3	3.5	0.0	1.4	1.8	3.4
Mansfield, Ohio MSA	175,818	90.8	7.1	0.2	0.5	0.0	0.3	1.1	0.9
McAllen–Edinburg–Mission, Texas MSA	569,463	77.7	0.5	0.4	0.6	0.0	18.6	2.1	88.3
Medford–Ashland, Oreg. MSA	181,269	91.6	0.4	1.1	0.9	0.2	2.9	2.9	6.7
Melbourne–Titusville–Palm Bay, Fla. MSA	476,230	86.8	8.4	0.4	1.5	0.1	1.1	1.8	4.6
Memphis, Tenn.–Ark.–Miss.MSA	1,135,614	52.9	43.4	0.2	1.4	0.0	1.1	1.0	2.4
Merced, Calif. MSA	210,554	56.2	3.8	1.2	6.8	0.2	26.1	5.7	45.3
Miami–Fort Lauderdale, Fla. CMSA	3,876,380	70.1	20.4	0.2	1.8	0.0	3.9	3.6	40.3
Fort Lauderdale, FL PMSA	1,623,018	70.6	20.5	0.2	2.3	0.1	3.0	3.4	16.7
Miami, FL PMSA	2,253,362	69.7	20.3	0.2	1.4	0.0	4.6	3.8	57.3
Milwaukee–Racine, Wis. CMSA	1,689,572	77.8	15.1	0.5	1.9	0.0	3.0	1.7	6.5
Milwaukee–Waukesha, WI PMSA	1,500,741	77.1	15.7	0.5	2.1	0.0	2.9	1.7	6.3
Racine, WI PMSA	188,831	83.0	10.5	0.4	0.7	0.0	3.7	1.7	7.9
Minneapolis–St. Paul, Minn.–Wis. MSA	2,968,806	86.1	5.3	0.7	4.1	0.0	1.6	2.1"	3.3
Missoula, Mont. MSA	95,802	94.0	0.3	2.3	1.0	0.1	0.4	1.9	1.6
Mobile, Ala. MSA	540,258	69.3	27.4	0.6	1.1	0.0	0.4	1.0	1.4
Modesto, Calif. MSA	446,997	69.3	2.6	1.3	4.2	0.3	16.8	5.4	31.7
Monroe, La. MSA	147,250	64.5	33.6	0.2	0.6	0.0	0.3	0.7	1.2
Montgomery, Ala. MSA	333,055	58.6	38.9	0.3	0.8	0.0	0.4	1.0	1.2
Muncie, Ind. MSA	118,769	90.7	6.7	0.2	0.7	0.1	0.5	1.1	1.1
Myrtle Beach, S.C. MSA	196,629	81.0	15.5	0.4	0.8	0.1	1.2	1.1	2.6
Naples, Fla. MSA	251,377	86.1	4.5	0.3	0.6	0.1	6.2	2.2	19.6
Nashville, Tenn. MSA	1,231,311	79.4	15.6	0.3	1.6	0.0	1.6	1.4	3.3
New London–Norwich, Conn.–R.I. MSA	293,566	88.0	4.7	0.9	1.9	0.1	1.8	2.5	4.7
New Orleans, La. MSA	1,337,726	57.3	37.5	0.4	2.1	0.0	1.2	1.4	4.4
New York–Northern New Jersey–Long Island, N.Y.–N.J.–Conn.–Pa. CMSA	21,199,865	64.1	17.2	0.3	6.8	0.0	8.2	3.4	18.2
Bergen–Passaic, NJ PMSA	1,373,167	72.7	8.1	0.3	8.2	0.0	7.9	2.9	17.3
Bridgeport, CT PMSA	459,479	78.1	11.5	0.2	2.3	0.0	5.3	2.5	12.4
Danbury, CT PMSA	217,980	88.6	3.0	0.2	3.2	0.0	3.0	2.0	7.0
Dutchess County, NY PMSA	280,150	83.7	9.3	0.2	2.5	0.0	2.4	1.9	6.4
Jersey City, NJ PMSA	608,975	55.6	13.5	0.4	9.4	0.1	15.5	5.6	39.8
Middlesex–Somerset–Hunterdon, NJ PMSA	1,169,641	73.9	8.0	0.2	11.2	0.0	4.4	2.2	11.2
Monmouth–Ocean, NJ PMSA	1,126,217	88.3	5.8	0.1	2.7	0.0	1.5	1.5	5.7
Nassau–Suffolk, NY PMSA	2,753,913	82.0	8.5	0.2	3.6	0.0	3.6	2.1	10.3
New Haven–Meriden, CT PMSA	542,149	77.4	13.1	0.2	2.7	0.0	4.3	2.1	9.8
New York, NY PMSA	9,314,235	48.8	24.6	0.5	9.1	0.1	12.3	4.6	25.1
Newark, NJ PMSA	2,032,989	65.9	22.3	0.2	4.0	0.0	4.9	2.7	13.3
Newburgh, NY–PA PMSA	387,669	84.8	7.5	0.3	1.4	0.0	3.8	2.1	10.8
Stamford–Norwalk, CT PMSA	353,556	81.0	9.2	0.1	3.9	0.0	3.5	2.2	10.8
Trenton, NJ PMSA	350,761	68.5	19.8	0.2	4.9	0.1	4.3	2.2	9.7
Waterbury, CT PMSA	228,984	82.2	8.3	0.3	1.3	0.0	5.5	2.3	11.5
Norfolk–Virginia Beach–Newport News, Va.–N.C. MSA	1,569,541	62.5	30.9	0.4	2.7	0.1	1.2	2.2	3.1
Ocala, Fla. MSA	258,916	84.2	11.5	0.4	0.7	0.0	1.7	1.4	6.0
Odessa–Midland, Texas MSA	237,132	75.5	5.8	0.7	0.8	0.0	14.8	2.4	35.8
Oklahoma City, Okla. MSA	1,083,346	75.7	10.6	4.2	2.5	0.1	3.2	3.9	6.7
Omaha, Nebr.–Iowa MSA	716,998	85.2	8.3	0.5	1.5	0.1	2.7	1.7	5.5
Orlando, Fla. MSA	1,644,561	75.0	13.9	0.3	2.7	0.1	5.1	2.9	16.5
Owensboro, Ky. MSA	91,545	93.7	4.3	0.1	0.4	0.0	0.4	0.9	0.9
Panama City, Fla. MSA	148,217	84.2	10.6	0.8	1.7	0.1	0.7	1.9	2.4
Parkersburg–Marietta, W.Va.–Ohio MSA	151,237	97.3	1.0	0.2	0.5	0.0	0.1	0.8	0.6
Pensacola, Fla. MSA	412,153	77.6	16.5	0.9	2.0	0.1	0.8	2.1	2.6
Peoria–Pekin, Ill. MSA	347,387	88.0	8.9	0.2	1.1	0.0	0.6	1.2	1.6

Metropolitan area	Total	White	Black	Indian/ Alaska Native	Asian	Pacific Islander	Other	Two or more races	Hispanic
Philadelphia–Wilmington–Atlantic City, Pa.–N.J.–Del.–Md. CMSA	6,188,463	72.5%	19.6%	0.2%	3.2%	0.0%	2.7%	1.7%	5.6%
Atlantic–Cape May, NJ PMSA	354,878	75.0	14.0	0.2	3.8	0.0	4.7	2.2	9.6
Philadelphia, PA–NJ PMSA	5,100,931	72.1	20.1	0.2	3.4	0.0	2.5	1.6	5.1
Vineland–Millville–Bridgeton, NJ PMSA	146,438	65.9	20.2	1.0	1.0	0.1	9.1	2.9	19.0
Wilmington–Newark, DE–MD PMSA	586,216	76.1	17.8	0.2	2.3	0.0	2.0	1.6	4.7
Phoenix–Mesa, Ariz. MSA	3,251,876	77.0	3.7	2.2	2.1	0.1	12.1	2.9	25.1
Pine Bluff, Ark. MSA	84,278	48.5	49.6	0.2	0.7	0.0	0.3	0.8	1.0
Pittsburgh, Pa. MSA	2,358,695	89.5	8.1	0.1	1.1	0.0	0.3	0.9	0.7
Pittsfield, Mass. MSA	84,699	94.8	2.3	0.1	0.9	0.0	0.6	1.2	1.7
Pocatello, Idaho MSA	75,565	91.3	0.6	2.9	1.0	0.2	2.1	2.0	4.7
Portland, Maine MSA	243,537	95.8	1.0	0.3	1.4	0.0	0.3	1.1	0.9
Portland–Salem, Oreg.–Wash. CMSA	2,265,223	84.3	2.4	1.0	4.1	0.3	4.6	3.3	8.7
Portland–Vancouver, OR–WA PMSA	1,918,009	84.5	2.7	0.9	4.6	0.3	3.8	3.3	7.4
Salem, OR PMSA	347,214	83.0	0.8	1.5	1.6	0.3	9.5	3.2	15.6
Providence–Fall River–Warwick, R.I.–Mass. MSA	1,188,613	86.2	4.0	0.4	2.2	0.0	4.5	2.6	7.9
Provo–Orem, Utah MSA	368,536	92.4	0.3	0.6	1.1	0.6	3.2	1.9	7.0
Pueblo, Colo. MSA	141,472	79.5	1.9	1.6	0.7	0.1	12.9	3.4	38.0
Punta Gorda, Fla. MSA	141,627	92.6	4.4	0.2	0.9	0.0	0.8	1.1	3.3
Raleigh–Durham–Chapel Hill, N.C. MSA	1,187,941	69.4	22.7	0.4	2.9	0.0	3.1	1.6	6.1
Rapid City, S.Dak. MSA	88,565	86.7	0.9	8.1	0.9	0.1	0.7	2.7	2.6
Reading, Pa. MSA	373,638	88.2	3.7	0.2	1.0	0.0	5.4	1.5	9.7
Redding, Calif. MSA	163,256	89.3	0.8	2.8	1.9	0.1	1.7	3.5	5.5
Reno, Nev. MSA	339,486	80.4	2.1	1.8	4.3	0.5	7.7	3.3	16.6
Richland–Kennewick–Pasco, Wash. MSA	191,822	80.0	1.3	0.8	2.1	0.1	12.7	3.1	21.3
Richmond–Petersburg, Va. MSA	996,512	64.9	30.2	0.4	2.1	0.0	1.1	1.3	2.3
Roanoke, Va. MSA	235,932	83.9	13.0	0.2	1.2	0.0	0.5	1.2	1.1
Rochester, Minn. MSA	124,277	90.3	2.7	0.3	4.3	0.0	0.9	1.5	2.4
Rochester, N.Y. MSA	1,098,201	84.0	10.3	0.3	1.8	0.0	1.9	1.7	4.3
Rockford, Ill. MSA	371,236	85.1	8.1	0.3	1.4	0.0	3.4	1.7	7.4
Rocky Mount, N.C. MSA	143,026	53.4	43.1	0.4	0.4	0.0	1.9	0.8	3.1
Sacramento–Yolo, Calif. CMSA	1,796,857	70.0	7.1	1.1	9.0	0.5	7.2	5.2	15.5
Sacramento, CA PMSA	1,628,197	70.2	7.7	1.1	8.9	0.5	6.5	5.2	14.4
Yolo, CA PMSA	168,660	67.7	2.0	1.2	9.9	0.3	13.8	5.2	25.9
Saginaw–Bay City–Midland, Mich. MSA	403,070	84.8	10.3	0.4	0.9	0.0	1.9	1.7	4.9
St. Cloud, Minn. MSA	167,392	96.0	0.8	0.3	1.5	0.0	0.4	0.8	1.3
St. Joseph, Mo. MSA	102,490	93.6	3.7	0.4	0.4	0.0	0.6	1.2	2.2
St. Louis, Mo.–Ill. MSA	2,603,607	78.3	18.3	0.2	1.4	0.0	0.5	1.2	1.5
Salinas, Calif. MSA	401,762	55.9	3.7	1.0	6.0	0.4	27.8	5.0	46.8
Salt Lake City–Ogden, Utah MSA	1,333,914	87.6	1.1	0.8	2.2	0.9	5.0	2.4	10.8
San Angelo, Texas MSA	104,010	79.1	4.1	0.7	0.9	0.1	12.8	2.4	30.7
San Antonio, Texas MSA	1,592,383	70.6	6.6	0.8	1.5	0.1	16.9	3.5	51.2
San Diego, Calif. MSA	2,813,833	66.5	5.7	0.9	8.9	0.5	12.8	4.7	26.7
San Francisco–Oakland–San Jose, Calif. CMSA	7,039,362	58.7	7.3	0.7	18.4	0.5	9.5	4.9	19.7
Oakland, CA PMSA	2,392,557	55.4	12.7	0.6	16.7	0.5	8.6	5.4	18.5
San Francisco, CA PMSA	1,731,183	58.6	5.3	0.4	22.7	0.8	7.7	4.5	16.8
San Jose, CA PMSA	1,682,585	53.8	2.8	0.7	25.6	0.3	12.1	4.7	24.0
Santa Cruz–Watsonville, CA PMSA	255,602	75.1	1.0	1.0	3.4	0.1	15.0	4.4	26.8
Santa Rosa, CA PMSA	458,614	81.6	1.4	1.2	3.1	0.2	8.4	4.1	17.3
Vallejo–Fairfield–Napa, CA PMSA	518,821	62.0	11.7	0.8	10.4	0.6	8.7	5.8	19.1
San Luis Obispo–Atascadero–Paso Robles, Calif. MSA	246,681	84.6	2.0	0.9	2.7	0.1	6.2	3.4	16.3
Santa Barbara–Santa Maria–Lompoc, Calif. MSA	399,347	72.7	2.3	1.2	4.1	0.2	15.2	4.3	34.2
Santa Fe, N.Mex. MSA	147,635	75.6	0.6	2.8	1.2	0.1	15.9	3.9	44.4
Sarasota–Bradenton, Fla. MSA	589,959	89.8	6.0	0.2	0.8	0.0	1.9	1.2	6.6
Savannah, Ga. MSA	293,000	61.2	34.9	0.3	1.5	0.1	0.8	1.3	2.2
Scranton–Wilkes-Barre–Hazleton, Pa. MSA	624,776	96.8	1.4	0.1	0.6	0.0	0.4	0.6	1.2
Seattle–Tacoma–Bremerton, Wash. CMSA	3,554,760	79.3	4.7	1.2	7.9	0.6	2.2	4.2	5.2

Metropolitan area	Total	White	Black	Indian/ Alaska Native	Asian	Pacific Islander	Other	Two or more races	Hispanic
Bremerton, WA PMSA	231,969	84.3%	2.9%	1.6%	4.4%	0.8%	1.4%	4.6%	4.1%
Olympia, WA PMSA	207,355	85.7	2.4	1.5	4.4	0.5	1.7	3.9	4.5
Seattle–Bellevue–Everett, WA PMSA	2,414,616	78.6	4.4	1.0	9.4	0.5	2.4	3.9	5.2
Tacoma, WA PMSA	700,820	78.4	7.0	1.4	5.1	0.8	2.2	5.1	5.5
Sharon, Pa. MSA	120,293	93.1	5.3	0.1	0.4	0.0	0.2	0.9	0.7
Sheboygan, Wis. MSA	112,646	92.7	1.1	0.4	3.3	0.0	1.5	1.1	3.4
Sherman–Denison, Texas MSA	110,595	87.2	5.9	1.3	0.6	0.0	2.9	2.1	6.8
Shreveport–Bossier City, La. MSA	392,302	59.7	37.4	0.4	0.8	0.0	0.5	1.1	1.8
Sioux City, Iowa–Nebr. MSA	124,130	86.1	1.8	1.7	2.5	0.0	5.8	2.1	11.3
Sioux Falls, S.Dak. MSA	172,412	93.7	1.4	1.7	0.9	0.0	0.9	1.4	1.9
South Bend, Ind. MSA	265,559	82.4	11.5	0.4	1.3	0.1	2.5	2.0	4.7
Spokane, Wash. MSA	417,939	91.4	1.6	1.4	1.9	0.2	0.8	2.8	2.8
Springfield, Ill. MSA	201,437	88.1	9.1	0.2	1.0	0.0	0.4	1.2	1.0
Springfield, Mo. MSA	325,721	94.4	1.8	0.6	0.9	0.1	0.6	1.6	1.7
Springfield, Mass. MSA	591,932	81.6	6.7	0.2	1.9	0.1	7.2	2.2	12.5
State College, Pa. MSA	135,758	91.4	2.6	0.1	4.0	0.1	0.7	1.1	1.7
Steubenville–Weirton, Ohio–W.Va. MSA	132,008	94.5	3.9	0.2	0.3	0.0	0.2	0.9	0.6
Stockton–Lodi, Calif. MSA	563,598	58.1	6.7	1.1	11.4	0.3	16.3	6.0	30.5
Sumter, S.C. MSA	104,646	50.1	46.7	0.3	0.9	0.1	0.8	1.2	1.8
Syracuse, N.Y. MSA	732,117	88.9	6.5	0.7	1.5	0.0	0.8	1.6	2.1
Tallahassee, Fla. MSA	284,539	62.0	33.6	0.3	1.6	0.0	1.1	1.4	3.9
Tampa–St. Petersburg–Clearwater, Fla. MSA	2,395,997	82.9	10.2	0.3	1.9	0.1	2.7	2.0	10.4
Terre Haute, Ind. MSA	149,192	92.9	4.4	0.3	0.9	0.0	0.3	1.2	1.0
Texarkana, Texas–Texarkana, Ark. MSA	129,749	73.5	23.3	0.6	0.4	0.0	0.9	1.2	3.6
Toledo, Ohio MSA	618,203	82.1	12.8	0.3	1.1	0.0	1.8	1.9	4.4
Topeka, Kans. MSA	169,871	82.9	9.0	1.2	1.0	0.0	3.2	2.7	7.3
Tucson, Ariz. MSA	843,746	75.1	3.0	3.2	2.0	0.1	13.3	3.2	29.3
Tulsa, Okla. MSA	803,235	76.0	8.8	6.9	1.2	0.0	2.1	4.8	4.8
Tuscaloosa, Ala. MSA	164,875	68.1	29.3	0.2	0.9	0.0	0.6	0.8	1.3
Tyler, Texas MSA	174,706	72.6	19.1	0.4	0.7	0.0	5.7	1.4	11.2
Utica–Rome, N.Y. MSA	299,896	91.8	4.6	0.2	1.0	0.0	0.9	1.4	2.7
Victoria, Texas MSA	84,088	74.2	6.3	0.5	0.8	0.0	15.9	2.2	39.2
Visalia–Tulare–Porterville, Calif. MSA	368,021	58.1	1.6	1.6	3.3	0.1	30.8	4.6	50.8
Waco, Texas MSA	213,517	72.2	15.2	0.5	1.1	0.0	9.2	1.8	17.9
Washington–Baltimore, D.C.–Md.–Va.–W.Va. CMSA	7,608,070	63.0	26.2	0.3	5.3	0.1	2.7	2.4	6.4
Baltimore, MD PMSA	2,552,994	67.3	27.4	0.3	2.7	0.0	0.7	1.5	2.0
Hagerstown, MD PMSA	131,923	89.7	7.8	0.2	0.8	0.0	0.5	1.0	1.2
Washington, DC–MD–VA–WV PMSA	4,923,153	60.1	26.0	0.3	6.7	0.1	3.9	2.9	8.8
Waterloo–Cedar Falls, Iowa MSA	128,012	88.4	8.0	0.2	1.0	0.0	0.9	1.5	1.8
Wausau, Wis. MSA	125,834	93.8	0.3	0.3	4.5	0.0	0.3	0.7	0.8
West Palm Beach–Boca Raton, Fla. MSA	1,131,184	79.1	13.8	0.2	1.5	0.1	3.0	2.4	12.4
Wheeling, W.Va.–Ohio MSA	153,172	95.6	2.9	0.1	0.4	0.0	0.1	0.8	0.5
Wichita, Kans. MSA	545,220	81.8	7.8	1.1	2.9	0.1	3.8	2.6	7.4
Wichita Falls, Texas MSA	140,518	79.8	9.6	0.9	1.7	0.1	5.3	2.6	11.8
Williamsport, Pa. MSA	120,044	93.9	4.3	0.2	0.4	0.0	0.3	0.9	0.7
Wilmington, N.C. MSA	233,450	80.7	16.2	0.5	0.7	0.1	1.0	1.0	2.2
Yakima, Wash. MSA	222,581	65.6	1.0	4.5	1.0	0.1	24.4	3.5	35.9
York, Pa. MSA	381,751	92.8	3.7	0.2	0.9	0.0	1.4	1.1	3.0
Youngstown–Warren, Ohio MSA	594,746	87.4	10.3	0.2	0.4	0.0	0.6	1.2	1.8
Yuba City, Calif. MSA	139,149	68.9	2.5	2.0	9.6	0.2	11.7	5.2	20.1
Yuma, Ariz. MSA	160,026	68.3	2.2	1.6	0.9	0.1	23.6	3.2	50.5
Aguadilla, PR MSA	146,424	87.1	3.9	0.2	0.1	0.0	5.8	2.8	98.8
Mayag,ez, PR MSA	253,347	85.7	4.4	0.3	0.2	0.0	4.9	4.6	99.1
Ponce, PR MSA	361,094	83.4	5.4	0.3	0.1	0.0	5.8	4.9	99.2
San Juan–Caguas–Arecibo, PR CMSA	2,450,292	78.2	9.5	0.4	0.3	0.0	7.3	4.4	98.6
Arecibo, PR PMSA	174,300	89.9	3.4	0.2	0.1	0.0	3.8	2.7	99.2
Caguas, PR PMSA	308,365	83.5	5.8	0.3	0.1	0.0	7.3	2.9	99.2
San Juan–Bayamon, PR PMSA	1,967,627	76.3	10.6	0.4	0.3	0.0	7.6	4.7	98.5

1. Hispanic persons may be of any race. **Source:** U.S Bureau of the Census, Press Release CB91-229

Population Change in the Top 100 Metropolitan Statistical Areas, 1990–2000

Since the 1990 Census, the Census Bureau has changed the boundaries of several dozen metropolitan statistical areas (MSAs), merging some areas and separating others. As a result, population statistics before and after 1990 are not directly comparable for more than 75 MSAs.

Metropolitan Statistical Area	Population 1990	Population 2000	Change, 1990–2000 Number	Change, 1990–2000 Percent
1. New York–Northern New Jersey–Long Island, N.Y.–N.J.–Conn.–Pa. CMSA	19,549,649	21,199,865	1,650,216	8.4%
2. Los Angeles–Riverside–Orange County, Calif. CMSA	14,531,529	16,373,645	1,842,116	12.7
3. Chicago–Gary–Kenosha, Ill.–Ind.–Wisc. CMSA	8,239,820	9,157,540	917,720	11.1
4. Washington–Baltimore, D.C.–Md.–Va.–WV CMSA	6,727,050	7,608,070	881,020	13.1
5. San Francisco–Oakland–San Jose, Calif. CMSA	6,253,311	7,039,362	786,051	12.6
6. Philadelphia–Wilmington–Atlantic City, Pa.–N.J.–Del.–Md. CMSA	5,892,937	6,188,463	295,526	5.0
7. Boston–Worcester–Lawrence, Mass.–N.H.–Maine–Conn. CMSA	5,455,403	5,819,100	363,697	6.7
8. Detroit–Ann Arbor–Flint, Mich. CMSA	5,187,171	5,456,428	269,257	5.2
9. Dallas–Fort Worth, Texas CMSA	4,037,282	5,221,801	1,184,519	29.3
10. Houston–Galveston–Brazoria, Texas CMSA	3,731,131	4,669,571	938,440	25.2
11. Atlanta, Ga. MSA	2,959,950	4,112,198	1,152,248	38.9
12. Miami–Fort Lauderdale, Fla. CMSA	3,192,582	3,876,380	683,798	21.4
13. Seattle–Tacoma–Bremerton, Wash. CMSA	2,970,328	3,554,760	584,432	19.7
14. Phoenix–Mesa, Ariz. MSA	2,238,480	3,251,876	1,013,396	45.3
15. Minneapolis–St. Paul, Minn.–Wisc. MSA	2,538,834	2,968,806	429,972	16.9
16. Cleveland–Akron, Ohio CMSA	2,859,644	2,945,831	86,187	3.0
17. San Diego, Calif. MSA	2,498,016	2,813,833	315,817	12.6
18. St. Louis, Mo.–Ill. MSA	2,492,525	2,603,607	111,082	4.5
19. Denver–Boulder–Greeley, Colo. CMSA	1,980,140	2,581,506	601,366	30.4
20. San Juan–Caguas–Arecibo, Puerto Rico CMSA	2,270,808	2,450,292	179,484	7.9
21. Tampa–St. Petersburg–Clearwater, Fla. MSA	2,067,959	2,395,997	328,038	15.9
22. Pittsburgh, Pa. MSA	2,394,811	2,358,695	-36,116	-1.5
23. Portland–Salem, Oreg.–Wash. CMSA	1,793,476	2,265,223	471,747	26.3
24. Cincinnati–Hamilton, Ohio–KY–Ind. CMSA	1,817,571	1,979,202	161,631	8.9
25. Sacramento–Yolo, Calif. CMSA	1,481,102	1,796,857	315,755	21.3
26. Kansas City, Mo.–Kans. MSA	1,582,875	1,776,062	193,187	12.2
27. Milwaukee–Racine, Wisc. CMSA	1,607,183	1,689,572	82,389	5.1
28. Orlando, Fla. MSA	1,224,852	1,644,561	419,709	34.3
29. Indianapolis, Ind. MSA	1,380,491	1,607,486	226,995	16.4
30. San Antonio, Texas MSA	1,324,749	1,592,383	267,634	20.2
31. Norfolk–Virginia Beach–Newport News, Va.–N.C. MSA	1,443,244	1,569,541	126,297	8.8
32. Las Vegas, Nev.–Ariz. MSA	852,737	1,563,282	710,545	83.3%
33. Columbus, Ohio MSA	1,345,450	1,540,157	194,707	14.5
34. Charlotte–Gastonia–Rock Hill, N.C.–S.C. MSA	1,162,093	1,499,293	337,200	29.0
35. New Orleans, La. MSA	1,285,270	1,337,726	52,456	4.1
36. Salt Lake City–Ogden, Utah MSA	1,072,227	1,333,914	261,687	24.4
37. Greensboro–Winston-Salem–High Point, N.C. MSA	1,050,304	1,251,509	201,205	19.2
38. Austin–San Marcos, Texas MSA	846,227	1,249,763	403,536	47.7
39. Nashville, Tenn. MSA	985,026	1,231,311	246,285	25.0
40. Providence–Fall River–Warwick, R.I.–Mass. MSA	1,134,350	1,188,613	54,263	4.8
41. Raleigh–Durham–Chapel Hill, N.C. MSA	855,545	1,187,941	332,396	38.9
42. Hartford, Conn. MSA	1,157,585	1,183,110	25,525	2.2
43. Buffalo–Niagara Falls, N.Y. MSA	1,189,288	1,170,111	-19,177	-1.6
44. Memphis, Tenn.–Ark.-Miss. MSA	1,007,306	1,135,614	128,308	12.7
45. West Palm Beach–Boca Raton, Fla. MSA	863,518	1,131,184	267,666	31.0
46. Jacksonville, Fla. MSA	906,727	1,100,491	193,764	21.4
47. Rochester, N.Y. MSA	1,062,470	1,098,201	35,731	3.4
48. Grand Rapids–Muskegon–Holland, Mich. MSA	937,891	1,088,514	150,623	16.1
49. Oklahoma City, Okla. MSA	958,839	1,083,346	124,507	13.0
50. Louisville, Ky.–Ind. MSA	948,829	1,025,598	76,769	8.1
51. Richmond–Petersburg, Va. MSA	865,640	996,512	130,872	15.1
52. Greenville–Spartanburg–Anderson, S.C. MSA	830,563	962,441	131,878	15.9
53. Dayton–Springfield, Ohio MSA	951,270	950,558	-712	-0.1
54. Fresno, Calif. MSA	755,580	922,516	166,936	22.1
55. Birmingham, Ala. MSA	840,140	921,106	80,966	9.6
56. Honolulu, Hawaii MSA	836,231	876,156	39,925	4.8
57. Albany–Schenectady–Troy, N.Y. MSA	861,424	875,583	14,159	1.6
58. Tucson, Ariz. MSA	666,880	843,746	176,866	26.5
59. Tulsa, Okla. MSA	708,954	803,235	94,281	13.3
60. Syracuse, N.Y. MSA	742,177	732,117	-10,060	-1.4
61. Omaha, Neb.-Iowa MSA	639,580	716,998	77,418	12.1
62. Albuquerque, NM MSA	589,131	712,738	123,607	21.0
63. Knoxville, Tenn. MSA	585,960	687,249	101,289	17.3

Metropolitan Statistical Area	Population 1990	Population 2000	Change, 1990–2000 Number	Change, 1990–2000 Percent
64. El Paso, Texas MSA	591,610	679,622	88,012	14.9%
65. Bakersfield, Calif. MSA	543,477	661,645	118,168	21.7
66. Allentown–Bethlehem–Easton, Pa. MSA	595,081	637,958	42,877	7.2
67. Harrisburg–Lebanon–Carlisle, Pa. MSA	587,986	629,401	41,415	7.0
68. Scranton–Wilkes-Barre–Hazleton, Pa. MSA	638,466	624,776	-13,690	-2.1
69. Toledo, Ohio MSA	614,128	618,203	4,075	0.7
70. Baton Rouge, LA MSA	528,264	602,894	74,630	14.1
71. Youngstown–Warren, Ohio MSA	600,895	594,746	-6,149	-1.0
72. Springfield, Mass. MSA	587,884	591,932	4,048	0.7
73. Sarasota–Bradenton, Fla. MSA	489,483	589,959	100,476	20.5
74. Little Rock–North Little Rock, Ark. MSA	513,117	583,845	70,728	13.8
75. McAllen–Edinburg–Mission, Texas MSA	383,545	569,463	185,918	48.5
76. Stockton–Lodi, Calif. MSA	480,628	563,598	82,970	17.3
77. Charleston–North Charleston, S.C. MSA	506,875	549,033	42,158	8.3
78. Wichita, Kans. MSA	485,270	545,220	59,950	12.4
79. Mobile, Ala. MSA	476,923	540,258	63,335	13.3
80. Columbia, S.C. MSA	453,331	536,691	83,360	18.4
81. Colorado Springs, Colo. MSA	397,014	516,929	119,915	30.2
82. Fort Wayne, Ind. MSA	456,281	502,141	45,860	10.1
83. Daytona Beach, Fla. MSA	399,413	493,175	93,762	23.5
84. Lakeland–Winter Haven, Fla. MSA	405,382	483,924	78,542	19.4
85. Johnson City–Kingsport–Bristol, Tenn.–Va. MSA	436,047	480,091	44,044	10.1
86. Lexington, Ky. MSA	405,936	479,198	73,262	18.0
87. Augusta–Aiken, Ga.–S.C. MSA	415,184	477,441	62,257	15.0
88. Melbourne–Titusville–Palm Bay, Fla. MSA	398,978	476,230	77,252	19.4
89. Lancaster, Pa. MSA	422,822	470,658	47,836	11.3
90. Chattanooga, Tenn.–Ga. MSA	424,347	465,161	40,814	9.6
91. Des Moines, Iowa MSA	392,928	456,022	63,094	16.1
92. Kalamazoo–Battle Creek, Mich. MSA	429,453	452,851	23,398	5.4
93. Lansing–East Lansing, Mich. MSA	432,674	447,728	15,054	3.5
94. Modesto, Calif. MSA	370,522	446,997	76,475	20.6
95. Fort Myers–Cape Coral, Fla. MSA	335,113	440,888	105,775	31.6
96. Jackson, Miss. MSA	395,396	440,801	45,405	11.5
97. Boise City, Idaho MSA	295,851	432,345	136,494	46.1
98. Madison, Wisc. MSA	367,085	426,526	59,441	16.2
99. Spokane, Wash. MSA	361,364	417,939	56,575	15.7
100. Pensacola, Fla. MSA	344,406	412,153	67,747	19.7

Note: CMSA = consolidated metropolitan statistical area; MSA = metropolitan statistical area. For component areas see "Population of Metropolitan Statistical Areas, 1990-2000." **Source:** U.S. Bureau of the Census, 2001.

Fastest Growing and Declining Metropolitan Statistical Areas, 1990-2000

Metropolitan Statistical Area	Population 1990	Population 2000	Change, 1990–2000 Number	Change, 1990–2000 Percent
FASTEST GROWING				
1. Las Vegas, Nev.-Ariz. MSA	852,737	1,563,282	710,545	83.3%
2. Naples, Fla. MSA	152,099	251,377	99,278	65.3
3. Yuma, Ariz. MSA	106,895	160,026	53,131	49.7
4. McAllen–Edinburg–Mission, Texas MSA	383,545	569,463	185,918	48.5
5. Austin–San Marcos, Texas MSA	846,227	1,249,763	403,536	47.7
6. Fayetteville–Springdale–Rogers, Ark. MSA	210,908	311,121	100,213	47.5
7. Boise City, Idaho MSA	295,851	432,345	136,494	46.1
8. Phoenix–Mesa, Ariz. MSA	2,238,480	3,251,876	1,013,396	45.3
9. Laredo, Texas MSA	133,239	193,117	59,878	44.9
10. Provo–Orem, Utah MSA	263,590	368,536	104,946	39.8
FASTEST DECLINING				
1. Steubenville–Weirton, Ohio–W.Va. MSA	142,523	132,008	-10,515	-7.4
2. Grand Forks, N.Dak,–Minn. MSA	103,181	97,478	-5,703	-5.5
3. Utica–Rome, N.Y. MSA	316,633	299,896	-16,737	-5.3
4. Binghamton, N.Y. MSA	264,497	252,320	-12,177	-4.6
5. Pittsfield, Mass. MSA	88,695	84,699	-3,996	-4.5
6. Elmira, N.Y. MSA	95,195	91,070	-4,125	-4.3
7. Alexandria, La. MSA	131,556	126,337	-5,219	-4.0
8. Wheeling, W.Va.–Ohio MSA	159,301	153,172	-6,129	-3.8
9. Johnstown, Pa. MSA	241,247	232,621	-8,626	-3.6
10. Anniston, Ala. MSA	116,034	112,249	-3,785	-3.3

Note: CMSA= consolidated metropolitan statistical area; MSA = metropolitan statistical area. For component areas see "Population of Metropolitan Statistical Areas, 1990-2000." **Source:** U.S. Bureau of the Census.

COUNTIES IN AMERICA

In 2001 there were 3,141 counties in the United States. While only 50 percent of Americans live in cities, almost every American lives in a county. Counties were originally the creation of state governments, which saw them as the local arm of state authority, with special responsibility for rural areas. Counties were intended more for the administrative convenience of the state than to meet the immediate needs of county residents and were not designed to have the intimate relationship with, or understanding of, the needs of localities theoretically characteristic of municipalities. But most states have loosened the reins on county governments in recent years, giving them more authority to meet the needs of population centers that have pushed beyond municipal limits. (Note that in Louisiana, counties are called parishes, and in Alaska and New York City, they are known as boroughs.)

Like cities and metropolitan areas, the fastest-growing counties are in the southern and western United States. Seven of the 10 fastest-growing counties in 2000 were in Colorado or Georgia; the other three were in Virginia, Utah and Idaho.

The counties with the largest numerical increase in population between 1990 and 2000 are all in the western U.S.: Maricopa County, Ariz. (950,048), Los Angeles County, Calif. (656,174), Clark County, Nevada (634,306), Harris County, Texas (582,379), and Orange County, Calif. (435,733).

In addition, most of the counties with greatest growth are those in or around major metropolitan areas. Colorado's Douglas and Elbert Counties, which border both the Denver and Colorado Springs metropolitan areas, ranked 1 and 3 in population growth between 1990 and 2000. Both more than doubled over that period. Forsyth County, Ga. (within the Atlanta metropolitan area) was the second-fastest-growing county, increasing by 123.2 percent.

The 50 Largest Counties, 1980–90

	Population		Change 1980–90		Rank
Rank, 1990/County	**1990**	**1980**	**Number**	**Percent**	**1980**
1. Los Angeles County, Calif.	8,863,164	7,477,238	1,385,926	18.5%	1
2. Cook County, Ill.	5,105,067	5,253,628	-148,561	-2.8	2
3. Harris County, Texas	2,818,199	2,409,547	408,652	17.0	3
4. San Diego County, Calif.	2,498,016	1,861,846	636,170	34.2	8
5. Orange County, Calif.	2,410,556	1,932,921	477,635	24.7	6
6. Kings County, N.Y.	2,300,664	2,231,028	69,636	3.1	5
7. Maricopa County, Ariz.	2,122,101	1,509,175	612,926	40.6	12
8. Wayne County, Mich.	2,111,687	2,337,843	-226,156	-9.7	4
9. Queens County, N.Y.	1,951,598	1,891,325	60,273	3.2	7
10. Dade County, Fla.	1,937,094	1,625,509	311,585	19.2	10
11. Dallas County, Texas	1,852,810	1,556,419	296,391	19.0	11
12. Philadelphia County, Pa.	1,585,577	1,688,210	-102,633	-6.1	9
13. King County, Wash.	1,507,319	1,269,898	237,421	18.7	20
14. Santa Clara County, Calif.	1,497,577	1,295,071	202,506	15.6	18
15. New York County, N.Y.	1,487,536	1,428,285	59,251	4.1	15
16. San Bernardino County, Calif.	1,418,380	895,016	523,364	58.5	30
17. Cuyahoga County, Ohio	1,412,140	1,498,400	-86,260	-5.8	13
18. Middlesex County, Mass.	1,398,468	1,367,034	31,434	2.3	16
19. Allegheny County, Pa.	1,336,449	1,450,195	-113,746	-7.8	14
20. Suffolk County, N.Y.	1,321,864	1,284,231	37,633	2.9	19
21. Nassau County, N.Y.	1,287,348	1,321,582	-34,234	-2.6	17
22. Alameda County, Calif.	1,279,182	1,105,379	173,803	15.7	22
23. Broward County, Fla.	1,255,488	1,018,257	237,231	23.3	23
24. Bronx County, N.Y.	1,203,789	1,168,972	34,817	3.0	21
25. Bexar County, Texas	1,185,394	988,971	196,423	19.9	26
26. Riverside County, Calif.	1,170,413	663,199	507,214	76.5	52
27. Tarrant County, Texas	1,170,103	860,880	309,223	35.9	34
28. Oakland County, Mich.	1,083,592	1,011,793	71,799	7.1	25
29. Sacramento County, Calif.	1,041,219	783,381	257,838	32.9	40
30. Hennepin County, Minn.	1,032,431	941,411	91,020	9.7	29
31. St. Louis County, Mo.	993,529	974,180	19,349	2.0	27
32. Erie County, N.Y.	968,532	1,015,472	-46,940	-4.6	24
33. Franklin County, Ohio	961,437	869,126	92,311	10.6	32
34. Milwaukee County, Wis.	959,275	964,988	-5,713	-0.6	28
35. Westchester County, N.Y.	874,866	866,599	8,267	1.0	33
36. Hamilton County, Ohio	866,228	873,203	-6,975	-0.8	31
37. Palm Beach County, Fla.	863,518	576,758	286,760	49.7	70
38. Hartford County, Conn.	851,783	807,766	44,017	5.4	37
39. Pinellas County, Fla.	851,659	728,531	123,128	16.9	45
40. Honolulu County, Hawaii	836,231	762,565	73,666	9.7	43
41. Hillsborough County, Fla.	834,054	646,939	187,115	28.9	57
42. Fairfield County, Conn.	827,645	807,143	20,502	2.5	38
43. Shelby County, Tenn	826,330	777,113	49,217	6.3	41
44. Bergen County, N.J.	825,380	845,385	-20,005	-2.4	36
45. Fairfax County, Va.	818,584	595,754	222,830	37.4	66
46. New Haven County, Conn.	804,219	761,325	42,894	5.6	44
47. Contra Costa County, Calif.	803,732	656,331	147,401	22.5	54
48. Marion County, Tenn.	797,159	765,233	31,926	4.2	42
49. DuPage County, Ill.	781,666	658,858	122,808	18.6	53
50. Essex County, N.J.	778,206	851,304	-73,098	-8.6	35

Source: U.S. Bureau of the Census release, 1991.

The 75 Largest Counties, 1990–2000

Rank, 2000/County	Population, 1990	Population, 2000	Change, 1990-2000	Percent Change
1. Los Angeles County, Calif.	8,863,164	9,519,338	656,174	7.4%
2. Cook County, Ill.	5,105,067	5,376,741	271,674	5.3
3. Harris County, Texas	2,818,199	3,400,578	582,379	20.7
4. Maricopa County, Ariz.	2,122,101	3,072,149	950,048	44.8
5. Orange County, Calif.	2,410,556	2,846,289	435,733	18.1
6. San Diego County, Calif.	2,498,016	2,813,833	315,817	12.6
7. Kings County, N.Y.	2,300,664	2,465,326	164,662	7.2
8. Miami-Dade County, Fla.	1,937,094	2,253,362	316,268	16.3
9. Queens County, N.Y.	1,951,598	2,229,379	277,781	14.2
10. Dallas County, Texas	1,852,810	2,218,899	366,089	19.8
11. Wayne County, Mich.	2,111,687	2,061,162	-50,525	-2.4
12. King County, Wash.	1,507,319	1,737,034	229,715	15.2
13. San Bernardino County, Calif.	1,418,380	1,709,434	291,054	20.5
14. Santa Clara County, Calif.	1,497,577	1,682,585	185,008	12.4
15. Broward County, Fla.	1,255,488	1,623,018	367,530	29.3
16. Riverside County, Calif.	1,170,413	1,545,387	374,974	32.0
17. New York County, N.Y.	1,487,536	1,537,195	49,659	3.3
18. Philadelphia County, Pa.	1,585,577	1,517,550	-68,027	-4.3
19. Middlesex County, Mass.	1,398,468	1,465,396	66,928	4.8
20. Tarrant County, Texas	1,170,103	1,446,219	276,116	23.6
21. Alameda County, Calif.	1,279,182	1,443,741	164,559	12.9
22. Suffolk County, N.Y.	1,321,864	1,419,369	97,505	7.4
23. Cuyahoga County, Ohio	1,412,140	1,393,978	-18,162	-1.3
24. Bexar County, Texas	1,185,394	1,392,931	207,537	17.5
25. Clark County, Nev.	741,459	1,375,765	634,306	85.5
26. Nassau County, N.Y.	1,287,348	1,334,544	47,196	3.7
27. Bronx County, N.Y.	1,203,789	1,332,650	128,861	10.7
28. Allegheny County, Pa.	1,336,449	1,281,666	-54,783	-4.1
29. Sacramento County, Calif.	1,041,219	1,223,499	182,280	17.5
30. Oakland County, Mich.	1,083,592	1,194,156	110,564	10.2
31. Palm Beach County, Fla.	863,518	1,131,184	267,666	31.0
32. Hennepin County, Minn.	1,032,431	1,116,200	83,769	8.1
33. Franklin County, Ohio	961,437	1,068,978	107,541	11.2
34. St. Louis County, Mo.	993,529	1,016,315	22,786	2.3
35. Hillsborough County, Fla.	834,054	998,948	164,894	19.8
36. Fairfax County, Va.	818,584	969,749	151,165	18.5
37. Erie County, N.Y.	968,532	950,265	-18,267	-1.9
38. Contra Costa County, Calif.	803,732	948,816	145,084	18.1
39. Milwaukee County, Wis.	959,275	940,164	-19,111	-2.0
40. Westchester County, N.Y.	874,866	923,459	48,593	5.6
41. Pinellas County, Fla.	851,659	921,482	69,823	8.2
42. DuPage County, Ill.	781,666	904,161	122,495	15.7
43. Salt Lake County, Utah	725,956	898,387	172,431	23.8
44. Shelby County, Tenn.	826,330	897,472	71,142	8.6
45. Orange County, Fla.	677,491	896,344	218,853	32.3
46. Bergen County, N.J.	825,380	884,118	58,738	7.1
47. Fairfield County, Conn.	827,645	882,567	54,922	6.6
48. Honolulu County, Hawaii	836,231	876,156	39,925	4.8
49. Montgomery County, Md.	757,027	873,341	116,314	15.4
50. Marion County, Ind.	797,159	860,454	63,295	7.9
51. Hartford County, Conn.	851,783	857,183	5,400	0.6
52. Hamilton County, Ohio	866,228	845,303	-20,925	-2.4
53. Pima County, Ariz.	666,880	843,746	176,866	26.5
54. New Haven County, Conn.	804,219	824,008	19,789	2.5
55. Fulton County, Ga.	648,951	816,006	167,055	25.7
56. Travis County, Texas	576,407	812,280	235,873	40.9
57. Prince George's County, Md.	729,268	801,515	72,247	9.9
58. Fresno County, Calif.	667,490	799,407	131,917	19.8
59. Essex County, N.J.	778,206	793,633	15,427	2.0
60. Macomb County, Mich.	717,400	788,149	70,749	9.9
61. Duval County, Fla.	672,971	778,879	105,908	15.7
62. San Francisco County, Calif.	723,959	776,733	52,774	7.3
63. Baltimore County, Md.	692,134	754,292	62,158	9.0
64. Ventura County, Calif.	669,016	753,197	84,181	12.6
65. Worcester County, Mass.	709,705	750,963	41,258	5.8
66. Middlesex County, N.J.	671,780	750,162	78,382	11.7
67. Montgomery County, Pa.	678,111	750,097	71,986	10.6
68. Monroe County, N.Y.	713,968	735,343	21,375	3.0
69. Essex County, Mass.	670,080	723,419	53,339	8.0
70. San Mateo County, Calif.	649,623	707,161	57,538	8.9
71. Pierce County, Wash.	586,203	700,820	114,617	19.6
72. Mecklenburg County, N.C.	511,433	695,454	184,021	36.0
73. Jefferson County, Ky.	664,937	693,604	28,667	4.3
74. Suffolk County, Mass.	663,906	689,807	25,901	3.9
75. El Paso County, Texas	591,610	679,622	88,012	14.9

Source: U.S. Bureau of the Census, 2001

The American People Today

The United States is the third most populous nation in the world, ranking behind only China and India. The 2000 Census reported a total U.S. population of 281,421,806, a growth rate of 13.2 pecent over the last decade. There were just under 250 million in 1990; the U.S. population has increased by more than 100 million since 1960, and has doubled since 1940.

The single most noteworthy characteristic of the U.S. population continues to be the "baby boom generation," the 75 million people born between 1946 and 1964. During these years the crude birth rate soared to as high as 24 live births per 1,000 population (compared to 20 or so in the years before World War II). Fertility rates, too, which had stood at about 75 live births per 1,000 women aged 15-44, jumped to as high as 121. As a result the population grew at an annual rate of between 1.4 percent and 1.8 percent.

The baby boom produced a generation of Americans much more populous than any other; the result has been that this generation attracts a great deal of attention as it passes through statistical age categories. Demographers sometimes refer to baby boomers, somewhat inelegantly perhaps, as the "pig in the python" in order to explain how this group has continued to distort the normal contours of the general body of the population. During the 1950's, their numbers required great capital outlays for new schools, and in the 1960's, for expanding colleges and universities. In the 1970's, they jammed the labor market causing higher unemployment rates, but helped the economy by increasing consumption and expanding the housing market.

The most troubling aspect of the 2000 Census is its stark revelation that the American population is very rapidly growing older. In 1970, 9.8 percent of the population was 65 or over; by 2000, 12.6 percent were. In 2030, the Census Bureau projects that fully 20 percent of Americans will 65 or over.

The impact of this change on the Social Security system cannot be taken seriously enough. In 2013, the first baby boomers turn 67 (the aging of the population has forced a deferral of the traditional retirement age from 65), and will begin collecting Social Security instead of paying into the fund. Ordinarily, this wouldn't be a remarkable fact. But the generation that followed the baby boom —the so-called baby bust generation, also known as generation X—was unusually small. By 1968 the population growth rate had sunk to 1.0 percent; the birth rate to fewer than 18 live births per 1,000 population, and fertility rates to about 85 live births per woman 15-44. As a result, the ratio of people working and paying into Social Security to those receiving payments will shrink dramatically. Today, that ratio is only 3.5-1, but by 2030 it will be closer to 2-1.

In the pages that follow, we have attempted to create a statistical portrait of the population. Note that the Census Bureau updates some information more often than every 10 years with annual population estimates.

THE CENSUS

Article I, section 2 of the U.S. Constitution requires Congress to undertake a census of the population every 10 years for the purpose of apportioning seats in the House of Representatives. Today the decennial census is also used to apportion federal and state funds totalling as much as $100 billion a year, so it is vitally important to local governments and individuals throughout the country. City and county planners, health care administrators, as well as the entire marketing and advertising industries are all strongly dependent on census data for their day-to-day operations. So it's not surprising that the 2000 census, officially taken on April 1, was the largest undertaking of its kind in our history. The first results—state population figures—were scheduled for release in December 2000, as required by law.

▶HIGHLIGHTS OF THE 2000 CENSUS

Population growth The resident U.S. population grew from 248.7 million people in 1990 to 281.4 million in 2000. For the first time in the 20th century, every state gained population. The total increase (32.7 million) is the largest numerical increase ever between censuses, though by percentage of total population (13.1), it still ranks below the 28 million person jump caused by the baby boom between 1950 and 1960 (an 18.5 percent increase), and far below the 35.1 percent increase between 1790 and 1800.

State and regional growth The greatest growth occurred in the West and South. The five fastest-growing states were all in the West: Nevada (which grew an astounding 66.3 percent since 1990), Arizona (40.0 percent), Colorado (30.6 percent), Utah (29.6 percent), and Idaho (28.5 percent). Overall, the West grew by 10.4 million people to a total of 63.2 million, or an increase of 19.7 percent. The South increased by 14.8 million, or 17.3 percent. Georgia was the fastest-growing state in the South, increasing by 26.4 percent.

The Midwest grew by 7.9 percent, while the Northeast experienced 5.5 percent growth. Minnesota, up 12.4 percent, was the fastest-growing state in the Midwest, while New Hampshire, which also grew by 12.4 percent, led the Northeast. The state with the lowest population growth was North Dakota, which increased only 0.5 percent. Still, that's a turnaround for the Peace Garden State, which lost 13,917 people between 1980 and 1990.

The center of U.S. population—the exact spot where an imaginary map of the U.S. would balance perfectly if all 281 million residents were of equal weight—was approximately 2.8 miles east of a town called Edgar Springs, Mo. This point is approximately 12.1 miles south and 32.5 miles west of Steelville, Mo., which was the 1990 center of population.

U.S. Resident Population and Population Change by State, 1990–2000

State	1990 Population	1990 Rank	2000 Population	2000 Rank	Change, 1990–2000 Number	Change, 1990–2000 Percent
United States	**248,709,873**	—	**281,421,906**	—	**32,712,033**	**13.2%**
Alabama	4,040,587	(22)	4,447,100	(23)	406,513	10.1
Alaska	550,043	(49)	626,932	(48)	76,889	14.0
Arizona	3,665,228	(24)	5,130,632	(20)	1,465,404	40.0
Arkansas	2,350,725	(33)	2,673,400	(33)	322,675	13.7
California	29,760,021	(1)	33,871,648	(1)	4,111,627	13.8
Colorado	3,294,394	(26)	4,301,261	(24)	1,006,867	30.6
Connecticut	3,287,116	(27)	3,405,565	(29)	118,449	3.6
Delaware	666,168	(46)	783,600	(45)	117,432	17.6
District of Columbia[1]	606,900	—	572,059	—	-34,841	-5.7
Florida	12,937,926	(4)	15,982,378	(4)	3,044,452	23.5
Georgia	6,478,216	(11)	8,186,453	(10)	1,708,237	26.4
Hawaii	1,108,229	(41)	1,211,537	(42)	103,308	9.3
Idaho	1,006,749	(42)	1,293,953	(39)	287,204	28.5
Illinois	11,430,602	(6)	12,419,293	(5)	988,691	8.6
Indiana	5,544,159	(14)	6,080,485	(14)	536,326	9.7
Iowa	2,776,755	(30)	2,926,324	(30)	149,569	5.4
Kansas	2,477,574	(32)	2,688,418	(32)	210,844	8.5
Kentucky	3,685,296	(23)	4,041,769	(25)	356,473	9.7
Louisiana	4,219,973	(21)	4,468,976	(22)	249,003	5.9
Maine	1,227,928	(38)	1,274,923	(40)	46,995	3.8
Maryland	4,781,468	(19)	5,296,486	(19)	515,018	10.8
Massachusetts	6,016,425	(13)	6,349,097	(13)	332,672	5.5
Michigan	9,295,297	(8)	9,938,444	(8)	643,147	6.9
Minnesota	4,375,099	(20)	4,919,479	(21)	544,380	12.4
Mississippi	2,573,216	(31)	2,844,658	(31)	271,442	10.5
Missouri	5,117,073	(15)	5,595,211	(17)	478,138	9.3
Montana	799,065	(44)	902,195	(44)	103,130	12.9
Nebraska	1,578,385	(36)	1,711,263	(38)	132,878	8.4
Nevada	1,201,833	(39)	1,998,257	(35)	796,424	66.3
New Hampshire	1,109,252	(40)	1,235,786	(41)	126,534	11.4
New Jersey	7,730,188	(9)	8,414,350	(9)	684,162	8.9
New Mexico	1,515,069	(37)	1,819,046	(36)	303,977	20.1
New York	17,990,455	(2)	18,976,457	(3)	986,002	5.5
North Carolina	6,628,637	(10)	8,049,313	(11)	1,420,676	21.4
North Dakota	638,800	(47)	642,200	(47)	3,400	0.5
Ohio	10,847,115	(7)	11,353,140	(7)	506,025	4.7
Oklahoma	3,145,585	(28)	3,450,654	(27)	305,069	9.7
Oregon	2,842,321	(29)	3,421,399	(28)	579,078	20.4
Pennsylvania	11,881,643	(5)	12,281,054	(6)	399,411	3.4
Rhode Island	1,003,464	(43)	1,048,319	(43)	44,855	4.5
South Carolina	3,486,703	(25)	4,012,012	(26)	525,309	15.1
South Dakota	696,004	(45)	754,844	(46)	58,840	8.5
Tennessee	4,877,185	(17)	5,689,283	(16)	812,098	16.7
Texas	16,986,510	(3)	20,851,820	(2)	3,865,310	22.8
Utah	1,722,850	(35)	2,233,169	(34)	510,319	29.6
Vermont	562,758	(48)	608,827	(49)	46,069	8.2
Virginia	6,187,358	(12)	7,078,515	(12)	891,157	14.4
Washington	4,866,692	(18)	5,894,121	(15)	1,027,429	21.1
West Virginia	1,793,477	(34)	1,808,344	(37)	14,867	0.8
Wisconsin	4,891,769	(16)	5,363,675	(18)	471,906	9.6
Wyoming	453,588	(50)	493,782	(50)	40,194	8.9

1. If the District of Columbia were included with the states, it would have ranked 48th in 1990 and 49th in 2000.
Source: U.S. Bureau of the Census, 2001.

Congressional representation Because each state's number of representatives in Congress is based on its population, the population shift to the South and West brought with it a corresponding shift in representation. A total of eight states gained representatives (four of them gained two), while 10 states lost representatives (two states lost two each). States cannot have fewer than one representative, so even though North Dakota experienced a much lower growth rate than New York, it did not lose its sole member of Congress, whereas New York lost two representatives.

Gainers		Losers	
Arizona	+2	New York	-2
Florida	+2	Pennsylvania	-2
Georgia	+2	Connecticut	-1
Texas	+2	Illinois	-1
California	+1	Indiana	-1
Colorado	+1	Michigan	-1
Nevada	+1	Mississippi	-1
Norh Carolina	+1	Ohio	-1
		Oklahoma	-1
		Wisconsin	-1

State Urban and Rural Percentage of Land Area and Population, 1990–2000

State	Land area, 2000			Population			
				1990		2000	
	Sq. miles	Urban	Rural	Urban	Rural	Urban	Rural
U.S. total	3,620,501	%	%	75.2%	24.8%	79.0%	21.0%
Alabama	50,753	6.3	93.7	60.4	39.6	55.4	44.5
Alaska	570,374	0.2	99.8	67.5	32.5	65.6	34.4
Arizona	113,609	2.5	97.5	87.5	12.5	88.2	11.8
Arkansas	52,079	2.2	97.8	53.5	46.5	52.5	47.5
California	156,062	6.0	94.0	92.6	7.4	94.4	5.6
Colorado	103,729	1.7	98.3	82.4	17.6	84.5	15.5
Connecticut	4,844	32.1	67.9	79.1	20.9	87.7	12.3
Delaware	1,978	14.1	85.9	73.0	27.0	80.1	19.9
District of Columbia	61.4	100.0	0.0	100.0	0.0	100.0	0
Florida	59,120	21.8	78.2	84.8	15.2	89.3	10.7
Georgia	58,051	6.3	93.7	63.2	36.8	71.6	28.4
Hawaii	6,425	4.1	95.9	89.0	11.0	91.5	8.5
Idaho	82,752	2.8	97.2	57.4	42.6	66.4	33.5
Illinois	55,588	7.4	92.6	84.6	15.4	87.8	12.2
Indiana	36,097	5.8	94.2	64.9	35.1	70.8	29.2
Iowa	57,853	1.9	98.1	60.6	39.4	61.1	38.9
Kansas	81,822	1.4	98.6	69.1	30.9	71.4	28.6
Kentucky	39,733	3.5	98.1	51.8	48.2	55.8	44.2
Louisiana	43,026	3.7	96.3	68.1	31.9	72.6	27.4
Maine	30,685	1.6	98.4	44.6	55.4	40.2	59.8
Maryland	9,833	17.5	82.5	81.3	18.7	86.1	13.9
Massachusetts	7,839	38.9	61.1	84.3	15.7	91.4	8.6
Michigan	56,804	6.3	93.7	70.5	29.5	74.7	25.3
Minnesota	79,617	2.3	97.7	69.9	30.1	70.9	29.1
Mississippi	46,918	2.5	97.5	47.1	52.9	48.8	51.2
Missouri	68,898	3.2	96.8	68.7	31.3	69.4	30.6
Montana	145,556	0.2	99.8	52.5	47.5	54.1	45.9
Nebraska	76,878	0.6	99.4	66.1	33.9	69.8	30.3
Nevada	109,806	0.8	99.2	88.3	11.7	91.5	8.5
New Hampshire	8,970	5.2	94.8	51.0	49.0	59.3	40.7
New Jersey	7,419	32.1	67.9	89.4	10.6	94.4	5.6
New Mexico	121,577	0.4	99.6	73.0	27.0	75.0	25.1
New York	47,224	11.6	88.4	84.3	15.7	87.5	12.5
North Carolina	48,715	6.6	93.4	50.4	49.6	60.2	39.8
North Dakota	68,994	0.3	99.7	53.3	46.7	55.9	44.1
Ohio	40,953	10.9	89.1	74.1	25.9	77.4	22.6
Oklahoma	68,680	2.7	97.3	67.7	32.3	65.3	34.7
Oregon	95,997	1.0	99.0	70.5	29.5	78.7	21.3
Pennsylvania	44,820	8.7	91.3	68.9	31.1	77.1	22.9
Rhode Island	1,045	50.5	49.5	86.0	14.0	90.9	9.1
South Carolina	30,111	4.7	93.4	54.6	45.4	60.5	39.5
South Dakota	75,898	0.3	99.7	50.0	50.0	51.9	48.1
Tennessee	41,219	6.6	93.4	60.9	39.1	63.6	36.4
Texas	261,914	3.4	96.6	80.3	19.7	82.5	17.5
Utah	82,168	1.1	98.9	87.0	13.0	88.2	11.8
Vermont	1,149	2.5	97.5	32.2	67.8	38.2	61.7
Virginia	39,598	6.3	93.7	69.4	30.6	73.0	27.0
Washington	66,581	3.3	96.7	76.4	23.6	82.0	18.0
West Virginia	24,664	1.8	98.2	36.1	63.9	46.1	54.0
Wisconsin	138,971	1.5	98.5	65.7	34.3	68.3	31.7
Wyoming	97,105	0.5	99.5	65.0	35.0	65.1	34.8

Source: U.S. Bureau of the Census, 2002.

Since 1960, California's representatives have increased from 38 to 53, Florida's have more than doubled from 12 to 25, and Texas's have grown from 23 to 32. Over the same period, New York has lost a total of 12 representatives while Illinois has lost 5.

Urban and rural population growth Since the 1920 census, more than one half of all Americans have lived in an urban area, which can be loosely defined as a place of 2,500 or more inhabitants. During the 1980's, the population of urban areas grew by 20 million people, from 167.1 to 187.1 million people, an increase of 12 percent. By 1990, the proportion of the U.S. population living in urban areas reached 75.2 percent, up from 73.7 percent in 1980. California had the highest proportion of urban population, at 92.6 percent. In comparison, the country's rural population grew by 3.6 percent, from 59.5 million in 1980 to 61.7 million in 1990. Only 11 states, however, had increased percentages of rural population in the 1980's (see the accompanying table) even though 32 states recorded an increase in the number of rural residents. Vermont had the highest rural percentage of population: 67.8 percent.

U.S. Population by State, 1790–1990

State	1790	1800	1810	1820	1830	1840	1850
Total U.S.	**3,929,214**	**5,308,483**	**7,239,881**	**9,638,453**	**12,860,702**	**17,063,353**	**23,191,876**
Alabama	—	1,250	9,046	127,901	309,527	590,756	771,623
Alaska	—	—	—	—	—	—	—
Arizona	—	—	—	—	—	—	—
Arkansas	—	—	1,062	14,273	30,388	97,574	209,897
California	—	—	—	—	—	—	92,597
Colorado	—	—	—	—	—	—	—
Connecticut	237,946	251,002	261,942	275,248	297,675	309,978	370,792
Delaware	59,096	64,273	72,674	72,749	76,748	78,085	91,532
District of Columbia	—	8,144	15,471	23,336	30,261	33,745	51,687
Florida	—	—	—	—	34,730	54,477	87,445
Georgia	82,548	162,686	252,433	340,989	516,823	691,392	906,185
Hawaii	—	—	—	—	—	—	—
Idaho	—	—	—	—	—	—	—
Illinois	—	—	12,282	55,211	157,445	476,183	851,470
Indiana	—	5,641	24,520	147,178	343,031	685,866	988,416
Iowa	—	—	—	—	—	43,112	192,214
Kansas	—	—	—	—	—	—	—
Kentucky	73,677	220,955	406,511	564,317	687,917	779,828	982,405
Louisiana	—	—	76,556	153,407	215,739	352,411	517,762
Maine	96,540	151,719	228,705	298,335	399,455	501,793	583,169
Maryland	319,728	341,548	380,546	407,350	447,040	470,019	583,034
Massachusetts	378,787	422,845	472,040	523,287	610,408	737,699	994,514
Michigan	—	—	4,762	8,896	31,369	212,267	397,654
Minnesota	—	—	—	—	—	—	6,077
Mississippi	—	7,600	31,306	75,448	136,621	375,651	606,526
Missouri	—	—	19,783	66,586	140,455	383,702	682,044
Montana	—	—	—	—	—	—	—
Nebraska	—	—	—	—	—	—	—
Nevada	—	—	—	—	—	—	—
New Hampshire	141,885	183,858	214,460	244,161	269,328	284,574	317,976
New Jersey	184,139	211,149	245,562	277,575	320,823	373,306	489,555
New Mexico	—	—	—	—	—	—	61,547
New York	340,120	589,051	959,049	1,372,812	1,918,608	2,428,921	3,097,394
North Carolina	393,751	478,103	555,500	638,829	737,987	753,419	869,039
North Dakota	—	—	—	—	—	—	—
Ohio	—	45,365	230,760	581,434	937,903	1,519,467	1,980,329
Oklahoma	—	—	—	—	—	—	—
Oregon	—	—	—	—	—	—	12,093
Pennsylvania	434,373	602,365	810,091	1,049,458	1,348,233	1,724,033	2,311,786
Rhode Island	68,825	69,122	76,931	83,059	97,199	108,830	147,545
South Carolina	249,073	345,591	415,115	502,741	581,185	594,398	668,507
South Dakota	—	—	—	—	—	—	—
Tennessee	35,691	105,602	261,727	422,832	681,904	829,210	1,002,717
Texas	—	—	—	—	—	—	212,592
Utah	—	—	—	—	—	—	11,380
Vermont	85,425	154,465	217,895	235,981	280,652	291,948	314,120
Virginia[2]	747,610	880,200	974,600	1,065,366	1,211,405	1,239,797	1,421,661
Washington	—	—	—	—	—	—	1,201
West Virginia	—	—	—	—	—	—	—
Wisconsin	—	—	—	—	—	30,945	305,391
Wyoming	—	—	—	—	—	—	—

Population growth in metropolitan areas The 2000 census revealed that more than 80 percent of all U.S. residents (226.0 million) lived in metropolitan areas, while just under 30 percent (84.1 million) lived in metro areas of 5 million people or more. Areas with populations between 2.0 million and 5.0 million grew the fastest: they increased by a total of 20 percent. Metro areas with more than 1 million but fewer than 2 million people grew by 17.7 percent. Nonmetropolitan areas grew slowest: a total of 10.2 percent between 1990 and 2000. That's better than the previous decade, however, when nonmetropolitan areas grew by only 3.9 percent.

The 10 fastest-growing metropolitan areas were all in the South or the West. Las Vegas, which leaped from 852,737 to 1.5 million, grew by an astounding 83.3 percent. Naples, Fla. was second, with 65.3 percent growth. Yuma, Ariz. (49.7), McAllen-Edinburg Mission, Texas (48.5) and Austin-San Marcos, Texas (47.7) rounded out the top five.

Race and Hispanic origin Since 1960, each Census has approached the issue of race in slightly different ways. The most important change for the 2000 Census was the ability of respondents to classify themselves as members of more than one race. In previous censuses, someone who was part black and part white had to choose one race or the other on Census forms. For the 2000 Census, however, people with more

State	1860	1870	1880	1890	1900	1910	1920
Total U.S.	**31,443,321**	**38,558,371**	**50,189,209**	**62,979,766**	**76,212,168**	**92,228,496**	**106,021,537**
Alabama	964,201	996,992	1,262,505	1,513,401	1,828,697	2,138,093	2,348,174
Alaska	—	—	33,426	32,052	63,592	64,356	55,036
Arizona	—	9,658	40,440	88,243	122,931	204,354	334,162
Arkansas	435,450	484,471	802,525	1,128,211	1,311,564	1,574,449	1,752,204
California	379,994	560,247	864,694	1,213,396	1,485,053	2,377,549	3,426,861
Colorado	34,277	39,864	194,327	413,249	539,700	799,024	939,629
Connecticut	460,147	537,454	622,700	746,258	908,420	1,114,756	1,380,631
Delaware	112,216	125,015	146,608	168,493	184,735	202,322	223,003
District of Columbia	75,080	131,700	177,624	230,392	278,718	331,069	437,571
Florida	140,424	187,748	269,493	391,422	528,542	752,619	968,470
Georgia	1,057,286	1,184,109	1,542,180	1,837,353	2,216,331	2,609,121	2,895,832
Hawaii	—	—	—	—	154,001	191,874	255,881
Idaho	—	14,999	32,610	88,548	161,772	325,594	431,866
Illinois	1,711,951	2,539,891	3,077,871	3,826,352	4,821,550	5,638,591	6,485,280
Indiana	1,350,428	1,680,637	1,978,301	2,192,404	2,516,462	2,700,876	2,930,390
Iowa	674,913	1,194,020	1,624,615	1,912,297	2,231,853	2,224,771	2,404,021
Kansas	107,206	364,399	996,096	1,428,108	1,470,495	1,690,949	1,769,257
Kentucky	1,155,684	1,321,011	1,648,690	1,858,635	2,147,174	2,289,905	2,416,630
Louisiana	708,002	726,915	939,946	1,118,588	1,381,625	1,656,388	1,798,509
Maine	628,279	626,915	648,936	661,086	694,466	742,371	768,014
Maryland	687,049	780,894	934,943	1,042,390	1,188,044	1,295,346	1,449,661
Massachusetts	1,231,066	1,457,351	1,783,085	2,238,947	2,805,346	3,366,416	3,852,356
Michigan	749,113	1,184,059	1,636,937	2,093,890	2,420,982	2,810,173	3,668,412
Minnesota	172,023	439,706	780,773	1,310,283	1,751,394	2,075,708	2,387,125
Mississippi	791,305	827,922	1,131,597	1,289,600	1,551,270	1,797,114	1,790,618
Missouri	1,182,012	1,721,295	2,168,380	2,679,185	3,106,665	3,293,335	3,404,055
Montana	—	20,595	39,159	142,924	243,329	376,053	548,889
Nebraska	28,841	122,993	452,402	1,062,656	1,066,300	1,192,214	1,296,372
Nevada	6,857	42,491	62,266	47,355	42,335	81,875	77,407
New Hampshire	326,073	318,300	346,991	376,530	411,588	430,572	443,083
New Jersey	672,035	906,096	1,131,116	1,444,933	1,883,669	2,537,167	3,155,900
New Mexico	93,516	91,874	119,565	160,282	195,310	327,301	360,350
New York	3,880,735	4,382,759	5,082,871	6,003,174	7,268,894	9,113,614	10,385,227
North Carolina	992,622	1,071,361	1,399,750	1,617,949	1,893,810	2,206,287	2,559,123
North Dakota	—	2,405	36,909	190,983	319,146	577,056	646,872
Ohio	2,339,511	2,665,260	3,198,062	3,672,329	4,157,545	4,767,121	5,759,394
Oklahoma	—	—	—	258,657	790,371	1,657,155	2,028,283
Oregon	52,465	90,923	174,768	317,704	413,536	672,765	783,389
Pennsylvania	2,906,215	3,521,951	4,282,891	5,258,113	6,302,115	7,665,111	8,720,017
Rhode Island	174,620	217,353	276,531	345,506	428,556	542,610	604,397
South Carolina	703,708	705,606	995,577	1,151,149	1,340,316	1,515,400	1,683,724
South Dakota	4,837	11,776	98,268	348,600	401,570	583,888	636,547
Tennessee	1,109,801	1,258,520	1,542,359	1,767,518	2,020,616	2,184,789	2,337,885
Texas	604,215	818,579	1,591,749	2,235,527	3,048,710	3,896,542	4,663,228
Utah	40,273	86,786	143,963	210,779	276,749	373,351	449,396
Vermont	315,098	330,551	332,286	332,422	343,641	355,956	352,428
Virginia[2]	1,596,318	1,225,163	1,512,565	1,655,980	1,854,184	2,061,612	2,309,187
Washington	11,594	23,955	75,116	357,232	518,103	1,141,990	1,356,621
West Virginia	—	442,014	618,457	762,794	958,800	1,221,119	1,463,701
Wisconsin	775,881	1,054,670	1,315,497	1,693,330	2,069,042	2,333,860	2,632,067
Wyoming	—	9,118	20,789	62,555	92,531	145,965	194,402

than one race in their heritage were permitted to identify all their racial backgrounds. More than 6.8 million people identified themselves as being of more than one race. Because it is impossible to know how people of more than one race identified themselves in the past, racial data from the 2000 Census is not strictly comparable with those from previous censuses.

The United States remains overwhelmingly white, though less so than in the past. There were 211 million white people in the U.S. in 2000, and 5 million more who were white and at least one other race. The white-only population was 75.1 percent of the total U.S. population in 2000, down from 80.3 percent 10 years earlier. In 1970, the white population of the U.S. was 87.5 percent of the total.

The black-only population was 34.7 million in 2000, up from just under 30 million in 1990. Another 1.8 million people were black and at least one other race. The black-only population is 12.3 percent of the total, up slighlty from 12.1 in 1990 and 11.1 percent in 1970.

The Asian population increased from 6.9 million in 1990 to 10.2 million (Asian-only) in 2000. Another 1.6 million people considered themselves Asian and at least one other race. The Asian-only population represented 3.6 percent of the total, up from 2.8 in 1990. For 2000, the Census Bureau separated out Native Hawaiian and other Pacific Islander from the Asian population for the first time.

People of Hispanic origin may be of any race. Hispanics or Latinos continue to be the fastest-growing segment of the population, primarily because of immigration and high birth rates. The Hispanic or Latino population grew 53 percent between 1980 and 1990 and another 58 percent

State	1930	1940	1950	1960	1970	1980[1]	1990
Total U.S.	**123,202,624**	**132,164,569**	**151,325,798**	**179,323,175**	**203,302,031**	**226,542,203**	**248,709,873**
Alabama	2,646,248	2,832,961	3,061,743	3,266,740	3,444,354	3,894,025	4,040,587
Alaska	59,278	72,524	128,643	226,167	302,583	401,851	550,043
Arizona	435,573	499.261	749,587	1,302,161	1,775,399	2,716,546	3,665,228
Arkansas	1,854,482	1,949,387	1,909,511	1,786,272	1,923,322	2,286,357	2,350,725
California	5,677,251	6,907,387	10,586,223	15,717,204	19,971,069	23,667,764	29,760,021
Colorado	1,035,791	1,123,296	1,325,089	1,753,947	2,209,596	2,889,735	3,294,394
Connecticut	1,606,903	1,709,242	2,007,280	2,535,234	3,032,217	3,107,564	3,287,116
Delaware	238,380	266,505	318,085	446,292	548,104	594,338	666,168
District of Columbia	486,869	663,091	802,178	763,956	756,668	638,432	606,900
Florida	1,468,211	1,897,414	2,771,305	4,951,560	6,791,418	9,746,961	12,937,926
Georgia	2,908,506	3,123,723	3,444,578	3,943,116	4,587,930	5,462,982	6,478,216
Hawaii	368,300	422,770	499,794	632,772	769,913	964,691	1,108,229
Idaho	445,032	524,873	588,637	667,191	713,015	944,127	1,006,749
Illinois	7,630,654	7,897,241	8,712,176	10,081,158	11,110,285	11,427,409	11,430,602
Indiana	3,238,503	3,427,796	3,934,224	4,662,498	5,195,392	5,490,214	5,544,159
Iowa	2,470,939	2,538,268	2,621,073	2,757,537	2,825,368	2,913,808	2,776,755
Kansas	1,880,999	1,801,028	1,905,299	2,178,611	2,249,071	2,364,236	2,477,574
Kentucky	2,614,589	2,845,627	2,944,806	3,038,156	3,220,711	3,660,324	3,685,296
Louisiana	2,101,593	2,363,880	2,683,516	3,257,022	3,644,637	4,206,116	4,219,973
Maine	797,423	847,226	913,774	969,265	993,722	1,125,043	1,227,928
Maryland	1,631,526	1,821,244	2,343,001	3,100,689	3,923,897	4,216,933	4,781,468
Massachusetts	4,249,614	4,316,721	4,690,514	5,148,578	5,689,170	5,737,093	6,016,425
Michigan	4,842,325	5,256,106	6,371,766	7,823,194	8,881,826	9,262,044	9,295,297
Minnesota	2,563,953	2,792,300	2,982,483	3,413,864	3,806,103	4,075,970	4,375,099
Mississippi	2,009,821	2,183,796	2,178,914	2,178,141	2,216,994	2,520,770	2,573,216
Missouri	3,629,367	3,784,664	3,954,653	4,319,813	4,677,623	4,916,762	5,117,073
Montana	537,606	559,456	591,024	674,767	694,409	786,690	799,065
Nebraska	1,377,963	1,315,834	1,325,510	1,411,330	1,485,333	1,569,825	1,578,385
Nevada	91,058	110,247	160,083	285,278	488,738	800,508	1,201,833
New Hampshire	465,293	491,524	533,242	606,921	737,681	920,610	1,109,252
New Jersey	4,041,334	4,160,165	4,835,329	6,066,782	7,171,112	7,365,011	7,730,188
New Mexico	423,317	531,818	681,187	951,023	1,017,055	1,303,302	1,515,069
New York	12,588,066	13,479,142	14,830,192	16,782,304	18,241,391	17,558,165	17,990,455
North Carolina	3,170,276	3,571,623	4,061,929	4,556,155	5,084,411	5,880,095	6,628,637
North Dakota	680,845	641,935	619,636	632,446	617,792	652,717	638,800
Ohio	6,646,697	6,907,612	7,946,627	9,706,397	10,657,423	10,797,603	10,847,115
Oklahoma	2,396,040	2,336,434	2,233,351	2,328,284	2,559,463	3,025,487	3,145,585
Oregon	953,786	1,089,684	1,521,341	1,768,687	2,091,533	2,633,156	2,842,321
Pennsylvania	9,631,350	9,900,180	10,498,012	11,319,366	11,800,766	11,864,720	11,881,643
Rhode Island	687,497	713,346	791,896	859,488	949,723	947,154	1,003,464
South Carolina	1,738,765	1,899,804	2,117,027	2,382,594	2,590,713	3,120,729	3,486,703
South Dakota	692,849	642,961	652,740	680,514	666,257	690,768	696,004
Tennessee	2,616,556	2,915,841	3,291,718	3,567,089	3,926,018	4,591,023	4,877,185
Texas	5,824,715	6,414,824	7,711,194	9,579,677	11,198,655	14,225,513	16,986,510
Utah	507,847	550,310	688,862	890,627	1,059,273	1,461,037	1,722,850
Vermont	359,611	359,231	377,747	389,881	444,732	511,456	562,758
Virginia	2,421,851	2,677,773	3,318,680	3,966,949	4,651,448	5,346,797	6,187,358
Washington	1,563,396	1,736,191	2,378,963	2,853,214	3,413,244	4,132,353	4,866,692
West Virginia	1,729,205	1,901,974	2,005,552	1,860,421	1,744,237	1,950,186	1,793,477
Wisconsin	2,939,006	3,137,587	3,434,575	3,951,777	4,417,821	4,705,642	4,891,769
Wyoming	225,565	250,742	290,529	330,066	332,416	469,557	453,588

Note: Excludes military and overseas population. Wherever possible, 1980 state boundaries are used in calculating populations of regions, areas, and territories prior to their statehoods. 1. 1980 figures are revised estimates issued by the Census Bureau in 1987. 2. The figures for Virginia through 1860 are from the 1960 census; in the 1980 summary, the Census Bureau gave separate figures for West Virginia between 1790 and 1860, even though it did not become a state until 1863. Since the result diminishes Virginia's population by over 300,000 in 1850 and 1860, a crucial period, we decided to keep the earlier breakdowns. Sources: U.S. Bureau of the Census, 1980 Census of Population: U.S. Summary, Number of Inhabitants (1981), and Release (1990).

between 1990 and 2000. Hispanics now make up 12.5 percent of the U.S. population, up from 9.0 percent in 1990 and 6.4 percent in 1980.

Undercounting the U.S. population in the 1990 and 2000 Censuses

The Census Bureau estimates it undercounted the original 1990 Census by about 1.6 percent nationwide. The Bureau concluded that it failed to enumerate 8 million people, and double-counted about 4 million others. That's a net difference of just over 4 million people, or a little more than the population within the Los Angeles city limits.

To prevent this problem in the 2000 Census, the Bureau planned to use statistical sampling methods to enumerate the hardest-to-count 10 percent of the population, and to conduct a follow-up survey of 750,000 households, which would point out inaccuracies in the initial count. But because census numbers are used to apportion Congressional districts and because blacks and Hispanics (who tend to vote Democratic) made up a signifi-

Portrait of the U.S. Population, April 1, 2000

Characteristic	Number	Percent
Total population	**281,421,906**	**100.0%**
SEX		
Male	138,053,563	49.1
Female	143,368,343	50.9
AGE		
Under 18 years	6,042,435	2.1
18 years and over	209,128,094	74.3
21 years and over	196,899,193	70.0
65 years and over	34,991,753	12.4
Median age	35.3	—
RACE		
One race, total	274,595,678	97.6
White only	211,460,626	75.1
Black only	34,658,190	12.3
American Indian and Alaska Native only	2,475,956	0.9
Asian only	10,242,998	3.6
Native Hawaiian and other Pacific Islander only	398,835	0.1
Other race	15,359,073	5.5
Two or more races, total	6,826,228	2.4
Hispanic or Latino (of any race)	35,305,818	12.5
HOUSEHOLD TYPE		
Total households	**105,480,101**	**100.0%**
Family households (families)	71,787,347	68.1
With own children under 18 years	34,588,368	32.8
Married-couple family	54,493,232	51.7
With own children under 18 years	24,835,505	23.5
Female householder[1]	12,900,103	12.2
With own children under 18 years	7,561,874	7.2
Nonfamily households	33,692,754	31.9
Householder living alone	27,230,075	25.8
65 years and over	9,722,857	9.2
Average household size (people)	2.59	—
Average family size (people)	3.14	—
HOUSING OCCUPANCY		
Total housing units	**115,904,641**	**100.0%**
Occupied housing units	105,480,101	91.0
Vacant housing units	10,424,540	9.0
For seasonal, recreational or occasional use	3,578,718	3.1
Homeowner vacancy rate (percent)		1.7
Rental vacancy rate (percent)		6.8
HOUSING TENURE		
Occupied housing units	**105,480,101**	**100.0%**
Owner-occupied	69,815,753	66.2
Renter-occupied	35,664,348	33.8

1. No husband present. **Source:** U.S. Bureau of the Census, 2001

U.S. Population by Region, 1990-2000

Region	1990 Census	2000 Census
United States	**248,790,925**	**281,421,906**
Northeast	**50,828,313**	**53,594,378**
New England	13,206,943	13,922,517
Middle Atlantic	37,621,370	39,671,861
Midwest	**59,669,320**	**64,392,776**
East North Central	42,009,114	45,155,037
West North Central	17,660,206	19,237,739
South	**85,455,793**	**100,236,820**
South Atlantic	43,571,473	51,769,160
East South Central	15,179,959	17,022,810
West South Central	26,704,361	31,444,850
West	**52,837,499**	**63,197,932**
Mountain	13,658,794	18,172,295
Pacific	39,178,705	45,025,637

Source: U.S. Census Bureau.

Population Growth by Region, 1790–2000 (in thousands)

Year	Northeast	Midwest[1]	South[2]	West
1790	1,968	N.A.	1,961	N.A.
1800	2,636	51	2,622	N.A.
1810	3,487	292	3,461	N.A.
1820	4,360	859	4,419	N.A.
1830	5,542	1,610	5,708	N.A.
1840	6,761	3,352	6,951	N.A.
1850	8,627	5,404	8,983	179
1860	10,594	9,097	11,133	619
1870	12,299	12,981	12,288	991
1880	14,507	17,364	16,517	1,801
1890	17,407	22,410	20,028	3,134
1900	21,047	26,333	24,524	4,309
1910	25,869	29,889	29,389	7,082
1920	29,662	34,020	33,126	9,214
1930	34,427	38,594	37,858	12,324
1940	35,977	40,143	41,666	14,379
1950	39,478	44,461	47,197	20,190
1960	44,678	51,619	54,973	28,053
1970	49,041	56,572	62,795	34,804
1980	49,135	58,866	75,372	43,172
1990	50,809	59,669	85,446	52,786
2000	53,594	64,393	100,237	63,198

1. Called North Central prior to 1980. 2. Includes black slave population through 1860.
Source: U.S. Bureau of Census, *The Statistical History of the U.S.* (1976) and 2000 Census of the U.S. www.census.gov.

cant portion of the 1990 undercount, Republicans in Congress challenged the plan, fearing that an accurate count of the country's minorities would erode GOP numbers. In August 1998 a federal court struck down the use of sampling, saying it violated 1957 and 1976 federal laws governing the census, and in July 1999 the Supreme Court rejected the Clinton administration's appeal of the decision.

As a result, the Census Bureau had to spend an additional $1.7 billion (over the $5 billion budgeted) to count each and every person in 2000, even those who didn't want to cooperate with pollsters; because of this additional cost, the size of the follow-up survey had to be cut to 314,000 interviews. By comparing this survey with results from traditional census-taking methods, the Census Bureau estimated in early 2001 that at least 6.4 million people were not counted in the 2000 census and at least 3.1 million were counted twice. The undercount rate of aproximately 1.2 percent was better than the 1.6 percent undercount in 1990, but controversy over the uncounted millions continued throughout 2001. In March 2001, the Census Bureau announced that it would recommend the use of unadjusted numbers for re-

U.S. Population, Population Density, and Area of Residence, 1790–2000

Year	Total population	Percent increase	Population per square mile	Percent urban	Percent rural
1790	3,929,214	N.A.	4.5	5.1%	94.9%
1800	5,308,483	35.1%	6.1	6.1	93.9
1810	7,239,881	36.4	4.3	7.3	92.7
1820	9,638,453	33.1	5.5	7.2	92.8
1830	12,866,020	33.5	7.4	8.8	91.2
1840	17,069,453	32.7	9.8	10.8	89.2
1850	23,191,876	35.9	7.9	15.3	84.7
1860	31,443,321	35.6	10.6	19.8	80.2
1870	39,818,449	26.6	13.4	25.7	74.3
1880	50,155,783	26.0	16.9	28.2	71.8
1890	62,947,714	25.5	21.2	35.1	64.9
1900	75,994,575	20.7	25.6	39.6	60.4
1910	91,972,266	21.0	31.0	45.6	54.4
1920	105,710,620	14.9	35.6	51.2	48.8
1930	122,775,046	16.1	41.2	56.1	43.9
1940	131,669,275	7.2	44.2	56.5	43.5
1950	150,697,361	14.5	50.7	64.0	36.0
1960	179,323,175	18.5	50.6	69.9	30.1
1970	203,302,031	13.4	57.4	73.5	26.5
1980	226,542,199	11.4	64.0	73.7	26.3
1990	248,718,302	9.8	70.3	75.2	24.8
2000	281,421,906	13.1	79.6	79.0	21.0

Note: Figures for 1980, 1990, and 2000 Censuses have been revised since publication. **Source:** U.S. Bureau of Census, *The Statistical History of the U.S.* (1976); *The Statistical Abstract of the United States* (annual).

drawing Congressional districts; several large cities planned to sue for the release of detailed data about regional and local undercounts, and debates over the use of adjusted census figures for allocation of other federal and state resources continued throughout the year.

Source: U.S. Bureau of the Census Executive Steering Committee for Accuracy and Coverage Evaluation Policy; www.census.gov.

U.S. POPULATION BY RACE AND HISPANIC ORIGIN

It is important to note that the Census Bureau's classification of the population by race, in its words, "reflects common usage not an attempt to define biological stock." Only since 1960, however, have the Census Bureau's race figures been based on self-identification, and only since 1980 has the Bureau reported statistics on Native Americans, Asians and persons of Hispanic origin.

The people of the United States are predominantly white, accounting for an estimated 80.7 percent of the total population in 2002—continuing a downward trend from 84.1 percent in the 1990 census and 81.1 in 2000. This dominance has been true since colonial days, although even then the indigenous peoples and the African slaves were significant racial minorities. In fact as slave labor became essential to the Southern economy so many slaves were brought here that just before the Civil War blacks constituted 15 percent of the U.S. population.

After the war, the proportion of whites rapidly increased as millions of immigrants from northern Europe settled throughout the country. The relentless movement of the population westward deprived the Native Americans of their lands and—with the assistance of several bloody wars—helped to reduce their numbers to a small fraction of what they were estimated to have been only a century before.

The black population, which represented between 9 and 12 percent of the total for many decades, remained the only significant minority group until the 1960's, when a surge of new immigrants from Puerto Rico, Mexico and Cuba made the Hispanic presence felt. So rapid and strong an impression did these groups make that the Census Bureau created a new population category, "Hispanic Origin." Since some Hispanics are black, some white, and still others Indian, this designation has nothing to do with race.

During the 1970's and 1980's, the arrival of several million Asians again caused a noticeable change in the composition of the population. The 1990 census was the first one to include a separate category for Asians and Pacific Islanders; in previous years, they had been included together with American Indians, Aleuts and Eskimos in the "other races" grouping.

The 2000 Census took an even more expansive approach. For the first time, it allowed people to identify themselves by more than one race. Although the vast majority of Americans (97.6 percent) still consider themselves of one race, a total of 6.8 million people said they were members of two or more races (2.4 percent). The most common mix was white and American Indian or Alaska Native; just over a million people identified themselves as such. Another 868,395 said they were a mix of white and Asian, and 784,764 said they were white and black or African-American. Another 2.2 million people said they were white and some other race. A total of 410,285 people identified themselves as members of three races, 38,408 said they were of four races, 8,637 were of five races, and 823 people were of six races.

The 2000 Census was also the first to separate out "Native Hawaiian and Other Pacific Islander" from the Asian category. This new category includes people who indicated their races as Guamanian, Chamorro, Samoan, Tahitian, Mariana Islander or Chuukese. The 2000 Census also included an "Other race" category, which includes people who did not identify their race, or who wrote in races such as Moroccan, South African or Belizean. This category also includes people who wrote in a Hispanic origin (e.g. Mexican, Cuban) instead of a race.

As a result of the expanded race categories, data from the 2000 Census is not directly comparable with information from previous censuses. Wherever possible, we have tried to provide two sets of race statistics for 2000: a) those who consider themselves members only of the race (i.e. white only or black only) and b) the aforementioned members of the race plus those who consider themselves members of the race and at least one other race as well (i.e. white and Asian, or black and Native American). We have also tried to provide more recent population estimates where they are available.

▶THE BLACK POPULATION

Ever since the Founding Fathers reached their famous "compromise" declaring a slave the equivalent of three-fifths of a person, the black population has had a less-than-equal standing in relation to the majority of Americans. Over the last two centuries, the struggle for equality, even in a nation pledged to that ideal, has proven long, hard, and in many cases, intractable, as so many contemporary facts and figures in this book make all too evident. From higher infant mortality rates and poverty rates to lower life expectancy and family income levels, the black population continues to suffer the effects of two centuries of slavery and one of institutionalized segregation.

Resident Population of the U.S., by Race and Hispanic Origin, 1990-2000

The 2000 Census was the first to allow people to identify themselves as of more than one race. In the table below, the fourth and fifth columns include people who described themselves only as the race shown. The last two columns includes all of those people, as well as people who described themselves as the race indicated, in addition to at least one other race. For example, 10.2 million Americans described themeselves as Asian alone, but an additional 1.7 million described themselves as part Asian and part some other race. Thus, a total of 11.9 million people may be considered at least partly Asian. Note that persons of Hispanic origin may be of any race.

	1990		2000			
Race/ Hispanic origin	Number	Percent	Race shown only	Percent	Race shown alone or in combination with other race(s)	Percent
Total population	**248,709,873**	**100.0%**	**281,421,906**	**100.0%**	**281,421,906**	**100.0%**
White	199,686,070	80.3	211,460,626	75.1	216,930,975	77.1
Black (African-American)	29,986,060	12.1	34,658,190	12.3	36,419,434	12.9
American Indian and Alaska Native	1,959,234	0.8	2,475,956	0.9	4,119,301	1.5
Asian	6,908,638	2.8	10,242,998	3.6	11,898,828	4.2
Native Hawaiian and other Pacific Islander	365,024	0.1	398,835	0.1	874,414	0.3
Other race	9,804,847	3.9	15,359,073	5.5	18,521,486	6.6
Two or more races	N.A.	N.A.	6,826,228	2.4	N.A.	N.A.
Hispanic origin[1]	22,354,059	9.0	35,305,818	12.5	35,305,818	12.5

1. Persons of Hispanic origin may be of any race. **Source:** U.S. Bureau of the Census.

Change in the Resident Population, by Race and Hispanic Origin, 1980-2000

	Change, 1980-90		Change, 1990-2000			
Race/ Hispanic origin	Number	Percent change	Number (race only)	Percent change	Race alone or in combination with other race(s)	Percent change
Total population	**22,164,068**	**9.8%**	**32,713,033**	**13.2%**	**32,713,033**	**13.2%**
White	11,314,448	6.0	11,774,556	5.9	17,244,905	8.6
Black (African-American)	3,491,035	13.2	4,672,130	15.6	6,433,374	21.5
American Indian and Alaska Native	538,834	37.9	516,722	26.4	2,160,067	110.3
Asian	3,773,223	107.8	3,334,360	18.3	4,990,190	72.2
Native Hawaiian and other Pacific Islander	([1])	([1])	33,811	9.3	509,390	139.5
Other race	N.A.	N.A.	5,554,226	56.6	8,716,639	88.9
Hispanic origin[2]	7,745,386	53.0	12,951,759	57.9	12,951,759	57.9

1. Native Hawaiian and other Pacific Islander included with Asian from 1980-90. 2. Persons of Hispanic origin may be of any race.
Source: U.S. Bureau of the Census.

According to the 2000 Census, 34,658,190 Americans identified themselves as black only. They represented 12.3 pecent of all Americans. An additional 1,761,244 were black and at least one other race (most often white), making a total of 36,419,434 people (12.9 percent of the population) at least partly black. The black-only population grew by 15.6 percent between the last two censuses, significantly faster than the overall population, which increased only by 13.2 percent. The number of people who are black or partly black has increased even faster: 6.4 million, or 21.5 percent from 1990 to 2000.

Most black Americans (54.8 percent of the black-only population) continue to live in the South, where they made up 18.9 percent of the

Resident Population of States by Race and Hispanic Origin, 2002

		One race only						
State	Total population	White	Black or African American	American Indian & Alaska Native	Asian	Native Hawaiian	Two or more races	Hispanic or Latino origin
United States	**288,368,698**	**80.7%**	**12.7%**	**1.0%**	**4.0%**	**0.2%**	**1.4%**	**13.4%**
Alabama	4,486,508	71.5	26.3	0.5	0.8	0.0	0.8	1.9
Alaska	643,786	71.0	3.7	15.6	4.2	0.6	4.9	4.4
Arizona	5,456,453	87.8	3.3	5.3	2.0	0.2	1.4	27.1
Arkansas	2,710,079	81.2	16.0	0.7	0.9	0.1	1.1	3.6
California	35,116,033	77.6	6.9	1.2	11.6	0.4	2.3	34.0
Colorado	4,506,542	90.4	4.1	1.1	2.5	0.1	1.7	18.2
Connecticut	3,460,503	85.5	10.0	0.3	2.8	0.1	1.2	10.0
Delaware	807,385	76.5	19.4	0.4	2.4	0.1	1.2	5.1
District of Columbia	570,898	35.4	59.9	0.4	3.1	0.1	1.2	9.2
Florida	16,713,149	80.8	15.8	0.4	1.9	0.1	1.1	18.1
Georgia	8,560,310	67.5	28.8	0.3	2.4	0.1	1.0	6.0
Hawaii	1,244,898	26.3	2.2	0.3	43.3	8.8	19.1	7.3
Idaho	1,341,131	95.5	0.5	1.4	1.0	0.1	1.4	8.5
Illinois	12,600,620	79.6	15.2	0.3	3.8	0.1	1..0	13.3
Indiana	6,159,068	89.0	8.5	0.3	1.1	0.0	1.0	3.8
Iowa	2,936,760	95.0	2.2	0.3	1.5	0.0	0.9	3.1
Kansas	2,715,884	89.4	5.9	1.0	2.0	0.1	1.6	7.6
Kentucky	4,092,891	90.5	7.5	0.2	0.9	0.0	0.9	1.7
Louisiana	4,482,646	64.3	32.9	0.6	1.4	0.0	0.8	2.6
Maine	1,294,464	97.1	0.6	0.6	0.8	0.0	0.9	0.8
Maryland	5,458,137	65.7	28.2	0.3	4.4	0.1	1.3	4.7
Massachusetts	6,427,801	87.5	6.7	0.3	4.2	0.1	1.2	7.3
Michigan	10,050,446	81.6	14.4	0.6	2.1	0.0	1.4	3.5
Minnesota	5,019,720	90.4	3.8	1.1	3.2	0.1	1.4	3.2
Mississippi	2,871,782	61.4	36.8	0.4	0.8	0.0	0.6	1.5
Missouri	5,672,579	85.5	11.5	0.5	1.3	0.1	1.2	2.2
Montana	909,453	91.0	0.4	6.4	0.6	0.1	1.6	2.1
Nebraska	1,729,180	92.2	4.2	0.9	1.5	0.1	1.1	6.0
Nevada	2,173,491	84.2	6.9	1.4	4.7	0.5	2.3	21.3
New Hampshire	1,275,056	96.5	0.9	0.3	1.5	0.0	0.9	1.8
New Jersey	8,590,300	77.6	15.5	0.3	6.3	0.1	1.1	14.2
New Mexico	1,855,059	85.1	2.2	9.9	1.3	0.1	1.4	42.9
New York	19,157,532	73.9	17.8	0.5	6.3	0.1	1.4	16.0
North Carolina	8,320,146	47.3	21.8	1.3	1.6	0.1	0.9	5.3
North Dakota	634,110	92.6	0.8	4.9	0.7	0.0	1.0	1.3
Ohio	11,421,267	85.5	11.7	0.2	1.4	0.0	1.2	2.0
Oklahoma	3,493,714	78.5	7.8	8.0	1.6	0.1	4.1	5.5
Oregon	3,521,515	91.0	1.8	1.4	3.3	0.3	2.3	8.9
Pennsylvania	12,335,091	86.6	10.3	0.2	2.0	0.0	0.9	3.4
Rhode Island	1,069,725	89.5	5.8	0.6	2.6	0.1	1.4	9.2
South Carolina	4,107,183	67.9	29.9	0.4	1.0	0.1	0.8	2.7
South Dakota	761,063	88.9	0.8	8.3	0.7	0.0	1.2	1.5
Tennessee	5,797,289	81.0	16.6	0.3	1.2	0.0	0.9	2.4
Texas	21,779,893	83.6	11.6	0.7	3.0	0.1	1.0	33.6
Utah	2,316,256	93.6	0.9	1.4	1.8	0.8	1.4	9.7
Vermont	616,592	96.9	0.6	0.4	1.0	0.0	1.1	0.9
Virginia	7,293,542	74.1	20.0	0.3	4.1	0.1	1.4	5.2
Washington	6,068,996	85.7	3.5	1.6	5.9	0.4	2.9	8.1
West Virginia	1,801,873	95.1	3.3	0.2	0.6	0.0	0.8	0.7
Wisconsin	5,441,196	90.3	5.9	0.9	1.9	0.0	1.0	3.8
Wyoming	498,703	94.8	0.9	2.3	0.7	0.1	1.2	6.7

Note: Persons of Hispanic origin may be of any race. **Source:** U.S. Census Bureau.

population in 2000. Blacks constituted 11.4 percent of the population in the Northeast, 10.1 percent in the Midwest, and just 4.9 percent in the West (down from 5.4 percent in 1990). The black population of the U.S. remains highly concentrated. The 10 states with the largest number of blacks (see the accompanying table) had 58 percent of all blacks in America (but only 49 percent of the total U.S. population). Blacks constituted more than 50 percent of the population in 96 counties; 95 of these counties were in the South (St. Louis City, Mo. was the only non-Southern county with a majority black population) and almost all of them were nonmetropolitan counties (with the exceptions of Baltimore City and Prince George's County, Md.). New York and Chicago alone accounted for 9 percent of the total black population. Among places with 100,000 or more in population, Gary, Ind. had the highest percentage of blacks, with 85 percent, followed by Detroit, Mich., which was 83 percent black.

Significant differences between the races also exist in other demographic categories, most notably in the high rates of divorce and single-motherhood for blacks. Compared to other single mothers, blacks are the least likely to be divorced

Black Population of the U.S., 1790–2000

Year	Number ('000s)	Percent of total population	Year	Number ('000s)	Percent of total population	Year	Number ('000s)	Percent of total population
1790	757	19.3%	**1920**	10,463	9.9%	**1995**	33,116	12.6%
1800	1,002	18.9	**1930**	11,891	9.7	**1996**	33,537	12.6
1850	3,639	15.7	**1940**	12,866	9.8	**1997**	33,989	12.7
1860	4,442	14.1	**1950**	15,042	10.0	**1998**	34,427	12.7
1870	4,880	12.7	**1960**[1]	18,872	10.5	**1999**	34,862	12.8
1880	6,581	13.1	**1970**	22,581	11.1	**2000**		
1890	7,489	11.9	**1980**	26,683	11.8	Black only	34,658	12.3
1900	8,834	11.6	**1985**	28,994	12.1	Black only or with other race(s)	36,419	12.9
1910	9,828	10.7	**1990**	30,517	12.3			

Note: Decennial census figures are as of April 1. Figures for 1995-99 are as of July 1. 1. Includes Alaska and Hawaii for first time. **Source:** U.S. Bureau of the Census, *The Black Population 2000*. (2001). www.census.gov.

Ten States With Largest Black Populations, 2002

Rank, State	Black only		Black only or in combination with other race(s)	
	Number	Percent	Number	Percent
1. New York	3,408,528	17.8%	3,562,800	18.6%
2. Florida	2,633,683	15.8	2,717,639	16.3
3. Texas	2,527,946	11.6	2,605,633	12.0
4. Georgia	2,462,419	28.8	2,502,870	29.2
5. California	2,435,921	6.9	2,662,082	7.6
6. Illinois	1,920,014	15.2	1,978,874	15.7
7. North Carolina	1,817,634	21.8	1,855,278	22.3
8. Maryland	1,536,785	28.2	1,577,600	28.9
9. Louisiana	1,473,150	32.9	1,488,712	33.2
10. Virginia	1,458,697	20.0	1,506,476	20.7

Note: States ranked by Black-only population. **Source:** U.S. Bureau of the Census. www.census.gov.

Ten States with Highest Percentage of Black Population, 2002

Rank, State	Total Population	Black only		Black only or in combination with other race(s)	
		Number	Percent	Number	Percent
1. Mississippi	2,871,782	1,057123	36.8%	1,065,067	37.1%
2. Louisiana	4,482,646	1,473,150	32.9	1,488,712	33.2
3. South Carolina	4,107,183	1,228,173	29.9	1,243,522	30.3
4. Georgia	8,560,310	2,462,419	28.8	2,502,870	29.2
5. Maryland	5,458,137	1,536,785	28.2	1,577,600	28.9
6. Alabama	4,486,508	1,181,698	26.3	1,194,672	26.6
7. North Carolina	8,320,146	1,817,634	21.8	1,855,278	22.3
8. Virginia	7,293,542	1,458,697	20.0	1,506,476	20.7
9. Delaware	807,385	156,942	19.4	162,640	20.1
10. New York	19,157,532	3,408,528	17:8	3,562,800	18.6

Note: States ranked by Black-only population. **Source:** U.S. Bureau of the Census. www.census.gov.

Black Population in the Largest U.S. Cities, 2000

	Total Population		Black-only population			Black only or in combination with other race(s) population		
City	Rank	Number	Rank	Number	Percent black	Rank	Number	Percent black
New York, N.Y.	1	8,008,278	1	2,129,762	26.6%	1	2,274,049	28.4%
Los Angeles, Calif.	2	3,694,820	7	415,195	11.2	6	444,635	12.0
Chicago, Ill.	3	2,896,016	2	1,065,009	36.8	2	1,084,221	37.4
Houston, Texas	4	1,953,631	5	494,496	25.3	5	505,101	25.9
Philadelphia, Pa.	5	1,517,550	4	655,824	43.2	4	672,162	44.3
Phoenix, Ariz.	6	1,321,045	60	67,416	5.1	53	76,065	5.8
San Diego, Calif.	7	1,223,400	36	96,216	7.9	32	109,470	8.9
Dallas, Texas	8	1,188,580	11	307,957	25.9	11	314,678	26.5
San Antonio, Texas	9	1,144,646	48	78,120	6.8	45	84,250	7.4
Detroit, Mich.	10	951,270	3	775,772	81.6	3	787,687	82.8
Baltimore, Md.	17	651,154	6	418,951	64.3	7	424,449	65.2
Memphis, Tenn.	18	650,100	8	399,208	61.4	8	402,367	61.9
Washington, D.C.	21	572,059	9	343,312	60.0	9	350,455	61.3
New Orleans, La.	31	484,674	10	325,947	67.3	10	329,171	67.9

Source: U.S. Bureau of Census, *The Black Population 2000* (2001). www.census.gov.

Black Population of Metropolitan Areas, 2000

Metropolitan Areas with Largest Black Population	Percent	Number
1. New York–Northern New Jersey–Long Island, NY–NJ–CT–PA CMSA	17.2%	3,646,377
2. Washington–Baltimore, DC–MD–VA–WV CMSA	26.2	1,993,314
3. Chicago–Gary–Kenosha, IL–IN–WI CMSA	18.6	1,703,302
4. Los Angeles–Riverside–Orange County, CA CMSA	7.6	1,244,397
5. Philadelphia–Wilmington–Atlantic City, PA–NJ–DE–MD CMSA	19.6	1,212,939
6. Atlanta, GA MSA	28.9	1,188,425
7. Detroit–Ann Arbor–Flint, MI CMSA	21.1	1,151,306
8. Miami–Fort Lauderdale, FL CMSA	20.4	790,782
9. Houston–Galveston–Brazoria, TX CMSA	16.9	789,158
10. Dallas–Fort Worth, TX CMSA	13.8	720,609
11. San Francisco–Oakland–San Jose, CA CMSA	7.3	513,873
12. New Orleans, LA MSA	37.5	501,647
13. Cleveland–Akron, OH CMSA	16.8	494,900
14. Memphis, TN–AR–MS MSA	43.4	492,856
15. Norfolk–Virginia Beach–Newport News, VA–NC MSA	30.9	484,988
16. St. Louis, MO–IL MSA	18.3	476,460
17. Charlotte–Gastonia–Rock Hill, NC–SC MSA	20.5	307,355
18. Richmond–Petersburg, VA MSA	30.2	300,947
19. Boston–Worcester–Lawrence, MA–NH–ME–CT CMSA	5.1	296,774
20. Birmingham, AL MSA	30.1	277,253

Metropolitan Areas with Highest Percentage Black Population	Percent	Number
1. Albany, GA MSA	51.0%	61,619
2. Pine Bluff, AR MSA	49.6	41,802
3. Sumter, SC MSA	46.7	48,870
4. Jackson, MS MSA	45.6	201,005
5. Memphis, TN–AR–MS MSA	43.4	492,856
6. Rocky Mount, NC MSA	43.1	61,644
7. Columbus, GA–AL MSA	40.4	110,948
8. Florence, SC MSA	39.3	49,424
9. Montgomery, AL MSA	38.9	129,558
10. New Orleans, LA MSA	37.5	501,647
11. Macon, GA MSA	37.5	120,956
12. Shreveport–Bossier City, LA MSA	37.4	146,721
13. Fayetteville, NC MSA	34.9	105,734
14. Savannah, GA MSA	34.9	102,257
15. Augusta–Aiken, GA–SC MSA	34.4	164,240
16. Tallahassee, FL MSA	33.6	95,605
17. Monroe, LA MSA	33.6	49,476
18. Greenville, NC MSA	33.6	44,956
19. Goldsboro, NC MSA	33.0	37,399
20. Danville, VA MSA	32.6	35,911

Note: Figures are for people identifying their race as black only; data on people identifying themselves as black and one or more other races is not available. **Source:** U.S. Bureau of the Census.

(17 percent) and most likely to never be married (65 percent). In 2002, less than half (48 percent) of all black families were married-couple families, compared with 82 percent of all non-Hispanic white families. (See also "The U.S. Economy" for information about black employment, income, wealth and poverty.)

▶THE HISPANIC POPULATION

The term Hispanic refers to people of Spanish or Latin American origin. American Hispanics are of diverse backgrounds. The vast majority trace their roots to Mexico (58.5 percent), followed by Puerto Rico (9.6 percent) Cuba (3.5 percent) and the Dominican Republic (2.2 percent). A mere 0.3 percent of Hispanic-Americans are from Spain. (These figures do not include Puerto Ricans living in Puerto Rico, which is a U.S. territory, but for which a separate census is issued. In recent years, the flow of Puerto Ricans to U.S. cities has been reversed, with more Puerto Ricans emigrating from the mainland to the island than the other way around.)

Contrary to popular opinion, Spanish-speaking countries are not culturally homogeneous, but varied and complex. They incorporate Spanish and other European influences, as well as Indian and African traits. In the Caribbean area, Panama, and the coasts of Venezuela, Colombia, Ecuador and sections of Peru, African culture has left a strong legacy. In Mexico, most of Central America and the Andean countries, diverse Indian cultures have had a major impact. Latin-American society varies greatly according to social class and vast differences exist between urban and rural areas. Since American Hispanics come from different countries and social backgrounds, they do not compose a uniform, cohesive population group.

U.S. Hispanics are of many races. In some areas, intermingling has made it impossible to distinguish one race from another, but in others, races are clearly defined. In Argentina, for example, there is a white majority of 85 percent—mostly of Italian, German or English extraction. Cuba, the Dominican Republic, Panama, Venezuela, and the coastal areas of Colombia, Ecuador and Peru all have significant black populations. In Bolivia, about one-half of the population is Indian and a third is mestizo (of mixed white and Indian ancestry). Both Peru and Cuba have concentrations of persons of Chinese ancestry, and Peru has a growing Japanese population. In Mexico, birthplace of the majority of most Hispanic-Americans, about 55 percent of the population is mestizo, 30 percent is Indian, and 15 percent is white.

Despite their diversity, the Hispanic peoples are united by many factors, among them language, religion, customs, and attitudes toward self, family and society. In the United States, these factors vary in importance according to the degree to which an individual has assimilated into the mainstream. For example, although language has traditionally been an important unifying factor, large numbers of second-generation Hispanics are English-dominant. About 85 percent of U.S. Hispanics speak English. Although the Spanish language continues to exert a strong emotional pull among U.S. Hispanics, it is difficult to assess to what extent Spanish will remain a unifying force among future generations.

Growth of the Hispanic population The Hispanic population is one of the fastest-growing segments of the U.S. population. Between 1980 and 2000, the number of Hispanics more than doubled, from 14.6 million to 35.3 million, according to the Census Bureau. According to numbers from the 2000 Census, the Hispanic population for the first time outnumbered the black-alone population (35.3 million to 34.7 million), although blacks alone or in combination with other races outnumbered Hispanics by just over one million. By July 2002, however, the total number of Hispanics of any race had increased to 38.8 million, finally exceeding the number of

Hispanic Population of Metropolitan Areas, 2000

Metropolitan Areas with Largest Hispanic Population	Percent	Number
1. Los Angeles–Riverside–Orange County, CA CMSA	40.3	6,598,578.94
2. New York–Northern New Jersey–Long Island, NY–NJ–CT–PA CMSA	18.2	3,858,375.43
3. Miami–Fort Lauderdale, FL CMSA	40.3	1,562,181.14
4. Chicago–Gary–Kenosha, IL–IN–WI CMSA	16.4	1,501,836.56
5. San Francisco–Oakland–San Jose, CA CMSA	19.7	1,386,754.31
6. Houston–Galveston–Brazoria, TX CMSA	28.9	1,349,506.02
7. Dallas–Fort Worth, TX CMSA	21.5	1,122,687.22
8. Phoenix–Mesa, AZ MSA	25.1	816,220.88
9. San Antonio, TX MSA	51.2	815,300.10
10. San Diego, CA MSA	26.7	751,293.41

Metropolitan Areas with Highest Percentage Hispanic Population	Percent	Number
1. Laredo, TX MSA	94.3	182,109.33
2. McAllen–Edinburg–Mission, TX MSA	88.3	502,835.83
3. Brownsville–Harlingen–San Benito, TX MSA	84.3	282,596.36
4. El Paso, TX MSA	78.2	531,464.40
5. Las Cruces, NM MSA	63.4	110,748.39
6. Corpus Christi, TX MSA	54.7	208,288.30
7. San Antonio, TX MSA	51.2	815,300.10
8. Visalia–Tulare–Porterville, CA MSA	50.8	186,954.67
9. Yuma, AZ MSA	50.5	80,813.13
10. Salinas, CA MSA	46.8	188,024.62

Source: U.S. Bureau of the Census.

Hispanic Population in the Largest U.S. Cities, 2000

City	Total Population Rank	Total Population Number	Hispanic population Rank	Hispanic population Number	Percent Hispanic
New York, N.Y.	1	8,008,278	1	2,160,554	27.0%
Los Angeles, Calif.	2	3,694,820	2	1,719,073	46.5
Chicago, Ill.	3	2,896,016	3	753,644	26.0
Houston, Texas	4	1,953,631	4	730,865	37.4
Philadelphia, Pa.	5	1,517,550	24	128,928	8.5
Phoenix, Ariz.	6	1,321,045	6	449,972	34.1
San Diego, Calif.	7	1,223,400	9	310,752	25.4
Dallas, Texas	8	1,188,580	8	422,587	35.6
San Antonio, Texas	9	1,144,646	5	671,394	58.7
Detroit, Mich.	10	951,270	72	47,167	5.0
El Paso, Texas	23	563,662	7	431,875	76.6
San Jose, Calif.	11	894,943	10	269,989	30.2

Source: U.S. Bureau of Census, *The Hispanic Population 2000* (2001). www.census.gov.

Resident Hispanic Population by Region and Origin, 2000

	Total, U.S. Number	Northeast Number	Northeast Percent	Midwest Number	Midwest Percent	South Number	South Percent	West Number	West Percent
All Hispanics	**35,305,818**	**5,254,087**	**14.9%**	**3,124,532**	**8.8%**	**11,586,696**	**32.8%**	**15,340,503**	**43.4%**
Mexican	20,640,711	479,169	2.3	2,200,196	10.7	6,548,081	31.7	11,413,265	55.3
Puerto Rican	3,406,178	2,074,574	60.9	325,363	9.6	759,305	22.3	246,936	7.2
Cuban	1,241,685	168,959	13.6	45,305	3.6	921,427	74.2	105,994	8.5
Other Hispanic	10,017,244	2,531,385	25.3	553,668	5.5	3,357,883	33.5	3,574,308	35.7

Source: U.S. Bureau of the Census, *The Hispanic Population 2000* (2001). www.census.gov.

blacks alone or in combination with other races, and officially becoming the largest minority population in the United States. Hispanics currently represent over 13 percent of the U.S. population.

The Hispanic population increased by 57.9 percent overall between 1990 and 2000. Mexicans increased by 52.9 percent, Puerto Ricans increased by 24.9 percent, and Cubans increased by 18.9 percent. The "other Hispanic" category, which includes people from Spain, people from all other Spanish-speaking countries in Latin America, and people who did not specify a detailed origin beyond "Hispanic," was the fastest-growing group of Hispanics, increasing by 96.9 percent.

The rapid growth of the Hispanic population is due primarily to immigration. For example, the number of people of Mexican background living in the U.S. more than doubled between 1980 and 1990, due in large part to the Immigration and Reform Control Act of 1986, which allowed immigrants living illegally in the United States to obtain legal U.S. citizenship. By 2002, 40.2 percent of the Hispanic population in the United States was foreign born. (See the section on immigration later in this chapter). Hispanics also have higher fertility rates than do the non-Hispanic population. In 1998, the overall fertility rate per 100,000 women ages 15-44 was 65.0, but for Hispanic women, it was 102.8. Mexican-American women had the highest fertility rates of all: 116.6 births per 100,000 women aged 15-44, or approximately double the rate for Cuban-American women.

Half of all Hispanics lived in two states in 2000: California and Texas. Hispanics represented 24.3 percent of the population in the West; they constituted more than 25 percent of the populations of Arizona, California, New Mexico and Texas. Mexicans were the biggest component of Hispanic populations in the South and West, but there were fewer than half a million Mexicans in the Northeast. The majority of Hispanics in the Northeast were of Puerto Rican origin. Over a million Puerto Ricans lived in New York alone; another half million lived in New Jersey and Connecticut. The vast majority of Cubans (67 percent) lived in Florida, where they represented 5.2 percent of the entire state population. The heaviest concentration of Hispanics in America is East Los Angeles, Calif., where 120,307 of the 124,283 residents (96.8 percent) are Hispanic. Laredo, Texas, is close behind, with a population that is 94.1 percent Hispanic.

States With Largest Hispanic Population, 2002

State	Hispanic population	Total population	Percentage Hispanic
1. California	35,116,033	11,936,707	34.0
2. Texas	21,779,893	7,314,341	33.6
3. New York	19,157,532	3,073,430	16.0
4. Florida	16,713,149	3,019,305	18.1
5. Illinois	12,600,620	1,681,402	13.3
6. Arizona	5,456,453	1,476,738	27.1
7. New Jersey	8,590,300	1,220,733	14.2
8. New Mexico	1,855,059	796,171	42.9
9. Colorado	4,506,542	818,274	18.2
10. Georgia	8,560,310	516,530	6.0

Note: Ranked by number of Hispanics. Nevada which is 19.7 percent Hispanic, has a total of 393,970 Hispanics.
Source: U.S. Bureau of the Census. www.census.gov.

▶THE ASIAN AND NATIVE HAWAIIAN/ OTHER PACIFIC ISLANDER POPULATION

In 1970 the Census Bureau counted about 1.5 million Asians and Pacific Islanders living in the U.S. By the 1980 census that figure had more than doubled to 3.4 million, thanks in large part to the more than 400,000 Southeast Asian refugees who came to America between 1975-80 under the Refugee Resettlement Program. By the 1990 Census, their numbers had doubled yet again, with Koreans and Vietnamese responsible for the majority of the increase.

The 2000 Census was the first to consider Native Hawaiians and Other Pacific Islanders (Guamanians, Chamorros and Samoans) separately from Asians. A total of 874,414 people identified themselves as at least partly Native Hawaiian. Unlike other races, the majority of Native Hawaiians (475,579) were also members of at least one other race. Only 398,835 people identified themselves as Native Hawaiian and Other Pacific Islander alone. The city with the largest number of Native Hawaiians was Honolulu, both alone (25,457, or 6.8 percent of the city population) or in combination with other races (58,130, or 15.6 percent).

Contrast that with the Asian population: 11,898,828 people said they were Asian or partly Asian in 2000. Of these, 10,242,998 (86.1 percent) said they were Asian only, while only 1,655,830 were Asian and another race. Chinese are still the largest group of Asians in the U.S., followed closely by Filipinos and Japanese.

▶THE AMERICAN INDIAN AND ALASKA NATIVE POPULATION

This race was known as the American Indian, Eskimo and Aleut population for the 1990 Census, which reported a total of 1,959,234 American Indians living in the United States (of these, 85,698 were Eskimos and Aleuts, a.k.a. Alaska Natives). For the 2000 Census, 2,475,956 people identified themselves as American Indian or Alaska Native only, and another 1,643,345 said they were this race and at least one other race. That makes for a total of 4,119,301 people who consider themselves at least partly American Indian or Alaska Native.

Not surprisingly, the state with the greatest percentage of American Indians and Alaska natives is Alaska, where people of this race constitute 15.6 percent of the population. New Mexico is second, with 9.5 percent, followed by South Dakota (8.3 percent) and Oklahoma (7.9 percent). The state with the most American Indians and Alaska Natives is California (333,346). Oklahoma is second, with 273,230, Arizona is third, with 255,879, and New Mexico is fourth, with 173,483. Washington, which had 102,940 Native Americans and Alaska Natives in 1990, saw this population drop to 93,301 for the 2000 Census. Meanwhile, the Amer-

Ten Cities With Largest Asian Population, 2000

Rank, State	Total Population	Asian only		Asian only or in combination with other race(s)	
		Number	Percent	Number	Percent
1. New York City	8,008,278	787,047	9.8%	872,777	10.9%
2. Los Angeles	3,694,820	369,254	10.0	407,444	11.0
3. San Jose	894,943	240,375	26.9	257,571	28.8
4. San Francisco	776,733	239,565	30.8	253,477	32.6
5. Honolulu	371,657	207,588	55.9	251,686	67.7
6. San Diego	1,223,400	166,968	13.6	189,413	15.5
7. Chicago	2,896,016	125,974	4.3	140,517	4.9
8. Houston	1,953,631	103,694	5.3	114,140	5.8
9. Fremont, Ca.	203,413	75,165	37.0	80,979	39.8
10. Seattle	563,374	73,910	13.1	84,649	15.0

Source: Ranked by number of Asian-only population. Seattle ranks 9th when states are ranked by number of Asians-only or Asians in combination with other races. **Source:** U.S. Bureau of the Census, *Census 2000*. www.census.gov.

Ten States With Largest Asian Population, 2002

Rank, State	Total Population	Asian only		Asian only or in combination with other race(s)	
		Number	Percent	Number	Percent
1. California	35,116,033	4,060,600	11.6%	4,461,295	12.7%
2. New York	19,157,532	1,206,600	6.3	1,297,712	6.8
3. Texas	21,779,593	648,519	3.0	722,535	3.3
4. New Jersey	8,590,300	544,139	6.3	581,057	6.8
5. Hawaii	1,244,898	538,818	43.3	726,171	58.3
6. Illinois	12,600,620	481,424	3.8	526,802	4.2
7. Washington	6,068,996	356,026	5.9	430,071	7.1
8. Florida	16,713,149	315,569	1.9	378,341	2.3
9. Virginia	7,293,542	297,661	4.1	340,258	4.7
10. Massachusetts	6,427,801	273,019	4.2	296,607	4.6

Source: Ranked by number of Asian-only population. **Source:** U.S. Bureau of the Census. www.census.gov.

ican Indian and Alaska Native population of Texas skyrocketed from 95,682 in 1990 to 118,362 in 2000. Almost half of all American Indians and Alaska Natives (1.2 million) live in the West. Only 162,558 American Indians and Alaska Natives live in the Northeast. Note: all the statistics cited in this paragraph refer to people who identified themselves as members of one race only.

There are 562 federally recognized Indian tribes in the U.S. and 554 federally identified areas associated with them, including reservations, which the federal government recognizes as territory in which American Indian tribes have jurisdiction, and "trust lands," which are held in trust by the federal government but consist of property associated with a particular tribe or reservation. The Bureau of Indian Affairs counted 314 reservations in 1997. Of the 2.4 million people who identified their race as American Indian or Alaska Native alone in the 2000 Census, the two tribes with the largest populations by far were the Cherokee (281,069) and the Navajo (269,202), followed at some distance by Canadian and Latin American Indians (108,802) and the Sioux (108,272) and Chippewa (105,907) tribes. 103,174 people identified themselves as American Indian alone without specifying a tribe.

States With Largest American Indian or Alaska Native Population, 2002

Rank, State	Total Population	American Indian or Alaska Native only		American Indian or Alaska Native only or in combination with other race(s)	
		Number	Percent	Number	Percent
1. California	35,116,033	410,501	1.2%	682,270	2.0%
3. Arizona	5,456,453	286,680	5.3	319,994	5.9
2. Oklahoma	3,493,714	278,124	8.0	395,219	11.3
4. New Mexico	1,855,059	183,972	9.9	199,186	10.7
5. Texas	21,779,893	145,954	0.7	237,751	1.1
6. North Carolina	8,320,146	106,454	1.3	137,639	1.7
9. New York	19,157,532	103,337	0.5	183,665	1.0
7. Alaska	643,786	100,494	15.6	121,532	18.9
8. Washington	6,068,996	99,446	1.6	164,338	2.7
10. South Dakota	761,063	63,390	8.3	69,233	9.1

Note: Ranked by American Indian or Alaska Native-only population. **Source:** U.S. Bureau of the Census. www.census.gov.

Population of Selected Reservations and Trust Lands, 1990

Rank/Reservation or Trust Land	Total population	American Indian, Eskimo or Aleut	
		Population	Percent of total
1. Navajo and Trust Lands, Ariz., N.Mex., Utah	148,451	143,405	96.6%
2. Pine Ridge and Trust Lands, Nebr.-S.Dak.	12,215	11,182	91.5
3. Fort Apache, Ariz.	10,394	9,825	94.5
4. Gila River, Ariz.	9,540	9,116	95.6
5. Papago, Ariz.	8,730	8,480	97.1
6. Rosebud and Trust Lands, S.Dak.	9,696	8,043	83.0
7. San Carlos, Ariz.	7,294	7,110	97.5
8. Zuni Pueblo, Ariz.-N.Mex.	7,412	7,073	95.4
9. Hopi and Trust Lands, Ariz.	7,360	7,061	95.9
10. Blackfeet, Mont.	8,549	7,025	82.2
11. Turtle Mountain and Trust Lands, N.Dak.-S.Dak.	7,106	6,772	95.3
12. Yakima and Trust Lands, Wash.	27,668	6,307	22.8
13. Osage, Okla.[1]	41,645	6,161	14.8
14. Fort Peck, Mont.	10,595	5,782	54.6
15. Wind River, Wyo.	21,851	5,676	26.0
16. Eastern Cherokee, N.C.	6,527	5,388	82.5
17. Flathead, Mont.	21,259	5,130	24.1
18. Cheyenne River, S.Dak.	7,743	5,100	65.9
19. Standing Rock, N.Dak.-S.Dak.	7,956	4,870	61.2
20. Crow and Trust Lands, Mont.	6,370	4,724	74.2
21. Mississippi Choctaw and Trust Lands, Miss.	4,073	3,932	96.5
22. Colville, Wash.	6,957	3,788	54.4
23. Laguna Pueblo and Trust Lands, N.Mex.	3,731	3,634	97.4
24. Red Lake, Minn.	3,699	3,602	97.4
25. Northern Cheyenne and Trust Lands, Mont.-S.Dak.	3,923	3,542	90.3

Note: Ranked by total American Indian, Eskimo, or Aleut population. 1. The Osage Reservation is coextensive with Osage County. **Source:** U.S. Bureau of the Census.

U.S. POPULATION BY AGE AND SEX

▶THE POPULATION BY AGE

With birth rates and fertility rates declining rapidly since 1965 it should come as no surprise that the average age of the U.S. population has been increasing almost as quickly. It will continue to rise for the foreseeable future in part because of the aging members of the baby boom generation.

During the baby boom years of the 1950s and 1960s, the median age of the population actually declined, the only time it has done so. Since then, however, the steady decline in the percentage of young people, especially those under 18 years of age (from 34.1 percent in 1970, to 25.6 percent in 1990), combined with the increase of those between 25 and 44 (they were 23.6 percent of the population in 1970, but 32.6 percent in 1990) has driven the median age from 28.0 in 1970 to 33.0 in 1990. A five-year increase in 20 years is unprecedented in U.S. history, but what's more revealing is that we will most likely duplicate that feat over the next 20 years. By 1999, the median age of the U.S. population had already increased to 35.5.

The other major factor in the "graying of America" is the increased life expectancy for older people. In 1950, the over-65 population totalled 7 percent of all Americans and numbered nine million. In 1990, 31.7 million Americans (12.3 percent of the population) were over 65; this represents a 24.1 percent increase since 1980 and a 1,000 percent increase since 1900. In 2000, there were 35 million people over 65.

As the population ages, 65 no longer seems old to most people. Especially when millions more people are living past the age of 80. There were 7 million people 80 or older in 1990, 3 million age 85 or older, nearly a million 90 years or older, and 36,000 people over the age of 100. By 2000, there were 16.7 million people over the age of 75 and 4.2 million age 85 or more.

Over the first decade of the 21st century, the over-65 population will grow another 13-14 percent—but between 2010 and 2030 the over-65 population will nearly double as the baby boom generation finally becomes senior citizens. In the year 2030, an estimated 20 percent of the population, or 70 million Americans, will be 65 years old or older.

Florida, and to a lesser degree, Pennsylvania, have long had the highest concentrations of retirees, but in the 1990s, several states saw dramatic growth in their over-65 population. Nevada's senior population grew by 55 percent between 1990 and 2000, while Alaska's increased 49 percent and Arizona's jumped 29 percent. Hawaii experienced 27 percent growth, Utah saw a 22 percent increase, and Colorado and New Mexico both had increases of 21 percent.

▶THE POPULATION BY SEX

In 2000, according to the Census Bureau, there were 39.0 million men and 47.1 million women 18 years and over who had never married or who were currently widowed, separated or divorced—a ratio of 83 unmarried men per 100 unmarried women. The popular interpretation of these figures—that there is a shortage of eligible men—fails to consider that women are more likely to live longer (and so be counted among the widowed) and less likely to remarry after a divorce. In fact, the surplus of women can be entirely attributed to the fact that there are 7 million more widows than widowers over the age of 65. But during the peak marrying ages, unmarried men actually outnumber unmarried women: among persons between

Number of Persons and Percent of Total Population, by Age Group, 1960–2050 (numbers in thousands)

Age in Years	1960	1970	1980	1990	2000	2010	2050
Under 5	20,341	17,166	16,458	18,765	19,176	20,099	26,914
Percent	11.3%	8.4%	7.2%	7.5%	6.8%	6.7%	6.7%
5-13	32,965	36,672	31,095	31,839	37,025	35,321	47,582
Percent	18.2	17.9	13.7	12.8	13.2	11.8	11.8
14-17	11,219	15,924	16,142	13,345	16,093	16,681	21,252
Percent	6.2	7.8	7.1	5.4	5.7	5.6	5.3
18-24	16,128	24,712	30,350	26,961	27,143	30,163	36,804
Percent	8.9	12.1	13.3	10.8	9.6	10.1	9.1
25-34	22,919	25,323	37,626	43,174	39,891	38,851	50,458
Percent	12.7	12.3	16.5	17.4	14.2	13.0	12.5
35-44	24,221	23,150	25,868	37,444	45,149	39,443	49,588
Percent	13.4	11.3	11.4	15.1	16.0	13.2	12.3
45-64	36,203	41,999	44,515	46,178	61,902	81,590	89,089
Percent	20.0	20.5	19.5	18.6	22.0	27.2	22.1
65 & over	16,675	20,107	25,704	31,084	34,992	39,715	81,999
Percent	9.2	9.8	11.3	12.5	12.4	13.2	20.3
85 & over	940	1,430	2,269	3,022	4,240	5,786	19,352
Percent	0.5	0.7	1.0	1.2	1.5	1.9	4.8
100 & over	3	5	15	N.A.	N.A.	129	1,095
Percent	—	—	—	—	—	—	0.3
Total U.S. population	**180,671**	**205,052**	**227,757**	**248,791**	**281,422**	**299,862**	**403,687**
Median age	**29.4**	**27.9**	**30.0**	**32.8**	**35.3**	**37.4**	**38.8**

Figures for 2010 and after are the projections the Census Bureau calls the "middle" or "most likely" series. **Source:** U. S. Bureau of the Census, *Projections of the Population of the U.S., by Age, Sex, and Race: 1995 to 2050* (2002).

Resident Population of States, by Age, 2002 (numbers in thousands)

State	Resident population	Under 18 years	18-24 years	25-44 years	45-64 years	65 years and over	Median age
U.S.							
Alabama	4,486,508	1,107,108	452,196	1,270,419	1,068,243	588,542	36.4
Alaska	643,786	192,428	58,738	188,661	164,759	39,200	33.8
Arizona	5,456,453	1,476,856	540,015	1,564,035	1,174,304	701,243	34.1
Arkansas	2,710,079	677,522	272,391	744,468	639,311	376,387	36.5
California	35,116,033	9,452,391	3,551,492	10,900,378	7,494,936	3,716,836	33.5
Colorado	4,506,542	1,151,118	447,869	1,411,030	1,062,053	434,472	34.6
Connecticut	3,460,503	872,853	287,412	993,016	834,908	472,314	37.8
Delaware	807,385	189,698	81,501	240,294	190,404	105,488	36.9
District of Columbia	570,898	112,128	66,003	193,731	130,502	68,534	35.1
Florida	16,713,149	3,882,271	1,403,624	4,603,097	3,969,319	2,854,838	39.1
Georgia	8,560,310	2,268,477	868,937	2,723,747	1,885,497	813,652	33.6
Hawaii	1,244,898	295,514	123,045	357,714	301,715	166,910	37.0
Idaho	1,341,131	370,439	149,036	366,279	304,236	151,141	33.6
Illinois	12,600,620	3,254,523	1,228,541	3,768,414	2,849,893	1,499,249	35.0
Indiana	6,159,068	1,594,857	628,691	1,755,704	1,422,365	757,451	35.4
Iowa	2,936,760	698,045	314,972	794,576	696,382	432,785	37.4
Kansas	2,715,884	696,519	291,509	756,291	616,471	355,094	35.5
Kentucky	4,092,891	931,588	419,536	1,220,845	1,011,446	509,476	37.0
Louisiana	4,482,646	1,185,674	495,811	1,255,113	1,025,602	520,446	34.5
Maine	1,294,464	279,058	118,126	367,062	343,835	186,383	39.8
Maryland	5,458,137	1,379,925	488,911	1,661,178	1,311,424	616,699	36.5
Massachusetts	6,427,801	1,463,340	597,865	1,974,544	1,528,357	863,695	37.4
Michigan	10,050,446	2,570,264	970,466	2,892,525	2,385,271	1,231,920	36.1
Minnesota	5,019,720	1,252,125	507,071	1,490,231	1,168,552	601,741	36.1
Mississippi	2,871,782	760,747	322,625	798,205	643,954	346,251	34.2
Missouri	5,672,579	1,397,461	567,574	1,613,247	1,337,100	757,197	36.7
Montana	909,453	216,320	92,915	236,459	240,953	122,806	38.7
Nebraska	1,729,180	439,393	184,586	480,041	393,026	232,134	35.7
Nevada	2,173,491	572,590	187,297	664,924	508,425	240,255	35.0
New Hampshire	1,275,056	308,371	114,725	379,088	320,295	152,577	37.9
New Jersey	8,590,300	2,127,391	693,034	2,584,742	2,063,936	1,121,197	37.5
New Mexico	1,855,059	500,506	191,698	506,918	434,483	221,454	35.1
New York	19,157,532	4,613,251	1,815,216	5,778,485	4,477,070	2,473,510	36.5
North Carolina	8,320,146	2,068,840	815,438	2,508,062	1,929,415	998,391	35.5
North Dakota	634,110	146,812	76,034	168,133	149,055	94,076	37.2
Ohio	11,421,267	2,879,927	1098,431	3,220,016	2,709,521	1,513,372	36.6
Oklahoma	3,493,714	873,560	377,256	961,461	820,978	460,459	35.9
Oregon	3,521,515	855,107	338,287	1,005,438	878,715	443,968	36.7
Pennsylvania	12,335,091	2,863,452	1,153,224	3,395,198	3,014,255	1,908,962	38.7
Rhode Island	1,069,725	239,248	114,090	311,721	252,380	152,286	37.6
South Carolina	4,107,183	979,163	429,425	1,197,588	997,751	503,256	36.3
South Dakota	761,063	195,625	82,635	200,515	173,966	108,322	36.6
Tennessee	5,797,289	1,404,661	553,941	1,709,712	1,409,798	719,177	36.6
Texas	21,779,893	6,102,316	2,287,194	6,568,300	4,669,187	2,152,896	32.7
Utah	2,316,256	713,012	321,169	666,010	417,024	199,041	27.7
Vermont	616,592	139,662	62,147	171,888	163,654	79,241	38.8
Virginia	7,293,542	1,779,408	720,847	2,232,643	1,743,203	817,441	36.0
Washington	6,068,996	1,513,360	593,628	1,822,158	1,462,318	677,532	35.8
West Virginia	1,801,873	389,171	173,743	483,168	479,817	275,974	39.7
Wisconsin	5,441,196	1,338,064	556,567	1,555,658	1,284,489	706,418	36.7
Wyoming	498,703	122,344	54,248	131,779	131,110	59,222	37.3

Note: Includes armed forces residing in each state. Figures as of 2003. **Source:** U.S. Bureau of the Census.

the ages of 18 and 24 there were 112 unmarried men for every 100 unmarried women; in the 25-to-34 age group, there were 120 men for every 100 women; and men 35-44 outnumber women 109 to 100. It's not until the 45-to-64 group that the reversal begins (68 unmarried men for every 100 available women), and among the 65-and-over there is a dramatic change, with only 32 unmarried men for every 100 unmarried women.

Growth of the Over-65 Population, 1900–2050

Year	Population 65 and over: Number ('000s)	Population 65 and over: Percent of total population	Population 85 and over: Number ('000s)	Population 85 and over: Percent of total population
1900	3,099	4.1%	N.A.	N.A.
1910	3,986	4.3	N.A.	N.A.
1920	4,929	4.7	N.A.	N.A.
1930	6,705	5.5	N.A.	N.A.
1940	9,031	6.9	N.A.	N.A.
1950	12,397	8.1	N.A.	N.A.
1960	16,675	9.2	940	0.5%
1970	20,107	9.8	1,430	0.7
1980	25,549	11.3	2,269	1.0
1990	31,242	12.5	3,080	1.2
2000	34,992	12.4	4,240	1.5
2010	39,715	13.2	5,786	1.9
2020	53,733	16.5	6,763	2.1
2030	70,319	20.0	8,931	
2040	77,177	20.5	14,284	
2050	81,999	20.3	19,352	4.8

Note: Prior to 1960, the Census Bureau did not count persons over 85 separately. Figures for 2010 through 2050 are Census Bureau projections based on their "most likely" series of estimates.
Source: U.S. Bureau of the Census, *Population Projections of the U.S by Age, Sex, Race, and Hispanic Origin.*

VITAL STATISTICS

The National Center for Health Statistics does a month-by-month tracking of four sets of numbers, which both it and the Census Bureau refer to as "vital": births, deaths, marriages, and divorces.

Births An estimated 4.02 million babies were born in the U.S. in 2001, up slightly from 4.06 million the year before. The crude birth rate (the number of live births per 1,000 total population) decreased slightly to 14.1, and the fertility rate (the number of births per 1,000 women aged 15-44) was 66.9, down slightly from 67.5 in 2000.

Deaths An estimated 2.42 million people died in 2001, up from 2.40 million in 2000. The crude death rate decreased from 8.7 to 8.5 per 1,000 population. In 1910, by comparison, the death rate was 14.7. (For infant mortality figures and for more specific information about death rates by cause see the section, "Health and Medicine.")

In 2001 there were 1,608,000 more births than deaths; this figure is called the natural increase, meaning the growth in population without immigration (which has accounted for close to 700,000 people per year in recent years).

Characteristics of Persons 65 or Older, 2002

Characteristic	Total	Male	Female
Total (millions)	**33.8**	**14.2**	**19.5**
Percent distribution	**100.0%**	**42.0%**	**58.0%**
Marital status:			
Never married	3.6%	3.7%	3.6%
Married	56.7	75.7	42.9
Spouse absent	2.3	2.6	2.1
Widowed	32.2	13.9	45.5
Divorced	7.4	6.7	8.0
Family status:			
In families[1]	66.7	79.2	57.6
Non-family householders	32.1	19.3	41.5
Secondary individuals	1.2	1.5	1.0
Educational Attainment			
High school graduate	54.4	73.1	40.8
Some college/associate deg.	35.3	30.2	39.0
Bachelor's/advanced deg.	16.7	22.0	12.8
Labor force participation:			
Employed	12.7	17.2	9.5
Unemployed	0.5	0.6	0.4
Not in labor force	86.8	82.1	90.2
Percent below poverty level	9.9	6.8	12.1

1. Excludes those living in unrelated subfamilies. **Source:** U.S. Bureau of the Census, *Statistical Abstract of the United States* (annual)

Marriages An estimated 2.33 million couples married during 2001, just slightly below 2000 levels; the marriage rate of 8.4 per 1,000 people equalled the 30-year-low recorded in 1998. In addition to getting married in fewer numbers, people are getting married at a later age In 1960, for example, about 40 percent of all 19-year-old women were married, but by 2001 only 6.2 percent were. Also in 1960, about 92 percent of all women were married before they reached age 30, but by 2001 only 77 percent were. In 2001, nearly 20 percent of 30-year-olds were never married, up from less than 6 percent in 1970.

Divorces The National Center for Health Statistics stopped publishing numbers of divorces in 2000 because four states no longer report divorce statistics. The latest available year for which data is available is 1998, when an estimated 1.13 million divorces were granted, down slightly from the

U.S. Population by Sex: Totals and Ratio of Males to Females, 1920–2001

Year	Male ('000s)	Female ('000s)	Males per 100 females: All ages	14-24	25-44	65+
1920	53,900	51,810	104.0	97.3	105.1	101.3
1930	62,137	60,638	102.5	98.4	101.8	100.5
1940	66,062	65,608	100.7	98.9	98.5	95.5
1950	74,833	75,864	98.6	98.2	96.4	89.6
1960	88,331	90,992	97.1	98.7	95.7	82.8
1970	98,926	104,309	94.8	98.7	95.5	72.1
1980	110,053	116,493	94.5	101.9	97.4	67.6
1990	122,049	127,875	95.1	104.6	98.9	67.2
1995	128,293	134,510	95.4	104.7	98.6	70.7
2000	138,054	143,368	96.3	105.1	100.2	70.0
2001	139,813	144,984	96.4	105.2	100.5	70.4

Source: U.S. Bureau of the Census, *Statistical Abstract of the United States* (annual)

Births and Deaths in the U.S., 1910–2002

Year	Live births ('000s)	Birth rate[1]	Deaths[2] ('000s)	Death rate[1]
1910	2,777	30.1	N.A.	14.7
1920	2,950	27.7	N.A.	13.0
1930	2,618	21.3	N.A.	11.3
1940	2,559	19.4	1,417	10.8
1950	3,632	24.1	1,452	9.6
1955	4,097	25.0	1,529	9.3
1960	4,258	23.7	1,712	9.5
1965	3,760	19.5	1,828	9.4
1970	3,731	18.4	1,921	9.5
1975	3,144	14.6	1,893	8.8
1980	3,612	15.9	1,990	8.8
1985	3,761	15.8	2,086	8.8
1990	4,158	16.7	2,148	8.6
1995	3,892	14.8	2,309	8.8
1997	3,882	14.5	2,294	8.6
1998	3,946	14.6	2,331	8.6
1999	3,965	14.5	2,396	8.8
2000	4,059	14.7	2,403	8.7
2001	4,026	14.1	2,418	8.5
2002[3]	4,019	13.9	N.A.	N.A.

1. Per 1,000 total population. 2. Excludes fetal deaths. 3. Preliminary. **Source:** U.S. National Center for Health Statistics, *Vital Statistics of the United States,* (annual) and *National Vital Statistics Report,* December 18, 2002.

Marriages and Divorces in the U.S., 1920–2001

Year	Marriages ('000s)	Rate per 1,000 population	Divorces ('000s)	Rate per 1,000 population
1920	1,274	12.0	171	1.6
1930	1,127	9.2	196	1.6
1940	1,596	12.1	264	2.0
1950	1,667	11.1	385	2.6
1955	1,531	9.3	377	2.3
1960	1,523	8.5	393	2.2
1965	1,800	9.3	479	2.5
1970	2,163	10.6	708	3.5
1975	2,153	10.0	1,036	4.8
1980	2,390	10.0	1,036	4.8
1985	2,413	10.1	1,190	5.0
1990	2,448	9.8	1,175	4.7
1995	2,336	8.9	1,169	4.4
1997	2,384	8.9	1,163	4.3
1998	2,244	8.4	1,135	4.2
1999	2,358	8.6	N.A.	4.1[1]
2000	2,329	8.5	N.A.	4.2[1]
2001	2,327	8.4	N.A.	4.0[1]

1. Based on reports from only 46 states; California, Colorado, Indiana, and Louisiana no longer report divorce data. **Source:** U.S. National Center for Health Statistics, *Vital Statistics of the United States* (annual) and *National Vital Statistics Report,* September 11, 2002.

previous year. The divorce rate per 1,000 population was 4.2, its lowest rate in more than 20 years. The divorce rate peaked in 1979 at 5.3 per 1,000 population. (In that year there were 22.8 divorced women for every 1,000 married women, up from 9.2 in 1960. While the divorce rate has stabilized, the ratio of divorced persons to married persons (with spouse present) has skyrocketed. Between 1970 and 2001, the proportion nearly quadrupled, from 47 divorced per 1,000 married to 180 per 1,000. For blacks, the rise was even greater, going from 83 per 1,000 to 330 per 1,000 in the same period.

In 2001, there were 21.0 million currently divorced persons in the U.S., 9.7 percent of the total adult population over 18. There are more divorced women (12.3 million) than men (8.7 million) because women are less likely to remarry.

A recent study by the National Center for Health Statistics revealed that 43 percent of all first marriages end in separation or divorce within 15 years. One in five ends in the first five years, and one in three ends within 10 years (see the accompanying table). The report also showed a link between the age of the woman and the duration of a marriage. Fifty-nine percent of first marriages involving women under 18 ended in separation or divorce within 15 years, compared with 36 percent of marriages where the bride was 20 or older.

▶FERTILITY RATES OF AMERICAN WOMEN

Population experts predict future trends by studying many factors including the crude birth rate (see "Vital Statistics") and the all-important fertility rates. The *general fertility rate* measures the ratio of live births to the total number of women aged 15 to 44. (Until 1990, the Census Bureau had reported based on the number of women 18 to 44, thus projecting a higher fertility rate but discounting the high number of teenage pregnancies.)

The *total fertility rate* is the number of births 1,000 women aged 10 to 50 would have in their lifetimes if, at each year of age, they experienced the birth rates occurring to women of that age in the specified calendar year. The total fertility rate is sometimes defined in the popular media as the number of *likely* births one woman will have in her lifetime; they do this by dividing by 1,000.

The total fertility rate is most helpful in measuring long-term trends, especially in determining whether or not the nation is sustaining a level of reproduction necessary for maintaining current population levels. That level, generally regarded as 2,100 per 1,000 women, was not achieved in the U.S. from 1971 through 1999, but by 2001 the figure had climbed to 2,115.

Fertility rates in 2001 were highest among women in their 20s. The fertility rate for women 20-24 was 109.9; for women 25-29 it was 121.3. American Indian women (70.8) had higher fertility rates overall than white women (66.3), Asian or Pacific Islander women (69.4), or black women (69.5). Women of Hispanic origin had an overall fertility rate of 107.4.

One clear indication that women are having children much later in life is the increasing fertility rate of women over 35. Since 1978, fertility rates of women 35-49 have more than doubled.

▶WOMEN AND CHILDBEARING: CURRENT TRENDS

Unmarried women According to the Census Bureau's Current Population Survey, a record 1,349,249 unmarried women gave birth in 2001. Births out of wedlock represented 33.5 percent of all births in 2001.

Births to teenagers Every year in the U.S., more than 450,000 teenagers give birth. Most of these women are unmarried. In 2001, 453,725 teenagers gave birth, down from 469,000 in 2000. The rate of teenage births is also in decline. The birth rate for women aged 15-19 hit a 20-year high of 62.1 in 1991, but has declined almost every year since then, to a record low of 45.8 in 2001.

Births and Birth Rates in the U.S., by Age, Race and Hispanic Origin, 2002

	All races	White, total	White, Non-Hispanic	Black	American Indian[1]	Asian/Pacific Islander	Hispanic[2]
BIRTHS							
Total, ages 10-54	**4,019,280**	**3,176,059**	**2,303,561**	**590,519**	**42,399**	**210,303**	**872,236**
10-14	7,318	3,879	1,502	3,195	131	113	2,406
15-19	424,670	305,749	180,039	103,221	7,707	7,993	127,055
20-24	1,021,182	783,248	520,581	193,621	14,361	29,952	263,924
25-29	1,060,133	851,680	616,551	135,921	10,141	62,391	234,974
30-34	951,555	780,503	621,790	94,550	6,337	70,166	157,196
35-39	453,338	369,685	297,627	48,078	2,986	32,588	71,156
40-44	95,627	76,884	61,857	11,363	705	6,675	14,765
45-54	5,456	4,430	3,613	569	31	426	760
BIRTH RATES							
Total, ages 15-44	**64.8**	**64.8**	**57.5**	**65.4**	**58.0**	**63.9**	**94.0**
10-14	0.7	0.5	0.2	1.8	0.9	0.3	1.4
15-19	42.9	39.4	28.6	66.2	53.8	18.3	82.9
20-24	103.5	101.6	84.5	126.4	112.7	60.2	163.5
25-29	113.6	117.5	109.6	98.5	91.8	105.2	138.7
30-34	91.6	95.6	94.7	64.1	56.4	109.3	94.7
35-39	41.4	42.3	40.9	31.3	25.4	56.3	47.6
40-44	8.3	8.2	7.6	7.4	5.9	12.4	11.5
45-54[3]	0.5	0.5	0.5	0.4	0.3	0.9	0.7

Notes: Figures are preliminary. 1. Includes births to Aleuts and Eskimos. 2. Hispanic persons may be of any race. 3. The birth rate is computed by relating the number of births to women aged 45-54 years to women aged 45-49 years; most of the births in this group are to women aged 45-49. **Source:** U.S. National Center for Health Statistics, *National Vital Statistics Report,* June 25, 2003.

Women and Childbearing in the U.S, by Age, 1976-2001

Characteristic	1976	1980	1990	1995	2000	2001[1]
Total number of women, 18-44 years old ('000s)	**41,618**	**45,652**	**58,381**	**60,225**	**60,133**	**62,044**
Births per 1,000 women						
All women 15-44 years old[2]	67.2	68.4	70.9	65.6	67.6	66.9
15-19 years	N.A.	53.0	59.9	56.8	48.7	45.8
20-24 years	93.22	115.1	116.5	109.8	112.5	109.9
25-29 years	104.8	112.9	120.2	112.2	121.7	121.3
30-34 years	56.4	61.9	80.8	82.5	94.2	95.2
35-39 years	22.6	19.8	31.7	34.3	40.3	41.3
40-44 years	6.5	3.9	5.5	6.6	7.9	8.1

1. Preliminary; figure for women 15-44 years old. 2. Women 18-19 included with women 20-24 years old. **Source:** U.S. National Center for Health Statistics, *National Vital Statistics Report,* December 18, 2002.

Percent of Population Never Married, by Age and Sex, 1960–2002

Age	1960	1970	1980	1990	2000	2002
MEN						
Total: 15 and over	**23.2%**	**28.1%**	**29.6%**	**29.9%**	**31.3%**	**32.0%**
15-17	98.8	99.4	99.4	99.8	98.7	98.6
18	94.6	95.1	97.4	98.5	98.2	97.9
19	87.1	89.9	90.9	95.3	(1)	(1)
20-24	53.1	54.7	68.8	79.3	83.7	85.4
25-29	20.8	19.1	33.1	45.2	51.7	53.6
30-34	11.9	9.4	15.9	27.0	30.1	34.0
35-39	8.8	7.2	7.8	14.7	20.3	21.1
40-44	7.3	6.3	7.1	10.5	15.7	16.7
45-54	7.4	7.5	6.1	6.3	9.4	10.9
55-64	8.0	7.8	5.3	5.8	5.5	6.6
65 and over	7.7	7.5	4.9	4.2	4.2	3.7
WOMEN						
Total: 15 and over	**17.3%**	**22.1%**	**22.5%**	**22.8%**	**25.1%**	**25.2%**
15-17	93.2	97.3	97.0	98.5	97.9	98.3
18	75.6	82.0	88.0	92.0	93.0	93.8
19	59.7	68.8	77.6	88.7	(1)	(1)
20-24	28.4	35.8	50.2	62.8	72.8	74.0
25-29	10.5	10.5	20.9	31.1	38.9	40.4
30-34	6.9	6.2	9.5	16.4	21.9	23.0
35-39	6.1	5.4	6.2	10.4	14.3	14.7
40-44	6.1	4.9	4.8	8.0	11.8	11.5
45-54	7.0	4.9	4.7	5.0	8.6	8.9
55-64	8.0	6.8	4.5	3.9	4.9	5.3
65 and over	8.5	7.7	5.9	4.9	3.6	3.5

1. Population aged 18-19 included under 18.
Source: U.S. Bureau of the Census, *Children's Living Arrangements and Characteristics* (March 2002). www.census.gov.

Marital Status, by Race and Hispanic Origin, 1970–2002

Year		Never married		Married		Widowed		Divorced		Separated	
and Race	Total	Number	Percent	Number	Percent	Number	Percent	Number	Percent	Number	Percent
All Races											
1970	132,507	21,443	16.2%	94,999	71.7%	11,784	8.9%	4,282	3.2%	N.A.	N.A.
1980	159,528	32,342	20.3	104,564	65.5	12,734	8.0	9,886	6.2	N.A.	N.A.
1990	181,849	40,361	22.2	112,552	61.9	13,810	7.6	15,125	8.3	N.A.	N.A.
2000	201,762	48,213	23.9	115,655	57.3	13,655	6.8	19,828	9.8	4,412	2.2%
2002	221,459	63,090	28.5	118,764	53.6	14,044	6.3	20,955	9.5	4,606	2.1
White											
1970	118,179	18,444	15.6	85,784	72.6	10,280	8.7	3,671	3.1	N.A.	N.A.
1980	139,480	26,405	18.9	93,800	67.2	10,938	7.8	8,338	6.0	N.A.	N.A.
1990	155,454	31,633	20.3	99,450	64.0	11,730	7.5	12,640	8.1	N.A.	N.A.
2000	168,140	36,017	21.4	101,159	60.2	11,529	6.9	16,507	9.8	2,928	1.7
2002	182,997	47,738	26.1	102,912	56.2	11,811	6.5	17,406	9.5	3,129	1.7
Black											
1970	12,972	2,668	20.6	8,310	64.1	1,427	11.0	567	4.4	N.A.	N.A.
1980	16,638	5,070	30.5	8,545	51.4	1,627	9.8	1,396	8.4	N.A.	N.A.
1990	20,320	7,141	35.1	9,302	45.8	1,730	8.5	2,146	10.6	N.A.	N.A.
2000	24,016	9,451	39.4	8,818	36.7	1,692	7.0	2,765	11.5	1,290	5.4
2002	26,137	11,334	43.4	9,162	35.1	1,673	6.4	2,727	10.4	1,241	4.7
Hispanic											
1970	5,066	943	18.6	3,637	71.8	286	5.6	200	3.9	N.A.	N.A.
1980	7,888	1,901	24.1	5,176	65.6	350	4.4	460	5.8	N.A.	N.A.
1990	13,560	3,694	27.2	8,365	61.7	548	4.0	952	7.0	N.A.	N.A.
2000	21,109	5,907	28.0	11,864	56.2	881	4.2	1,619	7.7	838	4.0
2002	26,332	9,557	36.3	13,278	50.4	875	3.3	1,734	6.6	889	3.4
Asian and Pacific Islander											
2000	7,859	2,241	28.5	4,792	61.0	332	4.2	360	4.6	135	1.7
2002	9,837	3,229	32.8	5,564	56.6						

Note: Note: Only those people 15 years old and over are included. Hispanic persons may be of any race.
Source: U.S. Bureau of the Census, *Children's Living Arrangements and Characteristics* (March 2002). www.census.gov.

New mothers in the labor force Being a stay-at-home mother is a luxury most American families can no longer afford. In June 2000, 61 percent of women with children under the age of three were in the labor force. That's nearly double the rate in 1975 (34.3 percent). 72.9 percent of all mothers with children under 18 were in the labor force in 2000, up from 47.4 percent in 1975.

▶ADOPTION

Between 1973 and 1994, the percent of ever-married women who have ever adopted a child declined from 2.1 percent to 1.3 percent, according to National Surveys of Family Growth from those years. The National Center for Health Statistics attributed the drop to several factors, including the legalization of abortion in 1973 and the development of new reproductive technologies that have reduced the number of unwanted pregnancies. Almost all of the decrease since 1973 has come in unrelated children; the percent of women adopting their nieces, nephews, stepchildren, boyfriend's children or other related (blood or otherwise) children has held steady.

Perhaps the greatest shift has come in the number of children available for adoption. Before 1973, never-married women under the age of 45 relinquished 8.7 percent of their children for adoption. In 1995, they gave up less than 1 percent. Almost all of this decrease has come among never-married white women, who relinquished nearly 20 percent of their children before 1973. Never-married black women have consistently kept their babies: Only 1.5 percent relinquished their children before 1973, and only 1.1 percent did between 1982 and 1988 (1995 figures were unavailable).

In 1995, there were 37.4 million ever-married women between the ages of 18 and 44. Of these, 9.9 million, or 26.4 percent, had considered adoption, 1.6 million had taken steps toward adoption, and 472,000 were currently looking to adopt a child. According to the survey, steps toward adoption include contacting an adoption agency or lawyer, placing a newspaper ad, or having previously adopted a child.

Marital Status of the Population by Sex and Age, 2002 (numbers in thousands)

Sex and Age	Total	Never married Number	Never married Percent	Married Number	Married Percent	Widowed Number	Widowed Percent	Divorced Number	Divorced Percent	Separated Number	Separated Percent
MALE											
Total 15+	**106,819**	**34,229**	**32.0%**	**59,470**	**55.7%**	**2,636**	**2.5%**	**8,686**	**8.1%**	**1,798**	**1.7%**
15-17	6,209	6,122	98.6	25	0.4	4	0.1	28	0.4	31	0.5
18-19	4,026	13,943	97.9	71	1.8	0	0	7	0.2	5	0.1
20-24	9,670	8,261	85.4	1,273	13.2	3	0	56	0.6	77	0.8
25-29	9,141	4,904	53.7	3,704	40.5	7	0.1	356	3.9	170	1.9
30-34	10,079	3,429	34.0	5,805	57.6	15	0.1	623	6.2	207	2.1
35-39	10,693	2,255	21.1	7,082	66.2	32	0.3	1,094	10.2	230	2.2
40-44	11,109	1,852	16.7	7,633	68.7	66	0.6	1,284	11.6	276	2.5
45-54	19,302	2,112	10.9	13,798	71.5	215	1.1	2,755	14.3	421	2.2
55-64	12,363	818	6.6	9,451	75.4	318	2.6	1,538	12.4	237	1.9
65-74	8,243	304	3.7	6,450	78.3	706	8.6	672	8.1	111	1.3
75-84	4,896	195	4.0	3,528	72.1	903	18.4	242	4.9	28	0.6
85+	1,088	33	3.1	649	59.6	368	33.8	33	3.0	5	0.5
FEMALE											
Total 15+	**114,639**	**28,861**	**25.2%**	**59,295**	**51.7%**	**11,408**	**10.0%**	**12,268**	**10.7%**	**2,808**	**2.4%**
15-17	5,927	5,826	98.3	38	0.6	4	0.1	32	0.5	28	0.5
18-19	3,880	3,640	93.8	200	5.2	2	0	16	0.6	22	0.6
20-24	9,722	7,195	74.0	2,230	23.0	8	0.1	164	1.3	124	1.3
25-29	9,158	3,700	40.4	4,613	50.4	33	0.4	524	3.1	288	3.1
30-34	10,270	2,362	23.0	6,541	63.7	75	0.7	946	3.4	347	3.4
35-39	10,947	1,613	14.7	7,362	67.2	102	0.9	1,402	4.3	469	4.3
40-44	11,506	1,320	11.5	7,892	68.6	215	1.9	1,677	3.5	403	3.5
45-54	20,209	1,799	8.9	13,518	66.9	672	3.3	3,566	3.2	654	3.2
55-64	13,497	715	5.3	8,687	64.4	1,407	10.4	2,384	2.3	305	2.3
65-74	9,876	346	3.5	5,345	54.1	3,018	30.6	1,053	1.2	114	1.2
75-84	7,291	230	3.2	2,566	35.2	4,010	55.0	441	0.6	44	0.6
85+	2,356	117	5.0	303	12.8	1,862	79.1	65	0.4	9	0.4

Note: Totals may not add up due to independent rounding.
Source: U.S. Bureau of the Census, *Children's Living Arrangements and Characteristics* (March 2002). **www.census.gov.**

Fertility Rates of U.S. Women, 1930-2001

Year	General fertility rate	Total fertility rate	Year	General fertility rate	Total fertility rate
1930	89.2	2,600	**1990**	70.9	2,081
1935	77.2	2,250	**1991**	69.2	2,073
1940	79.9	2,301	**1992**	68.9	2,073
1945	85.9	2,491	**1993**	67.6	2,065
1950	106.2	3,091	**1994**	66.7	2,036
1955	118.3	3,574	**1995**	65.6	2,019
1960	118.0	3,654	**1996**	65.3	2,027
1965	96.6	2,928	**1997**	65.0	2,032
1970	87.9	2,480	**1998**	65.6	2,058
1975	66.0	1,774	**1999**	65.9	2,075
1980	68.4	1,840	**2000**	67.5	N.A.
1985	66.3	1,84	**2001**	66.9	2,115

Source: U.S. National Center for Health Statistics, *National Vital Statistics Report,* December 18, 2002.

Median Age at First Marriage, by Sex, 1890-2000

Year	Male	Female	Year	Male	Female
1890	26.1	22.0	**1991**	26.3	24.1
1900	25.9	21.9	**1992**	26.5	24.4
1910	25.1	21.6	**1993**	26.5	24.5
1920	24.6	21.2	**1994**	26.7	24.5
1930	24.3	21.3	**1995**	26.9	24.5
1940	24.3	21.5	**1996**	27.1	24.8
1950	22.8	20.3	**1997**	26.8	25.0
1960	22.8	20.3	**1998**	26.7	25.0
1970	23.2	20.8	**1999**	26.9	25.1
1980	24.7	22.0	**2000**	26.8	25.1
1990	26.1	23.9			

Source: U.S. Bureau of the Census, *America's Families and Living Arrangements 2000* (2001). www.census.gov.

Black-White Married Couples in the U.S., 1960–2000 (thousands)

Year	Total married couples	Total black-white couples	Husband black, wife white	Wife black, husband white
1960	40,491	51	25	26
1970	44,598	65	41	24
1980	49,714	167	122	45
1990	53,256	211	150	61
1995	54,937	328	206	122
1997	54,666	311	201	110
1998	55,305	330	210	120
1999	55,849	364	240	124
2000	56,497	363	268	95

Source: U.S. Bureau of the Census, *America's Families and Living Arrangements 2000* (2001). www.census.gov.

Divorced Persons per 1,000 Married Persons by Sex and Race 1960–2001

Sex/race	All races	White	Black	Hispanic[1]
Both sexes:				
1960	35	33	62	N.A.
1970	47	44	83	61
1980	100	92	203	98
1990	142	133	282	129
2000	175	166	330	145
2001	180	172	314	139
Male:				
1960	28	27	45	N.A.
1970	35	32	62	40
1980	79	74	149	64
1990	118	112	208	103
2000	151	145	257	120
2001	150	146	217	115
Female:				
1960	42	38	78	N.A.
1970	60	56	104	81
1980	120	110	258	132
1990	166	153	358	155
2000	200	187	406	168
2001	211	198	415	162

Note: Persons 18 years and over. Per 1,000 married persons with spouse present. 1. Persons of Hispanic origin may be of any race.
Source: U.S. Bureau of the Census, *Children's Living Arrangements and Characteristics* (March 2002). www.census.gov

Percent of First Marriages Ending in Separation or Divorce by Length of Marriage and Age of Wife

Length of Marriage (years)	Percent ending in separation or divorce				
		Wife's age at first marriage			
	Total	Under 18	18-19	20-24	25 and over
1	3%	4%	4%	2%	2%
2	7	10	9	6	5
3	12	17	15	10	08
4	16	23	20	14	11
5	20	29	24	17	15
6	23	34	28	19	17
7	26	39	32	22	19
8	29	42	35	25	20
9	31	45	37	27	22
10	33	48	40	29	24
11	35	49	42	31	26
12	38	52	44	33	29
13	39	54	46	33	30
14	41	57	47	35	31
15	43	59	49	36	35

Source: National Center for Health Statistics, *Advance Data: First Marriage Dissolution, Divorce, and Remarriage: United States,* May 31, 2001.

HOUSEHOLDS AND FAMILIES

Since the very first census in 1790, the federal government has not only attempted to count every individual, it has also tried to determine where those individuals live and with whom. While the definition of *household* has changed somewhat over the years, it has remained a central element in understanding the basic structure of American society. Since 1970, changes in the size and composition of the household unit have revealed the extent of social change more clearly than any other measure. Note that data on households and families is from the Census Bureau's annual Current Population Survey, not from the decennial census.

▶HOUSEHOLDS

Virtually all Americans are part of a household. As of March 2000, the Census Bureau determined that 274 million persons belonged to a household, even if that household consisted of only one person. A small number of people in institutions or in unique group living arrangements do not belong to households. According to the official Census Bureau definition, a household consists of all persons who occupy a housing unit. A house, an apartment or other group of rooms, or a single room, is regarded as a housing unit when it is occupied or intended for occupancy as separate living quarters; that is when the occupants do not live and eat with any other persons in the structure and there is direct access from the outside or through a common hall.

There are two major categories of households identified by the Census Bureau: family and nonfamily. A family or family household requires the presence of at least two persons, the householder (i.e. the person in whose name the housing unit is owned or rented) and one or more additional family members related to the householder through birth, adoption or marriage. A nonfamily household consists of a householder who either lives alone or exclusively with persons who are not related to the householder. Since 1970 the rapid growth of nonfamily households has led to a continuous increase in the number of households and a fall in the average number of persons in each.

In 2002, there were 109.3 million households in the U.S., the largest number ever, with an average of 2.58 persons in each. This continues a trend begun during the 1970's when the number of households increased by more than 20 percent and over 17.3 million units, nearly double the growth of the 1940's and 1950's and over 60 percent more than the relatively explosive 1960's. The most significant change helping to ignite this surge was the unprecedented increase in the number of nonfamily households, which grew by 77.7 percent in the 1970's and 28.4 percent during the 1980's.

Several factors help to account for this change, including the rapid rise in the divorce rate, as well as an increase in the number of young single people living on their own and deciding to postpone marriage. In 2002, nearly 29 million people, or one in 10, lived alone—a considerable increase even since the 2000 Census figure of 26.7 million. The number of people living alone grew 59 percent during the 1970's, 21 percent during the 1980's, but only 16 percent from 1990 to 2000.

An additional 4.9 million unmarried-couple households were another large segment of the nonfamily population. Unmarried couples made up only a small percentage of all U.S. couples, but their numbers have continued to skyrocket since their sudden appearance on the American social landscape during the 1970's. There were only 523,000 unmarried couples living together in 1970, but their numbers had tripled to 1.6 million in 1980. A growing number of unmarried couples (1.7 million in 2000) have children under 15 years old in their households. This doesn't necessarily mean more children are being born out of wedlock, however, since this category includes children from previous marriages living with an un-remarried parent. As currently defined by the Census Bureau, an unmarried-couple household is two persons of the opposite sex who share living quarters. Although a close personal relationship is implied, other types—including tenancy—are included. But no more than two unrelated adults are present in an unmarried-couple household although children under age 15 may be present.

Despite all the attention given to the growth of nonfamily households, the fact remains that the overwhelming majority of Americans live in some

U.S. Households, Number and Size, 1940–2000

Year	Number of households ('000s)	Average number per household: All ages	Under 18 years	18 years and older
1940	34,949	3.67	1.14	2.53
1950	43,544	3.37	1.06	2.31
1960[1]	52,799	3.33	1.21	2.12
1970	63,401	3.14	1.09	2.05
1980	80,776	2.76	0.79	1.97
1990	93,347	2.63	0.69	1.94
1995	98,990	2.65	0.71	1.93
1996	99,627	2.65	0.71	1.94
1997	101,018	2.64	0.71	1.93
1998	102,528	2.62	0.70	1.92
1999	103,874	2.61	0.69	1.92
2000	104,705	2.62	0.69	1.93

1. Alaska and Hawaii included for first time. **Source:** U.S. Bureau of the Census, *The Statistical History of the U.S.* (1976); *America's Families and Living Arrangements 2000* (2001). www.census.gov.

Unmarried Couple Households, 1960–2000

Year	Total	Without children under 15	With children under 15
1960	439,000	242,000	197,000
1970	523,000	327,000	196,000
1980	1,589,000	1,159,000	431,000
1990	2,856,000	1,966,000	891,000
1995	3,668,000	2,349,000	1,319,000
1996	3,958,000	2,516,000	1,442,000
1997	4,130,000	2,660,000	1,470,000
1998	4,236,000	2,716,000	1,520,000
1999	4,486,000	2,981,000	1,505,000
2000	4,736,000	3,061,000	1,675,000

Note: Figures may not add to total due to rounding. **Source:** *America's Families and Living Arrangements: 2000* (2001).

kind of family situation. This is not to say that the size and structure of the family hasn't undergone major revamping in recent decades but rather to emphasize its inherent strength as the basic social unit despite the presence of powerful forces for change.

▶FAMILIES

In 2002 there were 74.3 million families in the U.S., up from 51.6 million in 1970. But the 21st-century American family bears less and less resemblance to the 20th-century family. Perhaps the greatest change is the drop in the percentage of nuclear families: married couples with their own children. These types of households represented 45 percent of the total in 1960; in 2000, they dropped below 25 for the first time (23.5 percent). Market researchers who once assumed the family consisted of four members now base their assumptions on families of three, reflecting a steady, dramatic decline in the average family size, from 3.58 in 1970 to 3.17 in 2000 (although the number rose slightly to 3.21 in 2002). These numbers indicate a growing number of families opting not to have children. They constituted 44.1 percent of all families in 1970, but since 1990, they have outnumbered families with children. In 2002, 35.7 million families had children under 18, compared to 38.7 million without children.

More important, perhaps, the proportion of married-couple families declined from 86.8 percent of all family households in 1970 to 76.3 percent in 2002, while the number of family households headed by females with no husbands present soared from 5.5 million, or 10.7 percent of all family households in 1970, to 13.1 million, or 17.7 percent in 2002 (A startling 43.4 percent of black families were headed by single women in 2002, up from 28.0 percent in 1970, but down from 47.2 percent in 2000.)

A related development, recently turned into a political issue by those advocating "family values," has been the rising number of single-parent situations. 27.8 percent of families with children under 18 were headed by a single parent in 2002, up from only 13 percent in 1970. The vast majority of these single-parent families were headed by women. The number of households headed by never-married women with children continues to grow. There were 248,000 such households in

Households and Families: Growth and Change, 1960–2000

Type of unit	Number ('000s) 1960	1970	1980	1990	2000	Percent change 1980–90	1990-2000
All Households	**52,799**	**63,401**	**80,776**	**93,347**	**104,705**	**15.5%**	**12.2%**
Average size	3.33	3.14	2.76	2.63	2.62	—	—
Families	**45,111**	**51,586**	**59,550**	**66,090**	**72,025**	**11.0%**	**9.0%**
Average size	3.67	3.58	3.29	3.17	3.17	—	—
Married couple	39,329	44,755	49,112	52,317	55,311	6.5	5.7
Male householder[1]	1,275	1,239	1,733	2,884	4,028	66.4	39.7
Female householder[1]	4,507	5,591	8,705	10,890	12,687	25.1	16.5
Unrelated subfamilies	**207**	**130**	**360**	**534**	**571**	**48.3%**	**6.9%**
Married couple	75	27	20	68	37	N.A.[2]	N.A.[2]
Father-child[1]	47	11	36	45	57	N.A.[2]	N.A.[2]
Mother-child[1]	85	91	304	421	477	38.5	13.3
Related subfamilies	**1,514**	**1,150**	**1,150**	**2,403**	**2,983**	**109.0%**	**24.1%**
Married couple	871	617	582	871	1,149	49.7	31.9
Father-child[1]	115	48	54	153	201	183.0	31.4
Mother-child[1]	528	484	512	1,378	1,633	169.1	18.5
Nonfamily households	**7,895**	**11,945**	**21,226**	**27,257**	**32,680**	**28.4%**	**19.9%**
Male householder	2,716	4,063	8,807	11,606	14,641	31.8	26.2
Female householder	5,179	7,882	12,419	15,651	18,039	26.0	15.3
One person	6,896	10,851	18,296	22,999	26,724	25.7	16.2

1. No spouse present. 2. Not shown; base less than 75,000.
Source: U.S. Bureau of the Census, *America's Families and Living Arrangements 2000* (2001). www.census.gov.

Families: Number, Average Size and Percent Distribution by Number of Children, 1970–2000

Year	Number of families ('000s)	Average size of family	Percent distribution by numberof own children under 18: None	1	2	3	4 or more
1970	51,586	3.58	44.1%	18.2%	17.4%	10.6%	9.8%
1980	59,550	3.29	47.9	20.9	19.3	7.8	4.1
1985	62,706	3.23	50.4	20.9	18.6	7.2	3.0
1990	66,090	3.17	51.1	20.5	18.5	7.0	2.8
1995	69,305	3.19	50.5	20.3	19.1	7.3	2.8
1996	69,594	3.20	50.9	20.2	19.0	7.1	2.9
1997	70,241	3.19	50.6	20.4	18.9	7.3	2.8
1998	70,880	3.19	51.0	20.3	18.5	7.6	2.7
1999	71,535	3.18	51.6	20.0	18.3	7.3	2.8
2000	72,025	3.17	50.4	21.5	18.5	6.9	2.8

Source: U.S. Bureau of the Census, *America's Families and Living Arrangements 2000* (2001)). www.census.gov.

Living Arrangements of Children Under 18, by Race, 1970–2000

Arrangement	1970 Number ('000s)	1970 Percent	1980 Number ('000s)	1980 Percent	1990 Number ('000s)	1990 Percent	2000 Number ('000s)	2000 Percent
All children								
Children under 18	69,162	100.0%	63,427	100.0%	64,137	100.0%	72,012	100.0%
Living with:								
Two parents	58,939	85.2	48,624	76.7	46,503	72.5	49,795	69.1
One Parent	8,199	11.9	12,466	19.7	15,867	24.7	19,220	26.7
Mother only	7,452	10.8	11,406	18.0	13,874	21.6	16,162	22.4
Father only	748	1.1	1,060	1.7	1,993	3.1	3,058	4.2
Other relatives	1,547	2.2	1,949	3.1	1,421	2.2	2,160	3.0
Nonrelatives only	477	0.7	388	0.6	346	0.5	837	1.2
White children								
Children under 18	58,791	100.0%	52,242	100.0%	51,390	100.0%	56,455	100.0%
Living with:								
Two parents	52,624	89.5	43,200	82.7	40,593	79.0	42,497	75.3
One Parent	5,110	8.7	7,901	15.1	9,869	19.2	12,192	21.6
Mother only	4,581	7.8	7,059	13.5	8,321	16.2	9,765	17.3
Father only	528	0.9	842	1.6	1,549	3.0	2,427	4.3
Other relatives	695	1.2	887	1.7	708	1.4	1,132	2.0
Nonrelatives only	362	0.6	254	0.5	220	0.4	634	1.1
Black children								
Children under 18	9,422	100.0%	9,375	100.0%	10,018	100.0%	11,412	100.0%
Living with:								
Two parents	5,508	58.5	3,956	42.2	3,781	37.7	4,286	37.6
One Parent	2,995	31.8	4,297	45.8	5,484	54.7	6,080	53.3
Mother only	2,783	29.5	4,117	43.9	5,132	51.2	5,596	49.0
Father only	213	2.3	180	1.9	353	3.5	484	4.2
Other relatives	822	8.7	999	10.7	655	6.5	879	7.7
Nonrelatives only	97	1.0	123	1.3	98	1.0	167	1.5
Hispanic children								
Children under 18	4,006	100.0%	5,459	100.0%	7,174	100.0%	11,613	100.0%
Living with:								
Two parents	3,111	77.7	4,116	75.4	4,789	66.8	7,561	65.1
One Parent	N.A.	N.A.	1,152	21.1	2,154	30.0	3,425	29.5
Mother only	N.A.	N.A.	1,069	19.6	1,943	27.1	2,919	25.4
Father only	N.A.	N.A.	83	1.5	211	2.9	506	4.4
Other relatives	N.A.	N.A.	183	3.4	177	2.5	431	3.7
Nonrelatives only	N.A.	N.A.	8	0.1	54	0.8	196	1.7

Note: N.A.= Not available. Hispanic children may be of any race. Excludes persons under 18 years who were maintaining households or family groups and spouses. **Source:** U.S. Bureau of the Census, *America's Families and Living Arrangements 2000* (2001).

1970; in 2000, there were 4.4 million of them, slightly less than the 4.6 million households headed by divorced women with children.

According to the Census Bureau, the period between 1990 and 2000 saw a general stabilizing of these trends; in the past 10 years, the percentage of married couple families and single-parent families has remained constant. The one startling change was the growth of single-parent homes headed by fathers. In 2000, they numbered 2.0 million, up from 1.8 million in 1998.

Another important though less vital sign of change is the growth in the number of so-called *subfamilies*. These are families who live in a household and are either related or not to the householder; the Census Bureau describes a *related subfamily* as a married couple with or without children, or one parent with one or more single (never married) children under 18, living in a household and related to the person who maintains the household. They are not counted in the total number of families. Related subfamilies have nearly tripled since 1980 and now stand at nearly 3 million.

An *unrelated subfamily* is a group of two persons or more who are related to one another by birth, marriage or adoption, but who are not related to the householder. Unrelated subfamilies numbered 474,000 in 2002.

▶SINGLE PARENTS AND GROWN CHILDREN LIVING AT HOME

Among the social changes that have taken place over the last 20 years, two of the most revealing are where children live, and how soon young people get to live on their own. Since 1970, the percentage of children under 18 living with only one parent has more than doubled. In 2002, 23 percent lived with only one parent, as compared to just under 12 percent in 1970 (4 percent lived with neither parent). This increase reflects not only a soaring divorce rate, but a startling increase in the number of children born to unwed mothers, especially among blacks. The numbers of households headed by unmarried black women and divorced black women were equal in 1970. In 2002, never-married black mother households outnumbered divorced-mother black households by more than two to one. Since 1990, more than half of all black children, one-fifth of white children, and 29 percent of Hispanic children under the age of 18 have lived with one parent only, usually the mother.

Inflation, soaring housing costs, stagnant wage rates, and postponement of marriage have helped to keep young adults of both sexes living at home with their parents for an increasingly long period. In 1970, 8.0 percent of 25-to-34-year-olds lived with their parents. By 1996, that number increased to nearly 12.3 percent, though it retreated to 10.6 percent in 2000. Because they marry younger, women aged 25-34 were much less likely (8.3 percent in 2000) as men (12.9 percent) to live with their parents. In 1996, a whopping 16.0 percent of men 25-34 lived at home.

▶LIVING WITH GRANDPARENTS

In 2002, the Census Bureau estimated that 3.7 million (5.1 percent of the nation's 73 million) children under age 18 lived in the home of their grandparents. This is up from 3.2 percent in 1970 and 3.6 percent in 1980, but down from the all-time high of 5.7 percent in 1996. Of those children, 65 percent had at least one parent in the household. Black chidren were more likely (9 percent) to live in their grandparents' household, compared with 6 percent of Hispanic children, 4 percent non-Hispanic white, and 3 percent Asian/Pacific Islanders.

Source: U.S. Bureau of the Census, *Children's Living Arrangements and Characteristics (March 2002).*

HOUSING

According to the Census Bureau's biannual American Housing Survey, there were 106.3 million occupied housing units in the U.S. in 2001, the latest year for which data are available. Of these units, 72.3 million (68 percent) were occupied by homeowners, while the remaining 34.0 million (32 percent) were occupied by renters.

Housing units The American ideal of the intact nuclear family may be somewhat tarnished in these days of high divorce rates and growing single-parent households, but U.S. housing patterns still reflect traditional values. Nearly two of every three occupied homes (62.1 million) were detached single unit structures. Mobile homes or trailers, numbering 7.2 million, are not included in those totals. Another 7.3 million were attached single-unit structures such as a brownstone or row house. Cooperatives and condominiums, totalling more than 5.2 million, are counted separately since they may include any number of dwellings.

Characteristics of Occupied Housing Units 1993-2001

Characteristic	1993 Units ('000)	1993 Percent of units	1995 Units ('000)	1995 Percent of units	1999 Units ('000)	1999 Percent of units	2001 Units ('000)	2001 Percent of units
Total occupied units	**94,724**	**100.0%**	**97,693**	**100.0%**	**102,803**	**100.0%**	**106,261**	**100%**
Owner occupied	61,252	64.7	63,544	65.0	68,796	66.9	72,265	68.0
Renter occupied	33472	35.3	34,150	35.0	31,007	30.2	33,996	32.0
Units in structure								
Single, detached	58,918	62.2%	60,826	62.3%	64,536	62.8%	67,129	63.2%
Single, attached	5,375	5.7	5,545	5.7	6,963	6.8	7,305	6.9
2 to 4	9,279	9.8	9,299	9.5	8,572	8.3	8,200	7.7
5 to 9	4,724	5.0	4,803	4.9	4,847	4.7	4,994	4.7
10 to 19	4,190	4.4	4,342	4.4	4,416	4.3	4,620	4.3
20 to 49	3,154	3.3	3,244	3.3	3,343	3.2	3,253	3.1
50 or more	3,429	3.6	3,470	3.6	3,341	3.2	3,543	3.3
Mobile home or trailer	5,655	5.9	6,164	6.3	6,785	6.6	7,219	6.8
Size								
Size of unit (sq. ft.)	1,725	N.A.	1,732	N.A.	1,730	N.A.	1,737	N.A.
Size of lot (acres)	0.43	N.A.	0.43	N.A.	0.34	N.A.	.36	N.A
Number of bedrooms								
One	11,279	11.9%	11,777	12.1%	11,986	11.7%	11,984	11.3%
Two	28,965	30.6	29,146	29.8	29,166	28.4	29,281	27.6
Three	38,504	40.6	40,302	41.2	43,103	41.9	44,786	42.1
Four or more	14,848	15.7	15,421	15.8	17,689	17.2	19,391	18.2
Number of bathrooms								
None	526	0.6%	465	0.5%	676	0.7%	681	0.6%
One	43,944	46.4	43,777	44.8	42838	41.7	42,113	39.6
One and a half	14,740	15.6	14,780	15.1	16189	15.8	16,548	15.6
Two or more	35,515	37.5	38,671	39.6	43100	41.9	46,920	44.2
Median age (years)	28	N.A.	28	N.A.	31	N.A.	31	N.A.
Mortgage status[1]								
None, owned free and clear	24,068	39.3%	24,518	38.6%	25,604	37.22%	25,675	35.5%
One mortgage	32,302	52.7	34,730	54.7	28,960	42.1	32,721	45.3
Two mortgages	3,975	6.5	4,244	6.7	6,884	10.0	8,470	11.7
Three or more mortgages	71	0.1	52	0.1	415	0.6	1,008	1.4
Median years remaining	19	N.A.	20	N.A.	20	N.A.	22	N.A.
Median amount outstanding	$48,357	N.A.	$48,466	N.A.	63,939	N.A.	69,227	N.A.

1. In this category, figures are perecentages of owner-occupied units only, which represent approximately two-thirds of all occupied units. Not all homeowners reported their mortgage status.
Source: U.S. Bureau of the Census, *American Housing Surveys* 1993, 1995, 1999 and 2001.

Size of housing units The size of the American house decreased slightly for the first time in a decade. The median size of all single, detached one-family houses (including mobile homes) was 1,737 square feet in 2001, down from 1,750 in 1997; for owner-occupied houses, the figure was 1,798 square feet, also down from 1,825. About 19 percent of single houses (14 million) had more than 2,500 square feet, and 11.7 percent (8.3 million) had less than 1,000 square feet. Although the typical American family is growing smaller, the typical American house is growing larger. The vast majority of houses in 2001 (75.9 percent) had between 4 and 7 rooms; most houses (60 percent) had 3 or more bedrooms, and 44.2 percent had two or more bathrooms.

Homeownership Rates, 1890–2001

Year	Homeownership rate	Year	Homeownership rate
1890	47.8%	**1980**	64.4%
1900	46.7	**1990**	64.2
1910	45.9	**1995**[1]	64.7
1920	45.6	**1996**[1]	65.4
1930	47.8	**1997**[1]	65.7
1940	43.6	**1998**[1]	66.3
1950	55.0	**1999**[1]	66.8
1960	61.9	**2000**[1]	67.4
1970	62.9	**2001**[1]	67.8

1. Figures from 1890-1990 are from the decennial census, which counts every home. Figures from 1995-2001 are from the Census Bureau's annual *Housing Vacancy Survey*, which uses statistical samples. **Source**: U.S. Census Bureau.

Equipment and fuel More houses had air conditioning (85 percent) than a dishwasher (58.7 percent), a washing machine (80.5 percent), or clothes dryer (76.8 percent). Natural gas was the fuel of choice for most houses: it heated 51.5 percent of houses. Electricity heated 30.7 percent, while 9.2 percent of houses had oil furnaces. Oil is most popular in the Northeast, where it is used to heat 37.7 percent of all houses; outside the Northeast, fewer than 4 percent of houses use oil heat. Gas heats 65.0 percent of the houses in the West and and 78.5 percent of the houses in the Midwest. Electricity heats 51.5 percent of houses in the South.

Growth of housing In 2001, the median age of all housing structures in the U.S. was 31 years (i.e. built in 1970). Only 8.6 million units built before 1919 were still in use. This reflects the extraordinary growth of the housing industry during the 1970's and 80's, when 35.8 million of extant units were built. By comparison, only 17.9 million of the

Homeownership Rates in the U.S. by Age, Race, and Hispanic Origin, 1982–2001

Characteristic	1982	1985	1990	1995	1999	2000	2001
U.S., total	**64.8%**	**63.9%**	**63.9%**	**64.7%**	**66.8%**	**67.4%**	**67.8%**
By age							
Under 25	19.3	17.2	15.7	15.9	19.9	21.7	22.5
Under 35	41.2	39.9	38.5	38.6	39.7	40.8	41.2
35 to 44	70.0	68.1	66.3	65.2	67.2	67.9	68.2
45 to 54	77.4	75.9	75.2	75.2	76.0	76.5	76.7
55 to 64	80.0	79.5	79.3	79.5	81.0	80.3	81.3
65 and over	74.4	74.8	76.3	78.1	80.1	80.4	80.3
By race and origin							
White	N.A.	N.A.	N.A.	68.7	70.5	71.1	71.6
Black	N.A.	N.A.	N.A.	42.7	46.3	47.2	47.7
Asian	N.A.	N.A.	N.A.	50.8	53.1	52.8	53.9
Hispanic (all races)	N.A.	N.A.	N.A.	42.0	45.5	46.3	47.3

Source: U.S. Bureau of the Census, *2001 Housing Vacancy Survey*, 2002.

Average Sales Prices of New One-Family Houses, by Region, 1965–2001

Year	Northeast	Midwest	South	West	United States: Amount	United States: Annual percent increase
1965	$22,900	$22,800	$18,900	$23,200	$21,500	N.A.
1970	32,800	28,000	24,000	26,900	26,600	N.A.
1975	47,000	43,400	39,600	44,300	42,600	N.A.
1980	80,300	74,400	69,100	89,400	76,400	6.4%
1985	121,900	95,400	88,900	111,800	100,800	3.3
1990	190,500	133,000	123,500	180,600	149,800	0.7
1995	216,600	157,200	142,000	169,800	158,700	2.7
1997	234,100	173,000	151,400	198,200	176,200	5.9
1998	240,100	179,200	159,700	200,500	181,900	3.2
1999	247,900	186,800	173,000	221,700	195,600	7.5
2000	274,800	199,300	179,000	238,900	207,000	5.8
2001	294,300	201,300	185,700	250,000	213,200	3.0

Note: Figures are in current dollars. **Source:** U.S. Bureau of the Census, *New One-Family Houses Sold* (March 2002).

housing units still in use were built between 1920 and 1950.

Home ownership Low mortgage rates, a strong economy and low unemployment continued to push home ownership rates to record levels. More than two-thirds of householders (67.4 percent) owned their own homes in 2000, up from 63.9 percent in 1990. (See the accompanying table). Of particular note is the increase in home ownership by those under 25 (21.7 percent in 2000, up from 15.9 percent five years earlier) and over 65 (80.4 percent, up from 78.1 percent in 1995). The growth in elderly homeownership rates reflects the growing independence of people over 65.

The overall increase in home ownership follows a decade—the 1980's—in which skyrocketing home prices prevented many people from buying homes. The decline in home-ownership rates in the 1980's was the first in 50 years.

Married couple families had the highest rates of home ownership (82.4 percent in 2000). Single people were less likely to own their own homes, especially single men. Their home-ownership rate in 2000 (47.8 percent) was lower than the rate for single women (53.0 percent). Home-ownership rates are consistently highest in the Midwest (72.6 percent in 2000) and South (69.6 percent) and lowest in the Northeast (63.4 percent) and West (61.7 percent).

Existing One-Family Houses Sold and Median Sales Price, by Region, 1970–2001

	Houses Sold ('000s)					Median Sales Price				
Year	United States	Northeast	Midwest	South	West	United States	Northeast	Midwest	South	West
1970	1,612	251	501	568	292	$23,000	$25,700	$20,100	$20,100	$24,300
1975	2,476	370	701	862	543	35,300	39,300	30,100	30,100	39,600
1980	2,973	403	806	1,092	672	62,200	60,800	51,900	51,900	89,300
1985	3,134	561	806	1,063	704	75,500	88,900	58,900	58,900	95,400
1990	3,219	458	809	1,193	759	92,000	126,400	75,300	75,300	129,600
1995	3,888	547	945	1,433	964	110,500	126,700	94,800	94,800	141,000
1998	4,970	662	1,130	1,868	1,309	128,400	135,900	114,300	114,300	164,800
1999	5,205	656	1,148	2,015	1,386	133,300	139,000	119,600	119,600	173,900
2000	5,152	643	1,119	2,015	1,376	139,000	139,400	123,600	128,300	183,000
2001	5,296	638	1,158	2,114	1,386	147,800	146,500	130,200	137,400	194,500

Source: National Association of Realtors, *Home Sales* (May 2002).

Median Sales Prices of Existing Single-Family Homes for Selected Metropolitan Areas, 1985–2002

Metropolitan area	1985	1995	2000	2001	2002[1]
Atlanta, Ga.	$66,200[2]	$ 97,500	$131,200	$138,800	$140,600
Baltimore, Md.	72,600	111,300	153,000	158,200	165,000
Boston, Mass.	134,200	179,000	314,200	356,600	358,000
Chicago, Ill.	81,100	147,900	171,800	198,500	198,000
Cincinnati, Ohio-Ky.-Tenn.	60,200	100,400	126,700	130,200	131,300
Cleveland, Ohio	64,400	104,700	N.A.	N.A.	N.A.
Dallas, Tex.	94,000	96,400	122,500	131,100	130,800
Denver, Colo.	84,300	127,300	196,800	218,300	223,800
Detroit, Mich.	51,700	98,200	N.A.	N.A.	N.A.
Honolulu, Hawaii	N.A.	349,000	295,000	299,900	310,000
Houston, Tex.	78,600	79,200	116,100	122,400	126,500
Kansas City, Mo.-Kans.	61,400	91,700	127,400	135,700	133,500
Las Vegas, Nev.	N.A.	113,500	137,400	149,100	153,100
Los Angeles area, Calif.	125,200	179,900	215,900	241,400	265,000
Miami-Hialeah, Fla.	80,500	107,100	144,600	162,700	172,500
Milwaukee, Wis.	67,500	114,700	140,700	149,400	159,000
Minneapolis-St. Paul, Minn.-Wis.	75,200	106,800	151,400	167,400	173,000
New Orleans, La.	N.A.	87,000	112,000	117,400	116,500
New York City area, N.Y.	134,000	169,700	230,200	258,200	285,600
Philadelphia, Pa-N.J.	74,000	118,700	125,200	134,800	122,000
Phoenix, Ariz.	74,800	96,800	134,400	139,400	141,700
Pittsburgh, Pa.	N.A.	82,100	93,600	97,800	94,400
St. Louis, Mo.-Ill.	65,700	87,700	108,400	116,200	N.A.
San Diego, Calif.	107,400	171,600	269,400	298,600	325,500
San Francisco Bay Area, Calif.	145,100	254,400	454,600	475,900	482,300
Seattle, Wash.	N.A.	159,000	230,100	245,400	247,600
Tampa-St. Petersburg-Clearwater, Fla.	58,400	78,300	110,800	123,600	129,700
Washington, D.C.-Md.-Va.	97,100	156,500	182,600	213,900	229,100
U.S. average	N.A.	$112,900	$139,000	$147,800	$151,000

1. First quarter only. 2. Figure is for 1984. **Source:** National Association of Realtors, *Home Sales* (May 2002).

Housing costs According to the most recent annual survey by the Chicago Title Insurance Company, the median price of a single-family home in 1999 was $175,400, up 4.5 percent from $167,900 in 1998. First-time buyers paid a median price of $150,300; they constituted 44.7 percent of all home buyers. Buyers who previously owned a home paid a median price of $195,000, up 3.1 percent from the previous year. San Francisco was by far the most expensive place to buy a house: the median price was $348,100 for all homes in the Bay Area (up more than 10 percent from the year before and 20 percent in 1997). That's more than double the median price in Atlanta ($151,600), Philadelphia ($144,000) and Denver ($156,300); and more than $100,000 over the medians in Chicago ($175,400), Los Angeles ($223,000) and even New York City ($192,700). Surprisingly, median sales prices in Washington D.C. ($203,400) and in Boston ($209,200) were both higher than in New York City. Housing prices in Memphis, Tenn. were cheapest

Fair Market Monthly Rents for Existing Housing for Selected Metropolitan Areas, 2002-03

Metropolitan area	2002 1 Bedroom	2002 2 bedrooms	2002 3 Bedrooms	2003 1 Bedroom	2003 2 bedrooms	2003 3 Bedrooms
Albuquerque, N.M	$505	$632	$871	537	671	925
Atlanta, Ga.	720	839	1,119	795	927	1,236
Austin-San Marcos, Tex.	645	858	1,192	684	911	1,265
Baltimore, Md.	542	661	875	691	844	1,117
Boston, Mass.	782	979	1,223	1,074	1,343	1,680
Charlotte–Gastonia–Rock Hill, N.C.	585	659	869	617	695	917
Chicago, Ill.	711	848	1,060	778	928	1,160
Cincinnati, Ohio	416	557	746	495	662	887
Cleveland-Lorain-Elyria, Ohio	555	687	874	603	748	951
Colorado Springs, Colo.	486	647	902	518	690	962
Columbus, Ohio	471	605	768	496	636	808
Dallas, Tex.	647	830	1,146	662	850	1,176
Denver, Colo.	625	832	1,154	710	945	1,311
Detroit, Mich.	598	723	904	638	771	964
El Paso, Tex.	451	534	739	479	567	785
Fort Lauderdale, Fla.	609	754	1,049	644	798	1,110
Fort Worth-Arlington, Tex.	521	675	943	572	741	1,035
Fresno, Calif.	433	517	720	973	564	786
Honolulu, Hawaii	713	839	1,134	717	844	1,142
Houston, Tex.	529	684	954	578	747	1,042
Indianapolis, Ind.	465	559	700	489	588	736
Jacksonville, Fla.	530	638	843	559	673	889
Kansas City, Mo.	526	633	875	582	701	970
Las Vegas, Nev.	636	757	1,054	694	827	1,150
Los Angeles-Long Beach, Calif.	618	782	1,055	683	865	1,167
Memphis, Tenn.–Ark.–Miss.	462	542	753	532	624	867
Miami, Fla.	616	768	1,054	652	813	1,116
Milwaukee-Waukeshau, Wis.	504	633	794	533	670	839
Minneapolis-St. Paul, Minn.	580	742	1,004	713	912	1,233
Nashville, Tenn.	520	641	873	548	676	921
New Orleans, La.	423	527	717	529	659	896
New York, N.Y.[1]	836	949	1,187	907	1,031	1,289
Oakland, Calif.	921	1,155	1,583	1,095	1,374	1,883
Oklahoma City, Okla.	422	547	760	448	581	807
Orange County, Calif.	845	1,046	1,455	934	1,155	1,607
Philadelphia, Pa	657	812	1,016	704	871	1,089
Phoenix-Mesa, Ariz.	544	683	950	641	806	1,121
Pittsburgh, Pa.	476	574	719	505	608	762
Portland-Vancouver, Oreg.-Wash.	592	730	1,015	625	771	1,073
Sacramento, Calif.	547	685	950	597	747	1,037
Saint Louis, Mo.	429	556	724	505	655	853
Salt Lake City–Ogden, Utah	550	698	971	586	744	1,036
San Antonio, Tex.	461	596	829	489	633	880
San Diego, Calif.	716	896	1,247	875	1,095	1,524
San Francisco, Calif.	1,154	1,459	2,001	1,535	1,940	2,661
San Jose, Calif.	1,199	1,481	2,030	1,425	1,760	2,412
Seattle-Bellevue-Everett, Wash.	639	809	1,123	710	899	1,249
Tampa-St. Petersburg, Fla.	557	690	917	601	745	989
Tucson, Ariz.	470	625	869	513	683	949
Tulsa, Okla.	427	559	778	454	593	826
Washington, D.C.-Md.-Va.	773	907	1,236	851	999	1,360
West Palm Beach-Boca Raton, Fla.	628	777	1,032	663	820	1,088

Note: Figures are projections made in the year prior to date shown. 1. Figures include areas outside Manhattan. **Source:** U.S. Dept. of Housing and Urban Development, Office of the Federal Housing Commissioner, *Fair Market Rents.*

of the 20 metropolitan areas surveyed; the median sales price was $110,000.

Average monthly mortgage payments for all homeowners rose from $1,212 in 1998 to $1,240 in 1999. These payments represented 32.3 percent of owners's incomes, about the same as the year before, but way up from 1976, when only 24.0 percent went to mortgage payments. Payments were higher among repeat buyers, but first-time buyers paid a larger percentage of their incomes toward their mortgages. Low interest rates were responsible for the popularity of fixed-rate mortgages, in which the consumer locks into a monthly payment for the life of the loan. Fixed-rate mortgages were the choice of 80 percent of mortgage buyers in 1999, up from 69 percent two years earlier, and up from and 55 percent as recently as 1995.

Adjustable, or variable rate mortgages, in which the monthly payment rises and falls based on the prevailing national interest rates, usually feature lower interest rates (as much as 3 percentage points) for the first several years, and higher rates toward the end of the loan. They were responsible for 14.3 percent of all mortgages in 1999, down from 23.4 percent in 1997, and the all-time high of 36.2 percent in 1995.

The average mortgage length was 28.5 years for first-time home buyers and 27.3 years for repeat buyers. Both numbers are down slightly from the year before. Meanwhile, the average down payment as a percentage of the purchase price continues to decline. In 1976, 26.9 percent of buyers put 10 percent or less down on a home purchase. In 1998, that number had skyrocketed to 50.7 percent. The average down payment was 19.5 percent, down from 25.2 percent in 1976.

Housing and the poor Two studies published in 1998, one by the Dept. of Housing and Urban Development, and one by the Center on Budget and Policy Priorities, revealed that despite the strong economic growth of recent years, the housing problems of the poor have grown worse. A severe shortage of affordable apartments has existed all around the nation for several years, forcing 4.4 million poor families to pay more than half their income on rent, usually 60 percent, or more than double what the government calls affordable rent.

The major reasons for this development are stagnating wages for the unskilled, rising real estate values, and the government's failure to supply enough subsidized housing. The number of new subsidized units fell to 70,000 a year during the Reagan-Bush years, down from 260,000 during the Carter administration. In 1995, when the Republicans took over Congress, the government actually stopped expanding the pool of subsidized housing for the first time in modern history.

About 15 million households currently qualify for federal housing assistance, but only 4.5 million families get it. Of those, about one-third live in conventional housing projects, while the rest receive subsidies that allow them to live in private housing. In each case, the tenants contribute 30 percent of their income toward the rent and the government provides the rest.

Moving In 2000, approximately 120 million people, or 46 percent of the population over five years old, lived in a different home than they did in 1995. Most people (25 percent) had moved within the same county; 10 percent had moved to a different county in the same state; eight percent moved between states; and three percent had moved to the U.S. from another country.

▶THE HOMELESS

Although homeless people have become a common sight in almost every community, their plight is always surrounded by some kind of controversy, one that is fueled by a wide range of opinions, some based on fact and others on stereotypes. The often shrill debate about just who the homeless are and what can or should be done for them has been hampered by a lack of reliable information on everything from the causes of homelessness to the actual number of people living on the streets or in shelters.

The number of homeless Because homelessness is a temporary circumstance, it is nearly impossible to measure the number of homeless. In

Characteristics of Recent Home Buyers, 1976–99

Item	1976	1980	1990	1995	1998	1999
Median purchase price	$43,340	$68,714	$131,200	$147,700	$167,900	$175,400
First-time buyers	37,670	61,450	106,000	128,300	142,200	150,300
Repeat buyers	50,090	75,750	149,400	164,300	189,800	195,700
Average monthly mortgage payment	$329	$599	$1,127	$1,062	$1,212	$1,240
First-time buyers	313	N.A.	N.A.	988	1,069	1,090
Repeat buyers	342	N.A.	N.A.	1,125	1,343	1,360
As percent of income	24.0%	32.4%	33.8%	32.6%	32.3%	32.3%
Percent buying:						
New houses	15.1%	22.4%	21.2%	21.5%	21.2%	22.7%
Existing houses	84.9	77.6	78.8	78.5	78.8	77.3
Single-family houses	88.8	82.4	83.8	83.1	82.3	83.0
Condominiums	11.2	17.6	13.1	14.0	14.7	13.5
For the first time	44.8	32.9	41.9	46.2	46.2	44.7
Down payment as percentage of sales price	25.2%	28.0%	23.3%	20.4%	19.3%	19.5%
First-time buyers	18.0	20.5	15.7	13.3	12.8	12.6
Repeat buyers	30.8	32.7	28.9	26.8	24.9	25.5
Average age (in years)						
First-time buyers	28.1	28.3	30.5	32.1	32.2	32.0
Repeat buyers	35.9	36.4	39.1	40.7	41.1	41.4

Source: Chicago Title and Trust Company, *Who's Buying Homes in America* (annual).

1990, the Census Bureau made the first comprehensive federal effort to count the homeless, and identified a total of 228,621 homeless persons on the night of March 21-22. In 2000, the Census Bureau counted 280,527 homeless, but said it would not release detailed statistics on the number of homeless by city and state because it believed the 1990 numbers it published had been inaccurate.

No one believes that any count of the homeless gives an accurate picture of the problem. A 1999 study by the Department of Housing and Urban Development counted 470,000 homeless people on an average night in February 1996, but suggested that this represented only about a quarter of all the people who were homeless at any time during the year. But the counts begin to provide insight into homelessness. Of those counted, 66 percent were single, and 69 percent were male. The vast majority were white (41 percent) or black (40 percent); only 11 percent of homeless people were Hispanic. More than half of the homeless counted in 1996 had suffered from mental illness at some point (39 percent within the past month). About a quarter had had problems with drug addiction in the past month, while 38 percent said they had been addicted to alcohol. Not surprisingly, most homeless said that insufficient income (30 percent of those surveyed) or lack of a job (24 percent) were the biggest impediments to finding housing.

On the positive side, the 1996 count found that the average homeless person had been without housing for an average of 32 months, down from 39 in 1987. And 30 percent had been homeless for three months or less, up from only 21 percent in 1987. Hunger was down too: only 28 percent of homeless said they "sometimes or often don't get enough to eat," down from 38 percent nine years earlier.

New York (44,794) and Los Angeles (26,554) had by far the most homeless people. The next biggest concentration of homeless were in Philadelphia (14,123) and Boston (13,483). The study also found that homeless populations don't correspond directly to a city's population or even to its population below the poverty line. Chicago, with a total population of 2.7 million, had almost the same number of homeless (13,307) as San Francisco (12,410 homeless among the total population of 735,315). Homeless as a percentage of the number of people below the poverty line was 1.59 in Chicago, 1.98 in Los Angeles, 2.30 in Philadelphia, 2.89 in Boston, 2.99 in New York, and 8.60 in San Francisco. Put another way, for every hundred poor people, there were five times as many homeless in San Francisco as in Chicago.

Federal funding The various federal government programs to assist the homeless are grouped under the Stewart B. McKinney Homeless Assistance Act, which became law in July 1987. The act includes 16 different provisions for emergency shelter, food, health care, mental health care, housing, educational programs, job training and other community services. Federal agencies providing services specifically for the homeless include the Federal Emergency Management Agency, and Departments of Agriculture, Education, Health and Human Services, Housing and Urban Development, Labor and Veterans' Affairs. An additional 34 programs, ranging from Medicaid and the Supplemental Security Income program to the Public and Indian housing program and the Ryan White CARE Act, provide general assistance to low-income people, including the homeless. The number of homeless people that these non-homeless-specific programs serve, however, is impossible to determine.

Since 1994, the federal government has budgeted more than $1 billion in funding for the McKinney program. Nevertheless, states and cities still foot the major part of the bill for caring for the homeless.

Funding for Federal Homeless Assistance Programs, 1995-98

Agency and Program	Budget (millions) 1995	1996	1997	1998
Dept. of Agriculture				
Homeless Children Nutrition Program	$1.7	$1.7	$2.1	$1.9
Dept. of Education				
Education for Homeless Children and Youth	28.8	23.0	25.0	28.8
Federal Emergency Management Agency				
Emergency Food and Shelter Program	130.0	100.0	100.0	100.0
Dept. of Health and Human Services				
Health Care for the Homeless	65.4	65.5	69.3	71.3
Projects for Assistance in Transition from Homelessness	29.5	20.0	20.0	23.0
Runaway and Homeless Youth Programs	54.1	64.2	66.6	73.5
Dept. of Housing and Urban Development				
Emergency Shelter Grants	155.0	115.0	115.0	165.0
Single-Room Occupancy Moderate Rehabilitation	N.A.	N.A.	10.1	23.5
Shelter Plus Care	162.0	89.0	61.0	116.9
Supportive Housing Program	602.0	577.0	620.0	574.2
Dept. of Labor				
Homeless Veterans Reintegration Project	N.A.	N.A.	N.A.	3.0
Dept. of Veterans' Affairs				
Domiciliary Care for Homeless Veterans	38.9	41.1	37.2	38.5
Homeless Chronically Mentally Ill Veterans	32.3	32.1	32.0	36.4
Homeless Providers Grant and Per Diem Program	6.3	6.3	6.1	5.9
Total	**$1,306.0**	**$1,134.9**	**$1,164.4**	**$1,261.9**

Source: General Accounting Office: *Report to Congressional Committee: Homelessness,* February, 1999.

IMMIGRATION

Over the last four centuries the mingling of peoples from all parts of the world has been a vital element in the formation of the United States both as a land of opportunity and in its emergence as a world power. In one relatively brief period between 1880 and 1920 the massive influx of more than 20 million European immigrants provided the continuous labor supply necessary to transform the nation from an agricultural society to an industrialized one with extraordinary rapidity.

Over the next 40 years, however, the flow of immigration slowed dramatically as the government decided to close the doors to most foreign groups. Motivated at first by a disconcerting kind of nativism, the nation's anti-immigration sentiments were later bolstered by the Great Depression and the need to provide work for those already living here. World War II and the subsequent national readjustment limited immigration for several decades.

Since 1960 a steadily increasing number of immigrants—both legal and illegal—has had a very noticeable impact on both the size and ethnic composition of the American population. The startling upsurge in the number of Asians and Hispanic immigrants during the 1970's, 80's, and 90's has been caused by a variety of factors from wars and political upheaval to the mundane fact of geographical proximity in the case of Mexico. Approximately 700,000 new legal immigrants are arriving annually and well over half are from those two ethnic backgrounds.

In 1998, total immigration hit a 10-year low of 660,477. Many demographers argue that if the immigration rate continues to fall, the effect on American population growth could be severe.

The Statue of Liberty

The Statue of Liberty was conceived and designed by Frédéric-Auguste Bartholdi (with Gustave Eiffel's help) and given to the U.S. by the French government in honor of the centennial of American independence in 1876. Funded by subscriptions from the French people, it was dedicated by President Grover Cleveland in 1886 and became a national monument in 1924.

Measuring 151 feet (46 m) to the top of her torch, Miss Liberty still stands guard over the entrance to New York harbor, the inscription on its base a poignant reminder of the vision Americans once had of their country:

Give me your tired, your poor,
Your huddled masses yearning to breathe free,
The wretched refuse of your teeming shore,
Send these, the homeless, tempest-tost to me:
I lift my lamp beside the golden door.

Immigration as a Percentage of Total Population Growth, 1901–2000

Period	Percent	Period	Percent
1901-10	39.6%	**1950-54**	10.6%
1911-20	17.7	**1955-59**	10.7
1921-30	15.0	**1960-64**	12.5
1931-34	-0.1	**1965-69**	19.7
1935-39	3.2	**1970-80**	19.4
1940-44	7.4	**1981-90**	32.8
1945-49	10.2	**1991-2000**	27.8

Source: U.S. Dept. of Justice, *1998 Statistical Yearbook of the Immigration and Naturalization Service* (2000).

U.S. Immigration Rate by Decade, 1820–2000

Period	Total immigrants	Rate per 1,000 U.S. population
1820-30	151,824	1.2
1831-40	599,125	3.9
1841-50	1,713,251	8.4
1851-60	2,598,214	9.3
1861-70	2,314,824	6.4
1871-80	2,812,191	6.2
1881-90	5,246,613	9.2
1891-1900	3,687,564	5.3
1901-10	8,795,386	10.4
1911-20	5,735,811	5.7
1921-30	4,107,209	3.5
1931-40	528,431	0.4
1941-50	1,035,039	0.7
1951-60	2,515,479	1.5
1961-70	3,321,677	1.7
1971-80	4,493,314	2.1
1981-90	7,338,062	2.9
1991-2000[1]	**9,095,417**	**3.2**
Total 1820-2000	**66,089,431**	**N.A.**

1. Includes more than 2 million aliens adjusting under the legalization provisions of the Immigration and Control Act (IRCA) of 1986. **Source:** U.S. Dept. of Justice, *2000 Statistical Yearbook of the Immigration and Naturalization Service* (2002).

Percent of Immigrants Admitted by Region, 1951–2002

Region	Total, 1951-2000	1951-60	1961-70	1971-80	1981-90	1991-2000	2002
Europe	20.0%	52.7%	33.8%	17.8%	10.4%	14.9%	16.7%
Asia	28.8	6.1	12.9	35.3	37.3	30.7	30.7
Africa	2.4	5.6	8.7	1.8	2.4	3.9	5.3
Oceania		0.5	0.8	0.9	0.6	0.6	0.6
America[1]	47.8	39.6	51.7	44.1	49.3	49.3	45.0
Caribbean	11.9	4.9	14.2	16.5	11.9	10.8	8.9
Central America	4.8	1.8	3.1	3.0	6.4	5.8	6.3
Other North America[1]	24.7	26.9	26.1	18.0	24.7	26.8	23.0
South America	6.2	3.6	7.8	6.6	6.3	5.9	6.9

Note: Data are for fiscal years. 1. Includes more than 2 million illegal immigrants from Mexico granted permanent legal residence under the 1986 Immigration Reform & Control Act. **Source:** U.S. Dept. of Justice, *2002 Yearbook of Immigration Statistics* (2003).

With the dramatic decline in its birth rates and fertility rates, the U.S. might very well begin to experience negative population growth by the year 2030; by 2020 immigration will add more population than natural increase will. According to the Office of Population Research at Princeton Uni-

Top 20 Countries of Birth for U.S. Immigrants, and Major Categories of Admission, 2002

Country of birth	Total immigrants[1]	Percent of total	Category of admission: Relative preferences	Occupational preferences	Immediate relatives	Refugees and asylees	IRCA legalization[2]
All countries	**1,063,732**	**100.0%**	**187,069**	**174,968**	**485,960**	**126,084**	**89,651**
1. Mexico	219,380	20.6	58,602	7,492	150,693	100	2,493
2. India	71,105	6.7	11,402	42,885	15,077	1,558	183
3. China, mainland	61,282	5.8	11,799	20,713	27,911	693	166
4. Philippines	51,308	4.8	12,060	12,566	26,470	68	144
5. Vietnam	33,627	3.2	12,810	297	12,984	6,926	610
6. El Salvador	31,168	2.9	4,748	1,670	8,763	187	15,800
7. Cuba	28,272	2.7	973	38	1,499	24,893	869
8. Bosnia-Herzegovina	25,373	2.4	24	65	235	25,033	16
9. Dominican Rep.	22,604	2.1	10,873	229	11,418	25	59
10. Ukraine	21,217	2.0	96	928	4,074	10,601	5,518
11. Korea	21,021	2.0	2,164	9,241	9,573	7	36
12. Russia	20,833	2.0	97	2,714	10,468	5,089	2,465
13. Haiti	20,268	1.9	6,732	141	7,436	769	5,190
14. Canada	19,519	1.8	735	9,530	8,825	26	403
15. Colombia	18,845	1.8	2,453	1,622	14,300	380	90
16. Guatemala	16,229	1.5	2,302	845	7,788	353	4,941
17. United Kingdom	16,181	1.5	627	7,511	7,847	23	173
18. Jamaica	14,898	1.4	4,803	557	9,503	6	29
19. Pakistan	13,743	1.3	2,930	3,334	5,871	467	1,141
20. Iran	13,029	1.2	1,684	1,514	4,292	4,806	733

1. Total includes Amerasians, Soviet and Indochinese parolees, foreign government officials, special immigrants, and admissions from nonpreference "underrepresented countries," suspension of deportation, and private law not shown separately. 2. Under the Immigration Reform and Control Act (IRCA) of 1986, illegal aliens with temporary resident status became eligible for permanent legal residence. **Source:** U.S. Dept. of Justice, *2002 Yearbook of Immigration Statistics* (2003).

Top 20 Metropolitan Areas of Intended Residence for U.S. Immigrants, 1995–2002

Rank, 2002 and State	Immigrants 1995 Number	1995 Percent of total	2000 Number	2000 Percent of total	2002 Number	2002 Percent of total
1. California	N.A.	N.A.	217,753	25.6%	291,216	27.4%
2. New York	N.A.	N.A.	106,061	12.5	114,827	10.8
3. Florida	N.A.	N.A.	98,391	11.6	90,819	8.5
4. Texas	N.A.	N.A.	63,840	7.5	88,365	8.3
5. New Jersey	N.A.	N.A.	40,013	4.7	57,721	5.4
6. Illinois	N.A.	N.A.	36,180	4.3	47,235	4.4
7. Massachusetts	N.A.	N.A.	23,483	2.8	31,615	3.0
8. Washington	N.A.	N.A.	18,486	2.2	25,704	2.4
9. Virginia	N.A.	N.A.	20,087	2.4	25,411	2.4
10. Maryland	N.A.	N.A.	17,705	2.1	23,751	2.2
Rank, 2002 and Metropolitan area	**Number**	**Percent of total**	**Number**	**Percent of total**	**Number**	**Percent of total**
1. Los Angeles-Long Beach, Calif.	54,669	7.6%	70,644	9.1%	108,613	10.2%
2. New York, N.Y.	111,687	15.5	85,867	12.3	91,275	8.6
3. Chicago, Ill.	31,730	4.4	32,300	4.7	43,810	4.1
4. Miami, Fla.	30,935	4.3	47,404	4.4	40,832	3.8
5. Washington D.C.-MD-Va.	25,717	3.6	29,394	3.9	38,468	3.6
6. Houston, Tex.	14,379	2.0	17,429	2.0	28,225	2.7
7. San Jose, Calif.	12,855	1.8	16,874	1.8	27,431	2.6
8. Orange County, Calif.	18,187	2.5	20,859	2.2	25,806	2.4
9. San Diego, Calif.	N.A.	N.A.	N.A.	N.A.	22,484	2.1
10. Boston-Lawrence-Lowell Mass.	16,750	2.3	16,469	2.0	21,535	2.01.

Includes other MSAs not shown separately. **Source:** U.S. Dept. of Justice, *2002 Yearbook of Immigration Statistics* (2003).

Immigration to the U.S. by Country of Last Residence, 1820-2002

Since 1820, Germany has sent more immigrants to the U.S. than has any other country, but Mexico is gaining fast. More than 6 million people immigrated to the U.S. from Mexico between 1820 and 2000, 64 percent of them since 1981, and the tide of Mexican immigration shows few signs of abating. More immigrants to the United States came from Mexico than from the next four countries combined in 2000. This table ranks the top 10 nations by the total number of U.S. immigrants since 1820.

Country	1820–2002 Number	1820–2002 Percent of total	1981–90 Number	1981–90 Percent of total	1991–2000 Number	1991–2000 Percent of total
All Countries	**68,217,481**	**100.0%**	**7,338,062**	**100.0%**	**9,095,417**	**100.0%**
Germany	7,219,222	10.6	91,961	1.2	92,606	1.0
Mexico	6,560,312	9.6	1,655,843	22.6	2,249,421	24.7
Italy	5,442,044	8.0	67,254	1.0	62,722	1.0
United Kingdom	5,309,331	7.8	159,173	2.2	151,866	2.0
Ireland	4,785,052	7.0	31,969	0.4	56,950	1.0
Canada	4,545,074	6.7	156,938	2.1	191,987	2.0
Former USSR	4,017,143	5.9	57,677	0.8	462,874	5.1
Austria	1,848,107	2.7	18,340	0.2	15,500	0.2
Hungary	1,679,815	2.5	6,545	0.1	9,382	0.1
Philippines	1,630,142	2.4	548,764	7.5	503,945	5.5

1. Austria and Hungary not counted separately for all years. **Source:** U.S. Dept. of Justice, *2002 Yearbook of Immigration Statistics* (2003).

Estimated Number of U.S. Immigrants, by Region and Selected Country of Last Residence, 1820-2002

Region/country	Total 1820–2002	2002
Europe	**38,816,282**	**177,652**
Austria[1]	1,848,107	2,657
Belgium	219,490	1,359
Czechoslovakia[2]	159,400	1,862
Denmark	377,887	655
France	833,434	4,596
Germany	7,219,222	21,058
Greece	734,145	1,516
Hungary[1]	1,679,815	1,359
Ireland	4,785,052	1,419
Italy	5,442,044	2,837
Netherlands	391,740	2,305
Norway[3]	759,949	464
Poland	795,742	13,304
Portugal	527,151	1,320
Romania	266,793	4,525
Soviet Union	4,017,143	55,464
Spain	305,797	1,603
Sweden[3]	1,263,129	1,633
Switzerland	374,579	1,503
United Kingdom	5,309,331	18,057
Yugoslavia[4]	252,865	28,100
Other Europe	261,964	10,573
Asia	**9,479,289**	**326,871**
China[5]	1,440,285	55,974
Hong Kong	430,268	7,952
India	951,556	66,854
Iran	261,200	7,730
Israel	186,800	4,938
Japan	549,800	9,150
Korea	846,461	20,114
Philippines	1,630,142	48,674
Turkey	457,950	3,934
Vietnam	811,495	32,425
Other Asia	1,913,332	69,116
America	**18,506,482**	**478,777**
Canada & Newfoundland	4,545,074	27,299
Mexico	6,560,312	217,318
Caribbean	3,873,162	94,240
Cuba	971,625	27,520
Dominican Republic	889,117	22,474
Haiti	456,125	19,189
Jamaica	628,393	14,567
Other Caribbean	927,902	10,490
Central America	1,486,126	66,520
El Salvador	552,058	30,539
Other Central America	934,068	35,981
South America	1,931,624	73,400
Argentina	165,032	3,811
Colombia	458,673	18,488
Ecuador	252,617	10,564
Other South America	1,055,302	40,537
Other America	110,184	3
Africa	**795,428**	**56,135**
Oceania	**274,256**	**6,536**
Not specified	**345,744**	**17,761**
All countries	**68,217,481**	**1,064,732**

Note: Because of changes in boundaries and government, figures for many countries, especially those in Asia, are not available for all years or were not reported separately for all years, and are therefore not strictly comparable throughout. Data for many countries are included with countries to which they belonged prior to World War I. 1. Data for Austria and Hungary not reported separately for all years. Total does not include 846,076 immigrants whose country of last residence is listed as Austria-Hungary. 2. No data available for Czechoslovakia until 1920. 3. Data for Norway and Sweden not reported separately until 1871. Total does not include 60,255 immigrants whose country of last residence is listed as Norway-Sweden. 4. Since 1922, includes immigrants from the Serb, Croat, and Slovene Kingdom. 5. Beginning in 1957, China includes Taiwan. **Source:** U.S. Dept. of Justice, *2002 Yearbook of Immigration Statistics* (2003).

Naturalization Rates for U.S. Immigrants by Nation, 1977–95

Almost half of the people who immigrated to the U.S. in 1977 had become naturalized U.S. citizens by 1995. The following table shows immigrants by country from 1977 and the number and percentage that had been naturalized by 1995.

Region and country of birth	Immigrants admitted, 1977	Naturalizations through 1995	
		Number	Rate
All countries	**352,070**	**161,438**	**45.9%**
Europe	**54,867**	**17,591**	**32.1%**
Austria	342	61	17.8
Belgium	300	67	22.3
Czechoslovakia	504	263	52.2
Denmark	362	55	15.2
Finland	231	40	17.3
France	1,283	391	30.5
Germany	4,899	824	16.8
Greece	6,577	2,208	33.6
Hungary	771	405	52.5
Ireland	1,076	297	27.6
Italy	5,843	1,131	19.4
Netherlands	828	152	18.4
Norway	283	32	11.3
Poland	3,468	1,656	47.8
Portugal	6,964	2,051	29.5
Romania	1,620	1,097	67.7
Soviet Union	4,535	2,965	65.4
Spain	2,086	427	20.5
Sweden	485	66	13.6
Switzerland	485	161	33.2
United Kingdom	8,981	2,032	22.6
Yugoslavia	2,256	959	42.5
Other Europe	688	251	36.5
Asia	**119,226**	**72,318**	**60.7%**
Bangladesh	460	317	68.9
Burma (Myanmar)	776	528	68.0
China, People's Republic	14,421	9,444	65.5
Cyprus	410	210	51.2
Hong Kong	3,146	2,404	76.4
India	15,033	8,877	59.1
Indonesia	658	330	50.2
Iran	3,404	1,855	54.5
Iraq	1,996	1,260	63.1
Israel	2,078	1,332	64.1
Japan	3,602	601	16.7
Jordan	2,187	1,379	63.1
Korea	19,824	11,745	59.2
Lebanon	3,900	2,551	65.4
Macau	248	182	73.4
Malaysia	387	231	59.7
Pakistan	2,563	1,655	64.6
Philippines	31,686	20,094	63.4
Singapore	226	119	52.7
Sri Lanka	314	194	61.8
Syria	1,342	857	63.9
Taiwan	2,460	1,922	78.1
Thailand	3,009	1,202	39.9
Turkey	1,546	623	40.3
Vietnam	2,724	1,911	70.2
Yemen	284	159	56.0
Other Asia	542	336	62.0
Africa	**7,713**	**4,528**	**58.7%**
Cape Verde	647	263	40.6
Egypt	1,964	1,319	67.2
Ethiopia	294	187	63.6
Ghana	392	238	60.7%
Kenya	418	257	61.5
Morocco	366	182	49.7
Nigeria	570	231	40.5
South Africa	1,331	856	64.3
Tanzania	256	175	68.4
Uganda	200	119	59.5
Other Africa	1,275	701	55.0
Oceania	**2,927**	**735**	**25.1%**
Australia	1,016	90	8.9
Fiji	551	274	49.7
New Zealand	449	97	21.6
Tonga	349	98	28.1
Western Samoa	369	136	36.9
Other Oceania	193	40	20.7
North America	**142,313**	**54,068**	**38.0%**
Canada	9,000	1,626	18.1
Mexico	30,967	6,869	22.2
Caribbean, total	89,885	39,662	44.1%
Anguilla	354	136	38.4
Antigua-Barbuda	614	307	50.0
Bahamas, The	238	61	25.6
Barbados	2,134	1,037	48.6
British Virgin Islands	367	78	21.3
Cuba	57,023	26,668	46.8
Dominica	392	194	49.5
Dominican Republic	8,955	2,561	28.6
Grenada	1,023	529	51.7
Haiti	4,268	1,841	43.1
Jamaica	7,896	3,587	45.4
St. Kitts & Nevis	699	349	49.9
St. Lucia	408	202	49.5
St. Vincent & Grenadines	456	224	49.1
Trinidad & Tobago	4,516	1,722	38.1
Other Caribbean	542	166	30.6
Central America	**12,381**	**5,890**	**47.6%**
Belize	660	285	43.2
Costa Rica	1,221	471	38.6
El Salvador	3,402	1,688	49.6
Guatemala	2,825	1,291	45.7
Honduras	1,228	640	52.1
Nicaragua	1,351	679	50.3
Panama	1,694	836	49.4
Other North America	80	21	26.3
South America	**25,024**	**12,198**	**48.7%**
Argentina	2,136	995	46.6
Bolivia	576	344	59.7
Brazil	1,128	299	26.5
Chile	2,047	958	46.8
Colombia	6,138	3,126	50.9
Ecuador	4,063	1,319	32.5
Guyana	4,115	2,439	59.3
Peru	3,158	1,902	60.2
Uruguay	947	529	55.9
Venezuela	485	175	36.1
Other South America	231	112	48.5

Source: U.S. Dept. of Justice, *1996 Statistical Yearbook of the Immigration and Naturalization Service* (1997).

versity, the U.S. will need 464,000 immigrants each year over the next century just to keep total population in 2100 at the same size as in 1980.

▶ELIGIBILITY

Prior to 1875 anyone from any foreign country could enter the U.S. freely and take up permanent residence here. Over the next 60 years, however, Congress passed laws restricting immigration on the basis of morality (no prostitutes or convicts), race (the Chinese Exclusion Act of 1882 was the first), and national origin (immigrants from Southern and Central Europe as well as Asia were severely limited during the 1920's). In 1952 Congress passed the Immigration and Nationality Act, which reaffirmed national origin as the central criterion for eligibility and in 1965, the Hart-Cellar Immigration Act established a preferential system for skilled workers and relatives of U.S. citizens, but restricted the total number of immigrants to 270,000 each year. However, the number of exceptions to this limit was far greater even than the 270,000 limit. An average of more than 700,000 immigrants legally entered the U.S. each year during the 1980's (not counting illegal aliens natural-

Foreign-Born Population by State, 1990-2000

	1990			2000[1]		
	Total population	Foreign-born population	Percent foreign-born	Total population	Foreign-born population	Percent foreign-born
United States	**248,709,873**	**19,767,316**	**7.9%**	**274,087,000**	**28,379,000**	**10.4%**
Alabama	4,040,587	43,533	1.1	4,434,000	71,000	1.6
Alaska	550,043	24,814	4.5	629,000	26,000	4.2
Arizona	3,665,228	278,205	7.6	4,874,000	630,000	12.9
Arkansas	2,350,725	24,867	1.1	2,560,000	47,000	1.8
California	29,760,021	6,458,825	21.7	33,958,000	8,781,000	25.9
Colorado	3,294,394	142,434	4.3	4,225,000	413,000	9.8
Connecticut	3,287,116	279,383	8.5	3,332,000	291,000	8.7
Delaware	666,168	22,275	3.3	767,000	36,000	4.7
District of Columbia	606,900	58,887	9.7	517,000	55,000	10.6
Florida	12,937,926	1,662,601	12.9	15,052,000	2,768,000	18.4
Georgia	6,478,216	173,126	2.7	7,810,000	345,000	4.4
Hawaii	1,108,229	162,704	14.7	1,215,000	196,000	16.1
Idaho	1,006,749	28,905	2.9	1,254,000	67,000	5.3
Illinois	11,430,602	952,272	8.3	12,166,000	1,155,000	9.5
Indiana	5,544,159	94,263	1.7	5,898,000	141,000	2.4
Iowa	2,776,755	43,316	1.6	2,834,000	110,000	3.9
Kansas	2,477,574	62,840	2.5	2,618,000	148,000	5.7
Kentucky	3,685,296	34,119	0.9	3,898,000	96,000	2.5
Louisiana	4,219,973	87,407	2.1	4,297,000	112,000	2.6
Maine	1,227,928	36,296	3.0	1,271,000	27,000	2.2
Maryland	4,781,468	313,494	6.6	5,055,000	457,000	9.0
Massachusetts	6,016,425	573,733	9.5	6,194,000	769,000	12.4
Michigan	9,295,297	355,393	3.8	10,127,000	518,000	5.1
Minnesota	4,375,099	113,039	2.6	4,804,000	243,000	5.1
Mississippi	2,573,216	20,383	0.8	2,763,000	26,000	0.9
Missouri	5,117,073	83,633	1.6	5,476,000	162,000	3.0
Montana	799,065	13,779	1.7	900,000	7,000	0.8
Nebraska	1,578,385	28,198	1.8	1,659,000	62,000	3.7
Nevada	1,201,833	104,828	8.7	1,932,000	294,000	15.2
New Hampshire	1,109,252	41,193	3.7	1,255,000	48,000	3.9
New Jersey	7,730,188	966,610	12.5	8,104,000	1,208,000	14.9
New Mexico	1,515,069	80,514	5.3	1,798,000	104,000	5.8
New York	17,990,455	2,851,861	15.9	18,508,000	3,634,000	19.6
North Carolina	6,628,637	115,077	1.7	7,510,000	333,000	4.4
North Dakota	638,800	9,388	1.5	616,000	9,000	1.5
Ohio	10,847,115	259,673	2.4	11,293,000	282,000	2.5
Oklahoma	3,145,585	65,489	2.1	3,269,000	105,000	3.2
Oregon	2,842,321	139,307	4.9	3,410,000	265,000	7.8
Pennsylvania	11,881,643	369,316	3.1	11,786,000	344,000	2.9
Rhode Island	1,003,464	95,088	9.5	983,000	77,000	7.8
South Carolina	3,486,703	49,964	1.4	3,818,000	61,000	1.6
South Dakota	696,004	7,731	1.1	704,000	9,000	1.3
Tennessee	4,877,185	59,114	1.2	5,537,000	99,000	1.8
Texas	16,986,510	1,524,436	9.0	20,044,000	2,443,000	12.2
Utah	1,722,850	58,600	3.4	2,151,000	118,000	5.5
Vermont	562,758	17,544	3.1	605,000	21,000	3.5
Virginia	6,187,358	311,809	5.0	6,842,000	526,000	7.7
Washington	4,866,692	322,144	6.6	5,697,000	422,000	7.4
West Virginia	1,793,477	15,712	0.9	1,757,000	16,000	0.9
Wisconsin	4,891,769	121,547	2.5	5,401,000	195,000	3.6
Wyoming	453,588	7,647	1.7	483,000	5,000	1.0

1. 2000 data rounded at source. **Source:** U.S. Bureau of the Census, 2000.

ized under provisions of the 1986 Immigration Reform and Control Act).

In 1992, the 270,000 limit was replaced with a sliding cap that is even less restrictive than previous immigration laws. The 1990 Immigration Act limited the total number of immigrants to 700,000 from 1992 to 1995, and to 675,000 thereafter. The act increased the number of openings for immigrants with valuable employment skills from 54,000 to 140,000 each year, and reserved 55,000 openings each year for immigrants from underrepresented countries. In addition, the new law

Selected Characteristics of Foreign-Born Population, 2002

The foreign-born population of the United States consists of naturalized citizens and more recent immigrants who have not obtained citizenship. As the following table illustrates, the foreign-born population is heavily represented in the West (19.2 percent of the population in the West was not born here) and the Northeast (14.1 percent) and lowest in the Midwest (5.4 percent). Note that race data for foreign-born residents has not been updated since 1999. See the accompanying table for race data.

		Foreign-born population			
Characteristic	Total U.S. population ('000s)	Total number ('000s)	As percent of U.S. population	Naturalized citizens ('000s)	Not citizens ('000s)
Total Population	**282,082**	**32,453**	**11.5%**	**11,962**	**20,491**
Age					
0 to 4 years	19,428	320	1.6%	55	265
5 to 9 years	20,026	694	3.5	89	605
10 to 14 years	21,037	1,100	5.2	144	956
15 to 19 years	20,045	1,706	8.5	247	1,459
20 to 24 years	19,404	2,841	14.6	431	2,410
25 to 29 years	18,310	3,492	19.1	648	2,844
30 to 34 years	20,360	3,999	19.6	999	2,999
35 to 44 years	44,284	7,005	15.8	2,628	4,377
45 to 54 years	39,545	4,931	12.5	2,524	2,408
55 to 64 years	25,874	3,054	11.8	1,863	1,191
65 to 74 years	18,123	1,922	10.6	1,251	671
75 to 84 years	12,191	1,076	8.8	828	249
85 years and over	3,456	310	9.0	254	56
Sex					
Male	137,871	16,352	11.9%	5,564	10,787
Female	144,211	16,101	11.2	6,398	9,703
Educational Attainment					
Not a high school graduate	28,948	8,460	29.2%	2,490	5,970
High school graduate or some college	104,498	10,500	10.0	5,095	5,505
Bachelors degree	32,282	4,381	13.6	2,215	2,166
Graduate/Professional degree	16,414	2,448	14.9	1,195	1,253
Economic Status					
Employed	135,154	18,933	14.0%	7,202	11,731
Unemployed	8,946	1,403	15.7	399	1,004
Not in labor force	72,787	9,654	13.3	3,997	5,657
Below poverty	32,907	5,209	15.8	1,186	4,023
Region of Residence					
Northeast	53,300	7,500	14.1%	3,119	4,381
Midwest	63,779	3,427	5.4	1,364	2,062
South	100,652	9,152	9.1	3,129	6,023
West	64,351	12,374	19.2	4,349	8,025

Source: U.S. Bureau of the Census, *Current Population Survey*, 2002.

Foreign-Born Population by Sex and Race, 1990–2000

Characteristic	1990[1]	1995	1999	2000
Total	**19,846,000**	**22,978,000**	**25,831,000**	**28,379,000**
Percent of U.S. population	**8.0%**	**8.7%**	**9.5%**	**10.4%**
By sex				
Male	9,737,000	11,173,000	12,472,000	14,200,000
Female	10,109,000	11805,000	13,360,000	14,179,000
By race				
White	13,428,000	14,930,000	16,575,000	14,100,000
Black	1,705,000	2117,000	2,517,000	2,200,000
American Indian, Eskimo, Aleut	86,000	120,000	150,000	N.A.
Asian and Pacific Islander	4,627,000	5,811,000	6,589,000	6,700,000
Hispanic Origin[2]	7,997,000	9,532,000	11,103,000	12,800,000

1. Figures are from the April 1990 Census. All other figures are as of July 1 of the year shown. 2. People of Hispanic origin may be of any race. **Source:** U.S. Bureau of the Census, *Foreign-Born Resident Population Estimates of the U.S., 1990-99*, (2000). www.census.gov.

introduced a sliding scale for admitting family-sponsored immigrants. As in previous years, there is no limit to the number of immediate family members admitted each year. However, beginning in 1995, the number of immediate family members admitted in the previous year is subtracted from 480,000 to determine the number of family-sponsored immigrants eligible for admission. The family-sponsored limit may not go below 226,000 in any year, however.

▶THE FOREIGN-BORN POPULATION

The strong increase in the number of immigrants since the 1970s has helped to reshape the makeup of American society. The percentage of the population that was born outside this country continues to increase. In 2000, according to the Census Bureau, 28.4 million U.S. residents (10.4 percent of the total population) were foreign-born. The last time the figure was higher was in 1930, when 11.6 percent of the population was born in an-

Foreign-Born Population by Place of Birth, 2000

Place of Birth	Number	Percent
All Foreign-born persons	**28,379,000**	**100.00%**
Europe	**4,355,000**	**15.35%**
Austria	65,000	0.23
Belgium	17,000	0.06
Czechoslovakia	71,000	0.25
Denmark	8,000	0.03
Finland	19,000	0.07
France	127,000	0.45
Germany	653,000	2.30
Greece	136,000	0.48
Hungary	87,000	0.31
Ireland	202,000	0.71
Italy	451,000	1.59
Latvia	11,000	0.04
Lithuania	39,000	0.14
Netherlands	93,000	0.33
Norway	18,000	0.06
Poland	445,000	1.57
Portugal	206,000	0.73
Romania	99,000	0.35
Spain	80,000	0.28
Sweden	49,000	0.17
Switzerland	29,000	0.10
United Kingdom	613,000	2.16
Yugoslavia	123,000	0.43
Other Europe	714,000	2.52
Soviet Union	**624,000**	**2.20%**
Asia	**7,246,000**	**25.53%**
Afghanistan	27,000	0.10
Cambodia	122,000	0.43
China	871,000	3.07
Hong Kong	195,000	0.69
India	1,007,000	3.55
Indonesia	53,000	0.19
Iran	306,000	1.08
Iraq	81,000	0.29
Israel	82,000	0.29
Japan	274,000	0.97
Jordan	39,000	0.14
Korea (South)	701,000	2.47
Laos	74,000	0.26
Lebanon	127,000	0.45
Malaysia	43,000	0.15
Burma	35,000	0.12
Pakistan	197,000	0.69
Philippines	1,222,000	4.31
Saudi Arabia	20,000	0.07
Syria	45,000	0.16
Taiwan	325,000	1.15
Thailand	147,000	0.52
Turkey	97,000	0.34
Vietnam	863,000	3.04
Other Asia	293,000	1.03
North America	**13,300,000**	**46.87%**
Canada	678,000	2.39
Caribbean, total	2,813,000	9.91
Bahamas	13,000	0.05
Barbados	54,000	0.19
Cuba	952,000	3.35
Dominican Republic	692,000	2.44
Grenada	42,000	0.15
Haiti	385,000	1.36
Jamaica	411,000	1.45
Trinidad/Tobago	173,000	0.61
Other Caribbean	91,000	0.32
Central America	9,789,000	34.49
Belize	59,000	0.21
Costa Rica	77,000	0.27
El Salvador	765,000	2.70
Guatemala	327,000	1.15
Honduras	250,000	0.88
Mexico	7,841,000	27.63
Nicaragua	245,000	0.86
Panama	69,000	0.24
Other Central America	157,000	0.55
Other North America	20,000	0.07
South America	**1,876,000**	**6.62%**
Argentina	89,000	0.31
Bolivia	44,000	0.16
Brazil	160,000	0.56
Chile	83,000	0.29
Colombia	435,000	1.53
Ecuador	281,000	0.99
Guyana	202,000	0.71
Peru	328,000	1.16
Uruguay	73,000	0.26
Venezuela	126,000	0.44
Other South America	55,000	0.19
Africa	**701,000**	**2.47%**
Egypt	126,000	0.44
Ethiopia	68,000	0.24
Ghana	80,000	0.28
Kenya	28,000	0.10
Morocco	38,000	0.13
Nigeria	87,000	0.31
South Africa	69,000	0.24
Other Africa	205,000	0.72
Oceania	**147,000**	**0.52%**
Australia	36,000	0.13
Fiji	33,000	0.12
New Zealand	20,000	0.07
Other Oceania	11,682	0.04
Not reported	**916,046**	**3.23%**

Note: The foreign-born population includes 1,864,285 persons who were born abroad of American parents.
Source: U.S. Bureau of the Census, 2000.

Foreign-Born Population by Region of Birth, 1850–2000

Year	Total population	Foreign-born population	Percent foreign-born	Region of birth: Europe	Asia	Africa	Oceania	Latin America	North America
1850[1]	23,191,876	2,244,602	9.7%	2,031,867	1,135	551	588	20,773	147,711
1860[1]	31,443,321	4,138,697	13.2	3,807,062	36,796	526	2,140	38,315	249,970
1870	38,558,371	5,567,229	14.4	4,941,049	64,565	2,657	4,028	57,871	493,467
1880	50,155,783	6,679,943	13.3	5,751,823	107,630	2,204	6,859	90,073	717,286
1890	62,622,250	9,249,547	14.8	8,030,347	113,383	2,207	9,353	107,307	980,938
1900	75,994,575	10,341,276	13.6	8,881,548	120,248	2,538	8,820	137,458	1,179,922
1910	91,972,266	13,515,886	14.7	11,810,115	191,484	3,992	11,450	279,514	1,209,717
1920	105,710,620	13,920,692	13.2	11,916,048	237,950	16,126	14,626	588,843	1,138,174
1930	122,775,046	14,204,149	11.6	11,784,010	275,665	18,326	17,343	791,840	1,310,369
1940	131,669,275	11,594,896	8.8	N.A.	N.A.	N.A.	N.A.	N.A.	N.A.
1950	150,216,110	10,347,395	6.9	N.A.	N.A.	N.A.	N.A.	N.A.	N.A.
1960	179,325,671	9,738,091	5.4	7,256,311	490,996	35,355	34,730	908,309	952,500
1970	203,210,158	9,619,302	4.7	5,740,891	824,887	80,143	41,258	1,803,970	812,421
1980	226,545,805	14,079,906	6.2	5,149,572	2,539,777	199,723	77,577	4,372,487	853,427
1990	248,709,873	19,767,316	7.9	4,350,403	4,979,037	363,819	104,145	8,407,837	753,917
2000	274,087,000	28,379,000	10.4	4,355,000	7,246,000	N.A.	N.A.	14,407,000	N.A.

1. In 1850 and 1860, information on nativity was not collected for slaves. The data in the table assume, as was done in 1870 census reports, that all slaves in 1850 and 1860 were native, even though 0.2 percent were foreign-born. 2. Numbers for 2000 rounded at source. **Source:** U.S. Bureau of the Census.

other country. More than half of the foreign-born population in America came from Latin America (14.4 million); of these, fully half (7 million) listed Mexico as their birthplace. Another 25.5 percent of the foreign-born population was from Asia. The remainder were divided between Europe (15.3 percent) and other regions (8.1 percent).

Most foreign-born residents come to the U.S. and stay. In 2000, naturalized citizens constituted more than one-third of the foreign-born population. More than 80 percent of foreign-born people who arrived before 1970 are now U.S. citizens. The percentage is 61.9 percent for foreign-born persons arrriving during the 1970's, 38.9 percent for immigrants arriving during the 1980's, and 8.9 percent for those immigrating in the 1990's.

SEX IN AMERICA

Pollsters scrutinize every angle of American life, including what goes on beyond closed bedroom doors. The research ranges from the statistical—the survey done by the National Center for Health Statistics—to the anecdotal, such as reader polls taken by popular magazines. Here's a summary of the two most serious studies, one conducted by the federal government, the other by a leading university.

▶WOMEN AND SEX

The National Survey of Family Growth is conducted periodically by the National Center for Health Statistics, with a national sample of women aged 15 to 44 years old. The most recent report, issued in May 1997, used data compiled in 1995. Questions concerned marriage and sexual activity. Some findings from the report:

- 75 percent of all married women had pre-marital intercourse; only 12 percent of women waited until marriage to have sex for the first time.
- 52 percent of women aged 20-44 had their first intercourse by age 18, and 75 percent were sexually experienced by age 20, up from 40 percent and 60 percent respectively in 1988.
- Nearly 14 percent of women aged 20-24 had sex before age 15; the median age at first intercourse for these women was 16.6 years old.
- 28 percent of women had an unintended birth; poor women and non-Hispanic black women were most likely to have had an unplanned birth.
- 20.4 percent of women reported having involuntary intercourse at some time in their lives; more than one-fourth of these women were under 15 when they were forced to have sex.
- 47 percent of unmarried women reported having just one sexual partner in the past year; 11.2 percent had two partners, and 34.5 percent said they had no partners. But over their lifetimes, women of all marital statuses reported many more sexual partners. More than half of all women had three or more sexual partners in their lifetimes.
- 64.2 percent of women currently use contraceptives; the remaining 35.8 percent are divided among women who are pregnant, seeking to have children, or abstinent. Only 5.2 percent of women admitted having unprotected sex. Among women using contraceptives, sterilization (27.7 percent) was the most popular method, followed by the pill (26.9 percent) and the condom (20.4). Women under the age of 30 were most likely to use the pill.

▶SEX PARTNERS AND FREQUENCY OF INTERCOURSE

The National Opinion Research Center at the University of Chicago (NORC) periodically conducts a study of the sexual behavior of adults. The Center interviews a nationwide representative sample of about 1,500 adults to collect accurate data on a wide range of topics dealing with sex. Here are some of the survey's primary findings.

Cohabitation As premarital sex becomes more commonplace and the average age at first marriage grows older, the number of couples living together out of wedlock continues to spiral. Just over 1.1 percent of all couples were living together in 1960; in 1997 (the latest year for which data are available), the rate was 7.0 percent. In 1988, 23.4 percent of married couples had lived together before marrying; by 1994, 28.0 percent had. Cohabiting was most popular among younger couples: 9.4 percent of people 18-29 were cohabiting in 1998, and 43.7 percent had cohabited with their current spouse before marriage. The exact same percentage of 30-39-year-olds cohabited before marriage, but only 7.6 percent of the people in this age group were currently cohabiting in 1998.

Extramarital sex Numbers regarding sex out of wedlock are usually unreliable, since most people are reluctant to admit their affairs to interviewers. The percentage of currently married people admitting to extramarital sex within the last year (3.6 percent in 1998) has fluctuated very little since 1988. More people were willing to admit having an affair at one point in their lives. In 1991, 14.6 percent of people who had ever been married admitted having at least one affair while married; in 1998, 16.5 percent said they had had extramarital sex. These figures are much higher than the one-year numbers because they include married people as well as those who are separated and divorced, perhaps as a result of one of these affairs. Men (4.9 percent in the last year, and 20.8 percent ever) were more likely than women (2.5 percent 13.4 respectively) to admit extramarital activity.

Gender of sex partners For the same reasons, many people are also reluctant to admit homosexual behavior. The percentage of sexually active adults admitting to homosexual behavior within the last year has remained steady at between 2 and 3.5 percent since 1988, but the actual number is probably somewhat higher. A smaller percentage (never more than 1 percent) of people claim to have had sex with partners of both genders. Men who attend church regularly (3.7 percent) were more likely to have had a same sex partner than those who attended church occasionally (3.0 percent) or rarely (3.5 percent).

Number of sex partners The average number of sex partners per person has remained fairly constant over the past few years. A majority of adults have had only one sexual partner in the past five years, and more than two-thirds had only one partner in the past year. Adults in 2000 had an average of 1.14 partners in the last 12 months, and 2.74 partners in the past five years.

Frequency of sexual intercourse Americans had intercourse an average of 62.5 times a year in 2000. That's up from 59.1 times a year in 1998, but not significantly different from data from surveys dating back to 1989. Not surprisingly, married people aged 18-29 had the most sex—99.3 times a year (or twice a week); unmarried people over 70 had the least sex: an average of 3.6 times annually. Just under 19 percent of adults had no sex at all in 2000, and 11 percent have not had sex for the past five years.

Frequency of Sexual Intercourse by Age, Race and Marital Status 1996-2000

Marital Status	Mean number of times per year: All Adults	By Race: White	By Race: Black	By Age: 18-29	30-39	40-49	50-59	60-69	70+
1996, Total	**65.3**	**61.2**	**64.7**	**83.7**	**79.7**	**63.4**	**47.4**	**28.1**	**9.8**
Married	N.A.	N.A.	N.A.	111.4	82.4	63.4	51.5	32.0	14.9
Unmarried	N.A.	N.A.	N.A.	71.8	76.9	63.4	43.5	23.7	6.4
1998, Total	**59.1**	**60.2**	**62.7**	**82.6**	**78.6**	**63.6**	**47.4**	**27.4**	**9.8**
Married	66.1	N.A.	N.A.	111.6	85.7	69.2	53.8	32.5	16.2
Unmarried	N.A.	N.A.	N.A.	69.1	65.6	49.8	31.2	15.7	2.6
2000, Total	**62.5**	**61.2**	**70.8**	**N.A.**	**N.A.**	**N.A.**	**N.A.**	**N.A.**	**N.A.**
Married	N.A.	N.A.	N.A.	99.3	84.2	71.7	54.8	30.7	16.9
Unmarried	N.A.	N.A.	N.A.	75.2	67.6	48.9	34.1	13.1	3.6

Source: National Opinion Research Center (NORC) *General Social Survey,* 1996, 1998, 2000.

Number of Sexual Partners by Adults, 1991-2000

Year	Number of sexual partners: None	1	2	3	4	5–9	10+	Mean
				Last 12 months				
1991	18.4%	71.2%	5.9%	1.9%	0.8%	1.4%	0.4%	1.12
1996	15.1	72.2	6.1	3.2	1.6	1.3	0.5	1.36
1998	17.4	70.7	6.0	2.2	1.5	1.4	0.4	1.24
2000	18.9	69.2	5.9	2.9	1.8	1.6	0.3	1.14
				Last five years				
1991	11.3%	60.3%	8.3%	6.7%	3.3%	6.0%	4.2%	2.70
1996	10.0	57.8	10.2	7.2	4.7	6.4	3.4	2.83
1998	11.2	59.0	9.2	6.0	4.7	5.7	2.9	2.50
2000	11.3	58.1	9.9	6.4	4.3	6.0	3.3	2.74

Source: National Opinion Research Center (NORC) *General Social Surveys,* 1991-2000.

Agriculture

In recent years, U.S. agriculture has become an integral part of the global economy. American farmers currently produce nearly 39 percent of the world's corn, 38 percent of its soybeans, and 8 percent of its wheat. Much of this they export to all parts of the world, but especially to Asia and Latin America. In 1990, U.S. agricultural exports totaled $39.4 billion, but by 2002, exports topped $53 billion. About 27 percent of that total was in grains and feeds; 22 percent was in animals and animal products.

This is a far cry from the small nation of "embattled farmers" who launched the American Revolution. In the early years of the Republic, agriculture, while vital (involving 95 percent of the population), remained relatively small-scale and in economic terms primitive, with the exception of large plantations in the South devoted to cotton, tobacco, and rice. The Civil War brought higher food prices and increased mechanization throughout the farming industry. It also led to federal legislation aimed at encouraging farming; the Homestead Act of 1862 and the Morrill Land Grant College Act were especially important. The decision to build a transcontinental rail system—undertaken by private enterprise abetted by government grants—opened up large areas of the Great Plains to farming, and the railroad companies recruited immigrants to buy and farm the land the government had given the companies.

In the early 20th century, machinery gradually replaced animal power. World War I stimulated agriculture, but the stimulus led to overproduction, which, with the coming of peace, depressed prices and land values. This decline both contributed to and was intensified by the Great Depression, one of the most paralyzing aspects of which was a near total cessation of world agricultural trade. The plight of farmers during the 1930's prompted considerable government remedies, including various forms of credit, price supports, rural electrification, and serious efforts at soil conservation. World War II again gave impetus to agriculture.

After the war, new machinery, new chemicals, and hybrid crops, more resistant to weather and biological enemies significantly increased crop yields. By the end of the 1940's, the United States had become the world's largest single producer of wheat, corn, and soybeans. One byproduct of this success was the creation of huge surpluses. U.S. agriculture proved a potent force in the world economy and in foreign policy, and in 1954, Public Law 480 provided for the export of surplus grains to poorer nations both to prevent starvation and stimulate economic development, and to alleviate the pressures on the domestic agriculture sector caused by the surpluses.

Since 1960, the number of American farms has declined as small units lose out to huge agribusinesses owned by corporations. Between 1980 and

Percent of U.S. Agricultural Exports by Region and Selected Nation, 1980–2002

Category	1980	1990	2000	2002
Total agricultural exports (billions)	**$41.2**	**$39.5**	**$51.2**	**$53.0**
Percent by region and nation				
Asia	36.5%	44.8%	43.3%	41.3%
Japan	14.9	20.6	18.1	15.8
Korea, South	4.4	6.7	5.0	5.0
Taiwan	2.7	4.2	3.9	3.7
China	5.6	2.1	3.3	3.7
Hong Kong	1.1	1.8	2.5	2.1
Western Europe	31.4	18.7	13.0	12.7
European Union	29.6	17.4	12.2	11.6
Latin America	15.0	13.0	20.8	22.3
Mexico	6.0	6.5	12.5	13.7
Canada	4.7	10.7	14.9	16.3
Africa	5.5	4.9	4.5	4.3

Source: U.S. Dept. of Agriculture, *Agricultural Statistics*, annual

U.S. Farms, Acreage and Population, 1850–2002

Year	Farms ('000s)	Acreage: Total ('000s)	Acreage: Per farm	Acreage: Percent of US	Farm Population: Total ('000s)	Farm Population: Percent of US
1850	1,449	293,561	203	15.6%	—	—
1860	2,044	407,213	199	21.4	—	—
1870	2,660	407,735	153	21.4	—	—
1880	4,009	536,082	134	28.2	21,973	43.8%
1890	4,565	623,219	137	32.7	24,771	42.3
1900	5,740	841,202	147	37.0	29,835	41.9
1910	6,366	881,431	139	38.8	32,077	34.9
1920	6,454	958,677	149	42.2	31,974	30.1
1930	6,295	990,112	157	43.6	30,529	24.9
1940	6,102	1,065,114	175	46.8	30,547	23.2
1950	5,388	1,161,420	216	51.1	23,048	15.3
1960	3,962	1,176,946	297	49.5[1]	15,635	8.7
1970	2,954	1,102,769	373	47.0[2]	9,712	4.8
1980	2,440	1,039,000	426	44.8	6,051	2.7
1990	2,146	987,000	460	42.7	4,801	1.9
1995	2,196	963,000	438	N.A.	N.A.	N.A.
2000	2,172	943,000	434	N.A.	N.A.	N.A.
2002	2,158	941,000	436	N.A.	N.A.	N.A.

Note: Acreage figures after 1980 rounded in source. 1. Figure for 1959. 2. Figure for 1969.
Source: U.S. Bureau of the Census, *Statistical History of the United States* (1970); *Statistical Abstract of the United States.*

2001, the number of farms fell from 2.44 million to 2.16 million, (a decline of 11 percent) while average acreage per farm rose from 426 to 436. Overall, the total land area devoted to farming dropped from 1.04 billion acres to 941 million, a decline of 10 percent. Meanwhile, improved technology has made farming less labor intensive, so the total farm population has also declined precipitously, and is now less than 2 percent of the total population, down from 42 percent at the turn of the century, and 15 percent in 1950.

The surpluses created by expanded and more efficient production required governments to prop up prices, often at the consumer's expense. In 1996, a Republican-led Congress pushed through the "Freedom to Farm" law, which was intended to remove price subsidies on most major crops. But in 2002, just as the program was to become fully effective, President George W. Bush signed legislation that instead raised farm susbisdies to $190 billion, an increase of $83 billion. The majority of the subsidy will go not to individual family farms, but to giant agribusinesses, continuing the trend of consolidation in the farming industry.

The worldwide nature of agricultural progress—the "green revolution"—has increased competition for markets, in some cases hurting

Farms–Number and Acreage, by State, 1980–2002

	Number of Farms ('000s)				Acreage (millions)				Acreage per farm			
State	1980	1990	2000	2002	1980	1990	2000	2002	1980	1990	2000	2002
U.S. total	**2,440**	**2,146**	**2,172**	**2,158**	**1,039**	**987**	**943**	**942**	**426**	**460**	**434**	**436**
Alabama	59	47	47	47	12	10	9	9	207	215	191	189
Alaska	(z)	1	1	1	2	1	1	1	3,378	1,707	1,586	1,559
Arizona	8	8	8	7	38	36	27	27	5,080	4,641	3,560	3,630
Arkansas	59	47	48	49	17	16	15	15	280	330	304	301
California	81	85	88	84	34	31	28	28	417	382	318	330
Colorado	27	27	30	30	36	33	32	31	1,358	1,249	1,071	1,043
Connecticut	4	4	4	4	(z)	(z)	(z)	(z)	117	108	92	92
Delaware	4	3	3	2	1	1	1	1	186	207	223	233
Florida	39	41	44	44	11	11	10	10	344	266	234	232
Georgia	59	48	50	50	15	13	11	11	254	260	222	220
Hawaii	4	5	6	5	2	2	1	1	458	357	262	272
Idaho	24	22	25	24	15	14	12	12	623	628	486	496
Illinois	107	83	78	76	29	28	28	28	269	342	355	364
Indiana	87	68	64	63	17	16	16	15	193	240	242	244
Iowa	119	104	95	93	34	34	33	33	284	322	345	352
Kansas	75	69	64	63	48	48	48	47	644	694	742	752
Kentucky	102	93	90	89	15	14	14	14	143	152	151	153
Louisiana	37	32	30	29	10	9	8	8	273	278	275	278
Maine	8	7	7	7	2	1	1	1	195	201	187	188
Maryland	18	15	12	12	3	2	2	2	157	148	169	172
Massachusetts	6	6	6	6	1	1	1	1	116	100	93	93
Michigan	65	54	52	52	11	11	10	10	175	200	200	200
Minnesota	104	89	79	79	30	30	29	28	291	337	362	359
Mississippi	55	40	43	43	15	13	11	11	265	325	258	256
Missouri	120	108	109	107	31	30	30	30	261	281	275	279
Montana	24	25	28	28	62	61	57	57	2,601	2,449	2,054	2,025
Nebraska	65	37	54	52	48	47	46	46	734	826	859	892
Nevada	3	3	3	3	9	9	7	7	3,100	3,560	2,267	2,267
New Hampshire	3	3	3	3	1	(z)	(z)	(z)	160	163	135	132
New Jersey	9	8	10	10	1	1	1	1	109	107	86	85
New Mexico	14	14	15	15	47	45	44	44	3,467	3,296	2,895	2,933
New York	47	39	38	37	9	8	8	8	200	218	203	205
North Carolina	93	62	57	56	12	10	9	9	126	156	161	163
North Dakota	40	34	30	30	42	41	39	39	1,043	1,209	1,300	1,313
Ohio	95	83	80	78	16	16	15	15	171	188	186	188
Oklahoma	72	70	85	87	35	33	34	34	481	471	400	391
Oregon	35	37	40	41	18	18	17	17	517	488	430	420
Pennsylvania	62	53	59	59	9	8	8	8	145	153	131	131
Rhode Island	1	1	1	1	(z)	(z)	(z)	(z)	87	95	86	86
South Carolina	34	25	24	25	6	5	5	5	188	208	200	196
South Dakota	39	35	33	33	45	44	44	44	1,169	1,266	1,354	1,354
Tennessee	96	87	90	90	14	12	12	12	142	139	130	130
Texas	196	196	226	230	138	132	130	131	705	673	575	570
Utah	14	13	16	15	12	11	12	12	919	856	748	773
Vermont	8	7	7	7	2	1	1	1	226	222	200	203
Virginia	58	46	49	49	10	9	9	9	169	193	178	178
Washington	38	37	40	39	16	16	16	16	429	432	393	403
West Virginia	22	21	21	21	4	4	4	4	191	180	176	176
Wisconsin	93	80	77	77	19	16	16	16	200	220	210	206
Wyoming	9	9	9	9	35	35	35	35	3,846	3,899	3,761	3,761

Note: z= Fewer than 500,000 acres. Source: U.S. Dept. of Agriculture, *Farm Numbers and Land in Farms,* 2003.

farmers who depend upon exporting a large share of their crop. Nevertheless, the U.S. continues to export agricultural products worth over $50 billion a year, almost half of the total to Asia. The 1997-98 financial crisis there drove down the price of all major commodities, and led to a decline in farm exports. Today's farmers face a difficult future. Record crops from 1996 to 1998 also pushed prices down, in some cases as low as during the Depression. Severe drought in the Southwest and part of the Southeast during 2000 also caused hardship. As a result, government subsidies have risen from $7.3 billion in 1996 to $22.7 billion in 2000. Further consolidation in the industry threatened to force even more family farmers from the business, and to continue the trend of agribusinesses swallowing up land once individually owned and farmed.

U.S. Agricultural Exports: Principal Commodities by Value and Percentage of Agriculture Exports, 1980–2002

Category	1980 Value (billions)	1980 Percent	1990 Value (billions)	1990 Percent	2000 Value (billions)	2000 Percent	2002 Value (billions)	2002 Percent
Total agricultural exports	**$41.2**	**100.0%**	**$39.5**	**100.0%**	**$50.7**	**100.0%**	**$53.3**	**100%**
Commodities								
Grains and feeds	$19.1	46.4%	$14.4	36.5%	$13.8	27.2%	14.1	26.5%
Oilseeds and products	9.4	22.8	5.7	14.4	8.4	16.6	9.7	18.2
Animals and animal products	3.8	9.2	6.7	16.9	11.5	22.7	11.6	21.8
Cotton	2.9	7.0	2.8	7.0	1.8	3.6	2.1	3.9
Tobacco, unmanufactured	1.3	3.3	1.4	3.6	1.2	2.4	1.2	2.3
Fruits and preparations	1.3	3.3	2.4	6.0	3.4	6.7	3.4	6.4
Vegetables and preparations	1.2	2.9	2.2	5.6	4.4	8.7	4.6	8.3
Nuts and preparations	0.8	1.9	1.0	2.5	1.2	2.4	1.5	2.8
Other	1.5	3.6	2.9	7.3	5.0	9.9	5.1	9.6

Source: U.S. Dept. of Agriculture, *Agricultural Statistics,* annual.

U.S. Production of Leading Farm Products as Percent of World Total, 1995–2002

Product	U.S. production (millions of metric tons) 1995	1999	2000	2002	As percent of world total 1995	1999	2000	2002
Total production								
Corn	188.0	240.0	252.0	229.0	36.5%	39.6%	43.1%	38.6%
Soybeans	59.0	72.0	75.0	74.0	47.4	45.3	44.1	38.3
Wheat	59.0	63.0	61.0	44.0	11.0	10.7	10.4	7.8
Cotton[1]	19.7	13.9	17.0	20.3	23.0	16.4	19.4	20.6
Rice, milled	5.6	6.6	5.9	6.5	1.5	1.6	1.5	1.7
Amount exported								
Corn	52.7	49.4	48.1	40.6	72.4%	67.5%	68.4%	54.4
Wheat	33.7	29.5	27.8	23.4	33.9	26.2	26.9	22.8
Soybeans	23.1	26.5	27.2	27.5	72.4	57.2	49.0	43.3
Cotton[1]	9.4	4.3	6.8	11.0	33.0	18.3	24.7	37.9
Rice, milled	3.1	2.6	2.8	3.6	14.8	10.4	12.3	12.9

1. Millions of bales. **Source:** U.S. Dept. of Agriculture, Foreign Agricultural Service, *Foreign Agricultural Commodity Circular Series.*

Top Agricultural States by Farm Marketings, 2002

Rank, State	Total Farm Marketings (millions)	Crops	Livestock and products	Principal commodities
1. California	$26,107	$19,865	$6,242	Dairy products, grapes, greenhouse, lettuce
2. Texas	12,665	4,577	8,088	Cattle, greenhouse, cotton, broilers
3. Iowa	10,834	5,759	5,075	Hogs, corn, soybeans, cattle
4. Nebraska	9,589	3,764	5,824	Cattle, corn, soybeans, hogs
5. Kansas	7,862	2,536	5,325	Cattle, wheat, corn, sorghum grain
6. Illinois	7,486	5,924	1,562	Corn, soybeans, hogs, cattle
7. Minnesota	7,478	3,833	3,645	Soybeans, hogs, corn, dairy products
8. Florida	6,848	5,609	1,239	Greenhouse, oranges, tomatoes, sugarcane
9. North Carolina	6,603	2,659	3,944	Hogs, broilers, greenhouse, tobacco
10. Wisconsin	5,319	1,551	3,768	Dairy products, cattle, corn, soybeans

Source: U.S. Dept. of Agriculture, Economic Research Service, *Agricultural Outlook,* August 2003.

Crime and Punishment

▶SERIOUS CRIME

Serious crime is the Justice Department's measure of the total number of violent crimes (murder, rape, robbery, and assault) plus property crimes (burglary, larceny/theft, motor vehicle theft, and arson). The number of serious crimes in the U.S. fell from an all-time high of close to 15 million in 1991 to just over 11.6 million in 2000, but rose again slightly to 11.8 million in 2001.

The number of violent crimes peaked at 1.93 million in 1992 and fell to 1.42 million in 2000, but rose again to 1.44 million in 2001. That's still significantly higher, however, than the 1.04 million violent crimes recorded in 1975. There were 15,980 murders reported to police in the U.S. in 2001, up 2.5 percent from 2000 but far below the 23,000 reported in 1990. Guns were the weapon of choice, used in about two-thirds of all homicides and in 46 percent of robberies; handguns alone accounted for more than half of all murders.

Property crime reached its all-time high in 1991, at 12.96 million total offenses reported to police. It too decreased through 2000 (to under 10.2 million), but increased again to 10.9 million in 2001. The number of burglaries is down 29.2 percent from 1990, to 2.1 million in 2001.

A strong economy throughout the 90's and a thriving job market were major reasons for the steadily declining number of serious crimes, especially the crimes of robbery, burglary, and motor vehicle theft, which have experienced some of the biggest drops. But it does not necessarily explain the equally impressive drop in the number of murders, which experts say is due to the aging of the population, as well as more police and better policing techniques. In addition, tougher sentencing laws have increased the number of people in prison. On the other hand, there has been an 80 percent increase in the number of aggravated assaults since 1978, though this number continues to decline from the all-time high of 1.14 million reached in 1994.

The number of forcible rapes is up 61 percent since 1975, but a portion of this significant jump is most likely the result of more women reporting this crime to police, rather than an increase in the number of incidents. The 90,491 rapes reported in 2001 were down from the 1992 high of 109,060, but up slightly from 90,178 in 2000.

The crime rate Raw numbers of crime do not necessarily tell the whole story. To account for population growth, criminologists use the crime rate per 100,000 population to compare crime statistics from different years. Because the population continues to grow, the rate of crime has in recent years dropped even more precipitously than the raw number of crimes. The total number of serious crimes fell nearly 18 percent since 1992, but the rate dropped 26.5 percent. In other words, the likelihood that you would become a victim of crime dropped even more quickly than the number of crimes committed. The crime rate rose 1 percent in 2001, however, the first increase since 1991.

The murder rate in 2001 was 5.6 per 100,000 population, a slight increase from 2000 but still down 39.8 percent from 1992. Property crime also seems to have reached a plateau. There were 504.4 violent crimes for every 100,000 people in 2001, down less than 1 percent from the year before. During the same period, property crimes per 100,000 inhabitants increased 1 percent.

Serious Crime in the U.S., 1975-2001

Crime	1975	1980	1990	1995	2000	2001	Percent change, 1992-2001
	Number of Offenses Reported to Police						
Violent crime	**1,039,710**	**1,344,520**	**1,820,127**	**1,798,792**	**1,425,486**	**1,436,611**	**-25.7%**
Murder	20,510	23,040	23,438	21,606	15,586	15,980	-32.7
Forcible rape	56,090	82,990	102,555	97,470	90,178	90,491	-17.0
Robbery	470,500	565,840	639,271	580,509	408,016	422,921	-37.1
Aggravated assault	492,620	672,650	1,054,863	1,099,207	911,706	907,219	-19.5
Property crime	**10,252,700**	**12,063,700**	**12,655,486**	**12,063,935**	**10,182,584**	**10,412,395**	**-16.7%**
Burglary	3,265,300	3,795,200	3,073,909	2,593,784	2,050,992	2,109,767	-29.2
Larceny/theft	5,977,700	7,136,900	7,945,670	7,997,710	6,971,590	7,076,171	-10.6
Motor vehicle theft	1,009,600	1,131,700	1,635,907	1,472,441	1,160,002	1,226,457	-23.9
Total serious crimes	**11,292,400**	**13,408,300**	**14,475,613**	**13,862,727**	**11,608,070**	**11,849,006**	**-17.9%**
	Rate per 100,000 inhabitants						
Violent crime	**487.8**	**596.6**	**729.6**	**684.5**	**506.5**	**504.4**	**-33.4%**
Murder	9.6	10.2	9.4	8.2	5.5	5.6	-39.8
Forcible rape	26.3	36.8	41.1	37.1	32.0	31.8	-25.7
Robbery	220.8	251.1	256.3	220.9	145.0	148.5	-43.7
Aggravated assault	231.1	298.5	422.9	418.3	324.0	318.5	-27.9
Property crime	**4,810.7**	**5,353.3**	**5,073.1**	**4,590.5**	**3,618.3**	**3,656.1**	**-25.4%**
Burglary	1,532.1	1,684.1	1,232.2	987.0	728.8	740.8	-36.6
Larceny/theft	2,804.8	3,167.0	3,185.1	3,043.2	2,477.3	2,484.6	-19.9
Motor vehicle theft	473.7	502.2	655.8	560.3	412.2	430.6	-31.8
Total serious crimes	**5,298.5**	**5,950.0**	**5,802.7**	**5,274.9**	**4,124.8**	**4,160.5**	**-26.5%**

Note: Totals may not add up due to independent rounding.
Source: Federal Bureau of Investigation, *Uniform Crime Reports: Crime in the United States 2001*, **www.fbi.gov/ucr/01cius.htm**

Serious Crime per 100,000 Population, by State, 2001[1]

State	All serious crime	Violent crime[2]				Property crime[2]		
		Murder	Forcible rape	Robbery	Aggravated assault	Burglary	Larceny/theft	Motor vehicle theft
U.S.								
Alabama	4,319.4	8.5	30.7	125.1	274.4	910.4	2,687.8	282.7
Alaska	4,236.2	6.1	78.9	81.0	422.3	605.9	2,629.6	412.4
Arizona	6,077.4	7.5	28.6	167.1	337.1	1,032.9	3,520.6	983.6
Arkansas	4,134.2	5.5	33.1	81.0	333.2	824.5	2,585.0	271.9
California	3,902.9	6.4	28.9	187.1	394.6	672.4	2,022.2	591.4
Colorado	4,218.9	3.6	43.7	80.5	222.9	645.9	2,747.1	475.2
Connecticut	3,117.9	3.1	18.7	122.1	191.7	501.0	1,920.0	361.4
Delaware	4,052.8	2.9	52.8	145.2	410.6	646.1	2,446.2	349.0
Dist. of Columbia[3]	7,709.6	40.6	32.9	689.6	973.7	876.3	3,755.2	1,341.3
Florida	5,569.7	5.3	40.5	200.5	550.9	1,073.7	3,150.4	548.4
Georgia	4,646.3	7.1	26.0	171.8	292.1	856.4	2,844.5	448.3
Hawaii	5,386.1	2.6	33.4	93.3	125.3	911.6	3,669.2	550.7
Idaho	3,133.4	2.3	32.2	18.5	190.1	568.3	2,141.2	180.8
Illinois[4]	4,097.8	7.9	31.5	199.2	398.3	631.6	2,438.3	390.8
Indiana	3,831.4	6.8	28.1	117.3	219.7	699.3	2,408.8	351.6
Iowa	3,301.2	1.7	22.2	39.5	205.7	577.6	2,266.2	188.3
Kansas	4,321.4	3.4	35.1	89.9	276.4	761.3	2,858.9	296.3
Kentucky[4]	2,938.1	4.7	27.8	80.7	143.8	651.9	1,799.3	229.8
Louisiana	5,338.1	11.2	31.4	176.1	468.3	1,040.2	3,125.2	485.7
Maine	2,688.2	1.4	25.3	20.5	64.2	536.1	1,910.7	129.9
Maryland	4,866.8	8.3	27.0	251.6	496.1	773.1	2,715.0	595.8
Massachusetts	3,098.6	2.3	29.1	101.5	346.6	508.4	1,674.5	436.2
Michigan	4,081.5	6.7	52.7	129.5	365.8	721.0	2,269.2	536.6
Minnesota	3,583.7	2.4	45.0	75.6	141.4	512.8	2,504.3	302.3
Mississippi	4,185.2	9.9	40.1	115.3	184.8	1,043.4	2,460.3	331.5
Missouri	4,776.1	6.6	24.6	138.0	372.1	763.4	2,973.9	497.6
Montana	3,688.7	3.8	20.8	25.4	302.4	405.8	2,729.2	201.3
Nebraska	4,329.6	2.5	25.2	65.8	210.8	569.7	3,076.8	378.8
Nevada	4,266.0	8.5	41.9	234.2	302.2	840.9	2,140.1	698.1
New Hampshire	2,321.6	1.4	36.4	35.3	97.2	388.3	1,593.1	170.0
New Jersey	3,225.3	4.0	15.1	166.3	204.7	551.7	1,839.0	444.4
New Mexico	5,324.0	5.4	46.5	147.3	581.9	1,068.9	3,083.7	390.2
New York	2,925.1	5.0	18.7	192.3	300.0	422.9	1,732.2	254.0
North Carolina	4,938.0	6.2	25.4	162.5	300.2	1,244.6	2,898.0	301.1
North Dakota	2,417.7	1.1	25.8	9.5	43.2	341.2	1,825.7	171.2
Ohio	4,177.6	4.0	39.3	151.2	157.4	852.1	2,602.3	371.3
Oklahoma	4,607.0	5.3	42.9	79.4	384.6	999.2	2,732.2	363.3
Oregon	5,044.1	2.4	33.8	79.2	191.3	767.3	3,542.7	427.4
Pennsylvania	2,961.1	5.3	28.2	142.4	234.5	442.3	1,817.8	290.7
Rhode Island	3,684.9	3.7	39.3	93.1	173.5	644.4	2,254.7	476.2
South Carolina	4,752.7	6.3	34.0	130.7	549.3	906.5	2,762.7	363.3
South Dakota	2,332.0	0.9	46.4	13.6	93.8	408.0	1,661.5	107.7
Tennessee	5,152.8	7.4	38.3	178.0	521.6	1,040.2	2,874.8	492.5
Texas	5,152.7	6.2	38.3	165.8	362.5	958.3	3,140.1	481.4
Utah	4,243.0	3.0	39.5	52.7	139.0	608.2	3,113.8	286.9
Vermont	2,769.3	1.1	17.5	17.5	69.0	513.8	2,026.8	123.6
Virginia	3,178.3	5.1	24.6	95.4	166.2	439.7	2,185.1	262.1
Washington	5,151.9	3.0	43.4	99.1	209.5	885.5	3,258.7	652.6
West Virginia	2,559.5	2.2	17.8	39.2	220.2	532.8	1,568.8	178.5
Wisconsin	3,321.2	3.6	21.1	82.3	124.2	498.5	2,319.1	272.5
Wyoming	3,517.6	1.8	30.9	17.0	207.5	501.8	2,617.8	140.8

Note: Offense totals are based on all reporting agencies and estimates for unreported areas. 1. The murder and nonnegligent homicides that occurred as a result of the events of September 11, 2001, were not included in this table. 2. Violent crimes are offenses of murder, forcible rape, robbery, and aggravated assault. Property crimes are offenses of burglary, larceny-theft, and motor vehicle theft. 3. Includes offenses reported by the Zoological Police. 4. Limited data for 2001 were available for Illinois and Kentucky; therefore, it was necessary that their crime counts be estimated.
Source: Federal Bureau of Investigation, *Uniform Crime Reports: Crime in the United States 2001*. **www.fbi.gov/ucr/01cius.htm**

The largest states, of course, had the most numbers of crimes. But the rate of crime was by far the greatest in Arizona (6,077.4 serious crimes per 100,000 residents, up 4.3 percent from 2000), Florida (5,569.7) and Louisiana (5,338.1). Meanwhile, New York, supposedly one of the most dangerous states, was at 2,925.1 crimes per 100,000 residents, significantly below the national average. The most dangerous place to live, however, was the nation's capital, with 7,709.6 serious

Serious Crime Per 100,000 Population, by Metropolitan Area, 2001[1]

Metropolitan area	All serious crime	Violent crime: Murder	Violent crime: Forcible rape	Violent crime: Robbery	Violent crime: Aggravated assault	Total violent crime[2]	Total property crime[2]
Albuquerque, N. Mex	7,014.3	6.1	44.8	266.2	704.9	1,022.1	5,992.2
Atlanta, Ga.[3]	4,825.7	7.9	27.2	235.1	299.9	570.1	4,255.6
Austin-San Marcos, Texas	4,842.6	3.2	35.8	107.0	218.4	364.4	4,478.1
Baltimore, Md.	5,464.8	11.7	29.5	326.1	658.7	1,026.0	4,438.7
Bergen-Passaic, N.J.	2,620.7	2.8	6.5	122.6	148.8	280.7	2,340.1
Birmingham, Ala.	4,856.2	11.9	38.6	187.6	317.9	556.1	4,300.1
Boston, Mass.-N.H.[4]	—	2.6	24.1	118.6	—	—	2,546.8
Buffalo–Niagara Falls, N.Y.	3,601.1	6.2	30.0	173.2	241.3	450.8	3,150.4
Dallas, Texas	5,825.4	8.7	36.3	283.6	368.7	697.3	5,128.1
Denver, Colo.	4,692.5	4.4	45.6	114.0	230.7	394.8	4,297.7
Detroit, Mich.	4,590.0	10.8	42.9	212.5	477.3	743.5	3,846.5
El Paso, Texas	4,852.3	3.5	34.2	116.8	544.1	698.7	4,153.7
Fort Lauderdale, Fla.	4,659.3	5.4	29.1	192.4	378.1	605.0	4,054.3
Ft. Worth-Arlington, Texas	5,517.4	6.0	41.1	140.1	275.9	463.0	5,054.4
Fresno, Calif.	5,971.6	8.0	37.5	196.3	508.3	750.1	5,221.6
Grand Rapids, Mich.	3,812.6	2.1	50.5	80.4	292.6	425.7	3,386.9
Greensboro–Winston–Salem–High Point, N.C.[3]	5,306.2	5.3	26.1	186.2	284.0	501.6	4,804.6
Harrisburg, Pa.	2,702.8	3.2	33.7	108.9	173.4	319.2	2,383.6
Hartford, Conn.	3,535.2	4.0	20.8	156.5	161.3	342.5	3,192.6
Honolulu, Hawaii	5,469.9	2.3	33.1	112.8	128.8	277.0	5,192.9
Houston, Texas	5,297.8	8.3	38.0	285.4	437.2	768.8	4,529.0
Jackson, Miss.	6,099.2	14.5	65.9	261.2	219.5	561.1	5,538.1
Jacksonville, Fla.	5,853.6	8.4	35.4	219.0	604.3	867.2	4,986.3
Jersey City, N.J.	4,005.6	5.5	18.9	305.8	340.9	671.1	3,334.4
Las Vegas, Nev.-Ariz.	4,474.9	10.5	37.8	267.4	301.0	616.8	3,858.1
Los Angeles–Long Beach, Calif.	4,033.2	11.1	28.8	312.0	574.8	926.6	3,106.6
Memphis, Tenn.[3]	7,416.4	15.3	53.4	413.6	622.2	1,104.4	6,312.0
Miami, Fla.	7,598.2	8.4	36.5	363.2	743.2	1,151.3	6,446.9
Milwaukee, Wisc.	4,626.7	8.9	26.3	216.0	171.5	422.6	4,204.1
Minneapolis-St. Paul, Minn.	4,093.6	2.6	46.2	114.4	168.8	332.0	3,761.6
Montgomery, Ala.	6,219.9	10.5	40.1	227.3	303.6	581.4	5,638.5
Nashville, Tenn.	5,984.3	6.6	49.7	233.1	681.5	970.9	5,013.4
Newark, N.J.	3,682.7	7.4	16.1	269.9	247.4	540.8	3,141.9
New Orleans, La.	5,748.1	20.0	30.8	297.6	438.3	786.7	4,961.4
New York, N.Y.	3,174.5	7.2	17.8	317.3	431.5	773.7	2,400.8
Oakland, Calif.	4,768.6	6.4	28.6	217.2	314.6	566.8	4,201.8
Oklahoma City, Okla.	6,082.6	5.9	54.0	124.2	364.0	548.1	5,534.5
Orange County, Calif.	2,756.5	2.2	15.2	109.9	168.2	295.5	2,461.0
Orlando, Fla.	6,073.9	4.1	41.5	199.6	632.8	878.1	5,195.8
Philadelphia, Pa.-N.J.	3,738.7	8.0	32.3	251.1	326.3	617.8	3,120.9
Phoenix-Mesa, Ariz.	6,426.8	8.9	26.6	197.0	334.0	566.5	5,860.3
Pittsburgh, Pa.	2,751.3	4.3	22.8	104.9	205.7	337.7	2,413.7
Portland–Vancouver, Oreg.–Wash.	5,357.3	2.4	40.1	104.2	243.0	389.6	4,967.7
Providence–Fall River–Warwick, R.I.–Mass.	3,684.4	3.5	39.2	100.3	208.6	351.5	3,332.9
Raleigh-Durham–Chapel Hill, N.C.	5,158.5	5.1	21.7	200.5	270.4	497.7	4,660.8
Richmond, Va.	4,728.7	10.9	27.1	213.9	231.9	483.7	4,244.9
Rochester, N.Y.	3,482.3	4.6	16.7	107.5	107.3	236.1	3,246.2
Sacramento, Calif.	4,636.8	5.2	33.5	160.7	300.4	499.8	4,137.0
Salt Lake City-Ogden, Utah	5,119.1	3.8	45.3	81.7	175.4	306.2	4,812.8
San Antonio, Texas	7,034.3	6.9	38.5	144.5	486.5	676.3	6,358.0
San Diego, Calif.	3,560.9	3.2	29.0	119.7	357.2	509.1	3,051.7
San Jose, Calif.	2,776.8	2.0	27.8	66.5	360.2	456.5	2,320.3
Seattle-Bellevue–Everett, Wash.	5,277.4	3.1	39.5	126.9	201.7	371.1	4,906.3
Syracuse, N.Y.	3,207.4	3.4	16.8	102.1	206.7	329.0	2,878.4
Tampa-St. Petersburg, Fla.	5,908.7	5.0	44.3	228.6	626.3	904.1	5,004.6
Tucson, Ariz.	7,599.1	6.1	47.2	219.3	399.1	671.6	6,927.4
Tulsa, Okla.	5,050.1	5.5	48.5	109.0	529.8	692.8	4,357.3
Washington, D.C.–Md.–Va.–W.Va.[5]	3,952.0	7.9	20.7	193.8	286.4	508.9	3,443.1
West Palm Beach, Fla.	6,213.6	4.4	42.4	204.8	484.2	735.8	5,477.8

Note: 1. The murder and nonnegligent homicides that occurred as a result of the events of September 11, 2001, were not included in this table. 2. Violent crimes are offenses of murder, forcible rape, robbery, and aggravated assault. Property crimes are offenses of burglary, larceny-theft, and motor vehicle theft. Data are not included for the property crime of arson. 3. Due to changes in reporting practices, annexations, and/or incomplete data, figures are not comparable to previous years' data. 4. Aggravated assault figures were found to be outside statistical parameters. 5. The data for anthrax assaults were not available.
Source: Federal Bureau of Investigation, *Uniform Crime Reports: Crime in the United States 2001*. **www.fbi.gov/ucr/01cius.htm**

crimes per 100,000 residents, nearly double the national average. By metropolitan area, Tucson (7,599.1), Miami (7,598.2), and Memphis (7,416.4) topped the list of dangerous cities. New Orleans was the murder capital of the United States for the fifth straight year in 2001, with 20 homicides per 100,000 residents, (up from 16.0 in 1999 but still down considerably from a high of 31.9 in 1996). The rate in New York City was 7.2.

Violent crime in other nations Although many reports and news stories have emphasized the continuing decline of serious crime, it is helpful to keep in mind that the U.S. remains far and away the most

Crimes per 100,000 Population in Metropolitan Areas, 1995-2001

Metropolitan area	All serious crimes[2]			Violent crimes[1]		
	1995	2000	2001	1995	2000	2001
Albuquerque, N. Mex	7,521.9	7,038.8	7,014.3	879.4	945.7	1,022.1
Anchorage, Alaska	7,220.9	4,931.4	5,013.1	990.1	584.1	663.2
Austin-San Marcos, Texas	6,051.2	4,688.5	4,842.6	579.6	383.7	364.4
Bergen-Passaic, N.J.	3,553.9	2,356.8	2,620.7	327.3	258.7	280.7
Birmingham, Ala.	6,494.0	5,142.7	4,856.2	1,071.3	578.7	556.1
Burlington, Vt.	5,656.0	4,433.1	3,847.8	155.9	182.3	155.3
Dallas, Texas	6,571.5	5,645.9	5,825.4	819.2	672.2	697.3
Denver, Colo.	5,591.3	4,273.6	4,692.5	513.4	356.4	394.8
Des Moines, Iowa	5,927.2	4,091.8	4,556.6	349.6	222.0	251.1
Detroit, Mich.	6,143.4	4,686.5	4,590.0	880.8	753.6	743.5
El Paso, Texas	6,623.4	5,192.2	4,852.3	802.0	655.9	698.7
Fort Lauderdale, Fla.	8,134.9	4,756.3	4,659.3	847.9	603.0	605.0
Ft. Worth-Arlington, Texas	5,892.0	5,182.5	5,517.4	684.8	468.9	463.0
Fresno, Calif.	8,566.2	5,877.7	5,971.6	1,189.0	761.3	750.1
Green Bay, Wis.	3,938.0	2,855.6	2,895.9	291.0	171.9	144.5
Greensboro–Winston–Salem–High Point, N.C.	6,435.1	5,199.3	5,306.2	702.3	555.1	501.6
Greenville, N.C.	7,638.5	7,018.4	7,152.7	805.8	661.9	635.7
Hartford, Conn.	4,749.3	3,750.1	3,535.2	482.6	325.5	342.5
Honolulu, Hawaii	7,627.8	5,280.4	5,469.9	327.4	260.5	277.0
Houston, Texas	5,633.8	5,046.3	5,297.8	856.1	717.3	768.8
Jacksonville, Fla.	7,557.8	5,942.4	5,853.6	1,168.6	936.2	867.2
Jersey City, N.J.	6,332.6	4,199.8	4,005.6	1,071.9	696.9	671.1
Las Vegas, Nev.-Ariz.	7,408.6	4,602.3	4,474.9	1,085.9	573.9	616.8
Lincoln, Nebr.	6,921.5	6,248.8	6,442.3	598.6	502.2	526.4
Los Angeles–Long Beach, Calif.	6,141.8	3,980.4	4,033.2	1,422.6	944.4	926.6
Miami, Fla.	12,319.2	8,063.3	7,598.2	1,886.3	1,207.4	1,151.3
Minneapolis-St. Paul, Minn.	5,287.2	4,111.6	4,093.6	489.9	358.0	332.0
Monmouth-Ocean, N.J.	3,417.3	2,293.5	2,447.7	239.7	186.2	199.0
Newark, N.J.	5,834.7	3,693.6	3,682.7	1,031.5	564.1	540.8
New Orleans, La.	8,210.5	5,817.0	5,748.1	1,334.5	772.9	786.7
New York, N.Y.	5,669.5	3,538.5	3,174.5	1,392.8	872.3	773.7
Oklahoma City, Okla.	7,905.8	6,351.3	6,082.6	808.5	521.8	548.1
Omaha, Nebr.-Iowa	5,602.6	5,319.2	5,700.5	623.7	546.0	476.0
Orange County, Calif.	4,672.2	2,633.7	2,756.5	513.2	304.8	295.5
Orlando, Fla.	7,123.5	6,016.8	6,073.9	1,007.0	892.7	878.1
Philadelphia, Pa.-N.J.	—	3,858.5	3,738.7	—	660.1	617.8
Phoenix-Mesa, Ariz.	8,808.5	6,205.2	6,426.8	765.0	560.4	566.5
Pittsburgh, Pa.	—	2,598.5	2,751.3	—	330.4	337.7
Portland–Vancouver, Oreg.–Wash.	6,738.1	5,047.1	5,357.3	726.9	452.2	389.6
Providence–Fall River–Warwick, R.I.–Mass.	4,370.3	3,502.7	3,684.4	389.2	306.4	351.5
Raleigh-Durham–Chapel Hill, N.C.	6,027.6	5,388.5	5,158.5	600.0	485.7	497.7
Riverside–San Bernardino, Calif.	6,409.2	3,848.8	4,159.6	945.5	574.5	595.4
Salt Lake City-Ogden, Utah	7,200.3	5,391.8	5,119.1	411.4	338.6	306.2
San Antonio, Texas	6,697.4	6,397.3	7,034.3	484.3	572.0	676.3
San Diego, Calif.	5,030.5	3,275.0	3,560.9	794.5	476.8	509.1
San Francisco, Calif.	5,833.8	3,926.4	—	884.3	533.8	—
San Jose, Calif.	4,244.6	2,628.6	2,776.8	614.5	426.1	456.5
Seattle-Bellevue–Everett, Wash.	—	5,221.2	5,277.4	—	383.6	371.1
Syracuse, N.Y.	3,673.6	2,846.4	3,207.4	301.9	312.3	329.0
Tampa-St. Petersburg, Fla.	7,127.8	5,821.0	5,908.7	1,120.4	886.8	904.1
Tucson, Ariz.	9,769.5	6,858.1	7,599.1	877.2	644.9	671.6
Tulsa, Okla.	5,386.7	4,658.6	5,050.1	737.8	662.6	692.8
West Palm Beach, Fla.	8,572.3	6,651.3	6,213.6	974.6	753.8	735.8

1. Violent crimes are offenses of murder, forcible rape, robbery, and aggravated assault. 2. Property crimes are offenses of burglary, larceny-theft, and motor vehicle theft. Data are not included for the property crime of arson.
Source: Federal Bureau of Investigation, *Uniform Crime Reports: Crime in the United States 2001.* **www.fbi.gov/ucr/01cius.htm**

violent industrialized nation. In 1999, the Bureau of Justice Statistics released a detailed comparison of crime rates in the U.S and England. Although violent crime was increasing in England while it was decreasing in the U.S., the rates of murder, rape, and robbery were still significantly higher in this country than in the U.K. The U.S. murder rate was six times as high as England's, the number of rapes per 100,000 population three times as high, and the robbery rate 40 percent higher. It is interesting to note, however, that the rate of assault was 13 percent higher in England, while the rates for burglary and motor vehicle theft were about double U.S. rates.

Homicide, Guns and Young People

Murders by youthful offenders have followed the same downward trend evidenced in the population at large, but still remain alarmingly high. The rate of homicides by 14- to 17-year-olds dropped from an all-time high of 24.4 per 100,000 in 1993 to about 9.2 murders per 100,000 population in 1998. But that's still almost double the rate in 1984, when the rate was 4.8 per 100,000. Similarly, the homicide rate for 18-24-year-olds was 31 per 100,000 in 1998, down from highs of more than 40 in 1991 and 1993, but still considerably higher than the 22 in 1985. Over the period 1976-98, the number of nongun homicides by offenders aged 14-24 has declined slightly, while the number of murders involving guns has more than doubled. By comparison, the number of gun homicides by offenders over the age of 25 has actually declined by more than 3,000 since 1976.

▶CRIME VICTIMS

Crime victimization statistics are a second measure of the so-called crime rate. Unlike reported crime statistics (above), which are based on reports to law enforcement authorities, crime victimization statistics are based on Bureau of Justice Statistics interviews with a sampling of people about their personal experience with crime. (The BJS does not ask about or keep statistics on homicides because it is impossible to question the victim). In most years, these different statistical methods have reported similar trends in criminal activity in the U.S. In 2001, however, a sharp difference emerged: while the FBI Uniform Crime Report suggests that serious crime rates increased slightly, the BJS survey shows a continued, steady drop in crime.

As the accompanying table shows, the victims of most kinds of crime are most likely to be black, young, poor, urban, single, and except for rape and domestic violence, male. People with family incomes of less than $7,500 were the most likely to be victimized by crime, especially violent crime. In general, the poorer a person is, the more likely he or she is to be the victim of a crime. And while senior citizens often feel most vulnerable to crime, it is teenagers who are most likely to be victimized by all kinds of crime. Children 12-19 years old are almost 20 times as likely to be the victims of violent crime as people over the age of 65.

▶LAW ENFORCEMENT

As of October 2001, there were 659,104 sworn police officers in the United States (up from 654,601 the year before) and an additional 279,926 civilians employed in police departments. This translates into 2.5 full-time police officers for every 1,000 residents. Including full-time civilian employees, the ratio was 3.5 per 1,000. In cities with more than one million residents, the ratio averaged 4.7 law enforcement employees per 1,000 residents. The ratio was 4.4 and 4.2 in rural and suburban counties, respectively.

Overall, civilians made up 29.8 percent of the law enforcement workforce in 2001. In cities, civilians comprised 23.2 percent of the workforce; in suburban and rural areas, they made up 39.3 percent, respectively. Northern states have the greatest number of sworn officers (2.8 officers per 1,000 inhabitants); the West has the fewest (1.7). By sex, 88.8 percent of sworn officers nationally and in cities collectively are male, but civilian police employees are overwhelmingly female (62.7 percent on average).

Arrests Nationwide, law enforcement agencies made an estimated 14 million arrests in 2000 for all criminal infractions except traffic violations, down 2.2 percent from 1999. This represents a rate of 5,010.4 arrests per 100,000 population. Among cities, those with populations under 10,000 had the highest rate of arrests, 6,460.1 per 100,000 population; those with populations from 25,000–49,999 had the lowest rate (4,600.1). The arrest rate was 4,021.5 per 100,000 for suburban counties, and 4,027.1 per 100,000 for rural counties. The greatest number of arrests were for drug abuse (1.6 million),

Criminal Victimization Rates, 1992-2001

	Victimizations ('000s)			Victimization rate per 1,000 persons		
Crime	1992	2000	2001	1992	2000	2001
All crimes[1]	**42,834**	**25,893**	**24,216**	**N.A.**	**N.A.**	**N.A.**
Violent crimes[1]	**10,249**	**6,323**	**5,744**	**49.0**	**27.9**	**25.1**
Simple assault	6,053	4,038	3,643	28.9	17.8	15.9
Aggravated assault	2,317	1,293	1,222	11.1	5.7	5.3
Robbery	1,272	732	631	6.1	3.2	2.8
Rape/sexual assault	607	261	248	2.9	1.2	1.1
Personal theft[2]	**369**	**274**	**188**	**1.8**	**1.2**	**0.8**
Property crime	**32,217**	**19,297**	**18,284**	**325.3**	**178.1**	**166.9**
Property thefts	24,579	14,916	14,135	248.2	137.7	129.0
Household burglary	5,803	3,444	3,140	58.6	31.8	28.7
Motor vehicle theft	1,835	937	1,009	18.5	8.6	9.2

Note: Rates per 1,000 people ages 12 or older. 1. The National Crime Victimization Survey cannot measure murder because it is impossible to question the victim. 2. Includes pocket picking, purse snatching, and attempted purse snatching.
Source: Bureau of Justice Statistics Bulletin, *Criminal Victimization 2001,* **www.ojp.usdoj.gov/bjs/abstract/cv01.htm**

Rates of Violent Crime and Personal Theft, by Sex, Age, Race, Hispanic Origin, Income,Residence, Marital Status and Region, 2001

Characteristic	Total	Crimes of violence[1] Rape/Sexual assault	Robbery	Assault	Theft
By sex					
Male	27.3	0.2	3.8	23.2	0.8
Female	23.0	1.9	1.7	19.4	0.9
By age					
12-15	55.1	1.7	5.2	48.3	0.5
16-19	55.8	3.4	6.4	46.1	3.0
20-24	44.7	2.4	4.2	38.1	1.8
25-34	29.3	1.1	3.6	24.6	1.0
35-49	22.9	1.0	2.1	19.7	0.4
50-64	9.5	0.2	1.2	8.2	0.3
65+	3.2	0.1	1.3	1.8	0.7
By race					
White	24.5	1.0	2.6	20.8	0.8
Black	31.2	1.1	3.6	26.4	0.8
Other	18.2	1.6	2.4	14.2	1.7
By Hispanic Origin					
Hispanic	29.5	1.1	5.3	23.1	0.7
Non-Hispanic	24.5	1.1	2.4	21.0	0.8
Family Income					
Less than $7,500	46.6	3.7	4.7	38.2	1.0
$ 7,500-$14,999	36.9	1.6	4.4	31.0	0.8
$15,000-$24,999	31.8	2.0	4.3	25.5	0.9
$25,000-$34,999	29.1	1.3	2.2	25.6	1.0
$35,000-$49,999	26.3	1.1	2.4	22.9	0.6
$50,000-$74,999	21.0	0.8	2.3	17.9	0.6
$75,000 or more	18.5	0.6	1.6	16.3	0.6
By Marital Status					
Never married	44.7	2.1	5.0	37.6	1.8
Married	11.4	0.3	1.1	10.0	0.2
Divorced/separated	42.0	2.0	4.8	35.2	0.8
Widowed	7.7	0.4	1.8	5.5	0.8

Note: Rates per 1,000 people ages 12 or older. 1. The National Crime Victimization Survey cannot measure murder because it is impossible to question the victim. **Source:** Bureau of Justice Statistics Bulletin, *Criminal Victimization 2001,* **www.ojp.usdoj.gov/bjs/abstract/cv01.htm**

driving under the influence of drugs or alcohol (1.5 million), simple assault (1.3 million) and larceny or theft (1.2 million), all of which remained relatively unchanged since from 1999.

By age, 5.5 percent of all people arrested nationwide in 2000 were under 15; 17.1 percent were under 18; 32.1 percent were under 21; and 46 percent were under 25. By sex, 77.8 percent of all those arrested were males. Females were most often arrested for larceny/theft. By race, 69.7 percent of all those arrested were white, 27.9 percent black. Whites accounted for 66.2 percent of all property crime arrests and 59.9 percent of violent crime arrests.

▶CORRECTIONS

The United States has more people in prison (as well as more people in prison per capita) than any other Western industrialized nation. In 2002 the Bureau of Justice Statistics reported a record 1.44 million inmates in federal and state prisons. However, the state prison population seems to be leveling off: it rose only 2 percent during 2002. Since 1980 the number of sentenced inmates per 100,000 residents has risen from 139 to 476.

During 2002, Maine reported the largest increase in its prison population (11.5 percent), followed by Rhode Island (8.6 percent), Colorado (7.9 percent), and Connecticut (7.9 percent). Excluding the District of Columbia, the states with the largest declines were Alaska (down 3.8 percent), Illinois (down 3.7 percent), and Delaware (down 3.2 percent).

The states with the highest incarceration rates (number of prisoners sentenced to more than one year per 100,000 residents) were all in the South. Louisiana led the way with 794 prisoners per 100,000 residents, followed by Mississippi (743) and Texas (692). The lowest rates were found in Maine (141), Minnesota (141), North Dakota (161), and Rhode Island (191). The national average was 476 prisoners per 100,000 residents.

Prison and race Blacks have made up the majority of the increase in the prison population. Between 1990 (the last year in which white prisoners outnumbered blacks) and 2002, the number of blacks behind bars jumped from 360,000 to 622,700, an increase of 73 percent. Meanwhile, the white prison population grew 31 percent, from 370,900 in 1990 to 485,400 in 2001; in 2002 it shrank slightly, to 472,200. Black males have the highest incarceration rates (3,437 per 100,000 residents in 2001) while white females have the lowest (35 per 100,000 residents). Put another way, about 3.5 percent of all black males are in prison. In the 25-29 age group, more than 10 percent of black males are in prison.

Arrests in the U.S., 1984–2001

Crime	Total Arrests 1984	1989	1995	2000	2001	Rate per 100,000 in 2001
Violent crime	400,877	487,673	619,230	415,573	434,391	225.6
Murder	15,126	16,146	16,701	8,709	9,426	4.9
Forcible rape	28,565	27,461	26,561	17,914	18,576	9.6
Robbery	115,522	123,317	137,811	72,320	76,667	39.8
Aggravated assault	241,664	320,749	438,157	316,630	329,722	171.2
Property crime	1,431,812	1,600,947	1,620,704	1,080,797	1,120,346	581.8
Burglary	338,737	320,470	292,315	189,343	198,883	103.3
Larceny/theft	981,812	1,102,112	1,164,371	782,082	806,093	418.6
Motor vehicle theft	96,975	165,317	149,053	98,697	102,607	53.3
Arson	14,288	13,048	14,965	10,675	12,763	6.6
All serious crimes	1,832,689	2,088,620	2,239,934	1,496,370	1,554,737	807.3
Other crimes	6,995,758	7,902,737	9,167,354	7,627,058	7,767,587	4,033.4
Total arrests	**8,828,447**	**9,991,357**	**11,407,288**	**9,123,428**	**9,322,324**	**4,840.7**

Note: Statistics for 2000 are based on a survey of approximately 9,511 law enforcement agencies representing 192,580,262 inhabitants. The number of agencies surveyed and the populations they represent changes from year to year.
Source: Federal Bureau of Investigation, *Uniform Crime Reports: Crime in the United States 2001.* **www.fbi.gov/ucr/01cius.htm**

Arrests by Race, 2001

Offense charged	Total	White Number	White Percent	Black Number	Black Percent	Other[1] Number	Other[1] Percent
All arrests	**9,306,587**	**6,465,887**	**69.5%**	**2,617,669**	**28.1%**	**223,031**	**2.4%**
Violent crime	**433,764**	**260,983**	**60.2**	**163,192**	**37.6**	**9,589**	**2.2**
Murder	9,416	4,561	48.4	4,585	48.7	270	2.9
Forcible rape	18,530	11,617	62.7	6,446	34.8	467	2.5
Robbery	76,610	34,099	44.5	41,228	53.8	1,283	1.7
Aggravated assault	329,208	210,706	64.0	110,933	33.7	7,569	2.3
Property crime	**1,118,460**	**738,080**	**66.0**	**350,879**	**31.4**	**29,501**	**2.7**
Burglary	198,648	137,887	69.4	56,527	28.5	4,234	2.1
Larceny/theft	804,605	531,521	66.1	250,912	31.2	22,172	2.7
Motor vehicle theft	102,462	58,869	57.5	40,806	39.8	2,787	2.7
Arson	12,745	9,803	76.9	2,634	20.7	308	2.4
All serious crimes	**1,552,224**	**999,063**	**64.4**	**514,071**	**33.1**	**39,096**	**2.5**

Note: Based on a survey of 9,511 law enforcement agencies representing 192,580,262 inhabitants. 1. Includes American Indian, Alaskan Native, Asian, and Pacific Islander.
Source: Federal Bureau of Investigation, *Uniform Crime Reports: Crime in the United States 2001,* **www.fbi.gov/ucr/01cius.htm**

Arrests and Convictions for Crimes Committed in the U.S., 2000

As the following table demonstrates, the number of police and the number of prisons have very little effect on the number of crimes committed because people who commit crimes have very little expectation of getting caught. Except for murder, most felonies rarely even result in an arrest, and result in a conviction even more infrequently. These statistics indicate neither a shortage of police nor leniency by judges, but simply the difficulty of solving a crime after it has been committed and proving who did it.

Offense	Number of crimes reported to police	Number of adults arrested	Arrests as percent of number of crimes	Number of felony convictions	Convictions as percent of number arrested	Convictions as percent of number of crimes
Murder[1]	15,517	11,997	77.3%	8,883	74.0%	57.2%
Rape	90,186	22,964	25.5	10,686	46.5	11.8
Robbery	407,842	79,279	19.4	38,379	48.4	9.4
Aggravated assault	910,744	411,917	45.2	79,653	19.3	8.7
Burglary	2,049,946	194,195	9.5	79,357	40.9	3.9
Motor vehicle theft	1,165,559	97,384	8.4	12,039	12.4	1.0
Drug trafficking	N.A.	261,402	N.A.	225,675	86.3	N.A.

1. Includes non-negligent manslaughter. **Source:** Bureau of Justice Statistics Bulletin, *Felony Sentences in State Courts, 2000,* June 2003.

Jails and prisons Although the terms tend to be used synonymously, "jails" and "prisons" differ in the types of inmates they house, their locations, their physical size and their programs. Jails are locally administered facilities that house inmates after arraignment, prisoners serving terms of less than one year, and prisoners who cannot be housed in state prisons due to overcrowding.

Prisons are administered by either state or federal government authority. Typically they hold convicted offenders sentenced to terms of confinement for more than one year. They tend to be located away from dense population centers, and they are usually larger than jails and have more rehabilitation programs.

Costs of prisons According to the Criminal Justice Institute, total U.S. expenditures for adult correctional facilities was $34.1 billion in 2000. In state prisons, the average cost per inmate was $57.92 per day in 2000.

Total U.S. prison capital costs increased from $538 million in 1980 to $2.8 billion in 2000. Operating costs surged from $3.1 billion in 1980. to $31.4 billion in 2000. In California, where over 20 new prisons were built during this period, expenditures on prisons rose from $336 million to $4 billion, with capital expenditures increasing by over 1,400 percent (in constant dollars). In Texas, capital expenditures rose over 1,500 percent.

Probation and Parole When an offender is convicted, the primary sentencing alternatives are incarceration or probation. Once imprisoned, the offender may become eligible for parole, a form of conditional release. The explosion in the prison population has understandably led to a corresponding increase in the number of prisoners released on probation or parole. At the end of 2002, according to the Bureau of Justice Statistics, a record 6.7 million people (3.1 percent of all U.S. adult residents, or 1 in every 32 adults) were under "correctional supervision" in the United States: in jail, in prison, on probation or on parole. More than half this population (nearly 4 million) were on probation; another 753,141 were on parole.

Recidivism In 2002 the Bureau of Justice Statistics released a study of recidivism among 272,111 inmates (from 15 different states) who were released in 1994. The study found that 67.5 percent were rearrested within 3 years; 46.9 percent were reconvicted for a new crime; 25.9 percent were resentenced to prison for a new crime; and 51.8 percent were back in prison within three years for

Prisoners in the U.S. by System, Sex, and Race, 1980–2002

	By system			By sex and race[1]			
Year	Total	Federal	State	White male	Black male	White female	Black female
Number							
1980	329,821	24,363	305,458	159,500	140,600	5,900	6,300
1985	502,507	40,223	462,284	242,700	210,500	10,800	10,200
1990	773,919	65,526	708,393	350,700	340,300	20,200	19,700
1995	1,125,874	100,250	1,025,624	487,400	509,800	30,500	31,900
2000	1,391,892	145,416	1,245,845	436,500	572,900	34,500	37,400
2002	1,440,655	163,528	1,277,127	436,800	586,700	35,400	36,000
Rate (Prisoners per 100,000 resident population)							
1980	139	9	130	168	1,111	6	45
1985	201	14	187	246	1,559	10	68
1990	292	20	272	338	2,234	19	117
1995	411	32	379	449	3,095	27	176
2000	469	44	425	449	3,457	34	205
2002	476	49	427	450	3,437	35	191

Note: Prisoners sentenced to more than one year. N/A = not available. 1. Prisoners of other races not shown.
Source: Bureau of Justice Statistics Bulletin, *Prisoners in 2002* (2003).

Jail Population, 1985–2002

Age and sex	1985	1990	1995	2000	2002
Number of inmates at midyear	**256,615**	**405,320**	**507,044**	**621,149**	**665,475**
Adults	254,986	403,019	499,300	613,534	658,228
Male	235,909	365,821	448,000	543,120	581,411
Female	19,077	37,198	51,300	70,414	76,817
Juveniles	1,629	2,301	7,800	7,615	7,248
Held as adults	—	—	5,900	6,126	6,112
Held as juveniles	1,629	2,301	1,800	1,489	1,136
Average daily population	**265,010**	**408,075**	**509,828**	**618,319**	**652,082**

Note: As of June 30 of each year. The average daily population is the sum of the number of inmates in a jail each day for a year, divided by 365. Juveniles are persons defined by state statute as being under a certain age, usually 18, and subject initially to juvenile court authority even if tried as adults. In 1994, the definition was changed to include all persons under age 18.
Source: Bureau of Justice Statistics, *Prison and Jail Inmates at Midyear 2002* (2003),**www.ojp.usdoj.gov/bjs/abstract/pjim02.htm**

either a new prison sentence or a violation of their original release. Prisoners with the highest rates of recidivism included those convicted of possessing or selling stolen property (77.4 percent), car thieves (78.8 percent), and larcenists (74.6 percent); prisoners with the lowest rates included those in prison for homicide (40.7 percent), sexual assault (41.4 percent), and rape (46.0 percent). Overall recidivism was up from 1983, when an earlier study estimated rearrests at 62.5 percent.

Number of Prisoners and Incarceration Rates by State, 2001-02

Region and jurisdiction	Total prisoners		Percent change, 2001–02	Total sentenced to more than one year		Incarceration rate, 2002
	2002	2001		2002[1]	2001	
U.S. total	**1,440,655**	**1,404,032**	**2.6%**	**1,380,370**	**1,345,217**	**476**
Federal	**163,528**	**156,993**	**4.2**	**143,040**	**136,509**	**49**
State	**1,277,127**	**1,247,039**	**2.4**	**1,237,330**	**1,208,708**	**427**
Alabama	27,947	26,741	4.5	27,532	26,138	612
Alaska[2]	4,398	4,571	-3.8	2,577	2,196	396
Arizona[4]	29,359	27,710	6.0	28,008	26,463	513
Arkansas	13,090	12,594	3.9	12,999	12,496	479
California	162,317	159,444	1.8	160,329	157,295	452
Colorado	18,333	17,448	7.9	18,833	17,448	415
Connecticut[2]	20,720	19,196	7.9	14,082	13,276	405
Delaware[2]	6,778	7,003	-3.2	3,659	4,033	453
District of Columbia[2,5]						
Florida[4]	75,210	72,404	3.9	75,204	72,404	450
Georgia[4]	47,445	45,937	3.3	47,424	45,904	552
Hawaii[2]	5,423	5,431	-0.1	3,840	3,670	308
Idaho	6,204	5,984	3.7	6,204	5,984	461
Illinois[3]	42,693	44,348	-3.7	42,693	44,348	336
Indiana	21,611	20,966	3.1	21,542	20,883	348
Iowa[3]	8,398	7,962	5.5	8,398	7,962	284
Kansas[3]	8,935	8,577	4.2	8,935	8,577	327
Kentucky	15,933	15,424	3.3	15,572	15,104	380
Louisiana	35,736	35,810	-0.2	35,736	35,810	794
Maine	1,900	1,704	11.5	1,817	1,641	141
Maryland	24,162	23,752	1.7	23,274	22,842	425
Massachusetts[6]	10,329	10,588	-2.4	8,947	9,355	234
Michigan	50,591	48,849	3.6	50,591	48,849	501
Minnesota	7,129	6,606	7.9	7,129	6,606	141
Mississippi	22,705	21,460	5.8	21,397	20,476	743
Missouri	30,099	28,757	4.7	30,080	28,736	529
Montana	3,290	3,328	-1.1	3,290	3,328	361
Nebraska	4,058	3,937	3.1	3,972	3,865	228
Nevada	10,478	10,233	2.4	10,478	10,233	483
New Hampshire	2,451	2,392	2.5	2,451	2,392	192
New Jersey[3]	27,891	28,142	-0.9	27,891	28,142	322
New Mexico	5,989	5,668	5.7	5,772	5,408	309
New York	67,065	67,533	-0.7	67,065	67,533	346
North Carolina	32,803	32,253	1.7	28,772	27,628	345
North Dakota	1,112	1,111	0.1	1,025	1,027	161
Ohio[3]	45,646	45,281	0.8	45,646	45,281	398
Oklahoma[3]	23,385	22,780	2.7	23,385	22,780	667
Oregon	12,086	11,410	5.9	12,075	11,368	342
Pennsylvania	40,168	38,062	5.5	40,164	38,057	325
Rhode Island[2]	3,520	3,241	8.6	2,045	1,926	191
South Carolina	23,715	22,576	5.0	22,837	21,606	555
South Dakota	2,898	2,790	3.9	2,891	2,781	378
Tennessee[3]	24,989	23,671	5.6	24,989	23,671	430
Texas[3]	162,003	162,070	0.0	151,782	153,056	692
Utah	5,567	5,339	4.3	5,461	5,254	233
Vermont[2]	1,863	1,741	7.0	1,321	1,313	214
Virginia	33,729	31,662	6.5	33,729	31,662	460
Washington	16,062	15,159	6.0	15,922	15,020	261
West Virginia	4,544	4,215	7.8	4,504	4,164	250
Wisconsin	22,133	21,495	3.0	21,324	21,033	391
Wyoming	1,737	1,684	3.1	1,737	1,684	348

Note: The incarceration rate is equal to the number of prisoners sentenced to more than 1 year per 100,000 residents. 1. Estimated. 2. Includes jail population. 3. Includes some inmates sentenced to one year or less. 4. Prisoner count based on custody counts. 5. Responsibility for sentenced felons was transferred to the Federal Bureau of Prisons. 6. Incarceration rate includes est. 6,200 inmates sentenced but held in local correctional facilities. **Source:** Bureau of Justice Statistics Bulletin, *Prisoners in 2002* (2003).

Lifetime Likelihood of Going to Prison by Age, Sex, Race and Hispanic Origin

One of every 20 people in the U.S. (5.1 percent) will serve time in a prison during their lifetime, according to a March, 1997, BJS report, if 1991 incarceration rates do not change dramatically. Men (9.0 percent) are much more likely than women (1.1 percent) to be incarcerated in prison at least once during their life, and black men (28.5 percent) are six times as likely as white men (4.4 percent) to be imprisoned. Sixteen percent of Hispanic men are likely to be imprisoned.

	Percent expected to go to prison at some time, by age[1]						
Category	**Birth**	**20**	**25**	**30**	**35**	**40**	**45**
Total	**5.1%**	**4.5%**	**3.1%**	**2.1%**	**1.4%**	**0.9%**	**0.6%**
By Sex							
Male	9.0	7.9	5.5	3.7	2.5	1.6	1.0
Female	1.1	1.0	0.8	0.6	0.3	0.2	0.1
By Race/Hispanic origin							
White (non-Hispanic)	2.5%	2.3%	1.7%	1.2%	0.9%	0.6%	0.4%
Male	4.4	4.1	3.0	2.1	1.5	1.1	0.8
Female	0.5	0.5	0.4	0.3	0.2	0.1	0.1
Black (non-Hispanic)	16.2	14.1	9.6	6.0	3.6	2.0	1.2
Male	28.5	25.3	17.3	10.8	6.5	3.6	2.1
Female	3.6	3.5	2.8	1.9	1.1	0.6	0.4
Hispanic	9.4	8.7	6.4	4.9	3.8	2.3	1.6
Male	16.0	14.8	11.1	8.6	6.8	4.3	3.0
Female	1.5	1.5	1.2	0.9	0.6	0.4	0.2

1. Among those not previously incarcerated.
Source: Bureau of Justice Statistics *Lifetime Likelihood of Going to State or Federal Prison*, March, 1997.

▶CAPITAL PUNISHMENT

The United States is the only Western industrialized nation that allows capital punishment. In the period 1930–2001, 4,608 executions were carried out under state or federal authority. The majority of those (3,859) occurred in the years before the Supreme Court ruled capital punishment unconstitutional in 1972. The Court reinstated the death penalty in 1976; since then, an additional 749 executions have been carried out; all but eight were males. Another 3,581 prisoners were on death row at the end of 2001 (all of whom had been convicted of murder).

The 66 prisoners executed in 2001 had been on death row an average of 11 years and 8 months, up from an average of 6 years in 1984. A positive aspect of this long delay is that it allows some death row prisoners to prove their innocence before they face the death chamber. According to the Death Penalty Information Center in Washington, D.C., at least 99 prisoners were released from death row in 24 states since 1973 because they were improperly convicted or because evidence of their innocence was discovered after they were sentenced to death. Among all prisoners sentenced to death between 1977 and 2001, 11.1 percent were executed and 35.9 percent received other dispositions.

Eighteen states have carried out 100 or more executions since 1930; as of 2001, 12 states and the District of Columbia did not authorize the death penalty for any crime. In Maine, Minnesota, and Wisconsin, there has been no death penalty statute in force since 1930, and Alaska and Hawaii have never had death penalty statutes. The death penalty was either abolished or declared unconstitutional in Michigan (1963), Iowa and West Virginia (1965), the District of Columbia (1973), Rhode Island (1979), Oregon (1981), and Massachusetts (1984). Kansas abolished the death penalty in 1973, but restored it in July, 1994. New York abolished it in 1984, but restored it in 1995. And South Dakota abolished the death penalty in 1915, restored it in 1939, abolished it again 1977, and restored it again 1979.

Prisoners Executed by Race, 1930–2001

Year	Total	White	Black	Other
1930-39	1,667	827	816	24
1940-49	1,284	490	781	13
1950-59	717	336	376	5
1960-67	191	98	93	0
Total, 1930-67	**3,859**	**1,751**	**2,066**	**42**
1977-79	3	3	0	0
1980-89	117	68	49	0
1990-99	478	303	164	11
2000	85	49	35	1
2001	66	48	17	1
Total, 1977-2001	**749**	**422**	**263**	**64**
Total, 1930-2001	**4,608**	**2,173**	**2,329**	**106**

Note: Executions under civil authority only. Does not include 160 executions carried out under military authority since 1930. There were no executions carried out between 1968 and 1977. **Source:** Bureau of Justice Statistics, *Sourcebook of Criminal Justice Statistics*, **www.albany.edu/sourcebook/** and *Capital Punishment 2001* (2002), **www.ojp.usdoj.gov/bjs/abstract/cp01.htm.**

Race and capital punishment Apart from the broad question of whether it is right for the state to take the life of an individual, the three major issues of concern to those opposed to capital punishment are whether it is a deterrent to crime, whether it violates the Eighth Amendment to the Constitution, prohibiting "cruel and unusual punishment" (the U.S. is the only industrialized democracy in the world that hasn't abolished it), and whether it is used fairly with respect to race.

Historically, blacks have been more likely to be executed than whites in proportion both to the general

Prisoners Executed by System, 1930–2001

System	Number executed: Since 1930	Since 1977	In 2001	On death row, 2001[1]	Method of execution	Minimum age authorized for execution
Alabama	158	23	0	186	Electrocution	16
Alaska	0	0	0	0	*No death penalty statute*	
Arizona	60	22	0	126	Gas; injection	none
Arkansas	142	24	1	40	Electrocution; injection	14
California[2]	301	9	1	603	Gas; injection	18
Colorado	48	1	0	6	Injection	18
Connecticut	21	0	0	7	Injection	18
Delaware	25	13	2	14	Injection; hanging	16
District of Columbia	40	0	0	0	*No death penalty statute*	
Federal system	35	2	2	0	Injection	18
Florida[2]	221	51	1	372	Electrocution; injection	16
Georgia[2]	393	27	4	116	Injection	17
Hawaii	0	0	0	0	*No death penalty statute*	
Idaho[2]	4	1	0	21	Injection; firing squad	none
Illinois	102	12	0	158	Injection	18
Indiana	50	9	2	36	Injection	16
Iowa	18	0	0	0	*No death penalty statute*	
Kansas[3]	15	0	0	4	Injection	18
Kentucky[2]	105	2	0	36	Electrocution	16
Louisiana[2]	159	26	0	88	Injection	none
Maine	0	0	0	0	*No death penalty statute*	
Maryland	71	3	0	16	Injection	18
Massachusetts	27	0	0	0	*No death penalty statute*	
Michigan	0	0	0	0	*No death penalty statute*	
Minnesota	0	0	0	0	*No death penalty statute*	
Mississippi[2]	158	4	0	62	Injection	16
Missouri	115	53	7	73	Gas; injection	16
Montana[2]	8	2	0	6	Injection	none
Nebraska	7	3	0	7	Electrocution	18
Nevada	38	9	1	86	Injection	16
New Hampshire	1	0	0	0	Hanging; injection	17
New Jersey[2]	74	0	0	16	Injection	18
New Mexico	9	1	1	3	Injection	18
New York[4]	329	0	0	6	Injection	18
North Carolina	284	21	5	216	Injection	17
North Dakota	0	0	0	0	*No death penalty statute*	
Ohio	174	2	1	203	Injection	18
Oklahoma	108	48	18	113	Electrocution; injection	16
Oregon	21	2	0	26	Injection	18
Pennsylvania	155	3	0	241	Injection	none
Rhode Island	0	0	0	0	*No death penalty statute*	
South Carolina	187	25	0	73	Electrocution; injection	none
South Dakota[2]	1	0	0	5	Injection	none
Tennessee	94	1	0	96	Electrocution; injection	18
Texas	553	256	17	453	Injection	17
Utah	19	6	0	11	Firing squad; injection	14
Vermont	4	0	0	0	*No death penalty statute*	
Virginia	175	83	2	26	Electrocution; injection	16
Washington	51	4	1	9	Hanging; injection	18
West Virginia	40	0	0	0	*No death penalty statute*	
Wisconsin	0	0	0	0	*No death penalty statute*	
Wyoming	8	1	0	2	Gas; injection	16
Total U.S.	**4,608**	**749**	**66**	**3,581**		

Note: 1. As of December 31. 2. State authorizes capital punishment for selected crimes other than murder. 3. Death penalty restored in 1994; no executions yet carried out. 4. Death penalty restored in 1995; no executions yet carried out. 5. Age defined by statute; effective age based on interpretation of U.S. Supreme Court decisions is 16.
Source: Bureau of Justice Statistics Bulletin, *Capital Punishment 2001* (2002),**www.ojp.usdoj.gov/bjs/ abstract/cp01.htm**

population and to the prison population. In the 1940s, for example, blacks made up less than 10 percent of the population, but more than 60 percent of prisoners executed were black. That's beginning to change, however. Since 1930, 51 percent of prisoners executed have been black, and since 1977, blacks constituted only 35 percent of executions.

Economy and Business

THE U.S. ECONOMY

▶GROSS NATIONAL PRODUCT AND GROSS DOMESTIC PRODUCT

The goal of an economic system is to transform resources into final products by business enterprises for consumption by society. This includes manufacturing goods such as cars, bread, furniture and so on, and providing services such as health care, education and motion pictures. The most commonly used measures associated with this goal are Gross National Product (G.N.P.) and Gross Domestic Product (G.D.P.). G.N.P. is the total national output of goods and services valued at market prices. G.N.P. in this broad context measures the output attributable to the factors of production—labor and property—supplied by a country's residents. G.N.P. differs from "national income" mainly in that G.N.P. includes allowances for depreciation and for indirect business taxes (sales and property taxes). G.D.P. is the measure of the output of production attributable to all factors of production (labor and property) physically located within a country. G.D.P., therefore, excludes net property income from abroad (such as the earnings of U.S. nationals working overseas), which is included in the G.N.P..

The word *final* serves to exclude intermediate goods sold to producers and used to make finished products eventually sold to consumers in the market. Auto parts such as batteries and tires are examples of intermediate goods and are included in G.N.P. or G.D.P. only through the price of a car when it is sold. G.N.P. and G.D.P., in terms of expenditure categories, comprise purchases of goods and services by consumers and government, gross private domestic investment (or business purchases), and net exports.

The assessment of G.N.P. and G.D.P. in current dollars is referred to as a nominal measure. Nominal measures may be misleading because G.N.P. and G.D.P. can appear to rise as average prices rise with inflation. An alternative method is to evaluate G.N.P. and G.D.P. by measuring the value of goods and services using constant prices for a given year; the government currently uses 1996 as the base year. Assessments based on constant prices are referred to as real measures because they indicate the change in quantity of output produced by the economy.

▶DEFINITIONS OF OUTPUT, INCOME, AND EXPENDITURE TERMS

Capital consumption adjustment Used for corporations, nonfarm sole proprietorships and partnerships, this is the difference between capital consumption claimed on income tax returns

G.D.P. in Current and Constant (1996) Dollars, 1960–2002 (billions)

Item	1960	1970	1980	1990	2000	2001	2002
CURRENT DOLLARS							
Gross domestic product (G.D.P.)	**$527.4**	**$1,039.7**	**$2,795.6**	**$5,803.2**	**$9,824.6**	**$10,082.2**	**$10,446.2**
Personal consumption expenditures	332.3	648.9	1,762.9	3,831.5	6,683.7	6,897.0	7,303.7
Durable goods	43.3	85.0	214.2	467.6	803.9	835.9	871.9
Nondurable goods	152.9	272.0	696.1	1,246.1	1,972.9	2,041.3	2,115.0
Services	136.1	292.0	852.7	2,117.8	3,906.9	4,109.9	4,316.8
Gross private domestic investment	78.9	152.4	477.9	861.7	1,755.4	1,586.0	1,593.2
Fixed investment	75.7	150.4	484.2	847.2	1,691.8	1,646.3	1,589.3
Change in private inventories	3.2	2.0	-6.3	14.5	63.6	-60.3	3.9
Net exports of goods and services	2.4	1.2	-14.9	-71.4	-365.5	-348.9	-423.6
Exports	25.3	57.0	278.9	557.2	1,101.1	1,034.1	1,014.9
Imports	22.8	55.8	293.8	628.6	1,466.6	1,383.0	1,438.5
Government consumption	113.8	237.1	569.7	1,181.4	1,751.0	1,858.0	1,972.9
Federal	65.9	116.4	245.3	508.4	589.2	628.1	693.7
National defense	55.2	90.9	169.6	374.9	374.9	399.9	447.4
State and local	47.9	120.7	324.4	673.0	1,161.8	1,229.9	1,279.2
CONSTANT (1996) DOLLARS							
Gross domestic product (G.D.P.)	**$2,376.7**	**$3,578.0**	**$4,900.9**	**$6,707.9**	**$9,191.4**	**$9,214.5**	**$9,439.9**
Personal consumption expenditures	1,510.8	2,317.5	3,193.0	4,474.5	6,223.9	6,337.2	6,576.0
Gross private domestic investment	272.8	436.2	655.3	907.3	1,762.9	1,574.6	1,589.6
Net exports of goods and services	—	—	—	-56.5	-398.8	-415.9	-488.5
Exports	87.5	159.3	334.8	575.7	1,137.2	1,076.1	1,058.8
Imports	108.0	223.1	324.8	632.2	1,536.0	1,492.0	1,547.4
Government consumption	661.3	931.1	1,020.9	1,387.3	1,582.5	1,640.4	1,712.8

Source: U.S. Bureau of Economic Analysis, *National Income and Product Accounts of the United States* (online edition: ww.bea.doc.gov).

and capital consumption allowances measured at straight-line depreciation, consistent service lives, and replacement cost. The tax return data are valued at historical costs and reflect changes over time in service lives and depreciation patterns as permitted by tax regulations.

Consumer expenditure Consumer expenditure statistics presented in the accompanying tables are arrived at from the findings of the Consumer Expenditure Survey program, designed to provide a continuous flow of data on the buying habits of American consumers, necessary for future revisions of the Consumer Price Index. One group of 5,000 consumers in 85 urban areas around the country keeps diaries of expenditures on small, frequently purchased items, such as food and beverages, tobacco, housekeeping supplies, nonprescription drugs, and personal care products and services. Another 5,000 consumers are interviewed quarterly for information about large expenditures, such as those for property, automobiles and major appliances, or expenditures occurring on a fairly regular basis, such as rent, utilities and insurance premiums.

Disposable personal income is that income after personal tax and nontax payments; this is the income available to persons for spending and saving. Personal tax and nontax payments are tax payments (except personal contributions for social insurance, net of refunds) by persons that are not chargeable to business expense, and also include certain personal payments to general government that are treated like taxes. Personal taxes include income, estate, gift, and personal property taxes and motor vehicle licenses. Nontax payments include passport fees, fines and penalties, donations, and tuitions and fees paid to schools and hospitals operated mainly by government.

Family income The term *family* refers to a group of two or more persons related by birth, marriage or adoption who reside together; all such persons are considered as members of one family. Family income refers to the sum of all income of the family members.

Gross domestic product (G.D.P.) see "Gross National Product and Gross Domestic Product," above.

Gross national product (G.N.P.) see "Gross National Product and Gross Domestic Product," above.

Gross state product (GSP) is the gross market value of the goods and services attributable to labor and property located in a state. It is the state counterpart of the nation's G.D.P..

Gross Domestic Product (G.D.P.), by Industry, in Current and Constant (1996) Dollars, 1987–2001 (billions)

Industry	Current dollars 1987	Current dollars 2000	Current dollars 2001	Constant (1996) dollars 1987	Constant (1996) dollars 2000	Constant (1996) dollars 2001
Gross Domestic Product (G.D.P.)	**$4,742.5**	**$9,824.6**	**$10,082.2**	**$6,113.3**	**$9,191.4**	**$9,214.5**
All Private industries	**4,081.4**	**8,606.9**	**8,800.8**	**5,212.0**	**8,157.8**	**8,189.4**
Agriculture, forestry, and fisheries	**88.9**	**134.3**	**140.6**	**110.3**	**166.7**	**163.9**
Farms	65.1	77.8	80.6	78.8	120.5	114.3
Agricultural services	23.8	56.5	60.1	31.8	47.6	49.1
Mining	**92.2**	**133.1**	**139.0**	**98.5**	**101.9**	**106.8**
Construction	**219.3**	**461.3**	**480.0**	**278.4**	**378.0**	**371.9**
Manufacturing	**888.6**	**1520.3**	**1423.0**	**1046.3**	**1,585.4**	**1,490.3**
Durable goods	516.8	886.4	812.8	541.0	1,044.3	990.1
Nondurable goods	371.8	633.9	610.2	512.0	558.0	518.3
Transportation and public utilities	**426.2**	**809.3**	**819.5**	**460.4**	**781.9**	**780.5**
Transportation	158.8	313.7	306.1	162.4	282.5	270.3
Communications	125.5	279.1	291.5	132.6	286.7	321.9
Electric, gas, and sanitary services	141.9	216.5	221.9	165.8	213.9	194.3
Wholesale trade	**308.9**	**696.8**	**680.7**	**353.5**	**750.2**	**748.7**
Retail trade	**434.5**	**887.3**	**931.8**	**512.1**	**909.2**	**951.2**
Finance, insurance, and real estate	**829.7**	**1,976.7**	**2,076.9**	**1,169.1**	**1,793.5**	**1,843.5**
Depository institutions	143.9	361.1	359.8	220.6	287.4	290.4
Nondepository institutions	17.9	69.5	88.8	22.4	79.0	91.9
Security and commodity brokers	41.3	150.8	175.0	41.5	216.760	245.1
Insurance carriers	43.6	182.4	170.1	109.8	146.0	141.2
Insurance agents, brokers, and service	30.4	61.6	66.5	66.3	51.9	53.5
Real estate	531.4	1,123.7	1,171.7	685.6	1,016.7	1,022.0
Services	**789.9**	**2,116.4**	**2,226.6**	**1,181.0**	**1,826.0**	**1,843.3**
Hotels and other lodging places	37.1	87.4	88.4	52.1	68.4	65.6
Personal services	31.0	59.3	62.7	44.0	52.9	53.3
Business services	145.0	534.4	544.1	187.1	460.1	459.4
Auto repair, services, and parking	40.8	94.9	99.5	57.1	84.8	87.5
Motion pictures	13.7	32.461	35.5	19.1	27.9	29.5
Amusement and recreation services	26.2	76.6	79.3	37.1	63.6	62.6
Health services	230.6	548.5	589.8	392.3	487.9	501.2
Legal services	61.8	134.4	145.6	97.8	116.8	120.2
Educational services	31.3	77.9	84.4	47.7	64.1	66.5
Social services	21.0	67.7	74.7	31.4	56.0	58.4
Other services	103.3	300.3	320.8	153.0	263.9	267.1
Government	**661.0**	**1,217.7**	**1,281.3**	**938.0**	**1,088.8**	**1,107.5**
Federal	258.9	389.5	396.2	369.5	355.0	350.9
State and local	402.1	828.2	885.1	569.2	733.6	756.1

Source: U.S. Bureau of Economic Analysis, *National Income and Product Accounts of the United States* (online edition: ww.bea.doc.gov).

Household income A household includes related family members and all unrelated persons, if any—such as lodgers, foster children, wards or employees—who share a house, an apartment or a single room when it is occupied or intended for occupancy as separate living quarters by that household; that is, when the members of the household do not live and eat with any other persons in the structure and there is direct access from the outside or through a common hall. Household income, therefore, is the sum of all income of household members. The *householder* (which replaced the term *head of household* beginning with the 1980 Current Population Survey) is the person in whose name the home is owned or rented. In the case of joint ownership, one person in each household is designated as the householder for statistical purposes.

Inventory valuation adjustment This represents the difference between the book value of inventories used in production and the cost of replacing them.

Mean vs. median income Mean (or average) income refers to the sum of all incomes of a group divided by the number of incomes in that group. Median income is the middle income when they are arranged in order of size—that is, there are the same number of incomes above and below the median. For example, consider incomes of $2,000, $3,000, $4,000, $15,000 and $95,000: the mean income is the sum of these divided by five, or $23,800; the median income is $4,000.

Money income This refers to income received (exclusive of certain money receipts such as capital gains) before payments for such things as personal income taxes, Social Security, union dues, and Medicare deductions. Money income does not include income in the form of noncash benefits such as food stamps, health benefits and subsidized housing; rent-free housing and goods produced and consumed on farms; or the use of business transportation and facilities, full or partial payments by business for retirement pro-

National Income, by Type of Income, 1960-2002 (billions of current dollars)

Type of Income	1960	1970	1980	1990	2000	2001	2002
National income	**$427.5**	**$837.5**	**$2,243.0**	**$4,642.1**	**$7,984.4**	**$8,122.0**	**$8,340.1**
Compensation of employees	**296.4**	**617.2**	**1,651.7**	**3,351.0**	**5,723.4**	**5,874.9**	**5,969.5**
Wages and salaries	272.8	551.5	1,377.4	2,754.6	4,836.3	4,950.6	4,996.4
Government	49.2	117.1	261.2	516.8	768.9	810.8	852.8
Other	223.7	434.3	1,116.2	2,237.9	4,067.4	4,139.8	4,143.6
Supplements to wages, salaries	23.6	65.7	274.3	596.4	887.1	924.3	973.1
Employer contributions for social insurance	9.3	23.8	88.9	206.5	342.9	353.9	362.5
Other labor income	14.4	41.9	185.4	390.0	544.2	570.4	610.6
Proprietors' income[1, 2]	**51.9**	**79.8**	**177.6**	**381.0**	**714.8**	**727.9**	**756.5**
Farm	11.4	14.3	13.1	31.1	22.6	19.0	12.9
Nonfarm	40.4	65.5	164.5	349.9	692.2	708.8	743.7
Rental income of persons[1]	**16.2**	**20.3**	**31.3**	**49.1**	**146.6**	**137.9**	**142.4**
Corporate profits[1, 2]	52.3	81.6	198.5	408.6	788.1	731.6	787.4
Corporate profits[2]	51.4	74.0	209.3	388.6	767.3	675.1	658.3
Profits before tax	51.5	80.6	251.4	401.5	782.3	670.2	665.2
Profits tax liability	22.7	34.4	84.8	140.6	259.4	199.3	213.3
Profits after tax	28.8	46.2	166.6	260.9	522.9	470.9	451.9
Dividends	13.4	24.3	64.1	165.6	376.1	409.6	434.3
Undistributed profits	15.5	21.9	102.6	95.3	146.8	61.2	17.6
Inventory valuation adjustment	-0.2	-6.6	-42.1	-12.9	-15.0	5.0	-6.9
Capital consumption adjustment	1.0	7.6	-10.8	19.9	20.8	56.5	129.1
Net interest	**10.7**	**38.4**	**183.9**	**452.4**	**611.5**	**649.8**	**684.2**

1. With capital consumption adjustment. 2. With inventory valuation adjustment.
Source: U.S. Bureau of Economic Analysis, *National Income and Product Accounts of the United States* (online edition: ww.bea.doc.gov).

Percent Distribution of National Income, by Type, 1960-2002

Type of income	1960	1970	1980	1990	2000	2001	2002
National income, total	**100.0%**	**100.0%**	**100.0%**	**100.0%**	**100.0%**	**100.0%**	**100.0%**
Compensation of employees	**69.3**	**73.7**	**73.6**	**72.2**	**71.6**	**73.1**	**71.5**
Wages and salaries	63.8	65.8	61.4	59.3	60.6	62.0	59.6
Supplements to wages, salaries	5.5	7.8	12.2	12.8	11.0	11.1	11.5
Proprietors' income[1]	**12.1**	**9.5**	**7.9**	**8.2**	**9.0**	**9.0**	**9.0**
Farm	2.7	1.7	0.6	0.7	0.4	0.3	.2
Non-farm	9.4	7.8	7.3	7.5	8.6	8.7	8.9
Rental income of persons[2]	**3.8**	**2.4**	**1.4**	**1.1**	**1.8**	**1.7**	**1.7**
Corporate profits[1]	**12.2**	**9.7**	**8.8**	**8.8**	**11.0**	**9.3**	**9.4**
Profits before tax	12.0	9.6	11.2	8.6	10.6	8.5	7.9
Profits after tax	6.7	5.5	7.4	5.6	7.2	5.9	5.4
Net interest	**2.5**	**4.6**	**8.2**	**9.8**	**6.7**	**6.8**	**8.2**

1. With inventory valuation and capital consumption adjustments (not shown separately). 2. With capital consumption adjustment (not shown separately). **Source:** U.S. Bureau of the Census, based on data from U.S. Bureau of Economic Analysis, *National Income and Product Accounts of the United States* (online edition: ww.bea.doc.gov).

grams, medical and educational expenses, and so on. These elements should be considered when comparing income levels. None of the aggregate income concepts (G.N.P., national income, or personal income) is exactly comparable with money income, although personal income is the closest. **National income,** the aggregate of labor and property earnings derived from the current production of goods and services, is the sum of employee compensation, proprietors' income, rental income, corporate profits and net interest. It measures the total factor costs of the goods and services produced by the economy. Income is measured before deduction of taxes.

Personal income is the current income received by persons from all sources minus their personal contributions for social insurance. *Persons* include individuals (including owners of unincorporated firms), nonprofit institutions serving individuals, private trust funds and private noninsured welfare funds. Personal income includes transfers (payments not resulting from current production) from government and business, such as Social Security benefits and public assistance, but ex-

Per Capita Personal Income by State, 1970–2002

State	Personal income (rank)				
	1970	1980	1990	2000	2002[1]
Alabama	$2,960 (49)	$7,720 (48)	$15,225 (43)	$23,521 (44)	25,128 (44)
Alaska	5,071 (2)	13,863 (1)	21,047 (10)	29,642 (15)	32,151 (15)
Arizona	3,810 (27)	9,328 (31)	16,542 (36)	24,988 (38)	26,183 (39)
Arkansas	2,841 (50)	7,457 (50)	14,032 (50)	21,995 (48)	23,512 (50)
California	4,777 (8)	11,792 (4)	21,287 (9)	32,149 (9)	32,996 (11)
Colorado	4,058 (17)	10,710 (14)	19,224 (19)	32,434 (8)	33,276 (10)
Connecticut	5,077 (1)	12,246 (3)	26,375 (1)	40,702 (1)	42,706 (1)
Delaware	4,611 (9)	10,614 (15)	21,696 (7)	31,012 (14)	32,779 (13)
District of Columbia	5,013 (3)	12,487 (2)	25,628 (2)	38,838 (2)	42,120 (2)
Florida	3,980 (20)	9,894 (22)	19,106 (20)	27,764 (24)	29,596 (24)
Georgia	3,395 (38)	8,395 (38)	17,378 (29)	27,794 (23)	28,821 (29)
Hawaii	4,995 (4)	10,860 (11)	21,333 (8)	27,851 (22)	30,001 (21)
Idaho	3,503 (35)	8,569 (37)	15,317 (42)	23,727 (42)	25,057 (45)
Illinois	4,587 (10)	10,986 (9)	20,494 (12)	31,856 (11)	33,404 (9)
Indiana	3,789 (30)	9,307 (32)	17,174 (31)	26,933 (31)	28,240 (33)
Iowa	3,839 (25)	9,505 (28)	16,959 (34)	26,431 (34)	28,280 (32)
Kansas	3,794 (29)	9,877 (23)	17,988 (23)	27,374 (28)	29,141 (27)
Kentucky	3,150 (44)	8,079 (42)	15,088 (44)	24,085 (40)	25,579 (40)
Louisiana	3,090 (47)	8,761 (35)	14,761 (46)	23,090 (46)	25,446 (42)
Maine	3,409 (37)	8,259 (39)	17,167 (32)	25,380 (37)	27,744 (34)
Maryland	4,519 (12)	10,889 (10)	22,483 (6)	33,482 (6)	36,298 (5)
Massachusetts	4,547 (11)	10,745 (13)	23,203 (4)	37,704 (3)	39,244 (4)
Michigan	4,145 (14)	10,273 (16)	18,710 (21)	29,127 (18)	30,296 (19)
Minnesota	4,012 (19)	10,149 (17)	19,374 (17)	31,935 (10)	34,071 (8)
Mississippi	2,608 (51)	6,915 (51)	12,710 (51)	20,900 (51)	22,372 (51)
Missouri	3,825 (26)	9,341 (30)	17,656 (26)	27,206 (30)	28,936 (28)
Montana	3,554 (34)	8,825 (34)	15,042 (45)	22,518 (47)	25,020 (46)
Nebraska	3,799 (28)	9,096 (33)	17,624 (27)	27,630 (27)	29,771 (23)
Nevada	4,889 (5)	11,577 (6)	20,124 (13)	29,506 (16)	30,180 (20)
New Hampshire	3,910 (23)	9,854 (26)	20,671 (11)	33,169 (7)	34,334 (7)
New Jersey	4,835 (7)	11,703 (5)	24,925 (3)	37,118 (4)	39,453 (3)
New Mexico	3,163 (43)	8,222 (40)	14,441 (47)	21,931 (49)	23,941 (48)
New York	4,866 (6)	11,003 (8)	23,132 (5)	34,689 (5)	36,043 (6)
North Carolina	3,255 (40)	8,067 (43)	16,664 (35)	26,882 (32)	27,711 (35)
North Dakota	3,145 (45)	7,825 (47)	15,324 (41)	24,708 (39)	26,982 (37)
Ohio	4,052 (18)	9,872 (25)	18,125 (22)	27,977 (21)	29,405 (26)
Oklahoma	3,456 (36)	9,444 (29)	15,584 (38)	23,650 (43)	25,575 (41)
Oregon	3,913 (21)	9,938 (19)	17,437 (28)	27,660 (26)	28,731 (30)
Pennsylvania	4,061 (16)	9,989 (18)	19,365 (18)	29,504 (17)	31,727 (16)
Rhode Island	4,086 (15)	9,646 (27)	19,691 (15)	29,113 (19)	31,319 (17)
South Carolina	3,027 (48)	7,624 (49)	15,421 (40)	24,000 (41)	25,400 (43)
South Dakota	3,215 (41)	7,866 (46)	15,538 (39)	25,958 (35)	26,894 (38)
Tennessee	3,168 (42)	8,123 (41)	16,295 (37)	25,946 (36)	27,671 (36)
Texas	3,651 (32)	9,922 (20)	17,219 (30)	27,752 (25)	28,551 (31)
Utah	3,324 (39)	8,003 (45)	14,204 (48)	23,436 (45)	24,306 (47)
Vermont	3,616 (33)	8,583 (36)	17,691 (25)	26,848 (33)	29,567 (25)
Virginia	3,771 (31)	9,918 (21)	19,996 (14)	31,120 (13)	32,922 (12)
Washington	4,188 (13)	10,755 (12)	19,583 (16)	31,230 (12)	32,677 (14)
West Virginia	3,098 (46)	8,041 (44)	14,177 (49)	21,738 (50)	23,688 (49)
Wisconsin	3,912 (22)	9,874 (24)	17,720 (24)	28,100 (20)	29,923 (22)
Wyoming	3,841 (24)	11,414 (7)	17,061 (33)	27,372 (29)	30,578 (18)
U.S. average	**$4,072**	**$10,029**	**$19,142**	**$29,469**	**$30,941**

1. Preliminary, subject to review when additional numbers from the 2000 Census become available..
Source: Bureau of Economic Analysis, Survey of Current Business, (monthly). www.bea.doc.gov.

cludes transfers among persons. Also included are certain nonmonetary types of income: estimated net rental value to owner-occupants of their homes, the value of services furnished without payment by financial intermediaries, and food and fuel produced and consumed on farms.

Poverty level is an estimate of the income necessary to purchase what society defines as a minimally acceptable standard of living. Families and unrelated individuals are classified as being above or below the poverty level according to their money income as a group and the number of peo-

Per Capita Personal Income by Metropolitan Area, 1970–2001

Metropolitan Statistical Area (ranked by 2001 income)	1970	1980	1990	2000	2001
United States	**$4,095**	**$10,183**	**$19,572**	**$29,760**	**$30,413**
Metropolitan portion	4,347	10,785	20,786	31,680	32,336
Nonmetropolitan portion	3,158	7,997	14,764	21,901	22,472
Highest per capita income, 2001					
1. San Francisco, Calif.[1]	6,206	15,833	31,494	58,702	57,714
2. San Jose, Calif.[1]	4,983	13,614	26,174	55,677	51,579
3. New Haven-Bridgeport-Stamford-Danbury-Waterbury, Conn.[1]	5,442	13,252	29,119	47,286	48,453
4. Bergen-Passaic, N.J.[1]	5,483	13,295	28,386	42,799	43,856
5. West Palm Beach-Boca Raton, Fla.	4,900	13,144	30,146	41,945	43,626
6. Middlesex-Somerset-Hunterdon, N.J.[1]	4,910	12,767	26,929	43,051	43,292
7. Newark, N.J. [1]	5,140	12,145	26,241	41,291	42,550
8. Trenton, N.J.[1]	4,858	12,136	26,342	40,911	42,317
9. Washington, D.C.-Md.-Va.-W.Va.[1]	5,175	12,884	26,790	40,536	41,754
10. Nassau-Suffolk, N.Y.[1]	5,305	12,938	27,782	40,978	41,559
11. Naples, Fla.	5,368	12,435	27,871	40,772	41,269
12. Seattle-Bellevue-Everett, Wash.[1]	4,686	12,686	24,018	41,025	41,229
13. Boulder-Longmont, Colo.[1]	4,284	11,603	22,186	40,447	40,840
14. New York, N.Y.[1]	5,391	11,842	25,794	39,501	40,450
15. Oakland, Calif.[1]	4,985	12,783	24,446	40,086	39,963
16. Boston-Worcester-Lawrence-Lowell-Brockton, Mass.-N.H.	4,515	10,806	23,545	39,125	39,873
17. Denver, Colo.[1]	4,561	12,110	22,026	37,924	38,513
18. Minneapolis-St. Paul, Minn.-Wisc.	4,666	11,840	22,853	37,152	38,131
19. Hartford, Conn.	4,924	12,033	25,358	36,915	37,819
20. Sarasota-Bradenton, Fla.	4,428	11,737	24,710	36,292	37,212
21. Reno, Nev.	5,327	13,418	23,595	35,781	36,988
22. Anchorage, Alaska	6,102	16,154	26,231	35,307	36,949
23. Santa Cruz-Watsonville, Calif. [1]	4,395	11,457	22,043	37,866	36,865
24. Orange County, Calif. [1]	4,952	13,453	25,606	35,446	36,647
25. Chicago, Ill.[1]	5,000	12,053	22,985	35,907	36,624
Lowest per capita income, 2001	**1970**	**1980**	**1990**	**2000**	**2001**
1. McAllen-Edinburg-Mission, Texas	$1,952	$5,365	$9,325	$13,238	$13,788
2. Brownsville-Harlingen-San Benito, Texas	2,178	5,765	9,946	14,954	15,334
3. Laredo, Texas	2,267	5,483	9,443	15,011	15,508
4. Yuma, Ariz.	3,432	8,227	13,446	15,819	16,839
5. Las Cruces, N.Mex.	2,985	6,906	12,660	17,090	17,984
6. Merced, Calif.	3,806	9,522	15,154	18,268	18,461
7. Auburn-Opelika, Ala.	2,685	7,408	14,207	18,714	18,923
8. El Paso, Texas	2,990	6,556	12,404	18,398	19,186
9. Provo-Orem, Utah	2,714	6,606	12,031	19,046	19,271
10. Visalia-Tulare-Porterville, Calif.	3,623	9,424	14,841	19,539	20,166
11. Pine Bluff, Ark.	2,826	7,712	14,035	19,745	20,387
12. Sumter, S.C.	2,638	6,476	13,177	20,519	21,009
13. Bakersfield, Calif.	3,933	11,080	16,566	20,543	21,021
14. Bryan-College Station, Texas	2,936	7,174	13,204	20,429	21,028
15. Danville, Va.	2,942	8,013	14,701	21,074	21,280
16. Fresno, Calif.	3,906	10,807	16,693	20,878	21,463
17. Cumberland, Md.-W.Va.	3,306	8,159	14,679	20,756	21,694
18. Goldsboro, N.C.	3,071	7,158	14,195	21,319	21,738
19. Pocatello, Idaho	3,326	8,723	14,161	21,081	21,780
20. Huntington-Ashland, W.Va.-Ky.-Ohio	3,158	8,313	14,747	21,021	21,793
21. Gadsden, Ala.	2,934	8,015	14,653	21,400	21,865
22. Jamestown, N.Y.	3,666	8,545	15,193	21,419	21,897
23. Yuba City, Calif.	3,940	9,667	15,395	22,130	21,983
24. Anniston, Ala.	2,808	7,650	14,870	21,486	22,035
25. Florence, Ala.	3,015	7,940	15,828	21,615	22,037

Note: in current dollars. 1. Primary Metropolitan Statistical Area.
Source: U.S. Bureau of Economic Analysis, Survey of Current Business, online edition. www.bea.doc.gov.

ple in the group (e.g. in 2002, a family of four with income less than $18,100 lived below the poverty level). Classification is based on the poverty index originated by the Social Security Administration in 1964 and revised in 1969 and 1980. The poverty index is based solely on money income and does not reflect the fact that many low-income persons receive noncash benefits such as food stamps, Medicaid and public housing. The poverty thresholds are updated every year to reflect changes in the Consumer Price Index.

Private domestic investment This consists of (1) non-residential fixed investment, i.e., firms' purchases of capital goods such as plants and equipment; (2) residential fixed investment (the building of single- and multi-family housing units); and (3) the change in business inventories, which are stocks on hand of raw materials and finished goods.

Per Capita Personal Income by County, 2001

Rank/County	Per capita income 2001	Percent of national average
Highest per capita income		
1. New York, New York	$92,984	305.7%
2. Pitkin, Colorado	67,547	222.1
3. Loving, Texas	64,636	212.5
4. Marin, California	63,083	207.4
5. Fairfield, Connecticut	60,839	200.0
6. Morris, New Jersey	58,151	191.2
7. San Mateo, California	57,906	190.4
8. Westchester, New York	56,691	186.4
9. Teton, Wyoming	56,417	185.5
10. San Francisco, California	55,816	183.5
11. Somerset, New Jersey	55,580	182.8
12. Hunterdon, New Jersey	53,815	176.9
13. Fairfax-Fairfax City-Falls Church, Virginia	53,721	176.6
14. Bergen, New Jersey	51,900	170.7
15. Santa Clara, California	51,579	169.6
16. Arlington, Virginia	51,221	168.4
17. Montgomery, Maryland	50,919	167.4
18. Alexandria City, Virginia	49,553	162.9
19. Chester, Pennsylvania	49,233	161.9
20. Lake, Illinois	48,794	160.4
21. Middlesex, Massachusetts	47,930	157.6
22. Montgomery, Pennsylvania	47,522	156.3
23. Nassau, New York	47,431	156.0
24. Norfolk, Massachusetts	47,302	155.5
25. Ozaukee, Wisconsin	47,122	154.9
Lowest per capita income		
1. Loup, Nebraska	$6,235	20.5%
2. Blaine, Nebraska	8,372	27.5
3. Arthur, Nebraska	8,852	29.1
4. Sherman, Oregon	8,928	29.4
5. Ziebach, South Dakota	9,610	31.6
6. Starr, Texas	9,769	32.1
7. Grant, Nebraska	10,164	33.4
8. McPherson, Nebraska	10,407	34.2
9. Sioux, Nebraska	10,944	36.0
10. Issaquena, Mississippi	11,249	37.0
11. Jefferson, Mississippi	11,267	37.0
12. Hooker, Nebraska	11,714	38.5
13. Zavala, Texas	12,004	39.5
14. Maverick, Texas	12,258	40.3
15. Todd, South Dakota	12,347	40.6
16. Union, Florida	12,385	40.7
17. Elliott, Kentucky	12,557	41.3
18. Echols, Georgia	12,620	41.5
19. Gilliam, Oregon	12,750	41.9
20. Willacy, Texas	12,760	42.0
21. Hoke, North Carolina	13,096	43.1
22. San Juan, Utah	13,108	43.1
23. Zapata, Texas	13,120	43.1
24. Greene, Mississippi	13,133	43.2
25. Long, Georgia	13,278	43.7

Source: U.S. Bureau of Economic Analysis, *Survey of Current Business* (online edition: www.bea.doc.gov).

Percent of Persons Below Poverty Level, by State, 1980–2001

State	1980	1990	2000	2001
United States	13.0%	13.5%	11.3%	11.7%
Alabama	21.2	19.2	13.3	15.9
Alaska	9.6	11.4	7.6	8.5
Arizona	12.8	13.7	11.7	14.6
Arkansas	21.5	19.6	16.5	17.8
California	11.0	13.9	12.7	12.6
Colorado	8.6	13.7	9.8	8.7
Connecticut	8.3	6.0	7.7	7.3
Delaware	11.8	6.9	8.4	6.7
District of Columbia	20.9	21.1	15.2	18.2
Florida	16.7	14.4	11.0	12.7
Georgia	13.9	15.8	12.1	12.9
Hawaii	8.5	11.0	8.9	11.4
Idaho	14.7	14.9	12.5	11.5
Illinois	12.3	13.7	10.7	10.1
Indiana	11.8	13.0	8.5	8.5
Iowa	10.8	10.4	8.3	7.4
Kansas	9.4	10.3	8.0	10.1
Kentucky	19.3	17.3	12.6	12.6
Louisiana	20.3	23.6	17.2	16.2
Maine	14.6	13.1	10.1	10.3
Maryland	9.5	9.9	7.4	7.2
Massachusetts	9.5	10.7	9.8	8.9
Michigan	12.9	14.3	9.9	9.4
Minnesota	8.7	12.0	5.7	7.4
Mississippi	24.3	25.7	14.9	19.3
Missouri	13.0	13.4	9.2	9.7
Montana	13.2	16.3	14.1	13.3
Nebraska	13.0	10.3	8.6	9.4
Nevada	8.3	9.8	8.8	7.1
New Hampshire	7.0	6.3	4.5	6.5
New Jersey	9.0	9.2	7.3	8.1
New Mexico	20.6	20.9	17.5	18.0
New York	13.8	14.3	13.9	14.2
North Carolina	15.0	13.0	12.5	12.5
North Dakota	15.5	13.7	10.4	13.8
Ohio	9.8	11.5	10.0	10.5
Oklahoma	13.9	15.6	14.9	15.1
Oregon	11.5	9.2	10.9	11.8
Pennsylvania	9.8	11.0	8.6	9.6
Rhode Island	10.7	7.5	10.2	9.6
South Carolina	16.8	16.2	11.1	15.1
South Dakota	18.8	13.3	10.7	8.4
Tennessee	19.6	16.9	13.5	14.1
Texas	15.7	15.9	15.5	14.9
Utah	10.0	8.2	7.6	10.5
Vermont	12.0	10.9	10.0	9.7
Virginia	12.4	11.1	8.3	8.0
Washington	12.7	8.9	10.8	10.7
West Virginia	15.2	18.1	14.7	16.4
Wisconsin	8.5	9.3	9.3	7.9
Wyoming	10.4	11.0	10.8	8.7

Source: U.S. Bureau of the Census, *Poverty in The United States, 2001* (2002).

Per Capita Money Income, by Race and Hispanic Origin, 1970-2001

Year	Current dollars				Constant (2001) dollars			
	All races	White	Black	Hispanic[1]	All races	White	Black	Hispanic[1]
1970	$3,177	$3,354	$1,869	N.A.	$12,543	$13,241	$7,379	N.A.
1975	4,818	5,072	2,972	$2,847	13,972	14,708	8,618	$8,256
1980	7,787	8,233	4,804	4,865	15,844	16,752	9,775	9,899
1985	11,013	11,671	6,840	6,613	17,280	18,313	10,733	10,376
1990	14,387	15,265	9,017	8,424	18,894	20,047	11,842	11,063
1995	17,227	18,304	10,982	9,300	19,871	21,113	12,667	10,727
2000	22,346	23,582	14,796	12,651	22,970	24,240	15,209	13,004
2001	22,851	24,127	14,953	13,003	22,851	24,127	14,953	13,003

Note: N.A. = Not available. 1. Hispanic persons may be of any race.
Source: U.S. Bureau of the Census, Current Population Survey. **www.census.gov/hhes/income/histinc.**

Median Income of Families by Race and Hispanic Origin, 2001

Characteristic	Number of families ('000s)				Median family income			
	All races[1]	White	Black	Hispanic[2]	All races[1]	White	Black	Hispanic[2]
All families	**74,340**	**61,647**	**8,847**	**8,516**	**$51,407**	**$54,067**	**$33,598**	**$34,490**
Type of family								
Married-couple families	56,755	49,612	4,234	5,778	60,335	61,000	51,514	40,614
Wife in paid labor force	34,917	30,230	2,914	3,250	70,834	71,687	60,693	50,437
Wife not in paid labor force	21,838	19,382	1,320	2,528	40,782	41,209	29,309	28,682
Male Householder[3]	4,440	3,394	775	817	36,590	37,488	31,512	31,635
Female Householder[3]	13,146	8,641	3,838	1,922	25,745	28,091	20,894	20,547
Number of earners								
No earners	10,120	8,491	1,264	825	21,958	24,089	10,404	11,657
One earner	22,518	17,685	3,583	2,994	34,517	36,878	23,739	23,041
Two earners	32,886	28,008	3,183	3,445	66,151	67,400	55,080	44,719
Three earners	6,702	5,639	674	892	78,290	79,731	70,098	57,946
Four or more earners	2,115	1,824	143	361	95,082	95,354	90,723	78,171

Note: 1. Includes other races not shown separately. 2. Hispanic persons may be of any race. 3. Spouse absent. **Source:** U.S. Bureau of the Census, Current Population Reports: *Money Income in the United States 2001*. www.census.gov/hhes/income/histinc/incfamdet.html

Persons Below Poverty Level, by Race, 1960–2001

Year	Number below poverty level (millions)					Percent below poverty level				
	All races[1]	White	Black	Hispanic[2]	Asian	All races[1]	White	Black	Hispanic[2]	Asian
1960	39.9	28.3	N.A.	N.A.	N.A.	22.2%	17.8%	N.A.	N.A.	N.A.
1970	25.4	17.5	7.5	N.A.	N.A.	12.6	9.9	33.5%	N.A.	N.A.
1980	29.3	19.7	8.6	3.5	N.A.	13.0	10.2	32.5	25.7%	N.A.
1990	33.6	22.3	9.8	6.0	0.9	13.5	10.7	31.9	28.1	12.2%
1995	36.4	24.4	9.9	8.6	1.4	13.8	11.2	29.3	30.3	14.6
1996	36.5	24.6	9.7	8.7	1.5	13.7	11.2	28.4	29.4	14.5
1997	35.6	24.4	9.1	8.3	1.4	13.3	11.0	26.5	27.1	14.0
1998	34.5	23.5	9.1	8.1	1.3	12.7	10.5	26.1	25.6	12.5
1999	32.3	21.9	8.4	7.4	1.2	11.8	9.8	23.6	22.8	10.7
2000	31.6	21.6	8.0	7.7	1.3	11.3	9.5	22.5	21.5	9.9
2001	32.9	22.7	8.1	8.0	1.3	11.7	9.9	22.7	21.4	10.2

1. Includes other races not shown separately. 2. People of Hispanic origin may be of any race.
Source: U.S. Bureau of the Census, *Poverty in The United States, 2001* (2002).

▶ECONOMIC INDICATORS

All market economies regularly go through cycles of recession—when output declines and unemployment rises—and expansion—when output and employment rise. These "business cycles" are one of the most important factors determining the socioeconomic conditions in any society. Although economists still have very little idea what actually causes recessions and what leads the economy to begin expanding again, they have had some success in predicting business cycles. Economic forecasting is the science of making these predictions. It is especially useful to be able to predict recessions sufficiently far in advance so that governments can take actions to stimulate the economy and reduce the severity of these downturns.

Economic indicators track developments in areas of the economy that are thought to be crucial to the future health of the economy, just as a barometer measures changes in air pressure that are crucial to changes in the weather. The development of economic indicators began around World War I but suffered a setback when the early forecasters failed to predict the Great Depression in 1929. During the depression the government asked a private research group, the National Bureau of Economic Research, to develop a set of measures that would help predict changes in business cycles. The group devised a list of measures based on analyses of previous business cycles. Since then, the list has been revised several times to reflect changes in the way the economy is structured.

Leading Indicators

There are currently 10 leading economic indicators, representing a broad spectrum of economic activity. These indicators are said to "lead" because their numbers change months in advance of a change in the general level of economic activity. They are as follows:

1. Average length of workweek of production workers in manufacturing.

2. Average weekly state unemployment insurance claims.

3. New orders for consumer goods and materials (in constant dollars).

4. Vendor performance (percent of companies receiving slower deliveries from suppliers).

5. Contracts and orders for plant and equipment (in constant dollars).

6. Index of new private housing units authorized by local building permits.

7. Index of stock prices, i.e., of 500 common stocks (Standard and Poor's 500).

8. Money supply-M2 in constant dollars. (See "Money and Banking" section.)

9. Interest rate spread.

10. Index of consumer expectations. (See "Note" below.)

This composite of leading economic indicators is published by the U.S. Department of Commerce, Bureau of Economic Analysis. The composite has a noteworthy record: since 1948 it has accurately predicted every downturn and upswing in the economy. One major reason for this success is that many of the indicators represent commitments to economic activity in the coming months. The average lead for the index is 9.5 months at business cycle peaks (indicating the end of a business cycle expansion and the beginning of a recession) and 4.5 months at business cycle troughs (indicating the end of a business cycle recession and the beginning of an expansion).

Coincident and Lagging Indicators

In addition to the leading economic indicators, two other sets of measures are used to track business cycles and the state of the economy. One set includes the coincident indicators, which measure how well the economy is doing at that moment (roughly, within three months of the business cycle turning points). These include the number of employees on nonagricultural payrolls; manufacturing and trade sales (in constant dollars); index of industrial production; and personal income less transfer payments (in constant dollars). The second set includes lagging economic indicators. These are the ratio of consumer installment credit outstanding to personal income; commercial and industrial loans outstanding (in constant dollars); the average prime interest rate charged by banks; the ratio of manufacturing and trade inventories to sales (in constant dollars); the average duration of unemployment in weeks (inverted); the change in index of labor cost per unit of output in manufacturing; and the change in the Consumer Price Index for services per unit labor costs. At business cycle peaks, the average lag of the index is 4.5 months, and at business cycle troughs 8.5 months. It seems reasonable to wonder what use there is for an indicator that tells you where you have already been. But in fact that is exactly their use: they provide another way of measuring whether turning points in the business cycle truly have occurred.

The government produces a wide variety of economic indicators in addition to those dis-

Composite Index of Economic Indicators, 1960–2003 (1996=100)

Year	Leading indicators	Coincident indicators	Lagging indicators
1960	72.7	37.2	82.2
1965	80.6	43.4	87.2
1970	83.1	53.1	96.9
1975	81.9	58.4	99.8
1980	88.0	70.8	100.4
1985	94.7	77.1	98.6
1990	97.8	88.1	101.7
1995	99.4	96.5	97.4
2000	106.4	114.2	103.4
2001	109.4	116.6	107.7
2002	112.2	115.4	102.6
2003	111.2	115.5	99.2

Note: As of January of each year.
Source: The Conference Board. www.tcb-indicators.org.

Employment Cost Index (ECI) 1985-2003 (1989=100)

Group	Index 1985	1995	2000	2002	2003	Percent Change 1984-85	2002-03
Civilian workers	84.3	124.8	146.5	158.4	164.5	4.7	3.9
White collar	83.0	125.5	148.4	160.5	166.7	5.3	3.9
Blue collar	86.5	123.6	142.7	153.7	159.8	3.8	4.0
Service occupations	84.5	125.0	146.0	158.4	164.1	4.7	3.6
Manufacturing	86.3	126.2	146.0	156.6	164.0	5.0	4.7
Non-manufacturing	83.5	124.4	146.6	158.7	164.5	4.6	3.7
Private Industry Workers	85.0	124.5	146.8	158.9	165.0	4.3	3.8
State & Local Government	81.0	126.4	145.5	156.1	162.6	6.3	4.1

Note: Figures are as of March of each year and are not seasonally adjusted. Excludes farm, household, and federal government workers.
Source: U.S. Bureau of Labor Statistics, *News, Employment Cost Index,* (quarterly)

cussed here for use in tracking more specific aspects of the economy, such as labor or capital markets.

The Employment Cost Index (ECI)

The ECI measures the *rate of change* in total employee compensation (wages, salaries, employer cost for employee benefits) in nonfarm private industry and in state and local governments. Provided quarterly by the Bureau of Labor Statistics, the ECI has become one of the most closely watched indices because any significant rise could signal an inflationary trend. The ECI grew annually by 4 to 5 percent in the late 1980s, fell below 3 percent in the 1990s, and has rebounded to 4 percent and higher since 2000.

▶PRICES AND INFLATION

Inflation

Inflation is a sustained rise in the general price level in the economy. It affects the level and timing of spending in the economy since it indicates the extent to which income will cover the purchase of a consumer's basket of goods (food, clothes, entertainment, medical services, housing, gasoline, and so on). For example, if a consumer is considering purchasing a television and inflation is high (that is, prices are rising rapidly), he or she will buy the television as soon as possible since savings may not cover the cost a month or a year from now. Inflation is closely watched to determine wage contracts and Social Security benefits that contain cost-of-living adjustment clauses. If wage contracts cover a long period of time and inflation is rapid, consumers' standard of living will fall in the interim before new contracts can be negotiated. Savings will tend to fall as consumers store their wealth in the form of commodities.

The cause of inflation is often described as "too much money chasing too few goods," brought about by the money supply rising rapidly or production of goods falling behind demand for them. Inflation may be due to (1) cost-push factors—that is, if the cost of inputs such as labor, raw materials, or other intermediate goods rises, the cost of the final product also rises; or (2) demand-pull factors—that is, if the demand for goods and services rises above the full employment level, wages rise as employers compete for labor, and the general price level of goods and services rises.

Consumer Price Index

Often referred to as the "cost of living index," the Consumer Price Index is the most commonly used measure of inflation. The index measures the average change in prices relative to an arbitrary base year of a common bundle of goods and services bought by the average consumer on a regular basis. The Bureau of Labor Statistics publishes two CPI's: (1) CPI-U for All Urban Consumers, which includes wage earners and clerical workers; professional, managerial, and technical workers; the self-employed; short-term workers; the unemployed; retirees and others not in the labor force—altogether covering 80 percent of the population—and (2) CPI-W for Urban Wage Earners and Clerical Workers, covering 32 percent of the population. Prices (including direct taxes) are collected from over 57,000 housing units and 19,000 establishments in 85 areas across the country. In calculating the index number, based on 100,000 price quotes a month, larger weights are assigned to goods that represent larger proportions of consumer expenditure. The index costs $26 million a year to produce and requires 40 economists and analysts tracking price changes in 365 categories.

Producer Price Index

The Producer Price Index measures average changes in prices received by producers of all commodities, at all stages of processing, produced in the United States. Prices used in constructing the index are collected from sellers and generally apply to the first significant large-volume commercial transaction for each commodity—i.e., the manufacturer's or other producer's selling price or the selling price on an organized exchange or at a central market. The weights used in the index represent the total net selling value of commodities produced or processed in the country. Values are f.o.b. (free on board) at the production point and are exclusive of excise taxes.

Purchasing Power of the Dollar, 1950–2001

Year	Annual average as measured by: Producer prices	Consumer Prices
1950	$3.546	$4.151
1955	3.279	3.732
1960	2.994	3.373
1965	2.933	3.166
1970	2.545	2.574
1975	1.718	1.859
1980	1.136	1.215
1985	0.955	0.928
1990	0.839	0.766
1991	0.822	0.734
1992	0.812	0.713
1993	0.802	0.692
1994	0.797	0.675
1995	0.782	0.656
1996	0.762	0.638
1997	0.759	0.623
1998	0.766	0.614
1999	0.752	0.600
2000	0.725	0.581
2001	0.711	N.A.

Source: U.S. Bureau of Economic Analysis, *Survey of Current Business* (monthly).

Consumer Price Index (CPI-U) 1915–2002 (1982–84=100)

Year	CPI-U	Year	CPI-U	Year	CPI-U
1915	10.1	1965	31.5	1995	152.4
1920	20.0	1970	38.8	1996	156.9
1925	17.5	1975	53.8	1997	160.5
1930	16.7	1980	82.4	1998	163.0
1935	13.7	1985	107.6	1999	166.6
1940	14.0	1986	109.6	2000	172.2
1945	18.0	1987	113.6	2001	177.1
1950	24.1	1988	118.3	2002	179.9
1955	26.8	1989	124.0		
1960	29.6	1990	130.7		

Source: U.S. Bureau of the Census, *Current Population Report*

Consumer Price Indexes for Selected Metropolitan Statistical Areas, 2002 (1982–84 = 100)

Area	All items	Food and beverages	Food	Housing	Fuel and utilities	Apparel	Transportation	Medical care
U.S. city average	**179.9**	**176.8**	**176.2**	**180.3**	**143.6**	**124.0**	**152.9**	**285.6**
Anchorage, Alaska	158.2	157.9	158.3	143.5	162.5	126.7	151.5	N.A.
Atlanta, Ga.	178.2	181.9	187.5	179.7	165.9	131.3	139.7	291.0
Boston, Mass.	196.5	184.8	185.5	200.3	134.3	138.0	149.9	383.4
Chicago-Gary Ill.-Ind.	181.2	178.1	177.0	186.7	124.5	99.8	148.5	280.8
Cincinnati-Hamilton, Ohio-Ky.-Ind.	170.0	162.7	161.0	162.2	127.4	119.7	150.0	281.2
Cleveland-Akron-Lorain, Ohio	173.3	180.1	182.5	172.5	135.2	119.7	152.6	245.6
Dallas-Ft. Worth, Tex.	172.7	176.5	173.3	162.5	149.9	136.2	153.9	267.6
Denver-Boulder-Greely, Colo.	184.8	184.4	174.4	184.4	139.7	85.0	190.9	332.1
Detroit-Ann Arbor-Flint, Mich.	178.9	171.9	171.4	170.8	144.1	125.2	168.3	283.8
Honolulu, Hawaii	180.3	171.9	171.6	181.2	142.6	102.6	170.9	N.A.
Houston-Galveston-Brazoria, Tex.	159.2	164.2	163.7	145.3	114.9	135.9	141.5	265.3
Kansas City, Mo.-Kans.	174.0	174.5	175.8	169.4	147.3	113.7	147.8	262.0
Los Angeles-Anaheim-Riverside, Calif.	182.2	184.9	183.1	188.1	187.0	109.0	154.5	281.2
Miami-Ft. Lauderdale, Fla.	175.5	183.9	184.3	167.8	122.7	151.7	157.5	263.4
Milwaukee, Wis.	174.0	176.0	176.9	174.6	129.3	110.0	147.7	283.2
Minneapolis-St. Paul, Minn.-Wis.	179.6	188.7	184.9	167.8	130.6	131.1	162.1	280.1
New York-Northern New Jersey-Long Island, N.Y.-N.J.-Conn.	191.9	180.3	179.0	199.9	122.0	115.4	159.8	299.7
Philadelphia-Wilmington-Trenton, Pa.-N.J.-Del.-Md.	184.9	171.8	171.3	188.1	142.6	100.7	156.7	326.0
Phoenix-Mesa, Ariz.[1]	101.2	101.7	101.6	101.5	108.9	104.2	101.6	101.5
Pittsburgh, Pa.	174.0	168.7	167.3	173.6	155.7	151.7	137.4	265.6
Portland, Oreg.	183.8	162.5	162.7	186.3	177.5	123.9	164.4	282.8
San Diego, Calif.	197.9	184.9	183.0	213.9	151.2	127.6	163.0	284.3
San Francisco-Oakland-San Jose, Calif.	193.0	186.2	186.1	221.4	180.1	109.0	141.0	265.8
Seattle-Tacoma, Wash.	189.3	185.1	186.2	200.0	158.5	128.2	161.3	270.2
St. Louis-East St. Louis, Mo.-Ill.	169.1	172.0	170.0	161.8	133.5	120.5	150.0	279.1
Tampa-St. Petersburg-Clearwater, Fla.	153.9	151.4	150.1	149.6	134.3	149.3	139.5	215.8
Washington-Baltimore, D.C.-Md.-Va.-W.Va.[2]	113.0	111.7	111.8	117.3	109.0	92.4	105.7	114.9

1. December 2001 = 100. 2. Nov. 1996 =100.
Source: U.S. Bureau of Labor Statistics, *Monthly Labor Review* and *CPI Detailed Report* (Jan. issues). www.bls.gov/data/home.htm

Implicit Price Deflator

The implicit price deflator (also called the GDP deflator) is derived from the ratio of current-to-constant dollar GDP (multiplied by 100) and measures the value of current production in current prices relative to the value of the same goods and services in prices for the base year. For example, in 2002, GDP in current dollars was $10,446.2 billion and GDP in constant (1996) dollars was $9,439.9 billion. Therefore, the GDP deflator for 2002 was (10,446.2 ÷ 9,439.9) x 100, or 110.7, which is simply a comparison between 1996 and 2002 prices. It is a weighted average of the detailed price indexes used in the deflation of GDP, but the indexes are combined using weights that reflect the composition of GDP in each period. Thus changes in the implicit price deflator reflect not only changes in prices, but also changes in the composition of GDP.

▶MONEY AND BANKING

Federal Reserve System

The government's interest in monitoring and controlling the banking industry and managing the money supply led to the Federal Reserve Act of 1913. The act created the Federal Reserve System (or the "Fed," as it is popularly known), the nation's central bank. There are 12 regional Fed banks located in major cities throughout the country (Boston, New York, Philadelphia, Cleveland, Richmond, Atlanta, Chicago, St. Louis, Minneapolis, Kansas City, Dallas and San Francisco). Commercial banks within each region select a majority of the directors who run each regional Fed bank. The president of the United States appoints a board of governors for the whole system, and the board is responsible for coordinating policies across the system. But the regional Feds play an important role in shaping those policies by representing regional interests and decentralizing the decision-making process.

The Fed has three main policy tools for managing the overall economy. First, it controls the *reserve requirements* at all depository institutions. These requirements determine what percentage of a bank's deposits must be held in reserve in the form of either deposits with Federal Reserve banks or vault cash. Raising the reserve requirements reduces the amount of loans available to borrowers and helps slow down the economy.

Producer Price Indexes for SelectedCommodities, 1970–2002 (1982=100)

Commodity group	1970	1980	1990	1995	2000	2001	2002
All commodities	38.1	89.8	116.3	124.7	132.7	134.2	131.1
Farm products	45.8	102.9	95.1	107.4	99.5	103.8	99.0
Processed foods and feeds	44.6	95.9	103.5	127.0	133.1	137.3	136.2
Industrial commodities	35.2	88.0	115.8	125.5	134.8	135.7	132.4
Textile products and apparel	52.4	89.7	114.9	120.8	121.4	121.3	119.9
Hides, skins, leather related products	42.0	94.7	141.7	153.7	151.5	158.4	157.6
Fuels, related products, power	15.3	82.8	82.2	78.0	103.5	105.3	93.2
Chemicals and allied products	35.0	89.0	123.6	142.5	151.0	151.8	151.9
Rubber and plastic products	44.9	90.1	113.6	124.3	125.5	127.2	126.8
Lumber and wood products	39.9	101.5	129.7	178.1	178.2	174.4	173.3
Pulp, paper, and allied products	37.5	86.3	141.3	172.2	183.7	184.8	185.9
Metals and metal products	38.7	95.0	123.0	134.5	128.1	125.4	125.9
Machinery and equipment	40.0	86.0	120.7	126.6	124.0	123.7	122.9
Furniture and household durables	51.9	90.7	119.1	128.2	132.6	133.2	133.5
Nonmetallic mineral products	35.3	88.4	114.7	129.0	142.5	144.3	146.2
Transportation equipment	41.9	82.9	121.5	139.7	143.8	145.2	144.6

Source: U.S. Bureau of Labor Statistics, *Producer Price Indexes*, monthly and annual.

Federal Reserve Bank, Discount Rates, 1914–2003

Year	Range	Year	Range	Year	Range	Year	Rate
1914	6.0-5.0%	**1940**	1.0%	**1968**	4.5-5.5%	**Feb. 1, 1995**	5.25%
1915	5.0-4.0	**1941**	1.0	**1969**	5.5-6.0	**Jan. 31, 1996**	5.00
1916	4.0-3.0	**1942**	1.0-0.5	**1970**	6.0-5.5	**Oct. 15, 1998**	4.75
1917	3-3.5.0	**1943**	0.5	**1971**	5.5-4.5	**Nov. 17, 1998**	4.50
1918	3.5-4.0	**1944**	0.5	**1972**	4.5	**Aug. 24, 1999**	4.75
1919	4.0-4.75	**1945**	0.5	**1973**	4.5-7.5	**Nov. 18, 1999**	5.00
1920	4.75-7.0	**1946**	0.5-1.0	**1974**	7.5-8.0-7.75	**Feb. 3, 2000**	5.25
1921	7.0-4.5	**1947**	1.0	**1975**	7.75-6.0	**Mar. 21, 2000**	5.50
1922	4.5-4.0	**1948**	1.0-1.5	**1976**	6.6-5.25	**May 19, 2000**	6.00
1923	4.0-4.5	**1949**	1.5	**1977**	5.25-6.0	**Jan. 4, 2001**	5.50
1924	4.5-3.0	**1950**	1.5-1.75	**1978**	6.0-9.5	**Jan. 31, 2001**	5.00
1925	3.0-3.5	**1951**	1.75	**1979**	9.5-12.0	**Mar. 20, 2001**	4.50
1926	3.5-4.0	**1952**	1.75	**1980**[1]	12.0-10.0-13.0	**Apr. 18, 2001**	4.00
1927	4.0-3.50	**1953**	1.75-2.0	**1981**[1]	13.0-14.0-12.0	**May 15, 2001**	3.50
1928	3.50-5.0	**1954**	2.0-1.5	**1982**	12.0-8.5	**June 27, 2001**	3.25
1929	5.0-6.0-4.5	**1955**	1.5-2.5	**1983**	8.5	**Aug. 21, 2001**	3.00
1930	4.5-2.0	**1956**	2.5-3.0	**1984**	8.5-9.0-8.0	**Sept. 17, 2001**	2.50
1931	2.0-1.5-3.5	**1957**	3.0-3.5-3.0	**1985**	8.0-7.5	**Oct. 2, 2001**	2.00
1932	3.5-2.5	**1958**	3.0-1.75-2.5	**1986**	7.5-5.5	**Nov. 6, 2001**	1.50
1933	2.5-3.2-2.0	**1959**	2.5-4.0	**1987**	5.5-6.0	**Dec. 11, 2001**	1.25
1934	2.0-1.5	**1960**	4.0-3.0	**1988**	6.0-6.5	**Nov. 6, 2002**	0.75
1935	1.5	**1961**	3.0	**1989**	6.5-7.0	**Jan. 9, 2003**[2]	2.25
1936	1.5-1.0	**1962**	3.0	**1990**	7.0-6.5	**June 25, 2003**	2.00
1937	1.0	**1963**	3.0-3.5	**1991**	6.5-3.5		
1938	1.0	**1964**	3.5-4.0	**1992**	3.5-3.0		
1939	1.0	**1966**	4.5	**1993**	3.00		
1939	1.0	**1967**	4.5-4.0-4.5	**1994**	3.0-4.75		

Note:1. The discount rates for 1980 and 1981 do not include the surcharge applied to frequent borrowings by large institutions. The surcharge reached 3% in 1980 and 4% in 1981, and was eliminated in November 1981. 2. The discount rate applied to short term adjustment credit until Jan. 9, 2003, when it was changed to primary credit, in an effort to eliminate the incentive for institutions to borrow for the purpose of exploiting the positive spread of money market rates over the discount rate. Latest rate in effect as of Sept. 20, 2003. **Source:** Board of Governors of the Federal Reserve System, *Federal Reserve Bulletin*, monthly, and *Annual Statistical Digest.*

A more frequently used instrument is *the discount rate*, the interest rate the Federal Reserve banks charge their commercial bank customers to borrow money. The Fed is known as the lender of last resort because of its responsibility to lend to banks in need, and it thus maintains the stability of the banking system. Raising the discount rate generally leads the commercial banks to raise the interest rates they charge their customers. This raises the costs of borrowing in the private sector and slows the economy. (Cutting the discount rate does the reverse and stimulates the economy.)

Most important, the Fed can also control the level of bank reserves through *open market operations*; that is, the direct sale on purchase of Treasury securities and other government debt instruments. When the Fed sells securities, it takes money from the buyer and holds it in its reserves, reducing the money supply; when it buys these instruments, it pays for them by taking money from its reserves, which then goes into circulation, increasing the money supply.

Controlling the money supply through open market operations is certainly the most common and, many would argue, the most important function of the Fed. The money supply shapes interest rates, through the supply and demand of money. Because the Fed is constantly involved in these open market operations (in order to keep the size of the money supply in proportion with a growing economy, for example), adjustments can be made subtly.

In addition, the Federal Reserve regulates banks through the Federal Deposit Insurance Corporation, influences foreign-currency exchange rates through the sale or purchase of foreign currencies, and coordinates international financial policy.

The money supply Money provides a medium of exchange as well as a way to store value. Traditionally, currency (paper money and coins) served that role exclusively. But over time, new financial instruments have developed that serve at least some of the functions of money. Checking accounts serve exactly the same role as currency, and to an extent, so do money market funds and other instruments.

The Fed uses three different measures of the money supply, which include different monetary instruments:

M1 is the original and most commonly reported measure of the money supply, which embraces currency and coins, demand deposits, traveler's checks, and other checkable deposits.

M2 is M1 plus money-market accounts, and savings and small time-deposits.

M3 is M2 plus money-market mutual-fund balances held by financial institutions, term repurchase agreements and term Eurodollars, and large time-deposits.

The U.S. Banking System

Commercial banks are the largest financial institutions in the country and are the principal vehicles for exchanging money. The nation's first commercial bank was the Bank of America (now First Pennsylvania Bank), established in Philadelphia in 1782. Commercial banks hold about two-thirds of the nation's money deposits. Savings and loans, the next-largest source of deposits, hold about half as much.

There are approximately 10,000 commercial banks in the country. They may be chartered either by the federal government or by individual states. While banks themselves may not operate across states, they may be owned by holding companies that can operate interstate, if state laws permit.

Commercial banks can make loans to individu-

The Money Supply, 1970–2002 (billions of dollars)

Item	1970	1980	1990	1995	2000	2001	2002
M1, total	**$214**	**$408**	**$824**	**$1,127**	**$1,085**	**$1,173**	**$1,211**
Currency[1]	49	115	246	372	531	581	627
Travelers' checks[2]	1	3	7	8	8	8	8
Demand deposits[3]	165	261	277	389	307	326	296
Other checkable deposits[4]	(z)	28	294	357	239	259	280
M2, total	**$628**	**$1,600**	**$3,277**	**$3,640**	**$4,927**	**$5,441**	**$5,796**
M1	214	408	824	1,127	1,085	1,173	1,211
Non-M1 components in M2	414	1,192	2,453	2,514	3,842	4,267	4,586
Money market funds, retail	(z)	64	357	448	925	991	944
Savings deposits (including money market deposit accounts)	261	400	923	1,134	1,874	2,303	2,758
Commercial banks	99	186	581	775	1,422	1,734	2,047
Thrift institutions	162	215	342	359	452	569	710
Small time deposits[5]	151	729	1,173	931	1,043	973	864
Commercial banks	79	286	611	575	699	634	584
Thrift institutions	72	442	563	357	344	339	300
M3, total	**$677**	**$1,996**	**$4,152**	**$4,626**	**$7,090**	**$7,994**	**$8,511**
M2	628	1,600	3,277	3,640	4,927	5,441	5,796
Non-M1 components in M3	49	396	875	985	2,164	2,553	2,715
Large time deposits[6]	45	260	480	428	820	786	800
Commercial banks[7]	44	215	358	355	717	671	683
Thrift institutions	1	45	121	74	103	115	117
Repurchase agreements[8]	4	58	151	198	363	375	469
Eurodollars[8]	(z)	61	103	94	192	202	213
Money market funds, institution only	(z)	16	140	264	788	1,190	1,233

Note: As of December of year shown. Adjusted seasonally. Figures may not add up because of independent rounding. Z = less than $500 million. 1. Currency outside U.S. Treasury, Federal Reserve Banks, and the vaults of depository institutions. 2. Outstanding amount of nonbank issuers. 3. At commercial banks and foreign-related institutions. 4. Consists of negotiable order of withdrawal (NOW) and automatic transfer service (ATS) accounts at all depository institutions, credit union share draft balances and demand deposits at thrift institutions. 5. Issued in amounts of less than $100,000. Includes retail repurchase agreements. Excludes individual retirement accounts (IRAs) and Keogh accounts. 6. Issued in amounts of $100,000 or more. Excludes those booked at international banking facilities.
7. Excludes those held by money market mutual funds, depository institutions, U.S. Government, foreign banks, and official institutions.
8. Excludes those held by depository institutions and money market mutual funds.
Source: Board of Governors of the Federal Reserve System, *Federal Reserve Bulletin*, monthly, and *Money Stock, Liquid Assets, and Debt Measures, Federal Reserve Statistical Release H.6*, weekly.

als and to commercial operations, establish checking or demand deposits, maintain "trust" departments that make investments for customers, and perform a variety of other functions such as issuing credit cards. Until the deregulation of the 1980's, commercial banks were the only ones permitted to issue checking accounts. Regulations that developed after bank failures in the Great Depression still keep these banks out of the investment business — largely to protect depositors and the solvency of banks from potential effects of bad investments. But deregulation of the banking industry in the 1980s is blurring many of these distinctions. In particular, investment companies are now permitted to issue demand deposits and to compete with banks in other areas as well. (As a result these companies are sometimes referred to as nonbanks.)

Consumer Credit Outstanding, 1980-2002 (billions of dollars)

Year	Total	Revolving[1]	Other[2]
1980	$349.4	$55.1	$294.3
1985	593.2	124.7	468.5
1990	789.1	238.6	550.5
1995	1,095.8	443.1	652.7
2000	1,560.2	668.0	892.1
2001	1,666.9	701.4	965.5
2002	1,725.7	712.9	1,012.8

1. Consists mainly of outstanding balances on credit card accounts, but also includes borrowing under check credit and overdraft plans, and unsecured personal lines of credit. 2. Includes automobile loans and all other loans not included in revolving credit, such as loans for mobile homes, trailers or vacations. noninstallment credit.
Source: Board of Governors of the Federal Reserve System, Federal Reserve Bulletin (monthly). www.federalreserve.gov.

Bank failures are especially serious problems because of the domino effect they may have on other financial institutions and businesses. Banks, and indeed all depository institutions, ultimately fail when many of their loans go bad and cannot be repaid. But even before that happens, depositors may get nervous about the security of their accounts and withdraw them all at once—a "run on the bank." Because banks loan out deposits and hold in reserve only a small percentage of the value of those deposits, banks experiencing a run would have to call in some of their loans (mainly those already due), putting sudden pressure on many commercial borrowers and causing some to fail. In addition the withdrawal of deposits and of loans reduces the money supply sharply. This process was an important cause of the Great Depression. Following the banking failures during the depression (2,293 banks failed in 1931, and 4,000 banks failed in 1933), the Federal Deposit Insurance Corporation (FDIC) was created in 1933 to protect the accounts of depositors and, more important, to help prevent bank failures. The FDIC charges banks a premium to pay for this coverage. The corporation is designed to prevent runs on banks by insuring deposits and lending to banks to prevent the need to call in loans.

But banks still fail because of bad loans. Between 1945 and 1980, U.S. banks failed at the rate of about six per year. Since then, hundreds of banks have failed each year. Most of these failures occurred in agricultural states where the failure of farms led to defaults on loans; more than half of all bank failures can be attributed to agriculture loans. Fraud also played an important role, especially in Tennessee, where more than 30 banks have failed since 1982. When a bank fails, the F.D.I.C. pays off each depositor and then sells the bank's assets. Sometimes the F.D.I.C. arranges for

Assets and Deposits of FDIC/BIF-Insured Banks, 2001-02

	2001			2002		
Charter class	Banks	Assets (millions)	Deposits (millions)	Banks	Assets (millions)	Deposits (millions)
All banks	**9,613**	**$7,868,249**	**$5,189,445**	**9,354**	**$8,434,686**	**$5,568,653**
Commercial banks	8,080	6,569,240	4,391,623	7,887	7,075,212	4,689,519
National banks	2,137	3,634,997	2,384,462	2,078	3,908,098	2,565,795
State banks (Fed members)	972	1,703,130	1,079,388	950	1,862,875	1,152,364
State banks (Fed nonmembers)	4,971	1,231,113	927,772	4,859	1,304,240	971,360
Savings banks	1,533	1,299,009	797,822	1,467	1,359,474	879,134
Federal charter	883	962,890	560,846	846	987,278	613,581
State charter	650	336,119	236,975	621	372,196	265,553

Note: As of Dec. 31 of each year. **Source:** Federal Deposit Insurance Corp., *Statistics on Banking, 2002* (2003).

Assets and Deposits of Deposit-Taking Institutions, 2002

Type of institution	Number of institutions	Percent share	Assets (millions)	Percent share	Deposits (millions)	Percent share
Commercial banks	7,887	39.4%	$7,075,212	70.8%	$4,689,519	70.6%
Savings banks[1]	1,467	7.3	1,359,474	13.6	879,134	13.2
Savings & Loans (thrifts)[2]	974	4.9	1,004,600	10.5	593,700	8.9
Credit unions[3]	9,688	48.4	557,200	5.6	484,200	7.3
Total	**20,016**	**100.0%**	**$9,996,486**	**100.0%**	**$6,646,553**	**100.0%**

1. Includes Federal and State-chartered Savings institutions. 2. Includes only thrifts regulated by the Office of Thrift Supervision. 3. Federally insured credit unions only. **Sources:** Federal Deposit Insurance Corp., Statistics on Banking, 2002 (2001); Office of Thrift Supervision. OTS Fact Book; National Credit Union Association, *2002 Year-End Statistics.*

Top 100 U.S. Banking Companies, 2002

Rank	Bank, City	Assets (millions)
1.	Citigroup Inc. New York	$1,097,190
2.	J.P. Morgan Chase & Co. New York	758,800
3.	Bank of America Corp. Charlotte	660,458
4.	Wells Fargo & Co. San Francisco	349,259
5.	Wachovia Corp. Charlotte	341,839
6.	Bank One Corp. Chicago	277,383
7.	*Washington Mutual Inc. Seattle	268,298
8.	FleetBoston Financial Corp. Boston	190,453
9.	U.S. Bancorp Minneapolis	180,027
10.	National City Corp. Cleveland	118,258
11.	SunTrust Banks Inc. Atlanta	117,322
12.	State Street Corp. Boston	85,794
13.	KeyCorp Cleveland	85,202
14.	Fifth Third Bancorp Cincinnati	80,894
15.	BB&T Corp. Winston-Salem, N.C.	80,216
16.	Bank of New York Co. Inc.	77,564
17.	*Golden West Financial Corp. Oakland	68,405
18.	PNC Financial Services Group Inc. Pittsburgh	66,377
19.	Comerica Inc. Detroit	53,301
20.	SouthTrust Corp. Birmingham, Ala.	50,570
21.	Regions Financial Corp. Birmingham, Ala.	47,938
22.	Charter One Financial Inc. Cleveland	41,896
23.	AmSouth Bancorp. Birmingham, Ala.	40,571
24.	UnionBanCal Corp. San Francisco	40,169
25.	*Sovereign Bancorp Inc. Philadelphia	39,524
26.	Northern Trust Corp. Chicago	39,478
27.	Mellon Financial Corp. Pittsburgh	36,231
28.	Union Planters Corp. Memphis	34,144
29.	Popular Inc. San Juan, Puerto Rico	33,660
30.	M&T Bank Corp. Buffalo	33,174
31.	Marshall & Ilsley Corp. Milwaukee	32,874
32.	Huntington Bancshares Inc. Columbus, Ohio	27,578
33.	Zions Bancorp. Salt Lake City	26,565
34.	Compass Bancshares Inc. Birmingham, Ala.	23,884
35.	First Tennessee National Corp. Memphis	23,823
36.	Banknorth Group Inc. Portland, Maine	23,418
37.	*GreenPoint Financial Corp. New York	21,814
38.	*Astoria Financial Corp. Lake Success, N.Y.	21,697
39.	National Commerce Financial Corp. Memphis	21,472
40.	North Fork Bancorp Inc. Melville, N.Y.	21,413
41.	Synovus Financial Corp. Columbus, Ga.	19,036
42.	Hibernia Corp. New Orleans	17,392
43.	Provident Financial Group Inc. Cincinnati	16,721
44.	Commerce Bancorp Inc. Cherry Hill, N.J.	16,403
45.	Colonial BancGroup Inc. Montgomery, Ala.	15,822
46.	Associated Banc-Corp Green Bay, Wis.	15,043
47.	*Hudson City Bancorp Inc. Paramus, N.J.	14,144
48.	*Webster Financial Corp. Waterbury, Conn.	13,468
49.	Commerce Bancshares Inc. Kansas City, Mo.	13,308
50.	*Commercial Federal Corp. Omaha	13,081
51.	*Westcorp Irvine, Calif.	12,410
52.	*People's Bank Bridgeport, Conn.	12,260
53.	BOK Financial Corp. Tulsa	12,245
54.	First Citizens BancShares Inc. Raleigh	12,231
55.	TCF Financial Corp. Wayzata, Minn.	12,202
56.	*Downey Financial Corp. Newport Beach, Calif.	11,978
57.	City National Corp. Beverly Hills	11,870
58.	*New York Community Bancorp Inc. Westbury, N.Y.	11,313
59.	First Virginia Banks Inc. Falls Church, Va.	11,227
60.	*Roslyn Bancorp Inc. Jericho, N.Y.	11,020
61.	Sky Financial Group Inc. Bowling Green, Ohio	11,013
62.	Mercantile Bankshares Corp. Baltimore	10,790
63.	FirstMerit Corp. Akron	10,688
64.	BancorpSouth Inc. Tupelo, Miss.	10,189
65.	First BanCorp Santurce, Puerto Rico	9,643
66.	Old National Bancorp Evansville, Ind.	9,612
67.	*IndyMac Bancorp Inc. Pasadena, Calif.	9,574
68.	Cullen/Frost Bankers Inc. San Antonio	9,552
69.	Bank of Hawaii Corp. Honolulu	9,516
70.	Valley National Bancorp Wayne, N.J.	9,134
71.	*Capitol Federal Financial Topeka, Kan.	8,688
72.	Doral Financial Corp. San Juan, Puerto Rico	8,421
73.	Fulton Financial Corp. Lancaster, Pa.	8,387
74.	W Holding Co. Inc. Mayaguez, Puerto Rico	8,205
75.	*Flagstar Bancorp Inc. Troy, Mich.	8,203
76.	Wilmington Trust Corp. Wilmington, Del.	8,131
77.	Greater Bay Bancorp Palo Alto, Calif.	8,075
78.	UMB Financial Corp. Kansas City, Mo.	8,035
79.	*Independence Community Bank Corp. Brooklyn, N.Y.	8,023
80.	South Financial Group Inc. Greenville, S.C.	7,941
81.	Hudson United Bancorp Mahwah, N.J.	7,651
82.	Citizens Banking Corp. Flint, Mich.	7,522
83.	*Washington Federal Inc. Seattle	7,359
84.	Investors Financial Services Corp. Boston	7,214
85.	Trustmark Corp. Jackson, Miss.	7,138
86.	Whitney Holding Corp. New Orleans	7,097
87.	F.N.B. Corp. Naples, Fla.	7,090
88.	Santander BanCorp Hato Rey, Puerto Rico	7,065
89.	*Staten Island Bancorp Inc. N.Y.	6,935
90.	Riggs National Corp. Washington	6,825
91.	Fremont General Corp. Santa Monica, Calif.	6,668
92.	International Bancshares Corp. Laredo, Tex.	6,495
93.	*BankUnited Financial Corp. Coral Gables, Fla.	6,372
94.	R & G Financial Corp. San Juan, Puerto Rico	6,277
95.	First Midwest Bancorp Inc. Itasca, Ill.	5,980
96.	*MAF Bancorp Inc. Clarendon Hills, Ill.	5,937
97.	Community First Bankshares Inc. Fargo, N.D.	5,827
98.	United Bankshares Inc. Charleston, W.Va.	5,792
99.	Susquehanna Bancshares Inc. Lititz, Pa.	5,544
100.	*Waypoint Financial Corp. Harrisburg, Pa.	5,425

Note: Institutions preceded by * are thrifts. **Source:** *© 2002 American Banker, April 15, 2003* another bank's acquisition of the failed bank by subsidizing the sale.

Thrifts are depository institutions including savings and loans (S&Ls), savings banks, and credit unions. The largest and most important thrifts are the S&Ls, which were created to provide home mortgages for borrowers and long-term savings deposits for individual investors. Until recently, thrifts were prohibited from engaging in riskier loans—including most commercial loans—and issuing checking deposits, and a ceiling was placed on the rate of interest they could pay depositors. Congress lifted the ceiling on interest payments to depositors in 1980 and in 1982 allowed the S&Ls to issue commercial loans and to invest directly in real estate developments. Unwise investment in these areas by many thrifts was a major cause of the savings and loan debacle of the late 1980's and early 1990's.

The Federal Home Loan Bank System was established in 1932 to serve some of the same functions for S&Ls that the Federal Reserve provides for banks. It has now been succeeded by the Office of Thrift Supervision (O.T.S.), which identifies institutions that may be financially distressed or likely to fail. All federally chartered S&Ls are regulated by the system (and must have the word *Federal* in their name). Less than half the thrifts are federally chartered, however; the rest are chartered by states, although most of these have joined the system as well. The F.S.L.I.C. (Federal Savings and Loan Insurance Corporation) insured deposits at member S&Ls until 1989, when it became insolvent and was dismantled.

Savings and loan crisis The S&Ls came under enormous economic pressure during the 1970s, when interest rates paid by banks and other financial institutions rose well above the rate ceiling for thrifts, and they started losing depositors. Further, they were in a financial bind because their outstanding loans were all in mortgages—long-term, 30-year loans issued at low interest. In part because of this, the thrifts were deregulated, released from many of the restrictions on their activities and allowed to pursue a more diverse market for loans. With this new freedom, however, many S&Ls took on loans at a higher level of risk in order to earn a higher rate of return. Some argue that the insurance on deposits provided by the Federal Home Loan Bank encouraged the S&Ls to make loans that were too risky.

Lending institutions fail mainly if a large percentage of their loans go bad and cannot be collected. And mortgage loans fail, not just because buyers cannot make their payments, but also because the collateral (the buildings) may decline in price so that it is less than the value of the loan. Especially in the Southwest, many of the loans for real estate development failed when the oil industry declined in the 1980s, taking local economies with it. S&Ls started to collapse at an alarming rate—517 thrifts closed between 1980 and 1988. With liabilities of $100 billion in excess of assets, the F.S.L.I.C. ran out of money. Its insurance obligations passed to the F.D.I.C., and the Resolution Trust Corporation (R.T.C.) was formed to dispose of (sell) approximately $400 billion of insolvent thrifts' assets. The government dealt with 205 insolvent S&Ls in 1988 alone by subsidizing their sale to more secure institutions.

Credit unions are employer-sponsored cooperative organizations that provide consumer and mortgage credit to their members. Employers often arrange for payroll-deduction savings plans through the credit union. Perhaps in response to the high rates charged by commercial banks for maintaining checking accounts, the number of people joining credit unions has jumped dramatically in recent years, from 61.4 million members in 1992 to 80.9 million in 2002.

Mortgage loans Mortgages are loans backed by buildings—either private dwellings or commercial buildings. Until the 1970s, virtually all mortgages had fixed-interest payments and 30-year terms. With the escalation of interest rates

Money Market Interest Rates and Mortgage Rates, 1970-2002

Type	1970	1980	1990	2000	2001	2002
Federal funds, effective rate	7.18%	13.35%	8.10%	6.24%	3.86%	1.67%
Prime rate charged by banks	7.91	15.26	10.01	6.23	6.91	4.67
Eurodollar deposits, 3-month	8.52	14.03	8.16	6.45	3.70	1.73
Large negotiable CDs, 3-month, secondary market	7.56	13.07	8.15	6.46	3.71	1.73
Federal Reserve discount rate[1]	5.50-6.00	10.00-13.00	6.50-7.00	5.00-6.00	1.25-6.00	0.75-1.25
Taxable money market funds[2]	N.A.	12.68	7.82	5.89	3.67	1.29
Tax-exempt money market funds[2]	N.A.	N.A.	5.45	3.54	2.24	0.94
U.S. Government securities:						
3-month Treasury bill[3]	6.39	11.39	7.50	5.82	3.40	1.61
6-month Treasury bill[3]	6.51	11.32	7.46	5.90	3.34	1.68
1-year Treasury bill[3]	6.48	10.85	7.35	5.78	3.84	N.A.
Home mortgages						
New home mortgage yields[4]	N.A.	12.70	10.05	7.52	7.00	6.43
Conventional, 15-year fixed[3]	N.A.	N.A.	9.73	7.76	6.53	6.02
Conventional, 30-year fixed[3]	N.A.	N.A.	9.97	8.08	7.01	6.56

N.A. = Not available. 1. Federal Reserve Bank of New York, low and high. The discount rate for 1980 does not include the 3% surcharge applied to frequent borrowings by large institutions. 2. 12-month return for Dec. 31 of year shown. 3. Annual averages. 4. Effective rate (in the primary market) on conventional mortgages, reflecting fees and charges as well as contract rate and assumed, on the average, repayment after 10 years.
Source: Except as noted, Board of Governors of the Federal Reserve System, *Federal Reserve Bulletin,* monthly.

beginning in the late 1970s, however, several alternative arrangements have developed. For example, in order to reduce the interest payments, many borrowers repay their loans in 15 years. Others use a *variable* or *adjustable rate mortgage* in which the interest rate varies with market rates. Some mortgages that hold payments down in the first few years and then increase them rapidly for the remaining term of the mortgage are known as balloon mortgages.

Money Instruments

Treasury bills, also called T-bills, are securities sold by the U.S. Treasury in denominations of $10,000 that mature at various dates, but all in less than one year. Treasury bills pay an interest rate that is adjusted by the Treasury according to supply and demand. The Treasury bill rate is thought to have the highest risk-free rate of return among all investments.

Federal funds are the reserves the Fed requires depository institutions such as commercial banks to hold on deposit at their regional Federal Reserve Bank as protection against withdrawals. Banks and other depository institutions can loan reserves in excess of those required by the Fed to each other. These Fed Fund loans can provide institutions with large amounts of liquid assets on very short notice, and most loans are for no more than one day.

Certificates of deposit (CDs) Customers who make these deposits at commercial banks or thrift institutions receive a certificate describing the maturity date of the deposit (e.g., a five-year CD). CDs guarantee a rate of return for as long as 10 years into the future. In addition, the fact that they can be purchased at local banks also makes them easy to secure. These factors make them appealing to the general public. The interest paid on CDs is set by the market and is generally the same across large institutions. Smaller institutions often offer higher rates to attract depositors.

Money-market accounts Customers pool their money into a fund that then purchases short-term debt such as Treasury bills and commercial paper in order to earn a high rate of return while maintaining liquidity (i.e., being able to convert assets quickly into cash). Customers typically can write checks on their money-market accounts, which are processed through cooperating banks, but checks generally have to be in large denominations—greater than $250—to prevent customers from using them as demand deposit accounts.

Capital Instruments

Stock, or equity, the most important source of capital for firms, represents a claim on the assets or equity of a business as well as on its earnings. See the chapter on U.S. Business later in this section.

Treasury bonds, or notes, have longer-term dates of maturity, from one to 10 years, than do Treasury bills. They are sold by the Treasury in denominations of $1,000 and are the principal means of funding government borrowing and the national debt. The interest on these bonds is paid out regularly. *Thirty-year Treasury Bonds,* commonly called the Long Bond, are also sold by the Treasury; their yield is watched closely because it forms the basis for all other interest rates, including mortgage-backed securities and fixed rates. Bond prices are determined by the relative number of investors willing to buy and sell them on the open market. Their decisions are in turn based on expectations about inflation. When the Federal Reserve announces that it will not change interest rates, indicating its belief that inflation will remain steady, more investors are willing to buy long-term investments, so bond prices rise, but result in a lower yield. When the economy heats up, however—that is, with increased business activity employing more workers—inflation is expected to rise, resulting in fewer investors willing to buy long-term instruments, and bond prices will fall as yields and other interest rates rise.

Other government securities Some agencies of the government that are involved in lending are permitted to sell securities in order to raise funds. The most important of these is the Federal National Mortgage Association—FNMA, or "Fanny Mae." It buys and sells mortgages insured by the federal government and stabilizes the market for those mortgages in the process.

Municipal bonds are issued by state and local governments to raise funds, usually to provide

Bonds Yields, 1970–2002

Type	1970	1980	1990	2000	2001	2002
U.S. Treasury, constant maturities:[1,2]						
1-year	N.A.	12.00%	7.89%	6.11%	3.49%	2.00%
5-year	7.38%	11.45	8.37	6.16	4.56	3.82
10-year	7.35	11.43	8.55	6.03	5.02	4.61
State and local govt. bonds, Aaa	6.12	7.86	6.96	5.58	5.01	4.97
State and local govt. bonds, Baa	6.75	9.02	7.30	6.19	5.75	5.64
High-grade municipal bonds (Standard & Poor's)	6.51	8.51	7.25	5.77	5.19	5.05
Municipal (Bond Buyer, 20 bonds)	6.35	8.55	7.27	5.71	5.15	5.04
Corporate Aaa seasoned	8.04	11.94	9.32	7.62	7.08	6.49
Corporate Baa seasoned	9.11	13.67	10.36	8.37	7.95	7.80
Corporate seasoned, all industries	8.51	12.75	9.77	7.98	7.49	7.10

1. Yields on the more actively traded issues adjusted to constant maturities by the U.S. Treasury. 2. Through 1990, yields are based on closing bid prices quoted by at least five dealers. Yields since 2000 are basd on closing idiciative prices quoted by secondary market participants. **Sources:** Board of Governors of the Federal Reserve System, *Federal Reserve Bulletin,* monthly; : U.S. Council of Economic Advisors, *Economic Indicators,* monthly (high-grade bonds); Moody's Investors Service (corporate bonds).

public works and other facilities. The federal government is prohibited by the Constitution from interfering in the ability of state and local governments to raise revenue, so income from municipal bonds is not subject to federal taxes. So-called revenue bonds are paid for by user fees—for example, tolls collected on a parkway are used to pay for the bonds used to build it. General-obligation bonds are paid for through general taxes. Municipal bonds tend to be very safe, although there have been occasions on which some state and local governments have had to take extraordinary actions to avoid default—most notably, New York City in 1975, which received a federal loan and sold new bonds to its municipal employee unions in order to avoid default.

▶GOVERNMENT DEBT

One of the most debated economic issues since the 1980's has been the importance of the government's budget deficit. The government raises most of its resources through taxes, but it can also raise money by borrowing. The government borrows by selling bonds (Treasury bonds, savings bonds, for example) which have increasingly been purchased by investors outside the U.S. The bonds raise money now but must be repaid in the future through revenues from taxes. The *budget deficit* in any year indicates the difference between what the government takes in through taxes and other forms of revenues, and the expenditures it makes. The deficit therefore suggests how much the government needed to borrow to fill that gap. The total amount of present and past borrowing, plus interest, constitutes the total *national debt.*

Governments routinely borrow to pay for long-term projects that will give benefits to the community into the future. It can be argued that because much of the benefit from projects such as highways and other public works will be enjoyed by the next generation of taxpayers, they should also bear much of the cost. And they can do that by paying off the government debt (paying the premiums on the government bonds) through taxes in the future. Controversy arises when the government borrows to pay for its more routine expenditures. One justification for such borrowing is that it can be used to manage business cycles in the economy: in other words, during recessions, the government can borrow in order to increase expenditures and expand the economy without raising taxes, which would slow it down.

When the total amount of government debt becomes large, some economists believe that it damages the economy in the following ways. First the fact that the government is selling large amounts of debt means that it is competing for limited investor dollars with private borrowers, driving up the cost of borrowing, and making it harder for private sector businesses to make investments for future growth. Second, the future taxes needed to pay off large amounts of government debt may place a serious drain on the future economy, again diverting resources from investment in the private sector. Politicians are concerned because debt payments must be funded from tax revenues so they must either raise taxes or reduce government spending in other areas (e.g. in defense, or in entitlement programs).

The debate over debt really turns on how much is "too much." Between 1935 and 1981 the only two significant increases in the deficit occurred during World War II and certain years of the Vietnam War, when deficits were about $25 billion. Between 1981 and 1989, however, the Reagan administration consistently ran annual deficits averaging $167 billion and increased the nation's total outstanding gross debt from just over $1 trillion to over $2.6 trillion.

The strong economy and prudent government accounting allowed the Clinton administration to wipe out the annual deficit in 1998 and post four straight years of surpluses (a feat not achieved since before the Depression). The total national debt, on the other hand, never decreased because the interest payments on the debt were higher than the annual surpluses. George W. Bush's tax

Deficits and the Debt, 1940–2003 (billions of dollars)

Year	Total receipts	Total outlays	Surplus or Deficit	Gross Federal Debt	Debt held by the public	Net interest paid[1] Total	Net interest paid[1] As percent of federal outlays
1940	$ 6.5	$ 9.5	$ -2.9	$ 50.7	$ 42.7	$ 1.0	9.5%
1945	45.2	92.7	-47.6	260.1	235.2	3.1	3.4
1950	39.4	42.6	-3.1	256.9	219.0	4.8	11.4
1955	65.5	68.4	-3.0	274.4	226.6	4.9	7.6
1960	92.5	92.2	0.3	290.5	236.8	6.9	8.5
1965	116.8	118.2	-1.4	322.3	260.8	8.6	8.1
1970	192.8	195.6	-2.8	380.9	283.2	14.4	7.9
1975	279.1	332.3	-53.2	541.9	394.7	23.2	7.5
1980	517.1	590.9	-73.8	909.0	711.9	52.5	10.6
1985	734.1	946.4	-212.3	1,817.4	1,507.3	129.5	16.2
1990	1,032.0	1,253.2	-221.2	3,206.3	2,411.6	184.3	16.1
1995	1,351.8	1,515.8	-164.0	4,920.6	3,604.8	232.1	15.8
1998	1,721.8	1,652.6	69.2	5,478.2	3,721.1	241.1	15.1
1999	1,827.5	1,701.9	125.6	5,606.5	3,632.4	229.8	13.8
2000	2,025.2	1,788.8	236.4	5,628.7	3,409.8	223.0	13.0
2001	1,991.2	1,863.9	127.3	5,769.9	3,319.6	206.2	11.6
2002	1,853.2	2,011.0	-157.8	6,198.4	3,540.4	171.0	8.9
2003[2]	1,922.0	2,229.4	-307.4	6,752.0	3,878.4	161.4	8.0

Note: For fiscal years ending in year shown. Public debt excludes debt held by Federal Government accounts. 1. Net interest is interest paid on debt held by the public. 2. Estimate. **Source:** *Budget of the United States Government, Fiscal Year 2004* (2003).

cut and the shrinking economy quickly turned a $127 billion annual surplus into a $158 billion deficit in 2002, pushing the total federal debt over the $6 trillion mark. In 2003, the deficit is expected to be a record $304 billion.

▶THE LABOR FORCE

Labor Force Participation Rate

The Labor Force Participation Rate (LFPR), often referred to simply as the labor force, is that proportion of the population that is either employed or actively seeking employment. It represents the supply of labor available to the economy. The LFPR is lower for young people because many are in school, and for older people because many have retired. It is highest for married men and for women who are heads of households.

Women in the work force One of the most important developments in the labor force has been the sharp increase in the LFPR of women, which has virtually doubled since the early 1960s. With higher levels of education than ever before, most women now opt for careers in the labor force rather than homemaking. Women are having fewer children, and are having them later in life, after they have started to establish their careers, and are returning to work sooner after childbirth. Furthermore, women are continuing to make inroads into professions like law and medicine that have previously been dominated by men.

Women have joined the labor force at an astounding rate since 1960. In 2002, 60 percent of women were in the labor force, up from 37.7 percent in 1960. Over the same period, the percentage of men in the labor force has actually dropped, from 83.3 percent to 74.1 percent. Women constituted 52 percent of the entire civilian population in 2002, about the same as in 1960, but only 33 percent of the labor force was female in 1960; in 2002, it was 47 percent.

Unemployment rate One of the most closely watched labor force statistics is the unemployment rate, which in 1997 fell below 5 percent for the first time in 30 years. It dropped all the way to 3.9 percent in April, 2000, before climbing slowly back over 5 percent in September, 2001. In 2002, the unemployment again surpassed 6 percent, its highest level since 1994. Contrary to popular opinion, the unemployment rate is only an indirect measure of the people without jobs, since it only measures the number of active (within the last four weeks) job seekers as a proportion of the total labor force. So the unemployment rate may rise as new job seekers enter the labor force. Every spring, for example, it rises slightly as school graduates enter the labor force and look for jobs. It may also fall as workers retire or otherwise leave the labor force. And when the economy is in a prolonged recession, the unemployment rate may actually drop slightly because some of the job seekers may give up trying to find a job and withdraw from the labor force.

The unemployment rate over time for the United States is a measure associated with identifying periods of expansion and recession. It reached a peak of 9.6 percent during the 1982-83 recession. The relatively high periods of unemployment beginning in the mid-1970s are in part due to the expansion of the labor force as the baby boom generation left school and began looking for work. Unemployment rates for women have paralleled those for men since 1990.

Hispanics People of Hispanic origin constitute the fastest-growing population group in the labor force, in large part due to immigration, with Mexicans making up the largest share. The proportion of Hispanic women working—historically, these women were more likely to stay at home—has boosted Hispanic participation in the labor force.

Occupations with Greatest Percentage of Women, Blacks, and Hispanics, 2002

Occupation	Percent women
Family child care providers	99.4%
Secretaries	98.6
Dental hygienists	98.1
Dental assistants	98.0
Prekindergarten and kindergarten teachers	97.7
Child care workers	97.6
Receptionists	97.1
Stenographers	95.2
Licensed practical nurses	94.9
Speech therapists	94.3

Occupation	Percent black
Nursing aides, orderlies, and attendants	34.1%
Postal clerks, except mail carriers	30.7
Health service occupations	30.6
Bus drivers	29.0
Barbers	29.0
Pressing machine operators	28.6
Correctional institution officers	28.1
Communications equipment operators	26.2
Guards	26.0
Telephone operators	25.9

Occupation	Percent Hispanic
Agricultural graders and sorters	71.1%
Farm workers	45.4
Tile setters	42.2
Pressing machine operators	42.0
Textile sewing machine operators	41.9
Cleaners and servants	40.7
Butchers and meat cutters	40.6
Drywall installers	40.6
Upholsterers	40.2
Concrete and terrazzo finishers	37.8

Source: U.S. Department of Labor, Bureau of Labor Statistics, *Employment and Earnings* January issues.

Unemployment Rate, 1947-2002

Year	Percent unemployed	Year	Percent unemployed
1947	3.9%	**1992**	7.5%
1950	5.3	**1993**	6.9
1955	4.4	**1994**	6.1
1960	5.5	**1995**	5.6
1965	4.5	**1996**	5.4
1970	4.9	**1997**	4.9
1975	8.5	**1998**	4.5
1980	7.1	**1999**	4.2
1985	7.2	**2000**	4.0
1990	5.6	**2001**	4.7
1991	6.8	**2002**	5.8

Source: U.S. Department of Labor, Bureau of Labor Statistics, *Employment and Earnings* January issues.

Employment Status of the Population by Sex, Race, and Hispanic Origin 1960–2002 (numbers in thousands)

		Civilian labor force				
Year	Civilian noninstitutional population[1]	Total	Percent of population	Number employed	Employment/ population ratio[2]	Percent unemployed
			Total			
1960	117,245	69,628	59.4%	65,778	56.1%	5.5%
1970	137,085	82,771	60.4	78,678	57.4	4.9
1980	167,745	106,940	63.8	99,303	59.2	7.1
1990	188,049	124,787	66.4	117,914	62.7	5.5
1995[3]	198,584	132,304	66.6	124,900	62.9	5.6
2000[3]	212,577	142,583	67.1	136,891	64.4	4.0
2001[3]	215,092	143,734	66.8	136,933	63.7	4.7
2002[3]	217,570	144,863	66.6	136,485	62.7	5.8
			Male			
1960	55,662	46,388	83.3%	43,904	78.9%	5.4%
1970	64,304	51,228	79.7	48,990	76.2	4.4
1980	79,398	61,453	77.4	57,186	72.0	6.9
1990	89,650	68,234	76.1	64,435	71.9	5.6
1995[3]	95,178	71,360	75.0	67,377	70.8	5.6
2000[3]	101,964	76,280	74.8	73,305	71.9	3.9
2001[3]	103,282	76,886	74.4	73,196	70.9	4.8
2002[3]	104,585	77,500	74.1	72,903	69.7	5.9
			Female			
1960	61,582	23,240	37.7%	21,874	35.5%	5.9%
1970	72,782	31,543	43.3	29,688	40.8	5.9
1980	88,348	45,487	51.5	42,117	47.7	7.4
1990	98,399	56,554	57.5	53,479	54.3	5.4
1995[3]	103,406	60,944	58.9	57,523	55.6	5.6
2000[3]	110,613	66,303	59.9	63,586	57.5	4.1
2001[3]	111,811	66,848	59.8	63,737	57.0	4.7
2002[3]	112,985	67,363	59.6	63,582	56.3	5.6
			White			
1975	134,790	82,831	61.5%	76,411	56.7%	7.8%
1980	146,122	93,600	64.1	87,715	60.0	6.3
1990	160,415	107,177	66.8	102,087	63.6	4.7
1995[3]	166,914	111,950	67.1	106,490	63.8	4.9
2000[3]	176,220	118,545	67.3	114,424	64.9	3.5
2001[3]	178,111	119,399	67.0	114,430	64.2	4.2
2002[3]	179,783	120,150	66.8	114,013	63.4	5.1
			Black			
1975	15,751	9,263	58.8%	7,894	50.1%	14.8%
1980	17,824	10,865	61.0	9,313	52.2	14.3
1990	21,300	13,493	63.3	11,966	56.2	11.3
1995[3]	23,246	14,817	63.7	13,279	57.1	10.4
2000[3]	24,902	16,397	65.8	15,156	60.9	7.6
2001[3]	25,138	16,421	65.3	15,006	59.7	8.6
2002[3]	25,578	16,565	64.8	14,872	58.1	10.2
			Hispanic[4]			
1975	N.A.	N.A.	N.A.	N.A.	N.A.	N.A.
1980	9,598	6,146	64.0%	5,527	57.6%	10.1%
1990	14,297	9,576	67.0	8,808	61.6	8.0
1995[3]	18,629	12,267	65.8	11,127	59.7	9.3
2000[3]	23,938	16,689	69.7	15,735	65.7	5.7
2001[3]	24,942	17,328	69.5	16,190	64.9	6.6
2002[3]	25,963	17,943	69.1	16,590	63.9	7.5

Note: N.A.=Not Available. 1. Age 16 and over. 2. Civilians employed as a percent of the civilian noninstitutional population. 3. Data for 1995-2002 are not directly comparable with data for previous years because of a major redesign of the Current Population Survey questionnaire and collection methodology and the introduction of 1990 census-based population controls, adjusted for the estimated undercount. 4. Hispanic persons may be of any race. **Source:** U.S. Bureau of Labor Statistics, *Employment and Earnings,* January issues.

But a doubling of the Hispanic population in the U.S. since 1980 has been responsible for most of the growth. In 2001, Hispanic workers made up 12.4 percent of the labor force, up dramatically from 1995, when they were only 9.3 percent of the labor force. Overall, however, Hispanic workers earn only 74 percent as much as the average for all workers. They also have a significantly higher unemployment rate, though not as high as the rate for blacks.

Productivity measures how much output an economy or organization can generate from a given amount of input. Higher levels of productivity suggest greater efficiency—doing more with the same amount of resources, just as an efficient or economical car goes farther on a gallon of gasoline. Increases in productivity, as the result of better tools or improved methods, provide the main mechanism for increasing output in an economy and ultimately for raising standards of living. Productivity is usually measured in terms of labor—output per worker or per hour of labor—not only because labor is the most important resource but also because it is one of the easiest to measure.

Average Earnings of Year-Round Full-Time Workers by Age and Educational Attainment, 2001

Age and Sex	All workers	Less than 9th grade	Some high school	High school graduate	Some college	Associate degree	Bachelor's degree or more
Male, total	**$51,590**	**$24,271**	**$28,890**	**$37,362**	**$44,377**	**$47,171**	**$80,170**
18 - 24 years old	24,315	16,656	20,109	23,416	23,525	28,673	39,390
25 - 34 years old	40,895	24,330	25,705	32,130	38,359	40,823	57,333
35 - 44 years old	56,265	24,802	32,348	39,535	48,305	49,061	87,941
45 - 54 years old	60,331	27,434	32,240	42,064	51,055	50,956	89,739
55 - 64 years old	60,682	24,330	35,951	41,961	51,427	56,882	90,671
65 years and over	55,244	24,281	28,807	54,640	46,734	40,311	76,746
Female, total	**$35,348**	**$18,049**	**$24,318**	**$26,660**	**$31,698**	**$34,031**	**$50,220**
18 - 24 years old	23,642	14,847	28,807	19,092	21,979	24,376	36,654
25 - 34 years old	34,273	16,862	33,131	25,353	28,784	30,206	44,615
35 - 44 years old	36,395	18,699	20,421	27,248	32,399	34,872	53,252
45 - 54 years old	38,439	18,548	21,586	29,238	34,549	36,399	54,375
55 - 64 years old	36,189	18,287	20,160	27,806	36,077	37,669	53,511
65 years and over	34,343	18,238	19,742	26,178	58,277	33,735	38,754

Note: High school graduate category includes equivalency.
Source: U.S. Bureau of the Census, *Current Population Reports.* www.census.gov/hhes/income/histinc/p32.html

Average Hourly and Weekly Earnings in Current and Constant (1982) Dollars, By Private Industry Group, 1970-2001

While average hourly and weekly wages (in current dollars) have more than quadrupled since 1970, the following table illustrates that when inflation is accounted for, real earnings (in constant dollars) have decreased steadily over the past two decades. Hourly earnings were slightly lower in 2001 than they were in 1970, and weekly earnings were down 8 percent. Thus, even though 2001 paychecks have more zeroes on the end, they don't go as far as a 1970 paycheck to cover living expenses.

	Current dollars					Constant (1982)[1] dollars				
Private industry group	1970	1980	1990	2000	2001	1970	1980	1990	2000	2001
Average hourly earnings	**$3.23**	**$6.66**	**$10.01**	**$13.75**	**$14.33**	**$8.03**	**$7.78**	**$7.52**	**$7.89**	**$8.00**
Mining	3.85	9.17	13.68	17.24	17.65	9.58	10.71	10.28	9.85	9.85
Construction	5.24	9.94	13.77	17.88	18.33	13.03	11.61	10.35	10.23	10.23
Manufacturing	3.35	7.27	10.83	14.38	14.84	8.33	8.49	8.14	8.25	8.29
Transportation, public utilities	3.85	8.87	12.92	16.22	16.89	9.58	10.36	9.71	9.31	9.43
Wholesale trade	3.43	6.95	10.79	15.20	15.80	8.53	8.12	8.11	8.72	8.82
Retail trade	2.44	4.88	6.75	9.46	9.82	6.07	5.70	5.07	5.43	5.48
Finance, insurance, real estate	3.07	5.79	9.97	15.07	15.83	7.64	6.76	7.49	8.65	8.84
Services	2.81	5.85	9.83	13.91	14.61	6.99	6.83	7.39	7.98	8.16
Average weekly earnings	**$120**	**$235**	**$345**	**$474**	**$490**	**$296**	**$275**	**$259**	**$272**	**$274**
Mining	164	397	603	743	766	409	464	453	426	428
Construction	195	368	526	703	719	486	430	395	403	401
Manufacturing	133	289	442	598	604	332	337	332	343	337
Transportation, public utilities	156	351	496	626	644	388	410	373	359	359
Wholesale trade	137	267	411	585	604	341	312	309	336	337
Retail trade	82	147	194	273	283	205	172	146	157	158
Finance, insurance, real estate	113	210	357	547	575	281	245	268	314	321
Services	97	191	319	455	478	240	223	240	261	267

Note: Constant dollar figures for 2000 are for June, and are not seasonally adjustted. 1. Earnings in current dollars divided by the Consumer Price Index on a 1982 base. **Source:** U.S. Bureau of Labor Statistics, *Employment and Earnings,* monthly.

Wages vary not only among the different professions but also between sexes and regions of the country. For example, women in year-round, full-time executive, administrative, and managerial positions have a median yearly income of only 61 percent of the median income for men in the same occupation group. This percentage is higher in the field of laborers, precision production, craft, and repair; but for all major occupation groups reported by the U.S. Bureau of the Census, women receive only a fraction of that received by their male counterparts. This may be due, in part, to the fact that women enter and leave the work force more times throughout their lives than do men and spend a smaller percentage of their lives economically active.

Another factor influencing the discrepancy between men's and women's wages is the concentration of women in occupations that pay less. As the accompanying table demonstrates, women made up 98 percent of child care workers and 97 percent of receptionists, two poorly paid positions.

Minimum wage in the nation was first enacted by the state of Massachusetts in 1912, covered only women, and was designed to shorten hours and raise pay in the covered industries. The nationwide minimum wage was established in 1938, and has grown in both dollar value and the types of employees it covers since then (see the accompanying table). Some states may establish minimum wages higher than the federal minimum.

Unions are organizations of workers who engage in collective bargaining with employers for higher wages, better working conditions, and increased benefits. In the United States, unions are organized at three levels: (1) labor federations or voluntary associations of national unions, which settle disputes between national unions, lobby for favorable labor legislation, and engage in public relations. There is only one labor foundation in the country—the American Federation of Labor and Congress of Industrial Organizations, or AFL-CIO—to which virtually all union members belong; (2) national unions, which coordinate agreements across local unions and conduct collective bargaining negotiations with industry employers; and (3) local unions, which administer labor contracts, serving individual members, employers, and in some cases, establishments directly. Unions can be divided into two groups: (1) industrial unions, representing workers of a particular firm or industry, such as autoworkers and steelworkers, and (2) craft unions, representing employees with a specific skill, such as pilots and musicians.

Many workers choose not to unionize because of the potential costs involved in membership, such as dues, lost pay during strikes, and possible retribution by employers. Union membership in

Work Stoppages, 1947-2002

	Number of work stoppages[1]	Workers involved[2] ('000s)	Days idle: Number[3] ('000s)	Days idle: Percent estimated working time[4]
1947	270	1,629	25,720	N.A.
1950	424	1,698	30,390	0.26%
1955	363	2,055	21,180	0.16
1960	222	896	13,260	0.09
1965	268	999	15,140	0.10
1970	381	2,468	52,761	0.29
1975	235	965	17,563	0.09
1980	187	795	20,844	0.09
1985	54	324	7,079	0.03
1990	44	185	5,926	0.02
1995	31	192	5,771	0.02
1999	17	73	1,996	0.01
2000	39	394	20,419	0.06
2001	29	99	1,151	N.A.
2002	19	46	660	N.A.

Note: Excludes work stoppages involving fewer than 1,000 workers and lasting less than 1 day. 1. Beginning in year indicated. 2. Workers counted more than once if involved in more than one stoppage during the year. 3. Resulting from all stoppages in effect in a year, including those that began in an earlier year. 4. Agricultural and government employees are included in the total working time; private household, forestry and fishery employees are excluded. **Source:** U.S. Bureau of Labor Statistics, *Compensation and Conditions,* monthly.

Federal Minimum Wage Rates, 1938–2003

The Fair Labor Standards Act of 1938 set a minimum wage of 25 cents per hour for employees engaged in interstate commerce or in the production of goods for interstate commerce. Over the years, the government has expanded the numbers of workers covered by the federal minimums (waiters and workers under age 20 in their first three months of work, for example, may be paid less than minimum wage) and has increased the minimum amount. But, as the following table shows, the increases have not always kept up with inflation.

Effective date	Hourly minimum (current dollars)	Purchasing power in constant (=1996) dollars
Oct. 24, 1938	$0.25	$2.78
Oct. 24, 1939	0.30	3.39
Oct. 24, 1945	0.40	3.49
Jan. 25, 1950	0.75	4.88
Mar. 1, 1956	1.00	5.77
Sept. 3, 1961	1.15[1]	6.03
Sept. 3, 1961	1.25	6.41
Feb. 1, 1967	1.40[2]	6.58
Feb. 1, 1968	1.60	7.21
May 1, 1974	2.00	6.37
Jan. 1, 1975	2.10	6.12
Jan. 1, 1976	2.30	6.34
Jan. 1, 1978	2.65	6.38
Jan. 1, 1979	2.90	6.27
Jan. 1, 1980	3.10	5.90
Jan. 1, 1981	3.35	5.78
Apr. 1, 1990	3.50	4.56
Apr. 1, 1991	4.25	4.90
Oct. 1, 1996	4.75	4.75
Sept. 1, 1997[3]	5.15	N.A.

Note: Purchasing power is based on the CPI-U Consumer Price Index. 1. A lower rate of $1.00 per hour was extended to employees in large retail and service enterprises as well as to local transit, construction, and gas service station employees. This rate was increased to $1.15 in 1964, and put on par with the higher rate on Sept. 3, 1965. 2. A lower rate of $1.00 was extended to state and local government employees of hospitals, nursing homes, and schools, and to laundries, dry cleaners, and large hotels, motels, restaurants, and farms. This rate continued to lag behind the rate guaranteed other workers until 1977 (1978 for farm workers). 3. Rate in effect as of Nov. 1, 2003
Source: U.S. Department of Labor.

the nation has held steady at around 16 million since 1990 (13.9 percent of the workforce) but that's down significantly from 1954, when 25.4 percent of the total labor force was unionized. As recently as 1983, more than 20 percent of the workforce was unionized. Notable examples of membership decline are among steelworkers, garment workers, and oil, chemical and atomic workers, which each fell by about 50 percent during 1979-90. Virtually all of these losses are due to the loss of jobs in unionized firms. Several factors may have contributed to this decline, such as changes in technology that displace workers, increased factor costs and international competition, and "downsizing," in which firms lay off large numbers of employees to keep the company's stock prices high.

U.S. Membership in AFL-CIO Affiliated Unions, 1979–2001

Labor organization	1979	1985	1995	2000	2001
Total[1]	**N.A.**	**N.A.**	**12,986,453**	**12,869,540**	**13,223,316**
Actors and Artists	75,000	100,000	75,893	69,000	69,000
Air Line Pilots	N.A.	N.A.	N.A.	43,633	46,048
Automobile, Aerospace and Agriculture (UAW)	N.A.	974,000	760,038	742,409	731,396
Bakery, Confectionery and Tobacco	131,000	115,000	95,186	108,250	103,939
Boilermakers	129,000	110,000	42,802	39,540	39,452
Bricklayers	106,000	95,000	84,000	63,784	62,275
Carpenters and Joiners	626,000	609,000	354,306	N.A.	N.A.
Communications Workers (CWA)	485,000	524,000	490,482	627,080	625,192
Electrical Workers (IBEW)	825,000	791,000	673,117	663,602	676,611
Electronic, Electrical, and Salaried	243,000	198,000	136,502	N.A.	N.A.
Engineers, Operating	313,000	330,000	295,833	281,167	280,000
Firefighters	150,000	142,000	151,000	175,000	193,750
Flight Attendants	N.A.	N.A.	31,776	40,671	42,657
Food and Commercial Workers (UFCW)	1,123,000	989,000	1,009,523	1,140,884	1,129,688
Garment Workers (ILGWU)	314,000	210,000	N.A.	N.A.	N.A.
Glass, Molders, Pottery, and Plastics	50,000	72,000	69,000	57,466	53,684
Government Employees (AFGE)	236,000	199,000	157,100	191,260	196,902
Graphic Communications	171,000	141,000	95,580	88,772	71,351
Hotel and Restaurant Employees	373,000	327,000	232,160	234,509	240,938
Ironworkers	146,000	140,000	80,485	86,294	90,546
Laborers	475,000	383,000	330,694	301,591	310,468
Letter Carriers (NALC)	151,000	186,000	210,000	210,000	210,000
Longshoreman's Association	63,000	65,000	60,595	61,601	61,997
Machinists and Aerospace (IAM)	688,000	520,000	431,619	458,008	446,078
Mine Workers	N.A.	N.A.	75,021	75,250	70,125
Needletrades, Industrial and Textile Employees	308,000	228,000	244,783	208,232	206,801
Nurses, United American	N.A.	N.A.	N.A.	N.A.	100,000
Office and Professional Employees	83,000	90,000	82,987	95,760	106,134
Oil, Chemical, Atomic Workers (OCAW)	146,000	108,000	82,080	N.A.	N.A.
Painters	160,000	133,000	90,000	102,044	101,617
Paper, Chemical and Energy Workers	262,000	232,000	235,302	262,816	283,916
Plumbing and Pipefitting	228,000	226,000	219,800	219,800	219,800
Postal Workers	245,000	232,000	265,757	275,915	266,002
Retail, Wholesale, Department Store	122,000	106,000	73,133	N.A.	N.A.
Rubber, Cork, Linoleum, Plastic	158,000	106,000	N.A.	N.A.	N.A.
School Employees Assocation, California	N.A.	N.A.	N.A.	N.A.	129,000
Seafarers	84,000	80,000	80,250	80,250	80,250
Service.Employees (SEIU)[2]	537,000	688,000	1,077,854	1,261,276	1,281,770
Sheet Metal Workers	120,000	108,000	103,042	93,000	93,000
Stage Employees, Moving Picture Machine Operators	50,000	50,000	50,900	55,788	57,150
State, County, Municipal (AFSCME)[2]	889,000	997,000	1,210,949	1,249,306	1,265,894
Steelworkers	964,000	572,000	516,880	450,436	438,908
Teachers (AFT)	423,000	470,000	631,529	822,191	893,453
Teamsters	N.A.	N.A.	1,286,371	1,226,300	1,217,880
Transit Union	94,000	94,000	96,340	108,117	112,142
Transport Workers	85,000	85,000	75,000	75,000	88,750
Transportation Union, United	121,000	52,000	59,575	90,725	92,300

Note: Membership figures based on average per capita paid membership to the AFL-CIO for the 12 months ending in June of the year shown. Figures reflect all mergers that have occurred since 1999. 1. Includes other AFL-CIO affiliated unions, not shown separately. 2. Figures for 1979 and 1985 exclude Hospital and Health Care Employees which merged with these unions in 1989.
Source: American Federation of Labor and Congress of Industrial Organizations, *Report of the AFL-CIO Executive Council* (annual).

Metropolitan Areas with Greatest Projected Job Growth, 2002-30

MOST JOBS ADDED Rank, Metropolitan statistical area	Number of jobs ('000s) 2002	 2030	Jobs added 2002-30
1. Atlanta	2,793	5,418	2,624
2. Houston	2,673	4,715	2,042
3. Phoenix-Mesa, Ariz.	2,010	4,029	2,018
4. Dallas	2,509	4,465	1,956
5. Washington, D.C.-Md.-Va.-W.Va.	3,447	5,317	1,869
6. Los Angeles-Long Beach, Calif.	5,296	7,104	1,809
7. San Diego.	1,765	3,315	1,550
8. Seattle-Bellevue-Everett, Wash	1,814	3,242	1,428
9. Chicago	5,000	6,413	1,413
10. Orange County, Calif.	1,904	3,307	1,403
11. Denver	1,538	2,917	1,379
12. Tampa-St. Petersburg-Clearwater, Fla.	1,484	2,800	1,316
13. Orlando	1,130	2,436	1,306
14. Boston[1]	3,881	5,100	1,219
15. Minneapolis-St. Paul	2,140	3,324	1,184
16. Riverside-San Bernardino, Calif.	1,388	2,391	1,003
17. Las Vegas	946	1,906	960
18. Sacramento	978	1,877	899
19. Austin-San Marcos, Texas	873	1,757	884
20. Portland-Vancouver, Oreg.-Wash.	1,265	2,128	863
21. Salt Lake City-Ogden, Utah	932	1,770	838
22. Fort Worth-Arlington, Texas	1,010	1,839	829
23. San Jose, Calif.	1,265	2,078	812
24. Raleigh-Durham-Chapel Hill, N.C.	867	1,594	727
25. Charlotte-Gastonia-Rock Hill, N.C.-S.C.	1,025	1,741	716
26. Philadelphia	2,824	3,533	709
27. Oakland	1,353	2,061	709
28. San Antonio	963	1,661	698
29. Miami	1,253	1,924	671
30. Fort Lauderdale	864	1,535	671
Total 30 MSA's	**57,189**	**93,694**	**36,505**

FASTEST JOB GROWTH Rank, Metropolitan statistical area	Number of jobs ('000s) 2002	 2030	Annual percent increase, 2002-30
1. Punta Gorda, Fla.	59	135	2.99%
2. Orlando	1,130	2,436	2.78
3. Naples, Fla.	146	312	2.74
4. Myrtle Beach, S.C.	140	287	2.60
5. Provo-Orem, Utah	208	425	2.59
6. Las Vegas	873	1,757	2.53
7. Laredo, Texas	90	182	2.53
8. Austin-San Marcos, Texas	946	1,906	2.53
9. Phoenix-Mesa, Ariz.	2,010	4,029	2.51
10. McAllen-Edinburg-Mission, Texas	215	428	2.50
11. Fort Collins-Loveland, Colo.	174	344	2.46
12. Fort Pierce-Port St. Lucie, Fla.	148	290	2.43
13. Sarasota-Bradenton, Fla.	374	730	2.42
14. Bryan-College Station, Texas	96	187	2.41
15. Atlanta	2,793	5,418	2.39
16. Ocala, Fla.	118	228	2.39
17. Fort Myers-Cape Coral, Fla.	227	438	2.38
18. Fayetteville-Springdale-Rogers, Ark.	202	390	2.38
19. Boulder-Longmont, Colo.	242	467	2.37
20. Yolo, Calif.	114	220	2.37
21. Sacramento	978	1,877	2.36
22. Boise City, Idaho	297	566	2.34
23. Olympia, Wash.	118	226	2.34
24. Fort Walton Beach, Fla.	120	227	2.32
25. Salt Lake City-Ogden, Utah	932	1,770	2.32
26. Tucson, Ariz.	455	863	2.31
27. Denver	1,538	2,917	2.31
28. Tampa-St. Petersburg-Clearwater, Fla.	1,484	2,800	2.29
29. West Palm Beach-Boca Raton, Fla.	657	1,240	2.29
30. San Diego	1,765	3,315	2.28

1. Includes Worcester, Lawrence, Lowell, Brockton, and portions of New Hampshire.
Source: NPA Data Services, Inc., *Regional Economic Growth in the U.S. Projections for 2002-30* (2003).

U.S. BUSINESS

The Office of Management and Budget (O.M.B.) classifies the entire national economy into industries, based on principal product or activity. There are nine industrial divisions, which are further classified into groups and subgroups. For example, under "manufacturing" would fall "food and kindred products," and beneath that, "meat-packing plants." The nine industrial divisions listed in the O.M.B.'s Standard Industry Classification (SIC) are agriculture, forestry and fishing; mining; construction; manufacturing; transportation and public utilities; finance, insurance and real estate; wholesale trade; retail trade; and services. In 2001, 7.1 million establishments employed 115 million workers with payrolls totaling $4.0 trillion.

Services and Manufacturing

Another way to view the economy is to divide it into manufacturing industries, producing tangible goods such as cars, shoes and furniture, and services industries, whose products are intangible, such as entertainment, tourism and banking. The manufacturing industries are further broken down into those that produce durable goods—that is, goods that are consumed over time, such as cars and houses—and nondurable goods that are consumed in the short run (food and soap). Services have played an increasingly important role in the economy, partly because companies in the manufacturing sector increasingly contract out services such as transportation, accounting, marketing and communications, previously performed in-house.

The service sector, which includes government, is responsible for approximately three-quarters of U.S. employment, and is expected to account for four of every five jobs by the year 2005. Seven of the 10 fastest-growing industries over the next 10 years are service industries. They include health services, computer and data processing services, and child day care services.

Financing Business

When an individual or a group of individuals decides to start a new company, they need money to rent or buy office space and equipment and to pay workers. Since there is a time lag between the day a business opens and the day a business sells its first good or service, funds must be borrowed from a bank or other financial institution or from individual investors to meet costs before revenues are generated. Additional funds may be needed throughout the life of the business to finance research and development of a new product or service or for the construction of new factories. Financing can take many forms, from short-term bank loans, commercial paper, or trade credit to long-term stocks and bonds.

Short-term Financing *Trade credit,* the largest category of short-term financing, is an arrangement between a company and its suppliers, whereby materials and supplies are delivered to the company with a promise to pay the invoice, plus interest, usually within a specified number of weeks. Commercial bank lending may take the form of a single loan with repayment in a lump sum or in installments over the life of the loan, or

Number of Business Establishments with Employees and Payroll, by Major Group, 2001

Major group	Number of establishments	Number of employees	Annual payroll ('000s)
Total	**7,095,302**	**115,061,184**	**3,989,086,323**
Forestry, fishing, hunting, and agriculture support	**26,447**	**183,476**	**4,791,849**
Forestry and logging	12,795	77,984	2,161,848
Fishing, hunting & trapping	2,636	9,954	340,916
Animal production support activities	1,553	15,173	373,066
Mining	**24,319**	**485,565**	**25,014,357**
Oil & gas extraction	437	9,586	724,419
Mining (except oil & gas)	17,702	654,484	41,942,303
Utilities	**698,898**	**6,491,994**	**247,211,475**
Construction	**215,806**	**1,616,973**	**64,956,985**
Building, developing & general contracting	40,476	901,207	39,801,624
Heavy construction	442,616	3,973,814	142,452,866
Special trade contractors	352,619	15,950,424	617,699,378
Manufacturing	**26,785**	**1,470,146**	**44,085,499**
Food	3,212	170,864	7,257,793
Beverage & tobacco products	4,452	308,490	8,402,974
Textile mills	6,966	202,022	5,059,415
Textile product mills	16,152	441,742	9,262,263
Apparel	1,763	60,567	1,495,667
Leather & allied products	17,289	557,507	15,829,400
Wood products	5,739	533,251	22,500,834
Paper	37,895	784,520	27,050,907
Printing & related support activities	34,172	713,855	24,539,045
Petroleum & coal products	2,253	103,570	6,335,924
Chemical	13,361	869,761	46,394,786
Plastics & rubber products	15,981	1,002,503	32,641,356
Nonmetallic mineral products	16,732	524,230	19,349,947
Primary metals	6,684	572,512	23,641,904
Fabricated metal products	60,791	1,761,358	61,803,349

Major group	Number of establishments	Number of employees	Annual payroll ('000s)
Machinery	28,922	1,332,854	54,713,649
Computer & electronic products	16,764	1,593,307	84,522,217
Electrical equipment, appliances & components	6,940	575,413	20,873,387
Transportation equipment	12,627	1,753,445	83,439,891
Furniture & related products	20,593	619,197	17,433,649
Miscellaneous	18,567	408,730	12,761,201
Wholesale trade	**438,924**	**6,142,089**	**275,899,416**
Wholesale trade, durable goods	283,435	3,633,480	173,196,447
Wholesale trade, nondurable goods	155,489	2,508,609	102,702,969
Retail trade	**1,119,950**	**14,890,289**	**314,756,961**
Motor vehicle & parts dealers	125,728	1,850,218	66,619,404
Furniture & home furnishing stores	65,766	567,318	13,644,132
Electronics & appliance stores	47,747	425,736	11,593,224
Building materials and garden supplies	94,135	1,249,126	34,701,139
Food & beverage stores	156,261	2,963,801	49,336,787
Health & personal care stores	81,898	958,072	20,634,666
Gasoline stations	118,892	927,284	13,455,657
Clothing & clothing accessories stores	151,668	1,392,626	21,117,525
Sporting goods, hobby, book & music stores	64,453	622,261	9,221,580
General merchandise stores	41,169	2,525,974	42,238,462
Miscellaneous store retailers	45,540	262,210	5,307,972
Nonstore retailers	42,922	566,279	18,316,560
Transportation & warehousing	**190,683**	**3,750,663**	**129,506,183**
Air transportation	5,451	608,986	28,780,671
Water transportation	1,871	70,462	3,342,061
Truck transportation	109,814	1,397,865	46,080,949
Transit & ground passenger transportation	16,466	391,561	7,558,748
Pipeline transportation	2,785	50,923	3,880,306
Scenic & sightseeing transportation	2,380	23,414	556,806
Transportation support activities	31,876	484,611	17,098,170
Couriers & messengers	12,855	577,575	17,815,332
Warehousing & storage	7,185	145,266	4,393,140
Information	**137,293**	**3,754,698**	**207,124,226**
Publishing industries	32,111	1,100,931	68,980,747
Motion picture & sound recording industries	22,782	297,143	11,986,269
Broadcasting & telecommunications	59,675	1,777,015	93,959,893
Information & data processing services	22,725	579,609	32,197,317
Finance & insurance	**425,028**	**6,248,400**	**373,569,819**
Credit intermediation & related activities	180,764	2,917,625	130,447,365
Security, commodity contracts & like activity	76,918	947,060	125,028,086
Insurance carriers & related activities	164,832	2,326,133	114,759,420
Real estate & rental & leasing	**307,003**	**2,013,673**	**64,009,540**
Real estate	241,115	1,335,298	44,422,141
Rental & leasing services	63,759	652,714	17,966,347
Professional, scientific & technical services	736,454	7,156,579	374,409,080
Management of companies & enterprises	47,559	2,879,223	213,123,787
Administrative, support, waste management, and remediation services	**362,665**	**9,061,987**	**221,385,956**
Administrative & support services	345,916	8,761,451	210,071,758
Waste management & remediation services	16,749	300,536	11,314,198
Educational services	**70,878**	**2,612,430**	**67,097,541**
Health care and social assistance	**671,370**	**14,534,726**	**465,712,029**
Ambulatory health care services	466,914	4,736,631	195,440,247
Hospitals	7,138	5,085,005	180,902,707
Nursing & residential care facilities	65,088	2,671,457	54,665,096
Social assistance	132,230	2,041,633	34,703,979
Arts, entertainment & recreation	**105,961**	**1,780,362**	**46,132,864**
Performing arts, spectator sports & related industries	34,840	361,745	20,393,467
Museums, historical sites & like institutions	6,032	113,545	2,781,408
Amusement, gambling & recreation industries	65,089	1,305,072	22,957,989
Accommodation & food services	548,569	9,972,301	128,649,922
Accommodation	60,196	1,752,782	34,096,205
Food services & drinking places	488,373	8,219,519	94,553,717
Other services (except public administration)	**719,402**	**5,370,479**	**115,218,331**
Repair & maintenance	230,867	1,343,180	38,242,761
Personal & laundry services	196,810	1,311,522	23,629,161
Religious, grantmaking, civic, professional & like organizations	291,725	2,715,777	53,346,409
Unclassified establishments	**78,644**	**105,228**	**2,355,804**

Note: Excludes most government employees, railroad employees, and self-employed persons. Totals include other categories not shown separately. **Source:** U.S. Bureau of the Census, *County Business Patterns 2001* (2003).

it may be a line of credit up to a maximum the bank will allow the company to overdraw on its account. *Commercial paper* is a promissory note of a well-established firm sold primarily to other business firms, with repayments made in two to six months. The only problem with commercial paper is that its resources are limited to the liquidity that corporations have at any given time for lending to other firms.

Intermediate-term financing, with a time frame of one to 15 years, may take the form of lease financing, whereby a company rents, rather than buys, the assets it uses; conditional sales contracts, by which equipment is bought over a period of time (the seller continues to have title of ownership until payment is completed); or term loans or business credit supplied by commercial banks and life insurance companies, repaid by amortization payments over the life of the loan (one to 15 years).

Long-term financing The issuance of stocks and bonds constitute the long-term source of finance for firms. *Bonds* are debt instruments (IOUs issued by a company to the bondholder) that obligate the firm to pay interest at specific times. Alternatively firms can raise money by issuing preferred and common stocks. Unlike bonds, *stocks* entitle the holder to share in ownership and profits made by the firm through dividends paid out for the entire period the investor owns the stock. However, if the business has low profits or limited funds, bondholders are paid first, preferred stockholders next, and common stockholders last.

▶WALL STREET

The U.S. stock market, commonly known as Wall Street, began in the late 19th century as a merchant-organized public auction in stocks and government bonds for the purpose of financing the government and expanding business and trade. At that time, brokers handed over securities to auctioneers who sold securities to the highest bidder. Today, while the form of the stock exchange has changed dramatically, the purpose remains the same.

The most commonly cited index of Wall Street's performance is the Dow Jones Industrial average (see "Glossary of Financial Terms"). From the Dow's inception in 1896 until the early 1980s, the 1,000 mark was considered the benchmark of a bull market. During that period, the Dow passed the 1,000 mark for the first time in 1972 and hovered around it in 1976 before eventually falling back below 1,000. The Dow soared high above 11,000 in the 1990s, but fell back below 8,000 in 2002 as companies like Enron, WorldCom, Tyco, Adelphia and others were forced to admit they had illegally inflated their profits.

The Dow's vicissitudes are of greater concern to larger numbers of people these days because many more people are invested in the stock market. The unprecedented growth of the 1990s, combined with easier access to trading due to online brokerages, attracted hundreds of thousands of new investors to the stock market. In 2002, almost half of all American households owned stocks, either directly or through pension plans or mutual funds (see related table). That was up from 31.7 percent in 1989 and 19 percent in 1983.

Even more startling is the percentage of the average American's wealth invested in the market. In 2001, stock investments made up a staggering 56 percent of Americans' household wealth, more even than the value of their homes. As recently as 1990, Americans had only 16 percent of their wealth invested in the stock market. Even during the bull market of the 1980's, the percentage of income invested in securities never topped 19 percent.

There are three major stock and bond markets in the U.S., all located in New York City. The growth of all three markets has been staggering. A total of 19.7 billion shares were traded on all three exchanges in 1980; by 2001, that number had soared to nearly 800 billion shares.

New York Stock Exchange (NYSE) The oldest exchange in the country was formally founded in 1817, when less than 100 shares were traded each day. In 2002, more than 360 billion shares were traded on the New York Stock Exchange. The growth in the value of those stocks has been equally impressive. The market value of all stocks traded on the NYSE doubled between 1987 and 1993, and then more than doubled again between 1993 and 2000, when it reached a staggering $12.3 trillion. In 2002, market value dropped all the way to $9.6 trillion.

NYSE: Daily Shares Traded, 1900–2002 (in thousands)

Year	Daily Average	Record High	Record Low
1900	505	1,627	89
1910	601	1,656	111
1920	828	2,008	227
1930	2,959	8,279	1,090
1940	751	3,940	130
1950	1,980	4,859	1,061
1960	3,042	7,077	2,184
1970	11,564	21,345	6,660
1980	44,871	84,297	16,132
1990	156,777	292,364	56,853
1995	346,101	652,829	117,723
2000	1,041,578	1,560,808	403,254
2001	1,239,957	2,367,955	413,825
2002	1,441,015	2,812,919	462,000

Source: New York Stock Exchange, Fact Book, *2002*

NYSE Listed Stocks, 1924–2002 (in millions)

Year	Shares (millions)	Market value (millions)	Average price[1]
1924	43	$27,072	$62.45
1945	1,592	73,765	46.33
1950	2,353	93,807	39.86
1960	6,458	306,967	47.53
1970	16,065	636,380	39.61
1980	33,709	1,242,803	36.87
1985	52,427	1,950,332	37.20
1990	90,732	2,819,778	31.08
1995	154,719	6,012,971	38.86
1999	280,930	12,296,057	43.77
2000	313,937	12,372,304	42.14
2001	341,509	11,713,707	34.11
2002	349,908	9,603,327	28.39

1. This average cannot be used as an index of price trend owing to changes in shares listed caused by new listing, suspensions, stock splits, and stock dividends.
Source: New York Stock Exchange, Fact Book, *2002*.

NASDAQ The National Association of Securities Dealers Automated Quotations was founded in 1971 and was the first to use computers and high-technology telecommunications to trade—and to monitor the trading of—millions of securities daily. Today, all the major stock markets have followed suit.

The American Stock Exchange (AMEX) The American Stock Exchange, also in downtown New York, is known as the stock market for the small investor and small companies because the stocks of organizations that do not meet the listing and size requirements of the NYSE are typically traded there. For years, the Amex was known as the "New York Curb Exchange" because its trading was conducted on the street outside the office buildings of many brokers. The exchange moved indoors in 1921. In 1998, the NASDAQ stock market bought the American Stock Exchange bringing the NASDAQ's advanced technology to the Amex's trading floor, but the two exchanges continue to operate as separate entities.

Online trading Internet, or online brokerages allow people to trade stocks directly without a broker for commissions as low as $5 per trade. According to Gómez, Inc., a Massachusetts Internet research firm, the number of online accounts at the nation's major brokerages increased from 1.5 million in 1997 to 12 million in 1999, and reached a plateau of 19.7 million at the end of 2001, the latest year for which figures are available. The popularity of online accounts has encouraged investors to make more trades, and to buy and sell more quickly to take advantage of short-term changes in market prices. Online trading has also sparked the creation of the day trader: an investor who buys and sells thousands of shares in hundreds of different stocks each day.

Mutual funds, in which investors pool their funds to purchase a variety of securities rather than investing in a single stock or bond, date back to 1924 in the U.S., but few Americans were aware of them until their popularity surged in the 1980s. In 2002, according to the Investment Company Institute, an estimated 95 million Americans in 54 million households owned some kind of mutual funds. Total assets of all mutual funds was $6.39 trillion in 2002, down slightly from the year before, but still nearly six times the amount invested in 1990 ($1.1 trillion). More money is invested in mutual funds today than in any other financial institution except for commercial banks, which held a total of $7.1 trillion in assets in 2002, according to the Federal Deposit Insurance Corporation (FDIC).

There are four kinds of mutual funds: stock (or equity), bond, hybrid, and money market. Funds can consist of stocks, bonds, gold, government securities or other assets. The share price of a mutual fund, called the *net asset value (NAV)*, is the

Milestones in the Dow Jones Industrial Average

Date	Average	Date	Average
Jan. 12, 1906	100	Nov. 21, 1995	5,000
Sept. 1, 1929	381	Oct. 14, 1996	6,000
Mar. 12, 1956	500	Feb. 13, 1997	7,000
Nov. 14, 1972	1,000	July 16, 1997	8,000
Jan. 8, 1987	2,000	April 6, 1998	9,000
April 17, 1991	3,000	Mar. 16, 1999	10,000
Feb. 23, 1995	4,000	May 3, 1999	11,000

Source: Dow Jones.

Performances of the Three Major Stock Exchanges, 1986–2002

Year	NYSE	AMEX	NASDAQ
Companies listed			
1986	1,575	796	4,417
1990	1,771	859	4,132
1995	2,675	791	5,122
2000	2,862	759	4,734
2001	2,798	691	4,109
2002	2,783	680	3,663
Shares traded (billions)			
1986	35,680	2,979	28,737
1990	39,665	3,329	33,380
1995	87,217	5,072	101,158
2000	262,478	13,318	442,752
2001	307,509	16,317	471,217
2002	363,136	N.A.	441,700
Dollar volume of shares traded (billions)			
1986	$1,388.8	$45.4	$378.2
1990	1,336.2	37.7	452.4
1995	3,110.2	72.7	2,398.2
2000	11,204.8	945.4	20,395.3
2001	10,644.5	817.0	10,934.6
2002	10,491.8	N.A.	7,254.0

Source: New York Stock Exchange, *Fact Book, 2002*, *NASDAQ Annual Report, 2002.*

Top U.S. Mutual Fund Managers, 2002-03, by Assets

Rank, Fund Manager	Assets (billions) 2002	2003
1. Fidelity Investments	$760.9	$752.0
2. Vanguard Group	590.0	618.1
3. Capital Research & Mgmt.	388.8	431.1
4. Merrill Lynch	199.0	191.2
5. Federated Investors	186.3	189.0
6. Morgan Stanley & Co.	199.8	182.8
7. Franklin Templeton Companies	176.1	179.8
8. Putnam Funds	200.6	165.4
9. Dreyfus Corporation	178.5	158.1
10. SchwabFunds/U.S. Trust	153.4	153.9
11. Citigroup Asset Management	163.6	149.6
12. TIAA-CREF	139.3	136.9
13. Banc of America Advisors LLC	148.3	134.4
14. PIMCO Funds	N.A.	131.6
15. OppenheimerFunds/ MassMutual	127.2	127.3
16. Deutsche Asset Management	93.4	115.6
17. AIM Investments	N.A.	115.4
18. Janus	130.3	113.1
19. Evergreen Funds	111.4	111.2
20. J.P. Morgan Chase & Co.	108.2	106.9
21. T. Rowe Price	100.2	104.2
22. One Group Mutual Funds	N.A.	100.0
23. Goldman Sachs & Co.	102.1	98.7
24. MFS Investment Management	97.0	90.2
25. Alliance Capital Mgmt. L.P.	99.8	88.5

Note: 2002 figures are as of May 31, 2002; 2003 figures are as of July 31, 2003. **Source:** Investment Company Institute.

market value of all the fund's securities, minus expenses, divided by the total number of shares outstanding, and rises or falls based on the performance of the securities in which the fund is invested. Each fund employs a professional fund manager, who chooses a diverse range of securities, so that a drop in the value of one security will not cause a shock to the entire portfolio. As securities prices rise or fall, the fund manager may seek to change the composition of the fund's portfolio. Like securities, but unlike investments offered by banks, mutual funds are not insured by the FDIC or any other government agency.

There were 8,256 different mutual funds in 2002, double the number in 1992, representing the full spectrum of investment objectives. *Aggressive growth funds* seek the maximum capital growth but also carry the greatest risk, because the stocks they invest in are very volatile. *Income-equity funds* forgo high growth rates in favor of a constant stream of income from stocks with a history of steady dividends. *Bond funds,* which invest in corporate bonds and government-issued securities, are generally more conservative than stock funds. *Hybrid funds* invest in both stocks and bonds. *Money market funds* are called short-term funds because they invest in securities that mature in a year or less, such as Treasury bills, CDs, and commercial paper. Many money market funds offer tax-exempt income (though their rate of return is often lower than taxable money market funds). *Special funds* meet the needs of specific investors by investing only in certain segments of financial markets (e.g. biotechnology, telecommunications, small-companies) or by pegging the fund's net asset value to one of several economic indexes (hence the name index fund). *Global equity funds* invest in the stock markets of other countries.

By far the largest segment of the mutual fund industry has been stock or equity funds. Assets of all equity funds in 2002 totaled $2.67 trillion, or 42

Assets of IRA Plans by Type of Investment, 1990–2002

Year	Total (billions)	Bank and thrift deposits[1] Amount (billions)	Bank and thrift deposits[1] Percent of total	Life insurance companies Amount (billions)	Life insurance companies Percent of total	Mutual funds Amount (billions)	Mutual funds Percent of total	Securities[2] Amount (billions)	Securities[2] Percent of total
1990	$637	$266	41.8%	$40	6.3%	$140	22.0%	$190	29.8%
1995	1,288	261	20.3	81	6.3	475	37.0	472	36.6
2000	2,629	252	9.6	202	7.7	1,247	47.4	929	35.3
2001	2,540	255	10.0	210	8.3	1,189	46.8	886	34.9
2002	2,333	263	11.3	208	8.9	1067	45.7	795	34.1

1. Includes Keogh deposits. 2. Stocks, bonds, CDs sold by brokers, and other investments held in brokerage accounts.
Source: Investment Company Institute, *Mutual Fund Fact Book* (2003).

Number of Funds, Accounts, and Total Assets of Mutual Funds, 1970–2002

Year	Total	Equity	Hybrid[1]	Bond & Income[1]	Money market Taxable	Money market Tax exempt
Number of Funds						
1970	361	323	N.A.	38	—	—
1978	505	294	N.A.	150	61	—
1980	564	288	N.A.	170	96	10
1990	3,079	1,099	193	1,046	506	235
1995	5,725	2,139	412	2,177	674	323
2000	8,155	4,385	523	2,208	703	336
2001	8,307	4,717	484	2,091	689	326
2002	8,256	4756	475	2036	679	310
Number of Accounts (millions)						
1978	8.7	6.8	N.A.	1.4	0.5	—
1980	12.1	5.8	N.A.	1.5	4.8	—
1990	61.9	22.2	3.2	13.6	21.6	1.4
1995	131.2	69.3	10.9	20.8	27.9	2.3
2000	244.7	164.1	13.1	19.5	45.5	2.7
2001	248.8	165.7	14.3	21.6	44.4	2.8
2002	251.0	164.4	15.5	25.6	42.7	2.7
Total Net Assets (billions)						
1970	$47.6	$45.1	N.A.	$2.5	—	—
1978	55.9	32.7	N.A.	12.3	10.9	—
1980	134.8	44.4	N.A.	14.0	74.5	$1.9
1990	1,065.2	239.5	36.1	291.3	414.7	83.6
1995	2,811.3	1,249.1	210.3	598.9	630.0	123.0
2000	6,964.7	3,962.3	349.7	811.1	1,607.2	238.1
2001	6,975.0	3,418.2	346.3	925.1	2,012.9	272.4
2002	6,391.6	2667.1	327.4	1,125.1	1,997.2	274.8

1. Bond and Income Funds were divided into Bond Funds and Hybrid Funds beginning in 1984. Data from before 1984 in all categories is not directly comparable to later years. **Source:** Investment Company Institute, *Mutual Fund Fact Book* (2003).

percent of all fund assets (down from 49 percent the year before). Declining stock prices sent many investors to the security of taxable money market funds, ($2.00 trillion in assets, or 31.2 percent of the total), and bond and income funds ($925.1 billion in assets, or 17.6 percent of the total).

Mergers and Acquisitions

Throughout the 1980s and 1990s, an ever-increasing number of companies sought to increase their power in the new global marketplace by buying rival companies or by merging with one. Because fierce competition tends to drive down prices, making profitability more difficult, and because one company needs fewer employees than two, the reasons for the current merger mania were obviously compelling. Not to mention the fact that the CEOs who brokered the deals also made huge cash profits on the mergers.

The accompanying table of the world's largest mergers now reads like a who's who of corporate scandal. In the summer of 2002, Qwest was under investigation by both the Justice Department and the Securities and Exchange Commission for grossly inflating its profits, while Worldcom's chief financial officer and controller were taken away in handcuffs for engineering a multibillion-dollar accounting fraud designed to hide the company's huge losses. And top executives at AOL and Vivendi were forced out in 2002 after failing to bolster their companies' falling stock prices.

▶GLOSSARY OF FINANCIAL TERMS

Arbitrage Simultaneous purchase and sale of a commodity or currency in at least two markets where price discrepancies exist. The arbitrageur makes a profit by buying an asset with a low price in one market and selling it in another market where the asset carries a higher price.

Bear/bull A bear is a speculator who expects prices to fall and sells stocks or bonds in order to buy them later at a lower price. A bull expects prices to rise and therefore buys now for resale later. Thus, a bearish (bullish) market is one in which prices are generally falling (rising).

Blue chip stock A stock that is considered a safe investment, with a low yield and a high price per share, issued by companies that are well known and have a history of good management and increasing profit levels.

Bond A debt obligation that requires the issuer to pay a fixed sum of money annually until maturity (interest payments) and then, at maturity, a fixed sum of money to repay the initial amount borrowed (principal). (See CORPORATE BONDS.)

Capital gain An increase in the market value of an asset above the price originally paid for it, realized when the asset is sold.

Capital loss A decrease in the market value of an asset below the price originally paid for it, realized when the asset is sold.

Common stock/equity A piece of paper that entitles the owner to a share of the firm's profits and a share of the voting power in shareholder elections. In other words, a shareholder is part owner of the firm. If he owns 50 percent of the issued shares of common stock (when no preferred stock is issued), he owns 50 percent of the company, and will receive 50 percent of profits paid out in dividends. Over 40 million Americans invest in common stocks.

Convertible bond A debt instrument which carries an option for the holder to convert it into a specified amount of company stock.

Corporate bonds Debt obligations that require the corporation to pay a fixed sum of money annually until maturity (interest payments) and then, at maturity, a fixed sum of money to repay the initial amount borrowed (principal). Bonds carry no claim to ownership and therefore pay no dividends, but payments to bondholders take priority over payments to stockholders.

Largest Mergers and Acquisitions in World History

Acquiring Company (Country)	Acquired Company (Country)	Date effective	Value (millions)
1. Vodafone AirTouch PLC (U.K.)	Mannesmann (Germany)	June 19, 2000	$202,785.1
2. America Online Inc. (U.S.)	Time Warner (U.S.)	Jan. 12, 2001	181,568.5
3. Pfizer Inc. (U.S.)	Warner-Lambert Co. (U.S.)	June 19, 2000	88,771.1
4. Exxon Corp. (U.S.)	Mobil Corp. (U.S.)	Nov. 30, 1999	86,398.8
5. GlaxoWellcome PLC (U.K)	SmithKline Beecham PLC (U.K.)	Dec. 27, 2000	77,255.2
6. Travelers Group (U.S.)	Citicorp (U.S.)	Oct. 8, 1998	72,558.2
7. SBC Communications Inc. (U.S.)	Ameritech Corp. (U.S.)	Oct. 8, 1999	72,356.5
8. Comcast Corp. (U.S.)	AT&T Broadband & Internet Svcs. (U.S.)	Nov. 18, 2002	72,041.2
9. Bell Atlantic Corp. (U.S.)	GTE Corp. (U.S.)	June 30, 2000	71,323.6
10. AT&T Corp. (U.S.)	Tele-Communications Inc. (U.S.)	Mar. 9, 1999	69,896.5
11. Vodafone Group PLC (U.K.)	AirTouch Communications (U.S.)	June 30, 1999	65,844.9
12. NationsBank Corp. (U.S.)	BankAmerica Corp. (U.S.)	Sept. 30, 1998	61,633.4
13. Pfizer Inc. (U.S.)	Pharmacia Corp. (U.S.)	April 15, 2003	60,704.0
14. Shareholders (Canada)	Nortel Networks Corp. (Canada)	May 1, 2000	59,973.6
15. Qwest Communications Intl. (U.S.)	US West Inc. (U.S.)	June 30, 2000	56,306.0
16. Total Fina SA (France)	Elf Aquitaine (France)	Mar. 27, 2000	55,339.8
17. British Petroleum Co. PLC (U.K.)	Amoco Corp. (U.S.)	Dec. 31, 1998	55,040.1
18. AT&T Corp. (U.S.)	MediaOne Group Inc. (U.S.)	June 15, 2000	51,873.9
19. Shareholders (U.S.)	Liberty Media Group (U.S.)	Aug. 10, 2001	46,050.0
20. Sumitomo Bank (Japan)	Sakura Bank Ltd. (Japan)	Apr. 1, 2001	45,494.4
21. Chevron Corp. (U.S.)	Texaco Inc. (U.S.)	Oct. 9, 2001	43,318.3
22. Vivendi SA (France)	Seagram Co. Ltd. (Canada)	Dec. 8, 2000	42,782.6
23. WorldCom Inc. (U.S.)	MCI Communications Corp. (U.S.)	Sept. 14, 1998	41,350.9
24. JDS Uniphase Corp. (U.S.)	SDL Inc. (U.S.)	Feb. 13, 2001	40,992.6
25. Viacom Inc. (U.S.)	CBS Corporation (U.S.)	May 4, 2000	40,882.2

Note: As of August 20, 2003. **Source:** Securities Data Company.

Securities Industry Revenues and Expenses, 1980-2001 (millions)

Type	1980	1985	1990	1995	2000	2001
Revenues, total	**$19,829**	**$49,844**	**$71,356**	**$143,414**	**$349,493**	**$280,096**
Commissions	6,777	10,955	12,032	23,215	54,107	44,764
Trading/investment gains	5,091	14,549	15,746	28,963	70,778	38,950
Underwriting profits	1,571	4,987	3,728	8,865	18,718	16,941
Margin interest	2,151	2,746	3,179	6,470	24,547	13,912
Mutual fund sales	278	2,754	3,242	7,434	19,395	16,396
Other	3,960	13,854	33,428	68,468	161,949	149,133
Expenses, total	**$16,668**	**$43,342**	**$70,566**	**$132,089**	**$310,390**	**$260,299**
Interest expense	3,876	11,470	28,093	56,877	131,877	98,947
Compensation	7,619	18,112	22,931	41,541	95,206	83,510
Commissions/clearance paid	1,055	2,314	2,959	5,700	15,523	14,043
Other	4,119	11,446	16,583	27,970	67,784	64,199
Net income, pretax	**$3,160**	**$6,502**	**$790**	**$11,325**	**$39,103**	**$19,397**

Source: U.S. Securities and Exchange Commission, *2002 Annual Report* (2003).

Debentures Debt securities issued by a company that pay a fixed interest rate, in order to raise finance for commercial or industrial operations.
Divestiture The sales by a company of a product line, subsidiary or division. The number of divestitures sold peaked in 1986, with a total of 1,316, for a record total price of $65.2 billion.
Dividends Payments made to common and preferred stockholders out of a firm's profits either in the form of cash or additional shares.
Dow Jones Industrial Average Dating back to 1893, this index of 30 blue chip stocks in industry traded on the New York Stock Exchange (and determined by the editors of the *Wall Street Journal*) is the most widely cited indicator of how the stock market is doing.
Establishment A physical place of business activity such as a factory, assembly plant, retail store, warehouse, etc. where goods are made, stored or processed, or where services are performed.
Eurocurrency Currency of the major industrial and financial countries held in the banks of major financial and industrial countries for the purpose of lending and borrowing. Most loans are for up to one year and are used for payments of deficits. Eurodollars are U.S. dollars held in foreign banks.
Firm A business organization that owns and/or operates one or more establishments. Also called a company, enterprise or business venture. Firms can be of three types: 1) sole proprietorships—firms owned directly by one person; 2) partnerships—firms whose ownership is shared by a fixed number of proprietors; and 3) corporations—firms created by a government charter, granting them greater accessibility to financial capital through the selling of common or preferred stock, greater accessibility to debt capital through the selling of bonds, and limited liability in the event of bankruptcy.
Futures market/forward market A market in which commodities or securities are bought and sold at prices fixed now, for delivery at specified future date. Futures are traded on the American Stock Exchange; the Chicago Board of Trade; Chicago Board Options Exchange; Chicago Mercantile Exchange; Chicago Rice and Cotton Exchange; Commodity Exchange, New York (COMEX); Kansas City Board of Trade; MidAmerica Commodity Exchange, Chicago; Minneapolis Grain Exchange; New York Coffee, Sugar, and Coca Exchange (including the Citrus Associates); New York Cotton Exchange; New York Futures Exchange; and New York Mercantile Exchange; New York Stock Exchange; Pacific Stock Exchange, Los Angeles and San Francisco; and Philadelphia Stock Exchange.

Top 25 Securities Firms by Capital, 2002-03

2003 Rank/Firm	2002	2003
1. Merrill Lynch & Co.[1]	96,580	101,399
2. Morgan Stanley Dean Witter[1, 2]	70,384	77,046
3. Goldman Sachs Group[1, 2]	49,247	57,714
4. Lehman Brothers Holdings[1, 2]	47,470	48,330
5. Citigroup Global Market Holdings, Inc.[1,3]	38,917	44,860
6. Credit Suisse First Boston[1]	22,550	30,811
7. Bear Stearns Companies[1, 2]	29,058	30,063
8. UBS Securities[4]	6,221	8,427
9. Alliance Capital Management	3,988	7,218
10. Deutsche Bank Securities	7,965	5,498
11. Banc of America Securities	4,699	5,369
12. Charles Schwab Corporation[1]	4,893	4,653
13. J.P. Morgan Securities Inc.	4,739	4,573
14. UBS Financial Services[5]	3,902	3,624
15. Wachovia Securities	2,156	2,222
16. TD Waterhouse Group	2,550	2,202
17. Legg Mason[1]	1,821	1,994
18. A.G. Edwards	1,678	1,668
19. Prudential Securities	2,020	1,654
20. ABN AMRO	1,913	1,648
21. CIBC World Markets Corp.	1,710	1,591
22. Nomura Securities International Inc.	1,549	1,576
23. Fidelity Brokerage	1,514	1,437
24. SG Cowen Securities Corp.[1]	1,643	1,370
25. LaBranche & Co.	1,317	1,276

Note: Data as of January 1 of year shown, except as noted. 1. Firm's capital is the sum of long-term borrowings and ownership equity. 2. Data as of Nov. 30 of previous year. 3. Formerly Salomon Smith Barney Holdings Inc. 4. Formerly UBS Warburg LLC. 5. Formerly UBS PaineWebber Inc.
Source: Securities Industry Association.

Greenmail Analogous to blackmail, greenmail is the practice of purchasing enough shares in a firm or trading company to threaten a takeover, thereby forcing the owners to buy them back at a higher rate in order to retain control of the business.
Individual Retirement Account (IRA) An account set up by individual investors to hold and invest funds until retirement. Under a traditional IRA,

which was established as an alternative for people not eligible for employee-sponsored pension plans, individuals may contribute up to $2,000 pre-tax per year to a tax-deferred retirement account. In 1997, Congress established the Roth IRA, which allows individuals to contribute $2,000 post-tax to a retirement account on which earnings are tax free forever in most cases.

Inital Public Offfering (IPO) A company's first sale of stock to the public (also known as "going public.") An IPO generates working capital in exchange for equity. A well-publicized IPO can drive up the stock price, making millionaires of company insiders who already own stock or options. For this reason, it is often difficult for outsiders to purchase shares in an IPO at the public offering price.

Insider trading Trading in the stock market based on information that has not been made public, and which is intended to remain confidential—for example, information that a small company is about to become part of a national corporation. The penalties paid by individuals and corporations for such activities in recent years have reached into the hundreds of millions of dollars. Drexel Burnham Lambert, Inc., was fined $650 million to settle six charges of securities law violations; and investor Ivan Boesky was fined $100 million and imprisoned for his insider trading activities.

Junk bond/high-yield bond Bonds with a rating below investment grade (at or below Ba1 (Moody's Investors Service), at or below BB+ (Standard & Poor's), or unrated. Issuers of junk bonds are usually small companies that in the past have been limited to borrowing from banks to raise capital for corporate growth. Although the major ratings services consider junk bonds risky (hence their name), they have a historically low default rate—only 1.5 percent between the mid 1970s and mid-1980s. The junk market grew considerably in the 1980s, and by 1987 accounted for over 25 percent of the value of all corporate bonds outstanding.

Leveraged buyout The purchase of a company by one of its employee groups (usually upper management) or a large shareholder with borrowed funds, usually using the company's assets as security for the loans. Leveraged buy-outs have been used to combat hostile takeover bids.

Mutual fund A pool of financial assets in which investors may buy shares and get the benefits (or share the losses) depending on the performance of the collective securities. Shares are sold publicly and can be redeemed at any time. Funds can consist of stocks, bonds, gold, government securities or other assets, and their names are descriptive of their primary purpose; for example, bonds funds, equity-fund portfolios, income funds, money market-mutual funds, and municipal funds. (See the section on mutual funds earlier in this chapter; see also MONEY MARKET ACCOUNTS in "Money and Banking.")

Option A contract to buy or sell commodities or securities within a given time period at a fixed price. For stocks, this period is usually three months. A contract to sell is a *put option* (or put); to buy, a *call option* (or call) and one to buy or sell is a *double option*. A buyer (seller) will gain if the trading price rises (falls) by more than the cost of entering into the contract. Options are traded on the same exchanges as futures contracts (see FUTURES MARKET).

Over-the-counter (OTC) stock A security not listed on an exchange that is traded between two individuals. The name stems from the eighteenth-century practice of merchants selling stocks over the counter in their own shops directly to investors without the use of stockbrokers or auctioneers.

Pension fund An arrangement whereby private or public-sector employers, unions, and—as in the case of individual retirement accounts (IRAs) and Keogh plans—individuals contribute to a fund from which money is paid out to the employees, union members, or contributors (or their dependents) upon death, disability or retirement. Contributions can be based on a percentage of salary or corporate profits; in some cases employees may make voluntary or mandatory contributions to the fund. Pension fund assets are usually held in the form of securities or property with a preference for long-term assets.

Preferred stock Similar to COMMON STOCK, except that owners of preferred stock have no voting rights, and preferred stock holders are paid their dividends at a fixed rate, before common stockholders receive any dividends.

Rating An agency evaluation of the quality of a debt instrument or a company issuing debt. Standard & Poor's and Moody's Investment Service are the two major credit ratings agencies in the U.S. The ratings measure the safety of interest and principal payments of bonds. S&P bond ratings are, from most to least secure: AAA, AA, A, BBB, BB, B, CCC, CC, C. Moody's ratings are: Aaa, Aa, A, Baa, Ba, B, Caa, Ca, C.

Russell Indexes These measure the performance of the largest U.S.-headquartered companies, based on total market capitalization. The Russell 3,000 Index measures the 3,000 largest U.S.-based companies (their total market capitalization represents approximately 98 percent of the investable U.S. equity market). The Russell 1,000 measures the largest 1,000 of these companies. The Russell 2,000 measures the smallest 2,000 companies in the Russell 3,000.

Securities Financial assets (usually long-term), such as equities/stocks and debentures/bonds; may also refer to shorter-term assets such as U.S. Treasury bills.

Securities and Exchange Commission (SEC) U.S. government agency that regulates the securities industry by requiring registration of brokers, dealers, and stock exchanges. The SEC also reviews the financial position of companies issuing

Venture Capital Investments, 1990–2002

Year	Total amount invested (millions)	Total number of companies invested in	Average investment per company (millions)
1990	$2,914.34	1,143	$2.55
1995	7,623.1	1,572	4.84
1996	11,610.1	2,117	5.48
1997	15,080.0	2,585	5.83
1998	21,446.9	3,458	6.20
1999	54,749.4	4,476	12.23
2000	106,224.7	6,427	16.53
2001	40,801.9	3,826	10.66
2002	21,188.9	2,537	8.35

Source: PricewaterhouseCoopers/Venture Economics/National Venture Capital Association MoneyTree Survey, July 24, 2003. www.ventureeconomics.com

securities for public sale, and investigates illegal activities such as insider trading.
Standard & Poor's 500 Composite Stock Price Index (S&P 500) A widely used measure of the movement of the U.S. stock market. The S&P 500 was introduced in 1957 and is one of 12 leading economic indicators used by the U.S. Commerce Department. The 500 issues include 400 industrial, 40 utility, 20 transportation and 40 financial companies—primarily those listed on the New York Stock Exchange (NYSE). The index is considered to be value-weighted because each stock is weighted according to its market value. As of December 31, 1987, the market value of issues tracked by the S&P 500 was equal to approximately 70 percent of the value of all publicly traded U.S. equities. Its value is calculated on a total return basis with dividends reinvested.
Stock exchange A market in which securities (other than bills and similar short-term instruments) issued by central and local government bodies, and public companies are traded (e.g., the New York Stock Exchange, the American Stock Exchange, the London Stock Exchange). Only members of a stock exchange may deal on it, and membership and arrangements for trading are strictly regulated. Stock exchanges in the United States are the American Stock Exchange (New York); Boston Stock Exchange; Cincinnati Stock Exchange; Intermountain Stock Exchange (Salt Lake City); Midwest Stock Exchange (Chicago); New York Stock Exchange; Pacific Stock Exchange (Los Angeles, San Francisco); Philadelphia Stock Exchange; and Spokane Stock Exchange.
Stock market An institution where stocks and shares are traded, existing in all advanced Western countries. Stock markets enable companies to more easily raise equity or loan capital from the public since investors can quickly realize their holdings because of the stock exchange share quotation. In other words, there is a ready market. The principal overseas stock markets are located in Amsterdam, Brussels, Frankfurt, Hong Kong, Johannesburg, London, Milan, Paris, Singapore, Stockholm, Sydney, Tokyo, Toronto and Zurich.
Stockbroker An individual who acts as an adviser and an agent (working on commission), to buy and sell stocks on behalf of a client on a particular stock exchange where the stockbroker is a member.
Venture capital Funds made available to start-up businesses that have excellent growth potential, but are unable to obtain more traditional methods of business financing. Also known as risk capital because these investments have a high risk and a high reward.
Wilshire 5000 Index The broadest measure of the U.S. stock market, containing some 5,000 issues including all publicly traded U.S. stocks for which daily pricing is available (i.e., includes all Amex, NYSE and OTC stocks).
Yield The annual return on a security, as a percentage of its current market price. A stock's dividend yield is the annual dividend divided by its current stock price.

▶BIG BUSINESS: THE *FORTUNE* 500

The ultimate measure of success in the business world is inclusion on *Fortune* magazine's annual list of the 500 biggest companies in America. In recent years, the global trend toward mega-mergers creating monolithic organizations has raised the bar for admission to this select circle. In 2002, Wal-Mart Stores again held the top slot, with nearly a quarter of a trillion dollars in revenues. Although the slumping economy battered most of the *Fortune* 500 in 2002, Wal-Mart increased its revenues by more than $25 billion. Wal-Mart's revenues were more than 30 percent higher than the second-place company, General Motors.

The accompanying tables list the top 100 companies of the *Fortune* 500 by revenues, the top three companies in several performance categories, and the top companies by industry.

▶SMALL BUSINESS

Small businesses account for 98 percent of the 5.65 million employer firms in the United States today. Nearly half of the small businesses in America had fewer than four employees. Small businesses create the vast majority of the net new jobs in America every year. Businesses with 100 employees or fewer employed 36 percent of the 114 million employees working for U.S. employer firms, according to the Census Bureau in 2000; 55.2 percent worked in businesses with fewer than 1,000 employees. According to the Small Business Administration, two-thirds of small businesses survive at least two years, and just over half make it four years. About three-quarters of

Fortune 500 Performance Leaders, 2002

Profits	(millions)
1. Citigroup (6)	$ 15,276.0
2. General Electric (5)	14,118.0
3. Exxon Mobil (3)	11,460.0

Market Value	(millions)
1. Microsoft (47)	$266,036.5
2. General Electric (5)	255,565.3
3. Exxon Mobil (3)	231,406.8

Fastest 1-year Revenue Growth	(percent)
1. AmerisourceBergen (24)	179.4%
2. ConocoPhillips (12)	141.4
3. Tyson Foods (72)	117.3

Return on Revenues	(percent)
1. USA Interactive (319)	37.1%
2. Wyeth (128)	30.5
3. Microsoft (47)	27.6

Return to Investors, 1 year	(percent)
1. Crown Holdings (268)	213.0%
2. Tenneco Automotive (453)	98.0
3. Providian Financial (393)	82.8

Return to Investors (10 years)	(percent)
1. AOL Time Warner (29)	49.9%
2. Dell Computer (36)	43.0
3. Qualcomm (489)	37.7

Note: Numbers in parentheses reflect overall *Fortune* 500 rank.

The Top U.S. Companies, by Industry and *Fortune* 500 Rank, 2002

Industry, Company, Rank	Revenues (millions)
Aerospace and Defense	
Boeing (15)	54,069
United Technologies (49)	28,212
Lockheed Martin (56)	26,806
Airlines	
AMR (104)	17,299
UAL (132)	14,286
Delta Air Lines (145)	13,305
Apparel	
Nike (188)	9,893
VF (322)	5,182
Jones Apparel Group (375)	4,341
Beverages	
Coca-Cola (92)	19,564
Coca Cola Enterprises (108)	16,889
Anheuser Busch (142)	13,566
Chemicals	
Dow Chemical (51)	27,609
DuPont (67)	24,522
PPG Industries (233)	8,067
Commercial Banks	
Citigroup (6)	100,789
Bank of America Corp. (23)	45,732
J.P. Morgan Chase (26)	43,372
Computer/Data Services	
Electronic Data Systems (80)	21,782
Computer Sciences (167)	11,426
First Data (242)	7,636
Computer Software	
Microsoft (47)	28,365
Oracle (190)	9,673
Computer Assoc. Intl. (497)	2,964
Computers, Office Equipment	
Intl. Business Machines (8)	83,132
Hewlett (14)	56,588
Dell Computer (36)	35,404
Consumer Food Products	
ConAgra Foods (50)	27,630
PepsiCo (62)	25,112
Sara Lee (101)	17,628
Diversified Financials	
General Electric (5)	131,698
Fannie Mae (16)	52,901
Freddie Mac (32)	39,663
Electronics	
Emerson Electric (138)	13,824
Whirlpool (173)	11,016
Eaton (258)	7,209
Energy	
American Electric Power (120)	15,583
TXU (134)	14,086
El Paso (152)	12,616
Engineering, Construction	
Fluor (186)	10,190
Jacobs Engineering Grp. (359)	4,556
Emcor Group (404)	3,968
Entertainment	
AOL Time Warner (29)	41,780
Walt Disney (61)	25,329
Viacom (66)	24,606
Food & Drug Stores	
Kroger (18)	51,760
Albertson's (35)	35,916
Safeway (41)	32,399
Food Production	
Archer Daniels Midland (71)	23,454
Tyson Foods (72)	23,367
Dean Foods (201)	9,213
Food Services	
McDonald's (124)	15,406
Yum Brands (240)	7,757
Darden Restaurants (372)	4,369
Forest & Paper Products	
International Paper (64)	24,976
Georgia Pacific (74)	23,271
Weyerhaeuser (96)	18,521
General Merchandisers	
Wal Mart Stores (1)	246,525
Target (25)	43,917
Sears Roebuck (30)	41,366
Health Care	
UnitedHealth Group (63)	25,020
Cigna (87)	19,915
Aetna (88)	19,879
Hotels, Casinos & Resorts	
Marriott International (175)	10,619
Park Place Entertainment (354)	4,652
Harrah's (386)	4,172
Household and Personal Products	
Procter & Gamble (31)	40,238
Kimberly-Clark (143)	13,566
Colgate-Palmolive (198)	9,294
Industrial & Farm Equipment	
Caterpillar (85)	20,152
Deere (135)	13,947
Illinois Tool Works (189)	9,812
Insurance	
American Intl. Group (9)	67,723
State Farm Insurance (21)	49,654
Berkshire Hathaway (28)	42,353
Mail, Package, Freight Delivery	
United Parcel Service (43)	31,272
FedEx (83)	20,607
Pittston (395)	4,043
Metals	
Alcoa (82)	20,618
United States Steel (264)	6,949
Nucor (342)	4,802
Mining, Crude Oil Production	
Occidental Petroleum (252)	7,429
Unocal (316)	5,297
Devon Energy (369)	4,396
Motor Vehicles & Parts	
General Motors (2)	186,763
Ford Motor (4)	163,630
Delphi (53)	27,427
Network Communications	
Motorola (59)	26,679
Cisco Systems (95)	18,915
Lucent Technologies (141)	13,568
Oil and Gas Equipment	
Halliburton (153)	12,572
Baker Hughes (320)	5,208
Smith International (480)	3,170
Petroleum Refining	
Exxon Mobil (3)	182,466
ChevronTexaco (7)	92,043
ConocoPhillips (12)	58,394
Pharmaceuticals	
Merck (17)	51,790
Johnson & Johnson (34)	36,298
Pfizer (37)	35,281
Publishing, Printing	
Gannett (275)	6,422
Tribune (312)	5,384
McGraw Hill (343)	4,788
Railroads	
Union Pacific (156)	12,491
Burlington No. Santa Fe (205)	8,979
CSX (231)	8,152
Real Estate	
Host Marriott (434)	3,680
Equity Office Properties (448)	3,506
Simon Property Group (637)	2,186
Savings Institutions	
Washington Mutual (94)	19,037
Golden West Financial (425)	3,744
Sovereign Bancorp (576)	2,492
Securities	
Morgan Stanley (40)	32,415
Merrill Lynch (48)	28,253
Goldman Sachs (75)	22,854
Semiconductors	
Intel (58)	26,764
Solectron (158)	12,276
Sanmina-SCI (214)	8,762
Specialty Retailers	
Home Depot (13)	58,247
Costco Wholesale (33)	38,763
Lowe's (60)	26,491
Telecommunications	
Verizon (10)	67,625
AT&T (22)	46,727
SBC Communications (27)	43,138
Tobacco	
Altria Group (11)	62,182
R.J. Reynolds Tobacco (281)	6,211
Universal (574)	2,500
Toys, Sporting Goods	
Mattel (337)	4,885
Hasbro (519)	2,816
Utilities	
Duke Energy (118)	15,663
Exelon (126)	14,955
PG&E Corp. (140)	13,784
Waste Management	
Waste Management (171)	11,142
Allied Waste Industries (307)	5,517
Republic Services (595)	2,365
Wholesalers: Food and Grocery	
Sysco (73)	23,351
Supervalu (81)	20,909
Fleming (102)	17,562

Source: *Fortune* magazine, 2003 Reprinted by permission.

Fortune 100 Largest U.S. Corporations, 2002

Rank	Company (2001 Rank)	Revenues (millions)	Rank	Company (2001 Rank)	Revenues (millions)
1.	Wal-Mart Stores (1)	$246,525.0	51.	Dow Chemical (60)	27,609.0
2.	General Motors (3)	186,763.0	52.	Marathon Oil (43)	27,470.0
3.	Exxon Mobil (2)	182,466.0	53.	Delphi (67)	27,427.0
4.	Ford Motor (4)	163,630.0	54.	Sprint (68)	27,180.0
5.	General Electric (6)	131,698.0	55.	Valero Energy (N.A.)	26,976.3
6.	Citigroup (7)	100,789.0	56.	Lockheed Martin (77)	26,806.0
7.	ChevronTexaco (8)	92,043.0	57.	Prudential Financial (62)	26,797.0
8.	Intl. Business Machines (9)	83,132.0	58.	Intel (65)	26,764.0
9.	American Intl. Group (12)	67,722.8	59.	Motorola (56)	26,679.0
10.	Verizon Communications (11)	67,625.0	60.	Lowe's (94)	26,490.9
11.	Altria Group (10)	62,182.0	61.	Walt Disney (73)	25,329.0
12.	ConocoPhillips (N.A.)	58,394.0	62.	PepsiCo (63)	25,112.0
13.	Home Depot (18)	58,247.0	63.	UnitedHealth Group (84)	25,020.0
14.	Hewlett-Packard (28)	56,588.0	64.	International Paper (66)	24,976.0
15.	Boeing (16)	54,069.0	65.	New York Life Insurance (69)	24,720.7
16.	Fannie Mae (20)	52,901.1	66.	Viacom (85)	24,605.7
17.	Merck (24)	51,790.3	67.	Du Pont (70)	24,522.0
18.	Kroger (22)	51,759.5	68.	CVS (93)	24,181.5
19.	Cardinal Health (23)	51,135.7	69.	American Express (89)	23,807.0
20.	McKesson (31)	50,006.0	70.	Wachovia Corp. (90)	23,591.0
21.	State Farm Insurance (25)	49,653.7	71.	Archer Daniels Midland (100)	23,453.6
22.	AT&T (15)	46,727.0	72.	Tyson Foods (177)	23,367.0
23.	Bank of America Corp. (19)	45,732.0	73.	Sysco (95)	23,350.5
24.	AmerisourceBergen (127)	45,234.8	74.	Georgia-Pacific (71)	23,271.0
25.	Target (34)	43,917.0	75.	Goldman Sachs Group (54)	22,854.0
26.	J.P. Morgan Chase (21)	43,372.0	76.	Ingram Micro (75)	22,459.3
27.	SBC Communications (27)	43,138.0	77.	BellSouth (82)	22,440.0
28.	Berkshire Hathaway (39)	42,353.0	78.	Honeywell Intl. (83)	22,274.0
29.	AOL Time Warner (37)	41,780.0	79.	Bank One Corp. (79)	22,171.0
30.	Sears Roebuck (32)	41,366.0	80.	Electronic Data Systems (97)	21,782.0
31.	Procter & Gamble (35)	40,238.0	81.	Supervalu (86)	20,908.5
32.	Freddie Mac (41)	39,663.0	82.	Alcoa (88)	20,618.0
33.	Costco Wholesale (44)	38,762.5	83.	FedEx (103)	20,607.0
34.	Johnson & Johnson (47)	36,298.0	84.	Mass. Mutual Life Insurance (N.A.)	20,247.1
35.	Albertson's (38)	35,916.0	85.	Caterpillar (98)	20,152.0
36.	Dell Computer (53)	35,404.0	86.	Johnson Controls (N.A.)	20,103.4
37.	Pfizer (49)	35,281.0	87.	Cigna (107)	19,915.0
38.	MetLife (51)	34,055.0	88.	Aetna (74)	19,878.7
39.	Kmart (40)	32,765.0	89.	TIAA-CREF (80)	19,791.0
40.	Morgan Stanley (29)	32,415.0	90.	HCA (N.A.)	19,729.0
41.	Safeway (45)	32,399.2	91.	Best Buy (131)	19,597.0
42.	J.C. Penney (50)	32,347.0	92.	Coca-Cola (99)	19,564.0
43.	United Parcel Service (55)	31,272.0	93.	AutoNation (N.A.)	19,478.5
44.	Allstate (57)	29,579.0	94.	Washington Mutual (116)	19,037.0
45.	Walgreen (78)	28,681.1	95.	Cisco Systems (92)	18,915.0
46.	Wells Fargo (64)	28,473.0	96.	Weyerhauser (140)	18,521.0
47.	Microsoft (72)	28,365.0	97.	Visteon (N.A.)	18,395.0
48.	Merrill Lynch (36)	28,253.0	98.	Bristol-Myers Squibb (96)	18,119.0
49.	United Technologies (59)	28,212.0	99.	Northrop Grumman (N.A.)	17,837.0
50.	ConAgra Foods (61)	27,629.6	100.	Abbott Laboratories (N.A.)	17,684.7

Source: *Fortune,* magazine, 2003. Reprinted by permission.

new business owners are still employed in a salaried job when they start their own business; 60 percent of new businesses start at home.

Franchising, a century-old tradition, continues to grow in popularity. The Department of Commerce estimates that franchising accounts for more than half of all sales in the U.S. The benefits to the franchisor are enormous: expansion with little or no risk, royalties and licensing revenue from the franchisee, and an initial franchise fee (usually around $25,000). The benefits to the franchisee are less obvious, but may include name recognition, a national advertising campaign, and training and financial assistance from the parent company. Although tales of self-made millionaires abound in franchising circles, far greater numbers of franchisees go bankrupt. As the accompanying table demonstrates, opening a franchised business is no simple proposition, often requiring hundreds of thousands (or even millions) of dollars in start-up costs.

Top 50 Franchises, by Number of Franchises, 2002

Rank	Franchise	Business	Number of franchises	Startup costs[1]	Franchise fees
1.	Kumon North America Inc.	Supplemental Education	22,043	$5,900-30,600	$1,000
2.	McDonald's	Hamburgers, chicken, salads	21,958	489,900-1.5 million	45,000
3.	7-Eleven Inc.	Convenience store	19,992	varies	varies
4.	Subway	Sandwiches	16,765	66,500-188,800	12,500
5.	Burger King Corp.	Hamburgers, chicken	10,425	294,000-2.8 million	50,000
6.	Jani-King	Commercial cleaning	9,594	11,300-34,100	8,600-16,300+
7.	Pizza Hut Inc.	Pizza	9,472	268,000-1.4 million	25,000
8.	KFC Corp.	Chicken	9,166	1.1 mil-1.7 million	25,000
9.	Coverall Cleaning Concepts	Commercial cleaning	6,730	6,300-35,900	6,000-32,200
10.	Century 21 Real Estate	Real estate	6,580	10,100-521,200	12,500/25,000
11.	Dairy Queen	Soft-serve dairy products/ sandwiches	5,739	234,200-640,800	20,000/35,000
12.	Dunkin' Donuts	Donuts & baked goods	5,537	255,700-1.1 million	50,000
13.	Jazzercise Inc.	Dance/exercise classes	5,456	1,800-20,600	325/650
14.	Taco Bell Corp.	Mexican fast food	5,348	3 million	45,000
15.	Baskin-Robbins USA Co.	Ice cream & yogurt	4,864	132,800-522,990	40,000
16.	Snap-On Tools	Hardware	4,641	20,700-247,700	5,000
17.	Mail Boxes Etc.	Postal/business/ communications services	4,591	123,700-228,100	29,950
18.	Choice Hotels Int'l.	Hotels, inns, suites & resorts	4,426	4.0-6.0 million	25,000-50,000
19.	ServiceMaster Clean	Commercial/residential contract cleaning	4,308	23,200-84,500	15,900-28,500
20.	RE/MAX Int'l. Inc.	Real estate	4,249	20,000-200,000	10,000-25,000
21.	Chem-Dry	Carpet, drapery & upholstery cleaning	3,857	22,600-63,100	9,950
22.	Curves for Women	Women's fitness & weight-loss centers	3,446	25,600-31,100	19,900
23.	Jackson Hewitt Tax Service	Computerized tax preparation/ electronic filing services	3,386	47,400-75,200	25,000
24.	Arby's	Roast beef sandwiches, chicken, subs	3,359	333,700-2.3 million	37,500/25,000
25.	Coldwell Banker Real Estate	Real estate	3,159	23,000-477,000	12,500-20,000
26.	Holiday Inn Worldwide	Hotels	3,102	varies	varies
27.	Midas Auto Service Experts	Auto maintenance services	2,597	379,400-528,000	20,000
28.	Novus Windshield Repair	Windshield repair, paint restoration	2,452	20,000-166,300	3,900
29.	ERA Franchise Systems Inc.	Real estate	2,414	42,700-205, 900	20,000
30.	RadioShack	Consumer electronics	2,094	60,000	25,000
31.	Super 8 Motels Inc.	Economy motels	2,088	288,100-2.3 million	Varies
32.	Sonic Drive In Restaurants	Drive-in restaurant	2,040	621,300-1.2 million	30,000
33.	Days Inn Worlwide	Hotels	1,942	407,000-5.4 million	Varies
34.	GNC Franchising Inc.	Vitamin & nutrition stores	1,892	132,700-182,000	40,000/30,000
35.	TCBY Systems LLC	Frozen Yogurt, ice cream, sorbet, smoothies	1,891	142,000-347,000	6,000-25,000
36.	Blimpie Int'l. Inc.	Submarine sandwiches, salads	1,887	72,800-338,200	18,000
37.	Merle Norman Cosmetics	Cosmetics studios	1,865	33,100-153,100	0
38.	Jiffy Lube Int'l. Inc.	Fast oil change	1,755	174,000-194,000	35,000
39.	Great Clips Inc.	Family hair salons	1,720	88,600-173,900	17,500
40.	Quizno's Franchise Co., The	Submarine sandwiches, soups, salads	1,663	208,400-243,800	25,000
41.	Hardee's	Burgers, chicken, biscuits	1,648	770,800-1.1 million	35,000
42.	Popeyes Chicken & Biscuits	Cajun-style fried chicken & biscuits	1,562	600,000-1.2 million	30,000
43.	Management Recruiters/Sales Consultants/MRI Worldwide	Personnel placement/search & recruiting services	1,362	114,950-162,200	77,000
44.	CleanNet USA Inc.	Commercial office cleaning	1,335	3,900-35,500	2,950-32,000
45.	Matco Tools	Automotive/professional tools & equipment	1,321	60,000-156,000	0
46.	The Medicine Shoppe	Pharmacy	1,297	76,800-152,500	10,000-18,000
47.	Jan-Pro Franchising Int'l. Inc.	Commercial cleaning	1,266	1,000-14,000+	1,000-14,000+
48.	Merry Maids	Residential cleaning	1,239	32,500-49,500	16,000-24,000
49.	Church's Chicken	Southern fried chicken and biscuits	1,157	203,000-750,000	10,000/15,000
50.	Hampton Inns & Suites	Hotels	1,153	4.9-8.7 million	45,000+

Note: Does not include franchises owned by the company. 1. Includes franchise fees.
Source: *Entrepreneur* (Jan. 2003). Reprinted by permission.

ADVERTISING

Few facts and figures reveal the extraordinary growth of the mass-consumption society as vividly as those dealing with the advertising business. In 1950, as the postwar economy began to heat up, American business spent $5.7 billion to advertise its goods and services; by 1960 that figure would double, and then almost double again by 1970. Between 1970 and 1990, as the Baby Boom generation entered the marketplace and the economy expanded, advertising expenditures grew at a spiraling rate, topping $100 billion in 1986. That rate of growth has not been sustained, but advertising spending continued to reach new highs every year until 2000. In 2001, however, the industry suffered its worst decline since 1987; total advertising expenditures dropped 6.5 percent, from $243 billion to $231 billion. Expenditures rebounded in 2002 to $236.8 billion.

Nearly 60 percent of all advertising dollars are spent to place ads in newspapers or magazines or to run commercials on radio and television. The Internet, meanwhile, represents only a tiny fraction of all advertising dollars spent. As the accompanying table shows, companies spent more than twice as much money to advertise in the Yellow Pages as they did on pop-up ads.

The biggest advertisers are the nation's largest manufacturers of automobiles, food, soft drinks, tobacco and beer. Most advertising dollars are filtered through about 13,000 advertising agencies, which mainly create the ads and buy the space or time from the media. The agency business has undergone a dramatic restructuring recently, as many of the largest agencies, most of them with worldwide connections, have merged to form enormous corporations. The largest such megacorporation is the New York-based Omnicom Group, which had a worldwide revenues of more than $7.5 billion in 2002. New York's Interpublic Group was a second with $6.2 billion, while the London-based WPP Group posted $5.8 billion. The combined revenues of the top three players were greater than the total revenues of the next 50-largest agencies combined.

Advertising Expenditures in the U.S., 1776–2002 (in millions)

Year	Amount[1]	Year	Amount[1]	Year	Amount[1]
1776	$0.2	**1890**	300	**1980**	54,780
1800	1	**1900**	450	**1985**	94,750
1820	3	**1909**	$1,000	**1990**	128,640
1840	7	**1915**	1,100	**1995**	160,930
1850	12	**1940**	2,110	**1999**	215,301
1860	22	**1950**	$5,700	**2000**	243,680
1867	40	**1960**	11,960	**2001**	231,300
1880	175	**1970**	19,550	**2002**	236,880

Source: *Advertising Age*. 1. These are estimated figures of the monies spent on placing advertising in all media; the costs of producing the advertising are not included.

Total U.S. Advertising Volume by Medium, 2001–02

Medium	2001 Expenditures (millions)	2001 Percent share	2002 Expeditures (millions)	2002 Percent share	Percent change 2001–02
Newspapers, total	**$44,300**	**19.2%**	**44,030**	**17.8%**	**-0.5%**
National	6,600	2.9	6,8100	2.9	2.9
Local	37,600	16.3	37,230	15.7	-1.1
Magazines, total	11,100	4.8	11,000	4.6	-0.9
Broadcast TV, total	38,900	16.8	42,070	17.8	8.2
Four TV networks	14,300	6.2	15,000	6.3	4.9
Syndication1	3,100	1.3	3,030	1.3	-2.2
Spot (national)	9,200	4.0	10,920	4.6	18.4
Spot (local)	12,300	5.3	13,110	5.6	7.0
Cable TV, total	15,500	6.7	16,300	6.9	3.6
Cable networks	11,900	5.1	12,070	5.1	2.5
Spot (local)	3,700	1.6	4,230	1.8	7.5
Radio, total	17,900	7.7	18,880	7.9	5.7
Network	700	0.3	780	0.3	9.0
Spot (national)	3,000	1.3	3,340	1.4	13.0
Spot (local)	14,200	6.1	14,760	6.2	4.0
Yellow pages, total	13,600	5.9	13,780	5.8	1.4
National	2,100	0.9	2,090	0.9	0.0
Local	11,500	5.0	11,690	4.9	1.6
Direct mail	44,700	19.3	46,070	19.4	3.0
Business papers	4,500	1.9	3,980	1.7	-11.0
Out of home, total	5,100	2.2	5,180	2.2	0.8
National	2,100	0.9	2,060	0.9	0.5
Local	3,100	1.3	3,110	1.3	1.0
Internet, total	5,800	2.5	4,880	2.1	-13.5
Miscellaneous, total	30,000	13.0	30,730	13.0	2.8
National	22,800	9.9	23,410	9.9	1.0
Local	7,200	3.1	7,320	3.1	6.6
Total national	141,800	61.3	145,430	61.4	2.6
Total local	89,500	38.7	91,450	38.6	2.2
Grand total	**$231,300**	**100.0%**	**236,880**	**100.0**	**2.4%**

1. Includes UPN and WB. 2. Includes billboards and other outdoor advertising. **Source**: Prepared for *Advertising Age* by Universal McCann's Robert J. Coen. www.adage.com

Top 25 U.S. Advertising Agencies, by Gross Domestic Income, 2002

Rank 2002/Agency, Headquarters (Rank 2001)	U.S. Revenues, 2002 (millions)	U.S. Percent change, 2001-02	Worldwide Reveneus 2002 (millions)	Worldwide Percent change, 2001-02
1. J. Walter Thompson Co., New York (1)	$393.7	-1.8 %	$996.9	-3.3%
2. Leo Burnett Worldwide, Chicago, 3)	379.0	8.0	801.9	6.5
3. McCann-Erickson Worldwide, New York (2)	327.1	-10.5	1,238.5	-8.0
4. BBDO Worldwide, New York (6)	251.8	7.1	1,062.7	9.8
5. DDB Worldwide Communications, New York (7)	236.0	7.3	815.0	9.7
6. Euro RSCG Worldwide, New York (5)	235.5	-1.9	976.0	-9.5
7. Grey Worldwide, New York (8)	229.4	6.1	586.0	-1.4
8. Ogilvy & Mather Worldwide, New York (10)	200.2	-0.2	589.4	-2.9
9. Foote, Cone & Belding Worldwide, New York (4)	193.2	-29.5	379.2	-31.9
10. Y&R Advertising, New York (9)	191.2	-7.8	442.0	-9.2
11. Saatchi & Saatchi, New York (11)	176.4	4.1	476.5	4.8
12. Deutsch, New York (13)	158.2	7.3	158.2	7.3
13. Campbell-Ewald, Warren, Mich. (12)	151.3	-2.9	151.3	-2.9
14. Publicis Worldwide, New York (16)	124.2	-7.6	909.9	0.2
15. Bates USA, New York (14)	118.1	-15.3	365.3	-9.0
16. TBWA Worldwide, New York (19)	114.0	7.9	665.9	10.2
17. Doner, Southfield, Mich. (20)	109.7	8.8	121.5	6.4
18. Arnold Worldwide, Boston (17)	105.6	-5.3	207.6	-9.1
19. Lowe & Partners Worldwide, New York (15)	104.0	-22.7	364.4	-20.8
20. Richards Group, Dallas (23)	101.0	19.5	101.0	19.5
21. Hill, Holliday, Connors, Cosmopulos, Boston (18)	100.9	-8.9	100.9	-8.9
22. Campbell Mithun, Minneapolis (21)	95.5	-5.2	95.5	-5.2
23. Rubin Postaer & Associates, Santa Monica, Calif. (22)	91.4	1.2	91.4	1.2
24. Zimmerman & Partners, Fort Lauderdale, Fla. (26)	80.3	10.6	80.3	10.6
25. Cramer-Krasselt, Chicago (25)	74.6	2.6	74.6	2.6

Note: Revenues are estimated by Advertising Age and do not include non-advertising specialty and subsidiary shops.
Source: *Advertising Age* (April 21,2003); reprinted by permission of Crain Communications, Inc. www.adage.com

The 100 Leading U.S. Advertisers, 1991-2002

2002 Rank, Company (2001 rank)	Total spending (milllions) 1991	1995	2000	2001	2002
1. General Motors Corp. (1)	$1,056.5	$1,499.6	$3,934.8	$3,374.4	$3,652.2
2. AOL Time Warner (2)	311.3	543.0	1,770.1	1,885.3	2,922.8
3. Procter & Gamble Co. (3)	1,166.4	1,507.4	2,363.5	2,540.6	2,673.4
4. Pfizer (5)	N.A.	N.A.	2,265.3	2,189.5	2,566.2
5. Ford Motor Co. (4)	517.7	891.8	2,345.2	2,408.2	2,251.8
6. DaimlerChrysler (6)	414.8	954.7	1,984.0	1,985.3	2,031.8
7. Walt Disney Co. (7)	257.3	777.8	1,757.5	1,757.3	1,083.0
8. Johnson & Johnson (9)	371.1	601.3	1,601.2	1,618.1	1,799.0
9. Sears, Roebuck & Co. (11)	462.3	557.8	1,455.4	1,480.1	1,661.2
10. Unilever (8)	371.4	442:7	1,453.6	1,483.6	1,640.0
11. Sony Corp. (16)	262.8	431.0	1,030.0	1,310.1	1,621.1
12. GlaxoSmithKline (10)	83.3	173.2	1,126.4	881.1	1,554.0
13. Toyota Motor Corp. (12)	442.5	513.4	1,273.9	1,399.1	1,552.7
14. Verizon Communications (13)	N.A.	N.A.	1,612.9	1,461.6	1,527.5
15. McDonald's Corp. (14)	87.4	586.4	1,273.9	1,194.7	1,335.7
16. Viacom (17)	N.A.	N.A.	1,220.9	1,282.8	1,259.8
17. Altria Group (15)	1,110.4	1,397.7	2,602.9	1,815.7	1,206.0
18. Honda Motor Co. (19)	242.5	388.8	1,035.0	1,102.9	1,192.0
19. Merck & Co. (18)	129.5	199.0	983.9	1,136.6	1,158.4
20. L'Oreal (22)	N.A.	N.A.	987.1	1,040.7	1,117.7
21. PepsiCo (23)	542.0	730.2	2,100.7	2,210.4	1,113.9
22. J.C. Penney Corp. (25)	105.2	273.9	1,011.2	1,085.7	1,108.0
23. SBC Communications (32)	N.A.	N.A.	786.0	943.1	1,091.6
24. U.S. Government (17)	123.4	219.9	1,246.3	1,056.8	1,082.8
25. Nestle (24)	307.6	490.1	637.7	967.1	1,073.2
26. Nissan Motor Co. (36)	212.0	367.7	813.8	774.7	966.7
27. Target Corp. (35)	N.A.	N.A.	826.7	925.7	960.0
28. General Mills (30)	419.1	367.7	639.2	883.5	954.1
29. Microsoft Corp. (27)	N.A.	147.7	854.8	973.8	909.1
30. Home Depot (34)	N.A.	96.6	651.6	919.7	885.2
31. AT&T Wireless (29)	N.A.	N.A.	616.3	887.7	872.9
32. Sprint Corp. (20)	N.A.	213.9	1,227.3	1,160.1	863.0

2002 Rank, Company (2001 rank)	Total spending (milllions)				
	1991	1995	2000	2001	2002
33. IBM Corp. (26)	$387.4	$490.6	$1,189.0	$993.5	$832.3
34. Best Buy Co. (54)	N.A.	94.0	446.7	542.7	818.7
35. AT&T Corp. (31)	391.7	675.2	1,415.7	1,371.9	815.1
36. Estee Lauder Cos. (35)	N.A.	N.A.	717.3	766.4	805.3
37. Diageo (39)	N.A	N.A	1,112.1	1,180.8	797.8
38. Anheuser-Busch Cos. (41)	327.9	320.5	707.6	655.6	792.9
39. Hewlett-Packard Co. (60)	N.A.	N.A.	791.4	898.7	736.1
40. Yum Brands (45)	N.A.	N.A.	N.A.	676.5	732.6
41. Cendant Corp. (40)	63.6	115.2	409.8	527.2	726.9
42. Wyeth (33)	N.A.	N.A.	N.A.	770.8	724.7
43. News Corp. (43)	358.6	275.9	923.2	670.4	715.9
44. Federated Department Stores (37)	111.4	407.6	1,127.6	746.1	715.1
45. ConAgra (44)	N.A.	N.A.	578.5	668.3	680.1
46. May Department Stores Co. (45)	194.0	339.4	570.1	552.8	655.9
47. Mars Inc. (49)	128.2	210.1	670.8	614.8	653.1
48. Burger King Corp. (46)	N.A.	N.A.	N.A.	N.A.	650.1
49. Kmart Corp. (47)	186.5	241.2	542.1	596.7	628.6
50. Nike (52)	109.5	146.3	613.5	576.6	623.5
51. Wal-Mart Stores (55)	76.7	143.2	497.8	573.4	618.1
52. Sara Lee Corp. (41)	N.A.	N.A.	617.1	812.1	604.7
53. Volkswagen (55)	N.A.	N.A.	551.3	595.8	602.4
54. Vivendi Universal (53)	N.A.	333.1	699.8	498.5	591.4
55. General Electric Co. (38)	N.A.	N.A.	1,310.1	663.8	579.0
56. Clorox Co. (38)	127.8	157.8	397.1	337.6	572.3
57. Novartis (56)	N.A.	N.A.	573.9	552.4	569.3
58. Coca-Cola Co. (48)	218.8	238.2	894.9	903.5	569.0
59. Bristol-Myers Squibb Co. (50)	184.0	219.4	1,190.7	973.8	563.5
60. American Express Co. (65)	156.2	210.4	538.2	444.5	542.1
61. Albertson's (59)	N.A.	N.A.	N.A.	457.7	524.9
62. Dell Computer Corp. (69)	N.A.	N.A.	429.5	302.2	510.6
63. Deutsche Telekom (95)	N.A.	N.A.	N.A.	289.0	509.3
64. Kroger Co. (57)	N.A.	N.A.	551.2	511.6	508.9
65. Schering-Plough Corp. (62)	95.9	104.0	510.5	497.8	507.6
66. Gillette Co. (63)	37.1	132.7	466.0	463.4	495.0
67. Aventis (75)	N.A.	N.A.	N.A.	421.0	486.0
68. SABMiller (68)	N.A.	N.A.	N.A.	N.A.	458.5
69. Campbell Soup Co. (78)	109.5	169.0	331.2	397.0	447.5
70. Lowe's Cos. (77)	N.A.	N.A.	206.7	233.5	444.3
71. Gap Inc. (72)	N.A.	N.A.	449.6	425.9	433.6
72. Kellogg Co. (74)	381.3	488.2	455.4	421.5	429.1
73. Visa International (71)	N.A.	N.A.	427.3	347.4	423.2
74. Adolph Coors Co. (70)	N.A.	N.A.	444.2	430.1	420.3
75. Limited Brands (73)	N.A.	N.A.	349.9	428.3	410.7
76. Berkshire Hathaway (70)	N.A.	N.A.	455.8	339.4	398.5
77. Cadbury Schweppes (76)	N.A.	N.A.	265.7	248.0	396.2
78. Mitsubishi Motors Corp. (92)	N.A.	N.A.	317.2	289.8	392.1
79. Mattel (81)	63.8	184.5	451.4	448.6	384.4
80. MCI (61)	N.A.	N.A.	N.A.	N.A.	371.2
81. Bayer (67)	55.8	160.5	648.9	567.1	370.6
82. Wendy's International (94)	61.1	179.4	296.3	312.2	359.5
83. MasterCard International (90)	N.A.	N.A.	311.1	288.1	358.0
84. Safeway (80)	N.A.	N.A.	397.7	440.5	356.2
85. Doctor's Associates (100)	N.A.	N.A.	N.A.	285.9	352.7
86. Kimberly-Clark Corp. (88)	111.7	133.1	297.3	304.3	352.5
87. Intel Corp. (66)	N.A.	N.A.	772.9	426.1	345.2
88. Morgan Stanley Dean Witter & Co. (79)	93.1	122.6	539.5	385.1	341.8
89. Circuit City Stores (65)	128.2	291.6	479.0	410.0	340.7
90. S.C. Johnson & Son (86)	93.1	115.6	464.8	478.8	340.7
91. Colgate-Palmolive Co. (90)	N.A.	N.A.	331.9	355.2	336.7
92. United Parcel Service (103)	N.A.	N.A.	155.9	200.7	331.4
93. Hershey Foods Corp. (84)	141.6	150.0	338.1	365.5	330.8
94. Nextel Communications (99)	N.A.	N.A.	197.9	284.1	319.6
95. Reckitt Benckiser (93)	N.A.	N.A.	289.2	316.2	318.0
96. Kia Motors Corp. (141)	N.A.	N.A.	N.A.	286.9	316.3
97. Kohl's Corp. (102)	N.A.	N.A.	231.7	268.0	316.0
98. Fortune Brands (106)	N.A.	N.A.	273.0	283.1	313.0
99. Eastman Kodak Co. (82)	N.A.	N.A.	343.2	323.9	312.3
100. Office Depot (97)	N.A.	N.A.	334.5	289.6	311.5
Total Top 100 companies	**N.A.**	**N.A.**	**$82,011**	**$80,941**	**$82,279**

Note: The top 100 companies in are not the same each year. **Source:** *Advertising Age,* 100 Leading National Advertisers, 2003

Education

The American people's unwavering commitment to public education dates back more than 150 years. Fueled by a demand for literacy from two different creeds, one described in the Bible, the other in the Declaration of Independence, the American system of education grew to be an essential element in our faith that this nation was uniquely the land of opportunity.

Today that belief has evolved into what is called equality of opportunity, and this vital idea has helped to create a school system whose size, scope and ambitions are unrivalled by any Western democracy. More than 69 million students and more than 4 million teachers, administrators, and support staff are directly involved in education. The cost of this undertaking is, of course, staggering: more than half a trillion dollars annually—nearly $9,000 per student—or 7.4 percent of the gross domestic product (G.D.P.), virtually all of it for public education. The portion of G.D.P. spent on education rose rapidly between 1959 and 1969, declined in the 1970s as enrollment in elementary and secondary schools fell, and began rising steadily again in 1984. Since 1990, it has remained relatively stable. And while some complain bitterly about the quality of the results, or about overt waste, mismanagement and even fraud, no one any longer questions the essential role of education in American life today.

Revenues for Public Elementary and Secondary Schools, 1920–2000

School year	Total revenues (millions)	Percentage Federal	State	Local[1]
1919–20	$970	0.3%	16.5%	83.2%
1929–30	2,089	0.4	16.9	82.7
1939–40	2,261	1.8	30.3	68.0
1949–50	5,437	2.9	39.8	57.3
1959–60	14,747	4.4	39.1	56.5
1969–70	40,267	8.0	39.9	52.1
1979–80	96,881	9.8	46.8	43.4
1989–90	208,548	6.1	47.3	46.6
1995–96	287,703	6.6	47.5	45.9
1996-97	305,065	6.6	48.0	45.4
1997-98	325,976	6.8	48.4	44.8
1998-99[2]	347,378	7.1	48.7	44.2
1999-2000	372,865	7.3	49.5	43.2

1. Includes a relatively small amount from nongovernmental sources (gifts and tuition and transportation fees from patrons). These sources accounted for 2.5 percent of total revenues in 1997–98. 2. Revised from previously published figures.
Source: U.S. Dept. of Education, National Center for Education Statistics, *Digest of Education Statistics, 2002.*

▶PUBLIC ELEMENTARY AND SECONDARY SCHOOLS

Expenditures on public elementary and secondary schools have been increasing faster than inflation in almost every year since figures were first kept in 1900. The exception was the period between 1978 and 1982, when inflation outpaced increases in expenditures. Total expenditures for public elementary and secondary schools topped $422 billion in 2001-02, or more than double what they were in 1989-90; expenditures per student were $8,745 in 2001-02. The accompanying table shows that even after adjusting for inflation, the amount spent to educate each student at public elementary and secondary schools continues to skyrocket.

In 1979, a historic shift occurred in the source of money to operate the American public school system. That was the year the state share of revenues rose above the local share for the first time. The federal share for elementary and secondary schools has always been relatively small.

Enrollment in public elementary schools declined dramatically from 1970 to 1985 (from 32.6 million to 27.0 million) as the number of young people decreased. That trend evidenced itself in secondary school populations between 1980 and 1990. Since 1990, however, populations of both elementary and secondary school populations have generally continued to rise. In 2002, the U.S.

Education Expenditures, 1950–2002

School year	All educational institutions: Total expenditures (millions)	As percentage of GDP	Elementary and Secondary schools, Public: Total (millions)	Public: Per pupil (constant dollars)[1]	Private (millions)[2]	Colleges and Universities: Public (millions)	Private (millions)
1949–50	$ 8,911	3.3%	$ 5,838	$1,738	$ 411	$ 1,430	$ 1,233
1959-60	23,860	4.7	15,613	2,668	1,100	3,904	3,244
1969-70	68,459	6.9	40,683	4,147	2,500	16,234	9,041
1979-80	165,627	6.5	95,962	5,255	7,200	41,434	21,031
1989-90	381,525	7.0	212,770	7,262	18,200	96,387	54,169
1995-96	529,596	7.2	293,646	7,431	24,600	132,752	78,597
1996-97	562,871	7.2	313,151	7,585	26,000	139,620	84,1002
1997-98	597,549	7.2	334,315	7,868	27,100	147,034	89,100
1998-99	633,532	7.2	355,838	8,158	28,200	155,294	94,200
1999-2000	678,399	7.3	381,729	8,454	29,700	167,670	99,300
2000-01[3]	712,800	7.3	398,500	8,464	30,500	178,500	105,300
2001-02[2]	745,200	7.4	422,100	8,745	32,000	182,500	108,600

1. Expenditure per pupil in fall enrollment, as measured in constant (2001-02) dollars, based on the Consumer Price Index. 2. Estimated. 3. Preliminary data for elementary and secondary schools and estimates for colleges and universities.
Source: U.S. Dept. of Education, National Center for Education Statistics, *Digest of Education Statistics,* 2002.

Number of Schools and Teachers in the U.S., Fall, 2000

School type	Schools Total	Schools Public	Schools Private	Teachers Total	Teachers Public	Teachers Private
Elementary and secondary	**N.A.**	**93,273**	**N.A.**	**3,355,386**	**2,952,911**	**402,475**
Elementary	N.A.	64,601	N.A.	1,867,083	1,673,469	193,614
Secondary	N.A.	21,994	N.A.	1,121,266	1,056,601	64,665
Combined	N.A.	5,096	N.A.	367,117	222,921	144,196
Other schools	N.A.	1,582	N.A.	N.A.	N.A.	N.A.
Colleges and universities	**4,182**	**1,698**	**2,484**	**1,063,000[1]**	**741,000[1,2]**	**322,000[1,2]**
4-year colleges	2,450	622	1,828	N.A.	N.A.	N.A.
2-year colleges	1,732	1,076	656	N.A.	N.A.	N.A.

1. Estimates. 2. Full- and part-time senior instructional faculty. **Source:** U.S. Dept. of Education, National Center for Education Statistics, *Digest of Education Statistics, 2002.*

School Enrollment, Kindergarten Through University Level, 1970–2002 (millions of students)

Year	Elementary (K-8) Public	Elementary (K-8) Private	Secondary (9-12) Public	Secondary (9-12) Private	Higher education Public	Higher education Private	Total
1970	32.6	4.1	13.3	1.3	6.4	2.2	**59.9**
1975	30.5	3.7	14.3	1.3	8.8	2.4	**61.0**
1980	27.6	4.0	13.2	1.3	9.5	2.6	**58.3**
1985	27.0	4.2	12.4	1.4	9.5	2.8	**57.2**
1990	29.9	4.1[1]	11.3	1.2[1]	10.8	3.0	**60.3**
1995	32.3	4.4	12.5	1.3	11.1	3.2	**64.8**
1997	33.1	4.6	13.1	1.2	11.2	3.3	**66.5**
1998	33.3	4.7[1]	13.2	1.2[1]	11.1	3.4	**67.0**
1999	33.5	4.8	13.4	1.3	11.3	3.5	**67.7**
2000	33.7	4.7	13.5	1.3	11.8	3.6	68.5
2001[2]	33.9[1]	4.7	13.7[1]	1.3	11.9	3.6	69.0
2002[2]	33.8	4.7	13.9	1.3	12.0	3.6	69.2

Note: Totals may not add up due to independent rounding. 1. Estimated. 2. Projected.
Source: U.S. Dept. of Education, National Center for Education Statistics, *Digest of Education Statistics, 2002.*

Department of Education projected a public elementary school population of 33.8 million; public secondary school enrollment reached an all-time high of 13.9 million. These numbers suggest that baby boomers started a baby boom of their own, the fruits of which are now starting to reach high school.

Teachers have more than kept pace with the growth in the number of students. There were 1.9 million elementary school teachers and 1.1 million secondary school teachers in 2000-01, more than double the number in 1955. The number of secondary school teachers has remained at about one million since 1975, while the number of public elementary school teachers has risen consistently every year since 1982, when they numbered 1.2 million. A more telling statistic, though, is pupil-teacher ratios. Despite constant complaints about overcrowded inner-city classrooms, the average number of pupils supervised by each teacher has declined dramatically in the past 30 years. Each elementary school teacher was responsible for 18 students in 2000-01, down from 24.3 in 1970, while secondary schools had a pupil-teacher ratio of 12 to 1, down from 19.8 to 1 in 1970.

According to a survey by the American Federation of Teachers, the average salary was $30,719 for first-year teachers in 2001-02, and $44,367 for teachers with an average of 16 years of experience. That's 2.7 percent higher than the year before, and after adjusting for inflation, slightly higher than 1972 levels ($40,350). Since 1995, teacher salaries have increased faster than inflation. Teachers, perhaps because their salaries come from tax revenues, earn significantly less than other college graduates. The survey found that teachers earn 58 percent as much as engineers, 60 percent of a computer analyst's paycheck, and 81 percent of what an accountant makes.

Nursery schools have increased dramatically in popularity since 1965, when 27.1 percent of 3-to-5-year-olds were enrolled in a kindergarten or pre-kindergarten program. That percentage has increased gradually ever since, reaching a high of 65.8 percent in 1999. (In 2001, it was 63.9 percent.) The percentage of youngsters attending full-time nursery school has also been on the rise. Only 17 percent of pre-primary students were in full-time programs in 1970; in 2000, 51.8 percent were full-time enrollees. Most nursery school students were in private schools, while most kindergarten students were enrolled in public schools.

School districts declined drastically between 1930, when there were 119,000 of them, and 1984, when there were a mere 15,747. Numbers since 1985 are not directly comparable with earlier years, but school districts have remained constant at about 15,000. There were 14,859 school districts in 2000-01. The greatest number

How the States Rank in Public Education, 2001–2002

State	Enrollment	Rank	Expenditures per pupil	Rank	Average teacher salary	Rank
U.S.	47,369,748[1]	—	$7,548[1]	—	$44,683[1]	—
Alabama	726,367	24	5,210[1]	48	37,194	40
Alaska	134,358	45	9,447	7	49,418	10
Arizona	915,656	16	5,099[1]	49	39,973	26
Arkansas	448,246	34	5,651	46	36,962	42
California	6,141,363	1	7,055	28	54,348	1
Colorado	742,145	22	6,912[1]	31	40,659	25
Connecticut	569,540	28	10,825	4	53,551	2
D.C.	68,449	51	13,993	1	47,049	13
Delaware	115,484	47	9,677[1]	6	48,363	11
Florida	2,495,969	4	6,143	43	39,275	30
Georgia	1,470,634	9	7,824	19	44,073	16
Hawaii	184,546	42	7,353	24	42,615	20
Idaho	246,415	39	6,469	39	39,591	29
Illinois	2,066,775	5	8,914[1]	10	49,435	9
Indiana	996,006	14	7,866[1]	17	44,195	15
Iowa	485,932	31	6,819	33	38,230	34
Kansas	470,205	33	7,354	23	37,093	41
Kentucky	631,117	26	7,085	27	37,951	36
Louisiana	730,252	23	6,560	37	36,328	45
Maine	205,586	41	8,831[1]	11	37,300	39
Maryland	860,640	20	7,658	21	48,251	12
Massachusetts	973,142	15	10,190	5	50,293	7
Michigan	1,720,570[1]	8	8,343[1]	15	52,676[1]	4
Minnesota	851,368	21	7,567	22	42,194	17
Mississippi	492,198	30	5,469	47	33,295	49
Missouri	890,195	18	6,759	35	37,996	35
Montana	151,947	44	7,130	26	34,379	48
Nebraska	283,791	37	6,811	34	36,236	46
Nevada	356,814	35	5,813	45	40,764[1]	24
New Hampshire	206,847	40	7,847	18	39,915	28
New Jersey	1,341,504	10	10,869	3	53,192	3
New Mexico	320,044	36	6,705	36	36,440	44
New York	2,839,536	3	11,023[1]	2	52,040	4
North Carolina	1,321,630[1]	11	6,364[1]	40	42,680	19
North Dakota	105,217	48	4,612[1]	51	32,253	50
Ohio	1,804,585	7	7,204	25	44,029	17
Oklahoma	622,154	27	6,237	42	34,744	47
Oregon	551,522	29	7,804	20	46,081	14
Pennsylvania	1,821,627	6	8,070[1]	16	50,599	6
Rhode Island	157,956	43	9,394[1]	8	49,758[1]	8
South Carolina	669,701	25	7,012[1]	29	39,923	27
South Dakota	125,612	46	6,540	38	31,295	51
Tennessee	907,774	17	5,947	44	38,515	33
Texas	4,146,653	2	6,850	32	39,232	32
Utah	477,801	32	4,674	50	37,414[1]	38
Vermont	100,867	49	9,352	9	39,240	31
Virginia	1,163,094	12	6,343[1]	41	41,731[1]	23
Washington	1,010,424	13	6,999	30	43,464	18
West Virginia	282,232	38	8,426	14	36,751	43
Wisconsin	879,361	19	8,604	13	42,232	21
Wyoming	87,897	50	8,813	12	37,837	37

1. Data estimated by NEA. **Source:** National Education Association, *Rankings of the States,* 2002.

of school districts had between 1,000 and 2,499 students in them, but school districts with 25,000 students or more were responsible for educating nearly one-third of public school students.

▶PRIVATE SCHOOLS

The U.S. Department of Education updates its data on private schools less frequently than it does for public institutions. The 1999-2000 school year is the latest year for which data is available for private elementary and secondary schools. (Data for teachers and tuitions are from 1993-94, the latest year available).

Schools and enrollment There were 27,223 private schools engaged in educating 5,126,684 students. Of these schools, 16,530 were elementary schools (responsible for educating 2,831,372 students), 2,538 were secondary schools (806,639 students), and 8,155 offered instruction in all 12 grades (1,524,673 students). Most private schools were religiously affiliated. One-third, or 8,102 schools, were affiliated with the Catholic Church; 13,232 were affiliated with other religious groups. Only 5,889 private schools were nonsectarian.

Tuition Average tuition for private school students was $3,116 per year. But that average is kept low by the large number of parochial schools offering free or low-cost private education. The average cost of all nonsectarian private schools (elementary and secondary) was $6,631, and more than half of such schools charge at least $5,000 per year in tuition. Average tuition for nonsectarian secondary schools was over $9,000 per year.

Teachers There were 378,365 full-time private school teachers; almost all of them were under the age of 50. The vast majority of these teachers (285,235) were women, and an even greater number (347,811) were white. The average teacher salary in private schools was $23,395, a fraction of the $35,924 earned by public school teachers. Male teachers earned substantially more than their female counterparts in both public and private schools, but the difference was most pronounced in private schools, where male compensation ($28,948) was 34 percent greater than female salaries ($21,657).

Catholic Schools, Pupils & Teachers, 1960–2003

Year	Schools	Pupils	Teachers: Total	Teachers: Religious	Teachers: Lay
Elementary schools					
1960	10,501	4,373,000	108,000	79,000	29,000
1970	9,362	3,355,000	112,000	52,000	60,000
1980	8,043	2,269,000	97,000	25,000	72,000
1990	7,291	1,883,906	91,039	10,837	80,202
1995	6,979	1,990,784	116,494	10,564	105,930
2000	6,923	2,013,084	109,404	6,862	102,542
2002	6,886	1,971,627	108,485	5,447	103,038
2003	6,785	1,923,143	112,884	5,479	107,405
Secondary schools					
1960	2,392	880,000	44,000	33,000	11,000
1970	1,981	1,008,000	55,000	29,000	26,000
1980	1,516	837,000	49,000	14,000	35,000
1990	1,296	591,533	40,159	6,579	33,580
1995	1,238	614,571	46,599	6,193	40,406
2000	1,221	639,954	47,730	4,149	43,581
2002	1,280	644,703	47,173	3,541	43,632
2003	1,215	630,134	50,120	3,694	46,426

Source: National Catholic Educational Association.

Average SAT and ACT Scores by Group, 1987–2002

Group	Composite scores: 1987	1990	1997	2000	2002	Total test-takers, class of 2001
SAT Scores						
American Indian, Alaskan Native	934	934	963	963	962	7,506
Asian American, Pacific Islander	1,020	1,029	1,060	1,064	1,070	103,242
Black	839	847	860	860	857	122,684
Mexican-American	912	917	913	913	903	48,225
Puerto Rican	868	872	899	907	906	14,273
Other Hispanic	926	923	927	928	922	41,627
White	1,038	1,034	1,054	1,058	1,060	698,659
Men	1,035	1,026	1,040	1,040	1,041	484,314
Women	983	989	998	1,002	1,002	590,899
National average[1]	**1,008**	**1,001**	**1,017**	**1,019**	**1,020**	**1,327,831**
ACT Scores						
American Indian, Alaskan Native	17.5	18.0	19.0	19.0	18.6	11,895
Asian American, Pacific Islander	21.9	21.7	21.8	21.7	21.6	36,732
Black	16.6	17.0	17.1	17.0	16.8	120,311
Mexican-American	18.1	18.3	18.5	18.6	18.2	45,762
Other Hispanic	19.3	19.3	19.6	19.5	18.8	21,008
White	21.3	21.2	21.7	21.8	21.7	773,933
Men	21.2	21.0	21.2	21.2	20.9	485,797
Women	20.1	20.3	20.9	20.9	20.7	623,128
National average[1]	**20.6**	**20.6**	**21.0**	**21.0**	**20.8**	**1,116,082**

1. Includes students of other ethnicities and students who did not identify their gender or their ethnicity.
Source: The College Board, American College Testing Program.

Race and ethnicity Private schools remain almost entirely white enclaves. Nearly half (13,231) of all private schools had minority enrollments of under 9 percent, and another quarter (6,435) had minority populations below 29 percent, even though almost half of private school students came from central cities.

Student-teacher ratios Students in private schools continue to get more teacher attention than do students in public schools. The average teacher in public elementary and secondary schools was responsible for 15.1 students, compared to 13.8 students for private school teachers. The difference was even more pronounced on the secondary school level, where private school teachers averaged 11.6 students, while each public school teacher was responsible for 14.2 pupils.

Average Cost of 4-Year Colleges in Current and Constant Dollars, 1971–2003 (tuition and fees)

Despite low rates of inflation, the cost of a college education continues to skyrocket. Tuition and fees in 2002-03 were nearly three times what they were as recently as 1985-86, and nearly 10 times what they were in 1971-72.

In constant dollars (which negate the effect of inflation), the cost of college has more than doubled since 1982-83. That's a departure from the trend during the 1970s, when the real cost of college actually decreased several times, and never reached $8,000.

Tuition and fees are in addition to room and board charges at most 4-year colleges (unless students commute). Room and board charges averaged $4,931 at public colleges, and $6,168 at private colleges, pushing the total cost of a private college education to more than $23,000 a year.

Meanwhile, according to a 2002 study by the Public Interest Research Group, the percentage of students who went into debt to finance their educations rose from 42 percent in 1992 to 64 percent in 2000. As a result, the average debt of graduating seniors nearly doubled, from $9,188 in 1992 to $16,928 in 2000.

	Tuition and fees			
	Current dollars		Constant dollars	
Year	Private	Public	Private	Public
1971-72	$1,820	$376	7,966	1,646
1975-76	2,272	433	7,378	1,406
1980-81	3,617	804	7,520	1,672
1985-86	6,121	1,318	10,131	2,181
1990-91	9,340	1,908	12,561	2,566
1991-92	9,812	2,107	12,786	2,746
1992-93	10,448	2,334	13,202	2,949
1993-94	11,007	2,535	13,558	3,122
1994-95	11,719	2,705	14,032	3,239
1995-96	12,216	2,811	14,240	3,277
1996-97	12,994	2,975	14,727	3,372
1997-98	13,785	3,111	15,350	3,464
1998-99	14,709	3,247	16,114	3,557
1999-2000	15,518	3,362	16,527	3,581
2000-01	16,233	3,487	16,697	3,587
2001-02	17,272	3,725	17,457	3,765
2002-03	18,273	4,081	18,273	4,081

Source: The College Board.

▶COLLEGE ENTRANCE EXAMINATION SCORES

SATs (Scholastic Assessment Tests) purportedly measure verbal and mathematical reasoning abilities. These tests are administered by the College Board, a nonprofit organization that provides tests and many other educational services for students, schools and colleges. The test is scored on a range from 400 to 1600, with average scores usually around 900. Male students consistently outscore females on the SAT, and whites and Asians typically score about 100 points higher than all other ethnic groups, and about 200 points higher than blacks. In response to criticisms of racial and gender bias, the College Board rewrote the SAT in 1994 to make it a test of aptitude, rather than of knowledge or test-taking techniques. The new test had more open-ended questions, which the College Board claimed made the test uncoachable. But scores on the new test suffered from the same gender and ethnicity gaps as the old test.

In 2001, the College Board announced another revision to the SAT, to go into effect beginning in March, 2005. The newest version will jettison the analogies section in favor of short reading sections, and will involve a written essay section. In addition, the math portion of the test will cover concepts taught in advanced high school algebra courses.

Most Popular Majors Among Incoming Freshmen, 1990–2001

	Percentage		
Major	1990	2000	2001
Arts and Humanities, total	**N.A.**	**N.A.**	**12.6%**
Art, fine and applied	2.0%	2.5%	2.9
English	1.0	1.7	1.7
Journalism	N.A.	1.7	1.6
Biological Science, total	**N.A.**	**N.A.**	**6.9**
General biology	1.8	3.6	4.0
Business, total	**N.A.**	**N.A.**	**16.6**
Accounting	5.3	2.3	2.2
Business administration	5.5	4.1	3.8
Finance	N.A.	1.7	1.7
Marketing	2.5	2.7	2.7
Management	4.0	3.3	3.6
Education, total	**N.A.**	**N.A.**	**10.1**
Elementary education	5.1	5.6	5.1
Secondary education	1.9	2.5	2.4
Engineering, total	**N.A.**	**N.A.**	**9.1**
Electrical engineering	2.5	2.0	2.0
Mechanical engineering	2.0	1.9	2.1
Physical Science, total	**N.A.**	**N.A.**	**2.6**
Professional, total	**N.A.**	**N.A.**	**12.0**
Premedicine, predental, preveterinary	3.2	4.4	4.3
Nursing	4.2	2.1	2.6
Therapy	2.3	1.9	1.9
Social Science, total	**N.A.**	**N.A.**	**10.3**
Political science	3.0	2.8	3.1
Psychology	4.2	4.8	4.8
Technical, total	**N.A.**	**N.A.**	**2.2**
Other fields, total	**N.A.**	**N.A.**	**17.9**
Communications	2.3	2.7	2.6
Computer science	1.7	3.7	3.3

Note: Totals include other categories not shown separately.
Source: Higher Education Research Institute, University of California, Los Angeles, *The American Freshman: National Norms for Fall, 2001.*

In 2002, the College Board published figures showing that scores generally reflect income levels (students from the poorest homes scored lowest; those from the wealthiest homes scored highest).

ACTs are administered by the American College Testing Program, a nonprofit educational organization headquartered in Iowa City, Iowa. Its use is more popular than the SAT in states west of the Mississippi River. The ACT composite score is the average of four tests that measure academic abilities in English, mathematics, social studies and natural sciences. Although similar numbers of students take each test, the ACT draws less criticism than the SAT, even though both tests evidence similar racial and gender biases.

Educational Attainment by State, 2001

State	Persons over 25 ('000s)	Completed 4 years high school or more (rank)	Completed 4 years college or more (rank)
U.S. Total	**182,142**	**84.1% (–)**	**26.7% (–)**
Alabama	2,784	78.9(48)	22.7(39)
Alaska	383	92.2(1)	25.6(27)
Arizona	3,182	84.6(34)	26.3(23)
Arkansas	1,692	81.0(40)	18.3(50)
California	20,958	80.2(42)	27.9(16)
Colorado	2,781	87.6(17)	35.7(5)
Connecticut	2,313	88.0(14)	32.6(7)
Delaware	518	88.5(11)	29.5(13)
Dist. of Columbia	382	83.5(36)	44.4(1)
Florida	11,051	83.3(37)	25.7(26)
Georgia	5,135	82.9(38)	25.0(30)
Hawaii	799	87.9(15)	26.8(20)
Idaho	811	86.8(24)	20.9(46)
Illinois	8,088	85.9(29)	27.3(17)
Indiana	4,058	85.3(32)	23.7(34)
Iowa	1,867	88.3(12)	23.1(38)
Kansas	1,747	87.5(18)	37.6(2)
Kentucky	2,620	80.8(41)	21.6(44)
Louisiana	2,709	78.8(49)	22.1(42)
Maine	916	87.4(21)	23.8(33)
Maryland	3,453	87.5(19)	37.6(3)
Massachusetts	4,357	87.5(20)	37.6(4)
Michigan	6,600	86.5(27)	22.5(40)
Minnesota	3,268	92.2(2)	30.5(10)
Mississippi	1,756	79.1(47)	20.9(47)
Missouri	3,551	88.1(13)	26.7(22)
Montana	595	89.7(8)	23.6(35)
Nebraska	1,063	89.8(7)	27.1(18)
Nevada	1,356	85.8(31)	22.1(43)
New Hampshire	873	90.2(6)	30.1(11)
New Jersey	5,894	85.9(30)	31.4(8)
New Mexico	1,113	81.6(39)	25.4(28)
New York	12,401	83.7(35)	28.8(14)
North Carolina	5,135	80.1(44)	22.4(41)
North Dakota	422	89.0(10)	25.3(29)
Ohio	7,509	87.3(23)	24.5(32)
Oklahoma	2,163	85.1(33)	20.4(48)
Oregon	2,216	87.7(16)	27.1(19)
Pennsylvania	8,205	86.1(28)	26.1(25)
Rhode Island	700	80.1(45)	30.1(12)
South Carolina	2,588	80.2(43)	23.3(37)
South Dakota	492	89.2(9)	23.6(36)
Tennessee	3,708	80.1(46)	21.5(45)
Texas	12,622	78.1(51)	26.2(24)
Utah	1,215	91.0(4)	26.8(21)
Vermont	421	87.4(22)	30.8(9)
Virginia	4,659	86.7(26)	34.6(6)
Washington	3,849	90.4(5)	28.3(15)
West Virginia	1,229	78.5(50)	15.9(51)
Wisconsin	3,520	86.8(25)	24.7(31)
Wyoming	523	91.6(3)	19.6(49)

Source: U.S. Bureau of the Census, *Current Population Survey, March 2002* (2003).

▶HIGHER EDUCATION

The accompanying figures give a startling picture of just how the coming of age of the baby boom generation transformed U.S. higher education. In just one decade (the 1960s) the number of undergraduate degrees conferred more than doubled, while the number of doctorates actually tripled. These extraordinary changes were matched in kind by dramatic shifts in what students wanted to study: during the late 1960s, for example, the number of degrees in sociology and psychology jumped by more than 15,000 each in just a few years (1966-1970), while interest in business soared during the 1980s. That trend has begun to reverse in the 1990s, as the need for social workers and other health and human service professionals has expanded.

College enrollment Between 1980 and 1992, college enrollment increased about 20 percent, from just over 12 million to a record 14.5 million. Since then, enrollment has increased only to 15.6 million, even though the traditional college-age population has dropped. Much of the growth in college enrollment was fueled by increases in older students, women and minorities on campus. Women have outnumbered men on college campuses since 1979, when there were just under 6 million of each in institutions of higher education. Since then, male enrollment has increased only to 6.7 million, while female enrollment has leapt to 8.6 million. Minorities, especially Hispanics and Asians, have increased from 15.7 percent of the campus population in 1976 to 28.2 percent in 2000, the latest year for which statistics are available. The percentage of blacks on campus fluctuated for many years, but began increasing again in 1990. In 2000, non-Hispanic blacks made up 11.3 percent of college students, up from 9.3 percent in 1990.

▶EDUCATIONAL ATTAINMENT

Despite complaints about the state of education in America, there can be no doubt that the general population continues to grow more educated every year. In 2001, more than 84 percent of all adults over the age of 25 had completed high school, and more than a quarter of American adults had a bachelor's degree or more. It's not surprising that those numbers were both much lower in 1940, when only 24 percent of adults had graduated from high school and college degrees belonged to fewer than 5 percent of the population. But even as recently as 1980, only 69 percent of adults over 25 had a high school diploma and only 17 percent had graduated from college. (See the accompanying table.)

The greatest proof of the importance of education is the correlation between years of schooling and higher salaries. In 2000 (the latest year available), the median annual income for adults with bachelor's degrees was $56,334 per year, compared with $34,303 for those with only high school diplomas. At the extreme ends of the spectrum, those with doctorates made $80,250 while those who failed to graduate from high school averaged only $25,095.

Number Of Degrees Conferred in U.S. by Type, 1950–2003

Year	All degrees[1]	Bachelor's	First professional[2]	Master's	Doctorate
1949–50	496,661	432,058[3]		58,183	6,420
1959–60	476,704	392,440[3]		74,435	9,829
1969-70	1,065,098	792,317	34,578	208,291	29,912
1979-80	1,330,244	929,417	70,131	298,081	32,615
1984-85	1,373,734	979,477	75,063	286,251	32,943
1989-90	1,485,004	1,051,344	70,988	324,301	38,371
1996-97	1,716,886	1,172,879	78,730	419,401	45,876
1997-98	1,739,178	1,184,406	78,598	430,164	46,010
1998-99	1,762,805	1,200,303	78,439	439,986	44,077
1999-2000	1,819,796	1,237,875	80,057	457,056	44,808
2000-01	1,837,258	1,244,171	79,707	468,476	44,904
2001-02[4]	1,875,700	1,282,000	80,800	468,000	44,900
2002-03[4]	1,894,700	1,301,000	80,200	468,000	45,000

1. Does not include associate of arts (A.A.) or associate of science (A.S.) degrees; more than 500,000 of these have been given each year since 1992. 2. Degrees are: medical doctor, law, dentistry, optometry, podiatry, pharmacy, theology, chiropractic, and veterinary medicine. 3. Prior to 1961, bachelor's and first professional degrees were listed together. 4. Projected.
Source: U.S. Dept. of Education, National Center for Education Statistics, *Digest of Education Statistics, 2002.*

Educational Attainment of the Population 25+ Years, 1940–2002

Year	Completed 4 years of high school or more			Completed 4 years of college or more		
	Both Sexes	Male	Female	Both Sexes	Male	Female
1940	24.5%	22.7%	26.3%	4.6%	5.5%	3.8%
1950	34.3	32.6	36.0	6.2	7.3	5.2
1959	43.7	42.2	45.2	8.1	10.3	6.0
1970	55.2	55.0	55.4	11.0	14.1	8.2
1980	68.6	69.1	68.1	17.0	20.8	13.5
1991	78.4	78.5	78.3	21.4	24.3	18.8
1995	81.7	81.7	81.6	23.0	26.0	20.2
2000	84.1	84.2	84.0	25.6	27.8	23.6
2001	84.1	84.1	84.2	26.2	28.2	24.3
2002	84.1	83.8	84.4	26.7	28.5	25.1

Source: Bureau of the Census, *Current Population Survey: Educational Attainment in the United States, March, 2002 (2003).*

Educational Attainment of the Population, Ages 25 and Over, 2001

Characteristic	Number of people	4 years high school or more	Some college or more	4 years college or more
All persons	**182,142,000**	**84.1%**	**52.0%**	**26.7%**
Sex:				
Male	86,996,000	83.8	52.8	28.5
Female	95,146,000	84.4	51.2	25.1
Race:				
White	151,942,000	83.8	52.4	28.5
Black	20,359,000	78.7	44.8	17.0
Hispanic origin[1]	19,670,000	57.0	28.0	10.6
Age groups:				
25 to 29 years	18,310,000	86.4	58.0	29.3
30 to 34 years	20,360,000	87.3	58.4	31.7
35 to 39 years	21,648,000	88.0	56.4	28.8
40 to 44 years	22,636,000	88.7	55.8	28.2
45 to 49 years	20,988,000	89.2	57.0	29.2
50 to 54 years	18,577,000	89.0	58.4	30.9
55 to 59 years	14,667,000	85.3	53.0	28.1
60 to 64 years	11,208,000	81.3	45.0	23.4
65 to 69 years	9,597,000	75.0	38.3	19.0
70 to 74 years	8,526,000	71.8	36.1	18.2
75 years or older	15,647,000	65.7	25.1	14.4
Residence				
Metropolitan area	147,239,000	85.0	54.5	29.1
Non-metropolitan area	34,904,000	80.2	41.3	17.0

Note: 1. People of Hispanic origin may be of any race. **Source:** Bureau of the Census, *Current Population Survey: Educational Attainment in the United States, March, 2002* (2003).

U.S. Energy

▶ENERGY PRODUCTION AND CONSUMPTION

Energy is usually measured in millions or larger quantities of British thermal units (Btu). One Btu is approximately equal to the energy released in burning a wooden match. An engine burning eight gallons of gasoline releases one million (10^6) Btu. One quadrillion (10^{15}) Btu is the equivalent of the energy released from an engine burning eight billion gallons of gasoline.

Total U.S. energy production was 71.4 quadrillion Btu in 2002. Natural gas and coal each accounted for more than one-quarter of domestic energy production. Fossil fuels, which also include crude oil, accounted for 80 percent of all energy production, down from 95 percent as recently as 1970. Nuclear energy (11 percent) and renewable energy forms like solar energy and wind power (7 percent) have made up the difference.

U.S. energy consumption hit an all-time of 98.94 quadrillion Btu in 2000 before declining slightly to 97.59 quadrillion Btu in 2002. Since the U.S. consumes more energy than it produces, it must import the difference.

Despite increasing prices for all forms of energy, American consumers continue to be lavish in their use, opting for convenience over energy efficiency at nearly every turn. The average home size increased by more than 500 square feet between 1973 and 1997 (bringing with it an attendant increase in heating costs), and is now packed with many more energy-sucking appliances than ever before, including whirlpool tubs, microwave ovens, toaster-ovens, washer-dryers, and central air-conditioning. In addition, Americans are driving bigger, less-efficient cars and trucks, and are driving them more total miles each year, thus consuming more gas than ever before. Since 1985, every energy-efficient form of commuting to work (carpooling, public transportation, biking, walking, and working at home) has declined in popularity, while the percentage of workers who drove to work alone continues to increase.

Petroleum continues to be the energy of choice among U.S. consumers. It accounted for 39 percent of all U.S. energy consumption in 2002, compared to 24 percent for natural gas and 23 percent for coal. Consumption of nuclear energy has grown steadily from nearly zero in 1960 to 8.14 quadrillion Btu in 2002. Renewable energy consumption grew similarly, from 1.66 quadrillion Btu, in 1960, to more than 7 quadrillion Btu in 1997; since then, it has fallen back to 5.9 quadrillion Btu in 2002.

The relationship between total energy consumption and real gross domestic product (GDP) is a primary indicator of the energy intensity of the economy. In 1949, the country used 20,630 Btu of energy per dollar of GDP (measured in constant 1996 dollars). Since then, energy consumption has tripled, but increases in energy efficiency, conservation, and the expansion of the service sector of the economy have propelled GDP six-fold. As a result, energy consumption now totals only 10,900 Btu per dollar of GDP, or approxi-

U.S. Energy Overview, 1960–2002

Activity and energy source	1960 (Quadrillion Btu)	1970	1980	1990	2000	2001	2002[1]	As percent of total, 2002[1]
Production, Total	**41.49**	**63.50**	**67.24**	**70.84**	**71.22**	**71.37**	**70.81**	**100.0%**
Coal	10.82	14.61	18.60	22.46	22.62	23.05	22.55	31.8
Natural gas (dry)	12.66	21.67	19.91	18.36	19.66	20.23	19.58	27.6
Crude oil[2]	14.93	20.40	18.25	15.57	12.36	12.28	12.16	17.1
Natural gas plant liquids	1.46	2.51	2.25	2.17	2.61	2.55	2.56	3.6
Nuclear electric power	0.01	0.24	2.74	6.16	7.86	8.03	8.15	11.5
Renewable energy[3]	1.61	4.08	5.49	6.14	6.16	5.32	5.90	8.3
Imports, Total	**4.23**	**8.39**	**15.97**	**18.95**	**28.97**	**30.15**	**29.40**	**100.0%**
Natural gas	0.16	0.85	1.01	1.55	3.87	4.12	N.A.	13.7
Petroleum[4]	4.00	7.47	14.66	17.12	24.53	24.88	N.A.	82.5
Other[5]	0.07	0.07	0.31	0.29	0.59	0.45	N.A.	1.3
Exports, Total	**1.48**	**2.66**	**3.72**	**4.87**	**4.00**	**3.76**	**3.66**	**100.0%**
Coal	1.02	1.94	2.42	2.77	1.53	1.27	N.A.	33.8
Petroleum	0.43	0.55	1.16	1.82	2.15	2.06	N.A.	54.8
Other[6]	0.03	0.18	0.14	0.27	0.17	0.20	N.A.	5.3
Consumption, Total	**43.80**	**67.86**	**78.44**	**84.34**	**98.94**	**96.32**	**97.59**	**100.0%**
Coal	9.84	12.26	15.42	19.25	22.58	21.90	22.18	22.7
Natural gas	12.39	21.79	20.39	19.30	23.95	22.89	23.08	23.6
Petroleum products[7]	19.92	29.52	34.20	33.55	38.40	38.33	38.40	39.5
Nuclear electric power	0.01	0.24	2.74	6.16	7.86	8.03	8.15	8.4
Renewable energy[3]	1.66	4.10	5.71	6.25	6.16	5.32	5.90	6.0

Note: Sum of components may not equal 100 percent due to independent rounding. 1. Preliminary. Percentages for imports and exports are from 2001. 2. Includes lease condensate. 3. Includes hydroelectric power, geothermal energy, solar energy, wind energy, and biofuels such as wood waste, landfill gases, fish oils, and other waste. 4. Includes imports of crude oil for the Strategic Petroleum Reserve, which began in 1977. 5. Includes coal, coal coke, and electricity. 6. Includes natural gas, coal coke, and petroleum products. 7. Petroleum products supplied include natural gas plant liquids and crude oil burned as fuel. **Source:** U.S. Dept. of Energy, *Annual Energy Review (2001)* 2002 and *Monthly Energy Review* (July 2003).

mately half what it was in 1970. In other words, the country is using much more energy, but not paying much more for it.

A second indicator is per capita consumption, which rose from 215 million Btu per capita in 1949 to a record 361 million Btu in 1978. Efforts at conservation persuaded people to decrease their consumption to 314 million Btu in 1983, but per capita use has rebounded since then, to 353 million Btu in 2000. Alaska is the biggest per capita consumer of energy. New York and Hawaii used the least energy per capita—Hawaii because so few houses need to be heated, and New York because so many people live in apartments, which require much less energy to heat and insulate.

(For information about energy consumption and production worldwide, see Part III: World Energy).

U.S. Energy Consumption, Total and Per Capita, 1950–2001

Year	Total energy consumption (million Btu)	Per capita consumption (million Btu)
1950	34,630,000,000	229
1955	40,240,000,000	244
1960	45,120,000,000	252
1965	54,016,000,000	279
1970	67,858,000,000	334
1975	72,040,000,000	334
1980	78,435,000,000	346
1985	76,705,000,000	322
1990	84,567,000,000	340
1995	91,501,000,000	344
2000	99,315,000,000	353
2001[1]	96,950,000,000	340

1. Preliminary.
Source: U.S. Dept. of Energy, *Annual Energy Review (2001)* 2002.

▶FOSSIL FUELS

Petroleum

Since 1958 the United States has consumed more energy than it produces; the difference has been met with energy imports. Net imports of energy (primarily petroleum) grew rapidly through 1973, when they totaled 13 quadrillion Btu, or 20 percent of consumption.

Despite the Arab oil embargo of 1973–74 and increases in the price of crude oil, petroleum net imports continued to grow, reaching a peak of nearly 19 quadrillion Btu in 1977. That year, U.S. dependence on petroleum net imports peaked at 47 percent of consumption. In 1985, petroleum net imports dropped to 9 quadrillion Btu and U.S. dependence on foreign oil fell to 27 percent of consumption, its lowest level since 1972.

But a drop in the worldwide price of oil ($12.52 per barrel in 1998, its lowest level in more than two decades) inhibited domestic production and caused U.S. reliance on imports to spring back. Oil prices spiked to $28.26 per barrel in 2000, and stayed high ($24.09) through 2002. In constant dollars, however, the price per barrel was less than half of what it was in 1981, when the price (in 1996 dollars) was $50.94. Dependence on imports reached a record high 55.5 percent in 2001 before retreating to 53.4 percent in 2002. Saudi Arabia, Venezuela, Canada and Mexico are the U.S.'s pri-

U.S. Fuel Consumption by Type and End-Use Sector, 1950-2002 (quadrillion Btu)

Year	Residential	Commercial	Industrial	Transportation	Electric utilities	Total
Petroleum						
1950	1.340	0.862	3.951	6.690	0.472	13.315
1960	2.265	1.228	5.747	10.126	0.553	19.919
1970	2.755	1.551	7.787	15.310	2.117	29.520
1980	1.748	1.287	9.525	19.008	2.634	34.202
1990	1.263	0.913	8.306	21.792	1.278	33.552
1995	1.356	0.710	8.552	23.181	0.755	34.554
2000	1.452	0.726	9.053	25.973	1.144	38.348
2001	1.511	0.737	9.069	25.739	1.277	38.333
2002	1.486	0.734	9.154	26.119	0.908	38.401
Natural Gas						
1950	1.240	0.401	3.546	0.130	0.651	5.968
1960	3.212	1.056	5.973	0.359	1.785	12.385
1970	4.987	2.473	9.536	0.745	4.054	21.795
1980	4.866	2.674	8.395	0.650	3.810	20.395
1990	4.523	2.701	8.502	0.680	3.321	19.727
1995	4.981	3.113	9.637	0.724	4.325	22.780
2000	5.126	3.301	9.535	0.672	5.316	23.950
2001	4.915	3.126	8.697	0.657	5.465	22.860
2002	5.057	3.204	8.468	0.663	5.664	23.056
Coal						
1950	1.261	1.542	5.781	1.564	2.199	12.347
1960	0.585	0.407	4.543	0.075	4.228	9.338
1970	0.209	0.165	4.656	0.007	7.227	12.264
1980	0.031	0.115	3.155	(2)	12.123	15.424
1990	0.028	0.128	2.756	(2)	16.245	19.157
1995	0.017	0.117	2.488	(2)	17.466	20.078
2000	0.011	0.092	2.256	(2)	20.220	22.579
2001	0.012	0.097	2.230	(2)	19.558	21.897
2002	0.012	0.097	2.092	(2)	19.985	22.186

1. Preliminary. 2. Small quantities consumed by transportation sector are included in industrial column.
Source: U.S. Dept. of Energy, *Monthly Energy Review* (July 2003)..

mary suppliers of foreign oil; each exports more than 1.4 million barrels of oil per day to the U.S.

Natural gas

Once considered a useless byproduct of oil well drilling (it was simply burned off at the site), natural gas is today the primary source of energy for space heating in 50 million U.S. households. U.S. natural gas trade was limited to the border countries of Mexico and Canada until shipping natural gas in liquefied form emerged as an alternative to pipelines. In 1969, the first shipments of liquefied natural gas (LNG) were sent to Japan, and U.S. imports from Algeria began the following year. In 2002, U.S. net imports of natural gas by all routes totaled 3.58 trillion cubic feet (the vast majority from Canada).

Coal

Since World War II coal has been the major U.S. energy export. Throughout most of the 1960s and 1970s, U.S. exports of coal increased, peaking at 113 million short tons in 1981. Exports have dropped steadily since 1991, when they totaled 109 million short tons; in 2002, exports were 49 million short tons, or less than half the 1991 total. Canada is the largest market for U.S. coal, importing close to 18 million tons in 2001. Japan, which imported more 25 million short tons as recently as 1982, imported just 2.1 million tons in 2001.

Electric utilities are the primary domestic consumers of coal. Their consumption grew from a 17 percent share in 1949 to a 90 percent share in 2002. Over the same period, consumption in all other sectors declined, most dramatically in the transportation sector, due primarily to railroads switching from coal to petroleum-driven trains. Transportation sector consumption, which topped 70 million short tons in 1949, has totaled fewer than 50,000 short tons every year since 1975. Consumption by the residential and commercial sector has also declined steadily, from a high of 117 million short tons in 1949 to 4.3 million short tons in 2002.

▶THE STRATEGIC PETROLEUM RESERVE

In an attempt to minimize the wild fluctuations in prices caused by the Arab oil embargoes of the 1970s, the U.S. in 1977 created the Strategic Petroleum Reserve, which permitted the storage of 580 million barrels of oil. The reserve proved useful in preventing additional oil price hikes during the Iraqi invasion of Kuwait in 1990.

The reserve can also be used as an emergency supply of oil in case of a complete oil embargo. In 1985, the reserve held enough oil to provide a normal level of petroleum to the U.S. for 115 days in the absence of any other petroleum imports. In the summer of 2000, President Bill Clinton released 30 million barrels from the reserve to alleviate a spike in oil prices, but in so doing, reduced the reserve to 53 days of oil. The 30 million barrels were to be repaid (with interest) in 2001-02, though at the end of 2001, only 10 million barrels had been replenished.

▶ELECTRICITY

Net generation of electricity by electric utilities topped 3.8 trillion kilowatthours (kWh) in 2002. Coal continued to fuel more than half the generation, accounting for 1.9 trillion kWh, while natural gas contributed 685.8 billion kWh. Petroleum-fired generation dropped dramatically, from 124.9 billion kWh in 2001 to 89.9 billion kWh in 2002. Nuclear-based generation continued to increase, reaching an all-time high of 780.1 billion kWh in 2002. Hydroelectric generation rebounded from an all-time low of 217.0 billion kWh in 2001 to 263.6 billion kWh in 2002.

The weighted average real price (based on 1996 dollars) of electricity to all sectors in 2001 was 6.64 cents per kWh, 30 percent below the price in 1982, but about the same as in 1974. But although prices of other major energy sources increased significantly during the same period, electricity remained by far the most expensive source of energy on a Btu basis.

▶NUCLEAR POWER

The number of nuclear power plants in operation in the U.S. skyrocketed from 18 in 1970 to 112 in 1990, and net nuclear generation of electricity jumped from 21.8 to 577 billion kWh. Since 1990, two new plants have opened and 10 have closed, but generation nonetheless increased to 780 billion kWh. More than three-quarters of the 104 nuclear power plants in the U.S. are located east of the Mississippi River. The U.S. has the highest number of reactors of any country in the world, but far fewer than the 236 that were in the stages of planning, construction or operation as recently as 1975.

Several factors have contributed to the decline in the number of planned nuclear units. Growth in electricity demand has been slower than expected; longer lead times for licensing and construction coupled during the 1980s with higher financing expenses increased costs; and rising interest rates and an uncertain economic environment eroded electric utilities' willingness to commission new plants. Furthermore, nuclear plant operators have been able to increase their generation of electricity steadily without increasing the number of reactors. Nuclear plants ran at a record high 90.4 percent of capacity in 2004, up from 66.0 percent in 1990 and 56.3 percent in 1980.

A further deterrent has been the increased public opposition to nuclear power plants because of concerns about their safety and the disposal of spent nuclear fuel. These were heightened in the wake of the 1979 accident at Three Mile Island near Harrisburg, Pennsylvania, and the far more devastating one at Chernobyl in Ukraine in 1986.

Gasoline and Heating Oil Retail Prices per Gallon, 1950–2001

Year	Motor gasoline (including taxes)[1] Current dollars	Constant (1996) dollars[3]	Residential heating oil[2] Current dollars
1950	$0.27	$1.54	N.A.
1960	0.31	1.40	$0.15
1970	0.36	1.23	0.18
1975	0.57	1.42	0.37
1980	1.19	2.09	0.97
1985	1.12	1.51	1.05
1990	1.15	1.33	1.06
1995	1.21	1.23	0.87
2000	1.56	1.46	1.31
2001	1.53	1.40	1.25

1. Prices are calculated from a sample of stations providing all types of services. Prices are for leaded regular gasoline only from 1950-75, and for an average of all grades of gasoline after 1975.
2. Prices derived by dividing sum of estimated national retail sales for residential heating oil (No. 2 fuel oil) by the estimated volume of retail sales for residential heating.
Source: U.S. Dept. of Energy, *Annual Energy Review 2001*, (2002).

▶ENERGY TRADING

Deregulation in the energy industry has led in the past decade to the the development of energy trading companies, large corporations that buy and sell power much like any other commodity. Because of an accounting procedure known as "mark-to-market," energy trading can produce huge paper profits overnight, even though it may take as much as 20 years for the revenues from these trades to appear, and fattens the company's debt load in the meantime. This arcane structure allowed energy traders at Enron to create fictitious trades that boosted profits even more (and triggered performance bonuses for top executives) before they were found out in the summer of 2002.

U.S. Net Generation of Electricity by Energy Source, 1950–2001 (billion kilowatthours)

Year	Coal	Natural gas	Petroleum[1]	Nuclear Power	Hydroelectric power	Geothermal and other[2]	Total
1950	155	45	34	0	101	([3])	329
1955	301	95	37	0	116	([3])	547
1960	403	158	48	1	149	([3])	756
1965	571	222	65	4	197	0.2	1,055
1970	704	373	184	22	251	0.8	1,532
1975	853	300	289	173	303	3.4	1,918
1980	1,162	346	246	251	279	5.6	2,286
1985	1,402	292	100	384	285	10.6	2,470
1990	1,591	369	124	577	291	60.8	3,024
1995	1,709	496	75	674	311	74.0	3,354
2000	1,966	601	109	754	276	80.9	3,802
2001[4]	1,904	613	126	768	218	79.8	3,720

1. Includes distillate fuel oil, residual fuel oil (including crude oil burned as fuel), jet fuel and petroleum coke. 2. Other is wood, waste, photovoltaic and solar thermal energy used to generate electricity for distribution. 3. Less than 0.5 billion kilowatthours. 4. Preliminary. **Source**: U.S. Dept. of Energy, *Annual Energy Review (2001)* 2002.

U.S. Commercial Nuclear Plants, 2003

There are 104 operable nuclear reactors in 31 states. The following table lists the states, with the total number of reactors in each, the names of the individual units and their location.

Alabama = 5
Browns Ferry 1, 2 & 3, Decatur
Joseph M. Farley 1 & 2, Dothan
Arizona = 3
Palo Verde 1, 2 & 3, Wintersburg
Arkansas = 2
Arkansas Nuclear 1 & 2, Russellville
California = 4
Diablo Canyon 1 & 2, Avila Beach
San Onofre 2 & 3, San Clemente
Connecticticut = 2
Millstone 2 & 3, Waterford
Florida = 5
Crystal River 3, Red Level
St. Lucie 1 & 2, Ft. Pierce
Turkey Point 3 & 4, Florida City
Georgia = 4
Hatch 1 & 2, Baxley
Vogtle 1 & 2, Waynesboro
Illinois = 11
Braidwood 1 & 2, Braidwood
Byron 1 & 2, Byron
Clinton 1, Clinton
Dresden 2 & 3, Morris
La Salle 1 & 2, Seneca
Quad Cities 1 & 2, Cordova
Iowa = 1
Duane Arnold, Palo
Kansas = 1
Wolf Creek, Burlington
Louisiana = 2
River Bend 1, St. Francisville
Waterford 3, Taft
Maryland = 2
Calvert Cliffs 1 & 2, Lusby
Massachusetts = 1
Pilgrim 1, Plymouth
Michigan = 4
Donald C. Cook 1 & 2, Bridgman
Fermi 2, Newport
Palisades, South Haven
Minnesota = 3
Monticello, Monticello
Prairie Island 1 & 2, Red Wing
Mississippi = 1
Grand Gulf 1, Port Gibson
Missouri = 1
Callaway 1, Fulton
Nebraska = 2
Cooper, Brownville
Fort Calhoun 1, Fort Calhoun
New Hampshire = 1
Seabrook 1, Seabrook
New Jersey = 4
Hope Creek 1, Salem
Oyster Creek 1, Forked River
Salem 1 & 2, Salem
New York = 6
Indian Point 2 & 3, Buchanan
James Fitzpatrick 1, Scriba
Nine Mile Point 1 & 2, Oswego
Robert E. Ginna, Rochester
North Carolina = 5
Brunswick 1 & 2, Southport
McGuire 1 & 2, Cowens Ford Dam
Shearon Harris 1, New Hill
Ohio = 2
Davis-Besse 1, Oak Harbor
Perry 1, North Perry
Pennsylvania = 9
Beaver Valley 1 & 2, Shippingport
Limerick 1 & 2, Pottstown
Peach Bottom 2 & 3, Lancaster
Susquehanna 1 & 2, Berwick
Three Mile Island 1, Middletown
South Carolina = 7
Catawba 1 & 2, Clover
H.B. Robinson 2, Hartsville
Oconee 1, 2 & 3, Seneca
Summer 1, Jenkinsville
Tennessee = 2
Sequoyah 1 & 2, Daisy
Watts Bar 1, Spring City
Texas = 4
Comanche Peak 1&2, Glen Rose
South Texas 1 & 2, Bay City
Vermont = 1
Vermont Yankee 1, Vernon
Virginia = 4
North Anna 1 & 2, Mineral
Surry 1 & 2, Surry
Washington = 1
Washington Nuclear 2, Richland
Wisconsin = 3
Kewaunee, Carlton
Point Beach 1 & 2, Two Creeks

Source: U.S. Nuclear Regulatory Commission, *Daily Power Reactor Status Report*, Aug. 1, 2003.

U.S. Health and Medicine

Milestones in the History of Medicine

B.C.

c. 2700 Chinese emperor Shen Nung develops principles of herbal medicine and acupuncture.

c. 1700 The Code of Hammurabi, king of Babylon, comprises regulations concerning physicians, including what they may treat and what their fees should be.

c. 1500 The Ebers Papyrus describes many remedies used in Ancient Egypt to treat dental ailments.

c. 400 Hippocrates of Cos (Greek: c. 460–c. 377), teacher and medical practitioner known as Father of Medicine, writes Hippocratic Oath, which sets ethical standards still followed by physicians throughout the world.

c. 300 Herophilus (Greek: c. 355–280) pioneers dissection of human body and founds first school of anatomy.

A.D.

c. 20 Aulus Cornelius Celsus (Roman: first cent.) writes first-known medical textbook.

c. 100 Romans develop a public medical service and appoint physicians to provide medical help to poor.

c. 180 Galen (Greek: c. 130–c. 201) writes *Methodus Medando*, which summarizes medical knowledge of ancient times. Galen's views on human physiology and disease would influence medical thought for more than 1,500 years.

c. 450 Susruta (Indian) notes relationship of malaria to mosquitoes and of bubonic plague to rats.

c. 900 Rhazes (Persian: c. 865–923/35) is first to describe smallpox and establish criteria for diagnosing and treating it.

1030 Ibn Sina (Avicenna; Persian: 980–1037) publishes *Canon of Medicine*, which becomes leading medical encyclopedia for centuries.

c. 1270–80 Spectacles are introduced by Venetian glassmakers.

1403 Venice imposes world's first quarantine of infected areas as safeguard against Black Death (bubonic plague).

1543 Andreas Vesalius (Flemish: 1514–64) publishes first accurate anatomy text and establishes foundations of modern anatomy.

1597 Gaspare Tagliacozzi (Italian) publishes first textbook of plastic surgery and revives operation of rhinoplasty (nose surgery).

1601 Sir James Lancaster (English: c. 1554–1618) writes that lemon juice helps prevent scurvy.

1628 William Harvey (English: 1578–1657) describes functions of the heart and how blood circulates throughout the body.

1658 Jan Swammerdam (Dutch: 1637–80) discerns red blood cells.

1670 Thomas Willis (English: 1621–75) rediscovers connection between sugar in urine and diabetes (known in antiquity by Greeks, Chinese, and Indians).

1751 Pennsylvania Hospital, first general hospital in U.S., founded in Philadelphia by Quakers.

1761 Leopold Auenbrugger von Auenbrugg (Australian: 1722–1809) discovers that fluid in chest cavity and other health problems can be detected by tapping gently on the chest.

Giovanni B. Morgagni (Italian: 1682–1771) establishes modern pathological anatomy with publication of *On the Seats and Causes of Disease*.

1796 Edward Jenner (English: 1749–1823) develops smallpox vaccine from cowpox serum.

1816 René T.H. Laënnec (French: 1781–1826) invents stethoscope and introduces practice of auscultation (monitoring sounds made by internal organs).

1818 James Blundel (English) performs first successful human blood transfusion.

1831 Samuel Guthrie (American: 1782–1848) discovers chloroform.

1833 William Beaumont (American: 1785–1853) provides first clear insight into nature of gastric digestion.

1839 Horace Hayden (American: 1769–1844) and Chapin Harris (1806–60) found world's first dental school, Baltimore College of Dental Surgery.

1842 Crawford Long (American: 1815–78) removes tumor from patient inhaling ether—first known operation under general anesthesia; publishes his findings in 1849, three years after William Morton (American: 1819–68) demonstrates effectiveness of ether as anesthetic.

1850 Hermann Helmholtz (German: 1821–94) invents ophthalmoscope, instrument used to examine interior of the eye.

1855 Manuel Garcia (Spanish: 1805–1906) invents modern laryngoscope, device used to inspect the throat, especially the larynx and vocal cords.

1863 International Red Cross established at Geneva, Switzerland.

1865 Joseph Lister (English: 1827–1912) introduces use of disinfectants to reduce infection.

Louis Pasteur (French: 1822–95) shows that spoilage of wine can be prevented by partial heat-sterilization; process, called pasteurization, soon applied to milk and other foods.

1866 Sir Thomas C. Allbutt (English: 1836–1925) invents clinical thermometer.

1868 Carl Wunderlich (German: 1815–77) establishes that fever is a symptom, not a disease, and introduces use of thermometer for taking body temperature.

1881 Pasteur produces vaccine that successfully prevents anthrax.

1890 Emil von Behring (German: 1854–1917) and Shibasaburo Kitasato (Japanese: 1852–1931) independently discover antitoxins.

1892 Dmitri Ivanovski (Russian: 1864–1920) discovers filterable viruses (viruses tiny enough to pass through fine filters previously believed to trap all living organisms).

1893 Felix Hofmann (German) develops a process for production of acetylsalicylic acid, the form of aspirin used today.

1895 Wilhelm Röntgen (German: 1845–1923) discovers X rays.

1900 Sigmund Freud (Austrian: 1856–1939), founder of psychoanalysis, publishes *The Interpretations of Dreams*.

Karl Landsteiner (Austrian-American: 1868–1943) discovers three blood groups, later named A, B, and O; fourth group, to be named AB, discovered in 1902.

Walter Reed (American: 1851–1902) establishes that yellow fever virus is transmitted by mosquitoes.

1901 Jokichi Takamine (Japanese-American: 1854–1922) isolates adrenaline, first hormone to be isolated.

1902 Eugene Opie (American: 1873-1971) establishes that diabetes results from destruction of specific portions of pancreatic tissue—the islets of Langerhans.

1905 Albert Einhorn (Austrian: 1856-1917) synthesizes procaine (novocaine), which becomes the most widely used dental anesthetic.

1906 August von Wassermann (German: 1866–1925) develops blood test for syphilis.

1910 Marie Curie (French: 1867–1934) isolates pure radium metal, which came to be used to treat cancer.

1913 Béla Schick (Hungarian-American: 1877–1967) perfects test for determining susceptibility to diphtheria.

1915 Death certificates come into general use in U.S.

Margaret Sanger (American: 1883–1966) founds the National Birth Control League, which in 1942 becomes Planned Parenthood.

1918 Francis Benedict (American: 1870–1957) devises basal metabolism test for measuring rate at which metabolism (total of all chemical reactions) occurs in the body.

1921 Sir Frederick G. Banting (Canadian: 1891–1941) and Charles H. Best (1899–1978) extract insulin from the pancreas.

1928 Sir Alexander Fleming (Scottish: 1881–1955) discovers penicillin, a substance in green mold *Penicillium notatum* that destroys certain bacteria.

1929 Hans Berger (German: 1873–1941) publishes his results of the first electroencephalograms (EEGs) of humans.

1935 Gerhard Domagk (German: 1895–1964) announces discovery of Prontosil (sulfonamide-crysoidin), the first useful sulfa drug.

1937 First blood bank is established, at Cook County Hospital in Chicago.

Alton Ochsner (American: 1896–1981) and Michael De Bakey (1908–) suggest that cigarette smoking is cause of lung cancer.

1944 Willem Kolff (Dutch-American: 1911–) develops first kidney dialysis machine.

Oswald Avery (Canadian: 1877–1955), Colin MacLeod, and Maclyn McCarty prove that DNA (deoxyribonucleic acid) is blueprint of heredity that determines how an organism develops.

First eye bank, Eye-Bank for Sight Restoration, founded in New York.

Albert Schatz (American: 1921–) and Selman Waksman (American: 1888–1973) isolate streptomycin, an antibiotic effective against bacterium that causes tuberculosis.

1945 Alfred Blalock (American: 1899–1964) introduces first operation to enable blue, or cyanotic, babies to survive (cyanosis, caused by poor circulatory flow or other problems, results in diminished oxygen in blood, causing bluish discoloration of the skin).

1947 Eugene Payne (American) uses chloromycetin, developed by Parke-Davis researchers, to treat typhus patients; first use of "broadspectrum" antibiotic.

1948 Philip S. Hench (American: 1896–1965) and Edward C. Kendall (1886–1972) synthesize cortisone and use it to treat arthritis victims.

1952 Jonas Salk (American: 1914–95) develops first vaccine against polio.

1953 John H. Gibbon, Jr. (American: 1903–73) uses heart-lung machine he invented in successful open-heart operation.

1954 Surgeons led by Joseph Murray (American: 1919-) perform first successful kidney transplant.

1957 Alick Isaacs (Scottish: 1921–67) and Jean Lindenmann (Swiss) discover interferon, a protein that interferes with viral reproduction.

1958 Wilson Greatbatch (American: 1919–) invents the implantable artificial pacemaker.

1961 Scientists at Bell Laboratories (Americans) announce first continuously operating laser, a tool having many surgical uses.

1963 Thomas Starzl (American: 1926–) performs first human liver transplant operation.

1964 James Hardy (American: 1918–) performs first human lung transplant.

1965 Medicare and Medicaid are established, guaranteeing medical insurance coverage for the aged and the poor.

1966 Paul Parkman and Harry Meyer (Americans) develop vaccine for rubella (German measles).

Insulin synthesized independently by U.S. and Chinese scientists—first hormone to be synthesized.

1967 Christiaan Barnard (South African: 1922–) performs world's first heart transplant.

Rene Favaloro (Argentinian: 1923–2000) performs first successful coronary bypass operation.

First modern hospice founded in London.

1969 Denton Cooley (American: 1920–) implants first temporary artificial heart in human being.

1972 Computerized axial tomography (CAT scan) is introduced in Great Britain.

1977 Scientists at Genentech Corporation (Americans) induce bacteria to make human-brain hormone somatostatin—first human chemical produced by recombinant-DNA techniques.

The first known human cases of cyclospora infection are diagnosed.

1978 First "test tube baby" (person conceived outside human body) is born, in England.

1981 Scientists identify acquired immune deficiency syndrome (AIDS) for the first time.

Surgeons at University of California at San Francisco perform first successful operation on a fetus.

1982 William DeVries (American) performs first complete replacement of human heart with artificial heart at University of Utah.

1984 First baby produced from frozen embryo is born, in Melbourne, Australia.

Luc Montagnier (French: 1933-) discovers virus believed to cause AIDS.

1990 R. Michael Blaese, W. French Anderson, and Kenneth W. Culver (Americans) develop procedure to infuse genetically engineered blood cells for treatment of immune system disorder—first gene therapy used in a human.

1993 The U.S. Environmental Protection Agency concludes that environmental tobacco smoke ("secondhand smoke") is a lung carcinogen and causes respiratory problems for infants and young children.

1996 British scientists announce the possibility that a new form of Creutzfeldt-Jakob disease is transmitted to humans through the meat of cattle infected with bovine spongiform encephalopathy ("mad cow disease").

1999 Surgeons at Vanderbilt University Medical Center perform first successful brain surgery on a fetus.

2000 Scientists announce they have deciphered most of the human genetic code, opening new frontiers in medicine.

2001 U.S. surgeons implant the first self-contained artificial heart.

2002 Doctors in Saudi Arabia perform first uterus transplant, which remains healthy for 90 days.

▶QUALITY OF HEALTH

Americans are living longer, healthier lives than ever before, yet many of the health problems they face could be avoided or alleviated with appropriate prevention or treatment. With this in mind, government health officials have three broad goals: increasing the span of healthy life, reducing health disparities, and achieving access to preventive services for everyone.

Health quality varies significantly by economic level, age group, and geographic region. Among the most persistent disparities are sickness and mortality rates for various racial and ethnic groups. These disparities are especially stark for white and black Americans. For example:

- A white baby can expect to live 77.4 years; a black baby, 71.8 years (2000 data).
- Whites can expect 63.8 years of healthy life; blacks, 55.6 years (1994).
- Whites experience 8.7 tuberculosis cases per 100,000 people; blacks, 23.9 (1995).
- The prevalence of diabetes is 9.9 percent among black adults, 6.2 percent among white adults. (1999)
- The age-adjusted death rate for prostate cancer for black men is 248 percent higher than for white men (1998).
- Blacks have a 38 percent greater risk of first strokes than whites. (1999.)
- The rate of adult/adolescent AIDS cases per 100,000 population is 84.2 among blacks, 9.0 among whites (1999).
- The age-adjusted homicide rate for black males is almost seven times the rate for white males (1998).
- The maternal mortality rate is 19.6 deaths per 100,000 for black pregnant women, 5.3 deaths for white pregnant women (1987-96).
- The infant mortality rate is 5.7 per 1,000 live births for whites, 14.0 for blacks (2000).
- The age-adjusted death rate for blacks is 32 percent higher than for whites (1999).

A growing body of evidence indicates that race, discrimination, and social and cultural factors influence the care that people receive and, consequently, their health.

▶HEALTH CARE EXPENDITURES

National health care spending exceeded $1.4 trillion in 2001, up 8.8 percent from 2000. This was the highest acceleration since 1988. As a share of gross domestic product (GDP), health spending increased slightly in 2000 to 14.1 percent. A 2002 report from the Centers for Medicare & Medicaid Services (formerly the Health Care Financing Agency) said that health care spending is projected to reach $2.8 trillion in 2011, growing at an average annual rate of 7.3 percent in the 2001-2011 period.

The United States spends more than any other developed nation on health care relative to its economy. The nation's 2001 health expenditures amounted to $5,035 per person, up from $2,737 in 1990—and only $143 in 1960. Close to 90 percent of these moneys were for personal health care; the remainder went to research, construction, program administration, the net cost of private health insurance, and public health activities.

A variety of factors contribute to the high costs of health care, including:

1. Use of sophisticated, expensive medical equipment.

2. New, higher priced prescription drugs and increased consumer demand induced by drug manufacturers' advertising.

3. Excessive and arguably unnecessary procedures, including duplication of tests and use of technologies that yield similar results.

4. Increasing elderly population, which use medical care more intensely than younger people.

5. Increasing number of accidents and other incidents that require emergency medical services.

6. Labor intensiveness and earnings growth for health care professionals and executives.

7. Malpractice insurance.

8. Administrative waste.

9. Fraud.

National Expenditures for Health Care, 1960–2001

Category	1960	1970	1980	1990	1995	1999	2000	2001
Total expenditures (billions)	**$26.7**	**$73.1**	**$245.8**	**$695.6**	**$987.0**	**$1,210.7**	**$1,310.0**	**$1,425.5**
Private	20.1	45.5	141.0	413.2	528.8	662.1	718.7	777.9
Public	6.6	27.6	104.8	282.4	458.2	548.5	591.3	646.7
Federal	2.8	17.6	71.3	196.6	323.9	384.7	415.1	454.8
State and local	3.8	10.0	33.5	89.8	134.3	163.9	176.2	191.8
Per capita expenditures	**$143**	**$348**	**$1,067**	**$2,737**	**$3,686**	**$4,358**	**$4,672**	**$5,035**
Private	108	216	612	1,626	1,975	2,384	2,563	2,749
Public	35	131	455	1,111	1,711	1,975	2,109	2286
Federal	15	84	309	758	1,210	1,385	1481	1608
State and local	20	48	146	353	502	590	628	678
Percent distribution	**100.0%**	**100.0%**	**100.0%**	**100.0%**	**100.0%**	**100.0%**	**100.0%**	**100.0%**
Private	75.2	62.3	57.4	59.4	53.6	54.7	54.9	54.6
Public	24.8	37.7	42.6	40.6	46.4	45.3	45.1	45.4
Federal	10.6	24.0	29.0	27.7	32.8	31.8	31.7	31.9
State and local	14.2	13.7	13.6	12.9	13.6	13.5	13.4	13.5
Health care expenditures as percent of GDP	**5.1%**	**7.0%**	**8.8%**	**12.0%**	**13.3%**	**13.0%**	**13.3**	**14.1**

Note: Figures may not add to totals because of rounding.
Source: U.S. Dept. of Health and Human Services, Centers for Medicare & Medicaid Services, Office of National Health Statistics.

Prescription Drugs

The fastest-growing health-care expenditure is prescription drugs. The Centers for Medicare & Medicaid Services reported that the rate of growth in prescription drug spending exceeded that of other health services by a wide margin, jumping 17.3 percent in 2000. It said that the increasing demand for drugs was related to an aging population, the introduction of new therapies for chronic conditions, and a shift in payment from out-of-pocket sources to third parties that paid for 41 percent of prescription drugs in 1990 and grew to 68 percent by 2000. These factors contributed to the number of retail prescriptions per capita rising to 10.5 per person in 2000, up from 8.3 in 1995.

A study issued by the National Institute for Health Care Management Foundation reported that the 50 top-selling drugs in 2000 accounted for 30 percent of all prescriptions and were almost twice as expensive as all other drugs. Retail pharmacies filled 2.9 billion prescriptions in 2000, an increase of 7.5 percent over 1999. But the number of prescriptions for the 50 best-selling drugs jumped 18.6 percent, to 866.6 million.

Health Care Spending by Category, 1999

Category	Amount (billions)	Change 1998–99
Hospital care	$390.9	3.7%
Physicians' services	269.4	6.0
Dental services	56.0	5.6
Other professional services	33.2	5.6
Drugs, other non-durables	99.6	16.9
Vision products, other durables	47.6	5.7
Nursing-home care	90.0	2.3
Home health care	33.1	-1.4
Other personal health care	33.2	9.9
Administration and net cost of private health insurance	72.0	7.4
Government public health activities	41.1	6.6
Research	22.2	8.2
Construction	17.6	-0.6
Total	**$1,210.7**	**5.6%**

Source: U.S. Dept. of Health and Human Services, Health Care Financing Administration, Office of the Actuary.

Health Expenditures as a Percent of G.N.P. for Selected Countries, 1960–98

Nation	1960	1970	1980	1990	1998
United States	**5.1%**	**7.1%**	**8.9%**	**12.2%**	**13.0%**
Germany	4.8	6.3	8.8	8.7	10.6
Switzerland	3.1	4.9	6.9	8.3	10.4
France	4.2	5.8	7.6	8.9	9.6
Canada	5.4	7.0	7.2	9.2	9.5
Netherlands	3.8	5.9	7.9	8.3	8.6
Australia	4.9	5.7	7.3	8.2	8.5
Sweden	4.7	7.1	9.4	8.8	8.4
Italy	3.6	5.2	7.0	8.1	8.4
Greece	3.1	5.7	6.6	7.6	8.3
New Zealand	4.3	5.2	6.0	7.0	8.1
Japan	3.0	4.6	6.5	6.1	7.6
Spain	1.5	3.7	5.6	6.9	7.1
United Kingdom	3.9	4.5	5.6	6.0	6.7

Source: U.S. Dept. of Health and Human Services, National Center for Health Statistics, *Health, United States, 2001.*

Hospital Care

In 2000, spending for hospital care reached $412 billion, up from $392 billion in 1999. However, hospital care comprised a steadily smaller share of overall health care spending. In 2000, it accounted for 32 percent of national health expenditures, down from 47.3 percent in 1980. The decline came as hospitals contained costs with shorter hospital stays and increased treatment on an outpatient basis.

In 1999, the average adult stay in community hospitals (excluding federal hospitals, psychiatric institutions, and long-term hospitals) was 5.9 days. The average costs to the hospital were $1,103 per day and $6,512 per stay. In contrast, the average stay in 1980 was 7.6 days; average costs were $245 per day and $1,851 per stay.

People age 65 and older are major consumers of inpatient care. They represented less than 13 percent of the U.S. population in 1999, but accounted for 40 percent of the estimated 32.1 million patient discharges from community hospitals. Their average length of stay was also higher (6.1 days) than for other age groups.

Nursing-Home Care

A study by the U.S. Department of Health and Human Services reported that people age 65 or older

Health Care Quality, by State, 1999

To measure the quality of health care across state lines, statisticians at Health Risk Management Inc. use a weighted average of 46 individual measures relating to population health, health care systems, and consumer health status, based on data contained in reports from various medical associations and U.S. government agencies. Examples of measures include drinking water quality, alcohol-related traffic deaths, public health expenditures, physician and dentist shortages, immunizations, infant mortality rate, and heart disease deaths. The average score is 100

Rank, State	Score
1. Minnesota	118.2
2. Hawaii	115.7
3. Wisconsin	114.6
4. New Hampshire	113.9
5. Vermont	113.1
6. Massachusetts	112.8
7. Connecticut	111.9
8. Washington	110.2
9. Maine	110.0
10. Iowa	109.3
11. Utah	108.8
12. Colorado	108.4
13. Alaska	108.3
14. Nebraska	108.1
15. No. Dakota	107.7
16. Rhode Island	107.2
17. New Jersey	107.0
18. Kansas	107.0
19. Virginia	106.7
20. Wyoming	106.6
21. So. Dakota	105.3
22. Oregon	105.0
23. Ohio	103.7
24. Pennsylvania	104.5
25t. California	103.2
25t. Montana	103.2
27. Illinois	102.8
28. Michigan	101.9
29. Maryland	101.6
30. New York	100.6
31. Indiana	99.8
32. Delaware	98.8
33. Idaho	98.1
34. Missouri	98.0
35. Florida	96.6
36. Georgia	95.8
37. No. Carolina	95.7
38. Nevada	93.9
39. Arizona	93.6
40. West Virginia	93.2
41. Kentucky	92.5
42. Texas	92.1
43. Alabama	91.0
44. New Mexico	90.4
45. So. Carolina	90.0
46. Oklahoma	88.9
47. Tennessee	87.1
48. Arkansas	86.6
49t. Mississippi	83.1
49t. Louisiana	83.1

Source: Health Risk Management Inc., *QualityFIRST Index*, 1999.

face a 40 percent lifetime risk of entering a nursing home. In 2002, approximately 1.6 million older adults were receiving care in some 17,000 nursing homes across the United States. Because of the dramatic growth in the number of Americans over age 75, the nursing home population is frailer than ever before and requires more specialized care.

Nursing-home prices are dependent on supply and demand and on the cost of living, with average charges higher in the Northeast and West and lower in the Midwest and South. According to a 2002 report from MetLife Mature Market Institute, the average cost of a nursing home stay was $168 per day for a private room. But there were large variations from one metropolitan area to another. The costliest metropolitan area surveyed was Stamford, Connecticut, at $347 per day; Shreveport, Louisiana, was lowest at $88 per day.

Americans spent $800 million on nursing-home care in 1960, $4.2 billion in 1970, $17.6 billion in 1980, and $50.9 billion in 1990. By 1999, the figure had reached $90 billion. Out-of-pocket payments, including personal savings and social security benefits, covered about one-third of this cost; Medicare and Medicaid covered most of the remaining costs.

Paying for Health Care

Medical care is usually paid for in one of three ways:

1. By patients; according to the U.S. Dept. of Health and Human Services, an estimated 17.6 percent of the nation's personal health care costs in 1999 were paid directly by patients.
2. By an insurance plan; employers, employees and individuals paid $355.3 billion for private health insurance premiums in 1999, funding one-third of all health care spending. Managed care plans enrolled 88.8 percent of employees in 1999—up from 48 percent in 1992.
3. As a public charge, which means that the government—and, ultimately, the taxpayer—pays the bill. In 1999, 43.3 percent of personal health care costs were paid for by federal, state, and local governments. In some instances, the percentage is even greater. For example, taxpayers pay 48 percent of the $2.3 billion spent each year to treat gunshot wounds according to a study published in the Journal of the American Medical Association in 1999, and 62 percent of nursing home care expenditures according to the Health Care Financing Administration.

Health insurance

There are five basic types of insurance:

1. Hospital expense insurance—pays costs of hospital room, X-rays, medicines, etc.
2. Surgical expense insurance—pays costs of an operation.
3. Medical expense insurance—pays for visits to a physician's office.
4. Major medical expense insurance—pays costs associated with extended sickness or injury.
5. Disability income insurance—pays a benefit when the person is unable to work because of illness or injury.

Federal insurance plans

Two government health programs, Medicare and Medicaid, financed $387.2 billion in health care services in 1998, one-third of the nation's total health care bill, and almost three-quarters of all public spending on health care. (The remaining federal health spending covers military and veterans' health care.)

Medicare is a federal health insurance plan for people age 65 and older, certain disabled people, and people with kidney failure. Medicaid is a health care program for poor people. It is funded

Nursing Home Residents Age 65 and Older, 1999

Characteristic	Number	Rate per 1,000 population
Total	**1,469,500**	**42.9**
65-74 years	194,800	10.8
75-84 years	517,600	43.0
85 years and over	757,100	182.5
Male	**377,800**	**26.5**
65-74 years	84,100	10.3
75-84 years	149,500	30.8
85 years and over	144,200	116.5
Female	**1,091,700**	**54.6**
65-74 years	110,700	11.2
75-84 years	368,100	51.2
85 years and over	612,900	210.5
White	**1,279,600**	**42.1**
65-74 years	157,200	10.0
75-84 years	440,500	40.5
85 years and over	681,700	181.8
Black	**145,900**	**51.1**
65-74 years	30,300	18.2
75-84 years	58,700	66.5
85 years and over	56,900	183.1

Source: Centers for Disease Control and Prevention, National Center for Health Statistics, *Health, United States, 2001*.

Hospital Facilities and Their Use, 1946–99

Year	Number of hospitals	Number of beds ('000s)	Admissions ('000s)	Average stay (days)	Outpatient visits ('000s)
1946	6,125	1,436	15,675	9.1	N.A.
1950	6,788	1,456	18,483	8.1	N.A.
1960	6,876	1,658	25,027	7.6	N.A.
1965	7,123	1,704	28,812	7.8	125,793
1970	7,123	1,616	31,759	8.2	181,370
1975	7,156	1,466	36,157	7.7	254,844
1980	6,965	1,365	38,892	7.6	262,951
1985	6,872	1,318	36,304	7.1	282,140
1990	6,649	1,213	33,774	7.3	368,184
1995	6,291	1,081	33,282	6.5	483,195
1999	5,890	994	34,181	5.9	573,461

Note: N.A.= Not Available. **Source:** American Hospital Association, *Hospital Statistics* (annual).

jointly by federal and state agencies. (See also Part II: "Social Insurance Programs.")

In 2001, Medicare had 40 million beneficiaries and total expenditures of $240.9 billion, an increase of 10.8 percent since 2000. Medicare traditionally consisted of two parts: Hospital Insurance, also known as Part A, and Supplementary Medicare Insurance, also known as Part B. A third, managed care part, the Medicare+Choice program, was established in 1997. In 2001, about 5.7 million of the 40 million Medicare enrollees chose to participate in a Medicare+Choice plan.

Managed care (HMOs, PPOs) A managed health care plan provides comprehensive health care coverage to enrolled members on a prepaid basis; that is, insurance and health care delivery are integrated within one system. The objective is to control costs, assure access to effective treatments, and eliminate inappropriate and duplicative services.

The oldest managed care providers are health maintenance organizations (HMOs), which started in the 1940s. They either employ physicians in clinics or hospital-like buildings, or contract with hundreds or even thousands of physicians who practice in their private offices.

HMO patients generally must use their HMO's physicians in order to be reimbursed. Preferred provider organizations (PPOs), a modified version of HMOs, permit enrollees to use non-plan providers (physicians and hospitals). However, patients who use services outside their PPO must pay a financial penalty.

HMO enrollment reached a high of about 81 million in 1999, then stalled and began to decline, dropping to about 78 million by mid-2001. Increasing concern about access to health care and demand for a choice in choosing physicians helped precipitate the decline. Enrollment in HMOs varied significantly from state to state in 2001, from lows in Alaska (0.0%), North Dakota

People With and Without Health Insurance Coverage, by State, 2002

State	People with coverage ('000s)	People without coverage ('000s)	Percent of people without coverage
United States	**242,360**	**43,574**	**15.2%**
Alabama	3,876	564	12.7
Alaska	516	119	18.7
Arizona	4,526	916	16.8
Arkansas	2,252	440	16.3
California	28,761	6,398	18.2
Colorado	3,756	720	16.1
Connecticut	3,027	356	10.5
Delaware	719	79	9.9
District of Columbia	498	74	13.0
Florida	13,586	2,843	17.3
Georgia	7,072	1,354	16.1
Hawaii	1,101	123	10.0
Idaho	1,067	233	17.9
Illinois	10,737	1,767	14.1
Indiana	5,303	797	13.1
Iowa	2,626	277	9.5
Kansas	2,404	280	10.4
Kentucky	3,498	548	13.6
Louisiana	3,627	820	18.4
Maine	1,125	144	11.3
Maryland	4,728	730	13.4
Massachusetts	5,827	644	9.9
Michigan	8,752	1,158	11.7
Minnesota	4,657	397	7.9
Mississippi	2,322	465	16.7
Missouri	4,939	646	11.6
Montana	767	139	15.3
Nebraska	1,530	174	10.2
Nevada	1,703	418	19.7
New Hampshire	1,141	125	9.9
New Jersey	7,408	1,197	13.9
New Mexico	1,452	388	21.1
New York	16,241	3,042	15.8
North Carolina	6,794	1,368	16.8
North Dakota	564	69	10.9
Ohio	9,938	1,344	11.9
Oklahoma	2,876	601	17.3
Oregon	2,999	511	14.6
Pennsylvania	10,809	1,380	11.3
Rhode Island	952	104	9.8
South Carolina	3,497	500	12.5
South Dakota	659	85	11.5
Tennessee	5,058	614	10.8
Texas	15,973	5,556	25.8
Utah	2,000	310	13.4
Vermont	553	66	10.7
Virginia	6,156	962	13.5
Washington	5,151	850	14.2
West Virginia	1,496	255	14.6
Wisconsin	4,938	538	9.8
Wyoming	402	86	17.7

Source: U.S. Bureau of the Census, *Current Population Survey*, March 2003.

Uninsured Americans, 2002

Category	Number('000s)	Percent uninsured
Total	**43,574[1]**	**15.2%**
Sex		
Male	23,327	16.7
Female	20,246	13.9
Age		
Under 18	8,531	11.6
18-24	8,128	29.6
25-34	9,769	24.9
35-44	7,781	17.7
45-64	9,106	13.5
65 and older	258	0.8
Race/Ethnicity		
White[2]	33,320	14.2
Black[2]	7,429	19.9
Hispanic[3]	12,756	32.4
Asian, Native Hawaiian, Other Pacific Islander[2]	2,447	18.1
Education level[4]		
No high school diploma	9,768	28.0
High school grad only	12,671	18.8
Some college	6,214	15.0
Associate degree	1,981	12.1
Bachelor's degree or higher	4,408	8.4
Region		
Northeast	7,057	13.0
Midwest	7,533	11.7
South	17,773	17.5
West	11,210	17.1
Annual household income		
Under $25,000	14,776	23.5
$25,000-$49,999	14,638	19.3
$50,000-$74,999	6,904	11.8
$75,000 or more	7,256	8.2

1. Not covered at any time during the year. 2. Alone or incombination with other races; non-Hispanic. 3. Persons of Hispanic origin may be of any race. 4. Persons age 18 and older.
Source: U.S. Bureau of the Census, *Current Population Survey*, March 2003.

(0.7%), and Mississippi (1.4%) to highs in California (51.6%), Massachusetts (44.7%), and Connecticut (39.7%).

The Uninsured In 2002 the number of Americans without health insurance showed its greatest increase in a decade. According to the Census Bureau, 15.2 percent of the population or 43.6 million people were without health insurance during all of 2002, up from 14.6 percent the year before. The number of uninsured children under 18 remained unchanged, at 8.5 million (11.6 percent).

Young adults (18-to-24 years old) remained the group least likely to have health insurance in 2001. Nearly 30 percent of people in this age group were without coverage. Close behind were people 25-to34 years old, 25 percent of whom had no coverage for all of 2002.

▶SURGERY

Increases in the number of surgical operations during recent years have been accompanied by dramatic changes in the rates of some procedures. An example is the incidence of cesarean sections—surgical incisions through the abdomen and uterus for removal of a baby, performed when normal vaginal delivery is deemed hazardous for the mother or child. Cesareans accounted for 22.9 percent of all live births in 2000—down from a high of 24.4 percent in 1988, but more than four times the rate in 1970 (5.5 percent) and among the highest rates for developed nations.

The frequency of certain procedures varies according to age, but, surprisingly, there may also be variations from one geographical region to another. For example, throughout the 1990s, cesarean rates were highest in the South and lowest in the Midwest and West. A survey by Dartmouth Medical Schools researchers released in 1996 also noted disparities in the treatment of choice. For example, they found that a person in Kingsport, Tennessee, with a herniated disk was seven times as likely to have back surgery as one in Provo, Utah.

Cardiovascular Operations in the U.S., 1999

	Sex		Age			
Operation	**Male**	**Female**	**Under 15**	**15–44**	**45–64**	**65 plus**
Total procedures	**3,498,000**	**2,634,000**	**179,000**	**569,000**	**2,170,000**	**3,215,000**
Cardiac catheterization	813,000	547,000	12,000	109,000	576,000	663,000
Angioplasty	708,000	361,000	—	58,000	505,000	504,000
Bypass	389,000	182,000	—	16,000	232,000	322,000
Endarterectomy	67,000	65,000	—	—	32,000	99,000
Pacemaker	77,000	86,000	—	—	17,000	141,000
Valve replacement	47,000	49,000	—	7,000	21,000	56,000
Defibrillator implants	26,000	10,000	—	—	9,000	13,000
Open heart surgery[1]	478,000	275,000	25,000	39,000	275,000	399,000

Note: Estimated figures. Breakdowns not available for some procedures, causing entries for some categories not to add up to the total. Does not include outpatient and other nonhospitalized procedures. 1. Includes valves, bypass, and "other" open heart procedures. **Source:** American Heart Association, *2002 Heart and Stroke Statistical Update*.

Common Operations and Procedures, 2000

Type of Operation	Total	Males	Females
All operations[1]	**39,981,000**	**15,654,000**	**24,328,000**
Endoscopy of large or small intestine	1,456,000	618,000	839,000
Cardiac catheterization	1,221,000	732,000	490,000
Repair of lacerations due to giving birth	1,136,000	—	1,136,000
Coronary artery obstruction: removal, stenting	1,025,000	655,000	370,000
Respiratory therapy	991,000	507,000	484,000
Diagnostic ultrasound	886,000	385,000	501,000
Cesarean section	855,000	—	855,000
CAT scan	754,000	345,000	409,000
Hysterectomy	633,000	—	633,000
Reduction of fracture	628,000	285,000	343,000
Coronary artery bypass	519,000	371,000	148,000
Removal of one or both ovaries	494,000	—	494,000
Hemodialysis	456,000	224,000	232,000
Gall bladder removal	419,000	134,000	284,000
Pacemaker insertion, removal or replacement	327,000	162,000	165,000
Destruction or closing off of fallopian tubes	315,000	—	315,000
Appendectomy	303,000	163,000	140,000
Knee replacement (total)	299,000	115,000	185,000
Spinal tap	296,000	156,000	141,000
Spinal disc operation	296,000	162,000	134,000
Nose, mouth, pharynx operations	261,000	158,000	103,000
Cancer chemotherapy	199,000	115,000	85,000
Prostatectomy	184,000	184,000	—

Note: Discharges of inpatients from non-Federal hospitals. Excludes newborn infants. 1. Includes operations not shown separately. **Source:** U.S. Dept. of Health and Human Services, National Center for Health Statistics, *2000 National Hospital Discharge Survey* (June 19, 2002).

Organ Transplantation

Transplant surgery is more successful than ever, thanks to improved surgical techniques, a better understanding of the body's immune system, and the development of drugs that combat rejection of implanted organs. Kidney transplants, for instance, enjoy a high rate of success and are much less expensive—and much more convenient—than maintaining a patient on dialysis. Unfortunately, a scarcity of donor organs keeps thousands of patients waiting, sometimes in vain. The number of donors has increased, but not as rapidly as the waiting list. On August 9, 2002, 80,374 patients were on the national patient waiting list for organ transplants. In 2001, 6,209 people died before they could receive the organs they needed.

In addition to organs, tissues—cornea, bone, and skin—can be transplanted. In fact, corneal transplants are the most frequently performed transplant surgery. According to the Eye Bank Association, there were 33,035 such operations in 2001, with a success rate averaging better than 90 percent. As with organs, the need for tissues frequently exceeds the supply.

There are 51 independent and 8 hospital organ procurement programs in the United States. Many have toll-free telephone numbers. The United Network for Organ Sharing (UNOS) operates the national waiting list (1-888-TX-INFO1).

To perform transplants, hospitals must be licensed. According to UNOS, 255 medical institutions operated organ transplant programs as of mid-2002. These can be separated into organ-specific programs, including:

248 kidney transplants
140 heart transplants
139 pancreas transplants
123 liver transplants
78 heart-lung transplants
75 lung transplants
38 intestine transplants

Number and Survival Rates of Transplant Operations, 2001

Organ	Year first performed	Number (2000)	Survival rates[1]
Heart	1967	2,202	85%
Heart-lung	1982	27	62
Intestine	1990	112	82
Kidney	1954	14,149	95
Cadaver	—	8,201	—
Living donor	—	5,948	—
Kidney-pancreas	1966	884	95
Liver	1963	5,117	86
Cadaver	—	4,663	—
Living donor	—	514	—
Lung	1963	1,071	77
Cadaver	—	1,034	—
Living donor	—	37	—
Pancreas	1966	468	96

1. One-year adult patient survival rates for operations from January 1999 through June 2001.
Source: Scientific Registry of Transplant Recipients.

Abortion

The deliberate termination of a pregnancy before the fetus is capable of living outside the womb has generally been legal in the United States since 1973, when the Supreme Court ruled (in *Roe v. Wade*) that abortion cannot be prohibited during the first three months of pregnancy. During most years from 1973 through 1984, the ratio of abortions to live births increased, peaking at 364 per 1,000 live births in 1984. Thereafter, the ratio declined, falling to 306 per 1,000 live births in 1997.

According to a report released by the Centers for Disease Control and Prevention (CDC) in 2002, women who obtained abortions in 1998 were predominantly 24 years of age or younger, white, unmarried, and had no live-born children. Slightly more than half were obtaining an abor-

Reported Abortions, 1972–98

Category	1972	1980	1990	1995	1997	1998[1]
NUMBER OF ABORTIONS						
Reported Abortions	586,760	1,297,606	1,429,577	1,210,883	1,186,039	884,273
Number per 1,000 live births	180	359	345	311	306	264
PERCENT OF TOTAL						
Race						
White	77.0%	69.9%	64.8%	59.5%	58.5%	58.8%
Black[2]	23.0	30.1	31.8	35.0	35.9	35.4
Other	—	—	3.3	5.4	5.7	5.8
Marital Status						
Married	29.7%	23.1%	21.7%	19.7%	19.0%	18.9%
Unmarried	70.3	76.9	78.3	80.3	81.0	81.1
Age						
Under 20	32.6%	29.2%	22.4%	20.1%	20.1%	19.8%
20-24	32.5	35.5	33.2	32.5	31.7	31.8
25 or older	34.9	35.3	44.4	47.4	48.2	48.4
Weeks of gestation						
Up to 8	34.0%	51.7%	51.6%	54.0%	55.4%	55.7%
9-10	30.7	26.2	25.3	23.1	22.0	21.5
11-12	17.5	12.2	11.8	10.9	10.7	10.9
13-15	8.4	5.1	6.4	6.3	6.2	6.9
16-20	8.2	3.9	4.0	4.3	4.3	4.1
21 or more	1.2	0.9	1.0	1.4	1.4	1.4

1. Data for 48 of 52 reporting areas. Alaska, California, New Hampshire, and Oklahoma did not report. 2. 1972 and 1980 include other nonwhite groups. **Source:** U.S. Dept of Health and Human Services, Centers for Disease Control and Prevention, *Morbidity and Mortality Weekly Report* (June 7, 2002).

tion for the first time. More than half of the abortions were performed during the first eight weeks of gestation; 88 percent were performed in the first 12 weeks. Curettage was the primary abortion procedure, accounting for 97 percent of all abortions.

▶DISEASE

Five of the most common categories of disease are:

1. Hereditary diseases—transferred from parent to child by genes. Examples: hemophilia, Down's syndrome, cystic fibrosis, sickle cell anemia.
2. Deficiency diseases—caused by lack of vitamins or other essential nutrients. Examples: scurvy, pellagra.
3. Infectious diseases—caused by viruses, bacteria, fungi, and other organisms and transferred from person to person. Examples: common cold, influenza, chicken pox, measles, tuberculosis, AIDS.
4. Diseases caused by chemical and physical agents such as radiation, smoke, drugs, and poisons. Examples: allergies, asbestosis, bysinosis, lead poisoning.
5. Degenerative diseases—resulting from natural aging processes. In some cases, cancer and high blood pressure are degenerative diseases.

Heart Disease

Cardiovascular diseases (diseases of the heart and blood vessels) are America's number one killer, claiming more lives each year than the next seven leading causes of death combined. Almost one in four Americans—an estimated 61.8 million people— suffer some form of cardiovascular disease.

Reported Cases of Common Infectious Diseases, 1950–2001

Disease	1950	1960	1970	1980	1990	2000	2001
Brucellosis (undulant fever)	3,510	751	213	183	85	63	136
Cholera	N.A.	N.A.	N.A.	9	6	2	5
Legionnellosis	N.A.	N.A.	N.A.	N.A.	1,370	1,127	1,085
Leprosy (Hansen's disease)	44	54	129	223	198	64	90
Malaria	2,184	72	3,051	2,062	1,292	1,560	1,266
Meningococcal infections	3,788	2,259	2,505	2,840	2,451	2,256	2,255
Mumps	N.A.	N.A.	104,953	8,576	5,292	338	266
Pertussis (whooping cough)	120,718	14,809	4,249	1,730	4,570	7,867	7,580
Plague[1]	N.A.	2	13	18	2	6	2
Poliomyelitis	33,300	3,190	33	9	6	0	0
Psittacosis	26	113	35	124	113	11	25
Rabies, in animals	7,901	3,567	3,224	6,421	4,826	6,934	7,150
Rabies, in humans	18	2	3	0	1	2	1
Rubella (German measles)	N.A.	N.A.	56,552	3,904	1,125	176	23
Tetanus	486	368	148	95	64	26	37
Toxic shock syndrome	N.A.	N.A.	N.A.	N.A.	322	125	125
Trichinosis	327	160	109	131	129	15	22
Tuberculosis[2]	121,742	55,494	37,137	27,749	25,701	15,976	15,989
Typhoid fever	2,484	816	346	510	552	317	368
Venereal diseases							
Gonorrhea	286,746	258,933	600,072	1,004,029	690,042	357,570	361,705
Syphilis[3]	23,939	16,145	21,982	27,204	50,578	5,978	6,130

1. Plague: disease caused by the bite of fleas infected with the bacterium Yersinia pestis. 2. Data after 1970 not comparable to prior years because of changes in reporting criteria effective in 1975. 3. Primary and secondary syphilis cases.
Sources: U.S. Dept. of Health and Human Services, Centers for Disease Control and Prevention, *Morbidity and Mortality Weekly Report,* Jan. 4, 2002, August 16, 2002; *Health, United States, 2000* (2000).

Heart Disease Death Rates, 1950–2000 (per 100,000 population)

Age	1950[1]	1960[1]	1970	1980	1990	1995	1999	2000
All ages								
Age adjusted	586.8	559.0	492.7	412.1	321.8	296.3	267.8	257.9
Crude	355.5	369.0	362.0	336.0	289.5	280.7	265.9	258.2
Under 1 year	3.5	6.6	13.1	22.8	20.1	17.1	13.7	12.8
1-4 years	1.3	1.3	1.7	2.6	1.9	1.6	1.2	1.2
5-14 years	2.1	1.3	0.8	0.9	0.9	0.8	0.7	0.7
15-24 years	6.8	4.0	3.0	2.9	2.5	2.9	2.8	2.7
25-34 years	19.4	15.6	11.4	8.3	7.6	8.5	8.1	7.9
35-44 years	86.4	74.6	66.7	44.6	31.4	32.0	30.3	29.4
45-54 years	308.6	271.8	238.4	180.2	120.5	111.0	97.7	95.5
55-64 years	808.1	737.9	652.3	494.1	367.3	322.9	274.3	264.5
65-74 years	1,839.8	1,740.5	1,558.2	1,218.6	894.3	799.9	709.5	673.8
75-84 years	4,310.1	4,089.4	3,683.8	2,993.1	2,295.7	2,064.7	1,861.8	1,787.1
85 and older	9,150.6	9,317.8	7,891.3	7,777.1	6,739.9	6,484.1	6,032.5	5,848.7

Note: Comparability between years is affected by changes in coding of the cause of death. 1. Includes deaths of nonresidents of the U.S.
Source: U.S. Dept. of Health and Human Services, Center for Health Statistics.

During 1999 these diseases claimed 958,775 lives. This represented 40.1 percent of all deaths—an average of a death every 33 seconds.

Death rates vary according to age, sex, race, even geographical location. Rates increase with age and are higher among men than among women. For both sexes, death rates are significantly higher among blacks than among whites.

In 1998, Hawaii had the lowest age-adjusted death rate from cardiovascular disease (295.7 per 100,000 population) followed by Utah, Colorado, Minnesota, and New Mexico. Mississippi had the highest rate (474.8) followed by Tennessee, West Virginia, Oklahoma, and South Carolina.

The good news is that the death rates from cardiovascular disease have declined dramatically, falling 15.6 percent from 1989 to 1999. This is due in part to improved drug treatments and other medical advancements. Another factor has been improved personal health habits: people have stopped smoking, lowered the fat content of their diets, and taken other steps that reduce the risks of cardiovascular disease.

Evidence suggests that further significant reductions in deaths from heart disease could be achieved through aggressive treatment of high cholesterol. In 2001, a U.S. government panel recommended that some 36 million Americans are candidates for cholesterol-lowering drugs and about 65 million should be on cholesterol-lowering diets.

Heart attacks A heart attack, or coronary event, occurs when the blood supply to the heart muscles is blocked. An uncomfortable pressure, fullness, squeezing, or pain in the center of the chest that lasts for two minutes or more may be a sign of a heart attack. Sweating, dizziness, nausea, fainting, or shortness of breath may also occur. Some 1.1 million people suffer heart attacks annually. According to the American Heart Association, about 650,000 of these are first attacks and 450,000 are recurrent attacks. Over 45 percent of the people who experience a heart attack in a given year will die from it. Among survivors, many develop congestive heart failure, which can leave the heart unable to pump blood effectively.

The American Heart Association estimates that 571,000 bypass operations were performed on 355,000 patients in 1999; 43.5 percent of the procedures were performed on people under age 65. In this operation a blood vessel from elsewhere in the body is used to reroute blood around a blocked coronary artery. The purpose: to reduce the person's risk of a heart attack. In 2001 it was announced that researchers from Massachusetts General Hospital had in 1999 successfully performed the first nonsurgical bypass, called percutaneous in-situ coronary venous arterialization. The procedure is considered safer and less painful than traditional bypass surgery.

Strokes Each year, approximately 600,000 Americans—72 percent of them age 65 or older—suffer a stroke; of these, more than 165,000 die. A stroke occurs when the blood supply to the brain is blocked, usually by a clot. The primary signal of a stroke is a sudden, temporary weakness or numbness of the face, arm, or leg on one side of the body. Other signals include temporary loss of speech, difficulty in speaking or understanding speech, temporary vision problems (particularly in one eye), unsteadiness, or unexplained dizziness.

Cancer

The nation's second leading cause of death is a group of diseases characterized by the unrestrained growth of cells. It afflicts people of all ages and races, although about 77 percent of all cancers are diagnosed at ages 55 and above. Cancers vary greatly in cause, symptoms, response to treatment, and possibility of cure.

A U.S. male has a 1 in 2 probability of developing invasive cancer at some time during his life; a female 1 in 3. The incidence of cancer varies from state to state. Between 1994 and 1998, the highest cancer death rates occurred in the District of Columbia (268.2 cancer deaths per 100,000 males and 165.2 per 100,000 females). The lowest cancer death rates were in Utah (143. for males, 102.3 for females.

5-Year Survival Rates for Cancer, by Race and Site, 1960-98

Cancer Site	1960-63	1970-73	1980-82	1992-98	1960-63	1970-73	1980-82	1992-98
	Whites				Blacks			
All sites	**39%**	**43%**	**52%**	**64%**	**27%**	**31%**	**40%**	**53%**
Brain	18	20	25	32	19	19	31	40
Breast (females)	63	68	77	88	46	51	66	73
Cervix	58	64	68	72	47	61	61	60
Colon	43	49	56	63	34	37	49	53
Leukemia	14	22	40	47	N.C.	N.C.	33	38
Liver	N.C.	N.C.	4	7	N.C.	N.C.	2	4
Lung (and bronchus)	8	10	14	15	5	7	12	12
Ovary	32	36	39	53	32	32	38	53
Pancreas	1	2	3	4	1	2	5	4
Prostate	50	63	75	98	25	55	65	93
Rectum	38	45	53	62	27	30	38	53
Stomach	11	13	16	21	8	13	19	20
Testis	63	72	92	96	N.C.	N.C.	90	85
Thyroid	83	86	94	96	N.C.	N.C.	95	93
Urinary bladder	53	61	79	82	24	36	59	65
Uterus	73	81	83	N.A.	31	44	55	N.A.

Note: Rates are an average of cases diagnosed in years shown. N.C.: valid rate could not be calculated. **Source:** U.S. Dept. of Health and Human Services, National Cancer Institute; published in American Cancer Society, *Cancer Facts and Figures.*

Cancer survival rates The National Cancer Institute estimates that approximately 8.9 million Americans alive today have a history of cancer. Chances of surviving cancer have steadily improved. In the 1930s, about one in four American cancer patients survived at least five years after diagnosis. In contrast, six out of 10 who get cancer this year will be alive five years after diagnosis.

Survival depends on many factors. Two of the most important are the site of the tumor and how much the cancer has spread before treatment is begun. Lifestyle choices are also important. The American Cancer Society estimated that 170,000 cancer deaths in 2002 would be caused by tobacco use, and that about one-third of all cancer deaths each year are related to nutrition, physical inactivity, obesity, and other lifestyle choices.

Cancer death incidence and rates After increasing steadily for most of the century, cancer incidence and death rates for all cancers combined and for most of the top ten cancer sites declined beginning in 1992. Overall incidence rates decreased an average of 1.1 percent per year between 1992 and 1998. During that same period, overall cancer death rates declined by 1.6 percent per year for men and 0.8 percent per year for women. The largest decrease, 2.5 percent per year, occurred in black men. Improved detection and treatment, coupled with healthier lifestyles, are believed to account for the declining rates.

The American Cancer Society estimated that about 555,500 Americans would die of cancer in 2002 — more than 1,500 people a day. Lung cancer is the leading cause of cancer deaths, killing an estimated 89,200 men and 65,700 women in 2002. Among women, breast cancer is the second most common killer, though if detected early and treated properly, it has a very high cure rate. Among men, prostate cancer causes the second greatest number of deaths. It, too, has a high survival rate if discovered while still localized within the general region of the prostate.

Cancer warning signs

Early detection is the key in fighting cancer. See your doctor if one of the following symptoms lasts longer than two weeks.

1. Unusual bleeding or discharge.
2. A sore that does not heal.
3. A change in a wart or mole
4. A lump or thickening in the breast or elsewhere.
5. A change in bowel or bladder habits.
6. Nagging cough or hoarseness.
7. Indigestion or difficulty in swallowing.

AIDS

Following the discovery of acquired immune deficiency syndrome (AIDS) in 1981, the disease spread rapidly around the world. In the United States, sharp rises in new infections with human immunodeficiency virus (HIV), which causes AIDS, were recorded throughout the 1980s and into the early 1990s. The number of deaths also jumped annually, reaching almost 50,000 in 1995. The introduction of powerful AIDS drugs around that time showed significant success in controlling HIV before it progressed into AIDS. But the rate of HIV infection remained stubbornly high, leveling

Estimated New Cancer Cases and Deaths by Site and Sex, 2003

	New cases			Deaths		
Site	Total	Male	Female	Total	Male	Female
All Sites	**1,334,100**	**675,300**	**658,800**	**556,500**	**285,900**	**270,600**
Skin[1]	58,800	32,300	26,500	9,800	6,200	3,600
Oral	27,700	18,200	9,500	7,200	4,800	2,400
Lung, bronchus, and other respiratory	185,800	102,200	83,600	159,900	88,600	71,300
Breast	212,600	1,300	211,300	40,200	400	39,800
Esophagus	13,900	10,600	3,300	13,000	9,900	3,100
Stomach	22,400	13,400	9,000	12,100	7,000	5,100
Small intestine	5,300	2,700	2,600	1,100	600	500
Colon, rectum, and anus	151,500	30,400	121,100	57,600	28,500	29,100
Liver and bile passages	17,300	11,700	5,600	14,400	9,200	5,200
Pancreas	30,700	14,900	15,800	30,000	14,700	15,300
Other digestive organs	4,500	1,400	3,100	1,900	700	1,200
Urinary (bladder, kidney, etc.)	91,700	63,300	28,400	25,100	16,400	8,700
Leukemia	30,600	17,900	12,700	21,900	12,100	9,800
Lymphoma	61,000	32,300	28,700	24,700	12,900	11,800
Multiple myeloma	14,600	7,800	22,400	10,900	5,400	5,500
Bone and joints	2,400	1,300	1,100	1,300	700	600
Endocrine system	23,800	6,600	17,200	2,300	1,100	1,200
Eye	2,200	1,100	1,100	200	100	100
Brain, other nervous system	18,300	10,200	8,100	13,100	7,300	5,800
Ovary	25,400	—	25,400	14,300	—	14,300
Uterus	52,300	—	52,300	10,900	—	10,900
Other genital, female	2,000	—	2,000	800	—	800
Prostate	220,900	220,900	—	28,900	28,900	—
Testis	7,600	7,600	—	400	400	—
Other genital, male	1,400	1,400	—	200	200	—
All other plus unspecified sites	30,300	14,100	16,200	42,300	21,700	20,600

Note: Except for bladder, figures for invasive cancer only. Carcinoma in situ of the breast accounts for about 54,300 new cases annually and melanoma carcinoma in situ accounts for about 34,300 cases annually. 1. Melanoma and other nonepithelial skin cancers only; highly curable basal cell and squamous cell skin cancers account for more than 1 million new cases annually.
Source: American Cancer Society, *Cancer Facts & Figures 2003*.

AIDS Cases and Deaths in the U.S., 1981–2001

Year	Cases diagnosed	Cases diagnosed to date	Known deaths	Known deaths to date
Pre-1981	100	100	30	30
1981	339	439	130	160
1982	1,199	1,638	465	625
1983	3,153	4,791	1,511	2,136
1984	6,368	11,159	3,526	5,662
1985	12,044	23,203	6,996	12,658
1986	19,404	42,607	12,183	24,841
1987	29,105	71,712	16,488	41,329
1988	36,126	107,838	21,244	62,573
1989	43,499	151,337	28,054	90,627
1990	49,546	200,883	31,836	122,463
1991	60,573	261,456	37,106	159,569
1992	79,657	341,113	41,849	201,418
1993	79,879	420,992	45,733	247,151
1994	73,086	494,078	50,657	297,808
1995	69,984	564,062	51,414	349,222
1996	61,124	625,186	38,074	387,296
1997	49,379	674,565	21,846	409,142
1998	41,829	716,394	18,148	427,290
1999	38,811	755,205	16,762	444,052
2000	36,087	791,292	14,499	458,551
2001	24,855	816,147	8,998	467,549

Note: Delays in reporting cases and deaths substantially impact data,particularly for recent years. In addition, there were 360 people known to have died but whose dates of death are unknown. **Source:** U.S. Dept. of Health and Human Services, Centers for Disease Control and Prevention, *HIV/AIDS Surveillance Report,* Vol. 13, No. 2 (2002).

off at about 40,000 new cases a year. The Centers for Disease Control and Prevention reported that AIDS had been diagnosed in 774,467 people in the United States and its territories by the end of 2000; of these, more than 448,000 had died.

HIV is spread through contact with infected body fluids such as blood and semen. Infected people may harbor the virus within their bodies for several years or even longer before developing symptoms of AIDS. Though symptomless, they still can infect others. AIDS experts stressed that preventive measures, including sex education, condom distribution, and needle-exchange programs for drug addicts, need to be emphasized. They also feared that the new AIDS drugs were making people complacent and careless about their sexual behavior. Indeed, it was reported in 2000 that the rate of new HIV infections among gay and bisexual men in San Francisco nearly tripled from 1997 to 1999.

An encouraging change of the 1990s was the steep reduction in mother-to-fetus transmissions of HIV. This resulted from the use of zidovudine (ZDV), taken by the pregnant woman beginning as early as the 14th week of pregnancy and continuing until labor; at birth, the baby takes ZDV for six weeks. In 1999, there were 232 reported cases of AIDS transmission from mothers to newborns, bringing the total to 7,943 since the epidemic began.

No cure for AIDS is known. Many in the medical community are pinning hopes on preventative AIDS vaccines now being developed. The drug therapies that have been extremely effective in controlling AIDS progression for some patients are very expensive, putting them beyond the

Adults and Adolescents With AIDS, 1981–2001

Exposure category	Males		Females		Total	
	Cases	Percent	Cases	Percent	Cases	Percent
Homosexual/Bisexual males	368,971	55%	--	--	368,971	46%
Intravenous (IV) drug abusers	145,750	22	55,576	39%	201,326	25
Homosexual male and IV drug abusers	51,293	8	--	--	51,293	6
Hemophilia/Coagulation disorder	5,000	1	292	0	5,292	1
Heterosexual contact	32,735	5	57,396	41	90,131	11
Blood transfusion, blood components, or tissue	5,057	1	3,914	3	8,971	1
Other/Undetermined[1]	57,220	9	23,870	17	81,091	10
Total[2]	**666,026**	**100%**	**141,048**	**100%**	**807,075**	**100%**

Note: Cases with more than one risk factor other than the combinations listed are tabulated only in the category listed first. 1. Includes patients whose mode of exposure to HIV is unknown; also includes 180 persons who acquired HIV infection perinatally but were diagnosed with AIDS after age 13. 2. Due to rounding, category totals may not total 100%. **Source:** U.S. Dept. of Health and Human Services, Centers for Disease Control and Prevention, *HIV/AIDS Surveillance Report,* Vol. 13, No. 2 (2002).

AIDS in the Cities, 2001

City	Number of cases	City	Number of cases	City	Number of cases
New York, N.Y.	126,237	**Boston, Mass.**	14,945	**New Orleans, La.**	7,252
Los Angeles, Calif.	43,488	**Ft. Lauderdale, Fla.**	13,594	**Seattle, Wash.**	7,006
San Francisco, Calif.	28,438	**Dallas, Texas**	13,119	**Nassau—Suffolk, N.Y.**	7,002
Miami, Fla.	25,357	**San Diego, Calif.**	11,070	**New Haven, Conn.**	6,913
Washington, D.C.	24,844	**Tampa—St. Petersburg, Fla.**	9,006	**Jersey City, N.J.**	6,855
Chicago, Ill.	22,703			**Orlando, Fla.**	6,540
Philadelphia, Pa.	20,369	**Oakland, Calif.**	8,347	**Orange County, Calif.**	5,925
Houston, Texas	19,898	**Detroit, Mich.**	8,196	**Denver, Colo.**	5,851
Newark, N.J.	17,796	**West Palm Beach, Fla.**	8,118	**Bergen-Passaic, N.J.**	5,691
Atlanta, Ga.	17,157	**Riverside—San Bernardino, Calif.**	7,319	**Phoenix, Ariz.**	5,662
Baltimore, Md.	15,792			**St. Louis, Mo.**	5,007

Note: Provisional data. **Source:** U.S. Dept. of Health and Human Services, Centers for Disease Control and Prevention, *HIV/AIDS Surveillance Report,* Midyear edition, Vol. 13, No. 2. (2002).

reach of the vast majority of the world's HIV-positive people.

(See also "World Health" for information on AIDS worldwide.)

AIDS patients Homosexual and bisexual males make up almost 50 percent of all adult and adolescent AIDS cases reported in the United States since 1981. During the 1990s, however, the epidemic shifted steadily toward a growing proportion of AIDS cases in blacks and Hispanics, and in women. In absolute numbers, blacks outnumbered whites in new AIDS diagnoses and deaths beginning in 1996, and in the number of persons living with AIDS beginning in 1998. The proportion of women with AIDS increased steadily; they accounted for 32 percent of the cases reported in 1999. In the 13-to-24 age group, women accounted for 49 percent of reported cases.

Heterosexuals most at risk are those with venereal disease and multiple sex partners. Evidence suggests that sexually transmitted diseases that cause genital ulcers, such as herpes and syphilis, are especially dangerous because they cause breaks in the skin through which HIV can enter. People with these diseases are three to five times more likely than usual to get HIV if they have sex with an HIV-infected person.

The overwhelming majority of AIDS cases are found in large cities and metropolitan areas. Through mid-2000, metropolitan areas with 500,000 or more population accounted for 632,344 of the 753,907 reported AIDS cases (83.9 percent).

Sexually Transmitted Diseases

Sexually transmitted diseases (STDs) have been around since the beginning of recorded history, and while the prevalence of some have declined, rates for others have exploded. Today, more than 65 million Americans have an incurable STD. An additional 15 million become infected with one or more STDs each year, roughly half of whom contract lifelong infections. Despite the widespread nature of STDs and their severe consequences, most Americans remain unaware of the risks and consequences of all but HIV (the AIDS virus). STDs are difficult to track—many infected people do not have symptoms and remain undiagnosed, though able to infect others. Even diagnosed cases frequently are not reported and counted.

The most prevalent STDs are the human papilloma virus, which causes warts and genital cancers (5.5 million new cases annually); trichomoniasis, caused by a protozoan (5.0 million); chlamydia, caused by a bacterium (3.0 million), genital herpes, caused by a virus (1.0 million), and gonorrhea, caused by a bacterium (650,000). People with these STDs have a significantly increased risk of becoming infected with HIV, in part because they may have open sores that provide the virus with an easy route of entry to the body.

Viral Hepatitis: A Major Cause of Liver Disease

Several viruses are responsible for viral hepatitis, a sometimes-fatal disease that attacks the liver. In the United States 97 percent of acute cases and 83 percent of chronic cases are accounted for by hepatitis viruses A, B, C, D, and E—particularly the first three.

Hepatitis A is spread primarily by fecal contamination of food and water and through person-to-person contact. The Centers for Disease Control and Prevention (CDC) estimates that the virus infects 150,000 Americans each year. Vaccines are available for prevention of hepatitis A infection in persons age 2 and older.

Hepatitis B is generally transmitted via contact with the blood of an infected person during sex, during birth, or through contaminated needles and syringes. People at high risk include intravenous drug users who share needles, homosexual men, and heterosexuals with multiple partners.

According to the CDC, an estimated 200,000 new infections of hepatitis B are diagnosed annually. Some of those infected become chronic carriers. An estimated one million Americans are believed to be chronic carriers, capable of transmitting the virus to other people. Furthermore, chronic carriers are at high risk of developing cirrhosis or liver cancer; each year in the United States, about 4,000 to 5,000 hepatitis B patients die of these illnesses. The CDC and medical associations recommend that all newborns be vaccinated against hepatitis B.

Hepatitis C is the leading reason for liver transplants in the United States and is believed to be responsible for much of the increase in liver cancer in recent years. An estimated 4 million Americans carry the virus, which is spread when blood or body fluids from an infected person enters the body of a person who is not infected. Therapies often are ineffective or cause serious side effects, and no vaccine is available.

Death Rates (per 100,000 population) by Sex and Race, 1940–2001

		All races		Whites		Black	
Year	Total	Male	Female	Male	Female	Male	Female
1940	1,076.4	1,197.4	954.6	1,162.2	919.4	N.A.	N.A.
1950	963.8	1,106.1	823.5	1,089.5	803.3	N.A.	N.A.
1960	954.7	1,104.5	809.2	1,098.5	800.9	1,181.7	905.0
1970	945.3	1,090.3	807.8	1,086.7	812.6	1,186.6	829.2
1980	878.3	976.9	785.3	983.3	806.1	1,034.1	733.3
1985	876.9	948.6	809.1	963.6	840.1	989.3	734.2
1990	863.8	918.4	812.0	930.9	846.9	1,008.0	747.9
1995	880.0	914.1	847.3	932.1	891.3	980.7	759.0
1999	877.0	882.0	872.2	911.2	924.1	880.0	761.3
2000	854.0	853.0	855.0	887.8	912.3	834.1	733.0
2001[1]	848.9	846.6	851.2	882.5	909.1	822.2	726.1

Note: Death rates are based on population estimates prepared by the U.S. Bureau of the Census. 1. Preliminary.
Source: U.S. Dept. of Health and Human Services, National Center for Health Statistics. *National Vital Statistics Report* (March 14, 2003).

Alzheimer's disease

Alzheimer's disease is a progressive degenerative condition characterized by forgetfulness in early stages and, as the disease progresses, increasingly severe debilitating symptoms that create demanding care-giving needs. An estimated 4 million Americans, most of them elderly, have Alzheimer's disease. It caused 49,044 deaths in 2000, making it the eighth-leading cause of death. Many more women than men die from Alzheimer's, but this mainly reflects the larger number of women alive at older ages. Death rates are much higher for whites than blacks, but the risk of acquiring Alzheimer's is higher for blacks than whites.

Stem Cell Therapies and the Treatment of Disease

Among the most significant scientific developments of recent years has been the discovery of stem cells and the ability to isolate these cells and use them in research. Stem cells are immature cells that can give rise to other types of cells. Embryonic stem cells, isolated from very early embryos, can differentiate into all types of cells. Stem cells from adult tissue are less versatile, though not tissue-specific; for example, some stem cells produced in bone marrow can differentiate into muscle, bone, cartilage, and tendon cells.

Scientists believe that stem-cell therapies have the potential to revolutionize treatment of disease, particularly degenerative diseases like Parkinson's and Alzheimer's. Animal experiments show that stem-cell transplants create new cells and tissues that are assimilated into the animals' own organs. For example, stem cells injected into the damaged hearts of mice that suffered heart attacks helped repair the hearts by developing into new muscle and blood vessel cells. The study of human embryonic stem cells is controversial, however, and strongly opposed by abortion opponents.

▶DEATH

In 2000, a record high total of 2,404,598 deaths were registered in the United States, an increase of 13,199 from the 1999 total. The age-adjusted death rate, which takes into account changes and variations in the age composition of the population, reached a record low of 872.4 per 100,000

Leading Causes of Death, 1970–2000

Cause of death	Deaths in 2000	Death rate per 100,000 1970	1980	1990	1999	2000[1]
All causes	**2,404,624**	**945.3**	**878.3**	**861.9**	**877.0**	**873.6**
Heart diseases	709,894	362.0	336.0	289.0	265.9	257.9
Cancer	551,833	162.8	183.9	201.7	201.6	200.5
Cerebrovascular diseases	166,028	101.9	75.1	57.9	61.4	60.3
Pulmonary diseases	123,550	15.2	24.7	35.5	45.5	44.9
Accidents	93,592	56.4	46.7	37.3	35.7	34.0
Diabetes mellitus	68,662	18.9	15.4	19.5	25.1	24.9
Pneumonia and influenza	67,024	30.9	24.1	31.3	23.4	24.3
Alzheimer's disease	49,044	N.A.	N.A.	N.A.	16.3	17.8
Kidney diseases	37,672	4.4	7.4	8.3	13.0	13.7
Septicemia	31,613	1.7	4.2	7.9	11.2	11.5
Suicide	28,332	11.6	11.9	12.3	10.6	10.3
Liver disease and cirrhosis	26,219	15.5	13.5	10.2	9.6	9.5
Hypertension	17,964	N.A.	N.A.	N.A.	6.2	6.5
Pneumonitis due to solids and liquids	16,659	N.A	N.A	N.A	5.6	6.1
Homicide and legal intervention	16,137	8.3	10.7	10.2	6.2	5.9

Note: Causes of death are classified by the International Classification of Diseases, which has been revised periodically, resulting in new cause-of-death titles and breaks in comparability of cause-of-death statistics. 1. Preliminary.
Source: U.S. Dept. of Health and Human Services, National Center for Health Statistics, *National Vital Statistics Reports.*

Deaths and Death Rates, 2001

Age	Total deaths	Rate per 100,000 population: Both sexes	Male	Female
All ages	**2,417,762**	**848.9**	**846.6**	**851.2**
Under 1 year	27,801	689.2	755.3	620.0
1-4 years	5,125	33.4	37.3	29.4
5-14 years	7,100	17.3	19.8	14.6
15-24 years	32,157	80.5	116.6	42.5
25-34 years	41,474	104.7	143.0	65.6
35-44 years	91,457	203.2	258.9	147.9
45-54 years	167,836	428.3	544.3	316.5
55-64 years	244,002	964.1	1,191.6	753.9
65-74 years	431,306	2,355.2	2,913.9	1,892.3
75-84 years	702,657	5,588.2	6,841.8	4,764.3
85 and older	666,456	15,133.8	16,760.0	14,453.4
Not stated	390	—	1,029.5	—

Note: Preliminary data.
Source: U.S. Dept. of Health and Human Services, National Center for Health Statistics. *National Vital Statistics Report* (March 13, 2003).

population, 1.1 percent lower than the 1999 rate of 881.9

Males experience greater numbers of deaths and higher death rates than females, with black males having significantly higher numbers and rates than white males. Age-adjusted death rates for 2000 were: white females, 723.4 deaths per 100,000 population; black females, 943.9; white males, 1,019.3; and black males, 1,371.3

Socioeconomic disparities in death rates also exist. A 1998 report from University of Michigan researchers said that adults in the lowest income group (less than $10,000 annual income) were 3.2 times more likely to die compared with those in the highest income bracket ($30,000 or more). Middle income adults ($10,000-$29,999) were 2.3 times as likely to die as those in the high-income group. Possible factors for higher death rates among the poor include depression, social isolation, a lack of optimism, low self-esteem, and chronic stress.

Causes of Death

For the purposes of national mortality statistics, every death is attributed to one underlying condition. The 15 leading cases of death in 2000 accounted for 83.4 percent of all deaths in the United States. During the 20th century the leading causes of death changed significantly. In 1900, infectious diseases took may lives; indeed, the leading causes of death were (1) pneumonia and influenza and (2) tuberculosis. By century's end, heart disease and cancer headed the list.

Changes in Leading Causes of Death, 1900–2000

Cause of death	Death rate (per 100,000 population)
1900: All causes	**1,719.1**
Pneumonia and influenza	202.2
Tuberculosis	194.4
Diarrhea, enteritis, and ulceration of the intestines	142.7
1920: All causes	**1,298.9**
Pneumonia and influenza	207.3
Heart disease	159.6
Tuberculosis	113.1
1940: All causes	**1,074.1**
Heart disease	291.3
Cancer	120.0
Cerebrovascular disease	90.8
1960: All causes	**954.7**
Heart disease	369.0
Cancer	149.2
Cerebrovascular disease	108.0
1980: All causes	**878.3**
Heart disease	336.0
Cancer	183.9
Cerebrovascular disease	75.1
1990: All causes	**863.8**
Heart disease	289.5
Cancer	203.3
Cerebrovascular disease	57.9
2000: All causes	**873.6**
Heart disease	257.9
Cancer	200.5
Cerebrovascular disease	60.3

Source: U.S. Dept. of Health and Human Services, National Center for Health Statistics.

Suicide

Each year, approximately 30,000 Americans kill themselves—about one person every 20 minutes. In addition, an estimated 500,000 people are treated in emergency rooms each year after attempting suicide. Although women make more attempts at suicide, men are four times more likely to succeed at it. In 1999, 23,458 men, but only 5,741 women committed suicide.

Particularly troublesome is the suicide rate for teens and young adults. Suicide is the eleventh-leading cause of death for all Americans and the third-leading cause for young people age 15-24. The causes of youth suicide are not fully known, although some evidence suggests that suicide is not as frequently associated with depression in young people as it is in adults. Many young suicide victims had a history of impulsive, aggressive, or antisocial behavior, often complicated by drug abuse. Having a parent who committed suicide also seems to increase a person's vulnerability.

Significant differences in suicide rates exist among the states. For 1999, the highest rates were reported for Nevada (22.3 per 100,000 population), Wyoming (20.4), Montana (18.4), New Mexico (18.3) and Arizona (16.0). The lowest were for the District of Columbia (5.8), New York (6.6), New Jersey (6.9), Massachusetts (7.0) and Connecticut (8.3).

The majority of Americans who commit suicide shoot themselves (56.8% in 1999). Other common methods are hanging, strangulation or suffocation (18.6%) and poisons (16.8%).

Many experts believe that suicide statistics are grimmer than reported. They contend that numerous suicides are categorized as accidents or other deaths to spare families.

▶ACCIDENTS

Every 10 minutes, two people are killed and about 370 suffer a disabling injury in accidents in the United States. Accidents are the nation's fifth most common cause of death. But for people between the ages of 1 and 44, accidents are the leading cause of death.

The accident death rate has declined significantly from the 1912 rate of 82.5 deaths per 100,000 population. In 1992 it reached a record low of 34.0. In 2000 the rate was 35.3, or a total of 97,300 accidental deaths, according to National Safety Council estimates. Accident rates vary significantly from one place to another. National

Suicide in the U.S., 1950–99

Age	Rate per 100,000 population					
	1950	1960	1970	1980	1990	1999
All ages[1]	**13.2**	**12.5**	**13.1**	**12.2**	**12.5**	**10.7**
0 - 4	—	—	—	—	—	—
5-14	0.2	0.3	0.3	0.4	0.8	0.6
15-24	4.5	5.2	8.8	12.3	13.2	10.3
25-34	9.1	10.0	14.1	16.0	15.2	13.5
35-44	14.3	14.2	16.9	15.4	15.3	14.4
45-54	20.9	20.7	20.0	15.9	14.8	14.2
55-64	26.8	23.7	21.4	15.9	16.0	12.4
65-74	29.6	23.0	20.8	16.9	17.9	13.6
75-84	31.1	27.9	21.2	19.1	24.9	18.3
85 & older	28.8	26.0	19.0	19.2	22.2	19.2

1. Age-adjusted. **Source:** U.S. Dept. of Health and Human Services, National Center for Health Statistics. *National Vital Statistics Reports* (Oct. 9, 2001).

Types of Accidental Deaths in U.S., 2000

Type	Number of deaths	Age group (years) 0–4	5–14	15–24	25–44	45–64	65–74	75+
All accidents	**97,300**	**2,700**	**2,700**	**13,800**	**26,600**	**19,500**	**7,600**	**24,400**
Motor vehicle	43,000	900	1,500	10,500	13,300	9,200	2,700	4,900
Falls	16,200	70	70	210	950	1,900	1,700	11,300
Poisoning by solids and liquids[1]	11,700	60	40	800	6,800	3,200	300	500
Drowning	3,900	450	350	700	1,250	650	230	270
Suffocation	3,400	100	20	30	250	400	500	2,100
Fires and burns	3,600	400	260	240	700	800	500	700
Firearms	600	20	60	150	190	110	30	40
Poisoning by gases	400	10	10	70	120	80	40	70
All other[2]	14,500	700	400	1,100	3,000	3,200	1,600	4,500

1. Deaths from poisons, drugs, medicines, mushrooms, and shellfish. Excludes poisonings from spoiled foods, salmonella, etc., which are classified as disease deaths. 2. Medical complications, air and water transport, machinery, excessive cold, etc.
Source: National Safety Council, *Injury Facts* (2001).

Estimated Number of Injuries in U.S. From Selected Products, 1999

Product group	Estimated injuries
Stairs, steps	1,048,257
Floors, flooring materials	1,033,938
Bicycles	627,164
Basketball	600,256
Beds	466,464
Knives	459,898
Football	399,501
Bathtubs, showers	201,465
Ladders, stools	197,309
Soccer	185,064
Nails, screws, tacks, bolts	158,982
Carpets, rugs	122,249
Fences, fence posts	118,603
Footwear	109,681
Trampolines	100,303
Drinking glasses	98,924
Wheelchairs	95,877
Power, hand saws	95,875
Skateboards	86,781
Lawn mowers	81,888
Bottles, jars	80,186
Swimming pools	80,110
Swings, swing sets	76,181
Fishing	72,751
Jewelry	72,300
Crutches, canes, walkers	69,349
Weightlifting	68,054
Snowboarding	67,979
Toilets	55,806
Golf, golf carts	54,137
Hot water	42,712
Hammers	40,707
Dancing	40,049
Razors, shavers	34,279
Scissors	31,512

Notes: These national estimates are based on injuries treated in hospital emergency rooms participating in the National Electronic Injury Surveillance System. Patients said their injuries were related to the products; this does not necessarily mean the injuries were caused by the products.
Source: Consumer Product Safety Commission, National Electronic Injury Surveillance System.

Accidental Deaths in the U.S., 1910–2000 (per 100,000 population)

Year	Death rate	Year	Death rate	Year	Death rate
1910	84.4	**1950**	60.3	**1990**	36.9
1920	71.2	**1960**	52.1	**1995**	35.5
1930	80.5	**1970**	56.2	**1999**	35.7
1940	73.4	**1980**	46.5	**2000**	34.0

Source: U.S. Dept. of Health and Human Services, National Center for Health Statistics.

Life Expectancy in U.S., 1950–2000

Year	All races Male	All races Female	Whites Male	Whites Female	Blacks Male	Blacks Female
At birth						
1950[1]	65.6	71.1	66.5	72.2	58.9	62.7
1960[1]	66.6	73.1	67.4	74.1	60.7	65.9
1970	67.1	74.7	68.0	75.6	60.0	68.3
1980	70.0	77.4	70.7	78.1	63.8	72.5
1990	71.8	78.8	72.7	79.4	64.5	73.6
1995	72.5	78.9	73.4	79.6	65.2	73.9
1998	73.8	79.5	74.5	80.0	67.6	74.8
2000	74.1	79.5	74.8	80.0	68.3	75.0
At age 65 (years remaining)						
1950[1]	12.8	15.0	12.8	15.1	12.9	14.9
1960[1]	12.8	15.8	12.9	15.9	12.7	15.1
1970	13.1	17.0	13.1	17.1	12.5	15.7
1980	14.1	18.3	14.2	18.4	13.0	16.8
1990	15.1	18.9	15.2	19.1	13.2	17.2
1995	15.6	18.9	15.7	19.1	13.6	17.1
1998	16.0	19.2	16.1	19.3	14.3	17.4
2000	16.3	19.2	16.3	19.2	14.6	17.5

1. Includes deaths of persons who were not residents of the 50 states and the District of Columbia.
Source: U.S. Dept. of Health and Human Services, National Center for Health Statistics, *Health United States 2000, National Vital Statistics Report* (Oct. 9, 2001).

Safety Council estimates indicate that the highest accidental death rates in 2000 were in Mississippi (61.7), Montana (56.3), and New Mexico (56.2); the lowest were in Massachusetts (21.3), New Jersey (22.5), and Hawaii and New York (24.9).

Approximately 20.5 million injuries disabled people for one or more days during 2000. The costs incurred from accidents totaled an estimated $512.4 billion in 2000—for medical care, wage loss, insurance administration, property damage, fire loss, and so on.

Motor Vehicle Deaths, 2000

Since the nation's first motor vehicle death (reportedly in New York City on September 13, 1899) some 2.9 million people have died in motor vehicle accidents. Over the years, however, the numbers of deaths per 100,000 population and per 100,000 registered vehicles have declined drastically. For example, noted the National Safety Council, there were 3,100 motor vehicle deaths in 1912, when the number of registered vehicles totaled only 950,000. In 2000, there were 43,000 fatalities, but registered vehicles had risen to more than 224 million. The motor vehicle death rate in 2000 was 1.6 deaths per 100 million vehicle miles. This ranged from a low of 0.8 deaths in Massachusetts to a high of 2.7 deaths in Mississippi. Here's how people died in motor vehicle accidents in 2000:

- 20,600 died in collisions between two or more motor vehicles
- 11,200 died in collisions with guardrails and other fixed objects
- 5,300 pedestrians were struck by motor vehicles
- 4,600 died in non-collision accidents
- 800 died in collisions with cyclists
- 400 died in collisions with railroad trains
- 100 died in other types of collisions, usually involving animals or animal-drawn vehicles.

Data suggest that safety belts, air bags, bicycle and motorcycle helmets, child safety seats, strict drunk-driving laws, and speed limits save thou-

Average Remaining Life Expectancy in U.S. (in years)

Age in	All races		White		Black		Age in	All races		White		Black	
1999	M	F	M	F	M	F	1999	M	F	M	F	M	F
At							50	27.7	31.7	28.0	32.0	24.0	28.7
birth	73.9	79.4	74.6	79.9	67.8	74.7	51	26.8	30.8	27.1	31.0	23.2	27.9
1	73.5	78.9	74.1	79.3	67.9	74.7	52	26.0	29.9	26.3	30.1	22.5	27.1
2	72.6	77.9	73.1	78.4	67.0	73.8	53	25.2	29.0	25.4	29.2	21.8	26.3
3	71.6	77.0	72.2	77.4	66.0	72.8	54	24.4	28.2	24.6	28.4	21.1	25.5
4	70.6	76.0	71.2	76.4	65.0	71.9	55	23.5	27.3	23.8	27.5	20.4	24.7
5	69.6	75.0	70.2	75.4	64.1	70.9	56	22.7	26.4	22.9	26.6	19.8	23.9
6	68.6	74.0	69.2	74.4	63.1	69.9	57	21.9	25.6	22.1	25.7	19.1	23.1
7	67.7	73.0	68.2	73.4	62.1	68.9	58	21.2	24.7	21.3	24.9	18.5	22.4
8	66.7	72.0	67.2	72.5	61.1	67.9	59	20.4	23.9	20.6	24.0	17.8	21.6
9	65.7	71.1	66.2	71.5	60.2	67.0	60	19.6	23.1	19.8	23.2	17.2	20.9
10	64.7	70.1	65.3	70.5	59.2	66.0	61	18.9	22.3	19.0	22.4	16.6	20.1
11	63.7	69.1	64.3	69.5	58.2	65.0	62	18.2	21.5	18.3	21.6	16.0	19.4
12	62.7	68.1	63.3	68.5	57.2	64.0	63	17.5	20.7	17.6	20.8	15.5	18.7
13	61.7	67.1	62.3	67.5	56.2	63.0	64	16.8	19.9	16.8	20.0	14.9	18.0
14	607	66.1	61.3	66.5	55.2	62.0	65	16.1	19.1	16.1	19.2	14.3	17.3
15	59.8	65.1	60.3	65.5	54.3	61.0	66	15.4	18.4	15.5	18.4	13.8	16.6
16	58.8	64.1	59.4	64.5	53.3	60.1	67	14.7	17.6	14.8	17.7	13.2	15.9
17	57.9	63.2	58.4	63.6	52.4	59.1	68	14.1	16.9	14.1	16.9	12.7	15.3
18	56.9	62.2	57.5	62.6	51.5	58.1	69	13.5	16.1	13.5	16.2	12.1	14.6
19	56.0	61.2	56.5	61.6	50.5	57.1	70	12.8	15.4	12.9	15.5	11.6	14.0
20	55.0	60.2	55.6	60.7	49.6	56.2	71	12.3	14.7	12.3	14.8	11.1	13.4
21	54.1	59.3	54.7	59.7	48.7	55.2	72	11.7	14.1	11.7	14.1	10.6	12.8
22	53.2	58.3	53.7	58.7	47.9	54.2	73	11.1	13.4	11.1	13.4	10.1	12.2
23	52.3	57.3	52.8	57.7	47.0	53.3	74	10.6	12.7	10.6	12.7	9.7	11.7
24	51.3	56.4	51.8	56.8	46.1	52.3	75	10.0	12.1	10.0	12.1	9.2	11.1
25	50.4	55.4	50.9	55.8	45.2	51.4	76	9.5	11.5	9.5	11.4	8.8	10.6
26	49.5	54.4	50.0	54.8	44.3	50.4	77	9.0	10.8	9.0	10.8	8.4	10.1
27	48.5	53.4	49.0	53.8	43.4	49.5	78	8.5	10.2	8.4	10.2	8.0	9.6
28	47.6	52.5	48.1	52.9	42.5	48.5	79	8.0	9.7	8.0	9.6	7.6	9.1
29	46.7	51.5	47.2	51.9	41.6	47.6	80	7.5	9.1	7.5	9.1	7.3	8.6
30	45.7	50.5	46.2	50.9	40.7	46.6	81	7.1	8.6	7.0	8.5	6.9	8.1
31	44.8	49.6	45.3	49.9	39.8	45.7	82	6.7	8.0	6.6	8.0	6.5	7.7
32	43.9	48.6	44.3	49.0	38.9	44.7	83	6.3	7.5	6.2	7.5	6.2	7.3
33	42.9	47.6	43.4	48.0	38.1	43.8	84	5.9	7.1	5.8	7.0	5.9	6.9
34	42.0	46.7	42.5	47.0	37.2	42.9	85	5.5	6.6	5.5	6.6	5.6	6.5
35	41.1	45.7	41.5	46.1	36.3	41.9	86	5.2	6.2	5.1	6.1	5.3	6.1
36	40.2	44.8	40.6	45.1	35.4	41.0	87	4.9	5.8	4.8	5.7	5.1	5.8
37	39.2	43.8	39.7	44.2	34.5	40.1	88	4.6	5.5	4.5	5.4	4.8	5.4
38	38.3	42.9	38.7	43.2	33.7	39.2	89	4.3	5.1	4.2	5.0	4.6	5.1
39	37.4	41.9	37.8	42.2	32.8	38.3	90	4.1	4.8	4.0	4.7	4.4	4.8
40	36.5	41.0	36.9	41.3	31.9	37.4	91	3.8	4.5	3.7	4.4	4.2	4.6
41	35.6	40.0	36.0	40.3	31.1	36.5	92	3.6	4.2	3.5	4.1	4.0	4.3
42	34.7	39.1	35.1	39.4	30.2	35.6	93	3.4	4.0	3.3	3.8	3.8	4.1
43	33.8	38.2	34.2	38.5	29.4	34.7	94	3.2	3.8	3.1	3.6	3.6	3.8
44	32.9	37.2	33.3	37.5	28.6	33.9	95	3.0	3.5	2.9	3.3	3.5	3.6
45	32.0	36.3	32.4	36.6	27.8	33.0	96	2.9	3.3	2.7	3.1	3.3	3.4
46	31.1	35.4	31.5	35.6	27.0	32.1	97	2.7	3.1	2.6	2.9	3.2	3.2
47	30.3	34.4	30.6	34.7	26.2	31.3	98	2.6	3.0	2.4	2.7	3.1	3.0
48	29.4	33.5	29.7	33.8	25.5	30.4	99	2.5	2.8	2.3	2.5	2.9	2.9
49	28.5	32.6	28.9	32.9	24.7	29.6	100+	2.4	2.7	2.2	2.4	2.8	2.7

Note: Based on an individual's age in 1999 For example, a white male age 27 in 1999 would be expected to live 49 more years, or to about 76 years old. A black female born in 1999 would be expected to live to almost 75 years of age **Source:** U.S. Dept. Health and Human Services, National Center for Health Statistics, *National Vital Statistics Reports*, March 21, 2002.

sands of lives each year. In 1999, 63 percent of people killed in crashes were not wearing seatbelts.

▶LIFE EXPECTANCY

Life expectancy figures represent the average number of years that infants are expected to live. Life expectancy has improved steadily over the years, due largely to a decline in deaths during childhood. The development of drugs to combat infectious diseases, plus improved nutrition and better environmental sanitation, have all played major roles in combating early deaths.

In 2000, the average length of life in the U.S. was 76.9 years. Whites were expected to outlive blacks by more than 5 years: 77.4 years versus 71.8 years. Homicides, killings in police confrontations, auto accidents, AIDS, tuberculosis, and several other diseases have had a disproportionate impact on black people's life expectancy rates in recent years.

▶INFANT MORTALITY

In 2000, there were 27,987 reported deaths of infants age one year or younger. The most commonly used index for measuring the risk of dying during the first year of life are infant mortality rates, which are calculated by dividing the number of infant deaths by the number of live births registered for the same period. The 2000 rate of 6.9 infant deaths per 1,000 live births was the lowest ever recorded for the United States.

The rate among white infants was less than half that of black infants: 5.7 infant deaths per 1,000 live births for whites in 2000, versus 14.0 per 1,000 for blacks. The reasons for this discrepancy are not clear, although an important factor is believed to be the quality of medical care received by people of different socioeconomic groups. For example, several studies of infant deaths have shown that adequate prenatal care is strongly associated with higher infant birth weight and survival. Many black mothers, who are far more likely to be poor than white mothers, do not have access to proper prenatal care. Poor nutrition, alcohol and drug abuse, ant other social factors also play significant roles.

Disproportionate poverty among minority groups is not the whole story, however. Studies have shown that even black infants born to college-educated mothers had nearly twice the mortality rate of comparable white infants.

The leading cause of infant mortality, congenital malformations and chromosomal abnormalities, accounted for 20.7 percent of all infant deaths in 2000. Disorders related to short gestation and low birth weight, the second leading cause of infant deaths, accounted for 15.4 percent.

(See also "World Health" for infant mortality rates in other nations.)

U.S. Infant Mortality Rate, 1940–2000 (per 1,000 live births)

Year	All races	White	Black
1940	47.0	43.2	72.9
1950	29.2	26.8	43.9
1960	26.0	22.9	44.3
1970	20.0	17.8	32.6
1980	12.6	11.0	21.4
1990	9.2	7.6	18.0
1995	7.6	6.3	15.1
1999	7.1	5.8	14.6
2000	6.9	5.7	14.0

Source: U.S. Dept. Health and Human Services, National Center for Health Statistics, *Monthly Vital Statistics Reports, National Vital Statistics Report,* Oct. 9, 2001

Childhood Vaccines: Recommended Immunization Schedule, 2002

Age	Vaccines
Birth	Hepatitis B
2 months	Hepatitis B; polio; diphtheria, tetanus, pertussis (DTaP); Haemophilus B (Hib), pneumonia and other pneumococcal bacteria (PVC)
4 months	Polio, DTaP, Hib, PVC
6 months	DTaP, Hib, PVC
6-18 months	Hepatitis B, Polio
12-15 months	Hib; measles, mumps, rubella (MMR#1); chicken pox, PVC
15-18 months	DTaP
4-6 years	Polio, DtaP, MMR#2
11-16 years	Tetanus

Note: It generally takes several doses of each vaccine for full protection. In some cases, there is a range of acceptable ages for vaccination. For example, the third dose of hepatitis B vaccine may be given between 6 and 18 months of age. Children who have not been vaccinated against Hepatitis B in infancy may begin the series during any childhood visit. For additional information, contact your physician.

Sources: American Academy of Pediatrics; American Academy of Family Physicians; and U.S. Dept. of Health and Human Services, Centers for Disease Control and Prevention.

▶SUBSTANCE ABUSE

Illicit Drugs

A significant portion of the American public uses illegal drugs. The 2000 National Household Survey on Drug Abuse estimated that 14.0 million Americans age 12 and older (6.3 percent of the population) were current users, meaning they had used an illicit drug in the month prior to interview. Males had a higher rate of current use than women: 7.7 percent versus 5.0 percent. Rates of drug use generally decline with age. Overall, 49 percent of current illicit drug users in 2000 were under age 26. However, 83 percent of hallucinogen users and 62 percent of inhalant users were under age 26. Conversely, only 32 percent of heroin users, 43 percent of cocaine users, and 45 percent of nonmedical psychotherapeutic users were under age 26.

A measure of the health consequences of drug use is the Drug Abuse Warning Network (DAWN), which collects information on patients seeking hospital emergency room treatment related to their abuse of legal and illicit drugs. An estimated 601,563 drug-related emergency-room episodes occurred in 2000. The four drugs mentioned most frequently in emergency room reports were alcohol-in-combination (204,510 mentions), cocaine (174,881), marijuana (96,416), and heroin (94,804). Males (259 episodes per 100,000 population) and young adults age 18-25 (426) had the highest rates of emergency room drug episodes in 2000.

Marijuana is the most commonly used illegal drug, used by 76 percent of current U.S. drug users; approximately 59 percent of current illicit drug users consume no drugs other than marijuana. It is made from the leaves and flowering tops of the hemp plant, *Cannabis sativa,* which contains psychoactive substances called cannabinoids. The primary psychoactive ingredient in marijuana and hashish (a resin e xuded from the flowering tops) is tetrahydrocannabinol, or THC. The amount of each cannabinoid varies markedly from one plant to another depending on climate, soil, and other factors.

Lifetime Experience With Illicit Drugs, 2000

Age	Used in lifetime	Used in past year	Used in past month
Total[1]	**38.9%**	**11.0%**	**6.3%**
By Age			
12-17	26.9	18.6	9.7
18-25	51.2	27.9	15.9
26 and older	38.5	7.1	4.2
By Sex			
Male	43.5	12.9	7.7
Female	34.7	9.2	5.0
By Race/Ethnicity			
White[2]	41.5	11.2	6.4
Black[2]	35.5	10.9	6.4
Hispanic	29.9	10.1	5.3
Asian	18.9	5.2	2.7

Note: Includes marijuana, cocaine, heroin, hallucinogens, inhalants, or prescription-type psychotherapeutic drugs (stimulants, sedatives, tranquilizers, and analgesics) for nonmedical purposes. 1. Age 12 and older. 2. Non-Hispanic. **Source:** U.S. Dept. of Health and Human Services, Substance Abuse and Mental Health Services Administration, *National Household Survey on Drug Abuse 2000.*

Marijuana is typically prepared as a tobacco-like mixture that is smoked in hand-rolled cigarettes or in pipes. It typically produces a "high"—a feeling of well-being, relaxation, and sleepiness. It also interferes with coordination and mental abilities. For instance, it distorts judgment and reaction time, which can be particularly dangerous when a user drives a car.

Possession or sale of marijuana has been illegal in the United States since 1937. Nonetheless, marijuana has legitimate medical uses. A significant body of evidence shows that marijuana combats nausea and weight loss in cancer and AIDS patients. It also helps reduce pressure within the eyes of glaucoma patients.

A study commissioned by the federal government confirmed in 1999 that marijuana has medical uses and that there is no evidence that giving the drug to sick people would increase illicit use in the general population. By 2002, at least eight states had enacted laws legalizing the possession of marijuana for medicinal uses. However, these laws conflict with federal policy, which prohibits doctors from recommending medical marijuana.

Cocaine is made from the leaves of the coca plant, a shrub native to South America. In the late 1800s and early 1900s, before its dangers were recognized, cocaine was used by doctors as an anesthetic because of its effectiveness in depressing nerve endings. It has since been replaced by less toxic, non-addictive anesthetics.

Drug Use by U.S. High School Seniors, 1975–2001

Drug	1975	1980	1985	1990	1995	1998	1999	2001
Alcohol	68.2%	72.0%	65.9%	57.1%	51.3%	52.0%	51.0%	49.8%
Cigarettes	36.7	30.5	30.1	29.4	33.5	35.1	34.6	29.5
Marijuana	27.1	33.7	25.7	14.0	21.2	22.8	23.1	22.4
LSD	2.3	2.3	1.6	1.9	4.0	3.2	2.7	2.3
Cocaine	1.9	5.2	6.7	1.9	1.8	2.4	2.6	2.1
Heroin	0.4	0.2	0.3	0.2	0.6	0.5	0.5	0.4

Note: Drug use during the 30 days preceding the survey.
Source: U.S. Dept. of Health and Human Services, National Institute on Drug Abuse, *Monitoring the Future Study*, 2002.

Commonly Abused Drugs

Drug	Primary Effect	Popular names
Alcohol	Depressant	Drink, booze
Amphetamines	Stimulant	Pep pills, uppers; *metamphetamines*: meth, speed, crystal, crank, ice
Amyl or butyl nitrites	Stimulant	Poppers, snappers rush, locker room
Barbiturates	Depressant	Sleeping pills, reds, yellowjackets
Cocaine	Stimulant	Coke, snow, lady; smokable form: crack
Ephedra	Stimulant	Ma huang; *brand names* Herbal Ecstasy, Euphoria, Buzz Tablets, Brain Wash
Heroin	Depressant	Snow, smack, horse, P-dope; *synthetic heroin*: China white, Persian heroin, gasoline dope; *combined heroin and cocaine*: speedball
D-lysergic acid diethylamide	Hallucinogen	LSD, acid, microdot, tabs, sugar cubes
Marijuana	Hallucinogen/depressant	Pot, grass, joint, dope, reefer, herb, weed, skunk
MDMA (combination of synthetic mescaline and an amphetamine	Stimulant/ hallucinogen	Ecstasy, E, Adam, love potion
Mescaline	Hallucinogen	Peyote, cactus
Morphine	Depressant	
PCP (phencyclidine)	Hallucinogen	Angel dust
Tranquilizers	Depressant	Downers

Alcohol Use in U.S. 2000

Characteristic	Total[1]	By Age 12-17	18-25	26 and older
Total	**46.6%**	**16.4%**	**56.8%**	**49.0%**
Race/Ethnicity				
White[2]	50.7	18.4	63.3	52.7
Black[2]	33.7	8.8	43.9	36.0
Hispanic	38.6	16.8	44.7	43.3
Asian	30.7	7.1	39.4	29.0
Sex				
Male	53.6	16.2	62.5	57.5
Female	40.2	16.5	51.3	41.4
Adult Education				
Less than high school	N.A.	N.A.	44.3	31.7
High school graduate	N.A.	N.A.	52.2	44.4
Some college	N.A.	N.A.	64.0	53.0
College graduate	N.A.	N.A.	74.4	62.3
Current Employment				
Full-time	N.A.	N.A.	61.7	56.6
Part-time	N.A.	N.A.	55.7	49.2
Unemployed	N.A.	N.A.	51.3	48.0
Other[3]	N.A.	N.A.	45.8	33.9

Notes: Percentages reporting use of alcohol in the previous month. N.A.=Not Applicable. 1. Age 12 and older. 2. Non-Hispanic. 3. Includes retired, disabled, homemaker, student, etc.
Source: U.S. Dept. of Health and Human Services, Substance Abuse and Mental Health Services Administration, *National Household Survey on Drug Abuse, 2000* (2001).

Cocaine causes a short-lived euphoria. It also suppresses appetite, interferes with sleep, and increases heart rate and blood pressure. Even small doses have been linked to heart attacks and cerebral hemorrhages. Repeated usage is required to maintain a "high." Abusers who try to abstain often experience a tremendous craving for the drug—a hallmark of addiction.

In 2000, an estimated 1.2 million Americans were current cocaine users. Of these, an estimated 265,000 were crack users. Crack is a highly addictive, smokable form of cocaine, sold in small beige chunks called pellets or rocks.

Heroin is a synthetic compound derived from morphine, which is made from opium poppies (Papaver somniferum). Highly addictive, heroin fell out of favor in the United States during the 1970's but there has been an increasing trend in new use since 1992. A large portion of new users smoked, snorted, or sniffed heroin, and most were under age 26. In 2000, an estimated 130,000 Americans were current heroin users.

Ecstasy, a synthetic drug with both stimulant and hallucinogenic properties, came onto the scene in the 1990's. Also known as MDMA, an acronym of its lengthy scientific name, it is available in pill form, with pills often embossed with smiley faces, shamrocks, and other enticing designs. Its popularity among young adults has grown dramatically in recent years. For example, according to the Monitoring the Future study, the proportion of 12th graders reporting use of ecstasy in the prior 12 months rose from 5.6 percent in 1999 to 8.2 percent in 2000. By 2000, an estimated 6.4 million people had tried ecstasy at least once in their lifetime.

Initially associated with dance venues such as raves, ecstasy now is being used in a variety of settings. However, a growing body of evidence indicates that its use can lead to severe overheating and dehydration, as well as stroke, heart attack, and neurological damage.

U.S. Alcohol Consumption, 1940–98 (gallons of ethanol, per capita)

Year	Beer	Wine	Spirits	All beverages
1940	0.73	0.16	0.67	1.56
1950	1.04	0.23	0.77	2.04
1960	0.99	0.22	0.86	2.07
1970	1.14	0.27	1.11	2.52
1980	1.38	0.34	1.04	2.76
1990	1.34	0.33	0.78	2.46
1995	1.25	0.29	0.64	2.17
1997	1.24	0.31	0.63	2.18
1998	1.25	0.31	0.63	2.19

Note: Based on population age 15 and older prior to 1970 and on population age 14 and older thereafter.
Source: U.S. Dept. of Health and Human Services, National Institute on Alcohol Abuse and Alcoholism, www.niaaa.nih.gov/databases/consum01.txt. (updated April 2001).

Alcohol

Consumption of alcohol constitutes the nation's most common drug abuse problem. Almost 20,000 deaths explicitly related to alcohol occur each year. In addition, alcohol is implicated in an additional 45,000 deaths. For example, in 1999, alcohol was involved in 12,547 traffic deaths (30.1 percent of all traffic deaths, a significant decline from 41.0 percent in 1990).

The 2000 National Household Survey on Drug Abuse reported that approximately 104 million people age 12 and older currently used alcohol (defined as any use in the previous month); 46 million engaged in binge drinking (defined as five or more drinks on at least one occasion in the past month), and 12.6 million were heavy drinkers (five or more drinks on the same occasion on at least five different days in the past month). The highest prevalence of both binge and heavy drinking in 2000 was among adults 18-25, with the peak rate occurring at 21.

Consumption According to the National Institute of Alcohol Abuse and Alcoholism (NIAAA), per capita consumption of beer, spirits, and wine grew slightly (1.0 percent) during the 1950's, rose rapidly (21.3 percent) during the 1960's, rose moderately (9.1 percent) in the 1970's, and decreased (12.0 percent) during the 1980's. The decline continued in the 1990's as annual per capita consumption from all alcoholic beverages dropped from 2.45 gallons in 1990 to a low of 2.15 gallons in 1995 before rising slightly to 2.1 gallons in 1999. Studies show that men are heavier drinkers than women, and much more likely to be binge drinkers. Younger people drink more than older people. Consumption was highest in New Hampshire (4.03 gallons of ethanol per capita), Nevada (3.90), and the District of Columbia (3.81). It was lowest in Utah (1.25), West Virginia (1.63), and Oklahoma (1.71).

Several factors have contributed to consumption declines, including the general aging of the population, increased state and federal taxes on alcoholic beverages, stricter penalties for drinking and driving, and the formation of minority advocacy groups to counter industry efforts to target minority populations.

Tobacco

Smoking is the leading cause of preventable death in the United States. It causes approximately 442,000 premature deaths annually—264,000 among men and 178,000 among women—and approximately $157 billion in annual health-related economic losses.

The percentage of adults who smoke decreased dramatically after 1964, the year the U.S. surgeon general first warned about the link between smoking and health problems such as cancer and heart disease. At that time, 40 percent of the adult population were smokers; in 2000, approximately 23.3 percent (46.5 million adults) smoked. The increased cost of cigarettes, a growing number of smoking restrictions in public places, and decreasing social acceptability of smoking also played roles in the decline. Cigarette smoking among adults was highest in Nevada, where 31.5 percent of the population age 18 and older were smokers in 1999. It was lowest in Utah (13.9 percent).

During 1993-2000, substantial decreases in current smoking prevalence were reported for all age groups except people age 18-24. Although cigarette smoking rates among high school students increased during most of the 1990s, they have declined significantly since 1997. In 2001, 27.7 percent of high school females and 29.2 percent of high school males were smokers. Surveys indicate that more than 90 percent of adults who are regular smokers began smoking while they were teenagers and that 32 percent of young people who become regular smokers will die of a smoking-related disorder.

U.S. Cigarette Consumption, 1900–2001

Year	Cigarettes (billions)	Per capita[1]	Year	Cigarettes (billions)	Per capita[1]
1900	2.5	54	**1970**	536.5	3,985
1910	8.6	151	**1980**	631.5	3,849
1920	44.6	665	**1990**	525.0	2,817
1930	119.3	1,485	**1998**	470.0	2,320
1940	181.9	1,976	**1999**	435.0	2,136
1950	369.8	3,552	**2000**	430.0	2,092
1960	484.4	4,171	**2001**	422.0	2,037

1. Among persons age 18 and older. **Source:** U.S. Dept. of Health and Human Services, Centers for Disease Control and Prevention; USDA, Economic Research Service.

Adult Cigarette Smokers in the U.S., 2000

Year	Men	Women	Total
Total	**25.7%**	**21.0%**	**23.3%**
Age			
18-24	28.5	25.1	26.8
25-44	29.7	24.5	27.0
45-64	26.4	21.6	24.0
65 and older	10.2	9.3	9.7
Race/Ethnicity			
White[1]	25.9	22.4	24.1
Black[1]	26.1	20.9	23.2
Hispanic	24.0	13.3	18.6
American Indian/Alaska Native	29.1	42.5	36.0
Asian	21.0	7.6	14.4
Education[2]			
8 years or less	26.1	14.2	20.0
9-11 years	37.6	30.8	33.9
12 years (diploma)	31.7	23.5	27.2
Undergraduate degree	14.2	12.4	13.2
Graduate degree	9.1	7.5	8.4

1. Non-Hispanic. 2. Among those age 25 and older.
Source: U.S. Dept. of Health and Human Services, Centers for Disease Control and Prevention, *Morbidity and Mortality Weekly Report* (July 26, 2002).

Health effects The major effects of smoking include:

- Shortened life span. Each year, some 440,000 Americans—and about 4 million people worldwide—die prematurely as a result of smoking
- Cancer of the lungs, mouth, esophagus, stomach, bladder, kidney, pancreas, and cervix. Smoking accounts for at least 30 percent of all cancer deaths in the United States each year, including 87 percent of lung cancer deaths.
- Cardiovascular disease, including heart attack, stroke, aneurysm, and the peripheral vascular disease. Smoking weakens the heart's ability to pump blood, promotes clot formation, and damages the inner lining of blood vessels.
- Pulmonary illness, including emphysema, pneumonia, and chronic bronchitis. Annually, more than 80,000 Americans die from non-cancerous chronic lung diseases linked to smoking.
- Spontaneous abortions. Women who smoke during pregnancy are 10 times more likely to miscarry than are nonsmokers.
- Underweight, sickly babies. Each year, the deaths of more than 2,000 children under a year old are attributed to the mothers' smoking while pregnant. Infants of smokers have a 50 percent higher risk of developing Sudden Infant Death Syndrome (SIDS) and are 74 percent more likely to be of low birth weight than are infants born to mothers who do not smoke. An infant exposed to *any* cigarette smoke is 3.5 times more likely to die of SIDS than an infant not exposed to smoke.
- Environmental smoking risks. Nonsmokers who are exposed to the tobacco smoke of other people are at increased risk for various diseases. Exposure to secondhand smoke is responsible for approximately 3,000 lung cancer deaths annually among nonsmokers and 150,000 to 300,000 cases of lower respiratory tract infections such as bronchitis and pneumonia in children up to 18 months old. It also doubles a person's risk of heart disease.

Teenage Tobacco Users, 1999

Category	Cigarettes	Cigars	Smokeless Tobacco
Total	**34.8%**	**17.7%**	**7.8%**
Sex			
Male	34.7	25.4	14.2
Female	34.9	9.9	1.3
Race/Ethnicity			
White[1]	38.6	18.8	10.4
Black[1]	19.7	13.7	1.3
Hispanic	32.7	16.7	3.9
High school grade			
9	27.6	13.7	6.8
10	34.7	17.8	7.1
11	36.0	18.2	8.4
12	42.8	22.0	8.9

Note: Used at least once during the 30 days preceding the survey. 1. Non-Hispanic. **Source:** U.S. Dept. of Health and Human Services, Centers for Disease Control and Prevention, *Morbidity and Morality Weekly Report*, June 9, 2000.

The Media

THE PRINT MEDIA

▶NEWSPAPERS

The mutual distrust between government and the media dates back to the very first American newspaper in 1690, when a three-page publication called *Publick Occurrences, Both Foreign and Domestick* was suppressed by the government after one issue. A number of newspapers sprang up during the pre-Revolutionary period and by 1775, the colonies, with a population of 2.5 million people, were served by 48 weekly newspapers, small in both size and circulation.

The first daily, the *Pennsylvania Evening Post and Daily Advertiser*, was not published until 1783. By 1800 there were 20 daily newspapers and more than 1,000 small-town and frontier weeklies. Most of the dailies, filled with political and business news, were expensive and aimed at educated, affluent readers. The first of the mass-circulation dailies, known as the penny press, was the *New York Sun*, started in 1833 and sold for the bargain price of one cent. The *Sun*, with its crime stories and soft features, marked a dramatic change in newspaper coverage.

The next major change in newspapers came in the era during and after the Civil War. Dramatic technological improvements like the transatlantic cable, the telephone, the electric light bulb, typewriters, web-fed presses, and typesetting machine made possible cheap, mass circulation newspapers. By 1900 the number of daily newspapers had jumped to 2,326. Over the next half century, the number of newspapers steadily declined while readership increased, due in part to the popularity of Sunday editions.

Newspapers today

In 2002, there were 1,457 daily newspapers published in the United States. Morning papers continued to outnumber evening papers (777 to 692). As recently as 1985, there were twice as many evening newspapers as morning papers in the U.S. The total number of newspapers has been declining for decades, in part because of radio, television and the Internet, but also because in the fight for readers and advertising, competing papers have battled until a single winner emerged. Fewer than 50 cities have competing newspapers today, a major change from the turn of the last century when most major cities had more than two newspapers. By contrast, 12 cities have competing newspapers only by virtue of a joint operating agreement that combines all of the two papers' operations except for their editorial staffs, which remain independent (in some cases fiercely) of each other.

Advertising expenditures on newspapers declined to 44.1 million in 2002, down from a record high of $48.7 billion in 2000.

The vast majority of newspapers have circulations of less than 50,000; 114 have circulations between 50,000 and 100,00; and 105 have a daily circulation of more than 100,000. The top six newspaper companies—Gannett, Knight-Ridder, Tribune Co., Advance Publications Inc., The New York Times Co., and Dow Jones & Co.—account for more than a third of all newspaper circulation. The newspapers with the greatest circulations in the world are all published in Japan and in Europe. The world's most widely read newspapers are Japan's *Yomiuri Shimbun*, with a circulation of over 14 million, and its rival, the *Asahi Shimbun*, read by more than 12 million people. By comparison, USA Today, tops in the U.S. in circulation, reaches just 2.1 million people.

Daily circulation for all newspapers dropped for the 14th consecutive year in 2002, to 55.2 million, according to the Newspaper Association of America. Morning, evening and Sunday newspapers all decreased in circulation. The percentage of people who read a daily newspaper increased slightly (for the first time in years) in 2002 to 55.4, up from 54.3 percent in 2001 but still below the 62.4 percent logged in 1990. Sunday edition readership was 63.1 percent in 2002, down from 63.7 percent in 2001, and 72.6 percent in 1995. Newspaper readership is highest among those with the most educa-

Daily Newspapers, Number and Circulation, 1900–2002

	Total		Morning		Evening		Sunday	
Year	Number of Daily papers	Daily circulation ('000s)	Number of papers	Daily circulation ('000s)	Number of papers	Daily circulation ('000s)	Number of papers	Daily circulation ('000s)
1900	2,226	15,102	—	—	—	—	—	—
1920	2,042	27,791	437	—	1,605	—	522	17,084
1930	1,942	39,589	388	—	1,554	—	521	26,413
1940	1,878	41,132	380	16,114	1,498	25,008	525	32,371
1950	1,772	53,829	322	21,266	1,450	32,563	549	46,582
1960	1,763	58,882	312	24,029	1,459	34,853	563	47,699
1970	1,748	62,108	334	25,934	1,429	36,174	586	49,217
1980	1,745	62,202	387	29,414	1,388	32,787	735	54,672
1990	1,611	62,324	559	41,308	1,084	21,015	863	62,634
1995	1,533	58,193	656	44,310	891	13,883	888	61,529
2000	1,480	55,773	766	46,772	727	9,000	917	59,421
2001	1,468	55,578	776	46,821	704	8,757	913	59,090
2002[1]	1,457	55,186	777	46,617	692	8,569	913	58,780

Note: All-day newspapers are listed in both morning and evening columns, but are counted only once in the total. 1. Preliminary.
Source: Newspaper Association of America, *Facts About Newspapers, 2003*.

Top 100 U.S. Daily Newspapers by Circulation, 2003

Rank	Newspaper	Average daily paid circulation	Rank	Newspaper	Average daily paid circulation
1.	USA Today	2,136,068	51.	Oklahoma City Daily Oklahoman	199,581
2.	Wall Street Journal	1,800,607	52.	Norfolk Virginian-Pilot	195,866
3.	New York Times	1,113,000	53.	St. Paul Pioneer Press	194,870
4.	Los Angeles Times	925,135	54.	Hartford Courant	190,312
5.	Washington Post	746,724	55.	Omaha World-Herald	190,218
6.	New York Daily News	715,070	56.	Cincinnati Enquirer	189,084
7.	Chicago Tribune	679,327	57.	Richmond Times-Dispatch	187,409
8.	New York Post	590,061	58.	Little Rock Democrat-Gazette	185,709
9.	Long Island Newsday	578,809	59.	Nashville Tennessean	184,106
10.	Houston Chronicle	552,052	60.	Austin American-Statesman	183,288
11.	San Francisco Chronicle	512,129	61.	Walnut Creek Contra Costa Times	182,196
12.	Dallas Morning News	505,724	62.	Riverside (Calif.) Press-Enterprise	178,994
13.	Chicago Sun-Times	479,584	63.	Bergen County Record	178,962
14.	Boston Globe	467,745	64.	Los Angeles Daily News	178,217
15.	Phoenix Arizona Republic	448,782	65.	Rochester Democrat and Chronicle	172,124
16.	Newark Star-Ledger	408,507	66.	Neptune Asbury Park Press	168,718
17.	Philadelphia Inquirer	373,892	67.	Jacksonville Times-Union	168,558
18.	Atlanta Journal-Constitution	371,161	68.	West Palm Beach Post	167,531
19.	Detroit Free Press	368,839	69.	Providence Journal	166,836
20.	Cleveland Plain Dealer	363,750	70.	Las Vegas Review-Journal	164,848
21.	Portland Oregonian	342,789	71.	Raleigh News & Observer	163,460
22.	Minneapolis Star Tribune	342,780	72.	Fresno Bee	158,286
23.	San Diego Union-Tribune	342,447	73.	Seattle Post-Intelligencer	157,558
24.	St. Petersburg Times	333,557	74.	Memphis Commercial Appeal	156,513
25.	Miami Herald	315,340	75.	Des Moines Register	152,633
26.	Denver Post	305,060	76.	Philadelphia Daily News	150,154
27.	Denver Rocky Mountain News	304,949	77.	Chicago Daily Herald	149,882
28.	Orange County Register	300,888	78.	Birmingham News	145,571
29.	Baltimore Sun	300,410	79.	Honolulu Advertiser	143,696
30.	St. Louis Post-Dispatch	287,424	80.	Toledo Blade	140,628
31.	Sacramento Bee	283,194	81.	Grand Rapids Press	140,135
32.	San Jose Mercury News	272,682	82.	Tulsa World	139,383
33.	Kansas City Star	269,188	83.	Westchester Co. Journal News	139,170
34.	Los Angeles Investor's Business Daily	264,699	84.	Salt Lake City Tribune	134,777
35.	Orlando Sentinel	256,520	85.	Akron Beacon Journal	134,774
36.	New Orleans Times-Picayune	255,994	86.	Dayton Daily News	131,435
37.	Indianapolis Star	254,624	87.	Tacoma News Tribune	128,739
38.	Columbus Dispatch	251,557	88.	Los Angeles La Opinion	126,189
39.	Pittsburgh Post-Gazette	243,091	89.	Syracuse Post-Standard	123,836
40.	Boston Herald	242,957	90.	Greensburg (Pa.) Tribune-Review	119,338
41.	Detroit News	242,391	91.	Wilmington (Del.) News Journal	119,163
42.	Milwaukee Journal Sentinel	242,234	92.	Allentown (Pa.) Morning Call	118,859
43.	Fort Lauderdale Sun-Sentinel	238,589	93.	Columbia (S.C.) State	115,959
44.	Charlotte Observer	235,759	94.	Knoxville News-Sentinel	112,017
45.	Seattle Times	224,140	95.	Lexington (Ky.) Herald-Leader	108,892
46.	Buffalo News	223,957	96.	Albuquerque Journal	108,344
47.	San Antonio Express-News	220,998	97.	Sarasota Herald-Tribune	106,594
48.	Fort Worth Star-Telegram	218,975	98.	Worcester (Mass.) Telegram & Gazette	102,978
49.	Louisville Courier-Journal	217,396	99.	Spokane Spokesman-Review	102,805
50.	Tampa Tribune	214,178	100.	Harrisburg Patriot-News	101,598

Source: *Editor and Publisher Yearbook, 2003*. Copyright © The Editor & Publisher Co. 2003. All Rights Reserved. www.mediainfo.com.

tion, the highest income, and the greatest job responsibilities. And the audience for newspapers continues to grow older: 72 percent of people over 65 read a daily paper, compared with 41 percent of 18-24-year-olds, a percentage that has risen slightly from 39 percent in 2001.

Newspapers tomorrow

The future heralds even greater drops in readership, as more and more people turn to the Internet for their news, rather than wait for the paper to come out the next day. America Online currently has more than 20 million subscribers, or more than the readership of the top 20 newspapers in America combined. Newspapers have rushed to create a presence on the Web in an effort to capture this audience, with varying degrees of success. More than 1,300 newspapers in the U.S. (including the top 100 in circulation) have Web sites; most of them can be accessed from the Newspaper Association of America's site: www.newspaperlinks.com.

▶MAGAZINES

Consumer magazines range from the very specialized (*Fly Fisherman*) to the general interest (*People*) and are sold either by subscription or through retail outlets (supermarkets, newsstands,

Weekly Newspapers in the U.S., 1960–2002

Year	Number of newspapers[1]	Average circulation	Total weekly circulation	Year	Number of newspapers[1]	Average circulation	Total weekly circulation
1960	8,174	2,566	20,974,338	**1985**	7,704	6,359	48,988,801
1965	8,061	3,106	25,036,031	**1990**	7,606	6,958	52,919,846
1970	7,612	3,660	27,857,332	**1995**[2]	8,453	9,425	79,668,266
1975	7,612	4,715	35,892,409	**2000**[2]	6,579	7,295	47,990,892
1980	7,954	5,324	42,347,512	**2002**[2]	6,699	7,467	50,023,378

1. Any newspaper published less than four times a week. 2. 1995 and later not comparable to prior years due to change in information collection procedures. 3. Preliminary. **Source:** Newspaper Association of America, *Facts About Newspapers, 2003.*

Top 100 U.S. Magazines by Circulation, 2002

Rank	Magazine	Average paid circulation per issue	Percent change 2001–02
1.	NRTA/AARP Bulletin	21,703,580	1.1%
2.	Modern Maturity	17,360,979	-5.5
3.	Reader's Digest	12,078,469	-3.8
4.	TV Guide	9,067,124	-2.1
5.	Better Homes & Gardens	7,605,204	0.0
6.	National Geographic	6,774,138	-12.5
7.	Good Housekeeping	4,699,736	3.7
8.	Family Circle	4,634,069	-4.6
9.	Woman's Day	4,205,049	1.3
10.	Time	4,111,927	-0.4
11.	Ladies' Home Journal	4,101,347	0.0
12.	My Generation	3,999,683	N.A.
13.	People Weekly	3,625,427	-2.4
14.	Rosie	3,420,788	-9.8
15.	Westways	3,369,799	7.0
16.	Home & Away	3,312,075	0.0
17.	Sports Illustrated	3,249,418	0.8
18.	Playboy	3,215,454	1.9
19.	Newsweek	3,183,008	-2.2
20.	Prevention	3,140,916	0.8
21.	Cosmopolitan	2,992,536	10.8
22.	Guideposts	2,702,124	0.1
23.	Via	2,643,896	-0.2
24.	The American Legion Magazine	2,639,097	1.0
25.	Southern Living	2,555,114	0.3
26.	Maxim	2,540,631	0.3
27.	Seventeen	2,445,539	4.0
28.	Glamour	2,406,859	10.9
29.	Redbook	2,387,297	3.3
30.	Martha Stewart Living	2,341,229	-3.3
31.	O, The Oprah Magazine	2,268,585	-14.1
32.	YM	2,231,752	-0.4
33.	AAA Going Places	2,202,555	2.8
34.	Parents	2,092,113	3.9
35.	Parenting Magazine	2,087,873	18.7
36.	Smithsonian	2,042,862	0.4
37.	U.S. News & World Report	2,025,890	-2.4
38.	Money	1,970,666	-4.4
39.	Ebony	1,863,227	4.5
40.	National Enquirer	1,788,210	-7.6
41.	Country Living	1,735,170	6.1
42.	V.F.W. Magazine	1,686,452	-0.4
43.	Men's Health	1,677,574	1.1
44.	Shape	1,668,253	2.1
45.	In Style	1,665,493	4.0
46.	Entertainment Weekly	1,640,989	6.9
47.	Woman's World	1,639,759	-1.3
48.	Teen People	1,627,431	0.1
49.	Cooking Light	1,587,597	0.3
50.	Golf Digest	1,571,362	0.5
51.	Endless Vacation	1,549,971	12.2
52.	ESPN	1,543,242	11.8%
53.	Field & Stream	1,591,660	-12.7
54.	Familyfun	1,508,819	9.5
55.	American Rifleman	1,492,011	-9.2
56.	Popular Science	1,477,129	-5.9
57.	Sunset	1,461,921	0.6
58.	First for Women	1,460,999	5.4
59.	Golf Magazine	1,418,153	1.3
60.	Star	1,410,116	-6.9
61.	Health	1,384,093	-0.8
62.	Car and Driver	1,378,481	0.7
63.	Boys' Life	1,323,678	3.4
64.	Self	1,308,693	-9.3
65.	Bon Appétit	1,292,856	1.4
66.	Motor Trend	1,277,657	1.2
67.	Rolling Stone	1,263,840	-0.3
68.	Vogue	1,251,639	8.9
69.	PC Magazine	1,231,822	0.2
70.	Popular Mechanics	1,229,696	0.3
71.	Fitness	1,225,515	4.3
72.	Scholastic Parent & Child	1,223,634	-2.1
73.	The Family Handyman	1,154,551	-0.3
74.	Stuff	1,150,511	10.6
75.	Vanity Fair	1,119,473	1.7
76.	PC World	1,106,573	-11.9
77.	The American Hunter	1,106,396	-9.9
78.	Country Home	1,103,081	9.4
79.	Real Simple	1,094,148	32.7
80.	US Weekly	1,084,622	17.3
81.	The Elks Magazine	1,078,955	-2.0
82.	Outdoor Life	1,078,609	-20.5
83.	Cosmo Girl!	1,062,271	30.4
84.	Scouting	1,061,718	2.0
85.	FHM	1,059,061	27.1
86.	Essence	1,057,303	0.5
87.	Discover	1,051,434	3.3
88.	Kiplinger's Personal Finance	1,048,670	-6.9
89.	Michigan Living	1,041,626	0.3
90.	Home	1,019,284	1.3
91.	Elle	995,183	2.4
92.	Soap Opera Digest	987,525	-3.7
93.	Business Week	982,349	1.1
94.	Victoria	963,409	-2.0
95.	Travel + Leisure	961,774	-4.3
96.	This Old House	957,340	1.9
97.	Food & Wine	954,795	1.2
98.	Jet	953,646	-1.2
99.	Allure	953,473	0.9
100.	Marie Claire	947,662	3.2
Total top 100*		**24,896,7368**	**1.2**

Note: Leading Audit Bureau of Circulation (ABC) magazines by average paid combined circulation per issue.
Source: Magazine Publishers of America, 2003.

Top 50 U.S. Magazines by Advertising Revenues, 2002

Rank, Magazine	Advertising revenues	Percent change 2001–02	Rank, Magazine	Advertising revenues	Percent change 2001–02
1. People Weekly	713,638,543	8.75%	**26.** ESPN Magazine	168,869,790	36.68%
2. Sports Illustrated	644,386,187	12.86	**27.** PC Magazine	165,554,249	-11.01
3. Parade	608,384,836	6.65	**28.** Glamour	159,288,176	6.36
4. Time	568,993,445	1.96	**29.** Rolling Stone	159,223,190	1.48
5. Better Homes & Gardens	554,785,628	12.93	**30.** Southern Living	156,591,293	5.59
6. Newsweek	389,328,521	14.96	**31.** Parents	151,360,573	16.25
7. USA Weekend	359,399,735	13.46	**32.** Golf Magazine	145,162,596	14.04
8. TV Guide	352,073,300	-9.46	**33.** Rosie	143,305,674	79.66
9. Business Week	351,561,105	-10.84	**34.** Vanity Fair	139,554,903	-1.07
10. Good Housekeeping	343,254,274	7.83	**35.** Parenting	133,532,348	18.58
11. Fortune	333,708,188	-12.01	**36.** Money	131,234,367	-9.75
12. Cosmopolitan	281,640,487	2.88	**37.** Redbook	127,944,255	10.14
13. Forbes	281,020,679	-8.11	**38.** The New Yorker	123,925,408	20.78
14. Woman's Day	267,267,492	-2.35	**39.** Seventeen	120,826,392	7.78
15. Reader's Digest	266,856,307	0.4	**40.** Car and Driver	115,681,196	7.44
16. In Style	264,470,598	10.92	**41.** Marie Claire	110,900,030	11.01
17. Family Circle	253,920,702	3.34	**42.** Motor Trend	110,505,494	28.02
18. Martha Stewart Living	234,363,153	11.4	**43.** Country Living	110,146,650	21.76
19. Entertainment Weekly	217,284,523	9.46	**44.** Elle	108,507,692	-11.54
20. New York Times Magazine	212,619,086	5.47	**45.** GQ	104,169,255	0.25
21. Ladies' Home Journal	200,831,257	5.91	**46.** W	102,536,185	-20.23
22. U.S. News & World Report	192,802,751	7.73	**47.** YM	100,208,047	48
23. Vogue	187,789,281	-6.89	**48.** Travel+Leisure	100,159,572	-13.08
24. Maxim	179,665,284	17.51	**49.** Harper's Bazaar	99,841,279	-5.42
25. O, The Oprah Magazine	179,078,602	23.28	**50.** Country Home	98,231,338	38.93

Source: Magazine Publishers of America, *Publishers Information Bureau Publications Ranked by Revenue, 2002* (2003).

etc.) The Audit Bureau of Circulations (ABC) monitors the sales of about 500 of the most popular consumer magazines. Trade publications are magazines with a narrow focus in a particular area of business (e.g. trucking, restaurants, computers). There are about 2,700 trade publications; they are sold either by subscription or distributed free.

Almost all magazines make money through revenues from both circulation and advertising. The most financially successful magazines are not necessarily the largest sellers, the difference being in the advertising fees they are able to obtain. *Fortune,* for example, is among the top 10 of all magazines in revenues, but does not even make the top-100 list in circulation.

▶BOOKS

Sales of books in the United States decreased in 2001 for first time in a decade, according to figures released by the Book Industry Study Group, which monitors the reading habits of American households. The number of books sold (down 3.1 percent) decreased faster than the dollar volume of book sales (down 1 percent), indicating that the average price of books continues to rise.

Ironically, it is the computer, predicted by many to be the book industry's death knell, which has been responsible for the overall increase in book production since 1990. Computers not only reduce publishers' production costs, enabling the publication of many more titles. Computers have also made possible the "superstore" in which computer indexes, rather than humans with encyclopedic knowledge, keep track of so many titles.

Steadily rising levels of educational attainment over two decades—more than 83 percent of the population had finished high school in 2001, compared with 68.1 percent in 1980, while more than 25 percent had finished college, compared with 17.0 percent in 1980—has created a growing audience for the printed word. It has also fueled a corresponding increase in the number of libraries in the U.S. Since 1980, the number of libraries has increased by more than 8 percent.

Number of Libraries in U.S. and Canada by Type, 1980–2000

Type of Library	1980	1990	1999	2000
Public	8,717	9,060	9,837	9,480
Branches of public libraries	5,936	5,833	6,376	6,957
Special	7,649	9,051	9,691	9,948
Medical	1,674	1,861	1,906	1,955
Religious	913	946	1,001	767
Law	417	647	1,136	1,172
Academic	4,591	4,593	4,723	3,491
Junior college	1,191	1,233	1,274	1,148
Colleges, universities	3,400	3,360	3,449	2,251
Departmental	1,489	1,454	1,467	1,454
Law, medical, religious	269	501	493	418
Government	1,260	1,735	1,874	1,411
Armed forces	485	489	352	341
Total, U.S.	**28,638**	**30,761**	**33,108**	**31,628**
Total, U.S. and Canada	**31,564**	**34,613**	**37,039**	**35,261**

Source: R.R. Bowker Co., *The Bowker Annual: Library and Book Trade Almanac.* (2001). Used with the permission of R.R. Bowker ® a Unit of Cahners Business Information.

Number and Value of U.S. Books Sold, 1990–2001 (in millions)

Type of publication and market area	Publishers' units			Domestic consumer expenditures		
	1990	2000	2001	1990	2000	2001
TYPE OF PUBLICATION						
Trade	730.7	903.9	845.7	$6,497.8	$11,514.4	$11,051.6
Adult trade	420.4	457.1	442.1	4,776.8	8,690.7	8,448.3
Juvenile trade	310.3	446.8	403.6	1,721.0	2,823.7	2,603.3
Mass market paperback	488.8	471.3	454.9	1,775.4	2,622.2	2,602.0
Book clubs	110.6	143.1	143.5	704.7	1,316.2	1,368.9
Mail order publications	142.6	65.3	52.0	751.7	590.3	551.4
Religious	137.7	170.8	174.0	1,361.9	2,295.4	2,413.4
Professional	148.6	186.7	168.1	2,956.8	5,292.7	4,869.9
University press	15.8	31.0	29.5	284.1	507.1	499.4
Elementary and high school	218.7	333.6	348.6	1,947.9	3,516.3	3,797.6
College	149.7	186.3	193.8	2,319.0	3,717.8	4,019.8
Subscription reference	1.1	1.2	1.2	443.6	678.7	705.9
All books	**2,144.3**	**2,493.2**	**2,411.3**	**$19,042.9**	**$32,051.1**	**$31,879.9**
MARKET AREA						
Domestic (total)	2,005.0	2,338.5	2,262.5	$19,042.9	$32,050.1	$31,879.9
General retailers	1,009.8	1,180.6	1,141.2	8,465.4	14,556.8	14,389.3
Colleges	254.6	301.3	293.5	3,403.2	5,698.5	5,717.7
Libraries and institutions	88.4	105.9	102.3	1,591.8	2,663.8	2,639.6
Schools and school libraries	244.1	343.3	341.0	2,365.0	4,234.3	4,351.1
Direct to consumers	304.1	303.5	285.6	2,901.0	4,447.5	4,344.3
Other	104.1	103.9	99.0	316.5	449.2	437.9
Export	139.4	154.7	148.8	—	—	—
Total	**2,144.3**	**2,493.2**	**2,411.3**	—	—	—

Note: Includes all titles released by publishers in the United States, and imports that appear under the imprint of American publishers. Multi-volume sets such as encyclopedias are counted as one unit. School libraries included with school, not libraries. Does not include standardized tests. **Source:** Book Industry Study Group, Inc., *Book Industry Trends 2002*, reprinted by permission.

Best-Sellers in America, 1917–2001

Year	Fiction	Nonfiction
1917	*Mr. Britling Sees It Through*, H.G. Wells	*Rhymes of A Red Cross Man*, Robert W. Service
1918	*The U.P. Trail*, Zane Grey	*Rhymes of A Red Cross Man*, Robert W. Service
1919	*The Four Horsemen of the Apocalypse*, V. Blasco Iañez	*The Education of Henry Adams*, Henry Adams
1920	*The Man of the Forest*, Zane Grey	*Now It Can Be Told*, Philip Gibbs
1921	*Main Street*, Sinclair Lewis	*The Outline of History*, H.G. Wells
1922	*If Winter Comes*, A.S.M. Hitchinson	*The Outline of History*, H.G. Wells
1923	*Black Oxen*, Gertrude Atherton	*Etiquette*, Emily Post
1924	*So Big*, Edna Ferber	*Diet and Health*, Lulu Hunt Peters
1925	*Soundings*, A. Hamilton Gibbs	*Diet and Health*, Lulu Hunt Peters
1926	*The Private Life of Helen of Troy*, John Erskine	*The Man Nobody Knows*, Bruce Barton
1927	*Elmer Gantry*, Sinclair Lewis	*The Story of Philosophy*, Will Durant
1928	*The Bridge on San Luis Rey*, Thornton Wilder	*Disraeli*, Andre Maurois
1929	*All Quiet on the Western Front*, Erich Maria Remarque	*The Art of Thinking*, Ernest Dimmet
1930	*Cimarron*, Edna Ferber	*The Story of San Michele*, Axel Munthe
1931	*The Good Earth*, Pearl S. Buck	*Education of a Princess*, Grand Duchess Marie
1932	*The Good Earth*, Pearl S. Buck	*The Epic of America*, James Truslow Adams
1933	*Anthony Adverse*, Hervey Allen	*Life Begins at Forty*, Walter Pitkin
1934	*Anthony Adverse*, Hervey Allen	*While Rome Burns*, Alexander Woollcott
1935	*Green Light*, Lloyd C. Douglas	*North to the Orient*, Anne Morrow Lindbergh
1936	*Gone With the Wind*, Margaret Mitchell	*Man the Unknown*, Alexis Carrel
1937	*Gone With the Wind*, Margaret Mitchell	*How to Win Friends and Influence People*, Dale Carnegie
1938	*The Yearling*, Marjorie Kinnan Rawlings	*The Importance of Living*, Lin Yutang
1939	*The Grapes of Wrath*, John Steinbeck	*Days of Our Years*, Piere von Paaseen
1940	*How Green Was My Valley*, Richard Llewellyn	*I Married Adventure*, Osa Johnson
1941	*The Keys of the Kingdom*, A.J. Cronin	*Berlin Diary*, William C. Shirer
1942	*The Song of Bernadette*, Franz Werfel	*See Here, Private Hargrove*, Marion Hargrove
1943	*The Robe*, Lloyd C. Douglas	*Under Cover*, John Roy Carlson
1944	*Strange Fruit*, Lillian Smith	*I Never Left Home*, Bob Hope
1945	*Forever Amber*, Kathleen Winsor	*Brave Men*, Ernie Pyle
1946	*The King's General*, Daphne du Maurier	*The Egg and I*, Betty MacDonald

Year	Fiction	Nonfiction
1947	*The Miracle of the Bells,* Russell Janney	*Peace of Mind,* Joshua L. Liebman
1948	*The Big Fisherman,* Lloyd C. Douglas	*Crusade in Europe,* Dwight D. Eisenhower
1949	*The Egyptian,* Mika Waltari	*White Collar Zoo,* Clare Barnes, Jr.
1950	*The Cardinal,* Henry Morton Robinson	*Betty Crocker's Picture Cookbook*
1951	*From Here to Eternity,* James Jones	*Look Younger, Live Longer,* Gayelord Hauser
1952	*The Silver Chalice,* Thomas B.Costain	*The Holy Bible: Revised Standard Version*
1953	*The Robe,* Lloyd C. Douglas	*The Holy Bible: Revised Standard Version*
1954	*Not As A Stranger,* Morton Thompson	*The Holy Bible: Revised Standard Version*
1955	*Marjorie Morningstar,* Herman Wouk	*Gift from the Sea,* Anne Morrow Lindbergh
1956	*Don't Go Near the Water,* William Brinkley	*Arthritis and Common Sense,* Dan Dale Alexander
1957	*By Love Possessed,* James Gould Cozzens	*Kids Say the Darndest Things!,* Art Linkletter
1958	*Doctor Zhivago,* Boris Pasternak	*Kids Say the Darndest Things!,* Art Linkletter
1959	*Exodus,* Leon Uris	*'Twixt Twelve and Twenty,* Pat Boone
1960	*Advise and Consent,* Allen Drury	*Folk Medicine,* D.C. Jarvis
1961	*The Agony and the Ecstasy,* Irving Stone	*The New English Bible: The New Testament*
1962	*Ship of Fools,* Katherine Anne Porter	*Calories Don't Count,* Dr. Herman Taller
1963	*The Shoes of the Fisherman,* Morris L. West	*Happiness Is a Warm Puppy,* Charles M. Schulz
1964	*The Spy Who Came in From the Cold,* John le Carré	*Four Days,* American Heritage
1965	*The Source,* James A. Michener	*How To Be a Jewish Mother,* Dan Greenburg
1966	*Valley of the Dolls,* Jacqueline Susann	*How to Avoid Probate,* Norman F. Dacey
1967	*The Arrangement,* Elia Kazan	*Death of a President,* William Manchester
1968	*Airport,* Arthur Hailey	*Better Homes & Gardens New Cook Book*
1969	*Portnoy's Complaint,* Philip Roth	*American Heritage Dictionary of the English Language,* ed. William Morris
1970	*Love Story,* Erich Segal	*Everything You Wanted to Know About Sex but Were Afraid to Ask,* David Reuben, M.D.
1971	*Wheels,* Arthur Hailey	*The Sensuous Man,* "M."
1972	*Jonathan Livingston Seagull,* Richard Bach	*The Living Bible,* Kenneth Taylor
1973	*Jonathan Livingston Seagull,* Richard Bach	*The Living Bible,* Kenneth Taylor
1974	*Centennial,* James A. Michener	*The Total Woman,* Marabel Morgan
1975	*Ragtime,* E. L. Doctorow	*Angels: God's Secret Agents,* Billy Graham
1976	*Trinity,* Leon Uris	*The Final Days,* Bob Woodward, Carl Bernstein
1977	*The Silmarillion,* J.R.R. Tolkien	*Roots,* Alex Haley
1978	*Chesapeake,* James A. Michener	*If Life is a Bowl of Cherries—What Am I Doing in the Pits?* Erma Bombeck
1979	*The Matarese Circle,* Robert Ludlum	*Aunt Erma's Cope Book,* Erma Bombeck
1980	*The Covenant,* James Michener	*Crisis Investing,* Douglas R. Casey
1981	*Noble House,* James Clavell	*The Beverly Hills Diet,* Judy Mazel
1982	*E.T. The Extra-Terrestrial Storybook,* William Kotzwinkle	*Jane Fonda's Workout Book,* Jane Fonda
1983	*Return of the Jedi Storybook,* Joan D. Vinge	*In Search of Excellence,* Thomas J. Peters, Robert H. Waterman Jr.
1984	*The Talisman,* Stephen King, Peter Straub	*Iacocca: An Autobiography,* Lee Iacocca with William Novak
1985	*The Mammoth Hunters,* Jean M.Auel	*Iacocca: An Autobiography,* Lee Iacocca with William Novak
1986	*It,* Stephen King	*Fatherhood,* Bill Cosby
1987	*The Tommyknockers,* Stephen King	*Time Flies,* Bill Cosby
1988	*The Cardinal of the Kremlin,* Tom Clancy	*The Eight-Week Cholesterol Diet,* Robert Kowalski
1989	*Clear and Present Danger,* Tom Clancy	*All I Really Need to Know I Learned in Kindergarten,* Robert Fulghum
1990	*The Plains of Passage,* Jean Auel	*A Life on the Road,* Charles Kuralt
1991	*Scarlett,* Alexandra Ripley	*Me: The Stories of My Life ,* Katharine Hepburn
1992	*Dolores Claiborne,* Stephen King	*The Way Things Ought to Be,* Rush Limbaugh
1993	*The Bridges of Madison County,* Robert James Walker	*See, I Told You So,* Rush Limbaugh
1994	*The Chamber,* John Grisham	*In the Kitchen with Rosie,* Rosie Daley
1995	*The Rainmaker,* John Grisham	*Men are From Mars, Women are From Venus,* John Gray
1996	*The Runaway Jury,* John Grisham	*Make the Connection,* Oprah Winfrey & Bob Greene
1997	*The Partner,* John Grisham	*Angela's Ashes,* Frank McCourt
1998	*The Street Lawyer,* John Grisham	*The Nine Steps to Financial Freedom,* Suze Orman
1999	*The Testament,* John Grisham	*Tuesdays with Morrie,* Mitch Albom
2000	*The Brethren,* John Grisham	*Who Moved My Cheese?* Spencer Johnson
2001	*Desecration,* Jerry B. Jenkins and Tim LaHaye	*The Prayer of Jabez,* Bruce Wilkinson

Sources: Alice Payne Hackett, *70 Years of Best Sellers; Publishers Weekly.*

New Books and Editions Published, by Subject, 1980–2002

Subject	1980	1990	2000	2002[1]
Agriculture	461	514	1,073	888
Art	1,691	1,262	4,980	4,481
Biography	1,891	1,957	3,899	5,049
Business	1,185	1,191	4,068	4,539
Education	1,011	1,039	3,378	3,652
Fiction	2,835	5,764	14,617	15,131
General works	1,643	1,760	1,318	1,468
History	2,220	2,248	7,931	6,818
Home economics	879	758	2,513	2,160
Juvenile	2,859	5,172	8,690	9,540
Language	529	649	2,536	2,419
Law	1,102	896	3,070	2,188
Literature	1,686	2,049	3,371	3,946
Medicine	3,292	3,014	6,234	5,933
Music	357	289	1,582	1,614
Philosophy, Psychology	1,429	1,688	5,556	6,006
Poetry, Drama	1,179	874	2,479	2,812
Religion	2,055	2,285	6,206	6,659
Science	3,109	2,742	8,464	7,032
Sociology, Economics	7,152	7,042	14,908	13,804
Sports, recreation	971	978	3,483	3,569
Technology	2,337	2,092	8,582	7,888
Travel	504	495	3,170	2,327
Total	42,377	46,748	122,108	119,923

Note: Comprises new books (published for the first time), and new editions (with changes in text or format). Includes mass-market paperbacks. Excludes government publications, books sold only by subscription, dissertations, periodicals, quarterlies, and pamphlets under 49 pages. 1. Preliminary. **Source:** R.R. Bowker Co., *The Bowker Annual Library and Book Trade Almanac,* copyright 2003 Reed Elsevier Inc. Used with the permission of R.R. Bowker ® a business unit of Reed Elsevier Inc.

The American Library Association's 75 Most Frequently Challenged Books of 1990–2000

Rank, Title, Author

1. *Scary Stories* (Series), Alvin Schwartz
2. *Daddy's Roommate,* Michael Willhoite
3. *I Know Why the Caged Bird Sings,* Maya Angelou
4. *The Chocolate War,* Robert Cormier
5. *Adventures of Huckleberry Finn,* Mark Twain
6. *Of Mice and Men,* John Steinbeck
7. *Harry Potter* (Series), J.K. Rowling
8. *Forever,* Judy Blume
9. *Bridge to Terabithia,* Katherine Paterson
10. *Alice* (Series), Phyllis Reynolds Naylor
11. *Heather Has Two Mommies,* Leslea Newman
12. *My Brother Sam is Dead,* James Lincoln Collier and Christopher Collier
13. *The Catcher in the Rye,* J.D. Salinger
14. *The Giver,* Lois Lowry
15. *It's Perfectly Normal,* Robie Harris
16. *Goosebumps* (Series), R.L. Stine
17. *A Day No Pigs Would Die,* Robert Newton Peck
18. *The Color Purple,* Alice Walker
19. *Sex,* Madonna
20. *Earth's Children* (Series), Jean M. Auel
21. *The Great Gilly Hopkins,* Katherine Paterson
22. *A Wrinkle in Time,* Madeleine L'Engle
23. *Go Ask Alice,* Anonymous
24. *Fallen Angels,* Walter Dean Myers
25. *In the Night Kitchen,* Maurice Sendak
26. *The Stupids* (Series), Harry Allard
27. *The Witches,* Roald Dahl
28. *The New Joy of Gay Sex,* Charles Silverstein
29. *Anastasia Krupnik* (Series), Lois Lowry
30. *The Goats,* Brock Cole
31. *Kaffir Boy,* Mark Mathabane
32. *Blubber,* Judy Blume
33. *Killing Mr. Griffin,* Lois Duncan
34. *Halloween ABC,* Eve Merriam
35. *We All Fall Down,* Robert Cormier
36. *Final Exit,* Derek Humphry
37. *The Handmaid's Tale,* Margaret Atwood
38. *Julie of the Wolves,* Jean Craighead George
39. *The Bluest Eye,* Toni Morrison
40. *What's Happening to my Body? Book for Girls: A Growing-Up Guide for Parents & Daughters,* Lynda Madaras
41. *To Kill a Mockingbird,* Harper Lee
42. *Beloved,* Toni Morrison
43. *The Outsiders,* S.E. Hinton
44. *The Pigman,* Paul Zindel
45. *Bumps in the Night,* Harry Allard
46. *Deenie,* Judy Blume
47. *Flowers for Algernon,* Daniel Keyes
48. *Annie on my Mind,* Nancy Garden
49. *The Boy Who Lost His Face,* Louis Sachar
50. *Cross Your Fingers, Spit in Your Hat,* Alvin Schwartz
51. *A Light in the Attic,* Shel Silverstein
52. *Brave New World,* Aldous Huxley
53. *Sleeping Beauty Trilogy,* A.N. Roquelaure (Anne Rice)
54. *Asking About Sex and Growing Up,* Joanna Cole
55. *Cujo,* Stephen King
56. *James and the Giant Peach,* Roald Dahl
57. *The Anarchist Cookbook,* William Powell
58. *Boys and Sex,* Wardell Pomeroy
59. *Ordinary People,* Judith Guest
60. *American Psycho,* Bret Easton Ellis
61. *What's Happening to my Body? Book for Boys: A Growing-Up Guide for Parents & Sons,* Lynda Madaras
62. *Are You There, God? It's Me, Margaret,* Judy Blume
63. *Crazy Lady,* Jane Conly
64. *Athletic Shorts,* Chris Crutcher
65. *Fade,* Robert Cormier
66. *Guess What?,* Mem Fox
67. *The House of Spirits,* Isabel Allende
68. *The Face on the Milk Carton,* Caroline Cooney
69. *Slaughterhouse-Five,* Kurt Vonnegut
70. *Lord of the Flies,* William Golding
71. *Native Son,* Richard Wright
72. *Women on Top: How Real Life Has Changed Women's Fantasies,* Nancy Friday
73. *Curses, Hexes and Spells,* Daniel Cohen
74. *Jack,* A.M. Homes
75. *Bless Me, Ultima,* Rudolfo A. Anaya

Source: American Library Organization.

THE ELECTRONIC MEDIA

▶TELEVISION

Few people doubt the pervasiveness of television's influence on America. Once a symbol of luxury, the color television set has found its way into almost every home in America, and a great majority of American households have two or more televisions. According to Nielsen Media Research, which monitors television viewership, at least one of these televisions was on in each household for 7 hours 22 minutes during the 2000-2001 television season. That's an hour and 21 minutes more than in 1971, when the average was just 6 hours 1 minute, but 9 minutes less than in 1999-2000. Average daily viewing per person is still much higher than 1970s levels. Women over the age of 18 watched longest; they averaged 4 hours 37 minutes per day, down 7 minutes from the year before, while men over 18 watched for 4 hours 1 minute, down 5 minutes from 1999-2000. Children aged 12-17 watched an average of 3 hours 17 minutes, up 11 minutes from a year ago. Viewing by children 2-11 has dropped from 3 hours 49 minutes in 1984-85 to three hours and 10 minutes in 2000-2001.

Top 50 Single Shows in TV History, by Rating

Rank/Program	Date	Network	Rating	Share
1. *M*A*S*H* Special (Last episode)	2/28/83	CBS	60.2%	77%
2. *Dallas* (Who Shot J.R.?)	11/21/80	CBS	53.3	76
3. *Roots,* part 8	1/30/77	ABC	51.1	71
4. Super Bowl XVI (San Francisco/Cincinnati)	1/24/82	CBS	49.1	73
5. Super Bowl XVII (Washington/Miami)	1/30/83	NBC	48.6	69
6. XVII Winter Olympics (Figure skating round 1)	2/23/94	CBS	48.5	64
7. Super Bowl XX (Chicago/New England)	1/26/86	NBC	48.3	70
8. *Gone With the Wind,* part 1	11/7/76	NBC	47.7	65
9. *Gone With the Wind,* part 2	11/8/76	NBC	47.4	64
10. Super Bowl XII (Dallas/Denver)	1/15/78	CBS	47.2	67
11. Super Bowl XIII (Pittsburgh/Dallas)	1/21/79	NBC	47.1	74
12. *Bob Hope Christmas Show*	1/15/70	NBC	46.6	64
13. Super Bowl XVIII (L.A. Raiders/Washington)	1/22/84	CBS	46.4	71
14. Super Bowl XIX (San Francisco/Miami)	1/20/85	ABC	46.4	63
15. Super Bowl XIV (Pittsburgh/L.A. Rams)	1/20/80	CBS	46.3	67
16. Super Bowl XXX (Dallas/Pittsburgh)	1/28/96	NBC	46.0	68
17. *ABC Theater "The Day After"*	1/20/83	ABC	46.0	62
18. *The Fugitive*	8/29/67	ABC	45.9	72
19. *Roots,* part 6	1/28/77	ABC	45.9	66
20. Super Bowl XXI (N.Y. Giants/Denver)	1/25/87	CBS	45.8	66
21. *Roots,* part 5	1/27/77	ABC	45.7	71
22. Super Bowl XXVIII (Dallas/Buffalo)	1/30/94	NBC	45.5	66
23. *Cheers* (Last episode)	5/20/93	NBC	45.5	64
24. *The Ed Sullivan Show*	2/9/64	CBS	45.3	60
25. Super Bowl XXVII (Dallas/Buffalo)	1/31/93	NBC	45.1	66
26. *Bob Hope Christmas Show*	1/14/71	NBC	45.0	61
27. *Roots,* part 3	1/25/77	ABC	44.8	68
28. Super Bowl XXXII (Denver/Green Bay)	1/25/98	NBC	44.5	67
29. Super Bowl XI (Oakland/Minnesota)	1/9/77	NBC	44.4	73
30. Super Bowl XV (Oakland/Philadelphia)	1/25/81	NBC	44.4	63
31. Super Bowl VI (Dallas/Miami)	1/16/72	CBS	44.2	74
32. XVII Winter Olympics (Figure skating finals)	2/25/94	CBS	44.1	64
33. *Roots,* part 2	1/24/77	ABC	44.1	62
34. *The Beverly Hillbillies*	1/8/64	CBS	44.0	65
35. *Roots,* part 4	1/26/77	ABC	43.8	66
36. *The Ed Sullivan Show* (with the Beatles)	2/16/64	CBS	43.8	60
37. Super Bowl XXIII (San Francisco/Cincinnati)	1/22/89	NBC	43.5	68
38. Academy Awards	4/7/70	ABC	43.4	78
39. Super Bowl XXXI (Green Bay/New England)	1/26/97	FOX	43.3	65
40. Super Bowl XXXIV (St. Louis/Tennessee)	1/30/00	ABC	43.3	63
41. *The Thorn Birds,* part 3	3/29/83	ABC	43.2	62
42. *The Thorn Birds,* part 4	3/30/83	ABC	43.1	62
43. NFC Championship game (San Francisco/Dallas)	1/10/82	CBS	42.9	62
44. *The Beverly Hillbillies*	1/15/64	CBS	42.8	62
45. Super Bowl VII (Miami/Washington)	1/14/73	NBC	42.7	72
46. *The Thorn Birds,* part 2	3/28/83	ABC	42.5	59
47. Super Bowl IX (Pittsburgh/Minnesota)	1/12/75	NBC	42.4	72
48. *The Beverly Hillbillies*	2/26/64	CBS	42.4	60
49. Super Bowl X (Pittsburgh/Dallas)	1/18/76	CBS	42.3	78
50. *Airport*	11/11/73	ABC	42.3	63

Note: As of August 2002. Does not include programs broadcast on more than one network, e.g. the Apollo moon landing or programs under 30 minutes scheduled duration. **Rating** is the number of people watching as a percentage of all television owners. **Share** is the number watching as a percentage of people with their TVs on at that particular time. **Source:** Nielsen Media Research.

▶CABLE TELEVISION

Cable television was originally designed as a means of improving TV reception in some rural areas. In the 1960s, operators realized that viewers were willing to pay for commercial-free programming, but their efforts to capitalize on the idea were hampered by stringent Federal Communications Commission restrictions. Not until 1975, when RCA put its first communications satellite into operation, did the industry really bloom. Under the name Home Box Office, the company started to transmit programming that could be received by independent operators around the country and then relayed to subscribers at minimal cost. With the dismissal of most of the FCC's regulations by a federal court in 1977, the door was opened for the development of what is now a multibillion-dollar industry.

As the accompanying table demonstrates, cable has changed the television broadcasting land-

Top 20 TV Shows of 2002–03

Rank, Program (Network)	Avg. rating	Avg. share
1. *CSI* (CBS)	16.3	25
2. *Friends* (NBC)	13.9	22
3. *Joe Millionaire* (FOX)	13.3	19
4. *E.R.* (NBC)	13.1	21
5. *American Idol* [Tuesday] (FOX)	12.6	19
6. *American Idol* [Wednesday] (FOX)	12.5	19
7. *Survivor: Thailand* (CBS)	12.1	19
8. *Everybody Loves Raymond* (CBS)	11.9	18
9. *Law and Order* (NBC)	11.7	19
9. *Survivor: Amazon* (CBS)	11.7	18
11. *NFL Monday Night Football* (ABC)	11.4	19
12. *CSI: Miami* (CBS)	11.0	18
12. *Will & Grace* (NBC)	11.0	17
14. *The Bachelorette* (ABC)	10.7	16
15. *Scrubs* (NBC)	10.3	16
16. *Law and Order: SVU* (NBC)	10.1	18
17. *Without a Trace* (CBS)	10.0	17
18. *60 Minutes* (CBS)	9.6	16
18. *The Bachelor* (ABC)	9.6	15
18. *Law and Order: CI* [10PM] (NBC)	9.6	16

Note: For the 2002–03 season through May 21, 2003. Does not include "movie of the week" programs or programs broadcast for fewer than 10 weeks. ***Rating*** is the percentage of all television owners watching that program. ***Share*** is the percentage of TVs that are on at the time of the program. For example, on a given Thursday night, 25 percent of the people watching TV at 9 P.M. were tuned to *CSI*, but because not every TV owner was watching television that night, only 16.3 percent of all TV owners were tuned in to *CSI*. **Source:** Nielsen Media Research.

Longest-Running National Network Series of All Time

Program	Seasons	Years[1]
60 Minutes	36	1968-
Walt Disney	33	1954-90
The Ed Sullivan Show	24	1948-71
Gunsmoke	20	1955-75
The Red Skelton Show	20	1951-71
Meet the Press	18	1947-65[2]
What's My Line?	18	1950-67
I've Got a Secret	17	1952-76
Lassie	17	1954-71
The Lawrence Welk Show	17	1955-71

Note: Includes prime-time (6-11 p.m.) shows only; sports broadcasts and movie series are not included. 1. Dates reflect the first and last broadcasts of each show. Programs did not necessarily run continuously throughout this period. 2. Ceased broadcasting in prime-time in 1965, though still on the air.

Primetime Viewing Shares of Free and Cable TV Networks, 1995–2000

	'95-96	'96-97	'97-98	'98-99	'99-00
DAYTIME					
Pay Cable	5%	6%	7%	6%	5%
Basic Cable	30	33	35	36	41
Public	3	3	3	3	3
Independents	11	11	11	11	11
Network Affiliates	51	47	44	42	40
PRIMETIME					
Pay Cable	5%	5%	6%	6%	5%
Basic Cable	26	30	33	36	36
Public	3	3	4	3	3
Independents	10	10	10	11	11
Network Affiliates	56	51	48	45	45

Note: Due to multiset use and independent roundings, totals add up to more than 100. **Source:** Nielsen Media Research.

Top 15 Cable Television Networks, 2002–03

Rank/Network	Subscribers (millions)	Launch date	Content
1. TBS Superstation	87.7	1976	Movies, sports, original & syndicated shows
2. ESPN	86.7	1979	Sports events and sports news
3. C-SPAN	86.6	1979	Public affairs, live Congressional coverage
4. The Discovery Channel	86.5	1985	Nonfiction, nature, science
5. USA Network	86.3	1980	Sports, family entertainment
6. Cable News Network (CNN)	86.2	1980	24-hour news, special interest reports
7. TNT (Turner Network Television)	86.2	1988	Movies, sports, and original programming
8. Lifetime Television	86.0	1984	Programming aimed at women
9. Nickelodeon/Nick at Nite	86.0	1979	Programming for kids
10. A&E Television	85.9	1984	Original programming, biographies, documentaries
11. Spike TV[1]	85.8	1983	Original programming, syndicated shows
12. The Weather Channel	85.3	1982	Weather updates
13. MTV (Music Television)	84.9	1981	Music videos
14. QVC	84.9[2]	1980	Televised shopping
15. ABC Family Channel	84.8	2001	Original and syndicated family programming

Notes: 1. Formerly TNN. 2. As of January 2003. **Source:** National Cable & Telecommunications Association, *Cable Developments 2003*.

scape, drawing away more than one-third of the total television viewing audiences. As a result, the fractured total television audience means that no single program will likely ever reach the kind of viewership numbers achieved during the 1960s and 70s, when viewers had only three or four choices. A case in point: the final episode of *Survivor II*, broadcast in the summer of 2001, was one of the most talked-about programs in a decade, but it didn't attract as many viewers as regular episodes of *The Beverly Hillbillies*.

The number of basic cable subscribers is currently increasing by about a half million per year (pay cable has grown at a more rapid rate of several million per year). But despite deregulation and increased competition from direct satellite providers, the average cable bill continues to increase. It was $7.69 in 1980; in 2002, it was $34.52. The number of digital cable subscribers has increased from 1.5 million in 1998 to 20 million in 2003. Over the same time period, the number of cable modem subscribers (allowing cable connections to the Internet) has increased from 500,000 to 12 million. The nation's two biggest cable providers are Comcast Cable Communications (21.3 million subscribers) and Time Warner Cable (10.9 million).

Top 5 Pay-Cable Services, 2000

Rank/Network	Subscribers	Content
1. The Disney Channel[1]	67,000,000	Movies, cartoons
2. HBO/Cinemax	37,000,000	Movies, variety, sports, documentaries
3. Showtime/The Movie Channel	25,500,000	Movies, variety, comedy, sports
4. Encore	24,500,000	On-demand movies
5. Spice	11,000,000	Adult movies

1. Disney is a basic cable service on some cable systems.
Source: National Cable Television Association, *Cable TV Developments* (Spring, 2001).

Basic and Pay Cable TV Systems and Subscribers, 1952–2002

Year	Number of systems	Basic cable: Subscribers	Basic cable: Percent of U.S. TV households	Pay cable: Subscribers	Pay cable: Percent of households with cable
1952	70	14,000	0.1%	N.A.	N.A.
1955	400	150,000	0.5	N.A.	N.A.
1960	640	650,000	1.4	N.A.	N.A.
1970	2,490	3,900,000	6.7	N.A.	N.A.
1975	3,506	9,196,690	13.2	469,000	23.6%
1980	4,225	17,671,490	22.6	9,144,000	50.6
1985	6,600	39,872,520	46.2	30,596,000	83.5
1990	9,575	54,871,330	59.0	39,900,000	77.1
2000	10,400	69,297,290	67.8	48,300,000	71.5
2001	9,924	72,958,180	69.2	50,600,000	72.8
2002	N.A.	73,525,150	68.9	53,200,000	72.4

Sources: National Cable & Telecommunications Association, *Cable Developments 2003*; Nielsen Media Research.

Video and Audio: Sales & Penetration in U.S. Homes, 1990–2003

Product	Sales (thousands of units) 1990	2000	2002	2003[1]	Percent of U.S. homes 1990	2000	2002	2003[1]
Video								
Analog color TV	20,384	24,175	22,469	21,350	96%	98%	98%	98%
Projection TV	351	1,708	2,485	3,140	6	15	16	18
Digital TV set[2]	N.A.	648	2,536	4,265	N.A.	N.A.	3	5
TV/VCR combination	424	4,964	4,870	3,243	N.A.	18	22	25
VCR[3]	11,986	35,117	20,687	12,559	68	93	94	89
DVD player	N.A.	8,499	17,090	22,277	N.A.	5	29	41
Camcorder[4]	2,962	5,848	5,790	5,915	10	36	43	45
Direct Satellite Receiver	N.A.	4,818	6,906	7,344	N.A.	15	20	22
Audio								
Home Radio	21,585	19,976	16,194	13,282	99%	98%	98%	98%
Home Theater-in-a-Box	N.A.	1,157	2,793	3,015	N.A.	22	27	30
Compact disc player[5]	9,155	54,374	42,914	35,461	19	57	57	57
Compact audio system	2,447	11,455	7,314	5,281	N.A.	42	43	41
MP3 Players	N.A.	510	1,737	1,916	N.A.	N.A.	N.A.	N.A.

N.A.= Not available. 1. Estimate. 2. Includes direct-view and projection digital TVs with integrated decoders and stand-alone digital TV displays. 3. Includes mono and stereo decks, but not machines that play but do not record. Does not include TV/VCR combinations. 4. Includes digital camcorders. 5. Sales represent total CD players; market penetration represents home CD players.
Source: Consumer Electronics Sales & Forecasts, © 2003 Consumer Electronics Association. Reprinted by permission.

▶RADIO

According to statistics compiled by the Radio Advertising Bureau, 98 percent of all U.S. households own at least one radio. Of Americans over age 12, 95.3 percent listen to radio for an average of 3 hours and 20 minutes each workday.

▶THE RECORDING INDUSTRY

In less than 10 years, the compact disc went from breakthrough to the music format of choice among most consumers. Along the way, it resuscitated an industry that many feared was sagging at the hands of video games, computers, and movies.

Fewer than 100,000 CDs were sold in 1983, the first year they were available, but the format quickly overtook LPs by 1988, and topped cassette sales in 1992. In 2002, CDs accounted for over 90 percent of all music sales, while cassettes and nearly obsolete vinyl LPs accounted for 2.4 percent and 0.7 percent, respectively. The CD revived the entire music industry, which in the late 1970s and early 80s was worried about losing young consumers to movies and videogames. The industry was also concerned that home taping was cutting into sales of records, but with CD's superior sound quality, that ceased to be a serious issue for many years. The total U.S. dollar value of all music sold in 2002 was $12.6 billion, down from $13.7 billion in 2001, and continuing a steady decline from 1999's peak of $14.6 billion.

Radio Stations by Primary Format, 1990–2001

Format	1990	1999	2001
Total commercial stations	**9,444**	**10,444**	**10,516**
Country	2,452	2,305	2,190
Adult contemporary	2,135	775	709
News, Talk, Business, Sports	405	1,159	1,139
Religion (teaching & music)	745	363	356
Oldies & Classic hits	659	766	786
Rock (Album, Modern, Classic)	419	730	760
Spanish & other ethnic	342	618	667
Adult standards	383	595	569
Top 40	824	401	468
R&B, Urban adult contemporary	N.A.	278	301
Jazz	N.A.	72	81
Variety	97	39	39
Classical, Fine arts	52	38	34
Easy listening	240	34	27
Pre-teen	3	51	55
Comedy	1	0	0
Off Air	210	96	113
Changing formats or not available	115	3	3
Total non-commercial stations	**1,636**	**2,366**	**2,542**
Total all stations	**11,080**	**12,810**	**13,058**

Note: As of November of each year.
Source: M Street Corporation, 2001.

U.S. Radio Stations and Radio Sales, 1946–2001

Year	Radio stations on air[1]	Unit sales to dealers[2]
1946	961	N.A.
1950	2,773	N.A.
1955	3,211	7,327
1960	4,133	18,031
1965	5,249	31,689
1970	6,760	34,049
1975	7,744	25,276
1980	8,566	27,104
1985	10,359	21,575
1990	10,788	21,585
1995	11,834	17,051
1998	12,641	18,734
1999	12,641	19,899
2000	N.A.	19,976
2001[3]	13,058	17,200

1. Includes AM and FM, commercial and noncommercial. 2. Includes table, clock, and portable—but not car—radios. 3. Estimate **Source:** M Street Corporation, 2001; Consumer Electronics Association, *U.S. Consumer Electronics Sales & Forecasts*, (2002).

Sales by Category

The sales of different types of music are in almost as constant a flux as the music types themselves. The category defined as rock accounted for nearly half of all music sales in 1987; in 2001, it was less than a quarter. Pop, Rap, Rhythm & Blues, and Country have made up the difference. For many years, the single largest group of recorded music consumers (as a percentage of total dollar value) was teenagers (buyers aged 15-19). But the high price of music and Internet music-sharing sites have cut into record sales among younger consumers. Since 1999, buyers over 45 have accounted for nearly 25 percent of annual music purchases, compared with just 12 to 13 percent by 15-19-year-olds. Women made more than half of the music purchases in the U.S. in 2001, and despite industry attempts to tap into online sales, digital downloads of music accounted for only 0.5 percent of 2002 music sales.

A decision in 1996 by Wal-Mart stores to restrict music sales of albums with controversial lyrics caused understandable consternation among record executives because of discount stores' increasing influence on the industry's bottom line. In 1989, 71.7 percent of all recorded music was sold in record stores, while 15.6 percent was sold in "other stores," which includes discount and consumer electronic stores. In 2002, record stores accounted for less than half of all music purchases (36.8 percent), while the Wal-Marts, Kmarts, and Targets of America made up 50.7 percent of music sales. In many remote areas, the local Wal-Mart is the only place to buy recorded music of any kind, forcing many top musical acts to release special Wal-Mart versions of their albums, with bowdlerized lyrics. Music purchases via the Internet grew from 0.3 percent in 1997 to 3.4 percent in 2002.

Top-Selling Albums of 2002

Title	Artist	Copies sold (millions)
1. *The Eminem Show*	Eminem	7.4
2. *Nellyville*	Nelly	4.8
3. *Let Go*	Avril Lavigne	3.9
4. *Home*	Dixie Chicks	3.4
5. *8 Mile* (Soundtrack)	Various Artists	3.2
6. *Missundaztood*	Pink	3.0
7. *Ashanti*	Ashanti	3.0
8. *Drive*	Alan Jackson	3.0
9. *O Brother Where Art Thou?* (Soundtrack)	Various Artists	2.7
10. *Up*	Shania Twain	2.6

Source: *Soundscan*, 2003

Recorded Music Sales by Genre, Format, and Age Group, 1987–2002

Characteristic	1987	1990	1995	1999	2000	2001	2002
Genre							
Rock	45.5%	36.1%	33.5%	25.2%	24.8%	24.4%	24.7%
Pop	13.5	13.7	10.1	10.3	11.0	12.1	9.0
Rap/Hip Hop	3.8	8.5	6.7	10.8	12.9	11.4	13.8
R&B/Urban1	9.0	11.6	11.3	10.5	9.7	10.6	11.2
Country	10.6	9.6	16.7	10.8	10.7	10.5	10.7
Religious/Gospel2	2.9	2.5	3.1	5.1	4.8	6.7	6.7
Jazz	3.8	4.8	3.0	3.0	2.9	3.4	3.2
Classical	3.9	3.1	2.9	3.5	2.7	3.2	3.1
Other3	6.2	8.8	10.1	11.5	11.0	11.6	11.0
Format							
CDs	11.5%	31.1%	65.0%	83.2%	89.3%	89.2%	90.5%
Cassettes	62.5	54.7	25.1	8.0	4.9	3.4	2.4
Singles (all types)	5.7	8.7	7.5	5.4	2.5	2.4	1.9
Music videos/ Video DVDs	N.A.	N.A.	0.9	0.9	0.8	1.1	0.7
DVD Audio	N.A.	N.A.	N.A.	N.A.	N.A.	1.1	1.3
Digital Download	N.A.	N.A.	N.A.	N.A.	N.A.	0.2	0.5
LPs	20.1	4.7	0.5	0.5	0.5	0.6	0.7
Age group							
10-14	7.3%	7.6%	8.0%	8.5	8.9%	8.5%	8.9%
15-19	24.2	18.3	17.1	12.6	12.9	13.0	13.3
20-24	19.1	16.5	15.3	12.6	12.5	12.2	11.5
25-29	14.5	14.6	12.3	10.5	10.6	10.9	9.4
30-34	10.8	13.2	12.1	10.1	9.8	10.3	10.8
35-39	8.2	10.2	10.8	10.4	10.6	10.2	9.8
40-44	4.8	7.8	7.5	9.3	9.6	10.3	9.9
45+	10.7	11.1	16.1	24.7	23.8	23.7	25.5

Note: Figures represent a percentage of that year's total U.S. dollar sales. 1. Inclues R&B, blues, dance, disco, funk, fusion, Motown, reggae, soul. 2. Includes Christian, Gospel, Inspirational, Religious, and Spiritual. 3. Includes soundtracks, children's music, and other categories not shown separately. Totals may not add to 100 percent due to "Don't Know/No Answer" Responses. **Source:** Recording Industry Association of America, *2002 Consumer Profile.*

Individual Record Sales

Up until 1958, the term **gold** album simply meant a hit album. But in that year, the Recording Industry Association of America codified the term to mean a record that had reached $1 million in sales. (Separate levels were established for singles, which have since been amended). The cast album from *Oklahoma!* was the first gold album. By 1975, inflation had diluted the importance of the award, so the RIAA also required gold records to sell at least 500,000 copies. The following year, it introduced the **platinum** record, awarded to albums that sell at least one million copies. The Eagles' *Their Greatest Hits 1971-1975* was the first platinum album, and is to date, the largest-selling album of all time, with 26 million copies sold. **Multi-platinum** awards go to albums selling more than two million copies. In 1999, the RIAA introduced the **diamond** award, for singles or records with U.S. sales of 10 million or more. As of August 2001, more than 80 titles had qualified for the award, in genres ranging from pop, R&B, and rock to rap, country, and instrumental. The Beatles have the most diamond records (five).

Peer-to-Peer File Sharing Napster, the online service that allowed users to copy music from other peoples' computers without paying for it, was forced to stop the process known as peer-to-peer (P2P) file sharing in 2000 because of a lawsuit brought by the music industry. Fearing that consumers would be able to share copies of DVDs, the movie industry joined the fight against file sharing. In 2002 some major record labels finally responded to the ongoing wave of music piracy by making more of their music legally available online, despite widespread fears that such a move will cannibalize more profitable CD sales. Perhaps the most successful new service was Apple Computer iTunes, which sold 10 million song downloads (for an average 99 cents each) in its first four months of operation in 2003. Despite these new efforts, P2P services like Kazaa remained active and extremely popular, and in 2003 the recording industry began filing lawsuits against several hundred file sharers (many of them young children) who were deemed to be the most serious violators of music copyright law. Some individual suits were settled quickly for relatively minor sums, but a larger battle loomed as some Internet service providers refused to divulge the identities of subscribers who had been targeted by the recording industry.

▶VIDEO

Video Cassette Recorders (VCRs) In 20 years, the video cassette recorder (VCR) has gone from a curiosity to a luxury to an appliance found in more than 90 percent of American homes. The vast majority of people continue to use their VCRs simply to watch pre-recorded videos from their local rental store. But a sizable number of owners have figured out how to program their VCRs and were responsible for the sale of 400 million blank cassettes in 2000.

DVD (Digital Video Disc) Players are the fastest-growing consumer electronics product in history, with 2002 sales of 17 million units, up 50 percent over the previous year. DVDs resemble CDs, but are capable of storing an entire feature-length film as well as additional features such as deleted scenes or the director's running commentary on the film. The average wholesale price for a DVD is $15 to $20; they are more durable than VHS tapes and take up much less space.

As of late 2003, sales of DVDs had overtaken videocassette sales, thanks to the increasing presence of DVD players in American homes (35 percent, up from 25 percent in 2002). In light of this change, video rental and retail stores have begun to show the signs of a permanent shift to DVDs, much as CDs supplanted vinyl albums and cassette tapes in the 1980s.

Top Selling and Renting Videos, 2002

VHS	DVD
SALES	
1. *Shrek*	1. *Fast and the Furious*
2. *Cinderella II: Dreams Come True*	2. *Training Day*
3. *Atlantis: Lost Empire*	3. *Shrek*
4. *Pearl Harbor (2001)*	4. *American Pie 2*
5. *Princess Diaries, The*	5. *A Knight's Tale*
6. *Rush Hour 2*	6. *Harry Potter and the Sorcerer's Stone*
7. *Harry Potter and the Sorcerer's Stone*	7. *Monsters Inc.*
8. *How the Grinch Stole Christmas (2000)*	8. *Rush Hour 2*
9. *Jurassic Park 3*	9. *Lord of the Rings: Fellowship of the Ring*
10. *Monsters Inc.*	10. *Spider-Man (2002)*
RENTALS	
1. *Fast and the Furious*	1. *Fast and the Furious*
2. *Training Day*	2. *Training Day*
3. *Harry Potter and the Sorcerer's Stone*	3. *Black Hawk Down*
4. *Shrek*	4. *Lord of the Rings: Fellowship of the Ring*
5. *Rush Hour 2*	5. *Pearl Harbor (2001)*
6. *Pearl Harbor (2001)*	6. *Harry Potter and the Sorcerer's Stone*
7. *Black Hawk Down*	7. *American Pie 2*
8. *Lord of the Rings: Fellowship of the Ring*	8. *Shrek*
9. *Ocean's Eleven (2001)*	9. *The Others*
10. *The Others*	10. *Monsters Inc.*

Note: Rental figures are based on number of transactions; sales figures are based on number of purchases, not dollar value.
Source: Alexander & Associates/Video Flash.

Personal Video Recorders (PVRs), also known as Digital Video Recorders (DVR) are touted by many as the next big thing in home entertainment, despite relatively lackluster sales (an estimated 205,000 in 2003) and falling prices (about $300, down from an average of $459 in 1999). PVRs perform the same basic function as VCRs—recording television shows—but instead of recording on removable videocassettes, a PVR uses an internal computer hard drive, generally 40 or 80 gigabytes, capable of holding up to 80 hours or more of television programming. Other features, depending on the model of PVR, include the ability to pause and rewind live TV and the ability to automatically record of future programs based on specific criteria (for example, every new episode of a particular sitcom). The most popular PVR, Tivo, is able to recommend or automatically record new shows based on its owner's viewing habits; and SonicBlue's ReplayTV offered an automatic commercial-skip feature—until 2003, when the company removed the feature in response to pressure from the advertising revenue-dependent television industry.

▶FILM

The motion picture industry grossed more than $9.5 billion in 2002, up 13 percent from 2001. A relatively small number of people are involved in this endeavor: only 582,900 in 2002. The various studios produce about 600 films per year; they submit most of these films to the Motion Picture Association of America for ratings and wide release in theaters. Two-thirds of these movies (67 percent in 2001) receive an R rating. Most of the rest receive a PG or PG-13 rating. Only 4 percent of 2001 movies were G-rated, and even fewer (less than 1 percent) received an NC-17 or X-rating. (Interestingly, in 2002 none of the top 20 grossing films had an R rating, compared with 20 percent of the top 20 in 2000.) Because many theaters simply refuse to show NC-17 movies, producers are loath to release a film with an NC-17 label. The number of movie screens has nearly doubled since 1985. Single-screen theaters made up 28 percent of all movie theaters; miniplexes accounted for 41 percent.

U.S. Film Box-Office Receipts, Screens, Admission, and Admission Charges, 1926–2002 (in current dollars)

Year	Box office receipts (millions)	Movie Screens			Annual admissions		Average admission charge	Number of $20 million hits
		Indoor	Drive-in	Digital	Total (millions)	Per person		
1926	$ 720.0	N.A.	N.A.	N.A.	2,600	N.A.	N.A.	N.A.
1930	732.0	N.A.	N.A.	N.A.	4,680	N.A.	N.A.	N.A.
1935	566.0	N.A.	N.A.	N.A.	3,900	N.A.	$0.24	N.A.
1940	735.0	N.A.	N.A.	N.A.	4,160	N.A.	0.24	N.A.
1950	1,376.0	N.A.	N.A.	N.A.	3,120	N.A.	0.53	N.A.
1960	951.0	N.A.	N.A.	N.A.	2,080	N.A.	0.69	N.A.
1970[1]	1,162.0	10,335	3,720	N.A.	920	N.A.	1.55	N.A.
1980	2,748.5	14,029	3,561	N.A.	1,022	4.5	2.69	N.A.
1990[2]	5,021.8	22,774	915	N.A.	1,189	4.8	4.23	N.A.
1995	5,493.5	26,958	847	N.A.	1,263	4.8	4.35	N.A.
2000	7,661.0	36,679	717	31	1,421	5.2	5.39	16
2001	8,412.5	36,110	654	45	1,487	5.3	5.66	16
2002	9,519.6	34,630	650	124	1,639	5.7	5.81	19

1. Theater figures are for 1971. 2. Beginning in 1990, admission totals and average prices are supplied by the National Association of Theater Owners and are not strictly comparable with data from previous years, which are based on the U.S. Department of Commerce's Consumer Price Index. **Source:** U.S. Dept. of Commerce; *Film Daily Yearbook;* Motion Picture Association of America, *2002 U.S. Economic Review.*

20 Top-Grossing Feature Films, 2002

Rank, Film	Distributor	Director	Gross
1. *Spider-Man*	Sony	Sam Raimi	$403,706,375
2. *Lord Of The Rings: The Two Towers*	New Line	Peter Jackson	$339,734,454
3. *Star Wars: Episode II*	Fox	George Lucas	$310,675,583
4. *Harry Potter And The Chamber Of Secrets*	Warners	Chris Columbus	$261,970,615
5. *My Big Fat Greek Wedding*	IFC Films	Joel Zwick	$241,437,427
6. *Signs*	Buena Vista	M. Night Shyamalan	$227,965,690
7. *Austin Powers In Goldmember*	New Line	Jay Roach	$213,117,789
8. *Men In Black 2*	Columbia	Barry Sonnenfeld	$190,418,803
9. *Ice Age*	Fox	Carlos Saldanha, Chris Wedge	$176,387,405
10. *Chicago*	Miramax	Rob Marshall	$170,684,505
11. *Catch Me If You Can*	Dreamworks	Steven Spielberg	$164,435,221
12. *Die Another Day*	MGM	Lee Tamahori	$160,201,106
13. *Scooby-Doo*	Warners	Raja Gosnell	$153,294,164
14. *Lilo & Stitch*	Buena Vista	Dean DeBlois, Chris Sanders	$145,771,527
15. *XXX*	Sony	Rob Cohen	$141,204,016
16. *Santa Clause 2, The*	Buena Vista	Michael Lembeck	$139,225,854
17. *Minority Report*	Fox	Steven Spielberg	$132,024,714
18. *Ring, The*	Dreamworks	Gore Verbinski	$128,579,698
19. *Sweet Home Alabama*	Buena Vista	Andy Tennant	$127,214,072
20. *Mr. Deeds*	Sony	Steven Brill	$126,293,452

Note: As of September 2003. **Source:** Exhibitor Relations Co., Inc.

Most Popular Films, By Decade

Title (Year)	Director	Rental (millions)
Pre-1930		
The Birth of a Nation (1915)	D.W. Griffith	$10.0
The Big Parade (1925)	K. Vidor	5.5
The Singing Fool (1928)	L. Bacon	4.0
1930–39		
Gone With the Wind (1939)	V. Fleming	$77.6
Snow White and the Seven Dwarfs (1937)	(Animated)	62.8
King Kong (1933)	M. Cooper	5.0
The Wizard of Oz (1939)	V. Fleming	4.5
San Francisco (1936)	W.S. Van Dyke	4.0
1940–49[1]		
Cinderella (1949)	(Animated)	$38.5
Pinocchio (1940)	(Animated)	32.9
Song of the South (1946)	H. Foster/ W. Jackson	29.2
Fantasia (1940)	(Animated)	28.5
Bambi (1942)	(Animated)	28.4
1950–59		
The Ten Commandments (1956)	C.B. DeMille	$43.0
Lady and the Tramp (1955)	(Animated)	40.2
Ben-Hur (1959)	W. Wyler	36.7
Around the World in 80 Days (1956)	M. Anderson	23.1
Sleeping Beauty (1959)	(Animated)	21.5
1960–69		
The Sound of Music (1965)	R. Wise	$79.98
Doctor Zhivago (1965)	D. Lean	60.96
Butch Cassidy and the Sundance Kid (1969)	G.R. Hill	45.95
Mary Poppins (1964)	R. Stevenson	45.00
The Graduate (1968)	M. Nichols	44.09
1970–79		
Star Wars (1977)	G. Lucas	$193.77
Jaws (1975)	S. Spielberg	129.55
Grease (1978)	R. Kleiser	96.30
The Exorcist (1973)	W. Friedkin	89.00
The Godfather (1972)	F. F. Coppola	86.30
1980–89		
E.T.—The Extra-Terrestrial (1982)	S. Spielberg	$228.17
Return of the Jedi (1983)	R. Marquand	168.19
Batman (1989)	T. Burton	150.50
The Empire Strikes Back (1980)	J. Kershner	141.67
Ghostbusters (1984)	I. Reitman	132.72
Raiders of the Lost Ark (1981)	S. Spielberg	115.60
Indiana Jones and the Last Crusade (1989)	S. Spielberg	115.50
Indiana Jones and the Temple of Doom (1984)	S. Spielberg	109.00
Beverly Hills Cop (1984)	M. Brest	108.00
Back to the Future (1985)	R. Zemeckis	105.50
1990–99		
Titanic (1997)	J. Cameron	$600.8
Star Wars: Episode One -The Phantom Menace (1999)	G. Lucas	431.1
Jurassic Park (1993)	S. Spielberg	357.1
Forrest Gump (1994)	R. Zemeckis	329.7
The Lion King (1993)	R. Allers/R. Minkoff	312.9
Independence Day (1996)	R. Emmerich	306.2
The Sixth Sense (1999)	M. Shyamalan	293.5
Home Alone (1990)	C. Columbus	285.7
Men in Black (1997)	B. Sonnenfeld	250.7
Toy Story 2 (1999)	A. Brannon	245.8

Note: Films from the 1990s are ranked according to their gross box office receipts. Films for previous decades are ranked according to film rentals, the portion of a film's box-office receipts paid by theater owners to the film's distribution company for renting the film. Figures include the U.S. and Canada. 1. All films listed for this decade were made by Disney studios and have been rereleased on a regular basis ever since. Their dominance on this chart is partly due to the fact that they are continually generating revenue.
Sources: *Variety,* Exhibitor Relations Co., Inc.

Top-Grossing Movies of All Time

Because of inflation and periodic re-releases, it is nearly impossible to compare the successes of films from different eras. What is simpler to compare is the number of people who went to see a film, regardless of when it was released, and regardless of how much they paid for their ticket. To arrive at this number, the Exhibitor Relations Co. divides domestic gross receipts by the average ticket prices for the year(s) in which the film was released. The estimated number of admissions is then multiplied by the average ticket price ($5.81 in 2002) to give an idea of what each film's domestic gross would be if it were released today. It is admittedly an imperfect measure, but it makes it quite clear that despite its $600 million gross, *Titanic* will have to be re-released several times to match the success of *Gone With the Wind*, which has made only $200 million over the years, but has been seen by 70 million more people.

Rank, Film, (Year of Release)	Estimated admissions	Inflation-adjusted domestic gross
1. *Gone With the Wind* (1939)[1]	202,044,569	$1,218,328,751
2. *Star Wars* (1977)[1]	178,119,595	1,074,061,158
3. *The Sound of Music* (1965)[1]	142,415,376[2]	858,764,717
4. *E.T. The Extra-Terrestrial* (1982)[1]	141,925,359	855,809,915
5. *The Ten Commandments* (1956)	131,000,000[2]	789,930,000
6. *Titanic* (1997)	129,201,761	779,086,618
7. *Jaws* (1975)[1]	128,078,818	772,315,271
8. *Snow White and the Seven Dwarfs* (1937)[1]	109,000,000[2]	657,270,000
9. *101 Dalmatians* (1961)[1]	99,917,251[2]	602,501,024
10. *The Empire Strikes Back* (1980)[1]	98,106,044	591,579,445

Note: As of September 2003. 1. Includes re-issues; ticket price used to calculate admissions is an average of ticket prices charged throughout the film's theatrical runs. 2. Gross estimated from the film rental, which is approximately 50 percent of the gross.
Source: Exhibitor Relations Co., Inc.

There were 1,437 multiplexes (8-15 screens) and 474 megaplexes (16 or more screens) in 2002. Only the number of megaplaxes grew in 2002, up 10 percent from 2001.

Movie Budgets

The cost of making movies has escalated dramatically in recent years. In 1988, the average price tag of a motion picture was $18.1 million. Today, that's less than the average marketing budget for a feature film. Rising actors' salaries, increased demand for special effects, and other spiraling costs drove the average cost of making a movie to a whopping $58.8 million in 2002. The cost of making a movie has skyrocketed since 1991 ($26.1 million), when the special effects of Terminator 2 were cutting edge. In addition to these production costs, studios spent an average of $30.6 million on advertising and publicity in 2001, or more than twice what they spent in 1993 ($14.1 million).

▶COMPUTER AND VIDEO GAMES

The computer and video game industry showed dramatic growth in recent years, shooting from sales of $3.7 billion in 1996 to $6.9 billion in 2002. Sales of computer games were $1.4 billion in 2002, down 0.2 percent from 2001, but video game sales shot up nearly 20 percent to $5.5 billion, resulting in overall industry growth of 8.7 percent for the year. Unit sales of computer games also declined in 2002, down 29.5 percent to 58.9 million units; but video game unit sales climbed 15 percent to 162.8 million units.

The stereotypical computer and video game player is a young male, but in 2002 women constituted 41.9 percent of the PC game-playing population and 28.5 percent of console gamers, while some 41.6 percent of PC game players and 22.7 percent of console gamers were over the age of 36. Among video game players, the best-selling game genres were action (25.1 percent) and sports (19.5 percent); computer gamers spent their money on strategy games (27.4 percent) and children's titles (15.9 percent).

Top-Selling Computer & Video Games, 2001

VIDEO GAMES

Rank, Title (Platform)	Publisher	Rating
1. Grand Theft Auto: Vice City (PS2)	Take 2	M
2. Grand Theft Auto 3 (PS2)	Take 2	M
3. Madden NFL 2003 (PS2)	EA	E
4. Super Mario Advance 2 (GBA)	Nintendo	E
5. Gran Turismo 3: A Spec (PS2)	Sony	E
6. Medal of Honor Frontline (PS2)	EA	T
7. Spider-Man (PS2)	Activision	E
8. Kingdom Hearts (PS2)	EA	E
9. Halo (XBX)	Microsoft	M
10. Super Mario Sunshine (GCN)	Nintendo	E

COMPUTER GAMES

Rank, Title (Platform)	Publisher	Rating
1. The Sims: Vacation	EA	T
2. The Sims: Unleashed	EA	T
3. Warcraft III: Reign of Chaos	Vivendi	T
4. Medal of Honor: Allied Assault	EA	T
5. The Sims	EA	T
6. The Sims: Hot Date	EA	T
7. The Sims Deluxe	EA	T
8. Zoo Tycoon	Microsoft	E
9. Harry Potter & The Sorceror's Stone	EA	E
10. Roller Coaster Tycoon 2	Hasbro	E

Note: Ranked by units sold in 2001. Platforms: GBA=Game Boy Advance; GCN=Nintendo GameCube; PS2=PlayStation2; XBX=Microsoft Xbox. Publishers: EA=Electronic Arts. Ratings: E=Everyone, suitable for age 6 and up; T=Teen, suitable for age 13 and up; M=Mature, suitable for age 17 and up.
Source: Interactive Digital Software Association, *2002 Essential Facts About the Video and Computer Game Industry*. www.idsa.com/pressroom.html.

Religion in America

▶RELIGIOUS AFFILIATION

As of 1999, approximately 168 million Americans claimed affiliation with a religious group. The vast majority of these, 158 million, claimed membership in a Christian church. The rest were Jews (5.8 million), Muslims (3 million), Buddhists, or members of other religions.

Because the U.S. Census Bureau does not ask questions about religious affiliation, all of these numbers can be regarded as educated approximations at best. Each year, the *Yearbook of American and Canadian Churches* asks more than 200 Christian religious bodies "How many members does your organization have?" The answers to these questions, which necessarily vary from denomination to denomination, are reflected in the accompanying table, which arranges Christian churches by their size and family. Denominations listed in the same family nearly always share common historical roots and some principal doctrines, but they should not be assumed to be similar in belief or practice. Denominations with 80,000 or more members are shown separately within their families.

The following are brief descriptions of each of the Christian denominational families and of major non-Christian faiths in the U.S. *(For information about religion internationally, see Part III: World Religions.)*

▶CHRISTIANITY

Roman Catholic Church

The Roman Catholic Church is the largest single Christian denomination in the United States. It claims nearly 37 percent of all religiously affiliated people—23 percent of the total population. Worldwide, there are nearly 900 million Roman Catholics (see "World Religions").

Many U.S. Catholics—descendants of immigrants from Ireland, Germany, Poland, Italy, and France—are concentrated in the Northeast and the industrial Midwest. Hispanic-Americans in Florida and the Southwest are also predominantly Catholic.

The church is hierarchically organized. Bishops, who administer church affairs in a given region, are appointed by higher authority. The world leader of the Roman church is the pope, who directs the church from Vatican City in Rome.

Priests are male and in most parts of the church must be and remain unmarried. Orders of nuns and monks provide many educational and charitable services. Many local churches operate parochial elementary schools. Regional bodies and religious orders operate high schools and help administer many seminaries and church-related colleges. In recent years the number of applicants for the priesthood and for religious orders has sharply decreased, even as membership in the church has continued to increase.

Catholic leaders have taken strong stands on many contemporary issues. The National Conference of Catholic Bishops has taken relatively liberal positions on efforts to bring about world peace and economic justice. In areas of personal conduct, the church is more conservative. It leads the campaign to outlaw abortion and opposes artificial means of birth control.

Baptist Churches

The Baptist family of churches is the largest Protestant family in the United States. Baptists trace their theological roots back to radical reformers in Europe in the 1500s, but the number of Baptists in the world was tiny until the 1800s, when Baptist faith and practice became predominant in the American South (both for whites and for blacks). Baptists are still most heavily represented in the southern and border states.

Local Baptist congregations have great independence, determining many of their own policies. At the same time, these churches share many practices. They agree that the rite of baptism should be administered only to those who have reached an age of independent judgment. Consequently, children are baptized no earlier than the age of six or seven, often by total immersion in the baptismal water. A Baptist child is not counted as a member until after baptism, which means that small children are not included in the membership totals reported above.

Most Baptists take a strong stand on the authority of the Bible, and many (though not all) believe that it should be interpreted literally. Baptists have traditionally been strong supporters of separation of church and state. Many Baptist denominations have mounted energetic missionary campaigns to bring the Christian message to people around the world.

The Southern Baptist Convention, a predominantly white church, is the largest Protestant denomination in the United States, but but has experienced division within its membership in recent years. The split, involving a moderate minority, was sparked by reluctance to accept the increasingly conservative church leadership's insistence that the Bible be interpreted literally and that women submit to their husbands and be barred from serving as pastors. As of September 2002, conventions had been organized by liberal and moderate Baptists to compete with mainstream state conventions in Missouri, Texas and Virginia..

The two National Baptist Conventions and the Progressive National Baptist Convention are predominantly black churches. Together they account for the religious affiliation of more blacks than any other family of churches.

Methodist Churches

Methodist churches trace their origins to John Wesley (1703-91), a minister in the Church of England who sought to bring a new sense of warmth and commitment to individuals' religious life. He urged his followers to set aside regular times to study the Bible and pray together. Wesley's opponents laughingly called his followers Methodists because of their discipline and seriousness. Wesley himself remained in the Church of England his whole life, but his followers began to develop independent organizations, both in England and the United States.

On the American frontier, Methodist "circuit riders" traveled from settlement to settlement, preaching and marrying, baptizing and burying members of pioneer families. Methodism grew with astonishing swiftness. By 1820 it was the largest religious family in the United States, and it remained the largest Protestant family until the 1920s.

The United Methodist Church accounts for nearly two-thirds of the Methodist family's total membership. This denomination is made up of not only traditional Methodists but also several churches of German origin whose beliefs and spirit accorded well with Methodism. The two "African" churches and the Christian Methodist Church are predominantly black churches, and they account for nearly all of the remaining third of the Methodist group.

Lutheran Churches

Lutherans trace their churches back to the German reformer Martin Luther (1483-1546). Luther sought to reform the doctrine and practice of the Roman Christian Church in Europe. He complained about corruption among the clergy and advocated worship in the language of the people rather than in Latin. He also came to favor a married, rather than a celibate, clergy. The Church of Rome considered Luther disloyal and eventually drove him out. He then helped establish independent churches in northern Germany.

Immigrants from Germany and Scandinavia brought the Lutheran faith to North America, concentrating first in Pennsylvania. Later immigrants settled in the upper Midwest. By 1900 scores of small Lutheran church bodies were divided from one another by language, theology, and degree of assimilation into American society. The Evangelical Lutheran Church in America represents a uniting of many of those earlier churches. The Lutheran Church-Missouri Synod, a national church despite its name, is more conservative theologically.

In July 2000, the Evangelical Lutheran Church announced a historic alliance with the Episcopal Church. The alliance, "Called to Common Mission," could play a significant role in helping both churches stem declines in membership.

Pentecostal Churches

The Pentecostal churches share a belief that God grants believers special spiritual gifts—especially the experience called "speaking in tongues," a common feature of Pentecostal services.

Pentecostal churches trace their origin to the day of Pentecost, described in the biblical book of Acts, when early Christians received ecstatic or mystical powers. Modern Pentecostalism began in the early 1900s, when members of some Holiness churches received the gift of tongues (see "Holiness Churches").

Pentecostal congregations tend to be small. They may meet in storefronts or in rented quarters on upper floors. Yet the Pentecostal faith, with its immediacy and emotional power, is perhaps the fastest-growing in the nation, attracting thousands of new adherents each year. In addition, Pentecostal beliefs have had an impact on Roman Catholic, Lutheran, Episcopal, and other denominations. These denominations report a growth among adherents of "charismatic renewal," a movement based on spiritual gifts.

The two Churches of God in Christ and the United Pentecostal Church are predominantly black denominations. The Assemblies of God is the largest predominantly white denomination. Many Pentecostal organizations are regional or purely local. Because of this loose organization, there are likely to be thousands of Pentecostal believers not counted here because their local congregations are not affiliated with a regional or national group.

Reformed Churches

Reformed churches trace their descent to the French-Swiss reformer John Calvin (1509-64). These churches were especially significant in the early settlement of the present-day United States. The Pilgrims and Puritans who settled in New England established the Congregational church, which is a main component of today's United Church of Christ. New York was settled by the Dutch, who established the present-day Reformed Church in America. Later, immigrants of Scottish and Scotch-Irish descent established a strong Presbyterian church. Presbyterians differed from Congregationalists in matters of church governance but shared many points of theology and practice.

Reformed church buildings are generally simple and sparsely adorned. Similarly, worship in these churches is austere and simple. Reformed churches generally value a well-educated clergy. In the past they helped found Harvard, Yale, and Princeton. Direct ties to these universities have ended, but Reformed organizations still support many colleges.

The Presbyterian Church (USA) is the result of several mergers between smaller Presbyterian churches that had been separated by regional and doctrinal differences. The United Church of Christ includes, in addition to Congregational churches, descendants of German Reformed churches and of the Evangelical and Reformed Church (also of German descent). The Reformed Church in America and the Christian Reformed Church are both of Dutch descent.

Orthodox Churches

The first great schism in the Christian church occurred in A.D.1054 between the Western church, centered at Rome, and the Eastern church, centered at Constantinople (present-day Istanbul). In 1054 Eastern Christianity was predominant in Greece and the Middle East, and missionaries had already introduced the faith in Russia. The Russian church celebrated its 1,000th anniversary in 1988. Immigrants from these countries brought Orthodox churches to the United States.

The two largest Orthodox churches in the U.S. today are Greek and Russian, respectively. The next largest represent Armenians and Syrians. Together these four churches have more than 80 percent of the Orthodox membership.

Orthodox churches are organized hierarchically. Archbishops and bishops possess special spiritual authority and administer church affairs. Religious observances tend to be solemn and elaborate. Ancient liturgies in the ancient languages have been carefully preserved. Orthodox clergy are male, and in most churches they are allowed to marry. Because of differences in calculating feast days, Easter and other movable feasts may occur on different dates in the Orthodox Church than in the Western churches.

In the U.S., many Orthodox churches have served as cultural centers for immigrants seeking to preserve their own ethnic heritage. At the same time, however, many denominations are active members of ecumenical groups such as the National Council of Churches.

Latter-day Saints (Mormons)

The Church of Jesus Christ of Latter-day Saints, known popularly as the Mormon church, was "established anew," according to Mormon doctrine, on Apr. 6, 1830, by a 19th-century American prophet named Joseph Smith (1805-44). Smith, who grew up in western New York State, reported direct revelations from God. The Book of Mormon, which Smith said he translated, tells of a visit by the resurrected Jesus Christ to pre-Columbian America.

Smith assembled a community of believers that settled first in western New York and later in Ohio, Missouri, and Illinois. Wherever they went, the Mormons aroused the antagonism of neighboring non-Mormons, in part because Mormons allowed men to take more than one wife. Persecution peaked with the murder of Smith himself in 1844.

The next great leader of the church was Brigham Young (1801-77), who led the majority of Mormons westward to settle in the then-uninhabited basin by the Great Salt Lake. There the church grew and prospered. To this day, the majority of religiously affiliated people in Utah are Mormons. There are also many adherents in surrounding states, especially Colorado and Idaho.

Most of the church's 10 million-plus members live in the United States, but the Mormons' legendary missionary work goes on around the globe. Since about 1900, the church has encouraged converts to stay in their own countries and organize congregations there. The National Council of Churches reports that in 2000 the Church of Jesus Christ of Latter-day Saints became the fifth largest church in the U.S., displacing the Evangelical Lutheran Church in America.

The Reorganized Church is the largest of the groups that did not make the trek to the Great Salt Lake. Its headquarters are in Independence, Missouri, which Smith had designated as the site of a great future temple. Members of the Reorganized Church do not consider themselves Mormons.

Christian Churches and Churches of Christ

This family of churches traces its origins to a great religious awakening in 1800 on the Pennsylvania and Kentucky frontiers. Discouraged by sectarian competition among Methodists, Presbyterians, and others, leaders of the revival did not seek to form a denomination but to reestablish a single nondenominational Christian church. In time they became a denomination themselves.

In the 1870s the Churches of Christ and the Christian Church (Disciples) split over questions of using musical instruments in worship and over the issue of centralizing some church functions. The Churches of Christ opposed both instrumental music and national organization. The Disciples allowed instrumental music and established a central missionary board to coordinate mission work. They are ecumenically minded and have a long history of cooperation and discussion with other denominations.

The third group, the Christian churches and Churches of Christ, split from the Disciples in the 1920s–30s. They allow instrumental music but are theologically more conservative than the Disciples.

Episcopal Family of Churches

The Episcopal churches are descendants of the Church of England, which was established as a separate church by King Henry VIII in 1534. Churches descending from the English church make up the worldwide Anglican Communion. The American church takes its name from the word *bishop*, which suggests its hierarchical organization.

In colonial times the Church of England was established in the southern colonies and had some influence in the middle colonies, but was not welcome in New England, where Reformed churches were predominant. During the American Revolution, most Church of England members and clergy remained loyal to England. Thousands migrated to Canada. Those who remained were under suspicion, and some were persecuted. The church almost ceased to function.

After the Revolution, a small group of Anglicans loyal to the United States gradually revived the church. It never grew as rapidly as the Methodist and Baptist families, but it did gain considerable influence. Especially in eastern cities, many families of wealth and power were Episcopalian.

The Episcopal Church accommodates a wide spectrum of belief and practice. It is usually considered Protestant and shares much with other Protestant denominations, yet its worship services retain much of pre-Reformation Catholic tradition. One wing of the church retains a strong emphasis on the church's Catholic heritage. In July 2000, the Episcopal Church announced an alliance with the Evangelical Lutheran Church.

Holiness Churches

The Holiness churches grew from a religious revival in the late 1800s, primarily in Methodist congregations. The originators of the movement objected to the excessive bureaucracy of established denominations and sought to refocus attention on the need for deep personal change. They placed great emphasis on the teachings of Methodism's founder, John Wesley, that those who are saved may aspire to the gift of complete sanctification, or holiness.

Around 1900, groups of especially intense Holiness worshipers began experiencing further "gifts of the Spirit." From these experiences grew the first Pentecostal churches with their emphasis on speaking in tongues. Many who began as adherents of Holiness churches became Pentacostalists. The Holiness churches rejected Pentecostal worship as extremist.

Jehovah's Witnesses

Jehovah's Witnesses are a remarkably active and dynamic sect, visible to most from street-corner or door-to-door encounters. They were founded by Charles Taze Russell (1852–1916) in western Pennsylvania in the 1870s. The Witnesses preach a slightly unorthodox form of the Christian message and look intently for the end of the present world. They claim three million members worldwide, of whom about a quarter live in the U.S.

Church of Christ, Scientist

Christian Scientists, as adherents are often known, follow the teaching of Mary Baker Eddy (1821–1910), who founded the church in 1879 in Boston and wrote *Science and Health with a Key to the Scriptures*, which remains a major sourcebook for the church. Christian Science asserts that sickness and other adversities exist only in the mind and that disciplined spiritual thinking can correct them. Thus, Christian Scientists refuse most or all medical treatment. Christian Science practitioners help adherents deal with illness but do not serve as clergy. The church operates many reading rooms open to the public.

The Adventist Family of Churches

Adventist churches sprang up in the U.S. in the 1840s with a wave of concern about prophecies of the end of the world. Adventists anticipate and prepare for the world's end and the second coming of Jesus Christ. The largest Adventist group, the Seventh-day Adventists, is one of the most dynamic religious groups in the world today, claiming a worldwide membership of five million and a growth rate of more than 7 percent annually. As their name suggests, they worship on Saturday rather than Sunday. They operate parochial schools, colleges, medical schools, and hospitals.

The Salvation Army

The Salvation Army is familiar to outsiders through its work among the homeless and the poor and its fund-raising on the streets, especially before Christmas. The church, which originated in England in 1865, is organized in quasi-military style, and many of its members devote their lives to its service.

Roman Rite Churches

The Roman Rite churches are those that have split from the Roman Catholic Church in recent times but have maintained many of its rituals and doctrines. The Polish church was established in Scranton, Pennsylvania, in the 1890s by church leaders of Polish descent. The Old Catholic churches had their origin in Europe after 1870.

Mennonite Churches

Mennonites trace their roots to a small group of Christians after 1530 who sought a reformation even more radical than those advocated by Lutherans and Calvinists. They were called Mennonites after Menno Simons (1469-1561), one of their early leaders. Their most distinctive practice is adult baptism, offered only to those who have made a decision to follow Christ's teachings.

Because they would not swear oaths and would not bear arms in the service of their temporal leaders, Mennonites were severely persecuted. Small bands were scattered to many corners of the world. Some settled in Pennsylvania beginning in the late 1600s. In the 1870s other groups arrived from Russia. Today more that 40 percent of the world's Mennonites live in the U.S. The next-largest group (estimated to be 150,000) lives in the nations of the former Soviet Union. In recent times Mennonites have become well known for their world relief work.

The Amish are groups with Mennonite beliefs who seek to remain quite aloof from the surrounding culture. The Old Order Amish, centered in Pennsylvania, wear "plain" clothing and still drive horses and buggies rather than automobiles.

Christian Churches in the United States by Size and Family

Family/Denomination	Local congregations	Total clergy	Total membership
Total Christian Churches	**349,506**	**534,913**	**158,294,022**
Roman Catholic Church	**19,584**	**47,199**	**62,018,436**
Baptist Churches	**64,026**	**123,249**	**28,293,420**
Southern Baptist Convention	40,870	97,783	15,729,356
National Baptist Convention, USA Inc.	N.A.	N.A.	N.A.
National Baptist Convention of America	2,500	N.A.	3,500,000
Progressive National Baptist Convention Inc.	2,000	N.A.	2,500,000
National Missionary Baptist Convention of America	N.A.	N.A.	2,500,000
American Baptist Churches in the USA	3,800	7,846	1,507,400
Baptist Bible Fellowship International	4,500	7,500	1,200,000
Baptist Missionary Association of America	1,334	3,055	234,732
National Association of Free Will Baptists	2,297	2,900	210,461
Conservative Baptist Association of America	236	541	38,996
Baptist General Conference	876	N.A.	141,445
General Association of Regular Baptist Churches	1,415	N.A.	101,854
Other (7 denominations)	4,198	3,624	599,176
Methodist Churches	**50,840**	**15,809**	**13,090,542**
United Methodist Church	36,170	N.A.	8,400,000
African Methodist Episcopal Church	6,200	8,000	2,500,000
African Methodist Episcopal Zion Church	3,098	2,767	1,252,369
Christian Methodist Episcopal Church	2,340	N.A.	718,922
Wesleyan Church	1,590	3,144	119,914
Other (6 denominations)	1,442	1,898	99,337
Pentecostal Churches	**47,575**	**92,794**	**11,326,188**
Church of God in Christ	15,300	33,593	5,499,875
Assemblies of God	11,937	32,337	2,525,812
Pentecostal Assemblies of the World	1,750	4,500	1,500,000
Church of God (Cleveland, Tenn.)	6,060	5,556	753,230
International Church of the Foursquare Gospel	1,851	7,300	238,065
Full Gospel Fellowship of Churches and Ministers Intl.	896	2,424	275,200
International Pentecostal Holiness Church	1,716	1,936	176,846
Pentecostal Church of God	1,237	1,802	104,300
Other (11 denominations)	6,828	3,346	252,860
Lutheran Churches	**19,224**	**28,642**	**8,316,331**
Evangelical Lutheran Church in America	10,862	17,589	5,178,225
Lutheran Church-Missouri Synod	6,218	8,316	2,594,404
Wisconsin Evangelical Lutheran Synod	1,240	1,648	411,295
Other (9 denominations)	904	1,089	132,407
Latter-day Saints Churches	**12,110**	**55,999**	**5,066,052**
Church of Jesus Christ of Latter-day Saints	10,811	36,418	4,923,100
Reorganized Church of Jesus Christ of Latter-day Saints	1,236	19,319	140,245
Church of Jesus Christ (Bickertonites)	63	262	2,707
Orthodox (Eastern) Churches	**2,040**	**2,800**	**4,013,497**
Orthodox Church in America	625	785	1,000,000
Greek Orthodox Archdiocese of North & South America	532	806	1,954,500
Diocese of the Armenian Church of America	72	70	414,000
Coptic Orthodox Church	85	68	180,000
Armenian Apostolic Church of America	28	31	200,000
Other (11 denominations)	698	1,040	264,997
Churches of Christ	**24,397**	**23,616**	**3,451,052**
Churches of Christ	15,000	16,350	1,500,000
Christian Churches and Churches of Christ	5,579	N.A.	1,071,616
Christian Church (Disciples of Christ)	3,818	7,266	879,436
Presbyterian Churches	**14,444**	**26,265**	**4,114,350**
Presbyterian Church (USA)	11,260	20,940	3,574,959
Presbyterian Church in America	1,340	2,665	279,549
Cumberland Presbyterian Church	774	835	87,198
Other (6 denominations)	1,070	1,825	172,644

Family/Denomination	Local congregations	Total clergy	Total membership
Episcopal Church	**7,390**	**14,925**	**2,364,559**
Reformed Churches	**7,894**	**13,523**	**1,948,167**
United Church of Christ	6,017	10,303	1,421,088
Reformed Church in America	902	1,784	295,651
Christian Reformed Church in North America	733	1,148	199,290
Other (5 denominations)	242	288	32,138
Jehovah's Witnesses	**11,064**	**N.A.**	**1,040,283**
Adventist Churches	**4,720**	**5,475**	**866,081**
Seventh-Day Adventists	4,405	5,044	839,915
Other (2 denominations)	315	431	26,166
Church of the Nazarene	**5,101**	**9,998**	**627,054**
Salvation Army	**1,388**	**5,248**	**471,416**
Mennonite Churches	**2,763**	**7,636**	**316,267**
Mennonite Church	926	2,688	92,161
General Conference of Mennonite Brethren Churches	368	N.A.	82,130
Old Order Amish Church	898	3,617	80,820
Other (5 denominations)	571	1,331	61,156
Christian and Missionary Alliance	**1,964**	**2,535**	**345,664**
Churches of God	**2,900**	**5,985**	**277,255**
Church of God (Anderson, Ind.)	2,353	5,468	234,311
Other (3 denominations)	547	517	42,944
International Council of Community Churches	**150**	**263**	**250,000**
Evangelical Free Church of America	**1,224**	**2,436**	**242,619**
Brethren Churches	**2,421**	**4,311**	**280,411**
Church of the Brethren	1,095	1,945	141,400
Other (7 denominations	1,326	2,366	139,011
Friends (Quaker) Churches	**2,413**	**552**	**186,280**
Religious Society of Friends (Conservative)	1,200	N.A.	104,000
Other (3 denominations)	1,213	552	82,280
Christian Congregation	**1,438**	**1,438**	**117,039**
Christian Brethren	**1,150**	**500**	**100,000**
Evangelical Covenant Church	**628**	**1,177**	**96,552**
Moravian Church in America	**94**	**177**	**26,641**
Church of Christ, Scientist	**2,200**	**N.A.**	**N.A.**
Other Christian Churches (39 denominations)	**5,297**	**8,152**	**480,479**

Note: Congregation, clergy and membership totals (in bold) do not include figures for denominations not reporting. **Source:** *2000 Yearbook of American and Canadian Churches.*

Christian Denominations in the U.S., 1999

The 30 largest churches in the U.S. (by membership) comprise almost 90 percent of all Christian church membership. But because not all churches report membership figures to the Yearbook of American and Canadian Churches every year, these figures must be considered an approximation at best.

Denomination	Membership, 1999	Percent of total
Roman Catholic Church	62,018,436	39.17%
Southern Baptist Convention	15,729,356	9.93
The United Methodist Church	8,400,000	5.30
Church of God in Christ	5,499,875	3.47
Evangelical Lutheran Church in America	5,178,225	3.27
Church of Jesus Christ of Latter-day Saints	4,923,100	3.11
Presbyterian Church (U.S.A.)	3,574,959	2.25
National Baptist Convention of America, Inc.	3,500,000	2.21
The Lutheran Church - Missouri Synod	2,594,404	1.63
Assemblies of God	2,525,812	1.59
African Methodist Episcopal Church	2,500,000	1.57
National Missionary Baptist Convention of America	2,500,000	1.57
Progressive National Baptist Convention, Inc.	2,500,000	1.57
Episcopal Church	2,364,559	1.49
Greek Orthodox Archdiocese of North and South America	1,954,500	1.23
American Baptist Churches in the U.S.A.	1,507,400	0.95%
Churches of Christ	1,500,000	0.94
Pentecostal Assemblies of the World	1,500,000	0.94
United Church of Christ	1,421,088	0.89
African Methodist Episcopal Zion Church	1,252,369	0.79
Baptist Bible Fellowship International	1,200,000	0.75
Christian Churches and Churches of Christ	1,071,616	0.67
Jehovah's Witnesses	1,040,283	0.65
Orthodox Church in America	1,000,000	0.63
Christian Church (Disciples of Christ)	879,436	0.55
Seventh-day Adventists	839,915	0.53
Church of God (Cleveland, Tenn.)	753,230	0.47
Christian Methodist Episcopal Church	718,922	0.45
Church of the Nazarene	627,054	0.39
The Salvation Army	471,416	0.29

Source: *2000 Yearbook of American and Canadian Churches.*

Churches of the Brethren

The Brethren, founded as a dissenting group in Germany in the early 1700s, immigrated to Pennsylvania in the 1720s to escape persecution. There they have remained. Brethren share many doctrinal points with their neighbors, the Mennonites. They practice adult baptism, refuse to swear oaths, and will not serve as combatants in war. The various Brethren denominations agree in basic theology but differ on less significant matters of interpretation.

Unitarian Universalist Association

Unitarianism was an outgrowth of New England Congregationalism in the late 1700s and early 1800s. Unitarians asserted God's unity and repudiated the doctrine of the Trinity. They also interpreted other Christian beliefs in a liberal, figurative manner. Universalism was a separate movement emphasizing the availability of God's care to all people, not only to a small chosen group. In 1961 Unitarian and Universalist organizations merged.

Friends (Quaker) Churches

Known popularly as Quakers, the Friends were established by the English religious mystic George Fox (1624–91) in the mid-1600s. They were persecuted in England for refusing to take oaths or to serve as combatants in war. Under the protection of William Penn (1644–1718), many settled in Pennsylvania. According to Fox, they were called Quakers because they were admonished to "tremble at the word of the Lord." In Pennsylvania the Quakers set themselves apart, dressing plainly and avoiding worldly amusements. In Philadelphia they became influential business people.

The most distinctive doctrine of the Friends is that of the Inner Light, the spark of God in each individual. Friends have avoided setting up formal church structures, and many groups have no clergy. Friends have organized remarkable world relief and peace organizations, by which they are perhaps best known to outsiders.

Other Christian Churches

Among the other denominations reported by the *Yearbook of American and Canadian Churches,* there is a wide variety of religious belief and practice. Many of the groups are radically congregational, making generalizations risky. Other groups are heterodox offshoots from the Pentecostal family. In many cases they depend on a single strong leader. The smallest denominations listed may actually be a single local congregation that reports as a separate church body.

Among the miscellaneous groups are spiritualist and other "New Age" groups. Some of these mix spiritualism with Christianity; others may not consider themselves Christian in any sense.

▶JUDAISM

Judaism is the largest non-Christian religious family in the United States. Jewish organizations report that there are 5.8 million American Jews. Of these, perhaps 3.8 million are religiously affiliated or observant. The remaining two million consider their Judaism to be more ethnic or cultural than religious.

As descendants of the Jews of biblical times, Jews worship one God and follow the religious precepts in the Hebrew scriptures, the writings called the Old Testament by Christians. Jews recognize Jesus as a religious teacher but do not acknowledge him as the Messiah or Son of God. Jews still await the coming of the Messiah as foretold by the prophets.

A handful of Jews arrived in North America in the 1600s. In the 1800s, Jews from Germany arrived with other immigrants. Then between 1890 and 1920, several million Jews arrived from eastern Europe, fleeing persecution and hard times in Russia and Poland. In the 1930s and 1940s, Jews reached America as refugees from the Nazi extermination campaigns. The slaughter of some six million Jews by the Germans, called the Holocaust, is one of two central facts of modern Jewish experience. The second is the establishment of Israel as an independent state in 1948. Today more Jews live in Israel than in any other country except the U.S.

There are three main branches of religious Judaism in the U.S. today: Orthodox, Reform, and Conservative. Orthodox Judaism is by far the most rigorous and smallest of the three branches, with an estimated 400,000 adherents. Orthodox Jews may keep entirely separate kitchens for milk and meat, refuse to operate electric and mechanical devices on the Sabbath, and often attend temple services or hold prayer sessions every day. Orthodox services are conducted in Hebrew, and require men and women to pray separately, even when not in temple. Many orthodox communities, especially self-contained communities such as the Hasidic Jews (located mainly in New York), impose strict dress codes, dictating not only the clothes, but also the hairstyles of their members.

Reform Judaism is the least strict branch. It flowered in the U.S. in the late 1800s, especially among immigrants from Germany. Reform Jews do not generally wear yarmulkes, don't usually observe the kosher dietary laws, and conduct their religious services primarily in English (though most of the prayers are recited in Hebrew). About 1.4 million Jews are affiliated with Reform temples.

Conservative Judaism rose in response to the Reform movement. It sought to preserve more of the ancient observances of the old orthodoxy, but without losing touch with American culture and behavior. As a middle road between Reform and Orthodox Judaism, Conservative Judaism has gained many adherents. About two million Jews are affiliated with Conservative institutions.

▶ISLAM

The Islamic faith, whose followers are called Muslims, is one of the three great theistic world religions, along with Judaism and Christianity. The first sizable group of Muslims arrived in the U.S. from Lebanon in the early 1900s. Later waves of immigration have brought Pakistanis, Indians, Arabs, and Iranians, among others.

There are about 1,200 mosques in the U.S. but membership estimates vary greatly, in part because many Muslims are new immigrants or recent converts. Some Muslim groups claim as many as six or seven million American Muslims; surveys conducted by academics and other church associations yield estimates between one and three million. Regardless of overall numbers, most Muslims are in cities in the Northeast and industrial Midwest. Observances may vary from one center to another, depending on the nationality of its adherents and their length of residence in the United States. In general, recent immigrants are more conservative and follow Islamic ritual and custom more closely.

▶BUDDHIST CHURCHES OF AMERICA

The Buddhist Churches of America is the oldest and largest U.S. Buddhist group. It represents the Jodo Shinshu sect of Buddhism, and many of its members are of Japanese descent. There are many other Buddhist organizations in the U.S., and there may be as many as 500,000 additional Americans who subscribe to Buddhist tenets.

Transportation

Americans spend more than $1 trillion annually on transportation products and services. Transportation expenditures (which include personal and governmental spending on motor vehicles and parts, gasoline and oil, airfares, and public transportation) accounted for 10.8 percent of gross domestic product in 2000, about the same as what the country spent on food, and much more than it spent on education. In 2000, the United States recorded 4.4 trillion passenger miles of travel and nearly 4 trillion revenue ton-miles of freight traffic. More than 200 million vehicles (most of them cars) were involved in domestic transportation, using nearly 200 billion gallons of fuel, and causing more than 40,000 fatalities.

The government has traditionally played a leading role in the development of the nation's trans-

Passenger Miles and Ton-Miles of Freight, by Mode of Transportation, 1970–2000 (numbers in millions)

Mode of transport	1970	1980	1990	1999	2000
Passenger miles, total[1]	**2,042,002**	**2,653,510**	**3,561,209**	**4,304,270**	**4,394,703**
Air carrier[2]	108,442	204,368	345,873	488,357	516,129
General aviation, intercity	9,100	14,700	13,000	13,500	N.A.
Highway:					
Passenger car and motorcycle	1,754,174	2,024,246	2,293,815	2,506,512	2,558,571
Truck	62,215	108,491	146,242	202,688	205,791
Transit	4,592	39,854	41,143	45,857	47,666
Amtrak	6,179	4,503	6,057	5,330	5,498
Ton-miles of freight, total	**2,207,000**	**2,989,000**	**3,196,000**	**3,814,000**	**N.A.**
Air carrier[3]	2,709	4,528	9,064	14,202	14,983
Intercity trucks	412,000	555,000	735,000	1,093,000	N.A.
Class I rail	764,809	918,958	1,033,969	1,433,461	1,465,960
Water transport	596,195	921,836	833,544	655,682	645,799
Oil pipeline	431,000	588,200	584,100	617,700	577,300

1. Includes mileage not shown separately. 2. Domestic, all services. 3. Includes revenue ton-miles, U.S. and foreign mail, and express, as reported on AIM Form 41. **Source:** U.S. Dept. of Transportation, *National Transportation Statistics 2002* (2003).

Number of Vehicles in the U.S., 1970–2000

Mode of Transport	1970	1980	1990	1999	2000
Air, total	**134,422**	**205,305**	**204,083**	**227,692**	**225,588**
Air carrier, certificated, all services	2,679	3,808	6,083	8,228	8,055
General aviation	131,743	211,045	198,000	219,464	217,533
Highway, total[1]	**111,242,295**	**161,490,159**	**193,057,376**	**220,461,056**	**225,821,841**
Passenger car & motorcycle	92,067,655	127,294,783	137,959,958	136,584,477	137,967,488
Other 2-axle 4-tired vehicle	14,210,591	27,875,934	48,274,555	75,356,376	79,084,979
Truck, total	4,586,487	5,790,473	6,195,876	7,791,426	8,022,649
Intercity bus	377,562	528,789	626,987	728,777	746,125
Local transit, total[2]	**61,298**	**75,388**	**92,961**	**128,516**	**131,493**
Motor bus	49,700	59,411	58,714	74,228	75,013
Light rail	1,262	1,013	913	1,297	1,577
Heavy rail	9,286	9,641	10,419	10,306	10,591
Trolley bus	1,050	823	832	859	951
Commuter rail	—	4,500	4,415	4,883	5,073
Demand response	—	—	16,471	31,884	33,080
Other	—	—	1,197	5,059	5,208
Rail, total[3]	**1,450,998**	**1,198,755**	**679,918**	**601,727**	
Class I Freight cars	1,423,921	1,168,114	658,902	579,140	560,154
Class I Locomotives	27,077	28,094	18,835	20,256	20,028
Amtrak[4]	—	2,547	2,181	2,331	2,272
Water transport, total	**5,155,716**	**8,817,509**	**11,036,334**	**12,780,500**	**12,823,951**
Non self-propelled vessels	19,337	31,662	31,209	33,387	33,152
Self-propelled vessels	6,455	7,126	8,236	8,379	8,202
Oceangoing ships[5]	1,579	864	636	463	454
Recreational boats	5,128,345	8,777,857	10,996,253	12,738,271	12,782,143

1. Registered vehicles. 2. Prior to 1984, excludes most rural and smaller transit systems. 3. Does not includes non-Class I freight cars or shippers' freight cars. 4. Includes passenger cars and locomotives. 5. Vessels 1,000 gross tons and over.
Source: U.S. Dept. of Transportation, *National Transportation Statistics 2002* (2003).

portation infrastructure. Technological, economic, and demographic changes all shape the government's priorities. In the 19th and early 20th centuries, for instance, the government made enormous direct and indirect contributions to the development of the nation's railroads. Today, the government spends vastly more on highways and aviation than on mass transit, railroad transportation or water transportation.

▶PASSENGER TRAVEL

In order to compare the costs of different modes of transportation, statisticians calculate the cost of carrying one passenger one mile. For modes of transportation that carry large numbers of passengers at once, these numbers are remarkably similar. It costs about 14 cents to carry a coach passenger one mile by plane, 15 cents by commuter rail, 18 cents by Amtrak, and 13 by intercity bus. By comparison, the average cost of operating a car in 2001 (including variable costs for gas and oil, maintenance and tires, and fixed costs for insurance, registration, depreciation and finance charges) was 50.2 cents per mile (down slightly from a high of 51 cents in 2000). The average fare in 2000 was $121 for an airline seat, $46 for a ride on Amtrak, $29 for an inter-city bus ticket, and $3.33 for a commuter rail trip. Fares are more than twice as high as they were in 1980 for all modes of transportation except flying. Airfares have risen 43 percent since 1980, and the average trip is now 824 miles by air (up from 791 in 1995), 248 miles on Amtrak, 143 miles by inter-city bus, and 23 miles by commuter rail.

World Motor Vehicle Production 2002

Country	Passenger cars	Commercial vehicles	Total vehicles
Australia	307,064	36,999	344,063
Belgium	936,903	119,414	1,056,317
Brazil	1,521,431	271,229	1,792,660
Canada	1,369,042	1,260,395	2,629,437
China	1,090,820	2,160,405	3,251,225
Czech Republic	441,312	5,765	447,077
France	3,283,775	408,963	3,692,738
Germany	4,798,643	346,071	5,144,714
India	706,061	185,885	891,946
Indonesia	231,670	47,517	279,187
Italy	1,125,768	301,179	1,426,947
Japan	8,618,728	1,638,962	10,257,690
Korea, South	2,651,273	496,311	3,147,584
Mexico	960,097	844,573	1,804,670
Poland	286,656	23,077	309,733
Portugal	182,573	68,259	250,832
Russia	980,736	238,898	1,219,634
South Africa	276,499	127,942	404,441
Spain	2,266,902	588,337	2,855,239
Sweden	237,975	38,218	276,193
Taiwan	245,000	91,699	336,699
Turkey	204,198	142,367	346,565
U.K.	1,628,020	193,064	1,821,084
U.S.	5,018,777	7,260,805	12,279,582
Total[1]	**41,215,063**	**17,757,439**	**58,972,502**

1. Includes other countries not shown separately. **Source:** Ward's Communications, *Ward's Motor Vehicle Facts & Figures, 2003.*

▶TRANSPORTATION SAFETY

Because they kill large numbers of people at once, plane crashes attract much more attention than do automobile accidents. But over the course of a year, air travel accounts for only a tiny percentage of transportation fatalities; in a typical year, more people die in boating accidents than in aviation mishaps. Between 1998 and 2000, the nation's major commercial carriers experienced a grand total of 105 fatalities; commuter airlines were responsible for 17 deaths over this period. The combined

Traffic Deaths by Selected Country, 1995-2001

Country	Deaths per 100,000 registered vehicles 1995	2000	2001
Austria	27.7	22.0	21.1
Belgium	30.5	27.1	27.6
Canada	20.1	16.9	16.4
China	N.A.	530.0	404.3
Denmark	28.9	22.3	18.6
Finland	20.2	18.0	17.5
France	27.8	22.3	21.8
Germany	21.7	17.9	14.5
Hungary	N.A.	51.1	44.0
Italy	19.8	18.9	17.9
Japan	16.0	12.4	11.9
Netherlands	21.2	16.1	14.1
Norway	14.8	14.7	11.7
Poland	175.3	53.1	51.0
Portugal	61.1	39.2	34.0
Spain	N.A.	29.4	25.9
Sweden	13.1	13.5	12.5
Switzerland	19.6	15.4	13.8
Turkey	148.6	84.1	48.2
U.K.	13.5	14.8	11.0
U.S.	21.5	19.5	18.1

Source: Ward's Communications, *Ward's Motor Vehicle Facts & Figures, 2003.*

World Motor Vehicle Production, 1950–2002 (numbers in thousands)

Year	United States	Canada	Europe	Japan	Other	World total	U.S. share of total
1950	8,006	388	1,991	32	160	10,577	75.7%
1960	7,905	398	6,837	482	866	16,488	47.9
1970	8,284	1,160	13,049	5,289	1,637	29,419	28.2
1980	8,010	1,324	15,496	11,043	2,692	38,565	20.8
1985	11,653	1,933	16,113	12,271	2,939	44,909	25.9
1990	9,783	1,928	18,866	13,487	4,496	48,554	20.1
1995	11,985	2,408	17,045	10,196	8,349	49,983	24.0
2000	12,771	2,962	17,161	10,145	14,490	57,528	22.2
2001	11,425	2,532	17,840	9,777	15,006	56,068	20.4
2002	12,280	2,629	17,295	10,258	16,511	58,973	20.8

Source: Ward's Communications, *Ward's Motor Vehicle Facts & Figures, 2003.*

total is approximately equal to the number of people killed each day in automobile accidents.

More than 90 percent of transportation fatalities and 99 percent of transportation injuries are a result of automobile accidents. In 2001, the latest year available, there were 6,322,896 automobile accidents, resulting in 3,032,672 injuries and 42,116 fatalities. Despite safety improvements to the production of automobiles, wider highway lanes, better lighting and lower speed limits, the annual number of automobile accidents, injuries and fatalities have not changed much since 1970. But over the same period, the number of miles traveled has more than doubled (from one trillion miles in 1970 to nearly 2.8 trillion miles in 2001), indicating that Americans are driving more miles without having any more accidents.

What has changed, though, is the number of accidents involving light trucks, minivans and sport-utility vehicles. Fewer than 4,000 crashes occurred between these vehicles and regular passenger cars in 1987; in 1995, there were 5,426. When someone is killed in such a crash, four out of five times it's the person in the car.

Another change is the number of people killed in accidents involving drunk drivers. In 1985, 23,167 people, or 52 percent of the total, died in alcohol-related auto accidents. In 2001, the total number of fatalities was about the same, but only 17,448, or 41 percent, involved a drunk driver. The number of non-motorists (pedestrians and cyclists) killed in auto accidents also decreased between 1985 and 2001, from 7,782 to 5,730.

▶MOTOR VEHICLES

Although the accompanying table would suggest that the average fuel efficiency of U.S. cars is on the rise, the statistics mask the explosion in the number of light trucks, minivans and sport utility vehicles favored by so many American drivers of the 1990s. These vehicles get much poorer gas mileage than most cars, but because they are classified as trucks, they are not held to the same fuel efficiency standards as cars. In 1980, over 80 percent of all new vehicles were cars (9.1 million), with an average fuel efficiency of 23 miles per gallon. In comparison, there were only 2.2 million new trucks, which got 18 miles per gallon. But 2001 sales figures told a different story. The number of cars sold had dropped to 8.4 million, while the number of gas-guzzling pickups, minivans and sport utility vehicles had quadrupled, to 9 million. Thus, despite government attempts to mandate improved fuel efficiency, the average

World Motor Vehicle Registrations, 1960–2001

Year	Registrations ('000s) Cars	Trucks and buses	Total vehicles	Population per car
1960	98,317	28,637	126,955	29
1970	193,516	52,852	246,368	18
1980	320,539	90,573	411,113	14
1985	374,727	112,816	487,544	13
1990	444,900	138,082	582,982	12
1995	477,010	169,749	646,759	12
1999	522,333	186,093	708,426	11
2000	547,147	203,274	750,420	11
2001	561,687	206,218	767,905	11

Source: Ward's Communications, *Ward's Motor Vehicle Facts & Figures, 2003* .

U.S. Retail Sales of Passenger Cars by Size and Country of Origin, 1983–2002

Category	1983	1990	1995	2000	2002
By size					
Small	38.8%	32.8%	27.1%	28.1%	28.6%
Middle	40.6	44.8	48.5	47.8	47.9
Large	10.7	9.4	10.8	7.0	6.1
Luxury	9.9	13.0	13.6	17.1	17.4
By origin					
U.S.	74.0%	74.2%	82.6%	77.2%	72.5%
Imports	26.0	25.8	17.4	22.8	27.5
Japan	20.9	18.5	11.4	9.8	11.4
Germany	3.0	2.9	2.4	5.8	6.7
Other	2.0	4.4	3.6	7.2	9.4

Source: Ward's Communications, *Ward's Motor Vehicle Facts & Figures, 2003.*

U.S. Motor Vehicle Sales and Registrations, 1900–2002

Year	Factory sales Passenger cars	Trucks and buses	Total	Motor vehicle registrations[1]
1900	4,192	—	4,192	8,000
1910	181,000	6,000	187,000	468,500
1920	1,905,560	321,789	2,227,349	9,239,161
1930	2,787,456	575,364	3,362,820	26,749,853
1940	3,717,385	754,901	4,472,286	32,453,233
1950	6,665,863	1,337,193	8,003,056	49,161,691
1960	6,674,796	1,194,475	7,869,271	73,857,768
1970	6,546,817	1,692,440	8,239,257	108,418,197
1980	6,400,026	1,667,283	8,067,309	155,796,219
1990	6,049,749	3,725,205	9,774,954	188,655,462
1995	6,309,836	5,713,469	12,023,305	201,530,021
1998	5,676,964	6,435,185	12,112,149	211,616,553
1999	5,427,746	6,699,113	12,126,859	216,308,623
2000	5,504,385	7,022,478	12,526,863	213,299,313
2001	4,884,313	6,223,586	11,107,899	216,682,937
2002	N.A.	6,963,720	N.A.	N.A.

1. Data exclude military vehicles as well as farm trucks registered at a nominal fee in certain states and restricted to use in the vicinity of owners' farms; in 1995, there were 60,490 such trucks. **Source:** Ward's Communications, *Ward's Motor Vehicle Facts & Figures, 2003.*

new vehicle gets worse mileage today (23.3 mpg in 1999, the latest year available) than it did in 1985 (26.3 mpg).

The popularity of larger vehicles, which up until 1999 were allowed to produce up to three times as much pollution per mile as standard cars, has also had implications for the environment. To remedy that situation, the Clinton administration in 1999 announced that minivans, pickup trucks, and sport utility vehicles would be subject to the

U.S. Motor Vehicle Registrations and Insurance Costs by State, 2001

State	Automobiles[1]	Buses	Trucks	Total motor vehicles	Average expenditure per insured vehicle
United States	**137,633,467**	**749,548**	**92,045,311**	**230,428,326**	**$717.70**
Alabama	1,765,088	8,826	2,461,175	4,235,089	605.32
Alaska	242,293	2,568	352,873	597,734	826.10
Arizona	2,263,970	4,725	1,698,422	3,967,117	822.35
Arkansas	975,531	6,936	883,331	1,863,798	620.90
California	17,918,760	49,041	10,812,255	28,780,056	688.89
Colorado	2,367,565	5,875	2,275,380	4,648,820	807.51
Connecticut	2,051,140	10,197	855,531	2,916,868	912.19
Delaware	410,464	2,062	240,559	653,085	850.56
District of Columbia	203,693	2,669	42,500	248,862	1,011.76
Florida	8,937,563	45,621	5,356,918	14,340,102	788.02
Georgia	4,084,746	18,538	3,201,501	7,304,785	703.07
Hawaii	528,622	4,640	334,811	868,073	705.10
Idaho	577,762	3,710	742,376	1,323,848	523.38
Illinois	6,424,601	17,987	3,418,902	9,861,490	682.59
Indiana	3,229,359	28,120	2,367,552	5,625,031	614.86
Iowa	1,870,457	8,316	1,439,536	3,318,309	512.66
Kansas	842,312	3,880	1,484,509	2,330,701	555.90
Kentucky	2,122,875	13,347	1,489,478	3,625,700	645.21
Louisiana	1,994,403	20,815	1,593,341	3,608,559	838.96
Maine	617,781	2,836	396,922	1,017,539	545.42
Maryland	2,595,892	11,923	1,331,033	3,938,848	783.77
Massachusetts	3,530,955	11,673	1,655,593	5,198,221	936.01
Michigan	4,903,195	26,060	3,524,396	8,453,651	735.12
Minnesota	2,564,940	15,397	1,973,849	4,554,186	735.20
Mississippi	1,147,240	9,234	797,299	1,953,773	637.62
Missouri	2,490,721	12,424	1,704,693	4,207,838	633.52
Montana	460,024	2,814	570,246	1,033,084	572.06
Nebraska	833,979	6,209	793,262	1,633,450	553.83
Nevada	679,137	1,904	598,787	1,279,828	851.15
New Hampshire	684,378	1,810	413,352	1,099,540	685.62
New Jersey	4,517,906	22,407	2,039,712	6,580,025	1,027.71
New Mexico	671,132	3,402	753,926	1,428,460	662.27
New York	7,597,371	55,698	2,543,399	10,196,468	1,014.96
North Carolina	3,713,667	31,226	2,434,858	6,179,751	564.76
North Dakota	347,620	2,291	357,674	707,585	497.79
Ohio	6,666,033	38,330	3,850,539	10,554,902	613.75
Oklahoma	1,748,889	17,039	1,515,152	3,281,080	621.58
Oregon	1,559,228	13,572	1,466,595	3,039,395	642.52
Pennsylvania	6,231,291	36,478	3,362,986	9,630,755	726.41
Rhode Island	536,246	1,860	226,372	764,478	880.06
South Carolina	1,919,405	16,630	1,206,704	3,142,739	616.87
South Dakota	389,032	2,598	411,866	803,496	510.42
Tennessee	3,011,787	17,080	2,109,976	5,138,843	610.65
Texas	7,724,309	79,531	6,554,917	14,358,757	735.46
Utah	924,021	1,262	826,451	1,751,734	640.12
Vermont	301,765	2,073	229,947	533,785	602.52
Virginia	3,976,364	18,260	2,176,757	6,171,381	610.14
Washington	2,903,201	9,719	2,266,177	5,179,097	749.74
West Virginia	786,539	3,120	662,393	1,452,052	706.90
Wisconsin	2,579,061	14,004	1,879,870	4,472,935	573.46
Wyoming	211,154	2,811	358,658	572,623	527.63

Note: Total includes privately owned vehicles and federal, state, and municipal vehicles; does not include vehicles owned by the military services. Farm trucks, registered at a nominal fee and restricted to use on farms, are not included. 1 Includes taxicabs.
Sources: U.S. Dept. of Transportation, *Highway Statistics 2001* (2002); National Association of Insurance Commissioners, *State Average Expenditures and Premiums for Personal Automobile Insurance* (annual).

same pollution standards as ordinary cars. In 2002, the Bush administration proposed a 7 percent improvement in the fuel economy of these vehicles by 2007, but critics complained that such a reduction was not enough, and was in fact no more than the auto industry had already committed to on its own.

Traffic

According to the Census Bureau, 90 percent of Americans have access to a motor vehicle, and half of the nation's households have two or more vehicles. In 2000, nearly 88 percent of all U.S. workers drove to work: 75.7 percent drove alone; only 12 percent were in car pools, up from 9 percent in 1999. (Of the remaining 12 percent, only 4.7 percent used mass transportation; 6.2 percent walked or worked at home, and 1.2 percent used bicycles, motorcycles, boats, etc. The average commute was 25.5 minutes in 2000, up from 21.7 minutes in 1980. The number of workers commuting more than 45 minutes each way increased from 10.9 million (11.6 percent of the total) to 13.9 million (12.5 percent) between 1980 and 1990.

It's no wonder, then, that traffic jams are routine. According to the Texas Transportation Institute's 2002 Mobility Study, the average rush hour driver in the 75 largest cities spent 62 hours stuck in traffic in 2000, up from 16 hours a year in 1982.

Top-Selling Passenger Cars and Trucks in the U.S., 2001-02

2002 rank, Cars (2001 rank)	Units sold, 2001	Units sold, 2002
1. Toyota Camry (2)	390,449	434,145
2. Honda Accord (1)	414,718	398,980
3. Ford Taurus (3)	353,560	332,690
4. Honda Civic (4)	331,780	313,159
5. Toyota Corolla (9)	245,023	254,360
6. Ford Focus (5)	264,414	243,199
7. Chevrolet Cavalier (7)	233,298	238,225
8. Nissan Altima (13)	148,345	201,822
9. Chevrolet Impala (8)	208,395	198,918
10. Chevrolet Malibu (10)	176,583	169,377
11. Buick Century (16)	142,157	163,739
12. Pontiac Grand Am (9)	182,046	150,818
13. Volkswagen Jetta (15)	145,221	145,604
14. Ford Mustang (11)	169,198	138,356
15. Buick Lesabre (14)	145,304	135,916
16. Pontiac Grand Prix (17)	128,935	130,141
17. Dodge Neon (x)	N.A.	126,118
18. Hyundai Elantra (19)	111,293	120,638
19. Saturn S (12)	162,110	117,533
20. BMW 3 Series (x)	N.A.	115,428

LIGHT TRUCKS	Units sold, 2001	Units sold, 2002
1. Ford F Series (1)	865,152	774,037
2. Chevy C/K Pickup/ Silverado (2)	708,386	648,040
3. Ford Explorer (3)	415,921	433,847
4. Dodge Ram Pickup (4)	344,538	396,934
5. Chevy Trailblazer (x)	N.A.	249,568
6. Dodge Caravan (6)	242,036	244,911
7. Ford Ranger (5)	272,460	226,094
8. Jeep Grand Cherokee (7)	223,612	224,233
9. Chevrolet Tahoe (9)	202,319	209,767
10. GMC Sierra (8)	206,390	200,146

Note: (x)=Not ranked in 2001. **Source:** Ward's Communications, *Ward's Motor Vehicle Facts & Figures, 2003.*

Delays were highest in, not surprisingly, Los Angeles, where drivers lost 136 hours a year to congestion. Drivers in San Francisco (92 hours), San Jose (74), and Dallas-Fort Worth (74), and Washington, D.C. (84) also lost nearly two hours a week sitting in traffic.

▶AVIATION

The September 11, 2001 terrorist attacks pushed

U.S. Roads and Streets, 1904–2000

	Mileage ('000s)			
Year	State control[1]	County & local control	Total[2]	Percent paved
1904	—	—	2,351	N.A.
1921	203	2,957	3,160	N.A.
1930	324	2,935	3,259	N.A.
1940	551	2,666	3,287	N.A.
1950	609	2,623	3,313	23.5%
1960	694	2,725	3,546	34.7
1970	755	2,762	3,731	44.5
1980	848	2,764	3,860	53.7
1990	798	2,889	3,867	58.4
1995	803	2,937	3,912	60.8
1999	774	3,039	3,932	62.4
2000	775	3,058	3,950	63.4

Note: Some years contain estimates by the Federal Highway Administration. 1. Reflects state highway agency roadways prior to 1980. Includes state park, state toll, and other state agency roadways beginning in 1980. 2. After 1930, includes mileage in federal parks, forests, and reservations not part of the state and local highway system and not shown separately.
Source: U.S. Department of Transportation, *Highway Statistics Summary to 1995* and *Highway Statistics 2000.*

Fuel Efficiency of U.S. Passenger Cars and Trucks, 1955–2000

Since 1980, the federal government has required car manufacturers to maintain a corporate average fuel efficiency (CAFE). Since 1985, the CAFE standard for cars has been 27.5 mpg, which automakers have exceeded by curtailing production of station wagons and full-size sedans. The CAFE standard for light trucks, minivans and sport utility vehicles, however, is much lower (20.7 mpg), yet the average new light truck has rarely attained even this lower level of fuel efficiency.

		Average New Vehicle (model year)		
Year	All passenger cars	Passenger cars[1]	Light trucks	Average vehicle
1955	14.5 mpg	16.0 mpg	–	–
1960	14.3	15.5	–	–
1965	14.3	15.4	–	–
1990	13.5	14.1	–	–
1975	13.5	15.1	–	–
1990	16.0	22.6	18.5 mpg	21.4 mpg
1985	17.5	26.3	20.7	24.0
1990	20.3	26.9	20.8	23.9
1995	21.1	27.7	20.5	23.8
1996	21.2	28.3	20.8	24.1
1997	21.5	27.8	20.6	23.3
1998	21.6	28.1	21.1	23.3
1999	21.4	28.3	20.9	23.3
2000	22.0	28.5	21.2	N.A.

Note: Calculated on the basis of 55% city and 45% highway miles sales weighted average. 1. Domestic vehicles only.
Source: U.S. Dept. of Transportation, *National Transportation Statistics 2000* (2001).

the already shaky airline industry to the edge of financial ruin. A $15 billion bailout by the federal government (a $5 billion giveaway and $10 billion in guaranteed federal loans) prevented a collapse of the industry, but most airlines remain in dire straits. U.S. Airways received a $900 million federal loan guarantee after emerging from bankruptcy in April 2003, but the company still expected no profits in 2003 or 2004. The federal government's denial of a $1.8 billion loan guarantee to United Airlines forced the airline to seek bankruptcy protection in 2002, and even American Airlines, the country's largest, teetered on the verge of bankruptcy in 2003.

After posting record profits of $5.6 billion in 1999, and $2.6 billion in 2000, the airline industry lost an astonishing $7.7 billion in 2001 and at least $10 billion in 2002. American Airlines posted a net loss of $3.51 billion in 2002—the largest single annual loss in airline history. The

On-time Performance and Mishandled Baggage by Major U.S. Airlines, 1987–2002

Airline	Percent of Flights Arriving On-Time 2002	Percent of Flights Arriving On-Time 1987-2002	Mishandled bags per 1,000 2002
Alaska	78.0%	75.9%	2.63
America West	82.9	78.6	3.55
American	83.8	79.1	4.27
Continental	83.5	78.8	3.14
Delta	80.0	77.6	3.57
Northwest	80.8	79.8	4.52
Southwest	82.6	82.4	3.52
United	84.0	75.7	3.76
US Airways	83.4	78.5	2.95
Average	**82.1**	**78.6**	**3.84**

Source: Federal Aviation Administration, Office of Aviation Enforcement and Proceedings, *Air Travel Consumer Report*, February, 2003. www. dot. gov/ airconsumer/

Top 25 Domestic Airline Routes, 2002

Rank	Cities		Passengers ('000s)
1.	New York	Fort Lauderdale	3,158
2.	New York	Chicago	2,707
3.	New York	Orlando	2,646
4.	New York	Los Angeles	2,401
5.	New York	Atlanta	2,215
6.	Honolulu	Kahului, Maui	2,019
7.	New York	Boston	1,637
8.	New York	Washington, DC	1,627
9.	Chicago	Los Angeles	1,521
10.	Dallas/ Fort Worth	Houston	1,520
11.	New York	San Francisco	1,500
12.	New York	Las Vegas	1,472
13.	Honolulu	Lihue, Kauai	1,430
14.	Chicago	Las Vegas	1,421
15.	New York	West Palm Beach	1,410
16.	New York	San Juan	1,393
17.	New York	Miami	1,345
18.	Los Angeles	Las Vegas	1,330
19.	New York	Tampa	1,272
20.	Honolulu	Kona, Hawaii	1,263
21.	Los Angeles	Oakland	1,241
22.	Chicago	Orlando	1,210
23.	New York	Dallas/Fort Worth	1,209
24.	Chicago	Phoenix	1,124
25.	Honolulu	Hilo, Hawaii	1,103

Source: Air Transport Association of America, *Air Transport 2002: The Annual Report of the U.S. Scheduled Airline Industry* (2003).

Top U.S. Airlines, 2002

Rank/Airline	Passengers ('000s)	Rank/Airline	Revenue Passenger Miles (millions)[1]	Rank/Airline	Cargo: Freight Ton Miles (millions)[2]
1. American	94,048	**1.** American	121,668	**1.** FedEx	9,094
2. Delta	90,799	**2.** United	109,395	**2.** UPS Airlines	4,534
3. Southwest	72,448	**3.** Delta	93,494	**3.** Atlas Air	2,376
4. United	68,350	**4.** Northwest	72,002	**4.** United	2,276
5. Northwest	51,743	**5.** Continental	57,003	**5.** Northwest	2,224
6. US Airways	47,155	**6.** Southwest	45,396	**6.** American	2,014
7. Continental	39,486	**7.** US Airways	40,024	**7.** Delta	1,458
8. America West	19,426	**8.** America West	19,855	**8.** Polar Air Cargo	1,349
9. Alaska	14,138	**9.** Alaska	13,178	**9.** Continental	859
10. American Eagle	11,835	**10.** American Trans Air	9,415	**10.** Airborne Express	685
11. AirTran	9,654	**11.** JetBlue	6,830	**11.** Gemini Air Cargo	440
12. Continental Express	9,212	**12.** AirTran	5,582	**12.** US Airways	406
13. Comair	8,732	**13.** Hawaiian	4,450	**13.** Evergreen Int'l	389
14. Atlantic Southeast	8,329	**14.** Spirit	4,096	**14.** Southern	249
15. American Trans Air	7,846	**15.** Continental Express	3,951	**15.** Tradewinds	225
16. JetBlue	5,672	**16.** Comair	3,748	**16.** DHL	218
17. Mesaba	5,587	**17.** American Eagle	3,673	**17.** Arrow	205
18. Hawaiian	5,183	**18.** Frontier	3,363	**18.** Air Transport Int'l	199
19. Horizon Air	4,815	**19.** Atlantic Southeast	3,296	**19.** Kalitta	178
20. Aloha	4,367	**20.** National	2,469	**20.** Express.Net	159
21. Frontier	3,722	**21.** Continental Micronesia	2,394	**21.** World	149
22. Spirit	3,672	**22.** Midwest Express	1,966	**22.** Kitty Hawk	140
23. Midwest Express	2,164	**23.** Mesaba	1,607	**23.** Southwest	128
24. Trans States	2,018	**24.** Aloha	1,605	**24.** Florida West	99
25. National	1,910	**25.** Horizon	1,515	**25.** Capital Cargo	86

Note: Carriers certificated under section 401, Federal Aviation Act. Figures for American include the former TWA. 1. One paying passenger traveling 1 mile generates 1 revenue passenger mile. 2. One ton of freight traveling 1 mile generates 1 freight-ton mile.
Source: Air Transport Association of America, *Air Transport 2002: The Annual Report of the U.S. Scheduled Airline Industry* (2002).

precipitous decline in passengers after September 11, 2001 was responsible for the vast majority of that loss. Revenue passenger miles (one passenger traveling 1 mile generates 1 revenue passenger mile) declined a record 5.9 percent in 2001. International passenger revenue fell even further, by 7.1 percent.

With the decline in air traffic came a sharp reduction in the number of airport delays. In 2000, 78.9 percent of flights departed on time, and 77.0 percent arrived on time. In 2002, those numbers improved to 82.1 percent and 81.0 percent respectively. New York's La Guardia, which was the worst airport for delays in 2000 (only 57.1 of flights arrived on-time) boosted its on-time arrival rate to 73.3 percent in 2001.

Once regarded as little more than a regional airline, Southwest flew 72,448 passengers in 2002,

On-time Arrival Rates at Major U.S. Airports, 1995-2002

City and Airport (Code)	Ontime Arrival Rate 1995	2000	2002
Atlanta/Hartsfield Intl.	74.6%	74.9%	72.1
Baltimore-Washington Intl.	N.A.	74.9	78.6
Boston/Logan International	74.3	65.5	77.7
Charlotte/Douglas Intl.	81.7	78.1	79.0
Chicago/Midway	N.A.	N.A.	80.1
Chicago/O'Hare Intl.	79.0	63.2	77.9
Cincinnati	82.3	79.8	81.3
Dallas-Fort Worth Intl.	80.7	78.0	81.7
Denver International1	81.2	68.2	87.3
Detroit Metropolitan	81.5	79.0	80.4
Fort Lauderdale Intl.	N.A.	N.A.	74.4
Houston Intercontinental	81.2	79.3	79.1
Las Vegas/ McCarran Intl.	79.2	70.5	78.7
Los Angeles International	70.8	66.6	80.8
Miami International	76.1	73.9	74.8
Minneapolis/St. Paul Intl.	81.7	79.5	84.8
New York/Kennedy Intl.	73.1	71.9	75.7
New York/La Guardia Intl.	80.6%	57.1%	73.3%
Newark Liberty Intl.	75.3	69.2	73.9
Orlando International	77.3	74.0	78.9
Philadelphia International	79.8	66.7	76.1
Phoenix/Sky Harbor Intl.	79.1	71.2	77.5
Pittsburgh International	81.0	76.4	81.3
Portland (Oreg.) Intl.	N.A.	71.9	77.4
Salt Lake City International	78.1	76.8	83.0
San Diego/Lindbergh Field	77.8	70.8	78.9
San Francisco Internationa	71.2	60.8	67.7
Seattle/Tacoma International	75.0	67.7	77.9
St.Louis/Lambert Intl.	75.9	77.6	80.9
Tampa International	75.9	73.4	77.1
Washington Dulles Intl.	N.A.	N.A.	82.4
Washington National	79.8	76.2	81.6
U.S. Average[2]	**78.0%**	**71.9%**	**82.1%**

1. Data for 1995 refers to Stapleton Airport. 2. Average of major U.S. airports only. **Source:** Federal Aviation Administration, Office of Aviation Enforcement and Proceedings, *Air Travel Consumer Report, Feb. 2003*. www.dot.gov/airconsumer

World's Busiest Airports, 2002

PASSENGERS Rank, Airport (Code)	Passengers	CARGO Rank, Airport (Code)	Metric tons
1. Hartsfield Atlanta Intl. (ATL)	76,876,128	**1.** Memphis Intl., Tennessee (MEM)	3,390,299
2. Chicago O'Hare Intl. (ORD)	66,501,496	**2.** Hong Kong Intl. (HKG)	2,516,441
3. Heathrow Intl., London (LHR)	63,338,649	**3.** Anchorage Intl., Alaska (ANC)	2,027,754
4. Tokyo-Haneda Intl. (HND)	61,079,478	**4.** Tokyo Intl.-Narita (NRT)	2,001,824
5. Los Angeles Intl. (LAX)	56,198,447	**5.** Los Angeles Intl. (LAX)	1,757,974
6. Dallas/Fort Worth Intl. (DFW)	52,826,304	**6.** Seoul ICN	1,705,880
7. Frankfurt/Main, Germany (FRA)	48,450,357	**7.** Changi, Singapore (SIN)	1,660,404
8. Charles de Gaulle, Paris (CDG)	48,303,439	**8.** Frankfurt/Main, Germany (FRA)	1,631,489
9. Schiphol, Amsterdam (AMS)	40,736,009	**9.** Miami Intl., Florida (MIA)	1,624,240
10. Denver Intl., Colo. (DEN)	35,651,098	**10.** Kennedy Intl., New York (JFK)	1,574,462
11. Sky Harbor Intl., Phoenix (PHX)	35,534,463	**11.** Standiford, Louisville, Ky. (SDF)	1,523,880
12. McCarran Intl., Las Vegas (LAS)	35,009,011	**12.** Charles de Gaulle, Paris (CDG)	1,397,000
13. Houston Intercontinental (IAH)	33,946,484	**13.** Chiang Kai Shek Intl., Taiwan (TPE)	1,380,748
14. Barajas, Madrid (MAD)	33,903,553	**14.** Heathrow Intl., London (LHR)	1,310,615
15. Hong Kong Intl. (HKG)	33,876,000	**15.** Schiphol, Amsterdam (AMS)	1,288,624
16. Minneapolis-St. Paul Intl. (MSP)	32,630,177	**16.** Chicago O'Hare Intl. (ORD)	1,279,176
17. Detroit Metropolitan (DTW)	32,436,999	**17.** Bangkok Intl. (BKK)	957,176
18. Bangkok Intl. (BKK)	32,177,245	**18.** Indianapolis Intl., (IND)	866,014
19. San Francisco Intl. (SFO)	31,447,750	**19.** Newark Liberty Intl., N.J. (EWR)	821,537
20. Miami Intl. Florida (MIA)	30,060,241	**20.** Osaka Intl., Osaka (KIX)	805,432
21. Gatwick Intl., London (LGW)	29,628,441	**21.** Dubai Intl. (DXB)	784,997
22. Changi, Singapore (SIN)	28,979,344	**22.** Hartsfield Atlanta Intl. (ATL)	732,532
23. Newark Liberty Intl., N.J. (EWR)	28,972,253	**23.** Tokyo-Haneda Intl. (HND)	707,074
24. Tokyo Intl.-Narita (NRT)	28,894,925	**24.** Dallas/Fort Worth Intl. (DFW)	669,507
25. Kennedy Intl., New York (JFK)	28,888,686	**25.** Peking Capital, Beijing (PEK)	668,733
26. Peking Capital, Beijing (PEK)	27,159,665	**26.** Oakland Intl., Calif. (OAK)	650,375
27. Sea-Tac Intl., Seattle (SEA)	26,688,127	**27.** Pu Dong, Shanghai (PVG)	634,966
28. Orlando Intl., Fla. (MCO)	26,650,975	**28.** San Francisco Intl. (SFO)	593,803
29. Pearson Intl., Toronto (YYZ)	25,930,293	**29.** Baiyun, Guangzhou (CAN)	592,554
30. Lambert-St. Louis Intl. (STL)	25,613,969	**30.** Philadelphia Intl. (PHI)	542,086

Source: Airports Association Council International, *Worldwide Airport Traffic Report—Calendar Year 2002* (2003). www.airports.org

more than any carrier other than American or Delta, and posted its 48th consecutive profitable quarter in early 2003. One major reason for Southwest's success is its focus on domestic routes, which produce an average of 13.41 cents per passenger mile, as compared with 9.65 cents for international flights. Southwest also flies only one kind of aircraft, meaning that all of its mechanics know how to fix all of its planes. Upstart airline JetBlue also saw profits in 2002 and had ambitious plans for expansion through 2003.

With more than 75 million people passing through its security detectors each year, Hartsfield Atlanta International Airport remained the busiest airport in the world in 2002, though air passenger travel was down considerably from 2001 because of Americans' unwillingness to fly after September 11 and new fears of SARS. Air cargo, however, suffered no such drop. Tennessee's Memphis International, home of Federal Express, logged more than 3.4 million metric tons of cargo in 2002, up from 2.6 million the year before.

World's Top Tourist Destinations 2001

2001 Rank/ Destination	International Arrivals (millions) 2000	2001	1985 rank	1990 rank
1. France	75.6	76.5	1	1
2. Spain	47.9	49.5	2	3
3. United States	50.9	45.5	4	2
4. Italy	41.2	39.0	3	4
5. China	31.2	33.2	13	12
6. United Kingdom	25.2	23.4	6	7
7. Russian Federation	21.2	N.A.	18	17
8. Mexico	20.6	19.8	9	8
9. Canada	19.7	19.7	7	10
10. Austria	18.0	18.2	5	6
11. Germany	19.0	17.9	8	9
12. Hungary	15.6	15.3	11	5
13. Poland	17.4	15.0	22	27
14. Hong Kong	13.1	13.7	19	19
15. Greece	13.1	N.A.	14	13
World Total	**696.7**	**692.7**	**N.A.**	**N.A.**

Note: Preliminary. Excludes same-day visitors but includes people who pass through a country for one or more nights en route to another country.
Source: World Tourism Organization, *Tourism Highlights 2002.*

Top 20 Destinations for U.S. Tourists, 1987–97

1997 Rank/ Destination	U.S. tourist arrivals 1987	1995	1997
1. Mexico	13,044,000	19,220,523	18,193,715
2. Canada	12,719,800	13,005,200	13,401,300
3. United Kingdom	2,800,000	3,146,000	3,432,000
4. Italy	1,956,153	2,570,704	3,074,000
5. France	1,802,000	2,184,000	2,660,000
6. Puerto Rico	1,550,250	2,246,778	2,444,918
7. Germany	2,071,647	1,548,618	1,760,099
8. Bahamas	1,299,215	1,328,925	1,310,420
9. Spain	865,592	877,467	1,020,000
10. Jamaica	545,476	760,304	804,315
11. China[1]	793,341	748,911	800,539
12. Switzerland	N.A.	783,069	786,359
13. Japan	550,261	539,899	621,737
14. Colombia	N.A.	451,176	533,473
15. Philippines	N.A.	514,850	427,431
16. South Korea	326,330	358,872	424,258
17. Singapore	211,369	345,611	376,418
18. India	134,876	203,343	244,239
19. Egypt	102,603	154,851	176,346
20. South Africa	37,750	103,466	142,781

1. Includes Hong Kong. **Source:** World Tourism Organization, *Tourism Market Trends, 1999 Edition.*

Tourists in the U.S., by Country of Origin, 1995–2001

2001 Rank/ Country	Arrivals in U.S. 1995	2000	2001
1. Canada	14,663,000	14,648,000	13,518,156
2. Mexico	8,016,000	10,322,000	9,558,000
3. United Kingdom	2,888,195	4,703,008	4,199,159
4. Japan	4,598,354	5,061,377	4,124,450
5. Germany	1,847,973	1,786,045	1,346,822
6. France	921,630	1,087,087	935,322
7. South Korea	592,327	661,844	626,669
8. Brazil	838,365	737,245	589,687
9. Venezuela	511,327	576,663	570,521
10. Italy	524,892	612,357	491,330
11. Australia	423,631	539,559	445,175
12. Argentina	381,904	533,936	443,134
13. Netherlands	408,153	553,297	432,403
14. Colombia	233,012	417,065	380,475
15. Taiwan	412,078	457,302	361,693
16. Spain	302,083	361,177	325,323
17. Switzerland	396,801	395,031	324,179
18. Bahamas	281,239	293,911	312,816
19. Israel	216,419	325,199	312,200
20. Ireland	149,430	285,697	281,638
21. India	123,499	274,202	270,769
22. Jamaica	196,175	242,903	235,408
23. Sweden	219,283	321,881	235,129
24. China	166,520	249,441	233,739
25. El Salvador	82,085	184,574	212,246
26. Peru	126,775	192,062	191,659
27. Belgium	206,134	249,957	191,352
28. Phillipines	109,583	168,053	181,431
29. Guatemala	131,105	185,677	179,796
30. Dominican Republic	175,878	197,298	177,231
31. Hong Kong	220,129	203,300	171,930
32. New Zealand	141,663	172,012	157,732
33. Chile	152,018	192,361	156,605
34. Costa Rica	118,119	176,058	154,156
35. Ecuador	97,770	129,938	152,078
Other	1,754,382	2,477,148	2,226,809
World Total	**4,3317,966**	**50,944,701**	**45,501,656**

Note: 2001 figures are preliminary. **Source:** World Tourism Organization.

Commuter and Rapid Rail Systems in the U.S., 2001

System	Passenger trips ('000s)	Passenger miles ('000s)	Stations	Route miles	Vehicles operated
Commuter Rail					
New York, Long Island RR	101,923.0	2,126,874.9	124	638.2	954
Chicago RTA-Metra	72,121.8	1,577,183.7	227	940.4	995
New York, Metro North	72,919.6	2,185,376.0	108	545.7	772
Newark, New Jersey Transit	63,970.7	1,357,374.5	167	1,091.4	733
Boston MBTA	36,992.6	784,413.0	121	710.0	376
Philadelphia SEPTA	30,781.9	388,882.7	177	449.2	291
Los Angeles, SCRRA	7,398.0	274,625.4	49	770.0	134
Indiana, NICTD	3,771.6	105,584.9	18	179.8	58
Rapid or Heavy Rail					
New York City TA	1,740,326.1	8,273,784.3	468	493.8	4,985
Washington Metro Area TA	235,731.7	1,362,866.3	83	206.6	628
Chicago RTA-CTA	181,692.2	1,009,234.0	144	206.3	988
Boston, MBTA	137,234.0	502,501.9	53	76.3	320
San Francisco, BART	103,919.4	1,263,667.8	39	190.1	507
Philadelphia, SEPTA	87,344.1	392,693.4	76	76.1	308
Atlanta, MARTA	82,388.6	563,016.8	38	96.0	186
New York, PATH	78,901.3	338,386.7	13	25.0	288
Los Angeles MTA-Metro	31,191.5	126,460.7	16	31.9	70
Miami/Dade Co. TA	13,735.3	107,648.8	21	42.2	86
Baltimore MTA	13,585.2	62,457.4	14	29.4	66
New Jersey/Port Authority TA	10,038.4	88,781.5	13	31.5	96
Cleveland RTA	8,232.2	61,606.8	18	38.2	28
New York, Staten Island MTA	3,968.0	24,985.1	23	28.6	44

Note: Rapid rail includes subways, elevated trains, and metros. BART = Bay Area Rapid Transit Authority; MBTA = Metropolitan Boston Transit Authority; PATH = Port Authority Trans Hudson; SCRRA = Southern California Railroad Authority; SEPTA = Southeastern Pennsylvania Transit Authority. **Source:** Federal Transit Administration, *2001 National Transit Database, Transit Summaries and Trends.*

U.S. Railroads: Mileage and Accident Rates, 2001–02

	2001			2002		
		Accidents			Accidents	
Railroad	Train-miles operated	Total	Per million train miles	Train-miles operated	Total	Per million train miles
Amtrak (National Railroad Passenger Corp.)	38,575,104	149	3.86	39,652,480	112	2.82
Burlington Northern Santa Fe	162,943,990	606	3.72	161,813,974	522	3.23
CSX Transportation	108,619,574	362	3.33	109,901,185	348	3.17
Grand Trunk Western Railroad Inc.	5,097,500	15	2.94	4,826,133	16	3.32
Illinois Central Railroad Co.	10,811,462	66	6.10	9,861,460	59	5.98
Kansas City Southern Railway Co.	7,659,908	92	12.01	8,551,673	93	10.88
Norfolk Southern Corp.	89,950,834	226	2.51	92,214,833	215	2.33
Soo Line Railroad Co.	8,292,477	30	3.62	8,449,125	17	2.01
Union Pacific Railroad Co.	172,712,098	896	5.19	186,750,216	824	4.41

Source: U.S. Dept. of Transportation, Federal Railroad Administration, Office of Safety, *Accident/Incident Bulletin Calendar Year 2002.* http://safetydata.fra.dot.gov/officeofsafety.

Amtrak Operating Statistics, 1985–2000

Category	1985	1990	1995	1999	2000
Ridership					
Passengers (millions)	20.8	22.2	20.7	21.5	22.5
Passenger miles (millions)	4,582	6,057	5,545	5,330	5,498
Passenger-Train Cars					
Operating fleet (active units)	1,854	1,863	1,722	1,992	1,894
Average age (years)	14.2	20.0	21.8	22.2	19.4
Train-miles operated (millions)	30	33	32	34	35
On-time performance	**81%**	**76%**	**76%**	**79%**	**78%**
Short Distance (<400 miles)	82	82	81	80%	81%
Long Distance (400+ miles)	78	53	57	61%	56%
Financial					
Revenues (millions)	$ 825	$1,308	$1,490	$2,011	$2,111
Expenses (millions)	1,600	2,012	2,257	2,660	2,876

Source: *Amtrak FY2000 Annual Report.*

Part III THE WORLD
World History

▶THE DAWN OF CIVILIZATION (c. 3000–1500 B.C.)

The transition from pre-historic Neolithic culture to civilization seems to have involved in every case two things combined: the establishment of settled agricultural communities instead of nomadic food-gathering communities and, in those settled communities, the development of urban centers with literate religious and social hierarchies in control of irrigation projects. The first condition is found (independently, so far as is now known) in at least four centers: Mexico and Central America; the great bend of the Niger River in Africa; the Yellow River valley in China; and in Mesopotamia (the "land between the waters" of the Tigris and Euphrates Rivers). Priority in time belongs to Mesopotamia. And there also the second condition of civilization, the urban center, first emerged.

Mesopotamia

The 600-mile-long plain of the Tigris and Euphrates valleys stretching to the Persian Gulf is the site of earliest civilization. The city-state of Sumer gives its name to this first flowering which blossomed about 3000 B.C. Each of the cities was a sacred temple city, the realm of a god whose regent on earth was the priest-king. To the Sumerians we owe: the calendar, the invention of writing (cuneiform), the plow, the potter's wheel and wheeled carts, boats using sails, and a host of other "firsts."

The separate and frequently warring city-states such as Lagash, Nippur, and Ur fell under the control of the more northerly *Empire of Akkad* whose greatest king was Sargon (c. 2250 B.C.) which in turn fell under the sway of the *Babylonian Empire* whose king Hammurabi (c. 1750 B.C.) conquered all of Mesopotamia and who is credited with the first known Code of Laws. Shortly before 1500 B.C. this empire fell under the domination of the more barbarous *Kassites* whose advantage lay in the use of horse-and-chariot manned by bowmen.

Egypt

The great valley of the Nile, a thin stream traversing the eastern Sahara desert, had given birth by about 3000 B.C. to no urban centers but to a network of farming villages whose population was of urban density. The legendary founder of Egypt was Menes whose conquest of Lower (i.e., northern) Egypt established the *Old Kingdom* (c. 3000–2200 B.C.). Political unification, quite different from the pattern of Sumer, permitted a rapid assimilation of Sumerian technology while the desert meant relative freedom from invasion. The pharaohs did not rule by permission of the gods, but were divine beings themselves; the building of their colossal tombs, the pyramids, were great religious works directed by the unitary state. The most famous is the Great Pyramid of Cheops at Gizeh (c. 2500 B.C.)

The older diversity of the valley reasserted itself during a century of dissolution and division called the *First Intermediate Period*, after which the traditions of Menes asserted themselves in the *Middle Kingdom* (c. 2100–1800 B.C.). Architecture and sculpture were consciously restorationist, modeled after the Old Kingdom, though temple architecture testifies to the importance of various priesthoods. In literature, it was Egypt's "classical age."

But this age ended with the invasion from Syria-Palestine of the barbarian charioteers known as Hyksos who ruled during the *Second Intermediate Period* (c. 1800–1600 B.C.). But the Eighteenth Dynasty, with its capital at Thebes, at last managed to drive out the Hyksos and re-establish royal authority throughout the valley, thereby initiating the *New Kingdom* (c. 1600–1100 B.C.).

Other Significant Centers

The *Indus Valley*, stretching from Tibet to the Arabian Sea, had become by about 3000 B.C. another locus of settled agriculture with obvious Sumerian influence. Innumerable small villages but only two cities have been excavated and the ancient Indian script remains a mystery to scholars. This Indian civilization flourished from about 2500 to about 1500 B.C. until it was conquered by Aryan tribesmen also utilizing chariots and arrows.

About the year 2000 B.C. three centers of civilization influenced by Mesopotamia and Egypt began to develop: the *Canaanites* in Syria and Palestine, the *Hittites* in Asia Minor, and the *Minoan civilization* on the island of Crete. It is not clear whether Minos was a name or, like "pharaoh" a title, but it was his palace, the Labyrinth, which dominated the trading city of Knossos, center of an elegant "sea empire" whose ships were in contact with Italy, Egypt, Asia Minor and mainland Greece. Yet by about 1500 B.C. Minoan trade was in decline and not long after a Greek prince was ruling at Knossos.

In China around 1875 B.C., the millet-based agricultural villages of the North China Plain gave rise to the semi-legendary Xia Dynasty, which ushered in the Bronze Age in East Asia. The Xia were overthrown around 1550 B.C. by Tang the Victorious, who established the Shang Dynasty, which endured for five hundred years. The Shang Dynasty is noted for its sophisticated bronze vessels, used in worship of the royal ancestors, and for oracle bones inscribed with an early form of Chinese script asking questions of the gods. Shang culture was enriched after around 1350 B.C. by new technologies from western Eurasia, including the chariot, the cultivation of wheat, and sheep-raising.

▶THE SPREAD OF CIVILIZATION (c. 1500–500 B.C.)

The impact of the chariot warriors from the steppes of Eurasia, a huge stretch of grassland stretching from the Black Sea almost to the Pacific Ocean, altered the earliest civilizations in different ways and to different degrees—least in the Near East, most in India. In the millennium from about 1500 to about 500 B.C., the area of civilized life continued to spread as the civilizations took on their classic form in the "heroic age" of the ancient world.

Egypt

Almost immediately after the hated Hyksos had been expelled from Egypt proper, the pharaohs of the *New Kingdom* (1570–1065 B.C.)—preeminently Thutmose III (c. 1500–1447 B.C.) and his regent queen Hatshepsut (d. 1468 B.C.)—created an empire in Palestine and Syria in which local princes ruled their peoples while Egyptian bureaucrats and garrison commanders oversaw imperial interests, especially the tribute payments. Egyptian control southward along the Nile into the Sudan and Nubia was also reestablished. The empire functioned well until ruled by a pharaoh whose interests lay elsewhere.

The pharaoh Amenhotep IV (ruled c. 1372–1354 B.C.) changed his name to Akhenaton and led a movement after 1370 B.C. to obliterate the name and memory of all the Egyptian gods save for the sun-god Aton (and his incarnation on earth, the pharaoh). This almost-monotheistic revolution absorbed the attention of the monarchy to such an extent that it helped the empire to crumble and the dynasty to be overthrown. A rigid traditionalism accompanied the painful recovery of the empire. Tutankhamen (whose famous tomb was discovered in 1922) was Akhenaton's son-in-law; his name shows the return of the god Amon and the eclipse of Aton. But by 1200 B.C. a series of invasions brought the Egyptians to withdraw from the empire to defend the Nile Valley, a withdrawal complete by about 1100.

The *Post-Empire Period* (1065-525 B.C.) saw Egypt's survival in a cultural and religious sense; but the state grew disunified and finally fell victim to conquests by the Assyrians (671 B.C.) and the Persians (525 B.C.).

Mesopotamia and Persia

The Kassite conquest of the First Babylonian Empire led to no great revolution since the conquerors adopted the culture and political structure of the conquered. To the north, the Assyrians were left under native rulers, then took advantage of a series of barbarian incursions against the Kassites to gain their independence in the *First Assyrian Empire* (c. 1150–728 B.C.). The Assyrians were fierce warriors, and they fell upon the south of Mesopotamia, upon Syria and Palestine, and even, briefly, Egypt, and they established the *Second Assyrian Empire* (728–612 B.C.).

The destruction of the great Assyrian capital of Nineveh (612 B.C.) was the work of the mobile strike force of the cavalry of the Medes who proceeded to conquer the Assyrian territory east of the Tigris as well as Armenia and eastern Iran, forming the short-lived *Median Empire* (625–559 B.C.). Assyria's fall permitted the *Second Babylonian Empire* (625–538 B.C.) to arise in Mesopotamia.

Both fell victim to the *Persian Empire* (559–331 B.C.). Cyrus the Great (550–533 B.C.) overturned his Median overlord (559 B.C.), conquered King Croesus of Lydia in Asia Minor (546 B.C.) and overthrew King Nebuchadnezzar III of Babylon (538 B.C.). It was his son who conquered Egypt and his grandson Darius I (521–485 B.C.)who brought the empire to its greatest extent, expanding eastward beyond the Indus by 519 B.C. Dividing his empire into 20 "satrapies" (administrative offices), Darius improved communications by building good roads and was farsighted enough to commence the construction of a Mediterranean war fleet.

Under this Persian dynasty's patronage, the religious doctrines of Zoroaster (c. 628–c. 551 B.C.) spread through its immense empire. Zoroaster taught a dualist doctrine of a cosmic struggle between the god Ahuramazda, the good god of light, truth and peace, and Ahriman, the evil god of darkness, lies, and discord. It was to prove one of the most profoundly influential teachings in the history of the world.

Israel and Judah

Amidst the ebb and flow of empire emerged the people of Israel. Tracing their origin to the ancient city of Ur in Mesopotamia and the covenant between their patriarch Abraham and their god Yahweh, they migrated to Canaan sometime after 1900 B.C. Entering Egypt, probably in the Hyksos period, they dwelt in the Egyptian delta until about 1280 B.C. when, against strong resistance from the pharaoh, Moses led the Hebrews out of Egypt into the desert of Sinai where, according to the Old Testament, they became Yahweh's chosen people in the Sinai covenant. Shortly before 1200 B.C. they occupied Canaan during the decline of Egyptian power there.

The religious league of clans was transformed into the *Kingdom of Israel* (c. 1020–922 B.C.) which flourished under the kings Saul (1028–1013 B.C.), David (1013–973 B.C.), and Solomon (973–933 B.C.) in the interstices of the great powers. But after the death of Solomon, the kingdom divided into Israel in the north and Judah in the south. The northern kingdom fell to the Assyrians under Sargon II (722–705 B.C.) in 721 B.C. Judah held on until the Second Babylonian Empire under Nebuchadnezzar II (c. 605–562 B.C.)destroyed the capital Jerusalem in 587 B.C.

While ethnic Israel fell, the spiritual Israel was preserved through the work of *the prophets*, especially Isaiah (c. 700 B.C.), Jeremiah (c. 600 B.C.) and the second Isaiah (c. 540) who taught an uncompromising monotheism: Yahweh not the god of the Jews alone, but the one God of mankind.

With the establishment of the Persian Empire, the Jews were permitted (538 B.C.) to return to Palestine and to build the second Temple, there to live under the great code of law, the *Torah*.

Greece

The Minoan culture of Crete had been in contact with the Greek mainland before 1650 B.C. The people of Greece (called Achaeans) had arranged themselves in small principalities of which Mycenae, located on the Greek mainland of the Peleponnesian peninsula, had pre-eminence. Adopting the courtly style of the life of Minoans and the war chariots of the Hyksos, the Achaeans expanded their settlements and with Cretan decline became heirs of Minoan trade with Egypt and Syria. This is the culture pictured for us in the epics of Homer's (c. 800 B.C.), *The Odyssey* and *The Iliad*.

About 1100 B.C., a second wave of Greek-speaking Dorians invaded from the north and the Achaeans were forced to migrate to the islands and the coast of Asia Minor. In defeat they performed their greatest work: the preservation of Mycenaean (and therefore also Minoan) traditions both socially and in the Homeric epics. Through these great poems the enterprise against Troy became the living symbol of the unity of the Greeks, the mythology of Mycenae provided a common religious background for local cults, and the language of the Achaeans became the norm for the whole Greek world.

By about 750 B.C. the Greek world had recovered. Colonies spread westward to Italy and Sicily and eastward to the northern Aegean and the Black Seas. The lyric poetry of Archilochus (c. 700 B.C.) and Sappho (c. 600 B.C.) flourished. The first philosophers (Thales, Heraclitus, Parmenides), later called the pre-Socratics, commenced their speculations on nature and the order of the universe; to this philosophy, the Pythagoreans added mathematical genius. And the characteristic unit of the city-state, the *polis* was created.

The greatest of these city-states were Athens and Sparta. *Sparta* emerged in 716 B.C. as conqueror of about 3,200 square miles of territory; by about 610 B.C. Sparta already had the formidable military organization based on strict education for citizenship to inculcate the "savage valor" that Spartans so esteemed. And by 540 B.C. Sparta had formed the Peloponnesian League, uniting all but two of the city-states of the peninsula.

The polis of *Athens* was, like other Greek cities, dominated by its aristocratic families. The grievous problem of increasing slavery for debt led the Athenian leaders to turn over power to Solon, a wealthy merchant and poet, descended from the old kings. Taking office in 594, he cancelled all debts, abolished debt-slavery, encouraged both agriculture and industry, and opened the assembly to all free men. But Athens remained divided among its landed wealth, its trading class and the poor peasants, the latter led by the nobleman Peisistratus who established a dictatorship in the name of the poor (546–528 B.C.). But its democratic constitution was not in place until it was imposed, in 508 B.C., by the aristocrat Cleisthenes.

India

The charioteers who invaded the civilization of the Indus valley called themselves Aryans, a word meaning "noble" in their Sanskrit language. Those they conquered were called Sudras, "slaves." The Aryans settled in villages along the Indus, organized in tribal principalities about which almost nothing is known. Over the half-millennium from about 800 B.C. to about 300 B.C. they moved south along the coast and east across the peninsula to the delta of the Ganges River. There, once the lush jungle vegetation was cleared (using the new tools of the iron age), rice could be cultivated in the rich soil, a food supply sufficient for a very dense and stable population.

Religiously, this is the classic age of Hinduism. The ancient *Vedas*, hymns to the gods, date back to about 1000 B.C.—though not written down until much later. The *Brahmanas* are a body of instructions for rituals, evidence of the rise of an important priestly body, composed over the years 800–600 B.C. Lastly, about 600 B.C. appeared the *Upanishads* with their stress on asceticism and mysticism.

Embodied in this classic religious literature are the germs of the later "caste" system, for they envision four *varnas* or castes: priests (brahmans), warriors (kshatriyas), peasants and artisans (vaisyas), and slaves (sudras).

China

The late Shang period, known for the extravagance of its royal burials, declined into misrule; the dynasty was overthrown around 1055 B.C. by the ruler of the state of Zhou, which controlled the Wei River Valley in northwestern China. The Duke of Zhou, regent for the third Zhou king, established a sort of feudal system in which the territory of China was parcelled out in small states governed by Zhou clansmen and supporters. These states gradually grew larger at the expense of the Zhou royal domain. The Zhou capital was forcibly moved eastwards from Chang'an (now Xi'an) to Luoyang around 770 B.C. but the Zhou kings continued to lose both territory and political authority. Zhou rule broke down altogether during the Warring States Period (c. 480–221 B.C.), when a handful of large feudal states swallowed up their smaller neighbors.

The principal states of northern China were known collectively as *zhongguo*, the "middle kingdoms"; the Chinese, isolated from the high cultures of western Eurasia and India, imagined their culture to be at the center of the world, surrounded by zones of ever-increasing barbarism. In this view, the Chinese ruler governed "all under heaven" by authority of the Mandate of Heaven (*tian ming*). This theory held that a dynastic founder, because of his own virtue, attracted the cosmic force of heaven itself in his support, bequeathing heaven's mandate to his descendants so long as they cherished the principle of virtuous rule. This poltical theory, which assumed that exhausted and corrupt dynasties would eventually be overthrown by righteous rebellions, was a force for renewal and long-term stability throughout Chinese history.

Confucius (c. 551–479 B.C.), China's first philosopher, sought a remedy for the political turmoil of his time in an attempted revival of the golden age of the Duke of Zhou. Thwarted in his search for a ruler who would put his ideas into practice, Confucius became a teacher whose disciples perpetuated his prescription for good government. Confucius looked to a natural aristocracy of virtue, rather than an hereditary elite, for social leadership; this led centuries later to the Chinese innovation of government by means of a professional civil service recruited through competitive examination. The Taoists, rivals of the Confucian school (and supposedly founded by Laozi, of whose life nothing is known) rejected government altogether in favor of individual self-cultivation.

The Warring States Period was an era of cultural brilliance in philosophy, technology, and the arts, a prelude to China's first great imperial age.

▶THE GROWTH OF WORLD EMPIRES (c. 500 B.C.–A.D. 500)

The millennium after 500 B.C. had as its most characteristic development the conquest of the earliest centers of civilization by certain small nations or tribes—Persians, Macedonians, Romans, Mauryans—on their peripheries. Territories of immense extent (the whole world as they knew it) were organized by these smaller nations, although without any attempt to integrate the conquered peoples into their own cultures. Rarely constructed according to any deliberate plan, these world empires grew up haphazardly.

Significant too was the extraordinary clustering in one generation (at about 500 B.C.) of Pythagoras and Heraclitus, the second Isaiah, Confucius, and the Buddha. And yet more so was the fourth century B.C. eruption of philosophic thought with Plato and Aristotle. Finally, at the middle of the millennium, appeared Jesus Christ.

The Persian Empire and the Greeks

The Persian Wars (499–479 B.C.) began with a failed revolt of the Greek cities of coastal Asia Minor against the Persian Empire (of which they had become a part in 546 B.C.). To punish the mainland Greek allies of the rebels, the city-states of Athens and Eretria, the Persian Empire made war on Greece, but unsuccessfully. From a Persian point of view the Athenian and Spartan victories were only a border issue of minor import; but to the Greeks, the battles of Marathon, Salamis, Plataea and Mycale were inspiring symbols of the superiority of their ideals of liberty and free citizenship over the servitude of Eastern despotism, with the unity of Athens and Sparta embodying what had been prefigured in the united Greek enterprise against Troy. The historian Herodotus first told this story.

Under the leadership of Pericles' (d. 429 B.C.) Athens transformed its naval league into an Athenian Empire, thus allowing Sparta to appear the defender of Greek liberties. The former allies, with their leagues, entered their death-struggle, the *Peloponnesian War* (431–404 B.C.) in which the Spartans won a crushing victory. The saga was told by the second great Greek historian, Thucydides (c. 460–400 B.C.) Spartan hegemony in Greece lasted only until 387 B.C. when a league of Greek cities with Persian assistance imposed a settlement which made all Greek poleis autonomous (and therefore weak) except for those in Asia under Persian rule. It was all but the end of the golden age of Greece.

But in just over a century the Greeks had created tragedy (Aeschylus, Sophocles, Euripides), philosophy (Socrates, Plato, Aristotle), history (Herodotus, Thucydides), and the imperishable glory of their monumental architecture (the Parthenon, the Acropolis) and the sculpture of Myron and Phidias.

The Macedonian Empire

Brooding above the disunited Greek city-states lay the small but militarily powerful kingdom of Macedon, militaristic but greatly influenced by Greek civilization. King Philip (356–330 B.C.), having conquered Illyria and Thrace on the northern Aegean, intervened in Greece and forced the formation of a Hellenic League which with Macedon began war against Persia (336 B.C.). No sooner had war began than Philip was assassinated, a death which occasioned the revolt of the Greek cities he dominated. But his son and successor, Alexander the Great (336–323 B.C.) ruthlessly crushed the revolt and plunged on into Asia; after his great victory in the battle of Issus (333 B.C.) over Darius III of Persia, Alexander declared himself successor to the last Persian emperor under the title King of Asia, continuing rule through the satrapies after the final defeat of the Persians in 330 B.C. In the meantime he added Egypt to his conquests (331 B.C.) and founded the great city of Alexandria. He pushed on into Bactria (modern Uzbekistan) and then to the Indus Valley beyond which his soldiers would not go. When he died of a fever in Babylon in 323 B.C. he had assembled in but a dozen years the largest empire the world had known; but his premature death meant the division of the empire among the *Diadochi* (Alexander's generals who claimed the succession) who battled for half a century before stabilizing into fragments, each a formidable military monarchy: descendants of Antigonus ruled Macedonia, those of Ptolemy Egypt, those of Seleucus most of Asia. The fringes, the western Mediterranean and India, were left to their own development.

Rome: From Republic to Empire

About the midpoint of the western side of the 650-mile long peninsula of Italy the primitive, devout, peasant community of Rome overturned their Etruscan rulers and established a republic shortly before the year 500 B.C. as the Greek golden age was just beginning. A century of patient expansion against neighboring tribes in central Italy was undone in 390 B.C. when Celts (or Gauls) from the Po Valley plundered and burnt the city. But the Romans commenced anew and within three generations had brought under their sway all of the peninsula except the Greek cities (Magna Graecia) in the south; and these they added by 272 B.C., just at the time the Diodochi were stabilizing their sectors of Alexander's empire.

The move into southern Italy involved Rome in a struggle with Carthage. Originally a Canaanite colony, the city of Carthage in north Africa had established a necklace of commercial colonies along the Mediterranean coast from Sicily across North Africa and Spain to the mouth of the valley of the Rhone, commanding the western seas. In a prodigious struggle called the *Punic Wars* (264–146 B.C.), during which Rome itself was almost brought to ruin by Hannibal (247–183 B.C.), the Romans utterly vanquished Carthage.

After the Second Punic War (218–201 B.C.) Rome became embroiled in the east as Pergamum, Rhodes and Athens appealed for help against the Diodochi. With the war against Macedon (100–196 B.C.) Rome's eastward expansions began. One by one, Greece, Macedonia, Asia Minor, Syria, Palestine, Egypt, and the whole north African coast came under Roman rule by 62 B.C. making the Mediterranean Sea truly what the Romans called *mare nostrum:* our sea.

But Asia did not beckon; rather the Romans embarked on that extraordinary experiment in the west, the conquest of Gaul by Julius Caesar (100–44 B.C.) in which almost 100 small Celtic principalities were brought into the civilization of the Roman Mediterranean. In time Gaul would lead to Britain (A.D. 43–84), while eastern defense considerations would lead to the annexation of Armenia, Mesopotamia and Assyria (A.D. 114–16). At its greatest extent, the Roman Empire stretched from the North Sea to the Sahara Desert, from the highlands of Scotland to the Persian Gulf.

But in winning their empire, the Romans lost their republic, with its freely elected assemblies and magistrates and its famous "council of elders," the Senate. The tremendous population losses in the Second Punic War, the increase in the slave population with every conquest, the transformation from a peasant agriculture to huge *latifundia* (plantations), the rise of a class of financiers (the *equites*), the rivalry of military commanders, the involvement of the military in politics—all conspired to strangle the old republican institutions. In the century from 298 B.C. to 133 B.C., the rivalry for power among demagogues and generals—the Gracchi brothers, Marius, Sulla, the triumvirate of Pompey, Caesar and Crassus, the dictatorship of Caesar, the second triumvirate of Lepidus, Octavian, and Antony—meant endless civil war leading to the final victory of the revolutionary adventurer Octavian who, renamed Augustus, initiated imperial rule in Rome itself and the *Pax Romana*, 200 years of peace in the Roman imperial orbit (27 B.C.–A.D. 180).

Christianity and the Roman Empire

More impressive than the military aspect of the work of Rome was the spread of the Mediterranean civic tradition into continental Europe: colonies of veterans such as Cologne, legionary headquarters such as York, imitated the old Italian, Greek, Phoenician and Syrian cities as well as the numerous foundations of Alexander. The empire became a network of administrative departments centered on cities with central power at Rome; with the external forms of civic life came economic prosperity and the intellectual culture of the Hellenized Roman civilization.

It was in this world that Christ and Christianity were born. In the reign of Augustus Jesus of Nazareth was born (c. 4 B.C.) and in the reign of Tiberius he died, crucified as a criminal (c. A.D. 30). His closest followers affirmed to his resurrection from the dead and his ascent to the one he always called "My Father" and they eagerly preached the "good news" (gospel) that God himself had become man and died for man's sins. This preaching and their communion in their liturgies were the focal points of the early Christians, as the Romans called them. Considering themselves the "second Israel" they nonetheless broke with the synagogue and through missionaries like Paul, Barnabas, and Timothy preached to the Gentiles. While numerically few, they spread through the cities of the Roman world: from Palestine to Syria, Anatolia and Greece, to Africa and Italy; in the second century to Gaul, Germany, Yugoslavia and Spain.

Because they met in secret societies and because they reused to worship the Roman imperial gods, the Christians were persecuted by Roman magistrates; after A.D. 110, adherence to Christianity became a capital offense. Yet the church continued to spread, not only among the poor and outcast but among the nobles and the philosophers (like Justin the Martyr who perished in A.D. 165). These Christians viewed the Pax Romana as providential.

When after the death of the Stoic emperor Marcus Aurelius (A.D. 180) the empire fell into civil war, economic decline, the exhaustion of civic life through excessive taxation and centralized government control, the frontiers became unsafe as well: for after A.D. 226 a revived Persian Empire grew aggressive in the east while great confederations of tribes (Goths, Vandals, Allemani, Franks) arose on the Rhine and Danube Rivers. The emperor Diocletian (284–305) attempted to stem the decline with a political and military reorganization; but it was the emperor Constantine (312–37) who saw that much more was needed.

He attempted to provide a new internal principal of spiritual unity to the Roman Empire through Christianity. His "new Rome" of Constantinople was a Christian city from the start; from persecution to toleration to favored position to state religion—such was the changed estate of the Catholic Church in less than one century. But it had become the religion of a state far gone in decline. Visigothic troops sacked Rome in 410 (for the first time in 800 years) then carved out a realm in southern Gaul and Spain by 450. Vandals tore north Africa away from Rome (429–39). Franks reached the Loire by 486. Saxons, Angles and Jutes ended the Roman province of Britain. Disintegration in the west seemed complete, under the impact of the so-called *Barbarian Invasions*.

Meanwhile in the Roman east, imperial control remained intact but the subject peoples asserted their nationality in religious, not political, forms, adopting one or another of the heresies that flourished after the formal definition of Christian orthodoxy at the Council of Chalcedon (450); that Christ was truly God and truly man.

India and Southeast Asia

The India that the armies of Alexander entered was a complex welter of tribal principalities and republics, of which a certain primacy attached to the kingdom of Magadha in the Ganges valley ruled by the Nanda dynasty. Resistance to the Macedonians was strongest among the Brahman caste: the Kshatriya princes proved more practical and accommodating. After the last Macedonian satrap left India in 317 B.C. Chandragupta Maurya, who has met Alexander, attacked and conquered Magadha with the aid of northwestern tribes, exterminating the house of Nanda and commencing the *Mauryan Empire* (317–184 B.C.). Married to a Macedonian princess, Chandragupta subdued the Indus valley as well and gained recognition from the Diadochus, Seleucus Nicator. By the reign of his grandson Asoka (269–232 B.C.), central and most of southern India had been added to the empire which extended north to the foothills of the Himalayas and west to the eastern reaches of Afghanistan.

Asoka was known as *the Buddhist Emperor*, personally devout and publicly the protector and propagator of the religion of the *Buddha*. Like Asoka, prince Siddhartha Gautama (563–483 B.C.) was not Brahman but Kshatriya; enlightenment came when he realized that desire is the source of all suffering and that salvation therefore means escape from existence into *nirvana* (or nothingness) through rightful living. (Buddha, in Sanskrit, is a title meaning "the enlightened one.") He founded no church but disciples lived in communities following his "eightfold path" to holiness. It was these communities that Asoka fostered and patronized. The more sternly ascetical *Jainism*, founded by Mahavira (probably a contemporary of the Buddha) had spread without political support amongst an elite; its characteristic doctrines were the eternity of everything that is, even matter, and the attainment of nirvana after nine reincarnations.

After the death of Asoka (233 B.C.) the Mauryan Empire began to crumble into its constituent parts, the last emperor being assassinated by one of his generals in 184 B.C. One of the successor states was the Graeco-Indian kingdom in the north and north-west founded by a general of the Diodoch king of Bactria; another was the Kushan Empire of the first and second centuries A.D., which proved to be the route by which Buddhism expanded into central Asia.

A second Chandragupta was the founder of the last great Indian imperial regime, the *Gupta Empire* (320–535 A.D.) which at its greatest extent stretched across the subcontinent from the mouth of the Indus to the mouth of the Ganges. The source of its unity was a revived Hinduism whose brahmans provided advisors to the emperors and drew up the great codes of Hindu law which articulated the structures of the caste system. It was the age also of the revival of the Sanskrit language both in the drama of Kalidasa

(c. 400–55) and in the final composition of the epic poems Mahabharata and Ramayana. The Gupta period was the golden age of Indian science, especially astronomy, and mathematics, to which we owe the decimal system and the invention of the number zero. The sway of the classic Indian civilization was spread far beyond the political borders of the Gupta realm by traders and missionaries to Burma, Thailand, and Indo-China, to the Malay peninsula and beyond into Indonesia. The shores of the Bay of Bengal and of the South China Sea thus became a kind of "greater India", as the Diodoch kingdoms had become a "greater Greece."

The Chinese Empire

In 246 B.C. the cavalry troops of the far western state of Qin, hardened by years of warfare with the barbarian nomads of the steppe, hurtled eastward to conquer and subjugate, one by one, all of the other feudal principalities in a quarter century of war that brought the period of the "warring states" to an abrupt halt. On this territorial basis arose the first *Chinese Empire* under the *Qin Dynasty* (221–206 B.C.) Qin Shihuangdi ("The First Emperor of Qin") proved more than just a conqueror: he oversaw the completion of the Great Wall along the edge of Inner Mongolia and provided a structure of government for the empire by dividing the land into regions of administration and war, governed by deputies responsible to himself alone. The old nobility he destroyed by land confiscations; the Confucian schools he closed, executing many prominent scholars, cowing the rest into submission. And while a weakling successor proved unable to stem rebellion and met his death by assassination (206 B.C.) the structure of imperial rule inaugurated by the Qin would endure for over two thousand years.

A rebel leader named Liu Bang emerged victorious in the confused and bloody uprisings that brought the Qin Dynasty to an end. Liu proclaimed himself emperor of the Han Dynasty, which was to endure (with a brief interregnum under the usurper Wang Mang) for four centuries, from 206 B.C. to A.D. 220. The Han founder retained the imperial structure of Qin rule, while moderating its punitive harshness; he opened the way for renewed Confucian participation in government. The greatest Han ruler, Emperor Wu (r. 140–87 B.C.) instituted the practice of choosing officials on the basis of learning and merit. He brought the rich ricelands of the Yangtze River Valley firmly under imperial control, and also greatly extended the boundaries of the empire, conquering south to the South China Sea, southwest to the borders of Burma and Tibet, northeast to northern Korea, and westward to the deserts of Central Asia. He pacified the northern frontier, defeating the Xiongnu tribes whose descendants the Huns would later invade Europe. In an early arms race, the powerful laminated compound bow and cavalry tactics of the northern nomads were countered by Chinese infantry armed with mass-produced crossbows—a refinement of a weapon of Southeast Asian origin. At this time trade increased along the Silk Route, a network of caravan trails that, through many intermediaries, brought Chinese silk to the Roman Empire and warhorses from Central Asia to China.

The "dynastic cycle" completed its course in the last decades of the Han period, when court corruption, peasant uprisings, and military insurrections led to the overthrow of the last Han emperor in A.D. 220. There followed the Three Kingdoms Period (220–265), when rival states tries without success to reunite the empire, and the period of the Northern and Southern Dynasties (265–589), when northern China was frequently ruled by short-lived dynasties of invaders from the steppes, and southern China was fragmented into equally short-lived and ineffectual kingdoms. During this period of disunion Buddhism, which had entered China via Central Asia in late Han times, began to establish itself as one of China's major religions. Especially successful were sects of Mahayana ("Greater Vehicle") Buddhism, which promised salvation to the faithful through the mediation of saints called *bodhisattvas*.

Japan and Korea

Around 300 B.C., invaders from northeastern Asia had invaded Japan via the Korean Peninsula. These invaders, equipped with horses, bronze weapons, and the wealth produced by rice agriculture, displaced the ancient Jomon culture of the original inhabitants of Japan. This bronze-age Yayoi civilization, which also shows evidence of influence from Austronesian culture via Taiwan and Okinawa, laid the foundations for the subsequent Japanese empire. But for several centuries Japan was fragmented into small states ruled by military clans (uji), with those associated with the Shinto shrines at Izumo and Ise claiming some degree of primacy.

In Korea, the decline of the Chinese colony at Lolang led to the establishment of indigenous kingdoms; three of these—Silla, Paekche, and Koguryo—predominated during the period 313-668 A.D. Chinese cultural influence, via Korea, helped to transform the Japanese petty states into a centralized kingdom by the 5th century A.D.

▶EUROPE'S "DARK AGE" AND THE IMPACT OF ISLAM (A.D. 500–1000)

The seventh-century eruption of Islam with its compact secular-religious civilization and its characteristic institution of the *jihad* (holy war), both rooted in the sacred writings of the Koran, created an empire stretching from the Iberian Peninsula to the Indus Valley but influencing events in far-off Ghana as well. It also provoked in response the formation of eastern and western Christendom.

Untouched by these developments, China underwent another dynastic cycle—one in which Chinese civilization spread to Korea and Japan. And in utter isolation, without iron or even the wheel, civilizations in Central America began.

The Roman Empire and Europe's "Dark Age"

The lapse of direct Roman rule in the west did not imply "the fall of the Roman Empire", for the Germanic barbarians lived in a "greater Rome" whose heir and representative was the Catholic Church while in the east Roman rule continued with enough vigor to experience a great revival under the emperor Justinian (527–65). Maintaining a rough alliance with the Christian Franks in Gaul under their *Merovingian* dynasty, Justinian's armies recovered the western provinces: Vandal Africa, Ostrogothic Italy and the Mediterranean sector of Visigothic Spain. Meanwhile his jurists codified and preserved the whole body of *Roman law* since the days of the republic. And under imperial patronage there grew up a magnificent cluster of churches whose pinnacle was the Hagia Sophia in Constantinople, constructed in 537.

But the cost was very great: the treasury was beggared and the eastern frontiers neglected so that the west might be rewon. After Justinian's death the empire had neither treasure nor troops enough to save Italy from new invaders, the Lombards. The city of Ravenna on its marshes kept its link with Constantinople and Rome itself was saved, principally through the work of the pope, Gregory the Great. In the 14 years of his papacy (590–604) he not only organized the defense of the city but oversaw the work of converting Visigothic Spain and began the restoration of Christianity in faraway Britain through the mission of St. Augustine to Kent. In this evangelizing effort Gregory relied upon the monks who followed the *Rule* of St. Benedict (480–547) who brought moderation and a Roman sense of order to the *monasticism* of the west. In a chaotic world, Benedict's *Rule* provided a uniform way of life for monks living as a community, including vows of poverty, chastity, and obedience, regular and frequent hours of prayer, study of the Bible, and manual work.

The empire, which barely held on in the east against Persia, met catastrophe at the hands of the armies of Islam (see next section). In half a dozen years (636–42) Syria, Egypt and Libya fell away; in a second wave of invasions (696–711) the rest of north Africa and Spain were lost as well; Frankish Gaul was only just saved by the cavalry of Charles Martel in the battle of Tours (732). The Mediterranean seemed on its way toward becoming a Moslem lake.

Two successor states to the old Roman empire emerged. In the east lay the empire proper, but now usually called the *Byzantine Empire* (610–1453). Its wealth and power were based in Asia Minor, its unity dependent upon three factors: Orthodox Christianity (slowly drifting away from Roman Catholicism until the final break with Rome in 1054); Hellenistic culture and the Greek language; and Roman law and administration. Missionary ventures carried Christianity and Byzantine influence to the Serbs and Croats in the Balkans, to the Moravians and Slovaks north of the Danube, and even as far as Kievian Rus, all in the ninth and tenth centuries.

In the west there arose the *Carolingian Empire* (751–888). The son of Charles Martel, Pepin III, cooperated with St. Boniface to reform the Frankish Church in close relation with Rome, deposed (with papal approval) the last Merovingian shadow-king, and was himself anointed king in 751. Before his death in 768 Pepin had made Frankish sovereignty felt southward to the Pyrenees and the Mediterranean. His son Charlemagne (768–814) conquered Lombardy, absorbed Bavaria, expanded into Saxony and beyond the Pyrenees, bringing under his sway an area equal in size to the old Roman Empire in the west. At the same time, to foster missionary endeavors, he ordered the creation of cathedral and monastic schools, drawing heavily for his scholars on Northumbria, the small English kingdom where Celtic and Roman monastic traditions had intermingled. The pinnacle of his work came on Christmas Day in the year 800 when in the city of Rome he was acclaimed and crowned as Roman Emperor, by the pope.

But with his death disintegration began. By 843 his grandsons divided his realm in three parts with a middle kingdom of the emperor Lothair separating the kingdoms of the East and West Franks (the nuclei of Germany and France yet to be). These realms faced deadly peril on all sides: Viking corsairs from the north (who also ravaged the British Isles and established commercial bases between the Baltic and Byzantium), Moslem pirates attacking from the south, and, just as these threats had abated, the fierce horsemen of the Hungarians, about the year 900. The family of the Carolingians proved unable to lead any effective resistance; that arose among the nobles of the empire who, inspired by the example of King Alfred the Great of Wessex (849–901) against the Danes in England, defended their people but demanded in return their obedience and support. This was the origin of that pattern of decentralized authority and allegiance known as *feudalism*. Not that monarchy died, but the medieval kings became "firsts amongst equals": Henry the Fowler (919–36) began the *Saxon Dynasty* of German kings while his son Otto I also assumed (962) the title of Emperor; and Hugh Capet in 987 began the *Capetian Dynasty* of France which ruled into the 19th century.

The aftermath of this terrible dark age was the creation of the new Christian monarchies on the fringe of the older Carolingian world: the restoration of the Empire in 962, replacing Charlemagne's empire, which barbarian tribes had destroyed; the consolidation and conversion of the Scandinavian monarchies about 990; the establishment of an independent and Catholic Poland (966) the already mentioned conversion of Kievian Rus (988) under St. Vladimir; and the founding in 1001 of a Catholic Hungarian kingdom under St. Stephen (997–1038).

The Islamic World

To the Roman Empire, the Arabs were a frontier annoyance, no menace as was Sassanid Persia; yet it was out of the Arabian Desert that the whirlwind of Islam arose. Its founder, Mohammed (or Muhammad) (570–632) was a religious prophet whose revelations came from God; these revelations form the heart of the Moslem sacred book, the *Koran*. Utter simplicity of doctrine (a stern monotheism and a focus on the world to come) and of moral code ("hard against the infidels, merciful among themselves") combine with an elaborate ceremonial (the strict fast of Ramadan, prayer five times daily, the Meccan pilgrimage). Driven out of Mecca to Yathrib (now Medina), Mohammed and his followers formed a religious and political community which, after eight years of desert warfare, returned to capture Mecca (630).

Within two years of Mohammed's death the armies of Islam were marching. From the Romans they wrested Syria, Mesopotamia, Egypt and Libya (636–46); the Persians they conquered outright (637–49). Not until 661 was the vexed question of the succession settled when the old tribal aristocracy triumphed over the family of the prophet and established *Umayyad Dynasty* (661–750) of caliphs ("successors") ruling not from Medina but from Damascus and utilizing the old Persian and Roman bureaucracies. For almost half a century Islam lay quiescent; then, with the conversion of the Berbers, Byzantine Africa was swept away (696) as was Visigothic Spain (711). In the same year a Moslem commander established himself in the lower Indus Valley.

A series of revolts protesting the purely Arabic dominance of the Umayyads led to the establishment of a new dynasty of caliphs, the *Abbasid Dynasty* (750–1258), descended from a cousin of Mohammed. Arab by descent, the Abbasids nonetheless moved the capital to the new city of Baghdad in Mesopotamia where Persian influence came to predominate in politics as in literature while the Islamic scientific and mathematical flowering owed as much to Gupta India and ancient Greece as to archaic Babylonian astral speculations, especially the decimal system of numeration and the use of the zero.

The Umayyads had not been totally overturned; Spain followed their rule when the rest of the empire turned to the house of Abbas; after about 800 there were independent Moslem states in Morocco, Tunis, and eastern Persia; and by about 875 in Egypt and Turkestan. Before the year 1000 the caliphs had lost almost all their political power, becoming largely a focus of religious unity, relying even then on the *ulema*, adepts of Islamic law and lore. To this day, ultimate authority in many Islamic states has remained with the religious leaders.

India and Africa on the Fringe of Islam

After the fall of the Gupta Dynasty in 535, India reverted to its older pattern of a large number of tribal principalities. The White Huns, whose incursion had overturned Gupta power, coexisted with the Hindu princes who knew them as *Rajputs* and established a feudal state across north India east of the Indus valley, the kingdom of Rajputana. The Sind (or lower Indus) was already in Moslem hands after 711. By the ninth century Buddhism had all but disappeared from India, absorbed into Hinduism; one exception was in the state of the Pala kings who ruled Bengal and Magadha into the 12th century. Buddhism remained influential in "greater India": in the small kingdoms of Burma, in the kingdom of Dvaravati in Siam, in Sri Lanka, and in the Sumatran state of Srivishaya under its Sailendra dynasty.

At the other extremity of the caliphate, Moslem traders from Morocco were in contact with the *Kingdom of Ancient Ghana* by about the year 800. Camel caravans crossed the Sahara to the grasslands between the upper Niger and Senegal rivers bearing salt and goods from the Mediterranean basin. There the king of Ghana supplied gold and ivory brought north from the southern reaches of the "shoulder" of Africa. Extracting import and export taxes and monopolizing the gold supply, the kings of Ghana exercised a kind of imperial control over the trading cities of the region, growing wealthy and powerful. Yet by 1076 the caliphs in Morocco were able to conquer the region.

At the opposite side of Africa, Moslem Arabs crossed the Red Sea and annexed the Somali coast (c. 1050) from the ancient Christian kingdom of Ethiopia.

China: Tang and Song Dynasties

Three centuries of disunion in China came to an end with the establishment of the *Sui Dynasty* in 589. Like the Qin, the Sui was a short-lived dynasty that paved the way for a long-enduring one. Extravagant expenditures on construction of the Grand Canal linking Hangzhou and Chang'an (a distance of over 1000 miles), a disastrous attempt to conquer Korea, and a Turkish invasion of northwestern China doomed the Sui. It was replaced in 618 by the *Tang Dynasty*, one of the most glorious eras in all of Chinese history. Buddhism flourished, as did poetry and the fine arts; Tang Chang'an was the largest and most cosmopolitan city in the world by around 700. But in 751 Chinese troops on the westernmost frontier were defeated by an Arab army in the Battle of Talas, and the Tang abandoned much of Central Asia; in 755, China's greatest general, An Lushan, rebelled against the throne. The rebellion was defeated, but the empire never recovered fully. An imperial persecution of Buddhism in the 840s, during which the wealth of many temples was confiscated, signaled the rise of Neo-Confucianism, reinvigorating China's oldest philosophical tradition. But with the imperial house in disarray, the Tang collapsed in 907.

After five decades of inconclusive attempts to restore central rule, the *Song Dynasty* was founded in 960, and endured until 1279. But the Song never had firm control of northern China. The northeast was controlled by the *Liao Dynasty* in the hands of the non-Chinese Khitan people (whose name gives us the world Cathay). They were replaced in the early 12th century by the *Jurchen Jin Dynasty*, which in 1127 conquered all of northern China, sending the Song emperors south to a new capital at Hangzhou. Although the Song were politically weak this was nevertheless a time of cultural brilliance, when Chinese landscape painting was perfected, poetry flourished, and urban life (rich with the wealth of overseas trade) attained new heights of sophistication. With the old northern aristocratic clans destroyed by the downfall of Tang and subsequent centuries of barbarian rule, the Song state was run by a surprisingly modern bureaucratic government recruited from a prosperous and well educated rural gentry.

Japan and Korea

In Korea, the state of Silla in 562 put an and to Japanese attempts to carve out colonial enclaves on the peninsula, and then, with Tang support, turned its attention to defeating its rivals Paekche and Koguryo. This process was completed by 670, and Silla grew prosperous with Tang support and cultural influence. But Silla in turn was defeated in 935 by the small western state of Koryo, which established a dynasty ruling all of Korea until 1392. Relatively isolated from Song influence by the intervening states of Liao, and later Jin, the Koryo state became culturally more independent of China.

In Japan, *the Yamato clan*, which had gradually pressed its claim to recognition as an imperial dynasty on the Chinese model, was firmly established on the throne by the fifth century A.D. Buddhism came to Japan in the following century, along with such continental innovations as the use of Chinese script to write (phonetically) the very different Japanese language. In 589 Prince Shotoku issued a 17-article "constitution" establishing imperial support for Buddhism and enjoining all aristocrats to respect the imperial throne. The throne thereupon came under the influence of the powerful *Soga clan* until 645; a restoration movement emphasized emulation of the Chinese model of government. But the principle of appointment to office on the basis of merit never caught on in Japan, which continued to be ruled by an hereditary aristocracy.

Japan's first permanent capital city was founded at Nara in 710; by 750 the city was wholly dominated by its rich and powerful Buddhist temples. In response the emperors moved the capital to the new city of Heian-kyo (now Kyoto) in 794; the emperors remained there for over a thousand years. Both Nara and Heian-kyo were built on a grid plan, modeled after Tang Chang'an; Heian-kyo especially boasted a glittering cultural life, supported by agrarian wealth from the provinces. The powerful *Fujiwara clan* gained control of the country's political life through the expedient of making sure that every emperor married a Fujiwara daughter, and abdicated the throne for a life of monastic retirement shortly after producing an heir; the head of the Fujiwara clan thus was always the father-in-law of one emperor and the legal guardian of the heir-apparent.

The Classic Age of Mayan Culture

Splendid archaeological remains wrapped in chronological obscurity give tantalizing hints of culture in central America before the year 1000. Sometime around 2500 B.C. (but perhaps a millennium earlier) the hybrid maize (or Indian corn) was developed on present-day Mexico's Gulf coast. Permanent agricultural settlements, stretching from Mexico's central plateau to the Guatemalan highlands, seem to date from about 1500 B.C. But it was not until the period A.D. 300–900 that Central America attained approximately to the cultural level of ancient Mesopotamia. From Guatemala to the Yucatan the Mayans developed temples, ritual calendars and a system of writing as yet not deciphered. Similarly, in the Mexican Plateau, there grew up a culture associated with the great city of Teotihuacan. Both seem to have been "empires" of city-states, but except for Teotihuacan itself the sites were not really cities, rather religious centers surrounded by agricultural hamlets. The Mexican development seems to have been cut short by invasions about A.D. 900, probably by the Toltecs. The abandonment about the same time of the Mayan temple sites may have been the result of drought, deforestation, and other environmental factors.

▶THE MOSLEMS, THE TURKS, AND THE RISE OF THE CHRISTIAN WEST (A.D. 1000–1500)

The four major centers of civilization that had been established by the year 1000—European Christendom, the Islamic world, India and China—all underwent tremendous challenges from confederations of warlike Turkish and Mongol tribes in the next 500 years. Of all the developments the most significant for world history proved to be the maturation of western Christendom which had already commenced, before the period closed, its expansion to the Americas, to Africa and to southern Asia as well.

Expansion of the Moslem World: Asia and Africa

The *Abbasid* dynasty of caliphs of Baghdad had long employed Turkish auxiliaries (rather as the Romans had used German tribes) in their Near Eastern armies; one such army, under their chieftain Mohammed of Ghazni, moved out of Afghanistan into the Punjab about the year 1000 and by 1030 established a Moslem dynasty there. Over the next 200 years they spread their conquests over the Rajputs eastward into the plain of the Ganges, establishing their capital at Delhi about the year 1200. The rich Hindu temples were plundered and, as "heathen," destroyed by these Moslem Turks. Under the sultan (="ruler") Ala-ud-din (1296–1316) most of the subcontinent was brought under one rule for the first time since Asoka.

Unable to break the caste tradition, the ruling Turks became yet another caste, a minority of warrior-aristocrats extracting heavy taxes but relying upon the Hindu princes for administration. Though the Hindu temples had been destroyed, the Turks had to permit a practical tolerance for a now less sacerdotal Hinduism. After the death of Ala-ud-din his empire dissolved into a medley of warring kingdoms ruled by Moslem generals or Hindu princes over whom the sultans at Delhi exercised greater or lesser control.

In the "greater India" of Southeast Asia, Islamic influence expanded through trade and Chinese influence through trade and warfare. In Burma, the Buddhist kingdom founded by Anawrata in 1044 was destroyed by the Mongol armies of Kublai Khan in 1287 and the land was divided into a number of small principalities. Dvaravati Siam (briefly annexed to Cambodia in the 11th century) was overrun by Thai tribesmen from China in the 13th century; by 1350 a Thai kingdom of Siam had established its capital at Ayutthaya, which was to remain its capital until the end of the 18th century. Over the next century, Siam subdued the independent kingdom of Cambodia to the east and expanded against Burma as well. In the archipelago of Indonesia and curving north into the Philippines, Moslem traders and missionaries had established 20 Islamic states by the year 1500. The Hindu aristocracy of Java took refuge on the island of Bali, which still preserves elements of pre-Islamic Indonesian culture.

Moslem expansion occurred in western Africa as well. The conquest of ancient Ghana by Moslem Berbers in 1076 (who had conquered Morocco as well 20 years earlier) led to no new empire but a series of successor states. One of these, Kangaba, had by the 13th century established another trading state of immense size, the *Kingdom of Mali* which stretched, in the 14th century, from the Atlantic coast eastward beyond Gao on the Niger. Under king Mansa Musa (c. 1312–37) Islam spread through the western savanna, the king himself making a pilgrimage to Mecca in 1324. Further east, the king of the Songhay people on the great bend of the Niger had already converted to Islam in the 11th century; thus, when the dominance of Mali was replaced in the 15th century by the *Kingdom of Songhay*, Islam dominated not only the northern coast of Africa but almost the entire belt of savanna south of the Sahara as well.

It was also in this period, but obscurely and beyond the range of Islam, that African tribes (speaking various languages of the Bantu family) continued their long migrations. In the previous period (c. 600-900) they had moved out of the Cameroon highlands east to the Great Lakes; from there they migrated in two streams: southwest to the Congo basin, and south to the savanna of modern Zambia. Now in the period from about 1000 to about 1500, they occupied Kenya and Tanzania on the east and the lands south to the edge of the Kalahari desert.

Transformation of the Moslem World: The Turks

No sooner had Mohammed of Ghazni established Turkish rule in the Punjab than two brothers of the Seljuk clan revolted and took Afghanistan (1037), then expanded into Persia and Mesopotamia (by 1055). After the battle of Manzikert (1071) they took most of Asia Minor from Byzantium. When Syria was added (1084) the *Seljuk Empire* (1037–1243) stretched from Egypt to India. During the 12th century, in the aftermath of the First Crusade (1096–99), their empire became a jumble of small emirates ruled by Seljuk princes or their generals. What brought the Seljuks low was the sudden appearance in the 1240s of the Mongols in the Near East; though menacing to both Moslems and Christians, Mongols power proved ephemeral and the true heirs of the Seljuks proved to be another clan of Turks, the Ottomans. In 1326 they drove Byzantine forces entirely out of Asia Minor, thus beginning the *Ottoman Empire* (1326–1920). By century's end they controlled all of Asia Minor and the Balkans as far north as Bosnia. Half a century later (1453) they took Constantinople, turning Hagia Sophia into a mosque in their re-named capital of Istanbul.

Eastern Christendom Submerged: Mongols and Turks

The 11th century was the apogee of the *Eastern Roman Empire* (Byzantium) as it conquered the Christian kingdom of Bulgaria (1018) and made Serbia a client state in the west, while to the east Armenia and the Crimea were annexed (1022). But by mid-century the Normans, descendants of Vikings who settled in the French province of Normandy, were establishing themselves in Byzantine Italy (and Moslem Sicily), and the battle of Manzikert (1071) proved a catastrophe from which the Empire never recovered, losing both its granary and its military recruiting ground to the Turks in a single blow. Although the first three crusades (1096–1192) were initially successful in wresting the Holy Land from Islam, the subsequent organization of the territory in the French pattern of small squabbling and isolated feudal statelets rendered them impotent and hence of only marginal help to Byzantium. The Fourth Crusade (1202-1204) was a disaster, for the crusaders took Constantinople, establishing what is called the *Latin Empire* (1204–61). In 1261, Michael Palaeologus (1261–82) restored a rump Byzantium along the shores of the Aegean and it was against this state that the Ottoman Turks expanded. The doom of Constantinople brought Turkish power right to the borders of Hungary, with the Balkans absorbed into the Ottoman Empire for 450 years.

In the northeast it was not the Turks but the Mongols whose arrival transformed Christendom. Hungary, Poland and Kievian Rus were weakened by dynastic struggles from the 11th century on, yet maintained their independence of the Holy Roman Empire to the west and the Turkish Cumans in the east. But the uniting of the Mongol federation under Genghis Khan (1206-27) created a power great enough to strike at China, the Near East, and Europe at the same time; by his death his realm extended from Korea to the borders of Persia and Rus. A decade later Mongol armies under Genghis Khan's grandson Batu (d. 1255) fell upon Europe (1237–40) attacking beyond Russia into Poland and Hungary and the lands of the German knights on the Baltic; but with the death of the Khan, the Mongols retreated. Still the "Golden Horde," an independent Mongol Khanate organized by Batu on the lower Volga River, ruled all of south Russia and reduced the north Russian principalities to vassal status.

Not until the late 15th century was the prince of Moscow sufficiently established to refuse tribute money to the Empire. His marriage to the niece of the last Byzantine emperor established the claim of Ivan III to imperial succession as he took the title "czar" (= Caesar or emperor) and his conquest of the principality of Novgorod (1478) established a large Russian state northeast of Poland. Poland had attained its status as the largest state in Christendom with the marriage (1386) of its queen Jadwiga (1384–99) to the Grand Duke Jagiello of Lithuania; in the 15th century the Jagellon Dynasty (1386–1572) controlled the entire region between the Baltic and Black Seas. But thereby it was exposed to a four-fold danger: from Ottomans to the south, Germans to the west, Swedes to the north and Russians to the northeast.

The Rise of Western Christendom

For 600 years out of the ruins of the western Roman Empire and the anarchy of barbarian invasions, Western Christendom slowly emerged, the process essentially completed with the conversion to Christianity of the Scandinavians, the Poles and the Magyars (950–1050). It was not a society associated with a great empire (for the Carolingian Empire had fallen in the ninth century) but with the feudal states of France and the tribal duchies of Germany. Its unity, such as it was, was religious and cultural as well as political.

Whether the leadership of this society should fall to the Popes or the Holy Roman Emperors was settled in the 11th century in the *Investiture Struggle* in which the papacy emerged victorious. From Pope Gregory VII (1073–85) to Boniface VIII (1294–1303) the papacy gave the lead to western Christendom often in alliance with reforming monastic leaders. In the 12th and 13th centuries the characteristic architecture and sculpture of medieval Europe (*Romanesque* and *Gothic*) spread across Europe under Church patronage while the Leagues of the Peace and the Crusades attempted to limit and channel to constructive use the warrior ethos of the feudal nobles.

Beginning in 11th century Italy and 12th century Netherlands, the commune movement, in which all the inhabitants of a town bound themselves by oath to obey their magistrates, keep the peace, and defend their liberties, revived town life and created the medieval city as a confederation of self-governing guilds. *Guilds* were associations of craftsmen of one trade or merchants bound together for mutual aid. In the west the fairs of Champagne and Burgundy provided ground for the re-establishment of trade while in the Mediterranean, the Italian cities (especially Venice and Genoa) linked the west with Byzantium and the Moslem Near East.

In these towns arose the great universities (Paris, Bologna, Salerno, Oxford) where Greek and Arab learning met with the Christian traditions of the Carolingian schools; the insights of Aristotle re-thought in Christian terms issued into the legal, philosophic, theological and scientific work of *scholasticism*, the work of men like Albertus Magnus, Thomas Aquinas, Bonaventure, Roger Bacon, and Duns Scotus—all members also of the new religious orders, Franciscans (St. Francis, 1182–1226) and Dominicans (St. Dominic, 1170–1221), which arose in the towns of the 13th century. Committed to evangelical poverty and combating heresy, they played a role in university life as well.

Late in the 12th century in Spain and Italy, in the 13th in Germany, England and France, in the 14th and 15th in Hungary, Poland and Scandinavia, the custom arose for monarchs to call the elected representatives of the towns to meet with prelates and nobles to render advice; such was the origin of *parliaments.*

The development of these social and cultural and religious institutions was accompanied by the expansion of western Christendom. One aspect was internal with the clearing of forests and the cultivation of new farmland able to support an increased population. The other was external, not so much the ephemeral Kingdom of Jerusalem (1099-1162) or Latin Empire of Constantinople (1204–61) as the reconquest of Spain from the Moslems (1085–1492), the conquest of Prussia and Livonia by the Teutonic Knights (1229–1466) and the conversion of Lithuania (1386 and after.)

The most significant check to population growth was the *Black Death*, an outbreak of bubonic plague that swept over Europe (1347–51), wiping out perhaps 25 million, a third of the population. The loose unity of western Christendom began to alter in the 14th century in significant ways. First of all, the universality of the papacy seemed compromised when seven popes in succession (1305–78) preferred to reside at Avignon rather than Rome, in too close an association with the kings of France; then, after the return to Rome arose that series of disputed elections to the papacy which is called the *Great Schism* (1378–1417); and third, with the end of the schism, the popes became more and more involved in the politics of Renaissance Italy.

Meanwhile, while theories of sovereignty derived from the study of Roman law exalted the authorities of kings, royal powers disastrously declined due to chronic feudal violence: the "age of princes" in Germany (1273-1493), the Hundred Years' War in England and France (1337–1453), and the dynastic Wars of the Roses in England (1455–85). Out of the turmoil arose the "new monarchies" of more unified states: the Tudors in England (1485), the Valois and in France (1328–1529), and in Spain the Spanish branch of the Habsburgs (1504–1700).

In the Italy of the 14th and 15th centuries, increasingly the plaything of the new monarchies, there began that great cultural transformation known as the *Renaissance*. Humanists like Petrarch (1304–74), and Boccaccio (1313–75) sought a revival of Latin antiquity, both pagan (Cicero, Virgil, Tacitus) and Christian (Augustine and the other Church fathers), in an educational movement that sought to unite the values of Hellenism with Christianity. At the same time artists, studying Roman architecture and Hellenistic sculpture on the one hand and the new sciences of anatomy and perspective on the other, created a new world of beauty. In painting, Botticelli and da Vinci, in architecture Brunelleschi (1377–1446), in sculpture Ghiberti (1378–1455) and Donatello (1386–1466)—these represent the output of the city of Florence alone.

Building on medieval foundations and new navigational discoveries (magnetic compasses, the astolabe, the quadrant), the Portuguese monarchy pioneered the exploration of the African coast; the Gulf of Guinea was reached by 1470, the Cape of Good Hope by 1487, and India itself by 1498. The Spanish monarchs sponsored the western route of Columbus whose four voyages (1492–1504) brought Europeans to the shores of the Caribbean (which he mistook for Japan and the Malay Peninsula). Finally, before the period closed, the new Tudor monarchy of England financed the more northerly westward explorations of the Cabots who reached Newfoundland and New England in 1497 and 1498. Like the humanists, by seeking a very old world, the explorers found something very new as well.

The Americas

The New World which Columbus discovered was dominated by two great empires. In Mexico, the Toltecs established an empire with its capital in the magnificent temple city of Tula; it included most of the old Mayan realm (c. 900–1200). But the 12th and 13th centuries saw a series of incursions of barbarian nomadic hunters from the south known collectively as Chichimecs whose armed might destroyed the Toltec civilization. In time, one of these tribes, the Aztecs, established a capital at Tenochtitlan and over the century from about 1360 to about 1470 conquered neighboring peoples and constructed the sanguinary *Aztec Empire* (c. 1360–1520). The king Montezuma I (died c. 1470) was a ruthless conqueror but a great builder as well, transforming the capital into a magnificent city of stone. By 1500 the Aztecs had reached Guatemala. For the subject peoples war and subjections were evil enough; worse was the Aztec worship of the sun god who required for his nourishment human blood.

Stretching thousands of miles along the west coast of South America lay the empire of the Incas with their capital at Cuzco. Unlike the military Aztec empire of subject states paying tribute including the blood tax, the *Inca Empire* was a centralized bureaucratic state which engaged in social engineering as well as road and bridge building and irrigation projects. Begun about 1200, the empire attained its greatest size under Huayna Capac (c. 1493–1527).

China and East Asia (1200–1500)

Genghis Khan (b. 1162–1227), leader of the Mongol federation, wished to unite all of the nomadic peoples of the Asian steppes under his rule. The Mongol conquest of northern China, ruled by Jurchen tribesmen from Manchuria, was completed by Genghis Khan's successors in 1234. The Mongols then turned their attention to Korea, which they conquered in 1231–36, and to the Chinese Song Dynasty in the Yangtze River Valley. The Song defended their territory vigorously, while the Mongols were slowed down as their horsemen learned to cope with wet ricefields and rivers defended by heavily armed ships; but in 1271 Kubilai Khan (b. 1215–94) proclaimed himself emperor of the *Yuan Dynasty* of China, and in 1279 the last Song emperor capitulated. During his reign Kubilai Khan tried twice to invade Japan; his fleets were stopped by *kamikaze*, "divine winds," i.e. typhoons. An attempt to conquer Java also met with only limited and temporary success.

In China the Mongols were seen as an alien occupying power; their habit of using foreign, Persian-speaking tax-collectors made them especially hated. The successors to Kubilai Khan were mediocre rulers; in 1368 a Chinese nativist rebellion led by a charismatic ex-Buddhist monk named Zhu Yuanzhang succeeded in overthrowing the Mongols and establishing the *Ming Dynasty* (1368–1644). The early Ming emperors were vigorous and forward-looking; they rebuilt the Great Wall, re-routed the Grand Canal to terminate near Beijing, built a new southern capital at Nanjing, and sent maritime expeditions on missions of exploration and diplomacy throughout the South China Sea and the Indian Ocean to the east coast of Africa. These expeditions, under Admiral Zheng He, were however abruptly terminated in 1433, criticized by the conservative Confucian bureaucracy as a waste of money and resources. Thus the Chinese missed by only three decades the chance to confront the Portuguese as rival maritime powers in the Indian Ocean.

In Korea, the *Koryo Dynasty* did not long outlast the rule of their Mongol patrons. The last Koryo king in 1388 sent his best general, Yi Songgye (famous for his victories over Japanese pirates), to invade China to try to overthrow the Ming Dynasty on behalf of the Mongols. General Yi instead turned back at the border, overthrew the Koryo king, and established his own dynasty, the *Kingdom of Choson*, which soon proclaimed its support for the Ming emperors. The third Choson (or Yi Dynasty) ruler, King Sejong (r. 1418–1450) was Korea's greatest sovereign, a patron of art, science and technology during whose reign Korean scholars and craftsmen perfected printing with moveable metal type, invented a syllabic script to write vernacular Korean, and equipped Seoul with what was, for a time, the best astronomical observatory in the world. The Choson monarchs tolerated Buddhism, promoted Confucianism, ruled through a very conservative aristocracy, and remained on the throne until 1910.

In Japan, the Fujiwara-dominated aristocrats of Heian-kyo ignored the rise of a provincial warrior aristocracy in the provinces until it was too late. The Fujiwaras were ousted by the western Taira clan in 1160; they in turn were defeated by Minamoto no Yoritomo at the naval battle of Dan-no-Ura in 1185. Yoritomo then took the hereditary title of *shogun* ("generalissimo"), and established a military capital at Kamakura, leaving the emperors to reign but not rule in Heian-kyo. The Minamoto were shunted aside by their own hereditary retainers, the *Hojo Clan*, in 1229. A crisis was precipitated in 1331 by Emperor Daigo II, who refused to abdicate on command of the shogun, and attempted to institute direct imperial rule. In 1333 another general, Ashikaga Takauji, helped Daigo II overthrow the Hojo, but Ashikaga then promptly proclaimed himself shogun, moved the military capital to the Muromachi district of Kyoto, and put the emperors firmly in their place once again. The *Muromachi* shogunate endured until 1568, though with little military power; the shoguns were better known as patrons of Zen Buddhism, Noh theater, and the tea ceremony. With the waning of central authority, Japanese merchants were more free to establish domestic and overseas trade routes (and to engage in piracy on the China coast), leading to economic prosperity amidst political instability.

▶ THE EXPANSION OF THE WEST AND THE ENDURANCE OF THE EAST (1500–1650)

During this period, the great empires of Asia—Ottoman Turkey, Safavid Persia, Mogul India and Ming China—remained intact and even expanded, but the dynamic power and movement of this extraordinary age were driven by the emerging nation-states of Europe. Despite severe internal divisions both religious (the Reformation) and national, which led to incessant warfare among all of them, the major powers managed to dominate the sea lanes of the globe and control the coasts and islands of Africa, southern Asia, and the Americas.

The Near East: Ottoman Empire and Safavid Persia

Under their sultans Selim I the Grim (1512–20) and Suleiman I the Magnificent (1520–66) the Ottoman Turks added Syria and Egypt to their domains, then from their fortress at Belgrade launched an invasion of Hungary which climaxed at the battle of Mohacs (1526), where over 20,000 Christian soldiers were slain and three-quarters of the realm fell under Turkish rule either directly or through Ottoman client princes of Transylvania. The Turks moved on to besiege Vienna (1529), halting the campaign because of troubles with Persia. On the seas Turkish fleets added Yemen and Aden on the Persian Gulf and Tripoli, Algeria, and Tunis on the southern shores of the Mediterranean.

But Suleiman's successor was Selim II (the Sot), the first in a series of weak sultans who came to the throne between 1566–1718 as a result of that perennial weakness of Moslem dynasties, harem intrigues of wives and eunuchs, and of the specifically Ottoman problem, the "praetorian guard" of Janissaries. In 1571, the Holy League (the Papacy, Venice, Tuscany and Spain) triumphed over the Turkish navy in the battle of Lepanto, though dissolution of the League after the victory meant that the Ottoman fleet could still raid almost at will through the Mediterranean.

Persia saw the revival of a native Iranian dynasty under the *Safavid Dynasty* (1501–1736). Its founder Shah Ismail seized power from the White Sheep Turks in 1501 and successfully defended Persia from Ottoman expansion into Mesopotamia, a work continued under his son and successor (1514–55). After the reign of the dynasty's greatest representative, Abbas I the Great (1587–1629), there began a period of harem intrigues which greatly weakened the dynasty. The Turks succeeded in taking Baghdad (1638).

Christian trading presence in Persia began with the Portuguese establishment at Hormuz in 1507; by 1622 the Portuguese were turned out by Abbas, English merchants supplanting them.

Mogul India and the Portuguese Spice Trade

In 1526, a descendent of Genghis Khan attacked the sultan at Delhi and established his dominance east of the Indus. Though a Turk, because of the long association of his family with the Mongols, his empire came to be called the *Mogul Empire* (1526–1857). Babur (b. 1483–1530), the founder then expanded east to the borders of Bengal. Although his son lost almost all Babur had conquered, his grandson Akbar (1556–1605), contemporary of Philip II of Spain and Elizabeth of England, restored Babur's realm and expanded it further until it included all of India north of the Deccan Plateau. Vigorous in warfare, gracious in victory, wise in administration, tolerant in religion, Akbar's empire knew peace and prosperity. Most of the Deccan was added in the reign of his grandson Shah Jahan (1628–58), who also built the Taj Mahal.

It seems almost miraculous that Portugal, a tiny state on the edge of the Atlantic, should create a seaborne empire dominating the Indian Ocean, but that is what Portugal did in the 16th century. In 1497, Vasco da Gama (c. 1469–1524) began a journey that took him around Africa's Cape of Good Hope and across the Indian Ocean to Calicut where he encountered the great riches of India's spice trade. After da Gama's second voyage (1502), the Moslem state of Gujerat, allied with Mameluke Egypt, declared a *jihad* against the Portuguese, but at Diu, the Portuguese won a complete victory (1508). The Portuguese viceroy organized the building of a "rosary" of over a dozen forts stretching form Hormuz on the Persian Gulf through Goa to Malacca on the Malay Peninsula. Thus the Portuguese could monopolize the carrying trade in the Indian Ocean as well as divert the spice trade around Africa. And from Malacca they established trading posts in the Spice Islands (Moluccas), China and Japan. This network provided the route for Christian missionaries as well.

But it proved all too much for Portugal. The English and the Dutch had established their East India Companies in 1600 and 1602 and in the 17th century the Dutch, piecemeal, took the place of the Portuguese by war and diplomacy. One portent for the future: by 1639 the English were at Madras.

East Asia: China, Korea, Japan

The late Ming emperors were great patrons of culture, but mediocre rulers. The former Chinese protectorate of Annam, while maintaining its mandarin culture, became independent, the first true monarchy of Vietnam. In 1557 the Portuguese established a trading colony at Macao (due to revert to Chinese rule in 1999). The danger to China from Mongolia, from where Altan Khan (1543–83) raided almost annually across the Great Wall, was kept in check by adroit Ming diplomacy, and further allayed by the Mongol acceptance of Tibetan religious authority; with the spread of Lamaism, monasteries absorbed surplus sons who might otherwise have become warriors. But danger lurked in the lands north of Korea, where descendants of the 12th-century Jurched rulers of the *Jin Dynasty* were forming a new tribal confederation of people who would become known as *Manchus*. Their chieftain Nurhachi took the title of emperor; his son brought all of Mongolia under his rule, overran Korea in 1627, and took the Ming northeastern outpost of Mukden in 1636.

Domestically in China, a combination of rising imperial expenditures and increasing land tax evasion by the rural gentry eventually destabilized even so rich an empire as the Ming. Factionalism and eunuch intrigues in the capital weakened the dynasty further; popular rebellions broke out and were not thoroughly suppressed. In desperation, the last Ming emperor invited a Manchu army to Beijing to expell a rebel band that had seized the city. Having expelled the rebels, the Manchus refused to leave. The Ming emperor hanged himself, and the Manchus proclaimed the founding of the *Qing Dynasty* (1644–1911). Ming resistance in southern China was quashed by 1661; all Chinese men were required to braid their hair in a queue as a sign of submission.

During the last decades of the Ming, China began to feel the first effects of European influence. The Jesuit missionary Matteo Ricci reached Macao in 1582 and Beijing in 1601. Adapting himself to local custom, he became an accomplished Confucian scholar and used that guise as a means of introducing to China such things as the astrolabe, the weight-driven clock, prisms, and the Mercator map of the world. For a brief time Christianity became a vogue among some members of the mandarin class, but imperial disapproval (exacerbated by factional disputes among the Christian missionary orders) discouraged conversions. Under Qing rule the Jesuits were prohibited from preaching, but allowed to remain in China for their technical skills in astronomy, mathematics, painting, and cannon-founding.

In Korea, the *Choson Dynasty* was badly shaken by a destructive invasion (1592–98) from Japan under the leadership of the shogun Toyotomi Hideyoshi. The invasion was finally repelled with Chinese aid, but Korea suffered long-term economic and social damage. Conquered by the Manchus in 1627, the Koreans had no difficulty in transferring their loyalty from the Ming to the Qing; Choson remained a loyal vassal of China, and isolated from the rest of the world, until the late 19th century.

Japan borrowed the old Chinese term "Warring States Period" to describe the century from 1467 to 1568, when Muromachi rule dissolved in a welter of mutually hostile feudal domains. Order was gradually restored after 1568 by three remarkable generals: Oda Nobunaga, who was the first Japanese general to use firearms extensively in battle; Toyotomi Hideyoshi, a peasant who rose to rule Japan, only to squander his resources in a fruitless invasion of Korea; and Tokugawa Ieyasu, who defeated Hideyoshi's army at the Battle of Sekigahara in 1600 and established the Tokugawa shogunate, military rulers of Japan until 1868. The Tokugawa period is sometimes known as the *Edo Period*, after its capital (now Tokyo).

Japan readily absorbed European influence in the sixteenth century. The Portuguese arrived as traders in 1543; another Jesuit, Francis Xavier (1506–52) began his mission to the Japanese in 1549. Within three decades the number of Catholic converts, including some members of the high military aristocracy, reached 150,000. Thereafter Hideyoshi began to suppress Christianity as a foreign threat, banishing Portuguese missionaries in 1587. The Tokugawa shoguns persecuted Christianity even more fiercely, executing thousands after 1612 and driving the church underground after the Christian Shimbara Uprising of 1637–38 ended in an appalling slaughter. Thereafter no foreigners were allowed in Japan except for a small number of Dutch traders, who were rigorously confined to an island in Nagasaki harbor.

Africa's Time of Troubles 1500–1650

The Portuguese sea route to the east diverted attention from the earlier trading contacts with Africa where Portuguese traders brought cotton goods and metal manufactures to exchange for ivory and gold as far as the delta of the Niger river, and where, further south, at the mouth of the Congo, a Bantu-speaking Christian state developed after 1483. And the new world of the Americas, the Spanish Caribbean and Portuguese Brazil, provided a large market for traffic in human beings: the *slave trade* which the Portuguese monopolized until the Dutch drove them out of the Gold Coast in 1642. African slavery, once the result of tribal warfare, now became its cause. First the Portuguese, then the Dutch and, after 1562, the English encouraged tributary states along the west coast to provide them with workers for new world plantations.

The trading *Kingdom of Songhay* which had reached its greatest extent under Askia Mohammed and Askia Dawud in the 16th century was smashed by a Moroccan invasion in 1591. The fall of Songhay brought decline further east to the *Kingdom of Kanem (Bornu)* in the savanna surrounding Lake Chad after 1617. The paradoxical result was the decline of Islamic influence for with the destruction of the Moslem towns the old caravan routes across the Sahara dwindled to a trickle. Further south, the Portuguese established themselves on the west and east coasts in *Angola* (1574) and Mozambique (1508) and after 1628 reduced to vassal status the *Kingdom of the Makaranga* which stretched from the Zambesi to the Limpopo with its capital at Great Zimbabwe. At Africa's southern tip the Dutch established themselves, founding Capetown in 1652.

The Americas: Europe's New Provinces

The Treaty of Tordesillas (1494) between Spain and Portugal divided the world by a line 370 leagues west of the Azores, establishing monopolies for Spain westward and Portugal eastward of the line, approximately 45 degrees west longitude. Thus Brazil, not discovered until 1500, accidentally, by Pedro Cabral (c. 1467–c. 1520) on a voyage to India, became Portuguese territory. But the new world seemed a dead end: the shores of the Caribbean were clearly not the islands and coasts of Asia, the Spanish westward route to the Indies bumped up against an apparently interminable barrier, the Americas.

What altered the picture entirely were the events of 1519–22. In 1520, Ferdinand Magellan (c. 1480-1521) sailed around the southern tip of South America, bringing the Spanish to the Philippines and the Moluccas across the Pacific. Then in 1521, the *conquistador* (conqueror) Hernando Cortez's (1485–1547) brutally subdued the Aztec Empire in 1521. When Francisco Pizarro (1476–1541) toppled the Inca Empire in 1534, Spain acquired a stupendous world empire the wealth of whose silver mines dwarfed the riches of the Indies.

Organized into two vice-royalties, the *Spanish Empire* granted *encomiendas* or plantations to the conquerors; although enslavement of the Indians was forbidden, the Spanish reduced them to serf-like status and forced them to work for their new lords. Christian missions were immediately established with such success that over 20 bishoprics had been created by the mid-16th century. Five universities were flourishing by the middle of the 17th century.

France also sent exploratory ventures to America led by Giovanni da Verrazano (1524) and Jacques Cartier (1534); but it was not until the 17th century that a permanent settlement was established by Samuel de Champlain (1567–1635) who founded New France (1608) with a capital at Quebec. Missions began in 1615 but the process of christianizing the Indians met with no such success as did the Spanish endeavor although Jesuits were involved here. Jean de Brébeuf's conversion of the Huron tribe only exposed them the more to the Iroquois savagery who undid his work and that of Isaac Jogues among the Mohawks. The establishment of Montreal made that more westward site the focus of the fur trade on which the economy of New France was based. Earlier the French began colonizing the Lesser Antilles, right on the fringe of the Spanish Empire and by 1656 had colonized a dozen.

England's Queen Elizabeth (1558–1603) limited herself to encouraging courtiers like Sir Humphrey Gilbert and Sir Walter Raleigh in their ill-fated attempts at early settlement (Roanoke I., 1585) and pirates and slave traders like Sir Francis Drake and Sir John Hawkins in their plundering Spanish ships. Not until the Stuart Dynasty (1603–49) did English settlement begin in earnest. Through grants to commercial companies and individual proprietors, the English established colonies from the Chesapeake to Maine broken only by the Swedes on the lower Delaware River and the Dutch in the Hudson Valley. The Chesapeake became the center of a thriving agricultural region based upon tobacco, while New England flourished as a haven for the English Calvinists known as Puritans.

Europe in the Age of the Reformation

The Europe whose sea-borne enterprise established the first truly world-wide empires was a civilization menaced from without by the Ottoman Turks and divided within both by dynastic-national rivalries and the sundering of Christian unity by the *Reformation*. For many years, leading members of the church had cried out for reform of the clergy, who often led scandalous lives amidst great wealth and who sold God's forgiveness (indulgences) for cash. But not even the powerful voices of the Dutch humanist Desiderius Erasmus (1466–1536) or the English statesman Sir Thomas More (1478–1535) had any impact.

In 1517, the call of the Augustinian monk Martin Luther (1483-1546) for a cleansing of the Church on the basis of his doctrine of "salvation by faith alone" (with its implication of the worthlessness of the priesthood and the sacramental system) swept across northern Germany from the Rhine to the Memel; the adherence of the Scandinavian monarchies to the new faith made the Baltic almost a Lutheran lake. The English king Henry VIII (1509–47), while anti-Lutheran, severed his realm from the Catholic Church after 1532. But what secured Protestantism's hold in Europe was the work of John Calvin (1509–64) who, from 1541 until his death, made Geneva a theocratic state and directed the spread of Calvinism to France, the Low Countries and the British Isles.

The attempts of the Holy Roman Emperor Charles V (1519–56) to halt the spread of Lutheranism were hampered by his need to defend the West against the Ottoman Turks (and thus not offend the Lutheran princes) and to maintain his dynastic territories against the kings of France who allied with the Turks against him. For he ruled the Netherlands and Spain in addition to holding the office of Emperor. At his abdication he willed the Empire to his brother Ferdinand along with Habsburg holdings in central Europe; Spain with its empire, both in the new world and Europe (Netherlands, Burgundy, Milan and Naples), he willed to his son Philip II (1556–98).

Philip faced rebellion in the Netherlands where by the end of his reign the northern provinces had all but won their independence while the southern provinces were held. His Armada (1588) against England met disaster, thereby confirming Queen Elizabeth's rule and the triumph of Protestantism in both England and Scotland. France was given over to the Wars of Religion (1562–98) in which Philip ineffectively intervened on the Catholic side against the Calvinists; the upshot was victory for the Calvinist claimant Henry IV (1589–1610) who, however, turned Catholic but issued the Edict of Nantes (1598) granting French Calvinists ("Huguenots") equal rights, even to the extent of maintaining their own armies.

Philip II considered himself the Catholic champion and it was during his reign that the Catholic *Counter-Reformation* made its greatest strides, not politically but ecclesiastically. Spanish religious leadership came from the new Jesuit Order founded in 1540 by Ignatius Loyola (1491–1556), a fertile source of missionaries, preachers, scholars and schoolmasters, and from the great mystic theologians Theresa of Avila and John of the Cross. Institutionally the *Council of Trent* (1545–63), while not healing the breach with the Protestants, managed to reform the most gratuitous abuses in the Church and provide a clear and authoritative expression of Catholic belief that would last for four centuries.

The uneasy balance between the opposing forces at the start of the 17th century broke down, provoking a time of great crisis. Germany and the Empire were devastated by the Thirty Years' War (1618–48) in which the triumph of the Catholic Habsburgs was prevented by the interventions of Lutheran Sweden and Catholic France personified by King Gustavus Adolphus of Lutheran Sweden and Cardinal Richelieu of France. Britain was shaken by the struggle between Anglicans and Puritans religiously, between the Stuart kings and Parliament politically, the climax coming in the English Civil Wars (1642–49) where the Puritan victory entailed the beheading of King Charles I and the establishment of a military dictatorship under Oliver Cromwell (1649–58).

In eastern Europe there was instability as well. After the long reign of Ivan IV the Terrible (1533–84) in which the entire Volga came under Russian rule and expansion began beyond the Ural Mountains, Russia underwent its "time of troubles." The nobles ("boyars") whose power he thought he had broken rose again to prominence under his weaker son Theodore and confusion as to the succession permitted Polish penetration deep into Russia until the national assembly in 1613 elected Michael Romanov, founder of the *Romanov Dynasty* (1613–1917). In Poland, under Sigismund II (1548–72), the spread of the Reformation was checked and Lithuania was united with Poland into a single state (1569). But Sigismund was the last of the Jagellonian dynasty and at his death the monarchy became in fact what it had always been in theory, elective and thus increasingly the plaything of other great powers. From 1587 to 1648 two members of the Catholic branch of Sweden's royal family, the Vasas, ruled in Poland. Their interventions in Swedish affairs and in Russia during the time of trouble made significant enemies for Poland.

It was a Polish priest, Copernicus (1473–1543) who stands at the beginning of the *Scientific Revolution*, overturning the ancient cosmology of Ptolemy for the heliocentric theory. Expanded by the work of the Dane Tycho Brahe (1546–1601) and his scientific heir, the German Johannes Kepler (1571–1630), the movement reached its first climax in the system of the Italian Galileo (1564–1642), the greatest scientist of the age.

It was also the age of the great flowering of the vernacular literatures of Europe, especially in epic poetry and the drama: in England, Spenser and Shakespeare; in Italy, Ariosto and Tasso; in Spain, Cervantes, Lope de Vega, and Calderon; in Portugal, Camoens. Ironically, this turbulent age also saw the magnificent flowering of painting and sculpture from the universal genius of Michelangelo (1475–1564), the sculptor Bernini (1598–1680), and the painters Raphael, Titian (c. 1490–1576), El Greco (c. 1541–1614), Velasquez (1599–1660), Rubens (1577–1640), and Rembrandt (1606–69).

▶EXPANSION OF THE EUROPEAN WORLD HEGEMONY (1650–1815)

The period in Europe was characterized by the predominance of France, absolutist at the start, revolutionary at the close—a dominance that was as much cultural as it was political. In the western hemisphere, the age saw the maturing of the colonial extensions of western civilization, with the British dominating the north and the Spanish the south. In Africa and the Middle East, western influence grew primarily through trade, principally British controlled. And in the great land mass of Eurasia, two huge empires grew, those of Russia and China.

Europe in Enlightenment and Revolution

The religious wars of the previous period had a double effect: the boundaries of religious division between Catholic and Protestant Europe solidified and there grew up, especially in northwest Europe, men whom the French called *politiques*, seeking peace beyond the reach of religious controversy and division. Parallel with the rise of the politique mentality there had arisen the philosophical movement known as *rationalism* which sought to reconstruct philosophy on the basis of "clear and distinct ideas" (Rene Descartes, 1596–1650). Then came the climax of the scientific revolution in the achievement of Isaac Newton (1642–1727), whose *Principia Mathematica* (1687) united the key ideas of inertia, gravitation, and centrifugal force.

These three streams flowed together in the movement known as the *Enlightenment* whose publicists, called "philosophes," skeptical of all things except reason (and reason understood as the application to all matters of the method of Newton), called all authority into question save their own and subjected all traditional institutions, including the Church, to the corrosive solvents of their argument and mockery.

The man who gave his name to the *Age of Louis XIV* (1661–1715) was no philosopher but an absolute monarch whose court at Versailles became the model for sovereigns across Europe, establishing a French cultural dominance more significant than her political power. Not that the latter was insignificant: in a series of four wars the "Sun King" expanded France's frontiers to the Rhine and his Bourbon dynasty to the throne of Spain. It took alliances of almost all Europe to limit him even to this, alliances organized principally by the Dutch stadtholder William of Orange who conspired as well with the Protestant English aristocracy to overturn their Catholic king James II, the second of the Stuarts restored after the Cromwellian dictatorship, and install him as William III of England. This event is known as the "Glorious Revolution" and it turned England essentially into an aristocratic republic dominated by Parliament.

Louis XIV's revocation of the Edict of Nantes (1685) forced the Protestant Huguenots to leave France for Holland, Britain, and Prussia where they became industrious businessmen and artisans; through their dominance of publishing, they laid the basis for the spread of the Enlightenment.

In eastern Europe the age of Louis XIV was principally the story of the decline of Polish and Ottoman power and the rise to dominance of Prussia and Russia in the Baltic region and the new *Habsburg Empire* in the southeast. With the Spanish Habsburgs sliding toward extinction and the Holy Roman Empire rendered ghostly by the Thirty Years' War, the Austrian Habsburgs drove the Ottomans out of Croatia and Hungary (1699) and added Galicia from helpless Poland (1772). Meanwhile, the War of the Spanish Succession (1702–13) which established the Bourbons on the throne of Spain also detached from Spain its holdings in the Netherlands (roughly modern Belgium) and Italy (Milan and Tuscany), awarding both to the Austrian Habsburgs. This unwieldy dynastic empire, so diverse as to lack even a name, is usually called the *Austrian Empire*, though that title was not taken until 1804. The heart of Catholic Baroque culture in art and architecture and music, Austria became in the reign of Joseph II (1765–80) the seat of an enlightened despotism as well.

More an army than a state, Brandenburg excelled in switching alliances: Frederick William the Great Elector gained sovereignty in the Duchy of Prussia from Poland (1660), and his son a royal title there from the Emperor (1701); thus the *Hohenzollern* dynasty's holdings are usually called *Prussia*. Under Frederick II the Great (1740–86), friend and patron of Voltaire, Prussia snatched Silesia from the Habsburgs (1748). Participating in the partitions of Poland (1772,1793,1795) the Hohenzollerns again doubled the size of their dynastic holdings.

Fought on three continents, the Seven Years' War (1756–63) was the first truly world war. In the European theater the alliances (Great Britain and Prussia against France, Austria and Russia) fought to a draw; the war was won overseas: in North America and in India the British drove out the French and established their hegemony. But in attempting to organize her new and gigantic North American holdings (the "new imperial system") Great Britain provoked into rebellion her old coastal colonies whose independence as the United States of America was recognized in the Peace of Paris (1783). (For North American developments afterward, see Part II: U.S. History.)

The French Revolution

A war for independence rather than, as its common name implies, a revolution, the American experience was an odd model for the tumultuous upheaval known as the *French Revolution*. France was the most prosperous state in Europe, but the long series of wars since 1660 combined with the clergy's and the aristocracy's exemption from taxation impoverished the monarchy. As a way out of the impasse, Louis XVI resurrected the old medieval Estates General (1789) but the representatives transformed themselves into a constitutional convention called the National Assembly. After abolishing serfdom, setting the peasants free, they remodeled the French state into a constitutional monarchy. But they also confiscated Church lands, dissolved the monasteries, and attempted to make the Church a department of the state, complete with elected bishops. This tore many devout Catholics away from the revolutionary cause.

The universal appeal of the French Revolution to so many people across Europe frightened the monarchs and encouraged the National Assembly to declare war on them all. The new mass armies of the French, fired by ideology and national pride, were a juggernaut against the old-fangled monarchical armies. At home, the war emergency and a revolt in a pro-royalist area (Vendee) against the newly declared republic were used to justify a Committee of Public Safety led by George Danton (1759–94) and Maximilien Robespierre (1758–94) and its *Reign of Terror* (1793–94); it's first victims were the royal family, including Louis XVI and his wife Marie Antoinette. The rule of the Directory (1795–99) that followed was overturned by its general, the Corsican adventurer and military genius Napoleon Bonaparte (1769–1821), who established a popular and military dictatorship (1799) first disguised as a republic, then under the name *French Empire* (1804–15).

Several coalitions of nations were formed to stop Napoleon, but he defeated all of them. Coalition after coalition broke up in defeat. At its peak, the Empire dominated all of Europe from the English Channel to the Ottoman Empire by incorporation into the Empire, or as satellites, or as allies. But a popular uprising in Spain, supported by Britain, and the failure of Napoleon's invasion of Russia (1812) began the breakup of his Empire. By 1814 the anti-French nationalisms that conquest had evoked and the recovery of the monarchs' courage brought Napoleon down and, when he returned in 1815, produced his final defeat at Waterloo (1815) at the hands of the first Duke of Wellington (1769–1852).

Scarcely noticed, another and perhaps more powerful revolution was already under way before the period ended. Enlightened British landowners were enclosing the commons (the village lands tenant farmers used to graze cattle) and developing new crops while inventors were creating the machinery (the spinning jenny, the waterframe, and the steam engine) which would provide the basis in the following period for the *Industrial Revolution*.

Europe Overseas: The Americas and Africa

Between the crises of the Cromwellian period (1643–60) and the Glorious Revolution (1688) the Stuart kings of England fostered new proprietary grants in the Hudson Valley, in Pennsylvania, and in the Carolinas. Thereafter the North American colonies became habituated to self-government under their elected assemblies in a period of "salutary neglect" by the home government. Legally colonies, they were in fact mature provinces of Britain overseas. When after the Seven Years' War the government attempted to limit settlement beyond the Appalachians, to tax the colonists for the costs of the enlarged British holdings, and to extend toleration to Catholics in Canada, the colonial resistance led to war and to independence.

The Spanish new world colonies, with new viceroyalties of New Granada (1717) (roughly modern Venezuela, Colombia, and Ecuador) and La Plata (1776) (Bolivia, Paraguay, Uruguay, and Argentina) remained essentially Indian states governed paternalistically by *Yo, el rey*—the king, in whose name all regulations were sent to the viceroys. After about 1650 Indian population grew rapidly. While rule remained in the hands of "peninsulares" from the home country and, to a lesser degree, in those of the "creoles," colonists of Spanish descent, in the towns, the Indians' chief contact with Spanish culture was in the Church whose missionaries and bishops provided a spiritual elite. Of special note were the Jesuit "reductions" on the upper Parana: self-governing, communistic Catholic Indian republics which fell victim to European politics and Brazilian incursions. Brazil by 1800 had a population larger than Portugal's.

To the viceroyalty of New Spain (Mexico) was attached the Philippines. No one was sure where in the Pacific lay the treaty line of 1494 so that while the Philippines were in fact on the Portuguese side, it was Spain which claimed them in 1565, founding Manila in 1571 which became the western terminus for the famous Manila galleons bearing Mexican silver. Through the whole period coasting voyages of English, Dutch and Spanish mariners discovered the islands of the South Pacific: the Carolines, the Marshalls, Tasmania, New Zealand and Australia; but no settlements disturbed the hunting and gathering culture of the Stone Age people who inhabited them.

It was otherwise in Africa where the slave trade continued until the end of the period, peaking in the 1780s but with demand dropping decade by decade thereafter. And in the early years of the 19th century Britain, Denmark and the United States abolished the trade, Britain actively but not always effectively blocking the trade along the African coast. In west Africa, there was an Islamic revival in the savanna as the *Fulbe people*, over the century after 1670, spread eastward toward Lake Chad in a series of *jihads* against *Hausa* cities. In south Africa, the *Zulu* nation, utilizing trained infantry units armed with spears established a small empire in the late 1700s over their neighbors who still relied on the hurling of javelins; while the Dutch at the southern tip, with its Mediterranean climate and its few Khoikhoi (Hottentots), built a Dutch-speaking, Calvinist, multi-racial colony which by 1815 had a population of about 80,000. The pioneering "trekboers" beyond the Cape found their expansion limited by the Xhosa people and when the colony passed from the Dutch to the British (1814), British governors attempted to halt the expansion in the name of peace. Finally, on the east coast trade reached inland as far as Lake Victoria, initiated by the Nyamwezi people of Tanzania but falling after 1800 into the hands of the trade network of Oman, an ally of Britain.

Two Eurasian Empires: Russian and Ottoman

In one aspect the development of the Russian Empire was an eastward expansion of Europe, in another it was the creation of a stupendous Oriental state menacing Europe. Russian pioneers had already reached the Pacific by 1637; expansion into Central Asia brought the Russians up against Chinese expansion westward into the same region, peace being established in 1689 by the Treaty of Nerchinsk which set the common boundary along the peaks of the Stanovoi Mountains, the Russians evacuating a fort they had constructed on the Amur. This shifted Russian interests to the northeast, leading eventually to Russian settlements in Canada and California (1805–1912).

A certain important but superficial "westernizing" of Russia took place under Peter the Great (1689–1725) who in a "revolution from above" autocratically imposed upon his land western modes in manufacturing, in political administration, in military techniques, in court manners and even in dress. Russia had already taken the eastern Ukraine including Kiev from Poland (1667), then the portion (1681) that their allies the Ottomans had won in that war. Peter's attempts to gain Azov—the warm-water port on the Black Sea that would provide access to the Mediterranean—from the Ottoman Empire proved ineffectual. But in the Great Northern War (1700-21) he proved more successful against Sweden, establishing Russia on the Baltic and founding a new capital at St. Petersburg.

Under Catherine II the Great (1762–96), another "enlightened despot" favored by Voltaire, Russia fought a war with the Ottoman Empire. The Treaty of Kuchuk Kainarji (1774) established Russia in the Crimea along the north of the Black Sea, granted navigation rights to Russia in Turkish waters, including the Straits into the Mediterranean, and provided a legal basis for Russia to intervene to protect Orthodox Christians in the provinces of Moldavia and Walachia—i.e. most of what Peter the Great wanted. Catherine also participated in the partitions of Poland (1772, 1793, 1795) which obliterated that ancient Christian state.

In a third stage of expansion Russia took Finland (1809) from Sweden and Bessarabia (1812) from the Ottomans during the Napoleonic Wars. After the invasion of Russia (1812) the czar Alexander I participated in the great coalition that at last brought Napoleon down. In 1815 Russian troops were participating in the occupation of Paris and the Polish Kingdom that emerged from the post-war settlement had Alexander as its king.

The Russian ascendancy was paralleled by Ottoman decline. Of the dozen sultans who ruled between 1648 and 1839 only Selim III (1789–1807) was a man of intelligence and vigor. The period began with misleading signs of strength, as the Turks took Podolia from Poland (1672) and advanced against the Habsburgs, climaxing in the siege of Vienna (1683). The failure of the siege proved a real turning point, the beginning of a long slow sag in Ottoman fortunes that made it by the 19th century "the sick man of Europe." Facing war after war against Austria and Russia (often in tandem) in the west and Persia in the east, the Empire yielded territory, strained its already chaotic finances, and developed a defensive mentality. Its domestic power waned as well as frontier garrisons meant for defense had to be used to suppress rebellions and endemic banditry.

The year after the siege of Vienna was lifted, the Austrians were victorious in the second Battle of Mohacs (1684) which reversed that of 1526, a victory confirmed by the Battle of Zenta (1697): Hungary and Croatia fell away. After the Treaty of Kuchuk Kainarji (1774), the Black Sea was no longer a Turkish lake and Russian ships sailed freely through Ottoman waters. Egypt, temporarily independent in 1769, gained its autonomy in 1805 while Serbia became the first Christian Balkan state to gain autonomy. Even Arabia, the original homeland of Islam, slipped from Ottoman rule as the Saud clan provided the political and economic support necessary for *Wahhabism* which sought a return to the primitive theocracy of the Prophet himself.

The Growth of British Influence in the Middle East and India

With the Portuguese control of the spice route in disarray and the Dutch diverted toward the Spice Islands, British commercial interests grew ascendant in India. Bombay became the headquarters of the *East Indian Company* (1661) from which Calcutta was founded (1690). But not uncontested: the French founded their East India Company in 1664 and established a trading post at Pondichery in 1674.

The Safavid Persian Empire with which the British East India Company had established trade in 1616 entered after 1664 a decline like that which had earlier begun in the Ottoman realm.

In the long reign of Mogul emperor Aurangzeb (1659–1707) the empire had reached its greatest territorial extent, principally through conquests in the Deccan plateau in south-central India. But within the empire his rule was weak as local governors grew increasingly independent. The Maratha people, under their raja Sivadi, established an independent Hindu state against which the emperor waged inconclusive war until his death, and the religious order of Sikhs (blending Hindu and Moslem beliefs) became under Govind Singh a military order.

After Aurangzeb's death Mogul decline became precipitous. Afghanistan became independent in 1709 then invaded Persia (1722) its leader, Mir Mohammed, becoming shah in 1725. With the death of the last Safavid in 1736 the general Nadir Shah reestablished rule over Afghanistan and even invaded India (1738). But all proved ephemeral. With his death Persia came under the rule of the *Zand Dynasty* (1750–94), then the *Kajar Dynasty* (1794-1925) under whom Great Britain gained the right by treaty (1814) to negate any Persian treaty contrary to her interests. The Afghans (1809) became British allies, bound to assist Britain were Persia or France to attack India.

In India during the 18th century the Maratha state became the dominant Indian body, collecting taxes (1720) in Southern India. Nadir Shah's invasion (1738) wrested the north and west from the Moguls. In the turmoil, the European companies began forming private armies of Indian troops ("sepoys") under European officers. After the War of the Austrian Succession (1746–48) French forces ruled virtually the entire south. But in the Indian theater of the Seven Years' War (1756–63) Robert Clive (1725–74) roundly defeated the French; the Treaty of Paris left but a few holdings to the French. In the aftermath, the East India Company gained from the *nawab* (viceroy) of Bengal landowner status over Calcutta, then pensioned off the *nawab* and ruled Bengal directly (1764).

During this struggle the Afghans invaded from the northeast establishing their rule over the Maratha and Sikhs (1761–62). Faced with the two foreign powers most Indian princes gravitated towards the British, a movement not halted by Parliament's India Act (1784) which brought the Company under government control and prohibited it from interfering in Indian affairs or from engaging in war. Still, between 1786 and 1813, the Company's governors-general began a judicial system, gained control over the foreign affairs of most southern principalities in return for British protection, and entered into the treaties with Persia and Afghanistan already mentioned.

In reality, there was no British empire. The Company ruled directly only certain territories whose princes could not secure peace and order and established treaty obligations with other princes. There were no missionaries, no conversions—not even British law: an odd combination of feelings of superiority with respect for Indian culture led to a hands-off policy. And to the Hindus, the British were but another caste.

Chinese Expansion, Japanese Isolation (1650–1800)

The Manchu emperors of China adapted themselves rapidly to the ancient system of empire government, maintaining the examination system for the bureaucracy (though sometimes doubling officials, one Manchu, one Chinese). So serene and sensible (and non-theological) did the Manchu state appear to the European mind that it almost rivaled England in their fantasies.

Taiwan was annexed in 1683, Tibet gradually brought under Chinese control (1705-51) with the emperor controlling succession of the Dalai Lamas. But the great expansion was into central Asia, settled diplomatically with the Russians in 1689 to China's advantage. All this was the work of Kang Xi, the contemporary of Louis XIV.

Under Qian Long, who ruled from 1736-95, Burma had to recognize Chinese overlordship (1769) as did Nepal (1792). Burma had only recently been re-united (1753) and that with British assistance to Alaungpaya, so the relationships became an avenue of British influence. At the same time Annam, largely Chinese in culture and recognizing its overlordship, nonetheless permitted Catholic missions which met with surprising success especially after Gia Long emerged as emperor in 1802.

The whole period was for China one of expansion, not only territorially. In agriculture new crops from the Americas (maize and yams) provided a larger and more diversified food supply, though by the end of the period population was pressing up against its limits. Trade with Europe and with Japan, carried in Portuguese ships, was based upon Chinese exports of tea, silk and porcelain, the latter increasingly produced on a mass basis in imperial and private kilns. But China showed little interest in the outside world. The late 19th-century mission of the British diplomat Lord George MacCartney was met with total indifference. China would soon suffer badly from this imperial self-satisfaction. The papacy's finding (1715) that reverence shown toward Confucius or toward one's ancestors was incompatible with Catholic belief led to the ban of Catholic missionaries in 1720.

In Japan the splendid isolation of the Tokugawa period continued. But the internal peace that they enforced left the samurai warriors functionless, increasingly dissolute and in debt to the thriving merchant class. The heyday of the latter in the *Genroku Period* (1688-1704) led to a flourishing of Japanese literature free of Chinese influence: the development of haiku poetry, especially under the master Matsui Basho (1644-94) and of the Kabuki drama. Late in the period there were signs of restiveness against the Tokugawa not only from the great clans excluded from power but from the imperial family as well, both merging patriotic feeling and imperial loyalty with the increasing vogue of the Shinto religion, both worried about the danger of the Westerners to Japan's isolated development.

▶TRIUMPH AND TRAGEDY OF WESTERN CIVILIZATION (1815-1945)

With the defeat of Napoleon in 1815, Europe entered 100 years of peace, the ending of serfdom, the extraordinary development of industrial capitalism, the spread of liberal and democratic institutions, and the apogee of her world-wide imperial influence. But then ensued 30 years of tumultuous upheaval: two world wars, waged with new weapons of mass destruction, flanking the subjection of most of Europe to grim totalitarian domination. At the end Europe lay broken and prostrate, its fate and the fate of the world in the hands of the two atomic superpowers, liberal-democratic America and Communist Russia.

Europe: The Rise of Nationalism

After a quarter-century of exhausting warfare the conservative monarchs and statesmen of Britain, Austria, Prussia and Russia made a generous peace with France, restoring the Bourbon dynasty but hedging her borders with an enlarged Netherlands to the north, the Prussians on the Rhine and the Habsburgs in northern Italy. To maintain the peace they established the Concert of Europe, a series of international conferences (to which France was soon admitted) to regulate European affairs, initiating the longest sustained general European peace since Rome's Antonine emperors in the second century A.D. Fearing revolution as the source of war and so a threat to themselves, they suppressed liberal and nationalist organizations and sent troops into Italy and Spain to prop up their tottering monarchies; but Britain, supporting the "Monroe Doctrine," prevented any intervention against the revolts in Latin America. With the devolution of the Ottoman Empire in the Balkans, the powers supported an independent Greece (1829) and autonomy for Serbia, Moldavia and Wałachia. Similarly, liberal revolts in Belgium and France (1830) led not to suppression but to independence for the first and a change of dynasty for the second; in the same year, however, Russia crushed a Polish revolt and absorbed that state into her empire. Britain herself, without revolution, carried out a liberal reform of her constitution (1832) abolishing "rotten" or underpopulated boroughs and expanding the electorate by 50 percent, especially in the new manufacturing centers.

The year 1848 saw a remarkable series of liberal and nationalist revolts in virtually all the capitals of the German and Italian principalities and of the Habsburg realms. Yet all proved stillborn, and the armies remained loyal to their sovereigns. Still they had lasting effects, as serfdom was abolished throughout central Europe. The liberal route to national unity, which combined political goals (representative government) with nationalist ones seemed discredited; and the 1848 revolt in Paris led to the establishment of a brief Second Republic, then, in a revival of Bonapartism, a *Second Empire* (1852-70) under Napoleon III (Louis Napoleon Bonaparte, 1808-73).

His assistance was essential in aiding Piedmont's conquests of all the Italian states save Venice and Rome; the *Kingdom of Italy* was proclaimed in 1861 and by 1870 it included Venice and Rome as well. The latter two it gained as an ally of Otto von Bismarck's (1815-98) Prussia, which in a series of three brief wars incorporated all of non-Habsburg Germany into the *German Empire*, proclaimed in 1871. The third of those wars (the Franco-Prussian war), took Alsace and Lorraine from France, toppled Napoleon III, and led to the formation of France's *Third Republic* (1871–1940). The second, which had excluded Austria from German affairs, led that empire to its own reform, the establishment in 1867 of the "Dual Monarchy" of *Austria-Hungary*.

In one decade the map of Europe had been transformed, its most powerful state the new Germany which, with rapid industrialization, became stronger still in the years which led up to the World War I.

Europe: Two World Wars, 1914–45

Bismarck attempted to keep France isolated. He encouraged her colonial expansion to compensate for her diminished status in Europe and in the hope that imperial rivalry with Britain would keep those western states apart. He hoped for similar results from Russian and British rivalry in Persia and Afghanistan. And he formed the Triple Alliance of Germany, Austria-Hungary, and Italy.

But France and Russia allied in 1894 and a decade later, after settling colonial issues that had nearly brought them to war, France and Britain came too a "friendly understanding." The triangle was completed in 1907 when Britain and Russia established spheres of influence in Persia. Bismarck's diplomacy was undone by Kaiser Wilhelm II's (r. 1888–1918) aggressive foreign policy and a naval arms race with Britain.

Not in the colonies but in the Balkans events moved beyond any statesman's ability. In the disintegration of Ottoman power there, Serbia, Romania and Montenegro became independent in 1878 and Bulgaria in 1908. The powers consistently checked Russian advances there while the influence of Austria-Hungary grew. Struggling for territory from the Ottomans and from each other, the Balkan states fought a series of three wars in 1912, 1913 and 1914. It was the third one, which began with the assassination of the Archduke Francis Ferdinand in Sarajevo by a Serbian nationalist that expanded into the catastrophe of World War I.

Outside Europe fighting was slight: German holdings in the Pacific and Africa were taken by British and French imperial forces; Russian and British forces engaged the Ottomans in

Mesopotamia and Armenia; and western-backed Arab revolts further weakened Ottoman strength. But in Belgium and northern France developed the horror of four years of trench warfare and on the gigantic eastern front immense armies clashed but without resolution until 1917 when the Bolsheviks, led by Vladimir I. Lenin (1870–1924), took Russia out of the war after their revolution (Nov. 6, 1917) toppled the Provisional Government that had succeeded the czarist collapse. But Russia's withdrawal in the east was balanced in the west by the American entry that same year, provoked by Germany's resumption of unrestricted submarine warfare in a futile attempt to escape the noose of Britain's naval blockade. The fighting at last ended November 11, 1918.

Besides its immense cost to blood (over eight million died in battle and six million civilians perished) and treasure, the war overturned the old European state system as four empires collapsed and were partitioned. Germany, under the Versailles Treaty (1919) emerged as the Weimar Republic with small territorial losses to France and to a resurrected Poland but burdened with the war guilt clauses and the immense financial reparations they were meant to justify. Russia lost all her western gains since Peter the Great, retreating eastward into the cruel experiment of Communist Revolution. Austria-Hungary disappeared utterly, two little republics maintaining the names at least of those once great states. And by 1923 in Asia Minor a one-party Turkish Republic emerged under Mustafa Kemal Ataturk (1818–1938).

The successor states in eastern Europe, whether republican or monarchical inform, readily adopted the parliamentary government of the victorious western Allies which, in the years after 1848, had steadily democratized the franchise. But most contained substantial ethnic minorities whose rivalries poisoned parliamentary life; tariff barriers which arose everywhere fragmented the old common markets of the empires they replaced, protecting inefficient, penalizing efficient industry; in agriculture depression was chronic.

To the east brooded the reduced but still vast Soviet Union where with the death of Lenin in 1924 the dictatorship of the party turned increasingly into the dictatorship of Joseph Stalin (1879-1953)who oversaw the murderous collectivization of agriculture and the forced industrialization of the Five Year Plans, then purged the party and the army and the secret police of all but his own men. Millions died.

Western and central Europe seemed sheltered from these grim developments by the "cordon sanitaire" of the new states of east-central Europe. After a period of post-war adjustment, prosperity returned to the western democracies, especially in Germany whose adherence to the Locarno Treaties (1925) presaged enduring peace. Yet in Italy whose wartime sacrifices seemed unrewarded by territorial gains and whose economy did not recover but rather seemed to dissolve into the chaos of socialist and anarchist and capitalist violence there arose in 1922 the second (after Lenin) of the dictators, Benito Mussolini (1883-1945). His fascist movement promised a halfway house between liberal individualism and communist class war, stressing a belligerent nationalism with a corporative economy. In fact it was little more than bombast.

But with the collapse of the world economy after 1929, the social and ethnic divisions of the successor states, their boundary grievances, and the real or imagined fear of communist revolution, most of Europe outside the monarchies of the north and west turned to right-wing authoritarian regimes which, though often called "fascist," resembled Italy less than they did Latin America. The very different and very grievous case was Germany where after 1933 Adolf Hitler (1889-1945) established the Nazi dictatorship in the heart of Europe.

The western democracies dithered, deluded themselves, and sought peace through appeasement (not that they had much alternative, unprepared as they were for military action) as Hitler, bent on overturning the Versailles settlement, successfully re-militarized the Rhineland (1936) and absorbed Austria (the Anschluss) and the ethnically German parts of Czechoslovakia (1938) then turned the remainder of Czechoslovakia into a satellite, took the city of Memel from Lithuania, and began demands on Poland (1939). In August 1939, Germany and Russia agreed to partition Poland yet again and with Hitler's invasion in September began World War II.

It was, until 1941, a European war with nonstop totalitarian triumphs; by June of 1940, when France fell, all of Europe outside Britain was neutral or an ally or a satellite of Germany. But in June of 1941 Hitler invaded Russia and in December Hitler's ally, Japan, attacked the U.S. in Hawaii. Japanese dominion reached as far as Burma in 1942, while German armies penetrated as far east as Stalingrad. Nevertheless, the grand alliance of Britain and the U.S. with the USSR caused Nazi Germany to fight a two-front war, which ultimately spelled utter defeat in May of 1945—but not before Germany killed six million Jews during the Holocaust. Three months later, atomic bomb attacks on Hiroshima and Nagasaki, major Japanese cities, hastened Japan's surrender and World War II came to its end. The United States and the Soviet Union, with Great Britain a very junior partner, bestrode the globe. The European Age in world history was at an end.

The Troubled Independence of Latin America

The impact of the Napoleonic wars upon Europe's trans-Atlantic provinces (and the newly independent United States as well) was profound. For one thing, Haiti's success in maintaining its independence, gained in 1794, against Napoleon's attempt to reconquer it led to his abandonment of any scheme for a New World empire: Louisiana was therefore sold to the United States. For another, placing his brother Joseph on the throne of Spain (1808) threw Spanish America into confusion: which king to obey? Juntas loyal to the Bourbon king Ferdinand VII, led by creoles such as Simon Bolivar (1783–1830) and Jose San Martin (1778–1850), resisted French rule at first, then turned against the absolutism of the restored Ferdinand in whose name they had first risen up. In colony after colony the juntas' armies fought for and won their independence: La Plata (1810), Chile (1818), New Granada (1819), Peru (1821). In separate and more complicated developments, Mexico and Brazil followed in 1822.

The *Monroe Doctrine* (1823) of the United States, instigated and given force by Great Britain, shielded the new states from Spanish repression. But nothing could shield them from the effects of their own inexperience in politics (an effect of Spanish imperial centralization) or from boundary disputes (for New World boundaries too were purely Spanish creations) or from the internal struggles of local leader (*caudillos*) seeking autonomy within the new republics. Thus independence was followed by a long period of wars, civil wars, insurrections and coups.

When the trade links with Spain were cut, the new states found a welcome from Great Britain for their products. British investment fostered mining and industrial development; American investment entered late in the 19th century. The development in the 1880s of adequate methods of refrigeration on steamships meant that beef could join wheat and sugar and coffee as exports. The needs of the Allies in World War I for massive increases in raw materials brought a great increase in trade; large-scale post-war investment from the United States both in industry and in plantation agriculture helped continue economic growth but with serious decline after 1929 in the rate of growth.

This expansion brought social tension through the growth of both a middle class and agricultural and industrial working classes, adding new elements to the older political instability. In the 1930s governments in Mexico and Argentina respectively followed the "popular front" or "corporate state" models of Europe but these were usually but trappings for a new breed of *caudillo*. In the Caribbean, the interests of the United States predominated whether as "policeman" or, as after 1934, "good neighbor."

European Empires in Africa

For 60 years after the Napoleonic wars, Europeans evinced only small interest in Africa. Liberal economic thought supported free trade rather than empire. Trading forts dotted the west African coasts while steamboats penetrated only somewhat further inland and missionaries began evangelization on a small scale. "Cash crop" agriculture was no European imposition: the profits from nuts and palm products, especially oil for lighting and machine lubrication, were enough encouragement to African kings and chiefs, especially with the drying up of the trade in slaves. In the south, the expansion of the Zulu nation after 1818 led to disruptions lasting into the 1850s while amongst the Boers in the south, the British ban on slavery provoked the Great Trek of some 10,000 settlers into the high veld, (or grassy plateau) depopulating the old Cape Colony except for some new British settlers. On the east coast the sultan of Oman moved his capital to Zanzibar the better to control his network of trade in cloves and slaves; the latter brought increasing British estrangement from their protegé. Along the Mediterranean coast, the Ottoman Empire was nominally sovereign though rule in fact was exercised by local beys and sultans who gladly countenanced piracy; this provoked the French in 1830 to occupy Algiers and a few coastal cities.

About 1880 a group of French projects—a railways scheme at Dakar, new trading posts on the Ivory Coast and north of the Congo river—alarmed the other powers into the witless "scramble for Africa" which brought Britain and Portugal and eventually even Germany into a contest to annex territory, principally to prevent the others from doing the same and gaining some unknown and unpredictable benefit. The Congress of Berlin (1885) sought to put some order into the competition and in 15 years the entire continent had been divided up, save for the colony of freed American slaves in Liberia and the ancient Christian empire of Ethiopia. Colonial theorists gained the ear of western governments for grand schemes of great belts of territory, the French to stretch from Dakar to the Red Sea, the British from Capetown to Cairo—all just after the construction of the Suez Canal (1859–69) had rendered such imaginings nugatory. One specific and concrete interest was the discovery of deposits of gold and diamonds in the republic of Transvaal which led to Britain's conquest of the Boer republics in the Boer War (1889-1901) and her formation (1910) of the Union of South Africa, which through elections Boers soon governed.

There was something illusory about it all: tiny armies setting up the national flag, treaties signed with hundreds of tribal chiefs who lacked authority, boundary lines drawn on maps in European capitals. But European administration did bring some measure of peace, some road and rail construction, some support for missionaries, some schools and hospitals, some westernizing of tribal leaders. The last would provide a certain leadership class in the independence movements after World War II which dismantled the empires even faster than they had been thrown together before World War I.

Europe's Asian Domination and the Rise of Japan

If Africa experienced European claims of sovereignty with only hints of the reality, Asia underwent the reverse as British rule was established in India, Burma and Malaya, Holland's in Indonesia, America's in the islands of the South Pacific (Hawaii, Samoa, and later the Philippines) and France's in Indochina. Two new provinces of western civilization grew in Australia and New Zealand. China underwent yet another cycle of imperial decline but with the new element of the presence of the "southern barbarians" (the Europeans) and the aggressive designs of a suddenly modernized Japan.

Three 19th century wars mark the decline of China's power and prestige. Her attempts to maintain Canton as the sole port for western trade and to end Britain's sale of opium led to the Opium War (1841–42) and a thorough British victory. The Treaty of Nanking opened four further cities to trade and ended the "tribute system," Westerners now accepted as China's equals, with a uniform tariff of 5 percent on trade; in addition Hong Kong was ceded to the United Kingdom. In the aftermath of the war, in 1844 and 1845, the United States gained the right of "extraterritoriality" (exemption from Chinese law) for its citizens, soon extended to all the western states, and the French gained toleration for Catholic Christianity, soon extended to Protestant Christians as well.

The social and economic dislocations caused by the Opium War in south China culminated in the *Taiping Rebellion* (1851-64), led by Hong Xiuquan, a failed examination candidate who, having read some Christian missionary pamphlets, imagined himself to be the younger brother of Jesus Christ. A charismatic figure, he raised a huge army and seized much of southern and central China, including the city of Nanjing. To put down the rebellion the Qing emperor resorted to the very dangerous expedient of allowing provincial governors-general to raise their own military units; these were effective but would prove destabilizing in the future. Some western military assistance helped keep the Taipings away from the trading port of Shanghai.

At the same time China experienced three other major rebellions: Moslem uprisings in the northwest and in Yunnan Province in the southwest, and the millenarian Nian Rebellion in the north-central plains. Total loss of life from these rebellions exceeded 20 million; the dynasty itself barely survived. In 1858, in the midst of this turmoil, the British provoked a small affray called the Arrow War, settled by the Treaty of Tientsin in 1860. The cost was the opening of yet another 11 ports, the legalization of the opium trade, and the collection of China's customs by Great Britain. Sir Robert Hart became, equivalently, China's finance minister through the years 1863–1908.

Japan's attempt to gain concessions like those of the western powers and to challenge Chinese control over the Manchu tributary state of Korea led to the Sino-Japanese War (1894-95): China had to cede Taiwan and certain mainland territories to Japan and recognize the independence of Korea, a prelude to that kingdom's incorporation into Japan in 1910.

Meanwhile in Indochina the French ignored Manchu protests and established protectorates over Annam (1883) and, right on China's border, Tonkin (1893).

After an unsuccessful attempt in 1898 to reform the imperial government, followed by the abortive, anti-western Boxer Rebellion (1900) discontent with the feebleness of the Manchu government led to the *Chinese Revolution* (1911). The new Chinese Republic's president, General Yuan Shih-k'ai, might have established yet another new dynasty but his death in 1916 permitted the republic to continue, at least in form. But in reality it was the return of feudal anarchy, this time with modern weapons and mass political organizations. Dr. Sun Yat-sen's party, the Kuo Min Tang (KMT), came after his death under the control of his brother-in-law, Chiang Kai-shek, the war lord who controlled south China and whose armies conquered the north in 1927. But the expelling of the Communists from the KMT in 1927 led to a failed series of Communist uprisings and their retreat to the northwest in *The Long March* In their new stronghold of Yan'an, Mao Zedong (1893–1976) emerged as the party leader and Chiang's chief rival. Their struggle was submerged in the 1930s by the need to oppose Japanese dominance; Japan in 1931–32 occupied Manchuria as a protectorate and invaded China in 1937. The great powers, especially America, kept up the illusion that China was a great power with Chiang its ruler, an illusion blown to pieces within four years after the end of World War II.

Japan's rise to great power status was rooted in an extraordinary adaptability. After the American Commodore Matthew Perry forced the opening of Japan to western trade in 1853 and 1854 patriotic sentiment, anti-foreign and pro-imperial, grew until in 1867, young patriots at the court of the emperor Mutsuhito felt strong enough to end the shogunate and restore imperial control. From his reigning name, Meiji, we speak of the *Meiji Restoration*. During his long rule until 1912, Japan embarked on a course of furious imitation of western ways, as earlier they had imitated the Chinese; western science, technology, industry and arms became the basis for attaining the goal of "wealthy land, strong army." The imitation reached the extent of inventing (1884) a Japanese peerage so that there might be an upper house on the British model when the Meiji Constitution (1889) established a Diet.

But it was the military (and industrial) aspects, not the political, that showed most rapid advance, providing the basis for triumphs over China (1895) and much more surprisingly Russia (1905), the take-over of some German holdings in the Pacific during World War I, and the incursions against China in the 1930s. The parliamentarianism of the west was repudiated in the reign of Mutsuhito's grandson Hirohito after 1926 as military cliques and gangs came to control government after government and political violence became the order of the day. The attack on Hawaii in December 1941 was designed to cripple the American Pacific fleet, protection for the invasion of southeast Asia which brought Japanese forces by mid-1942 to occupy the American Philippines, the Dutch East Indies, British Hong Kong, Malaya, Singapore and Burma while French Indochina and independent Thailand collaborated. By August 1945 however this whole proud bubble had burst and Japan itself was occupied by American forces.

In India the British kept up the fiction of Mogul rule but proceeded to act more and more like a sovereign power: commencing the repair of the Mogul system of canals (1818) and later building roads and irrigation projects; replacing Persian as the language of law courts with English in the higher courts and local tongues in local courts; founding schools whose curriculum was European and whose language of instruction was English; suppressing, in the 1830s, the funerary suicide of widows, banditry, and murder.

In the 1840s warfare in Afghanistan, in the Sind and against the Sikhs made Britain a true imperial power, the ruling authority in India, protecting Indian princes from subversion and aggression, annexing territory when princely families died out. After the *Great Mutiny* (1857–58) of the sepoys, Britain banished the last of the Moguls. Twenty years later came the symbolic climax, the proclamation (1877) of Queen Victoria as *Empress of India*.

But at the same time the British were establishing executive and legislative councils with Indians represented and courts with Indian justices sitting on the bench. And between the world wars, in which Indian troops fought loyally and with valor on the British side, the Indian National Congress, first established in 1885, came increasingly under the influence of Mahatma Gandhi. His campaigns of civil disobedience in 1921 and in 1930, which only a very liberal empire would have tolerated, presaged the post-war demands that would signal the end of British rule.

More enduring than British India or British rule in Singapore (1819) or Burma (1886) as vehicles of European influence were Australia, a convict colony founded in 1788 which was gradually transformed by generous land grants into the Commonwealth of Australia (1901) and New Zealand where assisted immigration after 1840 and land grants brought dominion status by 1907, both loyally supporting Britain in both of the world wars.

▶THE COLD WAR (1945–PRESENT)

The wartime alliance of Great Britain, France, the United States, and the Soviet Union was one of expediency rather than long-term mutual interest; suspicion and misunderstandings characterized the alliance even during the war. Soon after the war, hostility and divergent interests between the United States and its Western allies, on the one hand, and the Soviet Union, on the other, led to the Cold War, a period of international danger, distrust, and nuclear standoff, during which direct armed conflict was avoided, but wars fought indirectly by proxy nations and movements were endemic.

As the only major power to emerge from World War II with its population, infrastructure, and economy largely intact, the United States saw itself as the leader of the entire postwar world. Its goals, backed by a monopoly on nuclear weapons, included the rapid reconstruction of Western Europe, the fostering of independent and democratic countries in Eastern Europe, rendering Japan harmless in East Asia, encouraging democratic reform in Nationalist China, and promoting peaceful decolonization in Asia and Africa. The United Nations, organized under American leadership in 1945, was to be the vehicle for a postwar *pax Americana*.

The Soviet Union, devastated by the war, its industrial base and agricultural economy in a shambles, reeling from military and civilian casualties that probably exceeded 20 million persons dead, sought on the other hand to insulate itself behind a band of friendly and submissive neighbors, vowing never again to suffer the kind of invasion that Germany had mounted against the USSR during the war. The Soviet Union also determined to make a concerted effort to match the United States in production of nuclear weapons and delivery systems; the resulting arms race eventually resulted in the production of enough nuclear weapons by the two powers to obliterate the entire population of the world. (Beginning in the 1960s, a series of agreements between the US and the USSR succeeded in limiting the testing and production of nuclear weapons, and greatly reducing their numbers.)

Sharply differing visions of a desirable postwar world thus set the stage for a prolonged conflict between America and the Soviet Union.

In Europe, the Soviet Union's interpretation of the wartime Yalta agreements enabled it to move rapidly to depose fledgling democratic governments in the Eastern European countries under Soviet Occupation; as early as 1946 Winston Churchill warned that an "Iron Curtain" was being drawn around a Soviet zone in Eastern Europe. Soviet power was made credible with the rapid development of atomic weapons, using both Russian research and atomic secrets stolen from America during the war. Pro-USSR communist governments were in place in Poland, Czechoslovakia, Hungary, Yugoslavia, Bulgaria, and Romania by 1947. Austria and Finland accepted a neutral status highly deferential to the Soviet Union; communist movements in Italy, Greece and Turkey were defeated with American and British support.

The United States moved rapidly, especially after the development of the Marshall Plan aid program in 1948, to rebuild the economic and political stability of Western Europe in part to counter Soviet expansionism. A Soviet attempt to blockade the Western occupied zone of Berlin was met with the Berlin Airlift, which preserved a Western presence in the city; thereafter West and East Germany became for the balance of the Cold War in effect two separate and mutually hostile states. The Berlin Wall was built in 1961 to stem a tide of illegal migration from East to West Germany; its fall in 1989 marked the end of the Cold War. Meanwhile the North Atlantic Treaty Organization (NATO) was founded under American leadership in 1949 as a Soviet-containment strategy; it was countered by the organization of the Eastern-bloc Warsaw Pact in 1955. Later popular anti-Soviet uprisings in Hungary (1956), Czechoslovakia (1968), and Poland (1981) were ruthlessly suppressed.

Part of the European price for bowing to American leadership was American acquiescence in the postwar reconstitution of the old colonial empires of Britain, France, the Netherlands, and others. These colonial empires were gradually relinquished during the course of the Cold War, sometimes peacefully, as with the British African colonies, sometimes after bloody nationalist uprisings, as in Portuguese Africa and the French colonies of Algeria and Vietnam. The United States tended to step into the power-vacuum of the post-colonial world, in large part to forestall Soviet influence. The hysteria of McCarthyism in the early 1950s ushered in a long period of reflexive anti-communism that led America to support a series of corrupt, unpopular and repressive—but anti-communist—regimes in various parts of the Third World.

In *Asia*, the simmering conflict between Communist and Nationalist forces in China broke out into open civil war by 1946, despite American efforts at mediation. With only grudging material support from the USSR, Chinese Communists under the leadership of Mao Zedong (1893-1976) defeated the far larger and better equipped Nationalists, whose corruption, ineptitude, and bourgeois orientation proved no match for the simple Communist slogan, 'Land to the tiller.' The Nationalists retreated to Taiwan in 1948–49, and Mao proclaimed the founding of the People's Republic of China in Beijing on October 1, 1949. A break between the USSR and the People's Republic of China in the late 1950s, over both geopolitical and ideological issues, did not alter American policy assumptions of a monolithic international communism until the U.S.-Chinese rapprochement of 1973 under the leadership of Pres. Richard M. Nixon.

In Korea, divided after the war into separate occupation zones, a Soviet-backed government led by the veteran communist Kim Il-sung rapidly took control in the north, whereas in the south an inept and ill-prepared American occupation squandered the opportunity for democratic development, and eventually backed the corrupt right-wing movement of Singman Rhee. When North Korean troops invaded the south on June 25, 1950, the United States successfully obtained United Nations backing to rescue the south; the Korean War ensued, fought to a bloody standoff over the next three years.

The "loss" of China and the Korean war transformed American policy in Japan, which was suddenly seen as the anchor of a democratic and capitalist pro-American security zone surrounding communist Asia. India and Pakistan were similarly wooed by Britain and America. Elsewhere in Asia, communist-inspired uprisings in Malaysia and the Philippines were defeated, while an indigenous anti-communist backlash led to the slaughter of tens of thousands of people in Indonesia in 1965. But it was Vietnam that would prove to be the Asian battleground of the Cold War. After the French withdrawal in 1954, America felt impelled to step in to halt what seemed to be a clear case of international communist subversion of a friendly country; the results were devastating to all concerned, and in retrospect the Vietnamese communist movement seems certainly not to have been merely a cat's-paw for the Soviet Union and Communist China. The Soviet Union found its own "Vietnam" in Afghanistan, where its long attempt to install a communist government met with utter failure.

In *Latin America*, the 1959 triumph of Fidel Castro's Cuban revolution struck the American government as an unacceptable provocation on its own doorstep. The failed Bay of Pigs invasion of anti-Castro partisans trained by the CIA was a humiliation for American policy (1961). In 1954 the Russians had exploded a hydrogen bomb, and in 1957 Sputnik proclaimed the success of Soviet rocketry; the 1960 U.S. presidential election was held in an atmosphere of fear of Russian nuclear missiles. In 1962 the Cuban Missile Crisis was the most potentially deadly confrontation of the entire Cold War. Emboldened by success in that face-off, America intervened militarily to counter what it regarded as communist subversion in Guatemala, El Salvador, Nicaragua, Grenada, and elsewhere in Latin America.

In *Africa*, both the US and the USSR supported client states in the post-colonial period; America had some success in preserving the unity of the Congo (Zaire) and Nigeria, though at the cost of supporting kleptocratic regimes; the Soviet Union maintained an African presence in Angola and Mozambique (both garrisoned with Cuban troops), among other places.

The *Middle East* was an area of strong Soviet initiatives throughout the Cold War. With Israel seen as a creature of the United States, its Arab neighbors readily accepted Soviet aid and advice. Britain's inept and humiliating loss of the Suez Canal to Egypt in 1956 bolstered Nasser's socialist regime there, already friendly to Russia for aid in building the Aswan High Dam. Iraq, Syria, and Libya became anti-Israeli Soviet clients, while the U.S. sought support among the more conservative Arab monarchies. Further east, the CIA-sponsored overthrow of the democratic Mossadegh regime in 1953 led to the return to power of the shah; in 1979 his unpopular and autocratic government fell to a fundamentalist Islamic revolution. The subsequent Iran-Iraq war led the U.S. into the anomalous position of supporting the former Soviet client, Iraq's Saddam Hussein.

America's strategy throughout the Cold War had been to use its economic power to intimidate the Soviet bloc militarily and tempt the uncommitted nations of the world commercially. In this sense, the dramatic images of Neil Armstrong walking on the moon on July 20, 1969 were a key element in American Cold War propaganda. Conversely, the image of Americans hastily evacuating Saigon at the end of the Vietnam War were devastating to American interests because it seemed to show American impotence in the face of communist-inspired nationalism, even if the reality of the situation was, of course, much more complicated.

The anti-Soviet rhetoric of Pres. Ronald Reagan in the 1980s seemed like a throwback to the Cold War paranoia of the 1950s, but it seems to have hastened the Cold War's end. With a restless population and a crumbling economy, Russia found itself unable to sustain the military expenditures needed to keep pace with the U.S. in Cold War competition around the world. With the domestic softening of policy of Mikahil Gorbachev's *glasnost* and *perestroika* in the mid-80s, people in Poland, East Germany, Czechoslovakia, and elsewhere in Eastern Europe, and also in the Baltic states, rapidly overthrew their governments and threw out Soviet troops. The fall of the Berlin Wall meant in effect the fall of international communism, and the end of the Cold War.

There was fallout, to be sure, in the Persian Gulf War (1990-91), in the turmoil of the ex-Soviet republics, in the struggle of Africa to emerge from the era of Cold War patronage and great-power rivalry. But in the end the Cold War did not seem to amount to much. For all its espionage and paranoia, all the arms races and space races, all the proxy wars in unhappy countries throughout the world, the Cold War passed away with only a whimper, an historical episode that had outlived its day. The U.S. emerged as the only superpower both militarily and economically. The challenges for the future were how to maintain peace around the world, helping poorer nations find prosperity, and still remaining faithful to its ideal of self-determination for all peoples of the world.

In the ensuing years, the U.S. response to these critical problems has centered on efforts to strengthen the world economy and to do so on its own terms by maintaining an overwhelming military dominance. Despite the absence of any serious threat from a large power or a coalition of smaller ones, American military budgets continued to exceed $250 billion a year, sufficient to maintain an advanced weaponry program and to keep 1.5 million men and women on active duty. Russia has nuclear weapons but its military is in disarray and its economy keeps hovering on the edge of collapse. Only China has a larger military force than the U.S., but it lacks anything like America's air and nuclear power.

Since 1990, China has been the focal point of U.S. foreign policy and economic strategy. Despite the Chinese government's overt acts of repression and manifest evidence of serious human rights abuses, Presidents Bush and Clinton have both aggressively pursued an economic alliance that has benefited both countries. Tens of billions of dollars have been invested in China in the last decade and, not surprisingly, China has become the chief supplier of low-cost consumer goods and other items to the U.S. In 1997, China sent exports worth $62 billion to the U.S. but imported only $13 billion.

During the 1990s, the U.S. and its allies have promulgated the idea that democracy and economic freedom are inseparable ideals that only market economy rules can bring to fruition. A central element in this creed is free trade, and the U.S. has led the fight to end tariffs and other barriers by helping to establish the 139-member World Trade Organization to develop international rules and policies for trade. In 1994, the North American Free Trade Agreement ended all trade barriers for Canada, Mexico, and the U.S. In Europe, the European Union moved nations closer to economic integration by regulating trade and establishing a single currency—the euro—that could rival the dollar in the not-too-distant future.

Rulers of the World

EMPERORS OF ROME 27 B.C.–A.D. 491

Augustus 27 B.C.–14 A.D.
Tiberius 14–37
Caligula 37–41
Claudius 41–54
Nero 54–68
Galba 68–69
Otho 69
Vitellius 69
Vespasian 69–79
Titus 79–81
Domitian 81–96
Nerva 96–98
Trajan 98–117
Hadrian 117–38
Antoninus Pius 138–61
Marcus Aurelius (co-emperor with Lucius Verus) 161–69
Marcus Aurelius alone 169–77
Marcus Aurelius (co-emperor with Commodus) 177–80
Comodus alone 180–92
Pertinax 193
Didius Julianus 193
Septimius Severus 193–98
Carcalla (co-emperor with Geta) 211–12
Caracalla alone 212–17
Macrinus 217–18
Heliogabalus 218–22
Severus Alexander 222–35
Maximinus 235–38
Gordian I (co-emperor with Gordian II) 238
Pupienus Maximus (co-emperor with Balbinus) 238
Gordian III 238–44
Philip ("The Arab") 244–49
Decius 249–51
Hostilianus 251
Gallus 251–53
Aemilianus 253
Valerian (co-emperor with Gallienus) 253–60
Gallienus alone 253–68
Claudius II ("Gothicus") 268–70
Aurelian 270–75
Tacitus 275–76
Florianus 276
Probus 276–82
Carus 282–83
Carinus (co-emperor with Numerianus) 283–84
Carinus alone 284–85

Between 270 and 283, there were seven emperors, all chosen by the army. Carus was killed in battle, and Numerianus died on the march. The other five were murderd by their soldiers. In an attempt to end the chaos of the "barracks emperors," Diocletian attempted to establish an orderly succession in the East and West halves of the Empire, the emperor in the East being the senior emperor. Dicocletian and Maximian both abdicated in 305, although Maximian was recalled in 306. Subsequently, the succession became disputed in both East and West, and between 305 and 474 there were 39 claimants to the imperial title, five of whom ruled both the East and the West, most notably Constantine (324–37). With the demise of the last emperor in the West (476), the eastern emperor, Zeno, reunited the imperial office in one person.

East		West
Diocletian 284–305		**Maximian** 286–308
Galerius 305–11		**Constantius I** 305–306
Licinius 311–24		**Severus** 306–307
		Maximin 307–13
	Constantine I ***312–37***	
Constantius II 337–61		**Constantine II** 337–40
		Constans 340–50
	Constantius II ***350–61***	
	Julian ***361–63***	
	Jovian ***363–64***	
Valens 364–78		**Valentinian I** 364–75
Theodosius I 378–92		**Gratian** 375–83
		Valentinian II 375–92
	Theodosius I ***392–95***	
Arcadius 395–408		**Honorius**[1] 395–423
Theodosius II 408–50		**Valentinian III** 425–55
Marcian 450–57		**Petronius Maximus** 455
Leo I 457–74		**Avitus** 455–56
Leo II 474		**Marjorian** 457–61
Zeno 474–91		**Libius Severus** 461–65
		Anthemius 467–72
		Olybrius 472–73
		Glycerius 473–74
		Julius Nepos 474–75
		Romulus Augustus 475–76

Note: Names in ***bold italics*** ruled in both the East and the West. These lists are designed to make history neater than it was, so they do not reflect the turmoil of the fourth and fifth centuries, when usurpers and pretenders were numerous.

1. Stilicho was regent until 408.

DYNASTIES OF EUROPE

▶THE CAROLINGIANS (751-887)

The first Carolingian king of the Franks was Pepin the Short who usurped the title from the Merovingian line in 751.Taking their dynastic name from Pepin's father, Charles (Carolus) Martel, the Carolingians divided their realm among surviving sons. It was in this family that the papacy revived the Roman imperial title in the year 800. The lists below cover only the major figures and ignore brief reigns and minor claimants.

Pepin the Short, King 751–68
Charlemagne and Carloman 768–71
Charlemagne, King 771–814
Charlemagne, Emperor 800–814
Louis the Pious, Emperor 814–40

West Franks

Charles the Bald 843–77 (Emperor 875–77)
Louis II, the Stammerer 877–879
Louis III 879–82
Carloman 879–84

Lotharingia

Lothair, Emperor 840–55
Louis II, Emperor 855–75
Charles, King of Provence 855–63
Lothair II, King of Lorraine 855–69

East Franks

Louis the German 843–76
Carloman 876–80
Louis 876–82
Charles the Fat 882–887, Emperor (881–87)

▶HOLY ROMAN EMPIRE (962–1806)

The Holy Roman Empire refers to the second medieval "revival" of the Roman Empire in the West, in the year 962. Though drained of most of its power after 1250 and virtually all of its power after 1648, the Empire endured until 1806 when it was abolished by the Emperor Francis II (though he had no power to do so) who thereafter ruled as Francis I of the Austrian Empire which had been founded in 1804. Whatever the power of the Emperor, the title was the most prestigious in all of Europe. Normally the king of Germany was emperor once he was crowned by the pope; in 1356 the Golden Bull established a seven-member electoral college to choose the Emperor but from the fifteenth century on it was traditional for the electors to choose the Habsburg candidate.

Saxon Dynasty

The dukes of Saxony were most able in combatting the Hungarian menace in the 10th century and thus were chosen kings of Germany. The first was Henry the Fowler (919–936). His son Otto was the first Holy Roman Emperor.

Otto I, King 936, Emperor 962–73
Otto II 973–83
Otto III 983–1002
Henry II 1002–24

Franconian (or Salian) Dynasty

When Henry II died without heirs, Conrad of Franconia (a great-great grandson of Otto I) secured the succession. The dynasty intervened in Rome to reform the papacy, perhaps too successfully, for the popes contended with the emperors for the leadership of the Christian world in the Investiture Controversy (1076–1122). Both the imperial office and the kingship of Germany were greatly weakened by the papal victory.

Conrad II 1024–39
Henry III 1039–56
Henry IV 1056–1106
Henry V 1106–25
Lothair II 1125–37

Hohenstaufen Dynasty

The Hohenstaufen of Swabia were nephews of Henry V but the Church tended to support candidates of the Guelph (also known as Welf) family of Saxony and Bavaria. The struggle of these families and the involvement of the papacy fatally weakened the empire ushering in the "Age of the Princes" in Germany and the "Great Interregnum" in the Empire.

Conrad III 1138–52
Frederick I "Barbarossa" 1152–90
Henry VI 1190–97
Philip of Swabia 1198–1208
Otto IV (Guelph) (anti-king) 1198–1208
Otto IV 1208–12
Frederick II 1212–50
Conrad IV 1250–54
Interregnum 1254–73

When kingship and the imperial office were restored in 1273 the princes refused to establish any one dynasty; for a century and a half candidates from four families were elected.

Rudolf I (Habsburg) 1273–91
Adolf (Nassau) 1292–98
Albert I (Habsburg) 1298–1308
Henry VII (Luxemburg) 1308–13
Louis IV (Wittelsbach) 1314–46
Charles IV (Luxemburg) 1346–78
Wenceslas (Luxemburg) 1378–1400
Rupert (Wittelsbach) 1400–1410
Sigismund (Luxemburg) 1410–37

The Habsburgs

The House of Habsburg (the name is a contraction of the name of their castle, Habichtsburg, in Switzerland) was the most illustrious of the European dynasties. From the 15th century they became hereditary rulers of the Empire and through a series of brilliant marriages gained, by inheritance, the Netherlands, the Spanish kingdoms and Spain's empire in the New World, and Hungary and Bohemia. (From the reign of Francis I, the official family name is Habsburg-Lorraine.)

Albert II 1440–93
Frederick III 1440–93
Maximilian I 1493–1519
Charles V 1519–56
Ferdinand I 1556–64
Maximilian II 1564–76
Rudolf II 1576–1612
Matthias 1612–19
Ferdinand II 1619–37
Ferdinand III 1637–57
Leopold I 1658–1705
Joseph I 1705–11
Charles VI 1711–40
Interregnum 1740–42
Charles VII 1742–45
Francis I 1745–65
Joseph II 1765–90
Leopold II 1790–92
Francis II 1792–1806

▶DYNASTIES OF FRANCE (987–1848)

In 987 the West Frankish nobles elected as their king Hugh Capet. His descendants ruled France continuously until the French Revolution and again from 1814 until 1848. The direct line died out in 1328, and the collateral *Valois* branch of the Capetian family succeeded. The Valois ruled with difficulty, as the Hundred Years' War (1337–1453) blighted the beginning and the Wars of Religion (1562–98) the end of their rule. The last three Valois produced no male heirs so the throne passed to the victor in the Wars of Religion, Henry of Navarre (a distant cousin in the male line of Louis IX), who began the reign of the *Bourbon* branch of the Capetians. (After 1700, the Bourbon family became, with many interruptions, kings of Spain.)

Direct Capetians

Hugh Capet 987–96
Robert II the Pious 996–1031
Henry I 1031–60
Philip I 1060–1108
Louis VI 1108–37
Louis VII 1137–80
Philip II Augustus 1180–1223
Louis VIII 1223–26
Louis IX 1226–70
Philip III 1270–85
Philip IV 1285–1314
Louis X 1314–16
John I the Posthumous 1316
Philip V 1316–22
Charles IV 1322–28

Valois Branch

Philip VI 1328–50
John 1350–64
Charles V 1364–80
Charles VI 1380–1422
Charles VII 1422–61
Louis XI 1461–83
Charles VIII 1483–98
Louis XII (Valois-Orléans) 1498–1515
Francis I (Valois-Angoulême) 1515–47
Henry II 1547–59
Francis II 1559–60
Charles IX 1560–74
Henry III 1574–89

Bourbon Branch

Henry IV 1589–1610
Louis XIII 1610–43
Louis XIV 1643–1715
Louis XV 1715–74
Louis XVI 1774–92
French Revolution and Napoleon 1792–1814

Restored Bourbons

Louis XVIII 1814–24
Charles X 1824–30
Louis Philippe (Bourbon-Orléans) 1830–48

▶DYNASTIES OF ENGLAND (871–PRESENT)

Saxons

With the end of Roman rule, seven Germanic kingdoms emerged in England. The leader of the resistance to the Vikings was Alfred the Great of Wessex (871–99) who began a reconquest of the island and is considered the first true king of England; his dynasty, with interruptions, continued until the Norman Conquest in 1066.

Alfred the Great 871–99
Edward the Elder 899–924
Aethelstan 924–39
Edmund 939–46
Eadred 946–55
Eadwig 955–59
Edgar 959–75
Edward 975–78
Aethelred "the Unready" 978–1016
Edmund Ironside 1016
Canute (of Denmark, by conquest) 1016–35
Harold Harefoot 1035–40
Hardicanute (of Denmark) 1040–42
Edward the Confessor 1042–66
Harold Godwinson 1066

Normans

Duke William of Normandy, a cousin of Edward the Confessor, made good his claim to the throne by conquest, bringing with him highly organized Continental feudalism and the French tongue which so enriched the English language.

William the Conqueror 1066–87
William II 1087–1100
Henry I 1100–1135
Stephen 1135–54

Angevins (Plantagenets)

The grandson of Henry I was Henry of Anjou who, by marrying the heiress Eleanor of Aquitaine, assembled for his family the greatest feudal state in 12th century Europe. In 1154 he established his family on the throne of England as well; the direct line continued until 1399 when Richard II was deposed and killed by his first cousin who then ruled as Henry IV and established the *Lancastrian Dynasty*. Another branch of the family, with a stronger claim than the usurping Lancastrians, contested the succession in the War of the Roses and after 1461 ruled briefly as the *Yorkist Dynasty*.

Henry II 1154–89
Richard I 1189–99
John I 1199–1216
Henry III 1216–72
Edward I 1272–1307
Edward II 1307–27
Edward III 1327–77
Richard II 1377–99

Lancastrian Kings

Henry IV 1399–1413
Henry V 1413–22
Henry VI 1422–61

Yorkist Kings

Edward IV 1461–83
Edward V 1483
Richard III 1483–85

Tudors

An obscure Welsh family and adherents of the Lancastrian line, the Tudors became champions of the faction supporting them. Richard III died in battle at Bosworth Field against Henry Tudor, who usurped the throne, ruling as Henry VII and founding the dynasty that brought the Reformation to England.

Henry VII 1485–1509
Henry VIII 1509–47
Edward VI 1547–53
Mary I 1553–58
Elizabeth I 1558–1603

Stuarts

Elizabeth never married and had no heirs, so the Tudor line died with her. Rule passed to Elizabeth's cousin, James VI of Scotland who ruled in England as James I. Serious troubles with the Puritans and Parliament twice turned the Stuarts from the throne: Charles I was beheaded and James II was betrayed by his daughters and the husband of one, William of Orange.

James I 1603–25
Charles I 1625–49
Interregnum—Oliver Cromwell 1649–58
Richard Cromwell 1658–59
Charles II 1660–85
James II 1685–88
William III and Mary II 1689–94
William III alone 1694–1702
Anne 1702–14

Hanoverians and Windsors

Queen Anne had 17 children but died without leaving an heir. Geneological and religious considerations (Anne's brother "James III," the Catholic pretender, was still alive) brought to the throne the German House of Hanover. After the reign of Victoria, the family is Saxe-Coburg-Gotha but in 1917, for political reasons, George V changed the name to Windsor.

George I 1714–27
George II 1727–60
George III 1760–1820
George IV 1820–30
William IV 1830–37
Victoria 1837–1901
Edward VII 1901–10
George V 1910–36
Edward VIII 1936
George VI 1936–52
Elizabeth II 1952–present

▶DYNASTIES OF SPAIN (1506–PRESENT)

Until 1808 there was no kingdom called Spain but a number of separate kingdoms of which Castile and Aragon were only the principal ones. With the deaths of Isabella, then Ferdinand, the crowns passed to their grandson, the Habsburg Charles of Ghent; in the Empire he was Charles V, in the Spanish kingdoms Charles I. His *Habsburg Dynasty* ruled until 1700 when the line died out and was replaced by the *Bourbon Dynasty* which has ruled with numerous interruptions until the present day.

Habsburgs

Charles I (Holy Roman Emperor as Charles V) 1506–56
Philip II 1556–98
Philip III 1598–1621
Philip IV 1621–65
Charles II 1665–1700

Bourbons

Philip V 1700–1746
Ferdinand VI 1746–59
Charles III 1759–88
Charles IV 1788–1808
Joseph Bonaparte 1808–13
Ferdinand VII 1814–33
Isabella II 1833–68
Interregnum 1868–70
Amadeo 1870–73
Republic 1873–75
Alphonso XII 1875–85
Alphonso XIII 1886–1931
Republic 1931–36
Civil War 1936–39
Franco regime 1939–75
Juan Carlos 1975–present

▶AUSTRIAN HABSBURGS

When Charls V retired, his world-wide empire was divided into two parts, one Spanish, one Austrian. The Austrian branch always supplied the Holy Roman Emperors except during the reign of Maria Theresa (1740–80) when Charles Albert of Bavaria, then her husband and son held the imperial title. In 1804 Emperor Francis II proclaimed an Austrian Empire which he ruled as Francis I; two years later he abolished the Holy Roman Empire.

Francis II & I 1792–1835
Ferdinand I 1835–48
Francis Joseph 1848–1916
Charles I 1916–18

▶HOHENZOLLERN DYNASTY

For centuries the Hohenzollern were electors of Brandenburg in northeastern Germany. In 1701, with permission of the emperor, they took the royal titles King in Prussia. (Prussia was a duchy of Poland which the family inherited in 1618.) In 1871 they added the title German Emperor. Both titles disappeared with Germany's loss in World War I.

Frederick William, the Great Elector 1640–88
Frederick III, Elector of Brandenburg 1688–1701
Frederick I, King of Prussia 1701–13
Frederick William I 1713–40
Frederick II 1740–86
Frederick William II 1786–97
Frederick William III 1797–1840
Frederick William IV 1840–61
William I (German Emperor after 1871) 1861–88
Frederick III 1888
William II 1888–1918

▶ROMANOV DYNASTY (RUSSIA)

At the end of Russia's "time of troubles" early in the 17th century, the national assembly elected Michael Romanov as czar in 1613. The dynasty died out in 1762 when at the death of czarina Elizabeth, her nephew Peter III briefly succeeded. His family ruled until the Russian Revolution. Their name was Holstein-Gottorp but ruled under the name Romanov.

Michael 1613–45
Alexius 1645–76
Theodore III 1676–82
Ivan IV and Peter I 1682–89
Peter I, the Great, alone 1689–1725
Catherine I 1725–27
Peter II 1727–30
Anna 1730–40
Ivan VI 1740–41
Elizabeth 1741–62
Peter III 1762
Catherine II the Great 1762–96
Paul 1796–1801
Alexander I 1801–25

Nicholas I 1825–55
Alexander II 1855–81
Alexander III 1881–94
Nicholas II 1894–1917

▶HOUSE OF SAVOY-CARIGNANO

The dukes of Savoy ruled in a personal union Piedmont, Nice, and Sardinia until 1831, when the line died out and a distant cousin, Charles Albert came to the throne. It was his son, Victor Emmanuel II of Savoy whose armies conquered the rest of Italy over the years 1858–71 and who was proclaimed King of Italy in 1861. The dynasty fell with the end of the Second World War.

Victor Emmanuel II 1861–78
Humbert I 1878–1900
Victor Emmanuel III 1900–46
Humbert II 1946

THE DYNASTIES AND EMPERORS OF CHINA

Dates for the Xia and Shang Dynasties, and for the beginning of the Zhou Dynasty, are uncertain. Rulers of these three dynasties were known as kings (*wang*); only a few notable individuals are listed below. The title "emperor" (*huangdi*) was instituted with the Qin Dynasty. As is customary, names of emperors prior to A.D. 1368 are given in the form of their posthumous "temple names" (*miaohao*); names of emperors for the Ming and Qing Dynasties are given as their reign-title names (*nianhao*).

Xia Dynasty c. 1875–1550 B.C.
Yü the Great (legendary?) c. 1875–1850 B.C.
King Jie c. 1560–1550 B.C.

Shang Dynasty c. 1550–1055 B.C.
Tang the Victorious c. 1550–1500 B.C.
King Zhou c. 1070–1055 B.C.

Zhou Dynasty c. 1055–256 B.C.
Western Zhou Period c. 1055–771 B.C.
King Wen (pre-conquest) c. 1060–1055 B.C.
King Wu c. 1055–1048 B.C.
Duke of Zhou, regent for
King Cheng c. 1048–1011 B.C.
Era of the Spring and Autumn Annals 722–481 B.C.
Warring States Period 481–256 B.C.

Qin Dynasty 221–206 B.C.
Shihuangdi 221–209 B.C.
Erhuangdi 209–207 B.C.

Han Dynasty 206 B.C.–A.D. 220
Western or Former Han 206 B.C.–A.D. 9
Gaozu 206–195 B.C.
Huidi 195–188 B.C.
Gaohou (Empress Lü) 188–180 B.C.
Wendi 180–157 B.C.
Jingdi 157–141 B.C.
Wudi 141–87 B.C.
Zhaodi 87–74 B.C.
Xuandi 74–48 B.C.
Yuandi 48–33 B.C.
Chengdi 33–7 B.C.
Aidi 7–1 B.C.
Pingdi 1 B.C.–A.D. 6
Wang Mang (usurper) A.D. 9–23
Eastern or Latter Han A.D. 23–220
Guangwudi 25–57
Mingdi 57–75
Zhangdi 75–88
Hedi 88–105
Shangdi 105
Andi 106–25
Shaodi 125
Shundi 125–44
Chongdi 144–45
Zhidi 145–46
Huandi 146–68
Lingdi 168–89
Shaodi 189
Xiandi 189–220

Period of Disunion
The fall of the Han Dynasty ushered in a period of 369 years of disunion during which no dynasty succeeded in bringing all of China under its control This period is divided into the brief Three Kingdoms Period and the longer Period of Northern and Southern Dynasties, of which only the three most important dynasties are listed below.

Three Kingdoms 220–65
Kingdom of Shu Han 220–64
Kingdom of Wei 220–65
Kingdom of Wu 220–65

Period of Northern and Southern Dynasties 265–589
Western Jin Dynasty 265–317
Eastern Jin Dynasty 317–419
Northern Wei Dynasty 424–535

Sui Dynasty 589–618
Wendi 589–604
Yangdi 604–17
Gongdi 617–18

Tang Dynasty 618–907
Gaozu 618–26
Taizong 626–49
Gaozong 649–83
Zhongzong 683–84
Ruizong 684–90
Wuhou 690–705
Zhongzong 705–10
Ruizong 710–12
Xuanzong 712–56
Suzong 756–62
Taizong 762–79
Dezong 779–805
Shunzong 805
Xianzong 805–20
Muzong 820–24
Jingzong 824–26
Wenzong 826–40
Wuzong 840–46
Xuanzong 846–59
Yizong 859–73
Xizong 873–88
Zhaozong 888–904
Jingzong 904–7

Five Dynasties 907–60

Song Dynasty 960–1279

Northern Song 960–1127

Taizu 960–76
Taizong 976–97
Zhenzong 997–1022
Renzong 1022–63
Yingzong 1063–67
Shenzong 1067–85
Zhezong 1085–1100
Huizong 1100–1125
Qinzong 1125–27

Southern Song 1127–1279

Gaozong 1127–62
Xiaozong 1162–89
Guangzong 1189–94
Ningzong 1194–1224
Lizong 1224–64
Duzong 1264–74
Gongzong 1274–76
Duanzong 1276–79

Yuan (Mongol) Dynasty 1279–1368

Shizu (Kubilai Khan) 1260–94
Chengzong (Temür) 1294–1307
Wuzong (Khaishan) 1307–11
Renzong (Buyantu) 1311–20
Yingzong (Sudhipela) 1320–23
Taiding (Yesen-Temür) 1323–28
Mingzong (Asikipa) 1328
Wenzong (Tog-Temür) 1328–33
Xunzong (Toghon-Temür) 1333–68

Ming Dynasty 1368–1644

Hongwu 1368–98
Jianwen 1398–1402
Yongle 1402–24
Hongxi 1424–25
Xuande 1425–35
Zhengtong 1435–49
Jingtai 1449–57
Tianshun 1457–64
Chenghua 1464–87
Hongzhi 1487–1505
Zhengde 1505–21
Jiaqing 1521–66
Wanli 1572–1620
Taichang 1620
Tianzhi 1620–27
Chongzhen 1627–44

Qing Dynasty 1644–1911

Shunzhi 1644–61
Kangxi 1661–1722
Yongzheng 1722–35
Qianlong 1735–96
Jiaqing 1796–1820
Daoguang 1820–50
Xianfeng 1850–61
Tongzhi 1861–75
Guangxu 1875–1908
Puyi 1908–11

CHRONOLOGICAL LISTING OF THE POPES

Peter, Apostle d. c. 64
Linus c.66–c.78
Anacletus c.79–c.91
Clement I c.91–c.101
Evaristus c.100–c.109
Alexander I c.109–c.116
Sixtus I c.116–c.125
Telesphorus c.125–c.136
Hyginus c.138–c.142
Pius I c.142–c.155
Anicetus c.155–c.166
Soter c.166–c.174
Eleutherius, or Eleutherus c.174–89
Victor I 189–98
Zephyrinus 198/9–217
Callistus I (often Calixtus) 217–22
Hippolytus (antipope) 217–35
Urban I 222–30
Pontian 230–35
Anterus 235–36
Fabian 236–50
Cornelius 251–53
Novatian (antipope) 251–58
Lucius I 253–54
Stephen I 254–57
Sixtus II 257–58
Dionysius 260–68
Felix I 269–74
Eutychian 275–83
Gaius, or Caius 283–96
Marcellinus 296–304?
Marcellus I 306–8
Eusebius 310
Miltiades, or Melchiades 311–31
Silvester I 314–35
Mark 336
Julius I 337–52
Liberius 352–66
Felix II (antipope)[1] 355–65
Damasus I 366–84
Ursinus (antipope) 366–67
Siricius 384–99
Anastasius I 399–401
Innocent I 401–17
Zosimus 417–18
Eulalius (antipope) 418–19
Boniface I 418–22
Celestine I 422–32
Sixtus (Xystus) III 432–40
Leo I 440–61
Hilarus 461–68
Simplicius 468–83
Felix III[1] 483–92
Gelasius I 492–96
Anastasius II 496–98
Symmachus 498–514
Lawrence (antipope) 498–99, 501–6
Hormisdas 514–23
John I 523–26
Felix III[1] 526–30
Dioscorus (antipope) 530
Boniface II 530–32
John II 533–35
Agapitus I 535–36
Silverius 536–37
Vigilius 537–55
Pelagius I 556–61
John III 561–74
Benedict I 575–79
Pelagius II 579–90
Gregory I 590–604
Sabinian 604–6
Boniface III 607
Boniface IV 608–15
Deusdedit (later Adeodatus I) 615–18
Boniface V 619–25
Honorius I 625–38
Severinus 640
John IV 640–42
Theodore I 642–49
Martin I 649–53
Eugene I 654–57
Vitalian 657–72
Adeodatus II 672–76
Donus 676–78
Agatho 678–81
Leo II 682–83
Benedict II 684–85
John V 685–86
Conon 686–87
Theodore (antipope) 687
Paschal (antipope) 687
Sergius I 687–701
John VI 701–5
John VII 705–7
Sisinnius 708
Gregory II 715–31
Gregory III 731–41
Zacharias 741–52
Stephen (II)[2] 752
Stephen II (III)[2] 752–57
Paul I 757–67
Constantine (antipope) 767–68
Philip (antipope) 768
Stephen III (IV)[2] 768–72
Hadrian I 772–95
Leo III 795–816
Stephen IV (V)[2] 816–17
Paschal I 817–24
Eugene II 824–27
Valentine 827
Gregory IV 827–44

John (antipope) 844
Sergius II 844–47
Leo IV 847–55
Benedict III 855–58
Anastasius Bibliothecarius (antipope) 855
Nicholas I 858–67
Hadrian II 867–72
John VIII 872–82
Marinus I 882–84
Hadrian III 884–85
Stephen V (VI)[2] 885–91
Formosus 891–96
Boniface VI 896
Stephen VI (VII)[2] 896–97
Romanus 897
Theodore II 897
John IX 898–900
Benedict IV 900–903
Leo V 903
Christopher (antipope) 903–4
Sergius III 904–11
Anastasius III 911–13
Lando 913–14
John X 914–28
Leo VI 928
Stephen VII (VIII)[2] 928–31
John XI 931–36?
Leo VII 936–39
Stephen VIII (IX)[2] 939–42
Marinus II 942–46
Agapitus II 946–55
John XII 955–64
Leo VIII 963–65
Benedict V 964
John XIII 965–72
Benedict VI 973–74
Boniface VII (antipope) 974, 984–85
Benedict VII 974–83
John XIV 983–84
John XV 985–96
Gregory V 996–99
John XVI (antipope) 997–98
Silvester II 999–1003
John XVII 1003
John XVIII 1003–1009
Sergius IV 1009–12
Benedict VIII 1012–24
Gregory (VI) (antipope) 1012
John XIX 1024–32
Benedict IX 1032–44, 1045, 1047–48
Silvester III 1045
Gregory VI 1045–46
Clement II 1046–47
Damasus II 1048
Leo IX 1049–54
Victor II 1055–57
Stephen IX (X)[2] 1057–58
Benedict X (antipope) 1058–59
Nicholas II 1058–61
Alexander II 1061–73
Honorius (II) (antipope) 1061–64
Gregory VII 1073–85
Clement III (antipope) 1080, 1084–1100
Victor III 1086–87
Urban II 1088–99
Paschal II 1099–1118
Theoderic (antipope) 1100–1101
Albert or Adalbert (antipope) 1101
Silvester IV (antipope) 1105–11
Gelasius II 1118–19
Gregory (VIII) (antipope) 1118–21
Callistus II 1119–24
Celestine (II) 1124
Honorius II 1124–30
Innocent II 1130–43
Anacletus II (antipope) 1130–38
Victor IV (antipope) 1138
Celestine II 1143–44
Lucius II 1144–45
Eugene III 1145–53
Anastasius IV 1153–54
Hadrian IV 1154–59
Alexander III 1159–81
Victor IV (antipope)[3] 1159–64
Paschal III (antipope) 1164–68
Callistus (III) (antipope) 1168–78
Innocent (III) (antipope) 1179–80
Lucius III 1181–85
Urban III 1185–87
Gregory VIII 1187
Clement III 1187–91
Celestine III 1191–98
Innocent III 1198–1216
Honorius III 1216–27
Gregory IX 1227–41
Celestine IV 1241
Innocent IV 1243–54
Alexander IV 1254–61
Urban IV 1261–64
Clement IV 1265–68
Gregory X 1271–76
Innocent V 1276
Hadrian V 1276
John XXI 1276–77
Nicholas III 1277–80
Martin IV 1281–85
Honorius IV 1285–87
Nicholas IV 1288–92
Celestine V 1294
Boniface VIII 1294–1303
Benecict XI 1303–4
Clement V 1305–14
John XXII 1316–34
Nicholas (V) (antipope) 1328–30
Benedict XII 1334–42
Clement VI 1342–52
Innocent VI 1352–62
Urban V 1362–70
Gregory XI 1370–78
Urban VI 1378–89
Clement (VII) (antipope) 1378–94
Boniface IX 1389–1404
Benedict (XIII) (antipope) 1394–1417
Innocent VII 1404–6
Gregory XII 1406–15
Alexander V (antipope) 1409–10
John (XXIII) (antipope) 1410–15
Martin V 1417–31
Clement (VIII) (antipope) 1423–29
Benedict (XIV) (antipope) 1425–?
Eugene IV 1431–47
Felix V (antipope) 1439–49
Nicholas V 1447–55
Callistus III 1455–58
Pius II 1458–64
Paul II 1464–71
Sixtus IV 1471–84
Innocent VIII 1484–92
Alexander VI 1492–1503
Pius III 1503
Julius II 1503–13
Leo X 1513–21
Hadrian VI 1522–23
Clement VII 1523–34
Paul III 1534–49
Julius III 1550–55
Marcellus II 1555
Paul IV 1555–59
Pius IV 1559–65
Pius V 1566–72
Gregory XIII 1572–85
Sixtus V 1585–90
Urban VII 1590
Gregory XIV 1590–91
Innocent IX 1591
Clement VIII 1592–1605
Leo XI 1605
Paul V 1605–21
Gregory XV 1621–23
Urban VIII 1623–44
Innocent X 1644–55
Alexander VII 1655–67
Clement IX 1667–69
Clement X 1670–76
Innocent XI 1676–89
Alexander VIII 1689–91
Innocent XII 1691–1700
Clement XI 1700–21
Innocent XIII 1721–24
Benedict XIII 1724–30
Clement XII 1730–40
Benedict XIV 1740–58
Clement XIII 1758–69
Clement XIV 1769–74
Pius VI 1775–99
Pius VII 1800–23
Leo XII 1823–29
Pius VIII 1829–30
Gregory XVI 1831–46
Pius IX 1846–78
Leo XIII 1878–1903
Pius X 1903–14
Benedict XV 1914–22
Pius XI 1922–39
Pius XII 1939–58
John XXIII 1958–63
Paul VI 1963–78
John Paul I 1978
John Paul II 1978–

Note: Antipopes, *listed in italics*, were appointed in opposition to the one canonically chosen by the college of cardinals, usually by a prince, king, or emperor. 1. Because Felix II was an antipope, subsequent Felixes were sometime misnumbered. 2. Although elected and installed as Pope, Stephen (II) died before his consecration. Though the Vatican's *Annuario Pontifico* has excluded him from the official list of Popes since 1961, subsequent Stephens have a dual numbering. 3. He should have been Victor V, but he used Victor IV because the previous Victor IV's tenure (1138) as antipope was largely ignored.

World Geography

▶ GLOSSARY OF GEOGRAPHICAL WORDS AND TERMS

(Note: See also Part IV: Science and Technology, Composition of the Earth)

Altitude How high a place or a thing is, usually measured from sea level or the surface of the land.

Archipelago A cluster of islands.

Arctic Circle An imaginary line drawn along approximately latitude 66° 30'N. The climate north of the Arctic Circle is very cold, and relatively few people live there.

Atmosphere The mass of air that extends outward from the surface of the earth into space. The atmosphere is divided into four layers: the troposphere, in which temperature decreases as altitude increases; the stratosphere, in which temperature is constant, then increases; the mesosphere, in which it decreases; and the thermosphere, in which it increases again.

Atoll A coral reef that partially or completely surrounds a lagoon.

Basin A portion of land that is lower than the surrounding area. Basins are created when vertical movement causes the earth's crust to warp. Also, the area drained by a river and its tributaries.

Bay Part of an ocean, sea, or other body of water which extends inland. Bays are generally smaller than gulfs.

Bight A bay formed by a bend in the coastline.

Caldera A huge crater formed when the top of a volcano collapses or is exploded away.

Canyon A narrow, deep valley with steep sides. Many canyons have a river on their floor.

Climate General weather conditions over a long period. (See "Climates of the World.")

Continent A large unbroken land mass, distinguished from an island or peninsula. The seven continents are North America, South America, Europe, Asia, Africa, Australia, and Antarctica, though Europe and Asia are a continuous land mass divided along the spine of the Ural Mountains running south from the Arctic Ocean.

Continental drift theory The theory, proposed in 1915 by Alfred Wegener, that all of the continents used to be joined in one supercontinent, Pangaea. Some 200 million years ago Pangaea began to break up, and the continents "drifted" through the oceans to their present locations. The continental drift theory has now largely been replaced by the *plate tectonics theory*. (See the section "Earth Sciences.")

Continental shelf The edge of a continent covered by shallow ocean water, up to about 100 fathoms (600 feet), beyond which is the continental slope, which decends to the deep-sea plain, about 13,000-20,000 feet (4,000-6,000 m).

Cove A small and sheltered bay or inlet. Also, a small valley in a mountain.

Crater The bowl-shaped depression at the top of a volcano. Also, the depression made when a meteorite hits the earth. (See also *caldera.*)

Delta A triangular-shaped piece of land formed by sediment at the mouth of a river.

Desert (See "The Great Deserts" later in this section).

Dune A hill or ridge of sand that has been deposited by wind.

Equator An imaginary line circling earth halfway between the Poles. The equator is at latitude 0°.

Equinox The two times during the year (on or about March 21 and September 23) when the sun's rays strike the equator vertically. At equinox, day and night are the same length everywhere in the world. (See also *Solstice.*)

Erosion The gradual wearing away of the surface of the land. For example, soil is eroded by wind and water; rock is eroded by freezing and thawing.

Estuary A valley at the mouth of a river where fresh water and sea water mix. Estuaries are created either when the land sinks or when the sea level rises, and are generally shaped like a funnel.

Fjord A long, narrow inlet of the ocean with steeply sloping sides.

Floodplain Flat, low-lying land along either side of a river that is subject to flooding.

Geyser A jet of hot water or steam periodically thrown up by a hot spring.

Glacier A large mass of slowly moving ice. Glaciers are formed on land when snow is compacted and recrystallizes.

Gorge An especially narrow and steep-walled canyon.

Gulf Part of an ocean or sea that extends inland. Gulfs are generally larger than bays.

Hemisphere One half of the earth's surface, however it is divided. For example, the northern hemisphere lies north of the equator; the southern hemisphere, south of the equator. By convention, the eastern hemisphere consists of the continents of Europe, Asia, and Africa; the western hemisphere, of North America and South America.

Inlet An indentation in the shore of a sea or an ocean or in the bank of a river. Also, a narrow waterway which connects a lagoon to a larger body of water or which passes between two peninsulas.

Island A land mass completely surrounded by water.

Isthmus A narrow strip of land that connects two larger land masses.

Lagoon A shallow pool or pond completely or almost completely separated from the sea.

Lake A body of water, often of considerable size, surrounded by land.

Latitude and Longitude Latitude is the angle (measured in degrees, minutes, and seconds) between a point on the earth's surface north or south of the equator, the center of the earth, and the equator (0°0'0" latitude). Longitude is the angle between a point on the earth's surface, the center of the earth, and the prime meridien (0°0'0" longitude). There are 90° of latitude between the equator and each of the poles (shown on a globe as parallel horizontal lines). There are 360° of longitude (shown as vertical lines) divided into 180° east and west of the prime meridien (180°E and 180°W are thus the same). Since 1884, Greenwich, England (near London), has been universally recognized as the point through which the prime meridien passes. A degree (°) is 1/360 of a circle, a minute (') 1/60 of a degree, and a second (") 1/60 of a minute.

Lava Magma which reaches the surface of the earth and from which most of the gases have escaped. (See *Magma, Volcano.*)

Leeward The direction or side sheltered from the wind. (See *Windward.*)

Magma Molten rock that lies deep within the earth. In a volcanic eruption, magma bursts through the outer surface of the earth's crust. (See *Lava, Volcano.*)

Mountain Land that rises above its surroundings. Mountains are higher than hills. Older mountain ranges, like the Appalachians, are rounded because they are old and worn down; younger ranges, like the Andes or the Himalayas, have jagged peaks because they are still rising.

North Pole The northernmost point of the Earth's axis, at latitude 90°N. From this point, the only direction is south. It is entirely surrounded by water, and usually covered by ice. The first successful expedition to the North Pole—there is some doubt as to whether they actually reached the pole—was led by by Adm. Robert E. Peary, Apr. 6, 1909.

Ocean (See "Oceans of the World," later in this section).

Peninsula A portion of land surrounded by water on three sides.

Plain A large portion of level or rolling land which is treeless.

Plate tectonics theory The theory, first proposed in 1968, that Earth's crust is made up of 20 sections or "plates," each of which consists of continental and ocean crust. The plates shift, moving continents, changing the size and shape of oceans, causing earthquakes, and creating volcanos and mountains. The plate tectonics theory has largely replaced the *continental drift theory.*

Plateau A portion of land, generally large and with a level surface, which is sharply elevated above the surrounding land. Plateaus are created when vertical movement causes the earth's crust to warp.

Pond A small body of water surrounded by land.

Prairie Level or rolling land generally covered with grasses, with few trees.

Rain shadow An area on the leeward side of a mountain range which receives little rainfall.

River A large stream.

Sahel The Arabic word for "shore," the Sahel is a dry region separating the Sahara desert from tropical and West Central Africa running from Senegal to Sudan. The meager rainfall (4-8 inches per year) supports limited crops and grazing.

Savanna A portion of land in the tropics or subtropics with only scattered trees but whose grasses can survive with scant rainfall.

Sea A large body of saltwater, generally considered smaller than an ocean.

Solstice The time when the sun's rays strike vertically the Tropic of Cancer or the Tropic of Capricorn. At solstice, the daylight hours reach their maximum or minimum. In the Northern Hemisphere, for example, summer solstice occurs on or about June 22; that is the "longest day of the year" and signals the beginning of summer. The winter solstice occurs on or about December 22; that is the "shortest day of the year" and signals the beginning of winter. In the southern hemisphere, the longest and shortest days of the year occur on December 22 and June 22, respectively. (See also *Equinox.*)

Sound A body of water which separates an island from the mainland; or which connects two oceans, seas, or other bodies of water. Sounds are generally long and narrow.

South Pole The southernmost point of the Earth's axis, at 90°S. First reached by Norwegian explorer Roald Admundsen in 1911, the South Pole lies in the South Polar region.

Steppe A portion of land with little rainfall, extreme temperature variations, and drought-resistant vegetation.

Strait A narrow body of water that connects two large bodies of water.

Stream Any body of running water that flows on or under the surface of the earth. Brooks and creeks are small streams; rivers are large streams.

Swamp A portion of wet, waterlogged, or flooded land.

Tide The rise and fall of the surface of the ocean and of bays, gulfs, and other bodies of water connected to the ocean. Tides are caused by the gravitational pull of the moon, which passes over the same meridian of the Earth about once every 24 hours and 50 minutes. The length of time between successive high (or low) tides is about 12 hours and 25 minutes.

Tributary A stream or river that flows into a larger stream or river.

Tropic of Cancer Latitude 23½°N, which marks the northernmost limit of the sun's vertical rays. The area between the Tropic of Cancer and the Tropic of Capricorn is known as the "tropics."

Tropic of Capricorn Latitude 23½°S, the southernmost limit of the sun's vertical rays.

Tundra An area of treeless plain near or above the Arctic Circle. Tundra subsoil is permanently frozen, but the soil thaws enough to support the growth of mosses, lichens, and some small flowering shrubs.

Valley A long and sometimes narrow depression on the surface of the earth, usually between two mountain ridges or ranges.

Volcano A mountain formed by lava and/or other materials which have burst forth from deep within the earth. (See *Caldera, Lava, Magma.*)

Windward The direction or side facing the wind.

World Land Area and Population by Selected Region

	Land Area			Population			
Region	Square miles	Square kilometers	Percent of world total	Total ('000s)	Percent of total	Per square mile	Per square kilometer
World total[1]	**57,308,738**	**148,429,000**	**100.0%**	**6,068,511**	**100.0%**	**99.5**	**38.4**
Africa	11,608,156	30,065,000	20.3	805,243	13.3	69.4	40.9
Antarctica	5,404,000	14,000,000	9.4	(2)	(2)	(2)	(2)
Asia	17,212,041	44,579,000	30.0	3,688,072	60.8	214.3	82.7
Australia	2,967,966	7,687,000	5.2	19,164	0.3	6.5	2.5
Europe	3,837,082	9,938,000	6.7	728,981	12.0	190.0	73.4
North America	9,365,290	24,256,000	16.3	480,545	8.0	51.3	19.8
South America	6,879,952	17,819,000	12.0	346,504	5.7	50.4	19.4

1. Land only. Includes small islands not shown separately. 2. Antarctica has no indigenous population.
Source: *National Geographic Atlas of the World* (1995); U.S. Census Bureau, midyear 2000 population estimates.

The Continents: Highest and Lowest Elevations

Continent	Highest point	Location	Feet above sea level	Meters above sea level
Africa	Mt. Kilimanjaro	Tanzania	19,340	5,895
Antarctica	Vinson Massif	Ellsworth Mts.	16,066	4,897
Asia	Mt. Everest	Nepal-China	29,028	8,848
Australia	Mt. Kosciusko	New South Wales	7,310	2,228
Europe	Mt. Elbrus	Russia	18,510	5,642
North America	Mt. McKinley	U.S. (Alaska)	20,320	6,194
South America	Mt. Aconcagua	Argentina	22,834	6,960

Continent	Lowest point	Location	Feet below sea level	Meters below sea level
Africa	Lake Assal	Djibouti	512	156
Antarctica	ice covered	—	8,327	2,538
Asia	Dead Sea	Israel-Jordan	1,339	408
Australia	Lake Eyre	South Australia	52	16
Europe	Caspian Sea	Russia, Kazakhstan	92	28
North America	Death Valley	U.S. (California)	282	86
South America	Valdes Peninsula	Argentina	131	40

Source: *National Geographic Atlas of the World* (1995).

The Oceans of the World

Name	Area ('000s)		Average depth		Maximum depth	
	Sq. km.	Sq. mi.	Meters	Feet	Meters	Feet
Arctic ocean	**14,090**	**5,440**	**1,205**	**3,950**	**5,450**	**17,881**
Greenland Sea	1,205	465	1,450	4,750	4,846	15,899
Hudson Bay	1,230	470	128	420	259	850
Atlantic ocean	**82,440**	**31,830**	**3,926**	**12,877**	**9,219**	**30,246**
w/ marginal seas	106,450	41,100	3,332	10,932	—	—
Caribbean Sea	2,754	1,063	—	—	7,680	25,197
Mediterranean Sea	2,505	967	—	—	5,020	16,470
Norwegian Sea	1,547	597	—	—	4,020	13,189
Gulf of Mexico	1,544	596	—	—	4,380	14,370
North Sea	575	222	94	310	659	2,170
Black Sea	461	178	—	—	2,237	7,360
Baltic Sea	422	163	55	180	437	1,440
Indian ocean	**73,440**	**28,360**	**3,890**	**12,760**	**7,450**	**24,442**
w/marginal seas	74,920	28,930	—	—	—	—
Arabian Sea	3,863	1,492	2,734	8,970	5,800	19,029
Bay of Bengal	2,172	839	2,600	8,500	5,258	17,251
Red Sea	438	169	—	—	2,240	7,370
Pacific Ocean	**165,250**	**63,800**	**4,270**	**14,000**	**11,034**	**36,200**
w/marginal seas	179,680	69,370	—	—	—	—
South China Sea	3,447	1,331	1,060	3,478	5,560	18,241
Bering Sea	2,270	876	1,440	4,720	4,191	13,750
Sea of Okhotsk	1,580	610	838	2,750	3,372	11,063
East China Sea	1,248	482	349	1,145	2,717	8,912
Yellow Sea	1,243	480	40	131	91	300
Sea of Japan	1,007	389	1,752	5,748	3,733	12,280

Sources: International Hydrographic Organization; U.S. Navy Oceanographer (6/23/00), **oceanographer.navy.mil**; Central Intelligence Agency, *World Factbook 2001*, **www.cia.gov/cia/publications/factbook/index.html.**

▶THE OCEANS OF THE WORLD

The water of the world's oceans covers more than 70 percent of the world's surface. While for most of the twentieth century the so-called World Ocean was divided into the Pacific, Atlantic, Indian and Arctic Oceans, a decision by the International Hydrographic Organization in 2000 delimited a fifth ocean, the Southern Ocean, extending from 60 degrees south latitude to the coast of Antarctica. Other large bodies of water such as the Caribbean Sea, the Gulf of Mexico, Hudson Bay, the Mediterranean and Black Seas, and the South China Sea are termed marginal seas. The International Hydrographic Organization identifies 66 seas, gulfs, bays, bights, straits, channels, and passages, many of which are further subdivided. For instance, the Mediterranean Sea is divided into western and eastern basins, and the western basin is subdivided into the Strait of Gibraltar, Aboran Sea, Balearic Sea, Ligurian Sea, Tyrrhenian Sea, Ionian Sea, Adriatic Sea, and Aegean Sea. The table (above) gives the area and maximum depths of the world's major oceans and selected marginal seas.

Great Deserts of the World

Desert	Location	Approximate size	
		Sq. mi.	Sq. km.
An Nafud[1]	N Saudi Arabia	40,000	103,600
Arabian	Arabian Peninsula	900,000	2,330,000
Atacama	N Chile	70,000	181,300
Australian	Australia	600,000	1,554,000
Black Rock	NW Nevada	1,000	2,600
Chihuahuan	Texas, New Mexico, Arizona; Mexico	140,000	362,600
Dasht-e-Kavir	Central Iran	30,000	77,600
Dasht-e-Lut	E Iran	20,000	51,800
Death Valley	E California, SW Nevada	3,000	7,800
Gibson[2]	W Australia	120,000	310,800
Gobi	Mongolia; China	500,000	1,295,000
Great Sandy[2]	NW Australia	150,000	338,500
Great Victoria[2]	SW Australia	150,000	338,500
Kalahari	S Africa	225,000	582,800
Kara Kum (Turkestan)	Turkmenistan	120,000	310,800
Kyzyl Kum	Uzbekistan	100,000	259,000
Libyan[3]	Libya; SW Egypt; Sudan	450,000	1,165,500
Mojave	S California, W Arizona	15,000	38,900
Namib	Namibia	52,000	135,000
Negev	S Israel	4,700	12,200
Nubian[3]	NE Sudan	100,000	259,000
Painted Desert	N Arizona	5,000	12,950
Rub al-Khali ("Empty Quarter")[1]	S Saudi Arabia	250,000	647,500
Sahara	N Africa	3,500,000	9,065,000
Simpson[2]	Central Australia	40,000	103,600
Sonoran	SW Arizona; SE California; NW Mexico	70,000	181,300
Syrian[1]	N Saudi Arabia; E Jordan; S Syria; W Iraq	100,000	259,000
Taklimakan	Xinjiang Uygur Autonomous Region, China	140,000	362,600
Thar (Great Indian)	NW India; Pakistan	100,000	259,000

1. Part of Great Arabian Desert. 2. Part of Great Australian Desert. 3. Part of Sahara Desert. 4. Length; width varies from 30-100 mi. (48-160 km). 5. Length; width varies from 15-30 mi. (24-48 km).

▶THE GREAT DESERTS OF THE WORLD

To many people, the word *desert* brings to mind images of shifting sand dunes, scorching sun, and occasional lush oases. But there are actually many kinds of deserts, because a desert is simply an area that receives little precipitation and has little plant cover. Thus polar areas can be considered deserts, for their precipitation is locked into ice and snow. So are places like the Taklimakan in China, which lies in a rain shadow on the leeward side of mountain ranges, and the Atacama, which is near cold ocean currents that cool the air and prevent the formation of rain clouds. But most deserts are found in the tropics, where giant high-pressure cells keep rain from forming. Some deserts are indeed flat and sandy, but others are solid rock, loose pebbles, or even mountain plateaus. One of the many fascinating characteristics of deserts is their strangely shaped rock formations, created by wind-whipped sand.

Altogether, arid lands cover about a fifth of the Earth's total land surface—a third if semi-arid areas are also included. About a billion people live in arid and semiarid areas, and more than 100 countries are facing problems associated with expanding deserts.

Uses of the desert Even the hot, sandy tropical deserts are not necessarily, as their name implies, deserted. Traders, herders, and farmers have called the desert home for thousands of years. Settlements have grown up around oases or in irrigated areas, from ancient times to the present. Deserts are important to historians, archaeologists, paleontologists, and other scientists, for the relics of the past that are preserved there. Dinosaur eggs have been found in the Gobi Desert, for instance, and whole cities are said to lie buried beneath the Taklimakan Desert.

Deserts are also important for extractive industries. The Negev was the site of the fabled King Solomon's mines. In the 19th century, borax was mined in Death Valley. Petroleum is found in the Sahara and in the deserts of the Arabian Peninsula. The Atacama is famed for its deposits of nitrate and copper. The Rub al-Khali, or "Empty Quarter" of Saudi Arabia, is thought to contain deposits of limestone and gravel—but no one is certain because it has never been fully explored.

Desert extremes

- The Sahara is the largest desert, with an area greater than the contiguous United States.
- The driest place on earth is in the Atacama Desert of Chile, where no rainfall at all was recorded between 1570 and 1971.
- The highest temperature ever recorded—136° F (58° C)—was at Al-Aziziya, in the Libyan Desert, but the Dalol, Denakil Depression in Ethiopia is consistently the hottest place on earth, with an annual average temperature of 93°F (34 °C)
- The lowest point in the world—1,339 feet (408 m) below sea level—is on the shores of the Dead Sea in the Negev Desert.
- The lowest point in the Western Hemisphere—282 feet (86 meters) below sea level—is in Death Valley, California.

The World's Highest Mountain Peaks

Mountain peak	Range	Location	Height Feet	Height Meters
Everest	Himalayas	Nepal-China	29,028	8,848
K2 (Godwin Austen)	Karakoram	Kashmir	28,250	8,611
Kanchenjunga	Himalayas	Nepal-India	28,208	8,598
Lhotse I	Himalayas	Nepal-China	27,923	8,511
Makalu I	Himalayas	Nepal-China	27,824	8,481
Lhotse II	Himalayas	Nepal-China	27,560	8,400
Dhaulagiri	Himalayas	Nepal	26,810	8,172
Manaslu I	Himalayas	Nepal	26,760	8,156
Cho Oyu	Himalayas	Nepal-China	26,750	8,153
Nanga Parbat	Himalayas	Kashmir	26,660	8,126
Annapurna	Himalayas	Nepal	26,504	8,078
Gasherbrum	Karakoram	Kashmir	26,470	8,068
Broad	Karakoram	Kashmir	26,400	8,047
Gosainthan	Himalayas	China	26,287	8,012
Annapurna II	Himalayas	Nepal	26,041	7,937
Gyachung Kang	Himalayas	Nepal-China	25,910	7,897
Disteghil Sar	Himalayas	Kashmir	25,858	7,882
Himalchuli	Himalayas	Nepal	25,801	7,864
Nuptse	Himalayas	Nepal-China	25,726	7,841
Masherbrum	Karakoram	Kashmir	25,660	7,821
Nanda Devi	Himalayas	India	25,645	7,817
Rakaposhi	Karakoram	Kashmir	25,550	7,788
Kanjut Sar	Karakoram	Kashmir	25,461	7,761
Kamet	Himalayas	India-China	25,447	7,756
Namcha Barwa	Himalayas	China	25,445	7,756
Kua-la-man-ta-t`a (Gurla Mandhata)	Himalayas	China	25,355	7,728
Wu-lu-k'o-mu-shih (Ulugh Muztagh)	Kunlun	China	25,340	7,724
Kung-ko-erh (Kungur)	Mu-ssu-t'a-ko-a-t'e (Muztagh Ata)	China	25,325	7,719
Tirich Mir	Hindu Kush	Pakistan	25,230	7,690
Saser Kangri	Karakoram	Kashmir	25,172	7,672
Makalu II	Himalayas	Nepal-China	25,120	7,657
Minya Konka (Gonggashan)	Daxue Shan	China	24,900	7,590
Kula Kangri	Himalayas	Bhutan-China	24,784	7,554
Chang-tzu	Himalayas	Nepal-China	24,780	7,553
Mu-ssu-t'a-ko-a-t'e (Muztagh Ata)	Mu-ssu-t'a-ko-a-t'e (Muztagh Ata)	China	24,757	7,546
Skyang Kangri	Himalayas	Kashmir	24,750	7,544
Communism Peak	Pamirs	Tajikistan	24,590	7,495
Jongsong Peak	Himalayas	Nepal-India	24,472	7,459
Pobeda Peak	Tien Shan	Kyrgyzstan-China	24,406	7,439
Sia Kangri	Himalayas	Kashmir	24,350	7,422
Haramosh Peak	Karakoram	Kashmir	24,270	7,397
Istoro Nal	Hindu Kush	Pakistan	24,240	7,388
Tent Peak	Himalayas	Nepal-India	24,165	7,365
Chomo Lhari	Himalayas	Bhutan-China	24,040	7,327
Chamlang	Himalayas	Nepal	24,012	7,319
Kabru	Himalayas	Nepal-India	24,002	7,316
Alung Gangri	Himalayas	China	24,000	7,315
Baltoro Kangri	Himalayas	Kashmir	23,990	7,312
Muztagh Ata	Kunlun	China	23,890	7,282
Mana	Himalayas	India	23,860	7,273
Baruntse	Himalayas	Nepal	23,688	7,220
Nepal Peak	Himalayas	Nepal-India	23,500	7,163
Amne Machin	Kunlun	China	23,490	7,160
Gauri Sankar	Himalayas	Nepal-China	23,440	7,145
Badrinath	Himalayas	India	23,420	7,138
Nunkun	Himalayas	Kashmir	23,410	7,135
Lenin Peak	Pamirs	Tajikistan	23,405	7,134
Pyramid	Himalayas	Nepal-India	23,400	7,132

Mountain peak	Range	Location	Height	
			Feet	Meters
Api	Himalayas	Nepal	23,399	7,132
Pauhunri	Himalayas	India-China	23,385	7,128
Trisul	Himalayas	India	23,360	7,120
Korzhenevski Peak	Pamirs	Tajikistan	23,310	7,105
Kangto	Himalayas	India-China	23,260	7,090
Nyainqentanglha	Nyainqentanglha Shan	China	23,255	7,088
Trisuli	Himalayas	India	23,210	7,074
Dunagiri	Himalayas	India	23,184	7,066
Revolution Peak	Pamirs	Tajikistan	22,880	6,974
Aconcagua	Andes	Argentina	22,834	6,960
Ojos del Salado	Andes	Argentina-Chile	22,572	6,880
Bonete	Andes	Argentina	22,546	6,872
Tupungato	Andes	Argentina-Chile	22,310	6,800
Moscow Peak	Pamirs	Tajikistan	22,260	6,785
Pissis	Andes	Argentina	22,241	6,779
Mercedario	Andes	Argentina	22,211	6,770
Huascaran	Andes	Peru	22,205	6,768
Llullaillaco	Andes	Argentina-Chile	22,057	6,723
El Libertador	Andes	Argentina	22,047	6,720
Cachi	Andes	Argentina	22,047	6,720
Kailas	Himalayas	China	22,027	6,714
Incahuasi	Andes	Argentina-Chile	21,720	6,620
Yerupaja	Andes	Peru	21,709	6,617
Kurumda	Pamirs	Tajikistan	21,686	6,610
Galan	Andes	Argentina	21,654	6,600
El Muerto	Andes	Argentina-Chile	21,457	6,540
Sajama	Andes	Bolivia	21,391	6,520
Nacimiento	Andes	Argentina	21,302	6,493
Illimani	Andes	Bolivia	21,201	6,462
Coropuna	Andes	Peru	21,083	6,426
Laudo	Andes	Argentina	20,997	6,400
Ancohuma	Andes	Bolivia	20,958	6,388
Ausangate	Andes	Peru	20,945	6,384
Toro	Andes	Argentina-Chile	20,932	6,380
Illampu	Andes	Bolivia	20,873	6,362
Tres Cruces	Andes	Argentina-Chile	20,853	6,356
Huandoy	Andes	Peru	20,852	6,356
Parinacota	Andes	Bolivia-Chile	20,768	6,330
Tortolas	Andes	Argentina-Chile	20,745	6,323
Ampato	Andes	Peru	20,702	6,310
El Condor	Andes	Argentina	20,669	6,300
Salcantay	Andes	Peru	20,574	6,271
Chimborazo	Andes	Ecuador	20,561	6,267
Huancarhuas	Andes	Peru	20,531	6,258
Famatina[1]	Andes	Argentina	20,505	6,250
Pumasillo	Andes	Peru	20,492	6,246
Solo	Andes	Argentina	20,492	6,246
Polleras	Andes	Argentina	20,456	6,235
Pular	Andes	Chile	20,423	6,225
Chani	Andes	Argentina	20,341	6,200
McKinley	Alaska	U.S. (Alaska)	20,320	6,194
Aucanquilcha	Andes	Chile	20,295	6,186
Juncal	Andes	Argentina-Chile	20,276	6,180
Negro	Andes	Argentina	20,184	6,152
Quela	Andes	Argentina	20,128	6,135
Condoriri	Andes	Bolivia	20,095	6,125
Palermo	Andes	Argentina	20,079	6,120
Solimana	Andes	Peru	20,068	6,117
San Juan	Andes	Argentina-Chile	20,049	6,111
(Sierra) Nevada	Andes	Argentina-Chile	20,023	6,103
Antofalla	Andes	Argentina	20,013	6,100
Marmolejo	Andes	Argentina-Chile	20,013	6,100

1. Formerly General Manuel Belgrano.

Major Natural Lakes of the World

Lake	Surface area		Location	Maximum depth		Elevation	
	Sq. mi.	Sq. km.		Feet	Meters	Feet	Meters
Caspian Sea[1]	143,240	370,992	Russia, Kazakhstan, Azerbaijan, Turkmenistan, Iran	3,363	1,025	- 92	- 28
Superior	31,700	82,103	Ontario, Canada; Mich., Wis., Minn.	1,333	406	600	183
Victoria	26,820	69,464	Uganda, Kenya, Tanzania	279	85	3,720	1,134
Aral Sea[1]	24,904	64,501	Uzbekistan, Kazakhstan	220	67	174	53
Huron	23,000	59,570	Ontario, Can.; Mich.	750	229	576	176
Michigan	22,300	57,757	Mich., Ind., Ill., Wis.	923	281	579	176
Tanganyika	12,350	31,987	Burundi, Tanzania, Zambia, Zaire	4,800	1,463	2,543	775
Baikal	12,160	31,494	Russia	5,315	1,620	1,493	455
Great Bear	12,028	31,153	Northwest Terr., Canada	1,356	413	512	156
Nyasa (Malawi)	11,150	28,879	Tanzania, Mozambique, Malawi	2,280	695	1,550	472
Great Slave	11,030	28,568	Northwest Terr., Canada	2,015	614	513	156
Erie	9,910	25,667	Ontario, Canada; N.Y., Pa., Ohio, Mich.	210	64	570	174
Winnipeg	9,417	24,390	Manitoba, Canada	92	28	713	217
Ontario	7,540	19,529	Ontario, Canada; N.Y.	802	244	245	75
Balkhash[1]	7,115[2]	18,428[2]	Kazakhstan	87	27	1,115	340
Ladoga	6,835	17,703	Russia	755	230	13	4
Chad	6,300	16,317	Chad, Nigeria, Niger	24	7	787	240
Maracaibo[3]	5,200	13,468	Venezuela	197	60	sea level	
Patos[3]	3,920	10,153	Brazil	15	5	([4])	([4])
Onega	3,720	9,635	Russia	394	120	108	33
Titicaca	3,200	8,288	Bolivia, Peru	990	302	12,500	3,810
Nicaragua	3,150	8,159	Nicaragua	230	70	102	31
Mai-Ndombe	3,100	8,029[2]	Zaire	36	11	1,116	340
Athabasca	3,064	7,936	Saskatchewan, Alberta, Canada	407	124	700	213
Eyre[1]	2,970[2]	7,692[2]	Australia	4	1	- 52	- 16
Reindeer	2,568	6,651	Saskatchewan, Manitoba, Canada	720	219	1,106	337
Tonle Sap	2,500[2]	6,475[2]	Cambodia	39	12	([4])	([4])
Rudolf[1]	2,473	6,405	Kenya, Ethiopia	720	219	1,230	375
Issyk-Kul[1]	2,355	6,099	Kyrghyzstan	2,303	702	5,279	1,609
Torrens[1]	2,230[2]	5,776[2]	Australia	0.5	0.2	92	28
Albert	2,160	5,594	Uganda, Zaire	168	51	2,030	619
Vanern	2,156	5,54	Sweden	325	99	144	44
Nettilling	2,140	5,543	Baffin Island, Canada	([4])	([4])	95	29
Winnipegosis	2,075	5,374	Manitoba, Canada	39	12	830	253
Bangweulu	1,930	4,999	Zambia	5	2	3,500	1,067
Nipigon	1,872	4,848	Ontario, Canada	541	165	1,050	320
Gairdner[1]	1,840[2]	4,763[2]	Australia	0.5	0.2	112	34
Urmia[1]	1,815[2]	4,701[2]	Iran	49	15	4,180	1,274
Manitoba	1,800	4,662	Manitoba, Canada	92	28	813	248
Kyoga	1,710	4,429	Uganda	26	8	4	4
Khanka	1,700	4,403	China, Russia	33	10	4	4
Lake of the Woods	1,695	4,390	Ontario, Manitoba, Canada; Minn.	55	17	1,060	323
Great Salt[1]	1,680	4,351	Utah	48	15	4,200	1,280
Mweru	1,680	4,351	Zambia, Zaire	10	3	3,008	917
Peipus	1,660	4,299	Estonia, Russia	41	12	98	30
Koko Nor (Tsing Hai)	1,650	4,274	China	125	38	10,515	3,205
Dubawnt	1,600	4,144	Northwest Terr., Canada	([4])	([4])	774	236
Tung-t'ing Hu	1,430[2]	3,704[2]	China	([4])	([4])	36	11
Van Golu[1]	1,420	3,678	Turkey	82	25	5,643	1,720
Tana	1,390	3,600	Ethiopia	30	9	6,003	1,830

1. Saltwater. A lake is a body of water surrounded by land. The Caspian Sea is thus a lake. It was called a "sea" by the Romans because of its salty water. 2. Subject to large seasonal variation in surface area. 3. Lagoon. 4 . No information available. **Source:** U.S. Department of Commerce, National Oceanic and Atmospheric Administration, *Principal Rivers and Lakes of the World* (1982).

Major Rivers of the World, by Length

River	Length: Miles	Length: km	Source	Outflow
Nile	4,145	6,673	Tributaries of Lake Victoria, E. Africa	Mediterranean Sea
Amazon	4,000	6,440	Andes Mts., Peru	Atlantic Ocean
Mississippi-Missouri	3,740[1]	6,021[1]	Confluence of Jefferson, Madison, and Galatin R., Montana	Gulf of Mexico
Changjiang (Yangtze)	3,720	5,989	Kunlun Mts., China	China Sea
Yenisei-Angara	3,650[2]	5,877[2]	Lake Baikal, Russia	Kara Sea (Arctic Ocean)
Amur-Argun	3,590[2]	5,780[2]	Khingan Mts., China	Tatar Strait
Ob-Irtysh	3,360[2]	5,410[2]	Altai Mts., China	Gulf of Ob (Arctic Ocean)
Plata-Parana	3,030[2]	4,878[2]	Confluence of the Paranaiba and Grande rivers, Brazil	Atlantic Ocean
Huang He (Yellow)	2,903	4,674	Kunlun Mts., China	Gulf of Chihli (Yellow Sea)
Congo (Zaire)	2,900	4,669	Confluence of the Luapula and Lualaba rivers, Zaire	Atlantic Ocean
Lena	2,730	4,395	Baikal Mts., Russia	Laptev Sea (Arctic Ocean)
MacKenzie	2,635[2]	4,242[2]	Headwaters of Finlay Rivers, British Columbia, Canada	Beaufort Sea (Arctic Ocean)
Mekong	2,600	4,186	T'ang-ku-la Mts., Tibet	South China Sea
Niger	2,600	4,186	Guinea	Gulf of Guinea
Missouri	2,315	3,725	Confluence of Jefferson, Madison, and Montana Galatin rivers, Montana	Mississippi River
Mississippi	2,348[3]	3,780[3]	Lake Itasca, northwestern Minnesota	Gulf of Mexico
Murray-Darling	2,330	3,751	Great Dividing Range, Australia	Indian Ocean
Volga	2,290	3,687	Valdai Hills, Russia	Caspian Sea
Madeira	2,013	3,241	Confluence of the Mamore and Beni rivers, Bolivia/Brazil	Amazon River
Sao Francisco	1,988	3,201	Minas Gerais State, Brazil	Atlantic Ocean
Yukon	1,979	3,186	Confluence of Lewes and Pelly rivers, Yukon Territory, Canada	Bering Sea
Rio Grande	1,885	3,035	San Juan Mts., southwestern Colorado	Gulf of Mexico
Purus	1,860	2,995	Andes Mts., Peru	Amazon River
Tunguska, Lower	1,860	2,995	North of Lake Baikal, Russia	Yenesei River
Indus	1,800	2,898	Himalayas, Tibet	Arabian Sea
Danube	1,776	2,859	Confluence of Breg and Brigach rivers, Germany	Black Sea
Brahmaputra	1,770	2,850	Himalayas, Tibet	Ganges River
Salween	1,750	2,818	Tibetan Plateau, Tibet	Bay of Bengal
Para-Tocantins	1,710[2]	2,753[2]	Goias State, Brazil	Atlantic Ocean
Zambezi	1,700	2,737	Northwestern Zambia	Mozambique Channel
Paraguay	1,610	2,592	Mato Grosso State, Brazil	Parana River
Kolyma	1,320	2,130	Kolyma Mts., Russia	Arctic Ocean
Nelson-Saskatchewan	1,600	2,576	Rocky Mts., Canada	Hudson Bay
Orinoco	1,600	2,576	Sierra Parima Mts., Venezuela	Atlantic Ocean
Amu Darya	1,578	2,541	Pamir Mts., Uzbekistan/Turkmenistan	Aral Sea
Ural	1,575	2,536	Ural Mountains, Russia	Caspian Sea
Ganges	1,560	2,512	Himalayas, India	Bay of Bengal
Euphrates	1,510	2,431	Confluence of the Murat Nehri and Kara Su rivers, Turkey	Shatt-al-Arab
Arkansas	1,450	2,335	Central Colorado	Mississippi River
Colorado	1,450	2,335	Northern Colorado	Gulf of California
Dneiper	1,420	2,286	Valdai Hills, Russia	Black Sea
Atchafalaya-Red	1,400	2,254	Eastern New Mexico	Gulf of Mexico
Syr Darya	1,370	2,206	Tien Shan, China/Kyrghyzstan	Aral Sea
Kasai	1,338	2,154	Central Angola	Congo (Zaire) River
Irrawaddy	1,300	2,093	Confluence of Mali and Nmai rivers, Myanmar	Bay of Bengal
Ohio-Allegheny	1,300	2,093	Pennsylvania	Mississippi River
Orange	1,300	2,093	Lesotho	Atlantic Ocean
Columbia	1,243	2,001	Columbia Lake, British Columbia, Canada	Pacific Ocean
Tigris	1,180	1,900	Eastern Turkey	Shatt-al-Arab
Rhine	820	1,320	Confluence of Hinterrhein and Vorderrhein rivers, Switzerland	North Sea
St. Lawrence	800	1,288	Lake Ontario	Gulf of St. Lawrence

1. From the mouth of the Mississippi, up the Missouri to the Red Rock River in Montana. 2. Includes the length of tributaries that are part of the main trunk stream. 3. From the mouth of the Mississippi, up to its source in Minnesota. **Source**: U.S. Dept. of Commerce, National Oceanic and Atmospheric Administration, *Principal Rivers and Lakes of the World* (1982).

World's 25 Largest Capacity Reservoirs

Reservoir	Capacity (mil.) Cubic yards[1]	Cubic meters[1]	River or basin and location	Year completed
1. Owen Falls[2]	3,537,000	2,700,000	Lake Victoria/Nile, Uganda	1954
2. Kariba	236,586	180,600	Zambezi, Zimbabwe/Zambia	1959
3. Bratsk	221,744	169,270	Angara, Russia	1964
4. Aswan High	211,765	162,000	Nile, Egypt	1970
5. Akosombo	196,078	150,000	Volta, Ghana	1965
6. Daniel Johnson	185,826	141,852	Manicouagan, Quebec	1968
7. Guri	176,470	135,000	Caroni, Venezuela	1986
8. Krasnoyarsk	96,023	73,300	Yenesei, Russia	1967
9. W.A.C. Bennett	92,105	70,309	Peace, British Columbia	1967
10. Zeya	89,604	68,400	Zeya, Russia	1978
11. Cabora Bassa	82,530	63,000	Zambezi, Mozambique	1974
12. La Grande 2	80,847	61,715	La Grande, Quebec	1978
13. La Grande 3	78,626	60,020	La Grande, Quebec	1981
14. Ust-Ilim	77,683	59,300	Angara, Russia	1977
15. Boguchany	76,242	58,200	Angara, Russia	1989
16. Volga-V.I. Lenin (Kuibyshev)	75,980	58,000	Volga, Russia	1955
17. Caniapiscau	70,478	53,800	Caniapiscau, Quebec, Canada	1981
18. Bukhtarma	65,238	49,800	Irtysh, Russia	1960
19. Atatürk	63,797	48,700	Euphrates, Turkey	1990
20. Irkutsk	60,260	46,000	Angara, Russia	1956
21. Tucurui	64,753	49,536	Tocantins, Brazil	1984
22. Lower Kama	58,858	45,000	Kama, Russia	1987
23. Vilyui	47,029	35,900	Vilyui, Russia	1967
24. Sanmenxia	46,374	35,400	Huanghe (Yellow River), China	1960
25. Wuluwati	45,359	34,700	Kalakashi, China	1999

Note: Uncompleted reservoirs are not officially ranked. 1. One cubic yard equals 0.765 cubic meters. 2. Capacity includes Lake Victoria, a large natural lake. **Source:** International Committee on Large Dams (1998).

World's 25 Largest Volume Dams

Reservoir	Volume ('000s) Cubic yards[1]	Cubic meters[1]	River or basin and location	Year completed
1. New Cornelia Tailings	274,445	209,500	Ten Mile Wash, Arizona	1973
2. Tarbela	138,297	106,000	Indus, Pakistan	1976
3. Fort Peck	125,825	96,050	Missouri, Montana	1937
4. Lower Usuma	121,830	93,000	Usuma, Nigeria	1990
5. Tucurui	111,612	85,200	Tocantins, Brazil	1984
6. Atatürk	111,350	84,500	Euphrates, Turkey	1990
7. Guri (Raul Leoni)	102,142	77,971	Caroni, Venezuela	1986
8. Oahe	87,137	66,517	Missouri, South Dakota	1958
9. Gardiner	85,726	65,400	South Saskatchewan, Saskatchewan	1968
10. Mangla	85,646	65,379	Jhelum, Pakistan	1967
11. Afsluitdijk	83,093	63,430	Zuider Zee, Netherlands	1932
12. Oroville	80,125	61,164	Feather, California	1968
13. San Luis	78,022	59,559	San Luis, California	1967
14. Nurek	75,980	58,000	Vakhsh, Tajikistan	1980
15. Garrison	66,607	50,845	Missouri, North Dakota	1956
16. Cochiti	65,801	50,230	Grande, New Mexico	1975
17. Oosterschelde	65,500	50,000	Vense Gat Oosterschelde, Netherlands	1986
18. Tabqua (Thawra)	60,260	46,000	Euphrates, Syria	1976
19. Aswan, High	58,033	44,300	Nile, Egypt	1970
20. W.A.C. Bennett	57,290	43,733	Peace, Canada	1967
21. Kiev	55,544	42,400	Dnieper, Ukraine	1964
22. Dantiwada	53,762	41,040	Banas, India	1965
23. Saratov	52,924	40,400	Volga, Russia	1967
24. Earthquake Lake	50,079	38,228	Madison, Montana	1959
25. Fort Randall	50,042	38,200	Missouri, South Dakota	1952

Note: Volume refers to amount of material (earth, concrete, etc.) used in construction of dam. Tailings dams are formed from waste ore (tailings) from mining. Uncompleted reservoirs are not officially ranked. 1. One cubic meter equals 1.31 cubic yards. **Source:** *International Water Power & Dam Construction Handbook 1993.*

▶ MAJOR ISLANDS AND ISLAND GROUPS

Admiralty Is.: see Bismarck Archipelago.

Åland Is. (Ahvenanmaa): 60°N, 20°E. Finnish archipelago of more than 6,000 islands between Finland and Sweden.

Aleutian Is.: 51°-55°N, 163°W-166°E. Chain between Pacific Ocean and Bering Sea stretching 2,700 km: Unimak, Fox Is., Andreanof Is., Rat Is. and Near Is. (Alaska) and Komandorskiye Ostrova (Russia).

Andaman and Nicobar Is.: 12°N, 93°E. Union Territory of India comprising some 300 islands in two major archipelagos stretching 725 km north-south in the Bay of Bengal off the coast of Myanmar.

Anglesey: 53°N, 4°W. Irish Sea island off Wales.

Anticosti: 50°N, 63°W. Canadian island in Gulf of St. Lawrence.

Antigua and Barbuda: 17°N, 62°W. Two-island Caribbean country.

Antilles. Name for the Caribbean islands from Cuba to Trinidad and Tobago, but not including the Bahamas. *Greater Antilles:* Cuba, Jamaica, Hispaniola, and Puerto Rico. *Lesser Antilles:* Leeward Is. Virgin Is., Antigua and Barbuda, and Dominica. *Windward Is.:* Martinique, St. Lucia, St. Vincent, Grenada, Barbados, Trinidad and Tobago, and Aruba.

Aran Is.: 53°N, 10°W. Three islands—Inishmore, Inishmaan and Inisheer—off western Ireland.

Aruba: 12°N, 70°W. Dutch Caribbean island 30 km N of Venezuela.

Ascension: 7°S, 14°W. Island of the British Crown Colony of St. Helena about 1,100 km northwest of St. Helena, 2,250 km east of Brazil and 2,500 km west of Africa

Auckland Is.: 51°S, 166°E. Group about 300 km south of New Zealand.

Azores/Açores: 37°-40°N, 25°-31°W. Portuguese Atlantic group 1,400 km west of Portugal: Faial, Flores, São Miguel; first settled in 1430's.

Baffin: 68°N, 70°W. Largest Canadian Arctic island, on Davis Strait opposite Greenland.

Bahamas: 21°-27°N, 71°-79°W. Chain of 2,700 islands and cays stretching 800 km southeast of Florida; shared by Bahamas, Turks, Caicos (British); Columbus's first American landfall in 1492.

Bahrain: Persian Gulf island 25 km off coast of Saudi Arabia; probable site of ancient Dilmun.

Balearic Is.: 39°N, 3°E. Sixteen Spanish Mediterranean islands: incl. Majorca, Minorca and Ibiza.

Bali: 9°S, 115°E. Predominantly Hindu Indonesian island east of Java.

Banks: 73°N, 121°W. Westernmost large Canadian Arctic island, on Beaufort Sea.

Bear: see Spitsbergen.

Barbados: 13°N, 60°W. Island nation about 150 km east of southern Antilles.

Bermuda: 32°N, 65°W. British dependency of 138 coral islands, 20 inhabited, 900 km east of North Carolina.

Bikini: see Marshall Is.

Bismarck Archipelago: 5°S, 150°E. Papua New Guinea archipelago: Admiralty Is., New Britain and New Ireland; formerly a German colony.

Block: 41°N, 72°W. Island between Long Island Sound and Atlantic Ocean, 15 km off Rhode Island.

Borneo: 0°N/S, 114°E. Large equatorial Southeast Asian island shared by Indonesia, Malaya and Brunei.

British Isles: Group off Northwest Europe: Great Britain, Ireland, Man, Wight, Hebrides, Shetlands, Orkneys and Anglesey.

Canary Is.: 28°N, 16°W. Spanish archipelago of seven islands 100 km west of Morocco: incl. Tenerife, Gomera, Gran Canaria, Fuertaventura, Lanzarote. Inhabited since antiquity (Latin: Fortunatae Insulae); colonized by the Spanish in 1400s.

Cape Verde Is.: 15°-17°N, 23°-25°W. Ten-island nation 500 km west of Senegal: incl. São Tiago, Fogo. Settled by Portuguese in 15th century.

Capri: 41°N, 14°E. Italian island in Bay of Naples.

Caroline Is.: 5°-10°N, 130°-166°E. Micronesian group of more than 600 islands: Belau (Palau), Kusaie, Ponape, Satawal, Truk and Yap.

Cayman Is.: 20°N, 81°W. British dependency of 3 main islands 240 km south of Cuba.

Chagos Archipelago: 6°S, 72°E. Part of the British Indian Ocean Territory 600 km south of the Maldives. Diego Garcia has been a UK/U.S. military base since the 1970's when its 1,500 inhabitants—the descendents of slaves—were deported.

Channel/Santa Barbara Is.: 34°N, 120°W. Eight-island group off Los Angeles.

Channel Is.: 49°N, 2°W. Group in English Channel near France: Jersey, Guernsey, Alderney and Sark. They are dependent territories of the English Crown, as successor to William the Conqueror, Duke of Normandy, but not part of the UK.

Chatham Is.: 44°S, 176°W. Polynesian group 860 km east of New Zealand from where they were settled around 1500.

Chincha Is.: 14°S, 76°W. Group of three Peruvian islands; important source of guano before synthetic fertilizers.

Christmas: 10°S, 106°E. Australian dependency 360 km south of Java.

Cocos/Keeling Is.: 12°S, 97°E. Australian archipelago of 27 coral atolls 2,800 km northwest of Perth, settled in 19th century.

Comoros: 12°S, 44°E. Indian Ocean nation of three islands about 325 km east of Mozambique.

Cook Is.: 8°-23°S, 156°-167°W. Group of 15 islands 3,200 km northeast of New Zealand: Rarotonga.

Corsica: 42°N, 9°E. French Mediterranean island; birthplace of Napoleon Bonaparte.

Cuba: 21°N, 80°W. Northernmost Caribbean island, 1,250 km east-west; largest of 1,200 islands in Cuban archipelago.

Cyclades/Kikláhdes: 37°N, 25°E. Greek Aegean archipelago of about 220 islands; so-called because they encircle sacred island of Delos.

Delos: see Cyclades.

Devil's: 5°N, 52°W. Island off French Guiana; used as penal colony until 1938.

Diego Garcia: see Chagos Archipelago.

Dodecanese/Sporádhes: 36°N, 27°E. Greek Aegean archipelago of 12 islands, including Samos, Kos and Ródhos.

Dominica: 16°N, 61°W. Caribbean island nation.

Easter Island/Isla de Pascua/Rapa Nui: 27°07'S, 109°22'W. The most remote island on earth, Rapa Nui is the eastern tip of Polynesia, about 3,700 km west of Chile, which administers it, and 1,600 km east of Pitcairn Island. Settled by Marquesans around the 4th century, it is famous for its thousand carved statues, some 10 meters tall.

Elba: 43°N, 10°E. Italian island where Napoleon was briefly exiled.

Ellesmere Island, Nunavut Territory: 79°N, 82°W. Cape Columbia (83°08'N) is the northernmost point in Canada; part of Queen Elizabeth group.

Faeroe Is.: 62°N, 7°W. Group of 18 islands about 118 km north-south, 320 km north of the Shetlands and halfway between Norway and Iceland; settled in 7th century they are an autonomous part of Denmark.

Falkland Is./Islas Malvinas: 51°-53°S, 57°- 62°W. British Crown Colony of 340 islands about 600 km east of Argentina. Claimed by French sailors from St. Mâlo (hence Malvinas), contested by Spanish, settled by English. An Argentine invasion in 1982 failed.

Faylakah: 29°N, 48°E. Persian Gulf island off Kuwait.

Fernando de Noronha: 4°S, 32°W. Atlantic island about 500 km east of Brazil.

Fernando Po: 3°S, 9°E. Former name for Bioko, Equatorial Guinea.

Fiji Is.: 16°-19°S, 178°W-177°E. Pacific nation of about 330 islands, a third inhabited, about 1,770 km north of New Zealand.

The World's Largest Islands

Island	Location	Flags	Area Sq. mi.	Area Sq. km.
Greenland	N. Atlantic Ocean	Denmark	840,000	2,175,600
New Guinea	S. Pacific Ocean	Indonesia, Papua New Guinea	306,000	792,540
Borneo	Pacific Ocean	Indonesia, Malaysia, Brunei	280,100	725,459
Madagascar	Indian Ocean	Madagascar	226,658	587,044
Baffin	Arctic Ocean	Canada	195,928	507,454
Sumatra	Indian Ocean	Indonesia	165,000	427,350
Honshu	N. Pacific Ocean	Japan	87,805	227,415
Great Britain	N. Atlantic Ocean	United Kingdom	84,200	218,078
Victoria	Arctic Ocean	Canada	83,896	217,291
Ellesmere	Arctic Ocean	Canada	75,767	196,237
Celebes	Pacific Ocean	Indonesia	69,000	178,710
South Island	S. Pacific Ocean	New Zealand	58,305	151,010
Java	S. Pacific Ocean	Indonesia	48,900	126,651
Cuba	Caribbean Sea	Cuba	44,218	114,525
North Island	S. Pacific Ocean	New Zealand	44,035	114,051
Newfoundland	N. Atlantic Ocean	Canada	42,030	108,858
Luzon	N. Pacific Ocean	Philippines	40,880	105,879
Iceland	N. Atlantic Ocean	Iceland	39,769	103,002
Mindanao	N. Pacific Ocean	Philippines	36,775	95,247
Novaya Zemlya	Arctic Ocean	Russia	35,000	90,650
Ireland	N. Atlantic Ocean	Irish Republic, United Kingdom	32,599	84,431
Hokkaido	N. Pacific Ocean	Japan	30,144	78,073
Hispaniola	Caribbean Sea	Haiti, Dominican Republic	29,530	76,483
Sakhalin	N. Pacific Ocean	Russia	29,500	76,405
Banks	Arctic Ocean	Canada	27,033	70,015
Tasmania	S. Pacific Ocean	Australia	26,178	67,801
Sri Lanka	Indian Ocean	Sri Lanka	25,332	65,610
Devon	Arctic Ocean	Canada	21,331	55,247

Florida Keys: 24°-25°N, 80°-82°W. Chain of coral islands running 240 km west from tip of Florida: Key Largo, Islamorada, Key West and Dry Tortugas.
Frisian Is.: 53°-55°N, 5°-8°E. Chain of North Sea islands, 18 inhabited, off The Netherlands, Germany, and Denmark: Rømø, Sylt, Terschelling, Vlieland and Texel.
Galápagos: 1°S, 91°W. Archipelago of 60 volcanic islands about 430 km across and 1,000 km west of Ecuador; known for its diverse flora and fauna and Charles Darwin's research there in 1835.
Gotland: 57°N, 18°E. Swedish Baltic island, thought to be the homeland of the Goths.
Great Britain: 54°N, 3°W. Principal island of British Isles; includes England, Scotland and Wales.
Greenland: 70°N, 40°W. Large North Atlantic island, settled about 2500 B.C.; first visited by Europeans around 1000.
Guadalcanal: see Solomon Is.
Guam: see Mariana Is.
Guernsey: see Channel Is.
Hainan: 19°N, 109°E. Chinese island between South China Sea and Gulf of Tonkin.
Hawaiian Is.: 19°-28°N, 155°-178°W. Polynesian chain comprising eight large and 124 smaller islands stretching 2,400 km from Hawaii to Midway and Kure. Settled in 8th century from the Marquesas. U.S. state: Hawaii, Maui, Lauai, Molokai, Oahu, Kaui and Nihau.
Hebrides/Western Isles: 57°N, 7°W. Islands off the west coast of Scotland. Inner Hebrides: Skye, Mull and Islay; 210-km-long Outer Hebrides: Lewis, North Uist and South Uist.
Hispaniola: 19°N, 71°W. Caribbean island divided between Haiti and Dominican Republic.
Hokkaido: 43°N, 143°E. Northernmost of main Japanese islands.
Hong Kong: 22°N, 114°E. Chinese island at mouth of Pearl River, 145 km southeast of Guangzhou (Canton).
Honshu: 36°N, 136°E. Largest of main Japanese islands; cities include Tokyo.
Ibiza: see Balearic Is.
Iceland: 65°N, 18°W. North Atlantic island 900 km west of Norway, settled in 9th century.
Indonesia: From the Greek meaning "Indian islands," the name applies to the archipelagic nation of 18,108 islands: Sumatra, Java, Sulawesi, Bali, Malaku Is., and parts of Borneo, Timor and New Guinea.
Ionian Is.: 39°N, 21°E. Greek Adriatic archipelago of seven islands: Kerkira (Corfu), Kefallinia, Zákinthos and Odysseus's Itháki.
Ireland: 53°N, 8°W. Second largest island in British Isles; divided between Republic of Ireland and Northern Ireland (which is still part of the U.K.).
Iwo Jima: see Volcano Is.
Jamaica: 18°N, 75°W. Caribbean island nation about 175 km south of Cuba.
Jan Mayen: 71°N, 8°W. Norwegian island 400 km east of Greenland.
Japanese islands: see Hokkaido, Honshu, Kyushu, Shikoku, Ryukyu Is., Tsushima and Volcano Is.
Java: 7°S, 110°E. Indonesian island east of Sumatra.
Jersey: see Channel Is.
Juan Fernandez Is.: 33°S, 80°W. Three-island group 650 km west of Chile. Alexander Selkirk, model for Daniel Defoe's Robinson Crusoe, was marooned on Más a Tierra 1705-1709.
Kerguelen/Desolation Is.: 49°-50°S, 69°-71°E. French Indian Ocean territory of 300 islands and islets, including Crozet Is., about 4,500 km southeast of South Africa.
Komandorskiye Ostrova: 55°N, 167°E. Russian group at western tip of Aleutians.
Krakatoa: 6°S, 105°E. Volcanic Indonesian island west of Java.
Kuril Is.: 44°-51°N, 146°-155°E. Chain of some 56 islands stretching about 1,200 km between Japan and Russia.

Kyushu: 33°N, 131°E. Southernmost of main Japanese islands.
Lakshadweep/Laccadive Is.: 8°-12°N, 71°-74°E. Indian archipelago of 12 atolls, 250 km west of India.
Leeward Is.: see Antilles.
Line Is.: 6°N-11°S, 162°-152°W. Group of islands straddling the Equator (Line) south of Hawaii and belonging variously to the U.S., Great Britain and Kiribati.
Lofoten Is.: 69°N, 15°E. Northern Norwegian archipelago.
Long Island: 41°N, 73°W. New York island, 190 km long, between Atlantic Ocean and Long Island Sound.
Luzon: see Philippines.
Madagascar: 20°S, 47°E. Indian Ocean island, about 400 km east of Mozambique.
Madeira: 33°N, 17°W. Portuguese Atlantic archipelago of four main islands about 500 km west of Morocco: incl. Madeira, Porto Santo; discovered in 15th century.
Madeleine, Iles de la: 47°N, 61°W. Canadian group in Gulf of St. Lawrence.
Majorca: see Balearic Is.
Maldive Is.: 7°N-1°S, 73°E. Country of 26 archipelagos stretching 823 km north-south about 670 km southwest of Sri Lanka; about 750 km southwest of India.
Malta: 36°N, 14°E. Strategic island nation in central Mediterranean south of Sicily.
Maluku (Moluccas)/Spice Is.: 2°N-8°S, 124°-131°E: Indonesian archipelago; in the 16th century, sole source of cloves, nutmeg and mace, and a major goal of European merchants.
Man, Isle of: 54°N, 4°W. Irish Sea crown dependency of Great Britain.
Manhattan: 41°N, 74°W. New York island at confluence of Hudson River Long Island Sound.
Manitoulin: 46°N, 83°W. Canadian island in Lake Huron.
Mariana Is.: 13°-20°N, 146°E. Micronesian archipelago 2,400 km east of the Philippines comprising Commonwealth of the Northern Mariana Is. (Saipan, 15°N, 146°E), and Guam (13°N, 144°E).
Marquesas Is.: 7°-10°S, 138°-141°W. French Polynesian archipelago of 12 islands about 1,200 km northeast of Tahiti.
Marshall Is.: 5°-15°N, 161°-172°E. Micronesian group of 34 atolls and islands including Ratak and Ralik chains. Bikini was a nuclear test site in the 1940-50's.
Martha's Vineyard: 41°N, 71°W. Massachusetts island south of Cape Cod.
Martinique: 15°N, 61°W. French Caribbean island.
Matsu (26°N, 120°E) and **Quemoy** (24°N, 118°E): Chinese coastal islands about 250 km apart; administered and garrisoned by Taiwan since 1950.
Mauritius: 20°S, 58°E. Indian Ocean island 800 km east of Madagascar. Part of Mascarene Archipelago, with Réunion.
Melanesia: From the Greek meaning "black islands;" Pacific islands south of Micronesia and west of Polynesia—including New Guinea, the Solomons, New Hebrides and Fiji.
Micronesia: From the Greek meaning "small islands;" Pacific islands north of the Equator between Hawaii and the Philippines.
Mindanao: see Philippines.
Nantucket, Massachusetts: 41°N, 70°W. Massachusetts island south of Cape Cod. Major 19th-century whaling port.
Nauru: 1°S, 167°E. Island nation 2,300 km northeast of Sydney, Australia.
New Caledonia: 18°-22°S, 163-168°E. Pacific island that forms, with Loyalty Is., French overseas territory.
New Guinea: 5°S, 140°E. Largest island in Melanesia, shared by Indonesia and Papua New Guinea.
Newfoundland: 48°N, 56°W. Large Canadian Atlantic island south of Labrador.
Novaya Zemlya: 74°N, 57°E. New Land; Russian archipelago comprising two main islands, 960 km long, between Barents and Kara Seas.
Novosibirskiye Ostrova: 75°N, 142°E. New Siberian Is.; Russian group between Laptev and East Siberian Seas.
Okinawa: see Ryukyu Is.
Orkney Is.: 59°N, 3°W. Group of more than 20 islands, 85 km north-south, 10 km north of Scotland.
Outer Banks, North Carolina: 35°N, 76°W. Barrier islands—Roanoke, Pea, Bodie, Hatteras, Ocracoke and Portsmouth—stretching 145 km north-south off North Carolina between the Atlantic Ocean and Albemarle and Pamlico Sounds.
Ouessant, Ile d' (Ushant): 48°N, 5°W. Atlantic island off northwest France at entrance to English Channel.
Paracel Is.: 17°N, 112°E. South China Sea group about 400 km east of Vietnam; also claimed by China and Taiwan.
Philippines: Southeast Asian nation of more than 7,000 islands: Luzon, Samar, Palawan, Mindanao, Sulu Archipelago, Zamboanga.
Pitcairn: 25°S, 130°W. British colony (with Ducie, Henderson and Oeno Is.) halfway between Tahiti and Easter Island. HMS Bounty mutineers arrived in 1790.
Polynesia: From the Greek meaning "many islands;" Pacific islands within a triangle drawn between Hawaii, New Zealand and Easter Island.
Pribilof Is.: 57°N, 170°W. Alaskan Bering Sea group.
Prince Edward: 46°N, 63°W. Canadian island province in Gulf of St. Lawrence and connected to Nova Scotia by bridge.
Puerto Rico: 18°N, 66°W. Easternmost and fourth largest of Greater Antilles.
Qeshm: 26°N, 56°E. Iranian island in Strait of Hormuz at the mouth of the Persian Gulf.
Queen Charlotte Is.: 51°N, 129°W. Canadian group off British Columbia.
Queen Elizabeth Is.: 74°-82°N, 60°-125°W. Northernmost Canadian Arctic archipelago: Ellesmere Is., Parry Group and Sverdrup Group.
Quemoy: see Matsu and Quemoy.
Réunion: 21°S, 56°E. French Indian Ocean island 690 km east of Madagsacar; part of Mascarene Archipelago, with Mauritius.
Ryukyu Is.: 24°-31°N, 123°-131°E. Japanese chain stretching 1,000 km between Taiwan and Kyushu. Okinawa was a major World War II battleground.
Saipan: see Mariana Is.
St. Helena: 15°S, 6°W. British Atlantic island where Napoleon was exiled and died.
St. Lawrence Is.: 64°N, 171°W. Alaskan Bering Sea island south of Bering Strait.
St. Lucia: 14°N, 61°W: Second largest of Windward Is.
St. Pierre & Miquelon: 47°N, 56°W. French Atlantic islands southwest of Newfoundland, Canada.
Sakhalin: 51°N, 143°E. Russian island, 950 km long, between Sea of Japan and Sea of Okhostk.
Samoa Is.: 13°-14°S, 168°-173°W. Pacific group divided between Western Samoa and American Samoa.
Sandwich Islands: Former name of the Hawaiian Islands.
Sardinia: 40°N, 9°E. Italian island in western Mediterranean.
Severnaya Zemlya: 80°N, 98°E. Russian group (four main islands) discovered in 1913, between Kara and Laptev Seas.
Seychelles: 4°-5°S, 56°E. Indian Ocean republic of 115 islands extending 1,200 km northeast-southwest about 1,600 km east of Kenya.
Shetland Is.: 61°N, 1°W. British group of about 100 islands 80 km northeast of the Orkneys.
Shikoku: 33°N, 133°E. Smallest of four main Japanese islands.
Sicily: 37°N, 14°E. Italian island in central Mediterranean.

Singapore: 1°N, 104°E. Island nation off tip of Malay Peninsula at east end of Strait of Malacca.
Skye: see Hebrides/Western Isles
Society Is.: 16°-18°S, 148°-154°W. French Polynesian archipelago, 750-km long, including Tahiti; settled around 500 B.C.
Socotra: 13°N, 54°E. Yemeni Indian Ocean island about 250 km northeast of Somalia.
Solomon Is.: 156°-171°E, 5°-13°S. Melanesian archipelago of about 1,000 islands stretching 1,400 km southeast from New Guinea. Guadalcanal was major World War II battleground.
South Georgia Is.: 54°S, 37°W; and South Sandwich Is.: 56°S, 26°W. British dependent territory 1,500 km east of the Falklands.
South Orkney Is.: 61°S, 44°-46°W. British group about 1,440 km southeast of South America.
South Shetland Is.: 61°-64°S, 54°-63°W. Four-group chain, 540-km long, about 120 km north of the Antarctic Peninsula.
Spitsbergen: 79°N, 20°E: Norwegian Atlantic island; forms, with Bear Island (74°N, 19°E), dependency of Svalbard.
Spratly Is.: 9°N, 112°E. South China Sea archipelago about 500 km southeast of Vietnam; also claimed by China, Taiwan, Malaysia and the Philippines.
Sulawesi (Celebes): 2°S, 121°E. Indonesian island between Borneo and Maluku Is.
Sulu Archipelago: 5°-7°N, 120°-122°E. Philippine archipelago of about 900 islands between Celebes and Sulu Seas.
Sumatra: 0°, 100°E. Largest and westernmost island in Indonesia.
Taiwan: 23°N, 121°E. South China Sea island about 130 km east of mainland China.
Tasmania: 43°S, 17°E. Indian Ocean island 500 km south of southeast Australia; Australian state.
Tierra del Fuego: 54°S, 69°W. Island shared by Chile and Argentina between the Atlantic and Pacific Oceans; separated from South America by Strait of Magellan, and north of Cape Horn (55°59'S, 67°16'W).
Tongan (Friendly) Is.: 15°-23°S, 173°-177°W. Polynesian country of 171 islands (36 inhabited) stretching 1,000 km north-south about 2,000 km northeast of New Zealand.
Trinidad, Isla: 39°S, 62°W. Brazilian island 1,200 east of Brazil.
Trinidad and Tobago: 10°N, 61°W. Caribbean nation group off Venezuela.
Tristan da Cunha: 37°S, 12°W. British Atlantic group about 2,800 km east southeast of South Africa.
Tsushima: 34°N, 129°E. Japanese island in Korean (or Tsushima) Strait.
Tuamotu Archipelago: 14°-23°S, 134°-149°W. French Polynesian chain of 80 islands, 1,700 km long, east of Tahiti.
Vancouver: 50°N, 126°W. Largest island on west coast of Canada; part of British Columbia.
Vanuatu (New Hebrides): 13°-20°S, 166°-170°E. Melanesian island nation, 900 km long.
Victoria: 71°N, 114°W. Canadian Arctic island.
Volcano Is. (Kazan-Retto): 25°N, 141°E. Japanese group of three islands 1,100 km southwest of Tokyo. Iwo Jima was a major World War II battleground.
Wake Is.: 19°N, 177°E. U.S. Pacific atoll, 1,900 km west of Midway: Wilkes, Wake and Peale Islands.
Wight, Isle of: 51°N, 1°W. British English Channel island off Portsmouth and Southampton.
Windward Is.: see Antilles.
Wrangel Island (Ostrov Vrangelia): 71°N, 180°E/W. Russian island in East Siberian Sea.

▶THE POLAR REGIONS

Antarctica

• **GEOGRAPHY** **Location:** continent mostly south of Antarctic Circle at 90°S. **Boundaries:** None. Bordered by South Atlantic, Indian and South Pacific oceans. **Total land area:** about 5,404,000 sq. mi. (14,000,000 sq. km.). **Coastline:** 11,165 mi. (17,968 km). **Comparative area:** twice the size of Australia. **Land use:** 98% continental ice sheet; 2% barren rock. **Natural Resources:** None presently exploited. Iron ore, chromium, copper, gold, nickel, platinum, and other minerals, as well as coal and hydrocarbons have been found in small uncommercial qualities. **Temperature:** Varies with location and altitude. East Antarctica is coldest; Antarctic Peninsula in the west is mildest; mean annual temperature of the interior regions is -57°C (-71°F); mean temperatures at the coastal McMurdo station range from-28°C (-18°F) in August to -3°C (27°F) in January. **Major cities:** none.

• **THE LAND** Some 200 million years ago Antarctica was joined to South America, Africa, India and Australia as one large continent. Geological changes caused the breakup into separate continents. Studies indicate that Antarctica once had a tropical environment, but that its present ice form is at least 20 million years old. Approximately 98 percent of the continent is covered by ice; contains about 90 percent of the world's ice and 70 percent of the fresh water. Elevations average from 6,600 ft. to 13,200 ft. (2,000-4,000 m); mountain ranges up to 16,066 ft. (4,897 m) high. Ice-free coastal areas include parts of southern Victoria Land, Wilkes Land and Ross Island. The Antarctic ice sheet averages 7,090 ft. (2,160 m) in depth and is 15,670 ft. (4,776 m) deep at its thickest point. Altitude at the South Pole is about 9,800 ft. (3,000 m)

• **LAND/SEA LIFE:** Land life includes bacteria, lichens, mosses, two kinds of flowering plants in the ice-free areas, penguins and some flying birds. Sea life includes several types of seals and whales many of which were hunted to near extinction but are now protected by international conventions.

• **EXPLORATION:** British Captain James Cook circumnavigated the continent without sighting land in 1772–75. U.S. Capt. John Davis made the first known landing on the continent on Feb. 7, 1821. In 1908 the U.K. became the first nation to claim a "slice" of the continent, subsequently followed by claims from New Zealand (1923), France (1924), Australia (1933), Norway (1939), Chile (1940) and Argentina (1943). The U.S. and Russia have never claimed any Antarctica territory. Claims made by other nations are not recognized by other countries nor by the U.N.

In 1911 Capt. Robert F. Scott and Roald Amundsen of Norway began a "race to the pole." Amundsen's party arrived at the South Pole on 14 December 1911 while Scott located the pole on 18 January 1912.

• **SCIENTIFIC RESEARCH:** The greatest scientific study ever conducted in Antarctica occurred in 1957–58 when 67 nations participated in the International Geophysical Year (IGY). Twelve countries established more than 50 stations to study the effects of the continent's huge ice mass on global weather, the oceans, the aurora australis and the ionosphere. During the late 1980s research was focused on the study of the ozone depletion in the stratosphere—called the "ozone hole"—which allows high levels of potentially harmful ultraviolet radiation to reach the earth's surface.

In 1998, 18 different countries maintained 42 research stations year-round. Argentina and the former Soviet Union each had six, the U.K. maintained five, Australia, Chile, South Africa and the U.S. kept three, China and Japan each had two, and Brazil, Finland, France, Germany, India, South Korea, New Zealand, Poland, and Uruguay each had one.

• **PEOPLE** **Population:** No indigenous inhabitants. Staffing of research stations varies seasonally; Summer (January) popuation: approximately 4,415; Winter (July) population: approximately 1,046

• **GOVERNMENT** **Antarctica Treaty:** Signed in 1959 by the 12 IGY nations (in force as of June 23, 1961), it establishes a legal framework for the management of Antarctica. The treaty was renewed in 1991 in Madrid, where 24 countries, including the United States, signed a protocol to ban mineral and oil exploration for 50 years and to provide wildlife protection. The treaty states that the area is to be used for peaceful purposes only and military activity such as weapons testing

The 50 Tallest Buildings in the World

The two towers of New York City's World Trade Center were, until their destruction by a terrorist plane attack on Sept. 11, 2001, the fifth- and sixth-tallest buildings in the world, at 1,368 and 1,362 feet.

Rank/Building	City, Country	Year	Stories	Height Meters	Height Feet
1. Petronas Tower 1	Kuala Lumpur, Malaysia	1998	88	452	1,483
2. Petronas Tower 2	Kuala Lumpur, Malaysia	1998	88	452	1,483
3. Sears Tower	Chicago	1974	110	442	1,450
4. Jin Mao Building	Shanghai, China	1999	88	421	1,380
5. Citic Plaza	Guangzhou, China	1996	80	391	1,283
6. Shun Hing Square	Shenzhen, China	1996	69	384	1,260
7. Empire State Building	New York	1931	102	381	1,250
8. Central Plaza	Hong Kong	1992	78	374	1,227
9. Bank of China Tower	Hong Kong	1989	70	369	1,209
10. Emirates Tower One	Dubai, U.A.E.	2000	55	355	1,165
11. The Center	Hong Kong	1998	79	350	1,148
12. T&C Tower	Kaoshiung, Taiwan	1997	85	348	1,140
13. Aon Centre	Chicago	1973	80	346	1,136
14. John Hancock Center	Chicago	1969	100	344	1,127
15. Burj al Arab Hotel	Dubai, U.A.E.	2000	60	321	1,053
16. Baiyoke Tower II	Bangkok, Thailand	1997	90	320	1,050
17. Chrysler Building	New York	1930	77	319	1,046
18. Bank of America Plaza	Atlanta	1993	55	312	1,023
19. Library Tower	Los Angeles	1990	75	310	1,018
20. Telekom Malaysia Headquarters	Kuala Lumpur, Malaysia	1999	55	310	1,017
21. Emirates Tower Two	Dubai, U.A.E.	2000	54	309	1,014
22. AT&T Corporate Center	Chicago	1989	60	307	1,007
23. Chase Tower	Houston	1982	75	305	1,000
24. Two Prudential Plaza	Chicago	1990	64	303	995
25. Pyongyang Hotel	Pyongyang, North Korea	1995	105	300	984
26. Commerzbank Tower	Frankfurt, Germany	1997	56	299	981
27. Wells Fargo Plaza	Houston	1983	71	296	972
28. Landmark Tower	Yokohama, Japan	1993	70	296	971
29. 311 South Wacker Drive	Chicago	1990	65	293	961
30. Kingdom Centre	Riyadh, Saudi Arabia	2001	72	292	958
31. SEG Plaza	Shenzen	2000	72	292	957
32. Bank of America Center	Seattle	1984	76	291	954
33. American International Building	New York	1932	67	290	952
34. Cheung Kong Center	Hong Kong	1999	70	290	951
35. First Canadian Place	Toronto, Canada	1975	72	290	951
36. Key Tower	Cleveland	1991	57	290	950
37. One Liberty Place	Philadelphia	1987	61	288	945
38. Plaza 66	Shanghai, China	2001	66	288	945
39. Sunjoy Tomorrow Square	Shanghai, China	1999	59	285	934
40. The Trump Building	New York	1930	72	283	927
41. Bank of America Plaza	Dallas	1985	72	281	921
42. Overseas Union Bank Plaza	Singapore	1986	66	280	919
43. United Overseas Bank Plaza	Singapore	1992	66	280	919
44. Republic Plaza	Singapore	1995	66	280	919
45. Citicorp Center	New York	1977	59	279	915
46. Scotia Plaza	Toronto	1989	68	275	902
47. Williams Tower	Houston	1983	64	275	901
48. Al Faisaliah Complex	Riyadh, Saudi Arabia	2000	30	274	899
49. Renaissance Tower	Dallas	1975	56	270	886
50. Trump World Tower	Atlanta	2001	72	269	881

Note: Height is measured from sidewalk level of main entrance to structural top of building. Television and radio antennas and flag poles are not included. **Source:** Council on Tall Buildings and Urban Habitat, Lehigh University (2002).

is prohibited; calls for freedom of scientific investigation and cooperation and a free exchange of information and personnel; nuclear explosions or disposal of radioactive wastes is forbidden; and, treaty-state observers have free access, including aerial observation, to any area and may inspect all stations, installations and equipment.

At the Treaty's 17th meeting in November, 1992, there were 26 consultative (voting) members and 15 acceding (non-voting) members. The 26 consultative members include the seven countries that claim part of Antarctica as national territory (Argentina, Australia, Chile, France, New Zealand, Norway, and the U.K.) as well as 15 nonclaimant nations. The claimant nations all signed the Antarctica Treaty in 1959; the 15 non-claimant nations (followed by the year they signed the treaty) are Belgium (1959), Brazil (1983), China (1985), Ecuador (1990), Finland (1989), Germany (1981), India (1983), Italy (1987), Japan (1959), South Korea (1989), Netherlands (1990), Peru (1989), Poland (1977), South Africa (1959), Spain (1988), Sweden (1988), Uruguay (1985), the U.S. (1959), and Russia (1959). The nonvoting members (and their year of accession) are Austria (1987), Bulgaria (1978), Canada (1988), Colombia (1988), Cuba (1984), Czechoslovakia (1962), Denmark (1965), Greece (1987), Guatemala (1991), Hungary (1984), North Korea (1987), Papua New Guinea (1981), Romania (1971), Slovakia (1993), Switzerland (1990), and Ukraine (1992).

The Arctic

• **GEOGRAPHY** **Location:** The Arctic Regions comprise all the lands north of the Arctic Circle—66°30'N—including the northern reaches of Asia, Europe, and North America, the Arctic Ocean, and its islands. In terms of climate, geography, and culture this demarcation is relatively insignificant, but within the Arctic Circle there is at least one 24-hour period during which the sun never sets (summer solstice), and one in which it never rises (winter solstice). The Arctic Ocean is the fourth largest after the Pacific, Atlantic and Indian; its primary marginal seas are Baffin Bay, the Barents Sea, the Beaufort Sea, the Chukchi Sea, the East Siberian Sea, the Greenland Sea, Hudson Bay, Hudson Strait, the Kara Sea, and the Laptev Sea. Some oceanographers consider the Arctic Ocean to be a marginal sea of the Atlantic Ocean. **Boundaries:** None. **Total area:** The Arctic Ocean is 5,440,000 sq. mi. (14,090,000 sq km). The main island groups are the Canadian Arctic Archipelago (550,000 sq. mi.; 1,424,483 sq km), Greenland (840,000 sq. mi.; 2,175,590 sq km), Novaya Zemlya (31,000 sq. mi.; 80,290 sq km), and Svalbard (24,000 sq. mi.; 62,160 sq km). **Coastline:** 17,525 sq. mi. (45,389 km). **Comparative area:** The Arctic Ocean is about 1.5 times the size of the United States. **Land use:** The central surface is covered by a perennial drifting polar ice cap which averages about 3 meters thick, although pressure ridges may be three times that size. It drifts in a clockwise pattern in the Beaufort Gyral Stream, but exhibits nearly straight-line movement from the New Siberian Islands (Russia) to the Denmark Strait (between Greenland and Iceland). The ice pack is surrounded by open seas during the summer, but more than doubles in size during the winter and extends to the encircling land masses; the ocean floor is about 50 percent continental shelf (the highest percentage of any ocean) with the remainder a central basin interrupted by three submarine ridges (the Alpha Cordillera, Nansen Cordillera, and Lomonsov Ridge). The maximum depth is 17,881 ft. (5,450 m) in the Fram Basin. **Natural resources:** In the Arctic Ocean there are sand and gravel aggregates, placer deposits, polymetallic nodules, oil and gas fields, fish, and marine mammals (seals and whales). **Climate:** The dominant fact of life is the frigid conditions: persistent cold and relatively modest annual temperature ranges; winters characterized by continuous darkness, cold and stable weather conditions and clear skies; summers characterized by continuous daylight, damp and foggy weather, and weak cyclones with rain or snow. Between 60°N and 75°N there is seasonal freezing, while north of 75°N there is permanent ice. In North America, temperatures during the colder months average -25°F (-31°C), while Siberia is somewhat colder at -35°F (-37°C). **Environment:** Endangered marine species include walruses and whales; ice islands occasionally break away from northern Ellesmere Island; icebergs calved from western Greenland and extreme northeastern Canada; maximum snow cover in March or April is about 20-50 cm over the frozen ocean and lasts about 10 months; permafrost in islands; virtually ice-locked from October to June; fragile ecosystem slow to change and slow to recover from disruptions or damage.

• **PEOPLE** **Population** Ethnologists distinguish three native cultural areas—the Western Arctic, including Eskimo peoples (from the east coast of Greenland to Alaska), and Aleuts; Paleo-Siberian, including the Chukchi and Eskimos of Eastern Asia; and Eurasian Arctic, including some Chukchi, Yakut, Nenets, and Lapps. Today, however, the vast majority of the people living and working within the Arctic Circle are non-native peoples in industry or scientific enterprises.

• **GOVERNMENT** Governments with territory north of the Arctic Circle are Canada, the United States, Russia, Finland, Sweden, Norway, and Denmark (Greenland). Svalbard is the focus of a maritime boundary dispute between Norway and Russia.

• **ECONOMY** While there is a fair amount of economic activity in the continental portions of the Arctic—principally extractive industries in Siberia, northern Canada, and Alaska's North Slope—conditions in the numerous Arctic islands all but prevent significant development there. Norwegian and Russian miners extract about 1 million tons of coal per year from mines on Svalbard, and in Greenland there are large deposits of cryolite, lead, and other minerals, but only lead can be mined economically. Economic activity in the Arctic Ocean is limited to the exploitation of natural resources including crude oil, natural gas, fishing and sealing.

• **COMMUNICATIONS** **Ports:** Churchill (Canada), Murmansk (Russia), Prudhoe Bay (U.S.). **Telecommunications:** No submarine cables. **Transportation:** There is a sparse network of air, ocean, river, and land routes. The Arctic provides the shortest marine link between the extremes of eastern and western Russia. The two major waterways are the Northwest Passage, in North America, and the Northern Sea Route, in Asia, but ships are subject to superstructure icing from October to May. The U.S. and Russia operate floating research stations. Access to the Arctic Ocean from the Pacific Ocean is through the Bering Strait; from the Atlantic, through the Davis Strait (between Canada and Greenland), the Denmark Strait (between Greenland and Iceland), or the Norwegian Sea (between Iceland and Norway).

Time Zones and Area Codes for Selected Nations and Territories

Country	Hours from EST	Country Code	City Codes
Afghanistan	+9.5	93	Not required
Albania	+6	355	Durres 52, Elbassan 545, Tirana 42
Algeria	+6	213	Adrar 7, Ain Defla 3, Bejala 5, Guerrar 9
American Samoa	-6	684	Not required
Andorra	+6	376	Not required
Angola	+6	244	Not required
Argentina	+2	54	Buenos Aires 11, Cordoba 51, Rosario 41, Santa Fe 42
Armenia	+8	374	Not required
Aruba	+1	297	All points 8
Ascension Island	+5	247	Not required
Australia[1]	+15	61	Brisbane 07, Canberra 02, Melbourne 03, Perth 08, Sydney 2
Austria	+6	43	Graz 316, Innsbruck 5122, Linz 70, Salzburg 662, Vienna 1
Azerbaijan	+8	994	Baku 12, Dashkasan 216, Sumgayit 264
Bahrain	+8	973	Not required
Bangladesh	+11	880	Chittagong 31, Dhaka 2, Khulna 41
Belarus	+8	375	Loev 2347, Minsk 172, Mogilev 22
Belgium	+6	32	Antwerp 3, Brussels 2, Ghent 9, Liege 4
Belize	-1	501	Belize City 2, Belmopan 8, Orange Walk 3
Benin	+6	229	Not required
Bhutan	+10.5	975	Not required
Bolivia	+1	591	Cochabamba 42, La Paz 2, Santa Cruz 33, Sucre 64
Bosnia/ Herzegovina	+6	387	Mostar 88, Sarajevo 71, Zenica 72
Botswana	+7	267	Jwaneng 380, Molepolole 320, Serowe 430
Brazil[2]	+2	55	Belo Horizonte 31, Brasília 61, Porto Alegre 512, Recife 81, Rio de Janeiro 21, Salvador 71, São Paulo 11
Brunei	+13	673	Bandar Seri Begawan 2, Kuala Belait 3, Tutong 4
Bulgaria	+7	359	Plovdiv 32, Sofia 2, Varna 52
Burkina Faso	+5	226	Not required
Burundi	+7	257	Bujumbura 2, Gitega 40, Muyinga 30
Cambodia	+12	855	Not required
Cameroon	+6	237	Not required
Canada	Similar to U.S. (See "Area Codes of the U.S., Canada, and the Caribbean")		
Cape Verde Islands	+4	238	Not required
Central African Rep.	+6	236	Not required
Chad	+6	235	Not required
Chile	+1	56	Concepcion 41, La Serena 51, Santiago 2, Valparaíso 32
China	+12	86	Beijing 10, Fuzhou 591, Ghuangzhou (Canton) 20, Shanghai 21
Colombia	0	57	Barranquilla 5, Bogotá 1, Cali 2, Cartagena 5, Medellín 4
Comoros	+9	269	Not required
Congo, Dem. Rep.[3]	+6	243	Kinshasa 12, Lubumbashi 2
Congo Republic	+6	242	Not required
Cook Islands	-5	682	Not required
Costa Rica	-1	506	Not required
Croatia	+6	385	Dubrovnik 20, Rijeka 51, Split 2, Zagreb 1
Cuba	0	53	Havana 78, Nuevitas 32
Cyprus	+7	357	Kyrenia 357, Larnaca 4, Limassol 5, Nicosia 2
Czech Republic	+6	420	Brno 5, Ostrava 69, Prague 2
Denmark	+6	45	Not required
Djibouti	+8	253	Not required
East Timor	+14	670	Not required
Ecuador	0	593	Cuenca 7, Guayaquil 4, Machala 7, Quito 2
Egypt	+7	20	Alexandria 3, Aswan 97, Cairo 2, Port Said 66
El Salvador	-1	503	Not required
Equatorial Guinea	+6	240	Bata 8, Malabo 9
Eritrea	+8	291	All locations 1
Estonia	+7	372	Rakvere 32, Tallinn 2, Tartu 7
Ethiopia	+8	251	Addis Ababa 1, Dire Dawa 5, Nazareth 2
Faeroe Islands	+5	298	Not required
Fiji	+17	679	Not required
Finland	+7	358	Espoo 9, Helsinki 9, Tampere 3, Turku 2
France[4]	+6	33	Bordeaux 56, Marseille 91, Nice 93, Paris 1, Toulouse 5
French Antilles	+1	596	Not required
French Guiana	+2	594	Not required
French Polynesia[5]	-5	689	Not required
Gabon	+6	241	Not required
Gambia	+5	220	Not required
Georgia	+8	995	Sukhumi 881, Tblisi 32
Germany	+6	49	Berlin 30, Cologne 221, Frankfurt (west) 69, Frankfurt (east) 335, Hamburg 40, Leipzig 341, Munich 89

Country	Hours from EST	Country Code	City Codes
Ghana	+5	233	Accra 21, Koforidua 81, Kumasi 51, Takoradi 31
Gibraltar	+6	350	Not required
Greece	+7	30	Athens 01, Patras 061, Thessaloniki 031
Greenland	+2	299	Not required
Guadeloupe	+1	590	Base Terre 81, Jarry 26, Point a Pitre 8 or 9
Guam	+15	671	Not required
Guatemala	-1	502	Guatemala City 2, Quezaltenango 9
Guinea	+5	224	Conakry 4, Faranah 81, Kindia 61, Labe 51, Mamou 68
Guinea-Bissau	+5	245	Not required
Guyana	+2	592	Georgetown 2, New Amsterdam 3
Haiti	0	509	Not required
Honduras	-1	504	Not required
Hong Kong	+13	852	Not required
Hungary	+6	36	Budapest 1, Miskole 46
Iceland	+5	354	Not required
India	+10.5	91	Bombay 22, Calcutta 33, Hyderabad 40, Madras 44, New Delhi 11
Indonesia[6]	+12	62	Bandung 22, Jakarta 21, Medan 61, Surabaya 31
Iran	+8.5	98	Isfahan 31, Mashad 51, Tehran 21
Iraq	+8	964	Baghdad 1, Basra 40, Kirkuk 50, Mosul 60
Ireland	+5	353	Cork 21, Dublin 1, Galway 91, Limerick 61, Waterford 51
Israel	+7	972	Haifa 4, Jerusalem 2, Tel Aviv 3
Italy	+6	39	Florence 055, Milan 02, Naples 081, Rome 06, Venice 041
Ivory Coast	+5	225	Not required
Japan	+14	81	Kyoto 75, Nagoya 52, Osaka 66, Sapporo 11, Tokyo 3, Yokohama 45
Jordan	+7	962	Amman 6, Irbid 2, Zarqa 9
Kazakhstan	+11	7	Chimkent 325, Guryev 312, Petropavlovsk 3152
Kenya	+8	254	Kisumu 35, Mombasa 11, Nairobi 2, Nakuru 37, Thika 151
Kiribati	+17	686	Not required
Korea, North	+14	850	Pyongyang 2
Korea, South	+14	82	Inchon 32, Kwangju 62, Pusan 51, Seoul 2, Taegu 53
Kuwait	+8	965	Not required
Kyrgyzstan	+11	7	Osh 332
Laos	+12	856	Not required
Latvia	+7	371	Daugav'pils 54, Jelgava 30, Liepaja 34, Riga 2
Lebanon	+7	961	Beirut 1, Tripoli 6, Zahleh 8
Lesotho	+7	266	Not required
Liberia	+5	231	Not required
Libya	+6	218	Benghazi 61, Misurata 51, Tripoli 21
Liechtenstein	+6	423	Not required
Lithuania	+7	370	Kaunas 7, Klaipeda 6, Panavezys 54, Siauliai 1, Vilnius 2
Luxembourg	+6	352	Not required
Macau	+13	853	Not required
Macedonia	+6	389	Bitola 97, Skopje 91
Madagascar	+8	261	Antananarivo 2, Finanrantsoa 7, Moramanga 4
Malawi	+7	265	Domasi 531, Likuni 766, Thornwood 486
Malaysia[7]	+13	60	Ipoh 5, Johor Bahru 7, Kuala Lumpur 3
Maldives	+10	90	Not required
Mali Republic	+5	223	Not required
Malta	+6	356	Not required
Marshall Islands	+17	692	Ebeye 329, Majuro 625
Mauritania	+5	222	Not required
Mauritius	+9	230	Not required
Mayotte Island	+8	269	Not required
Mexico[8]	-1	52	Acapulco 744, Cancun 998, Guadalajara 43, Mexico City 55, Monterrey 81, Puebla 222, Tampico 833, Tijuana 666
Micronesia	+16	691	Kosrae 370, Truk 330, Yap 350
Moldova	+8	373	Benderi 32, Kishinev 2
Monaco	+6	377	Not required
Mongolia	+13	976	Ulan Bator 1
Morocco	+4	212	Casablanca 2, Fes 5, Marrakech 4, Rabat 7, Tangiers 99
Mozambique	+7	258	Maputo 1 Matola 4, Nampula 6
Myanmar	+11.5	95	Bassein 42, Mandalay 2, Yangon (Rangoon) 1
Namibia	+7	264	Swakopmund 64, Windhoek 61
Nauru	+17	674	Not required
Nepal	+10.5	977	Gorkha 64, Kathmandu 1
Netherlands	+6	31	Amsterdam 20, Rotterdam 10, The Hague 70, Utrecht 30
Netherlands Antilles	+1	599	Bonaire 7, Curaçao 9, St. Maarten 5
New Caledonia	+16	687	Not required
New Zealand	+17	64	Auckland 9, Christchurch 3, Hamilton 7, Wellington 4
Nicaragua	-1	505	Granada 552, León 311, Managua 2, Masaya 522
Niger Republic	+6	227	Not required
Nigeria	+6	234	Abuja 9, Kaduna 62, Lagos 1, Port Harcourt 84

Country	Hours from EST	Country Code	City Codes
Niue	-6	683	Not required
Norfolk Island	+16.5	672	Not required
Norway	+6	47	Not required
Oman	+9	968	Not required
Pakistan	+10	92	Faisalabad 41, Islamabad 51, Karachi 21, Lahore 42
Palau	+14	680	Not required
Panama	0	507	Not required
Papua New Guinea	+15	675	Not required
Paraguay	+2	595	Asunción 21, Encarnacion 71, Pedro Juan Caballero 36
Peru	0	51	Arequipa 54, Callao 14, Cuzco 84, Lima 14, Trujillo 44
Philippines	+13	63	Cebu 32, Davao 82, Iloilo 33, Manila 2
Poland	+6	48	Gdansk 58, Krakow 12, Lodz 42, Warsaw 22
Portugal	+5	351	Coimbra 239, Lisbon 21, Porto 22, Setubal 265
Qatar	+8	974	Not required
Reunion Island	+9	262	Not required
Romania	+7	40	Bucharest 1, Constanta 41, Iasi 32, Timisoara 56
Russia[9]	+8	7	Magadan 413, Moscow 095, St. Petersburg 812
Rwanda	+7	250	Not required
St. Helena	+5	290	Not required
St. Pierre/ Miquelon	+2	508	Not required
San Marino	+6	378	All points 549
São Tomé	+5	239	Not required
Saudi Arabia	+8	966	Jeddah 2, Mecca 2, Medina 4, Riyadh 3
Senegal	+5	221	Not required
Seychelles	+9	248	Not required
Sierra Leone	+5	232	Not required
Singapore	+13	65	Not required
Slovakia	+6	421	Bratislava 7, Presov 91
Slovenia	+6	386	Llubljana 61, Maribor 62
Solomon Islands	+16	677	Not required
Somalia	+8	252	Not required
South Africa	+7	27	Cape Town 21, Durban 31, Johannesburg 11, Pretoria 12
Spain	+6	34	Barcelona 93, Bilbao 94, Madrid 91, Seville 95, Valencia 96
Sri Lanka	+10.5	94	Colombo 1, Kandy 8
Sudan	+7	249	Not required
Suriname	+2	597	Not required
Swaziland	+7	268	Not required
Sweden	+6	46	Göteburg 31, Malmö 40, Stockholm 8, Uppsala 18
Switzerland	+6	41	Basel 61, Berne 31, Geneva 22, St. Moritz 82, Zurich 1
Syria	+8	963	Aleppo 21, Damascus 11, Hama 33, Homs 31, Latakia 41
Taiwan	+13	886	Kaohsiung 7, Taichung 2, Tainan 6, Taipei 2
Tajikistan	+11	7	Dushanbe 3772
Tanzania	+8	255	Dar Es Salaam 22, Dodma 61, Mwanza 68, Tanga 53
Thailand	+12	66	Bangkok 2, Chiang Mai 53, Chon Buri 39
Togo	+5	228	Not required
Tonga	+18	676	Not required
Tunisia	+6	216	Bizeria 2, Kef 8, Tunis 1, Sousse 3
Turkey	+7	90	Adana 322, Ankara 312, Istanbul 216 (Asia) or 212 (Europe), Izmir 232
Turkmenistan	+10	993	Chardzou 422
Tuvalu	+17	688	Not required
Uganda	+8	256	Entebbe 42, Jinja 43, Kampala 41
Ukraine	+8	380	Kharkov 57, Kiev 44
UnitedArab Emir.	+9	971	Abu Dhabi 2, Dubai 4, Sharjah 6
United Kingdom	+5	44	Belfast 2890, Birmingham 121, Glasgow 141, Leeds 1532 London: inner 207, outer 208, Manchester 161, Sheffield 114
Uruguay	+2	598	Montevideo 2, Paysandu 722, Punta del Este 42
Uzbekistan	+11	998	Not required
Vanuatu	+16	678	Not required
Vatican City	+6	39	All points 6
Venezuela	+1	58	Caracas 212, Maracaibo 61, Maracay 243, Valencia 241
Vietnam	+12	84	Da Nang 51, Hai Phong 31, Hanoi 4, Ho Chi Minh City 8
Wallis & Futuna Isl.	+17	681	Not required
Western Samoa	-6	685	Not required
Yemen	+8	967	Aden 2, San'a 1, Taiz 4
Yugoslavia	+6	381	Belgrade 11, Novi Sad 21,Titograd 81
Zambia	+7	260	Kitwe 2, Lusaka 1, Ndola 2
Zimbabwe	+7	263	Bulawayo 9, Harare 4, Mutare 20

1. More than one time zone; difference based on Sydney. 2. More than one time zone; difference based on Rio de Janeiro. 3. Formerly known as Zaire. 4. All codes in Paris are 1 + 8 digits beginning with 3, 4, or 6. 5. More than one time zone; difference based on Tahiti. 6. More than one time zone; difference based on Jakarta. 7. More than one time zone; difference based on Kuala Lumpur. 8. More than one time zone; difference based on Mexico City 9. More than one time zone; difference based on Moscow.
Source: *The AT&T Guide to Calling the World* (2002). **www.att.com/traveler/tools/codes.html**

Climate and Weather

▶CLIMATES OF THE WORLD

Knowing the similarities and differences between climates in various parts of the world helps us understand many things about our planet: why people live where they do; how they make their living; the problems and potentials of their land. Climates are very complex, however, and no climatic classification is ideal. The most commonly used classification was developed more than 50 years ago by a German climatologist, Wladimir Koppen. The Koppen system uses temperature and precipitation as the major criteria for grouping climates. Boundaries between climatic zones are determined by the limits of where certain plants grow. The five major climatic zones are known by the capital letters **A**, **B**, **C**, **D**, and **E**; each major zone has subzones. High-altitude areas are sometimes shown with the letter **H** because their climates are so complex that small maps cannot show all the detail.

(Note: In the following chart, **R** stands for the annual rainfall in centimeters; **T** is the average annual temperature in degrees Celsius.)

A Humid tropical climates. The average temperature of every month is 64° F (18° C) or higher. There is no winter.
Af *Rain forest.* The driest month has at least 2.4 inches (6 cm) of rain. The Amazon Basin is an example of an **Af** climate.
Am *Monsoon.* Similar to **Af** but with a short dry season. The amount of rainfall in the driest month is less than 2.4 inches (6 cm) but equal to or greater than 10 - (R/25). The southwestern coast of India is an example of an **Am** climate.
Aw *Savanna.* There is a well-defined dry season in the winter. The amount of rainfall in the driest month is less than 10 - (R/25). The Brazilian Highlands are a large area with an **Aw** climate.
As (Rare) There is a well-defined dry season in the summer.

B Dry climates. Annual rainfall is less than annual potential evaporation. The boundary between dry areas and humid areas is $R < 2T + 28$ when at least 70% of the rainfall occurs in the warmer six months; $R < 2T$ when at least 70 percent of the rainfall occurs in the cooler six months; or $R < 2T + 14$ when neither half of the year receives at least 70 percent of the total annual rainfall.
BS *Steppe.* The boundary between steppe and desert is half of the dry/humid boundary. Steppes border many of the world's large deserts.
BSh *Low-latitude steppe.* The average annual temperature is at least 64° F (18° C).
BSk *Mid-latitude steppe.* The average annual temperature is less than 64° F (18° C).
BW *Desert.* The boundary between desert and steppe is half of the dry/humid boundary. The Sahara Desert is the largest area with a **BW** climate.
BWh *Low-latitude desert.* The average annual temperature is at least 64° F (18° C).
BWk *Mid-latitude desert.* The average annual temperature is less than 64° F (18° C).

C Subtropical climates. The average temperature of the coldest month is between 64° F (18° C) and 27° F (-3° C). These are mainly humid mid-latitude areas with mild winters. The principal natural vegetation is broad-leafed forest.
Cw (Rare) The wettest month occurs in summer and has at least ten times as much rainfall as the driest month in winter. **Cw** zones are mainly areas of evergreen forest in mountainous **Aw** zones.
Cs *Dry summer.* The wettest month occurs in winter and has at least three times as much rainfall as the driest month in summer. Less than 1.5 inches (4 cm) of rain falls during the driest summer month.
Csa *Warm, dry summer.* The average temperature of the warmest month is more than 72° F (22° C), and for at least four months the average temperature is more than 50° F (10° C). Italy and other Mediterranean countries have a **Csa** climate.
Csb *Cool, dry summer.* In no month is the average temperature more than 72° F (22° C), but for at least four months the average temperature is more than 50° F (10° C). **Csb** climates are found near San Francisco, California; on the coast near Santiago, Chile; and in Portugal.
Cf *Humid summer.* Areas that cannot meet the criteria for **Cw** and **Cs**.
Cfa *Humid, warm summer.* The average temperature of the warmest month is more than 72° F (22° C), and for at least four months the average temperature is more than 50° F (10° C). Much of the eastern United States is in a **Cfa** zone.
Cfb *Marine west coast.* In no month is the average temperature more than 72° F (22° C), but for at least four months the average temperature is more than 50° F (10° C). Great Britain, New Zealand, and the west coast of Alaska are all examples of **Cfb** climates.

D Continental climates. The average temperature of the warmest month is more than 50° F (10° C), and the average temperature of the coldest month is 27° F (-3° C) or below. Forests are the principal natural vegetation.
Dfa *Humid, warm summer.* All seasons have some precipitation. The average temperature of the warmest month is more than 72° F (22° C), and for at least four months the average temperature is more than 50° F (10° C). The northern Great Plains of the United States have a **Dfa** climate.
Dwa *Humid, warm summer.* The wettest month occurs in summer and has at least ten times as much rainfall as the driest month in winter. The average temperature of the warmest month is more than 72° F (22° C), and for at least four months the average temperature is more than 50° F (10° C). The land around the northern part of the Yellow Sea has a **Dwa** climate.
Dfb *Humid, cool summer.* All seasons have some precipitation. In no month is the average temperature more than 72° F (22° C), but for at least four months the average temperature is more than 50° F (10° C). A large **Dfb** area stretches from eastern Europe into Asia.
Dwb *Humid, cool summer.* The wettest month occurs in summer and has at least ten times as much rainfall as the driest month in winter. In no month is the average temperature more than 72° F (22° C), but for at least four months the average temperature is more than 50° F (10° C). Much of the area between Manchuria and the Sea of Okhotsk has a **Dwb** climate.
Dfc *Subpolar.* All seasons have some precipitation. For one to three months, the average temperature is 50° (10° C) or more. A huge **Dfc** area is in Siberia and adjacent parts of the Soviet Union.

E Polar climates. The average temperature of the warmest month is less than 50° F (10° C). There is no summer, and no trees grow.

ET *Tundra.* The average temperature of the warmest month is less than 50° F (10° C) but more than 32° F (0° C). Vast areas of northern North America, Europe, and Asia lie in the **ET** climate zone.

EF *Ice cap.* The average temperature of the warmest 8 month is 32° F (0° C) or less. The **EF** climate is found at the North and South Poles and in interior Greenland.

▶WEATHER EXTREMES

Hottest: Dalol Danakil Depression, Ethiopia. Average annual temperature: 35°C/95°F.

Coldest: Plateau Station, Antarctica. Average annual temperature: -56.7°C/-71.7°F.

Wettest: Mawsynram, Assam, India. Average annual rainfall: 11.873 m/38.925 ft.

Driest: Atacama Desert, Chile. Average annual rainfall: too small to measure.

▶EL NIÑO AND LA NIÑA

The two ends of a natural, very complex climatic balancing act, caused by the interaction between the surface layers of the tropical Pacific Ocean and the atmosphere above it, with winds and planetary-scale ocean waves shipping the changing conditions from one side of the ocean to the other.

The sheer size and breadth of the Pacific allow El Niños and La Niñas time to develop and to have widespread effects. During La Niñas, tropical ocean temperatures become colder in the eastern and central Pacific regions and warmer in the west; tradewinds are stronger and normally wet regions become drier. During El Niños the shift is exactly the opposite: weaker tradewinds, colder tropical water in the west and warmer water in the east off the coast of South America, and much more rain in dry areas—and more frequent and more intense hurricanes in the eastern Pacific. These systemic changes also noticeably affect winters in the continental U.S.: La Niñas bring warmer than normal winters to the Southeast and colder than normal to the Northwest, while El Niños generally cause warmer winters in the North Central states and colder winters in the Southeast and Southwest.

Fishermen off the coasts of Peru, Ecuador and Colombia first noticed and named El Niño for the tendency of its very warm waters to arrive around Christmastime. Before the 1982-83 El Niño, scientists had no ability to forecast these massive weather changes, and, despite great advances in the field, still missed the rapid onset, the great magnitude and sudden demise of the 1997-98 El Niño. Yet once forecasters had some of the data, they were able to predict six months in advance the unusual 1997-98 winter in the U.S. season and government, business and individuals were better prepared for disaster. La Niñas often (but not always) occur after El Niños. Typically, La Niñas occur less frequently than El Niños, which occur irregularly every 2-7 years (1976-77, 1982-83, 1986-87, 1991-94, 1997-98) and last 12-18 months. In between these extremes is "normal" weather.

So far, researchers have been unable to link El Niños-La Niñas to sunspots or volcanic eruptions. Scientists are studying the compelling question of whether there is a relationship between El Niños-La Niñas and the greenhouse effect. And there is still considerable disagreement and contending theories about exactly what constitutes these phenomena, what their effects are and what role they play in Earth's complex climate and ecology.

Source: National Oceanic and Atmospheric Administration (2000), **www.noaa.gov**.

Determining the Wind-Chill Factor

Sometimes called a wind-chill index, this is a measure of the cooling power of air movement and low temperature on the human body. Because heat passes directly from a warm body to the cooler air surrounding it—a process known as convection—wind produces a continuing source of cooler air and a chilling effect that is equivalent to a lower temperature. The effect on a warm day is pleasant, but as temperatures approach freezing, wind chill is not only unpleasant, but can be dangerous. As the table below shows, a temperature of 5°F combined with a breeze of 20 mph produces a wind-chill temperature of -15°F—a temperature at which frostbite occurs much sooner than at 5°F. Wind speeds above 45 mph have little additional cooling effect.

				Wind speed					
Actual Temperature	**5 mph**	**10 mph**	**15 mph**	**20 mph**	**25 mph**	**30 mph**	**35 mph**	**40 mph**	**45 mph**
35°F	31°F	27°F	25°F	24°F	23°F	22°F	21°F	20°F	19°F
30°F	25	21	19	17	16	15	14	13	12
25°F	19	15	13	11	9	8	7	6	5
20°F	13	9	6	4	3	1	0	-1	-2
15°F	7	3	0	-2	-4	-5	-7	-8	-9
10°F	1	-4	-7	-9	-11	-12	-14	-15	-16
5°F	-5	-10	-13	-15	-17	-19	-21	-22	-23
0°F	-11	-16	-19	-22	-24	-26	-27	-29	-30
–5°F	-16	-22	-26	-29	-31	-33	-34	-36	-37
–10°F	-22	-28	-32	-35	-37	-39	-41	-43	-44
–15°F	-28	-35	-39	-42	-44	-46	-48	-50	-51
–20°F	-34	-41	-45	-48	-51	-53	-55	-57	-58
–25°F	-40	-47	-51	-55	-58	-60	-62	-64	-65
–30°F	-46	-53	-58	-61	-64	-67	-69	-71	-72
–35°F	-52	-59	-64	-68	-71	-73	-76	-78	-79
–40°F	-57	-66	-71	-74	-78	-80	-82	-84	-86
–45°F	-63	-72	-77	-81	-84	-87	-89	-91	-93

▶GLOSSARY OF WEATHER WORDS

Air mass A large body of air that, at a given elevation, has about the same temperature and humidity throughout.

Barometric pressure The weight of a column of air at a particular place is determined by measuring the height of a column of mercury under a vacuum. The instrument for making such a measurement is called a barometer. At sea level, the standard barometric pressure is 29.92 inches (76 cm). In the International System, air pressure is measured in bars or in kiloPascals. A bar is slightly less than the standard air pressure at sea level, and a kiloPascal is one-hundredth of a bar. At any location, however, barometric pressure is affected by changes in temperature, humidity, or elevation. When the barometric pressure is falling, the air pressure is decreasing, usually a sign of a storm. When the barometer is rising, fairer weather is on its way.

Climate General weather conditions over a long period of time.

Cold front The place where cold air that is advancing meets warm air that is retreating before it. This kind of weather not only lowers temperature as it passes but also causes high winds and may cause thunderstorms.

Cyclone A region of low atmospheric pressure (see "Depression"). Severe cyclones are known as hurricanes, tropical cyclones, and typhoons.

Degree-days A degree-day is one degree of deviation of the daily mean temperature from a given norm, usually 65°F. Cooling degree-days are the number of degrees Fahrenheit by which the mean temperature exceeds 65°F, while heating degree-days are the number of degrees the mean temperature is below 65°F. During a year, keeping track of the total number of degree days for each day is used to keep track of cooling or heating needs. For example, oil companies use heating degree-days

Worst Hurricanes in U.S. History

Measuring the cost of hurricanes is an imperfect science, primarily because of the difficulty in determining whether different kinds of damages are directly attributable to a particular storm. The following table ranks hurricanes by the amount of insured losses they cause (in constant 1996 dollars, to discount the effects of inflation). Insured losses are the amount claimed by property owners against their insurance policies. It is impossible to calculate the costs incurred by those without insurance. Note that even after discounting inflation, most of the costliest hurricanes have come within the past 30 years, as more and more people have built homes closer to shore, and harm's way. Improved meteorology, however, has insured that while the financial cost of hurricanes has increased, the loss of human life has declined. The 25 deadliest hurricanes in U.S. history all occurred before 1975.

The most intense hurricane (as measured by atmospheric pressure) was an unnamed storm that hit the Florida Keys in 1935 with winds greater than 155 mph.

COSTLIEST HURRICANES

Rank, Hurricane (year)	Location of primary damage	Insured losses (billions)[1]	Deaths
1. Andrew (1992)	Florida, Louisiana	$26.5	26
2. Hugo (1989)	South Carolina	7.0	<30
3. Floyd (1999)	Northeat states	4.5	56
4. Fran (1996)	N.C.	3.2	34
5. Opal (1995)	Fla., Ala.	3.0	59
6. Georges (1998)	Fla., Miss., Ala.	2.3	N.A.
6. Frederic (1979)	Ala., Miss.	2.3	31
8. Agnes (1972)	NE states	2.1	122
9. Alicia (1983)	Texas	2.0	<30
10. Bob (1991)	N.C., Northeast states	1.5	600
10. Juan (1985)	La.	1.5	<30

DEADLIEST HURRICANES

Rank, Hurricane (year)	Deaths
1. Galveston, Texas (1900)	8,000[2]
2. Lake Okeechobee, Fla. (1928)	1,836
3. Florida Keys /S. Texas (1919)	600[3]
4. New England (1938)	600
5. Florida Keys (1935)	408
6. Audrey, SW La., N. Texas (1957)	390
7. Northeast states (1944)	390[4]
8. Grand Isle, La. (1909)	350
9. New Orleans, La. (1915)	275
10. Galveston, Texas (1915)	275

1. Estimate. 2. Includes 500 lost at sea. 3. Includes 344 lost at sea.
Source: National Oceanic and Atmospheric Administration, National Hurricane Center. **www.nhc.noaa.gov.**

Worst Tornadoes in U.S. History

COSTLIEST TORNADOES

Rank, Location	Date	Damages (millions)[1]
1. Oklahoma City, Okla.	May 3, 1999	$963
2. Wichita Falls, Texas	April 10, 1979	884
3. Omaha, Neb.	May 6, 1975	745
4. Lubbock, Texas	May 11, 1970	558
5. Topeka, Kansas	June 8, 1966	494
6. Windsor Locks, Conn.	Oct. 3, 1979	442
7. St. Louis, Mo.- East St. Louis, Ill.	May 27, 1896	380
8. Xenia, Ohio	April 3, 1974	325
9. Conyers, Ga	Mar. 31, 1973	321
10. Worcester, Mass.	June 9, 1953	311

DEADLIEST TORNADOES

Rank, Location	Date	Deaths
1. Missouri-Illinois-Indiana	Mar. 18, 1925	695
2. St. Louis, Mo.- E. St. Louis, Ill.	May 27, 1896	255
3. Tupelo, Miss.	April 5, 1936	216
4. Gainesville, Ga.	April 6, 1936	203
5. Woodward, Okla.	April 9, 1947	181
6. Louisiana-Missisippi	April 24, 1908	143
7. New Richmond, Wisc.	June 12, 1899	117
8. Flint, Mich.	June 8, 1953	115
9. Goliad, Texas	May 18, 1902	114
10. Waco, Texas	May 11, 1953	114

1. In constant (1997) dollars. **Source:** NOAA/National Severe Storms Laboratory, *Normalized Damage from Major Tornadoes in the United States: 1890-1999.* www.nssl.noaa.gov/~brooks/damage/tdam1.html

to estimate how much oil their customers have used and when they might need a refill.

Depression Any region of low air pressure. In temperate regions over land, the typical depression is a *low*. The often more powerful depression occurring over tropical waters is called a *tropical depression*. If the air pressure in a tropical depression continues to fall, it becomes a tropical storm, or, lower still, a *hurricane*.

Dew point The temperature at which dew (drops of water) begins to form as air cools. Air can hold only a certain amount of water vapor at a given temperature. When the temperature falls, excess water vapor must turn into a liquid.

El Niño (see above)

Front The boundary between two different air masses.

High An air mass characterized by higher-than-normal air pressure; usually this is a fair-weather system. Some highs are typically found in the same place each year, such as the one that occurs over Bermuda in most summers.

Hurricane A huge tropical rainstorm with winds that swirl rapidly around a calm, dry central "eye." To be classified a hurricane, a tropical storm must have wind speeds of more than 74 mph (119 km/hr). The average hurricane is 375 miles (600 km) in diameter and extends up 40,000 feet (12,000 m) above the surface of the ocean. The eye averages 12.5 miles (20 km) in diameter. When a hurricane hits land, its fierce winds and floods can do great damage. On average five hurricanes each year threaten the eastern and southern United States.

Jet stream A strong river or two of high winds in the upper atmosphere (but below the stratosphere) that travels from west to east at between 75 and 150 mph (120-240 km/hr), most often in the middle latitudes. Discovered by American bomber pilots in World War II, it is now known to have significant effects on weather.

La Niña (see above)

Low An air mass characterized by lower-than-normal air pressure; usually this is the heart of a storm system. Some lows are found in the same region most of the year, such as the low in the Pacific just off the coast of Alaska.

Mean temperature Technically, this should be the average of all temperatures during the day. Sometimes it is the average of 24 temperatures taken once each hour, but most often the mean temperature is simply the average of the high and low for the day.

Monsoon A wind system in which the prevailing direction of the wind reverses itself from season to season. Southeast Asia is the most typical monsoon region. The summer (southwest) monsoon, characterized by hot, moist air and heavy rains lasts from April to September. The winter (northeast) monsoon lasts from October to March and is characterized by cool, dry air.

Occluded front When a cold front overtakes a warm front, the denser cold air flows under the less dense warm air.

Prevailing winds Throughout the world, winds follow regular patterns. In some places winds are so light and infrequent as to scarcely exist, such as in the doldrums along the equator and in the horse latitudes near latitude 30° north and south. In other places the winds tend to come from a particular direction and are called prevailing winds.

Rain shadow An area on the leeward side of a mountain range that receives little rainfall.

Relative humidity The amount of moisture (water vapor) in the air compared with the total amount it can hold expressed as a percent. Warm air can hold more water vapor than cold air, so a relative humidity of 75 percent on a warm summer day is moister than a relative humidity of 75 percent on a cool winter day. However, because evaporation is greater on warm days, the relative humidity is generally higher in summer than in winter.

Secondary cold front A cold front that sometimes forms behind another cold front and that is often even colder than the first front.

Secondary depression A low that forms to the south or east of a low that is a storm center.

Squall line A line of instability that often precedes a cold front, marked by wind gusts and often by heavy rain.

Stationary front A front that stays in the same place.

Storm surge The rise in water levels in the ocean or a large lake that comes from a combination of wind and low pressure during a storm, especially pronounced during a hurricane.

Temperature-humidity index A number derived from a formula relating temperature and humidity to discomfort. When it is 75, many are uncomfortable, while at 80 or above, almost everybody is uncomfortable. Temperatures are less comfortable at high humidities because cooling by sweating is less efficient (see also "The Heat Index," later in this section).

Temperature inversion A layer of warm air on top a layer of cooler surface air. Such layering, usually occurring at night, can prevent air pollutants near the surface from rising into the upper air. A long-lasting inversion, especially in industrial areas, can cause an excessive concentration of pollutants to accumulate in the surrounding air.

Tornado A small and short-lived but very severe windstorm. Tornadoes are whirling columns of air that reach down from a cloud, and they often accompany thunderstorms, rain, and hail. With wind speeds up to 300 mph (480 km/hr), tornadoes can do tremendous damage. The diameter of the average tornado is between 500 and 2,000 feet (150-600 m). The average tornado moves along the ground at 28 mph (45 km/hr) and has a "path" that is 16 miles (26 km) long. In the United States, some 750 tornadoes are reported every year, most frequently between April and June.

Tropical storm A storm that forms over the ocean in the tropics and often moves onto land, where it loses strength. Technically, a storm is designated a tropical storm only when winds are between 39 and 73 miles per hour. If winds become greater, a tropical storm becomes a hurricane.

Trough A low that is long, rather than nearly circular.

Typhoon A hurricane formed in the western Pacific Ocean.

Warm front The boundary of a moving warm air mass.

Weather The condition of the atmosphere—temperature, rain, and wind, for example—in a particular place. A climate is defined by weather conditions over a long period of time.

Wind Any current of air, measured on land in miles per hour, and at sea in knots. The direction of a given wind is determined from the point of the compass from which it blows (e.g., northeast, south). In various regions of the world, names are given to seasonal winds of particular quality. Among these are the *bora*, a cold usually dry north/northeast wind along the eastern Adriatic; *brickfielder*, a hot north wind of southeastern Australia; *buran*, a cold, violent north/northeast wind of Siberia and Central Asia, common in winter; *chinook*, a dry winter or spring wind which blows down the eastern slopes of the Rocky Mountains often warm enough to melt the snow; *harmattan*, a hot, dry north wind in West Africa which cools as it evaporates the moist air of the coast; *mistral*, a cold, strong north/northwest wind of the western Mediterranean with a surface strength of 60 km/hour, frequent in winter; *pampero*, a sudden, cold south or west wind in Argentina and Uruguay frequent in summer; *Santa Ana* a hot, dry wind that blows from the north or east in Southern California; *sirocco*, a hot south wind of North Africa and southern Italy; *southerly burster*, a cold, violent south wind of southeastern Australia; *williwaw*, a violent squall that blows in the Strait of Magellan (South America); and *zonda*, a hot, dry north wind of Argentina and Uruguay.

Beaufort Wind Scale

In 1806 Adm. Francis Beaufort devised a scale for recording wind force at sea based on the effect of the wind on a full-rigged ship. In 1838, this scale was adopted by the British Admiralty, and in 1874 it was adopted for international use. It is now the chief scale for specifying the force of the wind and is used in all parts of the world, both on land and at sea. Originally, there were no specific wind speeds corresponding to various force numbers on the Beaufort Wind Scale. Since 1946, wind speed has been determined according to measurements made by an anemometer (a device for measuring wind) at 10m (30 ft) above the ground.

Force	Description of wind	Mean wind speed in knots[1]	Specification for use on land and at sea
Force 0	Calm	Less than 1	Calm, smoke rises vertically. Sea like a mirror.
Force 1	Light air	1-3	Direction of wind shown by smoke drift, but not by wind vanes. Ripples with appearance of scales are formed, but without foam crests.
Force 2	Light breeze	4-6	Wind felt on face; leaves rustle; ordinary vane moved by wind. Small wavelets, still short but more pronounced; crests have a glassy appearance and do not break.
Force 3	Gentle breeze	7-10	Leaves and small twigs in constant motion; wind extends light flag. Large wavelets; crests begin to break; foam of glassy appearance; perhaps scattered white horses.
Force 4	Moderate breeze	11-16	Raises dust and loose paper; small branches are moved. Small waves becoming longer; fairly frequent white horses.
Force 5	Fresh breeze	17-21	Small trees in leaf begin to sway; crested wavelets form on inland waters. Moderate waves, taking a more pronounced long form; many white horses are formed (chance of some spray).
Force 6	Strong breeze	22-27	Large branches in motion; whistling heard in telegraph wires; umbrellas used with difficulty. Large waves begin to form; the white foam crests are more extensive everywhere (probably some spray).
Force 7	Moderate gale, near gale	28-33	Whole trees in motion; inconvenience felt when walking against wind. Sea heaps up and white foam from breaking waves begins to be blown in streaks along the direction of the wind.
Force 8	Fresh gale, gale	34-40	Breaks twigs off trees; generally impedes progress. Moderately high waves of greater length; edges of crests begin to break into spindrift; foam is blown in well-marked streaks.
Force 9	Strong gale	41-47	Slight structural damage occurs (chimney pots and slate removed). High waves; dense streaks of foam; crests of waves begin to topple, tumble and roll over.
Force 10	Whole gale, storm	48-55	Seldom experienced inland; trees uprooted; considerable structural damage occurs. Very high waves with long overhanging crests; the resulting foam, in great patches, is blown in dense white streaks; the sea takes a white appearance; the tumbling of the sea becomes heavy and shock like; visibility affected.
Force 11	Storm, violent storm	56-63	Very rarely experienced; accompanied by widespread damage. Exceptionally high waves at sea (medium-sized ships might be lost to view behind the waves); the sea is completely covered with white patches of foam; visibility affected.
Force 12+	Hurricane[2]	64 and above	The air is filled with foam and spray; sea completely white with driving spray; visibility very seriously affected.

1. Nautical miles-per-hour; 1 nautical mile = 1.151 statute miles. 2. Force 13: 72-80 knots; force 14: 81-89; force 15: 90-99; force 16: 100-108; force 17: 109-118. **Source**: Smithsonian Institution, *Smithsonian Meteorological Tables* (1966); Hydrographer of the Navy (U.K.), *Ocean Passages for the World* (1977).

Climate of Selected U.S. Cities

The first line following each city lists the normal daily high temperatures for each month (in degrees Fahrenheit); the second line lists the normal monthly precipitation (rain, snow, and melted ice).

	Jan.	Feb.	Mar.	Apr.	May	June	July	Aug.	Sept.	Oct.	Nov.	Dec.
Atlanta,	51.9°	56.8°	65.0°	72.9°	80.0°	86.5°	89.4°	87.9°	82.3°	72.9°	63.3°	54.6°
Georgia	5.02"	4.68"	5.38"	3.62"	3.95"	3.63"	5.12"	3.67"	4.09"	3.11"	4.10"	3.82"
Baltimore,	41.2°	44.8°	53.9°	64.5°	73.9°	82.7°	87.2°	85.1°	78.2°	67.0°	56.3°	46.0°
Maryland	3.47"	3.02"	3.93"	3.00"	3.89"	3.43"	3.85"	3.74"	3.98"	3.16"	3.12"	3.35"
Boston,	36.5°	38.7°	46.3°	56.1°	66.7°	76.6°	82.2°	80.1°	72.5°	61.8°	51.8°	41.7°
Massachusetts	3.92"	3.30"	3.85"	3.60"	3.24"	3.22"	3.06"	3.37"	3.47"	3.79"	3.98"	3.73"
Charlotte,	51.3°	55.9°	64.1°	72.8°	79.7°	86.6°	90.1°	88.4°	82.3°	72.6°	62.8°	54.0°
North Carolina	4.00"	3.55"	4.39"	2.95"	3.66"	3.42"	3.79"	3.72"	3.83"	3.66"	3.36"	3.18"
Chicago,	29.6°	34.7°	46.1°	58.0°	69.9°	79.2°	83.5°	81.2°	73.9°	62.1°	47.1°	34.4°
Illinois	1.75"	1.63"	2.65"	3.68"	3.38"	3.63"	3.51"	4.62"	3.27"	2.71"	3.01"	2.43"
Cleveland,	32.6°	35.8°	46.1°	57.3°	68.6°	77.4°	81.4°	79.2°	72.3°	60.8°	48.7°	37.4°
Ohio	2.48"	2.29"	2.94"	3.37"	3.50"	3.89"	3.52"	3.69"	3.77"	2.73"	3.38"	3.14"
Columbus,	36.2°	40.5°	51.7°	62.9°	73.3°	81.6°	85.3°	83.8°	77.1°	65.4°	52.4°	41.0°
Ohio	2.53"	2.20"	2.89"	3.25"	3.88"	4.07"	4.61"	3.72"	2.92"	2.31"	3.19"	2.93"
Dallas-Fort Worth,	54.1°	60.1°	68.3°	75.9°	83.2°	91.1°	95.4°	94.8°	87.7°	77.9°	65.1°	56.5°
Texas	1.90"	2.37"	3.06"	3.20"	5.15"	3.23"	2.12"	2.03"	2.42"	4.11"	2.57"	2.57"
Denver,	43.2°	47.2°	53.7°	60.9°	70.5°	82.1°	88.0°	86.0°	77.4°	66.0°	51.5°	44.1°
Colorado	0.51"	0.49"	1.28"	1.93"	2.32"	1.56"	2.16"	1.82"	1.14"	0.99"	0.98"	0.63"
Detroit,	31.1°	34.4°	45.2°	57.8°	70.2°	79.0°	83.4°	81.4°	73.7°	61.2°	47.8°	35.9°
Michigan	1.91"	1.88"	2.52"	3.05"	3.05"	3.55"	3.16"	3.10"	3.27"	2.23"	2.66"	2.51"
El Paso,	57.2°	63.4°	70.2°	78.1°	86.7°	95.3°	94.5°	92.0°	87.1°	77.9°	65.5°	57.4°
Texas	0.45"	0.39"	0.26"	0.23"	0.38"	0.87"	1.49"	1.75"	1.61"	0.81"	0.42"	0.77"
Gainesville,	66.2°	69.3°	75.1°	80.4°	86.5°	89.9°	90.9°	90.1°	87.4°	81.0°	74.4°	68.1°
Florida	3.51"	3.39"	4.26"	2.86"	3.23"	6.78"	6.10"	6.63"	4.37"	2.50"	2.17"	2.56"
Honolulu,	80.4°	80.7°	81.7°	83.1°	84.9°	86.9°	87.8°	88.9°	88.9°	87.2°	84.3°	81.7°
Hawaii	2.73"	2.35"	1.89"	1.11"	0.78"	0.43"	0.50"	0.46"	0.74"	2.18"	2.26"	2.85"
Houston,	62.3°	66.5°	73.3°	79.1°	85.5°	90.7°	93.6°	93.5°	89.3°	82.0°	72.0°	64.6°
Texas	3.68"	2.98"	3.36"	3.60"	5.15"	5.35"	3.18"	3.83"	4.33"	4.50"	4.19"	3.69"
Indianapolis,	34.5°	39.9°	51.4°	62.9°	73.5°	82.1°	85.6°	83.7°	77.4°	65.6°	51.6°	39.2°
Indiana	2.48"	2.41"	3.44"	3.61"	4.35"	4.13"	4.42"	3.82"	2.88"	2.76"	3.61"	3.03"
Jacksonville,	64.2°	67.3°	73.4°	78.6°	84.3°	88.7°	90.8°	89.4°	86.1°	79.1°	72.5°	65.8°
Florida	3.69"	3.15"	3.93"	3.14"	3.48"	5.37"	5.97"	6.87"	7.90"	3.86"	2.34"	2.64"
Kansas City,	36.0°	42.6°	54.4°	65.2°	74.6°	83.9°	88.8°	87.1°	79.0°	67.6°	52.0°	40.0°
Missouri	1.15"	1.31"	2.44"	3.38"	5.39"	4.44"	4.42"	3.54"	4.64"	3.33"	2.30"	1.64"
Las Vegas,	57.1°	63.0°	69.5°	78.1°	87.8°	98.9°	104.1°	101.8°	93.8°	80.8°	66.0°	57.3°
Nevada	0.59"	0.69"	0.59"	0.15"	0.24"	0.08"	0.44"	0.45"	0.31"	0.24"	0.31"	0.40"
Los Angeles,	68.1°	69.6°	69.8°	73.1°	74.5°	79.5°	83.8°	84.8°	83.3°	79.0°	73.2°	68.7°
California	3.33"	3.68"	3.14"	0.83"	0.31"	0.06"	0.01"	0.13"	0.32"	0.37"	1.05"	1.91"
Memphis,	48.6°	54.4°	63.3°	72.4°	80.4°	88.5°	92.1°	91.2°	85.3°	75.1°	62.1°	52.2°
Tennessee	4.24"	4.31"	5.58"	5.79"	5.15"	4.30"	4.22"	3.00"	3.31"	3.31"	5.76"	5.68"
Miami,	76.5°	77.7°	80.7°	83.8°	87.2°	89.5°	90.9°	90.6°	89.0°	85.4°	81.2°	77.5°
Florida	1.88"	2.07"	2.56"	3.36"	5.52"	8.54"	5.79"	8.63"	8.38"	6.19"	3.43"	2.18"
Milwaukee,	28.0°	32.5°	42.6°	53.9°	66.0°	76.3°	81.1°	79.1°	71.9°	60.2°	45.7°	33.1°
Wisconsin	1.85"	1.65"	2.59"	3.78"	3.06"	3.56"	3.58"	4.03"	3.30"	2.49"	2.70"	2.22"
Minneapolis-St. Paul,	21.9°	28.4°	40.6°	57.0°	70.1°	79.0°	83.3°	80.4°	71.1°	58.4°	40.1°	26.4°
Minnesota	1.04"	0.79"	1.86"	2.31"	3.24"	4.34"	4.04"	4.05"	2.69"	2.11"	1.94"	1.00"
New Orleans,	61.8°	65.3°	72.1°	78.0°	84.8°	89.4°	91.1°	91.0°	87.1°	79.7°	71.0°	64.5°
Louisiana	5.87"	5.47"	5.24"	5.02"	4.62"	6.83"	6.20"	6.15"	5.55"	3.05"	5.09"	5.07"
New York City,	38.0°	41.0°	49.8°	60.7°	70.9°	79.0°	84.2°	82.4°	74.7°	63.5°	53.1°	42.9°
New York	4.13"	3.15"	4.37"	4.28"	4.69"	3.84"	4.62"	4.22"	4.23"	3.85"	4.36"	3.95"
Oklahoma City,	47.1°	53.5°	62.5°	71.2°	78.9°	87.2°	93.1°	92.5°	84.1°	73.4°	59.6°	49.8°
Oklahoma	1.28"	1.56"	2.90"	3.00"	5.44"	4.63"	2.94"	2.48"	3.98"	3.64"	2.11"	1.89"
Philadelphia,	39.0°	42.1°	51.3°	62.0°	72.1°	80.6°	85.5°	84.0°	76.7°	65.7°	54.8°	44.2°
Pennsylvania	3.52"	2.74"	3.81"	3.49"	3.88"	3.29"	4.39"	3.82"	3.88"	2.75"	3.16"	3.31"
Phoenix,	65.0°	69.4°	74.3°	83.0°	91.9°	102.0°	104.2°	102.4°	97.4°	86.4°	73.3°	65.0°
Arizona	0.83"	0.77"	1.07"	0.25"	0.16"	0.09"	0.99"	0.94"	0.75"	0.79"	0.73"	0.92"
Pittsburgh,	35.1°	38.8°	49.5°	60.7°	70.8°	79.1°	82.7°	81.1°	74.2°	62.5°	50.5°	39.8°
Pennsylvania	2.70"	2.37"	3.17"	3.01"	3.80"	4.12"	3.96"	3.38"	3.21"	2.25"	3.02"	2.86"
Portland,	45.6°	50.3°	55.7°	60.5°	66.7°	72.7°	79.3°	79.7°	74.6°	63.3°	51.8°	45.4°
Oregon	5.07"	4.18"	3.71"	2.64"	2.38"	1.59"	0.72"	0.93"	1.65"	2.88"	5.61"	5.71"
Salt Lake City,	37.0°	43.4°	52.8°	60.9°	70.6°	82.2°	90.6°	88.7°	77.6°	64.0°	48.7°	38.0°
Utah	1.37"	1.33"	1.91"	2.02"	2.09"	0.77"	0.72"	0.76"	1.33"	1.57"	1.40"	1.23"
San Antonio,	62.1°	67.1°	74.3°	80.4°	86.0°	91.4°	94.6°	94.7°	90.0°	82.0°	71.4°	64.0°
Texas	1.66"	1.75"	1.89"	2.60"	4.72"	4.30"	2.03"	2.57"	3.00"	3.86"	2.58"	1.96"
San Francisco,	58.1°	61.4°	62.5°	64.5°	65.4°	67.7°	68.2°	69.2°	71.3°	70.4°	64.1°	58.6°
California	4.72"	4.15"	3.40"	1.25"	0.54"	0.13"	0.04"	0.09"	0.28"	1.19"	3.31"	3.18"
Seattle,	46.9°	50.5°	54.5°	59.3°	64.9°	69.5°	74.5°	74.9°	69.9°	60.3°	51.5°	46.5°
Washington	5.24"	4.09"	3.92"	2.75"	2.03"	1.55"	0.93"	1.16"	1.61"	3.24"	5.67"	6.06"
St. Louis,	37.9°	44.3°	55.4°	66.7°	76.5°	85.3°	89.8°	87.9°	80.1°	68.3°	53.8°	42.0°
Missouri	2.14"	2.28"	3.60"	3.69"	4.11"	3.76"	3.90"	2.98"	2.96"	2.76"	3.71"	2.86"
Washington,	41.4°	45.5°	55.0°	65.9°	74.6°	82.8°	87.4°	85.9°	78.9°	67.7°	56.5°	45.9°
D.C.	3.05"	2.77"	3.55"	3.22"	4.22"	4.07"	3.57"	3.78"	3.82"	3.37"	3.31"	3.07"

Source U.S. Department of Commerce, National Oceanic and Atmospheric Administration, *Climatic Averages and Extremes for U.S. Cities* (2003).

Climate of Selected World Cities

Average low and high temperatures for selected months in degrees Fahrenheit. Precipitation is the average monthly amount in inches of rainfall equivalent.

	January			April			July			October		
	Temp.		Avg.	Temp.		Avg.	Temp.		Avg.	Temp.		Avg.
City	Max.	Min.	precip.	Max.	Min.	precip.	Max.	Min.	precip.	Max.	Min.	precip.
Accra, Ghana	87°	73°	0.6″	88°	76°	3.2″	81°	73°	1.8″	85°	74°	2.5″
Amsterdam, Netherlands	40	34	2.0	52	43	4.6	69	59	2.6	56	48	2.8
Athens, Greece	54	42	2.2	67	52	0.8	90	72	0.2	74	60	1.7
Auckland, New Zealand	73	60	3.1	67	56	3.8	56	46	5.7	63	52	4.0
Baghdad, Iraq	60	39	0.9	85	57	0.5	110	76	t	92	61	0.1
Bangkok, Thailand	89	67	0.2	95	78	2.3	90	76	6.9	88	76	9.9
Beirut, Lebanon	62	51	7.5	72	58	2.2	87	73	t	81	69	2.0
Berlin, Germany	35	26	1.9	55	38	1.7	74	55	3.1	55	41	1.7
Bogotá, Colombia	67	48	2.3	67	51	5.8	64	50	2.0	66	50	6.3
Bombay, India	88	62	0.1	93	74	t	88	75	24.3	93	73	2.5
Budapest, Hungary	35	26	1.5	62	44	2.0	82	61	2.0	61	45	2.1
Buenos Aires, Argentina	85	63	3.1	72	53	3.5	57	42	2.2	69	50	3.4
Cairo, Egypt	65	47	0.2	83	57	0.1	96	70	0.0	86	65	t
Calcutta, India	80	55	0.4	97	76	1.7	90	79	12.8	89	74	4.5
Cape Town, South Africa	78	60	0.6	72	53	1.9	63	45	3.5	70	52	1.2
Caracas, Venezuela	75	56	0.9	81	60	1.3	78	61	4.3	79	61	4.3
Casablanca, Morocco	63	45	2.1	69	52	1.4	79	65	0.0	76	58	1.5
Copenhagen, Denmark	36	29	1.6	50	37	1.7	72	55	2.2	53	42	2.1
Dakha, Bangladesh	77	56	0.3	92	74	5.4	89	79	13.0	88	75	5.3
Dakar, Senegal	79	64	t	81	65	t	88	76	3.5	89	76	1.5
Dublin, Ireland	47	35	2.7	54	38	1.9	67	51	2.8	57	43	2.7
Geneva, Switzerland	39	29	1.9	58	41	2.5	77	58	2.9	58	44	3.8
Hanoi, Vietnam	68	58	0.8	80	70	3.6	92	79	11.9	84	72	3.5
Hong Kong	64	56	1.3	75	67	5.4	87	78	15.0	81	73	4.5
Istanbul, Turkey	45	36	3.7	61	45	1.9	81	65	1.7	67	54	3.8
Jakarta, Indonesia	84	74	11.8	87	75	5.8	87	73	2.5	87	74	4.4
Jerusalem, Israel	55	41	5.1	73	50	0.9	87	63	0.0	81	59	0.3
Kabul, Afghanistan	36	18	1.3	66	43	3.3	92	61	0.1	73	42	0.4
Karachi, Pakistan	77	55	0.5	90	73	0.1	91	81	3.2	91	72	0.1
Kinshasa, Congo, Dem. Rep.	87	70	5.3	89	71	7.7	81	64	0.1	88	70	4.7
Lagos, Nigeria	88	74	1.1	89	77	5.9	83	74	11.0	85	74	8.1
Lima, Peru	82	66	0.1	80	63	t	67	57	0.3	71	58	0.1
Lisbon, Portugal	56	46	3.3	64	52	2.4	79	63	0.2	69	57	3.1
London, United Kingdom	44	35	2.0	56	40	1.8	73	55	2.0	58	44	2.3
Madrid, Spain	47	33	1.1	64	44	1.7	87	62	0.4	66	48	1.9
Manila, Philippines	86	69	0.9	93	73	1.3	88	75	17.0	88	74	7.6
Melbourne, Australia	78	57	1.9	68	51	2.3	56	42	1.9	67	48	2.6
Mexico City, Mexico	66	42	0.2	78	52	0.7	74	54	4.5	70	50	1.6
Montreal, Canada	21	6	3.8	50	33	2.6	78	61	3.7	54	40	3.4
Moscow, Russia	21	9	1.5	47	31	1.9	76	55	3.0	46	34	2.7
Nairobi, Kenya	77	54	1.5	75	58	8.3	69	51	0.6	76	55	2.1
New Delhi, India	71	43	0.9	97	68	0.3	95	80	7.1	93	64	0.4
Osaka, Japan	47	32	1.7	65	47	5.2	87	73	5.9	72	55	5.1
Oslo, Norway	30	20	1.7	50	34	1.6	73	56	2.9	49	37	2.9
Paris, France	42	32	1.5	60	41	1.7	76	55	2.1	59	44	2.2
Prague, Czechoslovakia	34	25	0.9	55	40	1.5	74	58	2.6	54	44	1.2
Rio de Janeiro, Brazil	84	73	4.9	80	69	4.2	75	63	1.6	77	66	3.1
Riyadh, Saudi Arabia	70	46	0.1	89	64	0.1	107	78	0.0	94	61	0.0
Rome, Italy	54	39	3.3	68	46	2.0	88	64	0.4	73	53	4.3
Santiago, Chile	85	53	0.1	74	45	0.5	59	37	3.0	72	45	0.6
São Paulo, Brazil	77	63	8.8	73	59	2.2	66	53	1.5	68	57	4.6
Seoul, South Korea	32	15	1.2	62	41	3.0	84	70	14.8	67	45	1.6
Shanghai, China	47	32	1.9	67	49	3.6	91	75	5.8	75	56	2.9
Singapore	86	73	9.9	88	75	7.4	88	75	6.7	87	74	8.2
Stockholm, Sweden	31	23	1.5	45	32	1.5	70	55	2.8	48	39	2.1
St. Petersburg, Russia	23	12	1.0	45	31	1.0	71	57	2.5	45	37	1.8
Sydney, Australia	78	65	3.5	71	58	5.3	60	46	4.6	71	56	2.8
Tahiti, French Polynesia	89	72	13.2	89	72	6.8	86	68	2.6	87	70	3.4
Taipei, Taiwan	66	53	3.8	77	64	5.3	92	76	8.8	80	68	5.5
Tehran, Iran	45	27	1.8	71	49	1.4	99	72	0.1	76	53	0.3
Tokyo, Japan	47	29	1.9	63	46	5.3	83	70	5.6	69	55	8.2
Toronto, Canada	30	16	2.7	50	34	2.5	79	59	3.0	56	40	2.4
Vienna, Austria	34	26	1.5	57	41	2.0	75	59	3.0	55	44	2.0
Warsaw, Poland	30	21	1.2	54	38	1.5	75	56	3.0	54	41	1.7

t= trace. **Source:** U.S. Department of Commerce, National Oceanic and Atmospheric Administration, *Climates of the World (1991).*

World Population

In 2003, world population reached 6.3 billion people. Of those, 1.2 billion were in developed countries and 5.1 billion were in developing regions. The United Nations Population Fund (UNFPA) estimates that world population will reach 8.9 billion by 2050.

World population grew by 77 million people in 2003. That's a growth rate of 1.2 percent, down significantly from the all-time high of around 2 percent. Almost all of the increase in world population (95 percent) came in less developed regions of Africa, Asia and Latin America. Six countries were responsible for half of the increase: India (21 percent), China (12 percent), Pakistan (5 percent), Bangladesh (4 percent), Nigeria (4 percent) and the United States (4 percent).

China and India both have more than a billion people (China has 1,304,196,000 people; India has 1,065,462,000). The United States has the third-largest population with 294,043,000 people, followed by Indonesia with 219,883,000, and Brazil with 178,470,000 people.

By 2016, the U.N. estimates that India will have a population of 1.22 billion, which will be larger than all the more developed countries combined, that is, all the countries of Europe, including Russia, Australia, New Zealand, Japan, Canada and the United States. It is projected that India will have a larger population than China by 2045, with a total of 1.501 billion people (compared to China's 1.496 billion).

▶WORLD POPULATION TRENDS

Four factors are now affecting future world population: birth and death rates, aging of the population, AIDS, and migration. While birth rates continue to decline and couples in developing regions have three children on average, the total population continues to increase, with 77 million persons added in 2003.

Life expectancy now averages 66 years; by 2050 the United Nations Population Division estimates that it will reach 76 years. However, life expectancy varies from an average of 75.9 years in developed nations to 56.8 years in less developed countries. The combination of longer life expectancy and AIDS is having a dramatic impact on median ages and the balance between the old and young worldwide. The median age increased from 23.5 years in 1950 to 26 years in 2002 and is estimated to reach 36 years in 2050. The proportion of youth less than 15 years of age was 34 percent in 1950, 30 percent in 2000, and will reduce to 21 percent in 2050. The proportion of people over the age of 60 was 8 percent in 1950, 10 percent in 1999 and is expected to reach 21 percent in 2050. In numbers, there were 629 million persons over 60 years of age in 2002 and by 2050 this figure is to nearly triple to two billion. Among the oldest old—those over 80 years of age—65 percent are women.

In 2000, Japan had the oldest median age population, 41.3 years, followed by Italy and Switzerland, each with an average age of 40.2. Germany

Distribution of the World's Population, 1950–2050

Area	1950	2000	2050[1]
More developed regions	32.3%	19.7%	12.7%
Less developed regions	67.7	80.3	87.3
Africa	8.8%	13.1%	21.5%
Asia	55.5	60.6	58.2
Latin America and the Caribbean	6.6	8.6	8.6
Europe	21.8	12.0	6.5
Northern America	6.8	5.2	4.7
Oceania	0.5	0.5	0.5
Total world population (millions)	**2,519**	**6,057**	**9,322**

1. Based on the U.N.'s medium population projections.
Source: U. S. Bureau of the Census, *World Population Prospects: The 2000 Revision Highlights* (2001).

Countries with Declining Population Estimates, 2000–25

Country	2000	2025	Decrease
Russia	146,900,000	137,900,000	9,000,000
Italy	57,300,000	51,300,000	6,000,000
Japan	126,700,000	121,200,000	5,500,000
Ukraine	50,500,000	47,700,000	2,800,000
Spain	39,900,000	36,700,000	2,900,000
Romania	22,300,000	19,900,000	2,400,000
Germany	82,200,000	80,200,000	2,000,000
Hungary	10,000,000	8,900,000	1,100,000
Bulgaria	8,200,000	7,000,000	1,200,000
Belarus	10,200,000	9,500,000	700,000
Czech Republic	10,200,000	9,500,000	700,000
Greece	10,600,000	9,900,000	700,000
Portugal	9,900,000	9,300,000	600,000
Estonia	1,600,000	1,100,000	500,000
Latvia	2,400,000	1,900,000	500,000
Croatia	4,500,000	4,200,000	300,000
Lithuania	3,700,000	3,400,000	300,000
Slovenia	2,000,000	1,800,000	200,000
Belgium	10,200,000	9,900,000	100,000
Denmark	5,300,000	5,200,000	100,000

Source: United Nations Population Fund (UNFPA), *The State of World Population 1998* (1998).

World Births, Deaths, and Population Growth, 2003

Characteristic	World	More Developed	Less Developed
Population	6,302,486,693	1,202,572,059	5,099,914,634
Births	131,903,973	13,216,000	119,563,000
Deaths	55,508,568	12,248,000	41,898,000
Natural increase	73,250,395	968,000	77,665,000
Births per 1,000 population	20.4	11	22.6
Deaths per 1,000 population	8.8	10	8.5
Growth rate (percent)	1.2%	0.11%	1.4%

Source: U.S. Bureau of the Census, International Data Base (2003), and *World Population Profile, 1998.*

had an average of 39.9 years, and Sweden had a population average age of 39.6 years. In contrast, Uganda had the youngest median age population, 15.1 years. The average age was 15.1 years in Niger, 15.4 years in Mali and Yemen, and 15..5 years in Burkina Faso.

The United Nations Population Division identified 53 countries as having populations highly affected by HIV/AIDS: 38 in Sub-Saharan Africa, 5 in Asia, 8 in Latin America and the Caribbean, 1 in Europe and 1 in North America. The U.N. estimates that population in these 53 countries in 2050 will be 479 million less than it would have been without AIDS. From 2000-50, some 278 million people will die because of AIDS, and 178 million will not be born because of the early deaths of women. Seven countries that have an HIV prevalence at or above 20 percent—Botswana, Lesotho, Namibia, South Africa, Swaziland, Zambia and Zimbabwe—will have 19 percent less population in 2015 than they would have had without AIDS. Even with population loss due to AIDS, overall population will continue to increase in most of Africa. However, Botswana, Lesotho, South Africa and Swaziland are projected to have fewer people in 2050 than they had in 2000.

Years to Reach Population Milestones

Milestone	Year Reached	Years to Reach	Milestone	Year Reached	Years to Reach
1 billion	1804	N.A.	**6 billion**	1999	12
2 billion	1927	123	**7 billion**	2012	13
3 billion	1960	33	**8 billion**	2026	14
4 billion	1974	14	**9 billion**	2043	17
5 billion	1987	13			

Source: U.S. Census Bureau, *World Population Profile: 1998* (1999).

World Vital Events per Time Unit, 2003

Time unit	Births	Deaths	Natural Increase
Year	128,758,963	55,508,568	73,250,395
Month	10,729,914	4,625,714	6,104,200
Day	352,764	152,078	200,686
Hour	14,699	6,337	8,362
Minute	245	106	139
Second	4.1	1.8	2.3

Source: U.S Bureau of the Census, *International Data Base* (2003).

Countries with Oldest and Youngest Populations, 2000 and 2050

Country	Median age, 2000	Country	Median age, 2050
Oldest Population			
1. Japan	41.3	1. Japan	53.2
2. Italy	40.2	2. Slovenia	53.1
3. Switzerland	40.2	3. Latvia	53.0
4. Germany	39.9	4. Italy	52.4
5. Sweden	39.6	5. Estonia	52.3
6. Finland	39.4	6. Singapore	52.0
7. Bulgaria	39.1	7. Spain	51.9
8. Belgium	39.1	8. Czech Republic	51.7
9. Greece	39.1	9. Armenia	51.5
10. Croatia	38.9	10. Greece	51.3
Youngest Population			
1. Uganda	15.1	1. Niger	20.0
2. Niger	15.1	2. Angola	22.0
3. Mali	15.4	3. Somalia	22.1
4. Yemen	15.4	4. Yemen	22.3
5. Burkina Faso	15.5	5. Uganda	22.5
6. Burundi	15.8	6. Mali	22.6
7. Somalia	16.0	7. Burkina Faso	22.7
8. Angola	16.3	8. Guinea-Bissau	23.1
9. Congo, Dem. Republic of	16.5	9. Liberia	23.3
10. Liberia	16.6	10. Burundi	23.4
World average	**26.4**	**World average**	**36.8**

Source: United Nations Population Division, *World Population Prospects The 2002 Revision: Highlights* (2002).

World's Largest Countries, by Population, 2003-50

2003		2015		2025		2050	
Rank, Country	Population	Rank	Population	Rank	Population	Rank	Population
1. China	1,304,196,000	1	1,402,321,000	1	1,445,100,000	2	1,462,100,000
2. India	1,065,462,000	2	1,246,351,000	2	1,369,284,000	1	1,572,100,000
3. United States	294,043,000	3	329,669,000	3	358,030,000	3	397,100,000
4. Indonesia	219,883,000	4	250,428,000	4	270,113,000	5	311,300,000
5. Brazil	178,470,000	6	201,970,000	6	216,372,000	8	247,200,000
6. Pakistan	153,578,000	5	204,465,000	5	249,766,000	4	344,200,000
7. Bangladesh	146,736,000	7	181,428,000	7	208,268,000	7	265,400,000
8. Russia	143,246,000	9	133,429,000	10	124,428,000	16	104,300,000
9. Japan	127,654,000	10	127,224,000	11	123,444,000	15	109,200,000
10. Nigeria	124,009,000	8	161,726,000	8	192,115,000	6	278,800,000
11. Mexico	103,457,000	11	119,618,000	9	129,866,000	10	146,700,000
12. Germany	82,476,000	16	82,497,000	18	81,959,000	19	70,800,000
13. Vietnam	81,377,000	13	94,742,000	14	104,649,000	12	123,800,000
14. Philippines	79,999,000	12	96,338,000	13	108,589,000	11	128,400,000
15. Egypt	71,031,000	15	89,996,000	15	103,165,000	14	113,800,000
16. Turkey	71,325,000	17	82,150,000	17	88,995,000	17	98,800,000
17. Ethiopia	70,678,000	14	93,845,000	12	116,006,000	9	186,500,000
18. Iran	68,920,000	18	81,422,000	16	90,927,000	13	121,400,000
10. Thailand	62,833,000	19	69,585,000	19	73,869,000	18	82,500,000
20. France	60,144,000	20	62,841,000	20	64,165,000	20	61,800,000

Source: United Nations Dept. of Economic and Social Affairs, Population Division, *World Population Prospects: The 2002 Revision Highlights (2002).*

▶URBANIZATION

According to the United Nations, 47 percent of the world's population resided in urban areas in 2000. Seventy-six percent of the people in developed countries lived in urban areas and 39.9 percent of the people in developing regions lived in cities. Worldwide, 2.9 billion of the world's 6.1 billion people (or 47.5 percent) lived in urban areas. Urbanites are expected to make up half the world's population by 2007, and by 2030, they are expected to increase to about 60 percent (4.9 billion out of a world population of 8.1 billion). Eighty-four percent of people in developed areas will live in urban areas and 56 percent of people in developing countries will be urbanized in 2030. The urban population of developing nations will nearly double by 2030, when developing countries reach a level of urbanization similar to that exhibited by the more developed regions in 1950.

Most of the population increase expected during 2000-2030 will take place in less developed countries where urban population will potentially increase from 1.9 billion in 2000 to 3.9 billion in 2030. The urban population of the more developed regions is expected to increase slowly, from 0.9 billion in 2000 to one billion in 2030.

Latin America and the Caribbean is one of the most highly urbanized developing regions in the world, with 75 percent of the people living in cities in 2000. Asia was 37 percent urbanized and Africa 38 percent in 2000. The UN projects that by 2030, Africa and Asia will be 55 and 53 percent urban respectively; Latin America and the Caribbean will be 83 percent urban.

As the accompanying table demonstrates, the world's largest cities have changed dramatically over the last 50 years. In 1950 New York was the only city with a population over 10 million, and London was the world's second-largest city with 8.7 million people. Eleven of the 15 largest cities were in developed regions. Berlin, the 15th largest city, had a population of 3.3 million.

In 2000, 19 cities had populations over 10 million, and five of them had more than 15 million people. Four cities have surpassed New York in population: Tokyo, Mexico City, Bombay, and São Paulo, each with more than 17 million people.

By 2015, at least five cities will exceed 20 million people and 23 cities will have more than 10 million people. With 26.4 million people, Tokyo will still be the world's largest city, followed by Bombay, Lagos, Dhaka, and São Paulo. New York will fall to eighth, while London, Paris, Moscow, and Chicago will all fall off the list of the top 20 cities.

▶FERTILITY

Across the world, women are having fewer children now than 20 years ago. The United Nations estimates world fertility per woman at 2.8 births from 1995-2000. In developed regions fertility rates dropped from an average of 2.6 per woman in 1970 to 1.59 births in 1995-2000. Births in less developed regions dropped to an average of 2.9 births per woman and to 5.1 in the least developed countries in this same time period.

Replacement level fertility represents the point at which each couple has only the number of births required to replace themselves in the population. The replacement level fertility rate is usually 2.1 births per woman. Most countries in Europe and North America have fertility rates at or below that level. For the period 1995-2000, eight countries will have average fertility levels of 1.2 or fewer children per woman; Hong Kong, with 1.0, has the lowest.

The United Nations reports that fertility rates are declining in sub-Saharan Africa and South-central Asia, where fertility levels have been very

The World's Largest Urban Areas, 1950-2015

	Population (millions)					Rank	
2000 Rank, Urban area	**1950**	**1970**	**1990**	**2000**	**2015[1]**	**1950**	**2015**
1. Tokyo, Japan	6.9	16.5	25.0	26.4	26.4	3	1
2. Mexico City, Mexico	3.1	9.1	15.1	18.1	19.2	13	7
3. Bombay, India	2.9	5.8	12.2	18.1	26.1	15	2
4. São Paulo , Brazil	2.4	8.1	14.8	17.8	20.4	18	5
5. New York, U.S.	12.3	16.2	16.1	16.6	17.4	1	8
6. Lagos, Nigeria	N.A.	N.A.	7.7	13.4	23.2	N.A.	3
7. Los Angeles, U.S.	4.0	8.4	11.5	13.1	14.1	11	14
8. Calcutta, India	4.4	6.9	10.7	12.9	17.3	9	9
9. Shanghai, China	5.3	11.2	13.5	12.9	14.6	6	13
10. Buenos Aires, Argentina	5.0	8.4	10.6	12.6	14.1	7	15
11. Dhaka, Bangladesh	N.A.	N.A.	5.9	12.3	21.1	N.A.	4
12. Karachi, Pakistan	N.A.	N.A.	8.0	11.8	19.2	N.A.	6
13. Delhi, India	N.A.	3.5	8.2	11.7	16.8	N.A.	11
14. Jakarta, Indonesia	N.A.	3.9	9.3	11.0	17.3	N.A.	10
15. Osaka, Japan	4.1	9.4	10.5	11.0	11.0	10	20
16. Metro Manila, Philippines	N.A.	3.5	8.0	10.9	14.8	N.A.	12
17. Beijing, China	3.9	8.1	10.9	10.8	12.3	12	18
18. Rio de Janeiro, Brazil	2.9	7.0	9.5	10.6	11.9	14	19
19. Cairo, Egypt	2.4	5.3	8.6	10.6	13.8	16	16
20. Istanbul, Turkey	N.A.	N.A.	6.5	9.3	12.5	N.A.	17
21. Tianjin, China	2.4	5.2	9.3	N.A.	10.7	17	21
22. Hyderabad, India	N.A.	N.A.	N.A.	N.A.	10.5	N.A.	22
23. Bangkok, Thailand	N.A.	N.A.	5.9	N.A.	10.1	N.A.	23
24. Paris, France	5.4	8.5	9.3	9.6	N.A.	5	N.A.
25. Moscow, Russia	5.4	7.1	9.0	9.3	N.A.	4	N.A.
26. London, U.K.	8.7	8.6	7.3	7.3	N.A.	2	N.A.
27. Chicago, U.S.	4.9	6.7	6.8	7.0	N.A.	8	N.A.

Note: An urban area is a central city or central cities, and the surrounding urbanized areas, also called a metropolitan area. 1. Projected. **Source:** United Nations Population Division, *World Urbanization Prospects: The 1999 Revision* (2000).

high for decades. From 1980-85 to 1995-2000 Tanzania's fertility rate dropped from 6.7 to 5.4 births per woman and Namibia's declined from 5.8 to 4.6. Bangladesh declined from 6.2 births per woman to 3.4, India from 4.5 to 3, and Nepal from 6.3 to 4.26.

China, Thailand and Mexico made the greatest fertility rate reductions from 1970 to 1995-2000. China's fertility rate went from 6.0 to 1.8, Thailand's from 6.1 to 1.9, and Mexico's from 6.7 to 2.5.

These reductions in family size are largely due to contraceptive use. The U.N. estimates that 18 million couples reached their childbearing years each year during the 1990s. Almost all research indicates that couples the world over want fewer children. Thirty years ago, less than 10 percent of couples in the developing world had access to family planning. Today 60 percent of those couples have access, causing family size to drop from an average of six children during the 1960s to less than three today.

Nevertheless, there are still close to 150 million women who want to limit or space their pregnancies, but cannot do so effectively. Some 350 million couples continue to lack information about contraception and access to a range of contraceptive services.

Nations with Highest and Lowest Fertility Rates, 2000-05

HIGHEST RATES Country	Fertility rate per woman	LOWEST RATES Country	Fertility rate per woman
Niger	8.00	Armenia	1.10
Yemen	7.60	Latvia	1.10
Somalia	7.25	Bulgaria	1.10
Angola	7.20	Ukraine	1.10
Uganda	7.10	Spain	1.13
Mali	7.00	Slovenia	1.14
Afghanistan	6.80	Russian Federation	1.14
Burkina Faso	6.80	Czech Republic	1.16
Burundi	6.80	China	1.17
Liberia	6.80	Belarus	1.20
Ethiopia	6.75	Estonia	1.20
Congo, Dem. Republic of	6.70	Hungary	1.20
Chad	6.65	Italy	1.20

Source: United Nations Population Fund (UNFPA), *The State of World Population 2002*. (2002)

Population Indicators by Region and Nation

Region/Country	Population estimate ('000s) 2003	Population estimate ('000s) 2050	Birth rate per 1,000, 2003[1]	Death rate per 1,000, 2003[1]	Life expectancy, 2000	Percent urban, 2001	Fertility rate per woman 2000-05
World Total	**6,301,500**	**8,918,700**	**20**	**9**	**65**	**48%**	**2.7**
More Developed Regions	**1,203,300**	**1,219,700**	**11**	**10**	**76**	**76**	**1.5**
Less Developed Regions	**5,098,200**	**7,699,100**	**23**	**9**	**63**	**41**	**2.9**
Least Developed Countries	**718,100**	**1,674,500**	**40**	**15**	**50**	**26**	**5.1**
Africa	**850,600**	**1,803,300**	**36**	**14**	**49**	**38**	**4.9**
Asia	**3,823,400**	**5,222,100**	**19**	**8**	**67**	**38**	**2.5**
Europe	**726,300**	**631,900**	**10**	**11**	**74**	**74**	**1.4**
Latin America and the Caribbean	**543,200**	**767,700**	**21**	**6**	**71**	**76**	**2.5**
North America	**325,700**	**447,900**	**14**	**8**	**77**	**78**	**2.0**
Oceania	**32,200**	**45,800**	**17**	**7**	**74**	**74**	**2.3**
Afghanistan	23,900	69,500	41	17	43	22	6.8
Albania	3,200	3,700	15	5	74	43	2.3
Algeria	31,800	48,700	22	5	70	58	2.8
Angola	13,600	43,100	46	26	40	35	7.2
Argentina	38,400	52,800	17	8	74	88	2.4
Armenia	3,100	2,300	13	10	74	67	1.2
Australia	19,700	25,600	13	7	79	91	1.7
Austria	8,100	7,400	9	9	79	67	1.3
Azerbaijan	8,400	10,900	19	10	72	52	2.1
Bahrain	663	1,008	19	4	73	93	2.3
Bangladesh	146,700	254,600	30	9	61	26	3.5
Belarus	9,900	7,500	10	14	69	70	1.2
Belgium	10,300	10,200	11	10	79	97	1.7
Belize	236	392	31	6	74	48	2.9
Benin	6,700	15,600	43	14	51	43	5.7
Bhutan	2,300	5,300	35	14	63	7	5.0
Bolivia	8,800	15,700	26	8	64	63	3.8
Bosnia and Herzegovina	4,200	3,600	13	8	74	43	1.3
Botswana	1,800	1,400	26	31	40	49	3.7
Brazil	178,500	233,100	18	6	68	82	2.2
Brunei Darussalam	341	565	20	3	76	73	2.5
Bulgaria	7,900	5,300	10	14	71	70	1.1
Burkina Faso	13,000	42,400	45	19	46	17	6.7
Burundi	6,800	19,200	40	18	41	9	6.8
Cambodia	14,100	29,600	27	9	57	18	4.8
Cameroon	16,000	24,900	35	15	46	50	4.6
Canada	31,500	39,100	11	8	79	79	1.5
Central African Republic	3,900	6,600	36	20	40	42	4.9
Chad	8,600	25,400	47	16	45	24	6.7

Region/Country	Population estimate ('000s) 2003	Population estimate ('000s) 2050	Birth rate per 1,000, 2003[1]	Death rate per 1,000, 2003[1]	Life expec-tancy, 2000	Percent urban, 2001	Fertility rate per woman 2000-05
Chile	15,800	21,800	16	6	76	86%	2.4
China	1,304,200	1,395,200	13	7	71	37	1.8
Colombia	44,200	67,500	22	6	72	76	2.6
Congo, Dem. Rep. of	52,800	151,600	45	15	42	31	6.7
Congo, Republic of	3,700	10,600	29	14	48	66	6.3
Costa Rica	4,200	6,500	19	4	77	60	2.3
Croatia	4,400	3,600	13	11	74	58	1.7
Cuba	11,300	10,100	12	7	76	76	1.6
Czech Republic	10,200	8,600	9	11	75	67	1.2
Denmark	5,400	5,300	12	11	77	85	1.8
Djibouti	652	1,068	41	20	38	84	5.8
Dominican Republic	8,700	11,900	24	7	66	66	2.7
East Timor	—	—	28	6	—	—	—
Ecuador	13,000	18,700	25	5	72	63	2.8
Egypt	71,900	127,400	24	5	69	43	3.3
El Salvador	6,500	9,800	28	6	70	62	2.9
Eritrea	4,100	10,500	39	13	53	19	5.4
Estonia	1,300	700	9	13	72	69	1.2
Ethiopia	70,700	171,000	40	20	45	16	6.0
Fiji	832	916	23	6	70	50	3.0
Finland	5,200	4,900	11	10	78	59	1.7
France	60,100	64,200	13	9	79	76	1.9
Gabon	1,300	2,500	37	11	57	82	4.0
Gambia	1,400	2,900	41	12	54	31	4.7
Georgia	5,100	3,500	12	15	74	57	1.4
Germany	82,500	79,100	9	10	78	88	1.4
Ghana	20,900	39,500	26	11	58	36	4.1
Greece	11,000	9,800	10	10	78	60	1.3
Guatemala	12,300	26,200	35	7	66	40	4.4
Guinea	8,500	19,600	43	16	49	28	5.8
Guinea-Bissau	1,500	4,700	38	17	45	32	7.0
Guyana	765	504	18	9	62	37	2.3
Haiti	8,300	12,400	34	13	53	36	4.0
Honduras	6,900	12,600	32	6	66	54	3.7
Hong Kong	7,000	9,400	11	6	80	100	1.0
Hungary	9,900	7,600	10	13	72	65	1.2
Iceland	283	333	14	7	79	93	1.9
India	1,065,500	1,531,400	23	8	64	28	3.0
Indonesia	219,900	293,800	21	6	67	42	2.4
Iran	68,900	105,500	17	6	70	65	2.3
Iraq	25,200	57,900	34	6	61	67	4.8
Ireland	4,000	5,000	14	8	77	59	2.0
Israel	6,400	10,000	19	6	79	92	2.7
Italy	57,400	44,900	9	10	79	67	1.2
Ivory Coast	16,600	27,600	40	18	41	44	4.7
Jamaica	2,700	3,700	17	5	76	57	2.4
Japan	127,700	109,700	10	9	82	79	1.3
Jordan	5,500	10,200	24	3	71	79	3.6
Kazakhstan	15,400	13,900	18	11	65	56	2.0
Kenya	32,000	44,000	29	16	45	34	4.0
Korea, North	22,700	25,000	18	7	63	61	2.0
Korea, South	47,700	46,400	13	6	76	83	1.4
Kuwait	2,500	4,900	22	2	77	96	2.7
Kyrgyzstan	5,100	7,200	26	9	69	34	2.6
Laos	5,700	11,400	37	12	55	20	4.8
Latvia	2,300	1,300	9	15	71	60	1.1
Lebanon	3,700	4,900	20	6	74	90	2.2
Lesotho	1,800	1,400	27	25	35	29	3.8
Liberia	3,400	9,800	45	18	41	46	6.8
Libya	5,600	9,200	27	3	73	88	3.0
Lithuania	3,400	2,500	10	13	73	69	1.3
Luxembourg	448	715	12	8	78	92	1.8
Macedonia	2,100	2,200	13	8	75	59	1.9
Madagascar	17,400	46,300	42	12	54	30	5.7
Malawi	12,100	25,900	45	23	38	15	6.1
Malaysia	24,400	39,600	24	5	73	58	2.9
Maldives	309	868	37	8	68	28	5.4
Mali	13,000	46,000	48	19	49	31	7.0
Malta	393	400	13	8	78	91	1.8
Mauritania	2,900	7,500	42	13	53	59	5.8

Region/Country	Population estimate ('000s) 2003	2050	Birth rate per 1,000, 2003[1]	Death rate per 1,000, 2003[1]	Life expectancy, 2000	Percent urban, 2001	Fertility rate per woman 2000-05
Mauritius	1,200	1,500	16	7	72	42%	2.0
Melanesia	7,500	14,000	32	9	59	24	3.9
Mexico	103,500	140,200	22	5	73	75	2.5
Moldova	4,300	3,600	14	13	67	41	1.4
Mongolia	2,600	3,800	21	7	64	57	2.4
Morocco	30,600	47,100	23	6	69	56	2.8
Mozambique	18,900	31,300	37	23	38	33	5.6
Myanmar	49,500	64,500	19	12	57	28	2.9
Namibia	2,000	2,700	34	19	44	31	4.6
Nepal	25,200	50,800	32	10	60	12	4.2
Netherlands	16,100	17,000	12	9	78	90	1.7
New Zealand	3,900	4,500	14	8	78	86	2.0
Nicaragua	5,500	10,900	26	5	69	57	3.8
Niger	12,000	53,000	50	22	46	21	8.0
Nigeria	124,000	258,500	39	14	51	45	5.4
Norway	4,500	4,900	12	10	79	75	1.8
Oman	2,900	6,800	38	4	73	77	5.0
Pakistan	153,600	348,700	30	9	61	33	5.1
Panama	3,100	5,100	21	6	74	57	2.7
Papua New Guinea	5,700	11,100	31	8	58	18	4.1
Paraguay	5,900	12,100	30	5	71	57	3.8
Peru	27,200	41,100	23	6	70	73	2.9
Philippines	80,000	127,000	26	6	70	59	3.2
Poland	38,600	33,000	11	10	74	63	1.3
Portugal	10,100	9,000	12	10	76	66	1.5
Puerto Rico	4,000	4,800	14	8	76	76	1.9
Qatar	584	831	16	4	70	93	3.3
Romania	22,300	18,100	11	12	71	55	1.3
Russian Federation	143,200	101,500	10	14	66	73	1.1
Rwanda	8,400	17,000	40	22	39	6	5.7
Saudi Arabia	24,200	54,700	37	6	72	87	4.5
Senegal	10,100	21,600	36	11	53	48	5.0
Sierra Leone	5,000	10,300	44	21	34	37	6.5
Singapore	4,300	4,500	13	4	78	100	1.4
Slovakia	5,400	4,900	10	10	74	58	1.3
Slovenia	2,000	1,600	9	10	76	49	1.1
Somalia	9,900	39,700	46	18	48	28	7.3
South Africa	45,000	40,200	19	18	48	58	2.6
Spain	41,100	37,300	10	9	79	78	1.2
Sri Lanka	19,100	21,200	16	6	73	23	2.0
Sudan	33,600	60,100	36	10	56	37	4.4
Suriname	421	418	19	7	71	75	2.1
Swaziland	1,100	900	29	21	34	27	4.5
Sweden	8,900	8,700	11	10	80	83	1.6
Switzerland	7,200	5,800	10	8	79	68	1.4
Syria	17,800	34,200	30	5	72	52	3.3
Tajikistan	6,200	9,600	33	8	68	28	3.0
Tanzania	37,000	69,100	40	17	43	33	5.0
Thailand	62,800	77,100	16	7	69	20	1.9
Togo	4,900	10,000	35	12	50	34	5.3
Trinidad and Tobago	1,300	1,200	13	9	75	75	1.6
Tunisia	9,800	12,900	17	5	73	66	2.0
Turkey	71,300	97,800	18	6	71	66	2.4
Turkmenistan	4,900	7,500	28	9	67	45	2.7
Uganda	25,800	103,200	47	17	46	15	7.1
Ukraine	48,500	31,700	10	16	68	68	1.2
United Arab Emirates	3,000	4,100	18	4	75	87	2.8
United Kingdom	59,300	66,200	11	10	78	90	1.6
United States	294,000	408,700	14	8	78	77	2.1
Uruguay	3,400	4,100	17	9	75	92	2.3
Uzbekistan	26,100	37,800	26	8	70	37	2.4
Vanuatu	207	462	24	8	69	22	4.3
Venezuela	25,700	41,700	20	5	74	87	2.7
Vietnam	81,400	117,700	20	6	69	25	2.3
Yemen	20,000	84,400	43	9	60	25	7.0
Yugoslavia	10,500	9,000	14	10	73	52	1.6
Zambia	10,800	18,500	40	24	32	40	5.6
Zimbabwe	12,900	12,700	30	22	33	36	3.9

Note: Totals may not add because of independent rounding. 1. Regional data is from 1998. **Source:** United Nations Population Fund (UNFPA), *The State of World Population 2003* (2003); U.S. Bureau of the Census, International Data Base, (2002).

▶GLOSSARY OF DEMOGRAPHIC TERMS

Birth rate The average annual number of births during a year per 1,000 population at midyear; also known as the crude birth rate.

Contraception Deliberate use of methods to prevent conception or pregnancy. Contraception is an important portion of family planning.

Death rate The average annual number of deaths during a year per 1,000 population at midyear; also known as the crude death rate.

Growth rate The average annual percent change in the population, resulting from a surplus (or deficit) of births over deaths and the balance of migrants entering and leaving a country. The rate may be positive or negative; also known as population growth rate or average annual rate of growth.

Infant mortality rate The number of deaths to infants under one year of age in a given year per 1,000 live births occurring in the same year.

Least developed countries Defined by the United Nations as the countries with the poorest living standards. In 2001, the UN counted 49 countries, most of them landlocked, among the least developed.

Less developed countries Defined by the U.N. as countries with poorer people than in a more developed country, with economies based on agricultural production, with low GNPs, and lacking in advanced technologies. Approximately 77 countries, including those in Africa, Latin America, and the Caribbean, Asia (except Japan), and regions of Melanesia, Micronesia, and Polynesia, are considered less developed.

More developed countries The U.N. defines developed countries as industrialized nations with a high gross national product (GNP), high per capita GNP, and advanced science and technology. Approximately 45 countries including those in Europe, North America, Japan, Australia, and New Zealand, are considered developed.

Projections Data on population and vital rates derived for future years based on statistics from population censuses, vital registration system or sample surveys pertaining to the recent past, and on assumptions about future trends.

Vital events Births and deaths.

Vital rates Birth rates and death rates.

World Health

The World Health Organization (WHO), a specialized agency of the United Nations, is the global intergovernmental directing and coordinating authority for international health work. Headquartered in Geneva, Switzerland, WHO gathers health statistics, sets international health standards, provides assistance to individual countries when invited, and issues publications. Most of the information here is from the World Health Organization (WHO). (For information on the United States, see the section "Health and Medicine" in Part II.)

In 2002 the World Health Organization released its assessment of health risks and steps to take to achieve a healthier life style that can extend life expectancy by up to 10 years. WHO reports that 10 risk factors cause the most diseases globally: underweight, unsafe sex, high blood pressure, tobacco consumption, alcohol consumption, unsafe water, sanitation and hygiene, iron deficiency, indoor smoke from solid fuels, high cholesterol, and obesity. These account for more than one-third of all deaths in the world. WHO notes that a relatively small number of risks cause a huge number of premature deaths. For example, less than five of the above named risks cause 30 percent of all diseases in Sub-Saharan Africa and South-East Asia.

The major premature death factors in poor countries include underweight, unsafe water, poor sanitation and hygiene, unsafe sex (especially related to HIV/AIDS), iron deficiency and indoor smoke. Risks associated with wealthy societies include high blood pressure and high blood cholesterol, tobacco and excessive alcohol consumption, obesity and physical inactivity. Of great concern is the discovery that these "western diseases" are now appearing in poor societies where they are adding to the existing problems of infectious diseases.

The world's challenge today is to confront life style diseases and encourage people in poor and rich societies to eat nutritious foods, exercise, reject tobacco, consume small amounts of alcohol, and maintain proper body weight.

▶THE GLOBAL SITUATION

The World Health Organization estimates that of the 56.6 million deaths that occurred in 2001, 29.3 percent, or 16.6 million were due to cardiovascular diseases (heart attacks and strokes), 19.3 percent, or 10.9 million, were due to infectious and parasitic diseases (tuberculosis, sexually transmitted diseases, diarrhoeal diseases, childhood diseases, tropical diseases, and other infectious diseases), 12.6 percent, or 7.1 million, were due to cancers, and 9 percent or 5.1 million, were due to injuries. Worldwide, infectious and parasitic diseases kill nearly 11 million people a year, or 19.3 percent of all deaths. Respiratory infections (including asthma and chronic obstructive pulmonary diseases such as emphysema) accounted for 3.9 million deaths, or 7 percent of the total, while lower respiratory infections caused another 3.9 million deaths. HIV/AIDS caused 2.9 million deaths or 5.1 percent of all deaths.

Communicable diseases, maternal and perinatal conditions, and nutritional deficiencies caused 18.4 million deaths in 2001 or 32.5 percent of total deaths. Noncommunicable conditions caused 33.1 million deaths, or 58.5 percent of the total. WHO estimates that noncommunicable diseases will be responsible for 73 percent of all deaths by the year 2020.

Global Health Risk Factors

Many of the world's health risks today concern consumption—either too little in poor countries, or too much in richer societies. Around the world people are changing their patterns of consumption, particularly of food, alcohol and tobacco. These changes are causing a shift in health risks for billions of people, especially in middle- and low-income countries. In addition, infectious disease control and reduced fertility is creating a shift from young societies to societies with increasing numbers of middle-aged and elderly people which brings larger health burdens.

In poor countries, 170 million children are underweight; over three million of them die each year as a result. In contrast, there are more than one billion overweight adults worldwide, and at least 300 million who are clinically obese. Among these, about 500,000 people in North America and Western Europe die each year from obesity-related diseases. The number of overweight young people in particular is causing growing alarm.

Poverty and lack of nutritious food creates a massive health problem—underweight—that is a major cause of premature death, especially among children. While all ages are at risk, underweight is most prevalent among children under five years of age. WHO estimates that approximately 27 percent of children under five are underweight. This caused an estimated 3.4 million child deaths in 2000, including about 1.8 million in Africa and 1.2 million in Asia. Underweight is a contributing factor in 60 percent of all child deaths in developing countries.

Overweight and obesity, a problem largely in wealthy societies, leads to increases in blood pressure, high cholesterol levels and increased resistance to insulin. They raise the risk of coronary heart disease, stroke, diabetes, and many forms of cancer. Obesity is killing about 220,000 people each year in the United States and Canada, and about 320,000 in 20 countries of Western Europe.

These noncommunicable diseases, which are currently responsible for 60 percent of world deaths, are clearly related to changes in global dietary patterns such as increased consumption of processed fatty, salty and sugary foods, and a large drop in physical activity. Eating fruits and vegetables can help prevent cardiovascular diseases and some cancers; low intake of them is responsible for almost three million deaths a year from those diseases. WHO also found that physical inactivity causes about 15 percent of some cancers, diabetes, and heart disease.

Missing nutrients are causing millions of people to suffer ill health and premature death. Iodine deficiency is the single most common preventable cause of mental retardation and brain damage. Over 2.2 billion people are at risk for iodine deficiency and over one billion people have some degree of goiter.

Iron is needed by all tissues of the body for basic cellular functions and is important in muscle, brain and red blood cells. Iron deficiency is a major cause of anemia and affects two billion people. In total, iron deficiency causes 800,000 deaths (1.5 percent of the total) worldwide.

Vitamin A is needed for proper eye health, vision and immune function. Vitamin A deficiency is the leading cause of acquired blindness in children. Approximately 21 percent of all children under five years of age and women of reproductive age are at highest risk. Just under 800,000 deaths (1.4 percent) worldwide result from vitamin A deficiency.

Zinc deficiency can be indicated by short stature, hyprogonadism, impaired immune function, skin disorders, cognitive dysfunction and anorexia. WHO estimates that about one-third of the world's population is zinc deficient. In total, 800,000 deaths (1.4 percent) worldwide are attributable to zinc deficiency.

Aging Populations Globally

The United Nations estimates that in 2002, there were 629 million people over the age of 60 and that by 2050 that number will increase to two billion. In 2050, for the first time in human history, the world will have more persons over 60 than under 15. The largest number of older persons live in Asia (54 percent); Europe has the next largest share (24 percent). In developed countries, persons over 60 are expected to increase from 20 percent of the population today to 33 percent by 2050. In less developed regions, eight percent of people are were 60 years old or older in 2000; by 2050, that percentage is estimated to increase to 20 percent.

Today the median age for the world is 26 years, a number that is expected to increase to 36 by 2050. Yemen has the youngest population, 15 years on average, and Japan has the oldest, 41 years on average. In 2050, Niger will have the youngest population, 20 years on average, and Spain will have the oldest, at 55 years on average.

Nations with Highest and Lowest Infant Mortality Rates, 2000–05

Country	Highest Infant Mortality Rate[1]	Country	Lowest Infant Mortality Rate[1]
Sierra Leone	177	Iceland	3
Afghanistan	162	Japan	3
Liberia	147	Singapore	3
Angola	140	Sweden	3
Niger	126	Belgium	4
Mozambique	122	Hong Kong	4
Congo, Dem. Rep.	120	Finland	4
Guinea Bissau	120	Australia	5
Mali	119	Austria	5
Somalia	118	Canada	5
Djibouti	117	Czech Republic	5
Chad	115	Denmark	5
Malawi	115	France	5
Rwanda	112	Germany	5
Burundi	107	Italy	5
Zambia	105	Luxembourg	5
Guinea	102	Netherlands	5
Ivory Coast	101	Norway	5
Ethiopia	100	Spain	5
Cent. African Rep.	100	Switzerland	5
Tanzania	100	United Kingdom	5

Note: Estimates. Rate is number of deaths per 1,000 live births. **Source:** United Nations Population Fund (UNFPA), *The State of World Population 2003*.

Infant Mortality Rates by Region, 2000–05

Region	Infant mortality rate (per 1,000 live births)
World	**56**
More developed regions	8
Less developed regions	61
Least developed countries	97
Africa	89
Asia	53
Arab States	44
Europe	9
Latin America and Caribbean	32
Northern America	7
Oceania	26
Former USSR	17

Note: Estimates. **Source:** United Nations Population Fund (UNFPA), *The State of World Population 2003*.

Killer Diseases, 2001

Cause	Estimated deaths	Percent of total
Cardiovascular diseases	16,585,000	29.3%
Ischaemic heart disease	7,181,000	12.7
Cerebrovascular disease	5,454,000	9.6
Cancer	7,115,000	12.6
Trachae/bronchus/lung	1,213,000	2.1
Stomach	850,000	1.5
Liver	616,000	1.1
Colon/rectum	615,000	1.1
Breast	479,000	0.8
Esophagus	438,000	0.8
Mouth/oropharynx	326,000	0.6
Acute lower respiratory infections[1]	3,871,000	6.8
Respiratory infections	3,947,000	7.0
HIV/AIDS	2,866,000	5.1
Diarrhoeal diseases	2,001,000	3.5
Perinatal conditions	2,504,000	4.4
Tuberculosis	1,644,000	2.9
Childhood diseases	1,318,000	2.3
Malaria	1,124,000	2.0

1. Includes chronic obstructive pulmonary disease, asthma, and other respiratory diseases. **Source:** World Health Organization, *The World Health Report 2002.*

Leading Worldwide Causes of Death, 2001

Cause	Estimated deaths (millions)	Percent of total
World total deaths	**56.6**	**100.0%**
Communicable diseases, maternal and perinatal conditions and nutritional deficiencies	18.4	33.5
Infectious and parasitic diseases	11.0	19.3
Respiratory infections	4.0	7.0
Noncommunicable conditions	32.9	59.0
Cardiovascular diseases	16.6	29.3
Cancers	7.1	12.6
Injuries	5.0	9.0
Respiratory diseases	3.6	6.3
Digestive diseases	2.0	3.5

Source: World Health Organization, *The World Health Report 2001.*

▶TOBACCO USE: A GLOBAL HEALTH PROBLEM

The World Health Organization estimated that in 2000 tobacco use—smoking and chewing or snuff—caused 4.9 million deaths worldwide or about 8.8 percent of all deaths. This was a million more deaths than in 1990 and shows the increasing spread of tobacco use, largely in developing countries. Worldwide, tobacco contributed to about 12 percent of vascular disease, 66 percent of trachea bronchus and lung cancers and 38 percent of chronic respiratory disease.

It is difficult to count tobacco use. The current prevalence of smoking cannot accurately indicate the cumulative hazards of smoking, which vary depending on when smoking began, the smoker's age when he or she started, the number of cigarettes smoked per day, the tar and nicotine content, and the type of filter. Smoking has been steadily declining in many industrialized countries but has been increasing in poorer regions, especially among the young.

Smoking increases the risk of death from lung cancer and several other cancers, heart disease, stroke, chronic respiratory disease, and a range of other medical causes. Second-hand smoke contains all the same toxic components as cigarette smoking, but in somewhat different amounts. Second-hand smoke is associated with lower respiratory infections, sudden infant death syndrome, asthma, ischaemic heart disease, lung cancer, and nasal-sinus cancer. Women who smoke during pregnancy have increased risk of a low birth weight baby and sudden infant death syndrome. In industrialized countries where smoking has been common for decades, smoking is estimated to cause over 90 percent of lung cancer in men and about 70 percent in women. Smoking also accounts for 56-80 percent of chronic respiratory disease and 22 percent of cardiovascular disease.

▶CIRCULATORY DISEASES

According to the World Health Organization, diseases of the heart and circulation (cardiovascular and cerebrovascular) such as heart attacks and stroke kill over 16 million people worldwide and account for 29.3 percent of the total number of deaths each year. Additional millions are disabled, frequently in their prime years. Worldwide, heart disease accounts for 6.5 million deaths and strokes kill another 5.1 million; in developing countries, strokes kill twice as many people as heart disease.

Coronary heart disease became an epidemic in North America, Europe and Australasia in the early 1900s, peaked in the 1960s and early 1970s, and has since declined dramatically—by over 50 percent in some countries. The world's highest rates are now in eastern and central Europe.

In developed countries, almost half of all deaths—5 out of 12 million each year—are due to circulatory diseases. As the developing nations adopt Western lifestyles, these diseases are increasing rapidly; they now account for about 25 percent of all deaths.

Decades of research show that lifestyle, beginning in childhood, is the main cause of coronary heart disease. The major risk factors are high blood pressure, cigarette-smoking, poor dietary habits, especially the intake of saturated fat, elevated blood cholesterol, lack of physical activity, obesity and diabetes. Lack of physical activity is the most common risk factor in industrialized countries than can be changed.

▶CANCER

The World Health Organization estimates that in 2002, more than 10 million people developed cancer and another 7.2 million died from it. Eight types of cancer caused 60 percent of all cancer deaths: lung, stomach, breast, colon/rectum, mouth, liver, cervix and esophagus. Several risk factors are linked to cancer: diet, tobacco, infections, alcohol and hormones.

In 1996 there were an estimated 17.9 million people with cancer surviving up to five years after diagnosis. Of these, 10.5 million women, 5.3 million of whom had cancer of the breast, cervix or colon-rectum. Among men, prostate, colorectal and lung cancers were the most prevalent.

Lung cancer is the biggest cancer killer, causing almost one million deaths a year and over 1.3 million new cases. Globally, about 85 percent of lung cancers in men and 46 percent in women are tobacco-related. In developed countries, the ratios are 91 percent for men and 62 percent in women.

Current World Health Indicators, by Nation

Country	Life expectancy at birth (years) 1970	Life expectancy at birth (years) 2000-05	Daily calorie supply, 1997	Infant mortality per 1,000 births[1] 2000-05	Population with access to: Sanitation, 2000	Safe water, 2000	Essential drugs, 1999
Afghanistan	37	43	1,523	162	13%	12%	—
Albania	67	74	2,523	25	—	—	60%
Algeria	53	70	3,020	44	94	73	95
Angola	37	46	1,983	140	38	44	20
Antigua & Barbuda	—	75	2,365	17	—	—	—
Argentina	67	74	3,136	20	79	85	70
Armenia	—	73	2,147	17	67[2]	84[2]	40
Australia	71	79	3,001	6	100	100	100
Austria	70	79	3,343	5	100	100	100
Azerbaijan	—	72	2,139	29	—	—	66
Bahamas	65	69	2,443	18	96	86	80
Bahrain	62	74	—	14	—	—	100
Bangladesh	45	61	2,105	64	97	53	65
Barbados	69	77	3,207	11	100	100[2]	100
Belarus	—	69	3,101	11	100	100	70
Belgium	71	79	3,543	4	—	—	99
Belize	—	74	2,862	31	76	42	80
Benin	44	54	2,415	93	63	23	77
Bhutan	42	63	—	54	62	69	85
Bolivia	46	64	2,170	56	79	66	70
Bosnia & Herzegovina	—	74	—	14	—	—	—
Botswana	50	36	2,272	57	—	—	90
Brazil	59	68	2,938	38	87	77	40
Brunei Darussalam	—	76	2,331	6	—	—	99
Bulgaria	70	71	2,756	15	100	100	88
Burkina Faso	40	48	2,137	93	29	—	60
Burundi	45	42	1,708	107	—	—	20
Cambodia	42	56	1,974	73	30	18	30
Cameroon	49	50	2,175	86	62	92	66
Canada	73	79	3,056	5	100	100	100
Cape Verde	56	71	3,135	30	74	71	80
Central African Republic	42	44	1,938	100	60	31	50
Chad	38	46	1,972	115	27	29	46
Chile	62	76	2,810	12	94	97	88
China	59	71	2,844	37	75	38	85
Colombia	59	80	2,800	26	91	85	88
Comoros	48	61	1,824	67	96	98	90
Congo	51	52	2,107	84	51	—	—
Congo, Democratic Republic	—	52	1,815	120	45	20	—
Costa Rica	67	77	2,822	11	98	96	100
Croatia	—	74	2,458	8	100[2]	95[2]	100
Cuba	70	76	2,357	7	95	95	92
Cyprus	71	78	3,102	8	100	100	100
Czech Republic	69	75	3,177	6	—	—	88
Denmark	73	77	3,808	5	100	—	99
Djibouti	40	41	1,920	102	100	91	80
Dominica	—	74	3,093	17	97	—	—
Dominican Republic	59	67	2,316	36	79	71	66
East Timor	58	71	2,592	41	71	59	40
Ecuador	—	50	—	124	—	—	—
Egypt	51	68	3,289	41	95	94	88
El Salvador	58	70	2,515	26	74	83	80
Equatorial Guinea	40	52	—	101	43	53	44
Eritrea	—	52	1,585	73	46	13	57
Estonia	—	71	3,004	9	—	—	100
Ethiopia	43	43	1,845	100	24	15	66
Fiji	64	70	3,038	18	47	43	100
Finland	70	78	2,916	4	100	100	98
France	72	79	3,551	5	—	—	99
Gabon	44	53	2,517	57	70	21	30
Gambia	36	47	2,332	81	62	37	90
Georgia	—	74	2,184	18	99[2]	76[2]	30
Germany	71	78	3,330	5	—	—	100
Ghana	49	57	2,560	58	64	63	44
Greece	72	79	3,575	6	—	—	100
Guatemala	53	66	2,191	41	92	85	50

Country	Life expectancy at birth (years)		Daily calorie supply, 1997	Infant mortality per 1,000 births[1] 2000-05	Population with access to:		
	1970	2000-05			Sanitation, 2000	Safe water, 2000	Essential drugs, 1999
Guinea	36	49	2,099	102	48%	58%	93%
Guinea-Bissau	36	45	2,381	120	49	47	44
Guyana	65	62	2,392	51	87	94	44
Haiti	48	53	1,855	63	46	28	30
Honduras	53	69	2,368	32	90	77	40
Hong Kong	—	80	3,282	4	—	—	—
Hungary	70	72	3,402	9	99	99	100
Iceland	74	79	3,104	3	—	—	100
India	48	64	2,415	65	88	31	35
Indonesia	47	67	2,930	42	76	66	80
Iran	55	70	2,824	33	95	81	85
Iraq	55	65	2,252	83	85	79	70
Ireland	71	77	3,636	6	—	—	99
Israel	71	79	3,272	6	—	—	99
Italy	72	79	3,504	5	—	—	99
Ivory Coast	—	48	2,421	101	77	—	80
Jamaica	67	76	2,575	20	71	84	95
Japan	72	82	2,905	3	—	—	100
Jordan	55	71	2,681	24	96	99	100
Kazakhstan	—	65	3,007	52	91	99	66
Kenya	50	49	1,971	69	49	86	36
Kiribati	—	56	—	60	47	48	—
Korea, North	—	71	2,834	45	100	99	—
Korea, South	60	75	3,336	5	92	63	99
Kuwait	66	77	3,075	11	—	—	99
Kyrgzstan	—	69	2,489	37	77	100	66
Laos	40	55	2,143	88	90	46	66
Latvia	—	71	2,861	14	—	—	90
Lebanon	—	74	3,279	17	100	99	88
Lesotho	49	40	2,209	92	91	92	80
Liberia	47	56	1,640	147	39[2]	46[2]	30
Libya	52	71	3,132	21	72	97	100
Lithuania	—	73	2,805	9	—	—	88
Luxembourg	70	78	—	5	—	—	99
Macedonia	—	74	2,336	16	93[2]	99[2]	66
Madagascar	45	54	2,001	91	47	42	65
Malawi	40	39	2,097	115	57	77	44
Malaysia	62	73	2,899	10	—	—	70
Maldives	—	68	2,495	38	100	56	50
Mali	40	52	2,027	114	65	69	60
Malta	70	79	3,417	7	100	100	100
Mauritania	39	54	2,653	97	37	33	66
Mauritius	62	72	2,952	16	100	100	100
Mexico	62	73	3,137	28	86	73	92
Micronesia	—	71	—	34	—	—	—
Moldova	—	67	2,562	18	100	—	66
Monaco	—	63	2,985	58	100	100	41
Mongolia	60	64	2,098	58	60	30	60
Morocco	52	69	3,244	42	82	75	66
Mozambique	41	38	1,799	122	60	43	50
Myanmar	51	56	2,752	83	68	46	60
Namibia	48	44	2,168	60	77	41	80
Nepal	42	60	2,339	71	81	27	20
Netherlands	74	78	3,259	5	100	100	100
New Zealand	72	78	3,405	6	—	—	100
Nicaragua	54	69	2,328	36	79	84	46
Niger	38	46	2,116	126	59	20	66
Nigeria	44	52	2,609	79	57	63	10
Norway	74	79	3,350	5	100	—	100
Oman	45	72	—	20	39	92	90
Pakistan	48	61	2,408	87	88	61	65
Panama	66	75	2,556	21	87	99	80
Papua New Guinea	47	58	2,253	62	42	82	90
Paraguay	65	71	2,485	33	79	95	44
Peru	54	70	2,310	37	77	76	60
Philippines	57	70	2,356	29	87	83	66
Poland	70	74	3,344	9	—	—	88
Portugal	—	76	3,658	6	—	—	100

Country	Life expectancy at birth (years) 1970	2000-05	Daily calorie supply, 1997	Infant mortality per 1,000 births[1] 2000-05	Population with access to: Sanitation, 2000	Safe water, 2000	Essential drugs, 1999
Qatar	61	70	—	12	—	—	99%
Romania	69	70	2,943	20	99%	—	85
Russian Federation	—	66	2,704	16	—	99%	66
Rwanda	48	41	2,142	112	41	8	44
Samoa	—	70	—	26	99	99	100
São Tomé & Principe	—	64	2,156	32	—	—	—
Saudi Arabia	52	72	2,735	21	95	100	99
Senegal	43	54	2,394	61	78	70	66
Seychelles	—	71	2,424	14	—	—	—
Sierra Leone	34	41	2,002	177	28	28	44
Singapore	68	78	—	3	100	100	100
Slovakia	—	74	3,030	8	100	100	100
Slovenia	—	76	3,117	6	100	—	100
Solomon Islands	40	69	2,103	21	71	34	—
Somalia	—	49	1,505	118	27[2]	37[2]	18
South Africa	53	47	2,933	48	86	86	80
Spain	72	79	3,295	5	—	—	100
Sri Lanka	64	73	2,240	20	83	83	95
St. Kitts & Nevis	—	70	2,263	30	98	96	—
St. Lucia	62	70	2,822	15	98	—	—
St. Vincent and The Grenadines	63	73	2,434	16	93	96	—
Sudan	—	57	2,391	77	75	62	15
Suriname	64	71	2,578	26	95	83	100
Swaziland	46	38	2,529	78	—	—	100
Sweden	75	80	3,160	3	100	100	99
Switzerland	73	79	3,280	5	100	100	100
Syria	56	72	3,339	22	80	90	80
Tajikistan	—	67	2,129	50	—	—	44
Tanzania	45	51	2,028	100	54	90	66
Thailand	58	71	2,334	20	80	96	95
Togo	45	52	2,155	82	54	34	70
Tonga	—	68	—	34	100	—	—
Trinidad and Tobago	66	75	2,751	14	86	88	77
Tunisia	54	71	3,250	23	—	—	51
Turkey	57	71	3,568	40	83	91	99
Turkmenistan	—	67	2,563	49	100	58	66
Uganda	47	46	2,110	86	50	75	70
Ukraine	—	68	2,753	14	—	—	66
United Arab Emirates	61	75	3,366	14	—	—	99
United Kingdom	72	78	3,237	5	100	100	99
United States	71	78	3,642	7	100	100	99
Uruguay	—	75	2,830	13	98	95	66
Uzbekistan	—	70	2,550	37	85	100	66
Vanuatu	—	69	2,624	29	88	100	—
Venezuela	65	73	2,398	19	84	74	90
Vietnam	—	69	2,502	34	56	73	85
Yemen	42	62	2,041	71	69	45	50
Yugoslavia	68	73	3,634	13	—	83[2]	63
Zambia	47	42	1,939	105	64	78	66
Zimbabwe	51	43	2,083	58	85	68	70

Note: Not every nation reports in all categories, and some do not report any information at all. Nonreporting nations do not appear in the table. 1. 1999 figure. 2.Rate for children under 5 per 1,000 live births. **Source:** United Nations Department for Economic and Social Affairs, Population Division, *World Population Prospects – The 2000 Revision Highlights* (2000), UN Department for Economic and Social Information and Policy Analysis, *World Population 1996;* United Nations Development Programme, *Human Development Report 2001* (2001, World Health Organization and United Nations Children's Fund, *Global Water Supply and Sanitation Assessment 2000 Report* (2000).

While there is no effective treatment for lung cancer, most cases can be prevented through diet and exercise. Only 7-12 percent of patients survive five years after diagnosis. Rates of lung cancer are increasing in most countries; however, in countries where smoking is declining—Finland, United Kingdom and the United States—lung cancer is also now declining.

▶MATERNAL DEATHS WORLDWIDE

Approximately 585,000 women—one every minute—die around the world each year from pregnancy-related causes, according to the World Health Organization. In parts of some developing countries, the chance of a woman dying this way is 100 times greater than in the industrialized countries.

The five major causes of maternal death are: hemorrhage (25 percent), indirect causes (19 percent), sepsis or postpartum infection (15 percent), hypertensive disorders of pregnancy and eclampsia (13 percent), and unsafe abortion (13 percent). About 70,000 women die each year from unsafe abortion—600 in developed countries and 69,000 in less developed countries—and an unknown but much larger number suffer infection, injury and trauma. There are an estimated 20 million unsafe abortions each year, 90 percent of them in developing countries.

Women who do not have adequate family planning materials and services have unwanted pregnancies and bear too many children, or they have children when they are too young or too old, or have children too close together. Virtually all studies report that most women would prefer using contraceptives and resort to abortion as a last resort.

▶DEATHS OF CHILDREN

In 1991 UNICEF and the World Health Organization certified that 80 percent of all the world's one-year-olds were immunized against the six deadly childhood diseases: diphtheria, whooping cough, measles, tuberculosis, polio and tetanus, thereby effectively stopping the spread of these diseases. An estimated 3.2 million infants in the developing world are now saved from measles, neonatal tetanus and pertussis, and 445,000 infants will not be paralyzed by polio. WHO announced the eradication of smallpox from all peoples on Earth in 1980 and expect to have polio eradicated from all countries by the year 2005.

In recent years UNICEF and WHO have turned their attention to promoting 80 percent (oral rehydration therapy) use, as part of controlling diarrheal disease, eliminating vitamin A deficiency, promoting universal iodization of salt in countries with iodine deficiency disorders, and eliminating guinea worm disease (also called river blindness).

Recent conflicts and wars have had tragic effects on children. It is estimated that in the past decade, wars have killed 2 million children, disabled at least 1 million, left 12 million homeless, and separated another million from their parents. That's not counting the thousands of children under the age of 16 who have fought in wars in more than 25 countries.

▶GLOBAL SEX FACTS

According to the World Health Organization, sexual intercourse occurs more than 100 million times a day around the world. As a result, approximately 910,000 conceptions take place, as well as 350,000 cases of sexually transmitted diseases.

WHO estimates that 1,440 women die each day (an average of one a minute) because of complications during pregnancy or childbirth. About 150,000 unwanted pregnancies end each day in abortion.

The number of people using contraception in Third World countries has increased sharply in recent years, rising from 31 million in the 1960–65 period to 381 million during 1985–90. Women in developing countries had, on average, 6.1 children in the years 1965–70, but the figure declined to 3.9 in 1985–90.

▶SEXUALLY TRANSMITTED DISEASES (STDs)

In 2001, some 189,000 people died of Sexually Transmitted Diseases other than HIV, including 167,000 from syphilis, 8,000 from chlamydia and 2,000 from gonorrhea. There are an estimated 333 million new cases of STDs each year. STDs area most frequent in young people aged 15 to 24. Women contract STDs five time more often than men. Almost two-thirds of all cases of infertility are due to STDs. WHO estimates that in 1995, there were 150 million cases of STDs in adults in Southern/South-easrtern Asia, 65 million cases in sub-Saharan Africa, 36 million in Latin America and the Caribbean, and 14 million in North America.

▶AIDS WORLDWIDE

The Joint United Nations Programme on HIV/AIDS (UNAIDS) and the World Health Organization estimated that 42 million people worldwide were living with HIV/AIDS at the end of 2002, two-thirds of them in Sub-Saharan Africa. An estimated five million people were newly infected during 2002; 800,000 of them were children under the age of 15. A total of 3.1 million people died from AIDS during 2002: 2.4 million adults and 610,000 children.

Since the first clinical evidence of HIV/AIDS was reported in 1981, more than 62 million people have been infected with HIV and over 23 million people have died of AIDS, two-thirds of them in Sub-Saharan Africa.

Sub-Saharan Africa has been the region hardest hit by the HIV/AIDS pandemic. During 2002 an estimated 3.5 million new infections occurred in the region bringing the total to 29.4 million people living with HIV/AIDS. Ten million young people, aged 15-24, and almost three million children under 15 are living with HIV/AIDS. During 2002, there were 2.4 million AIDS-related deaths in the region. Fifty-five percent of women in Sub-Saharan Africa have HIV/AIDS making it the only region where more women than men have the infection. An estimated nine percent of African adults aged 15 to 49 are HIV-positive.

South Africa continues to have the highest number of HIV/AIDS cases in the world: 5 million people, or 20.1 percent of the population. Seven countries, all of them in Africa, have an HIV infection over 20 percent: Botswana (38.8 percent), Zimbabwe (33.7 percent), Swaziland (33.4 percent), Lesotho (31.0 percent), Namibia (22.5 percent), Zambia (21.5 percent), and South Africa (20.1 percent). The infection rate in Uganda, which reached a high of 14 percent a few years ago, declined to five percent in 2002.

South and South-East Asia had approximately six million people living with HIV/AIDS in 2002, including 700,000 new infections and 440,000 deaths. Cambodia (2.7 percent) and Thailand (1.8 percent) have the highest infection rates. China and India, with 36 percent of the world's population, have large numbers of people with HIV/AIDS, but the infection rate in those countries is less than one percent. India's 4.0 million HIV/AIDS cases translates into 0.8 percent of the population, while China's 850,000 cases represent 0.1 percent of the country's total population. UNAIDS estimates that unless effective responses are implemented, 10 million Chinese will have HIV by 2010.

The most rapid spread of the disease is in Eastern Europe and Central Asia, where 250,000 new infections in 2002 took the total to 1.2 million people living with HIV/AIDS. Ukraine remains the most affected country in all of Europe, with 250,000 people infected or an estimated infection rate of 1 percent. In Central Asia, the vast majority of reported HIV infections are among young people, mainly among those who inject drugs.

In high-income countries, 76,000 people became infected with HIV in 2002, raising their total to 1.6 million people living with the virus. Western Europe had 8,000 deaths and 30,000 new infections, bringing the total to 570,000 cases. Spain had 130,000 people, or 0.5 percent of its population, living with the infection. North America had 15,000 deaths and 45,000 new infections in 2002, bringing its total to 980,000.

At the end of 2001, Zimbabwe had the largest number of children (under age 15) living with HIV/AIDS: 400,000. Nigeria had 270,000 infected children, South Africa had 250,000, and India had 170,000. By contrast, Brazil had 13,000 children and young people with HIV/AIDS, and the United States had 10,000.

The number of orphans due to the loss of parents to AIDS is growing rapidly. At the end of 2001, Nigeria had one million living orphans and Ethiopia had 990,000. The Democratic Republic of the Congo had 930,000, Kenya had 890,000 orphans, and Zimbabwe had 780,000.

HIV/AIDS is so devastating that it is severely reducing life expectancy in most African countries. Because of AIDS, 10 countries in Sub-Saharan Africa now have a life expectancy of less than 40 years. In Zimbabwe, life expectancy would be 67.6 years without AIDS; because of AIDS, it is instead 33.1 years. AIDS has similarly reduced life expectancy in Botswana from 68.1 to 39.7 years, and in Swaziland from 62.2 to 34.4 years.

AIDS is also turning food emergencies into serious crises. The United Nations Food and Agricultural Organization (FAO) reports that seven million agricultural workers in 25 severely affected African countries have died from AIDS since 1985, causing a decrease in food production. For example, in Kenya, the death of a household head caused a 60 percent drop in farming production. The death of an adult female can also

HIV/AIDS Worldwide,2002 (numbers in millions)

	Total	Adult males	Adult females	Children under 15
New infections in 2002	5.0	2.2	2.0	0.8
People living with HIV/AIDS	41.8	19.4	19.2	3.2
AIDS deaths in 2002	3.1	1.3	1.2	0.6
Cumulative AIDS deaths	24.9	9.9	10.0	5.0

Source: Joint United Nations Programme on HIV/AIDS (UNAIDS) and World Health Organization, *AIDS Epidemic Update*, December 2002 (2002).

HIV/AIDS Estimates By Region, 2002

Region	New infections in 2002	Number living with HIV/AIDS	Deaths in 2002
Sub-Saharan Africa	3,500,000	29,400,000	2,400,000
South and Southeast Asia	700,000	6,000,000	440,000
East Asia and the Pacific	270,000	1,200,000	45,000
Eastern Europe and Central Asia	250,000	1,200,000	25,000
Latin America	150,000	1,500,000	60,000
Middle East and North Africa	83,000	550,000	37,000
Caribbean	60,000	440,000	42,000
North America	45,000	980,000	15,000
Western Europe	30,000	570,000	8,000
Australia and New Zealand	500	15,000	100
World Total	**5,000,000**	**42,000,000**	**3,100,000**

Source: Joint United Nations Programme on HIV/AIDS (UNAIDS) and World Health Organization, *AIDS Epidemic Update*, December 2002 (2002).

Nations with the Greatest Number of People with HIV/AIDS, 2001

Country	HIV/AIDS cases: Adults and children	Adults (15-49)	Children (under 15)	Deaths in 2001	Living orphans in 2001	Adult infection rate
South Africa	5,000,000	4,700,000	250,000	360,000	660,000	20.1%
India	3,970,000	3,800,000	170,000	NA	NA	0.8
Nigeria	3,500,000	1,700,000	270,000	170,000	1,000,000	5.8
Kenya	2,500,000	2,300,000	220,000	190,000	890,000	15.0
Zimbabwe	2,300,000	2,000,000	400,000	200,000	780,000	33.7
Ethiopia	2,100,000	1,900,000	230,000	160,000	990,000	6.4
Tanzania	1,500,000	1,300,000	17,000	140,000	810,000	7.8
Congo, Democratic Republic of	1,300,000	1,100,000	170,000	120,000	930,000	4.9
Zambia	1,200,000	1,000,000	150,000	120,000	570,000	21.5
Mozambique	1,100,000	1,000,000	80,000	60,000	420,000	13.0
Cameroon	920,000	860,000	69,000	53,000	210,000	11.8
USA	900,000	890,000	10,000	15,000	NA	0.6
China	850,000	850,000	2,000	30,000	76,000	0.1
Ivory Coast	770,000	690,000	84,000	75,000	420,000	9.7
Russia	700,000	700,000	N.A.	9,000	NA	0.9
Thailand	670,000	650,000	21,000	55,000	290,000	1.8
Brazil	610,000	600,000	13,000	8,400	130,000	0.7
Uganda	600,000	510,000	110,000	84,000	880,000	5.0
Rwanda	500,000	430,000	85,000	49,000	260,000	8.9
Sudan	450,000	410,000	30,000	23,000	62,000	2.6
Burkina Faso	440,000	380,000	61,000	44,000	270,000	6.5

Note: UNAIDS/WHO defines living orphans as living children under age 15 in 2001, who have lost at least one parent to AIDS.
Source: Joint United Nations Programme on HIV/AIDS (UNAIDS) and World Health Organization, Global HIV/AIDS & STD Surveillance, *Epi fact sheets by country*, 2002 updates.

threaten a family's food supply and lead to the dissolution of the family. A survey in two Zimbabwean districts in 2000 showed that two-thirds of households that had lost a key adult female had disintegrated and dispersed.

Local wars are also accelerating the spread of HIV/AIDS. Countries in conflict have a higher incidence of HIV/AIDS, largely caused by rape and the fact that soldiers tend to have higher rates of HIV/AIDS than the general population. For example, a 1997 study in Uganda found that the adult population had a 9.5 percent HIV/AIDS rate while soldiers had an infection rate of 27 percent.

World Religions

In 1996, 4.7 billion, or an estimated 80 percent of the world's population, identified themselves as adherents of one religion or another. Four religions—Christianity, Islam, Hinduism and Buddhism—claim 4.2 billion adherents, or 72 percent of the world's population, Approximately 19 percent of the world's people are atheist or nonreligious.

This section describes the major religions of the world, their basic tenets, scriptures, schools and sects, and their history. (Additional details may be found in the section "Religion in America.")

▶JUDAISM

Origins Judaism is the oldest of the world's three major monotheistic religions and a forerunner of Christianity and Islam. The Hebrew Bible recounts the story of the world and mankind from the creation, through the flood, and the work of the patriarch Abraham who brought his people from Mesopotamia to Canaan—the Promised Land. His descendants were enslaved in Egypt until Moses led them out of captivity. During the exodus, Moses received from God the Ten Commandments that form the bedrock of Jewish law. Jewish custom and law further evolved from the 10th century B.C. and the conquest of Canaan to the destruction of Jerusalem by the Romans in A.D. 70.

Scripture The sacred scripture of the Hebrew Bible, or Masorah, consists of 24 books. (The Christian Old Testament divides the same text into 39 books.) The *Torah*, or Law, was composed between the 10th and 5th centuries B.C. These five books—Genesis, Exodus, Leviticus, Numbers and Deuteronomy—are also known by their Greek name, *Pentateuch*. The later history of Israel and the divided kingdom is told in two separate but overlapping traditions known as the Prophets (13th-6th centuries B.C.) and the Writings (11th-2nd centuries B.C.). The Hebrew Bible is also known by the Greek name *Septuagint* ("seventy"), a reference to the number of authors engaged in its translation from Hebrew to Greek in the 3rd century B.C. In addition to scripture, there is a rich ancient tradition of rabbinical commentary called the *Talmud*, a huge compilation of the Oral Law and the accepted authority for Orthodox Jews. First codified around A.D. 200, the Talmudic tradition continued through the centuries and constitutes not only commentary on the law (*Halakah*), but also stories from the Bible and parables, legends, etc. (*Haggadah*) illustrating religious principles.

Beliefs Central to Jewish belief is the idea of a single God—Yahweh—who made a covenant (i.e. an agreement or contract) with His chosen people that He would protect them and provide for them if they swore Him love and obedience. Yahweh shapes history (the end of which is the kingdom of God) and imposes His will upon mankind; He saves, and He judges. The people of *Israel* have a unique relationship with God affirmed on the one hand by His covenant, and on the other, by His law. While Yahweh the creator guides human destiny, the humanity of mankind is defined by the ability of individuals to make ethical choices in keeping with His law. The failure to act according to His law—that is, to know God—is sin, and a basic tenet of Jewish faith is that sin is a willful act; so, too, is turning, or returning, to God.

The book of Isaiah (8th century B.C.) brings to the fore a messianic tradition identifying a future Israel under a divine ruler descended from the house of David as a restoration of paradise and the attainment of salvation.

Practice Jews worship in synagogues in congregations led by a rabbi—a teacher or master. The Sabbath is observed from sunset Friday to sunset Saturday; worship consists of readings from scripture, prayer, and singing. The most important holidays in the Jewish calendar are Rosh Hashanah (New Year), Yom Kippur (Day of Atonement), Hanukah (Festival of Lights), and Pesach (Passover). (See Part I: " Holidays and Holy Days").

Schools and sects There are three main branches of modern Judaism. Orthodox Jews rigorously observe Jewish law, ritual and custom. Reform Judaism professes a more liberal interpretation of Jewish doctrine and ritual, and is especially prevalent in the United States. Conservative Judaism combines elements of doctrinal reform with more traditional observance. Hasidism is today a branch of Orthodox Judaism with origins in a mystical movement in 18th-century Poland that stressed prayer over studying the Torah. Hasidim are very strict observers of the Jewish religious laws.

History The Bible recounts the history of the Jewish people from the creation, through the flood and the covenant of the rainbow, the patriarchs Abraham, Isaac and Jacob, and the story of the tribe of Israel in Egypt. The foundation of Jewish faith began with the exodus from Egypt, and the transmission of the Ten Commandments (the Decalogue) from God to his people through Moses, probably sometime between 1450 and 1290 B.C. The people of Israel conquered and settled in Canaan—the promised land—and were ruled by a succession of judges. The monarchical period under Samuel and David dates to the 11th and 10th centuries B.C. Israel and Judah continued under separate rulers until the fall of Israel in 722 B.C. Judah was conquered by Babylonians, and the Temple of David in Jerusalem was destroyed in 586 B.C. at the start of the Babylonian captivity, which also marks the start of the Jewish Diaspora, or dispersal. Exile lasted until 538 B.C., and the Second Temple was dedicated in 516 B.C. Under Seleucid rule the Maccabees successfully resisted efforts to suppress Judaism (168-142 B.C.). Under Roman rule (63 B.C.–A.D. 135), there were several revolts, the first of which resulted in the destruction of the Second Temple (A.D. 70). It was at around this time that Christianity began to diverge sharply from its Jewish sectarian origins.

The early Middle Ages saw the rise of the Talmudic tradition. Following the rise of Islam, Judaism evolved into two distinct strains, the Sephardim, centered in Spain, and the Ashkenazim, found mainly in France and Germany. Organized persecution of European Jewry began with their expulsion from France (1306) and Spain (1492), and culminated in the Nazi regime in Germany's attempt to eradicate all Jews during the Holocaust (1933-45). The Jewish enlightenment (*Haskala*) in 18th-century Germany gave rise to Reform Judaism and Conservative Judaism (1845). The nationalistic Zionist movement, a reaction to extreme anti-Semitism, led eventually to the birth of the State of Israel in 1948. Though Israel is a secular republic, religious parties play an active role in politics.

Geography and numbers There are an estimated 15 million Jews in 134 countries, the overwhelming majority of whom live in the United States (5.8 million) and Israel (4.3 million). There are an estimated 2.4 million Jews in Europe.

▶CHRISTIANITY

Origins Christianity is based on the acts and sayings of Jesus of Nazareth as related by his followers and apostles. Jesus was born a Jew in Bethlehem in about 4 B.C., but details of his life before about 26-28 A.D. are obscure. In his early 30s, Jesus was baptized by John the Baptist, whose ministry prophesied the coming judgment of God, and who recognized Jesus as the Messiah (Greek for the Christ, or anointed one). Jesus' ministry, chiefly among the poor and dispossessed, lasted only a few years before he was crucified by Roman authorities. According to Christian belief, Jesus rose from the dead three days after his crucifixion, and 40 days later he ascended to heaven to sit at the right hand of God.

Scripture The Bible consists of the Old Testament (the Hebrew Bible), originally written in Hebrew and Aramaic, and the New Testament (first written in Greek in the first century), which relates the life and teachings of Jesus and his early followers. A 3rd-century translation of the Bible into Latin is called the Vulgate. The central portion of the New Testament consists of the Four Gospels (each attributed to one of Christ's earliest followers: Matthew, Mark, Luke, and John). While each tells the story of Jesus' life and death, they differ in details, with Luke and John providing more stories and greater emphasis on Christ's divinity. The story of the spread of Christianity in the first century is told in the Acts of the Apostles and the epistles (letters) of St. Paul. The Roman Catholic canon also includes 15 books found in the Greek Septuagint but not in the Hebrew Bible. The Orthodox Church accepts four of these Apocryphal books; Protestants accept none.

Beliefs Christian belief is rooted in three basic ideas: incarnation—Christ was the human embodiment of God; atonement—mankind was reconciled to God through the agency of Christ; and the Trinity—the belief that the one God has three natures, God the Father, God the Son (Jesus), and God the Holy Spirit.

Practice Central to the practice of most Christians are the seven sacraments: baptism, confirmation, holy matrimony, holy orders, sacrament of the sick, reconciliation (confession), and the Eucharist, (or communion), the sacramental offering and consumption of bread and wine representing the body and blood of Christ. Christians are organized into congregations and worship in churches led by priests or ministers who administer the sacraments. Most denominations designate Sunday as the sabbath and the day for special observance and worship.

Schools and sects Christianity has three major branches: Eastern Orthodoxy, Roman Catholicism, and Protestantism. The division between Eastern Orthodoxy and Roman Catholicism came in 1054. In the sixteenth century, reform-minded priests broke with Rome and there emerged a number of distinct denominations known collectively as Protestantism.

The hierarchical authority of the Catholic Church starts with the Pope, and includes cardinals, bishops, and priests, all celibate men. In addition there are a number of Catholic lay and priestly orders for men and/or women.

The Eastern Orthodox Church embraces a number of national or regional churches. The laity are invested with more authority than are Catholics, and the bishop of Constantinople, titular head of the eastern church, is regarded as "first among equals."

Protestant denominations number in the hundreds. There is no single governing authority for all of them. (See Part II: "Religion in America" for a summary of the major sects).

History At the time of his death, Jesus had a small handful of followers among Jews. His teachings were not widely accepted among the larger Jewish community, however, and his disciples preached to non-Jewish gentiles throughout the Roman Empire. Jesus' teachings were gathered in a collection of books known as the Gospel, or New Testament. Christians were widely persecuted until the Emperor Constantine legalized the religion in 313; in 380 Christianity became the official religion of the Roman Empire. Christianity also reached northern Ethiopia.

Disputes over theological issues such as the nature of the Trinity and the person of Christ were resolved at a series of ecumenical councils. In 1054 the Eastern and Western churches split over differences of theology, politics, geography and language. The papacy in Rome acquired the nature of a civil authority and within the Western church ascetic, spiritual traditions competed with secular ones. In the sixteenth century, papal authority was challenged by such reform-minded priests as Martin Luther and John Calvin, abetted by England's King Henry VIII, who transferred authority over the church in England from the Pope to himself. Sectarian wars engulfed Europe for more than a century as Catholics and Protestants vied for temporal and spiritual power.

European explorers and colonists spread Christianity to the Americas, Asia and Africa. The Spanish and Portuguese brought Catholicism to Latin America, while North America became a haven for Protestant denominations from northern Europe. Since the mid-1800s, Protestant and Catholic evangelists have carried out energetic missionary programs to Africa and East Asia.

Geography and numbers Christianity is the most populous and most widespread religion in the world, with almost 2 billion adherents in 260 countries. Europe is home to more than 555 million Christians (76 percent of the region's population), but Latin America has proportionally the highest number of Christian adherents—93 percent of the population. There are more Christians in Africa (360 million, or 48 percent of the population) and Asia (303 million) than in North America (255 million).

▶ISLAM

Origins The precepts of Islam were revealed through Mohammed, the last of a line of prophets including Abraham, Moses and Jesus. Mohammed was born about 570 at Mecca (in western Saudi Arabia) and died in 632 in the nearby city of Medina.

Scripture The Koran ("recitation") consists of 114 chapters. The text is the infallible word of God as revealed to Mohammed and transcribed by his followers over the course of 23 years.

Beliefs Islam is a monotheistic religion with explicit links to Judaism and Christianity. The Koran's narrative includes stories of Abraham and Isaac, and Moses and the Ten Commandments. Unlike Jews, who trace their descent from Abraham through Isaac, the son of Sarah, Muslims trace their decent through Ishmael, Abraham's son by Hagar. The Koran recounts the virgin birth of Jesus, but does not accept his divinity.

The word Islam comes from the Arabic root *s-l-m*, meaning "peace" and "submission," and a hallmark of Islam is obedience to God.

Practice A Muslim's relations with God are regulated by the Five Pillars of Islam: the Shahadah, or profession of faith—"There is no God but God, and Mohammed is his prophet;" public and collective prayer five times daily; charity to the poor; fasting during the holy month of Ramadan; and pilgrimage to Mecca, the most holy place in the Muslim world, at least once in one's lifetime.

Islam has strict dietary laws and prohibitions against promiscuity, theft, gambling and lying. Muslims worship in mosques led by imams. The principal weekly worship is on Friday at midday.

Schools and sects The overwhelming majority of Muslims are Sunnites, or "traditionalists" (83 percent, or 934 million people). Shi'ites, or "partisans," represent another 16 percent (180 million) and smaller sects make up the rest. The Shi'ite/Sunnite schism reflects differences about who should have succeeded Mohammed. Shi'ites follow somewhat different rites than Sunnites, and recognize additional holy days and places.

History Mohammed was born in Arabia in about 570 A.D. Raised by his uncle, at the age of 25 he became a trader, and later married his employer, the widow Khadija. In 610, an angel descended on Mohammed and ordered him to proclaim the word of God. Rebuked in Mecca, in 622 he was invited to Medina to help bring order to the city. He accepted on the condition that the citizens worship Allah—the one God—and accept the precepts of Islam. This move—the *hegira*—is the year from which the Muslim calendar dates. Eight years later Mohammed returned to Mecca, and by the time of his death in 632, most Arabs were Muslims.

Under a succession of secular and theocratic caliphates, Islam swept east and west from Arabia. Muslims reached the Indus River in 713, and their advance in France was only stopped in 733 at the Battle of Tours; Muslims remained in Spain until 1492. Islamic armies captured the Byzantine capital of Constantinople in 1453, and controlled much of southeastern Europe until the 19th century. In the east, Muslims swept through India at the end of the 10th century and reached the East Indies in the 15th century.

The arts, architecture and technology flourished in the golden age of Islam and Islamic learning and culture was responsible for the transmission of much of classical philosophy and science to the West.

From the 18th to 20th centuries, traditionally Islamic countries came under Western cultural and political influence. In the 20th century, some traditionally Islamic countries like Turkey opted for a secular state; others such as Saudi Arabia and Iran came under strict fundamentalist rule.

Geography and numbers With 1.3 billion adherents in 184 countries, Islam is the second largest religion in the world. It is the dominant religion throughout the Middle East, North Africa, Central Asia, Afghanistan, Pakistan, and Indonesia, the country with the largest number of adherents (172 million people). There are 104 million Muslims in India—11 percent of that country's population.

▶HINDUISM

Origins Hinduism is a complex of polytheistic religion and philosophy that evolved from Vedism, an ancient Indian religion of Indo-European origin dating from the second millennium B.C.

Scripture Different Hindu sects rely on different holy texts, but common to the majority are the Vedic texts called the *Upanishads*. The *Svetasvatara Upanishad* describes Siva, the creator, preserver and destroyer of the universe. Sources for Hindu mythology include the *Mahabharata*, *Ramayana* (concerning Rama, the incarnation of the great god Vishnu), and the *Puaranas*. The *Bhagavad Gita* ("Lord's song," a part of the *Mahabharata*), is a dialogue between Krishna (another incarnation of the god Vishnu) and Prince Arjuna in which are described the three paths to union with God.

Beliefs Hinduism is rooted in the belief that individuals should connect their selves (Atman) with Brahman, or Godhead, the spiritual source of the tangible universe. Hindus also believe in reincarnation—*samsara*—one's subsequent status being dependent on one's actions (*karma*) and duties (*dharma*) in this life. The cycle of reincarnation is broken when one attains liberation (moksha) from the finite world through self-discovery—the union of self with the Godhead, or *Atman-Brahman*. There are four paths to union with Brahman: *jnana yoga*, based on knowledge; *bhakti yoga*, based on service to God; *karma yoga*, based on work for God (as opposed to oneself); and *raja yoga*, based on psychophysical exercise.

Hinduism has three primary theistic traditions revolving around the cults of anthropomorphic gods. Vishnu is a loving god incarnated as Krishna; Siva is a god at once protective and destructive; and Brahma is creator. Saktism is a form of worship dedicated to the female consorts of Vishnu and Siva.

Hindus have a deep respect for all living things; the most revered animal is the cow.

Practice Hindu worship is largely an individual and family matter. Hindu temples are devoted to a particular god or group of gods. Worship in temples or before domestic shrines includes prayers and offerings to an image of the god. Such rituals are intended to bring the worshipper and the god closer together.

Hindu pilgrimage sites include seven sacred cities, among others, where thousands or even millions of Hindus worship at annual festivals. Some of the most famous temples are on the banks of the Ganges River, which is sacred to Hindus, in northern India. Important festival days include Dipavali, "festival of lights," sacred to Lakshmi, goddess of prosperity; holi, a spring festival; and Dashara, a harvest festival.

Individuals follow a code of moral and religious conduct called *dharma*. Traditional Hinduism observes complex societal divisions into four primary (and thousands of subsidiary) castes defined by occupation and social standing: *brahmins:* leaders, philosophers, artists and their families; *kshatriyas:* princes, soldiers and administrators; *vaishyas:* merchants and landowners; and *shudras,* or laborers. Beyond the caste system are untouchables, or outcasts. India's modern constitution outlawed the caste system.

Schools and sects Hinduism comprises myriad religious cults and various schools of philosophy. The principle of religious toleration is reflected in the Hindu belief that Christianity, Islam and other religions offer alternative paths to the same goal. Among the more prominent modes of belief are *yoga* and *tantrism,* both of which evolved in both Hinduism and Buddhism, and *bhakti*. *Tantrism* emphasizes meditation and ritual involving mystical diagrams (mandalas) and chants (mantras) as a means to enlightenment. *Yoga* emphasizes an eightfold path to enlightenment through physical and mental training. *Bhakti* focuses on the primacy of love for a deity.

History Hinduism is the oldest of the world's great religions. Originating in India, it spread to Nepal and southeast Asia. The oldest Hindu writings are actually Vedic texts brought by Aryan invaders in the second millennium B.C. To the Vedic concept of future life, Hinduism attached the ideas of karma, reincarnation and ultimately release from the cycle of life, death and rebirth. Following the rise of rival religions such as Buddhism and Jainism in the 6th century B.C., ritual sacrifice to Vedic deities overseen by priests gave way to polytheistic worship intended to unite the worshipper with the god worshipped.

The classical period of Hinduism dates from the 6th century B.C. to the 10th century A.D., when the major theistic sects emerged and many of the classic works of Hinduism were composed, including the epic *Mahabharata* and *Ramayana* and a variety of works that discuss the duties of caste, advice to rulers, the attainment of pleasure and the attainment of liberation, or moksha. Hindu princes successfully resisted Muslim encroachment from the West until the 10th century. The Muslim ascendancy was coupled with the rise of *bhakti*, a devotional Hinduism that stresses love for the deity, and the adoption of vernacular languages for worship rather than Sanskrit.

Since the 18th century there have been several movements to strip Hinduism of its polytheistic practices, and in this century, great emphasis has been laid on Hindu prescriptions for non-violence and social equality, especially as practiced by the founder of modern India, Mahatma Gandhi.

Geography and numbers Hinduism has an estimated 793 million adherents worldwide. With deep roots in India, and lacking a missionary tradition, it is found almost nowhere outside of India and neighboring countries except in expatriate Indian communities.

▶BUDDHISM

Origins Buddhism was established by the followers of Siddhartha Gautama (ca. 563-483 B.C.), who was born into a kshatriya caste Hindu family in present-day Nepal. At the age of 29, he left his wife and young son in search of enlightenment. This he attained, according to tradition, while sitting under a bodhi tree near Patna. After 49 days of rapture, and withstanding the temptations of the devil Mara, Buddha—the enlightened one—inspired an order of monks and went forth to preach his philosophy of enlightenment for 45 years before passing into nirvana, in which "ideas and consciousness cease to be."

Scripture Of primary importance to all Buddhists is the *Tipitaka* ("Three baskets"), a record of the Buddha's teachings set down set down by Buddha's early followers after his death. These tell the story of his life (Buddha), his laws (Dharma) for personal conduct, and the guidelines for the monastic order (Sangha). There is a large body of other writings peculiar to individual sects and schools. The Buddhist canon continued to evolve over many centuries.

Beliefs Buddhists share with Hinduism a belief in the cycle of reincarnation and that this cycle could be broken. Buddha's teachings are predicated on the Four Noble Truths. Life is impermanent and fundamentally produces suffering, or *dukkha,* perpetuated due to the endless cycle of life, death, and rebirth. This suffering results from the pursuit of mortal desires. Desire can be overcome by attaining *nirvana*. *Nirvana* can be reached by adhering to the Eightfold Path. This path, or Middle Way, consists of right belief, thought, speech, action, livelihood, effort, mindfulness and concentration. These are the backbone of Buddhist ethics.

Practice A hallmark of Buddhist practice is the monastic order, to which monks withdraw from the everyday world and live austere lives of meditation either for a few years or for a lifetime. Mendicants also live on alms contributed by lay Buddhists. In certain sects, adolescents spend time in a monastery as part of a rite of passage into adulthood.

Buddhist temples are primarily for individual meditation, and collective rituals play a smaller part in the life of a Buddhist than in the lives of Jews, Christians and Muslims, or even of Hindus.

Schools and sects There are three main sects in Buddhism. Theravada (or Hinayana) Buddhism, which predominates today in Sri Lanka, Myanmar and Thailand, adheres most closely to the tenets of the early Buddhist sects. In this tradition, attainment of nirvana for oneself is the goal. Mahayana Buddhism, which became the larger sect, spread along the Silk Road from India to China and East Asia. This includes the worship of Buddha and Buddhist saints (*bodhisattvas*). Stressing compassion for others, *boddhisatvas*—literally "wisdom beings"—withhold themselves from attaining nirvana in order to help others attain enlightenment. In Zen Buddhism, a sect of Mahayana, adherents strive for enlightenment through mental conditioning and meditation. The third sect of Tantric Buddhism (Vajrayana), most common in Tibet and Mongolia, attempts to identify the initiate with a visualized deity. The Tantric canon includes esoteric texts, and meditation engages both the mind and the senses with the use of *mantras* (chants), *mudras* (hand gestures) and *mandalas* (visible icons of the universe). The spiritual and temporal leader of Tibetan Buddhists is the Dalai Lama.

History Following Buddha's death, his *sutras* (sermons) and *vinaya* (regulations) were written down by his disciples. Originally, Buddhist mendicants taught for nine months and held retreats during the monsoon. These retreats led to the establishment of monasteries and the rise of differing interpretations of Buddha's teaching. The Mahayana school more easily absorbs (and is absorbed by) different cultures. It received its greatest impetus in India from the Buddhist emperor Ashoka (272-232 B.C.), who sent missionaries to Ceylon, Southeast Asia and China, from where it was carried to Korea and Japan in the 6th century A.D.

The 7th century saw the rise of Zen Buddhism in China and Japan, and of Tantric Buddhism in Tibet. Chinese Buddhism reached its height in the 9th century during the T'ang Dynasty, when it was partially suppressed. Buddhism flourished in Japan until the 19th century, when Shintoism gained imperial favor.

Buddhism lost its influence in India beginning in the 8th century, partly through absorption of its ideas into Hinduism, and partly because of the rise of Islam. By the 13th century, Buddhism was all but extinct there.

Geography and numbers There are an estimated 350 million people in 92 countries who adhere to Buddhist beliefs and practices. Mahayana Buddhists account for about 53 percent (185 million) of all Buddhists, mostly in Japan, Korea and China; Theravada Buddhists account for 35 percent (124 million), in Southeast Asia and Sri Lanka. Lamaist Buddhists account for about 6 percent (21 million) in Tibet and Mongolia. Buddhist practice in Tibet is under threat from the Chinese government.

▶OTHER ORGANIZED RELIGIONS

Baha'i Founded by Baha'Ullah ("glory of God") in Iran in 1844, Baha'i teaches that the revealed religions of the world are in agreement and that the respective prophet-founders of each revealed the will of God for a particular time and place in history. There are approximately 6 million members of the Baha'i faith; the center of the Baha'i faith is in Haifa, Israel. A major temple in Wilmette, Illinois, attracts many visitors.

Chinese folk religions Chinese folk religions consist of a blend of ancient ancestor worship with elements of Buddhism, Confucianism, and Taoism. Taoism is a philosophy or religion based on the teachings of Lao-tzu, another great teacher of Confucian times. The vast majority of the world's 215 to 220 million adherents of Chinese folk religions live in China; the remainder live in scattered Chinese settlements around the world.

Confucianism As much a code of ethical conduct as a religion, Confucianism takes its name from the 6th-century B.C. scholar and civil servant Kung Fu-Tzu (Confucius), whose *Analects* prescribe the proper conduct for life. His impact on China has been enormous, and at times his cult has attained the status of a quasi-official religion. There are about 5 million Confucianists in the world; most of them live in South Korea.

Jainism Jainism is a polytheistic religion established in India by Vardhamana in the 6th century B.C. Its primary features are a belief in the perfection of the soul and in non-injury to living creatures. Almost all of the world's 5 million Jainists live in India.

New Religion This term applies to a variety of more or less organized religious systems that have grown up, primarily in East Asia, since the turn of the century. These religions are characterized by a synthesis of indigenous folk religion with various major Asian traditions (Hinduism, Buddhism, Confucianism and/or Taoism) overlaid with modern Western philosophy. There are more than 100 million people professing adherence to these religions, the majority of them in the Philippines, Indonesia, and Japan.

Parsiism This religion has its roots in Zoroastrianism, an ancient Iranian religion whose central focus is the struggle between good and evil. Its monotheistic tendencies are thought to have influenced the development of Judaism and Christianity. Parsis emigrated to India between the 10th and 15th centuries, and prospered as merchants, especially in Bombay.

Shintoism Evolved from ancient Japanese religious traditions, Shintoism became a state religion under the Meijis in the 19th century. Although some sacred Shinto (literally "way of the gods") texts date from the 8th century, none is considered authoritative. There are three strains of Shinto practice: State Shinto, Shrine Shinto, and Folk Shinto.

Sikhism The Sikh religion was founded by Guru Nanak in the early 16th century. A hybrid of Hindu and Islamic beliefs, it advocates a search for eternal truth and, while believing in reincarnation, rejects the notion of divine incarnation. It was led by a succession of ten gurus, the last of whom declared himself the last human guru. Sikhs now follow the sacred text known as Guru Granth Singh, or Collection of Sacred Wisdom. There are almost 19 million Sikhs in the world; almost all of them live in the Punjab region of India.

▶NONRELIGIOUS AND ATHEISTS

An estimated 887 million people (15 percent of the world's population) profess no religion, are agnostic or are indifferent to religion. Another 222 million people (4 percent) are declared atheists who do not believe in God. More than three-quarters (852 million) of these nonreligious and atheists live in China, where religious observance is sharply curtailed by the government. An estimated 12 percent of people in Europe are nonreligious, compared with 9.8 percent in Oceania, 7.2 percent in North America, and 3.3 percent in Latin America.

▶CHRONOLOGY OF WORLD RELIGION

B.C.

3000 Earliest elements of Hinduism develop in India.

c. 2500 Egyptian pyramids at Giza completed.

c. 1500 Aryan peoples invade India; bring additional elements of Hinduism.

c. 1290 Moses leads Israelites out of Egypt.

1010-922 Reigns of Hebrew kings David and Solomon. A great temple built at Jerusalem.

740 Hebrew prophet Isaiah flourishes.

628 Traditional birth date of Zoroaster, religious teacher in Persia. Followers today are Parsees in India.

587 Babylonians destroy Hebrew temple at Jerusalem and take many Hebrews as slaves. Fifty years later, Hebrews are freed and begin to rebuild temple.

560 Birth of Siddartha Gautama in northern India; later known as Buddha. Dies c. 480. His teachings, on which Buddhism is based, gain many followers in India, later spread to Southeast Asia.

551 Birth of Chinese teacher Confucius. Dies c. 479.

200 Mahayana Buddhism begins to spread in China and Japan.

4 Birth of Jesus Christ. The Western calendar dates from the supposed year of his birth.

A.D.

30 Death and resurrection of Jesus Christ.

66-70 Jewish revolt against Romans ends in destruction of second temple and scattering of Jews (a.k.a. The First Diaspora).

175 Apostles' Creed, a brief statement of Christian beliefs, formulated.

303-12 In final organized program of persecution, Romans kill estimated 500,000 Christians.

313 The emperor Constantine decrees toleration for Christianity in Roman Empire. In 325, he calls synod of Nicaea, which formulates Nicene Creed. By end of 300s, Christianity is official religion of empire.
354 Birth of St. Augustine, influential Christian teacher, in North Africa. Dies 430.
451 Council of Chalcedon (fourth ecumenical council) formulates long-held Christian understanding of Christ, the union in one person of two distinct natures, human and divine.
570 Muhammad, founder of Islam, born in Mecca (now in Saudi Arabia). Dies in 632 in nearby city of Medina.
600+ Tantrism, a Hindu school, grows up, emphasizing special rituals as means of enlightenment; uses mystical diagrams (mandalas) and chants (mantras).
650+ Islam enters India, gains many converts.
700+ Development in China of Zen, a school of Buddhism, which later attracted particular attention in the modern Western world.
711-715 Muslim Arabs settle in Spain.
800 Roman Empire revived in the West with the coronation of Charlemagne as emperor on Christmas Day, in St. Peter's in Rome.
988 Christianity reaches Russia through missionaries from eastern churches.
1054 Eastern (or Orthodox) and Western (or Roman) churches go separate ways after disputes about doctrine and authority.
1096 Christians in Europe go on first Crusade to take Holy Land from Muslims. Seven other major Crusades pursued between 1100 and 1300. Christian warriors temporarily occupy Jerusalem and other cities, but soon lose them again to Muslims.
1216 Pope Innocent III approves formation of Franciscans and Dominicans.
1227 Thomas Aquinas, great Christian theologian, born in Italy.
1300+ Bhakti, a Hindu sect, develops emphasizing primacy of love for a deity and using love between humans as illustration; rejects caste, ritual, and creeds, and emphasizes need for sincerity.
1309 The papacy moves from Rome to Avignon, France, where it remains until 1377 ("The Babylonian Captivity of the Church").
1377 English theologian and religious reformer John Wycliffe accused of heresy by Pope Gregory XI for attacks on worldliness of the church.
1378-1417 The Great Western Schism, during which first two, then three, claimants sought recognition as pope.
1415 Excommunication and execution of Czech religious leader Jan Hus, who protested sale of indulgences and other papal excesses, sets off Hussite Wars, which end with Compactata of Prague.
1453 Ottoman Turks (Muslims) conquer capital of Eastern Roman Empire, Constantinople. Turks push westward into Europe.
1454 Johannes Gutenberg prints first Bible with moveable type.
1469 Birth of Nanak, founder of Sikhism, in Punjab region of India.
1492 Muslims overthrown in Spain; Spanish Inquisition begins.
1517 Martin Luther, a German priest, posts 95 theses on cathedral door, questioning church teachings. Luther refuses to recant; is excommunicated from Catholic church. With cooperation of north German princes, he forms new Protestant churches. This begins Reformation, which ultimately divides European Christianity into two warring camps.
1534 King Henry VIII of England denies power of pope over church in England and establishes Church of England responsible to monarch. New church gradually adopts Protestant beliefs but maintains many practices of earlier Catholic era.
1536 John Calvin, a young French scholar, publishes *Institutes of the Christian Religion*, and becomes second major leader of Protestant Christianity; helping to create Presbyterian and other Reformed churches.
1540 Ignatius Loyola, a Spaniard, establishes the Jesuits (Society of Jesus) with papal approval. This order becomes powerful instrument of Catholic church in disputes with Protestants, in missionary efforts around world, and in education.
1545-63 Council of Trent makes major reforms in Catholic church and defines disagreements with Protestants. Its work begins Catholic Reformation, or Counter-Reformation.
1598 In the Edict of Nantes, Henry IV proclaims "peaceful coexistence" of Catholics and Calvinists in France. Revoked in 1685 by Louis XIV.
1618-48 Thirty Years War, caused in part by Protestant-Catholic hatreds, decimates central Europe. Calvinist leaders in England overthrow monarchy and execute king in civil war (1642-49). Monarchy is restored in 1660.
1620 Pilgrims, a small group of English Calvinists, establish colony at Plymouth in North America to escape persecution in England.
1683 Muslim Turks defeated near Vienna, Austria, in their last attempt to establish foothold in western Europe.
1734 The Great Awakening, a religious revival, sweeps New England, begun by prominent Massachusetts preacher Jonathan Edwards. English evangelist George Whitefield tours American colonies beginning in 1738, preaching to outdoor gatherings.
1738 Christian conversion experienced by brothers John and Charles Wesley in England. They begin evangelical activities, leading to development of independent Methodist church.
1789 U.S. Constitution guarantees separation of church and state.
1792 Second Awakening sweeps new United States, lasting more than 20 years. Revivals in Kentucky in 1800 result in formation of new denominations, ancestors of Disciples of Christ, Churches of Christ, and Christian churches.
1830 American Joseph Smith has religious visions that lead him to organize the Church of Jesus Christ of the Latter-Day Saints (Mormons).
1844 Baha'i established in Iran.
1869-79 Vatican Council I, convened by Pope Pius IX, declares that teachings of pope in matters of faith and morals are infallible.
1875 Mary Baker Eddy publishes *Science and Health with Key to the Scriptures* in Boston; it becomes basis of Church of Christ, Scientist.
1900 First documented modern Pentecostal experience—worshipers speak in unknown tongues during prayer meeting in Kansas. Within 20 years, Pentecostal churches form major new Christian denomination.
1935-45 Nazi government in Germany carries out destruction of estimated six million European Jews. This event known as the Holocaust.
1945-46 Compulsory adherence to Shintoism ended in Japan; Emperor Hirohito disavows his divinity to Japanese people.
1947 U.N. approves creation of the new state of Israel in Middle East for settlement by Jews.
1948 World Council of Churches established at huge assembly in Amsterdam. This ecumenical

organization supported by many Protestant, Anglican, and Orthodox denominations. Headquarters are in Geneva, Switzerland.

1962-65 Vatican Council II, convened by Pope John XXIII, announces many liberalizing changes in Roman Catholic liturgy and practice; supports cautious involvement in ecumenical discussions with other Christians.

1978 Karol Josef Wojtyla, archbishop of Krakow, Poland, elected to papacy as John Paul II, the first non-Italian pope since Hadrian VI in 1523.

1988 For the first time, a woman is elected to a bishopric in U.S. Episcopal church.

1991 Religious freedom granted in U.S.S.R.

The Books of the Bible

The first five books of the Bible are known as the Torah ("to teach" in Hebrew) in the Jewish faith. Roman Catholic canon recognizes additional "deuterocanonical" books, as well as additional parts of other books. Together, they are known as the Apocrypha. They are listed in *italics* following the Old Testament.

Old Testament
Genesis
Exodus
Leviticus
Numbers
Deuteronomy
Joshua
Judges
Ruth
First Samuel
Second Samuel
First Kings
Second Kings
First Chronicles
Second Chronicles
Ezra
Nehemiah
Esther
Job
Psalms
Proverbs
Ecclesiastes
Song of Solomon
Isaiah
Jeremiah
Lamentations
Ezekiel
Daniel
Hosea
Joel
Amos
Obadiah
Jonah
Micah
Nahum
Habakuk
Zephaniah
Haggai
Zechariah
Malachi

The Apocrypha
Tobit
Judith
Additions to Esther
Wisdom of Solomon
Ecclesisasticus (Sirach)
Baruch
The Letter of Jeremiah
The Prayer of Azariah and the Song of the Three Young Men
Susanna
Bel and the Dragon
First Maccabees
Second Maccabees
First Esdras
The Prayer of Manasseh
Psalm 151
Third Maccabees
Second Esdras
Fourth Maccabees

New Testament
Matthew
Mark
Luke
John
Acts
Romans
First Corinthians
Second Corinthians
Galatians
Ephesians
Philippians
Colossians
First Thessalonians
Second Thessalonians
First Timothy
Second Timothy
Titus
Philemon
Hebrews
James
First Peter
Second Peter
First John
Second John
Third John
Jude
Revelation

The Ten Commandments

Significant differences exist among the Protestant, Catholic, and Jewish versions of the Ten Commandments, both in wording and in numbering. Even within the King James Bible, the Commandments are presented twice, first in Exodus and later in Deuteronomy. The Exodus version (Exodus 20: 2-17) is the most familiar, and is reprinted here. Numbers refer to commandment numbers, not Biblical verses.

1 I am the Lord thy God, which have brought thee out of the land of Egypt, out of the house of bondage.

2 Thou shalt have no other gods before me.

Thou shalt not make unto thee any graven image, or any likeness of any thing that is in heaven above, or that is in the earth beneath, or that is in the water under the earth:

Thou shalt not bow down thyself to them, nor serve them: for I the Lord thy God am a jealous God, visiting the iniquity of the fathers upon the children unto the third and fourth generation of them that hate me;

And showing mercy unto thousands of them that love me and keep my commandments.

3 Thou shalt not take the name of the Lord thy God in vain; for the Lord will not hold him guiltless that taketh his name in vain.

4 Remember the sabbath day, to keep it holy.

Six days shalt thou labor, and do all thy work:

But the seventh day is the sabbath of the Lord thy God: in it thou shalt not do any work, thou, nor thy son, nor thy daughter, thy manservant, nor thy maidservant, nor thy cattle, nor thy stranger that is within thy gates:

For in six days the Lord made heaven and earth, the sea, and all that in them is, and rested the seventh day: wherefore the Lord blessed the sabbath day, and hallowed it.

5 Honor thy father and thy mother: that thy days may be long upon the land which the Lord thy God giveth thee.

6 Thou shalt not kill.

7 Thou shalt not commit adultery.

8 Thou shalt not steal.

9 Thou shalt not bear false witness against thy neighbor.

10 Thou shalt not covet thy neighbor's house, thou shalt not covet thy neighbor's wife, nor his manservant, nor his maidservant, nor his ox, nor his ass, nor any thing that is thy neighbor's.

The Koran

The sacred book of Islam was revealed by God to the prophet Mohammed over his life at Mecca and Medina. Its various versions were reconciled in the 7th century by Uthman, the third Caliph. It is divided into 114 chapters of verses, with chapters appearing in size order from longest to shortest, rather than in chronological order.

The Seven Deadly Sins

1	Pride
2	Envy
3	Anger
4	Sloth
5	Greed
6	Gluttony
7	Lust

Major Languages of the World

There are approximately 100 languages designated as "official" by national governments around the world. These run the gamut from Chinese and English—with hundreds of millions of speakers worldwide—to local languages whose speakers may number only in the tens of thousands.

Chinese This is the mother tongue of more than one billion people. Although spoken dialects of Chinese are not mutually intelligible, they share the same writing system—Chinese characters, or *hanzi*—and two people can speak different dialects and still be able to read each other's writing. This is possible because *hanzi* characters represent words independently of their pronunciation (just as Arabic numerals can represent the words for numbers in any language), and also because written Chinese has diverged less from a common standard than have the various spoken dialects.

Based on the dialect spoken in northern China around Beijing, Mandarin is an official language in China, Taiwan, and Singapore, where it is the primary language of more than 800 million people. The other principal dialects are Cantonese (or *Yue*), spoken in southern China and Hong Kong; *Wu*, spoken in Shanghai and nearby provinces in eastern China; *Min*, found in southeastern China, Taiwan and Malaysia; and *Xiang*, *Kan*, and *Hakka*, all spoken in southeastern China and Taiwan. Chinese is also an official language of the U.N.

English Although there are fewer native speakers of English than of Chinese, English is by far the most commonly found language outside of China. Some estimates suggest that as many as one-third of the world's people can speak English—which means four billion people can't. From the island kingdom in northwest Europe, the language spread throughout the British Empire to the Americas, Africa, India and Oceania. Today, 58 countries and the U.N. designate English as an official language, and these countries account for more than 460 million speakers. The main concentrations of English speakers are the United States (258 million), United Kingdom (57 million), Philippines (37 million), India (31 million), Canada (18 million), Australia (17 million) and Nigeria (16 million).

Hindi Spoken by an estimated 430 million people in India alone, Hindi is one of that country's two official languages, the other being English. There are significant numbers (relative to the local population) of Hindi speakers in Trinidad, Guyana, South Africa, Mauritius and other countries with large Indian expatriate communities.

Spanish Carried by Spanish conquistadors from Europe to the Americas and Asia, Spanish is now an official language of 21 nations, territories and colonies in which it is the mother tongue of more than 300 million people. By far the greatest number of Spanish speakers live in Mexico (85 million), followed by Colombia (35 million), Argentina (34 million), Spain (29 million) and Venezuela (21 million). Although the United States does not recognize an official language per se, the U.S. ranks sixth in the number of people who consider Spanish a first language with 20 million. Spanish is also an official language of the U.N.

Arabic Twenty-five countries around the world have adopted Arabic as an official language, more than any other language but English and French. These 25 countries alone represent nearly 200 million Arabic speakers. Arabic is also the language of the Koran—and thus, for many Muslims, of God. For this reason, it is the second language of many Indians, Indonesians, Iranians and other inhabitants of largely Muslim countries. Arabic is also an official language of the U.N.

Portuguese The transmission of Portuguese paralleled that of Spanish, but today it is used as an official language in only seven countries outside of Portugal (where there are a scant 10 million speakers): five in Africa, one in Latin America, and one in Macau, a special administrative region of China. Of the 168 million native Portuguese speakers worldwide, the vast majority of them live in Brazil (154 million). In Angola, there are just over 4 million.

Russian There are an estimated 130 million people who claim Russian as their mother tongue in the two countries where it is an official language, Russia (127 million) and Belarus (3 million). There are still significant numbers of people claiming Russian as a first language in the former republics of the Soviet Union, especially Ukraine (17 million) and Kazakhstan (8 million), Uzbekistan (2.5 million), and Kyrgyzstan and Moldova (1 million each). Russian is an official language of the U.N.

Japanese The official language of only one country, Japanese is spoken by more than 125 million. The most significant Japanese-speaking minorities outside of Japan are found in Brazil (600,000 people) and the United States (490,000). Modern Japanese employs four writing systems: *kanji* (adapted from the Chinese *hanzi*), *hiragana*, *katakana* and *romaji*.

Bengali The official language of Bangladesh, where it is the mother tongue of more than 120 million people, Bengali is also the first language of an estimated 72 million Indians, chiefly the state of West Bengal.

German An official language of six European countries (Germany, Austria, Switzerland, Luxembourg, Liechtenstein, and Belgium), German is spoken by more than 117 million in those countries. There are also significant German-speaking minorities in Eastern Europe (500,000 in Poland and 350,000 in Russia), Brazil (870,000) and the United States (1.8 million).

French Although there are fewer speakers of French than of other languages—fewer than 100 million people claim it is as a first language worldwide—its significance stems from the fact that it is an official language of 32 countries—more than any other language except English—and of the U.N. (These countries account for 88 million native speakers of French.) The most important in terms of numbers are France (55 million), Canada (7 million), Ivory Coast (Côte d'Ivoire) (5 million). Democratic Republic of the Congo, Belgium, Cameroon, Niger, Madagascar and Switzerland also have more than 1 million each claiming French as a first language.

Malay Variants and dialects of Malay are used as an official language in Indonesia (where it is known as *Bahasa Indonesia*), Malaysia (*Bahasa Nalaysia*), and Singapore and Brunei (*Bahasa Melayu*). Although these four countries have a combined population of more than 220 million people, Malay is not the mother tongue of the majority in any of them. A mere 33 million people claim Malay as their first language. In Indonesia, Malay runs a distant third to Javanese (78 million speakers) and Sundanese (31 million).

World Energy

The world's primary energy sources in 2001 were crude oil and natural gas liquids, natural gas, coal, and electricity from hydroelectric and nuclear power. In order to compare the energy produced by different sources, energy is measured in British thermal units (Btu). Energy production and consumption worldwide increased drastically during the 1980s, but their growth slowed somewhat in the 1990s. Petroleum production and consumption continues to increase, but whereas petroleum once constituted almost half the world's energy, it now accounts for less than 40 percent. Natural gas and nuclear power have made up most of the difference.

Petroleum World production of petroleum (which includes crude oil and natural gas plant liquids) was 74.7 million barrels per day in 2001, up slightly from 74.3 million in 2000. The United States, Russia and Saudi Arabia are the world's largest producers of petroleum; the three countries together account for nearly one-third of the world's petroleum production.

Consumption of petroleum has kept pace with the increase in production. But the United States is by far the biggest consumer. The U.S. consumes 19.6 million barrels of petroleum per day, more than one-fourth the world's total. That's more than double the amount the U.S. produces each day, forcing America to import nearly 12 million barrels of petroleum each day. No other country consumes even half as much oil as the United States. Japan was second in world consumption with 5.4 million barrels (most of which it imported), followed by China (5.0 million barrels), Germany (2.8 million), and Russia (2.6 million). Saudi Arabia, the world's largest petroleum producer, consumed a mere 1.5 million barrels per day, or 1.9 percent of the world total.

Dry natural gas World production of dry natural gas continued to set all-time highs; in 2001, production was more than 90 trillion cubic feet. Russia is the world's largest producer of natural gas (20.51 trillion cubic feet, or 23 percent of the

World Energy Production by Region, 1980–2001

Region	1980	1985	1990	1995	2000	2001
Crude oil (thousand barrels/day)	**59,599**	**53,981**	**60,566**	**62,335**	**68,342**	**68,057**
North America	11,968	13,187	11,461	10,982	10,811	10,988
Central & South America	3,647	3,602	4,318	5,481	6,602	6,300
Western Europe	2,531	3,847	4,125	5,878	6,168	6,060
Eastern Europe & Former USSR	12,038	11,909	11,216	7,017	7,898	8,580
Middle East	18,442	10,307	16,545	18,979	21,825	21,126
Africa	6,125	5,371	6,432	6,954	7,507	7,516
Far East & Oceania	4,848	5,758	6,468	7,043	7,533	7,487
Dry Natural Gas (trillon cubic ft)	**53.19**	**62.17**	**73.57**	**77.96**	**88.09**	**90.72**
North America	23.17	20.45	22.56	25.16	26.77	27.25
Central & South America	1.20	1.76	2.01	2.58	3.43	3.61
Western Europe	7.32	7.22	7.24	8.80	10.19	10.31
Eastern Europe & Former USSR	17.04	24.50	30.13	25.93	26.22	26.48
Middle East	1.33	2.38	3.72	4.99	7.57	8.25
Africa	0.69	1.86	2.46	3.01	4.44	4.58
Far East & Oceania	2.44	4.00	5.44	7.50	9.48	10.24
Coal (million short tons)	**4,196.13**	**4,869.40**	**5,386.18**	**5,161.04**	**4,995.16**	**5,266.01**
North America	877.37	955.77	1,113.01	1,125.80	1,162.36	1,211.82
Central & South America	16.66	21.31	32.86	39.07	56.95	61.67
Western Europe	845.33	928.34	872.60	555.04	492.10	500.55
Eastern Europe & Former USSR	1,282.36	1,331.37	1,339.45	892.80	787.69	817.65
Middle East	0.99	1.38	1.21	1.25	1.54	1.54
Africa	137.91	197.48	201.77	236.06	255.30	257.26
Far East & Oceania	1,035.51	1,433.75	1,825.27	2,311.03	2,239.23	2,415.53
Hydroelectric power (bil. kWh)	**1,735.2**	**1,973.1**	**2,167.4**	**2,474.7**	**2,625.8**	**2,571.1**
North America	546.9	611.1	606.6	667.6	657.6	564.8
Central & South America	199.3	285.7	364.8	471.5	545.0	513.4
Western Europe	431.7	453.2	453.4	503.7	557.5	554.1
Eastern Europe & Former USSR	211.3	230.7	253.6	271.8	253.5	271.5
Middle East	9.6	9.5	12.5	15.4	13.8	14.3
Africa	60.2	46.7	55.5	57.3	69.8	73.1
Far East & Oceania	276.2	336.4	420.9	487.3	528.7	579.8
Nuclear power (billion kWh)	**684.4**	**1,425.7**	**1,905.1**	**2,206.0**	**2,434.2**	**2,520.7**
North America	287.0	440.8	649.0	774.4	830.4	850.0
Central & South America	2.2	8.4	9.0	9.5	10.9	20.8
Western Europe	219.2	572.5	707.5	793.0	849.4	875.4
Eastern Europe & Former USSR	83.2	200.3	251.3	224.3	265.7	277.3
Middle East	0.0	0.0	0.0	0.0	0	0
Africa	0.0	5.5	8.4	11.3	13.0	10.7
Far East & Oceania	92.7	198.2	279.9	393.6	464.7	486.5

1. Preliminary. **Source:** Energy Information Administration, *International Energy Annual, 2001* (2003).

world total in 2001), followed by the United States (19.36 trillion cubic feet. The United States was responsible for 25 percent of world consumption, while Russia accounted for 16 percent.

Coal After more than a decade of decline, world coal production jumped in 2001 to more than 5.2 billion short tons. China continues to lead the world in production, with more than 1.4 billion short tons per year. The United States, the world leader until 1987, produced just over 1.1 billion short tons in 2001. Together, the U.S. and China account for close to half the world's production. They also accounted for the bulk of coal consumption in 2001. China consumed 1.38 billion short tons (26 percent of world consumption) and the U.S. consumed 1.06 million short tons (21 percent).

Hydroelectric power Generation of hydroelectric power worldwide dropped 2.1 percent between 2000 and 2001, to a total of 2.57 trillion kilowatthours (kWh). Canada (328 billion kWh), Brazil (266 billion kWh) and China (263 billion kWh) together produced 33 percent of the worldwide total. They were also the three biggest users of hydroelectric power, together making up 33

Top 10 Producers of Primary Energy, by Source, 2001

Crude oil[1]	(thousand barrels per day)	Natural gas plant liquids[2]	(thousand barrels per day)	Dry natural gas	(trillion cubic feet)
1. Saudi Arabia	8,031	1. United States	1,868	1. Russia	20.51
2. Russia	7,049	2. Canada	709	2. United States	19.36
3. United States	5,801	3. Saudi Arabia	680	3. Indonesia	2.44
4. Iran	3,724	4. Mexico	433	4. Uzbekistan	2.23
5. China	3,300	5. Norway	291	5. Iran	2.17
6. Mexico	3,157	6. United Arab Emirates	290	6. United Arab Emirates	1.59
7. Norway	3,117	7. United Kingdom	258	7. Argentina	1.31
8. Venezuela	2,880	8. Algeria	250	8. Mexico	1.30
9. Iraq	2,432	9. Russia	237	9. Australia	1.17
10. United Kingdom	2,282	10. Venezuela	200	10. Qatar	1.14

Coal[3]	(million short tons)	Hydroelectric power[4,5]	(billion kWh)	Nuclear electric power[5]	(billion kWh)
1. China	1,459.02	1. Canada	327.9	1. United States	768.8
2. United States	1,121.33	2. Brazil	265.5	2. France	400.9
3. Australia	356.85	3. China	263.4	3. Japan	309.0
4. India	338.62	4. United States	208.7	4. Germany	162.6
5. Russia	299.50	5. Russia	173.5	5. Russia	125.4
6. South Africa	250.28	6. Norway	119.2	6. Korea, South	106.5
7. Germany	225.66	7. Japan	87.0	7. United Kingdom	85.6
8. Poland	178.94	8. Sweden	77.6	8. Canada	72.9
9. Korea, North	105.27	9. India	77.4	9. Ukraine	71.7
10. Indonesia	99.64	10. France	72.7	10. Sweden	65.8

Note: Preliminary. **1.** Includes lease condensate. 2. Does not include China, for which data are unavailable. 3. Includes anthracite, subanthracite, bituminous, subbituminous, lignite, and brown coal. 4. Net generation; excludes generation from pumped storage. 5. Data consist of both utility and non-utility sources. Net generation; excludes energy consumed by the generating unit.
Source: U.S. Dept. of Energy, *International Energy Annual, 2001* (2003).

World Crude Oil Production, 1960–2002 (million barrels per day)

Country	1960	1970	1980	1990	2000	2001	2002
Organization of Petroleum Exporting Countries (OPEC)[1]	**8.70**	**23.30**	**26.61**	**23.20**	**29.26**	**28.32**	**26.37**
Iran	1.07	3.83	1.66	3.09	3.70	3.72	3.44
Iraq	0.97	1.55	2.51	2.04	2.57	2.43	2.02
Kuwait	1.69	2.99	1.66	1.18	2.08	2.00	1.89
Nigeria	0.02	1.08	2.06	1.81	2.16	2.26	2.12
Saudi Arabia	1.31	3.80	9.90	6.41	8.40	8.03	7.63
United Arab Emirates	0.00	0.78	1.71	2.12	2.37	2.28	2.08
Venezuela	2.85	3.71	2.17	2.14	3.16	2.88	2.60
Non-OPEC countries[1]	**12.29**	**22.59**	**32.99**	**37.37**	**36.33**	**38.29**	**39.03**
Canada	0.52	1.26	1.44	1.55	1.98	2.03	2.17
China	0.10	0.60	2.11	2.77	3.25	3.30	3.34
Mexico	0.27	0.49	1.94	2.55	3.01	3.16	3.18
Norway	0.00	0.00	0.53	1.70	3.20	3.12	2.99
Russia[2]	2.91	6.99	11.71	10.98	6.48	7.05	7.41
United Kingdom	(3)	(3)	1.62	1.82	2.28	2.28	2.29
United States	7.04	9.64	8.60	7.36	5.82	5.80	5.74
Total world	**20.99**	**45.89**	**59.60**	**60.57**	**68.34**	**68.06**	**68.84**

1. Includes other countries not shown separately. In addition to those listed separately, current OPEC members are: Algeria, Indonesia, Libya, and Qatar. 2. Figures for Russia before 1995 refer to the former Soviet Union. 3. Fewer than 5,000 barrels per day.
Source: U.S. Dept. of Energy, *Monthly Energy Review.*

Leading Suppliers of U.S. Oil, 1990-2002

The United States imports about half of the oil it consumes, or more than 10 million barrels a day. Since 1993, the U.S. has imported more of its oil from non-OPEC countries than from OPEC countries.

	U.S. imports, (thousand barrels/day)		
Country	**1990**	**2000**	**2002**
Canada	934	1,807	1,971
Saudi Arabia	1,339	1,572	1,552
Mexico	755	1,373	1,547
Venezuela	1,025	1,546	1,398
Nigeria	800	896	621
United Kingdom	189	366	478
Iraq	518	620	459
Total OPEC countries	4,296	5,203	4,605
Non-OPEC countries	3,721	6,257	6,925
Total imports	**8,018**	**11,459**	**11,530**

Source: Energy Information Administration, *Petroleum Supply Monthly.*

World Crude Oil Reserves, 1980-2002

	Reserves(billion barrels)	
Country	**1980**	**2002**
1. Saudi Arabia	166.5	261.8
2. Iraq	31.0	112.5
3. United Arab Emirates	29.4	97.8
4. Kuwait	68.5	96.5
5. Iran	58.0	89.7
6. Venezuela	17.9	77.7
7. Russia	N.A.	48.6
8. Libya	23.5	29.5
9. Mexico	31.2	26.9
10. Nigeria	17.4	24.0
World Total	**644.9**	**1,032.0**

Source: Energy Information Administration; *Oil and Gas Journal*, annual.

World Energy Consumption by Type and Region, 1986–2001

	Consumption (quadrillion Btu)					
Energy Type and Region	**1986**	**1990**	**1995**	**1999**	**2000**	**2001**
Petroleum	**126.70**	**134.87**	**142.58**	**153.42**	**155.89**	**156.48**
North America	38.35	40.39	41.49	45.86	46.37	45.92
Central & South America	7.02	7.34	9.04	10.42	10.58	10.52
Western Europe	26.54	27.42	29.63	30.41	30.36	30.70
Eastern Europe & Former USSR	21.99	20.32	11.94	10.42	10.39	10.53
Middle East	6.25	7.08	8.58	9.41	9.65	9.80
Africa	3.67	4.17	4.66	5.04	5.16	5.30
Asia & Oceania	22.88	28.15	37.23	41.86	43.39	43.71
Dry Natural Gas	**62.37**	**74.51**	**80.96**	**87.70**	**91.39**	**93.11**
North America	19.80	22.73	26.79	27.52	28.85	27.63
Central & South America	1.86	2.20	2.80	3.41	3.57	3.80
Western Europe	9.08	10.12	12.89	15.11	15.60	15.90
Eastern Europe & Former USSR	23.22	28.51	23.38	22.65	23.14	23.66
Middle East	2.65	3.77	4.96	6.75	7.14	7.64
Africa	1.21	1.52	1.87	2.03	2.20	2.46
Asia & Oceania	4.55	5.67	8.26	10.23	10.89	12.03
Coal	**86.39**	**89.96**	**91.23**	**91.52**	**93.65**	**95.94**
North America	18.57	20.52	21.64	23.42	24.52	23.93
Central & South America	0.63	0.60	0.66	0.87	0.86	0.80
Western Europe	14.40	13.95	10.11	9.55	9.79	9.98
Eastern Europe & Former USSR	20.74	19.85	12.67	11.11	11.61	11.78
Middle East	0.13	0.15	0.23	0.30	0.34	0.32
Africa	4.01	2.98	3.39	3.67	3.73	3.81
Asia & Oceania	27.91	31.92	42.53	42.60	42.80	45.32
Hydroelectric power	**21.34**	**22.66**	**25.89**	**27.12**	**27.52**	**26.85**
North America	6.85	6.40	7.19	7.31	7.05	5.99
Central & South America	3.21	3.79	4.80	5.36	5.67	5.34
Western Europe	4.57	4.74	5.26	5.52	5.80	5.76
Eastern Europe & Former USSR	2.47	2.64	2.83	2.72	2.64	2.82
Middle East	0.09	0.13	0.16	0.15	0.14	0.15
Africa	0.51	0.58	0.59	0.72	0.73	0.76
Far East & Oceania	3.63	4.38	5.06	5.34	5.50	6.03
Nuclear electric power	**16.34**	**20.37**	**23.21**	**25.08**	**25.52**	**26.45**
North America	5.25	6.99	8.21	8.49	8.72	8.93
Central & South America	0.06	0.10	0.11	0.12	0.12	0.22
Western Europe	6.47	7.43	8.30	8.90	8.88	9.15
Eastern Europe & Former USSR	2.17	2.89	2.46	2.74	2.93	3.06
Middle East	N.A.	N.A.	0.00	0.00	0.00	0.00
Africa	0.09	0.09	0.11	0.13	0.13	0.11
Asia & Oceania	2.29	2.87	4.02	4.70	4.74	4.98
Geothermal, solar, wind, wood & waste electric power	**0.37**	**1.72**	**2.25**	**2.76**	**2.97**	**3.11**
Total energy consumption	**313.48**	**346.18**	**368.25**	**389.58**	**398.88**	**403.92**

Source: Energy Information Administration, *International Energy Annual, 2001* (2003).

percent of world consumption. U.S. production dropped from 273 to 209 billion kWh in 2001.

Nuclear electric power World generation of nuclear electric power nearly quadrupled between 1980 and 2001 from 684.4 billion to 2.5 trillion kWh. In 2001, the U.S. alone produced more nuclear power (768.8 billion kWh) than the entire world total in 1980. France (400.9 billion kWh) and Japan (309.0 billion kWh) followed the U.S. in total nuclear production in 2001, as well as in the total number of reactors.

World Primary Energy Production By Source, 1980-2000 (quadrillion Btu)

Source	1980	1985	1990	1995	1999	2000
Petroleum[1]	133.22	121.21	136.35	141.48	155.86	155.34
Natural gas	52.65	61.38	75.91	80.26	90.82	93.53
Coal	74.48	85.77	91.87	90.59	91.17	96.02
Hydroelectric power	18.05	20.56	22.57	25.61	27.25	26.70
Nuclear electric power	7.58	15.37	20.37	23.21	25.52	26.45
Total, all sources[2]	**286.38**	**304.89**	**351.04**	**365.93**	**395.95**	**403.44**

Note: Totals may not add up due to rounding. 1. Includes natural gas plant liquids. 2. Includes geothermal, solar, wind, wood and waste electrical power not shown separately. **Source:** Energy Information Administration, *International Energy Annual, 2001* (2003).

World Nuclear Power Generation, by Region and Country, 1980–2001

Region and country	Generation (billion killowatthours)						Operable reactors
	1980	1985	1990	1995	2000	2001	in 2002
North America	**287.0**	**440.8**	**649.0**	**774.4**	**830.4**	**850.0**	**120**
Canada	35.9	57.1	69.2	93.0	68.7	72.9	14
Mexico	—	—	2.8	8.0	7.8	8.3	2
United States	251.1	383.7	577.0	673.4	753.9	768.8	104
Central and South America	**2.2**	**8.4**	**9.0**	**9.5**	**10.9**	**20.8**	**4**
Argentina	2.2	5.4	7.0	7.1	6.0	6.5	2
Brazil	0.0	2.9	1.9	2.4	4.9	14.3	2
Western Europe	**207.4**	**572.5**	**707.5**	**793.0**	**849.4**	**875.4**	**147**
Belgium	11.9	32.7	40.6	39.3	45.7	44.0	7
Finland	6.6	18.0	18.3	18.3	21.3	21.7	4
France	63.4	211.2	298.4	358.4	394.4	400.9	59
Germany[1]	55.0	138.6	145.1	145.4	161.2	162.6	19
Italy	2.1	6.6	0.0	0.0	0.0	0.0	0
Netherlands	4.0	3.7	3.3	3.8	3.7	3.8	1
Slovenia[2]	0.0	4.0	4.4	4.5	4.5	5.0	1
Spain	5.2	28.0	51.6	52.7	58.9	60.5	9
Sweden	25.3	55.8	64.8	66.4	54.1	65.8	11
Switzerland	12.9	20.1	22.4	23.7	23.7	25.5	5
United Kingdom	32.3	53.8	58.7	80.6	81.7	85.6	31
Eastern Europe	**90.7**	**200.3**	**251.3**	**240.9**	**265.7**	**277.3**	**67**
Bulgaria	5.9	12.4	13.5	16.1	17.3	182	4
Former Czechoslovakia	4.3	11.9	23.4	N.A.	N.A	N.A.	N.A
Czech Republic	N.A.	N.A.	N.A.	11.6	12.9	14.0	6
Slovakia	N.A.	N.A.	N.A.	10.8	13.1	16.2	6
Hungary	0.0	6.1	13.0	13.3	13.5	13.4	4
Former USSR	69.3	170.0	201.3	N.A.	N.A.	N.A.	N.A.
Armenia	N.A.	N.A.	N.A.	0.0	1.8	2.0	1
Kazakhstan	N.A.	N.A.	N.A.	0.1	0.0	0.0	0
Lithuania	N.A.	N.A.	N.A.	10.6	8.4	11.4	2
Russia	N.A.	N.A.	N.A.	94.3	122.5	125.4	30
Ukraine	N.A.	N.A.	N.A.	67.0	71.1	71.7	13
Romania	N.A.	N.A.	N.A.	0.0	5.2	5.0	1
Middle East	**0.0**	**0.0**	**0.0**	**0.0**	**0.0**	**0.0**	**0**
Africa	**0.0**	**5.5**	**8.4**	**11.3**	**13.0**	**10.7**	**2**
South Africa	0.0	5.5	8.4	11.3	13.0	10.7	2
Far East and Oceania	**92.6**	**198.2**	**279.9**	**393.6**	**464.7**	**486.5**	**101**
China	N.A.	N.A.	N.A.	12.4	16.0	16.7	7
India	2.7	4.7	5.6	6.5	14.1	18.2	14
Japan	78.7	149.7	192.2	276.7	293.8	309.0	54
Korea, South	3.3	15.8	50.2	63.7	103.5	106.5	18
Pakistan	0.1	0.3	0.4	0.5	0.4	2.0	2
Taiwan	7.8	27.8	31.6	33.9	37.0	34.1	6
World total[3]	**684.4**	**1,425.7**	**1,905.1**	**2,206.0**	**2,434.2**	**2,520.7**	**439**

Note: Net generation; does not include energy consumed by the generating unit. 1. Data before 1995 includes both the former East Germany and West Germany. 2. Data before 1995 refers to the former Yugoslavia. 3. Totals include other countries not shown separately. **Source:** Energy Information Administration, *International Energy Annual, 2001* (2003) and International Atomic Energy Agency, *Nuclear Power Reactors in the World* (2003).

The Global Military Situation

With the end of the cold war, the world entered a period of demilitarization marked by steady declines in global military spending and the ranks of active-duty military personnel. Beginning in 2001, however, several factors contributed to modest growth in overall defense spending that was expected to accelerate in succeeding years. This new phase in global military affairs was signaled by the U.S. commitment to strengthening what the administration of President George W. Bush characterized as an aging, underinvested armed forces; the rise in international terrorism and antiterrorist campaigns; the wars in Afghanistan and later Iraq; and ongoing regional conflicts.

According to the London-based International Institute for Strategic Studies (IISS), global defense spending in 2001 totaled $835.2 billion—an increase of 1.1 percent over the $825.7 billion spent in 2000. As a percentage of national gross domestic product (GDP), the 2001 figure represented 3.5 percent of the global average, roughly unchanged from 2000. As a matter of total spending and percentage of GDP, the 2001 figures were still well below the peaks of 1985 ($1.26 trillion and 6.7 percent), before the demise of the Soviet Union and Communist bloc.

The ranks of the world's active-duty military personnel continued to decline in 2001, reflecting economic pressures on many governments and the continuing shift from strategic reliance on conventional forces. At the end of 2001, according to the IISS, active-duty military personnel totaled 20.4 million worldwide, down from 22.2 million the year before and some 28 million in 1985.

The latest worldwide totals, however, conceal notable regional differences and shifts in military priorities. Strategic interventions on the part of the United States and NATO allies; concern over the spread of chemical, biological, and nuclear weapons; antiterrorist initiatives; and local conflicts yielded a major redistribution of military resources—even before the 2003 Iraq War.

The United States led the military buildup with 39 percent of global spending in 2001. U.S. defense spending exceeded $322 billion—up 6 percent from 2000—and represented 3.2 percent of GDP (up fractionally). The ranks of active-duty U.S. military rose slightly to 1.37 million.

As a candidate for the U.S. presidency in 2000, President Bush had advocated a modernization of U.S. defense forces, better wages for military personnel, and a higher standard of readiness. The terrorist attacks of September 11, 2001, and Bush's declaration of war against global terrorism at once reinforced those priorities and marked a major shift in national strategic policy. The war on terrorism would be the cornerstone of U.S. foreign relations and international diplomacy, as well as the guiding principle of its military affairs. The U.S. action in Afghanistan and heightened military readiness everywhere forced budget increases of tens of billions of dollars annually, contributing to a return to deficit spending. The 2003 war on Iraq was financed by Congressionally approved off-budget funding that also ran into tens of billions of dollars.

Nuclear weapons aside, naval strength remains a cornerstone of U.S. military superiority. The nation's 370,000 Navy personnel and fleet of 126 "principal surface combatants" (surface ships with 1,000 tonnes of displacement and non-defensive weapon systems) far exceed those of any other nation. The largest area of new military investment, however, remains aviation, with airpower procurements reaching $62 billion in 2001.

Collectively reluctant to follow the U.S. lead in 2001, the European NATO nations decreased military spending in 2001. Their combined outlay dropped 4.4 percent from 2000, to $165.4 billion. Active-duty armed forces declined by about 100,00 (4 percent), to 2.3 million.

The non-NATO European nations, excluding Russia, reduced defense spending by more than 10 percent (to a combined $23.2 billion), while increasing military personnel slightly to 1.15 million. The notable exception to both trends was Russia, which increased its 2001 defense outlay by more than 20 percent over the previous year, to $63.8 billion, while pursuing President Vladimir Putin's goal of reducing the nation's military personnel by up to 20 percent by 2005.

In other regions of the world, political developments and ongoing security issues fueled rises in military commitment. In the Middle East and North Africa, the prospect of U.S. action in Afghanistan and a heightened sense of alert in Iran, Saudi Arabia, and elsewhere contributed to an 11.4 percent increase in defense expenditure in 2001, to $66.7 billion.

In Central and South Asia combined national spending on defense declined in 2001, despite the war brewing in Afghanistan. Economic recession and an easing of political violence in Sri Lanka and elsewhere yielded an aggregate decrease of some $850 million (3.7 percent) to $22.1 billion.

In East Asia and Australasia, relatively removed from the post-September 11 antiterrorist campaign, estimated military spending decreased 7.9 percent in 2001, to $132 billion. Ongoing tensions between North and South Korea and between China and Taiwan had forced sharp increases in previous years. In Central America, South America and the Caribbean, economic difficulties squeezed defense spending, which declined more than 10 percent in 2001, to just over $32 billion.

Strategic Missile Forces and Nuclear Stockpiles in the Major Nuclear Powers, 2001

Country	ICBMs[1]	SLBMs/ SSBNs[2]	Estimated Total Deployed Strategic Nuclear Warheads
United States	550	432/18	6,500
Russia	740	280/17	5,600
China	20+	12/1	200–250
France	—	64/4	470
Great Britain	—	58/4	190
Total	**1,300+**	**846/44**	**13,000**

1. Intercontinental Ballistic Missiles. 2. Submarine-Launched Ballistic Missiles and nuclear-fueled ballistic-missile submarines.
Source: *The Military Balance, 2001/2002,* The International Institute for Strategic Studies; Center for Strategic and International Studies; Natural Resources Defense Council.

Defense Expenditures and Military Personnel, by Country, 2001

Country	Defense Expenditures			Military Personnel ('000s)		
	Total (millions)[1]	Per Capita[1]	Percent of GDP	Active	Reserve	Paramilitary
North America						
Canada	7,745	250	1.1	56.8	35.4	9.3
United States	322,365	1,128	3.2	1,367.7	1,200.6	53.0
NATO Europe						
Belgium	3,017		293	1.3	100.5	n.a.
Czech Republic	1,167	113	2.2	53.6	n.a.	5.6
Denmark	2,409	454	1.5	21.4	64.9	n.a.
France	32,909	553	2.6	273.7	419.0	100.7
Germany	26,902	328	1.5	308.4	363.5	n.a.
Greece	5,517	520	4.8	159.2	291.0	4.0
Hungary	909	92	1.8	33.8	90.3	14.0
Italy	20,966	365	2.0	230.4	65.2	252.2
Netherlands	6,257	394	1.7	50.4	32.2	5.2
Norway	2,967	659	1.8	26.7	222.0	n.a.
Poland	3,408	88	2.0	206.0	406.0	22.0
Portugal	2,226	223	2.0	43.6	210.9	46.4
Spain	6,938	174	1.2	143.5	328.5	71.2
Turkey	7,219	107	5.0	515.1	378.7	150.0
United Kingdom	34,714	583	2.5	211.4	247.1	n.a.
Non-NATO Europe						
Albania	106	34	2.6	27.0	n.a.	13.5
Armenia	637	168	6.5	42.0	210.0	1.0
Austria	1,471	182	0.8	34.6	72.0	n.a.
Azerbaijan	833	103	3.7	72.1	575.5	15.0
Belarus	1,960	194	2.2	82.9	289.5	110.0
Bosnia	141	34	2.6	27.0	n.a.	13.5
Bulgaria	365	46	2.8	77.3	303.0	34.0
Croatia	512	109	2.6	58.3	140.0	10.0
Cyprus	315	350	3.6	10.0	60.0	0.8
Finland	1,432	275	1.2	32.3	485.0	3.1
Ireland	623	164	0.5	10.5	14.8	n.a.
Romania	969	43	2.5	103.0	470.0	75.9
Russia	63,684	440	4.3	977.1	2,400.0	409.1
Serbia-Montenegro	609	58	6.3	105.5	400.0	93.0
Slovakia	386	71	2.0	33.0	20.0	4.7
Slovenia	277	139	1.5	7.6	61.0	4.5
Sweden	3,898	443	1.9	33.9	262	35.6
Switzerland	2,840	394	1.2	26.8	351.2	n.a.
Ukraine	4,899	100	2.2	303.8	1,000.0	116.6
Middle East and North Africa						
Algeria	3,149	102	6.3	124.0	150.0	181.2
Bahrain	364	520	4.8	11.0	n.a.	10.2
Egypt	4,318	62	4.7	443.0	254.0	325.0
Iran	4,698	66	5.8	513.0	350.0	40.0
Iraq	1,372	58	9.3	424.0	650.0	43.0
Israel	10,375	1,673	9.5	163.5	425.0	8.0
Jordan	740	145	8.5	100.2	35.0	10.0
Kuwait	5,029	2,514	12.1	15.5	23.7	5.0
Lebanon	576	160	3.5	71.8	n.a.	13.0
Libya	546	1.1	4.1	76.0	40.0	0.5
Morocco	1,315	43	4.2	198.5	150.0	48.0
Oman	2,831	1,089	14.4	43.4	n.a.	4.4
Qatar	1,243	2,072	7.1	12.3	n.a.	n.a.
Saudi Arabia	24,266	1,156	14.1	201.2	n.a.	16.0
Syria	1,884	114	10.9	321.0	354.0	108.0
Tunisia	377	39	1.9	35.0	n.a.	12.0
UAE	3,070	1,137	4.6	65.0	n.a.	1.0
Yemen	531	28	8.1	54.0	40.0	70.0
Central and Southern Asia						
Afghanistan	245	11	12.2	n.a.	n.a.	n.a.
Bangladesh	639	5	1.4	137.0	n.a.	63.2

Country	Defense Expenditures: Total (millions)[1]	Per Capita[1]	Percent of GDP	Military Personnel ('000s): Active	Reserve	Paramilitary
India	14,167	14	2.9	1,263.0	535.0	1089.7
Kazakhstan	1,274	79	1.3	64.0	237.0	34.5
Pakistan	2,395	17	4.4	620.0	513.0	288.0
Sri Lanka	786	41	5.1	121.0	4.2	88.6
Uzbekistan	1,764	70	2.6	52.0	n.a.	20.0
East Asia and Australasia						
Australia	6,752	350	1.9	50.7	21.3	1.0
Brunei	279	833	5.5	5.9	0.7	3.8
Cambodia	188	14	5.8	140.0	n.a.	67.0
China	46,049	36	4.0	2,310.0	550.0	1,500.0
Indonesia	860	4	0.6	297.0	400.0	195.0
Japan	39,513	310	1.0	239.8	47.4	12.3
Korea, North	2,049	91	11.6	1,082.0	4,700.0	189.0
Korea, South	11,165	237	2.7	683.0	4,500.0	4.5
Malaysia	3,249	144	3.8	100.5	42.8	20.1
Myanmar	1,088	22	2.4	344.0	n.a.	100.3
New Zealand	664	175	1.4	9.2	5.5	n.a.
Philippines	1,065	14	1.5	107.0	131.0	44.0
Singapore	4,280	1,044	5.1	60.5	312.5	94.0
Taiwan	10,432	472	3.7	370.0	1,657.5	26.7
Thailand	1,831	29	1.7	306.0	200.0	104.0
Vietnam	2,351	30	7.2	484.0	3,000.0	40.0
Caribbean and Central America						
Cuba	735	66	4.1	46.0	39.0	26.5
El Salvador	165	26	1.2	16.8	11.0	12.0
Guatemala	186	16	0.9	31.4	35.0	19.0
Haiti	40	5	1.1	3.0	n.a.	5.3
Honduras	96	15	1.5	8.3	60.0	6.0
Mexico	5,733	57	0.9	192.8	300.0	11.0
Panama	132	46	1.3	n.a.	n.a.	11.8
South America						
Argentina	4,408	118	1.7	70.1	n.a.	31.2
Bolivia	135	16	1.7	31.5	n.a.	37.1
Brazil	10,511	61	2.1	287.6	1,115.0	385.6
Chile	2,841	181	4.4	87.5	50.0	34.7
Colombia	2,861	67	3.5	158.0	60.7	104.6
Ecuador	507	39	2.9	59.5	100.0	0.3
Paraguay	76	14	1.1	18.6	164.5	14.8
Peru	896	34	1.7	100.0	188.0	77.0
Uruguay	352	103	2.0	23.9	n.a.	0.9
Venezuela	1,896	77	1.5	82.3	8.0	23.0
Sub-Saharan Africa						
Angola	1,470	109	17.0	130.5	n.a.	15.0
Botswana	203	127	3.8	9.0	n.a.	1.0
Cameroon	120	8	1.3	22.1	n.a.	9.0
Congo	80	26	3.0	10.0	n.a.	2.0
Dem. Rep. of Congo	392	7	8.9	81.4	n.a.	n.a.
Eritrea	173	45	20.9	171.9	120.0	n.a.
Ethiopia	580	9	9.8	252.5	n.a.	n.a.
Gabon	120	93	2.4	4.7	n.a.	2.0
Ghana	34	2	0.7	7.0	n.a.	n.a.
Kenya	308	10	3.1	24.4	n.a.	5.0
Nigeria	516	4	1.3	78.5	n.a.	82.0
Rwanda	98	12	5.8	70.0	n.a.	9.0
South Africa	1,829	41	1.7	61.5	89.2	5.5
Sudan	588	18	4.3	117.0	n.a.	7.0
Tanzania	140	4	1.6	27.0	80.0	1.4
Uganda	126	5	2.2	55	n.a.	1.8
Zimbabwe	267	23	2.9	39.0	n.a.	21.8
Total, World	**835,242**	**226**	**3.5**	**20,415.7**	**34,156.4**	**7,839.4**

1. In constant (2001) U.S. dollars.
Source: *The Military Balance, 2002/2003,* The International Institute for Strategic Studies. Reprinted by permission.

▶NUCLEAR AND CHEMICAL WEAPONS

The demise of the Soviet Union and compliance with disarmament agreements have resulted in large-scale reductions in the global nuclear arsenal. Although the precise size of national nuclear stockpiles and number of deployment vehicles remain official secrets, treaty compliance protocols and estimates from a variety of sources provide some reliable figures for the major nuclear powers. The arsenals of more recent members of the nuclear-weapons "community," such as Israel, India and Pakistan, are less known. By common estimates, the total number of nuclear warheads in the world declined by 100 percent in about 15 years—from approximately 70,000 in the mid-1980s to fewer than 35,000 by 2001-02.

Moreover, less than half of the world's warhead stockpile is operational. The five major nuclear powers—the United States, Russia, China, France and Great Britain—had a combined 13,000 deployed nuclear warheads in 2001. The U.S. accounted for a reported 6,500 of these, and Russia accounted for an estimated 5,600, down 4,600 from three years earlier.

The first years of the new century brought notable progress and changes in the course of global nuclear disarmament. The destruction of stockpiles in Ukraine, Belarus and Kazakhstan, mandated by treaty, was completed by year-end 2001. The United States and Russia, meanwhile, began SALT III talks in 2000, shortly after approval by the Duma (Russian parliament) of SALT II. But the U.S. still had not approved SALT II, which would reduce the deployed missile stockpiles of both nations to 3,500 by 2007, and had rejected the Comprehensive Test Ban Treaty (CTBT), which would prohibit nuclear testing.

The direction of nuclear disarmament took a new turn in 2001 with the installation of the Bush administration. To protect against future attack by outlaw nuclear nations, Bush called for the development of a space-based national missile defense (NMD) system. China, Russia, and even European allies expressed grave misgivings, fearing that such an initiative could undermine international stability and risk starting a new arms race. Building NMD, moreover, would violate the 1972 ABM treaty, the cornerstone of cold-war arms control.

Bush openly disavowed the ABM treaty in 2001, calling it a relic of the cold war, and the lack of U.S. interest in rescuing SALT II raised further questions about Bush's commitment to the spirit and goals of nuclear disarmament. The administration's strategy of leapfrogging Salt II and ABM, however, became clear in 2002, as it reached agreement with Russia on what Bush called "the most dramatic nuclear arms reduction in history." The Treaty of Moscow, called for a 65 percent cut in each nation's store of strategic warheads over ten years—from about 6,000 to between 1,700 and 2,200. The accord also called for mutual efforts in developing a missile defense shield. The U.S. Senate ratified the treaty in March 2003 and the Russian Duma in May.

At the same time, however, new threats to national security in 2003 led the Pentagon to begin discussing the prospect of developing a new stockpile of "low-yield" nuclear weapons, or "mini-nukes," and the Department of Energy proposed Congressional repeal of a nine-year ban on the development of such weapons. The first months of the year also saw a new round nuclear-capable missile tests by India and Pakistan, carried out against a backdrop of mounting political tensions.

The U.S. search for weapons of mass destruction (WMDs) in Afghanistan, the principal argument for U.S. military intervention, continued to prove fruitless months after the regime of Saddam Hussein had been defeated. In August 2003, in compliance with a longstanding international treaty, the United States began destroying its own stockpile of cold-war-era chemical weapons.

▶ARMS SALES DECLINE

According to the IISS and Congressional Research Service, the value of global arms transfer agreements fell significantly in 2001, from $40.0 billion to $26.4 billion—a drop of more than 34 percent from the peak year of 2000. The decline in weapons contracts, according to the latter organization, reflected suppressed demand due to the global economy and the economic absorption of prior purchases.

The United States remained the largest arms dealer, with some 46 percent of the world total. Still, U.S. sales of $14.2 billion were nearly $7 billion (36 percent) lower in 2001 than in 2000. Russia, the second-biggest dealer with $5.8 billion, was down $2.6 billion (31 percent). Every other major supplier—France, Germany, China and Great Britain—also showed declines.

Developing nations remained the largest market for U.S. weapons, accounting for about 60 percent of the 2001 total. The United Arab Emirates and India were the leading purchasers among developing countries Purchases by Saudi Arabia, which totaled $12.4 billion during the period 1994-97, fell to $1.7 billion for the years 1998-2001. The Bush administration reiterated its position that any arms exports to countries harboring or supporting terrorists in any way would make the exporting nation an enemy of the United States.

International Arms Sales, 1998–2001 (millions of dollars)[1]

Country	1998	% of total	1999	% of total	2000	% of total	2001	% of total
United States	$11,130	35.6%	$12,662	35.7%	$18,930	47.3%	$12,088	45.8%
Russia	2,621	8.4	4,480	12.6	8,432	21.0	5,800	22.0
France	3,603	11.5	1,600	4.5	4,263	10.6	2,900	11.0
Germany	5,460	17.5	3,840	10.8	1,444	2.9	1,000	3.8
China	1,202	3.8	2,666	7.5	624	1.6	600	2.3
Great Britain	2,184	7.0	1,387	3.9	624	1.6	400	1.5
Others	5,023	16.1	8,853	24.9	6,031	15.1	3,600	13.6
Total	**$31,222**		**$35,488**		**$40,039**		**$26,388**	

1. Value of arms transfer agreements, U.S. dollars, 2001 constant prices. **Source:** *The Military Balance, 2002/2003*, The International Institute for Strategic Studies. Reprinted by permission.

The Global Economy

(Note: for definitions of G.D.P., G.N.P., etc. see Part II, "The U.S. Economy")

During the boom years of the 1990s, the efficient and rapid movement of capital around the globe and a surging increase in world trade led many economists to believe that an integrated global economy would be a reality in the not-too-distant future. From 1983 to 1995, world output grew steadily at about 3 percent. In 1996, however, it rose to 4.0 percent, driven in large part by rapid growth in developing nations such as China (10 percent growth), Singapore and Malaysia (7-8 percent), and Chile (6 percent). The advanced economies (U.S., Japan and Germany) grew at only 2 to 3 percent, but it was capital from these wealthy nations that fueled the rapid growth of the poorer ones, especially in Asia. The 1997 Asian financial crisis resulted when growth in these countries returned to normal rates, and investors and currency speculators withdrew rapidly. The world output growth rate retreated to 2.8 percent in 1998, and the International Monetary Fund was forced to make enormous loans to keep these economies from collapse.

In the intervening years, the growth rate rebounded to a staggering 4.7 percent in 2000, but the effects of recession were already felt in 2001, as the rate dropped to 2.5 percent. In 2001, the IMF had projected an ambitious growth rate of 4.0 percent for 2003, but by April of 2003, it revised that estimate down to a more modest 3.2 percent.

G.N.P. Per Capita, by World Regions, 2001

Region	G.N.P. per Capita
South Asia	$450
Sub-Saharan Africa	460
East Asia and the Pacific	900
Middle East and North Africa	2,220
Eastern Europe and Central Asia	1,970
Latin America and the Caribbean	3,580
Western Europe, U.S. Japan, and other high-income areas	20,680

Source: The World Bank, *The World Bank Atlas 2003.*

Countries With Highest and Lowest G.N.P. Per Capita, 2001 (in U.S. dollars)

Country	Highest G.N.P. per capita	Country	Lowest G.N.P. per capita
Luxembourg	$39,840	Congo, Dem. Rep.	80
Switzerland	38,330	Burundi	100
Norway	35,630	Ethiopia	100
Japan	35,610	Liberia	140
United States	34,280	Sierra Leone	140
Denmark	30,600	Eritrea	160
Iceland	28,910	Guinea-Bissau	160
Sweden	25,400	Malawi	160
Hong Kong	25,330	Niger	180
United Kingdom	25,120	Tajikistan	180
Netherlands	24,330	Chad	200
Austria	23,940	Mozambique	210
Belgium	23,850	Burkina Faso	220
Finland	23,780	Rwanda	220
Germany	23,560	Mali	230
Ireland	22,850	Nepal	250
France1	22,730	Central African Rep.	260
Canada	21,930	Madagascar	260
Singapore	21,500	Uganda	260
Australia	19,900	Cambodia	270
Italy	19,390	Tanzania2	270
Kuwait	18,270	Togo	270
French Polynesia2	17,290	Kyrgyzstan	280
Israel	16,750	São Tomé & Principe	280
New Caledonia2	15,060	Ghana	290
		Nigeria	290

Note: Rankings based on countries reporting GNP per capita to The World Bank. Does not include countries for which GNP per capita has been estimated. If estimated data were included Lichtenstein would be ranked 2nd, Bermuda 6th, the Cayman Islands 9th, San Marino 11th, and Monaco 15th. 1. Includes French territories in the Caribbean. 2. Data for 2000. 3. Mainland only. **Source:** *The World Bank Atlas 2003.*

World G.N.P. Per Capita, by Type of Economy, 2001

More than 75 percent of the world's 6.1 billion people live in areas where per capita GNP is less than $2,975 according to these World Bank statistics, while only 15 percent live in economies whose GNP per capita is over $9,206.

Type of Economy (Number of Economies)	Population	G.N.P. per Capita
High-income (52)	957,000,000	$26,510
Upper-middle (38)	503,600,000	4,550
Lower-middle (54)	2,163,500,000	1,230
Low-income (63)	2,505,900,000	430
Total (207)	**6,130,100,000**	**5,120**

Source: The World Bank, *The World Bank Atlas 2002.*

Change in World Economic Output, 1983-2003

Category	Annual percent change 1983–92	1995	2000	2003[1]
World Total	**3.4%**	**3.6%**	**4.7%**	**3.2%**
Advanced economies	**3.3**	**2.7**	**3.9**	**1.9**
United States	3.4	2.7	4.1	2.2
European Union	2.6	2.4	3.4	1.1
Japan	3.9	1.6	2.2	0.8
Other economies	4.7	5.0	5.3	2.5
Developing countries	**4.7**	**6.1**	**5.7**	**5.0**
Africa	2.0	2.9	3.0	3.9
Developing Asia	7.3	9.0	6.7	6.3
Middle East, Malta, and Turkey	3.4	4.3	5.8	5.1
Western Hemisphere	2.3	1.7	4.0	1.5
Countries in transition	**–0.4**	**–1.5**	**6.6**	**4.0**
Central & Eastern Europe	—	5.5	3.8	3.4
Commonwealth of Independent States and Mongolia	—	–5.5	8.3	4.4
Russia	—	–4.2	9.0	4.0

Note: Output is the value of production minus the cost of inputs by all businesses. 1. Projection. **Source:** International Monetary Fund, *World Economic Outlook*, , April, 2003

▶THE HIERARCHY OF NATIONS

Most contemporary analyses of the global economy begin with the assumption that the nations of the world are divided into two basic categories, developed and developing. The developed ones are those with the highest G.N.P. figures, and are characterized by high per capita income, low rates of population growth and illiteracy, as well as having a low proportion of their labor force in agriculture and/or mining.

The wealthiest nations are at the center of the global economy and are responsible for promoting international trade, for helping to finance development in the poorer countries, and for maintaining a stable economic world. They attempt to do this through several organizations including:

Group of Seven (G-8): a loosely knit group of the largest economic powers who meet once a year to discuss policy in what has become a well-publicized media event. **Members:** Canada, France, Germany, Italy, Japan, Russia, U.K., U.S.

Organization of Economic Cooperation and Development (OECD) HQ: 2 rue André Pascal, F-75775 Paris Cedex 16, France. OECD Washington Center, 2001 L St. NW, Washington D.C. 20036. **www.oecdwash.org.** Estab. 1961, "... to help member countries promote economic growth, employment, and improved standards of living through the coordination of policy (and) ... to help promote the sound and harmonious development of the world economy and improve the lot of the developing countries, particularly the poorest." **Members (30):** Australia, Austria, Belgium, Canada, Czech Republic, Denmark, Finland, France, Germany, Greece, Hungary, Iceland, Ireland, Italy, Japan, Luxembourg, Mexico, Netherlands, New Zealand, Norway, Poland, Portugal, Slovakia, South Korea, Spain, Sweden, Switzerland, Turkey, U.K., U.S.

Net Foreign Direct Investment in Developing Countries, 1990-2001

Region and country	Billions of U.S. dollars 1990	1995	1998	1999	2000	2001
All developing countries	**$24.1**	**$105.4**	**$155.0**	**$185.4**	**$166.7**	**$171.7**
By region						
East Asia and the Pacific	$11.1	$52.0	$61.0	$56.0	$52.1	$48.9
Latin America and the Caribbean	8.2	30.7	57.9	90.4	75.1	69.3
Europe and Central Asia	1.1	17.0	20.9	26.5	28.5	30.1
Sub-Saharan Africa	0.8	3.5	4.8	8.0	6.7	13.8
South Asia	0.5	2.9	4.4	3.1	3.1	4.1
Middle East and North Africa	2.5	-0.7	5.9	1.5	1.2	5.4
10 leading nations						
China	$3.5	$35.8	$45.0	$38.8	$38.4	$44.2
Mexico	2.6	9.5	10.2	11.8	13.3	24.7
Brazil	1.0	4.9	24.0	32.7	32.8	22.6
South Africa	N.A	N.A	N.A	N.A	N.A	7.2
Poland	0.1	3.7	5.5	7.3	9.3	5.7
Czech Republic	0.2	N.A	N.A	5.1	4.6	4.9
Chile	0.6	3.0	4.8	9.2	3.7	4.5
Thailand	2.4	2.1	6.8	6.2	3.4	3.8
Venezuela	0.4	N.A	N.A	3.3	4.5	3.4
India	N.A	N.A	N.A	N.A	N.A	3.4

Note: Developing countries includes countries in transition. **Source:** The World Bank, *Global Development Finance* (2003)

Total External Debt by Region and Nation, 1970-2002 (billions of dollars)

Region and nation	1970	1980	1990	2000	2001	2002
All developing countries	**$70.2**	**$579.6**	**$1,421.6**	**$2,362.6**	**$2,332.1**	**$2,384.2**
By Region						
East Asia and the Pacific	8.6	64.6	239.0	497.4	504.1	509.5
Latin America and the Caribbean	32.6	257.4	475.4	782.9	764.9	789.4
Europe and Central Asia	5.0	75.6	217.9	503.6	497.8	511.8
Sub-Saharan Africa	6.9	60.8	176.9	211.4	203.0	204.4
South Asia	12.3	37.8	129.5	165.1	161.7	166.8
Middle East and North Africa	4.8	83.4	182.9	202.1	200.6	202.3
10 Most Indebted Nations, 2001						
Brazil	5.7	71.5	120.0	238.8	226.4	N.A.
China	N.A.	N.A.	55.3	145.7	170.1	N.A.
Mexico	7.0	57.4	104.4	158.5	158.3	N.A.
Russia	N.A.	N.A.	59.3	160.1	152.6	N.A.
Argentina	5.8	27.2	62.2	145.9	136.7	N.A.
Indonesia	4.5	20.9	69.9	144.1	135.7	N.A.
Turkey	2.7	19.1	49.4	118.3	115.1	N.A.
India	8.4	20.7	83.6	99.1	97.3	N.A.
Thailand	1.0	8.3	28.1	79.7	67.4	N.A.
Poland	N.A.	N.A.	49.4	63.3	62.4	N.A.

Note: Developing countries includes countries in transtition. **Source:** The World Bank, *Global Development Finance* (2003).

U.S. Merchandise Trade Partners, 2002 (millions of dollars)

Country	U.S. exports to	U.S. imports from	U.S. net balance of trade
TOTAL[1]	**$681,874**	**$1,164,746**	**$-482,872**
Belgium and Luxembourg	13,623	10,099	3,524
France	18,869	28,273	-9,404
Germany	26,024	62,477	-36,453
Italy	9,810	24,198	-14,388
Netherlands	18,108	9,798	8,310
United Kingdom	32,091	40,467	-8,376
Canada	160,895	211,761	-50,866
Japan	49,664	121,428	-71,764
Australia	12,760	6,446	6,314
Brazil	12,266	15,781	-3,515
Mexico	97,282	135,502	-38,220
Venezuela	3,966	15,093	-11,127
China	22,038	125,189	-103,151
Hong Kong	12,539	9,330	3,209
South Korea	21,755	35,570	-13,815
Singapore	15,973	14,789	1,184
Taiwan	17,886	32,152	-14,266

1. Includes other countries not shown separately. **Source:** U.S. Dept. of Commerce, *Survey of Current Business*, July, 2003.

The International Monetary Fund (I.M.F.) and The World Bank Both of these organizations are specialized agencies of the United Nations (see the separate section on the U.N. below) charged with making loans to nations having trouble with debt (I.M.F.) or for long-term growth and development among poorer nations (World Bank).

I.M.F. Classification of Countries

Advanced economies (28): These include the seven largest countries by G.D.P., all the other members of the E.U., the four "tigers" of Asia (Singapore, South Korea, Hong Kong, and Taiwan), and Australia, New Zealand and Israel.

Countries in transition (28): These are almost all industrialized countries that are moving from a centrally planned economy to one based on free market principles. All of the former republics of the Soviet Union (including Kazakhstan and Ukraine), the nations of central and eastern Europe (including Poland, the Czech Republic, and Estonia) and Mongolia are included.

Developing countries (127): These include the burgeoning economies of China, India, Brazil and Chile as well as the poorest nations of sub-Saharan Africa (Mozambique, Ethiopia, Niger, for example) and Asia (Bangladesh, Cambodia, Vietnam).

World's Leading Exporters and Importers in Merchandise Trade, 2001

Rank and country	Value 2001 (billions)	Share of world trade	Change in value, 2000-01
EXPORTERS			
1. United States	$730.8	11.9 %	-6%
2. Germany	570.8	9.3	3
3. Japan	403.5	6.6	-16
4. France	321.8	5.2	-1
5. United Kingdom	273.1	4.4	-4
6. China	266.2	4.3	7
7. Canada	259.9	4.2	-6
8. Italy	241.1	3.9	0
9. Netherlands	229.5	3.7	-2
10. Hong Kong	191.1	3.1	-6
11. Belgium	179.7	1.8	-5
12. Mexico	158.5	1.6	-5
13. South Korea	150.4	1.5	-13
14. Taiwan	122.5	1.3	-17
15. Singapore	121.8	1.2	-12
16. Spain	109.7	1.8	-5
17. Russia	103.1	1.7	-2
18. Malaysia	87.9	1.4	-10
19. Ireland	82.8	1.3	7
20. Switzerland	82.1	1.3	1
21. Sweden	75.3	1.2	-14
22. Austria	70.3	1.1	4
23. Saudi Arabia[1]	68.2	1.1	-12
24. Thailand	65.1	1.1	-6
25. Australia	63.4	1.0	-1
26. Brazil	58.2	0.9	6
27. Norway	57.9	0.9	-3
28. Indonesia	56.3	0.9	-9
29. Denmark	51.9	0.8	1
30. India	43.6	0.7	3
World Total[2]	**$6,155.0**	**100.0%**	**-4%**

Rank and country	Value 2001 (billions)	Share of world trade	Change in value, 2000-01
IMPORTERS			
1. United States	$1,180.2	18.3 %	-6%
2. Germany	492.8	7.7	-1
3. Japan	349.1	5.4	-8
4. United Kingdom	331.8	5.2	-3
5. France	325.8	5.1	-2
6. China	243.6	3.8	8
7. Italy	232.9	3.6	-2
8. Canada	227.2	3.5	-7
9. Netherlands	207.3	3.2	-5
10. Hong Kong	202.0	3.1	-6
11. Mexico	176.2	2.7	-4
12. Belgium	168.7	2.6	-5
13. South Korea	141.1	2.2	-12
14. Spain	142.7	2.2	-9
15. Singapore	116.0	1.8	-14
16. Taiwan	107.3	1.7	-23
17. Switzerland	84.1	1.3	1
18. Austria	74.4	1.2	3
19. Malaysia	74.1	1.2	-10
20. Australia	63.9	1.0	-11
21. Sweden	62.6	1.0	-14
22. Thailand	62.1	1.0	0
23. Brazil	58.3	0.9	0
24. Russia	53.9	0.8	20
25. Ireland	50.7	0.8	-1
26. Poland	50.3	0.8	3
27. India	49.6	0.8	-3
28. Denmark	45.4	0.7	0
29. United Arab Emirates	41.7	0.6	9
30. Turkey	40.6	0.6	-26
World Total[2]	**$6,441.3**	**100.0%**	**-4%**

1. Estimate. 2. Includes significant re-exports or imports for re-export and other countries not shown separately.
Source: World Trade Organization, International Trade Statistics 2002 (2003). www.wto.org

▶INTERNATIONAL FINANCE–BASIC CONCEPTS

Exchange rates Because countries have their own currencies, trade between them also involves exchanging or trading currencies. The *exchange rate* between currencies represents the ratio at which they can be exchanged or the price of one currency in terms of the other. For example, if the exchange rate between the British pound and the U.S. dollar is $1.50, then one British pound can be purchased at that price.

The exchange rate for almost all world currencies is now determined by the market. The exchange rate of a currency rises or appreciates when the demand for it rises and/or the supply falls. This may happen because foreign buyers want to buy more of a nation's goods or because consumers within the country decide to buy fewer imports. It may also happen because the country reduces its money supply. Finally, the central banks of countries can manipulate their exchange rates slightly by buying and selling their own and other currencies (see also Part II: "The Federal Reserve").

The gold standard Before World War I, exchange rates for world currencies were fixed, artificially, by tying them to a certain amount of gold—$32, for example, might equal one ounce of gold. Central banks would then buy and sell gold in order to equalize supply and demand for the currencies and maintain the fixed exchange rates. For this reason, the central banks maintained enormous gold stockpiles, like the one the U.S. had at Fort Knox. People therefore referred to currencies as being "backed by gold." Long-term changes in trading relationships and in the demand for various currencies eventually made the fixed exchange rates of the gold standard impossible to support. In 1944, the Bretton Woods agreement established the U.S. dollar as the world standard, but the U.S. still backed its dollars with gold and used gold to settle its debts. After 1973, the U.S. abandoned that role, and most of the world's exchange rates were set by the market.

Balance of payments The balance of payments account is the list of transactions between a country and the rest of the world. This account has three parts: *the current account:* a record of exports and imports of goods (e.g. oil, clothing) and services (e.g. tourism); *the capital account:* a record of exports and imports of assets such as bank loans and corporate stock purchases; and *the official-reserves account:* a record of a country's sales and purchases of official reserve assets at the central bank.

Balance of trade When a country imports goods from another country worth more than the value of its exports to it, there is said to be a deficit in the balance of trade between the countries.

Foreign Exchange Rates: Currency Units Per Dollar, 1975–2003

Country/currency	1975	1990	1995	2000	2001	2002	2003[1]
Australia/dollar	0.77	1.28	1.35	1.72	1.93	1.84	1.53
Austria/schilling[2]	17.44	11.33	10.08	N.A.	N.A.	N.A.	N.A.
Belgium/franc[2]	36.80	33.42	29.47	N.A.	N.A.	N.A.	N.A.
Brazil/real	N.A.	N.A.	N.A.	1.83	2.35	2.92	3.00
Canada/dollar	1.02	1.17	1.37	1.49	1.55	1.57	1.41
China/yuan	N.A.	4.79	8.37	8.28	8.28	8.28	8.28
Denmark/krone	5.75	6.19	5.60	8.10	8.33	7.89	6.84
European Community/euro	N.A.	N.A.	0.78	1.08	1.12	1.05	0.92
Finland/markka[2]	3.67	3.83	4.38	N.A.	N.A.	N.A.	N.A.
France/franc[2]	4.29	5.45	4.99	N.A.	N.A.	N.A.	N.A.
Germany/deutsche mark[2]	2.46	1.62	1.43	N.A.	N.A.	N.A.	N.A.
Greece/drachma[2]	32.30	158.59	231.68	365.92	N.A.	N.A.	N.A.
Hong Kong/dollar	4.94	7.79	7.74	7.79	7.80	7.80	7.80
India/rupee	8.40	17.49	32.41	45.00	47.22	48.63	45.88
Ireland/pound[2]	0.45	0.60	0.62	N.A.	N.A.	N.A.	N.A.
Italy/lira[2]	653.10	1,198.27	1,629.45	N.A.	N.A.	N.A.	N.A.
Japan/yen	296.79	145.00	93.96	107.80	121.57	125.22	117.58
Malaysia/ringgit	2.40	2.70	2.51	3.80	3.80	3.80	3.80
Mexico/peso	12.64	2,813.00	6.45	9.46	9.34	9.66	10.86
Netherlands/guilder[2]	2.53	1.82	1.60	N.A.	N.A.	N.A.	N.A.
New Zealand/dollar	0.82	1.68	1.52	2.19	2.38	2.15	1.71
Norway/krone	5.23	6.26	6.34	8.81	9.00	7.98	7.65
Portugal/escudo[2]	25.51	142.70	149.88	N.A.	N.A.	N.A.	N.A.
Singapore/dollar	2.37	1.81	1.42	1.72	1.79	1.79	1.74
South Africa/rand	0.74	2.59	3.63	6.95	8.61	10.52	7.48
South Korea/won	484.00	710.64	772.69	1,130.90	1,292.01	1,250.31	1,168.00
Spain/peseta[2]	57.43	101.96	124.64	N.A.	N.A.	N.A.	N.A.
Sri Lanka/rupee	6.98	40.08	51.05	76.96	89.60	95.77	96.75
Sweden/krona	4.15	5.92	7.14	9.17	10.34	9.72	8.51
Switzerland/franc	2.58	1.39	1.18	1.69	1.69	1.56	1.42
Taiwan/dollar	38.00	26.92	26.50	31.26	33.82	34.53	34.21
United Kingdom/pound	0.45	0.56	0.64	0.65	0.69	0.67	0.63
Venezuela/bolivar	N.A.	N.A.	174.85	680.52	724.10	1,161.19	1,600.00

Note: Averages of certified noon buying rates in New York for cable transfers. 1. Figures are for Aug. 22, 2003. 2. Country converted its currency to euros as of January 3, 2001. A euro is worth 13.76 Austrian schillings, 40.34 Belgian francs, 5.95 Finnish markkas, 6.56 French francs, 1.96 German marks, 340.75 Greek drachmas, 0.79 Irish pounds, 1,936.27 Italian lire, 2.20 Netherlands guilders, 200.48 Portuguese escudos, or 166.39 Spanish pesetas. **Source:** *Federal Reserve Bulletin,* monthly.

Changes in exchange rates tend to equalize the supply and demand for currencies and the balance of trade; in the above case, the exchange rate for the first country's currency should fall relative to the second country's, reducing imports by making them more expensive and encouraging exports by making them cheaper. But this equalization may take a long time to occur since consumers and producers in the two countries must change their behavior. And central banks may want to slow the pace at which exchange rates adjust to slow the effects on trading sectors within their economies.

The balance of trade is an important issue because it indicates something about how a nation's economy is changing and, ultimately, about its competitiveness vis-à-vis other countries. A rising balance of trade deficit indicates that an economy is not able to sell its goods abroad and that consumers are favoring imports over domestically produced goods.

Over the last five years, as the economy has grown increasingly robust, the U.S. *trade deficit* has continued to widen, climbing from $19.4 billion in 1990 to $164 billion in 1998. The entire U.S. trade deficit is in the manufactured goods sector; the U.S. runs a small surplus in the services sector. U.S. exports of goods have not kept up with imports in part because the strength of the dollar makes American goods more expensive for foreign nations to buy, while people in the U.S. have more money to spend on cheaper imports.

▶GLOBAL CAPITAL MOVEMENT

The current dynamic interaction among these very disparate economies—aided greatly by the technological revolution—has set in motion an unprecedented global movement of capital from the wealthiest nations to developing ones. Because holders of capital always seek greater returns on their investments, they will put their money in economies that show potential growth;

U.S. International Trade Balance (millions of U.S. dollars) 1960–2002

	Exports		Imports		Balance		
Year	Goods[1]	Services[2]	Goods[1]	Services[2]	Goods[1]	Services[2]	Total
1960	$19,650	$6,290	$14,758	$7,674	$4,892	$-1,385	$3,508
1970	42,469	14,171	39,866	14,520	2,603	-349	2,254
1980	224,250	47,584	249,750	41,491	-25,500	6,093	-19,407
1985	215,915	73,155	338,088	72,862	-122,173	294	-121,880
1990	387,401	147,832	498,435	117,659	-111,034	30,173	-80,861
1995	575,204	218,521	749,374	139,420	-174,170	79,101	-95,069
2000	771,994	298,060	1,224,417	221,021	-452,423	77,039	-375,384
2001	718,712	288,868	1,145,927	219,472	-427,215	69,396	-357,819
2002	681,874	292,233	1,164,746	227,399	-482,872	64,834	-418,038

Note: The balance is equal to exports minus imports. 1. Adjusted, excluding military. 2. Includes some military goods.
Source: U.S. Bureau of Economic Analysis, Foreign Trade Division, *U.S. International Transactions, Table 1.* www.bea.doc.gov.

10 Largest U.S. Merchandise Imports and Exports, 1990-2002

	Volume (millions)				
Product Group	1990	1995	2000	2001	2002
TOTAL TOP TEN EXPORTS	**$213,249**	**$324,510**	**$473,256**	**$436,477**	**$407,507**
1. Electrical machinery and appliances	31,554	65,638	110,095	88,557	82,657
2. Motor vehicles	30,524	49,222	59,992	56,703	60,329
3. Transportation equipment	32,346	27,720	43,399	48,025	46,148
4. Office and ADP machines	27,766	41,947	57,595	49,404	39,744
5. Power generating machinery	15,885	22,430	34,345	36,181	34,381
6. Miscellaneous manufactured articles	20,903	28,515	35,538	35,431	33,226
7. General industrial machinery	16,032	25,148	34,455	33,748	31,839
8. Professional scientific instruments	12,601	19,372	32,326	31,274	29,210
9. Specialized machinery	15,737	24,286	32,529	27,491	25,091
10. Telecommunications equipment	9,901	20,332	32,980	29,664	24,882
TOTAL TOP TEN IMPORTS	**$258,293**	**$420,911**	**$676,962**	**$624,659**	**$643,246**
1. Motor vehicles	73,017	100,254	161,682	157,409	168,173
2. Electrical machinery and appliances	33,601	75,169	108,813	84,710	81,225
3. Office and ADP machines	26,917	62,824	92,165	75,861	76,970
4. Telecommunications equipment	22,288	34,384	70,487	62,821	66,268
5. Apparel and clothing	25,533	39,526	64,296	63,862	63,810
6. Miscellaneous manufactured articles	25,028	36,467	56,718	57,538	62,044
7. General industrial machinery	14,484	24,113	34,709	33,258	35,201
8. Power generating machinery	14,591	20,486	33,815	36,127	34,032
9. Organic chemicals	N.A.	13,325	28,563	29,626	30,213
10. Nonmetallic minerals	N.A.	N.A.	25,714	23,446	25,310

Note: In current U.S. dollars. **Source:** U.S. Dept. of Commerce, International Trade Administration, *U.S. Foreign Trade Highlights 2002* (2003). www.ita.doc.gov/td/industry/otea/usfth/aggregate/H02T22.html.

if they own or run corporations, they will look for ways to reduce the costs of manufacturing, especially labor costs, so they realize a greater profit. By investing in foreign companies or by establishing their businesses in foreign nations, the power of capital can rapidly transform the economies of poorer nations while rearranging the patterns of daily life for millions.

The increase in the total amount of private capital going overseas (*net private capital flows*) from the U.S., Japan and the E.U. nations to developing countries has exploded from $43.9 billion in 1990 to $201.5 billion in 1995, and an estimated $299 billion in 1997. Over 80 percent of it came in two categories: foreign direct investment and portfolio investment.

Foreign Direct Investment (F.D.I) is simply investment by private companies of one nation in the territory of another nation. The investment can be in an existing enterprise of the host nation or the building of new facilities for the investing foreign company (which would then be known as a multinational enterprise). The amount of money flowing from the wealthy nations to the developing ones in this way increased from $24.5 billion in 1990 to $166 billion in 2000.

According to the U.N. *World Investment Report*, total F.D.I. inflows averaged $254 bil. between 1991-96, but soared to a record high $1.4 trillion in 2000. With the decline of the U.S. stock market, that figure receded to $651 bil. in 2002. All regions of the world except Central and Eastern Europe experienced declines: North America, 71 percent; Africa, 41 percent; Latin America, 33 percent; Asia, 11 percent; E.U. countries, 4 percent.

Portfolio Investment is investing in the stocks and bonds of foreign nations. In 1990 only $5.5 billion was invested in the markets of developing nations, about 12 percent of total private capital flows. By 1996, $91.8 billion (38 percent) was so invested. In the U.S. alone the number of mutual funds investing in stocks and bonds of emerging nations grew from 3 in 1990 to over 70 in 1997. The Asian financial collapse of 1997-98 curtailed this growth quickly, as stock markets in Asia plunged by as much as 50 percent, followed by strong declines in Latin American markets.

▶INTERNATIONAL TRADE

International trade takes place because some nations have an advantage in producing certain kinds of products either because they have a comparative wealth of resources (capital, labor, natural resources) or more efficient production techniques. Even an economy with the most efficient technology has a limit on its resources, and rather than using them to produce all variety of products, it concentrates its resources on what it makes most efficiently. It then trades that good for other commodities, importing those that it produces least efficiently. As a result, all countries are better off because specialization results in the expansion of the total supply of goods, and the cost of acquiring them then falls.

Just which commodities a country will export and import depends on the relative prices of the factors used in production. A country like India has abundant labor and low wages. It therefore exports labor-intensive products such as garments. A country like Canada, which has abundant natural resources, specializes in agriculture and raw materials. Countries such as Canada and India then import goods for which the factors of production are in relatively short supply.

Of course, there are political reasons why countries do not completely specialize their production. No country, for example, wants to import all of its military equipment for fear that supplies would be cut off in the event of international conflict. Similarly, even inefficient producers, such as farmers in Japan, where land is scarce and expensive, may have political power that forces their governments to subsidize them.

U.S. Exports and Imports in Services, by Type, 1986-2002 (millions)

Category	1986	1990	1995	2000	2001	2002
EXPORTS, TOTAL	**$77,545**	**$137,232**	**$203,060**	**$283,484**	**$275,498**	**$279,495**
Travel	20,385	43,007	63,395	82,400	71,893	66,547
Passenger fares	5,582	15,298	18,909	20,687	17,926	17,046
Other transportation	15,438	22,042	26,081	29,803	28,442	29,166
Royalties and license fees	8,113	16,634	30,289	43,233	41,098	44,142
Other private services[1]	28,027	40,251	64,386	107,361	116,139	122,594
Education	3,495	5,126	7,515	10,348	11,478	12,759
Financial	3,301	4,417	7,029	15,522	15,228	15,859
Insurance	1,385	230	588	2,486	2,399	2,839
Telecommunications	1,827	2,735	3,228	3,883	4,504	4,137
Business, professional, & technical	4,813	7,752	16,078	25,318	28,611	28,799
IMPORTS, TOTAL	**$64,731**	**$98,210**	**$126,754**	**$204,665**	**$201,615**	**$205,234**
Travel	25,913	37,349	44,916	64,705	60,200	58,044
Passenger fares	6,505	10,531	14,663	24,274	22,633	19,969
Other transportation	17,766	24,966	27,034	41,425	38,682	38,527
Royalties and license fees	1,401	3,135	6,919	16,468	16,713	19,258
Other private services[1]	13,146	22,229	33,222	57,793	63,387	69,436
Education	433	658	1,125	2,034	2,269	2,466
Financial	1,769	2,475	2,472	4,564	4,049	3,665
Insurance	2,200	1,910	3,272	7,598	11,613	15,348
Telecommunications	3,253	5,583	7,305	5,428	4,756	4,180
Business, professional, & technical	1,303	2,093	4,822	8,769	10,034	10,732

1. Includes other services not shown separately.
Source: U.S. Bureau of Economic Analysis, Foreign Trade Division, *U.S. International Transactions.* www.bea.doc.gov..

Tariffs and Quotas

One way to protect a country's own producers, especially where they are inefficient compared with the international competition, is with import tariffs—taxes on goods that are produced abroad. Import tariffs raise the price of imports relative to domestic alternatives and discourage demand for the former. If one country is the sole importer or even the main importer of another's exports, it is possible that an import tariff will simply force the exporter to cut its selling price (in order to keep the price to consumers—including the tariff—from rising sharply and cutting off demand). In this case, the exporter pays virtually the whole cost of the tariff. If, on the other hand, the importer badly needs the import and there are few substitutes, raising the tariff simply raises the costs to one's own consumers. Critics of U.S. trade policy have pointed out that because Japan has become virtually the sole supplier of many consumer electronic products in the U.S., any tariffs against those products would simply raise their prices and fuel U.S. inflation.

Import quotas attempt to achieve a restriction on imports without the price rises associated with tariffs by setting direct limits on the number of items imported. So-called trade wars start when one country imposes a tariff on imports from a second country, and the latter responds with tariffs of its own against the first country. The arguments presented above about the benefits of trade have led to efforts to restrict the use of tariffs and maintain free trade, i.e. trade without any restrictions. Economists argue that unrestricted trade will always promote economic growth by forcing domestic prices to reflect world prices, thereby encouraging the efficient allocation of resources. Over the last 50 years, i.e. since the end of World War II, many of the leading nations have made a strong and continuous effort to lower or eliminate tariffs, first regionally, then around the world. The most successful regional organization has been the European Union, which has encouraged the formation of many other such alliances in all parts of the world.

Global trade has grown rapidly over the last decade, in large part because of the General Agreement on Tariffs and Trade (GATT) and its successor organization, the World Trade Organization (WTO).

GATT The General Agreement on Tariffs and Trade was first established in 1948. In an attempt to regulate the world's trade, the representatives of 23 leading nations agreed to find ways to lower tariffs, lower quotas, and to make free trade, i.e. trade without restrictions of any kind, their final goal. The United Nations provided headquarters for the group in Geneva, Switzerland. Over a period of almost 50 years the most important trading nations met regularly to discuss specific trade matters and to continue to remove restrictions from trade. Each series of negotiations called "rounds" lasted several years. By 1975 tariffs on manufactured goods had been reduced from 40 percent to 10 percent and world trade more than tripled. By the 1980s, however, the nature of world trade had changed. In 1986 the so-called Uruguay Round of GATT (now with 92 nations represented) addressed these and other issues over a period of eight years. The results—lowering of tariffs of all kind, banning quotas, and protecting copyrights and patents—have been projected to add $500 billion annually to the global economy; the E.U. nations were projected to receive $164 billion of this total, the U.S. $122 billion, Japan $275 billion. Nations at the next level of development including the former Communist-ruled ones in Eastern Europe should realize $116 billion.

World Trade Organization Potentially the most important accomplishment of the 1994 GATT Agreement was the establishment of the World Trade Organization (W.T.O.), a permanent institution with real power to oversee trade agreements, enforce trade rules, and settle disputes. When it was approved by the U.S. Congress (Jan. 1, 1995), the organization became a reality, with 110 members. The basic principles of the W.T.O., derived from the GATT negotiations are the encouragement of fair competition and increased access to markets as well as the development of trade without discrimination (MFN, "most favored nation" status, i.e. no nation will be given preferential trading terms). **HQ:** Centre William Rappard, 154 rue de Lausanne, CH-1211 Geneva 21, Switzerland. **Internet Address: www.wto.org** **Membership:** (146) Albania, Angola, Antigua and Barbuda, Argentina, Armenia, Australia, Austria, Bahrain, Bangladesh, Barbados, Belgium, Belize, Benin, Bolivia, Botswana, Brazil, Brunei Darussalam, Bulgaria, Burkina Faso, Burundi, Cameroon, Canada, Central African Republic, Chad, Chile, China, Colombia, Congo, Congo (Democratic Rep.), Costa Rica, Croatia, Cuba, Cyprus, Czech Republic, Denmark, Djibouti, Dominica, Dominican Republic, Ecuador, Egypt, El Salvador, Estonia, EU, Fiji, Finland, France, Gabon, The Gambia, Georgia, Germany, Ghana, Greece, Grenada, Guatemala, Guinea, Guinea Bissau, Guyana, Haiti, Honduras, Hong Kong, Hungary, Iceland, India, Indonesia, Ireland, Israel, Italy, Ivory Coast, Jamaica, Japan, Jordan, Kenya, Kuwait, Kyrgyzstan, Latvia, Lesotho, Liechtenstein, Lithuania, Luxembourg, Macao, Macedonia, Madagascar, Malawi, Malaysia, Maldives, Mali, Malta, Mauritania, Mauritius, Mexico, Moldova, Mongolia, Morocco, Mozambique, Myanmar, Namibia, Netherlands , New Zealand, Nicaragua, Niger, Nigeria, Norway, Oman, Pakistan, Panama, Papua New Guinea, Paraguay, Peru, Philippines, Poland, Portugal, Qatar, Romania, Rwanda, Saint Kitts & Nevis, Saint Lucia, Saint Vincent & the Grenadines, Senegal, Sierra Leone, Singapore, Slovak Republic, Slovenia, Solomon Islands, South Africa, South Korea, Spain, Sri Lanka, Suriname, Swaziland, Sweden, Switzerland, Tanzania, Taiwan, Thailand, Togo, Trinidad & Tobago, Tunisia, Turkey, Uganda, United Arab Emirates, United Kingdom, United States, Uruguay, Venezuela, Zambia, Zimbabwe. **Observers and applicants:** (29): Algeria, Andorra, Azerbaijan, Bahamas, Belarus, Bhutan, Bosnia & Herzegovina, Cambodia, Cape Verde, Equatorial Guinea, Ethiopia, Holy See, Kazakhstan, Laos, Lebanon, Nepal, Russian Federation, Samoa, São Tome & Principe, Saudi Arabia, Seychelles, Sudan, Tajikistan, Tonga, Ukraine, Uzbekistan, Vanuatu, Vietnam, Yemen. *(With the exception of the Holy See, observers must start accession negotiations within five years of becoming observers.)*

▶EUROPEAN UNION

In 1997, the 40th year since its founding, the European Union appeared successful beyond the dreams of its founders: the world's largest economic superpower, a gigantic market of over 370 million people in 15 nations with ever more countries aspiring to join. Yet, at the same time, it faced two daunting major projects: the introduction of a common currency and the inclusion of many of the countries of post-Communist east-central Europe.

Many people in government have expressed great caution, if not skepticism, about both ideas. The very notion of replacing the traditional drachma, escudo, franc, guilder, krone, lire, mark, peseta, pound and schilling with a new single currency (the "euro") has aroused emotional opposition; and more serious difficulties surround the schedule of its introduction, agreed to in the 1991 Maastricht Treaty. And while enthusiasm for membership seems high in east-central Europe, the task of integrating their relatively backward economies with those of the highly developed West still appears almost Herculean.

Origins Out of the wreckage of World War II, with generous American Marshall Plan aid after 1948, western Europe commenced reconstruction; by 1954, several "economic miracles" occurred. Yet without economic integration, the recoveries of the separate nations involved duplications, inefficiencies, diminished competition, and the threats of local gluts and shortages. A small sign of what might be achieved was Benelux, the customs union between Belgium, the Netherlands and Luxembourg, constructed even before war's end in 1944 and a going concern by 1948 despite the very unequal status of the three economies.

On May 9, 1950, France's foreign minister, Robert Schuman, proposed that German and French coal and steel production (the sinews of war) be placed under a supra-national, not intergovernmental, "high authority"; the West German chancellor, Konrad Adenauer, responded positively that very evening. By May 1952, ratification of the six-nation European Coal and Steel Community was complete, with Italy and the Benelux countries joining the French and Germans. The dramatic successes of the ECSC led the six toward broader integration, with negotiations culminating in the March 1957 Treaties of Rome which established the European Economic Community (EEC) and the European Atomic Energy Commission (Euratom).

The EEC was designed to reduce and eventually abolish all tariffs among the six; to establish a single external tariff for the Community; and to foster the free movement of not only goods but of labor and capital as well. Euratom was intended for the common peaceful development of nuclear power, though common action proved subsequently difficult to agree on. In 1958 the United Kingdom, which had refused to join the original negotiations, proposed that the EEC be expanded into an Atlantic free-trade area, but France, under her new president, Charles de Gaulle, exercised the veto. The rebuff led Britain with Portugal, Austria, Switzerland and the Scandinavian kingdoms to form in 1959 the European Free Trade Association. The EFTA's successes were real but no match for the burgeoning EEC. So in 1961 Britain sought EEC membership. But de Gaulle, fearing American influence and objecting to the special terms that Britain sought for Commonwealth countries, again exercised the veto.

At the same time, de Gaulle was pushing for agricultural integration to match the EEC's industrial unity: the huge German market beckoned for France's chronic farm surpluses, yet Germany hesitated to sacrifice her own farmers in return for cheaper food. In fact, a serious crisis impended since each of the Six had its own system of protectionist duties, farm subsidies and crop controls. But the Dutch ("Mansholt") proposals met with relatively easy and rapid agreement. The Common Agricultural Policy of 1962 eventually established a highly bureaucratized, centrally financed common market with managed prices, common duties upon imports, and subsidies for exports.

The European Community (E.C.) With agricultural integration, the stage was set for the Brussels treaty of 1965 (often called the "The Second Treaty of Rome"), which founded the European Community. The earlier three communities (ECSC, EEC and Euratom) were merged into one and were provided with a four-part structure of Commission, Council, Parliament and Court.

It was this "refounded" E.C. that the United Kingdom was at last permitted to join in 1973 (after another Gaullist veto in 1967). As in its earlier attempts, it was accompanied by Ireland, Denmark and Norway (though Norwegian voters subsequently rejected admission in a referendum). The Nine subsequently became the Twelve with the admission of Greece (1981), Spain and Portugal (1986).

Twenty years after the Brussels Treaty, with the accession of Jacques Delors as president of the European Commission, the E.C. received new impetus toward what the Treaty of Rome had envisioned: a single market free of all barriers to the free movement of goods, services, capital and labor. The first result was the Single European Act of 1987, an unwieldy compendium of almost 300 rules and directives to bring about by 1992 a "Europe without frontiers." Even a decade later, its full meaning remains unclear, although both families and giant corporations have been able to hunt for bargains across national borders, tax and interest rates have been leveled, and trans-national regional ties have developed. The abolition of capital controls in 1990 has proven decisive in the movement toward monetary union, the second result of the Delors presidency (and of the strong support given by Helmut Kohl's Germany).

The European Union

Year admitted	Member countries
1957	Belgium, France, Germany, Italy, Luxembourg, Netherlands
1973	Denmark, Ireland, United Kingdom
1981	Greece
1986	Portugal, Spain
1995	Austria, Finland, Sweden
2004 (scheduled)	Cyprus, Czech Republic, Estonia,Hungary, Latvia, Lithuania, Malta, Poland, Slovakia, Slovenia
Current Applicants	Bulgaria, Romania, Turkey

The European Union (E.U.) In December 1991, the E.C. approved its third foundational treaty, the Treaty of Maastricht. Its three "pillars" were: monetary union, common foreign and security policies, and cooperation in justice and "home affairs." The latter two "pillars" are intergovernmental, not supranational affairs, and have not been dealt with since 1991, as the E.U.'s clumsy responses to the Bosnian and Albanian crises attest.

Following the simple idea that a single market requires a single currency, the Maastricht Treaty established a three-stage (1991, 1994, 1997) creation of the *European Monetary Union* (EMU). During the first two stages, the E.U. members were to converge according to five criteria: inflation rates, interest rates, currency exchange, rate stability (variation within 2.25 percent), budget deficits (less than 3 percent of G.D.P.), and public indebtedness (a debt-to-G.D.P. ratio of less than 60 percent). During the second stage would occur the transition from central bank financing of government spending to creation of the European Central Bank. With the third stage, the European Central Bank would propose and carry out the E.U.'s monetary policies and the "euro" would circulate as "bank money"—all preparatory to the actual introduction of the monetary union.

A tone of unreality attended attempts to establish the EMU. When Danish voters rejected Maastricht in a June 1992 referendum (unanimous approval being required for the treaty to take force), the E.U., at the time still called the E.C., permitted Denmark a sort of *à la carte* membership: Denmark could ratify while opting out of the single currency (and other treaty matters). Danish voters in May 1993 thereupon reversed themselves and approved the treaty. German ratification in November 1993 brought the treaty into effect. But between those two votes, the exchange rate variation was altered from 2.25 percent to 15 percent lest the French withdraw from the pact.

It was this oddly flexible E.U. that Austria, Finland and Sweden joined on January 1, 1995. The Norwegian government had sought membership and been approved, but Norwegian voters, as they had in 1973, said no.

The European Monetary Union The EMU had a strong domestic political impact in the member states. The European Commission forecast, April 23, 1997, of 1997 member deficits, claimed that only Italy and Greece would top the permitted 3 percent; but the very same day, the I.M.F. predicted that four others would as well: Spain, Britain, France and (embarrassingly) Germany.

What permitted the E.U. finance ministers to insist (in September, 1997) that they would hold to the Maastricht timetable was an informal agreement to scrap four of the five criteria and retain only the 3 percent deficit-to-GDP ratio. On this score, Greece was the only applicant of 12 to fall short. In March 1998, the European Commission recommended, and in May the Brussels summit formally endorsed, participation in the EMU by the following countries: Austria, Belgium, Finland, France, Germany, Ireland, Italy, Luxem-

Hourly Compensation Costs in U.S. Dollars For Production Workers, Selected Countries, 1975–2001

Country	1975	1980	1985	1990	1995	2000	2001
Australia	$5.62	$8.47	$8.21	$13.24	$15.56	$14.47	$13.15
Austria	4.51	8.88	7.58	17.75	25.32	19.46	19.40
Brazil	6.41	13.11	8.97	19.17	27.62	21.59	21.04
Belgium	N.A.	N.A.	N.A.	N.A.	N.A.	3.58	3.02
Canada	5.96	8.67	10.95	15.95	16.10	16.05	15.64
Denmark	6.28	10.83	8.13	18.04	24.98	21.49	21.98
Finland	4.66	8.33	8.25	21.25	24.32	19.45	19.94
France	4.52	8.94	7.52	15.49	19.35	15.66	15.88
Germany[1]	6.29	12.21	9.50	21.81	30.27	22.99	22.86
Greece	1.69	3.73	3.66	6.76	9.06	N.A.	N.A.
Hong Kong	0.76	1.51	1.73	3.23	4.91	5.63	5.96
Ireland	3.05	6.03	5.99	11.81	13.78	12.50	13.28
Israel	2.25	3.79	4.06	8.55	10.54	12.86	13.53
Italy	4.67	8.15	7.63	17.45	16.22	14.01	13.76
Japan	3.00	5.52	6.34	12.80	23.82	22.00	19.59
Korea, South	0.32	0.96	1.23	3.71	7.29	8.48	8.09
Luxembourg	6.26	11.54	7.49	16.04	23.45	17.70	17.37
Mexico	1.47	2.21	1.59	1.58	1.65	2.08	2.34
Netherlands	6.58	12.06	8.75	18.06	24.12	19.07	19.29
New Zealand	3.15	5.22	4.38	8.17	9.91	8.13	7.74
Norway	6.77	11.59	10.37	21.47	24.38	22.44	23.13
Portugal	1.58	2.06	1.53	3.77	5.37	4.75	N.A.
Singapore	0.84	1.49	2.47	3.78	7.33	7.42	7.77
Spain	2.53	5.89	4.66	11.38	12.80	10.78	10.88
Sri Lanka	0.28	0.22	0.28	0.35	0.48	0.48	N.A.
Sweden	7.18	12.51	9.66	20.93	21.44	20.14	18.35
Switzerland	6.09	11.09	9.66	20.86	29.30	21.24	21.84
Taiwan	0.38	1.02	1.49	3.90	5.85	5.85	5.70
United Kingdom	3.37	7.56	6.27	12.70	13.78	16.45	16.14
United States	**$6.36**	**$9.87**	**$13.01**	**$14.91**	**$17.19**	**$19.72**	**$20.32**

Note: Hourly compensation includes wages, premiums, bonuses, vacation, holidays and other leave, insurance, and benefit plans. 1. Prior to 1991, data for Germany were for West Germany. **Source:** U.S. Bureau of Labor Statistics, *International Comparisons of Hourly Compensation Costs for Production Workers in Manufacturing*, September, 2002.

bourg, Netherlands, Portugal and Spain. (Of the 11, only Finland, France and Luxembourg can meet the 60 percent indebtedness-to-GDP limit; Belgium and Italy had ratios in excess of 120 percent.) Despite failing the debt criterion, Greece was permitted to join the common currency on January 1, 2001, bringing the number of member states back to 12.

On Jan. 1, 1999, the E.U. introduced the euro. Initially well received in world financial markets, the euro sagged over the next six months, losing almost 20 percent of its value against the dollar. One reason for the flop was the E.U.'s decision to permit Italy's budget deficit to substantially exceed the target 2 percent of GDP; one member's excessive spending was dragging the whole currency down. By September, it had lost about 27 percent of its value against the dollar, prompting voters in Denmark to reject the new currency and instead keep their krone.

On Jan. 1, 2002, 50 billion new euro coins and 14.5 billion euro notes went into circulation in the 12 member countries, and on Feb. 28, 2002, all other currencies were withdrawn from circulation in the member nations. The two-month overlap period caused more than a little bit of confusion throughout Europe, but it bolstered the value of the euro to about even with the U.S. dollar.

Expansion and Constitution In 2004, the E.U. will expand southward and eastward to include (the Greek part of) Cyprus, the Czech Republic, Estonia, Hungary, Latvia, Lithuania, Malta, Poland, Slovakia and Slovenia. The 10 additional countries makes the E.U. truly "One Europe," some 450 million people with an economy about the size of that of the U.S.

Bulgaria and Romania are expected to be included a few years later; Turkey is also a candidate for admission. To ensure that the E.U. can continue functioning efficiently with 25 or more members, the Treaty of Nice set up rules governing the size of the E.U. institutions, streamlining the way they work. It became effective in Feb. 2003.

The addition of the new states poses a possible nightmare for E.U. farm subsidies, which already account for half of the E.U. budget. By the terms of an Oct. 2002 agreement, the new members will receive 25 percent of the older states' subsidies until 2007, when the subsidy grows to 40 percent; full parity is achieved in 2013. The aggregate expenditure on farm subsidies will be allowed to rise no more than 1 percent per year between 2007 and 2013. In June 2003, the E.U.'s agricultural ministers agreed to begin a reform of the Common Agricultural Policy, planning to sever the link between subsidies and production, linking them instead to farm size.

On Feb. 8, 2002, the 105 delegates of the Convention of the Future of Europe assembled in Brussels to present the draft of a new constitution for the E.U. The document contains over 400 articles and largely repeats existing E.U. treaties, but with several major innovations, including: 1) a written bill of rights; 2) a single foreign minister; 3) introduction of majority voting in many policy areas such as energy, agriculture and immigration (while maintaining unanimity in such areas as taxation and foreign policy); 4) a Council presidency elected by heads of state for a term of up to five years; 5) streamlining the Commission by abolishing each state's right to at least one member; and 6) creation of zones of E.U. criminal law to deal with terrorism, corruption and fraud.

Additional information about the European Union (in 11 languages) can be found at the EU Web server. The address is **http://europa.eu.int.**

Structure of the E.U.

The Commission is composed of 20 commissioners appointed by member governments. The five largest countries, France, Germany, Italy, Spain and the United Kingdom, appoint two commissioners each. The remaining 10 countries each appoint one commissioner. The treaties direct Commission members to act independently of their governments and represent the entire community's interests. The Commission supervises implementation of E.U. treaties, initiates and implements E.U. policy, transacts negotiations with nonmember states, and manages E.U. funds. The Commission can be forced to resign by two-thirds majority vote of the European Parliament. The Commission headquarters are in Brussels. The president, who is appointed by the Council, serves a two-year term.

The Council of the European Union consists of the foreign ministers of the 15 member governments and is the chief decision-making body of the E.U., passing legislation on the major issues affecting all members. Each country takes the presidency for six months, and votes are by majority, though each country's vote is weighted differently. Germany, France, Italy and the United Kingdom each have 10 votes; Spain has 8; Belgium, Greece, the Netherlands and Portugal have five votes; Austria and Sweden have four votes; Ireland, Denmark and Finland have three votes; and Luxembourg has two. The Council meets in Brussels.

Unemployment Rates in Leading Developed Nations, 1960-2002

Nation	1960	1970	1980	1990	1995	2000	2001	2002
Australia[1]	1.6%	1.6	6.1	6.7	8.2	6.3	6.7	6.3
Canada	6.5	5.7	7.3	7.7	8.6	6.1	6.4	7.0
France[2]	1.5	2.5	6.5	9.1	11.3	9.1	8.5	8.8
Germany[2, 3]	1.1	0.5	2.8	5.0	8.2	8.1	8.0	8.4
Italy	3.7	3.2	4.4	7.0	11.8	10.7	9.6	9.1
Japan[2]	1.7	1.2	2.0	2.1	3.2	4.8	5.1	5.4
Netherlands	N.A.	N.A.	6.0	5.9	6.7	2.7	2.4	N.A.
Sweden[1, 2]	1.7	1.5	2.0	1.8	9.1	5.8	5.0	5.2
United Kingdom 2	2.2	3.1	7.0	6.9	8.7	5.5	5.1	5.2
United States	5.5	4.9	7.1	5.6	5.6	4.0	4.7	5.8

Note: Seasonally adjusted. 1. Data for 1960 are estimated. 2. Data for 2002 are preliminary. 3. Data for Germany before 1991 refer to the former West Germany. **Source:** U.S. Bureau of Labor Statistics. ftp.bls.gov/pub/special.requests/ForeignLabor/flslforc.txt

The European Parliament The 625 deputies of the European Parliament are elected directly by the citizens of the individual countries. The Parliament oversees the E.U. budget and passes on Commission proposals to the Council of Ministers. The Parliament also passes on new applications to the E.U. Deputies are elected to five-year terms and meet monthly in Strasbourg.

The Court of Justice is the court of last resort for the E.U., interpreting E.U. treaties and legislation and hearing complaints about member-government violations. The Court also resolves differences between E.U. legislation and national laws. The 13 justices are appointed by the member governments and serve six-year terms.

The Economic and Social Committee is composed of 222 members representing labor, farmers and consumer groups. Through consultation, the Committee presents its views to the Council of Ministers and the E.U. Commission.

▶MAJOR REGIONAL TRADING GROUPS

Africa

Common Market for Eastern and Southern Africa (COMESA) HQ: Lotti House, Cairo Rd. Box 30051, 10101 Lusaka, Zambia. www.comesa.int. **Founded:** 1994. **Purpose:** To create an environment for foreign and domestic investment by developing rational production and marketing structures. Help to maintain peace and stability among member states. **Members:** (20) Angola, Burundi, Comoros, Congo, Djibouti, Egypt, Eritrea, Ethiopia, Kenya, Madagascar, Malawi, Mauritius, Namibia, Rwanda, Seychelles, Sudan, Swaziland, Uganda, Zambia, Zimbabwe.

Economic Community of West African States (ECOWAS) HQ: 6 King George V Rd. PMB 12745, Lagos, Nigeria. www.ecowas.int. **Founded:** 1975. **Purpose:** to promote the regional economic cooperation; in recent years it has also created joint military force to deal with the civil war in Liberia. **Members:** (16) Benin, Burkina Faso, Cape Verde, The Gambia, Ghana, Guinea, Guinea-Bissau, Ivory Coast, Liberia, Mali, Mauritania, Niger, Nigeria, Senegal, Sierra Leone, Togo.

Southern African Development Community (SADC) HQ: Private Bag 0095, Gaborone, Botswana. www.sadc.int. **Founded:** 1992. **Purpose:** To promote regional economic development and integration. **Members:** (13) Angola, Botswana, Lesotho, Malawi, Mauritius, Mozambique, Namibia, Seychelles, South Africa, Swaziland, Tanzania, Zambia, Zimbabwe.

Asia

Asia Pacific Economic Cooperation (APEC) HQ: 35 Heng Mui Terrace, Singapore 119616, Singapore. www.apecsec.org. **Founded:** 1989. **Purpose:** an alliance of nations from east and west seeking to promote trade and investment in the Pacific Basin. **Members:** (21) Australia, Brunei, Canada, Chile, China, Hong Kong, Indonesia, Japan, Malaysia, Mexico, Papua New Guinea, New Zealand, Philippines, Singapore, South Korea, Taiwan, Thailand, United States, Vietnam.

Association of South East Asian Nations (ASEAN) HQ: P.O. Box 2072, 70 A Jalan Sisingamangaraja, Jakarta 12110, Indonesia. www.aseansec.org. **Founded:** 1967. **Purpose:** to promote political and economic cooperation among states in region by coordinating policies in trade,

World's 50 Largest Banking Companies by Assets, 2002

Rank, Company, City	Assets (millions)
1. Mizuho Holdings, , Tokyo	$1,135,553
2. Citigroup , New York	1,097,190
3. Sumitomo Mitsui Financial Group, Tokyo	872,962
4. UBS AG, Zurich	852,190
5. Allianz AG, Munich	850,356
6. Deutsche Bank, Frankfurt	791,674
7. J.P. Morgan Chase & Co. , New York	758,800
8. HSBC Holdings PLC , London	757,406
9. ING Group NV, Amsterdam	751,711
10. BNP Paribas, Paris	744,627
11. Mitsubishi Tokyo Financial Group	742,896
12. Bayerische Hypo-und Vereinsbanken, AG, Munich	704,626
13. Credit Suisse Group, Zurich	682,602
14. Royal Bank of Scotland Group, Edinburgh	663,279
15. Bank of America Corp., Charlotte	660,458
16. Barclays PLC, London	648,807
17. UFJ Holdings Osaka, Japan	590,898
18. ABN Amro Holding NV, Amsterdam	581,850
19. HBOS PLC, Edinburgh	571,616
20. Credit Agricole SA, Paris	530,144
21. Societe Generale, Paris	525,994
22. Fortis Utrecht, Netherlands	509,227
23. Axa, Paris	466,134
24. Commerzbank AG, Frankfurt	437,407
25. Norinchukin Bank, Tokyo	433,630
26. Lloyds TSB Group PLC, London	406,886
27. Rabobank Group Utrecht, Netherlands	392,819
28. Dexia, Brussels	367,874
29. Wells Fargo & Co., San Fransicso	349,259
30. Wachovia Corp., Charlotte	341,839
31. Reasona Holdings Inc., Osaka, Japan	332,892
32. Abbey National PLC, London	331,121
33. Banco Santander Central Hispano, Madrid	324,378
34. BBV Argenteria Bilboa, Spain	293,156
35. Intesa Milan, Italy	280,733
36. Bank One Corp., Chicago	277,383
37. Washington Mutual Corp., Seattle	268,298
38. Nordea AB, Stockholm	261,241
39. Credit Lyonnais SA, Paris	256,729
40. Westdeutsche Landesbank Girozentrale, Dusseldorf	249,810
41. Almanij NV Antwerp, Belgium	249,391
42. Royal Bank of Canada, Toronto	240,154
43. Eurohypo AG, Frankfurt	237,166
44. KBC Bank, Brussels	232,670
45. Danske Bank SA, Copenkagen	230,579
46. UniCredito Italiano SpA, Milan	223,674
47. San Paolo Imi SpA, Turin, Italy	213,615
48. National Australia Bank, Melbourne	204,349
49. Norddeutsche Landesbank Hanover, Germany	206,675
50. FleetBoston Financial Corp.	190,453

Source: *American Banker,* Sept. 17, 2003.

transportation, communications, agriculture, science, finance and culture. **Members:** (10) Brunei, Cambodia, Indonesia, Laos, Malaysia, Myanmar, Philippines, Singapore, Thailand, Vietnam.

The Americas

Caribbean Community and Common Market (CARICOM) HQ: Bank of Guyana Building, P.O. Box 10827, 1 Avenue of the Republic, Georgetown, Guyana. www.caricom.org. **Founded:** 1973. **Purpose:** to create greater unity in Caribbean, and to formulate policies and cooperation in services such as education, health, labor matters and foreign policy. **Members:** (16) Antigua and Barbuda, Bahamas, Barbados, Belize, Dominica, Granada, Grenada, Guyana, Haiti, Jamaica, Montserrat, Saint Kitts and Nevis, Saint Lucia, Saint Vincent and the Grenadines, Suriname, Trinidad and Tobago.

Central American Common Market (CACM) HQ: c/o SIECA, Apart Postal 1237, 4a Avenida 10-25, Zona 14, Guatemala 01901, Guatemala. www.sice.oas.org. **Founded:** 1961. **Purpose:** to promote the establishment of a Central American Common Market and to liberalize

The *Fortune* 100 World's Largest Industrial Corporations, 2002

2002 Rank	Company, Country (2001 rank)	Sales (millions)
1.	Wal-Mart Stores, U.S. (1)	246,525.0
2.	General Motors, U.S. (3)	186,763.0
3.	Exxon Mobil, U.S. (2)	182,466.0
4.	Royal Dutch/Shell Group, Netherlands (8)	179,431.0
5.	BP, Britain (4)	178,721.0
6.	Ford Motor Company, U.S. (5)	163,871.0
7.	DaimlerChrysler, Germany (7)	141,421.1
8.	Toyota Motor, Japan (10)	131,754.2
9.	General Electric, U.S. (9)	131,698.0
10.	Mitsubishi, Japan (12)	109,386.1
11.	Mitsui, Japan (13)	108,630.7
12.	Allianz Holding, Germany (18)	101,930.2
13.	Citigroup, U.S. (11)	100,789.0
14.	Total Fina Elf, France (15)	96,944.9
15.	ChevronTexaco, U.S. (14)	92,043.0
16.	Nippon Telegraph & Telephone, Japan (16)	89,644.0
17.	ING Group, Netherlands (20)	88,102.3
18.	Itochu, Japan (17)	85,856.4
19.	IBM, U.S. (19)	83,132.0
20.	Volkswagen, Germany (21)	82,203.7
21.	Siemens, Germany (22)	77,205.2
22.	Sumitomo, Japan (23)	75,745.2
23.	Marubeni, Japan (25)	72,164.8
24.	Verizon Communications, U.S. (26)	67,625.0
25.	American Intl. Group, U.S. (34)	67,482.0
26.	Hitachi, Japan (32)	67,228.0
27.	U.S. Postal Service1 (29)	66,463.0
28.	Honda Motor, Japan (41)	65,420.4
29.	Carrefour, France (35)	64,978.6
30.	Altria Group, U.S. (24)	62,182.0
31.	AXA, France (30)	62,050.8
32.	Sony, Japan (37)	61,334.6
33.	Nippon Life Insurance, Japan (33)	61,174.5
34.	Matsushita Electric Japan (45),	60,744.3
35.	Royal Ahold, Netherlands (38)	59,454.6
36.	ConocoPhillips, U.S. (188)	58,384.0
37.	Home Depot, U.S. (46)	58,247.0
38.	Nestlé, Switzerland (55)	57,279.1
39.	McKesson HBOC, U.S. (57)	57,129.2
40.	Hewlett-Packard, U.S. (70)	56,588.0
41.	Nissan Motor, Japan (58)	56,040.8
42.	Vivendi Universal, France (51)	54,977.1
43.	Boeing, U.S. (42)	54,069.0
44.	Assicurazioni Generali, Italy (50)	53,598.9
45.	Fannie Mae, U.S. (52)	52,901.1
46.	Fiat, Italy (49)	52,612.5
47.	Deutsche Bank, Germany (27)	52,133.2
48.	Credit Suisse Group, Switzerland (31)	52,121.7
49.	Munich Re Group, Germany (79)	51,980.0
50.	Merck, U.S. (62)	51,790.3
51.	Kroger, U.S. (56)	51,759.5
52.	Peugeot, France (65)	51,465.7
53.	Cardinal Health, U.S. (61)	51,135.7
54.	BNP Paribas, France (44)	51,127.3
55.	Deutsche Telekom, Germany (75)	50,759.5
56.	State Power Corporation, U.S. (60)	49,653.7
57.	Aviva, U.K. (48)	49,533.3
58.	Metro Holding, Switzerland (72)	48,714.5
59.	Samsung Electronics, S. Korea (105)	47,605.6
60.	Vodafone, U.K. (123)	46,987.0
61.	AT&T, U.S. (40)	46,727.0
62.	Toshiba, Japan (77)	46,415.8
63.	ENI, Italy 1 (71)	46,328.2
64.	Bank of America, U.S. (47)	45,732.0
65.	Électricité De France, France (102)	45,720.3
66.	Unilever, Britain/Netherlands (68)	45,636.2
67.	AmerisourceBergen , U.S. (319)	45,234.8
68.	E.ON, Germany (28)	44,941.3
69.	China National Petroleum, China (81)	44,864.4
70.	Sinopec, China (86)	44,503.2
71.	France Télécom, France 7(97)	44,085.7
72.	Target, U.S. (89)	43,917.0
73.	Fortis, U.S. (85)	43,597.5
74.	Suez, France (99)	43,574.9
75.	J.P. Morgan Chase, U.S. (54)	43,372.0
76.	SBC Communications, U.S. (69)	43,138.0
77.	Dai-Ichi Mutual Life Insurance, Japan (76)	43,134.2
78.	Berkshire Hathaway, U.S. (101)	42,353.0
79.	UBS, Switzerland (59)	42,329.7
80.	AOL Time Warner, U.S. (98)	41,676.0
81.	Sears Roebuck, U.S. (83)	41,366.0
82.	RWE Group, Germany (53)	41,114.1
83.	Zurich Financial Services, Switzerland (96)	40,638.0
84.	Tesco, U.K. (114)	40,387.2
85.	Tokyo Electric Power, Japan (80)	40,370.1
86.	Procter & Gamble, U.S. (93)	40,238.0
87.	BMW, Germany (112)	39,974.9
88.	Deutsche Post, Germany (130)	39,956.0
89.	HSBC Holdings, U.K. (64)	39,730.0
90.	Freddie Mac, U.S. (108)	39,663.0
91.	Tyco International, U.S. (103)	38,971.3
92.	Costco Wholesale, U.S. (111)	38,762.5
93.	NEC, Japan (84)	38,531.2
94.	Hyundai Motor, South Korea (133)	38,458.5
95.	Pemex, Mexico (92)	37,973.9
96.	Nissho Iwai, Japan (74)	37,907.8
97.	Fujitsu, Japan (88)	37,895.5
98.	Crédit Agricole, France (107)	36,745.3
99.	HypoVereinsbank, Germany (91)	36,355.8
100.	Sumitomo Life Insurance, Japan (126)	36,304.5

Source: *Fortune*, July 21, 2003. Reprinted by permission.

trade with other nations including the U.S. **Members:** (5) Costa Rica, El Salvador, Guatemala, Honduras, Nicaragua.

Mercado Comun del Cono Sur (MERCOSUR) HQ: Rincon 575 P12, 11000 Montivideo, Uruguay. www.mercosur.org.uy. **Founded:** 1991 (established 1995). **Purpose:** to establish a free trade area and a customs union, and to negotiate free trade agreements with other Latin American countries that will eventually produce a Latin American Free Trade Area (LAFTA). **Members:** (4) Argentina, Brazil, Paraguay, Uruguay. **Associate Members:** Bolivia, Chile.

North American Free Trade Agreement (NAFTA) Founded: 1994. **Purpose:** to remove all barriers to trade among the three nations. **Members:** (3) Canada, Mexico, U.S.

World Economic Indicators, 2001

Country	G.N.P. (millions of U.S. dollars) 2001	G.N.P. per capita (in U.S. dollars) 2001	G.N.P. per capita Real growth rate 1980-91	G.N.P. per capita Real growth rate 1990-2001	Average inflation rate 1990-2001	Agriculture's share in G.D.P. 1970	Agriculture's share in G.D.P. 2001	Net private capital flows (millions) 2001[1]	Foreign direct investment as percent of G.D.P. 2001
Albania	$4,114	$1,340	—	4.3%	34.4%	—	50%	$203	5.0%
Algeria	54,680	1,650	-0.8%	0.1	17.0	10%	10	243	2.2
Angola	9,471	500	—	-1.1	658.8	45	8	1,924	22.7
Antigua and Barbuda	682	9,150	3.8	2.7	2.2	—	4	—	—
Argentina	268,638	6,940	-1.5	2.3	4.3	13	5	-3,897	1.2
Armenia	2,118	570	2.1	-1.3	172.0	N.A.	28	74	3.3
Australia	368,726	19,900	1.2	2.7	1.7	6	4	—	1.2
Austria	188,546	23,940	2.1	1.8	1.8	7	2	—	3.1
Azerbaijan	5,585	650	0.4	-1.3	96.9	N.A.	17	216	4.1
Bahamas	4,818	14,860	1.3	0.1	2.7	—	—	—	5.2
Bahrain	7,935	11,130	-3.8	1.9	0.8	—	—	—	—
Bangladesh	46,706	360	1.9	3.1	3.9	55	23	304	0.2
Barbados	2,757	9,750	1.3	2.1	2.9	11	6	171	0.6
Belarus	12,219	1,290	3.3	-0.6	318.1	N.A.	11	83	0.8
Belgium	229,610	23,850	2.1	1.9	1.9	4	2	—	32.1
Belize	805	2,940	2.5	1.6	1.8	—	23	125	4.2
Benin	2,372	380	-1.1	1.9	8.2	49	36	131	5.5
Bhutan	533	640	6.8	3.5	9.3	—	33	0	0.0
Bolivia	7,969	950	-2.0	1.4	8.0	17	16	637	8.3
Bosnia & Herzegovina	4,769	1,240	N.A.	—	2.7	N.A.	15	226	4.7
Botswana	5,196	3,100	5.8	2.5	9.0	33	2	55	1.1
Brazil	502,509	3,070	0.4	1.4	168.2	12	9	23,336	4.5
Brunei	—	—	—	-0.7	1.1	—	—	—	—
Bulgaria	13,553	1,650	1.7	-0.6	93.4	—	14	1,043	5.1
Burkina Faso	2,486	220	1.3	2.0	4.5	44	38	26	10
Burundi	689	100	1.4	-4.3	12.6	71	50	0	0.0
Cambodia	3,404	270	—	2.2	21.7	—	37	113	3.3
Cameroon	8,501	580	-0.9	-0.3	4.9	31	43	-16	0.9
Canada	694,475	21,930	2.1	2.1	1.5	—	—	—	4.0
Cape Verde	588	1,340	2.2	3.5	4.8	—	11	8	0.1
Central African Rep.	967	260	-1.5	-0.3	4.2	35	55	8	0.8
Chad	1,600	200	3.8	-0.5	6.7	43	39	80	5.0
Chile	66,450	4,590	1.7	4.7	7.5	7	9	5,727	6.7
China	1,159,031	890	7.8	8.8	6.2	35	15	43,238	3.8
Colombia	82,411	1,890	1.2	0.8	20.0	25	13	3,597	2.8
Comoros	221	380	-1.0	-1.4	3.6	—	41	2	0.7
Congo, Dem. Republic	5,187	80	-0.2	-7.7	846.2	18	56	32	0.6
Congo Republic	2,751	640	-1.6	-7.7	8.8	16	6	59	2.1
Costa Rica	16,108	4,060	1.0	2.8	16.3	23	9	630	2.8
Croatia	20,260	4,550	N.A.	2.1	72.2	N.A.	9	2,236	7.5
Cuba	—	—	—	3.7	1.1	—	7	—	—
Cyprus	9,131	12,320	4.9	3.2	3.4	—	—	—	1.8
Czech Republic[2]	56,784	5,310	0.4	1.3	10.6	—	4	5,194	8.7
Denmark	161,542	30,600	2.1	2.0	2.2	—	3	—	4.5
Djibouti	576	890	—	-3.6	3.6	—	4	3	0.6
Dominica	263	3,200	4.7	1.7	2.8	—	17	24	4.5
Dominican Republic	21,211	2,230	-0.2	4.2	9.1	20	11	1,729	5.6
Ecuador	17,982	1,080	-0.3	-0.3	1.7	24	11	1,444	7.4
Egypt	98,476	1,530	2.0	2.5	7.8	29	17	2,068	0.5
El Salvador	13,739	2,040	-0.3	2.4	6.8	28	9	674	1.9
Equatorial Guinea	1,846	700	3.4	18.8	16.8	—	8	88	4.8
Eritrea	688	160	—	2.5	9.0	—	19	34	5.0
Estonia	5,525	3,870	2.1	1.6	46.1	N.A.	6	624	9.8
Ethiopia	6,233	100	-1.6	2.4	6.1	56	52	10	0.3
Fiji	1,684	2,150	0.0	1.7	3.1	29	18	-9	-0.2

Country	G.N.P. (millions of U.S. dollars) 2001	G.N.P. per capita (in U.S. dollars) 2001	G.N.P. per capita Real growth rate 1980-91	G.N.P. per capita Real growth rate 1990-2001	Average inflation rate 1990-2001	Agriculture's share in G.D.P. 1970	Agriculture's share in G.D.P. 2001	Net private capital flows (millions) 2001[1]	Foreign direct investment as percent of G.D.P. 2001
Finland	$120,855	$23,780	2.5%	2.6%	1.9%	—	3%	—	3.1%
France[3]	1,309,807	22,730	1.8	1.5	1.5	—	3	—	4.0
Gabon	4,334	3,160	-4.2	-0.1	5.6	17%	8	$170	4.6
Gambia	390	320	-0.1	0.1	4.1	33	40	36	9.1
Georgia	3,138	590	2.2	-5.5	279.0	N.A.	21	173	5.1
Germany[4]	1,846,069	23,560	2.2	1.2	1.8	3	1	—	1.7
Ghana	5,301	290	-0.3	1.9	26.6	47	36	244	1.7
Greece	117,169	11,430	1.2	2.0	8.5	18	8	—	1.4
Grenada	398	3,610	5.3	2.9	2.3	—	8	30	8.6
Guatemala	20,496	1,680	-1.8	1.4	9.9	—	23	403	2.2
Guinea	2,989	410	—	1.6	5.1	—	24	1	0.1
Guinea-Bissau	199	160	1.3	-1.3	28.7	47	56	30	15.1
Guyana	699	840	-4.2	1.6	11.9	19	31	55	8.0
Haiti	3,737	480	-2.4	-2.5	20.3	—	—	3	0.1
Honduras	6,386	900	-0.7	0.3	18.0	32	14	126	3.1
Hong Kong	161,896	25,330	—	2.1	3.3	0	0	—	14.1
Hungary	51,926	4,830	0.7	2.1	18.3	18	—	3,952	4.7
Iceland	7,702	28,910	1.3	2.1	3.4	—	—	—	1.7
India	477,942	460	3.3	4.0	7.6	47	25	3,534	0.7
Indonesia	145,306	690	3.9	2.3	15.8	45	16	-7,312	-2.3
Iran	114,052	1,680	-1.1	2.0	25.7	19	19	1,049	0.0
Iraq	—	—	—	—	—	17	—	—	—
Ireland	103,298	22,850	2.2	6.8	3.5	—	4	—	9.6
Israel	108,325	16,750	1.8	2.0	9.3	—	—	—	3.0
Italy	1,088,754	19,390	2.1	1.4	3.6	8	3	—	1.4
Ivory Coast	10,411	630	-3.4	0.1	8.4	40	24	137	2.4
Jamaica	7,784	2,800	-0.3	-0.5	22.1	7	6	1,385	7.9
Japan	4,141,431	35,610	3.7	1.0	-0.1	6	1	—	0.1
Jordan	8,829	1,750	-3.3	0.9	2.9	10	2	-11.4	1.1
Kazakhstan	22,389	1,350	0.9	-1.9	168.5	N.A.	9	4,947	12.3
Kenya	11,396	350	0.3	-0.6	13.4	33	19	-37	0.0
Kiribati	40	830	0.5	0.6	3.3	—	—	—	—
Korea, South	422,167	9,460	8.8	4.7	4.5	26	4	9,279	0.8
Kuwait	32,806	18,270	—	-1.0	1.9	0	—	—	-0.1
Kyrgyzstan	1,525	280	2.1	-3.9	95.2	N.A.	38	-73	0.3
Laos	1,761	300	1.2	3.9	28.5	—	51	24	1.4
Latvia	7,549	3,230	2.8	-1.0	42.0	N.A.	5	880	2.3
Lebanon	16,709	4,010	—	3.6	15.1	9	12	2,757	1.5
Lesotho	797	530	0.0	2.1	9.5	35	16	113	14.7
Liberia	523	140	—	3.5	53.3	24	—	13	2.4
Libya	34,137	—	—	—	—	2	—	—	—
Lithuania	11,992	3,350	2.5	-1.6	63.3	N.A.	7	521	3.7
Luxembourg	18,540	39,840	3.8	4.2	2.2	4	1	—	—
Macedonia	3,426	1,690	N.A.	-0.9	66.0	N.A.	11	466	12.9
Madagascar	4,604	260	-2.4	-0.6	17.9	30	30	9	0.2
Malawi	1,749	160	0.1	1.5	33.0	44	34	58	3.3
Malaysia	88,041	3,330	2.9	3.9	3.6	29	9	855	0.6
Maldives	548	2,000	6.7	2.5	5.8	—	—	12	2.0
Mali	2,647	230	0.1	1.6	6.9	61	38	103	3.9
Malta	3,623	9,210	3.8	3.8	2.8	7	—	381	8.1
Marshall Islands	96	2,190	—	-3.5	5.3	N.A.	13	—	—
Mauritania	1,007	360	-1.8	1.2	6.2	29	21	27	3.0
Mauritius	4,500	3,830	6.1	3.9	6.2	16	6	-75	-1.1
Mexico	617,820	5,530	-0.5	1.5	18.2	12	4	28,079	4.0
Micronesia	237	2,150	N.A.	-1.3	3.0	N.A.	—	—	—
Moldova	1,479	400	1.8	-8.2	103.1	N.A.	26	70	6.3
Mongolia	1,049	400	—	0.0	51.4	—	30	62	6.0
Morocco	34,219	1,190	1.6	0.7	2.7	20	16	2,633	7.8
Mozambique	3,607	210	-3.6	4.3	29.6	—	22	450	13.3
Myanmar	—	—	—	5.7	24.6	38	57	145	—
Namibia	3,100	1,960	-1.5	2.2	8.5	—	11	—	—
Nepal	5,562	250	2.1	2.4	7.8	67	39	19	0.3
Netherlands	380,137	24,330	1.5	2.3	2.1	6	3	—	13.5
New Zealand	50,425	13,250	0.2	2.0	1.6	—	—	—	3.4
Nicaragua	—	—	-4.6	-0.1	45.2	25	—	13	—
Niger	1,954	180	-4.1	-0.9	5.8	65	40	7	0.7
Nigeria	41,373	290	-1.7	-0.3	26.5	40	30	920	2.7

Country	G.N.P. (millions of U.S. dollars) 2001	G.N.P. per capita (in U.S. dollars) 2001	G.N.P. per capita Real growth rate 1980-91	G.N.P. per capita Real growth rate 1990-2001	Average inflation rate 1990-2001	Agriculture's share in G.D.P. 1970	Agriculture's share in G.D.P. 2001	Net private capital flows (millions) 2001[1]	Foreign direct investment as percent of G.D.P. 2001
Norway	$166,145	$35,630	2.2%	2.9%	3.2%	6%	2%	—	1.3%
Oman	19,826	6,180	4.5	0.6	1.8	16	—	$-867	0.4
Pakistan	58,668	420	3.2	1.2	9.6	37	25	-308	0.7
Palau	122	6,780	—	—	2.8	—	4	—	—
Panama	10,171	3,260	-1.8	2.1	1.9	15	7	1,799	5.0
Papua New Guinea	2,959	580	-0.7	1.0	7.3	37	26	2	2.1
Paraguay	7,206	1,350	-0.8	-0.6	12.0	32	20	-14	1.1
Peru	54,047	1,980	-2.6	2.4	23.3	19	9	1,400	2.0
Philippines	71,438	1,030	-1.2	1.0	8.2	30	15	2,076	2.5
Poland	176,256	4,230	0.5	4.4	21.3	—	4	9,611	3.2
Portugal	109,803	10,900	2.7	2.6	5.1	—	4	—	5.4
Qatar	16,454	—	-10.9	—	—	—	—	—	—
Romania	38,718	1,720	-0.1	-0.1	91.0	—	15	2,633	3.0
Russian Federation	309,951	1,750	1.3	-3.5	139.6	N.A.	7	1,488	0.8
Rwanda	1,703	220	-2.6	-1.3	13.1	62	40	5	0.3
Saint Kitts and Nevis	343	6,630	5.8	3.9	3.0	—	3	110	24.2
Saint Lucia	662	3,950	2.9	0.7	2.9	—	7	58	7.7
Saint Vincent and the Grenadines	353	2,740	5.2	2.5	2.1	—	10	35	10.1
Samoa	255	1,490	5.1	2.0	3.8	—	17	1	0.5
São Tomé and Principe	47	280	-3.5	-0.6	46.7	37	20	6	11.7
Saudi Arabia	186,489	8,460	-4.2	-1.1	3.7	6	—	—	—
Senegal	4,714	490	0.0	1.1	4.2	24	18	167	2.7
Seychelles	570	6,530	2.5	0.1	3.9	—	3	56	10.4
Sierra Leone	749	140	-1.3	-6.6	29.2	28	50	4	0.5
Singapore	85,648	21,500	4.9	4.4	0.9	2	0	—	10.1
Slovak Republic	20,459	3,760	N.A.	1.9	10.4	N.A.	4	303	7.2
Slovenia	18,810	9,760	N.A.	3.0	18.3	N.A.	3	—	2.7
Solomon Islands	264	590	3.5	-1.4	8.2	—	—	-9	-1.9
Somalia	—	—	—	—	—	59	—	0	—
South Africa	113,274	2,820	0.9	0.2	9.3	8	3	6,627	6.3
Spain	581,823	14,300	2.9	2.2	3.9	—	4	—	3.7
Sri Lanka	15,911	880	2.5	3.6	9.1	28	19	243	1.1
Sudan	12,525	340	-2.4	3.2	58.2	43	39	574	4.6
Suriname	757	1,810	-4.5	2.6	82.8	7	11	—	—
Swaziland	1,255	1,300	3.1	0.1	12.3	33	17	35	1.7
Sweden	209,814	25,400	1.7	1.7	2.0	—	2	—	6.2
Switzerland	247,091	38,330	1.6	0.3	1.2	—	—	—	3.5
Syria	19,495	1,040	-2.1	1.9	7.4	20	22	204	1.1
Tajikistan	1,056	180	-0.1	-9.9	202.4	N.A.	29	39	2.1
Tanzania[5]	9,341	270	-1.1	0.4	3.9	41	45	197	2.4
Thailand	114,681	1,940	5.9	3.0	3.9	26	10	-3,052	3.3
Togo	1,259	270	-1.7	-0.6	6.6	34	39	67	5.3
Tonga	142	1,530	1.5	2.1	2.2	—	29	1	0.7
Trinidad and Tobago	8,842	5,960	-5.2	2.9	5.4	5	2	830	9.4
Tunisia	19,990	2,070	1.2	3.1	4.3	20	12	1,108	2.3
Turkey	147,683	2,530	2.9	1.7	74.2	30	14	906	2.2
Turkmenistan	5,962	950	0.7	-6.1	328.0	N.A.	29	—	—
Uganda	5,675	260	3.3	3.6	10.9	54	36	147	2.5
Ukraine	37,588	720	2.3	-7.4	220.9	—	17	426	2.1
United Arab Emirates	—	—	-5.8	-1.6	2.3	—	—	—	—
United Kingdom	1,424,094	25,120	2.6	2.5	2.8	—	1	—	4.4
United States	10,065,265	34,280	2.1	2.1	2.0	3	2	—	1.3
Uruguay	18,666	5,710	-0.4	2.1	27.8	13	6	796	1.7
Uzbekistan	11,270	550	0.8	-1.5	210.7	N.A.	34	46	0.6
Vanuatu	213	1,050	-0.2	-1.1	2.9	—	19	18	8.5
Venezuela	124,948	4,760	-1.5	-0.6	42.8	6	5	2,644	2.8
Vietnam	32,723	410	—	6.0	13.8	—	24	710	4.0
Yemen	9,276	450	—	2.4	21.1	52	16	-210	-2.2
Yugoslavia[6]	10,861	930	-1.4	—	—	18	15	10	0.0
Zambia	3,639	320	-2.9	-1.7	48.1	11	22	126	2.0
Zimbabwe	9,057	480	0.2	-0.2	28.4	15	18	-28	0.1

Note: The World Bank reports data on Gross Domestic Product and per capita Gross National Income (GNI) rather than Gross National Product (GNP). Some figures are for years other than those specified. 1. Data are shown for low and middle income countries only. 2. Data for years before 1990 refer to Czechoslovakia. 3. Data includes French Guiana, Guadeloupe, Martinique, and Réunion. 4. Data for years before 1990 refer to West Germany. 5. Data refers to mainland Tanzania only. 6. Former Yugoslav Republics of Serbia and Montenegro. **Source:** The World Bank, *The 2002 World Bank Atlas.*

NATIONS OF THE WORLD

The following section presents major facts about all the nations of the world, including statistics on each nation's geography, people, government, economy, and written text describing highlights of the country's history.

The commonly used name for each country is listed first, followed by the formal name. A list of colonial and other former names is found in the following section, "Territories of the World." Geographical descriptions are listed in both miles and kilometers, and the latitude and longitude of most islands are given.

Sources of information include the annual *World Factbook* published by the Central Intelligence Agency of the United States, the United Nations, the U.S. Bureau of the Census, and the U.S. Department of State. Names of heads of government are from the United Nations official protocol office and are valid as of Sept. 2003.

▶AFGHANISTAN

Transitional Islamic State of Afghanistan

• GEOGRAPHY **Location:** landlocked country in southwestern Asia. **Boundaries:** Turkmenistan to NW, Tajikistan to N, China to NE, Pakistan to E and S, Iran to W. **Total area**: 250,000 sq. mi. (647,500 sq km). **Coastline**: none. **Comparative area**: slightly smaller than Texas. **Land use:** 12% arable land; negl. % permanent crops; 88% other. **Major cities**: (1982 est.) Kabul (capital) 1,036,407; Qandahar 191,345; Herat 150,497; Mazar-i-Sharif 110,367; Jalalabad 57,824.

• PEOPLE **Population:** 28,717,213 (July 2003 est.). **Nationality:** noun—Afghan(s); adjective—Afghan. **Ethnic groups:** 44% Pashtun, 25% Tajik, 10% Hazara, 8% Uzbek. **Languages:** 50% Afghan Persian (Dari), 35% Pashtu, 11% Turkic langs. (primarily Uzbek and Turkmen), 4% minor langs. (30, primarily Balochi and Pashai); much bilingualism. **Religions:** 84% Sunni Muslim, 15% Shi'a Muslim, 1% other.

• GOVERNMENT **Type:** transitional government. **Independence:** Aug. 19, 1919 (from U.K.). **Constitution:** In progress. **National holiday:** Independence Day, Aug.19. **Heads of government:** Hamid Karzai, president (since June 2002).

• ECONOMY **Monetary unit:** afghani. **Budget:** ***income:*** N.A.; ***expend.:*** N.A. **GDP:** (2002 est.) $19 bil., $700 per capita. **Chief crops:** wheat, fruits, nuts, karakul pelts; wool, mutton. **Natural resources:** natural gas, crude oil, coal, copper, talc. **Major industries:** small-scale production of textiles, soap, furniture, shoes, fertilizer, and cement; hand-woven carpets; natural gas, coal, and copper. **Labor force:** 10 mil.; 80% agriculture and animal husbandry, 10% services and other, 10% industry (2000 est.). **Exports:** $1.2 bil. (2001); opium, fruits and nuts, hand-woven carpets, wool, and cotton. **Imports**: $1.3 bil. (2001); food supplies, petroleum products. **Major trading partners:** Pakistan, Japan, India.

Mountainous and landlocked, Afghanistan has been a crossroads of trans-Asian trade and conquest since antiquity. A part of the Persian Empire, Bactria was conquered by Alexander the Great, and became independent in the third century B.C. before falling to the Parthians in the next century. In the seventh century A.D., a flourishing Buddhist civilization there fell to Islamic conquests. Genghis Khan overthrew the 11th-century empire of Mahmud of Gazni in the early 13th century, and Afghanistan was the center of Tamerlane's empire in the late 14th century. Thereafter, the region was divided among various tribes and petty kingdoms.

Modern Afghan history began with the establishment of a united emirate by Ahmed Shah Durrani in 1747. In the 19th century, Russia and Great Britain contested domination of Afghanistan. The British Afghan Wars of 1838-42 and 1878-80 left Afghanistan unconquered but within Britain's sphere of influence. Afghanistan achieved full independence from Britain in 1919 under Amanullah Khan, who proclaimed himself king in 1926. Modern reforms were instituted by Amanullah and his successors Mohammed Nadir Shah (1929-33) and Mohammed Zahir Shah (1933-73).

The monarchy fell to a military coup in 1973, and Mohammed Daud Khan established a republic. In 1978 pro-Soviet leftists took power in a coup, and, ostensibly at the government's invitation, Soviet troops invaded Afghanistan in December 1979 to put down widespread popular revolts against Communist rule. In the ensuing civil war, the government's forces and their Soviet allies (with an eventual troop strength of more than 100,000) controlled the cities and main transportation routes, but guerrilla forces contested the countryside. In 1988 the Soviet Union began a withdrawal of its troops, completed by February 1989. The rebel factions failed to achieve a united front and the pro-Soviet government confounded predictions that it would fall soon after the Soviet departure.

The government fell on Apr. 15, 1992, and rebel troops entered Kabul. A respected religious leader, Sibghatullah Mujaddidi, was named interim president, with the backing of a coalition of forces dominated by rebel commanders. However, Gulbaddin Hekmatyar, leader of the fundamentalist Hizbe Islami faction, declined to join the coalition, and fighting broke out in and around Kabul.

On June 28 Mujaddidi turned over his power to the Leadership Council, which then elected Burhanuddin Rabbani as president. Fighting for control of Kabul continued between forces loyal to the Rabbani government and those backing Hekmatyar. Other factions later joined the fighting, and Kabul was subjected to continual rocket attacks in late 1992 and into the spring of 1993. Hekmatyar was named prime minister in an attempt to make peace. Fighting broke out again in early 1994 with Rabbani's followers getting the upper hand after fierce battles in Kabul.

By early 1995, the U.N. had brokered a scheme uniting the nine major factions in a council to which Rabbani would turn over power. But it was quickly undone by the emergence of a fundamentalist Islamic militia called the Taliban, 20,000 strong and composed of students from the Islamic schools. Taliban forces took over most of the country and established a fundamentalist regime based on Islamic law. In Oct. 1996, three remaining groups of opposition forces formed a loose Northern Alliance and kept up sporadic fighting; but by 1999 the Taliban controlled over 90 percent of Afghanistan's territory.

The Taliban then consolidated its power and began to enforce a strict Muslim code of behavior. In 2001, the U.N. reported a precipitate drop in opium poppies grown in Afghanistan (producer of 75 percent of the world's opium). A second ban, in Feb. 2001, on all statues in the country led to the destruction in March of 1,400-year-old Buddhist cliff carvings in the region of Bamiyan, despite a wave of world protest. In Sept. 2001 Afghanistan became the focus of world attention when the U.S. demanded the Taliban turn over the terrorist leaders suspected of plotting the attack on the World Trade Center.

The Anglo-American air strikes that began Oct. 7 led to the fall (Nov. 13) of Kabul to the Northern Alliance. The interim government under Hamid Karzai organized a Grand Council of about 1,600 members which elected Karzai to lead a transitional government until elections in 2004 for a permanent government. In Aug. 2003, NATO forces took command of the international peacekeepeers; the Karzai government seemed to be holding on amidst the rivalries of tribal chieftains and warlords. But a U.N. report of Oct. 2002 noted that Afghanistan had again become the world's foremost opium producer.

▶ALBANIA

Republic of Albania

• **GEOGRAPHY** **Location:** southeastern Europe. **Boundaries**: Yugoslavia to N, Macedonia to E, Greece to S, and Adriatic and Ionian Seas (parts of Mediterranean Sea) to W. **Total area**: 11,100 sq. mi. (28,750 sq km). **Coastline**: 225 mi. (362 km). **Comparative area**: slightly smaller than Maryland. **Land use:** 21% arable land; 4% permanent crops; 75% other. **Major cities**: (1990 est.) Tiranë (Tirana; capital) 244,200; Durrës (Durazzo) 85,400; Elbasan 83,300; Shkodër (Scutari) 81,900; Vlorë (Vlonë or Valona) 73,800.

• **PEOPLE** **Population:** 3,582,205 (July 2003 est.). **Nationality:** noun—Albanian(s); adjective—Albanian. **Ethnic groups:** 95% Albanian, 3% Greek, 2% Vlach, Gypsy, Serb, and Bulgarian (1989 est.). **Languages:** Albanian (Tosk is official dialect), Greek. **Religions:** 70% Muslim, 20% Albanian Orthodox, 10% Roman Catholic (all churches and mosques were closed in 1967 and religious observances prohibited; in November 1990, Albania began allowing private religious practice).

• **GOVERNMENT** **Type:** emerging democracy. **Independence:** Nov. 28, 1912 (from Ottoman Empire). **Constitution:** Nov. 28, 1998. **National holiday:** Independence Day, Nov. 28. **Heads of Government:** Alfred Moisiu, president (since July 2002); Fatos Nano, prime minister (since July 2002). **Structure:** executive—president, prime minister, Council of Ministers; legislative—unicameral People's Assembly; judicial—Supreme Court.

• **ECONOMY** **Monetary unit:** lek. **Budget:** (2002 est.) ***income:*** $697 mil.; ***expend.:*** $1.5 bil. **GDP:** (2002 est.) $14 bil., $4,500 per capita. **Chief crops:** vegetables, wheat, potatoes, fruits, sugar beets, corn. **Natural resources:** crude oil, natural gas, coal, chromium, copper. **Major industries:** food processing, textiles and clothing, lumber. **Labor force:** 1.3 mil. (2002 est.); 50% agriculture, 50% industry and services. **Exports:** $340 mil. (f.o.b., 2002 est.); textiles, footwear, asphalt, metals and ores, electricity, crude oil, vegetables, fruits, tobacco. **Imports**: $1.5 bil. (f.o.b., 2002 est.); machinery, consumer goods, grains. **Major trading partners:** Italy, Greece, Germany, Turkey.

The city of Epidamnus (Durrës) was colonized by Greeks from Corinth and Corcyra in 625 B.C. Later the Roman province of Illyricum, Albania was a much-coveted area after the fall of Rome and was in turn ruled by Byzantines, Normans, Venetians, Slavs, and the kings of Naples. Under the leadership of Skanderbeg (1405-68), Albania repelled repeated Turkish invasions. But Albania was part of the Ottoman Empire from 1478 until 1912. Ottoman rule succeeded in converting most of the populace to Islam (with Catholic minorities in the north and Greek Orthodox in the south) but did not destroy the Albanian sense of national identity, based on ties of tribe, clan, and family.

Independence came in 1912 as a result of the First Balkan War, when Austria-Hungary and Italy fostered the creation of an Albanian state. Occupied by its sponsors during World War I, Albania emerged from the war in a state of near-anarchy. With Yugoslav support, Ahmed Zogu became president of the republic in 1924; he proclaimed himself King Zog I in 1928.

In 1939 Italy invaded and annexed Albania. During World War II, partisan resistance was dominated by Communist forces under the leadership of Enver Hoxha. In 1944 Hoxha seized control of the government. A socialist republic was established in 1946: foreigners were expelled and their assets nationalized; churches were closed; agriculture and industry were collectivized. Albania under Hoxha became one of the world's most thoroughly totalitarian states.

A doctrinaire Stalinist, Hoxha broke with Khruschev's Soviet Union in 1961 and became a client state of China. But with liberalization in China after 1977, Hoxha broke that link as well. Albania became almost totally isolated from world affairs.

Hoxha died in 1985 and was succeeded as president and first secretary of the Albanian Communist party by Ramiz Alia. In 1990, Alia eased restrictions on religion, tourism, and foreign investment, and allowed the formation of an opposition Democratic party. But he scheduled elections to the National Assembly for 1991, before awareness had spread of the old regime's faltering power. The Communists carried the rural districts and formed a coalition government with the Democrats, who carried the cities.

In 1992, the Democrats completed the rout of the Communists, winning 92 of the 140 seats in the Assembly, and replacing Alia with Sali Berisha, a heart surgeon. But by the end of the year, factions within the Democratic party were already complaining about Pres. Berisha's "autocratic rule." Meanwhile, anarchy plagued much of the country, with food riots in the cities and armed brigandage in the countryside. EC and U.N. grants helped pay for needed imports and Italy provided invaluable assistance to the Albanian police forces. By 1993, zones of law and order were being established, churches were reopening, and 90 percent of farming had been privatized. But in November 1994, voters rejected (54-42) a new constitution proposed by Pres. Berisha.

In 1996 Berisha's Democratic Party won a major electoral victory amidst complaints of fraud, but he and his followers were driven from office in 1997 after a series of pryamid schemes collapsed ruining the finances of tens of thousands of families who had participated in them. Violence and looting occured in many areas and a multi-national force of 7,000 was sent in to help restore order. The Socialists (formerly Communists) returned to power under Fatos Nano. In the spring of 1998 NATO advisors began to train Albania's tiny army as ethnic Albanians in the Kosovo province of Yugoslavia began a violent rebellion. Yugoslavia's suppression of the rebellion drove thousands of ethnic Albanians out of Kosovo into Albania. Amidst this further tumult, internal struggles continued between supporters of the Democratic Party and the Socialists, erupting into serious violence in Sept. 1998. Though Nano resigned as prime minister late in

1998, he has continued to dominate Albanian politics as Socialist Party chairman, while prime ministers come and go.

▶ALGERIA

People's Democratic Republic of Algeria

• GEOGRAPHY **Location:** northern coast of Africa. **Boundaries**: Mediterranean Sea to N, Tunisia and Libya to E, Mali and Niger to S, Morocco, Western Sahara, Mauritania to W. **Total area**: 919,591 sq. mi. (2,381,740 sq km). **Coastline**: 620 mi. (998 km). **Comparative area**: slightly less than 3.5 times size of Texas. **Land use:** 3% arable land; negl. % permanent crops; 97% other. **Major cities**: (1984 est.) Algiers (capital) 1,721,607; Oran 663,504; Constantine 448,578; Annaba 348,322; Blida 191,314.

• PEOPLE **Population:** 32,818,500 (July 2003 est.). **Nationality:** noun—Algerian(s); adjective—Algerian. **Ethnic groups:** 99% Arab-Berber, less than 1% European. **Languages:** Arabic (official), French, Berber dialects. **Religions:** 99% Sunni Muslim (state religion), 1% Christian and Jewish.

• GOVERNMENT **Type:** republic. **Independence:** July 5, 1962 (from France). **Constitution:** Nov. 19, 1976, effective Nov. 22, 1976. **National holiday:** Revolution Day, Nov. 1. **Heads of Government:** Abdelaziz Bouteflika, head of state (since Apr. 1999), Ali Benflis, prime minister (since Aug. 2000). **Structure:** executive; bicameral legislature; judicial—Supreme Court.

• ECONOMY **Monetary unit:** Algerian dinar. **Budget:** (2001 est.) ***income:*** $20.3 bil.; ***expend.:*** $18.8 bil. **GDP:** $167 bil., $5,300 per capita. **Chief crops:** wheat, barley, oats, grapes, olives. **Natural resources:** crude oil, natural gas, iron ore, phosphates, uranium. **Major industries:** petroleum, light industries, natural gas, mining. **Labor force:** 9.4 mil. (2001 est.); 29% government, 25% agriculture, 15% construction and public works, 11% industry, 20% other (1996 est.). **Exports:** $19.5 bil. (f.o.b., 2001 est.); petroleum and natural gas. **Imports**: $10.6 bil. (f.o.b., 2002 est.); capital goods, food, beverages, consumer goods. **Major trading partners:** ***exports:*** 23% Italy, 15% France, 14% Spain. ***imports:*** 40% France, 11%U.S., 10% Italy.

From around 3000 B.C. nomadic ancestors of the Berbers inhabited Algeria, as the expanding Sahara desert displaced prehistoric grasslands and forests. The Phoenicians established trading centers in the Mediterranean coastal plain around 1200 B.C. Those centers were taken over by the Romans beginning around 200 B.C. With Roman support the Berber chief Masinissa formed the kingdom of Numidia in what is now northern Algeria. From 46 B.C. to about A.D. 640, the area was controlled successively by the Romans, Germanic Vandal tribes, and the Byzantine Empire.

In the eighth century A.D., the Islamic conquests spread Arab culture to Numidia. Most of the Berbers converted to Islam. The blend of Berber and Arab culture in Algeria gave rise to a flourishing and rich Islamic civilization in the coastal plain, while Tuareg and other nomadic peoples controlled the sparsely inhabited interior.

Around 1500 the Christian kingdom of Spain captured Algiers and other coastal cities. In 1518 Barbarossa, a Turkish sea captain, captured Algiers and drove the Spanish out. In so doing, he joined Algeria to the expanding Turkish Ottoman Empire. Piracy became a key source of income for the Ottoman cities of Algeria. In the early 1800's, France, along with England and the U.S., began military operations to suppress piracy in the Mediterranean. In 1830 France invaded Algeria, putting an end to Ottoman rule and establishing their own administration. Algeria was ruled as part of France itself. Many French settlers (colons) migrated to Algeria. Both they and the native Algerians were considered citizens of France, but the colons were granted substantial political and economic advantages over the indigenous population.

In 1847 a rebellion led by Abd-al-Qadir, a powerful Muslim leader, was suppressed by the French. In 1848, all of Algeria was conquered by the French and legally confirmed as part of France. During World War II, many Algerians joined the Free French, hoping that their display of loyalty would be rewarded with greater self-rule after the war. Those hopes were disappointed, as French administration was resumed in 1945.

In 1954 the Front de Liberation Nationale (FLN) began a guerrilla war against the French in Algeria. They were opposed by French police and military forces and by the Secret Army Organization (OAS), an underground movement of colons who favored continued French rule. As the FLN gained strength, by 1958 French premier Charles de Gaulle established a policy designed to prepare Algeria for self-rule.

Algerian independence was proclaimed on July 3, 1962; a million colons fled to France. A power struggle within the new Algerian government was resolved when Ahmed Ben Bella became the country's first premier in 1963. In 1965 Ben Bella was deposed by Col. Houari Boumidienne, who ruled as the head of a military government. In 1967 Algeria declared war on Israel, broke with the West, and established close relations with the U.S.S.R. Since the early 1970's, relations with the West, and particularly with France, have improved (mainly because of oil).

The first free, multiparty elections were held on June 12, 1990. The Islamic Salvation Front, which advocates turning Algeria into an Islamic Republic, won overwhelming control of local assemblies. In 1991 it won 188 seats in Parliament out of 231 up for election and seemed poised to win control of the government when the army interceded to keep the old power structure in place. On June 19, 1992, Pres. Mohammed Boudiaf was assassinated, presumably by Islamic fundamentalists.

The military's High Security Council, knowing the Islamic parties would win any free election, postponed a return to democracy. In January 1994 the High Security Council replaced the collective presidency of the High State Council with Gen. Liamine Zeroual. November 1995 saw the first contested presidential election since 1962, with Gen. Zeroual winning over 60 percent of the vote as major opposition groups boycotted the election. Elections in June 1997 produced Algeria's first mutli-party parliament since 1962, but the ruling military council still remained in control and in August Islamic fundamentalists killed over 300 in one night of terror. These vicious assasinations continued into 1998 with hundreds more having their throats cut over several nights. Civil strife and assassinations have claimed the lives of over 40,000 since 1992. In Sept. 1998 Gen. Zeroual announced that elections would be held in Feb. 1999 and he would not be a candidate.

By the time the elections were held in April, all candidates had withdrawn from the race save one, the army-backed Abdelaziz Bouteflika. His new government reached an accord with the rebel Islamic Salvation Front: in return for the end of the uprising, Pres. Bouteflika pledged to release thousands of militant Islamic prisoners on July 5, Algeria's national holiday, and to submit the peace agreement to a referendum. In Sept., 98 percent of voters favored the agreement that gave amnesty to militants who surrendered. When the amnesty period ended (Jan. 2000), the government claimed that 80 percent of the rebels had surrendered—probably an exaggeration—then commenced a major army offensive against remaining rebels, now organized as the "Armed Islamic Group" (GIA). While the GIA remained unconquered into 2002, the government was mending fences with the Berber people (who constitute about 1/3 of Algeria's population), recognizing their Tamazight language as a legal language in April. In May, the FLN won 199 seats in the 389-seat National Assembly.

▶ANDORRA

Principality of Andorra

• **GEOGRAPHY** **Location:** Pyrenees Mountains, southwestern Europe. **Boundaries**: France to N and E, Spain to S and W. **Total area**: 174 sq. mi. (450 sq km). **Coastline**: none. **Comparative area**: 2.5 times size of Washington, D.C. **Land use:** 2% arable land; 0% permanent crops; 98% other. **Major cities**: (1989) Andorra la Vella (capital) 19,566.
• **PEOPLE** **Population:** 69,150 (July 2003 est.). **Nationality:** noun—Andorran(s); adjective—Andorran. **Ethnic groups:** 43% Spanish, 33% Andorran, 11% Portuguese, 7% French, 6% other. **Languages:** Catalan (official); many also speak some French and Castilian. **Religions:** virtually all Roman Catholic.
• **GOVERNMENT** **Type:** parliamentary democracy (since March 1993) that retains as head of state a co-principality; the two princes are the president of France and Spanish bishop of Seo de Urgel, who are represented locally by officials called veguers. **Independence:** 1278. **Constitution:** March 1993. **National holiday:** Mare de Deu de Meritxell, Sept. 8. **Heads of Government:** French co-prince Jacques Chirac, president of France (since 1995) and Spanish co-prince Episcopal Msgr. Joan Enric Vives Siclia (since May 12, 2003); Don Marc Forne Molne, prime minister (since Dec. 1994). **Structure:** executive—co-princes, executive council; unicameral legislature; judiciary—Supreme Court at Perpignan, France.
• **ECONOMY** **Monetary unit:** euro. **Budget:** (1997) ***income:*** $385 mil.; ***expend.:*** $342 mil. **GDP:** $1.3 bil., $19,000 per capita (2000 est.). **Chief crops:** sheep raising; small quantities of tobacco, rye, wheat, barley, oats, and vegetables. **Natural resources:** hydropower, mineral water, timber, iron ore, lead. **Major industries:** tourism (particularly skiing), cattle raising, timber, tobacco, banking. **Labor force:** 33,000. (2001 est.). **Exports:** $58 mil. (f.o.b., 1998); tobacco products, furniture. **Imports**: $1.077 bil. (1998). **Major trading partners:** ***exports:*** 34% France, 58% Spain; ***imports:*** France, Spain, 2.8% U.S.

Set high in the Pyrenees, the tiny state of Andorra has been both a medieval relic and a modern capitalist land. Since 1278 Andorra has owed feudal allegiance to two co-rulers, the bishop of Seo de Urgel in Spain and, now, the president of France. Until 1993, Andorra had no constitution, so the exact rights of the corulers remained vague. Foreign affairs were handled by France.

Andorra's traditional economic mainstay had been the "transshipment of goods" (i.e., smuggling) between France and Spain. Andorra attracts tourists drawn by bargain shopping, and it is a banking center. Spain's 1986 entry into the E.U. led Andorra to seek a customs union with the E.U. The March 1990 treaty was Andorra's first in over 700 years. In the same year, the co-princes introduced Andorra's first penal code and a sales tax, soon followed by the adoption of the E.U.'s external tariff. In March 1993 voters—of whom there are only 9,123—adopted a modern constitution that will reduce the power of the co-princes and establish a government of three branches that will have authority to tax and to make foreign policy. In 1997 Premier Molne's party won a majority of seats in the General Council ending the coalition government.

▶ANGOLA

Republic of Angola

• **GEOGRAPHY** **Location:** southwestern Africa. **Boundaries**: Zaire to N and NE, Zambia to E, Namibia to S, South Atlantic Ocean to W; Cabinda district separated from rest of country by Congo to N, Zaire to S. **Total area**: 481,352 sq. mi. (1,246,700 sq km). **Coastline**: 994 mi. (1,600 km). **Comparative area**: slightly less than twice size of Texas. **Land use:** 2% arable land; negl. % permanent crops; 97% other. **Major cities**: Luanda (capital) 1,200,000 (1982 est.); Huambo (Nova Lisboa) 61,885; Lobito 59,258; Benguela 40,996; Lubango (São da Bandeira) 31,674 (1970 census).
• **PEOPLE** **Population:** 10,766,741 (July 2003 est.). **Nationality:** noun—Angolan(s); adjective—Angolan. **Ethnic groups:** 37% Ovimbundu, 25% Kimbundu, 13% Bakongo, 2% Mestiço, 1% European, 22% other. **Languages:** Portuguese (official), Bantu and other African languages. **Religions:** 47% indigenous beliefs, 38% Roman Catholic, 15% Protestant.
• **GOVERNMENT** **Type:** republic (nominally). **Independence:** Nov. 11, 1975 (from Portugal). **Constitution:** Nov. 11, 1975 (last revised Aug. 26, 1992). **National holiday:** Independence Day, Nov. 11. **Heads of Government:** José Eduardo dos Santos, president (since Sept. 1979); Fernando van Dunem, prime minister (since June 1996). **Structure:** executive; unicameral legislature; judiciary.
• **ECONOMY** **Monetary unit:** kwanza. **Budget:** (1992 est.) ***income:*** $928 mil.; ***expend.:*** $2.5 bil. **GDP:** $16.9 bil. (2002 est.), $1,600 per capita. **Chief crops:** bananas, sugarcane, coffee, sisal, corn, cotton, manioc (tapioca), vegetables. **Natural resources:** petroleum, diamonds, iron ore, phosphates, copper. **Major industries:** petroleum, mining (diamonds, iron ore, phosphates), food processing. **Labor force:** 5 mil. (1997 est.); 85% agriculture, 15% industry. **Exports:** $8.6 bil. (f.o.b., 2002 est.); oil, diamonds, petroleum products, gas, coffee. **Imports**: $4.1 bil. (f.o.b., 2002 est.); machinery, electrical equipment, vehicles and spare parts, medicines, food, textiles; substantial military deliveries. **Major trading partners:** ***exports:*** 44% U.S., 19% China; ***imports:*** 15% Portugal, 12% South Africa.

Bantu peoples have occupied Angola for 2,000 years. Portuguese explorers searching for a sea route to India founded Luanda (1575) and Benguela (1617). Portugal, in alliance with the Angolan kingdom of Bakongo, engaged in an extensive trade of slaves to Brazil—3 million in 300 years.

In the late 19th century, Angola was organized as a Portuguese colony, sometimes called Portuguese West Africa. Portuguese settlers dominated local government, and trade, organized plantation-style cultivation of cotton, palm oil, bananas, and coffee. A railroad was built to transport exports of metal from the Katanga region of the Belgian Congo (now Zaire) to the coast.

By the 1950's non-Portuguese Angolans began to agitate for independence. The National Front spearheaded the liberation movement. Guerrilla warfare began in 1961, with several feuding factions fighting the Portuguese. Following the Portuguese revolution of 1974, factional warfare intensified and most Portuguese settlers fled the country. Independence came on Nov. 11, 1975.

Civil war between the National Front, the Popular Movement for the Liberation of Angola (MPLA), and the National Union for the Total Independence of Angola (UNITA) led, in 1976, to the victory of the MPLA, which organized a Marxist state with Soviet backing and Cuban technical support including 37,000 soldiers. Large portions of the country remained in the hands of UNITA, which continued the civil war with Chinese and American support through the 1980's.

Direct clashes between Angolan and South African troops occurred during the 1980's, as Angola gave shelter to SWAPO guerrilla forces seeking independence for Namibia. Cuban troops withdrew from Angola between January 1989 and May 1991, and a cease-fire between the government and UNITA was also concluded in May 1991. While agreeing to recognize the dos Santos government, UNITA called for elections to be held by Sept. 1992, Angola's first since 1975.

In the elections, MPLA's candidate, José Eduardo dos Santos, decisively defeated UNITA's leader, Jonas Savimbi, but Savimbi's refusal to honor the results led to renewed fighting. The presence of thousands of U.N. peacekeepers from Feb. 1994 until Feb. 1999 made little dent in the continuing struggle which claimed perhaps 100,000 lives. The government succeeded, in 2000, in taking two diamond-mining provinces as well as the town of Cazombo from UNITA, capping the year with an offer of amnesty, in a gesture of reconciliation. But it was not until after Savimbi's death in a gun battle in Feb. 2002 that UNITA could be brought to sign a cease-fire in April which may signal an end to the long civil war. UNITA demobilization, a blanket amnesty, and recognition of UNITA as a legitimate political party are the main provisions.

▶ANTIGUA AND BARBUDA

• GEOGRAPHY **Location:** eastern Caribbean Sea approximately 300 mi. (480 km) SE of Puerto Rico. Antigua 17°06'N, 61°50'W; Barbuda 17°38'N, 61°48'W. **Boundaries**: Atlantic Ocean to N and E, Caribbean Sea to S and W. **Total area**: 170 sq. mi. (440 sq km). **Coastline**: 95 mi. (153 km). **Comparative area**: 2.5 times size of Washington, D.C. **Land use:** 18% arable land; 0% permanent crops; 82% other. **Major cities**: (1986 est.) St. John's (capital) 36,000.

• PEOPLE **Population:** 67,897 (July 2003 est.). **Nationality:** noun—Antiguan(s), Barbudan(s); adjective—Antiguan, Barbudan. **Ethnic groups:** almost entirely of black African origin; some of British, Portuguese, Lebanese, and Syrian origin. **Languages:** English (official), local dialects. **Religions:** Anglican (predominant), other Protestant sects, some Roman Catholic.

• GOVERNMENT **Type:** constitutional monarchy with U.K.-style parliament. **Independence:** Nov. 1, 1981 (from U.K.). **Constitution:** Nov. 1, 1981. **National holiday:** Independence Day, Nov. 1. **Heads of Government:** Dr. James B. Carlisle, governor-general (since June 1993); Lester B. Bird, prime minister (since Mar. 1994). **Structure:** executive—governor general, prime minister, and cabinet; bicameral legislature; judiciary—East Caribbean Supreme Court.

• ECONOMY **Monetary unit:** East Caribbean (EC) dollar. **Budget:** (2000) ***income:*** $123.7 mil.; ***expend.:*** $145.9 mil. **GDP:** $750 mil., $11,000 per capita (2002 est.). **Chief crops:** cotton, fruits and vegetables, sugar. **Natural resources:** negl.; pleasant climate fosters tourism. **Major industries:** tourism, construction, light manufacturing (clothing, alcohol, household appliances). **Labor force:** 30,000 (1983); 82% commerce and services, 11% agriculture, 7% industry; 11% unemployment (2001 est.). **Exports:** $40 mil. (2000); 48% petroleum products, 23% manufactures, 17% machinery and transportation equipment, 4% food and live animals. **Imports**: $357 mil. (2000); food and live animals, machinery and transport equipment, manufactures, chemicals, oil. **Major trading partners: *exports:*** 26% OECD, 15% Barbados, 4% Guyana, 2% Trinidad and Tobago; ***imports:*** 27% U.S., 16% U.K., 4% Canada.

Columbus visited and claimed Antigua for Spain in 1493. It was settled by the British in 1632, who grew tobacco, and later sugar. The island's economy was hobbled by abolition of slavery in 1834, a succession of natural disasters in the 1840's, and the closing of the Royal Dockyard in 1854. Today, tourism is a mainstay of the economy, fostered by the ruling Antigua Labor Party, which won its sixth consecutive parliamentary victory in March 1999. But its second economic mainstay, offshore banking, has been shaken by a U.S. Treasury warning in April 1999 that lax standards make it susceptible to money-laundering.

▶ARGENTINA
Argentine Republic

• GEOGRAPHY **Location:** southern South America. **Boundaries**: Bolivia, Paraguay, Brazil to N.; Uruguay, South Atlantic Ocean to E.; Chile to W. **Total area**: 1,068,298 sq. mi. (2,766,890 sq km) (figures exclude Falkland Islands and Antarctic territory claimed by Argentina). **Coastline**: 3,099 mi. (4,989 km). **Comparative area**: slightly less than three-tenths the size of the United States. **Land use:** 9% arable land; 1% permanent crops; 90% other. **Major cities**: (1991 census) Buenos Aires (capital) 12,960,976; Córdoba 1,148,305; La Matanza 1,111,811; Rosario 894,645; Morón 641,541.

• PEOPLE **Population:** 38,740,807 (July 2003 est.). **Nationality:** noun—Argentine(s); adjective—Argentine. **Ethnic groups:** 97% white, 3% mestizo, Indian, and other nonwhite groups. **Languages:** Spanish (official), English, Italian, German, French. **Religions:** 92% Roman Catholic (less than 20% practicing), 2% Protestant, 2% Jewish, 4% other.

• GOVERNMENT **Type:** republic. **Independence:** July 9, 1816 (from Spain). **Constitution:** May 1, 1853 (revised Aug. 1994). **National holiday:** Revolution Day, May 25. **Head of Government:** Néstor Carlos Kirchner, president (since May 25, 2003). **Structure:** executive; bicameral legislature; judiciary.

• ECONOMY **Monetary unit:** nuevo peso argentino. **Budget:** (2000 est.) ***income:*** $44 bil.; ***expend.:*** $48 bil. **GDP:** (2002 est.) $391 bil., $10,200 per capita. **Chief crops:** wheat, corn, soybeans. **Natural resources:** fertile plains of the pampas, lead, zinc, tin, copper, iron ore, petroleum. **Major industries:** food processing (especially meat packing), motor vehicles, consumer durables. **Labor force:** 15 mil. (1999 est.); 57% services, 31% industry, 12% agriculture; 21.5% unemployment (2002 est.). **Exports:** $25.3 bil. (f.o.b., 2002 est.); edible oils, cereals, feed, motor vehicles. **Imports**: $9 bil. (f.o.b., 2002 est.); motor vehicles and parts, chemicals, plastics. **Major trading partners: *exports:*** 27% Brazil, 12% U.S., 11% Chile; ***imports:*** 25% Brazil, 19% U.S., 5% Germany.

The indigenous nomads of the area around the river La Plata resisted Spanish intrusion, which began with the first founding of Buenos Aires by Pedro de Mendoza in 1536. Argentina was part of Spain's Viceroyalty of Peru until reforms in the Bourbon dynasty and a need to defend against Portuguese encroachment from Brazil led to the formation of the Viceroyalty of La Plata, including Argentina, Bolivia, Paraguay, and Uruguay, in 1776. Following the relaxation of trade restrictions two years later, Buenos Aires grew from a small town to a city of 50,000 by 1800. A provisional junta of the Provinces of Río de la Plata was established in 1810 after the Napoleonic occupation of Spain, and in 1816 the United Provinces of the Río de la Plata declared their independence.

After independence the question of political relations among the United Provinces was settled by a federalist solution in which the provinces dissolved into a number of practically independent republics. In 1824, a constituent assembly created the office of president, first held by Bernardino Rivadavia. However, the failure to ratify a workable constitution caused Rivadavia to resign.

Juan Manuel de Rosas became governor of Buenos Aires in 1829 and presided over the construction of a federal agreement between the provinces in 1831. Rosas governed Buenos Aires with an iron hand until his expulsion in 1852. The other provinces formed the Argentine Federation, based on a federal constitution of 1853, but Buenos Aires refused to join. Buenos Aires and the Argentine Federation entered into war (1859-1861) but reached an agreement on the inclusion of Buenos Aires in the Argentine Republic in 1862.

Argentina joined Brazil and Uruguay in a war (1865-70) against Paraguay. During the latter part of the 1870's, the government took the initiative against the indigenous populations of Patagonia and Tierra del Fuego, which were partitioned with Chile. Immigration from Europe, especially Spain and Italy, resulted in enormous growth. In 1869, there were 2 million inhabitants; by 1914, 8 million; by 1955, 19 million; and by 1990, 32 million.

The Argentine military, led by Lt. Gen. José F. Uriburu, ousted the civilian government of the Radical party in 1930 with the intention of following the European model of politics. In 1946 Juan Domingo Perón won the presidential election and constructed a populist political alliance that included workers, industrialists, and the armed forces. The Perón-inspired populist ideology of *justicialismo* included extension of the franchise to women and redistribution of income to workers and the poor. The activities of Perón's charismatic wife, Eva, bolstered *justicialismo* through her effort to distribute goods to the poor through the Social Aid Foundation.

Tied in with Perón's populist strategy was his policy of nationalist economic development, whereby state-led development was financed through extraction of capital from the old export-agricultural elite and politically supported through populism. The Perón government incurred great expense to gain control over foreign-owned economic infrastructure, including railway systems, telephone companies, and dock facilities. A number of events led to Perón's downfall in 1955. The market for Argentine goods deteriorated after World War II. As Perón shifted his strategy to encourage foreign investment and impose economic austerity, repression against the political opposition grew. The death of Eva Perón in 1952 robbed Perón of an important political resource, and when the government challenged the Catholic church on a number of issues, the military ousted Perón.

After a brief period of military rule, in which an attempt was made to roll back "Perónismo," Arturo Frondizi of the "Intransigent" faction of the Radical party won the presidency in 1958. In the following years, the military repeatedly attempted to keep the Perónistas from returning to power. In 1962 the military forced Frondizi to annul Perónist victories in provincial elections and removed him from office. Pres. Arturo Illia was ousted from office in 1966 for the same reason.

A military bureaucratic authoritarian regime led by a series of Argentine officers was established during 1966-73. Extreme violence by factions on the Left and Right led the military to accept Perón's return to the presidency in 1973. Perón died the following year, and his third wife, Isabel, replaced him but the military removed her in 1976 in the midst of economic and political upheaval.

Determined to deal with what they saw as a leftist threat, the armed forces launched what was later called the "dirty war," during which up to 20,000 people disappeared and were never heard from again. The authoritarian government collapsed after the 1982 Falkland/Malvinas Islands War against Britain led to the resignation of the junta and the holding of elections. Raúl Alfonsín, of the Radical Union party, was elected president in 1983. In 1989, he was succeeded by Carlos Saúl Menem, who agreed to take office early, in the midst of an economic crisis during which inflation reached 3,000 percent and foreign debt $58 billion.

Menem encouraged free enterprise and good relations with the U.S. Government controls on foreign investment and trade were relaxed, and the government sold off many state enterprises. In 1993 Argentina's 11-year debt crisis officially ended, and by 1995 inflation was down to 4 percent. In 1995 the government introduced an austerity plan to fight the budget deficit and to cushion the shocks of Mexico's devaluation. As Argentina's economy began to flourish, Menem was reelected, and his party won majorities in both houses of the legislature and control of more than half of Argentina's provincial governments.

But in May 1997, violent protests erupted in several major cities, as unemployment rose to nearly 20 percent. In October, the Peronistas lost control of the Chamber of Deputies, for the first time since 1983, to a left-wing coalition known as The Alliance. Presidential elections in October 1999 brought the first-ever Peronista defeat, as Alliance's Fernando de la Rúa defeated Eduardo Duhalde, while further Alliance legislative victories brought them within five seats of an absolute majority in the House of Deputies.

Throughout 2000, the rather fragile Alliance managed to move gingerly to fight corruption, to reform certain privileges of organized labor, and to balance the federal and state budgets. This was sufficient to gain a pledge from the I.M.F. and other international lenders for a $40 billion bailout, but by the middle of 2001 the recession had grown worse and the government put a severe austerity plan in place. Strikes and rioting at last drove de la Rua to resign in December, and his successor, interim president Rodriguez, resigned after only a week. A second interim president, but with a two-year term, was chosen by Parliament: Senator Duhalde. His decoupling of the peso from the dollar and its subsequent devaluation brought some relief but no solution to the crisis.Only a January 2003 roll-over by the IMF prevented a third major default, private investors and the World Bank having been stiffed earlier.

In the 2003 presidential election Menem withdrew from the run-off, leaving the presidency to Duhalde's protege, Nestor Kirchner.

▶ARMENIA

Republic of Armenia

• GEOGRAPHY **Location:** southwest Transcaucasia between Europe and Asia. **Boundaries**: Georgia to N, Azerbaijan to E, Iran to S, Turkey to W. Nakhichevan Autonomous Republic, an Azerbaijan territory, is an enclave within Armenian territory. **Total area**: 11,506 sq. mi. (29,800 sq km). **Coastline**: none. **Comparative area**: slightly smaller than Maryland. **Land use:** 18% arable land; 2% permanent crops; 80% other. **Major cities**: (1990 est.) Yerevan (capital) 1,202,000; Kumayri (formerly Leninakan) 123,000; Kirovakan 76,000.

• PEOPLE **Population:** 3,326,448 (July 2003 est.). **Nationality:** noun—Armenian(s); adjective—Armenian. **Ethnic groups:** 93% Armenian, 1% Azeri, 2% Russian. **Languages:** 96% Armenian, 2% Russian, 2% other. **Religions:** 94% Armenian Orthodox.

• GOVERNMENT **Type:** republic. **Independence:** Sept. 21, 1991 (from U.S.S.R.). **Constitution:** July 5, 1995. **National holiday:** Independence Day, Sept. 21. **Heads of Government:** Robert Kocharian, president (since April 1998); Andranik Markaryan, prime minister (since May 2000). **Structure:** executive; unicameral legislatiure; judiciary.

• ECONOMY **Monetary unit:** dram. **Budget:** (1999 est.) ***income:*** $402 mil.; ***expend.:***$482 mil. **GDP:** $12.6 bil., $3,800 per capita (2002 est.). **Chief crops:** fruit (especially wine grapes), vegetables, livestock. **Natural resources:** small deposits of gold and copper. **Major industries:** Industrial machinery, electrical equipment, tires, textiles (much of industry). **Labor force:** 1.4 mil. (2001). **Exports:** $525 mil. (f.o.b., 2001 est.); diamonds, mineral products, foodstuffs. **Imports**: $991 mil. (f.o.b., 2001 est.); natural gas, petroleum, tobacco products, foodstuffs. **Major trading partners:** Russia, U.S., Belgium.

Armenia, a small landlocked country just south of the great Caucasus mountain range, is but a fragment of ancient Armenia, one of the world's oldest civilizations dating back to the sixth century B.C. In about A.D. 300, Armenia adopted Christianity, which today is still an important component of Armenian national identity. Because Armenia forms part of a land bridge between the Black and the Caspian Seas, and between Turks and Slavs, it has long been overrun and controlled by the Byzantine, Arab, Ottoman, Mongol, and Russian Empires. In 1236 the Tatar and Mongol invasion spelled the end of Armenia as a separate state. In 1639, after the conclusion of a major war between Turkey and Iran, the territory of Armenia was partitioned. By the end of the 17th century, czarist Russia was also involved in Armenia, and in 1828 eastern Armenia was ceded to the Russian empire by the Treaty of Turkmenchai.

During the First World War, those Armenians living in the western part of the country under Ottoman rule were increasingly subjected to persecution by the Turks. In April 1915, the Turks forcibly removed the Armenians from the border area, during which more than a million of them either starved or were killed. In 1918, an Armenian republic emerged as the Russian empire collapsed, but this entity was short-lived, as Turkey, Russia, and later Britain fought for control. Finally, the Soviet Red Army moved into the territory and on Nov. 29, 1920, declared it a Soviet republic. Armenia was made part of the Transcaucasian Soviet Federal Socialist Republic of the U.S.S.R. in 1922, and in 1936, it became one of the Soviet Union's constituent union republics.

Armenian Christians have been subjected to many years of persecution by various invaders, causing a great diaspora of Armenians, especially to the United States and Europe. This large expatriate community has helped Armenia from abroad through difficult times.

Since 1988, Armenia's most pressing issue has been the war over Nagorno-Karabakh, the Armenian Christian enclave of Muslim Azerbaijan. Fighting broke out when 180,000 ethnic Armenians in Azerbaijan demanded that their homeland become part of Armenia. The war continued even as both nations declared their independence from the Soviet Union (Armenia on Sept. 23, 1991; Azerbaijan a month later). In October 1991, Levon Ter-Petrossian was elected president of independent Armenia, and in December, Armenia was one of 11 former Soviet republics to sign the Alma-Ata Declaration, creating the Commonwealth of Independent States. Since independence, Armenia has remained committed to the war over Nagorno-Karabakh, even though it has hindered the functioning of the stagnant Armenian economy.

In 1995, a new "strong president" constitution was approved by 68 percent in a referendum and Pres. Ter-Petrossian's six-party Republic Coalition carried a majority of seats in the first elections for the 190-seat National Assembly. He was reelected in 1996 but resigned in February 1998 in a dispute over policy toward Nagorno-Karabakh with his hard-line premier Robert Kocharian. In March, Kocharian easily won the presidential election over Soviet-era ruler Karen Demirchyan. In October 1999, gunmen entered Parliament, murdering premier Vazgen Sargissian and seven others. President Kocharian named Sargissian's brother, Aram, a political neophyte, as new premier. In March 2003, Kocharian was elected to a second five-year term as president, taking over 60% of the disputed vote; in May, his coalition won 70 of 131 parliamentary seats.

▶AUSTRALIA

Commonwealth of Australia

• GEOGRAPHY **Location:** continent of Australia, between Indian and Pacific Oceans. **Boundaries**: nearest neighbor is Papua New Guinea, to N. **Total area**: 2,967,897 sq. mi. (7,686,850 sq km). **Coastline**: 16,010 mi. (25,760 km). **Comparative area**: slightly smaller than U.S. **Land use:** 7% arable land; negl. % permanent crops; 93% other. **Major cities**: (1993 est.) Canberra (capital) 325,400; Sydney 3,719,000; Melbourne 3,187,500; Brisbane 1,421,700; Perth 1,221,300.

• PEOPLE **Population:** 19,731,984 (July 2003 est.). **Nationality:** noun—Australian(s); adjective—Australian. **Ethnic groups:** 92% Caucasian, 7% Asian, 1% aboriginal and other. **Languages:** English, native langs. **Religions:** 26.1% Anglican, 26% Roman Catholic, 24.3% other Christian, 11% non-Christian.

• GOVERNMENT **Type:** democratic, federal-state system. **Independence:** Jan. 1, 1901 (from federation of U.K. colonies). **Constitution:** July 9, 1900; effective Jan. 1, 1901. **National holiday:** Australia Day, Jan. 26. **Heads of Government:** Dr. Peter Hollingworth, governor general (since June 2001); John Howard, prime minister (since Mar. 1996). **Structure:** executive—governor general (appointed by the Queen), prime minister, and cabinet; bicameral legislature; independent judiciary.

• **ECONOMY** **Monetary unit:** Australian dollar. **Budget:** (FY01/02 est.) ***income:*** $86.8 bil.; ***expend.:*** $84.1 bil. **GDP:** (2002 est.) $528 bil.; $27,000 per capita. **Chief crops:** wheat, barley, sugarcane, fruits; cattle. **Natural resources:** bauxite, coal, iron ore, copper, tin. **Major industries:** mining, industrial and transportation equipment, food processing. **Labor force:** 9.2 mil. (2001); 73% services, 22% industry, 5% agriculture, 6.3% unemployment (2002). **Exports:** $66.3 bil. (f.o.b., 2002 est.); coal, gold, meat, wool. **Imports**: $68 bil. (f.o.b., 2002 est.); machinery and transport equipment, computers and office machines, telecommunication equipment and parts. **Major trading partners:** ***exports:*** 46% developing countries, 20% Japan, 13% ASEAN; ***imports:*** 32% developing countries, 22% E.U., 20% U.S.

The continent-nation of Australia is distinguished by its geographical isolation and by the unique flora and fauna that isolation fostered. The ancestors of today's aborigines arrived from Southeast Asia as much as 40,000 years ago. Thereafter, aborigine culture evolved in isolation except for some contact between the peoples of the northern coast and New Guinea. Australia was first sighted by Europeans at the beginning of the 17th century. In the 18th century, it was visited by the Dutch, who named it New Holland. The eastern coast was systematically explored in 1770 by Capt. James Cook, who claimed it for Great Britain.

British settlement began in 1788, with the landing of about 700 convicts near Sydney. Australia remained a penal colony during the first half of the 19th century, during which time the continent was explored and separate colonies established. Aboriginal populations were displaced and in some areas (most notably the island Tasmania) totally exterminated. Discovery of gold in Victoria in 1851 created a gold rush that greatly accelerated immigration. By 1900, the three mainstays of the Australian economy—livestock, mining, and wheat growing—were firmly established.

In 1901, a commonwealth was established consisting of a confederation of the various states except for the Northern Territory, which was added in 1911. The British Crown is represented by an appointed governor-general; the national government is a parliamentary system, but much local authority resides in the separate states. Comprehensive social welfare legislation was passed by the state and national governments soon after the commonwealth's formation. The population is highly educated and enjoys a generally high standard of living, but most aborigines are detribalized and live in considerable poverty.

Australian troops fought with distinction in both world wars. A Japanese threat to Australia in 1942 was averted by Allied victory in the Battle of the Coral Sea. Australia and the United States are firm allies, and Australian troops joined U.S. forces in Korea, Vietnam, the Persian Gulf War and the invasion of Iraq. Australia administers several external island groups and claims territory in Antarctica.

The abandonment of discriminatory immigration practices in 1973 led to a new wave of immigration, particularly from Asia. In the process Australian economic ties to Asia and the Pacific Rim have expanded considerably. New exploitation of mineral resources has in many cases been accomplished with Japanese investment or with long-term export contracts to Japan. Australia has undergone considerable industrial development in the past three decades.

After 10 years in office, Prime Minister Bob Hawke was ousted by his own Labour party in 1991 and replaced by Paul Keating. Keating's government was reelected in 1993 elections, despite a persistent economic slump. But continued high spending and taxes took their toll, and in 1996, 13 years of Labour rule ended. A coalition of the more conservative Liberal and Nationalist parties captured 94 of 148 seats in the House of Representatives. The popular Liberal party leader John Howard became the new prime minister.

In Oct. 1998 elections, the Liberal-Nationalist coalition maintained its control of the House of Representatives. In the interim, Australia's Constitutional Convention voted (in Feb. 1998) to proclaim Australia a republic, severing its residual ties to the British Crown. But in a 1999 referendum, voters rejected the republic 55 to 45 percent. With respect to aboriginal claims to Australian land, the government carried a Native Title Bill in July 1998, giving Australia's state governments authority to rule on the issue.

Howard and the Liberal-Nationalist coalition gained a third straight term in Nov. 2001 elections, although Labour gained control of every state government. The Howard government's decision to participate in the Iraqi war brought a (purely symbolic) vote of "no confidence" in the Senate; the real "no confidence" vote in the House failed by 82-63. By April 2003 Australian troops were already withdrawing, refusing to take part in any peacekeeping force.

▶AUSTRIA
Republic of Austria

• **GEOGRAPHY** **Location:** landlocked country in central Europe. **Boundaries**: Germany and Czech Republic to N, Hungary and Slovak Republic to E, Slovenia and Italy to S, Switzerland and Liechtenstein to W. **Total area**: 32,377 sq. mi. (83,858 sq km). **Coastline**: none. **Comparative area**: slightly smaller than Maine. **Land use:** 17% arable land; 1% permanent crops; 82% other. **Major cities**: (1991 census) Vienna (capital) 1,533,176; Graz 232,155; Linz 202,855; Salzburg 143,971; Innsbruck 114,996.

• **PEOPLE** **Population:** 8,188,207 (July 2003 est.). **Nationality:** noun—Austrian(s); adjective—Austrian. **Ethnic groups:** 97% German, Croatian, Slovene, other. **Languages:** German. **Religions:** 78% Roman Catholic, 5% Protestant, 17% Muslim or other.

• **GOVERNMENT** **Type:** federal republic. **Constitution:** 1920; revised 1929; reinstated May 1945. **National holiday:** National Day, Oct. 26. **Heads of Government:** Thomas Klestil, president (since July 1992); Dr. Wolfgang Schüssel, chancellor (since Feb. 2000). **Structure:** executive; bicameral legislature; directly elected president whose functions are largely representational; independent federal judiciary.

• **ECONOMY** **Monetary unit:** euro. **Budget:** (2001 est.) ***income:*** $53 bil.; ***expend.:*** $54 bil. **GDP:** (2002 est.) $226 bil., $27,700 per capita. **Chief crops:** grain, fruits, potatoes, sugar beets. **Natural resources:** iron ore, crude oil, timber, magnesite, lead. **Major industries:** construction machinery, vehicles and parts, food. **Labor force:** 4.3 mil. (2001); foreign laborers number 298,000; 67% services, 29% industry and crafts, 4% agriculture and forestry; 4.8% unemployment (2002 est.). **Exports:** (2001 est.) $70 bil.; machinery and equipment, paper and cardboard, metal goods.. **Imports**: (2001 est.) $74 bil.; vehicles, machinery and equipment, apparel, metal goods. **Major trading partners:** (2000) ***exports:*** 63% E.U., 5% Switzerland; ***imports:*** 68% E.U., 6% U.S., 3% Switzerland.

The Celtic tribes in what is now Austria were conquered by Rome under Emperor Augustus. After the fall of Rome, it was overrun by Huns, Lombards, Ostrogoths, and Bavarians. In 788 it was incorporated into the empire of Charlemagne. From the 9th to the 13th century, its territory was divided among a variety of feudal domains. In the late 13th century, Austria was reunited under Rudolph I of Habsburg, whose dynasty became synonymous with Austrian history for the next seven centuries. Rudolph's successors steadily enlarged their domain by conquest and marital diplomacy until, by the reign of Charles V (1500-58), they ruled not only the Holy Roman Empire (encompassing most of central Europe) but also the Netherlands, Spain, and all of its colonies.

After the reign of Charles V, the Habsburg Empire was split into two branches, one governing Spain, the other the Holy Roman Empire. Habsburg power in Germany declined after the Thirty Years' War (1618-48) but was affirmed in the Danube valley after the defeat of the Turkish siege of Vienna in 1683 and the subsequent reconquest of Hungary from the Turks. The marriage of Maria Teresa to Francis of Lorraine gave rise to the House of Habsburg-Lorraine in 1745. In 1804 the Austrian empire was founded, and two years later, the defunct Holy Roman Empire was abolished. The Ausgleich ("compromise") of 1867 transformed the empire into the Dual Monarchy of Austria-Hungary.

In 1914 the assassination of Archduke Franz Ferdinand, the heir to the Austrian throne, led to the outbreak of World War I, which resulted in a wholesale redrawing of national boundaries in Central Europe. Austria emerged as a small Alpine republic, with about 12 percent of the territory of the old Dual Monarchy. The new republic faced a severe postwar economic crisis, as well as a political stalemate between the Christian Social party and the Social Democratic party, each with the support of about half of the electorate, and each with its own paramilitary organization.

In 1933, as Hitler's National Socialists rose to power in Germany, Austrian Chancellor Engelbert Dollfuss, leader of the Christian Social party, instituted rule by decree and began building a corporate state modeled on Italian fascism. His attempt to disarm the Social Democratic militia led to civil war. The government triumphed, but Dollfuss was assassinated in an attempted coup by Austrian Nazis in July 1934. Hitler finally forced Austrian union with Germany (the Anschluss) in 1938, after which Austria was considered a part of Greater Germany.

Conquered by American and Soviet troops early in 1945, Austria was divided into French, British, American, and Russian zones of occupation after World War II. But the occupying powers permitted the formation of a unified national government, formed in November 1945 and recognized by the Western powers in 1946. The occupation ended in 1955 with the signing of the Austrian State Treaty. The four powers withdrew their forces, and Austria pledged itself to a policy of permanent neutrality, with no foreign military alliances or military bases on Austrian territory.

The coalition government continued to 1966, when the People's party under Josef Klaus gained a parliamentary majority. In 1970 the Socialist party under Bruno Kreisky came to power. Socialist dominance continued until 1983, when the Socialists had to form a coalition with the right-wing Freedom party in order to stay in power. Kreisky resigned and was succeeded by Fred Sinowatz.

From 1986 to 1997, a "Grand Coalition" of the Socialist and People's Parties governed Austria under Socialist Chancellor Franz Vranitzky. In ten years, the government cautiously privatized state-owned enterprises of the mild Austrian form of socialism, while tourism, a highly developed maunfacturing sector, and substantial petroleum reserves contributed to the country's prosperity. The government dramatically cut taxes and began promoting regional trade with the newly-independent states of East-Central Europe. On Jan. 1, 1995, Austria entered the European Union.

Tensions arising from increasing unemployment and growing immigration of "economic refugees" from Asia and Africa as well as from Eastern Europe led to some worrisome results: amending Austria's asylum law, consideration of immigration quotas, and the growing strength of the right-wing Freedom Party. The desire to meet the E.U.'s single currency standards led to welfare spending cuts which provoked further voter dissatisfaction. In Oct. 1996 Austrian voters (participating for the first time in European Parliament elections), gave Freedom Party candidates, who were opposed to Austria's participation in EMU, 27.6 percent of their votes, while Socialists garnered only 29.1 percent and the People's Party took 29.6 percent.

Chancellor Vranitzky resigned in Jan. 1997 and was succeeded by Socialist Finance Minister Viktor Klima. In the Oct. 1999 elections to the National Council, the Social Democrats received only one-third of the votes, while the People's Party and the Freedom Party each took 27 percent. When it proved impossible to reconstruct the "Grand Coalition," the latter two parties, together controlling 104 of 183 seats, formed their own coalition government, taking office on February 4, 2000 with Wolfgang Schuessel of the People's Party as chancellor.

With the Freedom Party (but not its now-resigned party leader Jörg Haider) entering the Austrian government, the other 14 E.U. governments cut off bilateral diplomatic contacts, as did Israel and the U.S. The E.U. lifted the sanctions after their investigative panel reported the superiority of Austria's treatment of immigrants to that of many other E.U. members; subsequently, the Freedom Party's share of the vote has shown slippage. In Nov. 2002 parliamentary elections, the party garnered but 10 percent of the vote while Chancellor Schluessler's People's Party won a surprising 43 percent. In Feb. 2003 a new People's-Freedom government was formed.

▶AZERBAIJAN
Azerbaijani Republic

• **GEOGRAPHY Location:** southern Transcaucasia between Europe and Asia. **Boundaries**: Georgia to NW, Russian Federation to N, Caspian Sea to E, Iran to S, Armenia to SW. Nakhichevan Autonomous Republic (ASSR) is part of Azerbaijan although it is inside Armenian territory. **Total land area**: 33,436 sq. mi. (86,600 sq km). **Coastline**: Caspian Sea. **Comparative area**: about the size of Maine. **Land use:** 19% arable land; 3% permanent crops; 78% other. **Major cities**: (1990 est.) Baku (capital) 1,149,000; Gyanja (formerly Kirovabad) 281,000; Sumgait 235,000.

• **PEOPLE Population:** 7,830,764 (July 2003 est.). **Nationality:** noun—Azerbaijani(s) or Azeri(s); adjective—Azerbaijani. **Ethnic groups:** 90% Azeri, 3.2% Dagestani Peoples, 2.5% Russian, 2% Armenian, 2.3% other. **Languages:** 89% Azeri, 3% Russian, 2% Armenian, 6% other. (1995 est.). **Reli-**

gions: 93.4% Muslim, 2.5% Russian Orthodox, 2.3% Armenian Orthodox, 1.8% other (1995 est.).
• **GOVERNMENT** **Type:** republic. **Independence:** Aug. 30, 1991 (from U.S.S.R.). **Constitution:** Nov. 12, 1995. **National holiday:** May 28. **Heads of Government:** Heydar Aliyev, president (since Oct. 1993); Ilham Aliyev, prime minister (since Aug. 4, 2003). **Structure:** executive; unicameral legislatiure; judiciary.
• **ECONOMY** **Monetary unit:** manat. **Budget:** (2001 est.) ***income:*** $786 mil.; ***expend.:*** $807 mil. **GDP:** $27 bil., $3,500 per capita (2002 est.). **Chief crops:** cotton, tea, tobacco, grain, fruit. **Natural resources:** petroleum, natural gas, iron ore. **Major industries:** petroleum and natural gas, construction materials, chemicals. **Labor force:** 3.7 mil. (2001). **Exports:** $2 bil. (f.o.b., 2002 est.); oil, gas, oil field equipment, textiles, cotton. **Imports**: $1.8 bil. (f.o.b., 2002 est.); machinery and parts, foodstuffs, metals. **Major trading partners:** Italy, U.S., Russia.

The territory of present-day Azerbaijan has been inhabited since Paleolithic times. The name Azerbaijan is derived (via Arabic and Turkish) from Atropates (a vassal of Alexander III of Macedonia), who founded an independent state here in the fourth century B.C. The population of Azerbaijan is approximately seven million, but nearly seven million additional Azeris with the same language and faith live across the border in Iran.

For much of its history, the territory of Azerbaijan, home to an indigenous nomadic people, has been occupied by Persians, Muslim Arabs, Turkic tribes from Mongolia, Ottoman Turks, Mongols, and in the 18th century, Russians. The capital city of Baku was an important outlet on the Volga River-Caspian Sea route; under Peter the Great, the Russians occupied Baku and Derbent, and for a while controlled the Caspian Sea. Command of this territory shifted between Ottomans, Persians, and Russians in the 18th and 19th centuries, with the Russians ultimately establishing military rule by 1828 with the Treaty of Turkmenchai. This treaty ceded the southern half of the country to Persia and the northern half to Russia.

Under the Russians, Azerbaijan became an industrial center and eventually a major oil producer. In 1883 the Russians finished building the Transcaucasian Railway, which linked Baku with the Black Sea coast and central Russia and made Baku one of the most important industrial hubs in the Russian empire. Baku became a revolutionary center around the turn of the century. In 1918 an independent republic was formed, but in 1920 it was overthrown by the Soviet Red Army, and in April 1920 the Azerbaijan Soviet Socialist Republic (SSR) was proclaimed. Two years later, it was joined with the Armenian and Georgian SSRs to form the Transcaucasian Soviet Federal Socialist Republic; in 1936, however, the three again became separate union republics.

While a Soviet republic, Azerbaijan was industrialized, its agriculture collectivized, and religious persecution was severe. It also entered into a war in 1988 with neighboring Armenia over the Nagorno-Karabakh region, which is largely populated with ethnic Armenians but lies within Azerbaijani territory. The local council of Nagorno-Karabakh petitioned the Armenian and Azerbaijani Supreme Soviets to transfer the region to Armenia in 1988, but Azerbaijan refused, spurring a war that lasts to this day.

In Jan. 1990, attacks on Communist party buildings and against Armenians in Azerbaijan precipitated a brutal Soviet Army intervention to restore order. A state of emergency was declared, and the first secretary of the Communist party was replaced by Ayaz Mutalibov. He was elected president in Sept. 1991, and on Oct. 18, 1991, Azerbaijan's Supreme Soviet declared the country's independence. On Dec. 21, 1991, Azerbaijan joined 10 other former Soviet republics in forming the Commonwealth of Independent States.

After the dissolution of the U.S.S.R., Azerbaijan had problems consolidating its own future. In 1992, Pres. Mutalibov was forced from office. His successor was in turn driven out of office by armed rebels after the fighting in Nagorno-Karabakh turned decisively in Armenia's favor. He was replaced by Heydar Aliyev, a former Communist party boss, in 1993. Aliyev survived two coup attempts and the country's flagging fortunes in Nagorno-Karabakh to complete a $7.4 billion deal with western companies to develop oil fields in the Caspian Sea in Sept. 1994. In parliamentary elections in 1995, Aliyev's New Azerbaijan party won 70 percent of the vote, amidst charges of vote-rigging. And in Jan. 1996, Aliyev negotiated an agreement to transport oil from the Caspian Sea via pipeline (through Chechnya) to the Russian port of Novorossiysk for export to the world market. The pipeline opened Nov. 12, 1997, soon after Aliyev met with Pres. Clinton in Washington to sign a treaty allowing transfer of profits and capital between U.S. and Azerbaijan.

In Oct. 1998, Aliyev held presidential elections which were boycotted by opposition parties and which European monitors declared to be seriously irregular. Aliyev took 76 percent of the vote. In parliamentary elections in Nov. 2000, his New Azerbaijan Party carried 70 percent of the vote, to no one's surprise. The ailing president, in Sept. 2002, oversaw the start of construction on a major oil pipeline from the Caspian through Georgia to Turkey (bypassing both Russia and Iran) and signed a treaty with Russia regularizing the Caspian border. But he was unable in August to prevent a presidential election in the secessionist, ethnically Armenian province of Nagorno-Karabakh.

▶BAHAMAS

Commonwealth of The Bahamas

• **GEOGRAPHY** **Location:** nearly 700 islands in an archipelago that extends 590 mi. (950 km) SE-NW between Florida and Haiti. Nassau 25°05'N, 77°20'W. **Boundaries**: western Atlantic Ocean to N, E, S, and W. **Total land area**: 5,382 sq. mi. (13,940 sq km). **Coastline**: 2,200 mi. (3,542 km). **Comparative area**: slightly larger than Connecticut. **Land use:** 1% arable land; negl. % permanent crops; 99% other. **Major cities**: (1990) Nassau (capital) 191,542.
• **PEOPLE** **Population:** 297,477 (July 2003 est.). **Nationality:** noun—Bahamian(s); adjective—Bahamian. **Ethnic groups:** 85% black, 12% white. **Languages:** English, some Creole among Haitian immigrants. **Religions:** 32% Baptist, 20% Anglican, 19% Roman Catholic; smaller groups of other Protestants, Greek Orthodox, and Jews.
• **GOVERNMENT** **Type:** constituional parliamentary democracy. **Independence:** July 10, 1973 (from U.K.). **Constitution:** July 10, 1973. **National holiday:** National Day, July 10. **Heads of Government:** Dame Ivy Dumont, governor-general (since Jan. 2002); Perry G. Christle, prime minister (since May 2002). **Structure:** executive—governor general (appointed by queen); bicameral legislature; judiciary.
• **ECONOMY** **Monetary unit:** Bahamian dollar. **Budget:** (FY01/02) ***income:*** $918.5 mil.; ***expend.:***

$956.5 mil. **GDP:** (2002 est.) $5.2 bil., $17,000 per capita. **Chief crops:** citrus fruits, vegetables; poultry. **Natural resources:** salt, aragonite, timber. **Major industries:** tourism, banking, cement. **Labor force:** 156,000 (1999); 50% tourism, 40% other services, 5% industry, 5% agriculture; 6.9% unemployment (2001 est.). **Exports:** $560.7 mil. (2002 est.); pharmaceuticals, cement, rum, crawfish. **Imports**: $1.86 bil. (2002 est.); foodstuffs, manufactured goods, crude oil. **Major trading partners:** ***exports:*** 28% U.S., 17% France, 14% Germany ***imports:*** 32% U.S., 18% South Korea, 17% Italy.

Christopher Columbus made his first landfall in the Americas in the Bahamas Oct. 12, 1492. Though the Spanish never settled the islands, they enslaved and removed to Hispaniola 40,000 of the indigenous Arawaks by 1508. Their shallow seas (baja mar) made the islands a haven for pirates in the 17th century—as well as during the Civil War, Prohibition, and for drug smugglers today. British colonization of the Bahamas began in 1629 and continued slowly over the next two centuries.

Tourism has been the mainstay of the economy in this century, but high unemployment is a continuing problem. Parliament relaxed restrictions on offshore banking to stem the flight of international capital prompted by allegations of government corruption and involvement in drug trafficking. In 1992 the government of Prime Minister Lynden Pindling was defeated after 25 years in office, largely because of corruption charges. In recent years the economy has grown and diversified but rising crime related to gangs of unemployed young men worries the electorate.

▶BAHRAIN
Kingdom of Bahrain

• **GEOGRAPHY** **Location:** group of 35 islands in western Persian Gulf. Manama 26°17'N, 50°33'E. **Boundaries**: Saudi Arabia about 15 mi. (24 km) to W and Qatar about 17 mi. (28 km) to SE. **Total land area**: 239 sq. mi. (620 sq km). **Coastline**: 161 mi. (259 km). **Comparative area**: slightly less than 3.5 times size of Washington, D.C. **Land use:** 4.35% arable land; 4.35% permanent crops; 91.3% other. **Major cities**: (1990 est.) Manama (capital) 138,784; Muharraq Town 75,906.

• **PEOPLE** **Population:** 667,238 (July 2003 est.). **Nationality:** noun—Bahraini(s); adjective—Bahraini. **Ethnic groups:** 63% Bahraini, 19% Asian, 10% other Arab, 8% Iranian. **Languages:** Arabic, English, Farsi, Urdu. **Religions:** 70% Sh'ia Muslim, 30% Sunni Muslim.

• **GOVERNMENT** **Type:** constitutional monarchy. **Independence:** Aug. 15, 1971 (from U.K.). **Constitution:** adopted late Dec. 2000. **National holiday:** Dec. 16. **Heads of Government:** Hamad Bin Isa Al-Khalifa, amir (since March 1999); Khalifa bin Salman al-Khalifa, prime minister (since 1971). **Structure:** executive—amir is traditional arab monarch, appoints cabinet led by prime minister; legislative—amir dissolved National Assembly (Aug. 1975), appointed Advisory Council Dec. 1992; independent judiciary.

• **ECONOMY** **Monetary unit:** Bahraini dinar. **Budget:** (2002 est.) ***income:*** $1.8 bil.; ***expend.:*** $2.2 bil. **GDP:** (2002 est.) $9.8 bil., $14,000 per capita. **Chief crops:** not self-sufficient in food production; produces some fruits and vegetables; engages in shrimping and fishing. **Natural resources:** oil, associated and nonassociated natural gas, fish. **Major industries:** petroleum processing and refining, aluminum smelting, offshore banking. **Labor force:** 295,000 (1998 est.); 79% industry, commerce and service (note: 44% of 15-64 age group is non-national). **Exports:** $5.8 bil. (f.o.b. 2002); petroleum, aluminum. **Imports**: $4.2 bil. (f.o.b., 2002). **Major trading partners: (2000)** ***exports:*** India, U.S., Saudi Arabia; ***imports:*** Saudi Arabia, U.S., U.K.

Bahrain has been an entrepôt of trade between Arabia and India since the second millenium B.C. The Portuguese fortified Bahrain in the 16th century but were driven out by the Persian shah Abbas I early in the 17th century. At the end of the 18th century, it became an Arab sheikhdom within the Ottoman Empire. Bahrain entered into treaty relations with Great Britain in 1820 and became a British protectorate in 1861. After British forces withdrew from the gulf, the nation became an independent emirate, in August 1971, under Amir Isa bin Sulman al-Khalifa, who had come to the throne in 1961. The U.S. has maintained a large military base here for many years.

Oil reserves—first discovered in 1932—were depleted by the mid-1970's. The economy diversified to include oil refining, aluminum smelting, international banking, and shipping. Bahrain has close relations with Saudi Arabia; a causeway permits direct communication between them.

In June 1995 social and political unrest caused by uneven distribution of wealth, high unemployment, and a repressive government erupted into serious rioting. Protests by the Shiite majority began again in early 1996; a government crackdown led to the arrest of over 600 dissidents. Bahrain's family-run, Sunni Muslim government continued with the March 1999 death of its founding emir and his replacement with his son, Hamad bin Isa al-Khalifa. The new emir, in Feb. 2001, fostered a trio of reform measures: extending amnesty to 400 political prisoners and repatriation to 100 exiles; repealing the State Security Law and abolishing the State Security Court, both of which had been designed to quash Shiite unrest; and sponsoring a referendum which approved (by 98 percent) the restoration of a parliament, the founding of an independent judiciary, and the extension of the right to vote to women. Then, in Feb. 2002, Sheik Hamad declared the state to be a constitutional monarchy, the Kingdom of Bahrain, with himself as king. Municipal elections were successfully held in May, with elections for the lower house of the legislature in Oct. giving Sunni candidates 19 of 40 seats. In Nov. the King appointed the upper house, including six women and one Jew.

▶BANGLADESH
People's Republic of Bangladesh

• **GEOGRAPHY** **Location:** southern Asia. **Boundaries**: India to N, E, and W; Myanmar to E, Bay of Bengal to S. **Total land area**: 55,598 sq. mi. (144,000 sq km). **Coastline**: 360 mi. (580 km). **Comparative area**: between Arkansas and Wisconsin. **Land use:** 61% arable land; 2% permanent crops; 37% other. **Major cities**: (1991 census) Dhaka (formerly Dacca) (capital) 3,637,892; Chittagong 1,566,070; Khulna 601,051; Rajshahi 324,532; Barisal 180,014.

• **PEOPLE** **Population:** 138,448,210 (July 2003 est.). **Nationality:** noun—Bangladeshi(s); adjective—Bangladesh. **Ethnic groups:** 98% Bengali, tribal groups, non-bengali muslims. **Languages:** Bangla (official); English widely used. **Religions:** 83% Muslim, 16% Hindu, 1% Buddhist, Christian, and other.

• **GOVERNMENT** **Type:** parliamentary democracy. **Independence:** Dec. 16, 1971 (from Pakistan). **Constitution:** Nov. 4, 1972, effective Dec. 16, 1972, suspended following coup of Mar. 24, 1982, restored

Nov. 10, 1986; amended many times. **National holiday:** March 26, Independence Day. **Heads of Government:** Iajuddin Ahmed, president (since Sept. 2002); Begum Khaleda Zia, prime minister (since Oct. 2001). **Structure:** executive—president appoints prime minister and Advisory Council; unicameral legislature dissolved by president following elections on Feb. 15, 1996 and named caretaker prime minister; judiciary.

• **ECONOMY** **Monetary unit:** taka. **Budget:** (FY99/00 est.) ***income:*** $4.9 bil.; ***expend.:*** $6.8 bil. **GDP:** (2002 est.) $239 bil., $1,700 per capita. **Chief crops:** large-scale subsistence farming, heavily dependent on monsoon rain; main crops are jute, rice, wheat, tea, sugarcane, and potatoes. **Natural resources:** natural gas, arable land, timber. **Major industries:** jute manufactures, cotton textiles, tea processing. **Labor force:** 64.1 mil. (1998); extensive export of labor to Saudi Arabia, UAE, and Oman; 63% agriculture, 26% services, 11% industry and mining. **Exports:** $6.2 bil. (2002); garments, jute, leather, seafood. **Imports**: $8.5 bil. (2002); machinery, chemicals, iron and steel, textiles. **Major trading partners:** (2001) ***exports:*** 29.6% U.S.; 10.3% Germany, 8.5% U.K.; ***imports:*** 13.1% India, 9.1% Singapore, 8.5% China.

Located on the alluvial plain of the Ganges River northeast of India, Bengal was ruled by Buddhist kings from the eighth to 12th centuries. Conquered by Muslim invaders around 1200, many inhabitants converted to Islam and Bengal became part of the Moghul Empire in the 16th century. The British East India Company established a settlement in 1642, and by 1750 all of Bengal was under British rule. The diverse agricultural economy became dominated by export crops of opium and jute, while rice continued to be grown in the fertile delta. The region's trade flowed through the British-built city of Calcutta.

With Indian independence in 1947, Bengal was partitioned along religious lines, Hindu West Bengal (including Calcutta) remaining with India and Muslim East Bengal becoming the eastern province of Pakistan. In the elections of 1971, the Bengali Awami League gained control of Pakistan's National Assembly. Seating of the new National Assembly was postponed, and riots broke out in East Pakistan. Troops from West Pakistan were sent to quell the riots on May 25; the following day East Pakistan declared its independence as Bangladesh. Civil war followed; 10 million refugees fled to India. Following Indian intervention, Pakistan acknowledged Bangladesh's independence on Dec. 15.

Since independence, Bangladesh has consistently been one of the world's poorest countries, plagued by violent political instability, military coups, overpopulation, a flagging economy, and frequent catastrophic floods (including one in 1975 that killed half a million people). The first president, Sheik Mujibur Rahman, was assassinated in 1975. Lt. Gen. Hossain Mohammad Ershad, who seized power in a coup in March 1982, was elected president in 1986, but resigned in 1990 in the face of opposition unrest.

In 1991, the Bangladesh Nationalist party (BNP) of Begum Khaleda Zia (widow of former president Ziaur Rahman, who was assassinated in 1981) won 138 of 330 parliamentary seats running on a platform of free enterprise and an Islamic state. In 1991, the constitution was amended to put the prime minister in charge of the government.

In 1994, nearly 150 opposition members of Parliament resigned en masse, eliciting a promise from Prime Minister Zia to hold general elections in June 1996. In those elections, the Awami League, led by Sheik Hasina Wazed, returned to power for the first time since 1975, when the military massacred most of her family, including her father, Pres. Sheik Mujibur Rahman. In 1998, fifteen were convicted and sentenced to death for their role in the assassinations. Zia's call for nation-wide protest strike went unanswered, but her BNP (in Jan. 1999) was one of three parties, with General Ershad's Jatiya and the Moslem Jamaat-e-Islami, to form a bloc seeking to force early elections upon prime minister Hasina. After completing Bangladesh's first-ever five-year term, premier Hasina and her Awami League faced the voters in Oct. 2001 only to be buried in a surprise landslide victory by former premier Khaleda Zia and her Nationalist party coalition.

▶BARBADOS

• **GEOGRAPHY** **Location:** easternmost of Caribbean islands, about 200 mi. (320 km) NE of Trinidad. Bridgetown 13°06'N, 59°36'W. **Boundaries**: Atlantic Ocean. **Total land area**: 166 sq. mi. (430 sq km). **Coastline**: 60 mi. (97 km). **Comparative area**: slightly less than 2.5 times size of Washington, D.C. **Land use:** 37% arable land; 2% permanent crops; 61% other. **Major cities**: (1990 census) Bridgetown (capital) 6,070.

• **PEOPLE** **Population:** 277,264 (July 2003 est.). **Nationality:** noun—Barbadian(s); adjective—Barbadian. **Ethnic groups:** 90% black, 4% white, 6% Asian and mixed. **Languages:** English. **Religions:** 67% Protestant, 4% Roman Catholic, 29% none or other.

• **GOVERNMENT** **Type:** parliamentary democracy recognizing Queen Elizabeth II as chief of state. **Independence:** Nov. 30, 1966 (from U.K.). **Constitution:** Nov. 30, 1966. **National holiday:** Independence Day, Nov. 30. **Heads of Government:** Sir Clifford Husbands, governor general (since June 1996); Owen Arthur, prime minister (since Sept. 1994). **Structure:** executive—governor general (appointed by the queen) prime minister; bicameral legislature; judiciary.

•**ECONOMY** **Monetary unit:** Barbadian dollar. **Budget:** (2000 est.) ***income:*** $847 mil.; ***expend.:*** $886 mil. **GDP:** (2002 est.) $4 bil., $14,500 per capita. **Chief crops:** sugarcane, vegetables, cotton. **Natural resources:** crude oil, fish, natural gas. **Major industries:** tourism, sugar, light manufacturing. **Labor force:** 128,500 (1998 est.); 75% services, 15% industry, 10% agriculture (1996 est.). **Exports:** $227 mil. (2002 est.); sugar and molasses, rum, other foods and beverages, chemicals. **Imports**: $987 mil. (2002 est.); consumer goods, machinery, foodstuffs. **Major trading partners: *exports:*** 43.2% CARICOM, 15.3% U.S. ***imports:*** 40.8% U.S., 19.8% CARICOM, 8.1% U.K.

Barbados is the only Caribbean island not to have changed hands prior to independence. Although the Spanish removed virtually all the indigenous Arawaks of Barbados by the mid1500's, the island was not claimed until the British arrived in the 1620's. Tobacco, cotton, and sugarcane—harvested by slaves until 1833—were mainstays of the economy. The 1966 constitution mandates the promotion of economic equality among Barbadians, and the country was fairly prosperous relative to other Caribbean states until recently, when declining tourism and record-low sugar production have had serious adverse effects. Still, the Barbados Labor Party retains its popularity, winning 26 of the parliament's 28 seats in Jan. 1999 elections.

▶BELARUS

Republic of Belarus

• **GEOGRAPHY** **Location:** northeastern Europe. **Boundaries**: Lithuania and Latvia to N, Russian Federation to NE and E, Ukraine to S, Poland to W, Lithuania and Latvia to NW. **Total land area**: 80,154 sq. mi. (207,600 sq km). **Coastline**: none. **Comparative area**: slightly smaller than Kansas. **Land use:** 30% arable land; 1% permanent crops; 69% other. **Major cities**: (1990 est.) Minsk (capital) 1,613,000; Gomel (Homel) 506,000; Mahilou (Mogilev) 363,000; Vitebsk 356,000; Grodno 277,000.

• **PEOPLE** **Population:** 10,322,151 (July 2003 est.). **Nationality:** noun—Belarusian(s); adjective—Belarusian. **Ethnic groups:** 81.2% Byelorussian, 11.4% Russian, 7.4% Polish, Ukrainian and other. **Languages:** Byelorusian (official), Russian. **Religions:** 80% Eastern Orthodox.

• **GOVERNMENT** **Type:** republic. **Independence:** Aug. 25, 1991 (from U.S.S.R.). **Constitution:** Adopted Nov. 1996. **National holiday:** Independence Day, July 3. **Heads of Government:** Aleksander Lukashenko, president (since July 1994); Gennady Novitsky, prime minister (since Oct. 2001). **Structure:** executive—president, prime minister, Council of Ministers; bicameral legislature—most members apointed by the president; judiciary.

• **ECONOMY** **Monetary unit:** Belarusian rubel. **Budget:** (1997 est.) ***income:*** 4 bil.; ***expend.:*** 4.1 bil. **GDP:** (2002 est.) $85 bil., $8,200 per capita. **Chief crops:** grain, potatoes, vegetables. **Natural resources:** forest, peat, oil, and natural gas. **Major industries:** tractors, metalworking, heavy-duty vehicles. **Labor force:** 4.8 mil. (2000). **Exports:** $7.7 bil. (f.o.b., 2002); machinery, transport equipment, chemicals, metals. **Imports**: $8.8 bil. (f.o.b., 2002); mineral products, machinery and equipment, metals, chemicals. **Major trading partners:** Russia, Ukraine, Latvia, Germany.

Belarus, also known as White Russia or Byelorussia, has been inhabited since the seventh century. In the 13th and 14th centuries, present-day Belarus became part of the Grand Duchy of Lithuania, which then became part of Poland in the 16th century. Between 1772 and 1795, Poland was partitioned, which resulted in Belarus becoming part of the Russian empire. After the Bolshevik revolution in 1917, Soviet troops came to Minsk, but they were forced to withdraw in the face of approaching German troops. The Treaty of Brest-Litovsk in March 1918 ceded to Germany most of the territory of Belarus. The same year, an independent Belarusian Democratic Republic was founded, but it had little real power. Once the Germans left, the Soviets easily retook Belarus, and on Jan. 1, 1919, the Belarusian Soviet Socialist Republic (SSR) was proclaimed.

This did not end the divisions of the traditional Belarusian lands. In February 1919 they were merged within the Soviet Union with Lithuania, but the Poles launched an attack in April of the same year and took both Lithuania and Belarus. In 1920 the Belarusian SSR was re-formed, but it included only the eastern portion of historical Belarusian lands. The Treaty of Riga in March 1921 granted the western territories of Belarus to Poland and the eastern portion to the Russian Federation. In 1924 and 1925 the eastern regions were returned to the Belarusian SSR.

After the Soviets invaded Poland in 1939, the lands that Belarus had lost in 1921 were returned to it. Between 1941 and 1945, the Germans occupied the Belarusian lands, and more than a million lost their lives, including most of the large Jewish population. After the war, the Belarusian SSR was restored with all of its historic lands, and Belarus was finally unified. However, when Stalin redrew the Soviet Union's borders, he included Belarus's capital of Vilnius in Lithuania.

Under Soviet rule, Belarus turned from a mainly agricultural to an industrial land. Large numbers of Belarusians fiercely fought Stalin's collectivization plan in the 1930's, and thousands were killed or deported. Both Stalin's purges of the 1930's and World War II, which devastated both its agriculture and industry, inflicted great losses on Belarus. After the war, Soviet policy in Belarus concentrated on rebuilding its economy and encouraging Russian immigration (Russian replaced Belarusian as the official language).

The Belarusian SSR was one of the more prosperous and stable of the union republics, so Mikhail Gorbachev's policy of glasnost, or openness, in the 1980's was relatively slow to have an impact. In 1987, however, two issues had come to the fore in the Belarusian SSR: the status of the Belarusian language and the ecological dangers of Chernobyl, the famous nuclear reactor that had exploded in nearby Ukraine in 1986, but which dropped almost three-quarters of its fallout on Belarus. In voicing these concerns, the Belarusians formed several new, non-Communist parties that challenged the authority of the ruling Communist party. On July 27, 1990, Belarus declared its sovereignty from the U.S.S.R.

After the fall of the Soviet government, Belarus was one of the strongest supporters of maintaining a union of republics. On Dec. 8, 1991, Belarus, Ukraine, and Russia hosted the talks leading to the Minsk Agreement, which created the Commonwealth of Independent States (CIS). On Dec. 21, 11 former Soviet republics joined the commonwealth by signing the Alma-Ata Declaration.

While Belarus at first seemed to view the CIS as a temporary expedient, Pres. Aleaksander Lukashenko fostered closer ties with Russia. A 1995 customs union was expanded by the 1996 Union Treaty to include a common currency, joint tax and legal systems, shared energy and transport networks, and common defense and foreign policies. Lukashenko tightened his dictatorial hold on Belarus with a new constitution (Nov. 1996) which permits presidential rule by decree and gives Lukashenko power to appoint half the members of the Constitutional Court and 20 of the 64 members of the Council of the Republic, the newly-created upper house of the legislature. In 1997, the U.S. announced it was cutting off $4 mil. in aid to protest the new authoritarian government.

In July 1999, 35 members of the disbanded parliament designated its former speaker, Semyon Sharetsky, as president. Sharetsky promptly fled to Lithuania for safety but claimed the presidency. October saw large demonstrations in Minsk protesting the disappearance of opposition leaders and the proposed reunion with Russia. That reunion was forestalled by a wary Pres. Yeltsin in Dec. 1999, but Pres. Lukashenko was gratified by his party's sweep of all the seats in Oct. 2000 elections for the Chamber of Representatives in what he described as an "absolutely democratic" vote, a stance he took in the presidential election he won overwhelmingly in Sept. 2001. Protests were vigorous but without effect.

▶BELGIUM

Kingdom of Belgium

• **GEOGRAPHY** **Location:** northwestern Europe. **Boundaries**: Netherlands to N, Luxembourg and

Germany to E, France to S, and North Sea to W. **Total land area**: 11,780 sq. mi. (30,510 sq km). **Coastline**: 40 mi. (64 km). **Comparative area**: slightly larger than Maryland. **Land use:** 25% arable land; 0% permanent crops; 75% other. **Major cities**: (1993) Bruxelles (Brussels—capital) 949,070; Antwerpen (Anvers, Antwerp) 462,880; Gent (Gand, Ghent) 228,490; Charleroi 206,898; Liège (Luik) 195,389.

• **People** **Population:** 10,289,088 (July 2003 est.). **Nationality:** noun—Belgian(s); adjective—Belgian. **Ethnic groups:** 58% Fleming, 31% Walloon, 11% mixed or other. **Languages:** 60% Dutch, 40% French, less than 1% German (all three official); legally bilingual (Dutch and French). **Religions:** 75% Roman Catholic, remainder Protestant or other.

• **Government** **Type:** federal parliamentary democracy under a constitutional monarch. **Independence:** Oct. 4, 1830 (from Netherlands). **Constitution:** Feb. 7, 1831; last revised July 14, 1993. **National holiday:** National Day, July 21. **Heads of Government:** Albert II, king (since Aug. 1993); Guy Verhofstadt, prime minister (since July 1999). **Structure:** executive—king, prime minister, and cabinet; bicameral legislature; independent judiciary.

• **Economy** **Monetary unit:** euro. **Budget:** (2000 est.) ***income:*** $113.4 bil.; ***expend.:*** $106 bil.. **GDP:** (2002 est.) $296.7 bil., $29,000 per capita. **Chief crops:** sugar beets, vegetables, fruit, grain. **Natural resources:** coal, natural gas. **Major industries:** engineering, metal products, motor vehicle assembly, processed food, beverages, chemicals. **Labor force:** 4.44 mil. (2001); 73% services, 25% industry; 2% agriculture (1999 est.). **Exports:** $162 bil. (f.o.b., 2002); machinery and equipment, chemicals, diamonds. **Imports**: $152 bil. (f.o.b., 2001); machinery and equipment, chemicals, metals. **Major trading partners: *exports:*** 73% E.U., 8% U.S.; ***imports:*** 71% E.U., 6% U.S.

The country now known as Belgium was, during the Middle Ages, part of the powerful duchy of Burgundy. By marriage and diplomacy, the "Low Countries" became part of the Habsburg Empire in 1482 (see "Austria"). In a struggle lasting from the late 16th century to the Treaty of Westphalia in 1648, the northern part of that region (Netherlands) became independent, but the southern portion remained part of the Habsburg Empire—under the Spanish branch until 1715, then under the Austrian branch until the French Revolution. The Congress of Vienna attached the lands to an enlarged Kingdom of the Netherlands in 1815.

In 1830 the Belgians revolted against the Dutch, and in 1831 the Treaty of London recognized an independent Kingdom of Belgium. Throughout the 19th century, its unity was precarious, as the country was divided politically between Catholic and Liberal parties, and ethnically between Dutch-speaking Flemings and French-speaking Walloons. In 1885 Belgium became a colonial power in Africa with Leopold II's establishment of the Congo Free State (later the Belgian Congo), which gained independence in 1960 as Zaire.

Belgium was a major battleground during World War I, but its boundaries were reestablished in 1919 by the Treaty of Versailles. When German troops overran Belgium in May 1940, King Leopold III quickly signed an armistice, hoping to placate Hitler and avert further fighting. But the Belgian government fled to England, repudiated the armistice, and joined the Allies. The Germans controlled Belgium until Sept. 1944.

Belgium made a swift postwar recovery. But the political atmosphere was poisoned by the issue of what to do about wartime collaborators up to and including the king. A referendum in 1950 narrowly approved Leopold III's return to the throne, but he was persuaded to abdicate in 1951 in favor of his son, Baudouin I.

Belgium has a flourishing economy with a modernized industrial sector complemented by tourism and agriculture. The issue of language dominates politics; since the 1960's, Belgium has devolved into a de facto confederation of Flemish-, French-, and German-speaking regions, with Brussels a multilingual region unto itself.

In the May 1995 election, the first under the new decentralized constitution of 1993, the Christian Democrat-Socialist coalition government retained a majority in the Chamber of Representatives. In Aug. 1996, the government was shaken by massive demonstrations against inept police and legal handling of a widespread child prostitution and pornography ring with possible links to prominent politicians. But it was the "poultry scandal" of early 1999 (the government's tardy reaction to the discovery of dioxin in Belgian meat and dairy products) that toppled the coalition of Prime Minister Jean-Luc Dehaene. June 1999 elections to the Chamber of Deputies resulted in a coalition government of Liberals, Socialists and Greens controlling a 19-seat majority under Flemish Liberal premier Guy Verhofstadt. The Greens were participants in government for the first time. In 2003 the liberals gained a slight majority.

▶BELIZE

• **Geography** **Location:** northeastern coast of Central America. **Boundaries**: Mexico to N, Caribbean Sea to E, Guatemala to S and W. **Total land area**: 8,865 sq. mi. (22,960 sq km). **Coastline**: 240 mi. (386 km). **Comparative area**: between Massachusetts and New Hampshire. **Land use:** 3% arable land; 1% permanent crops; 96% other. **Major cities**: (1993 est.) Belmopan (capital) 3,852; Belize City 47,723; Orange Walk 11,922; San Ignacio 9,702; Corozal 7,644.

• **People** **Population:** 266,440 (July 2003 est.). **Nationality:** noun—Belizean(s); adjective—Belizean. **Ethnic groups:** 49% mestizo, 25% Creole, 11% Maya, 6.1% Garifuna. **Languages:** English (official), Spanish, Mayan, Garifuna (Carib). **Religions:** 50% Roman Catholic, 27% Protestant.

• **Government** **Type:** parliamentary democracy. **Independence:** Sept. 21, 1981 (from U.K.). **Constitution:** Sept. 21, 1981. **National holiday:** Independence Day, Sept. 21. **Heads of Government:** Sir Colville Norbert Young, governor general (since Nov. 1993); Said Musa, prime minister (since Aug. 1998). **Structure:** executive—governor general (appointed by Queen Elizabeth II, who is recognized as the head of state), prime minister, cabinet; bicameral legislature; judiciary.

• **Economy** **Monetary unit:** Belizean dollar. **Budget:** (2002 est.) ***income:*** $224 mil.; ***expend.:*** $209 mil. **GDP:** $1.28 bil., $4,900 per capita (2002 est.). **Chief crops:** bananas, coca, citrus, sugarcane; cultured shrimp; illegal producer of cannabis for international drug trade. **Natural resources:** arable land potential, timber, fish. **Major industries:** garments, food processing, tourism. **Labor force:** 90,000 (2001 est.); 27% agriculture, 18% industry, 55% services; shortage of skilled labor and all types of technical personnel; 9.1% unemployment (2002 est.). **Exports:** $290 mil. (f.o.b., 2002 est.); sugar, citrus, bananas, clothing. **Imports**: $430 mil. (c.i.f., 2002 est.); machinery and transportation equipment, manufactured goods, food, fuels, chemicals.

Major trading partners: (2001) ***exports:*** 54% U.S., 23% U.K., 6% CARICOM; ***imports:*** 47% U.S., 11% Mexico, 5% Central America.

During the 1700's, Spain held sovereignty over Belize but never attempted to settle it. The British gradually did settle there, however, and in 1862, British Honduras, as it was called, became a Crown colony. Although Britain granted Belize independence in 1981, Guatemala claimed sovereignty over the area until 1992, when it finally recognized Belize's independence. But as British defense forces withdrew in 1994, Guatemala reasserted its old claims but without consequence.

▶BENIN

Republic of Benin

• **GEOGRAPHY** **Location:** western coast of Africa. **Boundaries**: Burkina Faso and Niger to N, Nigeria to E, Gulf of Guinea to S, Togo to W. **Total land area**: 43,483 sq. mi. (112,620 sq km). **Coastline**: 75 mi. (121 km). **Comparative area**: between Tennessee and Pennsylvania. **Land use:** 15% arable land; 1% permanent crops; 84% other. **Major cities**: (1985 est.) Porto-Novo (capital) 208,258; Cotonou 402,290.

• **PEOPLE** **Population:** 7,041,490 (July 2003 est.). **Nationality:** noun—Beninese (sing., pl.); adjective— Beninese. **Ethnic groups:** 99% African (predominantly Fon, Adja, Yoruba, Bariba); 5,500 Europeans. **Languages:** French (official); Fon and Yoruba in south; at least six major tribal languages in north. **Religions:** 50% indigenous beliefs, 20% Muslim, 30% Christian.

• **GOVERNMENT** **Type:** Multiparty democratic republic since Apr. 4, 1991. **Independence:** Aug. 1, 1960 (from France). **Constitution:** Dec. 2, 1990. **National holiday:** National Day, Aug. 1. **Head of Government:** Mathieu Kérékou, head of state (since Apr. 2001). **Structure:** executive—president, executive council; unicameral legislature; judiciary.

• **ECONOMY** **Monetary unit:** Communauté Financiere Africaine franc. **Budget:** (2001 est.) ***income:*** $377.4 mil.; ***expend.:*** $561.8 mil. **GDP:** (2002 est.) $7.3 bil., $1,070 per capita. **Chief crops:** corn, cotton, cassava, yams. **Natural resources:** small offshore oil deposits, limestone, marble, timber. **Major industries:** textiles, food processing, beverages. **Labor force:** 1.9 mil. (1987); 60% agriculture, 2% industrial sector, remainder employed in transport, commerce, and public services. **Exports:** $207 mil. (f.o.b., 2002); cotton, crude oil, palm products, cocoa. **Imports**: $479 mil. (f.o.b., 2002); foodstuffs, beverages, tobacco, petroleum products. **Major trading partners: *exports:*** India, Italy, Thailand; ***imports:*** China, France, U.K.

Although the early history of Benin is sketchy, a number of kingdoms had appeared in the region by the 11th century, and it was a center of wealth and power by the 1300's. In the 16th century, the Allada kingdom was founded in the south. In 1625, three brothers divided their power between Allada, Adjatché (Porto Novo), and Abomey. Under Ouegbadja (r. 1645-85) the latter, known as Dahomey, predominated. Much of its wealth derived from contact with Europeans, and especially the slave trade, which continued until 1885.

European contact began with the arrival of the Portuguese in 1485. Although traders and missionaries were established at Ouidah and Porto Novo in the 1500's, European influence remained slight. Dahomey expansion continued well into the 19th century. A commercial treaty with the French was signed in 1842, but relations between Dahomeyans and Europeans soon worsened. Outright hostilities began under Behanzin (r. 1858-89), who was defeated by the French, and in 1893 the French assimilated Abomey, Allada, and Porto Novo into the colony of Dahomey.

Independence from French rule came in 1960, followed by several coups until Mathieu Kerekou came to power in 1972. Kerekou established a Marxist regime, nationalizing large private businesses and abolishing opposition parties.

By December 1989, with the economy in a shambles and most trade conducted on the black market, there were demonstrations calling for Kerekou's resignation. A new constitution was approved in a Nov. 1990 referendum, and Nicéphore Soglo, a former World Bank official, was named prime minister. Soglo defeated the Marxist Kerekou in the 1991 presidential election, and appealed to western nations for a "Marshall Plan" for Africa. But in a rematch four years later, Kerekou regained the presidency with 53 percent of the vote. Yet, only three years later, in April elections for the National Assembly, it was Soglo's Renaissance of Benin Party that carried the majority. In March 2001 Kerekou won again over Soglo, this time with 84 percent of the vote.

▶BHUTAN

Kingdom of Bhutan

• **GEOGRAPHY** **Location:** Himalaya Mountains in southern Asia. **Boundaries**: China to N and W, India to S and E. **Total land area**: 18,147 sq. mi. (47,000 sq km). **Coastline**: none. **Comparative area**: between Maryland and West Virginia. **Land use:** 3% arable land; negl. % permanent crops; 97% other. **Major cities**: (1990 est.) Timphu (capital) 27,000.

• **PEOPLE** **Population:** 2,139,549 (July 2003 est.). **Nationality:** noun—Bhutanese (sing., pl.); adjective— Bhutanese. **Ethnic groups:** 50% Bhote, 35% ethnic Nepalese, 15% indigenous or migrant tribes. **Languages:** Dzongkha (official), various Tibetan dialects, various Nepalese dialects. **Religions:** 75% Lamaistic Buddhism, 25% Indian- and Nepalese-influenced Hinduism.

• **GOVERNMENT** **Type:** monarchy; special treaty relationship with India. **Independence:** Aug. 8, 1949 (from India). **Constitution:** no written constitution or bill of rights. **National holiday:** Dec. 17. **Head of Government:** Jigme Singye Wangchuk, king (since July 1972); Dr. Kinzang Dorji, prime minister (since 2002). **Structure:** executive—king, Royal Advisory Council, Council of Ministers; indirectly elected unicameral National Assembly consisting of 105 village elders, 10 monastic representatives, and 35 designated by the king; judicial—Supreme Court is the king.

• **ECONOMY** **Monetary unit:** ngultrums and Indian rupees are legal tender. **Budget:** (FY95/96) ***income:*** $146 mil.; ***expend.:*** $152 mil. **GDP:** (2002 est.) $2.7 bil., $1,300 per capita. **Chief crops:** rice, corn, root crops, citrus. **Livestock:** cattle, poultry, pigs, sheep, yaks. **Natural resources:** timber, hydropower, gypsum, calcium carbide. **Major industries:** cement, wood products, fruits. **Labor force:** N.A.; (1983) 93% agriculture, 5% services, 2% industry and commerce. **Exports:** $154 mil. (f.o.b., 2000 est.); cardamom, gypsum, timber, handicrafts. **Imports**: $196 mil. (c.i.f., 2000 est.); fuels and lubricants, grain, machinery and parts, vehicles. **Major trading partner:** India (95% of exports, 82% of imports).

A Tibetan-style Lamaistic Buddhist theocracy was established in this Himalayan enclave in the 16th century. The region came under the domination of the British raj in India in 1865, and Britain established a protectorate in 1910. A 1949 treaty with India granted independence to Bhutan. The present Druk Gyalpo, or Precious Ruler of the Dragon People, is the fourth in a dynasty dating from 1907. During the early years of his reign, he introduced reforms into this feudal, medieval country by broadening educational opportunities and compelling Buddhist monks to take up social work outside their monasteries.

From 1998 to 1999, King Wangchuk ruled through a rubber-stamp National Assembly, passing a series of laws aimed at driving out Nepalese and Indian settlers even if their families have resided in Bhutan for decades. More than 70,000 refugees have been registered by the U.N. high commissioner for refugees since 1991, and the numbers continue to grow. A "Gorkha Liberation Movement" has carried out raids in Bhutan from sanctuaries in India and Nepal.

In 1998 King Wangchuk began a second wave of reform, permitting the National Assembly to elect members of the Council of Ministers and even, by two-thirds vote, to call for the King's abdication. 1999 saw a mass amnesty of political prisoners.

▶BOLIVIA

Republic of Bolivia

• GEOGRAPHY Location: landlocked country in central South America. **Boundaries**: Brazil to N and E, Paraguay and Argentina to S, Chile and Peru to W. **Total land area**: 424,162 sq. mi. (1,098,580 sq km). **Coastline**: none. **Comparative area**: between Texas and Alaska. **Land use:** 2% arable land; negl. % permanent crops; 98% other. **Major cities**: (1992 est.) La Paz (administrative capital) 1,115,403; Sucre (legal capital and seat of judiciary) 130,952; Santa Cruz de la Sierra 694,616; Cochabamba 404,102; Oruro 183,194.

• PEOPLE Population: 8,586,443 (July 2003 est.). **Nationality:** noun—Bolivian(s); adjective—Bolivian. **Ethnic groups:** 30% Quechua, 25% Aymara, 30% mixed, 15% white. **Languages:** Spanish, Quechua, and Aymara (all official). **Religions:** 95% Roman Catholic; active Protestant minority, especially Methodist.

• GOVERNMENT Type: republic. **Independence:** Aug, 6, 1825 (from Spain). **Constitution:** Feb. 2, 1967. **National holiday:** Independence Day, Aug. 6. **Head of Government:** Gonzalo Sánchez de Lozada, president (since Aug. 2002). **Structure:** executive; bicameral legislature; judiciary.

• ECONOMY Monetary unit: boliviano. **Budget:** (2002 est.) ***income:*** $4 bil.; ***expend.:*** $4 bil. **GDP:** (2002 est.) $21 bil., $2,500 per capita. **Chief crops:** soybeans, coffee, coca, cotton, corn, sugarcane, rice, potatoes. **Natural resources:** tin, natural gas, crude oil, zinc, tungsten. **Major industries:** mining, smelting, petroleum. **Labor force:** 2.5 mil.; NA% agriculture, NA% services and utilities. **Exports:** $1.3 bil. (f.o.b., 2002 est.); soybeans, natural gas, zinc, gold. **Imports**: $1.6 bil. (f.o.b., 2002 est.); capital goods, chemicals, petroleum. **Major trading partners:** (2001 est.) ***exports:*** Brazil, Colombia, U.S. ***imports:*** Brazil, Argentina, U.S.

The Incan Empire conquered the region that is now Bolivia in the 13th century. The Spanish discovered the fabulous silver deposits of the region and established their presence in the area in the cities of Sucre (1538) and Potosí (1545). From the early colonial period on, Bolivia—then called Upper Peru and part of the Viceroyalty of Peru—depended heavily on the export of minerals. The exploitation of tin and later oil and natural gas has had an important economic and political impact on the country's development.

In 1776, Upper Peru was transferred to the new Viceroyalty of La Plata centered in Buenos Aires. Upper Peru began agitating for independence in 1809, but it was not until liberation by Símon Bolívar (for whom the country was renamed) in 1825 that Bolivia became the last Spanish possession in South America to achieve independence. During 1836-39, Peru formed a brief union with Bolivia, until Chile broke up the confederation.

Bolivia has lost much of its original territory to its neighbors. The dictator Mariano Melgarejo sold large chunks of territory from 1865 to 1871. After the War of the Pacific (1879-84), Bolivia lost its access to the sea. And in the 1932-35 Chaco War with Paraguay, Bolivia lost more territory in the east.

Bolivia has suffered from Indian/non-Indian racial and cultural divisions, and political rivalry between the elites from the Potosí region and those from La Paz and Santa Cruz. Conservatives of the silver-mining southern region of Potosí controlled the government until their ouster in 1898 by the Liberal tin interests of the La Paz region, who presided over a period of stable republican politics that lasted until the Great Depression and the Chaco War.

One of the results of the Chaco War was the fragmentation of the Bolivian military into competing factions in the struggle for power between conservative landowners and middle-class reformers. In 1941 the National Revolutionary Movement (MNR) was formed with the aim of transferring control of the country from conservative landowning elites to the middle sectors. The leadership of the movement found itself outpaced by revolts sponsored by workers and peasants; the MNR incorporated these elements into its program. When the 1952 revolution brought the MNR to power, its leadership, which included the future four-time president Victor Paz Estenssoro, embarked on a reformist political program. The military overthrew the MNR in 1964, and civilian rule was not restored until 1982. Paz Estenssoro was again elected to the presidency in 1985. Jaime Paz Zamora, leader of the Movement of the Revolutionary Left, gained the presidency in 1989.

In June 1993, MNR candidate Gonzalo Sanchez de Lozada won the presidential election. An advocate of free-market economic reform, as planning minister (1986-88) he reduced the country's hyperinflation rate from 25,000 percent to 15 percent. In January 1995, Bolivia sought membership in the newly-formed Southern Common Market (of Argentina, Brazil, Paraguay, and Uruguay). But opposition to free-market reforms brought a general strike by the leftist Bolivian Workers' Confederation. The government declared a state of siege in April 1995, and suspended civil liberties. Further privatization plans led to another general strike in 1996, with 50,000 demonstrators in the streets of La Paz. Faced with widespread rioting and looting, the government granted large raises to government employees.

Presidential elections in 1997 led to a run-off (settled in Congress) in which retired general Hugo Banzer Suarez, military dictator from 1971 to 1978, was elected president, pledging to continue economic reforms while ensuring that the poor benefit from the reforms. His government was confronted in April 2000 with nationwide riots over a planned increase in water rates and a general strike by the Workers Confederation. Timely retreats ended the protests. Banzer's resignation in August 2001 for reasons of health brought elections in June, with Congress again having to choose between the top two finishers; by the narrowest of margins, ex-president Sánchez de Lozada topped Socialist Evo Morales, head of the coca workers' union.

▶BOSNIA AND HERZEGOVINA

Republic of Bosnia and Herzegovina

• **Geography** **Location:** southeastern Europe. **Boundaries**: Croatia to N, W, Yugoslavia to S, E, and SE, Adriatic Sea to SW. **Total land area**: 19,776 sq. mi. (51,233 sq km). **Coastline**: 13 mi. (20 km). **Comparative area**: About half the size of Ohio. **Land use:** 10% arable land; 3% permanent crops; 87% other. **Major cities**: Bosnia: (1991) Sarajevo (capital) 525,980, Banja Luka 195,139. Herzegovina: (1991) Mostar 126,067.

• **People** **Population:** 3,989,018 (July 2003 est.) Note: all population data is subject to considerable error due to dislocations caused by military actions and ethnic cleansing. **Nationality:** noun—Bosnian(s); adjective—Bosnian; noun—Herzegovine(s) or Herzegovinian(s); adjective—Herzegovine or Herzegovinian. **Ethnic groups:** 37% Serb, 48% Bozniak, 14% Croat. **Languages:** Croatian, Serbian, Bosnian. **Religions:** 40% Muslim, 31% Orthodox, 15% Catholic, 4% Protestant, 10% other.

• **Government** **Type:** emerging democracy. **Independence:** Mar. 1, 1992. **Constitution:** Dayton agreement, signed Dec. 1995, included a new constitution now in force. **National holiday:** National Day, Nov. 25 **Heads of Government:** Dr. Dragan Čović (since June 27, 2003); Adnan Terzić, prime minister (since Jan. 13, 2003). **Structure:** executive—3-member rotating presidency, prime minister, cabinet; bicameral legislature; judiciary.

• **Economy** **Monetary unit:** convertible marka. **Budget:** (1999 est.) ***income:*** $1.9 bil.; ***expend.:*** $2.2 bil. **GDP:** (2002 est.) $7.3 bil.; $1,900 per capita. **Chief crops:** corn, wheat, fruits, vegetables; livestock. **Natural resources:** coal, iron, bauxite, manganese, timber. **Major industries:** steel production, mining, manufacturing, armaments. **Labor force:** 1.026 mil (2002 est.). **Exports:** $1.5 bil. (f.o.b., 2002 est.). **Imports**: $2.8 bil. (f.o.b., 2002 est.). **Major trading partners:** Croatia, Switzerland, Slovenia, Germany, Italy.

Bosnia-Herzegovina has been in the middle of European power struggles since the 14th century. Its constantly changing boundaries have meant that its population has always been a hodgepodge of races and ethnicities. The name Bosnia comes from the region's geographic location on the Bosna River; Herzegovina was originally an Austrian border duchy (Herzog means "duke" in German). The two lands were conquered by the Ottoman Empire in the 15th century, Bosnia in 1463, Herzegovina 20 years later. The conquered peoples, united into one administrative district by the Turks, were Roman Catholic Croatians and Orthodox Serbs. Over the centuries, a number of Slavic families, Croatians more than Serbs, gave up their Christianity and adopted the religion of their conquerors: Islam.

A peasant uprising (1875) over Turkish refusal to institute reforms ultimately led to the Russo-Turkish War of 1877-78. In 1878, the Congress of Berlin put Bosnia-Herzegovina under the control of Austria-Hungary. Sarajevo, the capital city, was the birthplace of World War I, where a Serbian nationalist assassinated the Austro-Hungarian archduke Francis Ferdinand in 1914. By 1918, Serbia had annexed Bosnia-Herzegovina and held it until World WarII, when Germany incorporated it into the state of Croatia. In 1946, Bosnia-Herzegovina was made one of Yugoslavia's six constituent republics, along with Serbia, Croatia, Slovenia, Montenegro, and Macedonia.

The constant redrawing of Bosnia-Herzegovina's borders has meant that ethnicity in the region came to be based on religion, rather than national origin. Thus a Serb who converted to Roman Catholic Christianity was considered a Croatian, while a Croatian who converted to Eastern Orthodoxy was considered a Serb. And to both groups, converts to Islam appeared to be collaborators with the Ottoman Turks.

Nevertheless, the three ethnic groups coexisted peacefully under the iron hand of president-for-life Marshall Tito (Josip Broz). And even after Tito's death in 1980, his rotating presidency scheme, in which the leaders of each republic took turns serving as "president of the presidency," worked smoothly, as long as Yugoslavia was dominated by communism. At times, the president was a Muslim, the prime minister was a Croatian, and the president of the Assembly was a Serb. But when communism fell in 1989, only Serbia and Montenegro returned Communist governments to power; the other four republics established non- and even anti-Communist governments, and quickly sought to establish political independence from the ultra-Marxist regime of Serbian president Slobodan Milosevic.

Milosevic rigged elections in the provinces of Kosovo and Vojvodina to keep them under Serbian control, but he was unsuccessful in ethnically Serbian areas of Slovenia, Croatia, and Bosnia-Herzegovina. Croatia and Slovenia declared their independence in 1991, forcing Bosnia to choose between independence or a diminished role in a Serb-dominated Yugoslavia.

Bosnia-Herzegovina voted for independence in March 1992. But the mostly Serbian military of the former Yugoslavian army refused to go along with the vote. Led by Radovan Karadzic, they gained control of the region's artillery and proclaimed the existence of the "Serbian Republic of Bosnia-Herzegovina." The siege of Sarajevo began a month after the vote for independence, with Serbia waging a ferocious war of "ethnic cleansing," in which they sought to rid Bosnia of Muslims and Croats. By July 1993, the Serbs surrounded the city, cutting off delivery of arms and supplies to Bosnian forces. Despite evidence that the Serbs were raping and torturing Muslims, the Bosnian Parliament in Sept. 1993 rejected a U.N.-sponsored peace plan that would have ended the war.

Several other cease-fire agreements were brokered throughout 1993 and 1994, but none led to a lasting peace until a 1995 pact brokered by U.S. negotiator Richard Holbrooke, in which the Bosnian Serbs agreed to follow the decisions of Yugoslavia's president Slobodan Milosevic in all peace talks. On Nov. 21, 1995, the presidents of Bosnia-Herzegovina, Croatia, and Serbia met in Dayton, Ohio, to sign a peace accord ending the civil war and dividing Bosnia-Herzegovina into two entities: a Serb republic and a Muslim-Croat federation. The two statelets would be governed by the same legislature and president.

The U.N. sent 60,000 peacekeeping troops (20,000 Americans) in Dec. 1995 to supervise the transition. Elections in Sept. 1996 selected a three-member collective presidency, chaired by Muslim Alijia Izetbegovic, and a legislature whose 42 members were selected in two separate elections, 28 from the Federation and 14 from the Srpska Republic. In Jan. 1997, parliament approved a cabinet with joint (Serb and Muslim) premiers.

Yugoslavia and Bosnia established diplomatic relations in Oct. 1996, with Yugoslavia agreeing to respect Bosnia's boundaries while Bosnia dropped charges of genocide. A new crisis arose when on the same day (March 5, 1999), the West's "High Authority" (under the Dayton Accords) deposed the President of the Serb Republic, who had just been elected, while a Western arbitrator awarded the strategic Sava River town of Brcko to the Moslem-Croat Federation, resulting in the Serb republic's effective withdrawal from Bosnia-Herzegovnia. Through 2000 and 2001 incidents of friction continued, provoking interventions by the High Authority and NATO troops, which themselves became sources of tension and even riots. In Oct. 2002, elections of bewildering complexity were held: for the three-man presidency, for the federation's parliament, and for the parliaments of the two member republics, with 57 parties taking part. Where true authority lay was made clear in April as Chairman of the Presidency, Mirko Sarovic, resigned before he could be sacked by the High Commissioner who, in the same month, transferred control of the armed forces from the republics to the central authority.

▶BOTSWANA

Republic of Botswana

• **GEOGRAPHY Location:** landlocked country in southern Africa. **Boundaries**: Namibia to N and W, Zimbabwe to NE, South Africa to SE and S. **Total land area**: 231,803 sq. mi. (600,370 sq km). **Coastline**: none. **Comparative area**: about size of Texas. **Land use:** 1% arable land; negl.% permanent crops; 99% other. **Major cities**: (1989 est.) Gaborone (capital) 110,973; Francistown 49,396; Selebi-Phikwe 46,490; Molepolole 29,212; Serowe 28,267.

• **PEOPLE Population:** 1,573,267 (July 2003 est.). **Nationality:** noun and adjective—Motswana (sing.), Batswana (pl.). **Ethnic groups:** 79% Tswana, 11% Kalanga, 3% Basarwa, 7% other. **Languages:** English (official), Setswana. **Religions:** 85% indigenous beliefs, 15% Christian.

• **GOVERNMENT Type:** parliamentary republic. **Independence:** Sept. 30, 1966 (from U.K.). **Constitution:** Mar. 1965, effective Sept. 30, 1966. **National holiday:** Independence Day, Sept. 30. **Head of Government:** Festus G. Mogae, MP, head of state (since April 1998). **Structure:** executive; bicameral legislature; judiciary.

• **ECONOMY Monetary unit:** pula. **Budget:** (FY01/02) ***income:*** $2.3 bil.; ***expend.:*** $2.4 bil. **GDP:** $15.1 bil., $9,500 per capita (2002 est.). **Chief crops:** sorghum, maize, millet, peanuts. **Natural resources:** diamonds, copper, nickel, coal, gold, salt, soda ash. **Major industries:** diamonds, copper, nickel, coal, salt, soda ash, potash. **Labor force:** (2000) 264,000 formal sector employees; 40% unemployment (2001 est.). **Exports:** $2.4 bil. (f.o.b., 2002 est.); 72% diamonds, copper and nickel, meat. **Imports**: $1.9 bil. (f.o.b., 2002 est.); foodstuffs, vehicles, textiles, petroleum products. **Major trading partners:** (2000) ***exports:*** 87% European Free Trade Association (EFTA), 7% South African Customs Union (SACU), 3% Zimbabwe; ***imports:*** 74% SACU, 17% EFTA, 4% Zimbabwe.

Botswana, occupying a high and relatively arid tableland in southern Africa, was traditionally occupied by diverse groups of farmers, pastoralists, and hunter-gatherers. European missionaries arrived from South Africa in the early 19th century. In the late 19th century, native peoples resisted the encroachment of Afrikaners from the Transvaal; in response the British government established a protectorate in what was then called Bechuanaland in 1886. The southern part of the protectorate was organized as a Crown Colony and ultimately passed under the control of South Africa. During the 20th century, the territory remaining in the protectorate saw a steady evolution of local rule.

In 1920 two advisory councils were established to represent the interests of native and European inhabitants. In 1934 British authorities promulgated regulations establishing the powers and jurisdictions of native chiefs and the functions of native councils and courts. Local fiscal powers were established soon thereafter. In 1951 a joint (native-European) advisory council was set up, and 10 years later an elected legislature met under the provisions of a new constitution.

In 1963-64 the British government accepted Botswanan proposals for self-government. A new capital was established at Gaborone in February 1965; a new constitution came into effect in the following month, and Botswana became fully independent on Sept. 30, 1966. Since independence, Botswana has been a multiparty, multiracial democracy that has remained untouched by the political turmoil affecting most of its neighbors. In Oct. 1999 National Assembly elections, voters gave the Botswana Democratic Party, the ruling party since 1966, 33 of the 40 seats, ensuring President Mogae of five more years.

Botswana is one of the most prosperous countries in Africa. It is the world's largest producer of diamonds; revenues from diamond exports have been wisely managed, leading to significant budgetary surpluses in recent years. Tourism, bolstered by Botswana's large herds of big game, is the country's major nonmining industry. But the nation's AIDS epidemic (30 percent of the adult population is in fected with H.I.V.) threatens to undermine the gains made over the past three decades.

▶BRAZIL

Federative Republic of Brazil

• **GEOGRAPHY Location:** central and northeastern South America. **Boundaries**: Colombia, Venezuela, Guyana, Suriname, French Guiana to N; Atlantic Ocean to E; Uruguay, Argentina, Paraguay to S; Peru, Bolivia to W. **Total land area**: 3,286,475 sq. mi. (8,511,965 sq km). **Coastline**: 4,652 mi. (7,491 km). **Comparative area**: slightly smaller than U.S. **Land use:** 6% arable land; 1% permanent crops; 93% other. **Major cities**: (1991 est.) Brasília (capital) 1,841,028; São Paulo 9,700,111; Rio de Janeiro 6,011,181; Belo Horizonte 2,339,039; Salvador 2,075,392.

• **PEOPLE Population:** 182,032,604 (July 2003 est.). **Nationality:** noun—Brazilian(s); adjective—Brazilian. **Ethnic groups:** Portuguese, Italian, German, Japanese, black, Amerindian; 55% white, 38% mixed, 6% black, 1% other. **Languages:** Portuguese (official), Spanish, English, French. **Religions:** 80% Roman Catholic.

• **GOVERNMENT Type:** federative republic. **Independence:** Sept. 7, 1822 (from Portugal). **Constitution:** Oct. 5, 1988. **National holiday:** Independence Day, Sept. 7. **Head of Government:** Luiz Inácio Lula da Silva, president (since Jan. 2003). **Structure:** strong executive with broad powers; bicameral legislature with growing powers; judiciary.

• **ECONOMY Monetary unit:** real. **Budget:** (2001) ***income:*** $100.6 bil.; ***expend.:*** $91.6 bil. **GDP:** $1.34 tril., $7,600 per capita (2002 est.). **Chief crops:** coffee, soybeans, wheat, rice; beef. **Natural resources:** bauxite, gold, iron ore, manganese, nickel. **Major industries:** textiles and other consumer goods, shoes, chemicals. **Labor force:** 79 mil. (1999 est.); 53% services, 23% agriculture, 24% industry; 6.4% unemployment (2001 est.). **Exports:** $59.4 bil. (f.o.b., 2002); iron ore, soybean bran, orange juice, footwear. **Imports**: $46.2 bil. (f.o.b., 2002); capital goods, chemical products, oil, electricity. **Major trading partners:** (2001) ***exports:*** 24% U.S., 12% Argentina, 5% Germany; ***imports:*** 27% U.S., 14% Argentina, 9% Germany.

The Portuguese arrived on the coast of what would become Brazil with the expedition of Pedro Alvares Cabral in 1500 and found an indigenous population of semisedentary and nonsedentary cultures. Many of the semisedentary Indians spoke the Tupian language and shared similar cultural features. The Tupians quickly formed economic relationships with the first Europeans, who were interested in the valuable dyewood that was so abundant in Brazil.

The transition of Indian-European economic relations from barter to slavery was given momentum by the introduction of sugar export agriculture, a trend that began in the region in the 1540's. The 1560's saw epidemics of smallpox and measles in the coastal areas, which greatly reduced the indigenous population. Although the European sugar growers initially favored the use of indigenous peoples over imported African slave labor, the shortage of labor resulting from the epidemics led to increasing use of African slave labor by the Portuguese.

The Portuguese vied with other European powers for control of Brazilian territory, and in 1630 the Dutch briefly seized the northeastern sugar-growing area. Brazil's southern regions were underpopulated during the early colonial period, and Portuguese activity was largely limited to cattle raising. With the discovery of gold (1690's) and diamonds (1729), European settlement of the Minas Gerais area in the southeast quickened.

In 1808, the Portuguese royal court escaped Napoleon's armies with the help of the British fleet; the prince regent, Dom João VI, sought refuge in Brazil and made it the seat of the Portuguese empire. Dom João returned to Portugal in 1821, leaving his son Dom Pedro behind as prince regent. In 1822, defying orders to return to Portugal and opposed to the reversion of Brazil to colonial status, Dom Pedro declared Brazil's independence and was crowned emperor. In 1825 an agreement mediated by the British led to Portuguese recognition of Brazil as a separate kingdom.

The early years of independence were rocky. Dom Pedro became increasingly estranged from his people and began losing control of the Brazilian political situation owing to a continuing series of landowner revolts and to the loss of a war with the United Provinces of Rio de la Plata over what would become Uruguay. In 1831 Dom Pedro abdicated in favor of his five-year-old son, Dom Pedro II; a regency governed Brazil until his accession to the throne in 1840.

The Brazilian empire found itself continually involved in the wars and internal politics of Uruguay, Argentina, and Paraguay in the 1850's and 1860's. The bloody five-year war with Paraguay that began in 1865 resulted in Paraguay's eventual defeat, but the process of the war had important consequences for the future of Brazil: the expansion of military power, the fragmentation of the political party system, and the undermining of the legitimacy of slavery. Slavery was abolished in 1888, and the following year, a military coup overthrew the emperor.

The "Old Republic," which lasted from 1889 to 1930, was a federal system in which much of the political control in Brazilian society was relegated to state-based political networks with local bosses. The presidency was assigned in a de facto rotation system called the "politics of the governors," in which the president's office was controlled by the most important state power networks. The world depression of 1929 hit the Brazilian agricultural export economy hard, and in 1930 the military overthrew the elected president; Getúlio Vargas, a politician from the state of Rio Grande do Sul, took over the presidency.

Vargas proceeded to centralize power in the presidency, diminishing states' rights dramatically. Civil unrest allowed Vargas to declare a state of siege with military backing, and in 1937 he declared the establishment of the Estado Novo, a state wherein Vargas had absolute power, in imitation of Portuguese and Italian regimes of the period. The military ousted Vargas in 1945, ushering in the period of the "Second Republic." Vargas again won re-election in 1950 but committed suicide in 1954. Juscelino Kubitschek, elected president in 1955, sought to develop the country and led the way for construction of the new capital of Brasília in the previously undeveloped interior.

His successor, Jânio da Silva Quadros, resigned in 1961 after only seven months in office, and the presidency passed to populist Vice Pres. João Goulart. The populist mobilization of peasants and workers endorsed by the Goulart government led to his overthrow by the military in 1964.

The Brazilian military governed the country until 1985. Military rule was not maintained in the form of a dictatorship; rather, the military ruled as a more or less cohesive institution. The succession of generals and their technocratic allies attempted to develop the country through a pattern of state-led growth from which civilian politics were excluded. In 1985, Tancredo Neves was elected president, but he died before taking office. José Sarney, the vice presidential candidate, became Brazil's first civilian president since 1964.

Promising to revitalize the economy with a free-market revolution, conservative Fernando Collor de Mello became president in 1990. The military's share of the budget was reduced from 6 to 2.2 percent, and some companies were privatized, but inflation and debt still strained the economy. The 1988 murder of environmental activist Chico Mendes had focused world attention on the rapidly accelerating deforestation of the Amazon River basin. Pres. Collor campaigned actively to halt the destruction and in June 1992 Rio De Janeiro was the site of a U.N.-sponsored conference on development and the environment.

Pres. Collor was forced to resign in Dec. 1992 because of charges he stole or misappropriated over $20 million (after a two-year investigation he was cleared of all charges). His successor, Vice Pres. Itamar Franco, worked to privatize industries and halt inflation, but a new corruption scandal involving at least 18 members of the legislature halted most government activity in 1994.

In presidential elections held in Oct. 1994, former finance minister Fernando Henrique Cardoso ran on an anti-inflation platform and won a landslide victory. The Cardoso government focused on establishing federal control over state banks and supporting land reform for peasants. The rewards were a dramatic drop in both inflation and unemployment and great popularity for Cardoso. In

1997 Congress passed a Constitutional Amendment permitting Cardoso to run for a second term.

In Oct. 1998 Cardoso easily won re-election for a four-year term. Despite an unexpected January 1999 devalutation of the *real*, the I.M.F. released the remainder of its 1998 aid package in March. In April, Brazil was able to sell $2 billion in bonds—a sign of continuing confidence by the world money markets. But Cardoso's popularity suddenly plummeted and in Oct. 2002 elections leftist Luiz da Silva swamped Cardoso-backed Jose Serra in the presidential run-off, while his Workers' Party won a plurality in the Chamber of Deputies and organized the cabinet.

▶BRUNEI

Negara Brunei Darussalam

• **GEOGRAPHY Location:** southeastern Asia, Kalimantan (Borneo) island. Bandar Seri Begawan 4°56'N, 114°58'E. **Boundaries**: surrounded on landward side by Sarawak, state, of Malaysia; South China Sea to N. **Total land area**: 2,228 sq. mi. (5,770 sq km). **Coastline**: 100 mi. (161 km). **Comparative area**: slightly larger than Delaware. **Land use:** 1% arable land; 1% permanent crops; 98% other. **Major cities**: Bandar Seri Begawan (formerly Brunei Town) (capital) 50,500 (1986 est.); Seria, Kuala Belait, Tutong.

• **PEOPLE Population:** 358,098 (July 2003 est.). **Nationality:** noun—Bruneian(s); adjective—Bruneian. **Ethnic groups:** 67% Malay, 15% Chinese, 6% indigenous, 12% other. **Languages:** Malay (official), English, Chinese. **Religions:** 67% Muslim (official), 13% Buddhist, 10% Christian, 10% indigenous and other.

• **GOVERNMENT Type:** constitutional sultanate. **Independence:** Jan. 1, 1984 (from U.K.). **Constitution:** Sept. 29, 1959 (some provisions suspended since Dec. 1962, others since independence). **National holiday:** National Day, Feb. 23. **Head of Government:** Sir Hassanal Bolkiah Mu'izzaddin Waddaulah, sultan and prime minister (since Aug. 1968). **Structure:** chief of state is sultan; unicameral legislature; judiciary.

• **ECONOMY Monetary unit:** bruneian dollar. **Budget:** (1997) ***income:*** $2.5 bil.; ***expend.:*** $2.6 bil. **GDP:** $6.5 bil., $18,600 per capita (2002 est.). **Chief crops:** rice, cassava, bananas. **Natural resources:** petroleum, natural gas, timber. **Major industries:** petroleum, petroleum refining, liquefied natural gas, construction. **Labor force:** 143,400 (1999 est.); 48% government, 42% oil, natural gas, services, and construction. **Exports:** $3 bil. (f.o.b., 2000 est.); crude oil, natural gas, petroleum products. **Imports**: $1.4 bil. (c.i.f., 2000 est.); machinery and transport equipment, manufactured goods, foodstuffs, chemicals. **Major trading partners:** (2002 est.) ***exports:*** 41% Japan, 13% South Korea, 12% Thailand; ***imports:*** 31% Singapore, 22% Japan., 18% Malaysia.

The Islamic sultanate of Brunei became dominant in northern Borneo in the 16th century but declined in power after the 17th century under pressure from the Dutch and other foreign powers. An Anglo-Dutch agreement of 1824 assigned North Borneo to Great Britain's sphere of influence in Asia. In 1841 a British adventurer, James Brooke, aided the sultan of Brunei in putting down a rebellion and was rewarded by being given the province of Sarawak, comprising more than half of the sultanate's area. Britain established a protectorate over Sabah, the eastern portion of Brunei, in 1881. That left the sultan with a tiny realm on the Brunei River, which was ultimately placed under British protection in 1888. The discovery of Southeast Asia's richest oilfield in Brunei and its offshore waters made the sultanate an enclave of tremendous wealth from the late 1920's onward.

Following Japanese occupation during World War II, British rule resumed in North Borneo. Sarawak and Sabah became part of Malaysia in 1963. Brunei was granted independence from Great Britain on Dec. 1, 1984. The sultan of Brunei, an absolute monarch, rules from the world's largest royal palace in Bandar Seri Begawan, the nation's capital. The economy is centered almost entirely on petroleum and international banking and investments.

▶BULGARIA

Republic of Bulgaria

• **GEOGRAPHY Location:** southeastern Europe. **Boundaries**: Romania to N, Black Sea to E, Turkey and Greece to S, Macedonia and Yugoslavia to W. **Total land area**: 42,822 sq. mi. (110,910 sq km). **Coastline**: 220 mi. (354 km). **Comparative area**: between Tennessee and Pennsylvania. **Land use:** 39% arable land; 2% permanent crops; 59% other. **Major cities**: (1992 est.) Sofia (capital) 1,114,476; Plovdiv 341,374; Varna 308,601; Burges 195,986; Ruse 170,203.

• **PEOPLE Population:** 7,537,929 (July 2003 est.). **Nationality:** noun—Bulgarian(s); adjective—Bulgarian. **Ethnic groups:** 83.6% Bulgarian, 9.5% Turk. **Languages:** Bulgarian; secondary languages closely correspond to ethnic breakdown. **Religions:** 83.8% Bulgarian Orthodox, 12.1% Muslim, 0.1% Jewish, 1.7% Roman Catholic, 2.3% Protestant, Gregorian-Armenian, and other.

• **GOVERNMENT Type:** parliamentary democracy. **Independence:** March 3, 1878 (from Ottoman Empire). **Constitution:** July 12, 1991. **National holiday:** Independence Day, Mar. 3. **Heads of Government:** Georgi Parvanov, president (since Jan. 2002); Simeon Saxe-Coburg-Gotha, prime minister (since July 2001). **Structure:** executive; unicameral legislature; judiciary.

• **ECONOMY Monetary unit:** lev. **Budget:** (2001 est.) ***income:*** $5.57 bil.; ***expend:*** $5.68 bil. **GDP:** $50.6 bil., $6,600 per capita (2002 est.). **Chief crops:** vegetables, fruits, tobacco; livestock. **Natural resources:** bauxite, copper, lead, zinc, coal. **Major industries:** machine building and metal working, food processing, chemicals. **Labor force:** 3.83 mil. (2000); 31% industry, 26% agriculture, 43% services; 18% unemployment (2002 est.). **Exports:** $5.3 bil. (f.o.b., 2002 est.); machinery and equipment, metals and ores, chemicals and plastics, food, textiles. **Imports**: $6.9 bil. (f.o.b., 2002 est.); fuels, minerals, and raw materials; machinery and equipment; food; textiles and apparel. **Major trading partners:** ***exports:*** 14% Italy, 10% Turkey, Germany, Greece; ***imports:*** 20% Russia, 10% Turkey, Germany, Greece.

Turkic Bulgars arrived at the west shore of the Black Sea in the seventh century, mingling with the indigenous Slavic population. The Bulgars accepted Eastern Orthodox Christianity in the ninth century and were conquered and incorporated into the Byzantine Empire by Basil II in the late 10th century. With the decline of Byzantium, Bulgaria became independent, but it was conquered by the Ottoman Turks in 1396 and remained part of the Ottoman Empire for the next 500 years.

In the Treaty of San Stefano, ending the Russo-Turkish War in 1878, a Bulgarian state was promised that was to stretch from the Adriatic to the Black Sea. But the Great Powers would not permit so large a Russian client state, and instead the Berlin Conference of 1878 sanctioned a much smaller Bulgarian state, under a German dynasty with the Ottoman sultan as nominal overlord. Bulgaria gained full independence in 1908.

The Balkan Wars of 1912 and 1913 led to a reduction of Bulgarian territory, and after World War I, Bulgaria, which had been allied with the Central Powers, lost its Aegean Coastline to Greece. A series of weak parliamentary governments under King Boris III (r. 1918-43) ended when the king established a dictatorship in 1935. Bulgaria joined the Axis powers in 1941 and declared war against the Western powers but not against Russia.

Russian troops entered Bulgaria in 1944 and organized a Communist government. The boy-king Simeon II remained on the throne until 1946, when the monarchy was abolished by a popular referendum. The People's Republic of Bulgaria was established in 1947.

Until the end of World War II, Bulgaria was a peasant society, with 80 percent of the population engaged in agriculture; industrial development was rudimentary. The People's Republic established a planned economy on the Soviet model; Russian credits and trade agreements permitted a rapid industrialization focused on machinery and equipment for export.

In 1954 Todor Zhivkov became first secretary of the Bulgarian Communist party. He served as premier in the 1960's and president from 1971 to 1990. In the 1960's Zhivkov promoted decentralization and responsiveness to market forces, but with the 1968 Russian invasion of Czechoslovakia, he returned the economy to central planning, collective farming, and giant state-industrial enterprises. In October 1985 Zhivkov met with Gorbachev and reforms based on Gorbachev's "self-management" policies were instituted.

Democratic reform began with Zhivkov's resignation in Nov. 1989. There followed a year of popular unrest and political turmoil with a succession of changes in the ruling hierarchy, culminating in the election of Zheliu Zhelev of the reform Union of Democratic Forces as president (Bulgaria's first non-Communist leader in 40 years), and the appointment in 1990 of Dimitar Popov as premier of a coalition government dominated by the Socialist (formerly Communist) party.

Elections in October 1991 ended the Socialist grip on power, as the Union of Democratic Forces formed a government under Philip Dimitrov. But within a year the government was bankrupt, inflation at 30 percent and unemployment 40 percent, and Dimitrov's government was ousted by Parliament. Lyuben Berov, an economic adviser to Zhelev, came to power for two years and then he was ousted in elections (Dec. 1994) by the Socialists, led by Zhan Videnov.

Under the Videnov-Zhelev "gridlock," matters only grew worse, with a food crisis developing atop growing unemployment and 300 percent inflation in 1996. Protests and riots marked the latter half of 1996, and in the Nov. presidential elections, the UDF candidate, Peter Stoyanov (who defeated Zhelev in a party primary) won easily. And in the April 1997 elections to parliament, the UDF coalition took 137 seats to the Socialists 58. With the promise of economic reform, the I.M.F. and the E.U. provided large new grants.

The new prime minister, Ivan Kostov, commenced some serious reforms of the all-but-insolvent economy, reforms that were on the one hand painful and on the other not radical enough to rid the economy of state control. In April 2001 Bulgaria's last king, Simeon II, founded a political movement which in the June parliamentary elections won half the seats and transformed the one-time king into the Republic's new prime minister. But in November presidential elections, voters rejected Simeon's preferred candidate and elected ex-Communist Georgi Parvanov.

▶BURKINA FASO

• **GEOGRAPHY** **Location:** landlocked country in western Africa. **Boundaries**: Mali to N and W, Niger to E, Benin, Togo, Ghana, Ivory Coast to S. **Total land area**: 105,869 sq. mi. (274,200 sq km). **Coastline**: none. **Comparative area**: between Colorado and Nevada. **Land use:** 12% arable land; negl.% permanent crops; 88% other. **Major cities**: (1985 census) Ouagadougou (capital) 441,514; Bobo-Dioulasso 228,668; Koudougou 51,926; Ouahigouya 38,902; Banfora 35,319.

• **PEOPLE** **Population:** 12,228,460 (July 2003 est.). **Nationality:** noun—Burkinabe (sing., pl.); adjective—Burkinabe. **Ethnic groups:** over 40% Mossi, Gurunsi, Senufo, Lobi, Bobo, Mande, Fulani. **Languages:** French (official); native African languages spoken by 90% of population. **Religions:** 50% Muslim, 40% indigenous beliefs, 10% Christian (mainly Roman Catholic).

• **GOVERNMENT** **Type:** parliamentary. **Independence:** Aug. 5, 1960 (from France). **Constitution:** June 2, 1991. **National holiday:** Republic Day, Dec. 11. **Heads of Government:** Blaise Compaore, president (since Dec. 1991); Paramanga Ernest Yonly, prime minister (since Nov. 2000). **Structure:** executive; bicameral legislature; judiciary.

• **ECONOMY** **Monetary unit:** Communauté Financière Africaine (CFA) franc. **Budget:** (2001) ***income:*** $316 mil.; ***expend.:*** N.A. **GDP:** $13.6 bil., $1,080 per capita (2002 est.). **Chief crops:** peanuts, shea nuts, sesame, cotton. **Natural resources:** manganese, limestone, marble; small deposits of gold, antimony, copper, nickel, bauxite. **Major industries:** cotton, beverages, agricultural processing. **Labor force:** 5 mil. (2002); 90% agriculture; a large part of male labor force migrates to neighboring countries for seasonal employment. **Exports:** $250 mil. (f.o.b., 2002 est.); cotton, gold, animal products. **Imports**: $525 mil. (f.o.b., 2002 est.); machinery, food products, petroleum. **Major trading partners:** (2001) ***exports:*** France, Italy, Singapore; ***imports:*** Ivory Coast, France, Nigeria.

The Mossi empire dominated the area of what is now Burkina Faso, a landlocked nation in western Africa with few natural resources and poor agricultural conditions, from as early as the 11th century. They ruled the region, often resisting Muslim invaders, until modern times.

The region was hardly visited by Europeans before the 1880's, but by 1896 the French had captured the Mossi capital city of Ouagadougou and established a protectorate over the area. The French created Upper Volta in 1919, naming it for the upper basin of the Volta River. Upper Volta became a self-governing state with the French Overseas Community in 1958 and gained independence Aug. 5, 1960.

After a brief period of military rule, the nation ratified a new constitution on June 14, 1970, and made a peaceful transition to civilian rule based on the French model. In 1980 the constitution was overthrown and a military government was set up. There was another coup on Aug. 4, 1983, and a government was established patterned after the

Libyan government of Muammar al-Qaddafi. On Aug. 14, 1984, Upper Volta officially changed its name to Burkina Faso.

Two attempted coups against the government of Capt. Blaise Compaore, in September and December 1989, were put down and the leaders executed. In 1992, as president, Compaore convened a National Reconciliation Forum followed by legislative elections that resulted in a new prime minister. In 1994 the World Bank reported significant economic progress in this desperately poor country.

▶BURUNDI

Republic of Burundi

• **GEOGRAPHY Location:** landlocked country on northeastern shore of Lake Tanganyika in central Africa. **Boundaries**: Rwanda to N, Tanzania to E and S, Zaire to W. **Total land area**: 10,745 sq. mi. (27,830 sq km). **Coastline**: none. **Comparative area**: slightly larger than Maryland. **Land use:** 30% arable land; 13% permanent crops; 57% other. **Major cities**: Bujumbura (capital) 215,243 (1987 est.); Gitega 15,943 (1978).

• **PEOPLE Population:** 6,096,156 (July 2003 est.). **Nationality:** noun—Burundian(s); adjective—Burundi. **Ethnic groups:** 85% Hutu (Bantu), 14% Tutsi (Hamitic), 1% Twa (Pygmy), 3,000 Europeans, 2,000 South Asians. **Languages:** Kirundi and French (both official), Swahili (along Lake Tanganyika and in Bujumbura area). **Religions:** 67% Christian (62% Roman Catholic, 5% Protestant), 23% indigenous beliefs, 10% Muslim.

• **GOVERNMENT Type:** republic. **Independence:** July 1, 1962 (from U.N. trusteeship under Belgian administration). **Constitution:** Mar. 13, 1992. **National holiday:** Independence Day, July 1. **Heads of Government:** Domitien Ndayizeye, president (since May 1, 2003); **Structure:** executive; unicameral legislature; judiciary. (Note: a miltary government took office during a 1996 coup, but the new leadership has not been officially recognized.)

• **ECONOMY Monetary unit:** Burundi franc. **Budget:** (2000 est.) ***income:*** $125 mil; ***expend.:*** $176 mil. **GDP:** $3.8 bil., $600 per capita (2002 est.). **Chief crops:** coffee, cotton, tea, corn, sorghum. **Natural resources:** nickel, uranium, rare earth oxide, peat, cobalt. **Major industries:** light consumer goods such as blankets, shoes, soap; assembly of imported components; public works construction. **Labor force:** (2000 est.) 3.7 mil.; 93% agriculture, 7% other. **Exports:** $26 mil. (f.o.b., 2002); coffee, tea, cotton, hides. **Imports**: $135 mil. (f.o.b., 2002); capital goods, petroleum products, foodstuffs. **Major trading partners:** ***exports:*** E.U., Switzerland, Kenya; ***imports:*** E.U., Tanzania, Kenya.

Burundi's population is divided between two ethnic groups, the majority Hutu and the minority, but politically powerful, Tutsi. The Hutu were the original settlers of the country and practiced agriculture; the cattle-herding Tutsi arrived several hundred years ago and established a form of feudal overlordship over the Hutu. The traditional government was monarchical, with a king (mwami) chosen from among a group of aristocratic families (ganwa).

European exploration of Burundi began in 1858, and the territory was incorporated into German East Africa in 1899. Following World War I, the League of Nations (1923) awarded Burundi, along with neighboring Rwanda, to Belgium as a mandated territory. Belgian rule over the Territory of Ruanda-Urundi, as it was then called, continued under a U.N. trusteeship after World War II.

Burundi became independent on July 1, 1962, as a constitutional monarchy under the traditional mwami. The country rapidly lapsed into political chaos. In 1966 Capt. Michel Micombero overthrew the monarchy and proclaimed a republic. A Hutu rebellion in 1972 against Tutsi political domination left 10,000 Tutsi dead; Tutsi reprisals in 1972-73 resulted in the slaughter of 150,000 Hutu. The Micombero government was overthrown in a bloodless coup, and on Nov. 1, 1976, Lt. Col. Jean-Baptiste Bagaza took control of the government.

Bagaza was overthrown in Sept. 1987, and his successor, Maj. Pierre Buyoya, proclaimed a policy of nonalignment, seeking closer links with the West, while maintaining relations with Libya and the eastern bloc. Domestically, the government pledged to eradicate Bagaza's record of persecution of the Catholic church (62 percent of Burundians are Catholic) and to seek ethnic reconciliation between Hutu and Tutsi, but renewed outbreaks of ethnic violence occurred in 1988. Buyoya led the country to its first free presidential elections in June 1993. Melchior Ndadaye, a Hutu, defeated Buyoya by a wide margin.

But in Oct. 1993 Ndadaye was assassinated, as was his Hutu successor (April 1994). The succeeding regime of Hutu president Ntibantunganya, unsuccesful in forming a stable, ethnically balanced goverment, was overturned in a military coup (July 1996) which dissolved parliament, outlawed all political parties, and named Pierre Buyoya to return as president. Vowing yet another return to democracy after the end of civil war, Buyoya faced economic sanctions by the Organization of African Unity. Meanwhile, the complicated civil war was only worsened by Zaire's attempt to expel almost half a million Tutsi (the Banyamulenge people, settled south on Lake Kivi since the 18th century) in 1996. The Tutsi succesful self defense had the paradoxical effect of driving yet more Hutu (50,000) into Burundi—and almost half a million more into neighboring Rwanda.

The civil war continued into 2000, with at least 200,000 dead, with 350,000 Hutu rebels "regrouped" into 50 camps, and with Burundian army involvement (unadmitted) in the Congo conflict. A promising peace accord, brokered by Nelson Mandela in Aug. 2000, collapsed in Feb. 2001 as the capital of Bujumbura fell to Hutu rebels. Government forces re-took it on March 1, and another accord again forged by Mandela was signed by all parties in July 2001. Based on a power-sharing arrangement for three years the new 14 Hutu/12 Tutsi cabinet began ruling Nov. 1. A year later (Dec. 2002) the rebel group "Force for the Defense of Democracy" signed a truce with the government and in April 2003 when (as agreed) Hutu Domitien Ndayizeye was sworn in as president. Yet in July rebels attacked the capital of Bujumbara, while fighting continued in provincial villages as the civil war entered its eleventh year.

▶CAMBODIA

Kingdom of Cambodia

• **GEOGRAPHY Location:** on Indochinese peninsula in Southeast Asia. **Boundaries**: Thailand to W and N, Laos to N, Gulf of Thailand to S, Vietnam to E. **Total land area**: 69,900 sq. mi. (181,040 sq km). **Coastline**: 275 mi. (443 km). **Comparative area**: between Missouri and Oklahoma. **Land use:** 21% arable land; 1 % permanent crops; 78% other. **Major cities**: (1991 est.) Phnom Penh (capital) 900,000.

• **PEOPLE Population:** 13,124,764 (July 2003 est.). **Nationality:** noun—Cambodian(s); adjective—Cambodian. **Ethnic groups:** 90% Khmer

(Cambodian), 5% Vietnamese, 1% Chinese, 4% other minorities. **Languages:** Khmer (official), French, English. **Religions:** 95% Theravada Buddhism.

• **GOVERNMENT** **Type:** multiparty liberal democracy under a constitutional monarchy. **Independence:** November 9, 1953 (from France). **Constitution:** promulgated Sept. 21, 1993. **National holiday:** Independence Day, November 9. **Heads of Government:** Norodom Sihanouk, king (reinstated Sept. 1993); Hun Sen, prime minister (since Nov. 1998). **Structure:** executive; bicameral legislature; judiciary.

• **ECONOMY** **Monetary unit:** new riel. **Budget:** (2001 est.) ***income:*** $396 mil.; ***expend.:*** $607 mil. **GDP:** $19.7 bil., $1,500 per capita (2002 est.). **Chief crops:** rice, rubber, corn, vegetables. **Natural resources:** timber, gemstones, some iron ore, manganese, phosphates, hydropower potential. **Major industries:** garments, rice milling, fishing, wood and wood products. **Labor force:** 6 mil.; 80% agriculture (2001 est.). **Exports:** $1.38 bil. (f.o.b., 2001 est.); timber, garments, rubber, soybeans, sesame. **Imports**: $1.73 bil. (f.o.b., 2001 est.); cigarettes, gold, construction materials, petroleum products. **Major trading partners:** U.S., Thailand.

The dominant power in Indochina from the Eighth through the 13th centuries, the Khmer Empire encompassed present-day Cambodia and much of western Thailand, southern Laos, and central and southern Vietnam. It built magnificent Buddhist temple cities at Angkor Wat and Angkor Thon. From the 14th century onward, the Khmer Empire came under increasing pressure from the expansionist Vietnamese state of Annam, which absorbed the territories east of the Mekong River. In the 18th century, the kingdom of Siam (Thailand) annexed three western provinces of the Khmer Empire. The remaining Khmer territory became the French protectorate of Cambodia in 1863, and a French colony as part of the Union of Indochina in 1887. In 1907 France forced Siam to return some territory to Cambodia.

During World War II, Cambodia was occupied by Japan from 1942 to 1945, when French control was restored. After the French defeat in Indochina, Cambodia became independent in 1953 under Prince Norodom Sihanouk, who had ascended the throne in 1941. In 1960 Sihanouk was named head of state under a constitutional monarchy. Shaken by the Vietnam War in the 1960's, Cambodia broke relations with the United States in 1965 because of South Vietnamese incursions across the border. In 1969 relations were restored when Sihanouk charged North Vietnam with arming the Khmer Rouge Cambodian Communist rebels. In the same year, American planes began secret bombing raids in Cambodia. In 1970 Sihanouk was ousted by a coup led by pro-U.S. Gen. Lon Nol; the monarchy was abolished, and Prince Sihanouk went into exile.

In April 1975 the Khmer Rouge, led by Pol Pot, captured the capital, Phnom Penh, and established a new government, the Kampuchean People's Republic. In an ensuing reign of terror, an estimated 3 million people died and hundreds of thousands more fled to refugee camps in Thailand. In 1978, Vietnamese troops invaded, capturing Phnom Penh on Jan. 7, 1979, and installing a new government led by Heng Samrin. The Kampuchean People's Republic continued to be recognized as the legal government of Cambodia in the United Nations and by most non-Soviet-bloc nations. A coalition dominated by the Khmer Rouge resisted the Vietnamese takeover, but by 1985 almost all of the country was under Vietnamese control with the Communist Party's Hun Sen as Prime Minister.

Most Vietnamese troops withdrew in 1989, and Prince Sihanouk emerged as the leader of a coalition of antigovernment forces. Starting in late 1988 conferences including representatives from all Cambodian factions were held to forge a political settlement to end the 20-year-old civil war. A peace agreement was signed on Oct. 23, 1991, providing for a cease-fire under U.N. supervision, the disarmament of all military factions, the formation of a coalition government, and the scheduling of a national election.

Despite bloody efforts by Khmer Rouge forces to disrupt the planned election, Cambodians went to the polls in large numbers on May 23, 1993. The Royalist party emerged with about 42 percent of the vote, ousting Hun Sen's Cambodian People's party. Hun Sen agreed to take part in a coalition cabinet as "second premier," with Sihanouk's son, Prince Ranariddh, as "first premier." Sihanouk took the title "king." In Jan. 1994, the united government went on the offensive and captured the Khmer Rouge stronghold of Pailin, driving 3,000 troops and 20,000 civilians into Thailand. Sihanouk succesfully negotiated international loans for rebuilding the country.

The coaltion government proved ineffective due to the inherent rivalry between the prince and Hun Sen, both of whom built up their security forces. When the Khmer Rouge leadership split in mid-1997, with Pol Pot either assasinated or imprisoned, Hun Sen seized the moment and his forces attacked those of his co-ruler's and drove the prince into exile. New elections were held in July 1998 and Hun Sen emerged victorious but agreed to form a coalition government. Hun Sen became "sole premier" with 12 cabinet posts while Ranariddh became President of the Assembly with 11 cabinet posts. In December, the last Khmer Rouge troops surrendered, and by March 1999, all of the remaining Khmer Rouge leaders had surrendered or were captured. In Jan. 2001 the Senate and National Assembly approved Hun Sen's agreement with the U.N. for an international tribunal to try the mass murderers.

▶CAMEROON
Republic of Cameroon

• **GEOGRAPHY** **Location:** western coast of central Africa. **Boundaries**: Nigeria to NW, Chad to NE, Central African Republic to E, Congo to SE, Gabon, Equatorial Guinea to S, Gulf of Guinea to W. **Total land area**: 183,568 sq. mi. (475,440 sq km). **Coastline**: 250 mi. (402 km). **Comparative area**: slightly larger than California. **Land use:** 13% arable land; 3% permanent crops; 84% other. **Major cities**: (1986 est.) Yaoundé (capital) 653,670; Douala 1,029,731; Nkongsamba (and environs) 123,149; Maroua (and environs) 103,653.

• **PEOPLE** **Population:** 15,746,179 (July 2003 est.). **Nationality:** noun—Cameroonian(s); adjective—Cameroonian. **Ethnic groups:** 31% Cameroon Highlanders, 19% Equatorial Bantu, 11% Kirdi, 10% Fulani, 8% Northwestern Bantu, 7% Eastern Nigritic, 13% other African; less than 1% non-African. **Languages:** English and French (both official); 24 major African language groups. **Religions:** 40% indigenous beliefs, 40% Christian, 20% Muslim.

• **GOVERNMENT** **Type:** unitary republic; multiparty presidential regime. **Independence:** Jan. 1, 1960 (from U.N. trusteeship under French administration). **Constitution:** May 20, 1972. **National holiday:** Republic Day, May 20. **Heads of Govern-**

ment: Paul Biya, president (since Nov. 1982); Peter Mafany Musonga, prime minister (since Sept. 1996). **Structure:** executive; unicameral legislature; judiciary.

• **ECONOMY** **Monetary unit:** Communauté Financière Africaine franc. **Budget:** (FY00/01 est.) ***income:*** $2.2 bil.; ***expend.:*** $2.1 bil. **GDP:** $27 bil., $1,700 per capita (2002 est.). **Chief crops:** coffee, cocoa, cotton, rubber. **Natural resources:** crude oil, bauxite, iron ore, timber, hydropower potential. **Major industries:** crude oil production and refinining, food processing. **Labor force:** (1983) 70% agriculture, 13% industry and transport, 17% other services. **Exports:** $1.9 bil. (f.o.b., 2002 est.); crude oil and petroleum products, lumber, cocoa beans, aluminum. **Imports**: $1.7 bil. (f.o.b., 2002 est.); machines and electrical equipment, transport equipment, fuel, food. **Major trading partners:** ***exports:*** 22% Italy, 12% Spain, 11% France; ***imports:*** 29% France, 12% Nigeria, 3% Italy.

Cameroon was settled by the Sao people about 1,000 years ago. In later times others, including the Bamileke, Bassa, Douala, and Fulani, migrated into the region. Portuguese trading stations were established along the coast beginning in the 15th century, and between 1500 and the early 19th century, the population was severely depleted by the slave trade in the hands of various European nations. European rivalries for domination in Cameroon were settled temporarily in 1884 when Germany established a protectorate.

British and French troops invaded German Cameroon during World War I, and following the war the League of Nations divided the protectorate into two mandated territories—French in the eastern sector and British in the west. French Cameroon rejected the Vichy government in World War II and became an important African base for Charles de Gaulle's Free French. In 1946 British and French rule in Cameroon was reaffirmed under U.N. trusteeships.

In 1958 the French trusteeship was abolished, and the Republic of Cameroon became independent on Jan. 1, 1960. In February 1961 a U.N.-supervised plebiscite was held in British Cameroon, allowing the people of that region to choose between union with Nigeria and union with the Republic of Cameroon. The northern two-thirds of the British territory elected union with Nigeria; the southern portion joined the Republic of Cameroon on Oct. 1, 1961, to form the Federal Republic of Cameroon. In 1972 the federal structure was abolished by a national referendum, and the United Republic of Cameroon was established. In 1984 the nation's name reverted to the Republic of Cameroon.

During the federal period, Cameroon had a multiparty political system, with party divisions coinciding with the old distinctions between west and east Cameroon. In 1966 all political parties were amalgamated to form the Cameroon National Union, which, with various changes in name, has dominated the political life of Cameroon ever since. In 1980 Pres. Ahidjo, the long-time political leader of Cameroon, was elected without opposition to a fifth five-year term in office. He resigned in 1982 and was replaced by Prime Minister Paul Biya, who was reelected in his own right in 1984. He instituted political reforms whereby multiple candidates ran for office within the structure of the country's single-party system. In 1992 he was elected president in the nation's first multiparty elections. His closest rival was put under house arrest.

The economy of Cameroon is based primarily on agriculture; it is self-sufficient in food and exports coffee, cocoa, rubber, cotton, palm oil, and timber. Oil is the principal export, however, accounting for 60 percent of export earnings.

▶CANADA

• **GEOGRAPHY** **Location:** northern North America (excluding Alaska and Greenland); second largest country in the world. **Boundaries**: Arctic Ocean to N, Greenland to NE across Baffin Bay, Atlantic Ocean to E, United States to S, Pacific Ocean and Alaska to W. **Total land area**: 3,851,794 sq. mi. (9,976,140 sq km). **Coastline**: 151,492 mi. (243,791 km). **Comparative area**: slightly larger than U.S. **Land use:** 5% arable land; negl.% permanent crops, 95% other. **Major cities**: (1991 census) Ottawa (capital) 912,100; Toronto 3,863,105; Montréal 3,091,115; Vancouver 1,584,115; Edmonton 832,155.

• **PEOPLE** **Population:** 32,207,113 (July 2003 est.). **Nationality:** noun—Canadian(s); adjective—Canadian. **Ethnic groups:** 28% British Isles origin, 23% French origin, 15% other European, 2% Amerindian, 6% other, mostly Asian, Arab, African. **Languages:** 59.3% English, 23.2% French (both official). **Religions:** 46% Roman Catholic, 36% Protestant, 17.5% other.

• **GOVERNMENT** **Type:** confederation with parliamentary democracy. **Independence:** July 1, 1867 (from U.K.). **Constitution:** amended British North America Act of 1867 transferred power and rights to Canada, Apr. 17, 1982; charter of rights and unwritten customs. **National holiday:** Canada Day, July 1. **Heads of Government:** Jean Chrétien, prime minister (since Nov. 1993); Adrienne Clarkson, governor-general (since Oct. 1999). **Structure:** executive—cabinet collectively responsible to House of Commons and headed by prime minister; legislative—bicameral Parliament with queen represented by governor general, Senate, and House of Commons; judiciary—judges appointed by governor general with Supreme Court as highest tribunal.

• **ECONOMY** **Monetary unit:** Canadian dollar. **Budget:** (FY00/01 est.) ***income:*** $178.6 bil.; ***expend.:*** $260.5 bil. **GDP:** $932 bil., $29,400 per capita (2002 est.). **Chief crops:** grain (principally wheat), oilseeds, tobacco. **Natural resources:** iron ore, nickel, zinc, copper, gold, lead. **Major industries:** processed and unprocessed minerals, food products, wood and paper products. **Labor force:** 16.4 mil.; 74% services, 15% manufacturing; 7.6% unemployment (2002 est.). **Exports:** $260.5 bil. (f.o.b., 2002 est.); motor vehicles and parts, wood pulp, timber, petroleum. **Imports**: $229 bil. (f.o.b., 2002 est.); machinery and equipment, petroleum, chemicals, motor vehicles. **Major trading partners:** U.S., Japan, U.K., other E.U..

Canada is geographically the second-largest country in the world, but most of its territory is very sparsely settled. The vast majority of the country's 32 million people live in a narrow band along the border with the U.S. Despite a long tradition of national independence, Canada's history has been dominated by relations with Great Britain, the U.S., and, to a lesser extent, France.

Canada's earliest inhabitants arrived via the Bering land bridge from Asia around 15,000 years ago and diversified to form the various Inuit (Eskimo), Northwest Indian, Plains Indian, and forest Indian cultures that still contribute significantly to Canada's national identity. The earliest-known European settlers of Canada were Vikings, who established a short-lived colony in Newfoundland around A.D. 1000. Other European explorers made numerous voyages to Canada during the 16th century, stimulated by Canada's rich resources of fish, forest products, and furs.

The first permanent European settlement in Canada was the French trading station at Quebec, founded by Samuel de Champlain in 1608. Fur traders rapidly spread into the interior along the St. Lawrence River and the Great Lakes; European diseases, particularly smallpox, decimated Native American populations as the explorers advanced. In 1663 New France was organized as a French Crown Colony, and royal governors replaced private commercial interests in governing Quebec.

The Hudson Bay Company was chartered by the British Crown in 1670, inaugurating a long period of commercial and territorial rivalry in Canada between Britain and France. In general, France sought to expand New France northward and westward, while Britain sought to expand its domination southward and westward from Hudson Bay. French and British interests clashed directly along the Atlantic coast, where both British and French settlements were established. Local and regional wars between the French and the British were endemic in Canada throughout the 17th and 18th centuries; each side enlisted Native American allies. These wars were often inconclusive, but in Queen Anne's War (1702-13), Britain gained a significant advantage by winning control of Acadia and Newfoundland, and by driving the French from Hudson Bay.

The French and Indian Wars of 1756-63, a North American extension of Europe's Seven Years' War, proved to be the decisive turning point in the Anglo-French rivalry in Canada. Prior to the outbreak of full-scale war, in 1755 the British deported some 7,000-10,000 French settlers from Acadia, in Nova Scotia, to the West Indies; many later settled in Louisiana. When war broke out in Europe in 1756, Britain employed its superior sea power to cut New France off from Europe and captured Quebec in the Battle of the Plains of Abraham in 1759. Montreal capitulated in 1760, leaving Britain in control of New France.

Faced with the problem of governing New France's large and rapidly growing French population (which far outnumbered Canada's English-speaking population), the British in 1774 passed the Quebec Act, which recognized the territory's legal code and manorial system of land tenure, and granted legal status to the Roman Catholic church. The act also extended Canadian territory south to the Ohio River, enraging the inhabitants of the 13 American colonies and helping to fuel the American Revolution.

During the American Revolution, nearly 40,000 loyalists fled to Canada from the rebellious colonies, establishing English-speaking settlements in New Brunswick and western Quebec. Friction between English- and French-speaking Canadians led the British in 1791 to divide Canada (west of the Atlantic maritime provinces) into two provinces, Upper Canada and Lower Canada. Each was granted a legislature; Upper Canada's was based on British institutions, Lower Canada's retained the French forms established by the Quebec Act of 1774.

During the War of 1812 between Great Britain and the U.S., Canada became a battleground; Toronto was captured and pillaged by the Americans in 1813. Many Americans hoped to expand the territory of the U.S. at the expense of Canada, or even to entice Canada into a continental American union, but Canadians, whether English- or French-speaking, showed no enthusiasm for joining the U.S. A small British garrison, with the support of Native American irregular forces, kept the Americans at bay. The Convention of 1818 established the border between Canada and the U.S. at latitude 49° north, as far west as the Rocky Mountains, and provided for joint U.S.-British control of Oregon (i.e., the entire Columbia River basin).

Following the War of 1812, British authorities encouraged British immigration to Canada, and between 1815 and 1855, one million Britons answered the call. This immigration radically altered Canada's ethnic balance, making French-speaking Canadians a minority population for the first time. The francophones of Lower Canada, hemmed in on all sides by English speakers, rose in rebellion under the leadership of the Parti Patriote in 1837-38. Lord Durham recommended in 1839 that Canada be united under a single government, and the Union of Canada was enacted in 1841. This move did not, however, quell the growing nationalism of French Canadians.

War with the U.S. threatened in 1844, as the U.S. claimed the entire Columbia River basin north to 54°40' ("fifty-four forty or fight"). But diplomacy triumphed in the end: In 1846 the boundary at 49° was extended westward to the Pacific Ocean. Meanwhile, gold was discovered in British Columbia in 1856, leading to a gold rush and a substantial increase in the population of western Canada.

Growing trade between Canada and the U.S. from the 1840's onward, and the development of a continental system of railroads in both Canada and the U.S. in the 1850's, led to a relative decline in British influence in Canada. The American Civil War had the indirect effect of prompting Canadians to seek self-government in a federal union. Previously, there had been little contact between the Canadas (Upper and Lower) and the maritime provinces, while the vast territories of the west were still privately administered by the Hudson Bay Company. A federal union was forged in a series of conferences beginning in 1864, and the federation of Quebec, Ontario, Nova Scotia, and New Brunswick was recognized by the British North America Act of July 1, 1867.

The Dominion of Canada thus established in 1867 became a self-governing entity within the British Empire; Sir J.A. Macdonald became Canada's first prime minister (1867-73). The dominion rapidly expanded. In 1869 it purchased the western territories of the Hudson Bay Company, and in 1870, in response to a rebellion of French-speaking Métis in Manitoba, Manitoba was granted provincial status within the federation. In 1871 the union of British Columbia with Canada was secured with the promise of a transcontinental railway; the Canadian Pacific Railway was completed in 1885. Prince Edward Island joined the federation in 1873, but neighboring Newfoundland remained a British colony outside the Canadian federation until 1949.

A second francophone rebellion broke out in Saskatchewan in 1885. Its leader, Louis Riel, was executed and became a symbol of French Canadian grievances against the English-speaking majority. Wilfred Laurier became Canada's first francophone prime minister in 1896, but he was unable to solve the problem of the rights of Catholics and French-speakers outside Quebec. Legislation restricting those rights had already been enacted in Manitoba in 1890.

The Klondike Gold Rush of 1897-98 brought Canada worldwide attention and indirectly helped promote the settlement of rich agricultural lands in the Canadian west. Immigrants to the prairie region came not only from eastern Canada, but also from Germany, Scandinavia, and the Ukraine. Japanese farmers and Chinese railroad and mining workers settled west of the Rockies, further increasing Canada's ethnic diversity, though Asian immigrants were denied citizenship. Alberta and Saskatchewan were granted provincial status in 1905; the Yukon Territory and the Northwest Territories continued to be governed by controllers appointed by the federal government and patrolled by the famous Royal Canadian Mounted Police.

Urbanization and industrialization were stimulated in the early 20th century by the exploitation of extensive mineral resources in western Canada and in northern Quebec, and by the development of hydroelectric projects and transportation facilities throughout the country. The long-lived Laurier government fell in 1911, when his proposal for free trade with the U.S. evoked widespread fears that Canada's nascent industries would suffer without protective tariffs.

Laurier's Conservative successor, Robert Borden, sent Canadian troops to fight in World War I in 1914 and bolstered Canada's war efforts in Europe through national conscription in 1917. The distinguished performance of Canada's armed forces in the war bought the country renewed international respect.

Borden's wartime English-speaking Conservative-Liberal coalition collapsed in 1921. He was succeeded by the Liberal leader William L. Mackenzie King, who was to be Canada's prime minister for over 20 years (1921-30, 1935-48). He skillfully managed the economic prosperity of the 1920's, which saw the establishment in Canada of branch plants of many American industrial firms.

The Statute of Westminster, which created the British Commonwealth in 1931, had the effect of granting full self-government to Canada within the Commonwealth.

Canada's federal structure was ill-equipped to manage the economic collapse of the 1930's, which brought both industrial depression and a drought-induced agricultural crisis. Efforts to deal with unemployment, land foreclosures, and other economic ills fell to the provincial governments, which were not up to the task.

Canada's recovery from the Great Depression was stimulated by the advent of World War II, which Canada entered in 1939. Although the war brought price controls, rationing, and other emergency measures, the overall effect of the war was to strengthen all sectors of Canada's economy and to enhance Canada's international status as a leading military and industrial power. A Liberal electoral victory of 1945 gave Mackenzie King a renewed mandate for the postwar era.

The two decades following the war saw the gradual expansion of federal financial responsibility for national welfare measures, including pensions, unemployment insurance, and comprehensive medical care, though the administration of such programs remained a provincial matter. These developments coincided with an increase in urbanization and industrialization in the major centers of Vancouver, Toronto, and Montreal. Formal "equalization payments" were enacted in the 1950's to reduce economic disparities between rich and poor provinces. The early stages of these developments played a part in persuading Newfoundland to join the federation as Canada's 10th province in 1949.

A landslide Conservative victory in 1958 brought John Diefenbaker to the prime ministership, but the Conservatives proved unable to offer a coherent political program and were ousted in the elections of 1963, which returned the Liberals to power. Canadian politics since the 1960's have been marked by increasing regionalization; the Liberal party is based largely in the east, while the New Democratic party, organized in 1961, has little support east of Ontario. The Conservatives offer a broad but insecure national alternative.

The language issue continues to divide Canada politically and ideologically. The rise of an aggressive Quebecois nationalism in the 1960's led directly to the Liberal prime ministership of Pierre Trudeau, a Quebecois known as a supporter of a strong federal constitution. Trudeau's efforts toward conciliation and for constitutional guarantees for Quebec within a strong federal structure proved unavailing, however. In 1970 he invoked the War Measures Act to send troops to Quebec to put down a wave of separatist terrorism, leaving the province subdued but sullen.

The 1976 electoral victory in Quebec of the Parti Québécois under René Lévesque provoked fears that Quebec would secede from Canada. Lévesque's plan for a separate "sovereignty-association" status for Quebec was rejected by a popular referendum in 1980, but only because of Trudeau's pledge to seek full autonomy for Canada in order to secure constitutional protection for Quebec's special interests.

In 1981, Canada's provincial governments reached agreement on proposals for constitutional change. The result was the passage by the British Parliament of the Canada Act, which came into effect on Apr. 17, 1982, granting full independence and constitutional autonomy to Canada and severing its last colonial ties to the British government. Canada's new 1982 Constitution more clearly delineated the powers of the federal and provincial governments, provided for Supreme Court review of legislation, and included a Charter of Rights to protect civil liberties.

A nationwide recession contributed to the defeat of Trudeau's Liberal government and to the election of the Conservative party leader Brian Mulroney (also a native of Quebec) as prime minister in 1984. The Mulroney government encouraged foreign investment and privatization as a means of revitalizing Canada's economy. But its most significant achievement was the negotiation and passage, in 1988-89, of a free-trade agreement with the U.S. (that also came to include Mexico).

The Meech Lake Agreement, containing a number of articles clarifying the 1982 Constitution, was worked out between Mulroney and Quebec's Liberal premier Robert Bourassa, along with the leaders of Canada's nine other provinces, and signed on June 23, 1987. Its provisions enhanced the power of the provinces; a key provision gave constitutional protection to Quebec's efforts to remain a "distinct society," linguistically and culturally French. But the aggressive measures of the Quebec government to eradicate the use of English in the public affairs of the province provoked a backlash against bilingualism. The Meech Lake Agreement failed to become law when the legislatures of Newfoundland and Manitoba declined to ratify it by the June 23, 1990, deadline. Canada plunged into the most serious constitutional crisis in its history.

An alternative agreement to restructure the federal government and give more power to the 10 provincial governments met initial opposition in Quebec, and was decisively defeated in a national referendum, leaving the nation to deal once again with the awkward status quo.

Faced with a decline in his popularity, Mulroney resigned in 1993. The Progressive Conservative party convention chose Kim Campbell to lead the government, the first woman to do so. In the 1993 general election, the Conservatives were routed by Jean Chrétien and the Liberals. The new government announced plans in early 1995 to cut the budget deficit through higher taxes and spending cuts on health care and social programs. Although they accomplished this goal, many Canadians were disconcerted because of high unemployment and a decrease in benefits. Chretien was also vulnerable on the problem of Quebec because he and the Liberal Party seemed to favor giving special status to the French province, where in 1995 a separatist referendum was only narrowly defeated. In 1997 elections, the Liberals lost 19 seats, but still held a slim majority. Since the other major parties (Reform, Bloc Quebecois) are not united, the Liberals have been able to govern. The issue of separatism rose again in Aug. 1998 when the Supreme Court ruled that a referendum on Quebec secession would be invalid without negotiations on the terms with both the provinces and the federation as a whole.

On April 1, 1999 the government officially created a new Arctic territory called Nunavut which is governed solely by the Inuit tribe (called Eskimos in Alaska and Greenland). In Nov. 2000 Chretien's Liberals won their third consecutive victory by a very large margin. The thorny issue of Quebec independence seems to have reached a settlement in April 2003 provincial elections in Quebec as the Liberals won 76 of 125 seats, denying another term to the Parti Quebecois, which carried 45 seats.

▶CAPE VERDE

Republic of Cape Verde

• GEOGRAPHY **Location:** archipelago of 15 islands in Atlantic Ocean, off northern Africa. **Boundaries:** Senegal about 300 mi. (500 km) to E. **Total land area:** 1,556 sq. mi. (4,030 sq km). **Coastline:** 600 mi. (965 km). **Comparative area:** slightly larger than Rhode Island. **Land use:** 11% arable land; 1. % permanent crops; 89% other. **Major cities:** (1990 census) Cidade de Praia (capital) 62,000.

• PEOPLE **Population:** 412,137 (July 2003 est.). **Nationality:** noun—Cape Verdean(s); adjective—Cape Verdean. **Ethnic groups:** 71% Creole (mulatto), 28% African, 1% European. **Languages:** Portuguese and Crioulo (blend of Portuguese and West African). **Religions:** Roman Catholicism fused with indigenous beliefs, Protestantism.

• GOVERNMENT **Type:** republic. **Independence:** July 5, 1975 (from Portugal). **Constitution:** Sept. 25, 1992. **National holiday:** Independence Day, July 5. **Heads of Government:** Pedro Verona Rodrigues Pires, president (since Mar. 2001); José Maria Neves, prime minister (since Feb. 2001). **Structure:** executive; unicameral legislature; judiciary.

• ECONOMY **Monetary unit:** Cape Verdean escudo. **Budget:** (2000 est.) ***income:*** $112 mil.; ***expend.:*** $198 mil. **GDP:** $600 mil., $1,400 per capita (2002 est.). **Chief crops:** bananas, corn, beans. **Natural resources:** salt, basalt rock, pozzolana, limestone, kaolin, fish. **Major industries:** food and beverages, fish processing, salt mining. **Labor force:** 102,000 (1985 est); 57% agriculture, 29% services, 14% industry (1981); 2% unemployment (200 est.). **Exports:** $30 mil. (f.o.b., 2002 est.); shoes, garments, fish, bananas. **Imports:** $220 mil. (f.o.b., 2002 est.); foodstuffs, consumer goods, industrial products. **Major trading partners: *exports:*** Portugal, U.K., U.S.; ***imports:*** Portugal, Netherlands, Italy, Germany.

In 1462 the Portuguese founded the first European city in the tropics at Ribeira Grande on Santiago, one of the 15 islands that compose the Republic of Cape Verde. Located 385 miles off the west coast of Africa, the Cape Verde Islands prospered during the slave trade in the 16th century and later served as supply stations on sea routes and trading lanes. The rise of whaling in the 19th century led to contact with the U.S., as American ships recruited crews from the islands. The United States set up an American consulate, headquarters for the U.S. Navy African Squadron, and a transatlantic cable station in the islands.

Portugal changed the status of the archipelago from colony to overseas province in 1951; in 1956, citizens of Cape Verde and Portuguese Guinea organized the African Party for the Independence of Guinea-Bissau and Cape Verde (PAIGC) to petition Portugal to improve living conditions. Beginning as a clandestine organization, the PAIGC became an overt political movement on the islands after the 1974 revolution in Portugal. An agreement between the PAIGC and Portugal, providing for a transitional government, paved the way for full independence in 1975.

In 1980 the PAIGC became the PAICV, which remained the "supreme expression" of Cape Verdeans' political will until the opposition party, Movement for Democracy, won a parliamentary majority in the nation's first multiparty elections in Jan. 1991. The new government instituted free market reforms, including privatization of industries. Voters approved of the reforms, giving the Movement for Democracy 50 of the 72 seats in Parliament in Dec. 1995 elections. Ten years of rule by the Movement for Democracy ended in 2001 as the opposition won a majority in the legislature and elected their candidate, Pedro Pires, as president.

▶CENTRAL AFRICAN REPUBLIC

• GEOGRAPHY **Location:** landlocked country in central Africa. **Boundaries:** Chad to N, Sudan to E, Zaire, Congo to S, Cameroon to W. **Total land area:** 240,533 sq. mi. (622,980 sq km). **Coastline:** none. **Comparative area:** slightly smaller than Texas. **Land use:** 3% arable land; negl.% permanent crops; 97% other. **Major cities:** (1988) Bangui (capital) 451,690; Berbérati 41,891; Bouar 39,676.

• PEOPLE **Population:** 3,683,538 (July 2003 est.). **Nationality:** noun—Central African(s); adjective— Central African. **Ethnic groups:** 33% Baya, 27% Banda, 13% Mandija, 10% Sara, 7% Mboum, 4% M'Baka; 2% other. **Languages:** French (official), Sangho (lingua franca and national language), tribal languages. **Religions:** 35% indigenous beliefs, 25% Protestant, 25% Roman Catholic, 15% Muslim; indigenous beliefs and practices strongly influence Christian majority.

• GOVERNMENT **Type:** republic. **Independence:** Aug. 13, 1960 (from France). **Constitution:** Adopted Jan. 7, 1995. **National holiday:** Republic Day, Dec. 1. **Heads of Government:** François Bozize, head of state (since March 31, 2003); Abel Goumba, prime minister (since March 31, 2003). **Structure:** executive; unicameral legislature; judiciary.

• ECONOMY **Monetary unit:** Communauté Financière Africaine (CFA) franc. **Budget:** (1994 est.) ***income:*** $638 mil.; ***expend.:*** $1.9 bil. **GDP:** $4.7

bil., $1,300 per capita (2002 est.). **Chief crops:** cotton, coffee, tobacco. **Natural resources:** diamonds, uranium, timber, gold, oil. **Major industries:** sawmills, breweries, diamond mining. **Labor force:** 775,413 (1986 est.); 85% agriculture, 9% commerce and services. **Exports:** $134 mil. (f.o.b., 2002 est.); diamonds, timber, cotton, coffee, tobacco. **Imports**: $102 mil. (f.o.b., 2002); food, textiles, petroleum products, machinery, electrical equipment, motor vehicles. **Major trading partners:** ***exports:*** 53% Belgium, Kazakhstan, Spain; ***imports:*** 26% France, Cameroon, Spain.

A landlocked country in Africa's central region, the Central African Republic is one of the least-developed countries in the world. Most of its people are farmers, and the nation has little manufacturing, few reliable roads, and no railroad. Europeans first came to the area in the early 1800's in their search for slaves, but it was not until 1889 that the French established an outpost as the current capital city of Bangui. The region was organized as the territory of Ubangi-Shari five years later. In 1910 it was incorporated into French Equitorial Africa along with what are now the countries of Chad, the Congo, and Gabon.

The country was granted internal selfgovernment by the French under its present name in 1958 and became a member of the French Overseas Community. Independence was achieved on Aug. 13, 1960. The first prime minister, Barthelemy Boganda, was killed in an airplane crash in 1959 and was succeeded by his nephew, David Dacko. Dacko was elected to a seven-year term in January 1964, but an army coup in 1966 overthrew his government. The head of the army, Jean-Bedel Bokassa, was installed as president. Named president for life in 1972, in 1976 Bokassa declared himself emperor and changed the name of the country to the Central African Empire.

Dacko returned to power in 1979, however, and Bokassa went into exile in France. The name of the country was changed back to the Central African Republic. A multiparty political system was reinstated in March 1981, but army officers threw Dacko out of office again six months later and banned all political parties. Opposition parties were legalized in 1991, and Bokassa was released shortly before elections in 1993, elections that made Ange Félix Patassé president. He tried to reduce the army's power but has been met with several rebellions requiring the intervention of peacekeepers from neighboring states. After surviving numerous coup attempts, Patassé was overturned in March 2003 by fired army head General Francois Bozize who suspended the constitution and proclaimed himself president.

▶CHAD
Republic of Chad

• **GEOGRAPHY** **Location:** landlocked country in north central Africa. **Boundaries**: Libya to N, Sudan to E, Central African Republic to S, Cameroon, Nigeria to SE, Niger to W. **Total land area**: 495,753 sq. mi. (1,284,000 sq km). **Coastline**: none. **Comparative area**: between Texas and Alaska. **Land use:** 3% arable land; negl. % permanent crops; 97% other. **Major cities**: (1988 est.) N'Djamena (capital) 594,000; Sarh 113,400; Moundou 102,000; Abéché 83,000.

• **PEOPLE** **Population:** 9,253,493 (July 2003 est.). **Nationality:** noun—Chadian(s); adjective—Chadian. **Ethnic groups:** 200 distinct ethnic groups, most of whom are Muslims (Arabs, Toubou, Fulbe, Kotoko, Hausa, Kanembou, Baguirmi, Boulala, and Maba) in north and center and non-Muslims (Sara, Ngambaye, Mbake, Goulaye, Moudang, Moussei, Massa) in south. **Languages:** French and Arabic (both official); Sara and Sango in south; more than 120 different languages and dialects. **Religions:** 51% Muslim, 35% Christian, 7% Animist, 7% other.

• **GOVERNMENT** **Type:** republic. **Independence:** Aug. 11, 1960 (from France). **Constitution:** Mar. 31, 1996. **National holiday:** Independence Day, Aug. 11. **Heads of Government:** Idriss Deby, president (since Dec. 1990); Moussa Faki Mahamat, prime minister (since June 24, 2003). **Structure:** executive; unicameral legislature; judiciary.

• **ECONOMY** **Monetary unit:** Communauté Financière Africaine (CFA) franc. **Budget:** (1998 est.) ***income:*** $198 mil.; ***expend.:*** $218 mil., **GDP:** $10 bil., $1,100 per capita (2002 est.). **Chief crops:** cotton, sorghum, millet, peanuts. **Natural resources:** small quantities of crude oil (unexploited but exploitation beginning), uranium, natron (sodium carbonate), kaolin, fish (Lake Chad). **Major industries:** oil, cotton textile mills, slaughterhouses, brewery, natron. **Labor force:** more than 80% agriculture—unpaid subsistence farming, herding and fishing. **Exports:** $197 mil. (f.o.b., 2002 est.); cotton, cattle, textiles. **Imports**: $570 mil. (f.o.b., 2002 est.); machinery and transport equipment, industrial goods, petroleum products, foodstuffs. **Major trading partners:** ***exports:*** 28% Portugal, 15% Germany, France; ***imports:*** 38% U.S., 26% France, 8% Cameroon.

The Sao and other ancient peoples built centers of civilization near Lake Chad that flourished for many centuries until they were displaced by the medieval kingdoms of Kanem-Bornu, Baguirmi, and Ouaddai. From about 1400 onward, Chad became a meeting ground between the Muslim cultures of the Sahara and the Sahel and the black African societies of the tropics. Between 1500 and 1800, Arab slave raiders were active around Lake Chad, supplying slaves for European traders on Africa's west coast.

French military forces reached Chad from West Africa in 1891 and fought a series of battles over the next two decades with the Arab rulers of the region. A French governorship of Chad was established in 1905 (based in Brazzaville, the Congo), but the country was not brought entirely under French control until 1914. Chad was incorporated into the federation of French Equatorial Africa in 1910 and was organized as a colony within the federation in 1920.

French Equatorial Africa was dissolved in 1959, and Chad became an autonomous member of the French Community. Full independence followed on Aug. 11, 1960; François Tombalbage became Chad's first president. In 1965 the Muslim northern and eastern parts of the country rebelled against the southern-led government; despite the aid of French troops, the government was unable to suppress the rebellion, and a long civil war ensued.

Tombalbage was overthrown in 1975 in a military coup led by Gen. Felix Malloum. Efforts to broaden the composition of the national government broke down, and in 1979 Prime Minister Hissein Habre broke with the government and led northern forces against the national army. A cease-fire was negotiated under international auspices, and a National Unity Transitional Government (GUNT) was installed in 1979, but civil war broke out again in 1980. Pres. Goukouni Oueddei sought Libyan aid in restoring order; a contingent of 7,000 Libyan troops occupied the country until 1981. They were replaced by an international peacekeeping force organized by the Organization of African Unity.

Civil war broke out again in 1982, and northern forces occupied the capital. A new republican government under the presidency of Hissein Habre was proclaimed on June 7. OAU forces withdrew, and Habre's government soon controlled all of the country except for a few northern areas held by GUNT. In 1983 GUNT launched a counterattack and regained some territory with the aid of Libyan forces. French and Zairian troops were sent to aid Habre's forces. In Sept. 1984 France and Libya agreed to the withdrawal of all foreign forces from Chad, but Libyan forces remained. GUNT forces controlled the country north of the 16th parallel; Libyan forces occupied the Aozou Strip, along the border, with the apparent intention of annexing it to Libya.

Between 1984 and 1986 Habre persuaded most Chadean dissident forces to rejoin the national government, and in Nov. 1986 he launched a campaign to recapture the north. The Chadean forces won a series of victories, and in May 1988 Libya's Col. Qaddafi declared an end to the 20-year war with Chad.

In Nov. 1990, forces led by renegade Gen. Idriss Deby launched attacks from Sudan and ousted Pres. Habre. Deby, who favors multiparty democracy, proclaimed a provisional government and suspended the constitution. A national charter calling for a new constitution and elections to be held within 30 months came into force in March 1991. Deby functioned as president after that, suppressing two attempted coups in 1992, and legalizing opposition parties. Deby's "Higher Transitional Council" remained in command until presidential elections were held in June 1996, which Deby won. He was re-elected in May 2001.

▶CHILE
Republic of Chile

• **Geography** **Location:** South Pacific coast of South America. **Boundaries**: Peru, Bolivia to N, Argentina to E, Pacific Ocean to W. **Total land area**: 292,259 sq. mi. (756,950 sq km). **Coastline**: 3,999 mi. (6,435 km). **Comparative area**: slightly larger than Texas. **Land use:** 3% arable land; negl. % permanent crops; 97% other. **Major cities**: (1995) Gran Santiago (capital) 5,076,808; Viña del Mar 322,220; Concepción 350,268; Valparaíso 282,168; Temuco 239,340.

• **People** **Population:** 15,665,216 (July 2003 est.). **Nationality:** noun—Chilean(s); adjective—Chilean. **Ethnic groups:** 95% white and white Amerindian, 3% Amerindian, 2% other. **Languages:** Spanish. **Religions:** 89% Roman Catholic, 11% Protestant, small Jewish population.

• **Government** **Type:** republic. **Independence:** Sept. 18, 1810 (from Spain). **Constitution:** Sept. 11, 1980, effective Mar. 11, 1981; modified by public referendum on July 30, 1989. **National holiday:** Independence Day, Sept. 18. **Head of Government:** Ricardo Lagos Escobar, president (since Mar. 2000). **Structure:** executive; bicameral legislature; judiciary.

• **Economy** **Monetary unit:** Chilean peso. **Budget:** (2001 est.) ***income:*** $17 bil.; ***expend.:*** $17 bil. **GDP:** $151 bil., $10,000 per capita (2002 est.). **Chief crops:** wheat, corn, grapes, beans, sugar beets. **Natural resources:** copper, timber, iron ore, nitrates, precious metals. **Major industries:** copper, other minerals, foodstuffs, fish processing. **Labor force:** 5.9 mil. (2002); 59% services, 27% industry and commerce, 14% agriculture, forestry, fishing; 9% unemployment (2002 est.). **Exports:** $17.8 bil. (f.o.b., 2002); copper, fish and fishmeal, other metals and minerals. **Imports**: $15.6 bil. (c.i.f., 2002); consumer goods, chemicals, motor vehicles, fuels. **Major trading partners:** ***exports:*** 18% U.S., 12% Japan, 6% U.K.; ***imports:*** 18% Argentina, 17% U.S., 9% Brazil.

Before the arrival of Europeans in the mid 1530's, indigenous habitation of the territory that would become Chile included the Araucanian population in the south and peoples under the influence of the Inca Empire in the north.

The Spanish founded the cities of Valparaíso in 1536, Santiago in 1541, and Concepción in 1550. Chile was under the authority of the Viceroyalty of Peru, established in 1544. Between 1810 and 1818, fortunes of the Chilean independence movement ebbed and flowed, culminating in the victory of Bernardo O'Higgins and the separatist forces in 1817. Independence was finally achieved in 1818.

From 1818 to 1833, Chile underwent a period of political instability due to power struggles among elite Chilean families. In 1833 a strong presidential-dominant constitution was written under the influence of leading political figure Diego Portales that set the form of government in Chile until 1891. Chile expanded its territory at the expense of Peru and Bolivia, first in a war with the Peruvian-Bolivian Confederation (1836-39) and later as a result of the War of the Pacific (1879-83).

A civil war was fought in 1890-91 between forces of the president, José Balmaceda, and the Chilean Congress over the issue of the limits of presidential authority. The defeat of the presidential forces led to the establishment of a congressional-dominant parliamentary system. The checks on policy initiative resulting from the parliamentary system left government deadlocked in the face of mounting social and political problems arising at the turn of the century. The occurrence of a number of bloody strike actions crystallized political debate around social issues such as better wages and working conditions. The immobilized parliamentary system was unable to respond to these problems. In 1925, when Congress failed to allocate funds for military pay, the forces overthrew the parliamentary government.

A new constitution was drawn up that same year that moved governmental structure toward presidential dominance. Nevertheless, political instability continued until 1933, when the new constitution was implemented. The Chilean balance of political power from 1958 until 1973 remained almost equally divided among parties representing the right, the center, and the left of the political spectrum. In order to prevent an electoral victory for the leftist parties, forces on the right allied themselves with the centrist Christian Democrats in the 1964 election, and this resulted in the victory of Christian Democratic presidential candidate Eduardo Frei Montalva.

The program of the Christian Democrats included agrarian reform and attempts to organize Chile's urban poor. It was believed that these stances would benefit the Christian Democrats at the polls in the 1970 presidential election. As in 1958, the 1970 election fielded three presidential candidates who represented the political right, center, and left. The leftist Popular Unity coalition candidate, Dr. Salvador Allende Gossens, won with 36.3 percent of the vote, but only after bitter debate did Congress recognize Allende's victory.

The Allende government nationalized the foreign-owned copper industry, but an international boycott of Chilean copper imposed in retaliation for this action seriously hurt the country's economy. The government also nationalized the coal and steel industries as well as 60 percent of private banking. The Popular Unity government found itself unable to control peasant seizures of land and factory takeovers by workers. The copper embargo, land and factory seizures, government subsidies to the poor for basic goods, and runaway inflation resulted in a deterioration of the national economy that particularly affected the middle classes. Members of congress from the center and right had hoped to gain enough seats in the 1973 elections to impeach Allende, but instead the Popular Unity made impressive electoral gains. In order to bolster the legitimacy of the Popular Unity administration in the eyes of political opponents, Allende resorted to inclusion of military officers in the government.

On Sept. 11, 1973, segments of the military led by commanders of three of Chile's four armed forces took control of the government, killing Allende in the process. Gen. Augusto Pinochet Ugarte emerged as the new president. The junta announced the arrest of some 13,000 persons, many of whom then lost their lives in a wave of brutal repression. (Mass graves were discovered in the desert in 1990, and in 1991 a commission reported that between 1973 and 1990, more than 2,000 people were killed by the government.) In March 1974 the dictatorship published its Declaration of Principles, which included a laissez-faire economic orientation, anti- Marxism, and nationalism.

A new constitution was approved by plebiscite in 1980. The two-phase evolution of Chile's political structure included an authoritarian "transitional period" between 1980 and 1989 and implementation of a new political structure thereafter. The constitution created a presidential system with very extensive executive powers and a "guardian" role for the military.

In an Oct. 1988 plebiscite, Chileans rejected continuation of Pinochet rule and called for an end to the dictatorship. On Dec. 14, 1989, Patricio Aylwin Azocar of the Christian Democratic party (one of a 17-party alliance) was elected president with over 55 percent of the vote; he took office in March 1990, ending 17 years of military dictatorship. He was succeeded by Eduardo Frei Ruiz-Tagle in March 1994.

In recent years, Chile's economy has expanded, exports have increased, and it has succeeded in lowering its large external debt. Although exports are still dominated by copper, other minerals and manufactures have gained in importance. In 1996, Chile joined Mercosur, a free trade agreement among six of the largest South American nations. In 1997 the U.S. agreed to sell Chile advanced fighter jets, ending a 20-year ban.

In March 1998 Gen. Pinochet resigned as head of the armed forces after 25 years and was sworn in as senator-for-life. In Oct., while in Britain, Pinochet was arrested after Spain sought his extradition for the murder of Spanish citizens. A long legal minuet ended in Jan. 2000 when Britain's Home Secretary declared Pinochet unfit to stand trial. Only days later, in a run-off presidential election, the candidate of the center-left Concertacion Coalition, Ricardo Lagos Escobar, took 51.3 percent of the vote. Though Lagos was the first Socialist president since Allende, he supports a market economy. In 2003 Chile and the U.S. signed a free trade agreement eliminating tarriffs on 85% of all goods.

▶CHINA

People's Republic of China

• **GEOGRAPHY Location:** covers vast area of eastern Asia. **Boundaries**: Russia, Mongolia to N; N. Korea to NE; Pacific Ocean to E; India, Nepal, Bhutan, Myanmar, Laos, and Vietnam to S; Afghanistan and Pakistan to W., Kazakhstan, Kyrgyzstan, and Tajikistan to NW. **Total land area**: 3,705,392 sq. mi. (9,596,960 sq km). **Coastline**: 9,112 mi. (14,500 km). **Comparative area**: between coterminous U.S. and Canada. **Land use:** 13% arable land;1% permanent crops, 86% other. **Major cities**: (1994 est.) Beijing (capital) 11,250,000; Shanghai 13,560,000; Tianjin 9,350,000; (1990 est.) Shenyang 4,540,000; Wuhan 3,750,000.

• **PEOPLE Population:** 1,286,975,468 (July 2003 est.). **Nationality:** noun—Chinese (sing., pl.); adjective—Chinese. **Ethnic groups:** 91.9% Han Chinese; 8.1% Zhuang, Uygur, Hui, Yi, Tibetan, Miao, Manchu, Mongol, Buyi, Korean, and numerous others. **Languages:** Standard Chinese or Mandarin (Putonghua based on the Beijing dialect); Yue (Cantonese), Wu (Shanghainese), Minbei (Fuzhou), Minnan (Hokkien-Taiwanese), Xiang, Gan, Hakka dialects, and minority langs. (see "Ethnic groups" above). **Religions:** officially atheist, but traditionally pragmatic and eclectic; Taoism, Buddhism, 1-2% Muslim, 3-4% Christian.

• **GOVERNMENT Type:** Communist state. **Constitution:** Dec. 4, 1982. **National holiday:** National Day, Oct. 1, (1949) **Heads of Government:** Hu jintao, president (since Mar. 15, 2003); Wen Jiabao, prime minister (since Mar. 16, 2003). **Structure:** executive; unicameral legislature; judiciary.

• **ECONOMY Monetary unit:** yuan. **Budget: (2002 est.)** ***income:*** $224.8 bil.; ***expend.:*** $267.1 bil. **GDP:** $5.7 trillion, $4,400 per capita (2002 est.). **Chief crops:** rice, potatoes, sorghum, peanuts. **Natural resources:** coal, iron ore, crude oil, mercury, tin; world's largest hydropower potential. **Major industries:** iron, steel, coal. **Labor force:** 700 mil. (2001 est.); 50% agriculture and forestry, 22% industry, 28% services. **Exports:** $325.6 bil. (f.o.b., 2002); machinery and equipment, textiles, clothing. **Imports**: $295.3 bil. (f.o.b., 2002); machinery and equipment, chemicals, plastics, iron and steel. **Major trading partners:** (1999) ***exports:*** Hong Kong, U.S., Japan, Germany, South Korea; ***imports:*** Japan, U.S., Taiwan, South Korea.

China is one of the world's oldest civilizations. Dynastic rule in the North China Plain began around 2000 B.C. The unifying Qin (221 B.C.) and Han (206 B.C.) dynasties greatly expanded the territory of the empire and established the basic pattern of imperial bureaucratic government that would endure until the beginning of the 20th century. Major dynasties during that period include the Han (206 B.C.—A.D. 220), Tang (618-907), Song (960-1279), Yuan or Mongol (1279-1368), Ming (1368- 1644), and Qing (1644-1911).

By the late 18th century, the Qing dynasty faced increasingly dangerous problems of explosive population growth, bureaucratic stagnation, and trade pressure from the West. Opium—introduced by Great Britain to balance its trade in tea, silk, porcelain, and other goods—created severe social problems. Western demands for free trade resulted in the Opium War (1839-42), in which China was humiliatingly defeated by the British. The treaties of Nanjing (1842) and Tianjin (1858) opened China to Western merchants and missionaries and created foreign-ruled enclaves on Chinese soil. At the same time, the Taiping Rebellion and other popular uprisings led to the deaths of at least 20 million Chinese between 1850 and 1870.

Such reform efforts as the Self-Strengthening Movement (1870's) and the 1898 Reform Movement proved inadequate to the task of strengthening and modernizing China's dynastic government. Japan, modernizing rapidly after the Meiji Restoration of 1868, joined the race for commercial access to China, decisively winning the Sino-Japanese War of 1894-95. The antiforeign Boxer Uprising of 1900 was put down by a joint foreign military force, dealing a mortal blow to Qing rule. On Oct. 10, 1911, the dynasty fell to a coalition of forces led by the veteran revolutionary nationalist Sun Yat-sen.

China's first attempt at republican government, under Pres. Yuan Shikai and subsequent presidents, quickly degenerated into factionalism and warlord control in the provinces. In 1915 Japan successfully demanded further concessions, provoking public outcries. When news reached China on May 4, 1919, that the Treaty of Versailles granted Japan all of Germany's former concessions in China, students rioted throughout the country, demanding reforms and modernization (the May Fourth Movement). Sun Yat-sen's Nationalist party (Kuomintang, or KMT) and the Chinese Communist party (CCP, founded in 1921 by Mao Zedong) joined forces in 1922 in an attempt to create a second republican revolution.

Sun Yat-sen died in 1925. His successor, Chiang Kai-shek, consolidated KMT forces in Guangzhou and mounted the Northern Expedition (1927-29) to defeat or co-opt the various provincial warlords and reunify the country. In the course of this successful effort, Chiang turned on his Communist allies. A series of failed Communist uprisings and KMT anti-Communist extermination campaigns between 1927 and 1934 nearly wiped out the CCP. Remnants of the party broke out of encirclement in Jiangxi Province in 1934 and undertook the 6,000-mile Long March to a secure base in Yan'an, Shanxi Province. There, under Mao, Zhou Enlai, and Zhu De, the CCP recovered its strength. In the Xi'an Incident of December 1936, Chiang was kidnapped by mutinous KMT allies and forced at gunpoint to agree to forming a United Front with the CCP against Japan.

Meanwhile Japan continued its penetration of China, with the assassination of Manchurian warlord and KMT ally Jiang Zuolin in 1928, the invasion of Manchuria on Sept. 18, 1931, and the establishment of the puppet state of Manchuguo in 1934. On July 7, 1937, fighting erupted between Japanese and Chinese troops near Beijing. The Japanese rapidly moved south to the Yangtse Valley, bombing and capturing Shanghai. The Nationalist capital at Nanjing fell in November 1937, amid widespread atrocities against civilians. The KMT army and government retreated to a wartime capital at Chongqing. The remainder of World War II in China was largely a stalemate, with Japan occupying most of the country. KMT-held areas opposed the Japanese with conventional forces (supported, after 1941, by the Americans), while the Communists harassed the Japanese with guerrilla tactics.

At the end of World War II, American forces ensured that the KMT would receive Japan's surrender throughout most of China, giving the Nationalists a commanding position while U.S. general George Marshall attempted to mediate the creation of a KMT-CCP coalition government. That effort failed, and civil war broke out. The KMT advantage was dissipated by ruinous inflation, corruption, mismanagement, and military ineffectiveness. At the end of 1947, with the Communist forces making continual advances, the United States pulled out of China. After losing several major battles throughout 1948-49, KMT forces retreated to Taiwan; in Beijing, Mao Zedong proclaimed the establishment of the People's Republic of China (PRC) on Oct. 1, 1949.

With U.S. backing, the Republic of China established a temporary capital at Taipei and continued to claim sovereignty over all of China, retaining China's seat in the U.N. The PRC was quickly granted diplomatic recognition by Soviet bloc nations and some Western nations, notably Great Britain, but was effectively isolated in most international affairs by American support for Nationalist China. Chinese troops entered the Korean War in November 1950, as U.N. forces approached the Sino-Korean border at the Yalu River. This direct confrontation between China and the United States forestalled any possibility of normal contacts for more than two decades.

Within China the CCP rapidly consolidated its control of the country and began rebuilding the nation after decades of warfare. Priority was given to land reform. Land was confiscated from landlords and returned to peasant ownership; landlords and other "class enemies" were tried and condemned by People's Courts set up under party auspices. Under the first five-year plan (1953), peasants were urged to set up rural cooperatives, while industrial recovery began with Soviet assistance. Artists, writers, and intellectuals were ordered to devote themselves to the service of the party and the nation. In 1956 Mao announced a policy of "let a hundred flowers bloom, let a hundred schools of thought contend," inviting criticism of the party and government. He was shocked by the vigor of the criticism; many critics were sent to labor camps in the ensuing Anti-Rightist Campaign of 1957.

Angered by the arrogance of Soviet advisers and by Soviet refusal to share nuclear weapons technology with China, Mao broke with the Soviet Union and expelled all Soviet personnel in 1958. At the same time, he announced the policy of the Great Leap Forward, under which China was to make progress on all fronts without outside aid. Huge rural communes took the place of peasant smallholdings and cooperatives, and agriculture was placed under the direction of centralized planning. In industry, labor and enthusiasm were expected to make up for a shortage of capital and technical expertise. The Great Leap was a catastrophic failure, causing widespread famine and social dislocation, as Mao admitted in a forced self-criticism in 1960. Mao withdrew into the background as a group of party pragmatists led by Liu Shaoqi assumed power in the early 1960's.

In foreign affairs Chinese shelling of the Nationalist-held offshore islands of Quemoy and Matsu in 1958 led to a crisis in the Taiwan Straits, patrolled by the U.S. Seventh Fleet to prevent a recurrence of China's civil war. A rebellion in Tibet in 1959 was suppressed with much bloodshed, and the dalai lama fled to India. Chinese troop movements into Tibet contributed to the outbreak in 1960 of a border war with India. Throughout the 1960's China worried about being drawn into the Vietnam War.

In late 1965 Mao made a bid to return to full power. His vehicle was the Great Proletarian Cultural Revolution, formally launched in 1966. Shock troops of teenage Red Guards were used to attack the entrenched party bureaucracy; Liu Shaoqi was placed under house arrest, and other prominent officials, including Deng Xiaoping, were exiled to rural areas. By 1968 internal disorder was so great that the military intervened to restore control in many areas. Most established organs of power were replaced under the Cultural Revolution by Revolutionary Committees; intellectuals, technical workers, and bureaucrats were severely persecuted. In 1971 Mao's second-in-command, Marshal Lin Biao, staged an abortive coup and died while attempting to flee the country. With Mao increasingly old and ill, most of his power was exercised by his wife, Jiang Qing, and her associates. Her rival, Premier Zhou Enlai, attempted to maintain orderly government functions in the face of this turmoil.

The 1968 Soviet invasion of Czechoslovakia convinced Mao that the U.S.S.R. was a greater threat to China than America, and he quietly encouraged the growth of better relations with the U.S. With tacit American approval, the PRC replaced the Republic of China (Taiwan) in the U.N. on Oct. 25, 1971. During Feb. 21-28, 1972, U.S. president Richard Nixon visited China. The Shanghai Communiqué, issued at the end of that visit, clarified the positions of both sides and paved the way for the resumption of U.S.-China relations short of formal diplomatic recognition.

Zhou Enlai died in January 1976, and Deng Xiaoping became acting premier. In April 1976 a rally in Beijing commemorating Zhou's birthday was dispersed by police on orders from Jiang Qing, and a riot ensued. Deng was dismissed from office. But when Mao died on Sept. 9, 1976, Deng reemerged as China's paramount leader, behind the new acting premier and acting party chairman, figurehead Hua Guofeng. Jiang Qing and three associates were arrested along with many of their allies. Labeled the Gang of Four, Jiang Qing's clique was blamed for all the ills of the Cultural Revolution; they were tried and convicted for crimes against the state in 1981.

China's post-Mao transformation took a decisive turn in 1978, with the announcement of the policy of the Four Modernizations (agriculture, industry, science and technology, and defense). Foreign investment and technology transfer were encouraged, and thousands of students were sent to study abroad. In the winter of 1978-79, the authorities tolerated the public posting of written critiques of the government ("Democracy Wall"). Deng consolidated power in his own hands, still acting behind the scenes; Hua Guofeng was dismissed from office, while Deng's allies Hu Yaobang and Zhao Ziyang were promoted to leadership of the party and government in 1982.

On Jan. 1, 1979, China and the United States entered into formal diplomatic relations; the United States rescinded its recognition of the Republic of China as China's legal government but maintained separate nongovernmental relations with the ROC under the Taiwan Relations Act. China's relations with Vietnam deteriorated in 1978 following Vietnam's invasion of Cambodia. In February 1979, China attempted, with little success, to "teach Vietnam a lesson" in a brief but violent border war. A conflict with Great Britain was resolved in 1984 as both sides agreed that Hong Kong would be returned to Chinese sovereignty, but with considerable local autonomy, in 1997. Relations with the Soviet Union remained strained, China insisting that no improvement could come before the U.S.S.R. reduced its troop concentrations on the Sino-Soviet border, withdrew from Afghanistan, and pressured Vietnam into withdrawing from Cambodia. China's overall foreign-policy stance in the post-Mao era has been low-key and nonconfrontational.

In the 1980's, China achieved spectacular improvements in agricultural production through dismantling rural communes and returning land to individual peasant holdings under long-term leases. Small-scale private enterprise has been encouraged in both rural and urban areas. Reform in industry and in the centrally controlled price structure has been harder to achieve and has led to such side effects as inflation and increased corruption. Within the overall context of reform, factions of relatively more conservative and reformist leaders have coexisted uneasily. A conservative drive against "spiritual pollution" in 1986 was quickly blunted by Deng, but in January 1987, the reformist party-secretary Hu Yaobang was ousted after student demonstrations calling for more democracy. The CCP 12th Party Congress in October 1987 forced the retirement of some older conservatives, named the reformist Zhao Ziyang as party secretary, and elevated the conservative pragmatist Li Peng as premier.

In April 1989 student demonstrators in Beijing mourning the death of Hu Yaobang launched a general movement for greater democracy. Demonstrators began a hunger strike and disrupted a summit visit by Soviet president Gorbachev. Martial law was proclaimed in May as demonstrations spread to other cities. Troops opened fire in Tienanmen Square on June 3-4, killing hundreds of demonstrators. In the aftermath, Zhao Ziyang was replaced as party secretary by Jiang Zemin, thousands of protesters and suspected dissidents were arrested (and an unknown number executed), and hard-liners in the government took firm control of the country.

World opinion was outraged by the Tienanmen incident; the United States and many other countries instituted sanctions against China, tourism plummeted, and the economy went into general decline. International trade resumed during 1989-90, and the U.S. renewed China's most-favored-nation status in June 1990 after several hundred dissidents were released from prison.

China strove to put Tienanmen Square behind it by holding speedy trials of those charged in connection with demonstrations. The government also made overtures to the former U.S.S.R., and from its permanent seat on the U.N. Security Council supported coalition efforts against Iraq in the Persian Gulf conflict. Economic sanctions were lifted by Western governments in 1991. China continued to pursue its economic reform policies while repressing all signs of political dissent. While national politics, dominated by an aging leadership, seemed torpid and adrift, the private-sector economy continued to grow vigorously.

In 1992-93 runaway growth made China's economy the world's fourth-largest by some standards of measurement. This resulted in higher wages and increased consumer spending, but also widening income disparities, increased corruption, smuggling, theft, etc.

Deng's long-expected death, in 1997, produced little immediate effect on the Chinese leadership, except for a new crackdown as leaders competed to seem tough on dissent. But the transition of power to Jiang Zemin, 71, went smoothly.

Domestic affairs in general were overshadowed by national jubilation over the return of Hong Kong to Chinese sovreignty on July 1, 1997. (Macao would follow, in December 1999, after 442 years as a Portuguese colony.) In June 1997, America's Congress voted to renew China's most-favored-nation trade status despite misgivings about its dismal human-rights record. Pres. Clinton made a long state visit in 1998 and appeared on Chinese TV criticizing China for human rights abuses and urged Mr. Jiang to open Chinese society. Undismayed, the Chinese government proceeded to crush the fledgling China Democracy Party, sentencing three of its leaders to long prison terms for subversion. In Feb. 1999, new missiles menaced Taiwan; tensions grew worse in July when Taiwan's president said publicly that his country was a separate Chinese state. When the U.S. accused China of nuclear spying in the U.S., China's response was: "typical racial prejudice".

In the face of not only these issues but also the newer "human rights" issue of China's ban on and persecution of the Falun Gong religious movement, the U.S. reached a trade agreement with China at the end of 1999 (as had Japan in July). In 2001 China signed a 20-year Friendship Treaty with Russia, the first since the end of the Cold War; short on details, it pledged peaceful settlement of border disputes and coordination against threats of aggression.

In Nov. 2002 the 16th Communist Party Congress named Hu Jintao as Party Secretary, replacing Jiang Zemin, and the National People's Congress formally ratified the Party decisions. Jiang remains as chairman of the Central Military Commission and unofficial eminence grise.

▶COLOMBIA
Republic of Colombia

• **GEOGRAPHY Location:** northwestern coast of South America. **Boundaries**: Caribbean Sea to N, Venezuela, Brazil to E, Peru, Ecuador to S, Panama, Pacific Ocean to W. **Total land area**: 439,734 sq. mi. (1,138,910 sq km). **Coastline**: 1,992 mi. (3,208 km). **Comparative area**: between Texas and Alaska. **Land use:** 2% arable land; 2% permanent crops;96% other. **Major cities**: (1995 est.) Bogotá (capital) 5,237,635; Cali 1,718,871; Medellín 1,621,356; Cartagena 745,689.

• **PEOPLE Population:** 41,662,073 (July 2003 est.). **Nationality:** noun—Colombian(s); adjective—Colombian. **Ethnic groups:** 58% mestizo, 20% white, 14% mulatto, 4% black, 4% other. **Languages:** Spanish. **Religions:** 90% Roman Catholic.

• **GOVERNMENT Type:** republic; executive branch dominates government structure. **Independence:** July 20, 1810 (from Spain). **Constitution:** July 5, 1991. **National holiday:** Independence Day, July 20. **Head of Government:** Álvaro Uribe Vélez, president (since Aug. 2002). **Structure:** executive; bicameral legislature; judiciary.

• **ECONOMY Monetary unit:** Colombian peso. **Budget:** (2001 est.) ***income:*** $24 bil.; ***expend.:*** $25.6 bil. **GDP:** $268 bil., $6,500 per capita (2002 est.). **Chief crops:** coffee, flowers, bananas, rice; illegal producer of coca and cannabis for international drug trade. **Natural resources:** crude oil, natural gas, coal, iron ore, nickel. **Major industries:** textiles, food processing, oil. **Labor force:** 18.3 mil. (1999 est.); 46% services, 30% agriculture, 24% industry (1990); 17.4% unemployment (2002 est.). **Exports:** $12.9 bil. (f.o.b., 2002 est.); petroleum, coffee, coal, bananas, flowers. **Imports**: $12.5 bil. (f.o.b., 2002 est.); industrial equipment, transportation equipment, consumer goods, chemicals. **Major trading partners: *exports:*** 43% U.S., 22% Andean Community of Nations; ***imports:*** 35% U.S., 16% E.U..

The territory that is now Colombia was home to various cultures prior to the arrival of Europeans. The Chibcha population of the Andean region might have numbered about one million prior to European contact. Portions of the area that make up modern Colombia fell under the authority of the Inca Empire.

In 1538 the colony of New Granada was established with its capital at Bogotá, and for most of the period up until 1740, the area was within the jurisdiction of the Viceroyalty of Peru. In that year a new viceroyalty was established that included modern-day Colombia, Ecuador, Panama, and Venezuela. During the wars of independence against Spain, forces under Simón Bolívar were victorious over the royalists at the Battle of Boyacá in 1819, and the region gained independence in 1821.

Colombian territory was a part of the federation of Gran Colombia until the collapse of the federal arrangement in 1830. Thereafter, the country—called New Granada—remained a separate political entity (which included the area of Panama). By the 1850's a federal system had been adopted for the country. But this arrangement rapidly disintegrated, and the practically semisovereign states were involved in a constant struggle with the central government for autonomy. The effort to define the political structure was largely resolved with the constitution of 1886, which ended federalist regional autonomy and made Colombia a unitary republic.

Colombian political struggle since the 1850's had been characterized by a rivalry between two groups that coalesced into the Liberal and Conservative parties. During much of the 19th century, the Liberal-Conservative ideological battle was influenced to a great extent by the definition of the role of the Roman Catholic church in political and social life. The 1887-88 Concordat gave the church "official protection," while the state was given authority over public education. The settlement left a central position for the church in Colombian society that was not substantially altered by the Concordat of 1942.

The Liberal-Conservative struggle led to at least six civil wars, which often ended in interparty compromise. A struggle in 1854 involved the issue of the future direction of the country's economic development and was followed by a settlement among elites. The Liberal-Conservative war of 1860-63 led to a Liberal victory and a period of Liberal political hegemony that lasted until 1886. The period of Conservative rule from 1886 until 1930 was punctuated by the "War of a Thousand Days" (1899-1902), in which the Conservatives defeated the Liberals. In 1903 the Colombian government rejected a U.S. offer for construction of a canal in Panama. Panama (backed by the U.S.) revolted against the Colombian government, ending in the separation of Panama from Colombia.

The world depression of 1929 disrupted both the economy and the politics of Colombia. The loss of popularity of the ruling Conservatives due to both the economic collapse and their brutal repression of the labor movement led to a Liberal victory in 1930. A new civil war between peasants loyal to the two parties also broke out that year. By 1934 Liberal president Alfonso López Pumarejo had inaugurated his "Revolution on the March" program of socioeconomic reform.

During the 1946 presidential election, Conservatives won the presidency with a minority of the overall vote, defeating a split Liberal party. Armed conflict originally instigated by the two party elites erupted. This marked the beginning of La Violencia (1948-57) during which more than 200,000 people died. In the summer of 1957, leaders of the Liberal and Conservative parties reached an agreement on constitutional reform in an attempt to end the violence. The agreement, known as the National Front, was to be in force for 16 years and included provisions for regular alternation of the presidency between the parties, as well as an accord on equal staffing of all political positions by both parties. The Liberal and Conservative parties agreed they alone would monopolize the arena of legitimate political competition for the 16-year period. The agreement held up until 1968 constitutional revisions allowed for other political groups to be officially recognized.

The emergence of terrorist and paramilitary groups on both the right and left—some with ties to the drug trade—in the 1960's and 1970's weakened the two-party power-sharing monopoly. In March 1990, one of the most notorious left-wing groups, M-19, elected to lay down its arms and enter the political mainstream and immediately captured 19 of 70 seats in a constitutional convention called to rewrite the constitution. Other groups followed suit in 1991.

Throughout the 1980's, narco-terrorists murdered government officials, journalists, and innocent bystanders with impunity. Despite the assassination of four presidential candidates prior to the 1990 election, the Liberal party's César Gaviria Trujillo won the election campaigning against the drug traffickers. In 1994 another Liberal party president (Ernesto Samper Pizano) took office pledging to continue the fight. Samper also promised to invest billions of dollars to improve the infrastructure with money from the newly discovered Cusiana oil field.

In the summer of 1995, the Samper government arrested three of the top seven members of the Cali drug cartel; by Sept. 1996, all seven had been apprehended. Meanwhile, Samper faced accusations that he knew of $6 million contributed by the Cali cartel. Formal charges instituted by Prosecutor General Valdivieso in Feb. 1996 were found groundless by the legislature's Accusations Committee. Still, the United States, which had decertified Colombia as a drug-war partner in March, revoked Samper's visa even as Colombian farmers protested government anti-coca and -poppy programs. In 1997 radical leftist terrorist groups began a wave of murders, kidnappings, and other violence against local government officials, and in 1998 attacked and defeated an army battalion. The election of Conservative Andres Pastrana in June 1998 held out promise of victory in the drug war despite violent outbursts during the remainder of 1998 and early 1999. Government meetings with FARC, the principal rebel group, and National Peace Council meetings with ELN, the second major insurgent group, continued into mid-1999. On Dec. 20, FARC announced a cease-fire (the first since 1984) until January 10. When, on Jan. 11, 2000, FARC forces attacked four towns, the Clinton administration approved a two-year aid package to Colombia of $1.4 billion.

Pastrana's patience gave out in 2002 and he again sent jets and ground troops against FARC, but too late to prevent independent ex-Liberal Álvaro Uride Vélez from winning the May 2002 presidential election. In 2003 the war entered its 35th year.

▶COMOROS

Federal Islamic Republic of the Comoros

• **Geography** **Location:** part of archipelago in Mozambique Channel; three main islands, Njazidja, Nzwami, and Mwali (formerly Grande-Comore, Anjouan, and Mohéli). Moroni, Njazidja Is., 11°40'S, 43°16'E. **Boundaries**: between Madagascar and southeast Africa. **Total land area**: 838 sq. mi. (2,170 sq km). **Coastline**: 211 mi. (340 km). **Comparative area**: slightly more than 12 times size of Washington, D.C. **Land use:** 35% arable land; 18% permanent crops; 47% other. **Major cities**: (1980 census) Moroni (capital) 17,267; Mutsamudu 13,000; Fomboni 5,400.

• **People** **Population:** 632,948 (July 2003 est.). **Nationality:** noun—Comoran(s); adjective—Comoran. **Ethnic groups:** Antalote, Cafre, Makoa, Oimatsaha, Sakalava. **Languages:** Arabic and French (both official), Shikomoro (a blend of Swahili and Arabic). **Religions:** 98% Sunni Muslim, 2% Roman Catholic.

• **Government** **Type:** independent republic. **Independence:** July 6, 1975 (from France). **Constitution:** Dec. 23, 2001. **National holiday:** Independence Day, July 6. **Heads of Government:** Colonel Azali Assoumani, head of state (since Apr. 1999). **Structure:** executive; bicameral legislature; judiciary.

• **Economy** **Monetary unit:** Comoran franc. **Budget:** (2001) ***income:*** $27.6 mil.; ***expend.:*** N.A. **GDP:** $441 mil., $720 per capita (2002 est.). **Chief crops:** vanilla, cloves, perfume essences. **Natural resources:** negligible. **Major industries:** tourism, perfume distillation. **Labor force:** 144,500 (1996); 80% agriculture; 20% unemployment (1996). **Exports:** $16.3 mil. (f.o.b., 2001 est.); vanilla, ylang-ylang, cloves, perfume oils. **Imports**: $39.8 mil. (f.o.b., 2001 est.); rice and other foodstuffs, consumer goods, petroleum products, cement. **Major trading partners:** ***exports:*** 31% France, 19% U.S., 19% Singapore; ***imports:*** 25% France, 17% South Africa, 7% Kenya.

Comoros is part of an archipelago composed of four prominent islands (the fourth, Mayotte, is a French dependency) and several smaller islands. Numerous groups from Africa, Europe, and Asia invaded the islands over the centuries. Shirazi Arabs introduced Islam to Comoros around the turn of the 16th century, and the French established colonial rule over the archipelago between 1841 and 1912 and developed a plantation-based economy. The islands remained a French territory until 1961 when political autonomy was granted. Comoros gained independence in 1975. Overthrown by foreign mercenaries in 1975, Pres. Ahmed Abdallah Abderemane returned to power in 1978 and helped establish the country's first constitution. In Nov. 1989 he was assassinated by a small group of rebels who quickly dispersed under pressure from the French government. A new constitution was approved in 1992, and the country's first democratic elections were held in Nov. 1992. An attempt, begun in 1997, by the islands of Anjouan and Moheli to gain independence or at least autonomy led to an army coup in April 1999 and Anjouan's claim of independence in Jan. 2000, a claim he soon renounced.

Much of the nation's soil is laden with lava, making it unsuitable for farming, especially on the island of Njazidja (Grand Comore), which is dominated by Mount Kartala, an active volcano. Poor transportation links between the islands and a harsh cyclone season add further to the country's problems. In an effort to end the series of coup attempts (over 20 since 1975), Comoros adopted a new constitution in Dec. 2001, which provides for a rotating presidency among the four islands in four-year terms, as well as a separate president and more autonomy for each of the four islands.

▶CONGO

Democratic Republic of the Congo (formerly Zaire)

• **GEOGRAPHY** **Location:** equatorial country in central Africa. **Boundaries**: Central African Republic, Sudan to N, Uganda, Rwanda, Burundi, Tanzania to E, Zambia to S, Angola to SW, Atlantic Ocean, Cabinda district of Angola, Congo to W. **Total land area**: 905,564 sq. mi. (2,345,410 sq km). **Coastline**: 23 mi. (37 km). **Comparative area**: about 1.5 times size of Alaska. **Land use:** 3% arable land; 1 % permanent crops; 96% other. **Major cities**: (1984 census) Kinshasa (capital) 2,653,558; Lubumbashi (Elizabethville) 543,268; Mbuji-Mayi (Bakwanga) 423,363; Kananga (Luluabourg) 290,898; Kisangani (Stanleyville) 282,650.
• **PEOPLE** **Population:** 56,625,039 (July 2003 est.). **Nationality:** noun—Zairian(s); adjective—Zairian. **Ethnic groups:** 45% of the people belong to one of four largest groups—Mongo, Luba, Kongo (all Bantu), and Mangbetu-Azande; over 200 other ethnic groups. **Languages:** French (official), Lingala, Kingwana, Kikongo, Tshiluba. **Religions:** 50% Roman Catholic, 20% Protestant, 10% Kimbanguist, 10% Muslim, 10% other syncretic sects and traditional beliefs.
• **GOVERNMENT** **Type:** dictatorship; presumably undergoing a transition to representative government. **Independence:** June 30, 1960 (from Belgium). **Constitution:** Transitional constitution promulgated Apr. 1994; draft constitution approved by former president Laurent Kabila in Nov. 1998, but not yet ratified by national referendum. **National holiday**: Independence Day, Nov. 24. **Heads of Government:** Joseph Kabila, president (since Jan. 2001). **Structure:** executive—president elected originally for seven-year term; legislative—300-member Transitional Constitutional Assembly est. Aug. 2000; judiciary.
• **ECONOMY** **Monetary unit:** zaire. **Budget:** (1996 est.) ***income***: $269 mil. ***expend.***: $244 mil. **GDP:** $34 bil., $610 per capita (2002 est.). **Chief crops:** coffee, sugar, palm oil, rubber, tea. **Natural resources:** cobalt, copper, cadmium, crude oil, industrial and gem diamonds. **Major industries:** mining, mineral processing, consumer products (incl. textiles, footwear, cigarettes). **Labor force:** 14.5 mil (1993 est.); 65% agriculture, 16% industry, 19% services. **Exports:** $1.2 bil. (f.o.b., 2002 est.); diamonds, copper, coffee, cobalt, crude oil. **Imports:** $890 mil. (f.o.b., 2002 est.); foodstuffs, mining and other machinery, transport equipment, fuels. **Major trading partners:** ***exports:*** 60% Belgium, 13% U.S., 7% Zimbabwe; ***imports:*** 18% South Africa, 16% Belgium, 12% Nigeria.

Pygmies were probably the earliest inhabitants of the Congo region, followed much later by Bantu and Nilotic peoples. By the eighth century A.D., a number of well-established kingdoms and empires occupied the lower reaches of the Congo (now Zaire) River and the coastal plain; these included Kongo (Bakongo), Kuba, Luba, and Lunda.

Portuguese explorers and merchants arrived along the coast in the 1480's and initially traded with these kingdoms on a basis of relative equality; an indigenous Catholic church became established. Soon, however, the Portuguese established a slave trade that brought turmoil and decline to the native states. Europeans did not penetrate the interior of Zaire until the 19th century, but the slave trade (partly in Arab hands, in inland regions) had repercussions everywhere.

Henry Stanley descended the Congo River from east to west in 1876, opening the area for further exploration. In 1878 Stanley was engaged by King Leopold II of Belgium to establish Belgian trading stations along the river. King Leopold established the Congo Free State in 1885, not as a Belgian colony but as a personal possession of which he was king as well as chief stockholder.

The management corporation that ran the Free State abolished slavery but instituted a harsh and exploitative regime that reduced native peoples to a condition of involuntary servitude. Forced labor and harsh suppression of rebellion resulted in the deaths of unnumbered thousands of people. Protests against these conditions, led by Great Britain and the United States, led to the transformation of the Free State into the colony of the Belgian Congo in 1908 with promises of reforms.

By the 1920's the Belgian Congo had become a major world producer of copper, diamonds, gold, rubber, palm oil, and other commodities. Railroads were developed to bring these goods to market, notably the line from Elizabethville (now Lubumbashi) in the Katanga region through Angola to the Atlantic coast. River navigation on the Congo was also developed. All mining, plantation agriculture, industry, and administration was in Belgian hands with no native participation in government except at the most local level.

In the 1950's agitation for increased native participation in government led, in 1957, to elections for local councils. In 1959 rioting against Belgian rule broke out. Elections were held on May 31 in anticipation of independence. Joseph Kasavubu became president, and Patrice Lumumba, head of the Congolese National Movement, became prime minister. On June 30, 1960, Belgium granted independence to the Congo; many Europeans fled the country. On July 4 the army mutinied, and on July 11 the southern province of Katanga (now Shaba), under the leadership of Moise Tshombe, seceded from the Congo and declared its independence. Belgium sent troops to quell the disorder.

On Aug. 9 the U.N. called on Belgium to withdraw its troops. Kasavubu removed Lumumba as prime minister. Lumumba, with the backing of Ghana, fought for control. He fled to Stanleyville (now Kisangani) but was kidnapped in January 1961 and taken to Katanga, where he was murdered, apparently with U.S. and Belgian complicity. Fighting continued in Katanga, where Tshombe's regime was supported by European mercenaries and opposed by U.N. peacekeeping forces. The Katangan rebellion ended in late 1963; rebels fled to Angola, and U.N. forces were withdrawn in June 1964. In a surprising political settlement, Tshombe became president of the Congo on June 30. On Sept. 7 leftist rebels attempted to establish a "people's republic" based in Stanleyville. Tshombe again resorted to the use of mercenaries and many white settlers, as well as Congolese, were killed in fighting and terrorist atrocities. The rebellion ended in July 1965. In Nov. 1965 Tshombe was deposed in a military coup led by Joseph Mobutu, whose government took steps to reduce European influence.

In 1971 Mobutu changed the country's name to Zaire and also changed the name of Leopoldville to Kinshasa. In 1972 he ordered all Zairians with European names to change them to African names; he became Mobutu Sese Seko. Attempts in 1974 to force foreign investors to sell their holdings to Zairians brought economic disruption, and foreign investors were invited back in 1977.

In 1977 another rebellion broke out in Katanga

(now Shaba) Province; the government put down the rebellion with the aid of France, Egypt, and Morocco. The rebels fled to Angola, but the province's rich mining economy was again disrupted; many European technical workers fled, and production plummeted.

Although Congo is rich with minerals, forest products, hydroelectric potential, and agriculture, most of these natural resources remain undeveloped and the country was impoverished by the nearly unprecedented corruption of the Mobutu regime. The president is estimated to have amassed a fortune of $3 billion. Rival leaders attempted to organize opposition to the Mobutu government in late 1987 and 1988, but most were arrested or driven into exile.

In June 1991, Mobutu agreed to draft a new constitution and end a 20-year ban on multiparty elections. Étiene Tshisekedi was elected prime minister by a national conference in 1992, but Mobutu fired him in 1993. France and Belgium dispatched troops to protect their nationals and together with the U.S. demanded that Mobutu transfer power to Tshisekedi. Mobutu did not comply, and as his nation's economy sank, he continued to live in luxury, protected by the army and police. In May, 1997, Mobutu was driven from office by the army of Laurent Kabila, who immediately changed the name of the country to Congo.

In the summer of 1998 a new military rebellion began—a rebellion joined by Uganda and Rwanda. By June 1999, a cease-fire seemed near, one that would involve the U.N. and the Organization of African Unity as peacemakers with a mandate to disarm the rebels. The cease-fire came in July 1999, but was not signed by the rebels, only by the six outside states. And an August split in the rebel group brought Rwanda and Uganda to war with each other, each supporting its "own" rebel faction. In 2000 Rwanda proved victorious over Uganda; and by June, the U.N. security council decided that peacekeepers would not be sent.

In Jan. 2001, Pres. Kabila was shot to death by a bodyguard; the (appointed) parliament chose his son, Joseph, as new president. Peace negotiations continued, on and off, through 2003, when Congo reached a series of peace accords with Rwanda,Uganda, and two main rebel groups. A transitional government of President Kabila and four vice presidents will rule till elections in 2005.

▶CONGO, REPUBLIC OF THE

• GEOGRAPHY Location: equatorial country on western coast of Africa. **Boundaries**: Cameroon to NW, Central African Republic to NE, Zaire to E and S, Angolan district of Cabinda to S, Gulf of Guinea to SW, Gabon to W. **Total land area**: 132,046 sq. mi. (342,000 sq km). **Coastline**: 105 mi. (169 km). **Comparative area**: between New Mexico and Montana. **Land use:** 1 % arable land; negl.% permanent crops; 99% other. **Major cities**: (1984 census) Brazzaville (capital) 596,200; Pointe-Noire 298,014; Pool 219,329; (1974) Bouenza 135,999; Cuvette 127,558.

• PEOPLE Population: 2,954,258 (July 2001 est.). **Nationality:** noun—Congolese (sing., pl.); adjective—Congolese or Congo. **Ethnic groups:** 48% Kongo, 20% Sangha, 17% Teke, 12% M'Bochi; about 8,500 Europeans (may be half that number following 1997 civil war). **Languages:** French (official); many African languages with Lingala and Kikongo most widely used. **Religions:** 50% Christian, 48% indigenous beliefs, 2% Muslim.

• GOVERNMENT Type: republic. **Independence:** Aug. 15, 1960 (from France). **Constitution:** Approved by referendum Jan. 2002. **National holiday:** National Day, Aug. 15. **Heads of Government:** Denis Sassou Nguesso, president (since 1997). **Structure:** executive; bicameral legislature; judiciary.

• ECONOMY Monetary unit: Communauté Financière Africaine (CFA) franc. **Budget:** (1997 est.) ***income:*** $870 mil.; ***expend.:*** $970 mil. **GDP:** $2.5 bil., $900 per capita (2002 est.). **Chief crops:** cassava, sugar, rice. **Natural resources:** petroleum, timber, potash, lead, zinc. **Major industries:** crude oil, cement, sawmills. **Labor force:** 79,100 (1985); 75% agriculture, 25% commerce, industry, government. **Exports:** $2.4 bil. (f.o.b., 2002); petroleum, lumber, plywood. **Imports**: $730 mil. (f.o.b., 2002); petroleum products, capital equipment, construction materials. **Major trading partners: *exports:*** 17% U.S., 13% South Korea, 10% China; ***imports:*** 21% France, 11% Italy, 10% U.S.

About 1,500 years ago, the lower reaches of the Congo River formed the focus of a number of well-organized states. The Kongo and Ndonga flourished south of the river; north of the river, in what is now the Congo, the Loango, Teke, and Bobangi were dominant. Some of these states were weakened beginning in the 16th century by the Portuguese slave trade, although the Loango benefited from it through the 19th century.

With the weakening of Portuguese power, the French became the dominant European power in western Africa. In 1883 they established a protectorate over the Teke kingdom, which they renamed Middle Congo. The treaty with the Teke king was concluded by Pierre Savorgnan de Brazza, for whom the capital was named.

In 1910 the French confederated their protectorates of Gabon, Middle Congo, Ubangi-Shari (later the Central African Republic), and Chad to form French Equatorial Africa. The territory became an important base of Free French activity during World War II, in acknowledgment of which Gen. Charles de Gaulle granted French citizenship to the territory's inhabitants in 1946, and local power was devolved upon advisory assemblies. The Republic of the Congo attained full autonomy upon the dissolution of the confederation of French Equatorial Africa in 1959, and the nation gained full independence on Apr. 15, 1960.

In 1963 Pres. Fulbert Youlou was driven from office by violent labor unrest; the military took control and installed a provisional civilian government led by Alphonse Massamba-Debat, who was elected president for a five-year term.

In 1968 Massamba-Debat was overthrown in a military coup and replaced by Capt. Marien Ngouabi, who in 1969 reorganized the Congo as a People's Republic. Despite its Marxist-Leninist stance, Congo remained strongly linked to France, its main source of trade, aid, and foreign investment. Ngouabi was assassinated in 1977 and replaced by a military committee of the Congolese Labor party led by Gen. Joachim Yhomby-Opango, who resigned and was arrested for treason in 1979. He was succeeded by Denis Sassou-Nguesso, who was reelected to a third five-year term in 1989.

In 1990, Congo began a relatively smooth transition to multiparty democracy and opposition parties were legalized as of Jan. 1, 1991. Pascal Lissouba was elected president in Aug. 1992. In June 1997, however, heavy fighting erupted in Brazzaville when Lissouba tried to have his rival, Sassou-Nguesso, arrested just weeks before a new election on the grounds that Sassou-Nguesso was planning a coup. He was and he succeeded, with oil money to buy arms and pay off rivals until by April 2001 a sort of peace and stability ensued, enough to elicit an E.U. loan. But ethnic civil war again broke out in June 2002.

▶COSTA RICA

Republic of Costa Rica

• GEOGRAPHY **Location:** Central American isthmus. **Boundaries**: Nicaragua to N, Caribbean Sea to E, Panama to S, and Pacific Ocean to W. **Total land area**: 19,730 sq. mi. (51,100 sq km). **Coastline**: 801 mi. (1,290 km). **Comparative area**: slightly smaller than West Virginia. **Land use:** 4% arable land; 5% permanent crops; 91% other. **Major cities**: (1995 est.) San José (capital) 318,765; Alajuela 171,840; Cartago 118,205; Puntarenas 100,266; Heredia 73,268.

• PEOPLE **Population:** 3,896,092 (July 2003 est.). **Nationality:** noun—Costa Rican(s); adjective—Costa Rican. **Ethnic groups:** 94% white (including mestizo), 3% black, 1% Amerindian, 1% Chinese. **Languages:** Spanish (official), Jamaican dialect of English spoken around Puerto Limón. **Religions:** 76.3% Roman Catholic, 13.7% Evangelical Protestant, other Protestant, Jehovah's Witness.

• GOVERNMENT **Type:** democratic republic. **Independence:** Sept. 15, 1821 (from Spain). **Constitution:** Nov. 7, 1949. **National holiday:** Independence Day, Sept. 15. **Head of Government:** Abel Pacheco de la Espriella, president (since May 2002). **Structure:** executive; unicameral legislature; judiciary.

• ECONOMY **Monetary unit:** Costa Rican colón. **Budget:** (2000 est.) ***income:*** $1.91 bil.; ***expend.:*** $2.35 bil. **GDP:** $32.3 bil., $8,500 per capita (2002 est.). **Chief crops:** coffee, bananas, sugarcane, corn, rice, cocoa. **Natural resources:** hydropower potential. **Major industries:** microprocessors, food processing, textiles, clothing, construction materials. **Labor force:** 1.9 mil. (1999 est.); 22% industry, 20% agriculture, 58% services; 6.3% unemployment (2002 est.). **Exports:** $5.1 bil. (f.o.b., 2002 est.); manufactured products, coffee, bananas, textiles, sugar. **Imports**: $6.4 bil. (f.o.b. 2002 est.); raw materials, consumer goods, capital equipment. **Major trading partners:** ***exports:*** U.S., Netherlands, Central America; ***imports:*** U.S., Mexico, Venezuela, Japan.

Costa Rica was under the jurisdiction of the Spanish colonial kingdom of Guatemala until it broke with Spain in 1821, along with other parts of Central America. With the collapse of the United Provinces of Central America in 1838, Costa Rica became an independent republic, and the country held its first democratic elections in 1889.

An attempt at electoral fraud in 1948 led to a brief civil war, which was won by the National Liberation forces under "Don Pepé" Jose Figueres Ferrer. The Costa Rican army was subsequently abolished.

In the 1980's, under Pres. Oscar Arias Sánchez, Costa Rica vigorously promoted the settlement of civil strife in Nicaragua and El Salvador and he was awarded the 1987 Nobel Peace Prize for his Central American peace plan.

Subsequent governments focused on economic matters. In 1994 Jose Maria Figueres Olsen, son of the legendary "Don Pepé," was elected president. But out-of-control public spending brought new debt and inflation. In 1998 Miguel Àngel Rodriguez captured the presidency, and his Social Christian Unity party carried an absolute majority in the Legislative Assembly. In 2002 the same party's candidate, Abel Pacheco, won the presidency.

▶COTE D'IVOIRE

(see Ivory Coast)

▶CROATIA

Republic of Croatia

• GEOGRAPHY **Location:** southeastern Europe. **Boundaries**: Slovenia and Hungary to N, Yugoslavia and Bosnia and Herzegovina to E, Adriatic Sea to S, Slovenia to W. **Total land area**: 21,824 sq. mi. (56,538 sq km). **Coastline**: 1,105 mi. (1,778 km). **Comparative area**: Slightly smaller than West Virginia. **Land use:** 24% arable land; 2% permanent crops; 74% other. **Major cities**: (1991 census) Zagreb (capital) 708,770; Split 189,388; Rijeka 167,064; Osijek 104,761; Zadar 76,343.

• PEOPLE **Population:** 4,422,248 (July 2003 est.). **Nationality:** noun—Croat(s); adjective—Croatian. **Ethnic groups:** 90% Croat, 5% Serb, 0.5% Bosniak. **Languages:** 96% Croatian. **Religions:** 87.8% Catholic, 4.4% Orthodox, 1.3% Slavic Muslim.

• GOVERNMENT **Type:** presidential/parliamentary democracy. **Independence:** June 25, 1991. **Constitution:** Dec. 22, 1990. **National holiday:** Statehood Day, May 30. **Heads of Government:** Stjepan Mesić, president (since Feb. 2000); Ivica Račan, prime minister (since Jan. 2000). **Structure:** executive; bicameral legislature; judiciary.

• ECONOMY **Monetary unit:** Croatian kuna. **Budget:** (2001 est.) ***income:*** $8.6 bil. ***expend.:*** $9 bil. **GDP:** $38.9 bil.; $8,800 per capita (2002 est.). **Chief crops:** wheat, corn, sugar beets, sunflowers, alfalfa. **Natural resources:** oil, coal, bauxite, low-grade iron ore, calcium. **Major industries:** chemicals and plastics, machine tools, fabricated metal, electronics, pig iron and rolled steel products. **Labor force:** 1.68 mil. (2000 est.); industry and mining, government, agriculture. **Exports:** $4.9 bil. (f.o.b., 2002); textiles, foodstuffs, fuels, chemicals. **Imports**: $10.7 bil. (c.i.f., 2002); machinery and transport equipment, chemicals, food and live animals, fuels and lubricants. **Major trading partners:** Germany, Italy, Bosnia and Herzegovina.

Croatia is one of Europe's most ancient states, King Tomaslav having created an independent Catholic realm in 924. In the sixth century the Croats, led by their eponymous chieftain Chrovatos, had migrated to the old Roman province of Illyricum, south of the Danube, where they dwelt in practical independence of the Byzantine Empire. Pope Gregory VII sent a papal crown, and therewith international recognition, to King Zvonimir (1076-89), but the king's death spelt the demise of the native dynasty. In 1102 Hungary's king Kalman was recognized as king of Croatia as well, in a dynastic union in which Croatia retained its own nobility and institutions. From the 14th century, Croatia (along with Hungary and Serbia) formed Europe's bulwark against the Ottoman Empire. After the Turkish victory at Mohacs (1526), the Hungarian and Croatian crowns were added to the Habsburg dynasty. Escaping Turkish sway, Croatia became controlled by Austrian military authorities as the frontier district against the Ottomans.

With the proclamation of the Austrian Empire in 1804, amalgamating the Habsburg possessions into one unified state, the estates of Croatia resisted the royal absolutism, stressing their autonomous status and ties to the Hungarian kingdom, but to slight avail, even after the Croat army of Baron Josip Jellacid proved essential in suppressing the Hungarian revolt of 1848. However, after the 1867 Ausleich ("compromise"), which established a practically independent Hungary within the Dual Monarchy, a further compromise (Nagoda) in the following year recognized Croatian autonomy within the Hungarian realm.

When the Habsburg monarchy collapsed during World War I, Croatia joined the new Yugoslavia, but since that state proved to be no federation but rather a greater Serbia, Croatia resisted Serbian dominance. And after the ferocious ethnic hostility provoked a royal dictatorship in 1929, Ante Pavelic formed the Ustase, a terrorist organization similar to and having ties with the Macedonian IMRO, with the aim of attaining Croatian independence. Just a week before the outbreak of World War II, Croatia was again granted autonomy, but with Hitler's 1941 conquest and dismemberment of Yugoslavia, an "Independent Croat State" was established under Italian protection. While Aimone, Duke of Spoleto was proclaimed king of Croatia under the preposterous name of Tomaslov II, he had the good sense never to enter "his" kingdom, whose governance was left to Pavelic and the Ustase. An "ethnic cleansing" of Croatia commenced, in which perhaps 100,000 Serbs and Jews lost their lives. Since the "chetniks" of Gen. Mihajlovic were Serbs and royalists, anti-Ustase Croats had nowhere to turn but to the Communist "partisans" of Tito (himself a Croat). Postwar vengeance against Tito's enemies, especially the Ustase, was severe but short-lived and Croatia in 1946 became one of the "republics" of the reconstituted Yugoslavia.

With Croatia's June 1991 secession from Yugoslavia, Serbian militias backed by the Yugoslavian army seized about one-third of Croatian territory, but by mid-1995 Croat forces had regained almost all of its land. President Franjo Tudjman also fostered the Muslim-Croat Federation in Bosnia to preserve a sort of Bosnian independence. The Yugoslav-Croat war came to an end in September 1996 with the establishment of diplomatic relations in which Yugoslavia recognized Croatia's boundaries, leaving ethnic Serbs in the lurch. And in Jan. 1998, a U.N. decision returned eastern Slavonia, part of historic Croatia captured by Serb militias in 1991, to Croatia.

Having won a third presidential term in January 1997, despite a stagnant economy, widespread corruption and complaints of autocracy, Tudjman succumbed to stomach cancer in Dec. 1999. Within a month, a six-party opposition coalition had captured 94 of 152 parliamentary seats, with Social Democrat Ivica Racan named premier. In a February 2000 presidential run-off, Stipe Mesic took over 56 percent of the votes.

▶CUBA

Republic of Cuba

• **GEOGRAPHY Location:** largest island in Caribbean Sea, about 100 mi. (160 km) S of Florida. **Boundaries**: North Atlantic Ocean to N, Windward Passage to E, Caribbean Sea to S, Yucatan Channel to W. **Total land area**: 42,803 sq. mi. (110,860 sq km). **Coastline**: 2,319 mi. (3,735 km). **Comparative area**: between Tennessee and Pennsylvania. **Land use:** 33% arable land; 8% permanent crops; 59% other. **Major cities**: (1993 est.) Havana (capital) 2,175,995; Santiago de Cuba 440,084; Camagüey 293,961; Holguín 242,085; Guantánamo 207,796.

• **PEOPLE Population:** 11,263,429 (July 2003 est.). **Nationality:** noun—Cuban(s); adjective—Cuban. **Ethnic groups:** 51% mulatto, 37% white, 11% black, 1% Chinese. **Languages:** Spanish. **Religions:** at least 85% Roman Catholic before Castro assumed power.

• **GOVERNMENT Type:** Communist state. **Independence:** Dec. 10, 1898 (from Spain; administered by the U.S. from 1898 to 1902). **Constitution:** Feb. 24, 1976. **National holiday:** Independence Day, Dec. 10. **Head of Government:** Fidel Castro Ruz, prime minister from February 1959, president (since Dec. 1976). **Structure:** executive; unicameral legislature; controlled judiciary.

• **ECONOMY Monetary unit:** Cuban peso. **Budget:** (2000 est.) ***income:*** $14.9 bil.; ***expend.:*** $15.6 bil. **GDP:** $25.9 bil., $2,300 per capita (2002 est.). **Chief crops:** sugar cane, tobacco, citrus, coffee, rice. **Natural resources:** cobalt, nickel, iron ore, copper, manganese. **Major industries:** sugar, petroleum, food and tobacco processing. **Labor force:** 4.3 mil. (2000); 51% services and government, 25% industry, 24% agriculture. **Exports:** $1.8 bil. (f.o.b., 2002 est.); sugar, nickel, shellfish, tobacco. **Imports**: $4.8 bil. (f.o.b., 2002 est.); petroleum, food, machinery, chemicals. **Major trading partners:** ***exports:*** 22% Netherlands, 13% Russia, 13% Canada; ***imports:*** 13% Spain, 7% France, 6% Canada.

At the time of Christopher Columbus's arrival in 1492, Cuba was home to Arawak, Ciboney, and Guanahatabey Indian people. Cuba served as a launching point for Spanish conquests in the Americas, and the early- 19th-century wars of independence that swept the rest of Spanish America did not overthrow the imposing Spanish garrison there. Slavery was abolished in 1886, but Spanish colonialism lingered until the 1890's.

Spanish control of the island began to deteriorate in the late 1860's with the beginning of the "Ten Years War" (1868-78). Under the terms of the 1898 Treaty of Paris, which ended the Cuban-U.S.-Spanish War, Cuba became a U.S. protectorate. The U.S.-sponsored Platt Amendment (1901) to the new Cuban constitution gave the United States the right to intervene in Cuban affairs.

Corruption and political repression plagued Cuban politics during the first half of the 20th century. Gerardo Machado won election to the presidency in 1925, but quickly turned his administration into a dictatorship that lasted until his ouster by a progressive coalition of students and labor in 1933. The "revolution" of 1933 installed Rámón Grau San Martín as the new head of the government, but the U.S. supported Grau's ouster, and army sergeant Fulgencio Batista replaced him. Batista ruled the country either directly or indirectly for the next quarter century.

In 1953 Fidel Castro Ruz led a failed attack on the Moncada army barracks in Santiago. In Dec. 1956 Fidel and Raúl Castro, Argentine physician Ernesto "Che" Guevara, and 79 others returned to Cuba and waged a guerrilla campaign against the government. Batista's military failed to defeat the guerrillas, and in the wake of increasing demonstrations of public antipathy for his government, the dictator fled the country. The Communist Fidelistas took control Jan. 1, 1959.

By mid-1959, revolutionary tribunals had tried and executed more than 500 political "enemies." The leaders announced an agrarian reform, and by 1960 the nationalization of the economy was in full swing. In 1961 U.S.-Cuban diplomatic relations were severed, and the U.S.-sponsored Bay of Pigs invasion by Cuban exiles failed. In 1962 the Cuban missile crisis brought the world to the brink of nuclear war when U.S. spy planes uncovered Soviet intentions to place nuclear weapons on the island. The Soviets agreed to the withdrawal of missiles in exchange for a U.S. pledge not to invade Cuba.

In its active foreign policy, Cuba provided assistance to a number of left-wing regimes in Africa and Latin America, most notably its military presence in Angola from 1975 to 1991. With the collapse of the Soviet Union in 1991, Cuba lost huge subsidies, forcing its economy into a downward spiral. In 1994, the worsening economy and a growing dissatisfaction with the Castro govenment fueled migration of Cubans to U.S. shores. With thousands of refugees arriving in Florida each day—aboard boats, homemade rafts, ferries—the U.S. and Cuba negotiated an agreement in which the United States would increase annual acceptance levels of Cuban immigrants to 20,000 in return for Cuba's promise to curb illegal migration.

Tensions flared between the U.S. and Cuba on Feb. 24, 1996, when Cuban MiGs shot down two private jets operating out of Miami. The U.S. responded by tightening economic sanctions, with penalties for foreigners investing in Cuba. Castro called for a renewed commitment to Marxism and met with Pope John Paul II who visited Cuba in 1999 and publicly confronted Castro on issues of freedom and religious liberty. But the regime remains changeless. In January 2003 "elections," 609 candidates ran unopposed for 609 National Assembly seats. In March, 78 dissidents and independent journalists were arrested; in April all 78 were found guilty in closed trials and given sentences of 6 to 28 years.

▶CYPRUS
Republic of Cyprus

• **GEOGRAPHY Location:** eastern Mediterranean Sea. Nicosia 35°11'N, 33°23'E. **Boundaries**: 62 mi. (100 km) S of Turkey, Syria to E. **Total land area**: 3,571 sq. mi. (9,250 sq km). **Coastline**: 403 mi. (648 km). **Comparative area**: between Delaware and Connecticut. **Land use:** 11% arable land; 5% permanent crops; 84% other. **Major cities**: Nicosia (capital) 149,100 (excludes Turkish-occupied portion); Limassol 107,200; Larnaca 48,300 (1982); Famagusta (Gazi Magusa) 39,500 (mid-1974); Phaphos 20,800 (1982).

• **PEOPLE Population:** 771,657 (July 2003 est.). **Nationality:** noun—Cypriot(s); adjective—Cypriot. **Ethnic groups:** 85% Greek, 12% Turkish. **Languages:** Greek, Turkish, English. **Religions:** 78% Greek Orthodox, 18% Muslim.

• **GOVERNMENT Type:** republic. **Independence:** Aug. 16, 1960 (from U.K.). **Constitution:** Aug. 16, 1960; negotiations have been held intermittently to create basis for new or revised constitution to govern the island and relations between Greek and Turkish Cypriots. **National holiday:** Independence Day, Oct. 1. **Heads of Government:** Tassos Papadopoulos, president (since Feb 1. 2003); Turkish sector—Rauf Denktash, president (since 1975). **Structure:** currently, government of Cyprus has effective authority over only Greek Cypriot community; headed by president of republic and comprising Council of Ministers, House of Representatives, and Supreme Court; Turkish Cypriots declared their own constitution and governing bodies within Turkish Federated State of Cyprus in 1975; state renamed Turkish Republic of Northern Cyprus in 1983.

• **ECONOMY Monetary unit:** Cypriot pound; Turkish lira. **Budget:** (2003 est.) ***income:*** $4.4 bil., Greek area; $231 mil., Turkish area; ***expend.:*** $3.7 bil., Greek area; $539 mil., Turkish area. **GDP:** (2002 est.) $9.4 bil., $15,000 per capita Greek area; $787 mil., $6,000 per capita Turkish area. **Chief crops:** potatoes, citrus, vegetables, barley, grapes. **Natural resources:** copper, pyrites, asbestos, gypsum, timber. **Major industries:** food, beverages, textiles, chemicals. **Labor force:** (2000) Greek area—291,000; 73% services, 22% industry, 5% agriculture; 3.6% unemployment; Turkish area—86,300; 56.4% services, 22.8% industry, 20.8% agriculture. **Exports:** Greek area (f.o.b., 2001 est.)—$1.03 bil.; citrus, potatoes, grapes; Turkish area (f.o.b., 2001)—$46 mil.; citrus, potatoes, textiles. **Imports:** Greek area (f.o.b., 2001 est.)—$3.9 bil.; consumer goods, petroleum and lubricants, foodstuffs; Turkish area (f.o.b., 2001)—$301 mil.; food, minerals, chemicals. **Major trading partners:** ***exports:*** Greek area—E.U., Syria, Russia; Turkish area—Turkey, U.K., Midle East; ***imports:*** Greek area—U.S., E.U.; Turkish area—Turkey, U.K., other E.U..

Recent excavations on Cyprus indicate a human presence at least 10,000 years ago. Mycenean (Greek) culture flourished in the second millenium B.C. Phoenicians colonized the island in the 10th century B.C., and it remained a major entrepôt for eastern Mediterranean trade. Annexed to Rome in 58 B.C. it was later part of the Byzantine Empire until the English Richard I (Lion Hearted) established a crusader state in A.D. 1191. The Lusignan dynasty ruled until 1489, when Cyprus was annexed by Venice. It was subsequently conquered by the Ottoman Empire in 1571.

In 1878 the Congress of Berlin placed Cyprus under British administration. In 1914 it was annexed outright by Great Britain and was made a British colony in 1925. From 1945 to 1948, the British used Cyprus as a detention area for "illegal" Jewish immigrants to Palestine.

After 1947 the Greek Cypriot community continued its long-standing agitation for union (enosis) with Greece, a policy strongly opposed by the Turkish Cypriot community. Communal violence broke out in 1954-55. In 1960 Cyprus was granted full independence under an agreement that forbade either enosis or partition and included guarantees of the rights of both Greeks and Turks. Attempts by the president, Archbishop Makarios, to alter the constitution to favor the Greek majority provoked further communal clashes in 1964, when a U.N. peacekeeping force was sent to the island. On July 15, 1974, a military coup by officers favoring union with Greece deposed the Makarios government. On July 20 Turkey invaded Cyprus and, after the collapse of cease-fire talks in August, occupied the northern two-fifths of the island. In 1975 the Turkish government announced a de facto partition of Cyprus; the northern territory was proclaimed the Turkish Federated State of Cyprus, under Pres. Rauf Denktash.

Makarios returned as president of the Republic of Cyprus, which was thus reduced in size, and remained in office until his death in 1977. He was succeeded by Spyros Kyprianou. Some 200,000 Greek Cypriots were expelled from the Turkish sector to the Republic; many Turks fled from the Republic to the Turkish sector. With a return of political stability, renewed foreign investment, and a customs union negotiated with the EEC, the Republic's economy has prospered, led by agriculture, light manufacturing, and tourism.

In the Turkish sector, the economy remains stagnant, hampered by the loss of population, wartime damage, and stringent economic controls. The Turkish sector proclaimed its independence as the Turkish Republic of Northern Cyprus in 1983, but the new republic has not gained international recognition.

The 1998 decision of the E.U. to invite Cyprus to apply for membership and to deny Turkey's application heightened tensions. In June, both Greece and Turkey sent aircraft to Cyprus and the newly-reelected government of Pres. Clerides sought anti-aircraft missiles from Russia. But by December Cyprus had cancelled plans for deployment, at the urging of Greek Premier Simitis. With the peaceful resolution of so serious a crisis, it became possible for Greek-Turkish relations (the key to reunification of Cyprus) to improve, as they did in the January 2000 accords on the Aegean environment, immigration, tourism and the like. Reunification talks continued through March 2003 but to no avail. So the E.U.'s treaty with Cyprus, signed in April 2003, concerns only the Greek portion of the island. (There, 83-year old Pres. Clerides had lost his re-election to Tassos Papadopoulos in February.) Still, Turkish Cyprus opened its border in April, while Greek Cyrus dropped its trade sanctions.

▶CZECH REPUBLIC

• **GEOGRAPHY Location:** Central Europe. **Boundaries**: Poland to N, Slovakia to E, Austria to S, Germany to W. **Total land area**: 30,387 sq. mi. (78,703 sq km). **Coastline**: none. **Comparative area**: about the size of South Carolina. **Land use:** 40% arable land; 3% permanent crops; 57% other. **Major cities**: (1994 est.) Prague (capital) 1,213,299; Brno 389,576; Ostrava 325,827; Pilsen (Plzen) 171,908; Olomouc 106,278.

• **PEOPLE Population:** 10,249,216 (July 2003 est.). **Nationality:** noun—Czech; adjective—Czech. **Ethnic groups:** 81.2% Czech, 13.2% Moravian, 3.1% Slovak. **Languages:** Czech. **Religions:** 39.8% atheist, 39.2% Roman Catholic, 4.6% Protestant.

• **GOVERNMENT Type:** parliamentary democracy. **Independence:** Oct. 29, 1918 (from Austro-Hungarian Empire); Jan. 2, 1993 (from Czechoslovakia). **Constitution:** Jan. 1, 1993. **National holiday:** Founding of the Republic, Oct. 28. **Heads of Government:** Václav Klaus, president (since Mar. 7, 2003), Vladimir Spidla, prime minister (since July 2002). **Structure:** executive; bicameral legislature; judiciary.

• **ECONOMY Monetary unit:** koruna. **Budget:** (2001 est.) ***income:*** $16.7 bil., ***expend.:*** $18 bil. **GDP:** $155.9 bil., $15,300 per capita (2003 est.). **Chief crops:** wheat, rye, barley, oats, corn, potatoes. **Natural resources:** coal, kaolin, clay, graphite. **Major industries:** fuels, metallurgy, machines. **Labor force:** (1999) 5.203 mil.; 40% industry, 55% services, 5% agriculture. **Exports:** $40.8 bil., (f.o.b., 2002); manufactured goods, machinery and equipment, chemicals, raw materials and fuels. **Imports**: $43.2 bil. (f.o.b., 2002); machinery and equipment, manufactured goods, chemicals. **Major trading partners:** (2001) Germany, Slovakia,Russia, U.K.

A Moravian empire, Christianized by Cyril and Methodius, existed in the ninth century until destroyed by the Magyars. From the 10th through the 14th century, Bohemia and Moravia, "lands of the crown of St. Vaclav," formed an independent kingdom within the Holy Roman Empire under the Czech Premsylid dynasty. In 1526 the crown lands came under Habsburg rule, a rule that lasted until World War I.

They were the richest crown lands of the Austro-Hungarian Empire. Prosperous agriculture in the central plains and mineral wealth in the hill country were supplemented in the 19th century by industrial development led by urban middle classes, who were largely German and Jewish.

With the crumbling of the Habsburg monarchy during the war, a new multinational state of Czechoslovakia emerged, founded by Eduard Beneŝ and Thomas Masaryk, in which the Czechs (only 45% of the population) ruled over Germans, Slovaks, Magyars, Poles, and Ukranians. Yet it was the most democratic state in Central Europe between the wars.

Following the Munich Pact of September 1938, Hitler annexed the German-speaking regions of the "Sudetenland," and in 1939 he established a "protectorate" over the Czech lands, while Slovakia became a self-governing satellite republic. With the collapse of Hitler's Reich, Czechoslovakia was reestablished (except for the Carpatho-Ukraine, which it was compelled to cede to the U.S.S.R.) with Beneŝ again as president and a socialist government, independent but pro-Soviet. Three million Germans were expelled, with tens of thousands killed either in mob violence or after hasty trials before "Special People's Courts." In 1948 a Communist coup forced Beneŝ to resign; he was replaced by the Communist leader Klement Gottwald. Jan Masaryk, the foreign minister, committed suicide or was murdered. Purges and persecutions followed.

With Stalin's death in 1953, Gottwald was replaced as party first secretary by Stalinist hardliner Antonin Novotny, who also became president in 1957. In 1968 Novotny was replaced as first secretary by a Slovak liberal, Alexander Dubcek. Czechoslovakia suddenly was in the vanguard of communist reform. The new regime abolished censorship, denounced Stalin, decentralized economic decision-making, and granted real power to the National Assembly.

The brief "Prague Spring" ended in Aug. 1968, when Warsaw Pact troops invaded. In 1969 Dubcek was replaced by Gustáv Husak. The party was purged, censorship restored, dissent repressed, and the centralized economy restored.

The 1970's brought inflation and economic stagnation but produced no change in policy. The rise of the Solidarity movement in Poland in the early 1980's provoked a backlash of preventive repression in Czechoslovakia, aimed especially at Charter 77, a human-rights organization, and at the Catholic church.

The pro-democracy movement began in earnest in October 1989, inspired by a lack of confidence in Communist rule and by reform movements throughout Eastern Europe. The resignation of Communist leaders throughout December culminated in the parliamentary election of Václav Havel, a dissident playwright and head of a loose coalition of opposition groups called Civic Forum, as president, and the vindicated Alexander Dubcek as chairman of Parliament.

Despite severe economic difficulties, revelations of state security abuses, environmental pollution, and other problems inherited from the Communist era, Czechoslovakia's "Velvet Revolution" seemed a resounding political and popular success. In 1990 Soviet troops left and Civic Forum and its Slovakian ally, Public Against Violence, won 47% of the vote in parliamentary elections, against 14% for the Communists and 12% for the Christian Democrats. Vaclav Havel was elected president, and Marian Calfa became prime minister.

But Slovak-Czech resentments and Slovakia's economic distress led to a separation of the two republics, effective Jan. 1, 1993. In June 1996, the first elections in the new Czech Republic gave 99 (out of 200) seats to the three-party center-right coalition (led by Prime Minister Vaclav Klaus and President Havel) which had guided the Czech Republic's successful transition to a market economy. After several years of prosperity, the Czech Republic suddenly fell on hard times in 1997, and

Klaus was forced to introduce austerity measures. Revelations of campaign finance irregularities brought Klaus' resignation in Nov. 1997. In the subsequent June 1998 elections, the Social Democrats won a plurality of seats and, with the Civic Democrats' agreement, formed a minority government for the next four years. The budget adopted in Jan. 1999 included the republic's first planned deficit as the nagging recession continued, with little economic growth forecast and unemployment rising to 9.5 percent. In the 2002 elections, the Social Democrats won a plurality but no majority in the Chamber of Deputies, necessitating a coalition with the Christian Democratic Union/Freedom Party and Vladimir Spidla remaining prime minister and Vaclav Klaus becoming president. In June, a referendum of Czech voters approved E.U. membership with a 77 percent "yes" vote.

▶DENMARK
Kingdom of Denmark

• **GEOGRAPHY Location:** northern Europe. **Boundaries**: Skagerrak channel to N, Baltic Sea to E, Germany to S, North Sea to W. **Total land area**: 16,629 sq. mi. (43,070 sq km). **Coastline**: 2,100 mi. (3,379 km). **Comparative area**: between Maryland and West Virginia. **Land use:** 56% arable land; negl. % permanent crops; 44% other. **Major cities**: (1995) København (Copenhagen—capital) 1,353,333; Århus (Aarhus) 277,477; Odense 182,617; Alborg (Aalborg) 159,056; Esbjerg 82,579.
• **PEOPLE Population:** 5,384,384 (July 2003 est.). **Nationality:** noun—Dane(s); adjective—Danish. **Ethnic groups:** Scandinavian, Inuit, Faeroese, German. **Languages:** Danish, Faroese, Greenlandic (Eskimo dialect); small German-speaking minority. **Religions:** 95% Evangelical Lutheran, Protestant and Roman Catholic, other.
• **GOVERNMENT Type:** constitutional monarchy. **Constitution:** June 5, 1953. **National holiday:** Constitution Day, Apr. 16. **Heads of Government:** Margrethe II, queen (since Jan. 1972); Anders Fogh Rasmussen, prime minister (since Nov. 2001). **Structure:** executive power vested in Crown, exercised by cabinet responsible to Parliament; unicameral legislature; Supreme Court.
• **ECONOMY Monetary unit:** Danish krone. **Budget:** (2001 est.) ***income:*** $52.9 bil.; ***expend.:*** $51.3 bil. **GDP:** $55.5 bil., $29,000 per capita (2002 est.). **Chief crops:** grain, potatoes; meat, dairy; fish. **Natural resources:** crude oil, natural gas, fish, salt, limestone. **Major industries:** food processing, machinery and equipment, textiles, clothing. **Labor force:** 2.856 mil.; 79% services, 17% industry; 5.1% unemployment (2002). **Exports:** $56.3 bil. (f.o.b., 2002); machinery and instruments, meat and meat products, fuels, dairy products. **Imports**: $47.9 bil. (f.o.b., 2002); machinery and equipment, petroleum, chemicals, grain and foodstuffs. **Major trading partners:** (2001) ***exports:*** 64.7% E.U., 6.9% Norway; ***imports:*** 69.9% E.U., 4.2% U.S.

Scandinavian by history, not geography, Denmark in the 11th century, under its second Christian king, Canute, ruled a great northern empire including Greenland, Iceland, the Faeroe Islands, Great Britain, and Norway. By 1387 Britain was long independent, but Denmark added Sweden and Finland to its domain. Yet it was never a great power. Its kings never really controlled the nobility, while in foreign affairs it was dominated by the Hansa, the league of German trading cities.

In the 16th century Denmark had to recognize the independence of Sweden and Finland. In the 19th century it lost Norway (to Sweden in 1814) and Schleswig-Holstein (to Prussia in 1864). In the 20th century Denmark sold the Virgin Islands to the United States in 1914 and had to recognize Iceland's independence in 1944.

In the 19th century, Denmark was transformed from a poor peasant society to one of Europe's richest agricultural nations by means of reforms that established agricultural cooperatives and emphasized intensive specialization in the production of dairy products and pork. These products remain a mainstay of the Danish economy.

Denmark remained neutral during World War I. In 1939 Denmark signed a 10-year nonaggression pact with Germany, but Germany nevertheless invaded Denmark in April 1940; the country surrendered without a fight. In 1941 Denmark's ambassador in Washington transferred defense of Greenland to the United States, and much of Denmark's merchant fleet joined the Allied war effort. Denmark was placed under German martial law in August 1943 and was treated as an enemy nation. Danish resistance succeeded in evacuating 7,000 Jews to neutral Sweden. Denmark was liberated by British troops in May 1945.

Although Denmark was not technically a participant on the Allied side in World War II, it became a U.N. member in 1946 and a founding member of NATO in 1949. By the latter year, the postwar recovery was complete, with industrial levels exceeding those of the prewar period. High taxes, unemployment, and inflation remained problems, but the economy was aided by the growth of trade with West Germany.

In 1953 the king assented to a constitutional reform that abolished the upper house of the legislature, leaving the Folketing as the sole legislative body. Proportional representation meant that it was impossible for any party to gain a parliamentary majority, so Denmark is always governed by coalition regimes. In the postwar period, these normally have been led by the Social Democrats.

In the 1950's Denmark adopted a characteristically Scandinavian program of free enterprise, high taxes, and extensive social welfare systems. A high rate of economic growth, spurred by agricultural exports, continued throughout the 1960's. Denmark joined the E.C. in 1972. The 1970's brought economic difficulties, as Danish oil exploration in the North Sea yielded disappointing results, and inflation reached double digits.

The elections of 1982 installed Denmark's first Conservative government since 1905. A Conservative four-party coalition formed in 1984 remained in office until 1993 when Prime Minister Schlüter resigned over charges of misleading the Folketing about restrictions on the immigration of Tamil refugees. Social Democrat Poul Nyrup Rasmussen formed a coalition government with only a one-seat majority.

The general revival of the world economy in the 1980's coupled with government austerity measures has led to renewed growth and lowered inflation. Although as recently as 1986 Danish voters renewed their commitment to the E.C., in the June 1992 referendum on the Maastricht Treaty—providing for common defense and foreign policy as well as a common currency and central bank—Denmark said "no." The E.U. quickly made concessions that guaranteed Denmark's right to opt out of any common E.U. citizenship, police force, defense policy, or judicial arrangement. In May 1993 Danish voters approved this different version of the treaty. In Sept. 2000 a referendum on the euro was defeated and later the Danes said they would not be part of the E.U.'s army. In Nov. 2001 Folketing elections, the Liberal Party, for the first time since 1920, outpolled the Social Democrats and the Liberal coalition organized a new government of the right under premier Anders Fogh Rasmussen. Within a week they had carried stronger immigration-control measures—the principal issue that had separated the two coalitions in the campaign.

▶DJIBOUTI
Republic of Djibouti

• **GEOGRAPHY** **Location:** northeastern Africa. **Boundaries**: Red Sea to N, Gulf of Aden to E, Somalia to SE, Ethiopia to S, W, and NW. **Total land area**: 8,494 sq. mi. (22,000 sq km). **Coastline**: 195 mi. (314 km). **Comparative area**: between Massachusetts and New Hampshire. **Land use:** 0% arable land; 0% permanent crops; 100% other. **Major cities**: Djibouti (capital) 200,000 (1981); Dikhil, Ali-Sabieh, Tadjourah, Obock.
• **PEOPLE** **Population:** 457,130 (July 2003 est.). **Nationality:** noun—Djiboutian(s); adjective—Djiboutian. **Ethnic groups:** 60% Somali, 35% Afar, 5% French, Arab, Ethiopian, and Italian. **Languages:** French and Arabic (official); Somali and Afar widely used. **Religions:** 94% Muslim, 6% Christian.
• **GOVERNMENT** **Type:** republic. **Independence:** June 27, 1977 (from France). **Constitution:** Sep. 4, 1992. **National holiday:** Independence Day, June 27. **Heads of Government:** Ismail Omar Guelleh, president (since May 1999); Deletia Mohamed Deletia, prime minister (since Mar. 2001). **Structure:** executive; unicameral legislature; judiciary.
• **ECONOMY** **Monetary unit:** Djiboutian franc. **Budget:** (1999 est.) ***income:*** $135 mil., ***expend.:*** $182 mil. **GDP:** $619 mil., $1,300 per capita (2002 est.). **Chief crops:** limited fruits and vegetables; goats, sheep, camels. **Natural resources:** geothermal areas. **Major industries:** limited to a few small-scale enterprises, such as construction and agricultural processing. **Labor force:** 282,000 (1991 est.); 75% agriculture, 14% services, 11% industry; over 50% unemployment (2000 est.). **Exports:** $70 mil. (f.o.b., 2002 est.); hides and skins and transit of coffee. **Imports**: $255 mil. (f.o.b., 2002 est.); foods, beverages, transport equipment, chemicals, petroleum. **Major trading partners:** ***exports:*** 56% Somalia, 24% Yemen, 6% France; ***imports:*** 18% Saudi Arabia, 10% France, 10% Ethiopia.

This small, arid region on the Horn of Africa near the southern mouth of the Red Sea became the object of British-French rivalry with the opening of the Suez Canal in 1869. The French sphere of influence, called French Somaliland, was affirmed by agreements with Ethiopia in 1897, 1945, and 1954. In the early 20th century, the French constructed a railroad from Addis Ababa to Djibouti, adding to the colony's strategic value.

French and Italian forces clashed at the border of Ethiopia and French Somaliland with the Italian invasion of Ethiopia in the 1930's. During World War II, the territorial administration at first sided with the Vichy government but in December 1942 established ties with the Free French and the Allies.

The colony was reorganized in 1957 and in 1958 became, by referendum, a French Overseas Territory. In July 1967 its name was changed to the Territory of the Afars and Issas. Growing nationalist sentiment led to a referendum in favor of complete independence. The Republic of Djibouti became independent on June 27, 1977. A new constitution was approved in 1992 and multiparty elections in December resulted in a clean sweep for Popular Rally for Democracy.

▶DOMINICA
Commonwealth of Dominica

• **GEOGRAPHY** **Location:** eastern Caribbean Sea, between Guadeloupe to N and Martinique to S. Roseau 15°18'N, 61°23'W. **Boundaries**: Dominica Passage to N, Atlantic Ocean to E, Martinique Passage to S, Caribbean Sea to W. **Total land area**: 290 sq. mi. (750 sq km). **Coastline**: 92 mi. (148 km). **Comparative area**: slightly more than four times size of Washington, D.C. **Land use:** 4% arable land; 16% permanent crops; 80% other. **Major cities**: (1991 census) Roseau (capital) 20,755.
• **PEOPLE** **Population:** 69,655 (July 2003 est.). **Nationality:** noun—Dominican(s); adjective—Dominican. **Ethnic groups:** black, Carib Amerindians, mixed, European, Syrian. **Languages:** English (official), French patois. **Religions:** 77% Roman Catholic, 15% Protestant.
• **GOVERNMENT** **Type:** parliamentary democracy. **Independence:** Nov. 3, 1978 (from U.K.). **Constitution:** Nov. 3, 1978. **National holiday:** Independence Day, Nov. 3. **Heads of Government:** Vernon Lorden Shaw, president (since Oct. 1998); Pierre Charles, acting prime minister (since Oct. 2000). **Structure:** executive; unicameral legislature; judiciary—East Caribbean Supreme Court.
• **ECONOMY** **Monetary unit:** East Caribbean (EC) dollar. **Budget:** (2001 est.). ***income:*** $73.9 mil.; ***expend.:*** $84.4 mil. **GDP:** $380 mil., $5,400 per capita (2002 est.). **Chief crops:** bananas, citrus, mangoes; forestry and fisheries. **Natural resources:** timber, hydropower, arable land. **Major industries:** soap, coconut oil, tourism. **Labor force:** 25,000 (1984); 40% agriculture, 32% industry and commerce, 28% services; 23% unemployment (2000 est.). **Exports:** $50 mil. (2002 est.); bananas, soap, bay oil. **Imports**: $135 mil. (2002 est.); manufactured goods, machinery and equipment, foodstuffs. **Major trading partners:** ***exports:*** 47% Caricom countries, 36% U.K., 7% U.S.; ***imports:*** 41% U.S., 25% Caricom, 13% U.K.

Pre-Columbian Dominica was a stronghold of Carib Indians, who had expelled the Arawaks in the 14th century, and today it is the only island in the Caribbean with a native Carib population. Dominica was visited by Columbus on his second American voyage; but though frequented by Spanish ships, it was not settled until French missionaries arrived in the 1630's. Carib resistance was so strong that the French and British agreed to consider the island neutral territory, until it passed under British control in 1763.

Later it was administratively joined to the Leeward and then the Windward Islands, and then became part of the West Indies Federation. It entered into political association with the United Kingdom in 1967. In 1978 Dominica gained independence from Britain. Prime Minister Mary Eugenia Charles's Freedom party has held power since 1980 on a program of economic reconstruction. Hurricanes in 1979-80 largely destroyed the island's agriculture. The government of Prime Minister Mary Eugenia Charles's Freedom party implemented a program of economic reconstruction and diversification after the disaster. In 1992 it began a controversial policy of granting citizenship to businessmen, Asians in particular, in exchange for investment in Dominica's economy. In 1995, Charles resigned after 15 years in office. The United Workers party took 11 of 21 seats in parliamentary elections and named its leader, Edison James, the new prime minister. But Jan. 2000 Assembly elections produced a coalition of the Labor and Freedom Parties, as the United Workers went again into opposition. Labor Party leader

Roosevelt "Rosie" Douglas was named prime minister, but he died unexpectedly on Oct. 2, leaving former Communications and Works minister Pierre Charles to serve as acting prime minister.

▶DOMINICAN REPUBLIC

• **Geography** **Location:** eastern Hispaniola, in Caribbean Sea. Santo Domingo 19°30'N, 70°42'W. **Boundaries**: North Atlantic to N, Mona Passage to E, Caribbean Sea to S, Haiti to W. **Total land area**: 18,815 sq. mi. (48,730 sq km). **Coastline**: 800 mi. (1,288 km). **Comparative area**: slightly more than four times size of Washington, D.C. **Land use:** 21% arable land; 10% permanent crops; 69% other. **Major cities**: (1981) Santo Domingo (capital) 1,313,172; Santiago de los Caballeros 278,638; La Romana 91,571; San Pedro de Macorís 78,562; San Francisco de Macorís 64,906.
• **People** **Population:** 8,715,602 (July 2003 est.). **Nationality:** noun—Dominican(s); adjective—Dominican. **Ethnic groups:** 73% mixed, 16% white, 11% black. **Languages:** Spanish. **Religions:** 95% Roman Catholic.
• **Government** **Type:** representative democracy. **Independence:** Feb. 27, 1844 (from Haiti). **Constitution:** Nov. 28, 1966. **National holiday:** Independence Day, Feb. 27. **Head of Government:** Hipólito Mejía Domínguez, president (since Aug. 2000). **Structure:** executive; bicameral legislature; judiciary.
• **Economy** **Monetary unit:** Dominican peso. **Budget:** (2001 est.) ***income:*** $2.9 bil.; ***expend.:*** $3.2 bil. **GDP:** $53 bil., $6,100 per capita (2002 est.). **Chief crops:** sugarcane, coffee, cotton, cocoa, tobacco; cattle, pigs. **Natural resources:** nickel, bauxite, gold, silver. **Major industries:** tourism, sugar processing, ferronickel and gold mining. **Labor force:** 2.3–2.6 mil. (1998 est.); 58.7% services and government, 24.3% industry, 17% agriculture. **Exports:** $5.3 bil. (f.o.b., 2002); ferronickel, sugar, gold, coffee. **Imports**: $8.7 bil. (f.o.b., 2002); foodstuffs, petroleum, cotton, fabrics, chemicals, pharmaceuticals. **Major trading partners:** (2000) ***exports:*** 87.3% U.S., 1.1% Netherlands, 0.7% Canada; ***imports:*** 60.5% U.S., 10.4% Japan, 4% Mexico.

The Dominican Republic takes up the eastern two-thirds of the island of Hispaniola, which it shares with Haiti. Christopher Columbus visited the island in 1492, and Santo Domingo is the oldest continually inhabited European settlement in the Americas, with the oldest cathedral, hospital, and monastery in the Western Hemisphere.

Western Hispaniola (Haiti) was ceded to France in 1697, and the eastern part of the island in 1795. Liberated with the Haitian slave revolts of 1801, it fell under Haitian rule from 1804 to 1808 (when it reverted to Spanish rule), and again from 1822 to 1844. It was again occupied by Spain from 1861 to 1865. Under Ulises Heureux (1882-99), the Dominican Republic enjoyed a period of independence and prosperity. The U.S. occupied the Dominican Republic between 1916 and 1924. In 1930 Rafael Trujillo set up a dictatorship lasting 31 years. Dominican political strife triggered another U.S. invasion (1965-66) to end the revolution. Reformist party candidate Joaquín Balaguer, president from 1966 to 1978, regained the presidency in 1986, was reelected in 1990, and again (at age 87) in 1994, but only for two years, a compromise arranged in the face of charges of election fraud.

The 1996 elections resulted in a runoff between Haitian-born Jose Pena Gomez and Leonel Fernandez—both center-left in politics, both committed to economic privatization. Fernandez was the winner. But even the small and halting steps towards economic reform provoked strikes by labor unions and students over low wages, chronic water and electric outages. The death in May 1998 of Pena one week before legislative elections added a sentimental boost to real opposition. His Dominican Revolutionary Party captured large majorities in both the Senate and Chamber of Deputies. And in May 2000, for the first time, the party's candidate for president won, Hipolito Mejia. (At 93, Balaguer tried one more time but finished third.)

▶EAST TIMOR

Democratic Republic of Timor-Leste

• **Geography** **Location:** eastern half of island of Timor. **Boundaries**: Banda Sea to N, Timor Sea to S, Indonesia to W. Coastline: 706 km. **Comparative area:** slightly larger than Connecticut. **Land use:** N.A. **Total land area**: 7,336 sq. mi. (19,000 sq km). **Major cities**: Dili (capital).
• **People** **Population:** 997,853 (2003 est.). **Nationality:** noun—Timorese; adjective—Timorese. **Ethnic Groups:** Austronesian (Malayo-Polynesian), Papuan, small Chinese minority. **Languages:** Tetum and Portuguese (official); English, Indonesian. **Religions:** 90% Roman Catholic, 4% Muslim, 3% Protestant.
• **Government** **Type:** Republic. **Independence:** May 20, 2002 (from Indonesia; Nov. 28, 1975 from Portugal). **Constitution:** March 22, 2002. **National Holiday:** Independence Day: Nov. 28. **Head of Government:** Jose Alexandre "Xanana" Gusamo, president; Mari Alkatiri, prime minister.
• **Economy** **Monetary unit:** Indonesian Rupiah. **Budget:** (2003) ***income:*** $36 mil., ***expend.:*** $97 mil. **GDP:** $440 mil., $500 per capita (2001 est.). **Chief crops:** coffee, rice, maize, cassava. **Natural resources:** gold, petroleum, natural gas, manganese, marble. **Major industries:** printing, soap manufacturing, handicrafts, woven cloth. **Labor force:** N.A., 50% unemployment. **Exports:** $8 mil. (2001 est.); coffee, sandalwood, marble. **Imports:** $6 mil (2001); mainly food. **Major trading partners:** N.A.

Early in the sixteenth century, Portuguese traders settled on some of the islands of the Malayan Archipelago, including Timor, and established trading posts there. In 1613 rival traders from the Netherlands settled in western Timor and began the slow process of pushing the Portuguese eastward. (The actual boundary on Timor was no settled by treaty until 1859.) As Dutch, and then British, power waxed through the 17th century, that of Portugal waned, leaving but a handful of fragments, like Goa and Macao and East Timor, of the Portuguese eastern sea empire.

But unlike the Dutch or English, the Portuguese sought to maintain close bonds among economic, political, and religious expansion. A missionary effort made East Timor something of a Catholic enclave amidst the predominantly Muslim Dutch East Indies (and, after 1949, Indonesia). Still, as late as 1975 only about one-third were Catholic; it was the independence struggle that brought the Catholic presence to its current 90 percent.

The leftist coup in Portugal in April 1974, with its socialist, democratic, but above all anti-imperialist ideology, led to the abandonment of East Timor; in Dec. 1975 Indonesia began its brutal conquest and annexation which led to an enduring guerilla warfare and eventually independence. The 1998 fall of Indonesia's dictator Suharto gave space for the 1999 U.N.-sponsored referendum on independence: 78 percent voted "yes." While Muslim militias, aided by segments of the Indonesian armed forces, ravaged the country, a U.N. trusteeship, run principally by Australia and Portugal, readied the new state for independence, finally celebrated May 20, 2002 under its first president, resistance leader Jose Gusmao.

▶ECUADOR

Republic of Ecuador

• **GEOGRAPHY** **Location:** northwestern South America. **Boundaries**: Colombia to N, Peru to E and S, Pacific Ocean to W. **Total land area**: 109,483 sq. mi. (283,560 sq km); incl. Galapagos Islands, 0°45'S, 90°19'W. **Coastline**: 1,389 mi. (2,237 km). **Comparative area**: between Colorado and Nevada. **Land use:** 6% arable land; 5% permanent crops; 89% other. **Major cities**: (1990 census) Quito (capital) 1,401,389; Guayaquil 1,877,031; Cuenca 239,896; Machala 184,588; Portoviejo 159,566.

• **PEOPLE** **Population:** 13,710,234 (July 2003 est.). **Nationality:** noun—Ecuadorian(s); adjective—Ecuadorian. **Ethnic groups:** 65% mestizo, 25% Amerindian, 7% Spanish, 3% black. **Languages:** Spanish (official), Amerindian languages, especially Quechua. **Religions:** 95% Roman Catholic.

• **GOVERNMENT** **Type:** republic. **Independence:** May 24, 1822 (from Spain). **Constitution:** Aug. 10, 1998. **National holiday:** Independence Day, Aug. 10. **Head of Government:** Lucio Gutiérrez Borbua, president (since Jan. 15, 2003). **Structure:** executive; unicameral legislature; independent judiciary.

• **ECONOMY** **Monetary unit:** U.S. dollar. **Budget:** (1999) ***income:*** 5.6 bil.; ***expend.:*** planned $5.6 bil. **GDP:** $41.7 bil., $3,200 per capita (2002 est.). **Chief crops:** bananas, coffee, cocoa, rice; cattle, sheep, pigs. **Natural resources:** petroleum, fish, timber. **Major industries:** petroleum, food processing, textiles. **Labor force:** 3.7 mil. (2001); 30% agriculture, 45% services and other activities, 25% industry; 13% unemployment (2002 est.). **Exports:** $4.9 bil. (f.o.b., 2002 est.); petroleum, bananas, shrimp. **Imports**: $6 bil. (f.o.b., 2002 est.); transport equipment, consumer goods, vehicles, machinery. **Major trading partners:** ***exports:*** 38% U.S., 7% Peru, 7% Colombia; ***imports:*** 25% U.S., 14% Colombia, 7% Japan.

The Inca Empire maintained control over the territory that is now Ecuador until the arrival of Spanish conqueror Francisco Pizarro in 1532. The Spanish conquistadores quickly dismantled the indigenous political structure, which had been weakened by a series of wars between the Inca chief Atahualpa and his half brother Huáscar. The Spaniards arrived in the Quito region in 1533 and established the city of Guayaquil shortly thereafter. The administrative center of Spanish rule was originally established through the viceroyalty of Peru in 1544, and an audiencia (a regional high court under the nominal authority of the viceroy) was established at Quito in 1563. Administrative control of the region was transferred to Bogotá and the viceroyalty of New Granada in 1718.

The local junta of Quito ousted the audiencia in 1809, but they did not achieve independence for the region until after the military victory of the rebel forces over the royalists at the battle of Pichincha in 1822. Ecuador formed a part of the Confederation of Gran Colombia until the confederation's collapse in 1830. The leader of the forces for independence, Gen. Juan José Flores, removed the country from the Gran Colombian confederation and ruled as dictator until his ouster in 1845. A political rivalry existed between the Liberals of Guayaquil and the Conservatives of Quito, but Conservative dominance of the government lasted until 1895.

During the rule of Conservative president Gabriel García Moreno (1861-75), the Roman Catholic church gained a central place in the political and cultural life of the country. García Moreno tied citizenship requirements to Catholic religious affiliation, brought in the Jesuits to "purify" the country through education, and dedicated the country to the Sacred Heart of Jesus. He was assassinated in 1875.

In 1895 the Radical Liberal (anticlerical) party seized power and held it until 1944. José María Velasco Ibarra, in and out of power until 1972, dominated the political scene. Political stability within the country had much to do with the state of the economy. The traditional reliance on cacao production was superseded in the 1950's by a "banana boom," and the discovery of large oil deposits by U.S. corporations in the 1960's led to a shift toward reliance on oil revenues by the 70's.

In 1988 Rodrigo Borja, of the Democratic Left party (ID), was elected to the presidency. In 1992 conservative Sixto Durán Ballén, an advocate of free market reforms, won the presidency and immediately moved to eliminate government subsidies and encourage foreign investment.

Duran's successor in 1996 was the bizarre Abdala Bucaram Ortiz, who was removed by Congress in Feb. 1997 for "mental incapacity." Not until July of 1998 was normality restored with the election of Quito mayor Jamil Mahuad Witt. While his austerity measures provoked widespread discontent, Congress passed most of the measures and the 50-year-long border dispute with Peru was peaceably settled in October 1998. In Sept. 1999, Ecuador defaulted on part of its international debt. And Witt was overturned in a brief army coup in Jan. 2000; his vice-president, Gustavo Noboa, was installed as president, a change ratified by Congress the next day. In March, Witt's plan to replace the sucre with the U.S. dollar as the national currency was adopted (though it had been the occasion of his overthrow). The 2002 presidential election was won by the somewhat leftist Lucio Gutierrez Borbua, a former army colonel and one of the leaders in the 2002 coup, Ecuador's sixth president in seven years.

▶EGYPT

Arab Republic of Egypt

• **GEOGRAPHY** **Location:** northeastern Africa and Asia (Sinai peninsula). **Boundaries**: Mediterranean Sea to N, Israel to NE, Red Sea to E, Sudan to S, and Libya to W. **Total land area**: 386,660 sq. mi. (1,001,450 sq km). **Coastline**: 1,523 mi. (2,450 km). **Comparative area**: slightly more than three times the size of New Mexico. **Land use:** 3% arable land; 0% permanent crops; 97% other. **Major cities**: (1992 est.) Cairo (capital) 6,800,000; El-Iskandriyah (Alexandria) 3,380,000; Giza 3,700,100; Shoubra el-kheima 834,000; Port Said 460,000.

• **PEOPLE** **Population:** 74,718,797 (July 2001 est.). **Nationality:** noun—Egyptian(s); adjective—Egyptian. **Ethnic groups:** 99% Eastern Hamitic stock. **Languages:** Arabic (official), English and French widely understood by educated classes. **Religions:** 94% Muslim (mostly Sunni), 6% Coptic Christian and other.

• **GOVERNMENT** **Type:** republic. **Independence:** Feb. 28, 1922 (from U.K.). **Constitution:** Sept. 11, 1971. **National holiday:** Anniversary of the Revolution, July 23. **Heads of Government:** Mohammed Hosni Mubarak, president (since 1981);

Dr. Atef Muhammad Muhammad Ebeid, prime minister (since Oct. 1999). **Structure:** executive—president nominated by parliament which is validated by popular referendum; bicameral legislature; judiciary.

• **ECONOMY Monetary unit:** Egyptian pound. **Budget:** (2001) ***income:*** $21.5 bil.; ***expend.:*** $26.2 bil. **GDP:** $268 bil., $3,900 per capita (2002 est.). **Chief crops:** cotton, rice, corn, wheat, beans, fruit, vegetables; cattle, water buffalo, sheep, goats. **Natural resources:** crude oil, natural gas, iron ore, phosphates, manganese. **Major industries:** textiles, food processing, tourism. **Labor force:** 20.6 mil. (2002 est.); 29% agriculture, 49% services, including government, 22% industry (2000); 12% unemployment (2001 est.). **Exports:** $7 bil. (f.o.b., 2002 est.); crude oil and petroleum products, cotton yarn, raw cotton, textiles, metal products, chemicals. **Imports**: $15.2 bil. (f.o.b., 2000 est.); machinery and equipment, foods, fertilizers, wood products, durable consumer goods, capital goods. **Major trading partners:** U.S., Italy, Germany.

Civilization began in the fertile valley of the Nile River around 5000 B.C. In about 3200 B.C., King Menes established the first of many dynasties of pharaohs that unified the country from the Nile Delta to Upper Egypt, creating a distinctive ancient civilization of great wealth and cultural brilliance.

The last pharaonic dynasty was overthrown by the Persians in 341 B.C. The Persians in turn were replaced by the Alexandrian and Ptolemaic Greek dynasties and then by the rule of the Roman Empire. Egypt was part of the Byzantine Empire from the third to the seventh centuries A.D., when it was conquered by the Arab Islamic expansion. Arab rule was ended around 1250 when the Mameluke dynasty, of Caucasian origin, established control. The Mamelukes were defeated by the Turks in 1517, and Egypt was incorporated into the Ottoman Empire.

The Suez Canal was built by a French corporation during 1859-69 but was taken over by the British in 1875. This, together with the expansion of the British Empire in East Africa and the Sudan, led to the establishment of de facto British rule in Egypt in 1882, although Egypt remained nominally part of the Ottoman Empire until 1914. A British protectorate in Egypt was established in that year, replaced by a League of Nations Mandate in 1922. The autonomy of the Egyptian monarchy was strengthened in an Anglo-Egyptian treaty of 1936, but Great Britain continued to maintain military forces in Egypt and controlled the Sudan as an Anglo-Egyptian condominium.

Egypt saw heavy fighting between British and Axis forces during WWII. After the war, a nationalist movement gained strength. The 1936 treaty was abrogated by Egypt in 1951. An uprising of the Society of Free Officers on July 23, 1952, forced King Farouk to abdicate. A republic was proclaimed on June 18, 1953. Lt. Col. Gamal Abdel Nasser became premier in 1954 and president in 1956.

British troops were withdrawn from the Suez Canal zone in June 1956. On July 26, 1956, Egypt announced the nationalization of the canal. Israel invaded the Sinai Peninsula at the end of October 1956. France and Great Britain landed forces and bombed Egyptian positions; a cease-fire went into effect under U.N. supervision on Nov. 17. A U.N. peacekeeping force patrolled the border between Egypt and Israel from 1957 to 1967.

Increasing Soviet involvement in Egypt was confirmed with its aid to Egypt in the construction of the Aswan High Dam. The dam, completed in 1971, provides both irrigation and hydropower but at the cost of extensive environmental damage. Egypt and Syria joined together as the United Arab Republic in 1958. Later joined by Yemen, the union was dissolved in 1961.

A full-scale war with Israel broke out on June 5, 1967. The Six-Day War ended on June 10 with Israel in full control of Gaza and the Sinai peninsula to the banks of the Suez Canal. Sporadic fighting between Egyptian and Israeli forces continued throughout 1969-70. The Suez Canal remained closed to shipping until 1975.

Nasser died in 1970 and was succeeded by Vice Pres. Anwar Sadat, who concluded a treaty of friendship with the U.S.S.R., but expelled all Soviet troops and advisers in 1972. On Oct. 6, 1973, Egyptian forces crossed the Suez Canal and attacked Israeli positions in the Sinai (Syrian forces also attacked Israeli positions in the Golan Heights). Israel drove back the attackers, and the Yom Kippur War ended in a cease-fire on Oct. 24.

In 1974 Sadat's government became increasingly friendly to the West, welcoming foreign investment and American aid. In 1974 and 1975 disengagement accords were signed with Israel, providing for the return of the Sinai to Egypt in stages. In November 1977 Sadat visited Jerusalem as a gesture of peace, and a peace treaty between Israel and Egypt was signed (after a series of talks mediated by Pres. Jimmy Carter) on Mar. 26, 1979. Formal diplomatic relations were established in 1982. Egypt was suspended from the Arab League—it was readmitted in 1989—and attacked by Libyan forces on several occasions along the Egyptian-Libyan border.

Popular unrest fomented by the Muslim Brotherhood in Sept. 1981 led to a military crackdown. Pres. Sadat was assassinated by members of a military conspiracy on Oct. 6, 1981, and was succeeded by Vice Pres. Mohammed Hosni Mubarak. The government has remained on friendly terms with Israel and the U.S. and has gradually improved relations with the rest of the Arab world. During the Persian Gulf War, it was a staunch member of the anti-Iraq coalition, in return for which the U.S. forgave $7 billion in debt.

Through the 1990's Egypt was troubled by bombings and assassinations by Moslem extremist groups such as Islamic Group and Islamic Jihad (the latter claiming to have killed Sadat). But late in the decade, government crackdowns seem to have been effective; Islamic Group in March 1999 announced a permanent cease-fire. In Sept. 1999 President Murabak ran virtually unopposed, winning a fourth six-year term.

▶EL SALVADOR
Republic of El Salvador

• **GEOGRAPHY Location:** Pacific coast of Central America. **Boundaries**: Honduras to N and E, Pacific Ocean to S, Guatemala to W. **Total land area**: 8,124 sq. mi. (21,040 sq km). **Coastline**: 191 mi. (307 km). **Comparative area**: about size of Massachusetts. **Land use:** 27% arable land; 12% permanent crops; 61% other. **Major cities**: (1992 census) San Salvador (capital) 422,570; Soyapango 251,811; Santa Ana 202,337; San Miguel 182,817; Mejicanos 145,000.

• **PEOPLE Population:** 6,470,379 (July 2003 est.). **Nationality:** noun—Salvadoran(s); adjective—Salvadoran. **Ethnic groups:** 90% mestizo, 1% Amerindian, 9% white. **Languages:** Spanish, Nahua (among some Amerindians). **Religions:** 83% Roman Catholic; extensive activity by Protestant groups throughout country.

• **GOVERNMENT** **Type:** republic. **Independence:** Sept. 15, 1821 (from Spain). **Constitution:** Dec. 23, 1983. **National holiday:** Independence Day, Sept. 15. **Head of Government:** Francisco Guillermo Flores Pérez (since June 1999). **Structure:** executive; unicameral legislature; judiciary.

• **ECONOMY** **Monetary unit:** U.S. dollar. **Budget:** (2001 est.) ***income:*** $2.1 bil.; ***expend.:*** $2.5 bil. **GDP:** $30 bil., $4,700 per capita (2002 est.). **Chief crops:** coffee, sugarcane, corn; beef, dairy; shrimp. **Natural resources:** hydropower and geothermal power, crude oil. **Major industries:** food processing, beverages, petroleum. **Labor force:** 2.35 mil. (1999); 30% agriculture, 55% services, 15% industry. **Exports:** $3 bil. (f.o.b., 2002); offshore assembly exports, coffee, sugarcane, shrimp. **Imports**: $4.9 bil. (f.o.b., 2002); raw materials, consumer goods, foodstuffs, capital goods. **Major trading partners:** ***exports:*** 65% U.S., 11% Guatemala, 8% Honduras; ***imports:*** 50% U.S., 10% Guatemala, 7% E.U..

A number of Indian tribes, of which the Pipil were dominant, originally inhabited the area now called El Salvador. The native population resisted the first attempt at Spanish colonization, begun in 1524, for almost 15 years. In 1821 El Salvador gained its independence from Spain, first as a jurisdiction under the Mexican empire and two years later as a member of the United Provinces of Central America. The Central American Federation collapsed in 1838, and in 1840 El Salvador emerged from a bloody two-year struggle as an independent republic.

The Salvadoran economy was dominated by coffee production from the 1860's onward, and a series of laws in the 1880's allowed for concentration of both land ownership and political power in the hands of a coffee oligarchy. In 1931 a reformist president won election, but the military subsequently dismissed him. A revolt ensued (1932) in which 10,000 to 20,000 Salvadorans—mostly peasants—were killed. The result of the massacre, which was called La Matanza, was a period of relative political stability that lasted until the 1970's.

In 1979 a political coup led by a group of junior military officers overthrew Pres. Gen. Carlos Humberto Romero. Owing to the polarization between conservative and reformist political groups, the first two civilian-military juntas resigned as a result of their failure to have their programs implemented by the military. A third government, which included Christian Democrat José Napoleón Duarte, took over on Mar. 5, 1980, on the basis of an armed forces' pledge to carry out an agrarian reform program. In 1980 the coalition of opposition political organizations became the Democratic Revolutionary Front (FDR), and five revolutionary military organizations consolidated under the banner of the Farabundo Marti Front for National Liberation (FMLN). Six social-democratic political leaders were assassinated in November 1980, further cementing the political opposition around the FMLN-FDR coalition.

A three-part agrarian reform program was initiated in 1980 in El Salvador, but the central part of the program—to redistribute most of the land involved in export agriculture—was dropped as a result of opposition from the agricultural elite.

In March 1982 elections for a constituent assembly, a majority of seats went to the rightist ARENA coalition. In December 1983 a new constitution went into effect, and in 1984 Christian Democrat José Napoleón Duarte assumed the presidency.

In 1989, Alfredo Cristiani of the conservative Alliance for National Renovation was elected president. On Nov. 11, 1989, FMLN guerrillas launched a new offensive that lasted for several weeks before fading away. The government's failure to prosecute military officers implicated in the murder of six Jesuit priests shortly thereafter jeopardized U.S. military aid, which totaled $6 billion between 1979 and 1992.

In January 1992, the government signed a peace treaty with the FMLN and the 12-year civil war, in which 70,000 people died, officially ended on December 15. The treaty called for the military to cut its forces by almost half (to 31,000 soldiers), and for the FMLN to lay down its arms and become a political party. A U.N.-sponsored Truth Commission found that 85 percent of all human-rights violations during the war were attributable to the Salvadoran army, security forces, or intelligence-unit death squads. Although the legislature narrowly passed a general amnesty for public officials, military officers, and political party leaders linked to human rights violations in March of 1993, the United States tried to link further military aid to the dismissal of the worst offenders in the military.

In the March 1994 elections, ARENA's candidate Armando Calderon Sol was elected president. ARENA also carried half the seats in the National Assembly. In the 1997 mid-term election, FMLN made a vary strong showing running virtually even with ARENA on the national level. In the March 1999 elections, ARENA and the FMLN carried almost the same number of seats in the National Assembly, but in the presidential election, ARENA easily won for the third straight time, their candidate (Francisco Flores Perez) gaining 51 percent of the vote, with the FMLN candidate winning only 29 percent.

▶EQUATORIAL GUINEA
Republic of Equatorial Guinea

• **GEOGRAPHY** **Location:** mainland territory of Río Muni in western Africa and five inhabited islands: Bioko (3°45'N, 8°50'E), Corisco, Great Elobey, Small Elobey, and Pagalu (Annabon). **Boundaries**: Cameroon to N, Gabon to E and S, Gulf of Guinea to W. **Total land area**: 10,830 sq. mi. (28,050 sq km). **Coastline**: 184 mi. (296 km). **Comparative area**: slightly larger than Maryland. **Land use:** 5% arable land; 4% permanent crops; 91% other. **Major cities**: (1983 census) Malabo (capital) 15,323; Bata 24,100.

• **PEOPLE** **Population:** 510,473 (July 2003 est.). **Nationality:** noun—Equatorial Guinean(s); adjective— Equatorial Guinean. **Ethnic groups:** Bioko (primarily Bubi, some Fernandinos); Río Muni (primarily Fang), less than 1,000 Europeans, mostly Spanish. **Languages:** Spanish (official), pidgin English, Fang. **Religions:** Christian, predominantly Roman Catholic; indigenous practices.

• **GOVERNMENT** **Type:** republic. **Independence:** Oct. 12, 1968 (from Spain). **Constitution:** Nov. 17, 1991. **National holiday:** Independence Day, Oct. 12. **Heads of Government:** Col. Teodoro Obiang Nguema Mbasogo, president (since Aug. 1979); Cándido Muatetema Rivas, prime minister (since Feb. 2001). **Structure:** executive; unicameral legislature; judiciary.

• **ECONOMY** **Monetary unit:** Communauté Financière Africaine (CFA) franc. **Budget:** (2001 est.) ***income:*** $200 mil.; ***expend.:*** $158 mil. **GDP:** $1.2 bil., $2,700 per capita (2002 est.). **Chief crops:** coffee, cocoa, rice, yams; livestock; timber. **Natural resources:** timber, crude oil, small unexploited deposits of gold, manganese, uranium. **Major industries:** petroleum, fishing, sawmilling. **Labor force:**

NA. **Exports:** $2.5 bil. (f.o.b., 2002 est.); petroleum, timber, cocoa. **Imports**: $562 mil. (f.o.b., 2002); petroleum, foodstuffs, beverages, clothing, machinery. **Major trading partners:** ***exports:*** 53% Spain, 26% China, 13% U.S.; ***imports:*** 33% U.S., 15% U.K., 12% Spain.

Equatorial Guinea consists of the Mbini River basin on the West African coast, and a number of offshore islands, chiefly Bioko and Pagalu (Annobón). Indigenous Pygmies were displaced beginning in the 17th century by migrations of various peoples that now inhabit the coastal region and by the Fang, who comprise 80 percent of the present population.

Bioko was discovered in 1473 by the Portuguese explorer Fernando Po, and until modern times the island bore his name. Portugal controlled the islands and adjacent mainland, exploiting them for the slave trade, until 1778 when the territory was ceded to Spain. Equatorial Guinea remained underdeveloped because of conflicting territorial claims and a lack of Spanish investment. Eventually, however, a plantation system was developed for the cultivation of cocoa, particularly on Bioko, using workers imported from Nigeria.

In 1959 the Spanish territories in the Gulf of Guinea were given status equivalent to a province of Spain. Investment in education, health care facilities, and other social programs, combined with the flourishing plantation economy, made the territory one of the most prosperous and best educated in West Africa. Local autonomy came in 1963, full independence in 1968.

Francisco Macias Nguema was elected Equatorial Guinea's first president in 1968. In 1970 he dissolved all opposition parties and declared a one-party state, and in 1972 proclaimed himself president for life and commenced rule by decree. During the next seven years, a reign of terror resulted in the death or exile of one-third of the country's people. Nigerian workers, along with other foreigners, were expelled from the country in 1976; without their labor and technical skills, the economy was quickly ruined.

Macias Nguema was overthrown in August 1979 in a military coup led by his nephew, Lt. Col. Teodoro Obiang Nguema Mbasogo. Macias Nguema was tried and executed a month later. The new leader moved to reduce Soviet influence and to improve relations with Spain. A new constitution was approved in a referendum in August 1982 and again in 1991, the latter calling for a multiparty political system. Nguema, however, retains firm control. Economic prospects have improved with the discovery of oil reserves estimated at over 65 million barrels a year.

▶ERITREA
State of Eritrea

• **GEOGRAPHY** **Location:** Horn of Africa (central-eastern Africa). **Boundaries**: Sudan to N and W, Red Sea to E, Djibouti and Ethiopia to S. **Total land area**: 46,842 sq. mi. (121,320 sq km). **Coastline**: 680 mi. (1,094 km) on Red Sea. **Comparative area**: about the size of New York. **Land use:** 4% arable land, negl.% permanent crops, 96% other. **Major cities**: (1993 est.) Asmara (capital) 400,000; Asseb, Massawa, Keren.

• **PEOPLE** **Population:** 4,362,254 (July 2003 est.). **Nationality:** noun—Eritrean(s); adjective—Eritrean. **Ethnic groups:** 50% Tigrinya, 40% Tigre and Kunama, 4% Afar, 3% Saho. **Languages:** Afar, Amharic, Arabic, Tigre and Kunama, Tigrinya, minor ethnic group languages. **Religions:** Muslim, Coptic Christian, Roman Catholic, Protestant.

• **GOVERNMENT** **Type:** transitional government. **Independence:** May 24, 1993 (from Ethiopia). **Constitution:** promulgated May 1997. **National holiday:** Independence Day, May 24. **Head of Government:** Isaias Afwerki, president (since May 1993). **Structure:** executive; unicameral legislature; judiciary.

• **ECONOMY** **Monetary unit:** birr. **Budget :** (2000 est.) ***income:*** $206.4 mil.; ***expend.:*** $615.7 mil. **GDP:** $3.3 bil; $740 per capita (2002 est.). **Chief crops:** sorghum, lentils, vegetables; livestock; fish. **Natural resources:** gold, potash, zinc, copper. **Major industries:** food processing, beverages, clothing and textiles. **Labor force:** N.A. **Exports:** $20 mil. (f.o.b., 2001); livestock, sorghum, textiles. **Imports**: $500 mil. (c.i.f., 2001); processed goods, machinery, petroleum products. **Major trading partners:** Sudan, Ethiopia, Italy, U.A.E.

In May 1993, after 30 years of fighting, leaders of the Eritrean People's Liberation Front (EPLF) formally declared this small area of north and northeast Ethiopia to be an independent state. Ethiopia, along with the U.S., the Sudan, and several other states, quickly recognized the authority of the new transitional government led by Issaias Afwerki, former head of the liberation movement.

During the early 20th century, the region of Eritrea was an outpost of the Italian empire, but it came under British rule during World War II. The British made Eritrea part of Ethiopia when independence was granted in 1952. The secessionist movement began immediately, first against Haile Selassie, then in the 1970's and '80's against the Marxist Mengistu Haile Mariam, who was finally driven from office by other forces in 1991. The new government quickly made peace with the Eritrean rebels, who promised continued access to the sea after independence became a fact. Late in 1995 Eritrea began to contest with Yemen control of Greater Hanish Island at the mouth of the Red Sea, a struggle serious enough to elicit U.N. mediation. Further troubles broke out in May 1998 when a small skirmish over the border with Ethiopia escalated into major military clashes in June. The U.S. was attempting to mediate. The bloody and incomprehensible border war continued, with much loss of life on both sides, into 2000 until June 18 when Eritrean and Ethiopian foreign ministers signed a cease-fire restoring the borders of May 1998. Both countries in April 2002 accepted the Hague Court of Arbitration's definition of the disputed 620-mile border.

▶ESTONIA
Republic of Estonia

• **GEOGRAPHY** **Location:** northeastern Europe. **Boundaries**: Gulf of Finland to N and NE, Russian Federation to SE, Latvia to SW, Baltic Sea to NW. **Total land area**: 17,413 sq. mi. (45,100 sq km). **Coastline**: Gulf of Finland. **Comparative area**: about twice the size of New Hampshire. **Land use:** 27% arable land; 0% permanent crops; 73% other. **Major cities**: (1994 est.) Tallinn (capital) 442,700; Tartu 105,800; Narva 79,100; Kohtla-Järve 56,600; Pärnu 52,000.

• **PEOPLE** **Population:** 1,408,556 (July 2003 est.). **Nationality:** noun—Estonian(s); adjective—Estonian. **Ethnic groups:** 65.3% Estonian, 28.1% Russian, 2.5% Ukrainian. **Languages:** Estonian (official), Russian, Ukrainian, English, Finnish, other. **Religions:** Lutheran, Orthodox Christian, others.

• **GOVERNMENT** **Type:** parliamentary democracy. **Independence:** Sep. 6, 1991. **Constitution:** June 28, 1992. **National holiday:** Independence Day,

Feb. 24. **Heads of Government:** Arnold Rüütel, president (since Oct. 2001); Juhan Parts, prime minister (since Apr. 9, 2003). **Structure:** executive; unicameral legislature; judiciary.

• **ECONOMY** **Monetary unit:** Estonian kroon. **Budget:** (2002) ***income:*** $1.89 bil.; ***expend.:*** $1.89 bil. **GDP:** $15.2 bil., $10,900 per capita (2002 est.). **Chief crops:** potatoes, vegetables, fruit; livestock and dairy products; fish. **Natural resources:** oil shale (world's number two producer), peat, phosphorites. **Major industries:** oil shale processing, shipbuilding, phosphates. **Labor force:** 608,600 (2001 est.). **Exports:** $3.4 bil. (f.o.b., 2002); 33% machinery and equipment, 15% wood and paper, 14% textiles, 8% food products. **Imports:** $4 bil. (f.o.b., 2000); 31% machinery and equipment, 13% chemical products. **Major trading partners:** Finland, Germany, Sweden, China.

Ethnic and linguistic "cousins" of the Finns, the Ests acquired their own independent state only in the 20th century. Previously they had been "colonized" by the Danes (who founded the capital, Tallinn), then in the 13th century by the Teutonic Knights, in the 16th century by the Swedes (who brought the Lutheran Reformation), in the 17th century by the Poles, and in the 18th century by the Russians. Through all these regimes the German element predominated, the "Baltic barons" forming a territorial aristocracy with German burghers ruling the towns. The Ests were restricted to farming, normally as serfs, with serfdom not abolished until 1819.

With that abolition there began a cultural revival with the study of folklore, the collecting of folk songs, the compilation of the national epic, Kalevipoeg, published between 1857 and 1861, and the circulation of newspapers in the Estonian language. Political expression of this revived national spirit came with the 1918 Treaty of Brest-Litovsk in which the new Soviet Union recognized the independence of Estonia. By 1920 Estonia was fully independent, under its own constitution adopted on June 15 of that year.

A radical land reform dispossessed German landowners of large estates, which were distributed to peasants. Dangers from extremists of Left (Communists) and Right ("liberators") were averted by the strong presidency of Constantice Päts, but the Hitler-Stalin Pact of 1939 spelled the end of Estonian independence. Allotted to Stalin's sphere of influence, Estonia was forced to accept Soviet garrisons larger than its national army in 1939, and 65,000 Germans were "repatriated" (after 700 years) to the Third Reich. Rigged elections in 1940 led to a government that "requested" incorporation into the U.S.S.R., an annexation never recognized by the U.S.

There followed nationalization of private property, amalgamation of Estonia's national forces into the Red Army, and a reign of terror against former political leaders and religious and cultural organizations. During and after the war the Estonian people suffered enormous losses through death in battle, murder, flight, and deportation.

Estonia's return to freedom began Mar. 30, 1990, when a freely elected government declared its intention to secede. Violence provoked by Russian "black berets," mass demonstrations, defiance of Gorbachev's economic sanctions and his January 1991 military crackdown, all marked stages toward the Kremlin's recognition in Sept. 1991 of Estonian independence. Estonia, like the other Baltic states, declined to sign the Dec. 1991 Alma-Ata Declaration that created the Commonwealth of Independent States.

Elections in Sept. 1992 produced a divided Parliament, with the majority a center-right coalition led by the Fatherland Alliance. Parliament in October chose as president Lennart Meri, a nationalist and devotee of free markets. The effective disenfranchisement of 40 percent of the population, mostly Russians, through laws requiring citizenship since 1940, provoked Russian ire. But by July 1994 the law was modified and Russian troops left by the end of August.

In March 1995, parliamentary elections brought into power a far-left alliance of parties led by the Coalition Party (the Communists' new name). Still, in 1998 the E.U. invited Estonia to apply for membership. In the March 1999 parliamentary elections, a coalition of three center-right parties regained control of the legislature, winning 53 of its 101 seats. Free-marketeer Mart Laar became Prime Minister for the second time. Interparty squabbling brought the coalition down in Dec. 2001 and in January Parliament elected former Finance Minister Siim Kallas to succeed Laar. Meanwhile, with Pres. Meri forbidden a third term, the Electoral College chose Arnold Routel, one-time Communist ruler, but a hero of Estonian independence.

▶ETHIOPIA

Federal Democratic Republic of Ethiopia

• **GEOGRAPHY** **Location:** Horn of Africa (central eastern Africa). **Boundaries:** Eritrea to N, Djibouti and Somalia to E, Kenya to S, Sudan to W. **Total land area:** 435,184 sq. mi. (1,127,127 sq km). **Coastline:** none. **Comparative area:** somewhat smaller than Alaska. **Land use:** 10% arable land; 1% permanent crops; 89% other. **Major cities:** (1993 est.) Addis Ababa (New Flower) 2,200,186; Dire Dawa 173,588; Harar 162,645; Gondar 146,777; Nazret 131,585.

• **PEOPLE** **Population:** 66,557,553 (July 2003 est.). **Nationality:** noun—Ethiopian(s); adjective—Ethiopian. **Ethnic groups:** 40% Oromo, 32% Amhara and Tigrean, 9% Sidamo, 6% Shankella. **Languages:** Amharic, Tigrinya, Orominga, Guaraginga, Somali, Arabic, English (major foreign language taught in schools). **Religions:** 45-50% Muslim, 35-40% Ethiopian Orthodox, 12% animist.

• **GOVERNMENT** **Type:** federal republic. **Independence:** oldest independent country in Africa and one of oldest in the world—at least 2,000 years. **Constitution:** Dec. 1994. **National holiday:** May 28. **Heads of Government:** Girma Wolde Giorgis, president (since Nov. 2001); Meles Zenawi, prime minister (since Aug. 1995). **Structure:** executive; bicameral legislature; judiciary.

• **ECONOMY** **Monetary unit:** birr. **Budget:** (FY96/97 est.) ***income:*** $1.8 bil.; ***expend.:*** $1.9 bil. **GDP:** $50.6 bil., $750 per capita (2002 est.). **Chief crops:** cereals, pulses, coffee, oilseed; hides, cattle. **Natural resources:** small reserves of gold, platinum, copper, potash. **Major industries:** food processing, beverages, textiles. **Labor force:** 80% agriculture and animal husbandry, 12% government and services. **Exports:** $433 mil. (f.o.b., 2001 est.); coffee, leather products, gold, oilseeds. **Imports:** $1.63 bil. (f.o.b., 2001); food and live animals, petroleum, chemicals, machinery (1994). **Major trading partners:** ***exports:*** 13% Djibouti, 9% Italy, 9% Japan; ***imports:*** 29% Saudi Arabia, 7% Italy, 7% India.

Ethiopia played an important role in the Red Sea trade of the classical world and was mentioned by the Greek historian Herodotus in the fifth century B.C. According to legend, the Ethiopian monarchy was founded by Melelik I, son of Israel's King Solomon and the Queen of

Sheba (Sab'a, i.e., North Yemen). Coptic Christianity became Ethiopia's dominant religion in the fourth century A.D. Ethiopia successfully resisted Islamic invasions in the seventh century except in areas along the Red Sea coast but was cut off from the rest of the Christian world by the Islamic states of North Africa and the Middle East.

Portugal established forts and trading stations on the Red Sea coast beginning in 1493, strengthening their domination of trade in the Indian Ocean. The Portuguese also sponsored Roman Catholic missionaries but with little success. A century of religious strife ended with the expulsion of all foreign missionaries in the 1630's. Ethiopia successfully resisted an attempted Italian invasion in 1880.

Ethiopia began to emerge into the modern world under Melelik II (r. 1889-1913). A period of instability after his death ended with the accession in 1930 of Haile Selassie. Italy invaded again in 1936 and soon conquered the entire country. Protests by the League of Nations had no effect; Haile Selassie fled to exile in England. The Italians were driven out during World War II by British and Ethiopian forces, and Haile Selassie returned to his throne.

Civil unrest broke out in February 1974, and Haile Selassie was deposed on Sept. 13, 1974. A coalition of urban elites and the armed forces took over, abolishing the monarchy in 1975 and curbing the power of the Coptic church. Land reform was instituted, and a socialist state proclaimed. In 1977-78 a period of "red terror" resulted in the arrest and execution of thousands of the regime's opponents. A provisional military council, the Dergue, was confirmed in power under Col. Mengistu Haile-Mariam's leadership.

A military assistance agreement in 1976 between Ethiopia and the U.S.S.R. ended an earlier military relationship with the U.S.; American military advisers were expelled. In 1977 Somalia, taking advantage of Ethiopia's shifting military situation, attacked across the Ogaden desert, aiming to restore certain disputed areas of Ethiopia to Somalia. A massive infusion of Soviet arms and Cuban troops expelled the Somalis in March 1978, but border clashes continued thereafter.

After the expulsion of the Italians during World War II, the province of Eritrea, under a U.N. plan, was to have become autonomous in a federation with Ethiopia. Instead, Eritrea was made a province of the Ethiopian Empire in 1962. A coalition of Marxist and non-Marxist liberation forces—most prominent among them the Eritrean People's Liberation Front (EPLF)— resisted the annexation from the beginning. By the spring of 1991, Eritrean forces had gained control of all of Eritrea, including Ethiopia's outlets to the sea.

Another rebel group, the Ethiopian People's Revolutionary Democratic Front (EPRDF), sought autonomy for Tigre, a northern region between Ethiopia and Eritrea. In February 1991, the EPRDF launched a major offensive, forcing Mengistu Haile Mariam's flight, a week before scheduled cease-fire talks were to start in London. The talks proceeded quickly under the auspices of the United States, and rebel forces under the leadership of the EPRDF entered Addis Ababa virtually unopposed at the end of May.

Years of civil war and devastating famines left Ethiopia in shambles. A transition government was installed to draft a constitution in July 1991, and acknowledged Eritrean independence without incident. But the country's first multiparty elections in June 1992 were so badly handled that the powerful OLF withdrew from the government.

In June 1994, the EPRDF won 484 of the 547 seats in the Constituent Assembly, which by November had drawn up a constitution for a parliamentary government over nine partially autonomous regions. But most opposition parties boycotted the country's first multiparty elections under the new constitution, resulting in decisive victories by the EPRDF, and its leader Meles Zenawi, who became premier. A small border war with Eritrea in May-June 1998 threatened the fragile political structure. By early 1999, the small war had ballooned into a major conflict with thousands of soldiers on each side struggling for control of some barren borderland near the outpost of Badme. It ended with a cease-fire, signed by the Ethiopian and Eritrean foreign ministers in June 2000, restoring the May 1998 borders. In May 2002 both countries accepted the Hague Court of Arbitration's delineation of the boundary.

▶FIJI
Republic of Fiji

• **GEOGRAPHY** **Location:** more than 300 islands (100 inhabited), in South Pacific Ocean. Suva 18°08'S, 178°25'E. **Boundaries**: South Pacific Ocean to N, S, and W; Koro Sea to E; nearest neighbor is Vanuatu, about 600 mi. (1,000 km) to W. **Total area**: 7,054 sq. mi. (18,270 sq km). **Coastline**: 702 mi. (1,129 km). **Comparative area**: slightly smaller than New Jersey. **Land use:** 11% arable land; 5% permanent crops; 84% other. **Major cities**: (1986 census) Suva (capital) 69,665; Lautoka, 29,000.

• **PEOPLE** **Population:** 868,531 (July 2003 est.). **Nationality:** noun—Fijian(s); adjective—Fijian. **Ethnic groups:** 51% Fijian, 44% Indian. **Languages:** English (official), Fijian, Hindustani. **Religions:** 52% Christian, 38% Hindu, 8% Muslim; Fijians are mainly Christian, Indians are Hindu with Muslim minority.

• **GOVERNMENT** **Type:** republic. **Independence:** Oct. 10, 1970 (from U.K.). **Constitution:** new constitution to allow a non-ethnic Fijian to become prime minister was signed by the president on July 25, 1997 and came into force July 28, 1998. **National holiday:** Independence Day, Oct. 10. **Heads of Government:** Ratu Josefa Holio, head of state (since July 2000); Laisenia Qarase, prime minister (since July 2000). **Structure:** executive; bicameral legislature; judiciary.

• **ECONOMY** **Monetary unit:** Fijian dollar. **Budget:** (2000 est.) ***income:*** $427.9 mil.; ***expend.:*** $531.4 mil. **GDP:** $4.7 bil., $5,500 per capita (2002 est.). **Chief crops:** sugar cane, coconuts, cassava; cattle, pigs, horses; fish. **Natural resources:** timber, fish, gold, copper, offshore oil potential. **Major industries:** sugar, tourism, copra. **Labor force:** 137,000 (1999); 70% agriculture (2001). **Exports:** $442 mil. (f.o.b., 2001); sugar, clothing, gold, processed fish. **Imports**: $642 mil. (f.o.b., 2001); machinery and transport equipment, petroleum products, food, chemicals. **Major trading partners:** ***exports:*** 25.6% Australia, 22.5% U.S., 15.1% U.K.; ***imports:*** 39.8% Australia, 18.7% New Zealand, 5.5% Singapore.

First reported to the West by the Dutch navigator Abel Tasman in 1643, the Fiji Islands were annexed as a British Crown Colony in 1874. Between 1879 and 1916, large numbers of Indian indentured laborers were imported to work on sugar plantations; eventually the original Melanesian inhabitants were outnumbered by persons of Indian descent. Fiji became an independent parliamentary democracy on Oct. 10, 1970, with most land ownership and political power vested in the

Fijian minority. A parliamentary election in 1987 brought the Indian party to power; the elected government was ousted in a military coup, and Lt. Col. Sitiveni Rabuka assumed control of the government on May 21, 1987. On June 2, 1992, he was sworn in as prime minister under a new constitution that guarantees a majority of seats for ethnic Fijians in the national legislature. He was reelected as the head of a coalition government in Feb. 1994.

Yet another constitution (1997) restored Indian political rights, and elections in May 1999 led to formation of a government with Fiji's first Indian prime minister, Mahendra Chaudhry. But in May 2000 a hostage crisis/coup led to the formation in July of an all-new, all-Fijian government which satisfied no one. Elections in 2001 resolved little: the (ethnic Fijian) Fiji United Party won a narrow victory over the (ethnic Indian) Fiji Labour Party but prime minister Lassenia Qarasa appointed only one Indian to his cabinet.

▶FINLAND

Republic of Finland

• GEOGRAPHY **Location:** northern Europe. **Boundaries**: Norway to N, Russian Federation to E, Baltic Sea to S, Gulf of Bothnia, Sweden to W. **Total area**: 130,127 sq. mi. (337,030 sq km). **Coastline**: 700 mi. (1,126 km) excluding islands and coastal indentations. **Comparative area**: slightly smaller than Montana. **Land use:** 7% arable land; 0% permanent crops; 93% other. **Major cities**: (1995) Helsinki (capital) 525,031; Espoo 191,247; Tampere 182,742; Vantaa 166,480; Turku 164,370.

• PEOPLE **Population:** 5,190,785 (July 2003 est.). **Nationality:** noun—Finn(s); adjective—Finnish. **Ethnic groups:** 93% Finn, 6% Swede, Sami, Roma, Tatar. **Languages:** 93.4% Finnish, 5.9% Swedish (both official); small Sami- and Russian-speaking minorities. **Religions:** 89% Evangelical Lutheran, 1% Russian Orthodox.

• GOVERNMENT **Type:** republic. **Independence:** Dec. 6, 1917 (from Russia). **Constitution:** Mar. 1, 2000. **National holiday:** Independence Day, Dec. 6. **Heads of Government:** Tarja Halonen, president (since Mar. 2000); Matti Vanhanen, prime minister (since June 24, 2003). **Structure:** executive; unicameral legislature; judiciary.

• ECONOMY **Monetary unit:** euro. **Budget:** (2000 est.) ***income:*** $36.1 bil.; ***expend.:*** $31 bil. **GDP:** $136.2 bil., $26,000 per capita (2002 est.). **Chief crops:** cereals, sugar beets, potatoes; dairy, cattle; fish. **Natural resources:** timber, copper, zinc, iron ore, silver. **Major industries:** metal manufacturing, shipbuilding, forestry and wood processing (pulp, paper), copper refining. **Labor force:** 2.6 mil. (2000 est.); 32% public services, 22% industry, 14% commerce; 8.5% unemployment (2002). **Exports:** $40.1 bil. (f.o.b., 2002); machinery, chemicals, paper and pulp. **Imports**: $31.8 bil. (f.o.b., 2002); foodstuffs, petroleum and petroleum products, chemicals, transport equipment. **Major trading partners:** ***exports:*** 12% Germany, 10% U.S., 10% U.K.; ***imports:*** 15% Germany, 10% Sweden, 9% Russia.

The Finns originated in the Ural Mountains, and their language is akin to Hungarian and closely similar to Estonian. Migrating from western Siberia to what is now Finland in the eighth century, they drove the indigenous Lapps to northernmost Scandinavia. Finland was conquered and Christianized by the Swedes in the 12th century and in the 16th century became a Swedish grand duchy. Ethnic Swedes make up about 7 percent of the present population. Finland was frequently a battleground in wars between Sweden and Russia; about one-third of the population perished in a war-induced famine in 1696. In 1721 Sweden ceded the province of Viborg to Russia, and all of Finland was taken over by Russia in 1809.

Under the Russians the czars became simultaneously grand dukes of Finland and ruled it as a semiautonomous province. Attempts to "Russify" Finland in the later 19th century provoked great popular resistance. When the Russian empire and then the Russian Republic fell in the 1917 Revolution, Finland lapsed into a fierce civil war between Communists and non-Communists. The "whites" under Baron Gustaf Mannerheim were the victors, and Finland became an independent country for the first time in its history.

In 1939 the U.S.S.R. attacked the Finnish Republic; Finland's resistance in the "Winter War" was heroic but unavailing. Defeated, it was forced to cede Western Keralia to the U.S.S.R. After the German invasion of Russia in 1941, fighting between Finland and Russia resumed; England, but not America, declared war on Finland as a cocombatant with Germany. Russia again defeated Finland in 1944 and obliged the Finns to wage war against the German occupying army in northern Finland; much of the country was devastated.

The terms of the 1944 armistice between Finland and the U.S.S.R. were very harsh: Finland ceded the Petsamo region to the Soviet Union, and thus was cut off from the Barents Sea; the Porkkala peninsula was leased to the Soviets for 50 years, and reparations amounting to 80 percent of Finland's exports were paid in kind. Soviet pressure forced Finland to reject Marshall Plan aid after World War II, but Finland benefited indirectly from the rapid postwar recovery of the Scandinavian region. The gross national product returned to prewar levels by 1947.

Finland's economy had traditionally been centered on timber and other forest products, including pulp and paper, and on small-scale, highly productive agriculture. In the postwar period, industrial development was emphasized; the production of heavy machinery became the country's leading industry.

In 1948 the Finns signed a mutual defense pact with the U.S.S.R., renewed in 1955, 1970, and 1983. Finland's presidents, Juho Paasikivi (1946-56), Urho Kekkonen (1956-81), and Mauno Koivisto (1982-94), although conservative and nationalistic, realized that the country's independence required the avoidance of any appearance of anti-Soviet moves in foreign policy. With the establishment of good Soviet-Finnish relations, the Porkkala peninsula was returned to Finland in 1956. Finland joined the Nordic Council and the United Nations in 1955. It became an associate member of the European Free Trade Association in 1961 and a full member in 1985.

With a strong presidency providing stability despite revolving-door coalition governments in the Eduskunta (parliament), and a prudent foreign policy in the shadow of the U.S.S.R., Finland preserved its free economy and civil liberties. The U.S.S.R.'s collapse struck a heavy blow to Finland's economy; through the 1980's 15-25 percent of Finland's exports had gone to the Soviet Union. Unemployment, recession and currency devaluation were constant reminders of these changes.

In politics the U.S.S.R.'s demise brought a rightward shift, with the first nonsocialist coalition government in 25 years being elected in April 1991 under Esko Aho of the Center party as prime minister. 1994 saw Finland's first direct election of a president with Social Democrat Martti Ahtisaari carrying 54 percent of the vote. In March, the E.U. voted to accept Finland as a member in 1995. Prime Minister Aho announced that Finland would join NATO's "partnership for peace" but not as a step to full membership, preferring to maintain Finland's neutrality.

The Finnish electorate and Parliament approved membership in the E.U. in late 1994. But years of recession and high unemployment led to the toppling of the Center party government in 1995 as the Social Democrats emerged as Finland's largest party, with Paavo Lipponen as prime minister. Presidential elections in 2000 gave victory to Social Democrat Tarja Halonen (Finland's first woman president) over ex-premier and Center Party candidate, Esko Aho. In June 2003, newly-installed prime minister Anneli Jaatteenmaki, who had just led her Center Party in March to a slender victory in parliamentary elections, resigned in a scandal in which she was accused of misusing leaked documents during the election campaign, alleging that Social Democrat Prime Minister Lipponen supported the war againstIraq. DefenseMinister, Matti Vanhanen, replaced her.

▶FRANCE

French Republic

• **Geography Location:** western Europe. **Boundaries**: English Channel to N, Belgium, Luxembourg, Germany, Switzerland, Italy to E, Mediterranean Sea, Spain to S, Atlantic Ocean to W. **Total area**: 176,460 sq. mi. (547,030 sq km). **Coastline**: 2,130 mi. (3,427 km). **Comparative area**: slightly less than twice the size of Colorado. **Land use:** 33% arable land; 2% permanent crops; 65% other. **Major cities**: (1990 census) Paris (capital) 2,152,423; Marseille (Marseilles) 800,000; Lyon (Lyons) 415,487; Toulouse 358,688; Nice 342,439.

• **People Population:** 60,180,529 (July 2003 est.). **Nationality:** noun—Frenchman (men), Frenchwoman (women); adjective—French. **Ethnic groups:** Celtic and Latin with Teutonic, Slavic, North African, Indochinese, and Basque minorities. **Languages:** French (100% of population); rapidly declining regional dialects (Provençal, Breton, Alsatian, Corsican, Catalan, Basque, Flemish). **Religions:** 83-88% Roman Catholic, 2% Protestant, 1% Jewish, 5-10% Muslim (North African workers), 4% unaffiliated.

• **Government Type:** republic. **Constitution:** Sept. 28, 1958, amended concerning election of president in 1962. **National holiday:** Bastille Day, July 14. **Heads of Government:** Jacques Chirac, president (since May 1995); Jean-Pierre Raffarin, prime minister (since May 2002). **Structure:** executive; bicameral legislature; judiciary.

• **Economy Monetary unit:** euro. **Budget:** (2002) ***income:*** $286 bil.; ***expend.:*** $330 bil. **GDP:** $1.54 trillion, $25,700 per capita (2002 est.). **Chief crops:** cereals, sugarbeets, potatoes, wine grapes (western Europe's foremost producer); beef, dairy products; fish. **Natural resources:** coal, iron ore, bauxite, fish, timber. **Major industries:** steel, machinery, chemicals, automobiles. **Labor force:** 26.6 mil. (2001); 71% services, 25% industry, 4% agriculture; 9.1% unemployment (2002 est.). **Exports:** $307.8 bil. (f.o.b., 2000 est.); machinery and transport equipment, chemicals, foodstuffs, agricultural products, iron and steel products. **Imports**: $303.7 bil. (f.o.b., 2002 est.); crude petroleum, machinery and equipment, vehicles, aircraft, chemicals, iron and steel products. **Major trading partners:** ***exports:*** 61% E.U., 9% U.S.; ***imports:*** 59% E.U., 9% U.S.

Pre-Roman France, known as Gaul, was populated by Celtic tribes. The Mediterranean coast, colonized by Phoenician and Greek traders, was conquered by Rome in the second century B.C. The Roman conquest of all of Gaul was carried out by Julius Caesar between 58 and 51 B.C. Gaul became a prosperous and thoroughly Latinized province of the Roman Empire and Christianity was introduced in the first century A.D.

Barbarian invaders including Visigoths, Franks, and Burgundii swept through France in the fifth century. In 486 Clovis, chief of the Franks, unified the country, accepted Christianity, and established the Merovingian dynasty. France was invaded by Muslim Saracens in the seventh century, but in 732 Charles Martel defeated the Saracens. His son, Pepin the Short, overthrew the last Merovingian ruler in 751 and proclaimed himself king. Pepin's son, Charlemagne, greatly expanded his kingdom and was crowned emperor of the West by the pope in 800.

Ninth-century Viking invasions greatly weakened the power of the Carolingians and France broke up into estates, some of them effectively independent countries, ruled by great aristocrats. Among the most important were the duke- doms of Aquitaine and Burgundy and the counties of Flanders, Blois, and Anjou. In 911 the Vikings, who had repeatedly raided the Atlantic coast of France, established the duchy of Normandy.

In 987 the Carolingian dynasty died out in France (although it survived in the Holy Roman Empire) and was replaced by a new line, the Capetians. Steadily expanding in both territory and power from their base in Paris, the Capetians solidified the foundations of the French monarchy. Paris became a great monastic and university city as well as a center of trade and manufacturing. Under the crusader-king Louis IX (St. Louis), France also became an international power.

During the 14th century, the Black Death, peasant rebellions, and the beginning of the Hundred Years' War (1337-1453) with England further weakened the French monarchy. The Norman conquest of England in 1066 had entwined the fortunes of the French and English monarchies, and with the Capetian line in decline, England pursued its claims in France. Henry V of England defeated the French at Agincourt in 1415, and in 1420 Charles IV made Henry heir to the throne of France. Henry's forces were defeated by French armies inspired by Joan of Arc, and in 1429 his claim to the French throne was overturned. In 1435 Burgundy allied itself with France, and in 1453 the English were driven out of France, except for an enclave at Calais.

Louis XI completed the consolidation of France under the French monarchy. France prospered as a center of commerce, industry, agriculture, learning, and culture throughout the 16th century but was disrupted by religious civil wars stemming from the Reformation. The Protestant Henry of Navarre, heir to the throne, was obliged to accept Catholicism before being crowned in 1594; he became founder of the Bourbon monarchy.

The consolidation of power under a highly centralized monarchy continued under Henry's heirs. With a foreign policy shaped by the powerful prime ministers Cardinal Richelieu and Cardinal Mazarin, France under Louis XIII and Louis XIV enhanced its stature in Europe by defeating the Habsburgs in the Thirty Years' War (1618-48). Louis XIV—the Sun King—moved the court from Paris to his new palace at Versailles and presided over the wealthiest and most powerful monarchy in Europe. His persecution of the Huguenots resulted in a great emigration of Protestants from France. A grand alliance of European states thwarted France's expansionist aims on the continent, but France became a major colonial power in North America, controlling Canada and Louisiana (including most of the Mississippi-Missouri valley), and pursued overseas ventures in Africa and Asia as well.

In the mid-18th century, France was weakened internationally by the expensive and fruitless Wars of the Austrian Succession and the Seven Years' War. Under the Treaty of Paris (1763), France ceded control of Canada to Great Britain. The Enlightenment made France a world center of intellectual activity but also led to the questioning of the political and social bases of the French monarchy. An increasingly wealthy but powerless bourgeoisie chafed under the restrictions of an archaic socioeconomic order.

France under Louis XVI supported the American colonies in the Revolutionary War, incurring a large public debt in the process. Combined with unrestrained extravagance on the part of the court and the aristocracy, poverty increased among the rural peasantry and the urban working class, while the bourgeoisie demanded a greater voice in government. These trends came to a head with the storming of the Bastille on July 14, 1789; soon thereafter, the Estates-General took control of the country, and France was in the throes of revolution.

Revolutionary leaders at first allowed Louis XVI to remain on the throne in a limited monarchy, but the king and Marie Antoinette were subsequently tried for treason and executed in 1793. Thousands died during the Reign of Terror which continued until July 1794, ending with the execution of its primary architects, Augustin Robespierre and Georges Danton. The Directory, with five heads of each division of government (1795-99), failed to maintain public order and suffered military reverses in foreign wars in which successive revolutionary governments had been embroiled since 1792. On Nov. 9, 1799, the Directory was overthrown by the Consulate, with Napoleon Bonaparte named first consul.

Napoleon proclaimed himself emperor of France in 1804. He transformed French law through the Code Napoleon and initially expanded the French empire in Europe and the Middle East. Suffering repeated reverses against British naval forces and disastrous losses in his 1812 invasion of Russia, Napoleon was defeated by the British under Wellington at Waterloo in 1815, and the French empire collapsed.

France restored its monarchy in 1815 but not its monarchical absolutism. Charles X, successor to Louis XVIII, was ousted in a coup d'état in 1830 and replaced by the liberal Louis Philippe. The monarchy came to an end in the wave of popular revolt that swept France, along with most of Europe, in 1848; Louis Napoleon (nephew of Bonaparte) became president of the Second Republic. In 1852 he created the Second Empire, ruling as Napoleon III and presiding over a court that set the standards of fashion for the wealthy bourgeois society of 19th-century Europe.

During the 19th century, France again became a major colonial power, acquiring important possessions in North and West Africa and Indochina. It also became a world leader in art, science, and literature and began its slow transformation into a major industrial power. Politically, however, France suffered from endemic weakness. The Second Empire ended disastrously with defeat in the Franco-Prussian War of 1870-71; the Paris Commune, formed during that war, was overthrown with great bloodshed. The Third Republic (1871-1914), despite the glittering pleasures of the Belle Epoque and France's prestige as a world power, was shaken by the Dreyfus Affair of 1894-1906.

France joined with Great Britain and Russia in forming the Triple Entente of 1907, a defensive agreement against the Triple Alliance of Germany, Italy, and the Austro-Hungarian empire. During World War I—in effect a war between these two alliances—France suffered millions of casualties and severe damage in the north. Although its role as a leader of the victorious alliance was confirmed at the Versailles Conference of 1919, France was seriously weakened by the war and played a diminished role as a world power.

France suffered badly in the world depression of the 1930's and could muster neither political nor military energy to offer effective opposition to the rise of Nazi Germany and fascist Italy. France was a participant in the Munich Agreement of 1938, which sealed the fate of central Europe. When World War II broke out in 1939, Hitler initially held off his attack on France, but when it came in May-June 1940, France was swiftly and ignominiously defeated.

During World War II, northern France was under German occupation, while in the south a collaborationist, semifascistic state was organized, with its capital at Vichy. Meanwhile, in London, Gen. Charles de Gaulle rallied the Free French forces, which fought on the Allied side in various campaigns. After the liberation of Paris a "provisional government" of various Resistance groups combined with de Gaulle's supporters drew up a constitution for the Fourth French Republic.

Although it suffered from inherent political weaknesses and often failed to provide stable cabinets, the Fourth Republic presided over postwar recovery, aided by the Marshall Plan; it promoted a mixed socialist-free enterprise economy and instituted social reforms such as women's suffrage and social security. It also led the way toward a united Europe, playing a leading role in the organization of the EEC in 1957. France became a founding member of NATO in 1949.

The Fourth Republic was unable, however, to withstand the strains of the dismantling of France's empire during the postwar wave of decolonization. France's recovery of Indochina in 1945 set off a war of national liberation there that lasted until France withdrew from the colony in 1954. Morocco and Tunisia won their independence in 1956; in Algeria, regarded as part of France itself, France fought on against Front de Liberation Nationale (FLN) rebels.

The Algerian War seriously polarized French public opinion, and, threatened with an army coup, the National Assembly voted in 1958 to grant Pres. Charles de Gaulle emergency powers for six months. De Gaulle outmaneuvered his army backers and negotiated to turn Algeria over to the FLN, a process completed in 1962. Meanwhile he also restored order at home and presided over the drafting of a new constitution that created the Fifth Republic in 1958.

The new constitution created a strong presidency, with powers to name the premier and the Council of Ministers and to preside over their meetings. The legislature was required to give priority to government initiatives and lacked authority over national defense, education, labor, and local government. Under the governments of premiers Michel Debré and Georges Pompidou, the Gaullist regime further advanced modernization of French industry and greatly benefited French agriculture by expanding the Common Market to include agricultural goods.

De Gaulle followed an independent foreign policy, pursuing European integration as well as closer relations with the Communist bloc and the Third World. He blocked British entry into the Common Market; developed an independent nuclear force, refusing to sign nuclear test-ban and nonproliferation treaties; pursued a historic rapprochement with Germany; recognized the People's Republic of China; established a leading French role in the former French colonies of Africa; and withdrew French forces from the NATO military command.

Reelected president in 1965, after a runoff election against the Socialist-Communist alliance candidate François Mitterrand, de Gaulle continued his independent policy until student riots in early 1968 provoked police repression, which led to further popular support for the students, especially in Paris. De Gaulle dissolved the National Assembly and, in an emotional campaign on behalf of national stability, won a large electoral majority. In 1969, however, following minor political reverses, de Gaulle resigned as president.

The elections of June 1969 gave the presidency to former premier Georges Pompidou, who died in office in April 1974. He was succeeded by the Independent Republican Valery Giscard d'Estaing, who served until May 1981. During these years the Gaullist heritage was developed and consolidated. In foreign policy the movement toward European unity continued with the development of the European Parliament and, in a reversal of policy in 1973, French support for British membership in the EEC. The economic shock of the OPEC price rises of 1973-74 led to a decision to stress new industrial ventures in high-technology fields, symbolized by the Anglo-French Concorde supersonic transport.

The 1970's were years of social ferment, with a relaxation of divorce laws and the legalization of contraception advertisements and abortion, and a decline in church membership and attendance. In 1978 disillusionment stemming from inflation and social difficulties under Giscard d'Estaing brought about a leftist electoral victory for the first time under the Fifth Republic.

The Gaullist era came to an end in 1981, when Socialist François Mitterrand defeated Giscard in a presidential election. He dissolved the National Assembly and led his party to an absolute majority. Socialist premier Pierre Mauroy formed a government which pursued an aggressive program of nationalization of banks and major industries and reform of local government. Continued economic difficulties led to a loss of popular support for Mitterrand's policies. In the elections of 1986, Jacques Chirac's coalition of Gaullists and Giscardists won an almost absolute majority in the National Assembly, and Chirac became premier—the first time since 1958 that the president and the premier were of opposing parties. An accommodation was worked out in which Mitterrand concentrated on foreign affairs, and Chirac on domestic matters. Mitterrand oversaw a restoration of French military cooperation with NATO and a continuation of Franco-German cooperation.

At home Chirac and his party reversed Mitterrand's policy of nationalization, cut taxes, and brought about a significant reduction in the inflation rate. Chirac ran for president against Mitterrand in 1988 but was defeated. Mitterrand's reelection with over 54 percent of the vote carried his Socialist party to a near majority in the assembly, where they constructed a coalition government. Persistent 9 percent unemployment and the growing appeal of Jean-Marie Le Pen's anti-immigrant National Front brought a cabinet shake-up in May 1991 and the designation of France's first female premier, Edith Cresson.

But the shake-up did nothing to stem voter dissatisfaction with the governing Socialists. Elections to regional councils in 1992 saw the Socialist vote drop to 18 percent, but not to the benefit of the center-right coalition Union for France, which gained only one-third of the vote. The National Front and the two rival "green" parties together gained 28 percent of the vote.

Mitterand strongly supported U.N. intervention in the Balkans and France's participation in the Maastricht Treaty. But not even the formidable Mitterand could prevent the Socialist rout in the March 1993 assembly elections. The Rally for France won the most lopsided victory in the republic's history, carrying 460 (of 577) seats while the left took only 93. Rejecting calls for his resignation, Mitterand reasserted his constitutional prerogatives in defense and foreign policy, vowing to stay on until 1995, when his unprecedented 14-year presidency ended as Jacques Chirac won over Lionel Jospin.

Pledged to tax and spending cuts and continued dismantling of state enterprises, Chirac and his followers met with limited success as unemployment reached its highest level ever. A giant truckers' strike blocked French highways without government action, and cutting social welfare spending (to meet the E.U.'s Euro conditions) proved elusive. So, seeking a public mandate for France's participation in the Euro, Chirac dissolved the Assembly a year early. But the result was yet another French "cohabitation": the left coalition took 319 seats and Lionel Jospin became prime minister. In May 1999 the Jospin government narrowly survived a censure motion over its handling of separatist unrest on Corsica. In a referendum in Sept. 2000, voters—only 30 percent of the electorate—gave their approval to reducing the term of the president from seven to five years.

Jospin's run for the presidency ended in embarrassment as he finished third to Pres. Chirac and the unimportant troublemaker Jean-Marie LePen, Chirac polling 82 percent in the run-off. In June Chirac's right wing coalition took 355 of the National Assembly's 577 seats, promising to support "law and order," cut taxes, and privatize the elephantine state pension system. In 2003 Chirac played a leading role in condemning the U.S.-led invasion of Iraq.

▶GABON

Gabonese Republic

• **GEOGRAPHY** **Location:** western coast of Africa. **Boundaries**: Equatorial Guinea to NW, Cameroon to N, Congo to E and S, Atlantic Ocean to W. **Total area**: 103,348 sq. mi. (267,670 sq km). **Coastline**: 550 mi. (885 km). **Comparative area**: slightly smaller than Colorado. **Land use:** 1% arable land; 1% permanent crops; 98% other. **Major cities**: (1993 census) Libreville (capital) 419,596; Port-Gentil 78,225; Masuku 75,000 (1988).

• **PEOPLE** **Population:** 1,321,560 (July 2003 est.). **Nationality:** noun—Gabonese (sing., pl.); adjective—Gabonese. **Ethnic groups:** Bantu tribes, including four major tribal groupings (Fang, Nzebi, Obamba, Bapounou); 154,000 other Africans and Europeans, including 10,700 French and 11,000 of dual nationality. **Languages:** French (official),

Fang, Myene, Bateke, Bapounou/Eschira, Bandjabi. **Religions:** 55-75% Christian, less than 1% Muslim, remainder indigenous beliefs.

• **Government** **Type:** republic; multi-party presidential regime since 1990. **Independence:** Aug. 17, 1960 (from France). **Constitution:** Mar. 14, 1991 **National holidays:** Founding of the Gabonese Democratic Party, Mar. 12 (1968). **Heads of Government:** El Hadj Omar Bongo, president (since Dec. 1967); Jean-François Ntoutoume-Emane, prime minister (since Jan. 1999). **Structure:** executive; bicameral legislature; independent judiciary.

• **Economy** **Monetary unit:** Communauté Financière Africaine (CFA) franc. **Budget:** (2002 est.) ***income:*** $1.8 bil.; ***expend.:*** $1.8 bil. **GDP:** $7 bil., $5,700 per capita (2002 est.). **Chief crops:** coffee, cocoa, sugar; rubber; wood; cattle; fishing. **Natural resources:** crude oil, manganese, uranium, gold, timber, iron ore. **Major industries:** petroleum, manganese, food, beverages. **Labor force:** 600,000; 60% agriculture, 15% industry, 25% services; 21% unemployment (1997). **Exports:** $2.6 bil. (f.o.b., 2002 est.); 77% crude oil, wood, manganese. **Imports**: $1.1 bil. (f.o.b., 2002 est.); machinery and equipment, foodstuffs, chemicals, petroleum products, construction materials. **Major trading partners:** ***exports:*** 50% U.S., 17% France, 8% China; ***imports:*** 65% France, 5% U.S., 4% Belgium.

Gabon, an equatorial nation largely covered by dense rain forest, is inhabited by a highly diverse mixture of people who migrated into the region over the course of the past 700 years; the now-dominant Fang arrived during the 19th century. The first Europeans to reach the area were the Portuguese in the 15th century; they were followed by Dutch, French, and British traders in the 16th century. All engaged in the slave trade.

France established an informal protectorate in 1839-41 and set about suppressing the slave trade. In 1849 a group of freed slaves settled near the American mission station at Baraka and renamed the town Libreville. France established a colonial administration in 1903 and in 1910 made it part of French Equatorial Africa. The territory became an important base of Free French activity during World War II, and in 1946 Gen. Charles de Gaulle granted French citizenship to the territory's inhabitants, and local power was devolved upon advisory assemblies. Gabon became fully independent on Aug. 17, 1960.

Gabon has remained politically stable under its 1961 constitution. Gabon's first president, Leon M'Ba, was briefly deposed by a military coup in 1964 but quickly reinstated with the aid of French troops. He died in 1967 and was succeeded by the vice president, Omar Bongo who combined all political parties into the Gabonese Democratic party in 1968; he was elected president in his own right in 1975, was reelected in each subsequent election through 1998 (which he won with a highly dubious 67 percent). Despite initial resistance from the government, Gabon has recently made the transition to multiparty democracy, thereby attracting more foreign investment. Bongo's Gabonese Democratic party remains in power.

Although its per capita income is much higher than almost every African nation, there is substantial income inequality and a good deal of poverty in Gabon.

▶THE GAMBIA
Republic of The Gambia

• **Geography** **Location:** narrow territory around Gambia River on northwestern coast of Africa. **Boundaries**: Senegal to N, E, and S, Atlantic Ocean to W. **Total area**: 4,363 sq. mi. (11,300 sq km). **Coastline**: 50 mi. (80 km). **Comparative area**: slightly less than twice the size of Delaware. **Land use:** 20% arable land; 1% permanent crops;79% other. **Major cities**: (1993 census) Banjul (capital) 43,326; Kombo St. Mary (surrounding urban area) 228,214.

• **People** **Population:** 1,501,050 (July 2003 est.). **Nationality:** noun—Gambian(s); adjective—Gambian. **Ethnic groups:** 42% Mandinka, 18% Fula, 16% Wolof, 10% Jola, 9% Serahuli, 1% non-African. **Languages:** English (official), Mandinka, Wolof, Fula, and others. **Religions:** 90% Muslim, 9% Christian, 1% indigenous beliefs.

• **Government** **Type:** republic under multiparty democratic rule. **Independence:** Feb. 18, 1965 (from U.K.). **Constitution:** Apr. 24, 1970, (suspended July 1994); rewritten, approved and reestablished in Jan. 1997. **National holiday:** Independence Day, Feb. 18. **Head of Government:** Colonel Yahya Jammeh, president (since July 1994). **Structure:** following the coup on July 22, 1994 all elective officers were dissolved; military leaders have promised to return control to a democratically-elected government.

• **Economy** **Monetary unit:** dalasi. **Budget:** (2001 est.) ***income:*** $90.5 mil.; ***expend.:*** $80.9 mil. **GDP:** $2.6 bil., $1,800 per capita (2002 est.). **Chief crops:** peanuts, millet, sorghum, rice, maize; cattle, goats, sheep. **Natural resources:** fish. **Major industries:** agricultural processing, tourism, beverages. **Labor force:** 400,000; 75% agriculture, 19% industry, commerce, and services, 6.1% government. **Exports:** $138 mil. (f.o.b., 2002); peanuts and peanut products, fish, cotton. **Imports**: $225 mil. (f.o.b., 2002 est.); foodstuffs, manufacturing, raw materials. **Major trading partners:** ***exports:*** Benelux, Brazil, U.K.; ***imports:*** China, Senegal, U.K.

Thirty miles across at its widest point, and 295 miles long, the serpentine republic of The Gambia was gerrymandered into being out of competing French and British colonial interests. Once the westernmost part of the kingdom of Mali, The Gambia was visited by the Portuguese in 1455. In 1588, they sold British traders exclusive rights to the Gambia River, and in 1660 British merchants established a trading fort. England and France struggled for 200 years to gain political and economic control over the territory, but in 1783 the French ceded to Great Britain possession of The Gambia. Its present boundaries were established in 1889 when it became a British Crown Colony. Between 1901 and 1906, legislative councils were established to encourage self-government, and slavery was abolished.

After World War II the country moved quickly toward constitutional government, achieving independence as a constitutional monarchy within the British Commonwealth of Nations in 1965. The Gambia became a republic on Apr. 24, 1970, and it had the same president, Sir Dawda K. Jawara, until 1994.

In 1994, Yahya Jammeh, a 29-year-old lieutenant fresh from a military police training course in the United States, led a bloodless coup deposing the government of Pres. Jawara. Jammeh pledged to restore civilian government "as soon as we have set things right." Later that year the United Kingdom, the United States, and the European Union cut off all economic and military aid pending a return to democracy. Pres. Jammeh was re-elected Oct. 2001 in a vote deemed fair by outside observers. He granted amnesty to Jawara, who returned from exile in 2002.

▶GEORGIA

• **GEOGRAPHY** **Location:** west and central Transcaucasia between Asia and Europe. **Boundaries**: Russian Federation to N and E, Azerbaijan, Armenia to S, Turkey to SW, Black Sea to W. **Total area**: 26,911 sq. mi. (69,700 sq km). **Coastline**: Black Sea. **Comparative area**: slightly smaller than South Carolina. **Land use:** 11% arable land; 4% permanent crops; 85% other. **Major cities**: (1994 est.) Tbilisi (capital) 1.3 mil.; Kutaisi 235,000; Rustavi 159,000; Batumi 136,000; Sukhumi 121,000.
• **PEOPLE** **Population:** 4,934,413 (July 2003 est.). **Nationality:** noun—Georgian(s); adjective—Georgian. **Ethnic groups:** 70.1% Georgian, 8.1% Armenian, 6.3% Russian, 5.7% Azeri, 3% Ossetian, 1.8% Abkhaz. **Languages:** 71% Georgian (official), 9% Russian, 7% Armenian, 6% Azeri. **Religions:** 65% Georgian Orthodox, 11% Muslim, 10% Russian Orthodox, 8% Armenian Apostolic.
• **GOVERNMENT** **Type:** republic. **Independence:** Apr. 9, 1991 (from Soviet Union). **Constitution:** Oct. 17, 1995. **National holiday:** Independence Day, May 26. **Heads of Government:** Eduard A. Shevardnadze, president (since 1992); Otar Patsatsia, prime minister. **Structure:** executive; unicameral legislature; judiciary.
• **ECONOMY** **Monetary unit:** lari. **Budget:** (2001 est.) ***income:*** $499 mil; ***expend.:*** $554 mil. **GDP:** $15 bil., $3,100 per capita (2002 est.). **Chief crops:** citrus, grapes, tea, vegetables. **Natural resources:** forests, hydropower, manganese. **Major industries:** steel, aircraft, machine tools. **Labor force:** 2.1 mil. (2001); 20% industry and construction, 40% agriculture and forestry, 40% other; 17% unemployment (2001 est.). **Exports:** $515 mil. (2002); citrus fruits, tea, wine. **Imports**: $750 mil. (2002); fuel, grain and other foods, machinery and parts. **Major trading partners:** Russia, Turkey, Germany, Azerbaijan.

Georgia is a land of rugged natural beauty, renowned for its famous war heroes and its hospitality. Georgia's most famous son, Iosif Djugashvili, known as Josef Stalin, was born in the mountain village of Gori in 1879. The name of Georgia derives from the Persian name for the native people, Gorj.

An independent state was founded in the fourth century B.C. following the conquest of the Persian Empire by Alexander III. Christianity became the state religion in the 4th century A.D. Both the Georgian language and the capital city of Tbilisi date from the fifth century A.D. The Georgian people, whose main occupation was cattle raising and agriculture, began to develop feudal states in the sixth century.

Georgia's later history, however, is one of almost continuous foreign domination. In the 12th century, Georgia gained independence from the Persian Empire, but it came under Mongol rule in 1236. For centuries Georgia was a battleground between Turks and Persians, and the territory was ultimately divided into principalities, some under the control of Persia and some under Turkey. In 1801, the Persian principalities were absorbed into the Russian empire, and by the end of the century the remaining Georgian state under Turkish domination was annexed to Russia.

Once the Russian Empire collapsed in 1917 with the Bolshevik revolution, independent Georgia was once again proclaimed in May 1918. It was dominated by Mensheviks (from the Russian word "minority," as opposed to Bolshevik, meaning "majority"), whose hold on power was short-lived. Although the Soviet Union and Georgia signed a treaty in May 1920 agreeing on their respective borders, the Soviet Red Army came into Georgia and forcibly incorporated it into the Soviet Union as a Socialist republic in early 1921. In 1922 it was made part of the Transcaucasian Soviet Federal Socialist Republic with Armenia and Azerbaijan, and in 1936 it became one of the U.S.S.R.'s union republics.

The Georgians have always been fiercely nationalistic, even in the face of the U.S.S.R.'s "one Soviet people" policy. Georgian pride was evident from the first demonstrations against "russification" in 1956, and again in 1978 when the rewritten U.S.S.R. constitution attempted to weaken the status of Georgian language. In 1988, during Gorbachev's policy of "glasnost," or openness, great numbers of Georgians began to call for sovereignty.

Even as Georgia fought for its independence from the U.S.S.R., the autonomous provinces of Abkhazia, Adzharia, and South Ossetia began fighting for independence from Georgia. Tensions continue to run high in Adzharia, where allegiances to Islam frighten many in Christian Georgia, and in South Ossetia, which is struggling to end its association with Georgia and to unite with North Ossetia in the Russian Federation.

But the greatest conflict raged in Abkhazia, the home region of Zviad Gamsakhurdia, who was elected the country's first president in May 1991, but ousted from office seven months later. Fighting between the Georgian army and troops loyal to Gamsakhurdia continued from 1991 to 1993, resulting in more than 2,000 casualties, including Gamsakhurdia, until Pres. Eduard Shevardnadze persuaded Parliament to give him emergency powers to quell the insurgency.

His political power consolidated, Shevardnadze began to renew ties to Russia. In 1994 he agreed to a cooperation pact to increase Russia's military influence in his country and, over the objections of the opposition National Radical party, Parliament ratified Georgia's membership in the Commonwealth of Independent States.

In Aug. 1995 Parliament overwhelmingly approved a new "strong president" constitution. And in Nov. 1995 Shevardnadze easily won election to a new five-year term, while his two-party coalition captured close to 80 percent of the seats in Parliament. But continued instability in Abkhazia, the presence of Russian troops, and several assasination attempts on Shevardnadze left future development in doubt. Still, Shevardnadze easily won reelection in April 2000 and in June, Georgia became the WTO's 137th member. After firing his entire cabinet in Nov. 2001, Shevardnadze announced that U.S. troops (to reach a total of 1,200) were arriving (Apr. 2002) to train Georgian troops in the struggle against Muslim separatists.

▶GERMANY

Federal Republic of Germany

• **GEOGRAPHY** **Location:** central Europe. **Boundaries**: Denmark, Baltic Sea to N, Poland, Czech Republic to E, Austria, Switzerland to S, France, Luxembourg, Belgium, Netherlands to W, North Sea to NW. **Total area**: 137,803 sq. mi. (356,910 sq km). **Coastline**: 1,385 mi. (2,389 km). **Comparative area**: slightly smaller than Montana. **Land use:** 34% arable land; 1% permanent crops; 65% other. **Major cities**: (1994) Berlin (capital) 3,477,900, Hamburg 1,703,800; München (Munich) 1,251,100; Köln (Cologne) 963,300; Frankfurt 656,200.

• **PEOPLE** **Population:** 82,398,326 (July 2003 est.). **Nationality:** noun—German(s); adjective—German. **Ethnic groups:** 91.5% German, 2.4% Turkish. **Languages:** German. **Religions:** 34% Protestant, 34% Roman Catholic, 3.7% Muslim, 28.3% unaffiliated or other.
• **GOVERNMENT** **Type:** federal republic. **Constitution:** May 23, 1949; provisional constitution known as Basic Law became constitution of reunited German state Oct. 3, 1990. **National holiday:** German Unity Day, Oct. 3. **Heads of Government:** Johannes Rau, president (since July 1999); Gerhard Schröder, chancellor (since Oct. 1988). **Structure:** president (titular head of state); bicameral parliament—Bundesrat (Federal Council, upper house), Bundestag (National Assembly, lower house); independent judiciary.
• **ECONOMY** **Monetary unit:** euro. **Budget:** (2001 est.) ***income:*** $802 bil.; ***expend.:*** $825 bil. **GDP:** $2.184 trillion, $26,600 per capita (2002 est.). **Chief crops:** wheat, barley, rye, potatoes, sugar beets, fruit; cattle, pigs, poultry. **Natural resources:** iron ore, coal, potash, timber. **Major industries:** among world's largest producers of iron, steel, coal, cement, chemicals, machinery, vehicles, machine tools, electronics, food and beverages; shipbuilding; textiles. **Labor force:** 41.9 mil. (2001 est.); 33.4% industry, 2.8% agriculture, 63.8% services. **Exports:** $608 bil. (f.o.b., 2002 est.); machinery, vehicles, chemicals. **Imports:** $487.3 bil. (f.o.b., 2002 est.); machinery, vehicles, chemicals, foodstuffs. **Major trading partners:** ***exports:*** 11.1% France, 10.6% U.S., 8.4% U.K.; ***imports:*** 9.4% France, 8.4% Netherlands, 8.3% U.S.

The ancient tribes of Germany resisted Roman conquest with mixed success. German federated troops served in the Roman legions, and Germanic invasions contributed to the fall of Rome. Most of Germany was united within the empire of Charlemagne. Divided among his three sons in 843, the empire's eastern regions became the heart of the Germanies. The Holy Roman Empire, founded in 962, gave some unity to the politically fragmented German territories, but its boundaries included more than Germany, and some Germans remained outside it. But that unity was fragile; the Holy Roman emperor was a feudal overlord rather than a ruler, and hundreds of separate political bodies coexisted within the imperial domain. Along the North Sea and Baltic coasts, the Hanseatic League controlled much of the commerce of northern Europe.

With the Reformation in the 16th century, religious divisions added to Germany's existing political fragmentation and local allegiances. The Thirty Years War (1618-48) resulted in the virtual extinction of the Holy Roman Empire and left Germany without even a shadow of unity.

After the Napoleonic Wars, in which much of Germany was conquered by France, the Congress of Vienna (1814-15) sanctioned the creation of a German League to succeed the Holy Roman Empire. The league consisted of 39 states, including five substantial kingdoms and the German parts of the Austrian empire. Prussia, one of the five kingdoms, had already risen to prominence under Frederick the Great in the 18th century. In a series of wars in the mid-19th century, Prussia conquered the other German states; after defeating France in the Franco-Prussian War of 1870-71, Prussia declared the establishment of the German empire. Under its chancellor, Otto von Bismarck, Germany became a major European power in the late 19th century, with a booming industrial economy, flourishing agriculture, a small colonial empire, and growing military might.

The German Empire reached its height under Kaiser Wilhelm II on the eve of World War I. Germany's disastrous defeat in that war was compounded by the harsh terms of the Treaty of Versailles (1919), which stripped Germany of its colonial empire, and returned part of Schleswig to Denmark, Alsace-Lorraine to France, and part of Prussia to Poland.

The Weimar Republic, established in 1919, gradually overcame economic difficulties, including ruinous inflation, to achieve a measure of recovery in the 1920's. The republic was disrupted by labor strife, political fragmentation, and the rise of armed extremist political movements on both left and right. After the onset of the world economic depression in 1929, Adolf Hitler's National Socialist movement gained increasing power, both at the polls and through open thuggery against its opponents. Hitler's appointment as chancellor in 1933 effectively put an end to the Weimar Republic as a functioning democracy.

The onset of World War II in Europe was presaged by Hitler's annexation of Austria and Czechoslovakia in 1938 and precipitated by the German invasion of Poland in 1939. Early military successes gave Germany control of most of Europe, but the eventual victory of the Allied powers in 1945 left the country exhausted and in ruins. Much of the Jewish population of Germany, and of other territories under German control, had been killed during the Holocaust. German cities were reduced to rubble, and a quarter of the country's homes were uninhabitable. Famine and fuel shortages added to the general misery.

Politically, Germany had essentially ceased to exist in 1945. The Allies divided the country into four zones of occupation, with a similar four-part division of Berlin. As the Cold War rift between the Western powers and the U.S.S.R. intensified during the late 1940's, so too the division of Germany hardened. In 1948 the U.S.S.R. imposed a blockade on West Berlin; the city was supplied by a massive airlift from the West for several months. In 1949 two Germanies were created: the German Democratic Republic in the Russian zone in the east, and the Federal Republic of Germany in the Allied zone in the west.

The Federal Republic was largely the creation of one man, Konrad Adenauer. A veteran pre-Hitler politician, he founded the Federation of Christian Democratic Parties (CDU-CSU) in 1945, and as president of the Parliamentary Council formed during the occupation, he virtually wrote the new constitution for West Germany. In the first elections held in the Federal Republic (August 1949), the "bourgeois coalition" led by the CDU-CSU won a parliamentary majority in the Bundestag, and Adenauer became chancellor, a post he held for 14 years. In 1951 the Western powers granted the new state autonomy in foreign affairs, and recognized its full sovereignty in 1954.

Even before the fighting in Germany subsided in 1945, the Soviet Air Force brought Walter Ulbricht, the exiled leader of the German Communist party, back to the U.S.S.R.'s zone of occupation in Germany. Backed by 20 Soviet divisions, Ulbricht and the party commenced the communization of the eastern zone. After local and state elections embarrassed the Communists, Stalin and Ulbricht forced all other parties into the National Front. With no other electoral lists permitted, voters gave a 99.7 percent approval to the

National Front in the first elections to East Germany's "People's Chamber" in 1950.

While Ulbricht attempted to collectivize agriculture and plan industrial development in the eastern zone, the Soviet Union extracted heavy reparations payments, bringing on an acute economic crisis. In June 1953, shortly after Stalin's death, strikes and riots erupted. The U.S.S.R. renounced further reparation payments and declared East Germany a sovereign state.

In foreign affairs Adenauer relied heavily on friendship with the United States and reconciliation with France. He also supported European integration: In 1951 West Germany joined both the Council of Europe and the Coal and Steel Community. West Germany was admitted to NATO in 1955 and in 1957 became one of the six founding members of the EEC.

In domestic affairs the political alliance between Adenauer and Ludwig Erhard led to political stability and the creation of a marketdriven economy. With a currency reform program and Marshall Plan aid in place by 1948 under occupation administration, the stage was set for Germany's "economic miracle" of the 1950's. Between 1949 and 1964, industrial production increased by 60 percent and gross national product tripled, while unemployment fell to 1 percent, even as millions of refugees from East Germany were integrated into the West German economy.

In 1963 Erhard succeeded Adenauer as chancellor. Economic growth slowed to an annual 3 percent rate, but West Germany was already one of Europe's strongest economic powers, even providing jobs for hundreds of thousands of "guest workers" from southern Europe and Turkey.

By 1963 East Germany had become the second-largest industrial power in Eastern Europe, and in 1968 it surpassed Czechoslovakia in output. A significant shift of labor to industry reduced the farm population to under 20 percent of total population by 1960. Though farming became mechanized, it remained relatively inefficient.

Although East Germany enjoyed prestige within the Eastern bloc as an industrial power, the steady stream of emigrants to West Germany told a different story. After a renewed collectivization policy was implemented in 1960, the stream became a flood, and East Germany responded by building the Berlin Wall. The wall was a visible sign of political failure, but it did slow the stream of emigration to a trickle.

Erhard resigned in 1966 when his coalition fell apart over the issue of a planned tax increase. He was succeeded by Kurt Kiesinger, who presided over a historic "great coalition" of Christian Democrats and Social Democrats. Under Willi Brandt (who served as deputy chancellor and foreign minister), the Social Democrats had shifted their orientation from a Marxist party to a reformist, market-oriented stance.

Elections in 1969 produced a majority for the coalition headed by the Social Democrats who governed until 1982. Brandt succeeded Kiesinger and pursued an Ostpolitik ("opening to the east"), regularizing relations with East Germany, signing a nonagression pact with the U.S.S.R., and recognizing the border between East Germany and Poland. But domestically, West Germany suffered serious dislocations from the OPEC oil price increases of the early 1970's; inflation reached almost 8 percent. Revelations that a Brandt aide was an East German spy led to his replacement as chancellor by Helmut Schmidt in 1974.

Schmidt continued Brandt's eastern policy but also pursued improved relations with the West. Economic difficulties persisted, however, and Schmidt's government fell in 1982. The Christian Democrats returned to power under chancellor Helmut Kohl. The improvement of the world economy in the 1980's led to economic recovery in Germany, boosting Kohl's popularity. Meanwhile, in East Germany an aging Ulbricht was replaced in May 1971 as party first secretary by Erich Honecker, who also became head of state in 1976. Honecker completed state ownership of all industry in 1972.

After Brandt's Ostpolitik, the two Germanies grew closer, at least economically. East Germany's trade with West Germany gave it access to the EC. However, East Germany resisted Mikhail Gorbachev's reform policies in the 1980's, trying to establish itself as a model of old-style communism in Eastern Europe. In the fall of 1989 tens of thousands of East Germans fled to West Germany through Hungary and Czechoslovakia, triggering a series of dramatic demonstrations and the dismantling of the Berlin Wall in October. Honecker's government collapsed as the momentum for unification became unstoppable. In March 1990 Christian Democrat Lothar de Maizière was elected prime minister on a unification platform.

In July an economic and fiscal union of the Germanies was completed, and in September the victorious wartime allies (the U.S., U.S.S.R., U.K., and France) agreed to a peace treaty that paved the way for political unification. On October 3, six regions of the former East Germany entered the Federal Republic as member states; eleven days later the Christian Democrats won elections in five of them, the Social Democrats winning one.

In December 1990, all-German elections to the Bundestag were held for the first time in 58 years. The CDU-CSU and the Free Democrats won 398 seats, the Social Democrats 239. Helmut Kohl was sworn in as chancellor Jan. 17, 1991. In June Parliament voted to move the capital back to Berlin.

In the years following unification, euphoria gave way to sober realism; economic restructuring would take many years, because the economy of East Germany proved to be in even worse shape than anyone imagined. Related to these economic woes was the wave of violent attacks by radical nationalists and neo-Nazi gangs upon immigrants and asylum seekers (who numbered over 2 million). In 1993 the government banned several violent groups and amended Germany's liberal asylum law to prevent refugees seeking economic betterment from entering the country.

In the Bundestag elections of 1994, the Kohl coalition (CDU, CSU, and FD)maintained its majority over the opposition, led by the Social Democrats. Kohl was reelected chancellor, for a fourth time, as the economy remained strong. By 1996, however, unemployment was at an all-time postwar high and the Kohl government announced that the budget deficit required sweeping spending cuts, especially in social welfare programs. The economy worsened in 1997 and rebounded in 1998 but not enough to give Kohl another electoral victory as he lost to the Social Democrats and their leader, Gerhard Schröder.

On Oct. 27, the Bundestag approved new Chancellor Schröder's "red-green" cabinet whose personnel and program appeared further left than Schröder. By March 1999, finance minister La-Fontaine, an old-style SD, had been replaced by "moderate" Hans Eichel, financial markets responding positively. Already, in the previous month, the government coalition lost control of the state government of Hesse, thereby losing its majority in the Bundesrat, the upper house whose members are elected by the states, apparently dooming the government's plan to loosen citizenship restrictions (a major and controversial plank in the "red-green" platform). Schröder's attempts to introduce an austerity budget led to further electoral setbacks in state elections in Sep. 1999.

The series of large Christian Democratic advances in state and municipal elections were brought to a halt with the revelations, at the end of 1999, of massive illegal contributions to the CDs over the years 1982–1998, leading to heavy fines upon the CDU and the ruin of the reputations of numerous CD politicians, preeminently of former chancellor Helmut Kohl. In return for a fine of 300,000 marks, prosecutors dropped charges against Kohl in 2001. In November the Schröder government narrowly (336-330) survived a vote of confidence over sending 4,000 troops to Afghanistan, but Schröder won re-election in Sept. 2002 in large part because of his opposition to a U.S. strike at Iraq. In 2003, faced with an enduring recession, growing unemployment and budget deficits, Schroeder proposed a reform package to cut unemployment benefits and government pensions, ease job-protection regulations and the Social Democrats grudgingly agreed to back him.

▶GHANA

Republic of Ghana

• **GEOGRAPHY** **Location:** western Africa. **Boundaries**: Burkina Faso to N, Togo to E, Gulf of Guinea to S, Ivory Coast to W. **Total area**: 92,100 sq. mi. (238,540 sq km). **Coastline**: 335 mi. (539 km). **Comparative area**: slightly smaller than Oregon. **Land use:** 16% arable land; 7% permanent crops; 77% other. **Major cities**: (1988 est.) Accra (capital) 949,113; Kumasi 385,192; Tamale 151,069; Tema 109,975; Sekondi-Takoradi 103,653.

• **PEOPLE** **Population:** 20,467,747 (July 2003 est.). **Nationality:** noun—Ghanaian(s); adjective—Ghanaian. **Ethnic groups:** 98.5% black African (major groups—44% Akan, 16% Moshi-Dagomba, 13% Ewe, 8% Ga), 1.5% European and other. **Languages:** English (official), Akan, Moshi-Dagomba, Ewe, Ga. **Religions:** 63% Christian, 21% indigenous beliefs, 16% Muslim.

• **GOVERNMENT** **Type:** constitutional democracy. **Independence:** Mar. 6, 1957 (from U.K.). **Constitution:** Apr. 28, 1992. **National holiday:** Independence Day, Mar. 6. **Head of Government:** John Agyekum Kufuor (since Jan. 2001). **Structure:** executive; unicameral legislature; judiciary.

• **ECONOMY** **Monetary unit:** new cedi. **Budget:** (2001 est.) ***income:*** $1.603 bil.; ***expend.:*** $1.975 bil. **GDP:** $42.5 bil., $2,100 per capita (2002 est.). **Chief crops:** cocoa, rice, coffee, timber. **Natural resources:** gold, timber, industrial diamonds, bauxite, manganese. **Major industries:** mining, lumbering, light manufacturing. **Labor force:** 9 million; 60% agriculture and fishing, 15% industry, 25% services; 20% unemployed (1997). **Exports:** $2.2 bil. (f.o.b., 2002); gold, cocoa, timber, tuna. **Imports**: $2.8 bil. (f.o.b., 2002); capital equipment, petroleum, consumer goods, food. **Major trading partners:** ***exports:*** Netherlands, U.S., U.K.; ***imports:*** U.K., Nigeria, U.S.

The connection between modern Ghana and the 10th century Ghana empire of southern Mali is obscure. In the 13th century, the Akan around the city of Kumasi were trading gold and other commodities with the Mande to the north. The number of competing states in the region grew rapidly after European contact. The Asante empire began in the early 17th century under Osei Tutu. By 1750 it controlled the northern part of Ghana, and by 1820 it had brought the coastal Fante empire, with its access to the European trade, under its control.

The Portuguese first explored the area, on Africa's west coast, in 1471, naming it the Gold Coast because of its gold deposits and its reserves of "black gold"—slaves. In the 16th and 17th centuries, the British, Danes, and Dutch established slave trading posts there, which is where most American slaves came from. The slave trade ended in the 1850's, and the British gained control of the Gold Coast, making it a protectorate in 1871 and a colony in 1886. Great Britain gave the colony a new constitution in 1946 under which Africans held a majority of seats in the legislature. Kwame Nkrumah became prime minister of the colony in 1952 and the first prime minister of the nation when it became independent in 1960.

At independence, Ghana boasted Africa's largest man-made deep-water port and the most productive gold mine in the world, and it was the second largest producer of industrial diamonds. Nkrumah began to court Communist bloc nations and exert absolute authority. In January 1964 all opposition parties were outlawed. A military council seized power in February 1966 and ousted Nkrumah.

Civilian governments ran the country briefly, but in 1981, Flt. Lt. Jerry Rawlings took power in a coup and ruled until 2000. Ghana suffered severe economic problems throughout the 1970's and 1980's, and many of Ghana's people left for Nigeria to find work. In 1983 Nigeria returned more than one million of these migrant workers, increasing Ghana's economic woes.

After five years of stagnation, Ghana achieved a 6 percent economic growth rate in 1989 under a World Bank restructuring program. But political unrest remained. A new constitution was approved in an April 1992 referendum, and in November Rawlings received 58 percent of the vote. His National Democratic Congress all but swept the legislative elections due to an opposition boycott. Under the constitution, Rawlings was not permitted to run for a third term and in Dec. 2000 John Kufuor of the opposition New Patriotic Party won the presidency in a run-off election.

▶GREAT BRITAIN (see United Kingdom)

▶GREECE

Hellenic Republic

• **GEOGRAPHY** **Location:** southeastern Europe. **Boundaries**: Albania, Macedonia, Bulgaria to N, Turkey to NE, Aegean Sea to E, Mediterranean Sea to S, Ionian Sea to W, Albania to NW; numerous islands surround mainland. **Total area**: 50,942 sq. mi. (131,940 sq km). **Coastline**: 8,500 mi. (13,676 km). **Comparative area**: slightly smaller than Alabama. **Land use:** 22% arable land; 8% permanent crops; 70% other. **Major cities**: (1991 census) Athinai (Athens, capital) 772,072; Thessaloniki 383,967; Piraeus 196,389; Patras 153,344; Iraklion 116,178.

• **PEOPLE** **Population:** 10,665,989 (July 2003 est.). **Nationality:** noun—Greek(s); adjective—Greek. **Ethnic groups:** 98% Greek, 2% other (note: Greek government states there are no ethnic divisions in Greece). **Languages:** Greek (official); English and French widely understood. **Religions:** 98% Greek Orthodox, 1.3% Muslim, 0.7% other.

• **GOVERNMENT Type:** parliamentary republic; monarchy rejected by referendum Dec. 8, 1974. **Constitution:** June 11, 1975. **National holiday:** Independence Day, Mar. 25. **Heads of Government:** Constantinos Stephanopoulos, president (since Mar. 1995); Konstandinos Simitas, prime minister (since Jan. 1996). **Structure:** executive—president elected by unicameral legislature; judiciary.

• **ECONOMY Monetary unit:** euro. **Budget:** (1998 est.) ***income:*** $45 bil.; ***expend.:*** $47.6 bil. **GDP:** $201.1 bil., $19,000 per capita (2002 est.). **Chief crops:** wheat, corn, barley, sugar beets, olives; meat, dairy products. **Natural resources:** bauxite, lignite, magnesite, crude oil, marble. **Major industries:** tourism, food and tobacco processing, textiles, chemicals. **Labor force:** 4.37 mil. (2002); 60% services, 20% agriculture, 20% industry; 10.3% unemployment (2002 est.). **Exports:** $12.6 bil. (f.o.b., 2002); manufactured goods, foodstuffs, fuels. **Imports**: $31.4 bil. (c.i.f., 2002); manufactured goods, foodstuffs, fuels. **Major trading partners:** ***exports:*** 52% E.U., 6% U.S.; ***imports:*** 66% E.U..

The Bronze Age and Iron Age cultures of Greece evolved to create the most glorious civilization of the ancient world. From the fifth to the third century B.C., the city-states of Greece led the world in art, philosophy, political culture, and science. Greece vied with the Persian Empire for control of Asia Minor and competed with the Phoenicians in maritime commerce in the Mediterranean. Alexander the Great, king of Macedonia, spread Greek civilization widely by conquering much of the Middle East and western Asia, but his empire did not long outlast his death in 323 B.C.

Greece was absorbed into the Roman Empire during the second and first centuries B.C. In the fourth century A.D., with the division of the Roman Empire, Greece became part of the Byzantine (Eastern Roman) Empire. Seven years after the Ottoman Turks captured Constantinople in 1453, they overran Greece and ruled it as part of the Ottoman Empire for 350 years.

Under Ottoman rule, much of the administration of Greece was left in local hands, keeping alive a sense of Greek nationhood and a tradition of Greek leadership, particularly through the clergy of the Greek Orthodox church. Inspired by the French Revolution, a romanticized ideal of the classical past, and the tradition of Greek orthodoxy, in 1821 Greece rebelled against Turkish rule. With the support of England, France, and Russia, Greek independence was won in 1827, although the country included only about half of its present territory.

The Western powers sponsored a monarchical government in Greece, ruled by a German prince. Deposed in a revolt, he was succeeded by King George I, a Danish prince who ruled from 1863 until his assassination in 1913. In the three Balkan Wars of 1912, 1913, and 1914, Greece expanded its borders to reach approximately its present size.

In 1923 a Greek Republic was established, but in 1935 King George II returned to his throne, placing government control in the hands of the patriotic but authoritarian Gen. Ioannis Metaxas. In 1940 Metaxas resisted Italy's attempt to conquer Greece, defeating Mussolini's armies so badly that Hitler sent crack troops to his ally's assistance. The German occupation of Greece was complete by June 1941. The Germans pillaged the country and massacred Jews; their Bulgarian allies colonized Macedonia.

During World War II, resistance grew among both Communist and anti-Communist groups. With the German withdrawal in October 1944, resistance groups battled each other; this led to full-scale civil war by 1946. British, and then American assistance (under the Truman Doctrine), enabled the Greek government to defeat the Communist forces when Stalin refused to intervene. King George II died in 1947, succeeded by his brother, King Paul I. Political instability—16 governments during 1946-52—prevailed until, under American pressure, the Greeks adopted a new constitution.

Until the postwar period, Greece's economy had been dominated by agriculture and livestock raising. Industry was limited largely to textiles and food processing; shipping was the major service industry. Under policies instituted in 1952 by the government of Marshall Alexandros Papagos, the industrial sector led a period of vigorous economic growth lasting into the 1960's. A market-oriented economy, tariff protection for Greek industry, tight internal security, and close ties with the West formed the mainstays of Greek policy.

Greece joined NATO in 1951, as did Turkey. Conflict over Cyprus divided the two nominal allies, however. The failure of the government of Constantine Karamanlis to resolve the Cyprus situation eroded his popularity, and he was replaced in 1964 by George Papandreou, who governed at the head of a left-center coalition. King Constantine, who succeeded his father in 1963, forced Papandreou to resign in 1964, after he and members of his government were accused of various improprieties. A military coup, led by Col. George Papadopoulos, toppled the government in 1967. A countercoup by King Constantine failed, and the king fled the country.

A military dictatorship ruled from 1967 to 1974. Its failed attempt to intervene in Cyprus in 1974 provoked a Turkish invasion of the island and led to the military regime's collapse. Karamanlis headed the government once again and a republic was established with the promulgation of a new constitution in 1975. Karamanlis's New Democracy party again received a majority in parliamentary elections in 1977.

Greece, an associate member of the EC since 1961, became a full member in 1981. Full military membership in NATO was restored in 1980. In 1981 the Panhellenic Socialist Movement under Andreas Papandreou won a parliamentary majority, renewed in 1984. The left-wing Papandreou government was outspokenly anti-NATO, anti-EC, and anti-American, but its policy was more moderate than its rhetoric, extending even to modest cooperation with Turkey in the Aegean. The Papandreou government was shaken by several pro-Palestinian terrorist incidents in Greece, and by a scandal involving the married Papandreou's relationship with a younger woman.

During 1989-90 Greece struggled through three parliamentary elections in less than a year. In the first two, no major party won a clear victory, leading to weak, short-lived coalition governments. The third, in the spring of 1990, resulted in a slim majority for the New Democracy party (headed by Prime Minister Constantine Mitsotakis) and the apparent decline of Papandreou's stature.

But Papandreou strengthened his grip on power in October 1993, leading his PASOK party to a landslide (47%) victory over the New Democrats (39%), as Greek voters expressed their displeasure with Mitsotakis's deficit-cutting "austerity" policies. Papandreou returned to office promising salary and pension increases and a halt to privatization. But serious illness forced him to resign in January 1996. His successor, Costas Simitas, promised to speed up the stalled privatization program, and his new cabinet removed most Papandreou loyalists. Elections later that year gave PASOK a smaller majority.

Greece's economy failed to meet the E.U.'s criteria for participating in the European Monetary Union in 1998, but the door was kept open for 2002. New tensions with Turkey over Cyprus, however, threatened to erupt into serious conflict during mid-year. Domestic discontent at what appeared to be Greek assistance in the Turks's capture of Kurdish rebel leader Ocalan in Nairobi led to a shakeup in the Simitis cabinet in Feb. 1999 but in March, government investigators were recommending trials for 18 Greek officials accused of assisting Ocalan's flight from the Turks.

In 1999 and 2000 a series of improvements occurred in Greek-Turkish relations: reciprocal earthquake assistance, agreements on sales of electricity (to Turkey) and water (to Cyprus, both Greek and Turkish, from Turkey) and foreign ministers' accords on crime, immigration, commerce, tourism and the Aegean environment. Greece even agreed to support Turkey's admission to the E.U. In April 2000, in Greece's closest parliamentary elections, PASOK became the first Greek party to win three consecutive elections.

The success of the government's austerity program led the E.U. to approve Greece's joining the E.M.U. in early 2001.

▶GRENADA

• **GEOGRAPHY** **Location:** southeastern Caribbean Sea, about 100 mi. (160 km) N of Trinidad. St. George's 12°03'N, 61°45'W. **Boundaries**: Atlantic Ocean to NE, E, and SE.; Caribbean Sea to SW, W, and NW. **Total area**: 131 sq. mi. (340 sq km). **Coastline**: 75 mi. (121 km). **Comparative area**: twice size of Washington, D.C. **Land use:** 6% arable land; 26% permanent crops; 68% other. **Major cities**: (1991 census) St. George's (capital) 4,439.

• **PEOPLE** **Population:** 89,258 (July 2003 est.). **Nationality:** noun—Grenadian(s); adjective—Grenadian. **Ethnic groups:** 83% black, 13% mixed, 5% European and East Indian. **Languages:** English (official), some French patois. **Religions:** 53% Roman Catholic, 13.8% Anglican, 33.2% other Protestant sects.

• **GOVERNMENT** **Type:** constitutional monarchy with Westminster-style parliament. **Independence:** Feb. 7, 1974 (from U.K.). **Constitution:** Dec. 19, 1973. **National holiday:** Independence Day, Feb. 7. **Heads of Government:** Sir Daniel C. Williams, governor-general (since Aug. 1996); Dr. Keith C. Mitchell, prime minister (since Jan. 1999). **Structure:** executive (cabinet led by prime minister); bicameral legislature; judiciary (West Indies Associate States Supreme Court).

• **ECONOMY** **Monetary unit:** East Caribbean (EC) dollar. **Budget:** (1997 est.) ***income:*** $85.8 mil.; ***expend.:*** $102.1 mil. **GDP:** $440 mil., $5,000 per capita (2002 est.). **Chief crops:** bananas, cocoa, nutmeg, mace. **Natural resources:** timber, tropical fruit, deep-water harbors. **Major industries:** food and beverages, textiles, light assembly operations. **Labor force:** 42,300 (1996); 62% services, 24% agriculture, 14% industry, 12.5% unemployment. **Exports:** $78 mil. (2000 est.); bananas, cocoa beans, nutmeg. **Imports**: $270 mil. (2000 est.); food, manufactured goods, machinery, chemicals, fuel (1989). **Major trading partners:** U.S., Caricom countries, U.K.

Dominated in the early 1600's by the warlike Carib Indians, Grenada alternated between French and British possession between 1650 and 1783, when British rule was established.

Independence came in 1974. The leftist New Jewel Movement seized power in a 1979 coup, but its leader, Maurice Bishop, was assassinated during a military coup in 1983. Shortly thereafter, the United States invaded and returned power to the governor-general until 1984. Prime Minister Nicholas Braithwaite of the National Democratic Congress party presided over a coalition government from 1990-95, when he was succeeded by George Brizan. In June 1995 the opposition New National party gained an absolute majority in Parliament and designated its leader, Keith Mitchell, as Prime Minister. It won all 18 seats in 1999.

▶GUATEMALA
Republic of Guatemala

• **GEOGRAPHY** **Location:** northern part of Central American isthmus. **Boundaries**: Mexico to N and W, Honduras and Belize to E, El Salvador to S. **Total area**: 42,042 sq. mi. (108,890 sq km). **Coastline**: 248 mi. (400 km). **Comparative area**: slightly smaller than Tennessee. **Land use:** 13% arable land; 5% permanent crops; 82% other. **Major cities**: (1994 est.) Guatemala City (capital) 1,150,452; Quezaltenango 100,983; Escuintla 67,958; Mazatenango 42,328; Puerto Barrios 39,267.

• **PEOPLE** **Population:** 13,909,384 (July 2003 est.). **Nationality:** noun—Guatemalan(s); adjective—Guatemalan. **Ethnic groups:** 55% Ladino (mixed Spanish and Amerindian), 43% Amerindian. **Languages:** 60% Spanish, 40% Amerindian languages (23 Amerindian dialects, including Quiche, Cakchiquel, Kekchi). **Religions:** predominantly Roman Catholic, some Protestant and traditional Mayan.

• **GOVERNMENT** **Type:** constitutional democratic republic. **Independence:** Sept. 15, 1821 (from Spain). **Constitution:** May 31, 1985, effective Jan. 1986. **National holiday:** Independence Day, Sept. 15. **Head of Government:** Alfonso Portillo Cabrera, president (since Jan. 2000). **Structure:** executive; unicameral legislature (113 seats, elected by popular vote to four-year terms); judiciary.

• **ECONOMY** **Monetary unit:** quetzal. **Budget:** (2002 est.) ***income:*** $2.3 bil.; ***expend.:*** $2.7 bil. **GDP:** $48 bil., $3,700 per capita (2002 est.). **Chief crops:** sugarcane, corn, bananas; cattle, sheep, pigs. **Natural resources:** crude oil, nickel, rare woods, fish, chicle. **Major industries:** sugar, textiles and clothing, furniture. **Labor force:** 4.2 mil. (1999 est.); 50% agriculture, 15% industry, 35% services; 7.5% unemployment (1999 est.). **Exports:** $2.7 bil. (f.o.b., 2002); coffee, sugar, bananas. **Imports**: $5.6 bil. (f.o.b., 2002); fuel and petroleum products, machinery, grain, fertilizers, motor vehicles. **Major trading partners:** ***exports:*** 55.3% U.S., 9.4% El Salvador, 4% Costa Rica; ***imports:*** 32.8% U.S., 9.3% Mexico, 8.2% South Korea.

Modern Guatemala was the heart of the Maya civilization that began early in the Christian era and flourished from the fourth to the 10th centuries. From the 11th century on there were two major powers, the Cakchiquel and the Quiché. They were overthrown by the Spanish who invaded from the north in 1524.

The captaincy general of Guatemala was the seat of Spanish military authority in Central America until the 19th century. After an earthquake destroyed Antiqua in 1773, the capital was moved to Guatemala City. Guatemala was the center of the United Provinces of Central America after independence was gained from Spain (1821) and Mexico (1823). The United Provinces collapsed after an uprising by Rafael Carrera, and Guatemala became a separate country in 1838.

The Liberal party held power from 1851 to 1944. There was considerable economic development under the repressive regimes of Manuel Estrada Cabrera (1898-1920) and Jorge Ubico (1931-44). Juan José Arévalo was elected president in 1945. He was succeeded, with strong Communist support, by Jacobo Arbenz, who was deposed in 1954 by a U.S.-backed coup led by Col. Carlos Castillo Armas. The military has ruled either directly or indirectly since then, although democratic rule resumed officially in 1986.

A civil war involving the army, right-wing death squads, and the antigovernment guerrilla group known as the Guatemalan National Revolutionary Union (URNG) began in 1960 and intensified through the 1980's, resulting in the deaths of more than 100,000 civilians.

In May 1993, Pres. Jorge Serrano Elias, backed by the military, suspended the constitution in an effort to crack down on labor and student strikes. Eight days later, in the face of overwhelming popular discontent and international protest, the military replaced Serrano with Atty. Gen. for Human Rights Ramiro de Leon Carpio. In March 1994, the URNG and the government reached an agreement to end the 30-year-old civil war, but talks stalled for a year until the two sides could agree on a pact amending the constitution to defend Indian rights. Meanwhile, the United States cut off military aid to Guatemala for its failure to prosecute security officers for crimes committed during the civil war.

In January 1996, URNG called a cease-fire during elections, in which Álvaro Arzú Irigoyen won a narrow but clear victory over a candidate considered a puppet of the military. The new government immediately purged the military of its most corrupt members, and made plans to privatize all aspects of the economy. The 36-year civil war seemed to end when the last 200 rebels turned in their arms in May 1997.

The April 1998 slaying of a Catholic bishop, a human rights advocate who had authored a report blaming 80 percent of the killings and kidnappings upon the military and right-wing paramilitary forces, remained unsolved a year later, as the lead prosecutor and two successive judges resigned in an atmosphere of threats. In Feb. 1999, an independent report, more comprehensive than Bishop Gerardi's, accused the army and paramilitaries of over 90 percent of the civil war abuses.

In May 1999, as the first prosecutions of military and security forces were beginning, Guatemalan voters rejected all the constitutional changes proposed in the 1996 peace. In November elections for Congress, they gave a majority to the Guatemalan Republican front; then, in December, they overwhelmingly elected its candidate as president.

▶GUINEA

Republic of Guinea

• **Geography** **Location:** western Africa. **Boundaries**: Guinea-Bissau to NW, Senegal to N, Mali to NE, Ivory Coast to SE, Liberia, Sierra Leone to S, Atlantic Ocean to W. **Total area**: 94,927 sq. mi. (245,860 sq km). **Coastline**: 199 mi. (320 km). **Comparative area**: slightly smaller than Oregon. **Land use:** 4% arable land; 2% permanent crops; 94% other. **Major cities**: (1983 est.) Conakry (capital) 656,000.

• **People** **Population:** 9,030,220 (July 2003 est.). **Nationality:** noun—Guinean(s); adjective—Guinean. **Ethnic groups:** 40% Peuhl, 30% Malinke, 20% Soussou, 10% smaller tribes. **Languages:** French (official), tribal languages. **Religions:** 85% Muslim, 8% Christian, 7% indigenous beliefs.

• **Government** **Type:** republic. **Independence:** Oct. 2, 1958 (from France). **Constitution:** Dec. 23, 1990. **National holiday:** Independence Day, Oct. 2. **Head of Government:** Lamine Sidimé, prime minister (since Mar. 1999). **Structure:** executive; unicameral legislature; judiciary.

• **Economy** **Monetary unit:** Guinean franc. **Budget:** (2000 est.) ***income:*** $395.7.; ***expend.:*** $472.4 mil. **GDP:** $15.9 bil., $2,000 per capita (2002 est.). **Chief crops:** rice, coffee, pineapples; cattle, sheep, goats; timber. **Natural resources:** bauxite, iron ore, diamonds, gold, uranium. **Major industries:** bauxite mining, alumina, diamond mining. **Labor force:** 3 mil. (1999); 80% agriculture, 20% industry and services. **Exports:** $835 mil. (f.o.b., 2002 est.); bauxite (the world's second largest producer), alumina, diamonds, coffee, fish. **Imports**: $670 mil. (f.o.b., 2002 est.); petroleum products, metals, machinery and transport equipment, foodstuffs, textiles. **Major trading partners: *exports:*** U.S., Belgium, Spain; ***imports:*** France, Ivory Coast, U.S., Belgium.

Guinea was formed out of the remains of a series of empires that flourished in West Africa between the 10th and 15th centuries. Situated to the southwest of the Sahara desert on the west coast of Africa, Guinea was a crossroads of West African trade long before Europeans arrived.

French merchants began trading in what is now Guinea in the early 17th century. France began acquiring land in the area in the mid19th century, and in 1845 the territories were organized as a separate colony. The colony received the name French Guinea in 1893.

Most high political posts were held by Europeans until after World War II. In 1946 French Guinea became a territory in the federation of French West Africa. In September 1958 Guinea became the only French colony to reject membership in the Fifth French Republic, resulting in the severance of political ties with France. The territorial assembly proclaimed Guinean independence on Oct. 2, 1958, and a new government headed by Sékou Touré was formed on the same day.

Touré was adamant in his rejection of French colonialism, severing ties with France (1960-63) and soliciting economic and other assistance from the U.S.S.R., China, and the United States. Touré remained in power until his death in April 1984. Within a week, a military government headed by Gen. Lansana Conte took power and by 1987 had improved relations with France while introducing market mechanisms into the command economy. Conte was elected president in 1993 and in June 1995, in Guinea's first-ever multiparty election, his Unity Progress party took 71 of the 114 legislative seats. He was succeeded by Sidia Toure a year later.

▶GUINEA-BISSAU

Republic of Guinea-Bissau

• **Geography** **Location:** northwestern coast of Africa. **Boundaries**: Senegal to N, Guinea to E and S, Atlantic Ocean to W. **Total area**: 13,946 sq. mi. (36,120 sq km). **Coastline**: 217 mi. (350 km). **Comparative area**: slightly less than three times the size of Connecticut. **Land use:** 11% arable land; 2% permanent crops; 87%% other. **Major cities**: (1979 census) Bissau (capital) 109,214; Bafatá 13,429; Gabú 7,803; Mansoa 5,390; Catió 5,170.

• **People** **Population:** 1,360,827 (July 2003 est.).

Nationality: noun—Guinean(s); adjective—Guinean. **Ethnic groups:** about 99% African (30% Balanta, 20% Fula, 14% Manjaca, 13% Mandinga, 7% Papel); less than 1% European and mulatto. **Languages:** Portuguese (official), Crioulo, numerous African languages. **Religions:** 50% indigenous beliefs, 45% Muslim, 5% Christian.

• **GOVERNMENT** **Type:** republic; multi-party since mid-1991. **Independence:** Sept. 24, 1973 (unilaterally declared by Guinea-Bissau); Sept. 10, 1974 (recognized by Portugal). **Constitution:** May 16, 1984, amended May 4, 1991, Dec. 4, 1991, Feb. 26, 1993, June 9, 1993, and 1996. **National holiday:** Independence Day, Sept. 24. **Heads of Government:** Kumba Yalá, president (since Feb. 2000); Alamara Intchia Nhassé, prime minister (since Dec. 2001). **Structure:** executive; unicameral legislature; no judiciary (Ministry of Justice).

• **ECONOMY** **Monetary unit:** Communauté Financière Africaine (CFA) franc. **Budget:** N.A. **GDP:** $1.1 bil., $800 per capita (2002 est.). **Chief crops:** rice, corn, beans; fishing, forestry. **Natural resources:** fish, timber, phosphates, bauxite, unexploited deposits of petroleum. **Major industries:** agricultural processing, beer, soft drinks. **Labor force:** 480,000. **Exports:** $71 mil. (f.o.b., 2002 est.); 70% cashews, fish, peanuts. **Imports**: $59 mil. (f.o.b., 2002 est.); foodstuffs, transport equipment, petroleum products. **Major trading partners:** ***exports:*** 41% Uruguay, 28% Thailand, 26% India; ***imports:*** 23% Portugal, 16% Senegal, 10% China.

The Portuguese began exploring and trading in what is now Guinea-Bissau in the 15th century and in 1630 began to exert administrative control over the territory. The area became the center of the Portuguese slave trade. When the slave trade declined in the 19th century, the coastal port of Bissau became a major commercial center. Later in the 19th century, the Portuguese began to conquer the interior of the territory and in 1879 consolidated the region into a territory called Portuguese Guinea, which in 1952 became an overseas province of Portugal.

A nationalist movement began in 1956 under the leadership of Amilcar Cabral and the African Party for the Independence of Guinea and Cape Verde (PAIGC). Armed insurrection broke out in 1961. By 1972 the PAIGC exerted influence over much of the country. Civilian rule was established in the territory that it controlled, and elections were held for a national assembly. Cabral was assassinated in 1973, but soon after the PAIGC National Assembly declared the independence of Guinea-Bissau from Portugal. Portugal acknowledged the country's new status on Sept. 24, 1973.

The civilian government was overthrown by a military coup in 1980, and the country was run by a Revolutionary Council headed by Brig. Gen. João Bernardo Vieira until a new constitution was adopted in May 1984. Under the new constitution, a new national assembly was selected, and Vieira was elected president in 1984 and 1989. In 1991 the government legalized opposition parties, but presidential elections were postponed.

In June 1998 a former army chief of staff, Ansumane Mane, launched a coup attempt against Vieira who was supported by loyalist troops and the Senegalese army. Hundreds of thousands fled the capital and the surrounding areas as the Senegalese shelled the city. By May 1999, General Mane had driven Vieira to seek asylum with the Portuguese and had installed the leader of the National Popular Assembly, Malan Sanha, as interim president until he was defeated in Jan. 2000 by Kumba Yala (who was overthrown by the army in Sept. 2003).

▶GUYANA

Co-operative Republic of Guyana

• **GEOGRAPHY** **Location:** northeastern South America. **Boundaries**: North Atlantic Ocean to N, Suriname to E, Brazil to S, Venezuela to W. **Total area**: 83,000 sq. mi. (214,970 sq km). **Coastline**: 285 mi. (459 km). **Comparative area**: slightly smaller than Idaho. **Land use:** 2% arable land; negl.% permanent crops; 97% other. **Major cities**: (1976 est.) Georgetown (capital) 72,049.

• **PEOPLE** **Population:** 702,100 (July 2003 est.). **Nationality:** noun—Guyanese (sing., pl.); adjective —Guyanese. **Ethnic groups:** 50% East Indian, 36% black, 7% Amerindian, 7% white, Chinese and mixed. **Languages:** English, Amerindian dialects. **Religions:** 50% Christian, 35% Hindu, 10% Muslim, 5% other.

• **GOVERNMENT** **Type:** republic within Commonwealth. **Independence:** May 26, 1966 (from U.K.). **Constitution:** Oct. 6. 1980. **National holiday:** Republic Day, Feb. 23. **Heads of Government:** Bharrat Jagdeo, executive president (since Aug. 2000); Samuel Hinds, prime minister (since Feb. 1998). **Structure:** executive—president (appoints and heads cabinet); unicameral legislature; judiciary.

• **ECONOMY** **Monetary unit:** Guyanese dollar. **Budget:** (2000 est.) ***income:*** $227 mil.; ***expend.:*** $235.2 mil. **GDP:** $2.7 bil., $4,000 per capita (2002 est.). **Chief crops:** sugarcane, rice, wheat; beef, pork, poultry. **Natural resources:** bauxite, gold, diamonds, hardwood timber, shrimp, fish. **Major industries:** bauxite mining, sugar, rice milling. **Labor force:** 418,000 (2001). **Exports:** $500 mil. (f.o.b., 2002); sugar, gold, bauxite/alumina, rice, shrimp, molasses. **Imports**: $575 mil. (c.i.f., 2002); manufactures, machinery, food, petroleum. **Major trading partners:** (2000 est.); ***exports:*** 23% U.S., 21% Canada, 14% U.K.; ***imports:*** 33% U.S., 19% Netherlands Antilles, 14% Trinidad and Tobago.

Although the region was visited by Europeans in the 15th century, Guyana was only colonized in the early 1600's by the Dutch. Rule in the area was contested by the French and the British, and it became the colony of British Guiana in 1831. After slavery was abolished, indentured servants from the East Indies were brought to work the land, and their descendants are in the majority today.

The People's National Congress was in power from 1964 to 1992, and socialist policies dominated the political landscape. Most of the country's large companies were nationalized, so despite its having the purest bauxite in the world, some gold, and conditions favorable to agriculture, it remains poor, dependent on foreign aid and remittances from overseas workers for much of its revenue.

In 1992 Cheddi Jagan of the People's Progressive party won the presidency, but attempts to privatize the sugar and bauxite industries have failed. In March 1997 Jagan died and Samuel Hinds, the prime minister became president while Jagan's widow took over as prime minister. In the presidential elections in Dec. 1997, Mrs. Jagan won election in her own right, with 56 percent of the vote, but her appointment of Hinds to be Prime Minister did nothing to stop the rioting and demonstrations by followers of the opposition People's National Congress. The PNC represents, principally, black, while the PPP does the same for East Indians. In Aug. 1999, Jagan resigned for health reasons and was succeeded by Bharrat Jagdeo, a 35-year-old Moscow-educated economist.

▶HAITI

Republic of Haiti

• **GEOGRAPHY** **Location:** western part of Hispaniola in northern Caribbean Sea. Port-au-Prince 18°33'N, 72°20'W. **Boundaries**: North Atlantic Ocean to N, Dominican Republic to E, Caribbean Sea to S; Windward Passage to W. **Total area:** 10,714 sq. mi. (27,750 sq km). **Coastline**: 1,100 mi. (1,771 km). **Comparative area**: slightly smaller than Maryland. **Land use:** 20% arable land; 13% permanent crops; 67% other. **Major cities**: (1984 est.) Port-au-Prince (capital) 738,342.

• **PEOPLE** **Population:** 7,527,817 (July 2003 est.). **Nationality:** noun—Haitian(s); adjective—Haitian. **Ethnic groups:** 95% black, 5% mulatto and European. **Languages:** French (official, but spoken by only 20% of population); all speak Creole. **Religions:** 80% Roman Catholic—of which majority also practice voodoo (called vodun), 16% Protestant.

• **GOVERNMENT** **Type:** republic. **Independence:** Jan. 1, 1804 (from France). **Constitution:** Mar. 1987, suspended June 1988; return to constitutional rule Oct. 1994. **National Holiday:** Independence Day, Jan. 1. **Heads of Government:** Jean Bertrand Aristide, president (since Feb. 2001); Yvon Neptune, prime minister (since Mar. 2002). **Structure:** executive; bicameral legislature; judiciary.

• **ECONOMY** **Monetary unit:** gourde. **Budget:** (FY 00/01) ***income:*** $273 mil.; ***expend.:*** $361 mil. **GDP:** $12 bil., $1,700 per capita (2002 est.). **Chief crops:** coffee, mangoes, sugarcane, rice, corn, sorghum. **Natural resources:** bauxite, copper, calcium carbonate, gold, marble, hydropower. **Major industries:** sugar refining, textiles, flour milling. **Labor force:** 3.6 mil. (1995); 66% agriculture, 25% services, 9% industry; shortage of skilled labor, unskilled labor abundant; widespread unemployment and underemployment. **Exports:** $185 mil. (f.o.b., 1999); light manufactures, coffee, other agriculture. **Imports**: $1.2 bil. (c.i.f., 1999); machines and manufactures, food and beverages, petroleum products. **Major trading partners: *exports:*** 89% U.S., 8% E.U.; ***imports:*** 60% U.S., 13% E.U..

The Arawak island of Haiti was discovered by Christopher Columbus, who renamed it Hispaniola, in 1492. In the next century many Arawaks were worked to death or killed by disease. The western third of the island was harassed by French pirates and was ceded to France in 1697. A slave revolt in 1791 led to abolition in 1794, and the island came under French rule the same year. Toussaint Louverture, an ex-slave, became governor-general in 1801, but he was deposed by the French. In 1803 a black army under Jean-Jacques Dessalines (Emperor Jacques I, 1804-6) and Henry Christophe (Henry I, 1806-20) defeated the French in 1803. Independence was declared in 1804. Under Jean-Pierre Boyer (1820-43), Haiti occupied Santo Domingo (which had been restored to Spain in 1808) from 1822 to 1844.

The next century was marked by political instability and an increased U.S. business and military presence in Haitian affairs. From 1905 to 1947, the United States had direct or indirect control of Haitian finances, and from 1915 to 1934 the country was under U.S. military occupation.

François "Papa Doc" Duvalier took power in 1957 and ruled Haiti with a stern hand. In 1971, he transferred power to his son, Jean-Claude (aka "Baby Doc"), whose regime was just as authoritarian. Most of Haiti's wealthy and educated population fled the country, leaving it the poorest and most illiterate nation in the Western Hemisphere.

In 1986, the military ousted Baby Doc, and imposed a succession of short-lived but brutal and incompetent governments. In 1989, Supreme Court Justice Ertha-Pascal Troillot was named interim president, and in 1990, Haiti held its first democratic national elections ever. The winner of those elections was the Rev. Jean-Bertrand Aristide, a 37-year-old Roman Catholic priest. But seven months into his five-year term, Aristide was overthrown in yet another military coup. Aristide fled to the U.S., which refused to recognize the junta and suspended aid to Haiti. But succesive trade embargoes by the U.S., Canada, and Western Europe only served to increase hardship among the poorest segments of the population. The junta leaders, propped up by Haiti's wealthy elite and by money from drug trafficking, began a campaign of violence against Aristide supporters, killing more than 3,000 of them.

After months of threats, the U.S. invaded on Oct. 15, 1994, forcing the junta's resignation and reinstating Aristide as president. Aristide disbanded the army, replacing it with a civilian police force. In mid-1995, Aristide's three-party coalition, Lavalas Political Organization, won overwhelming victories; in December, the Lavalas candidate, René Préval, took 88 percent in Haiti's first peaceful presidential election since independence.

By 1997 Lavalas and Pres. Préval had split. From June of that year, Haiti was without a government until Jan. 1999 when Préval announced he would rule by decree, and appointed his own prime minister. The U.S. and the U.N. ended their military mission in early 2000. Senate elections were held in May, giving 16 of 17 contested seats to Lavalas candidates. But in run-off elections held in July, opposition candidates and international observers refused to participate because of irregularities in the earlier election. In November, with the opposition and international monitors boycotting, the presidential election returned Aristide with 92 percent, while in remaining run-offs, Lavalas won all 9 Senate races and took 80 percent of the Assembly votes. When in March 2001 Jean-Marie Cherestal was sworn in as prime minister, his cabinet included some opposition members, though the opposition Democratic Convergence coalition had named its own "parallel" president a month earlier. After an attack on the presidential palace by 33 gunmen was thwarted in Dec. 2001, Aristide loyalists meted out savage reprisals to opposition groups (though the whole affair may have been staged). OAS-sponsored talks of the government with the opposition "Democratic Convergence" have gone nowhere.

▶HOLY SEE

The Holy See (State of the Vatican City)

• **GEOGRAPHY** **Location:** entirely within city of Rome, Italy; outside Vatican City, 13 buildings in Rome and Castel Gandolfo (the pope's summer residence) enjoy extraterritorial rights. **Boundaries**: surrounded by Italian territory. **Total area:** 0.17 sq. mi. (0.44 sq km). **Coastline**: none. **Comparative area**: about seven-tenths size of the Mall in Washington, D.C. **Land use:** 0% arable land; 0% permanent crops; 100% other. **Major cities**: Vatican City (capital).

• **PEOPLE** **Population:** 911 (July 2003 est.). **Nationality:** N.A. **Ethnic groups:** Italians, Swiss, other. **Languages:** Italian, Latin, various other languages. **Religion:** Roman Catholic.

• **GOVERNMENT** **Type:** monarchical-sacerdotal state. **Independence:** Feb. 11, 1929 (from Italy). **Constitution:** Apostolic Constitution of 1967 (effective Mar. 1, 1968). **National holiday:** Installation Day of Pope John Paul II, Oct. 22. **Heads of Government:** John Paul II, supreme pontiff (Karol Wojtylla, elected pope Oct. 16, 1978); Cardinal Angelo Sodano, Pro-Secretary of State of the Holy See. **Structure:** pope possesses full executive, legislative, and judicial powers; he delegates these powers to president of Pontifical Commission, who is subject to pontifical appointment and recall; Secretariat of State and Council of Public Affairs (which handles Vatican diplomacy) and Prefecture of Economic Affairs; College of Cardinals acts as chief papal adviser.

• **ECONOMY** **Monetary unit:** euro. **Budget:** (2001 est.) ***income:*** $173.5 mil.; ***expend.:*** $176.6 mil., supported financially by contributions (known as Peter's Pence) from Roman Catholics throughout world; some income derived from sale of Vatican postage stamps and tourist mementos, fees for admission to museums, and sale of publications. **GDP:** N.A. **Chief crops:** N.A. **Natural resources:** N.A. **Major industries:** consists of printing and production of small amount of mosaics and staff uniforms; worldwide banking and financial activities. **Labor force:** N.A.; dignitaries, priests, nuns, guards, and 3,000 lay workers who live outside the Vatican; Vatican City employees are divided into three categories—executives, office workers, and salaried employees. **Exports:** N.A. **Imports**: N.A. **Major trading partners:** N.A.

The Holy See is the smallest sovereign state in the world both in size and in population. It is a remnant of the "Patrimony of St. Peter," the secular state donated to the popes in the eighth century by Pepin the Short, father of Charlemagne. One of the major political powers on the Italian peninsula throughout the Middle Ages and into modern times, the States of the Church were conquered in 1870 by the new kingdom of Italy, which made Rome its capital.

In 1929 Mussolini's government made peace with the papacy in the Lateran Treaty, which recognized the Holy See as an independent state. The treaty was incorporated into the Italian Constitution of 1947. Under the terms of the treaty, the pope is pledged to perpetual neutrality and may intervene in international affairs as a mediator only upon request.

The pope is the sovereign of the Holy See in his capacity as bishop of Rome, and in that capacity, he accepts the credentials of foreign ambassadors assigned to the Holy See. The United States opened diplomatic relations with the Holy See in 1984, following the repeal of an 1867 law forbidding such relations. Pope John Paul II, a native of Poland, has been a source of spiritual leadership especially for Catholics in Eastern Europe. Since the collapse of communism in Eastern Europe, many countries there have renewed diplomatic relations with the Holy See. In a historic breakthrough the Holy See established diplomatic relations with Israel on Dec. 30, 1993.

As sovereign of the Holy See, the pope is an elected absolute monarch who appoints a Pontifical Council to govern the city on his behalf. The council meets only a few times each year. The economy is based on service industries, including printing; its revenues come from museum fees, philatelic sales, and sales of publications.

▶HONDURAS
Republic of Honduras

• **GEOGRAPHY** **Location:** Central America. **Boundaries**: Caribbean Sea to N, Nicaragua to E, El Salvador, Nicaragua to S, Guatemala, El Salvador to W. **Total area**: 43,278 sq. mi. (112,090 sq km). **Coastline**: 509 mi. (820 km). **Comparative area**: slightly larger than Tennessee. **Land use:** 15% arable land; 3% permanent crops; 82% other. **Major cities**: (1994 est.) Tegucigalpa (capital) 775,300; San Pedro Sula 368,500; El Progreso 81,200; Danli 43,300; Choluteca 72,800.

• **PEOPLE** **Population:** 6,669,789 (July 2003 est.). **Nationality:** noun—Honduran(s); adjective—Honduran. **Ethnic groups:** 90% mestizo, 7% Amerindian, 2% black, 1% white. **Languages:** Spanish, Amerindian dialects. **Religions:** 97% Roman Catholic, small Protestant minority.

• **GOVERNMENT** **Type:** democratic constitutional republic. **Independence:** Sept. 15, 1821 (from Spain). **Constitution:** Jan. 11, 1982 (effective Jan. 20, 1982). **National holiday:** Independence Day, Sept. 15. **Head of Government:** Ricardo Maduro Joest, president (since Jan. 2002). **Structure:** executive—elected president; unicameral legislature (128-seat National Congress); elected judicial branch.

• **ECONOMY** **Monetary unit:** lempira. **Budget:** (1999 est.) ***income:*** $607 mil.; ***expend.:*** $411.9 mil. **GDP:** $17.6 bil., $2,600 per capita (2002 est.). **Chief crops:** bananas, coffee, citrus; beef; timber; shrimp. **Natural resources:** timber, gold, silver, copper, lead. **Major industries:** agricultural processing (sugar and coffee), textiles, clothing. **Labor force:** 2.3 mil. (1997); 34% agriculture, 45% services, 21% industry; 28% unemployment (2002). **Exports:** $1.3 bil. (f.o.b., 2002 est.); bananas, coffee, shrimp, lobster. **Imports**: $2.7 bil. (f.o.b., 2002 est.); machinery and transport equipment, chemicals, basic manufactures. **Major trading partners:** ***exports:*** 45.7% U.S., 10.2% El Salvador; ***imports:*** 46.2% U.S., 9.9% Guatemala, 6.2% El Salvador.

Early in the Christian era, the Mayan civilization extended south to the pre-Columbian city of Copán in what is now northwestern Honduras. The territory was also home to the Lenca Indians and the indigenous people of the Moskitia area.

A silver strike in the 1570's prompted the first major influx of Spanish. The region was also celebrated for its tropical hardwood forests. Although the British controlled the Caribbean coast in the late 1700's, Honduras was a province of the Spanish captaincy of Guatemala. It became a member of the United Provinces of Central America after independence from Spain and Mexico, and an independent republic after the 1838 collapse of the Central American Federation.

Conservatives dominated Honduran politics until the 1870's, when the Liberals came to power and adopted a new constitution that reduced the influence of the church, among other things. Economic development came especially from a number of U.S. firms whose efforts were regarded as exploitative rather than beneficial; in 1912, U.S. president William Taft sent marines to protect U.S. interests.

Political unrest continued until the presidency of Gen. Tuburcio Carías Andino (1932-49), who was followed by a succession of pro-labor presidents. In 1963, a coup led by Col. Osvaldo López Arellano deposed the civilian president, and the military ruled almost uninterrupted until 1982. In 1969, the expulsion of thousands of Salvadoran peasants who had immigrated during the 1950's and 1960's led to the Soccer War with El Salvador. An armistice was negotiated by the OAS.

During the 1980's, Honduras was threatened by civil wars in El Salvador and Nicaragua. Honduran territory was used by Nicaraguan Contras, for which Honduras received substantial U.S. military and other aid. Demobilization of the Contras alleviated tensions between Left and Right, and in Jan. 1994 the new president, Carlos Roberto Reina Idiaquez, took office with the promise of controlling and reducing the power of the military which was more easily accomplished when the U.S. made severe cuts in military aid. In late 1997 the same Liberal Party easily won reelection, maintaining their control of the National Congress, while their candidate, Carlos Roberto Flores, won election as president.

In Oct. 1999, Honduras was devastated by Hurricane Mitch: 7,000 were dead, 600,000 homeless, and 70 percent of its crops destroyed — losses somewhat mitigated by international aid and debt reductions. In Jan. 1999, the legislature unanimously voted to place the autonomous military under civilian control. The Liberal Party was unseated in Nov. 2001 as the National Party elected only its second president since 1981, Ricardo Maduro.

▶HUNGARY

Republic of Hungary

• **GEOGRAPHY** **Location:** landlocked country in eastern Europe. **Boundaries**: Slovakia to N, Ukraine to NE, Romania to E, Yugoslavia to SE, Croatia to SW, Slovenia to W, Austria to NW. **Total area**: 35,919 sq. mi. (93,030 sq km). **Coastline**: none. **Comparative area**: slightly smaller than Indiana. **Land use:** 52% arable land; 3% permanent crops; 45% other. **Major cities**: (1994) Budapest (capital) 1,995,696; Debrecen 217,706; Miskole 189,655; Szeged 178,878; Pécs 172,177.

• **PEOPLE** **Population:** 10,045,407 (July 2003 est.). **Nationality:** noun—Hungarian(s); adjective—Hungarian. **Ethnic groups:** 89.9% Hungarian, 4% Roma, 2.6% German, 2% Serb, 0.8% Slovak, 0.7% Romanian. **Languages:** 98.2% Hungarian, 1.8% other. **Religions:** 67.5% Roman Catholic, 20.0% Calvinist, 5.0% Lutheran, 7.5% atheist and other.

• **GOVERNMENT** **Type:** parliamentary democracy. **Constitution:** Aug. 18, 1949; effective Aug. 20, 1949; revised Oct. 18, 1989; 1997 amendment streamlined judicial system. **National holiday:** St. Stephen's Day, Aug. 20. **Heads of Government:** Ferenc Mádl, president (since Aug 2000); Péter Medgyessy, prime minister (since May 27, 2002). **Structure:** executive—president elected by National Assembly; unicameral legislature—National Assembly (elected by direct suffrage); judicial—elected by Parliament.

• **ECONOMY** **Monetary unit:** forint. **Budget:** (2000 est.) ***income:*** $13 bil.; ***expend.:*** $14.4 bil. **GDP:** $134.7 bil., $13,300 per capita (2002 est.). **Chief crops:** corn, wheat, sunflower seeds, potatoes, sugar beets; chickens, pigs, cattle. **Natural resources:** bauxite, coal, natural gas, fertile soils. **Major industries:** mining, metallurgy, construction materials. **Labor force:** 4.2 mil. (1997); 65% services; 27% industry; 8% agriculture; 5.8% unemployment (2002). **Exports:** $31.4 bil. (f.o.b., 2002); 57.6% machinery and equipment, 31.0% other manufactures, 7.5% agriculture and food products. **Imports**: $33.9 bil. (f.o.b., 2002); 51% machinery and equipment, 35.3% other manufactures, 8.2% fuels and electricity, 2.9% agricultural and food products, 2.0% raw materials. **Major trading partners:** ***exports:*** Germany, Austria, Italy.

The Magyars, a tribe of Central Asian horsemen, terrorized Europe in the ninth century A.D. and settled in the Hungarian plain where, under their chieftain Arpad, they displaced earlier Germanic and Slavic settlers and organized a kingdom in 896. The Hungarians converted to Christianity late in the 10th century, and King Stephen (later St. Stephen) received a royal crown from Pope Sylvester II in 1001.

After the Battle of Mohacs in 1526, most of Hungary fell under Ottoman rule. The Turks were driven out in a series of battles with the Habsburg Holy Roman emperors at the end of the 17th century. Thereafter Hungary was part of the Habsburg Empire until 1867, when the Dual Monarchy of Austria-Hungary was organized, making Hungary independent of Austria in all but finance, the military, and foreign affairs.

During the 18th and 19th centuries, Hungary experienced extensive immigration of Romanians and Slovaks; by 1900 Magyars formed only a bare majority of the population. The pre-World War I economy was largely agricultural. Agriculture-related industry (beet sugar factories, breweries, tanneries, textile mills) developed in the late 19th century, along with some heavy industry.

In the dismemberment of Austria-Hungary following the defeat of the Central Powers in World War I, Hungary surrendered extensive territories to Romania, Yugoslavia, and Czechoslovakia. With the Treaty of Trianon ("Bloody Trianon") in 1920, the country lost 70 percent of its territory and 60 percent of its population; one-third of the Magyar people lived on foreign soil.

Short-lived governments—a republic under Michael Karolyi, and a Bolshevist state under Bela Kun—were replaced in 1920 by a new regime, with Adm. Miklós Horthy serving as regent. The Horthy regime was authoritarian but not fascist; its main objective was the recovery of Hungary's lost territories. Hungary established common cause with Germany in 1938 and 1940, recovering some territory from Czechoslovakia and Romania in the bargain, but at the price of participating in Hitler's war with the Soviet Union. Germany occupied Hungary in 1944 and set up a Hungarian Nazi regime. Late in 1944 the Russian army drove out the Germans and set up their own occupation.

The establishment of a full-scale Soviet-satellite regime was relatively slow. A republic was declared in February 1946, and the non-Communist Zoltan Tildy was elected president. Tildy was forced out in 1947, however, and replaced by the Stalinist dictator, Matias Rakosi. After the death of Stalin in 1953, the moderate Imre Nagy became premier and introduced some economic reforms. Nagy was forced out of office in 1955.

Nikita Khrushchev's denunciation of Stalin in 1956, combined with rising expectations for reforms in Hungary, led to a popular uprising in October 1956. Nagy, backed by the army, formed a coalition government on Oct. 23, proclaimed Hungary's neutrality, ended censorship, opened the borders, and withdrew from the Warsaw Pact. On Nov. 4, Soviet troops launched a massive invasion that crushed the rebellion. The Soviet army installed János Kádár as premier; Nagy was executed. About 200,000 Hungarians fled the country, and many more were imprisoned.

After several years of repressive rule, the Kádár regime announced, in 1963, amnesty for participants in the 1956 rebellion. Stalinists were gradually removed from the government, economic reforms emphasizing profit and productivity were introduced, and trade with the West was expanded. Hungary reluctantly took part in the suppression of Czechoslovakia's "Prague Spring" in 1968. In the same year, it announced the New Economic Mechanism (NEM) policy, ending central economic planning and introducing semifree enterprise under bureaucratic control.

After a brief return to central planning in the 1970's, the NEM was reintroduced in 1979 and expanded in 1982, when Hungary joined the World Bank and the I.M.F. Private ownership of subsidiaries of state-owned enterprises was permitted. In 1987 a pro-Gorbachev premier, Karoly Grosz, took office and in 1988 became head of the Communist party as well.

In 1989 the boundary with Austria was opened, making Hungary a key escape point for refugees from East Germany and Czechoslovakia. Nagy's reburial was attended by 300,000. Free elections were held in 1990, and the Democratic Forum, led by Jozsef Antall, won a plurality and formed a coalition government with the Smallholders and Christian Democratic parties. Having already achieved substantial perestroika-style economic reforms under communism, Hungary was well-placed to make a rapid transition to free enterprise and was seeking admission to the E.U. Sluggish production reduced tax revenues, resulting in serious deficits and an austerity budget.

Hungarian voters signaled just how painful they found the transition in the 1994 parliamentary elections by giving the Communists (now renamed Socialists) an absolute majority in Parliament. Privatization moved at a snail's pace, though the new government did appoint a committee to arrange the selling off of about 1,000 state-owned enterprises and soon foreign investment increased faster than anywhere in Central Europe. In 1997 Hungary was one of three eastern European nations invited to apply for admission to NATO and it was admitted in 1999.

Elections in 1998 gave the Socialists only 134 seats (of 386) in Parliament; the new government was formed by Civic Party which won 148 seats of its own, in coalition with the Smallholders and other parties of the right. The 2002 elections returned the Socialists (in coalition with the Free Democrats) to power, toppling the government of Victor Orban and replacing him with Peter Medgyessy. In a 2003 referendum voters gave 84 percent approval to joining the E.U.

▶ICELAND
Republic of Iceland

• **GEOGRAPHY Location:** near Arctic Circle in North Atlantic Ocean. Reykjavík 64°09'N, 21°58'W. **Boundaries**: Greenland about 190 mi. (300 km) to NW, Norway about 620 mi. (1,000 km) to E, U.K. 500 mi. (800 km) to S. **Total area**: 39,768 sq. mi. (103,000 sq km). **Coastline**: 3,100 mi. (4,988 km). **Comparative area**: slightly smaller than Kentucky. **Land use:** 1% arable land; 0% permanent crops; 99% other. **Major cities**: (1994 est.) Reykjavík (capital) 103,020.

• **PEOPLE Population:** 280,798 (July 2003 est.). **Nationality:** noun—Icelander(s); adjective—Icelandic. **Ethnic groups:** 94% homogeneous mixture of descendants of Norwegians and Celts, 6% of foreign origin. **Languages:** Icelandic (official). **Religions:** 87% Evangelical Lutheran, other Protestant and Roman Catholic, no affiliation.

• **GOVERNMENT Type:** constitutional republic. **Independence:** June 17, 1944 (from Denmark). **Constitution:** June 16, 1944; effective June 17, 1944. **National holiday:** Anniversary of the Establishment of the Republic, June 17. **Heads of Government:** Ólafur Ragnar Grímsson, president (since Aug. 1996); David Oddsson, prime minister (since Apr. 1991). **Structure:** executive power vested in president but exercised by cabinet responsible to Parliament; unicameral legislature; judiciary (Supreme Court justices appointed for life by president).

• **ECONOMY Monetary unit:** Icelandic króna. **Budget:** (1999 est.) ***income:*** $3.5 bil.; ***expend.:*** $3.3 bil. **GDP:** $7 bil., $25,000 per capita (2002 est.). **Chief crops:** potatoes, turnips; cattle, sheep; fish. **Natural resources:** fish, hydroelectric and geothermal power, diatomite. **Major industries:** fish processing, aluminum smelting, ferrosilicon production. **Labor force:** 159,000 (2000); 12.9% manufacturing; 11.8% fishing and fish processing; 10.7% construction, 5.1% agriculture, 59.5% other services; 2.8% unemployment (2002). **Exports:** $2.3 bil. (f.o.b. 2002); 70% fish and fish products, animal products, aluminum, ferrosilicon, diatomite. **Imports**: $2.1 bil. (f.o.b., 2002); machinery and equipment, petroleum products, foodstuffs, textiles. **Major trading partners: *exports:*** 18% U.K., 15% Germany, 11% Netherlands; ***imports:*** 12% Germany, 11% U.S., 9% Denmark.

The volcanic island of Iceland was settled in the ninth century A.D. by Vikings, who established Europe's oldest body of representative government, the Althing, in 930. Christianity was introduced around 1000. In the 13th century, Iceland acknowledged Norwegian rule. In 1380 Denmark, by then in control of all of Scandinavia, conquered Iceland as well. Iceland gained its independence in 1918 but shared a common king, Christian X, with the Danes. During World War II, first British, and then American, troops garrisoned the island; in 1944, with Denmark occupied by the Nazis, Iceland deposed its king and proclaimed itself a republic.

Iceland became a U.N. member in 1946 and a member of NATO in 1949. Lacking its own armed forces, it grudgingly tolerated the presence of an American air base at Keflavik. The republic developed a Scandinavian-style welfare state, with comprehensive social benefits that have produced one of the world's healthiest and best-educated peoples.

Less than 1 percent of Iceland's territory is arable; the island imports grain and vegetables but is self-sufficient in meat and dairy products. Fishing is the principal industry, accounting for 75 percent of exports, 20 percent of GDP, and engaging one-seventh of the work force.

Multiparty representation in the Althing has created a trend of government by coalitions or minority cabinets. Politically stable, the republic recently faced economic problems brought on by high taxes, chronic inflation, and a huge national debt. In 1997 and 1998, however, the economy made a strong recovery with GDP growing by 5 percent a year.

Iceland maintains close ties with Scandinavia and actively participates in the Nordic Council, but not the E.U., membership in which the government views as harmful to Iceland's all-important fishing industry.

▶INDIA
Republic of India

• **GEOGRAPHY Location:** Asian subcontinent, with Himalayan mountain range to N. **Boundaries**: Pakistan to NW; China, Bhutan, Nepal to N; Myanmar to NE; Bangladesh to E (surrounded by Indian territory except for short frontier with Myanmar); Bay of Bengal to E; Sri Lanka to SE across Palk Strait; Arabian Sea to W. **Total area**: 1,269,340 sq. mi. (3,287,590 sq km). **Coastline**: 4,350 mi. (7,000 km). **Comparative area**: slightly more than one-third the size of U.S. **Land use:** 54% arable land; 3% permanent crops; 43% other.

Major cities: (1991 census) New Delhi (capital) 7,174,755; Greater Bombay 9,909,547; Calcutta 4,388,262; Madras 3,795,208; Hyderabad 3,005,496.

• **PEOPLE** **Population:** 1,049,700,118 (July 2001 est.). **Nationality:** noun—Indian(s); adjective—Indian. **Ethnic groups:** 72% Indo-Aryan, 25% Dravidian, 3% Mongoloid and other. **Languages:** Hindi, English, and 14 other official languages; 24 languages spoken by a million or more persons each; numerous other languages and dialects; Hindi is national language and primary tongue of 30% of the people; English enjoys associate status but is the most important language for national, political, and commercial communication; Hindustani, a variant of Hindi/Urdu, is spoken throughout northern India. **Religions:** 81.3% Hindu, 12% Muslim, 2.3% Christian, 1.9% Sikh.

• **GOVERNMENT** **Type:** federal republic. **Independence:** Aug. 15, 1947 (from U.K.). **Constitution:** Jan. 26, 1950. **National holiday:** Anniversary of the Proclamation of the Republic, Jan. 26. **Heads of Government:** Avul P.J. Abdul Kalam, president (since July 2002); A. B. Vajpayee, prime minister (since March 1998). **Structure:** executive; bicameral parliament—Council of States, 250 members, up to 12 appointed by pres., remainder chosen by regionally elected officials; judiciary.

• **ECONOMY** **Monetary unit:** Indian rupee. **Budget:** (FY 01/02 est.) ***income:*** $48.3 bil.; ***expend.:*** $78.2 bil. **GDP:** $2.66 trillion, $2,540 per capita (2002 est.). **Chief crops:** rice, wheat, oilseed, cotton; cattle, water, buffalo, sheep; fish. **Natural resources:** coal (4th largest reserves in world), iron ore, manganese, mica, bauxite. **Major industries:** textiles, chemicals, food processing, steel. **Labor force:** 406 mil.; 60% agriculture, 23% services, 17% industry. **Exports:** $44.5 bil. (f.o.b., 2002 est.); clothing, gems and jewelry, engineering goods, chemicals. **Imports**: $53.8 bil. (f.o.b., 2002 est.); petroleum, machinery, gems, fertilizer. **Major trading partners: *exports:*** 21% U.S., 5% U.K., 4% Germany, 4% Japan; ***imports:*** 6% U.S., 6% U.K., 6% Belgium, , 4% Japan.

Indian civilization is one of the oldest in the world. Neolithic agricultural communities had appeared in the Indus River valley by 3000 B.C. and cities at Harappa and Mohenjo-Daro were founded around 2500 B.C. Around 1500 B.C. Indo-Europeans (Aryans) from Central Asia imposed their religion and political system on the indigenous population and generated population movements toward southern India.

Indo-European civilization was characterized by caste; everyone was a member of one of four fundamental divisions of society: Brahmins, hereditary priests responsible for higher learning and rituals; Ksatrias, warriors and administrators; Vaisas, merchants; and Sudras, farmers and subjugated peoples. At the bottom were casteless people, known later as untouchables.

By the mid-first millennium B.C., Brahminism had declined into a state of religious formalism. That situation prompted two reformations around 600 B.C., the first of which produced the Jain religion; the second, Buddhism. Jainism remained confined largely to India, while Buddhism eventually influenced most of the cultures of Asia, though it died out in India itself. Buddhism was adopted as a state religion by Asoka, third and greatest emperor of the Mauryan empire (325-184 b.c) under which much of India was united for the first time. Following the collapse of the Mauryan empire, Hinduism evolved out of Buddhism, Brahminism, and other local cults and became the dominant religion of India.

South India in the post-Mauryan period was divided into numerous states, the most prominent of which was Chola, a Tamil kingdom in the southeast that had extensive trade connections throughout the Indian Ocean.

The Gupta dynasty (c. A.D. 320-544), based in the Ganges River valley, established its rule over most of northern India and created what is generally regarded as a golden age of north Indian culture, with flourishing cities and significant achievements in art, literature, and science.

In the seventh century, King Sri Harsha created a short-lived feudal empire that united most of the petty states in the upper Ganges valley, while the Chalyuka dynasty dominated southern India. In the early eighth century, the Indus River valley was invaded by Arabs who introduced Islam to the region. The empire of Sri Harsha fell apart, replaced by the petty kingdoms of the Rajputs.

The 11th century saw the ascendency of Islam throughout northern India, which came under the shadow of the empire of Mamud of Ghazni, based in Afghanistan. In 1192 the Ghaznavid general Kutb ud-din Aibak defeated a coalition of Rajput states; in 1206 he founded the Sultanate of Delhi, which in the 13th century held off Mongol invasions in northwestern India and brought all of the subcontinent, except for the southernmost states, under its control. While the rulers of the sultanate were Muslims, most of their subjects remained Hindu.

Internal rebellions combined with the sacking of Delhi by Timur Leng (Tamerlane) in 1398 weakened the Sultanate of Delhi. In 1526 Babur, a descendant of Timur Leng, conquered all of northern India and established the Moghul empire. Under Akbar the Great, the empire flourished; Moghul culture gave rise to new styles of architecture, painting, and music.

In the 17th century, the Moghul emperors were threatened by the Hindu Marathas, whose kingdom on the west-central coast rapidly encompassed most of south India. By the late 18th century, Maratha power had spread to the north, and most of the petty kingdoms of the Moghul empire became part of a Maratha confederacy, owing only nominal allegiance to Delhi. By that time all of India was threatened by the expansion of the European powers.

Vasco da Gama had landed at Calicut in 1498, and in 1510 the Portuguese founded a colony at Goa. Dutch traders competed with the Portuguese during the 16th century, and British and French merchants followed in the 17th century. British trading stations were established at Surat (1612), Bombay (1661), and Calcutta (1690). In the mid-18th century, war broke out between British and French forces in India, and the French were confined to a few small enclaves. The growing instability of the Moghul empire in the face of Marathan and Rajput revolts and the expansion of the southern kingdom of Mysore encouraged the British to seek further control of Indian territory. Robert Clive's victory at Plassey in 1757 brought Orissa, Bihar, and Bengal under British control; British rule was extended to the upper Ganges in 1775. Victory over the maharaja of Mysore in 1792 paved the way for British control over the south.

British parliamentary acts of 1773 and 1784 placed these acquisitions firmly under government control, and in 1803 the Moghul emperor accepted the offer of a protectorate, and British suzerainty in India was assured. After a protracted war, 1812-23, Marathan resistance to British control was broken. The first Anglo-Afghan War, 1838-42, was inconclusive in Afghanistan but led to consolidation of British control of the Punjab.

In 1833 Parliament assumed political control of British interests in South Asia, while private merchants had unrestricted access to the economy. Plantation crops, such as opium and cotton, began to displace agriculture, which made India more dependent on imported goods.

In 1857 Indian troops in the British colonial forces staged a mutiny in north-central India that lasted 14 months. In 1858 the Moghul empire was dissolved, as was the East India Company. The government of India was made directly subject to the British Crown, which exercised control through a viceroy and through the British Colonial Office. Queen Victoria was crowned empress of India in 1877.

British sovereignty in India—the raj—was a patchwork of direct and indirect rule. In general, coastal areas, river valleys, and strategic frontier regions were ruled by British authorities, while interior states continued as British protectorates controlled by British advisers to native princes. In 1861 Indians were appointed to advisory councils of the viceroy and provincial governors.

The Indian National Congress was organized in 1885. In the wake of popular demonstrations in 1905, elections were instituted to choose Indian members of the viceroy's legislative council. Separate electorates were created for the Muslim and Hindu communities, formalizing a divisive force in Indian politics and weakening opposition to British rule. In 1914, with Chinese loss of control in Tibet, India's northern boundary was pushed forward to the McMahon Line, following the highest peaks in the Himalayas. This set the stage for numerous later boundary disputes between China and India, Pakistan, and Burma.

The Government of India Act of 1919 transferred some political power to elected provincial officials but left the appointed British governors firmly in control. In that year Mohandas K. Gandhi organized the first passive-resistance campaigns and was imprisoned. In 1935 the Government of India Act created elected provincial legislatures. In the first elections (1937) the Congress party under Jawaharlal Nehru won control of seven of the 11 provinces. Nehru's goal of a united Indian opposition to British rule was thwarted by Mohammed Ali Jinnah's Muslim League, which demanded the creation of a separate Muslim state.

During World War II, the British military position in South Asia was complicated by calls for Indian independence. An offer of local autonomy, with independence to follow, was spurned by Nehru, and an Indian National army under Subhas Bose fought with the Japanese. Jinnah's call for an independent Pakistan was greatly enhanced by his support of the British.

In 1947, the British raj became two independent nations, predominantly Hindu India and predominantly Muslim Pakistan. Despite its considerable stature in the international community at large, India has been troubled by a number of disputes with its neighbors and separatist movements within its own borders. Following independence hundreds of semiautonomous princely states were brought under control of the central government. The French ceded their remaining trading colonies in the 1950's, and Portugal gave up Goa in 1961. In 1962, India warred with China in a still unresolved dispute over their border along Kashmir and Assam. The state of Bhutan was granted independence in 1971, and in 1974 Sikkim was annexed and its monarchy abolished.

India's most intractable disputes have been with Pakistan. Immediately after independence, Hindus in Pakistan and Muslims in India were set upon by the majority populations; hundreds of thousands were killed, and at least 12 million refugees fled over the border in both directions. On Jan. 30, 1948, Gandhi was assassinated by a Hindu extremist who blamed him for partition.

In granting independence, Britain had divided states of Bengal and Punjab between the two countries, but fighting erupted over the status of Jammu and Kashmir, and a cease-fire line negotiated by the U.N. in 1949 has never been ratified as a formal national boundary. In 1989, separatists in the Indian part of Kashmir began calling for an end to Indian rule, and relations with Pakistan have worsened as India accused its neighbor of providing support for the guerrillas. In 1971, after 10 million refugees poured across its border, India intervened in the Pakistani civil war in an action that prompted an almost immediate cease-fire and the creation of an independent Bangladesh.

India's main separatist movement involves Sikh separatists in the Punjab who seek the formation of an independent state of Khalistan, but who are thought to be supported by Pakistan. The government is also contending with separatist movements in the northeastern states of Assam and its neighbor Nagaland.

The British legacy in India included a sizable national elite, well educated and committed to principles of parliamentary democracy. The English language linked the elites of India's linguistically diverse regions, easing minorities' fears of domination by a Hindi-speaking majority. India's economy had seen some industrial development under the British, but its infrastructure was geared to integration in a colonial empire rather than to independence. Port cities, heavy industry, and plantation agriculture coexisted with widespread rural poverty and the years following independence saw a massive migration of the rural poor into overburdened cities.

Under Prime Minister Jawaharlal Nehru, India assumed a leadership role in the world movement of nonaligned nations and followed a policy of neutrality in international affairs. The development of good relations between the United States and Pakistan led to correspondingly difficult U.S.-India relations. In August 1971 India signed a 20-year friendship treaty with the Soviet Union.

Nehru died on May 27, 1964, and was succeeded by Lal Bahadur Shastri. Nehru's daughter, Mrs. Indira Gandhi, was named prime minister on Jan. 19, 1966. In 1967 the dominant Congress party faced electoral setbacks; in 1969 it split into "Old" and "New" wings. Mrs. Gandhi's New Congress party won control of the legislature.

Faced with protests and strikes after the New Congress party was convicted of voting irregularities in 1975, Mrs. Gandhi declared a state of emergency in June; censorship was imposed, thousands were arrested for political offenses, and various economic-control measures were adopted. An opposition coalition led by the Janata Dal party won a massive victory in parliamentary elections in 1977. Mrs. Gandhi was driven from office, and the state of emergency was annulled. Mrs. Gandhi's party was returned to power in 1980, and she resumed the prime ministership. After an army attack on the Sikhs' Golden Temple in Amritsar, Gandhi was assassinated by Sikh bodyguards in October 1984. She was succeeded in office by her son, Rajiv, who placed the Punjab under direct control of the federal government.

On Dec. 3, 1984, methyl isocyanate gas leaked from a Union Carbide plant in Bhopal, killing over 2,500 people. The accident prompted a broad inquiry into industrial safety standards in India.

In November 1989, Rajiv Gandhi's Congress party was voted out of office in general elections after people close to the government were accused of taking kickbacks in a government arms purchase scandal. Gandhi was succeeded by V.P. Singh of the Janata Dal party, whose government collapsed after 11 months over a dispute involving Hindu plans to build a temple on the site of a mosque in Ayodhya. (Hindus contend the mosque was built on the site of Rama's birthplace.) Middle-class Hindus also protested an affirmative action policy to set aside federal government jobs for members of lower castes.

Singh was followed by Chandra Shekhar, whose minority government served only with the backing of the Congress party. After a parliamentary boycott by the Congress party instigated by Rajiv Gandhi, Shekhar quit the government in March 1991, agreeing to stay on as a caretaker until the May election. The election, postponed two weeks following the assassination of Gandhi, was won by the Congress party, and P.V. Narasimha Rao became prime minister. The Rao government attempted to foster economic growth by relaxing the centralized planning and controls on international trade and investment. This policy produced impressive economic gains despite a concurrent rise in corruption-related scandals.

A rise in Hindu extremist feeling, however, strengthened the hand of the opposition Bharatiya Janata party. On Dec. 6, 1992, a Hindu mob demolished a mosque built several hundred years earlier on a Hindu sacred site in the city of Ayodhya; in the ensuing turmoil, riots broke out in dozens of cities, most notably Bombay, leading to the deaths of hundreds of Muslims at the hands of Hindu attackers. A series of bomb explosions killed hundreds in Bombay on Mar.12, 1993, while dozens more were killed by an explosion in Calcutta four days later. Further riots followed, amid unsubstantiated accusations that Muslims, aided by Pakistan, were responsible for the explosions.

In 1993 separatist movements in Punjab and Assam waned, but violence in Kashmir and Jammu increased dramatically; despite several attempts by India and Pakistan to institute effective talks on the issue, violence continued unabated with loss of life in the hundreds if not thousands.

The Rao government's economic policies produced good results, but as India's economy strengthened its political stability weakened. The Congress Party continued to lose power to the Hindu Baratiya Janata Party. Congress was defeated in parliamentary elections in May 1996, ushering in an era of short-lived, weak coalition governments under Pres. K. R. Narayanan. Inder Kumer Gurjal formed a government in April, 1997 that fell in November. The BJP won a plurality of seats in March 1998 elections, but, to govern (under Prime Minister Vajapyee) required a 19-party coalition. Fragile authority need not exclude vigorous policy: it was the BJP coalition that carried out underground tests of five nuclear devices in May, vigorously asserted India's claims in Kashmir, and cut food subsidies as a means of reducing the deficit. It was the latter that dislodged the coalition and in April 1999, Pres. Narayanan dissolved the Lok Sabha, preparatory to India's third election campaign in three years. Perhaps sensing weakness, Muslim insurgents launched attacks against Indian forces in Kashmir. But India retaliated forcefully and peace was restored in July, although India continued to blame Pakistan for the violence. In the election results, the National Democratic Alliance, a 24-party coalition led by the Bharatiya Janata Party, won an absolute majority; so, for the first time in 27 years, an incumbent prime minister won re-election.

Despite this recent instability, India has enjoyed significant domestic and international achievements in the first 50 years after independence. The nation's territory was consolidated, and separatist movements in various provinces successfully resisted. The federal parliamentary system has proved workable, and the federal government has established its constitutional right to intervene in state affairs under some conditions. India's armed forces are large, well trained, and well equipped, with some nuclear capability. India has maintained watchful, but generally peaceful, relations with two unfriendly neighbors, Pakistan and China. The Green Revolution of the 1970's made the country self-sufficient in food for the first time since the 19th century. India has a large, well-educated middle class and a growing industrial economy.

The Dec. 13, 2001 attack on the Parliament in New Delhi by five Pakistan-based terrorists greatly heightened existing tensions between the two countries. While Hindu mobs killed Muslims in Gujarat, Muslim attacks continued, though at a diminished rate in 2002, in Jammu-Kashmir. Upwards of a million troops stood poised on the border with almost daily artillery exchanges. Several terrorist attacks in Kashmir led to U.S. and British diplomatic intervention that eased tensions considerably during 2003.

▶INDONESIA
Republic of Indonesia

• **GEOGRAPHY** **Location:** archipelago of about 18,108 islands stretching from Malay peninsula to New Guinea between mainland of Southeast Asia and Australia. Jakarta 6°08'S, 106°45'E. **Boundaries**: land borders with Papua New Guinea, to E of Irian Jaya, and with Malaysian states of Sarawak and Sabah in northern Borneo. **Total area**: 741,097 sq. mi. (1,919,440 sq km). **Coastline**: 34,006 mi. (54,716 km). **Comparative area**: slightly less than three times the size of Texas. **Land use:** 10% arable land; 7% permanent crops; 783% other. **Major cities**: (1990 census) Jakarta (capital) 8,222,515; Surabaya 2,473,272; Bandung 2,056,915; Medan 1,730,052; Semarang 1,249,230.

• **PEOPLE** **Population:** 234,893,453 (July 2003 est.). **Nationality:** noun—Indonesian(s); adjective—Indonesian. **Ethnic groups:** 45% Javanese, 14% Sundanese, 7.5% Madurese, 7.5% coastal Malays. **Languages:** Bahasa Indonesia (modified form of Malay; official); English and Dutch, leading foreign languages; local dialects, most widely spoken of which is Javanese. **Religions:** 88% Muslim, 5% Protestant, 3% Roman Catholic, 2% Hindu, 1% Buddhist.

• **GOVERNMENT** **Type:** republic. **Independence:** Aug. 17, 1945 (from Netherlands). **Constitution:** Aug. 1945, abrogated by Federal Constitution of 1949 and Provisional Constitution of 1950, restored July 5, 1959. **National holiday:** Independence Day, Aug. 17. **Head of Government:** Ms. Megawati Soekarnopurti, president. (since July 2001). **Structure:** executive—headed by president who is chief of state and head of cabinet; cabinet selected by president; unicameral legislature (DPR, or House of Representatives) of 500 members (100 appointed, 400 elected); second body (MPR, or People's Consultative Assembly) of 1,000 members includes legislature and 500 other members (chosen by several processes but not directly elected); judicial—Supreme Court Judges appointed by president.

• ECONOMY **Monetary unit:** Indonesian rupiah. **Budget:** (2000 est.) ***income:*** $26 bil.; ***expend.:*** $30 bil. **GDP:** $663 bil., $3,100 per capita (2002 est.). **Chief crops:** rice, cassava, peanuts, rubber, cocoa; poultry, pork, beef. **Natural resources:** crude oil, tin, natural gas, nickel, timber. **Major industries:** petroleum and natural gas, textiles, mining. **Labor force:** 99 mil. (1999 est.); 45% agriculture, 16% industry, 39% services; 10.6% unemployment (2002 est.). **Exports:** $52.3 bil. (f.o.b., 2002); textiles/garments, gas, plywood, rubber. **Imports**: $32.1 bil. (c.i.f., 2002 est.); manufactures, chemicals, foodstuffs, fuels. **Major trading partners:** ***exports:*** 19% Japan, 15% U.S., 12% Singapore; ***imports:*** 18% Japan, 10% South Korea, 8% Singapore.

The precolonial East Indies consisted of several Islamic and Hindu kingdoms in the western islands and tribal societies in the easterly ones. The Portuguese established trading posts in the 16th century; by the 17th century, control had largely passed to the Dutch East India Company. With the company's bankruptcy in 1799, the Dutch established direct colonial rule. Several 19th-century anticolonial uprisings, though costly to the Dutch, failed to dislodge them. Nationalist sentiment grew in the early 20th century, organized around Islamic groups, the Indonesian Communist party (PKI, founded 1920), and the Indonesian Nationalist party (PNI, founded 1927). Sukarno, founder of the PNI, achieved prominence as a nationalist leader and was jailed by the Dutch.

The Dutch East Indies fell quickly to the Japanese early in 1942. Some nationalists at first hailed the Japanese as liberators but quickly turned against their harsh occupation. On Aug. 17, 1945, Sukarno proclaimed Indonesia's independence. With British aid, the Dutch returned and tried to reestablish colonial rule; in 1949, threatened with a cutoff of American Marshall Plan aid, they withdrew and acknowledged Indonesia's independent status. Under Sukarno Indonesia took a leading role in international affairs among the nonaligned nations of the Third World.

In 1963 Indonesia gained control of the last Dutch outpost in the Indies, Irian Jaya (western New Guinea). Sukarno's politics moved steadily to the left, and Indonesia became hostile to the West and friendly with China. The influence of the PKI grew steadily. On Sept. 30, 1965, the army crushed an attempted coup by the PKI, setting off a popular reaction in which several hundred thousand people were killed as suspected Communists. Sukarno was shunted aside, and power devolved to Gen. Suharto, who became president in 1968. The PKI was banned, and Indonesian policy swung sharply in favor of the West.

The economy grew rapidly, aided by oil revenue, timber exports to Japan, and the Green Revolution in rice agriculture. Foreign investment aided industrial development, which was hampered, however, by domestic content laws and other trade restrictions. A policy of "transmigration" attempted, with mixed success, to move farmers from overcrowded Java and Bali to underdeveloped areas in Sumatra, Borneo, Sulawesi, and Irian Jaya. In 1975 Indonesia invaded the former Portuguese colony of East Timor, which was annexed in 1976. More than 100,000 East Timorese have been killed and the annexation was never recognized internationally.

In recent years declining oil revenues have been partly offset by the growth of industry and tourism. Pres. Suharto remained in power, at the head of the Golkar united-front party, and was reelected president for a fifth term in 1993. Despite the most violent campaign in Indonesia's history, the ruling Golkar Party was returned to power with nearly 75 percent of the vote in the 1997 parliamentary elections. But Suharto's regime faced serious problems, including continuing unrest in East Timor and rising public dissatisfaction with the alleged corruption of Suharto's family and close associates. The economy boomed in recent years and per capita income steadily grew but in 1998 the financial crisis that swept through Asia revealed the hollowness of the Indonesian approach. Strikes, protests, and riots forced Suharto to resign in May and his trusted aide, Vice-Pres. Habibie took power promising reforms and new elections in 1999. Habibie dropped half of Suharto's cabinet, began reforming the banking system, initiated inquiries into Suharto family wealth, and agreed with Portugal to hold a referendum on the status of East Timor. Elections were held in June 1999 with Golkar taking about 25 percent of the votes; an anti-Golkar coalition headed by Sukarno's daughter, Megawati Sukarnoputri, held a plurality. The people of East Timor voted overwhelmingly for independence from Indonesia, leading to violent attacks by militia groups and the sending of U.N. troops.

On Oct. 20, the Assembly approved the East Timor referendum and elected, not Megawati, but ailing Moslem cleric Abdurrahman Wahid as president, with Megawati as vice president. Under attack for his bumbling governance in a time of crisis, Wahid turned over day-to-day management to Megawati in mid-2000. On July 23, 2001 Wahid was formally impeached and replaced by Megawati, as the military refused to act in his behalf. In Feb. 2002 a fragile peace was brokered in the Moluccas between Muslims and Christians with arrests of some of the militia leaders. On May 20, East Timor became independent for the first time in 500 years.

In August 2002, the People's Consultative Assembly amended the constitution and established direct election of the president and abolished the military's 38 seats in Parliament. In Oct. terrorists linked to Al Qaeda bombed a Bali nightclub killing 180. In Dec. talks in Geneva with the separatist rebels in Aceh province appeared to have reached success; but in May, 2003 Pres. Megawati delcared martial law in Aceh and another army offensive began against the rebels.

▶IRAN

Islamic Republic of Iran

• GEOGRAPHY **Location:** western Asia. **Boundaries**: Armenia and Azerbaijan to N, Caspian Sea and Turkmenistan to NE, Pakistan and Afghanistan to E, Persian (Arabian) Gulf and Gulf of Oman to S, and Turkey and Iraq to W. **Total area**: 636,294 sq. mi. (1,648,000 sq km). **Coastline**: 1,516 mi. (2,440 km); Iran also borders the Caspian Sea (740 km). **Comparative area**: slightly larger than Alaska. **Land use:** 10% arable land; 1% permanent crops; 89% other. **Major cities**: (1991 census) Tehran (Teheran, capital) 6,475,527;

Mashad (Meshed) 1,759,155; Isfahan (Esfahan) 1,127,050; Tabriz 1,088,985; Shiraz 965,117.

• **People** **Population:** 68,278,826 (July 2003 est.). **Nationality:** noun—Iranian(s); adjective—Iranian. **Ethnic groups:** 51% Persian, 24% Azerbaijani, 8% Gilaki and Mazandarani, 7% Kurd. **Languages:** 58% Persian, 26% Turkic, 9% Kurdish. **Religions:** 89% Shi'a Muslim; 10% Sunni Muslim; 1% Zoroastrian, Jewish, Christian, and Baha'i.

• **Government** **Type:** theocratic republic. **Constitution:** Dec. 2-3, 1979; revised 1989 to expand powers of the presidency and eliminate the prime minister. **National holiday:** Islamic Republic Day, April 1. **Head of Government:** Seyed Mohammed Khatami, president (since Aug. 1997). **Structure:** executive; unicameral legislature (Islamic Consultative Assembly); judicial.

• **Economy** **Monetary unit:** Iranian rial. **Budget:** ***income:*** $29.5 bil.; ***expend.:*** $31.6 bil. **GDP:** $456 bil., $7,000 per capita (2002 est.). **Chief crops:** wheat, rice, sugar beets; dairy, wool; caviar. **Natural resources:** petroleum, natural gas, coal, chromium. **Major industries:** petroleum, petrochemicals, textiles. **Labor force:** 21 mil. (1998 est.); 33% agriculture, 25% industry, 45% services; 16.3% unemployment (2003). **Exports:** $24.8 bil. (f.o.b., 2002 est.); 85% petroleum; carpets, fruits, nuts, hides. **Imports**: $21.8 bil. (f.o.b., 2002 est.); machinery, military supplies, metal works, foodstuffs, pharmaceuticals. **Major trading partners:** ***exports:*** Japan, China, Italy; ***imports:*** Germany, Italy, France.

In 549 B.C. Cyrus the Great established the Persian empire by uniting Persia and conquered Babylonia. Alexander the Great conquered Persia in 333 B.C., but the Persians regained their independence after his death. The Persian Sassanian empire, established in A.D. 226, was the principal eastern rival of the Roman Empire. In 641 the Sassanians were defeated by invading Arabs, and Islam replaced the indigenous Zoroastrian religion. Persia reasserted its national identity—though not its political independence—under Islam and became a major center of Shia Muslim culture. In the early 13th century, Persia was conquered by the Mongols, who ruled the country until 1502.

The brilliant Safavid dynasty (1499-1736) was followed by two centuries of decline. During the 19th century, Persia lost control over Afghanistan and the Caucasus, while internal affairs came increasingly under British and Russian control. In 1907 an Anglo-Russian agreement formally divided Persia into spheres of influence. Following World War I, Persia was recognized as an independent nation, but was virtually a British protectorate. The Soviet Union renounced all claims to Persia in 1921.

In 1921 Reza Khan established a military dictatorship and had himself declared a hereditary monarch, Reza Shah Pahlavi, in 1925. In March 1935, the country's name was formally changed to Iran. In 1941 Great Britain, anxious over access to Iran's rich oil fields, charged Iran with pro-Axis activity, occupied Iran, and forced the abdication of Reza Shah in favor of his son, Mohammad Reza Shah Pahlavi. In 1945 Iran became a charter member of the United Nations.

Under Mohammed Mossadegh the National Front gained power in 1951. Parliament nationalized the oil industry; Britain responded with an economic blockade. The shah was briefly driven from power, but in August 1953, monarchist elements with clandestine British and American support ousted Mossadegh and restored the shah to the throne. The shah pursued a pro-Western policy of modernization and anticommunism and was rewarded with massive military and economic aid. His combination of secular, authoritarian rule and economic and social modernization was popular with the urban business sector but deeply resented by the rural and urban poor. Unrestrained use of the secret police to suppress dissent led to widespread disaffection.

Religiously inspired protests resulted in widespread violence in late 1978. A military government was installed by the shah on Nov. 6, with Prime Minister Shahpur Bakhtiar given sweeping powers. The shah went into exile on Jan. 16, 1979. On Jan. 31 Iran's dominant religious leader, Ayatollah Ruhollah Khomeini, returned to Iran from his exile in France. Government forces were routed by Khomeini's supporters, and Bakhtiar's government fell on Feb. 11. In 1979 clashes took place between rival religious factions, between religious parties and secular leftists, and between the urban middle class and the disenfranchised poor. Thousands were arrested and executed by the religious militia forces.

On Nov. 4, 1979, militants seized the U.S. embassy in Tehran and held 62 Americans hostage, provoking a long international crisis. An American military raid in April 1980 failed in an attempt to free the hostages. The hostages were finally freed on Jan. 21, 1981, minutes after Ronald Reagan's inauguration. The following day Iran's president, Abolhassan Bani-Sadr, was dismissed and the Ayatollah Khomeini took over executive power. A new wave of executions followed, with political moderates and non-Islamic religious believers among the principal victims.

On Sept. 22, 1980, a dispute between Iran and Iraq over the Shatt al-Arab waterway flared into open warfare. The war severely crippled Iran. Estimates on casualties range from 450,000 to over a million dead on both sides, and the war absorbed nearly all Iran's revenue from oil exports, leaving it nearly bankrupt. The U.S. was also drawn into the conflict. In 1986, Reagan administration officials attempted to secure the release of hostages in Lebanon by trading arms to the Iranians; and on July 3, 1988, an American ship patrolling in the Persian Gulf accidently shot down an Iranian civilian airliner, killing all aboard.

In Sept. 1988, a U.N. initiative led to a cease-fire between Iran and Iraq and to the opening of negotiations to find a permanent settlement to the war. Largely isolated from the world community, Iran's domestic priority was rebuilding the nation's economy. On June 3, 1989, Ayatollah Khomeini died, but the dire predictions that his death would cause turmoil within the Iranian political hierarchy proved wrong. Ali-Akbar Rafsanjani assumed the presidency.

In elections held Apr. 10, 1992, supporters of Rafsanjani's moderate policies wrested a parliamentary majority from the radical fundamentalist Islamic factions that had controlled the Iranian Parliament for 13 years. But "moderation" proved elusive, as Rafsanjani's party was subjected to pressure from religious extremists.

Although Iran had condemned the presence of Western troops in the Middle East during the Persian Gulf conflict, it abided by U.N. sanctions against Iraq and grounded Iraqi planes that sought refuge from Allied bombing raids. In 1995 the U.S. accused Iran of beginning a strategic military buildup and forbade all trade with Iran.

Iran has remained mired in economic and political stagnation with evidence of popular discontent for several years. In the 1997 elections the religious authorities gave the voters a genuine choice of presidential candidates and they shockingly chose (in a landslide) a moderate reformist, Mohammed Khatami. Since May 1997 Khatami has carefully maneuvered for moderate reforms in the face of Islamic clerical opposition, opening non-governmental dialogue with the American "great Satan", quietly replacing provincial governors with reformers, reining in secret police agents and the like. In Feb. 1999, the religious leaders permitted the first local elections in twenty years: Khatami's new party, formed only in December, swept all 15 seats in the Tehran city council, winning large victories nationwide.

In July 1999, a militant Islamic group attacked pro-democracy students in Tehran, killing several. Student demonstrations against the government erupted in many cities across the country and in Tehran the police dispersed the crowd with severe violence after students attacked buildings and burned cars. Pres. Khatami condemned the riots, leaving questions about the future of reform.

In Feb. 2000 parliamentary elections, voters gave about two-thirds of the seats in the 290-seat Majlis to reformers. But authorities closed most reform newspapers. In June 2001, Khatami won a landslide victory for re-election but his all his reforms have been rejected by the Council of Guardians and all demonstrations violently suppressed. In the wake of the Sept. 11th attacks on the U.S., Pres. Bush included Iran in the "axis of evil" that threatened civilization.In 2003 the U.S. accused Iran of trying to develop nuclear weapons.

▶IRAQ
Republic of Iraq

• **GEOGRAPHY** **Location:** western Asia with narrow outlet to Persian (Arabian) Gulf. **Boundaries**: Turkey to N, Iran to E, Saudi Arabia and Kuwait to S, Syria and Jordan to W. **Total area**: 168,754 sq. mi. (437,072 sq km). **Coastline**: 36 mi. (58 km). **Comparative area**: slightly more than twice the size of Idaho. **Land use:** 12% arable land; 1% permanent crops; 87% other. **Major cities**: Baghdad (capital) 3,236,000 (1987 census); Basra (Basia) 1,540,000; Mosul 1,220,000; Kirkuk 535,000 (1977 census).

• **PEOPLE** **Population:** 24,683,313 (July 2003 est.). **Nationality:** noun—Iraqi(s); adjective—Iraqi. **Ethnic groups:** 75-80% Arab, 15-20% Kurdish, 5% Turkoman, Assyrian, and other. **Languages:** Arabic (official), Kurdish (official in Kurdish areas), Assyrian, Armenian. **Religions:** 97% Muslim (60-65% Shi'a, 32-37% Sunni), 3% Christian and other.

• **GOVERNMENT** **Type:** in transition. **Independence:** Oct. 3, 1932 (from League of Nations mandate under British administration). **Constitution:** in transition. **National holiday:** Anniversary of the Revolution, July 17. **Heads of Government:** Saddam Hussein, president (since July 1979); Ahmed Hussein Khudair, prime minister (since 1994). **Structure:** executive; unicameral legislature (National Assembly)—Kurdish assembly elected in Kurdish areas, but unrecognized by Baghdad.

• **ECONOMY** **Monetary unit:** Iraqi dinar. **Budget:** N.A. **GDP:** $58 bil., $2,400 per capita (2002 est.). **Chief crops:** wheat, barley, rice, cotton; cattle, sheep. **Natural resources:** crude oil, natural gas, phosphates, sulphur. **Major industries:** petroleum, chemicals, textiles, construction materials. **Labor force:** 6.5 mil. (2002); 48% services, 30% agriculture, 22% industry. **Exports:** $13 bil. (2002 est.); crude oil. **Imports**: $7.8 bil. (2002 est.); food, medicine, manufactures. **Major trading partners:** (2001) ***exports:*** 61% U.S., 9% France, 7% Netherlands; ***imports:*** 19% France, 14% Australia, 11% Italy.

The fertile lands of Mesopotamia, between the Tigris and Euphrates rivers, were the site of one of the world's oldest civilizations. The city-states of Sumer were founded before 3000 B.C. and later became the heart of the Babylonian empire. Babylon became subject to the Assyrian empire after 1350 B.C. and was conquered by the Persians under Cyrus and Darius in the mid-sixth century B.C. Mesopotamia remained under the control of various Persian dynasties for the next 1,000 years.

In the seventh century A.D., the region was rapidly incorporated into the expanding Islamic world. The battle of Basra in 656 decisively established Arab control. In 762 the Caliphate, the center of Islamic rule, was moved from Damascus to the newly founded city of Baghdad, near the ruins of ancient Babylon. Mongol invaders sacked Baghdad in 1258 and destroyed its irrigation works; thereafter the region entered a period of long-term decline. Baghdad fell to the Ottoman Turks in 1534, and Iraq remained a province of the Ottoman Empire until the 20th century.

British troops occupied Iraq in 1915, and Great Britain governed the country under a League of Nations mandate after World War I. A Hashemite monarchy was organized under British protection in 1921. The kingdom of Iraq was granted independence in 1932 but remained closely tied to Great Britain by treaties guaranteeing British interests in petroleum and regional defense. Iraqi oil flowed through British-controlled pipelines traversing Jordan to Haifa (in Israel) and through a French-controlled pipeline traversing Syria.

After 1932 several attempted coups by anti-British factions were put down with the aid of British troops. One such coup in April 1941 sought aid from Italy and Germany; British troops landed at Basra in May and restored the pro-British monarchy. Iraq declared war against the Axis powers in 1943. In 1948 Iraq joined the Arab League and participated in the first Arab-Israeli War. Most of Iraq's 85,000 Jews emigrated to Israel after the war ended.

In 1952 a new agreement with Great Britain gave the Iraq Petroleum Company greater control over the country's oil, and a greater share of oil revenues. While remaining part of the Arab League, Iraq in 1955 broke ties with Egypt and also expelled the Soviet ambassador. Iraq signed a mutual defense treaty with Turkey.

A leftist pan-Arab revolutionary coup overthrew the monarchy in 1958 and established a republic, reversing Iraq's former pro-Western stance in international affairs. Oil resources and other industries were nationalized, and large landholdings were broken up. In 1968 a local branch of the international Ba'ath Socialist party came to power and established rule by decree within the republican framework of government. In 1972 the Soviet Union sent arms and advisers to Iraq. In the 1973 Arab-Israeli War, Iraq sent troops to aid Syrian forces on the front lines.

Iranian aid to a long-standing Kurdish rebellion in Iraq's northern mountains strained relations between the two countries. The Kurds were defeated in a bloody campaign in 1975, though the rebellion continued, leading to Iraq's bombing of Kurdish villages in 1979 and other incidents.

The execution of 21 alleged Communist conspirators in 1978 disrupted relations between Iraq and the U.S.S.R. Trade relations with the West were resumed. On July 16, 1979, Gen. Saddam Hussein at-Takriti assumed control of the government and purged leftist elements in the Ba'ath movement.

Several months of fighting in 1980 between Iraq and Iran for control of the Shatt al-Arab waterway in southern Iraq led to the outbreak of open warfare on Sept. 22, when each country launched bombing attacks on the other's cities. Warfare quickly spread along the entire Iraq-Iran border. The Iran-Iraq War produced eight years of fierce but generally stalemated fighting, with reports of the use of poison gas by both sides. On June 7, 1981, Israeli war planes destroyed a nuclear reactor near Baghdad, claiming it was capable of producing nuclear weapons. The war spread to the gulf in 1984, as both Iran and Iraq attacked tankers using each other's ports.

On May 17, 1987, the USS Stark, an American frigate on station in the gulf, was struck by missiles fired by an Iraqi fighter; 37 American sailors were killed. Iraq claimed that the attack was inadvertent and apologized to the United States.

In September 1988, a U.N. conference led to a cease-fire in the Iran-Iraq War. In the autumn of 1988, refugees in Turkey reported that poison gas had been used against Kurdish villages in northeastern Iraq as the Kurdish rebellion there continued. During 1989-90 Iraq's repressive internal policies and arms buildup provoked international criticism. Iraqi agents were caught attempting to smuggle components of nuclear weapons from the U.S. and Great Britain.

On Aug. 2, 1990, 120,000 Iraqi troops invaded and later annexed neighboring Kuwait. The invasion was met with almost universal disapproval, led by the U.N. Security Council, and U.S. troops were deployed to Saudi Arabia to defend it against a possible invasion. Coalition forces eventually totaled 500,000 troops from 13 countries.

After a six-week air war that destroyed most of Iraq's military capabilities and much of the country's infrastructure, Allied ground forces liberated Kuwait and occupied much of southern Iraq in only four days. Emboldened by the proximity of such overwhelming force, Kurdish and Sunni minorities in Iraq began a civil war that was put down with surprising speed and resulted in the displacement of hundreds of thousands of refugees to Turkey and Iran.

During 1992 Saddam Hussein solidified his hold on the military and remained in total control of the nation. However, U.N. inspectors discovered his secret plans to build nuclear weapons, and he was forced to destroy the program.

Throughout 1992-93 American warplanes provided protection for Kurdish areas in the north and Sunni Muslim areas in the southern marshlands. U.N. arms inspectors continued to press for access to Iraqi weapons plants and military research centers. On June 19, 1993, American missiles destroyed the Baghdad headquarters of Iraq's military intelligence service, in retaliation for a 1992 Iraq-backed plot to assassinate Pres. George Bush.

In Nov. 1994 Iraq formally recognized the sovereignty and territorial integrity of Kuwait. Nonetheless, the U.N. retained sanctions against Iraq until two conditions were met: destroying its stockpiles of weapons of mass destruction and improving its treatment of minorities. In May 1996 the U.N. agreed to ease sanctions on Iraq, permitting the sale of $2 billion worth of oil to purchase food and medical supplies. In late 1997 Iraq reneged on its agreement to allow U.N. weapons inspectors free access to all sites causing new tension in the region. Hussein's on-again, off-again cooperation with international inspection teams climaxed in the Dec. 1998 U.S./U.K. air strikes against Iraq. U.S. and U.K. patrols in the "no fly" zones regularly clashed with Iraqi MIGs. After the Security Council decision to review all aspects of U.N.-Iraqi relations in Jan. 1999, U.S. influence was further diminished by revelations that its intelligence agents had infiltrated the U.N. Special Commission and used UNSCOM to spy on Iraq. Three compromise recommendations by U.N. panels now met Iraqi rejection in April; nonetheless, the Security Council in May extended "oil-for-food" sales for six more months.

Iraq continuously rejected U.N. arms-monitoring schemes unless sanctions were lifted first. Yet, "oil-for-food" sales were renewed. British and U.S. airstrikes continued through 2001. Iraqi overtures (May 2002) and invitations to the U.N. to resume arms inspections came with conditions evoking a negative response and a serious threat of war by the U.S. (See "Major News Stories.")

▶IRELAND

• **GEOGRAPHY** **Location:** 26 of 32 counties comprising island of Ireland, in North Atlantic Ocean. Dublin 53°20'N, 6°15'W. **Boundaries:** Northern Ireland (U.K.) to N, Great Britain 50 mi (80 km) to E. **Total area:** 27,135 sq. mi. (70,280 sq km). **Coastline:** 900 mi. (1,448 km). **Comparative area:** slightly larger than W. Virginia. **Land use:** 20% arable land; negl. % permanent crops; 80% other. **Major cities:** (1991 census) Dublin (capital) 915,516; Cork 173,694; Limerick 75,436; Galway 50,853; Waterford 41,853.

• **PEOPLE** **Population:** 3,924,140 (July 2003 est.). **Nationality:** noun—Irishman (men), Irishwoman (women), Irish (collective pl.); adjective—Irish. **Ethnic groups:** Celtic, with English minority. **Languages:** Irish (Gaelic) and English (official); English widely spoken. **Religions:** 91.6% Roman Catholic, 2.5% Church of Ireland, 5.9% other.

• **GOVERNMENT** **Type:** republic. **Independence:** Dec. 6, 1921 (from U.K.). **Constitution:** Dec. 29, 1937. **National holiday:** St. Patrick's Day, Mar. 17. **Heads of Government:** Mary McAleese, president (since Oct. 1997); Bertie Ahern, prime minister (since June 1997). **Structure:** executive; bicameral parliament (Seanad, Dail); judiciary appointed by president on advice of government.

• **ECONOMY** **Monetary unit:** euro. **Budget:** (2002) ***income:*** $30.7 bil.; ***expend.:*** $30.5 bil. **GDP:** $118.5 bil., $30,500 per capita (2002 est.). **Chief crops:** turnips, barley, potatoes, sugar beets, wheat; meat, dairy. **Natural resources:** zinc, lead, natural gas, barite, copper. **Major industries:** food products, brewing, textiles, clothing. **Labor force:** 1.8 mil. (2001 est.); 63% services, 29% manufacturing and construction, 8% agriculture, forestry, fishing; 4.5% unemployment (2001). **Exports:** $86.6 bil. (f.o.b., 2002); chemicals, computers, industrial machinery. **Imports:** $48.6 bil. (c.i.f., 2002 est.); data processing equipment, chemicals, petroleum and petroleum products. **Major trading partners:** ***exports:*** 24% U.K., 18% U.S., 7% Germany; ***imports:*** 36% U.K., 16% U.S., 14% Belgium.

Ireland, a collection of warring Celtic chieftainships, was converted to Christianity by St. Patrick in the fifth century. Over the next two centuries, Ireland became a great center of monastic Christianity, sending missionaries to Scotland, England, and the Continent. While the Roman Empire decayed, Ireland was a center of peace, culture, and learning. Viking invasions in the ninth and 10th centuries caused substantial damage and overturned the rule of the great monasteries and their secular allies. By the time an Irish monarchy was reestablished by Brian Boru in 1014 and the surviving invaders were integrated into Irish society, Ireland had become an isolated, poor backwater on the periphery of Europe.

Trade gave rise to English commercial interests in Ireland and to Henry II's claim to overlordship of Ireland in the 12th century. Henry VIII declared himself king of Ireland and introduced the Reformation there. Large-scale Scottish immigration to Ulster began during the reign of Elizabeth I. Penal laws were applied, banning Catholics from public life and making the Mass an act of treason. A rebellion in 1641 was crushed by Oliver Cromwell over the course of a decade, ending with a massacre of thousands of Irish at Drogheda. After William of Orange's "Glorious Revolution" of 1688, the Irish supported James II, who was defeated at the Battle of the Boyne in 1690.

Following these events, British economic sanctions destroyed Ireland's flourishing export trade in wool. "Plantations" were established by British and Scottish Presbyterian landlords and farmers on lands seized from Irish Catholics. Much of the native aristocracy fled into exile, and the Gaelic language declined to near extinction.

A separate Irish Parliament, dominated by the Anglo-Irish establishment, was instituted in 1782, but it had little power. In 1798 a popular uprising led by Wolfe Tone, with inspiration and aid from revolutionary France, was put down with great loss of life. In 1800 Ireland and England were joined by the Act of Union, whereby Ireland was ineffectively represented in the British Parliament. After popular agitation led by Daniel O'-Connell, the Catholic Emancipation Act was enacted by Parliament in 1829, though mandatory tithes continued to support the established Anglican church until 1869.

Under absentee landlords, the Irish population was reduced to a subsistence diet based largely on potatoes. When a potato blight struck the country in the 1840's, disaster ensued. Between 1846 and 1851, one million people starved to death, and 1.6 million emigrated, most to America.

In the late 19th century, a home-rule movement under Charles Stewart Parnell won wide popular support. A Home Rule Act finally was passed by Parliament in 1914, but its effect was postponed for the duration of World War I. The Land Purchase Acts of the early 20th century enabled dispossessed peasants to buy land from absentee landlords, creating a rural economic basis for an independent Ireland. The country's economy, based largely on agriculture and pasturage, began to recover. (Industry, principally shipbuilding and textiles, was largely confined to Northern Ireland.)

The postponement of home rule led to the Easter Rebellion of 1916; brutally suppressed, it was followed by the "Troubles," a period of guerrilla warfare lasting to 1920. In that year the Government of Ireland Act established six of Ulster's nine counties as Northern Ireland, an integral part of the United Kingdom but with its own home-rule Parliament. The south's refusal of similar status led to the passage on Dec. 11, 1922, of the Irish Free State Act, by which Ireland became an independent dominion within the British Commonwealth.

The Fine Gael (People of Ireland) party governed until 1932, when Eamon De Valera, as the head of the Fianna Fail (Soldiers of Destiny) party, was elected president, holding that office until 1948. In 1938 the Constitution was revised to sever all connections with the British government except for an "external association" with the British monarchy. The outlawed Irish Republican Army (I.R.A.) pressed for forcible reunification of Ireland and carried out attacks on British interests in both Ireland and Northern Ireland.

Ireland remained neutral during World War II, and its government objected to British military activities in Northern Ireland. But it was generally sympathetic to the Allied war effort, especially after the United States entered the war in 1941.

In 1949 Ireland severed all ties to the British Crown, becoming a fully independent republic. The Fianna Fail won a majority in the republic's first elections, and De Valera became prime minister. In 1954 a coalition government under John Costello took power. De Valera was elected president of the republic in 1959.

During the 1950's, Ireland developed a moderate welfare state with the support of both the Fianna Fail and Fine Gael. In the 1960's attention turned to industrial development: zinc and lead mining, and export-oriented production of textiles, ceramics, and machinery. Ireland was admitted to the E.C. in 1973.

Beginning in the late 1960's, civil rights demonstrations led frequently to civil disorders and an increase in I.R.A. guerrilla activity in the north. While the 1970's were a boom period for the Irish Republic, sectarian violence and terrorism in the north left over 2,500 dead. The 1980's saw the establishment of an Anglo-Irish Intergovernmental Council (1981) and the Hillsborough accords (1985) between the Thatcher government and the Fine Gael-Labour coalition, which gave Ireland a consultative role in Northern Irish disputes.

The government of Charles Haughey, leader of Fianna Fail, elected in 1987, faced economic problems, including high inflation and unemployment, forcing Haughey to form a coalition government in the spring of 1989. After serious losses in June 1991 local elections, and amid charges of corruption, Haughey resigned in 1992. His successor, Albert Reynolds, faced a deep recession with unemployment rates of about 20 percent. In June 1992, a national vote strongly supported the E.C.'s Maastricht Treaty. Reynolds' coalition fell in Nov. 1992, but he created a new coalition between Fianna Fail and Labour.

In 1993, Reynolds and U.K. prime minister John Major announced the "Downing Street Declaration" that Sinn Fein, the political arm of the I.R.A., would be invited to participate in negotiations on Northern Ireland in return for the I.R.A.'s promise to halt terrorism and violence. In 1994, the I.R.A. announced a cease-fire in its 25-year-old effort to expel British troops from Northern Ireland.

Preliminary talks began optimistically, but bogged down over the British demand that the IRA disarm and the I.R.A. demand that Britain withdraw its forces from Ulster. In 1996, the I.R.A. announced an end to the 17-month-old cease-fire less than an hour before setting off a powerful bomb in East London, injuring 100 people. And in June, an even stronger bomb exploded in Manchester, injuring 200 and casting serious doubt on Sinn Fein leader Gerry Adams's ability to control the more militant members of his party.

Meanwhile, Ireland's governing coalition fell in Nov. 1995, and was replaced by an odd coalition with John Bruton of Fine Gael as prime minister. The new government passed legislation permitting Irish doctors to provide information about foreign abortion providers and sponsored a referendum that overturned the consitutional ban on divorce with remarriage. The Dail elections of June 1997 turned Bruton's coalition out of office, replaced by a new coalition of Fianna Fail and the Progressive Democrats with Fianna Fail's Bertie Ahern as prime minister.

In April 1998 came the breakthrough agreement (overwhelmingly approved in referendums in Northern Ireland and the Republic in May): extensive home rule in a Northern Ireland remaining part of the U.K. with some Republic of Ireland participation and with all paramilitary groups disarmed. When the deadline of Feb. 1, 2000 came and went without the I.R.A. or any other armed group disarming, Great Britain suspended the government that had been functioning for only 10 weeks (since Dec. 2). But when the I.R.A. in May pledged to put its arms "beyond use" and permit inspections, the Ulster Unionist Party accepted and the new government was functioning again by May 29. On July 26, the inspectors reported to Tony Blair that inspections had begun and that arms dumps were secure against use. Yet the refusal of the I.R.A. and other paramilitary groups to disarm led (on July 1, 2001) to the resignation of Protestant leader David Trimble as first minister, once again jeopardizing the peace accord.

But Trimble and the U.U.P. returned with confirmation that the I.R.A. had decommissioned some weapons in October and April—June was marred by militia violence in Belfast. Meanwhile, in the Republic, Fianna Fail became the first ruling party since 1969 to win re-election. In the spring of 2003 the issue of I.R.A. disarmament again caused Britain to suspend the Northern Assembly yet again.

▶ISRAEL

State of Israel

• **Geography** **Location:** western Asia, on eastern shore of Mediterranean Sea; has outlet to Red Sea via Gulf of Aqaba. **Boundaries**: Lebanon to N, Syria to NE, Jordan to E, Egypt to SW, Mediterranean Sea to W. **Total area**: 8,019 sq. mi. (20,770 sq km). **Coastline**: 170 mi. (273 km). **Comparative area**: slightly smaller than New Jersey. **Land use:** 17% arable land; 4% permanent crops; 79% other. **Major cities**: (1993 est.) Jerusalem (capital) 567,100; Tel Aviv-Jaffa 357,400; Haifa 246,500; Holon 162,800; Petach-Tikva 151,100.

• **People** **Population:** 6,116,533 (July 2003 est.). **Nationality:** noun—Israeli(s); adjective—Israeli. **Ethnic groups:** 80.1% Jewish, 19.9% non-Jewish (mostly Arab). **Languages:** Hebrew (official), Arab (official for Arab minority); English most widely used foreign language. **Religions:** 80.1% Judaism, 14.6% Islam (mostly Sunni Muslim), 2.1% Christian, 3.2% other.

• **Government** **Type:** parliamentary democracy. **Independence:** May 14, 1948 (from League of Nations Mandate under British administration). **Constitution:** no formal constitution; some functions of constitution are filled by Declaration of Establishment (1948), the basic laws of the Knesset (legislature)— relating to the Knesset, Israeli lands, the president, government—and Israeli citizenship law. **National holiday**: Israel declared independence on May 14, 1948; because Jewish calendar is lunar, however, holiday varies from year to year; all major Jewish religious holidays are also observed as national holidays. **Heads of Government:** Moshe Katsav, president (since Aug. 2000); Ariel Sharon, prime minister (since Mar. 2001). **Structure:** executive-president has largely ceremonial functions, except for authority to decide which political leader should try to form ruling coalition following election or fall of previous government, power vested in cabinet; unicameral legislature (Knesset); judiciary-legal system based on combination of English common law, British Mandate regulations, and religious law.

• **Economy** **Monetary unit:** new Israeli shekel. **Budget:** (2002 est.) ***income:*** $38.5 bil.; ***expend.:*** $45.1 bil. **GDP:** $122 bil., $19,000 per capita (2002 est.). **Chief crops:** citrus and other fruits, vegetables, cotton; beef, poultry, dairy products. **Natural resources:** copper, phosphates, bromide, potash, clay. **Major industries:** food processing, diamond cutting and polishing, high-tech projects. **Labor force:** 2.5 mil. (2002 est.); 31.2% public services; 20.2% manufacturing; 13.1% finance and business, 12.8% commerce, 7.5% construction, 6.4% personal and other services, 6.2% transport, storage, and communications, 2.6% agriculture, forestry, and fishing; 10.4% unemployment (2002 est.). **Exports:** $28.1 bil. (f.o.b., 2002); machinery, software, cut diamonds, chemicals, textiles and clothing. **Imports**: $30.8 bil. (f.o.b., 2002); raw materials, military equipment, investment goods, rough diamonds, oil. **Major trading partners:** U.S., E.U., Hong Kong.

In ancient times called the Land of Canaan, the region between the Jordan River and the Mediterranean Sea was one of the earliest sites of agricultural civilization in the Middle East. Hebrew exiles from Egypt arrived c. 1200 B.C.; their kingdom, Eretz Israel, was well established by 1000 B.C., with its capital at Jerusalem. The kingdom expanded under Kings Saul and David, who extended domination over the Philistines, a local seafaring people, and established the norms of Jewish religious worship at the great temple of Jerusalem.

After the reign of King Solomon, the kingdom split into two parts, Israel and Judah. Israel was conquered by the Assyrians in 722 B.C., and Judah by the Babylonians in 586 B.C. A locally autonomous state was reestablished under the Persian empire in the fifth century B.C. And in the fourth century B.C., Alexander the Great conquered the region, beginning a period of Hellenizing influence.

A new Jewish state was established in 141 B.C. after the revolt of the Maccabees against hellenic rule, the state falling to the Roman Empire around 70 B.C. Roman rule was exerted through the puppet kings of the Herodian dynasty. Christianity, a messianic religion centering on the teachings of Jesus of Nazareth, was suppressed in Israel by both the Herodian kings and the Jewish priesthood but spread widely in the eastern Mediterranean in the early first century A.D.

A Jewish rebellion against Rome in A.D. 66 was forcibly suppressed, and the temple at Jerusalem was destroyed by the Romans in A.D. 70. Large numbers of Jews were expelled from Judea, beginning the Jewish Diaspora throughout the Roman world and beyond. A second rebellion of Jews in Israel was quelled in A.D. 132.

The territory of the kingdoms of Israel and Judah became generally known as Palestine, after the name of its ancient inhabitants, the Philistines. With the official toleration of Christianity in the Roman Empire under Constantine I (early 4th century), Palestine became a major center of Christian pilgrimage. Politically, Palestine was administered as part of the Byzantine Empire.

Expansion of Islam from Arabia brought Palestine under Islamic rule in 636. Thereafter the region was ruled by the Caliphates of Damascus (661-750) and Baghdad (762-1258). Part of Palestine was captured in 1099 by European Crusaders, who established the short-lived Latin Kingdom of Jerusalem. The region was conquered by the Mongols in 1258; defeat of the Mongols in 1260 at the battle of Ain Jalyut, near Nazareth, prevented a Mongol invasion of Egypt.

Palestine next became part of the Mamluk empire and was incorporated into the Ottoman Empire in 1516. The Ottoman period was one of administrative decline, although the holy places of Judaism, Christianity, and Islam were maintained by local religious authorities.

The emigration of Jews from Europe to the homeland of Israel began around 1870, under the influence of the Zionist movement. Zionism, traceable in part to the thought of Moses Mendelssohn (1729-86), originally emphasized the need to maintain Jewish identity and religious consciousness as well as to promote Jewish assimilation into European culture. By the time of the First World Zionist Congress, convened in Basel by Theodor Herzl in 1897, emphasis had shifted to the need for a specific Jewish homeland. After 1905, under the leadership of Chaim Weizmann, Jewish emigration to Palestine increased as Weizmann attempted to win Turkish approval for a new state of Israel.

With the collapse of the Ottoman Empire during World War I, Palestine came under British rule in 1917. In that year the British government issued the Balfour Declaration, committing Britain to aiding the establishment of a Jewish homeland in Palestine. After Britain received a League of Nations Mandate to govern Palestine (as well as Transjordan) in 1923, Jewish immigration into Palestine increased significantly. Faced with rising Palestinian Arab opposition to a further increase in Jewish immigration, Britain reinterpreted the Balfour Declaration in restricted terms and attempted to limit the number of Jewish arrivals.

The crisis lasted until the outbreak of World War II. During the war the Palestinian Jewish community (then about 500,000) generally supported the British war effort, while some Palestinian Arab leaders translated anti-Zionist sentiments into sympathy for the Axis. Despite the horrible revelations about the Holocaust—the systematic killing of six million Jews during the War—in 1946 British authorities refused a recommendation of the Anglo-American Committee of Inquiry that they permit resettlement of 100,000 European Jews in Palestine and they limited further immigration to 2,000 per month. Jewish leaders pressed their cause at the United Nations, while in Palestine, Zionist terrorist organizations waged covert war against the British authorities.

In 1947 a U.N. Special Committee on Palestine, boycotted by Palestinian Arabs, recommended the partition of Palestine into Jewish and Arab sectors, with Jerusalem to be administered under international control. The U.N. adopted the recommendations on Nov. 29, 1947, and the British began to withdraw their forces, while Palestinian Jews and Arabs prepared for war.

On May 14, 1948, the independent state of Israel was established, with its capital at Tel Aviv. On the same day, troops from the Arab League nations attacked Israel. Fighting and cease-fires alternated throughout 1948; Israel lost control of the Old City of Jerusalem but retained the New City, and elsewhere consolidated its territorial control. Separate armistices between Israel and the Arab nations were concluded in 1949; Jordan retained control of the West Bank, and Egypt occupied Gaza. Large numbers of Palestinian Arab refugees departed for camps in Jordan, Lebanon, and Syria, while equally large numbers of Jews from Arab countries resettled in Israel.

Elections to the Knesset (Parliament) were held in Jan. 1949 and resulted in a coalition government. Chaim Weizmann was elected president, and David Ben-Gurion became prime minister. Laws were enacted to ensure religious control of education and civil law and to affirm the "Right of Return" of all Jews to Israel. The role of labor was protected by law, as was the establishment of agricultural collectives (kibbutzim).

Taking advantage of the Suez Crisis involving Great Britain, France, and Egypt, Israel invaded Egypt's Sinai Peninsula on Oct. 29, 1956. Israeli forces withdrew under the terms of a U.N. cease-fire on Nov. 6 but retained control of Gaza.

Throughout this period Israel's population continued to swell with immigrants from Europe, the U.S. and also from the dwindling Jewish communities of the Arab world. Israel's economy, aided by foreign aid and private remittances, grew rapidly, while foreign military aid and the growth of a substantial domestic armaments industry increased its military preparedness.

On May 19, 1967, U.N. peacekeeping forces withdrew from the Egypt-Israel border on the insistence of Egypt's president Gamal Abdel Nasser. Egyptian forces then reoccupied Gaza and closed the Gulf of Aqaba to Israeli shipping. In the Six-Day War, June 5-10, Israel recaptured Gaza, occupied the Sinai Peninsula to the Suez Canal, and captured the West Bank and the Old City of Jerusalem from Jordan and the Golan Heights from Syria. Another U.N.-supervised cease-fire went into effect.

Egypt and Syria, backed by Soviet airlifts, invaded Israel on Yom Kippur, Oct. 6, 1973. Israel, with strong U.S. support, counterattacked, driving back the Syrian forces and crossing the Suez Canal from the Sinai into Egypt. Fighting ceased on Oct. 24, and a disengagement agreement was signed on Jan. 18, 1974. Israeli forces withdrew from the west bank of the Suez Canal and, in stages, from the Sinai Peninsula, completing the withdrawal in 1982.

The government of Prime Minister Golda Meir fell after the Yom Kippur War, and a new coalition took power. A period of domestic and international difficulties followed, with severe inflation in the economy and a marked rise in Palestinian and other terrorist attacks against Israeli targets. Israeli forces repeatedly attacked Palestinian bases in southern Lebanon and aided the Christian militia forces in the Lebanese civil war of 1975-76. On July 3, 1976, Israeli commandos raided the airport at Entebbe, Uganda, to rescue 103 hostages held by Arab and German hijackers.

The 1977 parliamentary elections brought a conservative coalition to power, with Menachem Begin elected prime minister. Egypt's president Anwar Sadat visited Jerusalem in November 1977, and Begin and Sadat met at a conference with U.S. president Jimmy Carter at Camp David in 1979. On Mar. 26, 1979, Egypt and Israel signed a formal peace treaty ending 30 years of war and establishing diplomatic relations between the two nations.

In July 1980 Israel affirmed the transfer of its national capital from Tel Aviv to Jerusalem and the incorporation of the (formerly Jordanian) Old City into Israeli territory. The Israeli government decided in 1980 to promote increased Jewish settlement in the West Bank, provoking protest from Palestinian leaders.

Israeli forces invaded southern Lebanon in March 1978. After a brief occupation, most Israeli forces withdrew and were replaced by a U.N. peacekeeping force, but Israel continued to cooperate with Lebanese Christian militia forces in anti-Palestinian operations.

Israeli and Syrian forces clashed briefly in April 1981. On June 7, 1981, Israeli jets destroyed a nuclear reactor near Baghdad, Iraq, that Israel claimed could have been used to manufacture materials for nuclear weapons. Prime Minister Begin was returned to office in a close election in 1981, and he retired in 1983.

Attacking Palestine Liberation Organization strongholds in Lebanon in May, 1982, Israel mounted a full-scale invasion of Lebanon in June. Israeli and Syrian forces fought in Lebanon's Bekaa Valley but disengaged after a few days. On June 14 Israeli forces surrounded and shelled Beirut, forcing the PLO to evacuate the city. On Sept. 14 Israeli forces occupied West Beirut, following the assassination of the newly elected Lebanese president, Bashir Gemayel. Lebanese Christian militia, with tacit Israeli permission, entered two Palestinian refugee camps at Sabra and Shatila on Sept. 16 and massacred hundreds of civilians, provoking an international outcry against Israel's occupation of Lebanon. Israeli forces withdrew from Lebanon in June 1985, except for a narrow "security zone" along the border.

Parliamentary elections in 1984 resulted in a coalition government, with power shared by Likud leader Yitzhak Shamir and Labor leader Shimon Peres.

In December 1987, Palestinian residents of Gaza and the West Bank launched a series of violent demonstrations against Israeli authorities. The *intifada*, or uprising, continued into 1991 in a cycle of protest and police reaction that led to the deaths of hundreds of demonstrators and a crisis of Israeli control in the occupied territories. Tensions were exacerbated by the immigration of hundreds of thousands of Soviet Jews to Israel.

Parliamentary elections in Nov. 1988 continued the Likud-Labor stalemate and brought increased power to the minor religious parties. A new grand-coalition government announced in Jan. 1989, with Yitzhak Shamir as prime minister and Shimon Peres as minister of finance, collapsed in mid-March because of disagreements over an American-backed plan for peace talks with the Palestinians. This plunged the country into a crisis, resolved in June 1990 with the formation of a coalition government of Likud and several right-wing religious parties. Shamir managed to survive several no-confidence votes, and his alliance with religious party Agudat Israel in Nov. solidified his party's power as the Persian Gulf crisis unfolded.

After months of diplomacy spearheaded by the U.S., direct talks between Israel and a (non-PLO) Jordanian-Palestinian joint delegation opened in Washington in December 1991. The talks broke down in stalemate as Israel refused to compromise over the key issue of new Jewish settlements on the West Bank. In the election of June 1992, the Labor party led by Rabin scored an upset victory over Shamir's Likud coalition government. Rabin disclosed that the Shamir government had pursued a deliberate policy of intransigence in the peace talks in order to allow the accelerated West Bank settlement program to continue.

The Palestinian *intifada* gained renewed momentum in Dec. 1992 when Israel deported 400 Palestinians to Lebanon on the grounds that they were responsible for acts of violence. Both the U. S. and the U.N. opposed the move, which impeded the peace talks. Israel launched a series of air and land attacks on suspected terrorist bases in Lebanon, resulting in many casualties.

The world was stunned only a few weeks later, when on Sept. 13, 1993, Prime Minister Yitzhak Rabin and PLO leader Yasir Arafat signed an agreement in principle for a peace settlement based on Palestinian recognition of Israel's right to exist, and Israel's acceptance of partial self-rule for the Palestinians. Soon, areas in Gaza and the West Bank were under Palestinian control.

By fall of 1995, Israeli troops had begun withdrawing from Palestinian settlements on the West Bank, but a month later an Israeli extremist assassinated Rabin. His successor, Shimon Peres, vowed to continue moves toward peace and moved elections forward from October to May. In early 1996 Israel faced the worst suicide bomber attacks in 20 years: in five days 60 people were dead. Hamas, the Palestinian resistance group, took responsibility for the attacks.

In Israel's first direct election of a prime minister, Likud's hard-line Benjamin Netanyahu narrowly defeated Peres as Israelis chose "security" over "peace." By 1997 the peace process came to a virtual standstill as the Netanyahu government pushed ahead with new settlements in the West Bank and in East Jerusalem. The first sign of a break in the impasse came in June 1998 when Pres. Weizman declared that Netanyahu was undermining peace talks. Negotiations with the Palestinians began anew in July and on Oct. 23, in Washington, Netanyahu and Arafat agreed to the Wye Memorandum by which Israel agreed to surrender about 13 percent of her West Bank holdings. But the Knesset toppled Netanyahu's government and rejected the agreement. Elections in May 1999 brought Ehud Barak, former army chief of staff, to the office of prime minister and his One Israel party to dominance.

The roller-coaster peace talks between the Barak government and the Palestinians lasted for a year but broke off bitterly (July 25, 2000); what was seen in the Knesset as excessive concessions, especially on Jerusalem, led to the unravelling of Barak's coalition and a call for new elections. In the interim, Israel completed a withdrawal from the security zone it had established in 1978 in Lebanon. In late Sept. renewed violence between Israeli troops and Palestinians forced Barak to resign in December and in Feb. 2001 hard-liner Ariel Sharon won 63 percent of the vote to become prime minister. Nearly 400 people, mainly Palestinians, had died since September and in March began a series of suicide bombings by Palestinians in Israel. The deadly cycle of Palestinian terror-bombings and Israeli reprisals has continued without abatement through 2003. Sharon remained firmly in power even after Labor left his coalition forcing new elections in 2003. (See "Major News Stories.")

Palestinian Territories

As a result of the 1993 peace talks sponsored by the U.S., Israel and the P.L.O. signed the Declaration of Principles on Interim Self-Government Arrangements (known as the D.O.P.) which provided for a transitional period of no more than five years of Palestinian self-government in two areas, the Gaza Strip and the West Bank. Israel agreed to transfer some powers to the Palestinian Authority and a Palestinian Legislative Council was elected in 1996. Israel, however, retained control over security in these areas. Several other minor agreements were readied over the next three years but direct negotiations for a permanent settlement did not begin again until 1999. When the talks failed a new *intifada* broke out in Sept. 2000 and, with the onset of suicide bombings, Israel took stern military measures and ended any talk about a permanent settlement of differences.

GAZA STRIP This area (totalling 139 sq. mi. or 360 sq. km.) borders the Mediterranean Sea between Egypt and Israel. Approximately 1.3 million people live here including more than 5,000 Israelis in 25 settlements. Major cities include Gaza, Dayr al Balah, Rafah, Khan Yunus, and Abasan.

WEST BANK This area (totalling 2,263 sq. mi. or 5,860 sq. km.) borders Israel and Jordan and includes East Jerusalem and Jerusalem No Man's Land, established after the 1967 war. Approximately 2.2 million people live here including 187,000 Israeli settlers in the West Bank and fewer than 177,000 in East Jerusalem. Major cities include Jericho, Hebron, Bethlehem and Nablus.

▶ITALY

Italian Republic

• **GEOGRAPHY** **Location:** peninsula, extending from southern Europe into Mediterranean Sea, with a number of adjacent islands, principally Sicily to SW, and Sardinia to W. **Boundaries**: Switzerland and Austria to N, Slovenia to NE, Adriatic Sea to E, Ionian Sea to SE, Mediterranean Sea to W, France to NW. **Total area**: 116,305 sq. mi. (301,230 sq km). **Coastline**: 4,723 mi. (7,600 km). **Comparative area**: slightly larger than Arizona. **Land use:** 28% arable land; 9% permanent crops; 63% other. **Major cities**: (1993) Roma (Rome; capital) 2,687,881; Milano (Milan) 1,334,171; Napoli (Naples) 1,061,583; Torino (Turin) 945,551; Palermo 694,749.

• **PEOPLE** **Population:** 57,998,353 (July 2003 est.). **Nationality:** noun—Italian(s); adjective—Italian. **Ethnic groups:** primarily Italian, but includes small clusters of German-, French-, and Slovene-Italians in north and Albanian-Italians in south; Sicilians. **Languages:** Italian; parts of Trentino-Alto Adige region (e.g., Bolzano) are predominantly German-speaking; significant French-speaking minority in Valle d'Aosta region; Slovene-speaking minority in Trieste-Gorizia area. **Religions:** predominantly Roman Catholic.

• **GOVERNMENT** **Type:** republic. **Constitution:** Jan. 1, 1948. **National holiday:** Anniversary of the Republic, June 2. **Heads of Government:** Carlo Azeglio Ciampi, president (since May 1999); Silvio Berlusconi, prime minister (since June 2001). **Structure:** executive—president empowered to dissolve Parliament and call national election; commander of armed forces presides over Supreme Defense Council; otherwise, authority to govern invested in Council of Ministers; bicameral legislature—popularly elected Parliament (315-member Senate, 630-member Chamber of Deputies); judiciary—independent.

• **ECONOMY** **Monetary unit:** Italian lira. **Budget:** (2001 est.) ***income:*** $504 bil.; ***expend.:*** $517 bil. **GDP:** $1.438 tril., $25,000 per capita (2002 est.). **Chief crops:** fruits, vegetables, grapes, potatoes, sugar beets, soybeans, grain, olives; meat and dairy products. **Natural resources:** mercury, potash, marble, sulfur, dwindling natural gas and crude oil reserves. **Major industries:** tourism, machinery and transport equipment, iron, steel, chemicals. **Labor force:** 23.6 mil.; 63% services, 32% industry, 5% agriculture (2001); 9.1% unemployment (2002 est.). **Exports:** $259.2 bil. (f.o.b., 2002); engineering products, textiles and clothing, production machinery, motor vehicles. **Imports**: $238.2 bil. (f.o.b., 2002); engineering products, chemicals, transport equipment, energy products. **Major trading partners:** ***exports:*** 53.8% E.U., 9.7% U.S.; ***imports:*** 56.5% E.U., 4.9% U.S.

Rome became the major power in Italy around 500 B.C., dominating the Etruscans in the north and Greek settlements in the south. The Roman Republic already dominated most of the Mediterranean and western Europe by the time imperial rule was established under Julius Caesar. The empire was divided between Rome and Byzantium in the fourth century A.D. The Roman Empire in the west was severely weakened by Germanic invasions in the fifth century and gradually dissolved, so that Italy became a disunited collection of aristocratic holdings and independent cities.

By the 10th century, the city-states, especially in the north, emerged as major powers, rivaling the Papal States of the central peninsula. Venice and Genoa emerged as major maritime powers during the medieval period, while Florence, Siena, and other cities developed into centers of agricultural and commercial wealth, impelling the successive renaissances of the 12th and 15th centuries. With the rise of the Habsburg empire, the monarchical powers of northern Europe vied for power in Italy, and the peninsula's small states became pawns of France, Spain, and Austria.

At the turn of the 19th century, Napoleon created the short-lived Kingdom of Italy as a French satellite, but after his fall, there was a general return to the old pattern, with Austria dominating the north. Metternich in 1815 called Italy a "geographic expression."

The 19th century saw a growing sense of nationalism in both politics and culture. The revolutionary military leader, Giuseppe Garibaldi, and the statesman, Conte Camillo di Cavour, brought about the establishment of the Kingdom of Italy in 1861. The kingdom wrested Venice away from Austria (1866) and absorbed the Papal States in 1870. Although united territorially, the kingdom was divided by conflict between church and state, north and south, modern urban industry versus semifeudal rural poverty. Parliamentary politics under the constitutional monarchy created a regime that was weak and venal, inspiring little popular support.

Italy joined the Allied powers in World War I, but its minor gains in the Peace of Paris scarcely seemed to justify its wartime suffering and one million dead. Postwar economic dislocation, fear of communism, and political disillusionment abetted the rise of fascism. Benito Mussolini took over the Italian government at the invitation of the king in 1922 and soon acquired dictatorial powers. Papal secular authority in Vatican City was reestablished by the Lateran Agreement of 1929. In the late 1920's and early 1930's, Italy appeared to be a major power, defending Austria from Germany, colonizing Ethiopia, supporting Francisco Franco in the Spanish civil war, and joining in an "axis" with Hitler's Germany.

Mussolini, the senior partner in the fascist axis, soon was eclipsed by Hitler, and Italy was drawn into the disaster of World War II in 1939. Italy annexed Albania and invaded Greece, but that campaign turned into a fiasco from which German troops had to save the Italian army. In 1943 Allied attacks on Italy began; the fascist Grand Council deposed Mussolini, and the king, Victor Emmanuel III, had him arrested. Hitler intervened in September 1943 and began the war in Italy anew, rescuing Mussolini who established another fascist regime in northern Italy, while the legal Italian government in the south switched sides and welcomed Italy's liberation.

The head of the first postwar government was a Christian Democrat, Alcide de Gasperi. The monarchy was abolished by plebiscite in 1946, and the Republic of Italy was established. The north supported the republic, while monarchism retained significant support in the south. This division reflected a roughly accurate generalization that sees Italy as a progressive commercial and industrial north and a backward agricultural/pastoral south. Despite such industrial giants as Fiat and Pirelli, however, Italy's manufacturing is primarily carried on by medium-size and small firms, while agriculture is characteristic of the whole country. As late as 1956, there were more Italian workers in agriculture than in industry.

In the first elections under the republic, in 1948, the Christian Democrats benefited from American patronage and a split in the ranks of the Left to win a parliamentary majority. Italy accepted Marshall Plan aid and membership in NATO; reintegration into the European mainstream found expression in membership in the Council of Europe and the Coal and Steel Community.

Domestically, reconstruction was the major task, with industrial and agricultural output severely hampered by damage from the war; inflation was rampant and basic social services impaired. The Christian Democrats, normally in Center-Right coalitions in the 1950's and Center-Left coalitions in the 1960's, adopted a policy directed at creating a stable currency, a free market, comprehensive social welfare programs, and occasional state intervention in the economy. This created an Italian "economic miracle," with industrial production doubling between 1953 and 1961 and increasing an additional 40 percent by 1966, led by steel, automobiles, machinery, and electrical equipment.

In the 1970's the Christian Democrats gradually declined in political influence, normally gaining less than 40 percent of the popular vote while continuing to provide premiers in often short-lived coalition cabinets. Left-wing terrorism became a major national problem. The Christian Democratic leader and former prime minister Aldo Moro was kidnapped and murdered in 1978, and U.S. Brig. Gen./NATO officer James Dozier was kidnapped (and subsequently rescued) in 1981. The government of Bettino Craxi, Italy's first Socialist premier, was severely shaken after it refused to cooperate with the United States in apprehending and trying the hijackers of the Achille Lauro in 1985. Craxi resigned in 1987.

Lacking effective political unity, Italy's coalition governments—there have been more than 60 since the war—tended to muddle along in the face of slow economic growth, inflation, and high unemployment. But awareness of Mafia assassinations and revelations of government corruption led to demands for dramatic changes. In April 1993 the electorate overwhelmingly approved reforms that changed the basic elements of Italian political life. The first elections under the reformed system (March 1994) ended half a century of Christian Democrat-led coalition governments. The Christian Democrats, hastily renamed the Italian Popular Party, won only 11 percent of the vote, while the Socialists, normally the second largest party, fell to 2 percent. What replaced the old guard was the right-wing Alliance for Freedom. In May, wealthy publishing executive Silvio Berlusconi was sworn in as prime minister but his government lasted only into December. Political disputes, union opposition to his austerity budget, and the announcement that magistrates were investigating charges he had bribed tax officials diminished his authority.

Rather than call new elections, Italy's president asked Lamberto Dini to form a new "nonparty" cabinet of businessmen, judges, and professors, a cabinet that won the requisite votes of confidence in the two chambers by Feb.1, 1995. The new government showed surprising staying power, successfully passing its budget and negotiating reform of Italy's bloated pension system with leading trade unions. It even began the politically touchy process of investigating the anticrime magistrates for possible violations of civil rights.

As corruption trials continued, the Dini government survived successive votes of confidence, the last on condition that he resign with the new year, which he did. New elections were not held until April 1996. The left-wing "Olive Tree Coalition," led by the once-Communist "Democratic Party of the Left," trounced the right-wing "Freedom Alliance." Its new prime minister was Professor Romano Prodi of the Popular party. Prodi concentrated on bringing the economy into line so Italy would be eligible for participation in the EMU which, with much manevering, including a stringent austerity budget, and a sudden economic upswing, he did – formal endorsement coming in May 1998. Yet, in October, the Prodi government lost a vote of confidence over budget's cuts in social spending, unacceptable to the "Reconstructed Communists". Prodi endorsed Massimo D'Alema of the Democratic Party of the Left (the old Communist Party).

The "Olive Tree" government muddled along until the May 2001 elections, convincingly won by the right-wing House of Freedom coalition, spearheaded by Forza Italia, and bringing back Silvio Berlusconi as prime minister. Berlusconi was under indictment for corruption when in June 2003 the legislature granted him immunity until he was out of office.

▶IVORY COAST
Republic of Côte d'Ivoire

• **GEOGRAPHY** **Location:** western coast of Africa. **Boundaries**: Mali and Burkina Faso to N, Ghana to E, Gulf of Guinea to S, Liberia and Guinea to W. **Total area**: 124,502 sq. mi. (322,460 sq km). **Coastline**: 320 mi. (515 km). **Comparative area**: slightly larger than New Mexico. **Land use:** 9% arable land; 14% permanent crops; 77% other. **Major cities**: (1988) Yamoussoukro (capital—not recognized by U.S., which recognizes Abidjan) 106,786; Abidjan 1,929,079; Bouaké 329,850.

• **PEOPLE** **Population:** 16,962,491 (July 2003 est.). **Nationality:** noun—Ivorian(s); adjective—Ivorian. **Ethnic groups:** 41% Akan, 18% Voltaiques or Gur, 17% Northern Mandes, 11% Krous, 10% Southern Mandes, 3% other (including 130,000 Lebanese and 20,000 French). **Languages:** French (official); over 60 African languages and dialects with Dioula most widely spoken. **Religions:** 35-40% Muslim, 20-30%% Christian, 25-40% indigenous beliefs.

• **GOVERNMENT** **Type:** republic; multiparty presidential regime established 1960. **Independence:** Aug. 7, 1960 (from France). **Constitution:** Nov. 3, 1960. **National holiday:** National Day, Aug. 7. **Heads of Government:** Laurent Gbagbo, president (since Oct. 2000); Seydou Elimane Diarra, prime minister (since Mar. 13, 2003). **Structure:** executive—president has broad powers; unicameral legislature—175-member National Assembly; judiciary.

• **ECONOMY** **Monetary unit:** Communauté Financière Africaine franc. **Budget:** (2001) ***income:*** $1.72 bil.; ***expend.:*** $2.4 bil. **GDP:** $24.5 bil., $1,500 per capita (2002 est.). **Chief crops:** coffee, cocoa, bananas, palm oil; cotton, rubber; timber. **Natural resources:** crude oil, diamonds, manganese, iron ore, cobalt. **Major industries:** foodstuffs, wood processing, oil refinery. **Labor force:** N.A. **Exports:** $4.4 bil. (f.o.b., 2002 est.); cocoa, coffee, tropical woods. **Imports**: $2.5 bil. (f.o.b., 2002 est.); food, consumer goods, capital goods, fuel. **Major trading partners:** ***exports:*** 13% France, 9% Netherlands, 8% U.S.; ***imports:*** 23% France, 23% Nigeria, 6% China.

The peoples of the Ivory Coast belong to various tribes that had established small and mutually hostile kingdoms prior to the 18th century. The dominant Baule migrated to the Ivory Coast from Ghana about 200 years ago. European contact began with the Portuguese, who established coastal trading stations in the 15th century. They were followed in rapid succession by the Dutch, British, and finally the French, who landed at Assinie in 1637. Dense tropical forests and a lack of good harbors retarded European exploration.

France established a protectorate over the coastal zone in 1842 and during the remainder of the 19th century expanded its control, by conquest and diplomacy, into the interior. In 1893 the Ivory Coast was organized as a French colony, and in 1904 it was made part of French West Africa.

France's Vichy government controlled French West Africa during World War II and harshly suppressed the region's growing nationalist movements. In 1946 a group of West African leaders, inspired by Félix Houphouet-Boigny, formed the African Democratic Assembly, which later cooperated with the French in the implementation of reforms, including, by 1956, universal suffrage and the formation of locally autonomous assemblies. Complete independence for the Ivory Coast came on Aug. 4, 1960 and Félix Houphouet-Boigny was unanimously elected the first president.

His Democratic party was the only one allowed so Houphouet-Boigny easily won reelection. But even after he liberalized the political process in 1990 he retained control, winning a new five-year term in multiparty elections held in 1990. Under his presidency, the Ivory Coast enjoyed both political stability and economic prosperity.

Houphouet-Boigny died in 1993, and was succeeded by his fellow Democrat Henri Konan Bedie, president of the National Assembly. Bedie won reelection in 1995, and continued the policies of his predecessor. In Sept. 1999, however, after he ordered the arrest of several hundred members of an opposition party, Rally of the Republicans, a military coup led by General Robert Gueï overturned the Bedie government on Christmas Eve 1999. But Gueï's attempt to rig the 2000 elections provoked demonstrations that forced him to flee. Laurent Gbagbo became president.

In Sept. 2002, another coup by Gueï, in which he was killed, precipitated a civil war pitting the Gbagbo government against several rebel movements. French troops, sent to protect foreigners, became involved in the fighting and the negotiating. In March 2003 a power-sharing agreement went into effect with Gbagbo appointing a Muslim premier at the head of a 41-member cabinet representing all factions. Rebel attendence was sporadic, and fighting continued into the summer.

▶JAMAICA

• **GEOGRAPHY** **Location:** northern Caribbean Sea. Kingston 17°58'N, 76°48'W. **Boundaries**: Cuba 87 mi. (145 km) to N. **Total area**: 4,243 sq. mi. (10,990 sq km). **Coastline**: 635 mi. (1,022 km). **Comparative area**: slightly smaller than Connecticut. **Land use:** 16% arable land; 9% permanent crops; 75% other. **Major cities**: (1982 census) Kingston (capital) 524,638; Spanish Town 89,097; Montego Bay 70,265.

• **PEOPLE** **Population:** 2,695,867 (July 2003 est.). **Nationality:** noun—Jamaican(s); adjective—Jamaican. **Ethnic groups:** 90.9% black, 1.3% East Indian, 0.2% white, 0.2% Chinese, 7.3% mixed, 0.1% other. **Languages:** English, patois English. **Religions:** 61.3% Protestant, 4% Roman Catholic, some spiritualist cults.

• **GOVERNMENT** **Type:** constitutional parliamentary democracy. **Independence:** Aug. 6, 1962 (from U.K.). **Constitution:** Aug. 6, 1962. **National holiday:** Independence Day, first Monday in August. **Heads of Government:** Gov. Gen. Howard F.H. Cooke, governor-general (since Aug. 1991); Percival James Patterson, prime minister (since Apr. 1993). **Structure:** cabinet headed by prime minister; bicameral legislature; judiciary follows British tradition under chief justice.

• **ECONOMY** **Monetary unit:** Jamaican dollar. **Budget:** (FY99/00 est.) ***income:*** $2.23 bil.; ***expend.:*** $2.56 bil. **GDP:** $10 bil., $3,900 per capita (2002 est.). **Chief crops:** sugarcane, bananas, coffee, citrus, potatoes, vegetables; poultry, goats, milk. **Natural resources:** bauxite, gypsum, limestone. **Major industries:** tourism, bauxite mining, textiles. **Labor force:** 1.13 bil. (1998); 60% services, 21% agriculture, 19% industry and commerce; 15.4% unemployment. **Exports:** $1.4 bil. (f.o.b., 2002 est.); alumina, bauxite, sugar, bananas, rum. **Imports**: $3.1 bil. (f.o.b., 2002 est.); machinery and transport equipment, construction materials, fuel; food; chemicals. **Major trading partners:** ***exports:*** 35.7% U.S., 15.9% E.U. (excluding U.K.), 13% U.K.; ***imports:*** 47.8% U.S., 8% E.U. (excluding U.K.), 12.4% Caricom.

Christopher Columbus visited Jamaica in 1494, and the Spanish ruled the island—exterminating the native Arawaks in the process—until it fell to British control in 1655. A haven for buccaneers, by the 18th century Jamaica was a major sugar producer and the site of one of the busiest slave markets in the world. Emancipation of the slaves in 1833 and abolition of tariff protection in 1846 contributed strongly to the subsequent downfall of the plantation economy.

In 1962 the island gained its independence. The country has been plagued by racial and class division set within the context of an underdeveloped economy. Michael Manley of the People's National party became prime minister in 1972. He nationalized some industry and established closer ties with Cuba. Edward Seaga's Jamaica Labour party came to power in 1980 and encouraged more private-sector involvement in developing the economy. Though Manley was reelected to office in 1989, he did not reverse this general trend; in 1992 he was succeeded by Percival James

Patterson, who led the People's National party to a landslide victory in violence-marred elections in March 1993. He was reelected in 1997 despite continuing economic problems.

▶JAPAN

• **GEOGRAPHY** **Location:** chain of more than 3,000 islands extending 1,300 mi. (2,200 km) NE to SW between Sea of Japan and western Pacific Ocean; southern Japan about 93 mi. (150 km) E of S. Korea; islands of Hokkaido, Honshu, Shikoku, and Kyushu account for 98% of land area. Tokyo 35°40'N, 139°45'E. **Boundaries**: Sea of Okhotsk to N, Pacific Ocean to E, East China Sea to SW, and Sea of Japan to W. **Total area**: 145,882 sq. mi. (377,835 sq km). **Coastline**: 18,487 mi. (29,751 km). **Comparative area**: slightly smaller than California. **Land use:** 12% arable land; 1% permanent crops; 87% other. **Major cities**: (1995 est.) Tokyo (capital) 7,836,665; Yokohama 3,273,609; Osaka 2,478,628; Nagoya 2,086,745; Sapporo 1,733,133.
• **PEOPLE** **Population:** 127,214,499 (July 2003 est.). **Nationality:** noun—Japanese (sing., pl.); adjective—Japanese. **Ethnic groups:** 99% Japanese, 1% other (mostly Korean). **Languages:** Japanese. **Religions:** most Japanese observe both Shinto and Buddhist rites; about 16% belong to other faiths, including 0.7% Christian.
• **GOVERNMENT** **Type:** constitutional monarchy. **Constitution:** May 3, 1947. **National holiday:** Birthday of the Emperor, Dec. 23. **Heads of Government:** Akihito, emperor (since Jan. 1989); Junichiro Koizumi, prime minister (since Apr. 2001). **Structure:** executive—emperor is symbolic head of state; power is vested in cabinet appointed by prime minister; bicameral legislature; judiciary.
• **ECONOMY** **Monetary unit:** yen. **Budget:** (FY01/02 est.) ***income:*** $441 bil.; ***expend.:*** $718 bil. **GDP:** $3.55 trillion, $28,000 per capita (2002 est.). **Chief crops:** rice, sugar beets, vegetables, fruits; chickens, pigs, cattle; world's largest fish catch. **Natural resources:** negl. mineral resources, fish. **Major industries:** metallurgical and engineering industries, electrical and electronic industries, motor vehicles. **Labor force:** 67.7 mil. (2000); 70% trade and services, 30% industry and agriculture. **Exports:** $383.8 bil. (f.o.b., 2002 est.); semiconductors, office machinery, chemicals, motor vehicles. **Imports:** $292.1 bil. (c.i.f., 2002); fuels, foodstuffs, chemicals, textiles, office machinery. **Major trading partners:** U.S., China, South Korea.

Japan's ancient Jomon civilization was displaced by proto-Japanese Yayoi migrants from mainland northeast Asia beginning in the fourth century B.C. In the early Yayoi period, a mounted military aristocracy dominated rice-growing commoners. The shamanic religion of the time was ancestral to Japan's later indigenous religion, Shinto. Yayoi society evolved into the Yamato protostate, c. A.D. 250-500. The Yamato kings were buried in large, elaborate tomb mounds together with haniwa clay sculptures. From the third century A.D., contact with the mainland increased. Korean missionaries introduced Buddhism and Chinese writing in the mid-sixth century. A centralized monarchy developed in the Yamato Plain, central Honshu Island; Prince Shotoku, a great patron of Buddhism, founded the Horyuji and other great temples in the early seventh century.

In 710 the Yamato kings established a permanent capital for the first time, at Nara; the city was modeled on the Chinese capital. In 785 the court, split by factionalism and dominated by Nara's large and wealthy Buddhist temples, abandoned the capital; in 794 the new capital at Heian (Kyoto) was completed. The ensuing Heian period was one of the most brilliant in Japanese history. A small civil aristocracy, dominated by the Fujiwara family, drew great wealth from provincial estates and created a metropolitan culture of extreme refinement. From the ninth through the 11th centuries, strong Chinese influences were incorporated into Japanese culture.

In the 12th century the power of the Heian court waned as the influence of the provincial military aristocracy (samurai) grew stronger. In 1156 the capital was seized by the Taira family; in 1185 the Taira were overthrown by their rivals, the Minamoto. The Minamoto established a military government under a shogun (generalissimo) at Kamakura; the emperor remained at Kyoto, stripped of all governmental authority. In Kamakura the Minamoto were soon displaced by their former vassals, the Hojo. During the Kamakura period, the Japanese drew away from Chinese influence in art, architecture, literature, and religion in the process of creating a more distinctively Japanese culture. In 1274 and again in 1281, Mongol invasions were repulsed with the aid of timely typhoons (*kamikaze*, "divine winds").

In the course of a failed attempt at imperial restoration, the Kamakura shogunate was overthrown, in the 1330's, by the Ashikaga family, which in 1338 established a new shogunal government at Muromachi, a precinct of Kyoto. The Muromachi period saw the flowering of a new warrior culture, marked by such military virtues as bravery, loyalty, personal honor, and skill with weapons and by adherence to Zen Buddhism and its associated arts (tea ceremony, flower arranging, calligraphy, etc.). With the Onin Wars of the mid-15th century, the Muromachi shogunate lost most of its power, and the country fell into a century of civil war.

The civil wars were brought to an end during the second half of the 16th century by three successive unifiers, Oda Nobunaga, Hideyoshi, and Tokugawa Ieyasu. At the same time, the Jesuit Francis Xavier and his successors established a short-lived Japanese Christian community. Hideyoshi made several attempts (1592-98) to conquer and annex Korea. In 1601 Tokugawa Ieyasu defeated his rivals in the Battle of Sekigahara. He established a shogunal government at Edo (later Tokyo) in 1603; he and his successors formalized the structure of Japanese feudalism, created a rigid class structure, suppressed Christianity, and enforced the isolation of Japan from virtually all outside influence. Some trade with the mainland and a small Dutch trading station at Nagasaki provided Japan's only windows to the outside world for the next 250 years. The Edo period was marked by urbanization and the development of urban culture (Kabuki theater, wood-block prints, etc.) as the merchant class prospered from internal trade.

The Tokugawa shogun's inability to repel the 1854 visit of American commodore Matthew Perry and subsequently to avoid establishing commercial and diplomatic relations with Western nations deeply shocked the samurai class. Patriotic young samurai from Choshu, Satsuma, and other outlying feudal domains began to call for the abolition of the shogunate and the restoration of imperial rule in order to confront the threat of contact with the West. Quickly realizing that isolationism was doomed, the young radicals' program changed from "respect the emperor, expel the barbarians" to "enrich the state, strengthen the military." With the accession of the Meiji emperor in 1868, shogunal government ended.

Under direct imperial rule, feudalism was abolished and a wide-ranging program of military, industrial, commercial, and social modernization was implemented. The Meiji Constitution of 1889 created a constitutional monarchy and a parliamentary system of government. Having avoided domination by Western nations, Japan itself became an imperialist power. Defeating China in the Sino-Japanese War of 1894-95 and Russia in the Russo-Japanese War of 1904-05, Japan gained a dominant position in Manchuria and in Korea, which became a Japanese colony in 1910.

Under the ineffectual Taisho emperor (reigned 1912-26), parliamentary government flourished. Japan sided with the Allied Powers in World War I, and the Treaty of Versailles advanced Japan's international interests, particularly in China. The general prosperity of the 1920's was threatened by the Tokyo earthquake of 1923, by labor strife, and by a stagnant agricultural economy. Militant right-wing nationalism began to play an important role in domestic politics.

During the international economic depression of the early 1930's, right-wing militants gained the upper hand; they assassinated many moderate political figures. Japan invaded Manchuria in 1931 and established the puppet state of Manchuguo in 1934. An attempted military coup in 1936 failed in its immediate objectives but led to the establishment of martial law, under which the Showa emperor (Hirohito; reigned 1926-89) became a pawn of the ultranationalists. An invasion and military takeover of eastern China in 1937 was seen as the first step in the creation of a "Greater East Asian Co-prosperity Sphere," designed to unite Asia under Japanese control.

In 1940 Japan entered the Tripartite Alliance with Italy and Nazi Germany. Japan occupied French Indochina in June 1941, provoking increased Allied resistance to Japanese imperial ambitions. Gen. Hideki Tojo became prime minister in Oct. 1941 and ordered simultaneous preemptive strikes against Pearl Harbor, the Philippines, and Malaya on Dec. 7-8. By mid 1942, Japan controlled most of Southeast Asia and the western Pacific, but American victories at the Battle of the Coral Sea in May 1942 and the Battle of Midway in June 1942 halted Japanese expansion. Thereafter, Japanese forces were steadily pushed back in "island-hopping" campaigns in the central Pacific and along the western Pacific rim, and by Allied counterattacks in Burma. Air attacks on Japan itself culminated in the atomic bombing of Hiroshima and Nagasaki in August 1945.

Following Japan's formal surrender on Sept. 2, 1945, an American army in Japan under Gen. Douglas MacArthur took control of the country. A new constitution was promulgated, relegating the emperor to purely symbolic status, renouncing the use of military force, and guaranteeing the civil rights of citizens. The industrial combines that had lent strength to Japan's empire were partially dismantled. An international tribunal tried many wartime leaders as war criminals in 1948. In 1949 considerable authority was returned to the conservative government of Premier Shigeru Yoshida. Japan served as a base for American forces during the Korean War, 1950-53, greatly accelerating Japan's postwar economic recovery. On Apr. 28, 1952, a peace treaty between Japan and the United States went into effect, ending the Occupation. On Mar. 8, 1954, the two nations signed a mutual defense assistance pact.

Japan was admitted to the United Nations in 1956. The success of Japan's postwar recovery was symbolized by the Tokyo Olympic Games of 1964 and Expo '70 at Osaka. Violent student-protest movements in 1968-69 had no clear political goals and no lasting effect. Politically stable under an unbroken succession of Liberal Democratic party governments, Japan emerged as a major and steadily expanding world industrial power.

In general, Japan has been reluctant to play an international political role consistent with its vast economic power. From the mid-1970's onward, the balance of trade between Japan and the U.S. has weighed heavily in Japan's favor, leading to strains in U.S.-Japan relations and American charges that Japan engages in unfair trade practices. Several times during the 1980's and 1990's, especially when the yen was appreciating rapidly against the dollar, Japan pledged to take measures to even the trade balance by improving foreign access to Japan's domestic economy.

Domestically, Japan in the 1980's enjoyed a very high standard of living, marred by the extremely high cost and relatively low quality of housing, and by underinvestment in the public infrastructure. A real estate boom led prices of commercial property in downtown Tokyo to increase as much as 200-fold in the span of a decade. This boom extended to the United States, where the rapidly declining dollar made Japanese investment in the United States especially attractive.

For most of its postwar history, Japan has been essentially a one-party state, run by political professionals of the Liberal Democratic party (LDP) according to a system of consensus. But by the end of the 1980's, the system started to crumble as the regime's widespread corruption was revealed. Prime Minister Noburu Takeshita was force to resign in May 1989 after a bribery scandal. His successor, Sousuke Uno, lasted only two months before resigning in a scandal over his sexual conduct. Public opinion turned sharply against the LDP, which lost control of the upper house of the Diet in July 1989 elections; the Socialist party, led by Takako Doi, posted significant gains.

Uno's successor, Toshiki Kaifu, emerged as an unexpectedly skillful leader who enhanced Japan's international reputation by offering aid to Eastern Europe and the former Soviet Union, and by pledging billions of dollars to support the Persian Gulf War. In Oct. 1991, Kaifu was replaced as LDP chairman by Kiichi Miyazawa, who succeeded in passing legislation authorizing the posting abroad of Japanese troops—for the first time since World War II—for peacekeeping missions in noncombat roles.

An economic slump and political scandals continued to buffet the LDP throughout 1992 and 1993. LDP kingmaker Shin Kanemaru and other party officials resigned after admitting ties to gangsters. The LDP was forced from office in 1993 for the first time in 38 years, and formed successive coalition governments with the Socialist Party and other parties. The weak coalition governments paved the way for a LDP return to power in 1994; the years since have brought continued economic stagnation, bank failures, scandals involving government and business ties to organized crime, and general malaise.

The city of Kobe was hit by a severe earthquake in January, 1995; the government was criticized for inneffective rescue and relief efforts. The country's confidence was further shaken in March, 1995, by a bizarre attack with poison gas in the Tokyo subway, perpetrated by a religious cult,

Aum Shinrikyo. Its leader, Shoko Asahara, was eventually arrested and convicted of murder.

Several instances of violent crime involving U.S. servicemen in Okinawa led Pres. Clinton and Prime Minister Hashimoto to sign an agreement in April, 1996, reducing the number of American bases in Okinawa.

Prime Minister Ryutaro Hashimoto, first elected in Jan. 1996, was re-elected leader of the LDP in Sept., 1997. But the Asian economic crisis took a toll on Japan, still in the midst of a long-term recession. In the spring of 1998 a plunge in the value of the yen doomed the Hashimoto government; he resigned and was replaced by party stalwart, Keizo Obuchi.

In 1999 Japan's economy rebounded slightly as the Obuchi government tried desperately to raise the levels of spending throughout the economy. In April 2000, Premier Obuchi suffered a stroke. His successor Yoshiro Mori led the Liberal Democrats to a near majority in parliamentary elections June 25, forming a coalition government with New Komeito and the Conservatives (a new party, composed of former Liberals). With Mori's resignation in April 2001, the Liberal Democrats (operating under new party rules) selected as their leader, and the lower house named as Prime Minister, Junichiro Koizumi, a man outside the old party "factions" and promising modernizing liberal economic reforms. Japan's economy grew worse during 2001 and 2002, but rebounded slightly in 2003.

▶JORDAN

Hashemite Kingdom of Jordan

• **GEOGRAPHY** **Location:** western Asia. **Boundaries**: Syria to N, Iraq to NE, Saudi Arabia to SE, Israel to W. **Total area**: 34,445 sq. mi. (89,213 sq km). **Coastline**: 16 mi. (26 km). **Comparative area**: slightly smaller than Indiana. **Land use:** 3% arable land; 2% permanent crops; 95% other. **Major cities**: (1991) Amman (capital) 965,000; Zarqa 359,000; Irbid 216,000; Russeita 115,500.

• **PEOPLE** **Population:** 5,460,265 (July 2003 est.). **Nationality:** noun—Jordanian(s); adjective—Jordanian. **Ethnic groups:** 98% Arab, 1% Circassian, 1% Armenian. **Languages:** Arabic (official); English widely understood among upper and middle classes. **Religions:** 92% Sunni Muslim, 6% Christian, 2% other.

• **GOVERNMENT** **Type:** constitutional monarchy. **Independence:** May 25, 1946 (from League of Nations Mandate under British administration). **Constitution:** Jan. 8, 1952. **National holiday:** Independence Day, May 25. **Heads of Government:** Abdullah Bin Al Hussein, king (since Feb. 1999); Ali Abul Ragheb, prime minister (since Jan. 2002). **Structure:** executive—king is chief of state, prime minister and cabinet are appointed by king; bicameral legislature—House of Representatives has been dissolved by the king several times since 1974; House of Notables appointed by the king; judiciary.

• **ECONOMY** **Monetary unit:** Jordanian dinar. **Budget:** (2002 est.) ***income:*** $2.7 bil.; ***expend.:*** $3 bil. **GDP:** $22.8 bil., $4,300 per capita (2002 est.). **Chief crops:** wheat, barley, citrus, tomatoes, melons, olives; poultry, goats, sheep. **Natural resources:** phosphates, potash, shale oil. **Major industries:** phosphate mining, petroleum refining, cement. **Labor force:** 1.36 mil (2002); 82.5% services, 12.5% industry, 5% agriculture; 25-30% unemployment (2001). **Exports:** $2.5 bil. (f.o.b., 2002 est.); phosphates, fertilizers, potash, agricultural products, manufactures. **Imports:** $4.4 bil. (f.o.b., 2002 est.); crude oil, machinery, transport equipment, food, live animals, manufactured goods. **Major trading partners:** ***exports:*** India, Saudi Arabia, Israel; ***imports:*** E.U., Iraq, U.S.

The present territory of the Kingdom of Jordan corresponds to the biblical lands of Edom, Gilead, and Moab. The ancient rock city of Petra was the capital of the Edomite and Nabataean kingdoms. The region was incorporated into the Roman Empire, and later the Latin Kingdom of Jerusalem; it was an important early center of Christianity.

In the 630's Jordan became one of the first areas outside Arabia to fall to the expansion of Islam. It became subject to the Caliphate, located at Damascus and later at Baghdad, and in the 11th century became part of the empire of the Seljuk Turks. The Crusades brought European invaders, but with little lasting impact. The Mongols conquered Jordan in the mid-13th century, and it later passed into the control of the Mamluk sultanate. In 1517 Jordan was incorporated into the Ottoman Empire.

Following the post-World War I breakup of the Ottoman Empire, Jordan came under British control as part of a League of Nations Mandate of Palestine. In 1921 Great Britain sponsored the establishment of a monarchy by Abdullah, son of Hussein ibn Ali, ruler of the Hejaz in Arabia. Britain recognized the independence of the Hashemite Kingdom of Transjordan in 1923; a 1928 treaty gave Britain the unrestricted right to station troops in the kingdom.

Transjordan supported the Allies in World War II and was rewarded with full independence in 1946, although strong military ties to Great Britain were maintained. In 1948 the kingdom joined the Arab League, changed its name to Jordan, and joined other Arab states in the first Arab-Israeli War. The war resulted in the occupation by Jordanian troops of the West Bank and the Old City of Jerusalem, which were annexed in 1950. King Hussein I came to the throne on Aug. 11, 1952. All British military forces were withdrawn from the kingdom in 1957.

Israel recaptured the West Bank and the Old City of Jerusalem in the Six-Day War of 1967, and large numbers of Palestinian refugees fled to Jordan. Jordan played no substantial role in the 1974 Arab-Israeli War. In 1974 Jordan accepted the decision of an Arab summit conference designating the Palestine Liberation Organization the sole representative of Palestinians in the West Bank. Jordan's role as a front-line opponent of Israel won it a large annual subvention from Arab oil states; King Hussein's reputation as an Arab moderate led to significant American support.

King Hussein strongly opposed the 1979 Camp David Accords and the Egypt-Israeli peace treaty; Jordan broke off diplomatic relations with Egypt in March 1979 but resumed full relations in 1984.

In July 1981 King Hussein, charging the Palestine Liberation Organization with subversion, forced the withdrawal of PLO troops and political headquarters from Jordan. While some hoped that Hussein would represent the Palestinians in talks with Israel, in 1988 the king flatly rejected any such role, implied that the PLO should declare an independent state on the West Bank and in the Gaza Strip, and declared that a settlement would require talks between Israel and the PLO.

The Persian Gulf War had a drastic impact on Jordan's economy. King Hussein actively backed Iraq, thus jeopardizing direct aid from Kuwait and Saudi Arabia. But the historic peace treaty signed with Israel in October 1994 restored Hussein's standing while returning some territory taken in the 1967 war. In August 1998, while in the U.S. for medical care, King Hussein made a dramatic visit to the PLO-Israeli talks to appeal for a settlement. Back in Jordan, Hussein deposed his brother Hassan as Crown Prince, swearing in his eldest son Abdullah instead. Twelve days later (Feb. 7), the king died. The new king, Abdullah, pledged to continue his father's policies, asking the current cabinet to stay on. King Abdullah moved cautiously against radical Muslim groups (winning Israeli praise) and restructured the army command in 1999. His first cabinet change came in June 2000, as he appointed reformer Ali Abu Ragher as prime minister.

▶KAZAKHSTAN

Republic of Kazakhstan

• **GEOGRAPHY** **Location:** central Asia. **Boundaries**: Russian Federation to N and NE, China to SE, Kyrgystan, Uzbekistan, and Turkmenistan to S, Caspian Sea to W. **Total area**: 1,049,151 sq. mi. (2,717,300 sq km). **Coastline**: 1,441 mi. (2,320 km) on Caspian Sea. **Comparative area**: slightly less than four times the size of Texas. **Land use:** 11% arable cropland; 1% permanent crops; 88% other. **Major cities**: (1993 est.) Astana (capital) 300,000; Almaty (formerly Alma-Ata) 1,176,000; Karaganda 596,000.

• **PEOPLE** **Population:** 16,763,795 (July 2003 est.). **Nationality:** noun—Kazakhstani(s); adjective—Kazakhstani. **Ethnic groups:** 53.4% Kazakh, 30% Russian, 3.7% Ukrainian, 2.5% Uzbek. **Languages:** 64.4 Kazakh (state language); 95% Russian (official, used in everyday business). **Religions:** 47% Muslim, 44% Russian Orthodox, 2% Protestant.

• **GOVERNMENT** **Type:** republic. **Independence:** Dec. 16, 1991 (from the Soviet Union). **Constitution:** Jan 28, 1993. **National holiday:** Day of the Republic, Oct. 25. **Heads of Government:** Nursultan A. Nazarbaev, president (since Dec. 1991); Danial K. Akhmetov, prime minister (since June 13, 2003). **Structure:** executive—president, prime minister, Council of Ministers; bicameral legislature; judicial.

• **ECONOMY** **Monetary unit:** tenge. **Budget:** (1999 est.) ***income:*** $4.2 bil.; ***expend.:*** $5.1 bil. **GDP:** $105 bil., $6,300 per capita (2002 est.). **Chief crops:** grains, cotton; wool, meat. **Natural resources:** major deposits of petroleum, natural gas, coal, iron ore, manganese. **Major industries:** oil, coal, iron ore, manganese. **Labor force:** 8.4 mil. (1999); 30% industry, 20% agriculture; 8.8% unemployment (2002). **Exports:** $10.2 bil. (f.o.b., 2002 est.); oil, ferrous and nonferrous metals, chemicals, grain, wool. **Imports:** $9.6 bil. (f.o.b., 2002 est.); machinery and parts, industrial materials, oil and gas. **Major trading partners:** ***exports:*** 20% Russia, 14% Bermuda,11% Italy; ***imports:*** 45% Russia, 7% Germany, 5% U.S.

Kazakhstan, the largest nation in central Asia, is a land of deserts and plateaus stretching across the rolling tablelands of the Eurasian landmass; approximately 20 percent is mountainous. The Kazakhs are descended from Mongol and Turkic tribes who settled in the area known as Kazakhstan about the 1st century B.C. In the sixth century A.D. the area formed part of the Turkish Khaganate, a loose federation of nomadic tribes, and in the seventh to ninth centuries Islam became established among the settled population. Although the Mongols ruled the area from 1219 to 1447, the Turkish subjects of the Mongol Horde were to play a decisive role in the future of the region.

In the 15th century, the Kazakhs emerged as a distinct people, but by the 17th century, due to internecine fighting, the Kazakhs split into three nomadic federations, known as the Larger, the Middle, and the Lesser Hordes. In the mid-17th century, the Mongols began to invade the region, and the Kazakhs, not being unified enough to repel them, sought protection from the Russians. By the mid-18th century, the Kazakh lands were completely under Russian control. With the freeing of serfs in 1861 in Russia, Kazakhstan experienced its first major influx of Russian and Ukrainian peasants, who were given Kazakh lands. Resentment over this grew until the Kazakhs rebelled against Russian rule in 1916. The Russians brutally repressed the uprising, but not before thousands of Kazakhs and many Russians were killed.

After the 1917 Communist revolution in Russia, a civil war ensued in Kazakhstan, from which the Bolsheviks emerged victorious. The Kazakh territory was incorporated into Russia in 1920, granted "autonomous" status in 1925, and in 1936 it formally became one of the U.S.S.R.'s union republics. Kazakhstan was industrialized, but it suffered enormously from the U.S.S.R.'s policies. In the 1930's, the traditionally nomadic Kazakh people were forcibly settled on collectivized farms, and more than a million died of starvation. In the 1950's, Khrushchev's failed "Virgin Lands" scheme and the Soviet government's repeated nuclear tests wreaked environmental havoc on Kazakhstan. As a result of years of Soviet economic development programs, the rate of Russian and Ukrainian immigration into Kazakhstan greatly increased. By 1979, 41 percent of Kazakhstan's population was Russian; 36 percent were native Kazakhs.

Under Mikhail Gorbachev's policy of glasnost, or openness, in the 1980's, the corrupt Communist party leader of Kazakhstan and Brezhnev crony Dinmukhamed Kunayev was deposed. He was ultimately replaced by Nursultan Nazarbayev, an ethnic Kazakh, who was elected in April 1990 to the new post of president.

Kazakhstan declared its independence in March 1991 and joined the Commonwealth of Independent States in December. It has pursued closer economic but not political ties with Russia and Belarus. The May 1995 customs union among the three was expanded in March 1996 to include coordination of agricultural and industrial policies and the establishment of joint transport, energy and information systems, with Kyrgystan added as a fourth member. Kazakhstan took part (April 1996) in a five-power non-agression treaty with Russia, China, Kyrgyzstan, and Tajikistan which was extended a year later to include reduction of military forces in border areas. The last remaining Soviet-era nuclear missle was detonated underground in May 1995 and the last ballistic missle silo was torn down in September 1996. In Feb. 1997 the supposedly tame legislature refused to ratify a Russian lease of four nuclear test sites in Kazakhstan.

Independent Kazakhstan's first presidential election was held in December 1991 with Nazarbayev the only candidate. An April 1995 referendum cancelled the 1996 election and extended Nazarbayev's term to 2000 with a gratifying 95 percent "yes" vote; and in August of the year 89 percent approved a new "strong president" constitution, making the president head of the Supreme Court and permitting him to dissolve parliament at will. Nazarbayev had already dissolved parliament in March 1995, a parliament in which his supporters held two-thirds of the seats, but whose pace of economic reform displeased him. He ruled by decree until new elections late in 1995 and early in 1996.

Kazakhstan's economic future looks bright because of its enormous untapped gas and oil reserves, perhaps 25 billion barrels. Several global corporations have negotiated development rights. In April 1996, Kazakhstan, Russia and Oman established a consortium with eight oil companies to build a 900-mile pipeline linking the Tengiz fields with Russia's Black Sea port of Novorossiyak. And in July of that year, the I.M.F. chipped in with a loan of $446 million.

In 1998 the capital was moved— ostensibly for security reasons—from Almaty to remote Akmola, which was renamed Astana, a word meaning "capital" in Kazakh. In July, Navarbayev signed a pact with Russia, settling the thorny question of dividing the northern Caspian Sea (with its petroleum riches). But with falling world oil prices, the Kazakh economy stalled, bringing Nazarbayev to call for presidential elections 18 months early, elections he not surprisingly won handily, this time with 80 percent of the votes, in January 1999.

▶KENYA
Republic of Kenya

• **GEOGRAPHY** **Location:** eastern Africa. **Boundaries**: Sudan to NW, Ethiopia to N, Somalia to E, Indian Ocean to SE, Tanzania to SW, Lake Victoria, Uganda to W. **Total area**: 224,962 sq. mi. (582,650 sq km). **Coastline**: 333 mi. (536 km). **Comparative area**: slightly more than twice the size of Nevada. **Land use:** 7% arable land; 1% permanent crops; 92% other. **Major cities**: (1989 est.) Nairobi (capital) 1,346,000; Mombasa 465,000; Nakuru 162,800; Kisumu 185,100; Thika 57,100.

• **PEOPLE** **Population:** 31,639,091 (July 2003 est.). **Nationality:** noun—Kenyan(s); adjective—Kenyan. **Ethnic groups:** 22% Kikuyu, 14% Luhya, 13% Luo, 12% Kalenjin, 11% Kamba, 6% Kisii, 6% Meru, 15% other African, 1% non-African (Asian, European, and Arab). **Languages:** English and Kiswahili (both official), indigenous languages. **Religions:** 45% Protestant, 35% Roman Catholic, 10% indigenous beliefs, 10% Muslim, 2% other.

• **GOVERNMENT** **Type:** republic. **Independence:** Dec. 12, 1963 (from U.K.). **Constitution:** Dec. 12, 1963. **National holiday:** Independence Day, Dec. 12. **Head of Government:** Mwai Kibaki, president (since Jan. 1, 2003). **Structure:** executive—president and cabinet; unicameral legislature—first multiparty election since repeal of one-party state law in 1991; judiciary.

• **ECONOMY** **Monetary unit:** Kenyan shilling. **Budget:** (2000 est.) ***income:*** $2.9 bil.; ***expend.:*** $2.97 bil. **GDP:** $32 bil., $1,020 per capita (2002 est.). **Chief crops:** coffee, tea, corn, wheat, sugarcane; cattle, pork, poultry. **Natural resources:** gold, limestone, soda ash, salt barites. **Major industries:** small-scale consumer goods (plastic, furniture, batteries, textiles, soap, cigarettes, flour), agricultural processing, oil refining. **Labor force:** 10 mil. (2001); 75-80% agriculture, 20-25% non-agriculture; 40% unemployment (2001). **Exports:** $2.1 bil. (f.o.b., 2002 est.); tea, coffee, petroleum products. **Imports:** $3 bil. (f.o.b., 2002 est.); machinery and transport equipment, consumer goods, petroleum and petroleum products **Major trading partners:** ***exports:*** 14% U.K., 13% Tanzania, 12% Uganda; ***imports:*** 12% U.K., 10% UAE, 7% Japan.

Kenya formed part of an ancient network of trade between the Red Sea and the coast of East Africa as early as the fourth century B.C. Persian and Arab trading posts were established on the coast by the eighth century A.D. At about the same time, the indigenous Cushitic people of Kenya had been joined by Bantu and Nilotic immigrants. Swahili, a mixture of Bantu and Arabic, developed as a language of trade throughout the region.

Portuguese explorers reached Kenya in 1498. Portuguese control of the coastal area ended in 1729, when the region came under the control of the sultans of Oman. British adventurers explored Kenya in the late 19th century. In 1885 the Berlin Conference divided East Africa into European spheres of influence. The British East Africa Company established a protectorate over the coastal region in 1890 and extended its control into the interior in 1895. British settlers established farms, mission stations, and towns, and Kenya was given colonial status in 1920.

During World War II, northern Kenya was briefly occupied by troops from the Italian colony of Ethiopia. After the British reasserted control, Africans were granted the right to participate in local government in 1944.

From 1952 to 1959, a state of emergency was declared in Kenya because of the "Mau Mau" rebellion against British colonial rule. In response to local unrest, British authorities widened African participation in government and Africans were elected to the Legislative Council in 1957.

Kenya became independent on Dec. 12, 1963, and in 1964 assumed the status of a republic within the British Commonwealth. Jomo Kenyatta, a member of the dominant Kikuyu population and leader of the main political party, the Kenya African National Union (KANU), was elected Kenya's first president. A leftist party, the Kenya People's Union (KPU) was organized in 1966, led by Oginga Odinga. In 1969 it was implicated in the assassination of Tom Mboya, a prominent political leader; its leaders were imprisoned and the party dissolved. From 1969 to 1992 KANU was Kenya's sole political party.

Kenyatta died on Aug. 22, 1978, and Vice Pres. Daniel arap Moi succeeded him. In 1982 the constitution was amended to make Kenya a one-party state. Moi was reelected president in 1983 and again in 1988, the latter being the first election conducted without secret ballots. Foreign observers accused the Moi government of widespread human rights abuses. Riots broke out in several cities in 1991, and sporadic ethnic violence cost thousands of lives.

In 1991, Odinga formed the opposition Forum for the Restoration of Democracy (FORD), in direct defiance of the government. With Western aid conditioned on economic reform, political pluralism, and improved human rights, Moi allowed presidential elections to be held in Dec. of 1992. The three opposition parties split, and Moi was returned to office for a fourth time.

Kenya has traditionally been viewed as the success story of postcolonial Africa, but by the 1990's, widespread government corruption, and economic inefficiency had taken a heavy toll. Tourism has fallen due to the rise in violence, and the economy was further strained by the presence of refugees from Ethiopia, Somalia, and Sudan.

Early in 1994 the government announced reforms aimed at restoring confidence in the economy, including lifting the restrictions on foreign investment. But Pres. Moi's (April 1995) arrest of two leading opposition figures (bringing the total arrested since 1993 to more than 50) led to frustration among his many political enemies. In mid-1997, large demonstrations demanding Moi reform the electoral system in time for Dec. presidential elections were broken up by police with a great amount of violence. In the face of international condemnation Moi agreed to the proposed reforms (July 15), but little progress was made in subsequent meetings between the government and the opposition leaders. In Jan. 1998 Moi barely won reelection. (In an unrelated story, the U.S. embassy was attacked by a terrorist truck-bomb August 7, with 250 deaths.)

In 2002 dissentions within Moi's KANU party obliged him not to run for president; his attempt to name his successor (Uhuru Kenyatta, son of Kenya's "founding father") split the party and allowed the opposition National Alliance Party's candidate Mwai Kibaki to win the Dec. 2002 election.

▶KIRIBATI

Republic of Kiribati

• GEOGRAPHY **Location:** 33 atolls, in three main groups (E to W: Line Is., Phoenix Is., Gilbert Is.) in mid-Pacific Ocean; about 2,400 mi. (3,870 km) E to W and 1,275 mi. (2,050 km) N to S. Tarawa (Gilberts) 1°30'N, 173°00'E. **Boundaries**: surrounded by Pacific Ocean; nearest neighbors are Nauru to W, and Tuvalu and Tokelau to S. **Total area**: 277 sq. mi. (717 sq km). **Coastline**: 710 mi. (1,143 km). **Comparative area**: four times the size of Washington, D.C. **Land use:** 0% arable land; 51% permanent crops; 49% other. **Major cities**: (1990 census) Tarawa (capital) 25,154.

• PEOPLE **Population:** 98,549 (July 2003 est.). **Nationality:** noun—I-Kiribati (sing., pl.); adjective—I-Kiribati. **Ethnic groups:** Micronesian. **Languages:** English (official), Gilbertese. **Religions:** 52% Roman Catholic, 40% Protestant (Congregational), some Seventh-Day Adventist, Church of God, Mormon and Baha'i.

• GOVERNMENT **Type:** republic. **Independence:** July 12, 1979 (from U.K.). **Constitution:** July 12, 1979. **National holiday:** Independence Day, July 12. **Head of Government:** Anote Tong, president (since July 8, 2003). **Structure:** executive; unicameral legislature; judiciary—all judges appointed by the president.

• ECONOMY **Monetary unit:** Australian dollar. **Budget:** (2000 est.) ***income:*** $28.4 mil.; ***expend.:*** $37.2 mil. **GDP:** $79 mil., $840 per capita (2002 est.). **Chief crops:** copra; taro, bread fruit, vegetables; fish. **Natural resources:** phosphate (production discontinued in 1979). **Major industries:** fishing and handicrafts. **Labor force:** 7,870 economically active (1985 est.). **Exports:** $6 mil. (f.o.b., 1998 est.); 62% copra, seaweed, fish. **Imports:** $44 mil. (c.i.f., 1999 est.); foodstuffs, machinery and quipment. **Major trading partners:** ***exports:*** U.S., Japan, Bangladesh; ***imports:*** Australia, Fiji, Japan.

In 1892 the British established a protectorate over the Gilbert Islands, inhabited principally by Micronesians. In 1915 Britain joined the islands administratively with the Polynesian-speaking Ellice Islands to the south to form a British colony, the Gilbert and Ellice Islands (later expanded to include other islands). The Japanese occupied the Gilberts in 1942; in 1943 the Allied forces recaptured them, and Tarawa was the scene of some of the fiercest combat in the Pacific.

In 1971 Britain granted the colony self-rule. The Ellice Islands broke away in 1975, becoming the independent nation of Tuvalu in 1978. On July 12, 1979, the Gilbert Islands became independent as Kiribati. United States claims to portions of the Line and Phoenix islands were settled by a friendship treaty in 1979.

Kiribati's economy is based on subsistence farming and on fishing. Copra exports and the sale of fishing rights (principally to Japan) are the main earners of hard currency. The islands were expected to join the United Nations in late 1999.

▶KOREA, NORTH

Democratic People's Republic of Korea

• GEOGRAPHY **Location:** northern part of Korean peninsula in eastern Asia. **Boundaries**: China to NW, Sea of Japan to E, Republic of Korea to S, Yellow Sea to SW. **Total area**: 46,541 sq. mi. (120,540 sq km). **Coastline**: 1,551 mi. (2,495 km). **Comparative area**: slightly smaller than Mississippi. **Land use:** 14% arable land; 2% permanent crops; 18% other. **Major cities**: (1986 est.) Pyongyang (capital) 2,000,000; Hamhung 670,000; Chongjin 530,000; Sinuju 330,000; Kaesong 310,000.

• PEOPLE **Population:** 22,466,481 (July 2003 est.). **Nationality:** noun—Korean(s); adjective—Korean. **Ethnic groups:** racially homogeneous, with a small Chinese community. **Languages:** Korean. **Religions:** Buddhism and Confucianism; autonomous religious activities now almost nonexistent.

• GOVERNMENT **Type:** authoritarian socialist; one-man dictatorship. **Constitution:** adopted 1948, revised Apr. 1992 and Sept. 1998. **National holiday:** Foundation Day, Sept. 9. **Heads of Government:** Kim Jong Il, president (since Oct. 1994); Hong Song San, prime minister (since Dec. 1992). **Structure:** executive—president is dominant figure in government; Supreme People's Assembly theoretically supervises legislative and judicial functions; State Administration Council (cabinet) oversees ministerial operations.

• ECONOMY **Monetary unit:** North Korean won. **Budget:** N.A.; **GDP:** $22 bil., $1,000 per capita (2002 est.). **Chief crops:** corn, rice, vegetables; pigs, cattle. **Natural resources:** coal, lead, tungsten, zinc, graphite. **Major industries:** machine building, military products, electric power, chemicals. **Labor force:** 9.6 mil.; 36% agricultural, 64% nonagricultural. **Exports:** $842 mil. (f.o.b., 2001 est.); minerals, metallurgical products, agricultural and fishery products, manufactures. **Imports:** $1.314 bil. (c.i.f., 2001 est.); petroleum, machinery and equipment, coking coal, grain. **Major trading partners:** ***exports:*** 20% China, 27% Japan, 21% South Korea; ***imports:*** 44% China, 11% Japan, 8% Thailand.

(For pre-1945 history, see "Republic of Korea.")

The Soviet Union's declaration of war against Japan in the waning days of World War II strengthened its position in northeast Asia, and particularly in Korea. After Japan's surrender, Korea was arbitrarily divided into zones of Soviet and American occupation, north and south of latitude 38° north. The Korean Communist party (KCP), founded in 1922, had functioned in exile in the U.S.S.R. during the Japanese occupation, and KCP workers were quickly moved into the Soviet zone in 1945.

U.S.-Soviet talks aimed at Korean reunification broke down, and in 1948 the establishment of separate regimes in North and South Korea formalized the postwar occupation zones. The Korean Democratic People's Republic was proclaimed on May 1, 1948. It inherited most of the industrial and hydroelectric power infrastructure built during the Japanese colonial period and enjoyed strong Soviet backing.

On June 25, 1950, North Korean troops crossed the 38th parallel in an effort to force the reunification of Korea under a communist regime. U.N. troops under American leadership came to the defense of the South. (For the Korean War, see "South Korea.") The war was fought to a stalemate, and a truce was signed on July 27, 1953.

Until 1994 North Korea had a single leader throughout its national history: Kim Il Sung, chairman of the KCP from 1945 and president from 1972. Under Kim Il Sung, North Korea was a typically Stalinist Soviet nation, concentrating its economic energies on heavy industry and imposing a strictly regimented political and social life on its citizens. Economic development was supported by aid from the Soviet Union and China. After an impressive program of postwar reconstruction in the 1950's and 1960's, the country fell into economic stagnation.

Relations between North and South Korea were implacably hostile; the North has made numerous attempts to infiltrate and sabotage the South. In 1983, 17 people, including four South Korean cabinet ministers, were killed in Rangoon by a bomb planted by North Korean agents. In 1990 the leaders of both countries held three cordial but unproductive meetings. Much of the goodwill accumulated was harmed by the assertions of the U.S. that North Korea was planning to build nuclear weapons.

In August 1992, China, North Korea's long-term ally established diplomatic relations with South Korea, leaving North Korea completely isolated. High-level contacts between North and South Korea continued, but reconciliation talks stalled in 1993 as the issue of North Korean nuclear weapons came to the fore. North Korean leaders refused to allow international arms inspectors access to some facilities and withdrew from the Nuclear Non-Proliferation Treaty. In June 1994 former U.S. president Jimmy Carter met with Kim Il Sung and arranged for a summit meeting with South Korea and for another with Pres. Clinton to resolve the nuclear weapons issue. Kim Il Sung's sudden death in July prevented immediate progress, but in 1995 an agreement was reached that called for North Korea to dismantle its nuclear facilities in exchange for two new reactors from which weapons-grade plutonium is hard to extract. In 1996 severe floods destroyed most of the rice crop, left half a million homeless, and forced North Korea to accept emergency grants of rice from Japan and South Korea.

Continued severe famine spurred North Korea to pursue reconciliation talks with the South, but those talks were repeatedly disrupted by strife over North Korean nuclear-weapons programs, incidents of clandestine landing of northern commandos in the south, and the defection of senior communist officials. In the fall of 1997 Kim Jung Il assumed his father's old position as general secretary of the Worker's Party. U.S. suspicions, voiced in 1998, of a new underground nuclear plant were proven baseless in May of 1999, the Great Leader permitting an inspection in return for food aid. (Estimates of 2.3 million deaths from the famine must have influenced the decision). Talks with South Korea in Beijing were broken off in June 1999 after South Korea sank a North Korean torpedo boat in the Yellow Sea. But talks in Geneva continued with South Korea, China and the U.S., supplemented in March 2000 with secret talks with South Korea, as diplomatic relations were opened with Italy and Australia. The secret talks led, in June, to a Pyongyang visit by South Korea's president Kim. The two pledged themselves to peace and reunification. Family visits across the border ensued. In 2002, a naval attack in the Yellow Sea, in which a North Korean vessel sank a South Korean patrol boat, seriously eclipsed the "sunshine policy." In Oct. North Korean officials admitted to the U.S. they had been secretly developing nuclear weapons and in Dec. they expelled U.N. monitors. (See "Major News Stories")

▶KOREA, SOUTH
Republic of Korea

• **GEOGRAPHY** **Location:** southern part of Korean peninsula in eastern Asia. **Boundaries**: North Korea to N, separated by frontier roughly following 38th parallel; Sea of Japan to E, East China Sea to S, and Yellow Sea to W. **Total area**: 38,023 sq. mi. (98,480 sq km). **Coastline**: 1,500 mi. (2,413 km). **Comparative area**: slightly larger than Indiana. **Land use:** 17% arable land; 2% permanent crops; 81% other. **Major cities**: (1995 est.) Seoul (capital) 10,776,201; Pusan 3,802,319; Taegu 2,228,843; Inchon 1,818,293; Kwangju 1,144,695.
• **PEOPLE** **Population:** 48,289,037 (July 2003 est.). **Nationality:** noun—Korean(s); adjective—Korean. **Ethnic groups:** homogeneous; small Chinese minority (about 20,000). **Languages:** Korean; English widely taught in high school. **Religions:** 49% Christianity, 47% Buddhism, 3% Confucianism; pervasive folk religion.
• **GOVERNMENT** **Type:** republic. **Constitution:** Feb. 25, 1988. **National holiday:** Liberation Day, Aug. 15. **Heads of Government:** Roh Moo-hyun (since Feb. 25, 2003); Goh Kun, premier (since Feb. 26, 2003). **Structure:** executive; unicameral legislature (National Assembly); judiciary.
• **ECONOMY** **Monetary unit:** South Korean won. **Budget:** (2000 est.) ***income:*** $118.1 bil.; ***expend.:*** $95.7 bil. **GDP:** $931 bil., $19,400 per capita (2003 est.). **Chief crops:** rice, root crops, barley, vegetables, fruit; cattle, pigs, chickens, milk, eggs; fish catch of 2.9 mil. metric tons, seventh largest in the world. **Natural resources:** coal, tungsten, graphite, molybdenum. **Major industries:** electronics, automobiles, chemicals, shipbuilding. **Labor force:** 22 mil. (2001); 69% services and other, 21.5% industry; 9.5% agriculture, fishing, and forestry; 3.1% unemployment (2002). **Exports:** $162.6 bil. (f.o.b., 2002); electronic and electrical equipment, electrical machinery, steel, automobiles. **Imports:** $148.4 bil. (f.o.b., 2002); machinery, electronics and electronic equipment, oil, steel, transport equipment, textiles. **Major trading partners:** U.S., Japan, China.

From ancient times Korea has struggled successfully to preserve its national independence. To the native culture—marked by a warrior aristocracy, shamanic religion, and a subject class of rice cultivators—was added, under continuous Chinese influence, a strong adherence to Buddhism and a system of government modeled on Chinese Confucian bureaucratism. The three rival kingdoms of Silla, Paekche, and Koguryo were united, through Chinese intervention, in the seventh century A.D.; unified dynastic rule was maintained thereafter.

The Yi dynasty (1392-1910), under which Korea was known as the Kingdom of Choson, was a staunch tributary ally of China under both the Ming (1368-1644) and Qing (1644-1911) dynasties. A Japanese invasion of Korea in 1592 conquered most of the country but was finally repelled by combined Chinese and Korean forces. From the late 17th century to the 1870's, all non-Chinese foreign influence was rigorously excluded from the country.

Korea's isolation, and its status as a Chinese tributary, ended in 1874, when Japan imposed on it the Treaty of Kangwha, guaranteeing Japanese commercial access and other interests. The Sino-Japanese War of 1894-95 was fought primarily over the status of Korea; following Japan's victory in that war, Korea was made a Japanese protectorate and was annexed as a Japanese colony in 1910. A harsh regime was established with the aim of eradicating Korean culture and incorporating Korea entirely into the Japanese empire.

During the colonial period, Korean resistance to the Japanese regime was violently suppressed, but resistance movements survived in exile—notably the Korean Communist party in the Soviet Union and a republican movement in China. During World War II, tens of thousands of Koreans were conscripted as forced laborers to work in Japan and in Japanese-occupied territories.

Following Japan's surrender, Korea was arbitrarily divided into zones of Soviet and American occupation, north and south of 38° north latitude. The dividing line split Korea economically as well as geographically and politically; Korea's industry and hydroelectric power was concentrated in the north, while the south was primarily agricultural. In contrast to well-laid Soviet plans for installing a Communist government in the north (see "North Korea"), American attempts to reunify the country under a republican regime were inept. By 1948 it had become clear that plans for reunification were hopeless. In May of that year, the Republic of Korea was organized in the south, with Dr. Syngman Rhee as president. The United States withdrew its occupation forces in June 1949.

On June 25, 1950, North Korean troops invaded the south in an apparent attempt to unify the country forcibly under the communist regime. An emergency session of the U.N. Security Council voted to send troops to Korea; the U.S.S.R., having boycotted the session, was unable to exercise its veto on North Korea's behalf. U.N. troops, dominated by American forces and commanded by Gen. Douglas MacArthur, launched a counterattack in September with a landing at Inchon and swept north, reaching the Chinese border by Nov. 20. On Nov. 26 the tide turned again when Chinese troops entered the war, ostensibly to defend the Chinese border but also to aid their North Korean allies in driving the U.N. forces south again. Seoul fell once more on Jan. 4, 1951. In February and March another U.N. counteroffensive drove the combined Chinese and North Korean forces back to the 38th parallel again. Thereafter, the battle lines remained generally stable, although fierce fighting continued at intervals for another two years. On Apr. 11, 1951, Gen. MacArthur was relieved of the Korean command for making unauthorized policy statements and was replaced by Gen. Matthew Ridgway.

Armistice talks began in July 1951 but broke down repeatedly. A truce was signed on July 27, 1953, creating a demilitarized zone along the 38th parallel and establishing a framework for talks on a permanent settlement of the war. Negotiations have continued fruitlessly at the Panmunjom armistice conference headquarters ever since.

Postwar reconstruction, with significant U.S. aid, was overseen by the government of Syngman Rhee. Pres. Rhee resigned in 1960 after a wave of student demonstrations charging him with corruption and undemocratic practices. On May 16, 1961, Gen. Park Chung Hee seized power in a military coup. The military government was given democratic trappings when in 1972 a referendum was passed allowing Gen. Park to run for an unlimited series of six-year presidential terms. Gen. Park was assassinated on Oct. 26, 1979, by the government's chief of intelligence. Gen. Chun Doo Hwan rose to power, continuing the military rule of Gen. Park. Gen. Chun's regime was marked by widespread violent political protests but the economy made great strides. The traditionally agrarian country was transformed into a modernized, urban, industrial nation. In 1986 South Korea for the first time achieved a favorable balance-of-payments ratio in foreign trade, and the favorable balance has increased rapidly, led by exports of automobiles, textiles and clothing, and consumer electronic goods.

After weeks of widespread demonstrations in mid-1987, Gen. Chun agreed to allow direct presidential elections to choose his successor. In the elections, the government candidate, Roh Tae Woo, achieved a plurality over the sharply divided opposition parties. Under Pres. Roh, the political situation calmed, although student demonstrations continued, calling for greater efforts for Korean reunification and protesting the presence of large numbers of American troops.

High-level talks between North and South began in 1990, and an agreement in principle was reached that reunification would take place in the near future, a wish that remains unfulfilled.

In 1992 South Korea was a strong economic power in Asia and North Korea would become increasingly isolated, the establishment of diplomatic relations with China was a clear signal that it would remain so.

Also in 1992, longtime political opposition leader Kim Young Sam won election as South Korea's first postwar civilian president. Although he was initially able to liberalize some aspects of civil rights, the renewed threat of war with North Korea became the overriding preoccupation of the government until late 1994, when an agreement was reached calling for North Korea to dismantle its nuclear facilities in exchange for new reactors.

The ruling Democratic Labor Party was plagued by scandals that hampered its effectiveness. Pres. Kim's predecessor, Pres. Roh, was arrested for bribe-taking, as was his predecessor. Several key businessmen, including Kim's own son, were jailed for corruption. In elections in April 1996 the party lost its parliamentary majority but continued to govern as part of a coalition.

South Korea's economy was battered by the Asian economic crisis of 1997-98, leading to severe hardship for many workers. On Dec. 18, 1997, long-time democracy advocate and dissident Kim Dae Jung was elected. In May 1999 (after promising economic figures suggested a rising GDP and falling unemployment) he was able to reshuffle the cabinet to more closely accord with his "sunshine policy" of reforming the great conglomerate business empires and of improving relations with North Korea. In June talks with the North, held in Beijing, were abbreviated after South Korea sank a North Korean torpedo boat in a fishing grounds dispute in the Yellow Sea. Yet talks in Geneva continued and secret talks began in March 2000, leading to a "summit" in Pyongyang in June between President Kim and Kim Jong Il which promised peace and reunification.

Domestically, financial scandals involving Pres. Kim's son and some of his aides led him to distance himself from the Millenium Party, resigning as its head in Nov. 2001 and from the party itself in May. October by-elections had seen the party lose three seats, leaving it one short of a majority. A June 2002 North Korean naval attack called the "sunshine policy" into serious question. In December's presidential election, the Millennium

Democrats' candidate, Rho Moo Hyun, defeated Lee Hoi Chang of the Grand National Party. His inaugural address stressed reconcilation through dialogue in the face of the grave threat of North Korea's nuclear blustering.

▶KUWAIT

State of Kuwait

• **GEOGRAPHY** **Location:** northeastern Arabian peninsula. **Boundaries**: Iraq to N, Saudi Arabia to S, Persian Gulf to E. **Total area**: 6,880 sq. mi. (17,820 sq km). **Coastline**: 310 mi. (499 km). **Comparative area**: slightly smaller than New Jersey. **Land use:** negl. % arable land; negl. % permanent crops; 100% other. **Major cities**: (1995 census); Kuwait City (capital) 28,859; Salmiya 130,215; Hawalli 82,238; Faranawiya 53,100; Abraq Kheetan 45,120.

• **PEOPLE** **Population:** 2,183,161 (July 2003 est.). **Nationality:** noun—Kuwaiti(s); adjective—Kuwaiti. **Ethnic groups:** 45% Kuwaiti, 35% other Arab, 9% South Asian, 4% Iranian, 7% other. **Languages:** Arabic (official), English widely spoken. **Religions:** 85% Muslim (30% Shi'a, 70% Sunni), 15% Christian, Hindu, Parsi, and other.

• **GOVERNMENT** **Type:** nominal constitutional monarchy. **Independence:** June 19, 1961 (from U.K.). **Constitution:** Nov. 11, 1962 (some provisions suspended since Aug. 29, 1962). **National holiday:** National Day, Feb. 25. **Head of Government:** Jaber al-Ahmad al-Jaber al Sabah, amir (since Dec. 1977); Sabah Al-Ahmad Al -Jaber Al-Sabah, prime minister (since July 13, 2003). **Structure:** executive; unicameral legislature; judiciary.

• **ECONOMY** **Monetary unit:** Kuwaiti dinar. **Budget:** (FY02/03) ***income:*** $11 bil.; ***expend.:*** $17.5 bil. **GDP:** $34.2 bil., $15,000 per capita (2002 est.). **Chief crops:** virtually none; extensive fishing; about 75% of potable water must be distilled or imported. **Natural resources:** petroleum, fish, shrimp, natural gas. **Major industries:** petroleum, petrochemicals, desalination. **Labor force:** 1.3 mil. (1998 est.); 50% government and social services, 40% services, 10% industry and agriculture; non-Kuwaitis make up 80% of the work force. **Exports:** $16 bil. (f.o.b., 2002 est.); oil and refined products, fertilizers. **Imports:** $7.3 bil. (f.o.b., 2002 est.); food, construction materials, vehicles and parts, clothing. **Major trading partners: *exports:*** 22% Japan, 16% India; ***imports:*** 13% U.S., 9% Germany, 9% Japan.

Kuwait, at the head of the Persian Gulf, was part of the Abbasid empire from the eighth century and was absorbed into the Ottoman Empire in the late 16th century. It was organized as a principality under the al-Sabah dynasty in 1756, but the Ottomans continued to assert sovereignty. Increasing British influence during the 19th century was formalized in 1899, when Kuwait became a British protectorate.

The discovery of oil, first exported from Kuwait after World War II, rapidly made the principality one of the wealthiest in the Middle East. The British protectorate ended in 1961, when Kuwait gained full independence. The great majority of oil field workers in Kuwait are non-Kuwaiti Arabs, including many Palestinians. Oil revenues have made possible a total welfare state for Kuwaiti citizens, who pay no taxes and enjoy a wide range of free social services.

Kuwait allied itself with Iraq in the Iran-Iraq War of 1980-88; Kuwaiti tankers came under heavy attack from Iranian warships in the gulf. In July 1987, Kuwaiti tankers were reflagged with the U.S. flag and placed under escort of American warships in an operation that continued into 1989. Most of Kuwait's territory is barren and sparsely inhabited but with proven crude oil reserves of 94 bil. barrels—10 percent of the world's reserves—other economic endeavors are not needed.

On Aug. 2, 1990, Kuwait was invaded, and later annexed, by Iraq. In February 1991 it was liberated by a coalition of Arab, non-Arab Muslim, and Western nations led by the United States. Much of the country was destroyed or looted by the Iraqis. After its return to power, the ruling al-Sabah family came under strong pressure to institute democratic reforms. Parliamentary elections were held in 1992, and opposition candidates won 30 of 50 seats. The sultan then announced a new cabinet with more nonroyal members than ever before.

A brief war-scare flared up in October 1994 as 20,000 Iraqi Republican Guards were moved to the Kuwaiti border, only to retreat in the face of U.S. military opposition. In November, Iraq formally recognized Kuwait's sovereignty.

▶KYRGYZSTAN

Kyrgyz Republic

• **GEOGRAPHY** **Location:** eastern central Asia. **Boundaries**: Kazakhstan to N and NE, China to SE and S, Tajikistan to SW, Uzbekistan to W. **Total area**: 76,641 sq. mi. (198,500 sq km). **Coastline**: none. **Comparative area**: slightly smaller than South Dakota. **Land use:** 7% arable land; 0% permanent crops; 93% other. **Major cities**: (1990) Bishkek (known as Frunze 1926-91) (capital) 626,900.

• **PEOPLE** **Population:** 4,892,808 (July 2003 est.). **Nationality:** noun—Kyrgyzstani(s); adjective—Kyrgyzstani. **Ethnic groups:** 52.4% Kirghiz, 18% Russian, 12.9% Uzbek, 2.5% Ukrainian, 2.4% German, 11.8% other. **Languages:** Kirghiz and Russian (both official), Kirghiz is a member of south Turkic language group written in Cyrillic since 1940. **Religions:** 75% Muslim; 20% Russian Orthodox.

• **GOVERNMENT** **Type:** republic. **Independence:** Aug. 31, 1991 (from Soviet Union). **Constitution:** adopted May 5, 1993. **National holiday:** National Day, Dec. 2; Independence Day, Aug. 31. **Heads of Government:** Askar A. Akayev, president (since Oct. 1991); Nikolai T. Tanayev, prime minister (since May 2002). **Structure:** executive—president, prime ministers, Cabinet of Ministers; bicameral legislature; judiciary.

• **ECONOMY** **Monetary unit:** som. **Budget:** (1999 est.) ***income:*** $207.4 mil.; ***expend.:*** $238.7 mil. **GDP:** $13.5 bil., $2,800 per capita (2002 est.). **Chief crops:** wool, tobacco, cotton; sheep, goats, cattle. **Natural resources:** hydroelectric potential; gold; coal, natural gas, petroleum, lead, zinc. **Major industries:** small machinery, textiles, food processing, cement. **Labor force:** 2.7 mil. (2000); 55% agriculture and forest, 30% services, 15% industry and construction. **Exports:** $488 mil. (f.o.b., 2002 est.); cotton, wool, meat, tobacco; ferrous and nonferrous metals. **Imports:** $587 mil. (f.o.b., 2002 est.); foodstuffs, fuel, machinery. **Major trading partners:** Switzerland, Kazakhstan, Russia.

Kyrgyzstan is largely mountainous, dominated by the massive Tien Shan range in the northeast and the Pamir-Alay range in the southwest. Most of the population lives in one of three major valleys, the Fergana, the Chu, and the Talas, since much of the country is permanently ice-capped and covered with glaciers. The Kyrgyz people are mentioned in early Turkic inscriptions that date back at least to the eighth century A.D.

They were one of the great nomadic tribes of central Asia, who until the 10th century settled around the Upper Yenisei River. With the Mongol invasions of the 13th century, they migrated to the areas of the Tien Shan range in present-day Kyrgyzstan, a territory that has been controlled variously by Mongols, Kalmyks, Manchus, the large tribal empire of the Kokand khanate (or state), and the Russians. In the mid-17th century, the Kyrgyz began to be converted to Islam, but at nearly the same time, the Manchus defeated the Mongols and the Kyrgyz people became Chinese subjects. The Chinese did not interfere with their nomadic life, but in the 19th century they were attacked and came under the control of the khanate of Kokand, during which time Islam was strengthened. In 1868 the khanate became a Russian protectorate and in 1876, the area was merged into the Russian empire as Fergana region. A large Russian influx followed, and many Kyrgyz migrated to China and Afghanistan.

The period immediately following the 1917 Bolshevik revolution was one of great confusion and fighting between the Kyrgyz, the Reds, the Whites, and foreign interventionists. Soviet power was established in 1919, although fighting continued in some parts until 1922. In 1918, Kyrgyzstan was included in the Russian republic's Turkestan Autonomous Soviet Socialist Republic; then, with the National Delimitation of Central Asian Republics in 1924, its name changed to Kara-Kirghiz Autonomous Province (also within the Russian republic). On Dec. 5, 1936, it became a full Soviet Socialist Republic (SSR) of the U.S.S.R.

As a Soviet republic, advances were made in literacy, education, and public health, although repression of nationalist Kyrgyz was also evident. In the 1920's and 1930's, land reform and collectivization ended the traditional nomadic way of life. Kyrgyz nationalists strongly opposed the changes that Soviet rule brought, but the central government won in the end, and the nationalists were repressed. From the 1930's, ethnic Russians held most of the leading Communist party and government positions in the Kyrgyz SSR.

Mikhail Gorbachev's policy of glasnost, or openness, was responsible for the first public discussion of corruption in government, the emergence of a more liberal Kyrgyz press by 1988, and the emergence of opposition parties and ethnic conflicts. In 1990 disputes over housing and land in the Osh region of the crowded Fergana Valley led to violent confrontations between the Kyrgyz and the republic's Uzbeks. Osh had been incorporated into Kyrgyzstan in 1924, even though the majority population was Uzbek, and at various times the Uzbeks had lobbied for the establishment of an autonomous Uzbek region in Osh.

In Feb. 1990 traditional Soviet-style elections brought into office many Communist party officials, and in April the Supreme Soviet elected Absamat Masaliyev, who had been the Kyrgyz republic's Communist party First Secretary. In Oct. 1990, however, largely due to the violence in Osh, Masaliyev did not receive enough Supreme Soviet votes, and the reformer Askar Akayev was elected as president. After the failed coup in Moscow in August 1991, Communist party activities were suspended, although most leaders were still party members. In Dec. 1991 Kyrgyzstan signed the Alma-Ata Declaration that founded the Commonwealth of Independent States.

In 1992, with the help of the I.M.F., Akayev embarked on a radical economic program that included lowering wages, raising prices, and abolishing tariffs with Central Asian neighbors Kazakhstan and Uzbekistan. Although the program initially caused hardship, it proved successful. In 1995, elections, Akayev was elected to a second term with 60 percent of the vote. This came six months after international lenders, led by the World Bank, agreed in June to $680 million in aid.

In 1996 Kyrgyzstan joined the common market among Russia, Belarus, and Kazakhstan as it expanded to include development of common energy, transport and information systems. The government signed a non-agression pact with Russia, China, Kazakhstan and Tajikistan and in Oct. 2000 Akayev won a third term with 75 percent of the vote and in Feb. 2003 a "Constitutional Referendum" gave him greatly expanded powers. A muslim terrorist movement brought Russian troops to help destroy it

▶LAOS

Lao People's Democratic Republic

• GEOGRAPHY **Location:** landlocked country in Southeast Asia. **Boundaries**: Myanmar to NW, China to N, Vietnam to E, Cambodia to S, and Thailand to W. **Total area**: 91,429 sq. mi. (236,800 sq km). **Coastline**: none. **Comparative area**: slightly larger than Utah. **Land use:** 3% arable land; negl. % permanent crops; 97% other. **Major cities**: (1985 census) Vientiane (capital) 377,409; (1973) Savannaket 50,690; Pakse 44,860; Luang Prabang 44,244; Saya Bury 13,775.

• PEOPLE **Population:** 5,921,545 (July 2003 est.). **Nationality:** noun—Lao or Laotian (sing. and pl.); adjective—Lao or Laotian. **Ethnic groups:** 68% Lao Loum, 22% Lao Theung, 9% Lao Soung including Hmong and Yao. **Languages:** Lao (official), French, English, ethnic languages. **Religions:** 60% Buddhist, 40% animist and other.

• GOVERNMENT **Type:** communist state. **Independence:** July 19, 1949 (from France). **Constitution:** Aug. 14, 1991. **National holiday:** Republic Day, Dec. 2. **Heads of Government:** Khamtai Siphandone, president (since Feb. 1998); Sisavath Keobounphanh, prime minister (since Feb. 1998). **Structure:** executive; unicameral legislature; independent judiciary.

• ECONOMY **Monetary unit:** new kip. **Budget:** (FY98/99) ***income:*** $211 mil.; ***expend.:*** $462 mil. **GDP:** $9.9 bil., $1,700 per capita (2002 est.). **Chief crops:** sweet potatoes, vegetables, coffee, sugarcane, cotton; water buffalo, pigs, cattle, poultry; tobacco. **Natural resources:** tin, timber, gypsum, hydropower potential. **Major industries:** timber, hydropower, tin and gypsum. **Labor force:** about 1-1.5 mil.; 80% agriculture; 5.7% unemployment (1997). **Exports:** $345 mil. (f.o.b., 2002 est.); electricity, wood products, coffee, tin. **Imports:** $555 mil. (f.o.b., 2002 est.); machinery and equipment, vehicles, fuel. **Major trading partners:** ***exports:*** Vietnam, Thailand, France; ***imports:*** Thailand, Vietnam, China.

Inhabited by the Thai-speaking Lao people in the river valleys and by Hmong and other tribal people in the highlands, Laos historically had little national cohesion and was dominated by its more powerful neighbors, Siam (Thailand) to the west and Vietnam to the east. In 1893 France forced Siam to recognize Laos as a French protectorate; the country was thereafter incorporated into the French Union of Indochina. Laos was occupied by Japan during World War II but saw little major fighting.

In 1946 Laos was united under the Luang Prabang dynasty and was granted local autonomy as a constitutional monarchy in 1949. During the final phases of the Indochina War against French colonialism in 1953-54, Vietnamese Communist (Vietminh) incursions reinforced the position of the Laotian Communist party (Pathet Lao) in Laotian politics. Following the French withdrawal in December 1954, Laos became an independent nation and was admitted to the United Nations in 1955.

The creation of a coalition government under Prince Souvana Phouma in 1962 temporarily resolved a turbulent political situation; an international agreement signed in Geneva that year guaranteed Laos's neutrality. The Pathet Lao withdrew from the coalition in 1964 and renewed its armed uprising against the government, with North Vietnamese support. American planes bombed Vietnamese supply lines along the Ho Chi Minh trail, and American agents recruited Hmong tribesmen as irregular troops to attack Pathet Lao positions. The Pathet Lao nevertheless made steady gains, especially after 1970. In 1973, Prince Souvana Phouma ordered a cease-fire, and in 1975 the Pathet Lao took control of the capital, Vientiane. The Lao People's Democratic Republic was proclaimed on Dec. 3, 1975. Large numbers of Hmong and other tribal people fled to Thailand.

Subsequently, Laos was strongly dominated by Vietnam, which stationed significant numbers of troops in the country. In 1989, in Laos's first election since the communist takeover, a Supreme People's Assembly was elected specifically to approve a new constitution, which it did in 1991; the constitution confirmed the Lao People's Revolutionary party as the sole legal political party. Single-party elections in 1992 did little to alter the country's political climate, though observers predicted changes as the Communists began to pass from the scene. In 1995 Laos signed a treaty with Cambodia, Thailand, and Vietnam to establish a Mekong Commission to regulate water use among the four nations. In 1997 Laos was admitted to the Association of Southeast Asian Nations.

▶LATVIA

Republic of Latvia

• **GEOGRAPHY** **Location:** eastern coast of Baltic Sea in northeastern Europe. **Boundaries**: Baltic Sea to N, Estonia to NE, Russian Federation, Belarus to S, Lithuania to W. **Total area**: 24,749 sq. mi. (64,100 sq km). **Coastline**: Baltic Sea. **Comparative area**: slightly larger than West Virginia. **Land use:** 29% arable land; negl.% permanent crops, 71% other. **Major cities**: (1994 est.) Riga (capital) 856,281; Daugav'pils 121,974; Liepãja 104,628; Jelgava 71,332; Jurmala 59,581.

• **PEOPLE** **Population:** 2,348,784 (July 2003 est.). **Nationality:** noun—Latvian(s); adjective—Latvian. **Ethnic groups:** 57.7% Latvian, 29.6% Russian, 4.1% Belarussian, 2.7% Ukrainian, 2.5% Polish. **Languages:** Latvian (official), Lithuanian, Russian, other. **Religions:** Lutheran, Roman Catholic, Russian Orthodox.

• **GOVERNMENT** **Type:** parliamentary democracy. **Independence:** Aug. 21, 1991 (from Soviet Union). **Constitution:** the 1991 Constitutional Law supplements the 1922 constitution and provides for basic rights and freedoms. **National holiday:** Independence Day, Nov. 18. **Heads of Government:** Vaira Vike-Freiberga, president (since July 1999); Einars Repse, prime minister (since Nov. 7, 2002). **Structure:** executive; unicameral legislature; judiciary.

• **ECONOMY** **Monetary unit:** lat. **Budget:** ***income:*** $2.4 bil.; ***expend:*** $2.6 bil. (2002 est.) **GDP:** $20 bil., $8,300 per capita (2002 est.). **Chief crops:** grain, potatoes, sugar beets, vegetables; meat, milk, eggs; fish. **Natural resources:** minimal; amber, peat, limestone, dolomite. **Major industries:** machine building, metalworking, chemical processing. **Labor force:** 1.1 mil. (2001); 25% industry, 15% agriculture, 60% services (2000); 7.6% unemployment (2001). **Exports:** $2.3 bil. (f.o.b., 2002 est.); timber, textiles, foodstuffs. **Imports:** $3.9 bil. (f.o.b., 2002 est.); fuels, machinery and equipment, chemicals. **Major trading partners:** ***exports:*** 17% Germany, 16% U.K., 10% Sweden; ***imports:*** 17% Germany, 9% U.K., 8% Lithuania.

Though the Letts ethnically and linguistically are quite distinct from their northern neighbors the Ests, Latvia's history parallels that of Estonia. German merchants, knights, and missionaries made Latvia a semi-ecclesiastical German colony in the 13th century; in the 16th century Latvia passed under first Swedish, then Lithuanian rule; in the 18th century Peter the Great's Russian empire absorbed the land.

A 19th-century cultural revival, inspired in part by Johann von Herder, a native of Riga, found expression in folkloric societies, archaeological research and the compilation of the epic poem, Lacplesis. Brest-Litovsk, the Soviet Union's 1918 peace treaty with Germany, granted Latvia's political independence for the first time in its history.

The constitution of 1922 established a one-house legislature in whose system of proportional representation about 20 different political parties participated. To avoid violence between left and right armed extremists, Prime Minister Karlis Umanlis dissolved the Parliament in May 1934 and ruled as dictator until a new constitution that provided for expanded presidential powers and a second house of the legislature, based on the conception of a corporate state, came into existence in 1938 just before the Hitler-Stalin Pact awarded Latvia to the Russian sphere of interest. Stalin garrisoned troops in Latvia, rigged elections, and incorporated the country as a new union republic of the U.S.S.R. in 1940.

For 50 years, harsh Soviet rule continued. The larger cities were Russianized and the highly educated middle and upper-middle classes were deported throughout Russia. Industrialization brought relative prosperity, but the national consciousness was never eradicated.

Mikhail Gorbachev's policy of glasnost, or openness, led to the creation of dissident groups who staged public demonstrations on the anniversaries of the Stalin-Hitler Pact and of the establishment of Latvian independence. After the head of the Latvian Communist party, Boris Pugo was transferred to Moscow, Latvia's Communist party came under the influence of the newly created Latvian Popular Front. With the new political influence of non-Communists, on Sept. 29, 1988, Latvian replaced Russian as the official language.

In March 1990, following Lithuania's example, Latvia announced its intention to secede, survived Gorbachev's January 1991 military crackdown, and after the failed August 1991 coup in Moscow, declared independence.

In June 1995 Latvia gained associate status with the E.U. Summer elections revealed deep political divisions as the three major political parties took half the seats. It was not until December that Andris Skele was able to become prime minister, heading a cabinet containing members of six of Latvia's nine parties. Skele was forced to resign in July 1997 because of corruption charges and over disappointment that the E.U. would not consider Latvia's application until the "second wave." Parliamentary elections in Oct. 1998 resulted in the same degree of party splintering, but Vilis Kristopans was able to form a government. More significantly, in a referendum voters eased the citizenship laws, making it simpler for ethnic Russians (one-third of the population) to become citizens. In June 1999 Pres. Ulmanis' second term ended; his successor, Vaira Vike Freiberga, became the first female president of an ex-Soviet republic. Coalition discord brought the end of the Kristopanis government in July 1999; the successor government, under Andris Skele collapsed in April 2000, with the mayor of Riga, Andris Berzins, nominated as his successor. In 2002 a four-party center-right coalition government was founded with Einers Repse as prime minister. In 2004 Latvia joins the E.U. and NATO.

▶LEBANON

Lebanese Republic

• **GEOGRAPHY** **Location:** western Asia. **Boundaries**: Syria to N and E, Israel to S, Mediterranean Sea to W. **Total area**: 4,015 sq. mi. (10,400 sq km). **Coastline**: 140 mi. (225 km). **Comparative area**: about 0.7 times the size of Connecticut. **Land use:** 18% arable land; 13% permanent crops; 69% other. **Major cities**: (1975 est.) Beirut (capital) 1,500,000; Tarabulus (Tripoli) 160,000; Zahleh 45,000; Saida (Sidon) 38,000; Sur (Tyre) 14,000.

• **PEOPLE** **Population:** 3,727,703 (July 2003 est.). **Nationality:** noun—Lebanese (sing., pl.); adjective— Lebanese. **Ethnic groups:** 95% Arab, 4% Armenian, 1% other. **Languages:** Arabic (official), French, Armenian, English. **Religions:** 70% Islam, 30% Christian, negl. Judaism.

• **GOVERNMENT** **Type:** republic. **Independence:** Nov. 22, 1943 (from League of Nations Mandate under French administration). **Constitution:** May 23, 1926 (amended). **National holiday:** Independence Day, Nov. 22. **Heads of Government:** Emile Lahoud, president (since Nov. 1998); Rafic Hariri, prime minister (since Oct. 2000). **Structure:** executive—by custom, president is Maronite Christian, prime minister is Sunni Muslim, and president of legislature is Shia Muslim; unicameral legislature; judiciary—three courts for civil and commercial cases, one court for civil cases.

• **ECONOMY** **Monetary unit:** Lebanese pound. **Budget:** (2001 est.) ***income:*** $3.1 bil.; ***expend.:*** $5.9 bil. **GDP:** $19.3 bil., $5,400 per capita (2002 est.). **Chief crops:** citrus, vegetables, potatoes, olives, tobacco, hemp (hashish); sheep, goats. **Natural resources:** limestone, iron ore, salt; water-surplus state in water-deficit region. **Major industries:** banking, food processing, textiles. **Labor force:** 1.5 mil. plus as many as 1 mil. foreign workers (2001 est.); 62% services, 31% industry, 7% agriculture; 18% unemployment (1997 est.). **Exports:** 1 bil. (f.o.b., 2002 est.); foodstuffs and tobacco, textiles, chemicals, metals. **Imports:** $6 bil. (f.o.b., 2002 est.); foodstuffs, machinery & transport equipment, consumer goods. **Major trading partners:** ***exports:*** 11% France, 10% Switzerland, 9% U.S.; ***imports:*** 11% Italy, 10% France, 9% Germany.

The ancient history of Lebanon is essentially coextensive with that of Syria, of which it was long a part. The port cities of Tripoli, Tyre, and Sidon were important centers of the Phoenician empire. The parallel ranges of the Lebanon and Anti-Lebanon mountains, crowned with the country's famous cedar trees, enclose the fertile Bekaa Valley. The coastal cities became strongholds of early Christianity, later fragmented into numerous sects, including Maronites (Syrian Catholic), Roman Catholic, Greek Orthodox, Syrian Orthodox, and others. The mountains of the south became the center of the Druze sect of Islam, while orthodox Sunni Islam dominated in the Bekaa Valley.

Lebanon came under French influence in the late 18th century, as France claimed the role of protector of Syria's Christian community. France intervened in Lebanon in 1841 and again in 1860 when fighting between Maronite and Druze communities led to the massacre of many Christians. Under pressure from France, the Ottoman Empire granted some local autonomy to the Maronites of greater Lebanon.

In the dismemberment of the Ottoman Empire after World War I, France was granted a League of Nations Mandate over the Levant States (Lebanon and Syria), ensuring French control of the Iraq Petroleum Company pipeline from Iraq to Tripoli. In 1926 Lebanon became a self-governing republic under the mandate, but internal unrest and anti-French sentiment continued.

In June 1940 the French administration in Lebanon declared its allegiance to the Vichy government. British and Free French forces occupied Lebanon in June 1941 and declared it an independent republic; but France retained control, and full independence did not come until Jan. 1, 1944.

Under a National Covenant in 1943, political power in the Lebanese parliament was apportioned among the nation's various communities. The president was always to be a Maronite Christian, the prime minister a Sunni Muslim. This provided a workable formula for power sharing but also ensured that the national government would always be hostage to the considerable power of separate communities and clans.

The years from the end of World War II to the early 1970's were a brief golden age for Lebanon. Beirut developed into a wealthy, cosmopolitan city, the center of Middle Eastern banking and trade, while agriculture and small-scale industry flourished in the rest of the country. A Syrian-backed Muslim uprising in 1958 had no significant impact; U.S. Marines landed in May 1958 to protect American interests and remained until October. By the late 1960's, however, Lebanon's stability was threatened by PLO attacks on Israel from refugee camps in southern Lebanon and by a shift in the country's demographic balance. Muslims had become a majority in Lebanon by the late 1960's and demanded a revision of the National Covenant, while Maronite Christians continued to cling to their position of political dominance.

Throughout the 1970's, Palestinian raids from Lebanon into Israel brought Israeli retaliatory strikes in southern Lebanon. Israeli troops occupied southern Lebanon in 1978 and again in 1980. The Palestinian-Israeli conflict polarized opinion within Lebanon, inflaming anti-Western feelings among Lebanon's Sunni Muslims.

Civil war broke out in 1975, with Palestinian and leftist Muslim militias battling militias of the Maronite community, the Christian Phalange party, and other groups. More than 60,000 died, and damage ranged into the billions of dollars. Syrian troops intervened in 1976, battling Palestinian forces in an attempt to restore the status quo. Arab League efforts to negotiate a cease-fire produced an unstable peace at the end of 1976, though Syrian troops remained in Lebanon.

Fighting broke out between Syrian forces and Christian militiamen near Zahle on Apr. 1, 1981. Other groups joined the fighting in a general war of each against all. Israel staged commando raids against Palestinian positions in Tyre and Tulin. Israeli air raids on Beirut caused extensive loss of life and property damage.

Israel invaded Lebanon in a full-scale air and sea assault on June 6, 1982, in an attempt to drive out the PLO. Israeli forces surrounded Beirut and began a heavy bombardment of the city. On Aug. 1, Palestinian forces withdrew from Beirut under international supervision. On Sept. 14 newly elected Pres. Bashir Gemayel, a Maronite Christian, was assassinated; Israeli troops occupied the Muslim quarters of West Beirut in response. With tacit Israeli approval, Christian militiamen invaded two refugee camps and slaughtered hundreds of Palestinian civilians.

Beirut remained a battle zone in 1983, divided by the "Green Line" into Christian and Muslim sectors. Terrorist bombings were common. The U.S., France, Italy, and other Western nations stationed troops in Beirut in an attempt to enforce a cease-fire. Fifty people were killed when a bomb partly destroyed the U.S. embassy on Apr. 18; separate attacks on military installations on Oct. 23 killed 241 U.S. Marines and 58 French soldiers.

Rashid Karami became premier with Syrian support on Apr. 26, 1984. The civil war continued, with fighting among various groups of Christian, Druze, Sunni, Shiite, and Palestinian militias. Kidnappings of foreign nationals at the hands of various terrorist factions became commonplace. War between Shiite and Palestinian forces broke out in May 1985. Israeli forces withdrew from most of Lebanon in June, but maintained a "security zone" in the southern part of the country. Premier Karami was assassinated on June 1, 1987, when a bomb destroyed his helicopter.

At an October 1989 Arab League-sponsored meeting, Christian and Muslim leaders agreed on a new national charter. The Taif accord was condemned by Christian militants, led by Gen. Michel Aoun, and Muslim militia leaders. Newly elected Pres. René Mowad, a Syrian-backed Christian, was assassinated on Nov. 22 and succeeded by Elias Hraoui.

In November 1990, rival Shiite militias—the Syrian-backed Amal and Iranian-backed Party of God—signed an agreement ending three years of fighting. In February 1991 Lebanese troops moved to defend the area for the first time in 13 years and called for Israel to abandon its "security zone" in southern Lebanon. In addition to leaving 150,000 dead, the civil war severely disrupted the economy, virtually wiping out the international sector and causing significant damage to the domestic sector.

The government of Christian prime minister Omar Karami collapsed in May 1992, after riots protesting widespread economic hardship. New elections were held under Syrian supervision with Hizbollah and other Islamic fundamentalist parties gaining the most seats in the new parliament, in part because the Christian parties called for an electoral boycott.

In early 1994, as Israeli-Hizbollah skirmishes continued in southern Lebanon, the government banned the Christian political party Lebanese Forces, arrested some of its leaders, and stopped all "political" broadcasts not government-controlled. In 1995, Syria-backed premier Rafik Hariri won a second term together with a 2-1 backing in Parliament. Although he sought to address economic reconstruction, he was hindered by repeated skirmishes between Israel and Hizbollah Shiite guerrillas in Israel's "security zone" in southern Lebanon. In April 1996 the fighting escalated as Israel launched 600 airraids and 24,000 artillery shells some of which hit a U.N. refugee camp near Tyre, killing over 100 and wounding 100 more. The U.N. voted 64-2 (with 65 abstaining) to condemn the attack.

By the following year order had been essentially restored but no peace agreement reached with Israel. With $3 bil. in U.S. and E.U. aid the government set about to rebuild this ravaged land. The U.S. officially lifted its ban on travel to Lebanon in July 1997. Deadly skirmishes still occured in the "security zone." In 1998 Lebanon held its first municipal elections in 35 years; no clear pattern emerged. In Oct., the (pro-Syrian) National Assembly unanimously elected General Emile Lahoud as president. He nominated Selim al-Hoss as prime minister after Hariri declined a fourth consecutive government. In 1999 the Israeli-Hizbollah warfare in south Lebanon intensified until, suddenly, Israel withdrew completely (May 24, 2000), accompanied by about 3,000 Christian militiamen of the South Lebanese Army to whom Israel offered haven. Apparently at Syria's behest, only a token force of Lebanese troops and police entered the border area, effectively under Hizbollah control. In early Sept. Hariri won a decisive victory in parliamentary elections.

▶LESOTHO
Kingdom of Lesotho

• **GEOGRAPHY** **Location:** landlocked country in southern Africa. **Boundaries**: entirely surrounded by South African territory. **Total area**: 11,718 sq. mi. (30,350 sq km). **Coastline**: none. **Comparative area**: slightly smaller than Maryland. **Land use:** 11% arable land; 0% permanent crops; 89% other. **Major cities**: (1976) Maseru (capital) 45,000.

• **PEOPLE** **Population:** 1,861,959 (July 2003 est.). **Nationality:** noun—Mosotho (sing.), Basotho (pl.); adjective—Basotho. **Ethnic groups:** 99.7% Sotho; 0.3% Europeans, Asians and other. **Languages:** Sesotho (southern Sotho), English (official), Zulu, Xhosa. **Religions:** 80% Christian, 20% indigenous beliefs.

• **GOVERNMENT** **Type:** parliamentary constitutional monarchy. **Independence:** Oct. 4, 1966 (from U.K.). **Constitution:** Apr. 2, 1993. **National holiday:** Independence Day, Oct. 4. **Heads of Government:** Letsie III, king (since Feb. 1996); Pakalitha Bethuel Mosisili, prime minister (since May 1998). **Structure:** executive—king is chief of state but has no power and can be deposed by College of Chiefs; legislature—bicameral legislature; judiciary.

• **ECONOMY** **Monetary unit:** loti. **Budget:** (FY99/00 est.) ***income:*** $76 mil.; ***expend.:*** $80 mil. **GDP:** $5.6 bil., $2,700 per capita (2002 est.). **Chief crops:** corn, wheat, pulses, sorghum, barley; livestock. **Natural resources:** some diamonds and other minerals, water, agricultural and grazing land. **Major industries:** tourism, food, beverages. **Labor force:** 838,000 economically active; 86% subsistence agriculture; 35% work in South Africa. **Exports:** $422 mil. (f.o.b., 2002 est.); 75% manufactures, wool and mohair, food and live animals. **Imports:** $738 mil. (f.o.b., 2002 est.); food, building materials, vehicles, machinery. **Major trading**

partners: ***exports:*** **70% U.S.,** 24% South African Customs Union, 5% E.U.; ***imports:*** 77% South African Customs Union, 14% Asia, 8% E.U..

Lesotho, formerly Basutoland, is an independent kingdom surrounded entirely by the Republic of South Africa. The area was sparsely populated by Bushmen until the 16th century when refugees from tribal wars in surrounding areas began to move in, an influx that continued through the 19th century. These immigrants coalesced into a homogenous cultural group, the Basothos.

Under King Moshoeshoe (1823-70), several Basotho groups were consolidated, but much land was lost in a series of wars with South Africa. Moshoeshoe appealed to Queen Victoria for aid, and in 1868 the nation became a British protectorate. Between 1884 and 1959 all executive and legislative authority was in the hands of a British high commissioner. In 1903 a Basotho consultative body was established, and in 1959 a new constitution gave the council power to legislate on internal affairs.

On Oct. 4, 1966, Basutoland achieved full independence as the Kingdom of Lesotho. The first elections after independence, in 1970, were nullified by the ruling Basutoland National party (BNP) when early returns indicated that the party might lose. A state of emergency was declared, the constitution was suspended, and parliament dissolved.

Elections in 1985 were boycotted by opposition parties, and in 1986 the BNP government was ousted in a coup. The nation was run by a military council, which in February 1990 stripped King Moshoeshoe II of his powers. Military rule ended in April 1993 when Ntsu Mokhehle was elected prime minister and his Basotholand Congress party (BCP) gained all 243 seats in the legislature. King Moshoeshoe II was restored in Jan. 1995 but died a year later in an auto accident. The Traditional College of Chiefs named his son Letsie III as his successor.

Elections in May 1998 kept the ruling party in power with a new prime minister, Pakalitha Mosisili, but the opposition and some outside observers said the elections were dishonest and when pro-opposition army officers mutinied the government pledged new and free elections. These were held in March 2003 and Mosisili and his party returned to power

▶LIBERIA

Republic of Liberia

• **GEOGRAPHY Location:** western Africa. **Boundaries**: Sierra Leone, Guinea to N, Ivory Coast to E, Atlantic Ocean to S and W. **Total area**: 43,000 sq. mi. (111,370 sq km). **Coastline**: 360 mi. (579 km). **Comparative area**: slightly larger than Tennessee. **Land use:** 2% arable land; 2% permanent crops; 96% other. **Major cities**: (1984) Monrovia (capital) 421,058.

• **PEOPLE Population:** 3,317,176 (July 2003 est.). **Nationality:** noun—Liberian(s); adjective—Liberian. **Ethnic groups:** 95% indigenous peoples, including Kpelle, Bassa, Gio, Kru, Grebo, Mano, Krahn, Gola, Gbandi, Loma, Kissi, Vai, Bella; 2.5% descendants of repatriated slaves from the U.S. known as Americo-Liberians, 2.5% descendents of repatriated slaves from the Carribean known as Congo-people. **Languages:** 20% English (official); more than 20 languages of Niger-Congo language group. **Religions:** 40% indigenous beliefs, 20% Muslim, 40% Christian.

• **GOVERNMENT Type:** republic. **Independence:** July 26, 1847. **Constitution:** Jan. 6, 1986. **National holiday:** Independence Day, July 26. **Head of Government:** Charles Taylor, president (since July 1997). **Structure:** executive—president, appointed cabinet; bicameral legislature; judiciary.

• **ECONOMY Monetary unit:** Liberian dollar. **Budget:** ***income:*** $85.4 mil.; ***expend.:*** $90.5 mil. **GDP:** $3.5 bil., $1,100 per capita (2002 est.). **Chief crops:** rubber, coffee, cocoa, rice, cassava, palm oil, sugarcane; sheep, goats; timber. **Natural resources:** iron ore, timber, diamonds, gold. **Major industries:** rubber processing, palm oil processing, diamonds. **Labor force:** 70% agriculture. **Exports:** $110 mil. (f.o.b., 2002 est.); diamonds, iron ore, rubber, timber, coffee. **Imports:** $165 mil. (f.o.b., 2002 est.); fuels, chemicals, machinery, transportation equipment. **Major trading partners:** ***exports:*** 52% Germany, 7% Italy, 5% U.S.; ***imports:*** **30% France,** 24% South Korea, 16% Japan.

Liberia was populated by migrants from the north and east beginning in the 12th century, but it remained relatively isolated from the remainder of West Africa and was not incorporated into any of the region's premodern kingdoms and empires. Portuguese explorers first reached the Liberian coast in 1461 to be followed by other European traders. Until the 19th century, Liberia was largely ignored by the world except for a small-scale coastal trade in slaves and forest products.

In 1816 the U.S. Congress granted a charter to the American Colonization Society, ACS, a private organization dedicated to the African repatriation of freed slaves. The first settlers landed in 1822 at the town that was later to become Monrovia. In 1838 the settlers organized the Commonwealth of Liberia under a governor appointed by the ACS. The commonwealth declared its independence as the Republic of Liberia in 1847 and adopted a constitution modeled after that of the United States. The new government, Africa's first independent republic, was granted diplomatic recognition by Great Britain in 1848, France in 1852, and the United States in 1862.

Bolstered by the moral backing of the U.S., Liberia in its first 100 years of independence succeeded in fending off British and French attempts to encroach on its territory from their neighboring colonies. Although descendants of freed American slaves are a minority in Liberia's ethnically diverse population, they have consistently dominated the country's political life.

William V.S. Tubman was elected president in 1944 and served until his death in 1971, successfully steering Liberia through the post War age of African nationalism and decolonization. He was succeeded by William R. Tolbert, Jr. On Apr. 12, 1980, Tolbert was deposed in a military coup led by Master Sgt. Samuel K. Doe. Doe suspended the constitution and imposed martial law but pledged a new constitution by 1985.

Presidential elections were held on Oct. 15, 1985, under the terms of a provisional constitution that for the first time enacted universal suffrage. Doe was elected and his party won 80 percent of the seats in the legislature. Despite allegations of fraud that led to a violent but unsuccessful coup attempt in November 1985, the Second Republic, under the new constitution, was inaugurated on Jan. 6, 1986.

On Dec. 24, 1989, about 150 antigovernment guerrillas of the National Patriotic Forces of Liberia (NPFL), led by Charles Taylor, crossed the border from the Ivory Coast. The fighting degenerated into ethnic warfare between the Krahn and Mandingo, in support of the government, and the Gio and Mano, who supported the rebels. Prince

Johnson split from Taylor's forces and took up fighting both government troops and Taylor. A peacekeeping force of the Economic Community of West African States (ECOWAS) landed at Monrovia on Aug. 24 to mediate a cease-fire and prepare for free elections. On Sept. 10 Pres. Doe was killed by Prince Johnson, but a cease-fire was not agreed upon until Nov. 28, 1990.

From 1990 to 1992 Charles Taylor solidified his hold on the country despite the establishment of a government (under Amos Sawyer) in Monrovia by the West African States. By 1993 the government and ECOWAS forces succeeded in containing Taylor's forces. In 1994 an interim coalition government representing the country's three major factions came into power as peace talks began. Elections were scheduled for Nov. 1995 but extensive fighting broke out continually through the end of 1996. Over 150,000 had died up to then.

In early 1997 ECOWAS, led by a Nigerian peacekeeping force, helped to restore order, disarm many of the militias, and arrange for elections in July. Charles Taylor won a landslide victory. Doubts arose about domestic peace when Pres. Taylor attempted to arrest opposition militia leader Roosevelt Johnson in September: 50 died in the fighting as Johnson fled to the U.S. Embassy for safety. In early 1999, Taylor faced broad international condemnation for Liberia's aid to rebels in Sierra Leone. But the U.N. agreed to Taylor's proposal to place international monitors along Liberia's border with Sierra Leone. In return for Pres. Taylor's support for the RUF rebels in Sierra Leone, he controled their illegal diamond trade, skimming as much as 90 percent of the profit. In Aug. 2003 Taylor was forced into exile by ECOWAS and international pressure. (See "Major News Stories".)

▶LIBYA

Socialist People's Libyan Arab Jamahiriya

• **GEOGRAPHY** **Location:** along Mediterranean coast of North Africa. **Boundaries**: Mediterranean Sea to N, Egypt to E, Sudan to SE, Niger, Chad to S, Tunisia, Algeria to W. **Total area**: 679,359 sq. mi. (1,759,540 sq km). **Coastline**: 1,100 mi. (1,770 km). **Comparative area**: slightly larger than Alaska. **Land use:** 1% arable land; 0% permanent crops; 99% other. **Major cities**: in Jan. 1987, Col. Qaddafi designated Hun, a town 404 mi. (650 km) SE of Tripoli, as administrative capital of country (population N.A.); (1985) Tripoli 858,000; Benghazi 368,000; Misurata 117,000.

• **PEOPLE** **Population:** 5,499,074 (July 2003 est.). **Nationality:** noun—Libyan(s); adjective—Libyan. **Ethnic groups:** 97% Berber and Arab; some Greeks, Maltese, Italians, Egyptians, Pakistanis, Turks, Indians, Tunisians. **Languages:** Arabic, Italian, and English widely understood in major cities. **Religions:** 97% Sunni Muslim.

• **GOVERNMENT** **Type:** Jamahiriya (a state of the masses) in theory, governed by populace through local councils; in fact, a military dictatorship. **Independence:** Dec. 24, 1951 (from Italy). **Constitution:** Dec. 11, 1969, amended Mar. 2, 1977. **National holiday:** Revolution Day, Sept. 1. **Head of Government:** Col. Muammar al-Qaddafi (no official title; runs country and is treated as chief of state) (since Sept. 1969); Imbarak Abdullah Al-Shamekh, prime minister (since March 2000). **Structure:** officially, paramount political power and authority rests with General People's Congress, which theoretically functions as a parliament with a cabinet called General People's Committee; elections are indirect.

• **ECONOMY** **Monetary unit:** Libyan dinar. **Budget:** (2002 est.) ***income:*** $13.7 bil.; ***expend.:*** $8.6 bil. **GDP:** $41 bil., $7,600 per capita (2002 est.). **Chief crops:** wheat, barley, olives, dates, citrus fruits; meat, eggs. **Natural resources:** crude oil, natural gas, gypsum. **Major industries:** petroleum, food processing, textiles. **Labor force:** 1.5 mil.; 29% industry, 54% services and government, 17% agriculture. **Exports:** $11.8 bil. (f.o.b., 2002 est.); petroleum. **Imports:** $6.3 bil. (f.o.b., 2002 est.) machinery and transport equipment, food. **Major trading partners:** ***exports:*** 40% Italy, 16% Germany, 14% Spain; ***imports:*** 29% Italy, 12% Germany, 7% U.K.

The coastal cities of Libya played an important cultural and commercial role in the Mediterranean in antiquity and were prized possessions of numerous empires. The Libyan coast was successively ruled by Phoenicians, Carthaginians, Berbers, Romans, and Vandals before being incorporated into the Byzantine Empire in the fourth century A.D.; nomadic tribes in the interior were beyond the reach of any government. The Islamic conquests of the seventh and eighth centuries brought Libya into the Muslim world.

Libya was incorporated into the Ottoman Empire shortly after the Ottoman conquest of Egypt in 1517 and was ruled by local Ottoman vassals until 1835 when direct Ottoman government was established. In 1911 Libya was invaded and conquered by Italy. After World War I, local resistance to Italian colonial rule was led by King Idris I, Emir of Cyrenaica. British troops drove Italian and German forces from Libya in 1943. King Idris returned from exile in 1944. Following World War II, most of Libya was ruled as a British protectorate with a smaller portion under French administration.

Libya became an independent constitutional monarchy on Dec. 24, 1951. In 1959 significant oil reserves were discovered, rapidly transforming Libya from one of the poorest states in North Africa to one of the wealthiest.

A military coup on Sept. 1, 1969, led by Col. Muammar al-Qaddafi, deposed the monarchy and declared the establishment of the Libyan Arab Republic. Qaddafi moved rapidly to nationalize foreign assets, expel foreign troops, and close foreign libraries and cultural centers. He also assumed full dictatorial powers under a political system that gives equal weight to Islamic law and his own political philosophy. Popular participation in elections is mandatory, although no government organization outside Qaddafi and his circle of advisers exerts any real authority.

Libya has given strong political and financial aid to various radical Palestinian groups and other enemies of Israel, sponsoring terrorist activities throughout Europe and the Middle East in support of the Palestinian cause. Numerous anti-Qaddafi Libyan exiles were assassinated in Europe. Libya also engaged in sporadic military campaigns against Egypt and the Sudan.

Relations between Libya and the U.S. were very hostile in the 1980's. On May 6, 1981, the U.S. closed the Libyan "People's Bureau" (embassy) in Washington. On Aug. 2, 1981, U.S. jets shot down two attacking Libyan warplanes during U.S. naval exercises in the Gulf of Sidra, which Libya claims as national waters. In 1986 the United States imposed economic sanctions on Libya, ordered all Americans to leave the country, and froze Libyan assets in the U.S. Another clash in March 1986 ended with the loss of two Libyan ships.

On Apr. 5, 1986, Libyan-sponsored terrorists bombed a nightclub in West Berlin, killing two U.S. soldiers; in response, American bombers attacked Tripoli and Benghazi on Apr. 14 in an apparent attempt to kill Col. Qaddafi himself. In 1990, investigators announced they had linked Libyan agents to the bombing of a Pan Am Jet over Lockerbie, Scotland, in 1988.

In January 1989 an international outcry arose when a West German company admitted selling equipment to Libya for a chemical weapons plant. Qaddafi's difficulties with the Western powers continued in 1992, as they demanded he release the suspected terrorists in the Lockerbie bombing. The U.N. imposed sanctions on Libya, including a prohibition on sales of military equipment and a ban on all flights in and out of the country. U.S. attempts to gain a worldwide embargo on Libyan oil failed in 1995. In Sept. 1995 Qaddafi began the expulsion of the 30,000 Palestinians in Libya, provoking fighting between Libyan security forces and Islamic militants. In 1997 as the Vatican announced that it would establish diplomatic relations, the U.S. listed Libya as one of several nations sponsoring terrorism.

Elaborate diplomatic maneuvers in 1998 and 1999 led finally in April to President Qaddafi's handing over two Libyans for trial in the 1988 bombing of Pan Am flight 103. U.N. sanctions were suspended but the U.S. announced that its anti-terrorism sanctions would continue. The U.S. later eased food and medicine sanctions. In Jan. 2001 the Pan Am 103 trial ended with one conviction (with life imprisonment) and one acquittal. Qaddafi denounced the conviction but in 2003 Libya accepted responsibility and agreed to pay victims' families $2.7 bil.

▶LIECHTENSTEIN

Principality of Liechtenstein

• **Geography** **Location:** landlocked country in central Europe. **Boundaries**: Austria to N and E, Switzerland to S and W. **Total area**: 62 sq. mi. (160 sq km). **Coastline**: none. **Comparative area**: about 0.9 times the size of Washington, D.C. **Land use:** 25% arable land; 0% permanent crops; 75% other. **Major cities**: (1994) Väduz (capital) 5,067; Schaan 5,143; Balzers 3,917; Triesen 3,789; Eschen 3,443.

• **People** **Population:** 33,145 (July 2003 est.). **Nationality:** noun—Liechtensteiner(s); adjective—Liechtenstein. **Ethnic groups:** 86% Alemannic, 14% Italian, Turkish and other. **Languages:** German (official), Alemannic dialect. **Religions:** 76.2% Roman Catholic, 7.0% Protestant.

• **Government** **Type:** hereditary constitutional monarchy. **Independence:** Jan 23, 1719. **Constitution:** Oct. 5, 1921. **National holiday:** Assumption Day, Aug. 15. **Heads of Government:** Hans-Adam II, prince (since Nov. 1989); Otmar Hasler, prime minister (since Apr. 2001). **Structure:** executive—hereditary prince; unicameral legislature; judiciary—independent.

• **Economy** **Monetary unit:** Swiss franc. **Budget:** (1998); ***income:*** $424.2 mil.; ***expend.:*** $414.1 mil. **GDP:** $825 mil., $25,000 per capita (1999 est.). **Chief Crops:** wheat, barley, maize, potatoes; livestock, dairy products. **Natural resources:** hydroelectric potential. **Major industries:** electronics, metal manufacturing, tourism. **Labor force:** 29,000 of which 19,000 are foreign workers (mostly from Switzerland and Austria); 51.3% services; 47.4% industry, trade, and building; 1.3% agriculture, fishing, forestry, and horticulture; 1.3% unemployment (2002). **Exports:** $2.47 bil. (f.o.b., 1996 est.); small specialty machinery, dental products, stamps, hardware, pottery. **Imports:** $917.3 mil. (c.i.f., 1996 est.); machinery, metal goods, textiles, foodstuffs, motor vehicles. **Major trading partners:** ***exports:*** 62.6% E.U., 18.9% U.S.; ***imports:*** E.U. countries, Switzerland.

The alpine principality of Liechtenstein, bordered by Austria and Switzerland, is a remnant of the Holy Roman Empire, an ancient constitutional monarchy with a modern industrial economy. The current dynasty was established in 1699; Prince Franz Josef II came to the throne in 1938, yielding his executive powers to his heir apparent, Hans Adam, in 1984.

Liechtenstein was tied to the Austro-Hungarian monarchy until 1918. Since then it has remained in a customs union with Switzerland, which also handles its foreign affairs. The single-chamber diet, the Landtag is elected by universal suffrage, women having won the right to vote in 1984. For almost 60 years the government was a coalition of the conservcative Progressive Citizens Party and the liberal Fatherland Union. Since April, 1997 Premier Mario Frick has governed with a cabinet of his own Fatherland Union with the PCP in opposition. Liechtenstein joined the U.N. in 1990.

A referendum in 2003 amended the constitution giving the prince authority to dismiss the government and veto legislation; citizens gained the right to vote "no confidence" in the prince. Liechtenstein is a corporate haven, with some 25,000 corporations maintaining nominal headquarters there. Foreign workers constitute about 40 percent of the work force.

▶LITHUANIA

Republic of Lithuania

• **Geography** **Location:** eastern coast of Baltic Sea in northeastern Europe. **Boundaries**: Latvia to N, Belarus to E and SE, Poland to SW, Russian Federation (Kaliningrad) to W, Baltic Sea to NW. **Total area**: 25,174 sq. mi. (65,200 sq km). **Coastline**: Baltic Sea. **Comparative area**: slightly larger than West Virginia. **Land use:** 45% arable land; 1% permanent crops; 54% other. **Major cities**: (1995 est.) Vilnius (capital) 575,700; Kaunas 415,300; Klaipeda 202,800; Siauliai 147,200; Panevezys 132,000.

• **People** **Population:** 3,592,561 (July 2003 est.). **Nationality:** noun—Lithuanian(s); adjective—Lithuanian. **Ethnic groups:** 80.6% Lithuanian, 8.7% Russian, 7% Polish, 1.6% Belarussian. **Languages:** Lithuanian (official), Russian, Polish. **Religions:** primarily Roman Catholic, also Lutheran, Russian Orthodox, Protestant, evangelical Christian Baptist, Islam, Judaism.

• **Government** **Type:** parliamentary democracy. **Independence:** Sept. 6, 1991 (from Soviet Union). **Constitution:** Oct. 25, 1992. **National holiday:** Statehood Day, Feb. 16. **Heads of Government:** Roland Pakass, president (since Feb. 2003); Algirdas Mykolas Brazauskas, premier (since July 2001). **Structure:** executive; unicameral legislature; judiciary.

• **Economy** **Monetary unit:** litas. **Budget:** (2001 est.). ***income:*** $1.59 bil.; ***expend.:*** $1.77 bil. **GDP:** $29.2 bil., $8,400 per capita (2002 est.). **Chief crops:** grain, potatoes, sugar beets, vegetables; meat, milk, eggs; fish; flax fiber. **Natural resources:** peat. **Major industries:** machine building, metalworking, food processing. **Labor force:** 1.5 mil. (2001 est.); 50% services, 30% industry, 20% agriculture and forestry. **Exports:** $5.4 bil. (f.o.b., 2002); 22% machinery and equipment, 15% mineral products, 12% chemicals. **Imports:** $6.8 bil. (f.o.b., 2002); 18% machinery and equipment, 16% mineral products, 10% chemicals. **Major trading**

partners: ***exports:*** 13.8% U.K., 12.6% Latvia, 12.6% Germany; ***imports:*** 25.3% Russia, 17.2% Germany.

Lithuanians and Latvians are closely related peoples whose languages are quite similar. But their histories, at least until 1795, were radically different. Fierce warriors able to stem the German tide during the Middle Ages, the Lithuanians repeatedly defeated the Teutonic knights, defending their independence and retaining their own religion.

In the 14th century, under Grand Duke Gediminas and his sons, Lithuania conquered White Russia (Belarus) and Ukraine and extended the dynasty from the Baltic almost to the Black Sea. The completion of Gediminas's policies came in 1386 when his grandson Jogaila was baptized, married the Polish heiress Jadwiga, and was crowned king of Poland under the title Wladislaw II, thereby creating the Poland-Lithuania Commonwealth. A condition of the union was that Lithuania had to adopt Christianity, which it did in 1387.

With the Third Partition of Poland in 1795, Lithuania was absorbed into Russia. The upper and educated classes took part in Poland's anti–Russian rebellions in 1830 and 1863. After the latter, the Russians required Lithuanians to use the Russian alphabet instead of the Latin as a move to stop any national renaissance; but after 1883 literature smuggled into the czarist empire from Prussia and secret Lithuanian schools and societies kept alive a national identity based on ethnic, religious, and linguistic grounds rather than on the medieval and Renaissance traditions of political independence.

In Jan. 1921 the victorious allies of World War I acknowledged a new Lithuanian republic in the Soviet-German Treaty of Brest-Litovsk of March 1918. Formal recognition came in 1922. The territory of Memel (Klaipeda in Lithuanian), separated from Germany in the Treaty of Versailles, was seized in Jan. 1923 and organized as an autonomous unit of the new republic. The city itself was largely German, but its countryside was Lithuanian and it was Lithuania's only possible outlet to the sea. With the historic capital Vilnius annexed by the new Polish state, the de facto capital became the university city of Kaunas.

Danger from communists and fascists led the army to dispense with Parliament in Dec. 1926; an authoritarian regime under Pres. Antana Smetona followed. In 1939 Lithuania was doomed by the "secret protocols" of the 1939 Nazi-Soviet Pact. In June 1940 the Soviet Army invaded Lithuania and a Soviet-approved "people's government" was formed. After an election in which only pro-Soviet candidates were permitted to run, the Lithuanian Soviet Socialist Republic was proclaimed on July 21, 1940.

Thousands of Lithuanians fled westward, while other thousands disappeared into Siberia. Stalin returned Vilnius (from Poland) and Klaipeda (which Hitler had taken) to Lithuania and fostered industrialization, which elevated living standards above most of the U.S.S.R. A high Lithuanian birth rate enabled the country to resist "Russification" more easily than Latvia or Estonia.

Mikhail Gorbachev's policy of glasnost, or openness, spurred the strong Lithuanian nationalist and dissident movement into action. It began with a public discussion of the "secret protocols" of the 1939 Nazi-Soviet Pact, which had permitted the U.S.S.R. to annex Lithuania and which the Soviet government long had denied existed. In 1987 the Soviet government tolerated demonstrations in Vilnius, but by Feb. 1988, Soviet troops prevented the Lithuanians from celebrating their 70th year of independence. The Soviet stance resulted in the founding of the new Lithuanian Movement for Reconstruction (Sajudis), which became the main political vehicle for Lithuanian independence from the U.S.S.R.

On Mar. 11, 1990, Lithuania declared its independence, and in response the Soviets began an economic blockade. On Jan. 13, 1991, the world watched as Soviet paratroopers and tanks attacked the radio and television centers, beginning a standoff between the Soviets and the Lithuanians that lasted until Sept. 6, 1991, when the U.S.S.R. recognized Lithuanian independence.

After independence, Lithuania struggled to break a political deadlock caused by its lack of a constitution. In November 1992 free elections were held. The Democratic Labor party (the renamed Communists) gained 47 percent of the vote and 77 seats in Parliament, while Sajudis gained only 22 percent of the vote and 28 seats. In February 1993 the Democratic Labor candidate, Algirdas Brazauskas, handily won the presidential election with 61 percent of the vote.

The last Soviet troops left Lithuanian soil Aug. 31, 1993 and the government moved on a path to a free economy and worked for good relations with Russia and the other former Soviet states. In 1996 the Communists were routed and the Homeland Union party took control of the government. Over the next few years Lithuania followed strict fiscal and monetary policies thereby attracting over $1 bil. in foreign investment and strong GDP growth of 6 to 7 percent. In 1997-1998 presidential elections, Brazauskas-backed Valdas Adamkus, after being trounced in the first round, won a close victory. While Oct. 2000 elections brought a center-right coalition to power, led by Rolandas Paksos, squabbles over tax-cutting and privatization of utilities broke the coalition in June. The upshot on July 3 was the return of Lithuania's last Communist dictator, Algirdas Brazauskas, as premier. Paskos became president in 2003 and voters gave 90 percent aproval to joining the E.U.

▶LUXEMBOURG

Grand Duchy of Luxembourg

• **GEOGRAPHY** **Location:** landlocked country in western Europe. **Boundaries**: Belgium to N and W, Germany to E, France to S. **Total area**: 998 sq. mi. (2,586 sq km). **Coastline**: none. **Comparative area**: slightly smaller than Rhode Island. **Land use:** 25% arable land; 0% permanent crops; 75% other. **Major cities**: (1995 est.) Luxembourg-Ville (capital) 76,446; Esch-sur-Alzette 24,255; Differdange 16,196; Dudelange 15,833.

• **PEOPLE** **Population:** 454,157 (July 2003 est.). **Nationality:** noun—Luxembourger(s); adjective—Luxembourg. **Ethnic groups:** Celtic base, with French and German blend; also, guest and worker residents from Portugal, Italy, and other European countries. **Languages:** Luxembourgish, German, French (both administrative languages), English. **Religions:** 87% Roman Catholic, 13% Protestant, Jewish, Muslim.

• **GOVERNMENT** **Type:** constitutional monarchy. **Independence:** 1839 **Constitution:** Oct. 17, 1868, occasional revisions. **National holiday:** Grand Duke's birthday, National Day, June 23. **Heads of Government:** Henri de Luxembourg, grand duke (since Oct. 2000); Jean-Claude Juncker, prime minister (since Aug. 1999). **Structure:** executive—prime minister appointed by Grand Duke but responsible to parliament; unicameral legislature—Chamber of Deputies, appointed for appointed for five-year term; judiciary.

• **ECONOMY** **Monetary unit:** Luxembourg franc. **Budget:** (2000 est.) ***income:*** $5.5 bil.; ***expend.:*** $5.5 bil. **GDP:** $20 bil., $44,000 per capita (2002 est.). **Chief crops:** barley, oats, potatoes, wheat, fruits, wine grapes; livestock products. **Natural resources:** iron ore (no longer exploited). **Major industries:** banking, iron and steel, food processing. **Labor force:** 262,000, of whom 87,400 are foreign (2000); 90.1% services, 8% industry, 1.9% agriculture. **Exports:** $10.1 bil. (f.o.b., 2002); finished steel products, chemicals, rubber products, glass, aluminum. **Imports:** $13.25 bil. (c.i.f., 2002); minerals, metals, foodstuffs, machinery, quality consumer goods. **Major trading partners:** ***exports:*** 85.6% E.U., 2.6% U.S.; ***imports:*** 78.6% E.U., 3.9% U.S.

One of hundreds of small principalities in the Holy Roman Empire, Luxembourg joined the German league when the empire was abolished in 1806. It shared a monarchy with the Netherlands, but the two countries remained distinct under a single sovereign. In 1831 Luxembourg lost its French-speaking territory to Belgium. The Treaty of London granted sovereignty to Luxembourg in 1867. When King William III died in 1890, different rules of succession severed the dual monarchy; Queen Wilhelmina succeeded him in the Netherlands, while Adolf of Nassau became grand duke of Luxembourg. The nation's full independence dates from that event.

During the 19th century, Luxembourg developed a balanced modern economy, with prosperous small farms being complemented by industry, particularly mining and steel production. As late as 1970, steel accounted for over 25 percent of the nation's GDP and five-eighths of export earnings, although rising international competition has led to a decline since then.

Luxembourg was overrun by Germany during World War I and again in May 1940, in the early stages of World War II. Archduchess Charlotte fled to London and returned with the Allied armed forces in 1944. The constitutional monarchy has enjoyed political stability since the war, with the Christian Social party normally the senior partner in a three-way coalition.

Luxembourg formed a customs union with Belgium in 1921 and joined the Benelux (Belgium, Netherlands, Luxembourg) union even before World War II had ended. A founding member of the United Nations in 1945, Luxembourg abandoned its traditional neutrality in 1948 and joined NATO in 1949. It was a founding member of the EEC under the 1956 Treaty of Rome and is now home to numerous European Union institutions. International banking accounts for over half of its gross national product. The country's chief problem is a shrinking and aging citizenry. After 35 years Grand Duke John abdicated in 2000, succeeded by his son Henri.

▶MACEDONIA
The Former Yugoslav Republic of Macedonia

• **GEOGRAPHY** **Location:** southern part of the Balkan Peninsula. **Boundaries**: Serbia to N, Bulgaria to E, Greece to S, Albania to W, Yugoslavia to NE and N. **Total area**: 9,781 sq. mi. (25,333 sq km.). **Coastline**: none. **Comparative area**: slightly larger than Vermont. **Land use:** 24% arable land; 2% permanent crops; 74% other. **Major cities**: (1994 census) Skopje (Skoplje or, in Turkish, Uskub) 440,577; Bitola 75,386; Kumanovo 66,237; Tetovo 50,376.

• **PEOPLE** **Population:** 2,063,122 (July 2001 est.). **Nationality:** noun—Macedonian(s); adj.—Macedonian. **Ethnic groups:** 66% Macedonian, 23% Albanian, 4% Turkish, 2% Serb, 7% other (includes gypsies). **Languages:** 70% Macedonian (official), 21% Albanian, 3% Turkish, 3% Serbo-Croatian, 3% other. **Religions:** 67% Macedonian Orthodox, 30% Muslim, 3% other.

• **GOVERNMENT** **Type:** parliamentary democracy. **Independence:** Sept. 8, 1991 (from Yugoslavia). **Constitution:** Nov. 17, 1991. **National holiday:** Independence Day, Sept. 8. **Heads of Government:** Boris Trajovski, president (since Dec. 1999); Branko Crvenkovski, prime minister (since Oct. 31, 2002). **Structure:** executive; unicameral legislature; judiciary.

• **ECONOMY** **Monetary unit:** denar. **Budget:** (2001 est.) ***income:*** $1.13 bil.; ***expend.:*** $1.02 bil. **GDP:** $10 bil.; $5,000 per capita (2002 est.). **Chief crops:** rice, tobacco, wheat, corn, millet; beef, pork, poultry, mutton. **Natural resources:** chrome, lead, marble, zinc. **Major industries:** metallurgy and metal processing, chemicals, textiles, timber. **Labor force:** 1.1 mil. (2000 est.); 40% industry and mining; 37% unemployed (2002 est.). **Exports:** $1.1 bil. (f.o.b., 2002 est.); food, beverage, tobacco, machinery and transport equipment, other manufactured goods. **Imports:** $1.9 bil. (f.o.b., 2002 est.); machinery and transport equipment, chemicals, fuels. **Major trading partners:** Germany, Yugoslavia, Greece.

Located at the center of the Balkan peninsula, Macedonia is an epitome of the entire region in its history and ethnic complexity as well. While there is a Macedonian language (a Slavic tongue more akin to Bulgarian than to Serbo-Croatian and codified in grammar and orthography only after World War II), the question of whether or not there is a Macedonian nation is contested: to Serbians, Macedonians are "south Serbs"; to Greeks, they are "Slavophone Greeks"; to Bulgars, they are kindred people, ethnic "cousins."

In any case, Macedonians are not related to the classical people of King Philip and Alexander the Great. Their realm had become a Roman province by 146 B.C. and remained part of the Byzantine Empire even after being invaded and settled by Slavic peoples in the sixth and seventh centuries. Contested in the Middle Ages by the Byzantine, Bulgarian, and Serbian empires, Macedonia fell at last to the Ottoman Turks in 1371. Well into the 19th century its population called itself "Christian" or "Slav," while Greek served as the language of culture and business until a literary awakening associated with folk songs and heroic poetry brought a Macedonian consciousness. This found significant political expression with the formation in 1893 of the IMRO (Internal Macedonian Revolutionary Organization) that sought to unify all non-Turks—Bulgars, Greeks, Albanians, Vlacha—in an independent state and which did not shrink from terrorism and revolution.

The peace treaties of Paris concluding World War I divided Macedonia among three states: Greece, Bulgaria, and the newly created Yugoslavia. IMRO turned against Serbian dominance in Yugoslavia and filled the 1930's with violent struggles against "denationalization." Bulgarian claims to Macedonia led that state to ally with Hitler's Germany and to occupy Macedonia in 1941. With the victory of Tito's partisans and the reconstruction of the Yugoslav state as a federation of Communist "republics," a Macedonian People's Republic was established in 1946.

After Tito's death in 1980, Macedonia took part in the "collegial rule" whereby the presidency of Yugoslavia and the chairmanship of the Communist party Presidium rotated annually among the republics. But as the separate republics declared independence in 1991 and civil war began, Macedonia declared its own independence in Jan. 1992. Greece's opposition to the new nation's name and flag—as menaces to the northern Greek province of the same name—prevented international recognition until a 1995 agreement between the two countries. Under the pact, Macedonia removed an ancient Greek symbol from its flag and changed its constitution so as to remove any suggestion of a claim on Greek Macedonia. With U.N. recognition came both U.N. "peacekeeping forces" to patrol the frontier with rump Yugoslavia and the painful need to comply with the U.N. embargo against Serbia, to whose economy Macedonia has been closely tied. An April 1996 treaty with Yugoslavia resolved border questions and renounced territorial claims.

Elections in 1998 saw the ruling Social Democrats ousted by the right-wing Coalition for Changes which organized a government under Ljuplo Georgievski. In April, NATO pledged to defend Macedonia from Yugoslav incursions in the latter's struggle again Albanian separatists in Kosovo. Refugees from Kosovo flooded Macedonia, straining its humanitarian capacities. The decision of "founding" president Gligorov not to seek a second term brought presidential elections (Oct.–Dec. 1999) won by Boris Trajkovski of the governing coalition. In March 2001 ethnic Albanians rose up to fight for equal rights, taking over one-third of the country. A cease-fire in August and NATO intervention led to a peaceful settlement. In Sept. 2002 elections, the ruling party lost to a coalition that included Ali Ahmeti, leader of the guerilla uprising and on the U.S. terrorist list.

▶MADAGASCAR
Republic of Madagascar

• **GEOGRAPHY Location:** off southeast Africa in western Indian Ocean. Antananarivo: 18°52'S, 47°30'E. **Boundaries**: about 300 mi. (500 km) E of Mozambique. **Total area**: 226,656 sq. mi. (587,040 sq km). **Coastline**: 3,000 mi. (4,828 km). **Comparative area**: slightly less than twice the size of Arizona. **Land use:** 4% arable land; 1% permanent crops; 95% other. **Major cities**: Antananarivo (capital) 662,585 (1985 est.); Antsirabé 78,941; Toamasina (Tamatave) 77,395; Fianarantsoa 68,054; Mahajanga (Majunga) 65,864 (1975 census).

• **PEOPLE Population:** 16,979,744 (July 2003 est.). **Nationality:** noun—Malagasy (sing., pl.); adjective— Malagasy. **Ethnic groups:** highlanders of predominantly Malayo-Indonesian origin (Merina and related Betsileo); coastal peoples collectively termed Cotiers, with mixed African, Malayo-Indonesian, and Arab ancestry (Betsimisaraka, Tsimihety, Antaisaka, Sakalava); French, Indian, Creole, Comoran. **Languages:** French and Malagasy (both official). **Religions:** 52% indigenous beliefs, 41% Christian, 7% Muslim.

• **GOVERNMENT Type:** republic. **Independence:** June 26, 1960 (from France). **Constitution:** Aug. 19, 1992. **National holiday:** Independence Day, June 26. **Heads of Government:** Marc Ravalomanana, president (since Apr. 2002); Jacques Sylla, premier (since July 2002). **Structure:** executive; unicameral legislature, scheduled to become bicameral —two-thirds of upper house will be filled from directly elected regional assemblies, rest by presidential appointment; judiciary.

• **ECONOMY Monetary unit:** Malagasy franc. **Budget:** (1998) ***income:*** $553 mil; ***expend.:*** $735 mil. **GDP:** $12.6 bil., $760 per capita (2002 est.). **Chief crops:** coffee, vanilla, cloves, sugar; livestock. **Natural resources:** graphite, chromite, coal, bauxite, salt. **Major industries:** agricultural processing (meat canneries, soap factories, brewery, tanneries, sugar refining), light consumer goods industries (textiles, glassware), cement. **Labor force:** (2000) 7.3 mil. **Exports:** $700 mil. (f.o.b., 2002 est.); coffee, vanilla, cloves, shellfish, sugar, petroleum products. **Imports:** $985 mil. (f.o.b., 2002); 30% intermediate manufactures, capital goods, petroleum, consumer goods, food. **Major trading partners:** ***exports:*** 29% France, 28% U.S., 6% Germany; ***imports:*** 24% France, 7% Hong Kong, 7% China.

The largest island nation, and fourth largest island, in the world, Madagascar was settled by Malayo-Indonesian migrants some 2,000 years ago. Although later waves of African and Arab migrants were absorbed into the population, to a large extent it is still ethnically and culturally Asian. A Portuguese attempt to colonize the island in the 16th century failed, and during the 18th and 19th centuries, a unified kingdom backed by the British ruled the country. Foreign interests—largely British and French—developed extensive coffee plantations, and the French made Madagascar a protectorate in 1885 and a colony in 1896.

During World War II Madagascar sided with the Free French, and French colonial rule was reestablished after the war. The Malagasy Republic was founded as an independent nation on June 26, 1960. A coup in 1972 brought a repressive anti-French government to power.

A new federal constitution was approved in 1992, and in 1993 elections, Albert Zafy defeated the 17-year incumbent Didier Ratsiraka for the presidency, but the results were reversed in 1997 and Ratsiraka immediately set out to cut inflation, and renegotiate the nation's many foreign loans. The presidential election of 2001 turned into (except for the bloodshed) an opera bouffa, as neither incumbent Didier Ratsiraka nor challenger Marc Ravalomanana would concede defeat and each set up his own government. The military successes of troops loyal to Ravalomanana led to Ratsiraka's July 5 flight to the Seychelles.

Madagascar's wildlife (a mixture of African species and others of domestic evolution) and its isolation make it of unique scientific interest. (In 1990, scientists discovered the smallest mammal known to science: the dwarf lemur.) But some 75 percent of the population live in poverty. Conditions greatly worsened in 2000 with severe cyclone damage.

▶MALAWI
Republic of Malawi

• **GEOGRAPHY Location:** landlocked country in southern central Africa. **Boundaries**: Tanzania to N, Mozambique to E, S, and SW, Zambia to W; Lake Malawi forms much of eastern boundary. **Total area**: 45,745 sq. mi. (118,480 sq km). **Coastline**: none. **Comparative area**: slightly smaller than Pennsylvania. **Land use:** 20% arable land; 1% permanent crops; 79% other. **Major cities**: (1994 est.) Lilongwe (capital) 395,500; Blantyre 446,800.

• **PEOPLE Population:** 11,651,239 (July 2003 est.). **Nationality:** noun—Malawian(s); adjective—Malawian. **Ethnic groups:** Chewa, Nyanja,

Tumbuko, Yao, Lomwe, Sena, Tonga, Ngoni, Asian, European. **Languages:** English and Chichewa (both official); Tombuka and other regional languages. **Religions:** 55% Protestant, 20% Roman Catholic, 20% Muslim, 3% indigenous beliefs.

• **GOVERNMENT** **Type:** multiparty democracy. **Independence:** July 6, 1964 (from U.K.). **Constitution:** May 18, 1994. **National holiday:** Republic Day, July 6. **Head of Government:** Elson Bakili Muluzi, president (since May 1994). **Structure:** executive; legislature—National Assembly of 193 members elected to five-year terms; judiciary.

• **ECONOMY** **Monetary unit:** Malawian kwacha. **Budget:** (FY99 est.) ***income:*** $490 mil.; ***expend.:*** $523 mil. **GDP:** $7.2 bil., $670 per capita (2002 est.). **Chief crops:** tobacco, tea, sugar, cotton; cattle, goats. **Natural resources:** limestone; hydropower; unexploited deposits of uranium, coal, bauxite. **Major industries:** agricultural processing (tea, tobacco, sugar), sawmilling, cement. **Labor force:** 4.5 mil. (2001 est.); 86% agriculture. **Exports:** $435 mil. (f.o.b., 2002); tobacco, tea, sugar, coffee, wood products. **Imports:** $505 mil. (f.o.b., 2002); food, petroleum products, semimanufactures, consumer goods. **Major trading partners:** ***exports:*** 17% U.K., 13% Germany, 8% South Africa,; ***imports:*** 48% South Africa, 14% U.K., 4% India.

Malawi derives its name from the Maravi, a Bantu people who settled in the region in the 13th century and whose descendants, the Chewas, make up a significant segment of the current population. In the 1830's, the Ngoni, driven from what is now South Africa by the Zulus, arrived in the area around Lake Nyasa. The arrival of the Scottish missionary David Livingstone in 1859 led to the establishment of the British-controlled Nyasaland Protectorate in 1891. In 1953 Nyasaland formed a federation with Northern and Southern Rhodesia (Zambia and Zimbabwe) and began to organize an independence movement. The fight for independence was led by Dr. H. Kamuzu Banda, an expatriate who assumed the presidency of the Nyasaland African Congress, later the Malawi Congress party, upon his return in 1958. The British granted Nyasaland self-governing status in 1962, and Banda was elected prime minister the following year. Malawi achieved full independence under its present name in 1964.

Banda soon introduced one-party rule and had himself declared president for life in 1971. All dissent was crushed while corruption and nepotism strangled the economy, leaving Malawi's citizens among the poorest in the world.

By 1990 internal unrest and the decline of Banda's popularity (he was now in his 90's) rapidly led to change. In 1992 a series of violent strikes by workers in the two largest cities resulted in more than 35 deaths. The United States, Great Britain, and Germany, hoping to push the Banda government to institute democratic reforms, cut off most of the $500 million they had been giving annually in aid. In June 1993 Malawians voted 2 to 1 to institute a multiparty system and in May 1994 Banda lost his nation's only free election in 30 years to Bakili Muluzi's United Democratic Front (UDF). In December 1995, Banda was acquitted of conspiring to murder four of his political rivals in 1983.

▶MALAYSIA

• **GEOGRAPHY** **Location:** 13 states in Southeast Asia; 11 are in Peninsular Malaysia and two, Sabah and Sarawak, lie about 400 mi. (640 km) across South China Sea on northern coast of island of Borneo (Kalimantan). **Boundaries**: Peninsular Malaysia—Thailand to N, South China Sea to E, Island of Singapore to S across Johor Strait, and Indonesian island of Sumatra to W across Strait of Malacca; Sabah and Sarawak—South China Sea to NW, Sulu Sea to NE, Celebes Sea to E, Indonesia to S; Brunei is enclosed within Sarawak on coast of South China Sea. **Total area**: 127,317 sq. mi. (329,750 sq km). **Coastline**: 2,905 mi. (4,675 km). **Comparative area**: slightly larger than New Mexico. **Land use:** 6% arable land; 18% permanent crops; 76% other. **Major cities**: (1991 census) Kuala Lumpur (capital) 1,145,075; Ipoh 382,633; Johor Baharu 328,646; Melaka (Malacca) 295,999; Petaling Jaya 254,849.

• **PEOPLE** **Population:** 23,092,940 (July 2003 est.). **Nationality:** noun—Malaysian(s); adjective—Malaysian. **Ethnic groups:** 58% Malay and other indigenous, 24% Chinese, 8% Indian. **Languages:** Bahasa Melayu (official); English, Chinese dialects, Tamil, Telugu, Malayalam, Panjabi, Thai; note – in addition, in East Malaysia several indigenous languages are spoken, the largest of which are Iban and Kadazan. **Religions:** Islam, Buddhism, Daoism, Hinduism, Christianity, Sikhism; note – in addition, Shamanism is practiced on East Malaysia.

• **GOVERNMENT** **Type:** constitutional monarchy; Peninsular Malaysian states—hereditary rulers in all but Melaka and Penang, where governors are appointed by Malaysian government, with powers of state governments limited by federal constitution; Sabah—self-governing state, holding 20 seats in House of Representatives, with foreign affairs, defense, internal security, and other powers delegated to federal government; Sarawak—self-governing state, which holds 24 seats in House of Representatives, with foreign affairs, defense, internal security, and other powers delegated to federal government. **Independence:** Aug. 31, 1957 (from U.K.). **Constitution:** Aug. 31, 1957, amended Sept. 16, 1963, when Federation of Malaya became Federation of Malaysia. **National holiday:** National Day, Aug. 31. **Heads of Government:** Sultan Sirajuddin ibni Al-Marhum Tuanku Syed Putra Jamalullail, king (since Dec. 2001); Dr. Mahathir Mohamad, prime minister (since July 1981). **Structure:** executive—paramount ruler chosen by and from the nine state rulers for five-year term; bicameral legislature; judiciary.

• **ECONOMY** **Monetary unit:** Malaysian ringgit. **Budget:** (2002 est.) ***income:*** $20.3 bil. ***expend.:*** $27.2 bil. **GDP:** $210 bil., $9,300 per capita (2002 est.). **Chief crops:** Peninsular Malaysia—natural rubber, palm oil, rice; Sabah—mainly subsistence, main crops are rubber, timber, coconut, rice; Sarawak—rubber, timber, pepper. **Natural resources:** tin, crude oil, timber, copper, iron ore. **Major industries:** Peninsular Malaysia—rubber and oil-palm processing and manufacturing, light manufacturing industry, electronics; Sabah—logging, petroleum production; Sarawak—agriculture processing, petroleum production and refining, logging. **Labor force:** 9.9 mil. (2001 est.); 27% manufacturing, 16% agriculture, forestry, and fisheries; 28% local trade and tourism. **Exports:** $95.2 bil. (2002 est.); electronic equipment, petroleum products, palm oil, wood products, rubber, textiles. **Imports:** $76.8 bil. (2002 est.); machinery and equipment, chemicals, food. **Major trading partners:** ***exports:*** 22% U.S., 19% Singapore, 11% Japan; ***imports:*** 16% Japan, 14% U.S., 22% Singapore.

From ancient times a group of petty principalities in the southern part of the Malay Peninsula, bordering the Strait of Malacca, maintained extensive ties of maritime commerce throughout Southeast Asia. The early Malay states were Hindu, under Indian influence; with the rise of the Kingdom of Malacca in the 15th century, conversion to Islam was widespread. European influence in the Spice Islands began in the 16th century; the Portuguese, initially dominant, gave way to the Dutch, who seized Malacca in 1641.

British influence grew during the 18th century, with the founding of a trading settlement at Penang in 1789. Singapore was founded in 1819, and the Dutch ceded Malacca to Britain in 1824. By a series of treaties in the late 19th century, the various Malay states became British protectorates; Britain controlled the entire southern peninsula after 1909. Under British rule, commercial tin mining and the establishment of extensive rubber plantations led to the importation of many Indian and Chinese laborers; eventually ethnic Chinese dominated Malaya's domestic economy.

In the 19th century, Great Britain also gained a dominant position in northern Borneo. (Borneo is divided among Brunei, Indonesia and Malaysia.)

Japan overran Malaya by February 1942. Following World War II, the various Malay states (except Singapore) organized into a federation, which replaced the confusing prewar regime of federated and unfederated protectorates. A Communist rebellion disrupted the country throughout the early 1950's. Following the suppression of the Communist movement, elections were held in mid-1955 for a home-rule government. The elections brought the Alliance party of Tungku Abdul Rahman to power, and the Federation of Malaya became independent in 1957.

The nation expanded on Sept. 16, 1963, with the creation of Malaysia, incorporating the Federation of Malaya as well as Singapore and the former British colonies of North Borneo (thereafter called Sabah) and Sarawak. Singapore seceded from Malaysia in 1965 and became an independent nation.

Malaysia has been ruled since 1981 by the coalition government of Mahathir Mohamad, who has transformed the country from an agriculture-based economy to one of the fastest-growing economies in Asia. The country sustained annual growth rates of 8 percent through the 1980's. In 1995 Malaysia received $5.8 bil. in foreign direct investment, the most in East Asia. The Asian financial crisis of 1997-98 hit Malaysia very hard as the currency and stockmarkets declined steeply.

Facing Malaysia's first recession in 13 years, Mahathir announced that the free market system had proven a failure and dismissed his finance minister, Anwar Ibrahim in Sept. 1998. Arrested and beaten by police, Anwar faced charges of sodomy and corruption in a nightmare trial. In April 1999 he was found guilty and sentenced to six years in prison. His wife, Azizah Ismail announced a new opposition National Justice Party. But when elections were suddenly called in November, her new party took only five of the 193 seats, as Mahathir's National Front carried 148. Mahathir announced in 2002, that after 21 years, he would resign effective Oct. 25; deputy P.M. Abdullah Badawi has been groomed to succeed.

▶MALDIVES
Republic of Maldives

• **Geography** **Location:** chain of more than 1,200 small coral islands (about 220 inhabited), 475 mi. (764 km) from N to S and 80 mi. (207 km) from W to E in Indian Ocean; northernmost atoll about 370 mi. (960 km) southwest of India. Malé 4°00'N, 73°28'E. **Boundaries**: Laccadive Sea to NE, Arabian Sea to N, Indian Ocean to S and W. **Total area**: 116 sq. mi. (300 sq km). **Coastline**: 400 mi. (644 km). **Comparative area**: about 1.7 times size of Washington, D.C. **Land use:** 3% arable land; 7% permanent crops; 90% other. **Major cities**: (1995) Malé (capital) 62,973.

• **People** **Population:** 329,684 (July 2003 est.). **Nationality:** noun—Maldivian(s); adjective—Maldivian. **Ethnic groups:** South Indian, Sinhalese, and Arab. **Languages:** Maldivian Divehi (dialect of Sinhala; script derived from Arabic); English spoken by most government officials. **Religions:** Sunni Muslim.

• **Government** **Type:** republic. **Independence:** July 26, 1965 (from U.K.). **Constitution:** Adopted Jan. 1998. **National holiday:** Independence Day, July 26. **Head of Government:** Maumoon Abdul Gayoom, president (since Nov. 1978). **Structure:** executive; unicameral legislature; judiciary.

• **Economy** **Monetary unit:** rufiyaa. **Budget:** (2002 est.) ***income:*** $224 mil.; ***expend.:*** $282 mil. **GDP:** $1.25 bil., $3,900 per capita (2002 est.). **Chief crops:** coconut, corn, sweet potatoes; fishing. **Natural resources:** fish. **Major industries:** fishing, tourism, shipbuilding, some coconut processing. **Labor force:** about 88,000 (2000 est.); 22% fishing industry and agriculture, 18% services, 60% industry. **Exports:** $110 mil. (f.o.b., 2001 est.); fish, clothing. **Imports:** $395 mil. (f.o.b., 2001 est.); intermediate and capital goods, consumer goods, petroleum products. **Major trading partners: *exports:*** Sri Lanka, U.S., U.K.; ***imports:*** Singapore, India, Sri Lanka.

The small sultanate of the Maldive Islands, with an Islamic population of Sinhalese descent, was made a British protectorate in 1887. The islands' tiny area and poor soil limited development; fishing and fish processing are the main industries, and copra (dried coconut meat for coconut oil) is the only significant crop. The Maldives became an independent nation on July 26, 1965. In 1968 the sultanate was abolished and replaced by a republic. Since independence, tourism has become economically important and now accounts for 18 percent of the GDP. Protests over the concentration of development on the island of Malé in recent years have led to political unrest in the other islands, while attempts to address the basic needs of those islands have strained the nation's tiny economic base.

The current president, Maumoon Abdul Gayoom, was elected to office in 1978 and subsequently reelected twice. The elections of September 1988 were marked by considerable unrest and demonstrations. An attempted coup against the Gayoom government on Nov. 4, 1988, was put down with the intervention of Indian troops.

▶MALI
Republic of Mali

• **Geography** **Location:** northwestern Africa. **Boundaries**: Algeria to N, Niger to E, Burkina Faso, Ivory Coast, Guinea to S, Senegal and Mauritania to W. **Total area**: 478,765 sq. mi. (1,240,000 sq km). **Coastline**: none. **Comparative area**: slightly less than twice the size of Texas. **Land use:** 4% arable land; negl. % permanent crops; 96% other. **Major cities**: (1976 census) Bamako (capital) 404,000; Ségou 65,000; Mopti 54,000; Sikasso 47,000; Kayes 45,000.

• **People** **Population:** 11,626,219 (July 2003 est.). **Nationality:** noun—Malian(s); adjective—Malian. **Ethnic groups:** 50% Mande (Bambara,

Malinke, Soninke), 17% Peul, 12% Voltaic, 6% Songhai, 10% Tuareg and Moor. **Languages:** French (official); Bambara spoken by 80% of population. **Religions:** 90% Muslim, 9% indigenous beliefs, 1% Christian.

• **GOVERNMENT** **Type:** republic. **Independence:** Sept. 22, 1960 (from France). **Constitution:** Jan. 12, 1992. **National holiday:** Anniversary of the Proclamation of the Republic, Sept. 22. **Heads of Government:** Amadou Toumani Touré, president (since June 2002); Ahmed Mohamed Ag Amani, prime minister (since 2002). **Structure:** executive; unicameral legislature; judiciary.

• **ECONOMY** **Monetary unit:** Communauté Financière Africaine (CFA) franc. **Budget:** (2002 est.) ***income:*** $764 mil.; ***expend.:*** $828 mil. **GDP:** $9.8 bil., $860 per capita (2002 est.). **Chief crops:** cotton, millet, rice, corn; goats, sheep, cattle. **Natural resources:** gold, phosphates, kaolin, salt, limestone, uranium; bauxite, iron ore, manganese, tin, and copper deposits are known but not exploited. **Major industries:** small local consumer goods and food processing, construction, phosphate, gold. **Labor force:** 3.93.; 80% agriculture, 19% services. **Exports:** $680 mil. (f.o.b., 2002 est.); cotton, livestock, gold. **Imports:** $630 mil. (f.o.b., 2002 est.); machinery and equipment, foodstuffs, construction materials, petroleum. **Major trading partners:** ***exports:*** 17% Thailand, 13% Brazil, 6% Italy; ***imports:*** 18% Ivory Coast, 14% France, 5% Germany.

Mali has been a center of West African civilization for over 4,000 years. Iron Age civilizations flourished on the middle reaches of the Niger River from about 200 B.C. The kingdom of Ghana arose about A.D. 750 on the strength of the gold trade with North African Berbers. Ghana was overthrown by the Muslim Almoravids, who ruled only 11 years, though Islam remained a major influence from that time. From 1200 to 1400, the Kingdom of Mali was dominant in the region and was renowned throughout Islam and even in Christian Europe for its wealth and power; when Mansa Musa's retinue stopped in Cairo en route to Mecca, it carried so much gold that the price of gold fell 20 percent. By the end of the 14th century, the Mali empire had been eclipsed by the Songhai (Soyinka) empire, centered on the Niger River cities of Gao and Timbuktu.

The Songhai empire collapsed after Timbuktu was sacked by Moroccans in 1591. It fragmented into a series of smaller states, and power shifted from the desert fringe back to the Niger valley, bringing with it a further spread of Islam.

French exploration of Mali led to conquest in 1896 and the creation of the colony of French Sudan in 1898, governed from Dakar, Senegal. Timbuktu declined in importance, and Bamako became the country's principal urban center.

Malians were granted French citizenship and limited self-rule in 1946. In 1958 the territory became autonomous within the French Overseas Community. In 1959, with French support, the French Sudan and Senegal formed the Federation of Mali, which became independent on June 20, 1960. Senegal seceded from the federation almost immediately, and Mali became an independent republic on Sept. 22, 1960. Modibo Keita was elected the country's first president.

Keita's program of radical control of society and the economy by the central government provoked discontent, and he was overthrown in 1968 by military officers led by Lt. Moussa Traore. Traore's Military Committee of National Liberation ruled until 1979 when it was reorganized under a new constitution as the Malian People's Democratic Union. Traore was ousted in a 1991 coup and a transitional government under a civilian prime minister, Soumana Sacko, set up multiparty elections for June 1992. Alpha Konaré was elected president and his Alliance for Democracy in Mali party won 76 of 116 legislative seats. In 1995, the government reached an agreement in its long-standing dispute with the ethnic Tuareg nomads in the northern part of the country.

Pres. Konaré's government has succeeded in reviving the economy (cotton and gold production rank among the top in Africa) and winning praise from the World Bank. Political opposition, though small, turned violent in 1997 and caused a cancellation of the results of elections in April. Opposition parties claimed the Government had fixed the elections and boycotted new ones held in May that gave Konare victory. He governs unopposed in the National Assembly and many fear political instability is possible. Yet Konare bowed to a constitutional provision barring a third term and voters in May 2002 gave 65 percent of the votes to Amadou Toure.

▶MALTA

Republic of Malta

• **GEOGRAPHY** **Location:** archipelago (largest islands are Malta, Gozo, and Comino) in central Mediterranean. Valletta 35°54'N, 14°32'E. **Boundaries**: Sicily 58 mi. (93 km) to N, Libya 180 mi. (290 km) to S, Tunisia to W. **Total area**: 124 sq. mi. (320 sq km). **Coastline**: 87 mi. (140 km). **Comparative area**: slightly less than twice the size of Washington, D.C. **Land use:** 31% arable land; 3% permanent crops; 66% other. **Major cities**: (1994 est.) Valletta (capital) 7,953, Birkirkara 21,551, Qormi 17,928, Sliema 13,823.

• **PEOPLE** **Population:** 400,420 (July 2003 est.). **Nationality:** noun—Maltese (sing., pl.); adjective—Maltese. **Ethnic groups:** Maltese (descendants of ancient Carthaginians and Phoenicians, with strong elements of Italian and other Mediterranean stock) **Languages:** Maltese and English (both official). **Religions:** 98% Roman Catholic.

• **GOVERNMENT** **Type:** parliamentary democracy. **Independence:** Sept. 21, 1964 (from U.K.). **Constitution:** Dec. 13, 1974. **National holiday:** Independence Day, Sept. 21. **Heads of Government:** Prof. Guido de Marco, president (since Apr. 1999); Dr. Edward Fenech Adami, prime minister (since Sept. 1998). **Structure:** executive; unicameral legislature—seats are given to largest popular party to ensure a majority, usually 65; judiciary.

• **ECONOMY** **Monetary unit:** Maltese lira. **Budget:** (2000 est.) ***income:*** $1.5 bil.; ***expend.:*** $1.6 bil. **GDP:** $7 bil., $17,000 per capita (2002 est.). **Chief crops:** potatoes, cauliflower, grapes, wheat, barley; milk, pork, poultry. **Natural resources:** limestone, salt. **Major industries:** tourism, electronics, ship repair yard, construction. **Labor force:** 160,000 (2002); 24% industry, 71% services, 5% agriculture; 7% unemployment (2002). **Exports:** $2 bil. (f.o.b., 2001); machinery and transport equipment, manufactures. **Imports:** $2.8 bil. (f.o.b., 2001); machinery and transport equipment, manufactured goods; food, drink and tobacco. **Major trading partners:** ***exports:*** 20.2% U.S., 14.1% Germany, 10.2% France; ***imports:*** 19.9% Italy, 15.0% France, 11.6% U.S..

Malta, an ancient crossroads of Mediterranean trade, was ruled successively by Phoenicians, Carthaginians, Greeks, Romans, and Byzantines before being conquered by Islamic Saracens from North Africa in the ninth century. In 1090 the Nor-

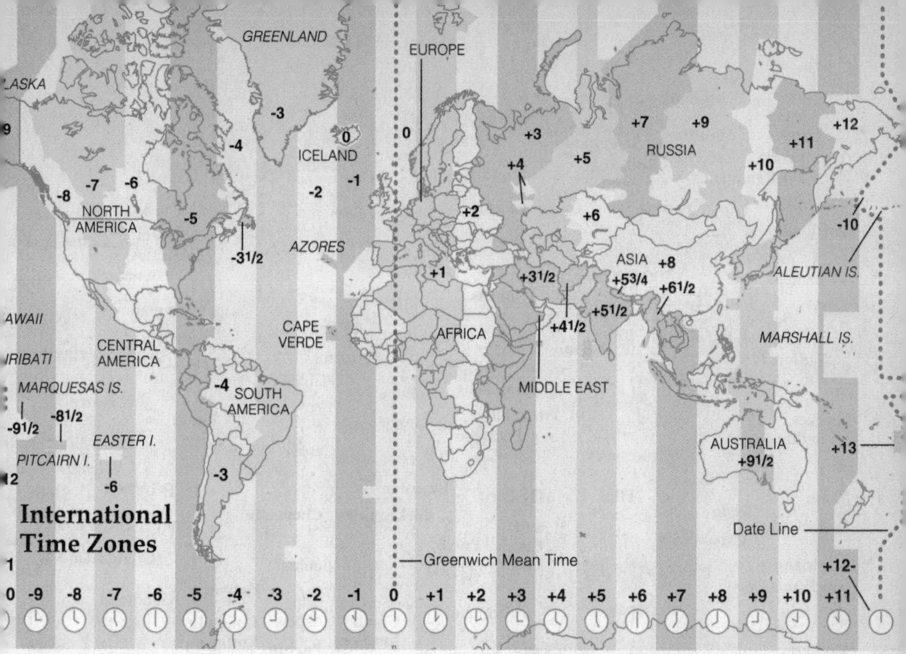
International Time Zones
GREENLAND
ALASKA
ICELAND
EUROPE
RUSSIA
NORTH AMERICA
AZORES
ASIA
ALEUTIAN IS.
HAWAII
KIRIBATI
CENTRAL AMERICA
CAPE VERDE
AFRICA
MIDDLE EAST
MARSHALL IS.
MARQUESAS IS.
SOUTH AMERICA
EASTER I.
PITCAIRN I.
AUSTRALIA
Date Line
Greenwich Mean Time
-3
-4
0
+3
+7
+9
+12
+11
+10
+4
+5
-10
-8
-7
-6
-5
-2
-1
+2
+6
-3 1/2
+1
+3 1/2
+8
+5 3/4
+6 1/2
+4 1/2
+5 1/2
-9 1/2
-8 1/2
-6
+13
+9 1/2
+12-
0 -9 -8 -7 -6 -5 -4 -3 -2 -1 0 +1 +2 +3 +4 +5 +6 +7 +8 +9 +10 +11

Canada
160° West
140°
120°
100°
0 Miles 500
Arctic Ocean
GREENLAND (DENMARK)
ICELAND
ALASKA
QUEEN ELIZABETH IS.
Beaufort Sea
BANKS I.
Baffin Bay
Inuvik
Mackenzie R.
Dawson
Great Bear Lake
VICTORIA I.
70° North
YUKON TERRITORY
Whitehorse
Cambridge Bay
BAFFIN I.
Davis Strait
NORTHWEST TERRITORIES
NUNAVUT
Iqaluit
Labrador Sea
60°
Yellowknife
ROCKY MTS
Great Slave Lake
Prince Rupert
Lake Athabasca
NEWFOUNDLAND
Prince George
ALBERTA
Churchill
Hudson Bay
LABRADOR
50°
SASKATCH-EWAN
CANADA
BRITISH COLUMBIA
Edmonton
MANITOBA
Vancouver
Saskatoon
ONTARIO
NEW BRUNSWICK
St. John's
Calgary
Lake Winnipeg
PRINCE EDWARD I.
VANCOUVER I.
Regina
QUEBEC
St. Lawrence R.
Sydney
Victoria
Winnipeg
Thunder Bay
Quebec
Fredericton
Halifax
Pacific Ocean
Lake Superior
Lake Huron
Montreal
Lake Michigan
Ottawa
NOVA SCOTIA
Toronto
Lake Ontario
UNITED STATES
Atlantic Ocean

CANADA
Bellingham
Port Angeles
Seattle
Olympia
Tacoma
Sandpoint
Spokane
WASHINGTON
Kalispell
Havre
Astoria
Yakima
Coeur d'Alene
Great Falls
Portland
Minot
NORTH DAKOTA
Grand Forks
Salem
Pendleton
MONTANA
Helena
Eugene
Bismarck
Fargo
Bend
Butte
IDAHO
Bowman
Fergus F
Billings
OREGON
SOUTH DAKOTA
Aberdeen
Boise
Sheridan
Medford
Gillette
Klamath Falls
Idaho Falls
Jackson
Pierre
Twin Falls
Rapid City
Eureka
Pocatello
WYOMING
Redding
Casper
Sioux Fall
Winnemucca
Valentine
NEBRASKA
Evanston
Ukiah
Elko
Ogden
Sioux Ci
Rock Springs
Cheyenne
Reno
Sidney
North Platte
Sacramento
Carson City
Salt Lake City
Provo
Oma
Grand Island
Boulder
Oakland
NEVADA
Ely
UTAH
Linc
San Francisco
Denver
Goodland
San Jose
Tonopah
Richfield
Grand Junction
Aspen
Colorado Springs
Top
Fresno
Moab
Salina
Monterey
Cedar City
Pueblo
KANSAS
Las Vegas
COLORADO
Hutchinson
Bakersfield
Dodge City
Wich
Santa Barbara
CALIFORNIA
Boulder City
Grand Canyon
Farmington
OKLAHOMA
ARIZONA
Las Vegas
Enid
Tu
Los Angeles
San Bernadino
Flagstaff
Santa Fe
Clinton
Prescott
Tucumcari
Long Beach
Winslow
Albuquerque
Amarillo
Oklahoma C
Phoenix
Mesa
San Diego
NEW MEXICO
Lawton
120° West
Yuma
Wichita Falls
Roswell
Tucson
Lubbock
Deming
Las Cruces
Dalla
Abilene
Ft. Wor
El Paso
Odessa
Midland
Waco
San Angelo
TEXAS
Hous
Del Rio
Austin
MEXICO
Rio Grande
San Antonio
Pacific Ocean
Laredo
Cor Chr
0 Miles 300
110°
Brownsv
HAWAII
Pacific Ocean
KAUAI
OAHU
MOLOKAI
NIHAU
MAUI
Honolulu
Hana
LANAI
KAHOOLAWE
Hilo
Miles
0 100
HAWAII
Barrow
Prudhoe Bay
Miles
0 400
Fairbanks
Nome
ALASKA
CANADA
Anchorage
Valdez
Homer
Juneau
Kodiak
Sitka
Pacific Ocean

United States: Political
CANADA
Gulf of St. Lawrence
International Falls
MINN.
Grand Rapids
Duluth
Lake Superior
Sault Ste. Marie
Lake Huron
Marquette
WISCONSIN
MICHIGAN
Minneapolis
St. Paul
Green Bay
Eau Claire
Lake Michigan
La Crosse
Rochester
Milwaukee
Grand Rapids
Flint
Madison
Lansing
Detroit
Waterloo
Rockford
Kalamazoo
Des Moines
Dubuque
Chicago
Cedar Rapids
Gary
South Bend
Fort Wayne
IOWA
Burlington
Peoria
Springfield
Decatur
Muncie
Indianapolis
INDIANA
Kansas City
Quincy
Columbia
Joplin
St. Louis
ILLINOIS
Jefferson City
Evansville
MISSOURI
Springfield
Fayetteville
ARKANSAS
Fort Smith
Little Rock
Hot Springs
Pine Bluff
Texarkana
Houlton
MAINE
Bangor
Augusta
Brunswick
Montpelier
Burlington
VT.
N.H.
MASS.
CAPE COD
N.Y.
CONN.
R.I.
N.J.
DEL.
MD.
Area of detail
40° North
Atlantic Ocean
L. Ontario
Syracuse
Rochester
Buffalo
L. Erie
Erie
PENNSYLVANIA
Cleveland
OHIO
Akron
Harrisburg
Pittsburgh
Columbus
Wheeling
Hagerstown
Dayton
Cincinnati
Washington D.C.
Clarksburg
Charleston
Huntington
Lexington
W.VA.
Frankfort
Louisville
KENTUCKY
Richmond
Lynchburg
Newport News
Norfolk
Roanoke
VIRGINIA
NORTH CAROLINA
Greensboro
Durham
Raleigh
Winston-Salem
Charlotte
Asheville
Fayetteville
Wilmington
Paducah
Bowling Green
Nashville
Knoxville
TENNESSEE
Memphis
Chattanooga
Spartanburg
Greenville
Huntsville
Columbia
SOUTH CAROLINA
Decatur
Atlanta
Oxford
Birmingham
Augusta
MISSISSIPPI
Tuscaloosa
Macon
Charleston
Montgomery
Savannah
Monroe
Vicksburg
GEORGIA
Shreveport
Jackson
Meridian
ALABAMA
Albany
Brunswick
LOUISIANA
Hattiesburg
Dothan
Baton Rouge
Mobile
Tallahassee
Jacksonville
Lake Charles
Biloxi
Pensacola
Gainesville
Daytona Beach
Lafayette
New Orleans
Panama City
FLORIDA
Orlando
Beaumont
Tampa
St. Petersburg
West Palm Beach
Sarasota
Fort Myers
Fort Lauderdale
Miami
Gulf of Mexico
Key West
CUBA
MEXICO
90° West
80°
70°
30°
20°
VERMONT
N.H.
Portland
Rutland
Portsmouth
Glens Falls
Concord
Manchester
Lowell
Schenectady
Brattleboro
Boston
Albany
Pittsfield
MASS.
Worcester
NEW YORK
Springfield
Providence
Kingston
CONN.
Hartford
R.I.
Binghamton
New London
Newburgh
New Haven
Newport
Paterson
Scranton
Newark
New York City
Allentown
Princeton
Trenton
Philadelphia
NEW JERSEY
PA.
Camden
Atlantic City
Wilmington
Baltimore
Dover
DELAWARE
Annapolis
Salisbury
MARYLAND

Mexico/Central America
UNITED STATES
Tijuana
Mexicali
Ensenada
Puerto Peñasco
San Quintin
Nogales
Ciudad Juárez
Rio Grande
30° North
Hermosillo
Ojinaga
Guaymas
Chihuahua
Piedras Negras
Santa Rosalía
Cuidad Obregón
Delicias
Monclova
Nuevo Laredo
Gulf of Mexico
Loreto
Hidalgo del Parral
BAJA CALIFORNIA
Los Mochis
Monterrey
Matamoros
Gulf of California
Culiacán
Torreón
Saltillo
La Paz
Durango
MEXICO
Cuidad Victoria
YUCATAN PENINSULA
Mazatlán
Cabo San Lucas
Zacatecas
Ciudad Mante
Cancún
Tampico
San Luis Potosí
Progreso
Tepic
León
Guanajuato
Mérida
Guadalajara
Pachuca
Poza Rica
20°
Morelia
Campeche
Xalapa
Colima
Mexico City
Chetumal
0 Miles 300
Manzanillo
Cuernavaca
Puebla
Veracruz
Belize City
Villahermosa
Coatzacoalcos
Chilpancingo
Tuxtla Gutiérrez
Belmopan
Oaxaca
Acapulco
Comitán
BELIZE
Puerto Escondido
Salina Cruz
GUATEMALA
Guatemala
Gulf of Tehuantepec
Tapachula
Pacific Ocean
San Salvador
EL SALVADOR
110° West
100°
90°

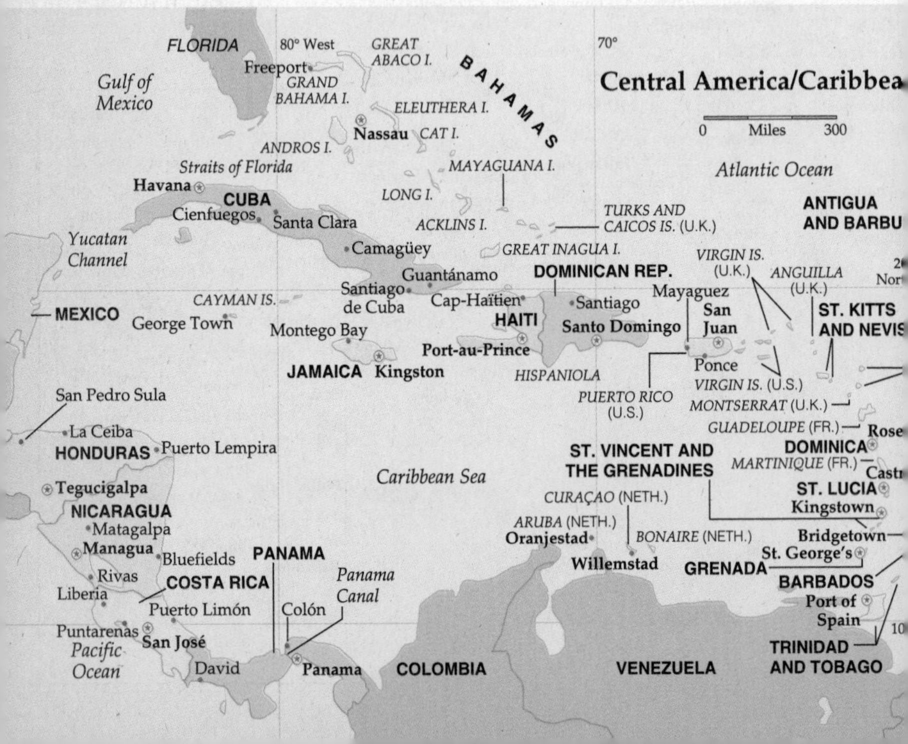
FLORIDA
80° West
GREAT ABACO I.
70°
Freeport
GRAND BAHAMA I.
BAHAMAS
Gulf of Mexico
Central America/Caribbea
ELEUTHERA I.
Nassau
CAT I.
0 Miles 300
ANDROS I.
Straits of Florida
MAYAGUANA I.
Atlantic Ocean
Havana
CUBA
LONG I.
TURKS AND CAICOS IS. (U.K.)
ANTIGUA AND BARBU
Cienfuegos
Santa Clara
ACKLINS I.
Yucatan Channel
Camagüey
GREAT INAGUA I.
VIRGIN IS. (U.K.)
ANGUILLA (U.K.)
Guantánamo
DOMINICAN REP.
CAYMAN IS.
Santiago de Cuba
Mayaguez
MEXICO
Cap-Haïtien
Santiago
San Juan
ST. KITTS AND NEVIS
George Town
HAITI
Santo Domingo
Montego Bay
Port-au-Prince
Ponce
JAMAICA
Kingston
HISPANIOLA
VIRGIN IS. (U.S.)
San Pedro Sula
PUERTO RICO (U.S.)
MONTSERRAT (U.K.)
GUADELOUPE (FR.)
La Ceiba
Rose
HONDURAS
Puerto Lempira
ST. VINCENT AND THE GRENADINES
DOMINICA
MARTINIQUE (FR.)
Castr
Tegucigalpa
Caribbean Sea
ST. LUCIA
Kingstown
NICARAGUA
CURAÇAO (NETH.)
Matagalpa
ARUBA (NETH.)
Oranjestad
BONAIRE (NETH.)
Bridgetown
Managua
Bluefields
PANAMA
Panama Canal
Willemstad
St. George's
GRENADA
Rivas
COSTA RICA
BARBADOS
Liberia
Puerto Limón
Colón
Port of Spain
Puntarenas
San José
Pacific Ocean
TRINIDAD AND TOBAGO
David
Panama
COLOMBIA
VENEZUELA

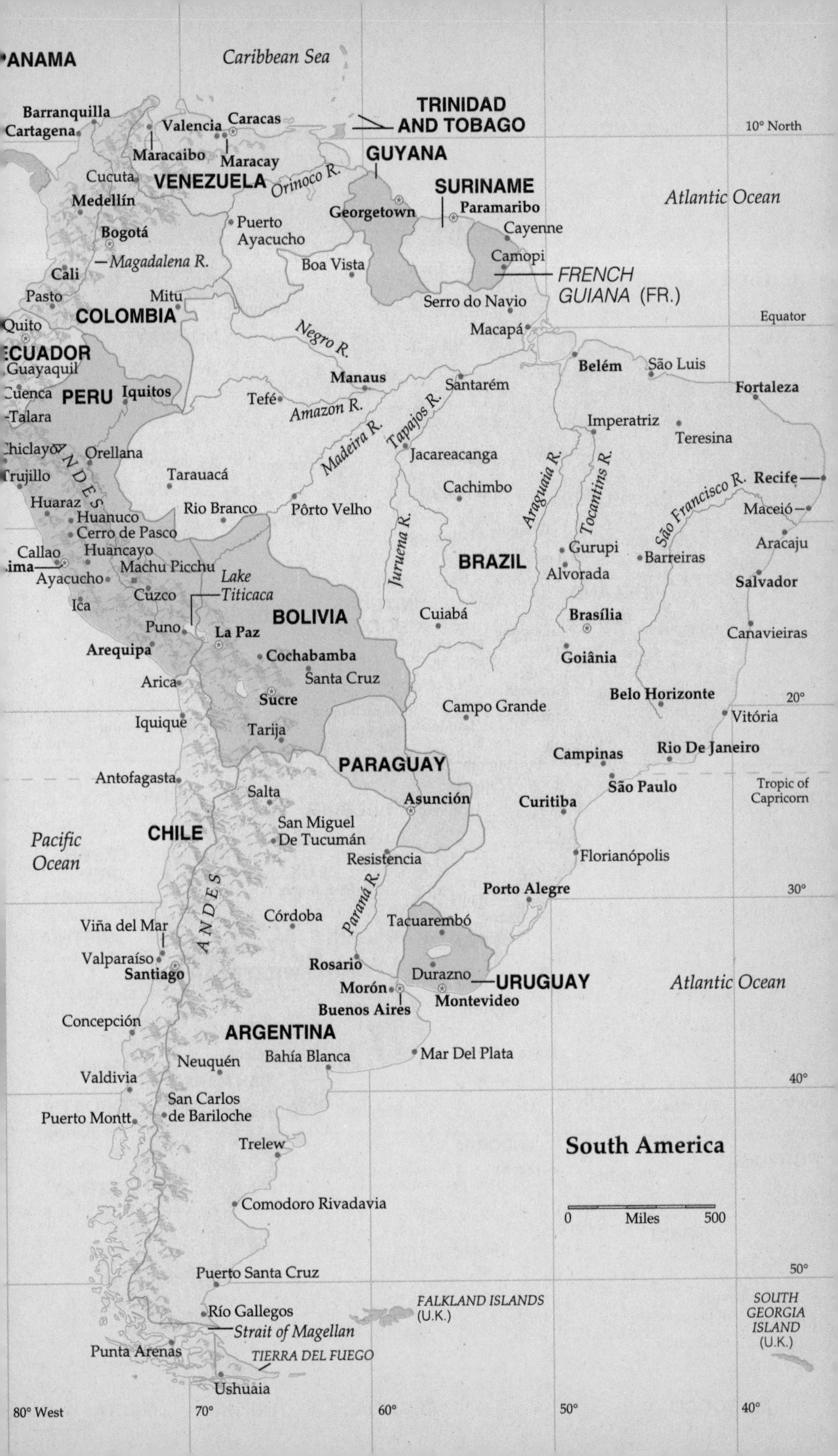

South America
ANAMA
Caribbean Sea
TRINIDAD AND TOBAGO
Barranquilla
Cartagena
Valencia
Caracas
Maracaibo
Maracay
GUYANA
Cucuta
VENEZUELA
Orinoco R.
SURINAME
Medellín
Georgetown
Paramaribo
Atlantic Ocean
Puerto Ayacucho
Cayenne
Bogotá
Camopi
Magadalena R.
Boa Vista
FRENCH GUIANA (FR.)
Cali
Pasto
Mitu
Serro do Navio
COLOMBIA
Quito
Macapá
Equator
ECUADOR
Negro R.
Guayaquil
Belém
São Luis
Manaus
Cuenca
PERU
Iquitos
Santarém
Fortaleza
Talara
Tefé
Amazon R.
Tapajos R.
Imperatriz
Teresina
Madeira R.
Chiclayo
ANDES
Orellana
Jacareacanga
Araguaia R.
Trujillo
Tarauacá
Tocantins R.
Cachimbo
São Francisco R.
Recife
Huaraz
Rio Branco
Pôrto Velho
Maceió
Huanuco
Juruena R.
Cerro de Pasco
Gurupi
Aracaju
BRAZIL
Barreiras
Callao
Huancayo
Lima
Machu Picchu
Alvorada
Ayacucho
Lake Titicaca
Salvador
Cuzco
Ica
BOLIVIA
Cuiabá
Brasília
Puno
La Paz
Canavieiras
Arequipa
Cochabamba
Goiânia
Santa Cruz
Arica
Sucre
Belo Horizonte
20°
Campo Grande
Vitória
Iquique
Tarija
Campinas
Rio De Janeiro
PARAGUAY
Antofagasta
São Paulo
Tropic of Capricorn
Salta
Asunción
Curitiba
San Miguel De Tucumán
CHILE
Pacific Ocean
Resistencia
Florianópolis
Paraná R.
Porto Alegre
30°
ANDES
Córdoba
Tacuarembó
Viña del Mar
Valparaíso
Rosario
Santiago
Durazno
URUGUAY
Atlantic Ocean
Morón
Montevideo
Buenos Aires
Concepción
ARGENTINA
Neuquén
Bahía Blanca
Mar Del Plata
Valdivia
40°
San Carlos de Bariloche
Puerto Montt
Trelew
Comodoro Rivadavia
0
Miles
500
Puerto Santa Cruz
50°
Río Gallegos
FALKLAND ISLANDS (U.K.)
SOUTH GEORGIA ISLAND (U.K.)
Strait of Magellan
Punta Arenas
TIERRA DEL FUEGO
Ushuaia
80° West
70°
60°
50°
40°
10° North

Europe
0 Miles 200
Reykjavik
ICELAND
Norwegian Sea
60° North
FAROE IS.
(DENMARK)
Torshavn
Bodo
Trondheim
SWEDEN
Alesund
Sundsvall
NORWAY
SHETLAND IS.
Lerwick
Bergen
Gavle
ORKNEY IS.
Oslo
Uppsala
Stockholm
HEBRIDES
Inverness
Stavanger
SCOTLAND
N. IRELAND
North Sea
Glasgow
Edinburgh
Alborg
Göteborg
Donegal
Viborg
Belfast
Arhus
Sunderland
IRELAND
Vejle
UNITED
KINGDOM
DENMARK
Copenhagen
Dublin
Limerick
Liverpool
Leeds
Manchester
15° West
Cork
Waterford
ENGLAND
NETHERLANDS
WALES
Hamburg
Birmingham
Leicester
Ouse R.
Cardiff
Amsterdam
GERMANY
POLAND
London
The Hague
Berlin
Atlantic
Ocean
Plymouth
Thames R.
Rotterdam
Poznan
Portsmouth
Essen
Elbe R.
English Channel
Brussels
Cologne
CHANNEL IS. (U.K.)
Le Havre
BELGIUM
Bonn
Rhine R.
Leipzig
Brest
Luxembourg
Frankfurt
Prague
Seine R.
Paris
Nürnberg
CZECH
REP.
Brno
LUX.
Strasbourg
Stuttgart
45°
Loire R.
Bratislava
Danube R.
Munich
Nantes
Vienna
Salzburg
Dijon
FRANCE
AUSTRIA
Zurich
Bay of Biscay
Bern
Vaduz (LIECH.)
Graz
Geneva
SWITZERLAND
Clermont-Ferrand
Ljubljana
ALPS
Bordeaux
Lyons
La Coruña
Milan
Venice
Zagreb
Po R.
Garonne R.
Bilbao
Bayonne
Genoa
SLOVENIA
Rhône R.
Toulouse
SAN MARINO
Porto
Valladolid
Duero R.
PYRENEES
Marseilles
Nice
MONACO
Florence
CROATIA
Coimbra
Salamanca
ANDORRA
Adriatic
Sea
Ebro R.
PORTUGAL
Zaragoza
CORSICA (FR.)
Madrid
Barcelona
Rome
APENNINES
ITALY
Tagus R.
Lisbon
Toledo
Bari
MALLORCA
Valencia
SPAIN
SARDINIA
(ITALY)
Naples
Palma
Córdoba
BALEARIC IS.
(SPAIN)
Guadalquivir R.
Tyrrhenian Sea
Seville
IBIZA
Strait of
Gibraltar
Málaga
15°
Mediterranean Sea
Palermo
Gibraltar
(U.K.)
0°
SICILY
Catania
MOROCCO
ALGERIA
TUNISIA
MALTA
Valletta

White Sea
Rovaniemi
Archangel
Syktyvkar
URAL MTS.
Lulea
FINLAND
Skelleftea
Severnaya Dvina
Sverdlovsk
Perm
Lake Onega
Vaasa
Kirov
Izhevsk
Vyatka R.
Lake Ladoga
Tampere
Belaya R.
Ufa
Vologda
Helsinki
Gulf of Finland
St. Petersburg
Kazan
60° North
Tallinn
Novgorod
Yaroslavl
Nizhniy Novgorod
ESTONIA
Samara R.
Pskov
Togliatti
Samara
Baltic Sea
LATVIA
Moscow
Moscow R.
Oka R.
Riga
Volga R.
Liepaja
Kaluga
LITHUANIA
Vitebsk
Smolensk
RUSSIA
Klaipeda
Saratov
Vilnius
Mogilev
RUSSIA
Orel
Lida
Minsk
Voronezh
KAZAKHSTAN
Olsztyn
Gomel
BELARUS
Don R.
Voronezh
Warsaw
Volgograd
Lodz
Chernobyl
Kharkov
Kiev
Astrakhan
POLAND
Lutsk
Poltava
UKRAINE
45°
Cracow
Dnepropetrovsk
Lviv
Vinnitsa
Dnieper R.
Rostov
Caspian Sea
SLOVAKIA
MOLDOVA
Sea of Azov
HUNG.
Chisinau
Grozny
Budapest
Krasnodar
Odessa
Vladikavkaz
Cluj
CRIMEA
CAUCASUS MTS.
Arad
ROMANIA
Galati
Yalta
Timisoara
Sevastopol
Braila
SERBIA
GEORGIA
Ploesti
Belgrade
Bucharest
Constanta
Black Sea
BOSNIA AND HERZ.
ARMENIA
Sarajevo
Varna
Trabzon
BULGARIA
YUGOSLAVIA
Sofia
IRAN
KOSOVO
Burgas
Bosporus
Zonguldak
MONTENEGRO
Lake Van
Istanbul
Tirana
Skopje
Xanthi
Ankara
GREECE
Thessaloniki
Bursa
Dardanelles
TURKEY
Aegean Sea
Tigris R.
MACEDONIA
Konya
Izmir
Adana
ALBANIA
Euphrates R.
Patrai
Athens
SYRIA
Antalya
LEBANON
Nicosia
CRETE
Ionian Sea
Khania
Iraklion
30° East
CYPRUS
IRAQ

0 Miles 500
Nations of Former Soviet Union
Arctic Circle
Arctic Ocean
20°
40°
60°
80°
100°
120°
140°
160°
80° North
180° East
70°
60°
50°
East Siberian Sea
Bering Sea
Barents Sea
Kara Sea
Laptev Sea
FRANZ JOSEF LAND
NORTH LAND
NEW SIBERIAN IS.
NOVAYA ZEMLYA
U.K.
North Sea
NORWAY
SWEDEN
DEN.
FINLAND
GER.
ESTONIA
Baltic Sea
POL.
LATVIA
Tallinn
Kaliningrad
RUSSIA
Riga
Vilnius
LITHUANIA
Pskov
St. Petersburg
Petrozavodsk
Murmansk
Archangel
MOLDOVA
BELARUS
Novgorod
RUSSIA
Minsk
Lviv
Smolensk
Tver
Vologda
Khmelnitskiy
Yaroslavl
Moscow
Kostroma
Kiev
Kaluga
Ivanovo
Syktyvkar
Bryansk
Tula
Vladimir
Chisinau
Kursk
Orel
Ryazan
Nizhniy Novgorod
Kirov
Odessa
Belgorod
Lipetsk
Perm
Dnepropetrovsk
Voronezh
Tambov
UKRAINE
Penza
Kazan
Simbirsk
Sevastopol
Saratov
Black Sea
Rostov
Volgograd
Yekaterinburg
Chelyabinsk
Tyumen
Orenburg
Kurgan
Irtysh R.
Volga R.
Stavropol
Petropavlovsk
Omsk
Novosibirsk
Tomsk
Krasnoyarsk
TURKEY
Sokhumi
Astrakhan
Aktyubinsk
GEORGIA
Guryev
KAZAKHSTAN
Pavlodar
Barnaul
Kemerovo
Abakan
Tbilisi
Yerevan
Astana
Semipalatinsk
Kyzyl
ARMENIA
Aral
Karaganda
Ganca
Aral Sea
Oskemen
Baku
Syr Darya R.
Lake Balkhash
AZERBAIJAN
Chimbay
Caspian Sea
Kzyl-Orda
Urganch
TURKMENISTAN
UZBEKISTAN
Dzhambul
Almaty
IRAQ
Ashgabat
Bukhoro
Tashkent
Bishkek
Charjew
Samarkand
KYRGYZSTAN
Osh
Dushanbe
IRAN
TAJIKISTAN
Salekhard
Ob R.
Khanty-Mansiysk
Dudinka
Norilsk
Yenisei R.
SIBERIA
Lena R.
Yakutsk
RUSSIA
Kolyma R.
Magadan
Anadyr
Palana
KAMCHATKA PENINSULA
Petropavlovsk Kamchatskiy
Sea of Okhotsk
KURILE IS.
SAKHALIN I.
Yuzhno-Sakhalinsk
Amur R.
Khabarovsk
Blagoveshchensk
Lake Baikal
Chita
Irkutsk
Ulan Ude
Vladivostok
JAPAN
Sea of Japan
MONGOLIA
NORTH KOREA
SOUTH KOREA
Yellow Sea
CHINA

Golan Heights, West Bank, and Gaza Strip are Israeli occupied areas. Current status of the latter two is subject to the Israeli - Palestinian Interim Agreement; permanent status to be determined.
Tripoli
LEBANON
Baalbek
Beirut
BEKAA
Damascus
Sidon
Mediterranean Sea
Tyre
GOLAN HEIGHTS
SYRIA
Nahariya
Jordan R.
Haifa
Sea of Galilee
As-Suwayda
Jordan R.
Nablus
Tel Aviv
WEST BANK
Az-Zarqa
Jericho
Amman
GAZA STRIP
Jerusalem
Bethlehem
Madaba
Hebron
Dead Sea
Gaza
Masada
Beersheba
Dimona
ISRAEL
JORDAN
NEGEV
EGYPT
Ma'an
Elat
Aqaba
SINAI PENINSULA
0 Miles 30

Middle East
0 Miles 200
TURKEY
Tabriz
Lake Urmia
Caspian Sea
TURKMENISTAN
Rasht
Mashhad
Aleppo
Mosul
Arbil
Al Ladhiqiyah
Tigris R.
Teheran
Mediterranean Sea
Hamah
Kirkuk
Hamadan
LEBANON
SYRIA
Euphrates R.
Qom
Bakhtaran
IRAN
AFGHAN.
SYRIAN DESERT
Baghdad
Isfahan
JORDAN
Karbala
Al Hillah
An Najaf
Yazd
ISRAEL
Kerman
IRAQ
Abadan
Area of detail
Basra
KUWAIT
Kuwait
Shiraz
PAK.
Suez Canal
Tabuk
Persian Gulf
Strait of Hormuz
Bandar-e Abbas
SAUDI ARABIA
Dhahran
Manama
QATAR
Al-Hufuf
Ad Dawhah
Dubai
EGYPT
Red Sea
Medina
Riyadh
UNITED ARAB EMIRATES
Abu Dhabi
Gulf of Oman
Muscat
BAHRAIN
Jeddah
Mecca
At Taif
ARABIAN PENINSULA
20° North
OMAN
Al-Jawarah
SUDAN
Arabian Sea
Sana
YEMEN
ERITREA
Al-Hudaydah
Al-Mukalla
ETHIOPIA
Aden
50°
SOCOTRA (YEMEN)
60° East

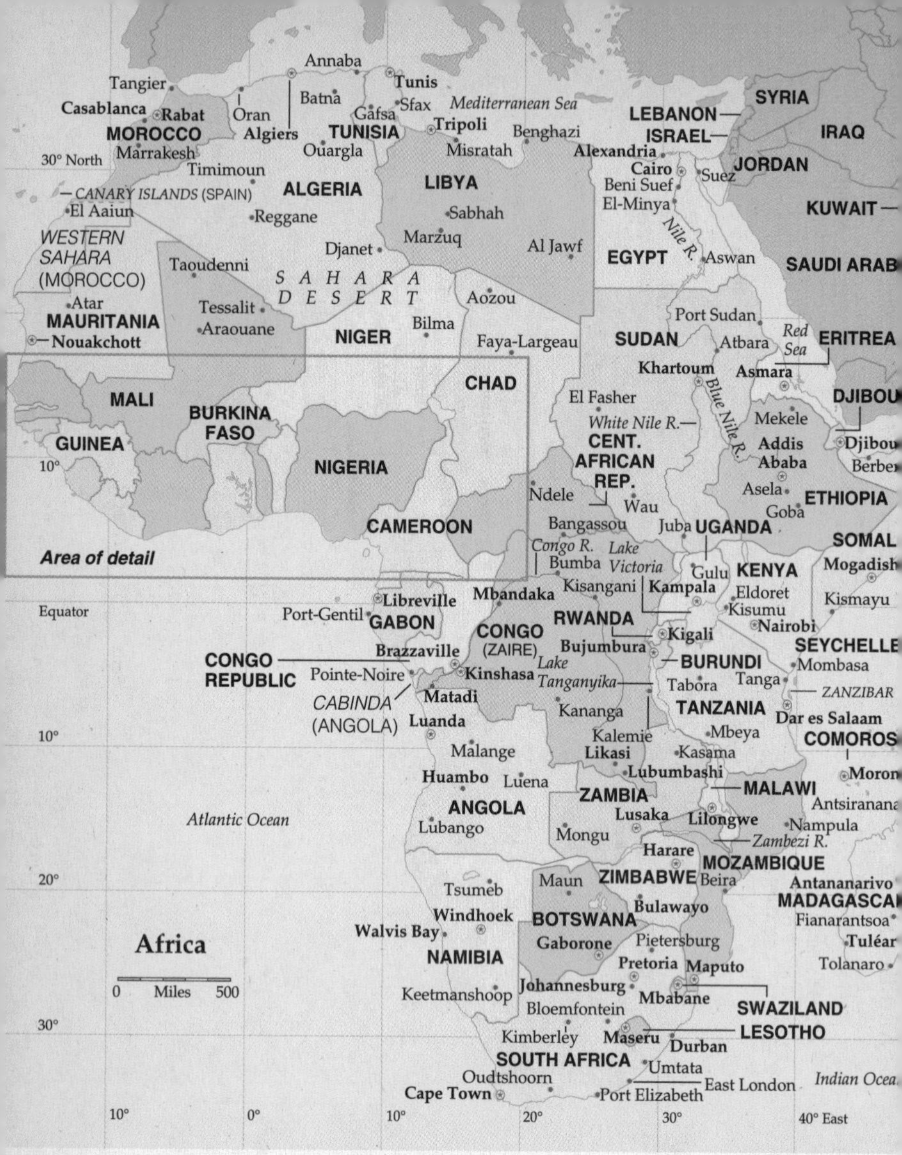
Africa
0 Miles 500
Tangier
Casablanca
Rabat
MOROCCO
Marrakesh
30° North
Oran
Algiers
Annaba
Batna
Tunis
Sfax
Gafsa
TUNISIA
Tripoli
Mediterranean Sea
Benghazi
Misratah
Timimoun
ALGERIA
Ouargla
LIBYA
CANARY ISLANDS (SPAIN)
El Aaiun
Reggane
Sabhah
WESTERN SAHARA (MOROCCO)
Djanet
Marzuq
Al Jawf
Taoudenni
SAHARA DESERT
Tessalit
Araouane
Atar
MAURITANIA
Nouakchott
NIGER
Bilma
Aozou
Faya-Largeau
Alexandria
Cairo
Suez
Beni Suef
El-Minya
Nile R.
EGYPT
Aswan
LEBANON
ISRAEL
SYRIA
IRAQ
JORDAN
KUWAIT
SAUDI ARAB
SUDAN
Port Sudan
Atbara
Red Sea
ERITREA
Khartoum
Asmara
Blue Nile R.
CHAD
MALI
BURKINA FASO
GUINEA
NIGERIA
CAMEROON
10°
Area of detail
El Fasher
White Nile R.
CENT. AFRICAN REP.
Ndele
Wau
Bangassou
Mekele
Addis Ababa
Asela
Goba
ETHIOPIA
DJIBOU
Djibou
Berbe
SOMAL
Mogadish
Kismayu
Juba
UGANDA
Congo R.
Bumba
Lake Victoria
Gulu
KENYA
Kisangani
Kampala
Eldoret
Kisumu
Nairobi
Equator
Libreville
GABON
Port-Gentil
Mbandaka
CONGO (ZAIRE)
RWANDA
Kigali
Bujumbura
BURUNDI
CONGO REPUBLIC
Brazzaville
Pointe-Noire
Kinshasa
Lake Tanganyika
CABINDA (ANGOLA)
Matadi
Luanda
Tabora
TANZANIA
Tanga
SEYCHELLE
Mombasa
ZANZIBAR
Dar es Salaam
Kananga
Kalemie
Mbeya
Likasi
Kasama
COMOROS
Moron
10°
Malange
Lubumbashi
Huambo
Luena
ZAMBIA
MALAWI
Antsiranana
ANGOLA
Lusaka
Lilongwe
Nampula
Atlantic Ocean
Lubango
Mongu
Zambezi R.
Harare
MOZAMBIQUE
20°
Tsumeb
Maun
ZIMBABWE
Beira
Antananarivo
MADAGASCA
Windhoek
BOTSWANA
Bulawayo
Fianarantsoa
Walvis Bay
Gaborone
Pietersburg
Tuléar
NAMIBIA
Pretoria
Maputo
Tolanaro
Johannesburg
Keetmanshoop
Mbabane
SWAZILAND
Bloemfontein
30°
Kimberley
Maseru
LESOTHO
Durban
SOUTH AFRICA
Umtata
Oudtshoorn
East London
Indian Ocea
Cape Town
Port Elizabeth
10°
0°
10°
20°
30°
40° East

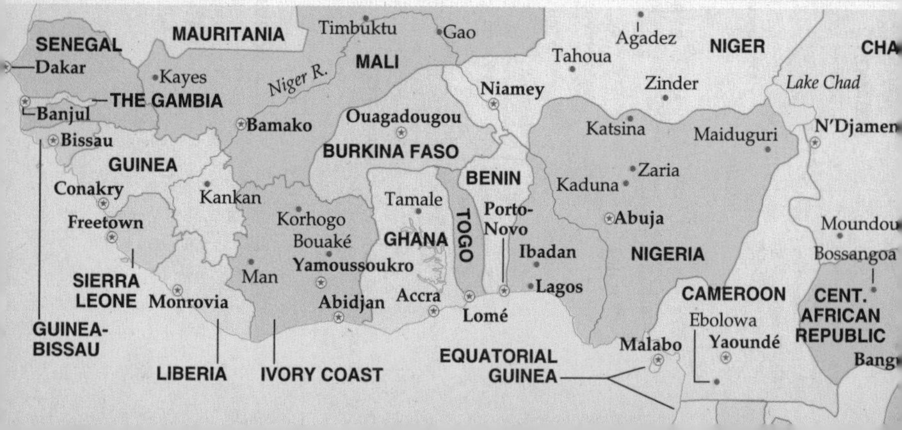
SENEGAL
MAURITANIA
Timbuktu
Gao
Agadez
NIGER
CHA
Dakar
Kayes
MALI
Niger R.
Tahoua
Zinder
Lake Chad
THE GAMBIA
Niamey
Banjul
Bamako
Ouagadougou
Katsina
Maiduguri
N'Djamen
Bissau
BURKINA FASO
GUINEA
Zaria
BENIN
Conakry
Kankan
Tamale
Kaduna
Korhogo
Porto-Novo
Abuja
Freetown
Moundou
Bouaké
GHANA
TOGO
Ibadan
NIGERIA
Bossangoa
Yamoussoukro
SIERRA LEONE
Man
Lagos
Monrovia
Abidjan
Accra
CAMEROON
CENT. AFRICAN REPUBLIC
Lomé
Ebolowa
GUINEA-BISSAU
Malabo
Yaoundé
Bang
LIBERIA
IVORY COAST
EQUATORIAL GUINEA

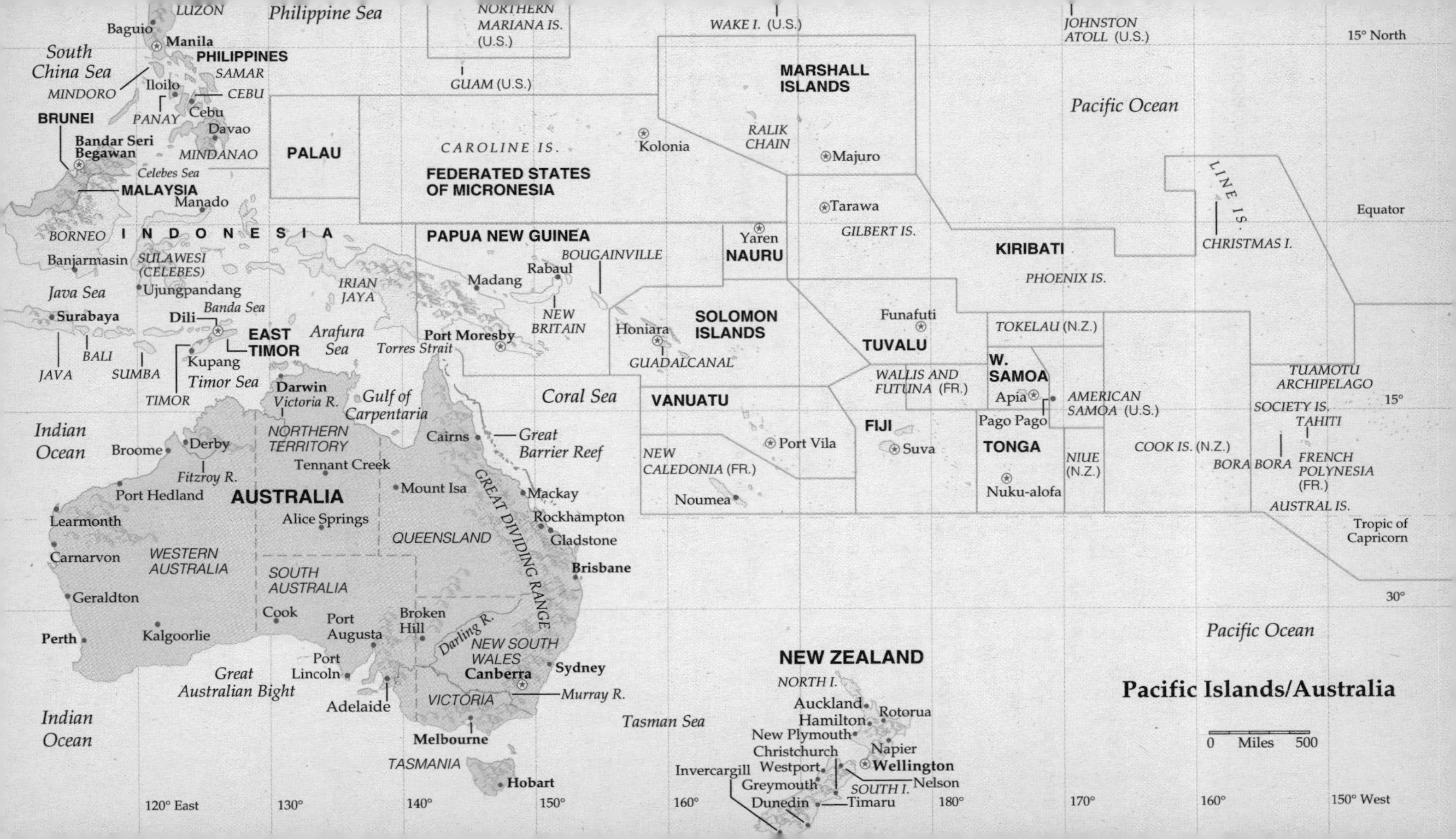
Pacific Islands/Australia
0 Miles 500
Philippine Sea
South China Sea
LUZON
Baguio
Manila
PHILIPPINES
SAMAR
MINDORO
Iloilo
CEBU
PANAY
Cebu
Davao
MINDANAO
BRUNEI
Bandar Seri Begawan
Celebes Sea
MALAYSIA
Manado
BORNEO
INDONESIA
Banjarmasin
SULAWESI (CELEBES)
Ujungpandang
Java Sea
Banda Sea
Surabaya
Dili
EAST TIMOR
JAVA
BALI
SUMBA
Kupang
TIMOR
Timor Sea
Arafura Sea
IRIAN JAYA
NORTHERN MARIANA IS. (U.S.)
GUAM (U.S.)
PALAU
CAROLINE IS.
FEDERATED STATES OF MICRONESIA
Kolonia
WAKE I. (U.S.)
MARSHALL ISLANDS
RALIK CHAIN
Majuro
Tarawa
GILBERT IS.
JOHNSTON ATOLL (U.S.)
Pacific Ocean
LINE IS.
CHRISTMAS I.
KIRIBATI
PHOENIX IS.
15° North
Equator
PAPUA NEW GUINEA
Madang
Rabaul
BOUGAINVILLE
NEW BRITAIN
Port Moresby
Torres Strait
Yaren
NAURU
SOLOMON ISLANDS
Honiara
GUADALCANAL
Funafuti
TUVALU
TOKELAU (N.Z.)
W. SAMOA
Apia
AMERICAN SAMOA (U.S.)
Pago Pago
WALLIS AND FUTUNA (FR.)
VANUATU
Port Vila
NEW CALEDONIA (FR.)
Noumea
FIJI
Suva
TONGA
Nuku-alofa
NIUE (N.Z.)
COOK IS. (N.Z.)
TUAMOTU ARCHIPELAGO
SOCIETY IS.
TAHITI
BORA BORA
FRENCH POLYNESIA (FR.)
AUSTRAL IS.
15°
Tropic of Capricorn
30°
Coral Sea
Gulf of Carpentaria
Darwin
Victoria R.
NORTHERN TERRITORY
Tennant Creek
Indian Ocean
Broome
Derby
Fitzroy R.
Port Hedland
AUSTRALIA
Learmonth
Carnarvon
WESTERN AUSTRALIA
Geraldton
Kalgoorlie
Perth
Alice Springs
SOUTH AUSTRALIA
Cook
Port Augusta
Port Lincoln
Great Australian Bight
Adelaide
Cairns
Great Barrier Reef
Mount Isa
QUEENSLAND
GREAT DIVIDING RANGE
Mackay
Rockhampton
Gladstone
Brisbane
Broken Hill
Darling R.
NEW SOUTH WALES
Sydney
Canberra
Murray R.
VICTORIA
Melbourne
TASMANIA
Hobart
Tasman Sea
NEW ZEALAND
NORTH I.
Auckland
Rotorua
Hamilton
New Plymouth
Napier
Christchurch
Wellington
Westport
Invercargill
Greymouth
SOUTH I.
Nelson
Dunedin
Timaru
120° East
130°
140°
150°
160°
180°
170°
160°
150° West

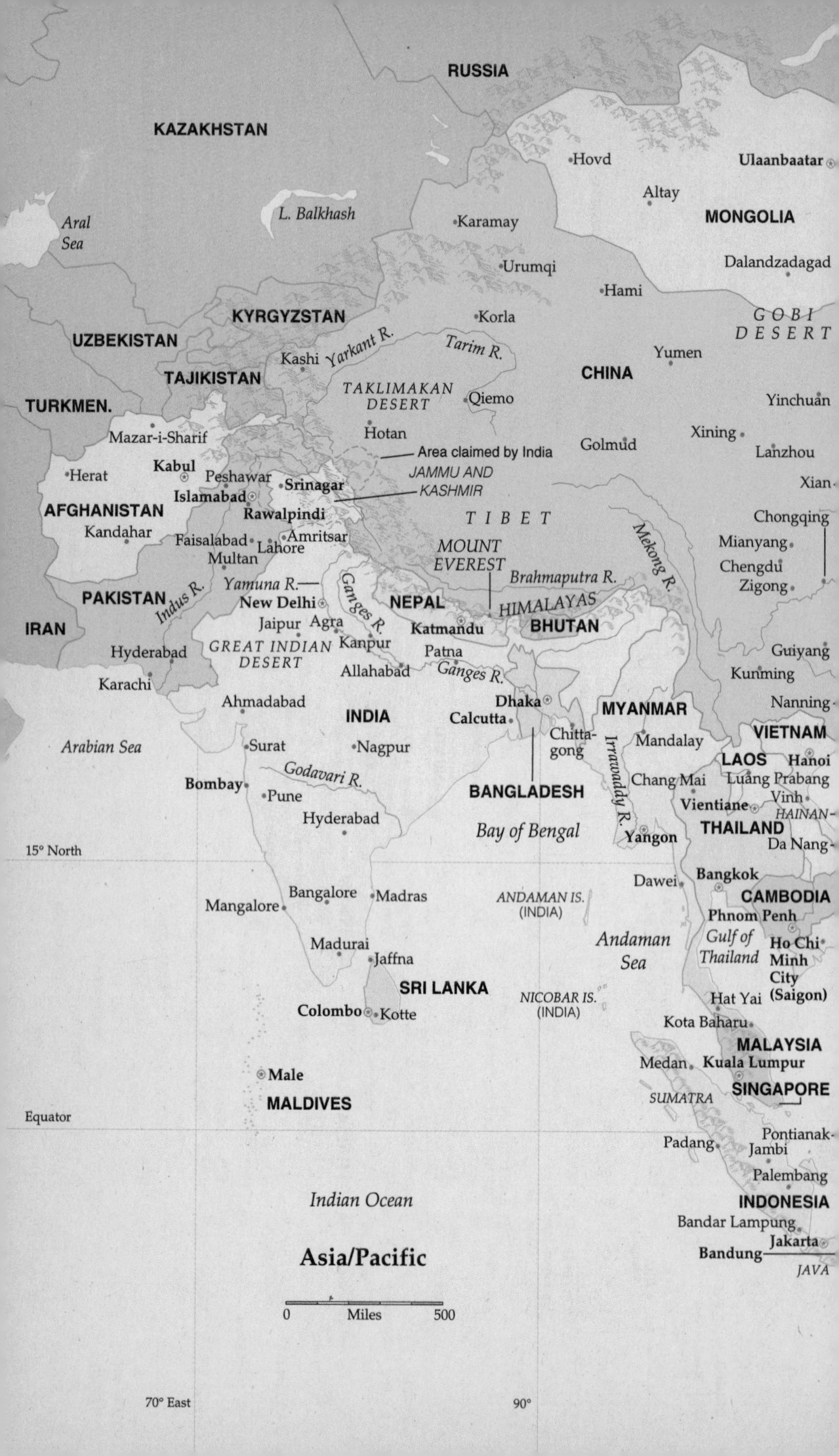
RUSSIA
KAZAKHSTAN
Aral Sea
L. Balkhash
Hovd
Ulaanbaatar
Altay
MONGOLIA
Karamay
Urumqi
Dalandzadagad
Hami
KYRGYZSTAN
Korla
GOBI DESERT
UZBEKISTAN
Yarkant R.
Tarim R.
Kashi
Yumen
TAJIKISTAN
CHINA
TAKLIMAKAN DESERT
Qiemo
Yinchuan
TURKMEN.
Hotan
Xining
Mazar-i-Sharif
Area claimed by India
Golmud
Lanzhou
Herat
Kabul
Peshawar
Srinagar
JAMMU AND KASHMIR
Xian
Islamabad
AFGHANISTAN
Rawalpindi
TIBET
Chongqing
Kandahar
Faisalabad
Amritsar
Lahore
Mekong R.
Mianyang
Multan
MOUNT EVEREST
Chengdu
Yamuna R.
Ganges R.
Brahmaputra R.
Zigong
PAKISTAN
Indus R.
New Delhi
NEPAL
HIMALAYAS
IRAN
Jaipur
Agra
Katmandu
BHUTAN
Hyderabad
GREAT INDIAN DESERT
Kanpur
Patna
Guiyang
Allahabad
Ganges R.
Kunming
Karachi
Ahmadabad
Dhaka
INDIA
Calcutta
MYANMAR
Nanning
Arabian Sea
Surat
Nagpur
Chitta-gong
Irrawaddy R.
Mandalay
VIETNAM
Godavari R.
LAOS
Hanoi
Bombay
Pune
BANGLADESH
Chang Mai
Luang Prabang
Vientiane
Vinh
Hyderabad
HAINAN
Bay of Bengal
Yangon
THAILAND
15° North
Da Nang
Dawei
Bangkok
Bangalore
Madras
ANDAMAN IS. (INDIA)
CAMBODIA
Mangalore
Phnom Penh
Gulf of Thailand
Madurai
Andaman Sea
Ho Chi Minh City (Saigon)
Jaffna
SRI LANKA
NICOBAR IS. (INDIA)
Hat Yai
Colombo
Kotte
Kota Baharu
MALAYSIA
Medan
Kuala Lumpur
Male
SUMATRA
SINGAPORE
MALDIVES
Equator
Padang
Pontianak
Jambi
Palembang
Indian Ocean
INDONESIA
Bandar Lampung
Jakarta
Asia/Pacific
Bandung
JAVA
0
Miles
500
70° East
90°

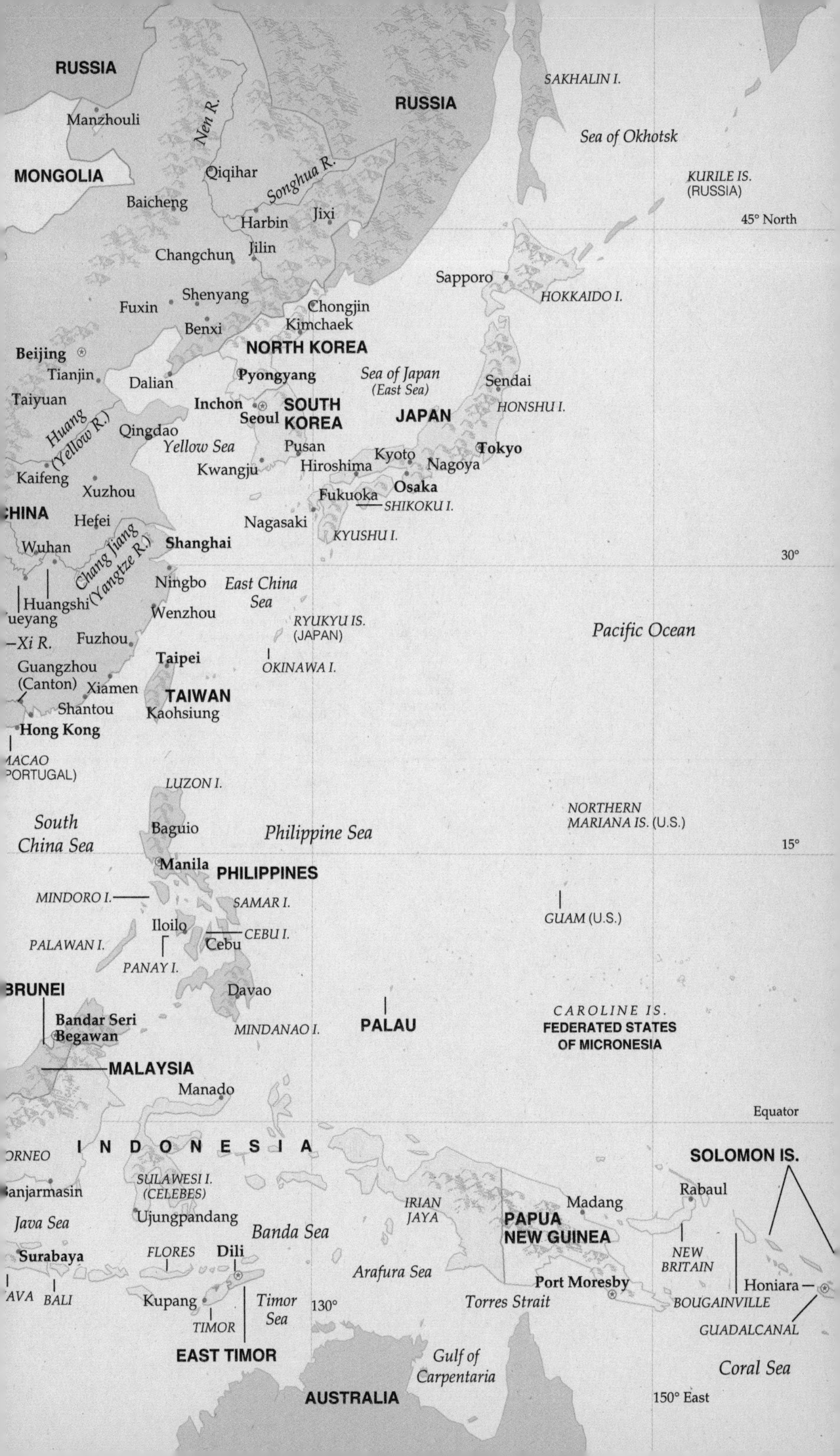
RUSSIA
Manzhouli
MONGOLIA
Nen R.
Qiqihar
Songhua R.
Baicheng
Harbin
Jixi
Jilin
Changchun
RUSSIA
SAKHALIN I.
Sea of Okhotsk
KURILE IS.
(RUSSIA)
45° North
Sapporo
HOKKAIDO I.
Fuxin
Shenyang
Benxi
Chongjin
Kimchaek
NORTH KOREA
Beijing
Tianjin
Dalian
Pyongyang
Sea of Japan
(East Sea)
Sendai
HONSHU I.
Taiyuan
Inchon
Seoul
SOUTH
KOREA
JAPAN
Huang
(Yellow R.)
Qingdao
Yellow Sea
Pusan
Tokyo
Kwangju
Hiroshima
Kyoto
Nagoya
Kaifeng
Xuzhou
Osaka
Fukuoka
SHIKOKU I.
CHINA
Hefei
Nagasaki
KYUSHU I.
Wuhan
Chang Jiang
(Yangtze R.)
Shanghai
30°
Ningbo
East China
Sea
Huangshi
Yueyang
Wenzhou
RYUKYU IS.
(JAPAN)
Pacific Ocean
Xi R.
Fuzhou
Taipei
OKINAWA I.
Guangzhou
(Canton)
Xiamen
TAIWAN
Shantou
Kaohsiung
Hong Kong
MACAO
(PORTUGAL)
LUZON I.
NORTHERN
MARIANA IS. (U.S.)
South
China Sea
Baguio
Philippine Sea
15°
Manila
PHILIPPINES
MINDORO I.
SAMAR I.
GUAM (U.S.)
Iloilo
CEBU I.
PALAWAN I.
Cebu
PANAY I.
BRUNEI
Davao
CAROLINE IS.
Bandar Seri
Begawan
MINDANAO I.
PALAU
FEDERATED STATES
OF MICRONESIA
MALAYSIA
Manado
Equator
INDONESIA
BORNEO
SOLOMON IS.
SULAWESI I.
(CELEBES)
Banjarmasin
Rabaul
IRIAN
JAYA
Madang
Ujungpandang
PAPUA
NEW GUINEA
Java Sea
Banda Sea
NEW
BRITAIN
Surabaya
FLORES
Dili
Arafura Sea
Port Moresby
Honiara
JAVA
BALI
Kupang
Timor
Sea
130°
Torres Strait
BOUGAINVILLE
TIMOR
GUADALCANAL
EAST TIMOR
Gulf of
Carpentaria
Coral Sea
AUSTRALIA
150° East

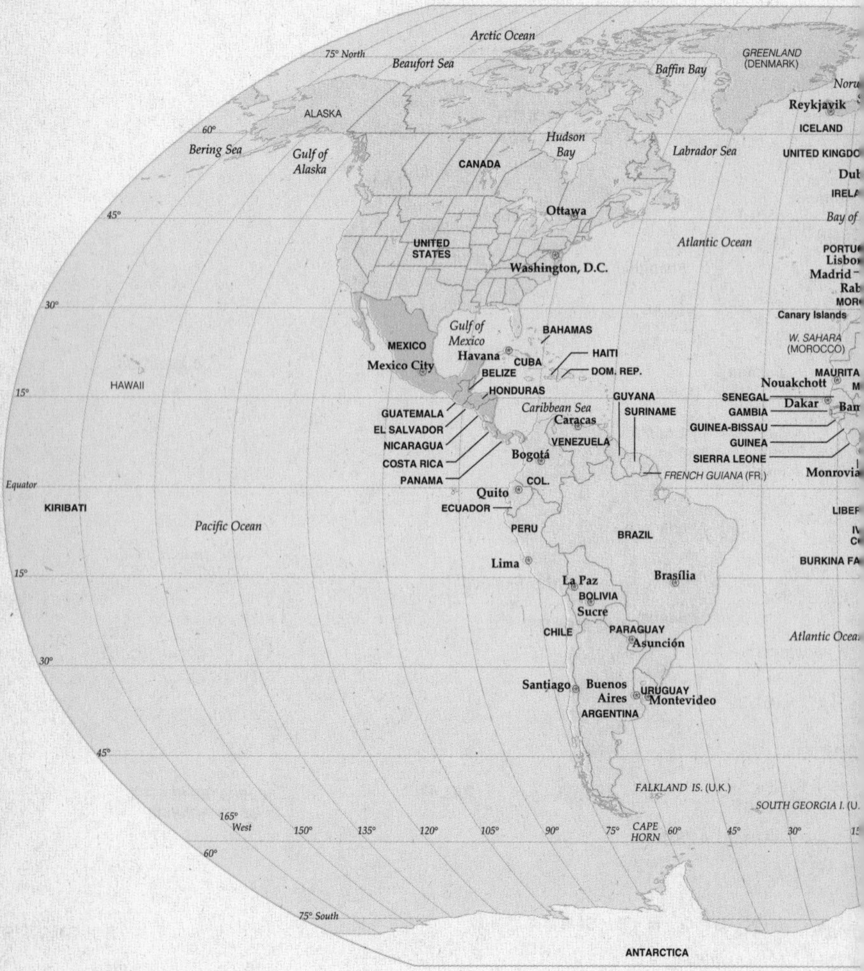

Arctic Ocean
75° North
Beaufort Sea
Baffin Bay
GREENLAND
(DENMARK)
Reykjavik
ICELAND
ALASKA
60°
Bering Sea
Gulf of
Alaska
Hudson
Bay
CANADA
Labrador Sea
UNITED KINGDO
IREL
45°
Ottawa
Bay of
Atlantic Ocean
UNITED
STATES
Washington, D.C.
PORTU
Lisbo
Madrid
Rab
MOR
30°
Canary Islands
Gulf of
Mexico
BAHAMAS
W. SAHARA
(MOROCCO)
MEXICO
Havana
CUBA
HAITI
Mexico City
BELIZE
DOM. REP.
MAURITA
Nouakchott
HAWAII
15°
HONDURAS
GUYANA
SENEGAL
Caribbean Sea
SURINAME
Dakar
GAMBIA
GUATEMALA
Caracas
EL SALVADOR
GUINEA-BISSAU
NICARAGUA
VENEZUELA
GUINEA
Bogotá
COSTA RICA
SIERRA LEONE
PANAMA
FRENCH GUIANA (FR.)
Monrovia
Equator
COL.
Quito
KIRIBATI
ECUADOR
LIBER
Pacific Ocean
PERU
BRAZIL
Lima
BURKINA FA
15°
La Paz
Brasília
BOLIVIA
Sucre
CHILE
PARAGUAY
Atlantic Ocea
Asunción
30°
Santiago
Buenos
Aires
URUGUAY
Montevideo
ARGENTINA
45°
FALKLAND IS. (U.K.)
SOUTH GEORGIA I. (U.
165°
West
150°
135°
120°
105°
90°
75°
CAPE
HORN
60°
45°
30°
60°
75° South
ANTARCTICA

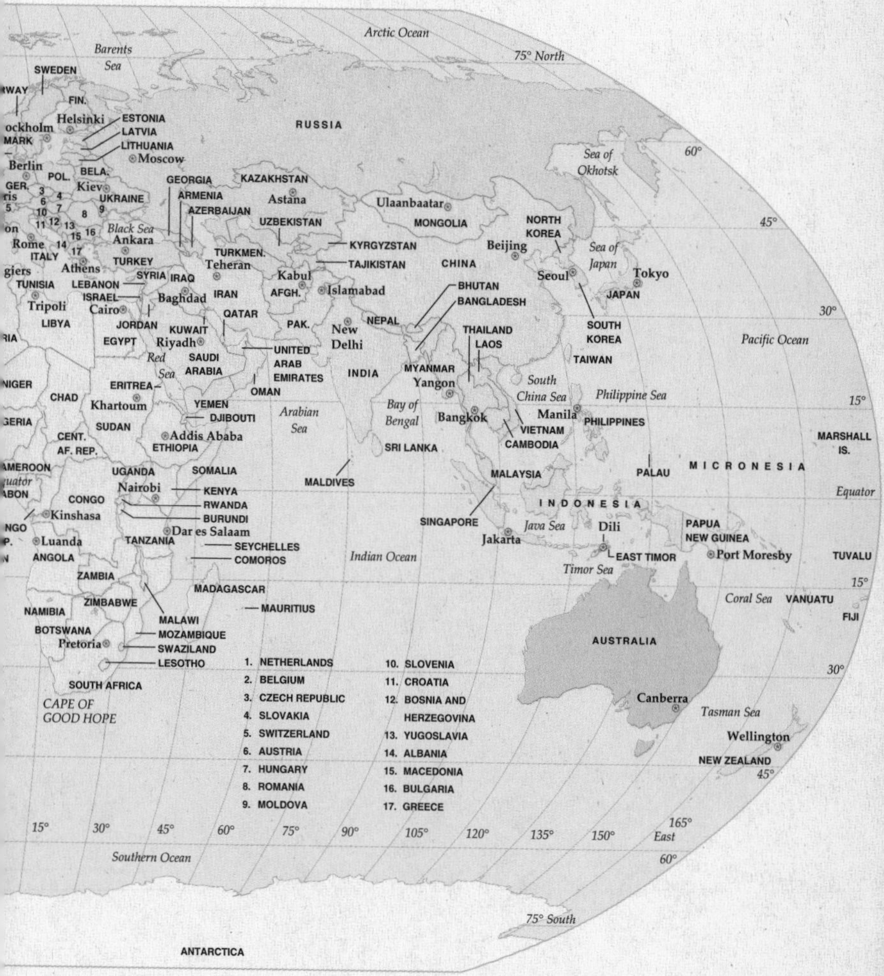

Arctic Ocean
Barents Sea
75° North
SWEDEN
FIN.
Helsinki
ESTONIA
LATVIA
LITHUANIA
Moscow
RUSSIA
Berlin
POL.
BELA.
Kiev
UKRAINE
GEORGIA
ARMENIA
AZERBAIJAN
KAZAKHSTAN
Astana
UZBEKISTAN
Ulaanbaatar
MONGOLIA
Sea of Okhotsk
60°
45°
NORTH KOREA
Sea of Japan
Black Sea
Ankara
Rome
ITALY
Athens
TURKEY
TURKMEN.
Teheran
KYRGYZSTAN
TAJIKISTAN
Beijing
CHINA
Seoul
Tokyo
JAPAN
TUNISIA
LEBANON
ISRAEL
SYRIA
IRAQ
Baghdad
IRAN
Kabul
AFGH.
Islamabad
BHUTAN
BANGLADESH
Tripoli
Cairo
LIBYA
JORDAN
KUWAIT
QATAR
PAK.
New Delhi
NEPAL
SOUTH KOREA
30°
Pacific Ocean
EGYPT
Riyadh
Red Sea
SAUDI ARABIA
UNITED ARAB EMIRATES
INDIA
MYANMAR
Yangon
THAILAND
LAOS
TAIWAN
South China Sea
Philippine Sea
NIGER
CHAD
ERITREA
Khartoum
SUDAN
YEMEN
DJIBOUTI
OMAN
Arabian Sea
Bay of Bengal
Bangkok
Manila
VIETNAM
CAMBODIA
PHILIPPINES
15°
CENT. AF. REP.
Addis Ababa
ETHIOPIA
SRI LANKA
MARSHALL IS.
UGANDA
SOMALIA
Nairobi
KENYA
RWANDA
BURUNDI
CONGO
Kinshasa
MALDIVES
MALAYSIA
PALAU
MICRONESIA
Equator
INDONESIA
SINGAPORE
Java Sea
Jakarta
Dili
EAST TIMOR
PAPUA NEW GUINEA
Port Moresby
Luanda
ANGOLA
TANZANIA
Dar es Salaam
SEYCHELLES
COMOROS
Indian Ocean
Timor Sea
TUVALU
ZAMBIA
MADAGASCAR
ZIMBABWE
NAMIBIA
MAURITIUS
Coral Sea
VANUATU
FIJI
MALAWI
BOTSWANA
MOZAMBIQUE
Pretoria
SWAZILAND
LESOTHO
AUSTRALIA
SOUTH AFRICA
CAPE OF GOOD HOPE
1. NETHERLANDS
2. BELGIUM
3. CZECH REPUBLIC
4. SLOVAKIA
5. SWITZERLAND
6. AUSTRIA
7. HUNGARY
8. ROMANIA
9. MOLDOVA
10. SLOVENIA
11. CROATIA
12. BOSNIA AND HERZEGOVINA
13. YUGOSLAVIA
14. ALBANIA
15. MACEDONIA
16. BULGARIA
17. GREECE
Canberra
Tasman Sea
Wellington
NEW ZEALAND
15°
30°
45°
60°
75°
90°
105°
120°
135°
150°
165° East
Southern Ocean
75° South
ANTARCTICA

United States: Physical

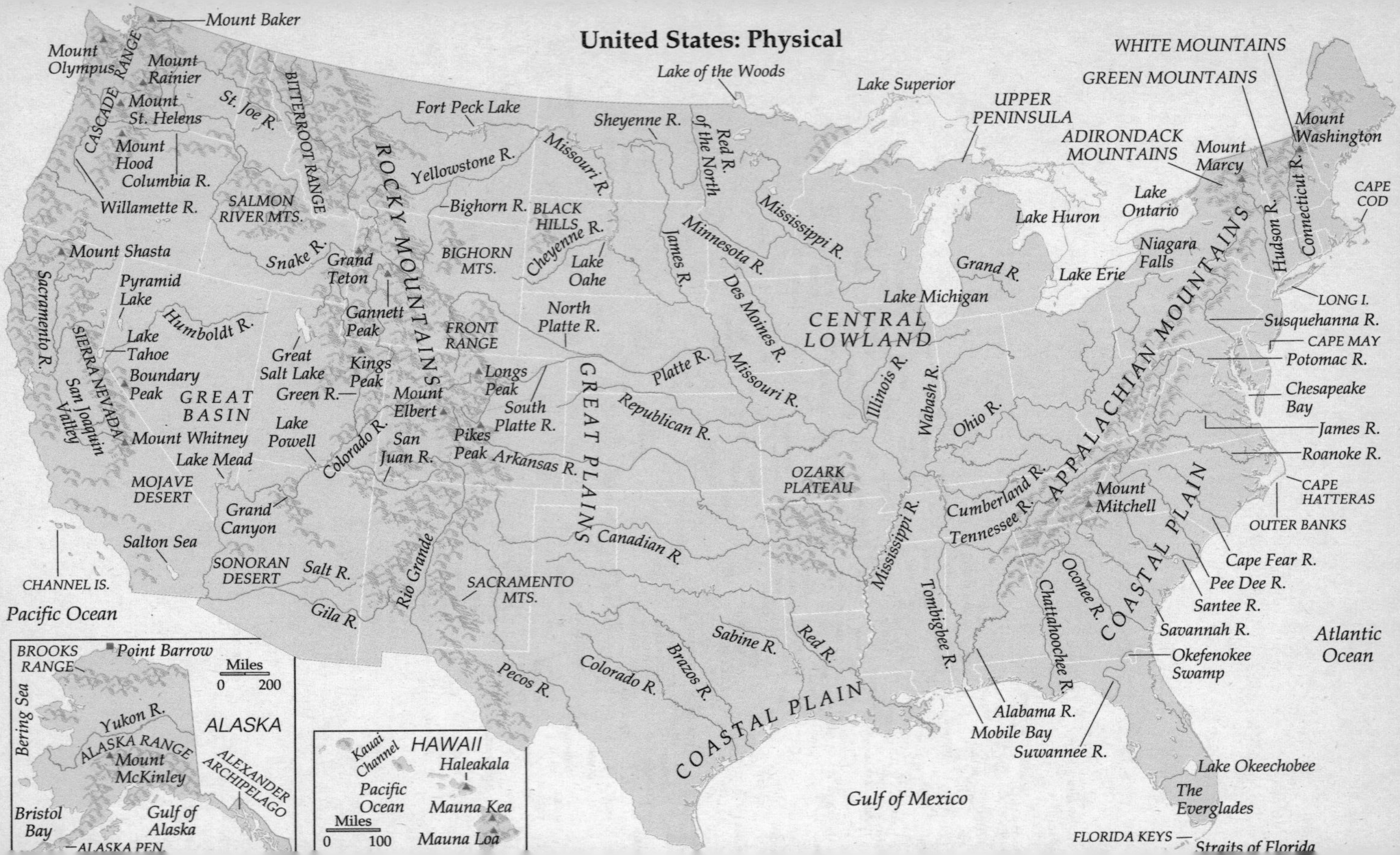

man kings of Sicily conquered it and made it a way station for the First Crusade. In 1530 Charles V gave the island to the Knights Hospitalers (the Knights of Malta). The island withstood a siege by the Ottoman Turks in 1565 and fell only to Napoleon in 1798.

Malta came under British rule in 1800, and was annexed in 1814. Limited self-rule was granted under the constitutions of 1921 and 1939. During World War II, Malta suffered devastating air raids by German and Italian forces; the entire population was awarded the George Cross for bravery.

In 1964 Malta was granted independence within the British Commonwealth, with Elizabeth II as its sovereign. Abrogating its mutual defense treaty with Great Britain in 1971, the Maltese government severed all ties to the British Crown, becoming a fully independent republic. British forces withdrew from the island in 1979.

Malta was governed by the leftist, anticlerical, and neutralist Labour party from 1971 to 1987, whose leader, the ardent nationalist Dominic Mintoff, was prime minister from 1971 to 1984, succeeded by Mifsud Bonnici. In 1997 the Catholic and pro-Western Nationalist party won a popular electoral majority but not a majority in Parliament. Under a 1987 constitutional amendment, it was granted sufficient extra seats in Parliament to allow it to organize a government under Prime Minister Eddie Fenech Adami.

The Nationalist party ruled for nine years until in 1996 elections the Labour party won a slim majority, but returned to power in Sept. 1998 with Adami returning as prime minister. In 2003 voters approved a move to enter the E.U.

▶MARSHALL ISLANDS

Republic of the Marshall Islands

• GEOGRAPHY **Location:** two groups of islands, the Ratak and Ralik chains, comprising 31 atolls in western Pacific. Majuro 7°09'N, 171°12'E. **Boundaries**: Guam about 1,300 mi. (2,100 km) to NW, Hawaii about 2,000 mi. (3,200 km) to NE, Kiribati to S, Federated States of Micronesia to W. **Total area**: 70 sq. mi. (181 sq km). **Coastline**: 230 (370 km). **Comparative area**: about the size of Washington, D.C. **Land use:** 17% arable land; 0% permanent crops; 83% other. **Major cities**: Majuro (capital—pop. N.A.).

• PEOPLE **Population:** 56,429 (July 2003 est.). **Nationality:** noun—Marshallese; adjective—Marshallese. **Ethnic groups:** Micronesian. **Languages:** English (official), two major Marshallese dialects from Malayo-Polynesian family, Japanese. **Religions:** Christian, mostly Protestant.

• GOVERNMENT **Type:** constitutional government in free association with U.S.; Compact of Free Association entered into force Oct. 21, 1986. **Independence:** Oct. 21, 1986 (from U.S.-administered U.N. trusteeship). **Constitution:** May 1, 1979. **National holiday:** Proclamation of the Republic of the Marshall Islands, May 1. **Head of Government:** Kessai Note, president (since Jan. 2000). **Structure:** executive; unicameral legislature; judiciary.

• ECONOMY **Monetary unit:** U.S. dollar. **Budget:** (1999) ***income:*** $42 mil.; ***expend:*** $40 mil. **GDP:** $115 mil., $1,600 per capita (2001 est.). **Chief crops:** coconuts, cacao, taro, breadfruit, fruits; pigs, chickens. **Natural resources:** phosphate deposits, marine products, deep seabed minerals. **Major industries:** copra, fish, tourism. **Labor force:** 28,698. **Exports:** $9 mil. (f.o.b., 2000 est.); coconut oil, fish, trochus shells. **Imports:** $54 mil. (c.i.f., 2000 est.); foodstuffs, machinery and equipment, fuels, beverages and tobacco. **Major trading partners:** U.S., Japan, Australia.

The Marshall Islands, part of the geographic region known as Micronesia, are made up of 31 atolls of the Ratak (Sunrise) and Ralik (Sunset) chains located between 4° and 14°N and 160° and 173°E. Although claimed by Spain in 1592, the islands were left undisturbed by the Spanish empire for 300 years. In 1885, Germany took over the administration on the islands of Jaluit and Ebon. At that time copra (dried coconut meat) trade was the primary industry. Japan assumed control of the Marshalls at the beginning of World War I and held them until 1944, when Allied forces occupied the islands. In 1947 the islands were included in the U.N. Trust Territory of the Pacific and placed under U.S. administration. In 1946 the U.S. government resettled the inhabitants of Bikini and Enewetak in order to begin nuclear tests, which continued through 1958. Residents began returning to Enewetak in 1980; but the estimated cost of a complete clean-up of Bikini is $100 million.

▶MAURITANIA

Islamic Republic of Mauritania

• GEOGRAPHY **Location:** northwestern Africa. **Boundaries**: territory of Western Sahara to N, Algeria to NE, Mali to E and S, Senegal to S, Atlantic Ocean to W. **Total area**: 397,954 sq. mi. (1,030,700 sq km). **Coastline**: 469 mi. (754 km). **Comparative area**: slightly larger than three times the size of New Mexico. **Land use:** negl. % arable land; negl. % permanent crops; 99% other. **Major cities**: Nouakchott (capital) 350,000 (1984 est.); Nouadhibou (Port Étienne) 21,961; Kaédi 20,848; Zouérate 17,474; Rosso 16,466 (1977 census).

• PEOPLE **Population:** 2,912,584 (July 2003 est.). **Nationality:** noun—Mauritanian(s); adjective—Mauritanian. **Ethnic groups:** 40% mixed Maur/black, 30% Maur, 30% black. **Languages:** Hassaniya Arabic (official), Wolof (official), Pular, Soninke, French. **Religions:** 100% Muslim.

• GOVERNMENT **Type:** republic. **Independence:** Nov. 28, 1960 (from France). **Constitution:** July 12, 1991. **National holiday:** Independence Day, Nov. 28. **Heads of Government:** Col. Maaouya Ould Sid' Ahmed Taya, president (since Dec. 1984); Cheikh El Avia Ould Mohamed Khouna, prime minister (since Nov. 1998). **Structure:** executive; bicameral legislature; judiciary.

• ECONOMY **Monetary unit:** ouguiya. **Budget:** (1996 est.) ***income:*** $329 mil.; ***expend.:*** $265 mil. **GDP:** $5.4 bil., $2,000 per capita (2000 est.). **Chief crops:** dates, millet, sorghum; cattle, sheep; fish. **Natural resources:** iron ore, gypsum, fish, copper, phosphate. **Major industries:** fish processing, mining of iron ore and gypsum. **Labor force:** 786,000 (2001 est.); 50% agriculture, 40% services, 10% industry and commerce; 21% unemployment (1999). **Exports:** $355 mil. (f.o.b., 2001); fish and fish products, iron ore, gold. **Imports:** $360 mil. (f.o.b., 2001); machinery and equipment, foodstuffs, consumer goods, petroleum products, capital goods. **Major trading partners:** ***exports:*** 15% Italy, 15% France, 12% Spain; ***imports:*** 23% France,8% Benelux, 6% Spain.

The population of Mauritania is divided between an Arab and Berber majority in the north and various black African peoples in the south and southwest. From the ninth through the 15th centuries, southern Mauritania was part of the kingdoms of, successively, Ghana, Mali, and Sanghay. In the 1050's, a puritanical Muslim sect, the Almoravids, arose in the Tidra Islands. Between 1054 and 1086 they conquered Ghana, Morocco,

Western Algeria, and Spain; they were eclipsed in the next century.

Portuguese trade on the Mauritania coast began in the early 15th century; the Portuguese remained dominant until about 1600 when their control was contested by the British, French, and Dutch. France established a protectorate in 1903, and the area was made a French colony in 1920.

In 1958 Mauritania became a self-governing republic within the French Overseas Community. In 1959 Mokhtar Ould Daddah was elected prime minister, and the country became fully independent on Nov. 28, 1960. A new constitution was adopted in 1961, establishing a presidential form of government. The four major political parties were combined into a single party in 1965.

Morocco claimed Mauritania as part of its sphere of influence; after talks about unifying the two countries broke down, Morocco recognized Mauritanian independence in 1970.

Spain relinquished its claim to the Spanish Sahara in 1976. The southern part of that territory was annexed by Mauritania, while the larger northern section was annexed by Morocco. Rebels of the Polisario Front proclaimed the independent state of Western Sahara, and in 1980 Mauritania relinquished its claims to its portion of the Western Sahara, signed a treaty with Polisario, and resumed relations with Algeria, Polisario's chief backer.

In 1978 Ould Daddah was removed from office in a military coup and was replaced as president by Lt. Col. Haidalla. He in turn was overthrown on Dec. 12, 1984, by Chief of Staff Maaouya Ould Sid' Ahmed Taya. Taya normalized relations with Morocco and held regional and local elections in 1986 and 1987 in a first step toward the restoration of democracy.

Border incidents erupted between Mauritania and Senegal in 1989 and Mauritania expelled 40,000 black Senegalese workers. Racial and religious strife has severely hampered the country's economy. Taya introduced multiparty elections in 1991 and a new constitution was approved; Taya and his Democratic and Social Republican party won the presidency and control of the legislature in 1992 and again in 1997

▶MAURITIUS
Republic of Mauritius

• **GEOGRAPHY** **Location:** southwestern Indian Ocean. Port Louis 20°09'S, 57°29'E. **Boundaries**: nearest neighbor is Réunion to SW. **Total area**: 718 sq. mi. (1,860 sq km). **Coastline**: 110 mi. (177 km). **Comparative area**: almost 11 times the size of Washington D.C.. **Land use:** 49% arable land; 3% permanent crops; 48% other. **Major cities**: (1994 est.) Port Louis (capital) 144,776; Beau Bassin/Rose Hill 96,621; Vacoas-Phoenix 94,042; Curepipe 76,610; Quatre Bornes 73,501.

• **PEOPLE** **Population:** 1,210,447 (July 2003 est.). **Nationality:** noun—Mauritian(s); adjective—Mauritian. **Ethnic groups:** 68% Indo-Mauritian, 27% Creole, 3% Sino-Mauritian, 2% Franco-Mauritian. **Languages:** English (official), Creole, French, Hindi, Urdu, Hakka, Bojpoori. **Religions:** 52% Hindu, 28.3% Christian (mostly Roman Catholic with a few Anglicans), 16.6% Muslim.

• **GOVERNMENT** **Type:** parliamentary democracy. **Independence:** Mar. 12, 1968 (from U.K.). **Constitution:** Mar. 12, 1968, amended Mar. 12, 1992. **National holiday:** Independence Day, Mar. 12. **Heads of Government:** Auguste Karl Offmann, president (since Feb. 2002); Sir Anerood Jugnauth, prime minister (since Sept. 2000). **Structure:** executive; unicameral legislature; judiciary.

• **ECONOMY** **Monetary unit:** Mauritian rupee. **Budget:** (1999 est.) ***income:*** $1.1 bil.; ***expend.:*** $1.2 bil. **GDP:** $13.2 bil., $11,000 per capita (2002 est.). **Chief crops:** sugarcane, tea, corn, potatoes; cattle, goats; fish. **Natural resources:** arable land, fish. **Major industries:** food processing (largely sugar milling), textiles, and wearing apparel. **Labor force:** 514,000 (1995); 36% construction and industry, 24% services, 14% agriculture and fishing, 16% trade, restaurants, hotels, 7% transportation and communication, 3% finance. **Exports:** $1.6 bil. (f.o.b., 2002); clothing and textiles, sugar. **Imports:** $1.8 bil. (f.o.b., 2002); manufactured goods, capital equipment, foodstuffs, petroleum products, chemicals. **Major trading partners:** ***exports:*** 26% U.K., 21% France, 16% U.S.; ***imports:*** 20% France, 19% South Africa, 9% India.

The volcanic island of Mauritius and its seven smaller neighbors lie about 500 miles east of Madagascar and 2,400 miles southwest of India. They were uninhabited when discovered by the Dutch in 1507. Following sporadic Dutch settlement in the 17th century, the French took over in 1721, establishing sugarcane plantations worked by slaves imported from Africa. Mauritius was captured by the British in 1810. Following the abolition of slavery in the British Empire (1834), Indian workers were imported to labor in the cane fields. A majority of the population is of Indian descent. On Mar. 12, 1968, Mauritius became an independent parliamentary democracy within the British Commonwealth. In 1992 it became a republic and the National Assembly elected Cassam Uteem as the country's first president.

In December 1995 the opposition party of Navinchandra Ramgoolam won 65.2 percent of the votes, and captured all 60 seats in Parliament defeating Anerood Jugnauth, PM for 13 years. These results were reversed in Sept. 2000.

Although sugar remains an important element in the economy, textile manufacturing and tourism have helped to make Mauritius one of the strongest economies in Africa.

▶MEXICO
United Mexican States

• **GEOGRAPHY** **Location:** southernmost state in North America. **Boundaries**: U.S. to N, Gulf of Mexico to E, Belize and Guatemala to S, Pacific Ocean to W. **Total area**: 761,603 sq. mi. (1,972,550 sq km). **Coastline**: 5,798 mi. (9,329 km). **Comparative area**: slightly less than three times the size of Texas. **Land use:** 13% arable land; 1% permanent crops;86% other. **Major cities**: (1990 census) Ciudad de México (Mexico City) (capital) 8,236,960; Guadalajara 1,628,617; Netzahualcóyotl 1,259,543; Monterrey 1,064,197; Heróica Puebla de Zaragoza (Puebla) 1,054,921.

• **PEOPLE** **Population:** 104,907,991 (July 2003 est.). **Nationality:** noun—Mexican(s); adjective—Mexican. **Ethnic groups:** 60% mestizo, 30% Amerindian or predominantly Amerindian, 9% white, 1% other. **Languages:** Spanish, various Mayan, Nahuatl, and other regional indigenous languages. **Religions:** 89% Roman Catholic, 6% Protestant.

• **GOVERNMENT** **Type:** federal republic. **Independence:** Sept. 16, 1810 (from Spain). **Constitution:** Feb. 5, 1917. **National holiday:** Independence Day, Sept. 16. **Head of Government:** Vincente Fox, president (since Dec. 2000). **Structure:** dominant executive; bicameral legislature (National Congress—Senate, Federal Chamber of Deputies); Supreme Court.

• **ECONOMY** **Monetary unit:** peso. **Budget:** (2001 est.) ***income:*** $136 bil.; ***expend.:*** $140 bil. **GDP:** $900 bil., $9,000 per capita (2002 est.). **Chief crops:** corn, wheat, soybeans, rice, beans, cotton, coffee, fruit, tomatoes; beef, poultry, dairy products; wood products. **Natural resources:** crude oil, silver, copper, gold, lead. **Major industries:** food and beverages, tobacco, chemicals. **Labor force:** 39.8 mil. (2000); 56% services; 20% agriculture, forestry, hunting, fishing; 24% industry; 3% urban unemployment (2000), plus considerable underemployment. **Exports:** $158.4 bil. (f.o.b., 2002); crude oil, oil products, coffee, silver, engines, cotton. **Imports:** $168.4 bil. (f.o.b., 2002); metal manufactures, agricultural machinery, electrical equipment. **Major trading partners:** (1999) ***exports:*** 88.4% U.S., 2% Canada, 0.9% Germany; ***imports:*** 68.4% U.S., 4.7% Japan, 3.6% Germany.

The pre-Columbian history of indigenous Mexican cultures is very rich and includes the high civilizations of the Olmecs, Mayas, Toltecs, and Aztecs, in addition to numerous nomadic cultures. In 1519 Hernán Cortés and several hundred Spanish soldiers entered Tenochtitlán (now Mexico City). A two-year campaign against the Aztecs under Montezuma II ended with the Spanish capture of the city. The Viceroyalty of New Spain—with its center at Mexico City—was proclaimed in 1535. At its height it encompassed the lands from California to Panama, Florida, Spain's Caribbean holdings, and the Philippines.

As was the case with the rest of Spanish America, the movement for independence in New Spain coincided with the weakening of the authority of the Spanish Crown as a result of the Napoleonic takeover of Spain in 1808. In 1810 Miguel Hidalgo led a failed uprising and was executed. Following in Hidalgo's footsteps, José María Morelos led another uprising in the south, and he in turn was captured and put to death. Agustín de Iturbide, leader of the royalist forces, defected to the side of those struggling for independence in 1821. Envisioning independent Mexico as a monarchy, military groups proclaimed Iturbide emperor of Mexico in 1822.

The Mexican empire did not last long, and the Central American counties seceded after Iturbide's ouster by Antonio de Santa Anna in 1823. A republic was declared and Guadalupe Victoria was the first president (1824-29). In 1836, Texas seceded from Mexico in a revolution that cost Santa Anna the presidency. Between 1845 and 1848, Mexico fought the United States over U.S. annexation of Texas, and in 1847 U.S. troops occupied Mexico City. Under the Treaty of Guadalupe Hidalgo (1848), Mexico sold about half its territory—including California, Nevada, Utah, most of Arizona, and parts of New Mexico, Colorado, and Wyoming to the United States—for $15 million.

Santa Anna ruled again, as dictator, from 1853 to 1855, before being toppled by the liberal movement, La Reforma. A new constitution was proclaimed in 1857, but Conservatives declared it void. Following the War of Reform (1858-61), France, Britain, and Spain all claimed compensation for destruction of their nations' property, and in 1862 they landed troops at Veracruz. Britain and Spain withdrew, but Napoleon III attempted to establish a dependent empire in Mexico and installed Archduke Ferdinand Maximilian of Austria on the Mexican throne in 1864. In the face of Mexican resistance and U.S. threats, France ended its Mexican adventure, and in 1867 Maximilian was captured and executed by Liberal forces.

Benito Juárez, who served as provisional president during the War of Reform, was a major force behind the liberal movement called La Reforma, which stressed the promotion of capitalism and the destruction of what were seen as vestiges of feudalism in Mexico. Juárez won a third presidential term in 1871 but died in office and was succeeded in office by Sebastián Lerdo de Tejada, who was in turn overthrown by Gen. Porfirio Díaz. During the stable dictatorship known as the Porfiriato (1876-1911), Mexico experienced economic growth, though wealthy landowners and the church benefited at the expense of the poor.

The Mexican Revolution began in 1910 after Porfirio Díaz had his electoral opponent, Francisco I. Madero, jailed. Madero formulated his Plan of San Luis Potosí, calling for armed resistance. Rebellions broke out in the northern state of Chihuahua under the leadership of Pancho Villa and in the southern state of Morelos led by Emiliano Zapata. The two states soon came under rebel control, and in 1911 Díaz left Mexico. Madero was elected president, but his failure to carry through promised reforms resulted in the continuation of the rebellion.

Backed by the U.S., Gen. Victoriano Huerta overthrew Madero in 1913. But the fighting continued, and Huerta lost the support of the U.S. and was forced from office by Zapata, Villa, and Venustiano Carranza, who became president (1914-20). Zapata and Villa continued their resistance, but by 1916 Gen. Alvaro Obregón had driven Villa back to Chihuahua and Zapata's armies had been contained. Carranza called for the election of delegates to a constitutional convention in 1916, and by the following year, the progressive Mexican Constitution of 1917 was in place.

Obregón deposed Carranza in 1920 and served as president until 1924. He was reelected to succeed Plutarco Elías Calles in 1928 but was assassinated before he could take office. In 1929 Calles founded the National Revolutionary party, which became the Institutional Revolutionary party (PRI) in 1946.

Lázaro Cárdenas won the presidency in 1934, sending Calles, the long-time power behind the scene, into exile. This, coupled with Cárdenas's decision to remove himself from politics at the end of his term, greatly stabilized the institutional structure created by the Mexican Revolution. Cárdenas was the last of the "revolutionary" leaders to make good on the promises to labor and the peasantry. He presided over extensive redistribution of land and in 1938 reorganized the ruling party into four constituencies: peasants, labor, the military, and the middle class. Cárdenas also used the national ownership of subsoil rights enshrined in the Mexican constitution to nationalize U.S. oil companies.

The political movement of Mexican presidents since Cárdenas has been away from its peasant and labor constituencies toward business and the popular sector, beginning with Miguel Alemán's election in 1946.

The PRI's stability was seriously challenged in the 1980's as a result of the economic crisis stemming from the severe decline in the price of oil. Mexico borrowed heavily from foreign creditors during the 1970's on the expectation that oil prices would remain high. The debt problem led to cutbacks in government spending, a catastrophic drop in the value of the currency, and capital and human flight out of the country. It also nearly caused the PRI's downfall. Carlos Salinas de Gortari, the PRI's candidate in the 1988 presidential election, won by one of the narrowest margins ever in a contest widely believed to have been rigged.

Pres. Salinas vigorously pursued economic reform and lobbied for passage of the North American Free Trade Agreement with the United States and Canada, which promised to bring more jobs and much-needed increases in capital investment. But the very day NAFTA went into effect, Jan. 2, 1994, a guerrilla group of poor Indians calling itself the Zapata Army of National Liberation declared war against the government and began fighting government troops in the southern state of Chiapas under the leadership of "Subcomandante Marcos."

The (unrelated) assassination of the PRI presidential candidate at a campaign stop in Tiajuana led Salinas to appoint the campaign manager Ernesto Zedillo, a member of the PRI's reform-minded wing, as the PRI's presidential candidate (over the objections of the "old guard").

With just over 50 percent of the vote (the lowest majority ever for the PRI), Zedillo won an election unusually free from fraud. The immediate crisis he faced was the collapse of the peso, which declined by 40 percent in less than two months. In 1995, in exchange for austere economic measures by the Zedillo government, the I.M.F. and U.S. offered an enormous bail-out aid package with Mexican oil revenues as collateral. By June 1996 Mexico managed the early repayment of $4.7 billion to the U.S. by privately refinancing the debt.

Zedillo was equally successful with the situation in Chiapas, arranging 1996 peace talks with the rebels to end fighting and increase Indian autonomy. The appearance of a similar group (the Popular Revolutionary army) in the state of Guerrero began troubles which continued into 1997.

The July 1997 elections, almost entirely free of fraud, saw the PRI lose its majority in the Chamber of Deputies, as it carried only 39 percent of the vote, with PAN second at 27 percent, and PRD third at 26 percent. In March 1999, Pres. Zedillo broke with tradition by not nominating a successor. Democracy entered the PRI itself with primary elections won by Francisco Labastida. But in the July 2000 presidential elections, it was the National Action Party (PAN) candidate, Vincente Fox, who triumphed with about 43 percent in a three-way race. (See Part I, "Major News Stories of the Year.")

▶MICRONESIA

Federated States of Micronesia

• GEOGRAPHY **Location:** forms (with Palau) archipelago of Caroline Islands, Ponape (6°52'N, 158°15'E), Yap (9°32'N, 138°08'E), Kosrae (5°19'N, 162°59'E), and Truk (7°22'N, 151°54'E), in western Pacific Ocean. **Boundaries**: Guam to NW, Marshall Islands to E, Papua New Guinea to S, Philippines about 497 mi. (800 km) to W. **Total area**: 271 sq. mi. (702 sq km). **Coastline**: 3,798 (6,112 km). **Comparative area**: about four times size of Washington, D.C. **Land use:** 6% arable land; 46% permanent crops; 48% other. **Major cities**: Palikir (capital—population N.A.).

• PEOPLE **Population:** 108,143 (July 2003 est.). **Nationality:** noun—Micronesian(s); adjective—Micronesian, Kosrae(s), Pohnpeian(s), Trukese, Yapese. **Ethnic groups:** nine ethnic Micronesian and Polynesian groups. **Languages:** English (official and common language), Trukese, Pohnpeian, Yapese, Kosrean. **Religions:** 50% Roman Catholic, 47% Protestant.

• GOVERNMENT **Type:** constitutional government in free association with U.S.; Compact of Free Association entered into force Nov. 3, 1986. **Independence:** Nov. 3, 1986 (from U.S.-administered U.N. Trusteeship). **Constitution:** May 10, 1979. **National holiday:** Constitution Day, May 10. **Head of Government:** Joseph Urusemal, president (since May 11, 2003). **Structure:** executive; unicameral legislature; judiciary.

• ECONOMY **Monetary unit:** U.S. dollar. **Budget:** (1998 est.) ***income:*** $161 mil.; ***expend.:*** $160 mil. **GDP:** $277 mil., $2,000 per capita (2002 est.). **Chief crops:** black pepper, tropical fruits and vegetables, coconuts, cassava, sweet potatoes; pigs, chickens. **Natural resources:** forests, marine products, deep seabed minerals. **Major industries:** tourism, construction, fish processing. **Labor force:** two-thirds are government employees. **Exports:** $22 mil. (f.o.b., FY99/00 est.); fish, garments, bananas, black pepper. **Imports:** $149 mil. (c.i.f., FY00/01 est.); food, manufactured goods, machinery and equipment, beverages. **Major trading partners:** U.S., Japan, Guam, Australia.

The Federated States of Micronesia extend 1,800 miles across an archipelago of the Caroline Islands in the larger island group of Micronesia. Ethnically diverse (there are eight primary languages, not including dialects), the islands are thought to be the first in the Pacific settled by argonauts from the Philippines and Indonesia, in about 1500 B.C. Ferdinand Magellan landed in the Marianas in 1521, and Spain claimed sovereignty from 1565 to 1899, when the Caroline Islands were sold to Germany. After World War I, the League of Nations mandated the islands to Japan, which developed agriculture (especially sugarcane), mining, and fishing. After World War II, the islands were included in the U.N. Trust Territory of the Pacific and placed under U.S. administration. A compact of free association between Micronesia and the United States was signed in 1986, and Micronesia's trust territory status with the U.N. trusteeship council was dissolved in December 1990.

▶MOLDOVA

Republic of Moldova

• GEOGRAPHY **Location:** southeastern Europe. **Boundaries**: Ukraine to N, E, S, Romania to W. **Total area**: 13,012 sq. mi. (33,700 sq km). **Coastline**: none. **Comparative area**: slightly more than twice the size of Hawaii. **Land use:** 54% arable land; 12% permanent crops; 34% other. **Major cities**: (1992 est.) Kishinev (Chisinău) (capital) 667,100; Tiraspol 186,200; Beltsy (Balti) 159,000.

• PEOPLE **Population:** 4,439,502 (July 2003 est.). **Nationality:** noun—Moldovan(s); adjective—Moldovan. **Ethnic groups:** 64.5% Moldovan/Romanian, 13.8% Ukrainian, 13% Russian, 1.5% Jewish, 2% Bulgarian, 5.2% Gaguaz and other. **Languages:** Moldovan (official), based on Romanian, but using a Cyrillic alphabet; Russian, Gagauz. **Religions:** 98% Eastern Orthodox, 1.5% Jewish.

• GOVERNMENT **Type:** republic. **Independence:** Aug. 27, 1991 (from Soviet Union). **Constitution:** July 28, 1994. **National holiday:** Independence Day, Aug. 27. **Heads of Government:** Vladimir Voronin, president (since Apr. 2001); Vasile Tarlev prime minister (since Apr. 2001). **Structure:** executive; unicameral legislature; judiciary.

• ECONOMY **Monetary unit:** leu. **Budget:** (1998 est.) ***income:*** $536 mil.; ***expend.:*** $594 mil. **GDP:** $11 bil., $2,500 per capita (2002 est.). **Chief crops:** sugar beets, grain, vegetables, wine grapes, other fruit. **Natural resources:** lignites, phosporites, gypsum. **Major industries:** food processing, agricultural machinery, foundry equipment, textiles, chemicals. **Labor force:** 1.7 mil. (1998); 46% services, 40% agriculture, 14% industry. **Exports:** $590 mil. (f.o.b., 2002); foodstuffs, wine, tobacco, textiles, footwear. **Imports:** $980 mil. (f.o.b., 2002); oil, gas, coal, steel, machinery. **Major trading partners:** Russia, Ukraine, Romania.

Historical Moldavia, of which present-day Moldova is only a small portion, encompassed territories that are now in Romania and Ukraine (including southern Bessarabia and northern Bukovina). Moldova is a hilly, fertile land, bounded by two great rivers, the Dniester and the Prut, that flow into the Black Sea. Its climate is very favorable to agriculture.

Moldavia was part of Scythia in the first millennium B.C. and later came under the Roman Empire. Lying on the gateway to Europe, it was invaded successively, but came under the control of Kievan Rus between the 10th and 12th centuries A.D., and in the 13th century it was invaded by the Mongolian empire. In the 16th century, eastern Moldavia, or Bessarabia, came under Turkish control but in 1812 was ceded to the Russian empire. Southern Bessarabia (now in Ukraine) was controlled variously by the Russian empire and by Romania, and in 1878 it again became part of Russia. After the Bolsheviks came to power in 1917 and created the U.S.S.R., a Moldavian Autonomous Soviet Socialist Republic (ASSR) was formed on the eastern side of the Dniester River, a territory claimed by Romania but populated by Ukrainians. In June 1940, as a result of the Nazi-Soviet Pact of 1939, Romania was forced to cede Bessarabia and northern Bukovina to the Soviet Union. These lands were made part of the Ukrainian Soviet Socialist Republic (SSR), and the remaining Bessarabian sections were merged with the old Moldavian ASSR to create on Aug. 2, 1940, the Moldavian SSR. Between 1941 and 1944, while Romania and the U.S.S.R. were at war, Bessarabia again became part of Romania, but in 1944 the Soviets retook the territory and reestablished it as a union republic.

While under Soviet control, Moldavians in the new republic were officially differentiated from their counterparts across the border in Romania. In 1940, the Cyrillic alphabet was imposed on the Romanian language; this official language was called "Moldavian." Contacts between the two countries were discouraged, and the U.S.S.R. encouraged Russian and Ukrainian immigration to the Moldavian SSR. While a part of the U.S.S.R., Moldavia created a diversified economy, which is based on agriculture and food processing, with a small industrial base.

Gorbachev's policy of glasnost, or openness, in the late 1980's gave vent to Moldavian complaints about "Russification" and immigration of non-Moldavians. In Sept. 1989, Romanian, now in a Latin script, was restored as the official language. Glasnost also gave birth to new political parties, the largest of which was the Popular Front of Moldavia, which organized protest demonstrations against Soviet power. Disturbances during the 1989 celebration of Soviet Revolution Day in the capital city of Kishinev led to the dismissal of the Slavic Communist party First Secretary, and his replacement by an ethnic Romanian.

The Communist party was banned in Moldova in 1990, and laws to develop the basics of a multiparty system were adopted in September 1991. Moldova officially declared its independence from the U.S.S.R. on Aug. 27, 1991, and in December, United Front-supported Mircea Snegur was elected president with 98.2% of the votes cast.

At the time Moldova declared its independence, sentiment was strong for reunification with Romania. So strong, in fact, that ethnic Russians and Ukrainians living in the Trans-Dniester region in eastern Moldova, fearing reunification with Romania, declared an independent Trans-Dniester republic, sparking ethnic violence there. But since then, most activity has focused on reestablishing ties with countries from the former U.S.S.R. In 1991, Moldova singed the Alma-Ata Declaration, joining the other former Soviet republics in the Commonwealth of Independent States. And in the country's first parlimantary elections, held in Feb. of 1994, two nationalist parties captured a combined 15 percent of the vote, while the pro-Russian Socialist party won 25 percent, and the Agrarian Democratic Party, led by former Communists, took 45 percent. Then, in a plebiscite held Mar. 6, 1994, an overwhelming majority (90 percent) of voters rejected reunification with Romania in favor of an independent Moldova. Two-thirds of Moldova's 2.3 million eligible voters cast ballots on the plebiscite. Snegur intended to use the referendum result to entice Trans-Dniester to rejoin Moldova.

In late 1996 Snegur lost the presidency to Petro Lucinschi who quickly recognized Trans-Dniester as autonomous within a single state and began a reform program to stimulate the weak economy. A strong Communist showing in 1998 legislative elections made this agenda more difficult to establish. The slow pace of reform led Prime Minister Ion Ciubuc to resign in Feb. 1999 (replaced by Ion Sturza) and Pres. Lucinschi to propose a referendum to increase the constitutional powers of the president, a model more in accord with the other ex-Soviet states.

Elections in Feb. 2001 gave the Communists a majority in parliament which selected Vladimir Voronin as president and Vasile Tarlev as prime minister. In November, Voronin and Russia's president Putin agreed to seek a "political" solution to the problem of Moldova's secessionist and Russian-dominated "Republic of Trans-Dniester."

▶MONACO
Principality of Monaco

• **GEOGRAPHY** **Location:** tiny enclave on Mediterranean coast of France. **Boundaries**: France to N, E, and W; Mediterranean Sea to S. **Total area**: 1.21 sq. mi. (1.95 sq km). **Coastline**: 2.6 mi. (4.1 km). **Comparative area**: about three times size of the Mall in Washington, D.C. **Land use:** 0% arable land; 0% permanent crops; 100% other. **Major cities**: Monaco (capital).

• **PEOPLE** **Population:** 32,130 (2003 est.). **Nationality:** noun—Monacan(s) or Monegasque(s); adjective—Monacan or Monegasque. **Ethnic groups:** 47% French, 16% Monegasque, 16% Italian, 21% other. **Languages:** French (official), English, Italian, Monegasque. **Religions:** 90% Roman Catholic.

• **GOVERNMENT** **Type:** constitutional monarchy. **Independence:** 1419. **Constitution:** Dec. 17, 1962. **National holiday:** National Day, Nov. 19. **Head of Government:** Prince Ranier III, chief of state (since Nov. 1949); Patrick Leclercq, prime minister (since Jan. 2000). **Structure:** executive—prince, minister of state (senior French civil servant appointed by prince), and Council of Government as cabinet; unicameral legislature—prince and National Council of 18 members; judiciary—authority delegated by prince to Supreme Tribunal.

• **ECONOMY** **Monetary unit:** euro. **Budget:** (1995

est.) ***income:*** $518 mil.; ***expend:*** $531 mil. **GDP:** $870 mil., $27,000 per capita (1999 est.). **Chief crops:** N.A. **Natural resources:** none. **Major industries:** Tourism, construction, small-scale industry and consumer products. **Labor force:** (1994 est.) 30,540. **Exports:** N.A. **Imports:** N.A. **Major trading partners:** full customs integration with France, which collects and rebates Monacan trade duties; also participates in E.U. market system through customs union with France.

Known to Phoenicians and Greeks from the beginning of the first millenium B.C., the history of the port of Monaco is coextensive with that of southeastern France for much of its history. A western colony of the great trading city-state of Genoa in the 13th century, Monaco in 1368 became an independent principality under the rule of the Matignon-Grimaldi family. At various times a protectorate of Spain, France, and Sardinia, it was restored to independence in 1861 by the Franco-Monegasque treaty.

In 1911 Monaco became a constitutional monarchy under the Matignon-Grimaldi dynasty. In 1918 France required the principality to conform to its national interests in all respects; by an agreement of 1919, should the dynasty fail to produce a male heir, Monaco would be absorbed into France. However, the family is allowed to adopt an heir if they so choose. The marriage of Prince Ranier III to the U.S film star Grace Kelly produced an heir apparent for this generation. The constitutional monarchy under its "Most Serene Prince" is essentially a one-party state in which the National and Democratic Union won all 18 seats in the National Council in 1968, 1978, 1983, and 1988, though in competition with the Socialist party. In 1993 Monaco became the smallest member nation of the U.N..

Despite the fame of the Monte Carlo casino, gambling accounts for only 4 percent of the principality's revenues. The principal industry is tourism, followed by light manufacturing. Monaco also supports a prominent institute of oceanography. Land reclamation projects, impelled by a real estate boom, have added about 20 percent to the nation's territory since World War II.

▶MONGOLIA

• **GEOGRAPHY** **Location:** landlocked country in central Asia. **Boundaries**: Russia to N, China to E, S, and W. **Total area**: 604,247 sq. mi. (1,565,000 sq km). **Coastline**: none. **Comparative area**: slightly larger than Alaska. **Land use:** 1% arable land; 0% permanent crops; 99% other. **Major cities**: (1994 est.) Ulan Bator (capital) 680,000; Darhan 85,800; Erdenet 63,000.

• **PEOPLE** **Population:** 2,712,315 (2003 est.). **Nationality:** noun—Mongolian(s) adjective—Mongolian. **Ethnic groups:** 85% Mongol, 7% Kazakh, 4.6% Tungusic, 3.4% other. **Languages:** Khalkha Mongol used by over 90% of population; Turkic, Russian, Chinese. **Religions:** predominantly Tibetan Buddhist, 4% Muslim, Shamanism and Christian.

• **GOVERNMENT** **Type:** republic. **Independence:** Mar. 13, 1921 (from China). **Constitution:** Feb. 12, 1992. **National holiday:** National Day, July 11. **Heads of Government:** Natsagiin Bagabandi, president (since June 1997); Nambar Enkhbayar, prime minister (since July 2000). **Structure:** executive; unicameral legislature; judiciary.

• **ECONOMY** **Monetary unit:** tughrik. **Budget:** (2001) ***income:*** $386 mil.; ***expend.:*** $427 mil. **GDP:** $5 bil., $1,840 per capita (2002 est.). **Chief crops:** livestock raising predominates; wheat, barley. **Natural resources:** oil, coal, copper, molybdenum, tungsten, phosphates. **Major industries:** copper, processing of animal products, building materials, foods and beverages. **Labor force:** 1.4 mil. (2001); primarily herding agricultural; over half adult population is in labor force, including large percentage of women; shortage of skilled labor. **Exports:** $501 mil. (f.o.b., 2002); copper, livestock, animal products, wool, hides, fluorospar, nonferrous metals. **Imports:** $659 mil. (c.i.f., 2002); machinery and equipment, fuels, food products, industrial consumer goods, chemicals. **Major trading partners:** ***exports:*** 48% China, 33% U.S., 9% Russia; ***imports:*** 34% Russia, 20% China, 12% South Korea.

Mongols under Genghis Khan conquered most of Eurasia in the early 13th century. The Mongol empire broke up in the mid-14th century, and Mongolia lapsed into tribal disunion and political insignificance. Chinese rule was established thereafter in Inner Mongolia and, in 1691, in Outer Mongolia (a province under local rule). With the 1911 Chinese Revolution, Outer Mongolia unsuccessfully proclaimed its independence from China. The nationalist religious leader, the Bogdo Lama, sought Russian support in 1920. Under the revolutionary leaders Sukhe Bataar and Khorloin Choibalsan, a "provisional people's government" again declared independence in 1921. Sukhe Bataar died in 1923; on Nov. 26, 1924, the Mongolian People's Republic (MPR) was established with Soviet sponsorship. The early years of the republic were marked by repeated Stalinist purges of Mongol revolutionary leaders and by disastrous attempts at centralized planning.

Choibalsan emerged as party leader and was confirmed as premier in 1940. In 1939 Soviet and Mongolian armies prevented a Japanese conquest of Mongolia. In 1945 the Republic of China recognized the MPR; recognition was reaffirmed by the People's Republic of China in 1949. In 1948 the first of a series of five-year plans began to bring industrial and agricultural development to Mongolia, with extensive Soviet aid and support. Choibalsan died in 1952 and was succeeded as premier by Yumjaagiyn Tsedenbal. Following the Sino-Soviet split of 1958, heavy concentrations of Soviet troops and missiles were stationed along the Chinese-Mongolian border. On Oct. 27, 1961, the MPR was admitted to the United Nations and diplomatic relations with various other non-Soviet bloc nations developed gradually. Tsedenbal was ousted in 1984 and replaced by Zhambyn Batmonh as party chairman and by Dumaagiin Sodnom as premier. The MPR established diplomatic relations with the United States in 1987.

Following widespread demonstrations calling for human rights, religious freedom, and an end to special privileges for Communist officials, the Communist party voted to give up its constitutional power in March 1990. After the resignation of Pres. Zhambyn Batmonh, Parliament elected Punsalmaagiin Ochirbat as president. That same year, in an attempt to strengthen economic ties with China, Ochirbat became the first Mongolian head of state to visit Beijing since 1962. But the Communists returned to power in 1992, when the ex-Communist Mongolian People's Revolutionary party, running on a platform of more moderate reform, won an overwhelming majority in Parliament. Nevertheless, the more reform-minded Ochirbat put together a coalition of opposing parties in 1993 to win reelection as president. He held office until 1997 when he was defeated by Natsagiin Bagabandi who won again in 2000.

With a young and rapidly growing population, an obsolete industrial base, and a shrinking economy, Mongolia has endured a painful transition to democracy and free markets. Aided by international loans, the government is pursuing a program of privatization, currency and banking reform. Trading on Mongolia's first stock exchange began in Aug. 1995. Since 1991 over 10,000 private businesses have been created, many of them small trading companies dealing with Russia and China. In Apr. 1997 parliament approved a decision to abolish all taxes on trade. U.S. Secretary of State Madeleine Albright visited in 1998 and pledged continued support and friendship.

▶MONTENEGRO

See "Serbia and Montenegro"

▶MOROCCO

Kingdom of Morocco

• **GEOGRAPHY** **Location:** northwestern Africa. **Boundaries**: North Atlantic Ocean to W and NW, Strait of Gibraltar to N, Mediterranean Sea to NE, Algeria to E and SE, Western Sahara to SW. **Total area**: 172,413 sq. mi. (446,550 sq km). **Coastline**: 1,140 mi. (1,835 km). **Comparative area**: slightly larger than California. **Land use:** 20% arable land; 2% permanent crops; 78% other. **Major cities**: (1990 census) Rabat (including Sale; capital) 1,385,872; Casablanca 2,940,623; Marrakech (Marrakesh) 745,541; Fès (Fez) 774,754; Oujda 678,778.
• **PEOPLE** **Population:** 31,689,265 (2003 est.). **Nationality:** noun—Moroccan(s); adjective—Moroccan. **Ethnic groups:** 99.1% Arab-Berber, 0.7% non-Moroccan, 0.2% Jewish. **Languages:** Arabic (official), several Berber dialects; French is language of business, government and diplomacy. **Religions:** 98.7% Muslim, 1.1% Christian, 0.2% Jewish.
• **GOVERNMENT** **Type:** constitutional monarchy. **Independence:** Mar. 2, 1956 (from France). **Constitution:** Mar. 10, 1972, revised Sept. 4, 1992, amended to create bicameral legislature Sept. 1996. **National holiday:** National Day, July 30. **Heads of Government:** Mohammed VI, king (since July 1999); Driss Jettou, prime minister (since Oct. 2002). **Structure:** executive—king has paramount powers; bicameral legislature—two-thirds of members are directly elected and one-third are indirectly elected; judiciary—independent of other branches.
• **ECONOMY** **Monetary unit:** dirham. **Budget:** (2001 est.) ***income:*** $13.8 bil.; ***expend.:*** $14.6 bil. **GDP:** $115 bil., $3,900 per capita (2002 est.). **Chief crops:** cereal farming and livestock raising predominant; barley, wheat, citrus fruit, wine, vegetables; livestock. **Natural resources:** phosphates, iron ore, manganese, lead, zinc, fish, salt. **Major industries:** phosphate rock mining and processing, food processing, leather goods. **Labor force:** 11 mil. (1999); 50% agriculture, 35% services, 15% industry; 19% unemployment (2002 est.). **Exports:** $7.5 bil. (f.o.b., 2002 est.); food and beverages, semiprocessed goods, consumer goods. **Imports:** $10.4 bil. (f.o.b., 2002 est.); semiprocessed goods, capital goods, food and beverages, fuel and lubricants. **Major trading partners:** France, Spain, U.K., Italy.

Neolithic inhabitants of Morocco were displaced by Berbers around 1000 B.C. Phoenician and Carthaginian settlements were established along the Mediterranean coast. Morocco came under Roman rule around 40 A.D. and was invaded via Spain by Germanic Vandals in the fifth century. The Islamic invasions of the mid-seventh century established Arab rule in Morocco, and most of the indigenous Berbers converted to Islam. Ethnic tension between Berbers and Arabs has been a basic element of Moroccan politics and society ever since.

In the late eighth century, King Idris ibn Adballah united Berbers and Arabs in a monarchy that lasted for 200 years and made the capital city of Fez one of the major religious and cultural centers of the Islamic world. In the 11th century, the Almoravid dynasty from Mauritania conquered Morocco, western Algeria, and Spain. It was ousted by another Muslin sect, the Almohads, led by Ibn Tumart. After about 1200 the tide of Moorish expansion in the Iberian Peninsula turned; in 1492 Ferdinand and Isabella expelled the last Moors from Grenada.

Naval conflict between Morocco, Spain, and Portugal continued in the western Mediterranean and along the Atlantic coast of Africa for several centuries more. In the mid-17th century, Morocco was reunited under the present Alawid dynasty. In the early 19th century, American and British forces combatted Moroccan piracy in the Mediterranean, and Spain established colonies in Tangier in the north and along the Atlantic coast between Morocco and Mauritania.

The attempts of Sultan Hassan I (r. 1873-94) to implement reforms to strengthen Morocco's independence were thwarted by European interests. By the early 20th century, France, securely established in Algeria, began exerting increasing control in Morocco. A multipower conference at Algeciras in 1906 affirmed Moroccan independence but upheld the special rights claimed by Spain and France. The Treaty of Fez, signed in 1912 between France and Sultan Abd-al-Hafidn, ended Moroccan independence by granting the country to France and reaffirming a Spanish sphere of influence in the southwest.

Nationalist unrest and tribal uprisings disrupted French administration in Morocco throughout the 1920's and 1930's. Morocco became a battleground during World War II between the Axis-supported Vichy French government and the Free French and their Allied backers. In 1943 Churchill and Roosevelt met at Casablanca to discuss wartime strategy; in the same year, the Istiqlal (Independence) party was founded to fight for independence from the French in the postwar era.

In 1947 Moroccan liberation forces began open warfare against the French. The exiled Sultan Mohammad V was allowed to return, and France promised independence by 1955.

With the withdrawal of French forces, Morocco became independent on Mar. 2, 1956. Tangier (under international administration since 1923) was incorporated into the newly independent state in October 1956, and the Spanish enclave of Ifni was ceded to Morocco in 1969.

A period of instability ensued after 1957 as newly formed political parties vied for power. King Mohammad I died in 1961 and was succeeded by his son, Hassan II. In 1962 an elected parliamentary government took power under the constitutional monarchy. Political unrest and economic difficulties led to the declaration of states of emergency in 1965 and 1970 and a new constitution in 1977.

Spain withdrew from its former territory of Spanish (now Western) Sahara, a phosphate-rich desert territory on Morocco's southern border, in Feb. 1976. On Apr. 14, 1976, Morocco annexed the northern two-thirds of the territory, while Mauritania claimed the remainder. The Polisario Spanish Saharan liberation movement, backed by Algeria and Libya, conducted guerrilla operations against Moroccan and Mauritanian forces. In 1979 Mauritania gave up its claims, and Morocco claimed the entire region.

In April 1987, Morocco completed construction of a 2,000-mile sand wall completely enclosing Western Sahara. Polisario forces control much of the Western Saharan countryside, while Morocco holds the cities and towns. In May 1987 a Moroccan-Algerian summit was held under the sponsorship of Saudi Arabia, which offered King Hassan $260 million to rebuild Morocco's war-torn economy in return for allowing a self-determination referendum in the Western Sahara. The king refused. By mid-1992 the situation was resolved as Polisario's leaders accepted an offer of anmesty, leaving the Moroccan government in possession of the territory although U.N. sponsored negotiations have failed to produce a settlement.

The Persian Gulf crisis made an already weak economy weaker, and riots during a general strike protesting low wages and poor job prospects in Fez left 100 dead and hundreds more injured in 1991. Although Morocco was an active member of the Allied coalition against Iraq, Moroccans also staged huge demonstrations in support of Saddam Hussein at the height of the war.

In 1992, demands of Muslim fundamentalist factions for greater political power threatened the stability of King Hassan II's government. In a gesture toward political reform, parliamentary elections were held in June 1993, but the results never posed any immediate challenge to the monarchy.

In March 1998 the king appointed Morocco's first opposition-led government, a coalition of seven political parties. Hassan died in July 1999 and was succeeded by his son Mohammed VI. A government trial balloon on women's rights produced a protest rally of 500,000 in March 2000. In may 2003, five simultaneous suicide bombings rocked Casablanca.

▶MOZAMBIQUE

Republic of Mozambique

• GEOGRAPHY **Location:** eastern coast of Africa. **Boundaries**: Zambia and Malawi to NW, Tanzania to N, Indian Ocean to E and SE, South Africa and Swaziland to SW, Zimbabwe to W. **Total area**: 309,494 sq. mi. (801,590 sq km). **Coastline**: 1,535 mi. (2,470 km). **Comparative area**: slightly less than twice size of California. **Land use:** 4% arable land; negl. % permanent crops; 96% other. **Major cities**: (1987 est.) Maputo (capital) 1,006,765.

• PEOPLE **Population:** 17,479,266 (2003 est.). **Nationality:** noun—Mozambican(s); adjective—Mozambican. **Ethnic groups:** 99.66% indigenous tribal groups (Shangaan, Chokwe, Manyika, Sena, Makua, and others). **Languages:** Portuguese (official), indigenous languages. **Religions:** 50% indigenous beliefs, 30% Christian, 20% Muslim.

• GOVERNMENT **Type:** republic. **Independence:** June 25, 1975 (from Portugal). **Constitution:** Nov. 30, 1990. **National holiday:** Independence Day, June 25. **Heads of Government:** Joachím Alberto Chissanó, president (since Nov. 1986); Dr. Pascoal Manuel Mocumbi, prime minister (since Nov. 1994.). **Structure:** executive; unicameral legislature; judiciary.

• ECONOMY **Monetary unit:** metical. **Budget:** (2001 est.) ***income:*** $393.1 mil.; ***expend:*** $1.025 bil. **GDP:** $19.2 bil., $1,000 per capita (2002 est.). **Chief crops:** cotton, cashew nuts, sugar, tea; beef, poultry. **Natural resources:** coal, natural gas, titanium. **Major industries:** food and beverages, chemicals (fertilizer, soap, paints), petroleum. **Labor force:** 9.2 mil. (2000 est.); 81% agriculture. **Exports:** $390 mil. (f.o.b., 2002 est.); shrimp; cashews, cotton, sugar. **Imports:** $1.18 bil. (c.i.f., 2002 est.); food, clothing, farm equipment, petroleum. **Major trading partners:** ***exports:*** 15% South Africa, 5% Zimbabwe, 4% Japan; ***imports:*** 41% South Africa, 8% Portugal, 2% U.S.

Mozambique has been inhabited since prehistoric times by a variety of Bantu peoples. Portuguese trading stations were established starting in 1505, and Portugal developed an extensive coastal trade in gold and ivory. Mozambique also served as a way station for Portuguese trade to East Asia.

Despite competition from other European nations, Portugal maintained control of the Mozambique coast. Settlement by sizable numbers of Portuguese immigrants began in the late 19th century. Mozambique was organized as a colony, sometimes called Portuguese East Africa, in 1885; boundaries in the interior were defined in 1891.

Economic development of Mozambique in the 20th century remained almost entirely in Portuguese hands. By the 1950's native peoples began to protest Portuguese rule; a rebellion of the Frelimo (Front for the Liberation of Mozambique) guerrilla movement began in 1961. Rebels controlled most of the northern part of the country by 1964. Fighting continued for another decade.

Following the Portuguese revolution of 1974, Portugal agreed to independence for Mozambique, and many Portuguese settlers returned to Portugal, leaving the country bereft of administrative personnel and infrastructure support. Mozambique became fully independent on June 25, 1975. A Marxist Frelimo government took office, with Samora Michel as the country's first president. The new government formed agricultural collectives and nationalized most private land and industry as well as all social services.

In the late 1970's, fighting broke out between Mozambique and Rhodesia. When Rhodesia achieved independence (and changed its name to Zimbabwe) in 1980, relations between the two governments improved. But a rebel movement, Renamo (Mozambique National Resistance), dedicated to overthrowing the Frelimo government grew stronger during the 1980's.

In 1986, following the death of Samora Michel, Joachím Chissanó became president. His government reintroduced some private agriculture, loosened ties to the Eastern bloc, and appealed to the West for economic assistance. In 1987 a U.N.-led relief effort began. In 1989 Mozambique signed a cooperation agreement with South Africa, which cut off its aid to the Renamo insurgents. But fighting continued into 1990.

In Nov. 1990, Mozambique adopted a new constitution widening individual rights and freedoms, including abolition of the death penalty, freedom of the press and speech, and an independent judiciary, as well as establishing multiparty democracy, a presidential regime, and free-market economy. On Oct. 4, 1992, Pres. Chissanó and Renamo leader Afonso Dhlakama signed a cease-fire; the U.N. dispatched 7,500 military and civilian personnel to oversee the disarmament and organize elections.

Mozambique's first multiparty elections were held in Oct. 1994. Pres. Chissanó was elected with 53 percent of the vote while his Frelimo party took 129 of the Parliament's 250 seats. (Renamo carried all but nine of the remaining seats.) Chissano was re-elected in Dec. 1999 with Frelimo taking 133 seats.

Mozambique is rich in agricultural land and mineral resources. Nevertheless, years of communism, drought, and civil war have left the country poor and dependent on foreign aid. In 1992 the worst drought in memory brought the nation to a virtual standstill, as an estimated 1.8 million people became dependent on donations of food from outsiders for survival. In recent years the I.M.F. has helped enormously with loans and planning advice but Mozambique remains one of the poorest nations. Devastating floods in March 2000 set back much of the progress that had been made.

▶MYANMAR
Union of Burma

• **GEOGRAPHY** **Location:** NW region of Southeast Asia. **Boundaries**: China and Laos to NE, Bangladesh, India to NW, Thailand to SE, Andaman Sea to S, and Bay of Bengal to SW. **Total area**: 261,969 sq. mi. (678,500 sq km). **Coastline**: 1,200 mi. (1,930 km). **Comparative area**: slightly smaller than Texas. **Land use:** 15% arable land; 1% permanent crops; 84% other. **Major cities**: (1983 census) Yangon (formerly Rangoon) (capital) 2,458,712; Mandalay 532,895; Bassein 335,000; Moulmein 219,991; Akyab 143,000.

• **PEOPLE** **Population:** 42,510,539 (2003 est.). **Nationality:** noun—Burmese (sing., pl.); adjective—Burmese. **Ethnic groups:** 68% Burman, 9% Shan, 7% Karen, 4% Rakhine, 3% Chinese, 2% Mon, 2% Indian, 5% other. **Languages:** Burmese, minority ethnic languages. **Religions:** 89% Buddhist, 4% Muslim, 4% Christian, 1% animist beliefs.

• **GOVERNMENT** **Type:** military regime. **Independence:** Jan. 4, 1948 (from U.K.). **Constitution:** Jan. 3, 1974; new constitution being drafted. **National holiday:** Independence Day, Jan.4. **Head of Government:** Gen. Than Shwe, chairman State Law and Order Restoration Council (SLORC) (since Apr. 1992). **Structure:** executive—military junta controls legislature—last election held in 1990, but never convened; judiciary—not independent, no guarantees.

• **ECONOMY** **Monetary unit:** kyat. **Budget:** (FY96/97) ***income:*** $7.9 bil.; ***expend.:*** $12.2 bil. **GDP:** $70 bil., $1,660 per capita (2002 est.). **Chief crops:** paddy rice, corn, oilseeds; hardwood. **Natural resources:** crude oil, timber, tin, copper, tungsten. **Major industries:** agricultural processing, textiles and footwear, wood and wood products. **Labor force:** 23.7 mil. (1999 est.); 70% agriculture, 7% industry, 23% services (2001 est.); **Exports:** $2.7 bil. (f.o.b., 2002); teak, rice, pulses, beans. **Imports:** $2.5 bil. (f.o.b., 2002); machinery, transport equipment, chemicals, food products. **Major trading partners: *exports:* Thailand, U.S.,** India; ***imports:*** Singapore, Thailand, China.

(Until the summer of 1989 this country was known as Burma.)

Burma, an independent Buddhist monarchy from the 11th century, fell to the Mongol empire in the 13th century, and after the 14th century was a satellite state of China. Anglo-French rivalry over trade left Burma under French influence in the early 19th century, but in a series of three wars (1824-26, 1852, 1885), Great Britain succeeded in bringing all of Burma into the British raj of India. The country became self-governing under a British protectorate in 1937.

Japanese occupation of Burma in early 1942 made the country a major theater of fighting during World War II. The Burma Road, built by the Allies to connect northeastern India with western China, was a key link in bringing supplies to the Chinese Nationalist army during the war.

Burma achieved independence as the Union of Burma on Jan. 4, 1948. Promises of autonomy for ethnic minority regions such as the Shan and Karen States have not been fulfilled, leading to armed separatist movements in those areas ever since. In 1962 a coup led by Gen. Ne Win overthrew the democratic government and established a one-party state under the Burmese Socialist Program party. The party's "Burmese Path to Socialism" resulted in self-imposed international isolation and economic stagnation at home despite the country's potential wealth in agriculture, timber, minerals, and gems.

In July 1988 Ne Win resigned from office in the face of mounting popular demonstrations. A series of short-lived successor governments were unable to restore public order and normal governmental functions; direct military rule was announced in September 1988 as demonstrations continued.

In the general election held on May 27, 1990 (the first multiparty free elections in three decades), the opposition National League for Democracy, led by Aung San Suu Kyi, won a decisive victory, but the results of the election were nullified by the State Law and Order Restoration Council (SLORC), and leaders of the elected government were placed under house arrest. In 1991 the continued political repression in Myanmar was brought to international attention when Aung San Suu Kyi was awarded the Nobel Peace Prize. This helped usher in a period of diminishing repression. A new leader of the ruling military junta, Gen. Than Shwe, began peace talks with the Karen rebels in early 1994, and released Aung San Suu Kyi in July 1995. In 1998, renewed pressure by NLD upon the junta (since Nov. 1997 renamed the State Peace and Development Council) to convene the 1990 parliament brought renewed repression and mass arrests; a committee of NLD delcared itself to be the legal parliament of Myanmar in September, asserting that all the junta legislation since 1990 was null and void. After releasing Aung from her 14-month arrest in May 2002, the junta "detained" Aung and 19 other NLD members in May 2003. In Sept. 2002 three grandsons of Ne Win and a son-in-law were sentenced to death for treason (an alleged coup attempt); Ne Win himself died suddenly shortly after.

▶NAMIBIA
Republic of Namibia

• **GEOGRAPHY** **Location:** southwest Africa. **Boundaries**: Angola to N, Botswana to E, South Africa to S, Atlantic Ocean to W. **Total area**: 318,259 sq. mi. (824,290 sq km). **Coastline**: 976 mi. (1,572 km). **Comparative area**: slightly more than half the size of Alaska. **Land use:** 1% arable land; negl. % permanent crops; 99% other. **Major cities**: (1990) Windhoek (capital) 125,000.

• **PEOPLE** **Population:** 1,927,447 (2003 est.). **Nationality:** noun—Namibian(s); adjective—Namibian. **Ethnic groups:** 87.5% black, 6% white, 6.5% mixed; 50% of the population belongs to the Ovambo tribe. **Languages:** Afrikaans common language, 32% German, and 7% English (official); several indigenous languages. **Religions:** 80%-90% Christian, 10%-20% indigenous religions.

• **GOVERNMENT** **Type:** republic. **Independence:** Mar. 21, 1990 (from South Africa). **Constitution:** Feb. 9, 1990. **National holiday:** Independence Day, Mar. 21. **Heads of Government:** Sam Nujoma, president (since Mar. 1990); Theo-Ben

Gurirab, prime minister (since Aug. 2002). **Structure:** executive; bicameral legislature; judiciary.

• **ECONOMY** **Monetary unit:** Namibian dollar. **Budget:** (1998) ***income:*** $883 mil.; ***expend.:*** $950 mil. **GDP:** $12.6 bil., $6,900 per capita (2002 est.). **Chief crops:** millet, sorghum, peanuts; livestock; fish. **Natural resources:** diamonds, copper, uranium, gold, lead. **Major industries:** meat packing, fish processing, dairy products, mining (copper, lead, zinc, diamonds, and uranium). **Labor force:** about 725,000; 47% agriculture, 20% industry and commerce, 33% services; 35% unemployment (1998 est.). **Exports:** $1.38 bil. (f.o.b., 2002 est.); diamonds, copper, gold, zinc, lead, uranium; meat, processed fish. **Imports:** $1.6 bil. (f.o.b., 2002 est.); foodstuffs, petroleum products, machinery and equipment, chemicals. **Major trading partners:** ***exports:*** 79% E.U., 4% U.S.; ***imports:*** 50% U.S., 31% E.U.

The Kalahari desert, on the Namibian plateau, has been inhabited since ancient times by San hunter-gatherers. Various Nama and Bantu peoples migrated into the area more recently. British and Dutch explorers and traders began to penetrate Namibia in the 18th century.

In 1872 Great Britain occupied the area around Walvis Bay and in 1884 annexed it to the Cape Colony. Also in 1884 Germany claimed most of South-West Africa; negotiations between the two powers resulted in German acceptance of Britain's claim of Walvis Bay and British acceptance of Germany's claim to the rest of the coastal region with a sphere of influence in the interior.

During World War I, British troops from South Africa occupied South-West Africa in 1915. In 1920 South Africa received a League of Nations mandate to administer the area. In 1946 when the United Nations succeeded the League, the United Nations proposed that South Africa continue its administration under a U.N. trusteeship. South Africa refused and annexed South-West Africa.

The proposed U.N. trusteeship was revoked by the United Nations in 1966. At the same time, the South-West Africa People's Organization (SWAPO), operating from bases in Zambia and Angola, began guerrilla actions against South African troops in the region. In 1968 the United Nations formally renamed the territory Namibia and appointed an 11-nation council to supervise its affairs and devise a plan leading to independence.

In 1971 the International Court of Justice upheld the U.N.'s authority over Namibia and ruled that South Africa's continued occupation of the territory was illegal. In 1975 South Africa convened the Turnhalle Conference, which proposed a plan for Namibian independence based on the racial-separation principles of apartheid. This was rejected by the United Nations, and in 1978 the U.N. Security Council approved Resolution 435, which called for a general cease-fire to be followed by U.N.-supervised elections.

In response, South Africa unilaterally held elections in Namibia, which were boycotted by SWAPO and other African organizations and rejected by the United Nations. In 1982 South Africa declared that it would enter into talks about the future of Namibia only after Cuban troops were withdrawn from Angola. In 1983 South Africa launched a major military operation against SWAPO forces in Angola.

In October 1984 Angolan president dos Santos agreed to work out a plan for withdrawal of Cuban troops as part of a settlement in Namibia. In June 1985 South Africa granted limited local authority to a Namibian government made up of a coalition of parties, excluding SWAPO. In 1987 South African troops occupied southern Angola (to aid Angolan rebels), and in early 1988, fighting between South African troops and Namibian rebels in northern Namibia and southern Angola intensified.

A new round of talks on the future of Namibia between South Africa, Cuba, and Angola, mediated by the United States, began in May 1988, and on Dec. 13, 1988, the three parties agreed on a plan for Namibian independence and a pullout of Cuban troops from Angola.

In January 1989 the Cuban withdrawal from Angola began. On Apr. 1 U.N. Resolution 435 went into effect in Namibia, and a U.N. peacekeeping force arrived to supervise the transition to independence. Elections were held in November 1989: SWAPO leader Sam Nujoma won an overwhelming victory, and opposition leaders pledged their support. A Western-style democratic constitution was adopted Feb. 16, 1990, and full independence came on Mar. 21. The first elections under the new constitution were held in December 1994 with SWAPO gaining even stronger control of Parliament. In November 1999 elections, Sam Nujoma won a third term as president with 77% percent of the vote while SWAPO took 76% of the votes for the National Assembly.

▶NAURU

Republic of Nauru

• **GEOGRAPHY** **Location:** central Pacific Ocean (0°32'S, 166°56'E), about 2,800 mi. (4,500 km) southwest of Hawaii. **Boundaries**: nearest neighbor is Banaba (Ocean Island), in Kiribati, about 185 mi. (300 km) to E. **Total area**: 8 sq. mi. (21 sq km). **Coastline**: 19 mi. (30 km). **Comparative area**: about one-tenth size of Washington, D.C. **Land use:** 0% arable land; 0% permanent crops; 100% other. **Major cities**: none as such; government offices in Yaren district.

• **PEOPLE** **Population:** 12,570 (2003 est.). **Nationality:** noun—Nauruan(s) adjective—Nauruan. **Ethnic groups:** 58% Nauruan, 26% other Pacific Islander, 8% Chinese, 8% European. **Languages:** Nauruan, a distinct Pacific Island language (official); English widely understood and spoken and used for most government and commercial purposes. **Religions:** Christian (two-thirds Protestant, one-third Catholic).

• **GOVERNMENT** **Type:** republic. **Independence:** Jan. 31, 1968 (from U.N. trusteeship under Australia, New Zealand, and U.K.). **Constitution:** Jan. 29, 1968. **National holiday:** Independence Day, Jan. 31. **Head of Government:** Rene R. Harris, president (since Aug. 2003). **Structure:** executive—president elected from and by Parliament for unfixed term; unicameral legislature; judiciary.

• **ECONOMY** **Monetary unit:** Australian dollar. **Budget:** (FY95/96) ***income:*** $23.4 mil.; ***expend.:*** $64.8 mil. **GDP:** $60 mil., $5,000 per capita (2002 est.). **Chief crops:** coconuts. **Natural resources:** phosphates. **Major industries:** phosphate mining (about 2 mil. tons per year), financial services, coconuts. **Labor force:** N.A. **Exports:** $27 mil. (f.o.b., 1995); phosphates. **Imports:** $33 mil. (c.i.f., 1995); food, fuel, manufactures, building materials, machinery. **Major trading partners:** Australia, New Zealand, U.K.

Nauru, formerly known as Pleasant Island, is an isolated island lying west of the Gilbert Islands. It became a German protectorate in 1888. After World War I, Nauru was administered by Australia under a League of Nations mandate. It was occupied by Japan throughout World War II. In 1947 it became a U.N. Trust Territory administered by Australia, and on Jan. 31, 1968, an independent republic. Nauru has a parliament of 18 members, who elect a prime minister and a cabinet. Most of the island's assets are owned by the state-controlled Nauru Phosphate Corporation and by the Nauru Cooperative Society.

Much of the island is covered by phosphate deposits. Phosphate mining and exports, under leases largely controlled by Australian interests, have given Nauru one of the world's highest per-capita incomes. In 1999 Nauru joined the United Nations.

▶NEPAL
Kingdom of Nepal

• **GEOGRAPHY** **Location:** central Asia, in Himalayan mountain range. **Boundaries**: China to N, India to E, S, and W. **Total area**: 54,363 sq. mi. (140,800 sq km). **Coastline**: none. **Comparative area**: slightly larger than Arkansas. **Land use:** 20% arable land; negl. % permanent crops; 79% other. **Major cities**: (1991 census) Kathmandu (capital) 419,073.

• **PEOPLE** **Population:** 26,469,569 (2003 est.). **Nationality:** noun—Nepalese (sing. and pl.); adjective—Nepalese. **Ethnic groups:** Newars, Indians, Tibetans, Gurungs, Magars, Tamangs, Bhotias, Rais, Limbus, Sherpas. **Languages:** Nepali (official); 20 other languages divided into numerous dialects. **Religions:** 86% Hindu, 8% Buddhist, 4% Muslim; only official Hindu kingdom in world, although no sharp distinction between many Hindu and Buddhist groups.

• **GOVERNMENT** **Type:** parliamentary democracy. **Constitution:** Nov. 9, 1990. **National holiday:** Birthday of King Gyanedra, July 7. **Heads of Government:** Gyanendra Bir Bikram Shah Dev, king (since June 2001), Surya Bahadur Thapa, prime minister (since June 4, 2003). **Structure:** executive—prime minister appointed by king from leading party in parliament; bicameral legislature—upper house (National Assembly) consists of 60 members, 50 appointed by lower house, 10 by the king; judiciary.

• **ECONOMY** **Monetary unit:** Nepalese rupee. **Budget:** (FY96/97 est.) ***income:*** $655 mil.; ***expend.:*** $1.1 bil. **GDP:** $36 bil., $1,400 per capita (2002 est.). **Chief crops:** rice, corn, wheat, sugarcane; milk, water buffalo meat. **Natural resources:** quartz, water, timber, hydroelectric potential, scenic beauty. **Major industries:** carpet and textiles, small rice, jute, sugar, and oilseed mills; cigarette and brick factories; tourism. **Labor force:** 10 mil. (1996 est.); 81% agriculture, 16% services, 3% industry; severe lack of skilled labor. **Exports:** $720 mil. (f.o.b., 2001) (does not include unrecorded border trade with India); clothing, carpets, leather goods, jute goods, grain. **Imports:** $1.6 bil. (f.o.b., 2001); gold, petroleum products, fertilizer, machinery. **Major trading partners:** ***exports:*** **48%** India, 26% U.S., 11% Germany; ***imports:*** **41%** India, 11% Singapore, 10% China.

The birthplace of Gautama Buddha (c. 600 B.C.), Nepal was for many centuries a collection of petty principalities, inhabited by various Tibeto-Burman peoples who mostly practiced Lamaistic Buddhism. In 1769 the country's three geographical zones—floodplain, foothills, and high mountains—were united under the Gurkhas, who made Hinduism the country's official religion. Nepal established treaty relations with Great Britain in 1792 and fought a border war with British India in 1814-16, but it was never incorporated into the British Empire.

A revolution in 1950 overthrew a government of heriditary rulers that had overthrown the Shah dynasty in the 19th century. King Tribuhavan (a Shah) was restored and tried to introduce democratic reforms, but his son Mahendra dissolved Parliament and introduced a tiered system of town, district, and national councils. Road and air links to India, Pakistan, and Tibet were improved, and Nepal began to emerge from its customary isolation. The successful climb of Mt. Everest by Sir Edmund Hillary and Tenzing Norgay in 1953 focused international attention on Nepal.

Mahendra was succeeded in 1972 by his son, Birendra. Antigovernment demonstrations in 1990 led to the shooting deaths of 63 civilians, so Birendra lifted a 30-year-old ban on political parties and ordered the constitution rewritten to establish multiparty democracy and human rights as essentials of the political system. The king retains control of the military and is still head of state.

The Nepali Congress Party formed the first government in 1991, but after 1994 a series of brief coalitions, often including the Communist Party, governed Nepal until the May 1999 elections permitted the Nepali Congress Party to govern without a coalition. But prime minister Krishna Prasad Bhattarai proved too ill to deal with Nepal's depressed economy and with the Maoist guerrilla force ("People's War") afflicting Nepal since 1996; he resigned in March 2000 to be replaced by Giriji Prasad Koirala.

On June 1, 2001 Crown Prince Dipendra murdered his parents and eight other members of the royal family, after which he shot himself. His uncle became King Gyanendra. In the turmoil, the Maoist rebels increased their depredations.

The accession of Sher Bahadur Deuba as prime minister in July 2001 brought a harder line against the Maoist rebels: no negotiations before surrender. (Both China and India support the government hard line.) In Oct. 2002, King Gyanendra suspended the constitution, appointed Lokendra Chand as interim prime minister to open dialogue with the Maoists. Secret talks and quickly-broken truces led nowhere. Chand resigned in May 2002 with the rebels holding about 4o percent of the country. Surya Bahadur Thapa replaced him.

▶NETHERLANDS
Kingdom of The Netherlands

• **GEOGRAPHY** **Location:** western Europe. **Boundaries**: North Sea to N and W, Germany to E, Belgium to S. **Total area**: 14,413 sq. mi. (37,330 sq km). **Coastline**: 280 mi. (451 km). **Comparative area**: slightly less than twice the size of New Jersey. **Land use:** 27% arable land; 0% permanent crops; 73% other. **Major cities**: (1994) Amsterdam (capital) 724,096; Rotterdam 598,521; The Hague 445,271; Utrecht 234,106; Eindhoven 196,130. The Hague is the seat of government.

• **PEOPLE** **Population:** 16,150,511 (2003 est.). **Nationality:** noun—Dutchman (men), Dutchwoman (women); adjective—Dutch. **Ethnic groups:** 83% Dutch, 17% other (9% of which are Moroccans,Turks, Antilleans, Surinamese and Indonesians). **Languages:** Dutch (official). **Religions:** 31% Roman Catholic, 21% Protestant, 40% unaffiliated, 3% Muslim.

• **GOVERNMENT** **Type:** constitutional monarchy. **Independence:** 1579 (from Spain). **Constitution:** 1814; last amended Feb. 17, 1983. **National holiday:** Queen's Day, Apr. 30. **Heads of Government:** Beatrix Wilhelmina Armgard, queen (since Apr. 1980); Dr. Jan Peter Balkenende, prime minister (since July 2002). **Structure:** executive—queen is constitutional monarch, prime minister is head of government; bicameral parliament; independent judiciary.

• **ECONOMY** **Monetary unit:** euro. **Budget:** (2001 est.) ***income:*** $134 bil.; ***expend.:*** $134 bil. **GDP:** $434 bil., $26,900 per capita (2002 est.). **Chief crops:** grains, potatoes, sugar beets; livestock. **Natural recources:** natural gas, crude oil, fertile soil. **Major industries:** agro-industries, metal and engineering products, electrical machinery and equipment. **Labor force:** 7.2 mil. (2002 est.); 73% services, 23% manufacturing and construction, 4% agriculture; 3.5% unemployment (1998). **Exports:** $243.3 bil. (f.o.b., 2002); machinery and equipment, chemicals, fuels, food and tobacco. **Imports:** $201.1 bil. (c.i.f., 2002 est.); machinery and transport equipment, chemicals, foodstuffs, fuels, clothing. **Major trading partners:** (2002) ***exports:*** 77% E.U..; ***imports:*** 53% E.U., 9% U.S.

Historically, the name Netherlands referred to the low-lying areas of the Holy Roman Empire near the mouths of the Rhine, Meuse, and Scheldt rivers. The Habsburg emperor Charles V willed these territories to his son Philip II of Spain in 1555, but by the end of the 16th century, the northern provinces—the Union of Utrecht, formed in 1579 by William the Silent, of the House of Orange—won their independence in a war that was both religious (Calvinist vs. Catholic) and constitutional (aristocratic/patrician vs. foreign monarchy). The independence of the Netherlands was recognized in the Treaty of Westphalia, which ended the Thirty Years' War in 1648.

Dutch prosperity, founded on the woolen trade with England, grew tremendously through trade and seafaring under the 17th-century republic. The Netherlands amassed a world empire, including the Indonesian archipelago, the island of Sri Lanka (then Ceylon), South Africa, Suriname, parts of the West Indies, and the Hudson valley in New Amsterdam (later New York); in addition it monopolized Western trade with Japan after 1637.

The Netherlands were incorporated into the Napoleonic empire. At the Congress of Vienna in 1815, a Dutch monarchy was established, which included Belgium until 1830. Land drainage and reclamation programs maintained the prosperity of the country's small-scale agriculture, while trade and colonial revenues were increasingly supplemented by industrial development in the 19th century. Dutch prosperity and the country's strategic position gave the Netherlands extraordinary influence and prestige in European affairs into the 20th century, despite the country's small size. It remained neutral in World War I.

Germany invaded the Netherlands in May 1940, taking control of the country after five days of fighting. Preparing to incorporate Holland into the Third Reich, Hitler installed a Nazi civilian government that ruled through totalitarian exploitation and cooperated in the persecution of Jews. But Queen Wilhelmina and the Dutch government escaped to England and maintained a government-in-exile throughout the war.

The final stages of fighting on the western front inflicted severe damage on the country, while in Asia the recovery of Indonesia from Japan led to a declaration of independence under Sukarno. Marshall Plan aid was intended to support a domestic postwar recovery; an equal amount was spent by the Dutch government in an attempt to recapture control of Indonesia before that country's independence was recognized in 1949.

Devastated by World War II and the loss of its empire, the country faced a bleak future in the postwar years. Forced to turn its attention to recovery at home, the Netherlands worked through the Benelux (Belgium, Netherlands, Luxembourg) union (founded in 1944) and the Common Market to create another European "economic miracle" between the early 1950's and the 1970's. The older bases of the economy—commerce, maritime industry, dairy farming, and flower farming—were expanded and modernized; Rotterdam was rebuilt to become Europe's most important port. Newer industries, such as chemicals and oil refining, electronics, and steel, relied on the country's highly skilled and productive labor force to turn imported raw materials into finished high-value exports. A huge impoundment project turned the Zuider Zee into a new province, increasing the country's land area by 10 percent.

This postwar prosperity has been based in large part on political stability. A coalition of the Catholic State party and the Labor (formerly Social Democratic) party governed for 10 years under Premier Willem Drees. After 1958 cabinets normally were formed from coalitions headed by three Christian parties (merged in 1980 to form the United Christian Appeal) or by the Liberal party; all pursued essentially the same policies of free enterprise, comprehensive social welfare programs, high taxation, and social liberalism.

From 1982 to 1989 a coalition of Christian Democrats and Liberals provided a cabinet headed by Prime Minister Ruud Lubbers; since 1989 the coalition has been of Christian Democrats and Labor. In 1994 Wim Kok, head of Labor, became prime minister, the first government to exclude the Christian Democrats since 1945.

Just 10 days before the May 15, 2002 elections, radical libertarian and anti-Muslim newcomer Pim Fortuyn was assassinated by an animal-rights activist. The election proved a nightmare for Kok's center-left coalition: the Christian Democrats topped the polls, followed by Fortuyn's party. These two put together an inexperienced coalition under CD prime minister Jan Peter Balkenende, but it lasted only three months. Balkendale cobbled together a new coalition after 2003 elections.

▶NEW ZEALAND

• **GEOGRAPHY** **Location:** South Pacific Ocean about 1,100 mi. (1,750 km) SE of Australia. **Boundaries**: South Pacific Ocean to N, E, and S; Tasman Sea to W. **Total area**: 103,738 sq. mi. (268,680 sq km). **Coastline**: 9,406 mi. (15,134 km). **Comparative area**: about size of Colorado. **Land use:** 6% arable land; 6% permanent crops; 88% other. **Major cities**: (1993 est.) Wellington (capital) 326,900; Auckland 910,200; Christchurch 312,600; Hamilton 151,800; Napier-Hastings 111,200.

• **PEOPLE** **Population:** 3,951,307 (July 2001 est.). **Nationality:** noun—New Zealander(s); adjective— New Zealand. **Ethnic groups:** 74.5% New Zealand European, 9.7% Maori, 4.6% other European, 3.8% Pacific Islander, 7.4% Asian and other. **Languages:** English (official) and Maori. **Religions:** 24% Anglican, 18% Presbyterian, 15% Roman Catholic, 5% Methodist, 2% Baptist, 3% other Protestant, 33% none or unspecified.

• **GOVERNMENT** **Type:** parliamentary democracy. **Independence:** Sept. 26, 1907 (from U.K.). **Constitution:** no formal, written constitution; consists of various documents, including certain acts of U.K. and New Zealand Parliaments. Constitution Act 1986 was to have come into force Jan. 1, 1987, but has not been enacted. **National holiday:** Waitangi Day, Feb. 6. **Heads of Government:** Dame Silvia Cartwright, governor-general (since

Apr. 2001); Helen Clark, prime minister (since Dec. 1999). **Structure:** executive—governor-general represents queen, prime minister is head of government; unicameral legislature; judiciary.

• ECONOMY **Monetary unit:** New Zealand dollar. **Budget:** (2002 est.) ***income:*** $29.2 bil.; ***expend.:*** $31.2 bil. **GDP:** $78.8 bil., $20,200 per capita (2002 est.). **Chief crops:** wheat, barley, potatoes, fruits; wool, meat, dairy. **Natural resources:** natural gas, iron ore, sand, coal, timber. **Major industries:** food processing, wood and paper products, textiles, aluminum smelting, tourism. **Labor force:** 1.92 mil. (2001); 65% services, 25% industry, 10% agriculture; 5.3% unemployment (2002). **Exports:** $15 bil. (f.o.b., 2002 est.); wool, lamb, mutton, beef, fruit, fish. **Imports:** $12.5 bil. (f.o.b., 2002 est.); machinery and equipment, vehicles and aircraft, petroleum, consumer goods, plastics. **Major trading partners:** ***exports:*** 19% Australia, 14% U.S., 12% Japan; ***imports:*** 24% Australia, 17% U.S., 12% Japan.

New Zealand was settled by Maori voyagers from Polynesia from about the ninth century A.D. The first European to sight it was the Dutch explorer Abel Tasman, in 1642; he named it, but did not take possession. In 1769, Capt. James Cook visited and claimed it for Britain. The first British missionaries arrived in 1814, and New Zealand became a full-fledged British colony in 1841. By the Treaty of Waitangi in 1840, the Maoris recognized Queen Victoria's protection and agreed to admit British settlers; in return, they were guaranteed possession of their lands. But in a series of bloody wars lasting until 1870, the Maoris were displaced from lands devoted to the expanding British settlements.

As a result of their defeat and of introduced diseases, the Maori population dwindled to about 40,000 by the 1890's. Their numbers have since recovered to over 400,000, and in recent decades, the Maoris have become a cohesive culture and significant political force, directly electing several members of Parliament. In 1985, the Waitangi Tribunal was given power to hear Maori claims for repayment for land taken without compensation since the 1840 treaty. Large financial settlements were negotiated by the government.

New Zealand was one of the first nations to introduce universal adult suffrage (1893) and to establish a comprehensive welfare state. Legislation beginning in 1898 regulates labor practices, and mandates universal old-age pensions, public sector medical care, and other social services. Since 1907, the country has been an independent member of the British Commonwealth. The crown is represented by a governor-general; government is drawn from a parliament and headed by a prime minister. Since the 1930's, government has alternated between the National and Labour parties.

New Zealand troops fought on the side of the Allies in both world wars, with U.N. forces in Korea, and with the U.S. in Vietnam. In 1951, New Zealand joined Australia and the U.S. in the ANZUS mutual-defense treaty, but was excluded from it in 1986 after denying port facilities to ships carrying nuclear weapons. New Zealand has also objected strenuously to French testing of nuclear weapons in the South Pacific and pressed for a comprehensive international nuclear test ban treaty.

Upon its election in 1984, the Labour government launched a profound economic restructuring program to transform the country from a protected agrarian economy to an open free-market economy. This program, continued by the National Party, which regained power in 1990, eliminated government subsidies, cut government spending, liberalized imports, deregulated financial markets, reduced tax rates, and deregulated the labor market, largely disempowering the unions. The reforms resulted in an expanding and competitive economy with low inflation, and, in 1993-94, the first budget surplus in 18 years. The government responded in 1995 by cutting taxes again. 1996 election results, however, forced the Nationalist Party into coalition with the new populist/zenophobic New Zealand First Party. The terms commit the new government to defer tax cuts, halt sales of state-owned businesses, freeze immigration levels, and increase spending on health and education. The coalition lasted 19 months until New Zealand First left the cabinet over government plans to privatize Wellington International Airport. Yet the government did not fall as votes of confidence in September 1998 and February 1999 permitted continuance of a minority government headed by New Zealand's first female prime minister, Jenny Shipley. Nine years of National Party rule ended in 1999 as a coalition government of Labor and Alliance established Helen Clark as prime minister. In June 2001 elections, the Nationalists garnered only 27 seats, their worse showing in their 66-year history. Clark's Labour Party gained 52 seats. Without a formal coalition, an alliance with the Greens yielded exactly 60 of the 120 votes.

▶NICARAGUA
Republic of Nicaragua

• GEOGRAPHY **Location:** Central American isthmus. **Boundaries**: Honduras to N, Caribbean Sea to E, Costa Rica to S, Pacific Ocean to W. **Total area**: 49,998 sq. mi. (129,494 sq km). **Coastline**: 565 mi. (910 km). **Comparative area**: slightly smaller than New York State. **Land use:** 20% arable land; 2% permanent crops; 78% other. **Major cities**: (1983) Managua (capital) 682,111; (1985 est.) León 100,982; Granada 88,636; Masaya 74,946; Chinandega 67,792.

• PEOPLE **Population:** 5,128,517 (2003 est.). **Nationality:** noun—Nicaraguan(s); adjective—Nicaraguan. **Ethnic groups:** 69% mestizo, 17% white, 9% black, 5% Amerindian. **Languages:** Spanish (official); English- and Amerindian-speaking minorities on Atlantic coast. **Religions:** 85% Roman Catholic, Protestant.

• GOVERNMENT **Type:** republic. **Independence:** Sept. 15, 1821 (from Spain). **Constitution:** Jan. 9, 1987 with reforms in 1995 and 2000. **National holiday:** Independence Day, Sept. 15. **Head of Government:** Enrique Bolaños Geyer, president (since Jan. 2002). **Structure:** executive branch; unicameral legislature; judiciary.

• ECONOMY **Monetary unit:** córdoba. **Budget:** (2000 est.) ***income:*** $726 mil.; ***expend.:*** $908 mil. **GDP:** $12.8 bil., $2,500 per capita (2002 est.). **Chief crops:** cotton, bananas, coffee, sugarcane, rice, corn, beans. **Natural resources:** gold, silver, copper, tungsten, lead. **Major industries:** food processing, chemicals, metal products. **Labor force:** 1.7 mil. (1999); 43% services, 42% agriculture, 15% industry; 24% unemployment (2002). **Exports:** $637 mil. (f.o.b., 2002 est.); coffee, seafood, cotton, tobacco, sugar, gold, bananas. **Imports:** $1.7 bil. (c.i.f., 2002 est.); consumer goods, machinery and equipment, petroleum products. **Major trading partners:** ***exports:*** U.S., Germany, Canada; ***imports:*** Central America, U.S.

Nicaragua gained independence from Spain in 1821 and formed a constituent part of the United Provinces of Central America in 1823. With the dissolution of the federation in 1838, Nicaragua became an independent republic. Throughout the United Provinces, an intra-elite struggle between Liberal and Conservative factions defined the political arena during the early 19th century. Nicaraguan Liberals invited the adventurer William Walker of Tennessee to take their part against their Conservative rivals in 1855. Walker took control of the country in 1856 but was driven out by a combined Central American force the following year.

The Conservatives held power in Nicaragua until 1893, when a planters' revolt brought Liberal José Santos Zelaya to the presidency. Because of Zelaya's intention to pursue an isthmian canal project, the U.S. government intervened in support of a Conservative uprising. The United States sent marines to Nicaragua in 1909, and Zelaya resigned in 1910. The marines occupied the country during 1909-25 and 1926-33.

Refusing to abide by a political settlement between the U.S. government and Nicaraguan Liberal forces in 1927, Augusto César Sandino, led a guerrilla war against U.S. occupation forces. In 1934, Anastasio Somoza García, head of the Nicaraguan National Guard, had Sandino assassinated and took over the presidency in 1937. Somoza and his sons Luis and Anastasio Somoza Debayle controlled Nicaragua until 1979.

A broad coalition of groups led by the Sandinista National Liberation Front (FSLN) overthrew the Somoza dictatorship in 1979. Elections were held in 1984 for the presidency, vice presidency, and a constituent assembly. The Sandinistas won the election for the presidency, captured a working majority in the National Assembly, and wrote a new constitution in 1987.

Between 1981 and 1990, the United States actively, but covertly supported Contra rebels fighting the Sandinista regime in a civil war that cost the country dearly. In 1989, Pres. Daniel Ortega announced elections for early 1990, which he lost in a stunning upset to Violeta Barrios de Chamorro, who headed a 17-party coalition, the United Nicaragua Opposition. Since then, the transition has been relatively peaceful, highlighted by Gen. Humberto Ortega's uneventful transfer of command of the army in 1995, the first peaceful transfer in Nicaragua's history. In late 1996 presidential elections the Liberal Alliance candidate, Arnoldo Alemán, won a decisive victory over former president Daniel Ortega and voters opted for a return to free enterprise and closer ties with the U.S. Limitations on the Aleman government's free enterprising policies were shown by student protests and transport workers' strikes which forced the government to boost university spending and abandon bus line deregulation while cutting back fuel taxes. In Nov. 2000 the Sandinistas and Daniel Ortega were again defeated as Liberal Alliance candidate Enrique Bolanos Geyer carried 54 percent of the presidential vote.

▶NIGER

Republic of Niger

• **GEOGRAPHY** **Location:** landlocked country in western Africa. **Boundaries**: Algeria and Libya to N, Chad to E, Nigeria to S, Benin, Burkina Faso to SW, Mali to W. **Total area**: 489,189 sq. mi. (1,267,000 sq km). **Coastline**: none. **Comparative area**: slighlty less than twice the size of Texas. **Land use:** 4% arable land; 0% permanent crops; 796% other. **Major cities**: (1988 census) Niamey (capital) 392,169; Zinder 119,838; Maradi 109,386; Tahoua 49,941; Agadez 49,361.

• **PEOPLE** **Population:** 11,058,590 (2003 est.). **Nationality:** noun—Nigerien(s); adjective—Nigerien. **Ethnic groups:** 56% Hausa, 22% Djerma, 8.5% Fula, 8% Tuareg, 4.3% Beri Beri (Kanouri); 1.2% Arab, Toubou, and Gourmantche; about 1,200 French expatriates. **Languages:** French (official), Hausa, Djerma. **Religions:** 80% Muslim, 20% indigenous beliefs and Christians.

• **GOVERNMENT** **Type:** republic. **Independence:** Aug. 3, 1960 (from France). **Constitution:** revised May 12, 1996 and July 18, 1999. **National holiday:** Republic Day, Dec. 18. **Heads of Government:** Tandja Mamadou, president (since Dec. 1999); Amadou Hama, prime minister (since Dec. 1999). **Structure:** executive; unicameral legislature; judiciary.

• **ECONOMY** **Monetary unit:** Communauté Financière Africaine (CFA) franc. **Budget:** (2002 est.) ***income:*** $320 mil.; ***expend.:*** $320 mil. **GDP:** $8.8 bil., $830 per capita (2002 est.). **Chief crops:** cowpeas, cotton, peanuts, millet, sorghum, cassava, rice; goats, sheep, cattle. **Natural resources:** uranium, coal, iron ore, tin, phosphates. **Major industries:** uranium mining, cement, brick, textiles. **Labor force:** 70,000 receive regular wages or salaries; 90% agriculture; 6% industry and commerce, 4% government. **Exports:** $293 mil. (f.o.b., 2002 est.); uranium ore, livestock, cowpeas, onions. **Imports:** $368 mil. (f.o.b., 2002); consumer goods, primary materials, machinery, vehicles and parts, petroleum, cereals. **Major trading partners:** ***exports:*** France, Nigeria, South Korea, U.S.; ***imports:*** France, Ivory Coast, U.S.

Most of Niger's territory is dominated by the Sahara and the Sahel (the "shore" of the desert), which have spread southward since prehistoric times. Much of the population lives in the narrow fertile belt south of the Niger River. Much of Niger was incorporated during medieval times in large empires centered in neighboring Mali, Chad, and Nigeria.

In the 18th century, Tuaregs migrating from the northern desert began to form tribal confederations in Niger. They united with local Hausa peoples to wage war against the Fulani empire. In the 19th century, British and German explorers explored the region. In the European rivalry that followed, the French, from bases in Mali and Chad, began to dominate Niger by 1900; Niger became a French colony in 1922, administered from Dakar, Senegal.

In 1946 the people of Niger, in common with other peoples in French Africa, were granted French citizenship, and limited self-rule began. This local autonomy was expanded in 1956, and in 1958 Niger became an autonomous state within the French Overseas Community. Full independence followed on Aug. 3, 1960; Niger maintained close ties to France.

Hamani Diori was elected Niger's first president in 1960, reelected in 1965 and 1970. He was overthrown in 1974 in a military coup led by Lt. Col. Seyni Kountche. In 1987, Pres. Kountche died and was succeeded by Col. Ali Saibou, who was elected president by the Supreme Military Council. The country began moving toward democracy again in 1989, and a new constitution was approved in 1992. Mahame Ousmane was elected president in 1993, but he and prime minister Hama Amadou were ousted in a violent military coup in Jan. 1996. The leader of the coup, Lt. Col. Ibrahim Barré, who criticized Ousmane's handling of the Taureg Liberation Front, became the new president. He survived an assasination attempt in Jan. 1998, but fell to another in April 1999. Junior army officers formed a junta, supported by all the civilian opposition parties, maintaining Ibrahim Mayaki in his post as prime minister. The junta promised a "nine-month transition", and presidential elections were held in Nov. 1999 in which Tandja Mamadou defeated former premier Mohamadou Issoufou.

▶NIGERIA

Federal Republic of Nigeria

• **GEOGRAPHY** **Location:** western coast of Africa. **Boundaries**: Niger to N, Cameroon to E, Gulf of Guinea to S, Benin to W. **Total area**: 356,668 sq. mi. (923,770 sq km). **Coastline**: 530 mi. (853 km). **Comparative area**: slightly more than twice the size of California. **Land use:** 31% arable land; 3% permanent crops; 66% other. **Major cities**: (1992) Abuja (capital) 305,900; Lagos 13,400,000; Ibadan 1,295,000; Kano 699,900; Ogbomosho 660,600.

• **PEOPLE** **Population:** 133,881,704 (2003 est.). **Nationality:** noun—Nigerian(s); adjective—Nigerian. **Ethnic groups:** 29% Hausa and Fulani, 21% Yoruba, 18% Ibo, 10% Ijaw, Kanuri, Ibibio, Tiv. **Languages:** English (official); Hausa, Yoruba, Ibo, Fulani. **Religions:** 50% Muslim, 40% Christian, 10% indigenous beliefs.

• **GOVERNMENT** **Type:** republic in transition from military rule. **Independence:** Oct. 1, 1960 (from U.K.). **Constitution:** New constitution adopted in 1999. **National holiday:** Independence Day, Oct. 1. **Head of Government:** Olusegun Obasanjo, president (since May 1999). **Structure:** executive; bicameral legislature; judiciary.

• **ECONOMY** **Monetary unit:** naira. **Budget:** (2000 est.) ***income:*** $3.4 bil.; ***expend:*** $3.6 bil. **GDP:** $113.5 bil., $875 per capita (2002 est.). **Chief crops:** peanuts, cocoa, palm oil, rubber, corn; goats, sheep, cattle, pigs; fish. **Natural resources:** crude oil, tin, columbite, iron ore, coal. **Major industries:** crude oil, coal, tin, columbite; palm oil, peanuts, cotton, rubber; textiles, cement, building materials. **Labor force:** 66 mil. (1999); 70% agriculture; 10% industry, 20% services; 28% unemployment (1992 est.). **Exports:** $17.3 bil. (f.o.b., 2002); 95% petroleum and petroleum products, cocoa, rubber. **Imports:** $13.6 bil. (f.o.b., 2002); machinery, chemicals, transportation equipment, manufactured goods, food and animals. **Major trading partners:** ***exports:*** 50% U.S., 10% Spain, 8% India; ***imports:*** 9% U.K., 9% U.S., 8% Germany.

The Nok culture of central Nigeria (500-200 B.C.) was one of the richest and most advanced ancient civilizations in western Africa. Around A.D. 1000, the Muslim Kanem civilization expanded into northern Nigeria; by the 14th century, the amalgamated kingdom of Kanem-Bornu took northern Nigeria as its political center, from which it dominated the Sahel and developed trade routes stretching throughout northern Africa and as far as Europe and the Middle East. During the 15th and 16th centuries, the Hausa Songhai empire rose to power. It was overthrown by the Fulani Muslim leader Uthman Dan Fodio, who created the Sokoto caliphate.

Southern Nigeria is dominated by the Yoruba, whose Oyo kingdom, centered at Ife, became a major power by A.D. 1000. Oyo gave rise to the Benin civilization, which flourished from the 15th to the 18th centuries and is famous for its brass, bronze, and ivory sculpture.

The Portuguese established trading stations on the Benin coast in the 15th century; initially, trade relations were cordial, and Benin became well-known in Europe as a powerful and advanced kingdom. With the rise of the slave trade (which began with the cooperation of the Benin kings, who brought slaves from the interior), relations became hostile, and Benin declined under European pressure. The Dutch, British, and other Europeans competed strenuously with Portugal for control of the slave trade, and by the 18th century, most of the coastal region of Nigeria was under British control. By the turn of the 19th century, Britain suppressed the slave trade; slaves captured aboard European ships were transported by the British to Freetown in Sierra Leone.

The British traded with Nigerians for agricultural and forest products and commenced exploration of the Niger River. Lagos came under British control in 1851, and in 1861 Nigeria was made a British colony. Despite native resistance the colony was expanded in 1906 to include territory east of the Niger River, which was called the Protectorate of Southern Nigeria, The two areas were administratively joined in 1914.

During the 1920's Britain began to respond to Nigerian demands for self-rule. In 1946 the colony was divided into three regions, each with an advisory assembly. In 1954 the colony was reorganized as the Nigerian Federation, and the assemblies were given more authority. Sir Akubar Tafawa Balewa became Nigeria's first prime minister.

The 1960's were marked by a struggle for political dominance among the major ethnic groups of Nigeria, including the Ibo (or Igbo), Yoruba, Hausa, and Fulani. Attempts to partition the country on tribal lines for administrative purposes provoked controversy, and charges of corruption and fraud in elections held in 1964 and 1965 led to violence and rioting.

In January 1966 civil war broke out when a group of Ibo army officers overthrew the central government. Prime Minister Balewa was killed, along with many other political leaders in the northern and western parts of the country. Gen. Johnson Aguiyi-Ironsi, leader of the Ibo forces, took control of the government.

Aguiyi-Ironsi abolished the country's federal structure and set up a strong central government, dominated by the Ibo. Anti-Ibo riots broke out in the north, and many Ibo were massacred. In July 1966 Aguiyi-Ironsi was assassinated by a group of northern army officers. Army Chief of Staff Yakubu Gowon became head of a new military government. In 1967 Gowon reapportioned Nigeria into 12 states. The Eastern Region rejected this plan and seceded from Nigeria to form the independent state of Biafra, provoking a civil war that lasted until January 1970, when Biafra was rejoined with Nigeria. An estimated one million Biafrans, mostly Ibos, died in the war.

Gowon tried to rebuild the Eastern Region and create a harmonious multitribal government, but he was overthrown in a coup in 1975. His successor was assassinated in 1976 and succeeded by Lt. Gen. Olusegun Obasanjo who increased the number of states from 12 to 19 and promised a return to civilian rule. Shehu Shagari was elected president in 1979 and reelected in 1983, but in Dec. 1983 the military again intervened.

Nigeria's crude oil resources fueled the economy and made it attractive for foreign investment. During the 1970's, petroleum exports helped Nigeria recover from the Biafran War. But corruption and overspending of projected petroleum revenues led to an economic crisis in the early 1980's as oil prices collapsed worldwide. Inflation, unemployment, and food shortages led to rioting in major population centers in 1986. And in 1987, religious violence broke out between the Christian south and the Muslim north.

The government of Maj. Gen. Ibrahim Babangida responded by announcing plans for a new constitution, various economic austerity measures, and the restoration of civilian rule by 1992. He also limited the number of political parties and dictated both party platforms in National Assembly elections held in 1992, and in 1993, he annulled the results of the presidential election, which international monitors said would have been won by opposition leader Moshood K. Abiola, who was taken prisoner for the "treason" of declaring himself the election winner. Babangida resigned in Aug. 1993, but his self-appointed successor was ousted in a November 1993 coup by Defense Minister Sani Abacha.

Abacha's tyrrany survived until his death in June 1998. A "transitional" military government led by army chief of staff, Abdusalem Abubakar, freed political prisoners (Abiola dying just before his release), held local, state, and national elections (Dec.– Feb.), and turned over power, May 29, 1999 to the first popularly-elected president in 16 years, former general and once military ruler, Olusegun Obasanjo. The new government faced formidable problems: increased Moslem-Christian violence as northern states attempted to impose Sharia (Koranic law); civil disorder and rioting in the face of increased fuel prices.

In July 2000, violence and bloodshed over the imposition of Sharia increased. Attempts to meet I.M.F. loan conditions, such as ending subsidies which kept oil prices low or reducing government payrolls, provoked riots and strikes. Hausa-Yoruba tribal conflict in Lagos left over 100 dead. Amidst religious, ethnic, and economic turmoil, Pres. Obasanjo (the first civilian president after almost 20 years of military rule) won a second term in 2003.

▶NORWAY

Kingdom of Norway

• **GEOGRAPHY** **Location:** western Scandinavian peninsula, northern Europe. **Boundaries**: Norwegian Sea to N and W, Russian Federation, Finland to NE, Sweden to E, North Sea to S and W. **Total area**: 125,182 sq. mi. (324,220 sq km). **Coastline**: 13,626 mi. (21,925 km)—2,125 mi. (3,419 km) mainland; 1,500 mi. (2,413 km) large islands; 10,002 mi. (16,093 km) long fjords, numerous small islands, and minor indentations. **Comparative area**: slightly larger than New Mexico. **Land use:** 3% arable land; negl.% permanent crops; n97% other. **Major cities**: (1995) Oslo (capital) 483,401; Bergen 221,717; Trondheim 142,927; Stavanger 103,590; Kristiansand 68,609.

• **PEOPLE** **Population:** 4,546,123 (2003 est.). **Nationality:** noun—Norwegian(s); adjective—Norwegian. **Ethnic groups:** Norwegian (Nordic, Alpine, Baltic), 20,000 Lapps (Sami). **Languages:** Norwegian (official), Lapp- and Finnish-speaking minorities. **Religions:** 86% Evangelical Lutheran (state church), 3% other Protestant and Roman Catholic, 1% other, 10% none and unknown.

• **GOVERNMENT** **Type:** constitutional monarchy. **Independence:** Oct. 26, 1905 (from Sweden). **Constitution:** May 17, 1814, and modified in 1884. **National holiday:** Constitution Day, May 17. **Heads of Government:** Harald V, king (since Jan. 1991); Kjell Magne Bondevik, prime minister (since Oct. 2001). **Structure:** executive—prime minister heads government; unicameral legislature—for certain purposes, *Storting* divides itself into two chambers and elects 25 percent of its members to an upper house; judiciary.

• **ECONOMY** **Monetary unit:** Norwegian kroner. **Budget:** (2000 est.) ***income:*** $71.7 bil.; ***expend.:*** $57.6 bil. **GDP:** $143 bil., $31,800 per capita (2002 est.). **Chief crops:** oats, feed grains; beef, milk; fish (among worlds top ten fishing nations). **Natural resources:** crude oil, copper, natural gas, pyrites, nickel. **Major industries:** petroleum and gas, food processing, shipbuilding. **Labor force:** 2.4 mil.; 74% services, 22% industry, 4% agriculture, forestry and fishing; 3.9% unemployment (1999). **Exports:** $68.2 bil. (f.o.b., 2002 est.); petroleum and petroleum products, metals, chemicals, ships, fish. **Imports:** $37.3 bil. (f.o.b., 2002 est.); machinery and equipment, chemicals, metals, foodstuffs. **Major trading partners:** ***exports:*** 78% E.U., 8% U.S.; ***imports:*** 67% E.U., 7% U.S.

The Viking age began in 793 with the sack of Lindisfarne in Ireland. By the 10th century, Norse and Danish Vikings had touched in almost every navigable river of Western Europe from Germany to Spain. In addition to coastal raiding, the Norse were beginning the first open-ocean voyages from Europe, sailing direct to Iceland (800 miles) and even to Greenland (2,200 miles), which they colonized in the 10th century.

At the beginning of the 10th century, Harold I united the petty kingdoms of western Scandinavia and extended his realm as far as the Orkney and Shetland islands. Viking nobles fleeing from his conquests consolided the Norse duchy of Normandy in France. Christianity was established under Olaf II at the beginning of the 11th century.

Under Magnus VI (1263-80), medieval Norway reached the height of its power and prosperity. Norwegian independence ended with the accession in 1319 of Magnus VII, who was king of Sweden as well. Under the Kalmar Union of 1397, the three kingdoms of Scandinavia were merged under Danish control; Norway ceased to exist as a nation-state and was governed by the Danes for the following four centuries.

In 1814 Denmark, which had sided with France in the Napoleonic wars, was forced by the victorious powers to cede Norway to Sweden. Under Sweden's military control Norway attempted to establish its own monarchy. The attempt failed, but in 1815 Sweden acknowledged the independence of Norway in perpetual union with the Swedish Crown.

Relations between Norway and Sweden remained strained throughout the 19th century. In 1905 the Norwegian legislature, the Storting, declared the union void and deposed Swedish King Oscar II as king of Norway. Sweden acquiesced, and Prince Charles of Denmark was enthroned as king of Norway, ruling as Haakon VII for 52 years.

During the 19th century, large numbers of Norwegians emigrated to North America. A rising tide of cultural nationalism was expressed in the flourishing Norwegian literature and art, as well as in a tradition of Arctic exploration. In the 20th century, industrialization, aided by the development of hydroelectric power, began to supplement Norway's traditional economic mainstays of fishing and seafaring.

Norway remained neutral during World War I and was relatively unaffected by the postwar upheavals. Norway attempted to remain neutral in World War II as well but was invaded by German troops in April 1940; the country fell after a brief resistance aided by a Franco-British expeditionary force. The king and government fled to London and established a government-in-exile there. The Norwegian merchant marine fleet was also largely transferred to Great Britain and contributed to the Allied cause in the North Atlantic.

At home, resistance grew to the collaborationist government of the Fascist leader Vidkun Quisling. As the Nazis retreated in 1945, King Haakon and his government returned home in triumph.

Elections in 1945 returned a majority Labor government in the Storting. Labor set about establishing a Scandinavian welfare state, emphasizing privately owned, free-market industry, publicly owned utilities, state planning to ensure ample housing as well as full employment through export-oriented industries, a comprehensive social welfare system, and high taxes.

Norway was a founding member of the United Nations and provided that body with its first secretary-general, Trygve Lie. With the hardening of the Cold War, Norway joined the NATO alliance in 1949. In 1959 Norway became one of the original members of the European Free Trade Association. Through the 1960's industrial development and exports continued to fuel an economic boom that led to great national prosperity and stability.

The 1970's were the decade of oil and gas, with extensive development of North Sea fields. As international energy prices rose, the government's petroleum monopoly, Statoil, seemed to provide an endless source of funds. Because Norway's hydroelectric plants made the country self-sufficient in electric power, almost all of the oil and gas was available for export; by 1981 energy exports amounted to one-third, and by 1985 one-half, of Norway's total exports. The government expanded the welfare state and encouraged large wage increases. Public spending swelled and government debt mounted; meanwhile Norway became an economic hostage to OPEC oil prices.

In the 1981 elections, the Conservative party formed a government for the first time since 1928; its austerity policy of holding down government spending while increasing taxes on consumer goods aroused popular opposition, and the government fell in 1986. The new Socialist coalition government faced even greater drops in oil revenues, combined with labor unrest and continued inflation. But in 1987 Norway negotiated the sale of gas to E.U. countries, and the recovery of energy prices brought a partial return to economic stability and prosperity. King Olav died in Jan. 1991; his son Harald V succeeded him in June.

In 1993 the government of Prime Minister Brundtland sought admission to the E.U.. On Mar. 29, 1994, the E.U. agreed to admit Norway to membership after long and intricate negotiations limiting Spanish and Portuguese fishing rights in Norwegian waters. But Norweigian voters in a Nov. 1994 referendum rejected E.U. membership. Brundtland resigned in Oct. 1996 and was replaced by Thorbjoern Jagland, but he remained prime minister less than a year. After 1997 elections to the Storting, a right-wing three-party coalition, which controlled only 24 of the 165 seats, formed a government under Christian Democrat Kjell Magne Bondevik. Even Bondevik's three-week leave of absence (to treat depression) in Sept. 1998 failed to shake the stability of Norway's politics. But a March 2000 no-confidence vote toppled the government, replacing it with a Labor-Conservative coalition under Labor's Jens Stoltenberg as prime minister.

Storting elections in Sept. 2001 brought another of western Europe's right-wing victories as Labor made its worst showing since 1924, losing 22 seats. Conservative Jens Stoltenberg became Norway's new prime minister.

▶OMAN

Sultanate of Oman

• GEOGRAPHY **Location:** southeastern Arabian peninsula. **Boundaries**: Gulf of Oman to N, Arabian Sea to E and S, Yemen to SW, Saudi Arabia to W, United Arab Emirates to NW; detached portion of Oman lies at tip of Musandam peninsula, on Strait of Hormuz. **Total area**: 82,031 sq. mi. (212,460 sq km). **Coastline**: 1,299 mi. (2,092 km). **Comparative area**: slightly smaller than Kansas. **Land use:** 0% arable land; negl. % permanent crops; 100% other. **Major cities**: (1993 census) Muscat (capital) 549,150; Al-Batinah 564,677; Al-Sharquia 258,344.

• PEOPLE **Population:** 2,807,125 (2003 est.). **Nationality:** noun—Omani(s); adjective—Omani. **Ethnic groups:** Arab, Baluchi, South Asian, African. **Languages:** Arabic (official), English, Baluchi, Urdu, Indian dialects. **Religions:** 75% Ibadhi Muslim, Sunni Muslim, Shi'a Muslim, Hindu.

• GOVERNMENT **Type:** monarchy. **Constitution:** none. **National holiday:** Birthday of the Sultan, Nov. 18. **Head of Government:** Qaboos bin Said, sultan and prime minister (since July 1970). **Structure:** executive—sultan is hereditary monarch; bicameral legislature-advisory powers only; judiciary—traditional Islamic judges in nascent civil court system; supreme court with non-Islamic judges.

• ECONOMY **Monetary unit:** Omani rial. **Budget:** (2000 est.) ***income:*** $9.2 bil.; ***expend.:*** $6.9 bil. **GDP:** $22.4 bil., $8,300 per capita (2002 est.). **Chief crops:** dates, limes, bananas, alfalfa, vegetables, cattle, camels; annual fish catch averages 100,000 metric tons. **Natural resources:** crude oil, copper, asbestos, some marble, limestone. **Major industries:** crude oil production and refining, natural gas production, construction. **Labor force:** 920,000 (2002 est.). **Exports:** $10.6 bil. (f.o.b., 2002 est.); petroleum, reexports, fish, metals, textiles. **Imports:** $5.5 bil. (f.o.b., 2002 est.); machinery, transportation equipment, manufactured goods, food, livestock, lubricants. **Major trading partners: *exports:*** 22% China, 19% Japan, 18% South Korea; ***imports:*** 28% UAE, 15% Japan, 8% U.K.

Oman occupies the southeastern corner of Arabia. From ancient times an important center of trade in the Persian Gulf and the Indian Ocean, Oman was frequently dominated by Persia prior to the mid-18th century. The principal port, Muscat, was captured by the Portuguese in 1508 and held by them until 1659, when the Ottoman Turks took possession. They were driven out in 1741 by Ahmed ibn Said of Yemen, who consolidated the sultanate of Oman in 1744 and founded the present royal line.

In the early 19th century, Oman was the most powerful state in Arabia, controlling Zanzibar, the southern coast of Iran, and much of Baluchistan (between Pakistan and Iran). Zanzibar was separated from Oman in 1856, and the Persian coast and much of Baluchistan was detached from Oman during the latter half of the 19th century. In 1958 Oman's sole remaining Baluchi possession, the city-state of Gwadar, was ceded to Pakistan in return for a monetary settlement.

Growing British influence was consolidated by the formation of a British protectorate in 1891, reconfirmed in 1951. In the 1950's Britain aided the sultanate in putting down rebellions in the desert interior. The British protectorate ended with Britain's withdrawal from the gulf in 1971. On July 23, 1970, Sultan Said ibn Taimur was overthrown by his son, Sultan Qaboos bin Said, who instituted a national development program and in 1975 defeated a leftist uprising in the western desert.

Petroleum makes up 95 percent of exports. Banking and shipping services are also important. The country is generally barren, with scattered flocks of sheep and camels. In April 1996 Oman joined with Russia and Kazakhstan to establish a consortium with eight oil companies to build a 900 mile pipeline to move oil to Russia's port in the Black Sea.

▶PAKISTAN

Islamic Republic of Pakistan

• GEOGRAPHY **Location:** southern Asia. **Boundaries**: Afghanistan to N, China to far NE, India to E, Arabian Sea to S, and Iran to W. **Total area**: 310,402 sq. mi. (803,940 sq km). **Coastline**: 650 mi. (1,046 km). **Comparative area**: slightly less than twice the size of California. **Land use:** 28% arable land; 1% permanent crops; 71% other. **Major cities**: (1991 est.) Islamabad (capital) 400,000; Karachi 7,000,000; Lahore 3,500,000; Faisalabad (Lyallpur) 2,000,000; Rawalpindi 800,000.

• PEOPLE **Population:** 150,694,740 (2003 est.). **Nationality:** noun—Pakistani(s); adjective—Pakistani. **Ethnic groups:** Punjabi, Sindhi, Pashtun (Pathan), Baloch, Muhajir (immigrants from India and their descendants). **Languages:** 48% Punjabi, 12% Sindhi, 10% Siraiki, 8% Pashtu, 8% Urdu (official), 3% Balochi, 2% Hindko, 1% Brahui, English (official and lingua franca of Pakistani elite and most government ministries), 8% Burushaski and other. **Religions:** 97% Muslim (77% Sunni, 20% Shi'a); 3% Christian, Hindu, and other.

• GOVERNMENT **Type:** federal republic. **Independence:** Aug. 14, 1947 (from U.K.). **Constitution:** Apr. 10, 1973; suspended July 5, 1977; restored Dec. 30, 1985; suspended Oct. 15, 1999, restored Dec. 31, 2002. **National holiday:** Republic Day, Mar. 23. **Heads of Government:** General Pervez Musharraf, president (since June 2001); Zafarullah Khan Jamali (since Nov. 22, 2002). **Structure:** executive—prime minister is head of government; bicameral legislature—dissolved after military takeover; judiciary.

• ECONOMY **Monetary unit:** Pakistani rupee. **Budget:** (FY02est.) ***income:*** $12.6 bil.; ***expend.:*** $14.8 bil. **GDP:** $311 bil., $2,100 per capita (2002 est.). **Chief crops:** wheat, rice, sugarcane, cotton; beef, milk, mutton, eggs. **Natural resources:** land, extensive natural gas reserves, limited petroleum, poor quality coal, iron ore. **Major industries:** cotton textiles, food processing. **Labor force:** 40.4 mil.; 44% agriculture, 17% mining and manufacturing, 39% services; extensive export of labor, mostly to the Middle East, and use of child labor. **Exports:** $9.8 bil. (f.o.b., FY02/03); cotton, textiles, clothing, rice, leather, carpets. **Imports:** $11.1 bil. (f.o.b., FY02); petroleum, petroleum products, machinery, transportation equipment, cooking oils. **Major trading partners:** ***exports:*** 27% U.S., 8% UAE; ***imports:*** **13% UAE,** 12% Saudi Arabia.

Pakistan occupies the heartland of ancient South Asian civilization, in the Indus River valley. Agricultural settlements in that area arose by 3000 B.C., and the great cities at Harappa and Mohenjo-Daro were founded some 500 years later. Indo-European (Aryan) invaders from Central Asia overthrew the ancient civilization around 1500 B.C. and established a new culture that spread throughout Pakistan and northern India. Brahmanism, the religious culture of the early Indo-European invaders, gave rise to Buddhism and Jainism around the sixth century B.C., and evolved into Hinduism in the early centuries A.D. The Indus valley was incorporated into the empire of Alexander the Great, c. 350 B.C., and then into the Mauryan empire of Asoka, which by the third century B.C. controlled all of South Asia except for the southernmost portion of India.

Under various rulers the Indus Valley and the areas to its northwest were a great center of Buddhist culture until the beginning of the eighth century, when the area fell to Muslim Arab invaders. Thereafter, Islam was firmly established throughout the region. But Baluchistan and the Northwest Frontier region became culturally allied to the Persian civilization of Iran and Afghanistan, while Sind and the Punjab were more closely akin to the culture of northern India.

Northern Pakistan was incorporated into the empire of Mahmud of Gazni in the 11th century, and fell to the Mongols in the 13th century. The Indus River became the boundary between the Mongol Inkhanate of Persia and the sultanate of Delhi. The region was conquered by Timur Leng at the end of the 14th century, and after the fall of the Timurid empire was divided between the kingdoms of Sind and Multan, in southern and central Pakistan, and the sultanate of Delhi, in the Punjab. All of Pakistan and northern India was reunited after 1526, when the conquests of Babur established the Mogul empire.

The expansion of British power in India during the 18th century left Pakistan largely untouched; the area was divided among various states, including Sind, the Punjab, Kashmir, and the western reaches of Rajputana. In the first half of the 19th century, British rule extended to the northwest; after the defeat of the Indian Mutiny of 1857, the entire Indus valley came under British rule. Sind and the Punjab were ruled directly by the British, while the native states were ruled as British protectorates.

From the beginning of the 20th century, various nationalist movements arose throughout British India. The Muslim League, under the leadership of Mohammad Ali Jinnah after 1916, advocated greater popular political participation, dominion status for India, and a strong Muslim voice in Indian administration. Muslims and Hindus were allied in the Non-Cooperation movement of the 1920's, but the alliance soon broke down and degenerated into communal frictions. With growing power of the Congress party in Hindu areas and Gandhi's civil disobedience movement in the 1930's, Jinnah's Muslim League charted an increasingly separate course and called for the creation of a separate Muslim state in 1940.

With the British withdrawal from India in 1947, Hindus in the Muslim majority areas of the Indus valley and in East Bengal fled to Hindu northern India, while Muslims in Hindu areas fled in the opposite direction. These massive population movements were accompanied by widespread violence leading to the loss of hundreds of thousands of lives. Jinnah, the father of modern Pakistan, died in 1948. Pakistan, encompassing Sind, the Punjab, Baluchistan, the Northwest Frontier Territories, part of Jammu and Kashmir, and adjacent areas in the west and East Bengal in the east, was granted dominion status within the British Commonwealth in 1947, becoming an independent republic in 1956.

Pakistan joined the Central Treaty Organization and became allied with the West, in contrast to the Soviet-leaning nonalignment of India. In 1958 Gen. Mohammad Ayub Khan seized power in a coup; he was elected president in 1960 and re-elected in 1965. Following border clashes with

India in 1962, Pakistan entered into friendly relations with China, which also had engaged in border warfare with India. Ayub Khan resigned as president in early 1969 after failing to put down widespread demonstrations in East Pakistan. A new government was formed under Gen. Yahya Khan, and martial law was declared. A parliamentary victory by the East Pakistani Awami League in December 1970 led to civil war and the secession of East Pakistan in 1971 (see "Bangladesh").

India's intervention on behalf of East Bengal had led to war on a western front with Pakistan. On July 3, 1972, India and Pakistan agreed to a mutual withdrawal of troops and entered into negotiations designed to settle border disputes and other problems. Diplomatic relations between India and Pakistan were resumed in 1976.

The elections of 1970 that had precipitated the civil war also brought Zulfikar Ali Bhutto to the presidency. He remained in office until July 1977, when he was overthrown in a military coup led by Gen. Mohammad Zia ul-Haq. He was convicted of complicity in a 1974 political murder and hanged in April 1979. Under Pres. Zia, Pakistan moved toward the implementation of Islamic law in parallel with the constitutional law of Pakistan's parliamentary system. In 1986 Bhutto's daughter, Benazir Bhutto, returned to Pakistan from exile in Europe to organize opposition parties against Pres. Zia, leading to widespread rioting.

On Aug. 17, 1988, Pres. Zia was killed in an airplane crash. From 1988 to 1999 the position of prime minister alternated between Benazir Bhutto as head of the Pakistan People's Party and Nawaz Sharif as leader of the Muslim League, each accusing the other in turn of tyranny and corruption, amidst endless tension with India over Jammu-Kashmir. The latter struggle lay at the root of the nuclear-test rivalry in May 1998, after which the prime ministers, Vajpayee and Sharif, attempted to lower the political temperature while not appearing to "cave in" to the other. Sharif's July 1999 agreement in Washington D.C. to withdraw support for Muslims in Kashmir made it appear that he was the one to blink first.

Sharif's dismissal of Gen. Musharraf over the army's support of Kashmir rebels led to a military coup and Sharif's trial on corruption charges which ended April 6, 2000 with a guilty verdict and a sentence of life imprisonment. Musharraf pledged a return to civilian rule within three years, but in June 2001 appointed himself president.

Musharraf has had to walk a delicate line after the Sept. 11th attacks on the U.S. Backing the U.S. in Afghanistan, he fired his three top generals (and closest advisers) for their ties to the Taliban and arrested leaders of demonstrations against the war in Afghanistan. In Dec. he denounced a murderous Pakistani Muslim attack on the Indian Parliament, even as he continued to deploy troops along the Indian border. By June 2002 India was admitting a sharp drop in the number of incursions and war seemed somewhat less likely. In Oct. Pakistan held its first elections since 1997, with Musharraf's party gaining a plurality and enough other support to elect Mir jamali as prime minister. In the same month both India and pakistan announced troop withdrawals from their borders (though not the Kasmir border). And in May 2003 Musharrif reciprocated India's dicision to restore diplomatic and rail links between the two countries.

▶PALAU

Republic of Palau

• **GEOGRAPHY** **Location:** more than 200 islands, in a chain about 400 mi. (650 km) long, in western central Pacific Ocean; Koror 71°21'N, 134°31'E. **Boundaries**: Guam 720 mi. (1,160 km) to NE, Federated States of Micronesia to E, island of New Guinea to S, Philippines 530 mi. (850 km) to NW. **Total area**: 177 sq. mi. (458 sq km). **Coastline**: 944 mi. (1,519 km). **Comparative area**: slightly more than 2.5 times size of Washington, D.C. **Land use:** 22% arable land; 0% permanent crops; 78% other. **Major cities**: (1990 census) Koror state 10,501; Koror is the current capital; a new capital is being built at Babelthuap, 20 km northeast.

• **PEOPLE** **Population:** 19,092 (2001 est.). **Nationality:** noun—Palauan(s); adjective—Palauan. **Ethnic groups:** composite of Polynesian, Malayan, and Melanesian races. **Languages:** English (official) in all 16 states; Palauan (official) in 13 states; Sonsoralese, Angaur, Japanese, Tobi in one state each. **Religions:** Christian (49% Roman Catholic, Seventh-Day Adventist, Jehovah's Witness, the Assembly of God, the Liebenzell Mission, and Latter-Day Saints), 33% Modekngei (indigenous faith).

• **GOVERNMENT** **Type:** constitutional government in free association with the U.S.; the Compact of Free Association entered into force Oct. 1, 1994. **Independence:** Oct. 1, 1994 (from U.S.-administered U.N. Trusteeship). **Constitution:** Jan. 1, 1981. **National holiday:** Constitution Day, July 9. **Heads of Government:** Tommy E. Remengesau, Jr., president (since Jan. 2001). **Structure:** executive—president and vice president popularly elected; legislative—bicameral legislature; judicial—Supreme Court headed by chief justice.

• **ECONOMY** **Monetary unit:** U.S. dollar. **Budget:** (FY98/99 est.) ***income:*** $57.7 mil.; ***expend.:*** $80.8 mil. **GDP:** $174 mil., $9,000 per capita (2001 est.). **Chief crops:** coconuts, copra, cassava, sweet potatoes. **Livestock:** N.A. **Natural resources:** forests, minerals (especially gold), marine products, deep-seabed minerals. **Major industries:** tourism, craft items (shell, wood, pearl), some commercial fishing and agriculture. **Labor force:** 9,845 (2000). **Exports:** $18 mil. (f.o.b., 2001); trochus, tuna, copra, handicrafts. **Imports:** $99 mil. (f.o.b., 2001). **Major trading partners:** U.S., Japan.

The first inhabitants of Palau (or Belau) probably arrived from Indonesia and the Philippines about 1500 B.C. The first European to visit the area was Ferdinand Magellan, in 1521. However, it was the British who dominated trade to Palau until 1885, when Pope Leo XIII acknowledged Spain's claims to the Carolines. Spain controlled Palau from 1885 to 1899, when it sold the territory to Germany. The Germans introduced coconut planting and phosphate mining, and introduced sanitary measures that arrested the deadly epidemics of dysentery and influenza, which over 120 years had reduced the population from 40,000 to 4,000.

Japan occupied Palau in 1914, and over the next 30 years increased the mining, agriculture, and fishing industries. In 1938, Palau became a closed military area, and it was the site of heavy fighting during World War II. On July 18, 1947, the United Nations Trusteeship Council placed the Trust Territory of the Pacific Islands, including Palau, under U.S. authority. This trusteeship ended on Oct. 1, 1994, when the Compact of Free Association with the United States (approved by the voters of Palau) went into effect, making Palau an independent country in association with the United States. The United States continues to provide for Palau's defense and to provide aid. In return, the

United States has the right to dock military vessels (including nuclear-powered vessels) in the islands for 50 years, and will consult closely on economic and environmental matters.

▶PANAMA

Republic of Panama

• GEOGRAPHY **Location:** southern Central America. **Boundaries**: Caribbean Sea to N, Colombia to E, Pacific Ocean to S, Costa Rica to W. **Total area**: 30,193 sq. mi. (78,200 sq km). **Coastline**: 1,546 mi. (2,490 km). **Comparative area**: slightly smaller than South Carolina. **Land use:** 7% arable land; 2% permanent crops; 91% other. **Major cities**: (1992 est.) Panamá (Panama City—capital) 625,150; Colón 137,825; David 99,811.

• PEOPLE **Population:** 2,960,784 (2003 est.). **Nationality:** noun—Panamanian(s); adjective—Panamanian. **Ethnic groups:** 70% mestizo, 14% Amerindian and mixed (West Indian), 10% white, 6% Amerindian. **Languages:** Spanish (official), 14% speak English as native tongue; many Panamanians are bilingual. **Religions:** 85% Roman Catholic, 15% Protestant.

• GOVERNMENT **Type:** constitutional democracy. **Independence:** Nov. 3, 1903 (from Colombia); became independent from Spain Nov. 28, 1821. **Constitution:** Oct. 11, 1972, with major reforms adopted in Apr. 1983 and in 1994. **National holiday:** Independence Day, Nov. 3. **Head of Government:** Mireya Elisa Moscoso Rodríguez, president (since Sept. 1999). **Structure:** executive—president, two vice presidents, cabinet; unicameral legislature; judiciary.

• ECONOMY **Monetary unit:** balboa. **Budget:** (2000) ***income:*** $1.9 bil.; ***expend.:*** $2 bil. **GDP:** $17.3 bil., $6,000 per capita (2002 est.). **Chief crops:** bananas, rice, sugarcane, coffee, corn; livestock, fishing. **Natural resources:** copper, mahogany forests, shrimp. **Major industries:** manufacturing and construction, petroleum refining, brewing, cement and other construction material. **Labor force:** 1.1 mil. (2000 est.); 20.8% agriculture, 18% industry, 61% services. **Exports:** $5.8 bil. (f.o.b., 2002 est.); bananas, shrimp, clothing, sugar, coffee. **Imports:** $6.7 bil. (f.o.b., 2000 est.); capital goods, crude oil, foodstuffs. **Major trading partners:** ***exports:*** 50% U.S., 5% Nicaragua, 5% Sweden; ***imports:*** 33% U.S., 7% Ecuador, 7% Venezuela.

The Spanish first arrived in what is now Panama in 1501. Vasco Nuñez de Balboa returned in 1510, and Pedro Arias Dávila founded the City of Panama in 1519. Panama became attached to the viceroyalty of New Granada after 1739 and left the Spanish empire with the rest of New Granada in 1821, becoming a part of Gran Colombia. The first canal company proposing the construction of a transisthmian passageway was formed in 1825-26. The completion of a U.S.-financed railway from Colón to Panama City by 1855 enhanced Panama's importance as a transoceanic passage.

Panamanian nationalists waged a "War of a Thousand Days" against the Bogotá government between 1899 and 1902. In 1903 Panama gained independence from Colombia with U.S. complicity. Within a month Panamanian officials accepted an agreement with the United States that created a canal zone under the control of the U.S. government "in perpetuity," and the Panama Canal was completed and opened in 1914.

Panama experienced protectorate status under U.S. control after independence insofar as the United States "guaranteed the independence" of Panama. The United States explicitly upheld its right of unilateral military intervention in Panama when in 1918 it sent troops there without the permission of the Panamanian government. The 1936 Hull-Alvaro Treaty eliminated protectorate status, and the U.S. dropped its claim to a right of intervention in the cities of Panama and Colón.

In 1968 a power struggle between Pres. Arnulfo Arias and the Panamanian National Guard led to the ouster of the president. A National Guard junta took control of the government, and Col. (later Gen.) Omar Torrijos Herrera became the ruler of the country the following year. In 1972 a new assembly under Torrijos's control offered him the title of Jefe Maximo (chief executive) in addition to drafting a new constitution for the country. Torrijos constructed a populist following through the creation of housing projects, a new labor code, an agrarian reform, and an increase in tax rates imposed on foreign banana-interests.

The Panamanian government and the U.S. concluded a new canal treaty in 1977, the key provisions of which included integration of the Canal Zone with the rest of Panamanian territory and full Panamanian control of the canal in 2000. In 1981 Omar Torrijos died in an air accident.

In 1988 the head of the military and de facto ruler of the country, Gen. Mañuel Noriega, was indicted in the U.S. on narcotics charges. But Noriega refused to submit to demands by the U.S. and by Panamanian president Eric Arturo Delvalle for his resignation. Delvalle was forced to go into hiding, and Manuel Solis Palma replaced him in the presidency. The United States responded by freezing Panamanian assets in the United States.

In May 1989 Gen. Noriega annulled election results that showed him losing to Guillermo Endara and assumed the role of dictator. After an unsuccessful coup attempt, the United States invaded Panama on December 20, captured Noriega, and brought him to Miami, where he was convicted on narcotics charges. Endara was restored to the presidency and in December 1990 U.S. forces helped put down a rebellion led by Noriega's former chief of the national police.

Endara's government was often accused of corruption but he left power peacefully in 1994. He helped to arrange honest elections that saw U.S.-educated businessman Ernesto Perez Balladares come to power with promises of improving the economy as Panama prepared to take over control of the canal. His free market reforms and a loosening of trade barriers (Panama joined WTO in 1998) have brought strong growth in GDP. An August 1998 referendum turned down (by 64 percent) Perez' seeking a second term. Voters in May 1999 chose Mireya Moscoso de Grubar, widow of three-time president Arnulfo Arias, over Martin Torrijos, son of the dictator who negotiated the 1977 Canal Treaty with the U.S., as Panama's new president.

▶PAPUA NEW GUINEA

Independent State of Papua New Guinea

• GEOGRAPHY **Location:** eastern section of island of New Guinea and about 600 smaller islands in Bismarck Archipelago (New Britain, New Ireland, and Manus) and northern part of Solomon Islands. Port Moresby 9°30'S, 147°07'E. **Boundaries**: Bismarck Sea to N, Solomon Sea to E, Australia to S, and Indonesia to W. **Total area**: 178,259 sq. mi. (461,690 sq km). **Coastline**: 3,202 mi. (5,152 km). **Comparative area**: slightly larger than California. **Land use:** negl.% arable land; 1% permanent crops; 99% other. **Major cities**: (1990 est.) Port Moresby (administrative capital) 173,500.

• PEOPLE **Population:** 5,295,815 (2003 est.). **Na-**

tionality: noun—Papua New Guinean(s); adjective—Papua New Guinean. **Ethnic groups:** predominantly Melanesian and Papuan; some Negrito, Micronesian, and Polynesian. **Languages:** 715 indigenous languages; English spoken by 1%-2%, pidgin English widespread, Motu spoken in Papua region. **Religions:** 22% Roman Catholic, 16% Lutheran, 28% other Christian, 34% indigenous beliefs.

• **GOVERNMENT** **Type:** parliamentary democracy. **Independence:** Sept. 16, 1975 (from U.N. trusteeship under Australian administration). **Constitution:** Sept. 16, 1975. **National holiday:** Independence Day, Sept. 16. **Heads of Government:** Silas Atopare, governor-general (since Nov. 1997); Sir Michael T. Somare, prime minister (since Aug. 2002). **Structure:** executive—British monarch (represented by governor general), chief of state, prime minister; unicameral legislature; judiciary.

• **ECONOMY** **Monetary unit:** kina. **Budget:** (2000 est.) ***income:*** $894 mil.; ***expend.:*** $1.1 bil. **GDP:** $1.2 bil., $2,300 per capita (2002 est.). **Chief crops:** cocoa, coffee, coconuts, rubber, palm kernels; pigs, chickens. **Natural resources:** gold, copper, silver, natural gas, timber. **Major industries:** copra crushing, palmoil processing, plywood processing. **Labor force:** 1.941 mil., 85% agriculture. **Exports:** $1.8 bil. (f.o.b., 2002 est.); gold, copper ore, oil, logs, coffee, palm oil, cocoa, lobster. **Imports:** $1.1 bil. (f.o.b, 2002 est.); machinery and transport equipment, manufactured goods, food, fuels, chemicals. **Major trading partners:** ***exports:*** 24% Australia, 10% Japan, 4% China; ***imports:*** 50% Australia, 20% Singapore, 5% New Zealand.

The island of New Guinea, the world's second-largest, was settled many thousands of years ago by waves of Papuan and Melanesian migrants who developed large numbers of linguistically diverse and mutually hostile tribes of hunters and small cultivators. In the 19th century, the island was divided between the Dutch (to the west, in what is now the Indonesian province of Irian Jaya), Germany, and the British. The German sector was occupied by Australia in 1914 and administered under a League of Nations mandate after World War I.

Japanese attempts to occupy New Guinea in 1942 met with only partial success. In a series of counteroffensives, the Allies regained control over the entire island by mid-1944.

Beginning in 1949 the former German and British colonies were administered by Australia under a U.N. mandate. The territories were made self-governing in 1973 and achieved full independence as Papua New Guinea on Sept. 16, 1975. The nation maintains close ties with Australia.

Most of the population is still engaged in small-scale agriculture. Mining is a major source of foreign investment and export earnings. In 1989 a rebellion on the mineral-rich island of Bougainville closed a large Australian-run copper mine, led to the deaths of many people and frightened away foreign investors. Violence lasted until 1998 and talks to resolve secessionist issues were still going in 2002.

An inexplicable decision to recognize Taiwan rather than mainland China, made in 1999 by prime minister Bill Skate, brought domestic (as well as Chinese) opposition, Skate's resignation, and the designation of Sir Mekere Morauta as the new prime minister. He immediately reversed the Taiwan agreement. In Feb. 2000 the government began a program of privatizing all state-owned enterprise within three years. In 2002 elections, violence kept the country without a government for three months until three-time prime minister Michael Somare was able to form a government.

▶PARAGUAY

Republic of Paraguay

• **GEOGRAPHY** **Location:** landlocked country in central South America. **Boundaries:** Bolivia to N, Brazil to E, Argentina to S and W. **Total area:** 157,046 sq. mi. (406,750 sq km). **Coastline:** none. **Comparative area:** slightly smaller than California. **Land use:** 6% arable land; 0% permanent crops; 94% other. **Major cities:** (1992 census) Asunción (capital) 637,737; Ciudad del Este (formerly Presidente Stroessner) 133,893; Pedro Juan Caballero (1982) 37,331; Encarnación (1982) 27,632; Villarrica (1982) 21,203.

• **PEOPLE** **Population:** 6,036,900 (July 2003 est.). **Nationality:** noun—Paraguayan(s); adjective—Paraguayan. **Ethnic groups:** 95% mestizo (mixed white and Amerindian). **Languages:** Spanish (official), Guaraní. **Religions:** 90% Roman Catholic, Mennonite and other Protestant denominations.

• **GOVERNMENT** **Type:** constitutional republic. **Independence:** May 14, 1811 (from Spain). **Constitution:** June 20, 1992. **National holiday:** Independence Day, May 14. **Head of Government:** Nicanor Duarte Frutos, president (since Aug. 15, 2003). **Structure:** president heads executive; bicameral legislature (Senate, Chamber of Deputies); judiciary.

• **ECONOMY** **Monetary unit:** guarani. **Budget:** (1999 est.) ***income:*** $1.3 bil.; ***expend.:*** $2 bil. **GDP:** $25 bil., $4,200 per capita (2002 est.). **Chief crops:** sugarcane, soybeans, cotton, wheat; beef, pork; timber. **Natural resources:** iron ore, manganese, limestone, hydropower, timber. **Major industries:** sugar, cement, textiles, beverages. **Labor force:** 2 mil. (2000 est.); 45% agriculture; 18% unemployment (2002 est.). **Exports:** $2 bil. (f.o.b., 2002 est.); cotton, soybeans, timber, vegetable oils, feed, tung oil. **Imports:** $2.4 bil. (f.o.b., 2002 est.); consumer goods, tobacco, raw materials, fuels. **Major trading partners:** ***exports:*** Brazil, Uruguay; ***imports:*** Brazil, Argentina, Uruguay.

When Europeans arrived in what is now Paraguay in the early 16th century, they encountered various groups of indigenous peoples. The Spanish entered into alliances with the Tupian semisedentary Guaraní against the nomadic Guaycuru Indians in the west of the region. Asunción, founded in 1537, was little more than a Spanish defense outpost against the Portuguese and a trading stopover between the silver mines of Potosí and Buenos Aires.

From early in the 17th century, the Jesuits established an extensive network of missions in the southern portion of the colony, and a rivalry grew between the Jesuits and the elites of Asunción over who would determine the colony's social and economic structure. The isolation of the settlers from the mainstream of Spanish colonial society combined with the lack of valuable resources led to the evolution of a relatively egalitarian social structure. The political elite of Asunción deposed Spanish authority in 1811, and Paraguayan independence was declared in 1813.

Authoritarian rule marked the period from independence until 1870. José Gaspar Rodríguez de Francia was declared ruler for life in 1816 and remained in power until his death in 1840. A period of political turmoil followed but was resolved in the election of Carlos Antonio López in 1844; in 1857 he was named president for life. López chose his son Francisco Solano López to succeed him in office in 1862. He intervened in a Brazilian attempt to control the fate of Uruguay, beginning the Paraguayan War, or the War of the Triple Alliance (Brazil, Argentina, Uruguay) from 1865 to 1870. The war was catastrophic for Paraguay, reducing the population from 450,000 to 220,000; and Paraguay lost 60,000 square miles of territory while being saddled with a war debt of 19 million gold pesos ($200,000,000), later dropped as unrealistic.

After the war the Colorado and Liberal parties developed, although the real political distinctions were dependent more on individuals and families than political ideology. Colorado-party general Bernardino Caballero, backed by Brazil, was the power behind the scenes of frequent changes in government personnel between 1874 and 1904. The Liberals, backed by Argentina, were in power from 1904 until 1936.

After 18 years of authoritarian military rule, Gen. Alfredo Stroessner, with the backing of Colorado party factions, began his rule in 1954. Stroessner held power until 1989, when Gen. Andrés Rodríguez overthrew him. Nevertheless, the Colorados maintained their hold on the presidency in hotly contested elections in 1993, when Juan Carlos Wasmosy gained 40 percent of the vote. However, a strong showing by the opposition Authentic Radical Liberal Party (PLRA) and National Encounter prevented a Colorado majority in Congress. A complex political struggle between Pres. Wasmosy and Lino Oviedo, one of the generals who overthrew Stroessner, led to Oviedo's imprisonment. His ally, Raul Cubas Grau, won the 1998 election by vowing to have Oviedo share power even from prison. Three days after taking office in August, however, Cubas released the popular general, causing an outburst of hostility among Congressional leaders.

In March 1999, the vice president was assassinated, Congress accusing Cubas and Oviedo. Impeached the next day, Cubas remanded Oviedo to state custody but refused to appear at his own trial in the Senate. Oviedo fled to Argentina, Cubas to Brazil. Congress named the president of the Senate, Luis Gonzalez Macchi, as president. Gonzalez appointed a cabinet with four opposition members among the 10, the first coalition since 1946. A coup attempt by Oviedo allies was foiled in May 2000. Three weeks later, Oviedo was arrested in Brazil.

In Feb. 2003 the senate tried, but failed, to impeach Gonzalez on corruption charges. Still the Colorado party candidate Nicanor Duarte Frutes won the presidential election in April thus continuing the political dominance of the party that has ruled Paraguay since 1947.

▶PERU

Republic of Peru

• **GEOGRAPHY** **Location:** western coast of South America. **Boundaries**: Ecuador, Colombia to N, Brazil, Bolivia to E, Chile to S, Pacific Ocean to W. **Total area**: 496,224 sq. mi. (1,285,220 sq km). **Coastline**: 1,546 mi. (2,414 km). **Comparative area**: slightly smaller than Alaska. **Land use:** 3% arable land; negl. % permanent crops; 97% other. **Major cities**: (1993 est.) Lima (capital) 5,706,127; Arequipa 619,156; Trujillo 509,312; Chiclayo 411,536; Callao 3699,768.

• **PEOPLE** **Population:** 28,409,897 (2003 est.). **Nationality:** noun—Peruvian(s); adjective—Peruvian. **Ethnic groups:** 45% Amerindian, 37% mestizo, 15% white, 3% black, Japanese, Chinese, and other. **Languages:** Spanish and Quechua (official), Aymara. **Religions:** 90% Roman Catholic.

• **GOVERNMENT** **Type:** constitutional republic. **Independence:** July 28, 1821 (from Spain). **Constitution:** Dec. 31, 1993. **National holiday:** Independence Day, July 28. **Heads of Government:** Alejandro Toledo Manrique, president (since July 2001); Beatriz Merino Lucero, prime minister (since July 28, 2003). **Structure:** executive; unicameral legislature; judiciary.

• **ECONOMY** **Monetary unit:** nuevo sol. **Budget:** (2002 est.) ***income:*** $10.4 bil.; ***expend.:*** $10.4 bil. **GDP:** $132 bil., $4,800 per capita (2002 est.). **Chief crops:** coffee, cotton, sugarcane, rice, poultry, meat, wool; fish. **Natural resources:** copper, silver, gold, petroleum, timber. **Major industries:** mining of metals, petroleum, fishing. **Labor force:** 7.6 mil. (1996); agriculture, mining and quarrying, manufacturing, construction, transport, services; 9.4% unemployment (2002 est.). **Exports:** $7.6 bil. (f.o.b., 2002 est.); copper, zinc, gold, petroleum. **Imports:** $7.3 bil. (f.o.b., 2002 est.); machinery, transport equipment, foodstuffs, petroleum. **Major trading partners:** ***exports:*** 25% U.S., 8% Switzerland, 6% China; ***imports:*** 24% U.S., 8% China, 6% Venezuela.

Peru was the site of the civilization of the Inca empire before the arrival of Europeans. The Incas had extended their control over most of the Andean region by the late 15th century. The civilization was advanced in terms of its ability to provide for the welfare of its subjects and was in possession of sophisticated knowledge in a number of fields, including medicine. By the time of the arrival of the Spanish conqueror Francisco Pizarro in 1532, the empire was already in decline, and a combination of plague and civil war in the decade prior to the appearance of Europeans no doubt made the empire more vulnerable to Spanish conquest. Inca resistance to Spanish domination was not quelled until the execution of Tupac Amarú in 1571. European-borne diseases such as smallpox and measles devastated the Indian population of the region.

Because of the great wealth of precious metals discovered by the Spanish and the adaptability of a sedentary indigenous civilization to the imposition of Spanish imperial control, Peru quickly became a major focal point of Spanish colonialism; they founded Lima in 1535. The viceroyalty of Peru, established in 1544, originally served as the political and administrative nerve center of Spanish colonization of South America. For nearly two centuries, Lima was the seat of power and wealth for the whole region. Peru was "liberated" by Simón Bolívar and José de San Martín in 1821 when Bolívar's army defeated the royalist forces at the battles of Junín and Ayacucho.

In the 40 years after independence, the presidency changed hands 35 times, and the country generated at least 15 different constitutions. Only four of the presidents of the period were constitutionally chosen, and the vast majority were military figures. In 1829 Peru tried and failed to annex Ecuador; in the 1830's an attempt at political federation between Peru and Bolivia collapsed with the Chilean invasion of 1839.

A political movement in favor of civilian rule, the Civilistas, began to organize by the 1860's. Chile defeated Peru in the War of the Pacific (1879-83), and Chileans occupied Lima and its port city of Callao for two years. The Peruvian government was deeply in debt after the war, resulting in the loss of ownership of much of Peru's infrastructure and natural resources to foreigners.

Peru experienced a period of civilian leadership between 1895 and 1930. Pres. Augusto B. Leguía (1908-12, 1919-30) extended his rule in an extra-constitutional manner until 1930, when Col. Luis Sánchez Cerro seized power; he ruled until his assassination in 1933. Gen. Oscar Benavides succeeded Cerro and managed to restore confidence in the economy. In 1939 civilian banker Manuel Prado was elected to the presidency, and the military allowed him to complete his term in office, which expired in 1945. During Prado's administration, Peru went to war with Ecuador and was victorious, seizing a great deal of territory.

Víctor Raúl Haya de la Torre founded Peru's most prominent political party, the American Popular Revolutionary Alliance (APRA), in 1924. As initiated, the party put forward an "anti-imperialist" platform aiming at nationalization of land and reconstruction of society in favor of oppressed people. Haya de la Torre was apparently fraudulently deprived of a presidential electoral victory in 1931. The following year Apristas (APRA supporters) seized Trujillo and killed some military personnel. By way of revenge, the army massacred 6,000 Apristas. The result was a continuing enmity between the Peruvian armed forces and the APRA party lasting until the 1980's. Although APRA clearly had majority support, the party was not allowed to take power until 1985.

The Peruvian military, led by Gen. Juan Velasco Alvarado, seized power in 1968 and embarked upon a course of reform that included the nationalization of Standard Oil's International Petroleum Company holdings. The Peruvian military took steps to restructure economic and political power in the country by joining the Andean Pact and undermining the power of the traditional agricultural elite in the country by sponsoring an agrarian reform that mobilized peasant sectors of the population.

The presidency of Peru returned to civilian leadership under Fernando Belaúnde Terry (1980-85). In 1985, the military allowed the APRA presidential candidate, Alan García Pérez, to take office. García promised to spend no more than 10 percent of the country's export earnings on payment of Peru's huge outstanding foreign debt and he was popular during his first years in office. But his public support was undermined by a growing insurgency sponsored by the Sendero Luminoso ("Shining Path") Maoist guerrillas and by runaway inflation.

On June 10, 1990, political novice Alberto Fujimori, the son of Japanese immigrants, defeated the well-known writer Mario Vargas Llosa for the presidency. Throughout 1991 and 1992, Shining Path's influence spread, demoralizing and almost paralyzing the government, and at a cost of 25,000 lives. But in April 1992, Fujimori implemented a "zero tolerance" policy toward terrorism, dissolving the legislature and proclaiming martial law. The capture in September of Abimael Guzmán Reynoso, Path's founder-leader, broke the back of the insurgency. The movement lived on, but diminished in numbers.

Meanwhile, economically, Fujimori pursued free-market reforms, taming runaway inflation and privatizing state-run dinosaurs, so that by 1994 the Peruvian economy was growing at a rate of 12 percent, fastest in the world. In April of that year, Fujimoro was elected to a second term with 64 percent of the vote.

The dramatic liberation in April 1997 of 600 prisoners held for ransom in the Japanese ambassador's compound by another radical terrorist group maintained the president's repute. In Nov. 1997, Peru completed negotiations with Ecuador (the treaty being signed in Oct. of 1998) ending a 50-year old border conflict. But all these achievements were accompanied by a rather ham-handed authoritarian streak which cost Fujimori much esteem. In elections for Congress, held in April 2000, his Peru 2000 party carried a plurality of seats but he himself just failed of a majority in the presidential race. A week before the May 28 run-off, his remaining opponent withdrew, claiming the election was a fraud; the final tally brought Fujimori only 51 percent. His July 28 inauguration was marred by serious rioting, with six dead and many public buildings in Lima burnt. While in Japan, Fujimori resigned, but Congress refused to accept, so it could remove him for abandoning office and dereliction of duty.

In June 2001, in a close run-off against former president Alan Garcia, Alejandro Toledo was elected president, the first Indian elected president in Peru's history. he was able to decentralize the government in 2002 and sucessfully prosecute Fujimori's right-hand ma, but strikes by teachers and farmers in 2003 led to a state of emergency and the use of troops to bring order.

▶PHILIPPINES

Republic of the Philippines

• **GEOGRAPHY Location:** archipelago of some 7,100 islands about 500 mi. (800 km) off southeastern Asia; about 1,100 mi. (2,800 km) from N to S and 650 mi. (1,684 km) from W to E; Luzon in N and Mindanao in S account for 66% of land area. Manila 14°36'N, 120°59'E. **Boundaries**: Luzon Strait to N, Philippine Sea to E, Celebes Sea to S, Sulu Sea to SW, and South China Sea to W. **Total area**: 115,830 sq. mi. (300,000 sq km). **Coastline**: 22,554 mi. (36,289 km). **Comparative area**: slightly larger than Arizona. **Land use:** 18% arable land; 15% permanent crops; 67% other. **Major cities**: (1990 census) Manila (capital) 1,598,918; Quezon City 1,666,766; Davao City 849,947; Caloocan City 761,011; Cebu City 610,417.

• **PEOPLE Population:** 84,619,974 (2003 est.). **Nationality:** noun—Filipino(s); adjective—Philippine. **Ethnic groups:** 91.5% Christian Malay, 4% Muslim Malay, 1.5% Chinese, 3% other. **Languages:** Pilipino (based on Tagalog) and English (both official). **Religions:** 83% Roman Catholic, 9% Protestant, 5% Muslim, 3% Buddhist and other.

• **GOVERNMENT Type:** republic. **Independence:** July 4, 1946 (from U.S.). **Constitution:** Feb. 2, 1987, effective Feb. 11, 1987. **National holiday:** Independence Day, June 12. **Head of Government:** Gloria Macapagal-Arroyo, president (since Jan. 2001). **Structure:** executive; bicameral legislature; judiciary.

• **ECONOMY Monetary unit:** Philippine peso. **Budget:** (2002) ***income:*** $10.9 bil.; ***expend.:*** $15 bil. **GDP:** $356 bil., $4,200 per capita (2002 est.). **Chief crops:** rice, corn, coconut, sugarcane, bananas; pork, eggs, beef; fish. **Natural resources:** timber, crude oil, nickel, cobalt, silver. **Major industries:** textiles, pharmaceuticals, chemicals. **Labor force:** 33.7 mil. (2002 est.); 39.8% agriculture, 19.4% government services, 17.7% services; 10.2% unemployment (2002). **Exports:** $35.1 bil. (f.o.b., 2002 est.); electronics and telecommunications, machinery and transport, garments. **Imports:** $33.5 bil. (f.o.b., 2002 est.); raw materials and intermediate goods, capital goods, consumer goods, fuels. **Major trading partners: *exports:*** 28% U.S., 16% Japan, 6% Taiwan; ***imports:*** 23% Japan, 20% U.S.

The Philippines were anciently settled by various Malayan peoples in several waves of migration from Southeast Asia. Tribal societies coexisted with petty principalities that had trade links to China, the East Indies, and countries in the Indian Ocean. The Philippines were visited by Magellan (who was killed there) in 1521, and Spanish conquest of the islands began in 1564. The Spanish colonial capital at Manila was founded in 1571 and became a key transit point for trade between Mexico and the Far East. Under Spanish rule a majority of Filipinos became Christian except in the southwestern islands, which remained Muslim. The Spanish period was marked by a torpid colonial administration and a rise in the power and wealth of the Catholic church.

In the late 19th century, a nationalist movement led by José Rizal gained a wide following. In 1896 an armed uprising began, led by Emilio Aguinaldo. The 1898 victory of Adm. George Dewey at the Battle of Manila Bay during the Spanish-American War led Spain to cede the Philippines to the U.S. in return for a payment of $20 million. Expecting immediate independence with U.S. support, Aguinaldo declared the islands a republic. When this was not recognized by the U.S., Aguinaldo led a new war for independence, which was bloodily suppressed by American troops in a six-year campaign, 1899-1905.

American policy in the Philippines combined military control with a desire to encourage home rule leading to independence. In 1935 the Commonwealth of the Philippines was established, with Manuel Quezon as its first president, beginning what was conceived of as a 10-year period of controlled autonomy leading to full independence on July 4, 1946. In November 1941, Quezon was reelected to the presidency. On Dec.8, 1941, Japan attacked Manila and destroyed the American bases there. American and Filipino troops, after weeks of fierce fighting, evacuated the islands in March 1942. The battle to recapture the Philippines began with the Battle of Leyte Gulf in October 1944 and was completed by July 1945.

In April 1946, Manuel Roxas was elected president of the Commonwealth. Independence came as scheduled on July 4 of that year, with the United States retaining military bases by treaty and establishing a special economic relationship with the Philippines. The leftist Hukbalahap Rebellion, originally a partisan campaign against the Japanese, caused severe difficulties for the new nation until it was finally defeated in military campaigns led by Ramon Magsaysay who was elected to the presidency in November 1953.

The early years of independence were marked by some economic development, but also great economic inequality. Most land was held by huge estates, and the economy depended primarily on plantation crops (sugar, copra), mining, and timber. Villagers fleeing the rural subsistence economy poured into the cities, leading to huge slums and a climate of urban poverty and violence.

In 1966 Ferdinand Marcos was elected president on a reform platform. Overwhelmed in the early 1970's by demonstrations, a new leftist guerrilla movement, and a separatist rebellion by Islamic Moros in Mindinao, Marcos declared martial law on Sept. 21, 1972. On Jan. 17, 1973, Marcos promulgated a new constitution giving unprecedented power to the presidency. His wife, Imelda, began to wield considerable influence, and the climate of unrest, poverty, and corruption worsened throughout the 1970's. Martial law was lifted, however, on Jan. 17, 1981, and Marcos was reelected to a new six-year term as president.

The airport assassination of opposition leader Benigno Aquino on his return to the Philippines on Aug. 21, 1983, led to a new phase in opposition to Marcos's rule. In a bitterly contested presidential election in February 1986, Marcos was officially declared the winner over Aquino's widow, Corazon. Mrs. Aquino also declared herself the winner, and her supporters took to the streets in massive anti-Marcos demonstrations. Deserted by key supporters in the military, church, and middle class, Marcos fled the country on Feb. 25, 1986. Mrs. Aquino took office pledging land reform, a new constitution, and a commission to recover the wealth Marcos had plundered.

Under Pres. Aquino the Philippines remained unsettled. Her former ally, Vice Pres. Salvadore Laurel, formed an opposition party. Military and political measures aimed at putting down the Communist insurrection yielded mixed results. The economy of the Philippines continued to be dependent on U.S. and international assistance, and sentiment against the continued presence of U.S. military bases (Clark Air Base, Subic Bay Naval Base, and four smaller installations) was strong. Ironically, an eruption of Mount Pinatubo in June 1991 caused massive devastations in central Luzon and destroyed Clark Air Base. In September, the national legislature voted not to renew the leases on American military bases; the United States moved to close Subic Bay Naval Base.

Aquino declined to run for re-election in 1992. Fidel Ramos won the presidency in a field of strong contenders, including Imelda Marcos. Lifted by a coalition that gave him a controlling majority in both houses of Congress after the 1994 legislative elections, Ramos made "national reconciliation" his highest domestic priority. In 1994 he proclaimed a cease-fire and amnesty for various insurgencies.

The Philippines' robust economic growth was slowed but not crippled by the Asian economic crisis of 1997-98. After some hesitation, Pres. Ramos decided not to seek re-election in 1998; in a crowded field of candidates, Joseph Estrada, a popular actor, won the presidential election of May 11, 1998, but the ruling LAKAS party elected the vice-president and took control of the lower house. In 1998 the long-running dispute with China over the Spratly Islands heated up, the Philippine Navy sequestering Chinese fishing boats. A series of hostage crises with Muslim rebels on Mindanao punctuated the year 2000 but became overshadowed by serious bribery charges against Pres. Estrada. As the House of Representatives moved toward impeachment, gigantic demonstrations for and against Estrada brought reminders of the fall of Pres. Marcos. When the Senate in Jan. 2001 suspended the president's trial, the protests expanded to a general strike; and when the heads of the armed forces joined the protests, Estrada's days were through. Vice-president Gloria Macagapal Arroyo was sworn in as Estrada resigned. By May the anti-Estrada coalition controlled the Congress and Estrada was under arrest.

The U.S. war on terrorism arrived here in 2001–02 as 4,000 troops landed in Mindanao to train Phillipine soldiers for the fight against the Abu Sayyaf Muslim insurgency.

▶POLAND
Republic of Poland

• **GEOGRAPHY Location:** eastern Europe. **Boundaries**: Baltic Sea to N, Russia and Lithuania to NE, Belarus and Ukraine to E, Czech Republic and Slovakia to S, Germany to W. **Total area**: 120,726 sq. mi. (312,680 sq km). **Coastline**: 305 mi. (491 km). **Comparative area**: slightly smaller than New Mexico. **Land use:** 46% arable land; 1% permanent crops; 53% other. **Major cities**: (1994 est.)

Warszawa (Warsaw, capital) 1,640,700; Lodz 828,500; Krakow (Cracow) 746,000; Wroclaw 642,900; Poznan 582,300.

• **People** **Population:** 38,622,660 (2003 est.). **Nationality:** noun—Pole(s); adjective—Polish. **Ethnic groups:** 97.6% Polish, 1.3% German, 0.6% Ukrainian, 0.5% Byelorussian. **Languages:** Polish. **Religions:** 95% Roman Catholic (about 75% practicing), 5% Eastern Orthodox, Protestant, and other.

• **Government** **Type:** republic. **Independence:** Nov. 11, 1918 (independent republic proclaimed) **Constitution:** Oct. 16, 1997; adopted by the National Assembly on Apr. 2, 1997; passed by national referendum May 23, 1997. **National holiday:** Constitution Day, May 3. **Heads of Government:** Aleksander Kwasniewski, president (since Dec. 1995); Leszek Miller, prime minister (since Oct. 2001). **Structure:** executive—prime minister is head of government; bicameral legislature—2 seats in lower house are constitutionally assigned to ethnic German parties; judiciary.

• **Economy** **Monetary unit:** zloty. **Budget:** (1999 est.) ***income:*** $49.6 bil.; ***expend.:*** $52.3 bil. **GDP:** $368.1 bil., $9,500 per capita (2002 est.). **Chief crops:** potatoes, milk, cheese, fruits, vegetables, wheat; poultry and eggs; pork, beef. **Natural resources:** coal, sulfur, copper, natural gas, silver. **Major industries:** machine building, iron and steel, extractive industries. **Labor force:** 17.6 mil. (2000 est.); 22.1% industry and construction, 27.5% agriculture, 50.4% services. **Exports:** $32.4 bil. (f.o.b., 2002); manufactured goods, chemicals; machinery and equipment; food and live animals. **Imports:** $43.4 bil. (f.o.b., 2002); manufactured goods, chemicals; machinery and equipment; mineral fuels. **Major trading partners:** ***exports:*** 34% Germany, 5% Italy; ***imports:*** 24% Germany, 8% Italy, 9% Russia.

The Slavic people known as Polonians accepted Christianity in the second half of the 10th century, during the reign of Duke Mieszko, whose close relationship with the papacy prevented the Holy Roman Empire from absorbing Poland. A strong and united Polish kingdom existed under the Piast dynasty until 1370, when the Anjou king of Hungary succeeded to the throne, followed by his daughter Jadwiga, who in 1386 married the grand duke of Lithuania, thus forming the great Commonwealth of Poland-Lithuania.

With the end of the Jagellonian line in 1572, the monarchy became elective. With a large nobility, equaling about 10 percent of the population, the monarchy grew weak, and Poland increasingly was subject to foreign intervention. The rise of the expansionist powers of Sweden, Prussia, Russia, and Austria came in part at the expense of the Poles. Jan Sobieski (1624-96), who ruled Poland as John III, saved Vienna from the Turks and briefly revived the Polish monarchy, but Polish royal power ended with his death. In a series of partitions in 1772, 1793, and 1795, Poland was dismembered and finally obliterated as a state.

Napoleon revived a Polish national entity with the Grand Duchy of Warsaw; with Napoleon's fall, the Congress of Vienna re-created a Kingdom of Poland in 1815, under the rule of the czar of Russia. After 1830 Poland was subjected to systematic Russification. The fall of Russia in World War I led to Poland's revival. The Lithuanian Socialist Józef Pilsudski led Poland in war against the new Bolshevik government of Russia until, in the 1921 Treaty of Riga, Poland emerged with its boundaries restored to those after the partition of 1793. It was ethnically about 70 percent Polish, a triumph for Polish nationalism but the end of Pilsudski's dream of a federation of northeastern Europe. Poland also had the largest Jewish population of any country in Europe.

With a strong legislature and a weak president, the new state seemed to Pilsudski too weak for its own defense. He became a virtual dictator in 1926 and ruled until his death in 1935. After his death a weak parliamentary government was controlled by military officers; the tentative revival of republicanism was halted by Hitler's and Stalin's aggression in 1939, yet another partition of Poland.

Poland was primarily an agricultural country, and the postwar republic attempted land reform, with some success; about 750,000 new private farm holdings were created by 1938. Mining—of coal and copper—was the principal traditional industrial activity in the 20th century, supplemented by extraction of natural gas. In the mid-1930's shipbuilding and railroad construction led the way toward a modern economy.

World War II commenced in September 1939, with attacks on Poland by Germany and the Soviet Union. The war brought severe destruction to Poland and the extermination of virtually its entire Jewish population. A government-in-exile was established in London, but the Soviet Union broke relations with it in 1943 when it requested a Red Cross investigation into the murder of 14,000 Polish officers whose bodies were discovered in Katyn Forest. (The Soviet government acknowledged responsibility for the massacre in 1990.) The Soviets established a puppet government in Lublin in 1944. In August the Red Army paused in its western advance on the outskirts of Warsaw, permitting the Nazis to obliterate the Polish Home Army. On Jan. 1, 1945, the U.S.S.R. recognized the Lublin regime as Poland's government.

By the time of the Allied Powers Conference in Yalta in February 1945, the Red Army was only 40 miles from Berlin and had total control of Poland. The Allies agreed to Stalin's proposal concerning the eastern boundary of Poland (allowing Russia to incorporate the eastern half of the country) and agreed that the government should be constituted from an enlargement of the Lublin regime. At Potsdam in Aug. 1945, Poland's borders were shifted approximately 200 miles westward from the prewar configuration, becoming once again those of the 10th century. The German population was expelled remorselessly.

The free elections promised in the Yalta Agreement were postponed until 1947, by which time a Communist victory could be assured. In 1948 the Socialists were forcibly merged into the Communist party; in 1949 Premier Boleslaw Bierut requested that Soviet general Konstantin Rokossovski be appointed minister of defense and commander in chief of the Polish army. All cultural periodicals and all writers' and artists' associations were taken over by the Communist party.

But there was little collectivization of Polish agriculture or forced industrialization on the Stalinist model. Intellectuals, bolstered by the Catholic church (which deeply resented a 1953 law requiring government approval for appointment of bishops), questioned the regime with some boldness. In 1956 both Bierut and Party Secretary Minc died, and Wladislaw Gomulka was elected party chairman in Oct. 1956. As Soviet warships sailed through the Baltic toward Poland, Nikita Khrushchev flew to Poland with a delegation of Soviet generals, where Gomulka assured them that Poland would follow the Soviet lead in foreign policy. Distracted by the crisis in Hungary, the Russians left Gomulka in power and even canceled Poland's debt and allowed the dismantling of agricultural collectives.

For a short time Gomulka permitted cultural and educational freedom, but by 1958 he had reverted to Stalinist form, imposing controls and pursuing a somewhat anti-Semitic Polish nationalism. Gomulka ruled until 1971, when he was replaced as party secretary by Edward Gierek. But moral leadership within Poland had clearly passed to Stefan Cardinal Wyszynski, leader of the increasingly vocal Catholic church; Gierek was forced to improve relations with the church in order to maintain his own credibility as a national leader.

Gierek presided over a decade of increasing unrest and growing discontent. Polish exports of ham and furniture to the West earned some hard currency but could not curb the rising national debt. The most significant event in Poland in the 1970's was the election of Karol Wojtyla, bishop of Krakow, as Pope John Paul II in October 1978. His visit to Poland in 1979 set the stage for the extraordinary events of the 1980's.

Gierek's austerity program of 1980 sent meat prices soaring. Strikes for wage adjustments, especially at the Lenin Shipyards in Gdansk, thrust Lech Walesa, a shipyard worker, into a position of national leadership. Walesa was elected chairman of the national coordinating committee of independent labor unions, Solidarity. Solidarity's demands went far beyond lower prices and higher wages; they included independent labor unions with the right to strike, freedom for political prisoners, and an end to censorship. In September Gierek resigned as party secretary and was replaced by Stanislaw Kania. By December, 40 independent trade unions had been formed, and a "rural Solidarity" movement was growing. In Feb. 1981 Soviet Army general Wojciech Jaruzelski was named prime minister. When in December Solidarity announced plans to hold a referendum on the Jaruzelski regime, martial law was declared; Solidarity leaders were arrested, all its activities banned, and the right to strike was abolished.

But the government was never able to suppress Solidarity as a popular force, and it was legalized in 1989. In 1989 elections Solidarity won 99 of 100 Senate seats and 299 of 460 seats in the lower house, although 65 percent had been reserved for the Communist party. Jaruzelski was elected president by Parliament and Solidarity leader Tadeusz Mazowiecki became prime minister.

The Communist party voted to disband on Jan. 28, 1990, and the Mazowiecki government announced a program of radical economic reform, winning promises of foreign aid and increased investment from Western governments. In June 1990, a commission was appointed to draft a new constitution. Jaruzelski resigned in September, and in presidential elections, Walesa, at the head of Solidarity's labor/Catholic faction, defeated Mazowiecki, representing Solidarity's political/technocrat faction.

The new prime minister, Krzysztof Bielecki, continued the reformist policies of curbing inflation and government spending, fostering foreign investment, and privatizing state enterprises. But the shock therapy, with its higher prices and unemployment (even while creating more than a million new jobs), led to disillusionment.

In the first fully free parliamentary elections, held in October 1991, only 42 percent of the voters participated, electing a fragmented 29-party Parliament. Reluctantly, Pres. Walesa named Jan Olszewski as prime minister of a coalition government. The Olszewski coalition collapsed in June 1992, replaced by an equally fragile seven-party coalition led by Hanna Suchocka, Poland's first female prime minister.

Despite high inflation (40 percent) and high unemployment (13 percent), under Poland's "iron lady" the private sector expanded and even the remaining state-owned enterprises responded to market demand, pushing exports from $8 bil. in 1988 to $14 bil. in 1992. And in May 1993, Parliament passed a bill privatizing 600 companies.

Still, at the end of May 1993, the Suchocka government fell, by one vote, to a Solidarity-sponsored no-confidence measure, in protest against her austerity budget. In new elections held in Oct. 1993, the Communist party (now called the Democratic Left Alliance) formed a coalition with the Peasants party to forge a surprising return to power. The Communist prime minister, Josef Oleksy, was joined by his party-mate Aleksander Kwasniewski, who defeated Walesa in presidential elections held in November 1995. Kwasniewski ran especially strong with younger voters, who regarded communism as an antiquated system that posed no threat of returning to Poland. A month after the presidential election, though, Oleksy was accused of spying for Russia, and although he protested his innocence, he resigned as premier.

Poland's economy had been among the fastest growing in Europe (a 7 percent rise in GDP in recent years and billions in direct foreign investment) although inflation ran high through 1997. In 1997, a new constitution and invitations to join NATO and eventually the E.U. gave the Poles a reason to believe the future looked very positive. The first elections under the new constitution produced a center-right coalition government. In 1999 Poland joined NATO, finally achieving security against the Russian expansion it always feared, but the economy slowed considerably.

Bucking western Europe's right-wing electoral tide, Poland's Democratic Left Alliance (the remnants of the Communists and their friends) captured control of the Sjem, garnering a near majority of the 460 seats. Leszek Miller became premier in coalition with the Polish Peasants' Party. In June 2003 voters gave overwhelming approval (77 percent) to joining the E.U.

▶PORTUGAL
Portuguese Republic

• **GEOGRAPHY** **Location:** Iberian Peninsula in southwest Europe; also two archipelagos in Atlantic Ocean: Azores (37°29'N, 25°40'W) and Madeira Islands (32°40'N, 16°55'W). **Boundaries:** Spain to N and E, Atlantic Ocean to S and W. **Total area:** 35,552 sq. mi. (92,080 sq km). **Coastline:** 1,114 mi. (1,793 km). **Comparative area:** slightly smaller than Indiana. **Land use:** 21% arable land; 8% permanent crops; 71% other. **Major cities:** (1991 census) Lisboa (Lisbon, capital) 681,063; Porto (Oporto) 309,485; Amadora 176,137; Setubal 103,241; Coimbra 147,722.

• **PEOPLE** **Population:** 10,102,022 (2003 est.). **Nationality:** noun—Portuguese (sing., pl.); adjective—Portuguese. **Ethnic groups:** homogeneous Mediterranean stock; citizens of African descent who immigrated during decolonization number less than 100,000. **Languages:** Portuguese. **Religions:** 94% Roman Catholic, Protestant, other.

• **GOVERNMENT** **Type:** parliamentary democracy. **Independence:** Oct. 5, 1910. **Constitution:** Apr. 25, 1976, revised Oct. 1982 and June 1989, Nov.

1992, Sept. 1997. **National holiday:** Day of Portugal, June 10. **Heads of Government:** Jorge Sampaio, president (since Feb. 1996); José Durão Barroso, prime minister (since Apr. 2002). **Structure:** executive—president and prime minister; unicameral legislature-(popularly elected 230-seat Assembly of the Republic); judiciary.

• **ECONOMY** **Monetary unit:** euro. **Budget:** (2001) ***income:*** $45 bil.; ***expend.:*** $48 bil. **GDP:** $182 bil., $18,000 per capita (2001 est.). **Chief crops:** grains, potatoes, olives, grapes for wine; livestock. **Natural resources:** fish, forests (cork), tungsten, iron ore, uranium ore. **Major industries:** textiles, footwear, wood pulp, paper, cork. **Labor force:** 5.1 mil. (2000); 60% services, 30% industry, 10% agriculture, forestry, fisheries, 4.7% unemployment (2001 est.). **Exports:** $25.9 bil. (f.o.b., 2002 est.); clothing and footwear, machinery, chemicals, cork and paper products, hides. **Imports:** $39 bil. (f.o.b., 2002 est.); machinery and transport equipment, chemicals, petroleum, textiles, agricultural products. **Major trading partners:** ***exports:*** 80% E.U., 6% U.S.; ***imports:*** 74% E.U., U.S., Japan.

Portugal traces its origins back to the warlike Lusitanian tribes of Roman times. The nation-state originated as a county of the kingdom of Leon-Castile, reconquered from the Moors in the 11th century. Portugal won recognition as an independent kingdom in 1143, and conquered Lisbon four years later. In 1267 the Algarve was conquered, and by then Portugal had expanded to its modern boundaries. Except for the period 1580-1640, when it was ruled by the Spanish Habsburgs, the Portuguese dynasty maintained its independence into the 20th century.

Portuguese fishermen had probably frequented the Grand Banks from before the time of Columbus, and the nation's tradition of seafaring gave rise to a world empire in the 15th and 16th centuries. Prince Henry the Navigator (1394-1460) colonized the Azores and the Madeiras and sponsored voyages of exploration along the west coast of Africa. Under his successors, Portugal controlled the west African coast, the shores of the Indian Ocean, and large stretches of southern Asia, as well as, in the Western Hemisphere, Brazil. Yet the rise of the empires of Spain and the Netherlands quickly reduced the Portuguese to second-rank status, leaving only Macao, Goa, and Timor in Asia; Portuguese Guinea (Guinea Bissau), Mozambique, and Angola in Africa; and the great territory of Brazil in Latin America.

In the 19th century, a series of dynastic civil wars weakened the monarchy, allowing Britain to gain control of the country's foreign policy (in addition to the wine trade of Oporto, long in British hands). Brazil declared its independence in 1822.

In 1910 Portugal became the first kingdom in the 20th century to be transformed into a republic. But in the next 15 years, chaos ensued: eight presidents, 44 governments, and a nearcollapse of the economy. Finally, the military established a dictatorship, lasting until recent times. In 1928 the military installed a civilian dictator, a professor of economics, Antonio Salazar. A firm believer in law and order, he managed to control the turbulence of political life and made the escudo one of Europe's most stable currencies, yet he could do nothing to alter Portugal's fundamental poverty. Although he ruled through civilian governments, his essential support always came from the army.

Portugal has long been Western Europe's poorest country. As late as 1960, almost half of the country's work force was engaged in agriculture, forestry, and fishing. In the north, agriculture was traditionally carried on in smallholdings; the south was characterized by large estates, remnants of feudal fiefs. Exports were traditionally cork, olive oil, port wine, and fish. Industrialization came late to Portugal, and today manufacturing is mostly carried on by small firms engaged in textile and clothing production and other labor-intensive production.

World War II affected Portugal very little. Salazar deftly managed to remain Britain's ally while keeping his country out of the war as a neutral state. In the postwar period, Portugal accepted Marshall Plan aid and became a member of NATO in 1949. Portugal was a founding member of the European Free Trade Association in 1959 and negotiated a special relationship with the EC in 1972 (when its trading partner and ally, Great Britain, joined that body).

Portugal joined the United Nations in 1955, just in time to become embroiled in the worldwide movement for decolonization. Protesting that Portugal had, not colonies, but "overseas provinces," Salazar refused to bow to the pressure of world opinion. In 1961 India forcibly annexed Goa and other Portuguese enclaves on the subcontinent. In the same year, nationalist revolts broke out in Angola, Guinea and Mozambique.

The colonial wars of the 1960's placed a terrible strain on Portugal's economy and resulted in severe military losses. Salazar, gravely ill, retired in 1968 and was replaced by Marcelo Caetano. In 1974 Caetano was deposed in a bloodless coup staged by the secret Armed Forces movement. The coup's leader, Antonio de Spinola, after reaching agreements on the independence of most of Portugal's old colonies, resigned as head of government in September 1974. Costa Gomes replaced Spinola, as a Revolutionary Council was instituted. The council survived two coup attempts, one by right-wing soldiers, the other by Communists, and it promulgated a Socialist constitution in 1976. Through a series of unstable governments (16 between 1974 and 1987), the old agrarian estates were expropriated, and banking, insurance, and large industrial concerns were nationalized. The shock of this economic transformation, along with the OPEC price rises, created a recession in the 1970's. In addition Portugal had to absorb a million Portuguese refugees from the former colonies.

Attempts by center-right coalitions in the 1980's to undo the nationalizations of the 1970's were thwarted by vetoes of the Constitutional Tribunal (successor to the Revolutionary Council), even when the free-market Social Democratic party held an absolute majority in the assembly. Portugal entered the EC on Jan. 1, 1986, pledging to reduce tariffs and end agricultural subsidies over a 10-year transitional period.

In 1987 the Social Democrats, running on a platform of spending cuts, privatization of state-owned firms, reversal of agricultural collectivism, and reliance on free enterprise, became the first party since 1974 to win an absolute majority in the legislative assembly. Per capita income tripled over the years 1985-92, so that Portugal was no longer the poorest country in the E.U. The 1992 sale of the huge state-owned Petrogal oil company was a harbinger of a return to free enterprise. In Oct. 1995, Antonio Guterres of the Socialist party displaced the Social Democrats. And in January 1996, Jorge Sampaio won the presidential election, giving Portugal both a Socialist president and prime minister for the first time since democracy was restored.

Portugal's economic stability was ratified in 1998 by the E.U. when the latter approved Portugal's membership in the Monetary Union. GDP growth averaged 3.5 percent through the late 1990's. In Dec. 1999 the colony of Macao was returned to Chinese rule after 442 years. In 2001 Sampaio was easily reelected. But the December loss by the Socialists of numerous municipal elections, including Lisbon and Oporto, led Sampaio to dissolve Parliament. March elections then brought another center-right coalition as the Social Democrats took 102 (of 230) seats, selecting Manual Durao Barroso as prime minister.

▶QATAR

State of Qatar

• **GEOGRAPHY** **Location:** occupies a peninsula projecting northward from Arabian mainland into western part of Persian (Arabian) Gulf. **Boundaries**: Persian Gulf to N, E, and W; Saudi Arabia and United Arab Emirates to S. **Total area**: 4,247 sq. mi. (11,000 sq km). **Coastline**: 350 mi. (563 km). **Comparative area**: slightly smaller than Connecticut. **Land use:** 1% arable land; 0% permanent crops; 99% other. **Major cities**: (1993) Doha (capital) 339,471; Al Rayyan 143,046; Al Wakrah 30,976.

• **PEOPLE** **Population:** 817,052 (2003 est.). **Nationality:** noun—Qatari(s); adjective—Qatari. **Ethnic groups:** 40% Arab, 18% Pakistani, 18% Indian, 10% Iranian, 14% other. **Languages:** Arabic (official), English commonly used as second language. **Religions:** 95% Muslim.

• **GOVERNMENT** **Type:** traditional monarchy. **Independence:** Sept. 3, 1971 (from U.K.). **Constitution:** provisional constitution enacted Apr. 19, 1972; permanent constitution approved by referendum Apr. 29, 2003. **National holiday:** Independence Day, Sept. 3. **Head of Government:** Hamad bin Khalifa al-Thani (since June 1995). **Structure:** executive—amir is head of government and chief of state; unicameral legislature—consultative, no elections since 1970, members terms extended every four years; judiciary.

• **ECONOMY** **Monetary unit:** Qatari riyal. **Budget:** (FY02 est.) ***income:*** $5 bil.; ***expend.:*** $5.5 bil. **GDP:** $17.2 bil., $21,500 per capita (2002 est.). **Chief crops:** fruits, vegetables; poultry, dairy products, beef; fish. **Natural resources:** crude oil, natural gas, fish. **Major industries:** crude oil production and refining, fertilizers, petrochemicals. **Labor force:** 280,122 (1997 est.). **Exports:** $10.9 bil. (f.o.b., 2002 est.); 80% petroleum products, steel, fertilizers. **Imports:** $3.9 bil. (f.o.b., 2002 est.); machinery, consumer goods, food, chemicals. **Major trading partners:** ***exports:*** 42% Japan, 18% South Korea, 5% Singapore; ***imports:*** 18% France, 9% Italy, 9% U.S.

The Qatar peninsula was ruled as part of the sheikhdom of Bahrain from the late 18th century until the mid-19th century. An informal British protectorate was established in 1868; the Ottoman Empire also asserted authority over the sheikhs of Qatar from 1872 to 1916. The Ottomans ceded authority to the British in that year, and a formal British protectorate was organized. When British forces withdrew from the Persian Gulf region in 1971, Qatar entered into negotiations with the emirates of the Trucial Coast to join the federation of the United Arab Emirates. When those negotiations broke down, Qatar declared its independence on Sept. 3, 1971. For over 30 years it has been politically stable under one ruler, Sheik Hamad bin Khalifa al-Thani, although he was deposed by his son in a bloodless coup in June 1995. He has claimed he wants to move the country toward democracy and has called for a free press, limited elections, and allowing women to vote.

Qatar's economy is dominated by oil, natural gas (Qatar has the world's third largest supply) banking, and shipping services in the port of Doha.

▶ROMANIA

• **GEOGRAPHY** **Location:** southeastern Europe. **Boundaries**: Ukraine to N, Moldova to NE, Black Sea to E, Bulgaria to S, Yugoslavia (Serbia) to SW, Hungary to NW. **Total area**: 91,699 sq. mi. (237,500 sq km). **Coastline**: 140 mi. (225 km). **Comparative area**: slightly smaller than Oregon. **Land use:** 41% arable land; 3% permanent crops; 21% meadows and pastures; 29% forest and woodland; 6% other; includes 11% irrigated. **Major cities**: (1993 est.) Bucharesti (Bucharest, capital) 2,066,723; Constanta 348,985; Iasi 337,643; Timisoara 325,359; Cluj-Napoca 321,850.

• **PEOPLE** **Population:** 22,271,839 (July 2003 est.). **Nationality:** noun—Romanian(s); adjective—Romanian. **Ethnic groups:** 89.5% Romanian, 6.6% Hungarian, 2.5% Roma, German, Ukrainian, Russian, Turk, other. **Languages:** Romanian, Hungarian, German. **Religions:** 87% Eastern Orthodox, 6% Roman Catholic, 7% Protestant.

• **GOVERNMENT** **Type:** republic. **Independence:** 1881 (from Turkey). **Constitution:** Dec. 8, 1991; republic proclaimed Dec. 30, 1947. **National holiday:** Unification Day, Dec. 1. **Heads of Government:** Ion Iliescu, president (since Dec. 2000); Adrian Nastase, prime minister (since Dec. 2000). **Structure:** executive; bicameral legislature; judiciary.

• **ECONOMY** **Monetary unit:** leu. **Budget:** (1999 est.): ***income:*** $11.7 bil.; ***expend.:*** $12.4 bil. **GDP:** $166 bil., $7,400 per capita (2002 est.). **Chief crops:** corn, wheat; milk, eggs, meat. **Natural resources:** crude oil (reserves declining), timber, natural gas, coal, iron ore. **Major industries:** mining, timber, construction materials. **Labor force:** 9.9 mil. (1999 est.). **Exports:** $13.7 bil. (f.o.b., 2002 est.); textiles and footwear, metals and metal products, machinery and equipment. **Imports:** $16.7 bil. (f.o.b., 2002 est.); 23% machinery and equipment, 12% fuels and minerals, 9% chemicals. **Major trading partners:** (2001) ***exports:*** 25% Italy, 16% Germany, 8% France; **imports:** 20% Germany, 15% Italy, 8% Russia.

The Roman province of Dacia was sufficiently Latinized to retain the name of Rome long after the legions withdrew in A.D. 27. Overrun by invading Bulgars in the eighth century, the Romanians retained their Latinate language and orthodox Christianity; Romania remained beyond the borders of the Byzantine Empire but was in close contact with it. The area was conquered by the Mongols in the 13th century and formed the independent principalities of Moldavia and Walachia after the Mongols withdrew.

By the 15th century, Moldavia and Walachia had become vassal states of the Ottoman Empire, though with some local autonomy that permitted retention of orthodox Christianity and the creation of a rich local culture. Attempts at national unity against Ottoman rule in 1601 and 1711 failed; in 1861 the provinces united as an autonomous state under the name Romania, within the Ottoman Empire, under Greek administration. Independence came in 1878.

Romania was for centuries the poorest country

in Europe. Thoroughly agricultural, it was a land of unfree peasants working the great estates of landowners who were generally wealthy, usually absentee, and often Greek. The peasants not only paid taxes but also were required to perform feudal labor services for the estate owners.

After enlarging itself at Bulgaria's expense in the Second Balkan War (1913), Romania switched sides three times in World War I, joining the Allies just before the war's end. Its reward was a huge expansion, doubling its territory with lands taken from Austria, Hungary, Russia, and Bulgaria.

The interwar period was one of political turbulence, marked by violence and assassinations. Twice King Carol II went into exile, leaving his throne to his son Prince Michael; the second time was in 1940, when Russia (in accordance with the Hitler-Stalin pact) reclaimed the territories of Bessarabia and northern Bukovina it had lost to Romania in 1920; Hitler required Romania to return about half of Transylvania to Hungary.

During World War II, the pro-Hitler dictator Marshall Ion Antonescu took power, supported by a semifascist "Iron Guard," but when the latter attempted a coup, the military crushed the uprising. Romanian troops participated in Hitler's invasion of Russia in 1941, and the country paid the price in 1944 when Russian troops "liberated" the country, with devastating results.

The country was quickly transformed into a Soviet satellite through rigged elections in which the communist National Democratic Front replaced the Peasant Alliance in power; a People's Republic was proclaimed on Dec. 30, 1947, and King Michael was forced to abdicate. A peace treaty in 1947 confirmed the loss of Bessarabia to Russia but returned Transylvania to Romania.

Under Russian occupation Romania was a virtual Soviet colony. The occupying armies did not leave until after reparation payments were completed in 1958, leaving the dictator Gheorghe Gheorghiu-Dej in power. Despite Council of Mutual Economic Assistance (COMECON) plans for Romania to become a major food supplier to the Soviet bloc, Gheorghiu-Dej pursued industrialization on the Stalinist model, in the process ruining Romanian agriculture while creating large, labor-intensive, and highly inefficient factories. The result was an economic depression; politically, however, it produced a de facto independence for Romania within the Soviet bloc. Russian troops were forbidden on Romanian soil, and Romania declined to participate in COMECON policies.

With the death of Gheorghiu-Dej in 1965, power passed to Nicolae Ceauşescu. He promulgated a new constitution and instituted a series of purges; he became party leader in 1965, prime minister in 1967, and president of the republic in 1974. Ceauşescu continued his predecessor's economic policy, deepening the country's misery; he also pursued a policy of "independence" from the U.S.S.R., refusing to go along with Soviet policies of de-Stalinization and liberalization.

Romania's "national communism" was expressed in militant nationalism, coupled with severe repression of ethnic minorities, especially Germans and Magyars in Transylvania. Hundreds of Hungarian villages were bulldozed into oblivion in the name of agricultural collectivization.

Ceauşescu's ambitions included the creation of a family dynasty in the Romanian leadership. In 1979 his wife Elena was named first deputy premier and elevated to the Council of Ministers. Her brothers were given important government positions; Ceauşescu's son, despite his reputation as a playboy, was groomed to replace his father.

Romania's transition from Communist rule was sudden and violent. On Dec. 16-18, 1989, demonstrations in Timisoara calling for Ceauşescu's ouster were put down with brute force by the Securitate (secret police), but they spread and citizens and regular army troops fought pitched battles with Securitate forces in Bucharest. Ceauşescu and his wife fled Bucharest but were captured, tried, and executed. The newly organized Council of National Salvation established a provisional government, consisting primarily of anti-Ceauşescu Communists in league with the Romanian army, with former Communist party official Ion Iliescu as president.

The Communist party was outlawed on Jan. 12, 1990. Despite the Council's domination by former Communists, no effective opposition movement emerged, and in hastily called and rigged elections on May 20, Iliescu was elected president in a landslide and the Council won 233 of 296 seats in the lower house.

In June 1990, many anti-Communist demonstrators were beaten and several killed by troops and armed miners brought to Bucharest by the government. Calls for Iliescu's resignation and a purge of Communists from government grew. Tensions were aggravated when the government's abrupt move to a market economy resulted in food shortages and price increases.

Continued rioting in 1991 led to the replacement of ex-Communist prime minister Petre Roman by the non-Communist Theodor Stolojan at the head of a "caretaker" coalition. More or less free elections in 1992 gave the National Salvation Front 28 percent of the seats in Parliament while the opposition Democratic Convention gained 20 percent; Iliescu defeated the Democratic Convention candidate in the presidential election with 61 percent of the vote. Both Iliescu and the prime minister he named (Nicolae Vacaroiu) were pledged to slowing the transition to a market economy but by 1994 with inflation at over 250 percent (leading to a massive workers' strike in Feb.) the government agreed to I.M.F.'s demand for increased privatization and fiscal austerity in order to receive a $700 mil. loan. Iliescu's presidency ended in Nov. 1996 with a coalition government headed by Emil Constantinescu immediately forging public links to the Romanian Orthodox Church ending decades of official atheism and taking action against corrupt banking officials, businessmen, and politicians. The economy remained in dire straits but in early 1997 loans were secured from the I.M.F. and the World Bank.

Elections in Nov. 1997 were won by Emil Constantinescu of the Democratic Convention party who became president and Victor Ciorbea the prime minister. Inflation and unemployment were falling but GDP growth was lagging and, with a patchwork tax system, international default looked likely. I.M.F. demands for restructuring as a condition of further loans produced government plans which included the closing of mines whose operation had lost $4 billion since 1990. But that in turn produced, in early 1999, widespread protest marches and violence by mine workers whose role in 1990 was not forgotten.

Parliamentary elections in Nov. 2000 gave a preponderance to the parties of the left, but the presidential election drew greater interest: Ion Iliescu, claiming now to be a reformer and a pro-westerner, carried two-thirds of the vote in the December run-off.

▶RUSSIA

Russian Federation

• **GEOGRAPHY** **Location:** northeastern Europe and northern Asia. **Boundaries**: Baltic Sea, Barents Sea, Kara Sea, East Siberian Sea to N, Bering Sea, Sea of Okhotsk, Sea of Japan to E, China, North Korea, Mongolia, Kazakhstan, Caspian Sea, Azerbaijan, Georgia, Black Sea to S, Ukraine, Belarus to W, Latvia, Estonia, Finland, Norway to NW. **Total area**: 6,592,745 sq. mi. (17,075,200 sq. km). **Coastline**: 23,402 mi. (37,653 km). **Comparative area**: slightly less than 1.8 times the size of the United States. **Land use:** 8% arable land, 0% permanent crops, 94% other. **Major cities**: (1995) Moscow (capital) 8,717,000; St. Petersburg 4,838,000; Nizhnyi Novgorod 1,383,000; Novosibirsk 1,369,000.

• **PEOPLE** **Population:** 144,526,278 (2003 est.). **Nationality:** noun—Russian(s); adjective—Russian. **Ethnic groups:** 81.5% Russian, 3.8% Tatar, 3% Ukrainian, 1.2% Chuvash. **Languages:** Russian, other. **Religions:** Russian Orthodox, Muslim, other.

• **GOVERNMENT** **Type:** federation. **Independence:** Aug. 24, 1991 (from Soviet Union). **Constitution:** Dec. 12, 1993. **National holiday:** Russia Day, June 12, celebrating first presidential election. **Heads of Government:** Vladimir V. Putin, president (since May 2000); Mikhail M. Kasyanov, prime minister (since May 2000). **Structure:** executive—president, premier, various advisory bodies; bicameral legislature; judiciary.

• **ECONOMY** **Monetary unit:** ruble. **Budget:** (2000 est.) ***income:*** $70 bil..; ***expend.:*** $62 bil. **GDP:** $1.35 tril., $9,300 per capita (2002 est.). **Chief crops:** grain, sugar beets, vegetables, sunflower seed; meat, milk. **Natural resources:** oil, natural gas, coal, timber. **Major industries:** extraction and processing raw materials, machine building from rolling mills to high-performance aircraft. **Labor force:** 71.8 mil. (2002). **Exports:** $104.6 bil. (2002 est.); petroleum and petroleum products, natural gas, wood and wood products, coal, metals, chemicals. **Imports:** $60.7 bil. (2002 est.); machinery and equipment, consumer goods, medicines, meat, grain, sugar, semifinished metal products. **Major trading partners:** Germany, U.S., Belarus.

Russia is the largest and most powerful of the states to emerge from the former Soviet Union. As the seat of the Soviet empire that existed for over 70 years, the Russians wielded tremendous power both within the U.S.S.R. and in the international sphere. Almost from their emergence as a separate people, the Russians have extended the boundaries of their country to include a wide variety of non-Russian people. Both the Russian Czars and the Bolsheviks who came to power in 1917 have a long history of expansionist policies, which explains why, even today, an important part of the Russian national identity is that of leader of a large empire.

In the ninth century A.D., Viking traders organized a state, which they called Rus, in the river valleys between the Baltic and the Black Seas, centered on the cities of Kiev and Novgorod. In time the Vikings were absorbed into the native Slavic population; in 998 a Ruthenian prince of Kiev accepted Christianity from Constantinople. In the 13th century, Mongols under Genghis Khan and his descendants conquered most of Russia, and the Mongol Golden Horde maintained its power through the 14th century, exercising loose control over Novgorod and Moscow.

From the mid-19th century, Moscow grew to become the center of a new state that gathered in other cities and territories as Mongol power waned. Ivan III (Ivan the Great, 1440-1505) consolidated the power of Moscow; his marriage to a Byzantine princess led him to regard his empire as a third Rome, heir to the religious tradition of Constantinople. His grandson, Ivan IV (Ivan the Terrible, 1530-84), adopted the title czar (from the Latin caesar). He broke the power of the aristocratic boyar class and greatly extended the power of Moscow through military conquest.

Over the next two centuries, Russia carried out a steady program of expansion eastward into Siberia and across the Bering Strait to Alaska, until the empire covered one-sixth of the land surface of the globe. Peter the Great (1672-1725) made Russia a Baltic and Black Sea naval power, brought Russia into the European state system, and instituted a sweeping, if superficial, Westernization of his realm. His new capital at St. Petersburg became one of the most splendid cities in Europe. At the end of the 18th century, Catherine the Great (1729-96) participated with Prussia and Austria in the partitions of Poland, and Russia thereby became a major power in central Europe.

Catherine's grandson Alexander I (1777-1825), member of the grand coalition that defeated Napoleon, was not only czar of Russia but also king of Poland and grand duke of Finland. His troops occupied Paris in 1815. The Russian aristocracy became ardent Francophiles in the 19th century, ignoring growing problems at home. After losing the Crimean War in 1856, Russia began to develop Siberia and the southern territories near the border of Persia. Alaska was sold to the United States in 1867. In a major reform of the agricultural system, serfdom was abolished under Alexander II in 1861, though the newly independent peasantry, organized into agricultural cooperatives, only slowly derived benefits from its freedom. The late 19th century also marked the beginning of modern industrialization in Russia and of extensive development in Siberia, aided by state investment in railroads and mining.

Under the last czar, Nicholas II (1868-1918), Russia was defeated by Japan in a war over Manchuria in 1905. The defeat sparked a naval mutiny and an abortive revolution, which led to the establishment of a constitutional monarchy and other limited political reforms. Further military losses in World War I set the stage for the monarchy's downfall in the revolution of 1917.

The initial revolution of March 1917 brought a relatively moderate socialist (Menshevik) group to power. Its principal leader, Aleksandr Kerensky, organized a republican government and tried to maintain the Russian war effort but failed to gain control of the many contending revolutionary factions of the time. The Germans allowed the radical Bolshevik leader, Vladimir I. Lenin, to return to Russia, where he and his followers organized workers' soviets (councils) hostile to the Menshevik republic. Bolshevik forces occupied Petrograd (St. Petersburg was renamed in 1914) on Nov. 7, 1917 (October in the old Byzantine calendar, hence the name October Revolution), arrested the cabiinet, and put in place a Council of People's Commissars, under Lenin's chairmanship. There followed four years of civil war between Bolshevik, Menshevik, and czarist forces, in the course of which Nicholas II and his family were executed by the Bolsheviks in 1918.

Decreeing land to the peasants, worker management in industry, and repudiation of czarist debts, the Bolsheviks won the survival of their regime by withdrawing from World War I. The

1918 Treaty of Brest-Litovsk, which gained peace with Germany, granted freedom to Finland, the Baltic republics, Poland, Ukraine, and Bessarabia. At the conclusion of the civil war in 1921, the Soviet state was established, with Ukraine reabsorbed into the Soviet Union. The Bolshevik victory also resulted in the creation in 1921 of the Mongolian People's Republic as a close Soviet ally.

The early 1920's are now remembered as a "golden age" of Soviet history. Lenin's New Economic Policy (NEP) allowed some role for market forces and private ownership and led to a brief burst of economic growth. Art, literature, and science flourished in an atmosphere of revolutionary enthusiasm and little censorship.

Lenin died on Jan. 21, 1924, and after a power struggle, was succeeded by Josef Stalin. Stalin supported Communist revolutions in China and elsewhere through the Communist International (Comintern) but generally withdrew from foreign engagements in order to concentrate on domestic affairs. Under Lenin, and even more under Stalin, the Communist party established a police state, condemning millions of people to internal exile in the 1920's and consolidating all power in the hands of the state. In 1929 agriculture was forcibly collectivized, leading to the starvation or execution of millions of peasants, while forced industrialization was carried out under a series of five-year plans. Under the guise of socialist revolution, the Russians continued in much the same manner as their czarist heirs. The Bolsheviks forcibly incorporated most of the territories of the old empire, and once in charge, insisted that Russian be the state language and that Russian Communist party officials run the republics.

On the national level, Stalin's chief rival, Leon Trotsky, was expelled from the U.S.S.R. in 1929 (and assassinated by Stalinist agents in Mexico in 1940). Stalin's obsession with eliminating all possible rivals for power led to a series of purges which saw the summary execution of an estimated seven million of presumed "enemies of the state" and the imprisonment in concentration camps of an estimated 12 million more.

Russia's reemergence as a world power was signaled by the signing in Aug. 1939 of the Hitler-Stalin Pact, a nonaggression treaty through which Stalin aimed to recover territories lost in 1918. Poland was partitioned, Bessarabia annexed (as the Moldavian republic), Finland conquered and partitioned, and the Baltic republics absorbed.

When in June 1941 Hitler turned against his ally and invaded Russia, unprepared Russian armies retreated. But Stalin emerged as a national leader in the "Great Patriotic War," restructuring the army and enlisting the support of the Orthodox church and relying on calls to Russian patriotism in rallying the population. In the early winter of 1942, the war changed course as Russia broke the German siege of Stalingrad, and Russian armies began their westward push that would carry them to the Elbe River by April 1945.

By the end of World War II, Stalin had reestablished the old czarist boundaries of Russia, and he had a ring of occupied states along his western boundary and a divided Germany beyond. Over the years 1945-48, he engineered a thorough communization of those occupied states, turning them into Russian satellites.

Stalin died in March 1953. He was succeeded by a collegial form of party and government leadership, from which Nikita Khrushchev, the party chairman, emerged as the paramount figure. In a secret speech to the party leadership in 1956, Khrushchev denounced Stalin for crimes against the party. He announced a set of new policies designed to bring about rapid modernization and consolidated his power when he became premier in 1958. The Khrushchev years brought a small but steady rise in living standards and a "thaw" in police state methods, the KGB (state security police) being brought under party control.

In foreign policy there was a thaw as well. In 1953 the Soviets agreed to an armistice in Korea and tolerated the formation of a more liberal government in Hungary. In 1955 Russia returned the Porkkala peninsula to Finland and agreed to the Austrian State Treaty, which created an independent and neutral Austria. But the limits of disengagement became clear in 1956 with the ruthless Soviet suppression of the Hungarian uprising. A summit conference between Khrushchev and Eisenhower in 1960 led to a propaganda victory for Russia when an American U-2 spy plane was shot down over Russian territory on May 1. And in 1962 Khrushchev tried to install Soviet missiles in Cuba, a reckless adventure from which he had to back down during the Cuban missile crisis.

While on vacation in 1964, Khrushchev was removed from office and replaced as party secretary by Leonid Brezhnev and as premier by Aleksei Kosygin. His failure to deliver on promises for domestic economic growth and his recklessness in foreign affairs seem to have been responsible for his downfall. The new leaders embarked on an ambitious program of military (especially naval) expansion and pressed ahead vigorously with a space program that had begun with the triumphant launching of Sputnik I in 1957.

Under Brezhnev and Kosygin the U.S.S.R. became more aggressive in foreign policy. The severe suppression of Czechoslovakia's "Prague Spring" in 1968 occasioned development of the Brezhnev Doctrine, whereby Russia claimed the right to intervene militarily in any socialist state. Soviet involvement in the Third World grew, with Russia supporting Vietnam against China; Syria and the PLO against Israel; leftist regimes in Angola, Ethiopia, and elsewhere in Africa; and the Sandinistas in Nicaragua. Cuba emerged as the principal Soviet proxy in supplying troops for leftist causes in the Third World. In 1979 Soviet troops moved into Afghanistan, allegedly at the invitation of its Marxist government, and remained bogged down there for a decade. Under American pressure, Brezhnev permitted the emigration of about 130,000 Jews and 40,000 ethnic Germans.

Domestically, the regime grew more oppressive; censorship was tightened and dissidents sentenced to terms in penal mental institutions. Elitism and nepotism created a self-perpetuating and interlocking network of power at the top, while the nation as a whole stagnated.

Brezhnev's death in 1982 brought about a rapid series of leadership transfers. Yuri Andropov, head of the KGB, succeeded Brezhnev as party secretary but died after only 15 months. He was succeeded by Konstantin Chernenko, who died 13 months later. In March 1985 Mikhail Gorbachev became party secretary, ushering in a new era.

Gorbachev first instituted a cautious shake-up of state and party bureaucrats, promoting younger men who were technocrats rather than party professionals. Under the slogan *glasnost* (openness, candor), censorship was relaxed, and policy was openly debated in the press. Jamming of broadcasts from the West was ended. By the end of 1990, freedom of the press and of religion had been approved, and private citizens were given limited rights to own small businesses.

Gorbachev's other slogan, *perestroika* (restructuring), addressed his aim to boost morale and increase economic efficiency by devolving responsibility for economic decisions away from the party and government and toward industrial and agricultural managers. Perestroika raised expectations but not output; the system remained sluggish, inefficient, and burdened with the vested interests of state planners. The nuclear power plant disaster of Chernobyl in April 1986 and a gas pipeline fire that killed hundreds of passengers in passing railroad trains in June 1989 exemplified the industrial mismanagement against which Gorbachev's policies were aimed. During 1989-91 there were strikes by coal miners, and shortages of food and consumer goods worsened.

In foreign policy Gorbachev pursued arms reduction agreements with the United States and withdrew Soviet forces from Afghanistan. His international stature exceeded that of any previous Soviet leader; but his problems at home made him increasingly unpopular. Foremost among his problems at home concerned the U.S.S.R.'s various ethnic nationalities. The southern Muslim regions of the U.S.S.R. were the scene of turmoil since the anti-Russian riots in Kazakhstan in 1986; in 1988 riots broke out in the Christian republic of Armenia over the status of ethnic Armenians in the neighboring Muslim republic of Azerbaijan. Fighting in Armenia and Azerbaijan worsened in 1989-90, leading to a breakdown of government control in some areas. Ethnic warfare between Uzbeks and Turks in Uzbekistan led to numerous deaths, and sporadic violence in other central Asian republics broke out in 1990.

The Baltic republics of Estonia, Latvia, and Lithuania raised their old national flags, enacted laws giving their native languages priority over Russian, and proclaimed the superiority of local republican law over the laws of the Soviet Union. Lithuania proclaimed its independence from the U.S.S.R. in Dec. 1989, provoking a confrontation with international ramifications; Lithuania finally agreed to postpone its independence in 1990 pending negotiations with the Soviet government. Within the U.S.S.R. itself, the Russian republic elected maverick Boris Yeltsin as president and pressed for greater autonomy; Yeltsin resigned from the Communist party in July 1990.

The total collapse of communist governments in Eastern Europe in 1989-90 added to Gorbachev's problems and led to the dissolution of the Warsaw Pact; the Berlin Wall fell in Nov. 1989; and the Council of Mutual Economic Assistance (COMECON) was dissolved in July 1990. Gorbachev responded by assuming the presidency of the U.S.S.R. and increasing the powers of that office, and he held off challenges to his leadership in 1990-91. Yet defections from the party by both right- and left-wing groups threw the party's future role in the U.S.S.R. itself in doubt. Demonstrations against Gorbachev and the Communist party took place in Moscow and elsewhere as the economy worsened and food supplies dwindled.

In June of 1991, Boris Yeltsin was elected president of the Russian republic in the first direct elections for the post. His stature soared when he rallied opposition to an unsuccessful coup to topple Gorbachev in August. In December 1991 Gorbachev and Yeltsin agreed that the U.S.S.R. would cease to exist as of Jan. 1, 1992.

In early December 1991, Ukraine, Belarus, and the Russian Federation signed the Minsk Agreement that created the Commonwealth of Independent States, and on Dec. 21, Ukraine and 11 other former union republics officially committed themselves to the union by signing the Alma-Ata Declaration. In Feb. 1992 Russian president Yeltsin agreed to begin dismantling the vast arsenal of Russian nuclear weapons, 80 percent of which were on Russia's territory, the rest being scattered across Ukraine, Belarus, and Kazkhstan. While Belarus agreed to allow Russia to control the weapons, Kazakhstan and Ukraine used their weapons as bargaining chips.

Throughout 1992, Pres. Yeltsin took center stage, first signing the historic second Strategic Arms Reduction Treaty (START II) with the U.S. in January, then in April rallying the people to support a referendum on government elections and to approve his policies, and finally in June calling together a Constitutional Assembly to write a new constitution. As the Russian economy continued to founder, however, Yeltsin became the target of attacks by former Communists. In Dec. 1992, Yeltsin barely survived a series of votes in Parliament that would have severely limited his control.

This struggle came to a violent head on Sept. 21, 1993, when Yeltsin declared Parliament dissolved and called for new elections to be held in December; Parliament then voted to impeach Yeltsin and appointed Vice Pres. Aleksandr V. Rutskoi to replace him. Anti-Yeltsin forces called for a national strike and barricaded themselves inside the Parliament building for two weeks. Anti-Yeltsin rallies escalated into serious violence when 10,000 protesters overwhelmed riot police and broke through government barricades, causing Yeltsin to summon military police. The leaders of the revolt surrendered after tanks fired directly on the Parliament building, and were immediately sent to prison. At least 100 people were killed in the exchange.

In the aftermath, Yeltsin moved quickly to parlay his victory into even greater political power, by banning several opposition parties, firing powerful opponents, and calling for new parliamentary elections. He announced he would stay in office until his term expired in 1996, and in Nov. 1993 he unveiled the country's first post-Soviet constitution, which centralized power in the executive presidency and limited the powers of the constituent regions. One of these regions, Chechnya, had long threatened secession from Russia and in 1994 its leaders took that action. In Dec. Yeltsin ordered the army to restore government control, but it took months of fighting before Grozny, the rebel capital, fell to Russian troops.

In 1996, unrest by Russia's nationalist faction eroded much of Yeltsin's support, forcing him into a runoff election against the Communist candidate Gennadi Zyuganov in May 1996. But in the runoff, Yeltsin decisively beat back the Communist challenger. In August, Yeltsin formed a cabinet of pro-business technocrats; in the Fall he chucked National Security advisor (and future rival) Lebed, and he agreed to the final withdrawl of Russia's Chechnya brigades.

Yeltsin met Pres. Clinton in Helsinki in March 1997 subsequently agreeing to NATO's eastward expansion in return for NATO's agreement neither to deploy nor to store nuclear weapons there. Economic difficulties reached serious proportions in 1998 and the I.M.F. and the U.S. pledged huge amounts to keep the economy from crumbling. In the spring, Yeltsin replaced many of his ministers with reform-minded bureaucrats. But in the summer, the economy turned down again, and Yeltsin was forced to devalue the ruble. As the economy worsened day-by-day and international lenders refused aid, Russia stood on the brink of collapse.

Even with Mr. Yeltsin's illnesses, personal volatility, and political capriciousness, the I.M.F. and various western investment "Clubs" managed to keep rescheduling Russian debt, so Russia was able to stumble on despite essentially defaulting on loan repayments. The August 1999 appointment of Vladimir Putin as prime minister made him the fifth in 18 months, the third in a row drawn from the secret police. One day after Putin's appointment, insurgents in the Federal Republic of Dagestan, operating out of Chechnya, proclaimed an independent Islamic state; hence, Putin's determination to have it out with Chechnya. Vigorously pursued and (unlike the 1994-96 debacle) very popular, the war went well for Russia and Putin's popularity soared as Grozny fell. Putin triumphed in the March presidential election occasioned by Yeltsin's December resignation. Putin consolidated his power and took a leading role in opposing U.S. plans to build a missile shield but cooperating with U.S. determination to end terrorism.

As 2001 drew to a close, three-pronged Russian American talks continued: American would support closer Russian ties with NATO; both would reduce by two-thirds their nuclear arms; and the U.S. would withdraw from the 1972 ABM pact. Meanwhile (in mid-July 2002) Russia and China signed a 20-year Friendship Treaty, the first since the end of the Cold War. In Nov. 2002 Russian troops began arriving in Kyrgystan, ostensibly to counter terrorism, but likely also to establish a military presence in the face of U.S. bases in Afghanistan. The war in Chechnya took a particularly nasty turn, from the Oct. 2002 Moscow theater hostage crisis to the eight suicide bombings of May-August 2003 which killed over 150.

▶RWANDA

Rwandese Republic

• **GEOGRAPHY** **Location:** landlocked country in central Africa. **Boundaries**: Uganda to N, Tanzania to E, Burundi to S, Zaire to W. **Total area**: 10,170 sq. mi. (26,340 sq km). **Coastline**: none. **Comparative area**: slightly smaller than Maryland. **Land use:** 32% arable land; 10% permanent crops; 158% other. **Major cities**: (1993) Kigali (capital) 234,500; Butare (1978) 21,691; Ruhengeri (1978) 16,025; Gisenyi (1978) 12,436.

• **PEOPLE** **Population:** 7,810,056 (2003 est.). **Nationality:** noun—Rwandan(s); adjective—Rwandan. **Ethnic groups:** 84% Hutu, 15% Tutsi, 1% Twa (Pygmoid). **Languages:** Kinyarwanda (official) universal Bantu vernacular, French and English (both official), Kiswahili (Swahili) used in commercial centers. **Religions:** 57% Catholic, 26% Protestant, 11% Adventist, 5% Muslim.

• **GOVERNMENT** **Type:** republic; presidential system; multiparty system. **Independence:** July 1, 1962 (from U.N. trusteeship under Belgian administration). **Constitution:** May 5, 1995, the Transitional National Assembly adopted a new constitution. **National holiday:** Independence Day, July 1. **Heads of Government:** Paul Kagame, president (since April 2000); Bernard Makuza, prime minister (since March 2000). **Structure:** executive—president; unicameral legislature; judiciary.

• **ECONOMY** **Monetary unit:** Rwandan franc. **Budget:** (2001 est.) ***income:*** $199.3 mil.; ***expend.:*** $445 mil. **GDP:** $9 bil., $1,200 per capita (2002 est.). **Chief crops:** coffee, tea, pyrethrum, bananas, beans, sorghum, potatoes; livestock. **Natural resources:** gold, cassiterite (tin ore), wolframite (tungsten ore), natural gas, hydropower. **Major industries:** agricultural products, small-scale beverage, soap, furniture industries, cement. **Labor force:** 4.6 mil. (2000); 90% agriculture. **Exports:** $68 mil. (f.o.b., 2002 est.); coffee, tea, hides, tin ore. **Imports:** $253 mil. (f.o.b., 2002 est.); foodstuffs, machines and equipment, petroleum products, cement and construction material. **Major trading partners:** ***exports:*** Germany, Pakistan; ***imports:*** Kenya, Belgium, U.S.

Tutsi cattle-breeders came to Rwanda, in the late 15th century and slowly conquered the native Hutu farmers. The Tutsi established a monarchy, forcing the Hutus into serfdom. Germans were the first Europeans to arrive in Rwanda and declared it a protectorate in 1899. After World War I Belgium was given a League of Nations mandate over the territory, which became a U.N. trusteeship after World War II.

Tutsi traditionalists resisted Belgian attempts in the 1950's to institute democratic institutions. In 1959 the Hutus revolted against the monarchy in a bloody conflict which led to a mass exodus of Tutsis. Two years later the Hutus won a U.N.-supervised referendum and were granted internal autonomy by Belgium on Jan. 1, 1962. Full independence came on July 1, 1962. Political unrest led to the overthrow of the government in 1973. Maj. Gen. Juvénal Habyarimana dissolved the National Assembly and banned all political activity.

In 1990 Tutsi refugees in Uganda fought with the army, and by 1993 as many as one million people were displaced. A cease-fire and amnesty paved the way for political reform, and a new constitution allowing for multi-party democracy, separation of powers, and presidential term limits went into effect in June 1992. Proposals to merge the armies of the government (Hutu) and the Tutsi Rwandan Patriotic Front were signed in 1993.

But in April 1994, the Hutu presidents of Rwanda and Burundi were both killed when rocket fire (perhaps launched by Hutu dissidents) shot down their plane as it returned from a peace conference in Tanzania. In renewed civil war, the Hutu dominated army of Rwanda and the Hutu militias were driven by the Tutsi-led Patriotic Front into Zaire, Tanzania, Uganda and Burundi; the Hutus reportedly slaughtered over 500,000 Tutsi and countless Hutu moderates as they went. The result was threefold: a million dead, three million refugees, and a Tutsi-dominated but multi-ethnic "government of national unity".

As the Mobutu regime collapsed in neighboring Zaire, the Zaire military attempted to expel a Tutsi community of 400,000 (the Banyamulenge people) who had been settled south of Lake Kivu since the 18th century. The Tutsi resistance gained support from the Rwandan government (Oct. 1996); thus commenced a de facto war between Rwanda and Zaire. The 500,000 Hutu militiamen and other refugees who, as a result, fled Zaire back to Rwanda joined another half million driven from Tanzania by the Tanzanian army. Yet another wave of killings by Hutu militants had begun in Rwanda. By 1999 the Hutu rebellion was petering out in small but vicious skirmishes and the government of Rwanda was continuing its military aid to insurgents in Congo while attacking Hutu bases in the eastern parts of that country, despite the July cease-fire. In April 2000, Paul Kagame was elected the first Tutsi president of Rwanda, and re-elected in 2003.

▶SAINT KITTS AND NEVIS

Federation of Saint Kitts and Nevis

• **Geography** **Location:** two islands in eastern Caribbean Sea, about 45 mi. (72 km) NW of Antigua. Nevis 17°08'N, 62°37'W; St. Kitts 17°17'N, 62°43'W. **Boundaries**: Caribbean Sea to N, E, S, and W. **Total area**: 104 sq. mi. (269 sq km). **Coastline**: 84 mi. (135 km). **Comparative area**: 1.5 times the size of Washington, D.C. **Land use:** 17% arable land; 3% permanent crops; 80% other. **Major cities**: (1994 est.) Basseterre (capital) 12,605.

• **People** **Population:** 38,763 (2003 est.). **Nationality:** noun—Kittitian(s), Nevisian(s); adjective—Kittitian, Nevisian. **Ethnic groups:** mainly of black African descent. **Languages:** English. **Religions:** Anglican, other Protestant sects, Roman Catholic.

• **Government** **Type:** constitutional monarchy. **Independence:** Sept. 19, 1983 (from U.K.). **Constitution:** Sept. 19, 1983. **National holiday:** Independence Day, Sept 19. **Heads of Government:** Cuthbert Sebastian, governor-general (since Jan. 1996); Denzil Douglas, prime minister (since July 1995). **Structure:** executive—cabinet headed by prime minister; unicameral legislature; judiciary—East Caribbean Supreme Court, based on Saint Lucia.

• **Economy** **Monetary unit:** East Caribbean (EC) dollar. **Budget:** (2003 est.) ***income:*** $89.7 mil.; ***expend.:*** $28.2 mil. **GDP:** $339 mil., $8,800 per capita (2002 est.). **Chief crops:** sugarcane, rice, yams, vegetables, bananas. **Natural resources:** negl. **Major industries:** sugar processing, tourism, cotton. **Labor force:** 18,172 (1995); 69% services, 31% manufacturing. **Exports:** $47 mil. (2001 est.); machinery, food, electronics, beverages, tobacco. **Imports:** $152 mil. (2001 est.); machinery, manufactures, food, fuel. **Major trading partners:** (1995) ***exports:*** 68.5% U.S., 22.3% U.K., 5.5% Caricom nations; ***imports:*** 42.4% U.S., 17.2% Caricom nations, 11.3% U.K.

The French settled St. Kitts in 1627; the English settled Nevis in 1628. In 1783 both became British possessions, and the two islands were united in 1882. Britain granted them independence in 1983. The country's economy is almost entirely based on sugar exports, so when Hurricane Hugo devastated sugar yields in 1990, the welfare of the entire population was affected. The reign of Kennedy Alphonse Simmonds, the only prime minister St. Kitts and Nevis had ever known, ended in July 1995, when Denzil Douglas's opposition Labour party defeated Kennedy's People's Action Movement. March 2000 elections confirmed the change: Labour took eight of the 11 seats, PAN took none. The continued fall of world sugar prices hurt the economy and in 1997 some leaders in Nevis started a movement to separate from St. Kitts because of high taxes. In 1998 a referendum on separation resulted in a majority yes-vote but not the two-thirds necessary.

▶SAINT LUCIA

• **Geography** **Location:** southeastern Caribbean Sea, between Martinique to N and St. Vincent to SW. Castries 14°01'N, 60°59'W. **Boundaries**: St. Lucia Channel to N, Atlantic Ocean to E, St. Vincent Passage to S, Caribbean Sea to W. **Total area**: 239 sq. mi. (620 sq km). **Coastline**: 98 mi. (158 km). **Comparative area**: 3.5 times size of Washington, D.C. **Land use:** 5% arable land; 23% permanent crops; 72% other. **Major cities**: (1992 est.) Castries (capital) 53,883.

• **People** **Population:** 162,157 (2003 est.). **Nationality:** noun—St. Lucian(s); adjective—St. Lucian. **Ethnic groups:** 90% black African descent, 6% mixed, 3% East Indian, 1% Caucasian. **Languages:** English (official), French patois. **Religions:** 90% Roman Catholic, 7% Protestant, 3% Anglican.

• **Government** **Type:** parliamentary democracy. **Independence:** Feb. 22, 1979 (from U.K.). **Constitution:** Feb. 22, 1979. **National holiday:** Independence Day, Feb. 22. **Heads of Government:** Perlette Louisy, governor-general (since Sept. 1997); Kenny D. Anthony, prime minister (since May 1997). **Structure:** executive—cabinet headed by prime minister; bicameral legislature—Senate, House of Representatives; judiciary—East Caribbean Supreme Court.

• **Economy** **Monetary unit:** East Caribbean (EC) dollar. **Budget:** (2000 est.) ***income:*** $141.2 mil.; ***expend.:*** $146.7 mil. **GDP:** $866 mil., $5,400 per capita (2002 est.). **Chief crops:** bananas, coconuts, vegetables, root crops, citrus, cocoa. **Natural resources:** forests, sandy beaches, minerals (pumice), mineral springs, geothermal potential. **Major industries:** clothing, assembly of electronic components, beverages. **Labor force:** 43,800 (1983 est.); 21.7% agriculture, 53.6% services, 24.7% industry and commerce; 16.7% unemployment (1997). **Exports:** $68.3 mil. (2000 est.); 41% bananas, clothing, cocoa, vegetables, fruits, coconut oil. **Imports:** $319.4 mil. (2000 est.); 23% food, 21% manufactured goods, 19% machinery and transport equipment, chemicals, fuels. **Major trading partners:** (1995) ***exports:*** 50% U.K., 24% U.S., 16% Caricom countries; ***imports:*** 36% U.S., 22% Caricom countries, 11% U.K.

In 1650 the French settled St. Lucia, which was ceded to Britain in 1783. A member of the Federation of the West Indies from 1958 to 1962, St. Lucia became internally self-governing in 1967 but was still under Great Britain's protection. In 1979 St. Lucia gained full independence and now enjoys stable competitive politics. Hurricane Allen destroyed many of the country's banana plantations in 1980, and the economy took years to recover from the disaster. The government of Prime Minister John Compton of the United Workers party worked for agrarian reform and proposed legalizing gambling to stimulate tourism but after 15 years in power lost the 1997 elections to the Labour Party led by Kenny B. Anthony.

▶SAINT VINCENT AND THE GRENADINES

• **Geography** **Location:** large island of St. Vincent (13°12'N, 61°14'W) and about 50 smaller islands in southeastern Caribbean Sea about 21 mi. (34 km) SW of St. Lucia and 100 mi. (160 km) W of Barbados. **Boundaries**: St. Vincent Passage to N, Atlantic Ocean to E and SE, Caribbean Sea to SW and W. **Total area**: 131 sq. mi. (340 sq km). **Coastline**: 52 mi. (84 km). **Comparative area**: twice size of Washington, D.C. **Land use:** 10% arable land; 18% permanent crops; 72% other. **Major cities**: (1991 census) Kingstown (capital) 15,670.

• **People** **Population:** 116,812 (2003 est.). **Nationality:** noun—St. Vincentian(s) or Vincentian(s); adjective—St. Vincentian or Vincentian. **Ethnic groups:** mainly of black African descent, remainder mixed, with some white, East Indian, and Carib Amerindian. **Languages:** English, French patois. **Religions:** Anglican, Methodist, Roman Catholic, Seventh-Day Adventist.

• **Government** **Type:** parliamentary monarchy. **Independence:** Oct. 27, 1979 (from U.K.). **Constitution:** Oct. 27, 1979. **National holiday:** Independence Day, Oct. 27. **Heads of Government:** Frederick Nathaniel Ballantyne, governor-general (since Sept. 2, 2002); Ralph E. Gonsalves, prime minister (since Mar. 2001). **Structure:** executive—prime minister is head of government; bicameral legislature—15-member elected House of Representatives and 6-member appointed Senate; judiciary—East Caribbean Supreme Court.

• **ECONOMY** **Monetary unit:** East Caribbean (EC) dollar. **Budget:** (2000 est.) ***income:*** $85.8 mil.; ***expend.:*** $94.6 mil. **GDP:** $339 mil., $2,900 per capita (2002 est.). **Chief crops:** bananas, coconuts, sweet potatoes, spices; small numbers of cattle, sheep, pigs, goats; small fish catch used locally. **Natural resources:** negl. **Major industries:** food processing (sugar, flour), cement, furniture. **Labor force:** 67,000 (1984 est.); 26% agriculture, 17% industry, 57% services; 22% unemployed (1997). **Exports:** $53.7 mil. (2000 est.); 39% bananas, eddoes and dasheen (taro), arrowroot starch, tennis racquets. **Imports:** $185.6 mil. (2000 est.); foodstuffs, machinery and equipment, chemicals and fertilizers, minerals and fuels. **Major trading partners:** ***exports:*** 49% Caricom countries, 16% U.K., 10% U.S.; ***imports:*** 36% U.S., 28% Caricom countries, 13% U.K.

Although ceded to Britain in 1763, St. Vincent was inhabited by the fierce Carib Indians, who continued fighting for control of the island until 1796, when they had all been either killed or deported. Just prior to its independence in 1979, St. Vincent and the Grenadines was a self-governing state in association with Great Britain. It is one of the poorest countries in the West Indies. Several natural disasters have plagued the economy, including a 1979 volcanic eruption and two destructive hurricanes in 1980 and 1986. Prime Minister James Mitchell of the New Democratic party currently governs the country, winning his fourth term after June 1997 elections gave his New Democratic Party a slender one-vote majority in the 15-seat legislature. But March 2001 elections overturned N.D.P. rule as united Labor won 12 of 15 parliamentary seats. The new left-wing government of Ralph Gonsalves has been seeking international accords with Libya and Cuba.

▶SAMOA
Formerly Western Samoa
Independent State of Samoa

• **GEOGRAPHY** **Location:** two large and seven small islands (five inhabited) in South Pacific Ocean, about 1,500 mi. (2,400 km) NE of New Zealand. Apia 13°49'S, 171°45'W. **Boundaries**: surrounded by Pacific Ocean; nearest neighbor is American Samoa to E. **Total area**: 1,104 sq. mi. (2,860 sq km). **Coastline**: 250 mi. (403 km). **Comparative area**: slightly smaller than Rhode Island. **Land use:** 19% arable land; 24% permanent crops; 57% other. **Major cities**: (1991 census) Apia (capital) 34,260.

• **PEOPLE** **Population:** 178,173 (2003 est.). **Nationality:** noun—Samoan(s); adjective—Samoan. **Ethnic groups:** 92.6% Samoan; about 7% Euronesians (persons of European and Polynesian blood), 0.4% Europeans. **Languages:** Samoan (Polynesian), English. **Religions:** 99.7% Christian (about half of population associated with London Missionary Society; includes Congregational, Roman Catholic, Methodist, Latter-Day Saints, Seventh-Day Adventist).

• **GOVERNMENT** **Type:** constitutional monarchy under native chief. **Independence:** Jan. 1, 1962 (from U.N. trusteeship administered by New Zealand). **Constitution:** Jan. 1, 1962. **National holiday:** Independence Day, Jun. 1. **Heads of Government:** Malietoa Tanumafili II, head of state (since 1962); Tuilaepa Sailele Malielegaoi, prime minister (since Nov. 1998). **Structure:** executive—chief of state appoints prime minister; unicameral legislature (47-member Legislative Assembly); judiciary.

• **ECONOMY** **Monetary unit:** tala. **Budget:** (2001/02 est.) ***income:*** $105 mil.; ***expend.:*** $119 mil. **GDP:** $1 bil., $5,600 per capita (2002 est.). **Chief crops:** coconuts, bananas, taro, yams. **Natural resources:** hardwood forests, fish. **Major industries:** timber, tourism, food processing. **Labor force:** 90,000 (2000 est.); 65% agriculture, 30% services. **Exports:** $15.5 mil. (f.o.b., 2002); coconut oil and cream, copra, fish, beer. **Imports:** $130.1 mil. (f.o.b., 2001); intermediate goods, food, capital goods. **Major trading partners:** ***exports:*** Australia, Indonesia; ***imports:*** **U.S.,** Australia, New Zealand.

The Polynesian island group of Samoa (Navigator's Islands) was partitioned in 1899 between the United States, which had established a naval base at Pago Pago on Tutuila in 1878, and Germany, which organized the westerly islands into a colony in 1894. In 1914 New Zealand troops occupied the German-held islands. New Zealand administered Western Samoa under a League of Nations mandate beginning in 1920 and continued to control the islands as a U.N. Trust Territory after 1945. In 1959 home rule was established under an elected local government. Western Samoa became an independent nation on Jan. 1, 1962. The constitution blends Western parliamentary government and traditional Samoan forms of rule. The parliamentary electorate is limited to the *matai*, heads of extended families; the malai are wholly responsible for local affairs. The local culture is similarly a blend of Samoan tradition with Christianity. The economy is based on subsistence agriculture, forestry, fishing, and tourism.

In November 1998, after 16 years of stable and peaceful rule, Prime Minister Tofilau Eti Alesana resigned for health reasons and was replaced by his deputy, Tuilaepa Sailele Malielegaoi.

▶SAN MARINO
Republic of San Marino

• **GEOGRAPHY** **Location:** on slopes of Mt. Titano, in the Apennines, within central Italian region of Emilia-Romagna. **Boundaries**: surrounded by Italian territory. **Total area**: 23 sq. mi. (60 sq km). **Coastline**: none. **Comparative area**: about three-tenths size of Washington, D.C. **Land use:** 17% arable land; 0% permanent crops; 83% other. **Major cities**: (1995 est.) San Marino (capital) 4,498.

• **PEOPLE** **Population:** 28,119 (2003 est.). **Nationality:** noun—Sammarinese (sing., pl.); adjective—Sammarinese. **Ethnic groups:** Sammarinese, Italian. **Languages:** Italian. **Religions:** Roman Catholic.

• **GOVERNMENT** **Type:** republic. **Independence:** 301 A.D. **Constitution:** Oct. 8, 1600; electoral law of 1926 serves some of functions of constitution. **National holiday:** Anniversary of the Foundation of the Republic, Sept. 3. **Heads of Government:** Giovanni Giannoni (Apr.-Sept. 2003) and Giovanni Francesco Ugolini (since Sept. 2002), president. **Structure:** executive—two captain-regents with six-month terms elected by and from the legislature, actual power wielded by secretary of state for foreign affairs; unicameral legislature—Great and General Council elected by popular vote for five-year terms; judicial—Council of Twelve is supreme judicial body.

• **ECONOMY** **Monetary unit:** Euro. **Budget:** (2000 est.) ***income:*** $400 mil.; ***expend:*** $400 mil. **GDP:** $940 mil., $34,600 per capita (2002 est.). **Chief crops:** wheat, grapes, maize, olives; cattle, pigs, horses, meat, cheese, hides. **Natural resources:**

building stones. **Major industries:** tourism, textiles, electronics. **Labor force:** 18,500 (1999); 57% services, 42% industry, 1% agriculture. **Exports:** trade data included with Italian statistics; commodity trade consisting primarily of exchanging building stone, lime, wood, chestnuts, wheat, and wine for a wide variety of consumer manufactures. **Imports:** see exports. **Major trading partners:** N.A.

The "Most Serene Republic" of San Marino, entirely surrounded by Italy near the city of Rimini, is the oldest republic in the world, with communitarian roots dating to the fourth century A.D. While Piedmont-Sardinia was conquering all of the rest of the Italian peninsula during the period 1860-70, it left San Marino independent; the new kingdom of Italy signed a treaty of friendship and cooperation with the republic in 1862.

Leftist coalitions governed from 1978 through 1986, giving San Marino the only Communist government west of the Soviet bloc. Since 1986 the government has been controlled by a coalition of Communists and Christian Democrats. In 1992 San Marino joined the United Nations.

The economy is balanced between small-scale agriculture (primarily wine grapes and livestock) and industry, including textiles, ceramics, and furniture. Philatelic sales and tourism are important sources of revenue. Lacking extremes of wealth and poverty and with low unemployment, the republic enjoys general prosperity.

▶SÃO TOMÉ AND PRÍNCIPE
Democratic Republic of Saõ Tomé and Príncipe

• **GEOGRAPHY** **Location:** two main islands, São Tomé (0°19'N, 6°43'E) and Príncipe, and Caroço, Pedras, Tinhosas (off Príncipe), and Rolas (off São Tomé), off west coast of Africa. **Boundaries**: west of Gabon in Gulf of Guinea. **Total area**: 371 sq. mi. (960 sq km). **Coastline**: 130 mi. (209 km). **Comparative area**: more than 5.5 times size of Washington, D.C. **Land use:** 2% arable land; 41% permanent crops; 57% other. **Major cities**: (1991) São Tomé (capital) 43,420.

• **PEOPLE** **Population:** 175,883 (2001 est.). **Nationality:** noun—São Toméan(s); adjective—São Toméan. **Ethnic groups:** mestiço, angolares (descendants of Angolan slaves), forros (descendents of freed slaves), servicais (contract laborers from Angola, Mozambique, and Cape Verde), tongas (children of servicais born on the islands), and Europeans (primarily Portuguese). **Languages:** Portuguese (official). **Religions:** Roman Catholic, Evangelical Protestant, Seventh-Day Adventist.

• **GOVERNMENT** **Type:** republic. **Independence:** July 12, 1975 (from Portugal). **Constitution:** Sept. 10, 1990. **National holiday:** Independence Day, July 12. **Heads of Government:** Fradique Bandeira Melo de Menezes, president (since Sept. 2001); Maris das Neves, prime minister (since Oct. 7, 2002). **Structure:** executive—president assisted by cabinet of ministers; unicameral legislature; judiciary.

• **ECONOMY** **Monetary unit:** dobra. **Budget:** (1993 est.) ***income:*** $58 mil.; ***expend.:*** $114 mil. **GDP:** $200 mil., $1,200 per capita (2002 est.). **Chief crops:** cocoa, copra, coconuts, coffee, palm kernels, bananas, cinnamon, pepper, papaya, beans; poultry, fish. **Natural resources:** fish. **Major industries:** light construction, textiles, soap, beer; fish processing. **Labor force:** most of population engaged in subsistence agriculture and fishing; labor shortages of skilled workers. **Exports:** $5.5 mil. (f.o.b., 2002 est.); 90% cocoa, copra, coffee, palm oil. **Imports:** $24.8 mil. (f.o.b., 2002 est.); machinery and electrical equipment, food products, fuels. **Major trading partners:** ***exports:*** 27% Netherlands, 18% Portugal, 9% Canada; ***imports:*** 39% Portugal, 22% U.S., 9% U.K.

The islands of São Tomé and Príncipe, located in the Atlantic Ocean 275 and 125 miles, respectively, off the northern coast of Gabon, make up the smallest nation in Africa. They were uninhabited when first discovered by the Portuguese in 1470 but by the mid-1500's became Africa's foremost exporter of sugar. As the sugar market declined, the islands became a major slave-trading center and producer of coffee and cocoa. By 1908 São Tomé was the world's largest cocoa producer.

Portugal did not abolish slavery until 1876, and abusive labor practices continued until well into the 20th century. In 1953 hundreds of workers were killed in clashes with the Portuguese. Soon after, a small number of São Toméans formed the Movement for the Liberation of São Tomé and Príncipe (MLSTP) with its base in Gabon. But the islands did not gain independence until July 12, 1975.

The MLSTP took over after independence and became the country's only official party. By 1986 the country relied on foreign aid for approximately 41 percent of its GNP. Although in the past it received military advisers from the former Soviet Union and economic advisers from Cuba, São Tomé and Príncipe has announced a foreign policy based upon nonalignment. Multi-party democracy was introduced in 1991. At the beginning of the new century oil was discovered and shortly later (July 2002) a military junta seized power.

▶SAUDI ARABIA
Kingdom of Saudi Arabia

• **GEOGRAPHY** **Location:** occupies four-fifths of Arabian peninsula in southwestern Asia. **Boundaries**: Jordan, Iraq, and Kuwait to N, Persian Gulf, Qatar, and United Arab Emirates to E, Oman to SE, Yemen to S and SE, Red Sea to W. **Total area:** 756,982 sq. mi. (1,960,582 sq km). **Coastline**: 1,641 mi. (2,640 km). **Comparative area**: slightly more than one-fifth the size of the U.S. **Land use:** 2% arable land; negl. % permanent crops; 98% other. **Major cities**: (1991 est.) Riyadh (capital) 1,800,000; Jid'dah 1,500,000; Mecca 630,000; Taif 410,000; Medina 400,000.

• **PEOPLE** **Population:** 24,293,844 (2003 est.). **Nationality:** noun—Saudi(s); adjective—Saudi or Saudi Arabian. **Ethnic groups:** 90% Arab, 10% Afro-Asian. **Languages:** Arabic. **Religions:** 100% Muslim.

• **GOVERNMENT** **Type:** monarchy. **Constitution:** none; governed according to Shari'a or Islamic law. **National holiday:** Unification of the Kingdom, Sept. 23. **Head of Government:** Fahd bin Abdul-Aziz al-Saud, king (since June 1982). **Structure:** king rules in consultation with royal family and Council of Ministers; no elected legislature; Supreme Council of Justice.

• **ECONOMY** **Monetary unit:** Saudi riyal. **Budget:** (2003 est.) ***income:*** $46 bil.; ***expend.:*** $56.5 bil. **GDP:** $242 bil., $10,500 per capita (2002 est.). **Chief crops:** wheat, barley, tomatoes, melons, dates, citrus; mutton, chickens, eggs, milk. **Natural resources:** crude oil, natural gas, iron ore, gold, copper. **Major industries:** crude oil production, petroleum refining, basic petrochemicals. **Labor force:** 7 mil.; 25% industry, 63% services, 12% agriculture. **Exports:** $71 bil. (f.o.b., 2001); 90% petroleum and petroleum products. **Imports:** $39.5 bil. (f.o.b., 2001); machinery and equipment, foodstuffs, chemicals, motor vehicles, textiles. **Major trading partners:** 19% U.S., 6% Japan, 10% South Korea; ***imports:*** 17% U.S., 10% Japan, 7% Germany.

In ancient times various cultures flourished in the Arabian peninsula, particularly along the western rim, in cities devoted to trade between the Gulf of Aden and the eastern Mediterranean, and in such agricultural and trading centers as Yemen and Oman. Cultural and political unity was lacking, however, until the rise of Mohammed, the prophet of Islam. In A.D. 622 Mohammed fled from Mecca, the center of Arabian paganism, to the nearby city of Medina; the Islamic era dates from that year. Preaching from Medina, Mohammed gained converts to Islam throughout Arabia. His army captured Mecca in 630, converting its sacred shrine, the Kaaba, to an Islamic place of worship. By 632, when Mohammed died, all of Arabia was unified under Islamic rule.

In 661 the Caliphate, the ruling body of early Islam, moved from Medina to Damascus. Thereafter Arabia was nominally unified under Islamic rule—but in practice was usually divided among various principalities in the arable areas and trading centers, and under tribal rule in the arid interior. Mecca fell to the Ottoman Empire in 1517, but Ottoman control of Arabia was never complete. The rise of the Wahabi sect of Islam in the 18th century posed a challenge to Ottoman rule. In the 19th century, the Saud family rose to leadership in the Wahabi movement and established a kingdom in Nejd, the central region of Arabia, with a capital at Riyadh.

In 1902 Ibn Saud (1880-1953) consolidated his family's control at Riyadh and in 1912-13 led a new Wahabi revolt against the Ottoman Turks. During World War I, the British aided Ibn Saud's rebellion in the Nejd, along with that of Ibn Saud's rival Hussein ibn Ali in the Hejaz, in the mountains of western Arabia along the coast of the Red Sea. A British protectorate was established in both regions in 1915, and Great Britain maintained a dominant position in Arabia after World War I.

In 1924 Ibn Saud captured Hussein ibn Ali's capital at Mecca, and he proclaimed himself king of Hejaz in 1926 and of Nejd in 1927. Ibn Saud consolidated his control over the following two years, and his kingdom was formally recognized by Great Britain in 1927. The country was renamed Saudi Arabia in 1932.

Saudi Arabia is an absolute monarchy based on Islamic law; it has no written constitution and no parliament. The king exercises sole authority and rules in consultation with a Council of Ministers. Islamic law is enforced; alcohol is prohibited and the public activities of women severely restricted. The Saudi kings have great power within the Islamic world through their control over the holy cities of Mecca and Medina and their administration of the annual Muslim pilgrimages to those cities.

The discovery of oil in eastern Arabia in the early 1930's rapidly transformed Saudi Arabia from an impoverished nation to a center of great wealth. In 1933 an exclusive concession for the exploitation of Saudi Arabian oil was granted to an American-chartered corporation, the Arabian-American Oil Company (Aramco). For many years wealth remained concentrated in the hands of the Saudi clan, and little change was felt in the desert interior, where Bedouin nomads continued to raise sheep and camels. Large numbers of Yemenis, Palestinians, Pakistanis, and other foreign workers are employed in the oil fields.

Saudi Arabia remained neutral during most of World War II but declared war on the Axis powers in March 1945; in the same year, it became a founding member of both the United Nations and the Arab League.

Ibn Saud became a leader of Arab anti-Zionism and contributed a small contingent of troops to the 1948 Arab-Israeli War. That policy was maintained by Ibn Saud's second son and successor, King Faisal, who instituted a policy of providing large annual subsidies to Egypt and other Arab League states following the 1967 Arab-Israeli War. In 1973 King Faisal sent Saudi units to fight in the Arab-Israeli War of that year. He played a leading role in organizing the 1973-74 Arab oil embargo in an effort to force the United States and its allies to take a harder line with Israel.

King Faisal was assassinated by his nephew, Prince Faisal, on Mar. 25, 1975, and was succeeded by King Khalid. Little change in policy resulted. In 1979 Saudi Arabia denounced the Camp David talks and the Egyptian-Israeli peace treaty and led the Arab League effort to ostracize Egypt within the Arab world.

Saudi Arabia has consistently opposed leftist and radical movements in the Arab world, sending troops to help put down leftist rebellions in North Yemen and Oman in the 1970's. Saudi kings have taken a moderate approach toward relations with the West. Following the transfer of Aramco assets to full Saudi Arabian ownership during 1973-76, Saudi Arabia used its leading position within the Organization of Petroleum Exporting Countries (OPEC) to argue for a policy of stable production and prices.

This moderate policy has been rewarded by the willingness of the U.S., Great Britain, France, and other Western nations to sell arms—including jet fighters, tanks, and other sophisticated weapons—to Saudi Arabia despite Israeli protests. The multibillion-dollar arms trade has helped to offset the Western oil trade deficit with Saudi Arabia.

Saudi Arabia experienced repeated disturbances in the 1980's. Muslim fundamentalist terrorists seized the Grand Mosque at Mecca on Nov. 20, 1979, provoking a crisis for the Saudi monarchy. On July 31, 1987, Iranian pilgrims rioted in Mecca and were fired upon by Saudi security forces; 402 persons died, including 275 Iranians. Iran's Ayatollah Khomeini denounced the Saudi government and said it was unworthy of being the guardian of Islam's sacred shrines.

A longtime supporter of the Palestine Liberation Organization, the Saudi government gave the PLO $850 million during the 1980's, but ceased when the PLO backed Saddam Hussein's invasion of Kuwait in 1990. During the Persian Gulf War, King Fahd granted permission to station U.S. troops in Saudi Arabia to guard against a possible Iraqi attack. The Saudis promised the United States $16.8 billion and Egypt $1.5 billion to defray the costs of the war. Little ground fighting took place on Saudi soil, but massive oil spills threatened the operation of crucial desalination plants in the Persian Gulf.

Since the war, Saudi Arabia has played a prominent and pivotal role in the diplomatic efforts of the United States and its allies to reach a permanent accord in the Middle East.

In 1996 King Fahd, ailing from a 1995 stroke, temporarily ceded power to his legal successor, Crown Prince Abdullah. In June, terrorists bombed an apartment complex in Dhahran, killing 19 American soldiers stationed there and wounding more than 300 people.

U.S.–Saudi relations were greatly strained when the 9/11 attacks were revealed to have been perpetrated by Saudi citizens. In May 2003 terrorist attacks in the form of four suicide bombings occurred in Riyad in two days. In Aug. a U.S. Congressional report on the 9/11 attacks appeared with 28 of its 850 pages deleted by the White House, pages reportedly describing support provided by Saudi government officials to the hijacker-terrorists.

▶SENEGAL

Republic of Senegal

• **GEOGRAPHY** **Location:** northwestern coast of Africa. **Boundaries**: Mauritania to N, Mali to E, Guinea and Guinea-Bissau to S, Atlantic Ocean to W; The Gambia forms narrow enclave extending 200 mi. (320 km) inland from Atlantic coast. **Total area**: 75,749 sq. mi. (196,190 sq km). **Coastline**: 330 mi. (531 km). **Comparative area**: slightly smaller than South Dakota. **Land use:** 12% arable land; negl.% permanent crops; 88% other. **Major cities**: (1992 census) Dakar (capital) 1,729,823; Thies 201,350; Kaolack 179,894.

• **PEOPLE** **Population:** 10,580,307 (2003 est.). **Nationality:** noun—Senegalese (sing., pl.); adjective—Senegalese. **Ethnic groups:** 43.3% Wolof, 23.8% Pular, 14.7% Serer, 3.7% Diola, 3% Mandink, 1.1% Soninke, 1% European and Lebanese. **Languages:** French (official), Wolof, Pulaar, Diola, Mandingo. **Religions:** 94% Muslim, 1% indigenous beliefs, 5% Christian (mostly Roman Catholic).

• **GOVERNMENT** **Type:** republic under multi-party democratic rule. **Independence:** Apr. 4, 1960 (from France). **Constitution:** a new constitution was adopted Jan. 7, 2001. **National holiday:** Independence Day, Apr. 4. **Heads of Government:** Abdoulaye Wade, president (since Apr. 2000); Mame Madior Boye, prime minister (since May 2001). **Structure:** executive—president; unicameral legislature; judiciary—Constitutional Court, Council of State, Court of Final Appeals, Court of Appeals.

• **ECONOMY** **Monetary unit:** Communauté Financière Africaine (CFA) franc. **Budget:** (2002 est.) ***income:*** $1.373 bil.; ***expend.:*** $1.373 bil. **GDP:** $16.2 bil., $1,500 per capita (2002 est.). **Chief crops:** peanuts, millet, corn, sorghum, rice, cotton, tomotoes, green vegetables; cattle, poultry, pigs; fish. **Natural resources:** fish, phosphates, iron ore. **Major industries:** fishing, agricultural processing, phosphate mining. **Labor force:** 60% agriculture. **Exports:** $1.15 bil. (f.o.b., 2002); fish, peanuts, petroleum products, phosphates, cotton. **Imports:** $1.2 bil. (f.o.b., 1998); foods and beverages, consumer goods, capital goods, petroleum products. **Major trading partners:** ***exports:*** 18% India, 16% France, 9% Italy; ***imports:*** 27% France, 19% Nigeria, 5% Germany.

Inhabited since ancient times, Senegal was dominated in the 13th and 14th centuries by the Mandingo and Jolof empires. Portuguese traders and explorers arrived in Senegal in the early 15th century and later competed with the British, Dutch, and French for domination in Senegal. The French established a trading station at Saint-Louis in 1659 and maintained possession thereafter, except for the British enclave along the Gambia River.

In the early 19th century, the French began a series of campaigns to bring the entire country under their control; the last independent sultanate surrendered in 1893. Senegal became a French colony in 1920, and Dakar became the capital of French West Africa. Senegal became a major contributor of African troops to the French armed forces.

In 1946 a territorial assembly was established, with a limited electorate and advisory powers, which were gradually expanded in subsequent years. With the creation of the French Community of Nations in 1958, Senegal achieved local self-rule within the community.

In 1959, with the encouragement of France, Senegal and French Sudan (now Mali) formed the Federation of Mali, which became fully independent on June 20, 1960. Senegal seceded from the federation on Aug. 20 and declared itself the Republic of Senegal. Leopold Sedar Senghor became Senegal's first president.

In 1962 Prime Minister Mamdou Dia attempted a coup against the Senghor government; it failed, and Dia was imprisoned. A new constitution was subsequently adopted, strengthening the power of the presidency. Senghor retired from office in 1981 and was succeeded by Adbou Diouf. He encouraged political pluralism and has presided over a generally stable government. Diouf was elected in his own right in 1983 and reelected in 1988. Following the 1988 elections, riots broke out over charges of electoral fraud, and a state of emergency was declared.

Diouf, who has taken a lead in African affairs, was reelected for the third time in 1993, but his Socialist party's legislative majority was diminished. At home, Diouf consolidated his power so well that in 1998 Parliament passed a law allowing him to become President for life. His involvement in the civil war in Guinea-Bissau, however, has caused dissension in the army. His January 1999 creation of a Senate as "upper house" to the National Assembly meant little for democracy since, with all opposition parties boycotting the election, his Socialist Party carried all 45 seats up for election. So the March 2000 presidential election was a surprise: Abdoulaye Wade of the Democratic Party (who had run four times since 1978) took 60 percent of the vote to become Senegal's third, and first non-Socialist, president.

Senegal remains closely tied to France commercially, culturally, and in foreign affairs. Senegal's economy is primarily agricultural. Industries include fishing and fish processing (the principal source of export earnings), food processing, light manufacturing, and phosphate mining. Senegalese merchants are active in commercial networks throughout West Africa.

▶SERBIA AND MONTENEGRO

• **GEOGRAPHY** **Location:** Southern central Europe. **Boundaries**: Hungary to N, Romania to NE, Bulgaria to E, Macedonia and Albania to S, Adriatic Sea, Bosnia and Herzegovina to W., Croatia to NW. **Total area**: 39,517 sq. mi. (102,350 sq km). **Coastline**: 124 mi. (199 km). **Comparative area**: Slightly smaller than Kentucky. **Land use:** 36% arable; 3% permanent crops, 61% other. **Major cities**: (mid-1992 est.) Belgrade (capital) 1,500,000; Nis 300,000; Kragujevac 250,000; Novi Sad 250,000; Podoricj 80,000.

• **PEOPLE** **Population:** 10,665,774 (2003 est.). **Nationality:** noun—Serb(s) and Montenegrin(s); adjective—Serbian and Montenegrin. **Ethnic groups:** 62.6% Serbian, 16.5% Albanian, 5% Montenegrin, 3.3% Hungarian, 12.6% other. **Languages:** 95% Serbian, 5% Albanian. **Religions:** 65% Orthodox, 19% Muslim, 4% Roman Catholic, 1% Protestant, 11% other.

• **GOVERNMENT** **Type:** republic. **Independence:**

Proclaimed itself successor to former Socialist Federal Republic of Yugoslavia Apr. 11, 1992. **Constitution:** Feb. 4, 2003. **National holiday:** Republic Day, Nov. 29. **Heads of Government:** Svetozar Marović, president (since Mar. 7, 2003); Dragisa Pesic, prime minister (since July 2001); **Structure:** executive—president; bicameral legislature; judiciary—judges elected by legislature.

• **ECONOMY** **Monetary unit:** Yugoslav new dinar. **Budget:** ***income:*** $3.9 bil., ***expend:*** $4.3 bil. **GDP:** $25.3 bil., $2,370 per capita (2002 est.). **Chief crops:** cereal, fruits, vegetables, tobacco, olives; cattle, sheep, goats. **Natural resources:** oil, gas, coal, antimony, copper. **Major industries:** machine building, metallurgy, mining, consumer goods, electronics, petroleum products, chemicals, pharmaceuticals. **Labor force:** 3 mil. (2001). **Exports:** $2.3 billion (2002); manufactured goods, food and live animals, raw materials. **Imports:** $6.3 bil. (2002); machinery and transport equipment, fuels and lubricants, manufactured goods, chemicals, food and live animals, raw materials. **Major trading partners:** Bosnia and Herzegovnia, Italy, Russia.

The lands that composed Yugoslavia until 1991 were incorporated into the Roman Empire as the province of Illyricum in the first century A.D. Christianity became dominant by A.D. 600. Its nucleus was Serbia, settled in the seventh century by South Slav migrants from the Over and Vistula, and converted to Christianity, in its Eastern Orthodox form, in the ninth century. Twice (in 1077 and again in 1202), the Vatican sent royal crowns to Serbian kings, emphasizing their independence, despite the religious differences. Serbia's medieval zenith came during the reign of Stephen Dushan (1331-55), who subjected Albania, Macedonia, Thessaly, and Epirus to his rule, and who gained the vassalage of Bulgaria in addition. But within 30 years of his death, the Ottoman Turks had overrun his realm, a dominance sealed by the Serbian catastrophe at the Battle of Kosovo (1389). Not until 1878 did Serbia regain independence.

The complexities of Balkan politics occupied European statesmen throughout the late 19th century, and the Balkan Wars of 1912 and 1913 led directly to the outbreak of World War I. After the collapse of the Austro-Hungarian Empire during the war, the multiethnic and multinational state of Yugoslavia was patched together in 1918-19. To Serbia were annexed the old Austro-Hungarian lands of Slovenia and Croatia, as well as the ethnically Croatian and Serbian lands of Bosnia and Herzegovina and Montenegro, Macedonia and Kosovo. The last three were Serbian, Bulgarian, and Albanian in nationality, respectively.

The nationalities coexisted in a state of mutual hostility, provoking a royal dictatorship, instituted by King Alexander in 1929 and enduring after his assassination in 1934. Hitler invaded Yugoslavia in 1941; German troops were welcomed in Croatia as liberators from the Serbs. Resistance began almost immediately, split into two mutually hostile groups: Draza Mihajlovic's Serbian royalist Chetniks, and the Partisans, a group of pan-Yugoslav Communists and non-Serbian anti-German forces led by Tito (a.k.a. Josip Broz). By the end of the war, over 2 million Yugoslavs had died, and 3.5 million were homeless. As marshal, backed by both Churchill and Stalin, Tito ruled over a ruined land: the newly created Federal People's Republic of Yugoslavia.

Tito imposed agricultural collectivization on the Stalinist model, and pushed for the development of industry under state ownership. Politically, harsh repression fell on members of the Chetnik resistance as well as on the Slovene Home Guard and the Croatian Ustasa. But the postwar period of tyranny was short-lived. Tito refused to permit Yugoslavia to become a Soviet satellite; in 1948 he expelled Russian military advisers, and was himself expelled from the Comintern.

In the face of economic pressure and military threats, Tito turned westward. Stalinism yielded to decentralized communism. The 1953 Agrarian Reform Law permitted private agricultural smallholdings, and over 80 percent of the land returned to private ownership; "self-management" rather than central control was encouraged in the industrial sector as well. Economic growth averaged over 7 percent per year for three decades, lifting Yugoslavia into the ranks of the semideveloped countries.

Despite a reconciliation with Khruschev's Soviet Union in 1955-56, Tito continued to chart an independent course, taking a leading role in the Third World Non-Aligned Movement and providing a political and economic alternative model for Eastern Europe. But Yugoslavian nationalism masked the development of separate nationalisms within the Yugoslavian federation.

The country's three major ethnic groups (Serbs, Croats, and Muslims) coexisted peacefully under Tito's iron hand, and even after Tito's death in 1980, his rotating presidency scheme, in which the leaders of each republic took turns serving as "president of the presidency," worked smoothly, as long as Yugoslavia was dominated by communism. But when communism fell in 1989, only Serbia and Montenegro voted for Communist governments, while the republics of Croatia, Slovenia, Macedonia, and Bosnia-Herzegovina sought independence.

A vicious civil war ensued in which Yugoslavia's Serbian president Slobodan Milosevic sought to keep all ethnically Serbian areas under Serbian control. While Serb militias captured about one-third of Croatia in 1991, the Croatian army won back most of the region in 1995. And Yugoslavia's attempt to keep Bosnia-Herzegovina within a "greater Serbia" failed as well, the failure ratified in the November 1995 "Dayton Accords," which brought NATO peacekeepers to the region. The year 1996 saw the formal end of the civil wars, as Milosevic endorsed treaties guaranteeing the boundaries of Macedonia, Croatia and Bosnia; additionally, a pact with the Albanians of Serbia's Kosovo province permitted Albanian as the language of instruction in Kosovo's schools.

Though Milosevic and his political allies won 84 of 138 seats in Yugoslavia's parliament in Nov. 1996, the political opposition, called Zajedno ("Together"), won control of 14 large cities. The annulments of these results by Yugoslav courts and electoral commissions provoked 11 weeks of popular protests until Milosevic conceded in Feb. 1997. In July, however, Milosevic maneuvered to take back the presidency by receiving a majority of votes in Parliament.

In 1998 ethnic Albanians in the Kosovo province of Serbia launched a terrorist campaign to secede from Serbia and join Albania. The Serbs put down the rebellion with unexpected ferocity. In the winter of 1999 Serbia launched a full-scale attack against Kosovo that drove 700,000 ethnic Albanians from their homes. Despite NATO warnings, Pres. Milosevic continued his ethnic cleansing of Serbia's province and at the end of March NATO began a bombing campaign that lasted 72 days. In June Serbia surrendered and Milosevic agreed to 50,000 NATO troops in Kosovo and the withdrawal of all Yugoslav troops. The U.N. supervised peace was slow to form and soon Serbs were being driven from Kosovo. In 2000 Milosevic managed to maintain his power but his attempt to rig elections in the summer led to mass protests.

In 2000, as NATO troops attempted to defend Serbia proper against Albanian incursions from Kosovo, opposition in Serbia to continuance of the Milosevic regime faced police-state measures. A coalition of 15 parties backed Vojislav Kostunica against Milosevic in the Sept. presidential elections. Hundreds of thousands protested the Milosevic attempts to force a run-off and Kostunica was sworn in Oct. 7. Milosevic was turned over to the U.N. for trial on war-crimes charges. In March 2002 the presidents of Serbia and Montenegro agreed to maintain foreign affairs and defense as the sole bonds in a loose federation. The very name "Yugoslavia" was dropped in favor of "Serbia and Montenegro."

▶SEYCHELLES

Republic of Seychelles

• **Geography** **Location:** more than 90 widely scattered islands in western Indian Ocean about 1,000 mi. (1,600 km) E of Kenya and Tanzania. Victoria (Mahé Is.) 4°37'S, 55°28'E. **Boundaries**: surrounded by Indian Ocean; nearest neighbor is Madagascar about 130 mi. (210 km) S of southernmost island group. **Total area**: 176 sq. mi. (455 sq km). **Coastline**: 305 mi. (491 km). **Comparative area**: 2.5 times the size of Washington, D.C. **Land use:** 2% arable land; 13% permanent crops; 85% other. **Major cities**: (1987) Victoria (capital) 24,325 (includes suburbs).

• **People** **Population:** 80,469 (2003 est.). **Nationality:** noun—Seychellois (sing., pl.); adjective—Seychelles. **Ethnic groups:** Seychellois (mixture of Asians, Africans, Europeans). **Languages:** English, French (both official); Creole. **Religions:** 87% Roman Catholic, 7% Anglican, 6% other.

• **Government** **Type:** republic. **Independence:** June 29, 1976 (from U.K.). **Constitution:** June 18, 1993. **National holiday:** National Day, June 18. **Head of Government:** France Albert René, president (since June 1977). **Structure:** executive—president; unicameral legislature; judiciary.

• **Economy** **Monetary unit:** Seychelles rupee. **Budget:** (1998 est.) ***income:*** $249 mil.; ***expend.:*** $262 mil. **GDP:** $626 mil., $7,800 per capita (2002 est.). **Chief crops:** coconuts, cinnamon, vanilla, sweet potatoes, cassava, bananas; broiler chickens; tuna fishing (expansion under way). **Natural resources:** fish, copra, cinnamon trees. **Major industries:** tourism is largest industry; processing of coconut and vanilla; fishing. **Labor force:** 30,900 (1996); 19% industry, 71% services, 10% agriculture, forestry, and fishing. **Exports:** $235 mil. (f.o.b., 2001); fish, cinnamon bark, copra, petroleum products (reexports). **Imports:** $380 mil. (c.i.f., 2001); food, petroleum products, machinery, transportation equipment. **Major trading partners:** ***exports:*** France, U.K., Italy; ***imports:*** France, Saudi Arabia, U.S.

The Seychelles Islands were occupied by France in the 18th century and seized by Great Britain in 1794. They were administered along with Mauritius until 1903, when the Seychelles became a separate British colony. African and Indian workers were brought in to work in coconut and spice plantations and in guano mining. The present population is of mixed African, Indian, and European descent.

In the post-World War II period, a home-rule government rejected independence as impracticable. At the urging of the Organization of African Unity and the United Nations, the Seychelles declared independence on June 29, 1976. Its first president was ousted in a socialist coup in 1977 led by Prime Minister France Albert René. A new constitution, promulgated in March 1979, formalized one-party Socialist rule. In July 1992 a commission was elected to rewrite the constitution before the end of the year, but the delegates defeated the first results.

Since independence, the economy of the Seychelles has become heavily dependent on the tourist industry, which accounts for 90 percent of the country's foreign exchange earnings. Fishing accounts for 40 percent of exports.

▶SIERRA LEONE

Republic of Sierra Leone

• **Geography** **Location:** west central Africa. **Boundaries**: Guinea to N and E, Liberia to S, Atlantic Ocean to W. **Total area**: 27,699 sq. mi. (71,740 sq km). **Coastline**: 250 mi. (402 km). **Comparative area**: slightly smaller than South Carolina. **Land use:** 7% arable land; 1% permanent crops; 92% other.; **Major cities**: Freetown (capital) 384,499 (1985 census); Koindu 82,474; Bo 59,768; Kenema 52,473; Makeni 49,474.

• **People** **Population:** 5,732,681 (2003 est.). **Nationality:** noun—Sierra Leonean(s); adjective—Sierra Leonean. **Ethnic groups:** over 90% African (30% Temne, 30% Mende), 10% creole. **Languages:** English (official); regular use limited to literate minority; principal languages are Mende in south and Temne in north; Krio is language of resettled ex-slave population of Freetown area and is lingua franca. **Religions:** 60% Muslim, 30% indigenous beliefs, 10% Christian.

• **Government** **Type:** constitutional democracy. **Independence:** Apr. 27, 1961 (from U.K.). **Constitution:** Oct. 1, 1991. **National holiday:** Independence Day, Apr. 27. **Heads of Government:** Alhaj Ahmad Tejan Kabbah, president (since Mar. 1996). **Structure:** executive—president; unicameral legislature-68 elected seats, 12 filled by paramount chiefs; judiciary.

• **Economy** **Monetary unit:** leone. **Budget:** (1996 est.) ***income:*** $96 mil.; ***expend.:*** $651 mil. **GDP:** $2.8 bil., $580 per capita (2002 est.). **Chief crops:** palm kernels, coffee, cocoa, rice, palm oil, peanuts; poultry, cattle, sheep, pigs; fish. **Natural resources:** diamonds, titanium ore, bauxite, iron ore, gold. **Major industries:** mining (diamonds, iron ore, bauxite, rutile), small-scale manufacturing (beverages, textiles, cigarettes, footwear), petroleum refinery. **Labor force:** 1.369 mil. (1981); 65% agriculture, 19% industry, 16% services; only small minority, some 65,000, earn wages. **Exports:** $35 mil. (f.o.b., 2002); diamonds, rutile, cocoa, coffee, fish. **Imports:** $190 mil. (c.i.f., 2002); foodstuffs, machinery and equipment, fuels and lubricants. **Major trading partners:** ***exports:*** **32% Greece,** 28% Belgium, 6% U.S., 8% U.S.; ***imports:*** 25% U.K., 10% Netherlands, 8% U.S.

Portuguese domination of the Sierra Leone coast began in 1462. English explorers, including Francis Drake, arrived in the late 16th century. Europeans traded for slaves in Sierra Leone, but in 1787 Freetown was founded by the British Sierra Leone Co. as a haven for freed slaves. The settlement was populated by former slaves from Great Britain, North America, and the Caribbean, and later by slaves liberated from slave trading ships by the British navy.

Sierra Leone was reorganized as a British

colony in 1808. The ex-slave population, from diverse tribal and national backgrounds, developed an English-speaking Creole culture unique in Africa. Freetown became the center of British colonial administration and trade in West Africa and was the focus of missionary-supported projects in health care and economic development.

The native peoples of Sierra Leone staged numerous rebellions against the British and the Creole elite; resentment focused on the tax system and on the privileges of the English-speaking descendents of ex-slaves. During the 20th century, home rule developed through an elected advisory legislature. In 1951 a constitutional framework had been developed as the basis of decolonization. Sir Milton Margei became chief minister in 1953, and prime minister in 1961. The last ties with the British Crown were cut on Apr. 27, 1961, when Sierra Leone became a republic. A referendum in 1978 created a one-party state. In 1984 and 1985 student and public employee protests against the government led to riots and the restoration of multi-party elections.

In April 1992, Momoh was ousted in a coup by Capt. Valentine Strasser. Despite the country's wealth of natural resources, Strasser's corruption and mismanagement threatened to derail the economy. Strasser was overthrown in Jan. 1996 by army officers who pledged to continue his plan for multi-party elections. Ahmad Tejan Kabbah of the People's party captured close to 60 percent of the votes.

In 1991 Sierra Leone was attacked by a murderous gang led by "rebel" Fodaj Sankoh, calling itself the Revolutionary United Front. By July 1999 it controlled perhaps half of the country, including diamond mines which they looted, then marketed through Liberia's president, Charles Taylor. In May 1997 regular army troops loyal to Major Johnny Paul Koroma briefly overthrew Pres. Kabbah until Nigerian-led west African troops restored Kabbah and assisted against the RUF gang. A July 1999 cease-fire brought four RUF killers into the government and an amnesty for Sankoh. But the RUF did not disarm, and continued the struggle into 2000. Sankoh was captured late in May. In 2001 Parliament, with U.N. and British approval, postponed the scheduled March elections and extended President Kabbah's term for six months. With Sankoh captured, more U.N. troops in the country, and, most importantly, diminished support from Pres. Taylor, RUF began in May to disarm and to release hundreds of its boy-soldiers. But fighting continued in the diamond-rich east.

The July 18, 2001 agreement of the U.N., Sierra Leone, and the RUF rebels was strong enough for the government to declare (Jan. 18, 2002) the 11-year civil war over. On March 4, Foday Sankah was chargedwith murder; and on May 19 elections brought overwhelming approval to both Pres. Kabbah and his Sierra Leone's People's Party (which gained 83 of the 112 parliamentary seats); 17,000 U.N. troops remained in Sierra Leone.

▶SINGAPORE
Republic of Singapore

• **GEOGRAPHY** **Location:** Singapore Island and some 57 islets off southern Malay peninsula (linked by a causeway). **Boundaries**: Johor Strait to N; Pacific Ocean to E; Strait of Malacca to SW, separating Singapore from Indonesian island of Sumatra; and Indian Ocean to W. **Total area**: 244 sq. mi. (633 sq km). **Coastline**: 120 mi. (193 km). **Comparative area**: slightly more than 3.5 times size of Washington, D.C. **Land use:** 2% arable land; 0% permanent crops; 98% other. **Major cities**: Singapore (capital).

• **PEOPLE** **Population:** 4,608,595 (2003 est.). **Nationality:** noun—Singaporean(s); adjective—Singapore. **Ethnic groups:** 77% Chinese, 14% Malay, 7.9% Indian, 1.4% other. **Languages:** Chinese, Malay, Tamil, and English (all official); Malay (national). **Religions:** majority of Chinese are Buddhists or atheists; Malays nearly all Muslim; minorities include Christians, Hindus, Sikhs, Taoists, Confucianists.

• **GOVERNMENT** **Type:** parliamentary republic. **Independence:** Aug. 9, 1965 (from Malaysia). **Constitution:** June 3, 1959, amended 1965; based on preindependence State of Singapore constitution. **National holiday:** Aug. 9. **Heads of Government:** S.R. Nathan, president (since Sept. 1999); Goh Chok Tong, prime minister (since Nov. 1990). **Structure:** executive—ceremonial president, power exercised by prime minister and cabinet; unicameral legislature; judiciary.

• **ECONOMY** **Monetary unit:** Singapore dollar. **Budget:** (FY00 est.) ***income:*** $27.9 bil.; ***expend.:*** $19.5 bil. **GDP:** $105 bil., $24,000 per capita (2002 est.). **Chief crops:** rubber, copra, fruits, vegetables; poultry. **Natural resources:** fish, deep-water ports. **Major industries:** financial services, petroleum refining, electronics, oil drilling equipment. **Labor force:** 2.19 mil. (2000 est.); 35% financial, business, and other services, 21% manufacturing, 13% construction, transportation and communication. **Exports:** $127 bil. (2002 est.); computer equipment, petroleum products, telecommunications equipment. **Imports:** $113 bil. (2002 est.); machinery and equipment, petroleum, chemicals, foodstuffs. **Major trading partners:** ***exports:*** 17% Malaysia, 15% U.S., 9% Hong Kong; ***imports:*** 17% Malaysia, 13% U.S., 12% Japan.

Singapore was founded in 1819 by Sir Thomas Stamford Raffles on land ceded to the East India Company by the sultanate of Johore (see "Malaysia"). An Anglo-Dutch treaty turned Singapore over to the British Crown in 1824, and eventually it was administered as part of the Straits Settlements. With its excellent harbor, Singapore eclipsed Penang and Malacca as the dominant port for trade through the Straits of Malacca.

Fortified as a bastion of British defense in Southeast Asia, Singapore was overrun by Japanese troops in Feb. 1942. The British reoccupied the city in Sept. 1945 and reorganized it as a British colony in 1946. On June 5, 1959, Singapore became a self-governing parliamentary democracy within the British Commonwealth. Lee Kwan Yew became prime minister. On Sept. 16, 1963, Singapore, along with Malaya, Sarawak, and Sabah, formed the Malaysian Federation. Singapore, ethnically Chinese, was uncomfortable within the Malay-dominated federation and seceded after two years, becoming an independent nation on Aug. 9, 1965.

Independent Singapore has enjoyed orderly, if authoritarian, government, economic growth, and a high standard of living. Still a major port, its economy now encompasses international banking, finance, communications, high-technology manufacturing, and tourism. On Nov. 26, 1990, Lee Kuan Yew, Singapore's only prime minister since independence and the longest serving prime minister in the world, resigned. He was succeeded by Goh Chok Tong, but he remains a force in Singapore's political life.

Measures in 2000 opened up segments of the economy to foreign firms, especially telecommunications and law, while the government ended its monopoly on broadcasting and newspapers. In 2001 Lee Kwan Yew's son, Lee Hsien Loong, currently chairman of the central bank and deputy prime minister, became prime minister.

▶SLOVAKIA
Slovak Republic

• **GEOGRAPHY Location:** Central Europe. **Boundaries**: Czech Republic and Poland to N, Ukraine to E, Hungary to S, Austria to W. **Total area**: 18,859 sq. mi. (48,845 sq km). **Coastline**: none. **Comparative area**: about twice the size of New Hampshire. **Land use:** 31% arable, 3% permanent crops, 66% other. **Major cities**: (1994 est.) Bratislava (capital) 450,776; Kosice 239,927; Nitra 87,127; Presov 92,013; Banská Bystrica 84,741.
• **PEOPLE Population:** 5,430,033 (2003 est.). **Nationality:** noun—Slovak(s); adjective—Slovak. **Ethnic groups:** 85.7% Slovak, 10.6% Hungarian, 1.6% Roma. **Languages:** Slovak (official), Hungarian. **Religions:** 60.3% Roman Catholic, 9.7% atheist, 8.4% Protestant, 4.1% Orthodox.
• **GOVERNMENT Type:** parliamentary democracy. **Independence:** Jan. 1, 1993 (from Czechoslovakia). **Constitution:** Jan. 1, 1993; changed Sept. 1996 to allow direct election of president. **National holiday:** Slovak Constitution Day, Sept. 1. **Heads of Government:** Rudolf Schuster, president (since Jun. 1999); Mikuláš Dzurinda, prime minister (since Oct. 1998). **Structure:** executive—president, prime minister, Council of Ministers; legislative—unicameral (National Council); judicial—Supreme Court.
• **ECONOMY Monetary unit:** koruna. **Budget:** (1999 est.) ***income:*** $5.2 bil.; ***expend.:*** $5.6 bil. **GDP:** $66 bil., $12,200 per capita (2002 est.). **Chief crops:** grains, potatoes, sugar beets, hops, fruit; hogs, cattle, poultry; forest products. **Natural resources:** brown coal and lignite; small amounts of iron ore, copper and manganese ore, salt. **Major industries:** metal working, food, beverages, fuels, chemicals. **Labor force:** 3 mil.; 29.3% industry, 8.9% agriculture, 8.0% construction, 8.2% transport and communication, 45.6% services. **Exports:** $12.9 bil. (f.o.b., 2002 est.); 39% machinery and transport equipment; 18% intermediate manufactured goods, 10% miscellaneous manufactured goods. **Imports:** $15.4 bil. (f.o.b., 2001 est.); 38% machinery and transport equipment; 18% intermediate manufactured goods, 13% fuels. **Major trading partners:** ***exports:*** 60% E.U., 17% Czech Republic; ***imports:*** 50% E.U., 15% Czech Republic, 15% Russia.

Though the Czech and Slovak languages are similar, the two peoples have always been far apart culturally and historically (much like the Letts and Lithuanians). The ninth-century Moravian Empire has been claimed as heritage by both peoples; but with the Magyar invasion of the Pannonian Plain in the 10th century, the Slovaks passed under Hungarian rule for 1,000 years. When in the 19th century a romantic-nationalist revival occurred, the Slovaks, under the leadership of Ludovit Štūr, decided to use their own language in literature (though some of the most prominent writers in the Czech tongue were of Slovak origin, such as the poet Jan Kollár and the historian P.J. Safarik). Unlike the Czechs, the Slovaks took no part in the revolutions of 1848. They lacked a native aristocracy; their national leadership came from wealthy peasants, small-town shopkeepers and, above all, their priests.

In the peacemaking at the end of World War I, as the Austro-Hungarian Empire collapsed, the Czech politicians Beneš and Masaryk claimed to speak for the (nonexistent) Czechoslovak nation. They carried the day despite apparent Slovak loyalty to Hungary and even the opposition of Fr. Hlinka's Slovak Populist party to union with the Czechs. The synthetic "nation" of Czechoslovakia was created, governed by a sort of benevolent democratic dictatorship of the Czechs over the other nations. With the Munich crisis of October 1939, Hitler imposed a federal structure giving Slovakia almost complete autonomy in the renamed Czecho-Slovakia; in the following March, when Hitler obliterated Czech independence, an "independent" Slovakia was formed with Hlinka's successor, Magr Tiso, as president.

But under the circumstances independence was illusory. German protection (against Hungarian revisionism) required complete Slovak accord with Reich foreign policy, including declarations of war on Poland (1939) and on the U.S.S.R., the United States, and Great Britain (1941). Domestically, Msgr. Tiso organized a one-party state with anti-Jewish legislation, half unwilling and half unable to resist the expulsion (and eventual extermination) of 60,000 Jews.

The cement for a restored Czechoslovakia after the war was the Communist tyranny imposed in 1948. But the "Velvet Revolution" in 1989 overturned Yalta and brought victory over the Communists. As the Czech premier Václav Klaus pushed for free-market "shock therapy," the Slovak premier Vladimír Meciar defended a slower "Slovak way" to capitalism. Economic differences inflamed by ancient Slovak resentment of the Czech majority led to a much-diminished federal government by the spring of 1992. In the summer the split became the "Velvet Divorce."

In July 1992 Slovak deputies to the federal Parliament blocked the reelection of Václav Havel to the presidency, and the Slovak National Council approved, by a vote of 113 to 24, a declaration of sovereignty. In September the two parliaments agreed to the terms. In accord with a two-to-one ratio of the republics' populations, the military and financial assets of Czechoslovakia were divided. By February even plans for a common currency had gone by the board, with only a customs union linking the two parts of the old state.

On Feb. 15, 1993, the Slovak Parliament elected its first president, Michal Kovác, with Meciar, as prime minister. Spiraling inflation and high unemployment coupled with a corruption scandal toppled the Meciar government early in 1994, but a coalition government including many former Communists restored him as prime minister later that year. In Sept. 1998, a four-party opposition coalition toppled Meciar's regime. Mikulás Dzurinda became prime minister, heading a government whose principal focus was NATO and E.U. membership.

On May 29, 1999, in Slovakia's first popular rather than parliamentary election of a president, Rudolf Schuster defeated Meciar in a run-off; but in July 2000, the cabinet, with Schuster incapacitated by illness, transferred presidential powers to the prime minister and parliament's speaker. Meciar was arrested on charges of fraud and abuse of power. Dzurinda put together a four-party coalition to stay in office and in May 2003 93 percent of voters approved, joining the E.U.

▶SLOVENIA
Republic of Slovenia

• **GEOGRAPHY Location:** southeastern Europe. **Boundaries**: Austria to N, Hungary to NE, Croatia to E and S, Adriatic Sea and Italy to W. **Total area**:

7,836 sq. mi. (20,296 sq km). **Coastline**: 20 mi. (32 km). **Comparative area**: Slightly smaller than New Jersey. **Land use:** 11% arable land, 3% permanent crops, 86% other. **Major cities**: (1994 est.) Ljubljana (capital) 269,972; Maribor 103,113; Celje 39,782; Kranj 36,770.

• **PEOPLE** **Population:** 1,935,677 (2003 est.). **Nationality:** noun—Slovene(s); adjective—Slovenian. **Ethnic groups:** 88% Slovene, 3% Croat, 2% Serb, 1% Bosniak. **Languages:** 91% Slovenian, 6% Serbo-Croatian. **Religions:** 70.8% Catholic, 1% Lutheran, 1% Muslim, 27.2% other.

• **GOVERNMENT** **Type:** parliamentary democratic republic. **Independence:** June 25, 1991 (from Yugoslavia). **Constitution:** Dec. 23, 1991. **National holiday:** National Statehood Day, June 25. **Heads of Government:** Janez Drnovšek, president of the presidency (four other members) (since Dec. 22, 2002); Anton Rop, prime minister (since 2002). **Structure:** executive—president, prime minister, cabinet; legislative—unicameral parliament-second chamber has only advisory powers; judicial—Supreme Court, Constitutional Court.

• **ECONOMY** **Monetary unit:** tolar (SIT). **Budget:** (1997 est.) ***income:*** $8.11 bil.; ***expend.:*** $8.32 bil. **GDP:** $36 bil., $18,000 per capita (2002 est.). **Chief crops:** potatoes, hops, wheat, sugar beets, corn, grapes; cattle, sheep, poultry. **Natural resources:** lignite coal, lead, zinc, mercury, uranium. **Major industries:** ferrous metallurgy and rolling mill products, aluminum reduction and rolled products, lead and zinc smelting, electronics, trucks, electric power equipment, wood products, textiles. **Labor force:** 857,400. **Exports:** $10.3 bil. (f.o.b., 2002); manufactured goods, machinery and transport equipment, chemicals. **Imports:** $11.1 bil. (f.o.b., 2002); machinery and transport equipment, other manufactured goods, chemicals. **Major trading partners:** ***exports:*** 26% Germany, 12% Italy, 9% Croatia; ***imports:*** 20% Germany, 18% Italy, 11% France.

In the sixth century, as part of the great Slavic migrations out of the Vistula and Oder basins, the Slovene people crossed the Carpathians into the Danube plain, penetrating as far as the eastern Alps. In the eighth and ninth centuries the lands they inhabited were subject to Bavarian colonization as part of the Ostmark (Eastern March) of the Carolingian Empire. It is probable, although contested, that most current Austrians are German-speaking Slovenes while the Slovenes are Slavophone Austrians. In any case, for 1,000 years, Slovene history was Austrian history. Thus, like the Croats, Christianity came in its western (Roman Catholic) form.

Lacking their own nobility and even a burgher class for most of their history, the Slovenes tended to look to their priests for leadership, regularly electing them as their representatives to the Reichstag in Vienna (as they did later to the Skupstina in Belgrade after Slovenia became part of Yugoslavia). The 19th-century rise of a national consciousness, associated with literary collections of legend and folklore, took a special turn in the Slovene case because of Napoleon's conquests. His "province of Illyria" was the first association of the Slovenes with Croats and Serbs and his minister of education there was the Slovene Franciscan Valentin Vodnik, so that Slovene "nationalism" had from a start a "Yugoslav" tinge.

In 1815 the Slovenes were again part of the Austrian Empire and were confirmed in the Ausgleich of 1867 as part of the Austrian, not Hungarian, part of the dual Monarchy. As that monarchy collapsed in World War I, it was the Slovene monsignor Anton Korosec who served as president of "The National Council of the Serbs, Croats, and Slovenes" out of which the new state of Yugoslavia emerged. Though the new Yugoslavia was a highly centralized, unitary state with no provision for Slovene autonomy, certain circumstances brought a kind of privileged position to Slovenia. Their distinct language made Serbian administration a practical impossibility and Serbian struggles against Croat separatism led them to favor the Slovenes to Croatia's north, forestalling any additional separatism there. Moreoever, as a part of the long Austrian connection, the Slovenes were better educated and more industrially advanced than any other part of Yugoslavia.

After the interlude of Hitler's break-up of Yugoslavia (in which Slovenia itself was partitioned between Germany and Italy) Slovenia became a constituent "republic" in Tito's reconstructed Yugoslavia and, despite the enduring emnity provoked by the Communist slaughter of the Slovene Domobranci (Home Guard), again assumed a kind of priviliged status in Yugoslavia. After the dictator's death in 1980, the Slovene Socialist Republic took part in the "collegial rule" of Yugoslavia, but with the end of Communist rule in 1990, Slovenia became the first of the republics to secede, in June 1991. After the Slovene militia inflicted a humiliating defeat on the Yugoslav army in July and with E.U. recognition in December, Slovenia became independent for the first time in its history. Forging economic ties with Austria, Hungary, and Italy, it has remained prosperously apart from the debacle to its south.

In Nov. 1996 elections, the center-right coalition calling itself Slovenian Spring captured 45 (of 90) seats in the Parliament with the Liberal Democrats and its allies controlling the other 45. After months of deadlock LD leader Janos Drnovsek was confirmed as prime minister. In 2002 he was elected president and Anton Rop became prime minister. In 2003 voters approved joining both the E.U. and NATO.

▶SOLOMON ISLANDS

• **GEOGRAPHY** **Location:** archipelago in South Pacific E of Papua New Guinea. Honiara (Guadalcanal Is.) 9°28'S, 159°57'E. **Boundaries**: South Pacific Ocean to N, E, and S, Solomon Sea to W; nearest neighbor is Santa Cruz Islands to SE. **Total area**: 10,985 sq. mi. (28,450 sq km). **Coastline**: 3,302 mi. (5,313 km). **Comparative area**: slightly smaller than Maryland. **Land use:** 2% arable land; 1% permanent crops; 97% other. **Major cities**: (1990 est.) Honiara (capital) 35,288.

• **PEOPLE** **Population:** 509,190 (2003 est.). **Nationality:** noun—Solomon Islander(s); adjective—Solomon Islander. **Ethnic groups:** 93% Melanesian, 4% Polynesian, 1.5% Micronesian, 0.8% European, 0.3% Chinese. **Languages:** 120 indigenous languages; Melanesian pidgin in much of country is lingua franca; English spoken by 1-2% of population. **Religions:** 34% Anglican, 19% Roman Catholic, 17% Baptist, 11% United (Methodist/Presbyterian), 11% Seventh-Day Adventist, 5% other Protestant, 4% traditional beliefs.

• **GOVERNMENT** **Type:** parliamentary democracy. **Independence:** July 7, 1978 (from U.K.). **Constitution:** July 7, 1978. **National holiday:** Independence Day, July 7. **Heads of Government:** Rev. John Inni Lapli, governor-general (since July 1999); Sir Allan Kemakeza, prime minister (since Dec. 2001). **Structure:** executive—authority in governor-general; unicameral legislature; judiciary.

• **ECONOMY** **Monetary unit:** Solomon Islands dollar. **Budget:** (2001 est.) ***income:*** $38 mil.; ***expend.:*** N.A. **GDP:** $800 mil., $1,700 per capita (2001 est.). **Chief crops:** cocoa, beans, coconuts, palm kernels, rice, potatoes, vegetables, fruits; cattle, pigs; timber; fish. **Natural resources:** fish, forests, gold, bauxite, phosphates. **Major industries:** fish (tuna), mining, timber. **Labor force:** 26,842 (1992 est.); 20% services, 75% agriculture, forestry, and fishing, 5% industry. **Exports:** $47 mil. (f.o.b., 2001 est.); timber, fish, palm oil, cocoa, copra. **Imports:** $82 mil. (c.i.f., 2001 est.); plant and equipment, manufactured goods, food and live animals, fuel. **Major trading partners:** (2000) ***exports:*** 20% Japan, 18% South Korea, 11% Phillipines; ***imports:*** 29% Australia, 18% Singapore, 7% U.S.

In 1893 Britain established a protectorate over the South Solomon Islands, including the large islands of Guadalcanal, San Cristobal, and Malata; the protectorate was extended to the smaller easterly islands of the chain in 1898. In 1900 Germany relinquished to Great Britain its claim to the North Solomons, including Choiseul and Santa Isabel; Bougainville Island was retained by Germany (see "Papua New Guinea"). The major islands were occupied by Japan in 1942 and retaken by the Allies in a series of battles in 1943.

The Solomon Islands were made self-governing in January 1976 and became an independent nation on July 7, 1978. The economy is based on subsistence agriculture and fishing. Some light manufacturing and craft industries have been established in recent years. Copra, cocoa, palm oil, and lumber are the principal exports. The sale of tuna fishing rights in the surrounding waters has given the nation a favorable balance of payments.

In June 1999 ethnic violence erupted on Guadalcanal against settlers from the island of Malaita, with perhaps 2,000 fleeing over the next year. Then, in June 2000, gunmen from the Malaita Eagle Force (MEF) placed the prime minister under house arrest and captured Honiara airport. On the eve of a parliamentary no-confidence vote, prime minister Ulufa'alu resigned June 14. On July 1 parliament elected opposition leader Mannasseh Sogavare to be prime minister. In 2001, a truce between militias brought no disarmament, but Sogavare used foreign aid to buy off the Eagle Force and other politicos. With Dec. 2001 elections, his rule was overturned, Sir Allen Kamekeza becoming prime minister after his People's Alliance won a majority in the legislature.

▶SOMALIA

• **Geography** **Location:** eastern coast of Africa. **Boundaries**: short frontier with Djibouti to NW, Gulf of Aden to N, long coastline on Indian Ocean to E, Kenya to SW, Ethiopia to W. **Total area**: 246,201 sq. mi. (637,660 sq km). **Coastline**: 1,880 mi. (3,025 km). **Comparative area**: slightly smaller than Texas. **Land use:** 2% arable land; negl. % permanent crops; 98% other. **Major cities**: (1987 est.) Mogadishu (capital) 1,000,000; Hargeysa 400,000; Kismayo 200,000; Merca 100,000.

• **People** **Population:** 8,025,190 (2003 est.). **Nationality:** adjective—Somali. **Ethnic groups:** 85% Somali, rest mainly Bantu; 30,000 Arabs. **Languages:** Somali (official), Arabic, Italian, English. **Religions:** almost entirely Sunni Muslim.

• **Government** **Type:** none. **Independence:** July 1, 1960 (from a merger of British Somaliland, which became independent from U.K. June 26, 1960, and Italian Somaliland, which became independent from Italian-administered U.N. trusteeship July 1, 1960, to form the Somali Republic). **Constitution:** Aug. 25, 1979, presidential approval Sept. 23, 1979. **National holiday:** N.A. **Heads of Government:** Abdikassim Salad Hassan, president (since Aug. 2000); Ali Khalif Galaydh, prime minister (since Aug. 2000).

• **Economy** **Monetary unit:** Somali shilling. **Budget:** N.A. **GDP:** $4.1 bil., $550 per capita (2001 est.). **Chief crops:** bananas, sorghum, corn, mangoes, sugarcane, sesame seeds, beans; cattle, sheep, goats; fishing potential largely unexploited. **Natural resources:** uranium, largely unexploited reserves of iron ore, tin, gypsum, bauxite. **Major industries:** a few small industries, including sugar refining, textiles, petroleum refining. **Labor force:** about 3.7 mil. (1993 est.); very few are skilled laborers; 71% agriculture (pastoral nomadism), 29% industry and services. **Exports:** $126 mil. (f.o.b., 2001 est.); livestock, bananas, hides, fish. **Imports:** $343 mil. (f.o.b., 2001 est.); manufactures, petroleum products, foodstuffs, construction materials. **Major trading partners:** (2001 est.) ***exports:*** 32% Saudi Arabia, 14% UAE, 17% Yemen; ***imports:*** 28% Djibouti, 13% Kenya, 10% India.

Arab trading settlements in Somalia were established in the seventh century and gradually evolved into independent sultanates. Portuguese traders established settlements and forts along the coast during the 15th and 16th centuries.

In the early 19th century, Great Britain arranged through local treaties to use harbors along the Somali coast and gained control over the northern part of the country by 1840. The border between Somalia and Ethiopia was demarcated by a treaty between Great Britain and Ethiopia in 1897. In 1885 the sultan of Zanzibar granted commercial advantages to Italy, and in 1897 and 1908 Italy gained control over southern Somalia.

During the early 20th century, an uprising against British rule was led by Mohamed Abdullah. Abdullah was defeated by the British with help from his local rivals but is now regarded as the father of Somali nationalism.

The Italian invasion of Ethiopia in 1936 gave Italy a dominant position in the Horn of Africa. In the early phases of World War II, Italian troops drove the British from British Somaliland, but a 1940 counterattack led to British occupation of all of Somalia by 1941. After World War II, as discussions of Somalia's future continued, Britain handed over the Ogaden and neighboring territories to Ethiopia.

A U.N. pact of 1949 created an Italian trusteeship in the former Italian Somaliland. Italy terminated its trusteeship and British Somaliland, a U.K. protectorate, achieved independence on June 26, 1960. On July 1 the two entities joined to become Somalia.

The new country was plagued by clan-based rivalries, with the Somali Youth League emerging as a unifying national force. In 1969 Maj. Gen. Mohamed Siad Barre took control, established a ruling Supreme Revolutionary Council, a socialist regime, and relations with the U.S.S.R.

In 1972 Somali forces began border raids into Ethiopia's Ogaden region, peopled largely by ethnic Somalis. The Somali army invaded the Ogaden in 1977. The Soviet Union switched its support to Ethiopia, and with Soviet aid and Cuban troops, Ethiopia drove back the Somali invasion. Over a million refugees fled from Ethiopia into Somalia. The United States was Somalia's principal source of military and economic aid after 1978.

In May 1988, the Somali National Movement captured a number of cities in the northwest and held them against the army. In the summer of

1990, the United Somali Congress began a peaceful antigovernment movement around Mogadishu. In Dec. 1990, this flared into a brief but bloody civil war that resulted in the ouster of Pres. Barre on Jan. 26. The Somali National Congress proclaimed a provisional government, but it was not recognized either by the United Somali Movement, which threatened secession, or the Somali Patriotic Movement, which controlled much of central and southern Somalia.

The continued unrest made it difficult to deliver humanitarian aid despite the efforts of Western governments and nongovernment organizations to do so. An estimated 50,000 people were killed between 1988-90.

Despite U.N. attempts to initiate peace talks, widespread clan and tribal warfare led to a complete breakdown of government authority in 1991-92. A severe drought helped to create over two million refugees, and widespread starvation gripped the nation. Relief workers were prevented by warring armed factions from distributing emergency food supplies. An estimated 300,000 people died in 1991-92.

In Dec. 1992, the United States began Operation Restore Hope, sending 28,000 troops to secure distribution of food and aid. The U.S. presence deterred the factions from further open hostilities and brought warring leaders to the peace table. The U.N. took over the operation but led by the followers of Gen. Mohammed Farah Aidid, Somali renegades ambushed U.S. troops and downed a helicopter leading to a U.S. withdrawal in March 1994. The last UN troops left Mogadishu a year later.

Clan warfare reignited in March 1995, and in June, Aidid declared himself president for life. However, no country recognized any Somali government and in Aug. 1996 Aidid was shot and killed. His son, a former U.S. Marine, replaced him but brutal clan violence continued. In Dec. 1997 a tentative peace agreement was reached among the major factions. Peace settled in during 1998, helped by the flooding that killed 2,000 and made 200,000 homeless. Increased inter-clan fighting in Sept. 1999 threatened to cause crop shortfalls and famine yet again. During the summer of 2000, however, a group of leaders met in Djibouti and formed a new government with Abdikassim Salad Hassan as president. But by March 2001 many warlords met in Ethiopia to form an opposition group and by May new clan warfare erupted. Thus Somalia has devolved into (at least) four separate states.

▶SOUTH AFRICA

Republic of South Africa

• **GEOGRAPHY** **Location:** southern Africa. **Boundaries**: Namibia to NW, Botswana, Zimbabwe to N, Mozambique to NE, Swaziland, Indian Ocean to E, Atlantic Ocean to W; Lesotho entirely surrounded by South African territory. **Total area**: 471,444 sq. mi. (1,221,040 sq km). **Coastline**: 1,739 mi. (2,798 km). **Comparative area**: slighlty less than twice the size of Texas. **Land use:** 12% arable land; 1% permanent crops;87% other. **Major cities**: (1991 census) Note: Figures are for metropolitan areas: Cape Town (legislative capital) 2,350,157; Pretoria (administrative capital) 1,080,187; Johannesburg 1,916,061; Durban 1,137,378; Port Elizabeth 853,205.

• **PEOPLE** **Population:** 42,768,678 (2003 est.). **Nationality:** noun—South African(s); adjective—South African. **Ethnic groups:** 75.2% black, 13.6% white, 2.6% Indian; 8.6% other. **Languages:** Afrikaans, English, Zulu, Xhosa, Sotho, Ndebele, Pedi, Swazi, Tsonga, Venda, Tswana (all official). **Religions:** 68% Christian (most whites and about 60% of blacks), 2% Muslim, 1.5% Hindu (60% of Indians), 28.5% traditional and animistic beliefs.

• **GOVERNMENT** **Type:** republic. **Independence:** May 31, 1910 (from U.K.). **Constitution:** signed Dec. 10, 1996 by then-President Mandela—being implemented in phases. **National holiday:** Freedom Day, Apr. 27. **Head of Government:** Thabo Mbeki, president (since June 1999). **Structure:** executive—president is head of govt. and chairman of cabinet; bicameral legislature—National Assembly, National Council of Provinces; judiciary—courts maintain substantial independence from government influence.

• **ECONOMY** **Monetary unit:** South African rand. **Budget:** (FY02/03 est.) ***income:*** $22.6 bil.; ***expend.:*** $24.7 bil. **GDP:** $432 bil., $10,000 per capita (2002 est.). **Chief crops:** corn, wheat, sugarcane, fruits, vegetables; beef, poultry, mutton, wool, dairy products. **Natural resources:** gold, chromium, antimony, coal, iron ore. **Major industries:** mining (world's largest producer of platinum, gold, chromium), automobile assembly, metalworking. **Labor force:** 17 mil. economically active (1997); 45% services, 30% agriculture, 25% industry and commerce; 37% unemployment (2001 est.). **Exports:** $31.8 bil. (f.o.b., 2002 est.); gold, minerals and metals, food, chemicals. **Imports:** $26.6 bil. (f.o.b., 2002 est.); machinery, chemicals, transport equipment. **Major trading partners:** ***exports:*** E.U., U.S., Japan; ***imports:*** E.U., U.S., Japan.

South Africa was originally inhabited by San and related peoples. Bantu peoples, including the Zulu and Xhosa, migrated to the region beginning around the 15th century and established large native kingdoms.

The Portuguese explorer Bartholomew Diaz discovered and named the Cape of Good Hope in 1488. The Dutch East India Company established a permanent settlement at Cape Town in 1652, which served as a supply and transshipment point for Dutch trade to the East Indies. It attracted Protestant settlers from throughout Western Europe. In a series of wars, the Xhosa people were expelled from the area under Dutch rule.

Great Britain began to dispute Dutch control of the Cape of Good Hope region in the late 18th century. To escape increasing British hegemony, in 1836 many Dutch farmers undertook the Great Trek, a northward migration to lands not under the control of any European power. These Afrikaner pioneers later became known as Boers (farmers). They came into conflict with the Zulu kingdom that, under King Shaka, had recently widened its dominion in the South African interior. The Zulus were defeated at the Battle of Blood River in 1838, but they retained substantial power and territory for another 40 years.

Great Britain formally took control of the Cape Colony in 1841 and annexed Natal in 1843. The other two Afrikaner provinces, the Orange Free State and the Transvaal, remained free of British control. But when diamonds were discovered in the Orange Free State in 1867 and gold in the Transvaal in 1886, an influx of British miners and entrepreneurs provoked Boer rebellions.

In 1878 the Zulu Kingdom under its last great king, Cetewayo, rebelled against British rule in Natal. British troops attacked Zululand in 1878 and crushed the rebellion in 1879.

The first Anglo-Boer War of 1881-82 led to total British victory. A renewed uprising led to the Boer War of 1899-1902, which was fought with great ferocity between British regular troops and Afrikaner guerrilla forces. The eventual British victory led to the establishment of British rule in all of South Africa and to the formation of the Union of South Africa in 1910. The union became a self-governing state within the British Empire in 1934.

South African politics became dominated by friction between British and Afrikaner whites; no effective black participation in government was permitted. The United South African party, led by Jan C. Smuts, advocated cooperation between the two groups and led South Africa to join World War II on the Allied side, over the opposition of the pro-Afrikaner Nationalist party.

After the war the Nationalists prevailed and won control of the government in 1948. Racial politics became the country's paramount concern, and the Nationalists introduced the policy of "apartheid" (separateness), under which racial groups were rigidly defined as white, black, Asian (primarily Indian), and colored (mixed ancestry). Each group was to be kept physically separate and develop its own political institutions within defined areas of residence; mixed neighborhoods, intermarriage, and other relations were prohibited. Blacks, in particular, were restricted by "pass laws" that allowed them only temporary access to white areas for employment.

International condemnation of these policies began almost immediately, as India broke relations with South Africa in 1946 over discrimination against Asians, and South Africa became the focus of mounting protest, U.N. resolutions, and international sanctions beginning in the 1960's. On May 31, 1961, South Africa gave up its dominion status and became a republic; its application for membership in the British Commonwealth was withdrawn in the face of strong opposition. The African National Congress (ANC), organized in 1912, was banned by South African authorities. The imprisonment of its leader, Nelson Mandela, provided a focus for black political protest and nationalist aspirations.

Homelands were established under the Promotion of Bantu Self-Government Act of 1959 to further the policy of apartheid by creating separate, but dependent, states for South Africa's blacks. Their form of government was set up in the Black Constitution Act of 1971. The South African government intended that the homelands be regarded as separate nations, but none was ever internationally recognized. The scattered homeland territories comprised only a tiny portion of the total area of South Africa, and tended to include marginal and underdeveloped lands. Residents of the homelands were not considered citizens of South Africa, but rather citizens only of their homeland. As such, they could be considered temporary migrant workers and were therefore ineligible for unemployment and other benefits.

An uprising in Soweto in 1976 was put down by South African police and armed forces with the loss of hundreds of lives, providing a further focus of black protest. Pieter Willem Botha was elected president in 1978, pledging to uphold apartheid while seeking solutions to racial problems. In 1983, a majority of white voters approved a new constitution that provided for limited power sharing by coloreds and Asians. Blacks, however, continued to be excluded.

In the early 1980's, South African troops intervened in civil wars in Angola and Mozambique and were deployed to counteract growing proindependence rebellions in Namibia. Within South Africa, terrorism and uprisings led by the African National Union grew in intensity in 1983-84. A state of emergency was declared in 1985, accompanied by renewed political and economic pressure from abroad. In 1986, Bishop Desmond Tutu, a leading black nationalist, addressed the United Nations and called for renewed sanctions. The Botha government announced an end to the pass laws and promised limited black participation in government. Fighting among black groups in 1986-87 further increased domestic tension.

On May 19, 1986, South African troops conducted raids against ANC bases in Zambia, Zimbabwe, and Botswana. A new national state of emergency was declared as strikes and riots marked the 10th anniversary of the Soweto uprising. The U.S. announced measures designed to end American investment in South Africa.

In early 1989, in anticipation of elections to be held in September, various proposals were put forward for constitutional reform. Most called for expanded power sharing but still within the context of defined racial groups. In July 1989 Pres. Botha had an unprecedented meeting with Nelson Mandela, amid strong suggestions that the white government was seeking an accommodation with the antiapartheid leadership. Botha's successor, F.W. de Klerk, continued that policy.

A series of measures in 1989-90 resulted in the partial dismantling of apartheid, against the vehement opposition of the white right wing, but violence between supporters of the ANC and the Zulu Inkatha movement in Natal led to the declaration of a state of emergency in the province.

Mandela was released from prison in the spring of 1990 and received a rapturous welcome from South Africa's blacks, and later made a triumphant tour of Western Europe and North America. His glory was short-lived, however, as the struggle for supremacy again erupted in murder and violence between Mandela's ANC and Mangosuthu Buthelezi's Inkatha Freedom party throughout the latter part of 1990 and 1991.

At the same time, Pres. de Klerk and Parliament continued to move the nation toward the ending of apartheid by repealing 60 years of segregation in hospitals, libraries, schools, and other public institutions. The government also released other political prisoners and completely repealed the legal foundations of apartheid: the Land Acts of 1913 and 1936, the Group Areas Act, and the Population Registration Act. The United States and other countries began lifting trade sanctions against South Africa in the summer of 1991.

In September 1991, de Klerk, Mandela, and Buthelezi, together with 20 smaller antiapartheid groups, signed an accord to end factional violence. De Klerk proposed a new constitution that would provide universal suffrage and create a two-chamber parliament open to all races. The new constitution abolished the black homelands, consolidating them into one large, multiracial South Africa. In March 1992 a referendum of white voters overwhelmingly approved a government proposal to dismantle all forms of apartheid and to conduct talks with black leaders designed to end white-only rule.

The new constitution was approved on Nov. 17, 1993, by all of the country's major political parties, except for Chief Mangosuthu Buthelezi's Zulu-based Inkatha Freedom party, which withheld its support until a week before the country's first-ever multiracial elections in April. More than 22 million voters cast ballots. An overwhelming majority chose the 75-year-old Mandela to lead a coalition government that included de Klerk's National party and Buthelezi's Inkatha Freedom party.

In May 1996 South Africa completed the transition to democracy when it approved a permanent constitution to replace the transitional one implemented three years earlier. It created a strong central government, an independent judiciary, and a bill of rights with one of the broadest guarantees of liberty in the world. In addition to freedom of speech, movement, and political activity, the South African Bill of Rights protects rights to adequate food, housing, water, education, and health care. The day after the new constitution was approved, de Klerk and his colleagues in the National party quit their cabinet posts, saying that the government was strong enough to handle "robust opposition."

In 1997 there were reminders that troubles remain: in February, riots in Johannesburg suburbs by coloreds against discrimination in favor of blacks and in March, a mass rally (which turned violent) in Johannesburg by still-unsatisfied Zulus. Bitter feelings between the Inkatha Freedom Party and Mandela's ANC surfaced again when the Truth and Reconciliation Committee reported testimony linking Inkatha leaders to assasination squads during the apartheid era.

On June 2, 1999, South Africa held its second post-apartheid elections: the ANC won a gigantic victory, taking 266 seats in the 400-seat Assembly. An "alliance" with the one member of the (Indian) Minority Front gave ANC the 2/3 majority that permits it to amend the Constitution. Thabo Mbeki, who replaced Nelson Mandela as party chief in December, was elected unopposed to be his successor as South Africa's president as well. There has been subsequent slippage in ANC popularity. As inflation heats up strikes grow more frequent. In Dec. 2000 local elections the ANC took only 59 percent and a serious bribery scandal is developing over a 1999 $3.5 billion arms deal. And the government's own report of March 2001 highlighted the gravity of South Africa's AIDS crisis.

South Africa has the continent's most highly developed economy; it is a fully-developed, capitalist industrial-commercial society with manufacturing, mining, agricultural, service, and other sectors. It remains the world's largest producer of gold, a key source of chromium and other strategic metals, and of gem-quality diamonds.

▶SPAIN

Kingdom of Spain

• GEOGRAPHY Location: Iberian Peninsula in southwest Europe; Canary Is. off West Africa (28°07'N, 15°26'W). **Boundaries**: Bay of Biscay and France to N; Mediterranean Sea to E; Morocco 19 mi. (30 km) to S, across Strait of Gibraltar; Portugal to W. **Total area**: 194,884 sq. mi. (504,750 sq km). **Coastline**: 3,085 mi. (4,964 km). **Comparative area**: slightly more than twice the size of Oregon. **Land use:** 29% arable land; 10% permanent crops; 261% other. **Major cities**: (1991 est.) Madrid (capital) 2,984,576; Barcelona 1,653,175; Valencia 777,427; Sevilla (Seville) 683,487; Zaragoza (Saragossa) 614,401.

• PEOPLE Population: 40,217,413 (2003 est.). **Nationality:** noun—Spaniard(s); adjective—Spanish. **Ethnic groups:** composite of Mediterranean and Nordic types. **Languages:** 74% Castilian Spanish (official); 17% Catalán, 7% Galician, 2% Basque. **Religions:** 94% Roman Catholic, 6% other.

• GOVERNMENT Type: parliamentary monarchy. **Independence:** 1492 (expulsion of Moors and unification). **Constitution:** Dec. 6, 1978, effective Dec. 29, 1978. **National holiday:** Oct. 12. **Heads of Government:** Juan Carlos I, king (since Nov. 1975); José María Aznar, prime minister (since May 1996). **Structure:** executive—king is chief of state, prime minister is head of government; bicameral legislature; judiciary— independent.

• ECONOMY Monetary unit: euro. **Budget:** (2000 est.) ***income:*** $105 bil.; ***expend.:*** $109 bil. **GDP:** $828 bil., $20,700 per capita (2002 est). **Chief crops:** grains, vegetables, olives, wine grapes, sugar beets, citrus; beef, pork, poultry, dairy products; fish. **Natural resources:** coal, lignite, iron ore, uranium, mercury. **Major industries:** textiles, apparel (including footwear), food and beverages, metals and metal manufacturing. **Labor force:** 17 mil. (2000); 64% services, 28% manufacturing, mining and construction, 8% agriculture. **Exports:** $122.2 bil. (f.o.b., 2002 est.); cars and trucks, manufactured goods, foodstuffs, other consumer goods. **Imports:** $156.6 bil. (f.o.b., 2002 est.); machinery, transport equipment, fuels, semifinished goods, foodstuffs, consumer goods, chemicals. **Major trading partners: *exports:*** 71% E.U., 6% Latin America, 4% U.S.; ***imports:*** 64% E.U., 7% OPEC, 5% U.S.

Prehistoric Spain was populated by Iberians, Basques, and Celts. Its Mediterranean ports were frequented by Phoenician traders, and part of the country was incorporated into the empire of Carthage. Spain fell under the Roman Empire around 200 B.C.; Roman rule ended when the Visigoths invaded and took control of the Iberian Peninsula in the fifth century. The Visigoths adopted Christianity but were in turn conquered by Moors from northwest Africa in A.D. 711. The Berber/Arab civilization of the Moors produced the most elegant and cultivated culture in medieval Europe, and was an important conduit for the reintroduction of Greek science into Europe in the 12th century.

The Christian reconquest of the Iberian Peninsula began almost immediately after the Moors had established themselves and proceeded slowly but steadily over a period of 750 years. The consolidation of the region's small, contentious Christian kingdoms came with the marital alliance of Ferdinand of Aragon and Isabella of Castile in 1469. Granada, the last Moorish outpost in Spain, fell to the forces of Ferdinand and Isabella in 1492, just as Columbus, with Isabella's sponsorship, was discovering the lands that were to become Spain's New World empire. Under the Inquisition, begun in 1478, Jews were expelled from Spain in 1492, and Muslims in 1502.

Under the Habsburg dynasty (1516-1700), Spain reached the zenith of its power and prestige around the year 1600 (despite the 1588 defeat of the Spanish Armada by England), controlling an empire that embraced nearly all of South America (except Brazil), Central America, Mexico, western North America, the Philippines, and smaller territories in Africa and Asia. But Spain's loss of the Netherlands, endless struggles with the French in Europe and the Turks in the Mediterranean, and relentless inflation caused by imports of New World silver—all took their toll. During the 18th century, the Bourbons ruled a declining but still powerful Spain, until Napoleon installed his brother as king in 1808.

After Napoleon's defeat, the Bourbons returned in 1814, but the loss of the South American colonies, three dynastic wars, and a brief republican interlude after 1868 were all signs of progressive weakness. The crowning blow to Spanish power and prestige was the loss of the Spanish-American War to the United States in 1898, leading to the independence of Cuba and the

American takeover of Puerto Rico and the Philippines.

Spain remained neutral in World War I. In 1923 Primo de Rivera established a dictatorship; he was forced out of office by King Alfonso XIII in 1930, but in 1931 the king was forced to abdicate. A republic replaced the monarchy. Its volatile mixture of socialism, anticlericalism, and decentralization provoked a right-wing reaction. The government moved to the Right, and in 1934 a miner's strike in Asturia was put down with great bloodshed. A left-wing government was elected in 1936 and deposed in a coup, which led to the terrible Civil War of 1936-39, in which Spain became a battleground for competing world ideologies. The Nationalists, aided by Hitler and Mussolini, defeated the Republicans, aided by Stalin and by leftist volunteers from many countries. Out of the wreckage emerged the dictatorship of the intensely patriotic and Catholic general Francisco Franco.

At the time of the Civil War, Spain was still an agricultural country, with small holdings in the north and great estates in the south. In the Basque country, the mining of iron, copper, and lead provided both exports and a domestic iron and steel industry, which had been the case since the 19th century. In the 20th century, shipbuilding and chemicals were added to the traditional textile industries of the Mediterranean coastal cities. The war largely destroyed this industrial base, which was not rebuilt until the 1950's.

Except for a contingent of troops sent to fight with the German invaders of the Soviet Union, Spain remained precariously neutral during World War II; Franco declined to repay Hitler for his support in the Civil War. But wartime Spain, despite its neutrality, could not muster the resources to undertake national reconstruction.

In postwar Europe, the Franco regime seemed like a remnant of the fascism of the 1930's; Stalin's active hostility led the United Nations to treat Spain as an international pariah. At home Franco represented peace and stability; few Spaniards were willing to risk a return to civil strife by opposing him. Over time the military and Catholic aspects of the regime grew more pronounced, while fascist elements were downplayed. In 1947 the Law of Succession made Spain a monarchy without a king, awaiting the restoration of the throne in the post-Franco era.

The Cold War led to friendlier American relations with Spain and the establishment of American military bases in 1953. U.N. membership followed in 1955. Despite some resultant growth in international trade, Spain's economy lagged, with industrialization barely beginning.

In 1958 Franco turned the direction of the economy over to a group of technocrats, mostly neoliberal members of the Opus Dei lay Catholic order. With U.S. economic and military aid, a growing tourist industry, increased foreign investment, and, especially, freer markets, the economy revived. Older industries like iron, steel, and textiles were rejuvenated, while newer ones, such as chemicals, plastics, automobile assembly, and power plants, were created. Agriculture was increasingly mechanized, and it shifted to export-oriented ranching and horticulture.

In 1967 Franco proclaimed the Organic Law, which, while confirming him as head of state, granted some independence to the Cortes (legislature) and permitted heads of families to vote for some of its delegates. This, along with a relaxation of censorship, softened the growing opposition to the regime among students, labor unions, and regional separatists. In 1969 Prince Juan Carlos was named heir apparent to the Spanish throne.

Franco died in 1975 and was duly succeeded by Juan Carlos. With the new prime minister, Adolfo Suarez, the king worked to liberalize the Franco inheritance: Political parties were legalized; the Cortes was transformed into a bicameral legislature, with both houses elected by universal suffrage; the first elections since 1936 were held; and a new constitution was promulgated—all by 1978.

In 1980, Catalonia and the Basque country were granted home rule, following overwhelming plebiscite victories. In the Basque lands, however, violent terrorist agitation for complete independence continues to this day.

Under the new monarchy, Spain became a full participant in the affairs of Europe. It joined the Council of Europe in 1977, NATO in 1982, and the E.U. in 1986. The Socialist Workers' party controlled both houses of the Cortes from 1982 to 1996, but the party abandoned both Marxism and the traditional labor radicalism of prewar Spain. Instead, it resembled the mainstream Social Democratic parties of Western Europe.

Under Prime Minister Felipe Gonzalez Marquéz, Spain was for a time the economic darling of Europe. GDP grew by an average of almost 5 percent between 1986 and 1990, and business investment jumped by over 10 percent a year. In 1992, the Summer Olympics in Barcelona and the Universal Exposition in Seville focused world attention on two very different parts of Spain.

But the economic growth slowed in 1992, unemployment reached 22 percent, and the conservative Popular party made strong gains in the Cortes in 1993. In 1994, Gonzalez's power eroded when several members of his government were indicted for their involvement with an antiterrorist death squad accused of assassinating 27 Basque separatists during the 1980's. After 10 years of Gonzalez and the Socialists, the May 1996 elections brought the Popular Party and its leader Jose Maria Aznar to governmental power (the Popular Party being supported by, though without a formal coalition with, Basque and Catalan nationalists). In July 1998, 12 officials of the Gonzalez government were sentenced to jail for crimes in the anti-Basque "dirty war," although Gonzalez himself was not implicated.

Spain's economy quickly reversed itself and annual growth surpassed three percent, so that Spain was able to meet the criteria for membership in the European Monetary Union.

Somewhat unexpectedly the E.T.A., the Basque terrorist organization, declared on September 16, 1998, a "total and indefinite" cease-fire. But despite talks with the Aznar government and the release of "political prisoners," the E.T.A., in late 1999, resumed its war with car-bombings and assassinations. In March 2000, the Popular Party won an unexpected majority (183 of 350 seats) in the Congresso (lower house). In Sept. 2002, two important leaders of E.T.A. were captured in France and government officials believed the group, responsible for over 800 deaths, would be crippled.

▶SRI LANKA

Democratic Socialist Republic of Sri Lanka

• **GEOGRAPHY** **Location:** Indian Ocean about 50 mi. (80 km) SE of India. Colombo 6°55'N, 79°52'E. **Boundaries**: Palk Strait to N, Bay of Bengal to E, Indian Ocean to S and SW, and Gulf of Mannar to NW. **Total area**: 25,332 sq. mi. (65,610 sq km). **Coastline**: 833 mi. (1,340 km). **Comparative area**: slightly larger than West Virginia. **Land use:** 13%

arable land; 16% permanent crops; 71% other. **Major cities**: (1990 est.) Colombo (capital) 615,000; Dehiwala-Mount Lavinia 196,000; Moratuwa 170,000.

• **People** **Population:** 19,742,439 (2003 est.). **Nationality:** noun—Sri Lankan(s); adjective—Sri Lankan. **Ethnic groups:** 74% Sinhalese; 18% Tamil; 7% Moor; 1% Burgher, Malay, and Veddah. **Languages:** Sinhala (official); Sinhala and Tamil listed as national languages; Sinhala spoken by about 74% of population, Tamil spoken by about 18%; English commonly used in government and spoken by about 10% of population. **Religions:** 70% Buddhist, 15% Hindu, 8% Christian, 7% Muslim.

• **Government** **Type:** republic. **Independence:** Feb. 4, 1948 (from U.K.). **Constitution:** Aug. 16, 1978. **National holiday:** Independence Day, Feb. 4. **Heads of Government:** Chandrika Bandaranaike Kumaratunga, president (since Nov. 1994); Ranil Wickremesinghe, prime minister (since Dec. 2001). **Structure:** executive—president is head of government and chief of state; unicameral legislature; judiciary—Supreme Court, Court of Appeals.

• **Economy** **Monetary unit:** Sri Lankan rupee. **Budget:** (2001) ***income:*** $2.8 bil.; ***expend.:*** $4.1 bil. **GDP:** $73.7 bil., $3,700 per capita (2002 est.). **Chief crops:** rice, sugarcane, grains, pulses, oilseed, roots, spices, coconuts, tea, rubber; milk, eggs, hides, meat. **Natural resources:** limestone, graphite, mineral sands, gems, phosphates. **Major industries:** processing of rubber, tea, coconuts, and other agricultural commodities; cement, petroleum refining. **Labor force:** 6.6 mil. (1998 est.); 45% services, 38% agriculture, 17% industry. **Exports:** $4.6 bil. (f.o.b., 2002); tea, textiles and garments, petroleum products, gems, rubber. **Imports:** $5.4 bil. (f.o.b., 2002 est.); machinery and equipment, textiles, petroleum. **Major trading partners:** ***exports:*** 39% U.S., 11% U.K., 4% Germany; ***imports:*** 10% India, 7% Singapore, 6% Hong Kong.

The ancient Veddah inhabitants of Sri Lanka were conquered by Sinhalese migrants from northern India in the sixth century B.C. The island's spices and precious stones and its position on the trans-Indian Ocean trade routes made it well known in ancient times. Sri Lanka was known to the Greeks as Tabrobane and to the Arabs as Serendip. From the third century A.D., Sri Lanka became a major center of Buddhist culture. Despite numerous invasions from India, the island was usually ruled by native kingdoms, but the invasions added a Tamil community to the premodern population.

The Portuguese conquered the coastal areas after 1505 and also introduced Roman Catholicism. The Dutch displaced the Portugese in 1648; the British expelled the Dutch in 1795. Great Britain was the first foreign power to extend its rule over the entire island, with the defeat of the central kingdom of Kandy in 1833. In that year all of Sri Lanka was incorporated into the British Crown colony of Ceylon. Under British rule, tea and rubber plantations were established in the island's interior, and coconut plantations in coastal areas were consolidated under foreign control.

Ceylon became an independent member of the British Commonwealth on Feb. 4, 1948; the Republic of Sri Lanka was proclaimed on May 22, 1972.

Prime Minister W.R.D. Bandaranaike was assassinated on Sept. 25, 1959. His widow, Sirimavo Bandaranaike, leader of the Freedom party, was elected as his successor. In 1962 her government expropriated the property of foreign oil companies. The conservative United National party won a majority in Parliament in 1965 and agreed to pay compensation for the expropriated assets. In May 1970 Mrs. Bandaranaike was again elected prime minister. Leftists secured the nationalization of foreign plantations in the mid-1970's. Mrs. Bandaranaike's party was ousted by the United National party in 1977. Constitutional reform in 1978 aimed at increasing stability by establishing a presidential form of government. Pres. J.R. Jayawardene was elected on Feb. 4, 1978.

But stability has eluded Sri Lanka because of the long struggle between Tamils and the Sinhalese. The political power acquired by the Tamil (mostly Hindu) middle class under the British was deeply resented by the Sinhalese (Buddhist) majority, which after independence slowly eroded Tamil rights. In 1957 the government proposed a Tamil state in a federal union and gave Tamil the status of a national (but not official) language. The pact was not fully implemented, and in the 1970's extremists began agitating for an independent Tamil state. The Tamils' minority status was reaffirmed in the constitution of 1972, the year the oldest insurgent group, the Liberation Tigers or Tamil Tigers, was founded.

In July 1987 Pres. Jayawardene accepted an offer from India's Prime Minister Rajiv Gandhi to supervise a truce in the Jaffna region under which the government pledged to hold a referendum aimed at granting self-rule to Tamil majority areas in the north. The plan failed, however; Indian troops became bogged down in battling the rebels, while the planned referendum was disrupted by fighting between separatists who demanded total independence for Tamil areas.

At the Sri Lankan government's request, India withdrew its forces in March 1989, and the Tamil Tigers agreed to a cease-fire as the government prepared its plan for Tamil-area autonomy. But this cease-fire soon broke down. The assassination of both the opposition political leader in April 1993 and Pres. Ranasinghe Pemadasa a month later left the nation in shock, although peaceful legislative elections were held later in May. In parliamentary elections held in 1994, the People's Alliance ended the United National party's 17-year rule. Prime Minister Chandrika Bandaranaike Kumaratunga won a landslide victory in presidential elections, and appointed her 78-year-old mother, Sirimavo Bandaranaike, as prime minister for a third time.

Hours after the new president's inauguration, the Tamil Tigers announced a cease-fire. The truce was formalized in Jan. 1995, but when the government offered a peace plan to divide Sri Lanka into autonomous regions, the Tamil rebels renewed the civil war which by 2000 had cost at least 60,000 lives and displaced at least a million people. Pres. Kumaratunga handily won re-election in Dec. 1999 but on the battlefield the Tamils grew more successful in 2000. A series of failed offensives against the Tigers in 2001 brought government to a halt and the loss of its majority. In Oct. 2001, Pres. Kumaratunga dissolved Parliament; resulting elections brought a three-party United Front to power. A Norway-negotiated truce in Feb. 2002 led to renewed peace talks in Thailand between the new government and the Tigers.

▶SUDAN

Republic of the Sudan

• **Geography** **Location:** northeastern Africa. **Boundaries**: Egypt to N, Red Sea, Eritrea, and Ethiopia to E, Kenya, Uganda, and Zaire to S, Central African Republic, Chad and Libya to W. **Total**

area: 967,495 sq. mi. (2,505,810 sq km). **Coastline:** 530 mi. (853 km). **Comparative area**: slightly more than one-quarter the size of the U.S. **Land use:** 7% arable land; negl. % permanent crops; 93% other. **Major cities**: (1993 census) Khartoum (capital) 924,505; Nyala 1,267,077; Shargen-Nil 879,105; Port Sudan 305,385; Omdurman 228, 778.

• **PEOPLE** **Population:** 38,114,160 (2003 est.). **Nationality:** noun—Sudanese (sing., pl.); adjective—Sudanese. **Ethnic groups:** 52% black, 39% Arab, 6% Beja, 2% foreigners. **Languages:** Arabic (official), Nubian, Ta Bedawie, diverse dialects of Nilotic, Nilo-Hamitic, and Sudanic languages, English; program of Arabization in progress. **Religions:** 70% Sunni Muslim (in north), 25% indigenous beliefs, 5% Christian (mostly in south).

• **GOVERNMENT** **Type:** transitional, previously military junta. **Independence:** Jan. 1, 1956 (from Egypt and U.K.). **Constitution:** Apr. 12, 1973, suspended following coup of Apr. 6, 1985; new constitution implemented June 1998, partially suspended Dec. 12 1999 by President Bashir. **National holiday:** Independence Day, Jan. 1. **Head of Government:** Lt. Gen. Omer Hassan Ahmed Al Bashir, president (since Jan. 1993). **Structure:** executive—president is head of government and chief of state; unicameral legislature; judiciary.

• **ECONOMY** **Monetary unit:** Sudanese pound. **Budget:** (2001 est.) ***income:*** $1.6 bil.; ***expend.:*** $1.9 bil. **GDP:** $52.9 bil., $1,420 per capita (2002 est.). **Chief crops:** cotton, peanuts,sorghum, millet, wheat, gum arabic, sesame; sheep. **Natural resources:** petroleum, reserves of iron oil, copper, chromium ore, zinc. **Major industries:** cotton ginning, textiles, cement. **Labor force:** 11 mil. (1996 est.); 80% agriculture, 7% industry and commerce, 13% government; labor shortages for almost all categories of skilled employment. **Exports:** $1.8 bil. (f.o.b., 2002 est.); cotton, sesame, livestock/meat. **Imports:** $1.5 bil. (f.o.b., 2002 est.); foodstuffs, petroleum products, manufactured goods, machinery and equipment, medicines and chemicals, textiles. **Major trading partners:** ***exports:*** **42% China, 145 Japan,** 7% Saudi Arabia; ***imports:*** 9% China, 8% Saudi Arabia, 7% Germany.

The northern Sudan, the ancient land of Nubia, was loosely controlled by Egypt in antiquity and incorporated into the Arab world by the Islamic expansion of the seventh century. The southern Sudan was part of tribal black Africa, under no external control but subject to continual raids by slave traders from the north.

Ottoman Egypt conquered the northern Sudan in 1820-21; British influence in Egypt in the 19th century extended into the Sudan as well. In 1881 Muhammed Ahmed ibn Abdalla, a religious leader known as the Mahdi, united northern and north-central Sudan and led a resistance movement against Anglo-Egyptian control. Khartoum, defended by British general Charles George Gordon, fell in 1885, but the Mahdi died soon thereafter, and his revolt came to an end. An Anglo-Egyptian force under Kitchener regained control in 1898; Anglo-Egyptian joint rule was established in the Sudan in 1899.

Great Britain and Egypt granted self-government and self-determination to the Sudan in 1953, and a Sudanese parliament was seated in 1954. Full independence came in 1956. Gen. Ibrahim Abboud took power in a bloodless coup in 1958 but was forced to resign after riots in 1964. In 1969 a new military coup installed a ruling Revolutionary Command Council and instituted a socialist regime. The council's leader, Gen. Muhammed Nimeiri, became prime minister. Disputes between Marxists and non-Marxists, and between arabized northerners and black southerners, led to continual difficulties. In 1972 Sudan's three black southern provinces were granted local autonomy. Another attempted coup in 1976 was put down by the Nimeiri government, and hundreds of prominent citizens were executed.

In 1983 attempts by the Nimeiri government to institute Islamic law throughout the Sudan led to riots in the south and the imposition of a nationwide state of emergency in 1984. Popular unrest was exacerbated by drought and famine in 1985. On Apr. 6, 1985, Nimeiri was overthrown in a coup by Gen. Suwar El Dahab. After a brief period of rule by a transitional military council, a civilian cabinet was installed, and free parliamentary elections were held in 1986.

In June 1989 the government was overthrown in a coup led by Lt. Gen. Omar Ahmed al-Bashir. The Bashir government renewed the fight against the southern rebels, and supported the imposition of Islamic law throughout the nation. Within three years the civil service, the military, the judiciary, and the educational system were under the control of Muslims and their political organization, the National Islamic Front headed by Hassan al-Turabi who was also the leader of parliament and the most powerful figure in Sudan. All opposition parties, newspapers, and unions were banned and a stepped up military campaign against christians in the South was launched.

In Oct. 1990, the U.S. government stopped aid to the Sudan, which openly supported Iraq during the Persian Gulf War. In 1991, the U.N. suspended relief efforts to help the estimated 7.1 million Sudanese threatened by famine. In 1993, the U.S. added Sudan to its list of states that sponsor terrorism, and in 1995, the U.N. endorsed an accusation that Sudan was sheltering the Islamic militants who attempted to assassinate Egyptian Pres. Hosni Mubarak. The government in 1995 announced plans to free all political prisoners and to hold national elections in 1996 but an increase in violence against the government by rebels in the south delayed them. In 1997 the government made peace with some rebel factions, promising a referendum on self determination. The main force of the Sudan People's Liberation Army (SPLA), led by John Garang, continued to fight.

Another famine in 1998 brought a ceasefire as aid workers transported huge amounts of food to over 300,000 in the south. In Aug. 1998 the U.S. launched cruise missiles at Khartoum to retaliate for the bombing of its embassies in Kenya and Tanzania and to destroy what it said was a chemical weapons plant. Since July 1998, both the SPLA and the Sudanese government have declared a series of cease-fires to permit international food relief. The rebels lost some international support as Uganda, Ethiopia and Eritrea became embroiled in wars of their own. The Sudanese government's "restoration" of a multi-party system at the start of 1999 was met with skepticism by the opposition. Throughout 1999 Pres. Bashir sought some sort of reconciliation with opposition parties and with the southern rebels. In December he struck against Turabi, declaring a state of emergency, dissolving parliament dismissing the entire government, and replacing it with his supporters. In Jan. 2002 a cease-fire and in July a peace accord signed in Nairobi brought hope at last that the war might end. Through the Fall of 2003 the peace accord has held.

▶SURINAME

Republic of Suriname

• **GEOGRAPHY** **Location:** northeastern coast of South America. **Boundaries**: North Atlantic Ocean to N, French Guiana to E, Brazil to S, Guyana to W. **Total area**: 63,039 sq. mi. (163,270 sq km). **Coastline**: 240 mi. (386 km). **Comparative area**: slightly larger than Georgia. **Land use:** negl. % arable land; negl. % permanent crops; 100% other. **Major cities**: (1993 est.) Paramaribo (capital) 200,970.

• **PEOPLE** **Population:** 435,449 (2003 est.). **Nationality:** noun—Surinamer(s); adjective—Surinamese. **Ethnic groups:** 31% Hindustani (East Indian), 31% Creole (black and mixed), 15% Javanese, 10% black. **Languages:** Dutch (official), English widely spoken, Sranang Tongo (Surinamese, sometimes called Taki-Taki, the native language of Creoles and much of younger population and lingua franca among others), Hindustani, Javanese. **Religions:** 27.4% Hindu, 25.2% Protestant (predominantly Moravian), 22.8% Roman Catholic, 19.6% Muslim.

• **GOVERNMENT** **Type:** constitutional democracy. **Constitution:** Sept. 30, 1987. **Independence:** Nov. 25, 1975 (from Netherlands). **National holiday:** Independence Day, Nov. 25. **Heads of Government:** Runaldo Ronald Venetiaan, president (since Aug. 2000); **Structure:** executive—president is chief of state and head of government, Commander in Chief of the National Army maintains significant power; unicameral legislature; judiciary.

• **ECONOMY** **Monetary unit:** Surinamese guilder. **Budget:** (1997 est.) ***income:*** $393 mil.; ***expend.:*** $403 mil. **GDP:** $1.5 bil., $3,500 per capita (2002 est.). **Chief crops:** rice, bananas, palm oil, timber. **Natural resources:** timber, hydropower potential, fish, shrimp, bauxite. **Major industries:** bauxite mining, alumina and aluminum production, lumbering. **Labor force:** 100,000; agriculture, industry, services; 17% unemployment (2000). **Exports:** $445 mil. (f.o.b., 2002); alumina, aluminum, crude oil, lumber, shrimp and fish, rice, bananas. **Imports:** $300 mil. (f.o.b., 2002); capital equipment, petroleum, foodstuffs, cotton, consumer goods. **Major trading partners:** (2001) ***exports:*** 31% U.S., 19% Norway, 9% Netherlands; ***imports:*** 59% U.S., 28% Netherlands.

In the early 17th century, the Dutch and English settled Suriname, which became a Dutch colony in 1667. Except for brief episodes of British rule, Suriname remained under Dutch control until its independence in 1975, shifting toward authoritarian military rule in 1980. The military created its own political party (the February 25 movement) and banned opposition organizations. The 1988 National Assembly election of Pres. Ramsewak Shankar ended direct military rule, but the restriction of civil liberties continued.

The Shankar government was overthrown in a bloodless coup led by Cmdr. Ivan Graanoogst in 1990, and civilian rule was restored in 1991 although the former military ruler, Col. Desi Bouterse, who led the coup and remains "Advisor of the State," is apparently still the defacto ruler. The current President, Jules Wijdenbosch, agreed in June 1999, after the National Assembly voted "no confidence," to resign—but to remain in office until after the May 2000 National Assembly elections, elections in which the four-party, labor-backed coalition, New Front, carried 33 of the 52 seats, one shy of the 2/3 needed to elect a president alone.

▶SWAZILAND

Kingdom of Swaziland

• **GEOGRAPHY** **Location:** landlocked country in southern Africa. **Boundaries**: South Africa to N, SE, S, and W; Mozambique to E. **Total area**: 6,703 sq. mi. (17,360 sq km). **Coastline**: none. **Comparative area**: slightly smaller than New Jersey. **Land use:** 11% arable land; negl. % permanent crops; 89% other. **Major cities**: (1996 census) Mbabane (capital) 38,290; Manzini 18,084.

• **PEOPLE** **Population:** 1,161,219 (2003 est.). **Nationality:** noun—Swazi(s); adjective—Swazi. **Ethnic groups:** 97% African, 3% European. **Languages:** English and siSwati (both official); government business conducted in English. **Religions:** 40% Zionist (mixture of Christianity and indigenous beliefs), 20% Roman Catholic, 10% Muslim, 10% other.

• **GOVERNMENT** **Type:** monarchy; independent member of Commonwealth. **Independence:** Sept. 6, 1968 (from U.K.). **Constitution:** suspended Apr. 12, 1973; new constitution promulgated Oct. 13, 1978, but not yet formally presented to people. **National holiday:** Somhlolo (Independence) Day, Sept. 6. **Heads of Government:** Mswati III, king (since Apr. 1986); Sibusiso Barnabas Dlamini, prime minister (since Aug. 1996). **Structure:** executive—king is hereditary monarch, appoints prime minister; bicameral legislature (lower house-10 members appointed by king, 55 elected; upper house-20 members appointed by king, 10 elected by lower house); judiciary—judges appointed by king.

• **ECONOMY** **Monetary unit:** lilangeni. **Budget:** (FY01/02) ***income:*** $448 mil.; ***expend.:*** $506.9 mil. **GDP:** $4.8 bil., $4,400 per capita (2002 est.). **Chief crops:** sugarcane, maize, cotton, maize, tobacco, rice, citrus fruits; cattle, goats, sheep. **Natural resources:** asbestos, coal, clay, cassiterite, hydropower. **Major industries:** mining (coal and asbestos), wood pulp, sugar. **Labor force:** 383,200. **Exports:** $820 mil. (f.o.b., 2002); soft drink concentrates, sugar, wood pulp, cotton yarn. **Imports:** $938 mil. (f.o.b., 2002); motor vehicles, machinery, transport equipment, foodstuffs, chemicals, petroleum products. **Major trading partners:** (1999) ***exports:*** 72% South Africa, 14% E.U., 4% Mozambique; ***imports:*** 89% South Africa, 6% E.U., 1% Japan.

The Kingdom of Swaziland, a landlocked African country, is surrounded on three sides by South Africa and on the fourth by Mozambique. The Swazi are of Bantu origin. They are believed to have migrated in the late 1700's, under their chief Ngwane II, into what is now southeastern Swaziland, finding several different peoples there. Ngwane II and his successors united these tribal clans by the beginning of the 19th century.

Although British and Boer traders began exploring the area in the 1830's, it was not until gold was discovered in the 1880's that settlers began coming in large numbers. They hoodwinked the illiterate Swazi leadership into signing away their rights to the land. The British and Boer governments agreed in 1894 that the Boers would control Swaziland, but power reverted to Great Britain after they defeated the Boers in the Boer War, which ended in 1902. Not until the 1967 did they give Swaziland authority over its internal affairs. Under the Britishauthored constitution, Swaziland gained its independence in September 1968 as a constitutional monarchy led by King Sobhuza II. He set aside the constitution in 1973 and disbanded the legislature. He ruled the country with the aid of a council of conservative ministers and named a committee to write a new constitution that was supposed to be more in keeping with Swazi traditions. A new legislature was created in 1979. The king died in 1982 and was replaced by his 18-year-old son, who took the name King Mswati III, in 1986.

In 1986 South African forces conducted raids into Swaziland, allegedly in pursuit of African National Congress activists. Swaziland maintains cooperative but cool relations with South Africa and Mozambique.

▶SWEDEN

Kingdom of Sweden

• **GEOGRAPHY** **Location:** Scandinavian peninsula, northwest Europe. **Boundaries**: Norway to NE and W, Finland to NE, Gulf of Bothnia to E, Baltic Sea to E and S, Skagerrak channel to SW. **Total area**: 173,731 sq. mi. (449,964 sq km). **Coastline**: 2,000 mi. (3,218 km). **Comparative area**: slightly larger than California. **Land use:** 7% arable land; 0% permanent crops; 93% other. **Major cities**: (1994 est.) Stockholm (capital) 703,627; Göteburg (Gothenburg) 444,553; Malmö 242,706; Uppsala 181,191; Linköping 130,489.

• **PEOPLE** **Population:** 8,878,085 (2003 est.). **Nationality:** noun—Swede(s); adjective—Swedish. **Ethnic groups:** homogeneous white population; small Lappish minority; about 12% foreign-born or first-generation immigrants (Finns, Yugoslavs, Danes, Norwegians, Greeks, Turks). **Languages:** Swedish, small Lapp- and Finnish-speaking minorities. **Religions:** 87% Lutheran, Roman Catholic, Orthodox, Baptist, other.

• **GOVERNMENT** **Type:** constitutional monarchy. **Constitution:** Jan. 1, 1975. **National holiday:** Day of the Swedish Flag, June 6. **Head of Government:** Carl XVI Gustaf, king (since Nov. 1973); Göran Persson, prime minister (since Mar. 1996). **Structure:** executive—prime minister is head of government; unicameral legislature; judiciary.

• **ECONOMY** **Monetary unit:** Swedish krona. **Budget:** (2000 est.) ***income:*** $119 bil.; ***expend.:*** $110 bil. **GDP:** $227.4 bil., $25,400 per capita (2002 est.). **Chief crops:** grain, sugar beets, potatoes; meat, milk. **Natural resources:** zinc, iron ore, lead, copper, silver. **Major industries:** iron and steel, precision equipment (bearings, radio and telephone parts, armaments), wood pulp. **Labor force:** 4.4 mil. (2000); 74% services, 24% industry, 2% agriculture. **Exports:** $80.6 bil. (f.o.b., 2002); 35% machinery, motor vehicles, paper products, pulp and wood, iron and steel products. **Imports:** $68.6 bil. (f.o.b., 2002); machinery, petroleum and petroleum products, chemicals, motor vehicles, foodstuffs. **Major trading partners:** ***exports:*** 55% E.U., 11% U.S., 9% Norway; ***imports:*** 66% E.U., 9% Norway, 7% U.S.

The earliest Swedes, the Svear, conquered and merged with their southern neighbors, the Gotar, by the sixth century. Organized into petty kingdoms, Swedes joined with other Norsemen in the Viking raids of the seventh through 11th centuries; in the 10th century, they began to dominate a trading empire that stretched through Russia to the Black Sea. Christianity was introduced by St. Ansgar in 829 but became fully established only in the 12th century, during the reign of Eric IX, who also conquered Finland. For centuries Sweden warred with its neighbors, Norway and Denmark, for control in the north, and it competed with the German Hanseatic League for control of the Baltic trade.

The Swedish and Norwegian monarchies were merged in 1319 by Magnus VII, and in 1397 Queen Margaret effected the Kalmar Union, which united Sweden, Denmark, and Norway under a single monarchy. Sweden resisted Danish rule, and in 1520 King Christian II responded with the massacre of the Swedish nobility at Stockholm. Sweden then rose against the Danish throne and in 1523 enthroned Gustavus Wasa as Gustavus I, founder of the Swedish monarchy. The Wasa dynasty slowly introduced Lutheran Christianity and in 1604 banned Catholicism.

Sweden became a European champion of Protestantism in the 17th century, intervening against the Habsburgs in the Thirty Years' War. Emerging among the victors after 1648, Sweden successfully waged wars with Denmark and Poland, built a great northern empire, and made the Baltic Sea virtually a Swedish lake. But in the late 17th century and into the 18th, the Russians deprived Sweden of the Baltic's eastern shore and, in 1808, of Finland, while the Prussians drove Sweden from the southern Baltic coast.

The kings of Sweden during the 18th century pursued a pointless despotism that weakened the country politically and socially. Sweden joined the European powers against Napoleon in 1813 and was rewarded with Norway in 1814. In 1905 Norway gained its independence, and Sweden took on its modern boundaries.

Sweden's natural resources—timber, iron ore, and hydroelectric power—were exploited by traditional industries, which supplemented other economic activities (fishing, maritime trade). All provided the basis for industrialization in the 19th and 20th centuries, leading to an economic prosperity that was enhanced by political neutrality.

Sweden's neutrality was largely respected by Hitler during World War II. Through the war Sweden continued to be ruled, under King Gustavus V, by a national coalition government lasting until 1945. Sweden's gross national product (GNP) rose by 20 percent during the war years.

The Social Democratic party dominated the Swedish government after 1936, and again after 1945, lasting until 1976 under the leadership of Tage Erlander. Sweden, like its Scandinavian neighbors, constructed an economy based on free enterprise, public ownership of utilities, exports, social welfare, and high taxes.

A U.N. charter member, Sweden accepted Marshall Plan aid and joined the Council of Europe in 1948. Sweden's plan for a Nordic Defense Alliance failed when Norway and Denmark joined NATO (Sweden refused to join), but the political and economic Nordic Council (Sweden, Norway, Denmark, Iceland, and, after 1956, Finland) was formed in 1952-53. This consultative body backed the establishment of SAS as the joint national airline of the first three members; coordination of the welfare programs of member states; and abolition of passport controls and controls on the migration of labor within Scandinavia.

Erlander retired as prime minister in 1969 and was succeeded by Olaf Palme, who pursued a more rigid socialist program than his predecessor. He advocated legislation to make incomes more equal, provoking some labor unrest. When King Gustav VI Adolf died in 1973 the Palme government passed the 1974 Instrument of Government Act, divesting the king of his role as commander in chief and of his right to appoint prime ministers.

Economic growth came to a virtual halt in the 1970's; lacking petroleum and gas resources, Sweden's oil import costs rose 700 percent between 1972 and 1979. Consumer prices rose sharply, and labor unrest grew. The Social Democrats were turned out of office by a conservative coalition in 1976 but returned with a minority cabinet in 1982.

Palme was assassinated in 1986, and he was succeeded by Ingvar Carlsson, whose Social Democratic program focused on a scheme whereby business profits are taxed to fund labor union purchases of sufficient stock to gain labor ownership of private enterprise.

Elections (Sept. 1991) unseated Carlsson and the Social Democrats, who had ruled for 53 of the last 59 years. A coalition government of four conservative parties pledged to cut taxes and phase out some welfare programs.

But in elections held in Sept. 1994, Carlsson returned to power as voters expressed dissatisfaction with inflation, unemployment, and an enormous public debt, all of which spiraled under the conservative coalition. The Social Democrats fell 13 votes short of a majority in Parliament, however, forcing them to seek the support of the right-centrist Liberal party in a coalition government. On Jan. 1, 1995, Sweden entered the European Union. In March 1996, Finance Minister Göran Persson succeeded Carlsson as prime minister. In 1998 Sweden announced it would not join the European Monetary Union, and in Sept. elections Persson's Government won enough votes to keep power by pledging more money for social welfare services. More significant for Sweden's future was the 1999 completion of the 10-mile, $2.6 billion bridge over (and under) the Baltic, linking Copenhagen with Malmoe (Sweden's third largest city). On Dec. 17, 1999, after almost 500 years, the Lutheran Church was disestablished. Persson and the Social Democrats beat back a concerted effort by four conservative parties and won the Sept. 2002 elections. In Sept. 2003 Foreign Minister Anna Lindh was assasinated just days before voters rejected participation in the European Monetary Union.

▶SWITZERLAND

Swiss Confederation

• **Geography** **Location:** landlocked country in central Europe. **Boundaries**: Germany to N, Austria to E, Italy to S, and France to W. **Total area**: 15,942 sq. mi. (41,290 sq km). **Coastline**: none. **Comparative area**: slightly less than twice the size of New Jersey. **Land use:** 11% arable land; 1% permanent crops; 88% other. **Major cities**: (1994 est.) Berne (Bern, capital) 128,422; Zürich 342,872; Basel 175,561; Genève (Geneva or Genf) 172,737; Lausanne 116,795.

• **People** **Population:** 7,318,638 (2003 est.). **Nationality:** noun—Swiss (sing., pl.); adjective—Swiss. **Ethnic groups:** 65% German, 18% French, 10% Italian, 1% Romansch, 6% other. **Languages:** 63.7% German, 19.2% French, 7.6% Italian (all official); 0.6% Romansch, 8.9% other. **Religions:** 46.1% Catholic, 40% Protestant.

• **Government** **Type:** federal republic. **Independence:** Aug. 1, 1291. **Constitution:** May 29, 1874. **National holiday:** Anniversary of the Founding of the Swiss Confederation, Aug. 1. **Head of Government:** Pascal Couchepin, president (since Jan. 2003). **Structure:** executive—president is head of government and chief of state; bicameral legislature—National Council, Council of States; judiciary left chiefly to cantons.

• **Economy** **Monetary unit:** Swiss franc. **Budget:** (2001 est.) ***income:*** $30 bil.; ***expend.:*** $30 bil. **GDP:** $231 bil., $31,700 per capita (2002 est.). **Chief crops:** grains, fruits, vegetables; meat, eggs. **Natural resources:** hydropower potential, timber, salt. **Major industries:** machinery, chemicals, watches. **Labor force:** 4 mil.; 69.1% services, 26.3% industry, 4.6% agriculture. **Exports:** $100.3 bil. (f.o.b., 2002); machinery, chemicals, metals, watches, agricultural products. **Imports:** $94.4 bil. (f.o.b., 2002); machinery, chemicals, vehicles, metals, agricultural products. **Major trading partners:** (2000 est.) ***exports:*** 61% E.U., 11% U.S., 4% Japan; ***imports:*** 80% E.U., 5% U.S.

Switzerland, the Roman province of Helvetia, began to assume its modern form in A.D. 1291, when three independent cantons formed a defensive league against the expansion of Habsburg power. The Swiss League grew to eight cantons in 1353, 13 in 1513, 22 in 1815. The league continues to evolve; it reached its present size of 20 cantons and six half-cantons with the creation of the Canton of Jura in 1979.

The Treaty of Westphalia, which ended the Thirty Years' War in 1648, gave international recognition to the independence of Switzerland from the Holy Roman Empire. Switzerland became a client state of France in the Napoleonic period; the European powers guaranteed Swiss independence and neutrality at the Congress of Vienna in 1815. Constitutional changes in 1848 and 1874 somewhat increased the power of the central government, but the individual cantons cling stubbornly to their independence within the confederation. This policy has helped ensure stability within a multilingual nation.

The Swiss government consists of an upper house, representing the cantons, and a lower house that is directly elected. No executive can veto, nor court disallow, a bill of the Swiss legislature. Executive power is vested in a seven-member committee chosen by the legislature, with a rotating presidency.

Swiss neutrality is defended by more than simply international guarantees. Switzerland is a highly militarized society; every male is required to serve in the citizen's militia until age 47, keeping an assault rifle and other equipment ready at home. The armed forces are equipped with modern weapons, and military spending amounts to 30 percent of the Swiss federal budget.

Landlocked, with little fertile farmland and lacking both natural resources and a colonial empire, Switzerland was traditionally one of Europe's poorest countries. Until the 19th century, its principal export was mercenaries who supplied military services to any European sovereign who could pay for them. (The pope's Swiss Guard is a remnant of this tradition.) With the spread in the late 18th century of the Romantic movement, Europeans learned to appreciate the Alpine scenery, and a tourist industry was born. It was expanded in the 20th century with the development of Alpine skiing. Tourism remains a conspicuous, though minor, part of the Swiss economy.

Swiss prosperity came in the 20th century with specialized manufacturing and free trade within the world economy. By 1940 half of the population was engaged in manufacturing, producing products requiring high degrees of skill: processed foods, watches, electrical machinery, engines, fine textiles, and the like.

Neutral in both world wars, Switzerland required no postwar recovery in the 1940's. It capitalized on the restructuring of European politics and economics to expand into the service sector, which now employs half of the work force (while manufacturing has declined to about 40 percent). Tourism, banking, insurance, and clerical/bureaucratic services to the many international organizations with headquarters in Switzerland help give the nation one of Europe's highest standards of living. Under pressure from the EC and the United States, Switzerland agreed to phase out its famous "Form B" (i.e., secret bank accounts).

In the postwar period, Switzerland has enjoyed both political and economic stability. A cautious approach to economic development led to annual growth rates of over 6 percent in the 1950's and early 1960's, declining to 2 percent in the 1970's; the world economic boom of the 1980's produced higher growth rates.

Referenda at this time brought overwhelming rejection of U.N. membership (it currently has observer status), and support for restrictive immigration legislation. The most significant political changes were the gradual extension of women's right to vote and the 1993 approval of casino gambling to fund social security.

In 1996 and 1997 the Swiss government, responding to international pressures, appointed a panel to examine what funds in Swiss banks the Nazis might have stolen or that Holocaust victims (or their families) might have deposited and were unable to retrieve. A less than rigorous accounting, however, resulted in several lawsuits which were settled in 1998 with the Swiss banks agreeing to pay $1.2 bil. On Dec. 9, 1998, Social Democrat Ruth Dreifuss became Switzerland's first female and first Jewish president. A June 1999 referendum (carried 70 percent–30 percent) to restrict refugee asylum prefigured a very strong showing in the October National Council elections by the nativist Swiss People's Party which had the largest total vote and won the second largest number of seats.

Recent referenda reflect divisions in Swiss minds over the country's identity and her role in the new Europe. In 2000, 64 percent refused to set a limit (18%) on the number of foreigners residing in Switzerland, and 74 percent refused to begin negotiations for E.U. membership. Yet in July, by a slender margin (50.9 percent), voters approved the arming of Swiss troops serving under international auspices as well as joint training of Swiss soldiers with foreign armies., and in 2002 Switzerland entered the U.N.

▶SYRIA

Syrian Arab Republic

• **GEOGRAPHY** **Location:** western Asia. **Boundaries**: Turkey to N, Iraq to E, Jordan to S, Lebanon and Israel to SW, Mediterranean Sea to W. **Total area**: 71,498 sq. mi. (185,180 sq km). **Coastline**: 193 mi. (193 km). **Comparative area**: slightly larger than North Dakota. **Land use:** 26% arable land; 4% permanent crops; 70% other. **Major cities**: (1994 est.) Damascus (capital) 1,444,138; Aleppo 1,542,000; Homs 558,000; Latakia 303,000; Hama 273,000.

• **PEOPLE** **Population:** 17,585,540 (2003 est.). **Nationality:** noun—Syrian(s); adjective—Syrian. **Ethnic groups:** 90.3% Arab, 9.7% Kurds, Armenians, and other. **Languages:** Arabic (official), Kurdish, Armenian, Aramaic, Circassian, French. **Religions:** 74% Sunni Muslim; 16% Alawite, Druze, and other Muslim sects; 10% Christian.

• **GOVERNMENT** **Type:** republic under military regime since Mar. 1963. **Independence:** Apr. 17, 1946 (from League of Nations Mandate under French administration). **Constitution:** Mar. 13, 1973. **National holiday:** National Day, Apr. 17. **Heads of Government:** Dr. Bashar Al-Assad, president (since July 2000); Dr. Mohammad Mostafa Miro, prime minister (since Mar. 2000). **Structure:** executive powers vested in president and Council of Ministers; unicameral legislature (People's Council); judiciary.

• **ECONOMY** **Monetary unit:** Syrian pound. **Budget:** (2002 est.) ***income:*** $6 bil.; ***expend.:*** $7 bil. **GDP:** $59.4 bil., $3,500 per capita (2002 est.). **Chief crops:** cotton, wheat, barley, lentils; beef, lamb, eggs, poultry, milk. **Natural resources:** crude oil, phosphates, chrome and manganese ores, asphalt, iron ore. **Major industries:** petroleum, textiles, food processing, beverages. **Labor force:** 5.2 mil. (2000 est.); 40% services, 40% agriculture, 20% industry. **Exports:** $4.8 bil. (f.o.b., 2000 est.); 65% petroleum, 10% textiles, 9% food and live animals. **Imports:** $4.9 bil. (f.o.b., 2002 est.); 21% machinery, 18% foodstuffs/animals, 15% metal and metal products, 10% chemicals. **Major trading partners:** (2001 est.) ***exports:*** 19% Germany, 16% Italy, 12% France; ***imports:*** 8% Italy, 7% Germany, 6% France.

The home of some of the world's most ancient centers of civilization, Syria was successively part of the Hittite, Assyrian, and Persian empires. At various times it was conquered by the Babylonians and the Egyptians. From about 1250 B.C., the coastal cities came under Phoenician rule. Alexander the Great brought Syria into the Hellenic world with his conquests in 332 B.C. After the fall of the Alexandrian empire, Syria came under the domain of the Seleucid empire but was constantly threatened by the Hellenic kingdom of Egypt, based in Alexandria.

In the classical period, Syria embraced a much larger territory than that of the present Syrian nation; it included the entire Levant and parts of present-day Turkey, Iraq, Iran, and Jordan. Greater Syria was conquered by Rome in 63 B.C. Under Roman rule the oasis region of Palmyra grew into a powerful semiautonomous kingdom. With the division of the Roman Empire in the fourth century A.D., Syria became part of the Eastern Roman (Byzantine) Empire. Throughout the Roman and Byzantine periods, the country was an important center of Christianity.

Syria was one of the first areas conquered when Islam began expansion from Arabia; Islamic rule was established by 636. From 661 to 751, Damascus was the center of the Caliphate, the ruling body of the Islamic world. By the late 11th century, the Seljuk Turks had conquered Syria. The large Syrian Christian population welcomed the European Crusaders as liberators from the Turks, but both Christians and Turks were defeated by the Arab general Saladin in the late 12th century. Saladin's rule was followed by that of the Mamluk empire of Egypt. During the Mamluk period, Mongol armies twice invaded Syria, in the mid-13th century and at the turn of the 15th century.

An Ottoman army defeated the Mamluks in Syria in 1516, making Syria part of the Ottoman Empire. In the 18th century, France declared itself the protector of Syria's Christian community against Ottoman abuses. Napoleon invaded Syria in 1799 but withdrew after a brief occupation. In the 1830's Egyptian troops occupied Syria but were forced to withdraw under pressure from the European powers.

Syrian nationalist aspirations emerged as the Ottoman Empire began to crumble before World War I. During the war the British encouraged Syrians to rebel against Turkish rule. After World War I, France governed both Syria and Lebanon under a League of Nations mandate. Under French rule, the region was divided into small territorial states along communal lines; Lebanon became independent in 1926. After prolonged negotiations much of Syria was organized into a semi-autonomous state in 1930-32.

In June 1940 the French administration in Syria declared its loyalty to the Vichy government. British and Free French forces invaded in June 1941, and an independent Syrian republic was established in September 1941. Separately administered territories were consolidated with the republic over the next two years, and full independence was declared on Jan. 1, 1944; foreign troops did not withdraw, however, until April 1946.

Syria became a founding member of the Arab League and participated in the first Arab-Israeli War in 1948. An armistice with Israel was signed in July 1949. Severe political instability marked the early years of Syrian independence; the government was overthrown by military coups three times in 1949 alone.

Most of Syria's Jews emigrated to Israel before or during 1948, and much of its once-substantial Christian population has emigrated also. Syrian politics remain dominated by communal concerns, however; the Arab majority is divided into Sunni, Shiite, Alawite, and Druze communities.

Syria and Egypt merged as the United Arab Republic in February 1958; Syria seceded from the federation on Sept. 30, 1961. In Mar. 1963 a military coup established the pan-Arab Socialist Baath party in power; all other political parties were abolished. The Baath party leadership is dominated by the minority Alawite community. Pres. Hafez al-Assad took power on Feb. 22, 1971.

In the 1967 Arab-Israeli War (the Six Day War), Israel seized and held the Golan Heights region of Syria, from which Syria had long shelled Israeli communities and military installations. The Golan Heights have since been incorporated into Israeli territory.

Syrian troops aided Palestinian forces fighting government troops in Jordan in September 1970. After the expulsion of Palestinian forces from Jordan in July 1971, Syria broke off relations with Jordan; relations were restored in 1975.

On Oct. 6, 1973, Syrian and Egyptian forces attacked Israel, touching off the third Arab-Israeli War, the Yom Kippur War. A cease-fire took effect on Oct. 24; Syria failed to regain territory lost to Israel in 1967. Following the 1973 war, Syria became a major recipient of economic aid from the Arab oil states and of military equipment from the Soviet Union.

In 1976 Syrian troops entered Lebanon in an attempt to mediate a civil war there and became enmeshed in that conflict. Major fighting between Syrian troops and Lebanese Christian militiamen broke out in April 1981. On June 6, 1982, Israeli troops invaded Lebanon and engaged Syrian troops in a five-day war in the Bekaa Valley. Following serious losses of aircraft and troops, Syria agreed to a cease-fire with Israel on June 11. Syrian troops continue to occupy parts of Lebanon.

An attempted coup, in February 1982, by the Muslim Brotherhood, led to serious fighting within Syria, but the rebellion was put down; casualties topped 5,000 on both sides.

From the time of the 1973 Arab-Israeli War (the Yom Kippur War), Syria consistently adopted a radical stance in Middle Eastern politics, rejecting the 1979 Egyptian-Israeli accord and all other attempts at Arab-Israeli reconciliation. Supporting radical movements within the Palestine Liberation Organization, Syria aided Palestinian militants in driving Yasir Arafat's centrist faction of the PLO from its headquarters in Tripoli in 1983. The government was implicated in various acts of international terrorism in support of Palestinian, Libyan, and Iranian causes.

Syria played a major role in the Lebanese peace process and accommodating a peace settlement between rival Shiite militias. Syria also took part in the anti-Iraq coalition in 1990-91, sending 20,000 troops to Saudi Arabia, as well as mobilizing forces on its common border with Iraq. Syria in 1994 made serious efforts toward achieving peace in the Middle East, including an offer to normalize relations in exchange for a return of the Golan Heights. But talks between the two countries were suspended after several bombings by the militant Islamic group Hamas.

In Oct. 1998, Syria reached an accord with Turkey; with 10,000 Turkish troops massed on Syria's border, Syria agreed to cease supporting Kurdish rebels. The legislative elections in Dec. 1998 contained no surprises: Assad's National Progressive Front won all 167 seats that they chose to contest. Then, in Feb. 1999, Assad himself won, with 99.95 percent approval in his sole candidacy, election to a fifth seven-year term as president. A cabinet shake-up in March 2000 produced 22 new members among the 36 under new premier Mohammed Mustafa Zubi just three months before the death of Assad. After his 30 years of rule, the government backed his son (and armed forces commander) Bashar al-Assad, 34.

▶TAIWAN

• **GEOGRAPHY** **Location:** one large and several smaller islands about 100 mi. (160 km) off SE coast of mainland China. Taipei 25°03'N, 121°30'E. **Boundaries**: East China Sea to N, Pacific Ocean to E, Bashi Channel to S, and Formosa Strait to W; separated from mainland by Formosa Strait. **Total area**: 13,892 sq. mi. (35,980 sq km). **Coastline**: 900 mi. (1,448 km). **Comparative area**: slightly smaller than Maryland. **Land use:** 24% arable land; 1% permanent crops;75% other. **Major cities**: (1992 est.) Taipei (capital) 2,696,073; Kaohsiung 1,405,909; Taichung 794,960; Tainan 694,630; Panchiao 543,982.

• **PEOPLE** **Population:** 22,603,001 (2003 est.). **Nationality:** noun—Chinese (sing., pl.); adjective—Chinese. **Ethnic groups:** 84% Taiwanese, 14% mainland Chinese, 2% aborigine. **Languages:** Mandarin Chinese (official); Taiwanese and Hakka dialects also used. **Religions:** 93% mixture of Buddhist, Confucian, and Taoist; 4.5% Christian, 2.5% other.

• **GOVERNMENT** **Type:** multi-party democratic regime headed by popularly elected president. **Constitution:** Jan. 1, 1947, amended 1992, 1994, and 1997. **National holiday:** National Day, Oct. 10. **Heads of Government:** Chen Shui-bian, president (since March 2000); Chang Chunsiung, premier (since Oct. 2000). **Structure:** executive—president appoints premier; two-chamber legislature—Legislative Yuan, National Assembly; judiciary—Judicial Yuan.

• **ECONOMY** **Monetary unit:** New Taiwan dollar. **Budget:** (2002 est.) ***income:*** $36 bil.; ***expend.:*** $36 bil. **GDP:** $406 bil., $18,000 per capita (2002 est.). **Chief crops:** rice, wheat, corn, soybeans, vegetables, fruit, tea; pigs, poultry, beef, milk; fish. **Natural resources:** small deposits of coal, natural gas, limestone, marble, and asbestos. **Major industries:** electronics, petroleum refining, textiles, clothing, chemicals. **Labor force:** 10 mil. (2002 est.); 35% industry and commerce, 58% services,

7% agriculture. **Exports:** $130 bil. (f.o.b., 2002); 54% electrical equipment and machinery, metals, textiles, plastics, chemicals, electronic products. **Imports:** $113 bil. (c.i.f., 2002); 44.5% machinery and electrical equipment, electronic products, minerals, precision instruments. **Major trading partners:** (2000) ***exports:*** 23% U.S., 22% Hong Kong,10% Japan; ***imports:*** 24% Japan, 16% U.S., 13% Europe.

Nominally part of the Chinese empire since the Song dynasty (960-1279), Taiwan was inhabited only by non-Chinese aboriginals before the 17th century. Around 1600 the Portuguese established a trading station on Taiwan; they named the island Ilha Formosa. In 1620 the Dutch built Fort Zeelandia near present-day Tainan, controlling the island until they were driven out by the Chinese pirate-patriot Koxinga (Zheng Chenggong). Remnants of the overthrown Ming dynasty (1368-1644) held out on the island until 1683, when it came under the sway of the Qing dynasty (1644-1911). Thereafter, substantial numbers of farmers from Fujian Province migrated to the fertile western lowlands of the island, driving the aboriginals into the central mountains. The Qing dynasty administered Taiwan as a semiautonomous subprovince of Fujian Province.

Following China's defeat by Japan in the Sino-Japanese War of 1894-95, Taiwan was ceded to Japan as a colony. The Japanese built roads and railroads to exploit Taiwan's resources of rice, timber, and minerals. In 1945, after Japan's defeat in World War II, Taiwan was returned to China.

As the Chinese civil war turned against the Nationalist party of Chiang Kai-shek (see "China"), Nationalist troops began to prepare Taiwan as a base for a retreat from the mainland.

In 1947 Nationalist agents executed several thousand students and others suspected of favoring Taiwan's independence from China. In 1949 approximately two million Nationalist soldiers, government officials, and civilian sympathizers retreated to Taiwan. The relocated Republic of China (ROC) continued to claim to be the legitimate government of all of China, now under Communist control. In addition to Taiwan proper, the Nationalists occupied the P'eng-hu Islands in the Taiwan Straits and the small islands of Quemoy and Matsu just off the coast of Fujian. Recovery of the mainland became a cornerstone of ROC policy, but no serious attempt was made to do so. U.S. policy in the Taiwan Straits was to defend Taiwan against Communist attack but also to keep the two rival governments of China separated.

A successful program of land reform in the early 1950's led to the creation of surplus capital, which fueled the development of an industrial base on the island. Foreign investment from Japan and the United States, and American military and economic aid, also enhanced economic development. By the early 1970's, the island had developed an export-oriented economy, producing textiles, cement, plastics, assembled electronic appliances, and other manufactured goods.

Chiang Kai-shek, president of the Republic of China since 1928, died in 1975 and was succeeded by his son, Chiang Ching-kuo. Under both father and son, the Nationalist party (Kuomintang, or KMT) controlled both the ROC and the Taiwan Provincial governments; mainland refugees and their descendants (15% of the population) dominated senior government posts and the military officer corps. Native Taiwanese played the leading role in agriculture, industry, and in local and county governments.

In 1971 China's seat in the United Nations was taken away from the ROC and awarded to the People's Republic of China, leaving Taiwan in international diplomatic limbo. On Jan. 1, 1979, the United States withdrew its recognition of the ROC and inaugurated mutual diplomatic relations with the People's Republic. Under the Taiwan Relations Act of 1979, nominally nongovernmental relations were maintained between the U.S. and Taiwan through the American Institute in Taipei and Taiwan's Coordination Council for North American Affairs in Washington, D.C. Taiwan's economy has continued to be one of the world's most vigorous; Taiwan enjoys a substantial favorable balance of trade with the U.S.

In 1986 Pres. Chiang Ching-kuo began a policy of liberalization; in 1987, he abolished martial law and allowed non-KMT political parties to function legally. Some barriers to travel and communication with the mainland by ROC citizens were eased, but Taiwan's government continued to rebuff all calls from the mainland for direct contacts and discussions of reunification. Chiang Ching-kuo died in Jan. 1988 and was succeeded by his vice president, Lee Teng-hui. In March 1990, Lee was overwhelmingly reelected by the National Assembly in the first election for the office.

The ruling KMT maintained its hold on power in legislative elections on Dec. 19, 1992, but the opposition Democratic Progressive party scored a stunning success, tripling its number of legislative seats and bringing the issue of Taiwanese independence to the forefront. Factional rivalry deepened in the KMT, with Pres. Lee's Wisdom Coalition challenged by the New Kuomintang Alliance of Prime Minister (and former general) Hau Pei-tsun. Hau reluctantly resigned on Feb. 3, 1993, to take responsibility for the electoral fiasco, but his faction, with military backing, continued to pose a threat to Pres. Lee's power.

During the campaign for Taiwan's presidential election in March, 1996, China held aggressive military exercises off the coast of Taiwan in an effort to influence the voting; the U.S. sent two aircraft carriers to the area. In a rebuke to Beijing, President Lee, who had campaigned for a more visible international role for Taiwan, was resoundingly re-elected; he was also re-elected as the head of the KMT in August, 1997. Since then, talks for cross-straits cooperation between Taiwan and the PRC have been inconclusive, and the ruling KMT saw its power eroded in local elections as voters protest against corruption and economic stagnation related to the Asia-wide economic crises of 1997-98. The KMT rebounded strongly in 1998 elections but tensions rose in 1999 with mainland China, when Pres. Lee's expressed interest in Taiwan's being included in a proposed anti-missile defense of its Asian allies (the "last straw" to Beijing). Later, Lee announced that Taiwan would conduct its relations with China on a "state-to-state" basis, meaning Taiwan was an independent state—to Beijing, an "extremely dangerous step". In March 2000, the KMT was peacefully voted out of power after 50 years. Chen Shui-Bian of the Democratic-Progressive Party was elected president. In Aug. 2002 Chen said he would seek legislation to authorize a referendum on Taiwanese independence.

▶ TAJIKISTAN

Republic of Tajikistan

• **GEOGRAPHY** **Location:** southeast central Asia. **Boundaries:** Kyrgyzstan to NE, China to E, Afghanistan to S and SW, Uzbekistan to NW and N. **Total area:** 55,251 sq. mi. (143,100 sq km). **Coastline:** none. **Comparative area:** slightly smaller than Wisconsin. **Land use:** 6% arable land; 1% permanent crops; 93% other. **Major cities:** (1990 est.) Dushanbe (Stalinabad 1929-61) (capital) 602,000; Khodzhent (formerly Leninabad), 163,000 (1989).

• **PEOPLE** **Population:** 6,863,752 (2003 est.). **Nationality:** noun—Tajikstani(s); adjective—Tajikstani. **Ethnic groups:** 64.9% Tajik, 25% Uzbek, 3.5% Russian, 6.6% other. **Languages:** Tajik (official) is closely related to Farsi (Persian) and was written in Cyrillic script since 1940; Russian widely used in government and business. **Religions:** 85% Sunni Muslim, 5% Shi'a Muslim.

• **GOVERNMENT** **Type:** republic. **Independence:** Sept. 9, 1991 (from Soviet Union). **Constitution:** Nov. 6, 1994. **National holiday:** National Day, Sept. 9. **Heads of Government:** Emomali Rakhmonov; head of state (since Nov. 1994); Akil Akilov, prime minister (since Dec. 1999). **Structure:** executive—popularly-elected president appoints prime minister and cabinet; bicameral legislature; judiciary.

• **ECONOMY** **Monetary unit:** Tajikistani ruble. **Budget:** (2002 est.) ***income:*** $502 mil.; ***expend.:*** $520 mil. **GDP:** $8 bil., $1,250 per capita (2002 est.). **Chief crops:** cotton, vegetables, fruit, grain, grapes; cattle, sheep, goats. **Natural resources:** significant hydropower potential, some petroleum, uranium, mercury, brown coal. **Major industries:** mineral processing, chemicals, fertilizers, cement. **Labor force:** 3.187 mil. (2000); 50% agriculture and forestry, 20% industry, 30% services. **Exports:** $710 mil. (f.o.b., 2002 est.); cotton, aluminum, electricity, fruits, vegetable oil, textiles. **Imports:** $832 mil. (f.o.b., 2002 est.); fuel, electricity, chemicals, machinery and transport equipment, foodstuffs. **Major trading partners:** ***exports:*** Europe, Russia; ***imports:*** Uzbekistan, Russia, Europe.

Tajikistan is a mountainous country, with over half of its territory above 10,000 feet. Its mountain ranges are the northern and southern Tian Shan and the Pamirs, where the former Soviet Union's highest points of Lenin Peak and Communism Peak are found. The dense river system and the many fertile valleys make habitation possible in such a mountainous country, although the entire territory is prone to earthquakes.

Tajikistan exemplifies the complexities of central Asia, since, unlike other ethnic groups on the region, the Tajiks were not nomadic but sedentary, and their language was Persian, not Turkic. They are a population that somehow escaped the waves of Turkish influence that swept through central Asia. As early as the eighth century A.D., the Tajiks probably formed a distinctive ethnic group, although they have never been a completely independent people. Despite the formation of several semi-independent states in their history, they have always been a small part of the larger Uzbek lands. In the mid-19th century, the Russian empire expanded southward, and the northern Tajik territories came under Russian rule. At the same time, the tribal state known as the Khanate of Bukhara controlled the southern Tajik territories.

In April 1918 northern Tajikistan came under Soviet control and was included in the Turkestan Autonomous Soviet Socialist Republic (ASSR). Three years later, the Red Army took the other regions that had been ruled by Bukhara. There was local opposition to Soviet rule, and the fighting meant that full Soviet authority over all of the area was not established until 1925. When the U.S.S.R. created the National Delimitation of the Central Asian Republics in 1924, it founded the Tajik ASSR as part of the Uzbek Soviet Socialist Republic (SSR); on Oct. 16, 1929, it became the Tajik SSR.

The Tajiks were fiercely opposed to the policies of land reform and collectivization, and during the ensuing Soviet repression of the 1930's, almost all native Tajiks were replaced by Russians in leading government and party positions. There have been reports of rising Islamic influence and increasing anti-Russian sentiment and even riots during the 1970's, evidence that the animosity toward the Russians that stemmed with its forced incorporation into the U.S.S.R. had not abated since the 1920's. Under Soviet rule, there was some economic and social progress,

However, living standards in Tajikistan are still among the lowest in the former union. Most people continue to live in rural qishlaqs, or settlements, consisting of 200-700 one-family houses built along an irrigation ditch or a river. The country is a major producer of cotton, and its industries are nonferrous metallurgy, cotton processing, fruit canning, and wine making.

Mikhail Gorbachev's glasnost, or openness, policy resulted in a campaign against corruption, a relaxation of censorship in the press, and increased ethnic tensions over alleged discrimination against Tajiks living in Uzbekistan. In June 1989 there were violent clashes between the two groups on the border between the two republics. There were also riots in February 1990 in Dushanbe, when the suggestion that Armenian refugees would be resettled there spurred the local Tajiks into action. Increased freedom of the press has given rise to a growing interest in Iran and Iranian culture, for even though they are closely related, contact between Iran and the Tajiks was severely limited during the Soviet period.

In large part due to the riots, opposition candidates were barred from the March 1990 elections and the Communist party won 94 percent of the seats. After the failed Aug. 1991 coup in Moscow, the Communist party was banned, and the president was forced to resign over his support of the coup. Since then, there have been several Communist party coups, and the party has been banned and reinstated several times. In the presidential elections, former Communist party leader Rakhmon Nabiyev won with 58 percent of the vote. But after a relatively tranquil six months, Islamic fundamentalists, armed allegedly by Iran and Afghanistan, rose up against the Nabiyev regime. Vicious fighting for almost four months led to Nabiyev's resignation at gunpoint and the launching of a fundamentalist government.

In 1992 the pro-Communist forces launched a successful counterattack in which thousands were killed and perhaps 300,000 displaced. Voters in Nov. 1994 approved by referendum a new (highly presidential) constitution with 90 percent of the vote, and elected as president Emomali Rakhmonov with 60 percent. But the civil war of the current, ex-Communist and Russian-backed government against Islamic rebels continues, despite U.N.-mediated cease-fires signed in Sept. 1994 and May 1995. Two renegade military commanders mutinied in Feb. 1996, but called off the coup when Rakhmonov dismissed several senior officials. Sporadic fighting between government troops and several rebel groups continued throughout 1997, and while the government appeared to be taking control, flareups continued into 2000. In Sept. 1999 voters amended the constitution to allow opposition Moslem parties and to extend the presidential term from 5 to 7 years. In November President Rakhmanov won a new term with 96 percent of the vote.

▶TANZANIA

United Republic of Tanzania

• **GEOGRAPHY** **Location:** Tanganyika, on eastern coast of Africa, and islands of Zanzibar and Pemba, about 25 mi. (40 km) off Tanganyika coast in Indian Ocean. **Boundaries**: Burundi, Rwanda to NW, Uganda, Kenya to N, Indian Ocean to E, Mozambique, Malawi to S, Zambia to SW, Zaire to W. **Total area**: 364,900 sq. mi. (945,090 sq km). **Coastline**: 885 mi. (1,424 km). **Comparative area**: slightly larger than twice size of California. **Land use:** 4% arable land; 1% permanent crops; 95% other. **Major cities**: (1985 est.) Dar es Salaam (capital) 1,096,000; Mwanza 252,000; Tabora 214,000; Mbeya 194,000; Tanga 172,000.

• **PEOPLE** **Population:** 35,922,454 (2003 est.). **Nationality:** noun—Tanzanian(s); adjective—Tanzanian. **Ethnic groups:** mainland—99% native Africans of over 130 groups; 1% Asian, European, and Arab; Zanzibar—Arab, native African, mixed Arab and native African. **Languages:** Kiswahili and Swahili and English (all official); English primary language of commerce, administration, higher education; Swahili widely understood, generally used for communication between ethnic groups; first language of most people is one of local languages; primary education generally in Swahili. **Religions:** mainland—30% Christian, 35% Muslim, 35% indigenous beliefs; Zanzibar—almost all Muslim.

• **GOVERNMENT** **Type:** republic. **Independence:** Tanganyika became independent Dec. 9, 1961 (from U.N. trusteeship under British administration); Zanzibar became independent Dec. 19, 1963 (from U.K.); Tanganyika united with Zanzibar Apr. 26, 1964. **Constitution:** Apr. 25, 1977, revised Oct. 1984 (Zanzibar has own constitution but remains subject to provisions of union constitution). **National holiday:** Union Day, Apr. 26. **Heads of Government:** Benjamin William Mkapa, president (since Nov. 1995); **Structure:** executive—president is head of government and chief of state; unicameral legislature (Zanzibar has its own House of Representatives to make laws especially for Zanzibar; judiciary.

• **ECONOMY** **Monetary unit:** Tanzanian shilling. **Budget:** (FY01/02 est.) ***income:*** $1.01 bil.; ***expend.:*** $1.38 bil. **GDP:** $22.5 bil., $630 per capita (2002 est.). **Chief crops:** cotton, coffee, sisal, vegetables, fruits, grain on mainland; cloves and coconuts on Zanzibar; cattle, sheep, goats. **Natural resources:** hydropower potential, tin, phosphates, iron ore and coal, gemstones. **Major industries:** agricultural processing (sugar, beer, cigarettes, sisal twine), diamond mining, oil refining. **Labor force:** 13.5 mil. (2000 est.); 80% agriculture, 20% industry and commerce. **Exports:** $836 mil. (f.o.b., 2000 est.); coffee, manufactured goods, cotton, sisal, cashew nuts, tobacco, cloves. **Imports:** $1.67 bil. (f.o.b., 2002 est.); consumer goods, machinery and transport equipment, crude oil. **Major trading partners:** ***exports:*** 15% India, 8% Germany, 7% Belgium; ***imports:*** 13% South Africa, 11% Japan, 6% U.K.

Formerly known as Tanganyika, Tanzania's indigenous population includes people of diverse ethnic background, including San, Bantu, and Nilotic peoples. It has been the site of a number of relatively advanced and well-organized societies.

Zanzibar and the neighboring island of Pemba have been a crossroads of trade in East Africa since ancient times. Trade via Zanzibar between the Tanganyika coast and the Middle East, primarily ivory, gold, and iron, dates to the late Roman Empire. The coast was dominated by various Arab and Persian powers, usually based in Zanzibar, from about the eighth century. Zanzibar and Tanganyika were visited by Vasco da Gama in 1498, and Portugal claimed Zanzibar in 1503 and the entire Tanganyika coast in 1506. The Portuguese established coastal trading stations but did not colonize the interior.

The Portuguese were driven from Zanzibar in 1652 by the sultanate of Oman, which soon expelled them from the mainland as well. Under Omani rule, trade in gold, ivory, and gems was supplemented by a sizable slave trade, and the clove plantations of Zanzibar became commercially important. Under Sultan Seyyid Said, the capital of the sultanate of Oman was transferred to Zanzibar in 1824, and Zanzibar became independent of Oman upon his death in 1856.

Both Germany and Great Britain became active in the region in the 19th century. Tanganyika was organized as the colony of German East Africa in 1884, while Zanzibar became a British protectorate in 1890. Tanganyika became a secondary battlefield of World War I, with frequent clashes between German and British troops.

Britain assumed control of Tanganyika in 1920 under a League of Nations Mandate and maintained control under a U.N. trusteeship after 1946. The temperate southern highlands were extensively colonized by British immigrants, and railroads and mines were developed by the British administration.

Elections for a local legislature were held in Zanzibar in July 1957. The island's politics were dominated by a split between Arab and African residents. Zanzibar became independent on Dec. 19, 1963. In January 1964 an African revolt overthrew the sultan of Zanzibar and resulted in the deaths of thousands of Arab residents and the emigration of many more. Political control shifted to the African party and Abeid Karume became president.

Tanganyika became independent in 1961. Julius K. Nyerere was Tanganyika's dominant political figure. Tanzania was formed from the union of Tanganyika and Zanzibar on April 26, 1964, with Zanzibar retaining local autonomy.

Nyerere advocated an "African socialist" form of development and formed close ties with China. Some British settlers left the country, but relations with Great Britain remained important. The Tan-Zan Railroad between Dar es Salaam and Lusaka, Zambia was built with Chinese aid between 1970 and 1975. The ruling parties of Tanganyika and Zanzibar were united in 1977 under Nyerere's leadership.

Political tensions eased and Tanzania adopted a more open political structure in the 1980's. Pres. Ali Hassan Mwinyi encouraged free-market economic reforms, including encouragement of foreign investment and strengthened ties with Kenya and Uganda (Tanzania invaded the latter in 1979 in an effort to depose Idi Amin). Tanzania's economy has great potential because of the country's extensive natural resources and one of Africa's best educational systems; literacy in both English and Swahili is relatively high.

Although only an estimated 20 percent of the population was found to be in favor of political pluralism, in 1992 the Revolutionary party of Tanzania voted in favor of a secular multiparty system, that is one based on neither ethnic nor regional lines. It won the country's first-ever multiparty elections in 1995. Benjamin Mkapa succeeded Mwinyi, who was barred by law from seeking a third term as president.

The elections of Oct. 2000 returned Mkapa to the presidency with 72 percent of the vote while the ruling party carried 167 of the National Assembly's 181 seats; similar results were reported from semiautonomous Zanzibar. The obviously rigged elections provoked demands for new elections from the opposition's Civic United Front and demonstrations in which over 40 were killed. In 2001, Tanzania formed, with Uganda and Kenya, the East African Community, a common market with stated but vague aspirations toward political unity.

▶THAILAND

Kingdom of Thailand

• **GEOGRAPHY Location:** extends southward, along isthmus of Kra, to Malay peninsula, in Southeast Asia. **Boundaries**: Myanmar to W and N, Laos to NE, Cambodia and Gulf of Thailand to E, Malaysia to S, Andaman Sea to SW. **Total area**: 198,456 sq. mi. (514,000 sq km). **Coastline**: 2,001 mi. (3,219 km). **Comparative area**: slightly more than twice the size of Wyoming. **Land use:** 33% arable land; 7% permanent crops; 70% other. **Major cities**: (1990 census), Bangkok metropolis (capital) 5,876,000; Songkhla 172,604; Chon Buri 115,350; Nakhon Si Thammarat 102,123; Chiang Mai 101,594.

• **PEOPLE Population:** 64,265,276 (2003 est.). **Nationality:** noun—Thai (sing., pl.); adjective—Thai. **Ethnic groups:** 75% Thai, 14% Chinese, 11% other. **Languages:** Thai; English is secondary language of elite; ethnic and regional dialects. **Religions:** 95% Buddhist, 3.8% Muslim, 0.5% Christianity, 0.1% Hinduism.

• **GOVERNMENT Type:** constitutional monarchy. **Constitution:** new constitution signed by King Phumiphon Oct. 11, 1997. **National holiday:** Birthday of His Majesty the King, Dec. 5. **Heads of Government:** Bhumibol Adulyadej, king (since June 1946); Thaksin Shinawatra, prime minister (since Feb. 2001). **Structure:** executive—king is head of state with nominal powers, prime minister is head of government; bicameral legislature (National Assembly—Senate appointed by king, to be phased into an elected body starting in 2000; elected House of Representatives); judiciary relatively independent except in important political subversion cases.

• **ECONOMY Monetary unit:** baht. **Budget:** (2000 est.) ***income:*** $19 bil. ***expend.:*** $21 bil. **GDP:** $429 bil., $6,900 per capita (2002 est.). **Chief crops:** rice, cassava, sugar, corn, rubber, manioc, coconuts, soybean. **Natural resources:** tin, rubber, natural gas, tungsten, tantalum. **Major industries:** tourism, textiles and garments, agricultural processing, beverages; world's second-largest tungsten producer and third-largest tin producer. **Labor force:** 33.4 mil. (2001 est.); 54% agriculture, 15% industry, 31% services including government; 2.9% unemployment (2002). **Exports:** $67.7 bil. (f.o.b., 2002 est.); computers and parts, textiles, rice. **Imports:** $58.1 bil. (f.o.b,. 2002 est.); capital goods, intermediate goods, consumer goods, fuels. **Major trading partners:** (2002) ***exports:*** 20% U.S., 15% Japan, 8% Singapore; ***imports:*** 23% Japan, 10% U.S., 8% Singapore.

Ethnic Thai migrating south from China after about A.D. 1000 created a number of petty states in the region, most notably the kingdom of Sukhothai. These came under the influence of Indian civilization from the adjacent states of Burma and the Khmer empire, and Buddhism became established as the dominant religion of the Thai. A unified kingdom of Siam was established c. 1350, with its capital at Ayutthaya. Portuguese and other European traders and missionaries were active in Siam after 1511.

In 1767 Ayutthaya was destroyed in a war with Burma. In 1782 the Chakkri dynasty was established at Bangkok and restored the power of the Thai monarchy. By skillfully playing off the European powers against one another, Kings Mongkut (r. 1851-68) and Chulalongkorn (r. 1868-1910) enabled Siam to be the only Southeast Asian nation to escape European colonization or political domination. In a series of treaties with Great Britain and France, however, King Chulalongkorn was forced to renounce Siam's claims to portions of Malaya, Laos, and Cambodia.

Absolute monarchy ended in 1932, when a military coup forced the granting of a constitution. Japanese troops occupied Siam in Dec. 1941. Siam concluded a nominal alliance with Japan in 1942 and declared war on Great Britain and the U.S, while the monarchy secretly supported a strong anti-Japanese resistance movement. A period of postwar political turmoil ended with the accession in 1950 of King Phumiphon, who instituted a reformist and pro-Western policy. Thai politics since World War II have been democratic but dominated by an oligarchy of military officers and civilians with strong military ties.

During the Vietnam War, Thailand was an important staging area for American forces. Since then, U.S. and other foreign investment contributed to significant industrialization and economic growth, making Thailand one of Asia's fastest-growing economies. Its prosperity has attracted a large number of refugees from Laos, Vietnam, and Cambodia.

On Dec. 8, 1990, Prime Minister Chatichai Choonhavan resigned amid charges of corruption. Reappointed by the king the next day, Chatichai was overthrown on Feb. 23 by military forces, who invited former diplomat Anand Panyarachun to serve as interim prime minister.

After parliamentary elections in March 1992, Gen. Suchinda Kraprayoon, who held no parliamentary seat, was named prime minister in a government dominated by the military. Mass demonstrations against the Suchinda government, led by former Bangkok governor Chamlong Srimuang, culminated on May 17-18, when troops fired on demonstrators, causing hundreds of fatalities. The king intervened and Suchinda resigned.Chamlong agreed to call off the demonstrations and Anand Panyarachun was invited to head another transitional government, and Parliament agreed in principle to a new constitution with a provision that the prime minister must be an elected member of Parliament.

Parliamentary elections in 1992 gained a majority for a five-party coalition headed by Chuan Leekpai that managed to govern for almost three years, liberalizing financial arrangements, spending heavily on infrastructure, and bringing Thailand to an 8 percent growth rate in 1994. In elections held in 1995, the Thai Nation party captured the largest number of seats; its leader, Banharn Silpa-Archa, became prime minister but the party lost the 1996 elections and a coalition government led by General Chavalit took over. Only six months later the Thai economy began a steep decline and the currency was devalued in June 1997. The U.S. and the I.M.F. agreed to provide loans of $4 bil. to stabalize the economy with more promised if the government took appropriate action. Chuan Leekpai returned as prime minister in Nov. 1997 but economic recovery was only slowly under way by mid-1998. Still the government survived a Dec. 1999 no confidence vote just before the Bank of Thailand announced a 4 percent rise in G.D.P. for the year.

Elections in Jan. 2001 brought a near majority to the Thai Rak Thai party of computer and telecommunications billionaire Thaksin Shinawatra, who was named prime minister but who faced serious legal charges of tax evasion. The Constitutional Court acquitted Thaksin by a vote of 8–7 and with no written opinion issued.

▶TOGO

Togolese Republic

• **Geography** **Location:** western coast of Africa. **Boundaries**: Burkina Faso to N, Benin to E, Gulf of Guinea to S, Ghana to W. **Total area**: 21,927 sq. mi. (56,790 sq km). **Coastline**: 35 mi. (56 km). **Comparative area**: slightly smaller than West Virginia. **Land use:** 41% arable land; 2% permanent crops; 57% other. **Major cities**: (1990 est.) Lomé (capital) 450,000; Sokodé 55,000; Kpalimé 31,000; Atakpamé 30,000; Tsevie 26,000.

• **People** **Population:** 5,429,299 (2003 est.). **Nationality:** noun—Togolese (sing., pl.); adjective—Togolese. **Ethnic groups:** 37 groups; largest are Ewe, Mina, and Kabre; under 1% European and Syrian-Lebanese. **Languages:** French (both official and language of commerce); Ewe and Mina in south, Dagomba and Kabyè in north. **Religions:** about 51% indigenous beliefs, 29% Christian, 20% Muslim.

• **Government** **Type:** republic under transition to multiparty democratic rule; **Independence:** Apr. 27, 1960 (from U.N. trusteeship under French administration). **Constitution:** Sept. 27, 1992. **National holiday:** Independence Day, Apr. 27. **Heads of Government:** Gen. Gnassingbé Eyadema, president (since 1992); Agbéyomé Messan Kodjo, prime minister (since Oct. 2000). **Structure:** executive—president appoints prime minister; unicameral legislature—National Assembly; judiciary.

• **Economy** **Monetary unit:** Communauté Financière Africaine (CFA) franc. **Budget:** (1997 est.) ***income:*** $232 mil.; ***expend.:*** $252 mil. **GDP:** $8 bil., $1,500 per capita (2002 est.). **Chief crops:** coffee, cocoa, cotton, yams, cassava, corn, beans, rice; meat, fish. **Natural resources:** phosphates, limestone, marble. **Major industries:** phosphate mining, agricultural processing, cement, handicrafts, textiles, beverages. **Labor force:** 1.74 mil. (1996 est.); 65% agriculture, 30% services, 5% industry. **Exports:** $449 mil. (f.o.b., 2002); cotton, phosphates, coffee, cocoa. **Imports:** $561 mil. (f.o.b., 2002); machinery and equipment, consumer goods, petroleum products. **Major trading partners:** (2001) ***exports:*** Nigeria, Benin, Ghana; ***imports:*** Ghana, France, Ivory Coast, China.

Ewe-speaking peoples began to migrate into what is now Togo, located on Africa's west coast, early in the 14th century. Portuguese explorers arrived in the late 15th century, turning the coast into a point of departure for slaves captured from nearby villages, and between the 1600's and 1800's, the region became known as the "Slave Coast." Germans started to explore and trade in the region in the mid-19th century and declared a protectorate over the area in 1884. After World War I, however, Britain and France divided the nation between them, Britain receiving the western third, France the eastern two-thirds. The League of Nations confirmed this arrangement, giving mandates to British Togoland (later a part of Ghana) and French Togoland.

In 1956 France made French Togo an autonomous republic but retained control of its foreign affairs, defense, and currency; Nicholas Grunitzky was prime minister. The United Nations rejected this plan and in elections in 1958 advocates of complete independence won control of the legislature. On Apr. 27, 1960, French Togo cut its ties with France and became the fully independent Republic of Togo. Sylvanus Olympio became the new nation's first prime minister. Grunitzsky went into exile but returned when Olympio was assassinated in January 1963. He led the new government and oversaw the writing of a new constitution allowing more political freedoms.

In 1967 army officers led by Lt. Col. Gnassingbé Eyadema overthrew Grunitzsky, suspended the constitution, and named Eyadema president. In 1990, Eyadema was forced out by democratic reformers, and Kokou J. Koffigoh was elected prime minister by a national conference in 1991. Eyadema resumed the presidency in 1992, but his refusal to embrace multiparty democracy and Koffigoh's weak leadership led to violence and public calls for the ouster of both men. Under a new constitution, ratified in 1992, General Eyadema's party, Rally of the Togolese People, always dominates, with prime ministers coming and going at his pleasure. In 2002, parliament amended the constitution, removing the two-term limit on the presidency.

▶TONGA

Kingdom of Tonga

• **Geography** **Location:** 172 islands in South Pacific Ocean, 36 permanently inhabited. Nuku'alofa 21°09'S, 175°14'W. **Boundaries**: surrounded by South Pacific Ocean; Fiji is about 400 mi. (650 km) to NW and Western Samoa lies N. **Total area**: 289 sq. mi. (748 sq km). **Coastline**: 260 mi. (419 km). **Comparative area**: four times the size of Washington, D.C. **Land use:** 24% arable land; 43% permanent crops; 33% other. **Major cities**: (1986 census) Nuku'alofa (capital) 28,899; Tongatapu 63,614; Vava'u 15,170; Ha'apai 8,979; Eua 4,393.

• **People** **Population:** 108,141 (2003 est.). **Nationality:** noun—Tongan(s); adjective—Tongan. **Ethnic groups:** Polynesian; about 300 Europeans. **Languages:** Tongan, English. **Religions:** Christian (Free Wesleyan Church claims over 30,000 adherents).

• **Government** **Type:** hereditary constitutional monarchy. **Independence:** June 4, 1970 (from U.K.). **Constitution:** Nov. 4, 1875; revised Jan. 1, 1967. **National holiday:** Independence Day, June 4. **Heads of Government:** Taufa'ahau Tupou IV, king (since Dec. 1965); Prince 'Ulukalala Lavaka Ata, premier (since Jan. 2000). **Structure:** executive—king, prime minister, cabinet; unicameral legislature—30-seat Legislative Assembly, 9 elected by popular vote, 12 are for cabinet ministers, 9 reserved for nobles; judiciary—appointed by king.

• **Economy** **Monetary unit:** pa'anga. **Budget:** (FY99/00) ***income:*** $39.9 mil.; ***expend.:*** $52.4 mil. **GDP:** $236 mil., $2,200 per capita (2001 est.). **Chief crops:** squash, coconut, copra, bananas, vanilla beans, cocoa, coffee, ginger, black pepper, fish. **Natural resources:** fish, fertile soil. **Major industries:** tourism, fishing. **Labor force:** 34,000

(1996 est.); 65% engaged in agriculture. **Exports:** $8.9 mil. (f.o.b., 2001); squash, fish, vanilla. **Imports:** $70 mil. (f.o.b., 2001); food products, machinery and transport equipment, fuels, chemicals. **Major trading partners:** (2001) ***exports:*** 42% Japan, 40% U.S., 6% New Zealand; ***imports:*** 33% New Zealand, 22% Fiji, 10% Australia.

The Polynesian islands that now compose Tonga were settled some 3,000 years ago. A highly stratified society evolved; the kings of Tonga dominated much of Polynesia by the 13th century. The islands were visited in 1643 by Abel Tasman, and in 1773 by Capt. James Cook, who named them the Friendly Islands. English missionaries arrived in 1797, and the islands came under British political influence. A code of laws was promulgated in 1862, and a constitutional monarchy established in 1875. A series of treaties with Western powers recognized Tonga's independence, but the kingdom became a British protectorate in 1900.

The islands were outside the Japanese perimeter in the Pacific theater of World War II. On June 4, 1970, the British dissolved their protectorate and the Kingdom of Tonga became independent as a member of the British Commonwealth. The present king, Taufa'ahau Tupou IV, came to the throne in 1965.

The Tongan economy is based on subsistence farming and fishing, with some handicraft industries and light manufacturing. The tourist industry is developing rapidly. Tonga joined the U.N. in late 1999.

▶TRINIDAD AND TOBAGO

Republic of Trinidad and Tobago

• Geography Location: two islands (Port of Spain, Trinidad Is., 10°38'N, 61°31'W; Tobago Is., 11°11'N, 60°45'W) in southeastern Caribbean Sea, off northeastern South America. **Boundaries**: Caribbean Sea to N and W, Atlantic Ocean to E and S. **Total area**: 1,981 sq. mi. (5,130 sq km). **Coastline**: 225 mi. (362 km). **Comparative area**: slightly smaller than Delaware. **Land use:** 15% arable land; 9% permanent crops; 26% other. **Major cities**: (1991) Port of Spain (capital) 51,076; San Fernando 30,115; Arima (borough) 29,483.

• People Population: 1,104,209 (2003 est.). **Nationality:** noun—Trinidadian(s), Tobagonian(s); adjective—Trinidadian, Tobagonian. **Ethnic groups:** 40% black, 40.3% East Indian, 14% mixed, 1% white, 1% Chinese. **Languages:** English (official), Hindi, French, Spanish, Chinese. **Religions:** 29.4% Roman Catholic, 23.8% Hindu, 10.9% Anglican, 14% other Protestant, 5.8% Muslim.

• Government Type: parliamentary democracy. **Independence:** Aug. 31, 1962 (from U.K.). **Constitution:** Aug. 1, 1976. **National holiday:** Independence Day, Aug. 31. **Heads of Government:** Arthur Napoleon Robinson, president (since Mar. 1997); Patrick Manning, prime minister (since Jan. 2002). **Structure:** executive—is cabinet led by prime minister; bicameral legislature (elected House of Representatives and appointed Senate); judiciary headed by chief justice and includes court of appeal, high court, and lower courts.

• Economy Monetary unit: Trinidad and Tobago dollar. **Budget:** (1998 est.) ***income:*** $1.54 bil.; ***expend.:*** $1.6 bil. **GDP:** $11.1 bil., $9,500 per capita (2002 est.). **Chief crops:** sugar, cocoa, coffee, rice, citrus, bananas; poultry. **Natural resources:** crude oil, natural gas, asphalt. **Major industries:** petroleum, chemicals, tourism. **Labor force:** 564,000 (2000 est.); 64.1% services, 14% manufacturing, mining, and quarrying, 12.4% construction and utilities, 9.5% agriculture. **Exports:** $4.2 bil. (f.o.b., 2002); petroleum and petroleum products, chemicals, steel products, fertilizer, sugar, cocoa, coffee, citrus, flowers. **Imports:** $3.8 bil. (f.o.b., 2002 est.); machinery, transport equipment, manufactured goods, food, live animals. **Major trading partners:** ***exports:*** 46.6% U.S., 8.5% Jamaica, 5.1% Barbados; ***imports:*** 34.2% U.S., 19.4% Venezuela, 8.0% Colombia.

Trinidad was a possession of Spain from 1498 to 1797, when it was surrendered to the British. England took control of Tobago in 1802. Together the two islands achieved independence from the U.K. in 1962. Prime Minister Arthur Robinson's National Alliance for Reconstruction currently governs the country. Civil and political rights are well respected, and political party competition tends to divide along ethnic (black, East Indian) lines. Agrarian reform designed to create tenable landholdings is a central political issue.

In 1990, militant Muslims seized Prime Minister A.N.R. Robinson and dozens of others in Parliament, paralyzing the government for five days. Peace was restored when the government promised reforms. People's National Movement candidate Carson Charles was elected prime minister in 1991, and in the interest of preserving the peace, he granted the Muslim militants amnesty in 1992. Robinson won the presidential election in 1997 in a landslide. Dec. 2001 elections produced an 18–18 tie between the (Indian-descent) United National Congress and the (African-descent) People's National Movement. Both parties agreed to allow Pres. Robinson to choose. His choice: Patrick Manning of the P.N.M.

▶TUNISIA

Republic of Tunisia

• Geography Location: northern coast of Africa. **Boundaries**: Mediterranean to N and E, Libya to SE, Algeria to W. **Total area**: 63,170 sq. mi. (163,610 sq km); includes land and inland waters. **Coastline**: 714 mi. (1,148 km). **Comparative area**: slightly larger than Georgia. **Land use:** 19% arable land; 13% permanent crops; 68% other. **Major cities**: (1994 census) Tunis (capital) 674,100; Sfax (Safaqis) 230,900; Ariana 152,700; Ehadhamen 149,200; Sousse 125,000.

• People Population: 9,924,742 (2003 est.). **Nationality:** noun—Tunisian(s); adjective—Tunisian. **Ethnic groups:** 98% Arab, 1% European, 1% Jewish and other . **Languages:** Arabic (official), Arabic and French (commerce). **Religions:** 98% Muslim, 1% Christian, 1% Jewish and other.

• Government Type: republic. **Independence:** Mar. 20, 1956 (from France). **Constitution:** June 1, 1959, amended July 12, 1988. **National holiday:** Independence Day, Mar. 20. **Heads of Government:** Zine el-Abidine Ben Ali, president (since Nov. 1987); Mohamed Ghannouchi, prime minister (since Nov. 1999). **Structure:** executive dominant; unicameral legislature (Chamber of Deputies) largely advisory; judiciary patterned on French and Koranic systems.

• Economy Monetary unit: Tunisian dinar. **Budget:** (2002 est.) ***income:*** $5.2 bil.; ***expend.:*** $5.7 bil. **GDP:** $63 bil., $6,500 per capita (2002 est.). **Chief crops:** olives, dates, oranges, almonds, grain, sugar beets, grapes; poultry, beef, dairy products. **Natural resources:** crude oil, phosphates, iron ore, lead, zinc. **Major industries:** petroleum, mining (particularly phosphates and iron ore), tourism, textiles. **Labor force:** 2.69 mil.; 55% services, 23% industry, 22% agriculture; 15.4% unemployment (2002 est.); shortage of skilled labor. **Exports:** $6.8 bil. (f.o.b., 2002 est.);

hydrocarbons, textiles, agricultural products, phosphates and chemicals. **Imports:** $8.7 bil. (f.o.b., 2002 est.); industrial goods, hydrocarbons, food. **Major trading partners:** ***exports:*** 29% France, 23% Italy, 13% Germany; ***imports:*** 28% France, 20% Italy, 10% Germany

The Phoenicians, an ancient seafaring people from the eastern Mediterranean, founded settlements in Tunisia dating back to 1000 B.C. The most important of these was Carthage, which dominated trade in the central Mediterranean until it was conquered and destroyed by Rome in 146 B.C. Tunisia remained part of the Roman Empire until it was conquered by the Vandals in the mid-fifth century A.D. The Byzantine Empire reconquered Tunisia in the sixth century.

Tunisia became part of the Arab world with the expansion of Islam in the seventh century and soon emerged as a principal center of Islamic culture in North Africa. Tunisia was incorporated into the Ottoman Empire in 1574 and was ruled from Constantinople by Turkish governors, or beys.

With the waning of Ottoman power in the 19th century, Tunisia became a French protectorate in 1881. Nationalist movements began in the early 20th century. During World War II Tunisia was under Vichy French rule and was the scene of fighting between the Axis and Allies in 1942-43. Nationalist unrest resumed when France reestablished its rule in the postwar period. Widespread popular unrest in the early 1950's led to a French grant of self-rule in 1954. Full independence was proclaimed on Mar. 20, 1956; large numbers of French settlers returned to France. The French-sponsored monarchy was abolished in 1957, and the Neo-Destour (New Constitution) party under the leadership of Habib Bourguiba took power. Bourguiba was elected president in 1959 without opposition and was named president for life. Under his rule, political parties ranging from Communist to monarchist flourished, leading to both democratic politics and political confusion.

Relations with France were strained in 1964 when Tunisia nationalized foreign assets but have since improved. The basic thrust of Tunisian government was socialist, with state ownership of principal industries and heavy subsidies of basic commodities. In foreign affairs Tunisia has been closely tied to France and has been a moderate voice within the Arab League.

Popular unrest and labor strife characterized Tunisia's internal situation in the 1980's, as political maneuvering began in anticipation of the end of the Bourguiba era, which came in 1987 when the aged leader was overthrown by Ben Ali. In 1989 new elections were planned as part of a political and economic restructuring. Ben Ali was elected president, twice winning 99 percent of the vote, while his party won virtually all the seats in the National Assembly. In 1994 and 1995, however, the political stability was threatened by radical Muslim groups both from within and from Algeria. Rumors of brutal repression were rife. In Oct. 1999, in Tunisia's first "multiparty" elections, Ben Ali was re-elected president, again with 99.42 percent of the vote while his Constitutional Union Party carried 148 of the 182 parliamentary seats.

Tunisia's economy, though plagued by labor difficulties, has developed rapidly, led by textiles, food processing and other light industry, tourism, phosphate mining, and other mineral processing. The large agricultural sector includes grain, olives, dates, and winter fruits and vegetables for export to Europe. In 1998 the government reached an accord with the E.U. to lower trade barriers.

▶TURKEY

Republic of Turkey

• GEOGRAPHY **Location:** partly in southeastern Europe and partly in western Asia. **Boundaries:** Black Sea to N; Georgia and Armenia to NE; Iran to E; Iraq, Syria, Mediterranean Sea to S; Aegean Sea, Greece to W; and Bulgaria to NW. **Total area:** 301,382 sq. mi. (780,580 sq km). **Coastline:** 4,471 mi. (7,200 km). **Comparative area:** slightly larger than Texas. **Land use:** 35% arable land; 3% permanent crops; 62% other. **Major cities:** (1993 est.) Ankara (capital) 2,719,981; Istanbul 7,331,927; Izmir 1,920,807; Adana 1,010,363; Bursa 949,810.
• PEOPLE **Population:** 68,109,469 (July 2003 est.). **Nationality:** noun—Turk(s); adjective—Turkish. **Ethnic groups:** 80% Turkish, 20% Kurdish. **Languages:** Turkish (official), Kurdish, Arabic. **Religions:** 99.8% Muslim (mostly Sunni), 0.2% other (mostly Christian and Jewish).
• GOVERNMENT **Type:** republican parliamentary democracy. **Independence:** Oct. 29, 1923 (from Ottoman Empire). **Constitution:** Nov. 7, 1982. **National holiday:** Independence Day. **Heads of Government:** Ahmet Necdet Sezer, president (since May 2000); Recep Tayyip Erdogan, prime minister (since Mar. 14, 2003). **Structure:** executive—president empowered to call new elections, promulgate laws (elected for seven-year term); unicameral legislature; independent judiciary.
• ECONOMY **Monetary unit:** Turkish lira. **Budget:** (2000) ***income:*** $54.5 bil.; ***expend.:*** $75.2 bil. **GDP:** $468 bil., $7,000 per capita (2002 est.). **Chief crops:** cotton, tobacco, grain, olives, sugar beets, pulses, citrus; livestock. **Natural resources:** antimony, coal, chromium, mercury, copper. **Major industries:** textiles, food processing, mining (coal, chromite, copper, boron minerals). **Labor force:** 23 mil.; 40% agriculture, 38% services, 22% industry; about 1.2 million Turks work abroad; 10.8% unemployment (2002 est.). **Exports:** $35.1 bil. (f.o.b., 2002 est.); 28% textiles and apparel, 17% foodstuffs, 9% iron and steel products. **Imports:** $50.8 bil. (c.i.f., 2002 est.); 29% machinery, fuels, minerals, foodstuffs. **Major trading partners:** ***exports:*** 17% Germany, 10% U.S., 8% Italy; ***imports:*** 13% Germany, 8% Italy, 8% Russia.

The Hittites, an Indo-European people, created an empire in Anatolia before 2000 B.C. and controlled most of what is modern-day Turkey for nearly 1,000 years. The rise of Troy and other Hellenic city-states on the coast of Asia Minor and the expansion of the Assyrian empire led to the collapse of Hittite power by around 900 B.C. Except for some Hellenic enclaves on the Aegean Coast (Ionia), all of Turkey was incorporated into the Persian empire of Cyrus and Darius in the sixth century B.C. Alexander the Great conquered Turkey, but it returned to Persian rule following the collapse of his empire, c. 300 B.C.

All of Turkey, comprising Thracia, Galatia, Cappadocia, Cilicia, and other provinces, was incorporated into the Roman Empire by the end of the first century A.D. Constantine the Great founded the city of Constantinople on the site of ancient Byzantium in 330 as the empire's eastern capital. Following the decline of the western Roman Empire in the seventh century, Constantinople became the capital of the independent Eastern Roman (Byzantine) Empire. The Byzantine Empire fought off repeated attacks by Arab Islamic forces in the seventh and eighth centuries but lost control of central Anatolia to the Seljuk Turkish rulers of Persia after 1038.

The 13th-century Mongol invasions left Turkey largely untouched but weakened both Byzantine and Seljuk power. At the end of the 13th century, the Ottomans, a small Turkish tribe, expanded from their stronghold in western Anatolia and within a century captured most of Turkey, Bulgaria, and Serbia. Constantinople fell to the Ottomans in 1453. By the middle of the 16th century, the Ottoman Empire extended from southeastern Europe into the Crimea and Iran and included most of the Middle East, Egypt, and Arabia.

At its height the Ottoman Empire was a great world power and a substantial participant in European international relations. But in the 18th century, the empire lost much of its autonomy through unequal treaties with European powers, and throughout the 19th century, parts of the empire were detached and either granted independence or placed under European protection. The Ottoman Empire became the "Sick Man of Europe." A liberal constitution was adopted in 1876 but largely ignored until the Young Turk Rebellion of 1908 forced the sultan to accept its provisions.

Siding with the Central Powers in World War I, the Ottoman Empire lost most of its non-Turkish possessions to the Allies. The Treaty of Sèvres (1920) reduced the Ottoman state to a small part of northern Anatolia. Before the treaty was ratified, however, Kemal Ataturk seized power and regained much territory in a series of campaigns with Soviet assistance. The Treaty of Lausanne (1923) established the present boundaries of Turkey, which was proclaimed a republic in October 1923. The Caliphate was renounced in 1924, ending the Ottoman claim of spiritual leadership in the Islamic world.

The Turkish Republic became officially a secular and multiethnic state. Large numbers of Armenians had been killed or driven from the country in widespread campaigns of persecution in the late 19th and early 20th centuries; after 1923 most Greek and Bulgarian residents were forcibly repatriated. The large minority of Kurds in southeastern Turkey were pressured to abandon their ethnic identity. Today more than 85 percent of the population is Turkish. Islam is widely practiced, but the veil and other Islamic dress are prohibited, as are religious political parties. In 1928 the Latin alphabet was adopted in place of Arabic script for writing Turkish. In 1930 Constantinople was officially renamed Istanbul.

Turkey joined the League of Nations in 1932. A series of treaties in the 1930's made small adjustments to Turkey's borders and confirmed Turkey's status as a European nation. Under Ismet Inonu, who became president upon Ataturk's death in 1938, Turkey remained neutral throughout most of World War II but declared war against Germany in Jan. 1945 and became a founding member of the United Nations at the end of the war.

Following World War II, Turkish relations with the Soviet Union cooled; Turkey became a major recipient of American aid under the Truman Doctrine. Turkish troops joined U.N. forces in the Korean War. Continuing the Europe-oriented policy, Turkey joined both NATO and the OECD and sought membership in the European Union.

In 1974, long-standing discord with Greece erupted over the status of Cyprus, an independent nation with strong ties to Greece. On July 20, 1974, Turkish troops invaded Cyprus, occupying the northeastern 40 percent of the island. The United States cut off military aid to Turkey in 1975. Turkey forced resettlement of Greek and Turkish Cypriot residents; the Turkish sector seceded from Cyprus and became a Turkish federated state on July 8, 1975. American aid was restored in 1978.

Politically, postwar Turkey has alternated between civil and military governments. In the wake of mounting violence, martial law was imposed in 1978, and a military takeover of the government occurred on Sept. 12, 1980. Civil government was restored in 1983, and martial law lifted in 1984.

Turkey tried to remain aloof from the political turmoil of the Middle East, but it was a crucial member of the anti-Iraq coalition in the Persian Gulf War. It supported the U.N. trade embargo and allowed the Allies to use Turkish bases. The Kurdish problem was aggravated after the war as Turkey tried to offer humanitarian assistance to Kurdish refugees from Iraq without encouraging Kurdish nationalists at home. A continuing insurgency in the southeast led to sporadic but serious violence in 1992-93. Muslim fundamentalists became more active and several violent episodes resulted in deaths and destruction.

Pres. Turgut Özal died in Apr. 1993. He was succeeded as president by Prime Minister Suleyman Demirel. On June 14 the ruling True Path party elected as the new prime minister, Mrs. Tansu Ciller, Turkey's first-ever woman prime minister. While the economy was her first concern (inflation hit 70 percent in 1994), military operations against the Kurdish rebels intensified with the launching of an attack into Iraq by 50,000 Turkish troops who aimed to end guerrilla raids by the Kurds.

The Ciller government collapsed in a corruption scandal, and elections held in Dec. 1995 gave Refah (Welfare), a pro-Islamic political party, its first national victory. The other parties, committed to the long tradition of secularism, refused to form a government with the Welfare party. After months of successive coalition governments, in June 1996 the Welfare party leader, Necmettim Erbakan, became prime minister of Turkey's first openly pro-Islamic government. A year later, he was forced from office by pressure from Turkey's military. In the wake of this de facto military coup, the new prime minister, Mesut Yilmaz, put together a fragile coalition government in July 1997 that closed some Islamic schools and banned traditional Muslim garb while the Supreme Court banned Erbakan from politics for five years.

Violence in Cyprus flared up in 1998 but the E.U.'s rejection of Turkey's application was the most serious event of the year. In 1999 Turkey finally wrung an accord from Syria not to aid Kurd rebels (with 10,000 Turkish troops poised on Syria's border), but the Yilmaz government still lost a vote of confidence on corruption charges. Pres. Demirel asked Bulent Ecevit to form a minority, interim government until the April elections. The results were splintered, and the president asked Ecevit to stay on as head of a coalition government. Meanwhile, Kurdish leader Ocalan was apprehended in Nairobi and, after trial, sentenced to death by hanging. From his cell, Ocalan renounced Kurdish independence and called upon his band to stop fighting.

In Aug. 1999 an earthquake brought great devastation and the loss of thousands of lives. It also brought aid from both the E.U. and Greece; Turkey reciprocated in the September earthquake in Greece—the two events initiating improved relations. In Feb. 2000 the Kurd leadership renounced all violence. In May, Parliament elected chief justice Ahmet Necdet Sezer president to succeed Demirel, constitutionally prohibited from a second term.

Faced with a mass hunger strike by political prisoners in December, Pres. Sezer announced an amnesty plan to release 72,000. A largely personal argument between Sezer and Ecevitin, in early 2001, provoked fears of government instability which led to a serious economic crisis as foreign investors pulled out of Turkey and the currency lost one-third of its value. While the I.M.F. signalled its approval of Ecevits's economic reforms in a series of loans in 2001 and 2002, parliament voted to hold new elections in Nov. 2002, 18 months early. Justice and Development (an offshoot of the Islamic Welfare Party) gained 363 of the 550 seats, the first majority government in 15 years. None of the cabinet formed by Abdullah Gul had any public association with Islam. In December, President Sezer first vetoed, then signed a constitutional amendment to allow the party's leader, Recip Erdogan, banned from holding office, to run for Parliament. He carried a March 2003 by-election with 85 percent of the vote and was named prime minister (Gul becoming foreign minister). Parliament refused to allow U.S. troops to deploy in preparation for the Iraq invasion (though use of Turkey's airspace was approved). In June Parliament, in an attempt to apease E.U. sentiment, voted certain civil rights for Kurds. An unhappy military chose not to intervene.

▶TURKMENISTAN

• **GEOGRAPHY** **Location:** southwestern central Asia. **Boundaries**: Kazakhstan to N, Uzbekistan to N and E, Iran to S, Afghanistan to SE, Caspian Sea to W. **Total area**: 188,456 sq. mi. (488,100 sq km). **Coastline**: Caspian Sea. **Comparative area**: slightly larger than California. **Land use:** 4% arable land; 0% permanent crops; 96% other. **Major cities**: (1994 est.) Ashkhabad (capital) 517,200; Chardzou (Carzou) 164,000.

• **PEOPLE** **Population:** 4,775,554 (2003 est.). **Nationality:** noun—Turkmen; adjective—Turkmen. **Ethnic groups:** 77% Turkmen, 9.2% Uzbek, 6.7% Russian, 2% Kazakh. **Languages:** 72% Turkmen (official), member of southern Turkic language group written in Cyrillic script since 1940; 12% Russian, 9% Uzbek, ethnic languages. **Religions:** 89% Muslim, 9% Eastern Orthodox, 2% unknown.

• **GOVERNMENT** **Type:** republic. **Independence:** Oct. 27, 1991 (from Soviet Union). **Constitution:** May 18, 1992. **National holiday:** Independence Day, Oct. 27. **Head of Government:** Saparmurat A. Niyazov, president (since Dec. 1991). **Structure:** executive—president, Council of Ministers; bicameral legislature; judicial—Supreme Court.

• **ECONOMY** **Monetary unit:** Turkmen manat. **Budget:** (1999 est.) ***income:*** $588.6 mil; ***expend.:*** $658.2 mil. **GDP:** $26 bil., $5,500 per capita (2002 est.). **Chief crops:** cotton, grain; livestock. **Natural resources:** petroleum, natural gas, coal, sulfur, sodium chloride. **Major industries:** natural gas, oil, petroleum products, textiles. **Labor force:** 2.34 mil. (1996). **Exports:** $2.97 bil. (f.o.b., 2002 est.); 63% oil and gas, 18% cotton. **Imports:** $1.65 bil. (c.i.f., 2002 est.); chemicals, foodstuffs, machinery and parts. **Major trading partners:** Ukraine, Turkey.

Turkmenistan, long a battleground for warring Asian empires, is bordered on the north by Uzbekistan and Kazakhstan, and on the west by the Caspian Sea. It also has a long international border with Iran and Afghanistan. About 90 percent of Turkmenistan is covered by the Kara Kum (Black Sand) desert, one of the largest in the world, and the southern areas are mountainous and prone to serious earthquakes.

A very remote and sparsely populated country, Turkmenistan has been inhabited since prehistoric times, first by Iranian-speaking people, then by Turkic tribes. In the 10th century A.D., Oghuz tribes (from Mongolia) arrived, bringing Islam with them. Although the Turkmen had emerged as a distinct ethnic group by the 15th century, they were ruled by the Persians in the south and the Uzbek khanates in the north for about 200 years. In the 19th century, Russian expansionism into Turkmen territory had begun, culminating in the Russian victory in the famous 1881 battle of Gok Tepe that killed 150,000 Turkmen.

In 1917 the Bolsheviks unsuccessfully attempted to seize power in Turkmen territory. By Apr. 30, 1918, the Soviets succeeded in creating the Turkestan Autonomous Soviet Socialist Republic (ASSR) as part of the Russian republic, but in July the ASSR was overthrown by nationalist elements with the help of the British. Once the British withdrew, however, the territory of Turkmen fell to the Soviets, and in 1924 the National Delimitation of Central Asian Republics took place. This created several central Asian republics, including the Turkmen Soviet Socialist Republic, which came into being on Oct. 27, 1924.

During the Soviet period, there were advances in medicine and public health, but the nomadic Turkmen people suffered enormously under forced collectivization and the many bloody antireligious campaigns. The purges of Turkmen intelligentsia in the 1930's were widespread. The Soviets undertook a small-scale industrialization campaign in Turkmenistan, but aside from the extraction of natural gas and petroleum, the majority of the population continued to work in agriculture, mainly growing cotton and fruits.

Under Gorbachev, the main issue for Turkmenistan became the environment. Large-scale cotton planting had led to serious environmental and health hazards. The Kara Kum Canal, which carries water from the Amu-Dar'ya to Turkmenistan's arid regions, is one of the main factors leading to the desiccation of the Aral Sea. Turkmenistan's main cultural issue was the status of the Turkmen language, for until May 1990 the official language had been listed as Russian (although only 25% of Turkmen people claimed to speak Russian). Due to its remoteness, Turkmenistan did not become involved in the democratic changes that engaged the other former union republics. Its Communist party dominated and still dominates Turkmen politics, although the Turkmen president, Saparmurat A. Niyazov, stood for popular election and was elected by direct ballot in Oct. 1990 by 98.3 percent of the population. However, the Turkmen government has banned demonstrations, picketing, and strikes, and it censors its media.

Turkmenistan was one of the early supporters of Gorbachev's proposal to form a new Union Treaty. When that led to the 1991 coup in Moscow, the Turkmen Supreme Soviet claimed independence on Oct. 27, 1991. Since then, Turkmenistan has begun to develop political and economic relations with Iran and Turkey. With vast oil and gas reserves Turkmenistan faces a brighter future than it ever expected.

Niyazov was overwhelmingly endorsed in a referendum, held Jan. 15, 1994 extending his mandate until 2002, bypassing a constitutional requirement for the reelection of a president every five years. In 1998 Niyazov visited the U.S., conferring with Pres. Clinton and concluding agreements with several U.S. energy firms to study the possibility of a cross-Caucasian gas pipeline to Turkey and the west (bypassing Iran). In Dec. 1999 the 50-member parliament elected (unanimously) Niyazov president-for-life (as recommended by the People's Council, headed by Niyazov). The cult of personality has grown to an incredible state as the Council renamed the month of January after him in 2002. His iron-fisted rule has led the U.S. State Dept. to say he governs in a "Soviet-era authoritarian style." In Nov. 2002 an assasination attempt by the former foreign minister failed and he was sentenced to life and 300 others were imprisoned.

▶TUVALU

• **GEOGRAPHY** **Location:** group of nine small atolls, about 350 mi. (560 km) from N to S, in South Pacific Ocean. Funafuti 8°30'S, 179°12'E. **Boundaries**: surrounded by South Pacific Ocean; Kiribati to N, Fiji to S, Solomon Islands to W. **Total area**: 10 sq. mi. (26 sq km). **Coastline**: 15 mi. (24 km). **Comparative area**: one-tenth size of Washington, D.C. **Land use:** 0% arable land; 0% permanent crops; 100% other. **Major cities**: (by atoll; 1985 census) Funafuti (capital) 2,810; Vaitupu 1,231; Niutao 904; Nanumea 879; Nukufetau 694.

• **PEOPLE** **Population:** 11,305 (2003 est.). **Nationality:** noun—Tuvaluan(s); adjective—Tuvaluan. **Ethnic groups:** 96% Polynesian. **Languages:** Tuvaluan, English. **Religions:** 97% Church of Tuvalu (Congregationalist), 1.4% Seventh-Day Adventists, 1% Baha'i.

• **GOVERNMENT** **Type:** constitutional monarchy with a parliamentary democracy; began debating republic status in 1992. **Independence:** Oct. 1, 1978 (from U.K.). **Constitution:** Oct. 1, 1978. **National holiday:** Independence Day, Oct. 1. **Heads of Government:** Sir Tomasi Puapua, governor-general; Saufatu Sopoaga, prime minister (since Aug. 2002). **Structure:** executive—prime minister and cabinet; unicameral legislature—12-member House of Assembly; judicial—high court, chief justice presides over sessions twice a year.

• **ECONOMY** **Monetary unit:** Tuvaluan dollar or Australian dollar. **Budget:** (2000) ***income:*** $22.5 mil.; ***expend.:*** $11.2 mil. **GDP:** $12.2 mil., $1,100 per capita (2002 est.). **Chief crops:** coconuts; fish. **Natural resources:** fish. **Major industries:** fishing, tourism, copra. **Labor force:** 7,000. **Exports:** $276,000 (f.o.b., 1997); copra. **Imports:** $7.2 mil. (c.i.f., 1998); food, animals, mineral fuels, machinery, manufactured goods. **Major trading partners:** Sweden, Fiji, Australia.

A British protectorate was established in 1892, and the islands were incorporated into the British colony of the Gilbert and Ellice Islands in 1915. The nine principal islands that make up the Ellice group escaped Japanese occupation in World War II and were used as Allied bases in the campaign to recapture the Pacific.

The Gilbert and Ellice Islands colony was granted self-rule in 1971. In 1975 the Ellice Islands, inhabited mainly by Polynesians, seceded from the other (mainly Micronesian) islands of the colony and became independent as Tuvalu on Oct. 1, 1978. (See also "Kiribati.") In a 1979 U.S.-Tuvalu friendship treaty, the United States relinquished claims, based on 19th-century guano mining, to the four southernmost islands, in return for access to World War II military airfields and veto power over other nations' use of the islands for military purposes.

The economy is based on subsistence farming and fishing. Exports include copra and woven palm-leaf products, and hydroponic agriculture and offshore fisheries are being developed. Tuvalu remains heavily dependent on foreign aid, principally from Australia, New Zealand, and the United Kingdom. In 2000, Tuvalu was admitted to the U.N.

▶UGANDA

Republic of Uganda

• **GEOGRAPHY** **Location:** landlocked equatorial country in eastern Africa. **Boundaries**: Sudan to N, Kenya to E, Tanzania to S, Rwanda to SW, Zaire to W. **Total area**: 91,135 sq. mi. (236,040 sq km). **Coastline**: none. **Comparative area**: slightly smaller than Oregon. **Land use:** 25% arable land; 9% permanent crops; 9% meadows and pastures; 266% other. **Major cities**: (1991 census) Kampala (capital) 773,463; Jinja 60,979; Mbale 53,634; Masaka 49,070; Gulu 42,841.

• **PEOPLE** **Population:** 25,632,794 (2003 est.). **Nationality:** noun—Ugandan(s); adjective—Ugandan. **Ethnic groups:** 17% Baganda, 8% Basogo, 8% Iteso, 7% Bakiga, 6% Langi, 6% Rwanda, 5% Bagisu, 4% Acholi, 4% Lugbara, 3% Bunyoro, 2% Karamojong. **Languages:** English (official), Luganda, Swahili, Arabic and other Niger-Congo languages. **Religions:** 33% Roman Catholic, 33% Protestant, 16% Muslim, 18% indigenous beliefs.

• **GOVERNMENT** **Type:** republic. **Independence:** Oct. 9, 1962 (from UK). **Constitution:** Oct. 8, 1995. **National holiday:** Independence Day, Oct. 9. **Heads of Government:** Yoweri Kaguta Museveni, president (since Jan. 1986); Prof. Apolo Nsibambi, prime minister (since Apr. 1999). **Structure:** executive—president is head of government and state; unicameral legislature; judiciary.

• **ECONOMY** **Monetary unit:** Ugandan shilling. **Budget:** (FY98/99) ***income:*** $959 mil.; ***expend.:*** $1.04 bil. **GDP:** $31 bil., $1,260 per capita (2002 est.). **Chief crops:** coffee, cotton, tobacco; beef, milk, poultry. **Natural resources:** copper, cobalt, limestone, salt. **Major industries:** sugar, brewing, tobacco. **Labor force:** 12 mil. (2001 est.); 82% agriculture, 13% services, 5% industry. **Exports:** $476 mil. (f.o.b., 2002); coffee, gold, fish. **Imports:** $1.14 bil. (f.o.b., 2002); transportation equipment, petroleum, medical supplies, cereals. **Major trading partners:** ***exports:*** Germany, Netherlands, U.S.; ***imports:*** Kenya, U.K., India.

Prior to 1800 Uganda was the site of several important kingdoms, notably Buganda, centered on Kampala on the northern shore of Lake Victoria. After 1830, Arabs from the sultanate of Oman, based in Zanzibar, asserted loose control over the region and dominated its trade. British explorers, seeking the source of the Nile, reached the Lake Victoria region in the mid-19th century. Mission stations were established in 1877; a Muslim rebellion destroyed the missions and occupied Kampala in 1888.

Buganda was brought under the control of the British East Africa Company in 1890, and Britain established a protectorate in 1894 that was expanded to include neighboring territories in 1896. In 1902 some of the protectorate's territory was transferred to Kenya. British immigrants extensively developed the agricultural potential of Uganda's fertile and temperate highlands, establishing large and prosperous farms. Lake Victoria was the scene of naval battles between Great Britain and Germany (established in neighboring Tanganyika) during World War I.

In 1955 the British administration created a local parliamentary government in which both whites and Africans held ministerial office. Talks on the terms for independence began in 1961 and after some difficulty arrived at a formula for a national structure in which Buganda and other traditional kingdoms would retain local autonomy. Several political parties competed for power; the Uganda People's Congress led by Milton Obote became dominant. Uganda became independent within the British Commonwealth on Oct. 9, 1962. Several constitutional changes in the early 1960's led to an end to the autonomy of the kingdoms and the effective concentration of all power in Obote's presidency. In 1967 a new constitution proclaimed Uganda an independent republic.

Obote was overthrown on Jan. 25, 1971, by Idi Amin Dada, commander of Uganda's armed forces. Amin declared himself president, dissolved the Parliament, and assumed absolute powers. In 1972 he expelled Uganda's Asians (primarily people of Indian and Pakistani descent), who controlled most of the country's small-scale commerce. The U.S. broke off diplomatic relations in 1973. In 1976 Amin declared himself president for life. His eight-year reign was marked by extreme violence and persecution of political and tribal opponents; as many as 300,000 may have been killed between 1971 and 1979. The country's prosperous agricultural, mining, and commercial economy was devastated, and its infrastructure, including a good road and rail network and Makerere University, fell into ruins.

On July 3, 1976, Israeli airborne troops landed at Entebbe and rescued 103 hostages who had been captured in a skyjacking carried out by Palestinian and German terrorists.

In 1978 Amin, with the aid of Libyan troops, invaded Tanzania. In the following year, Tanzanian troops countered by invading Uganda; they captured Kampala on Apr. 11, 1979, and drove Amin into exile. Diplomatic relations with the United States resumed. After a series of interim governments, elections in 1981 returned Obote to power. Obote's new regime was marked by repression of opponents and by rebellion in the northern part of the country by the National Resistance Army (NRA) under Yoweri Museveni.

Obote fled into exile in 1985 and was succeeded by Lt. Gen. Basilio Olara-Okello, but the NRA rebellion continued. Kenyan president Daniel arap Moi mediated peace talks between Olara-Okello and the NRA in late 1985; in Jan. 1986 Olara-Okello fled, and Museveni organized a new government. Despite continued insurgencies by rival military factions and a rebellion led by the charismatic religious leader Alice Lakwena, the Museveni government restored order and, with aid from the World Bank and the I.M.F., began to rebuild Uganda's shattered society.

A constituent assembly was elected in 1994. In 1995, it enacted a new constitution, which extended for five years a ban on political parties, and scheduled presidential elections for 1996, elections Museveni won with 74 percent of the vote. By 1997 Uganda had the fastest growing economy in Africa and in 1998 Pres. Clinton's visit helped to create interst among foreign investors. In a June 2000 referendum voters extended the "no party" system Museveni advocates. Museveni won re-election as president in March 2001 with 69 percent of the vote and announced in April that although Uganda was withdrawing from the Congo peace accord, its troops were withdrawing also, since they had accomplished their aim of defeating the Hutu extremists who threatened Uganda's borders

▶UKRAINE

• **Geography** **Location:** east-central Europe. **Boundaries**: Belarus to N, Russian Federation to NE and E, Sea of Azov and Black Sea to S, Moldova and Romania to SW, Hungary, Slovakia, Poland to W. **Total area**: 233,089 sq. mi. (603,700 sq km). **Coastline**: Black Sea. **Comparative area**: slightly smaller than Texas. **Land use:** 57% arable land; 2% permanent crops, 41% other. **Major cities**: (1995 est.) Kiev (capital) 2,635,000; Kharkov (Kharkiv) 1,576,000; Dnepropetrovsk 1,162,000; Donetsk (Donetske) 1,102,000; Odessa (Odesa) 1,060,000.

• **People** **Population:** 48,055,439 (2003 est.). **Nationality:** noun—Ukrainian(s); adjective—Ukrainian. **Ethnic groups:** 78% Ukrainian, 17% Russian, 5% other. **Languages:** Ukrainian, Russian, Romanian, Polish, Hungarian. **Religions:** Ukrainian Orthodox—Moscow Patriarchate, Ukrainian Orthodox—Kiev Patriarchate, Ukrainian Autocephalous Orthodox, Ukrainian Catholic, Protestant; Jewish.

• **Government** **Type:** republic. **Independence:** Aug. 24, 1991 (from Soviet Union). **Constitution:** June 28, 1996. **National holiday:** Independence Day, Aug. 24. **Heads of Government:** Leonid Kuchma, president (since Nov. 21, 2002); Victor F. Yanukovich, prime minister (since May 2001). **Structure:** executive—president, Cabinet of Ministers; legislative—Supreme Council (450 deputies); judicial—Supreme Court.

• **Economy** **Monetary unit:** hryvnia. **Budget:** (1999) ***income:*** $10.2 bil.; ***expend.:*** $10.2 bil. **GDP:** $218 bil., $4,500 per capita (2002 est.). **Chief crops:** grain, sugar beets, sunflower seeds, vegetables; meat, milk. **Natural resources:** coal, iron ore, manganese, natural gas, oil. **Major industries:** coal, electric power, metals, machinery and transport, chemicals. **Labor force:** 22.8 mil. (1997); 32% industry and construction, 24% agriculture and forestry, 44% services, 32% industry. **Exports:** $18.1 bil. (2002 est.); energy, chemicals, machinery and transport equipment. **Imports:** $18 bil. (2002 est.); energy, machinery and parts, transportation equipment, chemicals. **Major trading partners:** Russia,Turkmenistan, Germany.

Ukraine is the center of the original Russian state, known as Kievan Rus, which came into existence in the ninth century A.D. In the 13th and 14th centuries, during the Mongol invasion, Ukraine was controlled by Lithuania and Poland, and in 1654 it first entered the Russian empire. In the latter half of the 17th century, Ukraine was divided, with the eastern regions becoming part of Russia and the western part annexed by Poland; when Poland was subsequently partitioned, the western sections were ceded to Austria.

Until 1917 eastern Ukraine was a province of Russia called "Little Russia," and for two centuries the dominant country tried to Russianize the Ukrainian clergy and upper classes, and ban the Ukrainian language. Nevertheless, secret societies for the study of Ukrainian history, language, and culture formed, and when in the 19th century the Russians exiled Ukrainians to Siberia, modern Ukrainian nationalism was born.

In 1917, when the Russian empire collapsed, Ukrainian nationalists demanded Ukraine's autonomy by establishing a Ukrainian People's Republic, but within a few months, Red Army troops had occupied Ukraine. For the next few years, however, Ukraine was in the middle of the civil war and was even ceded to Germany under the Brest-Litovsk treaty of 1918, but in December 1920 a Ukrainian Soviet Socialist Republic (SSR) was established. Ukraine again was divided under the 1921 Treaty of Riga, which gave western Ukraine to Poland, Czechoslovakia, and Romania, while eastern Ukraine formed the Ukrainian SSR. Ukraine became one of the original members of the U.S.S.R. in December 1922.

The Ukrainians strongly opposed Stalin's policy of forced collectivization of agriculture in the 1930's, and the resulting chaos, famine, and deportation resulted in the deaths of millions of Ukrainians. Likewise, Stalin's great terror of the 1930's hit Ukraine hard, with the first victims being Ukrainian nationalists. World War II largely devastated Ukraine and killed millions of Ukrainians, but as a result of the war, Ukraine regained its old territories from Romania and Poland and was enlarged by the addition of historical Tatar lands in 1954. (The native Tatar inhabitants were forcibly deported to central Asia in the 1940's.)

Mikhail Gorbachev's policy of glasnost was slow to take root in Ukraine, largely because the head of the Communist party in Ukraine was a loyal Brezhnev crony, Vladimir Shcherbitsky. Outwardly, he appeared to agree with Gorbachev's policies, but Ukraine dissidents were still being arrested and cultural groups harassed by secret police. In 1986 a deadly nuclear power explosion at Chernobyl—and Soviet attempts at covering it up—turned international attention to Ukraine and gave rise to a number of new, powerful opposition movements. Rukh (the Ukrainian People's Movement for Restructuring), the most important of these, was founded in Kiev by a prominent group of intellectuals. By 1989 branches of Rukh had been organized in most parts of Ukraine. At the same time, Ukrainian miners became active in strikes, and the Ukrainian Catholic church and the Ukrainian Orthodox church became politically active. Shcherbitsky's failure to contain these groups led to his dismissal in 1989.

On July 16, 1990, the Ukrainian Supreme Soviet adopted a declaration of sovereignty, and Communist party Second Secretary Leonid Kravchuk became chairman of the Supreme Soviet. In March 1991 Ukraine participated in the negotiations to form a new union treaty, despite more radical demands by Rukh for complete independence. The Ukrainian Communist party's failure to denounce the attempted coup in Moscow in August 1991 led to significant changes in Ukraine's political situation. After the coup collapsed, the Communist party was banned, and on Aug. 24, 1991, Ukraine adopted a declaration of total independence. In December, Kravchuk was elected president.

Ukraine, Belarus, and the Russian Federation signed the Minsk Agreement that created the Commonwealth of Independent States, and on Dec. 21, Ukraine and 10 other former union republics officially committed themselves to the union by signing the Alma-Ata Declaration.

Potentially dangerous conflicts with Russia remained, however, including control of the powerful Black Sea fleet. Soon after the fall of the Soviet government armed conflict erupted in April 1994, when Russia removed a ship from Odessa laden with marine-research and navigational equipment valued at more than $10 million. A compromise was reached in 1995 that divided the 635-vessel fleet equally, with Russia then buying 32 percent of the ships from the Ukraine and paying rent for use of the naval base at Sevastopol.

The other conflict involved 2,000 nuclear warheads present in Ukraine. In Jan. 1994, Kravchuk, Boris Yeltsin, and Bill Clinton negotiated an agreement to dismantle Ukraine's 175 long-range missiles and more than 1,800 warheads. But Ukraine's Parliament refused to approve the agreement, even after Clinton made a $350 million U.S. aid package conditional on total disarmament. Parliament's intransigence was seen as an embarrassment to Kravchuk, and in July 1994 he lost the presidential election to reformer Leonid Kuchma. In Nov. Parliament overwhelmingly approved the Nuclear Nonproliferation Treaty and loans from the U.S. and the I.M.F. ensued. The U.S. also pledged $400 million to help dismantle the missiles.

In July 1996 the Rada approved a new "strong president" Constitution which guaranteed rights to own property and to engage in business, abolished local councils ("soviets"), and made Ukrainian the only legal language (although Russian is the language of about one-fifth of the population). The May 1997 Friendship Treaty with Russia settled the Black Sea fleet division, guaranteed Russia's right to rent part of the port facilities of Sevastopol to service the fleet, and confirmed Ukrainian sovereignty over all of Crimea.

In Aug. 1998 the I.M.F. agreed to loans totalling $2.2 bil. to assist the government despite its inability to make reforms. Kuchma easily won re-election in Nov. 1999 and in April 2000 his referendum to expand presidential power was approved.

Soon after, Kuchma's authority began to unravel: in November, charges, backed by tape recordings, surfaced that he had connived in the murder of an opposition journalist; the tapes also held evidence of election tampering and bribery. An odd alliance of the Communists with the business parties in Parliament toppled Prime Minister Yushchenko's government in April 2001; his replacement was the business coalition's Anatoly Kinakh. Although Kuchma's future seemed shaky, a coalition government emerged that supported him. Large public protests continued.

▶UNITED ARAB EMIRATES

• **Geography** **Location:** eastern Arabian peninsula. **Boundaries**: Persian Gulf to N, Gulf of Oman to NE, Oman to E, Saudi Arabia to S and W, short frontier with Qatar to NW. **Total area**: 31,969 sq. mi. (82,880 sq km). **Coastline**: 819 mi. (1,318 km). **Comparative area**: slightly smaller than Maine. **Land use:** negl.% arable land; negl.% permanent crops; 99% other. **Major cities**: (1995 est.) Abu Dhabi (capital) 928,360; Dubai 674,100; Sharjah 400,400.

• **People** **Population:** 2,484,818 (2003 est.). **Nationality:** noun—Emirian(s); adjective—Emirian. **Ethnic groups:** 19% Emirian, 23% other Arab and Iranian, 50% South Asian, 8% other expatriates (includes Westerners and East Asians); less than 20% of population are UAE citizens (1982). **Languages:** Arabic (official), Persian, English, Hindi, Urdu. **Religions:** 96% Muslim (16% Shia), 4% Christian, Hindu, and other.

• **Government** **Type:** federation with specified powers delegated to UAE central government and other powers reserved to member emirates. **Independence:** Dec. 2, 1971 (from UK). **Constitution::** Dec. 2, 1971; made permanent 1996. **National holiday:** National Day, Dec. 2. **Heads of Government:** Sheikh Zayed bin Sultan al-Nahyan of Abu Dhabi, president (since Dec. 1971); Maktoum al-Maktoum, prime minister (since Oct.1990). **Structure:** executive—Supreme Council of Rulers (seven members), from which president and vice president are elected; prime minister and Council of Ministers; unicameral legislature—Federal National Council; judicial—Union Supreme Court.

• **Economy** **Monetary unit:** Emirian dirham.

Budget: (2000 est.) ***income:*** $20 bil.; ***expend.:*** $22 bil. **GDP:** $53 bil., $22,000 per capita (2002 est.). **Chief crops:** dates, vegetables, watermelons; poultry, eggs, dairy products; fish. **Natural resources:** crude oil, natural gas. **Major industries:** petroleum, petrochemicals. **Labor force:** 1.6 mil. (2000 est.); 78% services, 15% industry and commerce, 7% agriculture. **Exports:** $44.9 bil. (f.o.b., 2002 est.); 45% crude oil, natural gas, re-exports, dried fish, dates. **Imports:** $30.8 bil. (f.o.b., 2002 est.); manufactured goods, machinery and transport equipment, chemicals, food. **Major trading partners: *exports:*** 29% Japan, 10% South Korea, 5% India; ***imports:*** 7% U.S., 7% Germany, 7% Japan.

In the 1820's Great Britain established protectorates over seven small sheikhdoms along the gulf coast between Qatar and Oman—Abu Dhabi, Dubai, Sharjah, Ajmar, Fujairah, and Umm al-Qaiwain. The region, which had been known as the Pirate Coast, then was generally referred to as the Trucial Coast or Trucial Oman. Under terms of a treaty in 1892, the sheikhdoms agreed not to enter into relations with any other country.

After Great Britain announced that it would withdraw its forces from the gulf in 1971, the seven sheikhdoms formed a federation and became independent as the United Arab Emirates on Dec. 2, 1971.

Just prior to his invasion of Kuwait in August 1990, Saddam Hussein threatened both the UAE and Kuwait for overproduction of petroleum, and the UAE was an integral part of the Allied coalition against Iraq. In 1995 the government signed a defensive alliance with France, who supplies the army with most of its weapons.

The economy is almost entirely dominated by petroleum. Citizens of the UAE receive extensive social services and enjoy one of the world's highest per capita incomes.

▶UNITED KINGDOM

United Kingdom of Great Britain and Northern Ireland

• **Geography** **Location:** northwestern Europe, occupying major portion of British Isles. **Boundaries**: Atlantic Ocean to NW and W, North Sea to E; separated from France by English Channel to S; Republic of Ireland to W. **Total area**: 94,525 sq. mi. (244,820 sq km). **Coastline**: 7,723 mi. (12,429 km). **Comparative area**: slightly smaller than Oregon. **Land use:** 26% arable land; negl. % permanent crops; 473% other. **Major cities**: (1994 est.) London (capital) 6,976,500; Birmingham 1,008,400; Leeds 724,400; Glasgow 680,000; Sheffield 530,100.

• **People** **Population:** 60,094,648 (2003 est.). **Nationality:** noun—Briton(s), British (collective pl.); adjective—British. **Ethnic groups:** 81.5% English, 9.6% Scottish, 2.4% Irish, 1.9% Welsh, 1.8% Ulster, 2.8% West Indian, Indian, Pakistani, and other. **Languages:** English, Welsh (about 26% of population of Wales), Scottish form of Gaelic (about 60,000 in Scotland). **Religions:** 40 mil. Anglican and Roman Catholic, 1.5 mil. Muslim, 800,000 Presbyterian, 760,000 Methodist, 500,000 Sikh, 500,000 Hindu, 350,000 Jewish.

• **Government** **Type:** constitutional monarchy. **Independence:** N.A. **Constitution:** unwritten; partly statutes, partly common law and practice. **National holiday:** Celebration of the Birthday of the Queen, second Saturday in June. **Heads of Government:** Elizabeth II, queen (since Feb. 1952); Tony Blair, prime minister (since May 1997). **Structure:** executive authority lies with collectively responsible cabinet led by prime minister; legislative authority rests with Parliament (House of Lords, House of Commons); House of Lords is supreme judicial authority and highest court of appeals.

• **Economy** **Monetary unit:** British pound. **Budget:** (FY01) ***income:*** $565 bil.; ***expend.:*** $540 bil. **GDP:** $1.52 trillion, $25,300 per capita (2002 est.). **Chief crops:** cereals, oilseed, potatoes, vegetables; cattle, sheep, poultry; fish. **Natural resources:** coal, crude oil, natural gas, tin, limestone. **Major industries:** machinery and transportation equipment, metals, food processing. **Labor force:** 29.7 mil. (2001); 74% services, 25% industry, 1% agriculture, 5.2% unemployment (2002 est.). **Exports:** $286.3 bil. (f.o.b., 2002); manufactured goods, machinery, fuels, chemicals. **Imports:** $330.1 bil. (f.o.b., 2002); manufactured goods, machinery, fuels, foodstuffs. **Major trading partners: *exports:*** 58% E.U. (13% Germany, 10% France, 8% Netherlands), 15% U.S.; ***imports:*** 52% E.U. (13% Germany, 9% France, 7% Netherlands, 5% Benelux), 13% U.S.

Early megalithic and Iron Age peoples of Britain, primarily Celtic, developed tribal states that were conquered by Roman invaders in A.D. 43. After Roman legions withdrew from Britain in 410, invasions of Jutes, Angles, and Saxons conquered much of England, while Celtic peoples flourished in Wales, Scotland, and especially Ireland. Viking invaders established settlements in the eighth century. A united Saxon kingdom fell to the Norman invasion of William the Conquerer in 1066.

An aristocratic rebellion against the royal absolutism of King John in 1215 led to the royal acceptance of the Magna Carta, guaranteeing legal rights and laying the foundations of parliamentary government. From the 12th to the 15th century, the Plantagenet dynasty ruled England and claimed overlordship over Ireland; Wales was conquered in 1283. The Plantagenets also controlled sizable territories in France.

The Hundred Years' War (1337-1453) cost England its French possessions; the War of the Roses, (1455-85) ended the Plantagenet dynasty and brought Henry Tudor (Henry VII) to the throne. The Tudors gradually centralized royal control by bringing pressure against both the church and the nobility. Henry VIII broke with Rome in 1534 and established the Church of England. Under Elizabeth I, the last of the Tudors, England defeated Spain at sea and laid the foundations of later worldwide English sea power. The English Renaissance began under Elizabeth I (1533-1603) with the works of Shakespeare and continued into the 17th century with Milton and Newton.

The Stuart dynasty was founded by James I (1566-1625), uniting the crowns of England and Scotland in 1603. The English Civil War (1642-49) culminated in the execution of Charles I and the proclamation of the Commonwealth (later the Protectorate) under Oliver Cromwell. The monarchy was restored with Charles II in 1660. In the bloodless Glorious Revolution (1688), James II fled before a Protestant army under the Dutch William of Orange, who married and ruled jointly with James's daughter Mary II. The English Bill of Rights established the supremacy of Parliament and made the government a model of constitutional monarchy.

In the last gasp of the Stuart claimants to the throne, Irish supporters of James II were defeated at the Battle of the Boyne (1690), which temporarily crushed Irish resistance to annexation by England. The United Kingdom was created when Scotland was joined with England in a common Parliament by the Act of Union in 1707. A Scottish uprising led by the Young Pretender, Charles Edward Stuart, was crushed at Culloden Moor in 1745. Ireland was made part of the United Kingdom in 1801.

In the 1700's the United Kingdom became the greatest sea power in the world, controlling an empire that included much of North America and India. Agrarian "enclosures" of the 18th century ruined the peasantry but created an entrepreneurial revolution in agriculture that ultimately led to greatly increased agricultural productivity. The capital created in the process contributed to the success of the Industrial Revolution, which over the next century made England the wealthiest land on earth.

Despite the loss of the 13 colonies after the American Revolution (1775-83), England consolidated its holdings in the Indian subcontinent, Australia and New Zealand, Malaya, Hong Kong, much of eastern Africa from "Cape to Cairo," and elsewhere. Britain's prosperity and moral purpose were embodied in the person of Victoria, Queen of Great Britain and Ireland (1836-1901) and Empress of India (from 1836).

The repeal of the protectionist Corn Laws in 1846 led to an agricultural depression and hastened the migration of labor from the countryside to the industrial cities. The rise of labor activism led in 1906 to laws granting privileged status to trade unions, which organized the Labour party to promote their interests.

Britain's involvement in the Triple Entente with France and Russia ensured its participation in World War I (1914-18) against Germany, Italy, and Austria-Hungary. Victory came at the cost of an entire generation of British youth, but Britain emerged from the war with its empire at a high point, adding Tanganyika, Jordan, Palestine, and Iraq as part of the postwar division of spoils. Most of Ireland became independent in 1921, however, leaving only Northern Ireland as part of the United Kingdom.

Between the two world wars, Britain's navy and air force were the largest in the world, its army the third largest. Yet its industry was aging, the Great Depression hit especially hard in the British Isles, strikes and labor unrest weakened the social fabric, and colonial ties began to weaken in the 1930's. Economic retrenchment led to a failure to rearm in the face of the rising threat of Hitler's Germany and Mussolini's Italy.

The Munich Pact of 1938 gave Hitler a license for war; his invasion of Poland in 1939 forced Britain into the conflict. When Winston Churchill became prime minister in 1940, Britain was under daily air attack and in danger of an invasion by sea, and the country was dependent on American friendship and lend-lease war materials. But 1941 brought alliance with the United States and the Soviet Union, and a slowly turning tide of war leading to victory in 1945. Still, postwar Britain dropped to the second rank of superpowers.

The coalition between the Conservative and Labour parties that had governed Great Britain during the war seemed no longer necessary in 1945 as the war wound down. Labour won a landslide victory in the 1945 elections; Churchill was recalled in the midst of the Potsdam Conference, and Clement Atlee became prime minister. A brief Labour flirtation with the U.S.S.R. quickly ended in the postwar 1940's; England became a founding member of the United Nations and also, in 1949, of NATO. As the Cold War took shape, Britain developed its own nuclear arsenal.

The Labour party nationalized the Bank of England along with railroads, public utilities, and heavy industry. A comprehensive welfare state apparatus was created, including a national health service, unemployment and retirement benefits, and free education at all levels. But Britain was in many respects too poor to afford such changes; in order to cut expenditures, the government hastened the process of withdrawal from colonies and military bases around the world. India was granted independence in 1947, and Palestine, Burma, and Ceylon in 1948-49.

The elections of 1951 brought Churchill back to the prime ministership at the head of a Conservative majority that would last for 13 years. The Conservatives returned steel and trucking to the private sector but in general refrained from undoing the social policies of their Labour predecessors. Economic growth began in the 1950's and held steady at about 2.5 percent per year, a significantly lower rate than in continental Europe; obsolescence, excessive wage and benefit settlements, and a low savings rate all took their toll. The coronation of Elizabeth II in 1953 added a much-needed element of national celebration.

Churchill retired in 1955 and was succeeded by Anthony Eden. Eden's government fell in 1956 over the failed Anglo-French invasion of Suez. Eden's fall in 1957 brought to power Harold Macmillan, who pursued close relations with the United States. Most important, he presided over the transformation of an empire to a commonwealth; in the early 1960's, Ghana, Nigeria, Malaya, Singapore, and numerous other colonies were granted independence and Commonwealth status. Immigrants from the Commonwealth promptly flocked to England, straining housing, social services, and the labor market and creating problems of assimilation that remain unsolved.

Britain under Macmillan was the moving force behind the European Free Trade Association in 1960. In 1961 Britain applied for membership in the EEC, but that application was humiliatingly vetoed by France's Charles de Gaulle in 1963. Macmillan's government fell with the Profumo Scandal of 1963, and Douglas Home became a caretaker prime minister pending new elections.

The 1964 elections brought the Labour party to power under Harold Wilson, whose moderate positions made him unpopular with his own party, especially when he sponsored legislation to ban wildcat strikes. Strikes, wage inflation, the steady growth of the public sector (including renationalization of the steel industry), and the rise of turmoil in Northern Ireland in 1968-69 combined to make public support for Labour evaporate.

The Conservative victory in the 1970 elections brought Edward Heath to the office of prime minister. Promising to cut expenditures and taxes, reward initiative, and curb union power, the Conservatives were able to accomplish none of those aims. Heath's government imposed ineffective wage controls in an attempt to slow inflation and passed the 1971 Industrial Relations Act to regulate unions. When unions defied that act, the government fell. Heath's major achievement was the United Kingdom's admission to the EC in 1973. Continued turmoil in Northern Ireland was met with the abolition of Ulster's Stormount Parliament in 1972 and the imposition of direct British rule—a policy that did nothing to stem the growing sectarian violence.

Wilson returned to the prime ministership in 1974 and retired in 1976, passing on the office to James Callaghan, who governed until 1979 at the head of a Labour-Liberal coalition. The continued power of trade unions was seen in the repeal of the Industrial Relations Act and the extension of union privileges. The left wing of the Labour party brought increasing pressure against defense spending, membership in NATO, and also loudly criticized American involvement in Vietnam.

The OPEC oil price rises of 1972-74 hurt Great Britain in the short run but also encouraged development of oil and gas fields in the North Sea, which made the nation a major petroleum exporter and helped revitalize its economy. Oil exploration in the North Sea also encouraged Scottish nationalism, with some damage to national unity, although in both Scotland and Wales, proposals in 1979 for separate parliaments were soundly defeated by plebiscites.

The 1979 elections brought the Conservatives to power again, behind Margaret Thatcher, Great Britain's (and Europe's) first female prime minister. She proved to be the only British prime minister in modern times to lead her party successfully in three elections. Thatcher took office with an agenda that involved undoing much of the course of postwar British history.

The first target was inflation, attacked through a freeze on expenditures and reduction of government borrowing. The policy was a success; inflation fell from 18 percent in 1980 to 3 percent in 1989. But the austerity program had a high cost in unemployment, which remained at 14 percent in the mid-1980's.

In 1982 national attention turned abruptly to overseas concerns, as Argentina invaded the Falkland ("Malvinas") Islands (only 300 miles east of Argentina), which it had long claimed as Argentine national territory, on Apr. 2. On May 21 British forces launched a counteroffensive, and the invading Argentine forces surrendered on June 14. The nation's success in mounting an amphibious operation 6,500 miles away provoked an upsurge of patriotism that swept Thatcher's party into a second term in 1983.

After the election the government turned to denationalization of industry. Over $30 billion in state property—from industrial giants, such as Britoil and British Gas, to individual apartments in municipal housing projects—was sold to private interests. This program was followed in 1986 by tax cuts, in which the top income-tax rate dropped from 98 percent to 40 percent. In foreign affairs, Britain agreed in 1985 to return Hong Kong to Chinese sovereignty in 1997.

The 1987 elections pitted the Conservatives against a weak Labour party that opposed NATO missile deployment in Great Britain, advocating unilateral disarmament and calling for renationalization of industry and a return to higher taxes for the wealthy. The Conservatives easily won their third straight election. By 1989 the "Thatcher Revolution" had produced a decisive long-term economic recovery, but one that was unevenly distributed: the southern part of the country enjoyed an economic boom, while the older industrial cities of the north remained stagnant. In 1990 an economic slowdown and rising inflation led to a strong decline in support for Mrs. Thatcher and her government. She resigned in November 1990.

Thatcher was replaced by Chancellor of the Exchequer John Major, whose greatest challenge has been Britain's role in a united Europe, to which Britain now has a land link via the 31-mile Channel Tunnel (Chunnel), completed in 1994.

In the April 1992 elections, the Conservatives, led by Major, won a comfortable 21-seat margin in Parliament despite a recession. Not since the Napoleonic Wars has a British political party been able to form four consecutive governments. Yet only 13 months later Major's ratings in the polls had fallen to 21 percent as the economy stalled and the Conservatives themselves split badly over some elements in the E.C.'s Maastricht Treaty. The Conservatives were further beset in 1994 with a series of tabloid scandals and allegations of political corruption concerning arms sales to Iraq and Malaysia. Conservative chances in parliamentary elections, due in the spring of 1997, were looking very slim, and they looked worse in March after the government clumsily handled the news that scientists had concluded that eating English beef could cause the fatal "mad-cow" disease. After insisting that there was no cause for alarm the government was forced to deal with an E.U. boycott.

The parliamentary election of May 1997 ended 18 years of Tory government with Labour winning its largest majority since 1935, 419 seats to the Conservatives 165. The new Prime Minister Tony Blair appointed a cabinet of political moderates. In 1997 Hong Kong was returned to China without incident and in April 1998 the Blair government succeeded in negotiating a settlement in Northern Ireland although problems still remain.

In May 1999 the first elections to the Scottish Parliament and the Welsh Assembly were held. Labour won a plurality in both (over nationalist parties). The two bodies have authority over education, environment, health care, housing, and law enforcement. The Scottish Parliament also possesses authority to tax. In the 2001 elections Blair's Labour Party won a huge victory, taking 413 of 659 seats, the first time Labour had won two consecutive victories. Still, in local elections in May 2002 and 2003, the Conservatives trounced labor. The vote on invading Iraq carried overwhelmingly (412-143); yet in the aftermath of victory serious troubles arose for the Blair government over the intelligence accounts used to justify British participation.

▶UNITED STATES OF AMERICA

• GEOGRAPHY **Location:** 48 conterminous states in North America, between Atlantic and Pacific Oceans; Alaska in northwest North America; Hawaiian Islands in Pacific Ocean about 3,000 miles W of California. **Boundaries**: Canada to N; Atlantic Ocean to E; Gulf of Mexico, Mexico to S; Pacific Ocean to W. Alaska bounded on E by Canada, on S and W by Pacific Ocean, on W and N by Arctic Ocean. **Total area**: 3,717,797 sq. mi. (9,629,091 sq km). **Coastline**: 11,954 mi. (19,924 km). **Comparative area**: slightly larger than Brazil; fourth-largest country. **Land use:** 19% arable land; negl. % permanent crops; 80% other. **Major cities**: (1994 est.) Washington, D.C. (capital) 567,094; New York 7,333,253; Los Angeles 3,448,613; Chicago 2,731,743; Houston 1,702,086; Philadelphia 1,524,249.

• PEOPLE **Population:** 290,342,554 (2003). **Nationality:** noun—American(s); adjective—American. **Ethnic groups:** 77.1% white, 12.9% black, 4.2% Asian, 1.5% Amerindian or Alaska native. **Languages:** predominantly English; sizable Spanish-speaking minority. **Religions:** 56% Protestant, 28% Roman Catholic, 10% none, 2% Jewish, 4% other.

• GOVERNMENT **Type:** federal republic; strong democratic tradition. **Independence:** July 4, 1776 (from U.K.). **Constitution:** Sept. 17, 1787, effective March 4,1789. **National holiday:** Independence Day, July 4. **Heads of Government:** George W.

Bush, president (since Jan. 2001); Richard Cheney, vice president (since Jan. 2001). **Structure:** executive—president, vice president, cabinet; legislative—bicameral Congress (House of Representatives and Senate); judicial—Supreme Court; branches, in principle, independent and maintain balance of power.

• **ECONOMY** **Monetary unit:** United States dollar **Budget:** (2002) ***income:*** $1.946 trillion; ***expend:*** $2.052 tril. **GDP:** $10.4 tril., $37,600 per capita (2002). **Chief crops:** wheat, other grains, corn, fruits, vegetables, cotton; beef, pork, poultry, dairy products; forest products; fish. **Natural resources:** coal, copper, lead, molybdenum, phosphates. **Major industries:** leading industrial power in the world, highly diversified; petroleum, steel, motor vehicles, aerospace, telecommunications, chemicals, electronics, food processing, consumer goods, fishing, lumber, mining. **Labor force:** 141.8 mil., includes unemployed (2001); 31.0% managerial and professional, 28.9% sales and administrative support, 13.6% services, 24.1% manufacturing, mining, transportation, and crafts, 2.5% farming, forestry, and fishing; 5.8% unemployment (2002). **Exports:** $687 bil. (f.o.b., 2002 est.); capital goods, automobiles, industrial supplies and raw materials, consumer goods, agricultural products. **Imports:** $1.165 tril. (f.o.b., 2002 est.); crude oil and refined petroleum, machinery, automobiles, consumer goods, industrial raw materials, food and beverages. **Major trading partners:** (2001) ***exports:*** 22% Canada, 14% Mexico, 8% Japan; ***imports:*** 19% Canada, 12% Mexico, 11% Japan.

(For current events and history see Part I: "Major News Stories of the Year," and Part II: "Chronology of American History.")

▶URUGUAY

Oriental Republic of Uruguay

• **GEOGRAPHY** **Location:** southeastern coast of South America. **Boundaries**: Brazil to N, Atlantic Ocean to E and S, Argentina to W. **Total area**: 68,039 sq. mi. (176,220 sq km). **Coastline**: 410 mi. (660 km). **Comparative area**: slightly smaller than Washington State. **Land use:** 7% arable land; negl. % permanent crops; 93% other. **Major cities**: (1992 census) Montevideo (capital) 1,383,660; Salto 77,400; Paysandú 75,200; Las Piedras 61,300; Rivera 55,400.

• **PEOPLE** **Population:** 3,413,329 (2003 est.). **Nationality:** noun—Uruguayan(s); adjective—Uruguayan. **Ethnic groups:** 88% white, 8% mestizo, 4% black. **Languages:** Spanish, Portunol, or Brazilero; Portuguese-Spanish mix on the Brazilian frontier. **Religions:** 66% Roman Catholic, 2% Protestant, 1% Jewish, 30% nonprofessing or other (less than half of the adult population attends church regularly).

• **GOVERNMENT** **Type:** republic. **Independence:** Aug. 25, 1825 (from Brazil). **Constitution:** Nov. 27, 1966; effective Feb. 1967; suspended June 27, 1973; constitutional reforms approved Jan. 7, 1997. **National holiday:** Independence Day, Aug. 25. **Head of Government:** Jorge Batlle Ibanez, president (since Mar. 2000). **Structure:** executive—headed by president; bicameral legislature (Senate and House of Deputies); national judiciary headed by Supreme Court.

• **ECONOMY** **Monetary unit:** Uruguayan peso. **Budget:** (2000 est.) ***income:*** $3.7 bil.; ***expend.:*** $4.6 bil. **GDP:** $26.5 bil., $7,800 per capita (2002 est.). **Chief crops:** wheat, rice, corn, sorghum; livestock; fishing. **Natural resources:** fertile soil, hydropower potential, minor minerals, fisheries. **Major industries:** meat processing, wool and hides, sugar. **Labor force:** 1.2 mil. (2001 est.); 70% services, 14% agriculture, 16% industry; 19.4% unemployment (2002). **Exports:** $2.1 bil. (f.o.b., 2002 est.); wool and textile manufactures, beef and other animal products, rice, fish. **Imports:** $1.87 bil. (f.o.b., 2002 est.); machinery and equipment, vehicles, chemicals, minerals, plastics, oil. **Major trading partners:** Brazil, Argentina, U.S.

Uruguay was known as the Banda Oriental del Uruguay (Eastern Shore of the Uruguay River) during the colonial period. Although the Spanish first explored the area in 1516, they did not immediately settle there. Instead, the Portuguese founded the Colonia de Sacramento, near Buenos Aires, in 1680. They did not permanently establish the settlement of Montevideo until 1726. Under the leadership of José Gervasio Artigas, Uruguayans fought against both the Portuguese and the junta of Buenos Aires between 1811 and 1814 in an effort to establish their independence; in 1815 they proclaimed the Autonomous Government of the Eastern Provinces.

In 1817 the Portuguese again took control of the region, but Uruguayan nationals ousted them in 1828. A new constitution for the country was promulgated in 1830; however, domestic rivalry among elites soon led to civil war. The two contending factions, Liberals (Colorados) and Conservatives (Blancos), wore red and white armbands, respectively. Civil war continued through the 1840's and 1850's, until the victory of the Colorados in 1865. In the War of the Triple Alliance (1865-70), Uruguay allied itself with Argentina and Brazil against Paraguay. The consequence of the war for Uruguay was independence from the other regional powers.

The Colorado party dominated Uruguayan government from 1865 until 1958. Waves of European immigrants transformed Uruguayan society during the latter half of the 19th century, and by 1880 immigrants made up almost half of the population. The last civil war between the Blancos and the Colorados took place in 1904; the Colorados won victory under Pres. José Batlle y Ordóñez, one of Uruguay's political legends.

Batlle inaugurated a labor and social-welfare reform program that created Latin America's first eight-hour working day as well as progressive legislation on women's rights. Impressed with the Swiss plural executive Federal Council during his stay in Switzerland, Batlle believed such a structure could help Uruguay avoid the Latin American hazard of caudillismo (authoritarian rule). Batlle proposed the idea of a plural executive, and a version of the idea became part of the constitution in 1919. The new constitution provided for both a president and a collegial National Council, both of which would make up the executive structure of the government.

In 1933 a military coup by Pres. Gabriel Terra sought to dissolve both the legislature and the National Council and to reestablish the single executive presidential system. He managed this by sponsoring a constituent assembly that drew up a new constitution in 1934. In a 1951 plebiscite, Uruguayan voters approved a return to the plural executive system, and a new constitutional order reflecting this went into effect the following year. The debate over the form of the executive was not over, however; in 1966 the public voted for yet another constitution, which once again established the single president as the executive power.

Uruguay's economy began to falter during the 1950's. This, combined with the expansion of governmental bureaucracy tied to the country's social welfare programs, led to increasing popular discontent. In 1958 the Blancos won two successive victories at the polls. A candidate from the conservative wing of the Colorado party, Jorge Pacheco Areco, regained the presidency for the traditional ruling party in 1967, but neither the Blancos nor the Colorados were able to deal with Uruguay's deteriorating economy or with its growing political unrest.

Uruguay's politics became increasingly polarized during the 1960's and into the 1970's. The leftist National Liberation Movement (MLN or Tupamaros), formed in 1967, began urban guerrilla activity that included robbery and kidnapping. The Tupamaros, many of whom were young and middle class, embarrassed government officials and were largely successful in eroding the public image of the civilian government. Tupamaro activity generated violence from the military and police, and as the political situation deteriorated in the early seventies, the government granted the military increasing authority.

By 1973 the military was in control of the country, and they dissolved the Congress. The military allowed Pres. Juan María Bordaberry to remain in office until 1976, at which time they installed Aparicio Méndez in the presidency. It was Bordaberry, however, who proposed the dismantling of the political parties in 1976. Uruguayan military rule was brutally repressive, and the armed forces perpetrated many human rights abuses. By some estimates, the Uruguayan military regime had the world's largest number of political prisoners in proportion to the population.

In 1980, Uruguayans rejected in a plebiscite the army's constitution, which would have amounted to continued de facto military control. So began a slow process in which the military tried to bargain with civilian political elites while promising to restore civilian rule. Finally, in 1984, Colorado party candidate Julio María Sanguinetti won a civilian presidential election.

Sanguinetti approved a general amnesty for the leaders of the military regime, but also had success in attracting foreign investment and righting the Uruguayan economy. He was unseated five years later by National party candidate Luis Alberto Lacalle, who further liberalized trade. But his austerity on social problems led voters to overturn some of his reforms by referendum. In 1994 elections, Sanguinetti won back the presidency. In Nov. 1999 the Colorado candidate, Jorge Batlle, pledged to continue the pro-market reforms of Sanguinetti, defeated in a run-off the (left-wing) Broad Front candidate, Tabare Vazquez, who had led in the first round.

▶UZBEKISTAN
Republic of Uzbekistan

• GEOGRAPHY **Location:** central Asia. **Boundaries**: Kazakhstan to N, NE, and NW, Kyrgyzstan to E, Tajikistan to SE, Afghanistan to S, Turkmenistan to SW and W. **Total area**: 172,741 sq. mi. (447,400 sq km). **Coastline**: Aral Sea. **Comparative area**: slightly larger than California. **Land use:** 11% arable land; 1% permanent crops; 88% other. **Major cities**: (1994 est.) Tashkent (capital) 2,100,000; Samarkand 370,000; Namangan 312,000; Andizhan 297,000; Bukhara 228,000.

• PEOPLE **Population:** 25,981,647 (2003 est.). **Nationality:** noun—Uzbekistani(s); adjective—Uzbekistani. **Ethnic groups:** 80% Uzbek, 5.5% Russian, 5% Tajik, 3% Kazakh, 2.5% Karakalpak, 1.5% Tatar. **Languages:** 74.3% Uzbek (official), member of Eastern Turk language group written in Cyrillic script since 1940; 14.2% Russian, 4.4% Tajik, 7.1% other languages. **Religions:** 88% Muslim (mostly Sunnis), 9% Eastern Orthodox, 3% other.

• GOVERNMENT **Type:** republic. **Independence:** Sept. 1, 1991 (from Soviet Union). **Constitution:** Dec. 8, 1992. **National holiday:** Independence Day, Sept. 1. **Heads of Government:** Islam A. Karimov, president (since Dec. 1991); Utkir T. Sultanov, prime minister (since Dec. 1995). **Structure:** executive—president, Cabinet of Ministers; legislative—Supreme Assembly; judicial—Supreme Court.

• ECONOMY **Monetary unit:** som. **Budget:** (1999 est.) ***income:*** $4 bil.; ***expend:*** $4.1 bil. **GDP:** $65 bil., $2,500 per capita (2002 est.). **Chief crops:** cotton, vegetables, fruits, grain; livestock. **Natural resources:** natural gas, coal, petroleum, gold, uranium. **Major industries:** textiles, food processing, machine building, metallurgy, natural gas. **Labor force:** 11.9 mil. (1998). **Exports:** $2.8 bil. (2002); cotton, gold, natural gas, mineral fertilizers, ferrous metals, textiles, food products, autos. **Imports:** $2.5 bil. (2002); machinery and parts, foodstuffs, chemicals, metals. **Major trading partners:** Russia, Switzerland, South Korea.

Uzbekistan, a land of deserts and steppe, lies in the heart of central Asia. Although the territory has been inhabited since prehistoric times, today's Uzbeks are actually descendants of nomadic Mongol, Iranian, and Turkic tribes who mixed with the populations there beginning in the 13th century A.D. The Uzbeks take their name from Khan Uzbek (1282-1342), the ruler responsible for converting the Mongol Golden Horde (the westernmost part of the Mongolian empire) to Islam. In the 18th and 19th centuries, the tribal states known as the Uzbek khanates of Bukhara, Samarkand, and Kokand were formed. Russian conquest of the Uzbek lands began in the 18th century and was completed in 1876 with the conquering of the khanate of Kokand. The Russian empire quickly built the Transcaucasian Railway to connect it with the region's major cities, thus sealing its hold on the area.

As with Kazakhstan, there was a large influx of Russians into Uzbekistan, mainly to its cities. Uzbek resentment of Russian immigrants precipitated a riot in 1898 in Andidzhan and again in 1916, when a decree that drafted central Asians into the Army was promulgated. At the time of the revolution, Soviet power was established in 1917 in the largely Russian city of Tashkent, and after some fighting, the region of Uzbekistan was incorporated into the Russian republic as the Turkestan Autonomous Soviet Socialist Republic (ASSR) in April 1918. In October 1924, the Uzbek Soviet Socialist Republic (SSR) came into being.

During 1924-25, the Soviet government initiated the National Delimitation of the Central Asian Republics to create Uzbek national symbols, to develop a new literary language, and to increase literacy among Uzbeks. It also conducted a brutal campaign against Islam and its believers. The Soviets modernized agriculture and industrialized the territory, although the native Uzbek population for the most part continued to live in rural areas and worked harvesting cotton, while the Russian population worked in industry. During World War II, Uzbekistan's industrial base expanded as many major factories and plants were moved there from the Russian areas to keep them safe from enemy attack.

Mikhail Gorbachev's policy of glasnost, or

openness, did not immediately result in political changes in Uzbekistan. In time, Uzbeks became politically active over many of the same issues that affected their Kazakh neighbors, such as the environmental problems causing the drying up of its rivers, the desiccation of the Aral Sea, and the salinization of the soil. They also demanded that Uzbek (and not Russian) be the official language of Uzbekistan.

In March 1990 the Supreme Soviet elected Islam Karimov as president, and in April 1991 Uzbekistan agreed to sign a new union treaty, which was derailed by the failed August 1991 coup in Moscow. On Aug. 31, 1991, Uzbekistan declared its independence, and in December signed the Alma-Ata Declaration and joined the Commonwealth of Independent States (CIS).

In December 1991 Islam Karimov won the presidential election, and he moved to reduce Uzbekistan's dependence on Russia. In 1994 he signed an economic free-trade agreement with Kazakhstan and Kyrgyzstan and he banned use of the ruble in order to strengthen the som, Uzbekistan's monetary unit. In December 1994 Karimov's supporters (calling themselves the Democratic party) won an overwhelming majority in Uzbekistan's first parliamentary elections. Since then the country has made a slow but steady economic recovery. In Feb. 1999, Uzbekistan refused to renew its collective security treaty with the CIS.

▶VANUATU

Republic of Vanuatu

• **Geography** **Location:** chain of 12 principal and some 60 smaller islands in Pacific Ocean, about 500 mi. (800 km) W of Fiji and 1,100 mi. (2,800 km) E of Australia. Port Vila 17°45'S, 168°18'E. **Boundaries**: surrounded by South Pacific Ocean; nearest neighbor is Santa Cruz Islands to N. **Total area**: 5,699 sq. mi. (14,760 sq km). **Coastline**: 1,571 mi. (2,528 km). **Comparative area**: slightly larger than Connecticut. **Land use:** 3% arable land; 7% permanent crops; 90% other. **Major cities**: (1989 census) Port Vila (capital) 19,311.

• **People** **Population:** 199,414 (2003 est.). **Nationality:** noun—Ni-Vanuatu (sing. and pl.); adjective—Ni-Vanuatu. **Ethnic groups:** 98% indigenous Melanesian, French, Vietnamese, Chinese, other Pacific Islanders. **Languages:** English and French (official); pidgin (known as Bislama or Bichelama). **Religions:** 36.7% Presbyterian, 15% Anglican, 15% Catholic, 7.6% indigenous beliefs, 6.2% Seventh-Day Adventist, 3.8% Church of Christ, 15.7% other.

• **Government** **Type:** republic. **Independence:** July 30, 1980 (from France and U.K.). **Constitution:** July 30, 1980. **National holiday:** Independence Day, July 30. **Heads of Government:** John Bani, president (since Mar. 1999); Nipake Edward Natapei, prime minister (since Apr. 2001). **Structure:** executive—president, prime minister, council of ministers; unicameral legislature; judiciary.

• **Economy** **Monetary unit:** vatu. **Budget:** (1996 est.) ***income:*** $94.4 mil. ***expend.:*** $99.8 mil. **GDP:** $563 mil., $2,900 per capita (2002 est.). **Chief crops:** copra, coconuts, cocoa, coffee, taro, yams, fruits, vegetables; fish, beef. **Natural resources:** manganese, hardwood forests, fish. **Major industries:** food and fish freezing, forestry processing, meat canning. **Labor force:** 65% agriculture, 30% services, 5% industry (2000 est.) **Exports:** $22 mil. (f.o.b., 2001); copra, beef, cocoa, timber, coffee. **Imports:** $93 mil. (f.o.b., 2001); machines and vehicles, food and beverages, fuels. **Major trading partners:** ***exports:*** 32% Japan, 8% Spain,14% Germany; ***imports:*** 52% Japan, 20% Australia, 8% Singapore.

Formerly known as the New Hebrides, Vanuatu is a rugged, volcanic island chain with heavily forested mountains; peaks rise to over 6,000 feet (on Espiritu Santo, the largest island). The people are Melanesians. In 1887 the islands were placed under the administration of an Anglo-French naval commission, becoming a joint Anglo-French colony (condominium) in 1906. The islands escaped Japanese occupation during World War II; they sided with the Free French and were used as bases for Allied campaigns in the Pacific. The New Hebrides were granted independence as Vanuatu on July 30, 1980, with membership in the British Commonwealth. The government is a parliamentary system, complemented by a National Council of Chiefs to decide matters of tradition and customary law.

The economy is based on subsistence agriculture, cattle raising, and fishing. Tourism is developing rapidly, and the sale of long-term tuna-fishing rights, principally to Japan, Australia, and the United States, is an important earner of foreign exchange.

▶VENEZUELA

Republic of Venezuela

• **Geography** **Location:** northern coast of South America. **Boundaries**: Caribbean Sea to N, Guyana to E, Brazil to S, Colombia to W. **Total area**: 352,144 sq. mi. (912,050 sq km). **Coastline**: 1,739 mi. (2,800 km). **Comparative area**: slightly more than twice the size of California. **Land use:** 3% arable land; 1% permanent crops; 96% other. **Major cities**: (1990 est.) Caracas (capital) 3,435,795; Maracaibo 1,400,643; Valencia 1,274,354; Maracay 956,656; Barquisimeto 787,359.

• **People** **Population:** 24,654,694 (2003 est.). **Nationality:** noun—Venezuelan(s); adjective—Venezuelan. **Ethnic groups:** Spanish, Italian, Portuguese, Arab, German, African, indigenous people. **Languages:** Spanish (official), native dialects (spoken by about 200,000 Amerindians in remote interior). **Religions:** 96% nominally Roman Catholic, 2% Protestant.

• **Government** **Type:** federal republic. **Independence:** July 5, 1811 (from Spain). **Constitution:** Dec. 30, 1999. **National holiday:** Independence Day, July 5. **Head of Government:** Hugo Chávez Frías, president (since Feb. 1999). **Structure:** executive (president); bicameral legislature (National Congress—Senate, Chamber of Deputies); judiciary.

• **Economy** **Monetary unit:** bolívar. **Budget:** (2000 est.) ***income:*** $21.5 bil.; ***expend.:*** $27 bil. **GDP:** $132.8 bil., $5,500 per capita (2002 est.). **Chief crops:** corn, sorghum, sugarcane, rice, bananas, vegetables, coffee; beef, pork, milk, eggs; fish. **Natural resources:** crude oil, natural gas, iron ore, gold, bauxite. **Major industries:** petroleum, iron ore mining, construction materials. **Labor force:** 9.9 mil. (1999); 64% services, 23% industry, 13% agriculture; 17% unemployment (2002). **Exports:** $28.6 bil. (f.o.b., 2001 est.); petroleum, bauxite, aluminum, steel, chemicals, agricultural products, basic manufactures. **Imports:** $18.8 bil. (f.o.b., 2001 est.); raw materials, construction materials, machinery and transport equipment. **Major trading partners:** (2000) ***exports:*** 60% U.S., 6% Brazil, 4% Colombia; ***imports:*** 36% U.S., 7% Colombia, 5% Brazil.

At the time of European contact in the early

16th century, coastal Venezuela was home to nearly 50,000 semisedentary Indians. Although the region was "discovered" by Christopher Columbus in 1498, European settlement of the area was slow in comparison with the neighboring region of New Granada. The Spaniards explored and exploited Venezuela in the 1520's, searching for gold and pearls.

Early attempts at agriculture by the Spaniards failed until they discovered that the area around Caracas (founded in 1567) could sustain the production of both wheat and cocoa. African slave labor was an important part of the economic structure, and as markets for cocoa expanded, Caracas grew in importance. Venezuela became a captaincy general (an administrative region below the level of viceroyalty) with an audiencia (high court) established at Caracas in 1777-78.

As early as 1797, Venezuelan society was in rebellion against the Spanish empire. A major hindrance to the revolutionary leadership of Simón Bolívar was the need to accommodate both conservative landowners and the pardos, lower class citizens of mixed African and European ancestry.

The wars of independence were particularly destructive in Venezuela, but in 1821 the region achieved independence and became part of the federation of Gran Colombia, which also included New Granada and Ecuador. By 1830 Gran Colombia was in a state of political collapse, and Venezuela became an independent republic.

The military caudillo (leader) José Antonio Páez controlled the country for three decades. With the demise of Páez and his conservative allies in the 1860's, the forces of liberalism under Antonio Guzmán Blanco took over. The Guzmán Blanco era ended during a brief civil war in 1889, won by Gen. Cipriano Castro, who proceeded to establish his own rule. In 1908 Gen. Juan Vicente Gómez occupied the presidency, and he controlled the politics of Venezuela until his death in 1935.

The shift from dictatorship to democracy began with the Generation of 28, a student movement that organized urban workers and peasants into a viable political opposition. The Generation of 28 later became the modern Democratic Action party. In 1945 a group of young military officers overthrew the conservative dictatorship and supported the Democratic Action group in writing a new democratic constitution. Democratic Action won the elections of 1947, but military elements overthrew the new government the following year. The coup brought Col. Marcos Pérez Jiménez to power until his ouster in 1958.

The election of Democratic Action candidate Romulo Betancourt as president marked the beginning of multiparty democratic politics in Venezuela. The stability of the system owed much to political possibilities provided by the country's petroleum revenues. Venezuela nationalized foreign-owned oil and iron firms in 1975 and 1976, but dependence on petroleum revenues still precipitated economic and political problems for the country in the 1980's. The downturn of the global oil market caused Venezuela's economic base to shrink, and the country's massive foreign debt hindered the expansion of populist political strategies.

The Christian Democrats defeated Democratic Action in 1968 and again in 1978. Pres. Luis Herrera Campíns's administration (1979-84) took the country in a more conservative direction but Democratic Action regained the presidency in 1983 under Jaime Lusinchi.

Venezuela's huge foreign debt in the 1980's led to tight economic controls and a reduction in social spending. The administration of Pres. Carlos Andrés Perez, elected in 1989, began with antigovernment riots in which hundreds died. In Feb. 1992, Latin America's oldest civilian government thwarted an attempted coup by soldiers angered over connections between high-ranking officers and drug traffickers; a second coup in November also failed. But in early 1993, Pres. Perez was suspended after the Senate ordered impeachment proceedings against him on charges he embezzled $17 million from the government; the Congress overwhelmingly elected Sen. Ramon Jose Valasquez Mujica to serve as interim president.

In early 1994 Rafael Caldera became president and immediately faced severe economic problems as the currency depreciated by more than 80 percent. Caldera imposed price and currency controls and suspended several constitutional guarantees. In July 1995, he restored those rights, except along Venezuela's borders with Colombia and Brazil, where crime and economic crises were most severe. Violent anti-government demonstrations continued into 1996 but Caldera persisted in austerity plans that resulted in a $1.4 bil. loan from I.M.F.. By early 1997 inflation seemed to be in check and the economy stabilizing although the continuing fall in worldwide oil prices added more pressure for budget cuts. By 1998 Venezuela's economy was caught in the worldwide financial crisis and spinning toward chaos as the presidential election approached.

In the December elections, the two old parties (Christian Democrats and Democratic Action) which had dominated for 40 years all but disappeared. The Patriotic Pole Coalition candidate, Hugo Chavez Frias (who had led the unsuccessful coup in 1992 against Perez) easily triumphed over Henrique Salas Romer. Two days later stock shares rose 22 percent despite Chavez' calls for redistribution of wealth, privatization of the government oil company and abolition of Congress. Chavez called for a Constitutional Assembly to rewrite the constitution (88 percent voted their approval in April 1999). In elections for the Assembly Chavez's supporters won all but seven of 128 seats. In December the Assembly adopted a new constitution (Venezuela's 26th) whose major features are a unicameral National Assembly and a six-year renewable presidential term.

Elections in Aug. 2000 confirmed Chavez for a new term and "Chavista" dominance of the Assembly. Chavez demanded OPEC cut production and travelled to major oil producers (including Iraq) to make his point. He agreed to sell oil to Castro's Cuba at bargain prices. In Nov. the new National Assembly gave him authority to rule by decree in 37 legislative areas.

But Chavez's excesses (such as decreeing 49 new laws in one day) provoked resistance by both business and labor, both of whom backed an army coup attempt on April 12, 2002. Within 48 hours, however, Chavez was back, the coup undercut by jealousy and divisions in the armed forces. A general strike, called in Oct. by business and labor groups, became a crisis for the regime when 30,000 oil workers joined. The O.A.S. brokered an agreement that both sides would disarm civilian supporters and recognize a constitutional right to a recall referendum. In Sept. 2003 the National Electoral Council rejected the petition signed by 3.2 million people demanding a recall referendum. The opposition, backed by the U.S., vowed to try again.

▶VIETNAM

Socialist Republic of Viet Nam

• **Geography** **Location:** Southeast Asia. **Boundaries**: China to N, Gulf of Tonkin to NE, South China Sea to E, Laos and Cambodia to W. **Total area**: 127,243 sq. mi. (329,560 sq km). **Coastline**: 2,140 mi. (3,444 km) excluding islands. **Comparative area**: slightly larger than New Mexico. **Land use:** 17% arable land; 5% permanent crops; 78% other. **Major cities**: (1989) Hanoi (capital) 1,088,862; Ho Chi Minh City (formerly Saigon) 3,169,135; Haiphong 456,049; Da Nang 370,670; Long Xuyen 217,171.

• **People** **Population:** 80,624,716 (2003 est.). **Nationality:** noun—Vietnamese (sing., pl.); adjective—Vietnamese. **Ethnic groups:** 85-90% Vietnamese, 3% Chinese; ethnic minorities include Muong, Thai, Meo, Khmer, Man, Cham. **Languages:** Vietnamese (official); French, Chinese, English, Khmer, ethnic langs. (Mon-Khmer and Malayo-Polynesian). **Religions:** Buddhist, Taoist, Roman Catholic, indigenous beliefs, Islam, Protestant, Cao Dai, Hoa Hao.

• **Government** **Type:** Communist state. **Independence:** Sept. 2, 1945 (from France). **Constitution:** Apr. 15, 1992. **National holiday:** Independence Day, Sept. 2. **Heads of Government:** Tran Duc Luong, president, (since Sept. 1997); Phan Van Khai, prime minister (since Sept. 1997). **Structure:** executive—president, prime minister, cabinet; unicameral legislature; judiciary—elected by legislature.

• **Economy** **Monetary unit:** new dong. **Budget:** (1999 est.) ***income:*** $5.3 bil.; ***expend.:*** $5.6 bil. **GDP:** $183 bil., $2,250 per capita (2002 est.). **Chief crops:** paddy rice, corn, potatoes, rubber, soybeans, coffee, tea, bananas; poultry, pigs; fish. **Natural resources:** phosphates, coal, manganese, bauxite, chromate. **Major industries:** food processing, textiles, machine building. **Labor force:** 38.2 mil. (1998 est.); 63% agriculture, 37% industry and services, 25% unemployment (1995 est.). **Exports:** $16.5 bil. (f.o.b., 2002 est.); crude oil, marine products, rice, coffee, rubber, tea, garments, shoes. **Imports:** $16.8 bil. (f.o.b., 2002 est.); machinery and equipment, petroleum products, fertilizer, steel products, raw cotton, grain, cement, motorcycles. **Major trading partners:** ***exports:*** Japan, U.S., Australia; ***imports:*** Singapore, South Korea, Japan.

The southward expansion of the Chinese empire in the first millennium B.C. drove the Vietnamese peoples southward into northern Vietnam (Tonkin). The area came under direct Chinese rule in 111 B.C. Chinese rule endured, with some interruptions, until A.D. 948; thereafter, Vietnam was independent under strong Chinese influence.

The Hindu-Buddhist kingdom of Annam, in central Vietnam, gradually increased in size and power at the expense of Tonkin and the Khmer empire and Champa, to the west and south. In 1558 the kingdom of Annam split, with independent courts established at Hanoi, controlling Tonkin and the Red River valley, and Hue, in central Vietnam. A remnant of the old Champa state remained independent in the Mekong delta in the south. In 1802 the monarchy was reunited, with the court at Hue controlling all of Vietnam and exercising hegemony over Cambodia.

European penetration of the region began in the 16th century; by the early 19th century, France was the dominant foreign power in Indochina. Efforts to establish French military control began in 1858-59 with the establishment of a colony in Cochin China, in southern Vietnam. Campaigns in the Red River valley in 1873 and 1882 were complicated by Chinese intervention and the determined resistance of the Vietnamese court. In 1884 separate protectorates were established in Tonkin and Annam; in 1887 those, along with Cochin China and Cambodia, were combined into the Union of Indochina under French colonial rule. Rubber plantations were established, and rice and timber exports were under French control. A nationalist rebellion under Phan Boi Chau was suppressed in the early 20th century.

Nationalist resistance to French colonialism continued, resulting in the creation in 1939 of the Vietminh, or Independence League. In 1940 Japanese troops occupied French Indochina, with the collaboration of colonial administrators loyal to the Vichy regime. The Vietminh spearheaded anti-Japanese guerrilla resistance and in 1945 forced the abdication of King Bao Dai, head of a pro-Japanese puppet state. In 1945 France reoccupied Indochina; in 1946 the leader of the Vietminh, Ho Chi Minh, became president of a separatist government at Hanoi. France ceded local autonomy to Tonkin and Annam but sought to retain Cochin China as a colony. Fighting between the French and the Vietminh resumed. On July 1, 1949, the French reinstalled Bao Dai as king of Vietnam, and in February 1950 recognized the independence of Vietnam within the French Union. Ho Chi Minh's republican government also claimed control of all of Vietnam.

Fighting between the two rivals culminated in the French defeat at Dienbienphu on May 7, 1954. An armistice was concluded according to which the country was partitioned at a demilitarized zone at latitude 17° north, the northern part going to the Communist-controlled Vietminh government, the southern to Bao Dai. Nearly one million refugees, including many ethnic Chinese, fled from the north to the south. An international conference in Geneva agreed that elections would be held throughout Vietnam in 1956. In June 1954 Ngo Dinh Diem became premier of South Vietnam; full sovereignty in the south was transferred by France to the Vietnamese government in December 1954. In October 1955 Diem held elections in the south that resulted in the dismissal of Bao Dai as king and the proclamation of an independent Republic of Vietnam.

The scheduled elections of 1956 were never held. French troops withdrew from South Vietnam in that year. Fighting continued in the south, as the Vietminh-backed National Liberation Front (Vietcong) sought to overthrow the Diem government. On Dec. 31, 1959, the Democratic Republic of Vietnam in the north adopted a new constitution calling for the reunification of the country; northern aid to the Vietcong increased significantly, as did American aid to the south. After 1962 American military advisers increased in number and combat exposure.

In 1963 widespread demonstrations, under Buddhist leadership, led to a coup on Nov. 1-2 in which Diem was deposed and assassinated. A series of short-lived military regimes followed until Sept. 1967, when Nguyen Van Thieu was elected president. U.S. air strikes against North Vietnam began in 1964. In the same year, the flow of troops and supplies from north to south increased. American combat troops entered the war in 1965. Despite U.S.-South Vietnamese superiority in arms and troops, and total control of the air, Vietcong control over the countryside increased. Both Operation Phoenix, in which antigovernment rural leaders were assassinated, and the establishment of fortified strategic hamlets to control the rural population, failed to reverse the tide.

The combined Vietcong-North Vietnamese Tet Offensive in early 1968 resulted in serious losses for South Vietnamese and American forces. The war spread to Laos and to Cambodia, the latter bombed in 1969. American air strikes in North Vietnam were stepped up, and U.S. troop strength reached a maximum of 543,000 in 1969. In July 1969 a series of U.S. troop withdrawals began, and secret talks were initiated in search of a negotiated settlement of the war. Following heavy U.S. bombardment of the north in 1972, a cease-fire agreement was signed in Paris by South Vietnam, North Vietnam, the Vietcong, and the United States on Jan. 27, 1973. It was never implemented, but the American withdrawal continued. In early 1975 South Vietnamese forces collapsed in the face of a series of North Vietnamese-Vietcong offensives. Remaining U.S. personnel were evacuated, and Saigon fell on Apr. 30, 1975. Hundreds of thousands of refugees ("boat people") fled the country over the next decade.

Following the fall of Saigon, the country was occupied by northern troops and administrators. Businesses were nationalized, agriculture collectivized, and tens of thousands of people sent to labor camps for "reeducation." A unified National Assembly met in 1976, and the country was officially reunified on July 2, 1976, under the existing government of the north. Saigon was renamed Ho Chi Minh City. A Soviet naval base was established at the former U.S. base at Cam Ranh Bay.

In 1978 Vietnamese troops occupied Cambodia ousting the government of Pol Pot and installing Heng Samrin as premier. In February 1979 China launched an unsuccessful attack over its border with Vietnam to display displeasure with the invasion of Cambodia and with the treatment of ethnic Chinese in Vietnam. In 1988 Vietnam pledged to withdraw its troops from Cambodia and completed the withdrawal in September 1989.

Vietnam's communist government ruled through the party's powerful Central Committee; no strong personalities emerged to replace the leaders of the wartime generation. The economy was functioning only at a basic level, with the infrastructure in disrepair and agriculture hampered by excessive collectivization. The collapse of the Soviet Union brought about a drastic reduction of the Soviet aid that had kept the Vietnamese economy afloat. Facing economic ruin, Vietnam's leadership eventually turned a blind eye to individual private enterprise. By 1992 the government was encouraging foreign investment.

Resumption of contacts with the U.S. had been precluded by American insistence that Vietnam account more fully for American prisoners of war and troops missing in action. But high-level talks on the normalization of relations and the Cambodian question opened in 1990, and the success of those negotiations helped to open diplomatic channels between Vietnam and the U.S.

In 1994, Pres. Clinton, satisfied with Vietnam's efforts to account for POWs and MIAs, ended the 19-year U.S. trade embargo against Vietnam; the following day, American firms were operating in Ho Chi Minh City. In July 1995, full diplomatic relations were established.

In October 1995, Vietnam's National Assembly adopted its first-ever national civil code under the Communist government. The document spelled out rights to land, personal property, inheritances, and raising capital. Close to 90 percent of the Assembly members voted in favor of the code, which went into effect in July 1996.

In recent years the Government has encouraged many Western companies to build factories and open businesses but poverty and the Asian financial crisis slowed progress. In July 2000 the U.S. and Vietnam signed a far-reaching trade agreement. In April 2001, the Central Committee of the Communist Party appointed a new Secretary General, Nong Duc Manh, with the aim of modernizing the economy (especially the industrial side) and ending corruption. By rumor, Nong is an illegitimate son of Ho Chi Minh. In Dec. 2001 Vietnam took two steps toward its goal of joining the W.T.O.: a trade agreement with the U.S. and the granting to private investors equal access to bank credit with the public sector. The the Communists had no intention of easing their political control, however, was made clear by the May 2002 "elections" to the National Assembly in which the Communists carried 447 of 498 seats.

▶WESTERN SAMOA

see "Samoa"

▶YEMEN

Republic of Yemen

• **GEOGRAPHY** **Location:** southern shore of Arabian peninsula and southwest corner of Arabian peninsula. **Boundaries**: Saudi Arabia to N, Oman to E, Gulf of Aden to S, Red Sea to W. **Total area**: 203,850 sq. mi. (527,970 sq km). **Coastline**: 1,184 mi. (1,906 km). **Comparative area:** slightly larger than twice the size of Wyoming. **Land use:** 3% arable land; negl. % permanent crops; 97% other. **Major cities**: (1995 est.) Sana'a (capital) 972,000; Aden 562,000; Hodeida 155,110; Mukalla 154,360; Taiz 178,043.

• **PEOPLE** **Population:** 19,349,881 (2003 est.). **Nationality:** noun—Yemini(s); adjective—Yemeni. **Ethnic groups:** predominantly Arab; Afro-Arab concentrations in western coastal locations; South Asians in southern regions; small European communities in major metropolitan areas. **Languages:** Arabic. **Religions:** Muslim including Shaf'i (Sunni) and Zaydi (Shia), small numbers of Jewish, Christian, and Hindu.

• **GOVERNMENT** **Type:** republic. **Independence:** May 22, 1990 (merger of North and South Yemen). **Constitution:** May 16, 1991: amended Sept. 29, 1994 and Feb. 2001. **National holiday:** Proclamation of the Republic, May 22. **Heads of Government:** Ali Abdullah Saleh, president (since May 1994); Abdulqader Bajammal, prime minister (since Apr. 2001). **Structure:** executive—president and cabinet; unicameral legislature; judicial—Supreme Court and lesser courts.

• **ECONOMY** **Monetary unit:** Yemeni rial. **Budget:** (2001 est.) ***income:*** $3 bil.; ***expend:*** $3.1 bil. **GDP:** $15.7 bil., $840 per capita (2002 est.). **Chief crops:** grain, fruits, vegetables, qat, coffee, cotton; dairy products, poultry, meat; fish. **Natural resources:** petroleum, fish, rocksalt, marble, small deposits of coal. **Major industries:** crude oil, petroleum refining, cotton textiles and leather goods, food processing, handicrafts, aluminum products, cement. **Labor force:** mostly agriculture and herding; also services, construction, industry, commerce. **Exports:** $3.4 bil. (f.o.b., 2002 est.);

crude oil, cotton, coffee, dried and salted fish. **Imports:** $2.9 bil., (f.o.b., 2002 est.); food and live animals, machinery and equipment, manufactured goods. **Major trading partners:** ***exports:*** 19% India, 17% Thailand, 12% China; ***imports:*** 11% Saudi Arabia, 8% UAE, 8% China.

Yemen—in ancient times Sheba or Saba—is strategically located in the southwestern corner of the Arabian peninsula, near the southern end of the Red Sea. In biblical times and for many centuries thereafter, Yemen dominated the caravan trade in spices, gold, and other luxury goods from India and Africa to the Middle East.

The Islamic unification of Arabia in 628 resulted in the incorporation of Yemen into Arabia as a whole, but many local uprisings broke out over the course of the following three centuries. In the 10th century, control passed to a line of Yemeni kings who were simultaneously imams of the Zaidi sect of Islam; the Zaidi imams ruled until 1962.

Aden was the most important port of the ancient kingdom of Sheba and retained that status under the Zaidi imams of Yemen. Portuguese activity around Aden began in the 15th century; from the mid-16th century, control of the port was disputed by the Portuguese, the Yemeni kings, the Ottoman Turks, and, later, the British.

In 1839, Aden was made a British Crown Colony; the Hadramaut region of southern Arabia, north and east of Aden, became the British Protectorate of Aden. The colony and protectorate were both administered as part of British India.

Yemen came under the control of the Ottoman Empire from the mid-16th to the mid-17th centuries, and again from 1849 to 1918. The Turks were expelled at the end of World War I, and Yemen became an independent kingdom in 1918. The kingdom's independence was threatened by a Saudi invasion in 1934 and by a 1954 dispute with Great Britain over the status of Aden, which was the key to British military power in the western Indian Ocean and Persian Gulf after India's independence in 1947.

Imam Ahmed came to the throne of Yemen in 1948, following the assassination of his predecessor. Most of Yemen's large Jewish population was evacuated to Israel in 1949-50. A palace coup against the imam in 1955 failed, but after his death in 1962, his successor was quickly ousted and the country was proclaimed the Yemen Arab Republic (North Yemen) under the leadership of Brig. Gen. Abdullah al-Salal.

A struggle for independence began in Aden and the protectorate in 1963, with two rival groups competing for power. The National Liberation Front (NLF) gained the upper hand over the Egyptian-backed Front for the Liberation of Occupied South Yemen, as both groups waged guerrilla war against the British. British forces withdrew in 1967, and South Yemen became independent. The nation's territory included Socotra and adjacent islands off the Horn of Africa, which had been British possessions since 1876.

In 1969 a leftist faction of the NLF seized power, nationalized key industries, and instituted a socialist regime. In the mid-1970's, South Yemeni troops aided leftist guerrillas in Oman, and fought in Ethiopia against Eritrean rebels. Subsequently Pres. Salem Robaye Ali took a more moderate stance and improved relations with Oman and Saudi Arabia. He was overthrown in a coup in June 1978 and executed. The succeeding government was overthrown on Jan. 13, 1986; on Feb. 8, Hasin Said Numan became prime minister.

In North Yemen, civil war between royalist and republican factions lasted until April 1970, when a coalition republican government was formed with the aid of Saudi mediation. Col. Ibrahim al-Hamidi came to power in a military coup in 1974; he was assassinated in 1977. Pres. Ali Abdullah Saleh assumed office in 1978, after the assassination of Pres. al-Gashmi.

Border skirmishes between North Yemen and South Yemen broke out during 1972-73. After several years of uneasy peace, South Yemen launched a full-scale war against the north on Feb. 24, 1979. Arab League pressure quickly led to a truce. Relations improved during the 1980's and North Yemen and South Yemen merged as the Republic of Yemen on May 22, 1990. Ali Abdullah Saleh, president of North Yemen, became the new country's president. San'a was proclaimed the capital of the United Yemen, though Aden remained its most important economic center.

The Gulf War forced the repatriation of tens of thousands of Yemeni workers from Kuwait and other Gulf states; later Saudi Arabia expelled 850,000 more to express its displeasure with Yemen's unenthusiastic stance toward the Gulf War. These repatriations deprived Yemen of a most important source of foreign exchange, and severely damaged the economy.

Yemen held its first general election since unification on Apr. 27, 1993, and a coalition government was formed. In Feb. 1994, fighting began and a full-scale civil war broke out in May. But in July the capture of Aden by government troops ended the conflict and Pres. Saleh has ruled in relative peace since. The first direct presidential electrion was held in Sept. 1999 but the Socialist Party was not allowed to field a candidate so Saleh won easily.

On Oct. 10, 2000, over 50,000 protested in Aden against U.S. support for Israel; two days later, the U.S. destroyer Cole, refueling in Aden, was attacked, leaving 17 dead and 39 wounded. The Saleh government permitted F.B.I. attendance at the questioning of witnesses; but the F.B.I. (and Navy) investigators became a new object of attack, by the terrorist "Islamic Army of Aden," in June. However, the F.B.I.'s response, attempts to arm its investigators with rifles and heavy weapons, provoked the U.S. ambassador's banning the F.B.I. team leader from Yemen.

▶YUGOSLAVIA (SEE SERBIA AND MONTENEGRO)

▶ZAIRE (SEE CONGO, DEMOCRATIC REPUBLIC)

▶ZAMBIA

Republic of Zambia

• **Geography** **Location:** landlocked country in southern central Africa. **Boundaries**: Zaire to N, Tanzania to NE, Malawi to E, Mozambique to SE, Zimbabwe to S, Namibia to SW, Angola to W. **Total area**: 290,583 sq. mi. (752,610 sq km). **Coastline**: none. **Comparative area**: slightly larger than Texas. **Land use:** 7% arable land; negl. % permanent crops; 93% other. **Major cities**: (1990 census) Lusaka (capital) 982,362; Kitwe 338,207; Ndola 376,311; Kabwe 166,519.

• **People** **Population:** 10,307,333 (2003 est.). **Nationality:** noun—Zambian(s); adjective—Zambian. **Ethnic groups:** 98.7% African, 1.1%

European, 0.2% other. **Languages:** English (official), major vernaculars—Bemba, Kaonda, Lozi, Lunda, Luvale, Nyanja, Tonga, and about 70 indigenous languages. **Religions:** 50-75% Christian, 24-49% Muslim and Hindu, 1% indigenous beliefs.
• **GOVERNMENT** **Type:** republic. **Independence:** Oct. 24, 1964 (from U.K.). **Constitution:** Aug. 2, 1991. **National holiday:** Independence Day, Oct. 24. **Heads of Government:** Levy Patrick Mwanawasa, president (since Jan. 2002). **Structure:** executive—modified presidential system; legislative—unicameral National Assembly; judiciary.
• **ECONOMY** **Monetary unit:** kwacha. **Budget:** (2001 est.) ***income:*** $1.2 bil.; ***expend.:*** $1.25 bil. **GDP:** $8.9 bil., $890 per capita (2002 est.). **Chief crops:** corn, sorghum, rice, peanuts, sunflower seed, tobacco, cotton, sugarcane, cassava; cattle, goats, pigs, poultry, beef, pork, milk, eggs, hides. **Natural resources:** copper, cobalt, zinc, lead, coal. **Major industries:** copper mining and processing, foodstuffs, construction. **Labor force:** 4.3 mil.; 85% agriculture, 9% services, 6% industry. **Exports:** $709 mil. (f.o.b., 2001 est.); copper, cobalt, zinc, lead, tobacco. **Imports:** $1.123 bil. (f.o.b., 2001 est.); machinery, transport equipment, foodstuffs, fuels, petroleum products, electricity. **Major trading partners:** South Africa, Switzerland, Zimbabwe.

Bantu peoples—including Luba, Lunda, Ngoni, and others—moved into what is now Zambia between the 15th and the 19th centuries, displacing or absorbing aboriginal populations. Occasional Portuguese explorers from Angola and Mozambique entered the region, and Angolan slave-raiders were active in the late 18th and early 19th centuries, but serious European influence did not begin until the mid-19th century. At that time British missionaries and merchants arrived, most notably David Livingstone and Cecil Rhodes.

Local rulers granted mineral concessions to Rhodes in both Northern and Southern Rhodesia (now Zambia and Zimbabwe). Rhodesia was declared a British sphere of influence in 1888; a British protectorate was established in 1891 and enlarged in 1894-95. The borders of Northern Rhodesia were established in 1911. The country was administered by the British South Africa Co. until 1924, when direct colonial rule began. Large numbers of British settlers arrived and developed farms and ranches and mined the region's substantial copper deposits. A railroad was built linking Northern Rhodesia with Elizabethville in the Belgian Congo (now Lubumbashi, Zaire).

In 1953 Northern and Southern Rhodesia (Zimbabwe) were joined with Nyasaland (now Malawi) to form the Federation of Rhodesia and Nyasaland. The country entered a period of unrest with native peoples demanding greater participation in government, while white settlers clung to their privileged positions.

As the result of an election in 1962, the federation was dissolved in 1963. A National Assembly was created on the basis of a broader, multiracial electorate. Northern Rhodesia became independent as the Republic of Zambia on Oct. 24, 1964. Relations between Zambia and white-ruled Rhodesia (formerly Southern Rhodesia) became strained in 1965 in a dispute over ownership and administration of the railway that spanned both countries. A new constitution was promulgated in 1973, creating a stronger presidency and a unicameral legislature; the United National Independence party was made the sole legal political party. Opposition parties were allowed to form again starting in December 1990.

Pres. Kenneth Kaunda, in office after Zambia's independence, led a moderate government that won the support of both whites and blacks. Zambia's economy did not fare well as the price of copper, the nation's main earner of foreign exchange, declined around the world causing massive foreign debt and labor unrest. The I.M.F. demanded reforms as a condition for future aid, and in 1987 Pres. Kaunda announced a program of economic restructuring. In 1990 his government survived an attempted coup precipitated by a doubling in the price of the staple food, maize meal.

At the end of 1991, Kaunda was defeated by Frederick Chiluba, head of the new Labor party. Chiluba's economic reforms helped Zambia repay more than $1.2 billion in outstanding debt, prompting the I.M.F. to restore its eligibility for international loans. But political problems resurfaced when Chiluba's government found a way to block Kaunda from winning in the 1996 presidential election. Kaunda was shot and wounded by a sniper in Aug. 1997 as he continued to criticize the government. In Oct. 1997 a failed coup attempt by junior army officers was blamed on Kaunda who was arrested in Dec. and put on trial in Jan. He was freed in June and all charges dropped probably on condition that he leave politics for good. In March 1999 Zambia's High Court declared him not a citizen. Pres. Chiluba honored his pledge not to run for re-election and the Dec. 2001 election was won by Levy Mwanawasa. The new president began a serious investigation into official corruption and Parliament (June 16, 2002) stripped Chiluba of his immunity and he was arrested in Feb. 2003 on charges of stealing millions of dollars.

▶ZIMBABWE

Republic of Zimbabwe

• **GEOGRAPHY** **Location:** landlocked country in southern Africa. **Boundaries**: Zambia to NW, Mozambique to E, South Africa to S, Botswana to SW. **Total area**: 150,803 sq. mi. (390,580 sq km). **Coastline**: none. **Comparative area**: slightly larger than Montana. **Land use:** 8% arable land; negl. % permanent crops; 91% other. **Major cities**: (1992) Harare (capital) 1,184,169; Bulawayo 620,936; Chitungwiza 274,035; Mutare 131,808; Gweru 124,735.
• **PEOPLE** **Population:** 12,576,742 (2003 est.). **Nationality:** noun—Zimbabwean(s); adjective—Zimbabwean. **Ethnic groups:** 98% African (82% Shona, 14% Ndebele, 2% other), 1% white, 1% mixed and Asian. **Languages:** English (official), Shona, Sindebele. **Religions:** 50% syncretic (part Christian, part indigenous beliefs), 25% Christian, 24% indigenous beliefs, 1% Muslim.
• **GOVERNMENT** **Type:** parliamentary democracy. **Independence:** Apr. 18, 1980 (from U.K.). **Constitution:** Dec. 21, 1979. **National holiday:** Independence Day, Apr. 18. **Head of Government:** Robert Gabriel Mugabe, president (since Dec. 1987). **Structure:** executive—cabinet led by president; unicameral legislature—120 of 150 members are popularly elected, others appointed; judiciary.
• **ECONOMY** **Monetary unit:** Zimbabwean dollar. **Budget:** (2000 est.) ***income:*** $2.5 bil.; ***expend.:*** $2.6 bil. **GDP:** $27 bil., $2,400 per capita (2002 est.). **Chief crops:** tobacco, corn, tea, sugarcane, cotton, wheat, coffee, peanuts; cattle, sheep, goats, pigs.

Natural resources: coal, chromium ore, asbestos, gold, nickel. **Major industries:** mining, steel, clothing and footwear. **Labor force:** 5.8 mil. (2000 est.). **Exports:** $1.57 bil. (f.o.b., 2001 est.); 23% tobacco, 14% gold, ferroalloys, cotton. **Imports:** $1.739 bil. (f.o.b., 2001 est.); 39% machinery and transport equipment, 18% manufactures, 15% chemicals, 10% fuels. **Major trading partners:** ***exports:*** 44% E.U., 12% South Africa,7% Japan; ***imports:*** 44% South Africa, 11% E.U., 6% U.S.

Massive stone structures at Great Zimbabwe give evidence of a sizable urban society that flourished from the ninth to the 13th centuries and dominated Iron Age trade in southeastern Africa. Bantu peoples migrated into the region beginning in the 15th century; the Mashona dominated until the early 19th century, when they were displaced by the Matebele.

Portuguese slave traders from Mozambique were active in Zimbabwe from the 16th to the mid-19th centuries. Mineral concessions were granted to Cecil Rhodes by local rulers in the late 19th century, and the region became a British protectorate in 1888. Salisbury (now Harare) was founded in 1890, and the territory comprising Zimbabwe and Zambia was named Rhodesia in 1895. Rhodesia was governed by the British South Africa Co. until 1923, when it was partitioned into Northern and Southern Rhodesia. Northern Rhodesia became a British colony; Southern Rhodesia, rejecting union with South Africa, became a self-governing (and whiteruled) state within the British Empire.

Southern Rhodesia had been heavily settled by whites from Great Britain, South Africa, and elsewhere, who developed extensive farms and ranches, forest products industries, and rich mines. The country prospered but with little native participation in government. In 1953 Northern Rhodesia, Southern Rhodesia, and Nyasaland were joined in the Federation of Rhodesia and Nyasaland. Increasing agitation for black participation in government, especially in the north and in Nyasaland, led to the dissolution of the federation in 1963; Northern Rhodesia subsequently became independent as Zambia, Nyasaland as Malawi. In 1961 Southern Rhodesia adopted a constitution that guaranteed the continuation of white rule. White resistance to black political demands led to the rise of the Rhodesian Front party, whose leader, Ian D. Smith, became prime minister of Rhodesia (formerly Southern Rhodesia). After British-led negotiations for a biracial political compromise broke down, the Smith government on Nov. 11, 1965, issued a unilateral declaration of independence, which was declared illegal and invalid by the British government. The U.N. condemned the Smith government and imposed economic sanctions,and in May 1968 voted to impose a trade embargo on Rhodesia.

In 1970 a new constitution effectively barred black participation in national politics. By 1974 mounting pressure from other African countries led the Smith government to enter into serious negotiations. Guerrilla warfare pitting black nationalist groups against white settlers and mercenaries raged sporadically throughout the country, and many white settlers emigrated. A 1977 British-American proposal for majority rule provided the basis for a settlement. An "internal settlement" was announced in April 1978 by Smith and three major nationalist leaders: Bishop Abel Muzorewa, leader of the United African National Congress, the Rev. Ndabaningi Sithole, former leader of the Zimbabwe African National Union (ZANU), and Chief Jeremiah Chirau. The settlement was rejected by the Patriotic Front that united ZANU (now led by Robert Mugabe) and Joshua Nkomo's Zimbabwe African People's Union (ZAPU).

Elections were held in April 1979 and Bishop Muzorewa assumed office on June 1 as prime minister of "Zimbabwe-Rhodesia," but the Patriotic Front continued to oppose the government. On Dec. 10 the "Zimbabwe-Rhodesia" Parliament dissolved itself, and the country reverted briefly to British colonial rule. On Dec. 21 all parties agreed to a cease-fire and to a period of transitional British rule leading to independence.

Elections held in 1980 resulted in a clear majority for Mugabe's ZANU party. Zimbabwe became independent, with Mugabe as prime minister, on April 18. As Mugabe embarked on an ambitious program of national reconstruction, Nkomo became leader of the opposition. Guerrillas linked to ZAPU, with Nkomo's tacit leadership and with alleged support from South Africa, continued to engage in sporadic warfare against Mugabe's government, and banditry disrupted the countryside.

The elections of 1985 increased ZANU's majority in Parliament. In 1987 the constitution was amended to strengthen the presidency and to end the separate role of blacks and whites in government; new elections were held for black members of Parliament to fill seats formerly reserved for whites. Guerrillas renewed attacks on white-owned farms.

In Dec. 1987 Mugabe and Nkomo agreed to merge ZANU and ZAPU (ZANU-PF), creating a de facto one-party state under Mugabe. A presidential election was scheduled for 1996, but in 1995, the Rev. Ndonga Sithole, leader of the opposition Zimbabwe African National Union, was arrested and charged with plotting to kill Mugabe.

Amidst a fuel crisis, 60 percent inflation and 50 percent unemployment, Zimbabwe voters in Feb. 2000 rejected a new constitution granting Mugabe 12 more years and power to seize white farmlands without compensation. But, with government approval, squatters began seizing white farms and preventing the tobacco harvest (30 percent of Zimbabwe's export earnings). June elections gave 57 of 120 seats contested to the opposition, sufficient to block any plan for a new constitution. But throughout 2001 Mugabe continued his plan to seize white-owned farms and began to arrest his political opponents. Court-packing, press controls, prohibition of assemblages, banning of non-governmental election-monitors, arrests of opponents—all preceded March 2002 presidential elections in which Mugabe claimed 1.7 million votes to 1.3 million for his principal opponent, Morgan Tsuangirai. Torture and rape by the army drove tens of thousands of Tsuangirai's supporters to flight. Mugabe seized further white farms amidst the worst famine in 60 years. A wave of arrests - over 300 members of opposition Movement for Democratic Change, including Tsuangirai, six members of Parliament, and the mayors of Zimbabwe's two largest cities - followed a weak attempt at a general strike in June 2003.

Selected Territories Of The World

NON-SELF-GOVERNING STATES

The community of nations has long recognized the existence of territories that do not have the status of independent states and that are subordinate in some degree to another power. The United Nations refers to these as "non-self-governing territories." Except for mandates and trusteeships specified by the League of Nations and the U.N., the relationships between more and less powerful states have tended to evolve outside any rigid legal framework, and none of the following terms has an absolutely fixed meaning.

Colonies are dependent possessions whose inhabitants are not constitutionally under the dominant state's system of government but whose inhabitants are nationals of that state.

Commonwealths are autonomous states equal in status, united in their allegiance to a central power but not subordinate either to it or to one another in internal or external affairs.

Dependencies are states, provinces, or other places subject to the control of another power of which they do not form an integral part. The best known is Hong Kong, which China ceded to the United Kingdom in perpetuity in 1842, but which reverted to Chinese rule in 1997. The governor is appointed by the British monarch and foreign relations and defense are the responsibility of the U.K., but Hong Kong has substantial autonomy in commercial relations.

Mandates were territories surrendered by Turkey and Germany after World War I and, according to the League of Nations, "inhabited by peoples not yet able to stand by themselves" and therefore placed under the "tutelage" of different members of the League as "mandatories on behalf of the League." The last mandate to gain independence was South West Africa, now Namibia.

Protectorates *(associated states)* are states or territories partly under the control of another state but autonomous in domestic and certain external affairs. Protectorates are established by treaties.

Territories are regions (especially of Australia, Canada, and the United States) administered by a federal government and having some degree of self-government but not organized as a province or a state.

AUSTRALIA

▶CHRISTMAS ISLAND

Territory of Christmas Island

• **Geography** **Location:** eastern Indian Ocean; 10°25'S, 105°39'E. **Boundaries:** Java Head, Indonesia, 224 mi. (360 km) to N, North West Cape, Australia, 875 mi. (1,408 km) to SE. **Total area:** 52 sq. mi. (135 sq km). **Coastline:** 86 mi. (138.9 km). **Comparative area:** about seven-tenths size of Washington, D.C. **Land use:** 0% arable land; 0% permanent crops; 100% other. **City:** The Settlement (capital).

• **People** **Population:** 433 (2003 est.). **Nationality:** noun—Christmas Islander(s); adjective—Christmas Island. **Ethnic groups:** 70% Chinese, 10% Malay, 20% European; no indigenous population. **Language:** English. **Religions:** 36% Buddhist, 18% Christian, 25% Muslim, 21% other.

• **Government** **Type:** territory of Australia. **Constitution:** Christmas Island Act of 1958. **National Holiday:** N.A. **Head of government:** Administrator (acting) Graham Nicholls (since N.A.). **Structure:** administrator appointed by the governor general of Australia; unicameral Christmas Island Shire Council; Supreme Court.

• **Economy** **Monetary unit:** Australian dollar. **Budget:** N.A. **GDP:** N.A. **Chief Crops:** N.A. **Natural resources:** phosphate. **Major industries:** tourism, phosphate extraction (near depletion). **Labor force:** N.A.; 400 people in tourism, 100 people in mining. **Exports:** phosphate. **Imports:** consumer goods. **Major trading partners:** Australia, NZ.

▶COCOS (KEELING) ISLANDS

Territory of Cocos (Keeling) Islands

• **Geography** **Location:** 27 islands in eastern Indian Ocean. West Island 12°05'S, 96°53'E. **Boundaries:** island of Sumatra (part of Indonesia) about 932 mi. (1,500 km) to NE; Perth, Australia 1,720 mi. (2,768 km) to SE. **Total area:** 5.4 sq. mi. (14.0 sq km). **Coastline:** 1.6 mi. (2.6 km). **Comparative area:** about 24 times size of the Mall in Washington, D.C. **Land use:** 0% arable land; 0% permanent crops; 100% other. **City:** West Island (capital).

• **People** **Population:** 630 (2003 est.). **Nationality:** noun—Cocos Islander(s); adjective—Cocos Islander. **Ethnic groups:** Europeans, Cocos, Malays. **Languages:** English, Malay. **Religions:** 80% Sunni Muslim, 20% other.

• **Government** **Type:** territory of Australia. **Constitution:** Cocos (Keeling) Islands Act of 1995. **National Holiday:** N.A. **Head of government:** Administrator (acting) Maureen Ellis (since N.A.). **Structure:** administrator appointed by the governor general of Australia; unicameral Cocos (Keeling) Islands Shire Council; Supreme Court.

• **Economy** **Monetary unit:** Australian dollar. **Budget:** N.A. **GDP:** N.A. **Chief crops:** vegetables, bananas, pawpaws, coconuts. **Natural resources:** vegetables, bananas, pawpaws, coconuts. **Major industries:** copra products. **Labor force:** N.A.; the Cocos Island Cooperative Society Ltd. employs construction workers, stevedores, and lighterage worker operations; tourism employs others. **Exports:** copra. **Imports:** foodstuffs. **Major trading partners:** Australia.

▶NORFOLK ISLAND
Territory of Norfolk Island

• GEOGRAPHY **Location:** island in western Pacific Ocean; 29°04'S, 167°57'E. **Boundaries:** Vanuatu to N, New Zealand to SE, Brisbane, Australia 870 mi. (1,400 km) to W. **Total area:** 13.3 sq. mi. (34.6 sq km). **Coastline:** 20 mi. (32 km). **Comparative area:** about one-fifth size of Washington, D.C. **Land use:** 0% arable land; 0% permanent crops;100% other. **City:** Kingston (capital).

• PEOPLE **Population:** 1,853 (2003 est.). **Nationality:** noun—Norfolk Islander(s); adjective—Norfolk Islander. **Ethnic groups:** descendants of Bounty mutineers; Australian, New Zealander, Polynesians. **Languages:** English (official), Norfolk (a mixture of 18th-century English and ancient Tahitian). **Religions:** 37.4% Anglican, 11.5% Roman Catholic, 14.5% Uniting Church in Australia, 3.1% Seventh-Day Adventist.

• GOVERNMENT **Type:** territory of Australia. **Constitution:** Norfolk Island Act of 1979. **National holiday:** Pitcairners Arrival Day Anniversary, June 8. **Head of government:** Assembly President and Chief Minister George Charles Smith, (since 1997). **Structure:** administrator appointed by the governor general of Australia; unicameral nine-member elected Legislative Assembly; Supreme Court.

• ECONOMY **Monetary unit:** Australian dollar. **Budget:** (FY92/93) ***income:*** $4.6 mil.; ***expend.:*** $4.8 mil. **GDP:** N.A. **Chief crops:** Norfolk Island pine seed, Kentia palm seed, cereals, vegetables, fruit; cattle, poultry. **Natural resources:** fish. **Major industries:** tourism. **Labor force:** 1,395 (1991 est.) **Exports:** $1.5 mil. (f.o.b., FY91/92); postage stamps, seeds of Norfolk Island pine and Kentia Palm, small quantities of avocados. **Imports:** $17.9 mil. (c.i.f., FY91/92). **Major trading partners:** Australia, Pacific Islands, New Zealand, Asia, Europe.

▶UNINHABITED TERRITORIES OF AUSTRALIA

Ashmore Is. (12°15'S, 123°05'E); Cartier Is. (12°30'S, 123°30'E); Coral Sea Is. (18°00'S, 158°00'E); Heard Is. (53°00'S, 73°35'E); McDonald Is. (52°29'S, 72°50'E).

DENMARK

▶FAEROE ISLANDS

• GEOGRAPHY **Location:** group of 18 islands (17 inhabited) in Atlantic Ocean SE of Iceland. Tórshavn 62°02'N, 6°47'W. **Boundaries:** Iceland to NW, Norwegian Sea to N, Norway to E, Shetland Islands to SE, U.K. to S. **Total area:** 541 sq. mi. (1,399 sq km). **Coastline:** 694 mi. (1,117 km). **Comparative area:** eight times size of Washington, D.C. **Land use:** 2% arable land; 0% permanent crops;98% other. **City:** (1991 est.) Tórshavn (capital) 16,223.

• PEOPLE **Population:** 46,345 (2003 est.). **Nationality:** noun—Faroese (sing., pl.); adjective—Faroese. **Ethnic groups:** homogeneous Scandinavian population. **Languages:** Faroese (derived from Old Norse), Danish. **Religions:** Evangelical Lutheran.

• GOVERNMENT **Type:** self-governing (since 1979) overseas administrative division of Denmark. **Constitution:** June 5, 1953 (Danish constitution). **National Holiday:** Olaifest, July 29. **Head of government:** Anfinn Kallsberg, prime minister (since Apr. 1998). **Structure:** executive—High Commissioner, Prime Minister; legislative—32-member Parliament (Lagting) islands elect 2 representatives to Danish parliament; no separate judiciary.

• ECONOMY **Monetary unit:** Danish krone. **Budget:** (1999 est.) ***income:*** $488 mil.; ***expend.:*** $484 mil. **GDP:** $1 bil., $22,000 per capita (2001 est.). **Chief crops:** milk, potatoes, vegetables, sheep; salmon farming; fish. **Natural resources:** fish, whales. **Major industries:** fishing. **Labor force:** 24,250 (2000 est.); fishing, manufacturing, transportation, commerce. **Exports:** $418 mil. (f.o.b., 2001 est.); 94% fish and fish products, animal feedstuffs, transport equipment. **Imports:** $469 mil. (c.i.f., 1999 est.); 29% machinery and transport equipment, 36% consumer goods, 32% raw materials and semimanufactures, fuels, fish, salt. **Major trading partners:** ***exports:*** 32% Denmark, 21% U.K., 9% France; ***imports:*** 49% Denmark, 21% Norway, 9% U.K.

▶GREENLAND

• GEOGRAPHY **Location:** North Atlantic Ocean, largely within Arctic Circle. Godthåb 64°11'N, 51°44'W. **Boundaries:** Iceland about 190 mi. (300 km) to E across Denmark Strait, Canada to SW and W across Baffin Bay and Davis Strait. **Total area:** 840,000 sq. mi. (2,175,600 sq km); land area 131,931 sq. mi. (341,700 sq km) ice free. **Coastline:** 27,400 mi. (44,087 km). **Comparative area:** slightly more than three times size of Texas. **Land use:** 0% arable land; 0% permanent crops; 100% other. **City:** (1992) Godthåb (Nuuk, capital), 12,233.

• PEOPLE **Population:** 56,385 (2003 est.). **Nationality:** noun—Greenlander(s); adjective—Greenlandic. **Ethnic groups:** 88% Greenlander (Eskimos and Greenland-born whites), 12% Danish and others. **Languages:** Eskimo dialects, Danish, Greenlandic (an Inuit dialect). **Religions:** Evangelical Lutheran.

• GOVERNMENT **Type:** parliamentary democracy with constitutional monarch. **Constitution:** June 5, 1953 (Danish constitution). **National Holiday:** June 21 (longest day). **Head of government:** Prime Minister Jonathan Motzfeldt (since Sept. 1997); named to post to replace Gunnar Martens, who retired ahead of scheduled election. **Structure:** prime minister is elected by the Parliament; unicameral Parliament or Landsting (31 seats); High Court or Landsrete.

• ECONOMY **Monetary unit:** Danish krone. **Budget:** (1999 est.) ***income:*** $646 mil.; ***expend:*** $629 mil. **GDP:** $1.1 bil., $20,000 per capita (2001 est.). **Chief crops:** forage crops, small garden vegetables; sheep, fish. **Natural resources:** zinc, lead, iron ore, coal, molybdenum. **Major industries:** mining, fishing. **Labor force:** 24,500 (1995 est.). **Exports:** $364 mil. (f.o.b., 2001 est.); fish and fish products. **Imports:** $403 mil. (c.i.f., 2001 est.); 25% machinery and transport equipment, 18% manufactured goods, 11% food and live animals, 6% petroleum products. **Major trading partners:** ***exports:*** 57% E.U., 16% Japan, 8% U.S.; ***imports:*** 65% Denmark, 18% Spain, 12% Norway.

FRANCE

▶FRENCH GUIANA
Department of Guiana

• **Geography** **Location:** NE coast of South America. **Boundaries:** North Atlantic Ocean to N, Brazil to E and S across Oyapock River, Suriname to W across Maroni River. **Total area:** 35,135 sq. mi. (91,000 sq km). **Coastline:** 235 mi. (378 km). **Comparative area:** slightly smaller than Indiana. **Land use:** negl. % arable land; negl. % permanent crops; 100% other. **City:** (1990) Cayenne (capital) 41,637.

• **People** **Population:** 186,917 (2003 est.). **Nationality:** noun—French Guianese (sing., pl.); adjective—French Guianese. **Ethnic groups:** 66% black or mulatto, 12% Caucasian, 12% East Indian, Chinese or Amerindian, 10% other. **Language:** French. **Religion:** predominantly Roman Catholic.

• **Government** **Type:** overseas department of France. **Constitution:** Sept. 28, 1958 (French constitution). **National Holiday:** Bastille Day, July 14. **Head of government:** President of the General Council Stephan Phinera (since March 1994); President of the Regional Council Antoine Karam (since March 1992). **Structure:** presidents of the General and Regional Councils are appointed by the members of those councils, who vote on party lines; unicameral 19-member General Council, 31-member Regional Council—both elected by popular vote to serve 6-year terms.; Court of Appeals.

• **Economy** **Monetary unit:** euro, French franc. **Budget:** (1996 est.) ***income:*** $225 mil.; ***expend.:*** $390 mil. **GDP:** $1.1 bil., $6,000 per capita (2002 est.). **Chief crops:** rice, corn, manioc, cocoa, vegetables, bananas, sugar; cattle, pigs, poultry. **Natural resources:** bauxite, timber, gold, cinnabar, kaolin. **Major industries:** construction, shrimp processing, forestry products. **Labor force:** 58,800 (1997); 60.6% services, government and commerce, 21.2% industry, 18.2% agriculture; 22% unemployment (2001). **Exports:** $155 mil. (f.o.b., 2001); shrimp, timber, gold, rum, rosewood essence, clothing. **Imports:** $625 mil. (c.i.f., 1997); food (grains, processed meat), machinery and transport equipment, fuels and chemicals. **Major trading partners:** ***exports:*** 62% France, 7% Switzerland; ***imports:*** 63% France, U.S., Trinidad and Tobago, Italy.

▶FRENCH POLYNESIA
Territory of French Polynesia

• **Geography** **Location:** five island groups or archipelagoes—Gambier, Marquesas, Society (includes Tahiti and Bora Bora), Tuamotu, and Tubuai (Austral Islands)—in South Pacific Ocean about halfway between South America and Australia. Papeete (Society Is.) 17°32'S, 149°34'W. **Boundaries:** Kiribati to NW, Cook Islands to W. **Total area:** 2,589 sq. mi. (4,167 sq km). **Coastline:** 1,569 mi. (2,525 km). **Comparative area:** slightly less than one-third size of Connecticut. **Land use:** 2% arable land; 6% permanent crops; 92% other. **Cities:** (1996) Papeete (capital) 25,553; Faa'a 25,888.

• **People** **Population:** 262,125 (2003 est.). **Nationality:** noun—French Polynesian(s); adjective—French Polynesian. **Ethnic groups:** 78% Polynesian, 12% Chinese, 6% local French, 4% metropolitan French. **Languages:** French, Tahitian (both official). **Religions:** 54% Protestant, 30% Roman Catholic, 16% other.

• **Government** **Type:** overseas territory of France. **Constitution:** Sept. 28, 1958 (French constitution). **National Holiday:** Bastille Day, July 14. **Heads of government:** President of the Territorial Government of French Polynesia Gaston Flosse (since April 4, 1991), President of the Territorial Assembly Justin Arapari (since May 13, 1996). **Structure:** presidents of the Territorial Government and Assembly are elected by the members of the assembly; unicameral Territorial Assembly (41-seats; members are elected by popular vote to serve five-year terms); Court of Appeal.

• **Economy** **Monetary unit:** Colonial Francs Pacifique (CFP). **Budget:** (1999) ***income:*** $1 bil.; ***expend.:*** $900 mil. **GDP:** $1.3 bil., $5,000 per capita (2001 est.). **Chief crops:** coconuts, vanilla, vegetables, fruits; poultry, beef, dairy products. **Natural resources:** timber, fish, cobalt. **Major industries:** tourism, pearls, agricultural processing. **Labor force:** 70,000 (1996); 13% agriculture, 19% industry, 68% services. **Exports:** $260 mil. (f.o.b., 2000); 53.8% cultured pearls, coconut products, mother-of-pearl, vanilla, shark meat. **Imports:** $1.2 bil. (c.i.f., 2000); fuels, foodstuffs, equipment. **Major trading partners:** ***exports:*** 53% Japan, 20% U.S.; ***imports:*** 45.8% France, 16.7% Australia.

▶GUADELOUPE
Department of Guadeloupe

• **Geography** **Location:** eastern Caribbean Sea: Guadeloupe 16°00'N, 61°42'W; St. Barthélemy 17°55'N, 63°50'W; Marie Galante 15°57'N, 61°20'W. **Boundaries:** Antigua to N, Dominica to S. **Total area:** 687 sq. mi. (1,780 sq km). **Coastline:** 190 mi. (306 km). **Comparative area:** 10 times size of Washington, D.C. **Land use:** 11% arable land; 4% permanent crops; 85% other. **Cities:** (1990 census) Basse-Terre (capital) 14,107; Les Abymes 62,809.

• **People** **Population:** 440,189 (2003 est.). **Nationality:** noun—Guadeloupian(s); adjective—Guadeloupe. **Ethnic groups:** 90% black or mulatto, 5% white, less than 5% East Indian, Lebanese, Chinese. **Languages:** 99% French (official), Creole patois. **Religions:** 95% Roman Catholic, 4% Hindu and pagan African, 1% Protestant sects.

• **Government** **Type:** overseas department of France. **Constitution:** Sept. 28, 1958 (French constitution). **National Holiday:** Bastille Day, July 14. **Head of government:** President of the General Council Marcellin Lubeth (since 1998), President of the Regional Council Lucette Michaux-Chevry (since March 1992). **Structure:** presidents of General and Regional Councils are elected by council members; unicameral General Council with 42 seats, members are elected by popular vote to serve 6-year terms; unicameral Regional Council with 41 seats, members are elected by popular vote by to serve 6-year terms; Court of Appeal.

• **Economy** **Monetary unit:** euro, French franc. **Budget:** (1996) ***income:*** $225 mil.; ***expend:*** $390 mil. **GDP:** $3.7 bil., $9,000 per capita (1997 est.). **Chief crops:** sugarcane, bananas, tropical fruits and vegetables; cattle, pigs, goats. **Natural resources:** cultivable land, beaches and climate that foster tourism. **Major industries:** construction, cement, rum. **Labor force:** 125,900; 68% services, 17% industry, 15% agriculture; 27.8% unemployment. **Exports:** $140 mil. (f.o.b., 1997); bananas, sugar, rum. **Imports:** $1.7 bil. (c.i.f.,

1997); foodstuffs, fuels, vehicles, clothing and consumer goods, construction materials. **Major trading partners:** (1999) ***exports:*** 60% France, 18% Martinique; ***imports:*** 63% France, 4% Germany.

▶MARTINIQUE
Department of Martinique

• **GEOGRAPHY Location:** eastern Caribbean Sea (14°36'N, 61°05'W). **Boundaries:** Dominica to N, St. Lucia to S. **Total area:** 425 sq. mi. (1,100 sq km). **Coastline:** 218 mi. (350 km). **Comparative area:** slightly more than six times size of Washington, D.C. **Land use:** 9% arable land; 11% permanent crops; 180% other. **City:** (1990 census) Fort-de-France (capital) 101,540.

• **PEOPLE Population:** 425,996 (2003 est.). **Nationality:** noun—Martiniquais (sing., pl.); adjective—Martiniquais. **Ethnic groups:** 90% African and African-Caucasian-Indian mixture, 5% Caucasian, 5% East Indian, Lebanese, Chinese. **Languages:** French, Creole patois. **Religions:** 85% Roman Catholic, 5% Hindu and pagan African beliefs.

• **GOVERNMENT Type:** overseas department of France. **Constitution:** Sept. 28, 1958. **National Holiday:** Bastille Day, July 14. **Head of government:** President of the General Council Claude Lise (since March 1992), President of the Regional Council Alfred Marie-Jeanne (since March 1998). **Structure:** presidents of General and Regional Councils elected by council members; unicameral 45-seat General Council and unicameral 41-seat Regional Assembly members are elected by popular vote to serve 6-year terms..

• **ECONOMY Monetary unit:** euro. **Budget:** (1996 est.) ***income:*** $900 mil.; ***expend.:*** $2.5 bil. **GDP:** $4.5 bil., $10,700 per capita (2001). **Chief crops:** bananas, pineapples, vegetables, avocados, flowers, sugarcane for rum. **Natural resources:** coastal scenery and beaches, cultivable land. **Major industries:** construction, rum, cement. **Labor force:** 165,900 (1998); 73% services, 17% industry, 10% agriculture (1997). **Exports:** $250 mil. (f.o.b., 1997); refined petroleum products, bananas, rum, pineapples. **Imports:** $2 bil. (c.i.f., 1997); petroleum products, crude oil, foodstuffs, construction materials, vehicles, clothing and other consumer goods. **Major trading partners:** (2000) ***exports:*** 45% France, 28 Guadeloupe, French Guiana; ***imports:*** 62% France, Venezuela, Germany.

▶MAYOTTE
Territorial Collectivity of Mayotte

• **GEOGRAPHY Location:** Comoros archipelago in eastern Indian Ocean (12°47'S, 45°12'E). **Boundaries:** Indian Ocean to N, Madagascar 300 mi. (480 km) to SE, Mozambique Channel to S, Mozambique to W. **Total area:** 145 sq. mi. (375 sq km). **Coastline:** 115 mi. (185.2 km). **Comparative area:** slightly more than twice size of Washington, D.C. **Land use:** N.A. **Cities:** (1985 census) Dzaoudzi (capital) 5,865; Mamoudzou 12,026

• **PEOPLE Population:** 178,347 (2002 est.). **Nationality:** noun—Mahorais (sing., pl.); adjective—Mahoran. **Ethnic groups:** N.A. **Languages:** Mahorian (a Swahili dialect), French. **Religions:** 97% Muslim, Christian (mostly Roman Catholic).

• **GOVERNMENT Type:** territorial collectivity of France. **Constitution:** Sept. 28, 1958 (French constitution). **National Holiday:** Bastille Day, July 14. **Heads of government:** President of General Council Younoussa Bamana (since 1977). **Structure:** president of the General Council elected by the members of the General Council for a six-year term; unicameral 16-seat General Council members elected by popular vote to serve 3-year terms; Supreme Court.

• **ECONOMY Monetary unit:** euro. **Budget:** (1991). ***income:*** N.A.; ***expend.:*** $73 mil. **GDP:** $85 mil., $600 per capita (1998 est.). **Chief crops:** vanilla, ylang-ylang, coffee, copra. **Natural resources:** negl. **Major industries:** newly created lobster and shrimp industry. **Labor force:** N.A. **Exports:** $3.44 mil. (f.o.b. 1997); ylang-ylang, vanilla, copra. **Imports:** $141.3 mil. (f.o.b. 1997); building materials, machinery and transportation equipment, metals, chemicals, rice, clothing, flour. **Major trading partners:** ***exports:*** 80% France, 15% Comoros, Reunion; ***imports:*** 66% France, 14% Africa, 20% Southeast Asia.

▶NEW CALEDONIA
Territory of New Caledonia and Dependencies

• **GEOGRAPHY Location:** one large and several smaller islands in western South Pacific. Nouméa 22°16'S, 166°26'E. **Boundaries:** Vanuatu to N, Australia about 930 mi. (1,500 km) to W. **Total area:** 7,359 sq. mi. (19,060 sq km). **Coastline:** 1,401 mi. (2,254 km). **Comparative area:** slightly smaller than New Jersey. **Land use:** negl. % arable land; negl. % permanent crops; 99% other. **City:** (1989) Nouméa (capital) 65,110.

• **PEOPLE Population:** 210,798 (2003 est.). **Nationality:** noun—New Caledonian(s); adjective—New Caledonian. **Ethnic groups:** 42.5% Melanesian, 37.1% European, 8.4% Wallisian, 3.8% Polynesian, 3.6% Indonesian, 1.6% Vietnamese, 3.0% other. **Languages:** French, Melanesian-Polynesian dialects. **Religions:** 60% Roman Catholic, 30% Protestant, 10% other.

• **GOVERNMENT Type:** overseas territory of France. **Constitution:** Sept. 28, 1958 (French Constitution). **National Holiday:** Bastille Day, July 14. **Heads of government:** President of the Territorial Congress Simon Loueckhote (since 1998). **Structure:** president of the Territorial Congress elected by the members of the congress; unicameral 54-seat Territorial Congress members are elected by popular vote to serve 6-year terms; Court of Appeal.

• **ECONOMY Monetary unit:** Colonial Francs Pacifique (CFP). **Budget:** (1996 est.) ***income:*** $861.3 mil.; ***expend.:*** $735.3 mil. **GDP:** $3 bil., $14,000 per capita (2002 est.). **Chief crops:** vegetables; beef, other livestock products. **Natural resources:** nickel, chrome, iron, cobalt, manganese. **Major industries:** nickel mining. **Labor force:** 79,395 (including 15,018 unemployed, 1996 est.); 40% services, 32% agriculture, 20% industry, 8% mining. **Exports:** $400 mil. (f.o.b., 2000); ferronickels, nickel ore. **Imports:** $1 bil. (c.i.f., 2000); food, transport equipment, machinery and electrical equipment, fuels and minerals. **Major trading partners:** ***exports:*** 30% Japan, 17% France, 113% Taiwan.; ***imports:*** 51% France, 14% Australia, 9% Singapore.

▶RÉUNION
Department of Réunion

• **GEOGRAPHY Location:** southwestern Indian Ocean (20°15'S, 55°27'E). **Boundaries:** 500 mi. (800 km) E of Madagascar. **Total area:** 969 sq. mi. (2,510 sq km). **Coastline:** 125 mi. (201 km). **Comparative area:** slightly smaller than Rhode Island. **Land use:** 13% arable land; 2% permanent crops; 85% other. **Cities:** (1990 census) Saint-Denis (capital) 121,999; Saint-Paul 71,669; Saint-Pierre 58,846.

• **PEOPLE** **Population:** 755,171 (2003 est.). **Nationality:** noun—Reunionese (sing., pl.); adjective—Reunionese. **Ethnic groups:** French, African, Malagasy, Chinese, Pakistani, Indian. **Languages:** French (official), Creole. **Religions:** 94% Roman Catholic, Hindu, Islam, Buddhist.
• **GOVERNMENT** **Type:** overseas department of France. **Constitution:** Sept. 28, 1958, (French constitution). **National Holiday:** Bastille Day, July 14. **Head of government:** President of the General Council Christophe Payet (since April 1994), President of the Regional Council Margarite Sudre (since June 25, 1993). **Structure:** presidents of General and Regional Councils elected by members of councils who vote on party lines; unicameral 47-seat General Council and unicameral 45-seat Regional Council members elected by direct popular vote to 6-year terms.; judiciary
• **ECONOMY** **Monetary unit:** French franc. **Budget:** (1998) ***income:*** $1.26 bil.; ***expend.:*** $2.62 bil. **GDP:** $3.6 bil., $4,800 per capita (1999 est.). **Chief crops:** sugarcane, vanilla, tobacco, tropical fruits and vegetables. **Natural resources:** fish, arable land. **Major industries:** sugar, rum, cigarettes, handicraft items. **Labor force:** 261,000 (1995); 73% services, 19% industry, 8% agriculture; 35% unemployment (1994). **Exports:** $214 mil. (f.o.b., 1997); 63% sugar, 4% rum and molasses, 3% lobster, 2% perfume essences. **Imports:** $2.5 bil. (c.i.f., 1997); manufactured goods, food, beverages, tobacco, machinery and transportation equipment, raw materials, petroleum products. **Major trading partners:** ***exports:*** 74% France, 6% Japan, 4% Comoros; ***imports:*** 67% France, 4% Bahrain, 3% Italy.

▶ST. PIERRE AND MIQUELON
Territorial Collectivity of St. Pierre and Miquelon

• **GEOGRAPHY** **Location:** North Atlantic off east coast of Canada. St. Pierre 46°46'N, 56°12'W. **Boundaries:** Newfoundland, Canada 16 mi. (25 km) to N, North Atlantic Ocean to E and S. **Total area:** 93 sq. mi. (242 sq km). **Coastline:** 75 mi. (120 km). **Comparative area:** 1.5 times size of Washington, D.C. **Land use:** 13% arable land; 0% permanent crops; 87% other. **Cities:** (1990 census) St. Pierre (capital) 5,683; Miquelon 709.
• **PEOPLE** **Population:** 6,976 (2003 est.). **Nationality:** noun—Frenchmen; adjective—French. **Ethnic groups:** Basques and Bretons (French fishermen). **Languages:** French. **Religions:** 99% Roman Catholic.
• **GOVERNMENT** **Type:** territorial collectivity of France. **Constitution:** Sept. 28, 1958 (French constitution). **National Holiday:** Bastille Day, July 14. **Heads of government:** Bernard Le Soavec, president of the General Council. **Structure:** president of the General Council is elected by members of the General Council; unicameral 19-seat General Council members are elected by popular vote to serve six-year terms; Superior Tribunal of Appeals.
• **ECONOMY** **Monetary unit:** euro. **Budget:** (1996 est.) ***income:*** $70 mil.; ***expend.:*** $60 mil. **GDP:** $74 mil., $11,000 per capita (1996 est.). **Chief crops:** vegetables; cattle, sheep, pigs; fish. **Natural resources:** fish, deep-water ports. **Major industries:** fishing, supply base for fishing fleets, tourism. **Labor force:** 3,261 (1999). **Exports:** $12 mil. (f.o.b., 1999); fish and fish products, fox and mink pelts. **Imports:** $55 mil. (c.i.f., 1999); meat, clothing, fuel, electrical equipment, machinery, building materials. **Major trading partners:** ***exports:*** 43% U.S., 14% Egypt, 11% Japan; ***imports:*** 44% France, 40% Canada.

▶WALLIS AND FUTUNA
Territory of the Wallis and Futuna Islands

• **GEOGRAPHY** **Location:** two island groups (Wallis to NE, Hooru, incl. Futuna Is., to SW) in South Pacific. Mata-Utu (Wallis group) 13°22'S, 176°12'W. **Boundaries:** Western Samoa to E, Fiji to SW. **Total area:** 106 sq. mi. (274 sq km). **Coastline:** 80 mi. (129 km). **Comparative area:** 1.5 times the size of Washington, D.C. **Land use:** 5% arable land; 20% permanent crops; 75% other. **City:** Mata-Utu (capital) (1983 census) 815.
• **PEOPLE** **Population:** 15,734 (2003 est.). **Nationality:** noun—Wallisian(s), Futunan(s), or Wallis and Futuna Islander(s); adjective—Wallisian, Futunan, or Wallis and Futuna Islander. **Ethnic groups:** Polynesian. **Languages:** French (official) Wallisian (indigenous Polynesian language). **Religions:** 99% Roman Catholic.
• **GOVERNMENT** **Type:** overseas territory of France. **Constitution:** Sept. 28, 1958 (French constitution). **National Holiday:** N.A. **Head of government:** President of the Territorial Assembly Victor Brial (since June 1, 1997). **Structure:** presidents of the Territorial Assembly and Government elected by the members of the assembly; unicameral 20-seat Territorial Assembly members elected by popular vote to 5-year terms; three traditional kings administer customary law; magistrate in Mata-Utu.
• **ECONOMY** **Monetary unit:** Colonial Francs Pacifique (CFP). **Budget:** (1998 est.) ***income:*** $20 mil.; ***expend.:*** $17 mil. **GDP:** $30 mil., $2,000 per capita (2000 est.). **Chief crops:** breadfruit, yams, taro, bananas; pigs, goats. **Natural resources:** negl. **Major industries:** copra, handicrafts. **Labor force:** N.A.; 80% agriculture, livestock, and fishing, 4% government. **Exports:** $250,000. (f.o.b., 1999 est.); copra, handicrafts. **Imports:** $300,000 mil. (c.i.f., 1999 est.); foodstuffs, manufactured goods, transportation equipment, fuel, clothing. **Major trading partners:** ***exports:*** Italy, Croatia, U.S.; ***imports:*** France, Australia, New Zealand.

▶UNINHABITED TERRITORIES OF FRANCE
Bassas da India (21°25'S, 39°42'E); Clipperton Is. (10°21'N, 109°13'W); Europa Is. (22°20'S, 40°22'E); French Southern and Antarctic Lands (Kerguelen Is. 49°20'S, 69°30'E); Glorioso Is. (11°30'S, 47°20'E); Tromelin Is. (15°52'S, 54°25'E).

MOROCCO

▶WESTERN SAHARA
• **GEOGRAPHY** **Location:** northwestern coast of Africa. **Boundaries:** Morocco to N, Algeria, Mauritania to E, Atlantic Ocean to W. **Total area:** 102,703 sq. mi. (266,000 sq km). **Coastline:** 690 mi. (1,110 km). **Comparative area:** about the size of Colorado. **Land use:** 19% arable land; 24% permanent crops; 0% meadows and pastures; 47% forest and woodland; 10% other. **City:** (1982) El Aaiun (capital) 93,785.

• **PEOPLE** **Population:** 261,794 (2003 est.). **Nationality:** noun—Sahrawi(s), Sahraoui; adjective—Sahrawian, Sahraouian. **Ethnic groups:** Arab, Berber. **Languages:** Hassaniya Arabic, Moroccan Arabic. **Religion:** Muslim.
• **GOVERNMENT** **Type:** legal status and sovereignty still unresolved. Morocco and Polisario Front have fought over this since 1976. A U.N.-sponsored ceasefire has been in effect since Sept., 1991. A U.N.-organized referendum has been repeatedly post-poned. **Constitution:** N.A. **National Holiday:** N.A. **Head of government:** N.A. **Structure:** N.A.
• **ECONOMY** **Monetary unit:** Moroccan dirham. **Budget:** N.A. **GDP:** N.A. **Chief crops:** fruits and vegetables in the few oases; camels, sheep, goats. **Natural resources:** phosphates, iron ore. **Major industries:** phosphate, fishing, handicrafts. **Labor force:** 12,000; 50% animal husbandry and subsistence farming. **Exports:** N.A.; 62% phosphates. **Imports:** N.A.; fuel for fishing fleet, foodstuffs. **Major trading partners:** Morocco claims administrative control over Western Sahara and controls all trade with country; trade figures are included in overall Moroccan accounts.

NETHERLANDS

▶ARUBA

• **GEOGRAPHY** **Location:** southern Caribbean Sea (12°32'N, 70°02'W), off NW Venezuela. **Boundaries:** Curaçao, Netherlands Antilles 42 mi. (68 km) to E, Venezuela 16 mi. (25 km) to S. **Total area:** 75 sq. mi. (193 sq km). **Coastline:** about 45 mi. (about 72 km). **Comparative area:** slightly larger than Washington, D.C. **Land use:** 11% arable land; 0% permanent crops; 89% other. **City:** Oranjestad (capital).
• **PEOPLE** **Population:** 70,744 (2003 est.). **Nationality:** noun—Aruban(s); adjective—Aruban. **Ethnic groups:** 80% mixed European/Caribbean Amerindian. **Languages:** Dutch (official), Papiamento (a Spanish-Portuguese-Dutch-English dialect); English widely spoken, Spanish. **Religions:** 82% Roman Catholic, 8% Protestant; also Hindu, Muslim, Confucian, Jewish minorities.
• **GOVERNMENT** Part of the Netherlands, but full autonomy in internal affairs obtained in 1986 upon separation from Netherlands Antilles. **Type:** parliamentary democracy. **Constitution:** Jan. 1, 1986. **National Holiday:** Flag Day, Mar. 18. **Head of government:** Prime Minister Jan. H. Eman (since July 29, 1994). **Structure:** prime minister elected by the Staten for a four-year term; unicameral 21-seat Legislature members elected by direct popular vote and serve 4-year terms; Joint High Court of Justice.
• **ECONOMY** **Monetary unit:** Aruban florin. **Budget:** (2000) ***income:*** $135.81. mil.; ***expend.:*** $147 mil. **GDP:** $1.94 bil., $28,000 per capita (2002 est.). **Chief crops:** aloes; livestock; fishing. **Natural resources:** negl.; white sandy beaches. **Major industries:** tourism, transshipment, oil refining. **Labor force:** 41,501 (1997 est.); mostly tourism. **Exports:** $1.88 bil. (2002); including oil re-exports; mostly petroleum products. **Imports:** $2.21 bil. (2002); including oil for processing and re-export, foodstuffs, consumer goods. **Major trading partners:** U.S., Venezuela.

▶NETHERLANDS ANTILLES

• **GEOGRAPHY** **Location:** two island groups in Caribbean Sea, about 500 mi. (800 km) apart. Curaçao Is. 12°12'N, 68°56'W; St. Maarten Is. 18°03'N, 63°05'W. **Boundaries:** southern group (Curaçao and Bonaire)—Venezuela to S; northern group (St. Eustatius, Saba, and St. Maarten)— Antigua to E, Virgin Islands to W. **Total area:** 371 sq. mi. (960 sq km). **Coastline:** 226 mi. (364 km). **Comparative area:** more than 5 times size of Washington, D.C. **Land use:** 10% arable land; 0% permanent crops; 90% other. **City:** Willemstad (capital).
• **PEOPLE** **Population:** 216,226 (2003 est.). **Nationality:** noun—Netherlands Antillean(s); adjective—Netherlands Antillean. **Ethnic groups:** 85% mixed African; remainder Carib Amerindian, European, East Asian. **Languages:** Dutch (official), Papiamento (Spanish-Portuguese-Dutch-English dialect) predominates; English widely spoken; Spanish. **Religions:** predominantly Roman Catholic; Protestant, Jewish, Seventh-Day Adventist.
• **GOVERNMENT** **Type:** autonomous part of Netherlands; parliamentary. **Constitution:** Dec. 29, 1954. **National holiday:** Queen's Day, April 30. **Head of government:** Miguel Pourier, prime minister (since Feb. 1994). **Structure:** leader of the majority party is usually elected prime minister by the Staten; unicameral 22-seat Staten members are elected by popular vote to serve 4-year terms; Joint High court of Jusice, appointed by the Netherlands monarch.
• **ECONOMY** **Monetary unit:** Netherlands Antillean guilder. **Budget:** (1997 est.) ***income:*** $710.8 mil.; ***expend.:*** $741.6 mil. **GDP:** $2.4 bil., $11,400 per capita (2002 est.). **Chief crops:** aloes, sorghum, peanuts. **Natural resources:** phosphates (Curaçao only), salt (Bonaire only). **Major industries:** tourism on Curaçao and St. Maarten; petroleum refining on Curaçao; petroleum transshipment facilities on Curaçao and Bonaire; light manufacturing on Curaçao. **Labor force:** 89,000; 84% services, 15% industry, 1% agriculture (1994 est.). **Exports:** $533 mil. (f.o.b, 2002); 98% petroleum products. **Imports:** $1.43 bil. (f.o.b., 2002); 64% crude petroleum, food, manufactures. **Major trading partners:** ***exports:*** 24.9% U.S., 15.3% Venezuela, 9.7% Guatemala; ***imports:*** 56.5 Venezuela, 12.6% Mexico, 10.9% U.S.

NEW ZEALAND

▶COOK ISLANDS

• **GEOGRAPHY** **Location:** 15 islands (13 inhabited) in South Pacific. Avarua 21°12'S, 159° 46'W. **Boundaries:** French Polynesia to E, American Samoa to W. **Total area:** 93 sq. mi. (240 sq km). **Coastline:** 75 mi. (120 km). **Comparative area:** 1.3 times size of Washington, D.C. **Land use:** 17% arable land; 13% permanent crops; 70% other. **City:** Avarua (capital).
• **PEOPLE** **Population:** 21,008 (2003 est.). **Nationality:** noun—Cook Islander(s); adjective—Cook

Islander. **Ethnic groups:** 81.3% Polynesian (full blood), 7.7% Polynesian and European, 7.7% Polynesian and non-European, 2.4% European, 0.9% other. **Languages:** English (official), Maori. **Religions:** Christian; majority of populace members of Cook Islands Christian church.

• **GOVERNMENT** **Type:** self-governing parliamentary democracy in free association with New Zealand; Cook Islands government is fully responsible for internal affairs and has right at any time to move to full independence by unilateral action; New Zealand responsible for external affairs, in consultation with Cook Islands government. **Constitution:** Aug. 4, 1965. **National holiday:** Constitution Day, Aug. 4. **Head of government:** Terepai Maoake, prime minister (since Nov. 1999). **Structure:** leader of the party that wins the most seats usually becomes prime minister; unicameral 25-seat Parliament members elected by popular vote to serve 5-year terms; High Court.

• **ECONOMY** **Monetary unit:** New Zealand dollar. **Budget:** (FY01/02) ***income:*** $28 mil; ***expend.:*** $27 mil. **GDP:** $105 mil., $5,000 per capita (2001 est.). **Chief crops:** copra, citrus fruits, pineapples, tomatoes, beans, pawpaws, bananas, yams, taro, coffee. **Labor force:** (1996) 8,000; 29% agriculture, 56% services, 15% industry. **Natural resources:** negl. **Major industries:** fruit processing, tourism. **Exports:** $9.1 mil. (f.o.b., 2000); copra, fresh and canned citrus fruit, coffee; fish; pearls and pearl shells; clothing. **Imports:** $50.7 mil. (c.i.f., 2000); foodstuffs, textiles, fuels, timber, capital goods. **Major trading partners:** ***exports:*** 34% Australia, New Zealand, Japan; ***imports:*** 61% New Zealand, Fiji, U.S.

▶NIUE

• **GEOGRAPHY** **Location:** coral island in western South Pacific (19°02'S, 169°55'W). **Boundaries:** Tonga 300 mi. (480 km) to W, southern Cook Islands 580 mi. (930 km) to E. **Total area:** 100 sq. mi. (260 sq km). **Coastline:** 40 mi. (64 km). **Comparative area:** 1.5 times size of Washington, D.C. **Land use:** 19% arable land; 8% permanent crops; 73% other. **City:** Alofi (capital).

• **PEOPLE** **Population:** 2,145 (2003 est.). **Nationality:** noun—Niuean(s); adjective—Niuean. **Ethnic groups:** Polynesian, with about 200 Europeans, Samoans, Tongans. **Languages:** Polynesian dialect closely related to Tongan and Samoan; English. **Religions:** 75% Ekalesia Niue (Niuean Church)—a Christian Protestant church closely related to London Missionary Society, 10% Latter-Day Saints, 15% Roman Catholic, Jehovah's Witnesses, Seventh-Day Adventist.

• **GOVERNMENT** **Type:** self-governing parliamentary democracy territory in free association with New Zealand. **Constitution:** Oct. 19, 1974. **National holiday:** Waitangi Day, Feb. 6. **Heads of government:** Sani Lakatani, premier (since Apr. 1999). **Structure:** executive—premier (elected by assembly); Legislative Assembly consists of 20 members (14 village representatives and six elected on a common roll); Supreme Court of New Zealand.

• **ECONOMY** **Monetary unit:** New Zealand dollar. **Budget:** N.A. **GDP:** $7.6 mil., $3,600 per capita (2000 est.). **Chief crops:** coconuts, passion fruit, honey, limes, taro, yams, cassava (tapioca), sweet potatoes; pigs, poultry, beef cattle. **Natural resources:** fish, arable land. **Major industries:** tourism, handicrafts. **Labor force:** 450 (1992 est.); most Niueans work on family plantations; paid work exists only in government service, small industry, and Niue Development Board. **Exports:** $137,200 (f.o.b., 1999); canned coconut cream, copra, honey, passion fruit products, pawpaw. **Imports:** $2.38 mil. (c.i.f., 1999); food, live animals, manufactured goods, machinery, fuels, lubricants, chemicals, drugs. **Major trading partners:** ***exports:*** New Zealand, Fiji, Cook Islands; ***imports:*** New Zealand, Fiji, Japan.

▶TOKELAU

• **GEOGRAPHY** **Location:** three atolls (Atafu, Nukunonu, Fakaofo) in South Pacific. Atafu 8°33'S, 172°30'W. **Boundaries:** northern Cook Islands to E, Western Samoa 300 mi. (480 km) to S, Tuvalu to W. **Total area:** 4 sq. mi. (10 sq km). **Coastline:** 62 mi. (101 km). **Comparative area:** about 17 times size of the Mall in Washington, D.C. **Land use:** 0% arable land; 0% permanent crops; 100% other. **City:** none; each atoll has own administrative center.

• **PEOPLE** **Population:** 1,418 (2003 est.). **Nationality:** noun—Tokelauan(s); adjective—Tokelauan. **Ethnic groups:** Polynesian. **Languages:** Tokelauan (a Polynesian language), English. **Religions:** 70% Congregational Christian church, 28% Roman Catholic; on Atafu, all Congregational Christian Church of Samoa; on Nukunonu, all Roman Catholic; on Fakaofo, both denominations.

• **GOVERNMENT** **Type:** territory of New Zealand. **Constitution:** administered under the Tokelau Islands Act of 1948, as amended in 1970. **National holiday:** Waitangi Day, Feb. 6. **Head of government:** Aliki Faipule Falimateao (since 1997). **Structure:** head of government is chosen from the Council of Faipule and serves a one-year term; unicameral 15-seat General Fono members chosen by each atoll's Council of Elders or Taupulega to serve 3-year terms; Supreme Court.

• **ECONOMY** **Monetary unit:** New Zealand dollar. **Budget:** (1987) ***income:*** $430,830; ***expend.:*** $2.8 mil. **GDP:** $1.5 mil., $1,000 per capita (1993 est.). **Chief crops:** coconuts, copra, breadfruit, papaya, bananas; pigs, poultry, goats. **Natural resources:** negl. **Major industries:** small-scale enterprises for copra production, woodwork, plaited craft goods, stamps, coins. **Labor force:** N.A. **Exports:** $98,000 (f.o.b., 1983); stamps, copra, handicrafts. **Imports:** $323,000 (c.i.f., 1983); foodstuffs, building materials, fuel. **Major trading partners:** New Zealand.

NORWAY

▶SVALBARD

• **GEOGRAPHY** **Location:** nine large and numerous smaller islands in Arctic Ocean. **Boundaries:** Longyearbyen (Spitsbergen Is.) 78° 13'N, 15°38'W; Bear Is. 74°30'N, 19°00'E. Norway to S, Greenland to W. **Total area:** 38,557 sq. mi. (62,049 sq km). **Coastline:** 2,229 mi.(3,587 km). **Comparative area:** slightly smaller than West Virginia. **Land use:** 0% arable land; 0% permanent crops; 100% other; no trees; only bushes are crowberry and cloudberry. **City:** Longyearbyen (capital).

• **People** **Population:** 2,811 (2003 est.). **Nationality:** N.A. **Ethnic groups:** 44.3% Russian and Ukrainian, 55.4% Norwegian. **Languages:** Russian, Norwegian. **Religions:** N.A.
• **Government** **Type:** territory of Norway. **Constitution:** N.A. **National holiday:** N.A. **Head of government:** Morten Ruud, governor (since Nov. 1998). **Structure:** governor responsible to the Polar Department of the Ministry of Justice
• **Economy** **Monetary unit:** Norwegian krone. **Budget:** (1998 est.) ***income:*** $11.5 mil.; ***expend.:*** $11.5 mil. **GDP:** N.A. **Chief Crops:** N.A. **Natural resources:** coal, copper, iron ore, phosphate, zinc. **Major industries:** coal mining; trapping of seal, polar bear, fox, walrus. **Labor force:** N.A. **Exports:** N.A. **Imports:** N.A. **Major trading partners:** N.A.

▶UNINHABITED TERRITORIES OF NORWAY

Bouvet Is. (54°26'S, 3°24'E); Jan Mayen Is. (71°00'N, 8°30'W).

UNITED KINGDOM

▶ANGUILLA

• **Geography** **Location:** island in northeastern Caribbean (18°03'N, 63°04'W). **Boundaries:** St. Martin 5 mi. (8 km) to S, St. Kitts 70 mi. (113 km) to SE. **Total area:** 35 sq. mi. (91 sq km). **Coastline:** 38 mi. (61 km). **Comparative area:** about one-half size of Washington, D.C. **Land use:** 0% arable land; 0% permanent crops; 100% other.; mostly rock with sparse scrub oak, few trees, some commercial salt ponds. **City:** The Valley (capital).
• **People** **Population:** 12,738 (2003 est.). **Nationality:** noun—Anguillan(s); adjective—Anguillan. **Ethnic groups:** mainly of black African descent. **Languages:** English. **Religions:** 40% Anglican, 33% Methodist, 7% Seventh-Day Adventist, 5% Baptist, 3% Roman Catholic.
• **Government** **Type:** dependent territory of U.K. **Constitution:** Apr. 1, 1982. **National holiday:** Anguilla Day, May 30. **Heads of government:** Chief Minister Hubert Hughes (since Mar. 16, 1994). **Structure:** chief minister appointed by the governor from among the members of the House of Assembly; unicameral 11-seat House of Assembly members elected by direct popular vote to serve 5-year terms; High Court.
• **Economy** **Monetary unit:** East Caribbean dollar. **Budget:** (2000) ***income:*** $22.8 mil.; ***expend.:*** $22.5 mil. **GDP:** $104 mil., $8,600 per capita (2001 est.). **Chief crops:** pigeon peas, corn, sweet potatoes; sheep, goats, cattle, poultry; fishing (including lobster). **Natural resources:** salt, fish, lobster. **Major industries:** tourism, boat building, off shore financial services. **Labor force:** 6,049 (2001); 6.7% unemployment (2001). **Exports:** $2.6 mil. (1999); lobsters, fish, livestock, salt. **Imports:** $80.9 mil. (1999). **Major trading partners:** U.S., U.K.

▶BERMUDA

• **Geography** **Location:** archipelago of about 150 islands, in southern North Atlantic Ocean (32° 18'N, 64°47'W). **Boundaries:** Cape Hatteras 580 mi. (933 km) to W. **Total area:** 19 sq. mi. (50 sq km). **Coastline:** 64 mi. (103 km). **Comparative area:** about three-tenths size of Washington, D.C. **Land use:** 6% arable land; 0% permanent crops; 94% other. **Cities:** (1990 est.) Hamilton (capital) 6,000; St. George's 3,000.
• **People** **Population:** 64,482 (2003 est.). **Nationality:** noun—Bermudian(s); adjective— Bermudian. **Ethnic groups:** 58% black, 36% white, 6% other. **Languages:** English (official), Portuguese. **Religions:** 39% non-Anglican protestant, 27% Anglican, 15% Roman Catholic, 19% other.
• **Government** **Type:** British dependent territory. **Constitution:** June 8, 1968. **National holiday:** Bermuda Day, May 24. **Heads of government:** Jennifer Smith, premier (since Nov. 1998). **Structure:** premier appointed by the governor; bicameral 11-seat Parliament members appointed by the governor, 40-seat House of Assembly members are elected by popular vote to serve 5-year terms; Supreme Court.
• **Economy** **Monetary unit:** Bermudian dollar. **Budget:** (FY01/02) ***income:*** $609.5 mil.; ***expend.:*** $574.6 mil. **GDP:** $2.25 bil., $35,200 per capita (2002 est.). **Chief crops:** bananas, vegetables, flowers, dairy products, citrus fruits. **Natural resources:** limestone, pleasant climate fostering tourism. **Major industries:** tourism, finance, structural concrete products. **Labor force:** 37,472 (2000); 22% clerical, 20% services, 17% laborers, 17% professional and technical, 13% administrative and managerial, 8% sales, 3% agriculture and fishing. **Exports:** $51 mil. (2000); reexports of pharmaceuticals. **Imports:** $719 mil. (2000); miscellaneous manufactured articles, machinery and transport equipment, food and live animals, chemicals. **Major trading partners:** ***exports:*** 78% E.U. (excluding U.K.), 4.5% U.S., 4.4% U.K., ***imports:*** 48.5% E.U., 26.9% Kazakhstan, 8.2% U.S.

▶BRITISH VIRGIN ISLANDS

• **Geography** **Location:** more than 40 mountainous islands (15 inhabited) in northeastern Caribbean. City of Road Town (on Tortola Is.), 18°26'N, 64°32'W. **Boundaries:** Puerto Rico about 100 mi. (161 km) to W. **Total area:** 58 sq. mi. (150 sq km). **Coastline:** 50 mi. (80 km). **Comparative area:** 0.9 times the size of Washington, D.C. **Land use:** 20% arable land; 7% permanent crops; 33% meadows and pastures; 73% other. **City:** (1987 est.) Road Town (capital), 2,500.
• **People** **Population:** 21,730 (2003 est.). **Nationality:** noun—Virgin Islander(s); adjective—British Virgin Islander. **Ethnic groups:** 83% black, remainder of white, Indian and Asian origin. **Languages:** English. **Religions:** 86% Protestant (33% Methodist, 17% Anglican, 9% Church of God, 6% Seventh-Day Adventist, 4% Baptist, 2% Jehovah's Witness, 2% other), 10% Roman Catholic, 2% none.
• **Government** **Type:** dependent territory of U.K. **Constitution:** June 1, 1977. **National holiday:** Territory Day, July 1. **Heads of government:** Ralph T. O'Neal, chief minister (since May 1995). **Structure:** chief minister appointed by the governor from among the members of the Legislative Council; unicameral 13-seat Legislative Council members are elected by direct popular vote to serve 5-year terms; Eastern Caribbean Supreme Court.
• **Economy** **Monetary unit:** U.S. dollar. **Budget:** (1997) ***income:*** $121.5 mil.; ***expend.:*** $115.5 mil. **GDP:** $320 mil., $16,000 per capita (2002). **Chief crops:** fruit, vegetables; livestock, poultry, fish. **Natural resources:** negl. **Major industries:** tourism, construction, rum. **Labor force:** 4,911 (1980).

Exports: $25.3 mil. (2002); rum, fresh fish, gravel, sand, fruits, vegetables. **Imports:** $187 mil. (2002); building materials, automobiles, foodstuffs, machinery. **Major trading partners:** Virgin Islands (U.S.), Puerto Rico, U.S.

▶CAYMAN ISLANDS

• **GEOGRAPHY** **Location:** three main and numerous smaller islands in western Caribbean. George Town (Grand Cayman Is.) 19°20'N, 81°23'W. **Boundaries:** Cuba to N, Jamaica 180 mi. (290 km) to SE. **Total area:** 100 sq. mi. (260 sq km). **Coastline:** 100 mi. (160 km). **Comparative area:** 1.5 times size of Washington, D.C. **Land use:** 0% arable land; 0% permanent crops; 100% other. **Cities:** (1989 census) Georgetown (capital) 12,921; West Bay 5,632.

• **PEOPLE** **Population:** 41,934 (2003 est.). **Nationality:** noun—Caymanian(s); adjective—Caymanian. **Ethnic groups:** 40% mixed, 20% white, 20% black, 20% expatriates of various ethnic groups. **Languages:** English. **Religions:** United Church (Presbyterian and Congregational), Anglican, Baptist, Roman Catholic, Church of God, other Protestant denominations.

• **GOVERNMENT** **Type:** British dependent territory. **Constitution:** 1959, revised 1972 and 1992. **National holiday:** Constitution Day, first Monday in July. **Head of government:** Peter Smith, governor and president of Executive Council (since May 1999). **Structure:** governor is appointed by the queen; unicameral 18-seat Legislative Assembly members elected by popular vote and serve 4-year terms; Grand Court, Cayman Islands Court of Appeals.

• **ECONOMY** **Monetary unit:** Caymanian dollar. **Budget:** (1997) ***income:*** $265.2 mil.; ***expend.:*** $248.9 mil. **GDP:** $1.27 bil., $65,000 per capita (2002 est.). **Chief crops:** fruits and vegetables; livestock, turtle farming. **Natural resources:** fish, climate and beaches that foster tourism. **Major industries:** tourism, banking, insurance, finance. **Labor force:** 19,820 (1995); 86% services, 12.6% industry, 1.4% agriculture. **Exports:** $1.2 mil. (1999); turtle products, manufactured consumer goods. **Imports:** $457.4 mil. (1999); foodstuffs, manufactured goods. **Major trading partners:** ***exports:*** mostly U.S.; ***imports:*** U.S., Trinidad and Tobago, U.K.

▶FALKLAND ISLANDS

Colony of the Falkland Islands

• **GEOGRAPHY** **Location:** two large and about 2,000 smaller islands in southwestern Atlantic Ocean. Stanley (East Falkland) 51°45'S, 57° 56'W. **Boundaries:** Cape Horn, South America, about 480 mi. (770 km) to SW. **Total area:** 4,699 sq. mi. (12,173 sq km). **Coastline:** 800 mi. (1,288 km). **Comparative area:** slightly smaller than Connecticut. **Land use:** 0% arable land; 0% permanent crops; 100% other. **City:** (1991 census) Stanley (capital) 1,557.

• **PEOPLE** **Population:** 2,697 (2003 est.). **Nationality:** noun—Falkland Islander(s); adjective—Falkland Island. **Ethnic groups:** British. **Languages:** English. **Religions:** predominantly Anglican, Roman Catholic, United Free Church, Evangelist Church, Jehovah's Witnesses, Lutheran, Seventh-Day Adventist.

• **GOVERNMENT** **Type:** colony of U.K. **Constitution:** Oct. 3, 1985. **National holiday:** Liberation Day, June 14. **Head of government:** Donald Lamont, governor (since May 1999). **Structure:** governor appointed by the queen; unicameral 10-seat Legislative Council members are elected by popular vote to serve 5-year terms; Supreme Court.

• **ECONOMY** **Monetary unit:** Falkland Island pound. **Budget:** (FY98) ***income:*** $66.2 mil.; ***expend.:*** $67.9 mil. **GDP:** N.A. **Natural resources:** fish, wildlife. **Major industries:** wool processing. **Labor force:** 1,100 (est.); 95% agriculture, mostly sheepherding. **Exports:** $7.6 mil. (1995); wool, hides, meat. **Imports:** $24.7 mil. (1995); food and drink, clothing, fuels, building materials. **Major trading partners:** U.K., Chile, Japan.

▶GIBRALTAR

• **GEOGRAPHY** **Location:** narrow peninsula running southward from southwest coast of Spain, to which it is connected by an isthmus. **Boundaries:** Spain to W and N, Mediterranean Sea to E, Morocco to S across Strait of Gibraltar. **Total area:** 3 sq. mi. (6.5 sq km). **Coastline:** 7.5 mi. (12 km). **Comparative area:** about 11 times size of the Mall in Washington, D.C. **Land use:** 0% arable land; 0% permanent crops; 100% other. **City:** Gibraltar (capital).

• **PEOPLE** **Population:** 27,776 (2003 est.). **Nationality:** noun—Gibraltarian(s); adjective—Gibraltar. **Ethnic groups:** Spanish, Italian, English, Maltese and Portuguese descent. **Languages:** English and Spanish are primary language;, Italian, Portuguese, Russian also spoken. English used in schools and for official purposes **Religions:** 76.9% Roman Catholic, 6.9% Church of England, 6.9% Muslim.

• **GOVERNMENT** **Type:** colony of UK. **Constitution:** May 30, 1969. **National holiday:** Commonwealth Day, second Monday of March. **Heads of government:** Peter Caruana, chief minister (since May 1996). **Structure:** chief minister appointed by the governor; unicameral 18-seat House of Assembly members elected by popular votes to serve 4-year terms; Supreme Court, Court of Appeals.

• **ECONOMY** **Monetary unit:** Gibraltar pound. **Budget:** (FY00/01) ***income:*** $307 mil.; ***expend.:*** $284 mil. **GDP:** $500 mil., $17,500 per capita (1997 est.). **Chief crops:** N.A. **Natural resources:** negl. **Major industries:** tourism, banking and finance, construction; support to large U.K. naval and air bases. **Labor force:** about 14,800 (including non-Gibraltar laborers); 60% services, 40% industry. **Exports:** $81.1 mil. (f.o.b., 1997); principally re-exports—51% petroleum, 41% manufactured goods, 8% other. **Imports:** $492 mil. (c.i.f., 1997); manufactured goods, fuels, foodstuffs. **Major trading partners:** ***exports:*** U.K., Morocco, Portugal; ***imports:*** U.K., Spain, Japan.

▶MONTSERRAT

(Two years of volcanic eruptions have left the southern half of this small island covered with ash and rock. More than half of its population had fled by mid-1997)

• **GEOGRAPHY** **Location:** eastern Caribbean Sea (16°44'N, 62°14'W). **Boundaries:** Guadeloupe 35 mi. (55 km) to S, Antigua 27 mi. (47 km) to NE. **Total area:** 39 sq. mi. (100 sq km). **Coastline:** 25 mi. (40 km). **Comparative area:** about three-fifths size of Washington, D.C. **Land use:** 20% arable land; 0% permanent crops; 80% other. **City:** (1980) Plymouth (capital) 3,500.

• **PEOPLE** **Population:** 8,995 (2000 est.); an estimated 8,000 refugees left the island following volcanic activity in 1995; some have returned. **Nationality:** noun—Montserratian(s); adjective—Montserratian. **Ethnic groups:** mostly black, with a few Europeans. **Languages:** English. **Religions:** Anglican, Methodist, Roman Catholic, Pentecostal, Seventh-Day Adventist, other Christian denominations.

• **GOVERNMENT** **Type:** colony of U.K. **Constitution:** present constitution came into force Dec.

19, 1989. **National holiday:** Celebration of the Birthday of the Queen, second Saturday of June. **Heads of government:** Chief Minister David Brandt (since Aug. 1997). **Structure:** the leader of the majority party ususally becomes chief minister; unicameral 11-seat Legislative Council members popularly elected to serve 5-year terms; Eastern Caribbean Supreme Court.

• **ECONOMY** **Monetary unit:** East Caribbean dollar. **Budget:** (1997 est.) ***income:*** $31.4 mil.; ***expend.:*** $31.6 mil. **GDP:** $29 mil., $3,400 per capita (2002 est.) **Chief crops:** cabbages, carrots, cucumbers, tomatoes, onions, peppers; livestock products. **Natural resources:** negl. **Major industries:** tourism, rum, textiles, electronic appliances. **Labor force:** 4,521 (1992 est.); 40.5% community, social, and personal services, 13.5% construction, 12.3% trade, restaurants, and hotels, 10.5% manufacturing. **Exports:** $700,000 mil. (2001); electronic components, plastic bags, apparel, hot peppers, live plants, cattle. **Imports:** $17 mil. (2001); machinery and transportation equipment, foodstuffs, manufactured goods, fuels, lubricants, related materials. **Major trading partners:** U.S., U.K.

▶PITCAIRN ISLANDS
Pitcairn, Henderson, Ducie, and Oeno Islands

• **GEOGRAPHY** **Location:** group of islands (one inhabited) in South Pacific. Pitcairn 25°04'S 130°04'W. **Boundaries:** about halfway between Panama and New Zealand; French Polynesia to NW. **Total area:** 18 sq. mi. (47 sq km). **Coastline:** 32 mi. (51 km). **Comparative area:** three-tenths size of Washington, D.C. **Land use:** N.A. **City:** Adamstown (capital).

• **PEOPLE** **Population:** 47 (2003 est.). **Nationality:** noun—Pitcairn Islander(s); adjective—Pitcairn Islander. **Ethnic groups:** descendants of Bounty mutineers and their Tahitian wives. **Languages:** English (official), also a Tahitian/English dialect. **Religion:** 100% Seventh-Day Adventist.

• **GOVERNMENT** **Type:** colony of U.K. **Constitution:** Local Government Ordinance of 1964. **National holiday:** Celebration of the Birthday of the Queen, second Saturday in June. **Head of government:** Island Magistrate and Chairman of the Island Council Jay Warren. **Structure:** magistrate elected by popular vote for a 3-year term; unicameral 10-seat Island Council members (6 popularly elected, 2 appointed) serve 1-year terms; Island Court.

• **ECONOMY** **Monetary unit:** New Zealand dollar. **Budget:** (FY94/95) ***income:*** $729,884; ***expend.:*** $878,119. **GDP:** N.A. **Chief crops:** wide variety of fruits and vegetables. **Natural resources:** miro trees (used for handicrafts), fish. **Major industries:** postage stamps, handicrafts. **Labor force:** 12 able-bodied men; no business community in usual sense; some public works; subsistence farming and fishing. **Exports:** fruits, vegetables, curios. **Imports:** fuel oil, machinery, building materials, flour, sugar, other foodstuffs. **Major trading partners:** N.A.

▶ST. HELENA

• **GEOGRAPHY** **Location:** eastern South Atlantic (15°56'S, 5°43'W). Dependencies are Ascension Is. (7°56'S, 14°25'W) 700 mi. to NW, and Tristan da Cunha (37°05'S, 12°17'W) 1,500 mi to SSW. **Boundaries:** Angola about 1,200 mi. (1,930 km) to E. **Total area:** 158 sq. mi. (410 sq km). **Coastline:** 37 mi. (60 km). **Comparative area:** slightly more than two times size of Washington, D.C. **Land use:** 13% arable land; 0% permanent crops; 87% other. **Cities:** (1987) Jamestown (capital) 1,413; Ascencion 1,152 (1996).

• **PEOPLE** **Population:** 7,367 (2003 est.). **Nationality:** noun—St. Helenian(s); adjective—St. Helenian. **Ethnic groups:** 50% African descent, 25% white, 25% Chinese. **Languages:** English. **Religions:** Anglican majority; also Baptist, Seventh-Day Adventist, Roman Catholic.

• **GOVERNMENT** **Type:** dependent territory of U.K. **Constitution:** Jan. 1, 1989. **National holiday:** Celebration of the Birthday of the Queen, second Saturday in June. **Head of government:** David Hollanby, governor and commander-in-chief. **Structure:** governor is appointed by the queen; unicameral 16-seat Legislative Council members elected by popular vote to serve 4-year terms; Supreme Court.

• **ECONOMY** **Monetary unit:** Saint Helenian pound. **Budget:** (FY92) ***income:*** $11.2 mil.; ***expend.:*** $11 mil. **GDP:** $18 mil.; $2,500 per capita (1998 est.) **Chief crops:** maize, potatoes, vegetables; timber production being developed; crawfishing on Tristan de Cunha. **Natural resources:** fish. **Major industries:** crafts (furniture, lacework, fancy woodwork), fish. **Labor force:** 3,500 (1998 est.); 6% agriculture and fishing, 48% industry, 46% services(1987). **Exports:** $704,000 (f.o.b., 1995); fish (frozen, canned, and salt-dried skipjack, tuna), handicrafts. **Imports:** $14.434 mil. (c.i.f., 1995); food, drink, tobacco, fuel oils, animal feed, building materials. **Major trading partners:** U.K., South Africa.

▶TURKS AND CAICOS ISLANDS

• **GEOGRAPHY** **Location:** more than 30 islands forming southeastern end of Bahamas Islands in Caribbean Sea. **Boundaries:** Haiti 90 mi (145 km) to S. **Total area:** 166 sq. mi. (430 sq km). **Coastline:** about 186 mi. (about 389 km). **Comparative area:** 2.5 times size of Washington, D.C. **Land use:** 2% arable land; 0% permanent crops; 98% other. **Cities:** Jamestown (capital).

• **PEOPLE** **Population:** 19,650 (2003 est.). **Nationality:** none. **Ethnic groups:** mostly African descent. **Languages:** English. **Religions:** 40% Baptist, 16% Methodist, 18% Anglican, 12% Church of God.

• **GOVERNMENT** **Type:** colony of U.K. **Constitution:** introduced on Aug. 30, 1976, suspended in 1986, restored and revised March 5, 1988. **National holiday:** Constitution Day, Aug. 30. **Head of government:** Derek Taylor, chief minister (since Jan. 1995). **Structure:** chief minister appointed by governor; unicameral 19-seat Legislative Council members (13 of which are popularly elected) serve 4-year terms; Supreme Court.

• **ECONOMY** **Monetary unit:** U.S. dollar. **Budget:** (1997/98 est.) ***income:*** $47 mil.; ***expend.:*** $33.6 mil. **GDP:** $231 mil., $9,600 per capita (2000 est.). **Chief crops:** corn, beans, cassava, citrus fruis, fish. **Natural resources:** spiny lobster, conch. **Major industries:** fishing, tourism, offshore financial services. **Labor force:** 4,848 (1990 est.); 33% government, 20% agriculture and fishing; significant numbers engaged tourist, financial and other industries. **Exports:** $169.2 mil. (2000); lobster, dried and fresh conch, conch shells. **Imports:** $175.6 mil. (2000); food and beverages, tobacco, clothing, manufactures, construction materials. **Major trading partners:** U.S., U.K.

▶UNINHABITED TERRITORIES OF THE UNITED KINGDOM

British Indian Ocean Territory (Diego Garcia 6°34'S, 72°24'E); South Georgia Is. (54°15'S, 36°45'W); South Orkney Is. (60°35'S, 45°30'W); South Sandwich Is. (56°00'S, 26°30'W); South Shetland Is. (62°00'S, 58°00'W).

The United Nations

▶STRUCTURE

Establishment Pres. Franklin D. Roosevelt coined the name "United Nations," which was first used in the "Declaration by United Nations" of Jan. 1, 1942, during World War II, when representatives of 26 countries pledged their governments to continue fighting together against the Axis Powers. From August to October 1944, representatives of China, the Soviet Union, the United Kingdom and the United States met at Dumbarton Oaks, a mansion in Washington, D.C., to discuss creating an international peacekeeping organization. Out of these meetings came a general outline for the United Nations.

At the United Nations Conference on International Organization, which met at San Francisco from Apr. 25 to June 26, 1945, representatives from 50 countries drew up the United Nations Charter and signed it on June 26, 1945. Poland, not present at the Conference, signed on October 15, 1945, and is considered one of the founding member states.

The United Nations officially came into existence on Oct. 24, 1945, when the charter was ratified by China, France, the Soviet Union, the United Kingdom, and the United States and by a majority of the other signatories.

U.N. Charter Full text of the Charter may be purchased for $3.00 from the United Nations, Sales Section, New York, NY 10017 U.S. The Preamble to the Charter sets forth the hopes for the United Nations: WE THE PEOPLES OF THE UNITED NATIONS DETERMINED

- to save succeeding generations from the scourge of war . . .
- to reaffirm faith in fundamental human rights, in the dignity and worth of the human person, in the equal rights of men and women and of nations large and small . . .
- to establish conditions under which justice and respect for the obligations arising from treaties and other sources of international law can be maintained . . .
- to promote social progress and better standards of life in larger freedom.

AND FOR THESE ENDS

- to practice tolerance and live together in peace with one another as good neighbors
- to unite our strength to maintain international peace and security
- to ensure, by the acceptance of principles and the institution of methods, that armed force shall not be used, save in the common interest
- to employ international machinery for the promotion of the economic and social advancement of all peoples.

HAVE RESOLVED TO COMBINE OUR EFFORTS TO ACCOMPLISH THESE AIMS. Accordingly, our respective Governments, through representatives assembled in the city of San Francisco, who have exhibited their full powers found to be in good and due form, have agreed to the present Charter of the United Nations and do hereby establish an international organization to be known as the United Nations.

Purposes The purposes of the United Nations are set forth in Article 1 of the Charter. They are: 1. To maintain international peace and security. 2. To develop friendly relations among nations based on respect for the principle of equal rights and self-determination of peoples. 3. To cooperate in solving international problems of an economic, social, cultural or humanitarian character, and in promoting respect for human rights and fundamental freedoms for all. 4. To be a center for harmonizing the actions of nations in the attainment of these common ends.

Official languages Originally, there were five official languages of the United Nations: Chinese, English, French, Russian and Spanish. Arabic was added to the General Assembly in 1973, to the Security Council in 1982 and to the Economic and Social Council in 1983. Major United Nations documents and all meetings of the General Assembly, the Security Council and the Economic and Social Council are translated into the six working languages.

United Nations headquarters United Nations, New York, NY 10017 U.S. U.N. headquarters covers a 16-acre site in New York City along the East River from 42nd to 48th Streets. It consists of the interconnected General Assembly, Secretariat and Dag Hammarskjöld Library buildings. Acquisition of the site was made possible by a gift of $8.5 million from John D. Rockefeller, Jr., and one-third of that amount from New York City. In 1951, the 39-story Secretariat building was completed and began functioning as the official home of the United Nations.

Permanent observers to the U.N. at New York headquarters cannot vote and do not have diplomatic privileges or immunities unless connected to the member nation's consulate. They do have free access to the public meetings and distribution of relevant documentation.

Non-member observers are the Holy See and Switzerland.

Intergovernmental and other observer organizations: More than 25 organizations have observer status at the U.N. Following is a representative sample: Caribbean Community, Commonwealth of Independent States; Council of Europe; International Federation of Red Cross and Red Crescent Societies; League of Arab States; Organization of African Unity; Organization of American States; Organization of Islamic Conference; Palestine.

PRINCIPAL ORGANS

General Assembly

The Assembly is the world's forum for discussing major issues facing the international community including world peace and security, human rights, global environment, disarmament, health issues including AIDS, and the rights of women and children.

The Assembly consists of all 191 member states, each having one vote. On important issues a two-thirds majority of those present and voting is required; other questions require a simple majority vote. It holds its annual session from September to December, and may call for extra sessions as needed. Its agenda of more than 150 matters for discussion is first dealt with in six main committees: Its agenda of more than 150 matters for discussion is first dealt with in six main committees: First Committee: Disarmament and International Security; Second Committee: Economic and Financial; Third Committee: Social, Humanitarian and Cultural; Fourth Committee: Special Political and De-colonization; Fifth Committee: Administrative and Budgetary; Sixth Committee: Legal. After discussing issues facing the world, it adopts recommendations (called resolutions) but has no power to enforce its decisions (resolutions), except the power of world opinion.

The Assembly considers and approves U.N. budget and assesses member states according to their ability to pay.

Security Council

The Council may investigate any dispute or situation that might lead to international friction, and may recommend methods for adjusting such disputes or terms for their settlement. While other organs of the U.N. make recommendations to governments, the Security Council alone has the power to take decisions that member states are obligated under the Charter to carry out.

The Security Council has 15 members: five permanent members, and the General Assembly elects 10 other members for two-year terms. They are not eligible for immediate re-election. The Council may be called into session at any time, and a representative of each member state must be present at U.N. headquarters at all times.

The five permanent members are China, France, Russia, the United Kingdom and the United States.

The terms of office of each non-permanent member ends on December 31 of the year indicated in parentheses: Angola (2004), Bulgaria (2003), Cameroon (2003), Chile (2004), Germany (2004), Guinea (2003), Mexico (2003), Pakistan (2004), Spain (2004), Syria (2003).

Decisions on matters of procedure require the approval of at least nine of the 15 members. Decisions on all other matters also require nine votes, including the concurring votes of all five permanent members. A negative vote by any permanent member on a non-procedural matter is often referred to as the "veto," which results in the rejection of the proposal. A state that is involved in a dispute may not vote.

Economic and Social Council (ECOSOC)

The Council is the principal organ to co-ordinate the economic and social work of the U.N. and its specialized agencies. It makes recommendations and initiates activities relating to world trade, industrialization, natural resources, human rights, the status of women, population, social welfare, education, health and related matters, science and technology and many other economic and social questions.

ECOSOC has 54 members elected for three-year terms by the General Assembly.

International Court of Justice (World Court) The Court is the judicial organ of the U.N. and sits in The Hague, Netherlands. All U.N. member states are automatically members of the Court. One country that is not a member of the U.N. is party to the Court–Switzerland. The Court is not open to individuals. It issues judgments on all questions that states refer to it and all matters provided for in the U.N. Charter or in treaties or conventions in force. Both the General Assembly and the Security Council can ask the Court for an advisory opinion on any legal question as can other organs of the U.N. or specialized agencies, when authorized to do so by the Assembly.

The Court has dealt with a wide variety of subjects, including territorial rights, the delimitation of territorial waters and continental shelves, fishing jurisdiction, questions of nationality and the right of individuals to asylum, territorial sovereignty, and the right of passage through foreign territory.

The judgment of the Court is final and without appeal. However, a revision may be applied for within ten years from the date of the judgment on the ground of a new decisive factor. If a party rejects the judgment, the other party may take the issue to the Security Council.

Judges: The ICJ has 15 independent judges, of different nationalities, elected by both the General Assembly and the Security Council. Judges hold 9-year terms and may be re-elected. All questions are decided by a majority of the judges present; the president votes only in case of a tie.

Secretariat

The Secretariat services the other organs of the U.N. and administers the programs and policies they develop. Headed by the Secretary-General, it consists of an international staff of more than 25,000 men and women from over 150 countries.

Secretaries-General: The General Assembly elects the Secretary-General to terms of office of five years (they may be re-elected). The Secretary-General, by tradition, does not come from one of the permanent member states of the Security Council–China, France, Russia, UK or the U.S. Those who have served in this post are:

Trygve Lie, Norway, Feb. 1, 1946, to Nov. 10, 1952;

Dag Hammarskjöld, Sweden, Apr. 11, 1953, to Sept. 17, 1961;

U Thant, Burma, Nov. 3, 1961, to Dec. 31, 1971;

Kurt Waldheim, Austria, Jan. 1, 1972, to Dec. 31, 1981;

Javier Perez de Cuellar, Peru Jan. 1, 1982 to Dec. 31,1991

Boutros Boutros-Ghali, Egypt, Jan 1, 1992, to Dec. 31, 1996;

Kofi Annan, Ghana, Jan. 1, 1997 to present.

▶UNITED NATIONS PROGRAMS

Each U.N. program was created by the General Assembly and reports to it through the Economic and Social Council (ECOSOC). Each member of the U.N. is a member of each Program.

International Research and Training Institute for the Advancement of Women (INSTRAW) Estab.: 1979. (made U.N. program in 1985); **HQ:** Calle Cesar Nicolas Penson, 102-A, Santo Domingo, Dominican Republic. Carries out research, training and information activities worldwide to show and increase women's key role in development.

United Nations Centre for Human Settlements (Habitat) Estab.: 1978; **HQ:** P.O. Box 30030, Nairobi, Kenya. Works to provide models and tools so people can improve their housing. Major concerns are planning, financing and management of human settlements—especially in developing countries.

U.S. Representatives to the U.N.

The U.S. representative to the UN holds the title of Ambassador Extraordinary and Plenipotentiary Permanent Representative and heads the U.S. Mission to the UN.

Year	Ambassador
1946	Edward R. Stettinius, Jr.
1946–47	Herschel V. Johnson (acting)
1947–53	Warren R. Austin
1953–60	Henry Cabot Lodge, Jr.
1960–61	James J. Wadsworth
1961–65	Adlai E. Stevenson
1965–68	Arthur J. Goldberg
1968	George W. Ball
1968–69	James Russell Wiggins
1969–71	Charles W. Yost
1971–73	George H.W. Bush
1973–75	John A. Scali
1975–76	Daniel P. Moynihan
1976–77	William W. Scranton
1977–79	Andrew Young
1979–81	Donald McHenry
1981–85	Jeane J. Kirkpatrick
1985–89	Vernon A. Walters
1989–92	Thomas J. Pickering
1992–93	Edward J. Perkins
1993–96	Madeleine K. Albright
1997–98	Bill Richardson
1999–2001	Richard C. Holbrooke
2001–	John D. Negroponte

United Nations Children's Fund (UNICEF) Estab.: 1946; **HQ:** UNICEF House, Three United Nations Plaza, New York, NY 10017, U.S. Provides care for children in developing countries by providing low-cost community-based services in maternal and child health, immunization, breastfeeding, growth monitoring, nutrition, clean water and sanitation, and education.

United Nations Conference on Trade and Development (UNCTAD) Estab.: 1964; **HQ:** Place des Nations, 8-14, Av. de la Paix, 1211 Geneva 10, Switzerland. Works to bring developing countries into global trade by formulating international trade policies, mediating multilateral trade agreements and providing assistance to governments.

United Nations Development Programme (UNDP) Estab.: 1965; **HQ:** One United Nations Plaza, New York, NY 10017, U.S. Coordinates development activities within the U.N. Operates over 5,000 projects in 150 countries and territories to facilitate development in economic and social sectors, including: farming, fishing, forestry, mining, manufacturing, power, transport, communications, housing, trade, health and environmental sanitation, economic planning and public administration.

United Nations Environment Programme (UNEP) Estab.: 1972; **HQ:** United Nations Avenue, Gigiri,P.O. Box 30552, Nairobi, Kenya. Coordinates international environment issues, including international environment conventions, monitors significant changes in environment and coordinates sound environmental practices.

United Nations Fund for Population Activities (UNFPA) Estab.: 1969; **HQ:** 220 E. 42nd Street, New York, NY 10017, U.S. Provides assistance to population programs in developing countries; promotes understanding of key population factors: population growth, fertility, mortality, spatial distribution and migration.

Office of the United Nations High Commissioner for Refugees (UNHCR) Estab.: 1950; **HQ:** Case Postale 2500, CH-1211 Geneve 2 Depot, Switzerland. Provides food, clothing and shelter for refugees and works with governments to establish safe conditions whereby refugees may return home and, when that is not possible, seeks to ensure that refugees receive asylum.

United Nations Institute for Training and Research (UNITAR) Estab: 1965; HQ: Palais des Nations, CH1211 Geneva 10, Switzerland. Provides training for members of U.N.'s permanent missions, including courses on international economics, workshops on drafting and negotiating international legal instruments, dispute settlement, and training on peace, security, human rights and humanitarian assistance.

United Nations University (UNU) Estab.: 1973; **HQ:** 53-70 Jingumae 5-chome, Shibuya-ku, Tokyo 150, Japan. UNU has no students of its own, no campus and no faculty. It is an international community of scholars engaged in research operating through worldwide networks of academic research institutions.

World Food Council (WFC) Estab.: 1974; **HQ:** Via delle Terme di Caracalla, 00100 Rome, Italy. Encourages developing countries to adopt a national food strategy whereby they assess their food situation needs, supply, potential for increasing production, storage, processing, transportation and distribution.

World Food Programme (WFP) (Joint program operated by U.N. and Food and Agriculture Organization (FAO) **Estab.:** 1963; **HQ:** Via C.G.Viola 68/70, Parco dei Medici, 00148 Rome, Italy. Provides food to support development activities and in times of emergencies. Operates projects in forestry, soil erosion control, irrigation, land rehabilitation and rural settlements.

▶SPECIALIZED AGENCIES OF THE U.N.

The specialized agencies associated with the United Nations are self-governing, independent organizations that work with the U.N. system and each other through the coordination machinery of the Economic and Social Council (ECOSOC). Each country affiliates with each agency on an individual basis. Membership in an agency is separate from U.N. membership. Nongovernmental organizations (NGOs) having expertise in the area may affiliate with each agency on a separate basis.

Food and Agriculture Organization of the United Nations (FAO) Member States: 174; **Estab.:** Oct. 16, 1945; **HQ:** Via delle Terme di Caracalla, 00100 Rome, Italy. Works to increase output of farmlands, forests and fisheries and to raise nutritional levels. Co-sponsors World Food Programme, which uses food, cash and services donated by member states for emergency situations.

International Atomic Energy Agency (IAEA) Member States: 127; **Estab.:** July 29, 1957; **HQ:** Vienna International Centre, P.O. Box 100, A-1400 Vienna, Austria. (Not regular specialized agency in that it does not report through ECOSOC but directly to General Assembly.) Fosters and guides development of peaceful uses of atomic energy, establishes standards for nuclear safety and environmental protection, aids member countries through technical cooperation, and fosters exchange of information on nuclear energy.

International Civil Aviation Organization (ICAO) Member States: 183; **Estab.:** Apr. 4, 1947; **HQ:** 999 University Street, Montreal, Quebec H3C 5H7, Canada. Works for safer air travel conditions worldwide. Establishes visual and instrument flight rules for pilots and crews; develops aeronautical charts for navigation; co-ordinates aircraft radio frequencies and works with customs procedures.

International Fund for Agricultural Development (IFAD) Member States: 160; **Estab.:** Nov. 30, 1977; **HQ:** Via del Serafico 107, 00142 Rome, Italy. Lends money to peoples in developing countries for agricultural development projects, including livestock, fisheries, processing and storage, irrigation, research and training.

International Labor Organization (ILO) Member States: 173; **Estab.:** 1919, under the Treaty of Versailles; (became U.N. specialized agency Dec. 14, 1946);. **HQ:** 4, route des Morillons, CH-1211 Geneva 22, Switzerland. Promotes social justice for working people everywhere by formulating international policies and programs to help improve working and living conditions; creates international labor standards as guidelines for governments and assists in vocational training, management techniques, occupational safety and health.

International Maritime Organization (IMO) Member States: 152; **Estab.:** Mar. 17, 1958; **HQ:** 4 Albert Embankment, London SE1 SR, England. Works to improve international shipping procedures and encourages highest standards in maritime safety; seeks to prevent and control marine pollution from ships and sets standards for training and certification of seafarers.

International Telecommunication Union (ITU) Member States: 184; **Estab.:** 1865, it became a U.N. specialized agency in Jan. 1949; **HQ:** Place des Nations, 1211 Geneva 20, Switzerland. Coordinates use of radio frequencies, tracks positions assigned by countries to geostationary satellites; coordinates modem and Internet standards.

United Nations Educational, Scientific and Cultural Organization (UNESCO) Member States: 186; **Estab.:** Nov. 4, 1946; **HQ:** 7, Place de Fontenoy, 75007 Paris, France. Promotes literacy through teacher training, building schools, and developing textbooks. Natural science programs include Man and the Biosphere and Intergovernmental Oceanographic Commission. Undertakes study and development of cultures, and conservation of world's inheritance of books, art and monuments.

United Nations Industrial Development Organization (UNIDO) Member States: 166; **Estab.:** 1966 (became U.N. specialized agency Jan. 1, 1986); **HQ:** P.O. Box 300, A-1400 Vienna, Austria. Promotes and accelerates industrialization of developing countries by providing technical assistance, training programs and advisory services.

Universal Postal Union (UPU) Member States: 189; **Estab.:** July 1, 1875 (became U.N. specialized agency July 1, 1948); **HQ:** International Bureau, Case postale 13, 3000 Berne 15, Switzerland. Establishes regulations for smooth exchange of mail worldwide.

World Bank Group Group of five closely related institutions. **HQ:** 1818 H Street, N.W., Washington, D.C. 20433 *International Bank for Reconstruction and Development (IBRD)* **Member States**: 178; **Estab.:** Dec. 27, 1945, to provide loans and technical assistance to developing countries to assist in their reconstruction and development. *International Finance Corporation (IFC)* **Member States: 165** (Membership is open only to World Bank members.); **Estab.:** July 20, 1956, to stimulate flow of private capital into productive investment in member countries. While closely associated with Bank, IFC is separate legal entity and its funds are distinct from those of Bank. *International Development Association (IDA)* **Member States**: 158; **Estab.:** Sept. 24, 1960. (Affiliate of the Bank, IDA has same directors and staff as Bank.) Lends money to poor countries with interest-free credits. Financial resources are from contributions by donor governments. *International Monetary Fund (IMF)* **Member States:** 181; Estab.: Dec. 27, 1945; HQ: 700 19th Street, N.W., Washington, D.C. 20431. Makes financing available to members in balance-of-payments difficulties and provides technical assistance to improve their economic management. *Multilateral Investment Guarantee Agency (MIGA)* **Member States:** 128; Estab.: 1988. Augments capacity of other insurers through coinsurance or reinsurance, thereby insuring investment in countries restricted or excluded by policies of other insurers.

World Health Organization (WHO) Member States: 190; **Estab.:** April 7, 1948; **HQ:** 20, avenue Appia, 1211 Geneva 27, Switzerland. Coordinates programs aimed at solving health problems by working with governments, other U.N. agencies and non-governmental organizations. See "World Health" section.

World Intellectual Property Organization (WIPO) Member States: 161; **Estab.:** 1883, (became U.N. specialized agency Dec. 17, 1974); **HQ:** 34, chemin des Colombettes, 121 Geneva 20, Switzerland. Promotes protection of intellectual property and cooperation in enforcement of agreements on matters such as copyrights, trademarks, industrial designs and patents.

World Meteorological Organization (WMO) Member States: 179; **Estab.:** 1873. (became U.N. specialized agency Mar. 23, 1950); **HQ:** 7 bis Avenue de la Paix, CP 2300, 1211 Geneva 2, Switzerland. Facilitates exchange of weather reports among countries; "World Weather Watch" tracks global weather conditions.

▶PEACEKEEPING OPERATIONS

United Nations peacekeeping is the use of multinational forces, under U.N. command, to keep disputing countries or communities from fighting while efforts are made to help them negotiate a solution. It is undertaken only with the agreement of both hostile parties. United Nations Peacekeeping Forces received the Nobel Peace Prize in 1988. As of June 2003, the U.N. had 14 peacekeeping operations, comprising 34,941 military and civilian police, 3,215 international civilian personnel, and 6,665 local civilian personnel. Eighty-nine countries contributed to the operations. Pakistan had the largest contribution: 206 civilian police, 72 military observers, and 3,940 troops for a total of 4,218. India had 483 civilian police, 38 military observers and 2,198 troops for a total of 2,719. Bangladesh had 97 civilian police, 63 military observers and

2,482 troops for a total of 2,642. The U.S. had 515 civilian police, 14 military observers and one troop for a total of 530. The total number of fatalities in peacekeeping operations from 1948 to June 2002 is 1,797. The approved budget for July 1, 2002 to June 30, 2003 was about $2.63 billion. Strength of the following operations is as of May 31, 2003.

Africa

Democratic Republic of the Congo – MONUC – U.N. Organization Mission in the Democratic Republic of the Congo. Since December 1991. Implements Lusaka Ceasefire agreement. **Strength:** 4,515 military; 60 civilian police; 630 international and 708 local civilian personnel.

Ethiopia and Eritrea – UNMEE – U.N. Mission in Ethiopia and Eritrea. Since July 2000. Monitors cease-fire and assists in observance of security commitments. **Strength:** 4,077 military personnel; 236 international and 260 local civilians.

Ivory Coast – MINUCI – U.N. Mission in Ivory Coast. Since May 2003. Mandated to implement Linas-Marcoussis Agreement, including complementing operations of French and ECOWAS forces. **Strength:** initially 26 military liaison officers and small civilian staff.

Sierra Leone – UNAMSIL – U.N. Mission in Sierra Leone. Since October 1999. Implements Lome Peace Agreement and assists in disarmament, demobilization and reintegration plan. **Strength:**13,084 military personnel, 119 civilian police, 310 international staff, 577 local civilians.

Western Sahara – MINURSO – U.N. Mission for the Referendum in Western Sahara. Since April 1991. Monitors cease-fire and is to organize and conduct a referendum which would allow people of Western Sahara to decide the Territory's future status. **Strength:** 229 military; 167 international civilians, 120 local civilians.

Asia

East Timor – UNMISET – U.N. Mission of Support in East Timor. Since May 2002. Provides assistance over two years until all operational responsibilities are fully managed by East Timor authorities. **Strength:** 3,497 military, 4,789 troops, 517 civilian police, 418 international civilians, 824 local civilians.

India-Pakistan – UNMOGIP – U.N. Military Observer Group in India and Pakistan. Since 1971. Stationed on both sides of Line of Control to observe cease-fire agreed upon by India and Pakistan under Simla Agreement of July 1972. **Strength:** 45 military, 24 international civilians, 47 local civilians.

Europe

Cyprus – UNFICYP – UN Peacekeeping Force in Cyprus. Since March 1964. Supervises cease-fire lines, maintains buffer zone, undertakes humanitarian activities. **Strength:** 1,248 military, 1,248 civilian police, 35 international civilian personnel, 105 local staff.

Georgia – UNOMIG – U.N. Observer Mission in Georgia. Since August 1993. Supervises 1994 Agreement on Ceasefire and Separation of Forces. **Strength:** 116 military observers, 99 international civilians, 176 local staff.

Kosovo - UNMIK – U.N. Interim Administration Mission in Kosovo. Since June 1999. Interim civilian administration supported by European Union and Organization for Security and Co-operation in Europe. **Strength:** 4,097 civilian police; 38 military; 1,005 international civilians; 3,184 local civilians.

Middle East

Golan Heights – UNDOF – U.N. Disengagement Observer Force. Since June 1974. Maintains an "area of separation" on Golan Heights between Israel and Syria and verifies arms limitation on both sides. **Strength:** 1,043 military; 37 international civilians, 87 local civilians.

Iraq/Kuwait – UNIKOM – U.N. Iraq-Kuwait Observation Mission. Since April 1991. Monitors demilitarized zone along the Iraq-Kuwait border. **Strength:** 13 military; 56 international civilians, 162 local civilians.

Lebanon – UNIFIL – U.N. Interim Force in Lebanon. Since March 1978. To confirm Israeli withdrawal from Lebanon, restore peace and security, help Lebanese government restore its authority. **Strength:** 2,029 military; 114 international civilians, 302 local staff.

Middle East – UNTSO – U.N. Truce Supervision Organization. Since May 1948. First U.N. peacekeeping operation. Monitors cease-fire, supervises armistice agreements, prevents isolated incidents from escalating and assists other U.N. peacekeeping operations in the region. **Strength:** 154 military, 102 international civilians, 113 local staff.

▶FURTHER U.N. INFORMATION

United Nations Bookstore Room GA-32, New York, NY, 10017; 212-963-7680; 1-800-553-3210; Fax: 212-963-4910. International publications issued by U.N. bodies and independent publishers.

▶U.N. INFORMATION ON-LINE

Official Web site for U.N. System:
http://www.unsystem.org
U.N. Headquarters: http://www.un.org

▶KEY EVENTS IN U.N. HISTORY

1946 (Jan. 10) First session of General Assembly begins at London with delegates of 51 member states.

1947 (Nov. 29) General Assembly passes Plan of Partition with Economic Union concerning future government of Palestine, thereby paving way for government of Tel Aviv to declare State of Israel on May 14, 1948.

1948 (Dec. 10) Universal Declaration of Human Rights adopted by General Assembly.

U.N. pioneers concept of peacekeeping observer missions and peacekeeping forces (1956).

1949 Mediates cease-fire between India and Pakistan, ending two years of fighting over Kashmir.

1950 Security Council calls members states to help South Korea repel invasion by North Korea.

Economic and Social Council adopts Standard International Trade Classification as basis for gathering world trade statistics.

1953 U.N. coordinates first global-census effort to establish earth's population for first time in history–2.4 billion people.

1955 First of ongoing congresses of criminologists and police officials draws up international principles and standards of criminal justice.

1959 U.N. General Assembly adopts Declaration on the Rights of the Child.

1960 Under de-colonization program, 17 territories become newly independent states; 16 in Africa join U.N.

1962 Secretary-General plays key role in resolving U.S.-Soviet confrontation over issue of nuclear missiles in Cuba.
1963 Security Council calls for arms embargo against South Africa. (Made mandatory in 1972.)
1967 After war erupts in Middle East, Security Council adopts Resolution 242, calling for withdrawal of forces from occupied territories, and recognizes right of all states in area to security.

Mediates settlement of Six-Day Arab-Israeli War.
1970 General Assembly adopts first international agreed-upon set of principles on seabed and ocean floor beyond national jurisdiction. Declares area "common heritage" of humanity.
1972 Security Council orders cease-fire in 17-day-old Middle East War and sends peacekeeping force to prevent further fighting between Israel and Arab states.
1975 U.N. conference at Mexico City launches Decade for Women to begin major effort toward women's equality worldwide.
1979 World Health Organization announces smallpox eradicated from all peoples on earth.
1987 First International Conference on Drug Abuse and Illicit Trafficking develops program on international coordination of illicit-drug issues.
1988 Mediates ending of Iran-Iraq War. Mediates Soviet withdrawal from Afghanistan.
1989 Mediates withdrawal of Cuban troops from Angola and South African troops from Namibia. U.N. sends peacekeeping troops and advisers to Namibia to supervise elections aimed at setting up self-government.
1990 Upon invitation, U.N. monitors demobilization of Nicaraguan rebel forces, and for first time monitors a presidential campaign and election in an independent nation.

Security Council Resolution 678 calls upon member states to restore peace and security in Kuwait by "all necessary means."

Responding to request by Haiti, U.N. supervises election of Haiti's first freely elected president.
1991 Security Council Resolution 687 sets terms of cease-fire in Gulf War and gives U.N. variety of duties to ensure peace.

Secretary-general negotiates cease-fire in 16-year-old civil war in Angola.

Secretary-general negotiates release of last six hostages held in Lebanon.

General Assembly rescinds Resolution 3379 of Nov. 10, 1975, equating Zionism with racism.
1992 Secretary-general completes peace negotiations between government of El Salvador and rebel Farabundo Marti National Liberation Front.
1993 145 nations co-sponsor Convention on Prohibition of the Development, Production, Stockpiling and Use of Chemical Weapons.

Human Rights Commission adopts Resolution 1993/8, which states that "abhorrent practice of rape and abuse of women and children in the former Yugoslavia....constitutes a ware crime:— this is first formal statement that declares rape, conducted during war, an international war crime under Geneva Convention.

General Assembly creates post of High Commissioner for Human Rights with power to intervene wherever basic freedoms are suppressed.
1994 Security Council removes South Africa from its agenda, declaring end of apartheid.

Security Council establishes International Tribunal for Rwanda to prosecute persons responsible for genocide and other violations of international humanitarian law.
1995 Secretary-general launches 50th anniversary commemoration. International Tribunal for Former Yugoslavia, established in 1993 to prosecute persons responsible for serious violations of international humanitarian law in former Yugoslavia since 1991, schedules first trials for September with 15 judges from 15 countries.

At request of government of Haiti, U.N. supervises free elections in the country.
1996 Upon request of the government, U.N. supervises free and fair elections in Sierra Leone that changes rule from military regime to democracy.

Hague-based International Criminal Tribunal for the former Yugoslavia begins trial for first war crimes in 50 years. Dusan Tadic, Bosnian Serb charged with torturing and murdering Bosnian Muslims and Croats at Omarska prison camp in Prijedor, Bosnia, in 1992. He is convicted in 1997 and sentenced to 20 years in prison.
1997 U.N. launches CyberSchoolBus to reach tens of thousands of students worldwide; provides lesson plans, global trends, quizzes; on-line Model U.N. discussion is first of its kind to reach 60,000 high schools and college students.

Thirteen nations ask for and receive U.N. assistance in holding their elections, including Algeria, Cambodia, Gambia, Guyana, Haiti, Honduras, Liberia, Mali and Yemen.
1998 1998 U.N. Conference on Rome adopts statute to create Permanent International Criminal Court to try individuals for genocide, war crimes, and crimes against humanity.
1999 Secretary-General issues Global Compact — enlisting businesses to advance universally agreed principles on human rights, labor and environment.

Security Council invests U.N. peacekeeping mission authority over Kosovo territory and people, including all legislative, executive, and judicial administration. First ever cooperation with non-U.N. organizations, including the EU and the Organization for Security in Europe.

Economic and Social Council holds first live broadcast of its high-level meeting over the Internet allowing global viewing.
2000 Millennium Summit, the largest single gathering of Heads of State and/or Government, brings 180 presidents, prime ministers and monarchs to the U.N. They issue the Millennium Declaration, which intends to solve humanity's most pressing problems, send every child to school, and deliver millions from poverty by 2015.
2001 (Sept. 28, 2001) Security Council establishes Counter Terrorism Committee and calls on all member states to cooperate in various measures to fight terrorism.
2002 (Jan.) Global Fund for fight AIDS, Tuberculosis and Malaria is launched.

(July 1) Statute of International Criminal Court enters into force. Anyone who commits any crimes under the Statute after this date will be liable for prosecution by the Court.
2003 (Sept.8, 9, 10) U.N. conducts first webcast of annual conference for nongovernmental organizations allowing people around the world to view and participate via e-mail. Daily live and on-demand webcasts of many U.N. meetings.

United Nations Member States (191)

Country	Joined U.N.
Afghanistan	1946
Albania	1955
Algeria	1962
Andorra	1993
Angola	1976
Antigua and Barbuda	1981
Argentina	1945
Armenia	1992
Australia	1945
Austria	1955
Azerbaijan	1992
Bahamas	1973
Bahrain	1971
Bangladesh	1974
Barbados	1966
Belarus	1945
Belgium	1945
Belize	1981
Benin	1960
Bhutan	1971
Bolivia	1945
Bosnia and Herzegovina	1992
Botswana	1966
Brazil	1945
Brunei Darussalam	1984
Bulgaria	1955
Burkina Faso	1960
Burundi	1962
Cambodia	1955
Cameroon	1960
Canada	1945
Cape Verde	1975
Central African Republic	1960
Chad	1960
Chile	1945
China	1945
Colombia	1945
Comoros	1975
Congo	1960
Congo, Democratic Republic of[1]	1960
Costa Rica	1945
Croatia	1992
Cuba	1945
Cyprus	1960
Czech Republic[2]	1993
Denmark	1945
Djibouti	1977
Dominica	1978
Dominican Republic	1945
East Timor	2002
Ecuador	1945
Egypt	1945
El Salvador	1945
Equatorial Guinea	1968
Eritrea	1993
Estonia	1991
Ethiopia	1945
Fiji	1970
Finland	1955
France	1945
Gabon	1960
Gambia	1965
Georgia	1992
Germany	1973
Ghana	1957
Greece	1945
Grenada	1974
Guatemala	1945
Guinea	1958
Guinea-Bissau	1974
Guyana	1966
Haiti	1945
Honduras	1945
Hungary	1955
Iceland	1946
India	1945
Indonesia	1950
Iran	1945
Iraq	1945
Ireland	1955
Israel	1949
Italy	1955
Ivory Coast	1960
Jamaica	1962
Japan	1956
Jordan	1955
Kazakhstan	1992
Kenya	1963
Kiribati	1999
Kuwait	1963
Kyrgyzstan	1992
Laos	1955
Latvia	1991
Lebanon	1945
Lesotho	1966
Liberia	1945
Libya	1955
Liechtenstein	1990
Lithuania	1991
Luxembourg	1945
Macedonia[3]	1993
Madagascar	1960
Malawi	1964
Malaysia	1957
Maldives	1965
Mali	1960
Malta	1964
Marshall Islands	1991
Mauritania	1961
Mauritius	1968
Mexico	1945
Micronesia	1991
Monaco	1993
Mongolia	1961
Morocco	1956
Mozambique	1975
Myanmar	1948
Namibia	1990
Nauru	1999
Nepal	1955
Netherlands	1945
New Zealand	1945
Nicaragua	1945
Niger	1960
Nigeria	1960
North Korea	1991
Norway	1945
Oman	1971
Pakistan	1947
Palau	1994
Panama	1945
Papua New Guinea	1975
Paraguay	1945
Peru	1945
Philippines	1945
Poland	1945
Portugal	1955
Qatar	1971
Moldova	1992
Romania	1955
Russian Federation	1945
Rwanda	1962
Saint Kitts and Nevis	1983
Saint Lucia	1979
Saint Vincent and the Grenadines	1980
Samoa	1976
San Marino	1992
São Tome and Principe	1975
Saudi Arabia	1945
Senegal	1960
Seychelles	1976
Sierra Leone	1961
Singapore	1965
Slovakia[2]	1993
Slovenia	1992
Solomon Islands	1978
Somalia	1960
South Africa	1945
South Korea	1991
Spain	1955
Sri Lanka	1955
Sudan	1956
Suriname	1975
Swaziland	1968
Sweden	1946
Switzerland	2002
Syria	1945
Tanzania	1961
Tajikistan	1992
Thailand	1946
Togo	1960
Tonga	1999
Trinidad and Tobago	1962
Tunisia	1956
Turkey	1945
Turkmenistan	1992
Tuvalu	2000
Uganda	1962
Ukraine	1945
United Arab Emirates	1971
United Kingdom	1945
United States	1945
Uruguay	1945
Uzbekistan	1992
Vanuatu	1981
Venezuela	1945
Viet Nam	1977
Yemen[4]	1947
Yugoslavia	1945
Zambia	1964
Zimbabwe	1980

Source: United Nations. 1. Formerly Zaire. 2. Czechoslovakia was an original member of the UN; when the nation split into separate Czech and Slovak Republics, both new republics were admitted as member states on Jan. 19, 1993. 3. Provisionally referred to for all purposes within the UN as "The former Yugoslav Republic of Macedonia" pending settlement of a difference with Greek Macedonia over the name. 4. Includes the former Democratic Yemen (admitted as a separate member in 1967), which merged with Yemen in 1990.

Major Political International Organizations

Commonwealth HQ: Marlborough House, Pall Mall, London, SW1Y 5HX, UK. **Estab.:** By some members of British Empire through evolutionary process formalized by Statute of Westminster on Dec. 31, 1931. As voluntary association of independent states, Commonwealth has no written constitution and no rigid contractual obligations. Emphasis is on consultation and exchange of views for cooperation, especially in economic affairs, drug trafficking, international terrorism and technical assistance to less developed states. Some countries that were part of British Empire are not part of Commonwealth. **Members** (54): Antigua and Barbuda, Australia, Bahamas, Bangladesh, Barbados, Belize, Botswana, Brunei, Cameroon, Canada, Cyprus, Dominica, Fiji, Gambia, Ghana, Grenada, Guyana, India, Jamaica, Kenya, Kiribati, Lesotho, Malawi, Malaysia, Maldives, Malta, Mauritius, Mozambique, Namibia, Nauru, New Zealand, Nigeria, Papua New Guinea, Saint Kitts and Nevis, Saint Lucia, Saint Vincent and the Grenadines, Samoa, Seychelles, Sierra Leone, Singapore, Solomon Islands, South Africa, Sri Lanka, Swaziland, Tanzania, Tong, Trinidad and Tobago, Tuvalu, Uganda, United Kingdom, Vanuatu, Western Samoa, Zambia, Zimbabwe.

Commonwealth of Independent States (CIS) HQ: Uliza Kirowa 17, Minsk 220000. **Estab.:** Dec. 8, 1991, by Byelorussia (Belarus), Russia, and Ukraine, which dissolved USSR and created CIS. Members agree to broad cooperation, including to cooperate in political, economic, ecological, humanitarian, and cultural fields. **Members** (12): Armenia, Azerbaijan, Belarus, Georgia, Kazakhstan, Kyrgyzstan, Moldova, Russia, Tajikistan, Turkmenistan, Ukraine, Uzbekistan.

European Union (EU, the Common Market), See Part III: "The Global Economy."

League of Arab States (LAS, the Arab League) HQ: Tahrir Square, Cairo, Egypt. **Estab.:** By treaty signed on Mar. 22, 1945 at Cairo, Egypt, to strengthen relations among members in financial, communications, cultural, health, social, nationality and social areas. **Members** (22): Algeria, Bahrain, Comoros, Djibouti, Egypt, Iraq, Jordan, Kuwait, Lebanon, Libya, Mauritania, Morocco, Oman, Palestine Liberation Organization, Qatar, Saudi Arabia, Somalia, Sudan, Syria, Tunisia, United Arab Emirates, Yemen.

North Atlantic Treaty Organization (NATO) HQ: B-1110 Brussels, Belgium. **Estab.:** By North Atlantic Treaty on Aug. 24, 1949, to maintain security among member states. NATO attempted to maintain military balance with countries of the Warsaw Pact: Bulgaria, Czechoslovakia, East Germany, Hungary, Poland, Romania, USSR. Since 1989 security challenges have shifted to possible adverse consequences from serious economic, social, and political difficulties, including ethnic rivalries and territorial disputes, arms proliferation, and terrorism. In 1997, leaders of NATO voted to admit Czech Republic, Hungary and Poland, and their official membership received final approval in 1999. In May 2002, Russia became a participant (but not a full-fledged member) of the organization. Russia is not bound by NATO's collective defense pact, nor will it have a veto over NATO decisions. **Members** (19): Belgium, Canada, Czech Republic, Denmark, France, Germany, Greece, Hungary, Iceland, Italy, Luxembourg, Netherlands, Norway, Poland, Portugal, Spain, Turkey, United Kingdom, U.S.

Organization of African Unity (OAU) HQ: African Unity Hall, POB 3243, Addis Ababa, Ethiopia. **Estab.:** By charter on May 25, 1963 at Addis Ababa, to promote unity and solidarity among African states. OAU works to eradicate all forms of colonialism from Africa and to defend their sovereignty and independence. **Members** (53): Algeria, Angola, Benin, Botswana, Burkina Faso, Burundi, Cameroon, Cape Verde, Central African Republic, Chad, Comoros, Congo, Democratic Republic of Congo, Djibouti, Egypt, Equatorial Guinea, Eritrea, Ethiopia, Gabon, Gambia, Ghana, Guinea, Guinea-Bissau, Ivory Coast, Kenya, Lesotho, Liberia, Libya, Madagascar, Malawi, Mali, Mauritania, Mauritius, Mozambique, Namibia, Niger, Nigeria, Rwanda, São Tomé and Principé, Senegal, Seychelles, Sierra Leone, Somalia, South Africa, Sudan, Swaziland, Tanzania, Togo, Tunisia, Uganda, Western Sahara, Zambia, Zimbabwe.

Organization of American States (OAS) HQ: 1889 F St., NW, Washington, DC 20006-4499, U.S. **Estab.:** By charter signed at Bogotá, Columbia, effective Dec. 13, 1951, to strengthen peace and security on continent, promote cooperation in human rights, education, economic and social development and scientific exchanges, and to seek solutions to political, juridical and economic problems. **Members** (35): Antigua and Barbuda, Argentina, Bahamas, Barbados, Belize, Bolivia, Brazil, Canada, Chile, Colombia, Costa Rica, Cuba (suspended from OAS activities but not membership in 1962), Dominica, Dominican Republic, Ecuador, El Salvador, Grenada, Guatemala, Guyana, Haiti, Honduras, Jamaica, Mexico, Nicaragua, Panama, Paraguay, Peru, Saint Kitts and Nevis, Saint Lucia, Saint Vincent and the Grenadines, Suriname, Trinidad and Tobago, U.S., Uruguay, Venezuela.

Organization of the Petroleum Exporting Countries (OPEC) HQ: Obere Donaustrasse 93, A-1020 Vienna, Austria. **Estab.:** Nov. 14, 1960 by resolution adopted at Baghdad Conference, to coordinate and unify petroleum policies and to stabilize international oil prices to prevent harmful fluctuations. **Members** (11): Algeria, Indonesia, Iran, Iraq, Kuwait, Libya, Nigeria, Qatar, Saudi Arabia, United Arab Emirates, Venezuela.

Organization for Security and Cooperation in Europe (OSCE) HQ: Kärtnerring 5-7, A-1010 Vienna, Austria. **Estab.:** by Final Act of Conference on Security and Cooperation in Europe in 1975. In 1990, CSCE members declared end of "era of confrontation and division of Europe" and beginning of "a new era of democracy, peace and unity." Serves as forum for dialogue, negotiation, cooperation, and direction in shaping new Europe. **Members** (55): Albania, Andorra, Armenia, Austria, Azerbaijan, Belarus, Belgium, Bosnia and Herzegovina, Bulgaria, Canada, Croatia, Cyprus, Czech Republic, Denmark, Estonia, Finland, France, Georgia, Germany, Greece, Holy See, Hungary, Iceland, Ireland, Italy, Kazakhstan, Kyrgyzstan, Latvia, Liechtenstein, Lithuania, Luxembourg, Macedonia, Malta, Moldova, Monaco, Netherlands, Norway, Poland, Portugal, Romania, Russia, San Marino, Slovakia, Slovenia, Spain, Sweden, Switzerland, Tajikistan, Turkmenistan, Ukraine, UK, U.S., Uzbekistan, Yugoslavia (suspended).

Part IV SCIENCE AND TECHNOLOGY
Science

ASTRONOMY

Astronomy is the oldest science, but it continues to be at the forefront of scientific thought. The ancients of the Northern Hemisphere knew the skies, probably better than most of us do. They recognized that most stars appear to rise in the east at night and travel in circular paths across the sky, and that a few are wanderers—planets—that move among the other stars. They named the groups of stars that we call constellations and recognized that constellations visible in winter are different from those visible in summer (although some are visible all year). They learned how to find the extremities of the sunrise and built giant stone structures, such as Stonehenge, probably to locate certain of the positions of the Sun or other stars.

In 1609 Galileo introduced the first artificial device for exploring the universe—the astronomical telescope. Even in that first year, he saw wonders the ancients never knew. Since then, we have built larger and better telescopes, devices for detecting radio waves, microwaves, X rays, infrared waves, and gamma rays from space, and have even traveled to our own Moon. We have sent space probes to eight of the nine planets of the solar system and to comets and asteroids.

▶THE SOLAR SYSTEM

Earth is a planet. A planet is a large, fairly cool body traveling in a path, called its orbit, around a star. All of the bodies under the gravitational influence of our local star, the Sun, together with the Sun, form the solar system. There are nine known planets in the solar system, as well as other planets around other stars, which are discussed below. Six of the nine solar-system planets were known to the ancients, and astronomers found the remaining three by early in the 20th century. Often smaller, cool bodies orbit planets. These are called satellites or moons.

Cool rocky or metallic bodies smaller than planets that orbit the Sun are called asteroids. Small icy bodies are called comets. Comets often have orbits that take them from the edge of the system to locations near the Sun (some actually hit the Sun and burn up). Very small objects in space are called meteoroids. A meteoroid that burns up in Earth's atmosphere is called a meteor. One that reaches Earth's surface without burning completely is a meteorite.

Major Events in Astronomy and Space

B.C.

585 Thales of Miletus (Greek: c. 625–c. 547) predicts solar eclipse in Asia Minor.

c. 480 Astronomer Oenopides of Chios (Greek: 5th cent.) discovers that Earth is tilted with respect to Sun.

352 Chinese report "guest star," or supernova, the earliest known sighting.

c. 340 Astronomer Kidinnu (Kidenas; Babylon: c. 379) discovers precession of equinoxes, the apparent change in position of stars caused by Earth's wobbling on its orbit.

c. 300 Chinese astronomers compile star maps.

c. 240 Chinese astronomers observe Halley's comet. Eratosthenes of Cyrene (Greek: c.276–c.194) correctly calculates Earth's size.

165 Chinese astronomers notice sunspots.

c. 130 Astronomer Hipparchus of Nicea (Greek: 147–127) correctly determines distance to Moon and rediscovers precession of equinoxes (see 340 B.C.).

A.D.

c. 140 *Almagest* of Ptolemy (Greek: c. 90–168) develops astronomy of solar system in form based on Sun and planets revolving about Earth.

1543 *De Revolutionibus* by Nicholas Copernicus (Polish: 1473–1543) presents convincing arguments that Earth and other planets orbit Sun.

1577 Tycho Brahe (Danish: 1546–1601) proves that comets are visitors from space, not weather phenomena as previously believed.

1592 David Fabricius (German: 1564–1617) discovers star, later named Mira, that gradually disappears; in studying it in 1638, Phocyclides Holawarda recognizes that it appears and reappears on regular basis—the first-known variable star.

1609 Johannes Kepler (German: 1571–1630) discovers that the planets move in elliptical orbits.

1610 Galileo observes Jupiter's moons, phases of Venus, and (although he does not recognize what they are) rings of Saturn.

1611 Several astronomers simultaneously discover sunspots for first time in West.

1671 Giovanni Domenico Cassini (Italian-French: 1625-1712) correctly determines distances of the planets from Sun.

1682 Edmond Halley (English: 1656–1742) describes comet now known by his name and in 1705 correctly predicts its return in 1758.

1718 Halley discovers that stars move with respect to each other.

1755 Immanuel Kant (German: 1724–1804) proposes that many nebulas are actually composed of millions of stars and that solar system formed when giant cloud of dust condensed.

1781 William Herschel (German-English: 1738–1822) discovers planet Uranus.

1785 Herschel demonstrates that Milky Way is disk- or lens-shaped group of many stars, one of which is the Sun.

1801 Guiseppe Piazzi (Italian: 1746–1826) discovers first-known asteroid, Ceres.

1838 Friedrich W. Bessel (German: 1784–1846) determines distance to star other than the Sun.

1846 Johann G. Galle (German: 1812–1910) discovers planet Neptune using predictions of Urbain J.J. Leverrier (French: 1811–77) and John Couch Adams (English: 1819–92).

1924 Edwin Hubble (American: 1889–1953) shows that galaxies are "island universes"—giant aggregations of stars as large as Milky Way.
1929 Hubble finds that universe is expanding.
1930 Clyde Tombaugh (American: 1906–97) discovers planet Pluto.
1931 Karl Jansky (American: 1905–50) discovers that radio waves are coming from space, leading to founding of radio astronomy.
1948 George Gamow (Russian-American: 1904–68), Ralph Alpher (American: 1921–), and Robert Herman (American: 1914–97) develop Big Bang theory of origin of universe.

Jan Hendrik Oort (Dutch: 1900–1992) proposes that comets come from a vast cloud of material orbiting far beyond Pluto; the material is now known as the Oort Cloud.
1957 USSR launches *Sputnik 1,* the first man-made satellite.
1961 Soviet cosmonaut Yuri A. Gagarin (Russian: 1934-68) is first human to orbit Earth.
1962 U.S. space probe *Mariner 2* is first to reach neighborhood of another planet, Venus.
1963 Maarten Schmidt (Dutch-American: 1929–) is first astronomer to recognize a quasar.
1964 Arno Penzias (German-American: 1933–) and Robert Wilson (American: 1936–) find radio waves pervading space, proving to most astronomers that Big Bang actually occurred.
1967 Jocelyn Bell-Burnell (English: 1943–) discovers first-known pulsar while working for Antony Hewish (English: 1924–); Hewish later gets Nobel Prize for discovery.
1969 Neil Armstrong (American: 1930–) and Edwin E. ("Buzz") Aldrin (American: 1930–) walk on Moon.
1971 American spacecraft, *Mariner 9,* is first to orbit another planet, Mars.
1975 Soviet space probe transmits pictures from surface of Venus.
1976 U.S. Viking space probes begin transmitting pictures of surface of Mars—unsuccessful in detecting life on planet.
1977 Rings of Uranus are discovered.
1979 U.S. space probe *Voyager 1* discovers that, like Saturn and Uranus, Jupiter has rings.
1980 Alan Guth (American: 1947–) develops theory of inflationary universe, an explanation of how Big Bang occurred.
1981 U.S. introduces reusable spacecraft, the space shuttle.
1987 The explosion of Supernova 1987A, the nearest supernova that has been visible from Earth since 1604, is observed.
1989 U.S. space probe *Voyager 2* flies by Neptune, farthest planet from the Sun at that time, imaging the planet, its rings, and its moons.
1990 The Hubble Space Telescope is launched.
1992 The Magellan Venus orbiter completes mapping 95 percent of the planet's surface with radar.

Observations from the *Cosmic Background Explorer Satellite (COBE)* confirm the Big Bang theory.
1993 Members of the crew of the Space Shuttle *Endeavour* successfully repair the main lens of the Hubble Space Telescope.
1994 Comet Shoemaker-Levy 9, broken into 21 fragments, some nearly half a kilometer in diameter, slams into the far side of Jupiter in July.
1995 Astronomers Michel Mayor (Swiss:) and Didier Queloz (Swiss: 1966–) announce the first planet to orbit an ordinary star other than the Sun.

The Hubble Space Telescope focuses on a single patch of the northern sky long enough to reveal previously unknown objects at great distances from Earth. The experiment, called the Hubble Deep Field, is repeated for the sky's southern hemisphere in 1998.
1996 Firm evidence is found for a massive black hole at the center of the Milky Way galaxy.
1997 Jupiter's moon Europa is found to have a sea of liquid water beneath a surface of ice crossed by giant fissures; astronomers conclude that it is possible that living organisms could exist in Europa's ocean.

The space probe *Pathfinder* lands safely on Mars on July 4. Pathfinder's rover, Sojourner, leaves the craft and sends to Earth reports of its close-up observation of Martian rocks in what appears to be an ancient flood plain.
1998 Astronomers conclude that there isn't enough matter in the universe to stop expansion; expansion may be accelerated by a small antigravity force.
1999 Two independent teams of astronomers determine that a system of at least three planets orbits the star Upsilon Andromedae.
2000 Studies using the Chandra X-Ray Observatory, a satellite launched in 1999, reveal that the pervasive X-ray background of the universe is caused by black holes that lurk in the hearts of most galaxies.

Permanent occupation of the International Space Station begins on May 19.

Calculations based on the US BOOMERANG (Balloon Observations of Millimetric Extragalactic Radiation and Geophysics) experiment, a balloon-borne study of the cosmic background radiation conducted in 1998, reveal that the universe is flat, not curved.
2001 Timothy Beers (American: 1957–) of Michigan State University and coworkers use uranium-238 to date the oldest stars in the universe at 12.5 billion years (with an uncertainty of 3 billion years), giving the minimum age for the universe.

In February the space probe *NEAR-Shoemaker* lands softly on asteroid 433 Eros, after orbiting it for a year.

The orbit of comet 200 CR-105 is calculated to be distorted as if by the presence of a planet larger than Pluto orbiting far beyond Neptune, now or at some time in the distant past—although the planet could have been Neptune itself if Neptune once occupied an orbit much farther from the Sun.

Geoffrey W. Marcy (American: 1954–) and R. Paul Butler (American) announce the discovery of an extrasolar planet slightly smaller than Jupiter orbiting star HD 4028 at a distance about equal to that of Mars about the Sun, suggesting a system of planets similar to the solar system might exist about HD 4028.
2002 Kenneth R. Sembach and coworkers report studies based on *FUSE (Far Ultraviolet Spectroscopic Explorer)* satellite observations show that the Milky Way is enveloped in a huge cloud of hot gas that extends almost to the nearest galaxies.

Studies of meteorites blasted off the surface of the Moon that have landed on Earth indicate that asteroids, not comets, bombarded the Moon (and Earth as well) about 3.9 billion years ago, causing thousands of giant craters.

The Martian *Odyssey* space probe determined that a large amount of water, frozen into ice, is just below the surface of both poles of Mars.

NASA Scientists propose that an unusual astronomical object named RXJ1856.6-3754 is a "quark star," a body so dense that the atomic nuclei have broken into constituent up and down quarks as well as some strange quarks.

A dozen unusual radio sources that appear as X patterns formed by giant jets of hot matter and radiation are recognized as the results of pairs of black holes colliding and merging.

Basic Facts About the Planets

	Terrestrial Planets				Gas Giants				
Characteristic	Mercury	Venus	Earth	Mars	Jupiter	Saturn	Uranus	Neptune	Pluto
Distance from Sun									
miles (millions)	36.0	67.2	93.0	141.6	483.78	890.75	1,784.86	2,793.0	3,647.23
km (millions)	57.9	108.2	149.6	227.9	778.57	1,433.53	2,872.46	4,495.1	5,869.66
Rotation period	59 days	243 days[1]	23.9 hrs	24.6 hrs	9.925 hrs	10.656 hrs	17.24 hrs	16.1 hrs	6.4 days
Orbital period (days)	88	224.7	365.256	686.98	4,331	10,747	30,589	59,800	90,588
Orbital velocity (miles/second)	29.74	21.76	18.51	14.99	8.12	6.02	4.23	3.37	2.93
Inclination of axis	0.01	3.39	23.45	25.19	3.13	26.73	97.77	28.32	122.53
Equatorial diameter									
miles	3,032	7,521	7,926	4,222	88,846	74,897	31,763	30,775	1,485
km	4,879	12,104	12,756	6,794	142,984	120,536	51,118	49,528	2,930
In relation to Earth:									
Diameter	38.3%	94.9%	100%	53.3%	1,121%	945%	401%	388%	18.7%
Mass	5.53%	81.5%	100%	10.7%	31,783%	9,516.2%	1,453.6%	1,714.7%	0.21%
Gravity	37.8%	90.7%	100%	37.7%	236.4%	91.6%	88.90%	112%	5.9%
Escape velocity									
miles/second	2.7	6.4	7.0	3.1	37.0	22.1	13.2	14.6	0.7
km/second	4.3	10.36	11.186	5.03	59.5	35.5	21.3	23.5	1.1
Average surface temperature	332.4°F 166.9°C	867.0°F 463.9°C	59°F 15°C	-85°F -65°C	-166°F -110°C	-220°F -140°C	-320°F -195°C	-330°F -200°C	-375°F -225°C
Planetary satellites	0	0	1	2	61	31	21	11	1

1. Venus's rotation is retrograde, or opposite the direction of other planets. **Source:** NASA: National Space Science Data Center (NSSDC) **http://nssdc.gsfc.nasa.gov.**

It is currently believed that the solar system formed when a cloud of gas condensed to form the Sun. Parts of the cloud formed small bodies similar to today's asteroids, comets, and meteoroids. Collectively, these small bodies are called planetesimals or planetoids. Early in the history of the solar system, about 4.6 billion years ago or even before, the planetoids frequently crashed into one another. While this sometimes resulted in one or more of the planetoids breaking up, often a small planetoid would stick to a larger one, making it larger still. The end products of this process, it is proposed, are the nine solar-system planets and their moons, along with the existing asteroids, comets, and meteoroids.

The solar system is located in a large system of stars called the Milky Way galaxy. The solar system is 28,000 light-years (defined below) from the center of the Milky Way and 67 light-years from the plane defined by the galactic spiral.

The Terrestrial Planets

In terms of distance from the Sun, these are the first four planets of the solar system— Mercury, Venus, Earth and Mars. Terrestrial planets all have a comparatively high density, a concentration of metallic elements, and hard, rocky surfaces. Earth is the largest of the terrestrial planets but is dwarfed by the enormous sizes of the outer "gas giant" planets (Jupiter, Saturn, Uranus and Neptune). Mercury, Earth and Mars have magnetic fields; Venus does not have a detectable magnetic field. Earth and Venus have thick atmospheres, Mars has a thin atmosphere, and Mercury's atmosphere is almost nonexistent.

Mercury

Main components of atmosphere: 98% helium, 2% hydrogen. Mercury is the planet closest to the Sun and in keeping with its namesake—Mercury, the winged messenger—moves the fastest in its orbit. Usually obscured from view from Earth by the Sun's glare, it is sometimes visible on Earth's horizon just after sunset, when it is called the Evening Star, or just before dawn, when it is called the Morning Star. About 14 times in each 100 years, Mercury can also be seen crossing directly in front of the Sun's disk.

Mercury was long thought to be the smallest planet, but better measurements of Pluto's size have shown that Pluto is even smaller. The U.S. *Mariner 10* space probe provided the first detailed pictures of Mercury's surface during flybys in 1974 and 1975. *Mariner 10* mapped about 35 percent of the planet's heavily cratered, moonlike surface. No space probe has visited the planet since.

Mercury is a waterless, airless world that alternately bakes and freezes as it orbits the Sun. Its tenuous atmosphere is thought to be one-trillionth the density of Earth's atmosphere and largely composed of helium. On Mercury's sunlit side temperatures reach 850°F (450°C) and plummet to -300°F (-180°C) on the dark side. These extremes are largely due to Mercury's slow rate of rotation: one single rotation is two-thirds of a Mercury year, or 59 days for a rotation compared

Glossary of Planetary Terms

Escape velocity The speed needed for an object to be propelled from the surface of a planet and not fall back. The escape velocity for Earth is 6.96 miles (11.2 km) per second, thus an object must travel at least that fast, or approximately 7 miles per second, to leave Earth's gravitational influence.

Inclination of axis The angle that the axis about which a planet rotates makes with the plane defined by its path around the Sun.

Orbital period The time it takes for a planet to orbit the Sun.

Orbital velocity The speed of a planet in its path around the Sun.

Rotation period The time it takes for a planet to rotate once about itself.

to 88 days for a revolution. Mercury's axis is almost perpendicular to its plane of rotation, so any single place on the planet sees dawn only once every 176 days—the planet must rotate three times and go through two of its "years" before a new day dawns.

Mercury's surface is scarred with hundreds of thousands of meteor craters. Many such craters were probably formed during the planetoid showers believed to have occurred soon after the formation of the solar system. Many areas have had the craters smoothed over by ancient lava flows, however. This indicates extensive volcanic activity on Mercury during and after the time of the planetoid showers. The surface is also crisscrossed by huge cliffs, or scarps. These probably formed as Mercury's surface cooled and shrank. Some of the scarps are up to 1.2 miles (1.9 km) high and 932 miles (1,500 km) long.

Mercury is so dense for its size that astronomers think that its rocky outer crust is very thin and that the planet is mostly iron. It probably was once larger. During the early bombardment, it is conjectured that one of the larger planetoids (about a sixth of the size of the early planet) hit Mercury so hard that it blasted most of the rocky crust away.

Venus

Main components of atmosphere: 96.5% carbon dioxide, 3.5% nitrogen. As seen in the night sky from Earth, Venus is second only to the Moon in brightness. Venus, named for the Roman goddess of love, is the planet that passes closest to Earth (24,000,000 mi., or 39,000,000 km). Since it is between Earth and the Sun, Venus, like Mercury, is seen either as the Morning Star or the Evening Star.

Because of its proximity to Earth and its position between Earth and the Sun, Venus became (in 1962) the first planet beyond Earth to be scanned by a space probe in its neighborhood (*Mariner 2*). The pull of the Sun's gravity makes Venus and Mercury "downhill" from the Earth; one must travel against the Sun's gravity to reach other planets. Since 1962 Venus has been visited by numerous U.S. and Soviet spacecraft. Soviet space probes *Venera 13* and *Venera 14* were the first to make a soft landing and send back pictures from the Venusian surface.

The Venusian atmosphere is thick with clouds that have shrouded the planet's surface from view, making the planet somewhat mysterious. The Venusian clouds range from about 28 to 37 miles (45 to 60 km) above the planet's surface and are differentiated into three layers. Droplets of sulfuric acid and water have been identified in the clouds.

The clouds and high level of carbon dioxide in the atmosphere have combined to trap heat in the lower atmosphere of Venus. This is an extreme form of the greenhouse effect and is responsible for high temperatures in the lower atmosphere, 870°F (460°C)—hot enough to melt lead. The atmospheric pressure at the surface is 92 times that of Earth. Radiation of heat from the lower atmosphere is so inefficient that there is little variation of temperature between night and day.

One feature of the Venusian upper atmosphere is markedly different from that of Earth. The atmosphere superrotates on Venus—that is, the atmosphere above the clouds moves 60 times faster than the planet rotates—whereas the Earth and its atmosphere rotate at the same speed. So, high winds and steady upper-atmosphere winds—100 mph (160 km/hr) or faster—are a dominant factor in Venusian weather. But at ground level, winds are calmer, with an average closer to 2 mph (3.6 km/hr).

Soviet space probes that soft-landed on Venus have provided photographs of the planet's surface. Radar maps of 99 percent of the Venusian surface, completed by the U.S. Pioneer spacecraft (from 1978 to 1993), and *Magellan* (from 1989 to 1994), now give a detailed picture of features as small as 350 ft. (100 m) in diameter. More than a thousand Venusian mountains, volcanoes, rifts, basins, impact craters, and other features have been identified.

About 10 percent of the surface is highland terrain, 70 percent rolling uplands, and 20 percent lowland plains. There are two major highland areas: one about half the size of Africa and located in the equatorial region and the other, about the size of Australia, located to the north. The highest mountain on Venus—Maxwell Montes—is in the northern highlands and is higher than Earth's Mt. Everest. Volcanic activity dominates Venus; the planet is covered with volcanic domes and lava channels.

Like Earth, Venus is thought to have an internal structure. The crust, however, is much thicker than that of Earth, perhaps twice as deep on the average, making the crust of Venus about 60 mi. (100 km) thick. Below the crust is a large layer called the mantle; below the mantle is a core thought to be molten nickel-iron, similar to Earth's outer core.

Earth

Main components of atmosphere: 78% nitrogen, 21% oxygen, 1% water, 0.93% argon. Earth is the third planet from the Sun and the only one in the solar system known to harbor life. From space, our planet appears as a bright, blue-and-white sphere—blue because some 70 percent of the surface is covered by water, and white because clouds cover about half the planet's surface.

Earth's atmosphere and composition are discussed in **Earth Science** below. Earth's mass is 6.583 x 10^{21} tons. (5.972 x10^{21} metric tons).

The Moon is Earth's only natural satellite. It is over one-quarter the size of Earth in diameter (2,160 mi. or 3,476 km). At an average distance of 238,000 mi. (380,000 km), it is the brightest object in Earth's nighttime sky. The Moon regularly changes in appearance as seen from Earth. See the discussion of these changes, called "Phases of the Moon," in Part I.

The Moon is slightly egg-shaped, and the same side of the satellite always faces Earth—this side being the elongated small end. As a result, the Moon rotates once during each revolution. The side we do not see is called the far side (not the dark side—all parts of the moon undergo 14 Earth days of light, followed by 14 days of darkness).

Over a decade of exploration of the Moon by space probes was capped by the landing of two U.S. astronauts on the Moon on July 20, 1969. A total of six two-man crews of American astronauts eventually landed on the Moon between 1969 and 1972, and they brought back some 842 pounds (382 kg) of samples of Moon rocks. The world these astronauts found was airless and devoid of life. Temperatures on the Moon range from up to 273°F (134°C) on the bright side to -274°F (-170°C) on the unlighted side.

A mixture of fine powder and broken rock blankets the Moon's surface. The near side also has large regions (called maria, or seas) of solidified lava. The lunar surface is pockmarked with craters up to 56 miles (90 km) across and is broken by huge mountain ranges. Some craters at the poles may contain frozen water in their depths.

Mars

Main components of atmosphere: 95% carbon dioxide, 3% nitrogen, 2% argon. Mars is the outermost of the four terrestrial planets and has a distinctive reddish coloring, coming from iron oxide in the Martian soil. The Romans named the planet after their god of war, and the two irregularly shaped satellites of Mars have been named after the horses—Deimos (terror) and Phobos (fear)—that pulled the war god's chariot. Mars is usually visible in Earth's nighttime sky and is lined up with Earth between it and the Sun once every 780 days, though its closest approach to Earth (33,800,000 mi., or 54,500,000 km) comes at 15- or 17-year intervals; 2003 will be the closest approach since 1986.

The so-called canals on Mars—later found to be optical illusions—were first observed by 19th-century astronomers and led to the widespread belief that there was life on Mars. (In 1900 the French Academy offered a prize to the first person to find life on any planet except Mars, presumably because everyone knew that there was life on that planet.) The planet thus became the target of numerous space probes, both U.S. and Soviet, from the early years of interplanetary exploration.

The first successful flyby of Mars was achieved by the U.S. spacecraft *Mariner 4* in 1965. The Soviets became the first to land a probe successfully on the surface of Mars in 1971, but the probe malfunctioned and stopped transmitting after only 20 seconds. It was not until 1976, when the U.S. *Viking 1* and *Viking 2* landers touched down on Mars, that extensive study of the planet from its surface became possible. The *Viking 1* lander continued to function until 1983. *Pathfinder* landed on Mars on July 4, 1997. Using a remote-controlled robot called *Sojourner,* whose travels to Martian rocks were televised, the *Pathfinder* mission reported the details of the weather and geology of Mars.

The big question of whether there is (or was) life on Mars has yet to be answered with certainty. The *Viking* landers conducted three experiments on Martian soil to check for biological processes. Some of the tests yielded positive results, but these could also be explained by the soil chemistry. The lack of other evidence of organic molecules adds to the case against life on Mars.

Orbiting satellites have mapped the entire planet down to a resolution of 500-1,000 ft. (150–300 m). The planet's surface is heavily cratered, and there is extensive evidence of once-active volcanoes. There are also such spectacular features as Olympus Mons (an extinct volcano three times as high as Earth's Mt. Everest); mammoth canyons, one of which is four times deeper than the Grand Canyon; and a gigantic basin (larger than Alaska) in the southern hemisphere that was probably created by a single, huge asteroid. The planet has ice caps at both poles (water ice with some frozen carbon dioxide), and the ice caps advance and recede with changes in the seasons.

But the most intriguing aspect of the Martian surface is that water once flowed there in great quantities. Parts of the terrain apparently have sedimentary origins, and there are many long channels, complete with smaller tributary channels and islands, that extend for hundreds of kilometers. Scientists speculate that Mars once had a much thicker atmosphere, made up of gases vented during volcanic eruptions, which would have made it possible for water in its liquid state to exist on the surface. Martian atmospheric pressure is now so low, however, that surface water would immediately vaporize. It is conjectured that in the past, water flowed through the channels to lowland areas and then sank into the Martian regolith, or upper soil layer, since there is no geologic evidence that standing bodies of water ever existed. In 2002 the orbiting Mars *Odyssey* detected signs of a large amount of water ice just below soil level in the south polar region.

Mars is too small to sustain continual volcanic activity. Its atmosphere apparently thinned out after volcanic activity ceased. Atmospheric pressure is now just seven one-thousandths of that on Earth at sea level, and the predominant gas is carbon dioxide, which is relatively heavy. A small amount of water vapor in the atmosphere is enough to form some clouds, small patches of fog in some valleys, and occasionally even patches of frost. Surface temperatures vary from a high of about 70°F (20°C) during summer at the equator to a low of about -220°F (-140°C) during winter at the poles.

By far the most pronounced feature of Martian weather is dust storms, which regularly engulf the entire planet for a period of several months.

The asteroids

Also called minor planets, the asteroids are very small bodies ranging from less than 1 to 600 miles in diameter. The name asteroid means "starlike" and was given to asteroids because they are so small they appear as points of light (as do stars) even in powerful telescopes. Otherwise, asteroids are not like stars at all.

The first four asteroids were discovered between 1801 and 1807. Today several hundred thousand asteroids are known and a million may exist in all. But the total mass of all known asteroids is less than that of Earth's Moon; only 26 asteroids are more than 130 miles (200 km) in diameter. Many asteroids occur in pairs that orbit each other. Some are thought to be solid bodies, while others may be collections of rocks held together by slight gravitational interactions.

Asteroids are found in several locations. The main belt is between Mars and Jupiter, but many inside the orbit of Mars are known as near-Earth asteroids. Asteroids that are thought to be larger than about 500 feet (150 m) in diameter that may travel as close as about 5 million miles (7.5 million km) to Earth are called potentially hazardous objects (PHOs). There are about 300 known PHOs, but none are expected to impact Earth in the foreseeable future. Two groups in the same orbit as Jupiter are called the Trojans because the larger ones are named for characters from Homer's *Iliad.*

The Outer Planets

Beyond Mars and the asteroid belt lie the five known outer planets of our solar system. Four of these planets—Jupiter, Saturn, Uranus, and Neptune—are the so-called gas giants. Many times larger than the terrestrial planets, these planets are huge, dense balls of hydrogen and other gases. Orbiting beyond them (most of the time) lies the solar system's outermost and smallest known planet, Pluto, which may be nothing more than a tiny ball of ice.

Jupiter

Main components of atmosphere: 90% hydrogen, 10% helium. Jupiter is the largest planet in the solar system. It has 2.5 times more mass than all the other planets of the solar system together and is 11 times as large as Earth in diameter. Jupiter is so large that scientists believe it almost became a star: as the gases and dust contracted to form the planet, gravitational forces created tremendous pressure and temperature inside the core—perhaps as high as tens of thousands of degrees. But there was not enough mass available to create the temperatures needed to start a fusion reaction such as that of the Sun (above 27,000,000°F, or 15,000,000°C, at the Sun's core); thus Jupiter has been slowly cooling down ever since. Even so, Jupiter still radiates about 2.5 times as much heat as it receives from the Sun.

The first object to reach Jupiter from Earth was *Pioneer 10.* It returned the first close-up pictures of the giant planet in 1973. Subsequently, the more sophisticated space probes *Voyager 1* and *Voyager 2* passed by Jupiter in 1979 and sent back images and more data on the planet. One of the most exciting discoveries by *Voyager 1* was that Jupiter has a faint but extensive ring system that extends almost 186,000 miles (300,000 km) out from the planet's surface. *Galileo* found another faint ring at 1 million miles (1.6 million km) in 1998. A probe from *Galileo* arrived at Jupiter on December 7, 1995, finding winds of 435 mph (700 km/hr) and much less water vapor than expected. Scientists later determined that the probe had arrived in what amounts to a Jovian desert. In September 2003, *Galileo's* mission ended with a final plunge into Jupiter's atmosphere.

Jupiter's thick atmosphere, which may extend above the planetary surface as much as 600 miles (1,000 km), is primarily made up of hydrogen, with some helium and traces of other gases. Because the planet spins so fast (one rotation in just under 10 hours), its clouds tend to form bands that give the planet a striped appearance. Darker bands are called belts, while light ones are zones. Clouds at higher altitudes are carried eastward by jet streams, while those at lower levels are blown westward.

There are numerous eddies and swirls in Jupiter's atmosphere, but none can compare with the Great Red Spot, apparently a massive hurricane (rotating counterclockwise) located in the southern hemisphere near the equator. The Great Red Spot was first observed some 300 years ago, and this storm continues unabated today. Since 1938 three smaller white ovals have been observed to the south of the Great Red Spot.

Jupiter's cloud tops are extremely cold (about -202°F, or -130°C), but temperatures increase deeper inside the atmosphere. Pressure also increases, and at about 600 miles (1,000 km) below the outermost atmospheric layers, great oceans of liquid hydrogen form Jupiter's surface. These may be some 12,000 miles (20,000 km) deep. Beneath them the hydrogen is so densely compacted it is thought to be in a metallic state. Within this is the core, thought to be an iron and silicate rock ball about the size of Earth.

Jupiter is now known to have 61 moons, many of them quite small (less than 6 miles in diameter). The four largest are the Galilean moons, so called because they were first observed by Galileo. The Galilean moons are Ganymede, Callisto, Europa, and Io—after the Roman god Jupiter's cupbearer (Ganymede) and three of Jupiter's inamorata. Ganymede is the largest moon in the solar system and is larger even than the planets Pluto and Mercury. It is a huge, cratered ball of ice and may have a core of solid silicate rock with liquid water between the thick ice covering and the core. Callisto, with an orbit outside that of Ganymede, is also covered with ice and is riddled with thousands of craters. Europa, which orbits inside Ganymede, is about the size of our Moon and has a smooth surface marked by networks of cracks. The most interesting of Jupiter's moons are Io, which orbits closest to Jupiter, and Europa.

Io undergoes the most intense volcanic activity known, heated it is thought by tidal energy from orbiting near Jupiter. One giant volcano may have been erupting for the past 19 years. Orange-red patches on Io's mottled surface are apparently molten sulfur beds, but most other parts of Io's surface are cold (about –229°F, or –145°C).

Europa, on the other hand, is covered in ice, but some have speculated that a liquid ocean beneath the ice could contain life. The liquid, which probably contains salts like oceans on Earth, could be heated by the same tidal forces that propel Io's volcanoes.

Saturn

Main components of atmosphere: 90% hydrogen, 3% helium. Saturn is the sixth planet of the solar system and the second largest, after Jupiter. The outermost of the planets that can be identified easily in Earth's nighttime sky with the unaided eye, Saturn has a pale yellowish color and is not nearly so bright as Mars. Saturn's spectacular ring system, which makes it one of the most interesting of the planets, is visible only through a telescope. Its rings are more extensive than those of any other planet.

Like Jupiter, Saturn is composed of densely compacted hydrogen, helium, and other gases. Liquid or metallic hydrogen probably exists underneath the planet's thick atmosphere, and scientists believe there is a solid core of rock about two times the size of Earth at its center. Saturn's high rotational speed (once every 10 hours, 12 minutes) makes it the most oblate (flattened) of all the planets; it is almost 6,800 miles (11,000 km) wider at the equator than on a line through the poles.

Exploration of Saturn began in 1979 with the first fly-by (*Pioneer 11*), but the *Voyager 1* (1980) and *Voyager 2* (1981) missions provided the first detailed look at the planet. Scientists have spent years sifting through the data gathered. Though there were important new findings, many questions about Saturn remain unanswered. The *Cassini-Hygens* probe, due to arrive in 2004, should provide many answers.

The *Voyagers* found a huge storm thousands of miles across on Saturn, along with a wide band of extremely high winds—up to 1,000 miles (1,600 km) per hour—at the equator. Winds in this band all travel in the direction of the planet's rotation (unlike bands of wind on Jupiter). The *Voyagers* also discovered a vast hydrogen cloud circling the planet above the equator.

The *Voyagers'* most exciting discoveries concern the planetary rings. Previously, about six different rings had been identified within the ring system, but *Voyager 1* pictures show as many as 1,000 separate rings. Narrow rings can even be seen within the Cassini Division, once thought to be an empty gap between the two major parts of the ring system. Some rings are not circular, and at least two rings are intertwined, or "braided." A strange new phenomenon was also discovered in the rings. *Voyager 1* pictures clearly show dark, radial fingers—"spokes"—moving inside the rings in the direction of rotation. Scientists speculate that they are made of ice crystals.

Voyager 2 pictures show that Saturn has far more than 1,000 rings—perhaps as many as a hundred thousand or more. One of the brightest rings is under 152 meters (500 ft.) thick. *Voyager 2* also found seasonal differences between the planet's two hemispheres and photographed a storm 4,000 miles (6,500 km) wide.

Twelve of Saturn's moons were known before the arrival of the *Voyagers*, and instruments aboard the space probe helped locate five new ones in the 1980s. In 1990 an 18th moon, later named Pan, was located in images made by *Voyager 2*. The discovery of 12 small moons of Saturn, found with ground-based telescopes, was reported in 2001, and another new moon was spotted in 2003, bringing the total number of moons to 31. Most of Saturn's moons are relatively small and composed of rock and ice. All but one of the small moons are pockmarked by meteor craters, and in some cases the moons appear to have been cracked by collisions with especially large meteors. But *Voyager* pictures show that one moon, Enceladus, is smooth in large regions apparently unmarked by collisions with meteors. Scientists believe that Enceladus is being pulled and stretched by the combined gravities of a nearby moon and Saturn itself. Tidal forces have apparently heated the core of Enceladus and made its surface soft enough to smooth over any craters formed by meteor impacts.

Titan, Saturn's largest moon (3,000 mi., or 4,800 km in diameter) is one of the few moons in the solar system known to have an atmosphere of any substance. Scientists suspect that at least some precursors of life may have formed there. For this reason *Voyager 1* was guided to within about 2,500 miles (4,000 km) of Titan during the Saturn flyby. Though Titan's surface was obscured by dense clouds, Voyager's sensors nevertheless returned a considerable amount of information about the moon and its atmosphere. Titan's atmosphere is composed mostly of nitrogen, like that of Earth, with only a small percentage of methane and carbon monoxide. Atmospheric pressure is at least 1.5 times that on Earth and temperatures range around -294°F (-181°C). Titan in fact appears to be a frozen version of Earth before life evolved.

The possibility of oceans of liquid methane (or of nitrogen or methane rain) on Titan was a matter of considerable controversy for some time after *Voyager 1* investigated the moon. But Titan is "dry," at least in the regions investigated. Pools of liquid methane might still exist in other low-lying regions, but it is unlikely that either methane or nitrogen condenses to liquid form on Titan.

Uranus

Main components of atmosphere: 82% hydrogen, 15% helium, 2% methane. Uranus is the seventh planet in the solar system and the third of the gas giants. The planet is barely visible in Earth's nighttime sky (it looks like a faint star) and for that reason, it went undiscovered until 1781.

Nearly the same size as Neptune and only about 5 percent of Jupiter's mass, Uranus is a faintly greenish color, perhaps because its atmosphere contains methane. The planet's axis of rotation is tipped over on its side. Astronomers discovered a system of nine faint rings in 1977, and *Voyager* found two more rings in 1986. There are thought to be 21 moons of Uranus. Among these, Caliban and Sycorax were found in 1997; a still-unnamed moon was noticed in 1999 by a researcher studying a 1986 photograph taken by *Voyager 2*. Three more discovered later in 1999 have been named Prospero, Setebos, and Stephano.

Uranus's atmosphere is very cold (-355°F, or -215°C). No clouds have been observed. Scientists speculate that, as on Jupiter and Saturn, temperatures and pressures increase dramatically down through the outer layer of atmosphere. At some point the hydrogen and helium would be sufficiently compressed to form a liquid or slushy surface "crust." Underneath this crust they believe is a mantle of solidified methane, ammonia, and water; and inside this mantle, a rocky core of silicon and iron about 15 times as massive as Earth. The core is thought to be hot, probably about 12,000°F (7,000°C).

Neptune

Main components of atmosphere: 80% hydrogen, 19% helium, 1% methane. The last of the gas giants, Neptune is the eighth planet in the solar system. It was discovered in 1846 after mathematical calculations based on irregularities in the orbit of Uranus provided astronomers with the correct location of the planet. Neptune, like Uranus, has been surrounded by considerable uncertainty because of its enormous distance from Earth. The 1989 visit by *Voyager 2* contributed greatly to improved understanding of the planet.

Neptune is a pale bluish color, but it has a clear atmosphere, and is very cold at the cloud tops (about -365°F or -220°C).

Scientists believe Neptune has a three-layered structure similar to that of Uranus: a crust of solidified or liquid hydrogen and helium that gradually thins outward into an atmosphere; a mantle of solidified gases and water; and a hot, rocky core (about 12,000°F or 7,000°C) some 15 times as massive as Earth. But one aspect of Neptune remains a mystery. Despite similarities with Uranus, Neptune has been found to radiate 2.7 times as much heat as it receives from the Sun (at a rate of 0.03 microwatts per ton of mass). Uranus, on the other hand, does not emit as much excess heat.

Neptune has 11 known moons, Triton and Nereid, discovered from Earth, six others discovered by *Voyager 2*, three more newly spotted in 2002. Triton is the largest moon and has an atmosphere. Triton is unusual in that it travels in a direction opposite that of Neptune's rotation, suggesting that it has a different origin from the planet. Triton also has volcanic activity: geysers of nitrogen rising as high as five miles (8 km).

Pluto

Main components of atmosphere: Methane and nitrogen (quantities unknown) The ninth and outermost (most of the time) known planet of the solar system is a ball of frozen gases probably only about the size of Earth's Moon. Pluto was discovered in 1930 as a result of an extensive search by Clyde Tombaugh. Because of its relatively small size and chaotic orbit (which at times crosses inside Neptune's orbit), some scientists think that Pluto is not really a planet at all. Instead, they theorize that Pluto is only one of the large comets in the Kuiper belt, discovered outside the orbit of Neptune over several years beginning in 1992.

Today Pluto is about as close to the Sun as it will ever get and possesses a thin atmosphere, but it is expected to freeze solid as the planet moves away from the Sun. Pluto has one known moon. Charon, discovered in 1978. Charon is about half the size of Pluto. Pluto and Charon rotate and revolve synchronously like a double planet system.

The Sun

Virtually all of the energy used by living things comes from the Sun. The Sun's light causes photosynthesis in green plants, and its heat causes winds. Fossil fuels, such as coal, oil, and natural gas, got their energy originally from photosynthesis, as does wood. Animals derive their energy from plants that photosynthesize, either directly or indirectly. The only natural nonsolar energy sources are nuclear reactions (which also produce geothermal energy); some bacteria that metabolize sulfur, and the tides, which on Earth are produced largely by the Moon, but in part by the Sun.

Because the Sun is a ball of gases, it does not rotate as a whole. The equator rotates in about 25 days, while gas near the poles rotates in about 30 days. The period of rotation at each latitude can be found by observing sunspots, which are magnetic storms. Sunspots appear and disappear in a mysterious 11-year cycle that many think influences weather on Earth, although convincing proof is lacking. Sometimes sunspots disappear for tens of years at a time, as during the period from 1645 to 1715. It may or may not be a coincidence that those years coincided with the "Little Ice Age" in Europe, when temperatures were far below average.

Like Earth, the Sun is composed of various layers. The part we see is called the photosphere. In the Sun's interior, energy is generated when hydrogen in the core fuses to become helium. Above the photosphere is a region of pinkish gases, the chromosphere. Above that is a large halo, visible only in eclipses, called the corona. Particles from the Sun, the solar wind, stream through the solar system, creating among other things auroras on Earth. Strong increases in solar wind during solar flares can interfere with radio communication.

▶ PLANETS OUTSIDE THE SOLAR SYSTEM

A detectable wobble, observed in more than 100 nearby stars, indicates that each such star is orbited by one or more planets, known as "extrasolar planets." The star Upsilon Andromedae is known to have at least three extrasolar planets, and six other stars show evidence of two. At least two pulsars have planets, and several stars are surrounded by dusty regions that may indicate planet formation.

In 1995 the first planet that orbits an ordinary star other than the Sun was established on the basis of regular changes in the position of the Sun-like star 51 Pegasi, which is nearly 50 light-years from the solar system. This discovery by Michel Mayor (Swiss:) and Didier Queloz (Swiss: 1966–) was soon followed by detection of many other ordinary stars that move back and forth in space. Such small movements indicate one or more large planets in orbit about the each star. This method works for relatively nearby stars orbited by very large planets—planets about half the size of Saturn to eleven times the size of Jupiter. The planets found generally orbit closer to their stars than the orbit of Mercury about the Sun, although one system discovered in 2001 has two planets in orbits about as far from the star as Mars and Jupiter are from the Sun. Some planets have also been detected as they reduce visible light from their stars by passing between the stars and Earth. In the next few years new equipment for existing telescopes and several newly built telescopes are expected to make it possible to observe smaller extrasolar planets than any found so far.

Changes in the pulses from a pulsar are easier to observe than the exact position of an ordinary star, so the first known extrasolar planet was found at a pulsar. In 1991, Aleksander Wolszczan (American: 1946–) observed that the pulsar PSR 1257+12 regularly changed the timing of its pulses as if being pulled back and forth in space by several bodies in orbit. Calculations since then show that two of the bodies, each about the size of Earth, move in small, swift orbits about the pulsar. A third planet is about the size of Earth's Moon and orbits inside the other two.

As early as 1983, infrared studies from space revealed dust clouds that might be the seeds of planets around such nearby stars as Vega and Fomalhaut. In 2001, astronomers studying a young star in the Orion nebula observed what appear to be larger clumps of dust, the predicted next step in planet building. In 2001 even larger clumps about the star Zeta Leopris—perhaps forming an asteroid belt—were proposed to explain its higher-temperature dust halo.

▶ STARS AND THE UNIVERSE

Astronomical Distances

The very large distances between stars and the even larger ones between the vast groups of stars called galaxies are usually expressed in terms of units of length that are peculiar to astronomy. The most familiar is the **light-year,** defined as the distance light travels through a vacuum in a year (approximately 365¼ days). Light travels through a vacuum at the rate of about 186,250 miles per second (exactly 299,792,458 m/s—exact because the

Characteristics of the Sun

Position in solar system	Center
Mean distance from Earth	92,960,000 mi. (149,600,000 km)
Distance from center of Milky Way galaxy	27,710 light-years
Period of rotation	25.45 days at 16° longitude
Inclination (relative to Earth's orbit)	7.25°
Equatorial diameter	865,000 mi. (1,392,000 km)
Diameter relative to Earth	109.2 times
Mass	2.192×10^{27} tons (1.9891×10^{30} kg)
Mass converted to energy each second	9,500 pounds (4,300 kg)
Surface gravity relative to Earth's	28 times
Temperature at core	28,280,000°F (15,710,000°C)
Temperature at bottom of photosphere	12,400°F (6,900°C)
Main components	Hydrogen and helium
Present age	4.6 billion years
Expected future life of hydrogen fuel supply	6.4 billion years

The Constellations

Name	Genitive	Abbr.	Translation	Remarks
Andromeda	Andromedae	And	Andromeda	Character in Greek myth
Antlia	Antliae	Ant	Air pump	Named by Nicolas Lacaille in 1750
Apus	Apodis	Aps	Swift, or Bird of Paradise	Named by Johann Bayer in 1603
Aquarius	Aquarii	Aqr	Water Bearer	In zodiac
Aquila	Aquilae	Aql	Eagle	Contains Altair
Ara	Arae	Ara	Altar	Part of the Centaurus group
Aries	Arietis	Ari	Ram	In zodiac
Auriga	Aurigae	Aur	Charioteer	Contains Capella
Boötes	Boötis	Boo	Herdsman	Contains Arcturus
Caelum	Caeli	Cae	Chisel, or graving tool	Lacaille, 1750
Camelopardalis	Camelopardalis	Cam	Giraffe	Named by Jakob Bartsch in 1661
Cancer	Cancri	Cnc	Crab	In zodiac
Canes Venatici	Canum Venaticorum	CVn	Hunting dogs	Named by Johannes Hevelius in 1687
Canis Major	Canis Majoris	CMa	Big Dog	Contains Sirius and Adhara
Canis Minor	Canis Minoris	CMi	Little Dog	Contains Procyon
Capricornus	Capricorni	Cap	Goat	In zodiac
Carina	Carinae	Car	Ship's Keel[1]	Lacaille, 1750; contains Canopus
Cassiopeia	Cassiopeiae	Cas	Cassiopeia	Character in Greek myth
Centaurus	Centauri	Cen	Centaur	Character in Greek myth; contains Rigil Kentaurus and Hadar/Agena
Cepheus	Cephei	Cep	Cepheus	Character in Greek myth
Cetus	Ceti	Cet	Whale	Sea monster slain by Perseus
Chamaeleon	Chamaeleontis	Cha	Chameleon	Bayer, 1603
Circinus	Circini	Cir	Compass	Lacaille, 1750
Columba	Columbae	Col	Dove	Bayer, 1603
Coma Berenices	Comae Berenices	Com	Berenice's Hair	Third Century B.C. Egyptian Queen
Corona Australis	Coronae Australis	CrA	Southern Crown	Also Sagittarius' crown
Corona Borealis	Coronae Borealis	CrB	Northern Crown	Also Ariadne's crown
Corvus	Corvi	Crv	Crow	Companion of Orpheus
Crater	Crateris	Crt	Cup	—
Crux[2]	Crucis	Cru	Southern Cross	Named by Augustine Royer in 1679; Contains Beta Crucis and Acrux
Cygnus	Cygni	Cyg	Swan	Contains Deneb
Delphinus	Delphini	Del	Dolphin	—
Dorado	Doradus	Dor	Goldfish	Bayer, 1603
Draco	Draconis	Dra	Dragon	Dragon slain by Hercules
Equuleus	Equulei	Equ	Little Horse	—
Eridanus	Eridani	Eri	River Eridanus	Contains Achernar
Fornax	Fornacis	For	Furnace	Lacaille, 1750
Gemini	Geminorum	Gem	Twins	In zodiac; contains Pollux
Grus	Gruis	Gru	Crane	Bayer, 1603
Hercules	Herculis	Her	Hercules	Character from Greek myth
Horologium	Horologii	Hor	Clock	Lacaille, 1750.
Hydra[3]	Hydrae	Hya	Hydra	Monster from Greek myth
Hydrus	Hydri	Hyi	Sea serpent	Bayer, 1603
Indus	Indi	Ind	Indian	Bayer, 1603
Lacerta	Lacertae	Lac	Lizard	Hevelius, 1687
Leo	Leonis	Leo	Lion	In zodiac; contains Regulus
Leo Minor	Leonis Minoris	LMi	Little Lion	Hevelius, 1687
Lepus	Leporis	Lep	Hare	Prey of Orion
Libra	Librae	Lib	Scales	In zodiac
Lupus	Lupi	Lup	Wolf	Part of Centaurus group
Lynx	Lyncis	Lyn	Lynx	Hevelius, 1687
Lyra	Lyrae	Lyr	Harp	Contains Vega
Mensa	Mensae	Men	Table (mountain)	Lacaille, 1750
Microscopium	Microscopii	Mic	Microscope	Lacaille, 1750
Monoceros	Monocerotis	Mon	Unicorn	Royer, 1679
Musca	Muscae	Mus	Fly	Bayer, 1603
Norma	Normae	Nor	Carpenter's Square	Lacaille, 1750
Octans	Octanis	Oct	Octant	Lacaille, 1750
Ophiuchus	Ophiuchi	Oph	Serpent Bearer	Character in Greek myth
Orion	Orionis	Ori	The Hunter	Character in Greek myth; contains Rigel, Betelgeuse, and Bellatrix
Pavo	Pavonis	Pav	Peacock	Bayer, 1603
Pegasus	Pegasi	Peg	Pegasus	Winged horse in Greek myth

Name	Genitive	Abbr.	Translation	Remarks
Perseus	Persei	Per	Perseus	Character in Greek myth
Phoenix	Phoenicis	Phe	Phoenix	Bayer, 1603
Pictor	Pictoris	Pic	Easel	Lacaille, 1750
Pisces	Piscium	Psc	Fish	In zodiac
Piscis Austrinus	Piscis Austrin	PsA	Southern Fish	Contains Fomalhaut
Puppis	Puppis	Pup	Ship's Stern[1]	Lacaille, 1750
Pyxis	Pyxidis	Pyx	Ship's Compass[1]	Lacaille, 1750
Reticulum	Reticuli	Ret	Net	Lacaille, 1750
Sagitta	Sagittae	Sge	Arrow	—
Sagittarius	Sagittarii	Sgr	Archer	In zodiac
Scorpius	Scorpii	Sco	Scorpion	In zodiac; contains Antares and Shaula
Sculptor	Sculptoris	Scl	Sculptor	Lacaille, 1750
Scutum	Scuti	Sct	Shield	Hevelius, 1687
Serpens	Serpentis	Ser	Serpent	Snake held by giant Ophiuchus
Sextans	Sextantis	Sex	Sextant	Hevelius, 1687
Taurus	Tauri	Tau	Bull	In zodiac; contains Aldebran and Elnath
Telescopium	Telescopii	Tel	Telescope	Lacaille, 1750
Triangulum	Trianguli	Tri	Triangle	Contains spiral galaxy M33
Triangulum Australe	Trianguli Australis	TrA	Southern Triangle	Bayer, 1603
Tucana	Tucanae	Tuc	Toucan	Bayer, 1603
Ursa Major	Ursae Majoria	UMa	Big Bear	Big Dipper
Ursa Minor	Ursae Minoris	UMi	Little Bear	Little Dipper
Vela	Velorum	Vel	Ship's Sails[1]	Lacaille, 1750
Virgo	Virginis	Vir	Virgin	In zodiac; contains Spica
Volans	Volantis	Vol	Flying Fish	Bayer, 1603
Vulpecula	Vulpeculae	Vul	Little Fox	Hevelius, 1687

1. Formerly part of the constellation Argo Navis, the Argonauts' ship. 2. Smallest constellation. 3. Largest constellation.

meter is defined in terms of the speed of light in a vacuum). A light-year is approximately 5,880 trillion miles (9,460 trillion km).

Astronomers also use a measure even larger than the light-year, the parsec, equal to about 3.26 light-years, or about 19,170 trillion miles (30,840 trillion km).

A smaller unit, for measurements within the solar system, is the astronomical unit, which is the average distance between the Earth and the Sun, or about 93 million miles (150 million km).

The Constellations

Constellations consist of several bright stars that are treated as a group. Long ago, before recorded history, people began naming these groups. By Sumerian times (3000-2500 B.C.), stories were already being told about how particular constellations were formed. Most of our present knowledge of such stories, however, comes from the ancient Greeks.

One group of constellations has exerted a special influence on human thought, at least since 1500 B.C. As the Sun, Moon, and planets move through the sky, they pass through a group of 12 constellations, called the constellations of the zodiac. The ancient belief that the presence of the Sun in one of these constellations at a person's birth influences happenings on Earth is called astrology.

Today astronomers use constellations for mapping the sky. Each part of the sky is named by a particular constellation. These constellations, especially in the southern hemisphere, may not be traditional ones, but rather, groups of stars astronomers have named so that for reference purposes all of the sky is labeled.

Star Names

While astronomers often use the traditional names of stars, most of which come to us from Latin or Arabic sources, they also use another system for naming objects in the sky that is based on constellations. Generally, the brightest star in a particular astronomical constellation is called alpha (∝), the next brightest beta (ß), and so on through several letters of the Greek alphabet; then numbers are used. All astronomers' constellations are named in Latin. When astronomers refer to a star within its constellation, they use the genitive case, meaning "of the thing." Thus the constellation Big Dog is officially Canis Major, and Sirius is alpha Canis Majoris, or "alpha of Big Dog," usually abbreviated to ∝CMa. This means it is the brightest star in the constellation Big Dog (Sirius has long been known as the dog star). Since Sirius is a binary star (see "Binary stars," below), the much brighter main star is officially ∝CMa A. Further along, numbers are used instead of Greek letters. Numbered stars in the news in the 1990s included 51 Pegasi and 71 Virginis.

Magnitude

The brightness of a star is designated by a number called its magnitude, although the relationship between size and brightness is complicated. When the magnitude system was first developed, by the early Greek astronomers Hipparchus (c. 190–c. 120 B.C.) and Ptolemy (c. 100–c. 170), astronomers did not know the actual distances to stars, so magnitude always referred to brightness as seen from Earth. They classed the brightest stars as the first magnitude and the dimmest they could see as the sixth. These numbers were somewhat arbitrary until 1856, when George Phillips Bond (American: 1825–65) determined that photographs of stars show magnitude in a way that is directly measurable—bright stars appear as larger spots than dim stars in photographs even though all stars appear as points to the naked eye. Astronomers could use accurate measures to compare two stars and thus measure magnitude with mathematical precision.

25 Brightest Stars: Magnitudes and Distances From Earth

The stars we see in the evening sky differ in how bright they appear because of a combination of two factors: 1) their total energy output, or **luminosity** (directly related to their absolute magnitude) and 2) their distance from Earth. Astronomers refer to this combination of effects as the **apparent magnitude** of a star, a measure of how bright the star appears in the nighttime sky. To separate the two effects, astronomers define **absolute magnitude** as the brightness of a star as measured from a fixed distance. Most of the stars we see in the sky have a large absolute magnitude but are relatively far away. If all the stars were placed the same distance from Earth, Deneb would be the brightest and the Sun would be the faintest (about 250,000 times fainter than Deneb). Note that negative magnitudes are higher than positive magnitudes.

Rank/ Common name	Star name	Apparent magnitude	Absolute magnitude	Distance from Earth (light-years)
1. **Sirius**	α CMa	-1.44	1.45	8.6
2. **Canopus**[1]	α Car	-0.62	-5.53	312.6
3. **Rigil Kentaurus**[2]	α Cen A	-0.28	4.07	4.4
4. **Arcturus**	α Boo	-0.05	-0.31	36.7
5. **Vega**	α Lyr	0.03	0.58	25.3
6. **Capella**	α Aur A	0.08	-0.48	42.2
7. **Rigel**[1]	β Ori	0.18	-6.69	772.5
8. **Procyon**	β CMi	0.40	2.68	11.4
9. **Achernar**	α Eri	0.45	-2.77	143.7
10. **Betelgeuse**[1]	α Ori	0.45	-5.14	427.3
11. **Hadar**[1]	β Cen	0.61	-5.42	525.0
12. **Altair**	α Aql	0.76	2.20	16.8
13. **Acrux**[1,3]	α Cru	0.77	(3)	320.6
14. **Aldebaran**	α Tau	0.87	-0.63	65.1
15. **Spica**	α Vir	0.98	-3.55	262.1
16. **Antares**[1]	α Sco	1.06	-5.28	603.7
17. **Pollux**	β Gem	1.16	1.09	33.7
18. **Fomalhaut**	α PsA	1.17	1.74	25.1
19. **Mimosa**	β Cru	1.25	-3.92	352.4
20. **Deneb**[1]	α Cyg	1.25	-8.73	3,227.7
21. **Regulus**	α Leo	1.36	-0.52	77.5
22. **Adhara**[1]	ε CMa	1.5	-4.10	430.6
23. **Castor**[1]	α Gem	1.58	0.59	51.5
24. **Gacrux**	γ Cru	1.59	-0.56	87.9
25. **Shaula**[1]	λ Sco	1.62	-5.05	702.6

Note: The magnitudes of many stars on this list vary slightly over time, although for most stars, the variation is quite small. Betelgeuse and Antares have the largest variations (about 1 magnitude). For consistency, median magnitudes are shown for all stars. 1. Stars more than 300 light-years away have an uncertainty of about 20 percent or more in their distances (and therefore in their absolute magnitudes as well). The distance of Deneb, in particular, may be wrong by half (i.e. only 1,600 light-years away). That would reduce Deneb's absolute magnitude to -7.22, still higher than any other star on this list. 2. A binary star, with both stars orbiting around each other. They appear to the naked eye to be the same star, with a combined apparent and absolute magnitude. 3. Acrux appears to the naked eye to be a single star, but in fact, it is the combined light of two stars, each at different distances from Earth. Its absolute magnitude, therefore, is impossible to define. **Source:** NASA.

Under Bond's system, stars with a magnitude of 1.00 are exactly 100 times as bright as those with a magnitude of 6.00. On this scale, the very brightest stars have negative magnitudes.

Roughly, each whole number difference in magnitude corresponds to 2.5 times the brightness.

By the time this system was introduced, astronomers already were able to determine the distances of some stars from Earth. Friedrich Wilhelm Bessel was the first to make such a measurement, which he announced in 1838. A closer star appears brighter than a similar star that is farther away. To better understand the relative brightness of stars as they actually are, astronomers imagine viewing all stars from the same distance away. A star's brightness from this distance, which is 10 parsecs or 32.6 light-years, is called its absolute magnitude.

If we could see it clearly, the star Cygnus OB2 #12 would be the brightest star in the Milky Way galaxy (absolute magnitude -9.9), but it is not only far from Earth but also is obscured by dust. The brightest single object known is not a star, but a quasar (see "The Universe," below), BR 1202-07, with an absolute magnitude of about -33. The Sun has the brightest apparent magnitude of any star, -26.8, but its absolute magnitude is only 4.75.

The Universe

Most of the universe was greatly misunderstood until the 20th century. The most common notion from the time of the ancient Greek philosophers until the end of the Middle Ages was that a number of crystal spheres revolved about Earth, and that each of the planets, the Sun, and Earth's Moon occupied one of these spheres. All the stars occupied the farthest sphere. There were only about 6,000 stars known, those visible to the naked eye (and about half of these were south of the equator, so few Europeans had ever seen them).

In 1609 Galileo of Italy turned the first astronomical telescope on the heavens. Galileo's early telescopes were good enough to show that the Milky Way was not merely a whitish band across the sky but consisted of a vast number of stars, far more than the few thousand visible with the naked eye. His observations also disproved the old idea of crystal spheres. People began to speculate about astronomical entities beyond a simple sphere of stars. Not until 1924 were telescopes sufficiently powerful to show that many cloudy patches in the sky consisted of millions of stars far away from the Milky Way. This discovery led to the recognition of the enormous complexity and diversity of the universe.

Big Bang The accepted theory of how the universe began is known as the Big Bang theory, since it proposes that the universe began as something like an explosion, which has caused all parts of the universe to rush away from one another (the expansion of the universe). Evidence for the Big Bang theory includes the discovery of cosmic background radiation, a radiation that seems to come equally from all directions. Cosmic background radiation has the characteristics expected if the universe resulted from a small, dense region exploding.

Binary stars Almost half the stars in the visible universe are actually pairs of stars that orbit each other. Astronomers can sometimes see both stars, but more commonly they recognize that a star is part of a binary because of the influence of the dimmer star's gravitational pull on the other star.

Black holes When a body becomes so dense for its size that not even light can escape the powerful gravitational pull it exerts, it is called a black hole. Black holes were predicted as early as 1784 (by John Michell) and invoked later by various astronomers and physicists to explain many strange astronomical phenomena. Black holes have been observed at the center of many galaxies, including our own Milky Way. Several smaller black holes, thought to be remains of supernova explosions, have also been located.

Brown dwarfs are bodies too small to be stars, but too large to be planets. They glow dimly as a result of energy released by gravitational contraction. A brown dwarf must be between 13 and 80 times the mass of Jupiter. The first brown dwarf to be definitely established orbits the star Gliese 229. Although about 50 times Jupiter's mass, its diameter is about the same as Jupiter's. Since then, a number of brown dwarfs have been located, including some not in orbit about other stars.

Clusters of stars Stars often form together, forming associations of hundreds or thousands or clusters of millions of stars. Open clusters, such as the Pleiades (Seven Sisters), contain several hundred to a thousand stars gathered in an irregular region perhaps tens of light years across. There are about a thousand open clusters in the Milky Way Galaxy. Globular clusters contain millions of stars, most very old, that have formed into a sphere a 100 to 200 light-years in diameter. There are about 125 known globular clusters associated with the Milky Way.

Dwarfs Dwarfs are small stars—the brightest are blue dwarfs, the dimmest red dwarfs. The Sun is a yellow dwarf; there are also white and brown dwarfs.

Expanding universe When Albert Einstein developed his general theory of relativity, he found it predicted that the universe would either expand as if it were exploding, or else collapse. He tried to correct this prediction by inserting a term in his equations to counteract the prediction, but in the 1920s, Edwin Hubble discovered that the universe actually is expanding. It is easier to measure the speed of recession than the distance, so astronomers commonly use the speed at which something is moving away as the measure of its distance from us. Of course, it is not just moving away from us. In the expanding universe, everything is moving away from everything else.

Galaxies are systems of very many stars separated from one another by largely empty space (sometimes galaxies are called island universes). In the 18th century, William Herschel concluded that many cloudy patches of light seen among the stars were actually giant systems of billions of stars, but so far away from Earth as to look like clouds. Better telescopes proved him right in the early 20th century, and these far-off, great masses of stars became known as galaxies, after our own Milky Way, the galaxy that includes the Sun. Observation with large telescopes in the 20th century has revealed two main types of galaxies—spiral and elliptical—although some galaxies are neither (irregular).

Milky Way This is the galaxy to which the Sun and Earth belong; it contains about 100 billion stars. If you are in a place unafflicted with much light pollution, when you look at the night sky, you can see a faint band crossing it. The ancient Greeks named this the Milky Way (galaxy in Greek). Early in the 19th century, William Herschel determined that our Sun was a star in a vast lens-shaped star system, and that the Milky Way was the part of the star system we see from our vantage point inside it. Today, recognizing there are very many other such star systems, scientists often call it the Milky Way galaxy.

Missing mass is matter that is apparently in the universe but that has not been observed. Astronomers note that galaxies are rotating as if they were embedded in larger, invisible bodies. Furthermore, there are theoretical reasons to believe there is even more matter in the universe than can be accounted for by the invisible matter surrounding galaxies. Ideas as to what this "missing mass" might be include everything from brown dwarfs to undiscovered subatomic particles.

Nebulae are patches of gas and dust observable in telescopes. Before Herschel discovered that some cloudy patches seen through telescopes were vast collections of stars, all such patches were called nebulae (meaning clouds). Some "clouds" turned out to be galaxies, but many did not. The patches of gas emit light, often by the same mechanism that a fluorescent light does; energy from stars ionizes the gas, which gives off visible light. Some patches of dust also glow, usually reflecting the light of nearby stars. Other patches of dust are opaque or nearly so, blocking out part of the sky. Some of the most striking nebulae consist of glowing gas surrounded by opaque dust or vice versa, which gives the nebula a definite shape, such as the North America Nebula (shaped like the continent of North America) or the Horsehead Nebula (which looks like a black horse's head against a glowing background). Herschel also studied a class of nebulae that looked to be giant spheres. He correctly concluded that these planetary nebulae were balls of gas produced when a star exploded.

Neutron stars are stars that have collapsed in a violent explosion, such as a supernova, so that the force keeping electrons apart is overcome. All the neutrons and protons can touch, forming the equivalent of a giant atomic nucleus. The star is electrically neutral because of the charge of the collapsed electrons. Such a star may be only a dozen miles in diameter but may have a mass twice that of the Sun.

Novae are stars that seem to appear out of nowhere. Later, they disappear. Early peoples were surprised from time to time by the appearance of a new (nova) star in the sky. Ancient Chinese astronomers called them guest stars. It is now clear that a truly new star does not appear; instead, a dim, existing star suddenly brightens. In early days, before the telescope, the dim stars could not be seen at all, so it looked as if a star came from nowhere. Today we know that there are two different types of "guest stars," and we reserve the name nova for one type and call the other a supernova (see below). The type referred to today as novae are less bright than supernovae and may appear more than once. It is thought that they occur when material from one star in a binary pair falls on the other star, causing it suddenly to flare up.

Pulsars are neutron stars that emit electromagnetic signals from their magnetic poles in a direction that reaches Earth. All neutron stars emit signals and rotate very rapidly (at least when they are first formed; they gradually slow down). These signals form a tight beam. If the beam intersects Earth, a radio telescope observes a fast pulsing on and off. The pulses are so regular that when they were first discovered, they were thought to be the work of extraterrestrial beings.

Quasars are distant sources of great energy. The name quasar is short for Quasi-Stellar Object, and the objects are so called because they seem to be about the size and general appearance of stars, but produce far too much energy to be stars. No one knows for sure what they are, but there is some evidence that quasars are caused by black holes in the central part of distant galaxies. The stars in the galaxies cannot be seen because of the great distance, so we see only the central part, which is the quasar.

Red giants are stars that have used their hydrogen fuel and expanded as a result. Young stars "burn" hydrogen in a nuclear fusion process that leads to helium. When a star has consumed the hydrogen in its core, new fusion reactions that start with helium begin, leading to carbon. The new reactions are hotter than the fusion of hydrogen to helium. This added energy causes the hydrogen and helium outside the core to expand. The star is red because the outer layers are relatively cool. When the Sun becomes a red giant in the distant future, it will expand almost to the orbit of Earth, completely engulfing Mercury and Venus, and charring Earth to a cinder.

Stars are bodies of gas large enough to undergo fusion reactions in their core. As a result of the energy produced by fusion, stars emit visible light, as well as electromagnetic radiation at other wavelengths. The Sun is a star. The hotter or larger a star is, the brighter it is.

Superclusters and clusters of galaxies are groups of galaxies associated in space. There may be just a few members of a cluster or as many as thousands. About two dozen galaxies near us form, with the Milky Way, our Local Group. The members of the Local Group also include the Andromeda galaxy and the Large and Small Magellanic Clouds. All are traveling through the universe together. The Local Group is a member of a supercluster of galaxies, called the Local Supercluster, that contains about 100 clusters. Clusters and superclusters are recognized because the average distance within a cluster or a supercluster from one galaxy or cluster to another is much less than the distance to other galaxies or clusters.

Supernovae are explosions of large stars. A supernova explosion is much more dramatic than the brightening of a nova. A supernova reported by Chinese astronomers from A.D. 1054 was visi-

Optical Telescopes

Telescopes were first developed in Holland about 400 years ago. The first telescopes used lenses to gather light and focus it. Later in the 17th century, scientists realized that curved mirrors could also gather and focus light. Since the light did not need to pass through the mirror (as light passes through a lens), mirrors proved to be more efficient than lenses for large telescopes.

Year	Type	Importance
1608	Lens	Hans Lippershey (Dutch: d. ca. 1916) applies for first patent on a telescope
1609	Lens	Galileo builds first astronomical telescopes, eventually reaching 30 power (or 30X enlargement)
1611	Lens	Johannes Kepler introduces convex eyepiece, producing greater power
1663	Mirror	James Gregory (Scottish: 1638-1676) is first to think that reflecting telescope can be made
1668	Mirror	Isaac Newton builds first telescope to use mirror to collect light, rather than lens
1723	Mirror	John Hadley (English: 1682-1744) invents reflecting telescope based on parabola, which concentrates light at a point
1789	Mirror	William Herschel builds telescope with 48-in. (122-cm) mirror, largest for many years
1895	Lens	Alvan Clark (American: 1832-1897) builds what is still world's largest telescope to use lens instead of mirror, 40 in. (102 cm)
1917	Mirror	Hooker Telescope at Mount Wilson in California is put into operation; at the time, it was world's largest (100 in., or 2.5 m)
1930	Combination	Bernard Schmidt (Estonian–German: 1879-1935) makes first telescopes combining lenses and mirrors; they become workhorse of astronomy
1948	Mirror	Hale Telescope (200 in., or 5 m) on Mt. Palomar, Calif., becomes largest and best on Earth
1962	Mirror	Largest telescope devoted to observing the Sun is erected at Kitt Peak in Arizona
1990	Mirror	Hubble Space Telescope (94 in., or 2.4 m) becomes first optical telescope in space
1993	Mirrors	Keck I Telescope in Hawaii uses world's largest mirror, 394 in. (10-m) in diameter; joined on May 8, 1996, with identical Keck II Telescope, both on Mauna Kea volcano
1999	Mirror	Japan's Subaru telescope begins operations on Mauna Kea; its 338-in (8.3m) mirror is the world's largest made from a single piece of glass
1999	Mirror	Gemini North is a 319-in (8.0 m) telescope on Mauna Kea, built by a seven-member consortium including the U.S. It was joined by its twin, Gemini South, in Chile, in 2000.
1999	Mirror	The Hobby-Eberly Telescope, dedicated primarily to spectroscopy, begins operation in October. It has the world's largest primary mirror—433 inches (11 m)—but is considered the world's third largest telescope (after the two Kecks), because only 362 inches (9.2 m) of its surface is available for use at any one time
2000	Mirror	All four 323 in. (8.2m) mirrors of the The Very Large Telescope (VLT) of the European Southern Observatory (ESO) in Chile are in operation

ble in the daytime. The remnants of this explosion are known today as the Crab Nebula. At its heart the Crab Nebula has a pulsar, all that is left of the star that exploded.

Variable stars Any star that periodically changes brightness is called a variable (a nova changes brightness but not at regular intervals). The period varies with the cause of the change and the individual star. Some variables are part of a binary system in which one star periodically passes in front of the other. Other kinds of variables are called Mira variables and Cepheid variables, after the first stars known of each type. It is not clear what causes the brightness to vary.

White dwarfs are stars whose cores have collapsed until all the atoms are pressed very close together. A single teaspoonful of the matter in a white dwarf weighs about five tons. The core collapses because a red giant has used all its helium for fuel, but the star is too small to start burning carbon.

Radio Telescopes

Before 1931, all telescopes were optical, i.e. they gathered and focused electromagnetic radiation in the range people can sense with their eyes. Stars, planets, and other objects in the universe also produce other wavelengths of radiation, however. A radio telescope gathers and focuses radiation at long wavelengths, the same kind of electromagnetic radiation used for transmission of radio signals. Several radio telescopes working together produce sharper images.

Year	Type	Importance
1931	Ordinary antenna	Karl Jansky accidentally discovers, in trying to track down sources of static, that radio waves are coming from space
1937	Parabolic dish	Grote Reber (American: 1911–) builds first intentional radio telescope dish, Wheaton Ill.
1957	Steerable dish	Parabolic dish (250 ft. or 75 m) at Jodrell Bank in England is first major radio telescope
1962	Steerable dish	Dish (300 ft., or 90 m) at Green Bank, W.Va., first used to search for extraterrestrial life; it collapsed on Nov. 15, 1988
1963	Fixed dish	Largest fixed-dish radio telescope, 1,000 ft. (305 m) across, is built in valley at Arecibo, Puerto Rico
1977	Several antennae	First Very Long Baseline Interferometry telescope begins operating at Cal Tech's Owens Valley Radio Observatory.
1980	27 antennae	Very Large Array (VLA) is built in 13-mi. (21 km) Y shape near Socorro, New Mexico.
1993	10 antennae	Very Long Baseline Array (VLBA) uses techniques that produce a resolution 500 times better than the best optical telescopes
1995	30 antennae	The Giant Meterwave Radio Telescope north of Pune, India, contains 30 parabolic 45-m (148-ft) antennae arranged in a 25-km (15-mi.) Y
2000	Steerable dish	The rebuilt Green Bank Telescope, often called "the 100-meter GBT" is, at 328 feet (100 m) by 361 feet (110 m), the worlds' largest fully steerable dish
2002	64 antennae	The Atacama Large Millimeter Array (ALMA) in Llano de Chajnanto, Chile, combines 64 antennae each 39 feet (12 m) in diameter and is also part of a worldwide network of radio telescopes.

Major Accomplishments of Satellites and Space Probes, 1957–2002

While much attention is focused on human beings in space, most of the serious scientific progress has been made by satellites or probes—the general name for space vehicles that neither carry humans nor orbit Earth—that are directed internally or from Earth.

10/4/57 ***Sputnik 1*** First satellite to orbit Earth (USSR).

11/3/57 ***Sputnik 2*** Carries Laika, first dog in space; burns in atmosphere 4/14/58.

1/31/58 ***Explorer 1*** First satellite to detect Van Allen radiation belts; first U.S. satellite.

3/17/58 ***Vanguard*** Demonstrates Earth is pear-shaped with a bulge in Southern Hemisphere (U.S.).

1/2/59 ***Mechta*** First space probe to go into orbit around Sun, passing 5,000 mi. from Moon (at which it was aimed) (USSR).

3/3/59 ***Pioneer 4*** First American probe aimed at Moon; like Mechta it misses and goes into orbit about Sun.

9/12/59 ***Lunik 2*** First space probe to reach Moon, where it crash-lands (USSR).

10/4/59 ***Lunik 3*** First space probe to return photographs of far side of Moon (USSR).

4/1/60 ***Tiros 1*** First weather satellite (U.S.).

6/22/60 ***Transit 1-B*** First navigational satellite (U.S.).

8/12/60 ***Echo 1*** First communications satellite—actually a large balloon off which radio signals could be bounced (U.S.).

8/18/60 ***Corona*** First U.S. spy satellite.

8/19/60 ***Sputnik 5*** Carries dogs Belka and Streika. Successfully returns them to Earth; 18 orbits.

12/12/61 ***Venera 1*** First space probe intended to reach another planet—Venus (USSR).

3/7/62 ***OSO 1*** Orbiting Solar Observatory—first major astronomical satellite (U.S.).

4/23/62 ***Ranger 4*** First U.S. space probe to reach Moon.

4/26/62 ***Cosmos 4*** First Soviet spy satellite.

7/10/62 ***Telstar*** First active communications satellite, allowing direct television between Europe and U.S. (U.S.).

8/27/62 ***Mariner 2*** First space probe to reach vicinity of another planet (Venus) and return scientific information (U.S.).

11/1/62 ***Mars 1*** First space probe aimed at Mars; contact lost about 66 million mi. from Earth (USSR).

6/26/63 ***Syncom 2*** First communications satellite to go into synchronous orbit with Earth (U.S.).

7/28/64 ***Ranger 7*** Returns close-up photographs of Moon, then crashes into it (U.S.).

8/28/64 ***Nimbus 1*** First weather satellite to be stabilized so that its cameras always point toward Earth (U.S.).
11/28/64 ***Mariner 4*** Flies by Mars and takes 21 pictures of its surface, successfully transmitting them back to Earth; its closest approach is 6,118 mi. (U.S.).
4/6/65 ***Early Bird*** First commercial satellite (U.S.).
7/16/65 ***Proton 1*** At 26,896 lbs., it is largest Earth satellite to this date (USSR).
11/16/65 ***Venera 3*** Crash-lands on Venus; first space probe to make physical contact with another planet; radio contact lost before it reaches immediate vicinity of planet (USSR).
11/26/65 ***A-1*** First satellite to be launched by nation other than the USSR or U.S. (France).
12/16/65 ***Pioneer 6*** Launched into solar orbit; still partially functions today (U.S.).
1/31/66 ***Luna 9*** Although main vehicle crash-lands, ejected capsule lands safely on Moon and transmits photographs to Earth (USSR).
5/30/66 ***Surveyor 1*** First soft landing of complete vehicle on Moon (U.S.).
3/31/66 ***Luna 10*** First space vehicle to go into orbit about Moon (USSR).
8/10/66 ***Lunar Orbiter 1*** First American space vehicle to go into orbit about Moon.
9/15/68 ***Zond 5*** First Soviet satellite to return to Earth from vicinity of Moon.
2/11/70 ***Ohsumi*** First satellite launched by Japan.
4/24/70 ***Mao 1*** First Chinese satellite; it broadcasts song "The East Is Red" once a minute, pausing at the end for other signals.
8/17/70 ***Venera 7*** First Venus probe to return signals from planet's surface (USSR).
9/12/70 ***Luna 16*** First space probe to land on Moon without humans aboard, scoop up samples, and return them to Earth (USSR).
11/10/70 ***Luna 17*** Carries roving vehicle to Moon's surface; vehicle roams for 2 weeks at a time (during daylight), then "sleeps"; as it roams, it returns photos and other data to Earth (USSR).
12/12/70 ***Uhuru*** First X-ray satellite telescope (U.S.).
5/28/71 ***Mars 3*** First space probe to soft-land on Mars; it quickly ceases functioning (USSR).
5/30/71 ***Mariner 9*** First space probe to orbit another planet (Mars); returns 7,329 photographs of planet (U.S.).
3/2/72 ***Pioneer 10*** First space probe to study Jupiter and, on June 13, 1983, first to leave solar system (U.S.); contact still maintained as of July 14, 2002.
7/23/72 ***Landsat I*** First Earth resources satellite (U.S.).
3/6/73 ***Pioneer 11*** First space probe to reach vicinity of Saturn (U.S.).
11/3/73 ***Mariner 10*** First space probe to observe 2 planets, Venus and Mercury, and only probe ever to observe Mercury (U.S.).
12/10/74 ***Helios*** First W. German space probe.
6/8/75 ***Venera 9*** Returns first photographs from surface of Venus (USSR).
8/20/75 ***Viking 1*** First American space probe to soft-land on Mars; returns data until Nov., 1982.
9/20/75 ***Viking 2*** Successfully soft-lands on Mars (U.S.).
8/20/77 ***Voyager 2*** After studying Jupiter and Saturn, it becomes first space probe to reach vicinities of Uranus and Neptune (U.S.).
9/5/77 ***Voyager 1*** After studying Jupiter, it becomes first space probe to reach vicinity of Saturn. Becomes furthest space probe from Sun on Feb. 17, 1998; by 2001 is more than 7 billion miles (12 billion km) from Earth (U.S.).
1/26/78 ***IUE*** International Ultraviolet Explorer — the first astronomical satellite to be placed in geosynchronous orbit; it sends back data until 1996 (European Space Agency, or ESA, U.S., and Britain).
5/20/78 ***Pioneer 12 (Venus 1)*** First space probe to go into orbit about Venus. (U.S.).
6/26/78 ***Seasat*** Analyzes ocean currents and ice flow (U.S.).
8/12/78 ***ISEE-3*** Originally the third International Sun-Earth Explorer. Renamed International Cometary Explorer when it is redirected to study tail of comet Giacobini-Zinner in 1983 (U.S.).
12/13/78 ***HEAO-2*** High-Energy Astronomy Observatory, also known as the Einstein Observatory—it makes high-resolution X-ray images of the universe (U.S.).
2/24/79 ***P78-1*** Studies solar radiation until purposely shot down by U.S. Air Force 9/13/85
2/14/80 ***Solar Max*** Studies solar radiation; after failure in Nov. 1980, it is repaired and relaunched from space shuttle in April 1984; finally pushed to its destruction by massive solar flare, 12/2/89 (U.S.).
1/25/83 ***IRAS*** Infrared Astronomical Satellite studies galactic and extragalactic infrared sources and discovers new planets forming (U.S.).
12/15/84 ***Vega 1*** First Soviet mission to study Halley's comet; along the way it drops balloon probe into atmosphere of Venus.
12/21/84 ***Vega 2*** Second Soviet mission to Halley's comet; releases a balloon probe at Venus.
1/7/85 ***Sakigake*** First Japanese mission to study Halley's comet (this one from far away).
7/2/85 ***Giotto*** Joint European mission to Halley's comet; passes closest to the comet—375 mi. (600 km)—and later is redirected to comet Grigg-Skjellerup, which it passes 7/10/92 at a distance of 125 mi. (200 km).
8/18/85 ***Suisei*** Japanese mission to Halley's comet.
2/21/86 ***SPOT*** French satellite; photographs surface details of Earth as small as 30 ft. across.
5/4/89 ***Magellan*** American probe orbits Venus and maps it in detail with radar.
10/18/89 ***Galileo*** After passing near Venus and Earth (twice), it reports on Jupiter's moons before crashing into Jupiter in Sept. 2003. (U.S.).
11/18/89 ***Cosmic Background Explorer (COBE)*** Studied cosmic background radiation in hopes of learning cause of galaxy formation.
4/24/90 ***Hubble Space Telescope*** Flawed optical telescope placed in orbit about Earth by U.S.; successfully repaired 12/10/93.
10/6/90 ***Ulysses*** Studying previously unobserved north and south poles of the Sun (U.S.-ESA).
4/5/91 ***Compton Gamma Ray Observatory*** A 17-ton telescope that observed the universe at very short wavelengths until June 4, 2000.
8/31/91 ***Yohkoh*** Japanese satellite that reports on X-rays and gamma rays from the Sun.
6/7/92 ***Extreme Ultraviolet Explorer (EUVE)*** American satellite studies high range of ultraviolet radiation in universe.
7/3/92 ***Solar Anomalous and Magnetospheric Particle Explorer (SAMPEX)*** American satellite that reports on particles in space, including space dust and the solar wind.
7/24/92 ***Geotail*** Japanese satellite launched by NASA to study Earth's magnetosphere.
10/6/92 ***Freja*** A Swedish satellite launched by a Chinese rocket from the Gobi Desert, Freja carries experiments from the U.S., Sweden, Canada, France, and Germany; The U.S. experiment measures Earth's magnetosphere.
2/9/93 ***Pegasus 3*** Brazilian satellite to monitor environment in Amazonia, launched by Orbital Sciences Corp. of Fairfax, Va.
2/20/93 ***ASCA*** Japanese X-ray telescope.

1/25/94 ***Clementine*** Joint U.S. military-science mission; maps the moon from lunar orbit and later visits the asteroid Geographos.
11/1/94 ***WIND*** Goes into a figure-8 orbit around the Earth and Moon at first, studying the solar wind; in 1996, moved to a point in Earth's orbit and orbits the Sun itself, staying in the same relation to the Earth as it revolves, a million miles from Earth.
3/18/95 ***Infrared Telescope in Space (IRTS)*** Japan's infrared space telescope surveys 7 percent of the sky over a period of 28 days.
11/17/95 ***Infrared Space Observatory (ISO)*** A European Space Agency satellite that extends the work of the earlier IRAS. Nicknamed "Europe's Hubble" (ESA).
12/2/95 ***Solar and Heliospheric Observatory (SOHO)*** Studies the sun from an orbit of about 930,000 miles (1.5 million km) from Earth (ESA/U.S.).
12/30/95 ***Rossi X-Ray Timing Explorer (XTE)*** First U.S. X-ray telescope since 1978; studies X-ray sources in Milky Way including stars, pulsars, and possible black holes.
2/17/96 ***Shoemaker Near Earth Asteroid Rendezvous (NEAR-Shoemaker)*** First of the new, less-expensive Discovery series of space probes. It passes close to asteroid 253 Mathilde in June 1999. *NEAR* orbits asteroid 433 Eros starting in February 2000, and lands on asteroid on February 12, 2001 (U.S.).
2/24/96 ***Polar*** Like WIND, Polar is reporting on the interaction of the solar wind and Earth's magnetic field, concentrating especially on the poles. It can take UV images of Earth's auroras and X-ray images of high-speed electrons in the solar wind (U.S.).
4/30/96 ***BeppoSAX (Satellite per Astronimica a Raggi X)*** This small orbiting observatory studies X-ray-emitting events from outer space. It scores a major triumph when it pinpoints the location of a gamma-ray burster for the first time, showing that these events are the most powerful explosions known (Italy/Netherlands/ESA).
8/21/96 ***FAST (Fast Auroral Snapshot)*** Smaller, cheaper satellite of the Small-Class Explorer series studies auroras from low-Earth orbit (U.S.).
11/7/96 ***Mars Global Surveyor*** A probe to Mars orbits the planet and surveys it from space for one Mars year (687 Earth days) starting in March, 1999, after delays caused by a defective solar panel. (U.S.).
12/4/96 ***Mars Pathfinder*** This probe bounces to the surface of Mars in the Ares Vallis region on 7/4/97, where it releases a rover named *Sojourner* to travel the surface during the day and report on Martian geology. (U.S.).
2/12/97 ***HALKA (VSOP)*** A radio observatory that adds a space component to radio telescopes on Earth, creating the Very Long Baseline Space Observatory for high-resolution astronomy (Japan).
4/21/97 ***Celestis 1*** Burials in space; small satellite contains some ashes of 24 individuals, notably Gene Roddenberry, creator of *Star Trek;* Gerard K. O'Neill, advocate of living in space; and Timothy Leary, LSD guru of the 1960s (U.S.).
8/25/97 ***Advanced Composition Explorer (ACE)*** Studies solar wind and particles from interstellar space (cosmic rays) as it orbits a stable point where the gravity from the Earth and Sun are in balance (U.S.)
10/15/97 ***Cassini-Huygens*** Mission to orbit Saturn and study its satellites; *Cassini* is the orbiter that will reach Saturn in July 2004 while *Huygens* is a probe into Saturn's atmosphere (U.S./ESA).
12/2/97 ***Equator-S*** A satellite orbiting the equatorial plane that studies Earth's magnetic field (Germany).
1/6/98 ***Lunar Prospector*** Confirms presence of water at the Moon's poles (U.S.).
4/2/98 ***Transition Regions and Coronal Explorer (TRACE)*** Uses ultraviolet telescope to study magnetism in the Sun's corona from a polar orbit about Earth. (U.S.).
7/4/98 ***Nozomi/Planet B Neutral Mass Spectrometer (NMS)*** Planned orbit about Mars begins October 1999; the satellite will study the Martian atmosphere and its interaction with the solar wind.
10/24/98 ***Deep Space 1*** Tests new technologies for space use including ion-propulsion system. (U.S.).
12/4/98 ***SAC-A*** Experiments in space with digital global positioning, a space camera, magnetosphere measurements, and whale tracking. (Argentina).
12/5/98 ***Submillimeter Wave Astronomy Satellite (SWAS)*** Space-based radio telescopes analyze microwaves to study chemical composition of interstellar gas clouds, the homes of new star formation. (U.S.)
2/7/99 ***Stardust*** The first mission to return materials from a comet, Stardust is due to reach comet Wild 2 in January 2004, gather samples there (as well as interstellar dust samples along the way), and parachute them back to Earth in 2006. (U.S.).
2/23/99 ***Ørsted*** Making a high-precision map of Earth's magnetic field (Denmark).
6/24/99 ***Far Ultraviolet Spectroscopic Explorer (FUSE)*** Exploring the universe at wavelengths slightly longer than X-rays, FUSE fills a significant gap in coverage of the electromagnetic spectrum (U.S./Canada/France).
7/23/99 ***Chandra X-Ray Observatory*** Its X-ray telescopes reveal previously unknown details of black holes, white dwarfs, neutron stars, and the X-ray background radiation. (U.S.).
12/10/99 ***X-Ray Multi-Mirror Telescope (XXM-Newton)*** The most powerful X-ray detector ever, XXM-Newton has 3 X-ray telescopes using 58 mirrors each as well as 2 X-ray spectrographs and an optical telescope. Its orbit takes it 1/3 the way to the Moon, giving it long periods for observation of active stars, galaxies, and black holes (ESA).
3/25/2000 ***Imager for Magnetopause-to-Aurora Global Exploration (IMAGE)*** The first satellite mission dedicated to imaging the Earth's magnetosphere, the region of space controlled by the Earth's magnetic field and containing extremely tenuous plasmas of both solar and terrestrial origin. (U.S.).
7/12/00 and **8/9/00** ***Cluster II*** Four spacecraft that maintain positions as the vertices of a pyramid as they orbit Earth in formation and study the interactions of Earth with the solar wind. (ESA).
10/9/00 ***High Energy Transient Explorer (HETE II)*** Observes, reports, and locates gamma-ray bursts for follow up by astronomers and surveys X-ray sources across the universe. (U.S., France, Japan, Italy).
4/7/01 ***Mars Odyssey*** Entered Mars orbit on October 23, 2001; primary mission from Feb. 2002 to Aug. 2004 is to search for water using instruments that recognize certain minerals and that detect hydrogen and also study the amount of radiation present; it will also be a communication relay for other Mars probes to be launched starting in 2003.
6/30/01 ***Microwave Anisotropy Probe (MAP)*** Mission to measure temperature fluctuations in the cosmic microwave background; will go into solar orbit at the L2 Lagrange point, keeping 1 million miles (1.6 million km) from Earth. Data will help us understand how and when galaxies formed. (U.S.)
8/8/01 ***Genesis*** A mission designed to spend three years in solar orbit, collecting particles from the solar wind, and then returning the material to Earth. (U.S.)
12/7/01 ***Jason 1*** Monitors ocean circulation to determine relationships between oceans and atmosphere and follow events such as El Niño. (U.S.-France)

12/7/01 ***Thermosphere-Ionosphere-Mesosphere-Energetics and Dynamics (TIMED)*** Studies the influence of the Sun and humans on the upper atmosphere. (U.S.)

12/16/01 ***Student-Tracked Atmospheric Research Satellite for Heuristic International Networking Experiment (STARSHINE 2)*** Each STARSHINE satellite is a ball the size of a beachball covered with mirrors. Elementary and high-school student teams observe the satellite in early morning or evening and use the time it takes to pass selected stars to calculate atmospheric density at various altitudes (U.S.)

2/5/02 ***Reuven Ramaty High Energy Solar Spectroscopic Imager (RHESSI)*** Explores the basic physics of particle acceleration and energy release by solar flares. (U.S.)

3/17/02 ***Gravity Recovery and Climate Experiment (GRACE)*** Two spacecraft flying in tandem make extremely precise measurements of Earth's gravitational field. (U.S.-Germany)

7/3/02 ***CONTOUR*** In a comet-chasing orbit around the sun. Encounters planned with comets Encke for Nov. 12, 2003 and Schwassmann-Wachmann 3 for June 18, 2006.(U.S.).

Spaceflights Carrying People, 1961–2003

The space programs of the former Soviet Union and the United States both had dramatic flights by human pilots as an important component, although many scientists felt that most goals of the space program could be achieved without risking lives. The *Vostok*, *Voskhod* and *Soyuz* missions were part of the Soviet program; *Mercury*, *Gemini*, *Apollo*, *Skylab* and the shuttle are part of the U.S. program.

Proving that People Can Venture into Space

4/12/61 ***Vostok 1*** (1 hr. 48 min.) Yuri A. Gagarin, First spaceflight by human.

5/5/61 ***Mercury 3*** (15 min.) Alan B. Shepard Jr. Suborbital.

7/21/61 ***Mercury 4*** (16 min.) Virgil "Gus" Grissom. Suborbital.

8/6/61 ***Vostok 2*** (25 hrs. 18 min.) Gherman S. Titov. First multiorbit flight; 17 orbits.

2/20/62 ***Mercury 6*** (5 hrs. 55 min.) John H. Glenn. First orbital flight by American; 3 orbits.

5/24/62 ***Mercury 7*** (4 hrs. 56 min.) M. Scott Carpenter. 3 orbits.

8/11/62 ***Vostok 3*** (94 hrs. 24 min.) Andrian G. Nikolayev. 64 orbits; landing by parachute.

8/12/62 ***Vostok 4*** (70 hrs. 57 min.) Pavel R. Popovitch. Dual launch with *Vostok 3*; 48 orbits.

10/3/62 ***Mercury 8*** (9 hrs. 13 min.) Walter Schirra. 6 orbits.

5/15/63 ***Mercury 9*** (34 hrs. 20 min.) Gordon Cooper. 22 orbits.

6/14/63 ***Vostok 5*** (119 hrs. 6 min.) V. Bikovsky. 81 orbits.

6/16/63 ***Vostok 6*** (70 hrs. 50 min.) Valentina V. Tereshkova. First woman cosmonaut; 48 orbits; dual launch with *Vostok 5*.

10/12/64 ***Voskhod 1*** (24 hrs. 17 min.) Vladimir M. Komarov, Konstantin P. Feoktistov, Boris B. Yegorov. First multihuman crew; 3 cosmonauts make 16 orbits.

Planning for Operations in Space

3/18/65 ***Voskhod 2*** (26 hrs.) A. Leonov, P. Belyayev. First extravehicular activity (EVA) by Leonov (20 min.); 17 orbits.

3/23/65 ***Gemini 3*** (4 hrs. 53 min.) Virgil "Gus" Grissom, John Young. First American multi-person crew; 3 orbits.

6/3/65 ***Gemini 4*** (97 hrs. 56 min.) James McDivitt, Edward White II. 62 orbits; first American EVA; first use of personal propulsion unit.

8/21/65 ***Gemini 5*** (190 hrs. 56 min.) Gordon Cooper, Charles Conrad 120 orbits; demonstrates feasibility of lunar mission; simulated rendezvous.

12/4/65 ***Gemini 7*** (330 hrs. 35 min.) Frank Borman, James Lovell. 206 orbits; extensions of testing and performance; target for first rendezvous.

12/16/65 ***Gemini 6A*** (25 hrs. 51 min.) Walter Schirra, Thomas Stafford. 15 orbits; rendezvous with *Gemini 7*.

3/16/66 ***Gemini 8*** (10 hrs. 42 min.) Neil Armstrong, David Scott. 6.5 orbits; first dual launch and docking; first Pacific landing.

6/3/66 ***Gemini 9A*** (72 hrs. 21 min. Thomas Stafford, Eugene Cernan. 44 orbits; unable to dock with target vehicle; 2 hrs. 7 min. of EVA.

7/18/66 ***Gemini 10*** (70 hrs. 47 min.) John Young, Michael Collins. 43 orbits; first dual rendezvous; docking maneuvers, umbilical EVA.

9/12/66 ***Gemini 11*** (71 hrs. 17 min.) Charles Conrad Jr., Richard Gordon Jr. 44 orbits; rendezvous and docking.

11/11/66 ***Gemini 12*** (94 hrs. 34 min.) James Lovell, Edwin "Buzz" Aldrin Jr. 59 orbits; final *Gemini* mission; 5 hours of EVA.

To the Moon and Beyond

4/23/67 ***Soyuz 1*** (26 hrs. 48 min.) Vladimir M. Komarov, 18 orbits; Komarov is killed when parachute fails; first fatality of space program.

10/11/68 ***Apollo 7*** (260 hrs. 8 min.) Walter Schirra, Donn Eisele, Walter Cunningham. 8 service propulsion firings; 7 live TV sessions with crew; rendezvous with S-IVB stage performed.

10/26/68 ***Soyuz 3*** (94 hrs. 51 min.) G. Beregovoi. 64 orbits; approaches unpiloted *Soyuz 2* to distance of 650 ft. (198 m).

12/21/68 ***Apollo 8*** (147 hrs.) Frank Borman, James Lovell, William Anders. First *Saturn-V* propelled flight; first lunar orbital mission (10 orbits); returns lunar photography.

1/14/69 ***Soyuz 4*** (71 hrs. 14 min.) V. Shatalov, 48 orbits; docks with *Soyuz 5* in first linkup of 2 space vehicles both carrying people.

1/15/69 ***Soyuz 5*** (72 hrs. 46 min.) B. Volynov, A. Yeliseyev, Y. Khrunov. 3 cosmonauts perform EVA, transferred to *Soyuz 4* in rescue rehearsal.

3/3/69 ***Apollo 9*** (241 hrs. 1 min.) James McDivitt, David Scott, Russell Schweickart. First flight of all lunar hardware in Earth orbit, incl. lunar module.

5/18/69 ***Apollo 10*** (192 hrs. 3 min.) Eugene Cernan, John Young, Thomas Stafford. Lunar mission development flight to evaluate lunar module performance in lunar environment; descent to within 50,000 ft. of Moon.

7/16/69 ***Apollo 11*** (165 hrs. 18 min.) Neil Armstrong, Michael Collins, Edwin "Buzz" Aldrin Jr. First lunar landing (July 20); limited inspection, photography, evaluation, and sampling of lunar soil.

10/11/69 ***Soyuz 6*** (118 hrs. 42 min.) G. Shonin, V. Kubasov. First triple launch (with *Soyuz 7* and *8*).

10/12/69 ***Soyuz 7*** (118 hrs. 41 min.) A. Filipchenko, V. Volkov, V. Gorbatko. With *Soyuz 6* and *8*, conducts experiments in navigation and photography.

10/13/69 ***Soyuz 8*** (118 hrs. 59 min.) V. Shatalov, A. Yeliseyev. 80 orbits.

11/14/69 ***Apollo 12*** (244 hrs. 36 min.) Charles Conrad Jr., Richard Gordon Jr., Alan Bean. Second lunar landing; demonstrates point landing capability; samples more area.
4/11/70 ***Apollo 13*** (142 hrs. 55 min.) James Lovell, Fred Haise Jr., John Swigert Jr. Third lunar landing attempt aborted owing to loss of pressure in liquid oxygen in service module and fuel cell failure.
6/2/70 ***Soyuz 9*** (424 hrs. 59 min. [17 days 16 hrs.]) A. Nikolayev, V. Sevastianov. Longest spaceflight to this time.
1/31/71 ***Apollo 14*** (9 days 42 min.) Alan Shepard, Stuart Roosa, Edgar Mitchell. Third lunar landing, returns 98 lbs. of material.
4/23/71 ***Soyuz 10*** (47 hrs. 46 min.) V. Shatalov, A. Yeleseyev, N. Rukavishnikov. Docks with *Salyut 1*, the first space station.
6/6/71 ***Soyuz 11*** (23 days 18 hrs. 22 min.) G. Dobrovolsky, V. Patsayev, V. Volkov. All 3 cosmonauts killed during reentry.
7/26/71 ***Apollo 15*** (12 days 7 hrs. 12 min.) David Scott, Alfred Worden, James Irwin. Fourth lunar landing; first to carry Lunar Roving Vehicle (LRV).
4/16/72 ***Apollo 16*** (11 days 14 hrs. 51 min.) John Young, Ken Mattingly, Charles Duke Jr. Fifth lunar landing; second to carry LRV. Returns 213 lbs. of material.
12/7/72 ***Apollo 17*** (12 days 13 hrs. 52 min.) Eugene Cernan, Ronald Evans, Harrison Schmitt. Last manned lunar landing; third with LRV; total EVA time: 44 hrs. 8 min.; returns 243 lbs. of material.

First Stations in Space

5/25/73 ***Skylab 2*** (28 days 49 min.) Charles. Conrad Jr., Joseph Kerwin, Paul Weitz. First *Skylab* launch; establishes *Skylab Orbital Assembly* in earth orbit; conducts medical and other experiments.
7/29/73 ***Skylab 3*** (59 days 11 hrs. 9 min.) Alan Bean, Owen Garriott, Jack Lousma. Second *Skylab*; crew performs systems and operational tests and thermal shield deployment.
9/27/73 ***Soyuz 12*** (47 hrs. 16 min.) V. Lazarev, O. Makarov. First Soviet spaceflight to carry humans since *Soyuz 11* tragedy.
11/16/73 ***Skylab 4*** (84 days 1 hr. 7 min.) Gerald P. Carr, Edward G. Gibson, William R. Pogue. Services unmanned Saturn workshop; obtains medical data for extending spaceflights.
12/18/73 ***Soyuz 13*** (7 days 20 hrs. 55 min.) P. Klimuk, V. Lebedev. Performs astrophysical and biological experiments.
7/3/74 ***Soyuz 14*** (15 days 17 hrs. 30 min.) P. Popovich, Y. Artyukhin. Crew occupies *Salyut 3* space station; studies Earth resources.
8/26/74 ***Soyuz 15*** (48 hrs. 12 min.) G. Sarafanov, L. Demin. Makes unsuccessful attempt to dock with *Salyut 3*.
12/2/74 ***Soyuz 16*** (5 days 22 hrs. 24 min.) A. Filipchenko, N. Rukavishnikov. Taken to check modifications to *Salyut* system.
1/10/75 ***Soyuz 17*** (29 days 13 hrs. 20 min.) A. Gubarev, G. Grechko. Docks with *Salyut 4;* sets Soviet endurance record.
4/5/75 ***Soyuz 18A*** (22 min.) V. Lazarev, O. Makarov. Separation from booster fails, and craft fails to reach orbit, but crew successfully lands in western Siberia.
5/24/75 ***Soyuz 18B*** (63 days) P. Klimuk, V. Sevastyanov. Docks with *Salyut 4*.
7/15/75 ***ASTP*** (9 days 1 hr. 30 min.) Thomas Stafford, Vance Brand, Donald Slayton. *Apollo-Soyuz* Test Project, cooperative U.S.-Soviet mission.
7/15/75 ***Soyuz 19*** (5 days 23 hrs. 31 min.) A. Leonov, V. Kubasov. Docks with *ASTP*, the U.S. *Apollo* capsule.

The Soviet Study of Human Biology in Space

11/17/75 ***Soyuz 20*** (90 days) No crew. Biological mission; docks with *Salyut 4*.
7/6/76 ***Soyuz 21*** (49 days) B. Volynov, V. Zholobov. Docks with *Salyut 5* and performs Earth resource work.
9/15/76 ***Soyuz 22*** (8 days) V. Bykovsky, V. Aksenov. Takes Earth-resources photo-graphs.
10/14/76 ***Soyuz 23*** (2 days) V. Zudov, V. Rozhdestvensky. Unsuccessful attempt to dock with *Salyut 5;* first landing in water (unplanned) for Soviet program (crew survives).
2/7/77 ***Soyuz 24*** (7 days) V. Gorbatko, Y. Glazkov. Docks with *Salyut 5* for 18 days of experiments.
10/9/77 ***Soyuz 25*** (2 days) V. Kovalyonok, V. Ryumin. Unsuccessful attempt to dock with *Salyut 6*.
12/10/77 ***Soyuz 26*** (96 days) Y. Romanenko, G. Grechko. Docks with *Salyut 6;* crew sets endurance record.
1/10/78 ***Soyuz 27*** (6 days) V. Dzhanibekov, O. Makarov. Carries second crew to dock with *Salyut 6* space station.
3/2/78 ***Soyuz 28*** (8 days) V. Remek, A. Gubarev. Carries third crew to board *Salyut 6*; Remek first non-Russian, non-American in space (Czech).
6/15/78 ***Soyuz 29*** (140 days) V. Kovalyonok, A. Ivanchenkov. Docks with *Salyut 6*; crew sets new endurance record.
6/27/78 ***Soyuz 30*** (8 days) P. Klimuk, M. Hermaszewski. Carries second international crew to *Salyut 6;* first Polish cosmonaut, Hermaszewski.
8/25/78 ***Soyuz 31*** (8 days) V. Bykovsky, S. Jahn. Carries third international crew to *Salyut 6*; first East German, Jahn.
2/25/79 ***Soyuz 32*** (175 days) V. Lyakhov, V. Ryumin. Carries crew to *Salyut 6*; sets new endurance record.
4/10/79 ***Soyuz 33*** (2 days) N. Rukavishnikov, Georgi Ivanov. Engine failure prior to docking forces early termination; first Bulgarian, Ivanov.
6/6/79 ***Soyuz 34*** (74 days) No crew. Launches with no crew; returns with crew from *Salyut 6*.
4/9/80 ***Soyuz 35*** (185 days) V. Ryumin, L. Popov. Carries 2 crew members to *Salyut 6*.
5/26/80 ***Soyuz 36*** (8 days) V. Kubasov, B. Farkas. Carries 2 crew members to *Salyut 6*; crew returns in *Soyuz 35*; first Hungarian, Farkas.
6/5/80 ***Soyuz T-2*** (4 days) Y. Malyshev, V. Aksenov. Test of modified *Soyuz* craft; docks with *Salyut 6*.
7/23/80 ***Soyuz 37*** (8 days) V. Gorbatko, P. Tuan. Exchanges cosmonauts in *Salyut 6;* returns *Soyuz 35* crew after 185 days in orbit; first Vietnamese in space, Tuan.
9/18/80 ***Soyuz 38*** (8 days) Y. Romanenko, A. Tamayo-Mendez. Ferries to *Salyut 6*; first Cuban in space, Tamayo-Mendez.
11/27/80 ***Soyuz T-3*** (13 days) L. Kizim, O. Makarov, G. Strekalov. Ferries to *Salyut 6*; first 3-person crew since *Soyuz 11*.
3/12/81 ***Soyuz T-4*** (75 days) V. Kovalyonok, V. Savinykh. Mission to *Salyut 6*.
3/22/81 ***Soyuz 39*** (8 days) V. Dzhanibekov, J. Gurragcha. Docks with *Salyut 6*; first Mongolian, Gurragcha.

The Space Shuttle: U.S. Reentry in Space

4/12/81 ***Columbia*** (2 days 6 hrs.) John Young, Robert Crippen. First flight of reusable space shuttle; first landing of U.S. spacecraft on land.
5/14/81 ***Soyuz 40*** (8 days) L. Popov, D. Prunariu. First Romanian (Prunariu), in space.
11/12/81 ***Columbia*** (2 days 6 hrs.) Joe Engle, Richard Truly. First reuse of space shuttle; ends early due to loss of fuel cell.
3/22/82 ***Columbia*** (8 days) Jack Lousma, Gordon Fullerton. Third shuttle flight; payload includes space science experiments.
5/13/82 ***Soyuz T-5*** (211 days) A. Berezovoy, V. Lebedev. First flight to *Salyut 7*; space station equipped to measure body functions.

6/24/82 ***Soyuz T-6*** (8 days) V. Dzhanibekov, J. Chrètien, A. Ivanchenkov. Mission to *Salyut 7*; Soviet/French team; first French cosmonaut, Chrétien.
6/27/82 ***Columbia*** (7 days 1 hr.) Ken. Mattingly Henry Hartsfield Jr. Fourth shuttle mission; first landing on hard surface.
8/16/82 ***Soyuz T-7*** (8 days) L. Popov, S. Savitskaya, A. Serebrov. Mission to *Salyut 7*; Svetlana Savitskaya, second Soviet woman in space.
11/11/82 ***Columbia*** (5 days 2 hrs.) Vance Brand, Robert Overmyer, Joseph Allen, William Lenoir. First operational mission; first 4-man crew; first deployment of satellites from shuttle.
4/4/83 ***Challenger*** (5 days) Paul Weitz, Karol Bobko, Donald Peterson, Story Musgrave. Second shuttle joins fleet; deploys TDRS tracking satellite; first shuttle EVA.
4/20/83 ***Soyuz T-8*** (48 hrs.) V. Titov, G. Strekalov, A. Serebrov. Planned rendezvous with *Salyut 7* fails.
6/18/83 ***Challenger*** (6 days) Robert Crippen, Frederick Hauck, John Fabian, Sally Ride, Norman Thagard. First 5-person crew; Ride is first U.S. woman in space; first use of Remote Manipulator Structure ("Arm") to deploy and retrieve satellite.
6/27/83 ***Soyuz T-9*** (150 days) V. Lyakhov, A. Aleksandrov. Crew spends 149 days in *Salyut 7* after *Soyuz 10* fails in relief mission.
8/30/83 ***Challenger*** (6 days) Richard Truly, Daniel Brandenstein, William Thornton, Guion Bluford, Dale Gardner. First night launch. Bluford is; first black American in space. Launches weather/communications satellite for India.
11/28/83 ***Columbia*** (10 days) John Young, Brewster Shaw Robert Parker, Owen Garriott, Byron Lichtenberg, Ulf Merbold. Launches *Spacelab;* crew performs experiments in astronomy and medicine.
2/3/84 ***Challenger*** (8 days) Vance Brand, Bruce McCandless, Robert Stewart, Ronald McNair, Robert Gibson. Jet-propelled backpacks carry 2 astronauts on first untethered space walks; 2 satellites lost; first landing at Kennedy Space Center.
2/8/84 ***Soyuz T-10B*** (237 days) L. Kizim, O. Atkov, V. Solovyev. Mission to *Salyut 7* to repair propulsion system; sets new duration-in-space record for crew.
4/2/84 ***Soyuz T-11*** (8 days) Y. Malyshev, G. Strekalov, R. Sharma. Docks with *Salyut 7*; first Indian cosmonaut, Sharma.
4/6/84 ***Challenger*** (7 days) Robert Crippen, Richard Scobee, Terry Hart, George Nelson, James van Hoften. Deploys Long Duration Exposure Facility for experiments in space durability; snares Solar Max satellite; repairs altitude-control system.
7/18/84 ***Soyuz T-12*** (12 days) S. Savitskaya, V. Dzhanibekov, I. Volk. Savitskaya becomes first woman to walk in space.
8/30/84 ***Discovery*** (7 days) Henry Hartsfield Jr., Michael Coats, Steven Hawley, Judith Resnik, Richard Mullane, Charles Walker. Third shuttle in fleet; deploys 3 satellites and tests a solar sail.
10/5/84 ***Challenger*** (8 days) Robert Crippen, Jon McBride, Kathryn Sullivan, Sally Ride, Marc Garneau, David Leestma, Paul Scully-Power. First Canadian astronaut, Garneau; deploys Earth Radiation Budget Satellite and uses Sir-B radar system to see beneath surface of sand.
11/8/84 ***Discovery*** (8 days) Frederick Hauck, David Walker, Anna Fisher, Joseph Allen, Dale Gardner. Salvages two inoperative satellites.
1/24/85 ***Discovery*** (4 days) Ken Mattingly, Loren Schriver, James Buchli, Ellison Onizuka, Gary Payton. Secret military mission.
4/12/85 ***Discovery*** (7 days) Karol Bobko, Donald Williams, Jake Garn, Charles Walker, Jeffrey Hoffman, David Griggs, Margaret Rhea Seddon. First U.S. senator in space, Garn.
4/29/85 ***Challenger*** (7 days) Robert Overmyer, Frederick Gregory, Don Lind, Taylor Wang, Lodewijk van den Berg, Norman Thagard, William Thornton. Carries European Spacelab module.
6/6/85 ***Soyuz T-13*** (112 days) V. Dzhanibekov, V. Savinykh. Successful mission to repair damage to *Salyut 7*, which had suffered power failure.
6/17/85 ***Discovery*** (7 days) John Creighton, Shannon Lucid, Steven Nagel, Daniel Brandenstein, John Fabian, Prince Salman al-Saud, Patrick Baudry. First Arabian in space, al-Saud; successfully launches 4 satellites.
7/29/85 ***Challenger*** (8 days) Roy Bridges, Anthony England, Karl Henize, Story Musgrave, Gordon Fullerton, Loren Acton, John-David Bartoe. Carries *Spacelab* 2, a group of scientific experiments.
8/27/85 ***Discovery*** (7 days) John Lounge, James van Hoften, William Fisher, Joe Engle, Richard Covey. Repairs satellite Syncom 3.
9/17/85 ***Soyuz T-14*** (65 days) V. Vasyutin, A. Volkov, G. Grechko. Takes supplies to *Salyut 7*.
10/3/85 ***Atlantis*** (4 days) Karol Bobko, Ronald Grabe, David Hilmers, William Pailes, Robert Stewart. Fourth shuttle.
10/30/85 ***Challenger*** (7 days) Henry Hartsfield Jr., Steven Nagel, Bonnie Dunbar, Guion Bluford, Ernst Messerschmid, Reinhard Furrer, Wubbo Ockels. Carries Spacelab 1-D; scientific experiments conducted by Germans.
11/26/85 ***Atlantis*** (7 days) Brewster Shaw, Bryan O'Conner, Charles Walker, Rudolfo Neri Vela, Jerry L. Ross, Sherwood C. Spring, Mary Cleave. First Mexican in space, Vela.
1/12/86 ***Columbia*** (5 days) Robert Gibson, Charles Bolden Jr., George Nelson, Franklin Chang-Diaz, Steven Hawley, Robert Cenker. First U.S. congressman in space, Nelson.
1/28/86 ***Challenger*** (73 seconds) Richard Scobee, Michael Smith, Robert McNair, Ellison Onizuka, Judith Resnik, Gregory Jarvis, Christa McAuliffe. O-rings in solid-fuel boosters wear through, and fuel supply explodes, killing all 6 regular astronauts and schoolteacher McAuliffe.

The First Space Station (Soyuz flight durations N.A.)

2/20/86 ***Mir*** Soviet space station, No crew.
3/13/86 ***Soyuz T-15*** V. Solovyev, L. Kizim. First cosmonauts to board *Mir* space station.
2/6/87 ***Soyuz TM-2*** Y. Romanenko, A. Laveykin. Cosmonauts begin marathon tours in space.
7/21/87 ***Soyuz TM-3*** A. Alexandrov, A. Viktorenko, M. Faris. First Syrian in space, Faris.
12/21/87 ***Soyuz TM-4*** V. Titov, M. Manarov, A. Levchenko. Cosmonauts set new record of a year in space, mostly in *Mir* space station: 366 days.
6/7/88 ***Soyuz TM-5*** A. Alexandrov, V. Savinykh, A. Solovyev. First Bulgarian in space, Alexandrov.
8/29/88 ***Soyuz TM-6*** V. Lyakhov, V. Polyakov, A. Ahad. Ahad first Afghan in space; on 9/6/88 Lyakhov and Ahad are stranded as they attempt to return in *Soyuz TM-5*, but land safely on 9/7/88.
9/29/88 ***Discovery*** (4 days) John Lounge, David Hilmers, Frederick Hauck, George Nelson, Richard Covey. Redesigned shuttle makes first flight since the *Challenger* disaster.
11/26/88 ***Soyuz TM-7*** A. Volkov, S. Krikalev, J. Chrétien. *Mir* temporarily abandoned for first time.
12/2/88 ***Atlantis*** (4 days) Robert Gibson, Jerry Ross, William Shepherd, Guy Gardner, Richard Mullane. Secret military mission known to have deployed radar spy satellite.
3/13/89 ***Discovery*** (5 days) Michael Coats, John Blaha, James Buchli, James Bagian, Robert Springer. Deploys NASA's third relay satellite and tests thermal control system for proposed U.S. space station.
5/4/89 ***Atlantis*** (4 days) David Walker, Ronald Grabe, Mary Cleave, Norman Thagard, Mark Lee. Launches probe *Magellan* to map Venus with radar.

8/9/89 ***Columbia*** (5 days) Brewster Shaw, Richard Richards, David Leestma, James Adamson, Mark Brown. Secret military mission to launch spy satellite.
9/5/89 ***Soyuz TM-8*** A. Viktorenko, A. Serebrov. Reoccupies *Mir.*
10/18/89 ***Atlantis*** (5 days) Donald Williams, Michael McCulley, Shannon Lucid, Franklin Chang-Diaz, Ellen Baker. Launches *Galileo* probe.
11/22/89 ***Discovery*** (5 days) Frederick Gregory, John Blaha, Story Musgrave, Kathryn Thornton, Manley Lanier Carter Jr. Secret military mission.
1/9/90 ***Columbia*** (11 days) Daniel Brandenstein, Bonnie Dunbar, Marsha Ivens, David Low, James Wetherbee. Launches communication satellite Syncom IV and retrieves the *Long Duration Exposure Facility* (see 4/6/84).
2/11/90 ***Soyuz TM-9*** A. Solovyev, A. Balandin. Relieves Viktorenko and Serebrov. Solovyev and Balandin briefly locked out of *Mir* by faulty hatch.
2/28/90 ***Atlantis*** (4 days) John Creighton, John Caspar, David Hilmers, Richard Mullane, Pierre Thuot. Secret military mission.
4/24/90 ***Discovery*** (5 days) Loren Shriver, Charles Bolden Jr., Bruce McCandless, Steven Hawley, Kathryn Sullivan. Launches Hubble Space Telescope.
8/1/90 ***Soyuz TM-10*** G. Manakov, G. Strekalov. Replace Solovyev and Balandin.
10/6/90 ***Discovery*** (4 days) Richard Richards, Robert Cabana, Bruce Melnick, William Shepherd, Thomas Akers. Launches *Ulysses* space probe into solar orbit.
11/15/90 ***Atlantis*** (5 days) Richard Covey, Frank Culbertson Jr., Charles Gemar, Carl Meade, Robert Springer. NASA announces this as last secret military mission.
12/2/90 ***Columbia*** (9 days) Vance Brand, Guy Gardner, Jeffrey Hoffman, John Lounge, Robert Parker, Samuel Durrance, Ronald Parise. Carries 3 UV and 1 X-ray telescope.
12/2/90 ***Soyuz TM-11*** V. Afansev, M. Manarov, T. Akiyama. Journalist Akiyama, sponsored by Japanese corporations; others replace Manakov and Strekalov on *Mir.*
4/5/91 ***Atlantis*** (6 days) Steven Nagel, Kenneth Cameron, Linda Godwin, Jerry Ross, Jerome Apt. Launches 17-ton *Gamma Ray Observatory;* unscheduled spacewalk required to open satellite's antenna properly.
4/28/91 ***Discovery*** (8 days) Michael Coats, Blaine Hammond Jr., Gregory Harbaugh, Charles Lacy Veach, Guion Bluford Jr., Richard Hieb, Donald McMonagle. Tests detection devices and recovers Star Wars satellite.
5/18/91 ***Soyuz TM-12*** S. Krikalev, A. Artsebarsky, H. Sharman. Political problems in Soviet Union result in Krikalev's spending an unexpected 313 days in space; Sharman is first Briton in space; returns with Manarov and Afansev.
6/5/91 ***Columbia*** (9 days) Bryan D. O'Connor, Sidney M. Gutierrez, James P. Bagian, Margaret Rhea Seddon, Francis A. Gaffney, Millie Hughes-Fulford, Tamara E. Jernigan. Performs human and animal space-adaptation experiments.
8/21/91 ***Atlantis*** (9 days) John Blaha, Michael Baker, Shannon Lucid, David Low, James Adamson. Performs 22 experiments and launches communications satellite.
9/12/91 ***Discovery*** (5 days) John Creighton, Kenneth Reightler Jr., Mark Brown, James Buchlim, Charles Gemar. Launches upper-atmosphere research satellite.
10/2/91 ***Soyuz TM-13*** A. Volkov, F. Viehboeck, T. Aubakirov. Viehboeck, first Austrian in space, returns with Artsebarsky and Aubakirov.
11/24/91 ***Atlantis*** (7 days) Frederick Gregory, Tom Henricks, James Voss, Mario Runco Jr., Story Musgrave, Thomas Hennen. First completely nonsecret military flight; studies how well military installations can be seen from space.
1/22/92 ***Discovery*** (8 days) Ronald Grabe, Stephen Oswald, Norman Thagard, William Readdy, David Hilmers, Roberta Bondar, Ulf Merbold. Performs experiments as the First International Microgravity Lab.
3/17/92 ***Soyuz TM-14*** K. Flade, A. Viktorenko, A. Kaleri. On March 25, Flade, a German, returns with Sergei Krikalev and Aleksandr Volkov.
3/24/92 ***Atlantis*** (9 days) Charles Bolden Jr., Brian Duffy, Kathryn Sullivan, David Leestma, Michael Foale, Byron Lichtenberg, Dirk Frimout. Inaugural flight of Mission to Planet Earth studies Earth's atmosphere and auroras.
5/7/92 ***Endeavour*** (9 days) Daniel Brandenstein, Kevin Chilton, Thomas Akers, Richard Hieb, Bruce Melnick, Kathryn Thornton, Pierre Thout. The first flight of the replacement for *Challenger* succeeds relaunching an erring communications satellite; first ever 3-person EVA.
6/25/92 ***Columbia*** (14 days) Richard Richards, Kenneth Bowersox, Bonnie Dunbar, Lawrence DeLucas, Ellen Baker, Eugene Trinh, Carl Meade. Sets record for duration of shuttle mission; carries U.S. Microgravity Laboratory.
7/27/92 ***Soyuz TM-15*** A. Solovyev, S. Avdeyev, M. Tognini. The third trip by a French astronaut, Tognini, to *Mir.*
7/31/92 ***Atlantis*** (8 days) Loren Schriver, Andrew Allen, Marsha Ivins, Jeffrey Hoffman, Franklin Chang-Diaz, Claude Nicollier, Franco Mallerba. Launches European Retrievable Carrier (Eureca) satellite. First Swiss astronaut (Nicollier); first Italian (Mallerba).
9/12/92 ***Endeavour*** (8 days) Robert Gibson, Curtis Brown Jr., Jay Apt, Jan Davis, Mae Carol Jemison, Mark Lee, Mamoru Mohri. First professional Japanese astronaut in space (Mohri); first married couple in space (Lee and Davis); first black female astronaut (Jemison). Japanese-sponsored mission to study biology in space.
10/22/92 ***Columbia*** (10 days) James Wetherbee, Michael Baker, Glenwood MacLean, Tamara Jernigan, William Shepherd, Charles Lacy Veach. Launches the Italian-made satellite *LAGEOS-2,* to provide information about Earth's gravitational field.
12/2/92 ***Discovery*** (7 days) Daniel Walker, Robert Cabana, Guion Bluford Jr., James Voss, Michael Clifford. Last scheduled military flight for the space shuttle; future military flights to use disposable rockets. Launches secret military satellite.
1/13/93 ***Endeavour*** (6 days) John Caspar, Gregory Harbaugh, Donald McMonagle, Susan Helms, Mario Runco Jr.. Observes X-rays and launches a TDRS (Tracking and Data Relay Satellite).
1/24/93 ***Soyuz TM-16*** A. Polishchuk, G. Manakov. Docks with *Mir* on Kristall module, using U.S.-compatible port first developed for the joint Soviet-U.S. mission in 1975; A. Solovyev and S. Avdeyev return after six months aboard *Mir.*
4/8/93 ***Discovery*** (9 days) Kenneth Cameron, Stephen Oswald, Kenneth Cockrell, Michael Foale, Ellen Ochoa. Launches and retrieves the *Spartan* Sun probe, used to study the solar corona, and observes Earth's ozone layer.
4/26/93 ***Columbia*** (10 days) Steven Nagel, Tom Henricks, Jerry Ross, Charles Precourt, Bernard Harris Jr., Ulrich Walter, Hans Schlegel. The European Spacelab with two German scientists (Walter and Schlegel) conducts experiments on weightlessness.
6/21/93 ***Endeavour*** (10 days) Ronald Grabe, Brian Duffy, Donald Low, Peter Wisoff, Nancy Jane Sherlock, Janice Voss. Recovers Europe's *Eureca* satellite; and conducts experiments using a pressurized laboratory called Spacehab.
7/1/93 ***Soyuz TM-17*** V. Tsiblyev, A. Serebrov, J. Haignere. Haignere is French astronaut who returns with A. Solovyev and S. Andreyev on July 29.
9/12/93 ***Discovery*** (10 days) Frank Culbertson Jr., William Readdy, James Newman, Daniel Bursch,

Carl Walz. Tests equipment and procedures to be used in repairing Hubble Space Telescope; first night landing at Kennedy.

10/18/93 ***Columbia*** (14 days) John Blaha, Richard Searfoss, William McArthur Jr., Shannon Lucid, Martin Fettman, Margaret Rhea Seddon, David Wolf. Conducts biological experiments on humans and rats; first dissection of animal in space.

12/2/93 ***Endeavour*** (11 days) Richard Covey, Kenneth Bowersox, Claude Nicollier, Story Musgrave, Thomas Akers, Kathryn Thornton, Jeffrey Hoffman. Repairs defective lens on Hubble Space Telescope.

1/8/94 ***Soyuz TM-18*** V. Afanasyev, Y. Usachyov, V. Polyakov. Trip planned to last 14 months for Polyakov, but Afanasyev and Usachyov return after six months. Previous *Mir* crew returns to Earth.

The U.S. and Russia Work Together in Space

2/3/94 ***Discovery*** (8 days) Charles Bolden Jr., Sergei Krikalev, Kenneth Reightler Jr., Jan Davis, Franklin Chang-Diaz, Ronald Sega. Krikalev first Russian on U.S. space shuttle mission.

3/4/94 ***Columbia*** (14 days) John Caspar, Andrew Allen, Charles Gemar, Marsha Ivins, Pierre Thuot. Develops techniques for use in space-station construction.

4/9/94 ***Endeavour*** (11 days) Sidney Gutierrez, Kevin Chilton, Michael Clifford, Linda Godwin, Jay Apt, Thomas Jones. Uses radar to map details of Earth in 3-D.

7/1/94 ***Soyuz TM-19*** Y. Malenchenko, T. Musabayev. Relieves Afanasyev and Usachyov on *Mir.*

7/8/94 ***Columbia*** (15 days) Robert Cabana, Leroy Chiao, James Halsell Jr., Richard Hieb, Chiaki Naito-Mukai, Donald Thomas, Carl Walz. Orbits Earth 236 times, a new record. First Japanese woman in space (heart surgeon Naito-Mukai).

9/9/94 ***Discovery*** (11 days) Richard Richards, Blaine Hammond Jr., Susan Helms, Mark Lee, J.M. Lineger, Carl Meade. Conducts laser experiments to measure pollution in atmosphere. Releases and recaptures satellite that collects data on solar wind; Meade and Lee use jet pack for untethered spacewalk.

9/30/94 ***Endeavour*** (11 days) Michael Baker, Daniel Bursch, Thomas Jones, Steven Smith, Jeff Wisoff, Terrence Wukcytt. The *Space Radar Laboratory* 2 mission is follow-up of nearly identical mission flown in the spring to detect seasonal changes.

10/4/94 ***Soyuz TM-20*** A. Viktorenko, Y. Kondakova, U. Merbold. Merbold, from the European Space Agency, studies space biology aboard *Mir* and returns to Earth on 11/4/94. Viktorenko and Kondakova relieve Malenchenko and Musabaye on *Mir.*

11/3/94 ***Atlantis*** (11 days) Curtis Brown, Donald McMonagle, Jean-François Clervoy (from ESA), Scott Parazynski, Joseph Tanner. Third shuttle flight since 1992 to carry the *Atlas* lab (Atmospheric Laboratory for Applications and Science).

2/3/95 ***Discovery*** (8 days) James Wetherbee, Eileen Collins, Michael Foale, Bernard Harris Jr., Vladimir Titov, Janice Voss. Carries Russian Titov to within 11 m (37 ft.) of *Mir.*

3/2/95 ***Endeavour*** (17 days) Stephen Oswald, Samuel Durrance, Tamara Jernigan, William Gregory, John Grunsfeld, Wendy Lawrence, Ronald Parise. Carries the lab *Astro 2,* used to study volcanic eruptions on Jupiter's moon Io.

3/14/95 ***Soyuz TM-21*** N. Thagard, V. Dezhurov, G. Strekalov. Thagard becomes the first U.S. astronaut to live aboard *Mir;* he studies the body's reaction to weightlessness; Polyakov, who returns on 3/22/95, with Kondakova and Viktorenko, sets endurance record of 14.5 months in space.

6/27/95 ***Atlantis*** (10 days) Robert Gibson, Charles Precourt, Ellen Baker, Gregory Harbaugh, Bonnie Dunbar, Anatoly Solovyev, Nikolai Budarin. Docks with *Mir* for 5 days. Spacelab on Atlantis and Spekter module of *Mir* used for biomedical research. Solovyev and Budarin relieve Thagard, Dezhurov, and Strekalov as crew of *Mir.*

7/13/95 ***Discovery*** (9 days) Tom Henricks, Kevin Kregel, Nancy Currie, Donald Thomas, Mary Ellen Weber. Launches Tracking and Data Relay Satellite (TDRS) to replace one lost when *Challenger* blew up.

9/3/95 ***Soyuz TM-22*** T. Reiter (Germany), Y. Gidzenko, S. Avdeyev. Replaces Solovyev and Budarin, who return to Earth 9/11/88.

9/7/95 ***Endeavour*** (11 days) Michael Gernhart, David Walker, Kenneth Cockrell, James Newman, James Voss. Uses an orbiting shield to produce a vacuum in its wake 10,000 times greater than any found on Earth.

10/20/95 ***Columbia*** (16 days) Ken Bowersox, Kent Rominger, Kathryn Thornton, Cady Coleman, Michael Lopez-Alegria, Fred Leslie, Albert Sacco Conducts microgravity experiments in Spacelab.

11/12/95 ***Atlantis*** (8 days) Kenneth Cameron, James Halsell Jr., Jerry Ross, William McArthur Jr., Chris Hadfield (Canada). Changes configuration of *Mir* to make docking easier in future missions.

1/11/96 ***Endeavour*** (9 days) Brian Duffy, Brent Jett Jr., Leroy Chiao, Winston Scott, Daniel Barry, Koichi Wakata (Japan). Recovers Japanese science-experiment orbiting platform, which had been launched by a Japanese H-2 rocket in March 1995.

2/21/96 ***Soyuz TM-23*** Y. Onufrienko, Y. Usachev. Relieves *Mir* crew.

2/22/96 ***Columbia*** (15 days) Nobie Stone, Jeffrey Hoffman, Andrew Allen, Doc Horowitz, Franklin Chang-Diaz, Claude Nicollier (ESA), Maurizio Cheli (ESA), Umberto Guidoni (Italian Space Agency).. Tethered satellite experiment partly successful, but satellite is mysteriously lost from end of tether.

3/22/96 ***Atlantis*** (9 days) Kevin Childon, Richard Seafoss, Ronald Sega, Michael Clifford, Shannon Lucid, Linda Godwin. Docks with *Mir.* Lucid stays behind on the space station.

5/19/96 ***Endeavour*** (10 days) John Caspar, Curtis Brown Jr., Daniel Bursch, Mario Runco Jr., Marc Garneau (Canadian), Andrew Thomas. Deploys first inflatable antenna from Spartan satellite. Conducts rendezvous studies of the *PAMS* satellite, a test of a system in which a satellite stabilizes itself without expending rocket fuel.

6/20/96 ***Columbia*** (17 days) Tom Henricks, Kevin Kregel, Rick Linnehan, Susan Helms, Charles Brady, Jean-Jacques Favier (Canada), Robert Thirsk. Carries the Life/Microgravity Spacelab, to study the effects of space flight on the human body, on rats, and on fish embryos; and SAREX-II.

8/17/96 ***Soyuz TM-24*** V. Korzun, A. Kaleri, C. Andre-Deshays (France). Korzun and Kaleri relieve Onufrienko and Usachev on *Mir.*

9/16/96 ***Atlantis*** (10 days) William Readdy, Terrence Wilcutt, Tom Akers, Jay Apt, Carl Walz, John Blaha, Shannon Lucid. Blaha relieves Lucid on *Mir.*

11/19/96 ***Columbia*** (18 days) Kenneth Cockrell, Kent Rominger, Story Musgrave, Thomas Jones, Tamara Jernigan. Deploys and retrieves *ORFEUS-SPAS,* a satellite gathering data about matter in space between the stars and the WSF-3/Wake Shield Facility, a satellite used in testing a method of producing a high vacuum to be used in manufacturing ultra pure semiconductor devices.

1/12/97 ***Atlantis*** (10 days) Mike Baker, Brent Jett, Jeff Wisoff, John Grunsfeld, Marsha Ivins, J.M. Linenger, John Blaha. Linenger relieves Blaha on *Mir.*

2/10/97 ***Soyuz TM-25*** V. Tsbliyev, A. Lazutkin, R. Ewald (Germany), V. Korzun, A. Kaleri. Tsbliyev and Lazutkin relieve Korzun and Kaleri on *Mir.*

2/11/97 ***Discovery*** (10 days) Ken Bowersox, Scott Horowitz, Joe Tanner, Steve Hawley, Greg Harbaugh, Mark Lee, Steve Smith. Replaces eight instruments in the Hubble Space Telescope and adds two new ones, greatly improving its abilities.

4/4/97 ***Columbia*** (4 days) Jim Halsell, Susan Still, Janice Voss, Mike Gernhardt, Don Thomas, Roger

Crouch, Greg Linteris. Carries the Microgravity Science Lab, but 85 percent of the experiments are canceled because of a problem with the fuel cells.
5/15/97 ***Atlantis*** (9 days) Charlie Precourt, Eileen Collins, Jean-François Clervoy, Carlos Noriega, Ed Lu, Elena Kondakova (Russia), Mike Foale, Jerry Linenger. Docks with Mir, taking Linenger back to Earth and leaving Foale. Brings needed supplies and replacement equipment to aging *Mir,* which has had problems with fires and failures.
7/1/97 ***Columbia*** (16 days) James Halsell, Susan Still, Janice Voss, Michael Gernhardt, Donald Thomas, Roger Crouch, Gregory Linteris. Replacement for flight of 4/4/97.
8/7/97 ***Discovery*** (11 days) Curt Brown, Kent Rominger, Jan Davis, Robert Curbeam, Steve Robinson, Bjarni Tryggvason. In the fourth cooperative German-American scientific mission, various experiments using infrared imagining, lasers, and cryogenic devices are conducted.
9/25/97 ***Atlantis*** (11 days) James Wetherbee, Mike Bloomfield, Vladimir Titov, Scott Parazynski, Jean-Loup Chrétien, Wendy Lawrence, David Wolf, Michael Foale. Takes Wolf to *Mir,* returns with Foale.
11/19/97 ***Columbia*** (16 days) Kevin Kregel, Steve Lindsey, Kalpana Chawla, Winston Scott, Takao Doi, Leonid Kadenyuk (first Ukranian to fly aboard a shuttle). Conducts microgravity experiments and attempts to launch *SPARTAN* solar research satellite; when *SPARTAN* malfunctions, astronauts retrieve it for a future attempt on a later flight.
1/22/98 ***Endeavour*** (9 days) Terrence Wilcutt, Joe Edwards, James Reilly, Michael Anderson, Bonnie Dunbar, Salizhan Sharipov, Andrew Thomas, David Wolf. Thomas relieves Wolf on *Mir.* Performs microgravity experiments with plants and crystals.
4/17/98 ***Columbia*** (16 days) Richard Searfoss, Scott Altman, Kathryn Hire, Richard Linnehan, Dave Williams, Jay Buckey, James Pawelczyk. Carries the *Neurolab* into space where the effects of space flight on the brains and reproduction of various species of animals and plants are studied.
6/2/98 ***Discovery*** (10 days) Charles Precourt, Dominic Gorie, Wendy Lawrence, Franklin Chang-Diaz, Janet Kavandi, Andrew Thomas, Valery Victorovitch Ryumin. Final U.S. astronaut mission on *Mir* completed as Thomas is returned to Earth.
11/20/98 ***Discovery*** (9 days) Curtis Brown Jr., Steven Lindsey, Scott Parazynski, Stephen Robinson, Pedro Duque, Chiaki Mukai, John Glenn. Glenn, first American to orbit Earth in 1962, becomes oldest astronau; studies effects of weightlessness on older humans.

Era of the International Space Station (ISS)

12/04/98 ***Endeavour*** (12 days) Robert Cabana, Frederick Sturckow, James Newman, Nancy Currie, Jerry Ross, Sergei Konstantinovich Krikalev (Russia). Crew docks with the Russian-built Functional Energy Block Zarya and adds Node-1 (Unity) to begin assembly of the International Space Station.
5/27/99 ***Discovery*** (10 days) Kent Rominger, Rick Husband, Tamara Jernigan, Ellen Ochoa, Daniel Barry, Julie Payette (Canada), Valery Ivanovich Tokarev (Russia). Brings cargo for outfitting (ISS), including Russian cargo crane to be mounted on exterior of Functional Energy Block.
7/22/99 ***Columbia*** (5 days) Eileen Collins, Jeffrey Ashby, Steven Hawley, Catherine Coleman, Michael Tognini (France). Collins first female commander. Launches Chandra X-ray Observatory.
12/19/99 ***Discovery*** (8 days) Curtis Brown Jr., Scott Kelly, John Grunsfeld, Michael Foales, Steven Smith, Jean-François Clervoy (France), Claude Nicollier (Switzerland). Captures, services, and re-launches Hubble Space Telescope.
2/11/00 ***Endeavour*** (11 days) Kevin Kregel, Dominic Gorie, Janet Kavandi, Janice Voss, Gerhard Thiele (German-ESA), Mamoru Mohri (Japan). The Shuttle Radar Topography Mission obtain the most detailed topographical map of the Earth to date.
5/19/00 ***Atlantis*** (10 days) James Halsell Jr., Scott Horowitz, Susan Helms, Mary Ellen Weber, Jeffrey Williams, James Voss, Yury Usachev (Russian). Carries supplies to ISS. Helms and Usachev remain on ISS as part of first crew.
9/8/00 ***Atlantis*** (12 days) Terry Wilcutt, Scott Altman, Dan Burbank, Ed Lu, Rick Mastracchio, Yuri Malenchenko (Russia), and Boris Morukov (Russia). Brings supplies to ISS and conducts space walk to perform station maintenance.
10/11/00 ***Discovery*** (13 days) Brian Duffy, Pamela Melroy, Leroy Chiao, Jeff Wisoff, Michael Lopez-Alegria, William McArthur, Jr., Koichi Wakata (Japan). Brings and installs parts needed for solar arrays, communications, and attitude control for ISS.
10/31/00 ***Soyuz TM-31*** (139 days) Bill Shepherd, Y. Gidzenko, S. Krikalev. This is Expedition 1, beginning the permanent occupation of ISS.
11/30/00 ***Endeavour*** (12 days) Brent Jett, Michael Bloomfield, Joseph Tanner, Carlos Noriega, Marc Garneau (Canada). Adds photovoltaic modules to the ISS's solar arrays; brings radiators for cooling photovoltaic cells; activates the S-band communications system.
2/7/01 ***Atlantis*** (13 days) Kenneth Cockrell, Mark Polansky, Robert Curbeam, Thomas Jones, Marsha Ivins. Installs ISS's "Destiny" laboratory module.
3/8/01 ***Discovery*** (13 days) Jim Wetherbee, Jim Kelly, Andy Thomas, Paul Richards. Brings Expedition 2 crew (Yury Usachev, James Voss, and Susan Helms) to ISS. Returns Expedition 1 crew (see 10/31/00). Brings additional laboratory equipment.
4/19/01 ***Endeavour*** (12 days) Kent Rominger , Jeffrey Ashby, Scott Umberto Guidoni (ESA), Scott Parazynski, Chris Hadfield (Canada), Yuri Lonchakov (Russia), John Phillips. Delivers the Italian "Raffaello" module and the Canadian mechanical arm to the ISS.
7/12/01 ***Atlantis*** (11 days) Steven Lindsey, Charles Hobaugh, Michael Gernhardt, Janet Kavandi, James Reilly. Delivers the Joint Airlock; resolves problems with the Canadian robotic arm.
8/10/01 ***Discovery*** (12 days) Scott Horowitz, Rick Sturckow, Daniel Barry, Patrick Forrester. Installs the Leonardo Multi-Purpose Module; launches Simplesat, a demonstration satellite built with "off-the-shelf" commercial hardware. Brings Expedition 3 crew (Frank Culbertson, Vladimir Dezhurov, and Mikhail Tyurin). Returns Expedition 2 crew (see 3/8/01).
10/21/01 ***Soyuz TM-33*** (165 days) Viktor Afanasyev (Russia), Konstantin Kozeev (Russia), Claudie Haignere (ESA). Conducts experiments in materials research, life sciences, meteorological phenomena. Emergency vehicle exchanged; crew returns on *Soyuz TM-32.*
12/5/01 ***Endeavour*** (12 days) Linda Godwin, Dominic Gorie, Mark Kelly, Daniel Tani. Brings Expedition 4 crew (Yury Onufrienko, Carl Walz, Daniel Bursh) and 3 tons (2.7 metric tons) of equipment and supplies. Returns Expedition 3 crew (see 8/10/01).
3/1/02 ***Columbia*** (11 days) Scott Altman, Duane Carey, Nancy Currie, John Grunsfeld, Richard Linnehan, Michael Massimino, James Newman. Fourth Hubble Space Telescope servicing mission; during five EVAs installs a new power control unit, new camera, new solar arrays.
4/8/02 ***Atlantis*** (11 days) Crew: Michael Bloomfield, Stephen Frick, Lee Morin, Ellen Ochoa, Jerry Ross, Steven Smith, Rex Walheim. Delivered and installed central truss segment to ISS, the first of nine parts of the space station's external frame.
4/25/02 ***Soyuz TM-34*** (11 days) Yuri Gidzenko (Russia), Roberto Vittori (ESA), Mark Shuttleworth (a pay-

ing tourist from South Africa). Exchange of *Soyuz* emergency vehicles; crew returned on *Soyuz TM-33*.
6/5/02 ***Endeavour*** (14 days) Franklin Chang-Diaz, Kenneth Cockrell, Paul Lockhart, Philippe Perrin (France). Delivers Microgravity Science Glovebox, enabling crew to work safely with experiments involving fluids, flames, fumes, etc. Delivers Expedition 5 crew (Peggy Whitson, Valery Korzun, Sergei Treschev), returns Expedition 4 crew (see 12/5/01)
10/7/02 ***Atlantis*** (11 days) Jeffrey Ashby, Pamela Melroy, David Wolf, Piers Sellers, Sandra Magnus, Fyodor Yurchikhin. Delivers S1 Truss.
10/30/02 ***Soyuz TMA-1*** (9 days) S. Zaletin, F. De Winne (Belgium), Y. Lonchakov, A. Lazutkin. Test flight of new *Soyuz TMA*. Conducts experiments with Microgravity Science Glovebox. Returns *Soyuz TM-34*
11/23/02 ***Endeavour*** (14 days) Jim Wetherbee, Paul Lockhart, Michael Lopez-Alegria, John Herrington. Delivers Expedition 6 crew (Peggy Whitson, Valery Korzun, Sergei Treschev) and parts to improve space station's thermal control system. Returns Expedition 5 crew (see 6/5/02)
1/16/03 ***Columbia*** (16 days) Rick Husband, Willie McCool, Michael Anderson, Kalpana Chawla, David Brown, Laurel Clark, Ilan Ramon. Shuttle explodes on re-entry minutes before its scheduled landing, killing all aboard *(See Part I: Major News Stories of the Year.)*
4/26/03 ***Soyuz TMA-2*** Yuri Milanchenko (Russia), Edward Lu. Retrieves Expedition 6 crew (see 11/23/02) trapped aboard ISS as Space Shuttle Program is grounded in wake of *Columbia* disaster. *(See Part I: Major News Stories of the Year.)*

The International Space Station

The International Space Station began at the end of the Cold War era with separate plans by the United States and Soviet Union. The Soviet Union had operated the successful space station *Mir* since 1986 and the U.S. was working with several other countries to launch its own space station, tentatively named Freedom. With the collapse of the Soviet Union in 1989-90, plans were altered and Russia joined the American-led effort, which was redesigned to replace *Mir*. Today there are 16 nations supporting the International Space Station (ISS)—the U.S., Russia, Japan, Canada, Italy, Belgium, the Netherlands, Denmark, Norway, France, Spain, Germany, Sweden, Switzerland, the United Kingdom, and Brazil.

Construction of the ISS is in modules, requiring some 45 different space flights to put all the parts in place. The first module, known as Zarya, was launched by Russia on Nov. 20, 1998. Other modules have included the U.S. Unity passageway and docking port (launched Dec. 4, 1998); Russia's Zvezda (installed Sept. 10, 2000), early living quarters for station crews; the U.S. Destiny workstation module (installed Feb. 10, 2001), and the Italian Raffaello multipurpose logistic module (MPLM). Other important components are trusses, the Canadian robot arm, and an airlock. Still to come are two more Italian MPLMs as well as modules from the European Space Agency, Japan, and Russia. The completed space station will weigh about a million pounds (453 metric tons) and be 356 feet (109 m) across by 290 feet (88 m) long. The interior working space will be somewhat larger than the volume of a Boeing 747 airliner, but there will be only four windows. ISS is powered by solar arrays that cover more than half an acre of space. Fifty-two separate computers will control operations.

EARTH SCIENCES

Earth sciences include geology (the study of Earth's rocks and interior), oceanography (the study of ocean water, currents, and the ocean floor), paleontology (the study of fossils and ancient lifeforms), parts of astronomy, and meteorology (the study of the atmosphere, including weather). Except for astronomy and weather, which are covered elsewhere, this section deals with all of these studies.

▶THE EARTH'S COMPOSITION

In their study of the Earth, scientists distinguish a number of distinct layers from the inner core—the center of which is about 6,400 km (roughly 4,000 mi.) below the surface—to the farthest limit of the atmosphere, about 1,000 km (600 mi.) above the surface. This section describes these layers, from the innermost to the outermost.

Core The core consists of two parts—one solid, the other liquid—both thought to be a mixture of iron and a lighter element, probably sulfur or oxygen. The solid inner core begins about 4,650 km (2,890 mi.) from the surface, and the liquid outer core at about 2,900 km (1,800 mi.) from the surface.

Mantle The bulk of the Earth—roughly two-thirds of its mass—is composed of the mantle, which extends from the outer core to within about 90 km (55 mi.) of the Earth's surface below the higher mountains, and to within only 5 to 8 km (3 to 5 mi.) of the Earth's surface below some areas of the oceans. Silicon dioxide constitutes almost half of the mantle, and there is an abundance of magnesium oxide, some iron oxide, and smaller amounts of oxides of other metals. (Although silicon dioxide is known as quartz when found in the Earth's crust, under the heat and pressure of the mantle it may have very different properties from the form we know.) Part of the upper mantle is somewhat fluid and is known as the asthenosphere.

Crust The crust is the outermost solid layer of the Earth. Under the continents, the crust varies from 30 to 90 km (19 to 55 mi.) in thickness, while under the oceans it is generally only 5 to 8 km (3 to 5 mi.) thick. Continental and oceanic crust differ from each other in thickness and composition. Continental crust consists of granite and other relatively light rocks, while oceanic crust is made up chiefly of basalt. The crust is separated from the mantle by the Mohorovičić discontinuity, or Moho. The crust that is accessible to accurate measurements contains the following principal elements:

Element	Percent	Element	Percent
Oxygen	45.6%	Magnesium	2.8%
Silicon	27.3	Sodium	2.3
Aluminum	8.4	Potassium	1.8
Iron	6.2	Hydrogen	1.5
Calcium	4.7	Titanium	0.6

Note: Adds to more than 100% due to independent rounding.

Hydrosphere Water—virtually all of it sea water—covers about 71 percent of the Earth's surface and thereby constitutes a distinct layer of the Earth. Sea water varies in composition from place to place, but on average it is about 3.5 percent salts—that is, evaporating 100 lb. of sea water would yield 3.5 lb. of salt. Sodium chloride (ordinary table salt) constitutes 2.7 percent of sea water, or 77.8 percent of total solids in sea water. The typical composition of solids in sea water is as follows:

Compound	Percent
Sodium chloride	77.8%
Magnesium chloride	10.9
Magnesium sulfide	4.7
Calcium sulfate	3.6
Potassium sulfate	2.5
Calcium carbonate	0.3
Magnesium bromide	0.2
Other compounds	trace

Atmosphere The atmosphere is the gaseous layer that envelopes the Earth. The lower atmosphere consists of the troposphere and the stratosphere. The *troposphere* has an average thickness of about 11 km (7 mi.), although it is only 8 km (5 mi.) at the poles and as much as 16 km (10 mi.) around the equator. Most clouds and weather phenomena occur in this region. The composition of dry air at sea level is: nitrogen, 78.08 percent; oxygen, 20.05

Geologic Time Scale

The history of the planet has been divided by geologists and other earth scientists into periods of varying length based on the fossils found in rock strata. Geologists often speak of the period before 545 million years ago as Precambrian Time. The eras after 545 million years ago are grouped into the Phanerozoic Eon.

Mass extinctions—brief periods when large numbers of species become extinct—often mark the boundaries between geologic time periods. In the greatest such extinction, known as the Final Permian (250 million years ago), perhaps as many as 80 to 90 percent of all species became extinct in less than a million years. No one knows what causes most mass extinctions, but the Final Cretaceous of 65 million years ago (also called the K-T extinction) and the Final Permian were almost certainly caused by impacts of asteroids. The most recent extinction, at the end of the last ice age (11,000 years ago), may have been caused by human hunting. Some biologists believe that human activities are causing a new mass extinction today as well.

Era or Eon, Period, Epoch	Organisms	Beginning of Interval (millions of years ago)
ARCHEAN EON	Monerans: bacteria and blue-green algae	**4,600**
PROTEROZOIC EON	Protists, algae, and soft-bodied creatures similar to jellyfish and worms	**2,500**
PHANEROZOIC EON		
PALEOZOIC ERA		
Cambrian period	Tiny fossils with skeletons followed by animals with shells, notably trilobites	**545**
Ordovician period	Brachiopods (shellfish similar to clams), corals, starfish, and some organisms that have no modern counterparts, called sea scorpions and conodonts	**500**
Silurian period	Snails, clams and mussels, ammonoids (similar to the nautilus), jawless fish, sea scorpions, land plants and animals (club mosses, land scorpions); modern groups of algae and fungi	**425**
Devonian period	Spiders, amphibians, jawed fish, lobe-finned fish, sharks, lungfish, and ferns	**395**
Carboniferous period	Insects, land snails, amphibians, early reptiles, sea lilies, giant club mosses, and seed ferns	**350**
Permian period	Mammal-like reptiles and fin-backed reptiles, cycads, ginkgoes, and conifers	**290**
MEZOZOIC ERA		
Triassic period	Marine reptiles (plesiosaurs and ichthyosaurs), crocodiles, frogs, turtles, early mammals, and early dinosaurs	**235**
Jurassic period	Dinosaurs (such as stegosaurs), pterosaurs (such as pterodactyl), early birds, dinoflagellates, diatoms, early flowering plants	**190**
Cretaceous period	Dinosaurs (such as tyrannosaurs, triceratops, and apatosaurs), salamanders, modern bony fishes, mosasaurs (marine lizards), flowering plants, placental and marsupial mammals	**130**
CENOZOIC ERA		
Tertiary period		
Paleocene epoch	Early primates, early horses, rodents, sycamores	**66.5**
Eocene epoch	Whales, penguins, roses, bats, camels, early elephants, dogs, cats, weasels	**57.8**
Oligocene epoch	Deer, pigs, saber-toothed cats, monkeys	**36.6**
Miocene epoch	Seals, dolphins, grasses, daisies, asters, sunflowers, lettuce, giraffes, bears, hyenas, early apes	**23.5**
Pliocene epoch	Apes, australopithecines (early hominids) *Homo habilis* (first human species), mammoths, giant sloths, and armadillos	**5.2**
Quaternary period		
Pleistocene epoch	*Homo erectus* and related human species, modern humans, and Neandertal humans; large mammals such as giant bison and beavers; many kinds of hoofed animals	**1.6**
Holocene epoch	Modern humans and flora and fauna of today	**0.01 (11,000 years)**

percent; argon, 0.93 percent; and carbon dioxide, 0.03 percent. There are also lesser amounts of neon, helium, krypton, and xenon. These proportions change with altitude, lighter gases being more common at higher altitudes, but they are approximately the same everywhere on Earth at the same altitude. There are also variable quantities of water vapor, dust particles, and other compounds whose proportions change from place to place at the same altitude—fewer dust particles being found over oceans, and less water vapor over deserts. Temperature decreases with altitude in the troposphere.

The *stratosphere* is found between 11 km and 50 km (7-30 mi.) out from the Earth's surface. Temperatures in this region rise slightly as altitude increases, to a maximum of about 0°C (32°F). Virtually coextensive with the stratosphere is the *ozonosphere*, or ozone layer, the region in which most of the atmosphere's ozone is found. Because ozone absorbs most of the sun's ultraviolet radiation, it is vital to the continued existence of life on the planet.

Beyond the stratosphere is the upper atmosphere, or *ionosphere*, so called because it is the layer in which atmospheric gases have been ionized by solar radiation. The ionosphere reflects certain wavelengths back to the surface, making it possible to transmit radio waves around the curve of the Earth. The ionosphere is further divided into the *mesosphere*, between 50 km and 80 km (30-50 mi.), in which the temperature decreases with altitude to -90°C (-130°F); and the *thermosphere*, from about 80 km to 450 km (50-280 mi.), in which the molecular temperature increases to as

Major Discoveries in Earth Sciences

B.C.

c.300 Dicaearchus (Greek: c. 320) develops map of Earth on a sphere using lines of latitude.

A.D.

132 Zhang Heng (Chinese: 78–139) develops first crude seismograph.

1600 William Gilbert (English: 1544–1603) suggests that Earth is giant magnet, which is why magnetic compasses indicate north.

1669 Nicolaus Steno (Niels Stensen; Danish: 1638–86) correctly explains origin of fossils.

1777 Nicolas Desmarest (French: 1725–1815) proposes that the rock basalt starts as lava.

1785 James Hutton (Scottish: 1726–97) explains features of Earth on basis of tiny changes taking place over long periods of time (uniformitarianism).

1795 Baron Georges Cuvier (French: 1769–1832) shows that giant bones found in Meuse River are remains of extinct giant reptile.

1797 Sir James Hall (Scottish: 1761–1832) shows that melted rocks form crystals upon cooling.

1822 Gideon A. Mantell (English: 1790–1852) and his wife, Mary Ann, discover and recognize dinosaur bones as those of a giant, extinct reptile.

1830 Sir Charles Lyell (Scottish: 1797–1875) begins to publish *Principles of Geology,* the work that convinced geologists that Earth is at least several hundred million years old.

1880 John Milne (English: 1850–1913) invents modern seismograph.

1896 Svante A. Arrhenius (Swedish: 1859–1927) calculates that global temperatures will rise with higher levels of carbon dioxide in atmosphere (greenhouse effect).

1902 Léon-Philippe Teisserenc de Bort (French: 1855–1913) discovers the stratosphere.

1906 Richard D. Oldham (English: 1858–1936) establishes existence of Earth's core.

1907 Bertram B. Boltwood (American: 1870–1927) shows that age of rocks containing uranium can be determined by measuring ratio of uranium to lead.

1909 Andrija Mohorovičić (Croatia: 1857–1936) discovers boundary between Earth's crust and mantle, now known as Mohorovičić discontinuity, or "Moho."

1912 Alfred L. Wegener (German: 1880–1930) proposes theory of continental drift, idea that a single continent—Pangaea—split into present-day continents, which have drifted away from each other.

1925 The German *Meteor* expedition discovers Mid-Atlantic Ridge, a giant mountain range in middle of the Atlantic Ocean.

1929 Motonori Matuyama (Japanese: 1884–1958) shows that Earth's magnetic field reverses every few hundred million years.

1958 James A. Van Allen (American: 1914–) discovers belts of radiation that surround Earth in space, now known as Van Allen belts.

1962 Harry H. Hess (American: 1906–69) develops theory of seafloor spreading—oceans become wider as new seafloor is formed at midocean ridges.

1979 American oceanographers discover hot vents in oceans, surrounded by exotic forms of life based on sulfur, not oxygen.

1980 Walter Alvarez (American: 1940–) and coworkers discover geologic layer of iridium in region identified with the demise of the dinosaurs; he attributes both iridium and extinction to a large comet or meteorite striking Earth.

1993 Ice cores from Greenland and Antarctica reveal the record of Earth's climate for the past 250,000 years.

Weather scientists discover unexpected displays of electromagnetism in Earth's upper atmosphere; the displays are named Sprites, ELVES, and blue jets.

1996 A farmer in Liaoning Province in China discovers a dinosaur whose skin is covered with a feathery down, the first major find at what proves to be an important fossil site that also includes dinosaurs with more highly developed feathers.

Scientists from the Scripps Institution of Oceanography at San Diego find evidence that life has existed on Earth for at least 3.85 billion years.

1998 Paul F. Hoffman (Canadian: 1941–) of Harvard University proposes that some 200 million years ago the surface of Earth was completely frozen from the poles to the equator, a condition that becomes known as "snowball Earth;" computer studies in 2000, however, indicate that a narrow band at the equator remained unfrozen.

2002 Thousands of fossils of large jellyfish, some 20 in. (50 cm) across, that had become stranded on a beach, are found near Mosinee, Wisconsin.

Laboratory studies reveal that Earth's mantle (the layer between the crust and core) could hold five times as much water as is in all the oceans.

Grant Yip of the University of California, Santa Barbara, and coworkers discover evidence of massive landslides in Baja California that occurred at precisely the same time as a giant object struck the Yucatán peninsula on the other side of the continent. The landslides were triggered by a magnitude 13 earthquake, thought to have been caused by the impact.

much as 1475°C (2690°F). To spacecraft traveling in the atmosphere, as the space shuttle does, however, the temperature seems cold because the molecules are so widely spaced. Beyond the thermosphere is the *exosphere*, extending to about 1,000 km (600 mi.). In this layer, temperature no longer has the customary meaning. (See also "Global Warming" and "The Ozone Layer.")

▶THE CHANGING EARTH

Despite its apparent solidity, the crust and interior of the Earth are constantly changing.

Plate tectonics The earth's outer crust is composed of about 20 lithospheric (or tectonic) plates that move from a few millimeters to several centimeters per year. Hundreds of millions of years ago, these plates formed a continuous landmass known as Pangaea, surrounded by ocean. Eventually the plates separated, until they reached the positions they occupy today.

As plates move away from each other, molten rock emerges from the mantle to form oceanic crust. Where they come together, one plate is usually forced under the other, forming either oceanic trenches or mountain ranges (such as the Himalayas) or both. In a few places, one plate slips by the other along a giant crack called a fault, such as the San Andreas Fault in California. These areas are also the site of greatest volcanic and earthquake activity.

Earthquakes and tsunamis Most earthquakes are caused when rock on one side of a fault (or crack) in the Earth's crust moves with respect to the rock on the other side of the fault. The motion causes vibrations in the crust that travel through the rock as shock waves. When these reach the surface, they cause it to move in various ways, which is called seismic motion. Small earthquakes that accompany volcanic eruptions are caused by the motion of liquid rock, or magma.

More than 800,000 earthquakes are registered by seismographs each year, but the overwhelming majority go unnoticed. However, large earthquakes are of great concern to many people living in regions of significant seismic activity. Although research on earthquake prediction has yielded no breakthroughs, death and destruction have been reduced somewhat by improvements in construction codes and techniques.

One common side effect of undersea earthquakes is tsunamis—or (incorrectly) tidal waves—against which there is little protection. Tsunamis are caused when an earthquake raises or lowers a section of seabed, thereby producing a wave that, while not generally noticeable at sea, can reach great heights as it approaches land. Similar to and as destructive as tsunamis, harbor waves are generated when a landslide falls into a bay, strait, or other confined body of water causing almost immediate flooding. High waves are also caused by volcanic explosions or collapses, such as the explosion and collapse of Krakatau in 1883.

Volcanoes are openings in the Earth's crust that emit molten or partially molten rock (lava), various hot gases, and ash. (A volcano is also the mountain formed by solidified lava or ash ejected from the opening.) If the opening is like a crack, it is called a vent. If it is larger and fairly circular, it is called a crater. A caldera is a basin formed by the settling of the top of a volcanic mountain, and it may have several vents or craters on its floor.

Most volcanoes are found where two tectonic plates meet, such as along the famous "Ring of Fire" around the Pacific Ocean. A few, such as the volcanoes of the Hawaiian Islands, appear to be over "hot spots" in the Earth's crust where liquid rock flows upward with sufficient force to burn through the crust.

Although volcanoes are associated with destruction, they have many positive effects. Minerals from deep within the Earth make the land around many volcanoes extremely fertile; volcanoes can create new landforms in the sea; and the study of volcanoes contributes enormously to our understanding of the Earth's interior.

Richter Scale and Effects Near the Epicenter

Note: The epicenter is the point on Earth's surface above the center of the quake

Below 2.5 Not felt except by a very few under specially favorable circumstances.
2.5 to 3.5 Felt only by a few persons at rest, especially on upper floors of buildings.
3.5 to 4.5 At lower levels or further from the quake, it is felt by many people, sometimes quite noticeably indoors, especially on upper floors of buildings, but many people do not recognize as an earthquake. At somewhat higher levels or nearer to the epicenter, during the day the quake is felt indoors by many; outdoors by few. Sensation is like heavy truck striking building. At the highest level, the earth movement is felt by nearly everyone; with many awakened if during the night. Disturbances of trees, telephone poles, and other tall objects sometimes can be noticed.
4.5 to 6.0 Felt by all; many frightened and run outdoors. Some heavy furniture moved; there will be a few instances of fallen plaster or damaged chimneys. Other slight local damage may occur. At higher level, however, everybody runs outdoors. At the upper level, while damage is still negligible in buildings of good design and construction, there can be moderate damage even to well-built ordinary structures; there will be considerable damage to poorly built or badly designed structures.
6.0 to 7.0 A destructive earthquake. Damage may still be slight in specially designed structures, but will be considerable in ordinary substantial buildings, often with partial collapse. Damage will be great in poorly built structures, including collapse of chimneys, factory stacks, columns, monuments, and walls. At the upper level, damage is likely to be considerable even in specially designed structures. Most ordinary buildings will be shifted off foundations. Even the ground will be cracked conspicuously.
7.0 to 8.0 A major earthquake. Worldwide, about 10 of these occur each year. Some well-built wooden structures will be destroyed. Most masonry and frame structures will be destroyed along with their foundations. Ground becomes badly cracked.
8.0 and above Great earthquakes. These occur once every five to 10 years. Few, if any masonry structures remain standing. Bridges are destroyed. Broad fissures appear in ground. At the highest levels and near the epicenter, damage total. Waves seen on solid ground. Heavy objects thrown upward into air.

Although geologists consider a volcano active if it has shown signs of activity in historic times, it is not usually clear whether a volcano is extinct or only dormant and could be active again. (Thus Tambora, which has not erupted since 1815, is considered active.) Some volcanoes once thought to be extinct have become active, and there are now about 600 volcanoes that are considered active. The accompanying list contains about a fourth of all volcanoes known to have been active in recent years, with special emphasis on volcanoes in the United States and volcanoes that have had famous eruptions.

The destruction caused by volcanoes is usually localized, but their effects can be felt around the world and take many forms. At their worst, volcanoes can blow themselves to pieces, as the island of Thera did about 1650 B.C. More often, volcanic ash blankets an area (as Mt. Vesuvius did at Pompeii), or clouds of hot gases and dust sweep down the side of the volcano poisoning the air. Lava generally moves too slowly to be a menace to people. Even more unpredictable, heat from a volcano can melt glaciers or snowcaps, triggering massive mud slides (as happened in Colombia in 1985) or releasing lakes of boiling water.

▶MEASURING EARTHQUAKES

The size of an earthquake is generally reported in the United States using the Richter scale, a system developed by seismologist Charles Richter (American: 1900-85) in 1935. The Richter scale measures the magnitude of an earthquake, that is, the size of ground waves generated by an earthquake as shown on a measuring device called a seismograph. Each whole number on the scale represents a tenfold increase (or decrease) in magnitude: a magnitude 6 earthquake produces a ground wave 10 times greater than a magnitude 5.

This does not mean, however, that a magnitude 6 earthquake has 10 times the energy as one of magnitude 5. Measuring the actual energy requires instruments placed at the site of the earthquake. Various methods have been developed for inferring energy from magnitude and these suggest that one change in magnitude corresponds to a thirty- to sixtyfold change in energy. Using these proportions, the energy of a magnitude 8 earthquake, a very serious event, can be as much as 1 million to 10 million times as much as that of a magnitude 4 earthquake, one that can be felt but causes almost no damage.

Major Earthquakes, 856-2002

Date	Location and remarks	Estimated deaths	Richter magnitude
856	Corinth, Greece	45,000	—
Dec. 22, 856	Iran	200,000	—
Mar. 23, 893	Iran	150,000	—
1036	Shansi	23,000	—
1057	Chihli (Hopeh), China	25,000	—
Aug. 9, 1138	Aleppo, Syria	230,000	—
1170	Sicily	15,000	—
1268	Silicia (Turkey)	60,000	—
Sept. 1290	Chihli, China	100,000	—
May 20, 1293	Kamakura, Japan	30,000	—
Jan. 26, 1531	Lisbon, Portugal	30,000	—
Jan. 23, 1556	Shansi, China	830,000	—
Nov. 1667	Shemakha, Azerbaijan	80,000	—
June 7, 1692	Port Royal, Jamaica	30,000	—
Jan. 11, 1693	Catania province, Sicily	60,000	—
1693	Naples, Italy	93,000	—
1707	Tsunami hits Japan	30,000	—
Nov. 18, 1727	Tabriz, Iran	77,000	—
Dec. 30, 1730	Hokkaido Island, Japan	137,000	—
1731	Beijing, China	100,000	—
Oct. 11, 1737	Calcutta, India	300,000	—
June 7, 1755	Northern Iran	40,000	—
Nov. 1, 1755	Lisbon, Portugal (earthquake, tsunami)	60,000	8.6
Feb. 4, 1783	Calabria, Italy	50,000	—
Feb. 4, 1797	Quito, Ecuador and Cuzco, Peru	41,000	—
Dec. 16, 1811	New Madrid, Missouri	<10	7.7
Feb. 7, 1812	New Madrid, Missouri	0	7.9
Sept. 5, 1822	Aleppo (Syria)	22,000	—
Dec. 28, 1828	Echigo, Japan	30,000	—
Dec. 24, 1854	Tokai, Japan	3,000	8.4
Oct. 1855	Tokyo, Japan	2,000+	—
Jan. 9, 1857	Fort Tejon, California	1	7.9
1857	East of Naples, Italy	10,000+	—
Aug. 13-15, 1868	Peru and Ecuador	40,000	—
May 16, 1875	Venezuela and Colombia	16,000	—
Aug. 31, 1886	Charleston, South Carolina	60	7.6
Oct. 28, 1891	Central Japan	7,300	—
June 15, 1896	Sanriku and Kamaishi, Japan (tsunami)	26,000	—
Apr. 4, 1905	Kangra, India	19,000	8.6
Apr. 18, 1906	San Francisco, California	3,000	7.7
Aug. 17, 1906	Santiago, Chile	20,000	8.6
1907	Tajikistan	40,000	—
Dec. 28, 1908	Messina, Sicily	75,000	7.5
Jan. 13, 1916	Avezzano, Italy	29,980	7.5
Dec. 16, 1920	Gansu, China	200,000	8.5
Sept. 1, 1923	Tokyo/Yokohama, Japan	143,000	8.3
Mar. 7, 1927	Tango, Japan	3,020	7.9
May 22, 1927	Nan-Shan, China	200,000	8.3
Dec. 25, 1932	Gansu, China	70,000	7.6
Mar. 2, 1933	Sanriku, Japan (tsunami)	2,990	8.9
Mar. 11, 1933	Long Beach, California	115	6.3
Jan. 15, 1934	Bihar, India and Nepal	10,700	8.4
May 30, 1935	Quetta, India (Pakistan)	50,000	7.5
Jan. 25, 1939	Chillan, Chile	30,000	8.3
Dec. 27, 1939	Erzincan, Turkey	30,000	8.0
Apr. 1, 1946	Earthquake at Unimak Island, Alaska, causes tsunami striking Hilo, Hawaii	165	7.3
Dec. 20, 1946	Tonankai, Japan	1,330	8.4
June 28, 1948	Fukui, Japan	5,390	7.3
Oct. 5, 1948	Ashkabad, Turkmenistan	110,000	7.3
Aug. 5, 1949	Pelileo, Ecuador	6,000	6.8
Aug. 15, 1950	Assam State, India	1,530	8.7
July 21, 1952	Kern County, California	12	7.5
June 10-17, 1956	Northern Afghanistan	2,000	7.7
July 2, 1957	Northern Iran	1,200	7.4
Dec. 13, 1957	Western Iran	1,130	7.3
Aug. 17, 1959	Hebgen Lake, Montana	28	7.3
Feb. 29, 1960	Agadir, Morocco	12,000	5.9
May 21-30, 1960	Southern Chile; tsunami strikes various Pacific islands, killing 61 in Hawaii; greatest earthquake ever recorded	5,700	9.5

Date	Location and remarks	Estimated deaths	Richter magnitude
Sept. 1, 1962	Northwestern Iran	12,230	7.3
Mar. 28, 1964	Southern Alaska	125	9.2
Aug. 19, 1966	Eastern Turkey	2,520	7.1
Aug. 31, 1968	Khurasan, Iran	12,000	7.3
July 25, 1969	Eastern China	3,000	5.9
Jan. 5, 1970	Yunnan Province, China	10,000	7.5
May 31, 1970	Yungay, Ranrahirca, and Huarás, Peru	66,000	7.8
Feb. 9, 1971	San Fernando Valley Calif.	65	6.6
Apr. 10, 1972	Ghir, Iran	5,054	7.1
Dec. 23, 1972	Managua, Nicaragua	5,000	6.2
Dec. 28, 1974	North Pakistan	5,300	6.2
Feb. 4, 1975	Liaoning Province, China (predicted)	10,000	7.4
Sept. 6, 1975	Lice, Turkey	2,300	6.7
Feb. 4, 1976	Guatemala City,	23,000	7.5
June 25, 1976	New Guinea and Irian Jaya, Indonesia	8,000+	7.1
July 27, 1976	Tangshan, China	655,000	8.0
Aug. 16, 1976	Mindanao, Philippines (earthquake and tsunami)	8,000	7.9
Nov. 24, 1976	Eastern Turkey	5,000	7.3
Sept. 16, 1978	Northeast Iran	15,000	7.8
Oct. 10, 1980	Northwestern Algeria	3,500	7.7
Nov. 23, 1980	Southern Italy	3,000	7.2
July 28, 1981	Kerman province, Iran	2,500	7.3
Dec. 13, 1982	Yemen	2,800	6.0
Sept. 19, 1985	Mexico City	9,500	8.1
Oct. 10, 1986	San Salvador, El Salvador	1,000+	5.5
Mar. 6, 1987	Ecuador	1,000+	7.0
Dec. 7, 1988	Armenia	25,000	7.0
Oct. 18, 1989	Loma Prieta, California (Santa Cruz Mountains), destructive in San Francisco and Oakland	63	7.2
June 20, 1990	Caspian Sea, Iran	50,000	7.7
July 16, 1990	Cabanatuan (Luzon I.), Philippines	1,621	7.8
Oct. 21, 1991	India and Nepal	2,000	7.0
Dec. 12, 1992	Flores Island, Indonesia (tsunami)	2,500	7.5
Sept. 29, 1993	Bombay, India	9,748	6.3
Jan. 17, 1994	Northridge, California	61	6.8
Oct. 4, 1994	Kuril Islands of Japan, Russia	190	8.3
Jan. 16, 1995	Near Kobe, Japan	5,502	6.9
May 27, 1995	Sakhalin Island, Russia	1,989	7.5
Feb. 17, 1996	Tsunamis in Irian Jaya, Indonesia	108	8.2
Feb. 28, 1997	Northwestern Iran	1,000+	6.1
May 10, 1997	Northeastern Iran	1,560	7.5
Feb. 4, 1998	Afghanistan	2,323	6.1
May 30, 1998	Afghanistan-Tajikistan border	4,000	6.9
July 17, 1998	Tsunamis strike Papua, New Guinea	2,183	7.1
Jan. 25, 1999	Armenia, Colombia	1,885	6.4
Aug. 17, 1999	Northwestern Turkey	17,118	7.4
Sept. 7, 1999	Athens, Greece	143	5.8
Sept. 20, 1999	Nantou, Taiwan	2,101	7.6
Oct. 5, 1999	Dodecanese Islands, Greece	103	4.6
Nov. 12, 1999	Turkey	843	7.5
June 4, 2000	Southern Sumatera, Indonesia	103	8.0
Jan. 1, 2001	Minandao, Philippines	0	7.5
Jan 13, 2001	El Salvador	844	7.7
Jan. 26, 2001	Southern India	20,005	7.7
Feb. 13, 2001	El Salvador	315	6.6
Feb. 23, 2001	Sichuan, China	10	5.4
Feb. 28, 2001	Washington State	1	6.8
May 4, 2001	Arkansas	0	4.2
June 3, 2001	Kermadec Islands, New Zealand	0	7.2
June 23, 2001	Coast of Peru	74	8.4
July 7, 2001	Near coast of Peru	1	6.6
Aug. 21, 2001	E. of North Island, New Zealand	0	7.1
Oct. 19, 2001	Banda Sea near Indonesia	0	7.5
Nov. 14, 2001	Qinghai, China	0	7.8
Dec. 12, 2001	South of Australia	0	7.1
Jan. 2, 2002	Vanuatu Islands	0	7.3
Jan. 10, 2002	Near north coast of New Guinea	1	6.7
Jan. 17–21, 2002	Lake Tanganyika region, Rwanda and Congo	10	4.7
Jan. 22, 2002	Crete	1	6.3
Feb. 3, 2002	Turkey	44	6.5
Mar. 3, 2002	Hindu Kush region, Afghanistan	163	7.4
Mar. 5, 2002	Minandao, Philippines	15	7.5
Mar. 25, 2002	Hindu Kush region, Afghanistan	1,000	6.1
Mar. 31, 2002	Taiwan	5	7.1
Apr. 1, 2002	New Guinea	36	5.0
Apr. 12, 2002	Hindu Kush region, Afghanistan	50	5.9
Apr. 20, 2002	New York State	0	5.0
Apr. 25, 2002	Northern Caucasus, Georgia and Russia	5	4.8
Apr. 26, 2002	Mariana Islands	0	7.1
May 15, 2002	Taiwan	1	6.2
June 18, 2002	Kentucky	0	4.4
June 22, 2002	Western Iran	227	6.5
June 26, 2002	Russia	0	7.3

Volcano Eruptions and Landslides, 1628 B.C.–A.D. 2002

Date	Event	Deaths
B.C.		
1628 or 1645	Mediterranean volcanic island of Thera (Santorini) explodes.	N.A.
A.D.		
Aug. 24–26, 79	Mt. Vesuvius, near Naples, Italy, erupts, destroying towns of Pompeii and Herculaneum.	2,000 +
260	Mt. Ilopango in El Salvador erupts, apparently destroying the early Maya civilization.	N.A.
Sept. 4, 1618	Landslides hit Chiavenna Valley, Italy.	2,420
Dec. 16, 1631	Mt. Vesuvius erupts.	4,000 +
Mar. 25, 1669	Mt. Etna at Catania, Sicily, erupts.	20,000
Jan. 11, 1683	Mt. Etna erupts, accompanied by earthquakes.	60,000
Aug. 11–12, 1772	Mt. Papandayan on Java explodes.	3,000 +
1782	Eruption of Mt. Unzen in Japan causes tidal wave.	15,000
June 1783–Feb. 1784	Laki fissure on Mt. Skaptar, Iceland erupts; poisonous gases kill crops and livestock, and thick haze interrupts fishing on oceans.	9,800
Sept. 2, 1806	Rossberg Peak collapses, causing landslides in Goldau Valley, Switzerland.	500
Apr. 5, 1815	Mt. Tambora on Sumbawa in East Indies begins series of eruptions that kill about 10,000 people; another 50,000 die of famine and disease locally	162,000

Date	Event	Deaths
Oct. 8 and 12, 1822	Mt. Galunggung on Java erupts, causing slides of mud and boiling water.	4,000
1845	Eruption of Nevada del Ruiz in northern Colombia causes mud slides from melting snow.	1,000
July 28, 1883	Epomeo volcano on Italian Isle of Ischia erupts, causing destructive earthquakes.	2,000 +
Aug. 26, 1883	Krakatau volcano in East Indies erupts, producing giant waves that strike nearby islands.	36,000
May 7, 1902	La Soufriére on St. Vincent in West Indies erupts.	1,500–2,000
May 8, 1902	Pelée volcano on neighboring Martinique erupts, pouring cloud of flaming gas on city of St. Pierre.	29,000
Aug. 30, 1902	Mt. Pelée erupts.	2,000
Apr. 18, 1906	Mt. Vesuvius near Naples erupts.	150 +
1911	Taal volcano, near Manila, Philippines, erupts.	1,300
May 1919	Crater lake of Mt. Kelut in Indonesia, boiling from volcanic activity, breaks through side of the mountain.	5,000 +
1937	Eruption of Rabaul caldera on New Britain, Papua New Guinea.	500 +
Jan. 15, 1951	Mt. Lamington on New Guinea produces cloud of hot gas and dust, similar to that at Mt. Pelée in 1902 and Mt. St. Helens in 1980.	3,000–5,000
Dec. 4, 1951	Mt. Catarman (Hibokhibok) in Philippines releases cloud of hot gas.	500
Sept. 24, 1952	Japanese research ship investigating undersea volcano is destroyed in eruptive event.	29
Dec. 25, 1953	Dam, created by 1945 eruption of Ruapehu volcano on New Zealand, gives way; avalanche of mud and snow strikes passenger train.	150
Jan. 10, 1962	Landslide on Mt. Huascarán, Peru.	3,000
Mar. 14, 1962	Two landslides near Paucartambno Hydroelectric Station in Peru.	204
Mar. 17-21, 1963	Mt. Agung volcano in Bali, Indonesia, erupts.	1,584
Aug. 10, 1963	Landslide in Nepal sweeps villages into Trisuli River.	200
Oct. 9, 1963	Flood occurs when Valont Dam near Langarone, Italy, overflows as result of landslide into its reservoir.	2,200
1965	Taal volcano near Manila in the Philippines erupts.	150
Aug. 30, 1965	Avalanche near Saas-Fee, Switzerland, from Allalin glacier strikes workers building dam.	40-100
1968	Eruption of Arenal in Costa Rica.	78
July 22, 1970	Landslide diverts Alaknanda River in India, causing sudden flood.	600
Mar. 18, 1971	Landslide into Lake Yanahuani, creates 60-foot wave that sweeps over Chungar, Peru.	200
July 29, 1971	Landslide into high lake in Hindu Kush mountains of Afghanistan causes instant flood.	1,000 +
June 28, 1974	Landslides along Quebrada Blanca Canyon in Eastern Colombia.	200
Jan. 10, 1977	Fast-moving stream of lava from volcano near Goma, Zaire, overtakes fleeing residents.	70
Feb. 21, 1979	Sinila volcano in Java, Indonesia	175 +
Apr. 30, 1979	Landslide covers side of Marapi volcano in Sumatra, Indonesia.	82 +
July 18, 1979	Landslide on Mt. Werung causes wave to strike beach areas on Lomblen Island, Indonesia.	539
May 18, 1980	Mt. St. Helens volcano erupts in Washington.	61
May 20, 1981	Landslides caused by eruption of Semeru in Java, Indonesia.	252
Mar. 28 and Apr. 3-4, 1982	El Chichón in Chiapas, Mexico, erupts, sending cloud of volcanic ash around world.	2,000
Aug. 16, 1984	Carbon dioxide emitted by Lake Monoun, Cameroon, spreads in region around lake.	37
Nov. 13, 1985	Eruption of Nevada del Ruiz in northern Colombia causes massive mud slide covering town of Armero.	25,000
Aug. 21, 1986	Carbon dioxide from Lake Nyos, Cameroon, spreads through region.	1,700 +
July 13, 1990	Earthquake triggers landslide in Pamir Mts., Tajikistan, USSR.	40+
Oct. 13, 1990	Geyserlike explosion in the Ahuachapán Geothermal Field, El Salvador, releases wave of carbon dioxide and water.	26
June 3, 1991	Eruption of Mt. Unzen, Kyushu, Japan.	43
June 9, 1991	Mount Pinatubo erupts, as predicted, in Luzon, Philippines; 358 killed by disease in evacuation camps.	754
Jan. 14, 1993	Galeras in Colombia unexpectedly erupts during a scientific workshop, killing six volcanologists who had been on the rim studying the volcano.	9
Feb. 2, 1993	An unexpected eruption of Mayon on Luzon, Philippines produces a cloud of hot gas and dust that rolls down the slope.	70
June 6, 1994	An earthquake at the Volcano Nevada de Huila in Colombia causes mud slides that destroy a dozen villages on its slopes.	650 +
Nov. 22, 1994	Various flows of hot ash and gases down the slope of Merapi volcano on Java in Indonesia kill workers at a water-treatment plant and sweep through villages where superstitious villagers ignored a call to evacuate.	64
Feb. 18, 1997	Mudslide caused by heavy rains destroys two Peruvian villages	300
May 5-6, 1998	Mudslides caused by heavy rains pour down Mount Sarno, east of Naples, Italy.	135
Oct. 30, 1998	Hurricane Mitch causes landslide on San Cristobal volcano in Nicaragua.	1600
Dec., 1999	Heavy rains cause floods and landslides in northern Venezuela.	20,000
Jan. 13, 2001	Landslides triggered by an earthquake near Santa Tecla, El Salvador bury villages,	585
Jan. 17, 2002	Lava flows from eruption of Nyirangongo volcano in the Congo.	45
Mar. 3, 2002	Landslide caused by earthquake in the Hindu Kush region of Afghanistan dams and floods Surkundara Valley.	150
Aug. 14, 2002	Landslides from heavy rains bury villages in Yunnan Province, China.	52

Major Active Volcanoes

Volcano	Location	Height (feet above sea level)	Last reported eruption
Africa and the Indian Ocean			
Cameroon	Cameroon	13,435	2000
Fogo	Cape Verde Islands	9,281	1995
Karthala	Comoros	7,746	1991
Ol Donyo Lengai	Tanzania	9,482	2001
Piton de la Fournaise	Réunion Island	8,632	2001
Nyamuragira	Zaire	10,033	2002
Nyirangongo	Zaire	11,384	2002
Asia			
Agung	Bali, Indonesia	10,308	1964
Akan	Hokkaido, Japan	4,918	1998
Alaid	Kuril Isl. Russia	7,674	1996
Asama	Honshu, Japan	8,339	1990
Aso	Kyushu, Japan	5,223	1995
Batur	Bali, Indonesia	5,633	2000
Bezymianny	Kamchatka, Russia	9,455	2001
Bulusan	Luzon, Philippines	5,134	1995
Chokai	Honshu, Japan	7,339	1974
Dieng Volc	Java, Indonesia	8,415	1996
Dukono	Halmahera, Indonesia	3,888	2002
Fuji	Honshu, Japan	12,388	1708
Galunggung	Java, Indonesia	7,113	1984
Gamalama	Ternate, Indonesia	5,627	1994
Karangetang	Siau Island, Indonesia	5,853	2002
Karymsky	Kamchatka, Russia	5,039	2002
Kelut	Java, Indonesia	5,679	1990
Kerenci	Sumatra,Indonesia	12,467	2002
Kliuchevskoi	Kamchatka, Russia	15,863	2000
Komaga-take	Hokkaido, Japan	3,740	2000
Koryaksky	Kamchatka, Russia	11,338	1957
Krakatau	Indonesia	2,667	2001
Lewotobi	Flores Isl., Indonesia	5,587	1999
Lokon-Empung	Sulawesi, Indonesia	5,184	2001
Mayon	Luzon, Philippines	8,077	2001
Merapi	Java, Indonesia	9,669	2002
Miyake-jima	Izu Islands, Japan	2,674	2002
Nasu	Honshu, Japan	6,289	1963
Nigata Yake-yama	Honshu, Japan	7,874	1989
On-take	Honshu, Japan	10,049	1980
Peuet Sague	Sumatra, Indonesia	9,190	2000
Pinatubo	Luzon, Philippines	4,875	1993
Raung	Java, Indonesia	10,932	2000
Rinjani	Lombok Island, Indonesia	12,224	1994
Sakura-jima	Kyushu, Japan	3,665	2002
Sangeang Api	Lesser Sunda, Indonesia	6,394	1988
Sarychev Peak	Kuril Islands, Russia	4,908	1989
Semeru	Java, Indonesia	12,060	2002
Shiveluch	Kamchatka, Russia	10,771	2002
Slamet	Java, Indonesia	11,260	1999
Suwanose-jima	Ryukyu Islands, Japan	2,621	2001
Taal	Luzon, Philippines	1,342	1977
Tambora	Sumbawa, Indonesia	9,350	1967
Tengger Caldera	Java, Indonesia	7,641	2001
Tiatia	Kuril Isl., Russia	5,968	1981
Unzen	Kyushu, Japan	4,921	1996
Usu	Hokkaido, Japan	2,398	2001
Europe and the Atlantic Ocean			
Askja	Iceland	4,974	1961
Beerenberg	Jan Mayen Island, Norway	7,470	1985
Etna	Italy	10,991	2001
Fogo	Cape Verde Islands	9,281	1995
Grímsvötn	Iceland	5,659	1998
Hekla	Iceland	4,892	2000
Krafla	Iceland	2,133	1984
Stromboli	Italy	3,058	2002
Tristan da Cunha	Tristan da Cunha, U.K.	6,758	1962
Vesuvius	Italy	4,203	1944
North America			
Akutan	Alaska	4,275	1992
Amukta	Alaska	3,497	1997
Atka	Alaska	5,029	1998
Augustine	Alaska	4,108	1986
Baker	Washington	10,777	1880
Carlisle	Alaska	5,315	1828
Cerberus	Alaska	2,539	1987
Cleveland	Alaska	5,676	2001
Colima	Mexico	12,631	2002
Crater Lake	Oregon	8,159	c.2290 B.C.
El Chichon	Mexico	3,773	1982
Fisher	Alaska	3,648	1830
Gareloi	Alaska	5,161	1989
Great Sitkin	Alaska	5,709	1974
Hood	Oregon	11,240	1866
Iliamna	Alaska	10,016	1876
Kagamil	Alaska	2,930	1929
Kanaga	Alaska	4,288	1995
Katmai	Alaska	6,716	1912
Kiska	Alaska	4,003	1990
Lassen Peak	California	10,456	1917
Little Sitkin	Alaska	3,852	1830
Makushin	Alaska	5,905	1995
Martin	Alaska	6,112	1953
Novarupta	Alaska	2,759	1912
Okmok	Alaska	3,520	1997
Parícutin	Mexico	1,500	1952
Pavlof	Alaska	8,264	1997
Pavlof Sister	Alaska	7,027	1786
Popocatépetl	Mexico	17,802	2002
Rainier	Washington	14,409	1825
Redoubt	Alaska	10,197	1990
St. Helens	Washington	8,363	1991
Seguam	Alaska	3,458	1993
Shasta	California	14,163	1786
Shishaldin	Alaska	9,373	1999
South Sister	Oregon	10,357	c 50 B.C.
Spurr	Alaska	11,069	1992
Tanaga	Alaska	5,925	1914
Trident	Alaska	6,115	1975
Veniaminof	Alaska	8,225	1994
Westdahl	Alaska	5,426	1992
Yunaska	Alaska	1,804	1937
Central America and the Caribbean			
Acatenango	Guatemala	13,044	1972
Arenal	Costa Rica	5,436	2002
Cerro Negro	Nicaragua	2,388	1999
Concepción	Nicaragua	5,577	1999
Fuego	Guatemala	12,346	2000
Irazú	Costa Rica	11,260	1994
Izalco	El Salvador	6,398	1966
Masaya	Nicaragua	2,083	2001
Pacaya	Guatemala	8,373	2001
Pelée	Martinique	4,583	1932
Poás	Costa Rica	8,884	1996

Volcano	Location	Height (feet above sea level)	Last reported eruption
Rincón de la Vieja	Costa Rica	6,286	1998
San Cristóbal	Nicaragua	5,725	2001
San Miguel	El Salvador	6,988	1997
Santa María	Guatemala	12,375	2002
Soufrière Hills	Montserrat	3,002	2002
Soufriere St. Vincent	St Vincent and the Grenadines	4,003	1979
Tacaná	Mexico/Guatemala	13,320	1986
Telica	Nicaragua	3,481	2000
South America			
Alcedo	Galápagos Islands, Ecuador	3,707	1993
Azul, Cerro	Galápagos Islands, Ecuador	5,381	1998
Copahué	Chile/Argentina	9,728	2000
Cotopaxi	Ecuador	19,393	1940
Galeras	Colombia	14,029	2000
Guagua Pichincha	Ecuador	15,695	2001
Guallatiri	Chile	19,918	1960
Hudson, Cerro	Chile	6,250	1991
Lascar	Chile	18,346	2000
Llaima	Chile	10,253	1998
Lonquimay	Chile	9,399	1990
Puracé	Colombia	15,256	1977
Reventador	Ecuador	11,686	1976
Ruiz, Nevado del	Colombia	17,457	1991
Sangay	Ecuador	17,159	2002
Tungurahua	Ecuador	16,479	2002
Villarrica	Chile	9,340	2002
Oceania—Australia, New Zealand, and the Pacific Islands			
Ambrym	Vanuatu	4,377	2002
Bagana	Bougainville Island, Papua New Guinea	5,741	2002
Haleakala	Hawaii	10,023	c.1790
Hualalai	Hawaii	8,277	1801
Karkar	Papua New Guinea	6,033	1979
Kilauea	Hawaii	4,009	2002
Langila	New Britain, Papua New Guinea	4,363	2002
Lopevei	Vanuatu	4.636	2001
Mauna Loa	Hawaii	13,681	1984
Manam	Papua New Guinea	5,928	2000
Ngauruhoe	North Island, New Zealand	6,489	1977
Pagan	Mariana Islands	1,870	1993
Rabaul	New Britain, Papua New Guinea	2,257	2001
Ruapehu	North Island, New Zealand	9,176	1997
Ulawun	New Britain, Papua New Guinea	7,657	2001
White Island	North Island, New Zealand	1,053	2001
Antarctica			
Big Ben	Heard Island	9,007	1993
Mount Erebus	Ross Island	13,444	2001

CHEMISTRY

Chemistry is concerned with the way substances interact with one another. These interactions are chiefly the result of outer electrons of an atom interacting with the outer electrons of another atom. It has increasingly become clear that the shapes of the various combinations of atoms (called molecules) also affect chemical reactions, and physical chemistry is one of the most vital parts of chemistry today. Another vital branch is biochemistry, the study of the chemistry of molecules in living organisms. Organic chemistry generally deals with chemicals formed by living organisms and other chemicals containing carbon, but it treats them as chemicals outside the organism. Inorganic chemistry is concerned with chemicals that do not contain carbon.

▶THE PERIODIC TABLE

In the 19th century, chemists began to determine how much one atom of an element weighed with respect to another—the atomic weight (also known as the atomic mass and measured in atomic mass units, or amu; in modern chemistry, one amu is equal to one-twelfth the weight of the most common form of carbon atom). The first comprehensive list of atomic weights was prepared by Jöns Jakob Berzelius in 1828. When chemists made lists of elements in the order of atomic weights, they noticed that every seven or eight elements in the list had similar properties. In 1869 Dmitri Mendeleyev boldly interchanged some elements in the list and left blanks for others to make sure the properties matched for every "period" of eight elements. This was the first periodic table. Mendeleyev had only 63 elements to work with, but he correctly predicted three more that would make his list more complete. Today the elements up to 116, with the exceptions of 113 and 115, have been identified. Claims for elements 116 and 118 were made in 1999 by Lawrence Berkeley National Laboratory in California and withdrawn in 2002, but element 116 was produced by the Joint Institute for Nuclear Research, Dubna, Russia, in 2000. Elements 110-112, 114 and 116 have not yet been named.

Early in the 20th century, atoms were discovered to consist of protons and electrons (in 1932 it was discovered that neutrons also are found in atoms). The number of protons is the atomic number, which is a different number for every element from hydrogen (atomic number 1) to the unnamed element 116 (elements 113 and 115 have yet to be synthesized). The periodic table was improved by arranging the elements in order of atomic number instead of atomic weight. This clearly showed where the blanks were.

Each column of the periodic table includes elements with similar properties, although hydrogen in the first column is less typical in this respect. But the other elements in the first column are all soft metals that are highly reactive. Similarly, the

Major Discoveries in Chemistry

B.C.

c. 450 Leucippus of Miletus (Greek: 5th cent.) introduces concept of atom, later expanded upon by his pupil Democritus of Abdera (c. 460–c. 370).

A.D.

1662 Robert Boyle (Anglo-Irish: 1627–91) announces what becomes known as Boyle's law: For gas kept at constant temperature, pressure and volume vary inversely.

1755 Joseph Black (Scottish: 1728–99) discovers carbon dioxide.

1778 Antoine-Laurent Lavoisier (French: 1743–94) discovers that air is mostly mixture of nitrogen and oxygen.

1784 Henry Cavendish (English: 1731–1810) announces water is compound of hydrogen and oxygen.

1789 Lavoisier explicitly states law of conservation of matter: In chemical change, matter is neither created nor destroyed.

1791 Jeremias Benjamin Richter (German: 1762–1807) shows that acids and bases always neutralize each other in same proportion.

1803 John Dalton (English: 1766–1844) establishes atomic theory of matter.

1811 Amedeo Avogadro (Italian: 1776–1856) proposes that equal volumes of gas at same temperature and pressure contain same number of molecules (Avogadro's law).

1824 Joseph-Louis Gay-Lussac (French: 1778–1850) discovers chemical isomers, chemicals with same formula but different structures.

1828 Friedrich Wöhler (German: 1800–1882) prepares organic compound from inorganic chemicals, showing that life is basically same as other matter.

1859 Gustav Robert Kirchhoff (German: 1824–87) and Robert Wilhelm Bunsen (German: 1811–99) introduce use of spectroscope to identify elements from light they give off when heated.

1869 Dmitry Ivanovich Mendeleyev (Russian: 1834–1907) publishes his first version of periodic table of elements.

1906 Mikhail Tsvett (Russian: 1872–1919) develops paper chromatography, the beginning of modern methods of chemical analysis.

1908 Fritz Haber (German: 1868–1934) develops cheap process for making ammonia from nitrogen in the air.

1962 Neil Bartlett (English: 1932–) creates a compound of xenon, platinum, and fluorine, showing that the noble gases can form compounds.

1984 Dany Schechtman (American) and coworkers discover first quasicrystal, a "crystal" that violates the symmetry rules of all other crystals.

1985 Richard E. Smalley (American: 1943–) and Harry Kroto (English: 1939–) discover buckminsterfullerene, a carbon molecule containing 60 carbon atoms arranged in a geodesic sphere (nicknamed "the bucky ball").

1991 Sumio Iijima (Japanese: 1939-) of NEC Corp. discovers that carbon forms tiny hollow cylinders called nanotubes.

1998 Research on carbon nanotubes shows that they conduct electricity with almost no resistance at room temperature (although they are not superconductors), emit light when carrying an electric current, and can behave either as semiconductors or metals depending on the alignment of atoms in the tube.

2000 Scientists at the Institute for Nuclear Research in Dubna, Russia, extend the periodic table to include element 116, created by bombarding curium with calcium ions.

2001 Researchers discover that the common mineral calcite (calcium carbonate) tends to segregate left-handed amino acids on one face and right-handed ones on another, suggesting a possible origin for all amino acids in living organisms being left-handed; similarly the handedness of amino acids affects crystal formation in calcite.

2002 Researchers at the University of California, Davis, discover that distributing molecules of gadolinium nitrate through porous silicon creates a form of silicon that explodes like gunpowder when scratched or when exposed to a spark from a low-power battery.

Mary P. Ryan of Imperial College of Science, Technology, and Medicine in London discovers that stainless steel develops pit corrosion because chromium atoms in the alloy migrate to zones that are then surrounded by regions of low chromium. Corrosion could be halted cheaply by processes that distribute chromium atoms uniformly on the steel's surface.

Scientists in Rome create molecules consisting of four nitrogen atoms (molecules of nitrogen in air contain two atoms only.

---

last column of the table contains the gases that react only minimally. In general, elements are metals on the left side of the table (hydrogen is a metal only under great pressure), becoming mostly nonmetals in the last six columns. These last columns include some elements that are metals, such as aluminum. (A broken, heavy line separates the metals from the nonmetals.)

The row of rare-earth elements beginning with lanthanum and the row of actinide elements beginning with actinium do not fit neatly into the rest of the table. Elements from atomic number 57 to 71 are all similar to lanthanum, while elements from atomic number 89 to 103 are similar to actinium. The rare earths are not generally rare, nor do they resemble soil. They are moderately common metals that, because of atomic structure, are very similar chemically. The actinide elements are radioactive metals.

The periodic table as shown here also includes the atomic mass as well as the atomic number. The atomic mass is a relative number; it shows the weight of an element as compared to the weight of an atom of carbon-12, which is assigned a weight of exactly 12. Most elements occur with several different atomic weights (in addition to carbon-12, for example, there are both carbon-13 and carbon-14; carbon-14 has 6 protons and 8 neutrons and is radioactive). These different forms are called isotopes. In the periodic table, the atomic mass given for most elements is the one that would be found by averaging the different isotopes in the amounts they naturally occur. Carbon is given an atomic mass of 12.01 because there is so much more carbon-12 than there is carbon-13 or carbon-14 in an ordinary sample of carbon. For some radioactive elements, natural abundance is meaningless, since there is no stable form. For these, the atomic mass of the most stable form is given, indicated by putting the atomic mass in parentheses.

THE PERIODIC TABLE OF THE ELEMENTS

6 C 12.01 Carbon	
6	atomic number
C	chemical number
12.01	atomic mass
Carbon	name of element

	alkali metals	alkaline earth metals	transition metals										nonmetals					noble gases
	I A	II A	III B	IV B	V B	VI B	VII B		VIII		I B	II B	III A	IV A	V A	VI A	VII A	O
Period 1	1 H 1.01 Hydrogen																	2 He 4.00 Helium
Period 2	3 Li 6.94 Lithium	4 Be 9.01 Beryllium											5 B 10.81 Boron	6 C 12.01 Carbon	7 N 14.01 Nitrogen	8 O 16.00 Oxygen	9 F 19.00 Fluorine	10 Ne 20.18 Neon
Period 3	11 Na 22.99 Sodium	12 Mg 24.31 Magnesium											13 Al 26.98 Aluminum	14 Si 28.09 Silicon	15 P 30.97 Phosphorus	16 S 32.07 Sulfur	17 Cl 35.45 Chlorine	18 Ar 39.95 Argon
Period 4	19 K 39.10 Potassium	20 Ca 40.08 Calcium	21 Sc 44.96 Scandium	22 Ti 47.88 Titanium	23 V 50.94 Vanadium	24 Cr 52.00 Chromium	25 Mn 54.95 Manganese	26 Fe 55.85 Iron	27 Co 58.93 Cobalt	28 Ni 58.70 Nickel	29 Cu 63.55 Copper	30 Zn 65.39 Zinc	31 Ga 69.72 Gallium	32 Ge 72.61 Germanium	33 As 74.92 Arsenic	34 Se 78.96 Selenium	35 Br 79.90 Bromine	36 Kr 83.80 Krypton
Period 5	37 Rb 85.47 Rubidium	38 Sr 87.62 Strontium	39 Y 88.91 Yttrium	40 Zr 91.22 Zirconium	41 Nb 92.91 Niobium	42 Mo 95.94 Molybdenum	43 Tc (98) Technetium	44 Ru 101.07 Ruthenium	45 Rh 102.91 Rhodium	46 Pd 106.4 Palladium	47 Ag 107.87 Silver	48 Cd 112.41 Cadmium	49 In 114.82 Indium	50 Sn 118.71 Tin	51 Sb 121.74 Antimony	52 Te 127.60 Tellurium	53 I 126.90 Iodine	54 Xe 131.29 Xenon
Period 6	55 Cs 132.91 Cesium	56 Ba 137.33 Barium	Lanthanide series (see below)	72 Hf 178.49 Hafnium	73 Ta 180.94 Tantalum	74 W 183.85 Tungsten	75 Re 186.21 Rhenium	76 Os 190.23 Osmium	77 Ir 192.22 Iridium	78 Pt 195.08 Platinum	79 Au 196.97 Gold	80 Hg 200.59 Mercury	81 Tl 204.38 Thallium	82 Pb 207.2 Lead	83 Bi 208.98 Bismuth	84 Po (209) Polonium	85 At (210) Astatine	86 Rn (222) Radon
Period 7	87 Fr (223) Francium	88 Ra 226.03 Radium	Actinide series (see below)	104 Rf (261) Rutherfordium	105 Db (262) Dubnium	106 Sg (263) Seaborgium	107 Bh (262) Bohrium	108 Hs (265) Hassium	109 Mt (266) Meitnerium	110 (269)	111 (272)	112 (277)		114 (281)		116 (292)		

rare earth elements—Lanthanide series	57 La 138.91 Lanthanum	58 Ce 140.12 Cerium	59 Pr 140.91 Praseodymium	60 Nd 144.24 Neodymium	61 Pm (145) Promethium	62 Sm 150.4 Samarium	63 Eu 151.96 Europium	64 Gd 157.25 Gadolinium	65 Tb 158.93 Terbium	66 Dy 162.50 Dysprosium	67 Ho 164.93 Holmium	68 Er 167.26 Erbium	69 Tm 168.93 Thulium	70 Yb 173.04 Ytterbium	71 Lu 174.97 Lutetium
Actinide series	89 Ac 227.03 Actinium	90 Th 232.04 Thorium	91 Pa 231.04 Protactinium	92 U 238.03 Uranium	93 Np 237.05 Neptunium	94 Pu (244) Plutonium	95 Am (243) Americium	96 Cm (247) Curium	97 Bk (247) Berkelium	98 Cf (251) Californium	99 Es (252) Einsteinium	100 Fm (257) Fermium	101 Md (258) Mendelevium	102 No (259) Nobelium	103 Lr (260) Lawrencium

Properties and Discovery of the Elements

All ordinary matter is made from one or more substances called elements (because they cannot be changed by chemical means). Ninety elements are found in nature, and people have created others, for a current total of 114. In this table each of the elements is listed in alphabetical order. The chemical symbol and the atomic number can be used to locate other information about the elements in the periodic table reprinted below. Many elements, known from ancient times, are labeled "prehistoric." Others are given with their first discovery—many elements having been independently rediscovered by others. In the following table, elements 110–12, 114, and 116, as yet unnamed, are listed as "Element 110" and so forth.

Element/Type[1]	Symbol/ Atomic number	Melting point[1]	Boiling point[1]	Derivation of name (Discoverer, Year)
Actinium	Ac	1924°F	5788°F	Greek *aktis*, a ray. (André-Louis Debierne, 1899)
Radioactive metal	89	1051°C	3198°C	
Aluminum	Al	1220°F	4566°F	Latin *alumen*, a substance with astringent taste (Hans
Metal	13	660°C	2519°C	Christian Oersted, 1825)
Americium	Am	2149°F	3652°F	Named for America (Glenn T. Seaborg & coworkers,1944)
Radioactive metal	95	1176°C	2011°C	
Antimony	Sb	1168°F	2889°F	Greek *antimonos*, opposed to solitude; symbol Sb from
Metal	51	631°C	1587°C	Latin *stibium*. (Rhazes, c. 900)
Argon	Ar	-308°F	-303°F	Greek *argus*, neutral inactive. (Sir William Ramsay, 1894)
Gas	18	-189°C	-186°C	
Arsenic[2]	As	N.A.	1117°F	Latin *arsenicum*; folk etymology connects with yellow
Nonmetal	33		603°C	and maleness. (Albertus Magnus, 1250)
Astatine	At	576°F	unk.	Greek *astatos*, unstable. (Emilio Segrè, D.R. Corson, &
Radioactive nonmetal	85	302°C		K.R. MacKenzie, 1940)
Barium	Ba	1341°F	3447°F	Greek *baros*, heavy, because of its dense compounds.
Metal	56	727°C	1897°C	(Humphry Davy, 1808)
Berkelium	Bk	1922°F	unk.	First made at Univ. of California. (Glenn T. Seaborg &
Radioactive metal	97	1050°C		coworkers,1949)
Beryllium	Be	2349°F	4480°F	Latin *beryllus*, Greek beryllos, gem. (Louis-Nicolas
Metal	4	1287°C	2471°C	Vauquelin,1798)
Bismuth	Bi	520°F	2847°F	German *weisse masse*, white mass; changed to *bismat*.
Metal	83	271°C	1564°C	(Claude J. Geoffrey, 1753
Bohrium	Bh	unk.	unk.	Named for Danish physicist Niels Bohr. (Russian
Radioactive metal	107			scientists at Dubna, 1977)
Boron	B	3767°F	7232°F	Arabic *borak* (borax); BORax + carbON. (Joseph-Louis
Nonmetal	5	2075°C	4000°C	Gay-Lussac & Louis-Jacques Thénard, 1808)
Bromine	Br	19°F	138°F	Greek *bromos*, a stench; because of odor of its vapors.
Liquid nonmetal	35	-7°C	59°C	(Antoine-Jérôme Balard, 1826)
Cadmium	Cd	610°F	1413°F	Greek *cadmia*, earthy. (Friedrich Strohmeyer, 1817)
Metal	48	321°C	767°C	
Calcium	Ca	1548°F	2703°F	Latin *calx, calcis*, lime. (Humphry Davy, 1808)
Metal	20	842°C	1484°C	
Californium	Cf	1652°F	unk.	First made at Univ. of California. (Glenn T. Seaborg &
Radioactive metal	98	900°C		coworkers, 1949)
Carbon[2]	C	N.A.	6917°F	Latin *carbo*, coal. (Prehistoric)
Nonmetal	6	N.A.	3825°C	
Cerium	Ce	1468°F	6229°F	Named for asteroid Ceres, discovered in 1801. (Martin
Rare earth	58	798°C	3443°C	Klaproth, 1803)
Cesium	Cs	84°F	1240°F	Latin *caesius*, bluish gray. (Gustav Kirchhoff & Robert
Metal	55	29°C	671°C	Bunsen, 1860)
Chlorine	Cl	-152°F	-29°F	Greek *chloros*, grass-green; from color of gas. (Humphry
Gas	17	-102°C	-34°C	Davy, 1810)
Chromium	Cr	3465°F	4840°F	Greek *chroma*, color; because many of its compounds
Metal	24	1907°C	2671°C	are colored. (Louis-Nicolas Vauquelin, 1797)
Cobalt	Co	2723°F	5301°F	German *Kobalt*, a goblin. (Georg Brandt, 1735)
Metal	27	1495°C	2927°C	
Copper	Cu	1985°F	4644°F	Latin *cuprum*; for island of Cyprus. (Prehistoric)
Metal	29	1085°C	2562°C	
Curium	Cm	2453°F	5612°F	Named after Pierre and Marie Curie. (Glenn T. Seaborg &
Radioactive metal	96	1345°C	3100°C	coworkers, 1944)
Dubnium	Db	unk.	unk.	Named for the Joint Institute for Nuclear Research at
Radioactive metal	105			Dubna,Russia. (Russian scientists at Dubna, 1967)
Dysprosium	Dy	2574°F	4653°F	Greek *dysprositos*, difficult of access. (Paul-Emile Lecoq
Rare earth	66	1412°C	2567°C	deBoisbaudran, 1886)
Einsteinium	Es	1580°F	unk.	Named after Albert Einstein. (Albert Ghiorso &
Radioactive metal	99	860°C		coworkers, 1952)

Element/Type[1]	Symbol/ Atomic number	Melting point[1]	Boiling point[1]	Derivation of name (Discoverer, Year)
Element 110 Radioactive metal	N.A. 110	unk.	unk.	(Society for Heavy Ion Research, Darmstadt, Germany, 1994)
Element 111 Radioactive metal	N.A. 111	unk.	unk.	(Society for Heavy Ion Research, Darmstadt, Germany, 1994)
Element 112 Radioactive metal	N.A. 112	unk.	unk.	(Society for Heavy Ion Research, Darmstadt, Germany, 1996)
Element 114 Radioactive metal	N.A. 114	unk.	unk.	(Dubna and Lawrence Livermore, 1998)
Element 116 Radioactive metal	N.A. 116	unk.	unk.	(Scientists at Dubna, 2000)
Erbium Rare earth	Er 68	2784°F 1529°C	5194°F 2868°C	Named for Ytterby, village in Sweden. (Carl Gustav Mosander, 1843)
Europium Rare earth	Eu 63	1512°F 822°C	2784°F 1529°C	Named for Europe. (Eugène-Anatole Demarçay, 1896)
Fermium Radioactive metal	Fm 100	2781°F 1527°C	unk.	Named after Italian physicist Enrico Fermi. (Albert Ghiorso & coworkers, 1952)
Fluorine Gas	F 9	-364°F -220°C	-306°F -188°C	Latin *fluere*, to flow. (Ferdinand-Frédéric-Henri Moissan, 1886)
Francium Radioactive metal	Fr 87	81°F 27°C	unk.	Named for France. (Marguerite Perey, 1939)
Gadolinium Rare earth	Gd 64	2395°F 1313°C	5923°F 3273°C	Named after gadolinite, mineral named for Johan Gadolin, Finnish chemist. (Jean-Charles Marignac, 1880)
Gallium Metal	Ga 31	86°F 30°C	3999°F 2204°C	Latin *Gallia*, France; also Latin *gallus*, a cock—a pun on Lecoq. (Paul-Emile Lecoq de Boisbaudran, 1875)
Germanium Metal	Ge 32	1721°F 938°C	5131°F 2833°C	Named for Germany. (Clemens Winkler, 1886)
Gold Metal	Au 79	1948°F 1064°C	5173°F 2856°C	Anglo-Saxon *gold*; Sanskrit *juel*, to shine; symbol from Latin *aurum*, shining dawn. (Prehistoric)
Hafnium Metal	Hf 72	4051°F 2233°C	8317°F 4603°C	From *Hafnia*, ancient name of Copenhagen. (Dirk Coster & György Hevesy, 1923)
Hassium Radioactive metal	Hs 108	unk.	unk.	Named for the German province of Hesse, where Darmstadt is located. (Society for Heavy Ion Research, Darmstadt, Germany, 1984)
Helium Gas	He 2	N.A. N.A.	-452°F -269°C	Greek *helios*, the Sun; first observed in Sun's atmosphere. (Pierre-Jules-César Janssen & Sir Joseph Norman Lockyer, 1868)
Holmium Rare earth	Ho 67	2685°F 1474°C	4892°F 2700°C	From *Holmia*, Latinized form of Stockholm. (Per Teodor Cleve, 1879)
Hydrogen Gas	H 1	-435°F -259°C	-423°F -253°C	Greek *hydor*, water, plus *gen*, forming. (Henry Cavendish, 1766)
Indium Metal	In 49	314°F 157°C	3762°F 2072°C	Latin *indicum*, indigo. (Ferdinand Reich & Hieronymus Theodor Richter, 1863)
Iodine[2] Nonmetal	I 53	237°F 114°C	364°F 184°C	Greek *iodes*, violet; from color of its vapor. (Bernard Courtois,1811)
Iridium Metal	Ir 77	4435°F 2446°C	8002°F 4428°C	Greek *iris*, a rainbow, from changing color of its salts. (Smithson Tennant , 1803)
Iron Metal	Fe 26	2800°F 1538°C	5182°F 2861°C	Anglo-Saxon *iren*; symbol from Latin *ferrum*. (Prehistoric)
Krypton[3] Gas	Kr 36	-251°F -157°C	-244°F -153°C	Greek *kryptos*, hidden. (Alexander Ramsay & Morris William Travers, 1898)
Lanthanum Rare earth	La 57	1684°F 918°C	6267°F 3464°C	Greek *lanthanein*, to be concealed. (Carl Gustav Mosander, 1839)
Lawrencium Radioactive metal	Lr 103	2961°F 1627°C	unk.	Named after American physicist Ernest Lawrence. (Albert Ghiorso & coworkers, 1961)
Lead Metal	Pb 82	621°F 327°C	3180°F 1749°C	Anglo-Saxon *lead*; symbol from Latin *plumbum*. (Prehistoric)
Lithium Metal	Li 3	351°F 181°C	2448°F 1342°C	Greek *lithos*, stony. (Johann A. Arfvedson, 1817)
Lutetium Rare earth	Lu 71	3025°F 1663°C	6159°F 3404°C	Latin *Lutetia*, ancient name for Paris. (Georges Urbain, 1907)
Magnesium Metal	Mg 12	1202°F 650°C	1994°F 1090°C	Latin *Magnesia*, a district in Asia Minor. (Humphry Davy, 1808)
Manganese Metal	Mn 25	2275°F 1246°C	3742°F 2061°C	Latin *magnes*, magnet; because of confusion with magnetic iron ores. (Johann Gottlieb Gahn, 1774)
Meitnerium Radioactive metal	Mt 109	unk.	unk.	Named for the Austrian-Swedish physicist Lise Meitner. (Society for Heavy Ion Research, Darmstadt, Germany, 1982)
Mendelevium Radioactive metal	Md 101	1521°F 827°C	unk.	Named after Russian chemist Dmitri Mendeléev. (Albert Ghiorso & coworkers, 1955)

Element/Type[1]	Symbol/ Atomic number	Melting point[1]	Boiling point[1]	Derivation of name (Discoverer, Year)
Mercury	Hg	-38°F	674°F	Named for Roman god Mercurius; symbol from Latin
Liquid metal	80	-39°C	357°C	*hydrargyrum.* (Prehistoric)
Molybdenum	Mo	4753°F	8382°F	Greek *molybdos,* lead. (Karl Wilhelm Scheele, 1778)
Metal	42	2623°C	4639°C	
Neodymium	Nd	1870°F	5565°F	Greek *neo,* new, plus *didymon,* twin (with the element
Rare earth	60	1021°C	3074°C	praseodymium). (Karl Auer (Baron von Welsbach), 1885)
Neon	Ne	-415°F	-411°F	Greek *neo,* new. (Alexander Ramsay & Morris William
Gas	10	-249°C	-246°C	Travers, 1898)
Neptunium	Np	1191°F	unk.	Named for planet Neptune. (Edwin McMillan & Philip
Radioactive metal	93	644°C		Abelson,1940)
Nickel	Ni	2651°F	5308°F	German *Nickel,* Satan (Old Nick). (Axel Cronstedt, 1751)
Metal	28	1455°C	2931°C	
Niobium	Nb	4491°F	8571°F	Latin *Niobe,* daughter of Tantalus. (Charles Hachett,
Metal	41	2477°C	4744°C	1801)
Nitrogen	N	-346°F	-320°F	Latin, forming *niter,* a compound of nitrogen. (Daniel
Gas	7	-210°C	-196°C	Rutherford, 1772)
Nobelium	No	1521°F	unk.	Named after Alfred Nobel; made at Nobel Institute.
Radioactive metal	102	827°C		(Albert Ghiorso & coworkers, 1958)
Osmium	Os	5491°F	9054°F	Greek *osme,* smell; for malodorousness. (Smithson
Metal	76	3033°C	5012°C	Tennant, 1803)
Oxygen	O	-362°F	-297°F	Greek *oxys,* sharp, plus *gen,* forming; from incorrect
Gas	8	-219°C	-183°C	belief that oxygen forms acids. (Joseph Priestley, 1774)
Palladium	Pd	2831°F	5365°F	Named for Greek goddess Pallas; from asteroid Pallas.
Metal	46	1555°C	2963°C	(William Hyde Wollaston, 1803)
Phosphorus	P	111°F	537°F	Greek *phosphoros,* light-bringer; glows because of rapid .
Nonmetal	15	44°C	281°C	oxidation(Hennig Brand, 1669)
Platinum	Pt	3215°F	6917°F	Diminutive of Spanish *plata,* silver, *platina.* (Antonio de
Metal	78	1768°C	3825°C	Ulloa, 1735)
Plutonium	Pu	1184°F	5842°F	Named for planet Pluto. (Glenn T. Seaborg & coworkers,
Radioactive metal	94	640°C	3228°C	1940)
Polonium	Po	489°F	1764°F	Named by Marie Curie for her native Poland. (Marie &
Radioactive metal	84	254°C	962°C	Pierre Curie, 1898)
Potassium	K	146°F	1398°F	Named for potash, a compound of potassium; symbol
Metal	19	64°C	759°C	from Latin *kalium.* (Humphry Davy, 1807)
Praseodymium	Pr	1708°F	6368°F	Greek *prasios,* green, plus *didymos,* twin (with
Rare earth	59	931°C	3520°C	neodymium). (Karl Auer (Baron von Welsbach), 1885)
Promethium	Pm	1908°F	5432°F	Named for Greek god Prometheus, who stole fire from
Radioactive	61	1042°C	3000°C	heaven. (J.A. Marinsky, L.E. Glendenin, & C.D.Coryell,
rare earth				1945)
Protactinium	Pa	2862°F	unk.	Latin *proto,* first, plus actinium, one of the elements.
Radioactive metal	91	1572°C		(Otto Hahn & Lise Meitner, 1918)
Radium	Ra	1292°F	unk.	Latin *radius,* ray. (Marie Curie & Pierre Curie, 1898)
Radioactive metal	88	700°C		
Radon	Rn	-96°F	-79°F	*Radium* plus *on,* as in *neon.* (Friedrich Ernst Dorn, 1900)
Radioactive gas	86	-71°C	-62°C	
Rhenium	Re	5767°F	10105°F	Latin *Rhenus,* Rhine. (Walter Noddack, Ida Tacke, & Otto
Metal	75	3186°C	5596°C	Berg, 1925)
Rhodium	Rh	3567°F	6683°F	Greek *rhodon,* rose; for red color of its salts. (William
Metal	45	1964°C	3695°C	Hyde Wollaston, 1803)
Rubidium	Rb	103°F	1270°F	Latin *rubidus,* red; from red lines in its spectrum. (Gustav
Metal	37	39°C	688°C	Kirchhoff & Robert Bunsen, 1861)
Ruthenium	Ru	4233°F	7502°F	Named for Ruthenia in Urals, where ore was first found.
Metal	44	2334°C	4150°C	(Carl Claus, 1844)
Rutherfordium	Rf	unk.	unk.	Named for the New Zealand-born English physicist Ernest
Radioactive metal	104			Rutherford. (Russian scientists at Dubna, 1964)
Samarium	Sm	1965°F	3261°F	Named for Scandinavian mineral samarskite. (Paul-Emile
Rare earth	62	1074°C	1794°C	Lecoq de Boisbaudran, 1879)
Scandium	Sc	2806°F	5137°F	Named for Scandinavia. (Lars Fredrik Nilson, 1879)
Metal	21	1541°C	2836°C	
Seaborgium	Sg	unk.	unk.	Named for American physicist Glenn T. Seaborg. (Russian
Radioactive metal	106			scientists at Dubna and U.S. team from Berkeley and
				Lawrence Livermore Laboratories, 1974)
Selenium	Se	429°F	1265°F	Greek *selene,* the Moon. (Jöns Jakob Berzelius, 1818)
Nonmetal	34	221°C	685°C	
Silicon	Si	2577°F	5909°F	Latin *silex,* flint. (Jöns Jakob Berzelius, 1824)
Nonmetal	14	1414°C	3265°C	
Silver	Ag	1763°F	3924°F	Anglo-Saxon *sealfor,* symbol is from Latin *argentum.*
Metal	47	962°C	2162°C	(Prehistoric)

Element/Type[1]	Symbol/ Atomic number	Melting point[1]	Boiling point[1]	Derivation of name (Discoverer, Year)
Sodium	Na	208°F	1621°F	English *soda*, a sodium compound; symbol from Latin
Metal	11	98°C	883°C	*natrium* (Humphry Davy, 1807)
Strontium	Sr	1431°F	2520°F	For Strontian, a town in Scotland. (Humphry Davy, 1808)
Metal	38	777°C	1382°C	
Sulfur	S	247°F	832°F	Sanskrit *solvere*, Latin *sulphur.* (Prehistoric)
Nonmetal	16	120°C	445°C	
Tantalum	Ta	5463°F	9856°F	For mythical king Tantalus, condemned to thirst; because
Metal	73	3017°C	5458°C	of its insolubility. (Anders Ekeberg, 1802)
Technetium	Tc	3915°F	7709°F	Greek *technetos*, artificial; first artificial element. (Emilio
Radioactive metal	43	2157°C	4265°C	Segrè,1937)
Tellurium	Te	841°F	1810°F	Latin *tellus*, the Earth. (Franz Joseph Müller, 1782)
Metal	52	450°C	988°C	
Terbium	Tb	2473°F	5846°F	For Ytterby, village in Sweden. (Carl Gustav Mosander,
Rare earth	65	1356°C	3230°C	1843)
Thallium	Tl	579°F	2683°F	Greek *thallos*, a green twig; after color of its spectrum.
Metal	81	304°C	1473°C	(William Crookes, 1861)
Thorium	Th	3182°F	8650°F	For Norse god Thor. (Jöns Jakob Berzelius, 1829)
Radioactive metal	90	1750°C	4788°C	
Thulium	Tm	2813°F	3542°F	Greek *Thule*, Greek name for land north of Britain. (Per
Rare earth	69	1545°C	1950°C	Teodor Cleve, 1879)
Tin	Sn	449°F	4716°F	Anglo-Saxon *tin*; symbol from Latin *stannum.* (Prehistoric)
Metal	50	232°C	2602°C	
Titanium	Ti	3034°F	5949°F	For Titans of classical mythology. (William Gregor, 1791)
Metal	22	1668°C	3287°C	
Tungsten	W	6192°F	10,031°F	Swedish *tung sten*, heavy stone; symbol from German
Metal	74	3422°C	5555°C	*Wolfram.* (Fausto and Juan José d'Elhuyar, 1783)
Uranium	U	2075°F	7468°F	For planet Uranus. (Martin Klaproth, 1789)
Radioactive metal	92	1135°C	4131°C	
Vanadium	V	3470°F	6165°F	For Scandinavian goddess Vanadis. (Andrès del Rio,
Metal	23	1910°C	3407°C	1801)
Xenon[3]	Xe	-169°F	-163°F	Greek *xenon*, stranger. (Alexander Ramsay & Morris
Gas	54	-112°C	-108°C	William Travers, 1898)
Ytterbium	Yb	1506°F	2185°F	For Ytterby, a village in Sweden. (George Urbain, 1907)
Rare earth	70	819°C	1196°C	
Yttrium	Y	2772°F	6053°F	For Ytterby, a village in Sweden. (Carl Gustav Mosander,
Rare earth	39	1522°C	3345°C	1843)
Zinc	Zn	787°F	1665°F	German *zink.* (Prehistoric)
Metal	30	420°C	907°C	
Zirconium	Zr	3371°F	7968°F	Arabic *zargun*, gold color. (Martin Klaproth, 1789)
Metal	40	1855°C	4409°C	

1. At a pressure of one atmosphere and, for type, at room temperature. 2. This element sublimes (goes directly from a solid to a gas). 3. Liquefaction also requires great pressure.

PHYSICS

Physics is the basis of the other sciences because it is concerned with the fundamental interactions of matter and energy. The first physicists studied how ordinary objects and very large objects (Moon, planets and stars) moved in response to forces. Their study was extremely successful. Near the end of the 19th century, physicists began to investigate radiation in detail, leading to the discovery of various forms of electromagnetic radiation (of which only forms of light, including infrared and ultraviolet, were known previously) and particles smaller than the atom (subatomic particles, such as the electron and proton). In the 20th century, the study of subatomic particles, called particle physics, became a major branch of the science. Many particle physicists limit their work to the particles in the nucleus of atoms and to the behavior of nuclei. Another major branch, condensed-matter physics, is concerned with the physical behavior of materials—for example, their electrical and magnetic properties. Major successes in condensed-matter physics include development of the transistor and related devices (chips) and superconductivity, a state in which electric currents can be transmitted with no resistance. Today many physicists are also cosmologists, who study how the universe began and is constructed, or astrophysicists, who study processes in stars.

Major Discoveries in Physics

1586 Simon Stevinus (Belgian-Dutch: 1548–1620) shows that two different weights dropped at same time from same height will reach ground at same time.

1604 Galileo (Italian: 1564–1642) announces his discovery that a body falling freely will increase its distance as the square of time.

1663 Blaise Pascal (French: 1623–62) proposes what becomes known as Pascal's law: pressure in fluid is transmitted equally in all directions

1675 Ole Rømer (Danish: 1644–1710) becomes first to measure speed of light, although his value is somewhat too slow by today's standards.

1676 Robert Hooke (English: 1635–1703) discovers what becomes known as Hooke's law: The amount a spring stretches varies directly with its tension.

1678 Christiaan Huygens (Dutch: 1629–95) introduces wave theory of light.

1687 Sir Isaac Newton's (English: 1642–1727) *Principia* is published, containing his laws of motion and theory of gravity.

1746 At least two experimenters in Leyden, the Netherlands, invent method for storing static electricity, which becomes known as Leyden jar.

1752 Benjamin Franklin (American: 1706–90) performs kite experiment, demonstrating that lightning is form of electricity.

1787 Jacques A.C. Charles (French: 1746–1823) discovers what is later known as Charles's law: All gases expand same amount with given rise in temperature; e.g., same rise in temperature that will cause hydrogen to double in volume will also cause air to double in volume.

1791 Luigi Galvani (Italian: 1737–98) announces his discovery that when two different metals touch in frog's muscle, they produce electric current.

1798 Benjamin Thompson, Count von Rumford (American-German: 1753–1814) shows that heat is form of motion.

Henry Cavendish (English: 1731–1810) determines gravitational constant and mass of Earth.

1800 William Herschel (German-English: 1738–1822) announces his discovery of infrared light.

1801 Johann W. Ritter (German: 1776–1810) discovers ultraviolet light.

1802 Thomas Young (English: 1773–1829) develops his wave theory of light.

1820 Hans Christian Oersted (Danish: 1777–1851) discovers that magnetism and electricity are two different manifestations of same force.

André-Marie Ampère (French: 1775–1836) formulates first laws of electromagnetism.

1831 Michael Faraday (English: 1791–1867) in England and Joseph Henry (American: 1797–1878) in U.S. (in 1830) independently discover principle of dynamo.

1842 Julius Robert von Mayer (German: 1814–78) is first scientist to state law of conservation of energy.

1848 William Thompson, Baron Kelvin (Scottish: 1824–1907), proposes concept of absolute zero, the lowest possible temperature (-460°F, or -273°C).

1850 Rudolf J.E. Clausius (German: 1822–88) makes first clear statement of second law of thermodynamics: Energy in closed system tends to degrade into heat.

1873 James Clerk Maxwell (Scottish: 1831–79) publishes complete theory of electromagnetism.

1888 Heinrich P. Hertz (German: 1857–94) produces and detects radio waves.

1895 Wilhelm Konrad Röntgen (German: 1845–1923) discovers X rays.

1896 Henri Becquerel (French: 1852–1908) discovers natural radioactivity.

1897 Sir Joseph John Thomson (English: 1856–1940) discovers electron.

1900 Max K.E.L. Planck (German: 1858–1947) explains behavior of electromagnetic radiation by proposing that there is smallest step a physical process can take, which he names quantum.

1905 Albert Einstein (German-American: 1879–1955) shows that photoelectric effect—ejection of electrons from metal by action of light—can be explained if light has particle nature as well as wave nature.

Einstein shows that motion of small particles in liquid ("Brownian motion") can be explained by assuming that the liquid is made of molecules.

Einstein develops his special theory of relativity and the law $E = mc^2$ (energy equals mass times square of speed of light).

1911 Heike Kamerlingh Onnes (Dutch: 1853–1926) discovers superconductivity.

Ernest Rutherford (British: 1871–1937) discovers the proton.

1915 Einstein completes his general theory of relativity, a theory of gravity more accurate than that of Sir Isaac Newton, and publishes it the following year.

1924 Louis-Victor de Broglie (French: 1892–1987) publishes his theory that particles, such as electrons, also have wave nature.

1925 Wolfgang Pauli (Austrian-American: 1900–1958) discovers exclusion principal: Two electrons or protons described by same numbers (called quantum numbers) cannot exist in same atom.

Werner Karl Heisenberg (German: 1901–76) develops matrix version of quantum mechanics, a mathematical treatment that explains behavior of electrons and protons.

1926 Erwin Schrödinger (Austrian: 1887–1961) develops wave version of quantum mechanics, a different mathematical treatment producing same results as Heisenberg's matrix mechanics.

1927 Heisenberg develops his uncertainty principle: It is impossible to measure accurately position and momentum of electron or proton at same time.

1932 Sir James Chadwick (British: 1891–1974) discovers neutron, a neutral particle about same mass as proton.

Carl D. Anderson (American: 1905–91) discovers positron, a positively charged analog of electron.

Sir John G. Cockcroft (English: 1897–1967) and Ernest Walton (Irish: 1903–95) develop first particle accelerator, a device for speeding subatomic particles, which causes them to react more intensely with atoms or other particles (often still known as "atom smasher").

1937 Carl Anderson, with other physicists, performs the work that culminates in the discovery of the muon.

1938 Otto Hahn (German: 1870-1968), in experiments interpreted by Lise Meitner (Austrian-Swedish: 1878-1968), splits uranium atom, opening way for nuclear bombs and nuclear power.

1945 Scientists funded by U.S. government and led by J. Robert Oppenheimer (American: 1904–67) detonate first nuclear-fission explosion (atomic bomb).

1947 Cecil Frank Powell (English: 1903–69) and coworkers discover pion, first-known meson, a subatomic particle involved in holding nucleus of atom together.

1955 Owen Chamberlain (American: 1920–) and Emilio Segrè (Italian-American: 1905–89) produce antiprotons, negatively charged analogs of proton.

1956 Clyde Cowan Jr. (American: 1919-74) and Frederick Reines (American: 1918-98) are first to observe neutrino, a subatomic particle with no mass or charge produced in certain forms of radioactive decay.

1957 Experiments by group led by Chien-Shiung Wu (Chinese-American: 1912–97) and quickly confirmed by others show that right and left are distinguished by behavior of electrons emitted in certain forms of radioactivity.

John Bardeen (American: 1908–91), Leon Cooper (American: 1930–), and Bob Schrieffer (American: 1931–) develop a theory explaining superconductivity.

1961 Murray Gell-Mann (American: 1929–) and, independently, Yu'val Ne'eman (Israeli: 1925–) and others develop method of classifying heavy sub-atomic particles that comes to be known as "eight-fold way."

1964 Murray Gell-Mann introduces concept of quarks as components of heavy subatomic particles, such as protons and mesons.

1967 Steven Weinberg (American: 1933–), Abdus Salam (Pakistani-British: 1926–96), and Sheldon Lee Glashow (American: 1932–) independently develop theory that combines electromagnetic force with weak force.

1980 Heinrich Rohrer (Swiss: 1933–) and Gerd Binnig (German: 1947–) invent the scanning tunneling microscope, with which it is possible to produce images of individual atoms on crystal surfaces.

1986 Karl Alexander Müller (Swiss: 1927–) and Johannes Georg Bednorz (German: 1950–) discover first "high-temperature" superconductor.

1995 Physicists at Fermilab in Batavia, Ill., announce the first observations of the sixth and last expected quark, known as top.

Eric Cornell of the U.S. National Institute of Standards and Technology and coworkers produce the first sample of the fifth state of matter, known as a Bose-Einstein Condensate (BEC), in which atoms huddle together in essentially the same place and condition.

Physicists at CERN (the European Laboratory for Particle Physics) produce the first few atoms of antihydrogen, with a positron orbiting an antiproton.

1997 Two groups of physicists, one in Austria and one in Rome, show that it is possible to entangle two particles so that measuring an exact quantum state of one of them will instantly determine the corresponding state of the other across any distance, a phenomenon known as "quantum teleportation."

1998 Scientists working with the Super-Kamiokande neutrino telescope in Japan establish indirectly that the neutrinos must have a nonzero, although small, mass.

2000 Experimenters at the European Laboratory for Particle Physics (CERN) produce short-lived clouds of free quarks and gluons.

An experiment at Fermilab creates and detects the tau neutrino, predicted in 1975 and associated with tauons the way that ordinary neutrinos are with electrons.

2001 Jun Akimitsu of Aoyama Gakuin University in Tokyo and coworkers discover that the common compound magnesium diboride is a superconductor at temperatures as high as -389°F (-234°C, or 39K), considerably higher than other simple materials (although not as high as some of the complex ceramics).

Physicists at Harvard University and the Harvard-Smithsonian Center for Astrophysics, both in Cambridge, MA, independently stop light completely for brief intervals as it travels through ultracold gases; a laser nudge starts the light wave on its way again.

2002 Robert C. Dynes of the University of California, San Diego, and coworkers have discovered that coating a superconductor with a very thin layer of silver raises the temperature at which it becomes superconducting, although thicker layers have the opposite effect.

Studies of a Fermilab experiment in which a particle called sigma minus was shot into a target revealed signs of previously unknown heavy particles that contain two charm quarks each, called twice-charmed baryons.

▶THE BASIC LAWS OF PHYSICS

Key Terms

Mass is a measure of the amount of matter; it is proportional to weight. Near the surface of Earth it is roughly equivalent to weight.

Velocity measures how an object changes position with time.

Acceleration is how an object changes velocity with time.

Momentum is the product of mass and velocity.

Energy is the ability to do work.

Law of Gravity

The gravitational force between any two objects is proportional to the product of their masses and inversely proportional to the square of the distance between them. If F is the force, G is the number that represents the ratio (the gravitational constant), m and M are the two masses, and r is the distance between the objects:

$$F = \frac{GmM}{r^2}$$

In metric measure, the gravitational constant is 0.0000000000667390 (6.67390×10^{-11}) newton m^2/kg^2, so another way of writing the basic law of gravity is

$$F = \frac{0.0000000000667390mM}{r^2}$$

This law implies that objects falling near the surface of Earth will fall with the same rate of acceleration (ignoring drag caused by air). This rate is 32.174 feet per second per second (ft./sec^2), or 9.8 m/sec^2, and is conventionally labeled g. Applying this rate to falling objects gives the velocity, v, and distance, d, after any amount of time, t, in seconds. If the object starts at rest and 32 ft./sec^2 is used as an approximation for g,

$$v = 32t$$
$$d = 16t^2$$

For example, after 3 seconds, a dropped object that is still falling will have a velocity of $32 \times 3 = 96$ feet per second and will have fallen a distance of $16 \times 3^2 = 144$ feet.

If the object has an initial velocity v_0 and an initial height above the ground of *a*, the equations describing the velocity and the distance, *d*, above the ground (a positive velocity is up and a negative velocity is down) become

$$v = v_0 - 32t$$

and

$$d = -16t^2 + v_0 t + a.$$

After 3 seconds, an object tossed in the air from a height of 6 feet with a velocity of 88 feet per second will reach a speed of 88 - 96 = -8 feet per second, meaning that it has begun to descend, and will have a height of (-16 x 9) + (88 x 3) + 6 = -144 + 264 + 6 = 126 feet above the ground.

The maximum height, *H*, reached by the object with an initial velocity v_0 and initial height *a* is

$$H = a + \frac{v_0^2}{64}$$

For the object tossed upward at 88 feet per second from a height of 6 feet, the maximum height reached would be 6 + 88^2/64 = 6 + 121 = 127 feet. Therefore, after 3 seconds, the object has just reached its peak and has fallen back only 1 foot.

Albert Einstein's general theory of relativity introduced laws of gravity more accurate than those just given, which were discovered by Sir Isaac Newton. Newton's gravitational theory is extremely accurate for most practical situations, however. For example, Newton's theory is used to determine how to launch satellites into proper orbits.

Newton's Laws of Motion

Newton's Laws of Motion apply to objects in a vacuum and are not easily observed in the real world, where forces such as friction tend to overwhelm the natural motion of objects. To obtain realistic solutions to problems, however, physicists and engineers begin with Newton's laws and then add in the various forces that also affect motion.

1. *Any object at rest tends to stay at rest. A body in motion moves at the same velocity in a straight line unless acted upon by a force.* This is also known as the law of inertia. Note that this law implies that an object will travel in a curved path only so long as a force is acting on it. When the force is released, the object will travel in a straight line. A weight on a string swung in a circle will travel in a straight line when the string is released, for the string was supplying the force that caused circular motion.

2. *The acceleration of an object is directly proportional to the force acting on it and inversely proportional to the mass of the object.* This law, for an acceleration *a*, a force *F*, and a mass *m*, is more commonly expressed in terms of finding the force when you know the mass and the acceleration. In this form it is written as

$$F = ma.$$

The implication of this law is that a constant force will produce acceleration, which is an increase in velocity. Thus, a rocket, which is propelled by a constant force as long as its fuel is burning, constantly increases in velocity. Even with an infinite supply of fuel, the rocket would eventually cease to increase in velocity, however, because Einstein's other relativity theory, the special theory of relativity, states that no object can exceed the speed of light in a vacuum (see "Conservation of mass-energy" below). Nevertheless, even a small force, constantly applied, can cause a large mass to reach velocities near the speed of light if enough time is allowed.

3. *For every action there is an equal and opposite reaction.*

Conservation Laws

Many results in physics come from various conservation laws. A conservation law is a rule that a certain entity must not change in amount during a certain class of operations. All such conservation laws treat closed systems. Anything added from outside the system could affect the amount of the entity being conserved.

Conservation of momentum In a closed system, momentum stays the same. This law is equivalent to Newton's third law. Since momentum is the product of mass and velocity, if the mass of a system changes, then the velocity must change. For example, consider a person holding a heavy anchor in a stationary rowboat in the water. The momentum of the system is 0, since the masses have no velocity. Now the person in the rowboat tosses the anchor toward the shore. The momentum of the anchor is now a positive number if velocity toward the shore is measured as positive. To conserve momentum, the rowboat is accelerated in the opposite direction, away from the shore. The positive momentum of the anchor is balanced by the negative momentum of the rowboat and its cargo. In terms of two masses, *m* and *M*, and matching velocities *v* and *V*,

$$mv = MV$$

Conservation of angular momentum

An object moving in a circle has a special kind of momentum, called angular momentum. As noted above, motion in a circle requires some force. Angular momentum combines mass, velocity, and acceleration (produced by the force). For a body moving in a circle, the acceleration depends on both the speed of the body in its path and the square of the radius of the circle. The product of this speed, the mass, and the square of the radius is the angular momentum of the mass.

In a closed system, angular momentum is conserved. This effect is used by skaters to change their velocity of spinning. Angular momentum is partly determined by the masses of a skater's arms combined with the rate of rotation and the square of the radius to the center of mass of each arm (the point that can represent the total mass of the arm). When skaters bring their arms close to their body, this would tend to reduce the angular momentum, because the center of mass is closer to the body. But, since angular momentum is conserved, the rate of rotation has to increase to compensate for the decreased radius. Because the rate depends on the square of the radius, the rate increases dramatically.

Conservation of mass *In a closed system, the total amount of mass appears to be conserved in all but nuclear reactions and other extreme conditions.*

Conservation of energy *In a closed system, energy appears to be conserved in all but nuclear reactions and other extreme conditions.* Energy comes in very many forms: mechanical, chemical, electrical, heat, and so forth. As one form is changed into another (excepting nuclear reactions and extreme conditions), this law guarantees that the total amount remains the same. Thus, when you change the chemical energy of a dry cell into electrical energy and use that to turn a motor, the total amount of energy does not change (although some becomes heat energy—see "Laws of Thermodynamics" below).

Conservation of mass-energy Einstein discovered that his special theory of relativity implies that energy and mass are related. Consequently, mass and energy by themselves are not conserved, since one can be converted into the other. Mass and energy appear to be conserved in ordinary situations because the effect of Einstein's discovery is very small most of the time. The more general law, then, is the law of conservation of mass-energy: *The total amount of mass and energy must be conserved.* Einstein found the following equation that links mass and energy:

$$E = mc^2$$

In this equation, E is the amount of energy, m is the mass, and c is the speed of light in a vacuum.

One instance of energy changing to mass occurs in Einstein's equation for how the mass increases with velocity. If m_0 is the mass of the object when it is not moving, v is the velocity of the object in relation to an observer who is considered to be at rest, and c is the speed of light in a vacuum, then the mass, m, is given by the equation

$$m = \frac{m_0}{\sqrt{1 - \frac{v^2}{c^2}}}$$

This accounts for the rule that no object can exceed the speed of light in a vacuum. As the object approaches this speed, so much of the energy is converted to mass that it cannot continue to accelerate.

In both nuclear fission (splitting of the atomic nucleus) and nuclear fusion (the joining of atomic nuclei, producing the energy of a hydrogen bomb), mass is converted into energy.

Conservation for particles Many properties associated with atoms and subatomic particles are also conserved. Among them are charge, spin, isospin, and a combination known as CPT for *charge conjugation, parity,* and *time.*

First and Second Laws of Thermodynamics

First law This is the same as the law of conservation of energy. It is a law of thermodynamics, or the movement of heat, because heat must be treated as a form of energy to keep the total amount of energy constant. All bodies contain heat as energy no matter how cold they are, although there is not much heat at temperatures close to absolute zero.

Second law *Heat in a closed system can never travel from a low temperature region to one of higher temperature in a self-sustaining process.* Self-sustaining in this case means a process that does not need energy from outside the system to keep it going. In a refrigerator, heat from the cold inside of the refrigerator is transferred to a warmer room, but energy from outside is required to make the transfer happen, so the process is not self-sustaining.

The second law has many implications. One of them is that no perpetual motion machine can be constructed. Another is that all energy in a closed system eventually becomes heat that is diffused equally throughout the system, so that one can no longer obtain work from the system.

The equations that describe the behavior of heat also can be applied to order and therefore to information. The word *entropy* refers to diffuse heat, disorder, or lack of information. Another form of the second law of thermodynamics is that in a closed system, entropy always increases.

Laws of Current Electricity

Key terms When electrons flow in a conductor, the result is electric current. The amount of current is based on an amount of electric charge called the *coulomb,* which is the charge of about 6.25 quintillion (6.25 x 10^{18}) electrons. When 1 coulomb of charge moves past a point in 1 second, it creates a current of 1 ampere. Just as a stream can carry the same amount of water swiftly through a narrow channel or slowly through a broad channel, the energy of an electric current varies depending on the difference in charge between places along the conductor. This is called *potential difference* and is measured in volts. The voltage is affected by the nature of the conductors. Some substances conduct an electric current much more easily than others. This resistance to the current is measured in ohms. *Electric power* is the rate at which electricity is used.

Ohm's law *Electric current is directly proportional to the potential difference and inversely proportional to resistance.* If you measure current, I, in amperes, potential difference, V, in volts, and resistance, R, in ohms, then the current is equal to the potential difference divided by the resistance.

$$I = \frac{V}{R}$$

Law of electric power If electric power, P, is measured in watts, then the power is equal to the product of the current measured in amperes and the potential difference measured in volts.

$$P = IV$$

Laws of Light and Electromagnetic Radiation

Key terms Light is a part of a general form of radiation known as *electromagnetic waves,* or, when thought of as particles, *photons.* Here, electromagnetic radiation is considered as a wave phenomenon for the most part. The velocity of a wave is how fast the wave travels as a whole. The *wavelength* is the distance between one crest of the wave and the next crest. The *frequency* is how many crests pass a particular location in a unit of time. One crest passing each second is called a hertz.

Law of electromagnetic energy The energy of an electromagnetic wave depends on a small number known as Planck's constant. Measured in joules per hertz (energy per frequency), Planck's constant is 6.67259 x 10^{-34}. *The energy is equal to the product of Planck's constant and the frequency.* Using E for energy, h for Planck's constant, and f for frequency,

$$E = hf$$

When thought of in terms of the particles called photons, the energy of a photon obeys the same law. The law of wave motion and the law of electromagnetic energy can be combined with the speed of light in a vacuum *(c)* to give

$$E = \frac{hc}{l}$$

The energy of a photon is the product of Planck's constant and the speed of light, divided by the wavelength *(l)* of the photon.

Inverse-square law All radiation obeys an inverse-square law, which is similar to the law of gravity. *The intensity of the radiation decreases as the inverse of the square of the distance from a point source of radiation.*

Two Basic Laws of Quantum Physics

When one considers effects on very small masses and at very small distances, it is necessary to recognize that objects behave differently from their action at sizes and distances one can observe directly. Since these effects occur in discrete steps based upon Planck's constant times the frequency, called the quantum—which is the size by which energy changes in steps (instead of continuously)—the science of such effects is called quantum physics. Small masses act sometimes like particles and sometimes like waves. Two laws in particular that describe the behavior of small masses are basic and easily stated.

Heisenberg's uncertainty principle *It is impossible to specify completely the position and momentum of a particle, such as an electron, at the same time.*

Pauli's exclusion principle *Two particles of matter cannot be in the same exact state.* Particles of matter include the electron, neutron, and proton. Bosons, particles of force, do not obey Pauli's exclusion principle. (See "Subatomic Particles.")

▶SUBATOMIC PARTICLES

The idea of an atom goes back to the ancient Greek philosophers, who thought that matter was composed of tiny indivisible particles. The concept was put on a scientific basis by John Dalton (English: 1766–1844) in 1803 and became the foundation of chemistry. Nearly a hundred years later, experiments by J.J. Thomson (English: 1856–1940) in 1899 were the first to show that atoms are not indivisible after all. In the past hundred years, physics at almost all levels has been completely revolutionized by the study of the particles that make up atoms or that are smaller than atoms. In the last decades of the 20th century physicists developed the standard model of elementary particles. This model incorporates three of the four fundamental forces in nature, the strong and weak nuclear forces and electromagnetic forces (the other force is gravity). In the model, bosons mediate the forces: gluons, for the strong nuclear force; the photon for electromagnetism, and W and Z particles for the weak nuclear force. Within this model, the weak and electromagnetic forces have been combined into electroweak theory. The standard model has thus far met all experimental challenges, but it has some gaps in addition to the omission of gravity: in particular, the strong and electroweak forces are not completely unified. Theories that attempt to unify the strong and electroweak forces are called Grand Unified Theories (GUTs). Beyond Grand Unified Theories, a great challenge for physicists is a Theory of Everything (TOE) that would account for all of the fundamental forces in nature. Below is a list of all the most important subatomic particles given in the chronological order of their discovery.

1897 Electron The first subatomic particle to be identified, also by J.J. Thomson, was the electron, a low-mass particle that can be found in the outer reaches of the atom. One property of the electron is charge, the response to electric or magnetic fields. The charge of a single electron is always the same, which is identified as –1 (negative one). Each atom consists of a cloud of electrons around a center of positive charge, which is called the nucleus.

1905 Photon The photon is the particle that carries the electromagnetic force. This concept began with Albert Einstein (German-American: 1879–1955) in 1905, when he established that light acts sometimes as a particle instead of as waves. Although we usually think of the photon as the particle of light, it is also the particle form of radio waves, X-rays, or gamma rays. The mass of the photon is 0.

1911 Proton At least one proton is always found in the nucleus of every atom. The proton has a charge that is the same in size as that of the electron, but responds in the opposite direction to an electric or magnetic field. This charge is +1 (positive one). Each proton is almost 2,000 times as heavy as an electron, or about the same as the mass of a single hydrogen atom.

1924 Bosons While matter is made from subatomic particles, the forces that act on matter are also produced by subatomic particles. The particles that create these forces are collectively called bosons because the mathematics of the behavior of this type of particle was worked out originally by Satyendranath Bose (Indian: 1894–1974) in 1924, although put into final form by Einstein. The observed bosons are the photon, pions, gluons, W particles, and Z particles. Bosons that are predicted, but that have not been observed, include the Higgs particle and the graviton.

1925–26 Quantum Mechanics The basic theory of subatomic particles, called quantum mechanics, was developed in two different forms, in 1925 by Werner Heisenberg (German: 1901–76) and in 1926 by Erwin Schrödinger (Austrian: 1887–1961). Although the two forms appear very different, they produce the same results.

1926 Fermions All the particles that make up matter are called fermions, as opposed to the bosons that create forces. The fermions include all the leptons and quarks as well as the particles made from quarks (see below). Fermions are named for Enrico Fermi (Italian-American: 1901–54), who first worked out the mathematics of their interactions in 1926. Fermions all obey the *Pauli exclusion principle* (see the section on *Basic Laws of Physics*, earlier in this chapter), which means that they occupy a definite space. Two fermions cannot be in the same place at the same time.

1930 Antiparticles When Paul A.M. Dirac (English-American: 1902-84) completed his mathematical version of the theory of the electron in 1930, he observed that one solution to his equations predicted a particle that would be a mirror image of the electron, exactly the same as the electron but with a positive charge instead of negative. The particle, discovered two years later in 1932, was named the positron. The same equations predicted mirror images for all subatomic particles. These particles are called the antiparticles, so another name for positron is antielectron.

1932 Neutron The neutron is very much like a neutral proton, with just slightly more mass. Neutrons are stable when they are found in atoms, but decay into other particles when left to themselves.

1935 Muon The muon is now recognized as a high energy analog to the electron with a mass about 200 times that of the electron.

1947 Pion A pion carries the strong force that holds the nucleus of atoms together, but since each pion appears and disappears almost instantly, the pions are not usually counted as part of the nucleus. (Predicted in 1935.) In the same year that the pion was found, theoreticians were able to work out a comprehensive theory of the electron, called quantum electrodynamics (QED).

1950 Strange particles Starting in 1950 experimenters observed a number of previously undetected particles that did not behave as particles were expected to do. Because these particles have masses greater than that of the proton and neutron, they were called hyperons. Other unexpected particles, about the size of the pion, were classed as mesons. A classification scheme for the hyperons developed in 1961 helped physicists understand them better, but their essential difference was already labeled "strangeness."

1955 Neutrinos Neutrinos are thought to be among the most common particles in the universe, but they interact with ordinary matter so weakly that they are very difficult to observe. Predicted in 1930, neutrinos were thought to have no rest mass, but Canadian experiments in 2001 indicate that they have a very small mass equal to less than about 10^{-7} of the mass of an electron. Different neutrinos are associated with electrons, muons, and tauons.

1964–95 Quarks Murray Gell-Mann (American: 1928–) and several other physicists determined that a way to explain the properties of protons, neutrons, mesons, and hyperons, is to think of the heavy particles as made from combinations of light ones, just as the atom is made from combinations of electrons, protons, and neutrons. The smaller particles are quarks; there are six of them in all. Two quarks, known as up and down, form protons and neutrons. The top quark is the most massive—about as heavy as an atom of gold—and the last to be detected. (First version of theory in 1964, evidence for top quark in 1995.)

1965–73 Gluons The eight different bosons that produce a force between quarks known as the color force are called gluons. The color force is also the basis of the strong force that holds the nucleus together. Because of the color force, the study of quarks and gluons is today called quantum chromodynamics (QCD).

1974 J/psi particle Like the strange hyperons, the J/psi particle is a heavy particle that appears at high energies. It also is produced by a different kind of quark, the charm quark. The odd name J/psi comes from the particle having been discovered independently by two investigators, one of whom called it J and the other of whom named it psi.

1983 W and Z particles The particles that produce the weak force are called W and Z. At high energies, however, the weak force merges with the electromagnetic force, so the W and Z are to some extent analogs to the photon, although they could not be more different, since the photon has a 0 rest mass and both W particles and the single Z particle are very massive.

1995 Antiatoms Since antiparticles have all the properties of ordinary particles except for being mirror images, it is possible to create an antiatom by combining subatomic antiparticles. This was accomplished in 1995 with the production of a few antiatoms of antihydrogen made by causing an antielectron (positron) to orbit an antiproton.

(Not yet observed) Graviton and Higgs particle A particle that produces gravitational force by its exchange between all kinds of particles is known as the graviton, but so far it is only known in theory. The Laser Interferometer Gravitational Wave Observatory (LIGO) that began operations in 2000 seeks to observe gravity waves, the wave version of the graviton. The Higgs particle is the main undetected particle of the standard model of subatomic particles. Physicists believe that the Higgs, named after Peter Higgs (English: 1919–) who predicted it in 1964, confers mass to all other particles.

LIFE SCIENCES

While the scientific study of living creatures seems to have begun with Aristotle, there was considerable practical experimentation with living things much earlier, going back to the domestication of a species, the dog, perhaps as early as 14,000 B.C. In the years that followed the Scientific Revolution of the 17th century, the science of biology came to include most of the then-known life sciences: zoology (the study of animals), botany (the study of plants), and taxonomy (the classification of living things). In the 19th century, biology began to fragment into other studies: microbiology (the study of creatures visible only through the microscope), genetics (the study of how traits are inherited), biochemistry (the study of molecules in living things), and so forth. At the same time, different ways of studying living organisms were developed, among them anthropology (the study of human beings), ecology (the study of interactions between different living things and their environment), and ethology (the study of animal behavior).

▶MAJOR GROUPS OF LIVING ORGANISMS

Biologists classify all living things (organisms) according to a system first introduced by Carolus Linnaeus in 1735. At that time Linnaeus and other scientists divided all life forms into two kingdoms: plants and animals. Since then, biologists have learned that there are fundamental differences among organisms that go beyond the differences between plants and animals and have added four kingdoms. The six kingdoms commonly recognized today are: Monera, Archaea, Protists, Fungi, Plants, and Animals.

Following Linnaeus, all classification terms are usually given in Latin. In the following list, English terms are substituted when they are an exact translation—for example, animals instead of Animalia and birds instead of Aves. If there is no exact translation, the Latin form is kept.

Each kingdom is divided into two or more phyla (singular: phylum). Organisms within one phylum are more closely related to one another than to members of other phyla.

The phyla are also divided into parts, which are then further divided, each time on the basis of closer and closer relationships. In descending order of size, the main divisions are as follows:

Kingdom
- Phylum
  - Class
    - Order
      - Family
        - Genus
          - Species

Many biologists add to this list by classifying groups of species with sub- or super-, as in subphylum or superfamily.

By convention, Latin names except for genus and species are given in Roman type; genus and species are italicized.

Kingdom: Monera One-celled organisms with simple cells that lack a membrane around the genetic material. Bacteria do not produce their own food; blue-green algae do.
Phylum: Bacteria (also called Eubacteria)
Phylum: Blue-green algae, also called blue-green bacteria or cyanobacteria

Kingdom: Archaea One-celled organisms, sometimes called Archaeobacteria, that are genetically more like the other kingdoms than they are like the Monera. The Archaea were first discovered as creatures living in hot springs and other high-temperature situations. They were later observed among the one-celled creatures that metabolize chemicals such as methane or sulfur instead of using oxygen. They also have been found in great abundance in the oceans and deep in the Earth's crust.

Kingdom: Protists One-celled or colonial; complex cells that have a membrane around their genetic material; protozoans and slime molds do not produce their own food; all other phyla in this kingdom can.
Phylum: Ciliated protozoans, such as Paramecium
Phylum: Protozoans with flagella, such as the trypanosome that causes African sleeping sickness.
Phylum: Amoebas and similar protozoans
Phylum: Protozoans that have no means of motion during most of their life, such as the plasmodia that cause malaria.
Phylum: Euglenas
Phylum: Golden algae and diatoms
Phylum: Fire or golden brown algae
Phylum: Green algae
Phylum: Brown algae
Phylum: Red algae
Phylum: Slime molds

Kingdom: Fungi One-celled or multicelled; cells have nuclei, which stream between cells, giving the appearance that cells have many nuclei; fungi do not produce their own food.
Phylum: Zygomycetes (e.g., black bread mold)
Phylum: Ascomycetes (includes Penicillium, truffles, yeasts)
Phylum: Basidiomycetes (includes mushrooms)

Kingdom: Plants Multicellular organisms that carry out photosynthesis; cells have nuclei and cell walls.
Phylum: Mosses and liverworts
Phylum: Club mosses
Phylum: Horsetails
Phylum: Ferns
Phylum: Conifers
Phylum: Cone-bearing desert plants
Phylum: Cycads
Phylum: The ginkgo
Phylum: Flowering plants
- Subphylum: Dicots (plants with two seed leaves—e.g., most fruits and vegetables, common flowers, and trees)
- Subphylum: Monocots (plants with a single seed leaf—e.g., onions, lilies, and grasses)

Kingdom: Animals Multicellular organisms that get their food by ingestion; most are able to move from place to place; cells have nuclei but not cell walls.
Phylum: Porifera (sponges)
Phylum: Cnidaria (jellyfish, anemones, corals)
Phylum: Platyhelminthes (flatworms)
Phylum: Nematodes (roundworms)
Phylum: Rotifers (microscopic wormlike or spherical animals)
Phylum: Bryozoa (moss animals)
Phylum: Brachiopods (lampshells)
Phylum: Phoronida (tube worms)
Phylum: Annelids (segmented worms, such as earthworms, leeches)
Phylum: Mollusks (soft-bodied animals with a mantle and foot)
- Class: Chitons
- Class: Bivalves (clams, oysters, mussels)
- Class: Scaphopoda (tooth or tusk shells)
- Class: Gastropods (slugs and snails)
- Class: Cephalopods (octopus, squid)

Phylum: Arthropods (segmented animals with an external skeleton)
- Class: Horseshoe crabs
- Class: Crustaceans (lobsters, crabs, shrimp)
- Class: Arachnids (scorpions, spiders, mites, ticks)
- Class: Insects
- Class: Millipedes and centipedes

Phylum: Cycliophora (known only as a tiny species growing in the mouths of lobsters)
Phylum: Echinoderms (starfish, brittle stars)
Phylum: Hemichordata (acorn worms)
Phylum: Chordates
- Subphylum: Tunicates
- Subphylum: Lancelets
- Subphylum: Vertebrates (animals with backbones)
  - Class: Agnatha (lampreys, hagfish)
  - Class: Sharks and rays
  - Class: Bony fish
  - Class: Amphibians
  - Class: Reptiles
  - Class: Birds
  - Class: Mammals
    - Subclass: Monotremes (egg-laying mammals)
    - Subclass: Marsupials
    - Subclass: Placentals
      - Order: Insectivores (shrews, moles, hedgehogs)
      - Order: Flying lemurs
      - Order: Bats
      - Order: Primates (lemurs, monkeys, apes, humans)
      - Order: Edentates (anteaters, sloths, armadillos)
      - Order: Pangolins

Order: Lagomorphs (rabbits, hares)
Order: Rodents (squirrels, rats, mice, porcupines)
Order: Cetaceans (whales, dolphins)
Order: Carnivores (wolves, cats, bears, raccoons, weasels, badgers, skunks, otters, hyenas)
Order: Seals
Order: The aardvark
Order: Elephants
Order: Hyraxes
Order: Sirenians (dugongs, manatees)
Order: Odd-toed ungulates (horses, tapirs, rhinoceroses)
Order: Even-toed ungulates (pigs, hippopotamuses, camels, deer, giraffes, pronghorns, cattle, goats, sheep)

▶CLASSIFYING HUMANS

KINGDOM: Animals Organisms that use other organisms for food and that sometimes move rapidly.
PHYLUM: Chordates Animals that are partially supported by a rod of cartilage or bone vertebrae and an internal skeleton.
SUBPHYLUM: Vertebrates Chordates that have vertebrae, such as fish, amphibians, reptiles, birds, and mammals.
CLASS: Mammals Vertebrates that have hair and suckle their young.
ORDER: Primates Mammals that use sight more than scent, have nails instead of claws on grasping hands and feet, are mostly active in daylight, and have relatively large brains.
SUPERFAMILY: Hominoids Primates that are tailless, generally large in size, can climb trees, and have relatively flat faces, such as *Sahelanthropus, Ardipithecus, Kenyapithecus,* australopithecines, and human beings.
FAMILY: Hominids Hominoids that walk upright, have small canines, and large brains; specifically, the australopithecines and human beings.
GENUS: *Homo* Hominids, with especially large brains, that speak and show other signs of culture; specifically, *Homo habilis, Homo erectus* and related species, and *Homo sapiens.*
SPECIES: *Homo sapiens* Modern human beings.

▶THE HUMAN GENOME PROJECT

On June 25, 2000, President Clinton, British Prime Minister Tony Blair, and Craig Venter of Celera Genomics jointly announced the completion of decoding all the bases that make up the genes in a human. Many assumed it meant that the Human Genome Project had succeeded in deciphering all human genes. But while the announcement marked a major milestone in biology, decoding the bases was actually just a step along the way. It was not until February 15-16, 2001, that scientists from the International Human Genome Sequencing Consortium and from Celera completed the original goal of the Human Genome Project: releasing lists of all the bases in order. And even then, the lists were still slightly incomplete. Yet to come is the recognition of which bases are identified with which genes, and what the function of each gene is. Also, scientists increasingly recognize that knowledge of genes alone is not the whole story.

Every organism is almost completely described by its own genes, combinations of triplets of four chemical building blocks, called bases, carried on long molecules of a chemical named deoxyribonucleic acid (DNA). Several different DNA molecules are found in every cell. Most human cells have 46 such molecules as the working parts of the chromosomes and additional DNA in small, energy-producing bodies called mitochondria. The total group of all the DNA for an organism is called its genome. The Human Genome Project has been a step-by-step process to determine the complete sequence of the more than 3 billion bases in human DNA, to identify the genes in that sequence, and to determine the immediate purpose of each gene. The DNA bases are usually known by their abbreviations, T, G, C, and A; thus, the goal of the project reached in February 2001 was to determine a giant string of the letters T, G, C, and A.

One of the surprises of the list so far has been that there appear to be only 30,000 to 40,000 human genes—fewer than half the number expected before sequencing. Ultimately other questions will need to be resolved, such as how genes interact with one another and with other molecules in the body. It appears the number of proteins encoded in the genes is much greater than the number of genes, so a new goal for researchers is to determine all the proteins—known as the proteome. Another task will be identification of variations from human to human called single-nucleotide polymorphisms (SNPs). Such variations are thought to be behind susceptibility to such complex diseases as cancer, diabetes, cardiovascular syndromes and some types of mental illnesses

The National Center for Human Genome Research was instituted on January 3, 1989, and with the participation of both the U.S. Department of Energy and National Institutes for Health, became the Human Genome Project in 1990. Scientists from the European Union, Japan and China also participate, forming together the International Human Genome Sequencing Consortium. Another group has developed out of this effort that plans to concentrate on the genomes of disease-causing organisms, primarily bacteria.

Along the way, the genomes of organisms other than human have been sequenced. Celera achieved the first, the small bacterium *Haemophilus influenzae,* in 1995. Since then, bacteria that cause syphilis, chlamydia, tuberculosis, cholera and staph infections, among some 60 different bacteria, have all had their genomes sequenced. In 1996 the gene of yeast, a more complex organism, was added to the list.

Scientists then targeted commonly used experimental organisms. Teams from the U.S. and Britain completed the genome of the first animal, *Caenorhabditis elegans,* a nematode worm, at the end of 1998. Celera concentrated on the fruit fly, *Drosophila melanogaster,* and established its sequence of 1.8 billion bases by September 9, 1999. In plants, the first success came at the end of 2000 with the mustard *Arabidopsis thaliana,* the common laboratory plant for botanists. In October, 2001, sequencing of the genome of the Japanese puffer fish was finished, the first fish. An international consortium had produced 98 percent of the map for the laboratory mouse genome by August 2002, but does not expect to have the complete sequence until 2005. The mouse genome is considered to be nearly as significant as that of the human because of the common use of mice in laboratory studies and a comparatively close relationship to humans—our common ancestor was only about 100 million years ago. The rat and the zebrafish will be the next laboratory animals. The genomes of the pig, dog, and vat are also being sequenced. The chimpanzee, thought to be genetically nearly identical to humans, is also under discussion.

Major Discoveries in Life Sciences

B.C.

c.9000 Agricultural Revolution starts in Near East with domestication of sheep and goats in Persia (Iran) and Afghanistan and of pigs in Anatolia (Turkey); and cultivation of wheat in Canaan (Israel and Jordan).

c.8000 Agricultural Revolution starts independently in what are now Peru, Central America, and Indochina.

c.350 Aristotle (Greek: 384–322 B.C.) classifies known animals in system that will continue to be used until 1735.

A.D.

1648 Jan Baptista van Helmont (Flemish: 1580–1644) shows that plants do not obtain large amounts of material for their growth from soil.

1665 Robert Hooke (English: 1635–1703) observes and names the cell.

1668 Francesco Redi (Italian: 1626–97) shows that maggots in meat do not arise spontaneously but are hatched from flies' eggs.

1669 Anton van Leeuwenhoek (Dutch: 1632–1723) discovers microorganisms—creatures too small to see with naked eye—and recognizes that sperm are part of reproduction.

1683 Leeuwenhoek is first to observe bacteria.

1735 Carolus Linnaeus (Carl Linné; Swedish: 1707–78) introduces system in use today for classifying plants and animals.

1779 Jan Ingenhousz (Dutch: 1730–99) discovers that plants release oxygen when exposed to sunlight and they consume carbon dioxide; this is first step in understanding photosynthesis.

1839 Theodor A.H. Schwann (German: 1810–82), building on work of Matthias Jakob Schleiden (German: 1804–81) in 1838, develops cell theory of life.

1856 First skeleton of what we now call Neandertals is found in cave in Neander Valley, near Düsseldorf (Germany).

Louis Pasteur (French: 1822–95) discovers that fermentation is caused by microorganisms.

1858 Charles R. Darwin (English: 1809–82) and Alfred R. Wallace (English: 1823–1913) announce their theory of evolution by natural selection to the Linnean Society.

1859 Darwin publishes *On the Origin of Species.*

1865 Gregor Johann Mendel's (Austrian: 1822–84) theory of dominant and recessive genes is published in obscure local journal.

1868 Workers building road in France discover skeletons of first-known Cro-Magnons in cave.

1894 Eugène Dubois (Dutch: 1858–1940) announces discovery of "Java ape-man," now known to be first specimen of *Homo erectus.*

1898 Mosaic disease of tobacco plants is recognized as being caused by virus, the first identification of a virus.

1900 Three different biologists rediscover laws of genetics originally found by Mendel.

1924 Raymond A. Dart (Australian-South African: 1893–1988) identifies first fossil of an australopithecine, a close relative of early humans.

1953 James D. Watson (American: 1928–) and Francis Crick (English: 1916–) determine structure of DNA, the basis of heredity.

1961 Louis S.B. Leakey (English: 1903–72) and Mary D. Leakey (English: 1913–96) discover a previously unknown ancestor of humans, *Homo habilis,* in the Olduvai Gorge of northern Tanzania.

Marshall W. Nirenberg (American: 1927–) learns to read one of the "letters" of genetic code.

1973 Stanley Cohen (American: 1922–) and Herbert Boyer (American: 1936–) put specific gene into bacterium, the first instance of true genetic engineering.

1974 Donald C. Johanson (American: 1943–) and coworkers discover Lucy in Afar region of Ethiopia, the nearly complete skeleton—but not the skull—of *Australopithecus afarensis,* an early relative of humans (more than 3 million years old).

1995 César Milstein (Argentine-English: 1927–) announces discovery of how to produce monoclonal antibodies, highly specific chemicals that can be made to react with particular proteins or other chemicals in the body.

1980 Martin Cline (American: 1934–) and coworkers succeed in transferring functioning gene from one mouse to another.

1983 Kary B. Mullis (American: 1945–) invents the use of the polymerase chain reaction to make copies of DNA sequences, a vital tool in finding specific genes.

1988 The complete developmental history of every cell in the nematode *Caenorhabditis elegans* published.

1994 Gen Suwa (Japanese), discovers the first fossil of *Ardipithecus ramidus,* the oldest known hominid, in Ethiopia.

1995 Craig Venter (American: 1946–) of the Institute for Genomic Research publishes the complete base sequences for all the genes of a free-living organism, the bacterium *Haemophilus influenzae.*

1997 Ian Wilmut (English: 1944–) succeeds in cloning a sheep from a cell from an adult ewe.

Svante Pääbo of the University of Munich, Germany, and coworkers clone DNA from the first discovered Neandertal fossil and compare the DNA to that of modern humans. They conclude that the Neandertal is a different species from our own.

1998 Elizabeth Gould and co-workers at Princeton University demonstrate that adult monkeys continue to grow new brain cells, a feat previously thought impossible for adult primates.

1999 Berhane Asfaw (Ethiopian: 1954-) and coworkers announce the discovery in Ethiopia of fossils of a new hominid species, *Australopithecus garhi* ("surprising southern ape").

2000 Tools are found at a Cactus Hill site in Virginia from 15,000 years ago, tending to disprove the theory that early Americans reached the continent through Alaska about 12,000 years ago.

The Human Genome Project and Celera Genomics announce jointly that they have developed a rough draft of the entire human genetic sequence.

2001 Meave G. Leakey (English-Kenyan: 1942-) of the National Museums of Kenya in Nairobi discovers the skull of a 3.5-million-year-old human ancestor, which she names *Kenyanthropus platyops* ("flat-faced man from Kenya").

2002 Biologists locate the first known nerve receptor to detect cold; it is also activated by menthol. Other scientists find a fifth taste receptor on the tongue, which responds to amino acids, including the glutamate of monosodium glutamate. Previously it was thought that there were only taste receptors for sweet, salt, bitter and sour.

For the first time in 87 years, a new order of insects is recognized (similar to Lepidoptera for butterflies and moths). Mantophasmatodea includes two genera and three species, popularly named gladiators, each somewhat like a cross between a mantis and a grasshopper.

Experiments conducted by two different groups of scientists show that amino acids, the building blocks of proteins, could form naturally in outer space from the action of ultraviolet radiation on simple, common molecules such as water, ammonia and methanol.

Michel Brunet and Martin Pickford discover in Chad the oldest hominid fossil found so far, the skull of *Sahelanthropus tchadensis,* who lived 6 to 7 million years ago in a setting of woods broken with patches of savanna.

Eckard Wimmer of the State University of New York at Stony Book uses the known sequence of genes in the poliovirus and laboratory-made DNA to create a completely synthetic version of the virus.

The Human Family Tree

EVOLUTION OF THE HUMAN FAMILY

New fossil finds since the start of 2000 have extended our knowledge of the ancestry of humans deep into the past. Anthropologists continue to argue as to the meaning of specific fossils; and new tools, such as DNA analysis, provide another framework for primate evolution. Several indicators now point to the first primate developing some 85 million years ago, long before the first fossil identified as a primate. The higher primates (monkeys, apes and humans), long thought to have evolved in Africa, may instead have split from the tarsier group in Asia.

Eosimis *c. 45 million years ago. Central and eastern China.* Evidence from fossils announced in 2000 strongly suggests that *Eosimis,* a small creature thought previously to be a tarsier, walked on all fours on tops of branches as monkeys do, which implies that it was a higher primate, the earliest known.

Catopithecus *c. 40 million years ago. Egypt.* For those anthropologists who think higher primates arose in Africa and that *Eosimis* is a tarsier ancestor, *Catopithecus* is the earliest representative of the higher primates.

Aegyptopithecus *c. 35 million years ago. Egypt.* A small, monkey-like, fruit-eating creature about the size of a house cat, *Aegyptopithecus* is sometimes called the "dawn ape" and may be the earliest known ancestor of the hominoids.

Afropithecus* and *Proconsul *c. 15 to 20 million years ago. East Africa.* Several different early apes lived in Africa and Asia about this time. Opinion is divided on whether *Afropithecus* or *Proconsul* is the ancestor to the hominids; other apes of this time are ancestral to gorillas and orangutans.

Sahelanthropus tchadensis *c. 6 to 7 million years ago. Chad.* Discovered by Ahounta Djimdoumalbaye and Michel Brunet on July 19, 2001, this is the earliest known hominid, combining a flat human-looking face with a brain the size of a chimpanzee's. It lived in a mixed region of woods and savanna near a large lake.

Orrorin tugenensis *c. 6 million years ago. Kenya (Tugen Hills).* Twelve fossils, including fragments of limb bone and jawbones as well as a few teeth, were found in 2000 by a French expedition headed by Brigette Senut and Martin Pickford. The name means "original man of Tugen," for the discoverers claim that this is the ancestor to the human line. This claim is disputed by many paleoanthropologists, although all admit that *Orrorin* is a hominid.

Ardipithecus ramidus kadabba *c. 5.5 million year ago. Ethiopia (Middle Awash River Valley).* Announced in 2001, these fossils include a jawbone with teeth, hand and foot bones, and fragments of other bones. The team was led by Ethiopians Yohannes Haile-Selassie and Giday WoldeGabriel. The discoverers label this as a subspecies of *Ardipithecus* (see below), but are not sure whether *Ardipithecus* is ancestral to australopithecines and humans or to chimpanzees.

Ardipithecus ramidus *c. 4.4 million years ago. Ethiopia.* Discovered in 1994 at Aramis, Ethiopia, *A. ramidus* lived in woodlands mixed with patches of savanna, rather than in the true savanna thought before this discovery to have been the home of ancestors to humans.

Australopithecus anamensis *c. 4.2 to 3.9 million years ago. Northern Kenya (Lake Turkana region)* These fossils, discovered in 1993 by Meave G. Leakey and Alan Walker, indicate that *A. anamensis* could walk upright on two legs.

Kenyapithecus platyops *c. 3.5 to 3.3 million years ago. Kenya.* Skull found in 2001 by Meave G. Leakey and coworkers and identified as a new genus. Leakey also thinks that some fossils previously identified as *Homo rudolfensis* may belong to *Kenyapithecus* genus.

Australopithecus afarensis *"Lucy" and "The First Family" c. 3.6 to 2.9 million years ago. Ethiopia and East Africa.* Many think *A. afarensis* is on the direct line to modern humans. A trail of footprints in volcanic ash at Laetoli, Tanzania, made by *A. afarensis* demonstrates that it walked upright, unlike any of the great apes.

Australopithecus africanus. *c. 3 to 2 million years ago. South Africa* First nonhuman hominid to be discovered, in 1924, although few anthropologists accepted it until the 1950s. Walked upright and, while large brained for a primate, had a brain that was much smaller than early *Homo* species. Thought to be on direct line to *Homo.*

Paranthropus (Australopithecus) aethiopicus *c. 2.7 to 2.3 million years ago. East Africa.* Thought to be the link between *A. africanus* and three "robust" species that many assign to the genus *Paranthropus* although at one time these species were considered to be australopithecines.

Australopithecus garhi *c. 2.5 million years ago. Ethiopia.* Fossils are found at same site as butchered animals and primitive stone tools, raising possibility that australopithecines used tools found at various early sites.

Homo habilis *c. 2.5 to 1.5 million years ago. Tanzania and South Africa—possibly Central Eurasia (Georgia).* Earliest known species of our own genus. *H. habilis* ("Handy Man") named for tools found at sites near fossil sites, although tools also could have been made by australopithecines whose contemporaneous fossils are also found nearby.

Homo rudolfensis *c. 2.4 to 1.5 million years ago. Kenya.* A different member of genus *Homo* that lived in the same general region at the same time as *H. habilis.*

Paranthropus (Australopithecus) robustus* and *P. bosei *c. 2.3 to 1.4 million years ago.* Although the *Paranthropus* line is now extinct, these robust hominids were successful contemporaries of *Homo* for about a million years.

Homo ergaster *c. 1.8 to 1.4 million years ago. Africa and Central Eurasia (Georgia).* Fossils once classed as African *H. erectus* are now often called *H. ergaster* ("Work Man"). Probable ancestor of *H. sapiens.*

Homo erectus *"Java Ape Man" and "Peking Man" c. 1.6 million to 40,000 years ago. Africa, Asia and Europe.* This successful maker of hand axes and user of fire has often been thought to be the immediate ancestor of *H. sapiens,* but the last groups of *H. erectus* ("Upright Man") were contemporaries of the earliest of our species.

Homo heidelbergensis *c. 600,000 years ago to 120,000 years ago. Europe and North Africa.* Some early members of this group, perhaps those in Spain or North Africa sometimes called *Homo* antecessor, appear to be ancestor to the Neandertals.

Homo neanderthalensis *c. 200,000 years ago to 30,000 years ago. Europe and the Near East.* This species was successful in the Ice Age, but became extinct shortly after *H. sapiens* spread across Europe. Although DNA studies indicate that *H. neanderthalis* and *H. sapiens* are different species, a few fossils have mixed characteristics that many think implies breeding across species lines.

Homo sapiens *c. 150,000 years ago to present. Worldwide.* Very early *H. sapiens,* sometimes termed "archaic," lived in Africa. DNA evidence suggests that about 100,000 years ago they spread into Asia and Europe. By 30,000 years ago they were the only remaining hominid (although some authorities include chimpanzees, and perhaps the gorilla, in the hominids).

Elements in a 150-Pound Person

Element/ Weight	Use by the body
Oxygen 97.5 lbs	Part of all major nutrients, which make up tissues of the body, but also vital to production of energy in the form of elemental oxygen obtained from air.
Carbon 27.0 lbs	Essential element for life—most compounds based on carbon are called organic, meaning "from life." An essential part of proteins, carbohydrates, and fats, the building blocks of human cells
Hydrogen 15.0 lbs	Part of each of major nutrients, and thus a building block of every cell. Unlike oxygen, has no part in respiration.
Nitrogen 4.5 lbs	Essential part of proteins, DNA, and RNA, the compounds most active in controlling cells; most of the body's functions depend on nitrogen compounds at one stage or another.
Calcium 3.0 lbs	Mostly locked into hard compounds that form nonliving parts of bone. One of principal messengers between cells, telling them when to act and when to stay quiet.
Phosphorus 1.8 lbs	Important element in bone building, but, like calcium, has another role: it is essential in producing energy in cell.
Potassium 0.3 lbs	Regulates contraction of muscle cells (and some other cell functions) along with sodium. Potassium is involved with muscle contractions and general maintenance of pressure a cell exerts on its covering membrane.
Sulfur 0.3 lbs	Essential to most forms of life. An important constituent of proteins.
Chlorine 0.3 lbs	Used in form of chloride ions to transport messages from the body to cells; helps regulate electrical activity.
Sodium 0.165 lbs	Required by vertebrates to control fluid pressure in cells.
Magnesium 0.06 lbs	Required by both plants (it is in chlorophyll) and animals. In humans, works with enzymes to speed chemical reactions, is involved in transmission of messages between nerves, and has a role in bone structure.
Iron 0.006 lbs	Essential for carrying oxygen to cells and carbon dioxide waste away. Lack of iron causes anemia.
Cobalt 0.00024 lbs	Part of vitamin B12, found in meats and dairy products; its exact role in the body is not well understood.
Copper 0.00023 lbs	Helps form red blood cells, maintain nervous system, and regulate cholesterol levels.
Manganese 0.00020 lbs	Aids in bone formation, helps regulate nervous system, and is part of sex hormones.
Iodine 0.00006 lbs	Part of thyroid hormone that controls rate at which food is burned for energy.
Zinc trace	Needed for some enzymes, for proper sex development, in healing wounds, for sense of taste, and for normal sperm count.
Fluorine trace	Strengthens teeth and bones.
Chromium trace	Used in metabolism of sugar and the regulation of fats.
Selenium trace	In small amounts, may reduce cell damage and promote growth.

Note: In addition, the body contains trace amounts of boron, aluminum, vanadium, molybdenum, and silicon. Their roles, however, are not fully understood.

MATHEMATICS

Strictly speaking, mathematics is not considered a science but a separate branch of learning on its own. Because the use of mathematics has been so important to science, however, it is generally treated along with sciences.

Mathematics consists of a set of abstract symbols and of rules for manipulating them, along with the results of that manipulation. Because of this, some have classified mathematics as a kind of language, while others view it as a kind of game. Many mathematicians believe there is a much deeper reality than those classifications, but it is one that is very difficult to explain. Even when mathematics is treated as a game, the results seem to be strongly connected to the real world.

The 20th century was an era of impressive progress in many fields of mathematics and statistics (see the discoveries listed in Milestones), and this progress continues today. Applied methods of statistical inference ("confidence intervals" and other techniques) based on the work of Sir R.A. Fisher (British, 1890-1962) and others have been highly developed and widely applied, through computer programs, in the sciences, engineering, and social sciences. There have also been dramatic advances in the ancient science of geometry, such as the development of fractal geometry (Benoit Mandelbrot, French-American, b. Poland, 1924-), in which patterns of smaller parts (such as a coastline seen very close up) relate in complex ways to the same coastline seen from a distance. Encryption methods have developed rapidly, spurred by the need to protect information sent by the Internet. An important class of such methods is based on the use of prime numbers (numbers divisible only by 1 and themselves). The largest prime identified as of August 2002 is $(2^{13,466,917})$-1, a number with more than 4 million digits. Another area in which important advances have been made is in computerizing numerical techniques for solving the equations in weather forecasting models, a use of mathematics that affects everyone's life. These and many other modern developments in mathematics and statistics mean that, while students today study some math that is thousands of years old—Greek geometry; and some that is hundreds of years old—the calculus of Leibniz and Newton; they also study, and their lives are affected by, up-to-date mathematical techniques embodied in powerful computational packages.

▶COMMONLY USED MATHEMATICAL FORMULAS

Most formulas needed in solving everyday problems are collected below, with special emphasis on formulas relating to measurements, as these are used in everything from sewing to building a house. However, some important formulas from algebra, graphing, and trigonometry are at the end. Additional formulas can also be found in "Basic Laws of Physics."

General

The **distance** *d*, given the rate *r* and the time *t*:

$$d = rt.$$

Length

The **perimeter (distance around)** *p* **of any polygon** (closed plane figure with straight sides that do not cross), given the lengths of the sides *a*, *b*, *c*, and so forth:

$$p = a + b + c + \dots$$

Perimeter *p* **of a rectangle,** given the length *l* and the width *w*:

$$p = 2l + 2w.$$

Perimeter *p* **of a square**, given the length of a side *s*:

$$p = 4s.$$

Circumference (distance around) *C* **of a circle,** given the diameter *d* (distance across) or the radius *r* (distance from the center to the circle):

$$C = \pi d$$
$$\text{or } C = 2\pi r.$$

The number π is an infinite decimal that begins 3.14159 . . . , which is often approximated as either 3.14 or as $\frac{22}{7}$.

Area

In each of the following, the area (amount of surface) is *A*. For three-dimensional figures, *A* is the total surface area.

Rectangle, given the length *l* and the width *w*:

$$A = lw.$$

Square, given the length of a side *s*:

$$A = s^2$$

Circle, given the radius *r*:

$$A = \pi r^2$$

Triangle, given the base *b* and the height *h*:

$$A = \tfrac{1}{2} bh$$

Right triangle, given the lengths *a* and *b* of the two sides (legs) that form the right angle:

$$A = \tfrac{1}{2} ab$$

Parallelogram, given the base *b* and the height *h*:

$$A = bh$$

Trapezoid, given the two bases *B* and *b* and the height *h*:

$$A = \tfrac{1}{2} h(B + b)$$

Kite, given the lengths of the two diagonals *D* and *d*:

$$A = \tfrac{1}{2} Dd$$

Regular polygon (polygon with all sides of equal length and all angles of equal measure), given the perimeter *p* and the apothem *a* (the distance from the center of the regular polygon to one of its sides):

$$A = \tfrac{1}{2} ap$$

Equilateral triangle (all sides the same length), given the length of a side *s*:

$$A = \frac{s^2\sqrt{3}}{4}$$

Heron's formula Any **triangle**, given half the length of the perimeter (the semiperimeter) *s* and the lengths of the sides *a*, *b*, and *c*:

$$A = \sqrt{s(s-a)(s-b)(s-c)}.$$

Right circular cylinder (a cylinder with a circular region as its base whose sides make a right angle with the base), given the radius *r* of the base and the height *h* of the cylinder:

$$A = 2\pi r(h + r)$$

Right circular cone (a cone with a circular region as its base and whose altitude makes a right angle with the base), given the radius *r* of the base and the slant height *l* of the cone (the shortest distance from the tip of the cone to the circle of the base):

$$A = \pi r(l + r).$$

Sphere, given the radius *r*:

$$A = 4\pi r^2$$

Volume

In each of the following, the volume (space enclosed) is *V*.

Cube, given the length of an edge *e*:

$$V = e^3$$

Right rectangular prism (box), given the length *l*, the width *w*, and the height *h*:

$$V = lwh$$

Prism, given the area of the base *B* and the height *h*:

$$V = Bh$$

Right circular cylinder, given the radius *r* of the base and the height *h*:

$$V = \pi r^2 h$$

Right circular cone, given the radius *r* of the base and the height *h*:

$$V = \tfrac{1}{3} \pi r^2 h$$

Pyramid, given the area of the base *B* and the height *h*:

$$V = \tfrac{1}{3} Bh$$

Sphere, given the radius *r*:

$$V = \tfrac{4}{3} \pi r^3$$

Algebra

If *a*, *b*, and *x* are any numbers or variables ("unknowns"):

$$(a + b)^2 = a^2 + 2ab + b^2$$
$$(a - b)^2 = a^2 - 2ab + b^2$$
$$x^2 - a^2 = (x + a)(x - a)$$
$$x^3 - a^3 = (x - a)(x^2 + ax + a^2)$$
$$x^3 + a^3 = (x + a)(x^2 - ax + a^2)$$

Milestones in the History of Mathematics

B.C.

c. 30,000 People in Europe begin using scratches or notches to record numbers.

c. 3500 Egyptians develop numeration system that can record very large numbers, with different symbols for ones, tens, hundreds, etc.

c. 2400 A numeration system based on place value (similar to Hindu-Arabic system) is introduced in Mesopotamia.

c. 2000 Mesopotamian mathematicians learn how to solve quadratic equations.

c. 1900 Mesopotamian mathematicians discover what we now call the Pythagorean theorem: The sum of the squares of the legs of a right triangle equals the square of the hypotenuse.

c. 470 Mathematician Hippasus of Metapontum (Greek: c. 500) discovers dodecahedron, a regular solid with 12 faces.

c. 450 Pythagoreans show that some lengths, such as the diagonal of a 1 x 1 square ($\sqrt{2}$), cannot be measured exactly using a side as a unit.

c. 300 Euclid's (Greek: c. 300) *Elements* shows that virtually all parts of mathematics known at the time can be proved from short list of assumptions.

c. 260 In Central America, Maya develop numeration system based on place value.

c. 250 Archimedes (Greek: c. 287–212) establishes important theorems about volumes of solids, calculates an excellent approximation of π, and develops a system for representing very large whole numbers.

c. 230 Apollonius of Perga (Greek: c. 262–190) writes *Conics*, an analysis of such curves as parabola, ellipse, and hyperbola.

A.D.

876 The first-known use of a symbol for zero as a number occurs in India.

c. 1100 Poet, mathematician, and astronomer Omar Khayyám (Persian: 1048-c. 1131) develops geometric methods for solving cubic equations.

1321 Levi ben Gershom (Gersonides; French: 1288–1344) is first to use mathematical induction.

c.1515 Scipione del Ferro (Italian: 1465–1526) discovers algebraic method for solving one form of cubic equations.

1536 Niccolò Tartaglia (Italian: 1499–1557) solves two types of cubic equations.

1545 Girolamo Cardano's (Italian: 1501–76) *Ars Magna* contains Lodovico Ferrari's (Italian: 1522–65) complete solution of the quartic, and a complete solution of the cubic based on Tartaglia's work.

1572 Rafael Bombelli (Italian: 1526–c. 1573) uses complex numbers to solve equations.

1614 John Napier (Scottish: 1550–1617) describes logarithms.

1637 René Descartes (French: 1596–1650) publishes first account of analytic geometry; also discovered by Pierre de Fermat (French: 1601–65).

1639 Gérard Desargues (French: 1591–1661) introduces projective geometry.

1654 Blaise Pascal (French: 1623–62) and Pierre de Fermat develop basic laws of probability.

1666 Sir Isaac Newton (English: 1642–1727) describes his invention of the calculus but does not have it published at this time.

1684 Gottfried Wilhelm Leibniz (German: 1646–1716) publishes first account of his independent discovery of the calculus.

1763 Gaspard Monge (French: 1746–1818) invents descriptive geometry, the mathematical techniques that are basis of mechanical drawing.

1799 Karl Friedrich Gauss (German: 1777–1855) proves fundamental theorem of algebra, which is that every polynomial equation has solution.

Paolo Ruffini (Italian: 1765–1822) offers first proof that not all polynomial equations of fifth degree can be solved by algebraic methods.

1826 Nikolai Ivanovich Lobachevski (Russian: 1793–1856) gives first public address concerning non-Euclidean geometry.

1854 Bernhard Riemann (German: 1826–66) shows that several non-Euclidean geometries are possible.

1877 Georg F.L.P. Cantor (German: 1845–1918) shows that number of points in a line segment is same as number in interior of a square.

1881 Josiah Willard Gibbs (American: 1839–1903) introduces vector analysis.

1882 Ferdinand von Lindemann (German: 1852–1939) proves that the circle cannot be squared with straightedge and compass.

1892 Cantor proves there are at least two types of infinities—specifically, that infinity of real numbers (including all infinite decimals) is bigger than infinity of counting numbers (1, 2, 3, . . .).

1900 David Hilbert (German: 1862–1943) proposes his famous list of 23 unsolved problems.

1931 Kurt Gödel (Austrian-American: 1906–78) shows that mathematical systems are either incomplete or inconsistent: *incomplete* if not all true theorems can be proved from within the system, or *inconsistent* if two contradictory theorems can be proved.

1936 Independently, Alan M. Turing (English: 1912–54) and Alonzo Church (American: 1903–95) discover there is no single infallible method for proving whether a mathematical statement in mathematics is true or false.

1948 Claude E. Shannon (American: 1916–2001) publishes his work on information theory, a general approach to handling communications.

1976 In first major computer-assisted proof, it is shown that any map can be colored with four colors in such a way that no two regions of the same color share common border.

1980 Classification of all finite simple groups, started in 1830, is completed, perhaps longest proof in history of mathematics.

1995 Andrew Wiles (English-American: 1953-) publishes a corrected version of his 1993 proof that the equation $x^n + y^n = z^n$ has no solution for n greater than 2 when x, y, and z are counting numbers—known as Fermat's last theorem.

1998 Thomas C. Hales of the University of Michigan uses a computer to establish that Johannes Kepler's 1611 conjecture that stacking spheres in a face-centered cubic pattern results in the densest concentration of spheres.

1999 Hales proves that, of all possible ways to cover a plane completely, a tiling of regular hexagons uses the least total amount of edge--known as the honeycomb conjecture since honeybees use hexagonal cells to store honey and have long been thought to do so in the way that requires the least wax.

2000 A computer at the University of Giessen in Germany verifies to 400 trillion the 1742 conjecture of Christian Goldbach (Russian: 1690-1764) that every even number greater than 2 is the sum of two primes.

Mathematicians from AT&T Laboratories develop formulas that identify the centers of all small circles packed into a large one provided that the curvature of each is an integral multiple of the smallest circle (curvature is the radius divided into 1).

If a, b, c, and d are any numbers or variables except that neither b nor d can be zero:

$$a/b + c/d = (ad + bc)/bd$$
$$a/b - c/d = (ad - bc)/bd$$
$$a/b \times c/d = ac/bd$$
$$a/b \div c/d = ad/bc\ (c \neq 0)$$

Quadratic formula for the solutions of a second degree polynomial equation in one variable of the form $ax^2 + bx + c = 0$:

$$x = \frac{-b \pm \sqrt{b^2 - 4ac}}{2a}$$

Laws of exponents, given that a, b, x, and y are numbers or variables:

$$a^x a^y = a^{x+y}$$
$$(a^x)^y = a^{xy}$$
$$(ab)^x = a^x b^x$$
$$(a/b)^x = a^x/b^x$$
$$a^x/a^y = a^{x-y}$$
$$a^{-x} = \frac{1}{a^x}$$
$$a^0 = 1$$
$$a^1 = a.$$

Laws of logarithms, given that a, b, x, and y are positive numbers, c is any real number, and $a \neq 1$, $b \neq 1$.

$$\log_a (xy) = \log_a x + \log_a y$$
$$\log_a 1/x = -\log_a x$$
$$\log_a (x/y) = \log_a x - \log_a y$$
$$\log_a (x^c) = c \log_a x$$
$$\log_b x = (\log_a x)/(\log_a b)$$
$$\log_a 1 = 0$$
$$\log_a a = 1$$
$$a^{\log_a x} = x$$
$$\log_a (a^c) = c$$

Graphs

In a rectangular (Cartesian) coordinate plane, where the horizontal axis is x and the vertical axis is y:

Slope of a line, m, given two particular points (x_1, y_1) and (x_2, y_2) where $x_1 \neq x_2$:

$$m = (y_2 - y_1)/(x_2 - x_1).$$

Point-slope equation of a line, given the slope m and a point on the nonvertical line (x_1, y_1):

$$y - y_1 = m(x - x_1).$$

Slope-intercept equation of a line, given the slope m and the y-intercept b (the number on the y axis where the line crosses the y axis):

$$y = mx + b.$$

Distance *d* between any two points, (x_1, y_1) and (x_2, y_2):

$$d = \sqrt{(x_2 - x_1)^2 + (y_2 - y_1)^2}.$$

Trigonometry

In a **right triangle** whose two shorter sides (or legs) are a and b, opposite angles A and B respectively, and whose longest side (or hypotenuse, always the side opposite the right angle, C) is c:

Pythagorean theorem:

$$c^2 = a^2 + b^2.$$

Trigonometric functions:

sine: $\sin A = a/c$
cosine: $\cos A = b/c$
tangent: $\tan A = a/b$
cotangent: $\cot A = b/a$
secant: $\sec A = c/b$
cosecant: $\csc A = c/a$.

In any triangle labeled such that side a is opposite angle A, side b is opposite angle B, and side c is opposite angle C:

Angle sum:

$$A + B + C = 180°$$

Fractions, Decimals, and Percents

To find the equivalent of a fraction in decimal form, divide the numerator (top number) by the denominator (bottom number). To change from a decimal to a percent, multiply by 100. To change from a percent to a decimal, divide by 100.

Fraction	Decimal	Percent
1/16	0.0625	6.25%
1/8 (= 2/16)	0.125	12.5
3/16	0.1875	18.75
1/4 (= 2/8; = 4/16)	0.25	25.0
5/16	0.3125	31.25
1/3	0.3 . . .	33 1/3
3/8 (= 6/16)	0.375	37.5
7/16	0.4375	43.75
1/2 (= 2/4; = 4/8; = 8/16)	0.5	50.0
9/16	0.5625	56.25
5/8 (= 10/16)	0.625	62.5
2/3	0.6 . . .	66 2/3
11/16	0.6875	68.75
3/4 (= 6/8; = 12/16)	0.75	75.0
13/16	0.8125	81.25
7/8 (= 14/16)	0.875	87.5
15/16	0.9375	93.75
1 (=2/2;=4/4;=8/8;=16/16)	1.0	100.0

Large Numbers

There are two primary naming systems for large numbers. The United States and France (among others) use one system, while Germany and Great Britain use the other. (Googol and googolplex, invented by the nephew of mathematician and author Edward Kasner, are rarely used outside the United States.) (See also "Standard Weights and Measures.")

Number of zeroes after 1	American name	British name
6	million	million
9	billion	milliard
12	trillion	billion
15	quadrillion	1,000 billion
18	quintillion	trillion
21	sextillion	1,000 trillion
24	septillion	quadrillion
27	octillion	1,000 quadrillion
30	nonillion	quintillion
33	decillion	1,000 quintillion
100	googol	googol
googol	googolplex	googolplex

Law of sines:

$$(\sin A)/a = (\sin B)/b = (\sin C)/c$$

Law of cosines:

$$c^2 = a^2 + b^2 - 2ab \cos C$$

If x is any real number or a measure of an angle in degrees, the following statements are true:

Defining trigonometric identities:

$\tan x = \sin x/\cos x$ $\csc x = 1/\sin x$
$\cot x = \cos x/\sin x$ $\cot x = 1/\tan x$
$\sec x = 1/\cos x$

Trigonometric identities of symmetry:

$\sin(-x) = -\sin x$ $\cos(-x) = \cos x$
$\tan(-x) = -\tan x$ $\cot(-x) = -\cot x$
$\sec(-x) = \sec x$ $\csc(-x) = -\csc x$.

Pythagorean identities:

$\sin^2 x + \cos^2 x = 1$
$\tan^2 x + 1 = \sec^2 x$
$\cot^2 x + 1 = \csc^2 x$

Sum and difference formulas: If x and y are any two real numbers or measures of angles:

$\sin(x + y) = \sin x \cos y + \cos x \sin y$
$\cos(x + y) = \cos x \cos y - \sin x \sin y$
$\tan(x + y) = (\tan x + \tan y)/(1 - \tan x \tan y)$
$\sin(x - y) = \sin x \cos y - \cos x \sin y$
$\cos(x - y) = \cos x \cos y + \sin x \sin y$
$\tan(x - y) = (\tan x - \tan y)/(1 + \tan x \tan y)$.

Prefixes Used in the International System of Units (SI)

Prefix	Abbreviation	Factor by which unit is multipled	Scientific Notation
Yotta-	Y	1,000,000,000,000,000,000,000,000	10^{24}
Zetta-	Z	1,000,000,000,000,000,000,000	10^{21}
Exa-	E	1,000,000,000,000,000,000	10^{18}
Peta-	P	1,000,000,000,000,000	10^{15}
Tera-	T	1,000,000,000,000	10^{12}
Giga-	G	1,000,000,000	10^{9}
Mega-	M	1,000,000	10^{6}
Kilo-	k	1,000	10^{3}
Hecto-	h	100	10^{2}
Deka-	da	10	10^{1}
Deci-	d	0.1	10^{-1}
Centi-	c	0.01	10^{-2}
Milli-	m	0.001	10^{-3}
Micro-	μ	0.000 001	10^{-6}
Nano-	n	0.000 000 001	10^{-9}
Pico-	p	0.000 000 000 001	10^{-12}
Femto-	f	0.000 000 000 000 001	10^{-15}
Atto-	a	0.000 000 000 000 000 001	10^{-18}
Zepto-	z	0.000 000 000 000 000 000 001	10^{-21}
Yocto-	y	0.000 000 000 000 000 000 000 001	10^{-24}

STANDARD WEIGHTS & MEASURES

▶SYSTEMS OF MEASUREMENT

There are two widely used measurement systems. Most of the world uses a system known as the metric system, or the International System, abbreviated SI from *Système Internationale,* its name in French. The United States continues to use a system called U.S. customary measure, which derives from (and differs from) the British imperial series of weights and measures. From time to time, our government has taken steps to change from the customary system to the International System, but these efforts have had limited success. Metric measure is legal in the United States, but nearly everyone continues to use the customary system in everyday use. The International System is generally used in scientific pursuits and increasingly in international trade.

The following tables show first the U.S. customary system, then the International System, and finally some important conversion factors between the two.

Length or Distance

U.S. customary system

1 foot (ft.)	=	12 inches
1 yard (yd.)	=	3 feet = 36 inches
1 rod (rd.)	=	5.5 yards = 16.5 feet
1 furlong (fur.)	=	40 rods = 220 yards
	=	660 feet
1 mile (mi.)	=	8 furlongs
	=	1,760 yards = 5,280 feet

An international nautical mile has been defined as 6,076.1155 feet.

International System

The basic unit for length is the meter, which is slightly longer than the customary yard. Other units of length are decimal subdivisions or multiples of the meter.

1 decimeter (dm)	=	10 centimeters
	=	0.1 meter
1 centimeter (cm)	=	0.01 meter
1 millimeter (mm)	=	0.1 centimeter
	=	0.001 meter
1 micrometer (μm)	=	0.001 millimeter
	=	0.0001 centimeter
	=	0.000001 meter
1 angstrom (Å)	=	0.0001 micrometers
	=	0.0000001 milimeter

1 dekameter (dam)	=	10 meters
1 hectometer (hm)	=	10 dekameters
	=	100 meters
1 kilometer	=	10 hectometers
	=	100 dekameters
	=	1,000 meters

Conversions

In 1959 the relationship between between customary and international measures of length was officially defined as follows:

0.0254 meter (exactly)	=	1 inch
0.0245 meter x 12	=	0.3048 meter
	=	1 international foot

This definition, which makes many conversions simple, defines a foot that is shorter (by about 6 parts in 10 million) than the survey foot, which had earlier been defined as exactly 1200/3937, or 0.3048006, meter.

Following the international foot standard, the major equivalents are as listed below:

1 in.	=	2.54 cm = 0.0254 m
1 ft.	=	30.48 cm = .3048 m
1 yd.	=	91.44 cm = 0.9144 m
1 mi.	=	1,609.344 m = 1.609344 km
1 cm	=	0.3937 in.
1 m	=	1.093613 yd. = 3.28084 ft.
1 km	=	0.62137 mi.

Area

U.S. customary system

Areas are derived from lengths as follows:

1 square foot	=	144 square inches
1 square yard	=	9 sq. ft.
1 square rod (rd.^{2})	=	30.25 square yards
	=	272.25 square feet
1 acre	=	160 square rods
	=	4,840 square yards
	=	43,560 sq. ft.
1 square mile	=	640 acres
1 section	=	1 mile square
1 township	=	6 miles square
	=	36 square miles

Simplified Conversion Table (alphabetical order)

To convert	to	multiply by:
centimeters	feet	0.0328
centimeters	inches	0.3937
cubic cm	cubic in.	0.061
cubic feet	cubic m	0.0283
degrees	radians	0.0175
feet	cm	30.5
feet	meters	0.305
gallons	liters	3.785
galon of water	pound of water	8.3
grams	ounces	0.035
inches	cm	2.54
kilograms	pounds	2.2
kilometers	feet	3,281
kilometers	miles	0.62
knots	mi./hr.	1.15
liters	gallons	0.264
liters	pints	2.1
meters	feet	3.28
miles	km	1.61
ounces	grams	28.35
pounds	kg	0.454

International System

1 sq. millimeter (mm^2)	=	1,000,000 sq. micrometers
1 sq. centimeter (cm^2)	=	100 mm^2
1 sq. decimeter (dm^2)	=	100 cm^2
1 sq. meter (m^2)	=	10,000 cm^2
1 are (a)	=	100 m^2
1 hectare (ha)	=	100 ares
	=	10,000 m^2
1 sq kilometer (km^2)	=	100 hectares
	=	1,000,000 m^2

Conversions

1 square inch	=	6.4516 cm^2
1 square foot	=	929.0304 cm^2
	=	0.09290304 m^2
1 square yard	=	8,361.2736 cm^2
	=	0.83612736 m^2
1 acre	=	4,046.8564 m^2
	=	0.40468564 hectares
1 square mile	=	2,589,988.11 m^2
	=	258.998811 hectares
	=	2.58998811 km^2
1 cm^2	=	0.1550003 sq. in.
1 m^2	=	1,550.003 sq. in.
	=	10.76391 sq. ft.
	=	1.195990 sq. yds.
1 hectare	=	107,639.1 sq. ft.
	=	11,959.90 sq. yds.
	=	2.4710538 acres
1 km^2	=	247.10538 acres
	=	0.3861006 sq. miles

Cubic Measure

U.S. customary system

1 cu foot (ft.^{3})	=	1,728 cubic inches (in.^{3})
1 cubic yard (yd.^{3})	=	27 cubic feet (ft.^{3})

International System

1 cubic centimeter (cm^3)	=	1,000 cubic millimeters (mm^3)
1 cubic decimeter (dm^3)	=	1,000 cubic centimeters (cm^3)
1 cubic meter (m^3)	=	1,000 cubic decimeters (dm^3)
	=	1,000,000 cubic centimeters (cm^3)

Cubic centimeter is sometimes abbreviated cc and is used in fluid measure interchangeably with milliliter (ml).

Conversions

1 in.^{3}	=	16.387064 cm^3
1 ft.^{3}	=	28.316846592 cm^3
	=	0.028316847 cm^3
1 yd.^{3}	=	764,554.857984 cm^3
	=	0.764554858 m^3
1 cm^3	=	0.06102374 in.^{3}
1 m^3	=	61,023.74 in.^{3}
	=	35.31467 ft.^{3}
	=	1.307951 yd.^{3}

Fluid Volume

U.S. customary system

A gallon is equal to 231 cubic inches of liquid or capacity.

1 tablespoon (tbs.)	=	3 teaspoons (tsp.)
	=	0.5 fluid ounce (fl. oz.)
1 cup	=	8 fl. oz.
1 pint (pt.)	=	2 cups = 16 fl. oz.
1 quart (qt.)	=	2 pt. = 4 cups
	=	32 fl. oz.
1 gallon (gal.)	=	4 qt. = 8 pt. = 16 cups
1 bushel (bu.)	=	8 gal. = 32 qt.

International System

Fluid-volume measurements are directly tied to cubic measure. One milliliter of fluid occupies a volume of 1 cubic centimeter. A liter of fluid (slightly more than the customary quart) occupies a volume of 1 cubic decimeter, or 1,000 cubic centimeters.

1 centiliter (cL)	=	10 mililiters (mL)
1 deciliter	=	10 cl = 100 mL
1 liter (L)	=	10 dl = 1,000 mL
1 dekaliter (daL)	=	10 L
1 hectoliter (hL)	=	10 daL = 100 L
1 kiloliter (kL)	=	10 hl = 1,000 L

Conversions

1 fluid ounce	=	29.573528 mL = 0.02957 L
1 cup	=	236.588 mL = 0.236588 L
1 pint	=	473.176 mL = 0.473176 L
1 quart	=	946.3529 mL = 0.9463529 L
1 gallon	=	3,785.41 mL = 3.78541 L
1 milliliter	=	0.0338 fluid ounce
1 liter	=	33.814 fluid ounces
	=	4.2268 cups = 2.113 pints
	=	1.0567 quarts = 0.264 gallon

Dry Volume

Conversions

1 pint, dry	=	33.600 cu. in. = 0.551 L
1 quart, dry	=	67.201 cu. in. = 1.101 L

Mass & Weight

Mass and weight are often confused. Mass is a measure of the quantity of matter in an object and does not vary with changes in altitude or in gravitational force (as on the Moon or another planet). Weight, on the other hand, is a measure of the force of gravity on an object and so does change with altitude or gravitational force.

U.S. customary system

In customary measure it is more common to measure weight than mass. The most common customary system of weight is avoirdupois:

1 pound (lb.)	=	16 ounces (oz.)
1 (short) hundred-weight (cwt.)	=	100 lb.
1 (short) ton	=	20 hundredweights
	=	2,000 lb.
1 long hundred-weight	=	112 lb.
1 long ton	=	20 long hundredweights
	=	2,240 lb.

A different system called troy weight is used to weigh precious metals. In troy weight the ounce is slightly larger than in avoirdupois, but there are only 12 ounces to the troy pound.

International System

Instead of weight, the International System uses measures of mass. The original basic unit was the gram, which was defined as the mass of 1 milliliter (= 1 cm3) of water at 4 degrees Celsius (about 39ºF). Today the official measure of mass is a specific metal object defined as the standard kilogram.

1 centigram (cg)	=	10 milligrams (mg)
1 decigram (dg)	=	10 cg = 100 mg
1 gram (g)	=	10 dg = 100 cg = 1000 mg
1 kilogram (kg)	=	10 hectograms (hg)
	=	100 dekagrams (dag)
	=	1,000 g
1 metric ton (t)	=	1000 kg

Conversions

Since mass and weight are identical at standard conditions (sea level on Earth), grams and other International System units of mass are often used as measures of weight or converted into customary units of weight. Under standard conditions:

1 ounce	=	28.3495 grams
1 pound	=	453.59 grams
	=	0.45359 kilogram
1 short ton	=	907.18 kilograms
	=	0.907 metric ton
1 milligram	=	0.000035 ounce
1 gram	=	0.03527 ounce
1 kilogram	=	35.27 ounces
	=	2.2046 pounds
1 metric ton	=	2,204.6 pounds
	=	1.1023 short tons

Time

Customary and International System

The International System in 1967 adopted a second that is based on the microwaves emitted by the vibrations of hot cesium atoms. A second (abbreviated sec. in customary usage, s in SI usage) is the time it takes the atoms to vibrate exactly 9,192,631,770 times. In the customary measure of time, the day is divided into 24 hours, the hour into 60 minutes, and the minute into 60 seconds. Since the Earth's rotation is gradually slowing, scientists must periodically add a second to a day to keep the year in sequence with their clocks. The change is so small that for almost all practical purposes an International System second and a customary second are the same.

Decimal fractions of time are used to measure smaller time intervals:

millisecond (ms)	=	0.001 second (10^{-3})
microsecond (μs)	=	0.000001 second (10^{-6})
nanosecond (ns)	=	0.000000001 second (10^{-9})
picosecond (ps)	=	0.000000000001 second (10^{-12})

Temperature

U.S. customary system

In the U.S, temperature is usually measured in degrees Fahrenheit: water freezes at 32°F and boils at 212°F. The basis of the Fahrenheit scale was 0°F, the coldest temperature that its originator, G.D. Fahrenheit (1686–1736), could obtain under laboratory conditions.

International System

The Swedish astronomer Anders Celsius (1701–44) devised the temperature scale that bears his name in 1742. On the Celsius scale, water freezes at 0°C and boils at 100°C. Very low temperatures are measured on the Kelvin scale, named for William Thomson, Baron Kelvin (1824–1907). It is also called the absolute scale because absolute zero—0°K (-273.15° C)—is the temperature at which no body can give up heat. The interval of a degree Kelvin equals the interval of a degree Celsius. At very high temperatures, differences between the Kelvin and Celsius scales are insignificant.

Conversions

Fahrenheit to Celsius: Subtract 32 from the temperature and multiply the difference by 5; then divide the product by 9. The formula is: $C = \frac{5}{9}(F-32)$

Fahrenheit and Celsius Temperature Conversions

You can roughly convert a Celsius temperature to Fahrenheit by doubling the number and adding 30. For example, 20°C Celsius is approximately 70°F. (Conversely, subtract 30 from Fahrenheit temperature and divide by two for a Celsius temperature.) For a closer equivalent, consult the table below.

Celsius	Fahrenheit	Fahrenheit	Celsius
-45°	= -49°	-45°	= -42.8°
-40°	= -40°	-40°	= -40.0°
-35°	= -31°	-35°	= -37.2°
-30°	= -22°	-30°	= -34.4°
-25°	= -13°	-25°	= -31.7°
-20°	= -4°	-20°	= -28.9°
-15°	= 5°	-15°	= -26.1°
-10°	= 14°	-10°	= -23.3°
-5°	= 23°	-5°	= -20.6°
0°	= 32°	0°	= -17.8°
5°	= 41°	5°	= -15.0°
10°	= 50°	10°	= -12.2°
15°	= 59°	15°	= -9.4°
20°	= 68°	20°	= -6.7°
25°	= 77°	25°	= -3.9°
30°	= 86°	30°	= -1.1°
35°	= 95°	32°	= 0.0°
40°	= 104°	35°	= 1.7°
45°	= 113°	40°	= 4.4°
50°	= 122°	45°	= 7.2°
55°	= 131°	50°	= 10.0°
60°	= 140°	55°	= 12.8°
65°	= 149°	60°	= 15.6°
70°	= 158°	65°	= 18.3°
75°	= 167°	70°	= 21.1°
80°	= 176°	75°	= 23.9°
85°	= 185°	80°	= 26.7°
90°	= 194°	85°	= 29.4°
95°	= 203°	90°	= 32.2°
100°	= 212°	95°	= 35.0°
125°	= 257°	100°	= 37.8°
150°	= 302°	105°	= 40.6°
175°	= 347°	110°	= 43.3°
200°	= 392°	212°	= 100.0°
225°	= 437°	225°	= 107.2°
250°	= 482°	250°	= 121.1°
275°	= 527°	275°	= 135.0°
300°	= 572°	300°	= 148.9°
325°	= 617°	325°	= 162.8°
350°	= 662°	350°	= 176.7°
375°	= 707°	375°	= 190.6°
400°	= 752°	400°	= 204.4°
425°	= 797°	425°	= 218.3°
450°	= 842°	450°	= 232.2°
475°	= 887°	475°	= 246.1°

Celsius to Fahrenheit: Multiply the temperature by 1.8 (or $\frac{9}{5}$), then add 32. The formula is: $F = \frac{9}{5}C + 32$
Celsius to Kelvin: Add 273.15 to the temperature The formula is: K= C+273.15

Force, Work/Energy, Power

U.S. customary system

The foot/pound/second system of reckoning includes the following units:

Kelvin, Celsius, and Fahrenheit Equivalents

Characteristic	K	C°	F°
Absolute zero	0	-273.15°	-459.7°
Freezing point, water	273.15	0°	32°
Traditional human body temperature	310.15	37°	98.6°
Boiling point, water	373.15	100°	212°

slug = the mass to which a force of 1 poundal will give an acceleration of 1 foot per second per second (= approximately 32.17 lbs.)
poundal = fundamental unit of force
foot-pound = the work done when a force of 1 poundal produces a movement of 1 foot
foot-pound/second = the unit of power equal to 1 foot/pound per second

Another common unit of power is horsepower, which is equal to 550 foot-pounds per second.

Thermal work or energy is often measured in British thermal units (Btu), One Btu is defined as the energy required to increase the temperature of 1 pound of water by 1 degree Fahrenheit. The Btu is equal to about 0.778 foot-pound.

International System

In physics, compound measurements of force, work or energy, and power are essential. There are two parallel systems using International System units: the centimeter/gram/second system (cgs) is used for small measurements, and the meter/kilogram/second system (mks) is used for larger measurements. The mks system is the official one for SI. They are described below.

Measurement of force

cgs unit	dyne (dy)	The force required to accelerate a mass of 1 g 1 cm/s² (cm/s² means "centimeter per second per second")
mks unit	newton (N)	The force required to accelerate a mass of 1 kg l m/s²

Measurement of work or energy

cgs unit	erg	The dyne-centimeter, i.e., the work done when a force of 1 dy produces a movement of 1 cm
mks unit	joule (j)	The newton-meter, i.e., the work done when a force of 1 N produces a movement of 1 m (=10,000,000 ergs)

Heat energy is also measured using the calorie (cal), which is defined as the energy required to increase the temperature of 1 cubic centimeter (1 ml) of water by 1 degree C. One calorie is equal to about 4.184 joules. The kilocalorie (Kcal or Cal) is equal to 1,000 calories and is the unit in which the energy values of food are measured. This more familiar unit, also commonly referred to as a Calorie, is equal to about 4,184 joules.

Measurement of power

cgs unit	erg/second	A rate of 1 erg per second
mks unit	watt (W)	The joule/second, i.e., a rate of 1 joule per second

Conversions

Measurement of force

1 poundal	=	13,889 dynes
	=	0.13889 newtons
1 dyne	=	0.000072 poundals
1 newton	=	7.2 poundals

Measurement of work or energy

1 foot-pound	=	1,356 joules
British thermal unit	=	1,055 joules
	=	252 calories
1 joule	=	0.0007374 ft.-lbs.
1 calorie	=	0.003968 Btu
1 Kilocalorie	≐	3.968 Btu

Measurement of power

1 foot-pound/second	=	1.3564 watts
1 horsepower	=	746 watts
	=	0.746 kilowatts
1 watt	=	0.73725 ft.-lb/sec.
	=	0.00134 horsepower
1 kilowatt	=	737.25 ft.-lb./sec.
	=	1.34 horsepower

Electrical Measure

Originally, the basic unit of quantity in electricity was the coulomb. A coulomb is equal to the passage of 6.25×10^{18} electrons past a given point in an electrical system.

The unit of electrical flow is the ampere, which is equal to a coulomb/second, i.e., the flow of 1 coulomb per second. The ampere is analogous in electrical measure to a unit of flow such as gallons-per-minute in physical measure. In SI, the ampere is taken as the basic unit.

The unit for measuring electrical potential energy is the volt, which is defined as 1 joule/coulomb, i.e., 1 joule of energy per coulomb of electricity. The volt is analogous to a measure of pressure in a water system.

The unit for measuring electrical power is the watt as defined in the previous section. Power in watts *(P)* is the product of the electrical flow in amperes *(I)* and the potential electrical energy in volts *(E)*:

$$P = IE.$$

Since the watt is such a small unit for practical applications, the kilowatt (= 1,000 watts) is often used. A kilowatt-hour is the power of 1,000 watts over an hour's time.

The unit for measuring electrical resistance is the ohm, which is the resistance offered by a circuit to the flow of 1 ampere being driven by the force of 1 volt. It is derived from Ohm's law, which defines the relationship between flow or current (amperes), potential energy (volts), and resistance (ohms). It states that the current in amperes *(I)* is proportional to potential energy in volts *(E)* and inversely proportional to resistance in ohms *(R)*. Thus, when voltage and resistance are known, amperage can be calculated by the simple formula

$$I = \frac{E}{R}$$

Measure of Angles and Arcs

Angles are measured by systems based on arcs (portions) of circles. Arcs of a circle can be measured by length, but they are also often measured by angles. In the latter case, the measure of the arc is the same as the measure of an angle whose vertex is at the center of the circle and whose sides pass through the ends of the arc. Such an angle is said to be subtended by the arc.

The most commonly used angle measure is degree measure. One degree is the angle subtended by an arc that is 1/360 of a circle. This is an ancient system of measurement probably originally developed by Sumerian astronomers. These astronomers used a numeration system based on 60 (60 × 6 = 360), as well as a 360-day year. They divided the day into 12 equal periods of 30 smaller periods each (12 × 30 = 360) and used roughly the same system for dividing the circle. Even when different years and numeration systems were adopted by later societies, astronomers continued to use a variation of the Sumerian system for angles.

1 degree (1°)	=	60 minutes (60')
	=	3,600 seconds (3,600")
1 minute	=	60 seconds

When two lines are perpendicular to each other, they form four angles of the same size, which are called right angles. Two right angles make up a line, which in this context is considered a straight angle.

1 right angle = 90°
1 straight angle = 180°

While this system is workable for most purposes, it is artificial. Mathematicians discovered that using a natural system of angle measurement produces results that make better sense in mathematical and many scientific applications. This system is called radian measure. Radian measure is considered a supplement to SI. One radian is the measure of the angle subtended by an arc of a circle that is exactly as long as the radius of the circle.

1 radian = about 57° 17' 45"

The circumference, *C*, of a circle is given by the formula $C = 2\pi r$, where π is a number (approximately 3.14159) and r is the radius. Therefore, a semicircle whose radius is 1 is π units long, which implies that there are π radians in a straight angle. Many of the angles commonly encountered are measured in multiples of π radians:

0° = 0 radians	90° = π/2 radians
30° = π/6 radians	180° = π radians
45° = π/4 radians	270° = 3π/2 radians
60° = π/3 radians	360° = 2π radians

To convert from radians to degrees, use the formula *t radians*= $(180/\pi)\ t°$. To convert from degrees to radians, use the formula

$$w° = (\pi/180)\,w \text{ radians.}$$

The U.S. artillery uses the mil to measure angles. A mil is the angle subtended by an arc that is 1/6400 of a circle.

1 mil = 0.05625°= 3' 22.5"
1 mil = almost 0.001 radian

The Environment

The modern environmental movement in the United States dates from Earth Day 1970 (April 22), when the American public first began to take stock of the ecological devastation going on around them. Then there were no pollution controls on cars; people and municipalities dumped untreated sewage into the nation's rivers, some of which were so saturated with chemical waste that they actually caught fire; and industrial cities were routinely shrouded with thick acrid smoke.

Many of these problems have been effectively addressed and dramatically diminished. Today the Environmental Protection Agency (EPA), established in 1970, routinely monitors air quality at thousands of sites around the country. Toxic emissions from smokestacks at smelters, factories, and garbage incinerators have been sharply reduced. Mandatory pollution control standards on automobiles have led to an overwhelming drop in lead emissions. Recycling as a way of reducing solid waste has taken hold in cities and towns throughout the country. Many people, however, oppose strong environmental safeguards on economic and other grounds, making it difficult to improve and enforce regulations. Growing population pressures also create environmental threats, particularly to natural habitats, arable soil, and drinking water supplies.

▶GLOBAL WARMING

Most climatologists are convinced that over the past century the Earth has begun to warm significantly—about 1.1°F (0.6°C)—and that at its current rate, it is likely to warm as much as 2.5° to 10°F (1.4° to 5.8°C) by the year 2100 (as compared to 1990). Analyses of data such as tree rings, ice cores, growth of corals, and historical records indicate that in the Northern Hemisphere it is likely that the 1990s were the warmest decade, and 1998 the warmest year, in the past 1,000 years. Globally, the Earth's average surface temperature in 1998 was the highest since thermometer records were first kept in the mid-19th century, as the effects of El Niño heightened the underlying warming trend. If global temperatures continue to increase, the potential devastation is staggering. Worldwide temperatures have risen only 9°F (5°C) since the end of the last ice age 12,000 years ago. Additional warming could cause melting of polar ice caps, setting off a chain of events that begins with a rise in sea level worldwide and could end with the destruction of water supplies, forests, and agriculture in many parts of the world.

Global warming occurs when certain gases in the atmosphere prevent sunlight from being reflected from the Earth. Ordinarily, sunlight that reaches the surface of the Earth is partly absorbed and partly reflected. The absorbed light heats the surface and is later emitted from the surface as infrared radiation. Gases that are not transparent to infrared radiation (carbon dioxide is one) collect this heat and keep it in the atmosphere, hence their name, greenhouse gases. The Earth's atmosphere is only 0.03 percent carbon dioxide, but combined with other gases, this is enough to trap 30 percent of the reflected heat (the rest is radiated out to space), and maintain the Earth's average temperature at about 59°F (15°C).

In a 1996 report, the Intergovernmental Panel on Climate Change (IPCC), a group of 2,500 scientists commissioned by the U.N., concluded that "the balance of evidence suggests that there is a discernible human influence on global climate." The most recent (2001) IPCC report reinforces this conclusion, asserting that "most of the observed warming over the last 50 years is likely to have been due to the increase in greenhouse gas concentrations."

The increased presence of carbon dioxide is due primarily to the burning of carbon fuels including oil, coal, and natural gas, as well as burning trees for deforestation. CFCs, now being phased out by many countries, are used as aerosols, in air-conditioning units, and in various industrial processes. Methane is emitted by decomposing organic wastes, natural-gas leaks, and fermenting rice paddies. The primary sources of nitrogen oxides are automobile exhaust and industrial smoke stacks. At a December 1997 conference in Kyoto, Japan, representatives of more than 150 countries reached tentative agreement to reduce greenhouse gases an average of 5 percent worldwide (from 1990 levels) by the year 2010. By September 2003, most of the world's industrialized nations had ratified the Protocol. President Bush, however, has emphatically refused to ratify the agreement, even though a 2002 report from his own administration stated that human actions were definitely contributing to global warming, and warned that several American ecosystems were in imminent danger of being destroyed by this trend.

Global warming produces complex and interrelated effects that could under some scenarios spell environmental disaster. Some of the elements of global warming are:

Weather patterns Climatologists think that higher global temperatures and changing precipitation patterns are already disrupting local weather in places around the world. For example, the IPCC (2001) reports that more intense precipitation events (storms) have likely increased in the Northern Hemisphere, including the United States, and are very likely to increase in most areas of the world in this century. The U.S. National Climatic Data Center in Asheville, NC reports that Northern Hemisphere snow cover has been below normal since 1987, and that extreme extratropical cyclone activity over the North Atlantic has increased since 1988.

Changed weather patterns can have a severe impact on crops and other forms of vegetation, as well as on the animals that depend on them. Rising temperatures also enable insects and fungal pests to migrate to previously unaffected regions. Long-lived plants, however, such as trees, spread much more slowly in the face of climate change.

Warming patterns Although global warming will cause an increase in average world temperatures, this increase is not expected to be uniform. In general, climatologists expect greater warming during winter months and at high latitudes (closer to the poles than to the equator). Some places will experience more severe effects than others. For example, the number of +95°F days in Rio de Janeiro would increase tenfold, from 5 to 52 days. Rome would go from 6 to 55 days and Tokyo from 5 to 41.

Higher temperatures have an even more dire effect than increased numbers of hot days. Increased heat expands the volume of ocean water,

Major Events in the History of the Environment

1775 Percival Pott observes that chimney sweeps develop cancer as a result of their contact with soot, the first recognition of environmental factors on cancer.
1864 George Perkins Marsh (American: 1801-81) publishes *Man and Nature*, the first textbook on conservation and the first detailed study of human influence on the environment.
1872 Robert Angus Smith (Scottish: 1817-84) describes acid rain.
1885 Yellowstone, world's first national park, opens.
1892 Canada establishes first national park at Banff, Alberta.
1895 Svante Arrhenius (Swedish, 1859-1927) is the first person to investigate effect of increasing carbon dioxide in the atmosphere on global climate.
1903 John Muir (Scottish-American: 1838-1914) founds the Sierra Club.
1905 U.S. president Theodore Roosevelt opens the first national refuge, Pelican Island in Florida, to protect nesting sites of brown pelicans.
U.S. Forest Service established.
National Audubon Society founded.
1911 Canada, Japan, Russia, and the United States sign treaty to limit the harvest of northern fur seals.
1916 National Park Service established.
1928 Boulder Canyon project (Hoover Dam) authorized to bring irrigation, electric power, and flood control system to western United States.
1933 Tennessee Valley Authority created to develop the Tennessee River for flood control, navigation, electric power, agriculture, and forestry.
1939 Paul Müller (Swiss: 1899-1965) discovers insecticidal properties of DDT.
1952 Smog blamed for 4,000 deaths in London.
1955 Link between exposure to asbestos and lung cancer established.
1957 Nuclear wastes stored by the Soviet Union in a remote mountain region of the Urals explode; radioactive contamination affects thousands of square miles; several villages permanently evacuated.
1961 Investigations in Scandinavia and the U.S. Adirondacks confirm that acid rain kills some species living in lakes.
1962 *Silent Spring* by Rachel Carson (American: 1907-64) attacks pesticide use and stimulates major environmental movement.
1963 Congress passes first Clean Air Act, allocating $95 million to local, state, and national air pollution control efforts.
1964 Congress passes Wilderness Act, setting up the National Wilderness Preservation System.
1965 Congress passes Highway Beautification Act, banning many highway billboards.
Congress passes Water Quality Act, giving federal government power to set water standards.
Congress passes the Solid Waste Disposal Act, its first major solid waste legislation.
1966 Congress passes Rare and Endangered Species Act.
1967 S. Manabe and R.T. Wetherald predict that increased amounts of carbon dioxide in the atmosphere will lead to global warming.
1968 Congress passes Wild and Scenic Rivers Act, identifying areas of scenic beauty for preservation and recreation.
1970 First Earth Day celebrated on April 22.
Environmental Protection Agency created.
1972 Congress passes Clean Water Act, forbidding discharges of pollutants into navigable waters.
Oregon passes the nation's first bottle recycling law.
The EPA bars registration and interstate sales of DDT because of its persistence in the environment and accumulation in the food chain.
1973 Representatives of 80 nations sign the Convention of International Trade in Endangered Species of Wild Fauna and Flora, which prohibits commercial trade in 375 endangered species of wild animals.
1974 F. Sherwood Rowland and Mario Molinas warn that chlorofluorocarbons (CFCs) are destroying the ozone layer.
1976 Congress passes Toxic Substances Control Act to control hazardous industrial chemicals.
1978 Community of Love Canal, near Niagara, N.Y., evacuated after hazardous waste dumps are uncovered. EPA declares site safe in 1990.
1979 Nuclear reactor at Three Mile Island, near Harrisburg, Pa., suffers partial meltdown; radiation confined to reactor dome.
1980 Congress passes Comprehensive Environmental Response, Compensation and Liability Act (the "Superfund") to clean up hazardous waste sites.
1984 More than 2,000 die and thousands more are injured by toxic gas from an accident at the U.S.-owned Union Carbide plant in Bhopal, India.
1985 British scientists discover that a "hole" in the ozone layer develops over Antarctica each winter.
The U.S. sets up a Conservation Reserve Program to remove environmentally sensitive farmland from agricultural use.
1986 A worldwide ban on whaling begins.
Chernobyl nuclear reactor number 4 explodes and burns, causing 31 deaths within days, shortening the lives of thousands, and forcing the evacuation of hundreds of square miles in Soviet Ukraine for an unknown length of time.
1988 The U.S. Ocean Dumping Ban Act mandates an end to ocean dumping of industrial waste and sewage sludge.
1989 Exxon *Valdez* grounds, leaking 35,000 tons of oil into Prince William Sound, Alaska.
Thirteen industrial nations agree to halt production of CFCs by the year 2000.
1991 Iraq dumps over a million tons of oil from occupied Kuwait into Persian Gulf.
1992 Representatives from 178 countries attend the first Earth Summit in Rio de Janeiro, where they sign treaties pledging to increase the diversity of animal and plant species and to halt global warming.
1994 U.S. Fish and Wildlife Service recommends that status of American bald eagle be reduced from "endangered" to "threatened" in most of the U.S..
1995 The United Nations Working Group I of the Intergovernmental Panel on Climate Change endorses global warming, reporting that "the balance of evidence suggests that there is a discernible human influence on global climate."
1996 The U.S. National Oceanic and Atmospheric Administration reports that measurements show that a global campaign to lower production of chemicals that damage the ozone layer has succeeded and that by 2010 the ozone layer will have begun to recover and by 2050 the Antarctic ozone "hole" will have closed.
1997 Representatives from more than 150 countries meet in Kyoto, Japan, where they agree to reduce emissions of greenhouse gases 5.2 percent worldwide by 2010.
2001 The Intergovernmental Panel on Climate Change (IPCC) reports that there is new and stronger evidence that most of the warming in the last half century is due to human activities.
2002 The United Nations World Summit on Sustainable Development in Johannesburg, South Africa, agrees on a program of sustainable development to reduce poverty while protecting the earth's natural resources.

and also increases flows to the oceans through melting of glaciers and ice caps, leading to a rise in sea level.

Sea level rise Climatologists generally expect the sea level to rise between 3.4 inches and almost three feet (.09 to .88 meters) by the end of this century (as compared to 1990). Generally speaking, a rise in sea level would be uniform, both geographically and seasonally, because sea level is a global phenomenon. The impact of such a rise, however, would vary greatly from place to place. A three-foot (1 m) rise would inundate 7,000 square miles (18,000 km^2) of dry land—an area the size of Massachusetts—in the United States, mostly in the Southeast. It would also destroy a comparable area of coastal wetlands, erode recreational beaches 100 to 200 meters, exacerbate coastal flooding, and increase the salinity of aquifers and estuaries. It is likely that the people of an industrialized continental nation such as the United States could sustain the population shifts caused by such climatic changes. However, an estimated one-third of the world's population—about 1.75 billion people, today—lives within 40 miles of the sea, mostly along low-lying floodplains and estuaries. How the low-lying Bangladesh or the island nations of the Pacific can or will respond to such forces is impossible to see.

Changing temperatures and precipitation patterns may also lead to basic changes in the deep circulation patterns of the oceans, the so-called thermohaline ("heat and salt") circulation, which brings heat to the North Atlantic region and keeps it considerably warmer than places at equal latitudes in the Pacific. Increased freshwater inflow to the oceans through more precipitation and glacier and ice cap melting could alter the balance that produces these patterns and shut them down, which is believed to have happened in the geologic past. If a shutdown occurs, extremely rapid temperature changes (cooling) would result. According to the 2001 IPCC report current climate models mostly show a weakening of the thermohaline circulation, but not a complete shutdown, over the course of this century.

▶THE OZONE LAYER

There are two distinct problems associated with the chemical ozone (O_3): ground-level ozone, the main component of smog (discussed under "Air Pollution," below), and stratospheric ozone. The primary difference between the two problems is that at ground level there is too much ozone, while in the stratosphere there is not enough.

The problem of stratospheric ozone depletion is closely related to global warming in that the chlorofluorocarbons (see below) that are its principal cause are greenhouse gases, but the science is different. Stratospheric ozone (sometimes referred to as upper-atmosphere or atmospheric ozone) absorbs most of the Sun's ultraviolet radiation. A significant reduction of the ozone layer would lead to sharp increases in the incidence of skin cancer and cataracts in humans. It is also thought that there would be serious losses of small ocean algae, which produce oxygen and break down carbon dioxide, and of bacteria important to crop production.

Complex natural forces are continually at work creating and destroying ozone in the atmosphere. This involves first the breakdown of individual molecules of oxygen (O_2) into atomic oxygen (O), through the absorption of ultraviolet radiation. In turn, each atomic oxygen normally combines with an additional molecule of O_2 to form ozone (O_3). Destruction of ozone can be caused by the occasional recombination of ozone with atomic oxygen to form two molecules of O_2. As long as the Earth's sunlit atmosphere contains molecular oxygen, as it has for more than one billion years, ozone will be maintained in this dynamic balance.

In 1974, scientists saw the first suggestion that a group of chemicals known as chlorofluorocarbons (CFCs) was destroying the ozone balance by adding chlorine to the atmosphere. Chemically inert, nontoxic, and easily liquefied, CFCs were developed in the 1930s as an ammonia substitute for use in refrigeration, but their use became widespread in air conditioning, packaging and insulation, as a solvent for cleaning electronic circuit boards, and as an aerosol propellant.

It is this very absence of chemical reactivity that makes CFCs so dangerous to the ozone layer. Unlike less inert compounds, CFCs are not destroyed or removed in the lower atmosphere by rain, oxidation, or sunlight, where their lifetimes have been estimated to be between 75 and 110 years. Instead they drift into the upper atmosphere, where their chlorine components are released into the atmosphere under the effects of ultraviolet radiation. Almost all of these freed chlorine atoms find and react with the ozone, creating chlorine monoxide and molecular oxygen. In a subsequent reaction, the chlorine monoxide releases its oxygen atom to form a second molecule of oxygen, and the chlorine atom is freed once again to repeat the process. Through this continuing cycle of reactions, each chlorine atom can destroy about 100,000 molecules of ozone before the chain reaction ends. In the Antarctic, ice crystals in the air speed up reactions, producing an "ozone hole," a region of extremely low levels of atmospheric ozone, over the south polar region during the Antarctic winter. A system of cold winds called the Antarctic Vortex amplifies this effect. NASA reported that the ozone hole on September 9, 2000, was the largest on record.

To combat ozone depletion, there have been stringent reductions in CFC use. The United States, Russia, Japan, and the nations of the European Union have eliminated CFC use and production, and there are further agreements for developing countries. Even so, adverse effects on the ozone layer from human-produced CFCs will likely continue until at least 2020.

▶AIR POLLUTION

Although we tend to think of air pollution as a local problem, studies reported in 1995 demonstrate that there are widespread effects. Air pollution, they report, is so pervasive in industrial regions of northeastern North America, central Europe, and eastern Asia that it partly blocks sunlight, counteracting global warming with regional cooling.

The U.S. Environmental Protection Agency (EPA) monitors air quality at about 3,000 sites for six pollutants: particulate matter (soot and dust), sulfur dioxide, carbon monoxide (mostly from automobiles), nitrogen oxides, lead, and ozone. In addition to health concerns, the effects of air pollution on vegetation, materials, and visibility are monitored.

The basic federal law dealing with air pollution is the Clean Air Act of 1990, which directs the EPA to set standards for air quality. The main pollutants are discussed here.

Particulate matter (PM_{10}) The EPA measures particulate matter with an aerodynamic diameter smaller than 10 micrometers down to 2.5 micrometers. This includes dust, dirt, soot, smoke, and liquid droplets directly emitted into the air from factories, power plants, cars, construction sites, fires, and natural erosion, as well as particles formed in the atmosphere by condensation or transformation of emitted gases such as sulfur dioxide and volatile organic compounds.

Particulate matter is responsible for most adverse health effects in the lower regions of the respiratory tract. People with chronic obstructive pulmonary or cardiovascular disease, individuals with influenza, asthmatics, the elderly, and children are especially sensitive.

Sulfur dioxide (SO_2) Ambient sulfur dioxide comes mostly from stationary-source coal and oil combustion, refineries, pulp and paper mills, and nonferrous smelters. The health hazards associated with exposure to SO_2 include impaired breathing, respiratory illness, alterations in the lungs' defenses, and aggravation of existing respiratory and cardiovascular disease. Those most sensitive to SO_2 include asthmatics and people with chronic lung disease or cardiovascular disease, children, and the elderly. Sulfur dioxide also damages leaves on trees and crops and it is an agent of acid rain.

Carbon monoxide (CO) Carbon monoxide is a colorless, odorless, and poisonous gas produced by incomplete burning of carbon in fuels. Carbon monoxide enters the bloodstream and disrupts delivery of oxygen to the body's organs and tissues. The health threat from carbon monoxide is serious for those who suffer from cardiovascular diseases. Healthy individuals are also affected, and exposure to elevated carbon monoxide levels is associated with impairment of visual perception and manual dexterity.

Federal regulations have succeeded in cleaning up much of the carbon monoxide pollution that

Unhealthy Days in Selected Metropolitan Areas, 1991-2001

To measure air quality in urban areas, the Environmental Protection Agency has developed an indicator called the Air Quality Index (AQI, formerly the Pollutant Standard Index, PSI). The AQI integrates into a single number emission levels of five major pollutants: particulate matter (PM_{10}). Sulfur Dioxide (SO_2), carbon monoxide (CO), ground level ozone (O_3) and nitrogen dioxide (NO_2). An AQI of 0-50 reflects good air, 51-100 denotes moderate air, and an AQI of over 100 is classified as unhealthy (201-300 signifies very unhealthy air; 301-500 is hazardous). The following chart lists the number of days in which the AQI exceeded 100 in metropolitan areas.

	Number of Unhealthy Days							
Metropolitan area (no. of trend sites)	1991	1995	1996	1997	1998	1999	2000	2001
Riverside-San Bernardino, Calif. (20)	154	124	118	105	94	96	100	94
Bakersfield, Calif. (7)	113	107	110	58	76	94	82	33
Fresno, Calif. (6)	83	61	70	75	67	81	78	85
Los Angeles-Long Beach, Calif. (14)	168	113	94	60	56	27	48	30
Houston, Texas (9)	36	66	28	47	29	52	41	28
Knoxville, Tenn. (7)	10	26	21	37	54	62	36	17
Sacramento, Calif. (10)	44	41	44	17	29	39	29	17
Ventura, Calif. (6)	87	66	62	45	29	22	27	18
Atlanta, Ga. (3)	23	35	25	31	50	61	26	8
Memphis, Tenn.-Ark.-Miss. (4)	9	21	19	17	26	35	24	13
Dallas, Texas (2)	2	28	10	20	26	23	20	14
Philadelphia, Pa.-N.J. (12)	49	38	38	38	37	32	18	22
Baltimore, Md. (7)	50	36	28	30	51	40	16	26
Nashville, Tenn. (6)	12	26	23	20	30	33	16	7
New Orleans, La. (6)	2	20	8	7	4	18	17	5
St.Louis, Mo.-Ill. (15)	24	36	20	15	23	29	14	15
San Diego, Calif. (9)	67	48	31	14	33	16	14	17
New York, N.Y. (4)	49	20	14	23	16	25	11	16
Washington, D.C.-Md.-Va.-W.V. (16)	48	32	18	30	47	39	11	22
Phoenix-Mesa, Ariz. (7)	11	22	15	12	14	10	10	6
Cleveland-Lorain-Elyria, Ohio (8)	23	27	19	13	22	21	5	17
Cincinnati, Ohio-Ky.-Ind. (5)	19	19	10	11	13	12	4	6
ndianapolis, Ind. (7)	12	21	16	12	19	24	4	8
Pittsburgh, Pa. (9)	21	26	11	20	39	24	4	18
Detroit, Mich. (7)	27	14	13	11	17	15	3	16
l Paso, Texas (4)	7	7	5	3	6	1	3	5
Oakland, Calif. (7)	4	12	11	0	12	6	3	3
Denver, Colo. (6)	6	5	1	0	9	4	2	2
Milwaukee-Waukesha, Wis. (9)	24	14	5	5	12	18	4	12
Boston, Mass.-N.H. (3)	13	7	4	7	8	8	1	14
eattle-Bellevue-Everett, Wash. (0)	4	2	6	1	3	1	1	0
Chicago, Ill. (19)	25	24	7	9	10	14	0	15
as Vegas, Nev.-Ariz. (3)	0	0	4	0	3	0	0	1
Miami, Fla. (4)	1	2	1	3	6	5	0	1
Minneapolis-St.Paul, Minn.-Wis. (2)	2	5	0	0	1	0	0	2
an Francisco, Calif. (0)	0	2	0	0	0	0	0	0

lote: Figures reflect data from selected EPA trend sites. Number of unhealthy days recorded by all active EPA monitoring sites may be ightly higher in some cities.

ource: Environmental Protection Agency, *National Air Quality and Emissions Trends Report 2001* (2003). www.epa.gov/airtrends.

plagued the U.S. in the 1980s. In 1990, 26 metropolitan areas exceeded the National Ambient Air Quality Standards for carbon monoxide at least once. Los Angeles exceeded the standard a whopping 47 times, while Las Vegas exceeded it 17 times. But in 1998, only six metropolitan areas exceeded the standard more than once. In 2000, only three cities exceeded it the standard: Calexico, Calif. (2 times), Los Angeles-Long Beach, Calif (2 times), and Fairbanks, Alaska (1 time).

Nitrogen oxides (NO_x) These highly reactive gases play a major role, together with volatile organic compounds, in the formation of ozone. Nitrogen oxides form when fuel is burned at high temperatures. When released into the atmosphere, they are one of the major causes of smog. The two major emissions sources are cars and trucks, and stationary fuel-combustion sources such as electric-utility and industrial boilers.

Nitrogen oxides can irritate the lungs and lower resistance to respiratory infections such as influenza. Prolonged exposure to higher than normal concentrations can cause pulmonary angina. Nitrogen dioxide (NO_2) is also an agent of acid rain and plays a key role in nitrogen loading of forests and ecosystems. Over the past decade, Los Angeles is the only urban area that has consistently recorded violations of the EPA's annual NO_2 standards. Many other urban areas violate the EPA's standards on occasional hot summer days, when the Sun cooks hydrocarbons and nitrogen oxides, thus producing smog.

Ozone (O_3) Ground-level ozone is a colorless gas and the main component of smog. Unlike most other air pollutants, ozone is not emitted by factories or automobiles, but is formed by the interaction of volatile organic compounds (VOCs) and nitrous oxide. These reactions are stimulated by sunlight and temperature so that peak ozone levels occur typically during the warmer times of year. The severity of a smog problem in a given locale is directly related to the temperature and ultraviolet radiation intensity in that area. While the problems associated with ozone depletion (see "The Ozone Layer," above) and ground-level ozone are usually viewed separately, it is worth noting that as upper-atmosphere ozone is depleted, more ultraviolet radiation reaches the Earth and stimulates the production of ozone/smog.

Both VOCs and nitrous oxide are emitted by transportation and industrial sources as diverse

Emissions Estimates for EPA-Monitored Pollutants, 1970–2001 (thousand short tons)

Year	Carbon monoxide (CO)	Nitrogen oxides (NO_x)	Volatile organic compounds	Sulfur dioxide (SO_2)	Particulate matter (PM_{10})	Lead (Pb)
1970	204,043	26,805	34,659	31,218	13,023	219,471
1975	188,398	26,304	30,765	28,043	7,556	N.A.
1980	185,407	27,079	31,106	25,925	7,013	74,956
1985	176,844	25,757	27,404	23,307	41,324	N.A.
1990	154,189	25,530	24,116	23,078	27,758	4,975
1995	126,777	24,956	22,041	18,619	25,819	N.A.
1998	115,382	24,349	18,783	18,947	22,900	3,973
1999	117,229	23,671	19,378	17,651	21,632	4,199
2000	123,568	23,199	19,704	16,317	24,699	N.A.
2001	120,759	22,349	17,963	15,790	24,104	N.A.

1.Particulate matter totals before 1990 do not include estimates for fugitive dust, which arises from construction activities, mining and quarrying and paved road resuspension. It is the leading source of PM_{10} emissions.
Source: Environmental Protection Agency, *Average Annual Emissions, All Criteria Pollutants,* August 2003.

Emissions Estimates for EPA-Monitored Pollutants By Source, 1970-2001 (thousand short tons)

Source	Carbon monoxide (CO)		Nitrogen oxides (NO_x)		Volatile organic compounds		Sulfur dioxide (SO_2)		Particulate matter (PM_{10})	
	1970	2001	1970	2001	1970	2001	1970	2001	1970	2001
Fuel Combustion										
Electric utility	237	492	4,900	4,891	30	63	17,398	10,821	1,775	663
Industrial	770	1,181	4,325	2,640	150	168	4,568	2,262	641	330
Other	3,625	2,919	836	1,068	541	953	1,490	549	455	511
Chemical/Allied Processing	3,397	381	271	117	1,341	305	591	329	235	54
Metals Processing	3,644	1,356	77	96	394	72	4,775	358	1,316	172
Petroleum/Related Industries	2,179	169	240	129	1,194	394	881	310	286	39
Other Industrial Processes	620	613	187	505	270	478	846	408	5,832	402
Solvent Utilization	N.A.	50	N.A.	4	7,174	5,053	N.A.	1	N.A.	5
Storage and Transport	N.A.	174	N.A.	11	1,954	1,150	N.A.	6	N.A.	86
Waste Disposal/Recycling	7,059	3,229	440	169	1,984	541	8	35	999	504
On-Road Vehicles	163,231	74,825	12,624	8,249	16,910	4,874	273	261	480	218
Non-Road Sources	11,371	24,677	2,652	4,156	1,616	2,622	278	440	164	316
Miscellaneous[1]	7,909	10,689	330	285	1,101	1,288	110	10	839	20,802
Total	204,043	120,759	26,805	22,349	34,659	17,963	31,218	15,790	13,023	24,104

Note: Some columns may not sum due to independent rounding. 1. Miscellaneous includes PM_{10} natural sources like fugitive dust, which arises from construction activities, mining and quarrying and paved road resuspension. It is the leading source of PM_{10} emissions.
Source: Environmental Protection Agency, August 2003. www.epa.gov/airtrends.

as autos, chemical manufacturing, dry cleaners, paint shops, and other solvent-using industries. High levels of ozone affect people with impaired respiratory systems, such as asthmatics, and exposure to relatively low concentrations of ozone for only a few hours has been found to significantly reduce lung function in normal, healthy people during exercise. This is generally accompanied by symptoms including chest pain, coughing, sneezing, and pulmonary congestion. Ozone is also responsible each year for several billion dollars worth of domestic crop yield losses, and it causes noticeable damage to leaves in many crops and species of trees.

World Carbon Dioxide Emissions from Consumption and Flaring of Fossil Fuels, 1992-2001

2001 Rank, Country	Millions of metric tons[1] 1992	2001
1. U.S.	1,379.62	1,565.31
2. China	667.90	831.74
3. Russia	573.50	440.26
4. Japan	285.77	315.83
5. India	175.97	251.33
6. Germany	241.59	223.24
7. Canada	124.71	156.19
8. United Kingdom	156.56	154.33
9. Italy	113.58	121.50
10. South Korea	77.55	120.80

Note: 1 metric ton is equal to 2,204.62 pounds. 1. Preliminatry figures. **Source:** U.S. Dept. of Energy, Energy Information Administration, *International Energy Annual, 2002.*

Ozone in Metropolitan Areas, 1992–2000

The following metropolitan areas are the most serious violators of ozone standards set by the Clean Air Act of 1990. They are ranked by the number of days they exceeded standards in 1998-2000.

Metropolitan area	Average number of days exceeding standards 1992 –94	1995 –97	1998 –2000
Los Angeles South Coast Air Basin, Calif.	103.3	56.7	35.4
San Joaquin Valley, Calif.	N.A.	N.A.	13.1
Atlanta, Ga.	N.A.	N.A.	10.6
Houston-Galveston-Brazoria, Tex.	6.5	14.9	10.2
Southeast Desert, Calif. (modified AQMD)	47.5	24.3	7.4
Sacramento Metro Area, Calif.	6.9	7.4	5.3
Knoxville, Tenn.	N.A.	N.A.	4.0
San Francisco-Bay Area, Calif.	N.A.	N.A.	3.4
Philadelphia, Pa-Wilmington, Del.-Trenton, N.J.	4.0	4.2	3.0
San Diego, Calif.	N.A.	N.A.	2.7
Washington, D.C.	N.A.	N.A.	2.7

Note: The National ambient air quality standard for ozone is 0.12 parts per million (ppm) daily maximum one-hour average. **Source:** Environmental Protection Agency Office of Air and Radiation, *1998-2000 Ozone and 1999-2000 Carbon Monoxide Air Quality Data Update.*

Lead (Pb) People can be exposed to lead via air, diet, and ingestion of lead in soil and dust. Lead accumulates in the body in blood, bone, and soft tissue, and because it is not readily excreted, it also affects the kidneys, nervous system, and blood-forming organs. Excessive exposure to lead may cause seizures, mental retardation, and/or behavioral disorders. Even at low doses, lead exposure is harmful; infants and children are especially susceptible to low doses of lead and often suffer central nervous system damage.

Lead gasoline additives, nonferrous smelters, and battery plants are the most significant contributors to atmospheric lead emissions. The decline in the share of lead emissions from internal-combustion engines of all kinds is due primarily to the introduction of unleaded gasoline in 1975, for use in automobiles equipped with catalytic control devices, which reduce emissions of carbon monoxide, VOCs, and nitrogen oxides. Today more than 99.8 percent of the lead once added to gasoline in the United States has been removed.

Air pollution worldwide The worst air pollution is undoubtedly in Asia. According to the World Health Organization, more than 1.5 million Asians die each year from the effects of air pollution alone, and another half million die from water pollution.

Anything over 100 micrograms of particles per cubic meter of air is considered dangerous, yet in cities like Taiyuan, China, and Delhi, India, the levels routinely top 500 micrograms. The threat is compounded by the fact that so many people in these areas cook indoors with coal briquettes. Particles in the air are a major cause of respiratory ailments in Asia; such ailments are a leading cause of death in China.

▶ACID RAIN

Acid rain refers to acidic precipitation of all kinds, including rain, snow, and fog, as well as acidic dust particles. The main component of acid rain is sulfuric acid, a product of reactions of sulfur dioxide released by industrial and power plants fueled by coal or oil. Another major agent of acid rain is nitrogen oxides, which form nitric acid and which are found in motor vehicle exhaust and in emissions from industrial plants that burn any fuel at high temperatures. Burning vegetation also produces nitric acid, as well as formic acid and acetic acid. Acid rain can travel great distances from its source: 10 percent to 80 percent increases in acidity have been detected as far away as 2,500 miles from a source.

Acid rain has been implicated in the destruction of lakes, the weathering of man-made structures, and the death of trees, crops, and animals. When acid rain ends up in lakes, it can increase the level of acidity to such an extent that the lake loses its ability to buffer the acidity with alkaline chemicals from the surrounding soil and rocks. How quickly this occurs is to some extent determined by the nature of the surrounding soil, which means that lakes in some regions are more vulnerable to the effects of acid rain than others. As lakes become more acidic, small invertebrates die off. This begins a reaction up the food chain: as the smallest organisms disappear, the food supply for larger vertebrates such as fish and frogs is depleted. Because lakes are not closed ecosystems, the demise of these organisms also affects land dwellers that depend on them, directly or indirectly, for survival.

A 1999 federal study revealed that regulation has succeeded in reducing harmful levels of sulfur dioxide in the air, but that the problem remains serious. At current rates, more than half of the 2,800 lakes in the Adirondacks will be too acidic to support life by the year 2040. The study also concludes that the San Gabriel Mountains near Los Angeles are already "saturated" with nitrogen, meaning that excess nitrogen is seeping into the surrounding waters.

▶WATER POLLUTION

Although the bad effect of air pollution on health was suspected even earlier, the first proven environmental cause of illness was water pollution. In England, a famous demonstration by physician John Snow in 1854 showed that removing the handle of a pump could reduce the incidence of cholera by depriving people living near a contaminated well from using the water. Chlorine used for water purification was already known at that time, and by the 20th century most major cities in the United States provided treated water.

Problems not directly connected to health also were recognized in the 19th century. Mining in California was, in some locations, polluting the water supply so greatly that crops could not be grown; a law against using water in extracting ores was instituted in the state in 1884. Industrial water pollution was also recognized, although not stopped. Five years after Dr. Snow's famous demonstration, a new source of water pollution was introduced when the first oil well was drilled.

The 20th century brought with it additional forms of water pollution. A series of revolutions in agriculture included use of artificial fertilizers, introduction of long-lasting pesticides, and concentration of animal wastes. Each change also introduced new forms of water pollution from runoff—water from rain or snow that fails to sink into the soil. "Point sources," such as sewage pipes and factory waste ponds, were now supplemented with the "nonpoint sources" of farming.

In 1999, the EPA released its first ever national index on the quality of the nation's 2,111 watersheds. The index asserts that 21 percent of the watersheds have serious problems, including fish-consumption advisories, pollution, and loss of wetlands. Another 36 percent are of only moderate quality.

The 1972 Clean Water Act was intended to solve many of the nation's water pollution problems, but it has been only partially effective in doing so. In 1972, only about a third of the nation's rivers were safe for fishing and swimming. That number improved to more than 50 percent during the 1970s and 1980s, but by 1998, the levels of pollution had crept back up again. The primary cause was no longer industrial pollution, residue from mining, and untreated sewage; instead, nonpoint sources from runoff, both agricultural and municipal, had taken over as the older point sources were eliminated.

Drinking Water

Americans have for many years taken their drinking water for granted. But despite this complacency, there are many threats to the water supply. These include biological threats to health from contamination, dangerous chemicals in the water supply from a variety of sources, and toxic elements introduced by water treatment or defects in plumbing. A related problem is that high water levels during storms overwhelm both industrial and municipal water treatment. This last source is somewhat more easily controlled than other nonpoint pollution, and revisions of the Clean Water Act in 1987, which went into effect in 1992, attack this problem for urban runoff at the city and county levels.

The Safe Drinking Water Act Amendments of 1996 further strengthened and expanded drinking water protections. They increased standards for microbial contamination such as cryptosporidium, which has been the source of several disease outbreaks, including a 1993 instance in Milwaukee, in which more than 100 people died.

Many municipal water supply systems regularly are found to contain levels of bacterial contamination that exceed EPA standards. Most, but not all bacterial contamination stems from the use of surface waters—rivers, lakes, and reservoirs. The other major source of water is groundwater—subsurface water contained for the most part in small cavities, or pores, in rock or soil. One common way to obtain unpolluted groundwater is to dig deep wells that find "fossil" water that has been at those levels for thousands of years. This source, however, is not renewable. Most shallow wells obtain their water from groundwater that recently was surface water and therefore subject to greater contamination.

Groundwater pollution is especially difficult to remedy. Almost all solutions are expensive and, in many cases, not feasible at any price. Such remedies include pumping detoxification agents into the ground or treating the water before use.

Groundwater can be contaminated by industrial pollutants stored or released in ways that put them in contact with the water supply; by leakage from underground storage of volatile chemicals, such as gasoline, cleaning fluid, or petroleum; and by seepage into the soil of agricultural pesticides. A privately funded review of federal and state water tests by the Environmental Working Group reported in 1994 that the water supplies used by 14.1 million Americans contain agricultural pesticides in amounts that would be banned if these levels were found in food.

Formerly one of the main sources of ground water contamination had been municipal landfills, but most of these are now sealed with clay liners to prevent seepage; and truly hazardous chemicals, such as mercury or lead from batteries or volatile organic compounds, are banned from landfills.

Some drinking water pollution takes place between the time the water comes from the well or from a surface source and the time it leaves faucets. For example, even though water from municipal plants is tested for lead and kept lead-free, service pipes, home plumbing, and some brass fixtures can leach lead into water, especially hot water. People who depend on private wells can have additional problems, as most of the pumps sold in recent years contain lead in brass or bronze parts that seeps into water contained in or surrounding the pump. Lead from plumbing or from pumps can be flushed from drinking or cooking water by letting the water run before use, but for water supplied by submerged pumps in deep wells, it may be necessary to run water for as long as 10 minutes to get to the lead-free supply.

Even municipal treatment of drinking water is suspected of potentially dangerous side effects. About 70 percent of all Americans drink water that has been disinfected by chlorination. But chlorine can react with organic material in water to form compounds such as chloroform that have

Major Ship Oil Spills

Date	Ship Name	Location	Oil Lost (metric tons)
1979	Atlantic Empress	off Tobago, West Indies	287,000
1991	ABT Summer	700 nautical miles off Angola	260,000
1983	Castillo de Bellver	off Saldanha Bay, South Africa	252,000
1978	Amoco Cadiz	off Brittany, France	223,000
1991	Haven	Genoa, Italy	144,000
1988	Odyssey	700 nautical miles off Nova Scotia	132,000
1967	Torrey Canyon	Scilly Isles, UK	119,000
1976	Urquiola	La Coruna, Spain	100,000
1977	Hawaiian Patriot	300 nautical miles off Honolulu	95,000
1979	Independenta	Bosphorus, Turkey	95,000

Note: One metric ton = 1.1 U.S. tons. Some spills did not impact coastlines, which is why some ship names are unfamiliar to the general public. The Exxon Valdez (1989) spill is estimated to be number 34 in the list of large spills.
Source: International Tanker Owners Pollution Federation.

been implicated in causing cancer in rats and mice. Except possibly for persons who have some reason for extra caution, however, the benefits of chlorination far outweigh any known danger.

Ocean Pollution

Pollution of the oceans disturbs marine ecosystems. It is thought to be the trigger for the algal growth that has all but eliminated the scallop fishery in Long Island Sound, for example. Other ocean fisheries in protected bays and sounds have also been damaged by pollution.

Ocean pollution from oil is primarily noted by the public when an oil well at sea is damaged or when an oil-carrying ship leaks large amounts of oil into the sea as a result of an accident like the 1989 Exxon *Valdez* disaster. Despite this perception, most oil pollution in the ocean actually comes from municipal and industrial runoff, cleaning of ships' bilges or tanks, and other routine events.

Ocean pollution is often in evidence on beaches. Tar balls from oil spills, plastic, and sometimes sewage wash up on beaches. Occasionally beaches have to be closed because of high bacteria counts in the water, making swimming hazardous.

Plastic, which generally does not break down in the ocean, is a hazard to larger organisms, such as endangered sea turtles. An international treaty prohibits disposal of plastic wastes that can kill or maim creatures that become entangled, but the treaty is very difficult to enforce.

▶SOLID WASTE

Many areas of the United States continue to face serious problems in safely and effectively managing the garbage they generate. As a nation, we are generating more trash than ever before, and as the generation of municipal solid waste (MSW) increases, the capacity to handle it is decreasing. Municipal solid waste is distinct from industrial wastes produced by factories, tailings from mines, construction and demolition waste, sludge from sewage treatment, and junked machinery.

Disposing of Solid Waste The average person disposed of 4.5 pounds of solid waste each day in 2000, up significantly from 1960, when per person disposal was 2.7 pounds. This waste consists of paper (37.4 percent), yard trimmings (12 percent), food scraps (11.2 percent), plastics (10.7 percent), metals (7.8 percent), rubber, leather, and textiles (6.7 percent), glass (5.5 percent), wood (5.5 percent), and other materials (3.2 percent). There are four primary methods of dealing with this waste: putting it in landfills, incinerating it; recycling it, and composting. But a fifth option, source reduction, may be the most effective way of reducing the nation's volume of MSW, which totals more than 200 million tons per year.

Landfills By far the greatest amount of MSW is sent to MSW landfills, of which there were 1,967 in 2000, a drop from nearly 8,000 in 1988. However, it is important to note that while the number of landfills has decreased, the average size has increased. Landfills are the cheapest method of disposing of MSW but they pose a number of environmental problems. Because most landfills are dry, they preserve garbage by cutting it off from the rotting influences of air and moisture. Even biodegradable materials do not decay; newspapers 40 years old can still be read and hot dogs thrown out years before look more or less unchanged.

EPA regulations favor dry landfills for two reasons. As biodegradation in wet landfills occurs there is a buildup of hazardous methane gas, and contaminated water leaching out of landfills (leachate) can pollute the surrounding groundwater. But wet landfills have their supporters, who argue that by enhancing decay, a landfill's biological life can be compressed from 40-to-50 years to 5-to-10 years. Since landfills can contain hundreds of hazardous chemicals, they require continuous monitoring anyway; so shortening their active biological life can yield significant savings. Moreover, by decreasing the volume of trash through biodegradation, landfills can be kept open longer. This is important because some estimates indicate that 80 percent of the nation's landfills will be closed within 20 years, and people are increasingly adamant about not having landfills in their communities, which makes it harder to site new landfills.

Incineration/combustion One popular method of disposing of municipal waste used to be simply to burn it. In the 1940s there were approximately 700 municipal incinerators in the United States. Despite the efficiency with which they reduced the volume of waste, they stank, their stacks emitted sizable particles of ash, and they produced noxious gases. For these aesthetic rather than environmental reasons, their numbers declined dramatically in the 1950s. By the time of the Clean Air Act of 1970, there were only

67 incinerators still in operation—most with no energy recovery and no air pollution controls.

Incinerator use increased in the 1980s and early 1990s as space for landfills became scarce, and as the energy produced by incineration became a valuable commodity. But in May, 1994, the U.S. Supreme Court ruled that waste from incinerators had to be treated as toxic on the same basis as any other waste. This was a blow because most incinerator ash contains dioxins that are produced by combustion and heavy metals such as lead, cadmium, and mercury, which do not burn.

In that same month, the Court ruled that localities could not prevent landfills from taking waste away from incinerators if the landfills offered better bargains. Because landfill was usually cheaper, few chose to incinerate their waste, and few municipalities could afford to subsidize the cost of incinerators. Within six months of the Court's decision, plans for 77 proposed incinerators were canceled.

Recycling/composting Recycling and composting recovered 30.1 percent (69.9 million tons) of waste generated in 2000. Recycling rates for paper and paperboard reached 45.4 percent (39.4 million tons), Metal recovery reached 35.4 percent (6.4 million tons), yard trimmings 56.9 percent (15.8 million tons), glass 23.0 percent (2.9 million tons), and plastics 5.4 percent (1.3 million tons). There were about 9,250 curbside recycling programs in the U.S. in 2000.

The EPA has set a nationwide recycling goal of 35 percent by the year 2005. In addition to significantly reducing the volume of wastes that winds up in landfills and incinerators, recycling and composting limit pollution and unnecessary depletion of natural resources. They also have the potential to generate revenues from the sale of secondary materials. According to the EPA, material recycled in 1996 had a value of $3.6 billion; with a 35 percent recycling rate, the value of material recycled in 2005 would be $5.2 billion. Costs of recycling are still high, but these are expected to decline as recycling programs mature and become fully integrated with the total MSW management system.

In July 2002 Congress began hearings on a national "bottle bill" that would require beverage companies to ensure that 80 percent of all cans and bottles are recycled within two years. According to a 2002 study by the the Container Recycling Institute, only 49 percent of aluminum cans were recycled in 2001, compared with 65 percent in 1992; more than 760,000 tons of aluminum cans were thrown away in 2001, the equivalent of two Empire State Buildings. Beverage companies, however, portrayed the bill as a new tax on consumers, who would have to pay a deposit of at least 10 cents on practically all bottles and cans.

Source reduction Many experts believe that the key to solving the municipal waste problem is source reduction—minimizing the volume of products used and the toxins they contain, and extending their lives in use. Removal of toxins enhances the safety of recycling, landfilling, and combustion, while volume reduction helps to extend the capacity of existing waste systems.

A broad variety of products and packaging that reduce waste and save money have been developed. By reducing the textured design on napkins, for example, the McDonald's Corporation found that it could fit 23 percent more napkins into a shipping container, saving 294,000 pounds of corrugated cardboard and 150 truckload shipments annually. The EPA estimates that since 1990, source reduction has kept 55.1 million tons of solid waste out of the waste stream in the U.S.

▶HAZARDOUS WASTE

Superfund In 1980, Congress enacted the Comprehensive Environmental Response, Compensation, and Liability Act (CERCLA), better known as the Superfund, a $1.6 billion, five-year program to clean up thousands of hazardous waste sites. The fund was renewed in 1986 by the Superfund Amendments and Reauthorization Act (SARA). The EPA, which administers the Superfund, estimated in 1996 that 70 million Americans lived within 4 miles of a toxic waste site.

The EPA evaluates hazardous waste sites for their levels of soil and water contamination, the mobility of toxins, and their proximity to human food supplies. (Contamination of petroleum, however, is excluded from this evaluation.) It then ranks the sites on a numerically based system that factors in risks to groundwater, surface water, and air. The highest ranking sites are placed on the EPA's National Priorities List (NPL). CERCLA also allows states and territories to designate one top-priority site regardless of its score; there are several such sites that would not make the NPL on the basis of their numerical score alone.

Once the EPA deems a site a national priority, it can take two types of action. It can remove the hazard in an emergency action limited to one year and/or $2 million. Or it can try to compel the individual or company responsible for the problem to provide a long-term solution.

But the second option is rarely exercised. Many of the original polluters are bankrupt or cannot be found when bills for the cleanup (which averages $25–$30 million, according to the EPA) are presented. And the EPA continues to add sites to the National Priorities List at least as fast as it cleans them up: the total number of superfund sites has remained close to 1,200 for over a decade.

Nuclear Waste Nuclear waste in the United States comes from nuclear weapons production facilities, nuclear power plants, medical equipment (primarily used in radiation treatments), industrial sources of radioactivity used as a more powerful alternative to X rays, and residues from uranium mining. Nuclear waste is often grouped into two categories, labeled "low-level" and "high-level." Low-level waste is slightly radioactive, often from exposure to a high-level source. High-level waste is often grouped as either civilian, mainly spent fuel from nuclear reactors, or military, wastes produced in the manufacture of nuclear weapons.

The problem with nuclear waste is that it is radioactive and can remain that way for years—in some cases, thousands of years. Early methods of disposal included dumping the wastes at sea and suspending them in a liquid or in cement and injecting the radioactive combination into wells. The United States was among the signatories of a 1976 international convention banning ocean dumping and stopped deep-well injection in 1984.

Current plans call for consortiums of states to develop sites for storage of low-level wastes. One such "temporary" site is in Barnwell County, S.C., which has handled low-level waste for 37 states since 1970. Meanwhile, the federal government continues to search for suitable sites for storage of high-level wastes from nuclear power plants and for very long-lived radioactive materials from weapons production. For the time being, these wastes remain on the sites where they were generated.

In 1998, the EPA certified the Department of Energy's Waste Isolation Pilot Plan in Carlsbad, N.M., the nation's first deep-underground facility for disposal of transuranic waste generated from defense activities. (Transuranic wastes consist primarily of sludges, tools, rags, glassware, and protective clothing that has been contaminated with radioactive elements from weapons production.) The facility is approximately 2,100 feet (640 meters) underground in excavated, natural salt formations. The first shipment of transuranic waste was delivered to the facility in March of 1999. By 2010, shipments from 23 military waste sites from across the nation to this site will reduce the number of Americans living within 50 miles of nuclear waste from 61 million to 4 million. Of course, the 113,000 people living within 50 miles of Carlsbad (as well as many New Mexicans beyond that radius) were understandably opposed, and fought its operation since the site was first proposed in 1974.

The Nuclear Regulatory Commission is the agency charged with monitoring the disposal of waste generated by civilian-operated nuclear reactors. However, most of the nuclear waste in the United States is the by-product of the federal government's nuclear weapons programs. Disposal and monitoring of this waste—which includes millions of cubic yards of contaminated soil and other debris at more than 100 sites in 32 states and the Marshall Islands—is the responsibility of the Department of Energy, the Department of Defense, the Nuclear Waste Technical Review Board, and the Office of the Nuclear Waste Negotiator. Total cost of the cleanup could be about $300-$400 billion over 30 years.

The difficulty of resolving nuclear waste disposal issues is illustrated by the saga of Yucca Mountain, Nevada, which was approved by Congress in 2002 as the nation's first long-term geologic repository for spent nuclear fuel and high-level radioactive waste. If the Nuclear Regulatory Commission grants the site a license, Yucca Mountain could begin accepting waste in 2010, with closure and decommissioning slated to begin in 2110. In the meantime, the site (about 100 miles northwest of Las Vegas) has been the subject of fierce opposition not only in Nevada, but also in states along proposed transportation routes for nuclear waste. (As of September 2003, the NRC had not yet granted a license.)

▶HABITATS

The place where a species lives and its surroundings, both living and non-living, is called a habitat. Broadly speaking, habitats include forests, grasslands, deserts, tundra, and wetlands. But there are many specific types of habitats within each of these categories. The habitat of a giant panda, for example, is a bamboo forest in China, not a pine forest in Canada; that of a tuna is the open ocean, not a Florida lake.

When a species' habitat is destroyed or altered, the species may suffer dramatic population declines. For example, because so much of North America's native grasslands have been replaced by farms and other developments, many songbirds have been left without homes and food, and their populations have decreased. Similarly, destruction of China's bamboo forests threaten the giant panda with extinction.

When a species becomes extinct, the Earth's biodiversity is diminished. Biodiversity is all the organisms in the world or in a particular habitat, including all their individual variations. Loss of biodiversity affects humans as well as the threatened species. For example, all major food crops depend on new genetic material from the wild to remain healthy and productive. Noted the 1992 U.N. Earth Summit report, "Our planet's essential goods and services depend on the variety and variability of genes, species, populations and ecosystems."

The major reasons for loss of biological diversity are habitat destruction and modification, overhunting and overfishing, climate change, pollution, and the introduction of so-called alien species (non-native species, such as African tulip trees in Hawaii and Amazon water hyacinths in Africa's Lake Victoria; native species often are unable to compete with the introduced species).

▶RAIN FORESTS

Rain forests are defined as forests that grow in regions that receive more than 70 inches (1.8 meters) of rain each year. Some rain forests occur in temperate places, such as southern Chile or the northwest coast of North America, but the majority are found in the tropics. Tropical rain forests cover more than 2 billion acres (0.8 billion

Superfund Hazardous Waste Sites, 1981–2003

Date	Number of sites	Date	Number of sites
Oct. 23, 1981[1]	115	**Feb. 23, 1994**	1,190
Dec. 30, 1982[1]	418	**Sept. 29, 1995**	1,232
Sept. 8, 1983	406	**June 17, 1996**	1,227
Oct. 15, 1984	538	**April, 1997**	1,208
June 10, 1986	703	**Feb. 1998**	1,197
July 22, 1987	802	**July 22, 1999**	1,226
Oct. 4, 1989	981	**July 31, 2000**	1,236
Feb. 21, 1990	1,081	**June 14, 2001**	1,236
Feb. 11, 1991	1,189	**March 2002**	1,223
Feb., 1992	1,183	**Sept. 2003**	1,233
May 10, 1993	1,201		

1. Proposed sites only. Final sites not calculated until release of first National Priorities list in 1983. **Source:** Environmental Protection Agency, National Priorities List. **www.epa.gov/superfund/sites**

States with the Most NPL Hazardous Waste Sites, 2003

State	Nonfederal	Federal	Total
New Jersey	104	8	112
California	72	24	96
Pennsylvania	89	6	94
New York	87	4	90
Michigan	67	0	67
Florida	46	6	51
Washington	32	14	47
Texas	37	4	41
Illinois	35	4	39
Wisconsin	39	0	39

Source: Environmental Protection Agency, *National Priorities List* (July 2003). **www.epa.gov/superfund/sites**

hectares) or about 7 percent of the Earth's land surface. They are found in Central and South America, equatorial Africa, Southeast Asia, and northeastern Australia.

It is estimated that the world may be losing more than 49 million acres (20 million hectares) of tropical forest each year. As the 1990s began, Brazil was losing 12.5-22.5 million acres (5-9 million hectares) of rain forest annually; India was losing 3.7 million acres (1.5 million hectares); and Indonesia was losing 2.2 million acres (0.9 million hectares). Other countries experiencing rapid losses included Myanmar, Costa Rica, Sri Lanka, Vietnam, Thailand, the Philippines, and Ghana.

Tropical rain forests are lush habitats, filled with a greater variety of organisms than any other type of habitat. According to a U.S. National Academy of Sciences report, a typical patch of rain forest covering four square miles (10.4 km^2) contains 750 species of trees, 750 species of other plants, 125 species of mammals, 400 species of birds, 100 species of reptiles, and 60 species of amphibians.

The dominant plants in a tropical rain forest are broad-leaved evergreens, while Northern Hemisphere temperate rain forests are filled with needle-leaved conifers. In both, the tallest trees form a dense canopy high above the forest floor. Vines climb up the trees in search of sunlight. In a tropical rain forest, nonparasitic plants grow high in the canopy, using the large trees as perches. In both types of forest, the floor is in deep shade; comparatively few shrubs and grasses grow there.

The rich plant life supports food chains that include many of the world's most spectacular animals: brightly colored frogs, fierce harpy eagles, agile monkeys, powerful tigers, slow-moving sloths, and huge columns of army ants, among many others.

While the diversity of plant life in rain forests is rich, the soil generally is not. The lush plants take up so much of the nutrients in rain forests that little is left for the soil below. A study of a rain forest in Venezuela found that 75 percent of the nutrients were in living organisms like plants and trees, 17 percent were in debris, and only 8 percent were in the soil. When an organism dies and decomposes in a rain forest, the nutrients in its cells are quickly absorbed by nearby plants.

Deforestation has many sources. Individuals often cut down rain forest trees for firewood and to clear land on which to raise crops, build ranches, and raise cattle. But erosion and poor soil fertility soon make these farms and ranches worthless. Large commercial operations deforest vast areas for lumber, paper, and other products, much of which are exported to pay debts owed to foreign governments and banks. Development projects such as roads, hydroelectric dams, and mines also destroy large areas of rain forest.

▶WETLANDS

A wetland is a location other than a river, lake, or open ocean in which the soil for at least part of the year contains as much water as it will hold (the soil is saturated with water). Saturated soil often slows decomposition of organic matter, resulting in a thin mud or muck, or in the decayed plant remains known as peat. Common names for wetlands include: **Potholes**, which are dry land most of the year, but seasonally become shallow ponds; **Tidal flats**, which are underwater at high tide but become muddy land at low tide; **Permafrost,** which is saturated soil that is frozen most of the year at the surface, and year-round below the surface; **Bogs,** which contain saturated soil and organic material all year, but have little or no standing water; **Marshes,** which contain standing shallow water and low vegetation; and **Swamps,** where trees grow on small hillocks surrounded by standing water. Often these informal categories overlap in a given wetland.

Wetlands produce numerous invaluable benefits. They provide a natural means of flood control, absorbing water from nearby rivers and lakes during periods of high runoff. This buffers the impact of storms and reduces shoreline erosion, thereby protecting against the loss of life and property. And by filtering out pollutants and trapping sediment, wetlands help maintain water quality.

Wetlands are the nurseries for many fish, almost all amphibians, and various birds and mammals. For instance, coastal wetlands are spawning grounds and nurseries for more than two-thirds of U.S. commercial fisheries, a $10 billion a year industry.

Despite all the benefits associated with wetlands, the definition of what is and is not a wetland is still a bone of contention among environmentalists (who would like to preserve the swampy areas), developers (who would like to drain them and erect housing complexes), and farmers (who would like to divert the water to their crops). In 1987, the U.S. Army Corp. of Engineers defined a wetland as "any ground that has mucky or peat-based soils, nourishes specific plant life, and is saturated with water at least seven days a year." Partisans on all sides of the issue have sought since then to modify that definition. Since colonial days, the contiguous United States has lost 53 percent of its wetlands, and now retains just under 104 million acres (42 million hectares). The rate of decline has slowed in recent years, but it is still significant: A 1997 report by the U.S. Fish and Wildlife Service estimated that the U.S. lost an average of 117,000 acres (47,000 hectares) of wetlands every year between 1985 and 1995.

The majority of the nation's wetlands are located in Alaska (170 to 200 million acres). Ohio, Indiana, Iowa, and California have lost the greatest percentage of their wetlands, but the wet states of Florida and Louisiana have lost the greatest total number of acres of wetlands.

ENDANGERED SPECIES

A species is a specific kind of organism, such as the common earthworm, the daffodil, the American opossum, or the human. There are about 1.75 million known species of all kinds, including plants, microorganisms, mammals, and fish. This is thought to represent no more than about 10 percent of all species. (And if the results of some surveys of rain forest canopies in Panama are correct, there may be as many as 30 million insect species alone.) Since life developed more than 600 million years ago, innumerable species have appeared and become extinct. Today, biological diversity faces a rate of species destruction greater than any since the mass extinctions of the dinosaurs 65 million years ago.

Animal and plant species are threatened on a number of fronts. Their natural habitats face destruction through deforestation, wetlands loss, and urban sprawl, and are also affected by processes that derive from global warming such as shifting climate and vegetation zones. Another problem is the shift to "monocultures" in agriculture, producing only one strain of crop for food. Some types of environments present special vulnerabilities. As an example, islands have small populations, limited habitats, and allow the introduction of new (alien) species easily

International controls

The U.S. Endangered Species Act of 1966 is the chief bulwark protecting species in the United States. The United States is also a signatory to international treaties that protect species. The Convention on International Trade in Endangered Species of Wild Fauna and Flora (CITES) has been in force since 1975. Signed by more than 120 nations, it lists species for which international trade in the live organisms, meat, lumber, or other parts of species is banned or restricted. While smugglers are thought to violate CITES restrictions regularly in what is believed to be a $5 billion annual illegal trade, CITES continues to be one of the main forces in species preservation.

Supplementing the CITES bans on international acts against species is the Convention on Biodiversity, agreed to at the 1992 Earth Summit in Rio de Janeiro. Ratified by 161 countries (though not the U.S.), this treaty commits nations to protect and preserve species and habitats within their own borders.

Other international treaties affect more limited interests. The International Whaling Commission, with 40 members currently, has been in business since 1949. The commission has probably saved whales from extinction with its near-total ban on whaling since the late 1980s. Other groups, such as the 10-nation Inter-American Tropical Tuna Commission, are modeled on the whaling group. Despite this moratorium, however, Norway and Japan have each killed hundreds of whales annually since the early 1990s; Norway, for example, authorized the killing of 425 minke whales in 1996. In 2003, Iceland began its first whale hunt in 14 years, claiming a scientific need to study the stomach contents of minke whales to measure their effect on important local fish stocks.

To reverse the trend toward species extinction, governments around the world have set aside a total of about 425 million hectares (about 16.4 million square miles) of protected lands in about 3,500 parks and preserves. In addition, many countries try to identify and improve the status of species threatened with extinction.

The efforts come none too soon. The World Conservation Union's list of threatened species of animals and plants worldwide, the "Red List" (www.redlist.org), contained 11,046 species of threatened plants and animals in 2002. These include 24 percent (one in four) of mammalian species, and 12 percent (1 in 8) of bird species. Indonesia, India, Brzil and China are among the countries with the most threatened mammals and birds; plant species are declining rapidly in South and Central America, Central and West Africa, and Southeast Asia. The list includes 5,714 threatened plants, but because only a small percentage (about 4 percent) of plant species have been evaluated for threat the number actually endangered is believed to be much larger. Among the most gravely affected types of animals and birds are primates: the number of critically endangered species went from 13 to 19 from 1996 to 2002. The number of threatened albatross species increased from 3 to 17 over the same period because of long-line fisheries, and the number of Critically Endangered freshwater turtle species, used for food and medicines in Asia, went from 10 to more than 20.

Endangered and Threatened Species, 2003

Group	Endangered U.S.	Endangered Foreign	Threatened U.S.	Threatened Foreign	Total Listed
Mammals	65	251	9	17	342
Birds	78	175	14	6	273
Reptiles	14	64	22	15	115
Amphibians	12	8	9	1	30
Fishes	71	11	44	0	126
Clams	62	2	8	0	72
Snails	21	1	11	0	33
Insects	35	4	9	0	48
Arachnids	12	0	0	0	12
Crustaceans	18	0	3	0	21
Total Animals	**388**	**516**	**129**	**39**	**1072**
Flowering Plants	571	1	144	0	716
Conifers and Cycads	2	0	1	2	5
Ferns and Allies	24	0	2	0	26
Lichens	2	0	0	0	2
Total Plants	**599**	**1**	**147**	**2**	**749**
Total Species	**987**	**517**	**276**	**41**	**1821**

Note: Separate populations of a species, listed both as endangered and threatened, are with few exeptions, tallied only once, for the endangered population only. (For details, see source.) Figures are as of Sept. 1, 2003.
Source: U.S. Fish and Wildlife Service, *Box Score of U.S. List of Endangered and Threatened Species,* http:ecos.fws.gov

▶SELECTED ENDANGERED MAMMALS OF THE WORLD

Although the list of endangered species includes plants and animals of every type, it is the growing group of endangered mammals that have been of special interest and concern to both conservationists and the general public. The World Conservation Union Red List of Endangered Animals indicated in 2000 that 1,130 mammals are considered threatened: 610 are listed as vulnerable, 340 as endangered, and 180 as critically endangered. The "critically endangered," a term indicating that a species' numbers have declined by at least 80 percent, include:

Bandicoot, eastern barred *(Perameles gunnii nova)* Range: Australia
Bat, Bulmer's fruit *(Aproteles bulmerae)* Range: Papua New Guinea
Bat, Pemba flying-fox *(Pteropus voeltzkowi)* Range: Tanzania
Bear, Baluchistan (*Ursus thibetanus gedrosianus)* Range: Iran, Pakistan
Chinchilla, short-tailed *(Chinchilla brevicaudata)* Range: Andes of South America
Cougar, Eastern (*puma concolor couguar*) Range: Canada, U.S.
Deer, Pere David's *(Elaphurus davidianus)* Range: China
Gazelle, acacia *(Gazella gazella acaciae)* Range: Israel
Gazelle, Przewalski's *(Procapra przewalskii)* Range: China
Gibbon, silvery (*Hylobates moloch)* Range: Indonesia

Goat, Chiltan *(Capra aegagrus chialtanensis)* Range: Pakistan
Hog, pygmy *(Sus salvanius)* Range: Himalayas of Asia
Hutia, large-eared *(Mesocapromys auritus)* Range: Cuba
Lemur, golden bamboo *(Hapalemur aureus)* Range: Madagascar
Leopard, North African *(Panthera pardus panthera)* Range: North Africa
Mole, Juliana's golden *(Amblysomus julianae)* Range: South Africa
Monkey, Northern brown howling *(Alouata guariba guariba)* Range: Brazil
Pika, Helan Shan *(Ochotona helanshanensis)* Range: China
Potoroo, Gilbert's *(Potorous gilbertii)* Range: Australia
Pronghorn, Baja California *(Antilocapra americana peninsularis)* Range: Mexico
Rabbit, Omiltemi *(Sylvilagus insonus)* Range: Mexico
Rhinoceros, black *(Diceros bicornis)* Range: Subsaharan Africa
Rhinoceros, Javan *(Rhinoceros sondaicus)* Range: Southeast Asia
Seal, Mediterranean monk *(Monachus monachus)* Range: Mediterranean and Black Sea
Shrew, Gansu *(Sorex cansulus)* Range: China
Sika, Ryukyu *(Cervus nippon keramae)* Range: China, Japan
Tamarin, black-faced lion *(Leontopithecus caissara)* Range: Brazil
Tamarin, golden lion *(Leontopithecus rosalia)* Range: Brazil
Tiger, Amur *(Panthera tigris altaica)* Range: Northeast Asia
Tiger, South China *(Panthera tigris amoyensis)* Range:China
Titi, northern Bahian blond *(Callicebus barbarabrownae)* Brazil
Vaquita *(Phocoena sinus)* Range: eastern central Pacific
Wombat, northern bairy-nosed *(Lasiorhinus krefftii)* Range: Australia

▶ENDANGERED ANIMALS IN THE UNITED STATES

Although the world's attention is often on large endangered mammals from Africa or the oceans, the United States is home to hundreds of endangered species and subspecies. A subspecies, sometimes called a race, is a local population of a given animal that has some distinctive trait, such as size or color, that sets it apart from the main species.

In the United States, species are classified as threatened or endangered by the U.S. Fish and Wildlife service in accordance with the 1973 Endangered Species Act. The list of endangered species maintained by the Department of the Interior goes back to the original Endangered Species Act of 1966. The first list of endangered species, in March 1967, included 78 species. Today's list contains more than 375 endangered animals and close to 600 endangered plants. Species listed are protected in various ways, most specifically by a prohibition against killing them. Also, a critical habitat can be protected against change if the change would contribute to species extinction. The animals and plants listed (www.endangered.fws.gov) range from the large and well-known, such as the Whooping Crane (Grus americana) and the Florida Panther (Felis concolor coryi), to the small and little-known plants and animals that are nonetheless important for the maintenance of the environment.

Since the Endangered and Threatened Wildlife and Plants listing was started in 1967, several listed species have become extinct, including the Tecopa pupfish (Cyprinodon nevadensis calidae, 1982), the blue pike (Stizostedion vitreum glaucum, 1983), the Santa Barbara song sparrow (Melospiza melodia graminea, 1983), Sampson's pearly mussel (Epioblasma (=Dysnomia) sampsoni, 1984), and the dusky seaside sparrow (Ammodramus (=Ammospiza) maritimus nigrescens, 1990).

There have also been success stories: several species listed as either threatened or endangered have recovered sufficiently to be removed from the list, including the Brown Pelican (Pelecanus occidentalis, 1985), the American Alligator (Alligator mississippiensis, 1987), and the American peregrine Falcon (Falco peregrinus anatum, 1999). Perhaps the most visible success has been the recovery of bald eagle populations, which had been severely threatened by the effects of the pesticide DDT in the food chain. (DDT is now banned in the United States.) Other causes included loss of habitat and lead in shot in waterfowl carcasses on which eagles and other birds of prey feed (the use of lead shot has been phased out in the U.S.) The bald eagle has not yet been delisted, but this step has been proposed. Even if it is removed from the Endangered Species List, it will remain protected under various other statutes.

Endangered and Threatened Species in the U.S., 1980–2003

Year	Endangered			Threatened			Total Species
	Animals	Plants	Total	Animals	Plants	Total	
1980	174	50	224	48	9	57	281
1985	207	93	300	59	25	84	384
1990	263	179	442	93	61	154	596
1995	324	432	756	113	93	206	962
1998	357	567	924	135	135	270	1,194
1999	358	581	939	126	140	266	1,205
2000	368	593	961	129	142	271	1,232
2001	386	595	981	128	145	273	1,254
2002	387	596	983	128	147	275	1,258
2003[1]	388	599	987	129	147	276	1,263

1. As of August 15, 2002. **Source:** U.S. Fish and Wildlife Service, U.S. Species listed per Calendar Year, 1980-present. http://endangered.fws.gov/stats/count.

Animals in the U.S. Officially Listed as Endangered

MAMMALS
Bat, gray
Bat, Hawaiian hoary
Bat, Indiana
Bat, lesser long-nosed
Bat, little Mariana fruit
Bat, Mariana fruit
Bat, Mexican long-nosed
Bat, Ozark big-eared
Bat, Virginia big-eared
Caribou, woodland
Deer, Columbian white-tailed
Deer, Key
Ferret, black-footed
Fox, San Joaquin kit
Jaguar
Jaguarundi, Gulf Coast
Jaguarundi, Sinaloan
Kangaroo rat, Fresno
Kangaroo rat, giant
Kangaroo rat, Morro Bay
Kangaroo rat, San Bernardino Merriam's
Kangaroo rat, Stephens'
Kangaroo rat, Tipton
Manatee, West Indian
Mountain beaver, Point Arena
Mouse, Alabama beach
Mouse, Anastasia Island beach
Mouse, Choctawhatchee beach
Mouse, Key Largo cotton
Mouse, Pacific pocket
Mouse, Perdido Key beach
Mouse, salt marsh harvest
Mouse, St. Andrew beach
Ocelot
Panther, Florida
Pronghorn, Sonoran
Puma, eastern
Rabbit, Lower Keys marsh
Rabbit, pygmy
Rabbit, riparian brush
Rice rat
Seal, Caribbean monk
Seal, Hawaiian monk
Sea-lion, Steller
Sheep, bighorn (2 species)
Shrew, Buena Vista Lake ornate
Squirrel, Carolina northern flying
Squirrel, Delmarva Peninsula fox
Squirrel, Mount Graham red
Squirrel, Virginia northern flying
Vole, Amargosa
Vole, Florida salt marsh
Vole, Hualapai Mexican
Whale, blue
Whale, bowhead
Whale, finback
Whale, humpback
Whale, right
Whale, Sei
Whale, sperm
Wolf, gray
Wolf, red
Woodrat, Key Largo
Woodrat, riparian

BIRDS
Akepa, Hawaii
Akepa, Maui
Akialoa, Kauai
Akiapola`au
Albatross, short-tailed
Blackbird, yellow-shouldered
Bobwhite, masked
Broadbill, Guam
Cahow
Condor, California
Coot, Hawaiian
Crane, Mississippi sandhill
Crane, whooping
Creeper, Hawaii
Creeper, Molokai
Creeper, Oahu
Crow, Hawaiian
Crow, Mariana
Crow, white-necked
Curlew, Eskimo
Duck, Hawaiian
Duck, Laysan
Elepaio, Oahu
Falcon, northern aplomado
Finch, Laysan
Finch, Nihoa
Flycatcher, southwestern willow
Goose, Hawaiian
Hawk, Hawaiian
Hawk, Puerto Rican broad-winged
Hawk, Puerto Rican sharp-shinned
Honeycreeper, crested
Kingfisher, Guam Micronesian
Kite, Everglade snail
Mallard, Mariana
Megapode, Micronesian
Millerbird, Nihoa
Moorhen, Hawaiian common
Moorhen, Mariana common
Nightjar, Puerto Rican
Nukupu`u
`O`o, Kauai
`O`u
Palila
Parrot, Puerto Rican
Parrotbill, Maui
Pelican, brown
Petrel, Hawaiian dark-rumped
Pigeon, Puerto Rican plain
Plover, piping
Po`ouli
Prairie-chicken, Attwater's greater
Pygmy-owl, cactus ferruginous
Rail, California clapper
Rail, Guam
Rail, light-footed clapper
Rail, Yuma clapper
Shrike, San Clemente loggerhead
Sparrow, Cape Sable seaside
Sparrow, Florida grasshopper
Stilt, Hawaiian
Stork, wood
Swiftlet, Mariana gray
Tern, California least
Tern, least
Tern, roseate
Thrush, large Kauai
Thrush, Molokai
Thrush, small Kauai
Vireo, black-capped
Vireo, least Bell's
Warbler, Bachman's
Warbler, golden-cheeked
Warbler, Kirtland's
Warbler, nightingale reed
White-eye, bridled
Woodpecker, ivory-billed
Woodpecker, red-cockaded

REPTILES
Anole, Culebra Island giant
Boa, Puerto Rican
Boa, Virgin Islands tree
Crocodile, American
Gecko, Monito
Lizard, blunt-nosed leopard
Lizard, St. Croix ground
Sea turtle, green
Sea turtle, hawksbill
Sea turtle, Kemp's ridley
Sea turtle, leatherback
Snake, San Francisco garter
Turtle, Alabama red-belly
Turtle, Plymouth redbelly

AMPHIBIANS
Frog, Mississippi gopher
Frog, Mountain yellow-legged
Salamander, Barton Springs
Salamander, California tiger
Salamander, desert slender
Salamander, Santa Cruz long-toed
Salamander, Shenandoah
Salamander, Sonoran tiger
Salamander, Texas blind
Toad, arroyo
Toad, Houston
Toad, Wyoming

FISHES
Cavefish, Alabama
Chub, bonytail
Chub, Borax Lake
Chub, humpback
Chub, Mohave tui
Chub, Oregon
Chub, Owens tui
Chub, Pahranagat roundtail
Chub, Virgin River
Chub, Yaqui
Cui-ui
Dace, Ash Meadows speckled
Dace, Clover Valley speckled
Dace, Independence Valley speckled
Dace, Kendall Warm Springs
Dace, Moapa
Darter, amber
Darter, bluemask
Darter, boulder
Darter, duskytail
Darter, Etowah
Darter, fountain
Darter, Maryland
Darter, Okaloosa
Darter, relict
Darter, vermillion
Darter, watercress
Gambusia, Big Bend
Gambusia, Clear Creek

Gambusia, Pecos
Gambusia, San Marcos
Goby, tidewater
Logperch, Conasauga
Logperch, Roanoke
Madtom, pygmy
Madtom, Scioto
Madtom, smoky
Minnow, Rio Grande silvery
Pikeminnow, Colorado
Poolfish, Pahrump
Pupfish, Ash Meadows Amargosa
Pupfish, Comanche Springs
Pupfish, desert
Pupfish, Devils Hole
Pupfish, Leon Springs
Pupfish, Owens
Pupfish, Warm Springs
Salmon, Atlantic
Salmon, chinook
Salmon, sockeye
Shiner, Cahaba
Shiner, Cape Fear
Shiner, palezone
Shiner, Topeka
Spinedace, White River
Springfish, Hiko White River
Springfish, White River
Steelhead
Stickleback, unarmored threespine
Sturgeon, Alabama
Sturgeon, pallid
Sturgeon, shortnose
Sturgeon, white
Sucker, June
Sucker, Lost River
Sucker, Modoc
Sucker, razorback
Sucker, shortnose
Topminnow, Gila
Trout, Gila
Woundfin

CLAMS
Acornshell, southern
Bean, Cumberland
Bean, purple
Blossom, green
Blossom, tubercled
Blossom, turgid
Blossom, yellow
Catspaw
Catspaw, white
Clubshell
Clubshell, black
Clubshell, ovate
Clubshell, southern
Combshell, Cumberlandian
Combshell, southern
Combshell, upland
Elktoe, Appalachian
Elktoe, Cumberland
Fanshell
Heelsplitter, Carolina
Higgins eye
Kidneyshell, triangular
Lampmussel, Alabama
Lilliput, pale
Mapleleaf, winged
Moccasinshell, Coosa
Moccasinshell, Gulf
Moccasinshell, Ochlockonee
Monkeyface, Appalachian
Monkeyface, Cumberland
Mucket, pink
Mussel, oyster
Mussel, scaleshell
Pearlymussel, birdwing
Pearlymussel, cracking
Pearlymussel, Curtis
Pearlymussel, dromedary
Pearlymussel, littlewing
Pigtoe, Cumberland
Pigtoe, dark
Pigtoe, finerayed
Pigtoe, flat
Pigtoe, heavy
Pigtoe, oval
Pigtoe, rough
Pigtoe, shiny
Pigtoe, southern
Pimpleback, orangefoot
Pocketbook, fat
Pocketbook, Ouachita rock
Pocketbook, shinyrayed
Pocketbook, speckled
Rabbitsfoot, rough
Riffleshell, northern
Riffleshell, tan
Ring pink
Spinymussel, James
Spinymussel, Tar River
Stirrupshell
Three-ridge, fat
Wartyback, white
Wedgemussel, dwarf

SNAILS
Ambersnail, Kanab
Campeloma, slender
Cavesnail, Tumbling Creek
Limpet, Banbury Springs
Lioplax, cylindrical
Marstonia, royal
Pebblesnail, flat
Riversnail, Anthony's
Rocksnail, plicate
Snail, armored
Snail, Iowa Pleistocene
Snail, Morro shoulderband
Snail, Snake River physa
Snail, tulotoma
Snail, Utah valvata
Snail, Virginia fringed mountain
Snails, Oahu tree
Springsnail, Alamosa
Springsnail, Bruneau Hot
Springsnail, Idaho
Springsnail, Socorro

INSECTS
Beetle, American burying
Beetle, Coffin Cave mold
Beetle, Comal Springs dryopid
Beetle, Comal Springs riffle
Beetle, Hungerford's crawling water
Beetle, Kretschmarr Cave mold
Beetle, Mount Hermon June
Beetle, Tooth Cave ground
Butterfly, Behren's silverspot
Butterfly, callippe silverspot
Butterfly, El Segundo blue
Butterfly, Fender's blue
Butterfly, Karner blue
Butterfly, Lange's metalmark
Butterfly, lotis blue
Butterfly, mission blue
Butterfly, Mitchell's satyr
Butterfly, Myrtle's silverspot
Butterfly, Palos Verdes blue
Butterfly, Quino checkerspot
Butterfly, Saint Francis' satyr
Butterfly, San Bruno elfin
Butterfly, Schaus swallowtail
Butterfly, Smith's blue
Butterfly, Uncompahgre fritillary
Dragonfly, Hine's emerald
Fly, Delhi Sands flower-loving
Grasshopper, Zayante band-winged
Ground beetle, [*Rhadine exilis*]
Ground beetle, [*Rhadine infernalis*]
Mold beetle, Helotes
Moth, Blackburn's sphinx
Skipper, Carson wandering
Skipper, Laguna Mountains
Tiger beetle, Ohlone

ARACHNIDS
Harvestman, Bee Creek Cave
Harvestman, Bone Cave
Harvestman, Cokendolpher Cave
Meshweaver, Braken Bat Cave
Meshweaver, Gov't Canyon Bat Cave
Meshweaver, Madla's cave
Meshweaver, Robber Baron Cave
Pseudoscorpion, Tooth Cave
Spider, [*Cicurina veni*]
Spider, Kauai cave wolf or pe'e pe'e maka 'ole
Spider, Madla's cave
Spider, spruce-fir moss
Spider, Tooth Cave

CRUSTACEANS
Amphipod, Hay's Spring
Amphipod, Illinois cave
Amphipod, Kauai cave
Amphipod, Peck's cave
Crayfish, cave (2 species)
Crayfish, Nashville
Crayfish, Shasta
Fairy shrimp, Conservancy
Fairy shrimp, longhorn
Fairy shrimp, Riverside
Fairy shrimp, San Diego
Isopod, Lee County cave
Isopod, Socorro
Shrimp, Alabama cave
Shrimp, California freshwater
Shrimp, Kentucky cave
Tadpole shrimp, vernal pool

Note: As of Sept. 1, 2003
Source: U.S. Fish and Wildlife Service, Threatened and Endangered Species System (TESS), *U.S. Listed Animal Species Reports,* 2003.

Technology

Major Discoveries in the History of Technology

(**See also "Chronology of Information Processing"** in "Computers" and "Satellites and Space Probes" and "Spaceflights Carrying People" in "Astronomy")

B.C.

2,400,000 Ancestors of human beings begin to manufacture stone tools.

1,000,000 Ancestors of human beings learn to control fire.

90,000 People from the Katranda culture in what is now Congo make barbed bone points, probably for use in harpoons.

25,000 People in what is now the Czech Republic begin weaving cloth.

23,000 Bow and arrow developed in Mediterranean regions of Europe and Africa.

10,000 The Jomon culture of Japan makes the first known pottery.

5000 Egyptians start mining and smelting copper ore.

3500 Potter's wheel and (shortly after) wheeled vehicles appear in Mesopotamia.

2900 Great Pyramid of Giza and first form of Stonehenge (a ditch and bank) are built.

2000 Interior bathrooms are built in palaces in Crete.

1500 Earliest glass vessels used in Egypt.

522 Eupalinus of Megara (Greek: 6th cent.) constructs 3,600-ft. tunnel on Samos to supply water from one side of Mt. Castro to other.

290 Pharos lighthouse at Alexandria is built.

260 Archimedes (Greek: c. 287–212 b.c.) develops mathematical descriptions of the lever and other simple machines.

200 Romans develop concrete.

140 Chinese start making paper but do not use it for writing.

100 In Illyria (now Yugoslavia and Albania), water-powered mills are introduced.

A.D.

c. 1 Chinese invent centerline rudder for ships and magnetic compass; neither found in West for 1,000 years.

190 Chinese develop porcelain.

600 First windmills are built in what is now Iran.

704 Between 704 and 751, Chinese start printing with woodblocks.

1040 Chinese develop gunpowder.

1041 Between 1041 and 1048, Chinese inventor Bi Sheng develops movable type.

1190 First-known reference to a compass in Europe.

1267 Book written by Roger Bacon (English: c. 1220–92) in 1267 mentions eyeglasses to correct far-sightedness.

1288 First-known gun, a small cannon, made in China.

1310 Mechanical clocks driven by weights begin to appear in Europe.

c. 1440 Johannes Gutenberg (German: c. 1398–1468) reinvents printing with movable type.

1450 Nicholas of Cusa (German: 1401–64) develops eyeglasses for the nearsighted.

1555 Georg Bauer (Georgius Agricola; German: 1494-1555) writes *De re metallica*, a handbook of mining techniques.

c. 1590 Compound microscope (using two lenses) developed in Holland.

1608 Telescope developed in Holland, probably by Hans Lippershey (German-Dutch: c. 1570–1619).

1620 Cornelis Jacobszoon Drebbel (Dutch: 1572–1633) builds first navigable submarine.

1643 Evangelista Torricelli (Italian: 1608–47) makes first barometer, thereby producing first vacuum known to science.

1654 Christiaan Huygens (Dutch: 1629–95) develops pendulum clock.

1658 Robert Hooke (English: 1635–1703) invents balance spring for watches.

1698 Thomas Savery (English: c. 1650–1715) patents the "Miner's Friend," first practical steam engine.

1701 Jethro Tull (English: 1674–1741), possibly inspired by Chinese devices, invents device for planting seeds called a seed drill.

1709 Daniel Gabriel Fahrenheit (German-Dutch: 1686–1736) invents alcohol thermometer; 1714, mercury thermometer.

1733 John Kay (English: 1704–64) invents flying-shuttle loom, which, along with the steam engine and improvements in making iron, is a key to the start of Industrial Revolution.

1751 Benjamin Huntsman (English: 1704–76) invents crucible process for casting steel.

1762 John Harrison (English: 1693–1776) designs a marine chronometer (clock) accurate enough to enable navigators to calculate longitude at sea.

1764 James Hargreaves (English: 1720–78) introduces spinning jenny, a machine that spins from 8 to 120 threads at once.

1765 James Watt (Scottish: 1736–1819) builds model of his improved steam engine.

1769 Sir Richard Arkwright (English: 1732–92) patents the water frame, a spinning machine that complements spinning jenny.

1783 Joseph-Michel and Jacques-Etienne Montgolfier (French: 1740-1810; 1745–99) develop first hot air balloon. Jacques A.C. Charles (French: 1746–1823) builds first hydrogen balloon.

1785 Edmund Cartwright (English: 1743–1823) invents first form of the power loom.

1792 William Murdock (Scottish: 1754–1839) is first to use coal gas for lighting.

1793 Eli Whitney (American: 1765–1825) invents cotton gin, a machine for separating cotton fibers from seeds.

1800 Alessandro G.A.A. Volta (Italian: 1745–1827) invents first form of chemical battery for producing electric current.

1804 Nicolas-François Appert (French: c.1750–1841) develops canning as means of preserving food.

1807 Robert Fulton (American: 1765–1815) introduces first commercially successful steamboat.

1816 Sir David Brewster (Scottish: 1781–1868) invents kaleidoscope.

1822 Joseph N. Niepce (French: 1765–1833) produces earliest form of the photograph.

1823 Charles Macintosh (Scottish: 1766–1843) patents a waterproof fabric.

1825 George Stephenson (English: 1781–1848) develops first steam-powered locomotive to carry both passengers and freight.

1835 William Henry Fox Talbot (English: 1800–77) invents photographic negative using silver chloride, essentially how black-and-white pictures are made today.

1837 Samuel Finley Breese Morse (American: 1791–1872) patents first commercially successful version of the telegraph.

1839 Louis J.M. Daguerre (French: 1789–1851) announces his process for making photographs, which come to be called daguerreotypes.

Charles Goodyear (American: 1800–60) discovers how to make rubber resistant to heat and cold, a process called vulcanization.

1842 Sir John Bennet Lawes (English: 1814–99) patents manufacture of superphosphate, the first manufactured fertilizer.

1843 Isambard Kingdom Brunel's (English: 1806–59) *Great Britain* is first iron-hulled screw-propellor ship to cross the Atlantic.

1846 Elias Howe (American: 1819–67) patents lockstitch sewing machine.

Richard March Hoe (American: 1812–96) invents rotary printing press.

1851 Isaac Merrit Singer (American: 1811–75) patents continuous-stitch sewing machine.

1852 Elisha Graves Otis (American: 1811–61) installs first elevator incorporating safety device that prevents cage from falling if the cable breaks.

1856 Henry Bessemer (English: 1813–98) develops method of making inexpensive steel (Bessemer process).

1859 Edwin L. Drake (American: 1819–80) drills first oil well, in Titusville, Pa.

1862 Richard Jordan Gatling (American: 1818–1903) invents first form of machine gun.

1866 Robert Whitehead (English: 1823–1905) invents naval torpedo. Georges Leclanché (French: 1839–82) develops first form of dry cell for producing electricity.

1867 Latham Sholes (American: 1819–90) and two others invent first practical typewriter.

1869 Hippolyte Mège Mouriés (French: 1817–80) patents margarine.

1866 Cyrus W. Field (U.S.: 1819–92) succeeds in laying the Trans-Atlantic Cable under the Atlantic Ocean, connecting Europe to America by telegraph wire.

1874 Joseph Farwell Glidden (American: 1813–1906) invents the kind of barbed wire used today.

1876 Alexander Graham Bell (Scottish-American: 1847–1922) invents telephone.

Karl von Linde (German: 1842–1934) invents first practical refrigerator.

1877 Nikolaus A. Otto (German: 1832–91) invents type of internal combustion engine still used in most automobiles.

Thomas Alva Edison (U.S.: 1847–1931) invents phonograph, which uses a tinfoil-covered cylinder.

1878 Louis-Marie-Hilaire Bernigaud (French: 1839–1924) develops rayon.

Carl Gustaf Patrik de Laval (Swedish: 1845–1913) invents turbine operated centrifugal cream separator.

1879 Edison and Sir Joseph W. Swan (English: 1828–1914) independently discover how to make practical electric lights.

1885 Karl Benz (German: 1844–1929) builds precursor of modern automobile.

Rover Safety Bicycle, built in England, is first bicycle with essentially modern features.

1886 George Westinghouse (American: 1846–1914) invents air brake for railroad cars.

1888 Emile Berliner (German: 1851–1929) invents phonograph disk.

John B. Dunlop (Scottish: 1840–1921) patents air-filled tire.

George Eastman (American: 1854–1932) develops first camera using roll film.

1889 Gustave Eiffel (French: 1832–1923) builds his famous tower in Paris; at 993 ft., it is tallest freestanding structure of the time.

1893 Rudolf Diesel (German: 1858–1913) describes diesel engine.

1895 First public showing of a motion picture, "Workers Leaving the Lumière Factory" by Auguste and Louis Lumière (French: 1862–1954; 1864–1948), in Paris.

Guglielmo Marconi (Italian: 1874–1937) transmits signals for a mile with his wireless telegraph (a precursor of radio) near Bologna, Italy.

1897 Karl Ferdinand Braun (German: 1850–1918) invents cathode-ray tube oscilloscope.

1898 Valdemar Poulsen (Danish: 1869–1942) invents magnetic wire recorder, the precursor to the modern tape recorder.

1902 Willis H. Carrier (American: 1876–1950) invents air conditioning.

1903 Orville and Wilbur Wright (American: 1871–1948; 1867–1912) fly the first successful airplane at Kitty Hawk, N.C.

1904 John Fleming (English: 1849–1945) develops first vacuum tube, a device for changing alternating current to direct.

1907 Lee De Forest (American: 1873–1961) patents Audion vacuum tube, a device for magnifying weak electronic signals.

1908 Henry Ford (American: 1863–1947) introduces Model T, the first affordable automobile.

1909 Leo Baekeland (Belgian-American: 1863–1944) patents Bakelite, the first truly successful plastic.

1912 Reginald Aubrey Fessenden (CanadianAmerican: 1866-1932) develops heterodyne circuit, an important improvement in radio reception.

1917 Clarence Birdseye (American: 1886–1956) develops freezing as a means of preserving food.

1919 Sir Arthur W. Brown (British: 1886–1948) and Sir John W. Alcock (British: 1892–1919) make first transatlantic flight, Newfoundland to Ireland.

1924 Vladimir Kosma Zworykin (Russian-American: 1889–1982) develops iconoscope, the beginning of modern television.

1929 Robert H. Goddard (American: 1882–1945) launches first instrumented, liquid-fueled rocket.

1930 Sir Frank Whittle (British: 1907–96) patents jet engine.

1931 Ernst A.F. Ruska (German: 1906–88) builds first electron microscope.

1934 Wallace Hume Carothers (American: 1896–1937) invents nylon, first marketed in 1938.

1935 Sir Robert Alexander Watson-Watt (Scottish: 1892-1973) begins work on radio detection and ranging (radar).

1937 Chester F. Carlson (American: 1906–68) invents xerography, the first method of photocopying.

1939 Paul H. Müller (Swiss: 1899–1965) discovers that DDT is potent and long-lasting insecticide.

Igor I. Sikorsky (Russian-American: 1889–1972) designs and flies first helicopter developed for mass production.

1940 Peter Carl Goldmark (Hungarian-American: 1906–77) demonstrates first successful color television system.

1941 John Rex Whinfield (British: 1901–66) invents Dacron.

1942 Enrico Fermi (Italian-American: 1901–54) builds first nuclear reactor.

1947 Dennis Gabor (Hungarian-British: 1900–79) develops holography, a method of recording and displaying a three-dimensional object.

1948 Goldmark develops the 33⅓ rpm long-playing phonograph record.

Georges de Mestral (Swiss: 1908–90) invents Velcro, patented in 1955.

John Bardeen (American: 1908–91), Walter H. Brattain (American: 1902–87), and William B. Shockley (English-American: 1910-89) invent the transistor.

1957 Gordon Gould (American: 1920–) develops basic idea for the laser, which he succeeds in patenting in 1986 after long struggle.

The Soviet spacecraft *Sputnik 1* becomes the first satellite to orbit Earth.

1958 United States opens first experimental nuclear power plant.

1959 First industrial robot is marketed.

1962 First active communications satellite, Telstar, goes into orbit.

1963 Audiocassettes introduced.

1964 Touch-tone telephones introduced.

1966 Engineers at ITT demonstrate fiber optics as a method of transmitting data.

1968 The first supersonic airliner, the Soviet Tupolev TU-144, is demonstrated on Dec. 31.
1969 ATMs and bar-code scanners introduced.
1970 Boeing 747 jets go into service.
1975 IBM introduces first laser printer.
1982 Compact disc players introduced.
1984 Motorola introduces first commercial version of cellular phone in U.S.
1989 The U.S. Defense Department launches the first satellite in the Global Positioning System.
1990 Leigh T. Canham (British) develops a method for producing light from stimulated silicon.
1991 Woo Paik and coworkers produce the first prototype of digital high-definition television.
1994 Channel Tunnel, also known as the Chunnel, connecting England and France beneath the English Channel, is officially opened.

Charles K. Rhodes of the University of Chicago develops an X-ray-emitting laser.
1995 Scientists at Los Alamos National Laboratory in New Mexico develop a flexible tape that is superconducting at the temperature of liquid nitrogen (about –325°F).

A group led by Junji Kido of Yamagata Univ. in Japan combines three different diode layers, including a blue-emitting diode that is a major advance of its own, to make white light.

Competing groups agree on standards for the Digital Video Disc (DVD), an improved compact disc that can store a complete motion picture on a disc the size of a CD.
1998 John A. Turner and Oscar Khaselev of the U.S. National Renewable Energy Laboratory in Golden, Colo. develop a solar cell that can split water into hydrogen and oxygen.

National Inventors Hall of Fame

In 1973 the U.S. National Council of Patent Law Associations (now the National Council of Intellectual Property Law) began the practice of naming inventors who hold U.S. patents to the National Inventors Hall of Fame. Although many of those honored have many patents, the committee selects one patent for each inventor (or group of inventors) as the occasion for the award, which they identify by the title of the original patent application. When an invention is the work of more than one person, the description of the invention is given only for one inventor. The date at the end of each of the following entries denotes the year of induction. The Hall is located in Akron, Ohio.

Edward Acheson (American: 1856–1931) CARBORUNDUM The hardest man-made surface, carborundum was integral to the development of interchangeable metal parts. It was cited by the Patent and Trademark Office as one of the inventions most responsible for the industrial age. (1997)
Ernst Alexanderson (Swedish-American: 1878–1975) HIGH FREQUENCY ALTERNATOR This device makes it possible for radio (and television) to transmit voices and music, not just dots and dashes. (1983)
Andrew Alford (Russian-American: 1904–92) LOCALIZER ANTENNA SYSTEM Alford developed the radio system for navigation as well as instrument landing systems for airplanes. (1983)
Luis Walter Alvarez (American: 1911–88) RADIO DISTANCE AND DIRECTION INDICATOR Alvarez is better known for developing methods of studying subatomic particles, which brought him a Nobel Prize for Physics in 1968. (1978)
Edwin Howard Armstrong (American: 1890–1954) METHOD OF RECEIVING HIGH FREQUENCY OSCILLATIONS Armstrong's several inventions connected with radio broadcasting and reception made possible the "radio days" of the 1920s. In 1939 he invented FM broadcasting and reception, which helped lead to another revolution in radio. (1980)
George H. Babcock (American: 1832–93) WATER TUBE STEAM BOILER The boilers designed by Babcock and Stephen Wilcox Jr. were much less likely to explode than the fire tube boilers that preceded them. To this day, nearly half the electricity produced in the U.S. comes from boilers based on Babcock and Wilcox's original design. (1997)
Leo Hendrik Baekeland (Belgian-American: 1863–1944) SYNTHETIC RESINS Baekeland's plastic (synthetic resin), which he named Bakelite, made people realize the potential of plastics. (1978)
Rodney Bagley (American: 1934-) CERAMIC SUBSTRATE FOR CATALYTIC CONVERTERS When coated with precious metal catalysts, this ceramic honeycomb enables 95 percent of the pollutants from automobile exhaust to be converted into harmless water vapor and carbon dioxide. (2002)
Robert L. Banks (American: 1921-89) POLYMERS Banks and Paul Hogan created high-density polyethylene (HDPE), which did not require the extremely high pressures used to manufacture low-density polyethylene. Products that use HDPE include milk jugs, laundry baskets, and artificial turf. (2001)
John Bardeen (American: 1908–91) TRANSISTOR The transistor is the essential semiconductor device used on microprocessors and other chips. (1974)
Arnold O. Beckman (American: 1900–) APPARATUS FOR TESTING ACIDITY Beckman developed a precise instrument to measure how acidic a substance is as well as other precision instruments. (1987)
S. Joseph Begun (Polish-American: 1905–95) MAGNETIC RECORDING. He built the first tape recorder used for broadcasting. (1998)
Alexander Graham Bell (Scottish-American: 1874–1922) TELEGRAPHY Bell's most famous of many inventions was the telephone. (1974)
Willard H. Bennett (American: 1903–87) RADIO FREQUENCY MASS SPECTROMETER This device measures the chemical composition of elements. (1991)
Emile Berliner (German-American: 1851–1929) MICROPHONE AND GRAMOPHONE. Berliner's microphone made it possible to use the telephone over long distances. Berliner also developed the gramophone, the forerunner of the record-player. (1994)
Henry Bessemer (English: 1813-98) BESSEMER STEEL PROCESS Bessemer's converter made it possible for unskilled workers to make vast quantities of steel cheaply, enabling the industrial age. (2002)
Gerd Karl Binnig (German: 1947–) SCANNING TUNNELING MICROSCOPE, which can trace details as small as 0.1 angstrom, or one-tenth the size of an atom. It opened entirely new views of the study of the structure of atoms and won Binnig and his partner Heinrich Rohrer the Nobel Prize for Physics in 1986. (1994)
Forrest Bird (American: 1921–) MEDICAL RESPIRATORS The little green box known as "The Bird" prevented thousands from dying from cardiopulmonary failure. Bird also developed the Babybird respirator for low birthweight babies, reducing mortality rates for infants with respiratory problems. (1995)
Harold Stephen Black (American: 1898–) NEGATIVE FEEDBACK AMPLIFIER The basic principle of the negative feedback amplifier has become fundamental to many other devices since Black first used it to control distortion. (1981)
Samuel Blum (American: 1920- EXCIMER LASER SURGERY (see Rangaswamy Srinivasan) (2002)

Baruch S. Blumberg (American: 1925–) HEPATITIS B VACCINE This vaccine (invented with Irving Millman) has protected hundreds of millions of people worldwide against the hepatitis B virus, still one of the leading causes of death worldwide. (1993)
Nils Bohlin (Swedish: 1920-) 3-POINT SAFETY BELT Bohlin, a Volvo engineer, developed the first lap and shoulder belt that was not only secure, but comfortable for automobile passengers to wear. (2002)
Robert A. Bower (American: 1936–) FIELD EFFECT DEVICE WITH INSULATED GATE, which gave semiconductors the speed necessary for modern microelectronic applications. It became the primary device used in almost all modern integrated circuits. (1997)
Herbert W. Boyer (American: 1936-) PROCESS FOR PRODUCING BIOLOGICALLY FUNCTIONAL MOLECULAR CHIMERAS When Boyer and Stan Cohen added genes from an organism to a simple cell, they discovered that the genes replicated themselves in the cell. Known as recombinant DNA, these experiments launched the biotechnology industry; Boyer and Cohen founded the biotechnology firm Genentech, Inc., which created the first genetically engineered human insulin. (2001)
Walter H. Brattain (American: 1902–87) TRANSISTOR (see John Bardeen) (1974)
Rachel Fuller Brown (American: 1898–1980) NYSTATIN (See Elizabeth Lee Hazen) (1994)
Luther Burbank (American: 1849–1926) PEACH Burbank's work in developing more than 800 new varieties of plants contributed to the development of the Plant Patent program in 1930. Burbank holds 16 plant patents, all issued posthumously. (1986)
Joseph H. Burckhalter (American: 1912–) FITC This yellow-green compound, known to doctors as fluorescein isothiocyanate, has proved invaluable in identifying different antibodies. In addition to helping identify the causes of AIDS, FITC has been used to speed the diagnosis of leukemia and lymphoma. (1995)
William Seward Burroughs (American: 1857–98) CALCULATING MACHINE Although the calculating machine dates from the 17th century, Burroughs's was the first that could be mass produced and easily used. (1987)
William Meriam Burton (American: 1865–1954) MANUFACTURE OF GASOLINE Burton developed the first commercially successful cracking process, which yielded twice the amount of gasoline from crude oil than the previous methods. (1984)
Donald L. Campbell (American: 1904–) FLUID CATALYTIC CRACKING This process revolutionized the petroleum industry by more efficiently transforming higher boiling oils into lighter, usable products. It is used to produce over half of the world's gasoline. (1999)
Marvin Camras (American: 1916–95) METHOD AND MEANS OF MAGNETIC RECORDING Before the tapes currently used to record sound and pictures, sound was recorded on the wire recorder that Camras invented in the 1930s. (1985)
Chester F. Carlson (American: 1906–68) ELECTROPHOTOGRAPHY Carlson invented the dry copying method called xerography. Although patented in 1940, the dry copier was not marketed until 1958, by which time Carlson had patented many improvements. (1981)
Wallace Hume Carothers (American: 1896–1937) DIAMINE-DICARBOXYLIC ACID SALTS AND PROCESS OF PREPARING SAME AND SYNTHETIC FIBER This is better known as nylon. Carothers also developed the first successful synthetic rubber. (1984)
Willis Haviland Carrier (American: 1876–1950) APPARATUS FOR TREATING AIR Carrier invented the first successful air-conditioning system, and many of the techniques used in modern refrigerators. (1985)
George Washington Carver (American: c. 1864–1943) PRODUCTS USING PEANUTS AND SWEET POTATOES A successful scientist in Iowa who later taught at the Tuskegee Institute, Carver developed over 300 uses for the peanut and 118 sweet-potato byproducts as an incentive for farmers to plant regenerative crops rather than the traditional soil-destroying cotton and tobacco. (1990)
Stanley N. Cohen (American: 1935-) PROCESS FOR PRODUCING BIOLOGICALLY FUNCTIONAL MOLECULAR CHIMERAS (see Herbert W. Boyer) (2001)
Frank B. Colton (Polish-American: 1923–) ORAL CONTRACEPTIVES Colton not only developed the first "pill" in 1960, but he also pioneered the development of anabolic steroids. (1988)
Lloyd H. Conover (American: 1923–) TETRACYCLINE Before Conover created tetracycline, no one thought that a natural drug could be chemically modified to improve its action; tetracycline remains the drug of choice for tick-spread disease such as Rocky Mountain spotted fever and Lyme disease. (1992)
William D. Coolidge (American: 1873–1974) VACUUM TUBE The "Coolidge tube" is actually an X-ray generator. Among his many other inventions was the modern tungsten-filament electric light. (1975)
Frederick G. Cottrell (American 1877–1948) ELECTROSTATIC PRECIPITATOR Cottrell's invention uses high-voltage electricity to capture the particulates, including fly ash, dust, and droplets of acid or other chemicals, found in smoke from the burning of fossil fuels and many industrial processes; the tons of waste can then be removed from smoke instead of being spread around the countryside. (1992)
Seymour Cray (American: 1925–96) SUPERCOMPUTER Cray's supercomputer processed information much faster than other computers because of its extraordinarily high number of integrated circuits. (1997)
Raymond V. Damadian (American: 1936–) APPARATUS AND METHOD FOR DETECTING CANCER IN TISSUE Damadian was the first to realize that the nuclear magnetic resonance technique could be used on living creatures and could detect cancer cells. (1989)
Mark Dean (American: 1957–) MICROCOMPUTER WITH BUS CONTROL MEANS FOR PERIPHERAL DEVICES Dean and Dennis Moeller, two IBM scientists, developed improvements in computer architecture that permitted rapid communication between internal and external components of IBM-compatible computers. (1997)
John Deere (American: 1804–86) PLOW Deere's vastly improved plow launched his commercial success,. (1989)
Lee De Forest (American: 1873–1961) AUDION AMPLIFIER De Forest's invention of the triode was the key to modern radio and later developments in the amplification of signals. (1977)
Robert H. Dennard (American: 1932–) DYNAMIC RANDOM ACCESS MEMORY (RAM) Dennard's dense, cost-effective memory system allowed computers to shrink dramatically from warehouse size to desktop size. RAM has been used as the memory system in all computers since the 1970s. (1997)
Rudolf Diesel (German: 1858–1913) INTERNAL COMBUSTION ENGINE The pressure-ignited heat engine is still called the diesel engine. (1976)
Walt Disney (American: 1901-66) MULTIPLANE CAMERA Years after he brought Mickey Mouse to the screen, his multiplane camera brought about richer animation. It was first used for a full-length feature in 1937's "Snow White and the Seven Dwarfs." (2000)
Carl Djerassi (Austrian-American: 1923–) ORAL CONTRACEPTIVES Djerassi's research into the chemistry of steroids and his synthesis of antihistamines are two of his many contributions to modern organic chemistry. (1978)
Herbert Henry Dow (Canadian-American: 1866–1930) BROMINE Besides new methods of extracting bromine and chlorine from naturally occurring salt deposits, Dow patented over 90 inventions and founded Dow Chemical. (1983)
Charles Stark Draper (American: 1901–87) GYROSCOPIC EQUIPMENT Draper's gyroscopic stabilizer helped antiaircraft guns and falling bombs hit their

targets during World War II. Later he developed gyroscopic systems for air and marine navigation and for guided missiles. (1983)
Graham J. Durant (British-American: 1934–) CIMETIDINE (TAGAMET) With John C. Emmet and C. Robin Ganellin, Durant developed the major drug used to suppress acid in stomach and intestinal ulcers. (1990)
George Eastman (American: 1854–1932) METHOD AND APPARATUS FOR COATING PLATES FOR USE IN PHOTOGRAPHY Eastman developed the dry plate negative and transparent roll film for still cameras, and a motion picture film for use in the newly invented cinema. (1977)
John Presper Eckert, Jr. (American: 1919-95) ENIAC DATA TRANSLATING DEVICE This 150-foot long, 30-ton computer required 200 people to operate, and can be outperformed by a 1970s calculator, but the Electronic Numerical Integrator and Computer is considered the prototype from which other modern computers evolved. (2002)

Utility Patents Issued for Inventions, 1790–2001

Period	Patents issued	Period	Patents issued
1790-1800	309	**1901-10**	315,193
1801-10	1,093	**1911-20**	383,117
1811-20	1,930	**1921-30**	423,089
1821-30	3,086	**1931-40**	439,863
1831-40	5,519	**1941-50**	308,436
1841-50	5,933	**1951-60**	430,120
1851-60	23,065	**1961-70**	585,115
1861-70	79,459	**1971-80**	687,818
1871-80	125,438	**1981-90**	737,017
1881-90	207,514	**1991-2000**	1,175,523
1891-1900	220,608	**2001**	166,039

Note: Excludes patents granted for designs and botanical plants.
Sources: U.S. Bureau of the Census, *The Statistical History of the United States* (1976) and U.S. Patent Office, *All Technologies Report* (February, 2002)

Harold E. Edgerton (American: 1903–90) STROBOSCOPE This device produced flashes that stopped action in a photograph at regular intervals. (His photograph of the crown produced by a drop of milk falling into a bowl of milk dates from the 1930s.) (1986)
Thomas Alva Edison (American: 1847–1931) ELECTRIC LAMP In addition to the carbon-filament electric lamp, Edison patented a phonograph, the mimeograph, the fluoroscope, and motion picture cameras and projectors. (1973)
Gertrude B. Elion (American: 1918–99) DNA-BLOCKING DRUGS Elion was the first woman elected to the Hall of Fame, for her discovery of drugs crucial to cancer treatment and anti-viral research. (1991)
John C. Emmet (British: 1938–) CIMETIDINE (TAGAMET®) (See Graham J. Durant). (1990)
Douglas Engelbart (American: 1925–) COMPUTER MOUSE Officially known as the X-Y Position Indicator for a Display System, this was the only patentable part of his pioneering work in computer design. (1998)
John Ericsson (American: 1803–89) PROPELLOR Ericsson's invention offered a highly efficient, difficult to damage, and easily maintained means of propulsion that sped the transition from wind to steam power (1993)
Oliver Evans (American: 1755-1819) HIGH PRESSURE STEAM ENGINE Although James Watt had already invented a low-pressure steam engine, Evans placed the cylinder and the crankshaft at the same end instead of at opposite ends, greatly reducing the overall weight (2001)
Federico Faggin (Italian-American 1941–) MICROPROCESSOR Faggin and Stanley Mazor refined Ted Hoff's microprocessor concept to produce the first single-chip central processing unit in 1971. All three men helped persuade Intel to make the new computers available to the general public. (1996)
Philo Taylor Farnsworth (American: 1906–71) TELEVISION SYSTEM Farnsworth patented many components of all-electronic television. He also worked on the electronic microscope, the use of ultraviolet light for seeing in the dark, and nuclear fusion. (1984)
James L. Fergason (American: 1934–) LIQUID CRYSTAL DISPLAY This invention is used in more than

Utility Patents Granted, 1901–2001

Utility patents, also known as patents for inventions, are issued for the invention of or improvement to a new and useful process, machine, manufacture, or composition of matter. They allow their owners to prohibit others from making, using or selling the invention for up to 17 years from the date of the grant. Utility patents represent about 90 percent of all patents. The other 10 percent are divided among plant patents, for a new and distinct, invented, or discovered asexually reproduced plant; and design patents, for a new, original, and ornamental design for an article of manufacture. Design patents last only 14 years.

		U.S. ownership			Foreign ownership		
Year	Total patents granted	Corporations	Government[1]	Individuals	Corporations	Government	Individuals
1901	25,546	4,370	N.A.	20,896[2]	280	N.A.	(2)
1921	37,798	9,860	N.A.	27,098[2]	840	N.A.	(2)
1930	45,226	19,700	N.A.	23,726[2]	1,800	N.A.	(2)
1940	42,238	22,165	40	17,627[2]	2,406	N.A.	(2)
1950	43,040	21,782	622	18,960[2]	1,660	N.A.	(2)
1960	47,170	28,187	1,244	13,069[2]	4,670	N.A.	(2)
1970	64,427	36,896	1,726	13,511[2]	12,294	N.A.	(2)
1980	61,819	27,640	1,237	9,956	18,874	254	3,858
1990	90,365	36,094	983	12,542	35,548	423	4,775
1995	101,419	44,035	1,028	12,885	38,688	245	4,538
1996	109,645	48,741	923	13,729	41,477	259	4,516
1997	111,983	50,220	944	12,914	42,907	273	4,725
1998	147,521	66,053	1,027	16,408	57,668	256	6,109
1999	153,485	69,390	983	16,698	60,168	162	6,084
2000	157,495	70,884	929	16,129	63,182	104	6,267
2001	166,039	74,327	957	15,205	68,942	92	6,516

1. Excludes patents issued to Alien Property Custodian until 1942. 2. Patents issued to foreign individuals before 1980 are included with U.S. individuals. **Source:** Department of Commerce, Patent and Trademark Office, *All Technologies Report,* Feburary, 2002.

five billion products annually, including computers, medical devices, and consumer electronics. (1998)

Enrico Fermi (Italian-American: 1901–54) NEUTRONIC REACTOR Fermi's nuclear reactor is the basis of nuclear power today. His many contributions to modern physics include basic theoretical work and experimental physics. (1976)

Reginald Aubrey Fessenden (American: 1866-1932) WIRELESS RADIO COMMUNICATION A disciple of both Alexander Graham Bell and Thomas Edison, he discovered the means for radio waves, which previously had carried only Morse Code, to transmit voice and other sounds directly. (2000)

Thomas J. Fogarty (American: 1934-) EMBOLECTOMY CATHETER This device, which utilizes a thin balloon to withdraw vascular occlusions, is still the most widely used technique for blood clot removal, and has encouraged advances for other minimally invasive surgeries, including angioplasty. (2001)

Henry Ford (American: 1863–1947) TRANSMISSION MECHANISM Best remembered for his innovative business practices, Ford also invented and patented numerous mechanisms used in automobiles. (1982)

Jay W. Forrester (American: 1918–) MULTICOORDINATED DIGITAL INFORMATION STORAGE DEVICE Forrester's main invention was the magnetic storage of information. Most computers today, from giant mainframes to lightweight laptops, still use magnetic storage to store data. (1979)

Alfred Free (American: 1913- 2000) and **Helen Murray Free** (American: 1923-) DIP-AND-READ TESTS FOR URINALYSIS These tests, developed by the husband and wife team of scientists, was the first to allow diabetics to easily and accurately monitor their blood glucose levels on their own. (2000)

C. Robin Ganellin (British: 1934–) CIMETIDINE (TAGAMET®) (See Graham J. Durant). (1990)

Edmund Germer (German-American: 1901–87) FLUORESCENT LIGHT Germer's high-pressure mercury-vapor lamp vastly increased the efficiency and safety of lighting while producing less heat. (1996)

Charles P. Ginsburg (American: 1920–) VIDEOTAPE RECORDER The VCR was originally developed by an engineering team led by Ginsburg. (1990)

Robert Hutchings Goddard (American: 1882–1945) CONTROL MECHANISM FOR ROCKET APPARATUS The father of American rocketry, Goddard devised successful rocket weapons and rocket-assisted take-off mechanisms for carrier-based airplanes for the military. (1979)

Charles Goodyear (American: 1800–60) IMPROVEMENT IN INDIA-RUBBER FABRICS In 1844 Goodyear discovered vulcanization, a process to make rubber resistant to heat and cold. (1976)

Gordon Gould (American: 1920–) OPTICALLY PUMPED LASER AMPLIFIERS Gould envisioned the basic idea for the laser in 1957, but did not win his first patent until 1977. (1991)

Wilson Greatbatch (American: 1919–) MEDICAL CARDIAC PACEMAKER Greatbatch's pacemaker has helped millions of people with heart disease. He also invented batteries to keep the pacemaker running without adverse effects from the battery chemicals. (1986)

Leonard M. Greene (American: 1918–) AIRPLANE STALL WARNING DEVICE Patented in 1949. (1991)

Charles Martin Hall (American: 1863–1914) MANUFACTURE OF ALUMINUM In 1886, Hall developed a cheap method to make aluminum (then selling at $5 a pound). (1976)

Robert N. Hall (American: 1919–) HIGH VOLTAGE HIGH POWER SEMICONDUCTOR PIN RECTIFIER This invention greatly reduced the waste of power and dangerous heat build-up that accompanies large-scale power transmission. Hall also invented the first semi-conductor laser, which is now commonly found in CD players. (1994)

W.E. "Butch" Hanford (American: 1908–) POLYURETHANE This 1942 patent (won with Donald F. Holmes) remains the basis for chemistry used in manufacture of all polyurethanes. (1991)

Elizabeth Lee Hazen (American: 1885–1975) NYSTATIN, the world's first non-toxic anti-fungal antibiotic. This medicine cures many disfiguring and disabling skin, mouth, and throat infections. Nystatin has also been used to treat Dutch elm disease and to rescue water-damaged artworks from mold. (1994)

M. Stephen Heilman (American: 1933-) IMPLANTABLE DEFIBRILLATOR (see Michel Mirowski) (2002)

William R. Hewlett (American 1913–) VARIABLE FREQUENCY OSCILLATION GENERATOR Hewlett's first invention was the audio oscillator in 1939, a device for generating high-quality audio frequencies that could be used for many different purposes; among the first uses was production of special sounds for the Disney movie *Fantasia*. (1992)

René Alphonse Higonnet (French: 1902–83) PHOTO COMPOSING MACHINE Along with Louis Marius Moyroud, Higonnet developed (in 1946) the first machine to set type by recording the images of letters on film. Film composition became the standard way of setting type, replacing type set from metal. (1985)

James Hillier (Canadian-American: 1915–) ELECTRON LENS CORRECTION DEVICE Although Hillier was not the first to make a microscope using electrons, his microscopes became the standard in the field. Electron microscopes can enlarge much smaller details than light microscopes because the wavelength of an electron is much smaller than the wavelength of a photon of visible light.

Marcian Edward "Ted" Hoff, Jr. (American: 1937–) MICROPROCESSOR CONCEPT AND ARCHITECTURE Hoff was the first to recognize the possibility of a single-chip CPU, thus helping to transform the computer from a machine that occupied an entire room to one that could fit onto a desk. (1996)

Felix Hoffmann (German: 1868- 1946) ASPIRIN Technically known as acetyl salicylic acid, aspirin is the closest thing to a miracle drug, not least for its contribution to the fight against heart attack and stroke. (2002)

Paul Hogan (American: 1919-) POLYMERS (see Robert L. Banks) (2001)

Herman Hollerith (American: 1869–1929) STORAGE AND PROCESSING OF NUMERICAL DATA Hollerith's punched cards and readers, developed for the 1890 U.S. Census, became the basis of modern data processing. (1990)

Donald Fletcher Holmes (American: 1910–80) POLYURETHANE (see W.E.Hanford). (1991)

Eugene J. Houdry (French: 1892–1962) CATALYTIC CRACKING OF PETROLEUM Houdry developed a process to make high-grade gasoline and airplane fuel from crude oil, as well as other catalytic processes and devices, including the basic catalytic converter used in mufflers. (1990)

J. Franklin Hyde (American: 1903-99) FUSED SILICA AND SILICONES Hyde discovered first new way of making glass in more than 3,000 years. His ultra-pure glass has many uses, including spacecraft windows, telescopes, and precision lenses for manufacturing equipment. It also provided the bases for the semiconductor and fiber optics industries. (2000)

Percy F. Julian (American: 1899–1975) SYNTHESIS OF CORTISONE AND OTHER HORMONES Julian discovered that soybeans could be used as the basis for synthesizing cortisone, an important hormone with many medical applications. (1990)

Donald B. Keck (American 1941–) FUSED SILICA OPTICAL WAVEGUIDE (See Robert D. Maurer). (1993)

Charles Franklin Kettering (American: 1875–1958) ENGINE STARTING DEVICES AND IGNITION SYSTEM Kettering's Delco company produced the self-starter for automobiles and a small generator for use in isolated farms. (1980)

Jack S. Kilby (American: 1923–) MINIATURIIZED ELECTRONIC CIRCUITS The monolithic integrated circuit that Kilby developed for Texas Instruments in 1959 was the beginning of the modern integrated circuit. (1982)
Willem J. Kolff (Dutch-American: 1911–) SOFT-SHELL MUSHROOM-SHAPED HEART The patent cited is for an early version of an artificial heart, but Kolff's most important work was the development of the artificial kidney dialysis machine. (1985)
William Justin Kroll (Luxembourgian 1889-1973) TITANIUM AND ZIRCONIUM PROCESSING Kroll discovered a process to produce metallic titanium, an abundant element that had previously proved difficult to obtain from its natural state, and when heated, had yielded a useless substance. He later applied the same process to zirconium. (2000)
Raymond Kurzweil (American: 1948-) KURZWEIL READING MACHINE Kurzweil's invention, which scans and reads printed material, is considered the most significant advancement for the blind since Braille. (2002)
Stephanie Kwolek (American: 1923–) KEVLAR This substance is five times as strong as steel and weighs 40% less than glass, making it ideal for use in aircraft construction, golf clubs and tennis racquets, fiber optic cables, and perhaps most important, bulletproof vests. (1995)
Irwin Lachman (American: 1930-) CERAMIC SUBSTRATE FOR CATALYTIC CONVERTERS (See Rodney Bagley) (2002)
Edwin Herbert Land (American: 1909–91) PHOTOGRAPHIC PRODUCT COMPRISING A RUPTURABLE CONTAINER CARRYING PHOTOGRAPHIC PROCESSING LIQUID Land's first success was the development and application of substances that polarize light. He also invented the instant Polaroid camera. (1977)
Alois Langer (American: 1945-) IMPLANTABLE DEFIBRILLATOR (see Michel Mirowski) (2002)
Irving Langmuir (American: 1881–1957) INCANDESCENT ELECTRIC LAMP In 1913, Langmuir realized that filling the original Edison-Swan lightbulb with a nonburning gas would result in a longer-lasting light. He later won a Nobel Prize (1932) for his work on the chemistry of surfaces. (1989)
Ernest Orlando Lawrence (American: 1901–58) METHOD AND APPARATUS FOR THE ACCELERATION OF IONS Although Lawrence did not develop the very first particle accelerator (known as an "atom smasher"), his 1930 cyclotron has been the basic pattern for the most successful and powerful machines of its kind ever since. (1982)
William P. Lear (American: 1902–78) AUTOMOBILE RADIO Though he was better known for inventing the Learjet, Lear's first claim to fame was in radio technology, with a company that went on to become Motorola. (1993)
Robert S. Ledley (American: 1926–) WHOLE-BODY C.A.T. SCANNER Ledley's device for making three-dimensional images of living tissues quickly became an established medical technique for looking inside the human body. (1990)
Ronald Lewis (American: 1936-) CERAMIC SUBSTRATE FOR CATALYTIC CONVERTERS (See Rodney Bagley) (2002)
Theodore Harold Maiman (American: 1927–) RUBY LASER SYSTEMS Although there has been much dispute about the invention of the laser, Maiman's ruby laser was the first to be recognized worldwide and to be commercially successful. (1984)
Guglielmo Marconi (Italian: 1874–1937) TRANSMITTING ELECTRICAL SIGNALS Marconi's patent for using radio waves to carry coded messages is best known as wireless telegraphy. (1975)
Homer Z. Martin (American: 1910–1993) FLUID CATALYTIC CRACKING (See Donald L. Campbell) (1999)
John Mauchly (American: 1907-80) ENIAC DATA TRANSLATING DEVICE (see John Presper Eckert, Jr.) (2002)
Robert D. Maurer (American: 1924–) FUSED SILICA OPTICAL WAVEGUIDE (With Donald B. Keck and Peter C. Schultz). This optical fiber helped launch the information age: it carries 65,000 times more information than copper wire 30-50 times farther without boosting the signal. (1993)
Stanley Mazor (American: 1941–) MICROPROCESSOR (See Federico Faggin) (1996)
Cyrus McCormick (American: 809–94) REAPER McCormick's machine for harvesting grain (patented in 1834) and other inventions revolutionized American agriculture. (1976)
Elijah J. McCoy (Canadian-American: 1844-1929) IMPROVEMENT IN LUBRICATORS FOR STEAM-ENGINES Until McCoy's invention, engines had to be stopped before they could be lubricated. McCoy's automatic lubricator, which saved time and therefore money, became known among heavy equipment users as "the real McCoy." (2001)
Ottmar Mergenthaler (German-American: 1854–99) MACHINE FOR PRODUCING PRINTING BARS Mergenthaler's invention, known as the Linotype, was the first major improvement in printing since Gutenberg's movable type in the 15th century. This machine, which is controlled by a keyboard, casts individual lines of type from melted lead. (1982)
George de Mestral (Swiss: 1907–1990) VELCRO® The success of his "hook and loop fastener" can be measured by the fact that the trademarked name is more commonly known than the generic name.
Irving Millman (American: 1923–) HEPATITIS B VACCINE (See Baruch S. Blumberg). (1993)
Michel Mirowski (Polish-American, 1924-90) IMPLANTABLE DEFIBRILLATOR This device, which monitors and corrects abnormal heart rhythms, is 99 percent effective in treating sudden cardiac arrest in more than 300,000 patients (2002)
Dennis Moeller (American: 1950–) MICROCOMPUTER WITH BUS CONTROL MEANS FOR PERIPHERAL DEVICES (See Mark Dean). (1997)
Bryan B. Molloy (American: 1939–) PROZAC Unlike other antidepressants, Prozac (fluoxetine hydrochloride) does not have undesirable side effects like grogginess and gastrointestinal problems. (1999)
Samuel F. B. Morse (American: 1791–1872) TELEGRAPH SIGNALS Morse developed the first commercially successful telegraph, with a dot-dash-dot code that made instantaneous long-distance communications possible. (1975)
Morton Mower (American: 1933-) IMPLANTABLE DEFIBRILLATOR (see Michel Mirowski) (2002)
Andrew J. Moyer (American: 1899–1959) METHOD FOR PRODUCTION OF PENICILLIN Moyer, a microbiologist for the U.S. Department of Agriculture, developed a way of producing penicillin in bulk during World War II. The basic method is still used in manufacture of antibiotics and other substances produced by micro-organisms. (1987)
Louis Marius Moyroud (French: 1914–) PHOTO COMPOSING MACHINE (see René Alphonse Higonet). (1985)
Eger V. Murphree (American: 1898–1962) FLUID CATALYTIC CRACKING (See Donald L. Campbell) (1999)
Kary Banks Mullis (American: 1944–) POLYMERASE CHAIN REACTION (PCR) This method has revolutionized the fields of microbiology, medical diagnostics, and forensics, by allowing scientists to identify a fragment of DNA genetic code and reproducing it infinitely. (1998)
Julius A. Nieuwland (Belgian-American : 1878–1936) SYNTHETIC RUBBER Known as Neoprene, Nieuwland's invention is superior to rubber because of its resistance to sunlight, abrasion, fluctuations in temperature, and corrosion by oil. (1996)
Alfred Nobel (Swedish: 1833–96) DYNAMITE Nobel's Improved Explosive Compound made explosives far safer to handle for use in mining and construction. (1998)

Robert N. Noyce (American: 1927–90) SEMICONDUCTOR DEVICE-AND-LEAD STRUCTURE Noyce was at the center of development for two important semiconductor producers, the Fairchild and Intel corporations. (1983)

Kenneth H. Olsen (American: 1926–) IMPROVED MAGNETIC CORE MEMORY Olsen founded Digital Equipment Corp. to manufacture computers based on his new memory devices. He has also contributed extensively to the development of the minicomputer. (1990)

Elisha Graves Otis (American: 1811–61) IMPROVEMENT IN HOISTING APPARATUS Otis devised the safety elevator in 1853, when his employer asked him to build a hoist to lift heavy equipment. Eight years later Otis installed the first passenger elevators. (1988)

Nikolaus August Otto (German: 1832–91) GAS MOTOR ENGINE Otto's four-stroke engine of 1876 is the basis of the modern internal combustion engine. (1981)

Louis W. Parker (Hungarian-American: 1906–) TELEVISION RECEIVER Parker invented the basic television receiver in common use today, and the type of color television transmission and reception that is most commonly used. (1988)

John T. Parsons (American: 1913–) NUMERICAL CONTROL OF MACHINE TOOLS This 1958 patent introduced automation to manufacturing and design and provided machines that can mill steel with an accuracy of one tenth the thickness of newsprint. (1993)

Louis Pasteur (French: 1822–95) BREWING OF BEER AND ALE Pasteur's work on beer and ale is generally considered unsuccessful, but his development of pasteurization, the heating process that protects food and beverages from microbe contamination, was a landmark contribution. (1978)

Charles J. Plank (American: 1915–89) CATALYTIC CRACKING OF HYDROCARBONS WITH A CRYSTALLINE ZEOLITE CATALYST COMPOSITE Along with Edward J. Rosinski, Plank discovered in the early 1960s that zeolites (various aluminum silicates, a fairly common kind of mineral) could be used to improve the production of gasoline and other petroleum products. (1979)

Roy J. Plunkett (American: 1910–94) TETRAFLUOROETHYLENE POLYMERS In 1938 Plunkett discovered the substance known as Teflon. He later developed many of the hydrofluorocarbons (freons) since found to be eroding the ozone layer. (1985)

Robert H. Rines (American: 1922–) CONTRIBUTIONS TO HIGH RESOLUTION IMAGE-SCANNING RADAR Rines's patents were the basis for almost all the high-definition radar used to provide the armed forces with early warning radar during the Persian Gulf War. (1994)

Heinrich Rohrer (Swiss: 1933–) SCANNING TUNNELING MICROSCOPE (See Gerd Karl Binnig) (1994)

Edward J. Rosinski (American: 1921–) CATALYTIC CRACKING OF HYDROCARBONS WITH A CRYSTALLINE ZEOLITE CATALYST COMPOSITE (see Charles J. Plank) (1979)

Benjamin A. Rubin (American: 1917–) BIFURCATED VACCINATION NEEDLE Rubin's needle enabled easy use of small amounts of smallpox vaccine, making it possible to stretch vaccine supplies and helping eliminate smallpox entirely as a disease by 1980. (1992)

Lewis Hastings Sarett (American: 1917–99) TREATING PREGENE COMPOUNDS In 1944, Sarett found a way to produce cortisones as an artificial steroid. By 1949, he and his collaborators had learned to make cortisone from simple inorganic chemicals. Cortisone and related steroids are used for treatment of conditions ranging from psoriasis to arthritis. (1980)

Arthur Schawlow (American: 1921–99) MASER Schawlow's work on masers dates back to 1954, continued through his invention of the laser (patented in 1960 with Charles Townes), and culminated with a 1981 Nobel Prize in physics. (1996)

Klaus K. Schmiegel (German-American: 1939–) PROZAC (See Bryan B. Molloy). (1999)

Peter C. Schultz (American: 1942–) FUSED SILICA OPTICAL WAVEGUIDE (See Robert D. Maurer). (1993)

Robert J. Seiwald (American: 1925–) RITC (See Joseph H. Burckhalter). (1995)

Waldo Semon (American 1898–1999) PVC PLASTISOLS Semon accidentally discovered the first synthetic rubber that bounces. It went on to become a $30 billion industry. (1995)

Gerhard M. Sessler (German: 1931–) FOIL ELECTRET MICROPHONE. This small, lightweight microphone combines high performance, accuracy, and reliability at a low cost. Nearly 90% of all microphones are based on the Foil Electret principle. (1999)

John C. Sheehan (American: 1915–92) SEMI-SYNTHETIC PENICILLIN Sheehan's research developed a synthetic penicillin that could be produced more cheaply and quickly than the natural way of producing it. (1995)

Patsy O. Sherman (American: 1930-) SCOTCHGARD™ The generic name for this trademarked stain repellent is "block and graft copolymers containing water solvatable polar groups and fluoroaliphatic groups." (2001)

William Bradford Shockley (English-American: 1910–89) TRANSISTOR (See John Bardeen). (1974)

Christopher L. Sholes (American: 1819-90) TYPEWRITER Sholes's typewriter was the first to arrange the keys in the QWERTY pattern (rather than alphabetically), so the levers wouldn't jam when frequently used letters were struck in quick succession. (2001)

Igor I. Sikorsky (Russian-American: 1889–1972) HELICOPTER CONTROLS Sikorsky in 1931 made a critical breakthrough in helicopter design. His continued developments led to the helicopter of today. (1987)

Samuel Smith (American: 1927-) SCOTCHGARD™ (See Patsy O. Sherman) (2001)

Percy L. Spencer (American: 1894 –1970) RADAR His contributions to radar research during World War II earned him the Distinguished Public Service Award. He also designed the first microwave oven. (1999)

Elmer A. Sperry (American: 1860–1930) SHIP'S GYROSCOPIC COMPASS Patented in 1917. (1991)

Rangaswamy Srinivasan (Indian-American: 1929 -) EXCIMER LASER SURGERY Better known as LASIK, this type of laser surgery permanently changes the shape of the cornea, eliminating the need for corrective lenses. (2002)

William Stanley (American: 1858–1916) ELECTRIC TRANSFORMER This invention allowed for the long-distance transmission of Alternating Current (AC), which was far less dangerous than transmitting Direct Current (DC) at very high voltages. (1995)

Charles Proteus Steinmetz (German-American: 1865–1923) SYSTEM OF ELECTRICAL DISTRIBUTION Steinmetz's most significant work was in developing the theory of alternating current that made power grids possible. Among his inventions was a machine that produced "lightning in the laboratory." (1977)

George R. Stibitz (American: 1904–95) COMPLEX COMPUTER Stibitz was one of several scientists who developed electromechanical computers in the late 1930s and during World War II. (1983)

Leo Szilard (Hungarian-American: 1898–1964) NUCLEAR REACTOR As chief physicist at the Manhattan Project in 1942, Szilard actively campaigned for the opportunity to set off the first controlled nuclear reaction. (1996)

Donalee L. Tabern (American: 1900–74) THIOBARBITURIC ACID DERIVATIVE This 1936 invention is better known as Pentothal, anesthetic of choice for short surgical procedures. He later introduced therapeutic use of radioactive chemicals. (1986)

Nikola Tesla (Croatian-American: 1857–1943) ELECTRO-MAGNETIC MOTOR Tesla's induction motor was simpler than previous electric motors and was powered by alternating current (AC), which can be distributed more easily over a long distance than direct current (DC). (1975)

Henry Timken (American: 1831–1909) TAPERED ROLLER BEARING This invention, now used on nearly every mode of transportation, releases the strong side pressures exerted on wheels and their bearings when a vehicle turns. (1998)

Max Tishler (American: 1906–) RIBOFLAVIN AND SULFAQUINOXALINE In the late 1930s, Tishler developed an economical method for synthesizing riboflavin (vitamin B2). Later he and his co-workers developed a commercial way to produce sulfaquinoxaline, an antibiotic that prevents common poultry diseases. (1982)

Charles Hard Townes (American: 1915–) MASERS The maser, which preceded the better-known laser, is essentially a laser that works at microwave wavelengths instead of at the shorter wavelength of visible light. (1976)

Charles W. Tyson (American: 1900–1977) FLUID CATALYTIC CRACKING (See Donald L. Campbell) (1999)

Ernest H. Volwiler (American: 1893–1992) THIOBARBITURIC ACID DERIVATIVES (see Donalee L. Tabern) (1986)

An Wang (Chinese-American: 1920–90) MAGNETIC PULSE CONTROLLING DEVICE Although best known for his state-of-the-art word processor of the 1960s, Wang contributed many ideas to the development of electronic computers, including the principle on which magnetic core memory is built. (1988)

James Edward West (American: 1931–) FOIL ELECTRET MICROPHONE (See Gerhard M. Sessler). (1999)

George Westinghouse (American: 1846–1914) STEAM-POWERED BRAKE DEVICES In 1869 Westinghouse patented an air brake for locomotives, his most important contribution to railroad safety. (1989)

Eli Whitney (American: 1765–1825) COTTON GIN By making it possible to remove seeds from cotton mechanically, the gin made large-scale cotton farming possible. Whitney also introduced interchangeable parts, the beginning of mass production. (1974)

Stephen Wilcox Jr. (American: 1830–93) WATER TUBE STEAM BOILER (See George H. Babcock). (1997)

Robert R. Williams (American: 1886–1965) ISOLATION OF VITAMIN B (THIAMINE) In 1935, Williams also synthesized thiamine for commercial production. (1991)

Steve Wozniak (American: 1950-) PERSONAL COMPUTER Apple Computer, the company he and Steve Jobs started from Wozniak's garage in 1976, helped to created the personal computer industry and shrink computers from room-size to desktop size. (2000)

Orville Wright (American: 1871–1948) & **Wilbur Wright** (American: 1867–1912) FLYING MACHINE The Wright brothers not only invented the first airplane in 1903, they also popularized, manufactured, and sold the new machines. (1975)

James Wynne (American: 1943- EXCIMER LASER SURGERY (see Rangaswamy Srinivasan) (2002)

Vladimir Kosma Zworykin (Russian-American: 1889–1982) CATHODE RAY TUBE The cathode ray tube that Zworykin invented in 1928 is the kinescope, the basic picture tube used in modern television. Ten years later he developed the iconoscope, the first practical television camera. (1977)

COMPUTERS

A computer is a machine for storing and processing information. It converts any information that it receives into a binary code—a string of signals, in which each signal is either 1 or 0. The basic working component of a computer is a series of switches, each of which can be set either "off" or "on" and thus represent 1 or 0 in the binary system. The history of computers is, to some extent, a history of the switching devices that have been used to represent 1 and 0. Early computers were based on mechanical switches; computers based on electronic switches proved much faster. These fall into three main categories: vacuum tubes, transistors, and integrated circuits.

The relative size and power of these three types are so disparate that it is almost impossible to compare them; there is no single scale against which they can be measured. In 1946 the ENIAC (Electronic Numerical Integrator and Calculator)—which occupied 2,000 square feet, weighed 50 tons, and used 18,000 vacuum tubes—could perform about 10,000 multiplications per second and had an internal memory capacity of 200 decimal digits, or about 20 words. The newest personal computers in 2003 could carry out more than 3.0 billion operations per second and store more than 200 billion bits of information. The world's fastest supercomputer, developed in Japan, could reach speeds of 35,600 gigaflops (billions of operations per second). Innovations in microprocessor and storage technologies promise quantum leaps in the speed and data capacity of the common computer.

▶A GLOSSARY OF COMPUTER TERMS

Application A computer *program* designed for a specific task or use, like word procesing, accounting, or missile guidance.

Artificial intelligence (AI) The underlying assumption of artificial intelligence is that machines can be programmed to perform human functions. The primary AI functions are *expert systems,* programs that contain a body of knowledge (contributed by experts) that the machine can draw on to solve specific types of problems; *natural language interfaces* that make it possible for users to access a computer's database with commands entered in ordinary written or spoken language (for example, "Give me a list of countries bordering the Atlantic Ocean"); *speech recognition, speech synthesis, and optical recognition systems* that enable computers to understand spoken commands, make speech, and interpret visible images (such as bar codes on retail goods); and *robotics,* machines whose design and systems enable them to imitate complex "eye-hand" coordination of humans.

ASCII (American Standard Code for Information Interchange) Computers work with numbers, not letters. ASCII is the numerical code used by personal computers. While many programs also use special codes of their own, data from one computer to another are best transmitted in "pure ASCII."

Baud rate A transmission rate used in sending data from one computer to another, with a baud approximately equal to one *bit* per second. Rates must be the same between *modems* for data to be transmitted.

Bit In the binary system, a bit (*bi*nary dig*it*) is either of the digits 0 or 1. It is the basic unit for storing data, with "off" representing 0 and "on" representing 1.

Buffer Any memory location where data can be stored temporarily while the computer is doing something else; specifically, a memory location in the computer, in a printer, or in a separate storage device (*peripheral*) that stores a file being printed so that the computer is not tied up waiting for the printing to finish.

Bug An error in a *software* program or the *hardware*.

Byte A group of eight *bits* that together represent one character, whether alphabetic, numeric, or other. A byte is the smallest accessible unit in a computer's memory.

Cathode ray tube (CRT) The display device, or *monitor*, similar to a television screen, used with most desktop computers.

CD-ROM A Compact Disc ("CD") used as a Read-Only-Memory ("ROM"). The CD, essentially the same as an audio CD, stores data in a form readable by a laser, resulting in a storage device of great capacity and quick accessibility.

Central processing unit (CPU) The group of circuits that directs the entire computer system by (1) interpreting and executing *program* instruction and (2) coordinating the interaction of input, output, and storage devices.

Computer-aided design (CAD), engineering (CAE) and manufacturing (CAM) Systems that automate many complex tasks such as drafting, computation, or repetitive actions.

Cursor A marker on the computer display that shows which region of the screen is active.

Database Either a *program* for arranging facts in the computer and retrieving them (the computer equivalent of a filing system) or a *file* set up by such a system. Databases may be stored on a standalone computer or network server and accessed online.

Directory An area or data structure in which information is stored regarding the location and contents of files or file structures.

Disk drive A mechanism for retrieving information stored on a magnetic disk. The drive rotates the disk at high speed and "reads" the data with a magnetic head similar to those used in tape recorders.

DVD Digital Versatile Disc, an improvement on the CD-ROM that is capable of storing an entire motion picture.

DOS Acronym for Disk Operating System and shorthand for MS-DOS, the standard operating system for 16-bit and most 32-bit IBM and IBM-compatible PCs.

File Any group of data treated as a single entity by the computer, such as a word processor document, a *program*, or a *database*.

Firewall A dedicated computer or software with special security features to safeguard a network server from damage by authorized or unauthorized users.

Floppy disk A thin, flexible magnetic disk encased in a protective jacket. On the disk's surface are a number of "tracks" on which data may be recorded in the form of magnetic spots.

GHz Gigahertz, now the standard measure of speed used for a *microprocessor*; 1 GHz equals 1 billion electrical cycles per second. Personal computers today typically come with 1.5–2.5 GHz chips.

Gigabyte (G) One billion *bytes*.

Graphical user interface (GUI) A system that uses icons (symbols) seen on the screen to represent available functions. These icons are generally manipulated by a mouse and/or a keyboard. This approach contrasts with the more traditional method of using typed commands.

Groupware Network programming that enables groups of users to work together by providing communication, workflow and task-sharing functions.

Hard disk A sealed cartridge containing magnetic storage disk(s) that holds much more memory—up to more than 100 *gigabytes*—than *floppy disks*. Usually a hard disk is built into the computer, but it can be a peripheral.

Hardware The physical equipment, as opposed to the programs and procedures, used in data processing. It covers not only computers themselves but also *peripherals* (see "Software").

Host The computer used to run programs and store files for remote users or in a LAN.

Icon A graphic symbol on the display screen that represents a file, peripheral, or some other object or function; for example, scissors are generally used to indicate cut-and-paste editing.

Integrated circuit An entire electronic circuit contained on one piece of material. Originally, electronic components (transistors, capacitors, etc.) were placed on a metal chassis and wired together. The first integrated circuit began with a single board (originally plastic), onto which strips of conducting material were sprayed. Electronic components could then be inserted directly onto the board (see "Silicon chip").

Kilobyte (K) A unit of measure for data storage or transmission equivalent to 1,024 *bytes*, but often rounded to 1,000.

Laptop A portable computer small enough to operate in one's lap. Generally a laptop weighs less than 15 pounds and uses a *liquid crystal display* monitor rather than a *cathode ray tube*.

Liquid crystal display (LCD) A type of flat-panel display monitor used in *laptop computers*.

Local area networks (LANs) Systems that allow users to connect PCs to one another or to *minicomputers* or *mainframes*.

Mainframe computer Generally the largest, fastest, and most expensive kind of computer, usually costing millions of dollars and requiring special cooling. Mainframe computers can accommodate hundreds of simultaneous users and normally are run around the clock; typically they are owned by large companies.

Massively parallel A form of computer architecture that uses hundreds or thousands of inexpensive *microprocessors* to perform many operations simultaneously.

Megabyte (M) One million *bytes*.

Menu-driven A *program* that uses a number of "menus," or lists of possible activities from which the operator chooses in order to activate the appropriate commands. This is the alternative to a command-driven program, for which the operator must remember a number of commands in order to tell the computer what to do.

MHz Megahertz, a measure of microprocessing speed; 1 MHz equals 1 million electrical cycles per second.

Microprocessor A complete central processing unit assembled on one single silicon chip.

MIPS (million instructions per second) A measure of computer processing speed.

Modem (modulator-demodulator) A device capable of converting a digital (computer-compatible) signal to an analog signal, which can be transmitted via a telephone line, reconverted, and then "read" by another computer.

Monitor The display device on a computer, similar to a television screen.

Motherboard The largest printed circuit board in a computer, housing the CPU chip and controlling circuitry.

Mouse A small box connected by cable to a computer and featuring one or more button-style switches. When moved around a desk, the mouse causes a symbol on the computer screen to make corresponding movements. By selecting items on the screen and pressing a button on the mouse, the user can perform certain functions much more quickly than by typing commands on the keyboard.

Network An interconnected group of computers that can exchange information or work together on different parts of the same problem.

Notebook A type of full-function portable computer that uses miniaturized components, weighs about 4-6 pounds, and can be carried in a briefcase.

Operating system A sequence of programming codes that instructs a computer about its various parts and peripherals and how to operate them. Operating systems deal only with the workings of the *hardware* and are separate from *software* programs.

Peripheral A device connected to the computer that provides communication or auxiliary functions. There are three types of peripherals: input devices, such as keyboards; output devices, such as *monitors* and printers; and storage devices, such as magnetic discs.

Personal computer A computer used by an individual at home or in the office.

Platform A fundamental layer of software required to make other systems run—used interchangeably with operating system, the most common type of platform. The Internet, local networks, Web browsers, and Java are all frequently viewed as platforms.

Program As a noun, a prepared set of instructions for the computer, often with provisions for the operator to choose among various options. As a verb, to create such a set of instructions.

Random-access memory (RAM) A temporary storage space in which data may be held on a chip rather than being stored on disk or tape. The contents of RAM may be accessed or altered at any time during a session, but will be lost when the computer is turned off (see "Read-only memory").

Read-only memory (ROM) A type of *chip* memory, the contents of which have been permanently recorded in a computer by the manufacturer and cannot be altered by the user (see "Random access memory").

RISC chip Reduced Instruction Set Computer chip, such as the Apple-IBM Power PC chip, which gains speed by using fewer instructions than the more familiar Complex Instruction Set chip.

Server The central computer in a network, providing a service or data access to client computers on the network.

Silicon chip A special kind of *integrated circuit* in which traditional electronic components have been replaced by chemicals. Tiny wafers (chips) of silicon are covered with layers of chemicals, each of which acts as an electrical component (a *transistor*, capacitor, etc.). The first chips, made in the early 1960s, contained two transistors. Chips today contain tens of millions of transistors.

Software The *programs* and procedures, as opposed to the physical equipment, used in data processing (see "Hardware").

Spreadsheet A *program* that performs mathematical operations on numbers arranged in large arrays; used mainly for accounting and other record keeping.

Supercomputer The fastest of the *mainframe* class of computers, usually used for complex scientific calculations.

Terabyte (TB) One trillion *bytes*.**Cache** A region of memory where frequently used data is stored for rapid access.

Transistor A small piece of semiconducting material (material that conducts electricity better than, say, wood but not as well as metal). Flows of electrons within the transistor can be controlled, enabling it to act as an electronic "switching" device. In other words, it can record information in the form of an "on" or an "off" signal. Early transistors were about one-hundredth the size of *vacuum tubes*, required very little energy, and generated no heat.

UNIX A multi-user, multitasking operating system designed to run on a wide variety of computers, from microcomputers to mainframes.

Virus A computer program segment or string of code that can attach itself to another program or file, reproduce itself, and spread from one computer to another. Viruses can destroy or change data and in other ways sabotage computer systems.

Window A portion of the screen display used to view simultaneously a different part of the file in use or a part of a different file than the one in use.

Workstation High-performance *computers* with advanced graphics capabilities designed for use by scientists and engineers.

Personal Computer Sales, 1985–2002

Year	Unit sales[1] (thousands)	Dollar sales [1] (millions)	Average unit price
1985	3,200	$2,175	$700
1990	4,000	4,187	1,050
1995	8,400	12,600	1,500
1997	11,000	15,950	1,450
1998	12,800	16,640	1,300
1999	14,900	16,390	1,100
2000	16,400	16,400	1,000
2001[2]	14,400	12,960	900
2002[3]	14,400	12,312	855

1. Sales to dealers. 2. Estimate. 3. Projection.
Sources: IDC; Consumer Electronics Association.

Personal Computer Households, 1994–2002

Year	Total U.S. households (millions)	Households with PCs (millions)	Percent of households with computers
1994	97.1	23.4	24.1%
1997	101.0	37.0	36.6
1998	102.5	43.2	42.1
1999	103.6	49.3	47.6
2000	104.7	53.7	51.0
2001	105.5	60.2	56.5
2002[1]	107.0	64.2	60.0

1. Estimate.
Source: U.S. Department of Commerce

Chronology of Information Processing

B.C.

500 Bead-and-wire abacus in use in Egypt.

A.D.

200 Computing trays in use in China and Japan.
1340 Double-entry bookkeeping originates in Lombardy.
c. 1621 Mathematician William Oughtred (English: 1574–1660) invents slide rule.
1642 Blaise Pascal (French: 1623–62) invents "pascaline"—the first calculating machine, capable of addition and subtraction.
1679 Gottfried Wilhelm Leibniz (German: 1646–1716) perfects binary system of notation that eventually will be used by all computers; also develops improved version of pascaline, capable of multiplication and division.
1801 Joseph-Marie Jacquard (French: 1752–1834) uses punched cards to control operation of his mechanical loom—precursor of cards used in early data-storage systems.
1822 Charles Babbage (English: 1792–1871) designs and builds prototype of "Difference Engine" for calculating logarithms.
1833 Babbage designs "Analytical Engine," a computing machine featuring printed card input, memory, and printed output, and capable of being programmed to perform different tasks. Forerunner of modern computer, it never goes beyond design stage.
1847 George Boole (English: 1815–64) publishes *Mathematical Analysis of Logic*, which treats logic as a branch of mathematics (Boolean Algebra).
1853 Pehr Georg Scheutz and his son Edvard G.R. Scheutz (Swedish: 1785–1873; 1821–81) complete version of Babbage's Difference Engine.
1886 William S. Burroughs (American: 1855–98) develops first commercially successful mechanical adding machine.
1887 U.S. Census Bureau holds competition for device to speed up computation of census information; Herman Hollerith (American: 1860-1929) designs winning tabulating machine. His Tabulating Machine Co. (founded 1911) becomes IBM in 1924.
1890 Hollerith's electromechanical machine processes U.S. Census results in six weeks—one-third the time taken in 1880.
1894 Otto Steiger develops "Millionaire," the first commercially successful machine capable of direct multiplication, as opposed to multiplication by repeated addition.
1931 Vannevar Bush (American: 1890–1974) completes "differential analyser," first computing machine to use electronic components (vacuum tubes in which values could be stored as voltages).
1936 Mathematician Alan M. Turing (English: 1912–54) publishes "On Computable Numbers," which describes hypothetical computer with infinite storage capacity, capable of performing any conceivable calculation.
1937 John V. Atanasoff (American: 1903–) starts work on first electronic computer.
1938 Konrad Zuse (German: 1910–95) builds "Z1," the first computing machine to use binary, instead of decimal, method of operation. Other features include keyboard to input information and system of electric bulbs to signal results of calculations.
1939 Atanasoff and Clifford Berry complete ABC device, first digital computer.
1940 Zuse's Z2 machine introduces electromagnetic relays (as used in telephone switching gear) to store numbers.

First Generation: Vacuum Tubes

1943 British government uses first fully electronic computer to crack German military codes. Designed by Turing, "Colossus" uses 2,000 vacuum tubes to perform calculations and digest information at rate of 5,000 characters per second.
1944 Completion of "Harvard Mark I," designed by Howard H. Aiken (American: 1900–1973) and built by IBM. Vast, over 50 ft. long, it was obsolete almost immediately because it used electromagnetic relays rather than vacuum tubes.
1946 At the University of Pennsylvania, the ENIAC (Electronic Numerical Integrator and Calculator) multiplies five-digit number by itself 5,000 times in half a second. Designed by J. Presper Eckert, Jr. (American: 1919–) and John W. Mauchly (American: 1907–80) to calculate ballistic trajectories, ENIAC occupies 2,000 sq. ft., weighs 50 tons, uses 18,000 vacuum tubes, and can store about 20 words in its memory.
John von Neumann (Hungarian-American: 1903–57) publishes paper suggesting that instructions given to computer—"programs"—can themselves be stored by computer in numerical form.
First use of term *bit* to mean binary digit.
1948 "Mark I," designed by Tom Kilburn (English: 1921–) and Sir Frederic C. Williams (English: 1911–77) at Manchester University, England, is first computer to utilize von Neumann's concept of stored programs.
John Bardeen (American: 1908–91), Walter H. Brattain (American: 1902–87), and William B. Shockley (English-American: 1910–89) invent the transistor, which will eventually replace vacuum tube and make computers faster.
IBM, Bell Telephone, and Sperry-Rand each begin production of commercial computers.
First chess-playing computer built at M.I.T.
1950 Eckert and Mauchly's EDVAC (Electronic Discrete Variable Automatic Computer) is first to use magnetic disks for storage.
1951 Lyons Tea Shop Co. in England uses specially designed computer ("LEO") to perform routine administrative functions.
Eckert and Mauchly's UNIVAC (Universal Automatic Computer) is installed at U.S. Bureau of Census. UNIVAC uses magnetic tape for input and becomes first commercially successful machine, selling over 50 models.
1952 One hour after polls close, CBS television network uses UNIVAC to predict Eisenhower's landslide victory in U.S. presidential election. Prediction was based on less than 10 percent of the votes.
1953 First high-speed printer linked to a computer.
IBM introduces its first stored-program computer, the vacuum-tube-based "701."
1956 First use of term artificial intelligence.

Second Generation: Transistors

1958 Control Data Corp. introduces first fully transistorized computer, the CDC 1604, designed by Seymour Cray (American: 1925–).
Jack St. C. Kilby (American: 1923–) of Texas Instruments and Robert Noyce (American: 1927–90) of Intel Corp. independently produce first integrated circuits.
1959 First commercially marketed program.
IBM markets its first transistorized computers.
1960 The PDP-1, developed by Digital Equipment Corp., is the first commercial computer to use a keyboard and monitor instead of punched cards.
Introduction of removable magnetic disks for data storage.

Third Generation: Integrated Circuits

1965 IBM markets its first integrated-circuit based computer, the 360.
Digital Equipment Corp. markets the first minicomputer, the PDP-8.
1969 Graduate student Alan Kay, later to become top designer with Apple Computer Co., writes doctoral thesis describing hypothetical "personal computer."

ARPANET, the first part of the Internet, is set up to link Defense Department contractors.
1970 Lexitron introduces first word processor, a computer designed specifically to handle written text. It features a cathode ray tube (CRT) terminal, as used in television sets, to display information.
Floppy disk is introduced for data storage.
1971 Intel Corp. announces first microprocessor, several integrated circuits contained on one silicon chip.
First electronic pocket calculator produced by Texas Instruments; it weighs about 2½ lbs. and costs about $150.
1973 Introduction of "bit-mapped" monitor capable of high-resolution graphics display.
Xerox markets first hand-held "mouse," a time-saving device for giving commands to computer.
Intel introduces 8080 microprocessor, which will become the central processing unit (CPU) of several microcomputers.
1975 First personal computer, the MITS Altair 8800, is marketed in kit form, with memory of 256 bytes.
Cray Research (founded 1972) announces the Cray-1 supercomputer, capable of 100 million operations per second.
1976 Apple Computer Co. founded by Stephen Wozniak and Steven Jobs (American: 1955–) in the Jobs family garage; first Apple "boards" (self-assembly personal computer kits) go on sale.
1977 Apple markets Apple II—the first widely accepted personal computer. Commodore and Tandy also begin to sell personal computers.
Microsoft Corp. founded by Bill Gates and Paul Allen.
1978 Hayes Microcomputer Products introduces Micromodem 100, the first microcomputer-compatible modem.
1979 Micropro International releases WordStar word processing program for personal computers.
1980 Microsoft adapts the UNIX operating system for use with microcomputers; paves way for personal computers to begin performing tasks associated with larger machines.
1981 IBM introduces its first personal computer, the IBM PC. Using operating system called PC-DOS, developed by Microsoft, it almost immediately becomes the industry standard.
Ashton-Tate introduces dBASE II, the first popular database program for microcomputers.
1982 Microsoft introduces MS-DOS, a version of the PC-DOS operating system designed for IBM PC; allows other manufacturers to produce copies ("clones") of the IBM machine.
Compaq announces its first portable computer (IBM-compatible).
1983 Apple introduces Apple IIe and "Lisa."
First IBM-compatible "laptop" computer introduced by Gavilan Corp.
Lotus Development Corp. introduces 1-2-3, a best-selling program for managing business spreadsheets.
Introduction of optical (laser-readable) disks.
1984 Apple introduces Macintosh. With list price of $2,495, it includes Apple's first "Mac" software programs, MacWrite (for text) and MacPaint (for graphics). Fifty thousand are sold within three months. IBM markets the PC AT (Advanced Technology) model.
1985 Apple's LaserWriter printer and Aldus Corp.'s PageMaker program usher in age of desktop publishing.
Introduction of erasable optical storage disks.
Toshiba markets first widely used laptop computer.
Cray 2 supercomputer is capable of 1.2 billion operations per second.
1986 IBM announces OS/2, a new operating system that allows personal computers to run several programs simultaneously (called multitasking).
1987 Apple introduces Macintosh SE and Macintosh II. IBM introduces Personal System/2 (PS/2), features of which include high-resolution VGA (Video Graphics Array) display.
1988 Computer security becomes an urgent issue when a "worm" program penetrates thousands of systems on Internet information network.
Motorola announces new microprocessor, the 88000, a 32-bit RISC (Reduced Instruction Set Computer) chip.
First IBM PS/2 "clones" announced.
IBM and Sears launch Prodigy, an on-line service enabling subscribers with a computer and modem to access a central information bank.
Parallel processing technique introduced that utilizes many inexpensive microprocessors to perform a large number of operations simultaneously.
1989 Intel announces the iPSC/860 chip, containing one million transistors; designed to give a microcomputer the power and speed normally associated with supercomputers.
IBM announces production of commercial quantities of four-megabyte chips.
First portable computers with color liquid crystal displays (LCDs) announced.
1990 Software writer Tim Berners-Lee writes the program for the World Wide Web to make the Internet easier to use for physicists at CERN in Geneva.
1991 The Thinking Machines Inc. CM-200 massively parallel supercomputer can perform 9.03 billion calculations per second.
1993 Intel begins shipping the Pentium chip with 3.1 million transistors on it; it operates twice as fast as the best previous Intel chip for personal computers.
Electrical engineers from the Univ. of Colorado claim the first fully optical computer that can store, transmit, and process data entirely in the form of light, with no electron intermediaries.
1994 Apple introduces the first personal computers to use the Power PC RISC Chip.
1995 Microsoft introduces its Windows 95 operating system software, featuring an improved interface and better multimedia support.
1997 In a six-game match, the IBM RS/6000 SP supercomputer (known as Deep Blue) defeats world chess champion Garry Kasparov, the first time a computer has beaten a player of this caliber.
Intel introduces a Pentium chip with MMX technology, enhancing multimedia capabilities on a PC.
1999 The total number of Internet users in the U.S. tops 100 million.
2000 The new century begins with minimal disruption from the much-feared Y2K programming bug.
Household penetration of personal computers in the United States surpasses 50 percent.
A U.S. federal circuit court judge finds the software giant Microsoft in violation of antitrust laws and orders the company broken up into two parts. Microsoft appeals.
2001 The U.S. high-tech industry hits hard times. The investment "bubble" in dot.com companies bursts, forcing numerous Web ventures to shut down. PC sales decline for the first time in decades. Still, the number of Internet users continues to climb, reaching 143 million—or 54 percent of the population.
A federal district judge issues an injunction against Napster, Inc., to halt the free exchange of copyright-protected music on the company's popular Internet site. Napster is later acquired by the German-based media giant Bertelsmann.
Microsoft and the U.S. Justice Department reach a settlement in their antitrust dispute by which the software company will be left intact in exchange for specific restrictions on anticompetitive behavior.
2002 A new Japanese supercomputer, called Earth Simulator, achieves a processing speed of 35,600 gigaflops (billions of calculations per second) — five times faster than its closest competitor.

TELECOMMUNICATIONS

Over the course of barely two decades, innovations in data transfer and information processing technologies have combined with increased satellite access, the spread of fiber optic cable, and the explosive growth of the Internet to fuel a communications revolution in North America, Europe and the industrialized nations of Asia. The proliferation of cellular phones, mobile radio phones, paging services and personal communication systems (PCS) has greatly expanded the communications capabilities of both consumers and business in terms of speed, accessibility and cost.

But for the telecommunications industry itself—including service providers, equipment manufacturers, and other support services—the enormous growth and promise of the late 1990s has given way to stagnation and unrealized expectations since the year 2000. That trend continued in 2002, as overall industry growth continued to slow. The total U.S. marketplace in 2002, according to the Telecommunications Industry Association (TIA), generated revenues of an estimated $668.3 billion, a mere 1.6 percent increase over 2001 (following 5.1 percent growth that year and 13.4 percent in 2000). Of total 2002 revenues, $325.3 billion (up 5.9 percent) derived from calling services—local exchange access, toll service and wireless service. The transition from conventional land-line usage to wireless usage, combined with continued price pressure, was reflected in a decline of 1.6 percent in toll service revenues, to $105.7 billion, and a concurrent 15.8 rise in wireless service revenues, to $86.3 billion. Service providers were not the only ones hit hard. Equipment manufacturers and software developers saw revenues drop by 15.4 percent in 2002, to $132.4 billion.

Largest U.S. Telephone Companies, 2002

Rank, Company	Access lines ('000s)	Operating revenues (millions)	Change in revenues, 2001-02
1. Verizon	135,800[1]	$67,625	+0.6%
2. SBC Communications	57,100	43,138	-6.0
3. AT&T	—	37,827	-10.4
4. Sprint	8,100	26,631	+4.4
5. BellSouth	24,500	22,440	-7.0
6. WorldCom/MCI	—	21,300[2]	N.A.
7. Qwest	16,900	15,487	-7.5
8. Alltel	2,572	7,983	+6.4

1. Equivalents. 2. 2001 figure, restated.
Source: U.S. Federal Communications Commission, *Statistics of Communications Common Carriers* (annual); annual reports.

U.S. Telecommunications Marketplace, 2000–2004 (millions of dollars)

Service	2000	2001	2002	2003[1]	2004[2]
Total Transport Services	$290,112	$307,851	$325,352	$345,281	$366,781
Local Exchange Services	118,795	125,916	133,350	141,100	149,000
Toll Service	109,615	107,400	105,700	107,500	110,000
Wireless Services	61,702	74,535	86,302	96,681	107,781
Specialized Services	5,801	10,372	15,558	21,312	27,308
Support Services	168,321	198,521	225,767	251,384	282,085
Equipment and Software	173,866	156,457	132,426	137,456	147,768
Industry Total[3]	**625,989**	**$658,022**	**$668,346**	**$735,693**	**$801,129**

1. Estimated. 2. Projected. 3. Installation charges included in both support services and equipment but only once in industry total.
Source: Telecommunications Industry Association (Arlington, Va.), *2003 Telecommunications Market Review and Forecast*. Reprinted by permission.

U.S. Telephone Systems, 1985–2001

Year	1985	1990	1995	1999	2000	2001
Local Exchange Carriers						
Carriers	55	51	53	52	52	52
Access lines (millions)	112	130	166	228	245	253
Business (millions)	31	36	46	57	58	54
Residential (millions)	79	89	101	115	115	112
Other (millions)	2	6	19	53	72	87
Local calls (billions)	365	402	484	554	537	515
Local service revenues (billions)	$32	$46	$52	$58	$60	$58
Long-Distance Carriers						
Carriers	N.A.	325	583	N.A.	700+	700+
Toll calls (billions)	N.A.	63	94	102	106	98
Toll service revenues (billions)	$43	$52	$74	$99	$100	$91
International Service						
U.S.-billed calls (millions)	411	984	2,821	5,215	5,269	5,627
U.S.-billed minutes (billions)	3.4	8.0	15.9	28.0	28.2	29.2
U.S.-billed revenues (billions)	$3.5	$8.0	$14.0	$14.4	14.5	$14.1

Source: U.S. Federal Communications Commission, *Statistics of Communications Common Carriers* (annual).

The TIA projects 10.0 percent growth for the U.S. telecommunications industry in 2003 and 8.9 percent in 2004. The increase in service revenues, however, is expected to lag that of the industry as a whole, and of wireless services most drastically, in the foreseeable future—to the great advantage of consumers.

Continued expansion of the Internet user base (still dominated by dial-up service) and competitive pricing in the long-distance market have steadily increased consumer demand for conventional phone service, even as usage has decline. As of year-end 2001, the total number of U.S. residential and business access lines exceeded 253 million, a nearly 11 percent rise from 1999. This did not even include the rapidly growing wireless segment. At the same time, however, Americans placed 515 billion land-line local calls in 2001 (down from 537 billion from 2000), generating an estimated $58 billion in revenues (down $2 billion). The decline in number of calls was due, in large part, to the transition of many home Internet users to broadband wireless alternatives. The rise in local call rates cannot be expected to be reversed until the much-discussed deregulation of local phone service becomes a reality.

The long-distance market remained the largest segment of the phone service industry, even as rates have declined dramatically. Americans placed an estimated 98 billion toll calls in 2001 (down 7.5 percent), spending $91 billion (down 9 percent). More than 20 years after the deregulation of the long-distance market, the effects are clear. The average price of a domestic long-distance call fell from 30 cents per minute in 1988 to about 12 cents per minute in 2001.

Wireless Communications By far the most rapid growth in the telecommunications service industry has come in the wireless segment. From 1995 through 2002, the total wireless market more than tripled in size, from $25.4 billion to $86.3 billion, with another 12 percent increase (to $96.7 billion) expected in 2003. Cellular phones continue to account for a majority of wireless service spending, but personal communications systems (PCSs)—handheld devices with fax capability and Internet access—and other equipment are expected to gain share. Some analysts expect wireless usage to account for half of all U.S. telecom service revenues within a few years.

From 1990 to 2001, the number of subscribers to a cellular phone system jumped from 5.3 million to more than 140 million. Some 12.4 million new subscribers were added in 2002 alone, an increase of

Wireless Communication Services Spending in U.S.,1997-2003 (in millions)

Year	Wireless Telephony	Paging	Total
1997	$29,038	$4,811	$33,849
1998	32,207	5,304	37,511
1999	40,626	5,429	46,055
2000	56,253	5,449	61,702
2001	69,103	5,432	74,535
2002	81,140	5,162	86,302
2003[1]	91,925	4,756	96,681

1. Projected. **Source:** The Strategis Group; Donaldson, Lufkin & Jenrette; Cellular Telecommunications and Internet Association; Telecommunications Industry Association.

Cellular Telephone Industry Growth in the U.S., 1990-2002

Year	Systems	Subscriber	Cell sites[1]	Employees	Service revenue (millions)	Average monthly bill
1990	751	5,283,000	5,616	21,382	$4,548	$80.90
1995	1,627	33,786,000	22,683	68,165	19,081	51.00
1996	1,740	44,043,000	30,045	84,161	23,635	47.70
1997	2,228	55,312,293	51,600	109,387	27,486	42.78
1998	3,073	69,209,321	65,887	134,754	33,133	39.43
1999	3,518	86,047,003	81,698	155,817	40,018	41.24
2000	2,440	109,478,031	104,288	188,449	52,466	45.27
2001	2,587	128,374,512	127,540	203,589	65,316	47.37
2002	2,846	140,766,842	139,338	192,410	76,508	48.40

1. A cell site is the basic geographic unit of a cellular system. A city or county is divided into smaller cells, each of which is equipped with a low-powered radio transmitter/receiver. The cells can vary in size depending on terrain, capacity, demands, etc. By controlling the transmission power, the radio frequencies assigned to one cell can be limited to the boundaries of that cell. When a cellular telephone moves from one cell to another, a computer at the switching office monitors the movement and transfers the phone call to the new cell and another radio frequency. **Source:** Cellular Telecommunications and Internet Association, annual wireless industry survey.

U.S. Paging and Messaging Market, 1990-2003

Year	Subscribers (millions)	Annual Percent Increase	Total Spending (millions)	Annual Percent Increase	Average Monthly Spending	Annual Percent Change
1990	9.9	22.2%	$1,744	17.8%	$14.68	-3.7%
1995	34.5	31.2	3,841	18.8	9.28	-9.4
1998	52.0	7.7	5,304	10.3	8.50	2.4
1999	52.3	0.6	5,429	2.4	8.65	1.8
2000	51.6	-1.3	5,449	0.4	8.80	1.7
2001	50.3	-2.5	5,432	-0.3	9.00	2.3
2002	46.5	-7.6	5,162	-5.0	9.25	2.8
2003[1]	41.5	-10.8	4,756	-7.9	9.55	3.2

1. Projected. **Source:** Telecommunications Industry Association, *2003 Telecommunications Market Review and Forecast.* Reprinted by permission.

nearly 10 percent. Service revenues skyrocketed from $4.5 billion at the start of the 1990s to $76.5 billion in 2002. The one-year increase was more than 17 percent, following 24 percent in 2001, and the explosion was expected to continue in coming years.

The paging and messaging market, which grew impressively throughout the 1990s, began to shrink in 2000 and has continued to do so. With cellular telephones serving the needs of many pager users, the number of paging/ messaging subscribers as well as total spending on such services has fallen each year since 2000.

New forms of wireless communication promise even greater versatility and broader usage. Personal communication systems, which transmit cellular calls digitally, provide superior reception. They allow users to download information from the Internet or a corporate data network right to wireless, phones. Local multipoint distributions systems are also expected to see rapid implementation.

Satellites The wireless revolution in telecommunications has been made possible, in large part, by the bandwidth capacity of geostationary satellites orbiting the Earth. As of 2002, more than 250 U.S. and European communications satellites were in place. But with launchings proceeding at record pace—reaching 40 in 2000—commercial satellite bandwidth began to exceed demand, and the number of commercial launchings declined to only 16 in 2001. The industry rebounded well in 2002, however, with more than 30 new satellites placed in orbit and a similar number expected in 2003. About 95 percent of commercial launchings are communications satellites, and about 85 percent are geostationary.

Growth in residential broadband service is likely to be dominated by the cable industry—as suggested by the failures of various global satellite-system ventures—but many analysts continued to predict a key role for satellites in the future. Digital radio may prove to be another major consumer electronics market served by satellite.

Telecom Industry Competition for the burgeoning wireless market, declining prices for long-distance service, an excess of optic fiber capacity, turbulence in the investment market, and improper or questionable accounting practices made the period 2000-2002 one of the most difficult ever for the U.S. telecom industry. Virtually every major company faced a squeeze on profits and declining share prices. In 2002, the Dow Jones Telecommunications Index fell a whopping 36 percent. Five of the eight largest U.S. phone companies showed declines in annual operating revenue and net income. WorldCom, after revelations of gross accounting errors, declared bankruptcy in July 2002—the biggest company (in terms of corporate assets) ever to do so. In April 2003, the company filed a reorganization plan with the U.S. Bankruptcy Court and announced that it was changing its name to MCI and moving its headquarters to Ashburn, Virginia—followed shortly by charges from competitors that it had inappropriately handled access fees.

U.S. Consumer Telecommunications Market, 1990–2003

Product	1990	1995	2000	2001	2002	2003[1]
Total Unit Shipments (millions)	**55.9**	**81.5**	**134.5**	**142.9**	**143.4**	**144.9**
Corded telephone	22.0	25.8	29.7	26.7	24.0	22.3
Cordless telephone	10.1	19.5	39.0	40.0	40.1	40.9
Cellular/PCS handset	8.7	15.9	43.2	52.6	56.3	58.2
Answering machine	13.6	17.5	19.9	21.0	20.7	21.5
Home fax machine	1.5	2.8	2.7	2.6	2.3	2.0
Total Dollar Sales (millions)	**$8,686**	**$8,501**	**$10,722**	**$11,584**	**$10,362**	**$9,575**
Corded telephone	765	668	463	384	317	290
Cordless telephone	1,170	1,913	1,953	2,450	2,105	2,045
Cellular/PCS handset	4,698	3,578	6,696	7,095	6,470	5,815
Answering machine	953	1,242	1,145	1,235	1,110	1,125
Home fax machine	1,100	1,100	465	420	360	300

1. Projected. **Source:** Telecommunications Association (Arlington, Va.), *2003 Telecommunications Market Review and Forecast.*

Percent of U.S. Homes with Telecommunications Equipment, 1990–2002

Product	1990	1995	1997	1998	1999	2000	2001	2002
Telephone answering device	31%	54%	65%	69%	72%	74%	77%	78%
Cordless telephone	25	52	66	70	75	78	81	81
Home computer	23	22	40	42	48	54	58	60
Fax and/or fax modems	N.A.	16	19	25	38	51	55	56
Wireless telephone	N.A.	20	34	39	44	51	59	66

Note: As of January of each year.
Source: Telecommunications Association (Arlington, Va.), *MultiMedia Telecommunications Market Review and Forecast* (2002).

Radios, Televisions, Telephones, and Computers per Capita, by Selected Nation, (number per 1,000 people), 2000

Nation	Radio receivers[1]	Television receivers[1]	Telephone main lines	Mobile telephones	Personal computers
Algeria	242	105	522	22	62
Argentina	681	223	215	1,212	51
Australia	1,391	554	524	446	465
Austria	751	525	474	786	276
Belgium	797	466	499	549	344
Brazil	434	223	1,492	136	44
Bulgaria	537	394	3,542	90	272
Canada	1,067	710	6,542	2,252	390
Chile	354	215	221	224	85
China	335	321	862	67	16
Colombia	524	115	1,602	752	342
Cuba	352	239	44	1	102
Czech Republic	803	531	3,712	422	122
Denmark	1,145	594	705	665	432
Dominican Republic	178	95	932	502	N.A.
Ecuador	348	130	912	312	202
Egypt	317	119	81	20	122
Finland	1,498	622	5,522	726	396
France	946	595	580	494	305
Germany	948	567	601	586	336
Ghana	236	93	12	6	32
Greece	475	240	5,282	559	70
Guatemala	79	61	57	302	102
Honduras	410	95	46	24	102
Hungary	690	435	3,712	293	85
India	120	65	32	4	5
Indonesia	155	68	31	17	10
Iran	263	71	149	15	562
Iraq	229	83	302	—[2]	N.A.
Ireland	697	402	4,782	597	365
Israel	524	288	463	702	254
Italy	880	528	4,622	737	209
Jamaica	483	183	199	142	432
Japan	956	686	5,582	526	315
Korea, South	1,039	348	464	567	190
Kuwait	678	505	2,402	1,582	1,212
Lebanon	907	375	2,012	1,942	462
Malaysia	434	172	211	155	105
Mexico	329	272	125	142	51
Morocco	247	115	50	83	112
Netherlands	980	519	6,072	671	395
New Zealand	997	512	4,962	3,662	360
Norway	917	462	729	703	491
Pakistan	94	22	222	22	42
Panama	299	187	1,642	832	322
Peru	273	126	64	402	362
Philippines	161	52	40	84	20
Poland	522	337	2,632	181	69
Portugal	306	336	431	665	105
Puerto Rico	714	270	3,332	2,092	N.A.
Romania	319	233	1,672	112	272
Russia	417	410	217	19	43
Saudi Arabia	321	262	1,292	402	572
Singapore	744	388	485	684	483
South Africa	355	134	1,252	1,202	62
Spain	331	409	421	609	143
Sweden	932	519	6,652	703	507
Switzerland	979	457	720	645	502
Syria	278	70	104	2	142
Taiwan	N.A.	N.A.	568	803	225
Thailand	234	254	862	44	24
Turkey	178	330	280	246	38
United Kingdom	1,443	521	5,672	670	338
United States	2,116	806	6,732	400	585
Uruguay	603	239	2,712	952	1,002
Venezuela	472	180	1,092	1,432	46

1. 1997 figures. 2. 1999 figures. **Source:** International Telecommunications Union, *World Telecommunication Indicators;* U.S. Census Bureau, *Statistical Abstract of the United States* (annual).

Area Codes of the United States and Canada, by State and Province

The continuing proliferation of fax machines, modems, pagers, and cellular phones has played havoc with the number of area codes in the U.S., Canada and the Caribbean. In 1990, there were 120 area codes, a number that increased only to 146 by 1996. But in 2002, there were more than 300. Several cities had two or more area codes in the exact same area (known as an overlay), requiring customers to dial 11 digits just to make a local call. At current growth rates, the North American area code system will run out of three-digit codes sometime between 2007 and 2012. (For International Dialing codes, see Part III: "The World.")

201 New Jersey (Jersey City)[1]
202 Washington, D.C.
203 Connecticut (Greenwich, New Haven)
204 Manitoba, Canada
205 Alabama (Birmingham, Tuscaloosa)
206 Washington (Seattle)
207 Maine
208 Idaho
209 California (Modesto, Stockton)
210 Texas (San Antonio)
212 New York City (Manhattan)[1]
213 California (Los Angeles)
214 Texas (Dallas)[1]
215 Pennsylvania (Philadelphia)[1]
216 Ohio (Cleveland)
217 Illinois (Decatur, Springfield)
218 Minnesota (Duluth)
219 Indiana (Gary)
224 Illinois (Des Plaines, Evanston)[1]
225 Louisiana (Baton Rouge)
228 Mississippi (Biloxi, Gulfport)
229 Georgia (Albany, Americus)
231 Michigan (Muskegon)
234 Ohio (Akron, Youngstown)[1]
239 Florida (Fort Myers)
240 Maryland (Rockville, Bethesda)[1]
242 Bahamas
246 Barbados
248 Michigan (Pontiac)[1]
250 British Columbia (Vancouver, Victoria)
251 Alabama (Mobile, Montgomery)[1]
252 North Carolina (Rocky Mount)
253 Washington (Tacoma)
254 Texas (Waco)
256 Alabama (Huntsville)
260 Indiana (Fort Wayne)
262 Wisconsin (Racine, Kenosha)
264 Anguilla
267 Pennsylvania (Philadelphia)[1]
268 Antigua/Barbuda
269 Michigan (Kalamazoo)
270 Kentucky (Bowling Green, Hopkinsville)
276 Virginia (Abingdon)
281 Texas (Houston)[1]
284 British Virgin Islands
289 Ontario (Hamilton, Niagara Falls)[1]
301 Maryland (Rockville, Bethesda)[1]
302 Delaware
303 Colorado (Denver, Englewood)[1]
304 West Virginia
305 Florida (Miami)[1]
306 Saskatchewan (Regina, Saskatoon)
307 Wyoming
308 Nebraska (North Platte)
309 Illinois (Moline, Peoria)
310 California (Santa Monica, Malibu)
312 Illinois (Chicago Loop)
313 Michigan (Detroit)
314 Missouri (St. Louis)
315 New York (Syracuse, Utica)
316 Kansas (Wichita)
317 Indiana (Indianapolis)
318 Louisiana (Shreveport)
319 Iowa (Cedar Rapids, Iowa City)
320 Minnesota (St. Cloud)
321 Florida (Melbourne, Orlando)[2]
323 California (Los Angeles, except downown)
330 Ohio (Akron, Youngstown)[1]
334 Alabama (Mobile, Montgomery)[1]
336 North Carolina (Greensboro)
337 Louisiana (Lafayette, Lake Charles)
339 Massachusetts (Arlington, Revere, Woburn)[1]
340 U.S. Virgin Islands
345 Cayman Islands
347 New York (Bronx, Brooklyn, Queens, Staten Island)[1]
351 Massachusetts (Andover, Salem)[1]
352 Florida (Gainesville, Ocala)
360 Washington (Bellingham, Vancouver)
361 Texas (Corpus Christi)
386 Florida (Lake City)
401 Rhode Island
402 Nebraska (Lincoln, Omaha)
403 Alberta (Calgary)
404 Georgia (Atlanta)
405 Oklahoma (Oklahoma City)
406 Montana
407 Florida (Orlando, Kissimmee)[2]
408 California (San Jose)
409 Texas (Galveston)
410 Maryland (Baltimore, Annapolis)[1]
412 Pennsylvania (Pittsburgh)[1]
413 Massachusetts (Pittsfield, Springfield)
414 Wisconsin (Milwaukee)
415 California (San Francisco)
416 Ontario (Toronto)[1]
417 Missouri (Joplin, Springfield)
418 Quebec (Quebec City)
419 Ohio (Sandusky, Toledo)[1]
423 Tennessee (Chattanooga, Bristol)
425 Washington (Bellevue, Redmond)
434 Virginia (Lynchburg, Danville)
435 Utah (Ogden)
440 Ohio (Cleveland suburbs)
441 Bermuda
443 Maryland (Baltimore, Annapolis)[1]
445 Pennsylvania (Philadelphia)[1]
450 Quebec (Montreal suburbs)
469 Texas (Dallas)[1]
473 Grenada
478 Georgia (Macon)
479 Arkansas (Fort Smith)
480 Arizona (Mesa, Scottsdale)
484 Pennsylvania (Allentown, Reading)[1]
501 Arkansas (Little Rock, Hot Springs)
502 Kentucky (Louisville)
503 Oregon (Portland, Salem)[1]
504 Louisiana (New Orleans)
505 New Mexico
506 New Brunswick, Canada
507 Minnesota (Rochester, Winona)
508 Massachusetts (Cape Cod, Plymouth, Worcester)[1]
509 Washington (Spokane, Yakima)
510 California (Berkeley, Oakland)
512 Texas (Austin)
513 Ohio (Cincinnati)[1]
514 Quebec (downtown Montreal)
515 Iowa (Ames, Des Moines)
516 New York (Western Long Island: Nassau County)
517 Michigan (Lansing, Saginaw)
518 New York (Albany, Schenectady)
519 Ontario, Canada (London)
520 Arizona (Tucson)
530 California (Chico, Redding)
540 Virginia (Roanoke, Winchester)
541 Oregon (Eugene, Medford)
551 New Jersey (Jersey City)[1]
559 California (Fresno)
561 Florida (West Palm Beach)
562 California (Long Beach)
563 Iowa (Davenport, Dubuque)
567 Ohio (Sandusky, Toledo)[1]
570 Pennsylvania (Scranton)
571 Virginia (Alexandria, Arlington)[1]
573 Missouri (Columbia, Jefferson City)
574 Indiana (South Bend)
580 Oklahoma (Lawton, Stillwater)
585 New York (Rochester)
586 Michigan (Roseville, Warren)
601 Mississippi (Jackson, Natchez)
602 Arizona (Phoenix, Tempe)
603 New Hampshire
604 British Columbia (Whistler)
605 South Dakota
606 Kentucky (Ashland, Middlesborough)
607 New York (Binghampton, Elmira)
608 Wisconsin (La Crosse, Madison)
609 New Jersey (Atlantic City, Long Branch)

610 Pennsylvania (Allentown, Reading)[1]
612 Minnesota (Minneapolis)
613 Ontario (Ottawa)
614 Ohio (Columbus)
615 Tennessee (Nashville)
616 Michigan (Grand Rapids)
617 Massachusetts (Boston)[1]
618 Illinois (Centralia, E. St. Louis)
619 California (downtown San Diego)
620 Kansas (Dodge City, Parsons)
623 Arizona (Glendale, Peoria)
626 California (Pasadena)
630 Illinois (Oak Brook)
631 New York (Eastern Long Island, Suffolk County)
636 Missouri (St. Louis suburbs)
641 Iowa (Mason City, Oskaloosa)
646 New York (Manhattan)[1]
647 Ontario (Toronto)[1]
649 Turks & Caicos Islands
650 California (Palo Alto, San Mateo)
651 Minnesota (St. Paul)
660 Missouri (Sedalia)
661 California (Bakersfield)
662 Mississippi (Yazoo City, Tupelo)
664 Montserrat
670 Northern Mariana Islands
671 Guam
678 Georgia (Marietta, Smyrna)[1]
682 Texas (Arlington, Fort Worth)[1]
701 North Dakota
702 Nevada (Las Vegas)
703 Virginia (Alexandria, Arlington)[1]
704 North Carolina (Charlotte, Gastonia)[1]
705 Ontario (North Bay)
706 Georgia (Augusta)
707 California (Eureka, Napa)
708 Illinois (Cicero, Oak Lawn)
709 Newfoundland
712 Iowa (Council Bluffs, Sioux City)
713 Texas (Houston)[1]
714 California (Huntington Beach, Santa Ana)
715 Wisconsin (Eau Claire, Wausau)
716 New York (Buffalo, Jamestown)
717 Pennsylvania (Harrisburg, Scranton)
718 New York Bronx, Brooklyn, Queens, Staten Island)[1]
719 Colorado (Colorado Springs, Pueblo)
720 Colorado (Denver, Englewood)[1]
724 Pennsylvania (New Castle)[1]
727 Florida (St. Petersburg)
731 Tennessee (Jackson, Union City)
732 New Jersey (New Brunswick)[1]
734 Michigan (Ann Arbor, Ypsilanti)
740 Ohio (Cambridge, Marietta)
754 Florida (Ft. Lauderdale, Hollywood)[1]
757 Virginia (Norfolk, Virginia Beach)
758 St. Lucia
760 California (Palm Springs)
763 Minnesota (Brooklyn Center, Fridley)
765 Indiana (Lafayette, Muncie)
767 Dominica
770 Georgia (Marietta, Smyrna)[1]
772 Florida (Fort Pierce, Stuart)
773 Illinois (Chicago except the Loop)
774 Massachusetts (Cape Cod, Plymouth, Worcester)[1]
775 Nevada (Carson City, Reno)
778 British Columbia (Whistler)
780 Alberta (Edmonton)
781 Massachusetts (Arlington, Revere, Woburn)[1]
784 St. Vincent and the Grenadines
785 Kansas (Topeka, Manhattan)
786 Florida (Miami)[1]
787 Puerto Rico[1]
801 Utah (Salt Lake City, Alta)
802 Vermont
803 South Carolina (Augusta, Columbia)
804 Virginia (Richmond)
805 California (Santa Barbara Lompoc,)
806 Texas (Amarillo)
807 Ontario (Fort William, Thunder Bay)
808 Hawaii
809 Dominican Republic
810 Michigan (Flint)
812 Indiana (Evansville, Terre Haute)
813 Florida (Tampa)
814 Pennsylvania (Altoona, Erie)
815 Illinois (Joliet, Rockford)
816 Missouri (Kansas City, St. Joseph)
817 Texas (Arlington, Fort Worth)[1]
818 California (Burbank, San Fernando)
819 Quebec (Sherbrooke)
828 North Carolina (Asheville, Morganton)
830 Texas (Fredericksburg)
831 California (Monterey, Salinas)
832 Texas (Houston)[1]
835 Pennsylvania (Allentown, Reading)[1]
843 South Carolina (Charleston)
845 New York (Kingston, Poughkeepsie)
847 Illinois (Des Plaines, Evanston)[1]
848 New Jersey (New Brunswick)[1]
850 Florida (Pensacola, Tallahassee)
856 New jersey (Camden, Trenton)[1]
857 Massachusetts (Boston)[1]
858 California (Northern San Diego, La Jolla)
859 Kentucky (Covington, Lexington)
860 Connecticut (Hartford)
862 New Jersey (Newark)[1]
863 Florida (Lakeland, Winter Haven)
864 South Carolina (Greenville-Spartanburg)
865 Tennessee (Knoxville)
867 Yukon and Northwest Territories
868 Trinidad & Tobago
869 St. Kitt's & Nevis
870 Arkansas (Jonesboro)
876 Jamaica
878 Pennsylvania (Pittsburgh, New Castle)[1]
901 Tennessee (Memphis)
902 Nova Scotia, Prince Edward Island
903 Texas (Sherman, Tyler)
904 Florida (Jacksonville, St. Augustine)
905 Ontario (Hamilton, Niagara Falls)[1]
906 Michigan (Upper Peninsula)
907 Alaska
908 New Jersey (Elizabeth)
909 California (Pomona, San Bernardino)
910 North Carolina (Fayetteville, Wilmington)
912 Georgia (Savannah)
913 Kansas (Kansas City)
914 New York (White Plains, Yonkers)
915 Texas (Abilene, El Paso)
916 California (Sacramento)
917 New York (New York City: cell phones and pagers)
918 Oklahoma (Muskogee, Tulsa)
919 North Carolina (Raleigh, Durham)
920 Wisconsin (Appleton, Green Bay)
925 California (Concord, Pleasanton)
928 Arizona (Flagstaff, Yuma)
931 Tennessee (Clarksville, Columbia)
936 Texas (Crocket, Nacogdoches)
937 Ohio (Dayton)
939 Puerto Rico[1]
940 Texas (Wichita Falls)
941 Florida (Bradenton, Sarasota)
947 Michigan (Pontiac)[1]
949 California (Irvine)
952 Minnesota (Bloomington, Minnetonka)
954 Florida (Ft. Lauderdale, Hollywood)[1]
956 Texas (Laredo, McAllen)
970 Colorado (Aspen, Grand Junction)
971 Oregon (Portland, Salem)[1]
972 Texas (Dallas)[1]
973 New Jersey (Newark)[1]
978 Massachusetts (Andover, Salem)[1]
979 Texas (Bryan, College Station)
980 North Carolina (Charlotte, Gastonia)[1]
985 Louisiana (Bogalusa, Houma)
989 Michigan (Alpena)

Note: When no cities are listed, area code is for entire state or province. 1. Area in which there is an overlay, or more than one area code for the area. 2. The 321 area code is an overlay on the 407 area code in the Orlando area only. Area codes in this area may be either 321 or 407, but all area codes in the Melbourne area are 321.
Source: Lockheed Martin, North American Numbering Plan Relief Letters, 2002. www.nanpa.com.

THE INTERNET

The Internet, an intricate global web of hundreds of thousands of computer networks linked by conventional telephone lines (and now such high-speed alternatives as cable modem and DSL), was created by the U.S. Defense Department in 1969 as a faster way for agencies to share information and as an emergency means of communications in case more traditional means were cut off. But the potential for consumer Internet use didn't occur until the 1980s, when the National Science Foundation created equipment that would allow other computer networks to connect to the government's larger network. From there, commercial services such as CompuServe, Prodigy, and America Online tapped into the ever-growing network and brought a wealth of information to anybody with a computer, a modem, and the monthly fee. In 1993 some three million people worldwide were connected to the Internet. By early 2003, according to one estimate, the total number of users exceeded 600 million.

Today, the Internet is the world's largest communications network. The number of names registered in the *domain name system*—Web sites of commercial enterprises, public institutions, and private individuals—exceeded 50 million by 2003. The networks and switches that make up the Internet carry data around the world in seconds, and link even the most remote user to a vast wealth of resources. The most popular network on the Internet is the *World Wide Web* (WWW, or simply, "the Web"), created in 1989 by CERN, the European Particle Physics Lab in Geneva and made available on the Internet in Aug. 1991. In 1993, the creation of software (Mosaic) that displayed the Internet in a format that resembled a magazine with text and graphics dramatically increased Net usage. In 1994, the Netscape browser came on the market, and since then, the Internet has become hugely popular, as computer users found they could navigate the Web quickly and easily.

In just a few short years, the Internet and the Web have quite literally transformed the way millions of people go about their daily lives. Everything from mundane tasks like banking or ordering tickets to more eventful activities like searching for a job or a date, planning a vacation, or buying a house, can all be done sitting in front of a computer. Physicians, lawyers, real estate agents and marketing specialists, among others, can get vital public documents and other information over the Net. Meanwhile, businesses can market products, purchase materials and services, and carry out other essential activities. For ordinary users, e-mail is by far the most popular online activity. As of 2003, up to half of the U.S. population used it regularly. Worldwide, more than 10 billion messages a day were being sent. If overhyped and overinvested in the 1990s, the Internet remains the fastest-growing and most versatile resource in media history.

25 Top Global Internet Properties, 2003

Rank, Site	Audience (000s)
1. Yahoo!	87,895
2. MSN	77,996
3. AOL Time Warner	67,928
4. Microsoft	51,634
5. Google	37,526
6. eBay	30,424
7. Amazon	30,230
8. About/Primedia	24,116
9. Lycos Network	23,582
10. Sony	17,463
11. Walt Disney Internet Group	16,409
12. Rakuten	15,235
13. CNET Networks	14,107
14. Nifty	14,087
15. AT&T	13,970
16. InfoSpace	13,007
17. Landmark Communications	12,466
18. NEC	11,968
19. Viacom International	11,626
20. Real Networks	10,919
21. eUniverse Network	10,229
22. Excite Network	9,811
23. Vivendi Universal	9,803
24. NTT Communications	9,751
25. CitySearch/Ticketmaster Online	9,523

Note: As measured in June 2003. 1. Unique audience. **Source:** Nielsen/NetRatings

Who Uses the Internet?

Almost unheard of before 1990, the Internet has entered the vocabulary of most Americans and the homes of a large number of them. Because Internet use is decentralized and almost completely unregulated, statistics on the number of users are difficult to verify and vary significantly among reporting services. By most accounts, however, the number of regular Internet users in the United States reached 50 million in 1998, about five years after the medium became viable for ordinary consumers. That narrow time frame easily eclipsed the 10 years for cable TV, 13 for television, and 38 for radio. And the user base continues to expand rapidly. An increase of nearly 40 percent from 2000 to 2003 put the number of U.S. Internet users at more than 162 million—some 56 percent of the total population. Even as evidence began to suggest that users were spending less time online, overall traffic continued to rise.

As the user base has expanded, the demographic profile of the average user has changed. According to several surveys, disparities in gender, age, income, education level, and race between Net users and non-users have continued to shrink. Children and teenagers still use the Internet more than any other age group. As of late 2001, according to a government study, 65 percent

Internet Users Worldwide, 2002

Region	Users[1] (millions)
Canada and United States	182.67
Europe	190.91
Asia/Pacific	187.24
Latin America	33.35
Middle East	5.12
Africa	6.31
World Total	**605.60**

1. Estimated as of September 2002.
Source: NUA Internet Surveys.

Guide to Domain Name Suffixes

Suffix	Used by
.aero	Air transport industry (***Reserved***)
.biz	Businesses (*alternative to .com*)
.com	Commercial entities
.coop	Business cooperatives (***Reserved***)
.edu	Educational institutions
.gov	Government bodies (*at any level*)
.info	General use (*alternative to .com*)
.museum	Museums (***Reserved***)
.name	Private individuals for personal sites
.net	Internet-related institutions
.org	Nonprofit organizations
.pro	Professionals

Note: Note: "Reserved for" domains are sponsored by an organization that represents the specific domain community and is responsible for policies concerning those sites. Unsponsored domains operate under policies established by the global Internet community through ICANN.

U.S. Online Households and Internet Users, 1997–2003

	Internet Users		Online Households	
Year	Number (millions)	Percent of Pop.	Number (millions)	Percent of Households
1997	56.8	22.2%	18.8	18.6%
1998	84.6	32.7	27.2	26.4
1999	102.0	39.1	34.6	33.3
2000	116.5	44.4	43.6	42.2
2001	142.8	53.9	53.3	50.5
2002	157.6	55.0	N.A.	N.A.
2003[1]	162.4	56.0	N.A.	N.A.

1. Estimated, spring. 2. Projection.
Source: U.S. Department of Commerce; Jupiter Media Metrix.

of 10–13 year-olds and 75 percent of 14–17 year-olds had Internet access. The median age of the average user, however, rose to 34. The gender gap also continued to close, as women surpassed men as a percentage of the over-18 user base (51 percent–49 percent) for the first time. Disparities remained in Internet access by income level; 79 percent of individuals with a family income of $75,000 or more had access, compared with only 19 percent of those with a family income under $15,000—but the latter group grew faster than the former. Likewise, access among blacks and Hispanics grew faster than among whites (33 percent and 30 percent versus 20 percent, respectively), though whites still accounted for 76 percent of users. The highest growth rate among types of households was single mothers with children.

In addition to the increases in the user base and overall traffic—and partly responsible for those increases—have come improvements in the means of access. As of late 2003, some 70 percent of U.S. Internet households still accessed the Net by telephone dial-up service, but such high-speed alternatives as cable modem and DSL (Digital Subscription Line) were growing rapidly. In 2003, according to industry monitor Jupiter Media Mextrix, more than 45 percent (40 million) of online households were expected to have a broadband connection by 2007.

▶THE WORLD WIDE WEB

The World Wide Web is a vast network of information within the Internet, which uses a hypertext system for quickly transmitting graphics, sound and video over phone lines. To read the information, users must have a *browser* (such as Netscape Navigator or Microsoft Internet Explorer). Because the hypertext system arranges information based on its relationship to other information rather than in linear or alphabetical order, the Web allows users to find information quickly, especially if they don't know exactly what they're looking for. Each piece of information, or *Web page,* can be connected to one or more other pages via a *link.* For example, the U.S. Census Bureau's Web site (www.census.gov) provides thousands of data tables produced by the Department of Commerce, and is also linked to data from 70 other government agencies.

The Web is divided into zones, which organize pages according to the type of information generally contained within them. There is of course some overlap, but generally, Web pages of educational institutions end in .edu; government Web pages end in .gov; Web pages of Internet-related institutions end in .net; commercial entities end with .com; and other organizations end with .org. In an attempt to relieve overcrowding in the .com and .net areas, the ICANN (Internet Corporation for Assigned Names and Numbers), the official governing body for domain names, created seven new suffixes (or TLDs, "Top-Level Domains") for use beginning in 2001: .aero, .biz, .coop, .info, .museum, .name, and .pro.

Growth of the Web It is becoming increasingly easy for companies, organizations, and even individuals to create their own Web sites. Millions of institutions, groups, and individuals have done so, resulting in such dramatic growth that the Web's 50 million sites in 2003 contained an estimated 6-8 billion pages (up to double the previous year's total) with 10K-20K of data per page. With so many sites throughout cyberspace, surfers would find it close to impossible to find what they were looking for without a *search engine.* Like a librarian who knows where in the library to find valuable information, search engines look through countless Web pages and create an index of what appears on each one. If you're looking for the rules of badminton, you can ask the search engine to sift hundreds of thousands of Web pages for the word badminton and it will return a list of Web pages that mention badminton. Google, MetaCrawler, AltaVista, and such newcomers as Teoma and WiseNut are some of the most popular search engines.

As the Internet has emerged as a mass medium, the major online service providers, search services, and other Web companies have competed ever more vigorously for user "audience." To attract the greatest number of visitors on a regular basis, many Web sites have expanded from their core services and established broad-based *portals*—whole arrays of services (such as e-mail, search, special-interest forums and bulletin boards, and chat rooms), information (news, weather, stock reports, reference resources), and links to other useful sites, all accessible from a single home page.

Business on the Web The increasing sophistication of both technology and users have made the World Wide Web a major and rapidly expanding business medium. No longer just a vehicle for publishing brochures and annual reports, the Web has emerged as a low-cost sales channel for producers of goods and services and as a highly convenient purchasing vehicle for end users.

Beginning late in 2000, however, a measure of reality came to the Internet industry, as the sky-high valuations of online ventures came back to earth, investors began demanding profitability, and a number of sites were simply shut down. Yet, while forecasts of e-commerce growth were scaled back, analysts reported strong increases.

A vast majority of all e-commerce is conducted between businesses, as the Internet has helped cut transaction costs, locate surplus or low-cost goods, and otherwise increase efficiencies. According to the research firm eMarketer, worldwide business-to-business net revenues were expected to reach $1.4 trillion in 2003, of which about half would be generated in the United States. The global figure was projected to nearly double in 2004, to $2.7 trillion, with the U.S. total exceeding $1 trillion.

Retail online purchasing, more familiar to the average consumer, suffered more severe setbacks in the dot-com shakeout, as numerous Net vendors were forced out of business. But reports of the death of online business-to-consumer merchandising were also premature. Retailers would be forced to show profits, but consumers continued to increase online spending. According to Jupiter Media Metrix, online retail revenues in the U.S. would reach $51.7 billion in 2003, up more than 50 percent from two years earlier, and were expected to reach $105 billion—or about 5 percent of all U.S. retail spending—in 2007. Jupiter estimated that some 97 million consumers, or nearly 60 percent of the total online population, would make an electronic purchase in 2003. The rate was only expected to increase as users become more comfortable with making online transactions. Travel, computers and consumer electronics, and books and music are the leading online retail categories.

One of the innovative and increasingly popular forms of e-commerce is online auctioning, which enables consumers to bid from their home computers on product offerings from private owners or original manufacturers and service providers. eBay, the largest person-to-person online trading community, claimed tens of millions of registered traders around the world and generated nearly $15 billion in gross merchandise sales in 2002.

Few industries have undergone more radical and rapid change as a consequence of online commerce than stock brokerage and financial services. Round-the-clock access, lower service fees, and push-button immediacy have made it easier, cheaper, and faster for ordinary consumers to buy stock or apply for a loan directly online.

Advertising on the Web Much as it has evolved as a communications and information medium, the World Wide Web, like television and and radio, has also emerged as a major vehicle of commercial advertising. The ads come in the form of banners, pop-up windows, and other Web-page design elements. E-mail has also proven to be viable as an advertising medium, giving birth to the next generation of direct-mail marketing.

The U.S. economic slowdown and shakeout in the dot-com industry in 2000-2002 slowed the growth of Internet advertising, but the rate of increase over the short life of the medium still far exceeded that of any other. And robust increases were expected in the years to come. Media analysts estimated global online ad spending in 2002 at $5-$6.0 billion, a significant decline from the previous year. Jupiter Media Metrix, however, predicted 10 percent growth in 2003 and an increase to $14 billion in 2007.

Privacy and Intellectual Property Rights As the popularity and purchasing power of the Internet have grown, and as monitoring tools have improved, many people have perceived a growing threat to their personal privacy. Software that tracks usage habits, network database technology, and the ability to transmit vast amounts of data have made it possible to collect and share detailed information about the browsing habits, interests and hobbies, buying patterns, financial history, and contact information of ordinary Internet-using citizens. The U.S. Congress in 2002 and 2003 considered various legislative measures to protect privacy and combat identity theft in the online environment.

In a similar vein, the data-sharing power of the Internet has undermined traditional protections for proprietary information and copyright materials. The issue came to the fore in 2000-2001, as the music industry successfully sued Napster.com, which enabled Web site visitors to swap MP3 music files of popular commercial recordings for free. But as millions of users continued to pirate digital songs, music and games through online file-sharing systems, copyright protection and intellectual property rights on the Internet loomed as major long-term issues.

▶A GLOSSARY OF COMMONLY USED INTERNET TERMS

Account Permission to use a computer on a network, or an access agreement with an Internet provider

Address The location of an Internet host. An e-mail address might take the form johndoe@xyz.com; a web address might look like www.xyztech.com. See also URL.

Applet A small program, typically embedded in an Web page, that a user can quickly download and launch, thus enhancing the Web page's content.

Bandwidth The amount of data, graphics, sound, and other information that can be transmitted through cyberspace at a certain time. Bandwidth is measured in kilobits per second (kbps). Most telephone modems have a bandwidth of 56 kbps (or simply 56k), though *cable modems* and *DSL* can offer bandwidths of more than 1 megabit per second (mbps).

Blog Short for "weblog." A diarylike Web site, usually containing the personal thoughts of the site's owner as well as links to other sites of interest.

Bookmark A browser feature (called "Favorites" in Microsoft Explorer) that stores a pointer to a Web site for easy access.

Browser A program that translates the hypertext markup language of the World Wide Web into languages ordinary people can understand. Netscape and Microsoft Internet Explorer are the two most common Web browsers.

Cable Modem A high-speed, broadband Internet connection via cable TV lines; services often include a selection of localized content.

Cache (Pronounced "cash") The place on a hard drive where a Web browser stores images a user has downloaded off the Internet. If the user wants to see the same Web page again, the browser loads it from the cache rather than retrieve it again from the Internet.

Chat line "talk" An electronic forum in which Internet users can communicate with each other online.

Cookie A small piece of information that a Web *browser* picks up from another site and stores. Such bits of information can be read and altered by another site, thereby making it possible to identify users who have been to the site before. Cookies allow you to add items to your "shopping cart" as you browse several pages in a virtual shopping mall.

Cyberspace An all-encompassing term for the digital world of computer networks.

Domain The identifying portion of an Internet address (which follows the @ in an e-mail address. Domain names are followed by a period and a zone that indicates the type of organization. Commercial entities end with *.com*; Educational institutions end with *.edu*; government bodies end with *.gov*; and other organizations end with *.org*.

Download A way to transfer files, graphics, or other information from the Internet to your computer. HTTP and FTP are the most common downloading methods.

DSL Digital Subscription Line, a high-speed Internet connection that uses the ultra-high frequency portion of ordinary telephone lines, allowing users to send and receive voice and data on the same line at the same time.

Emoticon A cluster of punctuation marks commonly used in online chat, postings and e-mail to signify a facial expression or emotional response. For example, :-) represents a smile, and :-(a frown.

Encryption A method of encoding files so only the recipient can read the information. Encryption is necessary for transmitting secure data like credit card numbers over computer networks.

FAQs Frequently Asked Questions. This is generally the first place to stop on a newsgroup or a Web site. It has the answers to the most common questions and indicators of where to go to find the answers to less frequently asked questions.

FTP File Transfer Protocol, the easiest way to download files not on the World Wide Web.

Freeware Free software available over the Internet. This is in contrast with *shareware*, which is available freely, but usually asks the user to send payment for using the software.

GIF Graphic Interchange Format (pronounced "jif"), a common file format for image files; best-suited for nonphotographic material.

Home page The first or main page of a Web site.

HTML HyperText Markup Language, the high-speed computer language used to create documents on the World Wide Web (WWW). To read documents written in HTML, one must have a browser.

HTTP HyperText Transport Protocol, the easiest way to transfer World Wide Web pages from one computer to another.

Hyperlink A connection between two tagged elements in a Web page, or separate sites, that makes it possible to click from one to the other.

Hypertext A system of organizing information based on its relationship to other information, rather than linear or alphabetical orders. Hypertext allows users to *link* related Web pages and to store information in more than one place. For example, in a hypertext almanac, the winners of the National Book Awards could be accessed either through the section on books or on awards.

Intranet A network of computers accessible only by members of the network, often members of one firm. Also known as an internal network.

ISDN Integrated Services Digital Network, a digital type of phone service that permits higher speed transmission of data than conventional phone lines. ISDN lines operate as fast as 128 kilobytes per second (kbps), compared with 28.8 or 56 kbps for the fastest modems.

ISP Internet Service Provider, a company that provides end-user access to the Internet via its central computers and local access lines. American Online (AOL), Earthlink, and Erols are some popular ISPs.

Java A computer language developed by Sun Microsystems that produces programs that run on almost any computer or operating system. Its compatibility and ease of use make it popular for for developing *applets*, tiny applications that can be sent quickly over the World Wide Web.

JPEG Joint Photographic Experts Group, a common file format for photographic images.

Link A hypertext connection that allows a user to jump from one Internet site to another by pointing and clicking. On the World Wide Web, links are often underlined or highlighted.

MIDI Musical Instrument Digital Interface, a file format for high-quality sound.

Mirror site An identical backup site that serves as an alternative for a busy web host.

MPEG Motion Picture Experts Group, a file format for high-quality video in small file sizes.

Newsgroups Discussion forums on the Internet, arranged by category of special interest. To read, respond to, or post information on a newsgroup, you must have a program known as a Newsreader.

Push technology Technology that pushes information onto a user's computer rather than requiring the user to navigate the Internet and "pull" the information from another computer network. E-mail and newsgroups are simple examples of push technology.

Search engine A tool used to look up Web pages. Also known as an index or a directory. Yahoo!, Excite, Lycos, and AltaVista are some of the most popular search engines.

Server The central computer in a network, providing a service or data access to client computers on that network. Frequently, a Web server is dedicated to a specific function, such as e-mail.

Shareware An honor system in which providers make their programs freely accessible over the Internet, with the understanding that those who use them will send payment to the provider after using them. See also *freeware*.

Spam Junk e-mail. As a verb, it means to send thousands of copies of a junk e-mail message.

Thumbnail A tiny picture on a Web page which, when clicked, is replaced by a larger version of the same image.

URL Uniform Resource Locator, the address that identifies a Web page to a browser. Also known as a Web address.

Usenet A system of thousands of newsgroups.

Web page An HTML file, containing text, graphics, and/or mini-applications, viewed with a Web *browser*.

Web site An organized, linked collection of *Web pages* stored on an Internet *server* and read using a Web *browser*. The opening page of a site is called a *home page*.

WebTV A commercial service that accesses the World Wide Web through a television and cable TV wires rather than through a computer and phone wires.

WWW The World Wide Web, or simply the Web, a vast network of information, particularly business, commercial, and government resources, that uses a hypertext system for quickly transmitting graphics, sound, and video over phone, cable TV, and fiber optic lines, allowing easy navigation among related subjects.

XML eXtensible Markup Language, a universal format for structured documents and data transmitted on the Web. XML is a "metalanguage," a system used for defining and creating specialized languages such as HTML.

Zip file A file that has been compressed for simpler transmission over the Internet. To read a ZIP file, you need a program to decompress the file, such as PKUNZIP or WinZip.

▶ A FIELD GUIDE TO SEARCHING THE WEB

To search the Web successfully, you need to pick the right engine and learn how to use it. Few people understand the fundamental difference between search engines and Web directories. The former use software agents called "spiders" or "crawlers" to index contents of individual Web pages, then follow links to other pages. Web directories such as Yahoo are compiled by humans who classify sites under topical headings. Most search sites now offer both options, along with information and other services, but topical directories that accompany powerful search engines may be weak, and vice-versa. Moreover, the various search engines themselves operate differently.

The first step in conducting an effective search is to pick an appropriate search site for the job. For a general search, a strong Web directory such as Yahoo or Look Smart is a good place to start. A directory-style search provides two ways to research broad topics: dive through a list of broad topics by clicking on the appropriate links or fill out a search box to find listings.

But directory searches are less effective when looking for specific information—things like the author of a book, the complete text of the Declaration of Independence or research on drug treatments for a medical condition. For this kind of information, search engines like Google and Alta Vista are the way to go. Because they search an index of keywords drawn by spiders from millions of Web pages, the chances are greater that they will find obscure terms in obscure Web pages.

There's a third kind of search site, one that includes popular sites like Metacrawler, Ask Jeeves and Dogpile. These sites—also called metasearch tools—issue search requests to fistfuls of other Web search sites. When Google, Excite, Alta Vista and the like return their results, the metasearch site collects them onto a single Web page for display.

Because no two search sites index exactly the same set of Web pages, metasearch tools give you a wider scope of results—but it's worth remembering that more does not necessarily equal better. What really counts is relevant results that are sorted in a relevant order. And that's the rub.

Simply picking one of two or three types of sites to search from is no guarantee of good results. Brad Hill, the author of World Wide Web Searching for Dummies (IDG), says most search sites deliver too much information. "Search engines do a good job on indexing," he said. "But because of that, they deliver more than you want."

So when you're faced with several hundred thousand results over dozens of pages, what should you do? "Don't go past the first page of results," Hill said. "If it doesn't have something of interest, you've probably entered the wrong search string."

Most people could get much more relevant results with a few simple tricks for constructing a search "string"—the words you enter in the search box. The most obvious is to type in several relevant words instead of just one or two. In general, the fewer words you enter, the more general your results will be.

AllTheWeb (www.alltheweb.com) A lesser known but superior search engine with a database of more than 2.1 billion indexed Web documents. Its "advanced search" option is a little difficult but well worth mastering.

Alta Vista (www.altavista.com) A powerful, highly rated search engine with a database of more than 600 million indexed documents. Accurate, well-integrated search results. The portal also includes a modest topical directory, links, tools, and services.

Ask Jeeves (www.askjeeves.com) A highly user-friendly metasearch site, with natural language querying and a basic subject directory. It helps you narrow your search through simple questions and simultaneously searches other engines for relevant Web pages. Results are organized under "Web," "News," and "Shopping" tabs. Ask Jeeves for Kids is also available from the home page.

Dogpile (www.dogpile.com) The most popular Internet metasearch site, Dogpile combs through about 15 search engines and directories. Results are sorted by the engine that found them—not the most useful presentation.

Google (www.google.com) The leading general Internet search engine, consistently a leader in user preference surveys and trade reviews. Fast and reliable, with more than 1.5 billion indexed documents. Known for yielding high-relevance results and few broken links.

Hotbot (http://hotbot.lycos.com) Now part of the Terra Lycos network, this search site remains a good choice for finding specific information. It features an easy-to-use interface, results listed by relevance, and a strong topical directory.

LookSmart (www.looksmart.com) An extensive and widely distributed (through licensing) subject directory of commercial listings. Geared to advertisers and pay-for-placement enterprises, it enables companies to reach general audiences and the business community through major portals and ISPs as well as its own home page.

Lycos (www.lycos.com) Part of the Terra Lycos network, this long-established portal site continues to offer a strong selection of search capabilities:a powerful Web search engine with access to a large database of indexed pages, a family-oriented topical directory, and extensive data and service options.

MSN Search (http://search.msn.com) The most frequently visited Internet search service, MSN Search uses the powerful Inktomi engine and database, and the LookSmart subject directory. The basic search screen presents limited options, but "Advanced Search" offers a number of useful functions.

Yahoo! (www.yahoo.com) One of the world's most popular portals and by all accounts the best directory index for broad general topics, Yahoo! features a comprehensive, hierarchical listing of selected sites—with limited ability to search the contents of individual pages. Reliable and easy to use, Yahoo! remains an excellent choice for basic research while offering a slate of customizable services.

▶ A WEB SITE DIRECTORY

The Internet provides users with an ever-expanding world of information and online services in virtually every field of interest. Along with the popular *search engines* and portals described above, the sites listed below may provide the beginnings of your personal index. Explore the sites yourself and add the ones you like to the "Bookmarks" or "Favorites" list in your *browser.*

Computer/Communication Services

CNET (www.cnet.com) An informative and well-designed technology portal. Product reviews, industry news, extensive selection of downloads.

eFax (www.efax.com) A free service that provides private fax numbers. Receive faxes by e-mail; send or forward them for a fee.

ICQ (web.icq.com) Free downloads for global private chat. Leave messages, alert friends to when you're online. Millions of subscribers.

TalkCity (www.talkcity.com) Chat, scheduled chat events, forums, member home pages, celebrity events—a Web community.

ZD Net (www.zdnet.com) Sponsored by Ziff-Davis Interactive, connects to a large worldwide network of computer sites and magazine; also has links, search, shareware. Now part of CNET.

Entertainment and Learning

Broadcast.com (broadcast.com) Live TV and radio broadcasts, CD jukebox of over 1,000 albums, movie trailers, audio books, and more. RealPlayer plug-in available. Now part of the Yahoo network.

Discovery.com (www.discovery.com) Fun, adventure, and learning for children and adults, from the producers of The Discovery Channel.

Disney.com (disney.go.com) Features games and activities for kids, content for parents, shopping for Disney merchandise.

eHow (www.howto.com) More than 15,000 how-to solutions for day-to-day living in easy, step-by-step instructions. Organized in 14 categories and 120 subcategories.

Electronic Zoo (netvet.wustl.edu/e-zoo.htm) A virtual zoological garden, with extensive animal information, online magazines, links, user groups, and multimedia galore.

How Stuff Works (www.howstuffworks.com) Engaging, clear, informative explanations of common devices and instruments, digital technologies, the human body, natural phenomena.

The Internet Movie Database (www.imbd.com) The biggest and best film resource on the Web, covering more than 200,000 movies, extensive filmographies, and hundreds of thousands of biographical profiles.

NASA (www.nasa.gov) The largest repository of space-related information on the Net. Rich in photos and the latest scoop on current and future missions, astronauts, etc.

National Geographic (www.nationalgeographic.com) Magazine articles, virtual museum exhibits, a mini-encyclopedia, and more, for kids and adults.

PBS Online (www.pbs.org) Educational and entertaining media presentations, transcripts, quizzes, learning guides, and more, based on public television programs and documentaries.

Smithsonian Institution (www.si.edu) "America's attic" comes to the Net. A vast and compelling collection of artifacts, exhibitions, special media presentations, research materials, and links to affiliated museums.

Spinner (www.spinner.com) Self-proclaimed "First and Largest Internet Music Service." Offers a RealAudio-based player, 150+ music channels, and 375,000 songs.

Family and Health

Genealogy.com (www.genealogy.com) Type in a name, begin your search. Take classes, post queries, find links to other sites. A great place to start a family tree. Subscription.

Healthfinder (www.healthfinder.gov) U.S. government site with thousands of documents, well-organized interface, medical news, databases, and links. A useful gateway.

Health Risk Assessment (www.youfirst.com) Tools and information for in-depth personal health assessment; create a confidential personal profile.

SeniorNet (www.seniornet.com) Online services and information for people over 50. Classes, chat, and more.

WebMD (www.webmd.com) Leader in providing services that help consumers, physicians, and health plans navigate the health care system. Medscape.com, accessible from the main page, provides in-depth clinical information.

Finance and Investment

E*Trade (www.etrade.com) The first and leading Internet trading/investment firm. Includes personalized portfolio management and news.

The Motley Fool (www.fool.com) Free, easy-to-understand financial information, including timely stock updates, portfolio tracker, and investor chat boards.

MSN MoneyCentral (moneycentral.msn.com) Portfolio management, stock screening, investment tracking and advice, financial headlines, real-time stock tracker, 401(k) planner, and more.

Quicken.com (quicken.com) Personal finance site, featuring interactive tools to help with insurance, home-loan, tax-preparation, investment, and retirement-planning needs.

TheStreet.com (thestreet.com) Extensive online financial information, including daily market analysis and real-time stock ticker.

General Information/Reference

About.com (www.about.com) A rich portal site and comprehensive Web directory for everyday use. More than 50,000 subjects and 1 million links to Net resources—well organized.

Britannica.com (www.britannica.com) The entire encyclopedia free, with links to related magazine articles and hundreds of thousands of Web sites.

FreeTranslation.com (www.freetranslation.com) Uses the Transparent Language translation engine for free translation of documents or Web pages—English, French, German, Italian, Portuguese, and Spanish.

OneLookDictionaries (www.onelook.com) Access to over 700 general and specialized dictionaries.

Virtual Reference Desk (refdesk.com) Vast collection of links to general and topical information sites.

Government

FedStats (www.fedstats.gov) A full range of statistics and information from more than 100 U.S. federal agencies.

Internal Revenue Service (www.irs.gov) Tax forms and instructions, advice, online filing.

The Library of Congress (www.loc.gov) Photos, documents, online exhibits, legislation text, and other resources make this site valuable for serious research or casual enjoyment.

Stamps.com (www.stamps.com) Users download software that allows them to print metered postage stickers from their desktop printers and pay for the cost of postage with a credit card account.

Thomas (thomas.loc.gov) Authoritative, in-depth information on federal legislation, a service of the Library of Congress.
U.S. Census Bureau (www.census.gov) Authoritative, extensive information on U.S. population, demographics, economy, industry and agriculture, education, law enforcement, etc.
The White House (www.whitehouse.gov) Write to the president, read documents and policy statements, take a tour, browse the archives, etc.

Jobs/Career Development

Career Builder (www.careerbuilder.com) Leading career management site for job seekers and employers.
HotJobs (www.hotjobs.com) Thousands of registered recruiters and over 500,000 resumes; no head-hunters allowed.
Jobs.com (www.jobs.com) Local job search, resume posting. Extensive listings.
Monster.com (www.monster.com) Online employment services, including job searches by location, a resume database available to recruiters, and online job application. Includes resources for freelancers.

News

ABCNews.com (www.abcnews.com) Headlines, online-only features, videos, instant polls, abundant links. Deep coverage with frequent updates.
BBC Online (www.bbc.co.uk) The vast international resources of BBC's news organization. World news with a unique perspective.
CNN Interactive (cnn.com) Late-breaking news and background: multimedia galleries, in-depth analysis, polls, searchable background material, links. Includes the CNNfn financial news network, and CNNSI, sports coverage with *Sports Illustrated*.
MSNBC (www.msnbc.com) The most interactive of all the news sites. Includes a personalized news page and compelling polls, chats, and discussions.
The New York Times (www.nytimes.com) Most of the daily paper is available online, as are extensive archives (for a small fee).

Shopping/Auctions

Alibris (www.alibris.com) Locate use, rare, and hard-to-find books. Millions of titles from a worldwide network of dealers.
Amazon.com (www.amazon.com) The "granddaddy"of consumer online shopping sites, it began with books, then moved into music, video, consumer electronics, and toys. Deep discounts.
CarsDirect (www.carsdirect.com) The leading direct online automobile buying service. Research, price, order, insure, and finance for virtually every make, model, and style of car available in the U.S.
Cooking.com (www.cooking.com) Top shopping site for chefs, offering a huge assortment of cookware, accessories, and specialty foods.
Dealtime (www.dealtime.com) A free online comparison-shopping service that lets you compare products, prices, and stores across the Web. Find the best deal for whatever you're looking for.
eBay (www.ebay.com) The largest online auction site, with millions of items at all times.
MSN CarPoint (www.carpoint.msn.com) Online car shopping service, with 2,000 affiliated dealers and 100,000 used car listings. Personal Auto Pages for tracking your car's service schedule.
Priceline.com (www.priceline.com) A popular buying service that asks you what you're willing to pay and seeks providers. Great for airline tickets, car rentals, hotel rooms and other products.
Ticketmaster (www.ticketmaster.com) One of most visited sites on the Web. Order tickets to concerts, sports competitions, and other events—more than 350,000 a year. Includes special deals.
uBid (www.ubid.com) A central (not person-to-person) online auction house. Great deals on discontinued consumer electronics and computing equipment and more typical auction items.

Sports and Games

CBS SportsLine (cbs.sportsline.com) In-depth, comprehensive, up-to-the-minute coverage. News, multimedia features, personalized information, live celebrity chats, forums, calendars and numerous links.
ESPN.com (msn.espn.go.com) Scores, stories, stats, schedules, standings, video, sound. Up-to-the minute analyses and features. GameCast lets you follow games on your screen as they happen.
Games Domain (www.gamesdomain.com) One of the Net's largest shareware directory sites, plus reviews, tips, contests, walkthroughs, industry news, and more.
GameSpot (gamespot.com) From ZDNet, a favorite with PC gaming enthusiasts—news, reviews, previews, free demo downloads, and more.
The Sporting News (www.sportingnews.com) Hardcore, in-depth coverage. Analysis by 30 well-known columnists. Abundant stats and links, with customizable team/score reporting.
Sportspages.com (www.sportspages.com) Fresh links to the world's best sports pages.

Travel and Weather

Expedia.com (expedia.com) Makes travel planning easy, from research to booking. Find special deals and unique vacations ideas on the Travel Network. Includes mapping features and a staff of travel agents.
Frommer's Online (www.frommers.com) Based on the popular book series, ideal for planning a low-cost excursion. Includes activity suggestions, guidebooks, message boards, and booking links.
National Park Service: ParkNet (www.nps.gov) Click on "Visit Your Parks" link for detailed maps and general information on the U.S. national parks.
National Weather Service (www.nws.noaa.gov) World, national, and regional forecasts—daily and long-term. Includes maps, satellite imagery, specialized data, and abundant links.
Smarter Living.com (www.smarterliving.com) A free online community dedicated to helping people save time and money on travel. Posts fare sales, special deals, and promotions. Members are eligible for special discounts on airfares, hotels, and more.
Travelocity.com (www.travelocity.com) Owned by Sabre Group, which maintains the largest worldwide reservation system. Best current fares and packages, e-mail and pager bulletins.
Mapquest.com (www.mapquest.com) Interactive maps and driving directions, customized mapping, and travel information for businesses and consumers.
Weather Channel (www.weather.com) The leading commercial weather site, and one of the most popular on the Web. Detailed national and local forecasts, with special details relating to travel, health, recreation, and special event locations. Comprehensive.

Part V AWARDS AND PRIZES
Awards in the Arts and Entertainment

Academy Awards 1928–2002

The "Oscars" are officially known as the Academy of Motion Picture Arts and Sciences Awards. They were inaugurated in 1928 as part of Hollywood's drive to improve its less-than-respectable image. Academy librarian and eventual executive director Margaret Herrick remarked that the statuette looked like her uncle Oscar, and the nickname has stuck ever since. Membership in the Academy (currently over 3,000) is by invitation only, with members divided into 13 branches. Each branch selects up to five nominees for awards in its area of expertise; the entire membership makes"Best Film" nominations and then votes on all the categories. Major awards are shown in the chart. Awards for Best Cinematography and for Best Foreign Language Film are shown in a separate table. Best Directors are named for films winning Best Picture except where otherwise indicated.

Year	Best picture	Best director	Best actor	Best actress	Best supporting actor	Best supporting actress
1928	*Wings*	Frank Borzage, *Seventh Heaven* Lewis Milestone, *Two Arabian Knights*	Emil Jannings, *The Way of All Flesh, The Last Command*	Janet Gaynor, *Seventh Heaven, Sunrise, Street Angel*	*No Awards Given*	*No Awards Given*
1929	*The Broadway Melody*	Frank Lloyd, *The Divine Lady*	Warner Baxter, *In Old Arizona*	Mary Pickford, *Coquette*	*No Awards Given*	*No Awards Given*
1930	*All Quiet on the Western Front*	Lewis Milestone	George Arliss, *Disraeli*	Norma Shearer, *The Divorcee*	*No Awards Given*	*No Awards Given*
1931	*Cimarron*	Norman Taurog, *Skippy*	Lionel Barrymore, *A Free Soul*	Marie Dressler, *Min and Bill*	*No Awards Given*	*No Awards Given*
1932	*Grand Hotel*	Frank Borzage, *Bad Girl*	Wallace Beery, *The Champ* Fredric March, *Dr. Jekyll and Mr. Hyde*	Helen Hayes, *The Sin of Madelon Claudet*	*No Awards Given*	*No Awards Given*
1933	*Cavalcade*	Frank Lloyd	Charles Laughton, *The Private Life of Henry VIII*	Katharine Hepburn, *Morning Glory*	*No Awards Given*	*No Awards Given*
1934	*It Happened One Night*	Frank Capra	Clark Gable, *It Happened One Night*	Claudette Colbert, *It Happened One Night*	*No Awards Given*	*No Awards Given*
1935	*Mutiny on the Bounty*	John Ford, *The Informer*	Victor McLaglen, *The Informer*	Bette Davis, *Dangerous*	*No Awards Given*	*No Awards Given*
1936	*The Great Ziegfeld*	Frank Capra, *Mr. Deeds Goes to Town*	Paul Muni, *The Story of Louis Pasteur*	Luise Rainer, *The Great Ziegfeld*	Walter Brennan, *Come and Get It*	Gale Sondergaard, *Anthony Adverse*
1937	*The Life of Emile Zola*	Leo McCarey, *The Awful Truth*	Spencer Tracy, *Captains Courageous*	Luise Rainer, *The Good Earth*	Joseph Schildkraut, *The Life of Emile Zola*	Alice Brady, *In Old Chicago*
1938	*You Can't Take It With You*	Frank Capra	Spencer Tracy, *Boys Town*	Bette Davis, *Jezebel*	Walter Brennan, *Kentucky*	Fay Bainter, *Jezebel*
1939	*Gone With the Wind*	Victor Fleming	Robert Donat, *Goodbye, Mr. Chips*	Vivien Leigh, *Gone With the Wind*	Thomas Mitchell, *Stagecoach*	Hattie McDaniel, *Gone With the Wind*
1940	*Rebecca*	John Ford, *The Grapes of Wrath*	James Stewart, *The Philadelphia Story*	Ginger Rogers, *Kitty Foyle*	Walter Brennan, *The Westerner*	Jane Darwell, *The Grapes of Wrath*
1941	*How Green Was My Valley*	John Ford	Gary Cooper, *Sergeant York*	Joan Fontaine, *Suspicion*	Donald Crisp, *How Green Was My Valley*	Mary Astor, *The Great Lie*
1942	*Mrs. Miniver*	William Wyler	James Cagney, *Yankee Doodle Dandy*	Greer Garson, *Mrs. Miniver*	Van Heflin, *Johnny Eager*	Teresa Wright, *Mrs. Miniver*

Year	Best picture	Best director	Best actor	Best actress	Best supporting actor	Best supporting actress
1943	*Casablanca*	Michael Curtiz	Paul Lukas, *Watch On The Rhine*	Jennifer Jones, *The Song of Bernadette*	Charles Coburn, *The More the Merrier*	Katina Paxinou, *For Whom the Bell Tolls*
1944	*Going My Way*	Leo McCarey	Bing Crosby, *Going My Way*	Ingrid Bergman, *Gaslight*	Barry Fitzgerald, *Going My Way*	Ethel Barrymore, *None But the Lonely Heart*
1945	*The Lost Weekend*	Billy Wilder	Ray Milland, *The Lost Weekend*	Joan Crawford, *Mildred Pierce*	James Dunn, *A Tree Grows in Brooklyn*	Anne Revere, *National Velvet*
1946	*The Best Years of Our Lives*	William Wyler	Fredric March, *The Best Years of Our Lives*	Olivia De Havilland, *To Each His Own*	Harold Russell, *The Best Years of Our Lives*	Anne Baxter, *The Razor's Edge*
1947	*Gentleman's Agreement*	Elia Kazan	Ronald Colman, *A Double Life*	Loretta Young, *The Farmer's Daughter*	Edmund Gwenn, *Miracle on 34th Street*	Celeste Holm, *Gentleman's Agreement*
1948	*Hamlet*	John Huston, *The Treasure of the Sierra Madre*	Laurence Olivier, *Hamlet*	Jane Wyman, *Johnny Belinda*	Walter Huston, *The Treasure of the Sierra Madre*	Claire Trevor, *Key Largo*
1949	*All the King's Men*	Joseph L. Mankiewicz, *A Letter to Three Wives*	Broderick Crawford, *All the King's Men*	Olivia De Havilland, *The Heiress*	Dean Jagger, *Twelve O'Clock High*	Mercedes McCambridge, *All the King's Men*
1950	*All About Eve*	Joseph L. Mankiewicz	José Ferrer, *Cyrano de Bergerac*	Judy Holliday, *Born Yesterday*	George Sanders, *All About Eve*	Josephine Hull, *Harvey*
1951	*An American in Paris*	George Stevens, *A Place in the Sun*	Humphrey Bogart, *The African Queen*	Vivien Leigh, *A Streetcar Named Desire*	Karl Malden, *A Streetcar Named Desire*	Kim Hunter, *A Streetcar Named Desire*
1952	*The Greatest Show on Earth*	John Ford, *The Quiet Man*	Gary Cooper, *High Noon*	Shirley Booth, *Come Back, Little Sheba*	Anthony Quinn, *Viva Zapata!*	Gloria Grahame, *The Bad and the Beautiful*
1953	*From Here to Eternity*	Fred Zinnemann	William Holden, *Stalag 17*	Audrey Hepburn, *Roman Holiday*	Frank Sinatra, *From Here to Eternity*	Donna Reed, *From Here to Eternity*
1954	*On the Waterfront*	Elia Kazan	Marlon Brando, *On the Waterfront*	Grace Kelly, *The Country Girl*	Edmond O'Brien, *The Barefoot Contessa*	Eva Marie Saint, *On the Waterfront*
1955	*Marty*	Delbert Mann	Ernest Borgnine, *Marty*	Anna Magnani, *The Rose Tattoo*	Jack Lemmon, *Mister Roberts*	Jo Van Fleet, *East of Eden*
1956	*Around the World in 80 Days*	George Stevens, *Giant*	Yul Brynner, *The King And I*	Ingrid Bergman, *Anastasia*	Anthony Quinn, *Lust for Life*	Dorothy Malone, *Written on the Wind*
1957	*The Bridge on the River Kwai*	David Lean	Alec Guinness, *The Bridge on the River Kwai*	Joanne Woodward, *The Three Faces of Eve*	Red Buttons, *Sayonara*	Miyoshi Umeki, *Sayonara*
1958	*Gigi*	Vincente Minnelli	David Niven, *Separate Tables*	Susan Hayward, *I Want to Live!*	Burl Ives, *The Big Country*	Wendy Hiller, *Separate Tables*
1959	*Ben-Hur*	William Wyler	Charlton Heston, *Ben-Hur*	Simone Signoret, *Room at the Top*	Hugh Griffith, *Ben-Hur*	Shelley Winters, *The Diary of Anne Frank*
1960	*The Apartment*	Billy Wilder	Burt Lancaster, *Elmer Gantry*	Elizabeth Taylor, *Butterfield 8*	Peter Ustinov, *Spartacus*	Shirley Jones, *Elmer Gantry*
1961	*West Side Story*	Jerome Robbins, Robert Wise	Maximilian Schell, *Judgment At Nuremberg*	Sophia Loren, *Two Women*	George Chakiris, *West Side Story*	Rita Moreno, *West Side Story*
1962	*Lawrence of Arabia*	David Lean	Gregory Peck, *To Kill a Mockingbird*	Anne Bancroft, *The Miracle Worker,*	Ed Begley *Sweet Bird of Youth*	Patty Duke, *The Miracle Worker*
1963	*Tom Jones*	Tony Richardson	Sidney Poitier *Lilies of the Field*	Patricia Neal, *Hud*	Melvyn Douglas, *Hud*	Margaret Rutherford, *The V.I.P.s*
1964	*My Fair Lady*	George Cukor	Rex Harrison, *My Fair Lady*	Julie Andrews, *Mary Poppins*	Peter Ustinov, *Topkapi*	Lila Kedrova, *Zorba the Greek*

Year	Best picture	Best director	Best actor	Best actress	Best supporting actor	Best supporting actress
1965	*The Sound of Music*	Robert Wise	Lee Marvin, *Cat Ballou*	Julie Christie, *Darling*	Martin Balsam, *A Thousand Clowns*	Shelley Winters, *A Patch of Blue*
1966	*A Man for All Seasons*	Fred Zinnemann	Paul Scofield, *A Man for All Seasons*	Elizabeth Taylor, *Who's Afraid of Virginia Woolf?*	Walter Matthau, *The Fortune Cookie*	Sandy Dennis, *Who's Afraid of Virginia Woolf?*
1967	*In the Heat of the Night*	Mike Nichols, *The Graduate*	Rod Steiger, *In the Heat of the Night*	Katharine Hepburn, *Guess Who's Coming to Dinner*	George Kennedy, *Cool Hand Luke*	Estelle Parsons, *Bonnie and Clyde*
1968	*Oliver!*	Carol Reed	Cliff Robertson, *Charly*	Katharine Hepburn, *The Lion in Winter,* Barbra Streisand, *Funny Girl*	Jack Albertson, *The Subject Was Roses*	Ruth Gordon, *Rosemary's Baby*
1969	*Midnight Cowboy*	John Schlesinger	John Wayne, *True Grit*	Maggie Smith, *The Prime of Miss Jean Brodie*	Gig Young, *They Shoot Horses, Don't They?*	Goldie Hawn, *Cactus Flower*
1970	*Patton*	Franklin J. Schaffner	George C. Scott, *Patton*	Glenda Jackson, *Women in Love*	John Mills, *Ryan's Daughter*	Helen Hayes, *Airport*
1971	*The French Connection*	William Friedkin	Gene Hackman, *The French Connection*	Jane Fonda, *Klute*	Ben Johnson, *The Last Picture Show*	Cloris Leachman, *The Last Picture Show*
1972	*The Godfather*	Bob Fosse, *Cabaret*	Marlon Brando, *The Godfather*	Liza Minnelli, *Cabaret*	Joel Grey, *Cabaret*	Eileen Heckart, *Butterflies Are Free*
1973	*The Sting*	George Roy Hill	Jack Lemmon, *Save the Tiger*	Glenda Jackson, *A Touch of Class*	John Houseman, *The Paper Chase*	Tatum O'Neal, *Paper Moon*
1974	*The Godfather, Part II*	Francis Ford Coppola	Art Carney, *Harry And Tonto*	Ellen Burstyn, *Alice Doesn't Live Here Anymore*	Robert De Niro, *The Godfather, Part II*	Ingrid Bergman, *Murder on the Orient Express*
1975	*One Flew Over the Cuckoo's Nest*	Milos Forman	Jack Nicholson, *One Flew Over the Cuckoo's Nest*	Louise Fletcher, *One Flew Over the Cuckoo's Nest*	George Burns, *The Sunshine Boys*	Lee Grant, *Shampoo*
1976	*Rocky*	John G. Avildsen	Peter Finch, *Network*	Faye Dunaway, *Network*	Jason Robards, *All the President's Men*	Beatrice Straight, *Network*
1977	*Annie Hall*	Woody Allen	Richard Dreyfuss, *The Goodbye Girl*	Diane Keaton, *Annie Hall*	Jason Robards, *Julia*	Vanessa Redgrave, *Julia*
1978	*The Deer Hunter*	Michael Cimino	Jon Voight, *Coming Home*	Jane Fonda, *Coming Home*	Christopher Walken, *The Deer Hunter*	Maggie Smith, *California Suite*
1979	*Kramer vs. Kramer*	Robert Benton	Dustin Hoffman, *Kramer vs. Kramer*	Sally Field, *Norma Rae*	Melvyn Douglas, *Being There*	Meryl Streep, *Kramer vs. Kramer*
1980	*Ordinary People*	Robert Redford	Robert De Niro, *Raging Bull*	Sissy Spacek, *Coal Miner's Daughter*	Timothy Hutton, *Ordinary People*	Mary Steenburgen, *Melvin and Howard*
1981	*Chariots of Fire*	Warren Beatty, *Reds*	Henry Fonda, *On Golden Pond*	Katharine Hepburn, *On Golden Pond*	John Gielgud, *Arthur*	Maureen Stapleton, *Reds*
1982	*Gandhi*	Richard Attenborough	Ben Kingsley, *Gandhi*	Meryl Streep, *Sophie's Choice*	Louis Gossett Jr., *An Officer and a Gentleman*	Jessica Lange, *Tootsie*
1983	*Terms of Endearment*	James L. Brooks	Robert Duvall, *Tender Mercies*	Shirley MacLaine *Terms of Endearment*	Jack Nicholson, *Terms of Endearment*	Linda Hunt, *The Year of Living Dangerously*
1984	*Amadeus*	Milos Forman	F. Murray Abraham, *Amadeus*	Sally Field, *Places in the Heart*	Haing S. Ngor, *The Killing Fields*	Peggy Ashcroft, *A Passage to India*
1985	*Out of Africa*	Sydney Pollack	William Hurt, *Kiss of the Spider Woman*	Geraldine Page, *The Trip to Bountiful*	Don Ameche, *Cocoon*	Anjelica Huston, *Prizzi's Honor*
1986	*Platoon*	Oliver Stone	Paul Newman, *The Color of Money*	Marlee Matlin, *Children of a Lesser God*	Michael Caine, *Hannah and Her Sisters*	Dianne Wiest, *Hannah and Her Sisters*

Year	Best picture	Best director	Best actor	Best actress	Best supporting actor	Best supporting actress
1987	*The Last Emperor*	Bernardo Bertolucci	Michael Douglas, *Wall Street*	Cher, *Moonstruck*	Sean Connery, *The Untouchables*	Olympia Dukakis, *Moonstruck*
1988	*Rain Man*	Barry Levinson	Dustin Hoffman, *Rain Man*	Jodie Foster, *The Accused*	Kevin Kline, *A Fish Called Wanda*	Geena Davis, *The Accidental Tourist*
1989	*Driving Miss Daisy*	Oliver Stone, *Born on the Fourth of July*	Daniel Day-Lewis, *My Left Foot*	Jessica Tandy, *Driving Miss Daisy*	Denzel Washington, *Glory*	Brenda Fricker, *My Left Foot*
1990	*Dances with Wolves*	Kevin Costner	Jeremy Irons, *Reversal of Fortune*	Kathy Bates, *Misery*	Joe Pesci, *Goodfellas*	Whoopi Goldberg, *Ghost*
1991	*The Silence of the Lambs*	Jonathan Demme	Anthony Hopkins, *The Silence of the Lambs*	Jodie Foster, *The Silence of the Lambs*	Jack Palance, *City Slickers*	Mercedes Ruehl, *The Fisher King*
1992	*Unforgiven*	Clint Eastwood	Al Pacino, *Scent of a Woman*	Emma Thompson, *Howards End*	Gene Hackman, *Unforgiven*	Marisa Tomei, *My Cousin Vinny*
1993	*Schindler's List*	Steven Spielberg	Tom Hanks, *Philadelphia*	Holly Hunter, *The Piano*	Tommy Lee Jones *The Fugitive*	Anna Paquin, *The Piano*
1994	*Forrest Gump*	Robert Zemeckis	Tom Hanks, *Forrest Gump*	Jessica Lange, *Blue Sky*	Martin Landau, *Ed Wood*	Dianne Wiest, *Bullets Over Broadway*
1995	*Braveheart*	Mel Gibson	Nicolas Cage *Leaving Las Vegas*	Susan Sarandon, *Dead Man Walking*	Kevin Spacey, *The Usual Suspects*	Mira Sorvino, *Mighty Aphrodite*
1996	*The English Patient*	Anthony Minghella	Geoffrey Rush, *Shine*	Frances McDormand, *Fargo*	Cuba Gooding Jr., *Jerry Maguire*	Juliette Binoche, *The English Patient*
1997	*Titanic*	James Cameron	Jack Nicholson, *As Good as it Gets*	Helen Hunt, *As Good as it Gets*	Robin Williams *Good Will Hunting*	Kim Basinger, *L.A. Confidential*
1998	*Shakespeare in Love*	Steven Spielberg, *Saving Private Ryan*	Roberto Benigni *Life is Beautiful*	Gwyneth Paltrow, *Shakespeare in Love*	James Coburn, *Affliction*	Judi Dench, *Shakespeare in Love*
1999	*American Beauty*	Sam Mendes	Kevin Spacey, *American Beauty*	Hilary Swank *Boys Don't Cry*	Michael Caine, *The Cider House Rules*	Angelina Jolie, *Girl, Interrupted*
2000	*Gladiator*	Steven Soderbergh, *Traffic*	Russell Crowe, *Gladiator*	Julia Roberts, *Erin Brockovich*	Benicio Del Toro, *Traffic*	Marcia Gay Harden, *Pollock*
2001	*A Beautiful Mind*	Ron Howard	Denzel Washington, *Training Day*	Halle Berry, *Monsters Ball*	Jim Broadbent, *Iris*	Jennifer Connelly, *A Beautiful Mind*
2002	*Chicago*	Roman Polanski, *The Pianist*	Adrien Brody, *The Pianist*	Nicole Kidman, *The Hours*	Chris Cooper, *Adaptation*	Catherine Zeta-Jones, *Chicago*

Source: Academy of Motion Picture Arts & Sciences. www. oscar.org

Academy Awards for Cinematography, 1928–2002

Year	Cinematographer, Film
1928	Charles Rosher, Karl Struss, *Sunrise*
1929	Clyde DeVinna, *White Shadows, In the South Seas*
1930	Joseph T. Rucker, Willard Van Der Veer, *With Byrd at the South Pole*
1931	Floyd Crosby, *Tabu*
1932	Lee Garmes, *Shanghai Express*
1933	Charles Bryant Lang Jr., *A Farewell to Arms*
1934	Victor Milner, *Cleopatra*
1935	Hal Mohr, *A Midsummer Night's Dream*
1936	Gaetano Gaudio, *Anthony Adverse*
1937	Karl Freund, *The Good Earth*
1938	Joseph Ruttenberg, *The Great Waltz*
1939	Gregg Toland, *Wuthering Heights*
	Ernest Haller, Ray Rennahan, *Gone With the Wind*
1940	George Barnes, *Rebecca*
	George Perinal, *Thief of Baghdad*
1941	Arthur Miller, *How Green Was My Valley*
	Ernest Palmer, Ray Rennahan, *Blood & Sand*
1942	Joseph Ruttenberg, *Mrs. Miniver*
	Leon Shamroy, *The Black Swan*
1943	Arthur Miller, *The Song of Bernadette*
	Hal Mohr, W. Howard Greene, *The Phantom of the Opera*
1944	Joseph LaShelle, *Laura*
	Leon Shamroy, *Wilson*
1945	Harry Stradling, *The Picture of Dorian Gray*
	Leon Shamroy, *Leave Her to Heaven*
1946	Arthur Miller, *Anna and the King of Siam*
	Charles Rosher, Leonard Smith, Arthur Arling, *The Yearling*

Year	Cinematographer, Film
1947	Guy Green, *Great Expectations*
1948	William Daniels, *The Naked City*
	Joseph Valentine, William V. Skall, Winton Hoch, *Joan of Arc*
1949	Paul C. Vogel, *Battleground*
	Winton Hoch, *She Wore a Yellow Ribbon*
1950	Robert Krasker, *The Third Man*
	Robert Surtees, *King Solomon's Mines*
1951	William C. Mellor, *A Place in the Sun*
	Alfred Gilks, John Alton (ballet), *An American in Paris*
1952	Robert Surtees, *The Bad and the Beautiful*
	Winton Hoch, Archie Stout, *The Quiet Man*
1953	Burnett Guffey, *From Here to Eternity*
	Loyal Griggs, *Shane*
1954	Boris Kaufman, *On the Waterfront*
	Milton Krasner, *Three Coins in the Fountain*
1955	James Wong Howe, *The Rose Tattoo*
	Robert Burks, *To Catch a Thief*
1956	Joseph Ruttenberg, *Sombody Up There Likes Me*
	Lionel Lindon, *Around the World in 80 Days*
1957	Jack Hildyard, *The Bridge on the River Kwai*
1958	Sam Leavitt, *The Defiant Ones*
	Joseph Ruttenberg, *Gigi*
1959	William C. Mellor, *The Diary of Anne Frank*
	Robert L. Surtees, *Ben-Hur*
1960	Freddie Francis, *Sons and Lovers*
	Russell Metty, *Spartacus*
1961	Eugene Shuftan, *The Hustler*
	Daniel L. Fapp, *West Side Story*
1962	Jean Bourgoin, Walter Wottitz, *The Longest Day*
	Freddie Young, *Lawrence of Arabia*
1963	James Wong Howe, *Hud*
	Leon Shamroy, *Cleopatra*
1964	Walter Lassally, *Zorba the Greek*
	Harry Stradling, *My Fair Lady*
1965	Ernest Laszlo, *Ship of Fools*
	Freddie Young, *Dr. Zhivago*
1966	Haskell Wexler, *Who's Afraid of Virginia Woolf?*
	Ted Moore, *A Man for All Seasons*
1967	Burnett Guffey, *Bonnie and Clyde*
1968	Pasqualino De Santis, *Romeo and Juliet*
1969	Conrad Hall, *Butch Cassidy and the Sundance Kid*
1970	Freddie Young, *Ryan's Daughter*
1971	Oswald Morris, *Fiddler on the Roof*
1972	Geoffrey Unsworth, *Cabaret*
1973	Sven Nykvist, *Cries and Whispers*
1974	Fred Koenekamp, Joseph Biroc, *The Towering Inferno*
1975	John Alcott, *Barry Lyndon*
1976	Haskell Wexler, *Bound for Glory*
1977	Vilmos Zsigmond, *Close Encounters of the Third Kind*
1978	Nestor Almendros, *Days of Heaven*
1979	Vittorio Storaro, *Apocalypse Now*
1980	Geoffrey Unsworth, Ghislain Cloquet, *Tess*
1981	Vittorio Storaro, *Reds*
1982	Billy Williams, Ronnie Taylor, *Gandhi*
1983	Sven Nykvist, *Fanny & Alexander*
1984	Chris Menges, *The Killing Fields*
1985	David Watkin, *Out of Africa*
1986	Chris Menges, *The Mission*
1987	Vittorio Storaro, *The Last Emperor*
1988	Peter Biziou, *Mississippi Burning*
1989	Freddie Francis, *Glory*
1990	Dean Semler, *Dances With Wolves*
1991	Robert Richardson, *JFK*
1992	Philippe Rousselot, *A River Runs Through It*
1993	Janusz Kaminski, *Schindler's List*
1994	John Toll, *Legends of the Fall*
1995	John Toll, *Braveheart*
1996	John Seale, *The English Patient*
1997	Russell Carpenter, *Titanic*
1998	Janusz Kaminski, *Saving Private Ryan*
1999	Conrad L. Hall, *American Beauty*
2000	Peter Pau, *Crouching Tiger, Hidden Dragon*
2001	Andrew Lesnie, *The Lord of the Rings: The Fellowship of the Ring*
2002	Conrad L. Hall, *Road to Perdition* (posthumous)

Academy Awards for Best Foreign Language Film, 1956–2002

Year	Film, Country	Director
1956	*La Strada,* Italy	Federico Fellini
1957	*The Nights of Cabiria,* Italy	Federico Fellini
1958	*Mon Oncle,* France	Jacques Tati
1959	*Black Orpheus,* France/Italy/Brazil	Marcel Camus
1960	*The Virgin Spring,* Sweden	Ingmar Bergman
1961	*Through A Glass Darkly,* Sweden	Ingmar Bergman
1962	*Sundays and Cybele,* France	Serge Bourgignon
1963	*8½,* Italy	Federico Fellini
1964	*Yesterday, Today, and Tomorrow,* Italy/France	Vittorio de Sica
1965	*The Shop on Main Street,* Czechoslovakia	Jan Kadar
1966	*A Man and a Woman* France	Claude Lelouch
1967	*Closely Watched Trains,* Czechoslovakia	Jiri Menzel
1968	*War and Peace,* USSR	Sergei Bondarchuk
1969	*Z,* France/Algeria	Constantin Costa-Gavras
1970	*Investigation of a Citizen Above Suspicion,* Italy	Elio Petri
1971	*The Garden of the Finzi-Continis,* Italy	Vittorio de Sica
1972	*The Discreet Charm of the Bourgeoisie,* France	Luis Buñuel
1973	*Day For Night,* France/Italy	François Truffaut
1974	*Amarcord,* Italy/France	Federico Fellini
1975	*Dersu Uzala,* USSR/Japan	Akira Kurosawa
1976	*Black and White in Color,* France/Switzerland/Ivory Coast	Jean-Jacques Annaud
1977	*Madame Rosa,* France	Moshe Mizrahi
1978	*Get Out Your Handkerchiefs,* France	Bertrand Blier
1979	*The Tin Drum,* Germany	Volker Scholondorff
1980	*Moscow Does Not Believe in Tears,* USSR	Vladimir Menshov
1981	*Mephisto,* Austria/ Germany/ Hungary	Istvan Szabo
1982	*To Begin Again,* Spain	Jose Luis Garcia
1983	*Fanny and Alexander,* Sweden	Ingmar Bergman
1984	*Dangerous Moves,* France	Richard Dembo
1985	*The Official Story,* Argentina	Luis Puenzo

Year	Film, Country	Director
1986	*The Assault,* Netherlands	Fons Rademakers
1987	*Babette's Feast,* Denmark	Gabriel Axel
1988	*Pelle the Conqueror,* Denmark	Bille August
1989	*Cinema Paradiso,* Italy	Giuseppe Tornatore
1990	*Journey of Hope,* Switzerland	Xavier Koller
1991	*Mediterraneo,* Italy	Gabriel Salvatores
1992	*Indochine,* France	Regis Wargnier
1993	*Belle Époque,* Spain	Fernando Trueba
1994	*Burnt by the Sun,* Russia	Nikita Mikhalkov
1995	*Antonia's Line,* Netherlands	Marlene Gorris
1996	*Kolya,* Czech Republic	Jan Sverak
1997	*Character,* Netherlands	Mike van Diem
1998	*Life is Beautiful,* Italy	Roberto Benigni
1999	*All About My Mother,* Spain	Pedro Almodóvar
2000	*Crouching Tiger, Hidden Dragon,* China	Ang Lee
2001	*No Man's Land,* Bosnia & Herzegovina	Danis Tanovic
2002	*Nowhere in Africa,* Germany	Caroline Link

Cannes Film Festival Best Film Awards, 1946–2003

The Festival International du Film was first held in 1946. The official name for the best film award was the Grand Prix (1949–54, 1964–74) and the Palme d'Or (1955–63, 1975–present)

Year	Film and director
1946	*La Bataille du Rail,* René Clément[1]
1949[2]	*The Third Man,* Carol Reed
1951	*Miracle in Milan,* Vittorio De Sica
	Miss Julie, Alf Sjöberg
1952	*Two Cents Worth of Hope,* Renato Castellani
	Othello, Orson Welles
1953	*The Wages of Fear,* Georges Clouzot
1954	*Gate of Hell,* Teinosuke Kinugasa
1955	*Marty,* Delbert Mann
1956	*The Silent World,* Jacques Cousteau, Louis Malle
1957	*Friendly Persuasion,* William Wyler
1958	*The Cranes are Flying,* Mikhail Kalatozov
1959	*Black Orpheus,* Marcel Camus
1960	*La Dolce Vita,* Federico Fellini
1961	*Viridiana,* Luis Buñuel
1962	*The Given Word,* Anselmo Duarte
1963	*The Leopard,* Luchino Visconti
1964	*The Umbrellas of Cherbourg,* Jacques Demy
1965	*The Knack, and How to Get It,* Richard Lester
1966	*A Man and a Woman,* Claude Lelouch
1967	*Blow-Up,* Michelangelo Antonioni
1969	*If . . . ,* Lindsay Anderson
1970	*M*A*S*H,* Robert Altman
1971	*The Go-Between,* Joseph Losey
1972	*The Working Class Goes to Heaven,* Elio Petri
	The Mattei Affair, Francesco Rosi
1973	*Scarecrow,* Jerry Schatzberg
	The Hireling, Alan Bridges
1974	*The Conversation,* Francis Ford Coppola
1975	*Chronique des Années de Braise,* M. Lakhdar Hamina
1976	*Taxi Driver,* Martin Scorsese
1977	*Padre Padrone,* Paolo and Vittorio Taviani
1978	*The Tree of Wooden Clogs,* Ermanno Olmi
1979	*The Tin Drum,* Volker Schlöndorff
1980	*Kagemusha,* Akira Kurosawa
1981	*Man of Iron,* Andrzej Wajda
1982	*Missing,* Costa-Gavras
	Yol, Yilmar Güney
1983	*The Ballad of Narayama,* Shohei Imamura
1984	*Paris, Texas,* Wim Wenders
1985	*When Father Was Away on Business,* Emir Kusturica
1986	*The Mission,* Roland Joffé
1987	*Under Satan's Sun,* Maurice Pialat
1988	*Pelle the Conqueror,* Bille August
1989	*sex, lies and videotape,* Steven Soderbergh
1990	*Wild at Heart,* David Lynch
1991	*Barton Fink,* Joel Coen
1992	*The Best Intentions,* Bille August
1993	*The Piano,* Jane Campion
	Farewell My Concubine, Chen Kaige
1994	*Pulp Fiction,* Quentin Tarantino
1995	*Underground,* Emir Kusturica
1996	*Secrets and Lies,* Mike Leigh
1997	*Taste of Cherries,* Abbas Kiarostami
	Unagi (The Eel), Shohei Imamura
1998	*Eternity and a Day,* Theo Angelopoulos
1999	*Rosetta,* Jean-Pierre and Luc Dardenne
2000	*Dancer in the Dark,* Lars von Trier
2001	*The Son's Room,* Nanni Moretti
2002	*The Pianist,* Roman Polanski
2003	*Elephant,* Gus Van Sant

1. Winner of the International Jury Prize. 2. In 1947, there was no "best film" award as such, but prizes were given instead to outstanding works in several categories, including "Psychological and Love Films," "Adventure and Police Films," and so on. The festival was cancelled in 1948 and 1950. **Source:** www.festival-cannes.org.

American Film Institute Life Achievement Awards, 1973–2003

Awarded to individuals whose "talent has fundamentally advanced the art of American film or television . . . and whose work has withstood the test of time."

Year	Recipient	Year	Recipient	Year	Recipient	Year	Recipient
1973	John Ford	1981	Fred Astaire	1989	Gregory Peck	1997	Martin Scorsese
1974	James Cagney	1982	Frank Capra	1990	David Lean	1998	Robert Wise
1975	Orson Welles	1983	John Huston	1991	Kirk Douglas	1999	Dustin Hoffman
1976	William Wyler	1984	Lillian Gish	1992	Sidney Poitier	2000	Harrison Ford
1977	Henry Fonda	1985	Gene Kelly	1993	Elizabeth Taylor	2001	Barbra Streisand
1978	Bette Davis	1986	Billy Wilder	1994	Jack Nicholson	2002	Tom Hanks
1979	Alfred Hitchock	1987	Barbara Stanwyck	1995	Steven Spielberg	2003	Robert De Niro
1980	James Stewart	1988	Jack Lemmon	1996	Clint Eastwood		

Source: American Film Institute. www.afionline.org

The National Film Registry

In 1988, the Library of Congress established the National Film Preservation Board to preserve 25 films each year to add to a National Film Registry. Films selected must be culturally, historically, or aesthetically significant, and they must be at least ten years old. Films are not limited to Hollywood movie releases; they include documentaries and other noncommercial films such as the Abraham Zapruder film of John F. Kennedy's assassination. Films in **bold type** were added in 2003.

Film (Year)

Abbott and Costello Meet Frankenstein (1948)
Adam's Rib (1949)
The Adventures of Robin Hood (1938)
The African Queen (1951)
***Alien* (1979)**
All About Eve (1950)
***All My Babies* (1953)**
All Quiet on the Western Front (1930)
All That Heaven Allows (1955)
All That Jazz (1979)
All the King's Men (1949)
America, America (1963)
American Graffiti (1973)
An American in Paris (1951)
Annie Hall (1977)
The Apartment (1960)
Apocalypse Now (1979)
The Awful Truth (1937)
***The Bad and the Beautiful* (1953)**
Badlands (1973)
The Band Wagon (1953)
The Bank Dick (1940)
The Battle of San Pietro (1945)
***Beauty and the Beast* (1991)**
Ben-Hur (1926)
The Best Years of Our Lives (1946)
Big Business (1929)
The Big Parade (1925)
The Big Sleep (1946)
The Birth of a Nation (1915)
The Black Pirate (1926)
***The Black Stallion* (1979)**
Blacksmith Scene (1893)
Blade Runner (1982)
The Blood of Jesus (1941)
Bonnie and Clyde (1967)
***Boyz N the Hood* (1991)**
Bride of Frankenstein (1935)
The Bridge on the River Kwai (1957)
Bringing Up Baby (1938)
Broken Blossoms (1919)
Cabaret (1972)
Carmen Jones (1954)
Casablanca (1942)
Castro Street (1966)
Cat People (1942)
Chan Is Missing (1982)
The Cheat (1915)
Chinatown (1974)
Chulas Fronteras (1976)
Citizen Kane (1941)
The City (1939)
City Lights (1931)
Civilization (1916)
Cologne: From the Diary of Ray and Esther (1939)
The Conversation (1974)
Cops (1922)

Film (Year)

A Corner in Wheat (1909)
The Cool World (1963)
The Crowd (1928)
Czechoslovakia 1968 (1968)
David Holzman's Diary (1968)
The Day the Earth Stood Still (1951)
Dead Birds (1964)
The Deer Hunter (1978)
Destry Rides Again (1939)
Detour (1946)
Do the Right Thing (1989)
The Docks of New York (1928)
Dodsworth (1936)
Dog Star Man (1964)
Don't Look Back (1967)
Double Indemnity (1944)
Dr. Strangelove (or, How I Learned To Stop Worrying and Love the Bomb) (1964)
Dracula (1931)
Duck Amuck (1953)
Duck Soup (1933)
E.T. The Extra-Terrestrial (1982)
Easy Rider (1969)
Eaux d'artifice (1953)
El Norte (1983)
The Emperor Jones (1933)
***The Endless Summer* (1966)**
Evidence of the Film (1913)
The Exploits of Elaine (1914)
The Fall of the House of Usher (1928)
Fantasia (1940)
Fatty's Tintype Tangle (1915)
Five Easy Pieces (1970)
Flash Gordon (Serial) (1936)
Footlight Parade (1933)
Force of Evil (1948)
The Forgotten Frontier (1931)
42nd Street (1933)
The Four Horsemen of the Apocalypse (1921)
Frank Film (1973)
Frankenstein (1931)
Freaks (1932)
The Freshman (1925)
***From Here to Eternity* (1953)**
From the Manger to the Cross (1912)
***From Stump to Ship* (1930)**
***Fuji* (1974)**
Fury (1936)
The General (1927)
Gerald McBoing Boing (1951)
Gertie the Dinosaur (1914)
Gigi (1958)
The Godfather (1972)
The Godfather, Part II (1974)
The Gold Rush (1925)
Gone With the Wind (1939)
Goodfellas (1990)
The Graduate (1967)
The Grapes of Wrath (1940)

Film (Year)

Grass (1925)
The Great Dictator (1940)
The Great Train Robbery (1903)
Greed (1924)
Gun Crazy (1949)
Gunga Din (1939)
Harlan County, U.S.A. (1976)
Harold and Maude (1972)
The Heiress (1949)
Hell's Hinges (1916)
Hindenburg disaster footage (1937)
High School (1968)
High Noon (1952)
His Girl Friday (1940)
The Hitch-hiker (1953)
Hoosiers (1986)
Hospital (1970)
The Hospital (1971)
The House in the Middle (1954)
How Green Was My Valley (1941)
How the West Was Won (1962)
The Hustler (1961)
I Am a Fugitive From a Chain Gang (1932)
The Immigrant (1917)
***In the Heat of the Night* (1967)**
In the Land of the Head-hunters (1914)
Intolerance (1916)
Invasion of the Body Snatchers (1956)
It Happened One Night (1934)
It's A Wonderful Life (1946)
The Italian (1915)
Jam Session (1942)
Jammin' the Blues (1944)
Jaws (1975)
Jazz on a Summer's Day (1959)
The Jazz Singer (1927)
Killer of Sheep (1977)
King: A Filmed Record. . . Montgomery to Memphis (1970)
King Kong (1933)
The Kiss (1896)
Kiss Me Deadly (1955)
Knute Rockne, All American (1940)
Koyaanisqatsi (1983)
The Lady Eve (1941)
***Lady Windermere's Fan* (1925)**
Lambchops (1929)
The Land Beyond the Sunset (1912)
Lassie Come Home (1943)
The Last of the Mohicans (1920)
The Last Picture Show (1972)
Laura (1944)
Lawrence of Arabia (1962)
The Learning Tree (1969)
Let's All Go to the Lobby (1957)

Film (Year)

Letter From an Unknown Woman (1948)
The Life and Death of 9413—a Hollywood Extra (1927)
The Life and Times of Rosie the Riveter (1980)
The Life of Emile Zola (1937)
Little Caesar (1930)
The Little Fugitive (1953)
Little Miss Marker (1934)
The Living Desert (1953)
The Lost World (1925)
Louisiana Story (1948)
Love Finds Andy Hardy (1938)
Love Me Tonight (1932)
M*A*S*H (1970)
Magical Maestro (1952)
The Magnificent Ambersons (1942)
The Maltese Falcon (1941)
The Manchurian Candidate (1962)
Manhatta (1921)
Manhattan (1979)
March of Time: Inside Nazi Germany—1938 (1938)
Marian Anderson: Th e Lincoln Memorial Concert (1939)
Marty (1955)
Master Hands (1936)
Mean Streets (1973)
Meet Me in St. Louis (1944)
Melody Ranch **(1940)**
Memphis Belle (1944)
Meshes of the Afternoon (1943)
Midnight Cowboy (1969)
Mildred Pierce (1945)
The Miracle of Morgan's Creek (1944)
Miss Lulu Bett (1922)
Modern Times (1936)
Modesta (1956)
Morocco (1930)
Motion Painting No. 1 (1947)
A Movie (1958)
Mr. Smith Goes to Washington (1939)
Multiple Sidosis (1970)
The Music Box (1932)
My Darling Clementine (1946)
My Man Godfrey (1936)
The Naked Spur (1953)
Nanook of the North (1922)
Nashville (1975)
National Lampoon's Animal House (1978)
Network (1976)
A Night at the Opera (1935)
The Night of the Hunter (1955)
Night of the Living Dead (1968)
Ninotchka (1939)
North by Northwest (1959)
Nothing but a Man (1964)
On the Waterfront (1954)
One Flew Over the Cuckoo's Nest (1975)
Out of the Past (1947)
The Ox-Bow Incident (1943)
The Outlaw Josey Wales (1976)
Pass the Gravy (1928)

Film (Year)

Paths of Glory (1957)
The Pearl **(1947)**
Peter Pan (1924)
Phantom of the Opera (1925)
The Philadelphia Story (1940)
Pinocchio (1940)
A Place in the Sun (1951)
Planet of the Apes (1968)
The Plow that Broke the Plains (1936)
Point of Order (1964)
The Poor Little Rich Girl (1917)
Porky in Wackyland (1938)
Powers of Ten (1978)
President McKinley Inauguation Footage (1901)
Primary (1960)
The Prisoner of Zenda (1937)
The Producers (1968)
Psycho (1960)
The Public Enemy (1931)
Pull My Daisy (1959)
Punch Drunks **(1934)**
Raging Bull (1980)
Raiders of the Lost Ark (1981)
Rear Window (1954)
Rebel Without a Cause (1955)
Red River (1948)
Regeneration (1915)
Republic Steel Strike Riot Newsreel Footage (1937)
Return of the Secaucus 7 (1980)
Ride the High Country (1962)
Rip van Winkle (1896)
The River (1937)
Road to Morocco (1942)
Roman Holiday (1953)
Rose Hobart (1936)
Sabrina **(1954)**
Safety Last (1923)
Salesman (1969)
Salome (1922)
Salt of the Earth (1954)
Scarface (1932)
The Searchers (1956)
Serene Velocity (1970)
Seventh Heaven (1927)
Shadow of a Doubt (1943)
Shadows (1959)
Shaft (1971)
Shane (1953)
She Done Him Wrong (1933)
Sherlock, Jr. (1924)
Sherman's March (1986)
Shock Corridor (1963)
The Shop Around the Corner (1940)
Show Boat (1936)
Singin' in the Rain (1952)
Sky High (1922)
Snow White (1933)
Snow White and the Seven Dwarfs (1937)
Some Like it Hot (1959)
The Sound of Music (1965)
Stagecoach (1939)
A Star is Born (1954)
Star Theatre **(1902)**
Star Wars (1977)
Steamboat Willie (1928)

Film (Year)

Stormy Weather (1943)
Stranger Than Paradise **(1984)**
A Streetcar Named Desire (1951)
Sullivan's Travels (1941)
Sunrise (1927)
Sunset Boulevard (1950)
Sweet Smell of Success (1957
Tabu (1931)
Tacoma Narrows Bridge Collapse (1940)
The Tall T (1957)
Taxi Driver (1976)
The Ten Commandments (1956)
Tevye (1939)
Theodore Case Sound Test: Gus Visser and his Singing Duck **(1925)**
The Thief of Bagdad (1924)
The Thin Blue Line (1988)
The Thin Man (1934)
The Thing From Another World (1951)
This is Cinerama **(1952)**
This is Spinal Tap **(1984)**
Through Navajo Eyes **(series) (1966)**
To Be or Not to Be (1942)
To Fly (1976)
To Kill a Mockingbird (1962)
Tootsie (1982)
Top Hat (1935)
Topaz (home movie footage taken at Japanese-American internment camp, the Topaz War Relocation Authority Center) (1943–45)
Touch of Evil (1958)
Trance and Dance in Bali (1938-39)
The Treasure of the Sierra Madre (1948)
Trouble in Paradise (1932)
Tulips Shall Grow (1942)
Twelve O'Clock High (1949)
2001: A Space Odyssey (1968)
Verbena Tragica (1939)
Vertigo (1958)
West Side Story (1961)
Westinghouse Works, 1904 (1904)
What's Opera, Doc? (1957)
Where Are My Children? (1916)
Why Man Creates **(1968)**
Why We Fight (series) (1943-45)
Wild and Woolly **(1917)**
The Wild Bunch (1969)
Wild River **(1960)**
Will Success Spoil Rock Hunter? (1957)
The Wind (1928)
Wings (1927)
Within Our Gates (1920)
The Wizard of Oz (1939)
Woman of the Year(1942)
A Woman Under the Influence (1974)
Woodstock (1970)
Yankee Doodle Dandy (1942)
Zapruder film (1963)

The Emmy Awards, 1951–2003

The Academy of Television Arts and Sciences, formed in 1946, presented the first Emmy Awards in 1949. The number and names of awards have changed over the years, but since 1965, the Academy has recognized an outstanding comedy and drama, as well as an actor and an actress in a comedy and in a drama.

Year	Comedy	Drama	Comedy Actor	Comedy Actress	Drama Actor	Drama Actress
1951	*The Red Skelton Show* (CBS)	*Studio One* (CBS)	Sid Caesar (NBC)	Imogene Coca (NBC)	(1)	(1)
1952	*I Love Lucy* (CBS)	*Robert Montgomery Presents* (NBC)	Thomas Mitchell	Helen Hayes	(1)	(1)
1953	*I Love Lucy* (CBS)	*The U.S. Steel Hour* (ABC)	Donald O'Connor, *Colgate Comedy Hour* (NBC)	Eve Arden, *Our Miss Brooks* (CBS)	(1)	(1)
1954	*Make Room for Daddy* (ABC)	*The U.S. Steel Hour* (ABC)	Danny Thomas, *Make Room for Daddy* (ABC)	Loretta Young, *The Loretta Young Show* (NBC)	(1)	(1)
1955	*The Phil Silvers Show* (CBS)	*Producers'* (NBC) *Showcase*	Phil Silvers, *The Phil Silvers Show* (CBS)	Lucille Ball, *I Love Lucy* (CBS)	(1)	(1)
1956	*The Phil Silvers Show* (CBS)	*Requiem for a Heavyweight* (CBS)	Sid Caesar, *Caesar's Hour* (NBC)	Nanette Fabray, *Caesar's Hour* (NBC)	Robert Young, *Father Knows Best* (NBC)	Loretta Young, *The Loretta Young Show* (NBC)
1957	*The Phil Silvers Show* (CBS)	*Gunsmoke* (CBS)	Robert Young, *Father Knows Best* (NBC)	Jane Wyatt, *Father Knows Best* (NBC)	(1)	(1)
1958 –59	*The Jack Benny Show* (CBS)	(2)	Jack Benny, *The Jack Benny Show* (CBS)	Jane Wyatt, *Father Knows Best* (NBC and CBS)	Raymond Burr, *Perry Mason* (CBS)	Loretta Young, *The Loretta Young Show* (NBC)
1959 –60	"Art Carney Special" (NBC)	*Playhouse 90* (CBS)	Robert Stack, *The Untouchables* (ABC)	Jane Wyatt, *Father Knows Best* (CBS)	(1)	(1)
1960 –61	*The Jack BennyShow* (CBS)	*"Macbeth,"* Hallmark Hall of Fame (NBC)	Raymond Burr, *Perry Mason* (CBS)	Barbara Stanwyck, *The Barbara Stanwyck Show* (NBC)	(1)	(1)
1961 –62	*The Bob Newhart Show* (CBS)	*The Defenders* (CBS)	E.G, Marshall, *The Defenders* (CBS)	Shirley Booth, *Hazel* (NBC)	(1)	(1)
1962 –63	*The Dick Van Dyke Show* (CBS)	*The Defenders* (CBS)	E.G. Marshall, *The Defenders*	Shirley Booth, *Hazel* (NBC) (CBS)	(1)	(1)
1963 –64	*The Dick Van Dyke Show* (CBS)	*The Defenders* (CBS)	Dick Van Dyke, *The Dick Van Dyke Show* (CBS)	Mary Tyler Moore, *The Dick Van Dyke Show*(CBS)	(1)	(1)
1964 –65	(3)	(3)	(3)	(3)	(3)	(3)
1965 –66	*The Dick Van Dyke Show* (CBS)	*The Fugitive* (ABC)	Dick Van Dyke, *The Dick Van Dyke Show* (CBS)	Mary Tyler Moore, *The Dick Van Dyke Show* (CBS)	Bill Cosby, *I Spy* (NBC)	Barbara Stanwyck, *The Big Valley* (ABC)
1966 –67	*The Monkees* (NBC)	*Mission: Impossible* (CBS)	Don Adams, *Get Smart* (NBC)	Lucille Ball, *The Lucy Show* (CBS)	Bill Cosby, *I Spy* (NBC)	Barbara Bain, *Mission: Impossible* (CBS)
1967 –68	*Get Smart* (NBC)	*Mission: Impossible* (CBS)	Don Adams, *Get Smart* (NBC)	Lucille Ball, *The Lucy Show* (CBS)	Bill Cosby, *I Spy* (NBC)	Barbara Bain, *Mission: Impossible* (CBS)
1968 –69	*Get Smart* (NBC)	*NET Playhouse* (NET)	Don Adams, *Get Smart* (NBC)	Hope Lange, *The Ghost and Mrs. Muir* (NBC)	Carl Betz, *Judd for the Defense* (ABC)	Barbara Bain, *Mission: Impossible* (CBS)
1969 –70	*My World & Welcome to It* (NBC)	*Marcus Welby, M.D.* (ABC)	William Windom, *My World & Welcome to It* (NBC)	Hope Lange, *The Ghost and Mrs. Muir* (ABC)	Robert Young, *Marcus Welby, M.D.* (ABC)	Susan Hampshire *The Forsyte Saga* (NET)

Year	Comedy	Drama	Comedy Actor	Comedy Actress	Drama Actor	Drama Actress
1970–71	*All in the Family* (CBS)	*The Senator* (segment), *The Bold Ones* (NBC)	Jack Klugman, *The Odd Couple* (ABC)	Jean Stapleton, *All in the Family* (CBS)	Hal Holbrook, *The Senator* (segment), *The Bold Ones* (NBC)	Susan Hampshire, *The First Churchills* (PBS)
1971–72	*All in the Family* (CBS)	*"Elizabeth R" Masterpiece Theatre* (PBS)	Carroll O'Connor, *All in the Family* (CBS)	Jean Stapleton, *All in the Family* (CBS)	Peter Falk, *Columbo* (NBC)	Glenda Jackson, *"Elizabeth R" Masterpiece Theatre* (PBS)
1972–73	*All in the Family* (CBS)	*The Waltons* (CBS)	Jack Klugman, *The Odd Couple* (ABC)	Mary Tyler Moore, *The Mary Tyler Moore Show* (CBS)	Richard Thomas, *The Waltons* (CBS)	Michael Learned, *The Waltons* (CBS)
1973–74	*M*A*S*H* (CBS)	*"Upstairs, Downstairs," Masterpiece Theatre* (PBS)	Alan Alda, *M*A*S*H* (CBS)	Mary Tyler Moore, *The Mary Tyler Moore Show* (CBS)	Telly Savalas, *Kojak* (CBS)	Michael Learned, *The Waltons* (CBS)
1974–75	*The Mary Tyler Moore Show* (CBS)	*"Upstairs, Downstairs," Masterpiece Theatre* (PBS)	Tony Randall, *The Odd Couple* (ABC)	Valerie Harper, *Rhoda* (CBS)	Robert Blake, *Baretta* (ABC)	Jean Marsh, *"Upstairs, Downstairs," Masterpiece Theater* (PBS)
1975–76	*The Mary Tyler Moore Show* (CBS)	*Police Story (NBC)*	Jack Albertson, *Chico & the Man* (NBC)	Mary Tyler Moore, *The Mary Tyler Moore Show*(CBS)	Peter Falk, *Columbo* (NBC)	Michael Learned, *The Waltons* (CBS)
1977–78	*All in the Family* (CBS)	*The Rockford Files* (NBC)	Carroll O'Connor, *All in the Family* (CBS)	Jean Stapleton, *All in the Family* (CBS)	Edward Asner, *Lou Grant* (CBS)	Sada Thompson, *Family* (ABC)
1978–79	*Taxi* (ABC)	*Lou Grant* (CBS)	Carroll O' Connor, *All in the Family* (CBS)	Ruth Gordon, *Taxi* (ABC)	Ron Leibman, *Kaz* (CBS)	Mariette Hartley, *The Incredible Hulk* (CBS)
1979–80	*Taxi* (ABC)	*Lou Grant* (CBS)	Richard Mulligan, *Soap* (ABC)	Cathryn Damon, *Soap* (ABC)	Ed Asner, *Lou Grant* (CBS)	Barbara Bel Geddes, *Dallas* (CBS)
1980–81	*Taxi* (ABC)	*Hill Street Blues* (NBC)	Judd Hirsch, *Taxi* (ABC)	Isabel Sanford, *The Jeffersons* (CBS)	Daniel Travanti, *Hill Street Blues* (NBC)	Barbara Babcock *Hill Street Blues* (NBC)
1981–82	*Barney Miller* (ABC)	*Hill Street Blues* (NBC)	Alan Alda, *M*A*S*H* (CBS)	Carol Kane, *Taxi* (ABC)	Daniel Travanti, *Hill Street Blues* (NBC)	Michael Learned, *Nurse* (CBS)
1982–83	*Cheers* (NBC)	*Hill Street Blues (NBC)*	Judd Hirsch, *Taxi* (NBC)	Shelley Long, *Cheers* (NBC)	Ed Flanders, *St. Elsewhere* (NBC)	Tyne Daly, *Cagney &Lacey* (CBS)
1983–84	*Cheers* (NBC)	*Hill Street Blues* (NBC)	John Ritter, *Three's Company* (ABC)	Jane Curtin, *Kate & Allie* (CBS)	Tom Selleck, *Magnum P.I.* (CBS)	Tyne Daly, *Cagney &Lacey* (CBS)
1984–85	*The Cosby Show* (NBC)	*Cagney & Lacey* (CBS)	Robert Guillaume, *Benson* (ABC)	Jane Curtin, *Kate & Allie* (CBS)	William Daniels, *St. Elsewhere* (NBC)	Tyne Daly, *Cagney &Lacey* (CBS)
1985–86	*The Golden Girls* (NBC)	*Cagney & Lacey (CBS)*	Michael J. Fox, *Family Ties* (NBC)	Betty White, *The Golden Girls* (NBC)	William Daniels, *St. Elsewhere* (NBC)	Sharon Gless, *Cagney &Lacey* (CBS)
1986–87	*The Golden Girls* (NBC)	*L.A. Law* (NBC)	Michael J. Fox, *Family Ties* (NBC)	Rue McClanahan, *The Golden Girls* (NBC)	Bruce Willis, *Moonlighting* (ABC)	Sharon Gless, *Cagney &Lacey* (CBS)
1987–88	*The Wonder Years* (ABC)	*thirtysomething* (ABC)	Michael J. Fox, *Family Ties* (NBC)	Beatrice Arthur, *The Golden Girls* (NBC)	Richard Kiley, *A Year in the Life* (NBC)	Tyne Daly, *Cagney &Lacey* (CBS)
1988–89	*Cheers* (NBC)	*L.A. Law* (NBC)	Richard Mulligan, *Empty Nest* (NBC)	Candice Bergen, *Murphy Brown* (CBS)	Carroll O'Connor, *In the Heat of the Night* (NBC)	Dana Delany, *China Beach*, (ABC)
1989–90	*Murphy Brown* (CBS)	*L.A. Law* (NBC)	Ted Danson, *Cheers* (NBC)	Candice Bergen, *Murphy Brown* (CBS)	Peter Falk, *Columbo* (ABC)	Patricia Wettig, *thirtysomething* (ABC)
1990–91	*Cheers* (NBC)	*L.A. Law* (NBC)	Burt Reynolds, *Evening Shade* (CBS)	Kirstie Alley, *Cheers* (NBC)	James Earl Jones, *Gabriel's Fire* (ABC)	Patricia Wettig, *thirtysomething* (ABC)

Year	Comedy	Drama	Comedy Actor	Comedy Actress	Drama Actor	Drama Actress
1991–92	*Murphy Brown* (CBS)	*Northern Exposure* (CBS)	Craig T. Nelson, *Coach* (ABC)	Candice Bergen, *MurphyBrown* (CBS)	Christopher Lloyd, *Avonlea* (Disney)	Dana Delany, *China Beach*, (ABC)
1992–93	*Seinfeld* (NBC)	*Picket Fences* (CBS)	Ted Danson, *Cheers* (NBC)	Roseanne Arnold, *Roseanne* (ABC)	Tom Skerritt, *Picket Fences* (CBS)	Kathy Baker, *Picket Fences* (CBS)
1993–94	*Frasier* (NBC)	*Picket Fences* (CBS)	Kelsey Grammer, *Frasier* (NBC)	Candice Bergen, *Murphy Brown* (CBS)	Dennis Franz, *NYPD Blue* (ABC)	Sela Ward, *Sisters* (NBC)
1994–95	*Frasier* (NBC)	*NYPD Blue* (ABC)	Kelsey Grammer, *Frasier* (NBC)	Candice Bergen, *Murphy Brown* (CBS)	Mandy Patinkin, *Chicago Hope* (CBS)	Kathy Baker, *Picket Fences* (CBS)
1995–96	*Frasier* (NBC)	*E.R.* (NBC)	John Lithgow, *Third Rock From the Sun* (NBC)	Helen Hunt, *Mad About You* (NBC)	Dennis Franz, *NYPD Blue* (ABC)	Kathy Baker, *Picket Fences* (CBS)
1996–97	*Frasier* (NBC)	*Law & Order* (NBC)	John Lithgow, *Third Rock From the Sun* (NBC)	Helen Hunt, *Mad About You* (NBC)	Dennis Franz, *NYPD Blue* (ABC)	Gillian Anderson, *The X-Files* (FOX)
1997–98	*Frasier* (NBC)	*The Practice* (ABC)	Kelsey Grammer, *Frasier* (NBC)	Helen Hunt, *Mad About You* (NBC)	Andre Braugher, *Homicide* (NBC)	Christine Lahti, *Chicago Hope* (CBS)
1998–99	*Ally McBeal* (FOX)	*The Practice* (ABC)	John Lithgow, *Third Rock From the Sun* (NBC)	Helen Hunt, *Mad About You* (NBC)	Dennis Franz, *NYPD Blue* (ABC)	Edie Falco, *The Sopranos* (HBO)
1999–2000	*Will and Grace* (NBC)	*The West Wing* (NBC)	Michael J. Fox, *Spin City* (ABC)	Patricia Heaton, *Everybody Loves Raymond* (CBS)	James Gandolfini, *The Sopranos* (HBO)	Sela Ward, *Once and Again* (ABC)
2000–01	*Sex and the City* (HBO)	*The West Wing* (NBC)	Eric McCormack, *Will and Grace* (NBC)	Patricia Heaton, *Everybody Loves Raymond* (CBS)	James Gandolfini, *The Sopranos* (HBO)	Edie Falco, *The Sopranos* (HBO)
2001–02	*Friends* (NBC)	*The West Wing* (NBC)	Ray Romano, *Everybody Loves Raymond*, (CBS)	Jennifer Aniston, *Friends* (NBC)	Michael Chiklis, *The Shield* (FX)	Allison Janney, *The West Wing* (NBC)
2002–03	*Everybody Loves Raymond* (CBS)	*The West Wing* (NBC)	Tony Shalhoub, *Monk* (USA)	Edie Falco, *The Sopranos* (HBO)	James Gandolfini, *The Sopranos* (HBO)	Debra Messing, *Will & Grace* (NBC)

Notes: 1. Before 1965, the Academy did always not give separate acting awards for comedy and drama. 2. *Playhouse 90* (CBS) was best drama of one hour or longer; *Alcoa-Goodyear Theatre* (NBC) was best drama of less than one hour. 3. In 1964, the Academy gave acting awards to Dick Van Dyke for *The Dick Van Dyke Show* (CBS), Lynn Fontaine and Alfred Lunt for *"The Magnificent Yankee" Hallmark Hall of Fame* (NBC), and Barbra Streisand for *My Name is Barbra* (CBS). It also gave Achievements in Entertainment awards to these programs. **www.emmys.tv**

Emmy Awards for Variety Shows, 1951–2003

Year	Show	Year	Show
1951	*Your Show of Shows* (NBC)	1977–78	*The Muppet Show (syndicated)*
1952	*Your Show of Shows* (NBC)	1978–79	"Steve & Eydie Celebrate Irving Berlin" (NBC)
1953	*Omnibus* (CBS)	1979–80	"IBM Presents Baryshnikov on Broadway" (ABC)
1954	*Disneyland* (ABC)	1980–81	"Lily: Sold Out "(CBS)
1955	*The Ed Sullivan Show* (CBS)	1981–82	"Night of 100 Stars" (ABC)
1956	*Caesar's Hour* (NBC)	1982–83	"Motown 25: Yesterday, Today, Forever" (NBC)
1957	*The Dinah Shore Show* (NBC)	1983–84	"The 6th Annual Kennedy Center Honors" (CBS)
1958–59	*The Dinah Shore Chevy Show* (NBC)	1984–85	"Motown Returns to the Apollo" (NBC)
1959–60	"The Fabulous '50s" (CBS)	1985–86	"The Kennedy Center Honors" (CBS)
1960–61	"Astaire Time" (NBC)	1986–87	"The 1987 Tony Awards" (CBS)
1962–63	*The Andy Williams Show* (NBC)	1987–88	"Irving Berlin's 100th Birthday Celebration" (CBS)
1963–64	*The Danny Kaye Show* (CBS)	1988–89	*The Tracey Ullman Show* (FOX)
1964–65	*My Name is Barbra* (CBS).	1989–90	*In Living Color* (FOX)
1965–66	*The Andy Williams Show* (NBC)	1990–91	"The 63rd Annual Academy Awards" (ABC)
1966–67	*The Andy Williams Show* (NBC)	1991–92	*The Tonight Show Starring Johnny Carson* (NBC)
1967–68	*Rowan & Martin's Laugh-In* (NBC)	1992–93	*Saturday Night Live* (NBC)
1968–69	*Rowan & Martin's Laugh-In* (NBC)	1993–94	*Late Show with David Letterman* (CBS)
1969–70	*The David Frost Show (syndicated)*	1994–95	*The Tonight Show with Jay Leno* (NBC)
1970–71	*The Flip Wilson Show* (NBC)	1995–96	*Dennis Miller Live* (HBO)
1971–72	Music: *The Carol Burnett Show* (CBS) Talk: *The Dick Cavett Show* (ABC)	1996–97	*Tracey Takes On . . .* (HBO)
		1997–98	*Late Show with David Letterman* (CBS)
1972–73	*The Julie Andrews Hour* (ABC)	1998–99	*Late Show with David Letterman* (CBS)
1973–74	*The Carol Burnett Show* (CBS)	1999-00	*Late Show with David Letterman* (CBS)
1974–75	*The Carol Burnett Show* (CBS)	2000-01	*Late Show with David Letterman* (CBS)
1975–76	*NBC's Saturday Night* (NBC)	2001-02	*Late Show with David Letterman* (CBS)
1976–77	*Van Dyke & Company* (NBC)	2002-03	*The Daily Show With Jon Stewart* (COM)

Source: Academy of Television Arts and Sciences. **www.emmys.tv**

The Tony Awards, 1947–2003

The Tony Awards are presented each year by the American Theatre Wing for distinguished achievement in the Broadway theater. Named for Antoinette Perry, an actress, producer, director, and chairman of the American Theatre Wing who died in 1946, the Tonys were first presented in 1947. Awards are given to performers, authors, producers, directors, composers, and choreographers, and scenic, costume, and lighting designers. Listed here is a selection of major awards for each year: best play (author), performance by an actor in a play, performance by an actress in a play, best musical (composer and lyricist), performance by an actor in a musical, performance by an actress in a musical. In 2001, *The Producers* won 12 Tony Awards, breaking the previous record of 10 set by *Hello, Dolly!* in 1964.

PLAYS

Year	Best Play	Best Actor	Best Actress
1947	no award	José Ferrer, *Cyrano de Bergerac*; Fredric March, *Years Ago*	Ingrid Bergman, *Joan of Lorraine*; Helen Hayes, *Happy Birthday*
1948	*Mister Roberts,* Thomas Heggen and Joshua Logan	Henry Fonda, *Mister Roberts*; Paul Kelly, *Command Decision*; Basil Rathbone, *The Heiress*	Judith Anderson, *Medea;* Katharine Cornell, *Antony and Cleopatra;* Jessica Tandy, *A Streetcar Named Desire*
1949	*Death of a Salesman,* Arthur Miller	Rex Harrison, *Anne of the Thousand Days*	Martita Hunt, *The Madwoman of Chaillot*
1950	*The Cocktail Party,* T. S. Eliot	Sidney Blackmer, *Come Back, Little Sheba*	Shirley Booth, *Come Back, Little Sheba*
1951	*The Rose Tattoo,* Tennessee Williams	Claude Rains, *Darkness at Noon*	Uta Hagen, *The Country Girl*
1952	*The Fourposter,* Jan de Hartog	José Ferrer, *The Shrike*	Julie Harris, *I Am a Camera*
1953	*The Crucible,* Arthur Miller	Tom Ewell, *The Seven Year Itch*	Shirley Booth, *Time of the Cuckoo*
1954	*The Teahouse of the August Moon,* John Patrick	David Wayne, *The Teahouse of the August Moon*	Audrey Hepburn, *Ondine*
1955	*The Desperate Hours,* Joseph Hayes	Alfred Lunt, *Quadrille*	Nancy Kelly, *The Bad Seed*
1956	*The Diary of Anne Frank* , Frances Goodrich and Albert Hackett	Paul Muni, *Inherit the Wind*	Julie Harris, *The Lark*
1957	*Long Day's Journey Into Night,* Eugene O'Neill	Fredric March, *Long Day's Journey Into Night*	Margaret Leighton, *Separate Tables*
1958	*Sunrise at Campobello,* Dore Schary	Ralph Bellamy, *Sunrise at Campobello*	Helen Hayes, *Time Remembered*
1959	*J.B.,* Archibald Macleish	Jason Robards, *The Disenchanted*	Gertrude Berg, *A Majority of One*
1960	*The Miracle Worker,* William Gibson	Melvyn Douglas, *The Best Man*	Anne Bancroft, *The Miracle Worker*
1961	*Becket,* Jean Anouilh	Zero Mostel, *Rhinoceros*	Joan Plowright, *A Taste of Honey*
1962	*A Man for All Seasons,* Robert Bolt	Paul Scofield, *A Man for All Seasons*	Margaret Leighton, *Night of the Iguana*
1963	*Who's Afraid of Virginia Woolf,* Edward Albee	Arthur Hill, *Who's Afraid of Virginia Woolf*	Uta Hagen, *Who's Afraid of Virginia Woolf*
1964	*Luther,* John Osborne	Alec Guiness, *Dylan*	Sandy Dennis, *Any Wednesday*
1965	*The Subject Was Roses,* Frank Gilroy	Walter Matthau, *The Odd Couple*	Irene Worth, *Tiny Alice*
1966	*Marat/Sade,* Peter Weiss	Hal Holbrook, *Mark Twain Tonight!*	Rosemary Harris, *The Lion in Winter*
1967	*The Homecoming,* Harold Pinter	Paul Rogers, *The Homecoming*	Beryl Reid, *The Killing of Sister George*
1968	*Rosencrantz and Guildenstern Are Dead,* Tom Stoppard	Martin Balsam, *You Know I Can't Hear You When the Water's Running*	Zoe Caldwell, *The Prime of Miss Jean Brodie*
1969	*The Great White Hope,* Howard Sackler	James Earl Jones, *The Great White Hope*	Julie Harris, *Forty Carats*
1970	*Borstal Boy,* Frank McMahon	Fritz Weaver, *Child's Play*	Tammy Grimes, *Private Lives (R)*
1971	*Sleuth,* Anthony Shaffer	Brian Bedford, *The School for Wives*	Maureen Stapleton, *Gingerbread Lady*
1972	*Sticks and Bones,* David Rabe	Cliff Gorman, *Lenny*	Sada Thompson, *Twigs*
1973	*That Championship Season,* Jason Miller	Alan Bates, *Butley*	Julie Harris, *The Last of Mrs. Lincoln*
1974	*The River Niger* Joseph A. Walker	Michael Moriarty, *Find Your Way Home*	Colleen Dewhurst, *A Moon for the Misbegotten (R)*
1975	*Equus,* Peter Shaffer	John Kani, *Sizwe Banzi Is Dead*; Winston Ntshona, *The Island*	Ellen Burstyn, *Same Time, Next Year*
1976	*Travesties,* Tom Stoppard	John Wood, *Travesties*	Irene Worth, *Sweet Bird of Youth (R)*
1977	*The Shadow Box,* Michael Cristofer	Al Pacino, *The Basic Training of Pavlo Hummel*	Julie Harris, *The Belle of Amherst*

Year	Best Play	Best Actor	Best Actress
1978	*Da*, Hugh Leonard	Barnard Hughes, *Da*	Jessica Tandy, *The Gin Game*
1979	*The Elephant Man*, Bernard Pomerance	Tom Conti, *Whose Life Is It Anyway?*	Constance Cummings, *Wings* Carole Shelley, *The Elephant Man*
1980	*Children of a Lesser God*, Mark Medoff	John Rubinstein, *Children of a Lesser God*	Phyllis Frelich, *Children of a Lesser God*
1981	*Amadeus*, Peter Shaffer	Ian McKellen, *Amadeus*	Jane Lapotaire, *Piaf*
1982	*The Life and Adventures of Nicholas Nickleby*, David Edgar	Roger Rees, *The Life and Adventures of Nicholas Nickleby*	Zoe Caldwell, *Medea* (R)
1983	*Torch Song Trilogy*, Harvey Fierstein	Harvey Fierstein, *Torch Song Trilogy*	Jessica Tandy, *Foxfire*
1984	*The Real Thing*, Tom Stoppard	Jeremy Irons, *The Real Thing*	Glenn Close, *The Real Thing*
1985	*Biloxi Blues*, Neil Simon	Derek Jacobi, *Much Ado About Nothing* (R)	Stockard Channing, *Joe Egg (R)*
1986	*I'm Not Rappaport*, Herb Gardner	Judd Hirsch, *I'm Not Rappaport*	Lily Tomlin, *The Search for Signs of Intelligent Life in the Universe*
1987	*Fences*, August Wilson	James Earl Jones, *Fences*	Linda Lavin, *Broadway Bound*
1988	*M. Butterfly*, David Henry Hwang	Ron Silver, *Speed-The-Plow*	Joan Allen, *Burn This*
1989	*The Heidi Chronicles*, Wendy Wasserstein	Philip Bosco, *Lend Me a Tenor*	Pauline Collins, *Shirley Valentine*
1990	*The Grapes of Wrath*, Frank Galati	Robert Morse, *Tru*	Maggie Smith, *Lettice and Lovage*
1991	*Lost in Yonkers*, Neil Simon	Nigel Hawthorne, *Shadowlands*	Mercedes Ruhl, *Lost in Yonkers*
1992	*Dancing at Lughnasa*, Brian Friel	Judd Hirsch, *Conversations with My Father*	Glenn Close, *Death and the Maiden*
1993	*Angels in America: Millennium Approaches*, Tony Kushner	Ron Leibman, *Angels in America: Millennium Approaches*	Madeline Kahn, *The Sisters Rosensweig*
1994	*Angels in America: Perestroika*, Tony Kushner	Stephen Spinella, *Angels in America: Perestroika*	Diana Rigg, *Medea (R)*
1995	*Love! Valour! Compassion!*, Terrence McNally	Ralph Fiennes, *Hamlet*	Cherry Jones, *The Heiress*
1996	*Master Class*, Terrence McNally	George Grizzard, *A Delicate Balance (R)*	Zoe Caldwell, *Master Class*
1997	*Last Night of Ballyhoo*, Alfred Uhry	Christopher Plummer, *Barrymore*	Janet McTeer, *A Doll's House*
1998	*Art*, Yasmina Reza	Anthony La Paglia, *A View From the Bridge*	Marie Mullen, *The Beauty Queen of Leenane*
1999	*Side Man*, Warren Leight	Brian Dennehy, *Death of a Salesman*	Judi Dench, *Amy's View*
2000	*Copenhagen*, Michael Frayn	Stephen Dillane, *The Real Thing*	Jennifer Ehle, *The Real Thing*
2001	*Proof*, David Auburn	Richard Easton, *The Invention of Love*	Mary-Louise Parker, *Proof*
2002	*The Goat or Who Is Sylvia?*, Edward Albee	Alan Bates, *Fortune's Fool*	Lindsay Duncan, *Private Lives*
2003	*Take Me Out*, Richard Greenberg	Brian Dennehy, *Long Day's Journey Into Night*	Vanessa Redgrave, *Long Day's Journey Into Night*

MUSICALS

Year	Best Musical	Best Actor	Best Actress
1947	no award	no award	no award
1948	no award	Paul Hartman, *Angel in the Wings*	Grace Hartman, *Angel in the Wings*
1949	*Kiss Me Kate*, Cole Porter (M&L)	Ray Bolger, *Where's Charley?*	Nanette Fabray, *Love Life*
1950	*South Pacific*, Richard Rodgers (M), Oscar Hammerstein (L)	Ezio Pinza, *South Pacific*	Mary Martin, *South Pacific*
1951	*Guys and Dolls*, Frank Loesser (M&L)	Robert Alda, *Guys and Dolls*	Ethel Merman, *Call Me Madam*
1952	*The King and I*, Richard Rodgers (M), Oscar Hammerstein (L)	Phil Silvers, *Top Banana*	Gertrude Lawrence, *The King and I*
1953	*Wonderful Town*, Leonard Bernstein (M), Betty Comden and Adolph Green (L)	Thomas Mitchell, *Hazel Flagg*	Rosalind Russell, *Wonderful Town*
1954	*Kismet*, Alexander Borodin (M), adapted by Robert Wright and George Forrest (L)	Alfred Drake, *Kismet*	Dolores Gray, *Carnival in Flanders*
1955	*The Pajama Game*, Richard Adler and Jerry Ross (M&L)	Walter Slezak, *Fanny*	Mary Martin, *Peter Pan*
1956	*Damn Yankees*, Richard Adler and Jerry Ross (M&L)	Ray Walston, *Damn Yankees*	Gwen Verdon, *Damn Yankees*

Year	Best Musical	Best Actor	Best Actress
1957	*My Fair Lady*, Frederick Loewe (M), Alan Jay Lerner (L)	Rex Harrison, *My Fair Lady*	Judy Holliday, *Bells Are Ringing*
1958	*The Music Man*, Meredith Willson (M&L)	Robert Preston, *The Music Man*	(tie) Thelma Ritter, Gwen Verdon, *New Girl in Town*
1959	*Redhead*, Albert Hague (M), Dorothy Fields (L)	Richard Kiley, *Redhead*	Gwen Verdon, *Redhead*
1960	(tie) *Fiorello*, Jerry Bock (M), Sheldon Harnick (L); *The Sound of Music*, Richard Rodgers (M), Oscar Hammerstein (L)	Jackie Gleason, *Take Me Along*	Mary Martin, *The Sound of Music*
1961	*Bye, Bye, Birdie*, Charles Strouse (M), Lee Adams (L)	Richard Burton, *Camelot*	Elizabeth Seal, *Irma la Douce*
1962	*How to Succeed in Business Without Really Trying*, Frank Loesser (M&L)	Robert Morse, *How to Succeed in Business Without Really Trying*	(tie) Anna Maria Alberghetti, *Carnival;* Diahann Carroll, *No Strings*
1963	*A Funny Thing Happened on the Way to the Forum*, Stephen Sondheim (M&L)	Zero Mostel, *A Funny Thing Happened on the Way to the Forum*,	Vivien Leigh, *Tovarich*
1964	*Hello, Dolly!* Jerry Herman (M&L)	Bert Lahr, *Foxy*	Carol Channing, *Hello, Dolly!*
1965	*Fiddler on the Roof*, Jerry Bock (M), Sheldon Harnick (L)	Zero Mostel, *Fiddler on the Roof*	Liza Minnelli, *Flora, the Red Menace*
1966	*Man of La Mancha*, Mitch Leigh (M), Joe Darion (L)	Richard Kiley, *Man of La Mancha*	Angela Lansbury, *Mame*
1967	*Cabaret*, John Kander (M), Fred Ebb (L)	Robert Preston, *I Do! I Do!*	Barbara Harris, *The Apple Tree*
1968	*Hallelujah, Baby!* Jule Styne (M), Betty Comden & Adolph Green (L)	Robert Goulet, *The Happy Time*	Patricia Routledge, *Darling of the Day* Leslie Uggams, *Hallelujah, Baby!*
1969	*1776*, Sherman Edwards (M&L)	Jerry Orbach, *Promises, Promises*	Angela Lansbury, *Dear World*
1970	*Applause*, Charles Strouse (M), Lee Adams (L)	Cleavon Little, *Purlie*	Lauren Bacall, *Applause*
1971	*Company*, Stephen Sondheim (M&L)	Hal Linden, *The Rothschilds*	Helen Gallagher, *No, No Nannette (R)*
1972	*Two Gentlemen of Verona* [best score: *Follies*, Stephen Sondheim (M&L)]	Phil Silvers, *A Funny Thing Happened on the Way to the Forum (R)*	Alexis Smith, *Follies*
1973	*A Little Night Music*, Stephen Sondheim (M&L)	Ben Vereen, *Pippin*	Glynis Johns, *A Little Night Music*
1974	*Raisin*, [best score: *Gigi*, Frederick Loewe (M), Alan Jay Lerner (L)]	Christopher Plummer, *Cyrano*	Virginia Capers, *Raisin*
1975	*The Wiz*, Charlie Smalls (M&L)	John Cullum, *Shenandoah*	Angela Lansbury, *Gypsy* (R)
1976	*A Chorus Line*, Marvin Hamlisch (M), Edward Kleban (L)	George Rose, *My Fair Lady (R)*	Donna McKechnie, *A Chorus Line*
1977	*Annie*, Charles Strouse (M), Martin Charnin (L)	Barry Bostwick, *The Robber Bridegroom*	Dorothy Loudon, *Annie*
1978	*Ain't Misbehavin'* [best score: *On the Twentieth Century*, Cy Coleman (M) Betty Comden and Adolph Green (L)]	John Cullum, *On the Twentieth Century*	Liza Minnelli, *The Act*
1979	*Sweeney Todd*, Stephen Sondheim	Len Cariou, *Sweeney Todd*	Angela Lansbury, *Sweeney Todd*
1980	*Evita*, Andrew Lloyd Webber (M), Tim Rice (L)	Jim Dale, *Barnum*	Patti LuPone, *Evita*
1981	*42nd Street*, [best score: *Woman of the Year*, John Kander (M), Fred Ebb (L)]	Kevin Kline, *The Pirates of Penzance*	Lauren Bacall, *Woman of the Year*
1982	*Nine*, Maury Yeston (M&L)	Ben Harney, *Dreamgirls*	Jennifer Holliday, *Dreamgirls*
1983	*Cats*, Andrew Lloyd Webber (M), T.S. Eliot (L)	Tommy Tune, *My One and Only*	Natalia Makarova, *On Your Toes*
1984	*La Cage Aux Folles*, Jerry Herman (M&L)	George Hearn, *La Cage Aux Folles*	Chita Rivera, *The Rink*
1985	*Big River*, Roger Miller (M&L)	No award	No award
1986	*The Mystery of Edwin Drood*, Rupert Holmes (M&L)	George Rose, *The Mystery of Edwin Drood*	Bernadette Peters, *Song and Dance*
1987	*Les Misérables*, Claude-Michel Schönberg (M); Herbert Kretzmer & Alain Boublil (L)	Robert Lindsay, *Me and My Girl*	Maryann Plunkett, *Me and My Girl*
1988	*The Phantom of the Opera* [best score: *Into the Woods*, Stephen Sondheim (M&L)]	Michael Crawford, *The Phantom of the Opera*	Joanna Gleason, *Into the Woods*
1989	*Jerome Robbins' Broadway* [best score: no award]	Jason Alexander, *Jerome Robbins' Broadway*	Ruth Brown, *Black and Blue*

Year	Best Musical	Best Actor	Best Actress
1990	*City of Angels,* Cy Coleman (M) David Zippel (L)	James Naughton, *City of Angels*	Tyne Daly, *Gypsy* (R)
1991	*The Will Rogers Follies,* Cy Coleman (M); Betty Comden and Adolph Green (L)	Jonathan Pryce, *Miss Saigon*	Lea Salonga, *Miss Saigon*
1992	*Crazy for You,* [best score: *Falsettos,* William Finn (M&L)]	Gregory Hines, *Jelly's Last Jam*	Faith Prince, *Guys and Dolls* (R)
1993	*Kiss of the Spider Woman* [best score: (tie) *Kiss of the Spider Woman,* John Kander (M) and Fred Ebb (L)' *Tommy,* Pete Townshend (M&L)]	Brent Carver, *Kiss of the Spider Woman*	Chita Rivera, *Kiss of the Spider Woman*
1994	*Passion,* Stephen Sondheim (M&L)	Boyd Gaines, *She Loves Me* (R)	Donna Murphy, *Passion*
1995	*Sunset Boulevard,* Andrew Lloyd Webber (M&L)	Matthew Broderick, *How to Succeed in Business Without Really Trying* (R)	Glenn Close, *Sunset Boulevard*
1996	*Rent,* Jonathan Larson (M&L)	Nathan Lane, *A Funny Thing Happened on the Way to the Forum* (R)	Donna Murphy, *The King and I* (R)
1997	*Titanic,* Maury Yeston (M&L)	James McNaughton, *Chicago* (R)	Bebe Neuwirth, *Chicago* (R)
1998	*The Lion King,* [best score: *Ragtime,* Stephen Flaherty & Lynn Ahrens (M&L)]	Alan Cumming, *Cabaret* (R)	Natasha Richardson, *Cabaret* (R)
1999	*Fosse,* [best score: *Parade,* Jason Robert Brown (M&L)]	Martin Short, *Little Me*	Bernadette Peters, *Annie Get Your Gun* (R)
2000	*Contact* [best score: *Aida,* Elton John (M) and Tim Rice (L)]	Brian Stokes Mitchell, *Kiss Me Kate*	Heather Headley, *Aida*
2001	*The Producers,* Mel Brooks (M&L)	Nathan Lane, *The Producers*	Christine Ebersole, *42nd Street* (R)
2002	*Thoroughly Modern Millie,* [best score: *Urinetown: The Musical,* Mark Hollmann (M); Mark Hollman and Greg Kotis (L)]	John Lithgow, *Sweet Smell of Success*	Sutton Foster, *Thoroughly Modern Millie*
2003	*Hairspray,* Scott Whittman, Marc Shaiman (M&L)	Harvey Fierstein, *Hairspray*	Marissa Jaret Winokur, *Hairspray*

M = music; L = lyrics, R = revival. **Note**: Since 1971 "Musical" and "Score" have been separate categories. However, the winner of the Tony for Best Musical usually wins the award for Best Score, except where otherwise indicated.
Source: Isabelle Stevenson, *The Tony Award* 1989; American Theatre Wing.

The Grammys, 1958–2002

The "Grammys" are officially known as the National Academy of Recording Arts and Sciences Awards. Winners (in almost 70 categories) are selected yearly by the 6,000 or so voting members of the academy. The five award categories listed below have remained fairly constant over the years, although the overall "Best Vocal Performance" awards were phased out in 1968. From that year on, we list "Best Pop Vocal Performance" (male and female), except where indicated.

Year	Record of the year	Album of the year	Song of the year	Best male vocal performance	Best female vocal performance
1958	Domenico Modugno, *Nel Blu Dipinto di Blu (Volare)*	Henry Mancini, *The Music from Peter Gunn*	Domenico Modugno, "Nel Blu Dipinto di Blu *(Volare)*"	Perry Como, *Catch a Falling Star*	Ella Fitzgerald, *Ella Fitzgerald Sings the Irving Berlin Songbook*[2]
1959	Bobby Darin, *Mack the Knife*	Frank Sinatra, *Come Dance with Me*	Jimmy Driftwood, "The Battle of New Orleans"	Frank Sinatra, *Come Dance with Me*	Ella Fitzgerald, *But Not for Me*
1960	Percy Faith, *Theme from a Summer Place*	Bob Newhart, *Button-Down Mind*	Ernest Gold, "Theme from Exodus"	Ray Charles, *Georgia on My Mind*	Ella Fitzgerald, *Mack the Knife*
1961	Henry Mancini, *Moon River*	Judy Garland, *Judy at Carnegie Hall*	Henry Mancini, Johnny Mercer, "Moon River"	Jack Jones, *Lollipops and Roses*	Judy Garland, *Judy at Carnegie Hall*[2]
1962	Tony Bennett, *I Left My Heart in San Francisco*	Vaughn Meader, *The First Family*	Leslie Bricusse, Anthony Newley, "What Kind of Fool Am I?"	Tony Bennett, *I Left My Heart in San Francisco*[2]	Ella Fitzgerald, *Ella Swings Brightly with Nelson Riddle*[2]
1963	Henry Mancini, *The Days of Wine and Roses*	Barbra Streisand, *The Barbra Streisand Album*	Henry Mancini, Johnny Mercer, "The Days of Wine and Roses"	Jack Jones, *Wives and Lovers*	Barbra Streisand, *The Barbra Streisand Album*[2]
1964	Stan Getz, Astrud Gilberto, *The Girl from Ipanema*	Stan Getz, Astrud Gilberto, *Getz/Gilberto*	Jerry Herman, "Hello, Dolly!"	Louis Armstrong, *Hello, Dolly!*	Barbra Streisand, *People*

Year	Record of the year	Album of the year	Song of the year	Best male vocal performance	Best female vocal performance
1965	Herb Alpert & the Tijuana Brass, *A Taste of Honey*	Frank Sinatra, *September of My Years*	Paul Francis Webster, Johnny Mandel, "The Shadow of Your Smile"	Frank Sinatra, *It Was a Very Good Year*	Barbra Streisand, *My Name is Barbra*[2]
1966	Frank Sinatra, *Strangers in the Night*	Frank Sinatra, *A Man and His Music*	John Lennon, Paul McCartney, "Michelle"	Frank Sinatra, *Strangers in the Night*	Eydie Gorme, *If He Walked into My Life*
1967	5th Dimension, *Up, Up and Away*	The Beatles, *Sgt. Pepper's Lonely Hearts Club Band*	Jim Webb, "Up, Up, and Away"	Glen Campbell, *By the Time I Get to Phoenix*	Bobbie Gentry, *Ode to Billie Joe*
1968	Simon & Garfunkel, *Mrs. Robinson*	Glen Campbell, *By the Time I Get to Phoenix*	Bobby Russell, "Little Green Apples"	Jose Feliciano[3], *Light My Fire*	Dionne Warwick[3], *Do You Know the Way to San Jose?*
1969	5th Dimension, *Aquarius/Let the Sunshine In*	Blood, Sweat & Tears, *Blood, Sweat & Tears*	Joe South, "Games People Play"	Harry Nilsson[4], *Everybody's Talkin'*	Peggy Lee[4], *Is That All There Is?*
1970	Simon & Garfunkel, *Mrs. Robinson*	Simon & Garfunkel, *Bridge over Troubled Water*	Paul Simon, "Bridge over Troubled Water"	Ray Stevens[4], *Everything is Beautiful*	Dionne Warwick[4], *I'll Never Fall in Love Again*[2]
1971	Carole King, *It's Too Late*	Carole King, *Tapestry*	Carole King, "You've Got a Friend"	James Taylor[5], *You've Got a Friend*	Carole King[5], *Tapestry*[2]
1972	Roberta Flack, *The First Time Ever I Saw Your Face*	George Harrison, Ravi Shankar, Bob Dylan et al, *Concert for Bangladesh*	Ewan McColl, "The First Time Ever I Saw Your Face"	Harry Nilsson, *Without You*	Helen Reddy, *I Am Woman*
1973	Roberta Flack, *Killing Me Softly with His Song*	Stevie Wonder, *Innervisions*	Norman Gimbel, Charles Fox, "Killing Me Softly with His Song"	Stevie Wonder, *You Are the Sunshine of My Life*	Roberta Flack, *Killing Me Softly with His Song*
1974	Olivia Newton-John, *I Honestly Love You*	Stevie Wonder, *Fulfillingness' First Finale*	Marilyn & Alan Bergman, Marvin Hamlisch, "The Way We Were"	Stevie Wonder, *Fulfillingness' First Finale*[2]	Olivia Newton-John, *I Honestly Love You*
1975	Captain & Tennille, *Love Will Keep Us Together*	Paul Simon, *Still Crazy After All These Years*	Stephen Sondheim, "Send in the Clowns"	Paul Simon, *Still Crazy after All These Years*[2]	Janis Ian, *At Seventeen*
1976	George Benson, *This Masquerade*	Stevie Wonder, *Songs in the Key of Life*	Bruce Johnston, "I Write the Songs"	Stevie Wonder, *Songs in the Key of Life*[2]	Linda Ronstadt, *Hasten Down the Wind*[2]
1977	The Eagles, *Hotel California*	Fleetwood Mac, *Rumours*	Barbra Streisand, Paul Williams, "Evergreen"	James Taylor, *Handy Man*	Barbra Streisand, *Evergreen*
1978	Billy Joel, *Just theWay You Are*	Various artists, *Saturday Night Fever*	Billy Joel, "Just the Way You Are"	Barry Manilow, *Copacabana (At the Copa)*	Anne Murray, *You Needed Me*
1979	The Doobie Brothers, *What a Fool Believes*	Billy Joel, *52nd Street*	Kenny Loggins, Michael McDonald, "What a Fool Believes"	Billy Joel, *52nd Street*[2]	Dionne Warwick, *I'll Never Love This Way Again*
1980	Christopher Cross, *Sailing*	Christopher Cross, *Christopher Cross*	Christopher Cross, "Sailing"	Kenny Loggins, *This Is It*	Bette Midler, *The Rose*
1981	Kim Carnes, *Bette Davis Eyes*	John Lennon/Yoko Ono, *Double Fantasy*	Donna Weiss, Jackie DeShannon, "Bette Davis Eyes"	Al Jarreau, *Breakin' Away*[2]	Lena Horne, *The Lady and Her Music Live on Broadway*[2]
1982	Toto, *Rosanna*	Toto, *Toto IV*	Johnny Christopher, Mark James, Wayne Carson, "Always on My Mind"	Lionel Richie, *Truly*	Melissa Manchester, *You Should Hear How She Talks About You*
1983	Michael Jackson, *Beat It*	Michael Jackson, *Thriller*	Sting, "Every Breath You Take"	Michael Jackson, *Thriller*[2]	Irene Cara, *Flashdance . . . What a Feeling*
1984	Tina Turner, *What's Love Got to Do with It?*	Lionel Richie, *Can't Slow Down*	Graham Lyle, Terry Britten, "What's Love Got to Do with It?"	Phil Collins, *Against All Odds (Take a Look at Me Now)*	Tina Turner, *What's Love Got to Do with It?*
1985	USA for Africa, *We Are the World*	Phil Collins, *No Jacket Required*	Michael Jackson, Lionel Richie, "We Are the World"	Phil Collins, *No Jacket Required*[2]	Whitney Houston, *Saving All My Love for You*

Year	Record of the year	Album of the year	Song of the year	Best male vocal performance	Best female vocal performance
1986	Steve Winwood, *Higher Love*	Paul Simon, *Graceland*	Various artists, "That's What Friends Are For"	Steve Winwood, *Higher Love*	Barbra Streisand, *The Broadway Album*[2]
1987	Paul Simon, *Graceland*	U2, *The Joshua Tree*	Linda Ronstadt, James Ingram, "Somewhere Out There"	Sting, *Bring on the Night*[2]	Whitney Houston, *I Wanna Dance with Somebody (Who Loves Me)*
1988	Bobby McFerrin, *Don't Worry, Be Happy*	George Michael, *Faith*	Bobby McFerrin, "Don't Worry, Be Happy"	Bobby McFerrin, *Don't Worry, Be Happy*	Tracy Chapman, *Fast Car*
1989	Bette Midler, *Wind Beneath My Wings*	Bonnie Rait, *Nick of Time*	Bette Midler, "Wind Beneath My Wings"	Michael Bolton, *How Am I Supposed to Live Without You*	Bonnie Raitt, *Nick of Time*
1990	Phil Collins, *Another Day in Paradise*	Quincy Jones, *Back on the Block*	Julie Gold, "From a Distance"	Roy Orbison, *Oh, Pretty Woman*	Mariah Carey, *Vision of Love*
1991	Natalie Cole, *Unforgettable*	Natalie Cole , *Unforgettable*	Irving Gordon, "Unforgettable"	Michael Bolton , *When a Man Loves a Woman*	Bonnie Raitt, *Something to Talk About*
1992	Eric Clapton, *Tears in Heaven*	Eric Clapton, *Unplugged*	Eric Clapton, "Tears in Heaven"	Eric Clapton, *Tears in Heaven*	k.d. Lang, *Constant Craving*
1993	Whitney Houston, *I Will Always Love You*	Whitney Houston, *The Bodyguard*	Alan Menken and Tim Rice, " A Whole New World" *(Aladdin's Theme)"*	Sting, *If I Ever Lose My Faith in You*	Whitney Houston, *I Will Always Love You*
1994	Sheryl *Crow*, *All I Wanna Do*	Tony Bennett, *MTV Unplugged*	Bruce Springsteen, "Streets of Philadelphia"	Elton John, *Can You Feel the Love Tonight*	Sheryl Crow, *All I Wanna Do*
1995	Seal, *Kiss From a Rose*	Alanis Morissette, *Jagged Little Pill*	Seal, "Kiss From a Rose"	Seal, *Kiss From a Rose*	Annie Lennox, *No More "I Love Yous"*
1996	Eric Clapton, *Change the World*	Celine Dion, *Falling Into You*	Wayne Kirkpatrick and Tommy Sims, "Change the World"	Eric Clapton, *Change the World*	Toni Braxton, *Unbreak My Heart*
1997	Shawn Colvin, *Sunny Came Home*	Bob Dylan, *Time Out of Mind*	Shawn Colvin and John Leventhal, "Sunny Came Home"	Elton John, *Candle in the Wind, 1997*	Sarah McLachlan, *Building a Mystery*
1998	Celine Dion, *My Heart Will Go On*	Lauryn Hill, *The Miseducation of Lauryn Hill*	James Horner and Will Jennings, "My Heart Will Go On"	Eric Clapton, *My Father's Eyes*	Celine Dion, *My Heart Will Go On*
1999	Santana, *Smooth*	Santana, *Supernatural*	Itaal Shur and Rob Thomas, "Smooth"	Sting, *Brand New Day*	Sara McLachlan, *I Will Remember You*
2000	U2, *Beautiful Day*	Steely Dan, *Two Against Nature*	U2 "Beautiful Day"	Sting, *She Walks This Earth*	Macy Gray, *I Try*
2001	U2, *Walk On*	Various artists, *O Brother, Where Art Thou?*	Alicia Keys, "Fallin'"	James Taylor, *Don't Let Me Be Lonely Tonight*	Nelly Furtado, *I'm Like a Bird*
2002	Norah Jones, *Don't Know Why*	Norah Jones, *Come Away With Me*	Norah Jones, "Don't Know Why"	John Mayer, *Your Body is a Wonderland*	Norah Jones, *Don't Know Why*

1. Awarded to the composer, rather than the performer, of the song. 2. Awarded for an album, rather than an individual song. 3. Award given for "Best Contemporary Pop Vocal Performance." 4. Award given for "Best Vocal Performance Contemporary." 5. From 1971 on, all awards are for "Best Pop Vocal Performance." **Source:** National Academy of Recording Arts and Sciences; www.grammy.com.

MTV Video Music Awards, 1984–2002

Each year MTV Networks recognizes outstanding achievement in the field of video music with the MTV Video Music Awards. In addition to those listed below, there are categories for rap, heavy metal and dance videos, as well as achievement in choreography, cinematography, and direction.

Year	Best video	Best male video	Best female video	Best group video	Best new artist
1984	The Cars, *You Might Think*	David Bowie, *China Girl*	Cyndi Lauper, *Girls Just Want to Have Fun*	ZZ Top, *Legs*	Eurythmics, *Sweet Dreams (are Made of This)*
1985	Don Henley, *The Boys of Summer*	Bruce Springsteen, *I'm on Fire*	Tina Turner, *What's Love Got to Do With It?*	USA for Africa, *We Are the World*	til' tuesday, *Voices Carry*
1986	Dire Straits, *Money for Nothing*	Robert Palmer, *Addicted to Love*	Whitney Houston, *How Will I Know?*	Dire Straits, *Money for Nothing*	a-Ha, *Take On Me*

Year	Best video	Best male video	Best female video	Best group video	Best new artist
1987	Peter Gabriel, *Sledgehammer*	Peter Gabriel, *Sledgehammer*	Madonna, *Papa Don't Preach*	Talking Heads, *Wild Wild Life*	Crowded House, *Don't Dream it's Over*
1988	INXS, *Need You Tonight/Mediate*	Prince, *U Got the Look*	Suzanne Vega, *Luka*	INXS, *Need You Tonight/Mediate*	Guns N' Roses, *Welcome to the Jungle*
1989	Neil Young, *This Note's for You*	Elvis Costello, *Veronica*	Paula Abdul, *Straight Up*	Living Color, *Cult of Personality*	Living Color, *Cult of Personality*
1990	Sinead O'Connor, *Nothing Compares to You*	Don Henley, *End of the Innocence*	Sinead O'Connor, *Nothing Compares to You*	B-52s, *Love Shack*	Michael Penn, *No Myth*
1991	R.E.M., *Losing My Religion*	Chris Isaak, *Wicked Game*	Janet Jackson, *Love Will Never Do Without You*	R.E.M., *Losing My Religion*	Jesus Jones, *Right Here, Right Now*
1992	Van Halen, *Right Now*	Eric Clapton, *Tears in Heaven*	Annie Lennox, *Why*	U2, *Even Better Than the Real Thing*	Nirvana, *Smells Like Teen Spirit*
1993	Pearl Jam, *Jeremy*	Lenny Kravitz, *Are You Gonna Go My Way*	k.d. lang, *Constant Craving*	Pearl Jam, *Jeremy*	Stone Temple Pilots, *Plush*
1994	Aerosmith, *Cryin'*	Tom Petty and the Heartbreakers, *Mary Jane's Last Dance*	Janet Jackson, *If*	Aerosmith, *Cryin'*	Counting Crows, *Mr. Jones*
1995	TLC, *Waterfalls*	Tom Petty and the Heartbreakers, *You Don't Know How it Feels*	Madonna, *Take a Bow*	TLC, *Waterfalls*	Hootie & the Blowfish, *Hold My Hand*
1996	Smashing Pumpkins *Tonight, Tonight*	Beck, *Where It's At*	Alanis Morissette, *Ironic*	Foo Fighters, *Big Me*	Alanis Morissette, *Ironic*
1997	Jamiroquai, *Virtual Insanity*	Beck, *Devil's Haircut*	Jewel, *You Were Meant For Me*	No Doubt, *Don't Speak*	Fiona Apple, *Sleep to Dream*
1998	Madonna, *Ray of Light*	Will Smith, *Just the Two of Us*	Madonna, *Ray of Light*	Backstreet Boys, *Everybody (Backstreet's Back)*	Natalie Imbruglia, *Torn*
1999	Lauryn Hill, *Doo-Wop*	Will Smith, *Miami*	Lauryn Hill, *Doo-Wop*	TLC, *No Scrubs*	Eminem, *My Name Is*
2000	Eminem, *The Real Slim Shady*	Eminem, *The Real Slim Shady*	Aaliyah, *Try Again*	Blink-182, *All The Small Things*	Macy Gray, *I Try*
2001	Various artists, *Lady Marmalade*	Moby *South Side*	Eve, *Let Me Blow Ya Mind*	'N SYNC *Pop*	Alicia Keys *Fallin'*
2002	Eminem, *Without Me*	Eminem, *Without Me*	Pink, *Get The Party Started*	No Doubt, *Hey Baby*	Avril Lavigne *Complicated*
2003	Missy Elliott, *Work It*	Justin Timberlake, *Cry Me a River*	Beyonce Knowles, *Crazy in Love*	Coldplay, *The Scientist*	50 Cent, *In Da Club*

Source: Press Department, MTV Networks. **www.mtv.com.**

Bollingen Prize for Poetry, 1949–2003

First awarded annually, and biennially since 1965, the Bollingen Prize for Poetry is offered by Yale University to an American citizen for a distinguished book of poetry, or in recognition of a poet's entire achievement.

Year	Recipient
1949	Wallace Stevens
1950	John Crowe Ransom
1951	Marianne Moore
1952	Archibald MacLeish William Carlos Williams
1953	W. H. Auden
1954	Leonie Adams Louise Bogan
1955	Conrad Aiken
1956	Allen Tate
1957	e.e. cummings
1958	Theodore Roethke
1959	Delmore Schwartz
1960	Ivor Winters
1961	Richard Eberhart John Hall Wheelock
1962	Robert Frost
1965	Horace Gregory
1967	Robert Penn Warren
1969	John Berryman Karl Shapiro
1971	Richard Wilbur Mona Van Duyn
1973	James Merrill
1975	A. R. Ammons
1977	David Ignatow
1979	W. S. Merwin
1981	May Swenson Howard Nemerov
1983	Anthony E. Hecht John Hollander
1985	John Ashbery Fred Chappel
1987	Stanley Kunitz
1989	Edgar Bowers
1991	Laura Riding Jackson Donald Justice
1993	Mark Strand
1995	Kenneth Koch
1997	Gary Snyder
1999	Robert W. Creeley
2001	Louise Glück
2003	Adrienne Rich

Source: Yale University.

The National Medal of Arts, 1985–2002

The National Medal of Arts is the highest award given to artists and arts patrons by the United States Government. It is awarded by the President of the United States to individuals or groups who "...are deserving of special recognition by reason of their outstanding contributions to the excellence, growth, support and availability of the arts in the United States."

1985
Elliott Carter, Jr., composer
Ralph (Waldo) Ellison, writer
Jose Ferrer, actor
Martha Graham, dancer, choreographer
Louise Nevelson, sculptress
Georgia O'Keeffe, painter
Leontyne Price, soprano
Dorothy Buffum Chandler, arts patron
Lincoln Kirstein, arts patron
Paul Mellon, arts patron
Alice Tully, arts patron
Hallmark Cards, Inc., corporate patron

1986
Marian Anderson, opera singer
Frank Capra, film director
Aaron Copland, composer
Willem de Kooning, painter
Agnes de Mille, choreographer
Eva Le Gallienne, actress, author
Alan Lomax, folklorist, scholar
Lewis Mumford, philosopher, critic
Eudora Welty, writer
Dominique de Menil, arts patron
Exxon Corporation, corporate patron
Seymour H. Knox, arts patron

1987
Romare Bearden, painter
Ella Fitzgerald, singer
Howard Nemerov, writer, scholar
Alwin Nikolais, dancer, choreographer
Isamu Noguchi, sculptor
William Schuman, composer
Robert Penn Warren, poet
J. W. Fisher, arts patron
Dr. Armand Hammer, arts patron
Mr. and Mrs. Sydney Lewis, arts patrons

1988
Saul Bellow, writer
Helen Hayes, actress
Gordon Parks, photographer, director
I.M. Pei, architect
Jerome Robbins, dancer, choreographer
Rudolf Serkin, pianist
Virgil Thomson, composer, music critic
Sydney J. Freedberg, art historian
Roger L. Stevens, arts administrator
(Mrs. Vincent) Brooke Astor, arts patron
Francis Goelet, music patron
Obert C. Tanner, arts patron

1989
Leopold Adler, preservationist
Katherine Dunham, dancer/choreographer
Alfred Eisenstaedt, photographer
Martin Friedman, museum director
Leigh Gerdine, arts patron, civic leader
John Birks "Dizzy" Gillespie, trumpeter
Walker Kirtland Hancock, sculptor
Vladimir Horowitz, pianist
Czelaw Milosz, writer
Robert Motherwell, painter
John Updike, writer
Dayton Hudson Corp., corporate patron

1990
George Francis Abbott, actor, director
Hume Cronyn, actor, director
Jessica Tandy, actress
Merce Cunningham, choreographer
Jasper Johns, painter, sculptor
Jacob Lawrence, painter
Riley "B.B." King, blues musician, singer
David Lloyd Kreeger, arts patron
Harris & Carroll Sterling Masterson, patrons
Ian McHarg, landscape architect
Beverly Sills, opera singer, director
Southeastern Bell Corporation, corporate arts patron

1991
Maurice Abravanel, conductor
Roy Acuff, country singer, bandleader
Pietro Belluschi, architect
J. Carter Brown, museum director
Charles "Honi" Coles, tap dancer
John O. Crosby, opera director
Richard Diebenkorn, painter
R. Philip Hanes, Jr., arts patron
Kitty Carlisle Hart, actress, singer, dancer
Pearl Primus, choreographer, anthropologist
Isaac Stern, violinist
Texaco Inc., corporate arts patron

1992
Marilyn Horne, opera singer
James Earl Jones, actor
Allan Houser, sculptor
Minnie Pearl, musical performer
Robert Saudek, television producer
Earl Scruggs, banjo player
Robert Shaw, conductor, choral director
Billy Taylor, jazz pianist
Robert Venturi & Denise S. Brown, architects
Robert Wise, film producer, director
AT&T, corporate arts patron
Lila Wallace-Reader's Digest Fund, patron

1993
Walter and Leonore Annenberg, patrons
Cabell "Cab" Calloway, singer
Ray Charles, singer, musician
Bess Lomax Hawes, folklorist
Stanley Kunitz, poet, educator
Robert Merrill, baritone
Arthur Miller, playwright
Robert Rauschenberg, artist
Lloyd Richards, theatrical director
William Styron, author
Paul Taylor, dancer, choreographer
Billy Wilder, movie director/producer

1994
Harry Belafonte, singer, actor
Dave Brubeck, pianist, composer
Celia Cruz, singer
Dorothy DeLay, violin teacher
Julie Harris, actress
Erick Hawkins, dance choreographer
Gene Kelly, dancer, singer, actor
Pete Seeger, musician
Catherine Filene Shouse, arts patron
Wayne Thiebaud, artist, teacher
Richard Wilbur, poet, teacher, critic
Young Audiences, arts presenter

1995
Licia Albanese, opera singer
Gwendolyn Brooks, poet
B. Gerald and Iris Cantor, arts patrons
Ossie Davis and Ruby Dee, actors
David Diamond, composer
James Ingo Freed, architect
Bob Hope, entertainer
Roy Lichtenstein, painter, sculptor
Arthur Mitchell, dancer, choreographer
William S. Monroe, bluegrass musician
Urban Gateways, arts organization

1996
Edward Albee, playwright
Sarah Caldwell, opera conductor
Harry Callahan, photographer
Zelda Fichandler, theater director
Eduardo "Lalo" Guerrero, musician
Lionel Hampton, musician, bandleader
Bella Lewitzky, dancer, choreographer
Vera List, arts patron
Robert Redford, actor, director
Maurice Sendak, author, illustrator
Stephen Sondheim, composer, lyricist
Boys Choir of Harlem, performing group

1997
Louise Bourgeois, sculptor
Betty Carter, jazz vocalist
Agnes Gund, arts patron
Daniel Urban Kiley, landscape architect
Angela Lansbury, actor
James Levine, opera conductor, pianist
Tito Puente, latin musician
Jason Robards, actor
Edward Villella, dancer, choreographer
Doc Watson, bluegrass musician
MacDowell Colony, artist colony

1998
Jacques d'Amboise, dancer, choreographer
Antoine "Fats" Domino, pianist, singer
Ramblin' Jack Elliott, singer, songwriter
Frank Gehry, architect
Barbara Handman, arts advocate
Agnes Martin, visual artist
Gregory Peck, actor, producer
Roberta Peters, opera singer
Philip Roth, writer
Sara Lee Corporation, corporate patron
Steppenwolf Theatre Company
Gwen Verdon, actress, dancer

1999
Irene Diamond, arts patron
Aretha Franklin, singer
Michael Graves, architect, designer
Odetta, singer, music historian
The Julliard School, arts school
Norman Lear, producer, writer, director
Rosetta LeNoire, actress, producer
Harvey Lichtenstein, arts administrator
Lydia Mendoza, singer
George Segal, sculptor
Maria Tallchief, ballerina

2000
Maya Angelou, poet and writer
Eddy Arnold, country singer
Mikhail Baryshnikov, dancer/director
Benny Carter, jazz musician
Chuck Close, painter
Horton Foote, playwright/screenwriter
Lewis Manilow, arts patron
National Public Radio, Cultural Programming Division, broadcaster
Claes Oldenburg, sculptor
Itzhak Perlman, violinist
Harold Prince, theater director/producer
Barbra Streisand, entertainer/filmmaker

2001
Alvin Ailey Dance Foundation, modern dance company and school
Rudolfo Anaya, writer
Johnny Cash, singer and songwriter
Kirk Douglas, actor and producer
Helen Frankenthaler, painter
Judith Jamison, artistic director, choreographer and dancer
Yo-Yo Ma, cellist
Mike Nichols, director/producer

2002
Florence Knoll Bassett, architect
Trisha Brown, choreographer, dancer
Philippe de Montebello, museum director
Uta Hagen, actress, drama teacher
Lawrence Halprin, architect
Al Hirschfeld, artist, illustrator
George Jones, country music composer, performer
Ming Cho Lee, theater designer
William "Smokey" Robinson, songwriter, musician

The National Book Awards, 1950–2002

The National Book Awards are given annually for outstanding literary works by American citizens. The number of prizes awarded has varied, including categories such as poetry, fiction, biography, science, philosophy, religion, and history.

FICTION

Year	Author, Title
1950	Nelson Algren, *The Man with the Golden Arm*
1951	William Faulkner, *The Collected Stories*
1952	James Jones, *From Here to Eternity*
1953	Ralph Ellison, *Invisible Man*
1954	Saul Bellow, *The Adventures of Augie March*
1955	William Faulkner, *A Fable*
1956	John O'Hara, *Ten North Frederick*
1957	Wright Morris, *Field of Vision*
1958	John Cheever, *The Wapshot Chronicle*
1959	Bernard Malamud, *The Magic Barrel*
1960	Philip Roth, *Goodbye, Columbus*
1961	Conrad Richter, *The Waters of Kronos*
1962	Walker Percy, *The Moviegoer*
1963	J. F. Powers, *Morte d'Urban*
1964	John Updike, *The Centaur*
1965	Saul Bellow, *Herzog*
1966	Katherine Anne Porter, *The Collected Stories*
1967	Bernard Malamud, *The Fixer*
1968	Thornton Wilder, *The Eighth Day*
1969	Jerzy Kosinski, *Steps*
1970	Joyce Carol Oates, *Them*
1971	Saul Bellow, *Mr. Sammler's Planet*
1972	Flannery O'Connor, *The Complete Stories*
1973	John Barth, *Chimera*
1974	Thomas Pynchon, *Gravity's Rainbow*
	Isaac Bashevis Singer, *A Crown of Feathers & Other Stories*
1975	Robert Stone, *Dog Soldiers*
	Thomas Williams, *The Hair of Harold Roux*
1976	William Gaddis, *JR*
1977	Wallace Stegner, *The Spectator Bird*
1978	Mary Lee Settle, *Blood Ties*
1979	Tim O'Brien, *Going After Cacciato*
1980	William Styron, *Sophie's Choice*
1981	Wright Morris, *Plains Song*
1982	John Updike, *Rabbit Is Rich*
1983	Alice Walker, *The Color Purple*
1984	Ellen Gilchrist, *Victory Over Japan*
1985	Don DeLillo, *White Noise*
1986	E. L. Doctorow, *World's Fair*
1987	Larry Heinemann, *Paco's Story*
1988	Pete Dexter, *Paris Trout*
1989	John Casey, *Spartina*
1990	Charles Johnson, *Middle Passage*
1991	Norman Rush, *Mating*
1992	Cormac McCarthy, *All the Pretty Horses*
1993	E. Annie Proulx, *The Shipping News*
1994	William Gaddis, *A Frolic of His Own*
1995	Philip Roth, *Sabbath's Theater*
1996	Andrea Barrett, *Ship Fever and Other Stories*
1997	Charles Frazier, *Cold Mountain*
1998	Alice McDermott, *Charming Billy*
1999	Ha Jin, *Waiting*
2000	Susan Sontag, *In America*
2001	Jonathan Franzen, *The Corrections*
2002	Julia Glass, *Three Junes*

POETRY

Year	Author, Title
1950	William Carlos Williams, *Paterson: Book III* and *Selected Poems*
1951	Wallace Stevens, *The Auroras of Autumn*
1952	Marianne Moore, *Collected Poems*
1953	Archibald MacLeish, *Collected Poems 1917–52*
1954	Conrad Aiken, *Collected Poems*
1955	Wallace Stevens, *The Collected Poems*
1956	W. H. Auden, *The Shield of Achilles*
1957	Richard Wilbur, *Things of this World*
1958	Robert Penn Warren, *Promises: Poems, 1954–56*
1959	Theodore Roethke, *Words for the Wind*
1960	Robert J. Lowell, *Life Studies*
1961	Randall Jarrell, *The Woman at the Washington Zoo*
1962	Alan Dugan, *Poems*
1963	William Stafford, *Traveling Through the Dark*
1964	John Crowe Ransom, *Selected Poems*
1965	Theodore Roethke, *The Far Field*
1966	James Dickey, *Buckdancer's Choice*
1967	James Merrill, *Nights and Days*
1968	Robert Bly, *The Light Around the Body*
1969	John Berryman, *His Toy, His Dream, His Rest*
1970	Elizabeth Bishop, *The Complete Poems*
1971	Mona Van Duyn, *To See, To Take*
1972	Howard Moss, *Selected Poems*
1973	A. R. Ammons, *Collected Poems: 1951–71*
1974	Allen Ginsberg, *The Fall of America: Poems of These States, 1965–71*
	Adrienne Rich, *Diving into the Wreck: Poems, 1971–72*
1975	Marilyn Hacker, *Presentation Piece*
1976	John Ashbery, *Self-Portrait in a Convex Mirror*
1977	Richard Eberhart, *Collected Poems, 1930–1976*
1978	Howard Nemerov, *The Collected Poems*
1979	James Merrill, *Mirabell: Books of Number*
1980	Philip Levine, *Ashes*
1981	Lisel Mueller, *The Need to Hold Still*
1982	William Bronk, *Life Supports*
1983	Galway Kinnell, *Selected Poems*
1984	Charles Wright, *Country Music*
1991	Philip Levine, *What Work Is*
1992	Mary Oliver, *New and Selected Poems*
1993	A. R. Ammons, *Garbage*
1994	James Tate, *Worshipful Company of Fletchers*
1995	Stanley Kunitz, *Passing Through*
1996	Hayden Carruth, *Scrambled Eggs and Whiskey: Poems 1991–1995*
1997	William Meredith, *Effort at Speech: New and Selected Poems*
1998	Gerald Stern, *This Time: New and Selected Poems*
1999	Ai, *New and Selected Poems*
2000	Lucille Clifton, *Blessing the Boats: New and Selected Poems 1988-2000*
2001	Alan Dugan, *Poems Seven: New and Complete Poetry*
2002	Ruth Stone, *In the Next Galaxy*

NONFICTION

Year	Author, Title
1950	Ralph L. Rusk, *Ralph Waldo Emerson*
1951	Newton Arvin, *Herman Melville*
1952	Rachel Carson, *The Sea Around Us*
1953	Bernard De Voto, *Course of Empire*
1954	Bruce Catton, *A Stillness at Appomattox*
1955	Joseph Wood Krutch, *The Measure of Man*
1956	Herbert Kubly, *An American in Italy*
1957	George F. Kennan, *Russia Leaves the War*
1958	Catherine Drinker Bowen, *The Lion and the Throne*
1959	J. Christopher Herold, *Mistress to an Age*
1960	Richard Ellman, *James Joyce*
1961	William L. Shirer, *The Rise and Fall of the Third Reich*
1962	Lewis Mumford, *The City in History*
1963	Leon Edel, *Henry James, vols. 2 and 3*
1964	Aileen Ward, *John Keats: The Making of a Poet*
1965	Louis Fisher, *The Life of Lenin*
1966	Arthur M. Schlesinger Jr., *A Thousand Days: JFK in the White House*
1967	Justin Kaplan, *Mr. Clemens and Mark Twain*
1968	Jonathan Kozol, *Death at an Early Age*
1969	Norman Mailer, *The Armies of the Night*
1970	Lillian Hellman, *An Unfinished Woman, a Memoir*
1971	James MacGregor Burns, *Roosevelt: The Soldier of Freedom*
1972	Joseph P. Lash, *Eleanor and Franklin*
1973	Frances Fitzgerald, *Fire in the Lake: The Vietnamese and the Americans in Vietnam*
1974	Pauline Kael, *Deeper into the Movies*
1975	Richard B. Sewall, *The Life of Emily Dickinson* Lewis Thomas, *The Lives of a Cell*
1976	Paul Fussell, *The Great War and Modern Memory*
1977	Bruno Bettelheim, *The Uses of Enchantment: The Meaning and Importance of Fairy Tales*
1978	Walter Jackson Bate, *Samuel Johnson*
1979	Arthur M. Schlesinger Jr., *Robert Kennedy and His Times*
1980	Tom Wolfe, *The Right Stuff*
1981	Maxine Hong Kingston, *China Men*
1982	Tracy Kidder, *The Soul of a New Machine*
1983	Fox Butterfield, *China: Alive in the Bitter Sea*
1984	Robert V. Remini, *Andrew Jackson and the Course of American Democracy, 1833–45*
1985	J. Anthony Lukas, *Common Ground: A Turbulent Decade in the Lives of Three American Families*
1986	Barry Lopez, *Arctic Dreams*
1987	Richard Rhodes, *The Making of the Atom Bomb*
1988	Neil Sheehan, *A Bright and Shining Lie: John Paul Vann and America in Vietnam*
1989	Thomas L. Friedman, *From Beirut to Jerusalem*
1990	Ron Chernow, *The House of Morgan*
1991	Orlando Patterson, *Freedom*
1992	Paul Monette, *Becoming a Man: Half a Life*
1993	Gore Vidal, *United States: Essays 1952-1992*
1994	Sherwin B. Nuland, *How We Die: Reflections on Life's Final Chapter*
1995	Tina Rosenberg, *The Haunted Land: Facing Europe's Ghosts After Communism*
1996	James Carroll, *An American Requiem: God, My Father and the War That Came Between Us*
1997	Joseph J. Ellis, *American Sphinx: The Character of Thomas Jefferson*
1998	Edward Ball, *Slaves in the Family*
1999	John W. Dower, *Embracing Defeat: Japan in the Wake of World War II*
2000	Nathaniel Philbrick, *In the Heart of the Sea: The Tragedy of the Whaleship Essex*
2001	Andrew Solomon, *The Noonday Demon: An Atlas of Depression*
2002	Robert A. Caro, *Master of the Senate: The Years of Lyndon Johnson*

YOUNG PEOPLE'S LITERATURE

Year	Author, Title
1996	Victor Martinez, *Parrot in the Oven: Mi Vida*
1997	Han Nolan, *Dancing on the Edge*
1998	Louis Sachar, *Holes*
1999	Kimberly Willis Holtt, *When Zachary Beaver Came to Town*
2000	Gloria Whelan, *Homeless Bird*
2001	Virginia Eumer Wollf, *True Believer*
2002	Nancy Farmer, *The House of the Scorpion*

Note: No award was given in poetry from 1985 to 1990. **Source**: National Book Awards, Inc.

The National Book Critics Circle Award, 1975–2002

Selected by a 24-member board of critics (who serve 3-year terms) from around the country; books are often recommended to the board by the more than 500 general members of the Circle.

FICTION

Year	Author, Title
1975	E.L. Doctorow, *Ragtime*
1976	John Gardner, *October Light*
1977	Toni Morrison, *Song of Solomon*
1978	John Cheever, *The Stories of John Cheever*
1979	Thomas Flanagan, *The Year of the French*
1980	Shirley Hazzard, *The Transit of Venus*
1981	John Updike, *Rabbit is Rich*
1982	Stanley Elkin, *George Mills*
1983	William Kennedy, *Ironweed*
1984	Louise Erdrich, *Love Medicine*
1985	Anne Tyler, *The Accidental Tourist*
1986	Reynolds Price, *Kate Vaiden*
1987	Phillip Roth, *The Counterlife*
1988	Bharati Mukherjee, *The Middleman and Other Stories*
1989	E.L. Doctorow, *Billy Bathgate*
1990	John Updike, *Rabbit at Rest*
1991	Jane Smiley, *A Thousand Acres*
1992	Cormac McCarthy, *All the Pretty Horses*
1993	Ernest J. Gaines, *A Lesson Before Dying*
1994	Carol Shields, *The Stone Diaries*
1995	Stanley Elkin[1], *Mrs. Ted Bliss*
1996	Gina Berriault, *Women in Their Beds*
1997	Penelope Fitzgerald, *The Blue Flower*
1998	Alice Munro, *The Love of a Good Woman*
1999	Jonathan Lethem, *Motherless Brooklyn*
2000	Jim Crace, *Being Dead*
2001	W.G. Sebald, *Austerlitz*
2002	Ian McEwan, *Atonement*

GENERAL NONFICTION

Year	Author, Title	Year	Author, Title
1975	R.W.B. Lewis, *Edith Wharton*	1990	Shelby Steele, *The Content of Our Character: A New Vision of Race in America*
1976	Maxine Hong Kingston, *The Woman Warrior: Memoirs of a Girlhood Among Ghosts*	1991	Susan Faludi, *Backlash*
1977	Walter Jackson Bate, *Samuel Johnson*	1992	Norman Maclean, *Young Men and Fire*
1978	Maureen Howard, *Facts of Life*	1993	Alan Lomax, *The Land Where Blues Began*
1979	Telford Taylor, *Munich: The Price of Peace*	1994	Lynn H. Nicholas, *The Rape of Europa: The Fate of Europe's Treasures in the Third Reich and the Second World War*
1980	Ronald Steel, *Walter Lippmann and the American Century*	1995	Jonathan Harr, *A Civil Action*
1981	Stephen Jay Gould, *The Mismeasure of Man*	1996	Jonathan Raban, *Bad Land: An American Romance*
1982	Robert A. Caro, *The Path of Power: The Years of Lyndon Johnson*	1997	Anne Fadiman, *The Spirit Catches You and You Fall Down*
1983	Seymour M. Hersh, *The Price of Power: Kissinger and the Nixon White House*	1998	Philip Gourevitch, *We Wish to Inform You That Tomorrow We Will Be Killed With Our Familes*
1984	Freeman Dyson, *Weapons and Hope*	1999	Jonathan Weiner, *Time, Love, and Memory, A Great Biologist and His Quest for the Origins of Behavior*
1985	J. Anthony Lukas, *Common Ground: A Turbulent Decade in the Lives of Three Americans*	2000	Ted Conover, *Newjack: Guarding Sing Sing*
1986	John W. Dower, *War Without Mercy: Race and Power in the Pacific War*	2001	Nicholson Baker, *Double Fold: Libraries and the Assault on Paper*
1987	Richard Rhodes, *The Making of the Atomic Bomb*	2002	Samantha Power, *A Problem From Hell: America and the Age of Genocide*
1988	Taylor Branch, *Parting the Waters: America in the King Years, 1954–63*		
1989	Michael Dorris, *The Broken Cord*		

BIOGRAPHY/AUTOBIOGRAPHY

Year	Author, Title	Year	Author, Title
1983	Joyce Johnson, *Minor Characters*	1993	Edmund White, *Genet*
1984	Joseph Frank, *Dostoevsky: The Years of Ordeal. 1850–1859*	1994	Mikal Gilmore, *Shot in the Heart*
1985	Leon Edel, *Henry James: A Life*	1995	Robert Polito, *Savage Art: A Biography of Jim Thompson*
1986	Theodore Rosengarten, *Tombee: Portrait of a Cotton Planter*	1996	Frank McCourt, *Angela's Ashes*
1987	Donald R. Howard, *Chaucer: His Life, His Works, His World*	1997	James Tobin, *Ernie Pyle's War: America's Eyewitness to World War II*
1988	Richard Ellman, *Oscar Wilde*	1998	Sylvia Nasar, *A Beautiful Mind*
1989	Geoffrey C. Ward, *A First-Class Temperament: The Emergence of Franklin Roosevelt*	1999	Henry Wiencek, *The Hairstons: An American Family in Black and White*
1990	Robert A. Caro, *Means of Ascent: The Years of Lyndon Johnson, Vol. 2*	2000	Herbert P. Bix, *Hirohito and the Making of Modern Japan*
1991	Philip Roth, *Patrimony*	2001	Adam Sisman, *Boswell's Presumptuous Task: The Making of the Life of Dr. Johnson*
1992	Carol Brightman, *Writing Dangerously: Mary McCarthy and Her World*	2002	Janet Browne, *Charles Darwin: The Power of Place, Vol. II*

CRITICISM

Year	Author, Title	Year	Author, Title
1975	Paul Fussell, *The Great War and Modern Memory*	1988	Clifford Geertz, *Works and Lives: The Anthropologist as Author*
1976	Bruno Bettelheim, *The Uses of Enchantment: The Meaning and Importance of Fairy Tales*	1989	John Clive, *Not by Fact Alone: Essays on the Writing and Reading of History*
1977	Susan Sontag, *On Photography*	1990	Arthur C. Danto, *Encounters and Reflections: Art in the Historical Present*
1978	Meyer Schapiro, *Modern Art: 19th and 20th Centuries, Selected Papers*	1991	Lawrence L. Langer, *Holocaust Testimonies*
1979	Elaine Pagels, *The Gnostic Gospels*	1992	Garry Wills, *Lincoln At Gettysburg: The Words That Remade America*
1980	Helen Vendler, *Part of Nature, Part of Us! Modern American Poets*	1993	John Dizikes, *Opera in America*
1981	Virgil Thompson, *A Virgil Thompson Reader*	1994	Gerald Early, *The Culture of Bruising: Essays on Prizefighting, Literature and Modern American Culture*
1982	Gore Vidal, *The Second American Revolution and Other Essays, 1976–82*	1995	Robert Darnton, *The Forbidden Best-Sellers of Pre-Revolutioary France*
1983	John Updike, *Hugging the Shore*	1996	William Gass, *Finding a Form*
1984	Robert Hass, *Twentieth Century Pleasures: Prose on Poetry*	1997	Mario Vargas Llosa, *Making Waves*
1985	William H. Gass, *Habitations of the Word: Essays*	1998	Gary Giddins, *Visions of Jazz*
1986	Joseph Brodsky, *Less Than One: Selected Essays*	1999	Jorge Luis Borges[1], *Selected Non-Fictions*
1987	Edwin Denby, *Dance Writings*	2000	Cynthia Ozick, *Quarrel & Quandary*
		2001	Martin Amis, *The War Against Cliché: Essays and Reviews, 1971–2000*
		2002	William H. Gass, *Tests of Time*

POETRY

Year	Author, Title
1975	John Ashbery, *Self-Portrait in a Convex Mirror*
1976	Elizabeth Bishop, *Geography III*
1977	Robert Lowell, *Day by Day*
1978	L.E. Sissman, *Hello Darkness: The Collected Poems of L.E. Sissman*
1979	Philip Levine, *Ashes and Seven Years from Somewhere*
1980	Frederick Seidel, *Sunrise*
1981	A.R. Ammons, *A Coast of Trees*
1982	Katha Pollitt, *Antarctic Traveler*
1983	James Merrill, *The Changing Light at Sandover*
1984	Sharon Olds, *The Dead and the Living*
1985	Louise Gluck, *The Triumph of Achilles*
1986	Edward Hirsch, *Wild Gratitude*
1987	C.K. Williams, *Flesh and Blood*
1988	Donald Hall, *The One Day*
1989	Rodney Jones, *Transparent Gestures*
1990	Amy Gerstler, *Bitter Angel*
1991	Albert Goldbarth, *Heaven and Earth*
1992	Hayden Carruth, *Collected Shorter Poems*
1993	Mark Doty, *My Alexandria*
1994	Mark Rudman, *Rider*
1995	William Matthews, *Time & Money*
1996	Robert Hass, *Sun Under Wood*
1997	Charles Wright, *Black Zodiac*
1998	Marie Ponsot, *The Bird Catcher*
1999	Ruth Stone, *Ordinary Words*
2000	Judy Jordan, *Carolina Ghost Woods*
2001	Albert Goldbarth, *Saving Lives*
2002	B.H. Fairchild, *Early Occult Memory Systems of the Lower Midwest*

1. Awarded posthumously. **Source:** The National Book Critics Circle.

The Newbery Medal, 1922–2003

The Newbery Medal, presented by the American Library Association, is awarded annually to the author of the most distinguished contribution to American literature for children published in the United States during the previous year. The award is named in honor of John Newbery (1713–67), the first English publisher of books for children.

Year	Author, Title
1922	Willem Van Loon, *The Story of Mankind*
1923	Hugh Lofting, *The Voyages of Doctor Dolittle*
1924	Charles Hawes, *The Dark Frigate*
1925	Charles Finger, *Tales from Silver Lands*
1926	Arthur Bowie Chrisman, *Shen of the Sea*
1927	Will James, *Smoky, The Cowhorse*
1928	Dhan Gopal Mukerji, *Gayneck, The Story of a Pigeon*
1929	Eric P. Kelly, *The Trumpeter of Krakow*
1930	Rachel Field, *Hitty, Her First Hundred Years*
1931	Elizabeth Coatsworth, *The Cat Who Went to Heaven*
1932	Laura Adams Armer, *Waterless Mountain*
1933	Elizabeth Foreman Lewis, *Young Fu of the Upper Yangtze*
1934	Cornelia Meigs, *Invincible Louisa*
1935	Monica Shannon, *Dobry*
1936	Carol Brink, *Caddie Woodlawn*
1937	Ruth Sawyer, *Roller Skates*
1938	Kate Seredy, *The White Stag*
1939	Elizabeth Enright, *Thimble Summer*
1940	James Daugherty, *Daniel Boone*
1941	Armstrong Sperry, *Call It Courage*
1942	Walter D. Edmonds, *The Matchlock Gun*
1943	Elizabeth Janet Gray, *Adam of the Road*
1944	Esther Forbes, *Johnny Tremain*
1945	Robert Lawson, *Rabbit Hill*
1946	Lois Lenski, *Strawberry Girl*
1947	Carolyn Sherwin Bailey, *Miss Hickory*
1948	William Pène du Bois, *The 21 Balloons*
1949	Marguerite Henry, *King of the Wind*
1950	Marguerite de Angeli, *The Door in the Wall*
1951	Elizabeth Yates, *Amos Fortune, Free Man*
1952	Eleanor Estes, *Ginger Pye*
1953	Ann Nolan Clark, *Secret of the Andes*
1954	Joseph Krumgold, *. . . And Now Miguel*
1955	Meindert DeJong, *The Wheel on the School*
1956	Jean Lee Latham, *Carry On, Mr. Bowditch*
1957	Virginia Sorensen, *Miracles on Maple Hill*
1958	Harold Keith, *Rifles for Watie*
1959	Elizabeth George Speare, *The Witch of Blackbird Pond*
1960	Joseph Krumgold, *Onion John*
1961	Scott O'Dell, *Island of the Blue Dolphins*
1962	Elizabeth George Speare, *The Bronze Bow*
1963	Madeleine L'Engle, *A Wrinkle in Time*
1964	Emily Cheney Neville, *It's Like This, Cat*
1965	Maia Wojciechowska, *Shadow of a Bull*
1966	Elizabeth Borten de Trevino, *I, Juan de Pareja*
1967	Irene Hunt, *Up a Road Slowly*
1968	E.L. Konigsburg, *From the Mixed-up Files of Mrs. Basil E. Frankweiler*
1969	Lloyd Alexander, *The High King*
1970	William H. Armstrong, *Sounder*
1971	Betsy Byars, *Summer of the Swans*
1972	Robert C. O'Brien, *Mrs. Frisby and the Rats of NIMH*
1973	Jean George, *Julie of the Wolves*
1974	Paula Fox, *The Slave Dancer*
1975	Virginia Hamilton, *M.C. Higgins the Great*
1976	Susan Cooper, *The Grey King*
1977	Mildred D. Taylor, *Roll of Thunder, Hear My Cry*
1978	Katherine Paterson, *Bridge to Terabithia*
1979	Ellen Raskin, *The Westing Game*
1980	Joan Blos, *A Gathering of Days: A New England Girl's Journal, 1830–32*
1981	Katherine Paterson, *Jacob Have I Loved*
1982	Nancy Willard, *A Visit to William Blake's Inn: Poems for Innocent and Experienced Travelers*
1983	Cynthia Voigt, *Dicey's Song*
1984	Beverly Cleary, *Dear Mr. Henshaw*
1985	Robin McKinley, *The Hero and the Crown*
1986	Patricia MacLachlan, *Sarah, Plain and Tall*
1987	Sid Fleischman, *The Whipping Boy*

Year	Author, Title
1988	Russell Freedman, *Lincoln: A Photobiography*
1989	Paul Fleischman, *Joyful Noise: Poems for Two Voices*
1990	Lois Lowry, *Number the Stars*
1991	Jerry Spinelli, *Maniac Magee*
1992	Phyllis Reynolds Naylor, *Shiloh*
1993	Cynthia Rylant, *Missing May*
1994	Lois Lowry, *The Giver*
1995	Sharon Creech, *Walk Two Moons*
1996	Karen Cushman, *The Midwife's Apprentice*
1997	Elaine Konigsburg, *The View From Saturday*
1998	Karen Hesse, *Out of the Dust*
1999	Louis Sachar, *Holes*
2000	Christopher Paul Curtis, *Bud, Not Buddy*
2001	Richard Peck, *A Year Down Yonder*
2002	Linda Sue Park, *A Single Shard*
2003	Avi, *Crispin: The Cross of Lead*

Source: American Library Association.

The Caldecott Medal, 1938–2003

The Caldecott Medal, presented by the American Library Association, is awarded annually to the illustrator of the most distinguished picture book for children published in the United States during the preceding year. The award is named in honor of the English illustrator Randolph Caldecott (1846–1886). In cases where only one name is given, the book was written and illustrated by the same person.

Year	Illustrator/Author/Title
1938	Dorothy Lathrop; Helen Dean Fish, *Animals of the Bible*
1939	Thomas Handforth, *Mei Li*
1940	Ingri and Edgar Parin d'Aulaire, *Abraham Lincoln*
1941	Robert Lawson, *They Were Strong and Good*
1942	Robert McCloskey, *Make Way for Ducklings*
1943	Virginia Lee Burton, *The Little House*
1944	Louis Slobodkin; James Thurber, *Many Moons*
1945	Elizabeth Orton Jones; Rachel Jones, *Prayer for a Child*
1946	Maude and Miska Petersham, *The Rooster Crows* (traditional Mother Goose)
1947	Leonard Weisgard; Golden MacDonald, *The Little Island*
1948	Roger Duvoisin; Alvin Tresselt, *White Snow, Bright Snow*
1949	Bert and Elmer Hader, *The Big Snow*
1950	Leo Politi, *Song of the Swallows*
1951	Katherine Milhous, *The Egg Tree*
1952	Nicolas Mordvinoff; Will Mordvinoff, *Finders Keepers*
1953	Lynd Ward, *The Biggest Bear*
1954	Ludwig Bemelmans, *Madeline's Rescue*
1955	Marcia Brown; Charles Perault, *Cinderella, or the Little Glass Slipper*
1956	Feodor Rojankovsky; John Langstaff, *Frog Went A-Courtin'*
1957	Marc Simont; Janice May Udry, *A Tree is Nice*
1958	Robert McCloskey, *Time of Wonder*
1959	Barbara Cooney (adapted from Geoffrey Chaucer), *Chanticleer and the Fox*
1960	Marie Hall Ets and Aurora Labastida, *Nine Days to Christmas*
1961	Nicolas Sidjakov; Ruth Robbins, *Baboushka and the Three Kings*
1962	Marcia Brown, *Once a Mouse . . .*
1963	Ezra Jack Keats, *The Snowy Day*
1964	Maurice Sendak, *Where the Wild Things Are*
1965	Beni Montresor; Beatrice Schenk de Regniers, *May I Bring a Friend?*
1966	Nonny Hogrogian; Sorche Nic Leodhas, *Always Room for One More*
1967	Evaline Ness, *Sam, Bangs & Moonshine*
1968	Ed Emberley; Barbara Emberley, *Drummer Hoff*
1969	Uri Shulevitz; Arthur Ransome, *The Fool of the World and the Flying Ship*
1970	William Steig, *Sylvester and the Magic Pebble*
1971	Gail E. Haley, *A Story—A Story*
1972	Nonny Hogrogian, *One Fine Day*
1973	Blair Lent; retold by Arlene Mosel, *The Funny Little Woman*
1974	Margot Zemach; Harve Zemach, *Duffy and the Devil*
1975	Gerald McDermott, *Arrow to the Sun*
1976	Leo and Diane Dillon; retold by Verna Aardema, *Why Mosquitoes Buzz in People's Ears*
1977	Leo & Diane Dillon; Margaret Musgrove, *Ashanti to Zulu: African Traditions*
1978	Peter Spier, *Noah's Ark*
1979	Paul Goble, *The Girl Who Loved Wild Horses*
1980	Barbara Cooney; Donald Hall, *Ox-Cart Man*
1981	Arnold Lobel, *Fables*
1982	Chris Van Allsburg, *Jumanji*
1983	Marcia Brown, *Shadow*
1984	Martin and Alice Provensen, *The Glorious Flight*
1985	Trina Schart Hyman, *Saint George and the Dragon*
1986	Chris Van Allsburg, *The Polar Express*
1987	Richard Egielski; Arthur Yorinks, *Hey, Al*
1988	John Schoenherr, *Owl Moon*
1989	Stephen Gammell; Karen Ackerman, *Song and Dance Man*
1990	Ed Young, *Lon Po Po: A Red-Riding Hood Story from China*
1991	David Macaulay, *Black and White*
1992	David Wiesner, *Tuesday*
1993	Emily Arnold McCully, *Mirette on the High Wire*
1994	Allen Say, *Grandfather's Journey*
1995	David Diaz; Eve Bunting, *Smoky Night*
1996	Peggy Rathman, *Officer Buckle and Gloria*
1997	David Wisniewski, *Golem*
1998	Paul O. Zelinsky, *Rapunzel*
1999	Mary Azarian; Jacqueline Briggs Martin, *Snowflake Bentley*
2000	Simms Taback, *Joseph Had a Little Overcoat*
2001	David Small, *So You Want to Be President?*
2002	David Wiesner, *The Three Pigs*
2003	Eric Rohmann, *My Friend Rabbit*

Source: American Library Association.

American Institute of Architects Gold Medalists, 1907–2002

The AIA medal recognizes outstanding lifetime achievement in architecture. It is not awarded every year.

Year	Medalist, Country	Year	Medalist, Country
1907	Sir Aston Webb, U.K.	**1964**	Pier Luigi Nervi, Italy
1909	Charles Follen McKim, U.S.	**1966**	Kenzo Tange, Japan
1911	George B. Post, U.S.	**1967**	Wallace K. Harrison, U.S.
1914	Jean Louis Pascal, France	**1968**	Marcel Breuer, U.S.
1922	Victor Laloux, France	**1969**	William Wilson Wurster, U.S.
1923	Henry Bacon, U.S.	**1970**	Richard Buckminster Fuller, U.S.
1925	Bertram Grosvenor Goodhue, U.S.	**1971**	Louis I. Kahn, U.S.
1925	Sir Edwin Landseer Lutyens, London	**1972**	Pietro Belluschi, U.S.
1927	Howard Van Doren Sha w, U.S.	**1977**	Richard Joseph Neutra, U.S.[1]
1929	Milton Bennett Medary, U.S.	**1978**	Philip Johnson, U.S.
1933	Ragnar Ostberg, Stockholm	**1979**	Ieoh Ming Pei, U.S.
1938	Paul Philippe Cret, U.S.	**1981**	Josep Lluis Sert, U.S.
1944	Louis Henri Sullivan, U.S.	**1982**	Romaldo Giurgola, U.S.
1947	Eliel Saarinen, U.S.	**1983**	Nathaniel A. Owings, U.S.
1948	Charles Donagh Maginnis, U.S.	**1985**	William Caudill, U.S.[1]
1949	Frank Lloyd Wright, U.S.	**1986**	Arthur Erickson, Canada
1950	Sir Patrick Abercrombie, U.K.	**1989**	Joseph Esherick, U.S.
1951	Bernard Ralph Maybeck, U.S.	**1990**	Fay Jones, U.S.
1952	Auguste Perret, France	**1991**	Charles Willard Moore, U.S.
1953	William Adams Delano,U.S.	**1992**	Benjamin Thompson, U.S.
1955	Willem Marinus Dudock, Netherlands	**1993**	Kevin Roche, U.S.
1956	Clarence S. Stein, U.S.		Thomas Jefferson, U.S.[1]
1957	Louis Skidmore, U.S.	**1994**	Sir Norman Foster, U.K.
1957	Ralph Walker, U.S.	**1995**	Cesar Pelli, U.S.
1958	John Wellborn Root, U.S.	**1997**	Richard Meier, U.S.
1959	Walter Gropius, U.S.	**1998**	No Award
1960	Ludwig Mies van der Rohe, U.S.	**1999**	Frank Gehry, U.S.
1961	Le Corbusier (Charles Edouard Jeanneret-Gris), France	**2000**	Ricardo Legorreta, Mexico
1962	Eero Saarinen, U.S.[1]	**2001**	Michael Graves, U.S.
1963	Alvar Aalto, Finland	**2002**	Tadao Ando, Japan

1. Awarded posthumously. **Source**: American Institute of Architects.

Pritzker Prize Winners, 1979–2003

Recognized as the most prestigious award in architecture, the Pritzker Prize is given annually by the Hyatt Hotel Foundation, and is named for its chairman, Jay Pritzker. The selection process is modeled after the Nobel Prizes, with secret voting by an international jury.

Year	Medalist, Country	Year	Medalist, Country
1979	Philip Johnson, U.S.	**1992**	Alvaro Siza, Portugal
1980	Luis Barragan, Mexico	**1993**	Fumihiko Maki, Japan
1981	James Stirling, U.K.	**1994**	Christian de Portzamparc, France
1982	Kevin Roche, U.S.	**1995**	Tadao Ando, Japan
1983	I.M. Pei, U.S.	**1996**	Rafael Moneo, Spain
1984	Richard Meier, U.S.	**1997**	Sverre Fehn, Norway
1985	Hans Hollein, Austria	**1998**	Renzo Piano, Italy
1986	Gottfried Boehm, Germany	**1999**	Norman Foster, U.K.
1987	Kenzo Tange, Japan	**2000**	Rem Koolhaas, Netherlands
1988	Gordon Bunshaft, U.S.	**2001**	Jacques Herzog, Switzerland
	Oscar Niemeyer, Brazil		Pierre de Meuron, Switzerland
1989	Frank O. Gehry, U.S.	**2002**	Glenn Murcutt, Australia
1990	Aldo Rossi, Italy	**2003**	Jørn Utzon, Denmark
1991	Robert Venturi, U.S.		

Templeton Prize Winners, 1973–2003

Believing that religion had been unfairly excluded from consideration by the Nobel Prize committee, John Marks Templeton in 1972 established the Templeton Prize for Progress in Religion for "those who seek new and different paths in advancing the world's understanding of God and/or spirituality." Templeton, a Tennessee-born financier, decreed that the monetary value of his prize should always exceed that of the Nobel Prize. The 2003 Prize was worth 700,000 pounds sterling (approx. $1.1 million).

Year Recipient

1973 Mother Teresa, for aiding the children of Calcutta.
1974 Brother Roger, founder of the Taize Community for orphaned children in France.
1975 Sarvepalli Radhakrishnan, Pres. of India (1962-67), and Oxford Prof. of Eastern Religions and Ethics.
1976 Leon Joseph Cardinal Suenens, Archbishop of Malines-Brussles.
1977 Chiara Lubich, founder of Italy's Focolare Movement.
1978 Thomas F. Torrance, Moderator of the Church of Scotland.
1979 Rev. Nikkyo Niwano, founder of Rissho Kosei-Kai (Japan), World Conference on Religion and Peace.
1980 Ralph Wendell Burhoe, founder and editor of *Zygon, Journal of Religion and Science*.
1981 Dame Cecily Saunders, founder of the Hospice and Palliative Care Movement.
1982 The Rev. Billy Graham, televangelist.
1983 Aleksandr Solzhenitsyn, Soviet dissident.
1984 The Rev. Michael Bourdeaux, founder of Keston College in England.
1985 Sir Alister Hardy, founder of the Sir Alister Hardy Research Centre at Oxford.
1986 The Rev. James McCord, Chancellor of the Center of Theological Inquiry in Princeton, N.J.
1987 The Rev. Stanley L. Jaki, professor of Astrophysics at Seton Hall University, N.J.
1988 Dr. Inamullah Khan, founder of Modern World Muslim Congress in Karachi, Pakistan.
1989 The very Rev. Lord MacLeod, founder of the Iona Community; and **Professor Carl Friedrich von Weizsacker**.
1990 Baba Amte, Hindu lawyer, and **L. Charles Birch**, Prof. of Biology at the University of Sydney.
1991 Lord Jakobovits, Chief Rabbi of Great Britain (1967-91).
1992 Rev. Dr. Kyung-Chik Han, founder of Seoul's Young Nak Presbyterian Church.
1993 Charles W. Colson, founder of the Prison Fellowship and Special Counsel to Pres. Nixon.
1994 Michael Novak, writer, professor, diplomat.
1995 Paul Charles William Davies, physicist.
1996 William R. "Bill" Bright, founder of Campus Crusade for Christ.
1997 Pandurang Shastri Athavale, founder of Bhagavad Gita–based self-study known as *swadhyaya*.
1998 Sir Sigmund Sternberg, Hungarian-born British philanthropist.
1999 Ian Barbour, professor emeritus at Carleton College in Northfield, Minn.
2000 Freeman J. Dyson, Princeton Univ. physicist.
2001 Arthur Peacocke, Oxford Univ. physical biochemist and Anglican priest, founder of the Society of Ordained Scientists (S.O.Sc.).
2002 John C. Polkinghorne, mathematical physicist and Anglican priest.
2003 Holmes Rolston III, professor at Colorado State University and a Presbyterian minister; widely known as the "father of environmental ethics."

Source: John Marks Templeton Foundation. **www.templeton.org.**

Fields Medal Winners, 1936–2002

The Fields Medal, named for Canadian mathematician J. D. Fields, is often described as the Nobel Prize for Mathematics. In agreement with Fields's wish that the awards recognize both existing work and the promise of future achievement, the medals are awarded to mathematicians no older than 40. Since 1950, medals have been awarded every four years.

Year	Winners
1936	**Lars Ahlfors,** Harvard Univ.; **Jesse Douglas,** MIT
1950	**Laurent Schwartz,** Universite de Nancy; **Atle Selberg,** Princeton/IAS
1954	**Kunihiko Kodaira,** Princeton Univ.; **Jean-Pierre Serre,** College de France
1958	**Klaus Roth,** Univ. of London; **Rene Thom,** Univ. of Strasbourg
1962	**Lars Hormander,** Univ. of Stockholm; **John Milnor,** Princeton Univ.
1966	**Michael Atiyah,** Oxford Univ.; **Paul Cohen,** Stanford Univ.; **Alex Grothendieck,** Univ. of Paris; **Stephen Smale,** Univ. of California
1970	**Alan Baker,** Cambridge Univ.; **Heisuke Hironaka,** Harvard Univ.; **Serge Novikov,** Moscow Univ.; **John Thompson,** Univ. of Chicago
1974	**Enrico Bombieri,** Univ. of Pisa; **David Mumford,** Harvard Univ.
1978	**Pierre Deligne,** IHES; **Charles Fefferman,** Princeton Univ.; **Gregori Margulis,** Moscow Univ.; **Daniel Quillen,** MIT
1982	**Alain Connes,** IHES; **William Thurston,** Princeton Univ.; **Shing-Tung Yau,** IAS
1986	**Simon Donaldson,** Oxford Univ.; **Gerd Faltings,** Princeton Univ.; **Michael Freedman,** Univ. of California at San Diego
1990	**Vladimir Drinfeld,** Phys.Inst.Kharkov; **Vaughan Jones,** Univ. of California; **Shigefumi Mori,** Univ. of Kyoto; **Edward Witten,** Princeton/IAS
1994	**Pierre-Louis Lions,** Universite de Paris-Dauphine; **Jean-Chrisophe Yoccoz,** Universite de Paris-Sud; **Jean Bourgain,** Princeton/IAS; **Efim Zelmanov,** Univ. of Wisconsin
1998	**Richard E. Borcherds,** Cambridge Univ.; **William T. Gowers,** Cambridge Univ.; **Maxim Kontsevich,** IHES and Rutgers Univ.; **Curtis T. McMullen,** Harvard Univ.
2002	**Laurent Lafforgue,** IHES; **Vladimir Voevodsky,** Princeton/IAS

Note: IAS= Institute of Advanced Study. IHES=Institut des Hautes Etudes Scientifiques.
Source: Fields Institute for Research in Mathematical Sciences. **www.fields.toronto.edu**

Pulitzer Prizes

THE 2003 PULITZER PRIZES

The Pulitzer Prize for Reporting is the oldest prize given in journalism and was first awarded in 1917 together with the Pulitzer Prizes for History and Biography. The changing nature and public perception of reporting can be seen in the various categories established over the years. Originally, the prize recognized excellence irrespective of the journalist's beat; it could be local, national or international, and it could be either reporting for a deadline or investigative reporting carried out over a longer period. In 1929 a Correspondence category was created to distinguish correspondents stationed either in Washington or abroad from local journalists. Separate categories for National and International Reporting were added in 1942, and the Correspondence category was absorbed by these categories in 1947.

Category, Winner, Description

PUBLIC SERVICE
The Boston Globe, for its courageous, comprehensive coverage of sexual abuse by priests, an effort that pierced secrecy, stirred local, national and international reaction and produced changes in the Roman Catholic Church.

BREAKING NEWS REPORTING
Staff, *The Eagle-Tribune (Lawrence, Mass.),* for its detailed, well-crafted stories on the accidental drowning of four boys in the Merrimack River.

INVESTIGATIVE REPORTING
Clifford J. Levy, *The New York Times,* for his vivid, brilliantly written series "Broken Homes" that exposed the abuse of mentally ill adults in state-regulated homes..

EXPLANATORY REPORTING
Staff, *The Wall Street Journal,* for its clear, concise and comprehensive stories that illuminated the roots, significance and impact of corporate scandals in America. .

BEAT REPORTING
Diana K. Sugg, *The Baltimore Sun,* for her absorbing, often poignant stories that illuminated complex medical issues through the lives of people.

NATIONAL REPORTING
Alan Miller and Kevin Sack, *Los Angeles Times,* for their revelatory and moving examination of a military aircraft, nicknamed "The Widow Maker," that was linked to the deaths of 45 pilots.

INTERNATIONAL REPORTING
Kevin Sullivan and Mary Jordan, *The Washington Post,* for their exposure of horrific conditions in Mexico's criminal justice system and how they affect the daily lives of people.

FEATURE WRITING
Sonia Nazario, *Los Angeles Times,* for "Enrique's Journey," her touching, exhaustively reported story of a Honduran boy's perilous search for his mother, who had migrated to the United States.

COMMENTARY
Colbert I. King, *The Washington Post,* for his against-the-grain columns that speak to people in power with ferocity and wisdom.

CRITICISM
Stephen Hunter, *The Washington Post,* for his authoritative film criticism that is both intellectually rewarding and a pleasure to read.

EDITORIAL WRITING
Cornelia Grumman, *Chicago Tribune,* for her powerful, freshly challenging editorials on reform of the death penalty.

EDITORIAL CARTOONING
David Horsey, *Seattle Post-Intelligencer,* for his perceptive cartoons executed with a distinctive style and sense of humor.

BREAKING NEWS PHOTOGRAPHY
Staff, *The Rocky Mountain News,* for its powerful, imaginative coverage of Colorado's raging forest fires.

FEATURE PHOTOGRAPHY
Don Bartletti, *Los Angeles Times,* for his memorable portrayal of how undocumented Central American youths, often facing deadly danger, travel north to the United States.

FICTION
Jeffrey Eugenides, *Middlesex*

DRAMA
Nilo Cruz, *Anna in the Tropics*

HISTORY
Rick Atkinson, *An Army at Dawn: The War in North Africa, 1942–43*

BIOGRAPHY OR AUTOBIOGRAPHY
Robert A. Caro, *Master of the Senate*

POETRY
Paul Muldoon, *Moy Sand and Gravel*

GENERAL NONFICTION
Samantha Power, *"A Problem From Hell": America and the Age of Genocide*

MUSIC
John Adams, *On the Transmigration of Souls*

PULITZER PRIZES IN JOURNALISM

Public Service, 1918–2003

Year Paper, Distinction

1918 ***New York Times,*** Reports, documents, and speeches relating to World War I.
1919 ***Milwaukee Journal,*** Campaign for Americanism.
1920 No award
1921 ***Boston Post,*** Articles exposing operations and leading to arrest of Charles Ponzi.
1922 ***New York World,*** Articles exposing operations of Ku Klux Klan.
1923 ***Memphis Commercial Appeal,*** News and cartoons about Ku Klux Klan.
1924 ***New York World,*** Exposure of Florida peonage evil.
1925 No award
1926 ***Columbus* (Ga.) *Enquirer Sun,*** Articles decrying Ku Klux Klan, dishonest public officials, lynching, and a law barring the teaching of evolution.
1927 ***Canton* (Ohio) *Daily News,*** Articles about collusion between city government and organized crime, resulting in assassination of editor, Don R. Mellett.
1928 ***Indianapolis Times,*** Exposure of political corruption in Indiana.
1929 ***New York Evening World,*** Campaign to correct evil and corruption in administration of justice.
1930 No award
1931 ***Atlanta Constitution,*** Municipal graft exposure leading to convictions.
1932 ***Indianapolis News,*** Campaign to eliminate waste in city management and reduce tax levy.
1933 ***New York World-Telegram,*** Series of articles on veterans' relief, real estate bond evil, and articles exposing lottery schemes of fraternal organizations.
1934 ***Medford* (Oreg.) *Mail Tribune,*** Campaign against unscrupulous politicians in Jackson County, Oreg.
1935 ***Sacramento Bee,*** Campaign against political machine influence in appointment of two federal judges in Nevada.
1936 ***Cedar Rapids Gazette,*** Crusade against corruption and misgovernment in state of Iowa.
1937 ***St. Louis Post-Dispatch,*** Exposure of registration fraud in St. Louis, resulting in invalidation of more than 40,000 fraudulent ballots and appointment of new election board.
1938 ***Bismarck* (N.D.) *Tribune,*** News reports and editorials entitled "Self Help in the Dust Bowl."
1939 ***Miami Daily News,*** Campaign for recall of Miami City Commission.
1940 ***Waterbury* (Conn.) *Republican & American,*** Campaign exposing municipal graft.
1941 ***St. Louis Post-Dispatch,*** Campaign against city smoke nuisance.
1942 ***Los Angeles Times,*** Campaign resulting in clarification and confirmation of freedom of press rights for all American newspapers.
1943 ***Omaha* (Nebr.) *World-Herald,*** Campaign for collection of scrap metal for war effort.
1944 ***New York Times,*** Survey of teaching of American history.
1945 ***Detroit Free Press,*** Investigation of legislative graft and corruption at Lansing, Mich.
1946 ***Scranton* (Pa.) *Times,*** Fifteen-year investigation of judicial practices in U.S. District Court, resulting in removal of the district judge and indictment of many others.
1947 ***Baltimore Sun,*** Series of articles by Howard M. Norton dealing with administration of unemployment compensation in Maryland, resulting in 93 criminal convictions and/or guilty pleas.
1948 ***St. Louis Post-Dispatch,*** Coverage of Centralia, Ill. mine disaster and follow-up articles resulting in reforms in mine safety laws and regulations.
1949 ***Nebraska State Journal,*** Campaign establishing "Nebraska All-Star Primary" that called attention to issues early in presidential campaign.
1950 ***Chicago Daily News* and *St. Louis Post-Dispatch,*** Work of George Thiem and Roy J. Harris, respectively, in exposing presence of 37 Illinois newspapermen on an Illinois state payroll.
1951 ***Miami Herald* and *Brooklyn Eagle,*** Crime reporting during the year.
1952 ***St. Louis Post-Dispatch,*** Investigation and disclosures of corruption in Internal Revenue Bureau and other government departments.
1953 ***Whiteville* (N.C.) *News Reporter* and *Tabor City* (N.C.) *Tribune,*** Campaign against Ku Klux Klan, culminating in the conviction of more than 100 Klansman and an end to terrorism in their communities.
1954 ***Newsday* (Garden City, N.Y.),** Exposé of New York State's racetrack scandals and labor racketeering, leading to imprisonment of racketeer William C. DeKooonig Sr.
1955 ***Columbus* (Ga.) *Ledger* and *Sunday Ledger-Enquirer,*** News coverage and editorial attack on corruption in neighboring Phenix City, leading to destruction of racket-ridden city government.
1956 ***Watsonville* (Calif.) *Register-Pajaronion,*** Exposure of corruption in public office leading to resignation of a district attorney and conviction of one of his associates.
1957 ***Chicago Daily News,*** Exposure of $2.5 million fraud in office of Illinois state auditor, resulting in his conviction.
1958 ***Arkansas Gazette,*** Civic leadership, journalistic responsibility, and moral courage during school integration crisis.
1959 ***Utica Observer-Dispatch* and *Utica Daily Press* (N.Y.),** Campaign against corruption, gambling, and vice.
1960 ***Los Angeles Times,*** Attack on narcotics traffic; reporting of Gene Sherman, which led to opening of negotiations between U.S. and Mexico to halt the flow of illegal drugs into California and other border states.
1961 ***Amarillo* (Tex.) *Globe-Times,*** Exposure of lax law enforcement resulting in punitive action sweeping officials from their posts and creating election of reform slate.
1962 ***Panama City* (Fla.) *News-Herald,*** Three-year campaign against entrenched power and corruption, resulting in reforms in Panama City and Bay County.
1963 ***Chicago Daily News,*** Articles calling public attention to providing birth control services in public health programs.
1964 ***St. Petersburg Times,*** Investigation of illegal activity within Florida Turnpike Authority, resulting in major reorganization of the state's road construction program.

Year	Paper, Distinction

1965 ***Hutchinson*** **(Kans.)** ***News,*** Campaign for more equitable reapportionment of Kansas legislature.
1966 ***Boston Globe,*** Campaign to prevent confirmation of Francis X. Morrissey as federal district judge in Massachusetts.
1967 ***Louisville Courier Journal*** **and** ***Milwaukee Journal,*** Campaign to control Kentucky strip-mining industry; campaign to stiffen water pollution laws in Wisconsin.
1968 ***Riverside*** **(Calif.)** ***Press-Enterprise,*** Exposure of corruption in courts in connection with handling of property and estates of an Indian tribe in California.
1969 ***Los Angeles Times,*** Exposure of wrongdoing within Los Angeles city government commissions, resulting in criminal convictions, resignations, and sweeping reforms.
1970 ***Newsday*** **(Garden City, N.Y.),** Three-year investigation and exposure of secret land deals in eastern Long Island, leading to criminal convictions, resignations, and discharges among public and political officials.
1971 ***Winston-Salem Journal and Sentinel,*** Coverage of environmental problems, as exemplified by campaign to block a strip-mining operation that would have caused irreparable damage to northwest North Carolina hill country.
1972 ***New York Times,*** Publication of Pentagon Papers.
1973 ***Washington Post,*** Investigation of Watergate case.
1974 ***Newsday*** **(Garden City, N.Y.),** Definitive report on illicit narcotics traffic in U.S. and abroad, entitled "The Heroin Trail."
1975 ***Boston Globe,*** Coverage of Boston school desegregation crisis.
1976 ***Anchorage Daily News,*** Disclosures of impact and influence of Teamsters Union on Alaska's economy and politics.
1977 ***Lufkin*** **(Tex.)** ***News,*** Obituary of local men who died in Marine training camp, which grew into investigation of that death and fundamental reform in Marine Corps' recruiting and training practices.
1978 ***Philadelphia Inquirer,*** Series of articles showing abuses of power by Philadelphia police.
1979 ***Point Reyes*** **(Calif.)** ***Light,*** Investigation of Synanon.
1980 ***Gannett News Service,*** Series on financial contributions to Pauline Fathers.
1981 ***Charlotte Observer,*** Series called "Brown Lung: A Case of Deadly Neglect."
1982 ***Detroit News,*** Series by Sydney P. Freedberg and David Ashenfelter exposing U.S. Navy's cover-up of circumstances surrounding deaths of seamen aboard ship and leading to significant reforms in naval procedures.
1983 ***Jackson*** **(Miss.)** ***Clarion-Ledger,*** Campaign supporting Gov. Winter in his legislative battle for reform of Mississippi's public education system.
1984 ***Los Angeles Times,*** In-depth examination of southern California's growing Latino community.
1985 ***Fort Worth Star-Telegram,*** Reporting by Mark J. Thompson revealing that nearly 250 U.S. servicemen died because of a design problem in helicopters built by Bell Helicopter—causing the army to ground almost 600 Huey helicopters pending their modification.
1986 ***Denver Post,*** In-depth study of "missing children," revealing that most are involved in custody disputes or are runaways, and helping to mitigate national fears stirred by exaggerated statistics.
1987 ***Pittsburgh Press,*** Reporting by Andrew Schneider and Matthew Brelis, revealing inadequacy of FAA's medical screening of airline pilots, and leading to reform.
1988 ***Charlotte Observer,*** Revealing misuse of funds by the PTL television ministry, despite massive campaign by PTL to discredit the newspaper.
1989 ***Anchorage Daily News,*** For series revealing high incidence of alcoholism and suicide among Native Alaskans.
1990 ***Philadelphia Inquirer,*** For series by Gilbert M. Gaul disclosing shortcomings in federal regulation of the nation's blood banks.
Washington **(N.C.)** ***Daily News,*** For series by Betty Gray and Mike Voss revealing contamination of the municipal water supply in the town of 9,000 and the eight-year cover-up by elected officials.
1991 ***Des Moines Register,*** For series by Jane Schorer about a rape and its aftermath that reopened debate over whether rape victims should be identified by name.
1992 ***Sacramento Bee,*** For series by Tom Knudson about pollution, overdevelopment and overpopulation along the Sierra Nevada mountain range.
1993 ***Miami Herald,*** For helping readers cope with Hurricane Andrew's devastation and for showing "how lax zoning, inspection and building codes had contributed to the destruction."
1994 ***Akron Beacon Journal,*** For two-part examination of race relations.
1995 ***Virgin Islands Daily News,*** For 10-part series on crime that examined crime on the islands and ultimately led to major reforms.
1996 ***Raleigh News and Observer,*** For stories revealing how agricultural corporations, unfettered by government regulation, were elbowing out small family hog farms and polluting the environment in the process.
1997 ***New Orleans Times-Picayune,*** For series analyzing the environmental, commercial, political, and social conditions that threaten the world's fish supply. It affected changes in Federal fisheries laws.
1998 ***Grand Forks*** **(N.D.)** ***Herald,*** For its coverage of the blizzard, flood, and fire that devastated the city and the newspaper's own plant.
1999 ***Washington Post,*** For its series that identified and analyzed patterns of reckless gunplay by city police officers who had little training or supervision.
2000 ***Washington Post,*** For a series by Katherine Boo about gross mistreatment of mentally retarded patients in District of Columbia group homes. The series prompted the city government to reform the system.
2001 ***The Oregonian*** **(Portland, Ore.),** For a series on inefficiency, misconduct and other systemic problems in the Immigration and Naturalization Service.
2002 ***New York Times,*** for "A Nation Challenged," a special section published regularly after the Sept. 11 terrorist attacks.
2003 ***The Boston Globe,*** for coverage of sexual abuse by priests.

Pulitzer Prizes for National Reporting, 1942–2003

Year	Winner, Newspaper
1942	Louis Stark, *New York Times*
1943	No award
1944	Dewey L. Fleming, *Baltimore Sun*
1945	James B. Reston, *New York Times*
1946	Edward A. Harris, *St. Louis Post-Dispatch*
1947	Edward T. Folliard, *Washington Post*
1948	Bert Andrews, *New York Herald Tribune*
	Nat S. Finney, *Minneapolis Tribune*
1949	C.P. Trussell, *New York Times*
1950	Edwin O. Guthman, *Seattle Times*
1951	No award[1]
1952	Anthony Leviero, *New York Times*
1953	Don Whitehead, Associated Press
1954	Richard Wilson, *Des Moines Register and Tribune*
1955	Anthony Lewis, *Washington Daily News*
1956	Charles L. Bartlett, *Chattanooga Times*
1957	James B. Reston, *New York Times*
1958	Relman Morin, Associated Press
	Clark Mollenhoff, *Des Moines Register and Tribune*
1959	Howard Van Smith, *Miami News*
1960	Vance Trimble , Scripps-Howard Newspaper Alliance
1961	Edward R. Cony, *Wall Street Journal*
1962	Nathan G. Caldwell and Gene S. Graham, *Nashville Tennessean*
1963	Anthony Lewis, *New York Times*
1964	Merriman Smith, United Press International
1965	Louis M. Kohlmeier, *Wall Street Journal*
1966	Haynes Johnson, *Washington Evening Star*
1967	Stanley Penn and Monroe Karmin, *Wall Street Journal*
1968	Howard James, *Christian Science Monitor*
	Nathan K. (Nick) Kotz, *Des Moines Register* and *Minneapolis Tribune*
1969	Robert Cahn, *Christian Science Monitor*
1970	William J. Eaton, *Chicago Daily News*
1971	Lucinda Franks and Thomas Powers, United Press International
1972	Jack Anderson, (Syndicated columnist)
1973	Robert Boyd and Clark Hoyt, Knight Newspapers
1974	James R. Polk, *Washington Star-News*
	Jack White, *Providence Journal and Evening Bulletin*
1975	Donald L. Bartlett and James B. Steele, *Philadelphia Inquirer*
1976	James Risser, *Des Moines Register*
1977	Walter Mears, Associated Press
1978	Gaylord D. Shaw, *Los Angeles Times*
1979	James Risser, *Des Moines Register*
1980	Bette Swenson Orsini and Charles Stafford, *St. Petersburg Times*
1981	John M Crewdson, *New York Times*
1982	Rick Atkinson, *Kansas City Times*
1983	Staff, *Boston Globe*
1984	John Noble Wilford, *New York Times*
1985	Thomas J. Knudson, *Des Moines Register*
1986	Arthur Howe, *Philadelphia Inquirer*
	Craig Flournoy and George Rodrigues, *Dallas Morning News*
1987	Staff, *Miami Herald*
	Staff, *New York Times*
1988	Tim Weiner, *Philadelphia Inquirer*
1989	Donald L. Bartlett and James B. Steele, *Philadelphia Inquirer*
1990	Ross Anderson, Bill Dietrich, Mary Ann Gwinn, and Eric Nalder, *Seattle Times*
1991	Marji Lundstrom and Rochelle Sharpe, Gannet News Service
1992	Jeff Taylor and Mike McGraw, *Kansas City Star*
1993	David Maraniss, *Washington Post*
1994	Eileen Welsome, *Albuquerque Tribune*
1995	Tony Horwitz, *Wall Street Journal*
1996	Alix M. Freedman, *Wall Street Journal*
1997	Staff, *Wall Street Journal*
1998	Russell Carollo and Jeff Nesmith, *Dayton (Ohio) Daily News*
1999	Staff, *New York Times*
2000	Staff, *Wall Street Journal*
2001	Staff, *New York Times*
2002	Staff, *Washington Post*
2003	Alan Miller and Kevin Sack, *Los Angeles Times*

1. The board decided that Arthur Krock of The *New York Times* deserved the prize but he could not accept because he was a board member.

Pulitzer Prizes for International Reporting, 1942–2003

Year	Winner, Newspaper
1942	Lawrence Edmund Allen, Associated Press
1943	Ira Wolfert, North American Newspaper Alliance, Inc.
1944	Daniel DeLuce, Associated Press
1945	Mark S. Watson, *Baltimore Sun*
1946	Homer William Bigart, *New York Herald Tribune*
1947	Eddy Gilmore, Associated Press
1948	Paul W. Ward, *Baltimore Sun*
1949	Price Day, *Baltimore Sun*
1950	Edmund Stevens, *Christian Science Monitor*
1951	Keyes Beech, *Chicago Daily News*
	Homer William Bigart, *New York Herald Tribune*
	Marguerite Higgins, *New York Herald Tribune*
	Relman Morin, Associated Press
	Fred Sparks, *Chicago Daily News*
	Don Whitehead, Associated Press
1952	John M. Hightower, Associated Press
1953	Austin Wehrwien, *Milwaukee Journal*
1954	Jim G. Lucas, Scripps-Howard Newspaper Alliance
1955	Harrison E. Salisbury, *New York Times*
1956	William Randolph Hearst Jr., Kingsbury Smith, and Frank Conniff, International News Service
1957	Russell Jones, United Press
1958	Staff, *New York Times*
1959	Joseph Martin and Philip Santora, *New York Daily News*
1960	A.M. Rosenthal, *New York Times*
1961	Lynn Heinzerling, Associated Press
1962	Walter Lippmann, *New York Herald Tribune Syndicate*
1963	Hal Hendrix, *Miami News*
1964	Malcolm W. Browne, Associated Press
	David Halberstam, *New York Times*
1965	J. A. Livingston, *Philadelphia Bulletin*
1966	Peter Arnett, Associated Press
1967	R. John Hughes, *Christian Science Monitor*
1968	Alfred Friendly, *Washington Post*
1969	William Tuohy, *Los Angeles Times*

Year	Winner, Newspaper
1970	Seymour M. Hersh, Dispatch News Service
1971	Jimmie Lee Hoagland, *Washington Post*
1972	Peter R. Kann, *Wall Street Journal*
1973	Max Frankel, *New York Times*
1974	Hedrick Smith, *New York Times*
1975	William Mullen (reporter), Ovie Carter (photographer), *Chicago Tribune*
1976	Sydney H. Schanberg, *New York Times*
1977	No award
1978	Henry Kamm, *New York Times*
1979	Richard Ben Cramer, *Philadelphia Inquirer*
1980	Joel Brinkley (reporter), Jay Mather (photographer), *Louisville Courier-Journal*
1981	Shirley Christian, *Miami Herald*
1982	John Darnton, *New York Times*
1983	Thomas L. Friedman, *New York Times* Loren Jenkins, *Washington Post*
1984	Karen Elliott House, *Wall Street Journal*
1985	Josh Friedman and Dennis Bell (reporters) and Ozier Muhammad (photographer), *Newsday* (Garden City, N.Y.)
1986	Lewis M. Simons, Pete Carey, and Katherine Ellison, *San Jose Mercury News*
1987	Michael Parks, *Los Angeles Times*
1988	Thomas L. Friedman, *New York Times*
1989	Glenn Frankel, *Washington Post* Bill Keller, *New York Times*
1990	Nicholas D. Kristof and Sheryl WuDunn, *New York Times*
1991	Caryle Murphy, *Washington Post* Serge Schmemann, *New York Times*
1992	Patrick J. Sloyan, *Newsday* (Garden City, N.Y.)
1993	John F. Burns, *New York Times* Roy Gutman, *Newsday* (Garden City, N.Y.)
1994	Team of reporters, *Dallas Morning News*
1995	Mark Fritz, Associated Press
1996	David Rohde, *Christian Science Monitor*
1997	John F. Burns, *New York Times*
1998	Staff, *New York Times*
1999	Staff, *Wall Street Journal*
2000	Mark Schoofs, *The Village Voice* (N.Y. City)
2001	Ian Johnson, *Wall Street Journal* Paul Salopek, *Chicago Tribune*
2002	Barry Bearak, *New York Times*
2003	Kevin Sullivan and Mary Jordan, *The Washington Post*

Pulitzer Prizes for Editorial Writing, 1917–2003

Year	Winner, Newspaper
1917	*Lusitania* editorial article, *New York Tribune*
1918	War editorials and articles, *Louisville Courier Journal*
1919	No award
1920	Harvey E. Newbranch, *Evening World Herald*
1921	No award
1922	Frank M. O'Brien, *New York Herald*
1923	William Allen White, *Emporia (Kans.) Gazette*
1924[1]	Coolidge editorial, *Boston Herald*
1925	"Plight of the South" editorial, *Charleston* (S.C.) *News and Courier*
1926	Edward M. Kingsbury, *New York Times*
1927	F. Lauriston Bullard, *Boston Herald*
1928	Grover Cleveland Hall, *Montgomery Advertiser*
1929	Louis Isaac Jaffe, *Norfolk Virginian-Pilot*
1930	No award
1931	Charles S. Ryckman, *Fremont* (Nebr.) *Tribune*
1932	No award
1933	series of editorials, *Kansas City Star*
1934	E.P. Chase, *Atlantic* (Iowa) *News-Telegraph*
1935	No award
1936	Felix Morley, *Washington Post* George B. Parker, Scripps-Howard Newspapers
1937	John W. Owens, *Baltimore Sun*
1938	William Wesley Waymack, *Des Moines Register and Tribune*
1939	Ronald G. Callvert, *Portland Oregonian*
1940	Bart Howard, *St. Louis Post-Dispatch*
1941	Reuben Maury, *New York Daily News*
1942	Geoffrey Parsons, *New York Herald Tribune*
1943	Forrest W. Seymour, *Des Moines Register and Tribune*
1944	Henry J. Haskell, *Kansas City Star*
1945	George W. Potter, *Providence Journal-Bulletin*
1946	Hodding Carter, *Delta Democrat-Times* (Greenville, Miss.)
1947	William H. Grimes, *Wall Street Journal*
1948	Virginius Dabney, *Richmond Times-Dispatch*
1949	John H. Crider, *Boston Herald* Herbert Elliston, *Washington Post*
1950	Carl M. Saunders, *Jackson* (Mich.) *Citizen Patriot*
1951	William Harry Fitzpatrick, *New Orleans States*
1952	Louis LaCoss, *St. Louis Globe Democrat*
1953	Vermont Connecticut Royster, *Wall Street Journal*
1954	Don Murray, *Boston Herald*
1955	Royce Howes, *Detroit Free Press*
1956	Lauren K. Soth, *Des Moines Register and Tribune*
1957	Buford Boone, *Tuscaloosa News*
1958	Harry S. Ashmore, *Arkansas Gazette*
1959	Ralph McGill, *Atlanta Constitution*
1960	Lenoir Chambers, *Norfolk Virginian-Pilot*
1961	William J. Dorvillier, *San Juan* (Puerto Rico) *Star*
1962	Thomas M. Storke, *Santa Barbara* (Calif.) *News Press*
1963	Ira B. Harkey Jr., *Pascagoula* (Miss.) *U. Chronicle*
1964	Hazel Brannon Smith, *Lexington* (Miss.) *Advertiser*
1965	John R. Harrison, *Gainesville* (Fla.) *Daily Sun*
1966	Robert Lasch, *St. Louis Post-Dispatch*
1967	Eugene Patterson, *Atlanta Constitution*
1968	John S. Knight, *Knight Newspapers*
1969	Paul Greenberg, *Pine Bluff* (Ark.) *Commercial*
1970	Philip L. Geyelin, *Washington Post*
1971	Horance G. Davis Jr., *Gainesville* (Fla.) *Daily Sun*
1972	John Strohmeyer, *Bethlehem* (Pa.) *Globe-Times*
1973	Roger B. Linscott, *Berkshire Eagle* (Pittsfield, Mass.)
1974	F. Gilman Spencer, *Trentonian* (Trenton, N.J.)
1975	John D. Maurice, *Charleston* (W.V.) *Daily Mail*
1976	Philip P. Kerby, *Los Angeles Times*
1977	Warren L. Lerude, Foster Church and Norman F. Cardoza, *Reno Evening Gazette and Nevada State Journal*
1978	Meg Greenfield, *Washington Post*
1979	Edwin M. Yoder Jr., *Washington Star*

Year	Winner, Newspaper
1980	Robert L. Bartley, *Wall Street Journal*
1981	No award
1982	Jack Rosenthal, *New York Times*
1983	Editorial Board, *Miami Herald*
1984	Albert Scardino, *Georgia Gazette*
1985	Richard Aregood, *Philadelphia Daily News*
1986	Jack Fuller, *Chicago Tribune*
1987	Jonathan Freedman, *San Diego Tribune*
1988	Jane Healy, *Orlando Sentinel*
1989	Lois Wille, *Chicago Tribune*
1990	Thomas J. Hylton, *Pottstown* (Pa.) *Mercury*
1991	Ron Casey, Harold Jackson, and Joey Kennedy, *Birmingham News*
1992	Maria Henson, *Lexington Herald-Leader*
1993	No award
1994	R. Bruce Dold, *Chicago Tribune*
1995	Jeffrey Good, *St. Petersburg Times*
1996	Robert B. Semple, Jr., *New York Times*
1997	Michael G. Gartner, *Daily Tribune* (Ames, Iowa)
1998	Bernard L. Stein, *Riverdale* (N.Y.) *Press*
1999	Editorial Board, *N.Y. Daily News*
2000	John C. Bersia, *Orlando Sentinel*
2001	David Moats, *Rutland* (Vt.) *Herald*
2002	Alex Raksin and Bob Sipchen, *Los Angeles Times*
2003	Cornelia Grumman, *Chicago Tribune*

1. A special prize was awarded to the widow of the late Frank I. Cobb of *The New York World* in recognition of his lifetime of editorial writing and service.

Pulitzer Prizes for Editorial Cartooning, 1922–2003

Year	Winner, Newspaper
1922	Rollin Kirby, *New York World*
1923	No award
1924	Jay Norwood Darling, *Des Moines Register and Tribune*
1925	Rollin Kirby, *New York World*
1926	Daniel R. Fitzpatrick, *St. Louis Post-Dispatch*
1927	Nelson Harding, *Brooklyn Daily Eagle*
1928	Nelson Harding, *Brooklyn Daily Eagle*
1929	Rollin Kirby, *New York World*
1930	Charles R. Macauley, *Brooklyn Daily Eagle*
1931	Edmund Duffy, *Baltimore Sun*
1932	John T. McCutcheon, *Chicago Tribune*
1933	H.M. Talburt, *Washington Daily News*
1934	Edmund Duffy, *Baltimore Sun*
1935	Ross A. Lewis, *Milwaukee Journal*
1936	No award
1937	C.D. Batchelor, *New York Daily News*
1938	Vaughn Shoemaker , *Chicago Daily News*
1939	Charles G. Werner, *Daily Oklahoman*
1940	Edmund Duffy, *Baltimore Sun*
1941	Jacob Burck, *Chicago Times*
1942	Herbert L. Block (Herblock), NEA Service
1943	Jay Norwood Darling, *Des Moines Register and Tribune*
1944	Clifford K. Berryman, *Washington Evening Star*
1945	Sergeant Bill Mauldin, United Feature Syndicate, Inc
1946	Bruce Alexander Russell, *Los Angeles Times*
1947	Vaughn Shoemaker , *Chicago Daily News*
1948	Reuben L. Goldberg, *New York Sun*
1949	Lute Pease, *Newark Evening News*
1950	James T. Berryman, *Washington Evening Star*
1951	Reg Manning, *Arizona Republic*
1952	Fred L. Packer, *New York Mirror*
1953	Edward D. Kuekes, *Cleveland Plain Dealer*
1954	Herbert L. Block (Herblock), *Washington Post & Times Herald*
1955	Daniel R. Fitzpatrick, *St. Louis Post-Dispatch*
1956	Robert York, *Lousiville Times*
1957	Tom Little, *Nashville Tennessean*
1958	Bruce M. Shanks, *Buffalo Evening News*
1959	Bill Mauldin, *St. Louis Post-Dispatch*
1960	No award
1961	Carey Orr, *Chicago Tribune*
1962	Edmund S. Valtman, *Hartford Times*
1963	Frank Miller, *Des Moines Register*
1964	Paul Conrad, *Denver Post*
1965	No award
1966	Don Wright, *Miami News*
1967	Patrick Oliphant, *Denver Post*
1968	Eugene Gray Payne, *Charlotte Observer*
1969	John Fischettii, *Chicago Daily News*
1970	Thomas F. Darcy, *Newsday* (Garden City, N.Y.)
1971	Paul Conrad, *Los Angeles Times*
1972	Jeffrey K. MacNelly, *Richmond News-Leader*
1973	No award
1974	Paul Szep, *Boston Globe*
1975	Garry Trudeau, Universal Press Syndicate
1976	Tony Auth, *Philadelphia Inquirer*
1977	Paul Szep, *Boston Globe*
1978	Jeffrey K. MacNelly, *Richmond News-Leader*
1979	Herbert L. Block (Herblock), *Washington Post*
1980	Don Wright, *Miami News*
1981	Mike Peters, *Dayton* (Ohio) *Daily News*
1982	Ben Sargent, *Austin* (Tex.) *American-Statesman*
1983	Richard Locher, *Chicago Tribune*
1984	Paul Conrad, *Los Angeles Times*
1985	Jeff MacNelly , *Chicago Tribune*
1986	Jules Feiffer, *Village Voice* (New York City)
1987	Berke Breathed, Washington Post Writers Group
1988	Doug Marlette, *Atlanta Constitution* and *Charlotte Observer*
1989	Jack Higgins, *Chicago Sun-Times*
1990	Tom Toles, *Buffalo News*
1991	Jim Borgman, *Cincinnati Enquirer*
1992	Signe Wilkinson, *Philadelphia Daily News*
1993	Stephen R. Benson, *Arizona Republic*
1994	Michael P. Ramirez, *Commercial Appeal* (Memphis)
1995	Mike Luckovich, *Atlanta Constitution*
1996	Jim Morin, *Miami Herald*
1997	Walt Handelsman, *New Orleans Times-Picayune*
1998	Stephen P. Breen, *Asbury Park* (N.J.) *Press*
1999	David Horsey, *Seattle Post-Intelligencer*
2000	Joel Pett, *Lexington Herald-Leader*
2001	Ann Telnaes, *Los Angeles Times Syndicate*
2002	*Clay Bennett, Christian Science Monitor*
2003	David Horsey, *Seattle Post-Intelligencer*

Pulitzer Prizes for Photography

PHOTOGRAPHY, 1942–67

Year	Winner, Newspaper
1942	Milton Brooks, *Detroit News*
1943	Frank Noel, *Associated Press*
1944	Frank Filan, *Associated Press*
	Earle L. Bunker, *World-Herald* (Omaha, Neb.)
1945	Joe Rosenthal, *Associated Press*
1946	No award
1947	Arnold Hardy, Amateur; photo distributed by Associated Press
1948	Frank Cushing, *Boston Traveler*
1949	Nathaniel Fein, *New York Herald Tribune*
1950	Bill Crouch, *Oakland Tribune*
1951	Max Desfor, *Associated Press*
1952	John Robinson and Don Ultang, *Des Moines Register and Tribune*
1953	William M. Gallagher, *Flint* (Mich.) *Journal*
1954	Mrs. Walter M. Schau, Amateur; photo published by *Akron Beacon Journal*
1955	John L. Gaunt Jr., *Los Angeles Times*
1956	Photography staff, *New York Daily News*
1957	Harry A. Trask, *Boston Traveler*
1958	William C. Beall, *Washington Daily News*
1959	William Seaman, *Minneapolis Star*
1960	Andrew Lopez, United Press International
1961	Yasushi Nago, *Manichi* (Tokyo); photo distributed by United Press International
1962	Paul Vathis, Associated Press
1963	Hector Rondon, *La Republica* (Caracas, Venezuela); photo distributed by Associated Press
1964	Robert H. Jackson, *Dallas Times-Herald*
1965	Horst Faas, Associated Press
1966	Kyoichi Sawada, United Press International
1967	Jack R. Thornell, Associated Press

SPOT NEWS PHOTOGRAPHY: 1968–1999

1968	Rocco Morabito, *Jacksonville Journal*
1969	Edward T. Adams, Associated Press
1970	Steve Starr, Associated Press
1971	John Paul Filo, *Valley Daily News* and *Daily Dispatch,* (New Kensington, Pa.)
1972	Horst Faas and Michael Laurent, Associated Press
1973	Hyunh Cong Ut, Associated Press
1974	Anthony K. Roberts, freelancer , Beverly Hills, Calif.
1975	Gerald H. Gay, *Seattle Times*
1976	Stanley Forman, *Boston Herald American*
1977	Neal Ulevich, Associated Press
	Stanley Forman, *Boston Herald American*
1978	John H. Blair, United Press International
1979	Thomas J. Kelly III, *Pottstown* (Pa.) *Mercury*
1980	Unnamed photographer, United Press Int'l
1981	Larry C. Price, *Fort Worth Star-Telegram*
1982	Ron Edmonds, Associated Press
1983	Bill Foley, Associated Press
1984	Stan Grossfeld, *Boston Globe*
1985	Photography Staff, *Register* (Santa Ana, Calif.)
1986	Carol Guzy and Michael duCille, *Miami Herald*
1987	Kim Komenich, *San Francisco Examiner*
1988	Scott Shaw, *Odessa* (Tex.) *American*
1989	Ron Olshwanger, freelancer, *St. Louis Post-Dispatch*
1990	Photography Staff, *Oakland Tribune*
1991	Greg Marinovich, Associated Press
1992	Photography Staff, Associated Press
1993	William Snyder and Ken Geiger, *Dallas Morning News*
1994	Paul Watson, *Toronto Star*
1995	Carol Guzy, *Washington Post*
1996	Charles Porter 4th, freelancer, Associated Press
1997	Annie Wells, *Press Democrat* (Santa Rosa, Calif.)
1998	Martha Rial, *Pittsburgh Post-Gazette*
1999	John McConnico, Associated Press

BREAKING NEWS PHOTOGRAPHY: 2000-2003

2000	Photography Staff, *Rocky Mountain News*
2001	Alan Diaz, Associated Press
2002	Staff, *New York Times*
2003	Staff, *The Rocky Mountain News*

FEATURE PHOTOGRAPHY: 1968–2003

1968	Toshio Sakai, United Press International
1969	Moneta Sleet Jr., *Ebony* Magazine
1970	Dallas Kinney, *Palm Beach Post* (West Palm Beach, Fla.)
1971	Jack Dykinga, *Chicago Sun-Times*
1972	Dave Kennerly, United Press International
1973	Brian Lanker, *Topeka Capital-Journal*
1974	Slava Veder, Associated Press
1975	Matthew Lewis, *Washington Post*
1976	Photography Staff, *Louisville Courier-Journal and Times*
1977	Robin Hood, *Chattanooga News-Free Press*
1978	J. Ross Baughman, Associated Press
1979	Photography Staff, *Boston Herald American*
1980	Erwin H. Hagler, *Dallas Times Herald*
1981	Taro M. Yamasaki, *Detroit Free Press*
1982	John H. White, *Chicago Sun-Times*
1983	James B. Dickman, *Dallas Times Herald*
1984	Anthony Suau, *Denver Post*
1985	Stan Grossfeld, *Boston Globe*
	Larry C. Price, *Philadelphia Inquirer*
1986	Tom Gralish, *Philadelphia Inquirer*
1987	David Peterson, *Des Moines Register*
1988	Michael duCille, *Miami Herald*
1989	Manny Crisostomo, *Detroit Free Press*
1990	David C. Turnley, *Detroit Free Press*
1991	William Snyder, *Dallas Morning News*
1992	John Kaplan, *Pittsburgh Post-Gazette,* Block Newspapers
1993	Staff, Associated Press
1994	Kevin Carter, freelancer, *New York Times*
1995	Staff, Associated Press
1996	Stephanie Welsh, freelancer, Newhouse News Service
1997	Alexander Zemlianichenko, Associated Press
1998	Clarence Williams, *Los Angeles Times*
1999	Susan Walsh, Associated Press
2000	Carol Guzy, Michael S. Williamson, and Lucian Perkins, *Washington Post*
2001	Matt Rainey, *Star-Ledger* (N.J.)
2002	Staff, *New York Times*
2003	Don Bartletti, *Los Angeles Times*

Pulitzer Prizes for Commentary, 1970–2003

Year	Winner, Newspaper	Year	Winner, Newspaper
1970	Marquis W. Childs, *St. Louis Post-Dispatch*	1986	Jimmy Breslin, *New York Daily News*
1971	William A. Caldwell, *The Record* (Hackensack, N.J.)	1987	Charles Krauthammer, *Washington Post*
1972	Mike Royko, *Chicago Daily News*	1988	Dave Barry, *Miami Herald*
1973	David S. Broder, *Washington Post*	1989	Clarence Page, *Chicago Tribune*
1974	Edwin A. Roberts Jr., *National Observer*	1990	Jim Murray, *Los Angeles Times*
1975	Mary McGrory, *Washington Star*	1991	Jim Hoagland, *Washington Post*
1976	Walter (Red) Smith, *New York Times*	1992	Anna Quindlen, *New York Times*
1977	George F. Will, Washington Post Writers Group	1993	Liz Balmaseda, *Miami Herald*
1978	William Safire, *New York Times*	1994	William Raspberry, *Washington Post*
1979	Russell Baker, *New York Times*	1995	Jim Dwyer, *New York Newsday*
1980	Ellen H. Goodman, *Boston Globe*	1996	E.R. Shipp, *New York Daily News*
1981	Dave Anderson, *New York Times*	1997	Eileen McNamara, *Boston Globe*
1982	Art Buchwald, *Los Angeles Times* Syndicate	1998	Mike McAlary, *New York Daily News*
1983	Claude Sitton, *Raleigh* (N.C.) *News & Observer*	1999	Maureen Dowd, *New York Times*
1984	Vermont Royster, *Wall Street Journal*	2000	Paul A. Gigot, *Wall Street Journal*
1985	Murray Kempton, *Newsday* (Garden City, N.Y.)	2001	Dorothy Rabinowitz, *Wall Street Journal*
		2002	Thomas Friedman, *New York Times*
		2003	Colbert I. King, *The Washington Post*

Pulitzer Prizes for Criticism, 1970–2003

Year	Winner, Newspaper	Year	Winner, Newspaper
1970	Ada Louise Huxtable, *New York Times*	1988	Tom Shales, *Washington Post*
1971	Harold C. Schonberg, *New York Times*	1989	Michael Skube, *Raleigh (N.C.) News and Observer*
1972	Frank Peters, *St. Louis Post-Dispatch*	1990	Allan Temko, *San Francisco Chronicle*
1973	Ronald Powers, *Chicago Sun-Times*	1991	David Shaw, *Los Angeles Times*
1974	Emily Genauer, *Newsday* Syndicate	1992	No award
1975	Roger Ebert, *Chicago Sun-Times*	1993	Michael Dirda, *Washington Post*
1976	Alan M. Kriegsman, *Washington Post*	1994	Lloyd Schwartz, *Boston Phoenix*
1977	William McPherson, *Washington Post*	1995	Margo Jefferson, *New York Times*
1978	Walter Kerr, *New York Times*	1996	Robert Campbell, *Boston Globe*
1979	Paul Gapp, *Chicago Tribune*	1997	Tim Page, *Washington Post*
1980	William A. Henry III, *Boston Globe*	1998	Michiko Kakutani, *New York Times*
1981	Jonathan Yardley, *Washington Star*	1999	Blair Kamin, *Chicago Tribune*
1982	Martin Bernheimer, *Los Angeles Times*	2000	Henry Allen, *Washington Post*
1983	Manuela Hoelterhoff, *Wall Street Journal*	2001	Gail Caldwell, *Boston Globe*
1984	Paul Goldberger, *New York Times*	2002	Justin Davidson, *Newsday* (Long Island, N.Y.)
1985	Howard Rosenberg, *Los Angeles Times*	2003	Stephen Hunter, *The Washington Post*
1986	Donal Henahan, *New York Times*		
1987	Richard Eder, *Los Angeles Times*		

Pulitzer Prizes for Feature Writing, 1979–2003

Year	Winner, Newspaper	Year	Winner, Newspaper
1979	Jon D. Franklin, *Baltimore Evening Sun*	1991	Sheryl James, *St. Petersburg Times*
1980	Madeline Blais, *Miami Herald*	1992	Howell Raines, *New York Times*
1981	Teresa Carpenter, *Village Voice* (New York)	1993	George Lardner, Jr., *Washington Post*
1982	Saul Pett, Associated Press	1994	Isabel Wilkerson, *New York Times*
1983	Nan Robertson, *New York Times*	1995	Ron Suskind, *Wall Street Journal*
1984	Peter Mark Rinearson, *Seattle Times*	1996	Rick Bragg, *New York Times*
1985	Alice Steinbach, *Baltimore Sun*	1997	Lisa Pollak, *Baltimore Sun*
1986	John Camp, *St. Paul Pioneer Press Dispatch*	1998	Thomas French, *St. Petersburg* (Fla.) *Times*
1987	Steve Twomey, *Philadelphia Inquirer*	1999	Angelo B. Henderson, *Wall Street Journal*
1988	Jacqui Banaszynski, *St. Paul Pioneer Press Dispatch*	2000	J.R. Moehringer, *Los Angeles Times*
1989	David Zucchino, *Philadelphia Inquirer*	2001	Tom Hallman Jr., *Oregonian* (Portland, Ore.)
1990	Dave Curtin, *Colorado Springs Gazette Telegram*	2002	Barry Siegel, *Los Angeles Times*
		2003	Sonia Nazario, *Los Angeles Times*

Pulitzer Prizes for Beat Reporting, 1991–2003

Year	Winner, Newspaper
1991	Natalie Anger, *New York Times*
1992	Deborah Blum, *Sacramento* (Calif.) *Bee*
1993	Paul Ingrassia and Joseph B. White, *Wall Street Journal*
1994	Eric Freedman and Jim Mitzelfeld, *Detroit News*
1995	David Shribman, *Boston Globe*
1996	Bob Keeler, *Newsday*
1997	Byron Acohido, *Seattle Times*
1998	Linda Greenhouse, *New York Times*
1999	Chuck Philips and Michael A. Hiltzik, *Los Angeles Times*
2000	George Dohrmann, *St. Paul Pioneer Press*
2001	David Cay Johnston, *New York Times*
2002	Gretchen Morgenson, *New York Times*
2003	Diane K. Sugg, *The Baltimore Sun*

Pulitzer Prizes for Explanatory Reporting, 1985–2003

Year	Winner, Newspaper
1985	Jon Franklin, *Baltimore Evening Sun*
1986	Staff, *New York Times*
1987	Jeff Lyon and Peter Gorner, *Chicago Tribune*
1988	Daniel Hertzberg and James B. Stewart, *Wall Street Journal*
1989	David Hanners, William Snyder, and Karen Blessen, *Dallas Morning News*
1990	David A. Vise and Steve Coll, *Washington Post*
1991	Susan C. Faludi, *Wall Street Journal*
1992	Robert S. Capers and Eric Lipton, *Hartford* (Conn.) *Courant*
1993	Mike Toner, *Atlanta Journal-Constitution*
1994	Ronald Kotulak, *Chicago Tribune*
1995	Leon Dash and Lucian Perkins, *Washington Post*
1996	Laurie Garrett, *Newsday*
1997	Michael Vitez, April Saul, and Ron Cortes, *Philadelphia Inquirer*
1998	Paul Salopek, *Chicago Tribune*
1999	Richard Read, *Oregonian*
2000	Eric Newhouse, *Great Falls* (Mont.) *Tribune*
2001	Staff, *Chicago Tribune*
2002	Staff, *New York Times*
2003	Staff, *The Wall Street Journal*

Note: From 1985 to 1997 this category was called "Explanatory Journalism".

Pulitzer Prizes for Breaking News Reporting, 1998–2003

Year	Winner, Newspaper
1998	Staff, *Los Angeles Times*
1999	Staff, *Hartford Courant*
2000	Staff, *Denver Post*
2001	Staff, *Miami Herald*
2002	Staff, *Wall Street Journal*
2003	Staff, *Eagle-Tribune* (Lawrence, Mass.)

Pulitzer Prizes for Investigative Reporting, 1985–2003

Year	Winner, Newspaper
1985	William K. Marimow, *Philadelphia Inquirer* Lucy Morgan and Jack Reed, *St. Petersburg* (Fla.) *Times*
1986	Jeffrey A. Marx and Michael M. York, *Lexington* (Ky.) *Herald Leader*
1987	John Woestendiek, *Philadelphia Inquirer* Daniel R. Biddle, H.G. Bissinger and Frederic N. Tulsky, *Philadelphia Inquirer*
1988	Dean Baquet, William Gaines and Ann Marie Lipinski, *Chicago Tribune*
1989	Bill Dedman, *Atlanta Journal and Constitution*
1990	Lou Kilzer and Chris Ison, *Star Tribune* (Minneapolis-St. Paul)
1991	Joseph T. Hallinan and Susan M. Headden, *Indianapolis Star*
1992	Lorraine Adams and Dan Malone, *Dallas Morning News*
1993	Jeff Brazil and Steve Berry, *Orlando Sentinel*
1994	Staff, *Providence Journal-Bulletin*
1995	Brian Donovan and Stephanie Saul, *Newsday*
1996	Staff, *Orange County Register*
1997	Eric Nalder, Deborah Nelson and Alex Tizon, *Seattle Times*
1998	Gary Cohn and Will Englund, *Baltimore Sun*
1999	Staff, *Miami Herald*
2000	Sang-Hun Choe, Charles J. Hanley and Martha Mendoza, *Associated Press*
2001	David Willman, *Los Angeles Times*
2002	Sari Horowitz, Scott Higham and Sarah Cohen, *Washington Post*
2003	Clifford J. Levy, *New York Times*

Special Awards and Citations

Year	Winner, Newspaper
1930	William O. Dapping, *Auburn* (N.Y.) *Citizen*, Prison reporting
1938	*Edmonton* (Alberta) *Journal*, Freedom of the Press editorials
1941	*New York Times*, Foreign news reporting
1944	Byron Price, Director of the Office of Censorship, Creation and administration of newspaper and radio codes.
1944	Mrs. William Allen White, Services to Advisory Board Graduate School of Journalism, Columbia Univ.
1945	American press cartographers, Maps of war fronts
1947	Columbia University and Graduate School of Journalism, Governing Pulitzer Prize awards
1947	*St. Louis Post Dispatch*, Adherence to ideals of journalism
1948	Dr. Frank Diehl Fackenthal, Interest and Service
1951	Cyrus L. Sulzberger, *New York Times*, Interview with Archbishop Stepinac
1952	Max Kase, *New York Journal-American*, Corruption in basketball
1953	*New York Times*, Sunday *Review of the Week* section
1958	Walter Lippman, *New York Herald Tribune*, Lifetime achievement
1964	Gannett Newspapers, *"Road to Integration"* program
1976	Professor John Hohenberg, Administration of Pulitzer Prizes
1978	Richard Lee Strout, *Christian Science Monitor*, Lifetime achievement
1987	Joseph Pulitzer Jr., Lifetime services to Pulitzer Board
1996	Herb Caen, *San Francisco Chronicle*, Lifetime achievement

PULITZER PRIZES IN LETTERS

The Pulitzer Prize for Fiction, 1918–2003

Year	Author, Title
1918	Ernest Poole, *His Family*
1919	Booth Tarkington, *The Magnificent Ambersons*
1920	No award
1921	Edith Wharton, *The Age of Innocence*
1922	Booth Tarkington, *Alice Adams*
1923	Willa Cather, *One of Ours*
1924	Margaret Wilson, *The Able McLaughlins*
1925	Edna Ferber, *So Big*
1926	Sinclair Lewis, *Arrowsmith*
1927	Louis Bromfield, *Early Autumn*
1928	Thornton Wilder, *The Bridge of San Luis Rey*
1929	Julia Peterkin, *Scarlet Sister Mary*
1930	Oliver LaFarge, *Laughing Boy*
1931	Margaret Ayer Barnes, *Years of Grace*
1932	Pearl S. Buck, *The Good Earth*
1933	T.S. Stribling, *The Store*
1934	Caroline Miller, *Lamb in His Bosom*
1935	Josephine Winslow Johnson, *Now in November*
1936	Harold L. Davis, *Honey in the Horn*
1937	Margaret Mitchell, *Gone With the Wind*
1938	John Phillips Marquand, *The Late George Apley*
1939	Marjorie Kinnan Rawlings, *The Yearling*
1940	John Steinbeck, *The Grapes of Wrath*
1941	No award
1942	Ellen Glasgow, *In This Our Life*
1943	Upton Sinclair, *Dragon's Teeth*
1944	Martin Flavin, *Journey in the Dark*
1945	John Hersey, *A Bell for Adano*
1946	No award
1947	Robert Penn Warren, *All the King's Men*
1948[1]	James A. Michener, *Tales of the South Pacific*
1949	James Gould Cozzens, *Guard of Honor*
1950	A.B. Guthrie Jr., *The Way West*
1951	Conrad Richter, *The Town*
1952	Herman Wouk, *The Caine Mutiny*
1953	Ernest Hemingway, *The Old Man and the Sea*
1954	No award
1955	William Faulkner, *A Fable*
1956	MacKinlay Kantor, *Andersonville*
1957	No award
1958	James Agee, *A Death in the Family*
1959	Robert Lewis Taylor, *The Travels of Jaimie McPheeters*
1960	Allen Drury, *Advise and Consent*
1961	Harper Lee, *To Kill a Mockingbird*
1962	Edwin O'Connor, *The Edge of Sadness*
1963	William Faulkner, *The Reivers*
1964	No award
1965	Shirley Ann Grau, *The Keepers of the House*
1966	Katherine Anne Porter, *Collected Stories*
1967	Bernard Malamud, *The Fixer*
1968	William Styron, *The Confessions of Nat Turner*
1969	N. Scott Momaday, *House Made of Dawn*
1970	Jean Stafford, *Collected Stories*
1971	No award
1972	Wallace Stegner, *Angle of Repose*
1973	Eudora Welty, *The Optimist's Daughter*
1974	No award
1975	Michael Shaara, *The Killer Angels*
1976	Saul Bellow, *Humboldt's Gift*
1977	No award
1978	James Alan McPherson, *Elbow Room*
1979	John Cheever, *The Stories of John Cheever*
1980	Norman Mailer, *The Executioner's Song*
1981	John Kennedy Toole[2], *A Confederacy of Dunces*
1982	John Updike, *Rabbit Is Rich*
1983	Alice Walker, *The Color Purple*
1984	William Kennedy, *Ironweed*
1985	Alison Lurie, *Foreign Affairs*
1986	Larry McMurtry, *Lonesome Dove*
1987	Peter Taylor, *A Summons to Memphis*
1988	Toni Morrison, *Beloved*
1989	Anne Tyler, *Breathing Lessons*
1990	Oscar Hijuelos, *The Mambo Kings Play Songs of Love*

Year	Author, Title
1991	John Updike, *Rabbit at Rest*
1992	Jane Smiley, *A Thousand Acres*
1993	Robert Olen Butler, *A Good Scent From a Strange Mountain*
1994	E. Annie Proulx, *The Shipping News*
1995	Carol Shields, *The Stone Diaries*
1996	Richard Ford, *Independence Day*
1997	Steven Millhauser, *Martin Dressler: The Tale of an American Dreamer*
1998	Philip Roth, *American Pastoral*
1999	Michael Cunningham, *The Hours*
2000	Jhumpa Lahiri, *Interpreter of Maladies*
2001	Michael Chabon, *The Amazing Adventures of Kavalier & Clay*
2002	Richard Russo, *Empire Falls*
2003	Jeffrey Eugenides, *Middlesex*

1. In 1948, the name of the category was changed from "The Novel" to "Fiction." 2. Awarded posthumously.

The Pulitzer Prize for Drama, 1918–2003

Year	Author, Title
1918	Jesse Lynch Williams, *Why Marry*
1919	No award
1920	Eugene O'Neill, *Beyond the Horizon*
1921	Zona Gale, *Miss Lulu Bett*
1922	Eugene O'Neill, *Anna Christie*
1923	Owen Davis, *Icebound*
1924	Hatcher Hughes, *Hell-Bent Fer Heaven*
1925	Sidney Howard, *They Knew What They Wanted*
1926	George Kelly, *Craig's Wife*
1927	Paul Green, *In Abraham's Bosom*
1928	Eugene O'Neill, *Strange Interlude*
1929	Elmer L. Rice, *Street Scene*
1930	Marc Connelly, *The Green Pastures*
1931	Susan Glaspell, *Alison's House*
1932	George S. Kaufman, Morrie Ryskind, and Ira Gershwin, *Of Thee I Sing*
1933	Maxwell Anderson, *Both Your Houses*
1934	Sidney Kingsley, *Men in White*
1935	Zoe Akins, *The Old Maid*
1936	Robert E. Sherwood, *Idiot's Delight*
1937	Moss Hart and George S. Kaufman, *You Can't Take It With You*
1938	Thornton Wilder, *Our Town*
1939	Robert E. Sherwood, *Abe Lincoln in Illinois*
1940	William Saroyan, *The Time of Your Life*
1941	Robert E. Sherwood, *There Shall Be no Night*
1942	No award
1943	Thornton Wilder, *The Skin of Our Teeth*
1944	No award
1945	Mary Chase, *Harvey*
1946	Russel Crouse and Howard Lindsay, *State of the Union*
1947	No award
1948	Tennessee Williams, *A Streetcar Named Desire*
1949	Arthur Miller, *Death of a Salesman*
1950	Richard Rodgers, Oscar Hammerstein II, and Joshua Logan, *South Pacific*
1951	No award
1952	Joseph Kramm, *The Shrike*
1953	William Inge, *Picnic*
1954	John Patrick, *The Teahouse of the August Moon*
1955	Tennessee Williams, *Cat on a Hot Tin Roof*
1956	Albert Hackett and Frances Goodrich, *The Diary of Anne Frank*
1957	Eugene O'Neill, *Long Day's Journey Into Night*
1958	Ketti Frings, *Look Homeward, Angel*
1959	Archibald MacLeish, *J.B.*
1960	Jerome Weidman and George Abbott (book); Jerry Bock (music); and Sheldon Harnick (lyrics), *Fiorello!*
1961	Tad Mosel, *All the Way Home*
1962	Frank Loesser and Abe Burrows, *How to Succeed in Business Without Really Trying*
1963	No award
1964	No award
1965	Frank D. Gilroy, *The Subject Was Roses*
1966	No award
1967	Edward Albee, *A Delicate Balance*
1968	No award
1969	Howard Sackler, *The Great White Hope*
1970	Charles Gordone, *No Place to Be Somebody*
1971	Paul Zindel, *The Effect of Gamma Rays on Man-in-the-Moon Marigolds*
1972	No award
1973	Jason Miller, *That Championship Season*
1974	No award
1975	Edward Albee, *Seascape*
1976	Michael Bennett; Nicholas Dante & James Kirkwood (book); Marvin Hamlisch (music); and Edward Kleban (lyrics), *A Chorus Line*
1977	Michael Cristofer, *The Shadow Box*
1978	Donald L. Coburn, *The Gin Game*
1979	Sam Shepard, *Buried Child*
1980	Lanford Wilson, *Talley's Folly*
1981	Beth Henley, *Crimes of the Heart*
1982	Charles Fuller, *A Soldier's Play*
1983	Marsha Norman, *'night Mother*
1984	David Mamet, *Glengarry Glen Ross*
1985	Stephen Sondheim (music and lyrics); James Lapine (book), *Sunday in the Park With George*
1986	No award
1987	August Wilson, *Fences*
1988	Alfred Uhry, *Driving Miss Daisy*
1989	Wendy Wasserstein, *The Heidi Chronicles*
1990	August Wilson, *The Piano Lesson*
1991	Neil Simon, *Lost in Yonkers*
1992	Robert Schenkkan, *The Kentucky Cycle*
1993	Tony Kushner, *Angels in America: Millennium Approaches*
1994	Edward Albee, *Three Tall Women*
1995	Horton Foote, *The Young Man From Atlanta*
1996	Jonathan Larson, *Rent*
1997	No award
1998	Paula Vogel, *How I Learned to Drive*
1999	Margaret Edson, *Wit*
2000	Donald Margulies, *Dinner With Friends*
2001	David Auburn, *Proof*
2002	Suzan-Lori Parks, *Topdog/Underdog*
2003	Nilo Cruz, *Anna In the Tropics*

The Pulitzer Prize for History, 1917–2003

Year	Author, Title
1917	J.J. Jusserand, *With Americans of Past and Present Days*
1918	James Ford Rhodes, *A History of the Civil War*
1920	Justin H. Smith, *The War with Mexico*
1921	William Sowden Sims, with Burton J. Hendrick, *The Victory at Sea*
1922	James Truslow Adams, *The Founding of New England*
1923	Charles Warren, *The Supreme Court in United States History*
1924	Charles Howard McIlwain, *The American Revolution*
1925	Frederic L. Paxson, *A History of the American Frontier*
1926	Edward Channing, *The History of the United States*
1927	Samuel Flagg Bemis, *Pinckney's Treaty*
1928	Vernon Louis Parrington, *Main Currents in American Thought*
1929	Fred Albert Shannon, *The Organization and Administration of the Union Army, 1861–1865*
1930	Claude H. Van Tyne, *The War of Independence*
1931	Bernadotte E. Schmitt, *The Coming of the War: 1914*
1932	John J. Pershing, *My Experiences in the World War*
1933	Frederick J. Turner, *The Significance of Sections in American History*
1934	Herbert Agar, *The People's Choice*
1935	Charles McLean Andrews, *The Colonial Period of American History*
1936	Andrew C. McLaughlin, *The Constitutional History of the United States*
1937	Van Wyck Brooks, *The Flowering of New England*
1938	Paul Herman Buck, *The Road to Reunion 1856–1900*
1939	Frank Luther Mott, *A History of American Magazines*
1940	Carl Sandburg, *Abraham Lincoln: The War Years*
1941	Marcus Lee Hansen, *The Atlantic Migration, 1607–1860*
1942	Margaret Leech, *Reveille in Washington*
1943	Esther Forbes, *Paul Revere and the World He Lived In*
1944	Merle Curti, *The Growth of American Thought*
1945	Stephen Bonsal, *Unfinished Business*
1946	Arthur Meier Schlesinger Jr., *The Age of Jackson*
1947	James Phinney Baxter III, *Scientists Against Time*
1948	Bernard DeVoto, *Across the Wide Missouri*
1949	Roy Franklin Nichols, *The Disruption of American Democracy*
1950	Oliver W. Larkin, *Art and Life in America*
1951	R. Carlyle Buley, *The Old Northwest*
1952	Oscar Handlin, *The Uprooted*
1953	George Dangerfield, *The Era of Good Feelings*
1954	Bruce Catton, *A Stillness at Appomattox*
1955	Paul Horgan, *Great River: The Rio Grande in North American History*
1956	Richard Hofstadter, *The Age of Reform*
1957	George F. Kennan, *Russia Leaves the War: Soviet American Relations, 1917–1920*
1958	Bray Hammond, *Banks and Politics in America*
1959	Leonard D. White, with Miss Jean Schneider, *The Republican Era: 1869–1901*
1960	Margaret Leech, *In the Days of McKinley*
1961	Herbert Feis, *Between War and Peace: The Potsdam Conference*
1962	Lawrence H. Gipson, *The Triumphant Empire: Thunder Clouds in the West*
1963	Constance McLaughlin Green, *Washington, Village and Capital, 1800–1878*
1964	Sumner Chilton Powell, *Puritan Village*
1965	Irwin Unger, *The Greenback Era*
1966	Perry Miller[1], *Life of the Mind in America*
1967	William H. Goetzmann, *Exploration and Empire*
1968	Bernard Bailyn, *The Ideological Origins of the American Revolution*
1969	Leonard W. Levy, *Origins of the Fifth Amendment*
1970	Dean Acheson, *Present at the Creation*
1971	James MacGregor Burns, *Roosevelt, The Soldier of Freedom*
1972	Carl N. Degler, *Neither Black Nor White*
1973	Michael Kammen, *People of Paradox*
1974	Daniel J. Boorstin, *The Americans: The Democratic Experience*
1975	Dumas Malone, *Jefferson and His Time*
1976	Paul Horgan, *Lamy of Santa Fe*
1977	David M. Potter[1] *The Impending Crisis*
1978	Alfred D. Chandler Jr., *The Visible Hand: The Managerial Revolution in American Business*
1979	Don E. Fehrenbacher, *The Dred Scott Case*
1980	Leon F. Litwack, *Been in the Storm So Long*
1981	Lawrence A. Cremin, *American Education*
1982	C. Vann Woodward (ed.), *Mary Chesnut's Civil War*
1983	Rhys L. Isaac, *The Transformation of Virginia, 1740–1790*
1985	Thomas K. McCraw, *Prophets of Regulation*
1986	Walter A. McDougall, *. . .the Heavens and the Earth*
1987	Bernard Bailyn, *Voyagers to the West*
1988	Robert V. Bruce, *The Launching of Modern American Science 1846–1876*
1989	Taylor Branch, *Parting the Waters*
	James M. McPherson, *Battle Cry of Freedom: The Civil War Era*
1990	Stanley Karnow, *In Our Image*
1991	Laurel Thatcher Ulrich, *A Midwife's Tale*
1992	Mark E. Neely Jr., *The Fate of Liberty*
1993	Gordon S. Wood, *The Radicalism of the American Revolution*
1995	Doris Kearns Goodwin, *No Ordinary Time: Franklin and Eleanor Roosevelt*
1996	Alan Taylor, *William Cooper's Town*
1997	Jack N. Rakove, *Original Meanings: Politics and Ideas in the Making of the Constitution*
1998	Edward J. Larson, *Summer for the Gods: The Scopes Trial and America's Continuing Debate Over Science and Religion*
1999	Edwin G. Burrows and Mike Wallace, *Gotham: A History of New York City to 1898*
2000	David M. Kennedy, *Freedom From Fear: The American People in Depression*
2001	Joseph P. Ellis, *Founding Brothers: The Revolutionary Generation*
2002	Louis Menand, *The Metaphysical Club: A Story of Ideas in America*
2003	Rick Atkinson, *An Army at Dawn: The War in North Africa, 1942–1943*

Notes: No award given in 1919, 1984, or 1994. 1. Awarded posthumously.

The Pulitzer Prize for Biography/Autobiography, 1917–2003

Year	Author, Title
1917	Laura E. Richards and Maude Howe Elliott, with Florence Howe Hall, *Julia Ward Howe*
1918	William Cabell Bruce, *Benjamin Franklin, Self-Revealed*
1919	Henry Adams, *The Education of Henry Adams*
1920	Albert J. Beveridge, *The Life of John Marshall*
1921	Edward Bok, *The Americanization of Edward Bok*
1922	Hamlin Garland, *A Daughter of the Middle Border*
1923	Burton J. Hendrick, *The Life and Letters of Walter H. Page*
1924	Michael Idvorsky Pupin, *From Immigrant to Inventor*
1925	M.A. DeWolfe Howe, *Barrett Wendell and His Letter*
1926	Harvey Cushing, *The Life of Sir William Osler*
1927	Emory Holloway, *Whitman*
1928	Charles Edward Russell, *The American Orchestra and Theodore Thomas*
1929	Burton J. Hendrick, *The Training of an American. The Earlier Life and Letters of Walter H.Page*
1930	Marquis James, *The Raven*
1931	Henry James, *Charles W. Eliot*
1932	Henry F. Pringle, *Theodore Roosevelt*
1933	Allan Nevins, *Grover Cleveland*
1934	Tyler Dennett, *John Hay*
1935	Douglas S. Freeman, *R.E. Lee*
1936	Ralph Barton Perry, *The Thought and Character of William James*
1937	Allan Nevins, *Hamilton Fish*
1938	Odell Shepard, *Pedlar's Progress*
	Marquis James, *Andrew Jackson*
1939	Carl Van Doren, *Benjamin Franklin*
1940	Ray Stannard Baker, *Woodrow Wilson, Life and Letters,* vols. 7 & 8
1941	Ola Elizabeth Winslow, *Jonathan Edwards*
1942	Forrest Wilson, *Crusader in Crinoline*
1943	Samuel Eliot Morison, *Admiral of the Ocean Sea*
1944	Carleton Mabee, *The American Leonardo: The Life of Samuel F.B. Morse*
1945	Russell Blaine Nye, *George Bancroft*
1946	Linnie Marsh Wolfe, *Son of the Wilderness*
1947	William Allen White, *The Autobiography of William Allen White*
1948	Margaret Clapp, *Forgotten First Citizen: John Bigelow*
1949	Robert E. Sherwood, *Roosevelt and Hopkins*
1950	Samuel Flagg Bemis, *John Quincy Adams and the Foundations of American Foreign Policy*
1951	Margaret Louise Coit, *John C. Calhoun*
1952	Merlo J. Pusey, *Charles Evan Hughes*
1953	David J. Mays, *Edmund Pendleton 1721-1803*
1954	Charles A. Lindbergh, *The Spirit of St. Louis*
1955	William S. White, *The Taft Story*
1956	Talbot Faulkner Hamlin, *Benjamin Henry Latrobe*
1957	John F. Kennedy, *Profiles in Courage*
1958	Douglas Southall Freeman[1], John Alexander Carroll, Mary Wells Ashworth, *George Washington,* vols. 1–4; and vol. 7, written after Dr. Freeman's death in 1953.
1959	Arthur Walworth, *Woodrow Wilson, American Prophet*
1960	Samuel Eliot Morison, *John Paul Jones*
1961	David Donald, *Charles Sumner and the Coming of the Civil War*
1962	No award
1963	Leon Edel, *Henry James*
1964	Walter Jackson Bate, *John Keats*
1965	Ernest Samuels, *Henry Adams*
1966	Arthur M. Schlesinger Jr., *A Thousand Days*
1967	Justin Kaplan, *Mr. Clemens and Mark Twain*
1968	George F. Kennan, *Memoirs*
1969	Benjamin Lawrence Reid, *The Man From New York: John Quinn and His Friends*
1970	T: Harry Williams, *Huey Long*
1971	Lawrance Thompson, *Robert Frost*
1972	Joseph P. Lash, *Eleanor and Franklin*
1973	W.A. Swanberg, *Luce and His Empire*
1974	Louis Sheaffer, *O'Neill, Son and Artist*
1975	Robert A. Caro, *The Power Broker*
1976	R.W.B. Lewis, *Edith Wharton: A Biography*
1977	John E. Mack, *A Prince of Our Disorder: The Life of T.E. Lawrence*
1978	Walter Jackson Bate, *Samuel Johnson*
1979	Leonard Baker, *Days of Sorrow and Pain*
1980	Edmund Morris, *The Rise of Theodore Roosevelt*
1981	Robert K. Massie, *Peter the Great*
1982	William S. McFeely, *Grant: A Biography*
1983	Russell Baker, *Growing Up*
1984	Louis R. Harlan, *Booker T. Washington*
1985	Kenneth Silverman, *The Life and Times of Cotton Mather*
1986	Elizabeth Frank, *Louise Bogan: A Portrait*
1987	David J. Garrow, *Bearing the Cross: Martin Luther King, Jr. and the Southern Christian Leadership Conference*
1988	David Herbert Donald, *Look Homeward: A Life of Thomas Wolfe*
1989	Richard Ellmann[1], *Oscar Wilde*
1990	Sebastian de Grazia, *Machiavelli in Hell*
1991	Steven Naifeh, Gregory White Smith, *Jackson Pollock*
1992	Lewis B. Puller Jr., *Fortunate Son*
1993	David McCullough, *Truman*
1994	David Levering Lewis, *W.E.B. DuBois*
1995	Joan D. Hedrick, *Harriet Beecher Stowe*
1996	Jack Miles, *God: A Biography*
1997	Frank McCourt, *Angela's Ashes*
1998	Katharine Graham, *Personal History*
1999	A. Scott Berg, *Lindbergh*
2000	Stacy Schiff, *Véra (Mrs. Vladimir Nabokov)*
2001	David Levering Lewis, *W.E.B. DuBois (vol. 2)*
2002	David McCullough, *John Adams*
2003	Robert A. Caro, *Master of the Senate*

1. Awarded posthumously.

The Pulitzer Prize for Poetry, 1922–2003

Pulitzer Prizes in poetry were first awarded in 1922. The Poetry Society awarded prizes in 1918 to Sara Teasdale for *Love Songs*, and in 1919 to Margaret Widdemer for *Old Road to Paradise* and to Carl Sandburg for *Corn Huskers*.

Year	Author, Title
1922	Edward Arlington Robinson, *Collected Poems*
1923	Edna St. Vincent Millay, *The Ballad of the Harp-Weaver; A Few Figs from Thistles; Eight Sonnets in American Poetry, 1922, A Miscellany*
1924	Robert Frost, *New Hampshire: A Poem with Notes and Grace Notes*
1925	Edward Arlington Robinson, *The Man Who Died Twice*
1926	Amy Lowell[1], *What's O'Clock*
1927	Leonora Speyer, *Fiddler's Farewell*
1928	Edward Arlington Robinson, *Tristram*
1929	Stephen Vincent Benét, *John Brown's Body*
1930	Conrad Aiken, *Selected Poems*
1931	Robert Frost, *Collected Poems*
1932	George Dillon, *The Flowering Stone*
1933	Archibald MacLeish, *Conquistador*
1934	Robert Hillyer, *Collected Verse*
1935	Audrey Wurdemann, *Bright Ambush*
1936	Robert P. Tristram Coffin, *Strange Holiness*
1937	Robert Frost, *A Further Range*
1938	Marya Zaturenska, *Cold Morning Sky*
1939	John Gould Fletcher, *Selected Poems*
1940	Mark Van Doren, *Collected Poems*
1941	Leonard Bacon, *Sunderland Capture*
1942	William Rose Benét, *The Dust Which Is God*
1943	Robert Frost, *A Witness Tree*
1944	Stephen Vincent Benét[1], *Western Star*
1945	Karl Shapiro, *V-Letter and Other Poems*
1947	Robert Lowell, *Lord Weary's Castle*
1948	W.H. Auden, *The Age of Anxiety*
1949	Peter Viereck, *Terror and Decorum*
1950	Gwendolyn Brooks, *Annie Allen*
1951	Carl Sandburg, *Complete Poems*
1952	Marianne Moore, *Collected Poems*
1953	Archibald MacLeish, *Collected Poems 1917–1952*
1954	Theodore Roethke, *The Waking*
1955	Wallace Stevens, *Collected Poems*
1956	Elizabeth Bishop, *Poems—North & South*
1957	Richard Wilbur, *Things of This World*
1958	Robert Penn Warren, *Promises: Poems 1954-1956*
1959	Stanley Kunitz, *Selected Poems 1928–1958*
1960	W.D. Snodgrass, *Heart's Needle*
1961	Phyllis McGinley, *Times Three: Selected Verse From Three Decades*
1962	Alan Dugan, *Poems*
1963	William Carlos Williams[1], *Pictures from Breughel*
1964	Louis Simpson, *At the End of the Open Road*
1965	John Berryman, *77 Dream Songs*
1966	Richard Eberhart, *Selected Poems*
1967	Anne Sexton, *Live or Die*
1968	Anthony Hecht, *The Hard Hours*
1969	George Oppen, *Of Being Numerous*
1970	Richard Howard, *Untitled Subjects*
1971	William S. Merwin, *The Carrier of Ladders*
1972	James Wright , *Collected Poems*
1973	Maxine Kumin, *Up Country*
1974	Robert Lowell, *The Dolphins*
1975	Gary Snyder, *Turtle Island*
1976	John Ashberry, *Self-Portrait in a Convex Mirror*
1977	James Merrill, *Divine Comedies*
1978	Howard Nemerov, *Collected Poems*
1979	Robert Penn Warren, *Now and Then*
1980	Donald Justice, *Selected Poems*
1981	James Schuyler, *The Morning of the Poem*
1982	Sylvia Plath[1], *The Collected Poems*
1983	Galway Kinnell, *Selected Poems*
1984	Mary Oliver, *American Primitive*
1985	Carolyn Kizer, *Yin*
1986	Henry Taylor, *The Flying Change*
1987	Rita Dove, *Thomas and Beulah*
1988	William Meredith, *Partial Accounts: New and Selected Poems*
1989	Richard Wilbur, *New and Collected Poems*
1990	Charles Simic, *The World Doesn't End*
1991	Mona Van Duyn, *Near Changes*
1992	James Tate, *Selected Poems*
1993	Louise Glück, *The Wild Iris*
1994	Yusef Komunyakaa, *Neon Vernacular*
1995	Philip Levine, *Simple Truth*
1996	Jorie Graham, *The Dream of the Unified Field*
1997	Lisel Mueller, *Alive Together: New and Selected Poems*
1998	Charles Wright, *Black Zodiac*
1999	Mark Strand, *Blizzard of One*
2000	C.K. Williams, *Repair*
2001	Stephen Dunn, *Different Hours*
2002	Carl Dennis, *Practical Gods*
2003	Paul Muldoon, *Moy Sand and Gravel*

Note: No award given in 1946. 1. Awarded posthumously.

The Pulitzer Prize for General Nonfiction, 1962–2003

Year	Author, Title
1962	Theodore H. White, *The Making of the President,1960*
1963	Barbara W. Tuchman, *The Guns of August*
1964	Richard Hofstadter, *Anti-Intellectualism in American Life*
1965	Howard Mumford Jones, *O Strange New World*
1966	Edwin Way Teal, *Wandering Through Winter*
1967	David Brion Davis, *The Problem of Slavery in Western Culture*
1968	Will and Ariel Durant, *Rousseau and Revolution*
1969	René Jules Dubos, *So Human An Animal*
	Norman Mailer, *The Armies of the Night*
1970	Erik H. Erikson, *Gandhi's Truth*
1971	John Toland, *The Rising Sun*
1972	Barbara W. Tuchman, *Stilwell and the American Experience in China, 1911–45*
1973	Robert Coles, *Children of Crisis, vols.2 & 3*
	Frances Fitzgerald, *Fire in the Lake*
1974	Ernest Becker[1], *The Denial of Death*
1975	Annie Dillard, *Pilgrim at Tinker Creek*
1976	Robert N. Butler, *Why Survive? Being Old in America*

Year	Author, Title
1977	William N. Warner, *Beautiful Swimmers*
1978	Carl Sagan, *The Dragons of Eden*
1979	Edward O. Wilson, *On Human Nature*
1980	Douglas R. Hofstadter, *Gödel, Escher, Bach: an Eternal Golden Braid*
1981	Carl E. Schorske, *Fin-de Siècle Vienna: Politics and Culture*
1982	Tracy Kidder, *The Soul of A New Machine*
1983	Susan Sheehan, *Is There No Place on Earth for Me?*
1984	Paul Starr, *The Social Transformation of American Medicine*
1985	Studs Terkel, *The Good War*
1986	Joseph Lelyveld, *Move Your Shadow*
	J. Anthony Lukas, *Common Ground*
1987	David K. Shipler, *Arab and Jew*
1988	Richard Rhodes, *The Making of the Atomic Bomb*
1989	Neil Sheehan, *A Bright and Shining Lie*
1990	Dale Maharidge, Michael Williamson, *And Their Children After Them*
1991	Bert Holldobler, Edward O. Wilson, *The Ants*
1992	Daniel Yergin, *The Prize: The Epic Quest for Oil, Money and Power.*
1993	Garry Wills, *Lincoln at Gettysburg*
1994	David Remnick, *Lenin's Tomb: The Last Days of the Soviet Empire*
1995	Jonathan Weiner, *The Beak of the Finch*
1996	Tina Rosenberg, *The Haunted Land*
1997	Richard Kluger, *Ashes to Ashes*
1998	Jared Diamond, *Guns, Germs, and Steel: The Fates of Human Societies*
1999	John McPhee, *Annals of the Former World*
2000	John W. Dower, *Embracing Defeat: Japan in the Wake of World War II*
2001	Herbert P. Bix, *Hirohito and the Making of Modern Japan*
2002	Diane McWhorter, *Carry Me Home: Birmingham, Alabama, the Climactic Battle of the Civil Rights Revolution*
2003	Samantha Power, *"A Problem From Hell": America and the Age of Genocide*

1. Awarded posthumously.

The Pulitzer Prize for Music, 1943–2003

Year	Author, Title
1943	William Schuman, Secular Cantata No. 2, *A Free Song*
1944	Howard Hanson, Symphony No. 4, Opus 34
1945	Aaron Copland, *Appalachian Spring*
1946	Leo Sowerby, *The Canticle of the Sun*
1947	Charles Ives, Symphony No. 3
1948	Walter Piston, Symphony No. 3
1949	Virgil Thomson, Music for the film, *Louisiana Story*
1950	Gian-Carlo Menotti, Music for the opera *The Consul*
1951	Douglas S. Moore, Music for the opera, *Giants in the Earth*
1952	Gail Kubik, *Symphony Concertante*
1953	No award
1954	Quincy Porter, Concerto for Two Pianos and Orchestra
1955	Gian-Carlo Menotti, *The Saint of Bleecker Street* (opera)
1956	Ernest Toch, Symphony No. 3
1957	Norman Dello Joio, *Meditations on Ecclesiastes*
1958	Samuel Barber, *Vanessa* (opera)
1959	John LaMontaine, Concerto for Piano and Orchestra
1960	Elliott Carter, Second String Quartet
1961	Walter Piston, Symphony No. 7
1962	Robert Ward, *The Crucible* (opera)
1963	Samuel Barber, Piano Concerto No. 1
1964	No award
1965	No award
1966	Leslie Bassett, Variations for Orchestra
1967	Leon Kirchner, Quartet No. 3
1968	George Crumb, *Echoes of Time and the River* orchestral suite
1969	Karel Husa, String Quartet No. 3
1970	Charles Wuorinen, *Time's Encomium*
1971	Mario Davidovsky, Synchronisms No. 6 for Piano and Electronic Sound
1972	Jacob Druckman, *Windows*
1973	Elliott Carter, String Quartet No. 3
1974	Donald Martino, *Notturno* (chamber music)
1975	Dominick Argento, *From the Diary of Virginia Woolf*
1976	Ned Rorem, *Air Music: Ten Etudes for Orchestra*
1977	Richard Wernick, *Visions of Terror and Wonder*
1978	Michael Colgrass, *Deja Vu* for Percussion Quartet and Orchestra
1979	Joseph Schwantner, *Aftertones of Infinity*
1980	David Del Tredici, *In Memory of a Summer Day*
1981	No award
1982	Roger Sessions, Concerto for Orchestra
1983	Ellen Taaffe Zwilich, Symphony No. 1
1984	Bernard Rands, "Canti del Sole" for Tenor and Orchestra
1985	Stephen Albert, Symphony *RiverRun*
1986	George Perle, Wind Quintet IV
1987	John Harbison, *The Flight Into Egypt*
1988	William Bolcom, 12 New Etudes for Piano
1989	Roger Reynolds, *Whispers Out of Time*
1990	Mel Powell, *Duplicates: A Concerto for Two Pianos and Orchestra*
1991	Shulammit Ran, *Symphony*
1992	Wayne Peterson, *The Face of the Night, The Heart of the Dark*
1993	Christopher Rouse, *Trombone Concerto*
1994	Gunther Schuller, *Of Reminiscences and Reflections*
1995	Morton Gould, *Stringmusic*
1996	George Walker, *Lilacs*
1997	Wynton Marsalis, *Blood on the Fields*
1998	Aaron Jay Kernis, *String Quartet No.2*
1999	Melinda Wagner, *Concerto for Flute, Strings, and Percussion*
2000	Lewis Spratalan, *Life is a Dream, Opera in Three Acts: Act II, Convert Version*
2001	John Corigliano, *Symphony No. 2 for String Orchestra*
2002	Henry Brant, *Ice Field*
2003	John Adams, *On the Transmigration of Souls*

Pulitzer Special Citations

SPECIAL CITATIONS IN LETTERS	
Year	**Recipient**
1944	Richard Rodgers and Oscar Hammerstein II, *Oklahoma!*
1957	Kenneth Roberts, for his historical novels
1960	Garret Mattingly, *The Armada*
1961	Publishers, *The American Heritage Picture History of the Civil War*
1973	James Flexner, *George Washington,* vols. 1–4
1977	Alex Haley, *Roots*
1978	E.B. White, Lifetime achievement
1984	Theodore Seuss Geisel (Dr. Seuss), Lifetime achievement
1992	Art Speigelman, *Maus*

SPECIAL CITATIONS IN MUSIC	
Year	**Recipient**
1974	Roger Sessions, Lifetime achievement
1976	Scott Joplin[1], Contributions to American music
1982	Milton Babbitt, Lifetime achivement
1985	William Schuman, Lifetime achievement
1998	George Gershwin[1], Contributions to American music
1999	Edward "Duke" Ellington[1], Contributions to American music

1. Awarded posthumously. **Source:** Columbia University.

The Nobel Prizes

First awarded in 1901, the Nobel Prizes were established through a bequest of $9.2 million from Alfred Bernhard Nobel (1833–1896), a Swedish chemical engineer and the inventor of dynamite and other explosives, and by a gift from the Bank of Sweden. Nobel's will directed that the interest from the fund be divided annually among people who have made significant discoveries or inventions in the fields of chemistry, physics, and physiology or medicine, as well as to that author who has "produced in the field of literature the most outstanding work of an idealistic tendency," and to that individual or group that has "done the most or the best work for fraternity between nations, for the abolition or reduction of standing armies and for the holding and promotion of peace congresses." In 1968, the 300th anniversary of the Bank of Sweden, an additional prize for outstanding work in the economic sciences was established; it was first granted the following year.

Today, all of the prizes are funded with the help of the Bank of Sweden. Final decisions are made for physics, chemistry and economics by the Royal Swedish Academy of Sciences, Stockholm; for physiology or medicine by the Nobel Assembly at the Karolinska Institute, Stockholm; for literature by the Swedish Academy, Stockholm; and for peace by the Norwegian Nobel Committee, Oslo.

The prizes are awarded annually on December 10, the anniversary of Nobel's death. The peace prize is presented in Oslo and other awards are given in Stockholm, by the king of Sweden. The amount of each prize varies according to the interest from the fund. In 2003, the award was worth 10 million Swedish crowns (approximately $1.33 million), up from $362,500 in 1987. No prizes were awarded between 1940 and 1942.

Note: For winners of the 2003 Nobel Prizes in all categories, see "Part I: The Almanac of the Year," or the Nobel Foundation web site: www.nobel.se.

Nobel Peace Prize Recipients

1901 Jean-Henri Dunant (Switzerland) Founder of International Committee of the Red Cross; **Frédéric Passy** (France) Founder of first French peace society.
1902 Elie Ducommun (Switzerland) Director of Permanent International Peace Bureau; **Charles Albert Gobat** (Switzerland) Secretary-General of Inter-Parliamentary Union.
1903 Sir William R. Cremer (U.K.) Founder of International Arbitration League.
1904 Institute of International Law Founded in 1873.
1905 Baroness Bertha S.F. von Suttner (Austria) Author of antiwar novel *Lay Down Your Arms.*
1906 Theodore Roosevelt (U.S.) President; mediated Russo-Japanese War.
1907 Ernesto T. Moneta (Italy) Founder of Lombard League of Peace; **Louis Renault** (France) Professor of International Law at Hague Peace Conference.
1908 Klas P. Arnoldson (Sweden) Founder of Swedish Peace and Arbitration League; **Fredrik Bajer** (Denmark) Writer and peace activist, Danish parliament member.
1909 Auguste M.F. Beernaert (Belgium) Prime minister and peace activist; **Paul H.B.B. D'Estournelles de Constant** (Baron Constant de Rebecque) (France) Founder of French parliamentary group for voluntary arbitration.
1910 Permanent International Peace Bureau Founded 1891.
1911 Tobias M.C. Asser (Netherlands) A founder of Institute of International Law; **Alfred H. Fried** (Austria) Journalist and founder of many peace publications.
1912 Elihu Root (U.S.) Former Secretary of state and originator of several arbitration treaties.
1913 Henri Lafontaine (Belgium) President of Permanent International Peace Bureau in Bern.
1914–1916 No awards given.
1917 International Committee of the Red Cross Founded 1863.
1918 No award.
1919 Woodrow Wilson (U.S.) President; instrumental in establishing League of Nations.
1920 Léon Victor A. Bourgeois (France) Drafted framework for League of Nations.
1921 Karl H. Branting (Sweden) Prime minister and pacifist; **Christian L. Lange** (Norway) A founder of Inter-Parliamentary Union.
1922 Fridtjof Nansen (Norway) Scientist; explorer; originator of "Nansen passports" for refugees.
1923–24 No award.
1925 Sir Austen Chamberlain (U.K.) Foreign secretary; worked for Locarno Pact; **Charles G. Dawes**

(U.S.) Vice president; drafted Dawes Plan settling German reparations issue.
1926 **Aristide Briand** (France) and **Gustav Stresemann** (Germany) Creators of Locarno Pact.
1927 **Ferdinand Buisson** (France) Human rights advocate; **Ludwig Quidde** (Germany) Peace activist.
1928 No award.
1929 **Frank B. Kellogg** (U.S.) Former Secretary of state; a creator of Kellogg-Briand Pact.
1930 **L.O. Nathan Söderblom** (Sweden) Archbishop; leader in the ecumenical movement.
1931 **Jane Addams** (U.S.) President of Women's International League for Peace and Freedom; **Nicholas M. Butler** (U.S.) Promoter of Kellogg-Briand Pact.
1932 No award.
1933 **Sir Norman Angell** (Ralph Lane) (U.K.) Author of antiwar book *The Great Illusion.*
1934 **Arthur Henderson** (U.K.) President of League of Nations World Disarmament Conference 1932.
1935 **Carol von Ossietzky** (Germany) Journalist and pacifist.
1936 **Carlos Saavedra Lamas** (Argentina) Secretary of state; president of League of Nations and mediator in conflict between Paraguay and Bolivia.
1937 **Lord Edgar Algernon R.G. Cecil** (U.K.) An architect of League of Nations.
1938 **Nansen International Office for Refugees** Founded 1921.
1939–1943 No awards given.
1944 **International Committee of the Red Cross** Founded 1863.
1945 **Cordell Hull** (U.S.) Former Secretary of state; instrumental in creating United Nations.
1946 **Emily G. Balch** (U.S.) Leader of international women's movement for peace; **John R. Mott** (U.S.) Leader of Christian ecumenical movement.
1947 **The Friends Service Council** (U.K.) and **The American Friends Service Committee** (U.S.) (The Quakers)
1948 No award.
1949 **Lord John Boyd Orr** (U.K.) Nutritionist; worked to eliminate world hunger.
1950 **Ralph Bunche** (U.S.) Mediator in Middle East war.
1951 **Léon Jouhaux** (France) Advocate of improved working-class conditions.
1952 **Albert Schweitzer** (France) Missionary surgeon/founder of Lambarene Hospital in Africa.
1953 **George C. Marshall** (U.S.) General; originator of Marshall Plan, which provided recovery loans and technical aid to Europe after World War II.
1954 **Office of the U.N. High Commissioner for Refugees** for their aid work for European refugees.
1955–1956 No awards given.
1957 **Lester B. Pearson** (Canada) Former Secretary of state; worked to resolve Suez Canal Crisis of 1956.
1958 **Georges Pire** (Belgium) Dominican priest and leader of relief organization for refugees, l'Europe du Coeur au Service du Monde.
1959 **Philip J. Noel-Baker** (U.K.) Lifelong worker for international peace through disarmament.
1960 **Albert J. Lutuli** (South Africa) President of the African National Congress; led peaceful resistance to apartheid.
1961 **Dag Hammarskjöld** (Sweden) United Nations Secretary General; worked for peace in the Congo.
1962 **Linus C. Pauling** (U.S.) Chemist; warned against dangers of radioactive fallout in nuclear weapons testing and war.
1963 **International Committee of the Red Cross and League of Red Cross Societies**
1964 **Martin Luther King, Jr.** (U.S.) Leader of American civil rights movement.
1965 **United Nations Children's Fund (UNICEF).**
1966–1967 No awards given.
1968 **René Cassin** (France) President of European Court for Human Rights.
1969 **International Labour Organization** United Nations agency involved in improving worldwide working and social conditions.
1970 **Norman Borlaug** (U.S.) Agricultural scientist and developer of high-yield grains credited with helping to alleviate world hunger.
1971 **Willy Brandt** (Federal Republic of Germany) Chancellor; champion of East-West détente.
1972 No award
1973 **Henry A. Kissinger** (U.S.) Secretary of state and **Le Duc Tho** (Democratic Republic of Viet Nam) Foreign minister; negotiated Vietnam cease-fire agreement. Mr. Tho declined the prize.
1974 **Seán MacBride** (Ireland) President of International Peace Bureau and United Nations commissioner for Namibia; **Eisaku Sato** (Japan) Prime minister of Japan and campaigner against nuclear weapons.
1975 **Andrei Sakharov** (USSR) Nuclear physicist and human rights campaigner.
1976 **Betty Williams and Mairead Corrigan** (Northern Ireland) Founder of Northern Ireland Peace Movement.
1977 **Amnesty International** for human rights work.
1978 **Anwar el-Sadat** (Egypt) President, and **Menachem Begin** (Israel) Prime minister; negotiated Israeli-Egyptian peace accord.
1979 **Mother Teresa** (India) Worker for the poor in Calcutta.
1980 **Adolfo Pérez Esquivel** (Argentina) Architect, sculptor, and human rights leader.
1981 **Office of the United Nations High Commissioner for Refugees** for aid work with Asian refugees.
1982 **Alva Myrdal** (Sweden) and **Alfonso Garcia Robles** (Mexico) Campaigners for disarmament.
1983 **Lech Walesa** (Poland) Leader of the Solidarity trade union federation.
1984 **Desmond M. Tutu** (South Africa) Bishop of Johannesburg; a leader of the anti-apartheid movement.
1985 **International Physicians for the Prevention of Nuclear War** Organization jointly headed by a Soviet and an American doctor.
1986 **Elie Wiesel** (U.S.) Writer on the Holocaust and Nazi death camp survivor.
1987 **Oscar Arias Sánchez** (Costa Rica) President of Costa Rica; creator of a peace plan for Central America.
1988 **United Nations Peacekeeping Forces**
1989 **Dalai Lama** (Tibet) Exiled religious and political leader of Tibet for his nonviolent campaign to end China's domination of his country.
1990 **Mikhail Gorbachev** (USSR) President of the Soviet Union, "for his role in the peace process which today characterizes important parts of the international community."
1991 **Aung San Suu Kyi** (Myanmar), leader of opposition National League for Democracy (under house arrest at the time) "for her nonviolent struggle for democracy and human rights."
1992 **Rigoberta Menchú** (Guatemala) A Quiché Indian and an outspoken advocate of human rights during the civil war in her country.
1993 **Pres. F. W. de Klerk** of South Africa and **Nelson Mandela,** black leader of the opposition African National Congress, for negotiating an end to the apartheid policies of the state and their collaboration on the formation of a democracy not based on race.
1994 **Yitzhak Rabin** (Israel) Prime Minister, **Shimon Peres** (Israel) Foreign Minister, and **Yasir Arafat,** leader of the Palestinian Liberation Organization, for negotiating the historic peace pact allowing Palestinian self-rule in the West Bank and Gaza Strip.

1995 **Joseph Rotblat** (U.K. b. Poland) and his **Pugwash Conferences on Science and World Affairs**. A former Manhattan Project physicist, Rotblat spent 40 years campaigning to eliminate nuclear weapons.
1996 **Bishop Carlos Ximenes Belo** (Australia, b. East Timor) and **Jose Ramos-Horta** (East Timor) for "sustained and self-sacrificing contributions for a small but oppressed people" in East Timor, a former Portuguese colony invaded by Indonesia in the 1970s.
1997 **The International Campaign to Ban Landmines** and its 47-year-old coordinator, **Jody Williams** (U.S.), for their efforts to outlaw land mines worldwide. The Nobel committee admitted that it was openly trying to persuade the U.S. to sign the international treaty banning landmines.
1998 **John Hume** (Ireland) and **David Trimble** (Ireland) the leaders of the largest Roman Catholic and Protestant political parties in Northern Ireland, who brought about the April 1998 peace agreement.
1999 **Doctors Without Borders** (Médecins Sans Frontières), whose independence and rapid intervention have helped " to form bodies of public opinion opposed to violations and abuses of power."
2000 **Kim Dae Jung,** President of South Korea, "for his work for democracy and human rights in South Korea and in East Asia in general, and for peace and reconciliation with North Korea in particular."
2001 **United Nations** and its Secretary General **Kofi Annan,** (Ghana), in equal portions, for "their work for a better organized and more peaceful world."
2002 **Jimmy Carter,** (U.S.), "for his decades of untiring effort to find peaceful solutions to international conflicts, to advance democracy and human rights, and to promote economic and social development." In presenting the award to Carter, the Nobel Committee expressly stated its opposition to the Bush Administration's rush to war in the Persian Gulf.
2003 See Part I: "The Almanac of the Year."

Nobel Prizes in Physiology or Medicine

1901 **Emil A. von Behring** (Germany) Marburg Univ. "for his work on serum therapy, especially its application against diphtheria, by which he has opened a new road in the domain of medical science and thereby placed in the hands of the physician a victorious weapon against illness and deaths."
1902 **Sir Ronald Ross** (U.K.) University College "for his work on malaria, by which he has shown how it enters the organism and thereby has laid the foundation for successful research on this disease and methods of combating it."
1903 **Niels R. Finsen** (Denmark) Finsen Medical Light Institute "in recognition of his contribution to the treatment of diseases, especially lupus vulgaris, with concentrated light radiation, whereby he has opened a new avenue for medical science."
1904 **Ivan P. Pavlov** (Russia) Military Medical Academy "in recognition of his work on the physiology of digestion."
1905 **Robert Koch** (Germany) Institute for Infectious Diseases "for his investigations and discoveries in relation to tuberculosis."
1906 **Camillio Golgi** (Italy) Pavia Univ., and **Santiago Ramon Y Cajal** (Spain) Madrid Univ. for "their work on the structure of the nervous system."
1907 **Charles L.A. Laveran** (France) Institute Pasteur "in recognition of his work on the role played by protozoa in causing diseases."
1908 **Il'ja I. Mecnikov** (Russia) Institut Pasteur (Paris), and **Paul Ehrlich** (Germany) Goettingen Univ. and Royal Institute for Experimental Therapy "in recognition of their work on immunity."
1909 **Emil R. Kocher** (Switzerland) Berne Univ. "for his work on the physiology, pathology, and surgery for the thyroid gland."
1910 **Albrecht Kossel** (Germany) Heidelberg Univ. "in recognition of the contributions to our knowledge of cell chemistry made through his work on proteins, including the nucleic substances."
1911 **Allvar Gullstrand** (Sweden) Uppsala Univ. "for his work on the dioptrics of the eye."
1912 **Alexis Carrel** (France) Rockefeller Institute for Medical Research (New York) "in recognition of his work on vascular suture and the transplantation of blood vessels and organs."
1913 **Charles R. Richet** (France) Sorbonne Univ. "in recognition of his work on anaphylaxis."
1914 **Robert Bárány** (Austria) Vienna Univ. "for his work on the physiology and pathology of the vestibular apparatus."
1915–1918 No awards
1919 **Jules Bordet** (Belgium) Brussels Univ. "for his discoveries relating to immunity."
1920 **Schack A.S. Krogh** (Denmark) Copenhagen Univ. "for his discoveries of the capillary motor regulating mechanism."
1921 No award
1922 **Sir Archibald V. Hill** (U.K.) London Univ. "for his discovery relating to the production of heat in the muscle"; **Otto F. Meyerhof** (Germany) Kiel Univ. "for his discovery of the fixed relationship between the consumption of oxygen and the metabolism of lactic acid in the muscle."
1923 **Sir Frederick G. Banting** (Canada) Toronto Univ. and **John J.R. Macleod** (Canada) Toronto Univ. "for the discovery of insulin."
1924 **Willem Einthoven** (Netherlands) Leyden Univ. "for his discovery of the mechanism of the electrocardiogram."
1925 No award
1926 **Johannes A.G. Fibiger** (Denmark) Copenhagen Univ. "for his discovery of the Spiroptera carcinoma."
1927 **Julius Wagner-Jauegg** (Austria) Vienna Univ. "for his discovery of the therapeutic value of malaria inoculation in the treatment of dementia paralytica."
1928 **Charles J.H. Nicolle** (France) Institut Pasteur "for his work on typhus."
1929 **Christiaan Eijkman** (Netherlands) Utrecht Univ. "for his discovery of the antineuritic vitamin"; **Sir Frederick G. Hopkins** (U.K.) Cambridge Univ. "for his discovery of the growth-stimulating vitamins."
1930 **Karl Landsteiner** (Austria) Rockefeller Institute of Medical Research (New York) "for his discovery of human blood groups."
1931 **Otto H. Warburg** (Germany) Kaiser-Wilhelm Institut "for his discovery of the nature and mode of action of the respiratory enzyme."
1932 **Sir Charles S. Sherrington** (U.K.) Oxford Univ. and **Lord Edgar D. Adrian** (U.K.) Cambridge Univ. "for their discoveries regarding the functions of neurons."
1933 **Thomas H. Morgan** (U.S.) California Institute of Technology "for his discoveries concerning the role played by the chromosome in heredity."
1934 **George H. Whipple** (U.S.) Rochester Univ., **George R. Minot** (U.S.) Harvard Univ., and **William P. Murphy** (U.S.) Harvard Univ. "for their discoveries concerning liver therapy in cases of anaemia."
1935 **Hans Spemann** (Germany) Univ. of Freiburg "for his discovery of the organizer effect in embryonic development."

1936 **Sir Henry H. Dale** (U.K.) National Institute for Medical Research, and **Otto Loewi** (Austria) Graz Univ. "for their discoveries relating to chemical transmission of nerve impulses."
1937 **Albert von Szent-Györgyi Nagyrapolt** (Hungary) Szeged Univ. "for his discoveries in connection with the biological combustion processes, with special reference to vitamin C and the catalysis of fumaric acid."
1938 **Corneille J.F. Heymans** (Belgium) Ghent Univ. "for the discovery of the role played by the sinus and aortic mechanisms in the regulation of respiration."
1939 **Gerhard Domagk** (Germany) Munster Univ. for "discovery of the antibacterial effects of prontosil."
1940–1942 No awards given.
1943 **Henrik C.P. Dam** (Denmark) Polytechnic Institut "for his discovery of vitamin K"; **Edward A. Doisy** (U.S.) St. Louis Univ. "for his discovery of the chemical nature of vitamin K."
1944 **Joseph Erlanger** (U.S.) Washington Univ. and **Herbert S. Gasser** (U.S.) Rockefeller Institute for Medical Research "for their discoveries relating to the highly differentiated functions of single nerve fibers."
1945 **Sir Alexander Fleming** (U.K.) London Univ., **Sir Ernst B. Chain** (U.K.) Oxford Univ., and **Lord Howard W. Florey** (U.K.) Oxford Univ. "for their discovery of penicillin and its curative effect in various infectious diseases."
1946 **Hermann J. Muller** (U.S.) Indiana Univ. "for his discovery of the production of mutations by means of X-ray irradiation."
1947 **Carl F. Cori** (U.S.) Washington Univ. and his wife **Gerty T. Cori** (U.S.) Washington Univ. "for their discovery of the course of the catalytic conversion of glycogen"; **Bernardo A. Houssay** (Argentina) Institute of Biology and Experimental Medicine "for his discovery of the part played by the hormone of the anterior pituitary lobe in the metabolism of sugar."
1948 **Paul H. Müller** (Switzerland) Laboratory of the J.R. Geigy Dye-Factory Co. "for his discovery of the high efficiency of DDT as a contact poison against several arthropods."
1949 **Walter R. Hess** (Switzerland) Zurich Univ. "for his discovery of the functional organization of the interbrain as a coordinator of the activities of the internal organs; **Antonio Caetano de Abreu F.E. Moniz** (Portugal) Univ. of Lisbon "for his discovery of the therapeutic value of leucotomy in certain psychoses."
1950 **Edward C. Kendall** (U.S.) Mayo Clinic, **Tadeus Reichstein** (Switzerland) Basel Univ., and **Philip S. Hench** (U.S.) Mayo Clinic "for their discoveries relating to the hormones of the adrenal cortex, their structure, and biological effects."
1951 **Max Theiler** (Union of South Africa) Laboratories Division of Medicine and Public Health, Rockefeller Foundation (New York) "for his discoveries concerning yellow fever and how to combat it."
1952 **Selman A. Waksman** (U.S.) Rutgers Univ. "for his discovery of streptomycin, the first antibiotic effective against tuberculosis."
1953 **Sir Hans A. Krebs** (U.K., b. Germany) Sheffield Univ. "for his discovery of the citric acid cycle"; **Fritz A. Lipmann** (U.S., b. Germany) Harvard Medical School and Massachusetts General Hospital "for his discovery of coenzyme A and its importance for intermediary metabolism."
1954 **John F. Enders** (U.S.) Harvard Medical School and Research Division of Infectious Diseases, Children's Medical Center; **Thomas H. Weller** (U.S.) Research Division of Infectious Diseases, Children's Medical Center; and **Frederick C. Robbins** (U.S.) Western Reserve Univ. "for their discovery of the ability of poliomyelitis viruses to grow in cultures of various types of tissue."
1955 **Axel H.T. Theorell** (Sweden) Nobel Medical Institute "for his discoveries concerning the nature and mode of action of oxidation enzymes."
1956 **Andre F. Cournand** (U.S., b. France) Cardio-Pulmonary Laboratory, Columbia Univ. Division. Bellevue Hospital; **Werner Forssman** (Germany) Mainz Univ. and Bad Kreuznach; and **Dickinson W. Richards** (U.S.) Columbia Univ. "for their discoveries concerning heart catheterization and pathological changes in the circulatory system."
1957 **Daniel Bovet** (Italy, b. Switzerland) Chief Institute of Public Health "for his discoveries relating to synthetic compounds that inhibit the action of certain body substances, and especially their action on the vascular system and the skeletal muscles."
1958 **George W. Beadle** (U.S.) California Institute of Technology, and **Edward L. Tatum** (U.S.) Rockefeller Institute for Medical Research "for their discovery that genes act by regulating definite chemical events"; **Joshua Lederberg** (U.S.) Wisconsin Univ. "for his discoveries concerning genetic recombination and the organization of the genetic material of bacteria."
1959 **Severo Ochoa** (U.S.) New York Univ. College of Medicine, and **Arthur Kornberg** (U.S.) Stanford Univ. "for their discovery of the mechanisms in the biological synthesis of ribonucleic acid and deoxyribonucleic acid."
1960 **Sir Frank M. Burnet** (Australia) Walter and Eliza Hall Institute for Medical Research, and **Sir Peter B. Medawar** (U.K.) Univ. College "for discovery of acquired immunological tolerance."
1961 **Georg von Békésy** (U.S., b. Hungary) Harvard Univ. "for his discoveries of the physical mechanism of stimulation within the cochlea."
1962 **Francis H.C. Crick** (U.K.) Institute of Molecular Biology, **James D. Watson** (U.S.) Harvard Univ., and **Maurice H.F. Wilkins** (U.K.) University of London "for their discoveries concerning the molecular structure of nuclear acids and its significance for information transfer in living material."
1963 **Sir John E. Eccles** (Australia) Australian National Univ. **Sir Alan L. Hodgkin** (U.K.) Cambridge Univ., and **Sir Andrew F. Huxley** (U.K.) University of London for their discoveries concerning the ionic mechanisms involved in excitation and inhibition in the peripheral and central portions of the nerve cell membrane."
1964 **Konrad Block** (U.S., b. Germany) Harvard Univ. and **Feodor Lymen** (Germany) Max-Planck-Institut fur Zellchemie "for their discoveries concerning the mechanism and regulation of the cholesterol and fatty acid metabolism."
1965 **Francois Jacob** (France), **André Lwoff** (France), and **Jacques Monod** (France), all from the Institut Pasteur "for their discoveries concerning genetic control of enzyme and virus synthesis."
1966 **Peyton Rous** (U.S.) Rockefeller Univ. "for his discovery of tumor-inducing viruses"; **Charles B. Huggins** (U.S.) Ben May Laboratory for Cancer Research, Univ. of Chicago "for his discoveries concerning hormonal treatment of prostatic cancer."
1967 **Ragnar Granit** (Sweden, b. Finland) Karolinska Institutet, **Haldan K. Hartline** (U.S.) Rockefeller Univ., and **George Wald** (U.S.) Harvard Univ. "for their discoveries concerning the primary physiological and chemical visual processes in the eye."
1968 **Robert W. Holley** (U.S.) Cornell Univ., **Har G. Khorana** (U.S., b. India) Univ. of Wisconsin, and **Marshall W. Nirenberg** (U.S.) National Institutes of Health "for their interpretation of the genetic code and its functions in protein synthesis."
1969 **Max Delbrück** (U.S., b. Germany) California Institute of Technology, **Alfred D. Hershey** (U.S.) Carnegie Institution of Washington, and **Salvador**

Luria (U.S., b. Italy) M.I.T. for their discoveries concerning the replication mechanism and the genetic structure of viruses."

1970 **Sir Bernard Katz** (U.K.) University College, **Ulf von Euler** (Sweden) Karolinska Institutet, and **Julius Axelrod** (U.S.) National Institutes of Health "for their discoveries concerning the humoral transmittors in the nerve terminals and the mechanism for their storage, release, and inactivation."

1971 **Earl W. Sutherland, Jr.** (U.S.) Vanderbilt Univ. "for his discoveries concerning the mechanisms of the action of hormones."

1972 **Gerald M. Edelman** (U.S.) Rockefeller Univ. and **Rodney R. Porter** (U.K.) Oxford Univ. "for their discoveries concerning the chemical structure of antibodies."

1973 **Karl von Frisch** (W. Germany) Zoologisches Institut der Universitat Munchen; **Konrad Lorenz** (Austria) Osterreichische Akademie der Wissenschaften, Institut fur vergleichende Verhaltensforschung, and **Nikolaas Tinbergen** (U.K.) University Museum for their discoveries concerning organization and elicitation of individual and social behavior patterns."

1974 **Albert Claude** (Belgium) Université Catholique de Louvain, **Christian de Duve** (Belgium) Rockefeller Univ. (New York), and **George E. Palade** (U.S., b. Romania) Yale Univ. "for their discoveries concerning the structural and functional organization of the cell."

1975 **David Baltimore** (U.S.) M.I.T., **Renato Dulbecco** (U.S., b. Italy) Imperial Cancer Research Fund Laboratory (London), and **Howard M. Temin** (U.S.) Univ. of Wisconsin "for their discoveries concerning the interaction between tumor viruses and the genetic material of the cell."

1976 **Baruch S. Blumberg** (U.S.) Institute for Cancer Research, and **D. Carleton Gajdusek** (U.S.) National Institutes of Health "for their discoveries concerning new mechanism for the origin and dissemination of infectious diseases."

1977 **Roger Guillemin** (U.S., b. France) Salk Institute, and **Andrew V. Schally** (U.S., b. Poland) Veterans Administration Hospital, New Orleans "for their discoveries concerning the peptide hormone production of the brain"; **Rosalyn Yalow** (U.S.) Veterans Administration Hospital, Bronx "for the development of radioimmunoassays of peptide hormones."

1978 **Werner Arber** (Switzerland) Biozentrum der Universitat, **Daniel Nathans** (U.S.) John Hopkins Univ., and **Hamilton O. Smith** (U.S.) John Hopkins Univ. "for the discovery of restriction enzymes and their application to problems of molecular genetics."

1979 **Alan M. Cormack** (U.S., b. South Africa) Tufts Univ., and **Sir Godfrey N. Hounsfield** (U.K.) Central Research Laboratories, EMI, "for the development of computer assisted tomography."

1980 **Baruj Benacerraf** (U.S., b. Venezuela) Harvard Medical School; **Jean Dausset** (France) Université de Paris, Laboratoire Immuno-Hemetologie; and **George D. Snell** (U.S.) Jackson Laboratory "for their discoveries concerning genetically determined structures on the cell surface that regulate immunological reactions."

1981 **Roger W. Sperry** (U.S.) California Institute of Technology "for his discoveries concerning the functional specialization of the cerebral hemispheres"; **David H. Hubel** (U.S., b. Canada) Harvard Medical School, and **Torsten T. Wiesel** (Sweden) Harvard Medical School "for their discoveries concerning information processing in the visual system."

1982 **Sune K. Bergström** (Sweden) Karolinska Institute, **Bengt I. Samuelsson** (Sweden) Karolinska Institute, and **Sir John R. Vane** (U.K.) Wellcome Research Laboratories "for their discoveries concerning prostaglandins and related biologically active substances."

1983 **Barbara McClintock** (U.S.) Cold Spring Harbor Laboratory "for her discovery of mobile genetic elements."

1984 **Niels K. Jerne** (Denmark) and **Georges J.F. Köhler** (W. Germany) of the Basel Institute for Immunology; and **César Milstein** (U.K. and Argentina) Medical Research Council Laboratory of Molecular Biology (Cambridge) for theories concerning the specificity in development and controls of the immune system and the discovery of the principle for production of monoclonal antibodies."

1985 **Michael S. Brown** (U.S.), and **Joseph L. Goldstein** (U.S.) both of the Univ. of Texas Health Science Center at Dallas "for their discoveries concerning the regulation of cholesterol metabolism."

1986 **Stanley Cohen** (U.S.) Vanderbilt Univ., and **Rita Levi-Montalcini** (Italy and U.S.) Institute of Cell Biology of the C.N.R. (Rome) "for their discoveries of growth factors."

1987 **Susumu Tonegawa** (U.S.) MIT "for discovery of the genetic principle for generation of antibody diversity."

1988 **Sir James W. Black** (U.K.) King's College Hospital Medical School, **Gertrude B. Elion** (U.S.) Welcome Research Laboratories, and **George H. Hitchings** (U.S.) Wellcome Research Laboratories "for their discoveries of Important Principles for Drug Treatment."

1989 **J. Michael Bishop** and **Harold E. Varmus** (U.S.) Univ. of California, San Francisco "for their discovery of the Cellular Origin of Retroviral Oncogenes."

1990 **Joseph E. Murray** (U.S.) Brigham and Women's Hospital (Boston) who performed the first kidney transplant (1954), and **E. Donnall Thomas** (U.S.), Fred Hutchinson Cancer Research Center (Seattle), who performed the first successful bone marrow transplant between two people who were not twins (1979).

1991 **Erwin Neher** (Germany) Max-Planck Institute for Biophysical Chemistry, Göttingen, and **Bert Sakmann** (Germany) Max-Planck Institute for Medical Research, Heidelberg, for establishing existence of ion channels by developing technique that allows detection of "incredibly small electrical currents that pass through a single ion channel."

1992 **Edmond H. Fischer** (U.S.) and **Edwin G. Krebs** (U.S.), both of the Univ. of Washington for a discovery in the 1950s of a regulatory mechanism in almost all human cells linked to some cancers, to the rejection of transplanted organs, and many other processes.

1993 **Richard J. Roberts** (U.K.), New England Bio Labs, and **Phillip A. Sharp** (U.S.), MIT, for their discovery in the 1970s that the composition of genes is of several segments, which led to gene splicing and to a better understanding of hereditary diseases and cancer.

1994 **Alfred G. Gilman** (U.S.) Univ. of Texas Southwestern Medical Center, and **Martin Rodbell** (U.S.) National Institute of Environmental Health Sciences, for their discovery of natural substances known as G-proteins and for showing how they help cells respond to stimuli like light and odors.

1995 **Edward B. Lewis** (U.S.) California Institute of Technology, **Eric F. Wieschaus** (U.S.) Princeton Univ., and **Christiane Nüsslein-Volhard** (Germany) Max-Planck Institute in Tübingen, for their discovery of how genes control structural development of the body. Their research, performed on fruit flies, helps explain birth defects in humans.

1996 **Peter C. Doherty** (Australia) St. Jude's Medical Center in Memphis, and **Rolf Zinkernagel** (Switzerland) University of Zurich, "for their discoveries concerning the specificity of the cell mediated immune

defense." Their work explained how the immune system recognizes and kills virus-infected cells.
1997 **Stanley B. Prusiner** (U.S.), Univ. of California, "for his discovery of Prions," disease-causing proteins that can be linked to degenerative brain diseases.
1998 **Robert F. Furchgott** (U.S.), SUNY Health Science Center; **Louis J. Ignarro** (U.S.), UCLA School of Medicine; and **Ferid Murad** (U.S.), Univ. of Texas, ""for their discoveries concerning nitric oxide as a signalling molecule in the cardiovascular system."
1999 **Günter Blobel** (U.S., b. Germany), Rockefeller Univ. "for the discovery that proteins have intrinsic signals that govern their transport and localization in the cel." Blobel found that many hereditary diseases are caused by mistakes in these signals.
2000 **Arvid Carlsson** (Sweden), Univ. of Gothenburg; **Paul Greengard** (U.S.), Rockefeller Univ., N.Y.; and **Eric Kandel** (U.S.), Columbia Univ., "for their discoveries concerning signal transduction in the nervous system," leading to greater understanding of neurological and psychiatric diseases like Parkinson's.
2001 **Leland H. Hartwell** (U.S.), Fred Hutchinson Cancer Research Center, Seattle, and **R. Timothy Hunt** (U.K.) and **Sir Paul M. Nurse** (U.K.), both of the Imperial Cancer Research Fund, London, "for their discoveries of key regulators of the cell cycle," which may lead to cures for irregular cell growth patterns like cancer.
2002 **Sydney Brenner,** (U.K.), Molecular Sciences Institute, **H. Robert Horvitz**, (U.S.), M.I.T., and **John E. Sulston,** (U.K.), Wellcome Trust Sanger Institute "for their discoveries concerning genetic regulation of organ development and programmed cell death." Their work has given scientists insights into cancer and the ways bacteria and viruses invade human cells.
2003 See Part I: "The Almanac of the Year."

Nobel Prizes in Economic Sciences

1969 **Ragnar Frisch** (Norway) Oslo Univ. and **Jan Tinbergen** (Netherlands) Netherlands School of Economics "for having developed and applied dynamic models for the analysis of economic processes."
1970 **Paul A. Samuelson** (U.S.) M.I.T. "for the scientific work through which he has developed static and dynamic economic theory and...contributed to raising the level of analysis in economic science."
1971 **Simon Kuznets** (U.S.) Harvard Univ. "for his empirically founded interpretation of economic growth which has led to new and deepened insight into the economic and social structure and process of development."
1972 **Sir John R. Hicks** (U.K.) All Souls College, and **Kenneth J. Arrow** (U.S.) Harvard Univ. "for their pioneering contributions to general economic equilibrium theory and welfare theory."
1973 **Wassily Leontief** (U.S.) Harvard Univ. "for the development of the input-output method and for its application to important economic problems."
1974 **Gunnar Mydal** (Sweden), **Friedrich A. von Hayek** (U.K.) "for their pioneering work in the theory of money and economic fluctuations and for their penetrating analysis of the interdependence of economic, social and institutional phenomena."
1975 **Leonid Kantorovich** (USSR) Academy of Sciences, and **Tjalling C. Koopmans** (U.S.) Yale Univ. "for their contributions to the theory of optimum allocation of resources."
1976 **Milton Friedman** (U.S.) Univ. of Chicago for "achievements in the fields of consumption analysis, monetary history and theory. . ."
1977 **Bertil Ohlin** (Sweden) Stockholm School of Economics, and **James E. Meade** (U.K.) Cambridge Univ. "for their pathbreaking contribution to the theory of international trade and international capital movements."
1978 **Herbert A. Simon** (U.S.) Carnegie-Mellon Univ. "for his pioneering research into the decision-making process within economic organizations."
1979 **Theodore W. Schultz** (U.S.) Univ. of Chicago, and **Sir Arthur Lewis** (U.K.) Princeton Univ. "for their pioneering research into economic development research with particular consideration of the problems of developing countries."
1980 **Lawrence R. Klein** (U.S.) Univ. of Pennsylvania "for the creation of econometric models and their application to the analysis of economic fluctuations and economic policies."
1981 **James Tobin** (U.S.) Yale Univ. "for his analysis of financial markets and their relations to expenditure decisions, employment, production, and prices."
1982 **George J. Stigler** (U.S.) Univ. of Chicago "for his seminal studies of industrial structures, functioning markets, and causes and effects of public regulation."
1983 **Gerard Debreu** (U.S.) Univ. of California, "for having incorporated new analytical methods into economic theory and for his rigorous reformulation of the theory of general equilbrium."
1984 **Sir Richard Stone** (U.K.) Cambridge Univ. "for having made fundamental contributions to the development of systems of national accounts and hence greatly improved [sic]the basis for empirical economic analysis."
1985 **Franco Modigliani** (U.S.) M.I.T. "for his pioneering analyses of saving and of financial markets.
1986 **James M Buchanan Jr.** (U.S.) Center for Study of Public Choice "for his development of the contractual and constitutional bases for the theory of economic and political decision-making."
1987 **Robert M. Solow** (U.S.) M.I.T. "for his contributions to the theory of economic growth."
1988 **Maurice Allais** (France) Centre d'analyse économique "for his pioneering contributions to the theory of markets and efficient utilization of resources.
1989 **Trygve Haavelmo** (Norway) Univ. of Oslo "for his clarification of the probability theory foundations of econometircs and his analyses of simultaneous economic structures."
1990 **Harry Markowitz** (U.S.) Baruch College (of the City Univ. of New York, for his Portfolio Theory; **William F. Sharpe** (U.S.) Stanford Univ., for his Capital Asset Pricing Model, and **Merton Miller** (U.S.) Univ. of Chicago, for his work on the Miller-Modigliani Theory. Together, their work revolutionized the financial/business industries.
1991 **Ronald H. Coase** (U.K.) Univ. of Chicago Law School, for his work on the role of firms in the economy and on social cost of industry, notably his articles "The Theory of the Firm" (1937) and "The Problem of Social Cost" (1960).
1992 **Gary S. Becker** (U.S.), Univ. of Chicago, for "having extended the domain of economic theory to aspects of human behavior . . ." including crime, family life, and racial bias. His book on education, *Human Capital* (1964), was cited by the Academy.
1993 **Robert W. Fogel** (U.S.), Univ. of Chicago, and **Douglass C. North** (U.S.), Washington Univ., for "applying economic theory and quarantine methods

to historical puzzles." Fogel's work on slavery as an efficient economic system caused great controversy.
1994 **John F. Nash** (U.S.) Princeton Univ., **John C., Harsanyi** (U.S., b. Hungary) Univ. of California, and **Reinhard Selten** (Germany) Univ. of Bonn, for their separate contributions to the field of game theory, which is used to predict how information and competition affect economic outcomes.
1995 **Robert E. Lucas, Jr.,** (U.S.) Univ. of Chicago, "the economist who has had the greatest influence on macroeconomic research since 1970." His work challenges the Keynesian belief that the government is able to fine-tune the economy.
1996 **James A. Mirrlees** (U.K.) Cambridge, Univ. and **William Vickrey** (U.S., b. Canada), Columbia Univ. for "their fundamental contributions to the economic theory of incentives." Their theories have been used in designing more efficient tax codes and eliciting the highest bids at auctions. **1997** **Robert Merton** (U.S.), Harvard University, and **Myron Scholes** (U.S.), Stanford University, for their work in creating "a pioneering formula for the valuation of stock options" and other derivatives. The Nobel committee cited their research as one of the principal reasons for the success of the derivatives markets.
1998 **Amartya Sen** (India), Cambridge Univ. and Harvard Univ., for his work on human rights, poverty, and inequality that has changed the way governments deal with famines, and for restoring "an ethical dimension to the discussion of vital economics problems."
1999 **Robert A. Mundell** (U.S.,b. Canada), Columbia University, "for his analysis of monetary and fiscal policy under different exchange rate regimes and his analysis of optimum currency areas." Although his work dates back several decades, "Mundell's contributions remain outstanding and constitute the core of teaching in international macroeconomics."
2000 **James J. Heckman** (U.S.), Univ. of Chicago "for his development of theory and methods for analyzing selective samples," and **Daniel L. McFadden** (U.S.), Univ. of California, "for his development of theory and methods for analyzing discrete choice."
2001 **George A. Akerlof** (U.S.) Univ. of California, **A. Michael Spence** (U.S.), Stanford Univ., and **Joseph E. Stiglitz** (U.S.), Columbia Univ. "for their analyses of markets with asymmetric information." Their work has applications in situations ranging from the elderly's inability to find low-cost medical insurance to the prices charged for used cars.
2002 **Daniel Kahneman,** (U.S. and Israel), Princeton University and **Vernon L. Smith,** (U.S.), George Mason University, whose achievements break new ground in incorporating experimental methods into the study of economics.
2003 See Part I: "The Almanac of the Year."

Nobel Prizes in Chemistry

1901 **Jacobus H. Van't Holt** (Netherlands) Berlin Univ. (Germany) for "the extraordinary services he has rendered by the discovery of the laws of chemical dynamics and osmotic pressure in solutions."
1902 **Hermann E. Fischer** (Germany) "in recognition of the extraordinary services he has rendered by his work on sugar and purine synthesis."
1903 **Svante A. Arrhenius** (Sweden) Stockholm Univ. "in recognition of the extraordinary services he has rendered to the advancement of chemistry by his electrolytic theory of dissociation."
1904 **Sir William Ramsay** (U.K.) London Univ. "in recognition of his services in the discovery of the inert gaseous elements in air; and his determination of their place in the periodic system."
1905 **Johann F.W.A. von Baeyer** (Germany) Munich Univ. "in recognition of his services in the advancement of organic chemistry and the chemical industry, through his work on organic dyes and hydroaromatic compounds."
1906 **Henri Moissan** (France) Sorbonne Univ. "in recognition of the great services rendered by him in his investigation and isolation of the element fluorine, and for the adoption in the service of science of the electric furnace called after him."
1907 **Eduard Buchner** (Germany) Agricultural College "for his biochemical researches and his discovery of cell-free fermentation."
1908 **Lord Ernest Rutherfold** (U.K.) Victoria Univ. "for his investigation into the disintegration of the elements, and the chemistry of radioactive substances."
1909 **Wilhelm Ostwald** (Germany) Leipzig Univ. "in recognition of his work on catalysis, and for his investigations into the fundamental principles governing chemical equilibria and rates of reaction."
1910 **Otto Wallach** (Germany) Goettingen Univ. "in recognition of his services to organic chemistry and the chemical industry by his pioneer work in the field of alicyclic compounds."
1911 **Marie Curie** (France) Sorbonne Univ. "in recognition of her services to the advancement of chemistry by the discovery of the elements radium and polonium, by the isolation of radium and the study of the nature and compounds of this remarkable element."
1912 **Victor Grignard** (France) Nancy Univ. "for the discovery of the so-called Grignard reagent, which in recent years has greatly advanced the progress of organic chemistry"; **Paul Sabatier** (France) Toulouse Univ., "for his method of hydrogenating organic compounds in the presence of finely disintegrated metals whereby the progress of organic chemistry has been greatly advanced in recent years."
1913 **Alfred Werner** (Switzerland) Zurich Univ. "in recognition of his work on the linkage of atoms in molecules by which he has thrown new light on earlier investigations and opened up new fields of research especially in inorganic chemistry."
1914 **Theodore W. Richards** (U.S.) Harvard Univ. for "his accurate determinations of the atomic weight of a large number of chemical elements."
1915 **Richard M. Willstätter** (Germany) Munich Univ. "for his researches on plant pigments, especially chlorophyll."
1916–1917 No awards given.
1918 **Fritz Haber** (Germany) Kaiser-Wilhelm Institut "for the synthesis of ammonia from its elements.
1919 No award
1920 **Walther H. Nernst** (Germany) Berlin Univ. "in recognition of his work in thermochemistry."
1921 **Frederick Soddy** (U.K.) Oxford Univ. "for his contributions to our knowledge of the chemistry of radioactive substances, and his investigations into the origin and nature of isotopes."
1922 **Francis W. Aston** (U.K.) Cambridge Univ. "for his discovery, by means of his mass spectrograph, of isotopes in a large number of nonradioactive elements, and for his enunciation of the whole-number rule."
1923 **Fritz Pregl** (Austria) Graz Univ. "for his invention of the method of microanalysis of organic substances."

1924 No award
1925 **Richard A. Zsigmondy** (Germany) Goettingen Univ. "for his demonstration of the heterogeneous nature of colloid solutions."
1926 **The (Theodor) Svedberg** (Sweden) Uppsala Univ. "for his work on disperse systems."
1927 **Heinrich O. Wieland** (Germany) Munich Univ. "for his investigations of the constitution of the bile acids and related substances."
1928 **Adolf O.R. Windaus** (Germany) Goettingen Univ. "for the services rendered through his research into the constitution of the sterols and their connection with the vitamins."
1929 **Sir Arthur Harden** (U.K.) London Univ., Hans K.A. von Euler-Chelpin (Sweden) "for their investigations on the fermentation of sugar and fermentative enzymes."
1930 **Hans Fischer** (Germany) Institute of Technology "for his researches into the constitution of haemin and chlorophyll, and especially for his synthesis of haemin."
1931 **Carl Bosch** (Germany) Heidelberg Univ. I.G. Farbenindustrie A.G., and **Fredrich Bergius** (Germany) Heidelberg Univ. and I.G. Farbenindustrie A.G. for "their contributions to the invention and development of chemical high pressure methods."
1932 **Irving Langmuir** (U.S.) General Electric Co., "for his discoveries and investigations in surface chemistry."
1933 No award
1934 **Harold C. Urey** (U.S.) Columbia Univ. "for his discovery of heavy hydrogen."
1935 **Frédéric Joliot** (France) Institut du Radium and his wife, **Iréne Joliot-Curie,** (France) Institut du Radium "in recognition of their synthesis of new radioactive elements."
1936 **Petrus (Peter) J.W. Debye** (Netherlands) Berlin Univ. and Kaiser-Wilhelm-Institut (now Max-Planck-Institut) "for his contributions to our knowledge of molecular structure through his investigations on dipole moments and on the diffraction of X-rays and electrons in gases."
1937 **Sir Walter N. Haworth** (U.K.) Birmingham Univ. "for his investigations on carbohydrates and vitamin C"; **Paul Karrer** (Switzerland) Zurich Univ. "for his investigations on carotenoids, flavins, and vitamins A and B-2."
1938 **Richard Kuhn** (Germany) Heidelberg Univ. and Kaiser-Wilhelm-Institut (now Max-Planck-Institut) "for his work on carotenoids and vitamins. (Compelled by the authorities of his country to decline the award, but later received diploma and medal.)
1939 **Adolf F.J. Butenandt** (Germany) Berlin Univ. and Kaiser-Wilhelm-Institut (now Max-Planck-Institut) "for his work on sex hormones. (Compelled by his country to decline the award, but later received diploma and medal); **Leopold Ruzicka** (Switzerland) Federal Institute of Technology "for his work on polymethylenes and higher terpenes."
1940–1942 No awards
1943 **George de Hevesy** (Hungary) Stockholm Univ. "for his work on the use of isotopes as tracers in the study of chemical processes."
1944 **Otto Hahn** (Germany) Kaiser-Wilhelm-Institut (now Max-Planck-Institut) "for his discovery of the fission of heavy nuclei."
1945 **Artturi I. Virtanen** (Finland) Helsinki Univ. "for his research and inventions in agricultural and nutrition chemistry, especially for his fodder preservation method."
1946 **James B. Sumner** (U.S.) Cornell Univ. "for his discovery that enzymes can be crystallized"; **John H. Northrop** (U.S.) Rockefeller Institute for Medical Research "for their preparation of enzymes and virus proteins in a pure form."
1947 **Sir Robert Robinson** (U.K.) Oxford Univ. "for his investigations on plant products of biological importance, especially alkaloids."
1948 **Arne W.K. Tiselius** (Sweden) Uppsala Univ. "for his research on electrophoresis and adsorption analysis, especially for his discoveries concerning the complex nature of the serum proteins."
1949 **William F. Giauque** (U.S.) Univ. of California, "for his contributions in the field of chemical thermodynamics, particularly concerning the behavior of substances at extremely low temperatures."
1950 **Otto P.H. Diels** (Germany) Kiel Univ. and **Kurt Alder** (Germany) Cologne Univ. "for their discovery and development of the diene synthesis."
1951 **Edwin M. McMillan** (U.S.) and **Glenn T. Seaborg** (U.S.) both of Univ. of California, "for their discoveries in the chemistry of the transuranium elements."
1952 **Archer J.P. Martin** (U.K.) Nations Institute for Medical Research, and **Richard L.M. Synge** (U.K.) Rowett Research Institute (Scotland) "for their invention of partition chromatography."
1953 **Herman Staudinger** (Germany) State Research Institute for Macromolecular Chemistry "for his discoveries in the field of macromolecular chemistry."
1954 **Linus C. Pauling** (U.S.) California Institute of Technology "for his research into the nature of the chemical bond and its application to the elucidation of the structure of complex substances."
1955 **Vincent du Vigneaud** (U.S.) Cornell Univ. "for his work on biochemically important sulphur compounds, especially for the first synthesis of a polypeptide hormone."
1956 **Sir Cyril N. Hinshelwood** (U.K.) Oxford Univ. and **Nikolaj N. Semenov** (USSR) Institute for Chemical Physics of the Academy of Sciences of the USSR "for their researches into the mechanism of chemical reactions."
1957 **Lord Alexander R. Todd** (U.K.) Cambridge Univ. "for his work on nucleotides and nucleotide co-enzymes."
1958 **Frederick Sanger** (U.K.) Cambridge Univ. "for his work on the structure of proteins, especially that of insulin."
1959 **Jaroslav Heyrovsky** (Czechoslovakia) Polaro-Institute of the Czechoslovakia Academy of Science for his discovery and development of the polarographic methods of analysis."
1960 **Willard F. Libby** (U.S.) Univ. of California, Los Angeles "for his method to use carbon-14 for age determination in archaeology, geology, geophysics, and other branches of science."
1961 **Melvin Calvin** (U.S.) Univ. of California, for research on carbon dioxide assimilation in plants."
1962 **Max F. Perutz** (U.K.) Laboratory of Molecular Biology, and **Sir John C. Kendrew** (U.K.) Laboratory of Molecular Biology, "for their studies on the structures of globular proteins."
1963 **Karl Ziegler** (Germany) Max-Planck-Institute for Carbon Research, and **Giulio Natta** (Italy) Institute of Technology "for their discoveries in the field of the chemistry and technology of high polymers."
1964 **Dorothy C. Hodgkin** (U.K.) Royal Society, Oxford Univ. "for her determinations by X-ray techniques of the structures of important biochemical substances."
1965 **Robert B. Woodward** (U.S.) Harvard Univ. "for his outstanding achievements in the art of organic synthesis."

1966 **Robert S. Mulliken** (U.S.) Univ. of Chicago "for his fundamental work concerning chemical bonds and the electronic structure of molecules by the molecular orbital method."

1967 **Manfred Eigen** (W. Germany) Max-Planck-Institut, **Ronald G.W. Norrish** (U.K.) Institute of Physical Chemistry, and **Sir George Porter** (U.K.) The Royal Institution "for their studies of extremely fast chemical reactions, effected by disturbing the equilibrium by means of very short pulses of energy."

1968 **Lars Onsager** (U.S.) Yale Univ. "for the discovery of the reciprocal relations bearing his name, which are fundamental for the thermodynamics of irreversible processes."

1969 **Sir Derek H.R. Barton** (U.K.) Imperial College of Science and Technology, and **Odd Hassel** (Norway) Kjemisk Institut "for their contributions to the development of the concept of conformation and its application in chemistry."

1970 **Luis F. Leloir** (Argentina) Institute for Biochemical Research for his discovery of sugar nucleotides and their role in the biosynthesis of carbohydrates."

1971 **Gerhard Herzberg** (Canada) National Research Council of Canada "for his contributions to the knowledge of electronic structure and geometry of molecules, particularly free radicals."

1972 **Christian B. Anfinsen** (U.S.) National Institutes of Health "for his work on ribonuclease, especially concerning the connection between the amino acid sequence and the biologically active conformation"; **Stanford Moore** (U.S.) Rockefeller Univ. and **William H. Stein** (U.S.) Rockefeller Univ. "for their contribution to the understanding of the connection between chemical structure and catalytic activity of the active center of the ribonuclease molecule."

1973 **Ernst O. Fischer** (W. Germany) Technical Univ. of Munich, and **Sir Geoffrey Wilkinson** (U.K.) Imperial College "for their pioneering work, performed independently, on the chemistry of the organometallic, so-called sandwich compounds."

1974 **Paul J. Flory** (U.S.) Stanford Univ. "for his fundamental achievements, both theoretical and experimental, in the physical chemistry of the macromolecules."

1975 **Sir John W. Cornforth** (Australia and U.K.) Univ. of Sussex "for his work on the stereo-chemistry of enzyme-catalyzed reactions"; **Vladimir Prelog** (Switzerland) Eidgenossische Technische Hochschule "for his research into the sterochemistry of organic molecules and reactions."

1976 **William N. Lipscomb** (U.S.) Harvard Univ. "for his studies on the structure of boranes illuminating problems of chemical bonding."

1977 **Ilya Prigogine** (Belgium) Université Libre de Bruxelles, (Univ. of Texas, U.S.) "for his contributions to nonequilibrium thermodynamics, particularly the theory of dissipative structures."

1978 **Peter D. Mitchell** (U.K.) Glynn Research Laboratories "for his contribution to the understanding of biological energy transfer through the formulation of the chemiosmotic theory."

1979 **Herbert C. Brown** (U.S.) Purdue Univ., and **Georg Wittig** (Germany) Univ. of Heidelberg "for their development of the use of boron-and-phosphorus-containing compounds, respectively, into important reagents in organic synthesis."

1980 **Paul Berg** (U.S.) Stanford Univ. "for his fundamental studies of the biochemistry of nucleic acids, with particular regard to recombinant-DNA"; **Walter Gilbert** (U.S.) Biological Laboratories, and **Frederick Sanger** (U.K.) MRC Laboratory of Molecular Biology "for their contributions concerning the determination of base sequences in nucleic acids."

1981 **Kenichi Fukui** (Japan) Kyoto Univ. and **Roald Hoffman** (U.S.) Cornell Univ. "for their theories, developed independently, concerning the course of chemical reactions."

1982 **Aaron Klug** (U.K.) MRC Laboratory of Molecular Biology "for his development of crystallographic electron microscopy and his structural elucidation of biologically important nucleic acid-protein complexes."

1983 **Henry Taube** (U.S.) Stanford Univ. "for his work on the mechanisms of electron transfer reactions, especially in metal complexes."

1984 **Robert B. Merrifield** (U.S.) Rockefeller Univ. "for his development of methodology for chemical synthesis on solid matrix."

1985 **Herbert A. Hauptman** (U.S.) Medical Foundation of Buffalo, and **Jerome Karle** (U.S.) U.S. Naval Research Laboratory "for their outstanding achievements in the development of direct methods for the determination of crystal structures."

1986 **Dudley R. Herschbach** (U.S.) Harvard Univ., **Yuan T. Lee** (U.S.) Univ. of California, and **John C. Polanyi** (Canada) Univ. of Toronto, "for their contributions concerning the dynamics of chemical elementary processes."

1987 **Donald J. Cram** (U.S.) University of California, Los Angeles, **Jean-Marie Lehn** (France) Université Louis Pasteur, and **Charles J. Pedersen** (U.S.) Du Pont Laboratory "for their development and use of molecules with structure-specific interactions of high selectivity."

1988 **Johann Deisenhofer** (U.S.) Howard Hughes Medical Institute, Robert Huber (W. Germany) Max-Planck-Institut, and **Hartmut Michel** (W. Germany) Max-Planck-Institut, "for their determination of the three-dimensional structure of a photosynthetic reaction centre."

1989 **Sidney Altman** (U.S.) Yale Univ., and **Thomas Cech** (U.S.) Univ. of Colorado for their separate discoveries of the catalytic properties of RNA.

1990 **Elias James Corey** (U.S.) Harvard Univ. for developing new ways to synthesize complex molecules ordinarily found in nature, work that has contributed to "the high standard of living and health, and the longevity enjoyed at least in the Western world."

1991 **Richard R. Ernst** (Switzerland) Eidgenössische Technische Hochschule, Zurich, for his work in refining nuclear magnetic resonance spectroscopy for use in chemical analysis.

1992 **Rudolph A. Marcus** (U.S., b. Canada), Cal Tech., for his mathematical explanation of chemical interactions involving the transfer of electrons between molecules.

1993 **Kary B. Mullis** (U.S.) for his discovery, in the 1970s, of the polymerase chain reaction (PCR) that allowed scientists to make trillions of copies of DNA. **Michael Smith** (Canada), Univ. of British Columbia, for developing the technique that alters the code of genetic molecules that will facilitate new medical therapies and plants that resist disease.

1994 **George A. Olah** (U.S., b. Hungary) Univ. of Southern California, for his discovery of new ways of breaking apart and rebuilding carbon and hydrogen compounds. He opened a wholly new field of hydrocarbon research, leading to improved fuels based on coal, methane, and petroleum.

1995 **F. Sherwood Roland** (U.S.) Univ. of California-Irvine, **Mario Molina** (U.S.) M.I.T., and **Paul Crutzen** (Netherlands) Max Planck Institute for Chemistry in Mainz, Germany, for their pioneering work in explaining how production and use of refrigerants and other chlorofluorocarbons deplete the

ozone layer, thus increasing the risk of skin cancer, cataracts, and damage to human immune systems.
1996 **Robert F. Curl, Jr.,** (U.S.) and **Richard E. Smalley** (U.S.), of Rice University, and **Harold W. Kroto** (U.K.) of Univ. of Sussex, for their 1985 discovery of buckminsterfullerene, or "buckyballs." Their work opened an entirely new branch of chemistry and gve scientists a greater understanding on how nature bonds carbon atoms together.
1997 **Paul D. Boyer** (U.S.), UCLA and **John E. Walker** (U.K.), Medical Research Council Laboratory of Molecular Biology, for demonstrating how all living things create adenosine triphosphate, a tiny molecule that stores energy and builds proteins, transmits nerve impulses, and contracts muscles. **Jens C. Skou** (Denmark), Aarhus Univ., for his discovery of sodium-potassium-stimulated adenosine triphosphate, an enzyme that maintains the balance of sodium and potassium ions in living cells.
1998 **Walter Kohn** (U.S., b. Austria), Univ. of California, Santa Barbara; **John A. Pople** (U.S., b U.K.), Northwestern Univ. Their achievements helped extend the mathematics of quantum mechanics to predicting specific chemical reactions and designing molecules for use in medicine and other applications.
1999 **Ahmed H. Zewail** (U.S., b. Egypt), CalTech, "for showing that it is possible with rapid laser technique to see how atoms in a molecule move during a chemical reaction," allowing scientists to study chemical reactions in extremely intricate detail.
2000 **Alan J. Heeger** (U.S.), Univ. of California at Santa Barbara; **Alan G. MacDiarmid** (U.S.), Univ. of Pennsylvania; and **Hideki Shirakawa** (Japan), Univ. of Tsukuba, for their discovery and development of a plastic that conducts electricity like a metal and may be used to increase the speed and decrease the size of computers.
2001 **William S. Knowles** (U.S.) and **Ryoji Noyori**, (Japan), Nagoya Univ. "for their work on chirally catalysed hydrogenation reactions." **K. Barry Sharpless** (U.S.), Scripps Research Institute, La Jolla, Calif., "for his work on chirally catalysed oxidation reactions," making possible the development of new drugs (including beta-blockers), as well as the production of insecticides and flavoring and sweetening agents.
2002 **John B. Fenn,** (U.S.), Virginia Commonwealth University, and **Koichi Tanaka,** (Japan), Shimadzu Corporation; and **Kurt Wüthrich,** (Switzerland), Swiss Federal Institute of Technology Zürich, and The Scripps Research Institute, La Jolla, Calif "for the development of methods for identification and structure analyses of biological macromolecules," through achievements in the fields of mass spectrometry and nuclear magnetic resonance spectrometry.
2003 See Part I: "The Almanac of the Year."

Nobel Prizes in Physics

1901 **Wilhelm C. Röntgen** (Germany) Munich Univ. "in recognition of the extraordinary services he has rendered by the discovery of remarkable rays subsequently named after him."
1902 **Hendrik A. Lorentz** (Netherlands) Leyden Univ., and **Pieter Zeeman** (Netherlands) Amsterdam Univ. "in recognition of the extraordinary service they rendered by their researches into the influence of magnetism upon radiation phenomena."
1903 **Antoine H. Becquerel** (France) Ecole Polytechnique "in recognition of the extraordinary services he has rendered by the discovery of spontaneous radioactivity"; **Pierre Curie** (France) Municipal School of Industrial Physics and Chemistry and his wife, **Marie Curie,** (France, b. Poland) "in recognition of the extraordinary services they have rendered by their joint researches on the radiation phenomena discovered by Professor Henri Becquerel."
1904 **Lord Rayleigh** (John W. Strutt) (U.K.) Royal Institution of U.K. "for his investigations of the densities of the most important gases and for his discovery of argon in connection with these studies."
1905 **Philipp E.A. Lenard** (Germany) Kiel Univ. "for his work on cathode rays."
1906 **Sir Joseph J. Thomas** (U.K.) Cambridge Univ. "in recognition of the great merits of his theoretical and experimental investigations on the conduction of electricity by gases."
1907 **Albert A. Michelson** (U.S.) Univ. of Chicago "for his optical precision instruments and the spectroscopic and meteorological investigations carried out with their aid."
1908 **Gabriel Lippman** (France) Sorbonne Univ. "for his method of reproducing colours photographically based on the phenomenon of interference."
1909 **Guglielmo Marconi** (Italy) Marconi Wireless Telegraph Co., Ltd., and **Carl F. Braun** (Germany) Strasbourg Univ. "in recognition of their contributions to the development of wireless telegraphy."
1910 **Johannes D. van der Waals** (Netherlands) Amsterdam Univ. "for his work on the equation of state for gases and liquids."
1911 **Wilhelm Wein** (Germany) Würzburg Univ. "for his discoveries regarding the laws governing the radiation of heat."
1912 **Nils G. Dalén** (Sweden) Swedish Gas-Accumulator Co. "for his invention of automatic regulators for use in conjunction with gas accumulators for illuminating lighthouses and buoys."
1913 **Heike Kamerlingh-Onnes** (Netherlands) Leyden Univ. "for his investigations on the properties of matter at low temperatures which led, inter alia, to the production of liquid helium."
1914 **Max von Laue** (Germany) Frankfurt-am-Main Univ. "for his discovery of the diffraction of X-rays by crystals."
1915 **Sir William Henry Bragg** (U.K.) London Univ. and his son **Sir William Lawrence Bragg** (U.K.) Victoria Univ. "for their services in the analysis of crystal structure by means of X-rays."
1916 No award.
1917 **Charles G. Barkla** (U.K.) Edinburgh Univ. "for his discovery of the characteristic Röntgen radiation of the elements."
1918 **Max K.E.L. Planck** (Germany) Berlin Univ. "in recognition of the services he rendered to the advancement of Physics by his discovery of energy quanta."
1919 **Johannes Stark** (Germany) Greifswald Univ. "for his discovery of the Doppler effect in canal rays and the splitting of spectral lines in electric fields."
1920 **Charles E. Guillaume** (Switzerland) International Bureau of Weights and Measurers "in recognition of the service he has rendered to precision measurements in physics by his discovery of anomalies in nickel steel alloys."
1921 **Albert Einstein** (Germany) Kaiser-Wilhelm-Institut für Physik (now Max-Panck-Institut) "for his services to theoretical physics, and especially for his discovery of the law of the photoelectric effect."
1922 **Niels Bohr** (Denmark) Copenhagen Univ. "for his services in the investigation of the structure of atoms and of the radiation emanating from them."

1923 Robert A. Millikan (U.S.) California Institute of Technology) "for his work on the elementary charge of electricity and on the photoelectric effect."
1924 Karl M.G. Siegbahn (Sweden) Uppsala Univ. "for his discoveries and research in the field of X-ray spectroscopy."
1925 James Franck (Germany) Goettingen Univ., and **Gustav Hertz** (Germany) Halle Univ. "for their discovery of the laws of governing the impact of an electron upon an atom."
1926 Jean B. Perrin (France) Sorbonne Univ. "for his work on the discontinuous structure of matter, and especially for his discovery of sedimentation equilibrium."
1927 Arthur H. Compton (U.S.) Univ. of Chicago "for his discovery of the effect named after him"; **Charles T.R. Wilson** (U.K.) Cambridge Univ. "for his method of making the paths of electrically charged particles visible by condensation of vapor."
1928 Sir Own W. Richardson (U.K.) London Univ. "for his work on the thermionic phenomenon and especially for the discovery of the law named after him."
1929 Prince Louis-Victor de Broglie (France) Sorbonne Univ. "for his discovery of the wave nature of electrons."
1930 Sir Chandrasekhara V. Raman (India) Calcutta Univ. "for his work on the scattering of light and for the discovery of the effect names after him."
1931 No award.
1932 Werner Heisenberg (Germany) Leipzig Univ. "for the creation of quantum mechanics, the application of which, has, inter alia, led to the discovery of the allotropic forms of hydrogen."
1933 Edwin Schrödinger (Austria) Berlin Univ. and **Paul A.M. Dirac** (U.K.) Cambridge Univ. "for the discovery of new productive forms of atomic theory."
1934 No award
1935 Sir James Chadwick (U.K.) Liverpool Univ. "for his discovery of the neutron."
1936 Victor F. Hess (Austria) Innsbruck Univ. "for his discovery of cosmic radiation"; **Carl D. Anderson** (U.S.) California Institute of Technology "for his discovery of the positron."
1937 Clinton J. Davisson (U.S.) Bell Telephone Laboratories, and **Sir George P. Thomson** (U.K.) London Univ. "for their experimental discovery of the diffraction of electrons by crystals."
1938 Enrico Fermi (Italy) Rome Univ. "for his demonstration of the existence of new radioactive elements produced by neutron irradiation, and for his related discovery of nuclear reactions brought about by slow neutrons."
1939 Ernest O. Lawrence (U.S.) Univ. of California, Berkeley "for the invention and development of the cyclotron and for results obtained with it, especially with regard to artificial redioactive elements."
1940–1942 No awards given.
1943 Otto Stern (U.S.) Carnegie Institute of Technology "for his contribution to the development of the molecular ray method and his discovery of the magnetic moment of the proton."
1944 Isidor I. Rabi (U.S.) Columbia Univ. "for his resonance method for recording the magnetic properties of atomic nuclei."
1945 Wolfgang Pauli (Austria) Princeton Univ. "for the discovery of the Exclusion Principle, also called the Pauli Principle."
1946 Percy W. Bridgman (U.S.) Harvard Univ. "for the invention of an apparatus to produce extremely high pressures, and for the discoveries he made therewith in the field of high-pressure physics."
1947 Sir Edward V. Appleton (U.K.) Dept. of Scientific and Industrial Research "for his investigations of the physics of the upper atmosphere, especially the so-called Appleton layer."
1948 Lord Patrick M.S. Blackett (U.K.) Victoria Univ. "for his development of the Wilson cloud chamber method, and his discoveries therewith in the fields of nuclear physics and cosmic radiation."
1949 Hideki Yukawa (Japan) Kyoto Imperial Univ. "for his prediction of the existence of mesons on the basis of theoretical work on nuclear forces."
1950 Cecil F. Powell (U.K.) Bristol Univ. "for his development of the photographic method of studying nuclear processes and his discoveries regarding mesons made with this method."
1951 Sir John D. Cockcroft (U.K.) Atomic Energy Research Establishment, and Ernest T.S. Walton (Ireland) Dublin Univ. "for their pioneer work on the transmutation of atomic nuclei by artificially accelerated atomic particles."
1952 Felix Block (U.S.) Stanford Univ., and **Edward M. Purcell** (U.S.) Harvard Univ. "for their development of new methods for nuclear magnetic precision measurements and discoveries in connection therewith."
1953 Frits (Frederik) Zernike (Netherlands) Groningern Univ. "for his demonstration of the phase contrast method, especially for his invention of the phase contrast microscope."
1954 Max Born (U.K.) Edinburgh Univ. "for his fundamental research in quantum mechanics, especially for his statistical interpretation of the wavefunction"; **Walther Bothe** (Germany) Heidelbery Univ., Max-Planck-Institut "for the coincidence method and his discoveries made therewith."
1955 Willis E. Lamb (U.S.) Stanford Univ. "for his discoveries concerning the fine structure of the hydrogen spectrum"; **Polykarp Kusch** (U.S.) Columbia Univ. "for his precision determination of the magnetic moment of the electron."
1956 William Shockley (U.S. Semiconductor Laboratory of Beckman Instruments, Inc., **John Bardeen** (U.S.) Univ. of Illinois, and **Walter H. Brattain** (U.S.) Bell Telephone Laboratories for research on semiconductors and discovery of "the transistor effect."
1957 Chen N. Yang (China) Institute for Advanced Study (Princeton, NJ) and **Tsung-Dao Lee** (China) Columbia Univ. "for their penetrating investigation of the so-called parity laws which has led to important discoveries regarding the elementary particles."
1958 Pavel A. Cherenkov (USSR) Physics Institute of USSR Academy of Sciences, **Il'ja M.Frank** (USSR) Academy of Sciences, and **Igor J. Tamm** (USSR) Univ. of Moscow and Physics Institute of USSR Academy of Sciences "for their discovery and the interpretation of the Cherenkov effect."
1959 Emillio G. Sergè (U.S.) Univ. of California, Berkeley, and **Owen Chamberlain** (U.S.) Univ. of California, Berkeley "for their discovery of the antiproton."
1960 Donald A. Glaser (U.S.) Univ. of California, Berkeley "for the invention of the bubble chamber."
1961 Robert Hofstadter (U.S.) Stanford Univ. "for his pioneering studies of electron scattering in atomic nuclei and for his thereby achieved discoveries concerning the structure of the nucleons"; **Rudolf L. Mössbauer** (Germany) Technische Hochschule (Munich), and California Institute of Technology "for his researches concerning the resonance absorption of gamma radiation and his discovery in this connection of the effect which bears his name."
1962 Lev D. Landau (USSR) Academy of Sciences "for his pioneering theories for condensed matter, especially liquid helium."
1963 Eugene P. Wigner (U.S.) Princeton Univ. "for his contributions to the theory of the atomic nucleus

and the elementary particles, particularly through the discovery and application of fundamental symmetry principles"; **Maria Goeppert-Mayer** (U.S.) Univ. of California, La Jolla, and **J. Hans D. Jensen** (Germany) Univ. of Heidelberg "for their discoveries concerning nuclear shell structure."

1964 Charles H. Townes (U.S.) M.I.T., **Nikolai G. Basov** (USSR) Lebedev Institute for Physics, and **Aleksandre M. Prochorov** (USSR) Lebedev Institute for Physics "for fundamental work in the field of quantum electronics, which has led to the construction of oscillators and amplifiers based on the maser-laser-principle."

1965 Schin'ichiro Tomonaga (Japan) Toyko Univ., **Julian Schwinger** (U.S.) Harvard Univ., and **Richard P. Feynman** (U.S.) California Institute of Technology "for their fundamental work in quantum electrodynamcis, with deep-ploughing consequences for the physics of elementary particles."

1966 Alfred Kastier (France) Ecole Normale Supérieure, Université de Paris "for the discovery and development of optical methods for studying hertzian resonance in atoms."

1967 Hans A. Bethe (U.S.) Cornell Univ. "for his contributions to the theory of nuclear reactions, especially his discoveries concerning the energy production in stars."

1968 Luis W. Alvarez (U.S.) Univ. of California, Berkeley "for his decisive contributions to elementary particle physics, in particular the discovery of a large number of resonance states, made possible through his development of the technique of using hydrogen bubble chamber and data analysis."

1969 Murray Gell-Mann (U.S.) California Institute of Technology "for his contributions and discoveries concerning the classification of elementary particles and their interactions."

1970 Hannes Alfvén (Sweden) Royal Institute of Technology "for fundamental work and discoveries in magneto-hydrodynamics with fruitful applications in different parts of plasma physics"; **Louis Neel** (France) Univ. of Grenoble "for fundamental work and discoveries concerning antiferromagnetism and ferrimagetism which have led to important applications in solid-state physics."

1971 Dennis Gabor (U.K.) Imperial College of Science and Technology "for his invention and development of the holographic method."

1972 John Bardeen (U.S.) Univ. of Illinois, **Leon N. Cooper** (U.S.) Brown Univ., and J. **Robert Schrieffer** (U.S.) Univ. of Pennsylvania "for their jointly developed theory of superconductivity, usually called the BCS-theory."

1973 Leo Esaki (Japan) IBM Thomas J. Watson Research Center (New York), and **Ivar Giaever** (U.S.) General Electric Co. "for their experimental discoveries regarding tunneling phenomena in semiconductors and superconductors, respectively"; **Brian D. Josephson** (U.K.) Cambridge Univ. "for his theoretical predictions of the properties of a supercurrent through a tunnel barrier, in particular those phenomena which are generally known as the Josephson effects."

1974 Sir Martin Ryle (U.K.) and **Antony Hewish** (U.K.), both of Cambridge Univ., "for their pioneering research in radio astrophysics: Ryle for his observations and inventions, in particular of the aperture synthesis technique, and Hewish for his decisive role in the discovery of pulsars."

1975 Aage Bohr (Denmark) Niels Bohr Institute, **Ben Mottelson** (Denmark) Nordita, and **James Rainwater** (U.S.) Columbia Univ. "for the discovery of the connection between collective motion and particle motion in atomic nuclei and the development of the theory of the structure of the atomic nucleus based on this connection."

1976 Burton Richter (U.S.) Stanford Linear Accelerator Center, and **Samuel C.C. Ting** (U.S.) M.I.T. "for their pioneering work in the discovery of a heavy elementary particle of a new kind."

1977 Philip W. Anderson (U.S.) Bell Laboratories, **Sir Nevill F. Mott** (U.K.) Cambridge Univ. and **John H. van Vleck** (U.S.) Harvard Univ. "for their fundamental theoretical investigations of the electronic structure of magnetic and disordered systems."

1978 Peter L. Kapitsa (USSR) Academy of Sciences "for his basic inventions and discoveries in the area of low-temperature physics, **Arno A. Penzias** (U.S.) Bell Laboratories, and **Robert W. Wilson** (U.S.) Bell Laboratories "for their discovery of cosmic microwave background radiation."

1979 Sheldon L. Glashow (U.S.) Lyman Laboratory, Harvard Univ., **Abdus Salam** (Pakistan) International Centre for Theoretical Physics (Italy) and Imperial College of Science and Technology (London), and **Steven Weinberg** (U.S.) Harvard Univ. "for their contributions to the theory of the unified weak and electromagnetic interaction between elementary particles, including, inter alia, the predictions of the weak neutral current."

1980 James W. Cronin (U.S.) Univ. of Chicago, and **Val L. Fitch** (U.S.) Princeton Univ. "for the discovery of violations of fundamental symmetry principles in the decay of neutral K-mesons."

1981 Nicolaas Bloembergen (U.S.) Harvard Univ., and **Arthur L. Schawlow** (U.S.) Stanford Univ. "for their contributions to the development of laser spectroscopy"; **Kai M. Siegbahn** (Sweden) Uppsala Univ. "for his contribution to the development of high-resolution electron spectroscopy."

1982 Kenneth G. Wilson (U.S.) Cornell Univ. "for his theory for critical phenomena in connection with phase transitions."

1983 Subrahmanyan Chandrasekhar (U.S.) Univ. of Chicago "for his theoretical studies of the physical processes of importance to the structure and evolution of the stars"; **William A. Fowler** (U.S.) California Institute of Technology for his "studies of the nuclear reactions of importance in the formation of the chemical elements in the universe."

1984 Carlo Rubbia (Italy) CERN (Switzerland), and **Simon van der Meer** (Netherlands) CERN (Switzerland) "for their decisive contributions to the discovery of the field particles W and Z, communicators of weak interaction."

1985 Klaus von Klitzing (W. Germany) Max-Planck-Institut for Solid State Research "for the discovery of the quantized Hall effect."

1986 Ernst Ruska (W. Germany) Fritz-Haber-Institut der Max-Planck-Gesellschaft "for his fundamental work in electron optics, and for the design of the first electron microscope"; **Gerd Binnig** (W. Germany) IBM Zurich Research Laboratory and **Heinrich Rohrer** (Switzerland) IBM Zurich Research Laboratory "for their design of the scanning tunneling microscope."

1987 Georg J. Bednorz (Switzerland) IBM Zurich research Laboratory, and **Dr. K. Alex Müller** (Switzerland) IBM Zurich Research Laboratory "for the discovery of new superconducting materials."

1988 Leon M. Lederman (U.S.) Fermi National Accelerator Laboratory, **Melvin Schwartz** (U.S.) Digital Pathways, Inc., and **Jack Steinberger** (Switzerland) "for the neutrino beam method and the demonstration of the doublet structure of the leptons through the discovery of the muon neutrino."

1989 **Norman R. Ramsey** (U.S.) Harvard Univ. "for the invention of the separated oscillatory fields method and its use in . . . atomic clocks"; **Hans G. Dehmelt** (U.S.) Univ. of Washington, and **Wolfgang Paul** (W. Germany) Univ. of Bonn "for the development of the ion trap technique," which allows detailed study of subatomic particles."
1990 **Richard E. Taylor** (Can.), Stanford U.; **Jerome I. Friedman** (U.S.) MIT; and **Henry W. Kendall** (U.S.) MIT, whose experiments between 1967 and 1973 confirmed the existence of quarks, the fundamental building blocks of matter.
1991 **Pierre-Gilles de Gennes** (France), Collège de France, Paris, for his discoveries about the ordering of molecules in a variety of substances but especially liquid crystals, where his work has helped in understanding superconductivity.
1992 **George Charpak** (France, b. Poland), affiliated with CERN, the accelerator complex, where he developed electronic detectors that traced the paths of subatomic particles with lightning speed.
1993 **Joseph H. Taylor** (U.S.), Princeton Univ., and **Russel A. Hulse** (U.S.), Princeton Plasma Physics Laboratory, for their discovery of a binary pulsar and their later success in measuring its pulse rate.
1994 **Clifford G. Shull** (U.S.) MIT, and **Bertram N. Brockhouse** (Canada) McMaster Univ., for experiments in the 1940s and '50s that exploited the penetrating power of low-energy neutron beams produced by nuclear reactors. Neutron beams are more powerful than other forms of radiation, and are now widely used to explore the atomic structure of matter.
1995 **Martin L. Perl,** (U.S.) Stanford Univ. Linear Accelerator Center, and **Frederick Reines** (U.S.) Los Alamos National Laboratory, for their separate discoveries of "two of nature's most remarkable subatomic particles," Perl's discovery of the tau in the 1970's and Reines's discovery of the neutrino in the 1950's.
1996 **Robert C. Richardson** (U.S.) and **David M. Lee** (U.S.) of Cornell Univ., and **Douglas S. Osheroff** (U.S.) Stanford Univ., for their 1972 discovery of superfluiditiy in a rare form of helium which may offer insights into the formation of galaxies.
1997 **Steven Chu** (U.S.) Stanford Univ., **Claude Cohen-Tannoudji** (France), Collège de France, and **William D. Phillips** (U.S.), National Institute of Standards and Technology, for development of a method to trap individual atoms, which allow them to be studied in greater detail.
1998 **Robert B. Laughlin** (U.S.), Stanford Univ., **Horst L. Störmer** (U.S.), Bell Laboratories; **Daniel Tsui** (U.S.), Princeton Univ., for their discovery of the fractional quantum Hall effect, the culmination of studies of magnetic fields dating back to 1897.
1999 **Gerardus 't Hooft** (Netherlands), Univ. of Utrecht, and **Martinus J.G. Veltman** (Netherlands) Univ. of Michigan, for placing the theory of particle physics on firm mathematical ground.
2000 **Jack S. Kilby** (U.S.), Texas Instruments, for his contribution to the invention of the integrated circuit, a.k.a. the computer chip; **Zhores I. Alferov** (Russia), A.F. Ioffe Physico-Technical Institute, St. Petersburg, and **Herbert Kroemer,** (U.S.), Univ. of California at Santa Barbara, for their invention of components called heterostructures, which are used in high-speed electronic devices like CD players, bar-code readers, and laser pointers.
2001 **Eric A. Cornell** (U.S.) and **Carl E. Wieman** (U.S.) both of the Joint Institute for Laboratory Astrophysics, Boulder, Colo., and **Wolfgang Ketterle** (Germany), M.I.T., "for the achievement of Bose-Einstein condensation in dilute gases of alkali atoms, and for early fundamental studies of the properties of the condensates."
2002 **Raymond Davis Jr.,** (U.S.), University of Pennsylvania and **Masatoshi Koshiba,** (Japan), University of Tokyo; and **Riccardo Giacconi,** (U.S., B. Italy), University of Milan, "for pioneering contributions to astrophysics." Davis and Koshiba's work led to the detection of cosmic neutrinos, tiny particles emitted by the Sun and other stars; Giacconi built the first X-ray telescopes, which have provided sharp images of the universe.
2003 See Part I: "The Almanac of the Year."

Nobel Prizes in Literature

1901 **Sully Prudhomme** (pen name of René F.A. Prudhomme) (France) "in special recognition of his poetic composition."
1902 **Christian M.T. Mommsen** (Germany) "the greatest living master of the art of historical writing, with special reference to his monumental work, *A History of Rome.*
1903 **Bjørstjerne M. Bjørnson** (Norway) for "his noble, magnificent, and versatile poetry which has always been distinguished by both the freshness of its inspiration and the rare purity of its spirit."
1904 **Frédéric Mistral** (France) "in recognition of the fresh originality and true inspiration of his poetic production, which faithfully reflects the natural scenery and native spirit of his people, and, in addition, his significant work as a Provençal philologist." **José Echegaray y Eizaguirre** (Spain) "in recognition of the numerous and brilliant compositions which, in an individual and original manner, have revived the great traditions of the Spanish drama."
1905 **Henryk Sienkiewicz** (Poland) "because of his outstanding merits as an epic writer.
1906 **Giosué Carducci** (Italy) "as a tribute to the creative energy, freshness of style, and lyrical force which characterize his poetic masterpieces."
1907 **Rudyard Kipling** (U.K.) "in consideration of the power of observation, originality of imagination, virility of ideas, and remarkable talent for narration which characterize the creations of this world-famous author."
1908 **Rudolf C. Eucken** (Germany) "in recognition of his earnest search for truth, his penetrating power of thought, his wide range of vision, and the warmth and strength in presentation. . ."
1909 **Selma O.L. Lagerlöf** (Sweden) "in appreciation of the lofty idealism, vivid imagination, and spiritual perception that characterize her writings."
1910 **Paul J.L. Heyse** (Germany) "as a tribute to the consummate artistry, permeated with idealism, which he has demonstrated during his long productive career as lyric poet, dramatist, novelist, and writer of world-renowned short stories."
1911 **Count Maurice (Mooris) P.M.B. Maeterlinck** (Belgium) "in appreciation of his many-sided literary activities, and especially of his dramatic works, which are distinguished by a wealth of imagination and by a poetic fancy."
1912 **Gerhart J.R. Hauptmann** (Germany) "primarily in recognition of his fruitful, varied, and outstanding production in the realm of dramatic art."
1913 **Rabindranath Tagore** (India) "because of his profoundly sensitive, fresh, and beautiful verse, by which, with consummate skill, he has made his poetic thought, expressed in his own English words, a part of the literature of the West."
1914 No award

1915 Romain Rolland (France) "as a tribute to the lofty idealism of his literary production and to the sympathy and love of truth with which he has described different types of human beings."
1916 Carl G.V. von Heidenstam (Sweden) "in recognition of his significance as the leading representative of a new era in our literature."
1917 Karl A. Gjellerup (Denmark) "for his varied and rich poetry, which is inspired by lofty ideals"; **Henrik Pontoppidan** (Denmark) "for his authentic descriptions of presentday life in Denmark."
1918 No award
1919 Carl F.G. Spitteler (Switzerland) "in special appreciation of his epic, *Olympian Spring*."
1920 Knut P. Hamsun (Norway) "for his monumental work, *Growth of the Soil*."
1921 Anatole France *(pen name of Jacques A. Thibault)* (France) "in recognition of his brilliant literary achievements, characterized as they are by a nobility of style, a profound human sympathy, grace, and a true Gallic temperament."
1922 Jacinto Benavente (Spain) "for the happy manner in which he has continued the illustrious traditions of the Spanish drama."
1923 William Butler Yeats (Ireland) "for his always inspired poetry, which in a highly artistic form gives expression to the spirit of a whole nation."
1924 Wladyslaw S. Reymont (pen name of Reyment) (Poland) "for his great national epic, *The Peasants*."
1925 George Bernard Shaw (U.K.) "for his work which is marked by both idealism and humanity, its stimulating satire often being infused with a singular poetic beauty."
1926 Grazia Deledda (pen name of Grazia Madesani (Italy) "for her idealistically inspired writings, which picture the life on her native island and with depth and sympathy deal with human problems."
1927 Henri Bergson (France) "in recognition of his rich and vitalizing ideas."
1928 Sigrid Undset (Norway) "principally for her powerful descriptions of Northern life during the Middle Ages."
1929 Thomas Mann (Germany) "principally for his great novel *Buddenbrooks*."
1930 Sinclair Lewis (U.S.) "for his vigorous and graphic art of description and his ability to create, with wit and humor, new types of characters."
1931 Erik A. Karlfeldt (Sweden) for his poetry.
1932 John Galsworthy (U.K.) "for his distinguished art of narration which takes its highest form in *The Forsyte Saga*."
1933 Ivan A. Bunin (stateless domicile in France) "for the strict artistry with which he has carried on the classical Russian traditions in prose writing."
1934 Luigi Pirandello (Italy) "for his bold and ingenious revival of dramatic art."
1935 No award
1936 Eugene G. O'Neill (U.S.) "for the power, honesty, and deep-felt emotions of his dramatic works, which embody an original concept of tragedy."
1937 Roger Martin du Gard (France) "for the artistic power and truth with which he has depicted human conflict as well as some fundamental aspects of contemporary life in his novel-cycle *Les Thibault*."
1938 Pearl Buck (pen name of Pearl Walsh) (U.S.) "for her rich and truly epic descriptions of peasant life in China and for her biographical masterpieces."
1939 Frans E. Sillanpää (Finland) "for his deep understanding of his country's peasantry and the exquisite art with which he has portrayed their way of life and their relationship with Nature."
1940–1943 No awards given.
1944 Johannes V. Jensen (Denmark) "for the rare strength and fertility of his poetic imagination."
1945 Gabriela Mistral (pen name of Lucila Godoy y Alcayaga) (Chile) "for her lyric poetry which, has made her name a symbol of the idealistic aspirations of the entire Latin American world."
1946 Hermann Hesse (Switzerland) "for his inspired writings which exemplify the classical humanitarian ideals and high qualities of style."
1947 André P.G. Gide (France) "for his writings in which human problems and conditions have been presented with a fearless love of truth and keen psychological insight."
1948 Thomas S. Eliot (U.K.) for his "outstanding, pioneer contribution to present-day poetry."
1949 William Faulkner (U.S.) ":for his powerful and artistically unique contribution to the modern American novel."
1950 Earl (Bertrand) Russell (U.K.) "in recognition of his varied and significant writings in which he champions humanitarian ideals and freedom of thought."
1951 Pär Fabian Lägerkvist (Sweden) "for the artistic vigour and true independence of mind with which he endeavours in his poetry to find answers to the eternal questions confronting mankind."
1952 François Mauriac (France) "for the deep spiritual insight and the artistic intensity with which he has in his novels penetrated the drama of human life."
1953 Sir Winston L.S. Churchill (U.K.) "for his mastery of historical and biographical description as well as for brilliant oratory in defending exalted human values."
1954 Ernest M. Hemingway (U.S.) "for his mastery of the art of narrative, most recently demonstrated in *The Old Man and the Sea*, and for the influence that he has exerted on contemporary style."
1955 Halldór K. Laxness (Iceland) "for his vivid epic power which has renewed the great narrative art of Iceland."
1956 Juan R. Jiménez (Puerto Rico, b. Spain) "for his lyrical poetry, which in Spanish language constitutes an example of high spirit and artistic purity."
1957 Albert Camus (France) "for his important literary production, which with clearsighted earnestness illuminates the problems of the human conscience in our times."
1958 Boris L. Pasternak (USSR) "for his important achievement both in contemporary lyrical poetry and in the field of the great Russian epic tradition." (Declined the prize.)
1959 Salvatore Quasimodo (Italy) "for his lyrical poetry, which with classical fire expresses the tragic experience of life in our own times."
1960 Saint-John Perse (pen name of Alexis Léger) (France) "for the soaring flight and the evocative imagery of his poetry which in a visionary fashion reflects the conditions of our time."
1961 Ivo Andric (Yugoslavia) "for the epic force with which he has traced themes and depicted human destinies drawn from the history of his country."
1962 John Steinbeck (U.S.) "for his realistic and imaginative writings, combining as they do sympathetic humour and keen social perception."
1963 Giorgos Seferis (pen name of Giorgos Seferiadis) (Greece) "for his eminent lyrical writing, inspired by a deep feeling for the Hellenic world of culture."
1964 Jean-Paul Sartre (France) "for his work which, rich in ideas and filled with the spirit of freedom and the quest for truth, has exerted a far-reaching influence on our age." (Declined the prize.)
1965 Michail A. Sholokhov (U.S.S.R.) "for the artistic power and integrity with which, in his epic of the Don, he has given expression to a historic phase in the life of the Russian people."

1966 Shmuel U. Agnon (Israel) "for his profoundly characteristic narrative art with motifs from the life of the Jewish people; **Nelly Sachs** (Germany, domiciled in Sweden) " for her outstanding lyrical and dramatic writing, which interprets Israel's destiny with touching strength."

1967 Miguel A. Asturias (Guatemala) "for his vivid literary achievement, deep-rooted in the national traits and traditions of Indian peoples of Latin America."

1968 Yasunari Kawabata (Japan) "for his narrative mastery, which with great sensibility expresses the essence of the Japanese mind."

1969 Samuel Beckett (Ireland) "for his writing, which—in new forms for the novel and drama—in the destitution of modern man acquires its elevation."

1970 Alexander Solzhenitsyn (USSR) "for the ethical force with which he has pursued the indispensable traditions of Russian literature."

1971 Pablo Neruda (pen name of Neftalí Ricardo Reyes Basoalto) (Chile) "for a poetry that brings alive a continent's destiny and dreams."

1972 Heinrich Böll (West Germany) "for his writing which through its combination of a broad perspective on his time and a sensitive skill in characterization has contributed to a renewal of German literature."

1973 Patrick White (Australia, b. U.K.) "for an epic and psychological narrative art which has introduced a new continent into literature."

1974 Eyvind Johnson (Sweden) "for a narrative art, far-seeing in lands and ages, in the service of freedom"; **Harry Martinson** (Sweden) "for writings that catch the dewdrop and reflect the cosmos."

1975 Eugenio Montale (Italy) "for his distinctive poetry which, with great artistic sensitivity, has interpreted human values under the sign of an outlook on life with no illusions."

1976 Saul Bellow (U.S.) "for the human understanding and subtle analysis of contemporary culture."

1977 Vincente Aleixandre (Spain) "for a creative poetic writing which illuminates man's condition in the cosmos and in present-day society, at the same time representing the great renewal of the traditions of Spanish poetry between the wars."

1978 Isaac Bashevis Singer (U.S., b. Poland) "for his impassioned narrative art which, with roots in a Polish-Jewish cultural tradition, brings universal human conditions to life."

1979 Odysseus Elytis (pen name of Odysseus Alepoudhelis) (Greece) "for his poetry, which against the background of Greek tradition, depicts man's struggle for freedom and creativeness."

1980 Czeslaw Milosz (U.S. and Poland) "who with uncompromising clear-sightedness voices man's exposed condition in a world of severe conflicts."

1981 Elias Canetti (U.K., b. Bulgaria) "for writings marked by a broad outlook, a wealth of ideas, and artistic power."

1982 Gabriel García Marquez (Colombia) "for his novels and short stories, in which the fantastic and the realistic are combined in a richly composed world of imagination, reflecting a continent's life and conflicts."

1983 William Golding (U.K.) "for his novels, which illuminate the human condition in the world of today."

1984 Jaroslav Seifert (Czechoslovakia) "for his poetry which, endowed with freshness, sensuality, and rich inventiveness, provides a liberating image of the indomitable spirit and versatility of man."

1985 Claude Simon (France) "who in his novel combines the poet's and the painter's creativeness with a deepened awareness of time in the depiction of the human condition."

1986 Wole Soyinka (Nigeria) "who in a wide cultural perspective and with poetic overtones fashions the drama of existence."

1987 Joseph Brodsky (U.S., b. U.S.S.R.) "for his all-embracing authorship imbued with clarity of thought and poetic intensity."

1988 Naguib Mahfouz (Egypt) "who through works rich in nuance, has formed an Arabian narrative art that applies to all mankind."

1989 Camilo José Cela (Spain) a novelist whose "rich and inventive prose, forms a challenging vision of man's vulnerability." His most famous work is *The Family of Pascual Duarte* (1942).

1990 Octavio Paz (Mexico) poet and social essayist. Volumes include *The Labyrinth of Solitude* (1950), *Sunstone* (1957), and *Sor Juana: Or, the Traps of Faith* (1990).

1991 Nadine Gordimer (South Africa) for her "involvement on behalf of literature and free speech in a police state where censorship and persecution of books and people exist."

1992 Derek Walcott (West Indies, b. St. Lucia), poet and playwright whose works evoke the cultural diversity of the Carribean "but through them he speaks to each and every one of us."

1993 Toni Morrison (U.S.), whose novels about racial prejudice are "characterized by visionary force and poetic import."

1994 Kenzaburo Oe (Japan), best known for his accounts of the atomic bombing of Hiroshima. The poetic force of his writing "creates an imagined world where life and myth condense to form a disconcerting picture of the human predicament."

1995 Seamus Heaney (Ireland), poet and essayist, "for works of lyrical beauty and ethical depth, which exalt everyday miracles and the living past."

1996 Wislawa Szymborska (Poland), a poet whose work contemplates the oddities of daily life.

1997 Dario Fo, (Italy), a leftist playwright, best known for biting political satires (*Can't Pay, Won't Pay* and *Accidental Death of an Anarchist*), which brought threats of censure and condemnation from the Italian government and the Catholic Church.

1998 José Saramago (Portugal), for his richly imaginative works that often use the supernatural and irrational to address questions of faith. Best known novels include: *Baltasar and Blimunda* (1982), *The Year of the Death of Ricardo Reis* (1984).

1999 Günter Grass (Germany) "whose frolicsome black fables portray the forgotten face of history." His epic 1959 novel, *The Tin Drum* addressed the uncomfortable issue of the German national identity through the Nazi era.

2000 Gao Xingjian (France, b. China), one of the most important Chinese dramatists of the 20th century, whose most significant works have been banned in China since the 1980s.

2001 V.S. Naipaul (U.K., b. Trinidad) His fiction, including *A House for Mr. Biswas* (1961) and *The Enigma of Arrival* (1987) is often highly autobiographical, exploring the challenges faced by postcolonial societies like his ancestral home of India.

2002 Imre Kertész, (Hungary) "for writing that upholds the fragile experience of the individual against the barbaric arbitrariness of history." His most important work is *Fateless,* a novel about a man who, like Kertész himself, is forced to spend his youth in a concentration camp.

2003 See Part I: "The Almanac of the Year."

THE NCAA

National Collegiate Athletic Association (NCAA)
One NCAA Place
700 W. Washington St.
Indianapolis, Ind. 46204
(317) 917–6222
www.ncaa.org

The NCAA acts as the governing body of intercollegiate athletics, setting the playing rules for each sport, and eligibility standards for athletes.

COLLEGE FOOTBALL

NCAA National Football Champions

For many years, college football selected its national champion through an arcane structure of bowl games and two press association polls (one of coaches, the other of writers), which often did not agree with each other, creating co-champions and arguments about which was the better team.

But in 1998, the NCAA adopted the Bowl Alliance, in which the top two teams (as determined by the same two polls) meet in a national championship game that rotates annually among the Rose, Fiesta, Orange, and Sugar Bowls. (Teams ranked 3–8 in the polls fill out the other bowl games).

Year	Team
1936	Minnesota
1937	Pittsburgh
1938	TCU
1939	Texas A&M
1940	Minnesota
1941	Minnesota
1942	Ohio State
1943	Notre Dame
1944	Army
1945	Army
1946	Notre Dame
1947	Notre Dame
1948	Michigan
1949	Notre Dame
1950	Oklahoma
1951	Tennessee
1952	Michigan St.
1953	Maryland
1954	Ohio State and UCLA
1955	Oklahoma
1956	Oklahoma
1957	Auburn and Ohio State
1958	Louisiana St.
1959	Syracuse
1960	Minnesota
1961	Alabama
1962	USC
1963	Texas
1964	Alabama
1965	Alabama and Michigan St.
1966	Notre Dame
1967	USC
1968	Ohio State
1969	Texas
1970	Nebraska and Texas
1971	Nebraska
1972	USC
1973	Notre Dame and Alabama
1974	USC and Oklahoma
1975	Oklahoma
1976	Pittsburgh
1977	Notre Dame
1978	Alabama and USC
1979	Alabama
1980	Georgia
1981	Clemson
1982	Penn State
1983	Miami (Fla.)
1984	BYU
1985	Oklahoma
1986	Penn State
1987	Miami (Fla.)
1988	Notre Dame
1989	Miami (Fla.)
1990	Colorado and Georgia Tech
1991	Miami and Washington
1992	Alabama
1993	Florida State
1994	Nebraska
1995	Nebraska
1996	Florida
1997	Michigan and Nebraska
1998	Tennessee
1999	Florida State
2000	Oklahoma
2001	Miami (Fla.)
2002	Ohio State

Source: NCAA.

NCAA National Championship Game Results, 1998–2002

Year	Bowl	Score
1998	Fiesta	Tennessee 23, Florida State, 16
1999	Sugar	Florida State 46, Virginia Tech 29
2000	Orange	Oklahoma 13, Florida State 2
2001	Rose	Miami (Fla.) 37, Nebraska 14
2002	Fiesta	Ohio State 31, Miami (Fla.) 24 (2OT)

Note: the National Championship game is played in January of the following year. Years shown refer to the year of the championship.

NCAA Football-Major Bowl Games, 1902–2003

ROSE BOWL (Pasadena, California)

1902	Michigan 49, Stanford 0
1916	Washington St. 14, Brown 0
1917	Oregon 14, Pennsylvania 0
1918	Mare Island 19, Camp Lewis 7
1919	Great Lakes 17, Mare Island 0
1920	Harvard 7, Oregon 6
1921	California 28, Ohio State 0
1922	Washington and Jefferson 0, Cal. 0
1923	USC 14, Penn State 3
1924	Navy 14, Washington 14
1925	Notre Dame 27, Stanford 10
1926	Alabama 20, Washington 19
1927	Alabama 7, Stanford 7
1928	Stanford 7, Pittsburgh 6
1929	Georgia Tech 8, California 7
1930	USC 47, Pittsburgh 14
1931	Alabama 24, Washington State 0
1932	USC 21, Tulane 12
1933	USC 35, Pittsburgh 0
1934	Columbia 7, Stanford 0
1935	Alabama 29, Stanford 13
1936	Stanford 7, Southern Methodist 0
1937	Pittsburgh 21, Washington 0
1938	California 13, Alabama 0
1939	USC 7, Duke 0
1940	USC 14, Tennessee 0
1941	Stanford 21, Nebraska 13
1942	Oregon State 20, Duke 16 (at Durham)
1943	Georgia 9, UCLA 0
1944	USC 29, Washington 0
1945	USC 25, Tennessee 0
1946	Alabama 34, USC 14
1947	Illinois 45, UCLA 14
1948	Michigan 49, USC 0
1949	Northwestern 20, California 14
1950	Ohio State 17, California 14
1951	Michigan 14, California 6
1952	Illinois 40, Stanford 7
1953	USC 7, Wisconsin 0
1954	Michigan State 28, UCLA 20
1955	Ohio State 20, USC 7
1956	Michigan State 17, UCLA 14
1957	Iowa 35, Oregon State 19
1958	Ohio State 10, Oregon 7
1959	Iowa 38, California 12
1960	Washington 44, Wisconsin 8
1961	Washington 17, Minnesota 7
1962	Minnesota 21, UCLA 3
1963	USC 42, Wisconsin 37
1964	Illinois 17, Washington 7
1965	Michigan 34, Oregon State7
1966	UCLA 14, Michigan State 12
1967	Purdue 14, USC 13
1968	USC 14, Indiana 3
1969	Ohio State 27, USC 16
1970	USC 10, Michigan 3
1971	Stanford 27, Ohio State 17
1972	Stanford 13, Michigan 12
1973	USC 42, Ohio State 17
1974	Ohio State 42, USC 21
1975	USC18, Ohio State 17
1976	UCLA 23, Ohio State 10
1977	USC 14, Michigan 6
1978	Washington 27, Michigan 20
1979	USC 17, Michigan 10
1980	USC 17, Ohio State 16
1981	Michigan 23, Washington 6
1982	Washington 28, Iowa 0
1983	UCLA 24, Michigan 14
1984	UCLA 45, Illinois 9
1985	USC 20, Ohio State 17
1986	UCLA 45, Iowa 28
1987	Arizona State 22, Michigan 15
1988	Michigan State 20, USC 17
1989	Michigan 22, USC 14
1990	USC 17, Michigan 10
1991	Washington 46, Iowa 34
1992	Washington 34, Michigan 14
1993	Michigan 38, Washington 31
1994	Wisconsin 21, UCLA 16
1995	Penn State 38, Oregon 20
1996	USC 41, Northwestern 32
1997	Ohio State 20, Arizona State 17
1998	Michigan 21, Washington State 16
1999	Wisconsin 38, UCLA 31
2000	Wisconsin 17, Stanford 9
2001	Washington 34, Purdue 24
2002	Miami (Fla.) 37, Nebraska 14
2003	Oklahoma 34, Washington St. 14

Year	ORANGE BOWL, Miami, Florida	SUGAR BOWL, New Orleans	COTTON BOWL, Dallas
1935	Bucknell 26, Miami (Fla.) 0	Tulane 20, Temple 14	—
1936	Catholic U. 20, Mississippi 19	Texas Christian 3, Louisiana St. 2	—
1937	Duquesne 13, Mississippi St. 12	Santa Clara 21, LSU 14	TCU 16, Marquette 6
1938	Auburn 6, Michigan State 0	Santa Clara 6, LSU 0	Rice 28, Colorado 14
1939	Tennessee 17, Oklahoma 0	TCU 15, Carnegie Tech 7	St. Mary's 20, Texas Tech 13
1940	Georgia Tech 21, Missouri 7	Texas A&M 14, Tulane 13	Clemson 6, Boston College 3
1941	Mississippi St. 14, Georgetown 7	Boston College 19, Tennessee 13	Texas A&M 13, Fordham 12
1942	Georgia 40, Texas Christian 26	Fordham 2, Missouri 0	Alabama 29, Texas A&M 21
1943	Alabama 37, Boston College 21	Tennessee 14, Tulsa 7	Texas 14, Georgia Tech 7
1944	Louisiana St. 19, Texas A&M 14	Georgia Tech 20, Tulsa 18	Texas 7, Randolph Field 7
1945	Tulsa 26, Georgia Tech 12	Duke 29, Alabama 26	Oklahoma A&M 34, TCU 0
1946	Miami (Fla.)13, Holy Cross 6	Okla. A&M 33, St. Mary's (Co. 13	Texas 40, Missouri 27
1947	Rice 8, Tennessee 0	Georgia 20, North Carolina 10	Arkansas 0, Louisiana State 0
1948	Georgia Tech 20, Kansas 14	Texas 27, Alabama 7	SMU 13, Penn State 13
1949	Texas 41, Georgia 28	Oklahoma 14, North Carolina 6	SMU 21, Oregon 13
1950	Santa Clara 21, Kentucky 13	Oklahoma 35, Louisiana State 0	Rice 27, North Carolina 13
1951	Clemson 15, Miami (Fla.)14	Kentucky 13, Oklahoma 7	Tennessee 20, Texas 14
1952	Georgia Tech 20, Baylor 14	Maryland 28, Tennessee 13	Kentucky 20, Texas Christian 7
1953	Alabama 61, Syracuse 6	Georgia Tech 24, Mississippi 7	Texas 16, Tennessee 0
1954	Oklahoma 7, Maryland 0	Georgia Tech 42, W. Virginia 19	Rice 28, Alabama 0
1955	Duke 34, Nebraska 7	Navy 21, Mississippi 0	Georgia Tech 14, Arkansas 6

Year	ORANGE BOWL, Miami, Florida	SUGAR BOWL, New Orleans	COTTON BOWL, Dallas
1956	Oklahoma 20, Maryland 6	Georgia Tech 7, Pittsburgh 0	Mississippi 14, Texas Christian 13
1957	Colorado 27, Clemson 21	Baylor 13, Tennessee 7	Texas Christian 28, Syracuse 27
1958	Oklahoma 48, Duke 21	Mississippi 39, Texas 7	Navy 20, Rice 7
1959	Oklahoma 21, Syracuse 6	Louisiana State 7, Clemson 0	Texas Christian 0, Air Force 0
1960	Georgia 14, Missouri 0	Mississippi 21, LSU 0	Syracuse 23, Texas 14
1961	Missouri 21, Navy 14	Mississippi 14, Rice 6	Duke 7, Arkansas 6
1962	Louisiana State 25, Colorado 7	Alabama 10, Arkansas 3	Texas 12, Mississippi 7
1963	Alabama 17, Oklahoma 0	Mississippi 17, Arkansas 13	Louisiana State 13, Texas 0
1964	Nebraska 13, Auburn 7	Alabama 12, Mississippi 7	Texas 28, Navy 6
1965	Texas 21, Alabama 17	Louisiana State 13, Syracuse 10	Arkansas 10, Nebraska 7
1966	Alabama 39, Nebraska 28	Missouri 20, Florida 18	Louisiana State 14, Arkansas 7
1967	Florida 27, Georgia Tech 12	Alabama 34, Nebraska 7	Georgia 24, SMU 9
1968	Oklahoma 26, Tennessee 24	LSU 20, Wyoming 13	Texas A&M 20, Alabama 16
1969	Penn State 15, Kansas 14	Arkansas 16, Georgia 2	Texas 36, Tennessee 13
1970	Penn State 10, Missouri 3	Mississippi 27, Arkansas 22	Texas 21, Notre Dame 17
1971	Nebraska 17, Louisiana State 12	Tennessee 34, Air Force 13	Notre Dame 24, Texas 11
1972	Nebraska 38, Alabama 6	Oklahoma 40, Auburn 22	Penn State 30, Texas 6
1973	Nebraska 40, Notre Dame 6	Oklahoma 14, Penn State 0	Texas 17, Alabama 13
1974	Penn State 16, Louisiana State 9	Notre Dame 24, Alabama 23	Nebraska 19, Texas 3
1975	Notre Dame 13, Alabama 11	Nebraska 13, Florida 10	Penn State 41, Baylor 20
1976	Oklahoma 14, Michigan 6	Alabama 13, Penn State 7	Arkansas 31, Georgia 10
1977	Ohio State 27, Colorado 10	Pittsburgh 27, Georgia 3	Houston 30, Maryland 21
1978	Arkansas 31, Oklahoma 6	Alabama 35, Ohio State 6	Notre Dame 38, Texas 10
1979	Oklahoma 31, Nebraska 21	Alabama 14, Penn State	Notre Dame 35, Houston 34
1980	Oklahoma 24, Florida State 7	Alabama 24, Arkansas 9	Houston 17, Nebraska 14
1981	Oklahoma 18, Florida State 17	Georgia 17, Notre Dame 10	Alabama 30, Baylor 2
1982	Clemson 22, Nebraska 15	Pittsburgh 24, Georgia 20	Texas 14, Alabama 12
1983	Nebraska 21, LSU 20	Penn State 27, Georgia 23	SMU 7, Pittsburgh 3
1984	Miami (Fla.) 31, Nebraska 30	Auburn 9, Michigan 7	Georgia 10, Texas 9
1985	Washington 28, Oklahoma 17	Nebraska 28, Louisiana State 10	Boston College 45, Houston 28
1986	Oklahoma 25, Penn State 10	Tennessee 35, Miami (Fla.) 7	Texas A&M 36, Auburn 16
1987	Oklahoma 42, Arkansas 8	Nebraska 30, Louisiana State 15	Ohio State 28, Texas A&M 12
1988	Miami (Fla.) 20, Oklahoma 14	Syracuse 16, Auburn 16	Texas A&M 35, Notre Dame 10
1989	Miami (Fla.) 23, Nebraska 3	Florida State 13, Auburn 7	UCLA 17, Arkansas 3
1990	Notre Dame 21, Colorado 6	Miami (Fla.) 33, Alabama 25	Tennessee 31, Arkansas 27
1991	Colorado 10, Notre Dame 9	Tennessee 23, Virginia 22	Miami (Fla.) 46, Texas 3
1992	Miami (Fla.) 22, Nebraska 0	Notre Dame 39, Florida 28	Florida St. 10, Texas A&M 2
1993	Florida State 27, Nebraska 14	Alabama 34, Miami 13	Notre Dame 28, Texas A&M 3
1994	Florida State 18, Nebraska 16	Florida 41, West Virginia 7	Notre Dame 24, Texas A&M 21
1995	Nebraska 24, Miami 17	Florida State 23, Florida 17	USC 55, Texas Tech 14
1996	Florida St. 31, Notre Dame 26	Virginia Tech 28, Texas 10	Colorado 38, Oregon 6
1997	Nebraska 41, Virginia Tech 21	Florida 52, Florida State 20	BYU 19, Kansas State 15
1998	Nebraska 42, Tennessee 17	Florida State 31, Ohio State 14	UCLA 29, Texas A&M 23
1999	Florida 31, Syracuse 10	Ohio State 24, Texas A&M 14	Texas 38, Mississippi State 11
2000	Michigan 35, Alabama 34	Florida State 46, Virginia Tech 29	Arkansas 27, Texas 6
2001	Oklahoma 13, Florida State 2	Miami 37, Florida 20	Kansas St. 35, Tennessee 21
2002	Florida 56, Maryland 23	Louisiana State 47, Illinois 34	Oklahoma 10, Arkansas 3
2003	USC 38, Iowa 17	Georgia 26, Florida State 13	Texas 35, Louisiana State 20

NCAA Football Career Leaders

Player, Team	Years	PASSING, Career yards Att.	Comp.	Int.	Pct.	Yards	TD
Ty Detmer, Brigham Young	1988-91	1,530	958	65	.626	15,031	121
Tim Rattay, Louisiana Tech	1997-99	1,552	1,015	35	.654	12,746	115
Chris Redman, Louisville	1996-99	1,679	1,031	51	.614	12,541	84
Kliff Kingsbury, Texas Tech	1999-02	1,883	1,231	40	.654	12,429	95
Todd Santos, San Diego State	1984-87	1,484	910	57	.613	11,425	70
Carson Palmer, USC	1998-02	1,515	895	49	.591	11,388	71
Tim Lester, Western Michigan	1996-99	1,507	875	49	.581	11,299	87
Peyton Manning, Tennessee	1994-87	1,381	863	33	.625	11,201	89
Eric Zeier, Georgia	1991-94	1,402	838	37	.598	11,153	67
Alex Van Pelt, Pittsburgh	1989-92	1,463	845	59	.578	10,913	64

CAREER POINTS (Nonkickers)

Player, Team	Years	TDs	Pts.
Travis Prentice, Miami (Ohio)	1996-99	78	468
Ricky Williams, Texas	1995-98	75	452
Brock Forsey, Boise State	1999-02	68	408
Anthony Thompson, Indiana	1968-69	65	394
Ron Dayne, Wisconsin	1996-99	63	378
Marshall Faulk, San Diego St.	1991-93	62	376
Eric Crouch, Nebraska	1998-01	59	374
Tony Dorsett, Pittsburgh	1973-76	59	356
Glenn Davis, Army	1943-46	59	354
Ken Simonton, Oregon State	1998-01	57	348

CAREER POINTS (Kickers)

Player, Team	Years	PAT	FG	Pts.
Roman Anderson, Houston	1988-91	213	70	423
Carlos Huerta, Miami (Fla.)	1988-91	178	73	397
Jason Elam, Hawaii	1988-92	158	79	395
Derek Schmidt, Florida St.	1984-87	174	73	393
Kris Brown, Nebraska	1995-98	217	57	388
Shayne Graham, Virginia Tech.	1996-99	167	68	371
Jeff Hall, Tennessee	1995-98	188	61	371
Jeff Chandler, Florida	1997-01	167	67	368
Luis Zendejas, Arizona St.	1981-84	134	78	368
Jeff Jaeger, Washington	1983-86	118	80	358

RUSHING, Career yards

Player, Team	Years	Carries	Yards
Ron Dayne, Wisconsin	1996-99	1,115	6,397
Ricky Williams, Texas	1995-98	1,011	6,279
Tony Dorsett, Pittsburgh	1973-76	1,074	6,082
Charles White, USC	1976-79	1,023	5,598
Travis Prentice, Miami (Ohio)	1996-99	1,138	5,596
LaDainian Tomlinson, TCU	1997-00	907	5,263
Herschel Walker, Georgia	1980-82	994	5,259
Archie Griffin, Ohio State	1972-75	845	5,177
Darren Lewis, Texas A&M	1987-90	909	5,012
Anthony Thompson, Indiana	1986-89	1,089	4,965

RECEIVING, Career catches

Player, Team	Years	Catches	Yards
Arnold Jackson, Louisville	1997-00	300	3,670
Trevor Insley, Nevada	1996-99	298	5,005
Geoff Noisy, Nevada	1995-98	295	4,249
Troy Edwards, Lousiana Tech.	1996-98	280	4,352
Aaron Turner, Pacific (Calif.)	1988-91	266	4,345
Chad Mackey, Lousiana Tech.	1988-91	264	3,789
Terance Mathis, New Mexico	1988-92	263	4,254
J. R. Tolver, San Diego St.	1999-02	262	3,572
Mark Templeton, Long Beach St.	1984-87	262	1,969
Howard Twilley, Tulsa	1981-84	261	3,343

Heisman Memorial Trophy

The Heisman Trophy honors the outstanding college football player in the U.S. Presented by the Downtown Athletic Club of New York, the award is named for John Heisman, former player, coach, and club director.

Year	Player	College	Pos.
1935	Jay Berwanger	Chicago	HB
1936	Larry Kelley	Yale	E
1937	Clint Frank	Yale	HB
1938	Davey O'Brien	Texas Christian	QB
1939	Nile Kinnick	Iowa	HB
1940	Tom Harmon	Michigan	HB
1941	Bruce Smith	Minnesota	HB
1942	Frank Sinkwich	Georgia	HB
1943	Angelo Bertelli	Notre Dame	QB
1944	Les Horvath	Ohio State	QB
1945	Doc Blanchard	Army	FB
1946	Glenn Davis	Army	HB
1947	John Lujack	Notre Dame	QB
1948	Doak Walker	SMU	HB
1949	Leon Hart	Notre Dame	E
1950	Vic Janowicz	Ohio State	HB
1951	Dick Kazmaier	Princeton	HB
1952	Billy Vessels	Oklahoma	HB
1953	John Lattner	Notre Dame	HB
1954	Alan Ameche	Wisconsin	FB
1955	Howard Cassady	Ohio State	HB
1956	Paul Hornung	Notre Dame	QB
1957	John David Crow	Texas A&M	HB
1958	Pete Dawkins	Army	HB
1959	Billy Cannon	Louisiana State	HB
1960	Joe Bellino	Navy	HB
1961	Ernie Davis	Syracuse	HB
1962	Terry Baker	Orgeon State	QB
1963	Roger Staubach	Navy	QB
1964	John Huarte	Notre Dame	QB
1965	Mike Garrett	USC	HB
1966	Steve Spurrier	Florida	QB
1967	Gary Beban	UCLA	QB
1968	O.J. Simpson	USC	HB
1969	Steve Owens	Oklahoma	HB
1970	Jim Plunkett	Stanford	QB
1971	Pat Sullivan	Auburn	QB
1972	Johnny Rodgers	Nebraska	WR
1973	John Cappelletti	Penn State	RB
1974	Archie Griffin	Ohio State	RB
1975	Archie Griffin	Ohio State	RB
1976	Tony Dorsett	Pittsburgh	RB
1977	Earl Campbell	Texas	RB
1978	Billy Sims	Oklahoma	RB
1979	Charles White	USC	RB
1980	George Rogers	South Carolina	RB
1981	Marcus Allen	USC	RB
1982	Herschel Walker	Georgia	RB
1983	Mike Rozier	Nebraska	RB
1984	Doug Flutie	Boston College	QB
1985	Bo Jackson	Auburn	RB
1986	Vinny Testaverde	Miami (Fla.)	QB
1987	Tim Brown	Notre Dame	WR
1988	Barry Sanders	Oklahoma State	RB
1989	Andre Ware	Houston	QB
1990	Ty Detmer	Brigham Young	QB
1991	Desmond Howard	Michigan	WR
1992	Gino Toretta	Miami (Fla.)	QB
1993	Charlie Ward	Florida State	QB
1994	Rashaan Salaam	Colorado	RB
1995	Eddie George	Ohio State	RB
1996	Danny Wuerffel	Florida	QB
1997	Charles Woodson	Michigan	CB
1998	Ricky Williams	Texas	TB
1999	Ron Dayne	Wisconsin	TB
2000	Chris Weinke	Florida State	QB
2001	Eric Crouch	Nebraska	QB
2002	Carson Palmer	USC	QB

COLLEGE BASKETBALL

NCAA Division I Men's Basketball Championship Final Four Results

Year	Champion	Score	Runner-up	Third place	Fourth place	Champion coach
1939	Oregon	46–33	Ohio State	Oklahoma[1]	Villanova[1]	Howard Hobson
1940	Indiana	60–42	Kansas	Duquesne[1]	USC [1]	Branch McCracken
1941	Wisconsin	39–34	Washington St.	Pittsburgh[1]	Arkansas[1]	Harold Foster
1942	Stanford	53–38	Dartmouth	Colorado[1]	Kentucky[1]	Everett Dean
1943	Wyoming	46–34	Georgetown	Texas[1]	DePaul[1]	Everett Shelton
1944	Utah	42–40[2]	Dartmouth	Iowa State[1]	Ohio State [1]	Vadal Peterson
1945	Oklahoma State	49–45	NYU	Arkansas[1]	Ohio State[1]	Henry Iba
1946	Oklahoma State	43–40	North Carolina	Ohio St.	California	Henry Iba
1947	Holy Cross	58–47	Oklahoma	Texas	CCNY	Alvin Julian
1948	Kentucky	58–42	Baylor	Holy Cross	Kansas State	Adolph Rupp
1949	Kentucky	46–36	Oklahoma State	Illinois	Oregon State	Adolph Rupp
1950	CCNY	71–68	Bradley	North Carolina State	Baylor	Nat Holman
1951	Kentucky	68–58	Kansas State	Illinois	Oklahoma State	Aldolph Rupp
1952	Kansas	80–63	St. John's	Illinois	Santa Clara	Forrest Allen
1953	Indiana	69–68	Kansas	Washington	Louisiana State	Branch McCracken
1954	LaSalle	92–76	Bradley	Penn State	USC	Kenneth Loeffler
1955	San Francisco	77–63	La Salle	Colorado	Iowa	Phil Woolpert
1956	San Francisco	83–71	Iowa	Temple	Southern Methodist	Phil Woolpert
1957	North Carolina	54–53[3]	Kansas	San Francisco	Michigan State	Frank McGuire
1958	Kentucky	84–72	Seattle	Temple	Kansas State	Adolph Rupp
1959	California	71–70	West Virginia	Cincinnati	Louisville	Pete Newell
1960	Ohio State	75–55	California	Cincinnati	NYU	Fred Taylor
1961	Cincinnati	70–65[2]	Ohio State	St. Joe's[4]	Utah	Edwin Jucker
1962	Cincinnati	71–59	Ohio State	Wake Forest	UCLA	Edwin Jucker
1963	Loyola (Ill.)	60–58[2]	Cincinnati	Duke	Utah	George Ireland
1964	UCLA	98–83	Duke	Michigan	Kansas State	John Wooden
1965	UCLA	91–80	Michigan	Princeton	Wichita State	John Wooden
1966	UTEP	72–65	Kentucky	Duke	Utah	Don Haskins
1967	UCLA	79–64	Dayton	Houston	North Carolina	John Wooden
1968	UCLA	78–55	North Carolina	Ohio State	Houston	John Wooden
1969	UCLA	92–72	Purdue	Drake	North Carolina	John Wooden
1970	UCLA	80–69	Jacksonville	New Mexico St.	St. Bonaventure	John Wooden
1971	UCLA	68–62	Villanova[4]	Western Kentucky[4]	Kansas	John Wooden
1972	UCLA	81–76	Florida State	North Carolina	Louisville	John Wooden
1973	UCLA	87–66	Memphis State	Indiana	Providence	John Wooden
1974	North Carolina State	76–64	Marquette	UCLA	Kansas	Norm Sloan
1975	UCLA	92–85	Kentucky	Louisville	Syracuse	John Wooden
1976	Indiana	86–68	Michigan	UCLA	Rutgers	Bob Knight
1977	Marquette	67–59	North Carolina	UNLV	UNC-Charlotte	Al McGuire
1978	Kentucky	94–88	Duke	Arkansas	Notre Dame	Joe Hall
1979	Michigan State	75–64	Indiana State	DePaul	Pennsylvania	Jud Heathcote
1980	Louisville	59–54	UCLA[4]	Purdue	Iowa	Denny Crum
1981	Indiana	63–50	North Carolina	Virginia	Louisiana State	Bob Knight
1982	North Carolina	63–62	Georgetown	Houston[1]	Louisville[1]	Dean Smith
1983	North Carolina State	54–52	Houston	Georgia[1]	Louisville[1]	Jim Valvano
1984	Georgetown	84–75	Houston	Kentucky[1]	Virginia[1]	John Thompson
1985	Villanova	66–64	Georgetown	St. John's[1]	Memphis[1,4]	Rollie Massimino
1986	Louisville	72–69	Duke	Kansas[1]	Louisiana State[1]	Denny Crum
1987	Indiana	74–73	Syracuse	UNLV[1]	Providence[1]	Bob Knight
1988	Kansas	83–79	Oklahoma	Arizona[1]	Duke[1]	Larry Brown
1989	Michigan	80–79[2]	Seton Hall	Illinois[1]	Duke[1]	Steve Fisher
1990	UNLV	103–73	Duke	Georgia Tech[1]	Arkansas[1]	Jerry Tarkanian
1991	Duke	72–65	Kansas	UNLV[1]	North Carolina[1]	Mike Krzyzewski
1992	Duke	71–51	Michigan	Cincinnati[1]	Indiana[1]	Mike Krzyzewski
1993	North Carolina	77–71	Michigan	Kansas[1]	Kentucky[1]	Dean Smith
1994	Arkansas	76–70	Duke	Arizona[1]	Florida[1]	Nolan Richardson
1995	UCLA	89–78	Arkansas	North Carolina[1]	Oklahoma State[1]	Jim Harrick
1996	Kentucky	76–67	Syracuse	Massachusetts[1,4]	Mississippi State[1]	Rick Pitino
1997	Arizona	84–79	Kentucky	Minnesota[1]	North Carolina[1]	Lute Olson
1998	Kentucky	78–69	Utah	North Carolina[1]	Stanford[1]	Tubby Smith
1999	Connecticut	77-74	Duke	Michigan State[1]	Ohio State[1]	Jim Calhoun
2000	Michigan State	89-76	Florida	North Carolina[1]	Wisconsin[1]	Tom Izzo
2001	Duke	82-72	Arizona	Maryland[1]	Michigan State[1]	Mike Krzyzewski
2002	Maryland	64-52	Indiana	Kansas[1]	Oklahoma[1]	Gary Williams
2003	Syracuse	81-78	Kansas	Marquette[1]	Texas[1]	Jim Boeheim

1. Tied for third place. 2. Overtime. 3. Triple overtime. 4. Later declared ineligible.

NCAA Basketball Career Leaders

Player, Team	POINTS
Pete Maravich, Louisiana State	3,667
Freeman Williams, Portland State	3,249
Lionel Simmons, LaSalle	3,217
Alphonzo Ford, Mississippi Valley	3,165
Harry Kelly, Texas Southern	3,066
Hersey Hawkins, Bradley	3,008
Oscar Robertson, Cincinnati	2,973
Danny Manning, Kansas	2,951
Alfredrick Hughes, Loyola (Ill.)	2,914
Elvin Hayes, Houston	2,884

Player, Team	REBOUNDS
Tom Gola, LaSalle	2,201
Joe Holup, George Washington	2,030
Charlie Slack, Marshall	1,916
Ed Conlin, Fordham	1,884
Dickie Hemric, Wake Forest	1,802
Paul Silas, Creighton	1,751
Art Quimby, Connecticut	1,716
Jerry Harper, Alabama	1,688
Jeff Cohen, William and Mary	1,679
Steve Hamilton, Morehead State	1,675

Player, Team	ASSISTS
Bobby Hurley, Duke	1,076
Chris Corchiani, N.Carolina State	1,038
Ed Cota, North Carolina	1,030
Keith Jennings, East Tennessee St.	983
Steve Blake, Maryland	972
Sherman Douglas, Syracuse	960
Tony Miller, Marquette	956
Greg Anthony, Portland/UNLV	950
Doug Gottlieb, Notre Dame/Oklahoma State	947
Gary Payton, Oregon State	938

National Invitation Tournament Champions

Year	Champion	Year	Champion
1938	Temple	**1971**	North Carolina
1939	Long Island	**1972**	Maryland
1940	Colorado	**1973**	Virginia Tech
1941	Long Island	**1974**	Purdue
1942	West Virginia	**1975**	Princeton
1943	St. John's	**1976**	Kentucky
1944	St. John's	**1977**	St. Bonaventure
1945	DePaul	**1978**	Texas
1946	Kentucky	**1979**	Indiana
1947	Utah	**1980**	Virginia
1948	St. Louis	**1981**	Tulsa
1949	San Francisco	**1982**	Bradley
1950	City College of New York	**1983**	Fresno State
1951	BYU	**1984**	Michigan
1952	LaSalle	**1985**	UCLA
1953	Seton Hall	**1986**	Ohio State
1954	Holy Cross	**1987**	Southern Mississippi
1955	Duquesne	**1988**	Connecticut
1956	Louisville	**1989**	St. John's
1957	Bradley	**1990**	Vanderbilt
1958	Xavier (Ohio)	**1991**	Stanford
1959	St. John's	**1992**	Virginia
1960	Bradley	**1993**	Minnesota
1961	Providence	**1994**	Villanova
1962	Dayton	**1995**	Virginia Tech
1963	Providence	**1996**	Nebraska
1964	Bradley	**1997**	Michigan
1965	St. John's	**1998**	Minnesota
1966	BYU	**1999**	California
1967	So. Illinois	**2000**	Wake Forest
1968	Dayton	**2001**	Tulsa
1969	Temple	**2002**	Memphis
1970	Marquette	**2003**	St. John's

NCAA Division I Women's Basketball Championship Results

Year	Champion	Score	Runner-Up	Coach	Outstanding player
1982	Louisiana Tech	76-62	Cheyney	Sonja Hogg	Janice Lawrence
1983	USC	69-67	Louisiana Tech	Linda Sharp	Cheryl Miller
1984	USC	72-61	Tennessee	Linda Sharp	Cheryl Miller
1985	Old Dominion	70-65	Georgia	Marianne Stanley	Tracy Claxton
1986	Texas	97-81	USC	Jody Conradt	Clarissa Davis
1987	Tennessee	67-44	Louisiana Tech	Pat Summitt	Tonya Edwards
1988	Louisiana Tech	56-54	Auburn	Leon Barmore	Erica Westbrooks
1989	Tennessee	76-60	Auburn	Pat Summitt	Brigitte Gordon
1990	Stanford	88-81	Auburn	Tara VanderVeer	Jennifer Azzi
1991	Tennessee	70-67	Virginia	Pat Summitt	Dawn Staley
1992	Stanford	78-62	Western Kentucky	Tara VanderVeer	Molly Goodenbour
1993	Texas Tech	84-82	Ohio State	Marcia Sharp	Sheryl Swoopes
1994	North Carolina	60-59	Louisiana Tech	Sylvia Hatchell	Charlotte Smith
1995	Connecticut	70-64	Tennessee	Geno Auriemma	Rebecca Lobo
1996	Tennessee	83-65	Georgia	Pat Summitt	Michelle Marciniak
1997	Tennessee	68-59	Old Dominion	Pat Summitt	Chamique Holdsclaw
1998	Tennessee	93-75	Louisiana Tech	Pat Summitt	Chamique Holdsclaw
1999	Purdue	62-45	Duke	Carolyn Peck	Ukari Figgs
2000	Connecticut	71-52	Tennessee	Geno Auriemma	Shea Ralph
2001	Notre Dame	68-66	Purdue	Muffet McGraw	Ruth Riley
2002	Connecticut	82-70	Oklahoma	Geno Auriemma	Swin Cash
2003	Connecticut	73-68	Tennessee	Geno Auriemma	Diana Taurasi

NCAA CHAMPIONS IN OTHER SPORTS

Men's Sports

CROSS COUNTRY
1938 Indiana
1939 Michigan State
1940 Indiana
1941 Rhode Island
1942 Indiana
1943 No Meet
1944 Drake
1945 Drake
1946 Drake
1947 Penn State
1948 Michigan State
1949 Michigan State
1950 Penn State
1951 Syracuse
1952 Michigan State
1953 Kansas
1954 Oklahoma St.
1955 Michigan State
1956 Michigan State
1957 Notre Dame
1958 Michigan State
1959 Michigan State
1960 Houston
1961 Oregon State
1962 San Jose State
1963 San Jose State
1964 W. Michigan
1965 W. Michigan
1966 Villanova
1967 Villanova
1968 Villanova
1969 UTEP
1970 Villanova
1971 Oregon
1972 Tennessee
1973 Oregon
1974 Oregon
1975 UTEP
1976 UTEP
1977 Oregon
1978 UTEP
1979 UTEP
1980 UTEP
1981 UTEP
1982 Wisconsin
1983 Vacated
1984 Arkansas
1985 Wisconsin
1986 Arkansas
1987 Arkansas
1988 Wisconsin
1989 Iowa State
1990 Arkansas
1991 Arkansas
1992 Arkansas
1993 Arkansas
1994 Iowa State
1995 Arkansas
1996 Stanford
1997 Stanford
1998 Arkansas
1999 Arkansas
2000 Arkansas
2001 Colorado
2002 Stanford

SOCCER
1959 St. Louis
1960 St. Louis
1961 West Chester
1962 St. Louis
1963 St. Louis
1964 Navy
1965 St. Louis
1966 San Franciso
1967 St. Louis, Michigan State
1968 Maryland. Michigan State
1969 St. Louis
1970 St. Louis
1971 Vacated
1972 St. Louis
1973 St. Louis
1974 Howard
1975 San Francisco
1976 San Francisco
1977 Hartwick
1978 Vacated
1979 So. Ill. Univ at Edwardsville
1980 San Francisco
1981 Connecticut
1982 Indiana
1983 Indiana
1984 Clemson
1985 UCLA
1986 Duke
1987 Clemson
1988 Indiana
1989 Santa Clara, Virginia
1990 UCLA
1991 Virginia
1992 Virginia
1993 Virginia
1994 Virginia
1995 Wisconsin
1996 St. John's (N.Y.)
1997 UCLA
1998 Indiana
1999 Indiana
2000 Connecticut
2001 North Carolina
2002 UCLA

WATER POLO
1969 UCLA
1970 UC Irvine
1971 UCLA
1972 UCLA
1973 California
1974 California
1975 California
1976 Stanford
1977 California
1978 Stanford
1979 UC Santa Barbara
1980 Stanford
1981 Stanford
1982 UC Irvine
1983 California
1984 California
1985 Stanford
1986 Stanford
1987 California
1988 California
1989 California
1990 California
1991 California
1992 California
1993 Stanford
1994 Stanford
1995 UCLA
1996 UCLA
1997 Pepperdine
1998 USC
1999 UCLA
2000 UCLA
2001 Stanford
2002 Stanford

FENCING[1]
1941 Northwestern
1942 Ohio State
1943 No Meet
1944 No Meet
1945 No Meet
1946 No Meet
1947 NYU
1948 CCNY
1949 Army, Rutgers
1950 Navy
1951 Columbia
1952 Columbia
1953 Pennsylvania
1954 Columbia, NYU
1955 Columbia
1956 Illinois
1957 NYU
1958 Illinois
1959 Navy
1960 NYU
1961 NYU
1962 Navy
1963 Columbia
1964 Princeton
1965 Columbia
1966 NYU
1967 NYU
1968 Columbia
1969 Pennsylvania
1970 NYU
1971 NYU, Columbia
1972 Detroit
1973 NYU
1974 NYU
1975 Wayne State
1976 NYU
1977 Notre Dame
1978 Notre Dame
1979 Wayne State
1980 Wayne State
1981 Pennsylvania
1982 Wayne State
1983 Wayne State
1984 Wayne State
1985 Wayne State
1986 Notre Dame
1987 Columbia
1988 Columbia
1989 Columbia

1. For champions after 1989, see "Men's and Women's Titles."

GYMNASTICS
1938 Chicago
1939 Illinois
1940 Illinois
1941 Illinois
1942 Illinois
1943-47 No Meet
1948 Penn State
1949 Temple
1950 Illinois
1951 Florida State
1952 Florida State
1953 Penn State
1954 Penn State
1955 Illinois
1956 Illinois
1957 Penn State
1958 Illinois, Michigan State
1959 Penn State
1960 Penn State
1961 Penn State
1962 USC
1963 Michigan
1964 So. Illinois
1965 Penn State
1966 So. Illinois
1967 So. Illinois
1968 California
1969 Iowa
1970 Michigan
1971 Iowa State
1972 So. Illinois
1973 Iowa State
1974 Iowa State
1975 California
1976 Penn State
1977 Indiana State, Oklahoma
1978 Oklahoma
1979 Nebraska
1980 Nebraska
1981 Nebraska
1982 Nebraska
1983 Nebraska
1984 UCLA
1985 Ohio State
1986 Arizona State
1987 UCLA
1988 Nebraska
1989 Illinois
1990 Nebraska
1991 Oklahoma
1992 Stanford
1993 Stanford
1994 Nebraska
1995 Stanford
1996 Ohio State
1997 California
1998 California
1999 Michigan
2000 Penn State
2001 Ohio State
2002 Oklahoma
2003 Oklahoma

ICE HOCKEY
1948 Michigan
1949 Boston College
1950 Colorado College
1951 Michigan
1952 Michigan
1953 Michigan
1954 Rensselaer
1955 Michigan
1956 Michigan
1957 Colorado College
1958 Denver
1959 North Dakota
1960 Denver
1961 Denver
1962 Michigan Tech.
1963 North Dakota
1964 Michigan
1965 Michigan Tech
1966 Michigan State
1967 Cornell
1968 Denver
1969 Denver
1970 Cornell
1971 Boston Univ.
1972 Boston Univ.
1973 Wisconsin
1974 Minnesota
1975 Michigan Tech
1976 Minnesota
1977 Wisconsin
1978 Boston Univ.
1979 Minnesota
1980 North Dakota
1981 Wisconsin
1982 North Dakota
1983 Wisconsin
1984 Bowling Green
1985 Rensselaer
1986 Michigan State
1987 North Dakota
1988 Lake Superior State
1989 Harvard
1990 Wisconsin
1991 N. Michigan
1992 Lake Superior State
1993 Maine
1994 Lake Superior State
1995 Boston Univ.
1996 Michigan

1997 North Dakota
1998 Michigan
1999 Maine
2000 North Dakota
2001 Boston College
2002 Minnesota
2003 Minnesota

SWIMMING
1937 Michigan
1938 Michigan
1939 Michigan
1940 Michigan
1941 Michigan
1942 Yale
1943 Ohio State
1944 Yale
1945 Ohio State
1946 Ohio State
1947 Ohio State
1948 Michigan
1949 Ohio State
1950 Ohio State
1951 Yale
1952 Ohio State
1953 Yale
1954 Ohio State
1955 Ohio State
1956 Ohio State
1957 Michigan
1958 Michigan
1959 Michigan
1960 USC
1961 Michigan
1962 Ohio State
1963 USC
1964 USC
1965 USC
1966 USC
1967 Stanford
1968 Indiana
1969 Indiana
1970 Indiana
1971 Indiana
1972 Indiana
1973 Indiana
1974 USC
1975 USC
1976 USC
1977 USC
1978 Tennessee
1979 California
1980 California
1981 Texas
1982 UCLA
1983 Florida
1984 Florida
1985 Stanford
1986 Stanford
1987 Stanford
1988 Texas
1989 Texas
1990 Texas
1991 Texas
1992 Stanford
1993 Stanford
1994 Stanford
1995 Michigan
1996 Texas
1997 Auburn
1998 Stanford
1999 Auburn
2000 Texas
2001 Texas
2002 Texas
2003 Auburn

WRESTLING
1928 Oklahoma St.[1]
1929 Oklahoma St.
1930 Oklahoma St.[1]
1931 Oklahoma St.[1]
1932 Indiana
1933 Iowa State,[1] Oklahoma St.[1]
1934 Oklahoma St.
1935 Oklahoma St.
1936 Oklahoma
1937 Oklahoma St.
1938 Oklahoma St.
1939 Oklahoma St.
1940 Oklahoma St.
1941 Oklahoma St.
1942 Oklahoma St.
1943 No Match
1944 No Match
1945 No Match
1946 Oklahoma St.
1947 Cornell College
1948 Oklahoma St.
1949 Oklahoma St.
1950 Northern Iowa
1951 Oklahoma
1952 Oklahoma
1953 Penn State
1954 Oklahoma St.
1955 Oklahoma St.
1956 Oklahoma St.
1957 Oklahoma
1958 Oklahoma St.
1959 Oklahoma St.
1960 Oklahoma
1961 Oklahoma St.
1962 Oklahoma St.
1963 Oklahoma
1964 Oklahoma St.
1965 Iowa State
1966 OklahomaSt.
1967 Michigan St.
1968 OklahomaSt.
1969 Iowa State
1970 Iowa State
1971 OklahomaSt.
1972 Iowa State
1973 Iowa State
1974 Oklahoma
1975 Iowa
1976 Iowa
1977 Iowa State
1978 Iowa
1979 Iowa
1980 Iowa
1981 Iowa
1982 Iowa
1983 Iowa
1984 Iowa
1985 Iowa
1986 Iowa
1987 Iowa State
1988 Arizona State
1989 Oklahoma St.
1990 Oklahoma St.
1991 Iowa
1992 Iowa
1993 Iowa
1994 Oklahoma St.
1995 Iowa
1996 Iowa
1997 Iowa
1998 Iowa
1999 Iowa
2000 Iowa
2001 Minnesota
2002 Minnesota
2003 Oklahoma

1. Unofficial champions.

INDOOR TRACK
1965 Missouri
1966 Kansas
1967 USC
1968 Villanova
1969 Kansas
1970 Kansas
1971 Villanova
1972 USC
1973 Manhattan
1974 UTEP
1975 UTEP
1976 UTEP
1977 Washington St.
1978 UTEP
1979 Villanova
1980 UTEP
1981 UTEP
1982 UTEP
1983 SMU
1984 Arkansas
1985 Arkansas
1986 Arkansas
1987 Arkansas
1988 Arkansas
1989 Arkansas
1990 Arkansas
1991 Arkansas
1992 Arkansas
1993 Arkansas
1994 Arkansas
1995 Arkansas
1996 George Mason
1997 Arkansas
1998 Arkansas
1999 Arkansas
2000 Arkansas
2001 Louisiana St.
2002 Tennessee
2003 Arkansas

OUTDOOR TRACK
1921 Illinois
1922 California
1923 Michigan
1924 No Meet
1925 Stanford
1926 USC
1927 Illinois
1928 Stanford
1929 Ohio State
1930 USC
1931 USC
1932 Indiana
1933 Louisiana St.
1934 Stanford
1935 USC
1936 USC
1937 USC
1938 USC
1939 USC
1940 USC
1941 USC
1942 USC
1943 USC
1944 Illinois
1945 Navy
1946 Illinois
1947 Illinois
1948 Minnesota
1949 USC
1950 USC
1951 USC
1952 USC
1953 USC
1954 USC
1955 USC
1956 UCLA
1957 Villanova
1958 USC
1959 Kansas
1960 Kansas
1961 USC
1962 Oregon
1963 USC
1964 Oregon
1965 Oregon, USC
1966 UCLA
1967 USC
1968 USC
1969 San Jose State
1970 BYU, Kansas
1971 UCLA
1972 UCLA
1973 UCLA
1974 Tennessee
1975 UTEP
1976 USC
1977 Arizona State
1978 UCLA, UTEP
1979 UTEP
1980 UTEP
1981 UTEP
1982 UTEP
1983 SMU
1984 Oregon
1985 Arkansas
1986 SMU
1987 UCLA
1988 UCLA
1989 Louisiana St.
1990 Louisiana St.
1991 Tennessee
1992 Arkansas
1993 Arkansas
1994 Arkansas
1995 Arkansas
1996 Arkansas
1997 Arkansas
1998 Arkansas
1999 Arkansas
2000 Stanford
2001 Tennessee
2002 Louisiana St.
2003 Arkansas

BASEBALL
1947 California
1948 USC
1949 Texas
1950 Texas
1951 Oklahoma
1952 Holy Cross
1953 Michigan
1954 Missouri
1955 Wake Forest
1956 Minnesota
1957 California
1958 USC
1959 Oklahoma St.
1960 Minnesota
1961 USC
1962 Michigan
1963 USC
1964 Minnesota
1965 Arizona State
1966 Ohio State
1967 Arizona State
1968 USC
1969 Arizona State
1970 USC
1971 USC
1972 USC
1973 USC
1974 USC
1975 Texas
1976 Arizona
1977 Arizona State
1978 USC
1979 Cal State—Fullerton
1980 Arizona
1981 Arizona State
1982 Miami (Fla.)
1983 Texas
1984 Cal State—Fullerton
1985 Miami (Fla.)
1986 Arizona
1987 Stanford
1988 Stanford
1989 Wichita State
1990 Georgia
1991 Louisiana St.
1992 Pepperdine
1993 Louisiana St.
1994 Oklahoma
1995 Cal State—Fullerton
1996 Louisiana St.
1997 Louisiana St.
1998 USC
1999 Miama (Fla.)
2000 Louisiana St.
2001 Miami (Fla.)
2002 Texas
2003 Rice

GOLF
1897 Yale
1898 Harvard (spring), Yale (fall)
1899 Harvard
1900 No tourney
1901 Harvard
1902 Yale (spring)
1903 Harvard
1904 Harvard
1905 Yale
1906 Yale
1907 Yale
1908 Yale

1909 Yale
1910 Yale
1911 Yale
1912 Yale
1913 Yale
1914 Princeton
1915 Yale
1916 Princeton
1917 No tourney
1918 No tourney
1919 Princeton
1920 Princeton
1921 Dartmouth
1922 Princeton
1923 Princeton
1924 Yale
1925 Yale
1926 Yale
1927 Princeton
1928 Princeton
1929 Princeton
1930 Princeton
1931 Yale
1932 Yale
1933 Yale
1934 Michigan
1935 Michigan
1936 Yale
1937 Princeton
1938 Stanford
1939 Stanford
1940 Louisiana St., Princeton,
1941 Stanford
1942 Louisiana St., Stanford
1943 Yale
1944 Notre Dame
1945 Ohio State
1946 Stanford
1947 Louisiana St.
1948 San Jose St.
1949 North Texas
1950 North Texas
1951 North Texas
1952 North Texas
1953 Stanford
1954 SMU
1955 Louisiana St.
1956 Houston
1957 Houston
1958 Houston
1959 Houston
1960 Houston
1961 Purdue
1962 Houston
1963 Oklahoma St.
1964 Houston
1965 Houston
1966 Houston
1967 Houston
1968 Florida
1969 Houston
1970 Houston
1971 Texas
1972 Texas
1973 Florida
1974 Wake Forest
1975 Wake Forest
1976 Oklahoma
1977 Houston
1978 Oklahoma St.
1979 Ohio State
1980 Oklahoma St.
1981 BYU
1982 Houston
1983 Oklahoma St.
1984 Houston
1985 Houston
1986 Wake Forest
1987 Oklahoma St.
1988 UCLA
1989 Oklahoma
1990 Arizona
1991 Oklahoma St.
1992 Arizona
1993 Florida
1994 Stanford
1995 Oklahoma St.
1996 Arizona State
1997 Pepperdine
1998 UNLV
1999 Georgia
2000 Oklahoma St.
2001 Florida
2002 Minnesota
2003 Clemson

LACROSSE
1971 Cornell
1972 Virginia
1973 Maryland
1974 Johns Hopkins
1975 Maryland
1976 Cornell
1977 Cornell
1978 Johns Hopkins
1979 Johns Hopkins
1980 Johns Hopkins
1981 North Carolina
1982 North Carolina
1983 Syracuse
1984 Johns Hopkins
1985 Johns Hopkins
1986 North Carolina
1987 Johns Hopkins
1988 Syracuse
1989 Syracuse
1990 Syracuse
1991 North Carolina
1992 Princeton
1993 Syracuse
1994 Princeton
1995 Syracuse
1996 Princeton
1997 Princeton
1998 Princeton
1999 Virginia
2000 Syracuse
2001 Princeton
2002 Syracuse
2003 Virginia

TENNIS
1946 USC
1947 William and Mary
1948 William and Mary
1949 San Francisco
1950 UCLA
1951 USC
1952 UCLA
1953 UCLA
1954 UCLA
1955 USC
1956 UCLA
1957 Michigan
1958 USC
1959 Notre Dame, Tulane
1960 UCLA
1961 UCLA
1962 USC
1963 USC
1964 USC
1965 UCLA
1966 USC
1967 USC
1968 USC
1969 USC
1970 UCLA
1971 UCLA
1972 Trinity (Tex.)
1973 Stanford
1974 Stanford
1975 UCLA
1976 USC, UCLA
1977 Stanford
1978 Stanford
1979 UCLA
1980 Stanford
1981 Stanford
1982 UCLA
1983 Stanford
1984 UCLA
1985 Georgia
1986 Stanford
1987 Georgia
1988 Stanford
1989 Stanford
1990 Stanford
1991 USC
1992 Stanford
1993 USC
1994 USC
1995 Stanford
1996 Stanford
1997 Stanford
1998 Stanford
1999 Georgia
2000 Stanford
2001 Georgia
2002 USC
2003 Illinois

VOLLEYBALL
1970 UCLA
1971 UCLA
1972 UCLA
1973 San Diego St.
1974 UCLA
1975 UCLA
1976 UCLA
1977 USC
1978 Pepperdine
1979 UCLA
1980 USC
1981 UCLA
1982 UCLA
1983 UCLA
1984 UCLA
1985 Pepperdine
1986 Pepperdine
1987 UCLA
1988 USC
1989 UCLA
1990 USC
1991 Cal State—Long Beach
1992 Pepperdine
1993 UCLA
1994 Penn State
1995 UCLA
1996 UCLA
1997 Stanford
1998 UCLA
1999 BYU
2000 UCLA
2001 BYU
2002 Hawaii
2003 Lewis

Men's and Women's Sports

FENCING
1990 Penn State
1991 Penn State
1992 Columbia
1993 Columbia
1994 Notre Dame
1995 Penn State
1996 Penn State
1997 Penn State
1998 Penn State
1999 Penn State
2000 Penn State
2001 St. John's (N.Y.)
2002 Penn State
2003 Notre Dame

RIFLE
1954 Seattle
1955 Dartmouth
1956 Dartmouth
1957 Colorado
1958 Denver
1959 Denver
1960 Denver
1961 Middlebury
1962 Colorado
1963 Colorado
1964 Dartmouth
1965 Utah
1966 W. Colorado
1967 Wyoming
1968 Denver
1969 Dartmouth
1970 Dartmouth
1971 Colorado
1972 Denver
1973 Wyoming
1974 Wyoming
1975 Vermont
1976 Colorado
1977 Wyoming
1978 Wyoming
1979 Utah
1980 Tennessee Tech
1981 Tennessee Tech
1982 Tennessee Tech
1983 West Virginia
1984 West Virginia
1985 Murray State
1986 West Virginia
1987 Murray State
1988 West Virginia
1989 West Virginia
1990 West Virginia
1991 West Virginia
1992 West Virginia
1993 West Virginia
1994 Alaska Fairbanks
1995 West Virginia
1996 West Virginia
1997 West Virginia
1998 West Virginia
1999 Alaska Fairbanks
2000 Alaska Fairbanks
2001 Alaska Fairbanks
2002 Alaska Fairbanks
2003 Alaska Fairbanks

SKIING
1954 Denver
1955 Denver
1956 Denver
1957 Denver
1958 Dartmouth
1959 Colorado
1960 Colorado
1961 Denver
1962 Denver

1963 Denver
1964 Denver
1965 Denver
1966 Denver
1967 Denver
1968 Wyoming
1969 Denver
1970 Denver
1971 Denver
1972 Colorado
1973 Colorado
1974 Colorado
1975 Colorado
1976 Dartmouth
1977 Colorado
1978 Colorado
1979 Colorado
1980 Vermont
1981 Utah
1982 Colorado
1983 Utah
1984 Utah
1985 Wyoming
1986 Utah
1987 Utah
1988 Utah
1989 Vermont
1990 Vermont
1991 Colorado
1992 Vermont
1993 Utah
1994 Vermont
1995 Colorado
1996 Utah
1997 Utah
1998 Colorado
1999 Colorado
2000 Denver
2001 Denver
2002 Denver
2003 Utah

Women's Sports

Year	Cross-Country	Field Hockey	Soccer	Volleyball	Indoor Track	Outdoor Track	Golf
1981	Virginia	Connecticut	N.A.	USC	N.A.	N.A.	N.A.
1982	Virginia	Old Dominion	North Carolina	Hawaii	N.A.	UCLA	Tulsa
1983	Oregon	Old Dominion	North Carolina	Hawaii	Nebraska	UCLA	TCU
1984	Wisconsin	Old Dominion	North Carolina	UCLA	Nebraska	Florida State	Miami (Fla.)
1985	Wisconsin	Connecticut	George Mason	Pacific	Florida State	Oregon	Florida
1986	Texas	Iowa	North Carolina	Pacific	Texas	Texas	Florida
1987	Oregon	Maryland	North Carolina	Hawaii	Louisiana St.	Louisiana St.	San Jose St.
1988	Kentucky	Old Dominion	North Carolina	Texas	Texas	Louisiana St.	Tulsa
1989	Villanova	North Carolina	North Carolina	Cal State Long Beach	Louisiana St.	Louisiana St.	San Jose St.
1990	Villanova	Old Dominion	North Carolina	UCLA	Texas	Louisiana St.	Arizona St.
1991	Villanova	Old Dominion	North Carolina	UCLA	Louisiana St.	Louisiana St.	UCLA
1992	Villanova	Old Dominion	North Carolina	Stanford	Florida	Louisiana St.	San Jose St.
1993	Villanova	Maryland	North Carolina	Long Beach St.	Louisiana St.	Louisiana St.	Arizona St.
1994	Villanova	James Madison	North Carolina	Stanford	Louisiana St.	Louisiana St.	Arizona St.
1995	Providence	North Carolina	Notre Dame	Nebraska	Louisiana St.	Louisiana St.	Arizona St.
1996	Stanford	North Carolina	North Carolina	Stanford	Louisiana St.	Louisiana St.	Arizona
1997	BYU	North Carolina	North Carolina	Stanford	Louisiana St.	Louisiana St.	Arizona St.
1998	Villanova	Old Dominion	Florida	Long Beach St.	Texas	Texas	Arizona St.
1999	BYU	Maryland	North Carolina	Penn State	Texas	Texas	Duke
2000	Colorado	Old Dominion	North Carolina	Nebraska	UCLA	Louisiana St.	Arizona
2001	BYU	Michigan	Santa Clara	Stanford	UCLA	USC	Georgia
2002	BYU	Wake Forest	Portland	USC	Louisiana St.	South Carolina	Duke
2003					Louisiana St.	Louisiana State	USC

Year	Gymnastics	Lacrosse	Softball	Swimming	Tennis	Fencing[1]	
1982	Utah	Massachusetts	UCLA	Florida	Stanford	N.A.	
1983	Utah	Delaware	Texas A&M	Stanford	USC	Wayne State	
1984	Utah	Temple	UCLA	Texas	Stanford	Penn State	
1985	Utah	New Hampshire	UCLA	Texas	USC	Yale	
1986	Utah	Maryland	Cal State Fullerton	Texas	Stanford	Yale	
1987	Georgia	Penn State	Texas A&M	Texas	Stanford	Pennsylvania	
1988	Alabama	Temple	UCLA	Texas	Stanford	Notre Dame	
1989	Georgia	Penn State	UCLA	Stanford	Stanford	Wayne State	
1990	Utah	Harvard	UCLA	Texas	Stanford	Wayne State	
1991	Alabama	Virginia	Arizona	Texas	Stanford		
1992	Utah	Maryland	UCLA	Stanford	Florida		
1993	Georgia	Virginia	Arizona	Stanford	Texas		
1994	Utah	Princeton	Arizona	Stanford	Georgia		
1995	Utah	Maryland	UCLA	Stanford	Texas		
1996	Alabama	Maryland	Arizona	Stanford	Florida		
1997	UCLA	Maryland	Arizona	USC	Stanford		
1998	Georgia	Maryland	Fresno State	Stanford	Florida		
1999	Georgia	Maryland	UCLA	Georgia	Stanford		
						Water Polo	**Ice Hockey**
2000	UCLA	Maryland	Oklahoma	Georgia	Georgia		
2001	UCLA	Maryland	Arizona	Georgia	Stanford	UCLA	Minn.Duluth
2002	Alabama	Princeton	California	Auburn	Stanford	Stanford	Minn.Duluth
2003	UCLA	Princeton	UCLA	Auburn	Florida	UCLA	Minn.Duluth

1. Since, 1990, the NCAA has recognized a joint fencing champion. See "Men's and Women's Titles" above.

International Sports

YACHTING: THE AMERICA'S CUP

In 1851, the Royal Yacht Squadron presented a "hundred guinea cup" to the winning yacht in a race around the Isle of Wight in the English Channel. The cup was won by the U.S. schooner *America* and thereafter became known as the America's Cup. In 24 challenges over the next 132 years the cup remained in the hands of U.S. yachtsmen.

In 2003, Switzerland became the first landlocked country to win the cup, when *Alinghi* defeated Team New Zealand 5-0 in Auckland.

The America's Cup, 1851–2003

Year	Winner	Loser
1851	America, U.S.	Aurora, England
1870	Magic, U.S.	Cambria, England
1871	Columbia, U.S	Livonia, England
1876	Madeline, U.S.	Countess of Dufferin, Canada
1881	Mischief, U.S.	Atalanta, Canada
1885	Puritan, U.S.	Genesta, Britain
1886	Mayflower, U.S.	Galatea, Britain
1887	Volunteer, U.S.	Thistle, Scotland
1893	Vigilant, U.S.	Valkyrie II, Britain
1895	Defender, U.S.	Valkyrie III, Britain
1899	Columbia, U.S.	Shamrock, Ireland
1901	Columbia, U.S.	Shamrock II, Ireland
1903	Reliance, U.S.	Shamrock III, Ireland
1920	Resolute, U.S.	Shamrock IV, Ireland
1930	Enterprise, U.S.	Shamrock V, Ireland
1934	Rainbow, U.S.	Endeavour, Britain
1937	Ranger, U.S.	Endeavour II, Britain
1958	Columbia, U.S.	Sceptre, Britain
1962	Weatherly, U.S.	Gretel, Australia
1964	Constellation, U.S.	Sovereign, Britain
1970	Intrepid, U.S.	Gretel II, Australia
1974	Courageous, U.S.,	Southern Cross, Australia
1977	Courageous, U.S.	Australia, Australia
1980	Freedom, U.S.	Australia, Australia
1983	Australia II, Australia	Liberty, U.S.
1987	Stars & Stripes, U.S.	Kookaburra III, Australia
1988	Stars & Stripes, U.S.	KZ, New Zealand
1992	America3, U.S.	Il Moro di Venezia, Italy
1995	Black Magic, New Zealand	Young America, U.S.,
2000	Team New Zealand, New Zealand	Prada, Italy,
2003	Alinghi, Switzerland,	Team New Zealand, New Zealand

THE WORLD CUP

The World Cup, modern soccer's crowning event, is staged every four years by the Federation Internationale de Football Association (FIFA). In 2002, teams from 198 nations competed for a bid to the 32-team round-robin first round; the top 16 teams advance to the single-elimination tournament. Players must represent their home country, regardless of where they regularly play. Millions attend the Cup's many contests, and the televised final is viewed by over a billion people worldwide.

The World Cup, 1930–2002

Year	Final Score	Leading scorer, country (goals)	Host country	Participating nations
1930	Uruguay 4, Argentina 2	Stabile, Argentina (8)	Uruguay	13
1934	Italy 2, Czechoslovakia 1 (OT)	Conen, Germany Nejedly, Czechoslovakia Schiavo, Italy (4)	Italy	31
1938	Italy 4, Hungary 2	Leonidas, Brazil (8)	France	36
1942	No tournament—World War II			
1946	No tournament—World War II			
1950	Uruguay 2, Brazil 1	Ademir, Brazil (7)	Brazil	33
1954	West Germany 3, Hungary 2	Kocsis, Hungary (11)	Switzerland	38
1958	Brazil 5, Sweden 2	Fontaine, France (13)	Sweden	53
1962	Brazil 3, Czechoslovakia 1	Jerkovic, Yugoslavia (5)	Chile	56
1966	England 4, West Germany 2 (OT)	Eusebio, Portugal (9)	England	71
1970	Brazil 4, Italy 1	Muller, West Germany (10)	Mexico	71
1974	West Germany 2, Netherlands 1	Lato, Poland (7)	West Germany	98
1978	Argentina 3, Netherlands 1 (OT)	Kempes, Argentina (6)	Argentina	106
1982	Italy 3, West Germany 1	Rossi, Italy (6)	Spain	109
1986	Argentina 3, West Germany 2	Lineker, England (6)	Mexico	121
1990	West Germany 1, Argentina 0	Schilacci, Italy (6)	Italy	112
1994	Brazil 0, Italy 0 (OT)[1]	Stoichkov, Bulgaria (6)	United States	144
1998	France 3, Brazil 0	Suker, Croatia (6)	France	173
2002	Brazil 2, Germany 0	Ronaldo, Brazil (8)	Korea/Japan	198

Source: FIFA. 1. Brazil won 3-2 on penalty kicks.

2002 World Cup, First Round

Group A	Wins-Losses-Ties	Points
Denmark	2-0-1	7
Senegal	1-0-2	5
Uruguay	0-1-2	2
France	0-2-1	1

Senegal 1, France 0 | Denmark 1, Senegal 1
Denmark 2, Uruguay 1 | Denmark 2, France 0
France 0, Uruguay 0 | Senegal 3, Uruguay 3

Group B	Wins-Losses-Ties	Points
Spain	3-0-0	9
Paraguay	1-1-1	4
South Africa	1-1-1	4
Slovenia	0-3-0	0

Paraguay 2 , South Africa 2 | South Africa 1, Slovenia 0
Spain 3, Slovenia 1 | Spain 3, South Africa 2
Spain 3, Paraguay 1 | Paraguay 3, Slovenia 1

Group C	Wins-Losses-Ties	Points
Brazil	3-0-0	9
Turkey	1-1-1	4
Costa Rica	1-1-1	4
China	0-3-0	0

Brazil 2, Turkey 1 | Costa Rica 1, Turkey 1
Costa Rica 2, China 0 | Brazil 5, Costa Rica 2
Brazil 4, China 0 | Turkey 3, China 0

Group D	Wins-Losses-Ties	Points
Korea	2-0-1	7
United Sates	1-1-1	4
Poland	1-2-0	3
Portugal	1-2-0	3

Korea 2, Poland 0 | Portugal 4, Poland 0
United States 3, Portugal 2 | Korea 1, Portugal 0
Korea 1, United States 1 | Poland 3, United States 1

Group E	Wins-Losses-Ties	Points
Germany	2-0-1	7
Ireland	1-0-2	5
Cameroon	1-1-1	4
Saudi Arabia	0-3-0	0

Ireland 1, Cameroon 1 | Cameroon 1, Saudi Arabia 0
Germany 8, Saudi Arabia 0 | Germany 2, Cameroon 0
Germany 1, Ireland 1 | Ireland 3, Saudi Arabia 0

Group F	Wins-Losses-Ties	Points
England	1-0-2	5
Sweden	1-0-2	5
Argentina	1-2-0	4
Nigeria	0-2-1	1

England 1, Sweden 1 | England 1, Argentina 0
Argentina 1, Nigeria 0 | Sweden 1, Argentina 1
Sweden 2, Nigeria 1 | Nigeria 0, England 0

Group G	Wins-Losses-Ties	Points
Mexico	2-0-1	7
Italy	1-1-1	4
Croatia	1-2-0	3
Ecuador	1-2-0	3

Mexico 1, Croatia 0 | Mexico 2, Ecuador 1
Italy 2, Ecuador 0 | Mexico 1, Italy 1
Croatia 2, Italy 1 | Ecuador 1, Croatia 0

Group H	Wins-Losses-Ties	Points
Japan	2-0-1	7
Belgium	0-0-3	3
Russia	1-2-0	3
Tunisia	0-2-1	1

Japan 2 , Belgium 2 | Tunisia 1, Belgium 1
Russia 2, Tunisia 0 | Japan 2, Tunisia 0
Japan 1, Russia 0 | Belgium 3, Russia 2

Note: A win is worth three points and a tie is worth one point. The top two teams in each group advance to the second round.

2002 World Cup, Second Round

Denmark 0 – England 3 → England 1
Brazil 2 – Belgium 0 → Brazil 2
Sweden 1 – Senegal 2 (OT) → Senegal 0
Japan 0 – Turkey 1 → Turkey 1 (OT)

England 1 – Brazil 2 → Brazil 1
Senegal 0 – Turkey 1 (OT) → Turkey 0

Germany 1 – Paraguay 0 → Germany 1
Mexico 0 – USA 2 → USA 0
Spain 1[1] – Ireland 1[1] → Spain 0[2]
South Korea 2 (OT) – Italy 1 → South Korea 0[2]

Germany 1 – USA 0 → Germany 1
Spain 0[2] – South Korea 0[2] → South Korea 0

Semifinals

Brazil 1 – Turkey 0
Germany 1 – South Korea 0

World Cup Final

Brazil 2 Germany 0

Third Place Game

Turkey 3 South Korea 2

1. Spain beat Ireland 3-2 on penalty kicks. 2. South Korea beat Spain 5-3 on penalty kicks.

The Women's World Cup, 2003

Germany became the first country to win both the men's and women's World Cup, when the German women beat Sweden 2-1 in overtime in the final. The tournament was originally supposed to be held in China, but was moved to the U.S. because of a fear of SARS, or severe acute respiratory syndrome, in Asia. The 2003 World Cup did not capture America's attention the way it did four years earlier, when the U.S. women won a thrilling championship game over China on penalty kicks.

FIRST ROUND

Group A	Wins-Losses-Ties	Points
x-United States	3-0-0	9
x-Sweden	2-1-0	6
North Korea	1-2-0	3
Nigeria	0-3-0	0

North Korea 3, Nigeria 0 — U.S. 5, Nigeria 0
United States 3, Sweden 1 — Sweden 3, Nigeria 0
Sweden 2, North Korea 0 — U.S. 3, North Korea 0

Group B	Wins-Losses-Ties	Points
x-Brazil	2-0-1	7
x-Norway	2-1-0	6
France	1-1-1	4
South Korea	0-3-0	0

Norway 2, France 0 — France 1, South Korea 0
Brazil 3, South Korea 0 — Norway 7, South Korea 1
Brazil 4, Norway 1 — France 1, Brazil 1

Group C	Wins-Losses-Ties	Points
x-Germany	3-0-0	9
x-Canada	2-1-0	6
Japan	1-2-0	3
Argentina	0-3-0	1

Germany 4, Canada 1 — Canada 3, Argentina 0
Japan 6, Argentina 0 — Canada 3, Japan 1
Germany 3, Japan 0 — Germany 6, Argentina 1

Group D	Wins-Losses-Ties	Points
x-China	2-0-1	7
x-Russia	2-1-0	6
Ghana	1-2-0	3
Australia	0-2-1	1

Russia 2, Australia 1 — China 1, Australia 1
China 1, Ghana 0 — Ghana 2, Australia 1
Russia 3, Ghana 0 — China 1, Russia 0

Note: A win is worth three points, and a tie is worth one point. The top two teams in each group advance to the second round.

2003 Women's World Cup, Second Round

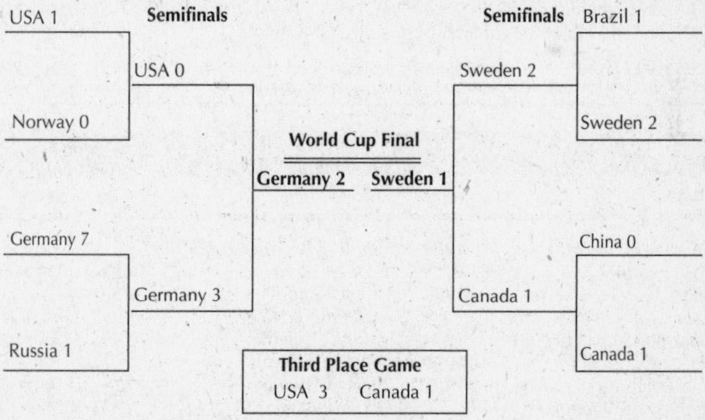

CYCLING

The Tour De France

Year	Champion	Year	Champion	Year	Champion	Year	Champion
1903	Maurice Garin	**1906**	Rene Pottier	**1909**	Francois Faber	**1912**	Odile Defraye
1904	Henri Cornet	**1907**	Lucien Petit-Breton	**1910**	Octave Lapize	**1913**	Philippe Thijs
1905	Louis Trousselier	**1908**	Lucien Petit-Breton	**1911**	Gustave Garrigou	**1914**	Philippe Thijs

Year	Champion
1919	Firmin Lambot
1920	Philippe Thijs
1921	Leon Scieur
1922	Firmin Lambot
1923	Henri Pelissier
1924	Lucien Petit-Breton
1925	Ottavio Bottecchia
1926	Lucien Buysse
1927	Nicolas Frantz
1928	Nicolas Frantz
1929	Maurice Dewaele
1930	Andre Leducq
1931	Antonin Magne
1932	Andre Leducq
1933	Georges Speicher
1934	Antonin Magne
1935	Romain Maes
1936	Sylvere Maes
1937	Roger Lapebie
1938	Gino Bartali
1939	Sylvere Maes
1947	Jean Robic
1948	Gino Bartali
1949	Fausto Coppi
1950	Ferdi Kubler
1951	Hugo Koblet
1952	Fausto Coppi
1953	Louison Bobet
1954	Louison Bobet
1955	Louison Bobet
1956	Roger Walkowiak
1957	Jacques Anquetil
1958	Charly Gaul
1959	Federico Bahamontes
1960	Gastone Nencini
1961	Jacques Anquetil
1962	Jacques Anquetil
1963	Jacques Anquetil
1964	Jacques Anquetil
1965	Felice Gimondi
1966	Lucien Aimar
1967	Roger Pingeon
1968	Jan Janssen
1969	Eddy Merckx
1970	Eddy Merckx
1971	Eddy Merckx
1972	Eddy Merckx
1973	Luis Ocana
1974	Eddy Merckx
1975	Bernard Thevenet
1976	Lucien Van Impe
1977	Bernard Thevenet
1978	Bernard Hinault
1979	Bernard Hinault
1980	Joop Zoetemelk
1981	Bernard Hinault
1982	Bernard Hinault
1983	Laurent Fignon
1984	Laurent Fignon
1985	Bernard Hinault
1986	Greg LeMond
1987	Stephen Roche
1988	Pedro Delgado
1989	Greg LeMond
1990	Greg LeMond
1991	Miguel Indurain
1992	Miguel Indurain
1993	Miguel Indurain
1994	Miguel Indurain
1995	Miguel Indurain
1996	Bjarne Riis
1997	Jan Ullrich
1998	Marco Pantini
1999	Lance Armstrong
2000	Lance Armstrong
2001	Lance Armstrong
2002	Lance Armstrong
2003	Lance Armstrong

CHESS

World Chess Champions

Year	Champion, Country
1886	Wilhelm Steinitz, Austria
1894	Emanuel Lasker, Germany
1921	José R. Capablanca, Cuba
1927	Alexander Alekhine, France
1935	Max Euwe, Netherlands
1937	Alexander Alekhine, France
1948	Mikhail Botvinnik, USSR
1957	Vassily Smyslov, USSR
1958	Mikhail Botvinnik, USSR
1960	Mikhail Tal, USSR
1961	Mikhail Botvinnik, USSR
1963	Tigran Petrosian, USSR
1969	Boris Spassky, USSR
1972	Bobby Fischer, USA
1975	Anatoly Karpov, USSR
1985[1]	Garry Kasparov, USSR/Russia
1993	Anatoly Karpov, Russia
1999	Alex Khalifman, Russia
2000	Visawanthan Anand, India
2002	Ruslan Ponomariov, Ukraine

1. In 1993, Kasparov started his own chess sanctioning body, the Professional Chess Association, leaving his World Chess Federation (FIDE) championship vacant, whereupon FIDE awarded the title to Karpov. **Source:** U.S. Chess Federation.

U.S. Chess Champions

Years	Name
1845–57	Charles Henry Stanley
1857–71	Paul Morphy
1871–90	Capt. George Mackenzie
1890–91	Jackson Showalter
1891–94	Solomon Lipschutz
1894	Jackson Showalter
1894-95	Albert Hodges
1895–97	Jackson Showalter
1897–1906	Harry Nelson Pillsbury
1906–09	Jackson Showalter
1909–36	Frank J. Marshall
1936-42	Samuel Reshevsky
1944	Arnold Denker
1946	Samuel Reshevsky
1948	Herman Steiner
1951-52	Larry Evans
1954	Arthur Bisguier
1957–61	Bobby Fischer
1961–62	Larry Evans
1962–66	Bobby Fischer
1968	Larry Evans
1969	Samuel Reshevksy
1972	Robert Byrne
1973	John Grefe, Lubomir Kavalek
1974-77	Walter Browne
1978	Lubomir Kavalek
1980	Walter Browne, Larry Evans, Larry Christiansen
1981	Walter Browne, Yasser Seirawan
1983	Walter Browne, Larry Christiansen, Roman Dzindzichashvili
1984-85	Lev Alburt
1986	Yasser Seirawan
1987	Joel Benjamin, Nick deFirmian
1988	Michael Wilder
1989	Roman Dzindzichashvili, Stuart Rachels, Yasser Seirawan,
1990	Lev Alburt
1991	Gata Kamsky
1992	Patrick Wolff
1993	Alexander Shabalaov, Alex Yermolinsky
1994	Boris Gulko
1995	Nick deFirmian, Alexander Ivanov, Patrick Wolf
1996	Alex Yermolinski
1997	Joel Benjamin
1998	Nick deFirmian
1999	Boris Gulko
2000	Joel Benjamin
2001	Joel Benjamin, Yasser Seirawan, Alexander Shabalaov
2002	Larry Christiansen
2003	Alexander Shabalaov,

Note: The U.S. championship is not held every year. **Source:** U.S. Chess Federation

FIGURE SKATING

U.S. and World Figure Skating Champions

	U.S. Champions		World Champions	
Year	Men	Women	Men, Country	Women, Country
1952	Richard Button	Tenley Albright	Richard Button, U.S.	Jacqueline du Bief, France
1953	Hayes Jenkins	Tenley Albright	Hayes Jenkins, U.S.	Tenley Albright, U.S.
1954	Hayes Jenkins	Tenley Albright	Hayes Jenkins, U.S.	Gundi Busch, W. Germany
1955	Hayes Jenkins	Tenley Albright	Hayes Jenkins, U.S.	Tenley Albright, U.S.
1956	Hayes Jenkins	Tenley Albright	Hayes Jenkins, U.S.	Carol Heiss, U.S.
1957	Dave Jenkins	Carol Heiss	Dave Jenkins, U.S.	Carol Heiss, U.S.
1958	Dave Jenkins	Carol Heiss	Dave Jenkins, U.S.	Carol Heiss, U.S.
1959	Dave Jenkins	Carol Heiss	Dave Jenkins, U.S.	Carol Heiss, U.S.
1960	Dave Jenkins	Carol Heiss	Alain Giletti, France	Carol Heiss, U.S.
1961	Bradley Lord	Laurence Owen	No champion	No champion
1962	Monty Hoyt	Barbara Roles Pursley	Don Jackson, Canada	Sjoukje Dijkstra, Netherlands
1963	Tommy Litz	Lorraine Hanlon	Don McPherson, Canada	Sjoukje Dijkstra, Netherlands
1964	Scott Allen	Peggy Fleming	Manfred Schnelldorfer, West Germany	Sjoukje Dijkstra, Netherlands
1965	Gary Visconti	Peggy Fleming	Alain Calmat, France	Petra Burka, Canada
1966	Scott Allen	Peggy Fleming	Emmerich Danzer, Austria	Peggy Fleming, U.S.
1967	Gary Visconti	Peggy Fleming	Emmerich Danzer, Austria	Peggy Fleming, U.S.
1968	Tim Wood	Peggy Fleming	Emmerich Danzer, Austria	Peggy Fleming, U.S.
1969	Tim Wood	Janet Lynn	Tim Wood, U.S.	Gabriele Seyfert, E. Germany
1970	Tim Wood	Janet Lynn	Tim Wood, U.S.	Gabriele Seyfert, E. Germany
1971	John Misha Petkevich	Janet Lynn	Ondrej Nepela, Czechoslovakia	Beatrix Schuba, Austria
1972	Ken Shelley	Janet Lynn	Ondrej Nepela, Czechoslovakia	Beatrix Schuba, Austria
1973	Gordon McKellen Jr.	Janet Lynn	Ondrej Nepela, Czechoslovakia	Karen Magnussen, Canada
1974	Gordon McKellen Jr.	Dorothy Hamill	Jan Hoffmann, E. Germany	Christine Errath, E. Germany
1975	Gordon McKellen Jr.	Dorothy Hamill	Sergei Volkov, USSR	Dianne de Leeuw, Netherlands/U.S.
1976	Terry Kubicka	Dorothy Hamill	John Curry, Great Britain	Dorothy Hamill, U.S.
1977	Charles Tickner	Linda Fratianne	Vladimir Kovalev, USSR	Linda Fratianne, U.S.
1978	Charles Tickner	Linda Fratianne	Charles Tickner, U.S.	Anett Potzsch, E. Germany
1979	Charles Tickner	Linda Fratianne	Vladimir Kovalev, USSR	Linda Fratianne, U.S.
1980	Charles Tickner	Linda Fratianne	Jan Hoffmann, E. Germany	Anett Potzsch, E. Germany
1981	Scott Hamilton	Elaine Zayak	Scott Hamilton, U.S.	Denise Biellmann, Switzerland
1982	Scott Hamilton	Rosalynn Sumners	Scott Hamilton, U.S.	Elaine Zayak, U.S.
1983	Scott Hamilton	Rosalynn Sumners	Scott Hamilton, U.S.	Rosalynn Sumners, U.S.
1984	Scott Hamilton	Rosalynn Sumners	Scott Hamilton, U.S.	Katarina Witt, E. Germany
1985	Brian Boitano	Tiffany Chin	Aleksandr Fadeev, USSR	Katarina Witt, E. Germany
1986	Brian Boitano	Debi Thomas	Brian Boitano, U.S.	Debi Thomas, U.S.
1987	Brian Boitano	Jill Trenary	Brian Orser, Canada	Katarina Witt, E. Germany
1988	Brian Boitano	Debi Thomas	Brian Boitano, U.S.	Katarina Witt, E. Germany
1989	Christopher Bowman	Jill Trenary	Kurt Browning, Canada	Midori Ito, Japan
1990	Todd Eldredge	Jill Trenary	Kurt Browning, Canada	Jill Trenary, U.S.
1991	Todd Eldredge	Tonya Harding	Kurt Browning, Canada	Kristi Yamaguchi, U.S.
1992	Christopher Bowman	Kristi Yamaguchi	Victor Petrenko, Russia	Kristi Yamaguchi, U.S.
1993	Scott Davis	Nancy Kerrigan	Kurt Browning, Canada	Oksana Baiul, Ukraine
1994	Scott Davis	Tonya Harding[1]	Elvis Stojko, Canada	Yuka Sato, Japan
1995	Todd Eldredge	Nicole Bobek	Elvis Stojko, Canada	Lu Chen, China
1996	Rudy Galindo	Michelle Kwan	Todd Eldredge, U.S.	Michelle Kwan, U.S.
1997	Todd Eldredge	Tara Lipinski	Elvis Stojko, Canada	Tara Lipinski, U.S.
1998	Todd Eldredge	Michelle Kwan	Alexi Yagudin, Russia	Michelle Kwan, U.S.
1999	Michael Weiss	Michelle Kwan	Alexi Yagudin, Russia	Maria Butyrskaya, Russia
2000	Michael Weiss	Michelle Kwan	Alexi Yagudin, Russia	Michelle Kwan, U.S.
2001	Tim Goebel	Michelle Kwan	Evgeni Plushenko, Russia	Michelle Kwan, U.S.
2002	Tim Goebel	Michelle Kwan	Alexi Yagudin, Russia	Irina Slutskaya, Russia
2003	Michael Weiss	Michelle Kwan	Evgeni Plushenko, Russia	Michelle Kwan, U.S.

1. Later stripped of title. **Source:** U.S. Figure Skating Association.

MARATHON RUNNING

Marathons are 26 miles, 385 yards long, the distance purportedly run by the Athenian messenger who announced his city-state's victory over the Persian Empire on the Plains of Marathon in 490 B.C. The oldest U.S. marathon covers a route from Hopkinton, Mass. to Boston.

Boston Marathon Champions

MEN'S CHAMPIONS

Year	Winner	Time
1897	John J. McDermott	2:55:10
1898	Ronald J. McDonald	2:42:00
1899	Lawrence J. Brignolia	2:54:38
1900	James J. Caffrey	2:39:44
1901	James J. Caffrey	2:29:23
1902	Samuel A. Mellor	2:43:12
1903	John C. Lorden	2:41:29
1904	Michael Spring	2:38:04
1905	Fred Lorz	2:38:25
1906	Timothy Ford	2:45:45
1907	Thomas Longboat	2:24:24
1908	Thomas P. Morrissey	2:25:43
1909	Henri Renaud	2:53:36
1910	Fred L. Cameron	2:28:52
1911	Clarence H. DeMar	2:21:39
1912	Michael J. Ryan	2:21:18
1913	Fritz Carlson	2:25:14
1914	James Duffy	2:25:01
1915	Edouard Fabre	2:31:41
1916	Arthur V. Roth	2:27:16
1917	William K. Kennedy	2:28:37
1918	Service team race won by Camp Devens	
1919	Carl W. A. Linder	2:29:13
1920	Peter Trivoulidas	2:29:31
1921	Frank Zuna	2:18:57
1922	Clarence H. DeMar	2:18:10
1923	Clarence H. DeMar	2:23:37
1924	Clarence H. DeMar	2:29:40
1925	Charles L. Mellor	2:33:00
1926	John C. Miles	2:25:40
1927	Clarence H. DeMar	2:40:22
1928	Clarence H. DeMar	2:37:07
1929	John C. Miles	2:33:08
1930	Clarence H. DeMar	2:34:48
1931	James P. Henigan	2:46:45
1932	Paul deBruyn	2:33:36
1933	Leslie Pawson	2:33:01
1934	Dave Komonen	2:32:53
1935	John A. Kelley	2:32:07
1936	Ellison M. (Tarzan) Brown	2:33:40
1937	Walter Young	2:33:20
1938	Leslie Pawson	2:35:34
1939	Ellison M. (Tarzan) Brown	2:28:51
1940	Gerard Cote	2:33:20
1941	Leslie Pawson	2:30:38
1942	Bernard Joe Smith	2:26:51
1943	Gerard Cote	2:28:25
1944	Gerard Cote	2:31:50
1945	John A. Kelley	2:30:40
1946	Stylianos Kyriakides	2:29:27
1947	Yun Bok Suh	2:25:39
1948	Gerard Cote	2:31:02
1949	Karle Gosta Leandersson	2:31:50
1950	Kee Yong Ham	2:32:39
1951	Shigeki Tanaka	2:27:45
1952	Doroteo Flores	2:31:53
1953	Keizo Yamada	2:18:51
1954	Veikko L. Karvonen	2:20:39
1955	Hideo Hamamura	2:18:22
1956	Antti Viskari	2:14:14
1957	John J. Delley	2:20:05
1958	Franjo Mihalic	2:25:54
1959	Eino Oksanen	2:22:42
1960	Paavo Kotila	2:20:54
1961	Eino Oksanen	2:23:39
1962	Eino Oksanen	2:23:48
1963	Aurele Vandendriessche	2:18:58
1964	Aurele Vandendriessche	2:19:59
1965	Morio Shigematsu	2:16:33
1966	Kenji Kimihara	2:17:11
1967	David McKenzie	2:15:45
1968	Ambrose Burfoot	2:22:17
1969	Yoshiaki Unetani	2:13:49
1970	Ron Hill	2:10:30
1971	Alavaro Mejia	2:18:45
1972	Olavi Suomalainen	2:15:39
1973	Jon Anderson	2:16:03
1974	Neil Cusack	2:13:39
1975	Bill Rodgers	2:09:55
1976	Jack Fultz	2:20:19
1977	Jerome Drayton	2:14:46
1978	Bill Rodgers	2:10:13
1979	Bill Rodgers	2:09:27
1980	Bill Rodgers	2:12:11
1981	Toshihiko Seko	2:09:26
1982	Alberto Salazar	2:08:52
1983	Gregory A. Meyer	2:09:00
1984	Geoff Smith	2:10:34
1985	Geoff Smith	2:14:05
1986	Robert de Castella	2:07:51
1987	Toshihiko Seko	2:11:50
1988	Ibrahim Hussein	2:08:43
1989	Abebe Mekonnen	2:09:06
1990	Gelindo Bordin	2:08:20
1991	Ibrahim Hussein	2:11:06
1992	Ibrahim Hussein	2:08:14
1993	Cosmas N'Deti	2:09:33
1994	Cosmas N'Deti	2:07:15
1995	Cosmas N'Deti	2:09:22
1996	Moses Tanui	2:09:16
1997	Lameck Aguta	2:10:34
1998	Moses Tanui	2:07:34
1999	Joseph Chebet	2:09:52
2000	Elijah Lagat	2:09:47
2001	Lee Bong-ju	2:09:43
2002	Rodgers Rop	2:09:02
2003	Robert Cheruiyot	2:10:11

WOMEN'S CHAMPIONS

Year	Winner	Time
1972	Nina Kuscsik	3:10:26
1973	Jacqueline Hansen	3:05:59
1974	Miki Gorman	2:47:11
1975	Liane Winter	2:42:24
1976	Kim Merritt	2:47:10
1977	Miki Gorman	2:46:22
1978	Gayle Barron	2:44:52
1979	Joan Benoit	2:35:15
1980	Jacqueline Gareau	2:34:28
1981	Allison Roe	2:26:46
1982	Charlotte Teske	2:29:33
1983	Joan Benoit	2:22:43
1984	Lorraine Moller	2:29:28
1985	Lisa Larsen-Weidenbach	2:34:06
1986	Ingrid Kristiansen	2:24:55
1987	Rosa Mota	2:25:21
1988	Rosa Mota	2:24:30
1989	Ingrid Kristiansen	2:24:33
1990	Rosa Mota	2:25:24
1991	Wanda Panfil	2:24:18
1992	Olga Markova	2:23:43
1993	Olga Markova	2:25:27
1994	Uta Pippig	2:21:45
1995	Uta Pippig	2:25:11
1996	Uta Pippig	2:27:12
1997	Fatuma Roba	2:28:03
1998	Fatuma Roba	2:23:21
1999	Fatuma Roba	2:23:25
2000	Catherine Ndereba	2:26:11
2001	Catherine Ndereba	2:21:50
2002	Margaret Okayo	2:20:43
2003	Svetlana Zakharova	2:25:20

New York Marathon Champions

MEN

Year	Winner	Time
1970	Gary Muhrcke	2:31:39
1971	Norman Higgins	2:22:55
1972	Sheldon Karlin	2:27:53
1973	Tom Fleming	2:21:55
1974	Norbert Sander	2:26:31
1975	Tom Fleming	2:19:27
1976	Bill Rodgers	2:10:10
1977	Bill Rodgers	2:11:28
1978	Bill Rodgers	2:12:12
1979	Bill Rodgers	2:11:42
1980	Alberto Salazar	2:09:41
1981	Alberto Salazar	2:08:13
1982	Alberto Salazar	2:09:29
1983	Rod Dixon	2:08:59
1984	Orlando Pizzolato	2:14:53
1985	Orlando Pizzolato	2:11:34
1986	Gianni Poli	2:11:06
1987	Ibrahim Hussein	2:11:01
1988	Steve Jones	2:08:20
1989	Jumo Ikangaa	2:08:01
1990	Douglas Waikihuri	2:12:39
1991	Salvador Garcia	2:09:28
1992	Willie Mtolo	2:09:29
1993	Andres Espinosa	2:10:04
1994	German Silva	2:11:21
1995	German Silva	2:11:00
1996	Giacomo Leone	2:10:09
1997	John Kagwe	2:08:12
1998	John Kagwe	2:08:45
1999	Joseph Chebet	2:09:14
2000	Abdelkhader el-Mouaziz	2:10:09
2001	Tesfaye Jifar	2:07:43
2002	Rodgers Rop	2:08:07

WOMEN

Year	Winner	Time
1970	No Finisher	—
1971	Beth Bonner	2:55:22
1972	Nina Kuscsik	3:08:42
1973	Nina Kuscsik	2:57:08
1974	Katherine Switzer	3:07:29
1975	Kim Merritt	2:46:15
1976	Miki Gorman	2:39:11
1977	Miki Gorman	2:43:10
1978	Grete Waitz	2:32:30
1979	Grete Waitz	2:27:33
1980	Grete Waitz	2:25:41
1981	Allison Roe	2:25:29
1982	Grete Waitz	2:27:14
1983	Grete Waitz	2:27:00
1984	Grete Waitz	2:29:30
1985	Grete Waitz	2:28:34
1986	Grete Waitz	2:28:06
1987	Priscilla Welch	2:30:17
1988	Grete Waitz	2:28:07
1989	Ingrid Kristiansen	2:25:30
1990	Wanda Panfil	2:30:45
1991	Liz McColgan	2:27:32
1992	Lisa Ondieki	2:24:40
1993	Uta Pippig	2:26:24
1994	Tegla Loroupe	2:27:37
1995	Tegla Loroupe	2:28:06
1996	Anuta Catuna	2:28:18
1997	Franziska Rochat-Moser	2:28:43
1998	Franca Fiacconi	2:25:17
1999	Adriana Fernandez	2:25:06
2000	Lyudmila Petrova	2:25:45
2001	Margaret Okayo	2:24:21
2002	Joyce Chepchumba	2:25:56

TRACK AND FIELD

Track and Field World Records (as of July 29, 2003)

These are the recognized records of the IAAF (International Amateur Athletic Federation). All walk records must have been made on a track, and all relay records must be made by teams composed of individuals from the same country. Indoor records must be performed on tracks no larger than 200m in circumference, and the meet must be subject to drug testing. Awards awaiting ratification are not shown.

MEN'S OUTDOOR TRACK RECORDS

Event	(min./sec.)	Record holder (country)	Date
100 m	9.78	Tim Montgomery(U.S.)	9/14/02
200 m	19.32	Michael Johnson (U.S.)	8/1/96
400 m	43.18	Michael Johnson (U.S.)	8/26/99
800 m	1:41.11	Wilson Kipketer (Denmark)	8/24/97
1,000 m	2:11.96	Noah Ngeny (Kenya)	9/5/99
1,500 m	3:26:00	Hicham el-Guerrouj (Morocco)	7/14/98
Mile	3:43.13	Hicham el-Guerrouj (Morocco)	7/7/99
2,000m	4:44.79	Hicham el-Guerrouj (Morocco)	9/7/99
3,000m	7:20.67	Daniel Komen (Kenya)	9/1/96
Steeple-chase	7:53.17	Brahim Boulami (Morocco)	8/16/02
5,000 m	12:39.36	Haile Gebrselassie (Ethiopia)	6/13/98
10,000 m	26:22.75	Haile Gebrselassie (Ethiopia)	6/1/98
Marathon	2:05:42	Khalid Khannouchi (Morocco)	10/24/99
110m hurdles	12.91	Colin Jackson (U.K.)	8/20/93
400m hurdles	46.78	Kevin Young (U.S.)	8/6/92
20 km walk	1:17:25.60	Bernardo Segura (Mexico)	5/7/94
50 km walk	3:40:57.90	Thierry Toutain (France)	9/29/96
4 x 100m	37.40	United States	8/8/92
	37.40	United States	8/21/93
4 x 200m	1:18.68	Santa Monica Track Club	4/17/94
4 x 400m	2:54.20	United States	7/22/98

WOMEN'S OUTDOOR TRACK RECORDS

Event	(min./sec.)	Record holder (country)	Date
100 m	10.49	Florence Griffith Joyner (U.S.)	7/16/88
200 m	21.34	Florence Griffith Joyner (U.S.)	9/29/88
400 m	47.60	Marita Koch (E. Germany)	10/6/85
800 m	1:53.28	Jarmila Kratochvilova (Czechoslovakia)	7/26/83
1,000m	2:28.98	Svetlana Masterkova (Russia)	8/23/96
1,500 m	3:50.46	Yunxia Qu (China)	9/11/93
Mile	4:12.56	Svetlana Masterkova (Russia)	8/14/96
2,000 m	5:25.36	Sonia O'Sullivan (Ireland)	7/9/94
3,000 m	8:06.11	Junxia Wang (China)	9/13/93
5,000 m	14:28.09	Bo Jiang (China)	10/23/97
10,000 m	29:31.78	Junxia Wang (China)	9/8/93
Marathon	2:20:43	Tegla Loroupe (Kenya)	9/26/99
100m hurdles	12.21	Yordanka Donkova (Bulgaria)	8/20/88
400m hurdles	52.61	Kim Batten (U.S.)	8/11/95
5 km walk	20:02.60	Gillian O'Sullivan (Ireland)	7/13/02
10 km walk	41:56.23	Nadezhda Ryashkina (USSR)	7/4/90
4 x 100m	41.37	East Germany	10/6/85
4 x 200m	1:27.46	United States	4/29/00
4 x 400m	3:15.17	Soviet Union	10/1/88

MEN'S OUTDOOR FIELD EVENTS

Event	Meters	Ft./In.	Recordholder (country)	Date
High jump	2.45	8 ft., 0.5 in.	Javier Sotomayor (Cuba)	7/27/93
Pole vault	6.14	20 ft., 1.75 in.	Sergey Bubka (Ukraine)	7/31/94
Long jump	8.95	29 ft., 4.5 in.	Mike Powell (United States)	8/30/91
Triple jump	18.29	60 ft., 0 in.	Jonathan Edwards (Great Britain)	8/7/95
Shot put	23.12	75 ft., 10.25 in.	Randy Barnes (United States)	5/20/90
Discus	74.08	243 ft., 0 in.	Jurgen Schult (East Germany)	6/6/86
Hammer	86.74	284 ft., 7 in.	Yuriy Syedikh (USSR)	8/30/86
Javelin	98.48	323 ft., 1 in.	Jan Zelezny (Czech Republic)	5/25/96
Decathlon	9,026 points		Roman Sebrle (Czech Republic)	5/27/01

WOMEN'S OUTDOOR FIELD EVENTS

Event	Meters	Ft./In.	Record Holder (country)	Date
High jump	2.09	6 ft., 10.25 in.	Stefka Kostadinova (Bulgaria)	8/30/87
Pole vault	4.81	15 ft., 9.25 in.	Stacy Dragila (United States)	6/09/01
Long jump	7.52	24 ft., 8.25 in.	Galina Chistyakova (USSR)	6/11/88
Triple jump	15.50	50 ft., 10.25 in.	Inessa Kravets (Ukraine)	7/10/95
Shot put	22.63	74 ft., 3 in.	Natalya Lisovskaya (USSR)	6/7/87
Discus	76.80	252 ft., 0 in.	Gabriele Reinsch (East Germany)	7/9/88
Hammer	76.07	249 ft., 7.25 in.	Michaela Melinte (Romania)	8/29/99
Javelin	71.54	234-8.5	Osleidys Menéndez (Cuba)	7/01/01
Heptathalon	7,291 points		Jackie Joyner-Kersee (United States)	9/24/88

MEN'S INDOOR TRACK EVENTS

Event	(min./sec.)	Record holder (country)	Date
50m	5.56	Donovan Bailey (Canada)	2/6/96
60m	6.39	Maruice Green (U.S.)	2/3/98
200m	19.92	Frank Fredericks (Namibia)	2/18/96
400m	44.63	Michael Johnson (U.S.)	3/4/95
800m	1:42.67	Wilson Kipketer (Denmark)	3/9/87
1,000 m	2:14.96	Wilson Kipketer (Denmark)	2/20/00
1,500 m	3:31.18	Hicham el-Guerrouj (Morocco)	2/2/97
Mile	3:48.45	Hicham el-Guerrouj (Morocco)	2/12/97
3,000 m	7:24.90	Daniel Komen (Kenya)	2/6/98
5,000 m	12:50.38	Haile Gebrselassie (Ethiopia)	2/14/99
50 m hurdles	6.25	Mark McKoy (Canada)	3/5/86
60 m hurdles	7.30	Colin Jackson (Great Britain)	3/6/94
5,000 m walk	18:07.08	Mikhail Shchennikov (Russia)	2/14/95
4 x 200 m	1:22.11	Great Britain	3/3/91
4 x 400 m	3:02.83	United States	3/7/99
4 x 800 m	7:13.94	United States	2/6/00

WOMEN'S INDOOR TRACK EVENTS

Event	(min./sec.)	Record holder (country)	Date
50 m	5.96	Irina Privalova (Russia)	2/9/95
60 m	6.92	Irina Privalova (Russia)	2/9/95
200 m	21.87	Merlene Ottey (Jamaica)	2/13/93
400 m	49.59	Jarmila Kratochvilova (Czechoslovakia)	3/7/82
800 m	1:55.82	Jolanda Ceplak (Slovakia)	3/3/02
1,000 m	2:30.94	Maria Mutola (Mozambique)	2/25/99
1,500 m	3:59.98	Regina Jacobs (U.S.)	2/1/03
Mile	4:17.14	Doina Melinte (Romania)	2/9/90
3,000 m	8:29.15	Berhane Adere (Ethiopia)	3/2/02
5,000 m	14:47.35	Gabriela Szabo (Romania)	2/13/99
50 m hurdles	6.58	Cornelia Oschkenat (East Germany)	2/20/88
60 m hurdles	7.69	Lyudmila Narozhilenko (USSR)	2/4/90
3,000 m walk	11:35.34	Gillian O'Sullivan (Ireland)	2/15/03
4 x 200 m	1:32.55	Germany	2/21/99
4 x 400 m	3:24.25	Russia	3/7/99
4 x 800m	8:18.71	Russia	2/4/94

MEN'S INDOOR FIELD EVENTS

Event	Meters	Ft./In.	Recordholder (country)	Date
High jump	2.43	7ft., 11.5 in.	Javier Sotomayor (Cuba)	3/4/89
Pole vault	6.15	20 ft., 2 in.	Sergey Bubka (Ukraine)	2/21/93
Long jump	8.79	28 ft., 10.25 in.	Carl Lewis (United States)	1/27/84
Triple jump	17.83	58 ft., 6 in.	Eliecer Urrutia (Cuba)	3/1/97
Shot put	22.66	74 ft., 4.25 in.	Randy Barnes (United States)	1/20/89
Heptathlon	6,476 points		Dan O' Brien (United States)	3/14/93

WOMEN'S INDOOR FIELD EVENTS

Event	Meters	Ft./In.	Record Holder (country)	Date
High jump	2.07	6 ft., 9.5 in.	Heike Henkel (Germany)	2/8/92
Pole vault	4.80	15-9	Svetlana Feofanova (Russia)	3/16/03
Long jump	7.37	24 ft., 2.25 in.	Heike Drechsler (East Germany)	2/13/88
Triple jump	15.16	49 ft., 8.75 in.	Ashia Hansen (Britain)	2/28/98
Shot put	22.50	73 ft., 10 in.	Helena Fibingerova (Czech.)	2/19/77
Pentathlon	4,991 points		Irina Belova (Unified Team)	2/15/92

Source: International Amateur Athletic Federation.

Olympic Sports

The 2002 Winter Olympics at Salt Lake City, Utah
February 8-24, 2002

Event	Gold medal winner, country, time	Silver medal winner, country, time	Bronze medal winner, country, time
ALPINE SKIING			
Men's Downhill	Fritz Strobl, Austria, 1:39.13	Lasse Kjus, Norway, 1:39.35	Stephan Eberharter, Austria, 1:39.41
Men's Slalom	Jean-Pierre Vidal, France, 1:41.06	Sebastien Amiez, France, 1:41.82	Alain Baxter, Great Britain, 1:42.32
Men's Giant Slalom	Stephan Eberharter, Austria, 2:23.28	Bode Miller, United States, 2:24.16	Lasse Kjus, Norway, 2:24.32
Men's Super-G	Kjetil Andre Aamodt, Norway, 1:21.58	Stephan Eberharter, Austria, 1:21.68	Andreas Schifferer, Austria, 1:21.83
Men's Combined	Kjetil Andre Aamodt, Norway, 3:17.56	Bode Miller, United States, 3:17.84	Benjamin Raich, Austria, 3:18.26
Women's Downhill	Carole Montillet, France, 1:39.56	Isolde Kostner, Italy, 1:40.01	Renate Goetschl, Austria, 1:40.39
Women's Slalom	Janica Kostelic, Croatia, 1:46.10	Laure Pequegnot, France, 1:46.17	Anja Paerson, Sweden. 1:47.09
Women's Giant Slalom	Janica Kostelic, Croatia, 2:30.01	Anja Paerson, Sweden, 2:31.33	Sonja Nef, Sitzerland, 2:31.67
Women's Super-G	Daniela Ceccarelli, Italy, 1:13.59	Janica Kostelic, Croatia, 1:13.64	Karen Putzer, Italy, 1:13.86
Women's Combined	Janica Kostelic, Croatia, 2:43.28	Renate Goetschl, Austria, 2:44.77	Martina Ertl, Germany, 2:45.16
BIATHLON			
Men's 10km Sprint	Ole Einar Bjoerndalen, Norway, 24:51.3	Sven Fischer, Germany, 25:20.2	Wolfgang Perner, Austria, 25:44.4
Men's 12.5km Pursuit	Ole Einar Bjoerndalen, Norway, 32:34.6	Raphael Poiree, France, +43.0	Ricco Gross, Germany, +56.0
Men's 20km	Ole Einar Bjoerndalen, Norway, 51:03.3	Frank Luck, Germany, 51:39.4	Victor Maigourov, Russia, 51:40.6
Men's 4x7.5km Relay	Norway, 1:23:42.3	Germany, 1:24:27.6	France, 1:24:36.6
Women's 7.5km Sprint	Kati Wilhelm, Germany, 20:41.4	Uschi Disl, Germany, 20:57.0	Magdalena Forsberg, Sweden, 21:20.4
Women's 10km Pursuit	Olga Pyleva, Russia, 31:07.7	Kati Wilhelm, Germany, +5.3	Irina Nikoultchina, Bulgaria, +8.1
Women's 15km	Andrea Henkel, Germany, 47:29.1	Liv Grete Poiree, Norway, 47:37.0	Magdalena Forsberg, Sweden, 48:08.3
Women's 4x7.5km Relay	Germany, 1:27:55.0	Norway, 1:28:25.6	Russia, 1:29:19.7
BOBSLED			
Two-Man	Germany, 3:10.11	Switzerland, 3:10.20	Switzerland, 3:10.62
Four-Man	Germany, 3:07.51	United States, 3:07.81	United States, 3:07.86
Two-Woman	United States, 1:37.76	Germany, 1:38.06	Germany 1:38.29
CURLING			
Men	Norway	Canada	Switzerland
Women	Great Britain	Switzerland	Canada
CROSS-COUNTRY SKIING			
Men's 1.5km Sprint	Tor Arne Hetland, Norway, 2:56.9	Peter Schlickenrieder, Germany, 2:57.0	Cristian Zorzi, Italy, 2:57.2
Men's 10km Pursuit	Johann Muehlegg, Spain, 49:20.4	Frode Estil, Norway, 49:48.9	*No bronze medal*
Men's 15km Classic	Andrus Veerpalu, Estonia, 37:07.4	Frode Estil, Norway, 37:43.4	Jaak Mae, Estonia, 37:50.8
Men's 30km Free	Johann Muehlegg, Spain, 1:09:28.9	Christian Hoffmann, Austria, 1:11:31.0	Mikhail Botvinov, Austria, 1:11:32.3
Men's 50km Classic	Mikhail Ivanov, Russia, 2:06:20.8	Andrus Veerpalu, Estonia, 2:06:44.5	Odd-Bjoern Hjelmeset, Norway, 2:08:41.5
Men's 4x10km Relay	Norway , 1:32:45.5	Italy, 1:32:45.8	Germany, 1:33:34.5
Women's 1.5km Sprint	Julija Tchepalova, Russia, 3:10.6	Evi Sachenbacher, Germany, 3:12.2	Anita Moen, Norway, 3:12.7

Event	Gold medal winner, country, time	Silver medal winner, country, time	Bronze medal winner, country, time
Women's 5km Pursuit	Olga Danilova, Russia, 24:52.1	Larissa Lazutina, Russia, 24:59.0	Beckie Scott, Canada, 25:09.9
Women's 10km Classic	Bente Skari, Norway, 28:05.6	Olga Danilova, Russia, 28:08.1	Julija Tchepalova, Russia, 28:09.9
Women's 15km Free	Stefania Belmondo, Italy, 39:54.4	Larissa Lazutina, Russia, 39:56.2	Katerina Neumannova, Czech Republic, 40:01.3
Women's 30km Classic	Gabriella Paruzzi, Italy, 1:30:57.1	Stefania Belmondo, Italy, 1:31:01.6	Bente Skari, Norway, 1:31:36.3
Women's 4x5km Relay	Germany, 49:30.6	Norway, 49:31.9	Switzerland, 50:03.6
FIGURE SKATING			
Men	Alexei Yagudin, Russia	Evgeni Plushenko, Russia	Timothy Goebel, U.S.
Women	Sarah Hughes, U.S.	Irina Slutskaya, Russia	Michelle Kwan, U.S.
Pairs	***Tie*** Elena Berezhnaya and Anton Sikharulidze, Russia ***and*** Jamie Sale and David Pelletier Canada		Hongbo Zhao and Xue Shen, China
Ice Dancing	Marina Anissina and Gwendal Peizerat, France	Irina Lobacheva and Ilia Averbukh, Russia	Barbara Fusar Poli and Maurizio Margaglio, Italy
FREESTYLE SKIING			
Men's Aerials	Ales Valenta, Czech Republic, 257.02	Joe Pack, United States, 251.64	Alexei Grichin, Belarus, 251.19
Men's Moguls	Janne Lahtela, Finland, 27.97	Travis Mayer, United States, 27.59	Richard Gay, France, 26.91
Women's Aerials	Alisa Camplin, Australia, 193.47	Veronica Brenner, Canada, 190.02	Deidra Dionne, Canada, 189.26
Women's Moguls	Kari Traa, Norway, 25.94	Shannon Bahrke, United States, 25.06	Tae Satoya, Japan, 24.85
ICE HOCKEY			
Men	Canada	United States	Russia
Women	Canada	United States	Sweden
LUGE			
Men's Singles	Armin Zoeggeler, Italy, 2:57.941	Georg Hackl, Germany, 2:58.270	Markus Prock, Austria, 2:58.283
Men's Doubles	Germany, 1:26.082	United States, 1:26.216	United States, 1:26.220
Women's Singles	Sylke Otto, Germany, 2:52.464	Barbara Niedernhuber, Germany, 2:52.785	Silke Kraushaar, Germany, 2:52.865
NORDIC COMBINED			
Individual 15km	Samppa Lajunen, Finland, 38:18.7	Jaakko Tallus, Finland, 39:36.4	Felix Gottwald, Austria, 37:23.5
Individual 7.5km Sprint	Samppa Lajunen, Finland, 16:40.1	Ronny Ackermann, Germany, 16:49.1	Felix Gottwald, Austria, 17:20.3
Team	Finland, 48:42.2	Germany, 48:49.7	Austria, 48:53.2
SHORT TRACK SPEED SKATING			
Mens 500m	Marc Gagnon, Canada, 41.802	Jonathan Guilmette, Canada, 41.994	Rusty Smith, United States, 42.027
Men's 1000m	Steven Bradbury, Australia, 1:29.109	Apolo Anton Ohno, United States, 1:30.160	Mathieu Turcotte, Canada, 1:30.563
Men's 1500m	Apolo Anton Ohno, United States, 2:18.541	Jiajun Li, China, 2:18.731	Marc Gagnon, Canada, 2:18.806
Men's 5000m relay	Canada, 6:51.579	Italy, 6:56.327	China, 6:59.633
Women's 500m	Yang Yang (a), China, 44.187	Evgenia Radanova, Bulgaria, 44.252	Chunlu Wang, China, 44.272
Women's 1000m	Yang Yang (a), China, 1:36.391	Gi-Hyun Ko, South Korea, 1:36.427	Yang Yang (S), China, 1:37.008
Women's 1500m	Gi-Hyun Ko, South Korea, 2:31.581	Eun-Kyung Choi, South Korea, 2:31.610	Evgenia Radanova, Bulgaria, 2:31.723
Women's 3000m Relay	South Korea, 4:12.793	China, 4:13.236	Canada, 4:15.738
SKELETON			
Men	Jim Shea, United States, 1:41.96	Martin Rettl, Austria, 1:42.01	Gregor Staehli, Switzerland, 1:42.15
Women	Tristan Gale, United States, 1:45.11	Lea Ann Parsley, United States, 1:45.21	Alex Coomber, Great Britain, 1:45.37

Event	Gold medal winner, country, time	Silver medal winner, country, time	Bronze medal winner, country, time
SKI JUMPING			
Individual K90	Simon Ammann, Switzerland, 269.0	Sven Hannawald, Germany, 267.5	Adam Malysz, Poland, 263.0
Individual K120	Simon Ammann, Switzerland, 281.4	Adam Malysz, Poland, 269.7	Matti Hautamaeki, Finland, 256.0
Team	Germany, 974.1	Finland, 974.0	Slovenia,946.3
SNOWBOARD			
Men's Halfpipe	Ross Powers, United States, 46.1	Danny Kass, United States, 42.5	Jarret Thomas, United States, 42.1
Men's Slalom	Philipp Schoch, Switzerland	Richard Richardsson, Sweden	Chris Klug, United States
Women's Halfpipe	Kelly Clark, United States , 47.9	Doriane Vidal, France, 43.0	Fabienne Reuteler, Switzerland, 39.7
Women's Slalom	Isabelle Blanc France	Karine Ruby France	Lidia Trettel Italy
SPEED SKATING			
Men's 500m	Casey Fitzrandolph United States, 69.23	Hiroyasu Shimizu Japan, 69.26	Kip Carpenter United States, 69.47
Men's 1000m	Gerard van Velde Netherlands, 1:07.18	Jan Bos Netherlands, 1:07.53	Joey Cheek United States, 1:07.61
Men's 1500m	Derek Parra United States, 1:43.95	Jochem Uytdehaage Netherlands, 1:44.57	Adne Sondral, Norway, 1:45.26
Men's 5000m	Jochem Uytdehaage Netherlands, 6:14.66	Derek Parra United States, 6:17.98	Jens Boden, Germany, 6:21.73
Men's 10,000m	Jochem Uytdehaage Netherlands, 12:58.92	Gianni Romme Netherlands, 13:10.03	Lasse Saetre, Norway, 13:16.92
Women's 500m	Catriona Lemay Doan, Canada, 74.75	Monique Garbrecht-Enfeldt, Germany, 74.94	Sabine Voelker, Germany, 75.19
Women's 1000m	Chris Witty, United States, 1:13.83	Sabine Voelker, Germany, 1:13.96	Jennifer Rodriguez, United States, 1:14.24
Women's 1500m	Anni Friesinger, Germany, 1:54.02	Sabine Voelker, Germany, 1:54.97	Jennifer Rodriguez United States, 1:55.32
Women's 3000m	Claudia Pechstein, Germany, 3:57.70	Renate Groenewold Netherlands, 3:58.94	Cindy Klassen, Canada, 3:58.97
Women's 5000m	Claudia Pechstein, Germany, 6:46.91	Gretha Smit Netherlands, 6:49.22	Clara Hughes, Canada, 6:53.53

Medal Count by Nation, 2002

Country	Gold	Silver	Bronze	Total	Country	Gold	Silver	Bronze	Total
Germany	12	16	7	35	**South Korea**	2	2	0	4
Norway	11	7	6	24	**Australia**	2	0	0	2
United States	10	13	11	34	**Spain**	2	0	0	2
Russia	6	6	4	16	**Estonia**	1	1	1	3
Canada	6	3	8	17	**Great Britain**	1	0	2	3
France	4	5	2	11	**Czech Republic**	1	0	1	2
Italy	4	4	4	12	**Sweden**	0	2	4	6
Finland	4	2	1	7	**Bulgaria**	0	1	2	3
Netherlands	3	5	0	8	**Japan**	0	1	1	2
Switzerland	3	2	6	11	**Poland**	0	1	1	2
Croatia	3	1	0	4	**Slovenia**	0	0	1	1
Austria	2	4	10	16	**Belarus**	0	0	1	1
China	2	2	4	8					

SUMMER OLYMPIC CHAMPIONS

Swimming and Diving, Men

50m Freestyle

		Time
1904	Zoltán Halmay, Hungary	0:28.00
1988	Matt Biondi, U.S.	0:22.14
1992	Aleksandr Popov, Unified Team	0:21.91
1996	Aleksandr Popov, Russia	0:22.13
2000	(tie) Anthony Ervin, U.S/Gary Hall Jr., U.S.	0:21.98

100m Freestyle

		Time
1896	Alfréd Hajós, Hungary	1:22.20
1904	Zoltán Halmay, Hungary (100 yds.)	1:02.80
1908	Charles Daniels, U.S.	1:05.60
1912	Duke Paoa Kahanamoku, U.S.	1:03.40
1920	Duke Paoa Kahanamoku, U.S.	1:00.40
1924	Johnny Weissmuller, U.S.	0:59.00
1928	Johnny Weissmuller, U.S.	0:58.60
1932	Yasuji Miyazaki, Japan	0:58.20
1936	Ferenc Csík, Hungary	0:57.60
1948	Walter Ris, U.S.	0:57.30
1952	Clarke Scholes, U.S.	0:57.40
1956	Jon Henricks, Australia	0:55.40
1960	John Devitt, Australia	0:55.20
1964	Donald Schollander, U.S.	0:53.40
1968	Michael Wenden, Australia	0:52.20
1972	Mark Spitz, U.S.	0:51.22
1976	Jim Montgomery, U.S.	0:49.99
1980	Jörg Woithe, East Germany	0:50.40
1984	Rowdy Gaines, U.S.	0:49.80
1988	Matt Biondi, U.S.	0:48.63
1992	Aleksandr Popov, Unified Team	0:49.02
1996	Aleksandr Popov, Russia	0:48.74
2000	Pieter van den Hoogenband, Netherlands	0:48.30

200m Freestyle

		Time
1900	Frederick Lane, Austria	2:25.20
1904	Charles Daniels, U.S.	2:44.20
1968	Michael Wenden, Australia	1:55.20
1972	Mark Spitz, U.S.	1:52.78
1976	Bruce Furniss, U.S.	1:50.29
1980	Sergei Kopliakov, U.S.S.R.	1:49.81
1984	Michael Gross, West Germany	1:47.44
1988	Duncan Armstrong, Australia	1:47.25
1992	Evgueni Sadovyi, Unified Team	1:46.70
1996	Danyon Loader, New Zealand	1:47.63
2000	Pieter van den Hoogenband, Netherlands	1:45.35

400m Freestyle

		Time
1896	Paul Neumann, Austria (500m)	8:12.60
1904	Charles Daniels, U.S. (440 yds.)	6:16.20
1908	Henry Taylor, Great Britain (440 yds.)	5:36.80
1912	George Hodgson, Canada	5:24.40
1920	Norman Ross, U.S.	5:26.80
1924	Johnny Weissmuller, U.S.	5:04.20
1928	Alberto Zorilla, Argentina	5:01.60
1932	Clarence "Buster" Crabbe, U.S.	4:48.40
1936	Jack Medica, U.S.	4:44.50
1948	William Smith, U.S.	4:41.00
1952	Jean Boiteux, France	4:30.70
1956	Murray Rose, Australia	4:27.30
1960	Murray Rose, Australia	4:18.30
1964	Donald Schollander, U.S.	4:12.20
1968	Michael Burton, U.S.	4:09.00
1972	Bradford Cooper, Australia	4:00.27
1976	Brian Goodell, U.S.	3:51.93
1980	Vladimir Salnikov, U.S.S.R.	3:51.31
1984	George DiCarlo, U.S.	3:51.23
1988	Ewe Dassler, East Germany	3:46.95
1992	Evgueni Sadovyi, Unified Team	3:45.00
1996	Danyon Loader, New Zealand	3:47.97
2000	Ian Thorpe, Australia	3:40.59

1,500m Freestyle

		Time
1896	Alfréd Hajós, Hungary (1,200m)	18:22.20
1900	John Arthur Jarvis, Great Britain (1,000m)	13:40.20
1904	Emil Rausch, Germany (1,609m)	27:18.20
1908	Henry Taylor, Great Britain	22:48.40
1912	George Hodgson, Canada	22:00.00
1920	Norman Ross, U.S.	22:23.20
1924	Andrew "Boy" Charlton, Australia	20:06.60
1928	Arne Borg, Sweden	19:51.80
1932	Kusuo Kitamura, Japan	19:12.40
1936	Noboru Terada, Japan	19:13.70
1948	James McLane, U.S.	19:18.50
1952	Ford Konno, U.S.	18:30.30
1956	Murray Rose, Australia	17:58.90
1960	John Konrads, Australia	17:19.60
1964	Robert Windle, Australia	17:01.7
1968	Michael Burton, U.S.	16:38.90
1972	Michael Burton, U.S.	15:52.58
1976	Brian Goodell, U.S.	15.02:40
1980	Vladimir Salnikov, U.S.S.R.	14:58.27
1984	Michael O'Brien, U.S.	15:05.20
1988	Vladimir Salnikov, U.S.S.R.	15:00.40
1992	Kieren Perkins, Australia	14:43.48
1996	Kieren Perkins, Australia	14:56.40
2000	Grant Hackett, Australia	14:48.33

100m Backstroke

		Time
1904	Walter Brack, Germany (100yds)	1:16.80
1908	Arno Bieberstein, Germany	1:24.60
1912	Harry Hebner, U.S.	1:21.20
1920	Warren Paoa Kealoha, U.S.	1:15.20
1924	Warren Paoa Kealoha, U.S.	1:13.20
1928	George Kojac, U.S.	1:08.20
1932	Masaji Kiyokawa, Japan	1:08.60
1936	Adolf Kiefer, U.S.	1:05.90
1948	Allen Stack, U.S.	1:06.40
1952	Yoshinobu Oyakawa, U.S.	1:05.40
1956	David Theile, Australia	1:02.20
1960	David Theile, Austalia	1:01.90
1964	Not held	
1968	Roland Matthes, East Germany	0:58.70
1972	Roland Matthes, East Germany	0:56.58
1976	John Naber, U.S.	0:55.49
1980	Bengt Baron, Sweden	0:56.33
1984	Richard Carey, U.S.	0:55.79
1988	Daichi Suzuki, Japan	0:55.05
1992	Mark Tewksbury, Canada	0:53.98
1996	Jeff Rouse, U.S.	0:54:10
2000	Lenny Krayzelburg, United States	0:53.72

200m Backstroke

		Time
1900	Ernst Hoppenberg, Germany	2:47.00
1964	Jed Graef, U.S.	2:10.30
1968	Roland Matthes, East Germany	2:09.60
1972	Roland Matthes, East Germany	2:02.82
1976	John Naber, U.S.	1:59.19
1980	Sándor Wladár, Hungary	2:01.93
1984	Richard Carey, U.S.	2:00.23
1988	Igor Poliansky, U.S.S.R.	1:59.37
1992	Martin Zubero, Spain	1:58.47
1996	Brad Bridgewater, U.S.	1:58.54
2000	Lenny Krayzelburg, United States	1:56.76

100m Breaststroke

		Time
1968	Donald McKenzie, U.S.	1:07.70
1972	Nobutaka Taguchi, Japan	1:04.94
1976	John Hencken, U.S.	1:03.11
1980	Duncan Goodhew, Great Britain	1:03.44
1984	Steve Lundquist, U.S.	1:01.65
1988	Adrian Moorhouse, Great Britain	1:02.04
1992	Nelson Diebel, U.S.	1:01.50
1996	Fred Deburghgraeve, Belgium	1:00.65
2000	Domenico Fioravanti, Italy	1:00.46

200m Breaststroke

		Time
1908	Frederick Holman, Great Britain	3:09.20
1912	Walter Bathe, Germany	3:01.80
1920	Haken Malmroth, Sweden	3:04.40
1924	Robert Skelton, U.S.	2:56.60
1928	Yoshiyuki Tsuruta, Japan	2:48.80
1932	Yoshiyuki Tsuruta, Japan	2:45.40
1936	Tetsuo Hamuro, Japan	2:41.50
1948	Joseph Verdeur, U.S.	2:39.30
1952	John Davies, Australia	2:34.40
1956	Masaru Furukawa, Japan	2:34.70
1960	William Mulliken, U.S.	2:37.40
1964	Ian O'Brien, Australia	2:27.80
1968	Felipe Muñoz, Mexico	2:28.70

1972	John Hencken, U.S.	2:21.55
1976	David Wilkie, Great Britain	2:15.11
1980	Robertas Zhulpa, U.S.S.R.	2:15.85
1984	Victor Davis, Canada	2:13.34
1988	Jozsef Szabo, Hungary	2:13.52
1992	Mike Barrowman, U.S.	2:10.16
1996	Norbert Rozso, Hungary	2:12.57
2000	Domenico Fioravanti, Italy	2:10.87

100m Butterfly

		Time
1968	Douglas Russell, U.S.	0:55.90
1972	Mark Spitz, U.S.	0:54.27
1976	Matt Vogel, U.S.	0:54.35
1980	Par Arvidsson, Sweden	0:54.92
1984	Michael Gross, West Germany	0:53.08
1988	Anthony Nesty, Suriname	0:53.00
1992	Pablo Morales, U.S.	0:53.32
1996	Denis Pankratov, Russia	0:52.27
2000	Lars Froelander, Sweden	0:52.00

200m Butterfly

		Time
1956	William Yorzyk, U.S.	2:19.30
1960	Michael Troy, U.S.	2:12.80
1964	Kevin Berry, Australia	2:06.60
1968	Carl Robie, U.S.	2:08.70
1972	Mark Spitz, U.S.	2:00.70
1976	Mike Bruner, U.S.	1:59.23
1980	Sergei Fesenko, U.S.S.R.	1:59.76
1984	Jon Sieben, Australia	1:57.04
1988	Michael Gross, West Germany	1:56.94
1992	Mel Stewart, U.S.	1:56.26
1996	Denis Pankratov, Russia	1:56.51
2000	Tom Malchow, United States	1:55.35

200m Individual Medley

		Time
1968	Charles Hickcox, U.S.	2:12.00
1972	Gunnar Larsson, Sweden	2:07.17
1984	Alex Baumann, Canada	2:01.42
1988	Tamas Darnyi, Hungary	2:00.17
1992	Tamas Darnyi, Hungary	2:00.76
1996	Attila Czene, Hungary	1:59.91
2000	Massimiliano Rosolino, Italy	1:58.98

400m Individual Medley

		Time
1964	Richard W. Roth, U.S.	4:45.40
1968	Charles Hickcox, U.S.	4:48.40
1972	Gunnar Larsson, Sweden	4:31.98
1976	Rod Strachan, U.S.	4:23.68
1980	Aleksandr Sidorenko, U.S.S.R.	4:22.89
1984	Alex Baumann, Canada	4:17.41
1988	Tamas Darnyi, Hungary	4:14.75
1992	Tamas Darnyi, Hungary	4:14.23
1996	Tom Dolan, U.S.	4:14.90
2000	Tom Dolan, U.S.	4:11.76

4x100m Freestyle Relay

		Time
1964	U.S.	3:33.20
1968	U.S.	3:31.70
1972	U.S.	3:26.42
1984	U.S.	3:19.03
1988	U.S.	3:16.53
1992	U.S.	3:16.74
1996	U.S.	3:15.41
2000	Australia	3:13.67

4x200m Freestyle Relay

		Time
1908	Great Britain	10:55.60
1912	Australia	10:11.60
1920	U.S.	10:04.40
1924	U.S.	9:53.40
1928	U.S.	9:36.20
1932	Japan	8:58.40
1936	Japan	8:51.50
1948	U.S.	8:46.00
1952	U.S.	8:31.10
1956	Australia	8:23.60
1960	U.S.	8:10.20
1964	U.S.	7:52.10
1968	U.S.	7:52.33
1972	U.S.	7:35.78
1976	U.S.	7:23.22
1980	U.S.S.R.	7:23.50
1984	U.S.	7:15.69
1988	U.S.	7:12.69
1992	Unified Team	7:11.95
1996	U.S.	7:14.84
2000	Australia	7:07.05

4x100m Medley Relay

		Time
1960	U.S.	4:05.40
1964	U.S.	3:58.40
1968	U.S.	3:54.90
1972	U.S.	3:48.16
1976	U.S.	3:42.22
1980	Australia	3:45.70
1984	U.S.	3:39.30
1988	U.S.	3:36.93
1992	U.S.	3:36.93
1996	U.S.	3:34.84
2000	U.S.	3:33.73

Platform Diving

1904	George E. Sheldon, U.S.
1908	Hjalmar Johansson, Sweden
1912	Erik Adlerz, Sweden
1920	Clarence Pinkston, U.S.
1924	Albert C. White, U.S.
1928	Pete DesJardins, U.S.
1932	Harold Smith, U.S.
1936	Marshall Wayne, U.S.
1948	Dr. Samuel Lee, U.S.
1952	Dr. Samuel Lee, U.S.
1956	Joaquin Capilla Perez, Mexico
1960	Robert Webster, U.S.
1964	Robert Webster, U.S.
1968	Klaus Dibiasi, Italy
1972	Klaus Dibiasi, Italy
1976	Klaus Dibiasi, Italy
1980	Falk Hoffmann, E. Germany
1984	Gregory Louganis, U.S.
1988	Gregory Louganis, U.S.
1992	Sun Shuwei, China
1996	Xiong Ni, China
2000	Liang Tian, China

Springboard Diving

1908	Albert Zürner, Germany
1912	Paul Günther, Germany
1920	Louis Kuehn, U.S.
1924	Albert C. White, U.S.
1928	Pete Desjardins, U.S.
1932	Michael Galitzen, U.S.
1936	Richard Degener, U.S.
1948	Bruce Harlan, U.S.
1952	David Browning, U.S.
1956	Robert L. Clotworthy, U.S.
1960	Gary Tobian, U.S.
1964	Kenneth R. Sitzberger, U.S.
1968	Bernard Wrightson, U.S.
1972	Vladimir Vasin, U.S.S.R.
1976	Philip Boggs, U.S.
1980	Aleksandr Portnov, U.S.S.R.
1984	Gregory Louganis, U.S.
1988	Gregory Louganis, U.S.
1992	Mark Lenzi, U.S.
1996	Dmitri Saoutine, Russia
2000	Xiong Ni, China

Swimming and Diving, Women

50m Freestyle

		Time
1988	Kristin Otto, E. Germany	0:25.49
1992	Yang Wenji, China	0:24.79
1996	Amy Van Dyken, U.S.	0:24.87
2000	Inge de Bruijn, Netherlands	0:24.32

100m Freestyle

		Time
1912	Fanny Durack, Australia	1:22.20
1920	Ethelda Bleibtrey, U.S.	1:13.60
1924	Ethel Lackie, U.S.	1:12.40
1928	Albina Osipowich, U.S.	1:11.00
1932	Helene Madison, U.S.	1:06.80
1936	Rie Mastenbroek, Netherlands	1:05.90
1948	Greta Andersen, Denmark	1:06.30
1952	Katalin Szoke, Hungary	1:06.80
1956	Dawn Fraser, Australia	1:02.00
1960	Dawn Fraser, Australia	1:01.20
1964	Dawn Fraser, Australia	0:59.50
1968	Jan Henne, U.S.	1:00.00
1972	Sandra Neilson, U.S.	0:58.59
1976	Kornelia Ender, East Germany	0:55.65
1980	Barbara Krause, East Germany	0:54.79
1984	Nancy Hogshead, U.S.	0:55.92
1988	Kristin Otto, East Germany	0:54.93
1992	Zhuang Yong, China	0:54.65
1996	Le Jingyi, China	0:54.50
2000	Inge de Bruijn, Netherlands	0:53.83

200m Freestyle

		Time
1968	Deborah Meyer, U.S.	2:10.50
1972	Shane Gould, Australia	2:03.56
1976	Kornelia Ender, East Germany	1:59.26
1980	Barbara Krause, East Germany	1:58.33
1984	Mary Wayte, U.S.	1:59.23
1988	Heike Friederich, East Germany	1:57.65
1992	Nicole Haislett, U.S.	1:57.90
1996	Claudia Poll, Costa Rica	1:58.16
2000	Susie O'Neill, Australia	1:58.24

400m Freestyle

		Time
1920	Ethelda Bleibtrey, U.S. (300 m)	4:34.00
1924	Martha Norelius, U.S.	6:02.20
1928	Martha Norelius, U.S.	5:42.80
1932	Helene Madison, U.S.	5:28.50
1936	Hendrika "Rie" Mastenbroek, Netherlands	5:26.40
1948	Ann Curtis, U.S.	5:17.80
1952	Valeria Gyenge, Hungary	5:12.10
1956	Lorraine Crapp, Australia	4:54.60
1960	S. Chris Von Saltza, U.S.	4:50.60
1964	Virginia Duenkel, U.S.	4:43.30
1968	Deborah Meyer, U.S.	4:31.80
1972	Shane Gould, Australia	4:19.44
1976	Petra Thümer, East Germany	4:09.89
1980	Ines Diers, East Germany	4:08.76
1984	Tiffany Cohen, U.S.	4:07.10

1988	Janet Evans, U.S.	4:03.85
1992	Dagmar Hase, Germany	4:07.18
1996	Michelle Smith, Ireland	4:07.25
2000	Brooke Bennett, U.S.	4:05.80

800m Freestyle		Time
1968	Deborah Meyer, U.S.	9:24.00
1972	Keena Rothhammer, U.S.	8:53.68
1976	Petra Thümer, East Germany	8:37.14
1980	Michelle Ford, Australia	8:28.90
1984	Tiffany Cohen, U.S.	8:24.95
1988	Janet Evans, U.S.	8:20.20
1992	Janet Evans, U.S.	8:25.52
1996	Brooke Bennett, U.S.	8:27.89
2000	Brooke Bennett, U.S.	8:19.67

100m Backstroke		Time
1924	Sybil Bauer, U.S.	1:23.20
1928	Maria Braun, Netherlands	1:22.00
1932	Eleanor Holm, U.S.	1:19.40
1936	Nida Senff, Netherlands	1:18.90
1948	Karen Harup, Denmark	1:14.40
1952	Joan Harrison, South Africa	1:14.30
1956	Judy Grinham, Great Britain	1:12.90
1960	Lynn Burke, U.S.	1:09.30
1964	Cathy Ferguson, U.S.	1:07.70
1968	Kaye Hall, U.S.	1:06.20
1972	Melissa Belote, U.S.	1:05.78
1976	Ulrike Richter, East Germany	1:01.83
1980	Rica Reinisch, East Germany	1:00.86
1984	Theresa Andrews, U.S.	1:02.55
1988	Kristin Otto, East Germany	1:00.89
1992	Krisztina Egerszegi, Hungary	1:00.68
1996	Beth Botsford, U.S.	1:01.19
2000	Diana Mocanu, Romania	1:00.21

200m Backstroke		Time
1968	Lillian "Pokey" Watson, U.S.	2:24.80
1972	Melissa Belote, U.S.	2:19.19
1976	Ulrike Richter, East Germany	2:13.43
1980	Rica Reinisch, East Germany	2:11.77
1984	Jolanda de Rover, Netherlands	2:12.38
1988	Krisztina Egerszegi, Hungary	2:09.29
1992	Krisztina Egerszegi, Hungary	2:07.06
1996	Krisztina Egerszegi, Hungary	2:07.83
2000	Diana Mocanu, Romania	2:08.16

100m Breaststroke		Time
1972	Catherine Carr, U.S.	1:13.58
1976	Hannelore Anke, East Germany	1:11.16
1980	Ute Geweniger, East Germany	1:10.22
1984	Petra van Staveren, Netherlands	1:09.88
1988	Tania Dangalakova, Bulgaria	1:07.95
1992	Elena Roudkovskaia, Unified Team	1:08.00
1996	Penny Heyns, South Africa	1:07.73
2000	Megan Quann, U.S.	1:07.05

200m Breaststroke		Time
1924	Lucy Morton, Great Britain	3:33.20
1928	Hilde Schrader, Germany	3:12.60
1932	Clare Dennis, Australia	3:06.30
1936	Hideko Maehata, Japan	3:03.60
1948	Nelly van Vliet, Netherlands	2:57.20
1952	Eva Szekely, Hungary	2:51.70
1956	Ursula Happe, Germany	2:53.10
1960	Anita Lonsbrough, Great Britain	2:49.50
1964	Galina Prozumenshikova, U.S.S.R.	2:46.40
1968	Sharon Wichman, U.S.	2:44.40
1972	Beverley Whitfield, Australia	2:41.71
1976	Marina Koshevaia, U.S.S.R.	2:33.35
1980	Lina Kaciusyte, U.S.S.R.	2:29.54
1984	Anne Ottenbrite, Canada	2:30.38
1988	Silke Hoerner, East Germany	2:26.71
1992	Kyoko Iwasaki, Japan	2:26.65
1996	Penny Heyns, South Africa	2:25.41
2000	Agnes Kovacs, Hungary	2:24.35

100m Butterfly		Time
1956	Shelly Mann, U.S.	1:11.00
1960	Carolyn Schuler, U.S.	1:09.50
1964	Sharon Stouder, U.S.	1:04.70
1968	Lynnette McClements, Australia	1:05.50
1972	Mayumi Aoki, Japan	1:03.34
1976	Kornelia Ender, East Germany	1:00.13
1980	Caren Metschuck, East Germany	1:00.42
1984	Mary T. Meagher, U.S.	0:59.26
1988	Kristin Otto, East Germany	0:59.00
1992	Qian Hong, China	0:58.62
1996	Amy Van Dyken, U.S.	0:59.13
2000	Inge de Bruijn, Netherlands	0:56.61

200m Butterfly		Time
1968	Ada Kok, Netherlands	2:24.70
1972	Karen Moe, U.S.	2:15.57
1976	Andrea Pollack, East Germany	2:11.41
1980	Ines Geissler, East Germany	2:10.44
1984	Mary T. Meagher, U.S.	2:06.90
1988	Kathleen Nord, East Germany	2:09.51
1992	Summer Sanders, U.S.	2:08.67
1996	Susan O'Neill, Australia	2:07.76
2000	Misty Hyman, U.S.	2:05.88

200m Individual Medley		Time
1968	Claudia Kolb, U.S.	2:24.70
1972	Shane Gould, Australia	2:23.07
1984	Tracy Caulkins, U.S.	2:12.64
1988	Daniela Hunger, East Germany	2:12.59
1992	Lin Li, China	2:11.65
1996	Michelle Smith, Ireland	2:13.93
2000	Yana Klochkova, Ukraine	2:10.68

400m Individual Medley		Time
1964	Donna De Varona, U.S.	5:18.70
1968	Claudia Kolb, U.S.	5:08.50
1972	Gail Neall, Australia	5:02.97
1976	Ulrike Tauber, East Germany	4:42.77
1980	Petra Schneider, East Germany	4:36.29
1984	Tracy Caulkins, U.S.	4:39.24
1988	Janet Evans, U.S.	4:37.76
1992	Krisztina Egerszegi, Hungary	4:36.54
1996	Michelle Smith, Ireland	4:39.18
2000	Yana Klochkova, Ukraine	4:33.59

4x100m Freestyle Relay					Time
1912	Great Britain	5:52.80	1964	U.S.	4:03.80
1920	U.S.	5:11.60	1968	U.S.	4:02.50
1924	U.S.	4:58.80	1972	U.S.	3:55.19
1928	U.S.	4:47.60	1976	U.S.	3:44.82
1932	U.S.	4:38.00	1980	E. Germany	3:42.71
1938	Netherlands	4:36.00	1984	U.S.	3:43.43
1948	U.S.	4:29.20	1988	E. Germany	3:40.63
1952	Hungary	4:24.40	1992	U.S.	3:39.46
1956	Australia	4:17.10	1996	U.S.	3:39.29
1960	U.S.	4:08.90	2000	U.S.	3:36.61

4x200m Freestyle Relay		Time
1996	U.S.	7:59.87
2000	U.S.	7:57.80

4x100m Medley Relay Time					
1960	U.S.	4:41.10	1984	U.S.	4:08.34
1964	U.S.	4:33.90	1988	E. Germany	4:03.74
1968	U.S.	4:28.30	1992	U.S.	4:02.54
1972	U.S.	4:20.75	1996	U.S.	4:02.88
1976	E. Germany	4:07.95	2000	U.S.	3:58.30
1980	E. Germany	4:06.67			

Platform Diving			
1912	Greta Johansson, Sweden	1964	Lesley Bush, U.S.
1920	Stefani Fryland-Clausen, Denmark	1968	Milena Duchkova, Czechoslovakia
1924	Caroline Smith, U.S.	1972	Ulrika Knape, Sweden
1928	Elizabeth Becker Pinkston, U.S.	1976	Elena Vaytsekhovskaya, U.S.S.R.
1932	Dorothy Poynton, U.S.	1980	Martina Jäschke, E. Germany
1936	Dorothy Poynton Hill, U.S.	1984	Zhou Jihong, China
1948	Victoria Draves, U.S.	1988	Xu Yahmei, China
1952	Patricia McCormick, U.S.	1992	Fu Mingxia, China
1956	Patricia McCormick, U.S.	1996	Fu Mingxia, China
1960	Ingrid Krämer, E. Germany	2000	Laura Wilkinson,U.S.

Springboard Diving			
1920	Aileen Riggin, U.S.	1968	Sue Gossick, U.S.
1924	Elizabeth Becker, U.S.	1972	Micki King, U.S.
1928	Helen Meany, U.S.	1976	Jennifer Chandler, U.S.
1932	Georgia Coleman, U.S.	1980	Irina Kalinina, U.S.S.R.
1936	Marjorie Gestring, U.S.	1984	Sylvie Bernier, Canada
1948	Victoria Draves, U.S.	1988	Gao Min, China
1952	Patricia McCormick, U.S.	1992	Gao Min, China
1956	Patricia McCormick, U.S.	1996	Fu Mingxia, China
1960	Ingrid Kramer, Germany	2000	Fu Mingxia, China
1964	Ingrid Kramer, E. Germany		

Track and Field, Men

100 Meter Dash

Year	Champion	Time
1896	Thomas E. Burke, U.S.	12.00
1900	Francis W. Jarvis, U.S.	11.00
1904	Archie Hahn, U.S.	11.00
1908	Reginald E. Walker, South Africa	10.80
1912	Ralph C. Craig, U.S.	10.80
1920	Charles W. Paddock, U.S.	10.80
1924	Harold M. Abrahams, Great Britain	10.60
1928	Percy Williams, Canada	10.80
1932	Eddie Tolan, U.S.	10.30
1936	Jesse Owens, U.S.	10.30
1948	Harrison Dillard, U.S.	10.30
1952	Lindy J. Remigino, U.S.	10.40
1956	Bobby J. Morrow, U.S.	10.50
1960	Armin Hary, Germany	10.20
1964	Robert L. Hayes, U.S.	10.00
1968	James Hines, U.S.	9.95
1972	Valery Borzov, U.S.S.R.	10.14
1976	Hasely Crawford, Trinidad & Tobago	10.06
1980	Allan Wells, Great Britain	10.25
1984	Carl Lewis, U.S.	9.99
1988	Carl Lewis, U.S.	9.92
1992	Linford Christie, Great Britain	9.96
1996	Donovan Bailey, Canada	9.84
2000	Maurice Greene, U.S.	9.87

200 Meters

Year	Champion	Time
1900	John W.B. Tewksbury, U.S.	22.20
1904	Archie Hahn, U.S.	21.60
1908	Robert Kerr, Canada	22.60
1912	Ralph C. Craig, U.S.	21.70
1920	Allen Woodring, U.S.	22.00
1924	Jackson V. Scholz, U.S.	21.60
1928	Percy Williams, Canada	21.80
1932	Eddie Tolan, U.S.	21.20
1936	Jesse Owens, U.S.	20.70
1948	Melvin Patton, U.S.	21.10
1952	Andrew W. Stanfield, U.S.	20.70
1956	Bobby J. Morrow, U.S.	20.60
1960	Livio Berruti, Italy	20.50
1964	Henry Carr, U.S.	20.30
1968	Tommie Smith, U.S.	19.83
1972	Valery Borzov, U.S.S.R.	20.00
1976	Donald Quarrie, Jamaica	20.23
1980	Pietro Mennea, Italy	20.19
1984	Carl Lewis, U.S.	19.80
1988	Joe DeLoach, U.S.	19.75
1992	Mike Marsh, U.S.	20.01
1996	Michael Johnson, U.S.	19.32
2000	Konstantinos Kenteris, Greece	20.09

400 Meters

Year	Champion	Time
1896	Thomas E. Burke, U.S.	54.20
1900	Maxey Long, U.S.	49.40
1904	Harry I. Hillman, U.S.	49.20
1908	Wyndham Halswelle, Great Britain	50.00
1912	Charles D. Reidpath, U.S.	48.20
1920	Bevil G.D. Rudd, South Africa	49.60
1924	Eric H. Liddel, Great Britain	47.60
1928	Ray Barbuti, U.S.	47.80
1932	William A. Carr, U.S.	46.20
1936	Archie Williams, U.S.	46.50
1948	Arthur Wint, Jamaica	46.20
1952	George Rhoden, Jamaica	45.90
1956	Charles L. Jenkins, U.S.	46.70
1960	Otis Davis, U.S.	44.90
1964	Michael D. Larrabee, U.S.	45.10
1968	Lee Evans, U.S.	43.86
1972	Vince Matthews, U.S.	44.66
1976	Alberto Juantorena, Cuba	44.26
1980	Viktor Markin, U.S.S.R.	44.60
1984	Alonzo Babers, U.S.	44.27
1988	Steven Lewis, U.S.	43.87
1992	Quincy Watts, U.S.	43.50
1996	Michael Johnson, U.S.	43.49
2000	Michael Johnson, U.S.	43.84

800 Meters

Year	Champion	Time
1896	Edwin H. Flack, Australia	2:11.00
1900	Alfred E. Tysoe, Great Britain	2:01.20
1904	James D. Lightbody, U.S.	1:56.00
1908	Melvin W. Sheppard, U.S.	1:52.80
1912	Ted Meredith, U.S.	1:51.90
1920	Albert G. Hill, Great Britain	1:53.40
1924	Douglas G.A. Lowe, Great Britain	1:52.40
1928	Douglas G.A. Lowe, Great Britain	1:51.80
1932	Thomas Hampson, Great Britain	1:49.70
1936	John Woodruff, U.S.	1:52.90
1948	Malvin Whitfield, U.S.	1:49.20
1952	Malvin Whitfield, U.S.	1:49.20
1956	Thomas W. Courtney, U.S.	1:47.70
1960	Peter Snell, New Zealand	1:46.30
1964	Peter Snell, New Zealand	1:45.10
1968	Ralph Doubell, Australia	1:44.30
1972	Dave Wottle, U.S.	1:45.90
1976	Alberto Juantorena, Cuba	1:43.50
1980	Steven Ovett, Great Britain	1:45.40
1984	Joaquim Cruz, Brazil	1:43.00
1988	Paul Ereng, Kenya	1:43.45
1992	William Tanui, Kenya	1:43.66
1996	Vebjoern Rodal, Norway	1:42.59
2000	Nils Schumann, Germany	1:45.08

1,500 Meters

Year	Champion	Time
1896	Edwin H. Flack, Australia	4:33.20
1900	Charles Bennett, Great Britain	4:06.20
1904	James D. Lightbody, U.S.	4:05.40
1908	Melvin W. Sheppard, U.S.	4:03.40
1912	Arnold N.S. Jackson, Great Britain	3:56.80
1920	Albert G. Hill, Great Britain	4:01.80
1924	Paavo Nurmi, Finland	3:53.60
1928	Harry E. Larva, Finland	3:53.20
1932	Luigi Beccali, Italy	3:51.20
1936	Jack Lovelock, New Zealand	3:47.80
1948	Henry Eriksson, Sweden	3:49.80
1952	Josy Barthel, Luxembourg	3:45.10
1956	Ronald Delany, Ireland	3:41.20
1960	Herbert Elliott, Australia	3:35.60
1964	Peter Snell, New Zealand	3:38.10
1968	Kipchoge Keino, Kenya	3:34.90
1972	Pekkha Vasala, Finland	3:36.30
1976	John Walker, New Zealand	3:39.17
1980	Sebastian Coe, Great Britain	3:38.40
1984	Sebastian Coe, Great Britain	3:32.53
1988	Peter Rono, Kenya	3:35.96
1992	Fermin Cacho Ruiz, Spain	3:40.12
1996	Noureddine Morceli, Algeria	3:35.78
2000	Noah Ngeny, Kenya	3:32.07

5,000 Meters

Year	Champion	Time
1912	Johannes Kolehmainen, Finland	14:36.60
1920	Joseph Guillemot, France	14:55.60
1924	Paavo Nurmi, Finland	14:31.20
1928	Ville Ritola, Finland	14:38.00
1932	Lauri Lehtinen, Finland	14:30.00
1936	Gunnar Höckert, Finland	14:22.20
1948	Gaston Reiff, Belgium	14:17.60
1952	Emil Zátopek, Czechoslovakia	14:06.60
1956	Vladimir Kuts, U.S.S.R.	13:39.60
1960	Murray Halberg, New Zealand	13:43.40
1964	Robert K. Schul, U.S.	13:48.80
1968	Mohamed Gammoudi, Tunisia	14:05.00
1972	Lasse Viren, Finland	13:26.40
1976	Lasse Viren, Finland	13:24.76
1980	Miruts Yifter, Ethiopia	13:21.00
1984	Said Aouita, Morocco	13:05.59
1988	John Ngugi, Kenya	13:11.70
1992	Dieter Baumann, Germany	13:12.52
1996	Venuste Niyongabo, Burundi	13:07.97
2000	Millon Wolde, Ethiopia	13:35.49

10,000 Meters

Year	Champion	Time
1912	Johannes Kolehmainen, Finland	31:20.80
1920	Paavo Nurmi, Finland	31:45.80
1924	Ville Ritola, Finland	30:23.20
1928	Paavo Nurmi, Finland	30:18.80
1932	Janusz Kusocinski, Poland	30:11.40
1936	Ilmari Salminen, Finland	30:15.40
1948	Emil Zatopek, Czechoslovakia	29:59.60
1952	Emil Zatopek, Czechoslovakia	29:17.00
1956	Vladimir Kuts, U.S.S.R.	28:45.60
1960	Pyotr Bolotnikov, U.S.S.R.	28:32.20
1964	William Mills, U.S.	28.24.40
1968	Naftali Temu, Kenya	29:27.40
1972	Lasse Viren, Finland	27:38.40

1976	Lasse Viren, Finland	27:40.38
1980	Miruts Yifter, Ethiopia	27:42.70
1984	Alberto Cova, Italy	27:47.54
1988	Brahim Boutaib, Morocco	27:21.46
1992	Khalid Skah, Morocco	27:46.70
1996	Haile Gebrselassie, Ethiopia	27:07.34
2000	Haile Gebrselassie, Ethiopia	27:18.20

Marathon		**Time**
1896	Spiridon Louis, Greece	2:58:50.00
1900	Michel Theato, France	2:59:45.00
1904	Thomas J. Hicks, U.S.	3:28:63.00
1908	John J. Hayes, U.S.	2:55:18.40
1912	Kenneth McArthur, South Africa	2:36:54.80
1920	Johannes Kolehmainen, Finland	2:32:35.80
1924	Albin Stenroos, Finland	2:41:22.60
1928	Boughéra El Quafi, France	2:32:57.00
1932	Juan Carlos Zabala, Argentina	2:31:36.00
1936	Kitei Son, Japan	2:29:19.20
1948	Delfo Cabrera, Argentina	2:34:51.60
1952	Emil Zátopek, Czechoslovakia	2:23:03.20
1956	Alain Mimoun O'Kacha, France	2:25:00.00
1960	Abebe Bikila, Ethiopia	2:15:16.20
1964	Abebe Bikila, Ethiopia	2:12:11.20
1968	Mamo Wolde, Ethiopia	2:20:26.40
1972	Frank Shorter, U.S.	2:12:19.80
1976	Waldemar Cierpinski, East Germany	2:09:55.00
1980	Waldemar Cierpinski, East Germany	2:11:03.00
1984	Carlos Lopes, Portugal	2:09:21.00
1988	Gelindo Bordin, Italy	2:10:32.00
1992	Young-Cho Hwang, S. Korea	2:13:23.00
1996	Josia Thugwane, South Africa	2:12:36.00
2000	Gezahgne Abera, Ethiopia	2:10:11

110-Meter Hurdles		**Time**
1896	Thomas P. Curtis, U.S.	17.60
1900	Alvin E. Kraenzlein, U.S.	15.40
1904	Frederick W. Schule, U.S.	16.00
1908	Forrest Smithson, U.S.	15.00
1912	Frederick W. Kelley, U.S.	15.10
1920	Earl J. Thomson, Canada	14.80
1924	Daniel C. Kinsey, U.S.	15.00
1928	Sydney Atkinson, South Africa	14.80
1932	George Saling, U.S.	14.60
1936	Forrest Towns, U.S.	14.20
1948	William Porter, U.S.	13.90
1952	Harrison Dillard, U.S.	13.70
1956	Lee Q. Calhoun, U.S.	13.50
1960	Lee Q. Calhoun, U.S.	13.80
1964	Hayes W. Jones, U.S.	13.60
1968	Willie Davenport, U.S.	13.30
1972	Rod Milburn, U.S.	13.24
1976	Guy Drut, France	13.30
1980	Thomas Munkelt, East Germany	13.39
1984	Roger Kingdom, U.S.	13.20
1988	Roger Kingdom, U.S.	12.98
1992	Mark McKoy, Canada	13.12
1996	Allen Johnson, U.S.	12.95
2000	Anier Garcia, Cuba	13.00

400-Meter Hurdles		**Time**
1900	John W. B. Tewksbury, U.S.	57.60
1904	Harry L. Hillman, U.S.	53.00
1908	Charles J. Bacon, U.S.	55.00
1920	Frank F. Loomis, U.S.	54.00
1924	F. Morgan Taylor, U.S.	52.60
1928	David Burghley, Great Britain	53.40
1932	Robert Tisdall, Ireland	51.70
1936	Glenn Hardin, U.S.	52.40
1948	Roy Cochran, U.S.	51.10
1952	Charles Moore, U.S.	50.80
1956	Glenn A. Davis, U.S.	50.10
1960	Glenn A. Davis, U.S.	49.30
1964	Warren "Rex" Cawley, U.S.	49.60
1968	David Hemery, Great Britain	48.12
1972	John Akii-Bua, Uganda	47.82
1976	Edwin Moses, U.S.	47.64
1980	Volker Beck, East Germany	48.70
1984	Edwin Moses, U.S.	47.75
1988	Andre Phillips, U.S.	47.19
1992	Kevin Young, U.S.	46.78
1996	Derrick Adkins, United States	47.55
2000	Angelo Taylor, U.S.	47.50

3,000-Meter Steeplechase		**Time**
1900	George Orton, Canada/U.S.	7:34.40
1904	James Lightbody, U.S.	7:39.60
1908	Arthur Russell, Great Britain	10:47.80
1920	Percy Hodge, Great Britain	10:00.40
1924	Ville Ritola, Finland	9:33.60
1928	Toivo A. Loukola, Finland	9:21.80
1932	Volmari Iso-Hollo, Finland (3,460m—extra lap by official error)	10:33.40
1936	Volmari Iso-Hollo, Finland	9:03.80
1948	Thore Sjöstrand, Sweden	9:04.60
1952	Horace Ashenfelter, U.S.	8:45.40
1956	Chris Brasher, Great Britain	8:41.20
1960	Zdzislaw Krzyszkowiak, Poland	8:34.20
1964	Gaston Roelants, Belgium	8:30.80
1968	Amos Biwott, Kenya	8:51.00
1972	Kipchoge Keino, Kenya	8:23.60
1976	Anders Gärderud, Sweden	8:08.20
1980	Bronislaw Malinowski, Poland	8:09.70
1984	Julius Korir, Kenya	8:11.80
1988	Julius Karuiki, Kenya	8:05.51
1992	Matthew Birer, Kenya	8:08.84
1996	Joseph Keter, Kenya	8:07.12
2000	Reuben Kosgei, Kenya	8:21.43

4x100-Meter Relay					**Time**
1912	Great Britain	42.40	**1964**	U.S.	39.00
1920	U.S.	42.20	**1968**	U.S.	38.20
1924	U.S.	41.00	**1972**	U.S.	38.19
1928	U.S.	41.00	**1976**	U.S.	38.33
1932	U.S.	40.00	**1980**	U.S.S.R.	38.26
1936	U.S.	39.80	**1984**	U.S.	37.83
1948	U.S.	40.60	**1988**	U.S.S.R.	38.19
1952	U.S.	40.10	**1992**	U.S.	37.40
1956	U.S.	39.50	**1996**	Canada	37.69
1960	W. Germany	39.50	**2000**	U.S.	37.61

4x400-Meter Relay					**Time**
1908	U.S.	3:29.40	**1964**	U.S.	3:00.70
1912	U.S.	3:16.60	**1968**	U.S.	2:56.16
1920	Great Britain	3:22.20	**1972**	Kenya	2:59.80
1924	U.S.	3:16.00	**1976**	U.S.	2:58.65
1928	U.S.	3:14.20	**1980**	U.S.S.R.	3:01.10
1932	U.S.	3:08.20	**1984**	U.S.	2:57.91
1936	Great Britain	3:09.00	**1988**	U.S.	2:56.16
1948	U.S.	3:10.40	**1992**	U.S.	2:55.74
1952	Jamaica	3:03.90	**1996**	U.S.	2:55.99
1956	U.S.	3:04.80	**2000**	U.S.	2:56.35
1960	U.S.	3:02.20			

Discus Throw		**Distance**
1896	Robert Garrett, U.S.	95′ 7½″
1900	Rezsö Bauer, Hungary	118′3″
1904	Martin Sheridan, U.S.	128′10½″
1908	Martin Sheridan, U.S.	134′2″
1912	Armas Taipale, Finland	148′3″
1920	Elmer Niklander, Finland	146′7″
1924	Bud Houser, U.S.	151′4″
1928	Bud Houser, U.S.	155′3″
1932	John Anderson, U.S.	162′4″
1936	W. Kenneth Carpenter, U.S.	165′7″
1948	Adolfo Consolini, Italy	173′2″
1952	Sim Iness, U.S.	180′6″
1956	Al Oerter, U.S.	184′11″
1960	Al Oerter, U.S.	194′2″
1964	Al Oerter, U.S.	200′1″
1968	Al Oerter, U.S.	212′6″
1972	Ludvik Danek, Czechoslovakia	211′3″
1976	Mac Wilkins, U.S.	221′5″
1980	Viktor Rashupkin, U.S.S.R.	218′8″
1984	Rolf Danneberg, West Germany	218′6″
1988	Jurgen Schult, East Germany	225′9¼″
1992	Romas Ubartas, Lithuania	213′8″
1996	Lars Riedel, Germany	227′ 8″
2000	Virgilijus Alekna, Lithuania	227′ 4″

Hammer Throw		**Distance**
1900	John Flanagan, U.S.	163′1″
1904	John Flanagan, U.S.	168′1″
1908	John Flanagan, U.S.	170′4″
1912	Matthew McGrath, U.S.	179′7″
1920	Patrick Ryan, U.S.	173′5″
1924	Frederick Tootell, U.S.	174′10″
1928	Patrick O'Callaghan, Ireland	168′7″
1932	Patrick O'Callaghan, Ireland	176′11″
1936	Karl Hein, Germany	185′4″
1948	Imre Nemeth, Hungary	183′11″
1952	Jozsef Csermak, Hungary	197′11″
1956	Harold V. Connolly, U.S.	207′3″
1960	Vasiliy Rudenkov, U.S.S.R.	220′2″

1964	Romuald Klim, U.S.S.R.	228′10″
1968	Gyula Zsivotzky, Hungary	240′8″
1972	Anatoly Bondarchuk, U.S.S.R.	247′8″
1976	Yuri Sedykh, U.S.S.R.	254′4″
1980	Yuri Sedykh, U.S.S.R.	268′4″
1984	Juha Tiainen, Finland	256′2″
1988	Sergei Litinov, U.S.S.R.	278′2½″
1992	Andrei Abduvaliyev, Unified Team	270′9″
1996	Balazs Kiss, Hungary	266′ 6″
2000	Szymon Ziolkowski, Poland	262′ 6″

High Jump		**Height**
1896	Ellery Clark, U.S.	5′11¼″
1900	Irving K. Baxter, U.S.	6′2¾″
1904	Samuel Jones, U.S.	5′11″
1908	Harry Porter, U.S.	6′3″
1912	Alma Richards, U.S.	6′4″
1920	Richmond Landon, U.S.	6′4″
1924	Harold Osborn, U.S.	6′6″
1928	Robert W. King, U.S.	6′4½″
1932	Duncan McNaughton, Canada	6′5½″
1936	Cornelius Johnson, U.S.	6′8″
1948	John Winter, Australia	6′6″
1952	Walter Davis, U.S.	6′8½″
1956	Charles E. Dumas, U.S.	6′11½″
1960	Robert Shavlakadze, U.S.S.R.	7′1″
1964	Valery Brumel, U.S.S.R.	7′1¾″
1968	Richard Fosbury, U.S.	7′4¼″
1972	Juri Tarmak, U.S.S.R.	7′3¾″
1976	Jacek Wszola, Poland	7′4½″
1980	Gerd Wessig, East Germany	7′8¾″
1984	Dietmar Mogenburg, West Germany	7′8½″
1988	Guennadi Avdeenko, U.S.S.R.	7′9½″
1992	Javier Sotomayor, Cuba	7′8″
1996	Charles Austin, U.S.	7′ 10″
2000	Sergey Kliugin, Russia	7′ 9″

Javelin		**Distance**
1908	Erik Lemming, Sweden	179′10″
1912	Erik Lemming, Sweden	198′11″
1920	Jonni Myyra, Finland	215′10″
1924	Jonni Myyra, Finland	206′7″
1928	Erik Lundquist, Sweden	218′6″
1932	Matti Jarvinen, Finland	238′6″
1936	Gerhard Stock, Germany	235′8″
1948	Kai Tapio Rautavaara, Finland	228′10″
1952	Cyrus Young, U.S.	242′1″
1956	Egil Danielson, Norway	281′2″
1960	Viktor Tsibulenko, U.S.S.R.	277′8″
1964	Pauli Nevala, Finland	271′2″
1968	Janis Lusis, U.S.S.R.	295′7″
1972	Klaus Wolfemann, West Germany	296′10″
1976	Miklos Nemeth, Hungary	310′4″
1980	Dainis Kula, U.S.S.R.	299′2″
1984	Arto Harkonen, Finland	284′8″
1988	Tapio Korjus, Finland	276′6″
1992	Jan Zelezny, Czechoslovakia	294′2″
1996	Jan Zelezny, Czech Republic	289′ 3″
2000	Jan Zelezny, Czech Republic	295′ 10″

Long Jump		**Distance**
1896	Ellery Clark, U.S.	20′ 10″
1900	Alvin Kraenzlein, U.S.	23′6¾″
1904	Meyer Prinstein, U.S.	24′1″
1908	Frank Irons, U.S.	24′6½″
1912	Albert Gutterson, U.S.	24′11¼″
1920	William Pettersson, Sweden	23′5½″
1924	De Hart Hubbard, U.S.	24′5″
1928	Edward Hamm, U.S.	25′4″
1932	Edward Gordon, U.S.	25′¾″
1936	Jesse Owens, U.S.	26′5½″
1948	Willie Steel, U.S.	25′8″
1952	Jerome Biffle, U.S.	24′10″
1956	Gregory C. Bell, U.S.	25′8¼″
1960	Ralph H. Boston, U.S.	26′7¾″
1964	Lynn Davies, Great Britain	26′5¾″
1968	Robert Beamon, U.S.	29′2½″
1972	Randy Williams, U.S.	27′½″
1976	Arnie Robinson, U.S.	27′4¾″
1980	Lutz Bombrowski, East Germany	28′¼″
1984	Carl Lewis, U.S.	28′¼″
1988	Carl Lewis, U.S.	28′7¼″
1992	Carl Lewis, U.S.	28′5½″
1996	Carl Lewis, U.S.	27′10¾″
2000	Ivan Pedroso, Cuba	28′ 1″

Pole Vault		**Height**
1896	William W. Hoyt, U.S.	10′10″
1900	Irving K. Baxter, U.S.	10′10″
1904	Charles E. Dvorak, U.S.	11′5¾″
1908	Albert C. Gilbert, U.S.; Edward T. Cook Jr., U.S.	12′2″
1912	Harry S. Babcock, U.S.	12′11½″
1920	Frank K. Foss, U.S.	13′5″
1924	Lee S. Barnes, U.S.	12′11½″
1928	Sabin W. Carr, U.S.	13′9¼″
1932	William Miller, U.S.	14′1¾″
1936	Earle Meadows, U.S.	14′3¼″
1948	O. Guinn Smith, U.S.	14′1¼″
1952	Robert Richards, U.S.	14′11″
1956	Robert Richards, U.S.	14′11½″
1960	Donald Bragg, U.S.	15′5″
1964	Fred M. Hansen, U.S.	16′8¾″
1968	Robert Seagren, U.S.	17′8½″
1972	Wolfgang Nordwig, East Germany	18′½″
1976	Tadeusz Slusarki, Poland	18′½″
1980	Wladyslaw Kozakiewicz, Poland	18′11½″
1984	Pierre Quinon, France	18′10¼″
1988	Sergei Bubka, U.S.S.R.	19′9¼″
1992	Maksim Tarassov, Unified Team	19′0¼″
1996	Jean Galfiore, France	19′5¼″
2000	Nick Hysong, U.S.	19′ 4″

Shot Put		**Distance**
1896	Robert Garrett, U.S.	36′9¾″
1900	Richard Sheldon, U.S.	46′3¼″
1904	Ralph Rose, U.S.	48′7″
1908	Ralph Rose, U.S.	46′7½″
1912	Patrick McDonald, U.S.	50′4″
1920	Ville Porhola, Finland	48′7¼″
1924	Bud Houser, U.S.	49′2¼″
1928	John Kuck, U.S.	52′¾″
1932	Leo Sexton, U.S.	52′6″
1936	Hans Woellke, Germany	53′1¾″
1948	Wilbur Thompson, U.S.	56′2″
1952	Parry O'Brien, Jr., U.S.	57′1½″
1956	Parry O'Brien, Jr., U.S.	60′11¼″
1960	William Nieder, U.S.	64′6¾″
1964	Dallas C. Long, U.S.	66′8½″
1968	James Randel Matson, U.S.	67′4¾″
1972	Wladyslaw Komar, Poland	69′6″
1976	Udo Beyer, East Germany	69′6¾″
1980	Vladimir Kiselyov, U.S.S.R.	70′½″
1984	Alessandro Andrei, Italy	69′9″
1988	Ulf Timmermann, East Germany	73′8¾″
1992	Mike Stulce, U.S.	71′2½″
1996	Randy Barnes, United States	70′ 11″
2000	Arsi Harju, Finland	69′ 10″

Triple Jump		**Distance**
1896	James B. Connolly, U.S.	44′ 11¾″
1900	Myer Prinstein, U.S.	47′5¾″
1904	Myer Prinstein, U.S.	47′1″
1908	Timothy Ahearne, Great Britain	48′11¼″
1912	Gustaf Lindblom, Sweden	48′5¼″
1920	Vilho Tuulos, Finland	47′7″
1924	Anthony Winter, Australia	50′11¼″
1928	Mikio Oda, Japan	49′11″
1932	Chuhei Nambu, Japan	51′7″
1936	Naoto Tajima, Japan	52′6″
1948	Arne Ahman, Sweden	50′6¼″
1952	Adhemar da Silva, Brazil	53′2¾″
1956	Adhemar da Silva, Brazil	53′7¾″
1960	Jozef Schmidt, Poland	55′2″
1964	Jozef Schmidt, Poland	55′3½″
1968	Viktor Saneyev, U.S.S.R.	57′¾″
1972	Viktor Saneyev,U.S.S.R.	56′11¼″
1976	Viktor Saneyev, U.S.S.R.	56′8¾″
1980	Jaak Uudmae, U.S.S.R.	56′11¼″
1984	Al Joyner, U.S.	56′7½″
1988	Hristo Markov, Bulgaria	57′9¼″
1992	Mike Conley, U.S.	57′10¼″
1996	Kenny Harrison, United States	59′4¼″
2000	Jonathan Edwards, Great Britain	58′ 1″

Decathlon		**Points**[1]
1904	Thomas Kiely, Ireland	6,036.00
1912	Jim Thorpe, U.S.[2]	8,412.00
1920	Helge Lovland, Norway	6,803.00
1924	Harold Osborn, U.S.	7,710.77
1928	Paavo Yrjola, Finland	8,053.29
1932	James Bausch, U.S.	8,462.23

1936	Glenn Morris, U.S.	7,900.00	1976	Bruce Jenner, U.S.	8,617.00
1948	Robert Mathias, U.S.	7,139.00	1980	Daley Thompson, Great Britain	8,495.00
1952	Robert Mathias, U.S.	7,887.00	1984	Daley Thompson, Great Britain	8,798.00
1956	Milton G. Campbell, U.S.	7,937.00	1988	Christian Schenk, East Germany	8,488.00
1960	Rafer Johnson, U.S.	8,392.00	1992	Robert Zmelik, Czechoslovakia	8,611.00
1964	Willi Holdorf, West Germany	7,887.00	1996	Dan O'Brien, U.S.	8,824.00
1968	Bill Toomey, U.S.	8,193.00	2000	Erki Nool, Estonia	8,641.00
1972	Nikolai Avilov, U.S.S.R.	8,454.00			

1. The scoring system was changed in 1936 and again in 1964. 2. Thorpe was disqualifed and forced to return his medals in the decathlon and pentathlon (a discontinued event) because he had played professional baseball. Sweden's Hugo Wieslander was the next highest finisher, with 7,724.49 points. The International Olympic Committee posthumously restored Thorpe's medals in 1982.

Track and Field, Women

100-Meter Dash		Time
1928	Elizabeth Robinson, U.S.	12.20
1932	Stanislawa Walasiewicz, Poland	11.90
1936	Helen Stephens, U.S.	11.50
1948	Fanny Blankers-Koen, Netherlands	11.90
1952	Marjorie Jackson, Australia	11.50
1956	Betty Cuthbert, Australia	11.50
1960	Wilma Rudolph, U.S.	11.00
1964	Wyomia Tyus, U.S.	11.40
1968	Wyomia Tyus, U.S.	11.00
1972	Renate Stecher, East Germany	11.07
1976	Annegret Richter, West Germany	11.08
1980	Lyudmila Kondratyeva, U.S.S.R.	11.06
1984	Evelyn Ashford, U.S.	10.97
1988	Florence Griffith-Joyner, U.S.	10.54
1992	Gail Devers, U.S.	10.82
1996	Gail Devers, U.S.	10.94
2000	Marion Jones, U.S.	10.75

200 Meters		Time
1948	Fanny Blankers-Koen, Netherlands	24.40
1952	Marjorie Jackson, Australia	23.70
1956	Betty Cuthbert, Australia	23.40
1960	Wilma Rudolph, U.S.	24.00
1964	Edith McGuire, U.S.	23.00
1968	Irena Kirszenstein Szewinska, Poland	22.50
1972	Renate Stecher, East Germany	22.40
1976	Bärbel Eckert, East Germany	22.37
1980	Bärbel Wöckel (Eckert), East Germany	22.03
1984	Valerie Brisco-Hooks, U.S.	21.81
1988	Florence Griffith-Joyner, U.S.	21.34
1992	Gwen Torrence, U.S.	21.81
1996	Marie-Jose Perec, France	22.12
2000	Marion Jones, U.S.	21.84

400 Meters		Time
1964	Betty Cuthbert, Australia	52.00
1968	Colette Besson, France	52.00
1972	Monika Zehrt, East Germany	51.08
1976	Irena Kirszenstein Szewinska, Poland	49.29
1980	Marita Koch, East Germany	48.88
1984	Valerie Brisco-Hooks, U.S.	48.83
1988	Olga Bryzgina, U.S.S.R.	48.65
1992	Marie-Jose Perec, France	48.83
1996	Marie-Jose Perec, France	48.25
2000	Cathy Freeman, Australia	49.11

800 Meters		Time
1928	Linda Radke-Batschauer, Germany	2:16.80
1960	Lyudmila Shevcova-Lysenko, U.S.S.R.	2:04.30
1964	Ann Packer, Great Britain	2:01.10
1968	Madeline Manning, U.S.	2:00.90
1972	Hildegard Falck, West Germany	1:58.55
1976	Tatyana Kazankina, U.S.S.R.	1:54.94
1980	Nadezhda Olizarenko, U.S.S.R.	1:53.42
1984	Doina Melinte, Romania	1:57.60
1988	Sigrun Wodars, East Germany	1:56.10
1992	Ellen Van Langen, Netherlands	1:55.54
1996	Svetlana Masterkova, Russia	1:57.73
2000	Maria Mutola, Mozambique	1:56.15

1,500 Meters		Time
1972	Lyudmila Bragina, U.S.S.R.	4:01.40
1976	Tatyana Kazankina, U.S.S.R.	4:05.48
1980	Tatyana Kazankina, U.S.S.R.	3:56.60
1984	Gabrielle Dorio, Italy	4:03.25
1988	Paula Ivan, Romania	3:53.96
1992	Hassiba Boulmerka, Algeria	3:55.30
1996	Svetlana Masterkova, Russia	4:00.83
2000	Nouria Merah-Bbenida, Algeria	4:05.10

3,000 Meters		Time
1984	Maricica Puica, Romania	8:35.96
1988	Tatyana Samolenko, U.S.S.R.	8:26.53
1992	Elena Romanova, Unified Team	8:46.04

5,000 Meters		Time
1996	Wang Junxia, China	14:59.88
2000	Gabriela Szabo, Romania	14:40.79

10,000 Meters		Time
1988	Olga Boldarenko, U.S.S.R.	31:44.69
1992	Derartu Tulu, Ethiopia	31:06.02
1996	Fernanda Ribeiro, Portugal	31:01.64
2000	Derartu Tulu, Ethiopia	30:17.49

Marathon		Time
1984	Joan Benoit, U.S.	2:24.52
1988	Rosa Mota, Portugal	2:25.40
1992	Valentina Yegorova, Unified Team	2:32.41
1996	Fatuma Roba, Ethiopia	2:26:05
2000	Naoko Takahashi, Japan	2:23:14

100-Meter Hurdles[1]		Time
1932	Babe Didrikson, U.S.	11.70
1936	Trebisonda Valla, Italy	11.70
1948	Fanny Blankers-Koen, Netherlands	11.20
1952	Shirley Strickland, Australia	10.90
1956	Shirley Strickland, Australia	10.70
1960	Irina Press, U.S.S.R.	10.80
1964	Karin Balzer, East Germany	10.50
1968	Maureen Caird, Australia	10.30
1972	Annelie Erhardt, East Germany	12.59
1976	Johanna Schaller, East Germany	12.77
1980	Vera Komisova, U.S.S.R.	12.56
1984	Benita Fitzgerald-Brown, U.S.	12.84
1988	Jordanka Donkova, Bulgaria	12.38
1992	Paraskevi Patoulido, Greece	12.64
1996	Ludmila Engquist, Sweden	12.58
2000	Olga Shishigina, Kazakhstan	12.65

400-Meter Hurdles		Time
1984	Nawal El Moutawakel, Morocco	54.61
1988	Debra Flintoff-King, Australia	53.17
1992	Sally Gunnell, Great Britain	53.23
1996	Deon Hemmings, Jamaica	52.82
2000	Irina Privalova, Russia	53.02

4x100-Meter Relay					Time
1928	Canada	48.40	1972	W. Germany	42.81
1932	U.S.	46.90	1976	E. Germany	42.55
1936	U.S.	46.90	1980	E. Germany	41.60
1948	Netherlands	47.50	1984	U.S.	41.65
1952	U.S.	45.90	1988	U.S.	41.98
1956	Australia	44.50	1992	U.S.	42.11
1960	U.S.	44.50	1996	U.S.	41.95
1964	Poland	43.60	2000	Bahamas	41.95
1968	U.S.	42.80			

4x400-Meter Relay					Time
1972	E. Germany	3:23.00	1988	U.S.S.R.	3:15.18
1976	E. Germany	3:19.23	1992	Unified Team	3:20.20
1980	U.S.S.R.	3:20.20	1996	U.S.	3:20.91
1984	U.S.	3:18.29	2000	U.S.	3:22.62

Discus Throw		Distance
1928	Halina Konopacka, Poland	129′11¾″
1932	Lillian Copeland, U.S.	133′2″
1936	Gisela Mauermayer, Germany	156′3″
1948	Micheline Ostermeyer, France	137′6″
1952	Nina Romaschkova, U.S.S.R.	168′8″
1956	Olga Fikotová, Czechoslovakia	176′1″
1960	Nina Ponomareva, U.S.S.R.	180′9″
1964	Tamara Press, U.S.S.R.	187′10″
1968	Lia Manoliu, Romania	191′2″
1972	Faina Melnik, U.S.S.R.	218′7″
1976	Evelin Schlaak, East Germany	226′4″
1980	Evelin Jahl (Schlaak), East Germany	229′6″
1984	Ria Stalman, Netherlands	214′5″
1988	Martina Hellmann, East Germany	237′2¼″
1992	Maritz Marten, Cuba	229′10″
1996	Ilke Wyludda, Germany	228′ 6″
2000	Ellina Zvereva, Belarus	224′ 5″

Hammer Throw		Distance
2000	Kamila Skolimowska, Poland	233′ 6″

High Jump		Height
1928	Ethel Catherwood, Canada	5′2½″
1932	Jean Shiley, U.S.	5′5¼″
1936	Ibolya Csak, Hungary	5′3″
1948	Alice Coachman, U.S.	5′6″
1952	Esther Brand, South Africa	5′5¾″
1956	Mildred McDaniel, U.S.	5′9¼″
1960	Iolanda Balas, Romania	6′0¾″
1964	Iolanda Balas, Romania	6′2¾″
1968	Miloslava Rezkova, Czechoslovakia	5′11½″
1972	Ulrika Meyfarth, West Germany	6′3½″
1976	Rosemarie Ackermann, East Germany	6′4″
1980	Sara Simeoni, Italy	6′5½″
1984	Ulrike Meyfarth, West Germany	6′7½″
1988	Louise Ritter, U.S.	6′ 8″
1992	Heike Henkel, Germany	6′7½″
1996	Stefka Kostadinova, Bulgaria	6′8¾″
2000	Yelena Yelesina, Russia	6′ 7″

Javelin		Distance
1932	Babe Didriksen, U.S.	143′4″
1936	Tilly Fleischer, Germany	148′3″
1948	Herma Bauma, Austria	149′6″
1952	Dana Zatopekova, Czechoslovakia	165′7″
1956	Inessa Janzeme, U.S.S.R.	176′8″
1960	Elvira Ozolina, U.S.S.R.	183′8″
1964	Mihaela Penes, Romania	198′7″
1968	Angela Nemeth, Hungary	198′0″
1972	Ruth Fuchs, East Germany	209′7″
1976	Ruth Fuchs, East Germany	216′4″
1980	Maria Colon Rueñes, Cuba	224′5″
1984	Theresa Sanderson, Great Britain	228′2″
1988	Petra Felke, East Germany	245′0″
1992	Silke Renke, Germany	224′2″
1996	Heli Rantanen, Finland	222′11″
2000	Trine Hattestad, Norway	226′ 1″

Long Jump		Distance
1948	Olga Gyarmati, Hungary	18′8¼″
1952	Yvette Williams, New Zealand	20′5¾″
1956	Elizbieta Krzesinska, Poland	20′10″
1960	Vyera Krepkina, U.S.S.R.	20′10¾″
1964	Mary Rand, Great Britain	22′2¼″
1968	Viorica Viscopoleanu, Romania	22′4½″
1972	Heidemarie Rosendahl, West Germany	22′3″
1976	Angela Voigt, East Germany	22′2¾″
1980	Tatiana Kolpakova, U.S.S.R.	23′0¾″
1984	Anisoara Cusmir-Stanciu, Romania	22′10″
1988	Jackie Joyner-Kersee, U.S.	24′3½″
1992	Heike Drechsler, Germany	23′5¼″
1996	Chioma Ajunwa, Nigeria	23′4½″
2000	Heike Drechsler, Germany	22′ 9″

Pole Vault		Distance
2000	Stacy Dragila, U.S.	15′ 1″

Shot Put		Distance
1948	Micheline Ostermeyer, France	45′1½″
1952	Galina Zybina, U.S.S.R.	50′1¾″
1956	Tamara Tyshkevich, U.S.S.R.	54′5″
1960	Tamara Press, U.S.S.R.	56′10″
1964	Tamara Press, U.S.S.R.	59′6¼″
1968	Margitta Gummel, East Germany	64′4″
1972	Nadezhda Chizhova, U.S.S.R.	69′0″
1976	Ivanka Hristova, Bulgaria	69′5¼″
1980	Ilona Slupianek, East Germany	73′6¼″
1984	Claudia Losch, West Germany	67′2¼″
1988	Natalya Lisovskaya, U.S.S.R.	72′11½″
1992	Svetlana Krivaleva, Unified Team	69′1¼″
1996	Astrid Kumbernuss, Germany	67′5½″
2000	Yanina Korolchik, Belarus	67′ 5″

Triple Jump		Distance
1996	Inessa Kravets, Ukraine	50′3½″
2000	Tereza Marinova, Bulgaria	49′ 10″

Pentathlon/Heptathlon[2]		Points
1964	Irina Press, U.S.S.R.	5,246
1968	Ingrid Becker, West Germany	5,098
1972	Mary Peters, Great Britain	4,801
1976	Siegrun Siegl, East Germany	4,745
1980	Nadezhda Tkachenko, U.S.S.R.	5,083
1984	Glynis Nunn, Australia	6,390
1988	Jackie Joyner-Kersee, U.S.	7,215
1992	Jackie Joyner-Kersee, U.S.	7,044
1996	Ghada Shouaa, Syria	6,780
2000	Denise Lewis, Great Britain	6,584

1. 80 meters until 1972. 2. In 1984, two additional events were added: the 800-meter run and the javelin throw.

Team Sports

Baseball
1988 U.S.
1992 Cuba
1996 Cuba
2000 U.S.

Basketball-Men
1936 U.S.
1948 U.S.
1952 U.S.
1956 U.S.
1960 U.S.
1964 U.S.
1968 U.S.
1972 U.S.S.R.
1976 U.S.
1980 Yugoslavia
1984 U.S.
1988 U.S.S.R.
1992 U.S.
1996 U.S.
2000 U.S.

Basketball-Women
1976 U.S.S.R.
1980 U.S.S.R.
1984 U.S.
1988 U.S.
1992 Unified Team
1996 U.S.
2000 U.S.

Soccer-Men
1900 Great Britain
1904 Canada
1908 Great Britain
1912 Great Britain
1920 Belgium
1924 Uruguay
1928 Uruguay
1936 Italy
1948 Sweden
1952 Hungary
1956 U.S.S.R.
1960 Yugoslavia
1964 Hungary
1968 Hungary
1972 Poland
1976 E. Germany
1980 Czechoslovakia
1984 France
1988 U.S.S.R.
1992 Spain
1996 Nigeria
2000 Cameroon

Soccer-Women
1996 U.S.
2000 Norway

Softball
1996 U.S.
2000 U.S.

Volleyball-Men
1964 U.S.S.R.
1968 U.S.S.R.
1972 Japan
1976 Poland
1980 U.S.S.R.
1984 U.S.
1988 U.S.
1992 Brazil
1996 Netherlands
2000 Yugoslavia

Volleyball-Women
1964 Japan
1968 U.S.S.R.
1972 U.S.S.R.
1976 Japan
1980 U.S.S.R.
1984 China
1988 U.S.S.R.
1992 Cuba
1996 Cuba
2000 Cuba

Water Polo
1900 Great Britain
1904 U.S.
1908 Great Britain
1912 Great Britain
1920 Great Britain/ Ireland
1924 France
1928 Germany
1932 Hungary
1936 Hungary
1948 Italy
1952 Hungary
1956 Hungary
1960 Italy
1964 Hungary
1968 Yugoslavia
1972 U.S.S.R.
1976 Hungary
1980 U.S.S.R.
1984 Yugoslavia
1988 Yugoslavia
1992 Italy
1996 Spain
2000 Hungary

Gymnastics-Men

Men's All-Around
1900 Gustave Sandras, France
1904 Julius Lenhart, Austria
1908 Alberto Braglia, Italy
1912 Alberto Braglia, Italy
1920 Giorgio Zampori, Italy
1924 Leon Stukelj, Yugoslavia
1928 Georges Miez, Switzerland
1932 Romeo Neri, Italy
1936 Alfred Schwarzmann, Germany
1948 Veikko Huhtanen, Finland
1952 Viktor Chukarin, U.S.S.R.
1956 Viktor Chukarin, U.S.S.R.
1960 Boris Shakhlin, U.S.S.R.
1964 Yukio Endo, Japan
1968 Sawao Kato, Japan
1972 Sawao Kato, Japan
1976 Nikolai Andrianov, U.S.S.R.
1980 Aleksandr Dityatin, U.S.S.R.
1984 Koji Gushiken, Japan
1988 Vladimir Artemov, U.S.S.R.
1992 Vitali Scherbo, Unified Team
1996 Li Xiaoshuang, China
2000 Alexei Nemov, Russia

Men's Floor Exercises
1932 István Pelle, Hungary
1936 Georges Miez, Switzerland
1948 Ferenc Pataki, Hungary
1952 K. William Thoresson, Sweden
1956 Valentin Muratov, U.S.S.R.
1960 Nobuyuki Aihara, Japan
1964 Franco Menichelli, Italy
1968 Sawao Koto, Japan
1972 Nikolai Andrianov, U.S.S.R.
1976 Nikolai Andrianov, U.S.S.R.
1980 Roland Brückner, E. Germany
1984 Li Ning, China
1988 Sergei Kharikov, U.S.S.R.
1992 Xiaosahuang Li, China
1996 Ioannis Melissanidis, Greece
2000 Igors Vihrovs, Latvia

Men's Horizontal Bar
1896 Herman Weingärtner, Germany
1904 Anton Heida, U.S.
Edward Hennig, U.S. (tie)
1924 Leon Stukelj, Yugoslavia
1928 Georges Miez
1932 Dallas Bixler, U.S.
1936 Aleksanteri Saarvala, Finland
1948 Josef Stalder, Switzerland
1952 Jack Günthard, Switzerland
1956 Takashi Ono, Japan
1960 Takashi Ono, Japan
1964 Boris Shakhlin, U.S.S.R.
1968 Akinori Nakayama, Japan
1972 Mitsuo Tsukahara, Japan
1976 Mitsuo Tsukahara, Japan
1980 Stoyan Deltchev, Bulgaria
1984 Shinji Morisue, Japan
1988 Vladimir Artemov, U.S.S.R.
Valeri Lioukine, U.S.S.R. (tie)
1992 Trent Dimas, U.S.
1996 Andreas Wecker, Germany
2000 Alexei Nemov, Russia

Men's Parallel Bars
1896 Alfred Flatow, Germany
1904 George Eyser, U.S.
1924 August Güttinger, Switzerland
1928 Ladislav Vácha, Czechoslovakia
1932 Romeo Neri, Italy
1936 Konrad Frey, Germany
1948 Michael Reusch, Switzerland
1952 Hans Eugster, Switzerland
1956 Viktor Chukarin, U.S.S.R.
1960 Boris Shakhlin, U.S.S.R.
1964 Yukio Endo, Japan
1968 Akinori Nakayama, Japan
1972 Sawao Koto, Japan
1976 Sawao Koto, Japan
1980 Aleksandr Tkachyov, U.S.S.R.
1984 Bart Conner, U.S.
1988 Vladimir Artemov, U.S.S.R.
1992 Vitali Scherbo, Unified Team
1996 Rustam Sharipov, Ukraine
2000 Xiaopeng Li, China

Men's Pommel Horse
1896 Jules Zutter, Switzerland
1904 Anton Heida, U.S.
1924 Josef Wilhelm, Switzerland
1928 Hermann Hänggi, Switzerland
1932 István Pelle, Hungary
1936 Konrad Frey, Germany
1948 Paavo Aaltonen, Finland
1952 Viktor Chukarin, U.S.S.R.
1956 Boris Shakhlin, U.S.S.R.
1960 Eugene Ekman, Finland
1964 Miroslav Cerar, Yugoslavia
1968 Miroslav Cerar, Yugoslavia
1972 Viktor Klimenko, U.S.S.R.
1976 Zoltán Magyar, Hungary
1980 Zoltán Magyar, Hungary
1984 Li Ning, China
1988 Lyubomir Gueraskov, Bulgaria
Dmitri Bilozertchev, U.S.S.R.
Zsolt Borkai, Hungary
1992 Vitali Scherbo, Unified Team
Gil Su Pae, North Korea
1996 Li Donghua, Switzerland
2000 Alexandre Moskalenko, Russia

Men's Rings
1896 Ioannis Mitropoulos, Greece
1904 Hermann Glass, U.S.
1924 Francesco Martino, Italy
1928 Leon Stukelj, Yugoslavia
1932 George Gulack, U.S.
1936 Alois Hudec, Czechoslovakia
1948 Karl Frei, Switzerland
1952 Grant Shaginyan, U.S.S.R.
1956 Albert Azaryan, U.S.S.R.
1960 Albert Azaryan, U.S.S.R.
1964 Takuji Haytta, Japan
1968 Akinori Nakayama, Japan
1972 Akinori Nakayama, Japan
1976 Nikolai Andrianov, U.S.S.R.
1980 Aleksandr Dityatin, U.S.S.R.
1984 Koji Gushiken, Japan
1988 Holger Behrendt, E. Germany
Dmitri Bilozertchev, U.S.S.R.
1992 Vitali Scherbo, Unified Team
1996 Yuri Chechi, Italy
2000 Szilveszter Csollany, Hungary

Men's Vault
1896 Karl Schumann, Germany
1904 George Eyser, U.S.
Anton Heida, U.S. (tie)
1924 Frank Kriz, U.S.
1928 Eugen Mack, Switzerland
1932 Savino Guglielmetti, Italy
1936 Alfred Schwarzmann, Germany
1948 Paavo Aaltonen, Finland
1952 Viktor Chukarin, U.S.S.R.
1956 Helmut Bantz, West Germany
1960 Takashi Ono, Japan
1964 Haruhiro Yamashita, Japan
1968 Mikhail Voronin, U.S.S.R.
1972 Klaus Köste, East Germany
1976 Nikolai Andrianov, U.S.S.R.
1980 Nikolai Andrianov, U.S.S.R.
1984 Lou Yun, China
1988 Lou Yun, China
1992 Vitali Scherbo, Unified Team
1996 Alexei Nemov, Russia
2000 Gervasio Deferr, Spain

Men's Team Combined

1908	Sweden	**1968**	Japan
1912	Italy	**1972**	Japan
1920	Italy	**1976**	Japan
1928	Switzerland	**1980**	U.S.S.R.
1932	Italy	**1984**	United States
1936	Germany		
1948	Finland	**1988**	U.S.S.R.
1952	U.S.S.R.	**1992**	Unified Team
1956	U.S.S.R.		
1960	Japan	**1996**	Russia
1964	Japan	**2000**	China

Women's All-Around
1952 Maria Gorokhovskaya, USSR
1956 Larissa Latynina, USSR
1960 Larissa Latynina, USSR
1964 Vera Cáslavská, Czechoslovakia
1968 Vera Cáslavská, Czechoslovakia
1972 Lyudmila Tourischeva, USSR
1976 Nadia Comaneci, Romania
1980 Yelena Davydova, USSR
1984 Mary Lou Retton, U.S.
1988 Elena Shushunova, USSR
1992 Tatiana Goutsou, Unified Team
1996 Lilia Popkopayeva, Ukraine
2000 Simona Amanar, Romania

Women's Balance Beam
1952 Nina Bocharova, U.S.S.R.
1956 Agnes Keleti, Hungary
1960 Eva Bosáková, Czechoslovakia
1964 Vera Cáslavská, Czechoslovakia
1968 Natalya Kuchinskaya, U.S.S.R.
1972 Olga Korbut, U.S.S.R.
1976 Nadia Comaneci, Romania
1980 Nadia Comaneci, Romania
1984 Simona Pauca, Romania
1988 Daniela Silivas, Romania
1992 Tatiana Lyssenko, UnifiedTeam
1996 Shannon Miller, United States
2000 Xuan Liu, China

Women's Floor Exercises
1952 Agnes Keleti, Hungary
1956 Agnes Keleti, Hungary
1960 Larissa Latynina, U.S.S.R.
1964 Larissa Latynina, U.S.S.R.
1968 Vera Cáslavská, Czechoslovakia
1972 Olga Korbut, U.S.S.R.
1976 Nelli Kim, U.S.S.R.
1980 Nadia Comaneci, Rom.
1984 Ecaterina Szabó, Romania
1988 Daniela Silivas, Romania
1992 Lavina Milosovici, Rom.
1996 Lillia Podkopayeva, Ukraine
2000 Elena Zamolodtchikova, Russia

Women's Uneven Bars
1952 Margit Korondi, Hungary
1956 Agnes Keleti, Hungary
1960 Polina Astakhova, U.S.S.R.
1964 Polina Astakhova, U.S.S.R.
1968 Vera Cáslavská, Czechoslovakia
1972 Karin Janz, East Germany
1976 Nadia Comaneci, Romania
1980 Maxi Gnauck, East Germany
1984 Ma Yanhong, China
1988 Daniela Silivas, Romania
1992 Li Lu, China
1996 Svetlana Khorkina, Russia
2000 Svetlana Khorkina, Russia

Women's Vault
1952 Yekaterina Kalinchuk
1956 Larissa Latynina, U.S.S.R.
1960 Margarita Nikolayeva, U.S.S.R.
1964 Vera Cáslavská, Czechoslovakia
1968 Vera Cáslavská, Czechoslovakia
1972 Karin Janz, East Germany
1976 Nelli Kim, U.S.S.R.
1980 Natalya Shaposhnikova, U.S.S.R.
1984 Ecaterina Szabó, Romania
1988 Svetlana Boguinskaya, U.S.S.R.
1992 Henrietta Onodi, Hungary
Lavinia Milosovici, Romania
1996 Simona Amanar, Romania
2000 Elena Zamolodtchikova, Russia

Women's Team Combined

1928	Holland	**1976**	U.S.S.R.
1936	W. Germany	**1980**	U.S.S.R.
1948	Czechoslovakia	**1984**	Romania
		1988	U.S.S.R.
1952	U.S.S.R.	**1992**	Unified Team
1956	U.S.S.R.		
1960	U.S.S.R.	**1996**	United States
1964	U.S.S.R.		
1968	U.S.S.R.	**2000**	Romania
1972	U.S.S.R.		

Boxing

Light Flyweight (106 pounds)
1968 Francisco Rodriguez, Venezuela
1972 Gyorgy Gedo, Hungary
1976 Jorge Hernandez, Cuba
1980 Shamil Sabyrov, Soviet Union
1984 Paul Gonzalez, USA
1988 Ivalio Hristov, Bulgaria
1992 Rogelio Marcelo, Cuba
1996 Daniel Petrov, Bulgaria
2000 Brahim Asloum, France

Flyweight (112 pounds)
1904 George Finnegan, USA
1920 Frank Genaro, USA
1924 Fidel LaBarba, USA
1928 Antal Kocsis, Hungary
1932 Istvan Enekes, Hungary
1936 Willy Kaiser, Germany
1948 Pascual Perez, Argentina
1952 Nathan Brooks, USA
1956 Terence Spinks, Great Britain
1960 Gyula Torok, Hungary
1964 Fernando Atzori, Italy
1968 Ricardo Delgado, Mexico
1972 Georgi Kostadinov, Bulgaria
1976 Leo Randolph, USA
1980 Petr Lesov, Bulgaria
1984 Steven McCrory, USA
1988 Kwang-Sun Kim, South Korea
1992 Su Choi-Choi, North Korea
1996 Maikro Romero, Cuba
2000 Wijan Ponlid, Thailand

Bantamweight (119 pounds)
1904 Oliver Kirk, USA
1908 Henry Thomas, Great Britain
1920 Clarence Walker, South Africa
1924 William Smith, South Africa
1928 Vittorio Tamagnimi, Italy
1932 Horace Gwynne, Canada
1936 Ulderico Sergo, Italy
1948 Tibor Csik, Hungary
1952 Pentti Hamalainen, Finland
1956 Wolfgang Behrendt, E. Germany
1960 Oleg Grigoryev, Soviet Union
1964 Takao Sakurai, Japan
1968 Valeri Sokolov, Soviet Union
1972 Orlando Martinez, Cuba
1976 Yong-Jo Gu, North Korea
1980 Juan Hernandez, Cuba
1984 Maurizo Stecca, Italy
1988 Kennedy McKinney, USA
1992 Joel Casamayor, Cuba
1996 Istvan Kovacs, Hungary
2000 Guillermo Rigondeaux, Cuba

Featherweight (125 pounds)
1904 Oliver Kirk, USA
1908 Richard Gunn, Great Britain
1920 Paul Fritsch, France
1924 John "Jackie" Fields, USA
1928 Lambertus "Bep" van Klaveren, Netherlands
1932 Carmelo Robledo, Argentina
1936 Oscar Casanovas, Argentina
1948 Ernesto Formenti, Italy
1952 Jan Zachara, Czechoslovakia
1956 Vladimir Safronov, USSR
1960 Francesco Musso, Italy
1964 Stanislav Stepashkin, USSR
1968 Antonio Roldan, Mexico
1972 Boris Kuznetsov, Soviet Union
1976 Angel Herrara, Cuba
1980 Rudi Fink, East Germany
1984 Meldrick Taylor, USA
1988 Giovanni Parisi, Italy
1992 Andreas Tews, Germany
1996 Somluck Kamsing, Thailand
2000 Bekzat Sattarkhanov, Kazakhstan

Lightweight (132 pounds)
1904 Harry Spanger, USA
1908 Frederick Grace, Great Britain
1920 Samuel Mosberg, USA
1924 Hans Nielsen, Denmark
1928 Carlo Orlandi, Italy
1932 Lawrence Stevens, South Africa
1936 Imre Harangi, Hungary
1948 Gerald Dreyer, South Africa
1952 Aureliano Bolognesi, Italy
1956 Richard McTaggart, Great Britain
1960 Kazimierz Pazdzior, Poland
1964 Jozef Grudzien, Poland
1968 Ronald Harris, USA
1972 Jan Szczepanski, Poland
1976 Howard Davis, USA
1980 Angel Herrera, Cuba
1984 Pernell Whitaker, USA
1988 Andreas Zuelow, E. Germany
1992 Oscar De La Hoya, USA
1996 Hocine Soltani, Algeria
2000 Mario Kindelán, Cuba

Light Welterweight (139 pounds)
1952 Charles Adkins, USA
1956 Vladimir Yengibaryan, Soviet Union
1960 Bohumil Nemecek, Czechoslovakia
1964 Jerzy Kulej, Poland
1968 Jerzy Kulej, Poland
1972 Ray Seales, USA
1976 Ray Leonard, USA
1980 Parizio Oliva, Italy
1984 Jerry Page, USA
1988 Viatcheslav Janovski, Soviet Union
1992 Hector Vinent, Cuba
1996 Hector Vinent, Cuba
2000 Mahamadkadyz Abdullaev, Uzbekistan

Welterweight (147 pounds)
1904 Albert Young, USA
1920 Albert "Bert" Schneider, Canada
1924 Jean Delarge, Belguim
1928 Edward Morgan, New Zealand
1932 Edward Flynn, USA
1936 Sten Suvio, Finland
1948 Julius Torma, Czechoslovakia
1952 Zygmunt Chychla, Poland
1956 Nicolae Linca, Romania
1960 Giovanni Benvenuti, Italy
1964 Marian Kaspryzk, Poland
1968 Manfred Wolke, East Germany
1972 Emilio Correa, Cuba
1976 Jochen Bachfeld, E. Germany
1980 Andres Aldama, Cuba
1984 Mark Breland, USA
1988 Robert Wangila, Kenya
1992 Michael Carruth, Ireland
1996 Oleg Saitov, Russia
2000 Oleg Saitov, Russia

Light Middleweight (156 pounds)
1952 Laszlo Papp, Hungary
1956 Laszlo Papp, Hungary
1960 Wilbert McClure, USA
1964 Boris Lagutin, Soviet Union
1968 Boris Lagutin, Soviet Union
1972 Dieter Kottysch, W.Germany
1976 Jerzy Rybicki, Poland
1980 Armando Martinez, Cuba
1984 Frank Tate, USA
1988 Si-Hun Park, South Korea
1992 Juan Lemus, Cuba
1996 David Reid, USA
2000 Yermakhan Ibraimov, Kazakhstan

Middleweight (165 pounds)
1904 Charles Mayer, USA
1908 John Douglas, Great Britain
1920 Harry Mallin, Great Britain
1924 Harry Mallin, Great Britain
1928 Piero Toscani, Italy
1932 Carmen Barth USA
1936 Jean Despeaux, France
1948 Laszlo Papp, Hungary
1952 Floyd Patterson, USA
1956 Gennady Schatkov, Soviet Union
1960 Edward Crook, USA
1964 Valeri Popenchenko, Soviet Union
1968 Christopher Finnegan, Great Britain
1972 Vyacheslav Lemeschev, Soviet Union
1976 Michael Spinks, USA
1980 Jose Gomez, Cuba
1984 Joon-Sup Shin, South Korea
1988 Henry Maske, East Germany
1992 Ariel Hernandez, Cuba
1996 Ariel Hernandez, Cuba
2000 Jorge Gutiérrez, Cuba

Light Heavyweight (178 pounds)
1920 Edward Eagan, USA
1924 Harry Mitchell, Great Britain
1928 Victor Avendanno, Argentina
1932 David Carstens, South Africa
1936 Roger Michelot, France
1948 George Hunter, South Africa
1952 Norvel Lee, USA
1956 James Boyd, USA
1960 Cassius Clay, USA
1964 Cosimo Pinto, Italy
1968 Dan Pozniak, Soviet Union
1972 Mate Parlov, Yugoslavia
1976 Leon Spinks, USA
1980 Slobodan Kacar, Yugoslavia
1984 Anton Josipovic, Yugoslavia
1988 Andrew Maynard, USA
1992 Torsten May, Germany
1996 Vassili Jirov, Kazakstan
2000 Aleksandr Lebziak, Russia

Heavyweight (201 pounds)
1904 Samuel Berger, USA
1908 A.L. Oldham, Great Britain
1920 Ronald Rawson, Great Britain
1924 Otto von Porat, Norway
1928 Arturo Rodriguez Jurado, Argentina
1932 Santiago Lovell, Argentina
1936 Herbert Runge, Germany
1948 Rafael Iglesias, Argentina
1952 H. Edward Sanders, USA
1956 Peter Rademacher, USA
1960 Franco De Piccolo, Italy
1964 Joe Frazier, USA
1968 George Foreman, USA
1972 Teofilo Stevenson, Cuba
1976 Teofilo Stevenson, Cuba
1980 Teofilo Stevenson, Cuba
1984 Henry Tillman, USA
1988 Ray Mercer, USA
1992 Felix Savon, Cuba
1996 Felix Savon, Cuba
2000 Felix Savon, Cuba

Super Heavyweight (Unlimited)
1984 Tyrell Biggs, USA
1988 Lennox Lewis, Canada
1992 Roberto Balado, Cuba
1996 Wladimir Klitschko, Ukraine
2000 Audley Harrison, Great Britain

WINTER OLYMPIC CHAMPIONS

Alpine Skiing (Men)

Downhill

Year	Name	Time
1948	Henri Oreiller, France	2:55.00
1952	Zeno Colo, Italy	2:30.80
1956	Anton Sailer, Austria	2:52.20
1960	Jean Vuarnet, France	2:06.00
1964	Egon Zimmerman, Austria	2:18.16
1968	Jean-Claude Killy, France	1:59.85
1972	Bernhard Russi, Switzerland	1:51.43
1976	Franz Klammer, Austria	1:45.73
1980	Leonhard Stock, Austria	1:45.50
1984	William Johnson, United States	1:45.59
1988	Pirmin Zurbriggen, Switzerland	1:59.63
1992	Patrick Ortlieb, Austria	1:50.37
1994	Tommy Moe, United States	1:45.75
1998	Jean-Luc Cretier, France	1:50.11
2002	Fritz Strobl, Austria	1:39.13

Slalom

Year	Name	Time
1948	Edi Reinalter, Switzerland	2:10.30
1952	Othmar Schneider, Austria	2:00.00
1956	Anton Sailer, Austria	3:14.70
1960	Ernst Hinterseer, Austria	2:08.90
1964	Josef Stiegler, Austria	2:11.13
1968	Jean Claude Killy, France	1:39.73
1972	Francisco Fernandez Ochoa, Spain	1:39.73
1976	Piero Gros, Italy	2:03.29
1980	Ingemar Stenmark, Sweden	1:44.26
1984	Philip Mahre, United States	1:39.41
1988	Alberto Tomba, Italy	1:39.47
1992	Finn Christian Jagge, Norway	1:44.39
1994	Thomas Stangassinger	2:02.02
1998	Hans-Petter Buraas, Norway	1:49.31
2002	Jean-Pierre Vidal, France	1:41.06

Giant Slalom

Year	Name	Time
1952	Stein Eriksen, Norway	2:25.00
1956	Anton Sailer, Austria	3:00.10
1960	Roger Staub, Switzerland	1:48.30
1964	Francois Bonlieu, France	1:46.71
1968	Jean Claude Killy, France	3:29.28
1972	Gustavo Thöni, Italy	3:09.62
1976	Heini Hemmi, Switzerland	3:26.97
1980	Ingemar Stenmark, Sweden	2:40.74
1984	Max Julen, Switzerland	2:41.18
1988	Alberto Tomba, Italy	2:06.37
1992	Alberto Tomba, Italy	2:06.98
1994	Markus Wasmeier, Germany	2:52.46
1998	Hermann Maier, Austria	2:38.51
2002	Stephan Eberharter, Austria	2:23.28

Super Giant Slalom

Year	Name	Time
1988	Frank Piccard, France	1:39.66
1992	Kjetil Andre Aamodt, Norway	1:13.04
1994	Markus Wasmeier, Germany	1:32.53
1998	Hermann Maier, Austria	1:34.82
2002	Kjetil Andre Aamodt, Norway	1:21.58

Combined (Downhill/Slalom)

1988	Hubert Strolz, Austria
1992	Josef Polig, Italy
1994	Lasse Kjus, Norway
1998	Mario Reiter, Austria
2002	Kjetil Andre Aamodt, Norway

Alpine Skiing (Women)

Downhill

Year	Name	Time
1948	Hedi Schlunegger, Switzerland	2:28.30
1952	Trude Jochum-Beiser, Austria	1:47.10
1956	Madeleine Berthod, Switzerland	1:40.70
1960	Heidi Biebl, Germany	1:37.60
1964	Christl Haas, Austria	1:55.39
1968	Olga Pall, Austria	1:40.87
1972	Marie-Theres Nadig, Switzerland	1:36.68
1976	Rosi Mittermaier, West Germany	1:46.16
1980	Annemarie Moser-Pröll, Austria	1:37.52
1984	Michela Figini, Switzerland	1:13.36[1]
1988	Marina Kiehl, West Germany	1:25.86
1992	Kerrin Lee-Gartner, Canada	1:52.55
1994	Katja Seizinger, Germany	1:35.93
1998	Katja Seizinger, Germany	1:28.89
2002	Carole Montillet, France	1:39.56

Slalom

Year	Name	Time
1948	Gretchen Fraser, United States	1:57.20
1952	Andrea Mead Lawrence, U.S.	2:10.60
1956	Renée Colliard, Switzerland	1:52.30
1960	Anne Heggtveigt, Canada	1:49.60
1964	Christine Goitschel, France	1:29.86
1968	Marielle Goitschel, France	1:25.86
1972	Barbara Cochran, United States	1:31.24
1976	Rosi Mittermaier, West Germany	1:30.54
1980	Hanni Wenzel, Liechtenstein	1:25.09
1984	Paoletta Magoni, Italy	1:36.47
1988	Vreni Schneider, Switzerland	1:36.69
1992	Petra Kronberger, Austria	1:32.68
1994	Vreni Schneider, Switzerland	1:56.01
1998	Hilde Gerg, Germany	1:32.40
2002	Janica Kostelic, Croatia	1:46.10

Giant Slalom

Year	Name	Time
1952	Andrea Mead Lawrence, U.S.	2:06.80
1956	Ossi Reichert, Germany	1.56.50
1960	Yvonne Rüegg, Switzerland	1:39.90
1964	Marielle Goitschel, France	1:52.24
1968	Nancy Greene, Canada	1:51.97
1972	Marie-Theres Nadig, Switzerland	1:29.90
1976	Kathy Kreiner, Canada	1:29.13
1980	Hanni Wenzel, Liechtenstein	2:41.66
1984	Debbie Armstrong, United States	2:20.98
1988	Vreni Schneider, Switzerland	2:06.49
1992	Pernilla Wiberg, Sweden	2:12.74
1994	Deborah Compagnoni, Italy	2:30.97
1998	Deborah Compagnoni, Italy	2:50.59
2002	Janica Kostelic, Croatia	2:30.01

Super Giant Slalom

Year	Name	Time
1988	Sigrid Wolf, Austria	1:19.03
1992	Deborah Compagnoni, Italy	1:21.22
1994	Diann Roffe-Steinrotter, U.S.	1:22.15
1998	Picabo Street, United States	1:18.02
2002	Daniela Ceccarelli, Italy	1:13.59

Combined (Downhill/Slalom)

1988	Anita Wachter, Austria
1992	Petra Kronberger, Austria
1994	Pernilla Wiberg, Sweden
1998	Katja Seizinger, Germany
2002	Janica Kostelic, Croatia

1. Race shortened by weather conditions

Biathlon (Cross-country skiing and riflery)

Men's 10-Kilometer (6.2 Miles)		Time
1980	Frank Ulrich, East Germany	32:10.69
1984	Eirik Kvalfoss, Norway	30:53.80
1988	Frank-Peter Roetsch, E. Germany	25:08.10
1992	Mark Kirchner, Germany	26:02.30
1994	Sergei Tchepikov, Russia	28:07.00
1998	Ole Bjorndalen, Norway	27:16.20
2002	Ole Einar Bjoerndalen, Norway	24:51.30

Men's 20-Kilometer (12.4 miles)		Time
1960	Klas Lestander, Sweden	1:33:21.60
1964	Vladimir Melanin, U.S.S.R.	1:20:26.80
1968	Magnar Solberg, Norway	1:13:45.90
1972	Magnar Solberg, Norway	1:15:55.50
1976	Nikolai Kruglov, U.S.S.R.	1:14:12.26
1980	Anatoli Alabyev, U.S.S.R.	1:08:16.31
1984	Peter Angerer, West Germany	1:11:52.70
1988	Frank-Peter Roetsch, E. Germany	0:56:33.33
1992	Evgueni Redkine, Unified Team	0:57:34.04
1994	Sergei Tarasov, Russia	0:57:25.30
1998	Halvard Hanevold, Norway	0:56:16.40
2002	Ole Einar Bjoerndalen, Norway	0:51:03.30

Men's 4x7.5 Kilometer (18.6 mile) Relay [1]		Time
1968	U.S.S.R., Norway, Sweden	2:13:02.40
1972	U.S.S.R., Finland, East Germany	1:51:44.92
1976	U.S.S.R., Finland, East Germany	1:57:55.64
1980	U.S.S.R., E. Germany, W. Germany	1:34:03.27
1984	U.S.S.R., Norway, West Germany	1:38:51.70
1988	U.S.S.R., West Germany, Italy	1:22:30.00
1992	Germany, Unified Team, Sweden	1:24:43.50
1994	Germany, Russia, France	1:30:22.10
1998	Germany, Norway, Russia	1:19:43.30
2002	Norway,Germany, France	1:23:42.30

Women's 7.5 Kilometer (4.6 miles)		Time
1992	Anfissa Restzova, Unified Team	24:29.2
1994	Myriam Bedard, Canada	26:08.8
1998	Galina Kukleva, Russia	23:08.0
2002	Kati Wilhelm, Germany	20:41.4

Women's 15 Kilometer (9.3 miles)		Time
1992	Antje Misersky	51:47.2
1994	Myriam Bedard, Canada	52:06.6
1998	Yekaterina Dafovska, Bulgaria	54:52.0
2002	Andrea Henkel, Germany	47:29.1

Women's 4x7.5 Kilometer (18.6 mile) Relay		Time
1992	France, Germany, Unified Team[2]	1:15:55.6
1994	Russia, Germany, France	1:47:19.5
1998	Germany, Russia, Norway	1:40:13.6
2002	Germany, Norway, Russia	1:27:55.0

1. 4x10km until 1980. 2. 22.5km (3x7.5km) in 1992 only.

Bobsled

Two Man		Time
1932	U.S.	8:14.74
1936	U.S.	5:29.29
1948	Switzerland	5:29.20
1952	Germany	5:24.54
1956	Italy	5:30.14
1964	Great Britain	4:21.90
1968	Italy	4:41.54
1972	W. Germany	4:57.07
1976	E. Germany	3:44.42
1980	Switzerland	4:09.36
1984	E. Germany	3:25.56
1988	U.S.S.R.	3:54.19
1992	Switzerland	4:03.26
1994	Switzerland	3:30.81
1998	Canada, Italy	3:37.24
2002	Germany	3:10.11

Four Man		Time
1924	Switzerland	5:45.54
1928	U.S.[1]	3:20.50
1932	U.S.	7:53.68
1936	Switzerland	5:19.85
1948	U.S.	5:20.10
1952	Germany	5:07.84
1956	Switzerland	5:10.44
1964	Canada	4:14.46
1968	Italy	2:17.39
1972	Switzerland	4:43.07
1976	E. Germany	3:40.43
1980	E. Germany	3:59.42
1984	E. Germany	3:20.22
1988	Switzerland	3:47.51
1992	Austria	3:53.90
1994	Germany	3:27.78
1998	Germany	2:39.41
2002	Germany	3:07.51

Two-Woman		Time
2002	U.S.	1:37.76

1. Five-man sled.

Ice Hockey

Year	Gold, Silver, Bronze
1920	Canada, United States Czechoslovakia
1924	Canada, United States, Great Britain
1928	Canada, Sweden, Switzerland
1932	Canada, United States, Germany
1936	Great Britain, Canada, United States
1948	Canada, Czechoslovakia, Switzerland
1952	Canada, United States, Sweden
1956	U.S.S.R., United States, Canada
1960	U.S., Canada, U.S.S.R.
1964	U.S.S.R., Sweden, Czechoslovakia
1968	U.S.S.R., Czechoslovakia, Canada
1972	U.S.S.R., United States, Czechoslovakia
1976	U.S.S.R., Czechoslovakia, West Germany
1980	U.S., U.S.S.R., Sweden
1984	U.S.S.R., Czechoslovakia, Sweden
1988	U.S.S.R., Finland, Sweden
1992	Unified Team, Canada, Czechoslovakia
1994	Sweden, Canada, Finland
1998	Czech Republic, Russia, Finland
2002	Canada, United States, Russia

Luge

Singles (Men)		Time
1964	Thomas Köhler, East Germany	3:26.77
1968	Manfred Schmid, Austria	2:52.48
1972	Wolfgang Scheidel, East Germany	3:27.58
1976	Dettlef Günther, East Germany	3:27.68
1980	Bernhard Glass, East Germany	2:54.79
1984	Paul Hildgartner, Italy	3:04.25
1988	Jens Mueller, East Germany	3:05.54
1992	Georg Hackl, Germany	3:02.36
1994	Georg Hackl, Germany	3:21.57
1998	Georg Hackl, Germany	3:18.44
2002	Armin Zoeggeler, Italy	2:57.94

Singles (Women)		Time
1964	Ortrun Enderlein, East Germany	3:24.67
1968	Erica Lechner, Italy	2:28.66
1972	Anna M. Müller, East Germany	2:59.18
1976	Margit Schumann, East Germany	2:50.62
1980	Vera Zozulya, U.S.S.R.	2:36.53
1984	Steffi Martin, East Germany	2:46.57
1988	Steffi Walter (Martin), East Germany	3:03.97
1992	Doris Neuner, Austria	3:06.69
1994	Gerda Weissensteiner, Italy	3:15.52
1998	Silke Kraushaar, Germany	3:23.78
2002	Sylke Otto, Germany	2:52.46

Two-seater (Men)		Time
1964	Austria	1:41.62
1968	East Germany	1:31.94
1972	(tie) Italy, East Germany	1:28.35
1976	East Germany	1:25.60
1980	East Germany	1:19.33
1984	West Germany	1:23.62
1988	East Germany	1:31.94
1992	Germany	1:32.05
1994	Italy	1:36.72
1998	Germany	1:41.10
2002	Germany	1:26.08

Nordic Skiing and Jumping (Men)

10-Kilometer (6.2 Miles) Pursuit method		Time
1992	Vegard Ulvang, Norway	27:36.00
1994	Bjorn Dahlie, Norway	24:20.10
1998	Bjorn Dahlie, Norway	27:24.50
2002	Johann Muehlegg, Spain	49:20.40

15-Kilometer (9.3 Miles) Cross-Country[1]		Time
1924	Thorleif Haug, Norway	1:14:31.00
1928	Johan Gröttumsbraaten, Norway	1:37:01.00
1932	Sven Utterstrom, Sweden	1:23:07.00
1936	Erik-August Larsson, Sweden	1:14:38.00
1948	Martin Lundström, Sweden	1:13:50.70
1952	Hallgeir Brenden, Norway	1:01:34.00
1956	Hallgeir Brenden, Norway	0:49:39.00
1960	Hakon Brusveen, Norway	0:51:55.50
1964	Eero Mäntyranta, Finland	0:50:54.10
1968	Harald Grönningen, Norway	0:47:54.20
1972	Sven-Ake Lundbäck, Sweden	0:45:28.24
1976	Nikolai Bazhukov, U.S.S.R.	0:43:58.47
1980	Thomas Wassberg, Sweden	0:41:57.63
1984	Gunde Svan, Sweden	0:41:25.60
1988	Mikhail Deviatiarov, U.S.S.R.	0:41:18.90
2002	Andrus Veerpalu, Estonia	0:37:07.40

30-Kilometer (18.6 Miles) Cross-Country		Time
1956	Veikko Hakulinen, Finland	1:44:06.00
1960	Sixten Jernberg, Sweden	1:51:03.90
1964	Eero Mäntyranta, Finland	1:30:50.70
1968	Franco Nones, Italy	1:35:39.20
1972	Vyacheslav Vedenin, U.S.S.R.	1:36:31.15
1976	Sergei Saveliev, U.S.S.R.	1:30:29.38
1980	Nikolai Zimyatov, U.S.S.R.	1:27:02.80
1984	Nikolai Zimyatov, U.S.S.R.	1:28:56.30
1988	Aleksei Prokourorov, U.S.S.R.	1:24:26.30
1992	Vegard Ulvang, Norway	1:22:27.80
1994	Thomas Alsgaard, Norway	1:12:26.40
1998	Mika Myllylae, Finland	1:33.55.80
2002	Johann Muehlegg, Spain	1:09:28.90

50-Kilometer (31.2 Miles) Cross-Country		Time
1924	Thorleif Haug, Norway	3:44:32.00
1928	Per Erik Hedlund, Sweden	4:52:03.00
1932	Veli Saarinen, Finland	4:28:00.00
1936	Elis Viklund, Sweden	3:30:11.00
1948	Nils Karlsson, Sweden	3:47:48.00
1952	Veikko Hakulinen, Finland	3:33:33.00
1956	Sixten Jernberg, Sweden	2:50:27.00
1960	Kalevi Hamalainen, Finland	2:59:06.30
1964	Sixten Jernberg, Sweden	2:43:52.60
1968	Ole Ellefsaeter, Norway	2:28:45.80
1972	Pål Tyldum, Norway	2:43:14.75
1976	Ivar Formo, Norway	2:37:30.05
1980	Nikolai Zimyatov, U.S.S.R.	2:27:24.60
1984	Thomas Wassberg, Sweden	2:15:55.80
1988	Gunde Svan, Sweden	2:04:30.90
1992	Bjorn Dahlie, Norway	2:03:41.50
1994	Vladimir Smirnov, Kazakhstan	2:07:20.30
1998	Bjorn Dahlie, Norway	2:05:08.20
2002	Mikhail Ivanov, Russia	2:06:20.80

40-Kilometer (24.8 Miles) Relay (4x10 km)		Time
1936	Finland, Norway, Sweden	2:41:33.00
1948	Sweden, Finland, Norway	2:32:08.00
1952	Finland, Norway, Sweden	2:20:16.00
1956	U.S.S.R., Finland Sweden	2:15:30.00
1960	Finland, Norway, U.S.S.R.	2:18:45.60
1964	Sweden, Finland, U.S.S.R.	2:18:34.60
1968	Norway, Sweden, Finland	2:08:33.50
1972	U.S.S.R., Norway, Switzerland	2:04:47.94
1976	Finland, Norway, U.S.S.R.	2:07:59.72
1980	U.S.S.R., Norway, Finland	1:57:03.46
1984	Sweden, U.S.S.R., Finland	1:55:06.30
1988	Sweden, U.S.S.R., Czechoslovakia	1:43:58.60
1992	Norway, Italy, Finland	1:39:26.00
1994	Italy, Norway, Finland	1:41:15.00
1998	Norway, Italy, Finland	1:40:55.70
2002	Norway, Italy, Germany	1:32:45.50

Nordic Combined

(15 km Cross-Country and 90-Meter Ski Jump[2])	
1924	Thorleif Haug, Norway
1928	Johan Gröttumsbraaten, Norway
1932	Johan Gröttumsbraaten, Norway
1946	Oddbjörn Hagen, Norway
1952	Simon Slåttvik, Norway
1956	Sverre Stenersen, Norway
1960	George Thoma, West Germany
1964	Tormod Knutsen, Norway
1968	Franz Keller, West Germany
1972	Ulrich Wehling, East Germany
1976	Ulrich Wehling, East Germany
1980	Ulrich Wehling, East Germany
1984	Torn Sandberg, Norway
1988	Hippolyt Kempf Switzerland
1992	Fabrice Guy, France
1994	Fred Lundberg, Norway
1998	Bjarte Engen Vik, Norway
2002	Samppa Lajunen, Finland

Nordic Combined, Team	
1988	W. Germany, Switzerland, Austria
1992	Japan, Norway, Austria
1994	Japan, Norway, Switzerland
1998	Norway, Finland, France
2002	Finland, Germany, Austria

90-Meter (293.5 ft.) Jump[2]		Points
1964	Veikko Kankkonen, Finland	229.90
1968	Jiri Raska, Czechoslovakia	216.50
1972	Yukio Kasaya, Japan	244.20
1976	Hans-Georg Aschenbach, E. Germany	252.00
1980	Anton Innauer, Austria	266.30
1984	Jens Weissflog, East Germany	215.20
1988	Matti Nykänen, Finland	229.10
1992	Ernst Vettori, Austria	222.80
1994	Espen Bredesen, Norway	282.00
1998	Jani Soininen, Finland	234.50
2002	Simon Ammann, Switzerland	269.00

120-Meter (393.7 ft.) Jump[3]		Points
1924	Jacob Tullin Thambs, Norway	18.960
1928	Alf Andersen, Norway	19.208
1932	Birger Ruud, Norway	228.10
1936	Birger Ruud, Norway	232.00
1948	Petter Hugsted, Norway	228.10
1952	Arnfinn Bergmann, Norway	226.00
1956	Antti Hyvarinen, Finland	227.00
1960	Helmut Recknagel, Germany	227.20
1964	Toralf Engan, Norway	230.70
1968	Vladimir Beloussov, U.S.S.R.	231.30
1972	Wojiech Fortuna, Poland	219.90
1976	Karl Schnabl, Austria	234.80
1980	Jouko Tormanen, Finland	271.00
1984	Matti Nykänen, Finland	231.20
1988	Matti Nykänen, Finland	224.00
1992	Toni Nieminen, Finland	239.50
1994	Jens Weissflog, Germany	274.50
1998	Kazuyoshi Funaki, Japan	272.30
2002	Simon Ammann, Switzerland	281.40

120-Meter (393.7 ft.) Jump, Team[3]		Points
1988	Finland, Yugoslavia, Norway	634.40
1992	Finland, Austria, Czechoslovakia	644.40
1994	Germany, Japan, Austria	970.10
1998	Japan, Germany, Austria	933.00
2002	Germany, Finland, Slovenia	974.10

1. 18-kilometers until 1956. Event not scheduled from 1992-1998. 2. 70 meters until 1992. 3. 90 meter until 1992.

Nordic Skiing (Women)

5-Kilometer (3.1 Miles) Cross-Country[1]		Time
1964	Claudia Boyarskikh, U.S.S.R.	17:50.50
1968	Toini Gustafsson, Sweden	16:45.20
1972	Galina Kulakova, U.S.S.R.	17:00.50
1976	Helena Takalo, Finland	15:48.69
1980	Raisa Smetanina, U.S.S.R.	15:06.92
1984	Marja-Liisa Hämäläinen, Finland	17:04.00
1988	Marjo Matikainen, Finland	15:04.00
1992	Marjut Lukkarinen, Finland	14:13.80
1994	Lyubov Egorova, Russia	14:08.80
1998	Larissa Lazutina, Russia	17:39.90
2002	Olga Danilova, Russia	24:52.1

10-Kilometer (6.2 Miles) Cross-Country[2]		Time
1952	Lydia Wideman, Finland	41:40.00
1956	Lyubov Kosyreva, U.S.S.R.	38:11.00
1960	Maria Gusakova, U.S.S.R.	39:46.60
1964	Claudia Boyarskikh, U.S.S.R.	40:24.30
1968	Toini Gustafsson, Sweden	36:46.50
1972	Galina Kolakova, U.S.S.R.	34:17.82
1976	Raisa Smetanina, U.S.S.R.	30:31.54
1980	Barbara Petzold, East Germany	30:31.54
1984	Marja-Liisa Hämäläinen, Finland	31:44.20
1988	Vida Ventsene, U.S.S.R.	30:08.20
2002	Bente Skari, Norway	28:05.60

1. Pursuit method in 2002. 2. Event not scheduled from 1992-98. 3. 20 Km until 1992. 4. 15 km (3 x 5 km) until 1976.

15-Kilometer (9.3 Miles) Cross-Country		Time
1992	Lyubov Egorova, Unified Team	42:20.8
1994	Manuela Di Centa, Italy	39:44.5
1998	Olga Danilova, Russia	46:55.4
2002	Stefania Belmondo, Italy	39:54.4

30-Kilometer (18.6 Miles) Cross-Country[3]		Time
1984	Marja Liisa Hämäläinen, Finland	1:01:45.0
1988	Tamara Tikhonova, U.S.S.R.	0:55:53.6
1992	Stefania Belmondo, Italy	1:22:30.1
1994	Manuela Di Centa, Italy	1:25:41.6
1998	Yuliya Chepalova, Russia	1:22:01.5
2002	Gabriella Paruzzi, Italy	1:30:57.1

20-Kilometer (12.4 Miles) Cross-Country Relay[4] (4x5Km)		
1956	Finland, U.S.S.R.,Sweden	1:09.01.00
1960	Sweden, U.S.S.R.,Finland	1:04.21.00
1964	U.S.S.R., Sweden, Finland	0:59:20.00
1968	Norway, Sweden, U.S.S.R.	0:57:30.00
1972	U.S.S.R., Finland, Norway	0:48:46.15
1976	U.S.S.R., Finland, E. Germany	1:07:49.75
1980	East Germany, U.S.S.R., Norway	1:02:11.10
1984	Norway, Czechoslovakia, Finland	1:06:49.70
1988	U.S.S.R., Norway, Finland	0:59:51.10
1992	Unified Team, Norway, Italy	0:59:34.80
1994	Russia, Norway, Italy	0:57:12.50
1998	Russia, Norway, Italy	0:55:13.50
2002	Germany, Norway, Switzerland	0:49:30.60

Figure Skating

MEN

1908 Ulrich Salchow, Sweden
1920 Gillis Grafstrom, Sweden
1924 Gillis Grafstrom Sweden
1928 Gillis Grafstrom, Sweden
1932 Karl Schafer, Austria
1936 Karl Schafer, Austria
1948 Richard Button, United States
1952 Richard Button, United States
1956 Hayes Alan Jenkins, United States
1960 David W. Jenkins, United States
1964 Manfred Schnelldorfer, Germany
1968 Wolfgang Schwartz, Austria
1972 Ondrej Nepela, Czechoslovakia
1976 John Curry, Great Britain
1980 Robin Cousins, Great Britain
1984 Scott Hamilton, United States
1988 Brian Boitano, United States
1992 Viktor Petrenko, Unified Team
1994 Aleksei Urmanov, Russia
1998 Ilya Kulik, Russia
2002 Alexei Yagudin, Russia

WOMEN

1908 Madge Syers, Great Britain
1920 Magda Julin-Mauroy, Sweden
1924 Herma von Szabo-Planck, Austria
1928 Sonja Henie, Norway
1932 Sonja Henie, Norway
1936 Sonja Henie, Norway
1948 Barbara Ann Scott, Canada
1952 Jeanette Altwegg, Great Britain
1956 Tenley Albright, United States
1960 Carol Heiss, United States
1964 Sjoukje Dijkstra, Netherlands
1968 Peggy Fleming, United States
1972 Beatrix Schuba, Austria
1976 Dorothy Hamill, United States
1980 Annett Pötzsch, East Germany
1984 Katarina Witt, East Germany
1988 Katarina Witt, East Germany
1992 Kristi Yamaguchi, United States
1994 Oksana Baiul, Ukraine
1998 Tara Lipinski, United States
2002 Sarah Hughes, United States

PAIRS

1908 Germany—Anna Hubler, Heinrich Burger
1920 Finland—Ludovika & Walter Jakobsson
1924 Austria—Helene Engelman, Alfred Berger
1928 France—Andree Joly, Pierre Brunet
1932 France—Andree & Pierre Brunet
1936 Germany—Maxie Herber, Ernst Baier
1948 Belgium—Micheline Lannoy, Pierre Baugniet
1952 Germany—Ria & Paul Falk
1956 Austria—Elisabeth Schwartz, Kurt Oppelt
1960 Canada—Barbara Wagner, Robert Paul
1964 U.S.S.R.—Ludmila Beloussova, Oleg Protopopov
1968 U.S.S.R.—Ludmila Beloussova, Oleg Protopopov
1972 U.S.S.R.—Irina Rodnina, Alexei Ulanov
1976 U.S.S.R.—Irina Rodnina, Aleksandr Zaitsev
1980 U.S.S.R.—Irina Rodnina, Aleksandr Zaitsev
1984 U.S.S.R.—Elena Valova, Oleg Vassiliev
1988 U.S.S.R.—Ekaterina Gordeeva, Sergei Grinkov
1992 Unified Team—Natalya Mishkutienok, Artur Dmitriev
1994 Russia—Ekaterina Gordeeva, Sergei Grinkov
1998 Russia—Oksana Kazakova, Artur Dmitriev
2002 **tie** Canada—Jamie Sale, David Pelletier **and** Russia—Elena Berezhnaya, Anton Sikharulidze

ICE DANCING

1976 U.S.S.R.—Lyudmila Pakhomova, Aleksandr Gorshkov
1980 U.S.S.R.—Natalia Linichuk, Gennadi Karponosov
1984 Great Britain—Jayne Torvill, Christopher Dean
1988 U.S.S.R.—Natalia Bestemianova, Andrei Bukin
1992 Unified Team—Marina Kimova, Sergei Ponomarenko
1994 Russia—Pasha Grishuk, Yevgeny Platov,
1998 Russia—Pasha Grishuk, Yevgeny Platov
2002 France—Marina Anissina, Gwendal Peizerat

Speed Skating, Men

500 Meters (1,641 Ft.)		Time
1924	Charles Jewtraw, U.S	0:44.00
1928	Clas Thunberg, Finland	0:43.40
	Bernst Evensen, Norway (tie)	
1932	John A. Shea, United States	0:43.40
1936	Ivar Ballangrud, Norway	0:43.40
1948	Finn Helgesen, Norway	0:43.10
1952	Ken Henry, United States	0:43.20
1956	Yevgeny Grishin, U.S.S.R.	0:40.20
1960	Yevgeny Grishin, U.S.S.R.	0:40.20
1964	Terry McDermott, United States	0:40.10
1968	Erhard Keller, West Germany	0.40.30
1972	Erhard Keller, West Germany	0.39.44
1976	Yergeny Kulikov, U.S.S.R.	0:39.17
1980	Eric Heiden, United States	0:38.03
1984	Sergei Fokichev, U.S.S.R.	0:38.19
1988	Uwe-Jens Mey, East Germany	0:36.45
1992	Uwe-Jens Mey, Germany	0:37.14
1994	Aleksandr Golubev, Russia	0:36.33
1998[1]	Hiroyasu Shimizu, Japan	1:11.35
2002	Casey Fitzrandolph United States	1:09.23

1,000 Meters (3,281 Ft.)		Time
1976	Peter Mueller, United States	1:19.32
1980	Eric Heiden, United States	1:15.18
1984	Gaétan Boucher, Canada	1:15.80
1988	Nikolai Guiliaev, U.S.S.R.	1:13.03
1992	Olaf Zinke, Germany	1:14.85
1994	Dan Jansen, United States	1:12.43
1998	Ids Postma, Netherlands	1:10.64
2002	Gerard van Velde Netherlands	1:07.18

1,500 Meters (4,922 Ft.)		Time
1924	Clas Thunberg, Finland	2:20.80
1928	Clas Thunberg, Finland	2:21.10
1932	John A. Shea, United States	2:57.50
1936	Charles Mathisen, Norway	2:19.20
1948	Sverre Farstad, Norway	2:17.60
1952	Hjalmar Andersen, Norway	2:20.40
1956	Yevgeni Grishin	2:08.60
	Yuri Mikhailov, U.S.S.R. (tie)	
1960	Roald Aas, Norway	2:10.40
	Yevgeni Grishin, U.S.S.R. (tie)	
1964	Ants Anston, U.S.S.R.	2:10.30
1968	Cornelis Verkerk, Netherlands	2:03.40
1972	Ard Schenk, Netherlands	2:02.96
1976	Jan Egil Storholt, Norway	1:59.38
1980	Eric Heiden, United States	1:55.44
1984	Gaétan Boucher, Canada	1:58.36
1988	Andre Hoffmann, East Germany	1:52.06
1992	Johann Olav Koss, Norway	1:54.81
1994	Johann Olav Koss, Norway	1:51.29
1998	Aadne Sondral, Norway	1:47.87
2002	Derek Parra United States	1:43.95

5,000 Meters (16,405 Ft.)		Time
1924	Clas Thunberg, Finland	8:39.00
1928	Ivar Ballangrud, Norway	8:50.50
1932	Irving Jaffee, United States	9:40.80
1936	Ivar Ballangrud, Norway	8:19.60
1948	Reidar Liaklev, Norway	8:29.40
1952	Hjalmar Andersen, Norway	8:10.60
1956	Boris Shilkov, U.S.S.R.	7:48.70
1960	Viktor Kosichkin, U.S.S.R.	7:51.30
1964	Knut Johannesen, Norway	7:38.40
1968	F. Anton Maier, Norway	7:22.40
1972	Ard Schenk, Netherlands	7:23.61
1976	Sten Stensen, Norway	7:24.48
1980	Eric Heiden, United States	7:02.29
1984	Sven Tomas Gustafson, Sweden	7:12.28
1988	Tomas Gustafson, Sweden	6:44.63
1992	Geir Karlstad, Sweden	6:59.97
1994	Johann Olav Koss, Norway	6:34.96
1998	Gianni Romme, Netherlands	6:22.20
2002	Jochem Uytdehaage Netherlands	6:14.66

10,000 Meters (32,810 Ft.)		Time
1924	Julien Skutnabb, Finland	18:04.80
1928	(ice thawed, event cancelled)	
1932	Irving Jaffee, United States	19:13.60
1936	Ivan Ballangrud, Norway	17:24.30
1948	Ake Seyffarth, Sweden	17:26.30
1952	Hjalmar Andersen, Norway	16:45.80
1956	Sigvard Ericsson, Sweden	16:35.90
1960	Knut Johannessen, Norway	15:46.60
1964	Jonny Nilsson, Sweden	15:50.10
1968	Johnny Hoeglin, Sweden	15:23.60
1972	Ard Schenk, Netherlands	15:01.35
1976	Piet Kleine, Netherlands	14:50.59
1980	Eric Heiden, United States	14:28.13
1984	Igor Malikov, U.S.S.R.	14:39.90
1988	Tomas Gustafson, Sweden	13:48.20
1992	Bart Veldkamp, Netherlands	14:12.12
1994	Johann Olav Koss, Norway	13:30.55
1998	Gianni Romme, Netherlands	13:15.33
2002	Jochem Uytdehaage Netherlands	12:58.92

1. Scoring system changed in 1998. Total is combined time from two performances.

Speed Skating, Women

500 Meters (1,641 Ft.)		Time
1960	Helga Haase, Germany	0:45.90
1964	Lydia Skoblikova, U.S.S.R.	0:45.00
1968	Ludmila Titova, U.S.S.R.	0:46.10
1972	Anne Henning, United States	0:43.30
1976	Sheila Young, United States	0:42.76
1980	Karin Enke, East Germany	0:41.78
1984	Christa Rothenburger, East Germany	0:41.02
1988	Bonnie Blair, United States	0:39.10
1992	Bonnie Blair, United States	0:40.33
1994	Bonnie Blair, United States.	0:39.25
1998[1]	Catriona Le May-Doan, Canada	1:16.60
2002	Catriona Le May Doan, Canada	1:14.75

1,000 Meters (3,281 Ft.)		Time
1960	Klara Guseva, U.S.S.R.	1:34.10
1964	Lydia Skoblikova, U.S.S.R.	1:33.20
1968	Carolina Geiissen, Netherlands	1:32.60
1972	Monika Pflug, West Germany	1:31.40
1976	Tatiana Averina, U.S.S.R.	1:28.43
1980	Natalia Petruseva, U.S.S.R.	1:24.10
1984	Karin Enke, East Germany	1:21.61
1988	Christa Rothenburger, East Germany	1:17.65
1992	Bonnie Blair, United States	1:21.90
1994	Bonnie Blair, United States	1:18.74
1998	Marianne Timmer, Netherlands	1:16.51
2002	Chris Witty, United States	1:13.83

1,500 Meters (4,922 Ft.)		Time
1960	Lydia Skoblikova, U.S.S.R.	2:25.20
1964	Lydia Skoblikova, U.S.S.R.	2:22.60
1968	Kaija Mustonen, Finland	2:22.40
1972	Dianne Holum, United States	2:20.80
1976	Galina Stepanskaya, U.S.S.R.	2:16.58
1980	Annie Borchink, Netherlands	2:10.95
1984	Karin Enke, East Germany	2:03.42
1988	Yvonne Van Gennip, Netherlands	2:00.68
1992	Jacqueline Boerner, Germany	2:05.87
1994	Emese Hunyady, Austria	2:02.19
1998	Marianne Timmer, Netherlands	1:57.58
2002	Anni Friesinger, Germany	1:54.02

1. Scoring system changed in 1998. Total is combined time from two performances.

3,000 Meters (9,843 Ft.) — **Time**

1960	Lydia Skoblikova, U.S.S.R.	5:14.30
1964	Lydia Skoblikova, U.S.S.R.	5:14.90
1968	Johanna Schut, Netherlands	4.56.20
1972	Christina Baas-Kaiser, Netherlands	4:52.14
1976	Tatiana Averina, U.S.S.R.	4:45.19
1980	Bjoerg Eva Jensen, Norway	4:32.13
1984	Andrea Schöne, East Germany	4:24.79
1988	Yvonne Van Gennip, Netherlands	4:11.94
1992	Gunda Niemann, Germany	4:19.90
1994	Svetlana Bazhanova, Russia	4:17.43
1998	Gunda Niemann-Stirnemann, Germany	4:07.29
2002	Claudia Pechstein, Germany	3:57.70

5,000 Meters (16,405 Ft.) — **Time**

1988	Yvonne Van Gennip, Netherlands	7:14.13
1992	Gunda Niemann, Germany	7:31.57
1994	Claudia Pechstein, Germany	7:14.37
1998	Claudia Pechstein, Germany	6:59.61
2002	Claudia Pechstein, Germany	6:46.91

The Summer Olympics

Olympiad	Year	Place	Competitors: Men	Competitors: Women	Nations represented	Events
I	1896	Athens, Greece	245	—	14	43
II	1900	Paris, France	1,206	19	24	87
III	1904	St. Louis, U.S.	681	8	13	94
IV	1908	London, U.K.	1,999	36	22	109
V	1912	Stockholm, Sweden	2,490	57	28	102
VI	1916	Berlin, Germany	— Canceled due to War —			
VII	1920	Antwerp, Belgium	2,591	78	29	154
VIII	1924	Paris, France	2,956	136	44	126
IX	1928	Amsterdam, Holland	2,724	290	46	109
X	1932	Los Angeles, U.S.	1,281	127	37	116
XI	1936	Berlin, Germany	3,738	328	49	129
XII	1940	Tokyo, Japan	— Canceled due to War —			
XIII	1944	London, Great Britain	— Canceled due to War —			
XIV	1948	London, Great Britain	3,714	385	59	136
XV	1952	Helsinki, Finland	4,407	518	69	149
XVI	1956	Melbourne, Australia	2,813	371	67	145
XVII	1960	Rome, Italy	4,738	610	83	150
XVIII	1964	Tokyo, Japan	4,457	683	93	163
XIX	1968	Mexico City, Mexico	4,750	780	112	172
XX	1972	Munich, W. Germany	6,065	1,058	121	195
XXI	1976	Montreal, Canada	4,781	1,247	92	198
XXII	1980	Moscow, USSR	4,093	1,124	80	203
XXIII	1984	Los Angeles, U.S.	5,230	1,567	140	221
XXIV	1988	Seoul, South Korea	6,279	2,186	159	237
XXV	1992	Barcelona, Spain	6,659	2,708	169	257
XXVI	1996	Atlanta, U.S.	6,797	3,523	197	271
XXVII	2000	Sydney, Australia	6,582	4,069	199	300
XXVII	2004	Athens, Greece				
XXIX	2008	Beijing, China				

The Winter Olympics

Olympiad	Year	Place	Competitors: Men	Competitors: Women	Nations represented	Events
I	1924	Chamonix, France	245	13	16	16
II	1928	St. Moritz, Switzerland	438	26	25	14
III	1932	Lake Placid, N.Y., U.S.	231	21	17	14
IV	1936	Garmisch-Partenkirchen, Germany	588	80	28	17
V	1948	St. Moritz, Switzerland	592	77	28	22
VI	1952	Oslo, Norway	585	109	30	22
VII	1956	Cortina D'Ampezzo, Italy	688	132	32	24
VIII	1960	Squaw Valley, Calif., U.S.	522	143	30	27
IX	1964	Innsbruck, Austria	891	200	36	34
X	1968	Grenoble, France	947	211	37	35
XI	1972	Sapporo, Japan	800	206	35	35
XII	1976	Innsbruck, Austria	892	231	37	37
XIII	1980	Lake Placid, N.Y., U.S.	839	233	37	38
XIV	1984	Sarajevo, Yugoslavia	1,000	274	49	39
XV	1988	Calgary, Canada	1,110	313	57	46
XVI	1992	Albertville, France	1,313	488	64	57
XVII	1994	Lillehammer, Norway	1,217	522	67	61
XVIII	1998	Nagano, Japan	1,488	814	72	68
XIX	2002	Salt Lake City, Utah, U.S.	1,513	886	77	78
XX	2006	Torino, Italy				

Source: International Olympic Committee.

PROFESSIONAL SPORTS

AUTOMOBILE RACING

A number of U.S. states and cities banned automobile racing on public roads during the early 1900s, leading to the development of closed-circuit courses. The Indianapolis Motor Speedway, a 2.5 mile macadam oval, was built in 1909. It was paved with brick in 1911, when the first Indy 500 was run. The American Automobile Association, troubled by a series of fatal crashes, stopped sanctioning races in 1956, whereupon the United States Auto Club (USAC) took over the Indy 500.

Indianapolis 500 Winners, 1911–2003

Year	Winner	Time	MPH
Under AAA Sanction			
1911	Ray Harroun	6:42.08	74.602
1912	Joe Dawson	6:21.06	78.719
1913	Juses Goux	6:35:05	75.933
1914	Rene Thomas	6:03:45	82.474
1915	Ralph DePalma	5:33:55	89.840
1916	Dario Resta	3:34:17[1]	84.001
1919	Howard Wilcox	5:40:42	88.050
1920	Gaston Chevrolet	5:38:32	88.618
1921	Tommy Milton	5:34:34	89.621
1922	Jimmy Murphy	5:17:30	94.484
1923	Tommy Milton	5:29:50	90.954
1924	L.L. Corum, Joe Boyer	5:05:23	98.234
1925	Peter DePaolo	4:56:39	101.127
1926	Peter Lockhart	4:10:14[2]	95.904
1927	George Souders	5:07:33	97.545
1928	Louis Meyer	5:01:33	99.482
1929	Ray Keech	5:07:25	97.585
1930	Billy Arnold	4:58:39	100.448
1931	Louis Schneider	5:10:27	96.629
1932	Fred Frame	4:48:03	104.144
1933	Louis Meyer	4:48:00	104.162
1934	William Cummings	4:46:05	104.863
1935	Kelly Petillo	4:42:22	106.240
1936	Louis Meyer	4:35:03	109.069
1937	Wilbur Shaw	4:24:07	113.580
1938	Floyd Roberts	4:15:58	117.200
1939	Wilbur Shaw	4:20:47	115.035
1940	Wilbur Shaw	4:22:31	114.277
1941	Floyd Davis, Mauri Rose	4:20:36	115.117
1946	George Robson	4:21:16	114.820
1947	Mauri Rose	4:17:52	116.338
1948	Mauri Rose	4:10:23	119.814
1949	Bill Holland	4:07:15	121.327
1950	Johnnie Parsons	2:46:55[3]	124.002
1951	Lee Wallard	3:57:38	126.244
1952	Troy Tuttman	3:52:41	128.922
1953	Bill Vukovich	3:53:01	128.740
1954	Bill Vukovich	3:49:17	130.840
1955	Bob Sweikert	3:53:59	128.209
Under USAC Sanction			
1956	Pat Flaherty	3:53.28	128.490
1957	Sam Hanks	3:41.14	135.601
1958	Jim Bryan	3:44:13	133.791
1959	Rodger Ward	3:40:49	135.857
1960	Jim Rathmann	3:36:11	138.767
1961	A.J. Foyt, Jr.	3:35:37	139.131
1962	Roger Ward	3:33:50	140.293
1963	Parnelli Jones	3:29:35	143.137
1964	A.J. Foyt, Jr.	3:23:35	147.350
1965	Jim Clark	3:19:05	150.686
1966	Graham Hill	3:27:52	144.317
1967	A.J. Foyt, Jr.	3:18:14	151.207
1968	Bobby Unser	3:16:13	152.882
1969	Mario Andretti	3:11:14	156.867
1970	Al Unser	3:12:37	155.749
1971	Al Unser	3:10:11	157.735
1972	Mark Donohue	3:04:05	162.962
1973	Gordon Johncock	2:05:26[4]	159.036
1974	Johnny Rutherford	3:09:10	158.589
1975	Bobby Unser	2:54:55[5]	149.213
1976	Johnny Rutherford	1:42:52[6]	148.725
1977	A.J. Foyt, Jr.	3:05:57	161.331
1978	Al Unser	3:05:54	161.363
1979	Rick Mears	3:08:47	158.899
1980	Johnny Rutherford	3:29:59	142.862
1981	Bobby Unser	3:35:41	139.084
1982	Gordon Johncock	3:05:09	162.029
1983	Tom Sneva	3:05:03	162.117
1984	Rick Mears	3:30:21	163.612
1985	Danny Sullivan	3:16:06	152.982
1986	Bobby Rahal	2:55:43	170.722
1987	Al Unser	3:04:59	162.175
1988	Rick Mears	3:27:10	144.809
1989	Emerson Fittipaldi	2:59:01	167.581
1990	Arie Luyendyk	2:41:18	185.984[7]
1991	Rick Mears	2:50:01	176.457
1992	Al Unser, Jr.	3:43:05	134.477
1993	Emerson Fittipaldi	3:10:50	157.207
1994	Al Unser, Jr.	3:06:29	160.872
1995	Jacques Villeneuve	3:15:18	153.616
1996	Buddy Lazier	3:22:46	147.956
1997	Arie Luyendyk	3:25:43	145.827
1998	Eddie Cheever	3:26:40	145.155
1999	Kenny Brack	3:15:51	153.176
2000	Juan Montoya	2:58.59	167.607
2001	Helio Castroneves	3:31.54	141.574
2002	Helio Castroneves	3:00:11	166.499
2003	Gil de Ferran	3:11:57	156.291

1. 300 miles (scheduled). 2. 400 miles (rain). 3. 345 miles (rain). 4. 332.5 miles (rain). 5. 435 miles (rain). 6. 255 miles (rain). 7. Track record. **Source:** Indianapolis Motor Speedway Hall of Fame and Museum.

Daytona 500 Winners, 1959–2003

Year	Winner	Year	Winner
1959	Lee Petty	1981	Richard Petty
1960	Junior Johnson	1982	Bobby Allison
1961	Marvin Panch	1983	Cale Yarborough
1962	Fireball Roberts	1984	Cale Yarborough
1963	Tiny Lund	1985	Bill Elliott
1964	Richard Petty	1986	Geoff Bodine
1965	Fred Lorenzen	1987	Bill Elliott
1966	Richard Petty	1988	Bobby Allison
1967	Mario Andretti	1989	Darrell Waltrip
1968	Cale Yarborough	1990	Derrike Cope
1969	LeeRoy Yarbrough	1991	Ernie Irvan
		1992	Davey Allison
1970	Pete Hamilton	1993	Dale Jarrett
1971	Richard Petty	1994	Sterling Marlin
1972	A.J. Foyt, Jr.	1995	Sterling Marlin
1973	Richard Petty	1996	Dale Jarrett
1974	Richard Petty	1997	Jeff Gordon
1975	Benny Parsons	1998	Dale Earnhardt
1976	David Pearson	1999	Jeff Gordon
1977	Cale Yarborough	2000	Dale Jarrett
1978	Bobby Allison	2001	Michael Waltrip
1979	Richard Petty	2002	Ward Burton
1980	Buddy Baker	2003	Michael Waltrip

Winston Cup Winners 1959–2002

Year	Winner	Year	Winner
1959	Lee Petty	1981	Darrell Waltrip
1960	Rex White	1982	Darrell Waltrip
1961	Ned Jarrett	1983	Bobby Allison
1962	Joe Weatherly	1984	Terry Labonte
1963	Joe Weatherly	1985	Darrell Waltrip
1964	Richard Petty	1986	Dale Earnhardt
1965	Ned Jarrett	1987	Dale Earnhardt
1966	David Pearson	1988	Bill Elliott
1967	Richard Petty	1989	Rusty Wallace
1968	David Pearson	1990	Dale Earnhardt
1969	David Pearson	1991	Dale Earnhardt
1970	Bobby Isaac	1992	Alan Kulwicki
1971	Richard Petty	1993	Dale Earnhardt
1972	Richard Petty	1994	Dale Earnhardt
1973	Benny Parsons	1995	Jeff Gordon
1974	Richard Petty	1996	Terry Labonte
1975	Richard Petty	1997	Jeff Gordon
1976	Cale Yarborough	1998	Jeff Gordon
1977	Cale Yarborough	1999	Dale Jarrett
1978	Cale Yarborough	2000	Bobby Labonte
1979	Richard Petty	2001	Jeff Gordon
1980	Dale Earnhardt	2002	Tony Stewart

BOWLING

PBA Leading Money Winners, 1959–2003

Year	Name	Amount	Year	Name	Amount	Year	Name	Amount
1959	Dick Weber	$ 7,672	1976	Earl Anthony	$110,833	1992	Marc McDowell	$174,215
1960	Don Carter	22,525	1977	Mark Roth	105,583	1993	Walter Ray. Williams Jr,	296,370
1961	Dick Weber	26,280	1978	Mark Roth	134,500	1994	Norm Duke	273,753
1962	Don Carter	49,972	1979	Mark Roth	124,517	1995	Mike Aulby	219,792
1963	Dick Weber	46,333	1980	Wayne Webb	116,700	1996	Walter Ray. Williams Jr,	241,330
1964	Bob Strampe	33,592	1981	Earl Anthony	164,735	1997	Walter Ray. Williams Jr,	240,544
1965	Dick Weber	47,675	1982	Earl Anthony	134,760	1998	Walter Ray Williams Jr.	238,225
1966	Wayne Zahn	54,720	1983	Earl Anthony	135,605	1999	Parker Bohn III	240,912
1967	Dave Davis	54,165	1984	Mark Roth	158,712	2000	Norm Duke	136,900
1968	Jim Stefanich	67,375	1985	Mike Aulby	201,200	2001	Parker Bohn III	245,200
1969	Billy Hardwick	64,160	1986	Walter Ray Williams Jr.	145,550	2002-03	Walter Ray Williams Jr.	419,700
1970	Mike McGrath	52,049	1987	Pete Weber	179,516			
1971	Johnny Petraglia	85,065	1988	Brian Voss	225,485			
1972	Don Johnson	56,648	1989	Mike Aulby	298,237			
1973	Don McCune	69,000	1990	Aurelio Monacelli	204,775			
1974	Earl Anthony	99,585	1991	David Ozio	225,585			
1975	Earl Anthony	107,585						

Note: Since 2001, the PBA season has started in October and ended in March. **Source:** Professional Bowlers Association.

Professional Women's Bowling Association, Career Money Leaders

Rank, Bowler	Earnings	Rank, Bowler	Earnings	Rank, Bowler	Earnings
1. Wendy MacPherson	$1,238,960	**8.** Lisa Wagner	$853,796	**15.** Dana Miller-Mackie	$636,672
2. Tish Johnson	1,098,562	**9.** Kim Adler	827,492	**16.** Nikki Gianulias	624,260
3. Aleta Sill	1,071,194	**10.** Cheryl Daniels	754,544	**17.** Liz Johnson	585,622
4. Leanne Barrette	1,028,993	**11.** Dede Davidson	753,859	**18.** Cindy Coburn-Carroll	576,023
5. Anne Marie Duggan	955,808	**12.** Robin Romeo	728,649	**19.** Carol Norman	571,867
6. Carol Gianotti-Block	918,777	**13.** Kim Terrell	713,586	**20.** Michelle Feldman	556,203
7. Carolyn Dorin-Ballard	916,476	**14.** Marianne DiRupo	664,073		

Note: As of July 13, 2003. Earnings do not include TV incentives. **Source:** Professional Women's Bowling Association.

BOXING

Although many governing bodies now issue and certify their own boxing championships, the three most widely accepted are the World Boxing Association (WBA), World Boxing Council (WBC), and the International Boxing Federation (IBF). Years given indicate the year the championship belt changed hands in a title bout. Champions who were awarded belts without a championship bout are not shown. Current champions (as of July 22, 2003) are shown in **boldface type.**

Heavyweights (over 190 lbs.)

Year	Name
1885	John L. Sullivan
1892	James J. Corbett
1897	Robert Fitzsimmons
1899	James J. Jeffries
1905	Marvin Hart
1906	Tommy Burns
1908	Jack Johnson
1915	Jess Willard
1919	Jack Dempsey
1926	Gene Tunney[1]
1928–30	vacant
1930	Max Schmeling
1932	Jack Sharkey
1933	Primo Carnera
1934	Max Baer
1935	James J. Braddock
1937	Joe Louis[1]
1949	Ezzard Charles
1951	Jersey Joe Walcott
1952	Rocky Marciano[1]
1956	Floyd Patterson
1959	Ingemar Johansson
1960	Floyd Patterson
1962	Sonny Liston
1964	Cassius Clay[1] (Muhammad Ali)
1965	Ernie Terrell (WBA)
1967	Muhammad Ali (unifies world title)
1968	Jimmy Ellis (WBA)
1970	Joe Frazier (unifies world title)
1973	George Foreman
1974	Muhammad Ali
1978	Leon Spinks, Larry Holmes[1], Muhammad Ali[1] (WBA)
1979	John Tate (WBA)
1980	Mike Weaver (WBA)
1982	Michael Dokes (WBA)
1983	Gerrie Coetzee (WBA)
1984	Tim Witherspoon (WBC), Pinklon Thomas (WBC), Greg Page (WBA)
1985	Tony Tubbs (WBA)
1986	Tim Witherspoon (WBA), Trevor Berbick (WBC), Mike Tyson (WBC), James "Bonecrusher" Smith (WBA)
1987	Mike Tyson (WBA), Tony Tucker (IBF)
1990	Buster Douglas (unifies world title), Evander Holyfield
1992	Riddick Bowe
1993	Evander Holyfield (WBA, IBF)
1994	George Foreman (WBA, IBF), Bruce Seldon (WBA), Frank Bruno[1] (WBC)
1996	Mike Tyson (WBC), Michael Moorer (IBF), Mike Tyson (WBA), Evander Holyfield (WBA)
1997	Lennox Lewis (WBC), Evander Holyfield (IBF)
1999	Lennox Lewis (WBA[1], IBF)
2001	Hasim Rahman (WBC, IBF), John Ruiz (WBA), **Lennox Lewis (WBC, IBF)**
2002	**Chris Byrd (IBF)**
2003	**Roy Jones Jr. (WBA)**

Light Heavyweights (169–175 lbs.)

Year	Name
1903	Jack Root, George Gardner
1903	Bob Fitzsimmons
1905	Philadelphia Jack O'Brien[1]
1912	Jack Dillon
1916	Battling Levinsky
1920	George Carpentier
1922	Battling Siki
1923	Mike McTigue
1925	Paul Berlenbach
1926	Jack Delaney[1]
1927	Tommy Loughran[1]
1930	Maxey Rosenbloom
1934	Bob Olin
1935	John Henry Lewis[1]
1939	Billy Conn[1]
1941	Gus Lesnevich
1948	Freddie Mills
1950	Joey Maxim
1952	Archie Moore[1]
1960	*Vacant*
1962	Harold Johnson
1963	Willie Pastrano
1965	Jose Torres
1966	Dick Tiger
1968	Bob Foster
1971	Vicente Rondon (WBA)
1972	Bob Foster (unifies world title)
1974	John Conteh (WBC), Victor Galindez (WBA)
1977	Miguel Angel Cuello (WBC)
1978	Mate Parlov (WBC), Mike Rossman (WBA), Marvin Johnson (WBC)
1979	Matthew Franklin (Matthew Saad Muhammad) (WBC), Marvin Johnson (WBA)
1980	Eddie Gregory (Eddie Mustafa Muhammad) (WBA)
1981	Michael Spinks (WBA), Dwight Braxton (Dwight Muhammad Qawi) (WBC)
1983	Michael Spinks (unifies world title)
1985	J.B. Williamson (WBC), Slobodan Kacar (IBF)
1986	Marvin Johnson (WBA), Dennis Andries (WBC), Bobby Czyz (IBF)
1987	Thomas Hearns[1] (WBC), Leslie Stewart (WBA), Virgil Hill (WBA), Prince Charles Williams (IBF), Don Lalonde (WBC)
1988	Sugar Ray Leonard (WBC)
1989	Dennis Andries (WBC), Jeff Harding (WBC)
1990	Dennis Andries (WBC)
1991	Thomas Hearns (WBA), Jeff Harding (WBC)
1992	Iran Barkley[1] (WBA), Virgil Hill (WBA)
1993	Henry Maske (IBF)
1994	Mike McCallum (WBC)
1995	Fabrice Tiozzo (WBC)
1996	Roy Jones Jr.[1] (WBC), Virgil Hill[1] (IBF),
1997	William Guthrie (IBF), Dariusz Michalczewski[1] (WBA), Lou Del Valle (WBA)
1998	Reggie Johnson (IBF), Graciano Rocchigiani (WBC), Roy Jones Jr. (WBA, WBC)
1999	Roy Jones Jr. (IBF)
2003	**Antonio Tarver (unifies world title)**

Note: WBC = World Boxing Council. WBA = World Boxing Association. IBF= International Boxing Federation.

Middleweights (155–160 lbs.)

Year	Name
1884	"Nonpareil" Jack Dempsey
1891	Bob Fitzsimmons[1]
1897	Kid McCoy[1], Tommy Ryan[1]
1907	Stanley Ketchel
1908	Billy Papke, Stanley Ketchel[1]
1911	*Vacant*
1913	Frank Klaus, George Chip
1914	Al McCoy
1917	Mike O'Dowd
1920	Johnny Wilson
1921	William Bryan Downey[1]
1923	Harry Greb
1926	Tiger Flowers, Mickey Walker
1931	Gorilla Jones
1932	Marcel Thil
1937	Fred Apostoli
1939	Ceferino Garcia
1940	Ken Overlin
1941	Billy Soose[1], Tony Zale
1947	Rocky Graziano
1948	Tony Zale, Marcel Cerdan
1949	Jake LaMotta
1951	Sugar Ray Robinson, Randy Turpin, Sugar Ray Robinson[1]
1953	Bobo Olson
1955	Sugar Ray Robinson
1957	Gene Fullmer (NBA), Sugar Ray Robinson, Carmen Basilio
1958	Sugar Ray Robinson
1960	Paul Pender
1961	Terry Downes
1962	Paul Pender
1963	Dick Tiger
1963	Joey Giardello
1965	Dick Tiger
1966	Emile Griffith
1967	Nino Benvenuti, Emile Griffith
1968	Nino Benvenuti
1970	Carlos Monzon
1977	Rodrigo Valdez
1978	Hugo Corro
1979	Vito Antuofermo
1980	Alan Minter, Marvin Hagler[1]
1987	Ray Leonard[1] (WBC), Frank Tate (IBF), Sumbo Kalambay (WBA), Thomas Hearns (WBC)
1988	Iran Barkley (WBC), Michael Nunn (IBF)
1989	Roberto Duran[1] (WBC), Mike McCallum[1] (WBA)
1990	Julian Jackson (WBC), James Toney[1] (IBF)
1991	Reggie Johnson[1] (WBA)
1993	Gerald McClellan[1] (WBC), Roy Jones[1] (IBF), John David Jackson (WBA)
1994	Jorge Castro (WBA)
1995	Julian Jackson (WBC), **Bernard Hopkins (IBF)**, Quincy Taylor (WBC), Shinij Takehara (WBA)
1996	Keith Holmes (WBC), William Joppy (WBA)
1997	Julio Cesar Green (WBA)
1996	William Joppy (WBA), Hassine Cherifi (WBC)
1999	Keith Holmes (WBC)
2001	Felix Trinidad (WBA), **Bernard Hopkins (WBA, WBC)**

Welterweights (141–147 lbs.)

Year	Name
1888	Paddy Duffy
1892	Mysterious Billy Smith
1894	Tommy Ryan[1]
1896	Kid McCoy[1]
1898	Mysterious Billy Smith
1900	Matty Matthews, Eddie Connolly, Rube Ferns, Matty Matthews
1901	Rube Ferns, Joe Walcott
1904	Dixie Kid[1]
1906	Honey Mellody
1907	Frank Mantell
1908	Harry Lewis[1]
1911–13	Vacant
1914	Waldemar Holberg, Tom McCormick, Matt Wells
1915	Mike Glover, Jack Britton, Ted (Kid) Lewis
1916	Jack Britton
1917	Ted (Kid) Lewis
1919	Jack Britton
1922	Mickey Walker
1926	Pete Latzo
1927	Joe Dundee
1929	Jackie Fields
1930	Young Jack Thompson, Tommy Freeman
1931	Young Jack Thompson, Lou Brouillard
1932	Jackie Fields
1933	Young Corbett, Jimmy McLarnin
1934	Barney Ross, Jimmy McLarnin
1935	Barney Ross
1938	Henry Armstrong
1940	Fritzie Zivic
1941	Fred Cochrane
1946	Marty Servo[1], Ray Robinson[1]
1951	Kid Gavilan
1954	Johnny Saxton
1955	Tony De Marco, Carmen Basilio
1956	Johnny Saxton, Carmen Basilio
1957	Carmen Basilio[1]
1958	Virgil Akins, Don Jordan
1960	Benny Paret
1961	Emile Griffith, Benny Paret
1962	Emile Griffith
1963	Luis Rodriguez, Emile Griffith[1]
1966	Curtis Cokes
1969	Jose Napoles
1970	Billy Backus
1971	Jose Napoles
1975	Angel Espada (WBA), John Stracey (WBC)
1976	Carlos Palomino (WBC), Jose Cuevas (WBA)
1979	Wilfredo Benitez (WBC), Sugar Ray Leonard (WBC)
1980	Roberto Duran (WBC), Thomas Hearns (WBA), Sugar Ray Leonard (WBC)
1981	Sugar Ray Leonard[1] (unifies world title)
1983	Donald Curry (WBA), Milton McCrory (WBC)
1985	Donald Curry (unifies world title)
1986	Lloyd Honeyghan[1]
1987	Mark Breland (WBA), Marlon Starling (WBA), Jorge Vaca (WBC)
1988	Simon Brown[1] (IBF), Thomas Molinares[1] (WBA)
1989	Marlon Starling (WBC), Mark Breland (WBA)
1990	Aaron Davis (WBA), Maurice Blocker (WBC)
1991	Meldrick Taylor (WBA), Simon Brown (WBC), Maurice Blocker (IBF), Buddy McGirt (WBC)
1992	Crisanto Espana (WBA)
1993	Pernell Whitaker (WBC), Felix Trinidad (IBF)
1994	Ike Quartey[1] (WBA)
1997	Oscar de la Hoya (WBC)
1998	James Page (WBA)
1999	Felix Trinidad[1] (WBC), Rawl Frank (IBF)
2000	Vernon Forrest (IBF), Oscar de la Hoya (WBC), Shane Mosley (WBC)
2001	Andrew Lewis (WBA)
2002	Vernon Forrest[1] (IBF), Michele Piccirillo (IBF), **Ricardo Mayorga (WBA),** Vernon Forrest (WBC)
2003	**Corey Spinks (IBF), Ricardo Mayorga (WBC)**

Lightweights (131–135 lbs.)

Year	Name
1896	Jack McAuliffe[1], Kid Lavigne
1899	Frank Erne
1902	Joe Gans[1]
1904	Jimmy Britt
1905	Battling Nelson
1906	Joe Gans
1908	Battling Nelson
1910	Ad Wolgast
1912	Willie Ritchie
1914	Freddie Welsh
1917	Benny Leonard[1]
1925	Jimmy Goodrich, Rocky Kansas
1926	Sammy Mandell
1930	Al Singer, Tony Canzoneri
1933	Barney Ross[1]
1935	Tony Canzoneri
1936	Lou Ambers
1938	Henry Armstrong
1939	Lou Ambers
1940	Lew Jenkins
1941	Sammy Angott
1942	Beau Jack
1943	Bob Montgomery, Beau Jack
1944	Bob Montgomery, Juan Zurita
1945	Ike Williams
1951	Jimmy Carter
1952	Lauro Salas, Jimmy Carter
1954	Paddy De Marco, Jimmy Carter
1955	Bud Smith
1956	Joe Brown
1962	Carlos Ortiz
1965	Ismael Laguna, Carlos Ortiz
1968	Teo Cruz
1969	Mando Ramos
1970	Ismael Laguna, Ken Buchanan[1]
1971	Pedro Carrasco (WBC)
1972	Mando Ramos (WBC), Roberto Duran[1] (WBA) Chango Carmona (WBC), Rodolfo Gonzalez (WBC)
1974	Ishimatsu Suzuki (WBC)
1976	Esteban De Jesus[1] (WBC)
1979	Jim Watt (WBC), Ernesto España (WBA)
1980	Hilmer Kenty (WBA)
1981	Sean O'Grady (WBA), Alexis Arguello (WBC), Claude Noel (WBA), Arturo Frias (WBA)
1982	Ray Mancini (WBA)
1983	Edwin Rosario (WBC)
1984	Charlie (Choo Choo) Brown (IBF), Livingstone Bramble (WBA), Jose Luis Ramirez (WBC)
1985	Jimmy Paul (IBF), Hector Camacho[1] (WBC)
1986	Edwin Rosario (WBA), Greg Haugen (IBF)
1987	Vinny Pazienza (IBF), Jose Luis Ramirez (WBC), Julio Cesar Chavez[1] (WBA)
1988	Greg Haugen (IBF), Julio Cesar Chavez[1] (WBC)
1989	Pernell Whitaker (IBF), Edwin Rosario (WBA), Pernell Whitaker (WBC)
1990	Juan Nazario (WBA), Pernell Whitaker[1] (unifies world title)
1991	Vacant
1992	Tony Lopez (WBA)
1993	Fred Pendleton (IBF), Dingaan Thobela (WBA), Orzubek Nazarov (WBA)
1994	Rafael Ruelas (IBF)
1995	Oscar de la Hoya[1] (IBF), Phillip Holiday (IBF)
1996	Jean-Baptiste Mendy (WBC)
1997	Steve Johnston (WBC), Shane Mosley[1] (IBF)
1998	Jean-Baptiste Mendy (WBA), Cesar Bazan (WBC)
1999	Julian Lorcy Fra (WBA), Steve Johnston (WBC), Stefano Zoff (WBA), Paul Spadafora[1] (IBF), Gilberto Serrano (WBA)
2000	Jose Luis Castillo (WBC)
2001	Raul Balbi (WBA)
2002	**Floyd Mayweather (WBC), Leonard Dorin (WBA)**

Featherweights (123–126 lbs.)

Year	Name
1900	Terry McGovern, Young Corbett[1]
1901	Abe Attell
1904	Tommy Sullivan[1]
1906	Abe Attell
1912	Johnny Kilbane
1923	Eugene Criqui, Johnny Dundee[1]
1925	Kid Kaplan[1]
1927	Benny Bass, Ton Canzoneri
1928	Andre Routis
1929	Battling Battalino[1]
1932	Tommy Paul
1933	Freddie Miller
1936	Petey Sarron
1937	Henry Armstrong[1]
1938	Joey Archibald
1940	Harry Jeffra, Joey Archibald
1941	Chalky Wright
1942	Wilie Pep
1948	Sandy Saddler
1949	Willie Pep
1950	Sandy Saddler[1]
1957	Hogan (Kid) Bassey
1959	Davey Moore
1963	Sugar Ramos
1964	Vicente Saldivar[1]
1968	Jose Legra[1] (WBA), Shojo Saijo (WBA)
1969	Johnny Famechon (WBC)
1970	Vicente Saldivar (WBC), Kuniaki Shibata (WBC)
1971	Antonio Gomez (WBA
1972	Clemente Sanchez (WBC), Ernesto Marcel[1] (WBA), Jose Legra (WBC)
1973	Eder Jofre[1] (WBC)
1974	Ruben Olivares (WBA), Bobby Chacon (WBC), Alexis Arguello[1] (WBA)
1975	Ruben Olivares (WBC), David Kotey (WBC)
1976	Danny Lopez (WBC)
1977	Rafael Ortega (WBA), Cecillio Lastra (WBA)
1978	Eusebio Pedrosa (WBA)
1980	Salvador Sanchez[1] (WBC)
1982	Juan LaPorte (WBC)
1984	Min Keun Oh (IBF), Wilfredo Gomez (WBC), Azumah Nelson (WBC)
1985	Barry McGuigan (WBA), Ki Yung Chung[1] (IBF)
1986	Steve Cruz (WBA)
1987	Antonio Esparragoza (WBA)
1988	Calvin Grove (IBF), Jeff Fenech[1] (WBC), Jorge Paez (IBF)
1990	Marcos Villasana (WBC)
1991	Yung Kyun Park (WBA)
1992	Troy Dorsey (IBF), Manuel Medina (IBF), Paul Hodkinson (WBC)
1993	Tom Johnson (IBF), Goyo Vargas (WBC), Kevin Kelley (WBC), Eloy Rojas (WBA)
1995	Alejandro Gonzalez (WBC), Manuel Medina (WBC), Luisito Espinosa (WBC)
1996	Wilfredo Vasquez[1] (WBA)
1997	Naseem Hamed (IBF), Hector Lizarraga (IBF)
1998	Fred Norwood (WBA), Manuel Medina (IBF), Antonio Cermeño Ven (WBA)
1999	Cesar Soto (WBC), Luisito Espinosa (WBC), Paul Ingle (IBF), Fred Norwood (WBA)
2000	Guty Espadas (WBC), **Derrick Gainer (WBA)**
2001	Frankie Toledo (IBF), Manuel Medina (IBF), **Erik Morales (WBC)**
2002	Johnny Tapia (IBF), Manuel Medina (IBF)
2003	**Juan Marquez (IBF)**

1. Stripped of title or abandoned belt. **Source:** International Boxing Hall of Fame.

GOLF

▶THE FOUR MAJOR TOURNAMENTS

No golfer has ever won the four major tournaments—the Masters, the U.S. Open, the British Open, and the PGA—in the same calendar year. The players to come closest were Ben Hogan, who won the first three tournaments in 1953, and Tiger Woods, who won them consecutively, but not in the same calendar year –he won the last three in 2000 and the Masters in 2001. Five players have won each of the four majors at least once over their entire careers: Hogan, Woods, Jack Nicklaus (who won each at least three times), Gary Player, and Gene Sarazen.

The Senior Tour began with two tournaments in 1980, which offered a total of $250,000 in prize money to qualified PGA members over the age of 50. By 1984, the tour had spiralled to 24 tournaments with prize money totalling $5 million. The arrival in 1990 of Jack Nicklaus and Lee Trevino on the senior tour helped propel the 50-and-over tour to unprecedented popularity, surpassing the Ladies' Professional Tour in both prize money and television ratings.

The Masters

Year	Winner	Year	Winner	Year	Winner	Year	Winner
1934	Horton Smith	1952	Sam Snead	1970	Billy Casper	1988	Sandy Lyle
1935	Gene Sarazen	1953	Ben Hogan	1971	Charles Coody	1989	Nick Faldo
1936	Horton Smith	1954	Sam Snead	1972	Jack Nicklaus	1990	Nick Faldo
1937	Byron Nelson	1955	Cary Middlecoff	1973	Tommy Aaron	1991	Ian Woosnam
1938	Henry Picard	1956	Jack Burke Jr.	1974	Gary Player	1992	Fred Couples
1939	Ralph Guldahl	1957	Doug Ford	1975	Jack Nicklaus	1993	Bernhard Langer
1940	Jimmy Demaret	1958	Arnold Palmer	1976	Ray Floyd	1994	José María Olazábal
1941	Craig Wood	1959	Art Wall Jr.	1977	Tom Watson	1995	Ben Crenshaw
1942	Byron Nelson	1960	Arnold Palmer	1978	Gary Player	1996	Nick Faldo
1943	Not held	1961	Gary Player	1979	Fuzzy Zoeller	1997	Tiger Woods
1944	Not held	1962	Arnold Palmer	1980	Seve Ballesteros	1998	Mark O'Meara
1945	Not held	1963	Jack Nicklaus	1981	Tom Watson	1999	José María Olazábal
1946	Herman Keiser	1964	Arnold Palmer	1982	Craig Stadler	2000	Vijay Singh
1947	Jimmy Demaret	1965	Jack Nicklaus	1983	Seve Ballesteros	2001	Tiger Woods
1948	Claude Harman	1966	Jack Nicklaus	1984	Ben Crenshaw	2002	Tiger Woods
1949	Sam Snead	1967	Gay Brewer Jr.	1985	Bernhard Langer	2003	Mike Weir
1950	Jimmy Demaret	1968	Bob Goalby	1986	Jack Nicklaus		
1951	Ben Hogan	1969	George Archer	1987	Larry Mize		

The U.S. Open Championship

Year	Winner	Year	Winner	Year	Winner	Year	Winner
1895	Horace Rawlins	1923	Robert T. Jones Jr.	1951	Ben Hogan	1979	Hale Irwin
1896	James Foulis	1924	Cyril Walker	1952	Julius Boros	1980	Jack Nicklaus
1897	Joe Lloyd	1925	W. MacFarlane	1953	Ben Hogan	1981	David Graham
1898	Fred Herd	1926	Robert T. Jones Jr.	1954	Ed Furgol	1982	Tom Watson
1899	Willie Smith	1927	Tommy Armour	1955	Jack Fleck	1983	Larry Nelson
1900	Harry Vardon	1928	Johnny Farrell	1956	Cary Middlecoff	1984	Fuzzy Zoeller
1901	Willie Anderson	1929	Robert T. Jones Jr.	1957	Dick Mayer	1985	Andy North
1902	Laurie Auchterlonie	1930	Robert T. Jones Jr.	1958	Tommy Bolt	1986	Ray Floyd
1903	Willie Anderson	1931	Billy Burke	1959	Billy Casper	1987	Scott Simpson
1904	Willie Anderson	1932	Gene Sarazen	1960	Arnold Palmer	1988	Curtis Strange
1905	Willie Anderson	1933	Johnny Goodman	1961	Gene Littler	1989	Curtis Strange
1906	Alex Smith	1934	Olin Dutra	1962	Jack Nicklaus	1990	Hale Irwin
1907	Alex Ross	1935	Sam Parks, Jr.	1963	Julius Boros	1991	Payne Stewart
1908	Fred McLeod	1936	Tony Manero	1964	Ken Venturi	1992	Tom Kite
1909	George Sargent	1937	Ralph Guldahl	1965	Gary Player	1993	Lee Janzen
1910	Alex Smith	1938	Ralph Guldahl	1966	Billy Casper	1994	Ernie Els
1911	John McDermott	1939	Byron Nelson	1967	Jack Nicklaus	1995	Corey Pavin
1912	John McDermott	1940	Lawson Little	1968	Lee Trevino	1996	Steve Jones
1913	Francis Ouimet	1941	Craig Wood	1969	Orville Moody	1997	Ernie Els
1914	Walter Hagen	1942	Not held	1970	Tony Jacklin	1998	Lee Janzen
1915	Jerome Travers	1943	Not held	1971	Lee Trevino	1999	Payne Stewart
1916	Charles Evans Jr.	1944	Not held	1972	Jack Nicklaus	2000	Tiger Woods
1917	Not held	1945	Not held	1973	Johnny Miller	2001	Retief Goosen
1918	Not held	1946	Lloyd Mangrum	1974	Hale Irwin	2002	Tiger Woods
1919	Walter Hagen	1947	Lew Worsham	1975	Lou Graham	2003	Jim Furyk
1920	Edward Ray	1948	Ben Hogan	1976	Jerry Pate		
1921	James M. Barnes	1949	Cary Middlecoff	1977	Hubert Green		
1922	Gene Sarazen	1950	Ben Hogan	1978	Andy North		

The British Open

Year	Winner	Year	Winner	Year	Winner	Year	Winner
1860	Willie Park	1896	Harry Vardon	1933	Denny Shute	1969	Tony Jacklin
1861	Tom Morris Sr.	1897	Harold H. Hilton	1934	Henry Cotton	1970	Jack Nicklaus
1862	Tom Morris Sr.	1898	Harry Vardon	1935	Alfred Perry	1971	Lee Trevino
1863	Willie Park	1899	Harry Vardon	1936	Alfred Padgham	1972	Lee Trevino
1864	Tom Morris Sr.	1900	John H. Taylor	1937	Henry Cotton	1973	Tom Weiskopf
1865	Andrew Strath	1901	James Braid	1938	R.A. Whitcombe	1974	Gary Player
1866	Willie Park	1902	Alexander Herd	1939	Richard Burton	1975	Tom Watson
1867	Tom Morris Sr.	1903	Harry Vardon	1940	Not held	1976	Johnny Miller
1868	Tom Morris Jr.	1904	Jack White	1941	Not held	1977	Tom Watson
1869	Tom Morris Jr.	1905	James Braid	1942	Not held	1978	Jack Nicklaus
1870	Tom Morris Jr.	1906	James Braid	1943	Not held	1979	Seve Ballesteros
1871	Not held	1907	Arnaud Massy	1944	Not held	1980	Tom Watson
1872	Tom Morris Jr.	1908	James Braid	1945	Not held	1981	Bill Rogers
1873	Tom Kidd	1909	John H. Taylor	1946	Sam Snead	1982	Tom Watson
1874	Mungo Park	1910	James Braid	1947	Fred Daly	1983	Tom Watson
1875	Willie Park	1911	Harry Vardon	1948	Henry Cotton	1984	Seve Ballesteros
1876	Bob Martin	1912	Edward (Ted) Ray	1949	Bobby Locke	1985	Sandy Lyle
1877	Jamie Anderson	1913	John H. Taylor	1950	Bobby Locke	1986	Greg Norman
1878	Jamie Anderson	1914	Harry Vardon	1951	Max Faulkner	1987	Nick Faldo
1879	Jamie Anderson	1915	Not held	1952	Bobby Locke	1988	Seve Ballesteros
1880	Robert Ferguson	1916	Not held	1953	Ben Hogan	1989	Mark Calcavecchia
1881	Robert Ferguson	1917	Not held	1954	Peter Thomson	1990	Nick Faldo
1882	Robert Ferguson	1918	Not held	1955	Peter Thomson	1991	Ian Baker-Finch
1883	Willie Fernie	1919	Not held	1956	Peter Thomson	1992	Nick Faldo
1884	Jack Simpson	1920	George Duncan	1957	Bobby Locke	1993	Greg Norman
1885	Bob Martin	1921	Jock Hutchison	1958	Peter Thomson	1994	Nick Price
1886	David Brown	1922	Walter Hagen	1959	Gary Player	1995	John Daly
1887	Willie Park Jr.	1923	Arthur G. Havers	1960	Kel Nagle	1996	Tom Lehman
1888	Jack Burns	1924	Walter Hagen	1961	Arnold Palmer	1997	Justin Leonard
1889	Willie Park Jr.	1925	James M. Barnes	1962	Arnold Palmer	1998	Mark O'Meara
1890	John Ball	1926	Robert T. Jones Jr.	1963	Bob Charles	1999	Paul Lawrie
1891	Hugh Kirkaldy	1927	Robert T. Jones Jr.	1964	Tony Lema	2000	Tiger Woods
1892	Harold H. Hilton[1]	1928	Walter Hagen	1965	Peter Thomson	2001	David Duval
1893	William Auchterlonie	1929	Walter Hagen	1966	Jack Nicklaus	2002	Ernie Els
1894	John H. Taylor	1930	Robert T. Jones Jr.	1967	Roberto DeVicenzo	2003	Ben Curtis
1895	John H. Taylor	1931	Tommy D. Armour	1968	Gary Player		
		1932	Gene Sarazen				

PGA Championship

Year	Winner	Year	Winner	Year	Winner	Year	Winner
1916	James M. Barnes	1938	Paul Runyan	1960	Jay Hebert	1982	Raymond Floyd
1917	Not held	1939	Henry Picard	1961	Jerry Barber	1983	Hal Sutton
1918	Not held	1940	Byron Nelson	1962	Gary Player	1984	Lee Trevino
1919	James M. Barnes	1941	Vic Ghezzi	1963	Jack Nicklaus	1985	Hubert Green
1920	Jock Hutchison	1942	Sam Snead	1964	Bobby Nichols	1986	Bob Tway
1921	Walter Hagen	1943	Not held	1965	Dave Marr	1987	Larry Nelson
1922	Gene Sarazen	1944	Bob Hamilton	1966	Al Geiberger	1988	Jeff Sluman
1923	Gene Sarazen	1945	Byron Nelson	1967	Don January	1989	Payne Stewart
1924	Walter Hagen	1946	Ben Hogan	1968	Julius Boros	1990	Wayne Grady
1925	Walter Hagen	1947	Jim Ferrier	1969	Ray Floyd	1991	John Daly
1926	Walter Hagen	1948	Ben Hogan	1970	Dave Stockton	1992	Nick Price
1927	Walter Hagen	1949	Sam Snead	1971	Jack Nicklaus	1993	Paul Azinger
1928	Leo Diegel	1950	Chandler Harper	1972	Gary Player	1994	Nick Price
1929	Leo Diegel	1951	Sam Snead	1973	Jack Nicklaus	1995	Steve Elkington
1930	Tommy Armour	1952	Jim Turnesa	1974	Lee Trevino	1996	Mark Brooks
1931	Tom Creavy	1953	Walter Burkemo	1975	Jack Nicklaus	1997	Davis Love III
1932	Olin Dutra	1954	Chick Harbert	1976	Dave Stockton	1998	Vijay Singh
1933	Gene Sarazen	1955	Doug Ford	1977	Lanny Wadkins	1999	Tiger Woods
1934	Paul Runyan	1956	Jack Burke	1978	John Mahaffey	2000	Tiger Woods
1935	Johnny Revolta	1957	Lionel Hebert	1979	David Graham	2001	David Toms
1936	Denny Shute	1958	Dow Finsterwald	1980	Jack Nicklaus	2002	Rich Beem
1937	Denny Shute	1959	Bob Rosburg	1981	Larry Nelson	2003	Shaun Micheel

PGA Leading Money Winners, 1934–2002

Year	Name	Winnings	Year	Name	Winnings	Year	Name	Winnings
1934	Paul Runyan	$6,767	**1957**	Dick Mayer	$65,835	**1980**	Tom Watson	$530,808
1935	Johnny Revolta	9,543	**1958**	Arnold Palmer	42,607	**1981**	Tom Kite	375,698
1936	Horton Smith	7,682	**1959**	Art Wall	53,167	**1982**	Craig Stadler	446,462
1937	Harry Cooper	14,138	**1960**	Arnold Palmer	75,262	**1983**	Hal Sutton	426,668
1938	Sam Snead	19,534	**1961**	Gary Player	64,540	**1984**	Tom Watson	476,260
1939	Henry Picard	10,303	**1962**	Arnold Palmer	81,448	**1985**	Curtis Strange	542,321
1940	Ben Hogan	10,655	**1963**	Arnold Palmer	128,230	**1986**	Greg Norman	653,296
1941	Ben Hogan	18,358	**1964**	Jack Nicklaus	113,284	**1987**	Curtis Strange	925,941
1942	Ben Hogan	13,143	**1965**	Jack Nicklaus	140,752	**1988**	Curtis Strange	1,147,644
1943	No statistics compiled		**1966**	Billy Casper	121,944	**1989**	Tom Kite	1,395,278
1944	Byron Nelson	37,967[1]	**1967**	Jack Nicklaus	188,998	**1990**	Greg Norman	1,165,477
1945	Byron Nelson	63,335[1]	**1968**	Billy Casper	205,168	**1991**	Corey Pavin	979,430
1946	Ben Hogan	42,556	**1969**	Frank Beard	164,707	**1992**	Fred Couples	1,344,188
1947	Jimmy Demaret	27,936	**1970**	Lee Trevino	157,037	**1993**	Nick Price	1,478,557
1948	Ben Hogan	32,112	**1971**	Jack Nicklaus	244,490	**1994**	Nick Price	1,499,927
1949	Sam Snead	31,593	**1972**	Jack Nicklaus	320,542	**1995**	Greg Norman	1,654,959
1950	Sam Snead	35,758	**1973**	Jack Nicklaus	308,362	**1996**	Tom Lehman	1,780,159
1951	Lloyd Mangrum	26,088	**1974**	Johnny Miller	353,021	**1997**	Tiger Woods	2,066,833
1952	Julius Boros	37,032	**1975**	Jack Nicklaus	298,149	**1998**	David Duval	2,591,031
1953	Lew Worsham	34,002	**1976**	Jack Nicklaus	266,438	**1999**	Tiger Woods	6,616,585
1954	Bob Toski	65,819	**1977**	Tom Watson	310,653	**2000**	Tiger Woods	9,188,321
1955	Julius Boros	63,121	**1978**	Tom Watson	362,428	**2001**	Tiger Woods	5,687,777
1956	Ted Kroll	72,835	**1979**	Tom Watson	462,636	**2002**	Tiger Woods	6,912,625

1. Paid in War Bonds. **Source:** Professional Golfers' Association. www.pgatour.com

PGA Leading Money Winners, 2003 and Career

2003		Career			
Rank, Golfer	**Earnings**	**Rank, Golfer**	**Earnings**	**Rank, Golfer**	**Earnings**
1. Davis Love III	$5,122,038	**1.** Tiger Woods	$37,936,348	**11.** Justin Leonard	$15,867,559
2. Tiger Woods	4,832,496	**2.** Davis Love III	25,172,888	**12.** Mark Calcavecchia	15,613,242
3. Vijay Singh	4,523,224	**3.** Phil Mickelson	23,559,850	**13.** Hal Sutton	15,090,458
4. Mike Weir	4,508,938	**4.** Vijay Singh	22,804,239	**14.** Fred Couples	14,906,315
5. Jim Furyk	4,474,313	**5.** Nick Price	18,753,677	**15.** Jeff Sluman	14,194,332
6. Kenny Perry	4,090,755	**6.** Ernie Els	18,386,902	**16.** Tom Lehman	13,936,013
7. David Toms	3,298,740	**7.** Jim Furyk	18,331,156	**17.** Greg Norman	13,890,429
8. Ernie Els	3,078,372	**8.** Scott Hoch	17,160,499	**18.** Kenny Perry	13,647,767
9. Chad Campbell	2,509,889	**9.** David Duval	16,235,305	**19.** Mark O'Meara	13,136,119
10. Jay Haas	2,239,502	**10.** David Toms	16,173,220	**20.** Brad Faxon	12,866,945

Note: Figures are as of August 17, 2003. **Source:** Professional Golfers' Association (www.pga.com).

LPGA Leading Money Winners 1956–2002

Year	Player	Winnings	Year	Player	Winnings	Year	Player	Winnings
1956	Marlene Hagge	$20,235	**1972**	Kathy Whitworth	$65,063	**1988**	Sherri Turner	$350,851
1957	Patty Berg	16,272	**1973**	Kathy Whitworth	82,864	**1989**	Betsy King	654,132
1958	Beverly Hanson	12,629	**1974**	JoAnne Carner	87,094	**1990**	Beth Daniel	863,578
1959	Betsy Rawls	26,774	**1975**	Sandra Palmer	76,374	**1991**	Pat Bradley	763,118
1960	Louise Suggs	16,892	**1976**	Judy T. Rankin	150,734	**1992**	Dottie Mochrie	693,335
1961	Mickey Wright	22,238	**1977**	Judy T. Rankin	122,890	**1993**	Betsy King	595,992
1962	Mickey Wright	21,654	**1978**	Nancy Lopez	189,813	**1994**	Laura Davies	687,201
1963	Mickey Wright	31,269	**1979**	Nancy Lopez	197,488	**1995**	Annika Sorenstam	666,533
1964	Mickey Wright	29,800	**1980**	Beth Daniel	231,000	**1996**	Karrie Webb	1,002,000
1965	Kathy Whitworth	28,658	**1981**	Beth Daniel	206,977	**1997**	Annika Sorenstam	1,236,789
1966	Kathy Whitworth	33,517	**1982**	JoAnne Carner	310,399	**1998**	Annika Sorenstam	1,092,748
1967	Kathy Whitworth	32,937	**1983**	JoAnne Carner	291,404	**1999**	Karrie Webb	1,591,959
1968	Kathy Whitworth	48,379	**1984**	Betsy King	266,771	**2000**	Karrie Webb	1,876,853
1969	Carol Mann	49,152	**1985**	Nancy Lopez	416,472	**2001**	Annika Sorenstam	2,105,868
1970	Kathy Whitworth	30,235	**1986**	Pat Bradley	492,021	**2002**	Annika Sorenstam	2,863,904
1971	Kathy Whitworth	41,181	**1987**	Ayako Okamoto	466,034			

Source: Ladies Professional Golfers' Association. www.lpga.com

LPGA Leading Money Winners

2003		Career			
Rank, Golfer	**Earnings**	**Rank, Golfer**	**Earnings**	**Rank, Golfer**	**Earnings**
1. Annika Sorenstam	$1,214,063	**1.** Annika Sorenstam	$12,384,431	**11.** Pat Bradley	$5,746,685
2. Grace Park	880,767	**2.** Karrie Webb	8,993,161	**12.** Patty Sheehan	5,513,409
3. Se Ri Pak	725,446	**3.** Juli Inkster	8,240,733	**13.** Nancy Lopez	5,320,876
4. Hilary Lunke	599,208	**4.** Betsy King	7,449,427	**14.** Kelly Robbins	5,314,477
5. Juli Inkster	573,897	**5.** Beth Daniel	7,436,246	**15.** Lorie Kane	4,704,827
6. Rachel Teske	566,385	**6.** Rosie Jones	6,942,508	**16.** Liselotte Neumann	4,567,489
7. Angela Stanford	559,634	**7.** Meg Mallon	6,764,774	**17.** Sherri Steinhauer	3,960,033
8. Lorena Ochoa	558,119	**8.** Dottie Pepper	6,717,702	**18.** Tammie Green	3,808,436
9. Patricia Meunier-Lebouc	556,467	**9.** Se Ri Pak	6,450,208	**19.** Jane Geddes	3,794,559
10. Rosie Jones	536,162	**10.** Laura Davies	6,235,392	**20.** Brandie Burton	3,746,494

Note: As of July 21, 2003. Source: Ladies' Professional Golfers' Association. www.lpga.com

U.S. Women's Grand Slam Champions, 1972–2003

Until 1979, women's golf had two major championships: The LPGA and the U.S. Women's Open. The duMaurier Classic became the third major in 1979, and the Nabisco Championship was added in 1983. In 2001, the Women's British Open replaced the duMaurier. In the table below, the tournaments are listed in the order in which they occur during the year.

Year	Nabisco Championship	LPGA Championship	U.S. Women's Open	du Maurier Classic[1]
1972		Kathy Ahern	Susie Berning	
1973		Mary Mills	Susie Berning	
1974		Sandra Haynie	Sandra Haynie	
1975		Kathy Whitworth	Sandra Palmer	
1976		Betty Burfeindt	JoAnne Carner	
1977		Chako Higuchi	Hollis Stacy	
1978		Nancy Lopez	Hollis Stacy	
1979		Donna Caponi	Jerilyn Britz	Amy Alcott
1980		Sally Little	Amy Alcott	Pat Bradley
1981		Donna Caponi	Pat Bradley	Jan Stephenson
1982		Jan Stephenson	Janet Anderson	Sandra Haynie
1983	Amy Alcott	Patty Sheehan	Jan Stephenson	Hollis Stacy
1984	Juli Inkster	Patty Sheehan	Hollis Stacy	Juli Inkster
1985	Alice Miller	Nancy Lopez	Kathy Baker	Pat Bradley
1986	Pat Bradley	Pat Bradley	Jane Geddes	Pat Bradley
1987	Betsy King	Jane Geddes	Laura Davies	Jody Rosenthal
1988	Amy Alcott	Sherri Turner	Liselotte Neumann	Sally Little
1989	Juli Inkster	Nancy Lopez	Betsy King	Tammie Green
1990	Betsy King	Beth Daniel	Betsy King	Cathy Johnston
1991	Amy Alcott	Meg Mallon	Meg Mallon	Nancy Scranton
1992	Dottie Pepper	Betsy King	Patty Sheehan	Sherri Steinhauer
1993	Helen Alfredsson	Patty Sheehan	Lauri Merten	Brandie Burton
1994	Donna Andrews	Laura Davies	Patty Sheehan	Martha Nause
1995	Nanci Bowen	Kelly Robbins	Annika Sorenstam	Jenny Lidback
1996	Patty Sheehan	Laura Davies	Annika Sorenstam	Laura Davies
1997	Betsy King	Chris Johnson	Alison Nicholas	Colleen Walker
1998	Pat Hurst	Se Ri Pak	Se Ri Pak	Brandie Burton
1999	Dottie Pepper	Juli Inkster	Juli Inkster	Karrie Webb
2000	Karrie Webb	Juli Inkster	Karrie Webb	Meg Mallon
				Women's British Open[1]
2001	Annika Sorenstam	Karrie Webb	Karrie Webb	Se Ri Pak
2002	Annika Sorenstam	Se Ri Pak	Juli Inkster	Karrie Webb
2003	Patricia Meunier-Lebouc	Annika Sorenstam	Hilary Lunke	Annika Sorenstam

1. The Women's British Open replaced the duMaurier Classic as the fourth major in 2001. **Source:** LPGA

U.S. Women's Open Champions, 1946–71

Year	Champion	Year	Champion	Year	Champion	Year	Champion
1946	Patty Berg	**1953**	Betsy Rawls	**1960**	Betsy Rawls	**1966**	Sandra Spuzich
1947	Betty Jameson	**1954**	Babe Zaharias	**1961**	Mickey Wright	**1967**	Catherine LaCoste
1948	Babe Zaharias	**1955**	Fay Crocker	**1962**	Murle Breer	**1968**	Susie Berning
1949	Louise Suggs	**1956**	Kathy Cornelius	**1963**	Mary Mills	**1969**	Donna Caponi
1950	Babe Zaharias	**1957**	Betsy Rawls	**1964**	Mickey Wright	**1970**	Donna Caponi
1951	Betsy Rawls	**1958**	Mickey Wright	**1965**	Carol Mann	**1971**	JoAnne Carner
1952	Louise Suggs	**1959**	Mickey Wright				

TENNIS

▸THE GRAND SLAM CHAMPIONSHIPS

The four tournaments that constitute the Grand Slam are the Australian, French, Wimbledon (officially known as the All-England Club's Lawn Tennis Championships), and U.S. championships. A challenge round system, in which the defending champion automatically qualified for the following year's final, was used at Wimbledon from 1877-1921 and at the U.S. Championships from 1884-1911. Prior to 1925, the French Open was restricted to members of French clubs, and from 1941-45, it was closed to all foreigners. Wimbledon, the French, and U.S. Championships became open to amateurs and pros in 1968; the Australian championships joined the open era a year later. Five players have achieved the Grand Slam, winning all four championships in the same year: Don Budge (1938), Maureen Connolly (with straight set victories in all four finals in 1953), Rod Laver (1962 and 1969), Margaret Court (1970) and Steffi Graf (1988). Martina Navratilova (1983-84) and Serena Williams (2002-03) have won the four tournaments consecutively, but not in the same calendar year.

Men's Grand Slam Champions 1920-2003

Year	Australian Champion	French Champion	Wimbledon Champion	U.S. Champion
1920	Pat O'Hara Wood	—	Bill Tilden	Bill Tilden
1921	Rhys H. Gemmell	—	Bill Tilden	Bill Tilden
1922	Pat O'Hara Wood	—	Gerald L. Patterson	Bill Tilden
1923	Pat O'Hara Wood	—	William M. Johnston	Bill Tilden
1924	James Anderson	—	Jean Borotra	Bill Tilden
1925	James Anderson	Rene Lacoste	Rene Lacoste	Bill Tilden
1926	John Hawkes	Henri Cochet	Jean Borotra	Rene Lacoste
1927	Gerald Patterson	Rene Lacoste	Henri Cochet	Rene Lacoste
1928	Jean Borotra	Henri Cochet	Rene Lacoste	Henri Cochet
1929	John C. Gregory	Rene Lacoste	Henri Cochet	Bill Tilden
1930	Gar Moon	Henri Cochet	Bill Tilden	John H. Doeg
1931	Jack Crawford	Jean Borotra	Sidney B.Wood Jr.	H. Ellsworth Vines
1932	Jack Crawford	Henri Cochet	Ellsworth Vines	H. Ellsworth Vines
1933	Jack Crawford	John H. Crawford	Jack Crawford	Fred Perry
1934	Fred J. Perry	Gottfried von Cramm	Fred Perry	Fred Perry
1935	Jack Crawford	Fred J. Perry	Fred Perry	Wilmer L. Allison
1936	Adrian Quist	Gottfried von Cramm	Fred Perry	Fred Perry
1937	Vivian B. McGrath	Henner Henkel	Don Budge	Don Budge
1938[1]	Don Budge	Don Budge	Don Budge	Don Budge
1939	John Bromwich	W. Donald McNeill	Bobby Riggs	Bobby Riggs
1940	Adrian Quist	No competition	Not Held	Donald McNeill
1941	Foreigners excluded	Bernard Destremau	Not Held	Bobby Riggs
1942	Foreigners excluded	Bernard Destremau	Not Held	Frederick Schroeder
1943	Foreigners excluded	Yvon Petra	Not Held	Joseph R. Hunt
1944	Foreigners excluded	Yvon Petra	Not Held	Frank Parker
1945	Foreigners excluded	Yvon Petra	Not Held	Frank Parker
1946	John Bromwich	Marcel Bernard	Yvon Petra	Jack Kramer
1947	Dinny Pails	Joseph Asboth	Jack Kramer	Jack Kramer
1948	Adrian Quist	Frank Parker	Bob Falkenburg	Pancho Gonzales
1949	Frank Sedgman	Frank Parker	Ted Schroeder	Pancho Gonzales
1950	Frank Sedgman	Budge Patty	Budge Patty	Arthur Larsen
1951	Richard Savitt	Jaroslav Drobny	Dick Savitt	Frank Sedgman
1952	Ken McGregor	Jaroslav Drobny	Frank Sedgman	Frank Sedgman
1953	Ken Rosewall	Ken Rosewall	Vic Seixas	Tony Trabert
1954	Mervyn Rose	Tony Trabert	Jaroslav Drobny	E. Victor Seixas Jr.
1955	Ken Rosewall	Tony Trabert	Tony Trabert	Tony Trabert
1956	Lew Hoad	Lew Hoad	Lew Hoad	Ken Rosewall
1957	Ashley Cooper	Sven Davidson	Lew Hoad	Malcolm Anderson
1958	Ashley Cooper	Mervyn Rose	Ashley Cooper	Ashley J. Cooper
1959	Alex Olmedo	Nicola Pietrangeli	Alex Olmedo	Neale Fraser
1960	Rod Laver	Nicola Pietrangeli	Neale Fraser	Neale Fraser
1961	Roy Emerson	Manuel Santana	Rod Laver	Roy Emerson
1962[1]	Rod Laver	Rod Laver	Rod Laver	Rod Laver
1963	Roy Emerson	Roy Emerson	Chuck McKinley	Rafael Osuna
1964	Roy Emerson	Manuel Santana	Roy Emerson	Roy Emerson
1965	Roy Emerson	Fred Stolle	Roy Emerson	Manuel Santana
1966	Roy Emerson	Tony Roche	Manuel Santana	Fred Stolle
1967	Roy Emerson	Roy Emerson	John Newcombe	John Newcombe
1968	Bill Bowrey	Ken Rosewall	Rod Laver	Arthur Ashe
1969[1]	Rod Laver	Rod Laver	Rod Laver	Rod Laver
1970	Arthur Ashe	Jan Kodes	John Newcombe	Ken Rosewall

Year	Australian Champion	French Champion	Wimbledon Champion	U.S. Champion
1971	Ken Rosewall	Jan Kodes	John Newcombe	Stan Smith
1972	Ken Rosewall	Andres Gimeno	Stan Smith	Ilie Nastase
1973	John Newcombe	Ilie Nastase	Jan Kodes	John Newcombe
1974	Jimmy Connors	Bjorn Borg	Jimmy Connors	Jimmy Connors
1975	John Newcombe	Bjorn Borg	Arthur Ashe	Manuel Orantes
1976	Mark Edmondson	Adriano Panatta	Bjorn Borg	Jimmy Connors
1977	Roscoe Tanner[2] Vitas Gerulaitis[2]	Guillermo Vilas	Bjorn Borg	Guillermo Vilas
1978	Guillermo Vilas	Bjorn Borg	Bjorn Borg	Jimmy Connors
1979	Guillermo Vilas	Bjorn Borg	Bjorn Borg	John McEnroe
1980	Brian Teacher	Bjorn Borg	Bjorn Borg	John McEnroe
1981	Johan Kriek	Bjorn Borg	John McEnroe	John McEnroe
1982	Johan Kriek	Mats Wilander	Jimmy Connors	Jimmy Connors
1983	Mats Wilander	Yannick Noah	John McEnroe	Jimmy Connors
1984	Mats Wilander	Ivan Lendl	John McEnroe	John McEnroe
1985	Stefan Edberg	Mats Wilander	Boris Becker	Ivan Lendl
1986	Moved to Jan. 1987	Ivan Lendl	Boris Becker	Ivan Lendl
1987	Stefan Edberg	Ivan Lendl	Pat Cash	Ivan Lendl
1988	Mats Wilander	Mats Wilander	Stefan Edberg	Mats Wilander
1989	Ivan Lendl	Michael Chang	Boris Becker	Boris Becker
1990	Ivan Lendl	Andrés Gomez	Stefan Edberg	Pete Sampras
1991	Boris Becker	Jim Courier	Michael Stich	Stefan Edberg
1992	Jim Courier	Jim Courier	Andre Agassi	Stefan Edberg
1993	Jim Courier	Sergi Bruguera	Pete Sampras	Pete Sampras
1994	Pete Sampras	Sergi Bruguera	Pete Sampras	Andre Agassi
1995	Andre Agassi	Thomas Muster	Pete Sampras	Pete Sampras
1996	Boris Becker	Yevgeny Kafelnikov	Richard Krajicek	Pete Sampras
1997	Pete Sampras	Gustavo Kuerten	Pete Sampras	Patrick Rafter
1998	Petr Korda	Carlos Moya	Pete Sampras	Patrick Rafter
1999	Yevgeny Kafelnikov	Andre Agassi	Pete Sampras	Andre Agassi
2000	Andre Agassi	Gustavo Kuerten	Pete Sampras	Marat Safin
2001	Andre Agassi	Gustavo Kuerten	Goran Ivanisevic	Lleyton Hewitt
2002	Thomas Johansson	Albert Costa	Lleyton Hewitt	Pete Sampras
2003	Andre Agassi	Juan Carlos Ferrero	Roger Federer	Andy Roddick

1. Grand Slam winner. 2. Two tournaments were held in 1977, the first in January, the second in December.

Women's Grand Slam Champions, 1920–2003

Year	Australian Champion	French Champion	Wimbledon Champion	U.S. Champion
1920	Not held	Suzanne Lenglen	Suzanne Lenglen	Molla Bjurstedt Mallory
1921	Not held	Suzanne Lenglen	Suzanne Lenglen	Molla Bjurstedt Mallory
1922	Margaret Molesworth	Suzanne Lenglen	Suzanne Lenglen	Molla Bjurstedt Mallory
1923	Margaret Molesworth	Suzanne Lenglen	Suzanne Lenglen	Helen Wills
1924	Sylvia Lance	Diddie Vlasto	Kathleen McKane	Helen Wills
1925	Daphne Akhurst	Suzanne Lenglen	Suzanne Lenglen	Helen Wills
1926	Daphne Akhurst	Suzanne Lenglen	Kathleen McKane Godfree	Molla Bjurstedt Mallory
1927	Edna Boyd	Kea Bouman	Helen Wills	Helen Wills
1928	Daphne Akhurst	Helen Wills	Helen Wills	Helen Wills
1929	Daphne Akhurst	Helen Wills	Helen Wills	Helen Wills
1930	Daphne Akhurst	Helen Wills Moody	Helen Wills Moody	Betty Nuthall
1931	Coral Buttsworth	Cilly Aussem	Cilly Aussem	Helen Wills Moody
1932	Coral Buttsworth	Helen Wills Moody	Helen Wills Moody	Helen Jacobs
1933	Joan Hartigan	Margaret Scriven	Helen Wills Moody	Helen Jacobs
1934	Joan Hartigan	Margaret Scriven	Dorothy Round	Helen Jacobs
1935	Dorothy Round	Hilde Sperling	Helen Wills Moody	Helen Jacobs
1936	Joan Hartigan	Hilde Sperling	Helen Jacobs	Alice Marble
1937	Nancye Wynne Bolton	Hilde Sperling	Dorothy Round	Anita Lizane
1938	Dorothy Bundy	Simone Mathieu	Helen Wills Moody	Alice Marble
1939	Emily Westacott	Simone Mathieu	Alice Marble	Alice Marble
1940	Nancye Wynne Bolton	Not Held	Not Held	Alice Marble
1941	Not Held	Not Held	Not Held	Sarah Palfrey Cooke
1942	Not Held	Not Held	Not Held	Pauline Betz
1943	Not Held	Not Held	Not Held	Pauline Betz
1944	Not Held	Not Held	Not Held	Pauline Betz Cooke
1945	Not Held	Not Held	Not Held	Sarah Palfrey Cooke

Year	Australian Champion	French Champion	Wimbledon Champion	U.S. Champion
1946	Nancye Wynne Bolton	Margaret Osborne	Pauline Betz	Pauline Betz
1947	Nancye Wynne Bolton	Patricia Todd	Margaret Osborne	Louise Brough
1948	Nancye Wynne Bolton	Nelly Landry	Louise Brough	Margaret Osborne duPont
1949	Doris Hart	Margaret Osborne duPont	Louise Brough	Margaret Osborne duPont
1950	Louise Brough	Doris Hart	Louise Brough	Margaret Osborne duPont
1951	Nancye Wynne Bolton	Shirley Fry	Doris Hart	Maureen Connolly
1952	Thelma Long	Doris Hart	Maureen Connolly	Maureen Connolly
1953[1]	Maureen Connolly	Maureen Connolly	Maureen Connolly	Maureen Connolly
1954	Thelma Long	Maureen Connolly	Maureen Connolly	Doris Hart
1955	Beryl Penrose	Angela Mortimer	Louise Brough	Doris Hart
1956	Mary Carter	Althea Gibson	Shirley Fry	Shirley Fry
1957	Shirley Fry	Shirley Bloomer	Althea Gibson	Althea Gibson
1958	Angela Mortimer	Zsuzsi Kormoczy	Althea Gibson	Althea Gibson
1959	Mary Carter Reitano	Christine Truman	Maria Bueno	Maria Bueno
1960	Margaret Smith	Darlene Hard	Maria Bueno	Darlene Hard
1961	Margaret Smith	Ann Haydon	Angela Mortimer	Darlene Hard
1962	Margaret Smith	Margaret Smith	Karen Hantze Susman	Margaret Smith
1963	Margaret Smith	Lesley Turner	Margaret Smith	Maria Bueno
1964	Margaret Smith	Margaret Smith	Maria Bueno	Maria Bueno
1965	Margaret Smith	Lesley Turner	Margaret Smith	Margaret Smith
1966	Margaret Smith	Ann Jones	Billie Jean King	Maria Bueno
1967	Nancy Richey	Francoise Durr	Billie Jean King	Billie Jean King
1968	Billie Jean King	Nancy Richey	Billie Jean King	Virginia Wade
1969	Margaret Smith Court	Margaret Smith Court	Ann Jones	Margaret Smith Court
1970[1]	Margaret Smith Court	Margaret Smith Court	Margaret Smith Court	Margaret Smith Court
1971	Margaret Smith Court	Evonne Goolagong	Evonne Goolagong	Billie Jean King
1972	Virginia Wade	Billie Jean King	Billie Jean King	Billie Jean King
1973	Margaret Smith Court	Margaret Smith Court	Billie Jean King	Margaret Smith Court
1974	Evonne Goolagong	Chris Evert	Chris Evert	Billie Jean King
1975	Evonne Goolagong	Chris Evert	Billie Jean King	Chris Evert
1976	Evonne Goolagong Cawley	Sue Barker	Chris Evert	Chris Evert
1977	Kerry Melville Reid[2] Evonne Goolagong Cawley[2]	Mima Jasuovec	Virginia Wade	Chris Evert
1978	Chris O'Neil	Virginia Ruzici	Martina Navratilova	Chris Evert
1979	Barbara Jordan	Chris Evert Lloyd	Martina Navratilova	Tracy Austin
1980	Hana Mandlikova	Chris Evert Lloyd	Evonne Goolagong Cawley	Chris Evert Lloyd
1981	Martina Navratilova	Hana Mandlikova	Chris Evert Lloyd	Tracy Austin
1982	Chris Evert Lloyd	Martina Navratilova	Martina Navratilova	Chris Evert Lloyd
1983	Martina Navratilova	Chris Evert Lloyd	Martina Navratilova	Martina Navratilova
1984	Chris Evert Lloyd	Martina Navratilova	Martina Navratilova	Martina Navratilova
1985	Martina Navratilova	Chris Evert Lloyd	Martina Navratilova	Hana Mandlikova
1986	Moved to Jan. 1987	Chris Evert Lloyd	Martina Navratilova	Martina Navratilova
1987	Hana Mandlikova	Steffi Graf	Martina Navratilova	Martina Navratilova
1988[1]	Steffi Graf	Steffi Graf	Steffi Graf	Steffi Graf
1989	Steffi Graf	Arantxa Sanchez	Steffi Graf	Steffi Graf
1990	Steffi Graf	Monica Seles	Martina Navratilova	Gabriela Sabatini
1991	Monica Seles	Monica Seles	Steffi Graf	Monica Seles
1992	Monica Seles	Monica Seles	Steffi Graf	Monica Seles
1993	Monica Seles	Steffi Graf	Steffi Graf	Steffi Graf
1994	Steffi Graf	Arantxa Sánchez Vicario	Conchita Martinez	Arantxa Sánchez Vicario
1995	Mary Pierce	Steffi Graf	Steffi Graf	Steffi Graf
1996	Monica Seles	Steffi Graf	Steffi Graf	Steffi Graf
1997	Martina Hingis	Iva Majoli	Martina Hingis	Martina Hingis
1998	Martina Hingis	Arantxa Sánchez Vicario	Jana Novotna	Lindsay Davenport
1999	Martina Hingis	Steffi Graf	Lindsay Davenport	Serena Williams
2000	Lindsay Davenport	Mary Pierce	Venus Williams	Venus Williams
2001	Jennifer Capriati	Jennifer Capriati	Venus Williams	Venus Williams
2002	Jennifer Capriati	Serena Williams	Serena Williams	Serena Williams
2003	Serena Williams	Justine Henin-Hardenne	Serena Williams	Justine Henin-Hardenne

1. Grand Slam winner. 2. Two tournaments were held in 1977, the first in January, the second in December.

THOROUGHBRED RACING

Thoroughbred Horse of the Year (Eclipse Award)

Year	Horse	Year	Horse	Year	Horse	Year	Horse
1936	Granville	**1953**	Tom Fool	**1970**	Personality	**1987**	Ferdinand
1937	War Admiral	**1954**	Native Dancer	**1971**	Ack Ack	**1988**	Alysheba
1938	Seabiscuit	**1955**	Nashua	**1972**	Secretariat	**1989**	Sunday Silence
1939	Challedon	**1956**	Swaps	**1973**	Secretariat	**1990**	Criminal Type
1940	Challedon	**1957**	Bold Ruler	**1974**	Forego	**1991**	Black Tie Affair
1941	Whirlaway	**1958**	Round Table	**1975**	Forego	**1992**	A.P. Indy
1942	Whirlaway	**1959**	Sword Dancer	**1976**	Forego	**1993**	Kotashaan
1943	Count Fleet	**1960**	Kelso	**1977**	Seattle Slew	**1994**	Holy Bull
1944	Twilight Tear	**1961**	Kelso	**1978**	Affirmed	**1995**	Cigar
1945	Busher	**1962**	Kelso	**1979**	Affirmed	**1996**	Cigar
1946	Assault	**1963**	Kelso	**1980**	Spectacular Bid	**1997**	Favorite Trick
1947	Armed	**1964**	Kelso	**1981**	John Henry	**1998**	Skip Away
1948	Citation	**1965**	Moccasin	**1982**	Conquistador Cielo	**1999**	Charismatic
1949	Capot	**1966**	Buckpasser	**1983**	All Along	**2000**	Tiznow
1950	Hill Prince	**1967**	Damascus	**1984**	John Henry	**2001**	Point Given
1951	Counterpoint	**1968**	Dr. Fager	**1985**	Spend a Buck	**2002**	Azeri
1952	Native Dancer	**1969**	Arts and Letters	**1986**	Lady's Secret		

Source: *The Jockey Club*

The Triple Crown Winners

Only 11 horses have won the Kentucky Derby, the Preakness, and the Belmont Stakes in the same year.

Year	Horse	Year	Horse	Year	Horse	Year	Horse
1919	Sir Barton	**1937**	War Admiral	**1946**	Assault	**1977**	Seattle Slew
1930	Gallant Fox	**1941**	Whirlaway	**1948**	Citation	**1978**	Affirmed
1935	Omaha	**1943**	Count Fleet	**1973**	Secretariat		

The Breeders' Cup

Thoroughbred racing's richest, most glamorous, and most exciting day of the year attracts the finest horses in the world for record purses as high as $4 million. The site changes from year to year.

BREEDER'S CUP JUVENILE

Purse: $1 million **Distance: 1⅛ miles**

Year	Winner	Jockey	Time
1984[1]	Chief's Crown	D. MacBeth	1:36.1
1985[1]	Tasso	L. Pincay Jr.	1:36.1
1986	Capote	L. Pincay Jr.	1:43.4
1987[1]	Success Express	J. Santos	1:35.1
1988[1]	Is It True	L. Pincay Jr.	1:36.3
1989	Rhythm	C. Perret	1:43.3
1990	Fly So Free	J. Santos	1:43.2
1991	Arazi	P. Valenzuela	1:44.78
1992	Gilded Time	C. McCarron	1:43.43
1993	Brocco	G. Stevens	1:42.99
1994	Timber Country	P. Day	1:44.55
1995	Unbridled's Song	M. Smith	1:41.60
1996	Boston Harbor	J. Bailey	1:43.40
1997	Favorite Trick	P. Day	1:41.47
1998	Answer Lively	J. Bailey	1:44.00
1999	Anees	G. Stevens	1:42.29
2000	Macho Uno	J. Bailey	1:42.05
2001	Johannesburg	M. Kinane	1:42.27
2002	Vindication	M. Smith	1:49.61

BREEDER'S CUP JUVENILE FILLIES

Purse: $1 million **Distance: 1⅛ miles**

Year	Winner	Jockey	Time
1984[1]	Outstandingly	W. Guerra	1:37.4
1985[1]	Twilight Ridge	J. Velasquez	1:35.4
1986	Brave Raj	P. Valenzuela	1:43.1
1987[1]	Epitome	P. Day	1:36.2
1988	Open Mind	A. Cordero Jr.	1:46.3
1989	Go For Wand	R. Romero	1:44.1
1990	Meadow Star	J. Santos	1:44.0
1991	Pleasant Stage	E. Delahoussaye	1:46.48
1992	Eliza	P. Valenzuela	1:42.93
1993	Phone Chatter	L. Pincay Jr.	1:43.08
1994	Flanders	P. Day	1:45.28
1995	My Flag	J. Bailey	1:42.55
1996	Storm Song	C. Perret	1:43.60
1997	Countess Diana	S. Sellers	1:42.11
1998	Silverbulletday	G. Stevens	1:43.68
1999	Cash Run	J. Bailey	1:36.32
2000	Caressing	J. Velasquez	1:42.77
2001	Tempera	D. Flores	1:41.49
2002	Storm Flag Flying	J. Velasquez	1:49.60

BREEDER'S CUP SPRINT

Purse: $1 million **Distance: 6 furlongs**

Year	Winner	Jockey	Time
1984	Eillo	C. Perret	1:10.1
1985	Precisionist	C. McCarron	1:08.2
1986	Smile	J. Vasquez	1:08.2
1987	Very Subtle	P. Valenzuela	1:08.4
1988	Gulch	A. Cordero Jr.	1:10.2
1989	Dancing Spree	A. Cordero Jr.	1:09.0
1990	Safely Kept	C. Perret	1:09.3
1991	Sheik Albadou	P. Eddery	1:09.36
1992	30 Slews	E. Delahoussaye	1:08.21
1993	Cardmania	E. Delahoussaye	1:08.76
1994	Cherokee Run	M. Smith	1:09.54
1995	Desert Stormer	K. Desormeaux	1:09.14
1996	Lit de Justice	C. Nakatani	1:08.60
1997	Elmhurst	C. Nakatani	1:08.01
1998	Reraise	C. Nakatani	1:09.07
1999	Artax	J. Chavez	1:07.89
2000	Kona Gold	A. Solis	1:07.77
2001	Squirtle Squirt	J. Bailey	1:08.41
2001	Orientate	J. Bailey	1:08.89

BREEDER'S CUP MILE

Purse: $1 million **Distance: 1 mile, turf.**

Year	Winner	Jockey	Time
1984	Royal Heroine	F. Toro	1:32.3
1985	Cozzene	W. Guerra	1:35.0
1986	Last Tycoon	Y. Saint-Martin	1:35.1
1987	Miesque	F. Head	1:32.4
1988	Miesque	F. Head	1:38.3
1989	Steinlen	J. Santos	1:37.1
1990	Royal Academy	L. Piggott	1:35.1
1991	Opening Verse	P. Valenzuela	1:37.59
1992	Lure	M. Smith	1:32.90
1993	Lure	M. Smith	1:33.58
1994	Barathea	L. Dettori	1:34.50
1995	Ridgewood Pearl	J. Murtagh	1:43.65
1996	Da Hoss	G. Stevens	1:35.80
1997	Spinning World	C. Asmussen	1:32.77
1998	Da Hoss	J. Velazquez	1:35.27
1999	Silic	C. Nakatani	1:34.26
2000	War Chant	G. Stevens	1:34.67
2001	Val Royal	J. Valdivia Jr.	1:32.05
2002	Domedriver	T. Thulliez	1:36.92

BREEDER'S CUP DISTAFF

Purse: $2 million **Distance: 1⅛ miles**

Year	Winner	Jockey	Time
1984[2]	Princess Rooney	E. Delahoussaye	2:02.2
1985[2]	Life's Magic	A. Cordero Jr.	2:02.0
1986[2]	Lady's Secret	P. Day	2:01.1
1987[2]	Sacahuista	R. Romero	2:02.4
1988	Personal Ensign	R. Romero	1:52.0
1989	Bayakoa	L. Pincay Jr.	1:47.2
1990	Bayakoa	L. Pincay Jr.	1:49.1
1991	Dance Smartly	P. Day	1:50.95
1992	Paseana	C. McCarron	1:48.17
1993	Hollywood Wildcat	E. Delahoussaye	1:48.35
1994	One Dreamer	G. Stevens	1:50.70
1995	Inside Information	M. Smith	1:46.15
1996	Jewel Princess	C. Nakatani	1:48.40
1997	Ajina	M. Smith	1:47.20
1998	Escena	G. Stevens	1:49.89
1999	Beautiful Pleasure	J. Chavez	1:47.56
2000	Spain	V. Espinoza	1:47.66
2001	Unbridled Elaine	P. Day	1:49.21
2002	Azeri	M. Smith	1:48.64

BREEDER'S CUP TURF

Purse: $2 million **Distance: 1½ miles**

Year	Winner	Jockey	Time
1984	Lashkari	Y. Saint-Martin	2:25.1
1985	Pebbles	P. Eddery	2:27.0
1986	Manila	J. Santos	2:25.2
1987	Theatrical	P. Day	2:24.2
1988	Great Communicator	R. Sibille	2:35.1
1989	Prized	E. Delahoussaye	2:28.0
1990	In the Wings	G. Stevens	2:29.3
1991	Miss Alleged	E. Legrix	2:30.95
1992	Fraise	P. Valenzuela	2:24.08
1993	Kotashaan	K. Desormeaux	2:25.16
1994	Tikkanen	M. Smith	2:26.50
1995	Northern Spur	C. McCarron	2:42.07
1996	Pilsudski	W. Swinburn	2:30.20
1997	Chief Bearhart	J. Santos	2:23.92
1998	Buck's Boy	S. Sellers	2:28.74
1999	Daylami	L. Dettori	2:24.73
2000	Kalanisi	J. Murtagh	2:26.96
2001	Fantastic Light	L. Dettori	2:24.36
2002	High Chaparral	M. Kinane	2:30.14

BREEDER'S CUP CLASSIC

Purse: $4 million **Distance: 1¼ miles**

Year	Winner	Jockey	Time
1984	Wild Again	P. Day	2:03.2
1985	Proud Truth	J. Velasquez	2:00.4
1986	Skywalker	L. Pincay Jr.	2:00.2
1987	Ferdinand	B. Shoemaker	2:01.2
1988	Alysheba	C. McCarron	2:04.4
1989	Sunday Silence	C. McCarron	2:00.1
1990	Unbridled	P. Day	2:02.1
1991	Black Tie Affair	J. Bailey	2:02.95
1992	A.P. Indy	E. Delahoussaye	2:00.20
1993	Arcangues	J. Bailey	2:00.83
1994	Concern	P. Day	2:02.41
1995	Cigar	J. Bailey	1:59.58
1996	Alphabet Soup	C. McCarron	2:01.00
1997	Skip Away	M. Smith	1:59.16
1998	Awesome Again	P. Day	2:02.16
1999	Cat Thief	P. Day	1:59.52
2000	Tiznow	C. McCarron	2:00.75
2001	Tiznow	C. McCarron	2:00.62
2002	Volponi	J. Santos	2:01.39

BREEDER'S CUP FILLIES AND MARES TURF

Purse: $1 million **Distance: 1¼ miles**

Year	Winner	Jockey	Time
1999	Soaring Softly	J. Bailey	2:13.89
2000	Perfect Sting	J. Bailey	2:13.07
2001	Banks Hill	O. Peslier	2:00.36
2002	Starine	J. Velasquez	2:03.57

BREEDER'S CUP LOCATIONS

1984	Hollywood	1994	Churchill Downs
1985	Aqueduct	1995	Belmont Park
1986	Santa Anita	1996	Woodbine
1987	Hollywood	1997	Hollywood
1988	Churchill Downs	1998	Churchill Downs
1989	Gulfstream	1999	Gulfstream
1990	Belmont Park	2000	Churchill Downs
1991	Churchill Downs	2001	Belmont Park
1992	Gulfstream	2002	Arlington Park
1993	Santa Anita	2003	Santa Anita

Note: Before 1991, decimals refer to fifths of a second. 1. One mile. 2. 1¼ miles

Kentucky Derby, 1875–2003

"The Run for the Roses," is the first leg of racing's Triple Crown for three-year-olds. It is always on the first Saturday in May. The distance was 1½ miles until 1896, 1¼ miles thereafter. **Site: Churchill Downs,** Louisville.

Year	Horse	Jockey	Time
1875	Aristides	O. Lewis	2:37¾
1876	Vagrant	R. Swim	2:38¼
1877	Baden-Baden	W. Walker	2:38.0
1878	Day Star	J. Carter	2:37¼
1879	Lord Murphy	C. Shauer	2:37.0
1880	Fonso	G. Lewis	2:37½
1881	Hindoo	J. McLaughlin	2:40.0
1882	Apollo	B. Hurd	2:40¼
1883	Leonatus	W. Donohue	2:43.0
1884	Buchanan	I. Murphy	2:40¼
1885	Joe Cotton	E. Henderson	2:37¼
1886	Ben Ali	P. Duffy	2:36½
1887	Montrose	I. Lewis	2:39¼
1888	MacBeth II	G. Covington	2:38¼
1889	Spokane	T. Kiley	2:34½
1890	Riley	I. Murphy	2:45.0
1891	Kingman	I. Murphy	2:52¼
1892	Azra	A. Clayton	2:41½
1893	Lookout	E. Kunze	2:39¼
1894	Chant	F. Goodale	2:41.0
1895	Halma	J. Perkins	2:37½
1896	Ben Brush	W. Simms	2:07¾
1897	Typhoon II	F. Garner	2:12½
1898	Plaudit	W. Simms	2:09.0
1899	Manuel	F. Taral	2:12.0
1900	Lieut.Gibson	J. Boland	2:06¼
1900	Lieut. Gibson	J. Boland	2:06¼
1901	His Eminence	J. Winkfield	2:07¾
1902	Alan-a-Dale	J. Winkfield	2:08¼
1903	Judge Himes	H. Booker	2:09.0
1904	Elwood	F. Prior	2:08½
1905	Agile	J. Martin	2:10¾
1906	Sir Huon	R. Troxler	2:08.4
1907	Pink Star	A. Minder	2:12.3
1908	Stone Street	A. Pickens	2:15.1
1909	Wintergreen	V. Powers	2:08.1
1910	Donau	F. Herbert	2:06.2
1911	Meridan	G. Archibald	2:05.0
1912	Worth	C. H. Shilling	2:09.2
1913	Donerall	R. Goose	2:04.4
1914	Old Rosebud	J. McCabe	2:03.2
1915	Regret	J. Notter	2:05.2
1916	George Smith	J. Loftus	2:04.3
1917	Omar Khayyam	C. Borel	2:04.0
1918	Exterminator	W. Knapp	2:10.4
1919	**Sir Barton**	J. Loftus	2:09.4
1920	Paul Jones	T. Rice	2:09.0
1921	Behave Yourself	C. Thompson	2:04.1
1922	Morvich	A. Johnson	2:04.3
1923	Zev	E. Sande	2:05.2
1924	Black Gold	J. D. Mooney	2:05.1
1925	Flying Ebony	E. Sande	2:07.3
1926	Bubbling Over	A. Johnson	2:03.4
1927	Whiskery	L. McAtee	2:06.0
1928	Reigh Count	C. Lang	2:10.2
1929	Clyde Van Dusen	L. McAtee	2:10.4
1930	**Gallant Fox**	E. Sande	2:07.3
1931	Twenty Grand	C. Kurtsinger	2:01.4
1932	Burgoo King	E. James	2:05.1
1933	Brokers Tip	D. Meade	2:06.4
1934	Cavalcade	M. Garner	2:04.0
1935	**Omaha**	W. Saunders	2:05.0
1936	Bold Venture	I. Hanford	2:03.3
1937	**War Admiral**	C. Kurtsinger	2:03.1
1938	Lawrin	E. Arcaro	2:04.4
1939	Johnston	J. Stout	2:03.2
1940	Gallahadion	C. Bierman	2:05.0
1941	**Whirlaway**	E. Arcaro	2:01.2
1942	Shut Out	W. D. Write	2:04.2
1943	**Count Fleet**	J. Longden	2:04.0
1944	Pensive	C. McCreary	2:04.1
1945	Hoop Jr.	E. Arcaro	2:07.0
1946	**Assault**	W. Mehrtens	2:06.3
1947	Jet Pilot	E. Guerin	2:06.3
1948	**Citation**	E. Arcaro	2:05.2
1949	Ponder	S. Brooks	2:04.1
1950	Middleground	W. Boland	2:01.3
1951	Count Turf	C. McCreary	2:02.3
1952	Hill Gail	E. Arcaro	2:01.3
1953	Dark Star	H. Moreno	2:02.0
1954	Determine	R. York	2:03.0
1955	Swaps	W. Shoemaker	2:01.4
1956	Needles	D. Erb	2:03.2
1957	Iron Liege	W. Hartack	2:02.1
1958	Tim Tam	I. Valenzuela	2:05.0
1959	Tommy Lee	W. Shoemaker	2:02.1
1960	Venetian Way	W. Hartack	2:02.2
1961	Carry Back	J. Sellers	2:04.0
1962	Decidedly	W. Hartack	2:00.2
1963	Chateaugay	B. Baeza	2:01.4
1964	Northern Dancer	W. Hartack	2:00.0
1965	Lucky Debonair	W. Shoemaker	2:01.1
1966	Kauai King	D. Brumfield	2:02.0
1967	Proud Clarion	R. Ussery	2:00.3
1968	Forward Pass[1]	R. Ussery	2:02.1
1969	Majestic Prince	W. Hartack	2:01.4
1970	Dust Commander	M. Manganello	2:03.2
1971	Canonero II	G. Avila	2:03.1
1972	Riva Ridge	R. Turcotte	2:01.4
1973	**Secretariat**[2]	R. Turcotte	1:59.2
1974	Cannonade	A. Cordero	2:04.0
1975	Foolish Pleasure	J. Vasquez	2:02.0
1976	Bold Forbes	A. Cordero	2:01.3
1977	**Seattle Slew**	J. Cruquet	2:02.1
1978	**Affirmed**	S. Cauthen	2:01.1
1979	Spectacular Bid	R. Franklin	2:02.2
1980	Genuine Risk	J. Vasquez	2:02.0
1981	Pleasant Colony	J. Velasquez	2:02.0
1982	Gato Del Sol	E. Delahoussaye	2:02.2
1983	Sunny's Halo	E. Delahoussaye	2:02.1
1984	Swale	L. Pincay	2:02.2
1985	Spend A Buck	A. Cordero	2:00.1
1986	Ferdinand	W. Shoemaker	2:02.4
1987	Alysheba	C. McCarron	2:03.2
1988	Winning Colors	G. Stevens	2:02.2
1989	Sunday Silence	P. Valenzuela	2:05.0
1990	Unbridled	C. Perret	2:02.0
1991	Strike the Gold	C. Antley	2:03.0
1992	Lil E. Tee	P.Day	2:03.0
1993	Sea Hero	J. Bailey	2:02.42
1994	Go for Gin	C. McCarron	2:03.72
1995	Thunder Gulch	G. Stevens	2:01.27
1996	Grindstone	J. Bailey	2:01.60
1997	Silver Charm	G. Stevens	2:02.44
1998	Real Quiet	K. Desormeaux	2:02.38
1999	Charismatic	C. Antley	2:03.29
2000	Fusaichi Pegasus	K. Desormeaux	2:01.12
2001	Monarchos	J. Chavez	1:59.97
2002	War Emblem	V. Espinoza	2:01.13
2003	Funny Cide	J. Santos	2:01.19

Note: Names in **bold** indicate Triple Crown winners. Before 1993, decimals refer to fifths of a second. 1. In 1968, Dancer's Image finished first, but was later disqualified from the purse money, and Forward Pass was declared winner. 2. Record. **Source:** *Daily Racing Form.*

Preakness Stakes Winners 1873–2003

The Preakness was first run in 1873, and the distance varied from 1 mile 70 yards to 1½ miles until 1925, when it was standardized at 1³⁄₁₆ miles. **Site: Pimlico Racetrack,** Baltimore, Maryland.

Year	Horse	Jockey	Time
1873	Survivor	G. Barbee	2:43.0
1874	Culpepper	Donohue	2:56½
1875	Tom Ochiltree	L. Hughes	2:43½
1876	Shirley	Barbee	2:44¾
1877	Cloverbrook	Holloway	2:45½
1878	Duke of Magenta	Holloway	2:41¾
1879	Harold	Hughes	2:40½
1880	Grenada	L. Hughes	2:40½
1881	Saunterer	Costello	2:40½
1882	Vanguard	Costello	2:44½
1883	Jacobus	Barbee	2:42½
1884	Knight of Ellerslie	Fisher	2:39½
1885	Tecumseh	M. McLaughlin	2:49.0
1886	The Bard	Fisher	2:45.0
1887	Dunboyne	W. Donohue	2:39½
1888	Refund	Littlefield	2:49.0
1889	Buddhist	Anderson	2:17½
1890	Montague	W. Martin	2:36¾
1891–93	Not run		
1894	Assignee	F. Taral	1:49¼
1895	Belmar	F. Taral	1:50½
1896	Margrave	H. Griffin	1:51.0
1897	Paul Kauver	Thorpe	1:51¼
1898	Sly Fox	W. Simms	1:49¾
1899	Half Time	R. Clawson	1:47.0
1900	Hindus	H. Spencer	1:48.2
1901	The Parader	F. Landry	1:47.1
1902	Old England	L. Jackson	1:45.4
1903	Flocarline	W. Gannon	1:44.4
1904	Bryn Mawr	E. Hildebrand	1:44.1
1905	Cairngorm	W. Davis	1:45.4
1906	Whimsical	W. Miller	1:45.0
1907	Don Enrique	G. Mountain	1:45.2
1908	Royal Tourist	E. Dugan	1:46.2
1909	Effendi	W. Doyle	1:39.4
1910	Layminister	R. Estep	1:40.3
1911	Watervale	E. Dugan	1:51.0
1912	Colonel Holloway	C. Turner	1:56.3
1913	Buskin	J. Butwell	1:53.2
1914	Holiday	A. Schuttinger	1:53.4
1915	Rhine Maiden	D. Hoffman	1:58.0
1916	Damrosch	L. McAtee	1:54.4
1917	Kalitan	E. Haynes	1:54.2
1918	Jack Hare Jr.	C. Peak	1:53.2
	War Cloud	J. Loftus	1:53.3
1919	**Sir Barton**	J. Loftus	1:53.0
1920	Man o'War	C. Kummer	1:51.3
1921	Broomspun	F. Coltiletti	1:54.1
1922	Pillory	L. Morris	1:51.3
1923	Vigil	B. Marinelli	1:53.3
1924	Nellie Morse	J. Merimee	1:57.1
1925	Coventry	C. Kummer	1:59.0
1926	Display	J. Maiben	1:59.4
1927	Bostonian	A. Abel	2:01.3
1928	Victorian	R. Workman	2:00.1
1929	Dr. Freeland	L. Schaefer	2:01.3
1930	**Gallant Fox**	E. Sande	2:00.3
1931	Mate	G. Ellis	1:59.0
1932	Burgoo King	E. James	1:59.4
1933	Head Play	C. Kurtsinger	2:02.0
1934	High Quest	R. Jones	1:58.1
1935	**Omaha**	W. Saunders	1:58.2
1936	Bold Venture	G. Woolf	1:59.0
1937	**War Admiral**	C. Kurtsinger	1:58.2
1938	Dauber	M. Peters	1:59.4
1939	Challedon	G. Seabo	1:59.4
1940	Bimelech	F. A. Smith	1:58.3
1941	**Whirlaway**	E. Arcaro	1:58.4
1942	Alsab	B. James	1:57.0
1943	**Count Fleet**	J. Longden	1:57.2
1944	Pensive	C. McCreary	1:59.1
1945	Polynesian	W. D. Wright	1:58.4
1946	**Assault**	W. Mehrtens	2:01.2
1947	Faultless	D. Dodson	1:59.0
1948	**Citation**	E. Arcaro	2:02.2
1949	Capot	T. Atkinson	1:56.0
1950	Hill Prince	E. Arcaro	1:59.1
1951	Bold	E. Arcaro	1:56.2
1952	Blue Man	C. McCreary	1:57.2
1953	Native Dancer	E. Guerin	1:57.4
1954	Hasty Road	J. Adams	1:57.2
1955	Nashua	E. Arcaro	1:54.3
1956	Fabius	W. Hartack	1:58.2
1957	Bold Ruler	E. Arcaro	1:56.1
1958	Tim Tam	I. Valenzuela	1:57.1
1959	Royal Orbit	W. Harmatz	1:57.0
1960	Bally Ache	R. Ussery	1:57.3
1961	Carry Back	J. Sellers	1:57.3
1962	Greek Money	J. L. Rotz	1:56.1
1963	Candy Spots	W. Shoemaker	1:56.1
1964	Northern Dancer	W. Hartack	1:56.4
1965	Tom Rolfe	R. Turncotte	1:56.1
1966	Kauai King	D. Brumfield	1:55.2
1967	Damascus	W. Shoemaker	1:55.1
1968	Forward Pass	I. Valenzuela	1:56.4
1969	Majestic Prince	W. Hartack	1:55.3
1970	Personality	E. Belmonte	1:56.1
1971	Canonero II	G. Avila	1:54.0
1972	Bee Bee Bee	E. Nelson	1:55.3
1973	**Secretariat**	R. Turcotte	1:54.2
1974	Little Current	M. Rivera	1:54.3
1975	Master Derby	D. McHargue	1:56.2
1976	Elocutionist	J. Lively	1:55.0
1977	**Seattle Slew**	J. Cruguet	1:54.2
1978	**Affirmed**	S. Cauthen	1:54.2
1979	Spectacular Bid	R. Franklin	1:54.1
1980	Codex	A. Cordero	1:54.1
1981	Pleasant Colony	J. Valasquez	1:54.3
1982	Aloma's Ruler	J. Kaenel	1:55.2
1983	Deputed Testamony	D. Miller	1:55.2
1984	Gate Dancer	A. Cordero	1:53.3
1985	Tank's Prospect	P. Day	1:53.2
1986	Snow Chief	A. Solls	1:54.4
1987	Alysheba	C. McCarron	1:55.4
1988	Risen Star	E. Delahoussaye	1:56.1
1989	Sunday Silence	P. Valenzuela	1:53.4
1990	Summer Squall	P. Day	1:53.3
1991	Hansel	J. Bailey	1:54.0
1992	Pine Bluff	C. McCarron	1:55.3
1993	Prairie Bayou	M. Smith	1:56.3
1994	Tabasco Cat	P. Day	1:56.2
1995	Timber Country	P. Day	1:54.2
1996	Louis Quatorze	P. Day	1:52.2
1997	Silver Charm	G. Stevens	1:54.4
1998	Real Quiet	K. Desormeaux	1:54.75
1999	Charismatic	C. Antley	1:55.32
2000	Red Bullet	J. Bailey	1:56.04
2001	Point Given	G. Stevens	1:56.51
2002	War Emblem	V. Espinoza	1:56.36
2003	Funny Cide	J. Santos	1:55.61

Note: Names in **bold** indicate Triple Crown winners. Before 1998, decimals refer to fifths of a second. **Source:** *Daily Racing Form*

Belmont Stakes Winners 1880–2003

The Belmont Stakes was first run in 1867. The distance of the race varied from 1¹⁄₁₈ miles to 1⅝ miles until 1926, when it was standardized at 1½ miles. **Site: Belmont Park,** New York. (The race was held at Jerome Park prior to 1890, at Morris Park from 1890 to 1904, at Aqueduct from 1963 to 1967.

Year	Horse	Jockey	Time
1880	Grenada	L. Hughes	2:47.0
1881	Saunterer	T. Costello	2:47.0
1882	Forester	J. McLaughlin	2:43.0
1883	George Kinney	J. McLaughlin	2:42.2
1884	Panique	J. McLaughlin	2:42.0
1885	Tyrant	P. Duffy	2:43.0
1886	Inspector B.	J. McLaughlin	2:41.0
1887	Hanover	J. McLaughlin	2:43.2
1888	Sir Dixon	J. McLaughlin	2:40.2
1889	Eric	W. Hayward	2:47.0
1890	Burlington	S. Barnes	2:07.6
1891	Foxford	E. Garrison	2:08.6
1892	Patron	W. Hayward	2:17.0
1893	Comanche	W. Simms	1:53.2
1894	Henry of Navarre	W. Simms	1:56.2
1895	Belmar	F. Taral	2:11.2
1896	Hastings	H. Griffin	2:24.2
1897	Scottish Chieftain	J. Scherrer	2:32.2
1898	Bowling Brook	F. Littlefield	2:32.0
1899	Jean Bereaud	R.R. Clawson	2:23.0
1900	Ildrim	N. Turner	2:21½
1901	Commando	H. Spencer	2:21.0
1902	Masterman	J. Bullman	2:22½
1903	Africander	J. Bullman	2:23.1
1904	Delhi	G. Odom	2:06.3
1905	Tanya	E. Hildebrand	2:08.0
1906	Burgomaster	L. Lyne	2:20.0
1907	Peter Pan	G. Mountain	No Time
1908	Colin	J. Notter	No Time
1909	Joe Madden	E. Dugan	2:21.3
1910	Sweep	J. Butwell	2:22.0
1911–12	Not run		
1913	Prince Eugene	R. Troxler	2:18.0
1914	Luke McLuke	M. Buxton	2:20.0
1915	The Finn	G. Byrne	2:18.2
1916	Friar Rock	E. Haynes	2:22.0
1917	Hourless	J. Butwell	2:17.4
1918	Johren	F. Robinson	2:20.2
1919	**Sir Barton**	J. Loftus	2:17.2
1920	Man o'War	C. Kummer	2:14.1
1921	Grey Lag	E. Sande	2:16.4
1922	Pillory	C. H. Miller	2:18.4
1923	Zev	E. Sande	2:19.0
1924	Mad Play	E. Sande	2:18.4
1925	American Flag	A. Johnson	2:16.4
1926	Crusader	A. Johnson	2:32.1
1927	Chance Shot	E. Sande	2:32.2
1928	Vito	C. Kummer	2:33.1
1929	Blue Larkspur	M. Garner	2:32.4
1930	**Gallant Fox**	E. Sande	2:31.1
1931	Twenty Grand	C. Kurtsinger	2:29.3
1932	Faireno	T. Malley	2:32.4
1933	Hurryoff	M. Garner	2:32.3
1934	Peace Chance	W. D. Wright	2:29.5
1935	**Omaha**	W. Saunders	2:30.3
1936	Granville	J. Stout	2:30.0
1937	**War Admiral**	C. Kurtsinger	2:28.3
1938	Pasteurized	J. Stout	2:29.2
1939	Johnstown	J. Stout	2:29.2
1940	Bimelech	F. A. Smith	2:29.3
1941	**Whirlaway**	E. Arcaro	2:31.0
1942	Shut Out	E. Arcaro	2:29.1
1943	**Count Fleet**	J. Longden	2:28.1
1944	Bounding Home	G. L. Smith	2:32.1
1945	Pavot	E. Arcaro	2:30.1
1946	**Assault**	W. Mehrtens	2:30.4
1947	Phalanx	R. Donoso	2:29.2
1948	**Citation**	E. Arcaro	2:28.1
1949	Capot	T. Atkinson	2:30.1
1950	Middleground	W. Boland	2:28.3
1951	Counterpoint	D. Gorman	2:29.0
1952	One Count	E. Arcaro	2:30.1
1953	Native Dancer	E. Guerin	2:28.3
1954	High Gun	E. Guerin	2:30.4
1955	Nashua	E. Arcaro	2:29.0
1956	Needles	D. Erb	2:29.4
1957	Gallant Man	W. Shoemaker	2:26.3
1958	Cavan	P. Anderson	2:30.1
1959	Sword Dancer	W. Shoemaker	2:28.2
1960	Celtic Ash	W. Hartack	2:29.3
1961	Sherluck	B. Baeza	2:29.1
1962	Jaipur	W. Shoemaker	2:28.4
1963	Chateaugay	B. Baeza	2:30.1
1964	Quadrangle	M. Ycaza	2:28.2
1965	Hail To All	J. Sellers	2:28.2
1966	Amberoid	W. Boland	2:29.3
1967	Damascus	W. Shoemaker	2:28.4
1968	Stage Door Johnny	H. Gustines	2:27.1
1969	Arts and Letters	B. Baeza	2:28.4
1970	High Echelon	J. L. Rotz	2:34.0
1971	Pass Catcher	W. Blum	2:30.2
1972	Riva Ridge	R. Turcotte	2:28.0
1973	**Secretariat**	R. Turcotte	2:24.0
1974	Little Current	M. Rivera	2:29.1
1975	Avatar	W. Shoemaker	2:28.1
1976	Bold Forbes	A. Cordero	2:29.0
1977	**Seattle Slew**	Jean Cruguet	2:29.3
1978	**Affirmed**	S. Cauthen	2:26.4
1979	Coastal	R. Hernandez	2:28.3
1980	Temperance Hill	E. Maple	2:29.4
1981	Summing	G. Martens	2:29.0
1982	Conquistador Cielo	L. Pincay	2:28.1
1983	Caveat	L. Pincay	2:27.4
1984	Swale	L. Pincay	2:27.1
1985	Creme Fraiche	E. Maple	2:27.0
1986	Danzig Connection	C. McCarron	2:29.4
1987	Bet Twice	C. Perret	2:28.1
1988	Risen Star	E. Delahoussaye	2:26.1
1989	Easy Goer	P. Day	2:26.0
1990	Go and Go	M. Kinane	2:27.1
1991	Hansel	J. Bailey	2:28.0
1992	A.P. Indy	E. Delahoussaye	2:26.0
1993	Colonial Affair	J. Krone	2:29.4
1994	Tabasco Cat	P. Day	2:26.4
1995	Thunder Gulch	G. Stevens	2:32.0
1996	Editor's Note	R. Douglas	2:28.4
1997	Touch Gold	C. McCarron	2:28.4
1998	Victory Gallop	G. Stevens	2:29.16
1999	Lemon Drop Kid	J. Santos	2:27.88
2000	Commendable	P. Day	2:31.19
2001	Point Given	G. Stevens	2:26.56
2002	Sarava	E. Prado	2:29.71
2003	Empire Maker	J. Bailey	2:28.26

Note: Names in **bold** indicate Triple Crown winners. Before 1998, decimals refer to fifths of a second. **Source:** *Daily Racing Form.*

FOOTBALL

National Football League
280 Park Avenue
New York, NY 10017
(212) 450-2000

www.nfl.com
Commissioner: Paul Tagliabue
Founded 1920.
Number of Teams: 32

2002 NFL Regular Season Final Standings

AMERICAN FOOTBALL CONFERENCE

AFC East	W-L-T	AFC North	W-L-T
New York Jets[1]	9-7-0	Pittsburgh[1]	10-5-1
New England	9-7-0	Cleveland[2]	9-7-0
Miami	9-7-0	Baltimore	7-9-0
Buffalo	8-8-0	Cincinnati	2-14-0

AFC South	W-L-T	AFC West	W-L-T
Tennessee[1]	11-5-0	Oakland[1]	11-5-0
Indianapolis[2]	10-6-0	Denver	9-7-0
Jacksonville	6-10-0	San Diego	8-8-0
Houston	4-12-0	Kansas City	8-8-0

NATIONAL FOOTBALL CONFERENCE

NFC East	W-L-T	NFC North	W-L-T
Philadelphia[1]	12-4-0	Green Bay[1]	12-4-0
New York Giants[2]	10-6-0	Minnesota	6-10-0
Washington	7-9-0	Chicago	4-12-0
Dallas	5-11-0	Detroit	3-13-0

NFC South	W-L-T	NFC West	W-L-T
Tampa Bay[1]	12-4-0	San Francisco[1]	10-6-0
Atlanta[2]	9-6-1	St. Louis	7-9-0
New Orleans	9-7-0	Seattle	7-9-0
Carolina	7-9-0	Arizona	5-11-0

1. Division champion. 2. Wild Card for playoffs.

2002 NFL Post-Season Playoff Results

AFC Wild Card Playoff
NEW YORK JETS 41, Indianapolis 0
PITTSBURGH 36, Cleveland 33

AFC Divisional Playoff
OAKLAND 30, New York Jets 10
TENNESSEE 34, Pittsburgh 31 (OT)

AFC Championship Game
OAKLAND 41, Tennessee 24

NFC Wild Card Playoff
Atlanta 27, GREEN BAY 7
SAN FRANCISCO 39, New York Giants 38

NFC Divisional Playoff
TAMPA BAY 31, San Francisco 6
PHILADELPHIA 20, Atlanta 6

NFC Championship Game
Tampa Bay 27, PHILADELPHIA 10

Super Bowl XXXVII at Qualcomm Stadium, San Diego
January 25, 2003
TAMPA BAY 48,Oakland 21

Note: Home team in CAPITAL LETTERS.

NFL First Round Draft Choices, 2003

Team	Selection, Position	School
1. Cincinnati	Carson Palmer, QB	USC
2. Detroit	Charles Rogers, WR	Michigan State
3. Houston	Andre Johnson, WR	Miami (Fla.)
4. N. Y. Jets	Dewayne Robertson, DT	Kentucky
5. Dallas	Terence Newman, CB	Kansas State
6. New Orleans	Johnathan Sullivan, DT	Georgia
7. Jacksonville	Byron Leftwich, QB	Marshall
8. Carolina	Jordan Gross, OT	Utah
9. Minnesota	Kevin Williams, DE	Oklahoma St.
10. Baltimore	Terrell Suggs, DE	Arizona State
11. Seattle	Marcus Trufant, CB	Washington St.
12. St. Louis	Jimmy Kennedy, DT	Penn State
13. New England	Ty Warren, DT	Texas A&M
14. Chicago	Michael Haynes, DE	Penn State
15. Philadelphia	Jerome McDougle, DE	Miami (Fla.)
16. Pittsburgh	Troy Polamalu, SS	USC
17. Arizona	Bryant Johnson, WR	Penn State
18. Arizona	Calvin Pace, DE	Wake Forest
19. Baltimore	Kyle Boller, QB	California
20. Denver	George Foster, OT	Georgia
21. Cleveland	Jeff Faine, C	Notre Dame
22. Chicago	Rex Grossman, QB	Florida
23. Buffalo	Willis McGahee, RB	Miami (Fla.)
24. Indianapolis	Dallas Clark, TE	Iowa
25. N. Y. Giants	William Joseph, DT	Miami (Fla.)
26. San Francisco	Kwame Harris, OT	Stanford
27. Kansas City	Larry Johnson, RB	Penn State
28. Tennessee	Andre Woolfolk, CB	Oklahoma
29. Green Bay	Nick Barnett, OLB	Oregon State
30. San Diego	Sammy Davis, CB	Texas A&M
31. Oakland	Nnamdi Asomugha, CB	California
32. Oakland	Tyler Brayton, DE	Colorado

NFL Leaders, 2002

RUSHING

AFC	No.	Yds.	Avg.	TDs
Ricky Williams, Miami	383	1,853	4.8	16
LaDainian Tomlinson, San Diego	372	1,683	4.5	14
Priest Holmes, Kansas City	313	1,615	5.2	21
Clinton Portis, Denver	273	1,508	5.5	15
Travis Henry, Buffalo	325	1,438	4.4	13
Jamal Lewis, Baltimore	308	1,327	4.3	6
Fred Taylor, Jacksonville	287	1,314	4.6	8
Corey Dillon, Cincinnati	314	1,311	4.2	7
Eddie George, Tennessee	343	1,165	3.4	12
Curtis Martin, New York Jets	261	1,094	4.2	7

NFC	No.	Yds.	Avg.	TDs
Deuce McAllister, New Orleans	325	1,388	4.3	13
Tiki Barber, New York Giants	304	1,387	4.6	11
Michael Bennett, Minnesota	255	1,296	5.1	5
Ahman Green, Green Bay	286	1,240	4.3	7
Shaun Alexander, Seattle	295	1,175	4.0	16
Duce Staley, Philadelphia	269	1,029	3.8	5
James Stewart, Detroit	231	1,021	4.4	4
Emmitt Smith, Dallas	254	975	3.8	5
Garrison Hearst, San Francisco	215	972	4.5	8
Marshall Faulk, St. Louis	212	953	4.5	8

RECEIVING

AFC	No.	Yds.	Avg.	TDs
Marvin Harrison, Indianapolis	143	1,722	12.0	11
Hines Ward, Pittsburgh	112	1,329	11.9	12
Eric Moulds, Buffalo	100	1,292	12.9	10
Troy Brown, New England	97	890	9.2	3
Peerless Price, Buffalo	94	1,252	13.3	9
Jerry Rice, Oakland	92	1,211	13.2	7
Charlie Garner, Oakland	91	941	10.3	4
Laveranues Coles, New York Jets	89	1,264	14.2	5
Rod Smith, Denver	89	1,027	11.5	5
Tim Brown, Oakland	81	930	11.5	2

NFC	No.	Yds.	Avg.	TDs
Randy Moss, Minnesota	106	1,347	12.7	7
Terrell Owens, San Francisco	100	1,300	13.0	13
Marty Booker, Chicago	97	1,189	12.3	6
Torry Holt, St. Louis	91	1,302	14.3	4
Joe Horn, New Orleans	88	1,312	14.9	7
Amani Toomer, New York Giants	82	1,343	16.4	8
Marshall Faulk, St. Louis	80	537	6.7	2
Isaac Bruce, St. Louis	79	1,075	13.6	7
Koren Robinson, Seattle	78	1,240	15.9	5
Keyshawn Johnson, Tampa Bay	76	1,088	14.3	5

PASSING RATING

AFC	Atttempts	Completions	Percentage	Yards	Touch-downs	Inter-ceptions	Rating
Chad Pennington, New York Jets	399	275	68.9	3,120	22	6	104.2
Rich Gannon, Oakland	618	418	67.6	4,689	26	10	97.3
Trent Green, Kansas City	470	287	61.0	3,690	26	13	92.6
Peyton Manning, Indianapolis	591	392	66.3	4,200	27	19	88.8
Drew Bledsoe, Buffalo	610	375	61.5	4,359	24	15	86.0
Tom Brady, New England	601	373	62.1	3,764	28	14	85.7
Mark Brunell, Jacksonville	416	245	58.9	2,788	17	7	85.7
Brian Griese, Denver	436	291	66.7	3,214	15	15	85.6
Jay Fiedler, Miami	292	179	61.3	2,024	14	9	85.2
Tommy Maddox, Pittsburgh	377	234	62.1	2,836	20	16	85.2

NFC	Atttempts	Completions	Percentage	Yards	Touch-downs	Inter-ceptions	Rating
Marc Bulger, St. Louis	214	138	64.5	1,826	14	6	101.5
Brad Johnson, Tampa Bay	451	281	62.3	3,049	22	6	92.9
Matt Hasselbeck, Seattle	419	267	63.7	3,075	15	10	87.8
Donovan McNabb, Philadelphia	361	211	58.4	2,289	17	6	86.0
Brett Favre, Green Bay	551	341	61.9	3,658	27	16	85.6
Jeff Garcia, San Francisco	528	328	62.1	3,344	21	10	85.6
Kerry Collins, New York Giants	545	335	61.5	4,073	19	14	85.4
Michael Vick, Atlanta	421	231	54.9	2,936	16	8	81.6
Aaron Brooks, New Orleans	528	283	53.6	3,572	27	15	80.1
Jim Miller, Chicago	314	180	57.3	1,944	13	9	77.5

Source: National Football League. **www.nfl.com**

NFL Number One Draft Picks, 1936–2003

Year	Player	Team	Pos.	College
1936	Jay Berwanger	Philadelphia Eagles	RB	Chicago
1937	Sam Francis	Philadelphia Eagles	RB	Nebraska
1938	Corbett Davis	Cleveland Rams	RB	Indiana

Year	Player	Team	Pos.	College
1939	Charles Aldrich	Chicago Cardinals	OL	Texas Christian
1940	George Cafego	Chicago Cardinals	QB	Tennessee
1941	Tom Harmon	Chicago Bears	RB	Michigan
1942	Bill Dudley	Pittsburgh Steelers	RB	Virginia
1943	Frank Sinkwich	Detroit Lions	RB	Georgia
1944	Angelo Bertelli	Boston Yanks	QB	Notre Dame
1945	Charley Trippi	Chicago Cardinals	RB	Georgia
1946	Frank Dancewicz	Boston Yanks	QB	Notre Dame
1947	Bob Fenimore	Chicago Bears	RB	Oklahoma A&M
1948	Harry Gilmer	Washington Redskins	QB	Alabama
1949	Chuck Bednarik	Philadelphia Eagles	OL	Pennsylvania
1950	Leon Hart	Detroit Lions	E	Notre Dame
1951	Kyle Rote	New York Giants	E/K	Southern Methodist
1952	Bill Wade	Los Angeles Rams	QB	Vanderbilt
1953	Harry Babcock	San Francisco 49ers	E	Georgia
1954	Bobby Garrett	Cleveland Browns	QB	Stanford
1955	George Shaw	Baltimore Colts	QB	Oregon
1956	Gary Glick	Pittsburgh Steelers	QB	Colorado State
1957	Paul Hornung	Green Bay Packers	RB	Notre Dame
1958	King Hill	St. Louis Cardinals	QB	Rice
1959	Randy Duncan	Green Bay Packers	QB	Iowa
1960	Billy Cannon	Los Angeles Rams	RB	Louisiana State
1961	Tommy Mason	Minnesota Vikings	RB	Tulane
1962	Ernie Davis	Washington Redskins	RB	Syracuse
1963	Terry Baker	Los Angeles Rams	QB	Oregon State
1964	Dave Parks	San Francisco 49ers	E	Texas Tech.
1965	Tucker Frederickson	New York Giants	RB	Auburn
1966	Tommy Nobis	Atlanta Falcons	LB	Texas
1967	Bubba Smith	Baltimore Colts	DL	Michigan State
1968	Ron Yary	Minnesota Vikings	OL	USC
1969	O.J. Simpson	Buffalo Bills	RB	USC
1970	Terry Bradshaw	Pittsburgh Steelers	QB	Louisiana Tech.
1971	Jim Plunkett	Boston Patriots	QB	Stanford
1972	Walt Patulski	Buffalo Bills	DL	Notre Dame
1973	John Matuzak	Houston Oilers	DL	Tampa
1974	Ed Jones	Dallas Cowboys	DL	Tampa
1975	Steve Bartkowski	Atlanta Falcons	QB	California
1976	Lee Roy Selmon	Tampa Bay Buccaneers	DL	Oklahoma
1977	Ricky Bell	Tampa Bay Buccaneers	RB	USC
1978	Earl Campbell	Houston Oilers	RB	Texas
1979	Tom Cousineau	Buffalo Bills	LB	Ohio State
1980	Billy Sims	Detroit Lions	RB	Oklahoma
1981	George Rogers	New Orleans Saints	RB	South Carolina
1982	Kenneth Sims	New England Patriots	DL	Texas
1983	John Elway	Baltimore Colts	QB	Stanford
1984	Irving Fryar	New England Patriots	WR	Nebraska
1985	Bruce Smith	Buffalo Bills	DL	Virginia Tech.
1986	Bo Jackson	Tampa Bay Buccaneers	RB	Auburn
1987	Vinny Testaverde	Tampa Bay Buccaneers	QB	Miami
1988	Aundray Bruce	Atlanta Falcons	LB	Auburn
1989	Troy Aikman	Dallas Cowboys	QB	UCLA
1990	Jeff George	Indianapolis Colts	QB	Illinois
1991	Russell Maryland	Dallas Cowboys	DT	Miami (Fla.)
1992	Steve Emtman	Indianapolis Colts	DT	Washington
1993	Drew Bledsoe	New England Patriots	QB	Washington State
1994	Dan Wilkinson	Cincinnati Bengals	DT	Ohio State
1995	Ki-Jana Carter	Cincinnati Bengals	RB	Penn State
1996	Keyshawn Johnson	New York Jets	WR	Southern California
1997	Orlando Pace	St. Louis Rams	OT	Ohio State
1998	Peyton Manning	Indianapolis Colts	QB	Tennessee
1999	Tim Couch	Cleveland Browns	QB	Kentucky
2000	Courtney Brown	Cleveland Browns	DL	Penn State
2001	Michael Vick	Atlanta Falcons	QB	Virginia Tech
2002	David Carr	Houston Texans	QB	Fresno State
2002	Carson Palmer	Cincinnati Bengals	QB	USC

The Sporting News' NFL Rookie of the Year, 1955–2002

Year	Player	Pos.	Team
1955	Alan Ameche	FB	Baltimore Colts
1956	J.C. Caroline	HB	Chicago Bears
1957	Jim Brown	FB	Cleveland Browns
1958	Bobby Mitchell	HB	Cleveland Browns
1959	Nick Pietrosante	FB	Detroit Lions
1960	Gail Codgill	E	Detroit Lions
1961	Mike Ditka	E	Chicago Bears
1962	Ronnie Bull	HB	Chicago Bears
1963	Paul Flatley	WR	Minnesota Vikings
1964	Charley Taylor	HB	Washington Redskins
1965	Gale Sayers	RB	Chicago Bears
1966	Tommy Nobis	LB	Atlanta Falcons
1967	Mel Farr	RB	Detroit Lions
1968	Earl McCullouch	WR	Detroit Lions
1969	Calvin Hill	RB	Dallas Cowboys
1970	NFC: Bruce Taylor	CB	San Francisco 49ers
	AFC: Dennis Shaw	QB	Buffalo Bills
1971	NFC: John Brockington	RB	Green Bay Packers
	AFC: Jim Plunkett	QB	New England Patriots
1972	NFC: Chester Marcol	PK	Green Bay Packers
	AFC: Franco Harris	RB	Pittsburgh Steelers
1973	NFC: Chuck Foreman	RB	Minnestoa Vikings
	AFC: Boobie Clark	RB	Cincinnati Bengals
1974	NFC: Wilbur Jackson	RB	San Francisco 49ers
	AFC: Don Woods	RB	San Diego Chargers
1975	NFC: Steve Bartkowski	QB	Atlanta Falcons
	AFC: Robert Brazile	LB	Houston Oilers
1976	NFC: Sammy White	WR	Minnesota Vikings
	AFC: Mike Haynes	CB	New England Patriots
1977	NFC: Tony Dorsett	RB	Dallas Cowboys
	AFC: A.J. Duhe	DT	Miami Dolphins
1978	NFC: Al Baker	DE	Detroit Lions
	AFC: Earl Campbell	RB	Houston Oilers
1979	NFC: Ottis Anderson	RB	St. Louis Cardinals
	AFC: Jerry Butler	WR	Buffalo Bills
1980	Billy Sims	RB	Detroit Lions
1981	George Rogers	RB	New England Patriots
1982	Marcus Allen	RB	Los Angeles Raiders
1983	Dan Marino	QB	Miami Dolphins
1984	Louis Lipps	WR	Pittsburgh Steelers
1985	Eddie Brown	WR	Cincinnati Bengals
1986	Rueben Mayes	RB	New Orleans Saints
1987	Robert Awalt	TE	St. Louis Cardinals
1988	Keith Jackson	TE	Philadelphia Eagles
1989	Barry Sanders	RB	Detroit Lions
1990	Richmond Webb	OL	Miami Dolphins
1991	Mike Croel	LB	Denver Broncos
1992	Santana Dotson	DE	Tampa Bay Buccaneers
1993	Jerome Bettis	RB	Los Angeles Rams
1994	Marshall Faulk	RB	Indianapolis Colts
1995	Curtis Martin	RB	New England
1996	Eddie George	RB	Houston Oilers
1997	Warrick Dunn	RB	Tampa Bay Buccaneers
1998	Randy Moss	WR	Minnesota Vikings
1999	Edgerrin James	RB	Indianapolis Colts
2000	Brian Urlacher	LB	Chicago Bears
2001	Kendrell Bell	LB	Pittsburgh Steelers
2002	Clinton Portis	RB	Denver Broncos

Note: From 1970–79, separate players were chosen for each conference. **Source:** *The Sporting News.*

NFL Most Valuable Player, 1957–2002

Year	Player,	Pos.	Team
1957	Jim Brown	RB	Cleveland Browns
1958	Gino Marchetti	DE	Baltimore Colts
1959	Charley Conerly	QB	New York Giants
1960	Norm Van Brocklin	QB	Philadelphia Eagles
	Joe Schmidt	LB	Detroit Lions
1961	Paul Hornung	RB	Green Bay Packers
1962	Jim Taylor	RB	Green Bay Packers
1963	Y.A. Tittle	QB	New York Giants
1964	Johnny Unitas	QB	Baltimore Colts
1965	Jim Brown	RB	Cleveland Browns
1966	Bart Starr	QB	Green Bay Packers
1967	Johnny Unitas	QB	Baltimore Colts
1968	Earl Morrall	QB	Baltimore Colts
1969	Roman Gabriel	QB	Los Angeles Rams
1970	John Brodie	QB	San Francisco 49ers
1971	Alan Page	DT	Minnesota Vikings
1972	Larry Brown	RB	Washington Redskins
1973	O.J. Simpson	RB	Buffalo Bills
1974	Ken Stabler	QB	Oakland Raiders
1975	Fran Tarkenton	QB	Minnesota Vikings
1976	Bert Jones	RB	Baltimore Colts
1977	Walter Payton	RB	Chicago Bears
1978	Terry Bradshaw	QB	Pittsburgh Steelers
1979	Earl Campbell	RB	Houston Oilers
1980	Brian Sipe	QB	Cleveland Browns
1981	Ken Anderson	QB	Cincinnati Bengals
1982	Mark Moseley	PK	Washington Redskins
1983	Joe Theismann	QB	Washington Redskins
1984	Dan Marino	QB	Miami Dolphins
1985	Marcus Allen	RB	Los Angeles Raiders
1986	Lawrence Taylor	LB	New York Giants
1987	John Elway	QB	Denver Broncos
1988	Boomer Esiason	QB	Cincinnati Bengals
1989	Joe Montana	QB	San Francisco 49ers
1990	Joe Montana	QB	San Francisco 49ers
1991	Thurman Thomas	RB	Buffalo Bills
1992	Steve Young	QB	San Francisco 49ers
1993	Emmitt Smith	RB	Dallas Cowboys
1994	Steve Young	QB	San Francisco 49ers
1995	Brett Favre	QB	Green Bay Packers
1996	Brett Favre	QB	Green Bay Packers
1997	Brett Favre	QB	Green Bay Packers
	Barry Sanders	RB	Detroit Lions
1998	Terrell Davis	RB	Denver Broncos
1999	Kurt Warner	QB	St. Louis Rams
2000	Marshall Faulk	RB	St. Louis Rams
2001	Kurt Warner	QB	St. Louis Rams
2002	Rich Gannon	QB	Oakland Raiders

Source: National Football League

All-Time Pro Football Records

SCORING (Total Points)	Years	Points	Touchdowns	PATs	Field Goals
1. Gary Anderson[1]	21	2223	0	741	494
2. Morten Andersen[1]	21	2153	0	695	486
3. George Blanda	26	2,002	9	943	335
4. Norm Johnson	18	1,736	0	638	366
5. Nick Lowery	18	1,711	0	562	383
6. Jan Stenerud	19	1,699	0	580	373
7. Eddie Murray	18	1,563	0	501	344
8. Al Del Greco	17	1,584	0	543	347
9. Pat Leahy	18	1,470	0	558	304
10. Jim Turner	16	1,439	1	521	304

RUSHING (Yards)	Years	Rushes	Yards	Avg.	TD
1. Emmitt Smith[1]	13	4,052	17,162	4.2	153
2. Walter Payton	13	3,838	16,726	4.4	110
3. Barry Sanders	10	3,062	15,269	5.0	99
4. Eric Dickerson	11	2,996	13,259	4.4	90
5. Tony Dorsett	12	2,936	12,739	4.3	77
6. Jim Brown	9	2,359	12,312	5.2	106
7. Marcus Allen	16	3,022	12,243	4.1	123
8. Franco Harris	13	2,949	12,120	4.1	91
9. Thurman Thomas	13	2,877	12,074	4.2	65
10. Jerome Bettis[1]	10	2,873	11,542	4.0	62

RECEPTIONS	Years	Receptions	Yards	Avg.	TD
1. Jerry Rice[1]	18	1,456	21,597	14.8	192
2. Cris Carter[1]	16	1,101	13,899	12.6	130
3. Tim Brown[1]	15	1,018	14,167	13.9	97
4. Andre Reed	16	951	13,198	13.9	87
5. Art Monk	16	940	12,721	13.5	68
6. Irving Fryar	17	851	12,785	15.0	84
7. Steve Largent	14	819	13,089	16.0	100
8. Henry Ellard	16	814	13,777	16.9	65
9. Larry Centers[1]	13	808	6,691	8.3	27
10. James Lofton	16	764	14,004	18.3	75

QUARTERBACK RATING	Yrs.	Attempts	Completions	Yards	TDs	Interceptions	Rating
1. Kurt Warner[1]	5	1,623	1,083	14,082	101	64	**98.2**
2. Steve Young	15	4,149	2,667	33,124	232	107	**96.8**
3. Joe Montana	15	5,391	3,409	40,551	273	139	**92.3**
4. Jeff Garcia[1]	4	1,968	1,224	13,704	95	43	**89.9**
5. Brett Favre[1]	12	5,993	3,652	42,285	314	188	**86.7**
6. Dan Marino	17	8,358	4,967	61,361	420	252	**86.4**
7. Peyton Manning[1]	5	2,817	1,749	20,618	138	100	**85.9**
8. Rich Gannon[1]	14	3,913	2,367	26,945	171	98	**85.3**
9. Mark Brunell[1]	9	3,561	2,142	25,309	142	86	**85.1**
10. Brad Johnson[1]	9	2,831	1,747	19,428	114	74	**84.6**

Passes Completed	
1. Dan Marino	4,967
2. John Elway	4,123
3. Warren Moon	3,988
4. Fran Tarkenton	3,686
5. Brett Favre[1]	3,652
6. Joe Montana	3,409
7. Dan Fouts	3,297
8. Vinny Testaverde[1]	3,211
9. Dave Krieg	3,105
10. Boomer Esiason	2,969
11. Drew Bledsoe[1]	2,919
12. Troy Aikman[1]	2,898
13. Steve DeBerg	2,874
14. Jim Kelly	2,874
15. Jim Everett	2,841

Yards Passing	
1. Dan Marino	61,361
2. John Elway	51,475
3. Warren Moon	49,325
4. Fran Tarkenton	47,003
5. Dan Fouts	43,040
6. Brett Favre[1]	42,285
7. Joe Montana	40,551
8. Johnny Unitas	40,239
9. Vinny Testaverde[1]	39,558
10. Dave Krieg	38,147
11. Boomer Esiason	37,920
12. Jim Kelly	35,467
13. Jim Everett	34,837
14. Jim Hart	34,665
15. Steve DeBerg	34,241

Touchdown Passes	
1. Dan Marino	420
2. Fran Tarkenton	342
3. Brett Favre[1]	314
4. John Elway	300
5. Warren Moon	291
6. Johnny Unitas	290
7. Joe Montana	273
8. Dave Krieg	261
9. Sonny Jurgensen	255
10. Dan Fouts	254
11. Boomer Esiason	247
12. John Hadl	244
12. Vinny Testaverde[1]	244
14. Len Dawson	239
15. Jim Kelly	237

Note: Through end of 2002 season. Includes players who played a portion of their careers in the American Football League. Quarterback rating is based on a combination of performances in the following four categories: percentage of completions, percentage of touchdown passes, percentage of interceptions and average gain per pass attempts. Minimum 1,500 attempts; through end of 2002 season.
1. Player active in 2002. **Source:** National Football League *2003 Record and Fact Book*.

NFL Champions, 1921–66

Year	Team (record)	Year	Team (record)	Year	Team (record)
1921	Chicago Staleys[1] (10-1-1)	**1937**	Washington Redskins (8-3-0)	**1952**	Detroit Lions (9-3-0)
1922	Canton Bulldogs (10-0-2)	**1938**	New York Giants (8-2-1)	**1953**	Detroit Lions (10-2-0)
1923	Canton Bulldogs (11-0-1)	**1939**	Green Bay Packers (9-2-0)	**1954**	Cleveland Browns (9-3-0)
1924	Cleveland Bulldogs[2] (7-1-1)	**1940**	Chicago Bears (8-3-0)	**1955**	Cleveland Browns (9-2-1)
1925	Chicago Cardinals (11-2-1)	**1941**	Chicago Bears (10-1-1)	**1956**	New York Giants (8-3-1)
1926	Frankford Yellowjackets (14-1-1)	**1942**	Washington Redskins (10-1-1)	**1957**	Detroit Lions (8-4-0)
1927	New York Giants (11-1-1)	**1943**	Chicago Bears (8-1-1)	**1958**	Baltimore Colts (9-3-0)
1928	Providence Steam Roller (8-1-2)	**1944**	Green Bay Packers (8-2-0)	**1959**	Baltimore Colts (9-3-0)
1929	Green Bay Packers (12-0-1)	**1945**	Cleveland Rams (9-1-0)	**1960**	Philadelphia Eagles (10-2-0)
1930	Green Bay Packers (10-3-1)	**1946**	Chicago Bears (8-2-1)	**1961**	Green Bay Packers (11-3-0)
1931	Green Bay Packers (12-2-0)	**1947**	Chicago Cardinals (9-3-0)	**1962**	Green Bay Packers (13-1-0)
1932	Chicago Bears (7-1-6)	**1948**	Philadelphia Eagles (9-2-1	**1963**	Chicago Bears (11-1-2)
1933	Chicago Bears (10-2-1)	**1949**	Philadelphia Eagles (11-1-0)	**1964**	Cleveland Browns (10-3-1)
1934	New York Giants (8-5-0)	**1950**	Cleveland Browns (10-2-0)	**1965**	Green Bay Packers (10-3-1)
1935	Detroit Lions (7-3-2)	**1951**	Los Angeles Rams (8-4-0)	**1966**	Green Bay Packers (12-2-0)
1936	Green Bay Packers (10-1-1)				

1. Later called the Chicago Bears. 2. Franchise moved from Canton.

Super Bowl Results

SUPER BOWL I

Jan. 15, 1967 Memorial Coliseum, Los Angeles

Green Bay Packers 35 Kansas City Chiefs 10

Green Bay's Max McGee was a surprise star, filling in for ailing Boyd Dowler. McGee had caught only four passes all year, but in Super Bowl I he caught seven for 138 yards and two touchdowns. Quarterback Bart Starr was the game's MVP, as he completed 16 of 23 passes for 250 yards and two touchdowns. Green Bay broke up the game with three second-half touchdowns, the first of which was set up by safety Willie Wood's 45-yard interception return.

SUPER BOWL II

Jan. 14, 1968, Orange Bowl, Miami

Green Bay Packers 33 Oakland Raiders 14

Bart Starr again dominated proceedings with 13 completions in 24 attempts, for 202 yards and a touchdown, winning his second straight MVP award. The Pack attack was in control all the way after building a 16–7 halftime lead. Don Chandler kicked four field goals and all-pro cornerback Herb Adderley capped the Green Bay scoring with a 60-yard interception return.

SUPER BOWL III

Jan. 12, 1969, Orange Bowl, Miami

New York Jets 16 Baltimore Colts 7

Quarterback Joe Namath guaranteed victory before the game and then he and the upstart AFL Jets easily dispatched the heavily favored Colts. Namath won MVP honors by completing 17 of 28 passes for 206 yards and directing a steady attack that racked up 337 total yards. Three times in the first half, the Jet defense intercepted Colts quarterback Earl Morrall, who was playing for an injured Johnny Unitas. With the Jets ahead 13–0 in the third quarter, Unitas came off the bench and later orchestrated Baltimore's sole touchdown.

SUPER BOWL IV

Jan. 11, 1970, Tulane Stadium, New Orleans

Kansas City Chiefs 23 Minnesota Vikings 7

MVP quarterback Len Dawson called a nearly flawless game for Kansas City, completing 12 of 17 passes and hitting Otis Taylor on a 46-yard pass for the final Chiefs touchdown. The Kansas City defense limited Minnesota's strong rushing game to 67 yards and had three interceptions and two fumble recoveries. The second consecutive victory by an AFL team proved that AFL teams could compete with NFL franchises, and assured a smooth merger between the two leagues.

SUPER BOWL V

Jan. 17, 1971, Orange Bowl, Miami

Baltimore Colts 16 Dallas Cowboys 13

Rookie Jim O'Brien's 32-yard field goal in the closing seconds broke a 13–13 tie and gave the Colts their first Super Bowl victory. Dallas led 13–6 at halftime, but two Colt interceptions set up a Baltimore touchdown and O'Brien's crucial kick. Baltimore's first touchdown came when a Johnny Unitas pass caromed off receiver Eddie Hinton's fingertips, bounced off Dallas defensive back Mel Renfro, and finally settled into the grasp of tight end John Mackey, who went 47 yards for the score. Dallas linebacker Chuck Howley was the MVP, the only time the MVP came from the losing team.

SUPER BOWL VI

Jan. 16, 1972, Tulane Stadium, New Orleans

Dallas Cowboys 24 Miami Dolphins 3

The Cowboys rushed for 252 yards and their defense limited the Dolphins to 185 total yards and no touchdowns. Dallas converted Chuck Howley's recovery of Larry Csonka's first fumble of the season into a 3–0 advantage. At halftime, Dallas led 10–3. An eight-play, 71-yard march made it a 17–3 game. Cowboys' quarterback Roger Staubach was voted MVP for his 12 completions in 19 attempts, 119 yards passing and two touchdowns.

SUPER BOWL VII

Jan. 14, 1973, Memorial Coliseum, Los Angeles

Miami Dolphins 14 Washington Redskins 7

In a game that wasn't as close as the score, the Dolphins thoroughly dominated the Redskins to complete the NFL's only undefeated season. Quarterback Bob Griese hit Paul Warfield for 18 yards, then delivered a 28-yard strike to Howard

Twilley for the Dolphins' first score. Just before the half, Dolphins linebacker Nick Buoniconti intercepted a Billy Kilmer pass and returned it to the Washington 27, setting up Miami's second touchdown. Safety Jake Scott led the Dolphin defense with two interceptions (one in the end zone killing a Redskin scoring drive) and was the MVP. The Redskins' sole touchdown resulted when Dolphin kicker Garo Yepremian tried to turn a botched field goal into a forward pass. Washington's Mike Bass picked the ball out of the air and returned it 49 yards for the score.

SUPER BOWL VIII

Jan. 13, 1974, Rice Stadium, Houston

Miami Dolphins 24 Minnesota Vikings 7

Miami scored on its first two possessions, on 62- and 56-yard marches. The initial 10-play drive was climaxed by a Larry Csonka touchdown bolt through right guard. Four plays later, Miami's Jim Kiick burst one yard through the middle for the second touchdown. By halftime Miami led 17–0. The Dolphins defense held off the Vikings on a crucial fourth-and-one play from the Miami 6-yard-line when middle linebacker Nick Buoniconti jarred the ball loose from Minnesota running back Oscar Reed and Jake Scott recovered for Miami. Csonka rushed 33 times for 145 yards, winning the MVP.

SUPER BOWL IX

Jan, 12, 1975, Tulane Stadium, New Orleans

Pittsburgh Steelers 16 Minnesota 6

Steeler Dwight White tackled Minnesota quarterback Fran Tarkenton in the end zone for a safety to put the Steelers on the board in the second quarter. They took advantage of another break in the second half, when Minnesota's Bill Brown fumbled the kickoff and Marv Kellum recovered for Pittsburgh on the Vikings' 30. From there, Franco Harris carried three straight times for the game's first touchdown. Minnesota blocked a Bobby Walden punt and Terry Brown recovered the ball for a touchdown to cut the lead to 9–6, but the Steelers roared back with a 66-yard march, climaxed by Terry Bradshaw's 4-yard scoring pass to Larry Brown. Pittsburgh's defense controlled the game, permitting Minnesota only 119 yards total offense. Franco Harris rushed 34 times for 158 yards to win MVP honors.

SUPER BOWL X

Jan. 18, 1976, Orange Bowl, Miami

Pittsburgh Steelers 21 Dallas Cowboys 17

Steeler quarterback Terry Bradshaw hurled a 64-yard touchdown pass to Lynn Swann to win the game, while the Steel Curtain defense stopped the Cowboys' last rally with an end-zone interception in the game's final play. It was a battle of quarterbacks with Bradshaw and Cowboy Roger Staubach each hurling two touchdowns. Swann earned MVP honors with 161 yards on four receptions. The Steelers blasted out in front with a 14-point fourth quarter.

SUPER BOWL XI

Jan. 9, 1977, Rose Bowl, Pasadena,California

Oakland Raiders 32 Minnesota Vikings 14

A record 81 million TV viewers watched the Raiders gain a record-breaking 429 yards, including running back Clarence Davis' 137 yards rushing. Wide receiver Fred Biletnikoff made four key receptions, which earned him the game's MVP trophy. Oakland scored on three successive possessions in the second quarter to build a 16–0 halftime lead. Minnesota's Fran Tarkenton passed for a touchdown in the third to cut the deficit, but two fourth-quarter interceptions clinched the title for the Raiders. One set up Pete Banaszak's second touchdown run, the other resulted in cornerback Willie Brown's 75-yard interception return.

SUPER BOWL XII

Jan. 15, 1978, Louisiana Superdome, New Orleans

Dallas Cowboys 27 Denver Broncos 10

The TV audience climbed to 102 million, as Dallas converted two interceptions into 10 points and a 13–0 Dallas halftime lead. Butch Johnson made a spectacular diving catch in the end zone of a Roger Staubach pass to make it 20–3. Dallas clinched the victory when running back Robert Newhouse threw a 29-yard touchdown pass to Golden Richards. Co-MVP's Harvey Martin and Randy White led the Cowboys' defense, which recovered four fumbles and intercepted four passes.

SUPER BOWL XIII

Jan, 21, 1979, Orange Bowl, Miami

Pittsburgh Steelers 35 Dallas Cowboys 31

MVP Terry Bradshaw hurled four touchdown passes to lead the Steelers to victory, making them the first team to win three Super Bowls. Bradshaw completed 17 of 30 passes for 318 yards. In the fourth quarter, the Steelers broke open the contest with two touchdowns in 19 seconds. Franco Harris rambled 22 yards up the middle to put Pittsburgh in front 28–17. The Steelers got the ball right back when Randy White fumbled the kickoff and Dennis Winston recovered. On first down, Bradshaw hit Lynn Swann with an 18-yard scoring pass to boost the lead to 35–17. The Cowboys came back with a Roger Staubach touchdown pass to Billy Joe DuPree and then recovered an onside kick, which led to another Staubach touchdown pass, this time to Butch Johnson. But Rocky Bleier smothered an onside kick with 17 seconds remaining to seal the victory.

SUPER BOWL XIV

Jan. 20, 1980, Rose Bowl, Pasadena, California

Pittsburgh Steelers 31 Los Angeles Rams 19

It was all Terry Bradshaw again as he completed 14 of 21 passes for 309 records, and set two passing records as the Steelers became the first team to win four Super Bowls. Despite three interceptions by the Rams, Bradshaw brought the Steelers back from behind twice in the second half. On Pittsburgh's first possession of the final period, Bradshaw lofted a 73-yard scoring pass to John Stallworth to put the Steelers in front to stay, 24–19. Franco Harris scored on a one-yard run later to seal the verdict. Bradshaw was the MVP for the second straight Super Bowl.

SUPER BOWL XV

Jan. 25, 1981, Louisiana Superdome, New Orleans

Oakland Raiders 27 Philadelphia Eagles 10

Jim Plunkett threw three touchdown passes, including an 80-yarder to Kenny King, to give Oakland a decisive 14-0 advantage nine seconds before halftime. Oakland linebacker Rod Martin intercepted three passes as the Raiders completely stifled Eagle quarterback Ron Jaworski's offense. Jaworski managed an 8-yard touchdown pass in the fourth quarter, but the issue had been decided by Plunkett, who completed 13 of the 21 pass attempts for 261 yards and was named MVP.

SUPER BOWL XVI

Jan. 24, 1982, Pontiac Silverdome, Pontiac, Mich.

San Francisco 49ers 26 Cincinnati Bengals 21

The 49ers led 20-0 at halftime, but barely hung on for the win. Ray Wersching kicked four field goals for San Francisco and quarterback Joe Montana engineered two touchdown drives, passing for one and scoring the other himself on a one-yard dive. The Bengals rebounded in the second half as quarterback Ken Anderson ran in a touchdown and passed for another. With 16 seconds remaining, the Bengals scored again, on a 3-yard pass to Dan Ross, but couldn't get the ball back a final time. Ross set a Super Bowl record with 11 receptions for 104 yards. Montana, the MVP, completed 14 of 22 passes for 157 yards.

SUPER BOWL XVII

Jan. 30, 1983, Rose Bowl, Pasadena, California

Washington Redskins 27 Miami Dolphins 17

Washington fullback John Riggins carried the ball for 166 yards on 38 carries to lead Washington to their first NFL title since 1942. Riggins, the MVP, and quarterback Joe Theismann, who passed 23 times for 15 completions, 143 yards, and two touchdowns paced the Redskins to 400 total yards of offense. Riggin's 43-yard touchdown run on fourth-and-one was the gamebreaker.

SUPER BOWL XVIII

Jan, 22, 1984, Tampa Stadium, Tampa, Florida

Los Angeles Raiders 38 Washington Redskins 9

This hopelessly lopsided victory set records. Raider reserve linebacker Jack Squirek intercepted a Joe Theismann pass at the Redskins five-yard line and ran the ball in for a touchdown with seven seconds left in the first half. Raiders' Marcus Allen rushed for 191 yards on 20 carries, including two touchdowns, one on a 74-yard run. Allen was voted game MVP.

SUPER BOWL XIX

Jan. 20, 1985, Stanford Stadium, Stanford, Calif.

San Francisco 49ers 38 Miami Dolphins 16

The Dolphins led 10-7 at the end of the first period, but 49er running back Roger Craig came back with three touchdowns. Joe Montana dominated the game with an MVP performance: 24 of 35 passes for yards and three touchdowns. He also rushed five times for 59 yards and a touchdown. Craig had 58 yards on 15 carries and caught seven passes for 77 yards. Wendell Tyler rushed 13 times for 65 yards, as San Francisco's running game racked up 211 yards..

SUPER BOWL XX

Jan 26, 1986 Louisiana Superdome, New Orleans

Chicago Bears 46 New England Patriots 10

The Patriots took a quick 3-0 lead on Tony Franklin's 36-yard field goal with 1:19 elapsed in the first period. But the Bears rebounded by mauling the Pats. Chicago tied the record for sacks (7), and limited the Pats to 7 yards rushing. Total yardage at intermission told the story: Chicago 236, New England -19. The Bears ran up a fat 23–3 lead in the first half. In the second, the Bears marched 96 yards in nine plays, capped by quarterback Jim McMahon's one-yard rush for a touchdown. Bears defensive end Richard Dent won the MVP after contributing 1 /2 sacks, and leading the ferocious Chicago defense.

SUPER BOWL XXI

Jan. 25, 1987, Rose Bowl, Pasadena, California

New York Giants 39 Denver Broncos 20

The Broncos held a 10–9 lead at halftime, backed by the passing of John Elway. He capped a 58 yard scoring drive on six plays with a four yard touchdown run. But in the second half, the Giants' defense took over, sacking Elway in his end zone for a safety. The Broncos had a first and goal, but failed to score on three plays and a field goal attempt. After that the Giants' offense rebounded, scoring 30 points in the second half. Giant quarterback Phil Simms passed for 268 yards and three touchdowns, and was named MVP.

SUPER BOWL XXII

Jan 31, 1988, Jack Murphy Stadium, San Diego

Washington Redskins 42 Denver Broncos 10

The Broncos jumped in front early as John Elway hurled a 56-yard touchdown pass to wide receiver Ricky Nattiel on the Broncos' first play from scrimmage. But the Redskins erupted for 35 points on five straight possessions. Redskins' quarterback Doug Williams led the assault, hurling four touchdown passes, including 80- and 50-yarders to wide receiver Rick Sanders. Washington scored five touchdowns in 18 plays in 5:47 of possession. MVP Williams completed 18 of 29 passes for 340 yards. Rookie running back Timmy Smith ran 22 times for 204 yards.

SUPER BOWL XXIII

Jan. 22, 1989, Joe Robbie Stadium, Miami

San Francisco 49ers 20 Cincinnati Bengals 16

San Francisco became the first NFC team to win three Super Bowls by defeating the Bengals in a rematch of Super Bowl XVI. Even though San Francisco held an advantage in total yards (453 vs. 229), they found themselves trailing when Jim Breech's field goal gave Cincinnati a 16-13 lead with 3:20 left in the game. The 49ers started their winning drive at their own 8-yard line. Over the next 11 plays, they drove 92 yards to the winning score, a 10-yard touchdown pass from Joe Montana to John Taylor with 34 seconds left. San Francisco's Jerry Rice won the MVP after catching 11 passes for 215 yards. Montana completed 23 of 36 passes for 357 yards and two touchdowns.

SUPER BOWL XXIII

Jan. 28,1990, Louisiana Superdome, New Orleans

San Francisco 49ers 55 Denver Broncos 10

San Francisco demolished the Broncos and became the first team to repeat as champions since the 1979–80 Steelers. Quarterback Joe Montana orchestrated the 49ers' diverse offense, completing 22 of 29 passes for 297 yards and five touchdowns, en route to winning the MVP. Montana raised his record to 122 straight Super Bowl pass attempts without an interception. His primary receiver was Jerry Rice, who hauled in seven passes for 148 yards and three touchdowns. Running backs Tom Rathman and Roger Craig ran for three more touchdowns. Meanwhile, the San Francisco defense completely dominated Denver's offense, limiting them to 167 total yards while sacking quarterback John Elway six times and intercepting two passes.

SUPER BOWL XXV

Jan. 27, 1991, Tampa Stadium, Tampa, Florida

New York Giants 20 Buffalo Bills, 19

The Giants edged the Bills in a nearly error-free game that was decided only when the Bills' Scott Norwood missed a field goal with eight seconds to play. Backup quarterback Jeff Hostetler and veteran running back Ottis Anderson directed the Giants' ball-control offense, holding the ball for a stunning 40:33. Anderson carried the ball 21 times for 102 yards and was named the MVP. After falling behind 12–3, the veteran Giants team refused to panic. Their defense slowed Buffalo's "hurry-up" offense to a crawl, surrounding Jim Kelly's receivers with extra defensive backs and linebackers. Kelly finished the day with 18 completions in 30 attempts for 205 yards, but could rarely convert on crucial third down opportunities. Hostetler, substituting for the injured Phil Simms, led the Giants on touchdown drives of 75 and 87 yards, while completing 20 of 32 passes for 214 yards and no turnovers.

SUPER BOWL XXVI

Jan. 26, 1992, The Metrodome, Minneapolis

Washington Redskins 37 Buffalo Bills 24

Washington jumped out to a 17-0 lead in the first half and never looked back. MVP quarterback Mark Rypien completed 18 of 33 passes for 292 yards and two touchdowns. Meanwhile, the blitzing Redskin defense intercepted Buffalo quarterback Jim Kelly four times and sacked the Bills' signal-caller five times. Buffalo's no-huddle offense was also plagued by several dropped passes, including two that would have gone for touchdowns. In all, Kelly threw a record 58 passes, 30 of which went incomplete. Brad Edwards, Washington's free safety, had two interceptions and broke up five passes, while linebacker Wilber Marshall forced two fumbles. Bills running back Thurman Thomas, the NFL's regular season MVP, was limited to 13 yards on 10 rushes.

SUPER BOWL XXVII

Jan. 31, 1993, Rose Bowl, Pasadena, California

Dallas Cowboys 52 Buffalo Bills 17

Buffalo lost its third straight Super Bowl and the second consecutive rout. The game's turning point came early in the second quarter, when Buffalo drove inside the Dallas five-yard-line twice but came away with only three points, and lost starting quarterback Jim Kelly in the process. Inspired by its defense's two goal line stands, the Cowboys' offense, which had been fairly inept up to this point, came alive for a long scoring drive. The Bills fumbled their first play from scrimmage on the ensuing drive, and one play later, the Cowboys had scored again, this time on a strike from Troy Aikman to Michael Irvin, giving Dallas a 28–10 halftime lead. Aikman passed for four touchdowns and was named MVP.

SUPER BOWL XXVIII

Jan. 30, 1994, Georgia Dome, Atlanta

Dallas Cowboys 30 Buffalo Bills 13

Buffalo became the first team in U.S. professional sports history to lose four consecutive championship games. The Bills actually led at halftime 13–6 on the strength of Thurman Thomas's 37 yards rushing and 54- and 28-yard field goals by Steve Christie. But Thomas fumbled on the opening drive of the second half and Dallas safety James Washington returned it 46 yards for a touchdown, tying the game at 13 Dallas then drove the length of the field on its next drive, with running back Emmitt Smith grinding out 61 yards. The Cowboys added another touchdown and a field goal to secure the victory. Smith, the league's regular season MVP, was named MVP of the Super Bowl as well.

SUPER BOWL XXIX

Jan. 29, 1995, Joe Robbie Stadium, Miami

San Francisco 49ers 49 San Diego Chargers 26

Favored by 20 points, (the largest margin in Super Bowl history), San Francisco scored early and often to capture a fifth Super Bowl championship. On the third play from scrimmage, Steve Young found Jerry Rice wide open inside the San Diego 10-yard line. Young threw six touchdowns and ran for 49 yards, making him the 49ers' leading rusher as well. Rice and running back Ricky Watters each scored three touchdowns. Young was named MVP for his 24-for-36 for 325 yard performance.

SUPER BOWL XXX

Jan. 28, 1996, Sun Devil Stadium, Tempe, Ariz.

Dallas Cowboys 27 Pittsburgh Steelers 17

Dallas scored on its first three possessions, but failed to dominate the game, and led only 13–7 at halftime. In the second half, the Steelers threatened to close the gap, but quarterback Neil O'Donnell stunted the drive by throwing an interception to Cowboy cornerback Larry Brown. Pittsburgh rallied again in the fourth quarter to cut Dallas' lead to 20–17. But O'Donnell threw another interception to Brown, who returned it to the Steeler 6-yard line, setting up the Cowboys' final touchdown. Brown was the obvious MVP choice.

SUPER BOWL XXXI

Jan. 26, 1997, Louisiana Superdome, New Orleans,

Green Bay Packers 35 New England Patriots 21

Packer quarterback Bret Favre hit Andre Rison for a 54-yard touchdown pass on Green Bay's second play from scrimmage, but the Patriots rallied for a 14-10 first quarter lead. The Packers recaptured the lead with a 17-points in the second quarter. In the second half, New England running back Curtis Martin scored to cut the lead to 27-21, but Desmond Howard returned the ensuing kickoff 99 yards for a touchdown. Howard's 154 yards on four kickoff returns and 90 yards on six punt returns earned him MVP honors.

SUPER BOWL XXXII

Jan. 25, 1998, Qualcomm Stadium, San Diego,

Denver Broncos 31 Green Bay Packers 24

The victory was Denver's first in five tries, and the AFC's first in 13 years. With the game tied at 24 late in the fourth quarter, Denver took over at midfield. A penalty and a pass moved the Broncos closer, and then running back Terrell Davis ran 17 yards to the one-yard-line. On the next play, he punched it in for his third touchdown. With less than two minutes left, the Packers drove into Denver territory but could not convert a 4th and 6. Davis earned MVP honors for his 30 carries, 157 yards, and three touchdowns.

SUPER BOWL XXXIII

Jan. 31, 1999, Pro Player Stadium, Miami

Denver Broncos 34 Atlanta Falcons 19

Denver quarterback John Elway completed 18 of 29 passes for 336 yards and MVP honors, as the Broncos cruised to their second straight Super Bowl victory. Broncos running back Terrell Davis added 102 yards rushing, and cornerback Darrien Gordon had interception returns of 50 and 58 yards, each setting up a Denver touchdown. Atlanta scored first on a Morten Andersen field goal to take a brief 3–0 lead. But despite driving deep into Denver territory several times, they could not crack the end zone until the fourth quarter, when the outcome was already decided.

SUPER BOWL XXXIV

Jan. 30, 2000, Georgia Dome, Atlanta

St. Louis Rams 23 Tennessee Titans 16

St. Louis dominated the first half, moving at will into Tennessee territory, but came away with only three field goals to show for it. The Rams extended their lead to 16-0 in the third quarter before the Titans put together three long scoring drives that tied the game with 2:12 remaining. On the very next play from scrimmage, quarterback Kurt Warner hit Isaac Bruce for a 73-yard touchdown pass to put St. Louis back up 23-16. With time running out, Tennessee quarterback Steve McNair engineered an 87-yard drive, but his last completion to Kevin Dyson left the Titans a yard short of a game-tying touchdown as time expired. Warner was named MVP on the strength of his 414 yards passing.

SUPER BOWL XXXV

Jan. 28, 2001, Raymond James Stadium, Tampa

Baltimore Ravens 34, New York Giants 7

Baltimore's vaunted defense pitched a shutout, as the Giants' only points came on special teams. The Ravens stymied New York's offense, constantly pinning the Giants deep inside their own territory, and creating five turnovers. Jermaine Lewis's 34-yard punt return set up Baltimore's first touchdown in the first quarter, and Duane Starks's interception return gave the Ravens a 17-0 lead late in the third quarter. Ron Dixon returned the ensuing kickoff 97 yards for the Giants' to cut the score to 17-7, but Lewis put the game out of reach on the very next play with an 84-yard kickoff return of his own. Middle linebacker Ray Lewis, the heart and soul of the Ravens defense, was the MVP.

SUPER BOWL XXXVI

Feb. 3, 2002, Louisiana Superdome, New Orleans

New England Patriots 20, St.Louis Rams 17

The Patriots, a 14-point underdog to the Rams and their high-flying offense, shocked the football world twice. First, they capitalized on three St. Louis turnovers to jump out to a 17-3 lead after three quarters. Then, after giving up the tying touchdown with 1:21 left in the game, New England marched 53 yards with no timeouts to set up Adam Vinatieri's game-winning 48-yard field goal. Patriots quarterback Tom Brady, who started the season as Drew Bledsoe's backup, completed his Cinderella season by completing five passes in eight attempts in the final drive, and was named MVP.

SUPER BOWL XXXVII

January 26, 2003, Qualcomm Stadium, San Diego

Tampa Bay Buccaneers 48, Oakland Raiders 21

The Buccaneers' defense dominated, intercepting five passes and returning three of them for touchdowns, and sacking Oakland quarterback Rich Gannon five times. Tampa Bay piled up 34 unanswered points on the strength of Michael Pittman's 124 rushing yards, and Joe Jurevicius' 78 receiving yards. The Raiders rallied for two touchdowns in the fourth quarter, but the Bucs dashed any hopes of a comeback by returning two interceptions for touchdowns. Dexter Jackson, who had the first two interceptions, was the MVP.

Pro Football Hall of Fame Members

Alphabetical listing of the members of the Professional Football Hall of Fame. Listing includes enshrinee's name, year of enshrinement, position, and the teams he played for.

Herb Adderley (1980) CB, Packers, Cowboys.
Lance Alworth (1978) WR, Chargers, Cowboys.
George Allen (2002) Coach, Rams, Redskins.
Marcus Allen (2003) RB, Raiders, Chiefs.
Doug Atkins (1982) DE, Browns, Bears, Saints.
Morris (Red) Badgro (1981) E, Yankees, Giants, Dodgers.
Lem Barney (1992) CB, Lions.
Cliff Battles (1968) RB, QB Braves, Redskins.
Sammy Baugh (1963) QB, Redskins.
Chuck Bednarik (1967) C, LB, Eagles.
Bert Bell (1963 Charter) Commissioner, NFL. Founder/coach, Eagles, Steelers.
Bobby Bell (1983) LB, DE, Chiefs.
Raymond Berry (1973) E, Colts.
Elvin Bethea (2003) DE, Oilers
Charles W. Bidwill, Sr. (1967) Owner/president, Cardinals.
Fred Biletnikoff (1988) WR, Raiders.
George Blanda (1981) QB, PK, Bears, Colts, Oilers, Raiders.
Mel Blount (1989) CB, Steelers.
Terry Bradshaw (1989) QB, Steelers.
Jim Brown (1971) FB, Browns.
Paul E. Brown (1967) Coach and GM, Browns, Bengals.
Roosevelt Brown (1975) OT, Giants.
Willie Brown (1984) CB, Broncos, Raiders.
Buck Buchanan (1990) DT, Chiefs.
Nick Buoniconti (2001) LB, Patriots, Dolphins.
Dick Butkus (1979) LB, Bears.
Earl Campbell (1991) RB, Oilers, Saints.
Tony Canadeo (1974) RB, Packers.
Joe Carr (1963) NFL President.
Dave Casper (2002) TE, Raiders, Oilers, Vikings.
Guy Chamberlin (1965) E, Bulldogs, Staleys, Yellowjackets, Cardinals. Coach, Bulldogs, Yellowjackets, Cardinals.
Jack Christiansen (1970) DB, Spartans, Lions.
Earl (Dutch) Clark (1970) DB, Spartans, Lions, Rams.
George Connor (1975) OT, DT, LB, Bears.
Jimmy Conzelman (1964) QB, Staleys, Independents, Badgers, Panthers. Owner, Steamrollers, Cardinals.
Lou Creekmur, (1996) OL, Lions.
Larry Csonka (1987) RB, Dolphins, Giants.
Al Davis (1992) President, Owner, General Manager, Coach, Raiders. Commissioner, American Football League.
Willie Davis (1981) DE, Browns, Packers.
Len Dawson (1987) QB, Steelers, Browns, Texans, Chiefs.
Joe DeLameielleure (2003) G, Bills, Browns.

Eric Dickerson, (1999) RB, Rams, Colts, Raiders, Falcons.
Dan Dierdorf, (1996) OT, Cardinals
Mike Ditka (1988) TE, Bears, Eagles, Cowboys.
Art Donovan (1968) DT, Colts, Yankees, Texans.
Tony Dorsett (1994) RB, Cowboys, Broncos.
John (Paddy) Driscoll (1965) QB, Pros, Staleys, Cardinals, Bears.
Bill Dudley (1966) RB, Steelers, Lions, Redskins.
Albert Glen (Turk) Edwards (1969) OT, Braves, Redskins.
Weeb Ewbank (1978) Coach, Colts, Jets.
Tom Fears (1970) E, Rams.
Jim Finks (1995) President, Vikings, Bears, Saints.
Ray Flaherty (1976) Coach, Redskins, Yankees.
Len Ford (1976) DE, E, Dons, Browns, Packers.
Dan Fortmann (1965) G, Bears.
Dan Fouts (1993) QB, Chargers.
Frank Gatski (1985) C, Browns, Lions.
Bill George (1974) LB, Bears, Rams.
Joe Gibbs (1996) Coach, Chargers, Redskins.
Frank Gifford (1977) RB, Giants.
Sid Gillman (1983) Coach, Rams, Chargers, Oilers.
Otto Graham (1965) QB, Browns.
Harold (Red) Grange (1963 Charter) RB, Bears, Yankees.
Bud Grant (1994) Coach, Vikings.
(Mean) Joe Greene (1987) DT, Steelers.
Forrest Gregg (1977) OL, Packers, Cowboys.
Bob Griese (1990) QB, Dolphins.
Lou Groza (1974) OT, PK Browns.
Joe Guyon (1966) RB, Bulldogs, Indians, Independents, Cowboys, Giants.
George Halas (1963) Founder, Coach, player, Staleys. President, Coach, player, Bears.
Jack Ham (1988) LB, Steelers.
Dan Hampton (2002) DE/DT, Bears
John Hannah (1991) G, Patriots.
Franco Harris (1990) RB, Steelers, Seahawks.
Mike Haynes (1997) CB, Patriots, Raiders.
Ed Healey (1964) OT, Independents, Bears.
Mel Hein (1963) C, Giants. Coach, Dons.
Ted Hendricks (1990) LB, Colts, Packers, Raiders
Wilbur (Pete) Henry (1963) OT, Bulldogs, Giants, Maroons.
Arnie Herber (1966) QB, Packers, Giants.
Bill Hewitt (1971) E, Bears, Eagles.
Clarke Hinkle (1964) RB, Packers.
Elroy (Crazylegs) Hirsch (1968) HB, E, Rockets, Rams.
Paul Hornung (1986) HB, Packers.
Ken Houston (1986) S, Oilers, Redskins.
Cal Hubbard (1963) OT, Giants, Packers, Pirates.
Sam Huff (1982) LB, Giants, Redskins.
Lamar Hunt (1972) Founder, AFL; Owner Texans, Chiefs.
Don Hutson (1963) E, Packers.
Jimmy Johnson (1994) CB, 49ers.
John Henry Johnson (1987) RB, 49ers, Lions, Steelers, Oilers.
Charlie Joiner (1996), WR, Oilers, Bengals, Chargers.
David (Deacon) Jones (1980) DE, Rams, Chargers, Redskins.
Stan Jones (1991) G, DT, Bears, Redskins.
Henry Jordan (1995) DT, Packers.
Sonny Jurgensen (1983) QB, Eagles, Redskins.
Jim Kelly (2002) QB, Bills
Leroy Kelly (1994) RB, Browns.
Walt Kiesling (1966) G, Eskimos, Maroons, Cardinals, Bears, Packers, Pirates. Coach, Pirates, Steelers.
Frank (Bruiser) Kinard (1971) OT, Dodgers, Yankees.
Paul Krause (1998) S, Vikings, Redskins.
Early (Curly) Lambeau (1963) Founder, Packers.. Coach, Packers, Cardinals, Redskins.
Jack Lambert (1990) LB, Steelers.
Tom Landry (1990) Coach, Cowboys.
Dick (Night Train) Lane (1974). DB, Rams, Cardinals, Lions.
Jim Langer (1987) C, Dolphins, Vikings.
Willie Lanier (1986) LB, Chiefs.
Steve Largent (1995) WR, Seahawks.
Yale Lary (1979) DB, Lions.
Dante Lavelli (1975) E, Browns.
Bobby Layne (1967) QB, Bears, Bulldogs, Lions, Steelers.
Alphonse (Tuffy) Leemans (1978) RB, Giants.
Marv Levy (2001) Coach, Chiefs, Bills.
Bob Lilly (1980) DT, Cowboys.
Larry Little (1993) G, Chargers, Dolphins.
James Lofton (2003) WR, Packers, Raiders, Bills, Rams.
Vince Lombardi (1971) Coach, GM, Packers, Redskins.
Howie Long (2000) DL, Raiders.
Ronnie Lott (2000) DB, 49ers, Raiders, Jets.
Sid Luckman (1965) QB, Bears.
William Roy (Link) Lyman (1964) T, Bulldogs, Yellowjackets, Bears.
Tom Mack (1999) OG, Rams.
John Mackey (1992) TE, Colts, Chargers.
Tim Mara (1963) Founder, President, Giants.
Wellington Mara (1997) Owner, Giants
Gino Marchetti (1972) DE, Texans, Colts.
George Preston Marshall (1963) Founder, President, Braves (Redskins).
Ollie Matson (1972) RB, Cardinals, Rams, Lions, Eagles.
Don Maynard (1987) WR, Giants, Titans, Jets, Cardinals.
George McAfee (1966) RB, Bears.
Mike McCormack (1984) OT, Yankees, Browns.
Tommy McDonald (1988) WR, Eagles, Cowboys, Rams, Falcons, Browns.
Hugh McElhenny (1970) RB, 49ers Vikings, Giants, Lions.
John (Blood) McNally (1963) RB, Badgers, Eskimos, Maroons, Packers, Pirates Packers.
Mike Michalske (1964) G, Yankees, Packers.
Wayne Millner (1968) E, Redskins. Coach Eagles.
Bobby Mitchell (1983) WR, RB Browns, Redskins.
Ron Mix (1979) OT, Chargers, Raiders.
Joe Montana (2000) QB, 49ers, Chiefs.
Lenny Moore (1975) WR, RB, Colts.
Marion Motley (1968) RB, Browns, Steelers.
Mike Munchak (2001) G, Oilers.
Anthony Muñoz (1998) T, Bengals.
George Musso (1982) OT, G, Bears.
Bronko Nagurski (1963) RB, Bears.
Joe Namath (1985) QB, Jets, Rams.
Earle (Greasy) Neale (1969) Coach, Eagles.
Ernie Nevers (1963) RB, Eskimos, Cardinals.
Ozzie Newsome (1999) TE, Browns.
Ray Nitschke (1978) LB, Packers.
Chuck Noll (1993) Coach, Steelers.
Leo Nomellini (1969) DT, 49ers.
Merlin Olsen (1982) DT, Rams.
Jim Otto (1980) C, Raiders.
Steve Owen (1966) T, Cowboys, Giants. Coach, Giants.
Alan Page (1988) DT, Vikings, Bears.

Clarence (Ace) Parker (1972) QB, Dodgers, Yankees.
Jim Parker (1973) OL, Colts.
Walter Payton (1993) RB, Bears.
Joe Perry (1969) RB, 49ers, Colts.
Pete Pihos (1970) E, Eagles.
Hugh (Shorty) Ray (1966) Supervisor of Officials.
Dan Reeves (1967) Owner, Rams.
Mel Renfro (1996), CB, Cowboys.
John Riggins (1992) RB, Jets, Redskins.
Jim Ringo (1981) C, Packers, Eagles.
Andy Robustelli (1971) DE, Rams, Giants.
Art Rooney (1964) Founder, President, Pirates, Steelers.
Dan Rooney (2000) President, Steelers.
Pete Rozelle (1985) Commissioner, NFL.
Bob St. Clair (1990) OT, 49ers.
Gale Sayers (1977) RB, Bears.
Joe Schmidt (1973) LB, Lions. Coach, Lions.
Tex Schramm (1991) GM, Cowboys.
Lee Roy Selmon (1995) DE, Buccaneers.
Billy Shaw (1999) OG, Bills.
Art Shell (1989) OT, Raiders.
Don Shula (1997) Coach, Colts, Dolphins.
Mike Singletary (1998) LB, Bears.
O.J. Simpson (1985) RB, Bills, 49ers.
Jackie Slater (2001) OT, Rams.
Jackie Smith (1994) TE, Cardinals, Cowboys.
John Stallworth (2002) WR, Steelers
Bart Starr (1977) QB, Packers.
Roger Staubach, (1985) QB, Cowboys.
Ernie Stautner (1969) DT, Steelers.
Jan Stenerud (1991) PK, Chiefs, Packers, Vikings.
Hank Stram (2003) Coach, Texans, Chiefs, Saints.
Dwight Stephenson (1998) C, Dolphins.
Ken Strong (1967) RB, Stapletons, Giants, Yankees.
Joe Stydahar (1967) OT, Bears.
Lynn Swann (2001) WR, Steelers.
Fran Tarkenton (1986) QB, Giants, Vikings.
Charley Taylor (1984) WR, RB, Redskins.
Jim Taylor (1976) RB, Packers, Saints.
Lawrence Taylor (1999) LB, Giants.
Jim Thorpe (1963) RB, Bulldogs, Indians, Maroons, Independents, Giants, Bulldogs, Cardinals.
Y.A. Tittle (1971) QB, Colts 49ers, Giants.
George Trafton (1964) C, Staleys, Bears.
Charley Trippi (1968) RB, QB, Cardinals.
Emlen Tunnell (1967) DB, Giants, Packers.
Clyde (Bulldog) Turner (1966) C, LB, Bears.
Johnny Unitas (1979) QB, Colts, Chargers.
Gene Upshaw (1987) G, Raiders.
Norm Van Brocklin (1971) QB, Rams, Eagles
Steve Van Buren (1965) RB, Eagles.
Doak Walker (1986) HB, Lions.
Bill Walsh (1993) Coach, 49ers.
Paul Warfield (1983) WR, Browns, Dolphins.
Bob Waterfield(1965) QB, Coach, Rams.
Mike Webster (1997) C, Steelers.
Arnie Weinmeister, (1984) DT, Yankees, Giants.
Randy White (1994) DT, Cowboys.
Dave Wilcox (2000) LB, 49ers.
Bill Willis (1977) G, MG, Browns.
Larry Wilson (1978) DB, Cardinals.
Kellen Winslow (1995) TE, Chargers.
Alex Wojciechowicz (1968) C, LB, Lions, Eagles.
Willie Wood (1989) S, Packers.
Ron Yary (2001) OT, Vikings.
Jack Youngblood (2001) DE, Rams.

BASKETBALL

National Basketball Association

Olympic Tower	**www.nba.com**
645 Fifth Avenue	**Commissioner: David Stern**
New York, NY 10022	**Founded: 1946**
(212) 826-7000	**Number of teams: 29**

Dr. James Naismith invented basketball in 1891, only after his indoor versions of lacrosse, rugby, and soccer proved too violent for the intended use in a YMCA fitness program. Yet even his "noncontact" amateur sport proved too rough for many YMCAs, which dropped basketball. Teams were forced to rent halls; they charged an admission fee to pay the rent, and split any leftover cash among the players.

The first pro game was played in 1896 in Trenton, N.J., and by 1898, the fledgling National Basketball League and several others were organized. The Buffalo Germans were the first powerhouse, winning 792 games against only 86 losses from 1895 to 1925. In 1914, the New York Celtics (later renamed the Original Celtics) were organized, playing a "modern" style of basketball using zone defenses, the fast break, and a pivot man.

Other "ethnic" teams dominated in the 1930's, including the Philadelphia SPHAs (South Philadelphia Hebrew Association) under Eddy Gottlieb, and the black barnstorming New York Rens. Several weak leagues continued to compete until the end of World War II. The Basketball Association of America was formed in 1946 by hockey arena managers seeking additional tenants. By 1949, it had merged with its biggest rival to form the modern NBA.

The American Basketball Association, an alternative pro league known for its three-point shots and its red, white and blue ball, lasted for nine seasons (1968–76) and featured such future NBA All-Stars as Julius Erving and Artis Gilmore. When the league folded after the 1975–76 season, four of its teams, the Denver Nuggets, Indiana Pacers, New York (now New Jersey) Nets, and San Antonio Spurs were admitted into the NBA.

The NBA expanded cautiously in the 1970s. Cleveland joined the league in 1970 along with Portland and the Buffalo Braves (now the Los Angeles Clippers); New Orleans received a franchise in 1974 but lost it to Utah in 1979; and in 1980, the NBA expanded to Dallas. Charlotte and Miami joined in 1988, followed by Orlando and Minnesota in 1989. The two Canadian expansion teams, Vancouver and Toronto, joined in 1995. The Vancouver franchise moved to Memphis for the 2001-02 season. And in 2002, after voters in North Carolina refused to finance a new stadium, the Charlotte Hornets moved to New Orleans

Under the current collective bargaining agreement, which is in effect until 2003–2004, player salaries are capped at 48 percent of gross income, individual salaries may not exceed $14 million per year ($9 million for players with less than 6 years experience; $11 million for players with 7–9 years service), and players in their first three years of service have severely limited contracts.

NBA Final Standings, 2002-03

EASTERN CONFERENCE	W-L	Pct.	Home	Away
Atlantic Division				
New Jersey Nets (2)	49-33	.598	33-8	16-25
Philadelphia 76ers (4)	48-34	.585	25-16	23-18
Boston Celtics (6)	44-38	.537	25-16	19-22
Orlando Magic (8)	42-40	.512	26-15	16-25
Washington Wizards	37-45	.451	23-18	14-27
New York Knicks	37-45	.451	24-17	13-28
Miami Heat	25-57	.305	16-25	9-32
Central Division				
Detroit Pistons (1)	50-32	.610	30-11	20-21
Indiana Pacers (3)	48-34	.585	32-9	16-25
New Orleans Hornets (5)	47-35	.573	29-12	18-23
Milwaukee Bucks (7)	42-40	.512	25-16	17-24
Atlanta Hawks	35-47	.427	26-15	9-32
Chicago Bulls	30-52	.366	27-14	3-38
Toronto Raptors	24-58	.293	15-26	9-32
Cleveland Cavaliers	17-65	.207	14-27	3-38

WESTERN CONFERENCE	W-L	Pct.	Home	Away
Midwest Division				
San Antonio Spurs (1)	60-22	.732	33-8	27-14
Dallas Mavericks (3)	60-22	.732	33-8	27-14
Minnesota Timberwolves (4)	51-31	.622	33-8	18-23
Utah Jazz (7)	47-35	.573	29-12	18-23
Houston Rockets	43-39	.524	28-13	15-26
Memphis Grizzlies	28-54	.341	20-21	8-33
Denver Nuggets	17-65	.207	13-28	4-37
Pacific Division				
Sacramento Kings (2)	59-23	.720	35-6	24-17
Los Angeles Lakers (5)	50-32	.610	31-10	19-22
Portland Trail Blazers (6)	50-32	.610	27-14	23-18
Phoenix Suns (8)	44-38	.537	30-11	14-27
Seattle SuperSonics	40-42	.488	25-16	15-26
Golden State Warriors	38-44	.463	24-17	14-27
Los Angeles Clippers	27-55	.329	16-25	11-30

Note: The numbers in parentheses reflect the team's seed for the playoffs. **Source:** NBA.

NBA Playoff Results, 2003

FIRST ROUND

EASTERN CONFERENCE
Detroit Pistons 4, Orlando Magic 3
New Jersey Nets 4, Milwaukee Bucks 2
Boston Celtics 4, Indiana Pacers 2
Philadelphia 76ers 4, New Orleans Hornets 2

WESTERN CONFERENCE
San Antonio Spurs 4, Phoenix Suns 2
Sacramento Kings 4, Utah Jazz 1
Dallas Mavericks 4, Portland Trail Blazers 3
L.A. Lakers 4, Minnesota Timberwolves 2

CONFERENCE SEMIFINALS

Detroit Pistons 4, Philadelphia 76ers 2
New Jersey Nets 4, Boston Celtics 0
San Antonio Spurs 4, Los Angeles Lakers 2
Dallas Mavericks 4, Sacramento Kings 3

CONFERENCE FINALS

New Jersey Nets 4, Detroit Pistons 0
San Antonio Spurs 4, Dallas Mavericks 2

NBA CHAMPIONSHIP SERIES

San Antonio Spurs defeat New Jersey Nets, 4 games to 2

Game 1: SAN ANTONIO 101, New Jersey 89
Game 2: New Jersey 87, SAN ANTONIO 85
Game 3: San Antonio 84, NEW JERSEY 79
Game 4: NEW JERSEY 77, San Antonio 76
Game 5: San Antonio 93, NEW JERSEY 83
Game 6: SAN ANTONIO 88, New Jersey 77

2003 NBA First Round Draft Picks

Rank, Team	Player, Position, College or High School
1. Cleveland	LeBron James, F, St. Vincent-St. Mary's High School
2. Detroit	Darko Milicic, F/C, Serbia and Montenegro
3. Denver	Carmelo Anthony, F, Syracuse
4. Toronto	Chris Bosh, F, Georgia Tech
5. Miami	Dwyane Wade, G, Marquette
6. L.A. Clippers	Chris Kaman, C, Central Michigan
7. Chicago	Kirk Hinrich, G, Kansas
8. Milwaukee	T.J. Ford, G, Texas
9. New York	Mike Sweetney, F, Georgetown
10. Washington	Jarvis Hayes, G/F, Georgia
11. Golden State	Mickael Pietrus, G/F, France
12. Seattle	Nick Collison, F, Kansas
13. Memphis	Marcus Banks, G, UNLV
14. Seattle	Luke Ridnour, G, Oregon
15. Orlando	Reece Gaines, G, Louisville
16. Boston	Troy Bell, G, Boston College
17. Phoenix	Zarko Cabarkapa, F/C, Serbia and Montenegro
18. New Orleans	David West, F, Xavier
19. Utah	Aleksandar Pavlovic , F, Serbia and Montenegro
20. Boston	Dahntay Jones, G/F, Duke
21. Atlanta	Boris Diaw-Riffiod, G/F, France
22. New Jersey	Zoran Planinic, G/F, Croatia
23. Portland	Travis Outlaw, F, Starkville HS
24. L.A. Lakers	Brian Cook, F, Illinois
25. Detroit	Carlos Delfino, G/F, Italy
26. Minnesota	Ndudi Ebi, F, Westbury Christian High School
27. Memphis	Kendrick Perkins, C, Clifton J. Ozen High School
28. San Antonio	Leandrinho Barbosa, G, Brazil
29. Dallas	Josh Howard , F, Wake Forest

NBA Leaders, 2002-03

SCORING	G	Pts.	Avg.
Tracy McGrady, Orlando	75	2,407	32.1
Kobe Bryant, L.A. Lakers	82	2,461	30.0
Allen Iverson, Philadelphia	82	2,262	27.6
Shaquille O'Neal, L.A. Lakers	67	1,841	27.5
Paul Pierce, Boston	79	2,048	25.9
Dirk Nowitzki, Dallas	80	2,011	25.1
Tim Duncan, San Antonio	81	1,884	23.3
Chris Webber, Sacramento	67	1,542	23.0
Kevin Garnett, Minnesota	82	1,883	23.0
Ray Allen, Seattle	76	1,713	22.5
Allan Houston, New York	82	1,845	22.5
Stephon Marbury, Phoenix	81	1,806	22.3
Antawn Jamison, Golden State	82	1,822	22.2
Jalen Rose, Chicago	82	1,816	22.1
Jamal Mashburn, New Orleans	82	1,772	21.6
Jerry Stackhouse, Washington	70	1,508	21.5
Shawn Marion, Phoenix	81	1,716	21.2
Steve Francis, Houston	81	1,703	21.0
Glenn Robinson, Atlanta	69	1,436	20.8
Jermaine O'Neal, Indiana	77	1,600	20.8

REBOUNDS	G	Reb.	Avg.
Ben Wallace, Detroit	73	1,126	15.4
Kevin Garnett, Minnesota	82	1,102	13.4
Tim Duncan, San Antonio	81	1,043	12.9
Jermaine O'Neal, Indiana	77	796	10.3
Brian Grant, Miami	82	837	10.2
Troy Murphy, Golden State	79	806	10.2
Dirk Nowitzki, Dallas	80	791	9.9
Shawn Marion, Phoenix	81	773	9.5
Jerome Williams, Toronto	71	650	9.2
P.J. Brown, New Orleans	78	701	9.0
Donyell Marshall, Chicago	78	699	9.0

ASSISTS	G	No.	Avg.
Jason Kidd, New Jersey	80	711	8.9
Jason Williams, Memphis	76	631	8.3
Gary Payton, Milwaukee	80	663	8.3
Stephon Marbury, Phoenix	81	654	8.1
John Stockton, Utah	82	629	7.7
Jamaal Tinsley, Indiana	73	548	7.5
Jason Terry, Atlanta	81	600	7.4
Steve Nash, Dallas	82	598	7.3
Andre Miller, L.A. Clippers	80	537	6.7
Eric Snow, Philadelphia	82	544	6.6

BLOCKED SHOTS	G	No.	Avg.
Theo Ratliff, Atlanta	81	262	3.23
Ben Wallace, Detroit	73	230	3.15
Tim Duncan, San Antonio	81	237	2.93
Elton Brand, L.A. Clippers	62	158	2.55
Adonal Foyle, Golden State	82	205	2.50
Shaquille O'Neal, L.A. Lakers	67	159	2.37
Jermaine O'Neal, Indiana	77	178	2.31
Andrei Kirilenko, Utah	80	175	2.19
Shawn Bradley, Dallas	81	170	2.10
Erick Dampier, Golden State	82	154	1.88

STEALS	G	No.	Avg.
Allen Iverson, Philadelphia	82	225	2.74
Ron Artest, Indiana	69	159	2.30
Shawn Marion, Phoenix	81	185	2.28
Doug Christie, Sacramento	80	180	2.25
Jason Kidd, New Jersey	80	179	2.24
Kobe Bryant, L.A. Lakers	82	181	2.21
Paul Pierce, Boston	79	139	1.76
Caron Butler, Miami	78	137	1.76
Steve Francis, Houston	81	141	1.74
Jamaal Tinsley, Indiana	73	125	1.71

FIELD GOAL PERCENTAGE	FGM	FGA	Pct.
Eddy Curry, Chicago	335	573	.585
Shaquille O'Neal, L.A. Lakers	695	1,211	.574
Carlos Boozer, Cleveland	331	618	.536
P.J. Brown, New Orleans	319	601	.531
Radoslav Nesterovic, Minnesota	400	762	.525
Nene Hilario, Denver	321	619	.519
Tim Duncan, San Antonio	714	1,392	.513
Matt Harpring, Utah	521	1,020	.511
Pau Gasol, Memphis	569	1,116	.510
Brian Grant, Miami	344	676	.509

FREE THROW PERCENTAGE	FTM	FTA	Pct.
Allan Houston, New York	363	395	.919
Ray Allen, Seattle	316	345	.916
Steve Nash, Dallas	308	339	.909
Troy Hudson, Minnesota	208	231	.900
Reggie Miller, Indiana	207	230	.900
Jason Terry, Atlanta	259	292	.887
Dirk Nowitzki, Dallas	483	548	.881
Chauncey Billups, Detroit	318	362	.878
Jerry Stackhouse, Washington	455	518	.878
Darrell Armstrong, Orlando	165	188	.878

3-PT FG PERCENTAGE	FGM	FGA	Pct.
Bruce Bowen, San Antonio	101	229	.441
Michael Redd, Milwaukee	182	416	.438
Wesley Person, Memphis	100	231	.433
David Wesley, New Orleans	134	316	.424
Wally Szczerbiak, Minnesota	61	145	.421
Steve Nash, Dallas	111	269	.413
Matt Harpring, Utah	66	160	.413
Anthony Peeler, Minnesota	87	212	.410
Mike Bibby, Sacramento	56	137	.409
Eddie Jones, Miami	98	241	.407
Jon Barry, Detroit	87	214	.407

MINUTES PER GAME	G	Min.	Avg.
Allen Iverson, Philadelphia	82	3,485	42.5
Cuttino Mobley, Houston	73	3,044	41.7
Shawn Marion, Phoenix	81	3,373	41.6
Kobe Bryant, L.A. Lakers	82	3,401	41.5
Antoine Walker, Boston	78	3,235	41.5
Steve Francis, Houston	81	3,318	41.0
Jalen Rose, Chicago	82	3,351	40.9
Kevin Garnett, Minnesota	82	3,321	40.5
Jamal Mashburn, New Orleans	82	3,321	40.5
Gary Payton, Milwaukee	80	3,208	40.1

NBA World Championship Series

Year	Winner	Loser	Games
1947	Philadelphia Warriors	Chicago Stags	4-1
1948	Baltimore Bullets	Philadelphia Warriors	4-2
1949	Minneapolis Lakers	Washington Capitols	4-2
1950	Minneapolis Lakers	Syracuse Nationals	4-2
1951	Rochester Royals	New York Knicks	4-3
1952	Minneapolis Lakers	New York Knicks	4-3
1953	Minneapolis Lakers	New York Knicks	4-1
1954	Minneapolis Lakers	Syracuse Nationals	4-3
1955	Syracuse Nationals	Fort Wayne Pistons	4-3
1956	Philadelphia Warriors	Fort Wayne Pistons	4-1
1957	Boston Celtics	St. Louis Hawks	4-3
1958	St. Louis Hawks	Boston Celtics	4-2
1959	Boston Celtics	Minneapolis Lakers	4-0
1960	Boston Celtics	St. Louis Hawks	4-3
1961	Boston Celtics	St. Louis Hawks	4-1
1962	Boston Celtics	Los Angeles Lakers	4-3
1963	Boston Celtics	Los Angeles Lakers	4-2
1964	Boston Celtics	San Francisco Warriors	4-1
1965	Boston Celtics	Los Angeles Lakers	4-1
1966	Boston Celtics	Los Angeles Lakers	4-3
1967	Philadelphia	San Francisco Warriors	4-2
1968	Boston Celtics	Los Angeles Lakers	4-2
1969	Boston Celtics	Los Angeles Lakers	4-3
1970	New York Knicks	Los Angeles Lakers	4-3
1971	Milwaukee Bucks	Baltimore Bullets	4-0
1972	Los Angeles Lakers	New York Knicks	4-1
1973	New York Knicks	Los Angeles Lakers	4-1
1974	Boston Celtics	Milwaukee Bucks	4-3
1975	Golden State Warriors	Washington Bullets	4-0
1976	Boston Celtics	Phoenix Suns	4-2
1977	Portland Trail Blazers	Philadelphia 76ers	4-2
1978	Washington Bullets	Seattle SuperSonics	4-3
1979	Seattle SuperSonics	Washington Bullets	4-1
1980	Los Angeles Lakers	Philadelphia 76ers	4-2
1981	Boston Celtics	Houston Rockets	4-2
1982	Los Angeles Lakers	Philadelphia 76ers	4-2
1983	Philadelphia 76ers	Los Angeles Lakers	4-0
1984	Boston Celtics	Los Angeles Lakers	4-3
1985	Los Angeles Lakers	Boston Celtics	4-2
1986	Boston Celtics	Houston Rockets	4-2
1987	Los Angeles Lakers	Boston Celtics	4-2
1988	Los Angeles Lakers	Detroit Pistons	4-3
1989	Detroit Pistons	Los Angeles Lakers	4-0
1990	Detroit Pistons	Portland Trail Blazers	4-1
1991	Chicago Bulls	Los Angeles Lakers	4-1
1992	Chicago Bulls	Portland Trail Blazers	4-2
1993	Chicago Bulls	Phoenix Suns	4-2
1994	Houston Rockets	New York Knicks	4-3
1995	Houston Rockets	Orlando Magic	4-0
1996	Chicago Bulls	Seattle SuperSonics	4-2
1997	Chicago Bulls	Utah Jazz	4-2
1998	Chicago Bulls	Utah Jazz	4-2
1999	San Antonio Spurs	New York Knicks	4-1
2000	Los Angeles Lakers	Indiana Pacers	4-2
2001	Los Angeles Lakers	Philadelphia 76ers	4-1
2002	Los Angeles Lakers	New Jersey Nets	4-0
2003	San Antonio Spurs	New Jersey Nets	4-2

NBA All-Time Career Leaders

Games		Points		Scoring average (min. 400 games)	
Robert Parish	1,611	Kareem Abdul-Jabbar	38,387	Michael Jordan[1]	30.1
Kareem Abdul-Jabbar	1,560	Karl Malone[1]	36,374	Wilt Chamberlain	30.1
John Stockton[1]	1,504	Michael Jordan[1]	32,292	Shaquille O'Neal[1]	27.6
Karl Malone[1]	1,434	Wilt Chamberlain	31,419	Elgin Baylor	27.4
Kevin Willis[1]	1,342	Moses Malone	27,409	Jerry West	27.0
Moses Malone	1,329	Elvin Hayes	27,313	Allen Iverson[1]	27.0
Buck Williams	1,307	Hakeem Olajuwon	26,946	Bob Pettit	26.4
Elvin Hayes	1,303	Oscar Robertson	26,710	George Gervin	26.2
Sam Perkins	1,286	Dominique Wilkins	26,668	Oscar Robertson	25.7
A.C. Green	1,278	John Havlicek	26,395	Karl Malone[1]	25.4

Assists		Rebounds		Free throw percentage (min. 1,200 made)	
John Stockton[1]	15,806	Wilt Chamberlain	23,924	Mark Price	.904
Mark Jackson[1]	10,215	Bill Russell	21,620	Rick Barry	.900
Magic Johnson	10,141	Kareem Abdul-Jabbar	17,440	Calvin Murphy	.892
Oscar Robertson	9,887	Elvin Hayes	16,279	Scott Skiles	.889
Isiah Thomas	9,061	Moses Malone	16,212	Reggie Miller[1]	.886
Rod Strickland[1]	7,704	Robert Parish	14,715	Larry Bird	.886
Gary Payton[1]	7,590	Karl Malone[1]	14,601	Bill Sharman	.883
Maurice Cheeks	7,392	Nate Thurmond	14,464	Ray Allen[1]	.882
Lenny Wilkens	7,211	Walt Bellamy	14,241	Jeff Hornacek	.877
Terry Porter	7,160	Wes Unseld	13,769	Ricky Pierce	.875

Note: Does not include statistics compiled in the ABA. Totals are as of the end of 2002-03 season. 1. Player active in 2002-03.
Source: NBA.

NBA Most Valuable Players, 1955–2003

Year	Most Valuable Player	Team	Year	Most Valuable Player	Team
1955-56	Bob Pettit	St. Louis Hawks	**1979-80**	Kareem Abdul-Jabbar	Los Angeles Lakers
1956-57	Bob Cousy	Boston Celtics	**1980-81**	Julius Erving	Philadelphia 76ers
1957-58	Bill Russell	Boston Celtics	**1981-82**	Moses Malone	Houston Rockets
1958-59	Bob Pettit	St. Louis Hawks	**1982-83**	Moses Malone	Philadelphia 76ers
1959-60	Wilt Chamberlain	Philadelphia Warriors	**1983-84**	Larry Bird	Boston Celtics
1960-61	Bill Russell	Boston Celtics	**1984-85**	Larry Bird	Boston Celtics
1961-62	Bill Russell	Boston Celtics	**1985-86**	Larry Bird	Boston Celtics
1962-63	Bill Russell	Boston Celtics	**1986-87**	Magic Johnson	Los Angeles Lakers
1963-64	Oscar Robertson	Cincinnati Royals	**1987-88**	Michael Jordan	Chicago Bulls
1964-65	Bill Russell	Boston Celtics	**1988-89**	Magic Johnson	Los Angeles Lakers
1965-66	Wilt Chamberlain	Philadelphia 76ers	**1989-90**	Magic Johnson	Los Angeles Lakers
1966-67	Wilt Chamberlain	Philadelphia 76ers	**1990-91**	Michael Jordan	Chicago Bulls
1967-68	Wilt Chamberlain	Philadelphia 76ers	**1991-92**	Michael Jordan	Chicago Bulls
1968-69	Wes Unseld	Baltimore Bullets	**1992-93**	Charles Barkley	Phoenix Suns
1969-70	Willis Reed	New York Knicks	**1993-94**	Hakeem Olajuwon	Houston Rockets
1970-71	Kareem Abdul-Jabbar	Milwaukee Bucks	**1994-95**	David Robinson	San Antonio Spurs
1971-72	Kareem Abdul-Jabbar	Milwaukee Bucks	**1995-96**	Michael Jordan	Chicago Bulls
1972-73	Dave Cowens	Boston Celtics	**1996-97**	Karl Malone	Utah Jazz
1973-74	Kareem Abdul-Jabbar	Milwaukee Bucks	**1997-98**	Michael Jordan	Chicago Bulls
1974-75	Bob McAdoo	Buffalo Braves	**1998-99**	Karl Malone	Utah Jazz
1975-76	Kareem Abdul-Jabbar	Los Angeles Lakers	**1999-00**	Shaquille O'Neal	Los Angeles Lakers
1976-77	Kareem Abdul-Jabbar	Los Angeles Lakers	**2000-01**	Allen Iverson	Philadelphia 76ers
1977-78	Bill Walton	Portland Trail Blazers	**2001-02**	Tim Duncan	San Antonio Spurs
1978-79	Moses Malone	Houston Rockets	**2002-03**	Tim Duncan	San Antonio Spurs

NBA Rookies of the Year, 1952–2003

Year	Rookie of the Year	Team	Year	Rookie of the Year	Team
1952-53	Don Meineke	Fort Wayne Pistons	**1978-79**	Phil Ford	Kansas City Kings
1953-54	Ray Felix	Baltimore Bullets	**1979-80**	Larry Bird	Boston Celtics
1954-55	Bob Pettit	Milwaukee Hawks	**1980-81**	Darrell Griffith	Utah Jazz
1955-56	Maurice Stokes	Rochester Royals	**1981-82**	Buck Williams	New Jersey Nets
1956-57	Tom Heinsohn	Boston Celtics	**1982-83**	Terry Cummings	San Diego Clippers
1957-58	Woody Sauldsberry	Philadelphia Warriors	**1983-84**	Ralph Sampson	Houston Rockets
1958-59	Elgin Baylor	Minneapolis Lakers	**1984-85**	Michael Jordan	Chicago Bulls
1959-60	Wilt Chamberlain	Philadelphia Warriors	**1985-86**	Patrick Ewing	New York Knicks
1960-61	Oscar Robertson	Cincinnati Royals	**1986-87**	Chuck Person	Indiana Pacers
1961-62	Walt Bellamy	Chicago Bulls	**1987-88**	Mark Jackson	New York Knicks
1962-63	Terry Dischinger	Chicago Bulls	**1988-89**	Mitch Richmond	Golden State Warriors
1963-64	Jerry Lucas	Cincinnati Royals	**1989-90**	David Robinson	San Antonio Spurs
1964-65	Willis Reed	New York Knicks	**1990-91**	Derrick Coleman	New Jersey Nets
1965-66	Rick Barry	San Francisco Warriors	**1991-92**	Larry Johnson	Charlotte Hornets
1966-67	Dave Bing	Detroit Pistons	**1992-93**	Shaquille O'Neal	Orlando Magic
1967-68	Earl Monroe	Baltimore Bullets	**1993-94**	Chris Webber	Golden State Warriors
1968-69	Wes Unseld	Baltimore Bullets	**1994-95**	Grant Hill	Detroit Pistons
1969-70	Kareem Abdul-Jabbar	Milwaukee Bucks		Jason Kidd	Dallas Mavericks
1970-71	Dave Cowens	Boston Celtics	**1995-96**	Damon Stoudamire	Toronto Raptors
	Geoff Petrie	Portland Trail Blazers	**1996-97**	Allen Iverson	Philadelphia 76ers
1971-72	Sidney Wicks	Portland Trail Blazers	**1997-98**	Tim Duncan	San Antonio Spurs
1972-73	Bob McAdoo	Buffalo Braves	**1998-99**	Vince Carter	Toronto Raptors
1973-74	Ernie DiGregorio	Buffalo Braves	**1999-00**	Elton Brand	Chicago Bulls
1974-75	Keith Wilkes	Golden State Warriors		Steve Francis	Houston Rockets
1975-76	Alvin Adams	Phoenix Suns	**2000-01**	Mike Miller	Orlando Magic
1976-77	Adrian Dantley	Buffalo Braves	**2001-02**	Pau Gasol	Memphis Grizzlies
1977-78	Walter Davis	Phoenix Suns	**2002-03**	Amaré Stoudamire	Phoenix Suns

Naismith Memorial Basketball Hall of Fame

The Basketball Hall of Fame elected its first members (including Dr. James Naismith, the game's originator) in 1959, but it did not have a physical home until February 17, 1968. In 1985 the Hall of Fame moved to larger quarters in Springfield. Mass. The Basketball Hall of Fame includes players from all basketball levels, including college, women's, and foreign leagues. Career statistics are given only for players who played some portion of their career in the NBA.

Player (Year Elected)	Games	Points	FG%	FT%	Rebs.	Assts.
Archibald, Nate (Tiny) (1991)	876	16,481	.467	.810	2,046	6,476
Averaged 18.8 ppg over 13 seasons; six-time All-Star.						
Arizin, Paul J. (1977)	713	16,266	.421	.810	6,129	1,665
NBA scoring leader in 1952 (25.4 ppg) and 1957 (25.6 ppg).						
Barry, Rick (1987)	794	18,395	.449	.900	5,168	4,017
(ABA Statistics)	226	6,884	.477	.880	1,695	935
NBA all-time free-throw percentage leader.						
Baylor, Elgin (1976)	846	23,149	.431	.780	11,463	3,650
Named to NBA All-Star First Team 10 times.						
Bellamy, Walt (1993)	1,043	20,941	.516	.632	14,241	2,544
NBA Rookie of the Year in 1962.						
Bing, Dave (1990)	901	18,327	.441	.775	3,420	5,397
NBA Rookie of the Year 1967, MVP 1976.						
Bird, Larry (1998)	897	21,791	.496	.886	8,974	5,695
NBA Rookie of the Year 1980. NBA MVP 1984, 1985, and 1986. 12-time All-star.						
Bradley, Bill (1982)	742	9,217	.448	.840	2,533	2,363
Averaged 30.2 ppg in 83 games at Princeton University.						
Chamberlain, Wilt (1978)	1045	31,419	.540	.511	23,924	4,643
Holds NBA single-game records for points (100) and rebounds (55); led league in scoring 1959-66.						
Cousy, Bob (1970)	924	16,960	.375	.803	4,786	6,955
Led NBA in assists eight consecutive seasons (1953-60)						
Cowens, Dave (1991)	766	13,516	.460	.783	10,444	2,950
Seven-time All-star; three-time All-defensive team						
Cunningham, Billy (1986)	654	13,626	.446	.720	6,638	2,625
(ABA Statistics)	116	2,684	.483	.791	1,343	680
Coached Philadelphia 76ers to 454-196 record in eight years						
Davies, Bob (1969)	462	6,594	.378	.759	980[1]	2,050
NBL MVP, 1947	(NBL)[2]	107	1177		.747	
DeBusschere, Dave (1982)	875	14,053	.432	.699	9,618	2,497
NBA All-Defensive team six consecutive seasons (1969-74)						
English, Alex (1997)	1,193	25,613	.507	.832	6,538	4,351
Eight-time all-star; Averaged 21.5 points per game over 15 seasons						
Erving, Julius (Dr. J) (1993)	836	18,364	.507	.777	5,601	3,224
(ABA Statistics)	407	11,662	.504	.778	4,924	1,952
ABA MVP 1974-76; NBA MVP, 1981.						
Frazier, Walt (Clyde) (1987)	825	15,581	.490	.786	4,830	5,040
NBA All-Defensive team seven consecutive seasons (1969-75)						
Fulks, Joe (1977)	489	8,003	.302	.766	1,382[1]	587
NBA scoring leader in 1947 (23.2 ppg)						
Gallatin, Harry (1991)	682	8,843	.398	.773	6,684	1,208
Seven-time All-Star						
Gervin, George (Iceman) (1996)	791	20,708	.511	.844	3,607	2,214
(ABA Statistics)	269	5,887	.480	.831	1,995	584
All-NBA team five years in a row (1978-82).						
Gola, Tom (1975)	698	7,871	.431	.760	5,605	2,953
One of only two major-college players with over 2,000 points and 2,000 rebounds in career						
Goodrich, Gail (1996)	1,031	19,181	.456	.807	3,279	4,805
Scored 42 points in 1965 NCAA Final; averaged 18.6 points per game over 14 years in NBA						
Greer, Harold (Hal) (1981)	1,122	21,586	.452	.801	5,665	4,540
Scored 19 points in one quarter of 1968 All-Star game						
Hagan, Cliff (1977)	746	13,447	.450	.798	5,019	2,236
(ABA Statistics)	94	1,423	.496	.807	436	398
Helped St. Louis to 1958 championship with 27.7 ppg in playoffs						
Havlicek, John J. (Hondo) (1983)	1,270	26,395	.439	.815	8,007	6,114
Averaged 20.8 ppg; Member of 8 NBA championship teams						
Hawkins, Connie (1992)	499	8,233	.467	.785	3,971	2,052
(ABA Statistics)	117	3,295	.515	.765	1,479	504
Four-time All-Star; ABA MVP 1969						
Hayes, Elvin (1990)	1,303	27,313	.452	.670	16,279	2,398
Led league in scoring (1969) and rebounds per game (1970,1974)						
Heinsohn, Tom (1986)	654	12,194	.405	.790	5,749	1,318
Played for eight NBA championship teams and coached two others						

Player (Year Elected)	Games	Points	FG%	FT%	Rebs.	Assts.
Houbregs, Robert J. (1987)	281	2,611	.404	.721	1,552	500
NCAA Player of the Year, 1953						
Issel, Dan (1993)	718	14,659	.506	.797	5,707	1,804
(ABA Statistics)	500	12,823	.488	.786	5,426	1,103
Averaged 33.7 points per game in senior year at Kentucky, 1969-70						
Jabbar, Kareem Abdul (1995)	1,560	38,387	.559	.721	17,440	5,660
Six-time NBA MVP. All-time NBA leader in scoring, games, minutes, field goals						
Jeannette, Buddy (1994) (BAA-NBA)	139	997	.341	.781	N.A.	287
Won NBL MVP three times						
Johnson, Earvin (Magic) (2002)	906	17,707	.520	.848	6,559	10,141
Led Lakers to five NBA championships; 3-time NBA MVP (1987, 1989, 1990); 12-time All-Star						
Johnston, Neil (1990)	516	10,023	.444	.768	5,856	1,269
Named to four straight all-NBA First Teams (1953-56)						
Jones, K.C. (1989)	676	5,011	.387	.647	2,399	2,908
High scorer in 1955 NCAA finals (24 pts); held Tom Gola scoreless for 21 mins.						
Jones, Sam (1983)	871	15,411	.456	.803	4,305	2,209
Member of 10 NBA championship teams						
Lanier, Bob (1992)	959	19,248	.514	.767	9,698	3,007
Eight-time All-Star; NBA MVP, 1974						
Lloyd, Earl (2003)	560	4,682	.356	.750	3,609	810
First African-American to play in a NBA game, 1950.						
Lovellette, Clyde (1988)	704	11,947	.443	.756	6,663	1,165
Three-time All-American at University of Kansas (1950-52)						
Lucas, Jerry Ray (Luke) (1979)	829	14,053	.499	.783	12,942	2,730
NBA Rookie of the Year and field-goal percentage leader (.527) in 1964						
Macauley, Edward (Easy Ed) (1960)	641	11,234	.436	.761	2,079	1,667
NBA All-Star Game MVP, 1951						
Malone, Moses (2001)	1,329	27,409	.491	.769	16,212	1,796
Three-time MVP, 12-time All-Star. Averaged 20 points per game 11 straight seasons.						
Maravich, Pete (Pistol) (1987)	658	15,948	.441	.820	2,747	3,563
NCAA career record holder for points scored (3667) and scoring avg. (44.2 ppg)						
Martin, Slater (1981)	745	7,337	.364	.762	2,302[1]	3,160
Played in seven straight All-Star Games, 1953-59						
McAdoo, Bob (2000)	852	18,787	.503	.754	8,048	1,951
NBA Rookie of the Year (1973); led league in scoring 1974, 1975, and 1976.						
McGuire, Dick (1993)	738	5,921	.389	.644	2,784	4,205
Averaged 8.0 ppg.						
McHale, Kevin (1999)	971	17,335	.554	.798	7,122	1,670
Seven-time All-Star; won Sixth Man Award twice; won 3 NBA Championships: 1981, 1984, 1986						
Mikan, George L. (1959)	439	10,156	.404	.782	4,167[1]	1,245
Three-time NBA scoring leader (1949, 1950, 1952).						
Mikkelson, Vern (1995)	699	10,063	.403	.766	5,940[1]	1,515
Six-time NBA All-Star; won 4 NBA Championships: 1950, 1952, 1953, & 1954						
Monroe, Earl (The Pearl) (1990)	926	17,454	.464	.807	2,796	3,594
NBA Rookie of the Year, 1968.						
Murphy, Calvin (1993)	1,002	17,949	.482	.892	2,103	4,402
Set single-season free throw percentage record with .958 in 1980-81.						
Parish, Robert (2003)	1,611	23,334	.537	.721	14,715	2,180
Nine-time NBA All-Star (1981-87, 1990-91). Won 3 NBA Championships (1981, 1984, & 1986)						
Petrovic, Drazen (2002)	290	4,461	.506	.841	669	701
Averaged 15.4 ppg and 43.7% from 3-pt range over 4 years before being killed in auto accident.						
Pettit, Bob (1970)	792	20,880	.436	.761	12,849	2,369
Led NBA in scoring (25.7 ppg) and rebounds (1164) in 1956						
Phillip, Andy (1961)	701	6,384	.368	.695	2,395[1]	3,759
Led NBA in assists, 1951 and 1952						
Pollard, Jim (1977)	438	5,762	.360	.750	2,487[1]	1,417
Started four NBA All-Star Games						
Ramsey, Frank (1981)	623	8,378	.402	.804	3,410	1,136
Member of seven NBA championship teams						
Reed, Willis (1981)	650	12,183	.476	.747	8,414	1,186
1970 NBA Most Valuable Player, All-Star Game MVP and Playoff MVP						
Risen, Arnie (1998)	637	7,633	.381	.699	5,011	1,058
Three-time NBA All-star (1953, 1954,and 1955)						
Robertson, Oscar (1979)	1,040	26,710	.485	.838	7,804	9,887
NBA MVP 1964; Member of All-NBA First team, 1961-69						
Russell, Bill (1974)	963	14,522	.440	.561	21,620	4,100
Five-time NBA Most Valuable Player; 32 rebounds in one half vs. Philadelphia, 1957						
Schayes, Adolph (Dolph) (1972)	996	18,438	.380	.849	11,256[1]	3,072
NBA Coach of the Year (1966)						
Sharman, Bill (1974)	711	12,665	.426	.883	2,779	2,101
Led NBA in free-throw percentage seven seasons						

Player (Year Elected)	Games	Points	FG%	FT%	Rebs.	Assts.
Thomas, Isiah, (2000)	979	18,822	.452	.759	3,478	9,061
NBA Rookie of the Year (1982); 12-time All-Star; MVP of the 1990 Finals.						
Thompson, David (1996)	509	11,264	.504	.778	1,921	1,631
(ABA Statistics)	83	2,158	.515	.794	525	308
NCAA player of the year 1974 and 1975; ABA Rookie of the Year, 1976.						
Thurmond, Nate (1984)	964	14,437	.421	.667	14,464	2,575
1,000+ rebounds 1964-69, 1970-73						
Twyman, Jack (1982)	23	15,840	.450	.778	5,421	1,969
Led NBA in field-goal percentage, 1958 (.452)						
Unseld, Wes (1988)	984	10,624	.509	.633	13,769	3,822
Named NBA Most Valuable Player and Rookie of the Year in same year (1969)						
Walton, Bill (1993)	468	6,215	.521	.660	4,923	1,590
MVP in 1976.						
Wanzer, Robert (1987)	502	5,891	.388	.800	1,652[1]	1,575
Free-throw percentage leader, 1952 (.904)						
West, Jerry Alan (1979)	932	25,192	.474	.814	5,376	6,238
NBA MVP in 1970; .805 free throw percentage in 13 years in the playoffs						
Worthy, James (2003)	926	16,320	.521	.769	4,707	2,791
MVP of 1988 NBA Finals. Won three NBA titles with L.A. Lakers (1985, 1987, and 1988).						
Wilkens, Lenny (1989)	1,077	17,772	.432	.774	5,030	7,211
600+ assists 6 consecutive seasons						
Yardley, George (1996)	472	9,063	.422	.780	4,220	815
First player in NBA history to score 2,000 points in a season						

Note: All statistics for NBA career unless otherwise noted. NBL = National Basketball League. ABA = American Basketball Association. NCAA (National Collegiate Athletic Association) 1. Does not include seasons played prior to 1950-51 when the NBA first began keeping statistics for rebounds. 2. The National Basketball League did not keep statistics for field-goal percentage, rebounds, or assists.

COACHES

Anderson, W. Harold 1984
Auerbach, Arnold J. "Red" 1968
Barry, Justin "Sam" 1978
Blood, Ernest A. 1960
Brown, Larry 2002
Cann, Howard G. 1967
Carlson, Dr. H. Clifford 1959
Carnesecca, Lou 1992
Carnevale, Ben 1969
Carril, Pete 1997
Case, Everett 1981
Chaney, John 2001
Conradt, Jody 1998
Crum, Denny, 1994
Daly, Chuck, 1994
Dean, Everett S. 1966
Diddle, Edgar A. 1971
Drake, Bruce 1972
Gaines, Clarence 1981
Gardner, James H. "Jack" 1983
Gill, Amory T. "Slats" 1967
Hannum, Alex 1998
Harshman, Marv 1984
Haskins, Don 1997
Hickey, Edgar S. 1978
Hobson, Howard A. 1965
Holzman, William "Red" 1985-86
Iba, Henry P. "Hank" 1968
Julian, Alvin "Doggie" 1967
Keaney, Frank W. 1960
Keogan, George E. 1961
Knight, Bob 1991
Krzyzewski, Mike 2001
Kundla, John 1995
Lambert, Ward L. 1960
Litwack, Harry 1975
Loeffler, Kenneth D. 1964
Lonborg, Arthur C. 1972
McCutchan, Arad A. 1980
McGuire, Al 1992
McGuire, Frank J. 1976
Meanwell, Dr. Walter E. 1959
Meyer, Raymond J. 1978
Miller, Ralph 1987
Moore, Billie 1999
Nikolic, Aleksandar 1998
Olson, Lute 2002
Ramsay, Jack 1992
Rupp, Adolph F. 1968
Sachs, Leonard D. 1961
Shelton, Everett F. 1979
Smith, Dean 1982
Summitt, Pat, 2000
Taylor, Fred R. 1985-86
Teague, Bertha 1984
Thompson, John 1999
Wade, L. Margaret 1984
Watts, Stanley H. 1985-86
Wilkens, Lenny, 1998
Wooden, John R. 1972
Woolpert, Phil 1992
Wootten, Morgan, 2000

WNBA Final Standings and Playoffs, 2003

EASTERN CONFERENCE Team	W-L	WESTERN CONFERENCE Team	W-L
Detroit Shock	25- 9	Los Angeles Sparks	24-10
Charlotte Sting	18-16	Houston Comets	20-14
Connecticut Sun	18-16	Sacramento Monarchs	19-15
Cleveland Rockers	17-17	Minnesota Lynx	18-16
Indiana Fever	16-18	Seattle Storm	18-16
New York Liberty	16-18	San Antonio Silver Stars	12-22
Washington Mystics	9-25	Phoenix Mercury	8-26

Conference Semifinals

Detroit Shock 2	Cleveland Rockers 1	Los Angeles Sparks 2	Minnesota Lynx 1
Connecticut Sun 2	Charlotte Sting 0	Sacramento Monarchs 2	Houston Comets 1

Conference Finals

Detroit Shock 2, Connecticut Sun 0	Los Angeles Sparks 2	Sacramento Monarchs1

WNBA Championship

Detroit Shock 2, Los Angeles Sparks 1

Note: The top four teams in each division made the playoffs. **Source:** WNBA. www.wnba.com.

ICE HOCKEY

National Hockey League
Commissioner: Gary Bettman
Founded: 1917
Number of Teams: 30
www.nhl.com

The NHL started with six franchises, and nearly went bankrupt in the 1970s due to lack of interest and financial mismanagement. But the sport and the league has started to thrive of late, winning national television broadcast deals and expanding to warm-weather cities like San Jose and Tampa Bay. Franchise relocation has also become common, as teams from Minnesota, Quebec, Winnipeg, and Hartford have moved, respectively, to Dallas, Colorado, Phoenix, and North Carolina.

In 1998, the NHL expanded to Nashville. And in 1999, Atlanta took its second crack at a franchise (its first, the Atlanta Flames, now plays in Calgary). In 2000, expansion teams were added in St. Paul, Minnesota and Columbus, Ohio.

The Stanley Cup

The oldest trophy competed for by professional athletes in North America, the Stanley Cup was donated by Frederick Arthur, Lord Stanley of Preston, in 1893. Lord Stanley purchased the trophy for 10 guineas (about $50) for presentation to the amateur hockey champions of Canada. Since 1910, when the National Hockey Association took possession of the Stanley Cup, the trophy has been the symbol of professional hockey supremacy. The National Hockey League took exclusive control of the cup in 1946, and now awards it annually to the team that wins the league's best-of-seven final playoff series.

Season	Champion	Finalist	GP in final
1917–18	Toronto Arenas	Vancouver Millionaires	5
1918–19	No decision[1]	No decision	5
1919–20	Ottawa Senators	Seattle Millionaires	5
1920–21	Ottawa Senators	Vancouver Millionaires	5
1921–22	Toronto St. Pats	Vancouver Millionaires	5
1922–23	Ottawa Senators	Edmonton	2
1923–24	Montreal Canadiens	Calgary	2
1924–25	Victoria Cougars	Montreal Canadiens	4
1925–26	Montreal Maroons	Victoria Cougars	4
1926–27	Ottawa Senators	Boston Bruins	4
1927–28	New York Rangers	Montreal Canadiens	5
1928–29	Boston Bruins	New York Rangers	2
1929–30	Montreal Canadiens	Boston Bruins	2
1930–31	Montreal Canadiens	Chicago Blackhawks	5
1931–32	Toronto Maple Leafs	New York Rangers	3
1932–33	New York Rangers	Toronto Maple Leafs	3
1933–34	Chicago Blackhawks	Detroit Red Wings	4
1934–35	Montreal Maroons	Toronto Maple Leafs	3
1935–36	Detroit Red Wings	Toronto Maple Leafs	4
1936–37	Detroit Red Wings	New York Rangers	5
1937–38	Chicago Blackhawks	Toronto Maple Leafs	4
1938–39	Boston Bruins	Toronto Maple Leafs	5
1939–40	New York Rangers	Toronto Maple Leafs	6
1940–41	Boston Bruins	Detroit Red Wings	4
1941–42	Toronto Maple Leafs	Detroit Red Wings	7
1942–43	Detroit Red Wings	Boston Bruins	4
1943–44	Montreal Canadiens	Chicago Blackhawks	4
1944–45	Toronto Maple Leafs	Detroit Red Wings	7
1945–46	Montreal Canadiens	Boston Bruins	5
1946–47	Toronto Maple Leafs	Montreal Canadiens	6
1947–48	Toronto Maple Leafs	Detroit Red Wings	4
1948–49	Toronto Maple Leafs	Detroit Red Wings	4
1949–50	Detroit Red Wings	New York Rangers	7
1950–51	Toronto Maple Leafs	Montreal Canadiens	5
1951–52	Detroit Red Wings	Montreal Canadiens	4
1952–53	Montreal Canadiens	Boston Bruins	5
1953–54	Detroit Red Wings	Montreal Canadiens	7
1954–55	Detroit Red Wings	Montreal Canadiens	7
1955–56	Montreal Canadiens	Detroit Red Wings	5
1956–57	Montreal Canadiens	Boston Bruins	5
1957–58	Montreal Canadiens	Boston Bruins	6
1958–59	Montreal Canadiens	Toronto Maple Leafs	5
1959–60	Montreal Canadiens	Toronto Maple Leafs	4
1960–61	Chicago Blackhawks	Detroit Red Wings	6
1961–62	Toronto Maple Leafs	Chicago Blackhawks	6
1962–63	Toronto Maple Leafs	Detroit Red Wings	5
1963–64	Toronto Maple Leafs	Detroit Red Wings	7
1964–65	Montreal Canadiens	Chicago Blackhawks	7
1965–66	Montreal Canadiens	Detroit Red Wings	6
1966–67	Toronto Maple Leafs	Montreal Canadiens	6
1967–68	Montreal Canadiens	St. Louis Blues	4
1968–69	Montreal Canadiens	St. Louis Blues	4
1969–70	Boston Bruins	St. Louis Blues	4
1970–71	Montreal Canadiens	Chicago Blackhawks	7
1971–72	Boston Bruins	New York Rangers	6
1972–73	Montreal Canadiens	Chicago Blackhawks	6
1973–74	Philadelphia Flyers	Boston Bruins	6
1974–75	Philadelphia Flyers	Buffalo Sabres	6
1975–76	Montreal Canadiens	Philadelphia Flyers	4
1976–77	Montreal Canadiens	Boston Bruins	4
1977–78	Montreal Canadiens	Boston Bruins	6
1978–79	Montreal Canadiens	New York Rangers	5
1979–80	New York Islanders	Philadelphia Flyers	6
1980–81	New York Islanders	Minnesota North Stars	5
1981–82	New York Islanders	Vancouver Canucks	4
1982–83	New York Islanders	Edmonton Oilers	4
1983–84	Edmonton Oilers	New York Islanders	5
1984–85	Edmonton Oilers	Philadelphia Flyers	5
1985–86	Montreal Canadiens	Calgary Flames	5
1986–87	Edmonton Oilers	Philadelphia Flyers	7
1987–88	Edmonton Oilers	Boston Bruins	4
1988–89	Calgary Flames	Montreal Canadiens	6
1989–90	Edmonton Oilers	Boston Bruins	5
1990–91	Pittsburgh Penguins	Minnesota North Stars	5
1991–92	Pittsburgh Penguins	Chicago Blackhawks	4
1992–93	Montreal Canadiens	Los Angeles Kings	5
1993–94	New York Rangers	Vancouver Canucks	7
1994–95[3]	New Jersey Devils	Detroit Red Wings	4
1995–96	Colorado Avalanche	Florida Panthers	4
1996–97	Detroit Red Wings	Philadelphia Flyers	4
1997–98	Detroit Red Wings	Washington Capitals	4
1998–99	Dallas Stars	Buffalo Sabres	6
1999–00	New Jersey Devils	Dallas Stars	6
2000-01	Colorado Avalanche	New Jersey Devils	7
2001-02	Detroit Red Wings	Carolina Hurricanes	5
2002-03	New Jersey Devils	Anaheim Mighty Ducks	7

1. In the spring of 1919 the Montreal Canadiens traveled to Seattle to meet Seattle, champs of the Pacific Coast Hockey League. After five games had been played—teams were tied at 2 wins and 1 tie—the series was called off by the local Department of Health because of the influenza epidemic. 3. Strike-shortened season. **Source:** National Hockey League.

NHL Standings, 2002–03

EASTERN CONFERENCE

Northeast Division	W	L	T	OTL	Pts.
Ottawa Senators[1]	52	21	8	1	113
Toronto Maple Leafs[3]	44	28	7	3	98
Boston Bruins[3]	36	31	11	4	87
Montreal Canadiens	30	35	8	9	77
Buffalo Sabres	27	37	10	8	72
Atlantic Division	**W**	**L**	**T**	**OTL**	**Pts.**
New Jersey Devils[2]	46	20	10	6	108
Philadelphia Flyers[3]	45	20	13	4	107
New York Islanders[3]	35	34	11	2	83
New York Rangers	32	36	10	4	78
Pittsburgh Penguins	27	44	6	5	65
Southeast Division	**W**	**L**	**T**	**OTL**	**Pts.**
Tampa Bay Lightning[2]	36	25	16	5	93
Washington Capitals[3]	39	29	8	6	92
Atlanta Thrashers	31	39	7	5	74
Florida Panthers	24	36	13	9	70
Carolina Hurricanes	22	43	11	6	61

WESTERN CONFERENCE

Central Division	W	L	T	OTL	Pts.
Detroit Red Wings[2]	48	20	10	4	110
St. Louis Blues[3]	41	24	11	6	99
Chicago Blackhawks	30	33	13	6	79
Nashville Predators	27	35	13	7	74
Columbus Blue Jackets	29	42	8	3	69
Northwest Division	**W**	**L**	**T**	**OTL**	**Pts.**
Colorado Avalanche[2]	42	19	13	8	105
Vancouver Canucks[3]	45	23	13	1	104
Minnesota Wild[3]	42	29	10	1	95
Edmonton Oilers[3]	36	26	11	9	92
Calgary Flames	29	36	13	4	75
Pacific Division	**W**	**L**	**T**	**OTL**	**Pts.**
Dallas Stars[1]	46	17	15	4	111
Anaheim Mighty Ducks[3]	40	27	9	6	95
Los Angeles Kings	33	37	6	6	78
Phoenix Coyotes	31	35	11	5	78
San Jose Sharks	28	37	9	8	73

1. Conference champion. 2. Division champion. 3. Earned playoff berth. **Source:** National Hockey League

Stanley Cup Playoffs 2002–03

(All rounds are seven-game series)

EASTERN CONFERENCE		WESTERN CONFERENCE	
ROUND 1			
Ottawa Senators 4	N.Y. Islanders 1	Dallas Stars 4	Edmonton Oilers 2
New Jersey Devils 4	Boston Bruins 1	Anaheim Mighty Ducks 4	Detroit Red Wings 0
Tampa Bay Lightning 4	Washington Capitals 2	Minnesota Wild 4	Colorado Avalanche 3
Philadelphia Flyers 4	Toronto Maple Leafs 3	Vancouver Canucks 4	St. Louis Blues 3
ROUND 2			
Ottawa Senators 4	Philadelphia Flyers 2	Anaheim Mighty Ducks 4	Dallas Stars 2
New Jersey Devils 4	Tampa Bay Lightning 1	Minnesota Wild 4	Vancouver Canucks 3
CONFERENCE CHAMPIONSHIPS			
New Jersey Devils 4	Ottawa Senators 3	Anaheim Mighty Ducks 4	Minnesota Wild 0

STANLEY CUP CHAMPIONSHIP

New Jersey Devils 4, Anaheim Mighty Ducks 3

Top Scorers, 2002-03

Player, Team	POINTS	Player, Team	GOALS	Player, Team	ASSISTS
Peter Forsberg, Colorado	106	Milan Hejduk, Colorado	50	Peter Forsberg, Colorado	77
Markus Naslund, Vancouver	104	Markus Naslund, Vancouver	48	Joe Thornton, Boston	65
Joe Thornton, Boston	101	Todd Bertuzzi, Vancouver	46	Mario Lemieux, Pittsburgh	63
Milan Hejduk, Colorado	98	Marian Hossa, Ott	45	Mike Modano, Dallas	57
Todd Bertuzzi, Vancouver	97	Glen Murray, Boston	44	Pavol Demitra, St. Louis	57
Pavol Demitra, St. Louis	93	Dany Heatley, Atlanta	41	Vaclav Prospal, Tampa Bay	57
Glen Murray, Boston	92	Ilya Kovalchuk, Atlanta	38	Brad Richards, Tampa Bay	57
Mario Lemieux, Pittsburgh	91	Brett Hull, Detroit	37	Markus Naslund, Vancouver	56
Dany Heatley, Atlanta	89	Mats Sundin, Toronto	37	Paul Kariya, Anaheim	56
Mike Modano, Dallas	85	Zigmund Palffy, Los Angeles	37	Al Macinnis, St. Louis	52

Source: National Hockey League.

Top 10 All-Time NHL Scoring Leaders

GOALS

Player	Seasons	Games	Goals	Goals/ Game
Wayne Gretzky	20	1,487	894	.601
Gordie Howe	26	1,767	801	.453
Marcel Dionne	18	1,348	731	.542
Phil Esposito	18	1,282	717	.559
Brett Hull[1]	18	1,183	716	.605
Mike Gartner	19	1,432	708	.494
Mario Lemieux[1]	16	879	682	.776
Mark Messier[1]	24	1,680	676	.402
Steve Yzerman[1]	20	1,378	660	.479
Luc Robitaille[1]	17	1,286	631	.491

ASSISTS

Player	Seasons	Games	Assists	Assists/ Game
Wayne Gretzky	20	1,487	1,963	1.320
Ron Francis[1]	22	1,651	1,222	.740
Ray Bourque	22	1,612	1,169	.725
Mark Messier[1]	24	1,680	1,168	.695
Paul Coffey	21	1,409	1,135	.806
Adam Oates[1]	18	1,277	1,063	.832
Gordie Howe	26	1,767	1,049	.594
Marcel Dionne	18	1,348	1,040	.772
Mario Lemieux[1]	16	879	1,010	1.149
Steve Yzerman[1]	20	1,378	1,010	.733

POINTS

Player	Seasons	Games	Goals	Assists	Points
Wayne Gretzky	20	1,487	894	1,963	2,857
Gordie Howe	26	1,767	801	1,049	1,850
Mark Messier[1]	24	1,680	676	1,168	1,844
Marcel Dionne	18	1,348	731	1,040	1,771
Ron Francis[1]	22	1,651	536	1,222	1,758
Mario Lemieux[1]	16	879	682	1,010	1,692
Steve Yzerman[1]	20	1,378	660	1,010	1,670
Phil Esposito	18	1,282	717	873	1,590
Ray Bourque	22	1,612	410	1,169	1,579
Paul Coffey	21	1,409	396	1,135	1,531

Note: As of end of 2002-03 season. 1. Player active in 2002-03. **Source:** *NHL Official Guide and Record Book, 2004.*

Hart Trophy Winners, 1924–2003

The league's most valuable player is chosen by a poll of the Professional Hockey Writers' Association.

Season	Player	Team
1924	Frank Nighbor	Ottawa Senators
1925	Billy Burch	New York Americans
1926	Nels Stewart	Montreal Maroons
1927	Herb Gardiner	Montreal
1928	Howie Morenz	Montreal
1929	Roy Worters	New York Americans
1930	Nels Stewart	Montreal Maroons
1931	Howie Morenz	Montreal
1932	Howie Morenz	Montreal
1933	Eddie Shore	Boston
1934	Aurel Joliat	Montreal
1935	Eddie Shore	Boston
1936	Eddie Shore	Boston
1937	Babe Siebert	Montreal
1938	Eddie Shore	Boston
1939	Toe Blake	Montreal
1940	Ebbie Goodfellow	Detroit
1941	Bill Cowley	Boston
1942	Tom Anderson	New York Americans
1943	Bill Cowley	Boston
1944	Babe Pratt	Toronto
1945	Elmer Lach	Montreal
1946	Max Bentley	Toronto
1947	Maurice Richard	Montreal
1948	Buddy O'Connor	New York Rangers
1949	Sid Abel	Detroit
1950	Charlie Rayner	New York Rangers
1951	Milt Schmidt	Boston
1952	Gordie Howe	Detroit
1953	Gordie Howe	Detroit
1954	Al Rollins	Toronto
1955	Ted Kennedy	Toronto
1956	Jean Béliveau	Montreal
1957	Gordie Howe	Detroit
1958	Gordie Howe	Detroit
1959	Andy Bathgate	New York Rangers
1960	Gordie Howe	Detroit
1961	Bernie Geoffrion	Montreal
1962	Jacques Plante	Montreal
1963	Gordie Howe	Detroit
1964	Jean Béliveau	Montreal
1965	Bobby Hull	Chicago
1966	Bobby Hull	Chicago
1967	Stan Mikita	Chicago
1968	Stan Mikita	Chicago
1969	Phil Esposito	Boston
1970	Bobby Orr	Boston
1971	Bobby Orr	Boston
1972	Bobby Orr	Boston
1973	Bobby Clarke	Philadelphia
1974	Phil Esposito	Boston
1975	Bobby Clarke	Philadelphia
1976	Bobby Clarke	Philadelphia
1977	Guy Lafleur	Montreal
1978	Guy Lafleur	Montreal
1979	Bryan Trottier	New York Islanders
1980	Wayne Gretzky	Edmonton
1981	Wayne Gretzky	Edmonton
1982	Wayne Gretzky	Edmonton
1983	Wayne Gretzky	Edmonton
1984	Wayne Gretzky	Edmonton
1985	Wayne Gretzky	Edmonton
1986	Wayne Gretzky	Edmonton
1987	Wayne Gretzky	Edmonton
1988	Mario Lemieux	Pittsburgh
1989	Wayne Gretzky	Los Angeles
1990	Mark Messier	Edmonton
1991	Bret Hull	St. Louis
1992	Mark Messier	New York Rangers
1993	Mario Lemieux	Pittsburgh
1994	Sergei Fedorov	Detroit
1995	Eric Lindros	Philadelphia
1996	Mario Lemieux	Pittsburgh
1997	Dominik Hasek	Buffalo
1998	Dominik Hasek	Buffalo
1999	Jaromir Jagr	Pittsburgh
2000	Chris Pronger	St. Louis
2001	Joe Sakic	Colorado
2002	Jose Theodore	Montreal
2003	Peter Forsberg	Colorado

Art Ross Trophy Winners, 1918–2003

The Art Ross Trophy goes "to the player who leads the league in scoring at the end of the regular season."

Season	Player	Team
1918	Joe Malone	Montreal
1919	Newsy Lalonde	Montreal
1920	Joe Malone	Quebec
1921	Newsy Lalonde	Montreal
1922	Punch Broadbent	Ottawa
1923	Babe Dye	Toronto
1924	Cye Denneny	Ottawa
1925	Babe Dye	Toronto
1926	Nels Stewart	Montreal Maroons
1927	Bill Cook	New York Rangers
1928	Howie Morenz	Montreal
1929	Ace Bailey	Toronto
1930	Cooney Weiland	Boston
1931	Howie Morenz	Montreal
1932	Harvey Jackson	Toronto
1933	Bill Cook	New York Rangers
1934	Charlie Conacher	Toronto
1935	Charlie Conacher	Toronto
1936	Dave Shriner	New York Americans
1937	Dave Shriner	New York Americans
1938	Gordie Drillon	Toronto
1939	Toe Blake	Montreal
1940	Milt Schmidt	Boston
1941	Bill Cowley	Boston
1942	Bryan Hextall	New York Rangers
1943	Doug Bentley	Chicago
1944	Herbie Cain	Boston
1945	Elmer Lach	Montreal
1946	Max Bentley	Chicago
1947	Max Bentley	Chicago
1948	Elmer Lach	Montreal
1949	Roy Conacher	Chicago
1950	Ted Lindsay	Detroit
1951	Gordie Howe	Detroit
1952	Gordie Howe	Detroit
1953	Gordie Howe	Detroit
1954	Gordie Howe	Detroit
1955	Bernie Geoffrion	Montreal
1956	Jean Béliveau	Montreal
1957	Gordie Howe	Detroit
1958	Dickie Moore	Montreal
1959	Dickie Moore	Montreal
1960	Bobby Hull	Chicago
1961	Bernie Geoffrion	Montreal
1962	Bobby Hull	Chicago
1963	Gordie Howe	Detroit
1964	Stan Mikita	Chicago
1965	Stan Mikita	Chicago
1966	Bobby Hull	Chicago
1967	Stan Mikita	Chicago
1968	Stan Mikita	Chicago
1969	Phil Esposito	Boston
1970	Bobby Orr	Boston
1971	Phil Esposito	Boston
1972	Phil Esposito	Boston
1973	Phil Esposito	Boston
1974	Phil Esposito	Boston
1975	Bobby Orr	Boston
1976	Guy Lafleur	Montreal
1977	Guy Lafleur	Montreal
1978	Guy Lafleur	Montreal
1979	Bryan Trottier	New York Islanders
1980	Marcel Dionne	Los Angeles
1981	Wayne Gretzky	Edmonton
1982	Wayne Gretzky	Edmonton
1983	Wayne Gretzky	Edmonton
1984	Wayne Gretzky	Edmonton
1985	Wayne Gretzky	Edmonton
1986	Wayne Gretzky	Edmonton
1987	Wayne Gretzky	Edmonton
1988	Mario Lemieux	Pittsburgh
1989	Mario Lemieux	Pittsburgh
1990	Wayne Gretzky	Los Angeles
1991	Wayne Gretzky	Los Angeles
1992	Mario Lemieux	Pittsburgh
1993	Mario Lemieux	Pittsburgh
1994	Wayne Gretzky	Los Angeles
1995	Jaromir Jagr	Pittsburgh
1996	Mario Lemieux	Pittsburgh
1997	Mario Lemieux	Pittsburgh
1998	Jaromir Jagr	Pittsburgh
1999	Jaromir Jagr	Pittsburgh
2000	Jaromir Jagr	Pittsburgh
2001	Jaromir Jagr	Pittsburgh
2002	Jarome Ignila	Calgary
2003	Peter Forsberg	Colorado

Conn Smythe Trophy Winners, 1965–2003

The Conn Smythe Trophy is awarded to the most valuable player in the playoffs.

Season	Player, Team
1965	Jean Béliveau, Montreal
1966	Roger Crozier, Detroit
1967	Dave Keon, Toronto
1968	Glenn Hall, St. Louis
1969	Serge Savard, Montreal
1970	Bobby Orr, Boston
1971	Ken Dryden, Montreal
1972	Bobby Orr, Boston
1973	Yvan Cournoyer, Montreal
1974	Bernie Parent, Philadelphia
1975	Bernie Parent, Philadelphia
1976	Reggie Leach, Philadelphia
1977	Guy Lafleur, Montreal
1978	Larry Robinson, Montreal
1979	Bob Gainey, Montreal
1980	Bryan Trottier, N.Y. Islanders
1981	Butch Goring, N.Y. Islanders
1982	Mike Bossy, N.Y. Islanders
1983	Bill Smith, N.Y. Islanders
1984	Mark Messier, Edmonton
1985	Wayne Gretzky, Edmonton
1986	Patrick Roy, Montreal
1987	Ron Hextall, Philadelphia
1988	Wayne Gretzky, Edmonton
1989	Al MacInnis, Calgary
1990	Bill Ranford, Edmonton
1991	Mario Lemieux, Pittsburgh
1992	Mario Lemieux, Pittsburgh
1993	Patrick Roy, Montreal
1994	Brian Leetch, N.Y. Rangers
1995	Claude Lemieux, New Jersey
1996	Joe Sakic, Colorado
1997	Mike Vernon, Detroit
1998	Steve Yzerman, Detroit
1999	Joe Nieuwendyk, Dallas
2000	Scott Stevens, New Jersey
2001	Patrick Roy, Colorado
2002	Nicklas Lidstrom, Detroit
2002	J.S. Giguere, Anaheim

James Norris Memorial Trophy, 1954–2003

The league's best defenseman is chosen by the Pro Hockey Writers' Association. The winner receives $10,000.

Season	Player, Team
1954	Red Kelly, Detroit
1955	Doug Harvey, Montreal
1956	Doug Harvey, Montreal
1957	Doug Harvey, Montreal
1958	Doug Harvey, Montreal
1959	Tom Johnson, Montreal
1960	Doug Harvey, Montreal
1961	Doug Harvey, Montreal
1962	Doug Harvey, N.Y. Rangers
1963	Pierre Pilote, Chicago
1964	Pierre Pilote, Chicago
1965	Pierre Pilote, Chicago
1966	Jacques Laperrière, Montreal
1967	Harry Howell, N.Y. Rangers
1968	Bobby Orr, Boston
1969	Bobby Orr, Boston
1970	Bobby Orr, Boston
1971	Bobby Orr, Boston
1972	Bobby Orr, Boston
1973	Bobby Orr, Boston
1974	Bobby Orr, Boston
1975	Bobby Orr, Boston
1976	Denis Potvin, N.Y. Islanders
1977	Larry Robinson, Montreal
1978	Denis Potvin, N.Y. Islanders
1979	Denis Potvin, N.Y. Islanders
1980	Larry Robinson, Montreal
1981	Randy Carlyle, Pittsburgh
1982	Doug Wilson, Chicago
1983	Rod Langway, Washington
1984	Rod Langway, Washington
1985	Paul Coffey, Edmonton
1986	Paul Coffey, Edmonton
1987	Ray Bourque, Boston
1988	Ray Bourque, Boston
1989	Chris Chelios, Montreal
1990	Ray Bourque, Boston
1991	Ray Bourque, Boston
1992	Brian Leetch, N.Y. Rangers
1993	Chris Chelios, Chicago
1994	Ray Bourque, Boston
1995	Paul Coffey, Detroit
1996	Chris Chelios, Chicago
1997	Brian Leetch, N.Y. Rangers
1998	Rob Blake, Los Angeles
1999	Al MacInnis, St. Louis
2000	Chris Pronger, St. Louis
2001	Nicklas Lidstrom, Detroit
2002	Nicklas Lidstrom, Detroit
2003	Nicklas Lidstrom, Detroit

Vezina Trophy Winners, 1927–2003

The Vezina Trophy is awarded to the league's best goalkeeper and is selected by a poll of the league's general managers. The winner receives $10,000.

Season	Player	Team
1927	George Hainsworth	Montreal
1928	George Hainsworth	Montreal
1929	George Hainsworth	Montreal
1930	Tiny Thompson	Boston
1931	Roy Worters	N.Y. Americans
1932	Charlie Gardiner	Chicago
1933	Tiny Thompson	Boston
1934	Charlie Gardiner	Chicago
1935	Lorne Chabot	Chicago
1936	Tiny Thompson	Boston
1937	Normie Smith	Detroit
1938	Tiny Thompson	Boston
1939	Frank Brimsek	Boston
1940	Dave Kerr	N.Y. Rangers
1941	Turk Broda	Toronto
1942	Frank Brimsek	Boston
1943	Johnny Mowers	Detroit
1944	Bill Durnan	Montreal
1945	Bill Durnan	Montreal
1946	Bill Durnan	Montreal
1947	Bill Durnan	Montreal
1948	Turk Broda	Toronto
1949	Bill Durnan	Montreal
1950	Bill Durnan	Montreal
1951	Al Rollins	Toronto
1952	Terry Sawchuk	Detroit
1953	Terry Sawchuk	Detroit
1954	Harry Lumley	Toronto
1955	Terry Sawchuk	Detroit
1956	Jacques Plante	Montreal
1957	Jacques Plante	Montreal
1958	Jacques Plante	Montreal
1959	Jacques Plante	Montreal
1960	Jacques Plante	Montreal
1961	Johnny Bower	Toronto
1962	Jacques Plante	Montreal
1963	Glenn Hall	Chicago
1964	Charlie Hodge	Montreal
1965	Terry Sawchuk/Johnny Bower	Toronto
1966	Lorne Worsley/Charlie Hodge	Montreal
1967	Glenn Hall/ Denis Dejordy	Chicago
1968	Lorne Worsley/Rogie Vachon	Montreal
1969	Jacques Plante/Glenn Hall	St. Louis
1970	Tony Esposito	Chicago
1971	Ed Giacomin/Gilles Villemure	N.Y. Rangers
1972	Tony Esposito/Gary Smith	Chicago
1973	Ken Dryden	Montreal
1974	Bernie Parent	Philadelphia
	Tony Esposito	Chicago
1975	Bernie Parent	Philadelphia
1976	Ken Dryden	Montreal
1977	Ken Dryden/Michel Larocque	Montreal
1978	Ken Dryden/Michel Larocque	Montreal
1979	Ken Dryden/Michel Larocque	Montreal
1980	Bob Sauvé/Don Edwards	Buffalo
1981	Richard Sevigny/Denis Herron/ Michel Larocque	Montreal
1982	Bill Smith	N.Y. Islanders
1983	Pete Peeters	Boston
1984	Tom Barrasso	Buffalo
1985	Pele Lindbergh	Philadelphia
1986	John Vanbiesbrouck	N.Y. Rangers
1987	Ron Hextall	Philadelphia
1988	Grant Fuhr	Edmonton
1989	Patrick Roy	Montreal
1990	Patrick Roy	Montreal
1991	Ed Belfour	Chicago
1992	Patrick Roy	Montreal
1993	Ed Belfour	Chicago
1994	Dominik Hasek	Buffalo
1995	Dominik Hasek	Buffalo
1996	Jim Carey	Washington
1997	Dominik Hasek	Buffalo
1998	Dominik Hasek	Buffalo
1999	Dominik Hasek	Buffalo
2000	Olaf Kolzig	Washington
2001	Dominik Hasek	Buffalo
2002	Jose Theodore	Montreal
2003	Martin Brodeur	New Jersey

Calder Memorial Trophy Winners, 1933–2003

The NHL rookie of the year, chosen by the Professional Hockey Writers' Association, receives $10,000.

Season	Player	Team	Season	Player	Team
1933	Carl Voss	Detroit	**1969**	Danny Grant	Minnesota
1934	Russ Blinko	Montreal Maroons	**1970**	Tony Esposito	Chicago
1935	Dave Schriner	New York Americans	**1971**	Gilbert Perreault	Buffalo
1936	Mike Karakas	Chicago	**1972**	Ken Dryden	Montreal
1937	Syl Apps	Toronto	**1973**	Steve Vickers	New York Rangers
1938	Cully Dahlstrom	Chicago	**1974**	Denis Potvin	New York Islanders
1939	Frank Brimsek	Boston	**1975**	Eric Vail	Atlanta
1940	Kilby MacDonald	New York Rangers	**1976**	Bryan Trottier	New York Islanders
1941	Johnny Quilty	Montreal	**1977**	Willie Plett	Atlanta
1942	Grant Warwick	New York Rangers	**1978**	Mike Bossy	New York Islanders
1943	Gaye Stewart	Toronto	**1979**	Bobby Smith	Minnesota
1944	Gus Bodnar	Toronto	**1980**	Ray Bourque	Boston
1945	Frank McCool	Toronto	**1981**	Peter Stastny	Quebec
1946	Edgar Laprade	New York Rangers	**1982**	Dale Hawerchuk	Winnipeg
1947	Howie Meeker	Toronto	**1983**	Steve Larmer	Chicago
1948	Jim McFadden	Detroit	**1984**	Tom Barrasso	Buffalo
1949	Pentti Lund	New York Rangers	**1985**	Mario Lemieux	Pittsburgh
1950	Jack Gelineau	Boston	**1986**	Gary Suter	Calgary
1951	Terry Sawchuk	Detroit	**1987**	Luc Robitaille	Los Angeles
1952	Bernie Geoffrion	Montreal	**1988**	Joe Nieuwendyk	Calgary
1953	Lorne Worsley	New York Rangers	**1989**	Brian Leetch	New York Rangers
1954	Camille Henry	New York Rangers	**1990**	Sergei Makarov	Calgary
1955	Ed Litzenberger	Chicago	**1991**	Ed Belfour	Chicago
1956	Glenn Hall	Detroit	**1992**	Pavel Bure	Vancouver
1957	Larry Regan	Boston	**1993**	Teemu Selanne	Winnipeg
1958	Frank Mahovlich	Toronto	**1994**	Martin Brodeur	New Jersey
1959	Ralph Backsrom	Montreal	**1995**	Petr Forsberg	Quebec
1960	Bill Hay	Chicago	**1996**	Daniel Alfredsson	Ottawa
1961	Dave Keon	Toronto	**1997**	Bryan Berard	New York Islanders
1962	Bobby Rousseau	Montreal	**1998**	Sergei Samsonov	Boston
1963	Kent Douglas	Toronto	**1999**	Chris Drury	Colorado
1964	Jacques Laperrière	Montreal	**2000**	Scott Gomez	New Jersey
1965	Roger Crozier	Detroit	**2001**	Evgeni Nabokov	San Jose Sharks
1966	Brit Selby	Toronto	**2002**	Dany Heatley	Atlanta Thrashers
1967	Bobby Orr	Boston	**2003**	Barret Jackman	St. Louis Blues
1968	Derek Sanderson	Boston			

BASEBALL

Major League Baseball,
245 Park Avenue
New York, N.Y. 10167
(212)-931-7800
www.mlb.com
Commissioner: Allan "Bud" Selig
Number of teams-30

▶THE 2003 BASEBALL SEASON

The 2003 baseball season looked a lot like the previous year. Five of the eight teams that made the playoffs in 2002 returned to the postseason in 2003. The three new arrivals were the Boston Red Sox, who replaced the World Champion Anaheim Angels as the A.L. Wild Card, the Florida Marlins, and the Chicago Cubs, who won the N.L. Central under new manager Dusty Baker after going 67-95 in 2002. The Minnesota Twins, slated by Baseball Commissioner Bud Selig for contraction in 2002, won their second-straight A.L. Central crown; the Atlanta Braves extended their record for division titles to 12 in a row.

Barry Bonds finished the season with 658 home runs, two shy of Willie Mays on the all-time list. His staggering .749 slugging percentage and 61 intentional walks made him a near-lock for an unprecedented third straight Most Valuable Player Award.

Major League Baseball All-Time Career Leaders

Hits (3,000 or more)	
1. Pete Rose	4,256
2. Ty Cobb	4,191
3. Hank Aaron	3,771
4. Stan Musial	3,630
5. Tris Speaker	3,514
6. Carl Yastrzemski	3,419
7. Cap Anson	3,418
8. Honus Wagner	3,415
9. Paul Molitor	3,319
10. Eddie Collins	3,315
11. Willie Mays	3,283
12. Eddie Murray	3,255
13. Nap Lajoie	3,242
14. Cal Ripken Jr.	3,184
15. George Brett	3,154
16. Paul Waner	3,152
17. Robin Yount	3,142
18. Tony Gwynn	3,141
19. Dave Winfield	3,110
20. Rickey Henderson[1]	3,055
21. Rod Carew	3,053
22. Lou Brock	3,023
23. Wade Boggs	3,010
24. Al Kaline	3,007
25. Roberto Clemente	3,000

Home Runs (450 or more)	
1. Hank Aaron	755
2. Babe Ruth	714
3. Willie Mays	660
4. Barry Bonds[1]	658
5. Frank Robinson	586
6. Mark McGwire	583
7. Harmon Killebrew	573
8. Reggie Jackson	563
9. Mike Schmidt	548
10. Sammy Sosa[1]	539
11. Mickey Mantle	536
12. Jimmie Foxx	534
13. Rafael Palmeiro[1]	528
14. Ted Williams	521
14. Willie McCovey	521
16. Eddie Mathews	512
16. Ernie Banks	512
18. Mel Ott	511
19. Eddie Murray	504
20. Lou Gehrig	493
21. Fred McGriff[1]	478
22. Ken Griffey Jr.[1]	481
23. Stan Musial	475
23. Willie Stargell	475
25. Dave Winfield	465
26. Jose Canseco	462
27. Carl Yastrzemski	452

Runs Batted In	
1. Hank Aaron	2,297
2. Babe Ruth	2,211
3. Lou Gehrig	1,990
4. Ty Cobb	1,961
5. Stan Musial	1,951
6. Jimmie Foxx	1,921
7. Eddie Murray	1,917
8. Willie Mays	1,903
9. Mel Ott	1,861
10. Carl Yastrzemski	1,844

Runs	
1. Rickey Henderson[1]	2,295
2. Ty Cobb	2,245
3. Babe Ruth	2,174
3. Hank Aaron	2,174
5. Pete Rose	2,165
6. Willie Mays	2,062
7. Cap Anson	1,996
8. Stan Musial	1,949
9. Barry Bonds[1]	1,941
10. Lou Gehrig	1,888

Average (minimum 4,000 at bats)	
1. Ty Cobb	.367
2. Rogers Hornsby	.358
3. Joe Jackson	.356
4. Ed Delahanty	.346
5. Tris Speaker	.345
6. Ted Williams	.344
6. Billy Hamilton	.344
8. Babe Ruth	.342
8. Dan Brouthers	.342
10. Willie Keeler	.341

Stolen Bases	
1. Rickey Henderson[1]	1,406
2. Lou Brock	938
3. Billy Hamilton	912
4. Ty Cobb	892
5. Tim Raines	808
6. Vince Coleman	752
7. Eddie Collins	743
8. Arlie Latham	739
9. Max Carey	738
10. Honus Wagner	703

Total Bases	
1. Hank Aaron	6,856
2. Stan Musial	6,134
3. Willie Mays	6,066
4. Ty Cobb	5,859
5. Babe Ruth	5,793
6. Pete Rose	5,752
7. Carl Yastrzemski	5,539
8. Eddie Murray	5,397
9. Frank Robinson	5,373
10. Barry Bonds[1]	5,253

Slugging Percentage[2]	
1. Babe Ruth	.690
2. Ted Williams	.634
3. Lou Gehrig	.632
4. Jimmie Foxx	.609
5. Hank Greenberg	.605
6. Barry Bonds[1]	.598
7. Manny Ramirez[1]	.588
8. Mark McGwire	.588
8. Joe DiMaggio	.579
10. Rogers Hornsby	.577

Extra Base Hits	
1. Hank Aaron	1,477
2. Stan Musial	1,377
3. Babe Ruth	1,356
4. Willie Mays	1,323
5. Barry Bonds[1]	1,268
6. Lou Gehrig	1,190
7. Frank Robinson	1,186
8. Carl Yastrzemski	1,157
9. Ty Cobb	1,137
10. Tris Speaker	1,131

Games Played	
1. Pete Rose	3,562
2. Carl Yastrzemski	3,308
3. Hank Aaron	3,298
4. Rickey Henderson[1]	3,081
5. Ty Cobb	3,035
6. Eddie Murray	3,026
6. Stan Musial	3,026
8. Cal Ripken	3,001
9. Willie Mays	2,992
10. Dave Winfield	2,973

Pitching-Wins	
1. Cy Young	511
2. Walter Johnson	417
3. Christy Mathewson	373
3. Grover Alexander	373
5. Pud Galvin	365
6. Warren Spahn	363
7. Kid Nichols	361
8. Tim Keefe	342
9. Steve Carlton	329
10. John Clarkson	328
11. Eddie Plank	326
12. Nolan Ryan	324
12. Don Sutton	324
14. Phil Niekro	318
15. Gaylord Perry	314
16. Tom Seaver	311
17. Roger Clemens[1]	310
18. Charles "Old Hoss" Radbourn	309
19. Mickey Welch	307
10. Lefty Grove	300
20. Early Wynn	300

Strikeouts	
1. Nolan Ryan	5,714
2. Steve Carlton	4,136
3. Roger Clemens[1]	4,099
4. Randy Johnson[1]	3,871
5. Bert Blyleven	3,701
6. Tom Seaver	3,640
7. Don Sutton	3,574
8. Gaylord Perry	3,534
9. Walter Johnson	3,508
10. Phil Niekro	3,342

Earned run average	
1. Ed Walsh	1.82
2. Addie Joss	1.88
3. Mordecai "Three Finger" Brown	2.06
4. Christy Mathewson	2.13
5. Rube Waddell	2.16
6. Walter Johnson	2.17
7. Orval Overall	2.24
8. Ed Reulbach	2.28
9. Jim Scott	2.32
10. Eddie Plank	2.34

Innings Pitched	
1. Cy Young	7,356
2. Pud Galvin	5,941
3. Walter Johnson	5,923
4. Phil Niekro	5,403
5. Nolan Ryan	5,387
6. Gaylord Perry	5,351
7. Don Sutton	5,280
8. Warren Spahn	5,244
9. Steve Carlton	5,217
10. Grover Cleveland Alexander	5,189

Shutouts	
1. Walter Johnson	110
2. Grover Cleveland Alexander	90
3. Christy Mathewson	80
4. Cy Young	76
5. Eddie Plank	69
6. Warren Spahn	63
7. Nolan Ryan	61
8. Tom Seaver	61
9. Bert Blyleven	60
10. Don Sutton	58

Note: As of the end of the 2003 season. 1. Active during the 2003 season. 2. (total bases divided by minimum 400 at-bats.).
Source: Major League Baseball.

Batting Champions 1901–2003

	NATIONAL LEAGUE			AMERICAN LEAGUE		
Year	Name	Team	Avg.	Name	Team	Avg.
1901	Jesse Burkett	St. Louis Cardinals	.382	Nap Lajoie	Philadelphia Athletics	.422
1902	C.H. Beaumont	Pittsburgh Pirates	.357	Ed Delahanty	Washington Senators	.376
1903	Honus Wagner	Pittsburgh Pirates	.355	Nap Lajoie	Cleveland Indians	.355
1904	Honus Wagner	Pittsburgh Pirates	.349	Nap Lajoie	Cleveland Indians	.381
1905	J. Bentley Seymour	Cincinnati Reds	.377	Elmer Flick	Cleveland Indians	.306
1906	Honus Wagner	Pittsburgh Pirates	.339	George Stone	St. Louis Browns	.358
1907	Honus Wagner	Pittsburgh Pirates	.350	Ty Cobb	Detroit Tigers	.350
1908	Honus Wagner	Pittsburgh Pirates	.354	Ty Cobb	Detroit Tigers	.324
1909	Honus Wagner	Pittsburgh Pirates	.339	Ty Cobb	Detroit Tigers	.377
1910	Sherwood Magee	Philadelphia Phillies	.331	Ty Cobb	Detroit Tigers	.385
1911	Honus Wagner	Pittsburgh Pirates	.334	Ty Cobb	Detroit Tigers	.420
1912	Heinie Zimmerman	Chicago Cubs	.372	Ty Cobb	Detroit Tigers	.410
1913	Jake Daubert	Brooklyn Dodgers	.350	Ty Cobb	Detroit Tigers	.390
1914	Jake Daubert	Brooklyn Dodgers	.329	Ty Cobb	Detroit Tigers	.368
1915	Larry Doyle	New York Giants	.320	Ty Cobb	Detroit Tigers	.370
1916	Hal Chase	Cincinnati Reds	.339	Tris Speaker	Cleveland Indians	.386
1917	Edd Roush	Cincinnati Reds	.341	Ty Cobb	Detroit Tigers	.383
1918	Zack Wheat	Brooklyn Dodgers	.335	Ty Cobb	Detroit Tigers	.382
1919	Edd Roush	Cincinnati Reds	.321	Ty Cobb	Detroit Tigers	.407
1920	Rogers Hornsby	St. Louis Cardinals	.370	George Sisler	St. Louis Browns	.407
1921	Rogers Hornsby	St. Louis Cardinals	.397	Harry Heilmann	Detroit Tigers	.394
1922	Rogers Hornsby	St. Louis Cardinals	.401	George Sisler	St. Louis Browns	.420
1923	Rogers Hornsby	St. Louis Cardinals	.384	Harry Heilmann	Detroit Tigers	.403
1924	Rogers Hornsby	St. Louis Cardinals	.424	Babe Ruth	New York Yankees	.378
1925	Rogers Hornsby	St. Louis Cardinals	.403	Harry Heilmann	Detroit Tigers	.393
1926	Bubbles Hargrave	Cincinnati Reds	.353	Heinie Manush	Detroit Tigers	.377
1927	Paul Waner	Pittsburgh Pirates	.380	Harry Heilmann	Detroit Tigers	.398
1928	Rogers Hornsby	Boston Braves	.387	Goose Goslin	Washington Senators	.379
1929	Lefty O'Doul	Philadelphia Phillies	.398	Lew Fonseca	Cleveland Indians	.369
1930	Bill Terry	New York Giants	.401	Al Simmons	Philadelphia Athletics	.381
1931	Chick Hafey[1]	St Louis Cardinals	.349	Al Simmons	Philadelphia Athletics	.390
1932	Lefty O'Doul	Brooklyn Dodgers	.368	Dale Alexander	Detroit-Boston	.367
1933	Chuck Klein	Philadelphia Phillies	.368	Jimmie Foxx	Philadelphia Athletics	.356
1934	Paul Waner	Pittsburgh Pirates	.362	Lou Gehrig	New York Yankees	.363
1935	Arky Vaughan	Pittsburgh Pirates	.385	Buddy Myer	Washington Senators	.349
1936	Paul Waner	Pittsburgh Pirates	.373	Luke Appling	Chicago White Sox	.388
1937	Joe Medwick	St. Louis Cardinals	.374	Charlie Gehringer	Detroit Tigers	.371
1938	Ernie Lombardi	Cincinnati Reds	.342	Jimmie Foxx	Boston Red Sox	.349
1939	Johnny Mize	St. Louis Cardinals	.349	Joe DiMaggio	New York Yankees	.381
1940	Debs Garms	Pittsburgh Pirates	.355	Joe DiMaggio	New York Yankees	.352
1941	Pete Reiser	Brooklyn Dodgers	.343	Ted Williams	Boston Red Sox	.406
1942	Ernie Lombardi	Boston Braves	.330	Ted Williams	Boston Red Sox	.356
1943	Stan Musial	St. Louis Cardinals	.357	Luke Appling	Chicago White Sox	.328
1944	Dixie Walker	Brooklyn Dodgers	.357	Lou Boudreau	Cleveland Indians	.327
1945	Phil Cavarretta	Chicago Cubs	.355	Snuffy Stirnweiss	New York Yankees	.309
1946	Stan Musial	St. Louis Cardinals	.365	Mickey Vernon	Washington Senators	.352
1947	Harry Walker	St. Louis-Philadelphia	.363	Ted Williams	Boston Red Sox	.343
1948	Stan Musial	St. Louis Cardinals	.376	Ted Williams	Boston Red Sox	.369
1949	Jackie Robinson	Brooklyn Dodgers	.342	George Kell	Detroit Tigers	.343
1950	Stan Musial	St. Louis Cardinals	.346	Billy Goodman	Boston Red Sox	.354
1951	Stan Musial	St. Louis Cardinals	.355	Ferris Fain	Philadelphia Athletics	.344
1952	Stan Musial	St. Louis Cardinals	.336	Ferris Fain	Philadelphia Athletics	.327
1953	Carl Furillo	Brooklyn Dodgers	.344	Mickey Vernon	Washington Senators	.337
1954	Willie Mays	New York Giants	.345	Bobby Avila	Cleveland Indians	.341
1955	Richie Ashburn	Philadelphia Phillies	.338	Al Kaline	Detroit Tigers	.340
1956	Hank Aaron	Milwaukee Braves	.328	Mickey Mantle	New York Yankees	.353
1957	Stan Musial	St. Louis Cardinals	.351	Ted Williams	Boston Red Sox	.388
1958	Richie Ashburn	Philadelphia Phillies	.350	Ted Williams	Boston Red Sox	.328
1959	Hank Aaron	Milwaukee Braves	.355	Harvey Kuenn	Detroit Tigers	.353
1960	Dick Groat	Pittsburgh Pirates	.325	Pete Runnels	Boston Red Sox	.320
1961	Roberto Clemente	Pittsburgh Pirates	.351	Norm Cash	Detroit Tigers	.361
1962	Tommy Davis	Los Angeles Dodgers	.346	Pete Runnels	Boston Red Sox	.326
1963	Tommy Davis	Los Angeles Dodgers	.326	Carl Yastrzemski	Boston Red Sox	.321
1964	Roberto Clemente	Pittsburgh Pirates	.339	Tony Oliva	Minnesota Twins	.323
1965	Roberto Clemente	Pittsburgh Pirates	.329	Tony Oliva	Minnesota Twins	.321
1966	Matty Alou	Pittsburgh Pirates	.342	Frank Robinson	Baltimore Orioles	.316
1967	Roberto Clemente	Pittsburgh Pirates	.357	Carl Yastrzemski	Boston Red Sox	.326
1968	Pete Rose	Cincinnati Reds	.335	Carl Yastrzemski	Boston Red Sox	.301

Year	NATIONAL LEAGUE Name	Team	Avg.	AMERICAN LEAGUE Name	Team	Avg.
1969	Pete Rose	Cincinnati Reds	.348	Rod Carew	Minnesota Twins	.332
1970	Rico Carty	Atlanta Braves	.366	Alex Johnson	California Angels	.329
1971	Joe Torre	St. Louis Cardinals	.363	Tony Oliva	Minnesota Twins	.337
1972	Billy Williams	Chicago Cubs	.333	Rod Carew	Minnesota Twins	.318
1973	Pete Rose	Cincinnati Reds	.338	Rod Carew	Minnesota Twins	.350
1974	Ralph Garr	Atlanta Braves	.353	Rod Carew	Minnesota Twins	.364
1975	Bill Madlock	Chicago Cubs	.354	Rod Carew	Minnesota Twins	.359
1976	Bill Madlock	Chicago Cubs	.339	George Brett	Kansas City Royals	.333
1977	Dave Parker	Pittsburgh Pirates	.338	Rod Carew	Minnesota Twins	.388
1978	Dave Parker	Pittsburgh Pirates	.334	Rod Carew	Minnesota Twins	.333
1979	Keith Hernandez	St. Louis Cardinals	.344	Fred Lynn	Boston Red Sox	.333
1980	Bill Buckner	Chicago Cubs	.324	George Brett	Kansas City Royals	.390
1981[2]	Bill Madlock	Pittsburgh Pirates	.341	Carney Lansford	Boston Red Sox	.336
1982	Al Oliver	Montreal Expos	.331	Willie Wilson	Kansas City Royals	.332
1983	Bill Madlock	Pittsburgh Pirates	.323	Wade Boggs	Boston Red Sox	.361
1984	Tony Gwynn	San Diego Padres	.351	Don Mattingly	New York Yankees	.343
1985	Willie McGee	St. Louis Cardinals	.353	Wade Boggs	Boston Red Sox	.368
1986	Tim Raines	Montreal Expos	.334	Wade Boggs	Boston Red Sox	.357
1987	Tony Gwynn	San Diego Padres	.370	Wade Boggs	Boston Red Sox	.363
1988	Tony Gwynn	San Diego Padres	.313	Wade Boggs	Boston Red Sox	.366
1989	Tony Gwynn	San Diego Padres	.336	Kirby Puckett	Minnesota Twins	.339
1990	Willie McGee	St. Louis Cardinals	.335	George Brett	Kansas City Royals	.329
1991	Terry Pendleton	Atlanta Braves	.319	Julio Franco	Texas Rangers	.341
1992	Gary Sheffield	San Diego Padres	.330	Edgar Martinez	Seattle Mariners	.343
1993	Andres Galarraga	Colorado Rockies	.370	John Olerud	Toronto Blue Jays	.363
1994[2]	Tony Gwynn	San Diego Padres	.394	Paul O'Neill	New York Yankees	.359
1995[2]	Tony Gwynn	San Diego Padres	.368	Edgar Martinez	Seattle Mariners	.356
1996	Ellis Burks	Colorado Rockies	.344	Alex Rodriguez	Seattle Mariners	.358
1997	Tony Gwynn	San Diego Padres	.372	Frank Thomas	Chicago White Sox	.347
1998	Larry Walker	Colorado Rockies	.363	Bernie Williams	New York Yankees	.339
1999	Larry Walker	Colorado Rockies	.379	Nomar Garciaparra	Boston Red Sox	.357
2000	Todd Helton	Colorado Rockies	.372	Nomar Garciaparra	Boston Red Sox	.372
2001	Larry Walker	Colorado Rockies	.350	Ichiro Suzuki	Seattle Mariners	.350
2002	Barry Bonds	San Francisco Giants	.370	Manny Ramirez	Boston Red Sox	.349
2003	Albert Pujols	St. Louis Cardinals	.359	Bill Mueller	Boston Red Sox	.326

1. Hafey led with .3489, Bill Terry, N.Y., second with.3486, Jim Bottomley, St. Louis, third with .3482. 2. Strike-shortened season.

Home Run Champions, 1919–2003

Year	NATIONAL LEAGUE Name, Team	Home Runs	AMERICAN LEAGUE Name, Team	Home Runs
1919	Gavvy Cravath, Philadelphia	12	Babe Ruth, Boston	29
1920	Cy Williams, Philadelphia	15	Babe Ruth, New York	54
1921	George Kelly, New York	23	Babe Ruth, New York	59
1922	Rogers Hornsby, St. Louis	42	Ken Williams, St. Louis	39
1923	Cy Williams, Philadelphia	41	Babe Ruth, New York	41
1924	Jack Fournier, Brooklyn	27	Babe Ruth, New York	46
1925	Rogers Hornsby, St. Louis	39	Bob Meusel, New York	33
1926	Hack Wilson, Chicago	21	Babe Ruth, New York	47
1927	Cy Williams, Philadelphia; Hack Wilson, Chicago	30	Babe Ruth, New York	60
1928	Jim Bottomley, St. Louis; Hack Wilson, Chicago	31	Babe Ruth, New York	54
1929	Chuck Klein, Philadelphia	43	Babe Ruth, New York	46
1930	Hack Wilson, Chicago	56	Babe Ruth, New York	49
1931	Chuck Klein, Philadelphia	31	Lou Gehrig, Babe Ruth, New York	46
1932	Chuck Klein, Philadelphia; Mel Ott, New York	38	Jimmie Foxx, Philadelphia	58
1933	Chuck Klein, Philadelphia	28	Jimmie Foxx, Philadelphia	48
1934	Ripper Collins, St. Louis; Mel Ott, New York	35	Lou Gehrig, New York	49
1935	Wally Berger, Boston	34	Jimmie Foxx, Philadelphia; Hank Greenberg, Detroit	36
1936	Mel Ott, New York	33	Lou Gehrig, New York	49
1937	Joe Medwick, St. Louis; Mel Ott, New York	31	Joe Dimaggio, New York	46
1938	Mel Ott, New York	36	Hank Greenberg, Detroit	58
1939	Johnny Mize, St. Louis	28	Jimmie Foxx, Boston	35
1940	Johnny Mize, St. Louis	43	Hank Greenberg, Detroit	41
1941	Dolph Camillia, Brooklyn	34	Ted Williams, Boston	37
1942	Mel Ott, New York	30	Ted Williams, Boston	36

Year	NATIONAL LEAGUE Name, Team	Home Runs	AMERICAN LEAGUE Name, Team	Home Runs
1943	Bill Nicholson, Chicago	29	Rudy York, Detroit	34
1944	Bill Nicholson, Chicago	33	Nick Etten, New York	22
1945	Tommy Holmes, Boston	28	Vern Stephens, St. Louis	24
1946	Ralph Kiner, Pittsburgh	23	Hank Greenberg, Detroit	44
1947	Ralph Kiner, Pittsburgh; Johnny Mize, New York	51	Ted Williams, Boston	32
1948	Ralph Kiner, Pittsburgh; Johnny Mize, New York	40	Joe DiMaggio, New York	39
1949	Ralph Kiner, Pittsburgh	54	Ted Williams, Boston	43
1950	Ralph Kiner, Pittsburgh	47	Al Rosen, Cleveland	37
1951	Ralph Kiner, Pittsburgh	42	Gus Zernial, Chicago-Philadelphia	33
1952	Ralph Kiner, Pittsburgh; Hank Sauer, Chicago	37	Larry Doby, Cleveland	32
1953	Eddie Mathews, Milwaukee	47	Al Rosen, Cleveland	43
1954	Ted Kluszewski, Cincinnati	49	Larry Doby, Cleveland	32
1955	Willie Mays, New York	51	Mickey Mantle, New York	37
1956	Duke Snider, Brooklyn	43	Mickey Mantle, New York	52
1957	Hank Aaron, Milwaukee	44	Roy Sievers, Washington	42
1958	Ernie Banks, Chicago	47	Mickey Mantle, New York	42
1959	Eddie Mathews, Milwaukee	46	Rocky Colavito, Cleveland; Harmon Killebrew, Washington	42
1960	Ernie Banks, Chicago	41	Mickey Mantle, New York	40
1961	Orlando Cepeda, San Francisco	46	Roger Maris, New York	61
1962	Willie Mays, San Francisco	49	Harmon Killebrew, Minnesota	48
1963	Hank Aaron, Milwaukee; Willie McCovey, San Francisco	44	Harmon Killebrew, Minnesota	45
1964	Willie Mays, San Francisco	47	Harmon Killebrew, Minnesota	49
1965	Willie Mays, San Francisco	52	Tony Conigliaro, Boston	32
1966	Hank Aaron, Atlanta	44	Frank Robinson, Baltimore	49
1967	Hank Aaron, Atlanta	39	Harmon Killebrew, Minnesota; Carl Yastrzemski, Boston	44
1968	Willie McCovey, San Francisco	36	Frank Howard, Washington	44
1969	Willie McCovey, San Francisco	45	Harmon Killebrew, Minnesota	49
1970	Johnny Bench, Cincinnati	45	Frank Howard, Washington	44
1971	Willie Stargell, Pittsburgh	48	Bill Melton, Chicago	33
1972	Johnny Bench, Cincinnati	40	Dick Allen, Chicago	37
1973	Willie Stargell, Pittsburgh	44	Reggie Jackson, Oakland	32
1974	Mike Schmidt, Philadelphia	36	Dick Allen, Chicago	32
1975	Mike Schmidt, Philadelphia	38	Reggie Jackson, Oakland George Scott, Milwaukee	36
1976	Mike Schmidt, Philadelphia	38	Graig Nettles, New York	32
1977	George Foster, Cincinnati	52	Jim Rice, Boston	39
1978	George Foster, Cincinnati	40	Jim Rice, Boston	46
1979	Dave Kingman, Chicago	48	Gorman Thomas, Milwaukee	45
1980	Mike Schmidt, Philadelphia	48	Reggie Jackson, New York; Ben Oglivie, Milwaukee	41
1981[1]	Mike Schmidt, Philadelphia	31	Tony Armas, Boston; Dwight Evans, Boston; Bobby Grich, California; Eddie Murray, Baltimore	22
1982	Dave Kingman, New York	37	Reggie Jackson, California; Gorman Thomas, Milwaukee	39
1983	Mike Schmidt, Philadelphia	40	Jim Rice, Boston	39
1984	Dale Murphy, Atlanta; Mike Schmidt, Philadelphia	36	Tony Armas, Boston	50
1985	Dale Murphy, Atlanta	37	Darrell Evans, Detroit	40
1986	Mike Schmidt, Philadelphia	37	Jesse Barfield, Toronto	40
1987	Andre Dawson, Chicago	49	Mark McGwire, Oakland	49
1988	Darryl Strawberry, New York Mets	39	Jose Canseco, Oakland	42
1989	Kevin Mitchell, San Francisco	47	Fred McGriff, Toronto	36
1990	Ryne Sandberg, Chicago	40	Cecil Fielder, Detroit	51
1991	Howard Johnson, New York Mets	38	Jose Canseco, Oakland	44
1992	Fred McGriff, San Diego	35	Juan Gonzalez, Texas	43
1993	Barry Bonds, San Francisco	46	Juan Gonzalez, Texas	46
1994[1]	Matt Williams, San Francisco	43	Ken Griffey Jr., Seattle	40
1995[1]	Dante Bichette, Colorado	40	Albert Belle, Cleveland	50
1996	Andres Galarraga, Colorado	47	Mark McGwire, Oakland	52
1997	Larry Walker, Colorado[2]	49	Ken Griffey Jr., Seattle[2]	56
1998	Mark McGwire, St. Louis	70	Ken Griffey Jr., Seattle	56
1999	Mark McGwire, St. Louis	65	Ken Griffey Jr., Seattle	48
2000	Sammy Sosa, Chicago Cubs	50	Troy Glaus, Anaheim	47
2001	Barry Bonds, San Francisco	73	Alex Rodriguez, Texas	52
2002	Sammy Sosa, Chicago Cubs	49	Alex Rodriguez, Texas	57
2003	Jim Thome, Philadelphia	47	Alex Rodriguez, Texas	47

1. Strike-shortened season 2. Mark McGwire hit 34 home runs with Oakland and 24 with St. Louis for a major-league-leading total of 58.

Rookie of the Year

Year	Name	Team
1947[1]	Jackie Robinson	Brooklyn Dodgers
1948[1]	Alvin Dark	Boston Braves

NATIONAL LEAGUE

Year	Name	Team
1949	Don Newcombe	Brooklyn Dodgers
1950	Sam Jethroe	Boston Braves
1951	Willie Mays	New York Giants
1952	Joe Black	Brooklyn Dodgers
1953	Junior Gilliam	Brooklyn Dodgers
1954	Wally Moon	St. Louis Cardinals
1955	Bill Virdon	St. Louis Cardinals
1956	Frank Robinson	Cincinnati Reds
1957	Jack Sanford	Philadelphia Phillies
1958	Orlando Cepeda	San Francisco Giants
1959	Willie McCovey	San Francisco Giants
1960	Frank Howard	Los Angeles Dodgers
1961	Billy Williams	Chicago Cubs
1962	Ken Hubbs	Chicago Cubs
1963	Pete Rose	Cincinnati Reds
1964	Richie Allen	Philadelphia Phillies
1965	Jim Lefebvre	Los Angeles Dodgers
1966	Tommy Helms	Cincinnati Reds
1967	Tom Seaver	New York Mets
1968	Johnny Bench	Cincinnati Reds
1969	Ted Sizemore	Los Angeles Dodgers
1970	Carl Morton	Montreal Expos
1971	Earl Williams	Atlanta Braves
1972	Jon Matlack	New York Mets
1973	Gary Matthews	San Francisco Giants
1974	Bake McBride	St. Louis Cardinals
1975	John Montefusco	San Francisco Giants
1976	Pat Zachry	Cincinnati Reds
	Butch Metzger	San Diego Padres
1977	Andre Dawson	Montreal Expos
1978	Bob Horner	Atlanta Braves
1979	Rick Sutcliffe	Los Angeles Dodgers
1980	Steve Howe	Los Angeles Dodgers
1981	Fernando Valenzuela	Los Angeles Dodgers
1982	Steve Sax	Los Angeles Dodgers
1983	Darryl Strawberry	New York Mets
1984	Dwight Gooden	New York Mets
1985	Vince Coleman	St. Louis Cardinals
1986	Todd Worrell	St. Louis Cardinals
1987	Benito Santiago	San Diego Padres
1988	Chris Sabo	Cincinnati Reds
1989	Jerome Walton	Chicago Cubs
1990	Dave Justice	Atlanta Braves
1991	Jeff Bagwell	Houston Astros
1992	Eric Karros	Los Angeles Dodgers
1993	Mike Piazza	Los Angeles Dodgers
1994	Raul Mondesi	Los Angeles Dodgers
1995	Hideo Nomo	Los Angeles Dodgers
1996	Todd Hollandsworth	Los Angeles Dodgers
1997	Scott Rolen	Philadelphia Phillies
1998	Kerry Wood	Chicago Cubs
1999	Scott Williamson	Cincinnati Reds
2000	Rafael Furcal	Atlanta Braves
2001	Albert Pujols	St. Louis Cardinals
2002	Jason Jennings	Colorado Rockies

AMERICAN LEAGUE

Year	Name	Team
1949	Roy Sievers	St. Louis Browns
1950	Walt Dropo	Boston Red Sox
1951	Gil McDougald	New York Yankees
1952	Harry Byrd	Philadelphia Athletics
1953	Harvey Kuenn	Detroit Tigers
1954	Bob Grim	New York Yankees
1955	Herb Score	Cleveland Indians
1956	Luis Aparicio	Chicago White Sox
1957	Tony Kubek	New York Yankees
1958	Albie Pearson	Washington Senators
1959	Bob Allison	Washington Senators
1960	Ron Hansen	Baltimore Orioles
1961	Don Schwall	Boston Red Sox
1962	Tom Tresh	New York Yankees
1963	Gary Peters	Chicago White Sox
1964	Tony Oliva	Minnesota Twins
1965	Curt Blefary	Baltimore Orioles
1966	Tommie Agee	Chicago White Sox
1967	Rod Carew	Minnesota Twins
1968	Stan Bahnsen	New York Yankees
1969	Lou Piniella	Kansas City Royals
1970	Thurman Munson	New York Yankees
1971	Chris Chambliss	Cleveland Indians
1972	Carlton Fisk	Boston Red Sox
1973	Al Bumbry	Baltimore Orioles
1974	Make Hargrove	Texas Rangers
1975	Fred Lynn	Boston Red Sox
1976	Mark Fidrych	Detroit Tigers
1977	Eddie Murray	Baltimore Orioles
1978	Lou Whitaker	Detroit Tigers
1979	John Castino	Minnesota Twins
	Alfredo Griffin	Toronto Blue Jays
1980	Joe Charboneau	Cleveland Indians
1981	Dave Righetti	New York Yankees
1982	Cal Ripken Jr.	Baltimore Orioles
1983	Ron Kittle	Chicago White Sox
1984	Alvin Davis	Seattle Mariners
1985	Ozzie Guillen	Chicago White Sox
1986	Jose Canseco	Oakland Athletics
1987	Mark McGwire	Oakland Athletics
1988	Walt Weiss	Oakland Athletics
1989	Greg Olson	Baltimore Orioles
1990	Sandy Alomar Jr.	Cleveland Indians
1991	Chuck Knoblauch	Minnesota Twins
1992	Pat Listach	Milwaukee Brewers
1993	Tim Salmon	California Angels
1994	Bob Hamelin	Kansas City Royals
1995	Marty Cordoba	Minnesota Twins
1996	Derek Jeter	New York Yankees
1997	Nomar Garciaparra	Boston Red Sox
1998	Ben Grieve	Oakland Athletics
1999	Carlos Beltran	Kansas City Royals
2000	Kazuhiro Sasaki	Seattle Mariners
2001	Ichiro Suzuki	Seattle Mariners
2002	Eric Hinske	Toronto Blue Jays

1. One player selected as Major League Rookie of the Year. Policy of naming a player from each league was inaugurated in 1949.
Source: Baseball Writer's Association.

Cy Young Award Winners

BOTH LEAGUES

Year	Name, Team	W–L,	ERA	Year	Name, Team	W–L,	ERA
1956	Don Newcombe, Brooklyn Dodgers	27– 7	3.06	1962	Don Drysdale, Los Angeles Dodgers	25– 9,	2.83
1957	Warren Spahn, Milwaukee Braves	21–11	2.69	1963	Sandy Koufax, Los Angeles Dodgers	25– 5,	1.88
1958	Bob Turley, New York Yankees	21– 7	2.97	1964	Dean Chance, Los Angeles Angels	20– 9,	1.65
1959	Early Wynn, Chicago White Sox	22–10	3.17	1965	Sandy Koufax, Los Angeles Dodgers	26– 8,	2.04
1960	Vernon Law, Pittsburgh Pirates	20– 9	3.08	1966	Sandy Koufax, Los Angeles Dodgers	27– 9,	1.73
1961	Whitey Ford, New York Yankees	25– 4	3.21				

NATIONAL LEAGUE

Year	Name, Team	W–L,	ERA
1967	Mike McCormick, San Francisco Giants	22–10	2.85
1968	Bob Gibson, St. Louis Cardinals	22– 9	1.12
1969	Tom Seaver, New York Mets	25– 7	2.21
1970	Bob Gibson, St. Louis Cardinals	23– 7	3.12
1971	Ferguson Jenkins, Chicago Cubs	24–13	2.77
1972	Steve Carlton, Philadelphia Phillies	27–10	1.97
1973	Tom Seaver, New York Mets	19–10	2.08
1974	Mike Marshall[1], Los Angeles Dodgers	15–12	2.42
1975	Tom Seaver, New York Mets	22– 9	2.38
1976	Randy Jones, San Diego Padres	22–1	2.74
1977	Steve Carlton, Philadelphia Phillies	23–10	2.64
1978	Gaylord Perry, San Diego Padres	21– 6	2.72
1979	Bruce Sutter[2], Chicago Cubs	6– 6	2.23
1980	Steve Carlton, Philadelphia Phillies	24– 9	2.34
1981	Fernando Valenzuela[3], Los Angeles Dodgers	13– 7	2.48
1982	Steve Carlton, Philadelphia Phillies	23–11	3.10
1983	John Denny, Philadelphia Phillies	19– 6	2.37
1984	Rick Sutcliffe, Chicago Cubs	20– 6	3.64
1985	Dwight Gooden, New York Mets	24– 4	1.53
1986	Mike Scott, Houston Astros	18–10	2.22
1987	Steve Bedrosian[4], Philadelphia Phillies	5– 3	2.83
1988	Orel Hershiser, Los Angeles Dodgers	23– 8	2.26
1989	Mark Davis[5], San Diego Padres	4– 3	1.85
1990	Doug Drabek, Pittsburgh Pirates	22– 6	2.76
1991	Tom Glavine, Atlanta Braves	20–11	2.55
1992	Greg Maddux, Chicago Cubs	20–11	2.18
1993	Greg Maddux, Atlanta Braves	20–10	2.36
1994	Greg Maddux[3], Atlanta Braves	16– 6	1.56
1995	Greg Maddux[3], Atlanta Braves	19– 2	1.53
1996	John Smoltz, Atlanta Braves	24– 8	2.94
1997	Pedro Martinez, Montreal Expos	17– 8	1.90
1998	Tom Glavine, Atlanta Braves	20– 6	2.47
1999	Randy Johnson, Arizona Diamondbacks	17 – 9	2.48
2000	Randy Johnson, Arizona Diamondbacks	19 – 7	2.64
2001	Randy Johnson, Arizona Diamondbacks	21– 6	2.49
2002	Randy Johnson, Arizona Diamondbacks	24– 5	2.32

AMERICAN LEAGUE

Year	Name, Team	W–L,	ERA
1967	Jim Lonborg, Boston Red Sox	22– 9	3.16
1968	Denny McLain, Detroit Tigers	31– 6	1.96
1969	Mike Cuellar, Baltimore Orioles	23–11	2.38
1970	Jim Perry, Minnesota Twins	24–12	3.03
1971	Vida Blue, Oakland Athletics	24– 8	1.82
1972	Gaylord Perry, Cleveland Indians	24–16	1.92
1973	Jim Palmer, Baltimore Orioles	22– 9	2.40
1974	Catfish Hunter, Oakland Athletics	25–12	2.49
1975	Jim Palmer, Baltimore Orioles	23–11	2.09
1976	Jim Palmer, Baltimore Orioles	22–13	2.51
1977	Sparky Lyle[6], New York Yankees	13– 5	2.17
1978	Ron Guidry, New York Yankees	25– 3	1.74
1979	Mike Flanagan, Baltimore Orioles	23– 9	3.08
1980	Steve Stone, Baltimore Orioles	25– 7	3.23
1981	Rollie Fingers[3,7], Milwaukee Brewers	6– 3	1.04
1982	Pete Vuckovich, Milwaukee Brewers	18– 6	3.34
1983	LaMarr Hoyt, Chicago White Sox	24–10	3.66
1984	Willie Henandez[8], Detroit Tigers	9– 3	1.92
1985	Bret Saberhagen , Kansas City Royals	20– 6	2.87
1986	Roger Clemens, Boston Red Sox	24– 4	2.48
1987	Roger Clemens, Boston Red Sox	20– 9	2.97
1988	Frank Viola, Minnesota Twins	24– 7	2.64
1989	Bret Saberhagen, Kansas City Royals	23– 6	2.16
1990	Bob Welch, Oakland Athletics	27– 6	3.06
1991	Roger Clemens, Boston Red Sox	18–10	3.06
1992	Dennis Eckersley[9], Oakland Athletics	7– 1	1.91
1993	Jack McDowell, Chicago White Sox	22–10	3.37
1994	David Cone[3], Kansas City Royals	16– 5	2.94
1995	Randy Johnson[3], Seattle Mariners	18– 2	2.48
1996	Pat Hentgen, Toronto Blue Jays	20–10	3.22
1997	Roger Clemens, Toronto Blue Jays	21 – 7	2.05
1998	Roger Clemens, Toronto Blue Jays	20 – 6	2.65
1999	Pedro Martinez, Boston Red Sox	23 – 4	2.07
2000	Pedro Martinez, Boston Red Sox	18 – 6	1.74
2001	Roger Clemens, New York Yankees	20 – 6	2.65
2002	Barry Zito, Oakland Athletics	23– 5	2.75

1. 21 saves in 1974. 2. 37 saves in 1979. 3. Strike-shortened season. 4. 40 saves in 1987. 5. 44 saves in 1989. 6. 26 saves in 1977. 7. 28 saves in 1981. 8. 32 saves in 1984. 9. 51 saves in 1992.

Most Valuable Player Award Winners

Between 1911 and 1914 the Chalmers Award was given to the player judged to be the most valuable in each league. It was not until 1922 that the American League began to select a league MVP. The National League began to do so as well two years later. By the end of the decade, though, both leagues failed to select an MVP. In 1931 the Baseball Writers Association of America began to select the league MVP's and has continued to do so through today.

NATIONAL LEAGUE

Year	Name	Team	HRs	RBIs	Avg.
1911	Frank Schulte	Chicago Cubs	21	121	.300
1912	Larry Doyle	New York Giants	10	90	.330
1913	Jake Daubert	Brooklyn Dodgers	2	52	.350
1914	Johnny Evers	Chicago Cubs	1	40	.279
1924	Dazzy Vance (Pitcher)	Brooklyn Dodgers	28W	6L	2.16 ERA
1925	Rogers Hornsby	St. Louis Cardinals	29	143	.403
1926	Bob O'Farrell	St. Louis Cardinals	7	68	.293
1927	Paul Waner	Pittsburgh Pirates	9	131	.380
1928	Jim Bottomley	St. Louis Cardinals	31	136	.325
1929	Rogers Hornsby	St. Louis Cardinals	39	149	.380
1931	Frankie Frisch	St. Louis Cardinals	4	82	.311
1932	Chuck Klein	Philadelphia Phillies	38	137	.348
1933	Carl Hubbell (Pitcher)	New York Giants	23W	12L	1.66 ERA
1934	Dizzy Dean (Pitcher)	St. Louis Cardinals	30W	7L	2.66 ERA
1935	Gabby Hartnett	Chicago Cubs	13	91	.344
1936	Carl Hubbell (Pitcher)	New York Giants	26W	6L	2.31 ERA
1937	Joe Medwick	St. Louis Cardinals	31	154	.374
1938	Ernie Lombardi	Cincinnati Reds	19	95	.342
1939	Bucky Walters (Pitcher)	Cinncinati Reds	27W	11L	2.29 ERA
1940	Frank McCormick	Cinncinati Reds	19	127	.309
1941	Dolph Camilli	Brooklyn Dodgers	34	120	.285
1942	Mort Cooper (Pitcher)	St. Louis Cardinals	22W	7L	1.78 ERA
1943	Stan Musial	St. Louis Cardinals	13	81	.357
1944	Marty Marion	St. Louis Cardinals	6	63	.267
1945	Phil Cavarretta	Chicago Cubs	6	97	.355
1946	Stan Musial	St. Louis Cardinals	16	103	.365
1947	Bob Elliott	Boston Braves	22	113	.317
1948	Stan Musial	St. Louis Cardinals	39	131	.376
1949	Jackie Robinson	Brooklyn Dodgers	16	124	.342
1950	Jim Konstanty (Pitcher)[1]	Philadelphia Phillies	16W	7L	2.66 ERA
1951	Roy Campanella	Brooklyn Dodgers	33	108	.325
1952	Hank Sauer	Chicago Cubs	37	121	.270
1953	Roy Campanella	Brooklyn Dodgers	41	142	.312
1954	Willie Mays	New York Giants	41	110	.345
1955	Roy Campanella	Brooklyn Dodgers	32	107	.318
1956	Don Newcombe (Pitcher)	Brooklyn Dodgers	27W	7L	3.06 ERA
1957	Hank Aaron	Milwaukee Braves	44	132	.322
1958	Ernie Banks	Chicago Cubs	47	129	.313
1959	Ernie Banks	Chicago Cubs	45	143	.304
1960	Dick Groat	Pittsburgh Pirates	2	50	.325
1961	Frank Robinson	Cincinnati Reds	37	124	.323
1962	Maury Wills	Los Angeles Dodgers	6	48	.299
1963	Sandy Koufax (Pitcher)	Los Angeles Dodgers	25W	5L	1.88 ERA
1964	Ken Boyer	St. Louis Cardinals	24	119	.295
1965	Willie Mays	San Francisco Giants	52	112	.317
1966	Roberto Clemente	Pittsburgh Pirates	29	119	.317
1967	Orlando Cepeda	San Francisco Giants	25	111	.325
1968	Bob Gibson (Pitcher)	St. Louis Cardinals	22W	9L	1.12 ERA
1969	Willie McCovey	San Francisco Giants	45	126	.320
1970	Johnny Bench	Cincinnati Reds	45	148	.293
1971	Joe Torre	St. Louis Cardinals	45	137	.363
1972	Johnny Bench	Cincinnati Reds	40	125	.270
1973	Pete Rose	Cincinnati Reds	5	64	.338
1974	Steve Garvey	Los Angeles Dodgers	21	111	.312
1975	Joe Morgan	Cincinnati Reds	17	94	.327
1976	Joe Morgan	Cincinnati Reds	27	111	.320
1977	George Foster	Cincinnati Reds	52	149	.320
1978	Dave Parker	Pittsburgh Pirates	30	117	.334
1979	Keith Hernandez	St. Louis Cardinals	11	105	.344
	Willie Stargell	Pittsburgh Pirates	32	82	.281

NATIONAL LEAGUE

Year	Name	Team	HRs	RBIs	Avg.
1980	Mike Schmidt	Philadelphia Phillies	48	121	.286
1981	Mike Schmidt[2]	Philadelphia Phillies	31	91	.316
1982	Dale Murphy	Atlanta Braves	36	109	.281
1983	Dale Murphy	Atlanta Braves	36	121	.302
1984	Ryne Sandberg	Chicago Cubs	19	84	.314
1985	Willie McGee	St. Louis Cardinals	10	82	.353
1986	Mike Schmidt	Philadelphia Phillies	37	119	.290
1987	Andre Dawson	Chicago Cubs	49	137	.287
1988	Kirk Gibson	Los Angeles Dodgers	25	76	.290
1989	Kevin Mitchell	San Francisco Giants	47	125	.291
1990	Barry Bonds	Pittsburgh Pirates	33	114	.301
1991	Terry Pendleton	Atlanta Braves	22	86	.319
1992	Barry Bonds	Pittsburgh Pirates	34	103	.311
1993	Barry Bonds	San Francisco Giants	46	123	.336
1994	Jeff Bagwell[2]	Houston Astros	39	116	.368
1995	Barry Larkin[2]	Cincinnati Reds	15	66	.319
1996	Ken Caminiti	San Diego Padres	40	130	.326
1997	Larry Walker	Colorado Rockies	49	130	.366
1998	Sammy Sosa	Chicago Cubs	66	158	.308
1999	Chipper Jones	Atlanta Braves	45	110	.319
2000	Jeff Kent	San Francisco Giants	33	125	.334
2001	Barry Bonds	San Francisco Giants	73	137	.328
2002	Barry Bonds	San Francisco Giants	46	110	.370

1. 22 saves in 1950. 2. Strike-shortened season. **Source:** Baseball Writers' Association.

AMERICAN LEAGUE

Year	Player	Team	HRs	RBIs	Avg.
1911	Ty Cobb	Detroit Tigers	8	144	.420
1912	Tris Speaker	Boston Red Sox	10	98	.383
1913	Walter Johnson (Pitcher)	Washington Senators	36W	7L	1.09 ERA
1914	Eddie Collins	Philadelphia Athletics	2	85	.344
1922	George Sisler	St. Louis Browns	8	105	.420
1923	Babe Ruth	New York Yankees	41	131	.393
1924	Walter Johnson (Pitcher)	Washington Senators	23W	7L	2.72 ERA
1925	Roger Peckinpaugh	Washington Senators	4	64	.294
1926	George Burns	Cleveland Indians	4	114	.358
1927	Lou Gehrig	New York Yankees	47	175	.373
1928	Mickey Cochrane	Philadelphia Athletics	10	57	.293
1931	Lefty Grove (Pitcher)	Philadelphia Athletics	31W	4L	2.06 ERA
1932	Jimmie Foxx	Philadelphia Athletics	58	169	.364
1933	Jimmie Foxx	Philadelphia Athletics	48	163	.356
1934	Mickey Cochrane	Detroit Tigers	2	76	.320
1935	Hank Greenberg	Detroit Tigers	36	170	.328
1936	Lou Gehrig	New York Yankees	49	152	.354
1937	Charley Gehringer	Detroit Tigers	14	96	.371
1938	Jimmie Foxx	Boston Red Sox	50	175	.349
1939	Joe DiMaggio	New York Yankees	30	126	.381
1940	Hank Greenberg	Detroit Tigers	30	125	.357
1941	Joe DiMaggio	New York Yankees	30	125	.357
1942	Joe Gordon	New York Yankees	18	103	.322
1943	Spud Chandler (Pitcher)	New York Yankees	20W	4L	1.64 ERA
1944	Hal Newhouser (Pitcher)	Detroit Tigers	29W	9L	2.22 ERA
1945	Hal Newhouser (Pitcher)	Detroit Tigers	25W	9L	1.81 ERA
1946	Ted Williams	Boston Red Sox	38	123	.342
1947	Joe DiMaggio	New York Yankees	20	97	.315
1948	Lou Boudreau	Cleveland Indians	18	106	.355
1949	Ted Williams	Boston Red Sox	43	159	.343
1950	Phil Rizzuto	New York Yankees	7	66	.324
1951	Yogi Berra	New York Yankees	27	88	.294
1952	Bobby Shantz (Pitcher)	Philadelphia Athletics	24W	7L	2.48 ERA
1953	Al Rosen	Cleveland Indians	43	145	.336
1954	Yogi Berra	New York Yankees	22	125	.307
1955	Yogi Berra	New York Yankees	27	108	.272
1956	Mickey Mantle	New York Yankees	52	130	.353
1957	Mickey Mantle	New York Yankees	34	94	.365
1958	Jackie Jensen	Boston Red Sox	35	122	.286
1959	Nelson Fox	Chicago White Sox	2	70	.306

AMERICAN LEAGUE

Year	Player	Team	HRs	RBIs	Avg.
1960	Roger Maris	New York Yankees	39	112	.283
1961	Roger Maris	New York Yankees	61	142	.269
1962	Mickey Mantle	New York Yankees	30	89	.321
1963	Elston Howard	New York Yankees	28	85	.287
1964	Brooks Robinson	Baltimore Orioles	28	118	.317
1965	Zoilo Versalles	Minnesota Twins	19	77	.273
1966	Frank Robinson	Baltimore Orioles	49	122	.316
1967	Carl Yastrzemski	Boston Red Sox	44	121	.326
1968	Dennis McLain (Pitcher)	Detroit Tigers	31W	6L	1.96ERA
1969	Harmon Killebrew	Minnesota Twins	49	140	.276
1970	Boog Powell	Baltimore Orioles	35	114	.297
1971	Vida Blue (Pitcher)	Oakland Athletics	24W	8L	1.82ERA
1972	Dick Allen	Chicago White Sox	37	113	.308
1973	Reggie Jackson	Oakland Athletics	32	117	.293
1974	Jeff Burroughs	Texas Rangers	25	118	.301
1975	Fred Lynn	Boston Red Sox	21	105	.331
1976	Thurman Munson	New York Yankees	17	105	.302
1977	Rod Carew	Minnesota Twins	14	100	.388
1978	Jim Rice	Boston Red Sox	46	139	.315
1979	Don Baylor	California Angels	36	139	.296
1980	George Brett	Kansas City Royals	24	118	.390
1981	Rollie Fingers (Pitcher)[1, 2]	Milwaukee Brewers	6W	3L	1.04 ERA
1982	Robin Yount	Milwaukee Brewers	29	114	.331
1983	Cal Ripken Jr.	Baltimore Orioles	27	102	.318
1984	Willie Hernandez (Pitcher)[3]	Detroit Tigers	9W	3L	2.48 ERA
1985	Don Mattingly	New York Yankees	35	145	.324
1986	Roger Clemens (Pitcher)	Boston Red Sox	24W	4L	2.48 ERA
1987	George Bell	Toronto Blue Jays	47	134	.308
1988	Jose Canseco	Oakland Athletics	42	124	.307
1989	Robin Yount	Milwaukee Brewers	21	103	.318
1990	Rickey Henderson	Oakland Athletics	28	61	.325
1991	Cal Ripken Jr.	Baltimore Orioles	34	114	.323
1992	Dennis Eckersley (Pitcher)[4]	Oakland Athletics	7W	1L	1.91 ERA
1993	Frank Thomas	Chicago White Sox	41	128	.317
1994	Frank Thomas[1]	Chicago White Sox	38	101	.353
1995	Mo Vaughn[1]	Boston Red Sox	39	126	.300
1996	Juan Gonzalez	Texas Rangers	47	144	.314
1997	Ken Griffey Jr.	Seattle Mariners	56	147	.304
1998	Juan Gonzalez	Texas Rangers	45	157	.318
1999	Ivan Rodriguez	Texas Rangers	35	113	.332
2000	Jason Giambi	Oakland Athletics	43	137	.333
2001	Ichiro Suzuki	Seattle Mariners	8	69	.350
2002	Miguel Tejada	Oakland Athletics	34	131	.308

1. Strike-shortened season. 2. 28 saves in 1981. 3. 32 saves in 1984. 4. 51 saves in 1992. **Source:** Baseball Writers' Association.

Triple Crown Winners

Only 11 players have led their league in home runs, runs batted in, and batting average in one season.

Year	Player, Team	HR	RBI	AVG.
1909	Ty Cobb, Detroit Tigers	9	115	.377
1912	Henry Zimmerman, Chicago Cubs	14	98	.372
1922	Rogers Hornsby, St. Louis Cardinals	42	152	.401
1925	Rogers Hornsby, St. Louis Cardinals	39	143	.403
1933	Chuck Klein, Philadelphia Phillies	28	120	.368
1933	Jimmie Foxx, Philadelphia A's	48	163	.356
1934	Lou Gehrig, New York Yankees	49	165	.363
1937	Joe Medwick, St. Louis Cardinals	31	154	.374
1942	Ted Williams, Boston Red Sox	36	137	.356
1947	Ted Williams, Boston Red Sox	32	114	.343
1956	Mickey Mantle, N.Y. Yankees	52	130	.353
1966	Frank Robinson, Baltimore Orioles	49	122	.316
1967	Carl Yastrzemski, Boston Red Sox	44	121	.326

A Most Valuable Team

Only 11 players have won the Most Valuable Player Award in consecutive seasons; oddly enough there is at least one from each fielding position. San Francisco's Barry Bonds has achieved this rare feat on two separate occasions. At the end of the 2003 season, Bonds seemed likely to win his sixth MVP award; no other player has won more than three.

Position	Player, Team	Years
1B	Jimmie Foxx, Philadelphia A's	1932–33
1B	Frank Thomas, Chicago White Sox	1993–94
2B	Joe Morgan, Reds	1975–76
3B	Mike Schmidt, Phillies	1980–81
SS	Ernie Banks, Cubs	1958–59
OF	Mickey Mantle, Yankees	1956–57
OF	Roger Maris, Yankees	1960–61
OF	Dale Murphy, Braves	1982–83
OF	Barry Bonds, Pirates/Giants	1992–93, 2001-02
C	Yogi Berra, Yankees	1954–55
P	Hal Newhouser, Tigers	1944–45

The Baseball Hall of Fame

National Baseball Hall of Fame and Museum
25 Main Street, Cooperstown, NY 13326.
888-HALL-OF-FAME (888-425-5633); www.baseballhalloffame.org
Open every day of the year except Thanksgiving, Christmas and New Year's.
Hours: 9am- 9pm, Memorial Day weekend to Labor Day; 9am-5pm the rest of the year.

The Hall of Fame was established in 1936 and opened in Cooperstown, N.Y. in 1939. From the start, there were two ways to be elected: by receiving 75 percent of the votes cast by the Baseball Writers Association of America or 75 percent of the votes cast by a Committee on Old Timers. In the first year, the writers picked the top five players of the post-1900 era: Ty Cobb, Walter Johnson, Christy Mathewson, Babe Ruth, and Honus Wagner. To be elected, a player must have played at least 10 years in the major leagues and been retired for at least five years. The Committee on Old Timers, originally created to consider 19th Century players, was replaced by a Special Veterans Committee whose scope includes all players retired for a minimum of 25 years who may have been overlooked when they were first eligible. In 1971 a Special Committee on the Negro Leagues was set up to consider ballplayers who played in the old Negro Leagues.

Player/Position/Year Inducted	Games	At Bats	HRs	Avg.	Hits	RBIs
Aaron, Henry (Hank) OF 1982	3,298	12,364	755	.305	3,771	2,297
All-time leader in home runs and RBI						
Anson, Adrian (Cap) 1B 1939	2,523	10,278	97	.333	3,418	2,076
Managed 20 years, 1879-98, winning five pennants						
Aparicio, Luis SS 1984	2,599	10,230	83	.262	2,677	791
Led AL in stolen bases nine years in a row (1955–64)						
Appling, Luke SS 1964	2,422	8,857	45	.310	2,749	1,116
Batted .388 in 1936						
Ashburn, Richie OF 1995	2,189	8,365	29	.308	2,574	586
Hit .300 or more nine times						
Averill, Earl OF 1975	1,669	6,358	238	.318	2,020	1,165
232 hits in 1936						
Baker, Frank (Home Run) 3B 1955	1,575	5,985	96	.307	1,838	1,013
Batted .363 in six World Series						
Bancroft, Dave SS 1971	1,913	7,182	32	.279	2,004	591
Handled 984 chances in 1922						
Banks, Ernie SS, 1B 1977	2,528	9,421	512	.274	2,583	1,636
Consecutive MVP awards, 1958–59						
Beckley, Jake 1B 1971	2,386	9,527	88	.308	2,931	1,575
244 career triples, mostly in 19th Century						
Bench, Johnny C 1989	2,158	7,658	389	.267	2,048	1,376
Hit .529 in 1976 World Series; NL MVP 1970, 1972						
Berra, Lawrence (Yogi) C, OF 1972	2,120	7,555	358	.285	2,150	1,430
Three MVP awards, 1951, 1954, 1955						
Bottomley, Jim 1B 1974	1,991	7,471	219	.310	2,313	1,422
12 RBI in one game, 1924						
Boudreau, Lou SS 1970	1,646	6,030	68	.295	1,779	789
MVP in 1948; managed 16 years						
Bresnahan, Roger C, OF 1945	1,430	4,478	26	.279	1,251	530
212 stolen bases; first catcher elected to Hall of Fame						
Brett, George 3B, 1B 1999	2,707	10,349	317	.305	3,154	1,595
Hit .300 11 times; 13-time all-star; hit .390 in 1980.						
Brock, Lou OF 1985	2,616	10,332	149	.293	3,023	900
938 stolen bases; batted .391 in three World Series						
Brouthers, Dan 1B 1945	1,673	6,711	106	.342	2,296	1,296
Seven slugging and five batting titles during 19th Century						
Burkett, Jesse OF 1946	2,072	8,430	75	.341	2,873	952
Led NL in batting three times and in hits four times						
Campanella, Roy C 1969	1,215	4,205	242	.276	1,161	856
Three MVP awards, 1951, 1953, 1955						
Carey, Max OF 1961	2,476	9,363	69	.285	2,665	800
738 stolen bases						
Carter, Gary C 2003	2,296	7,971	324	.262	2,092	1,225
11-time All-Star (1975, 1979-88); won three gold gloves						
Cepeda, Orlando 1B 1999	2,124	7,927	379	.297	2,351	1,365
Seven-time All-star; NL MVP 1967; .499 career slugging percentage						
Chance, Frank 1B 1946	1,286	4,295	20	.297	1,274	596
Managed Chicago (NL) to four pennants in five years, 1906–10						
Clarke, Fred OF 1945	2,245	8,588	67	.315	2,708	1,015
223 career triples, hit .300 or better 11 times						
Clemente, Roberto OF 1973	2,433	9,454	240	.317	3,000	1,305
Career average of over 18 outfield assists per season						
Cobb, Ty OF 1936	3,035	11,429	117	.367	4,191	1,938
Batted .320 or better in 23 straight years						

Player/Position/Year Inducted	Games	At Bats	HRs	Avg.	Hits	RBIs
Cochrane, Micky C 1947 Two MVP awards, 1928 and 1934	1,482	5,169	119	.320	1,652	832
Collins, Eddie 2B 1939 Hit .340 or better 10 times; led AL in fielding nine times	2,826	9,949	47	.333	3,315	1,300
Collins, Jimmy 3B 1945 Led NL in home runs, 1898	1,728	6,796	64	.294	1,997	982
Combs, Earle OF 1970 Averaged 127 runs scored per season	1,454	5,748	58	.325	1,866	629
Connor, Roger 1B 1976 Held all-time HR record before Babe Ruth	1,998	7,798	136	.318	2,480	1,078
Crawford, Sam OF 1957 312 triples, best ever	2,517	9,580	97	.309	2,964	1,525
Cronin, Joe SS 1956 MVP in 1930; managed 1933-47	2,124	7,579	170	.301	2,285	1,424
Cuyler, Hazen (Kiki) OF 1968 Led NL in runs scored twice, stolen bases four times	1,879	7,161	127	.321	2,299	1,065
Davis, George SS 1998 Hit over .300 nine years in a row (1893–1901)	2,376	9,035	73	.295	2,665	1,435
Delahanty, Ed IF, OF 1945 Batted .410 in 1899	1,835	7,505	101	.346	2,596	1,464
Dickey, Bill C 1954 Catcher on eight AL-pennant-winning teams	1,789	6,300	202	.313	1,969	1,209
DiMaggio, Joe OF 1955 56 game hitting streak in 1941	1,736	6,821	361	.325	2,214	1,537
Doby, Larry OF 1998 Led AL in HR twice; seven-time all-star (1949–55); first black man to play in AL	1,533	5,348	253	.283	1,515	969
Doerr, Bobby 2B 1986 Led AL in slugging 1944	1,865	7,093	223	.288	2,042	1,247
Duffy, Hugh OF 1945 Batted .438 in 1894	1,736	7,062	103	.328	2,314	1,299
Evers, Johnny 2B 1946 NL MVP in 1914	1,783	6,134	12	.270	1,658	538
Ewing, Buck C, IF, OF 1939 Regarded as the greatest player of the 19th Century	1,315	5,363	70	.303	1,625	733
Ferrell, Rick C 1984 Led AL catchers at times in putouts, assists, fielding average, and double plays	1,884	6,028	28	.281	1,692	734
Fisk, Carlton C 2000 Hit 20 or more home runs 8 times	2,499	8,756	376	.269	2,356	1,330
Flick, Elmer OF 1963 Led AL in triples 1905–07	1,484	5,603	47	.315	1,767	756
Fox, Nellie 2B 1997 Led AL in putouts, 1951–60	2,367	9,232	35	.288	2,663	790
Foxx, Jimmie 1B, 3B 1951 Slugged over .700 three seasons	2,317	8,134	534	.325	2,646	1,921
Frisch, Frank 2B, 3B 1947 Hit .300 or better 11 years in a row (1921–31)	2,311	9,112	105	.316	2,880	1,244
Gehrig, Lou 1B 1939 Played in 2,130 consecutive games; first player to hit 4 HRs in one game	2,164	8,001	493	.340	2,721	1,990
Gehringer, Charlie 2B 1949 60 doubles in 1936	2,323	8,860	184	.320	2,839	1,427
Goslin, Leon (Goose) OF 1968 100+ RBI 11 years	2,287	8,655	248	.316	2,735	1,609
Greenberg, Hank 1B 1956 58 home runs in 1938; 63 doubles in 1934	1,394	5,193	331	.313	1,628	1,276
Hafey, Charles (Chick) OF 1971 NL batting title (.349) in 1931	1,283	4,625	164	.317	1,466	833
Hamilton, Billy OF 1961 Scored 196 runs in 1894, with a .509 on-base average and 99 stolen bases	1,591	6,269	40	.344	2,159	739
Hartnett, Charles (Gabby) C 1955 Played on four NL pennant winners, managed one	1,990	6,432	236	.297	1,912	1,179
Heilmann, Harry OF, 1B 1952 Batted .403 in 1923	2,147	7,787	183	.342	2,660	1,539
Herman, Billy 2B 1975 57 doubles in 1935	1,922	7,707	47	.304	2,345	839
Hooper, Harry OF 1971 375 career stolen bases	2,308	8,785	75	.281	2,466	817
Hornsby, Rogers 2B, IF 1942 Batted .424 in 1924; won nine slugging titles	2,259	8,173	301	.358	2,930	1,584
Jackson, Reggie 1993 Played in 5 World Series and 11 divisional playoffs in 21 years; World Series MVP 1977	2,820	9,864	563	.262	2,584	1,702
Jackson, Travis SS 1982 Batted over .300 six times in 1920's and 1930's	1,656	6,086	135	.291	1,768	929
Jennings, Hugh SS 1945 Batted .398 in 1896	1,285	4,905	18	.312	1,531	840

Player/Position/Year Inducted	Games	At Bats	HRs	Avg.	Hits	RBIs
Kaline, Al OF 1980	2,834	10,116	399	.297	3,007	1,583
3,007 career hits						
Keeler, Willie OF 1939	2,123	8,591	33	.341	2,932	810
Batted .424 in 1897; 495 career stolen bases						
Kell, George 3B 1983	1,795	6,702	78	.306	2,054	870
AL batting champ (.343) in 1949						
Kelley, Joe OF 1971	1,845	7,018	65	.319	2,242	1,193
Averaged 151 runs scored, 1894–96						
Kelly, George 1B 1973	1,622	5,993	148	.297	1,778	1,020
Led NL in RBI, 1920 and 1925						
Kelly, Mike (King) OF, C 1945	1,463	5,923	69	.307	1,820	794
Two batting titles, 1884 and 1886; 315 career stolen bases						
Killebrew, Harmon 1B, 3B, OF 1984	2,435	8,147	573	.256	2,086	1,584
40+ home runs eight years						
Kiner, Ralph OF 1975	1,472	5,205	369	.279	1,451	1,015
Second highest home run per at bat ratio of all-time						
Klein, Chuck OF 1980	1,753	6,486	300	.320	2,076	1,201
44 outfield assists in 1930						
Lajoie, Napoleon 2B 1937	2,480	9,589	82	.338	3,242	1,599
Batted .422 in 1901						
Lazerri, Tony IF 1991	1,740	6,297	178	.292	1,840	1,191
Batted .300 or better five times; clutch hitter in World Series						
Lindstrom, Fred 3B, OF 1976	1,438	5,611	103	.311	1,747	779
231 hits in 1928						
Lombardi, Ernie C 1986	1,853	5,855	190	.306	1,792	990
Two NL batting titles, 1938 and 1942						
Mantle, Mickey OF 1974	2,401	8,102	536	.298	2,415	1,509
52 home runs in 1956, 54 in 1961						
Manush, Heinie OF 1964	2,009	7,653	110	.330	2,524	1,173
Hit .378 in 1926						
Maranville, Rabbit SS, 2B 1954	2,670	10,078	28	.258	2,605	884
23 year career; hit .308 in two World Series						
Mathews, Eddie 3B 1978	2,388	8,537	512	.271	2,315	1,453
1,444 career walks						
Mays, Willie OF 1979	2,992	10,881	660	.302	3,283	1,903
Slugged over .600 six seasons						
Mazeroski, Bill 2B 2001	2,163	7,775	138	.260	2,016	853
Eight-time gold glove winner. Turned a record 1,706 double plays.						
McCarthy, Tommy OF 1946	1,275	5,128	44	.292	1,496	666
Averaged 122 runs scored, 1888–94						
McCovey, Willie 1B, OF 1986	2,588	8,197	521	.270	2,211	1,555
Hit 18 career grand slams						
McPhee, Bid 2B 2000	2,135	8,291	53	.279	2,250	727
Considered greatest second baseman of the 19th century, though he played without a glove						
Medwick, Joe OF 1968	1,984	7,635	205	.324	2,471	1,383
Won NL triple crown in 1937						
Mize, Johnny 1B 1981	1,884	6,443	359	.312	2,011	1,337
Four-time NL home run champ						
Morgan, Joe 2B 1990	2,649	9,277	268	.271	2,517	1,133
Won back-to-back MVP Awards (1975–76)						
Murray, Eddie 1B 2003	3,026	11,336	504	.287	3,255	1,917
Third player ever with 3,000 hits and 500 HRs						
Musial, Stan OF, 1B 1969	3,026	10,972	475	.331	3,630	1,951
725 doubles and 177 triples						
O'Rourke, Jim OF 1945	1,774	7,435	51	.310	2,304	830
Batted .300+ eleven times in the 19th Century						
Ott, Mel OF 1951	2,732	9,456	511	.304	2,876	1,860
Averaged 121 RBI 1929–38						
Perez, Tony 1B 2000	2,777	9,778	379	.279	2,732	1,652
His 1,652 RBIs are the most ever by a Latin player.						
Puckett, Kirby OF 2001	1,783	7,244	207	.318	2,304	1,085
Led Minnesota Twins to World Series wins in 1987 and 1991. Won AL batting title in 1989.						
Reese, Harold (Pee Wee) SS 1984	2,166	8,058	126	.269	2,170	885
Finished in the top ten of MVP balloting nine times						
Rice, Sam OF 1963	2,404	9,269	34	.322	2,987	1,078
Only 18 strikeouts per 154 games						
Rizzuto, Phil SS 1994	1,661	5,816	38	.273	1,588	563
AL MVP in 1950; Played in 9 World Series						
Robinson, Brooks 3B 1983	2,896	10,654	268	.267	2,848	1357
16 consecutive Gold Gloves, 1960–75						
Robinson, Frank OF 1982	2,808	10,006	586	.294	2,943	1812
MVP in both leagues; AL triple crown in 1966						
Robinson, Jackie 2B 1962	1,382	4,877	137	.311	1,518	734
First black player in MLB; Rookie of the Year 1947; MVP and batting champ 1949						

Player/Position/Year Inducted	Games	At Bats	HRs	Avg.	Hits	RBIs
Roush, Edd OF 1962	1,967	7,363	68	.323	2,376	981
Two NL batting titles, 1917 and 1919						
Ruth, George (Babe) OF, P 1936	2,503	8,399	714	.342	2,873	2211
Slugged .847 1920–21						
Schalk, Ray C 1955	1,760	5,306	12	.253	1,345	594
176 stolen bases						
Schmidt, Mike 3B 1995	2,404	8,352	548	.267	2,234	1,595
Led NL in homers 8 times; won 10 Gold Gloves						
Schoendienst, Albert (Red) 1989	2,216	8,479	84	.289	2,449	773
Managed Cardinals to two pennants and 1967 World Series crown						
Sewell, Joe SS, 3B 1977	1,902	7,132	49	.312	2,226	1,051
Only 22 strikeouts in his last 2,500 at bats, 1929–33						
Simmons, Al OF 1953	2,215	8,761	307	.334	2,927	1,827
Drove in over 100 runs in each of his first 11 years, 1924–34						
Sisler, George 1B 1939	2,055	8,267	100	.340	2,812	1,175
Batted .400 1920–22						
Slaughter, Enos OF 1985	2,380	7,946	169	.300	2,383	1,304
52 doubles in 1939						
Smith, Ozzie SS 2002	2,573	9,396	28	.262	2,460	793
Won 13 Gold Gloves; 15-time All-Star						
Snider, Edwin (Duke) OF 1980	2,143	7,161	407	.295	2,116	1,333
Averaged 41 home runs, 1953–57						
Speaker, Tris OF 1937	2,789	10,195	117	.345	3,514	1,529
Led AL in doubles eight times						
Stargell, Willie OF, 1B 1988	2,360	7,927	475	.282	2,232	1,540
MVP in 1979						
Terry, Bill 1B 1954	1,721	6,428	154	.341	2,193	1,078
Hit .401 in 1930						
Thompson, Sam OF 1974	1,410	6,005	128	.331	1,986	1,299
166 RBI in 1887, 165 in 1895						
Tinker, Joe SS 1946	1,805	6,441	31	.263	1,695	782
Played in four World Series with Chicago Cubs						
Traynor, Pie 3B 1948	1,941	7,559	58	.320	2,416	1,273
100+ RBI seven years						
Vaughan, Joseph (Arky) SS 1985	1,817	6,622	96	.318	2,103	926
.385 in 1935						
Wagner, Honus SS 1936	2786	10,427	101	.329	3,430	1,732
Eight batting titles, four in a row 1906–09						
Wallace, Bobby SS 1953	2,386	8,652	35	.267	2,314	1,121
Handled 6.1 chances per game at shortstop.						
Waner, Lloyd OF 1967	1,992	7,772	28	.316	2,459	598
234 hits in 1929						
Waner, Paul OF 1952	2,549	9,459	112	.333	3,152	1,309
62 doubles in 1932						
Wheat, Zack OF 1959	2,410	9,106	132	.317	2,884	1,261
Batted .375 at age 36 in 1924						
Williams, Billy OF 1987	2,488	9,350	426	.290	2,711	1,475
30+ home runs in five seasons						
Williams, Ted OF 1966	2,292	7,706	521	.344	2,654	1,839
Last .400 hitter in majors, .406 in 1941						
Wilson, Lewis (Hack) OF 1979	1,348	4,760	244	.307	1,461	1,062
56 home runs and 190 RBI in 1930						
Winfield, Dave OF 2001	2,973	11,003	465	.283	3,110	1,833
Member of both the 3,000-hit and 400-home run club.						
Yastrzemski, Carl (Yaz) OF, 1B 1989	3,308	11,988	452	.285	3,419	1,844
Won Triple Crown in 1967; won batting titles in 1963, 1967, and 1968						
Youngs, Ross OF 1972	1,211	4,627	42	.322	1,491	592
Killed at age 30; .398 on-base average in four World Series, 1921–24.						
Yount, Robin SS, OF 1999	2,856	11,008	251	.285	3,142	1,406
Won AL MVP awards at shortstop (1982) and center field (1989), the only player ever to do so.						

Source: Major League Baseball.

▶FUTURE HALL OF FAMERS

While there are no specific criteria for election in to the Hall of Fame, certain benchmark numbers almost guarantee enshrinement. For example, every eligible player with 3,000 hits—Pete Rose, banned for life from baseball, is ineligible—is in the Hall of Fame. At one time, the benchmark number of home runs was 400, but given the ease with which players are hitting homers these days, the bar will probably be raised to 500 homers or more to keep out one-dimensional players like Jose Canseco (462 career home runs).

Assuming the status quo, however, several players who have retired in the past several years should start booking hotel reservations in Cooperstown. **Paul Molitor** (3,319 hits) becomes eligible in 2004, and **Wade Boggs** (3,010 hits) is due up in 2005. Two other members of the 3,000-hit club, **Tony Gwynn,** and **Cal Ripken Jr.,** become eligible in 2006, along with **Mark McGwire** (583 homers).

Hall of Fame Pitchers

Player/Year Inducted	W	L	ERA	Games	Innings	Strikeouts
Alexander, Grover Cleveland 1938	373	208	2.56	696	5,190	2,198
Won 30 games three years; led NL in ERA five times						
Bender, Charles (Chief) 1953	210	127	2.46	459	3,017	1,711
Led AL in winning percentage three seasons						
Brown, Mordecai (Three-Finger) 1949	239	130	2.06	481	3,172	1,375
1.04 ERA in 1906						
Bunning, Jim 1996	224	184	3.27	591	3,760	2,855
Struck out 1,000 batters in each league						
Carlton, Steve (Lefty) 1994	329	244	3.22	741	5,217	4,136
Four-time Cy Young Award winner (1972, 1977, 1980, 1982)						
Chesbro, Jack 1946	198	132	2.68	392	2,897	1,265
41 wins in 1904						
Clarkson, John 1963	326	177	2.81	531	4,536	2,015
53 wins in 1885, with 623 innings pitched						
Coveleski, Stan 1969	215	142	2.88	450	3,093	981
Led AL in ERA in 1925, 2.84						
Cummings, Williams (Candy) 1939	21	22	2.78	43	372	37
Inventor of the curveball						
Dean, Jay (Dizzy) 1953	150	83	3.03	317	1,966	1,155
30 wins in 1934						
Drysdale, Don 1984	209	166	2.95	518	3,432	2,486
56 2/3 consecutive scoreless innings, 1968						
Faber, Urban (Red) 1964	254	212	3.15	669	4,088	1,471
Led AL in ERA in 1921 and 1922						
Feller, Bob 1962	266	162	3.25	570	3,827	2,581
Led AL in wins six times, in shutouts seven						
Rollie Fingers 1992	114	118	2.90	944	1,701	1,299
341 saves over 17 years; AL MVP in 1981						
Ford, Edward (Whitey) 1974	236	106	2.75	498	3,170	1,956
25–4 in 1961, 24–7 in 1963						
Galvin, James (Pud) 1965	365	310	2.85	705	6,003	1,807
46 wins in 1883 and 1884						
Gibson, Bob 1981	251	174	2.91	528	3,885	3,117
1.12 ERA in 1968, seven straight wins in World Series play						
Gomez, Vernon (Lefty) 1972	189	102	3.34	368	2,503	1,468
Led AL in shutouts three years						
Grimes, Burleigh 1964	270	212	3.53	617	4,180	1,512
Last legal spitball pitcher, he won 20+ five times						
Grove, Robert (Lefty) 1947	300	141	3.06	616	3,941	2,266
Led AL in ERA nine times, in strikeouts seven						
Haines, Jesse 1970	210	158	3.64	555	3,209	981
Twice led NL in shutouts, 1921 and 1927						
Hoyt, Waite 1969	237	182	3.59	674	3,763	1,206
1.83 in 84 World Series innings						
Hubbell, Carl 1947	253	154	2.97	535	3,589	1,678
26–6 in 1936; 1.66 ERA in 1933						
Hunter, Jim (Catfish) 1987	224	166	3.26	500	3,448	2,012
21 or more wins, 1971–75						
Jenkins, Ferguson 1991	284	226	3.34	664	4,499	3,192
Cy Young Award winner in 1971; three-time all-star						
Johnson, Walter 1936	417	279	2.17	802	5,914	3,508
36-7, 1.14 ERA in 1913						
Joss, Addie 1978	160	97	1.89	286	2,327	920
Averaged 21–11, 1.66 ERA in years 1904–08						
Keefe, Tim 1964	342	225	2.62	600	5,049	2,564
Averaged 37 wins 1883–85						
Koufax, Sandy 1972	165	87	2.76	397	2,324	2,396
95–27, 1.85 ERA for seasons 1963-66						
Lemon, Bob 1976	207	128	3.23	460	2,850	1,277
Won 20 or more seven times						
Lyons, Ted 1955	260	230	3.67	594	4,161	1,073
Pitched 27 shutouts, but never won 20 games.						
Marichal, Juan 1983	243	142	2.89	471	3,509	2,303
Only 1.8 walks per nine innings over career						
Marquard, Richard (Rube) 1971	201	177	3.08	536	3,307	1,593
73–23 in years 1911–13						
Mathewson, Christy 1936	373	188	2.13	635	4,780	2,502
79 career shutouts						
McGinnity, Joe 1946	247	144	2.64	466	3,459	1,068
35–8 in 1904, with an ERA of 1.61						
Newhouser, Hal 1992	207	150	3.06	488	2,993	1,796
Led AL in victories three years in a row (1944–46)						

Player/Year Inducted	W	L	ERA	Games	Innings	Strikeouts
Nichols, Charles (Kid) 1949	361	208	2.95	620	5,056	1,873
Won 30 or more games seven times, 1891-94, 1896-98						
Niekro, Phil 1997	318	274	3.35	864	5,404	3,342
Knuckleballer pitched until age 48; five-time all-star						
Palmer, Jim 1990	268	152	2.86	558	3,948	2,212
Won Cy Young Award 1973, 1975, 1976						
Pennock, Herb 1948	240	162	3.61	617	3,558	1,227
162–90 as a New York Yankee, 1923–33						
Perry, Gaylord 1991	314	265	3.10	777	5,352	3,534
Won Cy Young Award in both leagues						
Plank, Eddie 1946	326	194	2.35	623	4,496	2,246
1.32 ERA in seven World Series games						
Radbourn, Charles (Old Hoss) 1939	309	195	2.67	528	4,535	1,830
60–12 in 1884, with 679 innings pitched						
Rixey, Eppa 1963	266	251	3.15	692	4,495	1,350
Won 25 games in 1922						
Roberts, Robin 1976	286	245	3.41	676	4,689	2,357
28–7 in 1952; five-time NL leader in complete games						
Ruffing, Charles (Red) 1967	273	225	3.80	624	4,344	1,987
.645 winning percentage as a New York Yankee						
Rusie, Amos 1977	243	160	3.07	462	3,770	1,957
Won 30+ games three years						
Ryan, Nolan 1999	324	292	3.19	807	5,386	5,714
Threw seven no-hitters; struck out 300 or more six times; struck out 200 or more 15 times						
Seaver, Tom 1992	311	205	2.86	656	4,782	3,640
Won 20 or more games five times; won Cy Young Award 1969, 1973, 1975						
Spahn, Warren 1973	363	245	3.09	750	5,244	2,583
Won 20 or more games 13 times, including 23 at age 42						
Sutton, Don 1998	324	256	3.26	774	5,280	3,574
Won 15 or more games eight years in a row (1969–76)						
Vance, Clarence (Dazzy) 1955	197	140	3.24	442	2,697	2,045
60–15 over two years—1924, 1925						
Waddell, George (Rube) 1946	193	143	2.16	407	2,961	2,316
349 strikeouts in 1904						
Walsh, Ed 1946	195	126	1.82	430	2,964	1,736
40–15 in 1908 with 11 shutouts; all-time ERA leader						
Ward, Monte 1964	161	101	2.10	291	2,462	920
47 wins in 1879; 40 wins in 1880; played 1,825 games as a hitter						
Welch, Mickey 1973	307	210	2.71	565	4,802	1,850
44–11 in 1885						
Wilhelm, Hoyt 1985	143	122	2.52	1070	2,254	1,610
227 career saves; first relief pitcher elected to Hall of Fame						
Willis, Vic 1995	249	205	2.63	513	3,996	1,651
Won 20 games eight times; 45 complete games in 1902						
Wynn, Early 1972	300	244	3.54	691	4,564	2,334
Led AL in shutouts at age 40 in 1960						
Young, Cy 1937	511	313	2.63	906	7,359	2,799
All-time leader in wins, losses, complete games, and innings pitched.						

Managers
Alston, Walter 1983
Anderson, Sparky 2000
Durocher, Leo 1994
Hanlon, Ned 1996
Harris, Bucky 1975
Huggins, Miller 1964
Lasorda, Tommy 1997
Lopez, Al 1977
Mack, Connie 1937
McCarthy, Joe 1957
McGraw, John 1937
McKechnie, Bill 1962
Robinson, Wilbert 1945
Selee, Frank, 1999
Stengel, Casey 1966
Weaver, Earl 1996

Umpires
Barlick, Al 1989
Chylak, Nestor, 1999
Conlan, Jocko 1974
Connolly, Tom 1953
Evans, Billy 1973
Hubbard, Cal 1976
Klem, Bill 1953
McGowan, Bill 1992

Pioneers and Executives
Barrow, Ed 1953
Bulkeley, Morgan 1937
Cartwright, Alexander 1938
Chadwick, Henry 1938
Chandler, Happy 1982
Comiskey, Charles 1939
Foster, Andrew (Rube) 1981
Frick, Ford 1970
Giles, Warren 1979
Griffith, Clark 1946
Harridge, William 1972
Hulbert, William 1995
Johnson, Ban 1937
Landis, Kenesaw Mountain 1944
MacPhail, Larry 1978
MacPhail, Lee 1998
Rickey, Branch 1967
Spalding, Albert Goodwill 1939
Veeck, Bill 1991
Weiss, George 1971
Wright, George 1937
Wright, Harry 1953
Yawkey, Tom 1980

Negro Leaguers
Bell, James "Cool Papa" 1974
Charleston, Oscar 1976
Dandridge, Ray 1987
Day, Leon 1995
Dihigo, Martin 1977
Foster, Bill 1996
Gibson, Josh 1972
Irvin, Monte 1973
Johnson, Judy 1975
Leonard, William "Buck" 1972
Lloyd, Pop 1977
Paige, Satchel 1971
Rogan, "Bullet" Joe 1998
Smith, Hilton 2001
Stearnes, Turkey 2000
Wells, Willie 1997
Williams, "Smokey Joe", 1999

The World Series

From 1882-90, the winners of the National League and American Association played each other in a championship series. After the A.A. folded, the top two N.L. clubs played for the "Temple Cup", but the idea never really caught on. The American League began operations in 1901, setting off bidding wars with the National League for the services of star players. Peace was established in 1903; toward the end of that season, the owners of the winning franchises in each league agreed to hold a "World Series" in October. Many were surprised that Boston, from the newer American League won the title.

There was no agreement to play such a series every year, however, and in 1904 the New York Giants refused to meet the Boston club, probably due to John McGraw's dislike of American League President Ban Johnson. But the baseball public wanted a championship series, and by 1905 Giants owner John Brush proposed rules governing a mandatory series to be played every year. With minute changes, those rules stand to this day.

1903 Boston (A) over Pittsburgh (N), 5–3. The upstart American league emerged victorious in the first World Series, a best of nine affair. The "Pilgrims" (Red Sox) staged one of the greatest comebacks in history by sweeping the final four games. Bill Dineen won three and Cy Young won two for Boston, and held Pirate immortal Honus Wagner to a .222 average.

1904 No series. New York Giant owner John T. Brush and manager John McGraw refused to play the World Champion Boston club, dismissing them as representative of an "inferior league."

1905 New York (N) over Philadelphia (A), 4–1. Every game was a shutout, with Cristy Mathewson throwing three for the Giants. In 27 innings, he allowed 14 hits, struck out 18 and walked one. The Athletics committed five errors in the pivotal Game 3.

1906 Chicago (A) over Chicago (N), 4–2. The first "subway series" was a stunning upset. The "Hitless Wonders" White Sox had batted .230 with 7 home runs during the season, while the Cubs were winning 116 games, still the all-time record. Utilityman George Rohe hit two game-winning triples for the Sox and Ed Walsh pitched two of their wins.

1907 Chicago (N) over Detroit (A), 4–0. The Cubs shut down Ty Cobb, Sam Crawford et al, behind a superb four-man pitching performance, and the hitting of Harry Steinfeldt (.471) and Johnny Evers (.350).

1908 Chicago (N) over Detroit (A), 4–1. Johnny Evers repeated his .350 average of 1907, player-manager Frank Chance hit .421, and outfielder Wildfire Schulte batted .389 in the Cub attack. Ty Cobb led Detroit (.368), to no avail.

1909 Pittsburgh (N) over Detroit (A), 4–3. The Tigers lost their third straight series, as Honus Wagner bested Ty Cobb. The Pirate shortstop hit .333 with six RBI and six stolen bases. Babe Adams pitched in with three complete game victories.

1910 Philadelphia (A) over Chicago (N), 4–1. Connie Mack's infielders combined to bat .364 as the A's rolled to an easy title. Jack Coombs pitched three wins and hit .385.

1911 Philadelphia (A) over New York (N), 4–2. The Athletics beat a strong New York club featuring Christy Mathewson and Rube Marquard. Frank "Home Run" Baker got his nickname from game-winning blasts in Games 2 and 3.

1912 Boston (A) over New York (N), 4–3. This thrill-a-minute series featured an 11-inning tie in Game 2. Errors by Giants Fred Merkle and Fred Snodgrass enabled Boston to score two runs in the bottom of the 10th inning of the final contest.

1913 Philadelphia (A) over New York (N), 4–1. Home Run Baker again hammered Giant pitching, batting .450 with seven RBI. Eddie Collins also starred for the A"s, hitting .421 with three stolen bases.

1914 Boston (N) over Philadelphia (A), 4–0. The red-hot "Miracle Braves" swept the heavily favored Athletics, who scored only six runs in the four games. Catcher Hank Gowdy (.545) and second baseman Johnny Evers (.438) led the Boston offense.

1915 Boston (A) over Philadelphia (N), 4–1. The famous Red Sox outfield of Speaker, Lewis, and Hooper combined to bat .364 while Rube Foster pitched two complete game wins. Foster also batted .500 and drove in the winning run in Game 2.

1916 Boston (A) over Brooklyn (N), 4–1. After three one-run games, Boston took charge with 6–2 and 4–1 victories. A young lefthander named Babe Ruth twirled a 14-inning six hitter in Game Two.

1917 Chicago (A) over New York (N), 4–2. The pitching of Red Faber (3-1, 2.33) and the hitting of Eddie Collins, Buck Weaver, and Joe Jackson were too much for the Giants in a sloppy (23 errors) series.

1918 Boston (A) over Chicago (N), 4–2. Every game was a pitchers' duel. The losing Cubs posted a 1.04 ERA over the six games. The Boston staff allowed but nine runs in the series, led by Babe Ruth who extended his consecutive scoreless inning streak to 29⅔.

1919 Cincinnati (N) over Chicago (A), 5–3. The results of this surprising World Series were declared invalid after eight members of the "Black Sox," including Shoeless Joe Jackson, were accused of throwing games for money. A court later found the Chicago players not guilty (most of them never even received the money from the gamblers with whom they conspired), but commissioner Kenesaw Mountain Landis nonetheless barred them from baseball forever.

1920 Cleveland (A) over Brooklyn (N), 5–2. Game 5 was surely the most freakish in series history. It featured a) the first World Series grand slam (Indians rightfielder Elmer Smith), b) the first World Series home run by a pitcher (Indians Jim Bagby), and c) the first and only unassisted triple play in series action (Indians second baseman Billy Wambsganss).

1921 New York (N) over New York (A), 5–3. Six Giants batted over .300, and their pitchers held Babe Ruth to a .500 slugging average. Giant hurler Jesse Barnes won two games and batted .444.

1922 New York (N) over New York (A), 4–0. The result was said to be final proof that "brains beat brawn." Giant pitching shut down Babe Ruth, allowing only 11 runs in the five contests (one tie).

1923 New York (A) over New York (N), 4–2. The Yankees took the last three to break the spell of their cross-river rivals, behind Babe Ruth's three homers and .368 average. Casey Stengel hit two home runs for the losers.

1924 Washington (A) over New York (N), 4–3. A 12-innning Game 7, won by Walter Johnson in relief, capped an exciting affair. Player-manager Bucky Harris starred for the Senators (.333, 7 RBIs), as did outfielder Goose Goslin (.344, 7 RBIs).

1925 Pittsburgh (N) over Washington (A), 4–3. Pirate centerfielder Max Carey had 11 hits and three stolen bases, as Pittsburgh became the first team since 1903 to come back from a three games to one deficit.

1926 St. Louis (N) over New York (A), 4–3. Babe Ruth hit three homers in Game 4, but in the seventh inning of Game 7, Grover Cleveland Alexander struck out Tony Lazzeri with the bases loaded, saving the game and the series for the Cardinals.

1927 New York (A) over Pittsburgh (N), 4–0. Generally regarded as the greatest team of all time, the "Murderers Row" Yankees disposed of the Pirates behind two Babe Ruth homers, plus the pitching of Wilcy Moore, Herb Pennock, and George Pipgrass.

1928 New York (A) over St. Louis (N), 4–0. Another Yankee sweep. Ruth and Lou Gehrig combined to bat .593, with seven home runs and 13 RBI. Waite Hoyt pitched two complete game victories.

1929 Philadelphia (A) over Chicago (N), 4–1. Trailing 8-0 in Game 4, the A's roared back to score 10 runs in the seventh inning. In the next contest, the Mackmen took the series with a three-run ninth inning.

1930 Philadelphia (A) over St. Louis (N), 4–2. Lefty Grove and George Earnshaw pitched well, while Al Simmons, Jimmie Foxx, and Mickey Cochrane combined for 11 extra-base hits. Cardinal regulars batted only .185 in the six games.

1931 St. Louis (N) over Philadelphia (A), 4–3. Cardinal centerfielder Pepper Martin set a record that stood for 33 years with his 12 hits. Martin also stole five bases and hit a home run. Bill Hallahan and Burleigh Grimes combined for a 4–0, 1.25 ERA.

1932 New York (A) over Chicago (N), 4–0. The Yankees completed a streak of 12 straight World Series victories in sweeping the Cubs. Babe Ruth and Lou Gehrig combined to bat .438, with five homers and 14 RBI.

1933 New York (N) over Washington (A), 4–1. Bill Terry's Giants defeated Joe Cronin's Senators in a battle of player-managers. Carl Hubbell won two for New York and did not allow an earned run.

1934 St. Louis (N) over Detroit (A), 4–3. Dizzy and Paul Dean hurled the Cardinals to the title, winning all four Redbird victories. A bad defensive series, with 27 errors and 13 unearned runs.

1935 Detroit (A) over Chicago (N), 4–2. The Cubs won 21 straight games in September, but came up short against Mickey Cochrane's Tigers. Charlie Gehringer and Tommy Bridges starred for Detroit, while Lou Warneke (2–0, 0.54) was superb for the losers.

1936 New York (A) over New York (N), 4–2. Joe McCarthy's "Windowbreakers" hammered Giant pitching for a record 18 runs in Games 2 and 43 runs for the series. Tony Lazzeri and Bill Dickey each drove in five runs in Game 2.

1937 New York (A) over New York (N), 4–1. Lefty Gomez pitched two of the Yankee wins and drove in the winning run with a single in the final game. The Yanks scored seven runs in the sixth inning of Game 1, then coasted to an easy championship.

1938 New York (A) over Chicago (N), 4–0. In a replay of 1932, the Bronx Bombers blew out an overmatched Cub squad. Cub fans are still waiting for their team's first series victory over the Yankees.

1939 New York (A) over Cincinnati (N), 4–0. New York won its fourth straight World Championship the same way they won the first three—easily. Charlie Keller batted .438 with three homers, and scored as many runs as the entire Reds team, eight.

1940 Cincinnati (N) over Detroit (A), 4–3. The Reds repeated as NL champs, then beat the Tigers when Paul Derringer beat Bobo Newsome 2–1 in Game 7. Derringer and Bucky Walters each won two games.

1941 New York (A) over Brooklyn (N), 4–1. With two outs in the ninth inning of Game Four, Dodger catcher Mickey Owen dropped a third strike on Tommy Henrich, allowing him to reach first base. The Yankees then scored four times to win the ballgame, and finished Brooklyn off the next day.

1942 St. Louis (N) over New York (A), 4–1. The Cardinals, winners of 106 games during the regular season, lost Game 1 with the tying run at bat. They then swept four in a row, behind the pitching of Johnny Beazley (2–0, 2.50) and Ernie White's shutout in Game 3.

1943 New York (A) over St. Louis (N), 4–1. In this rematch of the 1942 series, the Yanks held St. Louis to nine runs in the five games. Joe Gordon and Bill Dickey homered, while third baseman Billy Johnson drove in three runs for New York.

1944 St Louis (N) over St. Louis (A), 4–2. In their lone World Series appearance, the Browns struggled valiantly before falling short against a strong Cardinal club left relatively intact by World War II. Ten Browns errors gave the Redbirds seven unearned runs.

1945 Detroit (A) over Chicago (N), 4–3. Tiger ace Hal Newhouser was hit hard in Game 1, but he bounced back to win Games 5 and 7. Doc Cramer (.379) and Hank Greenberg (2 HR, 7 RBIs) led the Detroit offense.

1946 St. Louis (N) over Boston (A), 4–3 Enos Slaughter scored from first on a base-hit by Harry Walker in the eighth inning of Game 7, giving St. Louis its third title in five years. Harry Brecheen won three games for the Cardinals, allowing but one run.

1947 New York (A) over Brooklyn (N), 4–3. Yankee pitcher Bill Bevens had a no-hitter for 8⅔ innings in Game 4, but lost the game on a double by Cookie Lavagetto. Tommy Henrich (.323) had the game winning RBI in Games 1, 2, and 7.

1948 Cleveland (A) over Boston (N), 4–2. The series featured fine pitching on both sides, including Game 1, when Boston's Johnny Sain beat Bob Feller 1–0. Cleveland's Gene Beardon pitched 10⅔ scoreless innings.

1949 New York (A) over Brooklyn (N), 4–1. Game 1 was 0–0 until Tommy Henrich led off the bottom of the ninth with a home run off Don Newcombe. Bobby Brown batted .500 with five RBIs.

1950 New York (A) over Philadelphia (N), 4–0. New York struggled to win the first three contests by scores of 1-0, 2-1, and 3–2, in a series that was closer than it looks. The "Whiz Kid" Phillies held the Yanks to a .222 batting average, but managed to hit only .203 themselves.

1951 New York (A) over New York (N), 4–2. A tired Giant pitching staff held the Yankees in check for three games, but the AL champs broke out to score 23 runs in the final three. Eddie Lopat (2–0, 0.50) starred for the Yankees.

1952 New York (A) over Brooklyn (N), 4–3. Allie Reynolds and Vic Raschi each won two games, combining for a 1.69 ERA. Johnny Mize hit three homers, and Mickey Mantle and Yogi Berra each hit two. Duke Snider batted .345 with four homers in a losing cause.

1953 New York (A) over Brooklyn (N), 4–2. The Yankees won their fifth straight World Championship as second baseman Billy Martin tied a record with 12 hits. Martin slugged .958 and drove in eight runs.

1954 New York (N) over Cleveland (A), 4–0. The Indians won 111 games during the season. But the Giants, sparked by a spectacular Willie Mays catch in Game 1, went on to beat Cleveland easily. Dusty Rhodes drove in seven runs on two homers and two singles in six at bats.

1955 Brooklyn (N) over New York (A), 4–3. The Dodgers finally won a World Series in their eighth try, behind the pitching of series MVP Johnny Podres (2–0, 1.00). Duke Snider hit four homers in a series for the second time, and Dodger leftfielder Sandy Amoros made a game-saving catch in Game 7.

1956 New York (A) over Brooklyn (N), 4–3. Yankee righthander and series MVP Don Larsen pitched a perfect game in the fifth contest, while Mickey Mantle and Yogi Berra each hit three homers for New York.

1957 Milwaukee (N) over New York (A), 4–3. Lew Burdette won three times for the Braves, allowing but two runs in 27 innings and won the MVP. Milwaukee's hitting was led by Hank Aaron (.393, 3 HR, 7 RBIs).

1958 New York (A) over Milwaukee (N), 4–3. Hank Bauer and Moose Skowron combined for six homers and 15 RBI, as the Bronx Bombers came back from a 3–1 deficit. Yankee pitcher "Bullet" Bob Turley earned MVP honors.

1959 Los Angeles (N) over Chicago (A), 4–2. Los Angeles enjoyed its first World Championship as the transplanted Dodgers prevailed. MVP Larry Sherry had two wins and two saves; Ted Kluszewski of the "Go-Go" Sox hit .391, with three homers and 10 RBI.

1960 Pittsburgh (N) over New York (A), 4–3. Pirate second baseman Bill Mazeroski's home run in the bottom of the ninth in Game 7 capped one of the most exciting contests in history. Ten of the runs in the 10–9 ballgame were scored in the last two innings. Yankee second baseman Bobby Richardson, a hitting star throughout the series, was named MVP.

1961 New York (A) over Cincinnati (N),4–1. Whitey Ford tossed two shutouts in winning the MVP, and the Yankee offense pounded out 16 extra-base hits in the five games. Bobby Richardson (.391) and John Blanchard (.400, 2 HR) starred for New York.

1962 New York (A) over San Francisco (N), 4–3. Ralph Terry's four-hit shutout won the seesaw affair for the Yanks, and earned him the MVP. Whitey Ford completed his series record 33⅔ consecutive scoreless innings in the first game. Chuck Hiller hit the first National League series grand slam in Game 4.

1963 Los Angeles (N) over New York (A), 4–0. Dodger pitchers held New York to four runs, led by Sandy Koufax's two wins and 23 strikeouts, including a record-breaking 15 in the first game. Koufax was the runaway choice for MVP.

1964 St. Louis (N) over New York (A), 4–3. Ten Yankee home runs were not enough to beat the Cardinals. Bob Gibson was the series MVP, and Tim McCarver (.478) also starred. Highlights included Ken Boyer's game-winning grand slam in Game 4, and Bobby Richardson's record 13 hits.

1965 Los Angeles (N) over Minnesota (A), 4–3. As in 1963, MVP Sandy Koufax again excelled for the Dodgers, allowing only two runs in 24 innings, striking our 29. Jim "Mudcat" Grant won two games and hit a three-run homer for the Twins.

1966 Baltimore (A) over Los Angeles (N), 4–0. The Orioles shone in their first World Series appearance, as their young pitchers did not allow a run after the third inning of Game 1. Slugger Frank Robinson capped a great year with the series MVP award.

1967 St. Louis (N) over Boston (A), 4–3. Bob Gibson pitched three complete game victories, added a home run in Game 7, and was named MVP. Lou Brock batted .414 and stole seven bases, tying Eddie Collins' record and pacing the Cards.

1968 Detroit (A) over St. Louis (N), 4–3. The Cardinals were rolling behind Bob Gibson's record 17 strikeouts in Game 1 and his record seventh straight series win in Game 4. Again Lou Brock joined him in the record books with 13 hits and seven stolen bases. But their feats couldn't stop the Tigers, led by the MVP pitching of Mickey Lolich (3–0, 1.67).

1969 New York (N) over Baltimore (A), 4–1. The Amazin' Mets stunned the baseball world by winning four in a row after dropping Game 1. Their young pitchers held the Orioles to nine runs, aided by great outfield catches by Ron Swoboda and Tommy Agee. Series MVP Donn Clendenon (.357, 3 HR) and Al Weis (.455, 1 HR) led the Met attack.

1970 Baltimore (A) over Cincinnati (N), 4–1. MVP Brooks Robinson almost singlehandedly beat the Reds with spectacular defense at third base and a .429 average with two homers and two doubles. Also chipping in for the Orioles were Paul Blair (.474), Frank Robinson, and Boog Powell (two homers each).

1971 Pittsburgh (N) over Baltimore (A), 4–3. Roberto Clemente played in 14 World Series games and hit safely in every one. Here he batted .414, slugged .759, and won MVP honors. Steve Blass, Nelson Briles, and Bruce Kison won all the Pirate victories with a combined ERA of 0.54.

1972 Oakland (A) over Cincinnati (N), 4–3. A's backup catcher Gene Tenace hit home runs in his first two series at bats, then went on to hit two more, becoming the surprise star and MVP Rollie Fingers relieved in six contests, winning one and saving two.

1973 Oakland (A) over New York (N), 4–3. The Mets had the worst record of any pennant winner ever (82–79), but they lasted till the Game 7 in a sloppy (19 errors) affair. Darold Knowles pitched in all seven games for the A's, saving two. Reggie Jackson slugged his way to his first series MVP award.

1974 Oakland (A) over Los Angeles (N), 4–1. The A's won their third straight Championship behind the two saves and one win of MVP Rollie Fingers. and the hitting of Joe Rudi (.333) and Bert Campaneris (.353).

1975 Cincinnati (N) over Boston (A), 4–3. Five games were decided by one run, including Game 6, a memorable 12-inning contest decided by Carlton Fisk's famous home run. Pete Rose, the heart and soul of the Big Red Machine, hustled his way to MVP honors.

1976 Cincinnati (N) over New York (A), 4–0. The Big Red Machine drove over the Yankees, slugging .522 as a team. Seven Reds hitters batted over .300, led by MVP Johnny Bench's .533 (1.133 slugging average).

1977 New York (A) over Los Angeles (N), 4–2. Reggie Jackson hit five homers, including three in the final game, to equal records set by Babe Ruth, and win his second MVP award. Mike Torrez won two for the Yanks.

1978 New York (A) over Los Angeles (N), 4–2. Shortstop Bucky Dent and backup infielder Brian Doyle batted .417 and .438 respectively, pacing New York in its second straight six-game triumph. Dent was named MVP. In the last four contests, the Yankees outscored L.A. 28–8.

1979 Pittsburgh (N) over Baltimore (A), 4–3. The Pirates overcame a three games to one deficit as Earl Weaver's Orioles waited for three-run homers that never came. Led by Willie Stargell (.400, 3 HR) and Phil Garner (.500), Pittsburgh batted .323 as a team. Willie "Pops" Stargell's leadership of the Pirates' "family" on and off the field earned him MVP honors

1980 Philadelphia (N) over Kansas City (A), 4–2. The two teams batted .292 in a series decided largely by the relief pitching of Tug McGraw (1–1, 2 saves) vs. Dan Quisenberry (1–2, 1 save). Mike Schmidt took MVP honors with a .381 average and seven RBI.

1981 Los Angeles (N) over New York (A), 4–2. Many observers called this sloppy series a fitting end to this strike-stricken 1981 season. Even the MVP award proved impossible to settle, as Pedro Guerrero, Steve Yeager, and Ron Cey shared the honor.

1982 St. Louis (N) over Milwaukee (A), 4–3. Joaquin Andujar won two games for the Cardinals, and Willie McGee had perhaps the greatest single series game by a rookie, with two homers and two great catches in Game 3. St. Louis' Darrell Porter won MVP honors for his clutch hitting and 5 RBI.

1983 Baltimore (A) over Philadelphia (N), 4–1. The Phillies couldn't hit Orioles' pitching, scoring but nine runs in the five games. Catcher Rick Dempsey hit four doubles and a home run, held the Phils to one stolen base, and was named MVP.

1984 Detroit (A) over San Diego (N), 4–1. The Tigers belted seven homers and backed them up with the pitching of Jack Morris (2–0, 2.00). Sparky Anderson became the first manager to win World Championships in both leagues. Alan Trammell, the Tigers' shortstop, hit two home runs to earn MVP honors.

1985 Kansas City (A) over St. Louis (N), 4–3. The Cards were one inning away from the title, but a disputed call at first base opened the door for the Royals in Game 6. They won that contest, then blew St. Louis away 11–0 in the finale. Bret Saberhagen won two for Kansas City, and the MVP.

1986 New York (N) over Boston (A), 4–3. The Red Sox were one out away from winning it all, when Bob Stanley's wild pitch let in the tying run, and Mookie

Wilson's grounder slipped between Bill Buckner's legs to score the winning run in Game 6. MVP Ray Knight hit a tie-breaking homer in Game 7 to send Boston to its fourth straight seven-game defeat.

1987 Minnesota (A) over St. Louis (N), 4–3. The Twins won their first championship by taking all four games in at the Metrodome. Cardinal pitching held Minnesota to five runs in the three games in St. Louis, but in Minnesota, the Twins could not be contained, scoring 33 times. Frank Viola (2–1,3.72) was the MVP.

1988 Los Angeles (N) over Oakland (A), 4–1. Series MVP Orel Hershiser (2–0, 17 K's) dazzled the powerful A's. Injured Dodger Kirk Gibson's dramatic two-out home run in the bottom of the ninth in Game 1 set the tone for the unexpected L.A. triumph.

1989 Oakland (A) over San Francisco (N), 4–0. The A's thoroughly dominated a weak Giants' pitching staff, pounding out 32 runs, 44 hits (including nine home runs) in only four games. Series MVP Dave Stewart and reliever Dennis Eckersley led the Oakland staff. This series will be long remembered for the major earthquake that struck the Bay area just before Game 3 and delayed the contest for 12 days.

1990 Cincinnati (N) over Oakland (A), 4–0. Cincinnati dominated the heavily favored A's in a stunning sweep. The Reds hit .317 as a team, while their pitchers, led by MVP José Rijo, held Oakland's vaunted offense to a mere .207 series average. Billy Hatcher broke Babe Ruth's World Series record by hitting .750, with seven consecutive hits and four doubles.

1991 Minnesota (A) over Atlanta (N), 4–3. No team in baseball had ever gone from worst to first. In 1991, it happened twice, as the Twins and Braves, both of whom had finished last the year before met in one of the most exciting fall classics ever. Five games were decided by one run, three went into extra innings, and four were decided on the last at bat. Best of all was Game 7, a scoreless affair until the 10th inning, when the Twins finally scored. Jack Moris pitched all 10 innings for Minnesota and earned MVP honors.

1992 Toronto (A) over Atlanta (N), 4–2. The Blue Jays became the first non-American team to win (or play in) the World Series. Braves closer Jeff Reardon gave up the winning hits in games 2 and 3, and Bobby Cox wasloath to use him again. Dave Winfield's double in the 11th-inning of Game 6 sent the Braves to their second straight World Series defeat. Toronto catcher Pat Borders was the MVP with a .450 average.

1993 Toronto (A) over Philadelphia (N), 4–2. The Blue Jays became the first team since the 1977–78 Yankees to repeat as champions, battering the Phillies for 45 runs (despite a Game 5 shutout). Joe Carter's homer in Game 6 marked only the second time the World Series had ended on a home run (Bill Mazeroski hit the other in 1960). DH Paul Molitor went 12 for 24 with six extra-base hits to win MVP honors.

1994 World Series canceled. The longest work stoppage in professional sports history, a 232-day dispute over a cap on player salaries, forced the first-ever cancellation of the World Series and playoffs .

1995 Atlanta (N) over Cleveland (A), 4–2. Good pitching beats good hitting as evidenced by this dramatic series. Baseball's best pitching staff (the Braves) held the game's most explosive offense (the Indians) to a .179 average and 19 runs. Five games were decided by one run, including the clincher: a dazzling 1–0 one-hitter by Atlanta's Tom Glavine, the series MVP.

1996 New York (A) over Atlanta (N), 4–2. The Braves shellacked the Yankees 12–1 and 4–0 in the first two games. But the Yankees struck back and won the next four. The turning point was in Game 4, when New York rallied from a 6–0 deficit to win 8–6 in 10 innings. Jim Leyritz provided the crushing blow: a three-run homer off Mark Wohlers to tie the game at 6–6. Yankee closer John Wetteland saved all four wins and was the MVP.

1997 Florida (N) over Cleveland (A), 4–3. This sloppy series was marked by porous defense and poor relief pitching. Game 3 alone involved 17 walks and 6 errors. Cleveland was two outs away from winning it all in Game 7, when Craig Counsell's sacrifice fly tied the game at 2–2. In the 11th, Edgar Renteria singled home the winning run. Florida rookie Livan Hernandez, winner of Games 1 and 5, was the MVP.

1998 New York (A) over San Diego (N), 4–0. The Yankees completed one of the greatest seasons in baseball history with a sweep that gave them a combined record of 125–50 and a .714 winning percentage. Homers by Chuck Knoblauch and Tino Martinez helped the Yankees come from behind in Game 1, while Scott Brosius's three-run blast off San Diego closer Trevor Hoffman in Game 3 broke the Padres' back. Brosius, the MVP, hit .471 with two homers.

1999 New York (A) over Atlanta (N), 4–0. The Yankees' World Series winning streak increased to 12 games with their second-straight sweep. Atlanta errors opened the door to big innings for New York in Games 1 and 2; the Yankees hit four homers in Game 3 to turn a 5-1 deficit into a 10-inning, 6-5 win. Mariano Rivera, who did not allow a run after July, saved Games 1 and 4, won Game 3 in relief, and took MVP honors.

2000 New York (A) over New York (N), 4-1. Every game of the first Subway Series in 45 years was decided by one or two runs. The Yankees rallied to tie Game 1 in the ninth inning, and won it in the 12th. Derek Jeter hit the first pitch of Game 4 over the center field fence and the Yankees never trailed again. Jeter batted .409 with two homers, and was the MVP.

2001 Arizona (N) over New York (A), 4-3. Curt Schilling and Randy Johnson powered Arizona to a 2-0 lead, but the Yankees came back with three straight one-run victories in New York. In *both* Game 4 *and* Game 5, the Yankees were down to their last out when they rallied with game-tying homers against closer Byung-Hyun Kim (by Tino Martinez and Scott Brosius, respectively). Arizona had the last laugh in Game 7; the Diamondbacks entered the ninth inning trailing 2-1, but they rallied for two runs against Mariano Rivera to win. Schilling and Johnson were co-MVPs.

2002 Anaheim (A) over San Francisco (N), 4-3. In the first matchup of two wild card teams, the glass slipper fit the Angels. Anaheim pitched carefully to Barry Bonds, and although he hit .471 with four homers and 13 walks, the batters before and after him hit .276 and .231 respectively, limiting the damage Bonds was able to inflict. The Angels batted .310 as a team, led by MVP third baseman Troy Glaus, who hit .385 with 3 homers and 8 RBIs. With the Giants six outs away from winning it all in Game 6, Glaus's eighth-inning double turned a 5-4 deficit into a 6-5 Anaheim victory.

2003 (See page 972 for game-by-game summaries)

Most Wins by Managers

Manager	Wins	Losses	Pct.
1. Connie Mack	3,731	3,948	.486
2. John McGraw	2,763	1,984	.586
3. Sparky Anderson	2,194	1,834	.545
4. Bucky Harris	2,157	2,218	.493
5. Joe McCarthy	2,125	1,333	.615
6. Walter Alston	2,040	1,613	.558
7. Tony La Russa[1]	2,009	1,789	.529
8. Leo Durocher	2,008	1,709	.540
9. Casey Stengel	1,905	1,842	.508
10. Bobby Cox[1]	1,906	1,465	.565

1. Manager active in 2003. **Source:** Major League Baseball.

World Series MVP Winners

Year	Name	Team
1955	Johnny Podres	Brooklyn Dodgers
1956	Don Larsen	New York Yankees
1957	Lew Burdette	Milwaukee Braves
1958	Bob Turley	New York Yankees
1959	Larry Sherry	Los Angeles Dodgers
1960	Bobby Richardson	New York Yankees
1961	Whitey Ford	New York Yankees
1962	Ralph Terry	New York Yankees
1963	Sandy Koufax	Los Angeles Dodgers
1964	Bob Gibson	St. Louis Cardinals
1965	Sandy Koufax	Los Angeles Dodgers
1966	Frank Robinson	Baltimore Orioles
1967	Bob Gibson	St. Louis Cardinals
1968	Mickey Lolich	Detroit Tigers
1969	Donn Clendenon	New York Mets
1970	Brooks Robinson	Baltimore Orioles
1971	Roberto Clemente	Pittsburgh Pirates
1972	Gene Tenace	Oakland Athletics
1973	Reggie Jackson	Oakland Athletics
1974	Rollie Fingers	Oakland Athletics
1975	Pete Rose	Cincinnati Reds
1976	Johnny Bench	Cincinnati Reds
1977	Reggie Jackson	New York Yankees
1978	Bucky Dent	New York Yankees
1979	Willie Stargell	Pittsburgh Pirates
1980	Mike Schmidt	Philadelphia Phillies
1981	Ron Cey, Pedro Guerrero, Steve Yeager	Los Angeles Dodgers
1982	Darrell Porter	St. Louis Cardinals
1983	Rick Dempsey	Baltimore Orioles
1984	Alan Trammell	Detroit Tigers
1985	Bret Saberhagen	Kansas City Royals
1986	Ray Knight	New York Mets
1987	Frank Viola	Minnesota Twins
1988	Orel Hershiser	Los Angeles Dodgers
1989	Dave Stewart	Oakland Athletics
1990	José Rijo	Cincinnati Reds
1991	Jack Morris	Minnesota Twins
1992	Pat Borders	Toronto Blue Jays
1993	Paul Molitor	Toronto Blue Jays
1994	No World Series	
1995	Tom Glavine	Atlanta Braves
1996	John Wetteland	New York Yankees
1997	Liván Hernández	Florida Marlins
1998	Scott Brosius	New York Yankees
1999	Mariano Rivera	New York Yankees
2000	Derek Jeter	New York Yankees
2001	Randy Johnson and Curt Schilling	Arizona Diamondbacks
2002	Troy Glaus	Anaheim Angels
2003	See page 972	

All-Star Game Results, 1933–2003

To revive interest in the midsummer classic, Major League Baseball decided in 2003 to award home field advantage in the World Series to the league that wins the All-Star Game.

Year	Winner, Score	Year	Winner, Score
1933	American, 4-2	1967	National, 2-1
1934	American, 9-7	1968	National, 1-0
1935	American, 4-1	1969	National, 9-3
1936	National, 4-3	1970	National, 5-4
1937	American, 8-3	1971	American, 6-4
1938	National, 4-1	1972	National, 4-3
1939	American, 3-1	1973	National, 7-1
1940	National, 4-0	1974	National , 7-2
1941	American, 7-5	1975	National, 6-3
1942	American, 3-1	1976	National , 7-1
1943	American, 5-3	1977	National, 7-5
1944	National , 7-1	1978	National, 7-3
1945	No game [1]	1979	National, 7-6
1946	American, 12-0	1980	National, 4-2
1947	American, 2-1	1981	National, 5-4
1948	American, 5-2	1982	National, 4-1
1949	American, 11-7	1983	American, 13-3
1950	National, 4-3	1984	National, 3-1
1951	National, 8-3	1985	National , 6-1
1952	National, 3-2	1986	American, 3-2
1953	National, 5-1	1987	National, 2-0 (10)
1954	American, 11-9	1988	American, 2-1
1955	National, 6-5	1989	American, 5-3
1956	National, 7-3	1990	American, 2-0
1957	American, 6-5	1991	American, 4-2
1958	American, 4-3	1992	American, 13-6
1959(1)[2]	National, 5-4	1993	American, 9-3
1959(2)	American, 5-3	1994	National, 8-7 (10)
1960(1)	National, 5-3	1995	National, 3-2
1960(2)	National , 6-0	1996	National, 6-0
1961(1)	National, 5-4	1997	American, 3-1
1961(2)	Tie[3], 1-1	1998	American, 13-8
1962(1)	National, 3-1	1999	American, 4-1
1962(2)	American, 9-4	2000	American, 6-3
1963	National, 5-3	2001	American, 4-1
1964	National, 7-4	2002	Tie[4], 7-7
1965	National, 6-5	2003	American, 7-6
1966	National, 2-1		

1. Wartime travel restrictions. 2. Two All Star games were played 1959–62. 3. Game was called because of rain after nine innings. 4. Game was called after nine innings because both managers had already used all their pitchers.

World Series Records

Total

Hits		Home runs	
Yogi Berra	71	Mickey Mantle	18
Mickey Mantle	59	Babe Ruth	15
Frankie Frisch	58	Yogi Berra	12
Runs batted in		**Runs scored**	
Mickey Mantle	40	Mickey Mantle	42
Yogi Berra	39	Yogi Berra	41
Wins		**Strikeouts**	
Whitey Ford	10	Whitey Ford	94

Note: Through the 2002 World Series.

In a Single Series

Hits	13	Home runs	5
Bobby Richardson, 1964		Reggie Jackson, 1977	
Lou Brock, 1968		RBIs	12
Marty Barrett, 1986			
Runs batted in	12		
Bobby Richardson, 1960			

Major League Baseball League Championship Series Results

AMERICAN LEAGUE

Year	Winner	Loser	MVP
1969	Baltimore Orioles-3	Minnesota Twins-0	
1970	Baltimore Orioles-3	Minnesota Twins-0	
1971	Baltimore Orioles-3	Oakland A's-0	
1972	Oakland Athletics-3	Detroit Tigers-2	
1973	Oakland Athletics-3	Baltimore Orioles-2	
1974	Oakland Athletics-3	Baltimore Orioles-1	
1975	Boston Red Sox-3	Oakland Athletics-0	
1976	New York Yankees-3	Kansas City Royals-2	
1977	New York Yankees-3	Kansas City Royals-2	
1978	New York Yankees-3	Kansas City Royals-1	
1979	Baltimore Orioles-3	California Angels-1	
1980	Kansas City Royals-3	New York Yankees-0	Frank White, Kansas City
1981	New York Yankees-3	Oakland Athletics-0	Graig Nettles, New York
1982	Milwaukee Brewers-3	California Angels-2	Fred Lynn, California
1983	Baltimore Orioles-3	Chicago White Sox-1	Mike Boddicker, Baltimore
1984	Detroit Tigers-3	Kansas City Royals-0	Kirk Gibson, Detroit
1985[1]	Kansas City Royals-4	Toronto Blue Jays	George Brett, Kansas City
1986	Boston Red Sox-4	California Angels-3	Marty Barrett, Boston
1987	Minnesota Twins-4	Detroit Tigers-1	Gary Gaetti, Minnesota
1988	Oakland Athletics-4	Boston Red Sox-0	Dennis Eckersley, Oakland
1989	Oakland Athletics-4	Toronto Blue Jays-1	Rickey Henderson, Oakland
1990	Oakland Athletics-4	Boston Red Sox-0	Dave Stewart, Oakland
1991	Minnesota Twins-4	Toronto Blue Jays-1	Kirby Puckett, Minnesota
1992	Toronto Blue Jays-4	Oakland Athletics-2	Roberto Alomar, Toronto
1993	Toronto Blue Jays-4	Chicago White Sox-2	Dave Stewart, Toronto
1994	No League Championship Series		
1995	Cleveland Indians-4	Seattle Mariners-2	Orel Hershiser, Cleveland
1996	New York Yankees-4	Baltimore Orioles-1	Bernie Williams, New York
1997	Clevland Indians-4	Baltimore Orioles-2	Marquis Grissom, Cleveland
1998	New York Yankees-4	Cleveland Indians-2	David Wells, New York
1999	New York Yankees-4	Boston Red Sox-1	Orlando Hernandez, New York
2000	New York Yankees-4	Seattle Mariners-2	David Justice, New York
2001	New York Yankees-4	Seattle Mariners-1	Andy Pettitte, New York
2002	Anaheim Angels-4	Minnesota Twins-1	Adam Kennedy, Anaheim
2003	New York Yankees-4	Boston Red Sox-3	Mariano Rivera, New York

NATIONAL LEAGUE

Year	Winner	Loser	MVP
1969	New York Mets-3	Atlanta Braves-0	
1970	Cincinnati Reds-3	Pittsburgh Pirates-0	
1971	Pittsburgh Pirates-3	San Francisco Giants-1	
1972	Cincinnati Reds-3	Pittsburgh Pirates-2	
1973	New York Mets-3	Cincinnati Reds-2	
1974	Los Angeles Dodgers-3	Pittsburgh Pirates-1	
1975	Cincinnati Reds-3	Pittsburgh Pirates-0	
1976	Cincinnati Reds-3	Philadelphia Phillies-0	
1977	Los Angeles Dodgers-3	Philadelphia Phillies-1	Dusty Baker, Los Angeles
1978	Los Angeles Dodgers-3	Philadelphia Phillies-1	Steve Garvey, Los Angeles
1979	Pittsburgh Pirates-3	Cincinnati Reds-0	Willie Stargell, Pittsburgh
1980	Philadelphia Phillies-3	Houston Astros-2	Manny Trillo, Philadelphia
1981	Los Angeles Dodgers-3	Montreal Expos-2	Burt Hooton, Los Angeles
1982	St. Louis Cardinals-3	Atlanta Braves-0	Darrell Porter, St. Louis
1983	Philadelphia Phillies-3	Los Angeles Dodgers-1	Gary Mathews, Philadelphia
1984	San Diego Padres-3	Chicago Cubs-2	Steve Garvey, San Diego
1985[1]	St. Louis Cardinals-4	Los Angeles Dodgers-2	Ozzie Smith, St. Louis
1986	New York Mets-4	Houston Astros-2	Mike Scott, Houston
1987	St. Louis Cardinals-4	San Francisco Giants-3	Jeff Leonard, San Francisco
1988	Los Angeles Dodgers-4	New York Mets-3	Orel Hershiser, Los Angeles
1989	San Francisco Giants-4	Chicago Cubs-1	Will Clark, San Francisco
1990	Cincinnati Reds-4	Pittsburgh Pirates-2	Rob Dibble, Rany Myers, Cincinnati
1991	Atlanta Braves-4	Pittsburgh Pirates-3	Steve Avery, Atlanta
1992	Atlanta Braves-4	Pittsburgh Pirates-3	John Smoltz, Atlanta
1993	Philadelphia Phillies-4	Atlanta Braves-2	Curt Schilling, Philadelphia
1994	No League Championship Series		
1995	Atlanta Braves-4	Cincinnati Reds-0	Mike Devereaux, Atlanta

Year	Winner	Loser	MVP
1996	Atlanta Braves-4	St. Louis Cardinals-3	Javier Lopez, Atlanta
1997	Florida Marlins-4	Atlanta Braves-2	Livan Hernández, Florida
1998	San Diego Padres-4	Atlanta Braves-2	Sterling Hitchcock, San Diego
1999	Atlanta Braves-4	New York Mets-2	Eddie Perez, Atlanta
2000	New York Mets-4	St. Louis Cardinals-1	Mike Hampton, New York
2001	Arizona Diamondbacks-4	Atlanta Braves-1	Craig Counsell, Arizona
2002	San Francisco Giants-4	St. Louis Cardinals-1	Benito Santiago, San Francisco
2003	Florida Marlins-4	Chicago Cubs-3	Luán Rodríguez, Florida

1. In 1985 the League Championship Series was switched to a best-of-seven format.

2003 Individual Leaders

AMERICAN LEAGUE

Batting average (min. 500 appearances)

Bill Mueller, Boston	.326
Manny Ramirez, Boston	.325
Derek Jeter, New York	.324
Magglio Ordóñez, Chicago	.317
Vernon Wells, Toronto	.317
Garret Anderson, Anaheim	.315
A.J. Pierzynski, Minnesota	.312
Ichiro Suzuki, Seattle	.312
Aubrey Huff, Tampa Bay	.311
Carlos Beltran, Kansas City	.307

Home runs

Alex Rodriguez, Texas	47
Carlos Delgado, Toronto	42
Frank Thomas, Chicago	42
Jason Giambi, New York	41
Rafael Palmeiro, Texas	38
Alfonso Soriano, New York	38
Manny Ramirez, Boston	37
Bret Boone, Seattle	35
Aubrey Huff, Tampa Bay	34
Vernon Wells, Toronto	33

Runs batted in

Carlos Delgado, Toronto	145
Alex Rodriguez, Texas	118
Bret Boone, Seattle	117
Vernon Wells, Toronto	117
Garret Anderson, Anaheim	116
Carlos Lee, Chicago	113
Rafael Palmeiro, Texas	112
Jason Giambi, New York	107
Aubrey Huff, Tampa Bay	107
Hideki Matsui, New York	106

Pitching-wins

Roy Halladay, Toronto	22- 7
Esteban Loaiza, Chicago	21- 9
Jamie Moyer, Seattle	21- 7
Andy Pettitte, New York	21- 8
Roger Clemens, New York	17- 9
Derek Lowe, Boston	17- 7
Mike Mussina, New York	17- 8
Tim Hudson, Oakland	16- 7
Ramon Ortiz, Anaheim	16-13
Joel Piñeiro, Seattle	16-11

Earned run average (min. 162 innings)

Pedro Martínez, Boston	2.22
Tim Hudson, Oakland	2.70
Esteban Loaiza, Chicago	2.90
Mark Mulder, Oakland	3.13
Roy Halladay, Toronto	3.25
Jamie Moyer, Seattle	3.27
Barry Zito, Oakland	3.30
Mike Mussina, New York	3.40
Ryan Franklin, Seattle	3.57
C.C. Sabathia, Cleveland	3.60

Strikeouts

Esteban Loaiza, Chicago	207
Pedro Martínez, Boston	206
Roy Halladay, Toronto	204
Mike Mussina, New York	195
Roger Clemens, New York	190
Andy Pettitte, New York	180
Bartolo Colón, Chicago	173
Johan Santana, Minnesota	169
Tim Wakefield, Boston	169
Tim Hudson, Oakland	162

NATIONAL LEAGUE

Batting average (min. 500 appearances)

Albert Pujols, St. Louis	.359
Todd Helton, Colorado	.358
Barry Bonds, San Francisco	.341
Edgar Renteria, St. Louis	.330
Gary Sheffield, Atlanta	.330
Jason Kendall, Pittsburgh	.325
Marcus Giles, Atlanta	.316
Luis Castillo, Florida	.314
Mark Grudzielanek, Chicago	.314
Mark Loretta, San Diego	.314
Scott Podsednik, Milwaukee	.314

Home runs

Jim Thome, Philadelphia	47
Barry Bonds, San Francisco	45
Richie Sexson, Milwaukee	45
Javy Lopez, Atlanta	43
Albert Pujols, St. Louis	43
Sammy Sosa, Chicago Cubs	40
Jeff Bagwell, Houston	39
Jim Edmonds, St. Louis	39
Gary Sheffield, Atlanta	39
Andruw Jones, Atlanta	36
Preston Wilson, Colorado	36

Runs batted in

Preston Wilson, Colorado	141
Gary Sheffield, Atlanta	132
Jim Thome, Philadelphia	131
Albert Pujols, St. Louis	124
Richie Sexson, Milwaukee	124
Todd Helton, Colorado	117
Andruw Jones, Atlanta	116
Javy Lopez, Atlanta	109
Chipper Jones, Atlanta	106
Aramis Ramirez, Chicago	106

Pitching-wins

Russ Ortiz, Atlanta	21- 7
Mark Prior, Chicago Cubs	18- 6
Woody Williams, St. Louis	18- 9
Jason Schmidt, San Francisco	17- 5
Greg Maddux, Atlanta	16-11
Hideo Nomo, Los Angeles	16-13
Steve Trachsel, New York	16-10
Randy Wolf, Philadelphia	16-10
Liván Hernández, Montreal	15-10
Al Leiter, New York Mets	15- 9
Jeriome Robertson, Houston	15- 9

Earned run average (min. 162 innings)

Jason Schmidt, San Francisco	2.34
Kevin Brown, Los Angeles	2.39
Mark Prior, Chicago Cubs	2.43
Brandon Webb, Arizona	2.84
Curt Schilling, Arizona	2.95
Hideo Nomo, Los Angeles	3.09
Carlos Zambrano, Chicago	3.11
Liván Hernández, Montreal	3.20
Kerry Wood, Chicago Cubs	3.20
Javier Vazquez, Montreal	3.24

Strikeouts

Kerry Wood, Chicago Cubs	266
Mark Prior, Chicago Cubs	245
Javier Vazquez, Montreal	241
Jason Schmidt, San Francisco	208
Curt Schilling, Arizona	194
Kevin Brown, Los Angeles	185
Liván Hernández, Montreal	178
Hideo Nomo, Los Angeles	177
Randy Wolf, Philadelphia	177
Brandon Webb, Arizona	172

Major League Baseball Final Standings, 2003

Division/Team	W	L	Pct.	GB
American League East				
New York Yankees[1]	101	61	.623	—
Boston Red Sox[2]	95	67	.586	6
Toronto Blue Jays	86	76	.531	15
Baltimore Orioles	71	91	.438	30
Tampa Bay Devil Rays	63	99	.389	38
American League Central				
Minnesota Twins[1]	90	72	.556	—
Chicago White Sox	86	76	.531	4
Kansas City Royals	83	79	.512	7
Cleveland Indians	68	94	.420	22
Detroit Tigers	43	119	.265	47
American League West				
Oakland Athletics[1]	96	66	.593	—
Seattle Mariners	93	69	.574	3
Anaheim Angels	77	85	.475	19
Texas Rangers	71	91	.438	25

Division/Team	W	L	Pct.	GB
National League East				
Atlanta Braves[1]	101	61	.623	—
Florida Marlins[2]	91	71	.562	10
Philadelphia Phillies	86	76	.531	15
Montreal Expos	83	79	.512	18
New York Mets	66	95	.410	34½
National League Central				
Chicago Cubs[1]	88	74	.543	—
Houston Astros	87	75	.537	1
St. Louis Cardinals	85	77	.525	3
Pittsburgh Pirates	75	87	.463	13
Cincinnati Reds	69	93	.426	19
Milwaukee Brewers	68	94	.420	20
National League West				
San Francisco Giants[1]	100	61	.621	—
Los Angeles Dodgers	85	77	.525	15½
Arizona Diamondbacks	84	78	.519	16½
Colorado Rockies	74	88	.457	26½
San Diego Padres	64	98	.395	36½

1. Division champion. 2. Wild card for playoffs.

2003 Division Series

AMERICAN LEAGUE

New York Defeats Minnesota, 3 games to 1

Minnesota 3, NEW YORK 1

Miscues by Soriano, Williams, and Hideki Matsui allowed the Twins to score three runs. Johan Santana left after four innings, but the bullpen held on.

NEW YORK 4, Minnesota 1

Alfonso Soriano scored two runs and drove in the game-winner. Andy Pettitte gave up a run and four hits over seven innings and Mariano Rivera pitched two innings of scoreless relief.

New York 3, MINNESOTA 1

The Yankees used the same formula again: a strong start from Roger Clemens and two shutout innings by closer Mariano Rivera. Hideki Matsui's two-run homer provided the offense.

New York 8, MINNESOTA 1

The Yankees exploded for six runs in the fourth inning against Santana. David Wells pitched a gem for the Yanks; Minnesota hit .198 overall.

Boston Defeats Oakland, 3 games to 2

Oakland 5, Boston 4 (12 innings)

Ramón Hernández drove home the game-winner with a surprise two-out bunt after the Boston bullpen blew a 4-3 lead in the ninth.

OAKLAND 5, Boston 1

In the second inning, the A's erupted for five runs on two hits and a Todd Walker throwing error. Barry Zito held the Red Sox to five hits over seven innings.

BOSTON 3, Oakland 1 (11 innings)

Obstruction calls gave the Red Sox a run in the second inning and cost the A's a run in the sixth. Trot Nixon's two-run homer in the 11th broke the 1-1 tie.

BOSTON 5, Oakland 4

David Ortiz's two-run double in the eighth off closer Keith Foulke rallied Boston from the brink of defeat.

BOSTON 4, Oakland 3

Manny Ramírez's three-run homer broke a 1-1 tie. The A's loaded the bases in the ninth but did not score. It was the ninth straight time Oakland failed to close out a Division Series.

NATIONAL LEAGUE

Chicago Cubs Defeat Atlanta, 3 games to 2

Chicago Cubs 4, ATLANTA 2

Kerry Wood struck out 11 and gave up just two hits over 7.1 innings; he also stroked a two-run double and scored in his own cause.

ATLANTA 5, Chicago Cubs 3

John Smoltz blew a 3-2 lead in the top of the 8th, but Mark DeRosa rescued him in the bottom half of the inning with a two-run double.

CHICAGO CUBS 3, Atlanta 1

Mark Prior threw a complete game, holding Atlanta to two hits. Randall Simon's first-inning single drove in two runs to provide all the offense Prior needed.

Atlanta 6, CHICAGO CUBS 4

Chipper Jones homered from both sides of the plate to power the Braves. With two outs and one on in the ninth, Sammy Sosa's long fly ball fell just short of a game-tying home run.

Chicago Cubs 5, ATLANTA 1

Kerry Wood shut down the Braves again. Alex González and Aramis Ramírez homered for the Cubs, who won their first postseason series in 95 years.

Florida Defeats San Francisco, 3 games to 1

SAN FRANCSICO 2, Florida 0

Jason Schmidt pitched a three-hit complete game shutout. Edgardo Alfonzo starred on offense, scoring one run and driving in the other.

Florida 9, SAN FRANCISCO 5

Marlins center fielder Juan Pierre went 4-for-5 with three singles, a double, three RBIs, and three runs scored, as the Marlins rallied from a 4-1 deficit.

FLORIDA 4, San Francisco 3 (11 innings)

Ivan Rodríguez drove in all four Marlins runs, the last two on a game winning single in the 11th after the Giants had rallied in the top half of the inning to take a 3-2 lead.

FLORIDA 7, San Francisco 6

After blowing a 5-1 lead, the Marlins scored two in the eighth to break a 5-5 tie when Yorvit Torrealba dropped a throw to the plate. In the ninth, Ivan Rodríguez held onto the ball and tagged out J.T. Snow for the final out of the series.

Note: Home teams in CAPITAL LETTERS.

2003 American League Championship Series

New York Yankees defeat Boston Red Sox, 4 games to 3

Boston 5, NEW YORK YANKEES 2
The Red Sox launched three homers against Mike Mussina; David Ortiz's two-run shot into the upper deck in the fourth inning was the big blow. Knuckleballer Tim Wakefield kept the Yankee hitters off balance all night, holding them to just two hits over six innings.

NEW YORK YANKEES 6, Boston 2
The Red Sox had six hits in the first two innings off Andy Pettitte, but managed only one run. Gabe Kapler was caught stealing as Bill Mueller struck out in the first inning; in the second, Kapler hit into a conventional double play. Pettitte allowed just one run on three hits over the next five innings. Nick Johnson broke a 1-for-33 slump with a two-run homer in the second inning, and Bernie Williams went 2-for-3 with two runs and an RBI.

New York Yankees 4, BOSTON 3
This classic was overshadowed by a near brawl when Pedro Martínez threw behind Karim Garcia's head. Both benches emptied again in the fourth when Manny Ramírez charged the mound because he thought a Roger Clemens fastball came too close. Nobody was ejected, and both starting pitchers bore down. The Red Sox cut the lead to one run in the seventh, but Mariano Rivera closed it out with two innings of scoreless relief.

BOSTON 3, New York Yankees 2
A rainout delayed this game a day, allowing for a Wakefield-Mussina rematch, with a similar result. Mussina was again plagued by home runs (solo shots by Todd Walker and Trot Nixon), while Wakefield continued his mastery of the Yankee hitters. Scott Williamson gave up a solo homer to Rubén Sierra in the ninth, but shut the door after that.

New York Yankees 4, BOSTON 2
David Wells bested Derek Lowe in this pitcher's duel. The Yankees took a 3-0 lead in the second on RBI singles by Karim Garcia and Alfonso Soriano. Manny Ramírez hit a solo homer in the fourth, but failed to deliver with the bases loaded in the sixth. The Yankees were buoyed by sparkling defensive plays from infielders Derek Jeter, Nick Johnson, and Alfonso Soriano.

Boston 9, NEW YORK YANKEES 6
The Red Sox offense finally awakened, rallying from behind twice. Nomar Garciaparra's fielding error allowed the Yankees to take a 5-4 lead in the fourth. But Garciaparra atoned with four hits in the game, including a triple that started Boston's three-run seventh inning. Boston relievers allowed just one run over the last five innings.

NEW YORK 6, Boston 5 (11 innings)
Roger Clemens and Pedro Martínez squared off again, but neither pitcher was involved in the decision. Clemens left after giving up four runs in three-plus innings; Martínez held the Yankees to two Jason Giambi solo homers until the eighth inning, when he finally faltered and allowed the tying runs to score. Aaron Boone led off the bottom of the 11th with a homer against Tim Wakefield to win the game. Mike Mussina kept the Yankees in it with three innings of scoreless relief, as did closer Mariano Rivera, who was the series MVP.

2003 National League Championship Series

Florida Marlins defeat Chicago Cubs, 4 games to 3

Florida 9, CHICAGO CUBS 8 (11 innings)
The Cubs took a 4-0 lead in the first, but Florida responded with three homers and five runs in the third. Sammy Sosa tied the game again in the ninth with a two-run homer. But Mike Lowell homered for Florida in the 11th for the deciding run.

CHICAGO CUBS 12, Florida 3
The Cubs again took the early lead, but this time they didn't let the Marlins back into the game. Sammy Sosa again led the charge, with a two-run homer in the third. Cubs shortstop Alex Gonzalez had two home runs, and Aramis Ramírez had one.

Chicago Cubs 5, FLORIDA 4 (11 innings)
This back-and-forth thriller was almost a replay of Game 1. The Cubs took the early lead, fell behind 3-2 in the seventh, took another lead on Randall Simon's two-run homer in the eighth, then gave it back when the bullpen couldn't hold it. In the 11th, Doug Glanville tripled home Kenny Lofton with the deciding run.

Chicago Cubs 8, FLORIDA 3
Aramis Ramírez hit a grand slam off Dontrelle Willis in the first inning, and the game was never close after that. The Marlins scored twice in the bottom of the fifth, but never seriously challenged starter Matt Clement. Ramírez went 3-for-4 with 6 RBIs.

FLORIDA 4, Chicago Cubs 0
Josh Beckett pitched a complete game shutout, holding the Cubs to two hits and striking out 11. Mike Lowell's two-run homer in the fifth broke a scoreless tie; Iván Rodríguez and Jeff Conine added solo shots in the 7th and 8th innings.

Florida 8, CHICAGO CUBS 3
The Cubs were five outs away from the World Series. But just as the Wrigley Field faithful started to hope, their dreams were crushed. Mark Prior, who had been cruising with a 3-0 lead, suddenly faltered; the normally sure-handed Alex Gonzalez booted an easy grounder to short; and a fan touched a foul popup that Moises Alou seemed sure to catch. When it was all over, the Marlins had scored eight runs and revived talk of a curse against the Cubs.

Florida 9, CHICAGO CUBS 6
Kerry Wood gave up a three-run homer to Miguel Cabrera in the first, then rebounded with a home run of his own in the second to tie the score. The Cubs took a 5-3 lead in the third on Moises Alou's homer, but the Marlins came back with three in the fifth, one in the sixth, and two in the seventh. Josh Beckett came back on two days' rest and threw four stellar innings of one-hit relief. Marlins Catcher Iván Rodríguez, who set an NLCS record with 10 RBIs in the series, was the runaway choice for MVP.

Note: Home teams in CAPITAL LETTERS.

The 2003 World Series

Florida Marlins defeat New York Yankees, 4 games to 2

Game 1 Florida 3, NEW YORK YANKEES 2
The Marlins used their speed to manufacture a run in the top of the first. Juan Pierre bunted for a base hit, went to third on Luis Castillo's hit-and-run single, and scored on Iván Rodríguez's sacrifice fly. The Yankees tied the game in the third, but ran themselves out of a big inning when Rodríguez picked Nick Johnson off third base with the go-ahead run. Pierre then drove in Florida's other two runs on a fifth-inning single. The Yankees put the winning runs on base in both the eighth and ninth innings, but could not convert their opportunities. Brad Penny got the win for Florida, but rookie Dontrelle Willis, who relieved him in the sixth, and closer Ugueth Urbina, who threw a four-out save, got the toughest outs.

	123	456	789	R	H	E
Florida	100	020	000	**3**	**7**	**1**
New York	001	001	000	**2**	**9**	**0**

W-Brad Penny (1-0) L-David Wells (0-1)
S-Ugueth Urbina (1)

Game 2 NEW YORK YANKEES 6, Florida 1
As he did in each of the previous postseason rounds, Andy Pettitte evened the series for the Yankees. The big lefthander pitched a gem; only an Aaron Boone error in the ninth inning prevented Pettitte from registering a complete game shutout. Pettitte held the Marlins to six hits, all singles; the Yankee defense turned three double plays behind him. Hideki Matsui led the Yankee offense with a three-run homer off Mark Redman in the first inning. The Yankees tacked on runs in the second inning, on Juan Rivera's double, and in the fourth, on Alfonso Soriano's two-run homer.

	123	456	789	R	H	E
Florida	000	000	001	**1**	**6**	**0**
New York	310	200	00x	**6**	**10**	**2**

W-Andy Pettitte (1-0) L-Mark Redman (0-1)

Game 3 New York Yankees 6, FLORIDA 1
For seven innings, this was a tight pitcher's duel between Marlins ace Josh Beckett and the Yankees' Mike Mussina, who had not won a postseason game in his last six starts despite pitching well. Florida scored in the first inning on a Juan Pierre bloop that fell between two outfielders, and a Miguel Cabrera single. The Yankees rallied to tie it in the fourth on a Derek Jeter double, two walks, and a hit batter. Then they took the lead in the eighth when Hideki Matsui singled home Jeter, who had doubled again. In the ninth, the Yankees broke it open against the Marlins bullpen, as both Aaron Boone and Bernie Williams went deep.

	123	456	789	R	H	E
New York	000	100	014	**6**	**6**	**1**
Florida	100	000	000	**1**	**8**	**0**

W-Mike Mussina (1-0) L- Josh Beckett (0-1)
S-Mariano Rivera (1)

Game 4 FLORIDA 4, New York Yankees 3 (12 innings)
Roger Clemens' swan song was nearly a disaster. He threw 41 pitches in the first inning, allowing three runs on five hits, all after he retired the first two batters. Miguel Cabrera's two-run homer was the big blow. But over the next six innings, the 41-year-old Clemens held the Marlins to three hits and no runs, and received a standing ovation from the Florida crowd as he left the mound for the last time in his career. Carl Pavano was even better, holding New York to one run over eight innings. But Ugueth Urbina couldn't nail down the save, giving up the tying runs on Rubén Sierra's two-out triple. In the 11th, Joe Torre called on Jeff Weaver, who hadn't pitched in a month. Weaver retired the side in order in the 11th, but in the 12th, he gave up a walk-off homer to Alex González.

	123	456	789	10	11	12	R	H	E
New York	010	000	002	0	0	0	**3**	**12**	**0**
Florida	300	000	000	0	0	1	**4**	**10**	**0**

W-Braden Looper (1-0) L-Jeff Weaver (0-1)

Game 5 FLORIDA 6, New York Yankees 4
Joe Torre dropped Jason Giambi and Alfonso Soriano from the lineup, and the revamped order paid dividends with a first-inning run. But a back injury forced starting pitcher David Wells from the game after one inning, leaving the Yankees to scramble for relief. José Contreras gave up four runs over the next three innings, and the Marlins scored two unearned runs on a Mike Lowell single in the fifth after Enrique Wilson's throwing error extended the inning. The Yankees rallied in the seventh and ninth, bringing the tying run to the plate each time, but the Florida bullpen held on each time.

	123	456	789	R	H	E
New York	100	001	002	**4**	**12**	**1**
Florida	030	120	00x	**6**	**9**	**1**

W-Brad Penny (2-0) L-Jose Contreras (0-1)
S- Ugueth Urbina (2)

Game 6 Florida 2, New York Yankees 0
Josh Beckett came back on three days' rest and dominated the Yankees, who went meekly. Beckett threw a complete game shutout, held New York to five hits, and did not permit a runner to reach third base. The Marlins manufactured a run in the fifth and added an insurance run in the sixth after a Derek Jeter throwing error. Andy Pettitte pitched well enough to win, but the Yankees went 0-12 with runners on base. Beckett was the MVP for the Marlins, who still have not lost a postseason series.

	123	456	789	R	H	E
Florida	000	011	000	**2**	**7**	**0**
New York	000	000	000	**0**	**5**	**1**

W-Josh Beckett (1-1) L-Andy Pettitte (1-1)

INDEX

A

Abortion, 372-373
By marital status and age, 372
Number reported, 372
By race, 372
Academy Awards, 813-818
Accidents, deaths from, 379-382
Account (Internet term), 808
Acid rain, 777-778
Acquired immune deficiency syndrome (see AIDS), 375-377
ACT (see American College Testing Program)
Adams, John
Administration, 114
Biography, 86
Election, 101
Vice President, 113
Adams, John Quincy
Administration, 114
Biography, 87-88
Election, 102
Administration for Children and Families (ACF), 133
Administration, Office of, 131
Administrative Office of the U.S. Courts, 125
Adoption, 282
Advent, 44
Adventist churches (U.S.), 403
Advertising, U.S., 351-353
Expenditures by year, 351
Top 100 advertisers, 352-353
Top 25 agencies, 352
Volume, by medium, 351
on the Web, 808
Aeronautics and Space Administration, National (NASA), 137-138
Employment and budget outlays, 141
AFDC (see Aid to Families with Dependent Children)
Afghanistan, description, 517-519
Area codes, 462
Economy, 517
Geography, 517
Government, 517
Health indicators, 481
Major cities in, 517
People, 517
Population indicators, 475
Time zones, 462
AFL-CIO, 337
Africa
Birth rate, 475
Death rate, 475
Elevation extremes, 449
Energy production/consumption, 494, 496
Fertility rate, 475
History, 423
Life expectancy, 475
Nuclear power generation, 497
Percent urban, 475
Population, 475
Population indicators, 475
Population, percentage of world, 472
African-American Population (see Black population)
African Development Foundation, 136
Age
U.S. population by, 276
U.S. population, median, 276
Age group
Homicide, guns, and young people, 309
Teenage Tobacco Users, 385
Aged persons
Medicaid benefits for, 159-160
Medicare benefits for, 157, 158-159
Old age, survivors and disability insurance (OASDI), 156-158
Social security for, 155-159
Supplemental insurance benefits for, 159
Agricultural services, forestry and fishing industries
Establishments with employees and payrolls, 339
Agriculture, U.S., 302-304
Exports by region and nation, 302
Exports: Principal Commodities, 304
Farms, acreage, and population in U.S., 302
Farms, number and acreage by state, 303
Production of Farm Products, 304
Agriculture, U.S. Dept. of (USDA), description, 132
Employment and budget outlays, 141
Aid to Families with Dependent Children (AFDC), 156
AIDS, 375-377
2002-03 Events, 35
Adolescents with, 376
Adults with, 376
Cases, 376
in Cities, 376
Deaths, 376
Heterosexuals and, 377
Nations with most AIDS patients, 485
Patients, 377
by World region, 485
Worldwide, 484-486
Air Force, U.S., description, 133, 150
Casualties, by conflict, 150
Major units, 149
Minorities in, 153
Women in, 153
Worldwide deployment, 151
Air mass, definition, 467
Air pollution, 774-777
Airlines, U.S., 412
On-time Performance and Mishandled Baggage by, 412
Airports
On-time Arrival and Departure Rates, U.S., 413
World's busiest, 413
Alabama, description, 169-170
Area codes, 804-805
Black population in, 270
Business, 170
Cities, major, population of, 169
Crime in, 306
Education expenditures per pupil, 356
Educational attainment, 359
Elected officials, 169
Elevations, 57
Emblems, 169
Executions in, 315
Famous natives, 170
Farms in, 303
Fortune 500 companies, 170
Health care quality, 368
Land area, 169
Land cover and use, 55
Memorable events, 170
Noteworthy places, 170
Nuclear plants in, 364
Parks and recreation areas, 53
Persons below poverty level, 321
Population by race and Hispanic origin, 269
Population by race/national origin, 169
Population estimates, 1990-2000, 169
Population, foreign-born, 297
Prisoners in, 313
Public school enrollment, 356
Resident population and population change, 261
Resident population by age, 2002, 277
Revenues and expenditures, 203
Taxation in, 204-207
Tourist information, 170
Web site, 170
Alaska, description, 170-171
Area codes, 804-805
Business, 171
Cities, major, population of, 171
Crime in, 306
Education expenditures per pupil, 356
Educational attainment, 359
Elected officials, 171
Elevations, 57
Emblems, 171
Executions in, 315
Famous natives, 171
Farms in, 303
Fortune 500 companies, 171
Health care quality, 368
Land area, 171
Land cover and use, 55
Memorable events, 171
Noteworthy places, 171
Parks and recreation areas, 53
Persons below poverty level, 321
Population by race and Hispanic origin, 269
Population by race/national origin, 171
Population estimates, 1990-2000, 169
Population, foreign-born, 297
Prisoners in, 313
Public school enrollment, 356
Resident population and population change, 261
Resident population by age, 2002, 277
Revenues and expenditures, 203
Taxation in, 204-207
Tourist information, 171
Web site, 171
Albania, description, 518-519
Area codes, 462
Economic Indicators, 514
Economy, 518
Geography, 518
Government, 518
Health indicators, 481
Major cities in, 518
Population indicators, 475
Time zones, 462
Albuquerque, N.Mex., description, 212
Area codes, 804-805
Crime in, 307, 308
Government, 212
Location, 212
Population, 212
Population by race/Hispanic origin, 235
Population, 1980-2000, 238
Rents in, 290
Tax burdens in, 242
Terrain and climate, 212
Visitor information, 212
Web site, 212
Alcohol
Consumption, U.S., 384
Alcohol, Tobacco and Firearms, Bureau of, 135
Algebra, 764-766
Algeria, description, 519-520
Area codes, 462
Economic indicators, 514
Economy, 519
Geography, 519
Government, 519
Health indicators, 481
Major cities in, 519
People, 519
Population indicators, 475
Time zones, 462
All Saints' Day, 44
Alzheimer's disease, 378
America's Cup, 879
American College Testing Program
Scores by sex, race and Hispanic origin, 357
American Film Institute Life Achievement Awards, 818
American Indian and Alaska Native population
Population of selected reservations and trust lands, 275
Resident population by state, 269
by State, 169-203
of U.S. cities, 1990, 235-238
of U.S. MSAs, 1990, 250-255
American Institute of Architects (AIA) Gold Medalists, 837
American People Today, 260-301
American Samoa, description, 207
Area codes, 462
Health indicators, 481
Population, 207
Population indicators, 475
Time zones, 462
American Stock Exchange, 342
Americas (see South America, Latin America, Central America, North America)
Discovery of, 426, 431-432
History, 429
Amish (see Mennonite Churches)
Amphibians, endangered in U.S., 785
AMTRAK, 136
Operating statistics, 415
Anchorage, Alaska
Cost of living index, 324
Crime in, 308
Population by race/Hispanic origin, 235
Population, 1980-2000, 238
Tax burdens in, 242
Tax Progressivity in, 240
Andorra, description, 520
Area codes, 462
Economy, 520
Geography, 520

Government, 520
Major cities, 520
People, 520
Population indicators, 475
Time zones, 462
Angles
Measurement of, 771
Angola, description, 520-521
Area codes, 462
Economic indicators, 514
Economy, 520
Geography, 520
Government, 520
Health indicators, 481
Major cities, 520
People, 520
Population indicators, 475
Time zones, 462
Anguilla, 705
Angular momentum, conservation of, 755-756
Animals
Endangered, 782-784
Endangered in the U.S., 784
Anniversaries, gifts for, 47
Annunciation, the, 44
Antarctica, description, 459-501
Antarctica Treaty, 460-461
Elevation extremes, 449
Exploration, 459
Geography, 459
Government, 460-461
Land/sea life, 459
People, 460
Scientific research on, 459-460
Antiatoms, 758
Antigua and Barbuda, description, 521
Economic indicators, 514
Economy, 521
Geography, 521
Government, 521
Health indicators, 481
Major cities, 521
People, 521
Antiparticles, 757-758
Applet (Internet term), 808
April Fool's Day, 42
Arabic lang., 493
Arachnids, endangered in U.S., 786
Arbitrage, definition, 344
Arbor Day, 42
Archaea, 759
Architect of the Capitol, 125
Architecture
American Institute of Architects (AIA) Gold Medalists, 837
Pritzker Prizes in Architecture, 837
Archipelago, 447
Archives and Records Administration, National (NARA), 138
Arctic, description, 461
Communications, 461
Economy, 461
Geography, 461
Government, 461
Population, 461
Area
Formulas for measuring, 764
Measures of, 768
Area codes
International, 462-464
United States and Canada, 804-805
Argentina, description, 521-523
2002-03 Events, 23
Area codes, 462
Economic indicators, 514
Economy, 521
Geography, 521
Government, 521
Health indicators, 481
Major cities, 521
Nuclear power generation, 497
People, 521
Population in U.S., 299
Population indicators, 475
Time zones, 462
U.S. immigrants from, 295
Arizona, description, 171-172
Area codes, 804-805
Business, 171
Cities, major, population of, 171
Crime in, 306
Education expenditures per pupil, 356
Educational attainment, 359
Elected officials, 171
Elevations, 57
Emblems, 171
Executions in, 315
Famous natives, 171-172
Farms in, 303
Fortune 500 companies, 171
Health care quality, 368
Land area, 171
Land cover and use, 55
Memorable events, 172
Noteworthy places, 172
Nuclear plants in, 364
Parks and recreation areas, 53
Persons below poverty level, 321
Population by race and Hispanic origin, 269
Population by race/national origin, 171
Population estimates, 1990-2000, 169
Population, foreign-born, 297
Prisoners in, 313
Public school enrollment, 356
Resident population and population change, 261
Resident population by age, 1999, 277
Revenues and expenditures, 203
Taxation in, 204-207
Tourist information, 172
Web site, 172
Arkansas, description, 172
Area codes, 804-805
Business, 172
Cities, major, population of, 172
Crime in, 306
Education expenditures per pupil, 356
Educational attainment, 359
Elected officials, 172
Elevations, 57
Emblems, 172
Executions in, 315
Famous natives, 172
Farms in, 303
Fortune 500 companies, 172
Health care quality, 368
Land area, 172
Land cover and use, 55
Memorable events, 172
Noteworthy places, 172
Nuclear plants in, 364
Parks and recreation areas, 53
Persons below poverty level, 321
Population by race and Hispanic origin, 269
Population by race/national origin, 172
Population estimates, 1990-2000, 169
Population, foreign-born, 297
Prisoners in, 313
Public school enrollment, 356
Resident population and population change, 261
Resident population by age, 1999, 277
Revenues and expenditures, 203
Taxation in, 204-207
Tourist information, 172
Web site, 172
Armed Forces Day, 42
Armed forces personnel by nation, 499-500
Armed forces, U.S., description, 147-149
Basic pay table, 155
Casualties, by conflict, 150
Employees, 147
Guard and reserve forces, 153
Minorities in, 153
Nuclear forces, 154-155
Personnel by state, 154
Personnel on active duty, 147
Reserve forces, 151-152
Salaries in, 155
Special operations forces, 150-151
Weapon systems and combat forces, 152
Women in, 153
Worldwide deployment, 151
Armenia, description, 523
Area codes, 462
Economic indicators, 514
Economy, 523
Geography, 523
Government, 523
Health indicators, 481
Major cities, 523
People, 523
Population indicators, 475
Time zones, 462
Army, U.S., description, 147-149
Casualties, by conflict, 150
Major forces, 148
Minorities in, 153
Women in, 153
Worldwide deployment, 151
Arrests
as Percent of number of crimes, 311
for Property crimes, 311
by Race, 311
for Violent crime, 311
Arson, arrests for, 311
Arthur, Chester A.
Administration, 116
Biography, 91
Vice President, 113
Artificial Intelligence, 795
Arts and entertainment, awards in
Aruba, description, 703
Area codes, 462
Population indicators, 475
Time zones, 462
Ascension Island
Area codes, 462
Population indicators, 475
Time zones, 462
ASEAN (Association of South East Asian Nations), 512-513
Ash Wednesday, 44
Asia
Area and population, 448
Birth rate, 475
Death rate, 475
Elevation extremes, 449
Fertility rate, 475
History, 420-437
Life expectancy, 475
Moslems in, 424
Nuclear power generation, 497
Percent urban, 475
Population indicators, 475
Population, 2000, 475
Population, percentage of world, 472
U.S. immigrants from, 295
Asia Pacific Economic Cooperation (APEC), 512
Asian or Pacific Islander population
Cities with largest population, 274
Resident population by state, 269
by State, 169-203
States with largest populations, 274
of U.S. cities, 235-238
of U.S. MSAs, 1990, 250-255
Assault, aggravated
Arrests for, 311
Rate, by state, 306
Association of South East Asian Nations (ASEAN), 512-513
Astrological Calendar, 47
Astronomical Distances, 723-724
Astronomical Events, 2003, 47-49
Astronomy, 716-729
2002-03 News, 36
Basic facts about the planets, 718
Atheists, 490-498
Atlanta, Ga., description, 212
Area codes, 804-805
Black population in, 271
Climate in, 470
Cost of living index, 243
Government, 212
Housing prices in, 290
Location, 212
Population, 212
Population by race/Hispanic origin, 235
Population, 1980-2000, 238
Rents in, 290
Tax burdens in, 242
Terrain and climate, 212
Visitor information, 212
Web site, 212
Atlantic Ocean (see Oceans of the World)
Atmosphere (geo.), 739-741
Atoms
Periodic table of elements, 746-747
Austin, Tx., description, 212-213
Area codes, 804-805
Crime in, 307, 308
Government, 213
Location, 213
Population, 213
Population by race/Hispanic origin, 235
Population, 1980-2000, 238
Rents in, 290
Terrain and climate, 213
Visitor information, 213
Web site, 213
Australia, description, 523-524 (see also Oceania)
Area codes, 462
Birth rate, 475
Currency exchange rates, 505
Death rate, 475
Economic indicators, 514
Economy, 524
Elevation extremes, 449
Fertility rate, 475
Geography, 523
Government, 523
Health indicators, 481
Life expectancy, 475
Major cities, 523
Motor vehicle production, 408
People, 523
Percent urban, 475
Population in U.S., 299
Population indicators, 475
Population, 2000, 475
Time zones, 462
Australian Open (tennis), 916-917
Austria, description, 524-525
Area codes, 462

Currency Exchange Rates, 505
Economic indicators, 514
Economy, 524
European Union Membership, 509
Geography, 524
Government, 524
Habsburg Dynasty, 443
Health indicators, 481
Major cities, 524
People, 524
Population in U.S., 299
Population indicators, 475
Time zones, 462
Traffic deaths, 408
U.S. immigrants from, 295
Autobiography
National Book Critics Circle Awards, 834-835
Pulitzer Prize, 851
Automobile Racing, 906
Aviation, 411-414
Airlines, U.S., 412
Domestic airline routes, 412
On-time Performance and Mishandled Baggage by Major U.S. Airlines, 412
World's busiest airports, 413
Aviation Administration, Federal (FAA), 135
Awards and Prizes, 813-868
Academy Awards, 813-818
American Film Institute Life Achievement Awards, 818
American Institute of Architects (AIA) Gold Medalists, 837
Bollingen Prize for Poetry, 830
Caldecott Medal, 836
Cannes Film Festival, 818
Eclipse Award (horse racing), 918
Emmy Awards, 821-823
Fields Medal, 838
Grammy Awards, 827-829
MTV Video Music Awards, 829-830
National Book Awards, 832-833
National Book Critics Circle Awards, 833-835
Newbery Medal, 835-836
Nobel Prizes, 854-868
Oscar awards (see Academy Awards)
Pritzker Prizes in Architecture, 837
Pulitzer Prizes, 839-854
Templeton Prize Winners, 838
Tony Awards, 824-827
Azerbaijan, description, 525-526
Area codes, 462
Economic indicators, 514
Economy, 526
Geography, 525
Government, 526
Health indicators, 481
Major cities, 525
People, 525-526
Population indicators, 475
Time zones, 462

B

Bachelor's degrees conferred, 1950-2001, 360
Baha'i, 490
Bahamas, description, 526-527
Economic indicators, 514
Economy, 526-527
Geography, 526
Government, 526
Health indicators, 481
Major cities, 526
People, 526
Bahrain, description, 527
Area codes, 462
Economic indicators, 514
Economy, 527
Geography, 527
Government, 527
Health indicators, 481
Major cities, 527
People, 527
Population indicators, 475
Time zones, 462
Baker and Howland Islands, 207
***Baker v. Carr* (1962), 122**
Balance of payments, definition, 505
Balance of trade, definition, 505-507
Baltimore, Md., description, 213
Area codes, 804-805
Black population in, 271
Climate in, 470
Cost of living index, 243
Crime in, 307
Government, 213
Housing prices in, 290
Location, 213
Population, 213
Population by race/Hispanic origin, 235
Population, 1980-2000, 238
Rents in, 290
Tax burdens in, 242
Terrain and climate, 213
Visitor information, 213
Web site, 213
Bandwidth, definition, 808
Bangladesh, description, 527-528
Area codes, 462
Economic indicators, 514
Economy, 528
Geography, 527
Government, 527-528
Health indicators, 481
Major cities, 527
People, 527
Population indicators, 475
Time zones, 462
Banks, 325-332 (see also Money and Banking)
Deposit-taking institutions, 328
Failures, 328-330
Federal Reserve, 325-327
Federal Reserve discount rates, 326
Number and deposits, 328
Top 100 banking companies, 329
Baptist churches (U.S.), 401
Barbados, description, 528
Economic indicators, 514
Economy, 528
Geography, 528
Government, 528
Health indicators, 481
Major cities, 528
People, 528
Population in U.S., 299
Barometric pressure, definition, 467
Baseball, NCAA champions, 876
Baseball, Olympic champions, 897
Baseball, professional, 947-972
2003 batting and pitching leaders, 969
2003 Division Series, 970
2003 Final Standings, 970
2003 League Championship Series, 971
2003 Season, 947
2003 World Series, 972
All-Time leaders, 948
Batting Champions 1901-2003, 949-950
Cy Young Award Winners, 1956-2002, 953
Hall of Fame, 957-962
Home Run Champions, 1919-2003, 950-951
League Championship Series , 1969-2003, 968-969
Managers, most wins by, 966
Most Valuable Players, 1911-2002, 954-956
Most Valuable Team, 956
Rookie of the Year, 1947-2002, 952
Triple Crown winners, 956
World Series, 1903-2002, 963-966
Basin, 447
Basketball, college, 873, 874
NCAA Career Leaders, 874
NCAA Men's Final Four Results, 873
NCAA Women's champions, 874
Basketball, Olympic champions, 897
Basketball, professional (NBA), 934-941
2002-03 Final Standings, 935
2002-03 Playoff Results, 935
2003 NBA First Round Draft Picks, 935
Naismith Hall of Fame, 939-941
NBA All-Time Career Leaders, 937
NBA Most Valuable Players, 938
NBA Rookies of the Year, 938
NBA World Championship Series, 937
WNBA, 941
Baud rate, 795
Bay, 447
Bear/bull, definition, 344
Beaufort wind scale, 469
Belarus, description, 529
Area codes, 462
Declining population, 472
Economic indicators, 514
Economy, 529
Geography, 529
Government, 529
Health indicators, 481
Major cities, 529
People, 529
Population indicators, 475
Time zones, 462
Belgium, description, 529-530
Area codes, 462
Currency exchange rates, 505
Economic indicators, 514
Economy, 530
European Union membership, 509
Geography, 529-530
Government, 530
Health indicators, 481
Major cities, 530
Motor vehicle production, 408
Nuclear power generation, 497
People, 530
Population in U.S., 299
Population indicators, 475
Time zones, 462
Traffic deaths, 408
U.S. immigrants from, 295
Belize, description, 530-531
Area codes, 462
Economic indicators, 514
Economy, 530-531
Geography, 530
Government, 530
Health indicators, 481
Major cities, 530
People, 530
Population in U.S., 299
Population indicators, 475
Time zones, 462
Belmont Stakes, 922
Bengali lang., 493
Benin, description, 531
Area codes, 462
Economic indicators, 514
Economy, 531
Geography, 531
Government, 531
Health indicators, 481
Major cities, 531
People, 531
Population indicators, 475
Time zones, 462
Bermuda, 705
Bhutan, description, 531-532
Area codes, 462
Economic indicators, 514
Economy, 531
Geography, 531
Government, 531
Health indicators, 481
Major cities, 531
People, 531
Population indicators, 475
Time zones, 462
Bible, books of the, 492
Big Bang, 726
Big business: the *Fortune* 500, 347
Bight, 447
Bill of Rights (See also Constitution, U.S.)**, 64-66**
Billings, Mont.
Tax burdens in, 242
Tax progressivity in, 240
Binary stars, 726
Biographies of U.S. Presidents, 86-100
Biography
National Book Critics Circle Awards, 834-835
Pulitzer Prize, 851
Birds, endangered in U.S., 785
Birmingham, Ala.
Black population in, 271
Crime in, 307, 308
Population by race/Hispanic origin, 235
Population, 1980-2000, 238
Tax burdens in, 242
Birth rate, definition, 478
by Region and nation, 475-477
in U.S., 279
Births
in U.S., 278, 279
to Teenagers, 280
Births and deaths, world, 472
Birthstones, 47
Black Lung Program, 159
Black population, description, 268-272
in Armed forces, 153
Arrests, 311
Below poverty level, 322
Cancer survival rates, 374
Crime victimization rates, 310
Death rates, 377
Divorced persons per 1,000 married persons, 283
Employment status of, 334
Interracial couples, 283
in Largest U.S. Cities, 271
Life expectancy, 380, 381
Lifetime likelihood of going to prison, 314
Marital status, 281
of Metropolitan areas, 271
Money income of families, 322
One-parent families, 286
as Percent of total population, 268
Prisoners, 312
Prisoners executed, 314
Resident population by state, 269
by State, 169-203

States with highest percentage of, 270
States with largest number of, 270
of the U.S., 1790-2000, 270
of U.S. cities, 235-238
of U.S. MSAs, 1990, 250-255
Blackout of 2003, 25-26
Blog, 808
Blue chip stock, definition, 344
Boise City, Idaho
Area codes, 804-805
Population by race/Hispanic origin, 235
Tax burdens in, 242
Tax progressivity in, 240
Bolivia, 532-533
2002-03 Events, iv
Area codes, 462
Economic indicators, 514
Economy, 532
Geography, 532
Government, 532
Health indicators, 481
Major cities, 532
People, 532
Population indicators, 475
Time zones, 462
Bollingen Prize for Poetry, 830
Bond, definition, 344
Bookmark (Internet term), 808
Books
Banned, 392
Best-sellers in America, 390-391
Bollingen Prize for Poetry, 830
Caldecott Medal, 836
Children's book awards, 835-836
National Book Awards, 832-833
National Book Critics Circle Awards, 833-835
New books and editions published, by subject, 392
Newbery Medal, 835-836
Nobel Prizes in Literature, 866-868
Number and value of U.S. books sold, 390
Pulitzer Prizes in Letters, 848-854
Bosnia and Herzegovina, description, 533-534
Area codes, 462
Economic indicators, 514
Economy, 533
Geography, 533
Government, 533
Health indicators, 481
Major cities, 533
People, 533
Population indicators, 475
Time zones, 462
Bosons, 757
Boston Marathon champions, 884, 885
Boston, Mass., description, 213-214
Area codes, 804-805
Black population in, 271
Climate in, 470
Crime in, 307
Cost of living index, 243
Government, 214
Housing prices in, 290
Location, 214
Population, 214
Population by race/Hispanic origin, 235
Population, 1980-2000, 238
Rents in, 290
Tax burdens in, 242
Terrain and climate, 214
Visitor information, 214
Web site, 214
Botanic Garden, U.S., 125
Botswana, description, 534
Area codes, 462
Economic indicators, 514
Economy, 534
Geography, 534
Government, 534
Health indicators, 481
Major cities, 534
People, 534
Population indicators, 475
Time zones, 462
***Bowers v. Hardwick* (1986), 123**
Bowl Games (College Football), 870-871
Bowling, 907
Ladies Pro Bowling Tour, 907
PBA Leading Money Winners, 907
Boxing, 908
Brazil, description, 534-536
2002-03 Events, 23
Area codes, 462
Economic indicators, 514
Economy, 534-535
Geography, 534
Government, 534
Health indicators, 481
Major cities, 534
Motor vehicle production, 408
Nuclear power generation, 497
People, 534
Population indicators, 475
Time zones, 462
Breeders' Cup, 918
Brethren churches (U.S.), 406
Bridgeport, Conn.
Population by race/Hispanic origin, 235
Tax burdens in, 242
Brightest stars: magnitudes and distances from Earth, 726
British Virgin Islands, 705-706
***Brown v. Board of Education of Topeka* (1954), 122**
Brown dwarfs, 727
Browser, 808
Brunei, description, 536
Area codes, 462
Economic indicators, 514
Economy, 536
Geography, 536-707
Government, 536-707
Health indicators, 481
Major cities, 536-707
People, 536-707
Population indicators, 475
Time zones, 462
Buchanan, James
Administration, 115
Biography, 89-90
Election, 103
Buddhism, description
in the U.S., 406
in World, 489-498
Budget authority, definition, 142
Budget deficit/surplus, definition, 142
Budget, U.S. Federal, 139-144
Congressional process, 142
Glossary of terms, 142-144
Office of Management and Budget, 131
Outlays by branch and agency, 141
Outlays for national defense functions, 143
Percent distribution, 143
Receipts by source, 142
Buffer, 795-796
Bug, 796
Buildings, world's 50 tallest, 460
Bulgaria, description, 536-537
Area codes, 462
Declining population, 472
Economic indicators, 514
Economy, 536
European Union membership, 509
Geography, 536
Government, 536
Health indicators, 481
Major cities, 536
Nuclear power generation, 497
People, 536
Population indicators, 475
Time zones, 462
Bureau (see rest of entry)
Burglary
Arrests for, 311
Rate, by metropolitan area, 307
Rate, by state, 306
Burkina Faso, description, 537-538
Area codes, 462
Economic indicators, 514
Economy, 537
Geography, 537
Government, 537
Health indicators, 481
Major cities, 537
People, 537
Population indicators, 475
Time zones, 462
Burlington, Vt.
Crime in, 308
Tax burdens in, 242
Burundi, description, 538
Area codes, 462
Economic indicators, 514
Economy, 538
Geography, 538
Government, 538
Health indicators, 481
Major cities, 538
People, 538
Population indicators, 475
Time zones, 462
Buses
Number in U.S., 407
Registrations, state, 410
Registrations, world, 409
Sales, U.S., 409
***Bush v. Gore* (2000), 123**
Bush, George H.
Administration, 119
Biography, 98
Election, 109
Vice President, 113
Bush, George W.
Administration, 119
Biography, 99-100
Bush v. Gore (U.S. Supreme Court Case), 123
Election, 110, 111
Business
on the Web, 807-808
Business establishments with employees and payroll, by major group, 339-340
Business, U.S., 339-351
2002-03 News, 32-34
Advertising, 351-353
Big business: *Fortune* 500 companies, 347
Small business, 347-351
by State, 169-203
Business, U.S. Economy and, 316-353
Bypass surgery, 374

C

Cabinet (see Administrations)
Cabinet Members, 1789-2001, 114-119
Cable Modem, 808
Cable television
Basic and pay systems and subscribers, 395
Cable networks, top 15, 394
Pay-cable services, top 5, 395
Primetime viewing shares of free and cable TV networks, 394
Cache, 808
Caldecott Medal, 836
Caldera, 447
Calendar of the Year, 37-49
Calendars
Astrological, 47
Chinese, 45
Christian Holy Days, 44
Gregorian, 38-49
Hindu, 46-47
Holidays and Holy Days, 42-47
Islamic, 46
Jewish, 45-46
Julian, 38
Lunar, 38
Perpetual, 39
Solar, 38
Understanding, 37-41
California, description, 172-173
2002-03 Events, v, 24-25
Area codes, 804-805
Black population in, 270
Business, 173
Cities, major, population of, 173
Crime in, 306
Education expenditures per pupil, 356
Educational attainment, 359
Elected officials, 173
Elevations, 57
Emblems, 173
Executions in, 315
Famous natives, 173
Farms in, 303
Fortune 500 companies, 173
Health care quality, 368
Land area, 173
Land cover and use, 55
Memorable events, 173
Noteworthy places, 173
Nuclear plants in, 364
Parks and recreation areas, 53
Persons below poverty level, 321
Population by race and Hispanic origin, 269
Population by race/national origin, 173
Population estimates, 1990-2000, 169
Population, foreign-born, 297
Prisoners in, 313
Public school enrollment, 356
Recall election, 24-25
Resident population and population change, 261
Resident population by age, 2002, 277
Revenues and expenditures, 203
Taxation in, 204-207
Tourist information, 173
Web site, 173
Cambodia, description, 538-539
Area codes, 462
Economic indicators, 514
Economy, 539
Geography, 538
Government, 539
Health indicators, 481
Major cities, 538
People, 538-539
Population in U.S., 299
Population indicators, 475
Time zones, 462
Cameroon, description, 539-540
Area codes, 462
Economic indicators, 514
Economy, 540
Geography, 539
Government, 539-540

Health indicators, 481
Major cities, 539
People, 539
Population indicators, 475
Time zones, 462
Campaign finance reform, 26-27
Canada, description, 540-543
Area codes, 462, 804-805
Currency exchange rates, 505
Economic indicators, 514
Economy, 540
Geography, 540
Government, 540
Health indicators, 481
Holidays in, 43
Major cities, 540
Motor vehicle production, 408
Nuclear power generation, 497
People, 540
Population in U.S., 299
Population indicators, 475
Time zones, 462
Traffic deaths, 408
U.S. immigrants from, 295
Cancer
Death rates, 375
New cases and deaths, by site and sex, 375
Survival rates, by race and site, 374
Warning signs, 375
Worldwide, 480-484
Cannes Film Festival, 818
Canyon, 447
Cape Verde, description, 543
Area codes, 462
Economic indicators, 514
Economy, 543
Geography, 543
Government, 543
Health indicators, 481
Major cities, 543
People, 543
Population indicators, 475
Time zones, 462
Capital consumption adjustment, 316-317
Capital gain, definition, 344
Capital Instruments, 331-332
Capital loss, definition, 344
Capital Planning Commission, National, 138
Capital punishment, 314-315
Executions by race, 314
Executions by state, 315
Race and, 314-315
Capitol, Architect of, 125
Carbon dioxide emissions, worldwide, 777
Cardiovascular operations, U.S., 371
Caribbean
Birth rate, 475
Death rate, 475
Fertility rate, 475
Life expectancy, 475
Percent urban, 475
Population indicators, 475
Population, 2000, 475
Population, percentage of world, 472
U.S. immigrants from, 295
Carolingians, 441
Cars
Fatalities, 408
Fuel efficiency of, 411
Production, world, 408
Registrations, by state, 410
Registrations, world, 409
Top selling, U.S., 411
Traffic deaths, 408
Carter, Jimmy
Administration, 119
Biography, 97
Election, 108-109
Casualties in Iraq War, 18
Catholic schools in the U.S., 357
Catholics (see Roman Catholic Church)
Cayman Islands, 706
CD (see Certificates of deposit)
Celsius scale (temp.), 769
Census, Bureau of the , 132
Census, U.S., 2000, 260-265
Accuracy of, 260-268
Undercount in, 265-267
Centers for Disease Control and Prevention (CDC), 133
Central African Republic, description, 543-544
Area codes, 462
Economic indicators, 514
Economy, 543-544
Geography, 543
Government, 543
Health indicators, 481
Major cities, 543
People, 543
Population indicators, 475
Time zones, 462
Central America
Birth rate, 475
Common Market (CACM), 513-514
Death rate, 475
Energy production/ consumption, 494, 496
Fertility rate, 475
Life expectancy, 475
Nuclear power generation, 497
Percent urban, 475
Population, 2000, 475
U.S. immigrants from, 295
Central Intelligence Agency (CIA), 136
Central Processing Unit, 796
Certificates of deposit, 331
Chad, description, 544-545
Area codes, 462
Economic indicators, 514
Economy, 544
Geography, 544
Government, 544
Health indicators, 481
Major cities, 544
People, 544
Population indicators, 475
Time zones, 462
***Charles River Bridge v. Warren Bridge* (1837), 120**
Charleston, W.Va.
Tax burdens in, 242
Charlotte, N.C., description, 214
Area codes, 804-805
Government, 214
Location, 214
Population, 214
Population by race/Hispanic origin, 235
Population, 1980-2000, 238
Rents in, 290
Tax burdens in, 242
Terrain and climate, 214
Visitor information, 214
Web site, 214
Chat line "talk", 808
Chemistry, 746-752
Major Discoveries in Chemistry, 747
Periodic table of elements, 748
Properties, abundance and discovery of the elements, 749-752
Chess, 882
Cheyenne, Wyo.
Tax burdens in, 242
Tax progressivity in, 240
Chicago, Ill., description, 214
Area codes, 804-805
Black population in, 271
Government, 215
Hispanic population in , 273
Housing prices in, 290
Location, 214
Population, 214
Population by race/Hispanic origin, 235
Population, 1980-2000, 238
Rents in, 290
Tax burdens in, 242
Terrain and climate, 214
Visitor information, 215
Web site, 215
Child care feeding program, 160
Childbearing, women and, current trends, 280-282
Children
Adoption, 282
AFDC, 156
Adolescents with AIDS, 376
Childhood deaths, causes, 484
Death and death rates, 378
Food assistance programs for, 160
Head Start, 161-162
Heart disease death rates, 373
Living arrangements of, 286
Suicide and, 379
Vaccines and immunization schedule, 382
Chile, description, 545-546
2002-03 Events, 22
Area codes, 462
Economic indicators, 514
Economy, 545
Geography, 545
Government, 545
Health indicators, 481
Major cities, 545
People, 545
Population in U.S., 299
Population indicators, 475
Time zones, 462
China, description, 546-549
2002-03 Events, v, 24, 32-33
Area codes, 462
Birth rate, 475
Currency exchange rates, 505
Death rate, 475
Dynasties and Emperors of, 444-445
Economic indicators, 514
Economy, 546
Geography, 546
Government, 546
Health indicators, 481
History, 418, 421, 423
Major cities, 546
Motor vehicle production, 408
Nuclear power generation, 497
People, 546
Population in U.S., 299
Population indicators, 475
Population, percentage of world, 472
Time zones, 462
Traffic deaths, 408
U.S. immigrants from, 295
Chinese calendar, 45
Chinese folk religions, 490
Chinese lang., 493
Christian Churches and Churches of Christ (U.S.), 403
Christian Holy Days, 44
Christian Science (see Church of Christ, Scientist)
Christianity, description, 487-498
History, 420, 421-422, 425-426, 429-430
Popes, chronological listing of , 445-446
in World, 487-498
in U.S., 401-406
Christmas, 42, 44
Christmas Island, 698
Chronologies
Astronomy and Space, 716-717
Chemistry, 747
Earth sciences, 740
Environment, 773
Geologic time scale, 739
Life sciences, 761
Mathematics, 765
Physics, 753-754
U.S. History, 68-85
United Nations, 712-715
World religions, 490-498
Church of Christ, Scientist (U.S.), 403
Churches of Christ, 403
Churches of the Brethren, 406
Cigarettes
Adult smokers, 385
Bureau of ATF, 135
Consumption, U.S., 385
Health effects, 385
Cincinnati, Ohio
Area codes, 804-805
Black population in, 271
Climate in, 470
Cost of living index
Housing prices in, 290
Rents in, 290
Cinematography, Academy Awards for, 816-817
Circulatory diseases, 480
Cities, U.S., 211-257
Area codes, 804-805
Climate of selected, 470
Cost of living index in, 243
Cost of living index in selected U.S. cities, 243
Fastest declining, 241
Fastest growing, 241
50 largest, 212-230
Land area of, 231-234
Largest in each state, 169-203
Mayors: 20 best paid, 1998, 243
Population by race and Hispanic origin, 2000, 235-238
Population change in 75 largest, 238-239
Population change, 1970-2000, and density of, 231-234
Population of 50 largest, 240
by Population size, 234
Tax burdens in, 242
Tax progressivity in, 240
Cities, world
Area codes of selected, 462-464
Climate of selected, 471
Time zones of selected, 462-464
Citizenship Day, 42
Civil Rights Cases (1883), 121
Civil Rights, U.S. Commission on , 139
Civil War, 150
Clams, endangered in U.S., 786
Class (bio.), 759
Cleveland, Grover
Administration (1893–97), 116
Biography, 91-92
Election, 104, 105
Cleveland, Ohio, description, 215
Area codes, 804-805
Black population in, 271
Climate in, 470
Cost of living index, 243
Government, 215
Housing prices in, 290
Location, 215
Population, 215
Population by race/Hispanic origin, 235
Population, 1980-2000, 238
Rents in, 290
Terrain and climate, 215
Visitor information, 215
Web site, 215
Climate, definition, 447, 467

Beaufort wind scale, 469
El Niño and La Niña, 466-498
Hurricanes, costliest in U.S. history, 467
of U.S. cities, selected, 470
Weather words, 467-501
Wind-chill factor, 466
World cities, selected, 471
World climates, 465-498
Clinton, Bill
Administration, 119
Biography, 98-99
Cabinet, 132
Election, 109-110
Coal, description, 363, 495
Top producers, 495
World consumption, 496
World production, 494
Coast Guard, U.S., description, 135, 150
and Homeland security, 26
Major commands, 149
Cocaine, 383-384
Cocos (Keeling) Islands, 698-699
***Cohens v. Virginia* (1821), 120**
Coincident economic indicators, 323-324
Cold front, definition, 467
Cold War, 438-439
College Sports, 869-878
Basketball, 873-874
Football, 869-872
NCAA, 869-878
Colleges and Universities
Average Cost, 358
College entrance examinations, 358-359
Degrees conferred, 360
Enrollment, 355
Majors of incoming freshmen, 358
Number, 355
Colombia, description, 549-550
2002-03 Events, 23
Area codes, 462
Economic indicators, 514
Economy, 549
Geography, 549
Government, 549
Health indicators, 481
Major cities, 549
People, 549
Population in U.S., 299
Population indicators, 475
Time zones, 462
U.S. immigrants from, 295
Colorado, description, 174
Area codes, 804-805
Business, 174
Cities, major, population of, 174
Crime in, 306
Education expenditures per pupil, 356
Educational attainment, 359
Elected officials, 174
Elevations, 57
Emblems, 174
Executions in, 315
Famous natives, 174
Farms in, 303
Fortune 500 companies, 174
Health care quality, 368
Land area, 174
Land cover and use, 55
Memorable events, 174
Noteworthy places, 174
Parks and recreation areas, 53
Persons below poverty level, 321
Population by race and Hispanic origin, 269
Population by race/national origin, 174
Population estimates, 1990-2000, 169
Population, foreign-born, 297
Prisoners in, 313
Public school enrollment, 356
Resident population and population change, 261
Resident population by age, 2002, 277
Revenues and expenditures, 203
Taxation in, 204-207
Tourist information, 174
Web site, 174
Colorado springs, Colo., description, 215
Area codes, 804-805
Government, 215
Location, 215
Population, 215
Population by race/Hispanic origin, 235
Population, 1980-2000, 238
Rents in, 290
Terrain and climate, 215
Visitor information, 215
Web site, 215
Columbia, S.C.
Population by race/Hispanic origin, 235
Tax burdens in, 242
Tax progressivity in, 240
Columbus Day, 42
Columbus, Ohio, description, 215-216
Area codes, 804-805
Climate in, 470
Government, 216
Location, 216
Population, 216
Population by race/Hispanic origin, 235
Population, 1980-2000, 238
Rents in, 290
Tax burdens in, 242
Terrain and climate, 216
Visitor information, 216
Web site, 216
Combat forces, U.S., 147-154
Commandments, Ten, 492
Commerce, U.S. Dept. of, description, 132
Employment and budget outlays, 141
Commercial banks, 327-328
Commercial paper, 330
Commission (see rest of entry)
Commodity Futures Trading Commission (CFTC), 136
Common Market for Eastern and Southern Africa, 512
Common stock, definition, 344
Commonwealth (international organization), 715
Commonwealth of Independent States (CIS), 715
Communications Commission, Federal (FCC), 137
Community Service, Corporation for National, 136
Commuter rail systems in the U.S., 415
Comoros, description, 550
Area codes, 462
Economic indicators, 514
Economy, 550
Geography, 550
Government, 550
Health indicators, 481
Major cities, 550
People, 550
Time zones, 462
Compensation costs for production workers, 510
Computers, 795-802
Games, 400
Websites about, 811
Computer-aided design, 796
Confucianism, 490
Congo, Democratic Republic of the, description, 551-552
Area codes, 462
Economic indicators, 514
Economy, 551
Geography, 551-707
Government, 551-707
Health indicators, 481
Major cities, 551-707
People, 551-707
Population indicators, 475
Time zones, 462
Congo, Republic of the, description, 552-553
Area codes, 462
Economic indicators, 514
Economy, 552
Geography, 552
Government, 552
Health indicators, 481
Major cities, 552
People, 552
Population indicators, 475
Time zones, 462
Congress, U.S.
2002-03 Events, 19, 27, 29
108th Congress, 126
Budget process, 142
House offices, 126
How a bill becomes law, 125
Library of Congress, 125
Reapportionment from 2000 Census, 261
Congressional Budget Office (CBO), 125
Connecticut, description, 174-175
Area codes, 804-805
Business, 175
Cities, major, population of, 175
Crime in, 306
Education expenditures per pupil, 356
Educational attainment, 359
Elected officials, 174
Elevations, 57
Emblems, 174
Executions in, 315
Famous natives, 175
Farms in, 303
Fortune 500 companies, 175
Health care quality, 368
Land area, 174
Land cover and use, 55
Memorable events, 175
Noteworthy places, 175
Nuclear plants in, 364
Parks and recreation areas, 53
Persons below poverty level, 321
Population by race and Hispanic origin, 269
Population by race/national origin, 175
Population estimates, 1990-2000, 169
Population, foreign-born, 297
Prisoners in, 313
Public school enrollment, 356
Resident population and population change, 261
Resident population by age, 2002, 277
Revenues and expenditures, 203
Taxation in, 204-207
Tourist information, 175
Web site, 175
Conservation Laws, 755
Constellations, 724-725
Constitution, U.S., 59-66
Amendments to, 64-66
Text of, 59-64
Construction industries
Earnings in, 335
Establishments with employees and payrolls, 339
Consumer credit outstanding, 328
Consumer expenditure
Consumer expenditure statistics presented, 317
Consumer Price Index (CPI), 324
Consumer prices, 324
Consumer Product Safety Commission (CPSC), 136
Continental drift theory, 447
Continental shelf, 447
Continents, definition, 447
Area and population, 448
Elevations of, 449
Contraception, definition, 478
Convertible bond, definition, 344
Convictions, as percent of crimes committed, 311
Cook Islands, description, 703-704
Area codes, 462
Health indicators, 481
Population indicators, 475
Time zones, 462
Cookie (Internet term), 808
Coolidge, Calvin
Biography, 93
Election, 106
Core, 738
Corporate bonds, definition, 344
Corporations, *Fortune* 100 largest, 349
Corpus Christi, 44
Corrections, 310-313
Incarceration rates by state, 313
Jails and prisons, 312
Prison and race, 310
Probation and parole, 312-313
Cost of living index (see Consumer Price Index)
Costa Rica, description, 553
Area codes, 462
Economic indicators, 514
Economy, 553
Geography, 553
Government, 553
Health indicators, 481
Major cities, 553
People, 553
Population in U.S., 299
Population indicators, 475
Time zones, 462
Cote d'Ivoire (see Ivory Coast)
Council (see rest of entry)
Counties
Personal income of selected, 321
Counties, U.S., 258-259
50 largest, by population, 1980-90, 258
75 largest, by population, 1990-98, 259
Types of government, 211
Courts, U.S.
U.S. Courts of Appeals, 124-125
U.S. District Courts, 125
U.S. Supreme Court, 124
Cove, 447
Crater, 447
Credit Union Administration, National (NCUA), 138
Credit unions, definition, 330
Number and deposits of, 328
Crime, 305-315
Arrests for, 311
Rate, by state, 306

Reported crime, by type of offense, 305
Serious crime, 305-309
Victims, 309
Violent crime in other nations, 308-309
Criticism
National Book Critics Circle Award for, 834-835
Pulitzer Prizes for, 846
Croatia, description, 553-554
Area codes, 462
Declining population, 472
Economic indicators, 514
Economy, 553
Geography, 553
Government, 553
Health indicators, 481
Major cities, 553
People, 553
Population indicators, 475
Time zones, 462
Cross-Country, NCAA champions, 875
Crude oil
Top producers, 495
World consumption, 496
World production, 494, 495
Crust, 738-739
Crustaceans, endangered in U.S., 786
Cuba, description, 554-555
Area codes, 462
Economic indicators, 514
Economy, 554
Geography, 554
Government, 554
Health indicators, 481
Major cities, 554
People, 554
Population in U.S., 299
Population indicators, 475
Time zones, 462
U.S. immigrants from, 295
Cubic Measure, 768
Currency exchange rates, by nation, 505
Current Electricity, 756
Cyberspace, 809
Cycling: Tour de France winners, 881
Cyclone, definition, 467
Cyprus, description, 555-556
Area codes, 462
Economic indicators, 514
Economy, 555
European Union membership, 509
Geography, 555
Government, 555
Health indicators, 481
Major cities, 555
People, 555
Population indicators, 475
Time zones, 462
Czars of Russia, 443-444
Czech Republic, description, 556-557
Area codes, 462
Declining population, 472
Economic indicators, 514
Economy, 556
European Union membership, 509
Geography, 556
Government, 556
Health indicators, 481
Major cities, 556
Motor vehicle production, 408
Nuclear power generation, 497
People, 556
Population indicators, 475
Population in U.S., 299
Time zones, 462
U.S. immigrants from, 295

D

Dallas, Texas, description, 216
Area codes, 804-805
Black population in, 271
Climate in, 470
Cost of living index, 243
Crime in, 307, 308
Government, 216
Hispanic population in , 273
Housing prices in, 290
Location, 216
Population, 216
Population by race/Hispanic origin, 235
Population, 1980-2000, 239
Rents in, 290
Terrain and climate, 216
Visitor information, 216
Web site, 216
Dams, world's largest by volume, 455
Dark Ages, 421-422
***Dartmouth College v. Woodward* (1819), 120**
Dasahra, 47
Database, 796
Day, 37
Daylight Saving Time, 42
Daytona 500, 907
Death
Births and, world, 472
Causes of, 379, 480
Childhood, 484-498
Death rates, 378
Life expectancy, 380, 381, 382
Maternal, 483-498
Motor vehicle, 381-382
Numbers of deaths, 378
Suicide, 379-380
in U.S., 279
Death rate, definition, 478
from Cancer, 375
from Heart disease, 373
by Nation, 475-477
by Sex and Race, 377
in U.S., 279, 378
Debentures, definition, 345
Debt, External, by Region and Nation, 503
Debt, government, 332-333
Decimals, fractions and, 766
Declaration of Independence, 58-59
Signers of, 60
Defense contractors
Awards by state, 154
Top 10, U.S., 152
Defense establishment, 146-147
Budget outlays for, 146
Contractors, top 10, 152
Employees, 147
Defense Nuclear Facilities Safety Board, 136-137
Defense, U.S. Dept. of (DOD), description, 133
Budget outlays for, 146
Chain of command, 147
Contract awards, by state, 154
Contractors, top 10, 152
Joint Chiefs of Staff, Chairmen, 147
Payroll, by state, 154
Personnel, by state, 154
Strategic offensive forces, 152
Deficits and the debt, 332
Degree-days, definition, 467
Delaware, description, 175
Area codes, 804-805
Black population in, 270
Business, 175
Cities, major, population of, 175
Crime in, 306
Education expenditures per pupil, 356
Educational attainment, 359
Elected officials, 175
Elevations, 57
Emblems, 175
Executions in, 315
Famous natives, 175
Farms in, 303
Fortune 500 companies, 175
Health care quality, 368
Land area, 175
Land cover and use, 55
Memorable events, 175
Noteworthy places, 175
Parks and recreation areas, 53
Persons below poverty level, 321
Population by race and Hispanic origin, 269
Population by race/national origin, 175
Population estimates, 1990-2000, 169
Population, foreign-born, 297
Prisoners in, 313
Public school enrollment, 356
Resident population and population change, 261
Resident population by age, 1999, 277
Revenues and expenditures, 203
Taxation in, 204-207
Tourist information, 175
Web site, 175
Delta, 447
Democrats
Presidential primary, 27-28
in State legislatures, 206
Denmark, description, 557-558
Area codes, 462
Currency exchange rates, 505
Economic indicators, 514
Economy, 557
European Union membership, 509
Geography, 557
Government, 557
Health indicators, 481
Major cities, 557
People, 557
Population in U.S., 299
Population indicators, 475
Time zones, 462
Traffic deaths, 408
U.S. immigrants from, 295
***Dennis v. United States* (1951), 122**
Denver, Colo., description, 216
Area codes, 804-805
Black population in, 271
Climate in, 470
Cost of living index, 243
Crime in, 307, 308
Government, 216
Housing prices in, 290
Location, 216
Population, 216
Population by race/Hispanic origin, 235
Population, 1980-2000, 239
Tax burdens in, 242
Terrain and climate, 216
Visitor information, 216
Web site, 216
Department (see rest of entry)
Deposit Insurance Corporation, Federal (FDIC), 137
Deposit-taking institutions, 328
Depression (weather), definition, 468
Des Moines, Iowa
Crime in, 308
Population by race/Hispanic origin, 235
Tax burdens in, 242
Desert, definition, 447
World's largest, 450
Detroit, Mich., description, 216-217
Area codes, 804-805
Black population in, 271
Cost of living index, 243
Crime in, 307, 308
Government, 217
Hispanic population in , 273
Housing prices in, 290
Location, 217
Population, 217
Population by race/Hispanic origin, 235
Population, 1980-2000, 239
Tax burdens in, 242
Terrain and climate, 217
Visitor information, 217
Web site, 217
Developed countries, definition, 478
Population, percentage of world, 472
Unemployment rates, 1975-2000, 511
Developing countries, definition, 478
Net foreign direct investment, 503
Population, percentage of world, 472
Dew point, definition, 468
Digital Video Recorders (see Personal Video Recorder)
Dipavali, 47
Disability insurance
Social Security insurance, 155-159
Temporary disability insurance, 156
Disabled persons
Medicaid benefits, 160
Medicare benefits, 157
Social security benefits for, 157
Supplemental insurance benefits for, 159
Discount rates, Federal Reserve Bank of New York, 326
Disease
AIDS, 375-377
Alzheimer's, 378
Cancer, 374
Common Infectious, 373
Heart disease, 373-374
Hepatitis, 377
Sexually transmitted, 377
Treatment of, 378-379
Disk drive, 796
Disposable personal income, 317
Distance, measurement of, 767-768
District of Columbia, description, 175-176
Area codes, 804-805
Business, 176
Crime in, 306
Education expenditures per pupil, 356
Educational attainment, 359
Elected officials, 176
Emblems, 176
Executions in, 315
Famous natives, 176
Fortune 500 companies, 176
Health care quality, 368
Land area, 176
Memorable events, 176
Noteworthy places, 176
Population by race and Hispanic origin, 269
Population by race/national origin, 176
Population estimates, 1990-2000, 169

Population, foreign-born, 297
Prisoners in, 313
Public school enrollment, 356
Resident population and population change, 261
Resident population by age, 1999, 277
Tourist information, 176
Web site, 176
Divestiture, definition, 345
Dividends, definition, 345
Divorces
Marriages and, 279
Rates, 279
by Sex and race/Hispanic origin, 281, 282, 283
Djibouti, description, 558
Area codes, 462
Economic indicators, 514
Economy, 558
Geography, 558
Government, 558
Health indicators, 481
Major cities, 558
People, 558
Population indicators, 475
Time zones, 462
Doctorate degrees conferred, 1950-2000, 360
Dollar
Foreign exchange rates, 505
Purchasing power of, 324
Domain, 809
Dominica, description, 558-559
Economic indicators, 514
Economy, 558
Geography, 558-707
Government, 558-707
Health indicators, 481
Major cities, 558-707
People, 558-707
Dominican Republic, description, 559
Economic indicators, 514
Economy, 559
Geography, 559
Government, 559
Health indicators, 481
Major cities, 559
People, 559
Population in U.S., 299
Population indicators, 476
U.S. immigrants from, 295
Dow Jones Industrial Average, definition, 345
Download, 809
Drama
Pulitzer Prize for, 849
Tony Awards, 824-827
***Dred Scott v. Sanford* (1857), 120**
Drinking water pollution, 778-779
Drug Control Policy, Office of National, 131
Drug Enforcement Administration (DEA), 134
Drugs and drug abuse (see also Substance abuse)
Cocaine, 383-384
Commonly Abused Drugs, 383
Lifetime experience, 383
Marijuana, 382-383
Prescription, 368
U.S. high school seniors and, 383
Dry natural gas, 494-495
Top producers, 495
DSL, 809
Dune, 447
DVD (Digital Video Discs), 397-398
DVR (see Personal Video Recorder)

E

Earnings
by Age and educational attainment, 335
by Industry group, 335
Federal minimum wage rates, 336
Earth
Composition of, 738-741
Earthquakes, 741
Plate tectonics, 741
Tsunamis (see Earthquakes), 741
Volcanoes, 741-742
Earth Sciences, 738-746
Discoveries in, 740
Earthquakes
Major, 742-743
Measuring, 742
East Timor, description, 559
Economy, 559
Geography, 559
Government, 559
Health Indicators, 481
People, 559
Population indicators, 476
Easter, 44
EC. (see European Union)
Eclipses, 2003, 49
Economic Advisers, Council of, 131
Economic and Social Council (ECOSOC), 709
Economic Community of West African States (ECOWAS), 512
Economic Cooperation and Development, Organization for (OECD), 503
Economic Development Administration (EDA), 132
Economic indicators, 322-324
by Nation, 514-516
Coincident, 323-324
Composite Index of, 323
Lagging, 323-324
Leading, 323
Economic output, change in world , 502
Economic Sciences, Nobel Prizes in, 859-863
Economy, Global, 502-516
ECOSOC, 709
Finance, 505-507
Trade, 507-508
Economy, U.S., 316-338
Ecstasy, 384
Ecuador, 560
2002-03 Events, 23
Area codes, 462
Economic indicators, 514
Economy, 560
Geography, 560
Government, 560
Health indicators, 481
Major cities, 560
People, 560
Population in U.S., 299
Population indicators, 475
Time zones, 462
U.S. immigrants from, 295
Education, 354-360
Government expenditures for, 354
Higher education, 359
Education, U.S. Dept. of, description, 133
Employment and budget outlays, 141
Educational attainment
by Age, sex, region, race and Hispanic origin, 360
by State, 359
Egypt, description, 560-561
Area codes, 462
Economic indicators, 514
Economy, 561
Geography, 560
Government, 560-561
Health indicators, 481
History, 416, 417
Major cities, 560
People, 560
Population in U.S., 299
Population indicators, 475
Time zones, 462
Eisenhower, Dwight D.
Administration, 118
Biography, 95
Election, 107, 108
El Nino, 466-498
El Paso, Texas, description, 217
Area codes, 804-805
Climate in, 470
Crime in, 307, 308
Government, 217
Hispanic population in , 273
Location, 217
Population, 217
Population by race/Hispanic origin, 235
Population, 1980-2000, 239
Rents in, 290
Terrain and climate, 217
Visitor information, 217
Web site, 217
El Salvador, description, 561-562
Area codes, 462
Economic indicators, 514
Economy, 562
Geography, 561
Government, 562
Health indicators, 481
Major cities, 561
People, 561
Population in U.S., 299
Population indicators, 475
Time zones, 462
U.S. immigrants from, 295
Elderly
Cancer death rates, 375
Death amd death rates, 378
Heart disease death rates, 373
Nursing home care and, 368-369
Suicide and, 379
Elderly persons (see Aged persons)
Elderly population
Characteristics of, 278
Growth of, 1900-2050, 276
Numbers of, 277, 278
Election Commission, Federal (FEC), 137
Election Day, 42
Elections, U.S. Presidential, 1796-2000, 101-110
Electoral College, 110-112
Electrical Measure, 771
Electricity, description, 363
Generation, by utilities, 364
Electromagnetic energy, law of, 756-757
Electron, 757
Electronic appliances, sales and penetration in U.S. homes, 395
Electronic media, 393-400
Cable TV, 394-395
Computer and video games, 400
Film, 398-400
Radio, 396
Recording industry, 396-397
Television, 393
Video, 397-398
Elementary schools
Catholic, 357
Enrollment, 354-355
Expenditures, 354
Number, 355
Revenues, 354
Elements (chem.)
Periodic table of, 746-747
Properties of, 749-752
Elevations, by state, 57
Emancipation Proclamation, 67
Emergency Management Agency, Federal (FEMA), 137
Emissions estimates for EPA-monitored pollutants, 776
Emmy Awards, 821-823
Emoticon, 809
Emperors
China, 444-445
Holy Roman Empire, 441
Rome, ancient, 440
Employees
Employment and budget outlays, 141
Federal government, 139-144
Employment
Cost Index (ECI), 323, 324
Federal minimum wage rates, 336
by Major industry, 339-340
Status by race/Hispanic origin, 334
Status, by sex, 334
Employment and Training Administration (Dept. of Labor, 134
Encryption, 809
Endangered species, 782-786
in the United States, 784, 785-786
in the World, 783-784
Endowment for the Arts, National (NEA), 138
Endowment for the Humanities, National (NEH), 138
Energy
Conservation of, 755-756
Measuring, 770-771
Energy, U.S., 361-364
Consumption per capita, 362
Overview, 361
Production and consumption, 361-362
Energy, U.S. Dept. of (DOE), description, 133
Employment and budget outlays, 141
Energy, world, 494-497
Consumption, by region, 496
Consumption, by type, 496
Nuclear power generation, by region and country, 497
Production by region, 494
Production, by source, 497
Top producers by source, 495
England (see also United Kingdom)
Dynasties and Kings of, 442-443
Expansion, 433
English lang., 493
Engraving and Printing, Bureau of, 136
Enlightenment, the, 430-431
Entertainment
Websites , 811
Environment, 772-786
Acid rain, 777-778
Air pollution, 774-777
Endangered species, 782-784
Global warming, 772-774
Habitats, 781
Hazardous waste, 780-781
Major events in the history of the environment, 773
Ozone layer, 774
Rain forests, 781-782
Solid waste, 779-780
Water pollution, 778-779
Wetlands, 782
Environmental Protection Agency
Emissions for EPA-monitored pollutants, 776

Environmental Protection Agency (EPA), 137
Employment and budget outlays, 141
Environmental Quality, Council on, 131
Episcopal Churches (U.S.), 403
Equal Employment Opportunity Commission (EEOC), 137
Equatorial Guinea, description, 562-563
Area codes, 462
Economic indicators, 514
Economy, 562-563
Geography, 562
Government, 562
Health indicators, 481
Major cities, 562
People, 562
Population indicators, 475
Time zones, 462
Equinoxes
2004, 37
Precession of, 37-42
Equity (see Common stock)
Eritrea, description, 563
Area codes, 462
Economic indicators, 514
Economy, 563
Geography, 563
Government, 563
Health indicators, 481
Major cities, 563
People, 563
Population indicators, 475
Time zones, 462
Erosion, 447
Escape velocity, 718
Establishment, definition, 345
Establishments, business, with employees and payroll, 339-340
Estonia, description, 563-564
Area codes, 462
Declining population, 472
Economic indicators, 514
Economy, 564
Geography, 563
Government, 563-564
Health indicators, 481
Major cities, 563
People, 563
Population in U.S., 299
Population indicators, 475
Time zones, 462
Estuary, 447
Ethiopia, description, 564-565
Area codes, 462
Economic indicators, 514
Economy, 564
Geography, 564
Government, 564
Health indicators, 481
Major cities, 564
People, 564
Population in U.S., 299
Population indicators, 475
Time zones, 462
EU (see European Union)
Eurocurrency, definition, 345
Europe
Birth rate, 475
Currency exchange rates, 505
Death rate, 475
Elevation extremes, 449
Energy consumption/production, 494, 496
European Union, 508-512
Fertility rate, 475
Life expectancy, 475
Motor vehicle production, 408
Nuclear power generation, 497
Percent urban, 475
Population indicators, 475
Population, 2000, 475
Population, percentage of world, 472
Traffic deaths, 408
U.S. immigrants from, 295
European Community (see European Union)
European Economic Community (EEC), 509
European Union (EU), 508-512
Economic and Social Committee of, 512
History, 509
Members and applicants, 509
Structure of, 511-512
Evangelical Free Church of America, 405
Evolution of the human family, 762
***Ex Parte Milligan* (1866), 120**
Exchange rates, definition, 505
by Nation, 505
Executive branch , 131-139
Cabinet, 132
Employment, 140
Employment and budget outlays, 141
Executive office of the president, 131-132
Independent establishments, corporations and agencies, 136-139
Salaries, 140
Executive Office of the President, 131-132
Executive schedule (EX), salaries in, 140
Export-Import Bank of the United States, 137
Exports
Largest U.S. merchandise, 506
U.S., in services, by type, 507
World's leading, in merchandise, 504
Exports, U.S.
Agricultural, 302
Express mail, rates for, 167

F

Faeroe Islands, 699
Area codes, 462
Time zones, 462
Fahrenheit scale (temp.), 769
Falkland Islands, 706
Families, definition, 285-286
Money income, 322
Number and average size, 285
Number and percent in poverty, by state, 321
One-parent, 285
Family (bio.), 759
Family income, 317
Fannie Mae mortgage, 331
FAQs (Frequently Asked Questions), 809
Far East
Energy production/.consumption, 494, 496
Nuclear power generation, 497
Fargo, N. Dak.
Tax burdens in, 242
Farm Credit Administration, 137
Farms, U.S.
Marketings, 304
Number and acreage by state, 303
Number, 1850–1999, 302
Population, 302
Production in U.S., 304
Fat Tuesday, 44
Father's Day, 42
FDIC
FDIC-insured banks, 328
Federal (see rest of entry)
Federal Bureau of Investigation (FBI), 134
Federal Deposit Insurance Corporation (FDIC), 137
Federal Election Campaign Act, 112
Federal funds, 331
Federal Government, U.S., 124-168
108th Congress, 126
Budget deficit, 332
Congressional budget process, 142
Debt of, 332-333
Deficits and the debt, 332
Education expenditures, 354
Employees and budget, 1901-2003, 139
Employment and population, 141
Executive branch, 131-139
Glossary of budget terms, 142-144
Health care expenditures, 367-373
Homeless programs funding, 292
Independent establishments, corporations and quasi-official agencies, 136-139
Internal Revenue Service, 163-166
Jobs and salaries, 139-142
Judicial branch, 124-125
Legislative branch, 125
National defense, 146-154
Outlays, 141, 143
Pay systems, 140
Postal Service, 167-168
Receipts by source, 142, 144-145
Social insurance programs, 155-163
Federal Holidays in the U.S., 42
Federal Home Loan Bank System, 330
Federal insurance plans, 369-370
Federal Reserve Act (1913), 325
Federal Reserve Bank, 325-327
and Commercial banks, 327-328
Discount rates, 326
Federal funds and, 325-327
Open market operations, 326
Federal Reserve System, 137, 325-332
Discount rates, 1976-99, 326
Federal Savings and Loan Insurance Corp. (F.S.L.I.C.), 330
Female population
Average earnings by age and educational attainment, 335
Childbearing trends, 280-282
Crime victimization rates, 310
Deaths and death rates of, 378
Divorced persons per 1,000 married persons, 283
Employment status of, 334
Frequency of sexual intercourse, 301
in Armed forces, 153
Life expectancy, 381
Lifetime likelihood of going to prison, 314
Males per 100 females in U.S., 279
Marital status of, 282
Never married, percent, 281
Number of sex partners, 301
Pregnancies of unmarried women, 280
Prisoners, 312
in Selected occupations, 333
Fencing
NCAA Champions, 875
Fermions, 757
Fertility, world, 474-478
Fertility rate
of American women, 279-280
Nations with highest and lowest, 475
by Region and nation, 475-477
Fiction
Best-sellers in America, 390-391
National Book Critics Circle Award for, 833
Nobel Prize in Literature, 866-868
Pulitzer Prize for, 848-849
Fields Medal, 838
Figure Skating
Olympic champions, 903
U.S. Champions, 883
World Champions, 883
Fiji, description, 565-566
Area codes, 462
Economic indicators, 514
Economy, 565
Geography, 565
Government, 565
Health indicators, 481
Major cities, 565
People, 565
Population in U.S., 299
Population indicators, 475
Time zones, 462
File sharing, peer-to-peer, 397
Fillmore, Millard
Administration, 115
Biography, 89
Vice President, 113
Film
Academy Awards, 813-818
American Film Institute Life Achievement Awards, 818
Box-office receipts, 398
Cannes Film Festival, 818
Most popular, by decade, 399
National Film Registry, 819-820
Top-grossing films, 2002, 399
Top-grossing movies of all-time, 400
Final Four (college basketball), 873
Finance
Glossary of terms, 344-347
Websites about, 811
Finance, insurance and real estate industries
Earnings in, 335
Finance, world, 505-507
Balance of payments, 505
Currency exchange rates, 505
World Bank, 504
World Bank Group, 711
Financial terms, glossary of, 344-347
Finland, description, 566-567
Area codes, 462
Currency exchange rates, 505
Economic indicators, 515
Economy, 566
European Union membership, 509
Geography, 566
Government, 566
Health indicators, 481
Major cities, 566
Nuclear power generation, 497

People, 566
Population in U.S., 299
Population indicators, 475
Time zones, 462
Traffic deaths, 408
Firm (bus.), definition, 345
Fiscal year, definition, 142
Fish and Wildlife Service, U.S., 133
Fishes, endangered in U.S., 785
Fjord, 447
Flag Day, 42
***Fletcher v. Peck* (1810), 120**
Floodplain, 447
Florida, description, 176-177
Area codes, 804-805
Black population in, 270
Business, 176
Cities, major, population of, 176
Crime in, 306
Education expenditures per pupil, 356
Educational attainment, 359
Elected officials, 176
Elevations, 57
Emblems, 176
Executions in, 315
Famous natives, 176
Farms in, 303
Fortune 500 companies, 176
Health care quality, 368
Land area, 176
Land cover and use, 55
Memorable events, 176-177
Noteworthy places, 176
Nuclear plants in, 364
Parks and recreation areas, 53
Persons below poverty level, 321
Population by race and Hispanic origin, 269
Population by race/national origin, 176
Population estimates, 1990-2000, 169
Population, foreign-born, 297
Prisoners in, 313
Public school enrollment, 356
Resident population and population change, 261
Resident population by age, 2002, 277
Revenues and expenditures, 203
Taxation in, 204-207
Tourist information, 177
Web site, 177
Food and Agriculture Organization (FAO), 710
Food and Drug Administration, 133
Food assistance programs, 160
Food Stamps, 160
Participants and cost, 160
Football, College, 869
Heisman Trophy winners, 872
NCAA career leaders, 871
NCAA Champions, 869
Rose Bowl, 870
Football, professional (NFL), 923-934
2002 Leaders, 924
All-Time Records, 927
First Round Draft Choices, 2003, 923
Hall of Fame Members, 932-934
Most Valuable Player, 1957-2002, 926
NFL Champions, 1921–66, 928
Number One Draft Picks, 1936–2002, 924-925
Rookie of the Year, 1955–2002, 926
Super Bowl Results, 928-932
Force, measurement of, 770-771
Ford, Gerald R.
Administration, 118
Biography, 96-97
Vice President, 113
Foreign born population (U.S.), 293-300
by Place of birth, 1990, 299
by State, 297
Characteristics of, 293-300
by Region of birth, 300
by Sex and race, 298
Foreign direct investment (FDI), 507
Foreign exchange rates, 505
Foreign Service, description, 134-135
Fort Worth, Texas, description, 217
Area codes, 804-805
Black population in, 271
Cost of living index, 243
Crime in, 307, 308
Government, 217
Housing prices in, 290
Location, 217
Population, 217
Population by race/Hispanic origin, 236
Population, 1980-2000, 239
Rents in, 290
Terrain and climate, 217
Visitor information, 217-218
Web site, 218
***Fortune* 100, 513**
***Fortune* 500 companies**
by State, 169-203
***Fortune* 500 corporations**
by Industry, 348
by Performance, 347
by Size, 349
Fossil fuels, description, 362-363
Foundation on the Arts and the Humanities, National, 138
Fractions and decimals, 766
France, description, 567-569
Area codes, 462
Currency exchange rates, 505
Dynasties and kings of, 442
Economic indicators, 515
Economy, 567
European Union membership, 509
Geography, 567
Government, 567
Health indicators, 481
Major cities, 567
Motor vehicle production, 408
Nuclear power generation, 497
People, 567
Population in U.S., 299
Population indicators, 475
Revolution, 431
Time zones, 462
Traffic deaths, 408
U.S. immigrants from, 295
Franchising, definition, 349-351
Top 50 franchises by number of outlets, 350
Freeware (Internet term), 809
French Antilles
Area codes, 462
Population indicators, 475
Time zones, 462
French Guiana, description, 700
Area codes, 462
Population indicators, 475
Time zones, 462
French lang., 493
French Open (tennis), 916-917
French Polynesia, description, 700
Area codes, 462
Population indicators, 475
Time zones, 462
Fresno, Calif., description, 218
Area codes, 804-805
Crime in, 307, 308
Government, 218
Location, 218
Population, 218
Population by race/Hispanic origin, 236
Population, 1980-2000, 239
Rents in, 290
Terrain and climate, 218
Visitor information, 218
Web site, 218
Fridays (Muslim Holy Day), 46
Friends Churches (U.S.), 406
Front, definition, 468
FTP (File Transfer Protocol), 809
Fuel consumption, U.S., 362
Fuel efficiency of U.S. cars, 411
Fungi, 759
Futures market, definition, 345

G

G.D.P. (see Gross domestic product)
G.N.P. (see Gross national product)
Gabon, description, 569-570
Area codes, 462
Economic indicators, 515
Economy, 570
Geography, 569
Government, 570
Health indicators, 481
Major cities, 569
People, 569-570
Population indicators, 475
Time zones, 462
Galaxies, 727
Gambia, the, description, 570-571
Area codes, 462
Economic indicators, 515
Economy, 570
Geography, 570
Government, 570
Health indicators, 481
Major cities, 570
People, 570
Population indicators, 475
Time zones, 462
Games, computer and video, 400
Garfield, James A.
Administration, 116
Biography, 91
Gasoline
Retail prices, 363
GATT, 508
Gaza Strip, 594
General Accounting Office (GAO), 125
General Agreement on Tariffs and Trade (GATT), 508
(See also WTO)
General schedule (GS), salaries in, 140
General Services Administration (GSA), description, 137
Employment and budget outlays, 141
Genus, 759
Geography, U.S., 50-57
U.S. Geographic Extremes, 50
Geologic Time Scale, 739
Geological Survey, U.S. (Dept. of Interior), 134
Georgia (U.S. State), description, 177
Area codes, 804-805
Black population in, 270
Business, 177
Cities, major, population of, 177
Crime in, 306
Education expenditures per pupil, 356
Educational attainment, 359
Elected officials, 177
Elevations, 57
Emblems, 177
Executions in, 315
Famous natives, 177
Farms in, 303
Fortune 500 companies, 177
Health care quality, 368
Land area, 177
Land cover and use, 55
Memorable events, 177
Noteworthy places, 177
Nuclear plants in, 364
Parks and recreation areas, 53
Persons below poverty level, 321
Population by race and Hispanic origin, 269
Population by race/national origin, 177
Population estimates, 1990-2000, 169
Population, foreign-born, 297
Prisoners in, 313
Public school enrollment, 356
Resident population and population change, 261
Resident population by age, 2002, 277
Revenues and expenditures, 203
Taxation in, 204-207
Tourist information, 177
Web site, 177
Georgia (Nation), description, 571
Area codes, 462
Economic indicators, 515
Economy, 571
Geography, 571
Government, 571
Health indicators, 481
Major cities, 571
People, 571
Population indicators, 475
Time zones, 462
German lang., 493
Germany, description, 571-574
Area codes, 462
Currency exchange rates, 505
Declining population, 472
Economic indicators, 515
Economy, 572
European Union membership, 509
Geography, 571
Government, 572
Health indicators, 481
Hohenzollern, 443
Major cities, 571
Motor vehicle production, 408
Nuclear power generation, 497
People, 572
Population in U.S., 299
Population indicators, 475
Time zones, 462
Traffic deaths, 408
U.S. immigrants from, 295
Gettysburg Address, 67
Ghana, description, 574
Area codes, 462
Economic indicators, 515
Economy, 574
Geography, 574

Government, 574
Health indicators, 481
Major cities, 574
People, 574
Population in U.S., 299
Population indicators, 475
Time zones, 462
***Gibbons v. Ogden* (1824), 120**
Gibraltar, description, 706
Area codes, 462
Population indicators, 475
Time zones, 462
***Gideon v. Wainwright* (1963), 123**
GIF, 809
Gifts for wedding anniversaris, 47
Global capital movement, 506-507
Global economy, 502-516
Global health situation, 478-498
Global military situation, 498-501
Global warming, 772-774
2002-03 Events, 35
Glossaries
Federal budget terms, 142-144
Financial terms, 344-347
Internet terms, 808-810
Output, income and expenditure terms, 316-321
Weather words, 467-498
Gluons, 758
Gold record, definition, 397
Gold standard, definition, 505
Golf, 911
LPGA Champions, 914
LPGA Leading Money Winners, 914
NCAA Champions, 876-877
PGA Champions, 912
PGA leading money winners, 913
Women's Grand Slam Champions, 914
Good Friday, 44
Government (see Federal Government)
Websites about, 811-812
Government debt, 332-333
Government Printing Office (GPO), 125
Government securities, 331
Governors of U.S. states
Salaries, 206
Grammy Awards, 827-829
Grand Slam (tennis), 916-917
Grandparents, living with, 287
Grant, Ulysses S.
Administration, 116
Biography, 90-91
Election, 104
Graphs, mathematical formulas for, 766
Graviton and Higgs particle, 758
Gravity, law of, 754-755
Great Britain (see United Kingdom)
Great Lakes, 54
Greece, description, 574-576
Area codes, 463
Currency exchange rates, 505
Declining population, 472
Economic indicators, 515
Economy, 575
European Union membership, 509
Geography, 574
Government, 575
Health indicators, 481
History, 417-418, 419
Major cities, 574
People, 574-575
Population in U.S., 299
Population indicators, 476
U.S. immigrants from, 295
Green Bay, Wis.
Crime in, 308
Greenland, description, 699-700
Area codes, 463
Health indicators, 481
Population indicators, 475
Greenmail, definition, 345
Greensboro, N.C.
Crime in, 307, 308
Greenwich mean time (GMT)., 49
Gregorian calendar, 38-49
Grenada, description, 576
Economic indicators, 515
Economy, 576
Geography, 576
Government, 576
Major cities, 576
People, 576
Population in U.S., 299
***Griswold v. Connecticut* (1965), 123**
Gross domestic product (G.D.P.), definition, 317
Agriculture's share in, by country, 514-516
Composition of, 316
in Current and constant dollars, 1960-99, 316
G.D.P. Deflator, 325
Gross national product (G.N.P.), definition, 317
by Country, 514-516
Health care as a percent of, by nation, 368
Highest and lowest by country, 502
per Capita, by type of economy, 502
per Capita, by world region, 502
Gross state product (G.S.P.), definition, 317
by State, 169-203
Ground Zero rebulding, 28-29
Groundhog Day, 43
Group of Seven (G-7), 503
Growth rate (population), definition, 478
Guadeloupe, description, 700-701
Area codes, 463
Health indicators, 481
Population indicators, 475
Guam, description, 207-208
Area codes, 463
Elevations, 57
Health indicators, 481
Population, 207
Population in U.S., 299
Population indicators, 475
Guatemala, description, 576-577
Area codes, 463
Economic indicators, 515
Economy, 576
Geography, 576
Government, 576
Health indicators, 481
Major cities, 576
People, 576
Population in U.S., 299
Population indicators, 476
U.S. immigrants from, 295
Guinea, description, 577
Area codes, 463
Economic indicators, 515
Economy, 577
Geography, 577
Government, 577
Health indicators, 481
Major cities, 577
People, 577
Population indicators, 476
Guinea-Bissau, description, 577-578
Area codes, 463
Economic indicators, 515
Economy, 578
Geography, 577
Government, 578
Health indicators, 481
Major cities, 577
People, 577-578
Population indicators, 476
Guyana, description, 578
Area codes, 463
Economic indicators, 515
Economy, 578
Geography, 578
Government, 578
Health indicators, 481
Major cities, 578
People, 578
Population indicators, 476
Gymnastics
NCAA Champions, 875
Olympic champions, 898

H

Habitats, 781
Habsburgs
Austrian, 443
Holy Roman Empire, 441
Haiti, description, 579
Area codes, 463
Economic indicators, 515
Economy, 579
Geography, 579
Government, 579
Health indicators, 482
Major cities, 579
People, 579
Population in U.S., 299
Population indicators, 476
U.S. immigrants from, 295
Halloween, 43
Halls of Fame
Baseball, 957-962
Basketball, 939-941
Pro Football, 932-934
Hanukkah, 45
Harding, Warren G.
Administration, 117
Biography, 93
Election, 106
Harrison, Benjamin
Administration (1889–93), 116
Biography, 92
Election, 105
Harrison, William Henry
Administration, 115
Biography, 88
Election, 102
Hartford, Conn.
Crime in, 307, 308
Hawaii, description, 177-178
Area codes, 804-805
Business, 178
Cities, major, population of, 178
Crime in, 306
Education expenditures per pupil, 356
Educational attainment, 359
Elected officials, 177
Elevations, 57
Emblems, 177
Executions in, 315
Famous natives, 178
Farms in, 303
Fortune 500 companies, 178
Health care quality, 368
Land area, 177
Land cover and use, 55
Memorable events, 178
Noteworthy places, 178
Parks and recreation areas, 53
Persons below poverty level, 321
Population by race and Hispanic origin, 269
Population by race/national origin, 177-178
Population estimates, 1990-2000, 169
Population, foreign-born, 297
Prisoners in, 313
Public school enrollment, 356
Resident population and population change, 261
Resident population by age, 1999, 277
Revenues and expenditures, 203
Taxation in, 204-207
Tourist information, 178
Web site, 178
Hayes, Rutherford B.
Administration, 116
Biography, 91
Election, 104
Hazardous waste
Superfund sites, 781
Waste sites, by state, 780
Head Start, 161-162
Health and Human Services, U.S. Dept. of (HHS), description, 133
Employment and budget outlays, 141
Health and Medicine, U.S., 365-385
2002-03 News, 34-36
Websites about, 811
Health care
Expenditures as percent of GNP for selected countries, 368
Expenditures for, U.S., 367
Health insurance, U.S., 369-371
Health Maintenance Organizations (HMOs), 370-371
People with and without insurance, by state, 370
Quality of, 367
Quality, by state, 368
Spending, by category, 368
Uninsured, 371
Health Care Financing Administration (HCFA), 133
Health insurance, 369-385
Americans without, 370
Health, National Institutes of (NIH), 133
Health, world, 478-486
AIDS, 484-498
Cancer, 480-498
Childhood deaths, 484-498
Circulatory disease, 480-498
Global situation, 478-498
Indicators, by nation, 481-483
Maternal deaths, 483-498
Smoking, 480-498
Heart Disease
Cardiovascular operations in U.S., 371
Death rates from, 373
Heart attacks, 374
Strokes and bypass surgery, 374
***Heart of Atlanta Motel, Inc. v. United States* (1964), 123**
Heating oil, retail prices, 363
Heisenberg's uncertainty principle, 757
Heisman Trophy, 872
Hepatitis, 377
Heroin, 384
Higgs particle, 758
High schools (see Secondary schools)
High, definition, 468
High-yield/junk bond, definition, 346
Higher Education, 359 (see also Colleges and Universities)
Highway Administration, Federal (FHWA), 135
Highway Traffic Safety Administration, National , 135
Hindi lang., 493
Hindu Year, 46-47

Hinduism, description, 488-498
Hispanic Population, description, 272-273
in Armed forces, 153
Below poverty level, 322
Divorced persons per 1,000 married persons, 283
Employment status, 334
Growth of, 272-273
in Largest U.S. Cities, 273
Marital status, 281
of Metropolitan areas, 272
Money income of families, 322
of U.S., 269
of U.S. cities, 235-238
of U.S. MSAs, 2000, 250-255
One-parent families, 286
by Region and Origin, 273
Resident population by state, 269
in Selected occupations, 333
by State, 169-203
States with largest populations, 273
in Work force, 333
Historic Documents, U.S., 58-67
Constitution, 59-66
Declaration of Independence, 58-59
Emancipation Proclamation, 67
Gettysburg Address, 67
Pledge of Allegiance, 67
History
Chronology of U.S., 68-85
Pulitzer Prize for, 850
U.S., 58-123
World, 416-439
HIV (see AIDS)
Infections (by world region), 485
Hockey (see Ice Hockey, professional)
Hohenzollern dynasty, 443
Holidays and Holy Days, 42-49
Christian, 44
Federal, in the U.S., 42
Jewish, 45-46
Muslim, 46
Holiness Churches (U.S.), 403
Holy (Maundy) Thursday, 44
Holy Days of Obligation, 44-45
Holy Roman Empire, 441
Holy Saturday, 44
Holy See, description, 579-580
Economy, 580
Geography, 579
Government, 579-580
Major cities, 579
People, 579
Home page, 809
Homeland Security, U.S. Dept. of, 26
Homeless, 291-292
Federal funding for, 292
Housing for, 161
Number, U.S., 291-292
Homeownership rates, U.S., 288
Homicide, guns, and young people, 309
Homosexuality in U.S., 300
2002-03 News, 31
Honduras, description, 580-581
Area codes, 463
Economic indicators, 515
Economy, 580
Geography, 580
Government, 580
Health indicators, 482
Major cities, 580
People, 580
Population in U.S., 299
Population indicators, 476
Hong Kong
2002-03 Events, 23-24
Area codes, 463
Currency exchange rates, 505
Economic indicators, 515
Health indicators, 482
Population indicators, 476
Population in U.S., 299
U.S. immigrants from, 295
Honolulu, Hawaii, description, 218
Area codes, 804-805
Climate in, 470
Crime in, 307, 308
Government, 218
Location, 218
Population, 218
Population by race/Hispanic origin, 236
Population, 1980-2000, 239
Rents in, 290
Tax burdens in, 242
Terrain and climate, 218
Visitor information, 218
Web site, 218
Hoover, Herbert
Administration, 117
Biography, 93-94
Election, 106
Horse Racing (see Thoroughbred Racing)
Hospital insurance, 157
Hospitals, 368
Admissions, 369
Facilities, 369
House of Representatives, U.S.
Address and phone number, 126
Officers, 126
Reapportionment from 2000 Census, 261
Salaries and allowances, 140
Speakers of, 113
Household income, definition, 318
Households, definition, 284
with selected Electronic appliances, 395
Growth and change, 285
Number and average size, 284
Unmarried couple, 284
Housing and Urban Development, U.S. Dept. of (HUD), description, 133
Employment and budget outlays, 141
Housing Finance Board, Federal, 137
Housing, U.S., 287-292
Characteristics of recent home buyers, 291
Costs, 290-291
Fair-market rents, selected MSAs, 290
Growth, 288-289
for the Homeless, 161
Homeownership rates, 288
Sales prices, 288, 289
Subsidies, 161
Units, by type and year built, 287
for Veterans, 163
Houston, Texas, description, 218
Area codes, 804-805
Black population in, 271
Climate in, 470
Cost of living index, 243
Crime in, 307, 308
Government, 218
Hispanic population in , 273
Housing prices in, 290
Location, 218
Population, 218
Population by race/Hispanic origin, 236
Population, 1980-2000, 239
Rents in, 290
Tax burdens in, 242
Terrain and climate, 218
Visitor information, 218-220
Web site, 218
How a bill becomes law, 125
How to contact your senator or representative, 126
Howland Island (see Baker and Howland Islands)
HTML (Hyper Text Markup Language), 809
HTTP (Hyper Text Transport Protocol), 809
Human family, evolution of, 762
Human genome project, 760-764
Humans
Classifying, 760
Elements in, 763
Hungary, description, 581-582
Area codes, 463
Declining population, 472
Economic indicators, 515
Economy, 581
European Union membership, 509
Geography, 581
Government, 581
Health indicators, 482
Major cities, 581
Nuclear power generation, 497
People, 581
Population in U.S., 299
Population indicators, 476
Traffic deaths, 408
U.S. immigrants from, 295
Hurricane, definition, 468
Worst in U.S. History, 467
Hussein, Saddam, 17-19
Hydroelectric power, 496
Net generation of electricity, 364
Top producers, 495
World consumption, 496
World production, 494
Hydrosphere (geo.), 739
Hyperlink, 809
Hypertext, 809

I

Ice Hockey, NCAA champions, 875
Ice Hockey, Olympic, 901
Ice Hockey, professional (NHL), 942-947
2002-03 final standings, 943
2002-03 top scorers, 943
All-time scoring leaders, 944
Calder Trophy winners, 1933–2003, 947
Hart Trophy winners, 1924–2003, 944
Norris Trophy winners, 1954–2003, 946
Ross Trophy winners, 1918–2003, 945
Smythe Trophy winners, 1965–2003, 945
Stanley Cup champions, 1917-2003, 942
Stanley Cup Playoffs 2002-2003, 943
Iceland, description, 582
Area codes, 463
Economic indicators, 515
Economy, 582
Geography, 582
Government, 582
Health indicators, 482
Major cities, 582
People, 582
Population indicators, 476
Id al-Adha, 46
Id al-Fitr, 46
Idaho, description, 178
Area codes, 804-805
Business, 178
Cities, major, population of, 178
Crime in, 306
Education expenditures per pupil, 356
Educational attainment, 359
Elected officials, 178
Elevations, 57
Emblems, 178
Executions in, 315
Famous natives, 178
Farms in, 303
Fortune 500 companies, 178
Health care quality, 368
Land area, 178
Land cover and use, 55
Memorable events, 178
Noteworthy places, 178
Parks and recreation areas, 53
Persons below poverty level, 321
Population by race and Hispanic origin, 269
Population by race/national origin, 178
Population estimates, 1990-2000, 169
Population, foreign-born, 297
Prisoners in, 313
Public school enrollment, 356
Resident population and population change, 261
Resident population by age, 2002, 277
Revenues and expenditures, 203
Taxation in, 204-207
Tourist information, 178
Web site, 178
Illicit Drugs (see Drugs and drug abuse)
Illinois, description, 178-179
Area codes, 804-805
Black population in, 270
Business, 179
Cities, major, population of, 178-179
Crime in, 306
Education expenditures per pupil, 356
Educational attainment, 359
Elected officials, 178
Elevations, 57
Emblems, 178
Executions in, 315
Famous natives, 179
Farms in, 303
Fortune 500 companies, 179
Health care quality, 368
Land area, 178
Land cover and use, 55
Memorable events, 179
Noteworthy places, 179
Nuclear plants in, 364
Parks and recreation areas, 53
Persons below poverty level, 321
Population by race and Hispanic origin, 269
Population by race/national origin, 178
Population estimates, 1990-2000, 169
Population, foreign-born, 297
Prisoners in, 313
Public school enrollment, 356
Resident population and population change, 261
Resident population by age, 2002, 277

Revenues and expenditures, 203
Taxation in, 204-207
Tourist information, 179
Web site, 179
Immigration and Naturalization Service (INS), 26, 134
***Immigration and Naturalization Service v. Chadha* (1983), 123**
Immigration, U.S., 293-300
as percentage of population growth, 293
Countries/region of origin, 295
Eligibility, 297-299
Foreign-born population by region of birth, 299, 300
Foreign-born population by sex and race, 298
Foreign-born population by state, 297
Metropolitan areas of residence, 294
Nations sending largest percentage, 294
Naturalization rates by nation, 296
Percent by region, 293
Population growth and, 293
Rate by decade, 293
Selected characteristics of foreign-born population, 298
States with most foreign-born, 297
Immunization schedule for children, 382
Implicit Price Deflator, 325
Imports
Largest U.S. merchandise, 506
U.S., in services, by type, 507
World's leading, in merchandise, 504
Incarceration rates, by state, 313
Incineration/combustion of solid waste, 779-780
Income
Federal poverty guidelines, 161
National, by type, 318
National, percent distribution, 318
Personal per capita, by MSA, 320
Personal per capita, by selected county, 321
Personal per capita, by state, 319
Support programs, 159-162
Income tax
Collections by state, 204
Individual rates, by state, 205
Income tax, federal
Deductions, average itemized, 166
Internal Revenue Service, 163-166
Returns filed and examined, 165
Returns processed, 164
Tax rate schedules, 164
Independence Day, 42
Independent establishments, corporations and quasi-official agencies, 136-139
India, description, 582-585
Area codes, 463
Currency exchange rates, 505
Economic indicators, 515
Economy, 583
Geography, 582-583
Government, 583
Health indicators, 482
History, 418, 420-421, 423
Major cities, 583
Motor vehicle production, 408
Nuclear power generation, 497
People, 583
Population in U.S., 299
Population indicators, 476
U.S. immigrants from, 295
Indian Affairs, Bureau of, 134
Indian Ocean (see Oceans of the World)
Indiana, description, 179
Business, 179
Cities, major, population of, 179
Crime in, 306
Education expenditures per pupil, 356
Educational attainment, 359
Elected officials, 179
Elevations, 57
Emblems, 179
Executions in, 315
Famous natives, 179
Farms in, 303
Fortune 500 companies, 179
Health care quality, 368
Land area, 179
Land cover and use, 55
Memorable events, 179
Noteworthy places, 179
Parks and recreation areas, 53
Population by race and Hispanic origin, 269
Population by race/national origin, 179
Population estimates, 1990-2000, 169
Population, foreign-born, 297
Prisoners in, 313
Public school enrollment, 356
Resident population and population change, 261
Resident population by age, 2002, 277
Revenues and expenditures, 203
Taxation in, 204-207
Tourist information, 179
Web site, 179
Indianapolis 500, 906
Indianapolis, Ind., description, 218-219
Area codes, 804-805
Black population in, 271
Climate in, 470
Cost of living index, 243
Government, 219
Housing prices in, 290
Location, 219
Population, 219
Population by race/Hispanic origin, 236
Population, 1980-2000, 239
Rents in, 290
Tax burdens in, 242
Terrain and climate, 219
Visitor information, 219-220
Web site, 219
Individual Retirement Account (IRA), definition, 346
Indonesia, description, 585-586
Area codes, 463
Economic indicators, 515
Economy, 586
Geography, 585
Government, 585-586
Health indicators, 482
Major cities, 585
Motor vehicle production, 408
People, 585
Population in U.S., 299
Population indicators, 476
Infant mortality, 382
Rates, by race, 382
Infant mortality rate, definition, 478
Nations with highest and lowest rates, 479
World, by nation, 481-483
World, by region, 479
Insects, endangered in U.S., 786
Insider trading, definition, 346
Institute (see rest of entry)
Inter-American Foundation, 137
Intergovernmental expenditure/revenue, definition, 142
Interior, U.S. Dept. of. description, 133-134
Employment and budget outlays, 141
Internal Revenue Service (IRS), description, 163-165
Returns filed and examined, 165
Returns processed, 164
Tax collections, 166
International Atomic Energy Agency (IAEA), 710-711
International Bank for Reconstruction and Development (IBRD) (see World Bank Group)
International Boxing Federation (IBF) (see Boxing)
International Civil Aviation Organization (ICAO), 711
International Court of Justice, 709
International Development Association (IDA) (see World Bank Group)
International Development, U.S. Agency for (AID), 139
International Finance Corporation (IFC) (see World Bank Group)
International finance, basic concepts, 505-507
International Fund for Agricultural Development (IFAD), 711
International Labor Organization (ILO), 711
International Maritime Organization (IMO), 711
International Monetary Fund (IMF), 504
Classification of countries, 504
see also World Bank Group
International political organizations, 715
International Research and Training Institute for the Advancement of Women (INSTRAW), 709
International Space Station, 738
International Sports, 879-886
International system (SI), converting to customary measure, 768
International Telecommunication Union (ITU), 711
International trade, 507-508
International Trade Administration (ITA), 132
International Trade Commission, U.S., 139
Internet, The, 806-812
Business on, 807-808
Directory of Websites, 810-812
Glossary of commonly used terms, 808-810
ISPs (Internet Service Providers), 809
Most visited sites, 806
Users, 806-807
World Wide Web, 807-808
Intracoastal Waterway, 54
Intranet, 809
Inventory valuation adjustment, 318
Inverse-square law, 757
Investment in developing countries, 503
Iowa, description, 180
Area codes, 804-805
Business, 180
Cities, major, population of, 180
Crime in, 306
Education expenditures per pupil, 356
Educational attainment, 359
Elected officials, 180
Elevations, 57
Emblems, 180
Executions in, 315
Famous natives, 180
Farms in, 303
Fortune 500 companies, 180
Health care quality, 368
Land area, 180
Land cover and use, 55
Memorable events, 180
Noteworthy places, 180
Nuclear plants in, 364
Parks and recreation areas, 53
Persons below poverty level, 321
Population by race and Hispanic origin, 269
Population by race/national origin, 180
Population estimates, 1990-2000, 169
Population, foreign-born, 297
Prisoners in, 313
Public school enrollment, 356
Resident population and population change, 261
Resident population by age, 2002, 277
Revenues and expenditures, 203
Taxation in, 204-207
Tourist information, 180
Web site, 180
Iran, description, 586-588
2002-03 events, v
Area codes, 463
Economic indicators, 515
Economy, 587
Geography, 586-587
Government, 587
Health indicators, 482
Major cities, 586-587
Oil reserves, 496
People, 587
Population in U.S., 299
Population indicators, 476
U.S. immigrants from, 295
Iraq, description, 588-589
2002-03 events, iv, 17-20
Area codes, 463
Economic indicators, 515
Economy, 588
Geography, 588
Government, 588
Health indicators, 482
Major cities, 588
Oil reserves, 496
People, 588
Population indicators, 476
War in, 17-20
Ireland, description, 589-591
Area codes, 463
Currency exchange rates, 505
Economic indicators, 515
Economy, 589

European Union membership, 509
Geography, 589
Government, 589
Health indicators, 482
Major cities, 589
People, 589
Population in U.S., 299
Population indicators, 476
U.S. immigrants from, 295
ISDN, 809
Islam, description, 488-498
in the U.S., 406
World history, 422-423
Islamic Calendar, 46
Islands, definition, 447
and Island groups, 456-459
World's largest, 457
ISPs (Internet Service Providers), 809
Israel, description, 591-594
2002-03 Events, 20-21
Area codes, 463
Economic indicators, 515
Economy, 591
Geography, 591
Government, 591
Health indicators, 482
History, 417
Major cities, 591
People, 591
Population in U.S., 299
Population indicators, 476
U.S. immigrants from, 295
Italy, description, 594-595
Area codes, 463
Currency exchange rates, 505
Declining population, 472
Economic indicators, 515
Economy, 594
European Union membership, 509
Geography, 594
Government, 594
Health indicators, 482
House of Savoy-Carignano, 444
Major cities, 594
Motor vehicle production, 408
Nuclear power generation, 497
People, 594
Population in U.S., 299
Population indicators, 476
Traffic deaths, 408
U.S. immigrants from, 295
Ivory Coast, description, 595-596
2002-03 Events, 22
Area codes, 463
Economic indicators, 515
Economy, 596
Geography, 595
Government, 596
Health indicators, 482
Major cities, 595
People, 595
Population indicators, 476

J

J/Psi particle, 758
Jackson, Andrew
Administration, 114
Biography, 88
Election, 102
Jackson, Miss.
Population by race/Hispanic origin, 236
Tax burdens in, 242
Jacksonville, Fla., description, 219
Area codes, 804-805
Black population in, 271
Climate in, 470
Crime in, 307, 308
Government, 219
Housing prices in, 290
Location, 219
Population, 219
Population by race/Hispanic origin, 236
Population, 1980-2000, 239
Rents in, 290
Tax burdens in, 242
Terrain and climate, 219
Visitor information, 219-220
Jails, 312
Jainism, 490
Jamaica, description, 596-597
Economic indicators, 515
Economy, 596
Geography, 596
Government, 596
Health indicators, 482
Major cities, 596
People, 596
Population in U.S., 299
Population indicators, 476
U.S. immigrants from, 295
Janmastami, 46-47
Japan, description, 597-599
Area codes, 463
Currency exchange rates, 505
Economic indicators, 515
Economy, 597
Geography, 597
Government, 597
Health indicators, 482
History, 421-424
Major cities, 597
Motor vehicle production, 408
Nuclear power generation, 497
People, 597
Population in U.S., 299
Population indicators, 476
Traffic deaths, 408
U.S. immigrants from, 295
Japanese lang., 493
Jarvis Island, 208
Java, 809
Jefferson, Thomas
Administration, 114
Biography, 86-87
Election, 101
Vice President, 113
Jehovah's Witnesses, 403
Jersey City, N.J.
Crime in, 307, 308
Population by race/Hispanic origin, 236
Population, 1980-2000, 239
Jet stream, definition, 468
Jewish Calendar, 45
Jewish Holy Days, 45-46
Jobs
Federal government, 139-142
Websites about, 812
Jobs and Occupations
Job growth, selected MSAs, 338
Johnson, Andrew
Administration, 115
Biography, 90
Vice President, 113
Johnson, Lyndon B.
Administration, 118
Biography, 95-96
Election, 108
Vice President, 113
Johnston Atoll, 208
Joint Chiefs of Staff
Chairmen of, 147
Organization of the, 133
Jordan, description, 599-600
Area codes, 463
Economic indicators, 515
Economy, 599
Geography, 599
Government, 599
Health indicators, 482
Major cities, 599
People, 599
Population in U.S., 299
Population indicators, 476
Journalism, Pulitzer Prizes in, 839
JPEG, 809
Judaism, description, 486-498
in the U.S., 406
Judicial Branch, 124-125
Appeals courts, 124-125
Cases before the courts, 124
Employment and budget outlays, 141
Salaries in, 140
U.S. Supreme Court, 124
Julian Calendar, 38
Julian Day Count, 38
July Fourth (Independence Day), 42
Junk bond/high-yield bond, definition, 346
Jupiter
Visibility, 2003, 48
Justice, U.S. Dept. of, description, 134
Employment and budget outlays, 141

K

Kansas, description, 180-181
Area codes, 804-805
Business, 180
Cities, major, population of, 180
Crime in, 306
Education expenditures per pupil, 356
Educational attainment, 359
Elected officials, 180
Elevations, 57
Emblems, 180
Executions in, 315
Famous natives, 180
Farms in, 303
Fortune 500 companies, 180
Health care quality, 368
Land area, 180
Land cover and use, 55
Memorable events, 180-181
Noteworthy places, 180
Nuclear plants in, 364
Parks and recreation areas, 53
Persons below poverty level, 321
Population by race and Hispanic origin, 269
Population by race/national origin, 180
Population estimates, 1990-2000, 169
Population, foreign-born, 297
Prisoners in, 313
Public school enrollment, 356
Resident population and population change, 261
Resident population by age, 1999, 277
Revenues and expenditures, 203
Taxation in, 204-207
Tourist information, 181
Web site, 181
Kansas City, Mo., description, 219
Area codes, 804-805
Black population in, 271
Climate in, 470
Cost of living index, 243
Government, 220
Housing prices in, 290
Location, 219
Population, 219
Population by race/Hispanic origin, 236
Population, 1980-2000, 239
Rents in, 290
Tax burdens in, 242
Terrain and climate, 219
Visitor information, 220
Web site, 220
Kazakhstan, description, 600-601
Area codes, 463
Economic indicators, 515
Economy, 600
Geography, 600
Government, 600
Health indicators, 482
Major cities, 600
Nuclear power generation, 497
People, 600
Population indicators, 476
Kelvin scale (temp.), 769
Kennedy, John F.
Administration, 118
Biography, 95
Election, 108
Kentucky, description, 181
Area codes, 804-805
Business, 181
Cities, major, population of, 181
Crime in, 306
Education expenditures per pupil, 356
Educational attainment, 359
Elected officials, 181
Elevations, 57
Emblems, 181
Executions in, 315
Famous natives, 181
Farms in, 303
Fortune 500 companies, 181
Health care quality, 368
Land area, 181
Land cover and use, 55
Memorable events, 181
Noteworthy places, 181
Parks and recreation areas, 53
Persons below poverty level, 321
Population by race and Hispanic origin, 269
Population by race/national origin, 181
Population estimates, 1990-2000, 169
Population, foreign-born, 297
Prisoners in, 313
Public school enrollment, 356
Resident population and population change, 261
Resident population by age, 1999, 277
Revenues and expenditures, 203
Taxation in, 204-207
Tourist information, 181
Web site, 181
Kentucky Derby, 920
Kenya, description, 601-602
Area codes, 463
Economic indicators, 515
Economy, 601
Geography, 601
Government, 601
Health indicators, 482
Major cities, 601
People, 601
Population in U.S., 299
Population indicators, 476
Killer diseases, 480
Kingdom (bio.), 759
Kingman Reef, 208
Kiribati, description, 602
Area codes, 463
Economic indicators, 515
Economy, 602
Geography, 602
Government, 602
Health indicators, 482
Major cities, 602

People, 602
Koran, 488, 492
Korea, North, description, 602-603
2002-03 Events, 21
Area codes, 463
Economy, 602
Geography, 602
Government, 602
Health indicators, 482
History, 421, 423-424
Major cities, 602
People, 602
Population indicators, 476
Korea, South, description, 603-605
Area codes, 463
Economy, 603
Geography, 603
Government, 603
Health indicators, 482
History, 421, 423-424
Major cities, 603
Motor vehicle production, 408
Nuclear power generation, 497
People, 603
Population in U.S., 299
Population indicators, 476
U.S. immigrants from, 295
Korean Conflict, 150
***Korematsu v. United States* (1944), 122**
Kuwait, description, 605
2002-03 Events, 17
Area codes, 463
Economic indicators, 515
Economy, 605
Geography, 605
Government, 605
Health indicators, 482
Major cities, 605
Oil reserves, 496
People, 605
Population indicators, 476
Kwanzaa, 43
Kyrgyzstan, description, 605-606
Area codes, 463
Economic indicators, 515
Economy, 605
Geography, 605
Government, 605
Health indicators, 482
Major cities, 605
People, 605
Population indicators, 476

L

La Nina, 466-498
Labor Day, 42
Labor force, U.S., 333-341
Hispanics in, 333-335
Participation rate, 333
Productivity, 335
Unemployment rate, 333
Unions, 336-337
Women in, 333
Work stoppages, 336
Labor Relations Authority, Federal (FLRA), 137
Labor Relations Board, National (NLRB), 138
Labor Statistics, Bureau of (BLS), 134
Labor, U.S. Dept. of, description, 134
Employment and budget outlays, 141
Lacrosse, NCAA champions, 877
Lagging economic indicators, 323-324
Lake, definition, 447
Major natural of world, 453
Lakes
in the U.S., 53-55
Laksmipuja, 47
Land Management, Bureau of (BLM), 134
Landfills, 779
Landslides, 743-744
Languages of the world
Principal world languages, 493
Laos, description, 606-607
Area codes, 463
Economic indicators, 515
Economy, 606
Geography, 606
Government, 606
Health indicators, 482
Major cities, 606
People, 606
Population in U.S., 299
Population indicators, 476
Larceny/theft
Arrests for, 311
Rate, by state, 306
Large numbers, 767
Las Vegas, Nev., description, 220
Area codes, 804-805
Black population in, 271
Climate in, 470
Crime in, 307, 308
Government, 220
Housing prices in, 290
Location, 220
Population, 220
Population by race/Hispanic origin, 236
Population, 1980-2000, 239
Rents in, 290
Tax burdens in, 242
Tax progressivity in, 240
Terrain and climate, 220
Visitor information, 220
Web site, 220
Latin America
Area and population, 448
Birth rate, 475
Death rate, 475
Fertility rate, 475
History, 424, 435-436
Life expectancy, 475
Percent urban, 475
Population indicators, 475
Population, 2000, 475
Population, percentage of world, 472
Latter-day Saints Churches (U.S.), 402-403
Latvia, description, 607-608
Area codes, 463
Declining population, 472
Economic indicators, 515
Economy, 607
Geography, 607
Government, 607
Health indicators, 482
Major cities, 607
People, 607
Population in U.S., 299
Population indicators, 476
Law enforcement, 309-310
Law of electric power, 756
Law of gravity, 754-755
Laws of thermodynamics, 756
Laws of conservation, 755
Laws of current electricity, 756
Lead emissions, 777-778
Leading economic indicators, 323
League of Arab States, 715
Least developed countries, definition, 478
Lebanon, description, 608-609
Area codes, 463
Economic indicators, 515
Economy, 608
Geography, 608
Government, 608
Health indicators, 482
Major cities, 608
People, 608
Population in U.S., 299
Population indicators, 476
Legislative Branch of the U.S. government, 125
106th Congress, 126
Congressional budget process, 142
Employment, 140
Employment and budget outlays, 141
How a bill becomes law, 125
How to contact your senator or representative, 126
Salaries in, 140
Length, measuring, 767-768
Lent, 44
Lesotho, description, 609-610
Area codes, 463
Economic indicators, 515
Economy, 609-610
Geography, 609
Government, 609
Health indicators, 482
Major cities, 609
People, 609
Population indicators, 476
Less developed countries, definition, 478
Letters, Pulitzer Prizes in, 848-854
Leveraged buyout, definition, 346
Liberia, description, 610-611
2002-03 Events, 21-22
Area codes, 463
Economic indicators, 515
Economy, 610
Geography, 610
Government, 610
Health indicators, 482
Major cities, 610
People, 610
Population indicators, 476
Libraries in U.S. and Canada by type, 389
Library of Congress, 125
Libya, description, 611-612
Area codes, 463
Economic indicators, 515
Economy, 611
Geography, 611
Government, 611
Health indicators, 482
Major cities, 611
Oil reserves, 496
People, 611
Population indicators, 476
Liechtenstein, description, 612
Area codes, 463
Economy, 612
Geography, 612
Government, 612
Major cities, 612
People, 612
Life expectancy
at Birth, 380
by Nation, 475-477
Remaining, 381
Life sciences, 758-760
Major discoveries in, 761
Lincoln, Abraham
Administration, 115
Biography, 90
Election, 103
Emancipation Proclamation, 67
Gettysburg Address, 67
Lincoln, Nebr.
Crime in, 308
Link (Internet term), 809
Literature, Nobel Prizes in, 866-868
Lithuania, description, 612-613
Area codes, 463
Declining population, 472
Economic indicators, 515
Economy, 612-613
Geography, 612
Government, 612
Health indicators, 482
Major cities, 612
People, 612
Population in U.S., 299
Population indicators, 476
Little Rock, Ark.
Population by race/Hispanic origin, 236
Tax burdens in, 242
Living arrangements
of Children, 286
of Elderly population, 278
with Grandparents, 287
Local government, forms of, 211
***Lochner v. New York* (1905), 122**
Long Beach, Calif., description, 220
Area codes, 804-805
Government, 220
Location, 220
Population by race/Hispanic origin, 236
Population, 1980-2000, 239
Terrain and climate, 220
Visitor information, 220
Web site, 220
Los Angeles, Calif., description, 220-221
Area codes, 804-805
Black population in, 271
Climate in, 470
Cost of living index, 243
Crime in, 307, 308
Government, 221
Hispanic population in , 273
Housing prices in, 290
Location, 221
Population, 221
Population by race/Hispanic origin, 236
Population, 1980-2000, 239
Rents in, 290
Tax burdens in, 242
Terrain and climate, 221
Visitor information, 221
Web site, 221
Louisiana, description, 181-182
Area codes, 804-805
Black population in, 270
Business, 182
Cities, major, population of, 182
Crime in, 306
Education expenditures per pupil, 356
Educational attainment, 359
Elected officials, 182
Emblems, 181
Executions in, 315
Famous natives, 182
Farms in, 303
Fortune 500 companies, 182
Health care quality, 368
Land area, 181-182
Memorable events, 182
Noteworthy places, 182
Nuclear plants in, 364
Persons below poverty level, 321
Population by race and Hispanic origin, 269
Population by race/national origin, 182
Population estimates, 1990-2000, 169
Population, foreign-born, 297
Prisoners in, 313
Public school enrollment, 356
Resident population and population change, 261
Resident population by age, 1999, 277
Revenues and expenditures, 203
Taxation in, 204-207
Tourist information, 182
Web site, 182
Louisville, Ky.

Population by race/Hispanic origin, 236
Population, 1980-2000, 239
Tax burdens in, 242
Low, definition, 468
Lunar Calendar, 38
Lunar Eclipses, 49
Lutheran Churches (U.S.), 402
Luxembourg, description, 613-614
Area codes, 463
Economic indicators, 515
Economy, 614
European Union membership, 509
Geography, 613
Government, 613-614
Health indicators, 482
Major cities, 613
People, 613
Population indicators, 476
Lynch, Jessica, 18

M

Macau
Area codes, 463
Macedonia, description, 419, 614-615
Area codes, 463
Economic indicators, 515
Economy, 614
Geography, 614
Government, 614
Health indicators, 482
Major cities, 614
People, 614
Population indicators, 476
Madagascar, description, 615
Area codes, 463
Economic indicators, 515
Economy, 615
Geography, 615
Government, 615
Health indicators, 482
Major cities, 615
People, 615
Population indicators, 476
Madison, James
Administration, 114
Biography, 87
Election, 101
Magazines, 387-389
by Circulation, top 100, 388
by Revenues, top 50, 389
Magnitude of stars, 725-726
Mahasivaratri , 47
Mahavisuva Day, 46
Mail (see Postal Service, U.S.)
Maine, description, 182
Area codes, 804-805
Business, 182
Cities, major, population of, 182
Crime in, 306
Education expenditures per pupil, 356
Educational attainment, 359
Elected officials, 182
Elevations, 57
Emblems, 182
Executions in, 315
Famous natives, 182
Farms in, 303
Fortune 500 companies, 182
Health care quality, 368
Land area, 182
Land cover and use, 55
Memorable events, 182
Noteworthy places, 182
Parks and recreation areas, 53
Persons below poverty level, 321
Population by race and Hispanic origin, 269
Population by race/national origin, 182
Population estimates, 1990-2000, 169
Population, foreign-born, 297
Prisoners in, 313
Public school enrollment, 356
Resident population and population change, 261
Resident population by age, 1999, 277
Revenues and expenditures, 203
Taxation in, 204-207
Tourist information, 182
Web site, 182
Makaraj-Samkranti, 46
Malawi, description, 615-616
Area codes, 463
Economic indicators, 515
Economy, 616
Geography, 615
Government, 616
Health indicators, 482
Major cities, 615
People, 615-616
Population indicators, 476
Malay lang., 493
Malaysia, description, 616-617
Area codes, 463
Currency exchange rates, 505
Economic indicators, 515
Economy, 616
Geography, 616
Government, 616
Health indicators, 482
Major cities, 616
People, 616
Population in U.S., 299
Population indicators, 476
Maldives, description, 617
Area codes, 463
Economic indicators, 515
Economy, 617
Geography, 617
Government, 617
Health indicators, 482
Major cities, 617
People, 617
Population indicators, 476
Male population
Average earnings by age and educational attainment, 335
Crime victimization rates, 310
Deaths and death rates of, 378
Divorced persons per 1,000 married persons, 283
Employment status of, 334
Frequency of sexual intercourse, 301
Life expectancy, 381
Lifetime likelihood of going to prison, 314
Marital status of, 282
Never married, percent, 281
Number in U.S., 279
Number of sex partners, 301
per 100 females in U.S., 279
Prisoners, 312
Mali Republic, description, 617-618
Area codes, 463
Economic indicators, 515
Economy, 618
Geography, 617
Government, 618
Health indicators, 482
Major cities, 617
People, 617-618
Population indicators, 476
Malta, description, 618-619
Area codes, 463
Economic indicators, 515
Economy, 618
European Union membership, 509
Geography, 618
Government, 618
Health indicators, 482
Major cities, 618
People, 618
Population indicators, 476
Mammals, endangered in U.S., 785
Managed care providers (health insurance), 370-371
Management and Budget, Office of (OMB), 131
Manchester, N.H.
Population by race/Hispanic origin, 236
Tax burdens in, 242
Mantle (geo.), 738
Manufacturing industries
Earnings in, 335
Establishments with employees and payrolls, 339-340
Marathon running, 884
***Marbury v. Madison* (1803), 120**
Mardi Gras, 44
Marijuana use, 382-383
Marine Corps, U.S., description, 149-150
Casualties, by conflict, 150
Major forces, 149
Minorities in, 153
Women in, 153
Worldwide deployment, 151
Marital fidelity, 301
Marital status, U.S.
by Age and sex, 282
Percent of population never married, by age and sex, 281
by Race and Hispanic origin, 281
Maritime Administration (MARAD), 135
Maritime Commission, Federal , 137
Marriages
and Divorces, U.S., 279
Fidelity, 301
Interracial, 283
Marital status by race and Hispanic origin, 281
Marital status by sex and age, 282
Rates, U.S., 279
Mars
Visibility, 2003, 48
Marshall Islands, description, 619
Area codes, 463
Economic indicators, 515
Economy, 619
Geography, 619
Government, 619
Major cities, 619
People, 619
Marshals Service, U.S., 134
Martin Luther King Day, 42
Martinique, 701
Maryland, description, 183
Area codes, 804-805
Black population in, 270
Business, 183
Cities, major, population of, 183
Crime in, 306
Education expenditures per pupil, 356
Educational attainment, 359
Elected officials, 183
Elevations, 57
Emblems, 183
Executions in, 315
Famous natives, 183
Farms in, 303
Fortune 500 companies, 183
Health care quality, 368
Land area, 183
Land cover and use, 55
Memorable events, 183
Noteworthy places, 183
Nuclear plants in, 364
Parks and recreation areas, 53
Persons below poverty level, 321
Population by race and Hispanic origin, 269
Population by race/national origin, 183
Population estimates, 1990-2000, 169
Population, foreign-born, 297
Prisoners in, 313
Public school enrollment, 356
Resident population and population change, 261
Resident population by age, 1999, 277
Revenues and expenditures, 203
Taxation in, 204-207
Tourist information, 183
Web site, 183
Mass
Conservation of, 755
Measurement of, 769
Mass-energy, conservation of, 756
Massachusetts, description, 183-184
Area codes, 804-805
Business, 184
Cities, major, population of, 184
Crime in, 306
Education expenditures per pupil, 356
Educational attainment, 359
Elected officials, 183-184
Elevations, 57
Emblems, 183
Executions in, 315
Famous natives, 184
Farms in, 303
Fortune 500 companies, 184
Health care quality, 368
Land area, 183
Land cover and use, 55
Memorable events, 184
Noteworthy places, 184
Nuclear plants in, 364
Parks and recreation areas, 53
Persons below poverty level, 321
Population by race and Hispanic origin, 269
Population by race/national origin, 184
Population estimates, 1990-2000, 169
Population, foreign-born, 297
Prisoners in, 313
Public school enrollment, 356
Resident population and population change, 261
Resident population by age, 1999, 277
Revenues and expenditures, 203
Taxation in, 204-207
Tourist information, 184
Web site, 184
Master's desgrees conferred in U.S., 1950-2000, 360
Maternal deaths, 483-484
Mathematics, 763-767
Commonly used equations and formulas, 764-767
Fields Medal, 838
History of, 765
Maundy Thursday, 44
Mauritania, description, 619-620
Area codes, 463
Economic indicators, 515
Economy, 619

Geography, 619
Government, 619
Health indicators, 482
Major cities, 619
People, 619
Population indicators, 476
Mauritius, description, 620
Area codes, 463
Economic indicators, 515
Economy, 620
Geography, 620
Government, 620
Health indicators, 482
Major cities, 620
People, 620
Population indicators, 477
Mayans in world history, 424
Mayors, 20 best paid, 1998, 243
Mayotte Island, 701
Area codes, 463
***McCulloch v. Maryland* (1819), 120**
McKinley, William
Administration, 116
Biography, 92
Election, 105
Mean temperature, definition, 468
Measurement, systems of, 767-771
Media, 386-400
Electronic, 393-400
Print, 386-392
Mediation and Conciliation Service, Federal, 137
Mediation Board, National, 138
Medicaid
Beneficiaries and payments, 155
Medicare
Beneficiaries and payments, 155
Recipients and benefits, 157
Medicine
Nobel Prizes in Physiology and, 856-863
Melanesia
Population indicators, 477
Memorial Day, 42
Memphis, Tenn., description, 221
Area codes, 804-805
Black population in, 271
Climate in, 470
Crime in, 307
Government, 221
Housing prices in, 290
Location, 221
Population, 221
Population by race/Hispanic origin, 236
Population, 1980-2000, 239
Rents in, 290
Tax burdens in, 242
Terrain and climate, 221
Visitor information, 221
Web site, 221
Mennonite Churches (U.S.), 404
Merchandise
U.S. exports and imports, 504, 506
U.S.trade partners, 504
Mercury
Visibility, 2003, 47-48
Mergers and acquisitions, largest, 344
Mesa, Ariz, description, 221
Area codes, 804-805
Government, 221
Location, 221
Population, 221
Population by race/Hispanic origin, 236
Population, 1980-2000, 239
Terrain and climate, 221
Visitor information, 221-222
Mesasamkranti, 46
Mesopotamia
History, 416, 417
Methodist Churches (U.S.), 401
Metric system
Converting to customary measure, 768
Prefixes used in, 767
Metropolitan Areas
Ozone in, 777
Unhealthy days in selected, 775
Metropolitan statistical area (MSAs)
Fastest-declining, 256
Job growth in selected, 338
Population of, 1990-2000, 244-249
Population of, by race and Hispanic origin, 250-255
Mexican War, 150
Mexico, description, 620-622
Area codes, 463
Currency exchange rates, 505
Economic indicators, 515
Economy, 621
Geography, 620
Government, 620-621
Health indicators, 482
Major cities, 620
Motor vehicle production, 408
Nuclear power generation, 497
Oil reserves, 496
People, 620
Population in U.S., 299
U.S. immigrants from, 295
Miami, Fla., description, 221-222
Area codes, 804-805
Black population in, 271
Climate in, 470
Crime in, 307, 308
Government, 222
Housing prices in, 290
Location, 222
Population, 222
Population by race/Hispanic origin, 236
Population, 1980-2000, 239
Terrain and climate, 222
Visitor information, 222
Web site, 222
Michigan, description, 184-185
Area codes, 804-805
Black population in, 270
Business, 184
Cities, major, population of, 184
Crime in, 306
Education expenditures per pupil, 356
Educational attainment, 359
Elected officials, 184
Elevations, 57
Emblems, 184
Executions in, 315
Famous natives, 184-185
Farms in, 303
Fortune 500 companies, 184
Health care quality, 368
Land area, 184
Land cover and use, 55
Memorable events, 185
Noteworthy places, 185
Nuclear plants in, 364
Parks and recreation areas, 53
Persons below poverty level, 321
Population by race and Hispanic origin, 269
Population by race/national origin, 184
Population estimates, 1990-2000, 169
Population, foreign-born, 297
Prisoners in, 313
Public school enrollment, 356
Resident population and population change, 261
Resident population by age, 2002, 277
Revenues and expenditures, 203
Taxation in, 204-207
Tourist information, 185
Web site, 185
Micronesia, description, 622
Area codes, 463
Economic indicators, 515
Economy, 622
Geography, 622
Government, 622
Health indicators, 482
Major cities, 622
People, 622
Middle East, 496
Energy production/consumption, 494, 496
History, 433
Nuclear power generation, 497
MIDI, 809
Midway Islands, 208
Military costs and armed forces personnel as percent of GDP, 499-500
Military personnel (see Armed forces)
Military situation, global, 498-501
Milky Way, 727
Milwaukee, Wisc., description, 222
Area codes, 804-805
Black population in, 271
Climate in, 470
Government, 222
Housing prices in, 290
Location, 222
Population by race/Hispanic origin, 236
Population, 1980-2000, 239
Rents in, 290
Tax burdens in, 242
Terrain and climate, 222
Visitor information, 222
Web site, 222
Minimum wage, 336
Mining industries
Earnings in, 335
Minneapolis, Minn., description, 222
Area codes, 804-805
Black population in, 271
Climate in, 470
Cost of living index, 243
Crime in, 307, 308
Government, 222
Housing prices in, 290
Location, 222
Population by race/Hispanic origin, 236
Population, 1980-2000, 239
Rents in, 290
Tax burdens in, 242
Tax progressivity in, 240
Terrain and climate, 222
Visitor information, 222
Web site, 222
Minnesota, description, 185
Area codes, 804-805
Business, 185
Cities, major, population of, 185
Crime in, 306
Education expenditures per pupil, 356
Educational attainment, 359
Elected officials, 185
Elevations, 57
Emblems, 185
Executions in, 315
Famous natives, 185
Farms in, 303
Fortune 500 companies, 185
Health care quality, 368
Land area, 185
Land cover and use, 55
Memorable events, 185
Noteworthy places, 185
Nuclear plants in, 364
Persons below poverty level, 321
Population by race and Hispanic origin, 269
Population by race/national origin, 185
Population estimates, 1990-2000, 169
Population, foreign-born, 297
Prisoners in, 313
Public school enrollment, 356
Resident population and population change, 261
Resident population by age, 2002, 277
Revenues and expenditures, 203
Taxation in, 204-207
Tourist information, 185
Web site, 185
Minority Business Development Agency (MBDA), 132
Mint, U.S., 136
***Miranda v. Arizona* (1966), 123**
Mirror site, 809
Mississippi, description, 185-186
Area codes, 804-805
Black population in, 270
Business, 186
Cities, major, population of, 186
Crime in, 306
Education expenditures per pupil, 356
Elected officials, 186
Elevations, 57
Emblems, 186
Executions in, 315
Famous natives, 186
Farms in, 303
Fortune 500 companies, 186
Health care quality, 368
Land area, 186
Land cover and use, 55
Memorable events, 186
Noteworthy places, 186
Nuclear plants in, 364
Parks and recreation areas, 53
Persons below poverty level, 321
Population by race and Hispanic origin, 269
Population by race/national origin, 186
Population estimates, 1990-2000, 169
Population, foreign-born, 297
Prisoners in, 313
Public school enrollment, 356
Resident population and population change, 261
Resident population by age, 2002, 277
Revenues and expenditures, 203
Taxation in, 204-207
Tourist information, 186
Web site, 186
Mississippi River system, 54
Missouri, description, 186-187
Area codes, 804-805
Business, 186
Cities, major, population of, 186
Crime in, 306
Education expenditures per pupil, 356
Educational attainment, 359
Elected officials, 186

Elevations, 57
Emblems, 186
Famous natives, 186
Farms in, 303
Fortune 500 companies, 186
Health care quality, 368
Land area, 186
Land cover and use, 55
Memorable events, 186-187
Noteworthy places, 186
Nuclear plants in
Parks and recreation areas, 53
Persons below poverty level, 321
Population by race and Hispanic origin, 269
Population by race/national origin, 186
Population estimates, 1990-2000, 169
Population, foreign-born, 297
Prisoners in, 313
Public school enrollment, 356
Resident population and population change, 261
Resident population by age, 2002, 277
Revenues and expenditures, 203
Taxation in, 204-207
Tourist information, 187
Web site, 187
Moldova, description, 622-623
Area codes, 463
Economic indicators, 515
Economy, 622-623
Geography, 622
Government, 622
Health indicators, 482
Major cities, 622
People, 622
Population indicators, 477
Momentum, conservation of, 755
Monaco, description, 623-624
Area codes, 463
Economy, 623-624
Geography, 623
Government, 623
Health indicators, 482
Major cities, 623
People, 623
Monerans, 759
Money income, definition, 318-319
Money Instruments, 331
Money supply, definition, 327
Federal Reserve, 325-327
Money-market accounts
Interest rates, 330
Mongolia, description, 624-625
Area codes, 463
Economic indicators, 515
Economy, 624
Geography, 624
Government, 624
Health indicators, 482
Major cities, 624
People, 624
Population indicators, 477
Mongols in World History, 425
Monroe, James
Administration, 114
Biography, 87
Election, 101
Monsoon, definition, 468
Montana, description, 187
Area codes, 804-805
Business, 187
Cities, major, population of, 187
Crime in, 306
Education expenditures per pupil, 356
Educational attainment, 359
Elected officials, 187
Elevations, 57
Emblems, 187
Executions in, 315
Famous natives, 187
Farms in, 303
Fortune 500 companies, 187
Health care quality, 368
Land area, 187
Land cover and use, 55
Memorable events, 187
Noteworthy places, 187
Parks and recreation areas, 52, 53
Persons below poverty level, 321
Population by race and Hispanic origin, 269
Population by race/national origin, 187
Population estimates, 1990-2000, 169
Population, foreign-born, 297
Prisoners in, 313
Public school enrollment, 356
Resident population and population change, 261
Resident population by age, 2002, 277
Revenues and expenditures, 203
Taxation in, 204-207
Tourist information, 187
Web site, 187
Montenegro (see Yugoslavia)
Months of the Year, 47
Montserrat, 706-707
Moon
Eclipses of the, 49
Phases of the, 47, 48
Mormons (see Latter-day Saints Churches)
Morocco, description, 625-626
Area codes, 463
Economic indicators, 515
Economy, 625
Geography, 625
Government, 625
Health indicators, 482
Major cities, 625
People, 625
Population in U.S., 299
Population indicators, 477
Mortgage loans, 330-331
Fannie Mae, 331
Moslems (see Islam)
Mother's Day, 43
Motion, laws of, 755
Motor vehicles (see also Cars)
Accidents and deaths from, 381-382
Fatalities, 408
Fuel efficiency, 411
Number in U.S., 407
Production, world, 408
Registrations, by state, 410
Registrations, U.S., 409
Registrations, world, 409
Sales, U.S., 409
Theft, arrests for, 311
Top-selling cars and light trucks in U.S., 411
Traffic, 411
Traffic deaths by selected nation, 408
Mountain, definition, 448
Highest, 451-452
Movies (see Film)
Mozambique, description, 626-627
Area codes, 463
Economic indicators, 515
Economy, 626
Geography, 626
Government, 626
Health indicators, 482
Major cities, 626
People, 626
Population indicators, 477
MPEG, 809
MTV Video Music Awards, 829-830
Multilateral Investment Guarantee Agency (MIGA) (see World Bank Group)
Municipal bonds, 331-332
Municipality government, 211
***Munn v. Illinois* (1877), 121**
Muon, 758
Murder
Arrests for, 311
Homicide, guns, and young people, 309
Rate, by state, 306
Music
Grammy Awards, 827-829
MTV Video Music Awards, 829-830
Pulitzer Prize for, 853
Radio, 396
Recording industry, 396-397
Sales of recorded music by genre and age group, 397
Top-selling albums of 1999, 396
Musicals, Tony Awards for, 825-827
Muslim Holy Days, 46
Muslims (see Islam)
Mutual funds, 342-344
Number of funds, accounts, and total assets, 343
Myanmar, description, 627
Area codes, 463
Economic indicators, 515
Economy, 627
Geography, 627
Government, 627
Health indicators, 482
Major cities, 627
People, 627
Population in U.S., 299
Population indicators, 477

N

Naismith Memorial Basketball Hall of Fame, 939-941
Namibia, description, 627-628
Area codes, 463
Economic indicators, 515
Economy, 628
Geography, 627
Government, 627-628
Health indicators, 482
Major cities, 627
People, 627
Population indicators, 477
Napster, 397
NASA, 137-138
Nashville, Tenn., description, 222-223
Area codes, 804-805
Crime in, 307
Government, 223
Location, 223
Population, 223
Population by race/Hispanic origin, 237
Population, 1980-2000, 239
Terrain and climate, 223
Visitor information, 223
Web site, 223
National (see rest of entry)
National Basketball Association (see Basketball, professional)
National Book Awards, 832-833
National Book Critics Circle Awards, 833-835
National Collegiate Athletic Association (see College Sports)
National Defense (U.S.) (see Defense, U.S. Dept. of)
National Film Registry, 819-820
National Football League. (see Football, professional)
National Guard and Reserve, 151-152
National Hockey League (see Ice Hockey, professional)
National income, 319
National Invitation Tournament Champions, 874
***National Labor Relations Board v. Jones & Laughlin Steel Corp.* (1937), 122**
National Maritime Day, 43
National park system, 51-53
Acreage of and visits to, 52
National Teacher Day, 43
Nationalization rates for U.S. immigrants, by nation, 296
Nations
Area codes for, 462-464
Currency exchange rates, 505
Economic indicators, 514-516
Fertility rates, highest and lowest, 475
G.N.P. per capita, highest and lowest, 502
Health indicators, 481-483
Hierarchy of, 503-514
Population indicators, 475-477
Time zones of, 462-464
of the World, 517-707
Native Americans (see American Indian population, Asian and Native Hawaiian population)
NATO (North Atlantic Treaty Organization), 715
Natural gas and plant liquids, description, 363
Natural gas and plant/dry liquids, 494-495
Top producers, 495
World consumption, 496
World production, 494
Nauru, description, 628-629
Area codes, 463
Economy, 628
Geography, 628
Government, 628
Major cities, 628
People, 628
Navassa, 208
Navy, U.S., description, 150
Casualties, by conflict, 150
Major forces, 149
Minorities in, 153
Women in, 153
Worldwide deployment, 151
NCAA (see College Sports)
Nebraska, description, 187-188
Area codes, 804-805
Business, 188
Cities, major, population of, 188
Crime in, 306
Education expenditures per pupil, 356
Educational attainment, 359
Elected officials, 187
Elevations, 57
Emblems, 187
Executions in, 315
Famous natives, 188
Farms in, 303
Fortune 500 companies, 188

Health care quality, 368
Land area, 187
Land cover and use, 55
Memorable events, 188
Noteworthy places, 188
Nuclear plants in, 364
Parks and recreation areas, 53
Persons below poverty level, 321
Population by race and Hispanic origin, 269
Population by race/national origin, 187
Population estimates, 1990-2000, 169
Population, foreign-born, 297
Prisoners in, 313
Public school enrollment, 356
Resident population and population change, 261
Resident population by age, 1999, 277
Revenues and expenditures, 203
Taxation in, 204-207
Tourist information, 188
Web site, 188

Nepal, description, 629
Area codes, 463
Economic indicators, 515
Economy, 629
Geography, 629
Government, 629
Health indicators, 482
Major cities, 629
People, 629
Population indicators, 477

Neptune
Visibility, 2003, 48-49

Netherlands, description, 629-630
Area codes, 463
Currency exchange rates, 505
Economic indicators, 515
Economy, 630
Geography, 629
Government, 629-630
Health indicators, 482
Major cities, 629
Nuclear power generation, 497
People, 629
Population in U.S., 299
Population indicators, 477
Traffic deaths, 408
U.S. immigrants from, 295

Netherlands Antilles, 703
Area codes, 463

Neutrinos, 758

Neutron, 758

Nevada, description, 188
Area codes, 804-805
Business, 188
Cities, major, population of, 188
Crime in, 306
Education expenditures per pupil, 356
Educational attainment, 359
Elected officials, 188
Elevations, 57
Emblems, 188
Executions in, 315
Famous natives, 188
Farms in, 303
Fortune 500 companies, 188
Health care quality, 368
Land area, 188
Land cover and use, 55
Memorable events, 188
Noteworthy places, 188
Parks and recreation areas, 53
Persons below poverty level, 321
Population by race and Hispanic origin, 269
Population by race/national origin, 188
Population estimates, 1990-2000, 169
Population, foreign-born, 297
Prisoners in, 313
Public school enrollment, 356
Resident population and population change, 261
Resident population by age, 1999, 277
Revenues and expenditures, 203
Taxation in, 204-207
Tourist information, 188
Web site, 188

New Caledonia, 701
Area codes, 463

New Hampshire, description, 188-189
Area codes, 804-805
Business, 189
Cities, major, population of, 189
Crime in, 306
Education expenditures per pupil, 356
Educational attainment, 359
Elected officials, 189
Elevations, 57
Emblems, 188
Executions in, 315
Famous natives, 189
Farms in, 303
Fortune 500 companies, 189
Health care quality, 368
Land area, 188-189
Land cover and use, 55
Memorable events, 189
Noteworthy places, 189
Nuclear plants in, 364
Parks and recreation areas, 53
Persons below poverty level, 321
Population by race and Hispanic origin, 269
Population by race/national origin, 189
Population estimates, 1990-2000, 169
Population, foreign-born, 297
Prisoners in, 313
Public school enrollment, 356
Resident population and population change, 261
Resident population by age, 1999, 277
Revenues and expenditures, 203
Taxation in, 204-207
Tourist information, 189
Web site, 189

New Jersey, description, 189-190
Area codes, 804-805
Business, 189
Cities, major, population of, 189
Crime in, 306
Education expenditures per pupil, 356
Educational attainment, 359
Elected officials, 189
Elevations, 57
Emblems, 189
Executions in, 315
Famous natives, 189
Farms in, 303
Fortune 500 companies, 189
Health care quality, 368
Land area, 189
Land cover and use, 55
Memorable events, 189-190
Noteworthy places, 189
Nuclear plants in, 364
Parks and recreation areas, 53
Persons below poverty level, 321
Population by race and Hispanic origin, 269
Population by race/national origin, 189
Population estimates, 1990-2000, 169
Population, foreign-born, 297
Prisoners in, 313
Public school enrollment, 356
Resident population and population change, 261
Resident population by age, 1999, 277
Revenues and expenditures, 203
Taxation in, 204-207
Tourist information, 190
Web site, 190

New Mexico, description, 190
Area codes, 804-805
Business, 190
Cities, major, population of, 190
Crime in, 306
Education expenditures per pupil, 356
Educational attainment, 359
Elected officials, 190
Elevations, 57
Emblems, 190
Executions in, 315
Famous natives, 190
Farms in, 303
Fortune 500 companies, 190
Health care quality, 368
Land area, 190
Land cover and use, 55
Memorable events, 190
Noteworthy places, 190
Parks and recreation areas, 53
Persons below poverty level, 321
Population by race and Hispanic origin, 269
Population by race/national origin, 190
Population estimates, 1990-2000, 169
Population, foreign-born, 297
Prisoners in, 313
Public school enrollment, 356
Resident population and population change, 261
Resident population by age, 1999, 277
Revenues and expenditures, 203
Taxation in, 204-207
Tourist information, 190
Web site, 190

New Orleans, La., description, 223
Area codes, 804-805
Black population in, 271
Climate in, 470
Crime in, 307, 308
Government, 223
Housing prices in, 290
Location, 223
Population, 223
Population by race/Hispanic origin, 237
Population, 1980-2000, 239
Rents in, 290
Tax burdens in, 242
Terrain and climate, 223
Visitor information, 223
Web site, 223

New Religion, 490

New Year's Day, 42

New York, description, 190-191
Area codes, 804-805
Black population in, 270
Business, 191
Cities, major, population of, 191
Crime in, 306
Education expenditures per pupil, 356
Educational attainment, 359
Elected officials, 190
Elevations, 57
Emblems, 190
Executions in, 315
Famous natives, 191
Farms in, 303
Fortune 500 companies, 191
Health care quality, 368
Land area, 190
Land cover and use, 55
Memorable events, 191
Noteworthy places, 191
Nuclear plants in, 364
Persons below poverty level, 321
Population by race and Hispanic origin, 269
Population by race/national origin, 190-191
Population estimates, 1990-2000, 169
Population, foreign-born, 297
Prisoners in, 313
Public school enrollment, 356
Resident population and population change, 261
Resident population by age, 1999, 277
Revenues and expenditures, 203
Taxation in, 204-207
Tourist information, 191
Web site, 191

New York City, N.Y., description, 223-224
Area codes, 804-805
Black population in, 271
Climate in, 470
Cost of living index, 243
Crime in, 307, 308
Government, 224
Hispanic population in , 273
Housing prices in, 290
Location, 224
Population, 224
Population by race/Hispanic origin, 237
Population, 1980-2000, 239
Rents in, 290
Tax burdens in, 242
Tax progressivity in, 240
Terrain and climate, 224
Visitor information, 224
Web site, 224

New York Stock Exchange (NYSE), 341

***New York Times Co. v. United States* (1971), 123**

New Zealand, description, 630-631
Area codes, 463
Currency exchange rates, 505
Economic indicators, 515
Economy, 631
Geography, 630
Government, 630-631
Health indicators, 482
Major cities, 630
People, 630
Population in U.S., 299
Population indicators, 477

Newark, N.J.
Area codes, 804-805
Black population in, 271
Crime in, 307, 308
Population by race/Hispanic origin, 237
Population, 1980-2000, 239
Tax burdens in, 242

Newbery Medal, 835-836
News
Websites about, 812
Newsgroups, 809
Newspapers, 386-387
Number and circulation, 386
Pulitzer Prizes in Journalism, 839
Top 100 U.S., 387
Weekly, 388
Newton's laws of motion, 755
Nicaragua, description, 631-632
Area codes, 463
Economic indicators, 515
Economy, 631
Geography, 631
Government, 631
Health indicators, 482
Major cities, 631
People, 631
Population in U.S., 299
Population indicators, 477
Niger, description, 632-633
2002-03 Events, 19
Area codes, 463
Economic indicators, 515
Economy, 632
Geography, 632
Government, 632
Major cities, 632
People, 632
Population indicators, 477
Nigeria, description, 633-634
2002-03 Events, 22
Area codes, 463
Economic indicators, 515
Economy, 633
Geography, 633
Government, 633
Health indicators, 482
Major cities, 633
Population indicators, 477
Oil reserves, 496
People, 633
Population in U.S., 299
Nitrogen oxides emissions, 776
Niue, 704
Area codes, 464
Nixon, Richard M.
Administration, 118
Biography, 96
Election, 108
Vice President, 113
Nobel Prizes, vi, 854-868
Nonfiction
Best-sellers in America, 390-391
National Book Critics Circle Award, 834
Pulitzer Prize, 852-853
Norfolk Island, 699
Area codes, 462, 464
Time zones, 462
North America
Birth rate, 475
Death rate, 475
Elevation extremes, 449
Energy production/consumption, 494, 496
Fertility rate, 475
Life expectancy, 475
Nuclear power generation, 497
Percent urban, 475
Population indicators, 475
Population, 2000, 475
Population, percentage of world, 472
U.S. immigrants from, 295
North American Free Trade Agreement (NAFTA), 514
North Atlantic Treaty Organization (NATO), 715
North Carolina, description, 191-192
Area codes, 804-805
Black population in, 270
Business, 191-192
Cities, major, population of, 191
Crime in, 306
Education expenditures per pupil, 356
Educational attainment, 359
Elected officials, 191
Elevations, 57
Emblems, 191
Executions in, 315
Famous natives, 192
Farms in, 303
Fortune 500 companies, 191
Health care quality, 368
Land area, 191
Land cover and use, 55
Memorable events, 192
Noteworthy places, 192
Nuclear plants in, 364
Parks and recreation areas, 53
Persons below poverty level, 321
Population by race and Hispanic origin, 269
Population by race/national origin, 191
Population estimates, 1990-2000, 169
Population, foreign-born, 297
Prisoners in, 313
Public school enrollment, 356
Resident population and population change, 261
Resident population by age, 2002, 277
Revenues and expenditures, 203
Taxation in, 204-207
Tourist information, 192
Web site, 192
North Dakota, description, 192
Area codes, 804-805
Business, 192
Cities, major, population of, 192
Crime in, 306
Education expenditures per pupil, 356
Educational attainment, 359
Elected officials, 192
Elevations, 57
Emblems, 192
Executions in, 315
Famous natives, 192
Farms in, 303
Fortune 500 companies, 192
Health care quality, 368
Land area, 192
Land cover and use, 55
Memorable events, 192
Noteworthy places, 192
Parks and recreation areas, 53
Persons below poverty level, 321
Population by race and Hispanic origin, 269
Population by race/national origin, 192
Population estimates, 1990-2000, 169
Population, foreign-born, 297
Prisoners in, 313
Public school enrollment, 356
Resident population and population change, 261
Resident population by age, 2002, 277
Revenues and expenditures, 203
Taxation in, 204-207
Tourist information, 192
Web site, 192
North Korea (see Korea, North)
Northern Ireland (see United Kingdom)
Northern Mariana Islands, description, 208-209
Population, 208
Norway, description, 634-635
Area codes, 464
Currency exchange rates, 505
Economic indicators, 516
Economy, 634
Geography, 634
Government, 634
Health indicators, 482
Major cities, 634
People, 634
Population indicators, 477
Traffic deaths, 408
U.S. immigrants from, 295
Novel/Fiction, Pulitzer Prize for, 848-849
Nuclear forces, U.S., 154
Nuclear power generation, description, 497
by Region/country, 497
Nuclear power, description, 363
Commercial plants in operation, by state, 364
Nuclear Waste, 780-781
Nuclear weapons
in North Korea, 21
Stockpiles and storage locations, 498
Numbers, large
Scientific notation, 767
Nursing home care, 368-369

O

Oakland, Calif., description, 224
Area codes, 804-805
Black population in, 271
Cost of living index, 243
Crime in, 307
Government, 224
Housing prices in, 290
Location, 224
Population, 224
Population by race/Hispanic origin, 237
Population, 1980-2000, 239
Rents in, 290
Terrain and climate, 224
Visitor information, 224
Web site, 224
OASDI (Old-age, survivors and disability insurance), 156-158
Beneficiaries and payments, 156
Obasanjo, Olusegun, 22
Occluded front, definition, 468
Occupational Safety and Health Administration (OSHA), 134
Ocean pollution, 779
Oceania
Birth rate, 475
Death rate, 475
Energy production/consumption, 494, 496
Fertility rate, 475
Life expectancy, 475
Nuclear power generation, 497
Percent urban, 475
Population in U.S., 299
Population indicators, 475
Population, 2000, 475
U.S. immigrants from, 295
Oceanic and Atmospheric Administration, National (NOAA), 132
Oceans of the world, definition, 449
Area and depth of, 449
Marginal seas of, 449
Off-budget/on-budget, definition, 143
Office (see rest of entry)
Offsetting collections, definition, 143
Ohio, description, 192-193
Area codes, 804-805
Business, 193
Cities, major, population of, 193
Crime in, 306
Education expenditures per pupil, 356
Educational attainment, 359
Elected officials, 193
Elevations, 57
Emblems, 193
Executions in, 315
Famous natives, 193
Farms in, 303
Fortune 500 companies, 193
Health care quality, 368
Land area, 193
Land cover and use, 55
Memorable events, 193
Noteworthy places, 193
Nuclear plants in, 364
Parks and recreation areas, 53
Persons below poverty level, 321
Population by race and Hispanic origin, 269
Population by race/national origin, 193
Population estimates, 1990-2000, 169
Population, foreign-born, 297
Prisoners in, 313
Public school enrollment, 356
Resident population and population change, 261
Resident population by age, 2002, 277
Revenues and expenditures, 203
Taxation in, 204-207
Tourist information, 193
Web site, 193
Ohm's law, 756
Oil
Major spills, 779
Oil Production, 495
Oil reserves, world, 496
Oil suppliers, 496
Oklahoma, description, 193-194
Area codes, 804-805
Business, 193-194
Cities, major, population of, 193
Crime in, 306
Education expenditures per pupil, 356
Educational attainment, 359
Elected officials, 193
Elevations, 57
Emblems, 193
Executions in, 315
Famous natives, 194
Farms in, 303
Fortune 500 companies, 193
Health care quality, 368
Land area, 193
Land cover and use, 55
Memorable events, 194
Noteworthy places, 194
Parks and recreation areas, 53
Persons below poverty level, 321
Population by race and Hispanic origin, 269
Population by race/national origin, 193
Population estimates, 1990-2000, 169

Population, foreign-born, 297
Prisoners in, 313
Public school enrollment, 356
Resident population and population change, 261
Resident population by age, 2002, 277
Revenues and expenditures, 203
Taxation in, 204-207
Tourist information, 194
Web site, 194
Oklahoma City, Okla., description, 224
Area codes, 804-805
Climate in, 470
Crime in, 307, 308
Government, 224
Location, 224
Population, 224
Population by race/Hispanic origin, 237
Population, 1980-2000, 239
Tax burdens in, 242
Terrain and climate, 224
Visitor information, 224
Web site, 224
Old-Age, Survivors and Disability Insurance (see OASDI)
Olympic Sports, 887-905
2000 Summer Olympics at Sydney, Australia September 15-October 1, 2000, 887-889
Alpine Skiing, 900
Baseball, 897
Basketball, 897
Biathlon, 901
Bobsled, 901
Figure Skating, 903
Gymnastics, 898
Ice Hockey, 901
Locations of Olympiads, 905
Luge, 901
Medal Count by Nation, 2000, 889
Nordic Skiing and Jumping, 902
Soccer, 897
Softball, 897
Speed Skating, 904
Swimming and diving, 890-891
Track and field, 893-896
Volleyball, 897
Water Polo, 897
Omaha, Neb., description, 224-225
Area codes, 804-805
Crime in, 308
Government, 225
Location, 225
Population, 225
Population by race/Hispanic origin, 237
Population, 1980-2000, 239
Tax burdens in, 242
Terrain and climate, 225
Visitor information, 225
Web site, 225
Oman, description, 635-636
Area codes, 464
Economic indicators, 516
Economy, 635
Geography, 635
Government, 635
Health indicators, 482
Major cities, 635
People, 635
Population indicators, 477
One-parent family groups, 285, 285-287
Online trading, 342
OPEC (Organization of the Petroleum Exporting Countries), 715
Operation Desert Storm, 150
Operations
Cardiovascular, 371
Common, 371
Optical telescopes, 728
Option (bus.), definition, 346
Orange County, Calif.
Crime in, 307, 308
Order (bio.), 759
Oregon, description, 194
Area codes, 804-805
Business, 194
Cities, major, population of, 194
Crime in, 306
Education expenditures per pupil, 356
Educational attainment, 359
Elected officials, 194
Elevations, 57
Emblems, 194
Executions in, 315
Famous natives, 194
Farms in, 303
Fortune 500 companies, 194
Health care quality, 368
Land area, 194
Land cover and use, 55
Memorable events, 194
Noteworthy places, 194
Parks and recreation area, 53
Persons below poverty level, 321
Population by race and Hispanic origin, 269
Population by race/national origin, 194
Population estimates, 1990-2000, 169
Population, foreign-born, 297
Prisoners in, 313
Public school enrollment, 356
Resident population and population change, 261
Resident population by age, 2002, 277
Revenues and expenditures, 203
Taxation in, 204-207
Tourist information, 194
Web site, 194
Organ Transplants, 372
Number and survival rates, 372
Organisms, major groups of, 758-760
Organization for Security and Cooperation in Europe (OSCE), 715
Organization of African Unity (OAU), 715
Organization of American States (OAS), 715
Organization of Economic Cooperation and Development (OECD), 503
Organization of the Petroleum Exporting Countries (OPEC), 715
Orlando, Fla.
Crime in, 307, 308
Orthodox Churches (U.S.), 402
Oscar awards. See Academy Awards
Ottoman Empire, 427, 432-433
Outlays, definition, 143-144
Over-the-counter (OTC) stock, definition, 346
Overseas Private Investment Corporation (OPIC), 138
Ozone emissions in metropolitan areas, 777
Ozone layer, 774

P

Pacific Islanders (see Asian and Native Hawaiian/other Pacific Islander population)
Pacific Ocean (see Oceans of the World)
Pakistan, description, 636-637
Area codes, 464
Economic indicators, 516
Economy, 636
Geography, 636
Government, 636
Health indicators, 482
Major cities, 636
Nuclear power generation, 497
People, 636
Population in U.S., 299
Population indicators, 477
Palau, description, 637-638
Area codes, 464
Economy, 637
Geography, 637
Government, 637
Major cities, 637
People, 637
Palestinian Territories, description, 593-594
2002-03 Events, 20-21
Palm Sunday, 44
Palmyra Atoll, 208
Panama, 638
Area codes, 464
Economic indicators, 516
Economy, 638
Geography, 638
Government, 638
Health indicators, 482
Major cities, 638
People, 638
Population in U.S., 299
Population indicators, 477
Panama Canal, 54-55
Papua New Guinea, description, 638-639
Area codes, 464
Economic indicators, 516
Economy, 639
Geography, 638
Government, 639
Health indicators, 482
Major cities, 638
People, 638-639
Population indicators, 477
Paraguay, description, 639-640
Area codes, 464
Economic indicators, 516
Economy, 639
Geography, 639
Government, 639
Health indicators, 482
Major cities, 639
People, 639
Population indicators, 477
Parcel post, rates for, 167
Parents, single, 286-287
Park Service, National, 133-134
Parks, National (see National park system)
Parole, 312-313
Parsiism, 490
Particle physics, 757-758
Particles
Conservattion for, 756
Subatomic, 757-758
Particulate matter emissions, 774-775
Passover (Pesach), 45, 46
Patents
Issued for inventions, 791
Utility patents granted by patentee, 791
Pauli's exclusion principle, 757
Pay Cable (see Cable television)
Peace Corps, 138
Peace, Nobel Prize for, 854-856
Peacekeeping operations (UN), 711-712
Peer-to-Peer File Sharing, 397
Pennsylvania, description, 194-195
Area codes, 804-805
Business, 195
Cities, major, population of, 195
Crime in, 306
Education expenditures per pupil, 356
Educational attainment, 359
Elected officials, 195
Elevations, 57
Emblems, 194-195
Executions in, 315
Famous natives, 195
Farms in, 303
Fortune 500 companies, 195
Health care quality, 368
Land area, 195
Land cover and use, 55
Memorable events, 195
Noteworthy places, 195
Nuclear plants in, 364
Parks and recreation area, 53
Persons below poverty level, 321
Population by race and Hispanic origin, 269
Population by race/national origin, 195
Population estimates, 1990-2000, 169
Population, foreign-born, 297
Prisoners in, 313
Public school enrollment, 356
Resident population and population change, 261
Resident population by age, 2002, 277
Revenues and expenditures, 203
Taxation in, 204-207
Tourist information, 195
Web site, 195
Pension Benefit Guaranty Corporation (PBGC), 138
Pension fund, definition, 346
Pentecost, 44
Pentecostal Churches (U.S.), 402
Perpetual Calendar, 39
Persia, 417, 419, 427
Personal income, definition, 319-320
by County, 321
Disposable, 317
by Metropolitan Area, 320
by State, 319
Personal Video Recorder, 398
Personnel Management, Office of (OPM), description, 138
Employment and budget outlays, 141
Special pay rates and, 142
Peru, description, 640-641
Area codes, 464
Economic indicators, 516
Economy, 640
Geography, 640
Government, 640
Health indicators, 482
Major cities, 640
People, 640
Population in U.S., 299
Population indicators, 477
Pesach (Passover), 45, 46
Petroleum and petroleum products, description, 362-363
Strategic Petroleum Reserve, 363

U.S. Consumption, 362
U.S. exports/imports, 362-363
PGA Championship (golf), 912
Phases of the Moon, 47
Philadelphia, Penn., description, 225
Area codes, 804-805
Black population in, 271
Climate in, 470
Cost of living index, 243
Crime in, 307, 308
Government, 225
Hispanic population in, 273
Housing prices in, 290
Location, 225
Population, 225
Population by race/Hispanic origin, 237
Population, 1980-2000, 239
Rents in, 290
Tax burdens in, 242
Terrain and climate, 225
Visitor information, 225
Web site, 225
Philippines, description, 641-642
Area codes, 464
Economic indicators, 516
Economy, 641
Geography, 641
Government, 641
Health indicators, 482
Major cities, 641
People, 641
Population in U.S., 299
Population indicators, 477
U.S. immigrants from, 295
Phoenix, Ariz., description, 225-226
Area codes, 804-805
Black population in, 271
Climate in, 470
Cost of living index, 243
Crime in, 307, 308
Government, 226
Hispanic population in, 273
Housing prices in, 290
Location, 226
Population, 226
Population by race/Hispanic origin, 237
Population, 1980-2000, 239
Rents in, 290
Tax burdens in, 242
Terrain and climate, 226
Visitor information, 226
Web site, 226
Photography, Pulitzer Prizes for, 845
Photon, 757
Phylum, 759
Physics, 752
Basic laws of, 754-757
Key terms, 754
Major discoveries in, 753-754
Nobel Prizes in, 863-866
Subatomic particles, 757-758
Physiology or Medicine, Nobel Prizes in, 856-863
Pierce, Franklin
Administration, 115
Biography, 89
Election, 103
Pion, 758
Pitcairn Islands, 707
Pittsburgh, Pa.
Area codes, 804-805
Black population in, 271
Climate in, 470
Crime in, 307, 308
Housing prices in, 290
Population by race/Hispanic origin, 237
Population, 1980-2000, 239
Rents in, 290
Planets
Timing Planetary Phenomena, 49
Visibility, 2003, 47-49
Plate tectonics, 741
Platinum record, definition, 397
Plays (see Drama)
Pledge of Allegiance, U.S., 67
***Plessy v. Ferguson* (1896), 122**
Poetry
Bollingen Prize, 830
National Book Awards, 832
Pulitzer Prize for, 852
Poland, description, 642-644
Area codes, 464
Economic indicators, 516
Economy, 643
European Union membership, 509
Geography, 642-643
Government, 643
Health indicators, 482
Major cities, 642-643
Motor vehicle production, 408
People, 643
Population in U.S., 299
Population indicators, 477
Traffic deaths, 408
U.S. immigrants from, 295
Polar regions
Antarctica, 459-501
Arctic, 461
Policy Development, Office of, 131
Polk, James K.
Administration, 115
Biography, 89
Election, 102-103
Pollution
Air, 774-777
in Metropolitan areas (Pollutant Standards Index), 775
Water, 778-779
Popes, Chronological Listing of, 445-446
Population
Jail, 312
Prison, state and federal, 312
Population, U.S.
by Age, 276-278
Alaska Native, 274-275
American Indian, 274-275
Asian, 274
Black, 268-272
by Race/Hispanic origin, 267-275
Change in 75 largest cities, 1980-2000, 238-239
Change in major cities, 1970-2000, 231-234
Change, by state, 1990-2000, 261
Cities, by population size, 1960-90, 234
Cities, by race and Hispanic origin, 235-238
Counties, 50 largest, 1980-90, 258
Counties, 75 largest, 1990-2000, 259
Density and area of residence, 267
Density in major cities, 1970-90, 231-234
Density of U.S. States, 1980-2000, 170
Farm, 302
Fastest-declining cities, 238
Fastest-declining MSAs, 256
Fastest-growing cities, 238
Federal government employment and, 141
Foreign-born, 297, 298, 299, 300
Growth, by region, 266
Hispanic, 272-273
Male-female ratio, 279
Marital status of, by race and Hispanic origin, 281
Marital status of, by sex and age, 282
Median age of, 276
MSAs, 1980-90, 244-249
MSAs, by race and Hispanic origin, 2000, 250-255
Native Hawaiian, 274
Never married, percentage, 281
Pacific Islander, 274
of Reservations and trust lands, 275
Rural, 262
by Sex, 276-277
by State, 1790-1990, 263-265
of States, 1990-99, 169
of Territories, 207-210
Urban, 262
Population, world, 472-478
Birth rate, 475-477
Births, 472, 473
Countries with oldest and youngest, 473
of largest Countries, 2000, 2025 and 2050, 473
Death rate, 475-477
Deaths, 472, 473
Distribution by major areas, 472
Fertility rate, 475-477
Growth, 472
Indicators, 475-477
Life expectancy, by nation, 475-477
Milestones, 473
Percent urban, 475-477
Trends, 472-498
Portfolio investment, 507
Portland, Maine
Tax burdens in, 242
Portland, Oreg., description, 226
Area codes, 804-805
Cost of living index, 243
Crime in, 307, 308
Government, 226
Location, 226
Population, 226
Population by race/Hispanic origin, 237
Population, 1980-2000, 239
Tax burdens in, 242
Terrain and climate, 226
Visitor information, 226
Web site, 226
Portugal, description, 644-646
Area codes, 464
Currency exchange rates, 505
Declining population, 472
Economic indicators, 516
Economy, 645
European Union membership, 509
Geography, 644
Government, 644-645
Health indicators, 482
History, 427-428
Major cities, 644
Motor vehicle production, 408
People, 644
Population in U.S., 299
Population indicators, 477
Traffic deaths, 408
U.S. immigrants from, 295
Portuguese Guinea (see Guinea-Bissau)
Portuguese lang., 493
Possessions (see Territories)
Post office (see Postal Service, U.S.)
Postage rates, 167
Postage stamps, 167
Postal abbreviations, 168
Postal Rate Commission, 138
Postal Service, U.S., description, 139
Poverty
Families below poverty level, by state, 321
Federal income guidelines, 162
Level, defined, 320-321
by Race/Hispanic origin, 322
Threshholds, U.S., 161
Power, measurement of, 770-771
Preakness Stakes, 921
Precession of the equinoxes, 37-42
Prefixes used in the metric system, 767
Presbyterian Churches (U.S.), 402
Prescription Drugs, 368
President's Day (see Washington's Birthday)
President, U.S.
Executive office of the, 131-132
Salary and allowances, 140
Presidential Elections
1796–2000, 101-110
2000, by State, 111
Campaign Contribution Limits, 112
Electoral College, 110-112
Federal Election Campaign Act, 112
Voter Turnout, 110
Presidential Order of Succession, 114
Presidents, U.S.
Administrations, 114-119
Biographies of, 86-100
Elections, 1796–2000, 101-112
Order of succession, 114
Prevailing winds, definition, 468
Prices
Consumer, 324
Gasoline, 363
Inflation, 324
Producer, 324-327
Print media, 386-389
Books, 389-393
Magazines, 387-389
Newspapers, 386-387
Priority mail, rates for, 167
Prisoners in the U.S.
Executed by race, 314
Executed by system, 315
Incarceration rate, by state, 313
by State, 313
by System, sex and race, 312
Prisons, Bureau of, 134
Prisons, definition, 312
Lifetime likelihood of going to prison, 314
Population, 312
Pritzker Prizes in Architecture, 837
Private domestic investment, 321
Private schools, 356-358
Number in U.S., 355
Prizes (see Awards and Prizes)
Probation, 312-313
Producer price index, 324-327
Production workers, hourly compensation costs for, by selected country, 510
Professional Bowlers Association (PBA), 907
Professional degrees conferred in U.S., 1950-2000, 360
Professional Golfers Association (PGA), 911
Professional sports, 906-972
Projections, definition, 478
Property crime
Arrests for, 311
Number and rate, by offense, 305
Rate, by state, 306
Property taxes
by State, 204
Protists, 759
Proton, 757
Providence, R.I.
Crime in, 307, 308

Population by race/Hispanic origin, 237
Tax burdens in, 242
Public Debt, Bureau of the , 136
Public schools
Enrollment, 354-355
Expenditures, 354
Number in U.S., 355
Puerto Rico, description, 209
Elevations, 57
Population, 209
Population indicators, 477
Pulitzer Prizes, 839-854
Punishment, capital, 314-315
Purchasing power of the dollar, 324
Purim, 45
Push technology, 809
PVR (see Personal Video Recorder)

Q

Qatar, description, 646
Area codes, 464
Economic indicators, 516
Economy, 646
Geography, 646
Government, 646
Health indicators, 483
Major cities, 646
People, 646
Population indicators, 477
Quakers (see Friends Churches)
Quantum Mechanics, 757
Quantum Physics, laws of, 757
Quarks, 758

R

Race and/or Hispanic origin
ACT and SAT scores, 357
in Armed forces, 153
Cancer deaths by, 375
Crime victimization rates, 310
Death rates, 377
Educational attainment by, 360
Employment status pf population, 334
Infant mortality by, 382
Life expectancy, 380, 381
Lifetime likelihood of going to prison, 314
Population of U.S. cities, 235-238
Population of U.S. Metropolitan areas, 250-255
Prisoners by, 312
Prisoners executed by, 314
Radio, 396
Ownership by selected nation, 803
Sales of radios, 396
Stations in U.S. by format, 396
Radio telescopes, 729
Railroad Administration, Federal (FRA), 135
Railroad Passenger Corporation, National (see AMTRAK)
Railroads, 415
AMTRAK, 415
Commuter and rapid rail systems, U.S., 415
Mileage and accident rates, 415
Rain forests, 781-782
Rain shadow, definition, 448, 468
Ramadan, 46
Ramanavami, 46
Rape, forcible
Arrests for, 311
Rate, by state, 306
Rathayatra, 46
Rating (bus.), definition, 346
Reagan, Ronald
Administration, 119
Biography, 97-98
Election, 109
Receipts, definition, 144
Receipts, Federal Government, by source, 142
Recidivism, 312-313
Recording industry, 396-397
Gold, platinum and diamond record definitions, 397
Grammy Awards, 827-829
MTV Video Music Awards, 829-830
Sales of recorded music by genre and age group, 397
Top-selling albums of 1999, 396
Recycling/composting of solid waste, 780
Red giants, 728
Reformation, the, 429-430
Reformed Churches (U.S.), 402
Regional trading groups, 512-514
Regulatory Commission, Nuclear (NRC), 138
Relative humidity, definition, 468
Religions, 486-492
Affiliations in the U.S., 401-406
Atheists, 490
Baha'i, 490
Buddhism, 489-498
Chinese folk, 490
Christianity, 487-498
Chronology of world, 490-501
Confucianism, 490
Hinduism, 488-498
Islam, 488-498
Jainism, 490
Judaism, 486-498
New religions, 490
Nonreligious, 490
Parsees, 490
Shintoism, 490
Sikhism, 490
Templeton Prize, 838
World, 486-492
Reptiles, endangered in U.S., 785
Republicans in state legislatures, 206
Reservations, population of, 275
Reserve forces, 151-152
Reserve System, Federal, 137
Reservoirs, world's largest, by capacity, 455
Retail trade industries
Earnings in, 335
Retired persons, Social Security benefits for, 157
Reunion Island, 701-702
Area codes, 464
Revolutionary War, 150
Rhode Island, description, 195-196
Area codes, 804-805
Business, 195
Cities, major, population of, 195
Crime in, 306
Education expenditures per pupil, 356
Educational attainment, 359
Elected officials, 195
Elevations, 57
Emblems, 195
Executions in, 315
Famous natives, 195-196
Farms in, 303
Fortune 500 companies, 195
Health care quality, 368
Land area, 195
Land cover and use, 55
Memorable events, 196
Noteworthy places, 196
Parks and recreation area, 53
Persons below poverty level, 321
Population by race and Hispanic origin, 269
Population by race/national origin, 195
Population estimates, 1990-2000, 169
Population, foreign-born, 297
Prisoners in, 313
Public school enrollment, 356
Resident population and population change, 261
Resident population by age, 1999, 277
Revenues and expenditures, 203
Taxation in, 204-207
Tourist information, 196
Web site, 196
Rhodesia (see Zimbabwe)
River, definition, 448
Length and source of, by world, 454
Rivers
Navigable U.S., 53-55, 56
Roads and streets in U.S., 411
Robbery
Arrests for, 311
Rate, by state, 306
***Roe v. Wade* (1973), 123**
Roman Catholic Church
Popes, Chronological listing of, 445-446
Roman Catholic Church (U.S.), 401
2002-03 scandals, 29-30
Roman Rite Churches (U.S.), 403
Romania, description, 646-647
Area codes, 464
Declining population, 472
Economic indicators, 516
Economy, 646
Geography, 646
Government, 646
Health indicators, 483
Major cities, 646
People, 646
Population in U.S., 299
RomaniaPopulation indicators, 477
U.S. immigrants from, 295
Romanov dynasty, 443-444
Rome
History, 419-420, 421-422
Holy Roman emperors, 441
Rulers of ancient, 440
Roosevelt, Franklin D.
Administration, 117
Biography, 94
Election, 107
Roosevelt, Theodore
Administration, 116-117
Biography, 92
Election, 105
Vice President, 113
Rose Bowl, 870
Rosh Hashanah (Jewish New Year), 45
Rural population, U.S., 262
Russell Indexes, definition, 346
Russia, description, 648-651
Area codes, 464
Declining population, 472
Dynasties and czars of, 432-433, 443-444
Economic indicators, 516
Economy, 648
Geography, 648
Government, 648
Health indicators, 483
Major cities, 648
Motor vehicle production, 408
Nuclear power generation, 497
Oil reserves, 496
People, 648
Population indicators, 477
Russian lang., 493
Rwanda, description, 651
Area codes, 464
Economic indicators, 516
Economy, 651
Geography, 651
Government, 651
Health indicators, 483
Major cities, 651
People, 651
Population indicators, 477

S

Sabbath, 45
Sacramento, Calif., description, 226
Cost of living index, 243
Crime in, 307
Government, 226
Location, 226
Population, 226
Population by race/Hispanic origin, 237
Population, 1980-2000, 239
Terrain and climate, 226
Visitor information, 226
Web site, 226
Saint Christopher (see Saint Kitts and Nevis)
St. Helena, 707
Area codes, 464
Saint Kitts and Nevis, description, 652
Economic indicators, 516
Economy, 652
Geography, 652
Government, 652
Health indicators, 483
People, 652
Saint Lawrence Seaway, 54-55
Saint Lawrence Seaway Development Corporation, 135
Saint Louis, Mo., description
Area codes, 804-805
Cost of living index, 243
Government, 229
Location, 229
Population, 229
Population by race/Hispanic origin, 238
Population, 1980-2000, 239
Terrain and climate, 229
Visitor information, 229
Web site, 229
Saint Lucia, description, 652
Economic indicators, 516
Economy, 652
Geography, 652
Government, 652
Health indicators, 483
Major cities, 652
People, 652
Saint Maarten (see Netherlands Antilles)
St. Pierre and Miquelon, 702
Area codes, 464
Saint Vincent and the Grenadines, description, 652-653
Economy, 653
Economic indicators, 516
Geography, 652
Government, 652-653
Health indicators, 483

Major cities, 652
People, 652
Salaries
in Armed forces, 155
in Federal government, 140
Salaries of state officials, 206
Sales taxes
by State, 204
Salt Lake City, Utah
Climate in, 470
Crime in, 307, 308
Population by race/Hispanic origin, 237
Tax burdens in, 242
Salvation Army, 403
Samoa, description, 653
Economic indicators, 516
Geography, 653
Government, 653
Health indicators, 483
judiciary. l Economy, 653
Major cities, 653
People, 653
San Antonio, Texas, description, 226
Area codes, 804-805
Black population in, 271
Climate in, 470
Cost of living index, 243
Crime in, 307, 308
Black population in, 271
Climate in, 470
Government, 227
Hispanic population in , 273
Housing prices in, 290
Location, 227
Population, 227
Population by race/Hispanic origin, 237
Population, 1980-2000, 239
Rents in, 290
Terrain and climate, 227
Visitor information, 227
Web site, 227
San Diego, Calif., description, 227
Area codes, 804-805
Black population in, 271
Climate in, 470
Cost of living index, 243
Crime in, 307, 308
Government, 227
Hispanic population in , 273
Housing prices in, 290
Location, 227
Population, 227
Population by race/Hispanic origin, 237
Population, 1980-2000, 239
Rents in, 290
Terrain and climate, 227
Visitor information, 227
Web site, 227
San Francisco. Calif., description, 227
Area codes, 804-805
Black population in, 271
Climate in, 470
Crime in, 308
Government, 228
Housing prices in, 290
Location, 227
Population, 227
Population by race/Hispanic origin, 237
Population, 1980-2000, 239
Rents in, 290
Terrain and climate, 227-228
Visitor information, 228
Web site, 228
San Jose, Calif., description, 228
Area codes, 804-805
Cost of living index
Crime in, 307, 308
Government, 228
Hispanic population in , 273
Location, 228
Population, 228
Population by race/Hispanic origin, 237
Population, 1980-2000, 239
Terrain and climate, 228
Visitor information, 228
Web site, 228
San Marino, description, 653-654
Area codes, 464
Economy, 653-654
Geography, 653
Government, 653
Major cities, 653
People, 653
Sao Tome and Principe, description, 654
Area codes, 464
Economy, 654
Economic indicators, 516
Geography, 654
Government, 654
Health indicators, 483
Major cities, 654
People, 654
SARS, 34-35
SAT (Scholastic Assessment Test)
Scores by sex, race and Hispanic origin, 357
Satellite communications, 802
Saturn
Visibility, 2003, 48
Saudi Arabia, description, 654-656
Area codes, 464
Economic indicators, 516
Economy, 654-655
Geography, 654
Government, 654
Health indicators, 483
Major cities, 654
Oil reserves, 496
People, 654
Population in U.S., 299
Population indicators, 477
Savings and loans (thrifts)
Crisis, 330
Savoy-Carignano, House of, 444
***Schechter Poultry Corp. v. United States* (1935), 122**
***Schenk v. United States* (1919), 122**
School Breakfast Program, 161
School district governments, 211
School Lunch Program, 161
Schools (see also Public schools, Private schools)
Catholic, 357
Government expenditures, 354
Nursery, 355
Private, 356-358
Public, 354-356
Schwarzenegger, Arnold, 24-25
Science
Nobel Prizes, 854-868
Science and Technology, 716-812
2002-03 News, 34-36
Science and Technology Policy, Office of , 131-132
Science Foundation, National, 138
Scotland (see United Kingdom)
Search engine, 809
Seattle, Wash., description, 228
Area codes, 804-805
Black population in, 271
Climate in, 470
Crime in, 307, 308
Government, 228
Housing prices in, 290
Location, 228
Population by race/Hispanic origin, 237
Population, 1980-2000, 239
Rents in, 290
Tax burdens in, 242
Tax progressivity in, 240
Terrain and climate, 228
Visitor information, 228
Web site, 228
Secondary cold front, definition, 468
Secondary depression, definition, 468
Secondary schools
Catholic, 357
Enrollment, 354-355
Expenditures, 354
Number in U.S., 355
Revenues, 354
Secret Service, U.S., 136
Securities and Exchange Commission (SEC), 138, 346-347
Securities, definition, 346
Security Council, National (NSC), 131
Selective Service System, 138
Senate, U.S.
108th Congress, 126
Address and phone number, 126
Officers, 126
Salaries, 140
Senegal, description, 656
Area codes, 464
Economic indicators, 516
Economy, 656
Geography, 656
Government, 656
Health indicators, 483
Major cities, 656
People, 656
Population in U.S., 299
Population indicators, 477
Senior executive service (ES), salaries in, 140
Serbia and Montenegro
Area codes, 464
Economy, 657
Economic indicators, 516
Geography, 656
Government, 656
Health indicators, 483
Major cities, 656
People, 656
Population in U.S., 299
Population indicators, 477
U.S. immigrants from, 295
Server (Internet term), 809
Service industries
Earnings in, 335
Seven Deadly Sins, 492
Seventh-day Adventists, 403
Sex
ACT and SAT scores by, 357
Educational attainment by, 360
Frequency of intercourse, 301
Global facts, 484-498
Homosexuality, 300
Marital fidelity, 301
for Money, 300
Number of partners, 301
U.S. population by, 279
Women and, 300
Seychelles, description, 658
Area codes, 464
Economic indicators, 516
Economy, 658
Geography, 658
Government, 658
Health indicators, 483
Major cities, 658
People, 658
Shabuoth (Feast of Weeks), 46
Shareware, 809
Shintoism, 490
Shrove Tuesday, 44
Sierra Leone, description, 658-659
Area codes, 464
Economic indicators, 516
Economy, 658
Geography, 658
Government, 658
Health indicators, 483
Major cities, 658
People, 658
Population indicators, 477
Sikhism, 490
Singapore, description, 659-660
Area codes, 464
Currency exchange rates, 505
Economic indicators, 516
Economy, 659
Geography, 659
Government, 659
Health indicators, 483
Major cities, 659
People, 659
Population indicators, 477
Single parents, 286-287
Sins, Seven Deadly, 492
Sioux Falls, S. Dak.
Population by race/Hispanic origin, 237
Tax burdens in, 242
Tax progressivity in, 240
Skiing
Olympic, 900
Slaughter-House Cases (1873), 120
Slovak Republic
Economic indicators, 516
Slovakia, description, 660
Area codes, 464
Economy, 660
Geography, 660
Government, 660
Health indicators, 483
Major cities, 660
Nuclear power generation, 497
People, 660
Population indicators, 477
Slovenia, description, 660-661
Area codes, 464
Declining population, 472
Economic indicators, 516
Economy, 661
Geography, 660-661
Government, 661
Health indicators, 483
Major cities, 661
Nuclear power generation, 497
People, 661
Population indicators, 477
Small business, 347-351
Small Business Administration (SBA), 139
Employment and budget outlays, 141
Smokers, Adult, in the U.S., 385
Smoking, 480-498
Snails, endangered in U.S., 786
Soccer (see also World Cup)
NCAA champions, 875
Olympic champions, 897
Social insurance programs, 155-163
Social Security, 155-159
Social Security Administration, description, 139
Softball
Olympic champions, 897
Solar Calendar, 38
Solar Phenomena, 37
Equinoxes, 37
Solstices, 37
Solid waste, 779-780
Solomon Islands, 661-662
Area codes, 464
Economic indicators, 516
Economy, 661-662
Geography, 661
Government, 661
Health indicators, 483
Major cities, 661
People, 661
Somalia, description, 662-663

Area codes, 464
Economic indicators, 516
Economy, 662
Geography, 662
Government, 662
Health indicators, 483
Major cities, 662
People, 662
Population indicators, 477
Source reduction of solid waste, 780-783
South Africa, description, 663-665
Area codes, 464
Currency exchange rates, 505
Economy, 663
Geography, 663
Government, 663
Health indicators, 483
Major cities, 663
Motor vehicle production, 408
Nuclear power generation, 497
People, 663
Population indicators, 477
South America
2002-03 Events, 22-23
Area and percent of world total, 448
Birth rate, 475
Death rate, 475
Elevation extremes, 449
Energy production/consumption, 494, 496
Fertility rate, 475
Life expectancy, 475
Nuclear power generation, 497
Percent urban, 475
Population, 2000, 475
Population, percentage of world, 472
U.S. immigrants from, 295
South Carolina, description, 196
Area codes, 804-805
Black population in, 270
Business, 196
Cities, major, population of, 196
Crime in, 306
Education expenditures per pupil, 356
Educational attainment, 359
Elected officials, 196
Elevations, 57
Emblems, 196
Executions in, 315
Famous natives, 196
Farms in, 303
Fortune 500 companies, 196
Health care quality, 368
Land area, 196
Land cover and use, 55
Memorable events, 196
Noteworthy places, 196
Nuclear plants in, 364
Parks and recreation area, 53
Persons below poverty level, 321
Population by race and Hispanic origin, 269
Population by race/national origin, 196
Population estimates, 1990-2000, 169
Population, foreign-born, 297
Prisoners in, 313
Public school enrollment, 356
Resident population and population change, 261
Resident population by age, 2002, 277
Revenues and expenditures, 203
Taxation in, 204-207
Tourist information, 196
Web site, 196
***South Carolina v. Katzenbach* (1966, 123**
South Dakota, description, 196-197
Area codes, 804-805
Business, 197
Cities, major, population of, 197
Crime in, 306
Education expenditures per pupil, 356
Educational attainment, 359
Elected officials, 197
Elevations, 57
Emblems, 196
Executions in, 315
Famous natives, 197
Farms in, 303
Fortune 500 companies, 197
Health care quality, 368
Land area, 196
Land cover and use, 55
Memorable events, 197
Noteworthy places, 197
Parks and recreation area, 53
Persons below poverty level, 321
Population by race and Hispanic origin, 269
Population by race/national origin, 197
Population estimates, 1990-2000, 169
Population, foreign-born, 297
Prisoners in, 313
Public school enrollment, 356
Resident population and population change, 261
Resident population by age, 2002, 277
Revenues and expenditures, 203
Taxation in, 204-207
Tourist information, 197
Web site, 197
South Korea (see Korea, South)
Currency exchange rates, 505
Economic indicators, 515
Southern African Development Community (SADC), 512
Soviet Union, former
Commonwealth of Independent States (CIS), 715
Energy consumption/production, 494, 496
Nuclear power generation, 497
U.S. immigrants from, 295
Space shuttles, 733-738
2002-03 Events, 34
Spaceflights carrying people, 732-738
Spain, description, 665-666
Area codes, 464
Currency exchange rates, 505
Declining population, 472
Dynasties and kings of, 443
Economic indicators, 516
Economy, 665
Geography, 665
Government, 665
Health indicators, 483
Major cities, 665
Motor vehicle production, 408
Nuclear power generation, 497
People, 665
Population in U.S., 299
Population indicators, 477
Traffic deaths, 408
U.S. immigrants from, 295
Spam (Internet term), 809
Spanish lang., 493
Spanish-American War, 150
Special district governments, 211
Special nutrition programs, 160-161
Special Operations Forces, 150-151
Species (bio.), 759
Endangered and threatened species in U.S., 784
Endangered mammals of the world, 783-784
Speed skating, Olympic, 904
Sports, 869-878
College, 869-878
International, 879-886
Olympic, 887-905
Professional, 906-972
Websites about, 812
Squall line, definition, 468
Sri Lanka, description, 666-667
Area codes, 464
Currency exchange rates, 505
Economic indicators, 516
Economy, 667
Geography, 666-667
Government, 667
Health indicators, 483
Major cities, 667
People, 667
Population indicators, 477
St. Louis, Mo.
Black population in, 271
Climate in, 470
Cost of living index
Housing prices in, 290
St. Patrick's Day, 43
Standard & Poor's 500, definition, 347
***Standard Oil Co. of New Jersey v. United States* (1911), 122**
Standard weights and measures, 767-771
Stanley Cup (see also Ice Hockey, professional)
Stars and the universe, 723-729
Bright stars, 726
Brightest as seen from Earth, 726
Constellations, 724-725
Variable, 729
State and local government
Education expenditures, 354
Health care expenditures by, 367
State government finances, 204-206
State legislatures, 206
State parks and recreation areas by state, 53
State tables
Crime rates, 306
Defense contracts, payroll and personnel, 154
Educational attainment, 359
Elevations, 57
Executions by, 315
Expenditures per public school pupil, 356
Farm Marketings, 304
Farms–Number and Acreage, 303
Finances of state governments, 205
Health care quality, 368
Individual income tax rates, 205
Land area, urban and rural, 262
Legislatures, composition of, 206
Motor vehicle registrations, 410
Nuclear plants in, 364
Parks and recreation areas, 53
People with and without health insurance, 370
Population by race and Hispanic origin, 269
Population change, 1980-90, 261
Population density, 1980-97, 170
Population, 1790-1990, 263-265
Population, 1990-2000, 169
Prisoners and incarceration rates, 313
Public school enrollment, 356
Public school teacher salaries, 356
Resident population by age, 2002, 277
Revenues and expenditures of state governments, 203
Salaries of administrative officials, 206
Tax collections, 204
Top priority Superfund Site, by state, 780
State, U.S. Dept. of, description, 134-135
Employment and budget outlays, 141
States, U.S.
2002-03 Events, 30
Area, 169-203
Area codes, 804-805
Borders, 169-203
Budget shortfalls, 30
Business, 169-203
Cities, 169-203
Descriptions, 169-203
Elected officials, 169-203
Emblems, 169-203
Famous natives, 170-203
Government finances, 205
Gross state product, 169-203
Lakes, 169-203
Memorable events, 170-203
Mountains, 169-203
Noteworthy places, 170-203
Postal abbreviations for, 168
Revenues and expenditures of state governments, 203
Taxation, 204, 205
Tourist information, 170-203
Web pages for, 170-203
Stationary front, definition, 468
Statue of Liberty, 293
Stem Cell Therapies, 378-379
Stock exchange, definition, 347
American (AMEX), 342
New York (NYSE), 341
Stockbroker, definition, 347
Storm surge, definition, 468
Strange particles, 758
Strategic Petroleum Reserve, 363
Strokes and bypass surgery, 374
Students
in Catholic schools, 357
in Private schools, 355, 356-357
in Public schools, 354-355
SAT scores of, 357
Subatomic particles, 757-758
Substance abuse (see also Alcohol, Drugs and drug abuse)
Alcohol, 384
Illicit drugs, 382-384
Tobacco, 385
Substance Abuse and Mental Health Services Administration, 133
Sudan, description, 667-668
Area codes, 464
Economic indicators, 516

Economy, 668
Geography, 667-668
Government, 668
Health indicators, 483
Major cities, 668
People, 668
Population indicators, 477
Suicide
Number and rate, by age, 379
Sukkoth (Tabernacles), 45
Sulfur dioxide emissions, 775
Summer feeding program, participants and cost, 160
Summer Olympics (see Olympic Sports)
Sun, eclipses of the, 49
Super Bowl results, 928-932
Superclusters, 728
Superfamily (bio.), 760
Superfund
Hazardous waste sites, 781
Top priority Superfund site by state, 780
Supernovae, 728-729
Supplemental Security Income (SSI), 159
Supreme Court of the U.S., 120-123
2002-03 Decisions, 31-32
Cases before the, 124
Chief Justices of, 120
Important decisions of, 120-123
Justices of, 121
Salaries of justices, 140
Surgery, 371-373
Abortions, 372
Cardiovascular operations, 371
Common operations, 371
Organ transplants, 372
Suriname, description, 669
Area codes, 464
Economic indicators, 516
Economy, 669
Geography, 669
Government, 669
Health indicators, 483
Major cities, 669
People, 669
Population indicators, 477
Susan B. Anthony Day, 44
Svalbard, 704-705
Swaziland, description, 669-670
Area codes, 464
Economic indicators, 516
Economy, 669
Geography, 669
Government, 669
Health indicators, 483
Major cities, 669
People, 669
Population indicators, 477
Sweden, description, 670-671
Area codes, 464
Currency exchange rates, 505
Economic indicators, 516
Economy, 670
European Union membership, 509
Geography, 670
Government, 670
Health indicators, 483
Major cities, 670
Motor vehicle production, 408
Nuclear power generation, 497
People, 670
Population in U.S., 299
Population indicators, 477
Traffic deaths, 408
U.S. immigrants from, 295
Swimming
NCAA champions, 876
Swimming and Diving
Men's Olympic Champions, 890-891
Women's Olympic Champions, 891-892
Switzerland, description, 671-672
Area codes, 464
Currency exchange rates, 505
Economic indicators, 516
Economy, 671
Geography, 671
Government, 671
Health indicators, 483
Major cities, 671
Nuclear power generation, 497
People, 671
Population in U.S., 299
Population indicators, 477
Traffic deaths, 408
U.S. immigrants from, 295
Syria, description, 672-673
Area codes, 464
Economic indicators, 516
Economy, 672
Geography, 672
Government, 672
Health indicators, 483
Major cities, 672
People, 672
Population in U.S., 299
Population indicators, 477
Systems of measurement, 767-771

T

Taft, William Howard
Administration, 117
Biography, 92-93
Chief Justice of the U.S. Supreme Court, 120
Election, 105-106
Justice of U.S. Supreme Court, 121
Taiwan, description, 673-674
Area codes, 464
Currency exchange rates, 505
Economy, 673-674
Geography, 673
Government, 673
Major cities, 673
Motor vehicle production, 408
Nuclear power generation, 497
People, 673
Population in U.S., 299
Tajikistan, description, 675-676
Area codes, 464
Economic indicators, 516
Economy, 675
Geography, 675
Government, 675
Health indicators, 483
Major cities, 675
People, 675
Population indicators, 477
Tampa-St. Petersburg, Fla.
Black population in, 271
Crime in, 307, 308
Housing prices in, 290
Rents in, 290
Tanzania, description, 676-677
Area codes, 464
Economic indicators, 516
Economy, 676
Geography, 676
Government, 676
Health indicators, 483
Major cities, 676
People, 676
Population indicators, 477
Tariffs and quotas, 508
Taxes and taxation
2002-03 News, 27
Burdens in major U.S. cities, 242
Deductions, average itemized, 166
Individual income tax rates, by state, 205
Internal revenue collections, 166
Internal Revenue Service, 163-166
Progressivity of U.S. Cities, 243
Property taxes by state, 204
Returns filed and examined, 165
Returns processed, 164
Sales taxes by state, 204
Tax rate schedules, 164
Taylor, Charles, 21-22
Taylor, Zachary
Administration, 115
Biography, 89
Election, 103
Teachers
in Catholic schools, 357
in Private schools, 355, 357
in Public schools, 355
Salaries, by state, 356
Technology, 787-812
Technology Administration, 132-133
Teenagers, births to, 280
Telecommunications, 800-805
Telephones
Long distance companies, U.S., 800
by Selected nation, 803
U.S. telephone systems, 800
Telephones, wireless, 801
Telescopes
Optical, 728
Radio, 729
Television, 393
Cable TV, 394-395
DVDs, 397-398
Emmy Awards, 821-823
Games, 400
Longest running series, 394
MTV Video Music Awards, 829-830
Primetime viewing shares of free and cable TV networks, 394
by Selected nation, 803
Top 15 shows 1999-2000, 394
Top 50 shows of all time, 393
Top selling and renting videos, 398
Temperature, 769-770
Celsius, Fahrenheit and Kelvin scales compared, 769
Temperature inversion, definition, 468
Temperature-humidity index, definition, 468
Templeton Prize Winners, 838
Temporary Assistance to Needy Families (TANF) (see Welfare)
Temporary Disability Insurance, 156
Ten Commandments, 492
Tennessee, description, 197
Area codes, 804-805
Black population in, 269
Business, 197
Cities, major, population of, 197
Crime in, 306
Education expenditures per pupil, 356
Educational attainment, 359
Elected officials, 197
Elevations, 57
Emblems, 197
Executions in, 315
Famous natives, 197
Farms in, 303
Fortune 500 companies, 197
Health care quality, 368
Land area, 197
Land cover and use, 55
Memorable events, 197
Noteworthy places, 197
Nuclear plants in, 364
Parks and recreation area, 53
Persons below poverty level, 321
Population by race and Hispanic origin, 269
Population by race/national origin, 197
Population estimates, 1990-2000, 169
Population, foreign-born, 297
Prisoners in, 313
Public school enrollment, 356
Resident population and population change, 261
Resident population by age, 1999, 277
Revenues and expenditures, 203
Taxation in, 204-207
Tourist information, 197
Web site, 197
Tennessee Valley Authority (TVA), 139
Tennis, 915
NCAA champions, 877
Women's Grand Slam Champions, 916-917
Territories
United States, 207-210
Territories of the World
Area codes for, 462-464
Time zones for, 462-464
Terrorism, 17-20, 26
Texas, description, 197-198
Area codes, 804-805
Black population in, 270
Business, 198
Cities, major, population of, 198
Crime in, 306
Education expenditures per pupil, 356
Educational attainment, 359
Elected officials, 198
Elevations, 57
Emblems, 198
Executions in, 315
Famous natives, 198
Farms in, 303
Fortune 500 companies, 198
Health care quality, 368
Land area, 198
Land cover and use, 55
Memorable events, 198
Noteworthy places, 198
Nuclear plants in, 364
Persons below poverty level, 321
Population by race and Hispanic origin, 269
Population by race/national origin, 198
Population estimates, 1990-2000, 169
Population, foreign-born, 297
Prisoners in, 313
Public school enrollment, 356
Resident population and population change, 261
Resident population by age, 1999, 277
Revenues and expenditures, 203
Taxation in, 204-207
Tourist information, 198
Web site, 198
Thailand, description, 677-678
Area codes, 464
Economic indicators, 516
Economy, 677
Geography, 677

Government, 677
Health indicators, 483
Major cities, 677
People, 677
Population in U.S., 299
Population indicators, 477
Thanksgiving, 42
Theater
Pulitzer Prize in Drama, 849
Tony Awards, 824-827
Theft
Arrests for, 311
Rate, by state, 306
Thermodynamics, laws of, 756
Thoroughbred Racing, 918
Belmont Stakes, 922
Breeders' Cup, 918
Horse of the Year (Eclipse Award), 918
Kentucky Derby, 920
Preakness Stakes, 921
Triple Crown winners, 918
Thrift institutions, definition, 330
Thrift Supervision, Office of (OTS), 136
Thumbnail (Internet term), 809
Tidal waves (see Earthquakes, Tsunamis), **741**
Time zones and area codes for nations and territories, 462-464
Time, measurement of, 769
Timing Planetary Phenomena, 49
Tivo (see Personal Video Recorder)
Tobacco
Bureau of Alcohol, Tobacco and Firearms, 135
Cigarettes, 385
Health effects, 385
Teenage users, 385
Use, 480-498
Togo, description, 678
Area codes, 464
Economic indicators, 516
Economy, 678
Geography, 678
Government, 678
Health indicators, 483
Major cities, 678
People, 678
Population indicators, 477
Tokelau, 704
Tonga, description, 678-679
Area codes, 464
Economic indicators, 516
Economy, 678-679
Geography, 678
Government, 678
Health indicators, 483
Major cities, 678
People, 678
Population in U.S., 299
Tony Awards, 824-827
Tornado, definition, 468
Worst in U.S. History, 467
Tour De France winners, 881
Tourism
Top destinations for U.S. tourists, 414
Tourists in U.S. by country of origin, 414
World's top destinations, 414
Tourist information, by state, 170-203
Town governments, 211
Track and Field
NCAA champions, 876
Olympic champions, 893-896
World Records, 885
Trade
U.S. merchandise partners, 504
Trade balance, 506
Trade Commission, Federal (FTC), 137
Trade Representative, Office of the U.S., 132
Trade, international, 507-508
GATT, 508
U.S. international trade balance, 506
Traffic, 411
Transit Administration, Federal, 135
Transplantation, organs, 372
Transportation and public utilities industries
Earnings in, 335
Transportation Safety Board, National (NTSB), 138
Transportation Statistics, Bureau of, 135
Transportation, U.S., 407-415
Aviation, 411-414
Fatalities, 408
Passenger travel, 408
Safety, 408-409
Traffic, 411
Transportation, U.S. Dept. of (DOT), description, 135
Employment and budget outlays, 141
Travel
Websites about, 812
Treasury bills, 331
Treasury bonds, 331
Treasury, U.S.
Bills, 331
Treasury, U.S. Dept. of, description, 135-136
Employment and budget outlays, 141
Trigonometry, 766-767
Trinidad and Tobago, description, 679
Economic indicators, 516
Economy, 679
Geography, 679
Government, 679
Health indicators, 483
Major cities, 679
People, 679
Population in U.S., 299
Population indicators, 477
Trinity Sunday, 44
Triple Crown winners
Baseball, 956
Thoroughbred Racing, 918
Tropical storm, definition, 468
Trough, definition, 468
Trucks
Number in U.S., 407
Registrations, by state, 410
Registrations, world, 409
Sales, U.S., 409
Top selling in U.S., 411
Truman, Harry S
Administration, 117-118
Biography, 94-95
Election, 107
Vice President, 113
Trust fund, definition, 144
Trust Territories of the Pacific Islands (see Palau)
Tsunamis, 741
Tucson, Ariz., description, 229
Area codes, 804-805
Crime in, 307, 308
Government, 229
Location, 229
Population, 229
Population by race/Hispanic origin, 238
Population, 1980-2000, 239
Terrain and climate, 229
Visitor information, 229
Web site, 229
Tulsa, Okla., description, 229
Area codes, 804-805
Crime in, 307, 308
Government, 230
Location, 230
Population by race/Hispanic origin, 238
Population, 1980-2000, 239
Terrain and climate, 230
Visitor information, 230
Web site, 230
Tunisia, 679-680
Area codes, 464
Economic indicators, 516
Economy, 679-680
Geography, 679
Government, 679
Health indicators, 483
Major cities, 679
People, 679
Population indicators, 477
Turkey, description, 680-682
Area codes, 464
Economic indicators, 516
Economy, 680
Geography, 680
Government, 680
Health indicators, 483
History (Ottoman empire), 425
Major cities, 680
Motor vehicle production, 408
People, 680
Population in U.S., 299
Population indicators, 477
Traffic deaths, 408
U.S. immigrants from, 295
and War in Iraq, 17
Turkmenistan, description, 682-683
Area codes, 464
Economic indicators, 516
Economy, 682
Geography, 682
Government, 682
Health indicators, 483
Major cities, 682
People, 682
Population indicators, 477
Turks and Caicos Islands, 707
Tuvalu, description, 683
Area codes, 464
Economy, 683
Geography, 683
Government, 683
Major cities, 683
People, 683
Tyler, John
Administration, 115
Biography, 88-89
Vice President, 113
Typhoon, definition, 468

U

U.N. (see United Nations)
U.S. (see rest of entry)
U.S. Customary measure, converting to metric measure, 768
U.S. Open (tennis), 916-917
U.S. Supreme Court (see Supreme Court of the U.S.)
U.S. Virgin Islands (see Virgin Islands, U.S.)
U.S. Women's Open (golf), 914
Uganda, description, 683-684
Area codes, 464
Economic indicators, 516
Economy, 683
Geography, 683
Government, 683
Health indicators, 483
Major cities, 683
People, 683
Population indicators, 477
Ukraine, description, 684-685
Area codes, 464
Declining population, 472
Economic indicators, 516
Economy, 684
Geography, 684
Government, 684
Health indicators, 483
Major cities, 684
Nuclear power generation, 497
People, 684
Population indicators, 477
Unemployment insurance and compensation, 162
Unemployment rates in leading developed nations, 511
UNESCO (United Nations Educational, Scientific and Cultural Organization), 711
Unhealthy days in selected metropolitan areas, 775
UNICEF (United Nations Children's Fund), 710
Union of Soviet Socialist Republics (see Soviet Union)
Unitarian Universalist Association, 406
United Arab Emirates, description, 685-686
Area codes, 464
Economic indicators, 516
Economy, 685-686
Geography, 685
Government, 685
Health indicators, 483
Major cities, 685
Oil reserves, 496
People, 685
Population indicators, 477
United Kingdom, description, 686-688
Area codes, 464
Currency exchange rates, 505
Dynasties and kings of England, 442-443
Economic indicators, 516
Economy, 686
Geography, 686
Government, 686
Health indicators, 483
Major cities, 686
Motor vehicle production, 408
Nuclear power generation, 497
People, 686
Population in U.S., 299
Population indicators, 477
Traffic deaths, 408
U.S. immigrants from, 295
United Nations, 708-715
2002-03 Events, 17-20
Address, 708
Chronology, 712-715
General Assembly, 708-709
Headquarters, 708
History, 712-715
Languages, 708
Member states, 714
Observers, 708
Peacekeeping operations, 711-712
Programs, 709-710
Purposes, 708
Secretariat, 709
Security Council, 709
Specialized agencies, 710-711
Structure, 708-709
U.S. Representatives to, 710
United States Mission to, 134
and War in Iraq, 17-20
Web site, 712
World Court (International Court of Justice), 709
United Nations Day, 44
United States (see also rest of entry)
2000 Census, 260-268
Agriculture, 302-304
AIDS cases reported, 376
Area codes, 804-805
Armed forces, 146-154
Cardiovascular operations in, 371

Cities and Counties, 211-259
Crime and punishment in, 305-315
Crime rates, by state, 306
Economic indicators, 516
Economy, 689
Economy and Business, 316-353
Education in, 354-360
Elevations by state, 57
Endangered species in, 784
Energy consumption/production, 361, 362
Exports, 506, 507
Farms, acreage, and population, 302-304
Foreign-born in, 298, 299, 300
Geography, 50-57, 688
Government, 688-689
Health and medicine in, 365-385
Health care as percent of GNP, 368
Health care expenditures in, 367
Health indicators, 483
Holidays, 43
Households and families, 284-287
Housing, 287-292
Immigration, 293-300
Imports, 506, 507
Incarceration rates. by state, 313
Independence Day, 42
Infant mortality rate, 382
Major cities, 688
Mission to the United Nations, 134
Money income of families, 322
Motor vehicle production, 408
Motor vehicle registrations, 410
National park system, 51-53
Nuclear plants in, 364
Nuclear power generation, 497
Passenger travel, 408
People, 688
Personal income per capita, 319, 320
Physiographic regions, 50-51
Political-geographic divisions, 50
Population 1790-1990, 263-265
Population indicators, 477
Prisoners executed, by state, 315
Religion in, 401-406
Rivers and lakes, 53-55
Roads and streets in, 411
Sex in, 300
State parks and recreation areas, 53
Territories of, 207-210
Top destinations for tourists, 414
Traffic deaths, 408
Transportation, 407-415
Vehicles, number, 407
Vital statistics, 278-283
***United States v. E.C. Knight Co.* (1895), 122**
***United States v. Nixon* (1974), 123**
Universal Postal Union (UPU), 711
Universities (see Colleges and Universities)
***University of California Regents v. Bakke* (1978), 123**
Upper Volta (see Burkina Faso)
Uranus
Visibility, 2003, 48-49
Urban population
by Region and nation, 475-477
Urban population, U.S., 262
(see also Rural population, U.S.)
Urbanization, world, 474
URL (Uniform Resource Locator), 809
Uruguay, description, 689-690
Area codes, 464
Economic indicators, 516
Economy, 689
Geography, 689
Government, 689
Health indicators, 483
Major cities, 689
People, 689
Population in U.S., 299
Population indicators, 477
Usenet (Internet term), 809
User charges, definition, 144
Utah, description, 198-199
Area codes, 804-805
Business, 199
Cities, major, population of, 199
Crime in, 306
Education expenditures per pupil, 356
Educational attainment, 359
Elected officials, 198
Elevations, 57
Emblems, 198
Famous natives, 199
Farms in, 303
Fortune 500 companies, 199
Health care quality, 368
Land area, 198
Land cover and use, 55
Memorable events, 199
Noteworthy places, 199
Parks and recreation area, 53
Persons below poverty level, 321
Population by race and Hispanic origin, 269
Population by race/national origin, 198
Population estimates, 1990-2000, 169
Population, foreign-born, 297
Prisoners in
Public school enrollment, 356
Resident population and population change, 261
Resident population by age, 2002, 277
Revenues and expenditures, 203
Taxation in, 204-207
Tourist information, 199
Web site, 199
Uzbekistan, description, 690-691
Area codes, 464
Economic indicators, 516
Economy, 690
Geography, 690
Government, 690
Health indicators, 483
Major cities, 690
People, 690
Population indicators, 477

V

Vaccination and immunization schedule for children, 382
Valentine's Day, 43
Van Buren, Martin
Administration, 115
Biography, 88
Election, 102
Vice President, 113
Vanuatu, description, 691
Area codes, 464
Economic indicators, 516
Economy, 691
Geography, 691
Government, 691
Health indicators, 483
Major cities, 691
People, 691
Population indicators, 477
Variable stars, 729
Variety Shows, Emmy Awards for , 823
Vatican City
Area codes, 464
Venezuela, description, 691-692
2002-03 Events, 22-23
Area codes, 464
Economic indicators, 516
Economy, 691
Geography, 691
Government, 691
Health indicators, 483
Major cities, 691
Oil reserves, 496
People, 691
Population in U.S., 299
Population indicators, 477
Venus
Visibility, 2003, 48
Vermont, description, 199
Area codes, 804-805
Business, 199
Cities, major, population of, 199
Crime in, 306
Education expenditures per pupil, 356
Educational attainment, 359
Elected officials, 199
Elevations, 57
Emblems, 199
Executions in, 315
Famous natives, 199
Farms in, 303
Fortune 500 companies, 199
Health care quality, 368
Land area, 199
Land cover and use, 55
Memorable events, 199
Noteworthy places, 199
Nuclear plants in, 364
Parks and recreation area, 53
Persons below poverty level, 321
Population by race and Hispanic origin, 269
Population by race/national origin, 199
Population estimates, 1990-2000, 169
Population, foreign-born, 297
Prisoners in, 313
Public school enrollment, 356
Resident population and population change, 261
Resident population by age, 2002, 277
Revenues and expenditures, 203
Taxation in, 204-207
Tourist information, 199
Web site, 199
Veteran's Employment and Training Service (VETS), 134
Veterans Affairs, U.S. Dept. of, description, 136
Employment and budget outlays, 141
Social insurance programs, 162-163
Veterans' benefits and, 163
Veterans Benefit Administration, 136
Veterans Health Administration, 136
Veterans' Day, 42
Vice President
Office of, 131
Salary, 140
Vice Presidents of the U.S., 112, 113
Victims, crime, 309
Video, 397-398
Video Music Awards, MTV, 829-830
Vietnam, description, 693-694
Area codes, 464
Economic indicators, 516
Economy, 693
Geography, 693
Government, 693
Health indicators, 483
Major cities, 693
People, 693
Population in U.S., 299
Population indicators, 477
U.S. immigrants from, 295
Vietnam Conflict, 150
Vietnam War (see Vietnam Conflict)
Violent crime
Arrests for, 311
Number and rate, by offense, 305
in Other nations, 308-309
Rate, by state, 306
Reported, 305
Victims of, 309
Virgin Islands, description, 210
Elevations, 57
Population, 210
Virginia, description, 199-200
Black population in, 270
Business, 200
Cities, major, population of, 200
Crime in, 306
Education expenditures per pupil, 356
Educational attainment, 359
Elected officials, 200
Elevations, 57
Emblems, 200
Executions in, 315
Famous natives, 200
Farms in, 303
Fortune 500 companies, 200
Health care quality, 368
Land area, 200
Land cover and use, 55
Memorable events, 200
Noteworthy places, 200
Nuclear plants in, 364
Parks and recreation area, 53
Persons below poverty level, 321
Population by race and Hispanic origin, 269
Population by race/national origin, 200
Population estimates, 1990-2000, 169
Population, foreign-born, 297
Prisoners in, 313
Public school enrollment, 356
Resident population and population change, 261
Resident population by age, 2002, 277
Revenues and expenditures, 203
Taxation in, 204-207
Tourist information, 200
Web site, 200
Virginia Beach, Va., description, 230
Area codes, 804-805
Cost of living index, 243
Government, 230

Location, 230
Population, 230
Population by race/Hispanic origin, 238
Population, 1980-2000, 239
Tax burdens in, 242
Terrain and climate, 230
Visitor information, 230
Web site, 230
Visibility of the Planets, 2003, 47-49
Vital events, definition, 478
per Time unit, 473
Vital rates, definition, 478
Vital statistics, U.S., 278-282
Marriages and divorces, 279
Volatile organic compounds emissions, 776-777
Volcanoes
Active, 745-746
Volleyball
NCAA champions, 877
Olympic champions, 897
Volume, measurement of, 768-769
Voter Turnout in Presidential Elections, 1928-2000, 110

W

W and Z particles, 758
Wages
Earnings by age and educational attainment, 335
Earnings by industry, 335
Federal minimum wage, 336
Wake Islands, description, 210
Wales (see United Kingdom)
Wall Street, 341-347
2002-03 News, 33
Wallis & Futuna Isl.
Area codes, 464
Wallis and Futuna, 702
War in Iraq, 17-20
War of 1812, 150
Warm front, definition, 468
Washington, description, 200-201
Area codes, 804-805
Business, 201
Cities, major, population of, 201
Crime in, 306
Education expenditures per pupil, 356
Educational attainment, 359
Elected officials, 201
Elevations, 57
Emblems, 200
Executions in, 315
Famous natives, 201
Farms in, 303
Fortune 500 companies, 201
Health care quality, 368
Land area, 200
Land cover and use, 55
Memorable events, 201
Noteworthy places, 201
Nuclear plants in, 364
Parks and recreation area, 53
Persons below poverty level, 321
Population by race and Hispanic origin, 269
Population by race/national origin, 201
Population estimates, 1990-2000, 169
Population, foreign-born, 297
Prisoners in, 313
Public school enrollment, 356
Resident population and population change, 261
Resident population by age, 1999, 277
Revenues and expenditures, 203
Taxation in, 204-207
Tourist information, 201
Web site, 201
Washington's Birthday, 42
Washington, D.C., description, 230
Area codes, 804-805
Black population in, 271
Climate in, 470
Cost of living index, 243
Crime in, 307
Educational attainment, 359
Government, 230
Housing prices in, 290
Location, 230
Persons below poverty level, 321
Population, 230
Population by race/Hispanic origin, 238
Population, 1980-2000, 239
Rents in, 290
Tax burdens in, 242
Terrain and climate, 230
Visitor information, 230
Web site, 230
Washington, George
Administration, 114
Biography, 86
Election, 101
Waste
Disposing of, 779
Hazardous, 780-781
Incineration/combustion, 779-780
Nuclear, 780-781
Recycling, 780
Solid, 779-780
Source reduction, 780
Water pollution, 778-779
Water Polo
NCAA champions, 875
Olympic champions, 897
Waterways, navigable U.S., 53-55
Weapons of mass destruction, 19-20
Weapons systems and combat forces, 152
Weather
Websites about, 812
Weather, definition, 468
Beaufort wind scale, 469
Hurricanes, worst in U.S. history, 467
Tornadoes, worst in U.S., 467
in selected U.S. cities, 470
Weather words, 467-498
Wind-chill factor, 466
in selected World cities, 471
Web page, 809
Web site, 809
Web, the (see World Wide Web)
Weblog, 808
WebTV, 809
Wedding anniversaries, gifts for, 47
Weight, measurement of, 769
Weights and measures, standard, 767-771
Welfare, 159-160
West Bank, 594
West Germany (see Germany, West)
West Palm Beach, Fla.
Black population in, 271
Crime in, 307, 308
Housing prices in, 290
West Virginia, description, 201
Area codes, 804-805
Business, 201
Cities, major, population of, 201
Crime in, 306
Education expenditures per pupil, 356
Educational attainment, 359
Elected officials, 201
Elevations, 57
Emblems, 201
Executions in, 315
Famous natives, 201
Farms in, 303
Fortune 500 companies, 201
Health care quality, 368
Land area, 201
Land cover and use, 55
Memorable events, 201
Noteworthy places, 201
Parks and recreation area, 53
Persons below poverty level, 321
Population by race and Hispanic origin, 269
Population by race/national origin, 201
Population estimates, 1990-2000, 169
Population, foreign-born, 297
Prisoners in, 313
Public school enrollment, 356
Resident population and population change, 261
Resident population by age, 1999, 277
Revenues and expenditures, 203
Taxation in, 204-207
Tourist information, 201
Web site, 201
***West Virginia Board of Education v. Barnette* (1943), 122**
Western Europe
Energy consumption/productio n, 494, 496
Nuclear power generation, 497
Western Sahara, 702-703
Western Samoa (see Samoa)
Area codes, 464
Population in U.S., 299
Wetlands, U.S., 782
White dwarfs, 729
White House Office, 131
White population
Arrests, 311
Cancer survival rates, 374
Crime victimization rates, 310
Death rates, 377
Divorced persons per 1,000 married persons, 283
Employment status of, 334
Family households headed by, 286
Interracial couples, 283
Life expectancy, 380, 381, 382
Lifetime likelihood of going to prison, 314
Marital status, 281
of U.S. MSAs, 1990, 250-255
One-parent families, 286
Prisoners, 312
Prisoners executed by, 314
Resident population by state, 269
WHO (World Health Organization), 711
Wholesale trade industries
Earnings in, 335
WIC (women-infants-children) program, 160
Wichita, Kans.
Area codes, 804-805
Government, 230
Location, 230
Population, 230
Population by race/Hispanic origin, 238
Population, 1980-2000, 239
Tax burdens in, 242
Terrain and climate, 230
Visitor information, 230
Web site, 230
Wilmington, Del.
Tax burdens in, 242
Wilshire 5000 Index, definition, 347
Wilson, Joseph C., 19-20
Wilson, Woodrow
Administration, 117
Biography, 93
Election, 106
Wimbledon, 916-917
Wind, definition, 468-469
Beaufort wind scale, 469
Wind-chill factor, 466
Winston Cup Winners, 907
Winter Olympics (see Olympic Sports)
Wisconsin, description, 201-202
Area codes, 804-805
Business, 202
Cities, major, population of, 202
Crime in, 306
Education expenditures per pupil, 356
Educational attainment, 359
Elected officials, 202
Elevations, 57
Emblems, 202
Executions in, 315
Famous natives, 202
Farms in, 303
Fortune 500 companies, 202
Health care quality, 368
Land area, 202
Land cover and use, 55
Memorable events, 202
Noteworthy places, 202
Nuclear plants in, 364
Parks and recreation area, 53
Persons below poverty level, 321
Population by race and Hispanic origin, 269
Population by race/national origin, 202
Population estimates, 1990-2000, 169
Population, foreign-born, 297
Prisoners in, 313
Public school enrollment, 356
Resident population and population change, 261
Resident population by age, 1999, 277
Revenues and expenditures, 203
Taxation in, 204-207
Tourist information, 202
Web site, 202
Women
in Armed forces, 153
in Labor force, 333
Women's Sports
Bowling, 907
Golf, 914
Olympic sports, 887-905
Tennis, 916-917
Track and Field, 885
World Cup, 881
Women-infants-children (WIC), 160
Work stoppages, 336
Work, measurement of, 770-771
Workers
Work stoppages and, 336
Workers' compensation, 162
World
Airports, busiest in the, 413
Area codes, 462-464
Births and deaths, 472
Buildings, tallest, 460
Climates of the, 465-498
Dams, largest, 455

Debt, external, by region and nation, 503
Deserts, largest, 450
Economic indicators, 514-516
Energy, 494-497
Fertility rates, 475-477
Fortune 100 largest corporations, 513
Health, 478-492
Health indicators, 481-483
International economy, 502-516
International organizations, 715
Islands, largest, 457
Lakes of, 453
Land Area, 448
Languages of, 493
Military situation, 498-501
Motor vehicle production, 408
Motor vehicle registrations, 409
Mountain peaks, highest, 451-452
Oceans of, 449
Population, 448, 472-492
Population indicators, 475-477
Population trends, 472-498
Religions, 486-492
Reservoirs, largest, 455
Rivers of, by length, 454
Rulers of, 440-446
Time Zones, 462-464
Top tourist destinations, 414
Traffic deaths, 408
Vital events, 473
World Bank, 504
World Bank Group, 711
World Boxing Association (WBA) (see Boxing)
World Boxing Council (WBC) (see Boxing)
World Court, 709
World Cup, 879, 880, 881
World economic output, change 1997-2001, 502
World energy, 494-497
World Figure Skating Champions, 883
World Food Council (WFC), 710
World Food Programme (WFP), 710
World Geography, 447-464
World health, 478-492
World Health Organization (WHO), 711
World Intellectual Property Organization (WIPO), 711
World Meteorological Organization (WMO), 711
World population, 472-492 (see also Population, world)
World religions, 486-492
World Series
MVPs, 1955-2002, 967
Records, 967
Winners, 1903-2002, 963-966
World Trade Organization (WTO), 508 (see also GATT)
2002-03 Events, 24
World War I, 150
World War I and World War II, 434-435
World War II, 150
World Wide Web
State home pages, 170-203
World Wide Web (WWW), 807-808
Business on, 807-808
Growth of, 807
Web TV, 809
Website directory, 810-812
Wrestling
NCAA champions, 876
WWW, 809
Wyoming, description, 52, 202-204
Area codes, 804-805
Business, 202
Cities, major, population of, 202
Crime in, 306
Education expenditures per pupil, 356
Educational attainment, 359
Elected officials, 202
Elevations, 57
Emblems, 202
Executions in, 315
Famous natives, 202
Farms in, 303
Fortune 500 companies, 202
Health care quality, 368
Land area, 202
Land cover and use, 55
Memorable events, 202-203
Noteworthy places, 202
Parks and recreation area, 53
Persons below poverty level, 321
Population by race and Hispanic origin, 269
Population by race/national origin, 202
Population estimates, 1990-2000, 169
Population, foreign-born, 297
Public school enrollment, 356
Resident population and population change, 261
Resident population by age, 2002, 277
Revenues and expenditures, 203
Taxation in, 204-207
Tourist information, 203-204
Web site, 203-204

X

XML, 809

Y

Yachting, 879
Year, 37
Yemen, description, 694-695
Area codes, 464
Economic indicators, 516
Economy, 694-695
Geography, 694
Government, 694
Health indicators, 483
Major cities, 694
People, 694
Population indicators, 477
Yield (bus.), definition, 347
Yom Kippur (Day of Atonement), 45
***Youngstown Sheet and Tube Co. v. Sawyer* (1952), 122**
Yugoslavia (see Serbia and Montenegro)

Z

Zaire (see Congo, Democratic Republic
Zambia, description, 695-696
Area codes, 464
Economic indicators, 516
Economy, 696
Geography, 695
Government, 696
Health indicators, 483
Major cities, 695
People, 695-696
Population indicators, 477
Zimbabwe, description, 696-698
2002-03 events, v
Area codes, 464
Economic indicators, 516
Economy, 696-697
Geography, 696
Government, 696
Health indicators, 483
Major cities, 696
People, 696
Population indicators, 477
Zip codes, 168
Zip file, 810
Zodiac (see Astrological Calendar)